LIST OF PART PROBLEMS REQUIRING THE USE OF THE IDES APPROACH

PART 1 **FOUNDATIONS OF LAW (P. 1)**
In the wake of political fund-raising controversies, AirTex, Inc. (a hypothetical business) needs to assess the legal and ethical ramifications surrounding the firm's $500,000 contribution to the Democratic National Committee.

PART 2 **THE AMERICAN LEGAL SYSTEM (P. 89)**
Albee started his own "investment" business, investing in stocks for himself and, for a fee, his clients. When the business fails, Albee's clients seek legal recourse.

PART 3 **CONTRACTS (P. 223)**
Sean, a college student, opened a computer consulting business. Because of certain business agreements, Sean faces a number of legal problems.

PART 4 **SALES AND LEASES (P. 405)**
Mildred has decided to make a little money from her favorite hobby, woodworking. Most customers like Mildred's work. However, a few dissatisfied customers cite Mildred as a merchant in wooden goods and claim that she has breached a contract or a warranty.

PART 5 **NEGOTIABLES (P. 529)**
Amir is National Bank's vice president for customer relations. Amir is not a lawyer, so he must be able to communicate efficiently with National's corporate legal department when problems arise.

PART 6 **DEBTOR-CREDITOR RELATIONS (P. 645)**
Donna has opened Suds 'n Duds, a combination laundromat and tavern, purchasing most of her equipment and materials on credit. When the business fails, Donna seeks legal help to discuss relief in bankruptcy.

PART 7 **AGENCY (P. 771)**
Koolin'-Aid is a manufacturer and seller of air-conditioning equipment. A freelance salesperson Koolin'-Aid no longer commissions has been misrepresenting himself as an agent of Koolin'-Aid, profiting by these acts. Also, a truck driver for Koolin'-Aid has caused a $100,000 tort liability lawsuit to be filed against Koolin'-Aid.

PART 8 **BUSINESS ORGANIZATIONS (P. 839)**
InterActive, a multimedia software developer, has recently encountered legal problems with a former manager and an owner.

PART 9 **GOVERNMENT REGULATION OF BUSINESS (P. 995)**
Healthtech, a health-care technology firm, wishes to expand, but the firm faces complaints under the Sherman and Clayton Acts. Also, advocacy groups have attacked Healthtech's workplace policies.

PART 10 **PROPERTY PROTECTION (P. 1141)**
Call-Image Technology (CIT), a videophone developer, is concerned about a number of real, personal, and intellectual property law issues for which it needs to seek legal help.

BUSINESS LAW

DANIEL V. DAVIDSON
RADFORD UNIVERSITY

BRENDA E. KNOWLES
INDIANA UNIVERSITY SOUTH BEND

LYNN M. FORSYTHE
CALIFORNIA STATE UNIVERSITY, FRESNO

WEST
WEST EDUCATIONAL PUBLISHING COMPANY
An International Thomson Publishing Company

PRINCIPLES AND CASES IN THE LEGAL ENVIRONMENT

SIXTH EDITION

Publisher/Team Director: Jack W. Calhoun
Acquisitions Editor: Rob Dewey
Developmental Editor: Kurt Gerdenich
Production Editor: Sharon L. Smith
Sr. Marketing Manager: Scott D. Person
Production House: Pre-Press Co., Inc.
Cover Design: Paul Neff Design
Cover Illustrator: Cathleen Toelke
Internal Design: Michael H. Stratton

Library of Congress Cataloging-in-Publication Data

Davidson, Daniel V.
Business law : principles and cases in the legal environment / Daniel V. Davidson, Brenda E. Knowles, Lynn M. Forsythe. —6th ed.
p. cm.
Includes index.
ISBN: 0-538-86856-2 (hardcover)
1. Commercial law—United States—Cases. I. Knowles, Brenda E. II. Forsythe, Lynn M. III. Title.
KF888.D28 1997
346.7307—DC21 97-15970
CIP

ISBN: 0-538-86856-2

1 2 3 4 5 6 7 8 VH 3 2 1 0 9 8 7

Printed in the United States of America

I(T)P®
International Thomson Publishing
West Educational Publishing is an ITP Company.
The ITP trademark is used under license.

To Dee, Jaime, and Tara. Thanks for your help and support.

Daniel V. Davidson

To Paul for challenging me to be better and for sustaining me with his unfailing love and support.

Brenda E. Knowles

To Jim and Mike Poptanich for their love and patience, and to Aileen and Robert Zollweg and to Mary Helen and John Poptanich.

Lynn M. Forsythe

P R E F A C E

A Business-Oriented Business Law Text

Business Law: Principles and Cases in the Legal Environment, Sixth Edition, offers students a business-oriented introduction to the legal and ethical topics that affect business. This may seem redundant. After all, doesn't a business law textbook by its nature adopt an orientation toward the practice of business? Textbooks that typically teach the law, often clearly and in great detail, can fail to show students how the law will affect their future careers in the business world. Our goal as business law and legal environment instructors is not to train lawyers. Rather, our goal is to train future businesspeople how to avoid legal problems or, should legal problems arise, how to recognize the nature of these problems and work with a lawyer to achieve solutions.

Our strategy in revising the sixth edition is threefold:

- To present, in an accessible style, a current and comprehensive introduction to the legal topics relevant to business
- To demonstrate how these topics apply to the practice of business
- To provide an approach to legal analysis—often termed *critical thinking*—for addressing legal problems encountered in the practice of business.

We have also tried to better support the teaching and learning process associated with using the text. Our association with West Education Publishing now allows us to offer a wide array of supplementary materials for instructors and students.

New Coverage in the Sixth Edition

As we mentioned, our first goal is to present, in an accessible style, a current and comprehensive introduction to the legal topics relevant to business. Toward this goal, the book is divided into ten parts based on traditional topical areas of undergraduate business law. The following content changes and updates were made to the sixth edition.

Part I Foundations of Law Part 1 presents an overview of law and the legal system. The sixth edition provides increased coverage of ethics and international law topics. In particular, Chapter 2, "Business Ethics," has an increased focus on the application of ethical theories in the practice of business.

Part 2 The American Legal System Part 2 examines the court system and the legal system used in the United States. New to the sixth edition is a full chapter devoted to alternative dispute resolution—Chapter 7, "Alternate Dispute Resolution."

Part 3 Contracts Part 3 examines the primary importance of contract law to business. The chapters contained here have been substantially updated.

Part 4 Sales and Leases Part 4 introduces the Uniform Commercial Code in significant detail and examines the law of sales from an international perspective. Part 4 now offers comparisons of Article 2A contracts with Article 2 contracts and the similarity in treatment between contracts for the sale of goods and contracts for the leasing of goods. Part 4 also provides a detailed examination of the international sale of goods, including increased coverage of the UN Convention on Contracts for the International Sale of Goods (CISG), INCOTerms, and ISO 9000 and 14000.

Part 5 Negotiables Part 5 discusses UCC Articles 3 (Revised), 4 (Revised), 4A, and 7. It also includes a discussion of electronic fund transfers. New coverage reflects the changes in negotiable instrument law with the revision of Articles 3 and 4 of the UCC.

Part 6 Debtor-Creditor Relations Part 6 examines secured transactions under Article 9 of the UCC and the federal protections available under the Bankruptcy Reform Act. This part includes increased coverage of the Bankruptcy Reform Act of 1994.

Part 7 Agency Part 7 explains the agency relationship and its use in the conduct of a business. Special emphasis is given to the liability of both the principal and the agent for contracts entered into by the agent and to the liability of both the principal and the agent for torts and crimes committed by the agent.

Part 8 Business Organizations Part 8 treats the various types of business organizations in a unique manner. Rather than have separate chapters dealing with the various organizations, the text treats the organizations in a compare-and-contrast fashion within the chapters. The emphasis is no longer on *how* the various types of business organizations should be implemented; rather, the text emphasizes *why* a particular form should be chosen.

Part 9 Government Regulation of Business Part 9 addresses regulatory topics. Part 9 now has an entire chapter devoted to consumer law—Chapter 41, "Consumer Protection"—and to environmental law—Chapter 42, "Environmental Protection."

Part 10 Property Protection Part 10 examines real and personal property law and "wealth protection." Part 10 also offers updated coverage on intellectual property law.

NEW AND IMPROVED APPLICATIONS

Our second goal for this revision is to demonstrate how the legal topics presented here apply to the practice of business. Toward this goal, *Business Law* offers the following features, many of which are unique to this text.

Court Cases

Each chapter contains four to five court cases in the language of the court. Cases are briefed in the following format:

- *Facts*—the facts of the case
- *Issue(s)*—the issues, in the form of questions, on which the decision hinges
- *Holding*—a summary, in the form of answers to the preceding questions, of the court decision
- *Reasoning*—the reasoning the court used in reaching its decision

We have made an effort in the sixth edition to include more court language in our briefed cases. Our selection of cases includes both classic, landmark opinions and current, cutting-edge cases. In addition, all of our court cases end with a Business Considerations and an Ethical Considerations section.

Call-Image Technology (CIT) Business Application Thread Case

An integrated, continuous business "thread" case, or scenario, profiles the experiences of a hypothetical videophone business, Call-Image Technology (CIT). Chapters begin with an Agenda that highlights the major legal issues relevant to CIT. Within chapters, Application Boxes address particular legal issues and call for students to offer the firm guidance. Each application box is categorized by the functional area of business—management, manufacturing, finance and accounting, sales, marketing, and international business—to which the scenario is most relevant. Finally, application boxes include Business Considerations and Ethical Considerations questions, asking the students to go beyond CIT's problem to decide how the type of problem faced might affect other business concerns. See pages 27–28 for an introduction to the CIT business application thread case.

Resources for Business Law Students

Resources for Business Law Students, included in every chapter, highlight World Wide Web sites of particular relevance to the study of business law and legal environment. For convenience, Web sites are listed by their name, the resources of particular interest, and the address:

http:// RESOURCES FOR BUSINESS LAW STUDENTS

NAME	RESOURCES	WEB ADDRESS
Business Law Web Site by West Publishing	The Business Law Web Site by West Publishing contains teaching and learning materials, case and current event updates, and resources from West Publishing. As well, you can communicate with the authors and the editors of *Business Law: Principles and Cases in the Legal Environment.*	http://www.westbuslaw.com/

Memos from Amy Chen

Memos from Amy Chen, included in most chapters, offer practical legal suggestions for business managers. Amy Chen, the hypothetical lawyer introduced in the Call-Image Technology (CIT) business application thread case, offers pragmatic comments on the topics discussed in the chapter.

You Be the Judge Boxes

You Be the Judge boxes, included in every chapter, highlight scenarios from the news in which legal or ethical problems are at play. Students, using the material in the chapter, are asked to decide the outcome of the scenario. Students have the opportunity to think critically and to discuss these problems in class; also, the problems provide potential writing assignments or team projects for students. Finally, You Be the Judge boxes include Business Considerations and Ethical Considerations questions, asking the students to go beyond the given scenario and decide how the type of problem faced might affect other business concerns.

Discussion Questions, Case Problems and Writing Assignments

Each chapter concludes with ten discussion questions, five legal case problems, one business applications case, one ethics applications case problem, and one IDES case problem based on the IDES approach to legal reasoning (discussed below). The legal case problems ask students to test their understanding of principles and terms covered in the chapter, and the business and ethics application problems and the IDES problem ask students to apply these concepts to business situations. All of the end-of-chapter materials can be used as study tools in reviewing the material, as class or small-group discussion material, or for writing assignments.

The IDES Approach to Legal Analysis

A new feature, and one that is exciting to us, is the inclusion of the IDES approach to legal analysis. IDES is an acronym for the following:

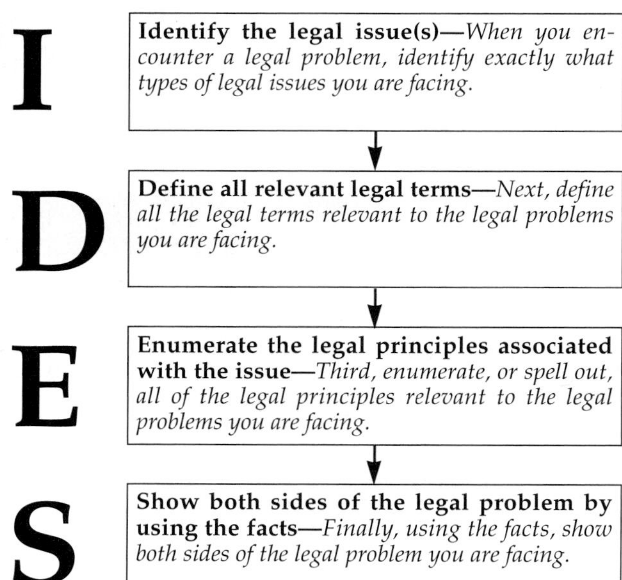

I
Identify the legal issue(s)—*When you encounter a legal problem, identify exactly what types of legal issues you are facing.*
D
Define all relevant legal terms—*Next, define all the legal terms relevant to the legal problems you are facing.*
E
Enumerate the legal principles associated with the issue—*Third, enumerate, or spell out, all of the legal principles relevant to the legal problems you are facing.*
S
Show both sides of the legal problem by using the facts—*Finally, using the facts, show both sides of the legal problem you are facing.*

Each part of the text contains a comprehensive business problem requiring the use of the IDES approach. Each chapter also contains a specific problem requiring the use of the IDES approach. By using IDES, students learn to analyze legal problems in an orderly and logical manner. As well, students engage in critical thinking and learn to see problems from the perspectives of all sides in a dispute.

IDES, as an approach to legal analysis, should not be confused with a method for briefing a case. While briefing a case allows one to comprehend the significance of a particular judicial decision, the IDES approach to legal analysis provides a framework within which to address larger legal problems.

SUPPLEMENTAL RESOURCES

NEW! The sixth edition of *Business Law,* as part of the Business Law Web Site from West Educational Publishing (http://www.westbuslaw.com/), now has a site on the

World Wide Web devoted to teaching and learning support for the text (http://davidson.westbuslaw.com). Come visit to see for yourself.

The following supplemental resources are available with the sixth edition:

- *Study Guide to Accompany Business Law: Principles and Cases in the Legal Environment (0-538-86857-0).*
- *Telecourse Study Guide* (0-538-86858-9)
- *Instructor's Manual* (0-538-86031-6)
- *Test Bank*—Thoroughly revised by Wayne Wells and Janell Kurtz, Saint Cloud State University (0-538-86863-5)
- WESTEST testing software (0-538-86861-9)
- PowerPoint Transparency Masters (0-538-86864-3)
- Telecourse Videos—30 half-hour telecourse videos, developed by Intellecom in conjunction with the third edition of *Business Law*, provide coverage for key topics in business law. (Contact your ITP/West sales representative for more details.)
- South-Western's Business Law Video Series
- Legal Tutor Software on Contracts and on Sales
- CNN Legal Issues Video Update—Update your coverage of legal issues by using the *CNN Legal Issues Update*. This video update is produced by Turner Learning, Inc., using the resources of CNN, the world's first 24-hour, all-news network. (0-538-86862-7)

The following supplements from West Educational Publishing are available to qualified adopters of *Business Law*. Contact your ITP/West sales representative for more details.

- Ten Free Hours of WestLaw
- Business Law and Legal Environment Video Library
- Business Law Videodisc
- U.S. Supreme Court Audiocassette Library
- West's Regional Reporters
- Contracts and UCC Article 2, Sales, Software
- You Be the Judge Software
- CD-ROM Resources for Business Law and Legal Environment

A Note on AACSB Curricular Standards

The AACSB curricular standards relevant to business law and the legal environment of business state that curricula should include ethical and global issues; the influence of political, social, legal and regulatory, environmental, and technology issues; and the impact of demographic diversity on organizations. We believe *Business Law: Principles and Cases in the Legal Environment* uniquely satisfies these standards.

First, global issues are treated in-depth in *two* chapters, Chapter 3, "International Law," and Chapter 20, "International Sales of Goods: CISG," (more than any other current business law text). Also, we have revised Chapter 2, "Business Ethics," to reflect more of the application of ethical theories than the theories themselves. Ethics questions also appear following court cases, You Be the Judge boxes, CIT business application boxes, and at the end of chapters.

Second, we have revised the text with the intent of creating a book that is intuitive, engaging, and oriented toward providing the legal skills students will need in the business world. Hence, the contents of the book stretch beyond the mere presentation of "legal topics" to encompass the spectrum of "political, social, legal, regulatory, environmental, and technological issues." The pedagogical features are designed to augment this content.

Finally, the attention to applications, evidenced in the CIT business application thread and the IDES approach to legal reasoning, uniquely satisfies the need to show how demographic diversity affects organizations. In the CIT case, the Kochanowskis—founders of a family business—must understand the cultural and political challenges that a larger domestic and international market (and work force) pose for them. By following the case, students are immersed in these problems and are asked to offer advice as questions arise. The IDES approach to legal reasoning mandates that the students examine each problem from *both* sides, or from the perspective of all of the parties involved. This encourages sensitivity and an understanding of other points of view.

On another level, the Kochanowskis (and, vicariously, the students) learn that successful businesses today are often cross functional. In this case, the Kochanowskis need to recognize how the law applies to marketing, sales, management, finance and accounting, and manufacturing, and they must be able to act on this knowledge. The students, by assuming an advisory role with CIT, have a unique glimpse at the cross-functional nature of many business activities today.

ACKNOWLEDGMENTS

Writing a textbook is always an arduous undertaking, even if the text is "merely" a revision of a previous edition. This edition has been no different, and in many ways it has been more difficult. There have been numerous substantive changes in the law since the last edition, and each of these needed attention. There are also several areas that are in a state of upheaval as we go into print, and trying to be as up-to-date as possible while meeting a production deadline can be a problem for the entire production team.

This edition of the book would not have been possible without the help, assistance, and guidance of our developmental editor Kurt Gerdenich. Kurt is always there when we need him. His good humor, his patience, and his support have been invaluable to us. Sharon Smith has also been tremendous. She has provided advice when needed and has assisted Kurt in helping us to put together this book. Robine Andrau of Pre-Press has worked diligently in making last minute corrections, updating materials as needed, and making our work look as professional as it looks. She and her staff were wonderful to us throughout the process.

Each of the authors owes a hearty "thank you" and a sincere "well done" to the other two authors. Each provided feedback, (positive) criticism, and support to the others during the hectic days of reading copyedited pages and page proofs. Each of us brings a unique personality to the process, and we have learned how and when to merge our talents to produce the best book possible. As authors, we have been a team for quite some time, working together through six editions of the text. We each write about an equal number of chapters, and we each have input into the chapters written by the other authors. We sincerely believe that our group effort has been successful and that the sum of our contributions is greater than the parts. We hope you enjoy using this book as much as we have enjoyed preparing it.

A special thanks to our families. They put up with the late nights, the short deadlines (and the shorter tempers) and provide support and input to help us get through the process every time we revise the text. Without their support, we would never be able to accomplish our goal.

Finally, a sincere thank you to the following reviewers, whose suggestions, criticism, questions, observations, and keen and insightful commentary on our work helped us to maintain our focus and to write a text that is user-friendly, readable, and enjoyable without losing content:

Deborah Ballam
Ohio State University

Marshall N. Bean
San Jose State University

Jeanne A. Calderon
New York University

Thomas D. Cavenaugh
North Central College

Meg Costello
Oakland Community College

Thomas Duda
SUNY, Canton

Robert Emerson
University of Florida

Joan T. A. Gabel
Georgia State University

Georgia Holmes
Mankato State University

Madelyn M. Huffmire
University of Connecticut

Ida Jones
California State University, Fresno

Jack Karns
East Carolina University

Barbara W. Kincaid
Southern Methodist University

Dan Levin
Mankato State University

Gerald A. Loy
Broome Community College

Arthur J. Marinelli
Ohio University

Howard L. Perry
Black Hills State University

George N. Plavac
Cuyahoga Community College

Stephen L. Poe
University of North Texas

Irving E. Richards
Cuyahoga Community College

Alan C. Roline
University of Minnesota, Duluth

Tom Rossi
Broome Community College

Martin E. Segal
University of Miami (FL)

John N. Sigler
University of Baltimore

Charles Solocher
University of Texas at Dallas

Edward L. Welsh, Jr.
Mesa Community College

BRIEF CONTENTS

CONTENTS

List of Exhibits

ABOUT THE AUTHORS

Daniel V. Davidson

Daniel V. Davidson received both his B.S. in Business Administration and his J.D. from Indiana University, Bloomington. He is an inactive member of the Connecticut Bar Association. He has taught at Central Connecticut State College in New Britain; St. Cloud State University in Minnesota; the University of Arkansas, Fayetteville; and California State University, Fresno. He recently finished serving as the Associate Dean of the College of Business and Economics at Radford University in Virginia and is Professor of Business Law.

Professor Davidson has published numerous articles on business law, the teaching of business law, and business ethics. He was named the Outstanding Teacher of the Year at Central Connecticut State College. In 1979 he received the Outstanding Faculty Award from Beta Alpha Psi, and in 1980 he was named the *Razorback Award* winner as the Outstanding Business Professor, both at the University of Arkansas. In 1984, Professor Davidson was awarded the Meritorious Performance Award at California State University, Fresno.

Professor Davidson is a member of Beta Gamma Sigma, Sigma Iota Epsilon, and Beta Alpha Psi. He is also a member of the Academy of Legal Studies in Business (formerly the American Business Law Association) and its Southern Regional. He has held all of the offices in the Southern Regional, including that of President, and is currently serving as the Senior Advisory Editor for the *Southern Law Journal* and the *Proceedings* of the region's annual meeting.

Brenda E. Knowles

Brenda E. Knowles received a B.A. *magna cum laude* from the University of Evansville, an M.A. from Miami University, and a J.D. from the Indiana University School of Law Bloomington. She is Professor of Business Law and Director of the Honors Program at Indiana University South Bend, where she has been the recipient of the Amoco Foundation Excellence in Teaching Award, a system-wide, all-university teaching award. She also has been active in FACET, the faculty colloquium on excellence in teaching, which is a system-wide, all-university effort to encourage effective teaching and learning in the academic community. In 1995, Professor Knowles was named Director of the Honors Program (a position theretofore always held by liberal arts faculty members). In 1997, the Student Association at Indiana University South Bend chose her as the campus's "Outstanding Educator."

Professor Knowles specializes in research on employment discrimination, pedagogy, and intellectual property law. She publishes her work in professional journals and has won an award for her research. In addition, she has been recognized both nationally and locally for her professional and civic accomplishments, most recently through the W. George Pinnell Award for outstanding service to Indiana University.

Professor Knowles is an active member of the Academy of Legal Studies in Business (formerly the American Business Law Association) and of several regionals. More specifically, having held every office, she is a past President of both the ALSB and the Tri-State Regional. Professor Knowles presently serves as the Chairperson of the ALSB's Research and Teaching Mentorship Programs, and, in 1994, she won the

ALSB's Master Teacher Award. Moreover, she is a member of Beta Gamma Sigma. She is licensed to practice law in Indiana and is a member of the American, Indiana State, and St. Joseph County Bar Associations.

Lynn M. Forsythe

Lynn M. Forsythe received her B.A. from the Pennsylvania State University and her J.D. from the University of Pittsburgh School of Law. She has passed the bar examination in the states of California and Pennsylvania. She is Professor of Business Law at the Craig School of Business at California State University, Fresno. Professor Forsythe has also held administrative positions, including Director of Graduate Business Programs, Interim Department Chair, and Co-Chair of the AACSB Reaccreditation Committee.

Professor Forsythe received the 1992 School of Business Faculty Award for Educational Innovation and previously was awarded a university Meritorious Performance Award. She has been an estate and gift attorney for the Internal Revenue Service and has taught business law, administrative law, government regulation of business, real estate law, business ethics, estate planning, and business and society. She is the author of numerous articles on business law and the teaching of business law. She has held the positions of Co-Editor, Staff Editor, and Reviewer for *The Journal of Legal Studies Education* and served as the Editor-in-Chief for the 1987–1989 term. She is currently Advisory Editor.

Professor Forsythe is a member of Beta Gamma Sigma and Alpha Kappa Psi. She has been active in the American Bar Association, for which she chaired subcommittees and panels, including an American Law Institute–American Bar Association advanced program. She is active in the Academy of Legal Studies in Business (formerly the American Business Law Association), for which she served as academic program coordinator for the 1983 meeting, liaison to the National Conference of Commissioners on Uniform State Laws, and as a member of the Executive Committee. She is currently the chairperson of its Business Ethics Section. She has held every office, including President, in the Western Regional.

Part 1

FOUNDATIONS OF LAW

Ignorance of the law is no excuse. The basic truth of this old adage seems simple and obvious. However, the simplicity of the truth hides the complexity of the law. Each citizen—and resident—of this country has "constructive notice" of the law. Each person is expected to be aware of, and to abide by, all the laws of the land. Yet the enormity of "the law" makes such an expectation futile. No one person can really know the law, but every person is expected to obey it. Thus, a built-in contradiction exists in the system.

Part I of this book will first help you understand what law is, how it operates in the United States, and how it affects business. Next, this part will introduce you to business ethics. Finally, it will introduce the international legal environment in which business operates.

Each part of this book will shed light on and offer insights into aspects of the law. A thorough knowledge of law takes years of specialized study, and this text will not provide it. But it will begin to open the doors of understanding for you, and it will help to remove the "ignorance of the law [that] is no excuse."

I D E S

Controversy has arisen over fund-raising activities of the Democratic party during the 1996 Presidential election. Did foreign interests, in making large contributions to the Democratic National Committee (DNC), attempt to influence Bill Clinton on foreign policy and/or trade policy issues? Did Vice President Al Gore's telephone calls from the White House possibly imply that favorable treatment would follow for those people who contributed? Consider the legal and ethical positions of the Democratic party and the firms and individuals making donations. Is this conduct allowable under the U.S. legal system? Given the needs of a legal system, should such conduct be allowed or forbidden? What are the ethical implications of such conduct? Many critics of campaign financing consider the Democratic party's actions reprehensible. Is there legal recourse, either under U.S. law or international law, against the Democratic party or the donors?

Consider these issues in the context of the chapter materials, and prepare to analyze them using the IDES model:

IDENTIFY the legal issues raised by the questions.

DEFINE all the relevant legal terms and issues involved.

ENUMERATE the legal principles associated with these issues.

SHOW BOTH SIDES by using the facts.

INTRODUCTION TO LAW

AGENDA

The Kochanowskis need to understand what type(s) of law will influence Call-Image Technology (CIT). Will CIT be subject to federal regulation? To state regulation? To administrative regulation? How will these types of regulations affect CIT? Most of the legal issues in business law involve civil law. Obviously, the family needs to concern itself with numerous civil law topics. In addition, should the family also be concerned with criminal law? How does criminal law influence business?

What happens when a person in a lawsuit asks the court for a particular action as the remedy? Why are lawyers and courts so interested in prior court decisions?

These and other questions need to be addressed as you cover the material in this chapter of the text. Be prepared! You never know when one of the Kochanowskis will need your advice.

OUTLINE

WHAT IS THE RELATIONSHIP AMONG LAW, ORDER, AND JUSTICE?

Law

This book is about understanding the law of business. Before we begin our study, however, we must answer a basic question: What is *law*? Many definitions exist, ranging from the philosophical to the practical. Plato (427–347? B.C.), a Greek philosopher who studied and wrote in the area of philosophical idealism, said law was *social control*. Sir William Blackstone (1723–1780), an English judge and legal commentator, said law was *rules specifying what was right and what was wrong*. For our purposes, however, we shall define law as *rules that must be obeyed*. People who disobey these rules are subject to sanctions that may result in their having to do something they would not voluntarily do such as paying a fine or going to jail. Our society has many kinds of rules, but not all rules can be considered "law." A rule in baseball, for example, says that after three strikes the batter is out. This rule, however, is not law. All laws are rules, but not all rules are laws. What differentiates a law from a rule? Simply stated, *enforceability* separates laws from rules. People who do not follow the rules in baseball are not arrested or taken to court. They are simply ejected from the game. In contrast, people who break laws can be held accountable for their actions through judicial imposition of sanctions.

Many different types of legal rules exist. One legal rule defines a specific way to create a legal document. A second forbids certain kinds of conduct; **criminal law** is an excellent example of this kind of legal rule. A third type of legal rule was created to compensate persons who have been injured because someone else breached a duty. For example, when an automobile manufacturer negligently builds a car, and the manufacturer's **negligence** is the direct cause of an injury, the manufacturer may have to pay the injured person monetary damages. Rules about creating legal documents, defining crimes, and specifying legal duties are generally rules about **substantive law.** Finally, rules exist that our legislative bodies and courts establish to take care of their everyday business. For example, all states have a rule concerning the maximum number of days defendants have before they must answer a civil lawsuit; this is an example of **procedural law.** The distinction between substantive law and procedural law is important and will be revisited throughout our discussion of business law.

We will view the law as a body of rules that establish a certain level of social conduct, or of *duties* that members of the society must honor. One way to view these duties is shown in Exhibit 1.1. Breaches of the laws, or duties, provide grounds for

Criminal law
The body of law dealing with public wrongs called crimes.

Negligence
Failure to do something a reasonable person would do, or doing something a reasonable and prudent person would not do.

Substantive law
The portion of law that creates and defines legal rights. It is distinct from the law that defines how laws should be enforced in court.

Procedural law
Methods of enforcing rights or obtaining compensation for the violation of rights.

EXHIBIT 1.1 Duties in a Society

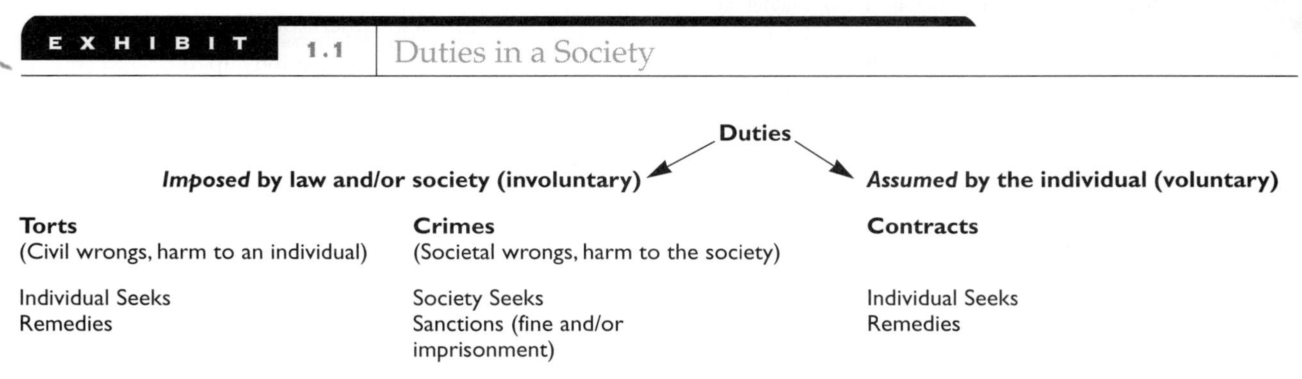

enforcement in courts of law by the party or parties who are harmed by the breaches. Enforcement consists of one of three legal remedies: (1) paying money as damages or as a fine, (2) being subject to a court order that directs a person to do or not do something (an injunction), or (3) going to jail or prison.

Order

The law usually considers an *order* as a legal command issued by a judge. But we are not concerned with order in that sense. Another definition of order is the *absence of chaos.* Chaos, as you know, is confusion and total disorganization. If the laws of a society were always followed and never broken, perfect order would result. No crime would exist, and everyone would be safe. History, however, tells us that no society with perfect order has ever existed.

The words *law* and *order* are often linked together. It is natural to link them because, when the law is followed, there will be order. However, precisely because the law is not followed all the time by all the people, perfect order does not exist. Society is always *somewhat* chaotic and disorganized. One of the reasons people do not always obey the law is that often they are not aware of what the law is. However, our legal system *presumes* that everyone *is* aware of the law and what it requires. If the society did not presume that everyone knows the law, society would be more chaotic than it already is. In that case, individuals accused of breaking the law would have an excellent defense: They could argue that they did not know they were breaking the law, and the society would then have to prove the *knowledge* of the person before sanctions could be imposed. The presumption that everyone knows the law, that "ignorance of the law is no excuse," creates an incentive for all citizens to study the law. Our educational system plays an important role in permitting us to learn the law.

Justice

Justice is a difficult term to define. When we speak of *justice,* we normally mean "fairness." Although perfect justice *is* fair, there is more to the concept of justice than merely being fair. Justice, as used in the Anglo-American legal system, refers to both a *process* and the *results* obtained in the process. Courts try to *administer* justice in conformity with the laws of the territory. From a social perspective, justice may be affected as much—or even more—by appearances than by results. Thus, lawyers are required to avoid the *appearance* of impropriety in their dealings. If the public perceives that the system is not just, they will be less likely to accept the results the system provides. This, in turn, might lead to the breaking down of the order developed in the society through its laws and their enforcement.

The ultimate goal of any legal system should be the attainment of justice by continually searching for fairness and equity. Fairness is less abstract than justice, and thus it is easier to address on a practical level. Most people have a basic concept of "fairness" that can be applied to any given situation, even though those same people may not have a similar concept of "justice." For example, when you see a bully pick on a victim, you probably believe that this conduct is not fair. In this type of situation, the conduct is clearly unfair, and it also is clearly unjust. In most situations, however, it is difficult to determine what a fair-and-just result would be. For example, suppose that a wealthy individual is accused of committing a crime. That wealthy individual hires the best attorneys he or she can find, and—in a very public trial—is found not guilty by the jury. Many people might question whether this result is *fair.* However, the process followed in the legal system assures —at least to some extent—that the result of the trial is *just.*

Different theories of justice exist, causing additional confusion. In Anglo-American law, there are two primary theories of justice: **commutative justice** and **distributive justice.** Each theory is followed in some situations, and not followed in others. By using both types of justice, the courts try to mete out a form of justice that is perceived as fair to the public, and which allows for some flexibility by the courts.

Commutative justice
The attempt to give all persons equal treatment based on the assumption that equal treatment is appropriate. Individual differences are not considered.

Distributive justice
The attempt to "distribute" justice in a way that considers inequalities among individuals.

Commutative justice attempts to give every person that which is due to him or her. It does this by placing everyone on an equal footing. In most situations, misdemeanors are punished under the concept of commutative justice. All speeders are treated the same, regardless of factors such as income, profession, type of automobile, and so forth. Contract law also operates to a meaningful extent from a commutative justice perspective.

Distributive justice attempts to treat each person as that person should be treated, taking into account the differences among people. Distributive justice recognizes that some people have more than other people, and that justice sometimes demands that some people should receive more than others. In criminal law, felony cases often use distributive justice, especially when the judge has a significant amount of discretion in sentencing. Suppose two people attempt an armed robbery, and get caught, arrested, tried, and convicted. One may be sentenced to a much longer jail term than the other. Why? Perhaps one person planned the crime, and the other person was convinced to go along. Perhaps one person is a first-time criminal, and the other has previously been convicted of five other armed robberies. Distributive justice might also be used as a philosophical basis for affirmative action programs, which attempt to make up for past unconstitutional discrimination.

The Nexus: Practicability

What we often refer to as "*the Law*" is really a system consisting of law, order, and justice. Combined, they make up the U.S. legal system. All the elements should balance in perfect equilibrium so that one element does not adversely affect any other. If we had total order, we would have very little justice; if we had total justice, we might have very little order. The *nexus* (link between elements) of the two concepts is the point of *practicability*. For example, to achieve perfect justice with respect to traffic violations, we need jury trials with counsel to ascertain precisely whether a driver did in fact violate the speed limit. However, the costs of such a venture are so prohibitive that no municipality or other local jurisdiction can afford to pay for it. As a result, most traffic courts tend to achieve "assembly line" justice rather than perfect justice.

THE LAW AS AN ARTIFICIAL LANGUAGE SYSTEM

Many terms used in the law are also used in everyday speech, but often they have totally different meanings in the law. This text will define the terms for you in the chapter, in notes in the margins, and/or in the glossary at the back of the book. The list of terms is seemingly endless: *offer, acceptance, consideration, guaranty,* and so on. Because terms may have different connotations within the law, be on guard for subtle shifts in meaning. If you are in doubt, read the passage again or check the glossary for a definition.

In addition, it is impossible to discuss the law intelligently without reference to some words that are only defined in the law. Examples of this specialized vocabulary include *estoppel, appellee, assignee, bailee, causa mortis, caveat venditor, quid pro quo,* and *codicil*. You make no assumptions when you study a foreign language; therefore, make none about the law. Remember these three rules about our artificial language system to ease your mastery of this material:

Law merchant
Those rules of trade and commerce used by merchants in England beginning in the Middle Ages.

1. Legal terms may appear to be synonyms with everyday words, but they are not.
2. Legal terms may have more than one legal meaning.
3. Some legal terms have no relation to everyday language.

THE LAW OF BUSINESS

The law of business began as a private system administered outside regular law courts in England. It was called the **law merchant** because it was administered in courts established in the various merchant guilds, commonly called Merchant Courts. Eventually, it was integrated into the English **common law** court system. Today, the law of business includes contracts, sales, negotiable instruments, secured transactions, agency, partnerships, and corporations, among other topics.

MANAGEMENT 1.1

CALL-IMAGE TECHNOLOGY

HEALTH INSURANCE FOR CIT EMPLOYEES

When the Kochanowskis first began the firm, they gave virtually no consideration to providing health insurance benefits for the employees of CIT. When the employees were family members who were covered under the family's health insurance plan, there was no need to give the matter any consideration. However, as the firm has grown and expanded, it has hired personnel who are not family members. The employees have asked Tom about a benefits package that would include health insurance coverage. They have also asked Tom to see if any health insurance coverage acquired for the employees can be made convertible into private coverage or portable to a new employer if any employee changes jobs. Tom has asked you whether the firm should provide health insurance for the employees, and what the consequences of providing—or not providing—such coverage would be. What advice will you give him?

BUSINESS CONSIDERATIONS Should the Kochanowskis provide health insurance as an employee benefit for their employees? What are the business implications—including taxation—if such coverage is provided? What are the legal implications if such coverage is not provided?

ETHICAL CONSIDERATIONS Would it be ethical for the family to provide coverage for family members, but not for other employees? What are the ethical implications of not offering insurance coverage for one's employees merely to increase profits for the firm?

WHY STUDY THE LAW OF BUSINESS?

This textbook may be called a primer in **preventive law**. The focus is how to avoid legal problems and when legal difficulties do arise, to resolve them as quickly as possible. *Remedial law* is also an important aspect of the law. When a particular problem begins to arise, courts or legislatures may anticipate its future development and attempt to resolve the problem. The law makers, however, cannot prevent every legal problem that may arise.

As a businessperson, you should understand the legal implications of what you are doing; as a consumer, you will find such understanding valuable. If you understand the issues raised here and can apply your knowledge to particular business situations, you may save yourself great expense later. In general, business is a very practical subject. As you will see, the law of business is just as practical.

Another reason to study the law of business is that it will help you develop valuable decision-making skills. It will also sensitize you to particular situations in which you may need the assistance of a lawyer. In the sale of commercial real estate, for example, you will discover that the buyer or seller needs the assistance of a lawyer *before*, rather than after, an earnest money contract is signed.

WHAT ARE THE NEEDS OF A LEGAL SYSTEM?

Common law
Unwritten law, which is based on custom, usage, and court decisions; different from statute law, which consists of laws passed by legislatures.

Preventive law
Law designed to prevent harm or wrongdoing before it occurs.

The Need to Be Reasonable

A legal system must be reasonable. The laws under which people live must be based on assumptions that are provable. These various assumptions can be proved through reliance on facts. Speeding laws are reasonable because one can prove that higher speeds on busy streets are related to higher numbers of accidents.

In addition to being reasonable, laws must be applied in a reasonable manner. A law stating that a person, for example, Juana, will have property taken away from her if she does not pay for the property is certainly reasonable; but it would be unreasonably applied if Juana stopped paying for the property and, without notice, Ramiro, the person to whom the money was owed, removed the property. Juana would first have to be told that the money was due and payable and then receive a chance to say why the money could or should not be paid. Then, if the money still was not paid, Ramiro could repossess the property through legal process.

The Need to Be Definite

The law must be definite, not vague. For example, a law stating that all contracts "for a lot of money" must be in writing would not clearly specify when a contract must be in writing, leading to confusion. The Statute of Frauds, however, states that all contracts for the sale of goods costing $500 or more must be in writing, which makes it very clear. If one has a contract for $499.99, it need not be in writing; a contract for $500.01 must be in writing.

Sometimes the law is unable to state precisely what one must do in all circumstances. In such cases, the law uses the word *reasonable* rather than set precise boundaries. If an automobile hits a pedestrian and causes injury, the pedestrian may sue the driver of the vehicle. In this situation, the law does not state that speed in excess of a particular amount is sufficient to find the driver at fault. If the only information you had was that the speed limit was 55 miles per hour and the car was going 50 miles per hour, would you find the driver at fault? Under these conditions, the law would ask the question: Was the driver's conduct reasonable under the circumstances? If so, it will be written off as an accident without civil liability; if not, the driver will be liable for any injury to the pedestrian. In the final analysis, the law provides an answer. Thus, the law is definite.

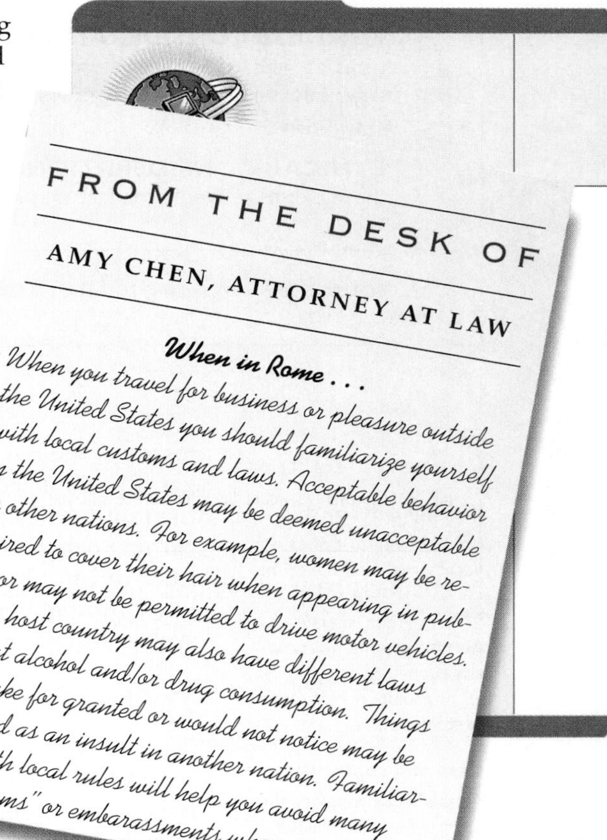
FROM THE DESK OF
AMY CHEN, ATTORNEY AT LAW

When in Rome . . .

When you travel for business or pleasure outside the United States you should familiarize yourself with local customs and laws. Acceptable behavior in the United States may be deemed unacceptable in other nations. For example, women may be required to cover their hair when appearing in public or may not be permitted to drive motor vehicles. The host country may also have different laws about alcohol and/or drug consumption. Things we take for granted or would not notice may be viewed as an insult in another nation. Familiarity with local rules will help you avoid many "problems" or embarassments when you travel.

The Need to Be Flexible

To say that the law must be both definite and flexible seems like a contradiction in terms. The law needs to be definite in order to establish a standard. In other

YOU BE THE JUDGE

Smithsonian Blocks Access to Nude Photos

The Smithsonian Institute has a collection of nude photographs taken of college freshmen from Ivy League and other elite schools. Schools involved include Harvard, Princeton, Swarthmore, Yale, Vassar, and Wellesley. Many of the universities and colleges involved required all freshmen to pose in the nude for a frontal and a profile picture. This practice began in the early 1900s. At first, the pictures were taken as part of physical education classes to study posture; poise and posture were considered important in health. The pictures were then continued as part of a research project by W. H. Sheldon who believed that there was a relationship between body shape and other traits such as intelligence. (His research is generally dismissed by scientists today.) Schools allowed Sheldon access to take pictures of their students from the 1940s through the 1960s. Many of the schools have destroyed their collections. How the Smithsonian received the collection and who is actually pictured in the Smithsonian collection is unclear.

Some prominent people were allegedly photographed during this period, including former President George Bush and President Clinton's wife, Hillary Rodham Clinton.[1] A number of people have filed suit seeking an injunction against any displays or other uses of these pictures without permission of the subject. The case has been brought in your court. How will you rule?

BUSINESS CONSIDERATIONS What should the Smithsonian or other museums or research institutes do when they receive property of this nature? Why? Should a business have a policy for handling sensitive information or photographs about its employees or customers? Who should have ownership rights in pictures such as these?

ETHICAL CONSIDERATIONS What should be the Smithsonian's ethical obligation in regard to these pictures? Would the fact that some prominent people may be included affect this ethical obligation?

SOURCE: Brigette Greenberg, *The Fresno Bee* (21 January 1995), pp. A1, A12.

Wrongful death
Unlawful death. It does not necessarily involve a crime.

Moot
Abstract; a point not properly submitted to the court for a resolution. Not capable of resolution.

Case and controversy
A case brought before the court where the plaintiff and defendant are really opposed to one another on significant issues.

respects, the law must be flexible so that it can be applied in many different *individual* situations. For example, if a family wage earner is killed by a drunk driver and the family files a **wrongful death** lawsuit, recovery would be based on the future earning capacity of the wage earner. It would not be based on a table of damages. If trees did not bend in the wind, they would break. Our legal system is like those trees: It must bend without breaking. However, because of this flexibility, our legal system loses some of its predictability.

The Need to Be Practical

Because people depend on the law to guide their actions, the law needs to be practical and oriented to action rather than to thought. However, there are thoughtful ideas supporting the legal system. The law must deal with real issues created by real people. For example, most courts will only decide real disputes between the parties. They will not decide hypothetical cases. Courts will also avoid cases where the issue is **moot** or where there is no real **case and controversy**.

The Need to Be Published

If we had the best set of laws imaginable but no one knew about them, they would be useless. In traffic law, for example, speed limits need to be posted so drivers know how fast they can legally drive. If no speed limits are posted, arbitrary enforcement would be the rule and drivers would not know how fast they can legally drive. In general, people cannot voluntarily comply with secret laws and rules. Therefore, all laws must be published. Once a law has been published, we can presume that all people know it. Consequently, ignorance of the law is no excuse.

The Need to Be Final

If a controversy exists and the legal system is used to resolve it, one thing is certain: At some point in the future, the matter will be resolved. It may not be resolved to the full satisfaction of the person who "won" the case, but it will be resolved. In this sense, the law is like a political election. On election day, someone wins and someone loses. The outcome is final. In criminal law, if the defendant wins the case in trial court, the matter ends. In most situations, the prosecutor cannot appeal. A defendant who is convicted in trial court, however, can appeal to the highest court in the state system. If the defendant does not gain a reversal, the matter ends unless the U.S. Supreme Court chooses to review the case. Exhibit 1.2 outlines the needs of a legal system.

WHAT ARE THE PURPOSES OF A LEGAL SYSTEM?

Achieving Justice

As previously discussed, justice is basically fairness. Sometimes we achieve it and sometimes we do not. In the law of business, we deal more with commutative justice—treating each person equally—than with distributive justice. In a contract, for

EXHIBIT 1.2 The Needs of a Legal System

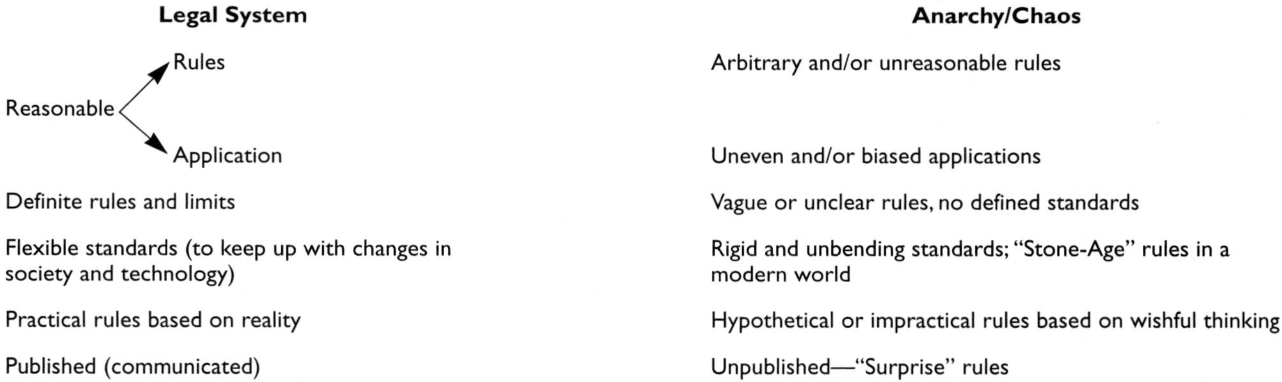

Legal System	Anarchy/Chaos
Reasonable → Rules	Arbitrary and/or unreasonable rules
Reasonable → Application	Uneven and/or biased applications
Definite rules and limits	Vague or unclear rules, no defined standards
Flexible standards (to keep up with changes in society and technology)	Rigid and unbending standards; "Stone-Age" rules in a modern world
Practical rules based on reality	Hypothetical or impractical rules based on wishful thinking
Published (communicated)	Unpublished—"Surprise" rules
Final—to put an end to a case at a particular time	Ongoing, continuous—never seeming to end

Unconscionability
Condition of being so unreasonably favorable to one party, or so one-sided, as to shock the conscience.

example, commutative justice gives each person what that person is entitled to under the contract—no more, no less. The rule of *caveat emptor* (let the buyer beware) is an example of how the law allocates risk in a business transaction. If the buyer does not thoroughly examine the goods before they are bought, the buyer cannot seek redress in the courts if what is bought does not conform to the buyer's expectations.

A trend exists, however, to introduce elements of distributive justice into the law of business. The courts, legislatures, and administrative agencies are attempting to reallocate the risks of business transactions by taking into account the status of the parties. For example, in 1976, the Federal Trade Commission established a rule concerning consumer transactions that resulted in more protection for the consumer.

Another limit placed on the doctrine of commutative justice is that of **unconscionability.** An eighteenth-century English case provides an excellent working definition of unconscionable contracts as contracts that are so unfair "no man in his senses and not under delusion would make [them] on the one hand, and no honest and fair man would accept [them] on the other."[2] Our legal system must always consider that some contracts ought not to be enforced even if they fully comply with all the rules concerning contract formation.

1.2

MANAGEMENT

CIT SECURITY ISSUES

Dan Kochanowski plans to visit Washington, D.C., next week for a conference on video technology, including a session at the White House. Anna and Tom recognize that this trip is important to CIT, but they are a little concerned because of several violent incidents at the White House over the last few years. For example, two individuals have fired shots at the White House and one individual apparently tried to crash a plane into the building. White House security and the D.C. police have strengthened security around the White House and have applied strict rules about people carrying weapons and/or acting in a suspicious manner. While Anna and Tom appreciate the extra security, they do not understand why different rules seem to apply to the White House than exist in their hometown. They have asked you to explain how or why this is permitted. What will you tell them?

BUSINESS CONSIDERATIONS Is it reasonable to have different legal rules about carrying weapons near the White House than in other areas? Should the police apply the rules differently in this area? Can a business impose different rules concerning the carrying of weapons on or around the workplace? What factors would cause a business to do so?

ETHICAL CONSIDERATIONS Is it ethical for the government to have different rules near the White House than it has in other areas? What are the ethical implications of having special rules in certain specified areas or under certain conditions?

Providing Police Power

Because justice is the ultimate purpose of a legal system, providing police power may be viewed as an intermediate purpose of a legal system. When most students see the term *police power*, they usually envision a uniformed police officer with a badge and gun. That, however, is just one part of what we call police power. Police power is inherent in all governments. This power allows for the creation and enforcement of laws designed to protect the public's health, safety, and general welfare.[3] Laws and ordinances concerning police, fire, sanitation, and social welfare departments in state and local governments stem from this power.

Maintaining Peace and the Status Quo

Ever since the days of ancient England, one of the clearest purposes of the law has been to "keep the King's peace." Most modern torts and crimes can trace their origin to a simple breaching of the King's peace. Today, laws that govern the relationships between private individuals, such as the laws governing assault, battery, trespass, and false imprisonment, are private forms of keeping the peace. Closely associated with keeping the peace is the concept of maintaining the status quo—that is, keeping things the way they are. It is natural for the law to maintain the status quo unless changing things will benefit society. In cases where irreparable injury is alleged, it is possible, upon a proper showing, to obtain a preliminary **injunction** from a court that will maintain the status quo until the matter is finally resolved.

Injunction
A court order prohibiting a person or persons from doing a certain thing or, on the other hand, ordering that some particular thing be done.

Providing Answers

On a philosophical level, the law should be just; but on a practical level, it should provide answers. Sometimes the answers the law provides are not satisfactory. If Melanie sues Troy, a neighbor, because Troy is allegedly creating a **nuisance** on his property, and Troy wins the case in the trial court, then Melanie can appeal the decision to the next higher court. In most states this higher court is called an **appellate court.** If an appellate court rules in favor of Troy, a further appeal may be taken to the state's highest court. In that court, Melanie may win and thereby receive a satisfactory answer. But whether she wins or loses, she and Troy will each be provided with an answer to the matter on completion of the appellate process.

Nuisance
Wrongs that arise from the unreasonable or unlawful use of a person's own property.

Appellate court
A court that has the power to review the decisions of lower courts.

Providing Protection

The law protects all kinds of interests. You have already seen that the law concerns itself with protecting individuals. The tort law of assault and battery is a classic example of protection of the individual. The law also protects persons less conspicuously when it protects their **civil rights.** Civil rights laws are extremely important in modern litigation and have their historical background in the first 10 amendments to the U.S. Constitution. (Refer to the Constitution in the Appendix A at the end of this book; it is worthwhile for you to refresh your memory about its features.) Persons are protected in the free exercise of their speech, are free to choose or not to choose a religion, can peacefully assemble, and may petition their government for a redress of grievances (a rarely used freedom). The right to keep and bear arms, the right to be free of unreasonable searches and seizures, the right against compulsory self-incrimination, the right to a grand jury, the right against double jeopardy, the right to a jury trial, and the right to bail are a few of the more important civil rights contained in the U.S. Constitution.

Civil rights
The rights in the first 10 amendments to the U.S. Constitution (the Bill of Rights) and due process and equal protection under the Fourteenth Amendment.

The government is also in the business of protecting *itself*. A government's self-protection is an ancient right that goes back to Roman law. It is based on the concept that if the **sovereign** is *truly* sovereign, it cannot be attacked legally. Because the sovereign is, by definition, supreme, it cannot be subject to attack nor can it be held liable to its inferiors. Thus, the rule of *sovereign immunity* was developed, shielding the sovereign from lawsuits against it, but permitting the sovereign to file lawsuits. This rule still stands, to some extent, although the federal government and many states have passed special statutes allowing suits for torts to be brought against them.

Sovereign
Above or superior to all others; that from which all authority flows.

Finally, the law is concerned with the protection of property. All property is characterized as either personal or real property. *Personal property* is all property with the exception of real property. In general, if property is movable, it is personal property. *Real property*, on the other hand, is land and whatever is affixed to land, such as a house. However, personal property can have dual meanings in law. It may also mean property that is owned by individuals, as opposed to public property that is owned by the government or the community. Our legal system has a variety of laws that protect both types of property.

Enforcing Intent

The law of contracts is based on *freedom of contract*. It is this rule that allows each of us to be our own "legislator" to a limited extent. We make our own "laws" of conduct, as long as the contracts into which we enter do not violate the general principles of contract law. For example, you may wish to enter into a contract with a supplier of goods. You may want to make the contract today so that it will immediately bind the other party. Perhaps you have found a good price and do not think you will find a better one. Your problem, however, is that you do not presently have the money to pay for the goods, but you know that you can easily resell them for an immediate cash profit within 10 days after delivery. You should, therefore, seek a provision in the contract stating that the buyer will pay the seller for the goods 11 days after receipt of the goods. Of course, if you cannot resell the goods within the 10 days as anticipated, you will have a financial problem. This is more a question of business judgment, however, than of law.

Providing Rehabilitation

Both criminal law and civil law are directed toward rehabilitation. Criminal law should, among other things, rehabilitate the criminal. Civil law is also involved in rehabilitation to some extent. Contract law provides rehabilitation for a party harmed by a breach of the contract. Tort law provides for a form of rehabilitation in the assessment of damages for the victim of the tort. The federal bankruptcy law is directed toward the rehabilitation of debtors.

Facilitating Commercial Transactions

One of the major characteristics of the U.S. legal system is that it facilitates commercial transactions. For example, if sellers demanded cash to sell an automobile, the number of automobiles sold in the United States would be reduced by millions. Our national economy is still very reliant on the automobile industry. The prosperity of the steel, energy, and transportation industries are directly related to that of the automobile. Thus, reducing the number of automobiles sold could be harmful to the national economy. Accordingly, the extension of credit for the purchase of automobiles greatly facilitates trade. The use of checks and credit cards also accelerates commercial transactions. The taking of a security interest in goods expedites trade to persons who might otherwise not be in a financial position to make the purchase. The U.S. legal system fosters free and open competition and facilitates trade. This characteristic of the legal system has done much to contribute to the business and financial power of the United States. Exhibit 1.3 outlines the purposes of a legal system.

JURISPRUDENCE

Jurisprudence is the study of the science or philosophy underlying the law. In Latin, jurisprudence means the "wisdom of the law." However, there are really many different "wisdoms" of the law reflected in a number of different philosophical views about how the law developed and what role it should play in society. The law continues to change, and knowledge of the legal philosophies will improve your

EXHIBIT 1.3 The Purposes of a Legal System

Purpose	Reason
Achieving justice	To provide "justice" so that the needs of the members of society are addressed.
Providing police power	To provide a social structure so that "wronged" individuals do not have to resort to self-help; to give society control of the system.
Maintaining peace and the status quo	To provide each member of society with a feeling of personal security and a structure on which each individual can rely.
Providing answers	To achieve practical justice; lets the members of society know what is expected of them and what they may reasonably expect from others.
Providing protection	To define and establish social guidelines and protect the entire society if any of these guidelines are not followed and obeyed.
Enforcing intent	To provide some method for permitting private agreements and for ensuring that these agreements are honored or enforced.
Providing rehabilitation	To allow a person who violates the guidelines of the society a second chance; recognizes that anyone can make a mistake.
Facilitating commercial transactions	To support freedom of contract and private ownership of property; each of these concepts encourages and promotes business transactions.

ability to understand the law and predict future trends. Here is a brief introduction to some of the philosophical approaches.

Natural Law Theory

The *natural law* theory believes that the law should be based on what is correct and moral. There are certain moral and legal values that do not change because their source is absolute. People use reason to discover these moral and legal values. Once the natural law is discovered, it nullifies any contradictory law created by humans.

This theory rests on some significant assumptions—the world is perceived as a rational order with values and purposes built into it; the laws of nature describe how things should be; and humans should use reason to grasp what should be done. Many early Greek philosophers were natural law theorists. In the history of Christian thought, the dominant theory of ethics has been the theory of natural law,[4] best exemplified by St. Thomas Aquinas.[5] The natural law theory focuses on fairness and justice, even though some disorder will result when individuals decide that the written law is not "natural law."

Legal Positivism

The *legal positivist* approach believes that the law is the result of lawmaking by a legitimate government. In the United States, this is primarily executive orders, legislation, court opinions, and administrative bodies. Under this theory, legality and morality are separated. The positive law approach promotes social stability and the supremacy of written laws.

Precedents
Decided cases that establish legal authority for later cases.

Sociological Theory

The *sociological* theory believes that the law is a technique to shape social behavior. The role of prior law in the form of **precedents** is minimized. The law's source should be contemporary opinion and customs. In creating statutes or court decisions, the maker should record community interests; familiarize himself or herself with the community standards and mores; and make a decision based on these standards. This theory has been criticized because law becomes less predictable given that contemporary opinion changes rapidly. In a court decision relying on this theory, the judge may discuss sociological factors and current customs.

Historical Theory

The *historical* theory believes that the law is primarily a system of customs and social traditions that have developed over time. Each nation develops its own individual consensus about what the law should be. The law is an evolving system, and precedents have a significant role. Legitimacy is obtained from the historical will of the people of a nation.

Law and Economics Theory

Law and economics theory applies classical economic theory and empirical methods to explain legal doctrines and to predict judicial decisions. This theory is commonly used in areas such as torts, contracts, and property law. The legal system should be viewed as a system to promote the efficient allocation of resources in society. Critics contend that this theory tends to be politically conservative and generally rests on one type of economic philosophy to the exclusion of others. Another criticism is that the theory could be descriptive and explain what the law is, but it is not helpful as a prescriptive theory. The law and economics theory is closely allied with the Chicago school, where it originated.

Feminist Legal Theory

The *feminist legal* theory believes that the law does not treat women equally. Followers assert that the current legal system is dominated by men, and that women are often victimized and their perspectives ignored. Thus, the law should consider the female perspective. Workplace behavior that may not seem harassing to men, for example, may seem harassing to women, and the law should address this accordingly.

Critical Legal Studies Theory

The *critical legal studies,* or *CRITS,* theory believes that in order to accomplish social and political change, the law must be examined and critiqued. The current law is a combination of legal and nonlegal beliefs that is used to maintain the status quo, especially in the political and economic spheres. This is accomplished by convincing others that those in power should remain in power. The legal system, including legal education, is a deceptive social mechanism for the preservation of power by those who currently have it. People can only free themselves of this perspective by critically examining these beliefs. Generally, people who subscribe to the CRITS view wish to overturn the status quo.

WHAT ARE THE SOURCES OF LAW IN THE U.S. LEGAL SYSTEM?

The U.S. legal system is based on the Constitution, treaties, statutes, ordinances, administrative regulations, common law, case law, and equity. Although each of the elements is separate, the elements are interdependent; together they constitute our system. These elements must be thought of as a system, since a change in one element cannot be considered in isolation. Such a change will affect one or more parts of the system. In a civil rights suit, a person may allege a violation of constitutional rights (Fourteenth Amendment), a statutory right (Civil Rights Act of 1964), an administrative regulation (Equal Employment Opportunity Commission guideline), past decisions of the court (***stare decisis***), and equity (if all else fails, the person should win because it is fair). The important thing to remember is that all the parts of the legal system are interconnected and that the whole is more than the sum of the parts.

Stare decisis
To abide by, or adhere to, decided cases; policy of courts to stand by decided cases and not to disturb a settled point of law.

Constitutions

A *constitution* is the fundamental law of a nation. It may be written or unwritten. The British constitution is said to be unwritten. Clearly, the U.S. Constitution *is* written. (See Appendix A to this text.) It allocates the powers of government and also sets limits on those powers. Our founding fathers knew that all tyrants had two powers: the power of the purse and the power of the sword. The Constitution places the power of the purse exclusively with Congress and the power of the sword with the Executive branch. Our third branch of government, the Judiciary, has neither the power of the purse nor the power of the sword, and yet it has the power to decide the constitutionality of the laws passed by Congress. In the case of *Marbury* v. *Madison*,[6] the U.S. Supreme Court for the first time applied the doctrine of **judicial review.** That case held that the Supreme Court has the power to decide whether laws passed by Congress comply with the Constitution. If they do not, they are unconstitutional and thus of no force or effect. We will discuss the unique nature of the Constitution, and the *Marbury* v. *Madison* case, in Chapter 4.

Judicial review
The power of the courts to say what the law is.

Our states also have constitutions, and they are the fundamental laws of those states. The U.S. Constitution, however, is the supreme legal document in the United States and thus will take precedence over state constitutions.

Treaties

Treaties, which are formal agreements between two or more nations, are the only elements of our legal system that do not stem from the Constitution. Treaties are made, not with the authority of the Constitution, but under the authority of the United States. This difference is important because the power to make a treaty is a function of sovereignty and not one of a constitution. In most cases, treaties require enabling legislation to be passed by Congress. The case of *Missouri* v. *Holland*[7] established that statutes passed in accordance with a valid treaty cannot be declared unconstitutional. Once made, treaties also become the supreme law of the land.

Statutes

Statutes are the acts of legislative bodies. They command or prohibit the doing of something. The word *statute* is preferred when one is referring to a legislative act to distinguish it from such other "laws" as ordinances, regulations, common law, and case law. The best example of state statutory law is found in the Uniform Commercial Code (UCC) (see Appendix B). All 50 states, the District of Columbia, and the U.S. Virgin Islands have adopted at least portions of the law. The UCC is very important and, accordingly, is the subject of many of the chapters contained in this book. The UCC covers the following subjects: sales, leases, negotiable instruments, bank deposits and collections, fund transfers, letters of credit, bulk transfers, documents of title, investment securities, and secured transactions.

Immemorial antiquity
Goes back to earliest memory.

Dictum
An observation or remark by a judge, which is not necessarily involved in the case or essential to its resolution. An aside written by the judge.

Ordinances

Ordinances are laws passed by municipal bodies. Cities, towns, and villages, if incorporated, have the power to establish laws for the protection of the public's health, safety, and welfare. These entities are to be distinguished from counties, which generally do not have legislative power. Counties usually have the power to enforce state laws within their boundaries.

Administrative Regulations

Administrative regulations are rules promulgated by governmental bodies created by the legislative branch of government such as the Federal Trade Commission (FTC) on the federal level and an insurance commission on the state level. These bodies have unusual powers, which will be discussed in Chapter 39. The rules and regulations of these entities have the full force and effect of law.

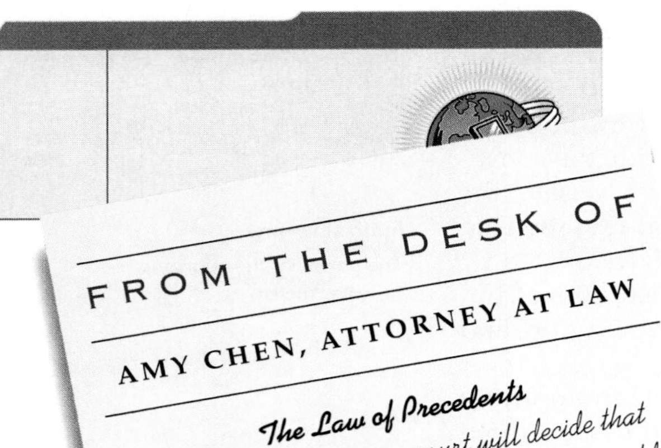

FROM THE DESK OF
AMY CHEN, ATTORNEY AT LAW

The Law of Precedents

Remember that sometimes a court will decide that precedents should be changed. However, it would be unfair to change the precedents for the parties currently before the court because they have relied on existing law. The court will then "hint" that a change is coming and that the next time the court examines the issue, a different result will occur. This, generally, is followed by a detailed discussion of what the new rule will be. Although this discussion will "technically" be considered ***dictum****, it provides important information about the future direction of the court.*

Common Law and Law Merchant

Common law consists of "those principles and rules of action, relating to the government and security of persons and property, which derive their authority solely from usages and customs of **immemorial antiquity**, or from the judgments and decrees of the courts recognizing, affirming, and enforcing such usages and customs."[8] *Law merchant* is the body of rules used by merchants, based on usage and custom; this law is the predecessor of the modern law of business.

Case Law

Case law derives from the many reported cases emanating from federal and state courts. Quite often the judges must interpret statutes in order to apply them to actual cases and controversies. These interpretations place what lawyers call a "judicial gloss" on the statute. You will not fully understand a particular statute until you have read not only the statute but also the cases that have interpreted it. *Case law*, then, is the law as pronounced by judges.

Stare decisis is an ancient doctrine that means the question has been decided. For example, if a particular legal point is well settled in a certain jurisdiction, a future case with substantially the same facts will be decided in accordance with the principle that has already been decided. This is one of the reasons that lawyers do a great deal of legal research. The doctrine of *stare decisis* is also called precedents. Even though a legal matter has been settled, it does not mean the legal system must remain static.

A precedent remains in effect until it is changed. (Precedents do not play a major role in all legal systems.) It must be remembered that the legal system evolves. Lawyers and petitioners in court are constantly asking to have precedents changed, and sometimes they are successful. Occasionally, the court will change or modify the precedents. When a court changes the precedents, it will generally support this decision with one of these three reasons:

1. The prior rule is out of date and not appropriate to present-day society.
2. The prior case is distinguishable because the facts are different in one or more significant details.
3. The judge or justice who made the prior ruling was incorrect or wrong.

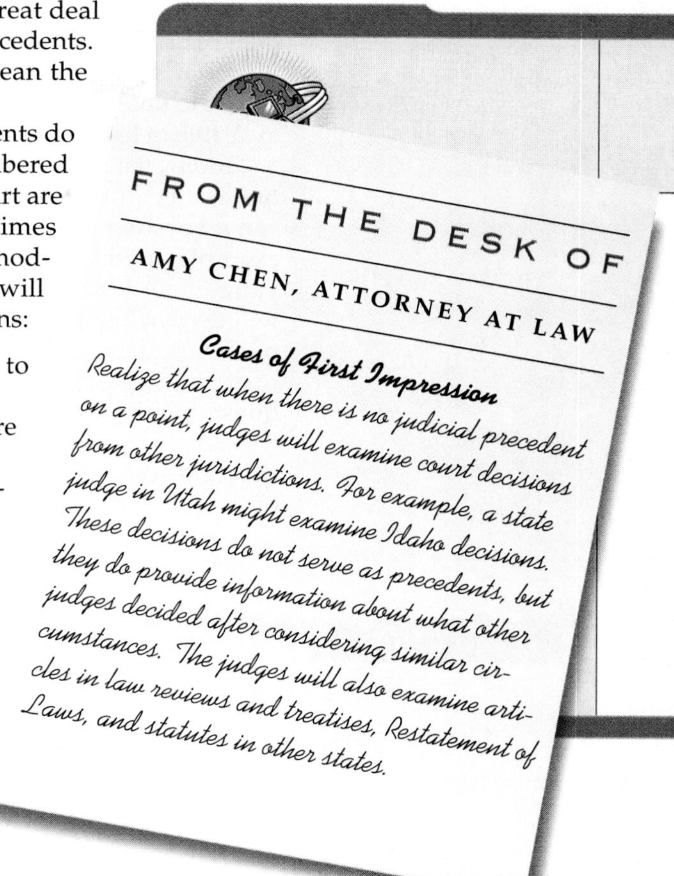

FROM THE DESK OF
AMY CHEN, ATTORNEY AT LAW
Cases of First Impression
Realize that when there is no judicial precedent on a point, judges will examine court decisions from other jurisdictions. For example, a state judge in Utah might examine Idaho decisions. These decisions do not serve as precedents, but they do provide information about what other judges decided after considering similar circumstances. The judges will also examine articles in law reviews and treatises, Restatement of Laws, and statutes in other states.

When a court follows precedent it is striving to make the law *definite*, satisfying one of the needs of a legal system. However, as times and situations change, courts need to be able to change. The law would not be *flexible*, another need of a legal system, if precedents could never be changed. Courts have a difficult time balancing these two needs—definite and flexible—in applying the law within the area of precedents. *Brown* v. *Board of Education*[9] is an example of a court overturning precedents. In that case, the U.S. Supreme Court decided, contrary to prior decisions, that providing separate schools for black and white children was unconstitutional.

Judges may be reluctant to state that the prior ruling was in error, especially if they participated in the prior ruling. It is easier to admit that someone else made an error. Judges *sometimes* do admit that the rule they fashioned earlier is not the preferred response to a particular legal problem.

An opportunity to "make law," as it is called, occurs when jurisdictions are in conflict over a point of law. For example, many states are divided into various judicial districts, and each of these districts may issue written legal opinions. If two or more districts have published conflicting opinions on a particular point, and the state's supreme court has *not* issued an opinion on the point, the time is ripe for the creation of a new rule, statewide, that will resolve the matter once and for all. Until the statewide rule is created, however, each court creates precedents for itself and for any courts directly under it. When there are no prior court decisions on a point of law, the court may state that the case is one of **first impression**.

First impression
Case is presented to the court for an initial decision when the case presents an entirely novel question of law for the court's decision. It is not governed by any existing precedent.

Equity

Equity is defined as a body of rules applied to legal controversies when no adequate remedy at law exists. These rules are based not on technicalities but rather on the principles outlined by Justinian during his reign as the Byzantine emperor of Rome

(A.D. 527–565): "to live honestly, to harm nobody, [and] to render to every man his due." These rules were developed outside the common law courts in England by an officer of the King called the chancellor. The primary reasons for their development were the unfair decisions made by the law courts and the limited types of remedies available in law courts.

Today, the rules of law and equity are joined into one system of law. The injunction is an equitable remedy, but before U.S. courts will issue an injunction, the person requesting it must show proof that the remedy at law would be inadequate. For example, if your neighbors are burning rubber tires on their property and the prevailing wind carries the obnoxious odor directly across your property, their action will destroy the peaceful use and enjoyment of your land. In general, no amount of monetary damages would be sufficient to allow them to continue to burn rubber tires. In that case, you would not have an adequate remedy at law, and you could request that the court issue an injunction to stop your neighbors from burning those tires. In a larger sense, however, equity may be viewed as a doctrine that results in the legal system's adhering to the principle of fairness. Exhibit 1.4 summarizes some of the differences between law and equity.

EXHIBIT 1.4 Distinctions Between Actions in Law and in Equity[a]

Characteristic	In Law	In Equity[b]
Type of relief	Money to compensate plaintiff for his or her losses	Action, either in the form of ordering the defendant to do or not to do something, or in the form of a decree about the status of something[cd]
Nature of proceeding	More restricted by precedents	More flexible and less restricted by precedents, supposed to create equity (justice)
Time limit for filing lawsuit	Applicable period fixed by the statute of limitations[e]	A reasonable period of time as determined by the judge on a case-by-case basis[f]
Decider of fact	Jury trial, if requested by a party	No jury trial, judge decides the facts[g]
Enforcing a decision	Plaintiff may begin an execution of the judgment[h]	Plaintiff may begin contempt proceedings if the defendant does not perform as directed; defendant may be placed in jail and/or fined[i]

[a]Actions at law and those in equity are no longer as distinct as they once were. As a result, many states allow "combined" trials with issues of law and issues of equity being tried together.

[b]Traditionally, courts of equity were called courts of chancery, and the judge was called the chancellor.

[c]Common equitable remedies include injunction, specific performance of a contract, rescission of a contract, and reformation (correction or rewriting of) a contract.

[d]Courts would prefer to award monetary damages. Equitable relief is only granted when the plaintiff can show the court that money would be inadequate.

[e]The statute of limitations period will depend on the state and the type of lawsuit. It will be a fixed period.

[f]If the plaintiff has waited too long to file suit under the circumstances, the judge will apply the doctrine of laches and the suit will be dismissed.

[g]Some states permit the use of an advisory jury.

[h]In an execution, the clerk of the court issues a formal document and the sheriff seizes the defendant's money and/or other property. If property is seized, the sheriff will sell it and use the proceeds to pay the plaintiff.

[i]The court is authorized to place the defendant in jail until he or she complies (or agrees to comply) with the court decree.

HOW IS THE LAW CLASSIFIED?

Federal Versus State Law

Our legal system is divided into two branches: federal and state. American lawyers must learn not only the law of their states but the law of the federal courts as well. In addition, lawyers should know the majority rule. The *majority rule* is simply the rule that most states have adopted. Quite often, a *minority rule,* which a smaller number of states follow, also exists. Rarely, if ever, do the states agree on all aspects of a law. Exhibit 1.5 outlines the sources of the U.S. legal system.

Common Versus Statutory Law

As discussed earlier, the legal system consists of both common and statutory laws. Judges in the United States and England generally have the power to "make law" by interpreting statutes or applying precedents, and those interpretations become "common" law. Judges also apply the statutory law. Statutory law refers to legislative enactments, the statutes passed by the legislative bodies of the state. Common law is "unwritten" law, law developed over time by judicial action. Common law fills the gaps where other sources of law do not cover a particular topic. Statutory enactments override common law, filling the gap with a statutory provision and eliminating the need for unwritten coverage.

EXHIBIT 1.5 The Sources of the U.S. Legal System

Authority	Source	Definition
F, S	Constitution	Supreme law of the land; fundamental basis of domestic law.
F	Treaties	Not based on the Constitution; formal agreements between nations; fundamental basis of international law/relations.
F, S	Statutes	Acts of the legislature; control of domestic conduct; subject to limits imposed by the Constitution.
S	Ordinances	Laws passed by municipal bodies and designed to control purely local problems, subject to any limits imposed by statutes or by the Constitution.
F, S	Administrative Regulations	Acts of administrative agencies; control of specific areas of conduct; subject to any limits imposed by statutes or by the Constitution.
S	Common Law and Law Merchant	Principles and rules that have developed over time and are based on custom and usage; provide rules when statutes and the Constitution do not.
F, S	Case Law	Precedent, established interpretations of areas of law in which the courts define what the law is.
F, S	Equity	Special rules and relief when "the law" does not provide a proper and/or adequate remedy.

Legend: F = federal; S = state

Civil Versus Criminal Law

The U.S. legal system also separates civil and criminal law. *Civil law* is private law wherein one person sues another person. *Criminal law* is public law in which a government entity files charges against a person. For example, if a person becomes violently abusive and attacks another individual, and thus inflicts bodily harm on the innocent individual, the district attorney, as the representative of a government entity, may prosecute the attacker for assault. If convicted, the attacker may go to jail or prison. In addition, the person who was injured may sue the attacker in court for money damages. The additional suit would not constitute **double jeopardy** or its civil law equivalent, **res judicata**, since two different theories of action exist: civil and criminal.

1.3

MANAGEMENT

CALL-IMAGE TECHNOLOGY

LOBBYING GOVERNMENT FOR CALL-IMAGING

A number of citizens are concerned that products, such as the Call-Image phone, will lead to the invasion of privacy for many customers who are merely using the telephone in their own homes. These citizens have lobbied members of the state legislature demanding a statutory approach to guarantee the privacy of people who own Call-Image or similar videophones. Responding to complaints from organized consumer groups and individuals, the state legislature is considering the enactment of a statute that prohibits the marketing of videophones in the state unless they have an on/off switch for the video function. CIT is currently developing such an on/off switch, but has not yet perfected it. As a result, the switch is not available for Call-Image phones, and may not be available for quite some time. CIT would obviously like to stop the state legislature from enacting this proposed legislation because such a statute would prevent CIT from selling any of its existing phones in the state. CIT and the Kochanowski family members wonder what they can do, and turn to you for advice. What advice can you give them?

BUSINESS CONSIDERATIONS What options are available to CIT under these circumstances? What can—or should—a business do when it feels that proposed legislation will have a serious impact on the firm's profitability?

ETHICAL CONSIDERATIONS Would it be ethical for a firm to attempt to influence potential legislation? What ethical considerations would come into play should a firm decide to attempt to influence members of the legislature?

Substantive Versus Procedural Law

Substantive law deals with rights and duties given or imposed by the legal system. *Procedural law* is devoted to how those rights and duties are enforced. For example, the law of contracts is substantive law. The law of pleadings describes the steps used to enforce those rights or duties. A controversy over the mental ability to form a valid contract is a substantive matter, but how one goes about getting the dispute into a court is a matter of procedure. Where one files the lawsuit, what must be alleged, how one notifies the defendant, and how long the defendant has to answer the allegations are all examples of procedural law. This book is devoted primarily to *substantive* law.

Legal Systems in Other Countries

Sometimes we assume that all countries have the same or similar legal systems. This ethnocentric view can result in a rude shock when a U.S. citizen traveling in a foreign country continues to act the same as he or she would act at home. The U.S. citizen may find that behavior that is tolerated in the United States constitutes a crime in a foreign country, and that many of the protections he or she expects in the United States do not apply abroad.

With the exception of England, most of Europe, including France, Germany, and Sweden, follows civil law. In this context *civil law* means that the legal system relies on statutory law. The statutes are grouped into codes, and the codes are administered by judges. Judges, therefore, do not make law to the degree that they do in the United States. The judge relies primarily on the code and secondarily on statutes passed by the legislative bodies.

Until recently, the former Union of Soviet Socialist Republics (U.S.S.R.) followed a unique version of civil law. Owing to its socialist philosophy, private ownership of property was limited. The primary goal of this legal system was to preserve state ownership of all means of production. Consequently, the Soviet Union's law primarily consisted of public law such as criminal law. The law of property, contracts, and business organizations did not play a role. Many of the former Soviet republics are now beginning to engage in privatization. Consequently, a body of private law is being developed as these countries move toward a more traditional civil law system.

In addition, the U.S. legal system is based on the law of precedents previously discussed in this chapter. However, there are other countries, such as Mexico, where precedent is not important. Each judge does his or her best to fashion a fair result in the particular case before the court. In civil law systems, precedent is not significant. In the European Union (EU), the role of precedents is increasing. Decisions made by the EU Court of Justice become precedents in all the member countries. Although the EU is primarily a code system, it is moving toward the use of precedents and more of a common law approach.

There are a number of legal systems based on religious teachings. The Hindu legal system is one example. Their system is a personal and religious law system which states that Hindus should act in accordance with this law wherever they live. The Hindu system has been recorded in law books called *smitris*. Most Hindu law applies to family matters. Anglo-Hindu law evolved in most Hindu countries while they were British colonies, where judges were applying a combination of English and Hindu laws. India replaced Anglo-Hindu law with a civil code primarily based on Hindu law when it gained its independence from England.

Muslims believe in Islamic law or *Shari'a*, which is based on the Koran and other religious writings. Saudi Arabia relies almost exclusively on Islamic law. Other countries apply Islamic law in some areas, such as family law, and supplement it with secular law. There are also legal systems in the Catholic and Jewish faiths.

Double jeopardy
A rule of criminal law that states that a person will not be tried in court more than once by the same government for the same criminal offense.

Res judicata
A rule of civil law that states that a person will not be sued more than once by the same party for the same civil wrong.

THE ATTORNEY–CLIENT RELATIONSHIP

Legal issues are critical in all businesses, even though some businesses are subjected to more government regulation than others. Whether the business is faced with litigation or is practicing preventive law and attempting to avoid legal problems, attorneys can be important "partners" in a business. One of the primary purposes of this text is to assist you in speaking intelligently with your attorney and to enable you to more fully understand what he or she says to you.

Hints for Hiring an Attorney

Attorneys are generally paid a flat fee (a one-time fee), an hourly fee (based on an hourly rate), or a contingent fee (based on a percentage of the settlement or award.) Contingent fees are not permitted in criminal cases; in some states, they may be disallowed for other types of cases too. The following should be helpful when you need to hire an attorney:

1. Generate a list of potential lawyers by asking personal and/or business contacts. Try to find friends who have had a similar type of legal difficulty. Use *Matindale-Hubbell* legal directories or directories maintained by your state bar association to discover additional information about the lawyers on your list.
2. Shop around and interview more than one attorney.
3. When interviewing, ask lawyers about their experience in this particular area of the law. Also ask, What are the probable outcomes of your dispute? How long will the legal matter take?
4. Find out how the attorney is going to charge and what services you as the client will receive for the fee. For example, it is common in litigation for a fee to include a trial, but no appellate work. Will a contingent fee be based on the award before or after expenses? If the attorney is going to charge an hourly rate, what is the smallest unit of time that is used for billing? In other words, will you be billed for 10 minutes or 15 minutes for a simple phone call to the lawyer? What is a realistic estimate for the total bill and expenses? You should realize that it is more difficult to make a realistic estimate for some types of cases than others, particularly when the workload may depend on the decisions of the opponent. How often will the attorney send you a bill? Will the attorney put the estimate in writing? Will the attorney enter into a written contract with a client?
5. Ask whether the fee will include private investigators, filing fees, expert witnesses, other attorneys, paralegals, photocopies, and so on. Generally, it does not. What other types of fees and expenses does the lawyer anticipate?
6. Find out if you can take steps to reduce the legal fees. For example, you may be able to do some tasks yourself.
7. Ask if the attorney will need additional information from you.
8. Find out the attorney's procedure for handling billing disputes. Will the attorney charge for the additional hours spent on the billing dispute? Will the attorney agree to mandatory arbitration of the fee if the parties cannot resolve the dispute?
9. What are the alternatives to litigation? (See Chapter 7.) Does the attorney recommend any of them for this case? Does the attorney know any mediators or arbitrators who would be appropriate?
10. Try to discern whether client complaints have been filed against this attorney. *Often* this information is made public and is available from the disciplinary agency for the state. This is generally the state bar association or the state supreme court.
11. Select the approach you plan to take with the case and choose a lawyer whose style is similar to the approach you selected. Do you want someone who is extremely aggressive or more conciliatory?
12. Do *not* hire an attorney who is unable to communicate effectively with you or is unwilling to answer questions.

Clients are sometimes dissatisfied with the services provided by their attorneys. In 1994, *Consumer Reports* surveyed members regarding their experiences with attorneys from 1991–1994 and discovered that of the 30,000 respondents, clients involved in adversarial cases were more likely to be displeased with the legal services they received than those involved in nonadversarial matters. For example, 27 percent of the people who had hired an attorney for an adversarial matter were dissatisfied with the work performed by the lawyer. The survey noted that *some* clients were unhappy

http:// RESOURCES FOR BUSINESS LAW STUDENTS

NAME	RESOURCES	WEB ADDRESS
The Legal Information Institute (LII)	LII, maintained by the Cornell Law School, provides Supreme Court decisions, opinions of the New York Court of Appeals, a hypertext version of the full U.S. Code and Uniform Commercial Code (UCC), treaties, statutes, and other legal documents.	http://www.law.cornell.edu/
Thomas: Legislative Information on the Internet	The U.S. Congress, via Thomas (for Thomas Jefferson) provides news and information on Congress, bills before Congress (text, summary, and status), the *Congressional Record*, and committee information.	http://thomas.loc.gov/
FedLaw	FedLaw, maintained by the U.S. General Services Administration (GSA), includes federal laws and regulations, executive orders, and Office of Management and Budget (OMB) circulars and bulletins.	http://www.legal.gsa.gov/
StateLaw	StateLaw, maintained by the Washburn School of Law, provides links for state legislative and governmental information—including court cases and statutes—as well as local information.	http://lawlib.wuacc.edu/washlaw/uslaw/statelaw.html
West's Legal Directory	West's Legal Directory, updated daily, offers over 800,000 profiles of lawyers and law firms in the United States and Canada, including international offices.	http://www.wld.com/

with an aspect of their case, including the manner in which the attorney expedited the resolution of the matter, kept them informed, charged fair fees and expenses, protected their rights and financial interests, informed them early about costs, and was polite and considerate.[10]

Resolving Problems with Legal Counsel

If a problem does arise from the attorney–client relationship, the client should first try to resolve the problem with the attorney and/or the law firm. Begin with a clear letter expressing your concern and what you would like the attorney to do. If the problem is not resolved at this stage, you can fire the attorney and hire another. However, it may be costly for the replacement to become familiar with the dispute, and replacing an attorney may postpone the ultimate resolution of the legal matter.

If you believe the attorney breached one of the codes of ethics, you can report him or her to the disciplinary board. The American Bar Association (ABA) has a code of ethics for attorneys; however, most states also have their own codes of ethics. Copies are usually available from the library or the state Bar Association or disciplinary board. Bar associations or disciplinary boards will not provide legal assistance to you, but may investigate and take punitive action against the attorney, if appropriate. Most states have established a fund for clients who lose money because the attorney takes it from them and uses it inappropriately (e.g., embezzles it). Practicing attorneys in the state are generally required to pay into the fund. As a last resort, you can sue the attorney for malpractice; however, then you will have to hire another attorney and begin a new litigation. In addition, it may be difficult for you to prove your damages, especially if you lost a lawsuit while the first attorney was representing you. Then the defendant will argue that even with another attorney, you still would have lost the suit.

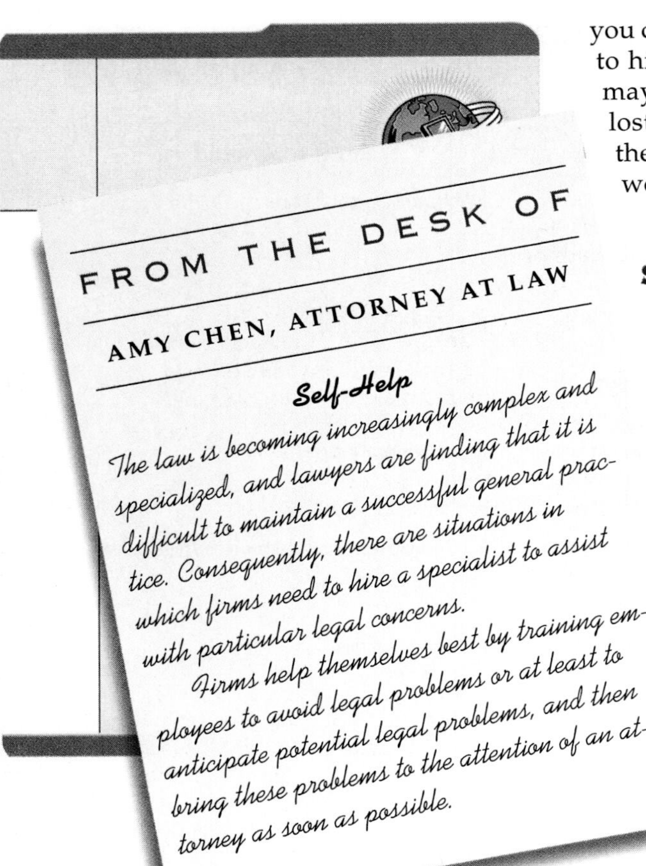

FROM THE DESK OF
AMY CHEN, ATTORNEY AT LAW
Self-Help
The law is becoming increasingly complex and specialized, and lawyers are finding that it is difficult to maintain a successful general practice. Consequently, there are situations in which firms need to hire a specialist to assist with particular legal concerns.
Firms help themselves best by training employees to avoid legal problems or at least to anticipate potential legal problems, and then bring these problems to the attention of an attorney as soon as possible.

SUMMARY

Law consists of rules that must be observed. These rules must be obeyed because they are enforceable in courts of law. Order is the absence of chaos. Our legal system strives to create and to maintain order. Justice is fairness. Commutative justice seeks to treat each person the same regardless of circumstances. Distributive justice seeks to vary treatment as appropriate in the situation. The goal of distributive justice is to balance the unequal distributions that exist in society. Our legal system seeks constantly to balance law, order, and justice. Its ultimate goal is to achieve equilibrium.

The law is an artificial language system. It includes everyday words but they have technical meanings. The law also uses words that are unique to the law. The law of business includes contracts, sales, negotiable instruments, secured transactions, agency, partnerships, and corporations. By studying the law of business, you will learn how to avoid legal problems. If legal problems should develop, however, this knowledge will sensitize you to their ramifications. As a result, you will know when an attorney should be consulted.

A legal system needs to be reasonable, definite, practical, published, and final. A legal system should be directed toward achieving justice. It does so by properly utilizing police power; by keeping the peace or maintaining the status quo when irreparable injury is threatened; by providing answers; by protecting people, property, and government; by enforcing intent; by rehabilitating people; and by facilitating commercial transactions.

Our legal system is like a three-dimensional chess game in which a move in one subsystem can affect other subsystems. The sources of the U.S. legal system are constitutions, treaties, statutes, ordinances, administrative regulations, common law, the law merchant, case law, and equity. The law is a multidimensional system, including common and statutory law, civil and criminal law, and substantive and procedural law. The legal system is also composed of two branches—federal law and state law.

DISCUSSION QUESTIONS

1. John Locke stated, "Where there is no law, there is no freedom."[11] What do you think he meant by this statement?
2. Which jurisprudential view do you most closely agree with? Why?
3. Why do you think St. Augustine said that states without justice are robber bands enlarged?
4. Are law, order, and justice equally weighted parts of our legal system, or do one or two outweigh the others? Explain.

5. What rational arguments can you make for *not* having a knowledge of the law? What rational arguments can you make for *having* a knowledge of the law?
6. Lenny Bruce once said, "They call it the Halls of Justice because the only place you get justice is in the halls." What do you think he meant? Do you agree or disagree? Why?
7. The philosopher John Rawls said, "Justice is the first virtue of social institutions, as truth is of systems of thought." Discuss this quote.
8. The Federal Tort Claims Act allows the U.S. government to be sued for acts of its employees under certain circumstances. It primarily deals with employee negligence (carelessness). Why do you think this statute was enacted? Why are intentional torts exceptions to the statute?
9. What is *stare decisis*? Once a question has been decided, is there any way for the rule to be changed? What are the advantages *and* disadvantages of a legal system that relies on *stare decisis* (precedents)?
10. Jeremy Bentham (1748–1832), an English lawyer, is best known for his utilitarian philosophy that the object of law should be to achieve the "greatest happiness of the greatest number." Discuss the implications of the following statement based on your knowledge of common versus statutory law:

    Do you know how they make [common law]? Just as a man makes laws for his dog. When your dog does anything you want to break him of, you wait until he does it and then beat him. This is the way you make law for your dog, and this is the way judges make laws for you and me. They won't tell a man beforehand. . . . The French have had enough of this dog-law; they are turning it as fast as they can into statute law, that everybody may have a rule to go by. . . .[12]

CASE PROBLEMS AND WRITING ASSIGNMENTS

1. On numerous occasions, Mochan telephoned a person and used language that was obscene, lewd, and filthy. After the person complained to the police, Mochan was indicted and convicted of a common law misdemeanor because there was no criminal statute covering obscene telephone calls at that time. Discuss the outcome of this case with respect to the rule that our laws need to be published. [See *Commonwealth* v. *Mochan*, 177 Pa.Super. 454, 110 A.2d 788 (1955).]

2. The Environmental Defense Fund (EDF) requested an injunction, a form of equitable relief. In 1966, the U.S. Army Corps of Engineers recommended increasing the width of the channel. There was public notice. As early as 1967, EDF knew about the plan to widen the channel. In 1976, EDF filed its complaint, and in 1978 the complaint was changed to include the legal question about lack of authority on the part of the Army Corps. A large amount of money was expended in the intervening time. A prompt hearing was not requested by EDF. Should EDF's lawsuit be barred because it waited too long to file the suit (laches)? [See *Environmental Defense Fund* v. *Alexander*, 614 F.2d 474 (5th Cir. 1980).]

3. The state of Oregon highly regulates landfills and waste disposal in the state. Oregon decided to impose an additional fee, called a surcharge, on solid waste that was generated outside the state and was disposed of in landfills inside the state. The amount of the fee was to be set by the Environmental Quality Commission. Following its rule-making process, the commission set the surcharge at $2.25 per ton. Is this a proper law or rule? Should Oregon be allowed to establish this type of rule? Why or why not? [See *Oregon Waste Systems, Inc.* v. *Department of Environmental Quality of the State of Oregon*, 128 L.Ed. 13 (1994).]

4. Margaret Beattie was seriously injured in an automobile accident in Delaware. She incurred medical expenses of nearly $300,000 and was a quadraplegic following the accident. She filed suit against her husband for damages, alleging that his negligence was the cause of her injuries. Because the Beatties had substantial liability insurance, Margaret Beattie would have received a large sum in damages if she was able to establish her case. Unfortunately, Delaware follows the precedent of not allowing one spouse to sue the other spouse in tort. Should this precedent prevent Margaret from being allowed to sue her husband for her damages in this case? [See *Beattie* v. *Beattie*, 630 A.2d 1096 (Del. 1993).]

5. Universal Studios and Walt Disney Productions filed suit against Sony Corporation for copyright infringement, alleging that the sale of videotape recorders, which allow the taping of shows from television, allowed and encouraged the infringement of copyrights. Sony denied that it was responsible for any copyright infringements and denied liability. How should the court resolve this case? What factors should the court consider in reaching its decision? [See *Sony Corporation of America* v. *Universal City Studios*, 464 U.S. 417 (1984).]

6. **BUSINESS APPLICATIONS CASE** The Italian federal corporate tax system is structured in a manner similar to that of the United States. However, there is a general practice in Italy by which corporations are expected to submit tax returns that understate income by 30 to 70 percent. After the corporate tax returns are filed, the tax authority asks the corporation to "discuss" the tax return. At this discussion, the firm and the tax authority haggle over the amount of tax actually owed, eventually reaching an agreement. A U.S. firm opened a division in Italy and filed its Italian return in the same manner as it would have done in the United States. When asked to "discuss" the return, the firm's manager refused. Instead, he wrote a letter to the tax authority informing it that the return was accurate and that there was nothing to discuss. Following receipt of this letter, the Italian tax authority filed a formal tax assessment in which the firm was told that its tax liability was three times the amount reflected on its return. What should the manager do in this case? Why did you recommend this particular course of action? [See *Case Study—Italian Tax Mores*, by Arthur L. Kelly, *Case Studies in Business Ethics* (Prentice-Hall, Inc., Englewood Cliffs, N.J., 1984).]

7. **ETHICS APPLICATION CASE** Michael Fay, an American teenager, aged 18, was found guilty of spray-painting and throwing eggs at cars and possessing street signs in his room in Singapore. After Fay confessed, he was sentenced to four months in jail, fined $2,215, and subjected to six blows with a cane. This is a standard penalty for this type of behavior. Caning involves blows with a soaked rattan cane that is one-half inch thick. Prisoners often become unconscious during canings; however, they are revived by a doctor before the flogging continues. Caning causes severe pain and can cause serious bleeding and leave permanent scars. Prior to the caning, President Clinton and the parents (George Fay and Randy Chan) requested clemency from Singapore's president, Ong Teng Cheong. Is Fay's punishment under the Singapore criminal justice system appropriate? Why or why not? Is this a reasonable method to obtain law and order? Should the U.S. President have intervened? Why or why not? [See William Murphy, "Boy's Parents Losing Hope on Flogging," *The Fresno Bee* (15 April 1994), p. A13; Jim Steinberg, "Fresnans Split on Flogging Penalty," *The Fresno Bee* (2 April 1994), pp. B1 and B2.]

8. **IDES CASE** Connecticut enacted a strong statute that went into effect 1 October 1993. Under the statute, police are permitted to seize a person's car if he or she patronizes prostitutes from the car. Police may arrest the person hiring the prostitute and impound the car. The person can recover his or her car for use prior to trial by posting a bond equal to the vehicle's book value. If the person is found innocent in court, he or she would be entitled to the return of the car and any bond that has been posted. If someone else owns the car and the owner did not realize the car would be used to solicit prostitutes, the owner is entitled to have the car returned. Is this Connecticut law fair or just? Apply the IDES model to answer these questions. [See "Police Hope to Drive Away Prostitutes by Confiscating Clients' Cars," *The Fresno Bee* (17 October 1993), p. A9.]

NOTES

1. Brigette Greenberg, "Smithsonian Blocks Access to Nude Photos," *The Fresno Bee* (21 January 1995), pp. A1 and A12.
2. *Earl of Chesterfield* v. *Janssen*, 28 Eng. Rep. 82, 100 (Ch. 1750).
3. *Drysdale* v. *Prudden*, 195 N.C. 722, 143 S.E. 530, 536 (1928).
4. James Rachels, *The Elements of Moral Philosophy*, 2nd ed. (New York: McGraw-Hill, 1993), p. 50.
5. Ibid.
6. 1 Cranch 137, 2 L.Ed. 60 (1803).
7. 252 U.S. 416, 40 S.Ct. 382, 64 L.Ed. 641 (1920).
8. *Western Union Tel. Co.* v. *Call Pub. Co.*, 181 U.S. 92, 21 S.Ct. 561, 45 L.Ed. 765 (1901).
9. 347 U.S. 483 (1954).
10. "When You Need a Lawyer," *Consumer Reports* (February 1996), pp. 34–39.
11. John Locke, *Second Treatise of Government*, Section 57, ed. and introduction by Thomas P. Perdon (New York: Liberal Arts Press, 1952).
12. Jeremy Bentham, *The Works of Jeremy Bentham* (New York: Russell and Russell, 1962), p. 231.

CALL-IMAGE TECHNOLOGY NEEDS YOU!

WHAT IS CALL-IMAGE TECHNOLOGY?

To own your own business, to be an entrepreneur, is the dream of many people, and Tom and Anna Kochanowski are living this dream through their own videophone company, Call-Image Technology (CIT). CIT began as a family business, with Tom and Anna's children being its first employees, but it has grown quickly. CIT now designs, produces, manufacturers, markets, and sells "Call-Image," its interactive videophone, in the United States and around the world.

While CIT has expanded, it still is a small business at heart, and relies on the services of its family and friends for help. Lately, Tom and Anna Kochanowski have found more and more of their time consumed by legal questions: What laws govern the sales of Call-Image? How can CIT protect its trade secrets? How should CIT handle employee and customer disputes? What elements does CIT need in its contracts? What does CIT need to be aware of when acquiring financing and capital? CIT retains the services of a lawyer, Amy Chen, a friend of the family, but Tom and Anna realize they cannot ask Amy to involve herself in every decision CIT makes. For this reason, Tom and Anna need a consultant with training in business law matters to help CIT avoid legal problems before they arise, identify legal problems when they do arise, and then communicate intelligently these legal problems to Amy Chen to find solutions. This consultant is you, and CIT needs your help!

YOUR ROLE IN CALL-IMAGE TECHNOLOGY

Call-Image Technology, of course, is a fictional company, but it does allow you to see how the legal concepts discussed in each chapter apply to the business world. Chapters begin with an "Agenda," which highlights the major issues relevant to a small business. This agenda introduces you to the key concepts in the chapter. Within chapters particular issues involving CIT, relevant to the discussion in the text, call for your help. As in the business world, you are asked to give your advice, based on what you have learned, on how to avoid legal problems, how to manage problems should they arise, and how to work with attorneys to solve problems. You are not asked to be a lawyer. Rather, you are asked to be an enlightened consultant on business law issues—which you will become, with hard work, as the course progresses—in conjunction with CIT's employees and lawyers. Finally, each chapter contains "Memos" from Amy Chen, CIT's attorney, offering practical legal advice on the topics discussed in the chapter.

The issues you are asked to help CIT with involve many different functional areas of business—management, manufacturing, finance and accounting, sales and marketing, international business—and even a few personal legal issues. Hence, the text, and this course, will help you not only understand the law, but will help you understand your other business courses as well.

THE PRODUCT AND PEOPLE BEHIND CIT

Call-Image Call-Image is a videophone that allows parties in a conversation to speak and to see each other simultaneously on a 6″ x 6″ monitor.

Anna Kochanowski Anna Kochanowski, a founder of CIT with her husband, Tom, is a former engineer for a major fiber optics firm and the primary designer of Call-Image. Anna works full time for CIT.

Tom Kochanowski Tom Kochanowski, a founder of CIT with his wife, Anna, is a 25-year veteran of the business world, working primarily in marketing and sales. Tom continues to work part time in the marketing department of a major telecommunications firm and devotes free time to planning the marketing strategy and managing the various other aspects of CIT.

Amy Chen Amy Chen, a successful attorney and friend of the Kochanowski family, provides legal advice and performs legal functions for CIT. Amy has a general practice.

Donna Kochanowski Donna Kochanowski, Anna and Tom's 27-year-old daughter, is a certified public accountant (CPA). Donna offers financial advice and works part time for CIT.

Julio Rodriguez Julio Rodriguez, Donna Kochanowski's fiancé, is also a CPA. Julio offers financial advice to CIT, although he is not an employee.

Dan Kochanowski Dan Kochanowski, Anna and Tom's 23-year-old son, works full time for CIT. Dan's background is in engineering, but he assists Tom and Anna in all aspects of the business.

John Kochanowski John Kochanowski, Anna and Tom's 20-year-old son, works part time for CIT. John is pursuing management/finance studies at a local college.

Lindsay Kochanowski Lindsay Kochanowski, Anna and Tom's 16-year-old daughter, attends high school. Lindsay works for CIT after school and on weekends.

THE "IDES" APPROACH TO LEGAL ANALYSIS

LEGAL ANALYSIS

A class in the legal environment of business or business law carries with it many benefits:

- Studying law enables you to understand more fully your rights and responsibilities as a citizen and/or as a businessperson.
- The complexity of the present-day legal environment makes such knowledge a critical component of a business or nonbusiness education.
- The law's emphasis on language requires you to master verbal data, just as accounting and finance classes require the mastery of financial data or economics classes require the mastery of graphical data. Law thus complements many of the substantive areas that comprise a typical business curriculum.
- Law provides a mode of analysis that permits you to recognize potential legal issues before they become problematic, and provides you with an objective way of marshaling facts and distinguishing among alternatives.

In short, the study of law supplies you with a powerful model for analyzing complex business (and other) decisions. Business law professors learn this skill—called legal analysis—in law school, and they in turn infuse this methodology into their teaching so that you can add this method of reasoning to your own arsenal of problem-solving skills.

I — **Identify the legal issue(s)**—*When you encounter a legal problem,* identify *exactly what types of legal issues you are facing.*

↓

D — **Define all relevant legal terms**—*Next,* define *all the legal terms relevant to the legal problems you are facing.*

↓

E — **Enumerate the legal principles associated with the issue**—*Third,* enumerate, *or spell out, all of the legal principles relevant to the legal problems you are facing.*

↓

S — **Show both sides of the legal problem by using the facts**—*Finally, using the facts,* show *both sides of the legal problem you are facing.*

THE "IDES" APPROACH TO LEGAL ANALYSIS

In this course, you should think of legal analysis as a four-step approach, known by the acronym "IDES":

Identify the legal issue(s). The legal problems you will encounter in the business environment (or in personal affairs) will not, unfortunately, be labeled as a "torts" problem, or as a "contracts" problem, or as an "antitrust" problem. Rather, you will need to survey the facts and categorize the legal question(s) within the appropriate substantive area(s)—torts, contracts, and antitrust law, for example. Unless you can properly categorize the question, you will be unable either to make the proper decisions or to take the appropriate preventive steps to avoid problems. Conversely, understanding legal rights and responsibilities allows you to avoid many costs and difficulties. Advance planning can save you and your firm a great deal of time, money, and trouble.

In short, when you encounter a problem with legal ramifications, your first step should be to identify *exactly what types of legal issues you are facing.*

Define all relevant legal terms. Since law is an artificial language system, it often uses words in specialized ways. Words like "consideration" and "battery" have meanings in law different from their meaning in "normal" life.

Supplying these definitions, therefore, helps you to focus on the problems at hand and to limit your analysis to the relevant issues involved in the problems.

In short, when you encounter a problem with legal ramifications, your second step should be to define *all the legal terms relevant to the problem you are facing.*

Enumerate the legal principles associated with the issue. Once you ascertain what the central issue is, you must acquaint yourself with any relevant subissues. Generally speaking, in our adversarial legal system, these principles include the elements of the plaintiff's *prima facie* case and any applicable *defenses* that the defendant can assert. To illustrate, if the issue is negligence, the elements of the plaintiff's prima facie case include a showing that the defendant owed a duty to the plaintiff, that the duty was *breached*, that the plaintiff suffered harm as a result of the breach, and the harm was *proximately* caused by the breach of duty. The defendant's possible defenses would include contributory negligence by the plaintiff, assumption of the risk, lack of foreseeability, and intervening causes.

This sort of analysis allows you to understand the legal issues involved in significant depth. This, in turn, will allow you to determine whether there is a case for you to pursue (as either the plaintiff or the defendant), or whether you would be better off settling the issue prior to trial. In addition, knowledge of such issues and principles will allow you to avoid conduct that might result in lawsuits, liability, or other legal problems.

In short, when you encounter a problem with legal ramifications, your third step should be to enumerate, *or spell out, all the legal principles relevant to the legal problem you are facing.*

Show both sides of the legal problem (the plaintiff's and the defendant's) by using the facts. The factual setting you may encounter in your legal environment can take on an almost infinite variety. Yet, by thinking about both sides of the issue, you can prepare the best possible argument to support your side of a controversy. By knowing the facts, you gain two important benefits: (1) you can analyze the facts in a more objective and complete manner, allowing you to present the strongest possible argument for your position; and (2) you can pinpoint those facts that the other side will be most likely to use, allowing for the preparation of rebuttal arguments by you.

Anticipating the other side's arguments is nearly as important as deciding what arguments best support your position. Moreover, learning to think of both sides of an issue leads to objectivity in thinking, and the ability to decide the best course of action in light of all the possible alternatives both in and out of court.

In short, when you encounter a problem with legal ramifications, your fourth step should be to show *both sides of the legal problem you are facing, using the facts.*

A FINAL NOTE

The greatest benefit of the IDES approach is its systematic strategy for approaching legal problems. Using IDES will increase and improve your ability to handle verbal data, it will sharpen your analytical abilities, and it will provide a useful "critical thinking" tool.

The IDES approach *will not substitute* for the advice of and need for attorneys. You will be better able to avoid legal problems in the first place, and work with your lawyer should legal problems arise, but you should still consult with a lawyer on legal problems you encounter.

Business Ethics

Outline

Ethics and Morality
Ethical Theories
A Synthesis for Ethical Decision Making
The Game Theory of Business
The Social Contract Theory
Multinational Ethics
A Recommendation for Business
Summary
Discussion Questions
Case Problems and Writing Assignments

Agenda

The Kochanowskis need to understand the ethical restrictions under which they will operate Call-Image Technology. Businesses today are expected to act ethically, even if they do not have any formulated ethical theory that provides guidance in this area. However, a business must also satisfy the social contract it has with society. In addition, the business must weigh decisions, taking into account the potential impact—both beneficial and harmful—on each of its constituents. How does a business know what the social contract theory demands of it? Who are the constituents of a business? These and other questions need to be addressed in covering the material in this chapter. Be prepared! You never know when one of the Kochanowskis will need your advice.

Ethics and Morality

It is fairly standard for people to equate ethics with morals. In so doing, they find it easier to discuss the topic of ethics. However, such an equation is not altogether accurate. *Ethics* refers to a guiding philosophy—the principles of conduct governing an individual or a group.[1] By contrast, *morals* relate to principles of right and wrong behavior as sanctioned by or operative on one's conscience.[2] From the perspective of an individual, ethics and morals may have the same meaning. However, from the perspective of a group—including a society—it is only appropriate to speak of ethics. Thus, when we speak of ethics, we are talking about societal values, the accepted conduct within a given society. In contrast, when we speak of morals, we are talking about individual values, the accepted conduct of an individual by that individual. Different societies may have different ethics, but the morals of any given individual should remain relatively constant no matter which society that person should happen to be in at any point in time. *Ethical conduct* is conduct that is deemed right—or at least accepted as *not* wrong—within a societal setting. *Moral conduct* is conduct that the individual considers right—or at least does *not* consider as wrong—without regard to the attitude of the society.

To further complicate this already complex issue, societies have standards that go beyond ethics. The ethical standards of a society reflect what is considered "right" and "wrong" within that society in a general manner. Some *wrong* behavior may be merely a matter of rude conduct, frowned on within the society, but not of sufficient seriousness or severity to merit more than a social dislike of the conduct. Other "wrong" conduct may be considered much more serious, calling for more than a societal frown; this conduct may be so inappropriate for the society that the person who acts in this "wrongful" manner may be subjected to a fine or even to incarceration. To help ensure that people within a society act in a socially acceptable manner, the society enacts laws and regulations, usually with penalties attached for conduct in violation of the law or regulation in question. These laws enacted by society provide an ethical *floor*—a minimum standard of behavior that is expected from each member of that society.

Although it is a broad generalization, conduct that violates a law or a regulation of a society is generally deemed unethical by that society. This is not to say that all unethical conduct is also illegal; rather it says that all illegal conduct is also unethical. Of course there are examples where some members of a society will act in a manner that violates a law or a regulation in order to force the society to reconsider its official position, with the aim of changing the law, and thereby changing the *official* social values the law affects. One such example involves Dr. Martin Luther King, Jr., and his encouragement of civil disobedience in the 1950s. His conduct was technically illegal at the time, but the Civil Rights movement changed the laws regarding equal rights and racial discrimination, officially changing the social values reflected by the laws governing human rights.

To take a simple, albeit controversial, example, let us examine the abortion issue in the United States. Since the Supreme Court's opinion in *Roe* v. *Wade*,[3] doctors in the United States have been able to legally and *ethically* perform abortions. Prior to that opinion, abortions were considered illegal in numerous states, and any doctor who performed an abortion was acting in an unethical—not to mention illegal—manner. In a similar vein, women now may ethically choose to have an abortion when they could not have so chosen prior to the *Roe* v. *Wade* decision. However, the fact that such a decision is ethical (acceptable to society) does not mean that it will be considered moral by everyone. Many women would not consider having an abortion because they view abortions as immoral. To have an abortion would be to violate their personal moral values. The fact that society considers such a procedure ethical would not affect how these women feel from a personal perspective. In other words, as long as their personal values—their morals—do not involve acting in a manner that calls for action prohibited by society's ethics, there is no problem with their adherence to their values.

If the personal morals of an individual call for conduct prohibited by society's ethics, however, there is a potential problem. For example, suppose a person feels that stealing is moral as long as the victim of the theft is wealthy. This person will encounter problems if he or she acts on the basis of this moral value by stealing from a wealthy victim. Our society has deemed theft to be an illegal and an unethical act, and the person whose morals conflict with this ethic will find that society has deemed the conduct both illegal and unethical even though, purely personally, the conduct may have been moral to the individual.

ETHICAL THEORIES

Before the topic of *business* ethics can be addressed, it is imperative to have at least an introductory exposure to some of the more widely cited ethical theories and principles. This section of the chapter introduces four of these ethical principles and compares them to one another. When we study these ethical theories, it is important to remember that there is no single "best" ethical theory everyone should follow. Each individual and each organization must choose the theory that best suits his, her, or its values and morals. The theory followed can be chosen in any fashion, even if that fashion seems entirely arbitrary. The theory chosen can even be a combination of features from several different theories. For example, some people base their ethical beliefs on the Golden Rule (Do unto others as you would have others do unto you) while others select an "ends" approach (the outcome of the conduct determines its ethical nature). The important point is that a theory has been chosen and is being followed.

The study of ethics and of ethical principles is well known in philosophy, but it is relatively new to business. Business students have long been used to "hard-and-fast" rules and theories in their classes. Some of these rules or theories, such as ***caveat emptor*** and ***laissez faire*** economics, were followed for a while and then discarded as society and its values changed. Others are still followed today. For example, "debits equal credits" is a given in accounting classes, and an accounting student can tell at a glance if the debits and the credits are equal. If they are not equal, that same accounting student knows that a problem exists, and will then endeavor to find the problem and to solve it. However, the mere fact that debits do, in fact, equal credits does not guarantee that there is not a problem. An error might still exist, but that error happens to be exactly offset by one or more other errors. Such errors are not as obvious as the one that exists when the debits and the credits do not match, but they are every bit as real, and they are more difficult to find. Business ethics is somewhat similar to this latter example.

Caveat emptor
Let the buyer beware.

Laissez faire
Let (the people) do as they choose; a doctrine opposing governmental interference in economic affairs beyond the minimum necessary for the maintenance of peace and property rights.

Studying ethical theories and principles is not nearly as "hard and fast" as most other business topics, and the problems are not nearly as obvious in an ethical setting as the problems from the examples here. Yet questions of ethics—particularly questions of business ethics—are among the most important questions the businessperson of the modern era will face in his or her career. The manager may face a "Hobson's choice" among bad alternatives; or the decision may entail a trade-off between short-term gains and long-term gains; or the decision may involve short-term gains (or losses) compared to longer-term losses (or gains).

While ethics can be defined as the system, or code, of morals of a particular person, religion, group, or profession,[4] such a definition does not provide much help in the area of business ethics. Why? Business does not fit neatly into any of the categories mentioned in the definition. Although a business may be recognized as a legal person, the business is not a "particular person," nor does any one individual influence business enough to provide moral or ethical modeling for the firm. Even though it is undoubtedly true that some businesspeople worship "the almighty dollar," business does not qualify as a religion in any realistic sense of the term. Likewise, the "group" to which business belongs is too diverse to have a single system or code of morals.

Similarly, "business" is not a single profession like medicine or law, susceptible to the adoption of a single code of professional conduct, or of ethics, if you will. Thus, for most people, the study of business ethics comes down to an analysis of the system or code of morals of a particular person, the specific businessperson whose conduct is being evaluated. Unfortunately, the ethical standard too often applied in this situation is the ethical standard of the observer, and not that of the person being observed. To properly treat the ethical issues of a businessperson, some kind of analysis framework must be established, and some basic understanding of the ethical parameters of business needs to be developed.

Consequential and Nonconsequential Principles

Before a framework for the analysis of business ethics can be developed, some decisions must be made as to what values and standards are being measured, and on what basis the measurement is being made. Two broad categories of ethical theories exist. Ethical theories may be based on either consequential (teleological) principles or on nonconsequential (deontological) principles.

Consequential principles judge the ethics of a particular action by the consequences of that action. Consequential ethics, therefore, determine the "rightness" or the "wrongness" of any action by determining the ratio of good to evil that a given action will produce. A person practicing consequential ethics needs to evaluate each of his or her possible alternative actions, measuring the good (and the evil) that may result from the alternatives. The "right" action is that action which produces the greatest ratio of good to evil of any of the available alternatives. The two major theories of ethical behavior under the consequential principles are egoism and utilitarianism.

Nonconsequential principles tend to focus on the concept of "duty" rather than on any concepts of right and/or wrong. Under the nonconsequential approach, a person acts ethically if that person is faithful to his or her duty, regardless of the consequences that follow from being faithful to that duty. If a person carries out his or her duties, the greatest good must occur because the duty of the individual was carried out. If each individual carries out his or her duty, society knows what to expect from each individual in any and every given situation. This provides for greater long-term continuity than would arise if each individual based every choice he or she made on the anticipated consequences of each particular action for that individual. In addition, society imposes duties to maximize the values society wants, and by meeting that duty the individual is furthering the interests of that society. The "categorical imperative" advanced by Immanuel Kant and the "veil of ignorance" advocated by John Rawls are two of the best-known theories in support of the non-consequential principles of ethics. Both of these theories will be discussed in detail later in this chapter.

Consequential Ethics

Egoism. The doctrine which posits that self-interest is the proper goal of all human action is known as *egoism*.[5] (Do not confuse an *egoist*, a person who follows the ethical theory of egoism, with an *egotist*, a person who has an exaggerated sense of self-importance.) In the doctrine of egoism each person is expected to act in a manner that will maximize his or her long-term interests. In so doing, society is expected to benefit because when each individual acts in a manner that produces the greatest ratio of good to evil, the sum of all of these individual "good-producing" actions within the society will produce the greatest total good for the society.

One common misconception of egoism is that all egoists are hedonistic seekers of pleasure who emphasize instant gratification. This concept treats one's pleasure as being equal to one's best interests. In fact, an egoist may well decide to act in a "selfless" manner because doing so will further the long-term self-interest of that person to a greater degree than will any short-term pleasures he or she might be able to enjoy. An egoist may be willing to make a personal sacrifice today to receive some benefit in the future, and doing so is perfectly consistent with the doctrine of egoism. Similarly, an egoist may obtain self-gratification from performing acts that benefit others so that such actions further one's long-term interests by increasing one's satisfaction.

In the same manner that an individual may follow egoism, so may an organization. From an organizational perspective, *egoism* involves those actions that best promote the long-term interests of the organization. Thus, a corporation may establish a minority hiring program or a college scholarship program, and in so doing the corporation may well be acting in a purely egoistic manner. These programs may advance the long-term interests of the corporation by improving its public image, by reducing social tensions, or by avoiding legal problems that might otherwise have arisen. The short-term expenses incurred in such programs are more than offset by the benefits to be derived in the future so that the programs may appear to be generous and public-spirited when in reality they are undertaken for purely "selfish" reasons—as befits the ethical theory of the particular firm.

Utilitarianism. The other major consequential approach to ethics is *utilitarianism.* To a utilitarian, the proper course of conduct to follow in any given setting is the course that will produce the greatest good (or the least harm) for the greatest number.[6] Rather than focusing on the interests of the individual (as an egoist would), the utilitarian focuses on the interests of the society. The ethical course of conduct is the one that best serves the interests of the social group as a whole, regardless of the impact on any individuals or any subgroups of the total social system. In theory, someone who is a utilitarian does not care if the "good" is immediately felt or if it is long term in nature. The only concern is whether the "good" to be derived—whenever it is derived—produces the greatest possible quantity of good available among the alternatives from which the choice was made.

There are two primary types of utilitarianism, act utilitarianism and rule utilitarianism. *Act utilitarianism* is concerned with individual actions and the effect of those actions on the social group as a whole. An act utilitarian expects each person to act in a manner that will produce the greatest net benefit for the social group, even if such actions require the breaking of a social "rule." While it is felt that rules should generally be followed, exceptional situations may compel an act utilitarian to break the rules for the greater good of the society. Thus, to an act utilitarian, telling a "little white lie" may be the most ethical course of conduct in a given situation if telling the lie produces more total good than would be obtained by telling the truth, by avoiding the answer, or by any other alternative.

A *rule utilitarian* believes that strict adherence to the rules of the society will, by definition, produce the greatest good for the greatest number. A rule utilitarian follows all of the rules of the society without exception. Further, if the rules of society change, the conduct of the rule utilitarian will also change to reflect the change in the rules. Rule utilitarians take the position that the ends justify the means and that the rules strictly define the means so that the proper and ethical course of conduct is simple. If one follows the rules, the proper ends will be attained automatically. This principle applies across-the-board, whether the acts are those of an individual or of an organization. The rules of a society reflect the social values of that society, and strict obedience of those rules maximizes social values and social good.

Nonconsequential Ethics

Kant and the Categorical Imperative. The nonconsequential principles of ethical theory are best exemplified by the categorical imperative developed by Immanuel Kant, an eighteenth-century German philosopher. Kant felt that certain universal moral standards existed without regard to the circumstances of the moment or the values of any particular society.[7] Under Kant's theory, when people follow these universal moral principles, they are acting morally and ethically. When people do not follow these universal principles, they are acting unethically. Individual variations and consequences are irrelevant. The universal moral principles impose a duty on each person, and the performance of that duty is what determines the "rightness" or "wrongness" of any given action.

Kant also posited perfect duties and imperfect duties. Perfect duties are those things a person must always do or refrain from doing such as the duty of a merchant never to cheat a customer. Imperfect duties involve things a person should do, but not necessarily things a person must do. For example, a person should contribute to charities, but a person should not necessarily contribute to all charities, nor should a person have to contribute to any particular charity every time that charity solicits contributions.

Based on his theories, Kant developed his categorical imperative. The *categorical imperative,* simply stated, says that each person should act in such a manner that his or her actions could become the universal law. In a perfectly ethical and moral world, each person is expected to act as every person ought to act. The rules to be followed are unconditional, and adherence to these rules is imperative. If each person carries out his or her duty by following these "universal rules," society will be properly served by each individual.

Kant's approach to ethics is also applicable to organizations. An organization is judged in the same manner as an individual; the organization is expected to obey the categorical imperative, just as an individual is expected to obey it. The organization is to act according to its duty, with its actions being judged against the "universal law" standard—would such conduct be proper if all organizations were to act in the same manner? The organization would be expected to act in a manner that discharges its duty to every aspect of society, which would include recognition of the rights of others and the duty owed to others.

Rawls and the Veil of Ignorance. John Rawls took the works of Locke, Rousseau, and Kant as a starting point to develop his own theory of justice.[8] Rawls viewed these earlier works as the foundation for a "contract theory" of justice, and he presented his conception of justice as a higher level of abstraction from the earlier theories. Rawls felt that a truly just society would be one where the rules governing the society were developed behind a *veil of ignorance*, behind which no person would know his or her personal characteristics. Since the people making the rules were making those rules while wholly ignorant of their unique combination of race, religion, color, gender, wealth, age, or education, they would enact rules they would be willing to live under regardless of which combination of factors they would have to live under once they stepped out from behind the veil of ignorance.

By creating a situation in which each member of the society is willing to live under the rules developed behind the veil, true justice can be obtained by the society. A proper constitution will be adopted; an appropriate method for legislation based on the constitution adopted will be created; a proper method for dispute resolution will be developed; and, finally, the application of rules to particular cases by judges and administrators, and the following of rules by citizens generally will be implemented.[9] These four theories are summarized and analyzed as they apply in a business setting in Exhibit 2.1.

A Synthesis for Ethical Decision Making

Each of these ethical theories provides a possible framework for evaluating the ethics of a business and for evaluating the ethics of the people who operate the business. Remember, there is no one universally accepted theory or approach to ethics in general, nor is there an accepted and universal approach to business ethics. Each firm in the business environment can select a theory of ethics to follow in developing its own ethical approach to conducting its business, whether it chooses a consequential theory, a nonconsequential theory, or a composite theory. Before choosing a theory, however, the businessperson should also take into account several other factors. These factors should include, but not be limited to, the short-term versus the long-term impact of any decisions, the constituent groups that will be affected by the decision being made (constituent groups are discussed later in the chapter), and the way in which the ethical decision fits within the laws and regulations affecting the business in this area.

Perhaps a business would be best advised to seek a synthesis of these different theories, as tempered by the social contract theory, to develop an approach to ethical issues. This approach would provide a structure for evaluating actions and options regardless of the ethical theory that most closely reflects the values of the business. One such synthesis is suggested by the work of Vincent Ruggerio.[10] Ruggerio suggests that there are three common concerns in ethical decision making: the way human relations affect the quality of ethical actions; the impact of actions on ideals; and the effects of actions. As a result, the firm should follow a two-step process. The first step is to identify the important considerations involved (obligations, ideals, and effects). The second step is to decide where the emphasis should lie among the three

EXHIBIT 2.1 A Comparison of Ethical Theories

Ethical Theory	Positive Aspects in a Business Context	Negative Aspects in a Business Context
Egoism		
(Consequential theory—an act is ethical when it promotes the best long-term interests of the firm.)	1. Provides a basis for formulating and testing policies. 2. Provides flexibility in ethical decision making for business. 3. Allows a business to tailor codes of conduct to suit the complexity of its particular business dealings.	1. May ignore blatant wrongs. 2. Incompatible with the nature and role of business. 3. Cannot resolve conflicts of egoistic interests. 4. Introduces inconsistency into ethical counsel.[11]
Utilitarianism		
(Consequential theory—the most ethical decision is the one that produces the greatest good, or the least harm, for the greatest number of people.)	1. Provides a basis for formulating and testing policies. 2. Provides an objective manner for resolving conflicts of self-interest. 3. Recognizes the four constituent groups of a business. 4. Provides the latitude in ethical decision making that business seems to need.	1. Utilitarians ignore conduct which appears to be wrong in-and-of itself. 2. The principle of utility may be in conflict with the principle of justice. 3. It is very difficult to formulate satisfactory rules.[12]
Categorical Imperative		
(Nonconsequential theory—only when we act from a sense of duty do actions have ethical worth.)	1. The categorical imperative takes the guesswork out of ethical decision making in business. 2. Introduces a needed humanistic dimension into business ethics decisions. 3. The concept of duty implies the ethical obligation to act from a respect for rights and the recognition of responsibilities.	1. Provides no clear way to resolve conflicts among duties. 2. There is no compelling reason that the prohibition against certain actions should hold without exception.[13]
Veil of Ignorance		
(Nonconsequential theory—rational agents, unaware of their personal characteristics or places in society, choose the principles they wish to have govern everyone in society.)	1. The veil of ignorance takes the guesswork out of ethical decision making in business. 2. Introduces a needed humanistic dimension into business ethics decisions. 3. Implies the ethical obligation to act from a respect for rights and the recognition of responsibilities.	1. Uses the better-off members of society to assume the welfare of the worst-off. 2. There is no compelling reason for following universal principles that might be agreed to in theory.[14]

considerations. This approach allows the firm to apply its ethical principles to an ethical problem while also taking into account the social contract *and* the relative positions of each of the four constituent groups of the business.

The following case was decided in the late nineteenth century. Although the case has nothing to do with business, it does provide an opportunity to examine some of the problems that can arise in the study of ethics. Compare the ethical stances of the defendants in this case with the ethical theories discussed earlier.

2.1 REGINA v. DUDLEY AND STEPHENS 14 Q.B.D. 273 (1884)

FACTS In July 1884 four British sailors were cast away in a storm 1,600 miles from the Cape of Good Hope in an open lifeboat. The only food the crew found aboard the lifeboat was two one-pound tins of turnips. They were able to catch a turtle on their fourth day at sea, but had no other food beyond the turnips and the turtle through the 20th day. All four of the seamen were suffering from hunger and thirst by this time, and the youngest was delirious from drinking seawater. At that point in time, Dudley proposed that the other three should kill the youngest so that the other three would have food and liquid, and Stephens agreed. The next day, while Brooks was sleeping, Dudley killed the boy. While Brooks did not condone the act, he shared in the "bounty," and for the next four days the three men fed on the body and blood of the boy. They were rescued by a passing ship on the 29th day and taken to England, where they were arrested and charged with murder.

ISSUE Was the killing of the boy an act of murder or an act of self defense?

HOLDING It was an act of murder.

REASONING The court granted "that if the men had not fed upon the body of the boy they would probably not have survived to be so picked up and rescued, but would within the four days have died of famine." It also agreed "that the boy, being in a much weaker condition, was likely to have died before them . . . [t]hat under these circumstances there appeared to the prisoners every probability that unless they then fed or very soon fed upon the boy or one of themselves they would die of starvation. That there was no appreciable chance of saving life except by killing some one for the others to eat. . . ."

The court addressed the self-defense issue by examining the words of Lord Hale. In the chapter in which he deals with the exemption to murder created by compulsion or necessity, he stated: "If a man be desperately assaulted and in peril of death, and cannot otherwise escape unless, to satisfy his assailant's fury, he will kill an innocent person then present, the fear and actual force will not acquit him of the crime and punishment of murder, for he ought rather to die himself than kill an innocent; but if he cannot otherwise save his own life the law permits him in his own defence to kill the assailant."

The court recognized the stress the sailors faced, and acknowledged that the temptations they faced were powerful, but denied that these things created a "necessity" justifying homicide. "Nor is this to be regretted. Though law and morality are not the same, and many things may be immoral which are not necessarily illegal, yet the absolute divorce of law from morality would be of fatal consequence; and such divorce would follow if the temptation to murder in this case were to be held by law an absolute defence of it. It is not so. To preserve one's life is generally speaking a duty, but it may be the plainest and the highest duty to sacrifice it. . . . It is not needful to point out the awful danger of admitting the principle which has been contended for. Who is to be the judge of this sort of necessity? By what measure is the comparative value of lives to be measured? Is it to be strength, or intellect, or what? It is plain that the principle leaves to him who is to profit by it to determine the necessity which will justify him in deliberately taking another's life to save his own. . . [I]t is quite plain that such a principle once admitted might be made the legal cloak for unbridled passion and atrocious crime. There is no safe path for judges to tread but to ascertain the law to the best of their ability and to declare it according to their judgment; and if in any case the law appears to be too severe for individuals, to leave it to the Sovereign to exercise that prerogative of mercy which the Constitution has intrusted to the hands fittest to dispense it. . . . It is therefore our duty to declare that the prisoners' act in this case was willful murder, that the facts as stated in the verdict are no legal justification of the homicide; and to say that in our unanimous opinion the prisoners are upon this special verdict guilty of murder."

[The court then proceeded to pass a sentence of death on the prisoners. Queen Victoria subsequently commuted the sentences, setting the punishment to be served by Dudley and Stephens at six months imprisonment.]

BUSINESS CONSIDERATIONS Assume that a business is facing serious economic problems. While there are several alternatives available, the easiest method of economic recovery for the business is to "cannibalize" (strip away the assets, leaving an empty shell) a subsidiary of the firm. What should the business do?

ETHICAL CONSIDERATIONS Is it possible to make a (superficially) persuasive ethical argument in support of the defendants on either an egoistic or a utilitarian basis, if one so desires? Can a persuasive argument be made under either the categorical imperative or the veil of ignorance?

This case illustrates how simple it is for a person to sometimes rationalize conduct that would generally be viewed as reprehensible.

THE GAME THEORY OF BUSINESS

Business as an Amoral Institution

Amoral
Being neither moral nor immoral; lying outside the sphere to which moral judgments apply.

Historically, business was viewed by many as an **amoral** institution. Since any given business was inanimate, and since only animate objects could be expected to possess "morality," it stood to reason that a business was not expected to possess

YOU BE THE JUDGE

Who Is Legally and Ethically Responsible?

Commencement exercises were held at Roanoke College in Salem, Virginia, with much of the standard pomp and circumstance, and with a couple of not-so-normal occurrences. The crowd that came out for the ceremony more than filled the parking spaces available on campus, forcing many of the proud parents and other guests to park on the streets around the campus. The Andersons were one such family, forced to park their 1995 Pontiac on the street near the library parking lot.

During the ceremony, the Salem police received an emergency call stating that there had been a possible heart attack at the college. Emergency crews were dispatched immediately, with both the city fire department and the city's volunteer rescue squad rushing to the scene. As it turned out, there was no heart attack, and the two crews left the scene soon thereafter. Unfortunately, on its way back to the fire station, the fire department vehicle sideswiped the Anderson's car, causing several hundred dollars worth of damages. When the Andersons returned to their car following the ceremony, they found a note on their windshield. The note, written by a Salem police officer, informed them that their car had been hit by one of the city's fire trucks.

The Andersons contacted the city manager to get information on how to file a claim with the city's insurer, expecting to get their car repaired under the city's liability coverage. At that point they learned that Salem denied any liability for the damages. According to the city manager, the city was immune from liability because the accident occurred while a city vehicle was performing a governmental service.

The Andersons have now brought their claim to *your* court, seeking a resolution to this matter. How would you decide this case? Explain your reasoning for each answer.

BUSINESS CONSIDERATIONS If the city of Salem is not held liable for the damages to the Anderson's car from the collision caused by the driver of the fire truck, the Andersons will be forced to seek compensation from their insurance carrier. Presume that the Andersons own a business and the car that was damaged is a business vehicle. How will the fact that they must pay for the damages directly or indirectly affect the business? Will the Andersons or the insurer be able to pass these costs on to their customers in some manner?

ETHICAL CONSIDERATION Without regard to the legal issue, *should* the city be responsible for this sort of claim?

SOURCE: *The Roanoke Times* (28 May 1996), p. C1.[15]

"morality." Because it could not be expected to be moral, it also could not be immoral. Morality and immorality were reserved for animate beings, and inanimate objects were amoral. When most businesses were relatively small and local in nature, this did not present much of a problem. The owners and operators of businesses were known in the community, and even though the *business* was viewed as amoral, the owner or operator was held to community standards. Thus most businesses were operated in an ethical manner in order to keep the local customers satisfied. However, as businesses grew increasingly larger and more complex, this local flavor was lost. Businesses no longer operated in a restricted geographic market, and no longer had to adhere to community standards. Eventually, society began to demand some minimal ethical standards for businesses. Included among these standards were the expectations of fair play and honesty, and the expectation that a business would seek profits for its investors. If a business did not meet these demands voluntarily, society sought direction from the legislature, which enacted statutes setting minimal business standards of behavior. If the business obeyed these laws, it met the duty of fair play; if the managers did not blatantly lie to the customers, the business met the duty of honesty; if the firm generated profits for its investors, it met this duty.

As an example, examine the court's reasoning in the following case. Notice what the court said a corporation is expected to do. Would such conduct by a corporation be considered ethical today?

2.2 DODGE v. FORD MOTOR CO. — 170 N.W. 668 (MICH. 1919)

FACTS Ford Motor Company was formed in June 1903. In its articles of incorporation, the capital stock was fixed at the sum of $150,000, with 1,500 shares of the par value of $100 each. The amount of capital stock subscribed was $100,000. The parties who signed the articles included Henry Ford, whose subscription was for 255 shares, John F. and Horace E. Dodge, who each subscribed for 50 shares, and several other persons. The company began business in June 1903. In 1908, its articles were amended and the capital stock was increased from $150,000 to $2,000,000, with the number of shares being increased to 20,000. At the time of the lawsuit, Ford Motor had assets in excess of $132 million, total liabilities of just over $18 million, and a capital surplus of nearly $112 million. Ford was, at that time, paying a dividend of 5% *per month*, and had also paid "special dividends" of $41 million in the previous five years, or $20 in dividends per $1 of stock. Henry Ford declared that, henceforth, there would be no special dividends paid, although the 5% per month dividend would continue. He also stated that certain socially beneficial programs would be started with the financial support of the Ford Motor Company. The Dodge brothers brought suit to compel the payment of special dividends, and for other relief under the laws of the state of Michigan.

ISSUE May the board of directors of a corporation place the interests of the public ahead of the interests of the stockholders of the corporation by discontinuing these special dividends and by rerouting funds for nonbusiness purposes?

HOLDING No. The directors have a duty to the business and to the stockholders and they must honor that duty. Directors may not change the goals of the business in order to devote themselves to other purposes.

REASONING Citing prior opinions, the court stated: "It is a well-recognized principle of law that the directors of a corporation, and they alone, have the power to declare a dividend of the earnings of the corporation, and to determine its amount. . . . Courts of equity will not interfere in the management of the directors unless it is clearly made to appear that they are guilty of fraud or misappropriation of the corporate funds, or refuse to declare a dividend when the corporation has a surplus of net profits which it can, without detriment to its business, divide among its stockholders, and when a refusal to do so would amount to such an abuse of discretion as would constitute a fraud, or breach of that good faith which they are bound to exercise toward the stockholders."

When plaintiffs made their complaint and demand for further dividends, the Ford Motor Company had concluded its most prosperous year of business. It could reasonably have expected a profit for the next year of upwards of $60

2.2 DODGE v. FORD MOTOR CO. *(cont)* **170 N.W. 668 (MICH. 1919)**

million. It had assets of more than $132 million, a surplus of almost $112 million, and its cash on hand and municipal bonds were nearly $54 million. Its total liabilities, including capital stock, was a little over $20 million. It had declared no special dividend during the business year except the October 1915 dividend. It had been the practice, under similar circumstances, to declare larger dividends. Considering only these facts, a refusal to declare and pay further dividends appears not to be an exercise of discretion on the part of the directors, but an arbitrary refusal to do what the circumstances required to be done. These facts and others called on the directors to justify their action, or failure or refusal to act.

The board "defended" its decision by pointing to a plan to *reduce* the selling price for a new Ford by $80, thus reducing gross income by $48 million for the year. As the court stated, "in short, the plan does not call for and is not intended to produce immediately a more profitable business, but a less profitable one; not only less profitable than formerly, but less profitable than it is admitted it might be made. The apparent immediate effect will be to diminish the value of shares and the returns to shareholders."

A business corporation is organized and carried on primarily for the profit of the stockholders. The powers of the directors are to be employed for that end. The discretion of the directors is to be exercised in the choice of means to attain that end, and does not extend to a change in the end itself, to the reduction of profits, or to the nondistribution of profits among stockholders in order to devote them to other purposes.

The decree of the court below, fixing and determining the specific amount to be distributed to stockholders, is affirmed. In other respects, except as to the allowance of costs, the said decree is reversed.

[Ford Motor Company had enjoyed spectacular success. The original $100,000 in capital stock had increased to $2,000,000 by means of stock dividends, so that the original $10,000 invested by the Dodge brothers had increased to $200,000. Special dividends of $41,000,000 had been paid between 1911 and 1915, together with the "regular" dividend of 5% per month. The Supreme Court of Michigan affirmed the lower court's order that a $19 million special dividend be paid by Ford Motor Company from its capital surplus on hand as of August 1, 1916. Thus, the Dodge brothers had received special dividends of $6 million plus regular dividends of $120,000 *per year* for the period from 1911 through 1916, a substantial return on an initial investment of $10,000.]

ETHICAL CONSIDERATIONS What does the Michigan Supreme Court's opinion say about the ethical expectations of corporations before the Great Depression? What were the ethical "rules of the game" under which Ford was expected to operate?

BUSINESS CONSIDERATIONS How could the Ford Motor Company justify to its stockholders a proposal to reduce the price of its new cars when it could sell every car it was capable of producing at the higher price than was being charged? What were the likely long-term effects of such a proposal?

The *Dodge* v. *Ford Motor Company* case is viewed as a landmark opinion, providing guidance for boards of directors in closely held corporations. While this opinion deals directly with the conflict between the desire of the Ford board to provide for the workers, and the challenge by shareholders who want dividends, the basic thrust of the opinion is that the board has a duty to the shareholders to maximize the return on their investments.

Many people have argued that the *Dodge* opinion, *supra*, prohibited any charitable contributions by a corporation, unless such contributions were expressly authorized in the corporation's charter or bylaws. However, courts have generally disagreed with this position, finding an implicit authority to make contributions, if such contributions are in the best long-term interests of the firm. The next case is the landmark opinion on this topic.

2.3 A.P. SMITH MFG. CO. v. BARLOW — 98 A.2d 581 (N.J. 1953)

FACTS The A.P. Smith Manufacturing Company was incorporated in 1896, and is engaged in the manufacture and sale of valves, fire hydrants, and special equipment, mainly for the water and gas industries. The plant is located in East Orange and Bloomfield, New Jersey. Over the years, the firm was a regular contributor to the local community chest, as well as to Upsala College in East Orange and to Newark College (now a part of Rutgers University). In 1951 the board of directors adopted a resolution to join in the Annual Giving to Princeton University, authorizing the payment of $1,500 to the university. The board's resolution stated that the contribution was "in the best interests of the company." Several stockholders questioned the propriety of this contribution, and the corporation instituted a declaratory judgment action in the Chancery Division to determine whether the contribution was ***intra vires*** (within the powers of the corporation) or ***ultra vires*** (outside the powers of the corporation).

ISSUE May a corporation legally make charitable contributions from corporate funds, or is such an issue an unlawful "wasting" of corporate assets?

HOLDING Yes. A corporation may—in fact, should—make charitable contributions under certain circumstances.

REASONING The president of the corporation testified that the contribution was a sound investment, that the public expects corporations to aid philanthropic and benevolent institutions, that such contributions create goodwill, and that the overall effect is to create a favorable environment in which to conduct business. He added that such contributions increase the likelihood that the firm will help to create a flow of properly trained personnel for potential future employment. He also asserted that the public "expected" business to contribute to the society, and that a failure to do so was not good business. To strengthen the president's assertions, the state of New Jersey enacted a statute in 1930 expressly authorizing corporations to make charitable contributions in many situations.

The challenges by the stockholders—that the contributions were a waste of corporate assets, and that the statute should not apply to A.P. Smith because it had been incorporated prior to the adoption of the statute—were deemed of lesser weight by the court. The public policy considerations involved, the statutory approval, and the size of the contribution all point to a positive effect on the community, without any harm to the corporation. The conduct of the firm was approved.

BUSINESS CONSIDERATION How can charitable contributions by a corporation be justified from a business perspective, presuming that the primary purpose of the business is to generate profits for its stockholders?

ETHICAL CONSIDERATIONS If the court's opinion reflects society's values in this case, what happened to social expectations concerning corporate conduct between the *Dodge* v. *Ford Motor Company* opinion and this opinion? How should this change have affected corporate decision making?

The "Game Theory"

As society and the courts began to recognize the existence of corporate duties, the concept of business as an amoral institution became untenable. If a business had duties, it had some ethical responsibilities. These responsibilities, however, tended to be based on adherence to "rules" and obeying those rules. If a business obeyed the rules and stayed within the law, it was deemed to be acting in an ethical manner. This approach to business ethics led to the development of the "game theory" as a means of judging the ethical stance of the business.[16] Basically, the *game theory* equates the operation of a business with playing a game, and the rules from various games were applicable to determine the ethics of the business. If a manager of a firm lied to his or her customers, the manager—and consequently, the business—had acted unethically. However, if the manager bluffed his or her customer, the manager—and the firm—may have acted in an ethical manner, presuming that bluffing

2.1

SALES/MANUFACTURING

IS BUSINESS A GAME?

A family friend was visiting the Kochanowskis over the weekend, and he seemed excited that the family was starting a business. He pointed out that he, too, had formed a business, and that he was now doing quite well for himself. He then offered the family some "free advice" for their business. He urged them to set their price high when they first enter the market, because there will be little competition, and the public will pay dearly for Call-Image. He also urged them to use the cheapest components possible, allowing them to maximize their profits early, before any other firms enter the market. As he pointed out, CIT can always increase its quality and lower its prices later. After all, business is "a game, just like *Monopoly*, only with real money." This advice bothered the Kochanowskis, and they have asked your advice. To what extent is business "just a game"? What are the rules (if any) to the game?

BUSINESS CONSIDERATIONS What business problems might arise for CIT if it adopts an attitude such as this?

ETHICAL CONSIDERATIONS Can the ethical theory the firm follows help the Kochanowskis in determining whether to listen to the advice of their friend? Explain your reasoning.

is an acceptable part of the game being played. Bluffing is, after all, an accepted part of several games, including poker. Of course, one person's bluffing may well be another person's lying, but such conundra were left for others to solve.

There is a basic flaw in the game theory of business ethics. Game theories and game rules are fair and equitable only if all of the participants in the game are aware a game is being played. If any of the participants do not realize a game is being played, they cannot be aware of the rules of that game, and thus will be at a disadvantage. To take advantage of people under such circumstances would not be ethical.

Under the game theory, a number of rules were developed and followed. For example, *caveat emptor* (let the buyer beware) was a rule of the business game for a substantial period in U.S. history. Similarly, *laissez faire* economic regulation was a rule of business in the United States. Business and its customers were aware of these rules, and played the business game accordingly. Eventually, however, business began to industrialize and to gain an increasing ability to produce for larger and larger markets. The game was no longer quite as fair as it had been before, and as the game became more one-sided in favor of business, the other players (the customers) began to seek new rules for the game. When business would not voluntarily change the rules, the customers asked the government to intervene. This led to government regulation of business, and eventually an entirely new playing field on which the game of business was to be conducted. This new playing field is the one on which business must operate today.

THE SOCIAL CONTRACT THEORY

Many business executives today argue that U.S. business is too regulated by the government. These people see domestic business drowning in a sea of bureaucratic red tape while less-regulated foreign firms are assuming control of the economy. They want to be unfettered, set free from the "excessive" regulations imposed by the government and allowed to compete freely with foreign producers. Although this attitude can be justified from a simplistic economic position, it fails to take into account two factors: the spillover costs society must pay when a business fails to act in a responsible and ethical manner, and the "social contract" between business and society. Recall the discussion of business as an amoral institution. When business became too large for local control, the society sought legislative intervention to force compliance with social demands. This is the gist of the social contract. Business must comply with the demands of the

Ultra vires
Acts beyond the scope of the power of a corporation.

Intra vires
Acts within the scope of the power of a corporation.

society if it wants to continue to exist and to operate within that society. The social contract defines the permissible scope of business conduct and goes beyond the purely economic issues. If society wants more from business than profits, business must accept this mandate in order to survive in society. To do otherwise is to breach the social contract.

Since the social contract theory basically posits that business can exist only because society allows it to exist, that business must satisfy the demands of the society if it is to be allowed to continue. If business does not satisfy the demands of society, society will change the "rules of the game," and in so changing the rules, the permission that business now has may well be revoked. Today, society expects (and demands) more from business than mere profits. Environmental concerns, consumer safety and protection, and quality of life, among other things, must also be provided for in the production process. If these added demands cause costs to rise, so be it. If business as we know it will not meet these demands voluntarily, these demands will be met by regulation—or by society's changing the form of business or the rules of doing business. Not only has the "game theory" of business been rejected by society, but the rules by which business is allowed to exist have also been changed by the social contract theory.

In dealing with the social contract theory and in evaluating the ethical stance of any given business, it is important to recognize that each business has a number of constituent groups—stakeholders, employees, customers, and the community in which it operates—and that each group of constituents will have different wants, needs, and desires. The business manager must base decisions affecting the business, at least in part, on the impact the decisions will have on the various constituents. Some decisions will affect all of the constituent groups, although not equally. Others will only affect some of the groups. Deciding how each group will be affected, and how much weight to give to each group, is essential in reaching ethical decisions. Exhibit 2.2 shows the constituent groups a corporation must consider.

EXHIBIT 2.2 Constituents of a Business

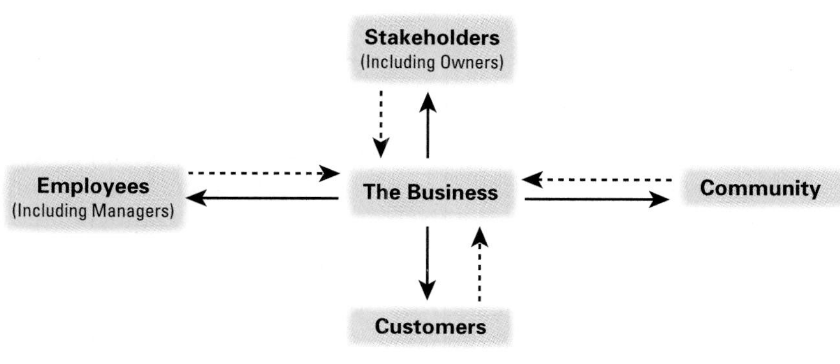

As an example of how these duties can affect a business in its decision process, consider the following example. A firm has developed a new production method that will lower costs (which will lead to increased profits) while simultaneously making safer products. To adopt this new method will benefit two constituent groups, stakeholders and customers. However, this new method will require relocating the plant, and it may produce a number of pollutants. Relocating the plant will cause harm to current employees who may be unable or unwilling to relocate, and to the current community, which will suffer economic harm from reduced employment. The possible increase in pollutants will harm the community at the site of the new plant, although this harm will be offset to some extent by the increase in employment and the economic "ripple effect" a new plant will cause. Somehow a balancing of these competing interests must be undertaken in reaching a decision that reflects the best short-term and long-term interests of the firm.

The Changing Social Environment

Over the years, business has changed, and with it the attitudes of society toward business. The early days of commerce featured primarily local trade, with mainly handcrafted goods produced and sold by local merchants and artisans. Under these circumstances, the rule of *caveat emptor* was followed, and the success of any business was, to a significant extent, dependent on the reputation of its owner/operator.

Eventually, business began to industrialize and to gain an increased capacity for productivity. As businesses began to produce more, they were able to expand their geographic markets from local to regional. This expansion caused some minor changes, although the buyer still had to beware. No longer could the buyer expect to be personally acquainted with the seller. Although the reputation of the seller remained important, much of the spread of that reputation was now by hearsay. The buyer and the seller were becoming separated by distance.

Industrialization continued to expand, and transportation and communication also grew and developed. The advent of the railroads allowed truly national business operations for the first time. With this opportunity to deal on a national scope, manufacturers became aware of "economies of scale." The age of "bigger is better" had arrived. Now *caveat emptor* took on more meaning. No longer could a buyer rely on a seller's reputation. Sellers were combining into trusts, and available substitutes for a seller's goods began to decline. Buyers were being thrust into a "take-it or leave-it" position.

For the first time, the public expectation of business made a drastic change. The public began to request government intervention to protect the consumer and the worker from "big business." The government responded with what business must have thought was a vengeance. The Interstate Commerce Commission, the antitrust statutes, the Securities and Exchange Commission, and a myriad of other agencies and acts were passed in relatively rapid succession.

Why did these changes occur? Fundamentally, because business was so busy meeting its own perceived needs that it ignored the expectations and the demands of the public. Was business acting illegally? In most cases, no. Was business acting unethically? From our contemporary perspective, probably; from a historic point of view, probably not. The key point to remember is that, in most cases, business was being conducted in a manner that had been socially and legally acceptable up to that time. However, as society changed and as the demands of society changed, business failed to respond. Then, when business failed to respond, society sought legislative intervention. The end of the nineteenth century saw the birth of the social contract as an essential element of conducting business.

One example of the changing social environment is the area of "employment at will." An *at-will* employee is one who works for the employer only so long as both parties agree to the employment. There is no fixed term of employment, and either party may terminate the employment relationship at any time merely by giving notice to the other party. Historically, courts upheld the right of the employer to discharge an at-will employee "for good cause, for no cause, or even for cause morally wrong. . . ."[17] The employer's unlimited right to discharge an employee was too often abused by the employer, which led to a reevaluation of the traditional "at-will" doctrine. In *Pierce* v. *Ortho Pharmaceutical Corporation,*[18] the court ruled that, generally speaking, an employer in an employment-at-will is free to terminate the employment relationship at any time, with or without cause. However, the court also stated that firing an employee for a reason that violates public policy would not be done in good faith and could result in liability for wrongful discharge.

The following case relies to a great extent on the *Pierce, supra,* opinion, as well as the New Jersey Conscientious Employee Protection Act (CEPA), in addressing the issue of wrongful discharge.

2.4 HAWORTH v. DEBORAH HEART AND LUNG CENTER

638 A.2d 1354 (N.J.Super. 1994)

FACTS Haworth was the blood bank supervisor at the Deborah Heart and Lung Center within the Deborah Hospital. Part of the responsibility of the blood bank was to collect blood samples from patients and to test those samples. The blood bank also ensured that there was an adequate supply of the proper blood type for the patient when the patient underwent surgery. Following an argument with his supervisor, Haworth destroyed an entire rack of patient blood samples. Following a leave of absence due to "stress," Haworth was offered a less stressful—but lower-level—job. Haworth refused to accept this reassignment, and the hospital discharged him at that time. Haworth claimed the discharge violated the Conscientious Employee Protection Act. He alleged that the destruction of the blood samples was a communicative act designed to show his objection to an allegedly defective blood identification system, and that the discharge was an illegal retaliatory act by the hospital.

ISSUE Was Haworth's conduct a communicative act, protected by the CEPA?

HOLDING No. His conduct was not communicative, and his dismissal was not a violation of the CEPA.

REASONING Haworth contended that the blood test and storage system presented problems for him and for the blood bank, and that he was merely attempting to communicate his concern over these problems to the hospital administration when he destroyed the blood samples. However, he never made these concerns known to any hospital officials or inspectors prior to the event in question. Nor did he apprise anyone of his decision to discard the samples until the next day. The court recognized and emphasized New Jersey's strong public policy protecting employees from wrongful discharge or retaliatory treatment by their employers. But the court also recognized that these considerations have limits, and stressed that its ruling was limited to the particular facts of this case. "Without notice to anyone, plaintiff unilaterally destroyed patients' blood samples. Less drastic avenues of protest or objection were readily available." The conduct was not protected by CEPA, and the discharge was not retaliatory.

BUSINESS CONSIDERATIONS How should a manager react when an employee takes actions that are contra to the firm's interests, but that may involve a legitimate protest by the employee? What if the manager believes the protest is not legitimate?

ETHICAL CONSIDERATIONS How should an employee make his or her protest of a firm's practices known without jeopardizing the employee's position or compromising the employee's morals? What protections should the firm provide for employees who sincerely have moral reservations about a firm's practices?

Problems with Business Ethics

A basic problem faces any business that seeks to act in an "ethical" manner. There are no fixed guidelines to follow, no formal code of ethics to set the standards under which the business should operate. Numerous professional organizations have their own codes of ethics or conduct. For example, the legal profession has the Code of Professional Responsibility; the medical profession has its Hippocratic Oath; the accounting profession has a code of ethics and also has generally accepted auditing standards (GAAS) and generally accepted accounting principles (GAAP); the real estate industry has a code of conduct; and various other groups or organizations have similar codes. However, business has no code, no "road map" of ethical conduct. The closest thing business has to an ethical guideline is the law. If a business is acting within the law, it is acting legally and is seemingly meeting its minimum social requirements. However, this forces business into a reactive posture, always responding to legislative demands. It would seem that a proactive position in which business establishes its own path would be preferable.

Given this overriding problem, what can be done to provide a solution? At the present time, probably nothing can be done in the global sense. But it may be possible for each industry to develop a code of ethics for that particular industry, in much the same manner that the real estate industry has developed a code for its members. If such an industry-wide approach does not prove feasible, each individual firm can develop its own personal code of ethics. Although such a microapproach may not be ideal, it at least gets business to embark on the journey toward formalizing its ethical posture.

MANAGEMENT

SHOULD CIT ADOPT A CODE OF ETHICS?

John recently took a business ethics seminar at his school, and he feels that CIT should adopt a "Code of Ethics" for the firm to follow. He asserts that such a code will help the company not only to respond to ethical dilemmas as they arise, but also to plan ahead in order to avoid ethical problems in the future. Dan argues to the contrary, pointing out that the business is run by the family and that the family is already ethical so that a code is not necessary. The family is seeking your advice on this matter.

BUSINESS CONSIDERATIONS Why might it be a good idea to adopt a code for the business now, even if it is family owned and operated, and the family is already ethical? Why might such a code be a bad idea?

ETHICAL CONSIDERATION If the firm is to adopt a code of ethics, what ethical theory should be selected as the foundation for the code? Explain your reasons.

The Human Factor. As was mentioned earlier, business was frequently viewed as an amoral institution in the past. Workers were expected to leave their personal values at the front gate when they reported to work, and then (presumably) to retrieve them at the close of the working day. At the same time, workers were expected to be loyal agents of the firm. Generally, this was interpreted to mean that if a course of conduct was beneficial to the employer, the employee was to follow that course. If a course of conduct was not beneficial to the employer, the employee was not to follow it. The attitudes and opinions of the employees were ignored.

The "loyal agent" attitude was described—and then rebutted—by Alex C. Micholos in his article "The Loyal Agent's Argument."[19] The loyal agent's argument presumes that the principal follows the ethical theory of egoism, and that the loyal agent must also act egoistically for the principal. The argument runs as follows:

1. As a loyal agent of the principal, I ought to serve his interests as he would serve them himself if he possessed my expertise.

2. The principal will serve his interests in a thoroughly egoistic manner.
3. Therefore, as a loyal agent of this principal, I must operate in a thoroughly egoistic manner on his behalf.

In order to operate in a thoroughly egoistic manner, a person acts in the way that best advances his or her interests, presuming that everyone else is doing the same thing. The underlying assumption here is that if each person maximizes his or her personal interests, society as a whole will be better off than it would be under any other approach.

The gist of the loyal agent's argument is that a truly loyal agent will put the principal first in any decisions between conflicting interests. The agent is more concerned with being first than he or she is concerned with being nice or with being right. Thus, the traditional argument posits that a loyal agent is expected to act without regard to ethical considerations as long as the conduct puts the principal first. There is a major flaw in this traditional loyal agent's argument, and Micholos spends a substantial portion of his article exposing this flaw. Too many people feel that a loyal agent, if acting in a truly egoistic manner, has license—if not a duty—to act immorally and unethically if doing so will advance the interests of the principal. Micholos argued that the truly loyal agent must exercise due care and skill in the performance of the agency duties, and must act in a socially acceptable manner while furthering the interests of the principal. To do otherwise will have a long-term detrimental impact on the principal, and will therefore be disloyal.

2.3

MARKETING/MANAGEMENT

OPERATING CIT ETHICALLY

Tom and Anna have each seen numerous examples of what they consider unethical conduct when they were working full-time for other firms. Tom knows several salespeople who believe that it is perfectly legitimate to say virtually anything short of an outright lie in order to close a sale with a customer. They frequently "push the envelope" to the edge, grossly exaggerating qualities of the product being marketed, often to the detriment of the purchasers of that product. Anna knew electrical engineers who would not hesitate to claim credit for the work of others, or who would even assert privileges due to seniority in order to gain credit for the work of others. (Of course, both knew even more people who did not act in this manner, but these others did not disturb them.) They feel that such conduct is generally harmful to a business and its reputation, especially with repeat customers. They also know they would like to operate the family business ethically, but they don't know how to verbalize this goal.

ETHICAL CONSIDERATIONS What might you suggest to Tom and Anna to help them operate CIT in an ethical manner?

BUSINESS CONSIDERATIONS Where might Tom and Anna look for examples of what they should or should not do? As one of the original entrants into this particular field, should CIT attempt to be proactive in establishing an ethical code, or should the firm wait for governmental guidance?

The Legal Aspect. The U.S. legal system contains numerous ethical components. For example, a person is presumed to be innocent until proven guilty in criminal law. Each person is entitled to due process of the law and to equal protection under the law. Protections exist against compulsory self-incrimination and cruel and unusual punishment. The constitution provides for free speech, free exercise of religion, and the right to counsel, among other rights and guarantees.

Business law also attempts to reflect the ethical standards of the society and to promote ethical conduct in the realm of business. The law of sales imposes a duty on each party to a sales contract to act in good faith. Bankruptcy is designed to give an honest debtor a fresh start. Agency law imposes the duties of loyalty and good faith on the agent.

The laws that regulate business have developed, to a significant extent, under the social contract theory. Governmental regulations of business were enacted initially, in many cases, in response to a public demand for protection from the abuses and excesses of "big business." Antitrust laws were intended to control business and to protect the ideal of a free-and-competitive economy, while the Federal Trade Commission was established to stop unfair and deceptive trade practices.

The apparent success of the antitrust laws encouraged both the public and the government in the use of statutes to force business to meet the demands of the public. The consumer movement of the 1960s led to a number of protective statutes by both the federal and state governments. The federal government was concerned with protecting consumer credit and consumer product safety. State governments tended to be more concerned with safety and with home solicitations. In either case, government became involved only after a perceived problem was identified, public demands for protection were raised, and the business community failed or refused to adequately meet the demands of the public.

The 1960s and 1970s also saw an increased public awareness of and concern about pollution of the environment. Again, a number of protests and a great deal of public action were ignored by the business community in general, and once again governmental intervention was the tool used to address the problem. Governmental environmental protection statutes were intended to clean up the environment in order to protect the quality of life for our population, for wildlife, and for future generations. Government involvement was triggered once more by the failure of the business community to address environmental issues the public had raised.

Similar steps were followed in other areas such as labor and fair employment. The public expressed a concern over how business was treating a perceived problem. However, the steps business took toward solving the problem were less than the public demanded. Consequently, the legislature was asked to intervene on behalf of the public.

In virtually every circumstance, though, the statutory treatment of the problems adopted by the legislature is relatively rigid and potentially expensive for business. Similar protections could have—and should have—been developed within the business community, with a great deal less rigidity and a great deal less expense, had business been willing to meet the challenge directly. Instead, by having waited until the government told it what to do, business now has a much stricter regulatory environment in which to operate.

In each of these areas, and in a number of others, the application of the social contract theory is apparent. Society perceived problems and demanded that certain corrective steps be taken to alleviate the problems. Business had an opportunity to take the corrective steps in a manner devised by business, but failed—or refused—to do so. At that point, the government stepped in to resolve the problem in a rigid, statutory manner when no satisfactory solutions were advanced by business. By failing to respond in a proactive manner, which would have permitted a custom-tailored, micro-focused solution by each affected business or industry, the business community was left with a reactive, macro-oriented solution that must, by definition, extend across industry lines and that is intended to control all aspects of the business community with one broad regulation.

Multinational Ethics

There is an old adage that states: "When in Rome, do as the Romans do." This adage is very appropriate when considering business ethics in a multinational setting. If business ethics tended to be Kantian in nature, with firms throughout the world seeking—and then following—a categorical imperative, there would not be any problem. Since a categorical imperative is a rule for which any and every exception has been developed, businesses would merely have to follow the resulting rules, and their actions would be ethical by definition. Unfortunately, there is no categorical imperative for business, nor are most businesses Kantian in their ethical perspectives. Thus, problems with business ethics exist, and these problems are compounded in an international environment.

A businessperson tends to follow his or her personal moral and ethical values and to apply these values in judging the ethics of others. While the "loyal agent's" argument stresses that a truly loyal agent will put the interests of the principal ahead of the interests of the agent, that same agent will normally only work for a principal whose interests and values can be reconciled with the interests and the values of the agent. If the demands and requirements of a job consistently conflict with the morals and the ethics of an employee, that employee is likely to give up the job before changing his or her ethical perspective. Similarly, the ethical stance of the firm is likely to be consistent with the ethical values of the society. If the firm does not conform to socially acceptable standards, the "social contract theory" is used to change the permissible scope of the firm's conduct.

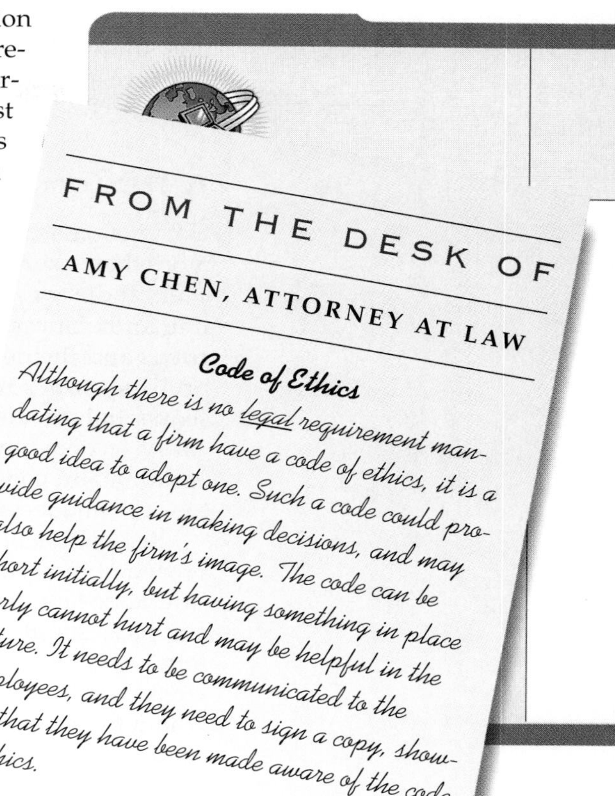

FROM THE DESK OF
AMY CHEN, ATTORNEY AT LAW
Code of Ethics
Although there is no legal requirement mandating that a firm have a code of ethics, it is a good idea to adopt one. Such a code could provide guidance in making decisions, and may also help the firm's image. The code can be short initially, but having something in place early cannot hurt and may be helpful in the future. It needs to be communicated to the employees, and they need to sign a copy, showing that they have been made aware of the code of ethics.

Even if a business has a formal stated objective of acting in a socially responsible and ethical manner, problems may occur. What happens when that firm expands its operations into another country? What happens when a truly loyal and ethical agent of the firm is reassigned to a foreign post within the company? This expansion and/or reassignment may have serious ethical implications. The social contract between the new location and its businesses may well be different from the social contract between the firm and its domicile state, calling for a reappraisal of what is acceptable—or even desirable—behavior. For instance, a firm may open a new plant in a nation with very lax environmental protection statutes. This same firm, in its domicile state, has been an environmentally concerned business that has taken many pro-environment steps to reduce pollution in its production. If the firm tries to be as environmentally active in its new location, it will be at a short-term competitive disadvantage. If it seeks to be economically competitive, it will be acting in a manner contrary to its stated company policy of environmental concern and protection. What should the firm do?

Although there is no perfect solution, any firm that is considering expansion into another country needs to make every effort to learn about the cultural differences that exist between the two nations, and to take steps to reduce any culture shock or conflict prior to the expansion. The firm may consider hiring citizens of the other nation, or it may consider requiring some form of educational exposure to prepare its employees for the move. The employees should be taught as much as possible about the new country, and they should also be urged to "watch and learn." The firm and its employees should be aware that they are visitors, guests in another nation, and should act as they would were they personal guests at the home of a new friend. Above all else, the firm and its employees should avoid being judgmental. New countries and new cultures may seem strange and exotic, or they may merely seem different, but the new country will provide the social values that drive the social contract under which the firm will now be conducting business. Assimilation and acceptance are essential!

A Recommendation for Business

U.S. businesses need to develop a model or a framework of ethical behavior. It is more than likely that no single model can be developed that will apply equally to every industry within the U.S. economy, but it is possible to suggest a general outline for business. This general outline can then be tailored by each industry to the needs and the demands of that particular industry. For example, business should probably lean toward the consequential ethical theories rather than the nonconsequential theories. Consequential theories are more readily understood and more easily accepted by the public than the more esoteric nonconsequential approaches. Additionally, consequential theories are more flexible, and thus are more responsive to social and technological changes.

Regardless of the overriding theory, business should adopt a "synthesis" approach of resolving ethical issues. The firm should first identify the important considerations involved (obligations, ideals, effects), and should then decide where the emphasis should lie among these three considerations, especially with respect to its four constituents (stakeholders, employees, customers, community). This approach works well with any ethical principle adopted, takes into account the people to whom the firm must answer, and provides a framework for decision making that is comparable to other types of business decisions regularly made by managers.

Business should also consider its public relations image in deciding how to proceed within the consequential area. A utilitarian approach, one that is most concerned with the greatest good for the greatest number, is more acceptable to society than an egoistic approach. Society already tends to view business as egoistic—perhaps excessively so—without formally adopting such a theory as the driving force behind ethical considerations. Also, many people seem incapable of distinguishing between egoistic and egotistic. (Egoists measure their conduct on the basis of self-interest, choosing the course of conduct that will provide the greatest benefit to themselves. Egotists are self-centered, characterized by excessive references to themselves.)

Next, business should avoid rigid rules that force specific actions or reactions, especially with the rapid changes of the modern technological age. This does not mean business should not have rules and standards, but, rather, that the rules and standards should be flexible enough to change as society and the business environment change. Business should also advocate the loyal agent's argument, while emphasizing that a truly loyal agent will act within the law while keeping the best interests of the principal in mind.

Whenever possible, businesses should learn to work with the government in establishing statutory regulations. By taking a proactive role in regulation, business can help to protect not only its own best interests, but also can show its concern for society and its various constituents.

The development of a comprehensive business ethic will not be easy, nor will it be greeted with open arms by all businesses or business leaders. The alternative, however, is excessive regulation, public distrust, and a general malaise in the business community. Steps can be taken to benefit both business and society, which can ultimately only be better for business.

http:// RESOURCES FOR BUSINESS LAW STUDENTS

NAME	RESOURCES	WEB ADDRESS
DePaul University Institute for Business and Professional Ethics	The DePaul University Institute for Business and Professional Ethics maintains materials on ethics, including articles, professional papers, an online journal, and book reviews.	http://condor.depaul.edu/ethics/
Ethics Connection	Ethics Connection, maintained by the Markkula Center for Applied Ethics at Santa Clara College, provides current and past issues of *Issues in Ethics*, case problems for ethics, and other ethics materials.	http://www.scu.edu/ethics/
Centre for Applied Ethics	The University of British Columbia's Centre for Applied Ethics provides working papers, research projects, and links for applied ethics sites.	http://www.ethics.ubc.ca/
Students for Responsible Business (SRB)	SRB, a network of business students dedicated to integrating social responsibility into business schools, provides a newsletter, media resources, press releases, and association information.	http://www.srbnet.org/
Ethics Update	Ethics Updates provides updates on current ethics literature, both popular and professional.	http://www.acusd.edu/ethics/
The Institute for Global Ethics	The Institute for Global Ethics, an independent, nonsectarian, and nonpolitical organization, provides general resources on ethics.	http://www.globalethics.org/

SUMMARY

It is important to distinguish ethics from morals. Ethics refers to either individual or group (including society) values, whereas morals refers to individuals' values and matters of conscience. Throughout this book we use *ethics* to refer to group or social values and *morals* to refer to individual values.

Over the history of this country, the social environment in which business operates has changed drastically. As the social environment has changed, the demands of society on business have also changed. Business, however, has been slow to recognize or to accept these changes.

For a substantial amount of time, business was judged by the "game theory." This theory does not take into account several factors, including the fact that the customers of a business may not be aware that a game is being played. For a substantial part of the twentieth century, business has been judged by the social contract theory. The *social contract theory* says that business must respond to the demands of the society, or the society will be permitted to change the "rules of the game" to ensure that business will comply. If business does not act as society demands, society will have the legislature enact rules to force compliance.

Even if businesses (and businesspeople) want to act ethically, it is difficult for them to do so. There are no clear-cut guidelines for most businesses to follow in adopting a code of ethics, and agreements among competing firms within an industry as to what should be done could be challenged as a conspiracy to restrain trade, a violation of antitrust laws. Still, some effort must be made. Business can make this effort by recognizing the human element—the fact that its employees are humans, with human wants, desires, and values. Business needs to recognize that unless it responds voluntarily, the legislature will often intervene. Business also needs to recognize that the courts are beginning to recognize ethical aspects to corporate conduct. Cases, such as *Pinto* and *Pennzoil-Texaco*, will help to establish a new line of precedents concerning business ethics and the liability of the firms that fail to toe the ethical line.

Finally, business must make these changes and develop these ethical standards in a more global setting. Multinational trade carries with it multinational responsibilities, including meeting the ethical standards and expectations of other nations. The social contract business must follow will become more confusing and more restrictive as more and more businesses discover the profits of international trade.

Discussion Questions

1. What is the "social contract theory," and how does this theory affect the ethical conduct of business within the society in which that business operates?
2. What are the advantages and the disadvantages for a business that decides to be "proactive" in the areas of ethics and social responsibility? What are the advantages and disadvantages for a business that decides to be "reactive" in these areas? Based on your responses, which option would better serve a business? Explain your reasoning.
3. Assume that a manager for a national business must make a decision between two alternatives. Alternative A would be very profitable for the company in the short term, but might have some long-term negative repercussions. Alternative B would have very positive long-term implications, but would not be profitable in the short term. Alternative A will make the manager look good immediately, while Alternative B will not enhance the manager's reputation in the near future. The manager's employment contract with the firm will expire in the near future, and she would like to negotiate a new contract for a longer time period. Presuming that this manager is to act as a truly "loyal agent," which alternative should be chosen? Explain.
4. Can the "game theory," which allows—and even encourages—bluffing, be reconciled with the basic social obligations and responsibilities a business is expected to perform? Should business follow the game theory in every situation, only in some situations, or in no situations? Explain and give examples where appropriate.
5. It has been established scientifically and medically that cigarette smoking is a health hazard, not only to the smoker, but also to those persons subjected to second-hand smoke. As a result, sales and profits for tobacco companies have declined substantially in the United States. Cigarette smoking is increasing in some parts of the world, especially in Asia, with a steadily increasing demand for American-made cigarettes. The sale of American cigarettes to this growing Asian market can generate literally billions of dollars in sales over the next few years. Many of the restrictions the tobacco companies face in the United States do not exist in these Asian nations, nor are there any restrictions on advertising. However, the health hazards posed by consumption of the product are the same as those faced in the United States. From an ethical perspective, what should American cigarette manufacturers do under these circumstances? Justify your answer and explain the theory under which you reached your conclusions.
6. Do you feel that the federal government should develop a "model code of business ethics" for all businesses in the United States to follow? If so, why? If not, why not?
7. A business has its headquarters in nation A and has plants in nations B and C. The ethical standards in nation A prohibit a certain business practice as illegal. That same practice is considered ethical in nation B while nation C views the practice as legal, but highly unethical. What position regarding this practice should the business follow? Should the business follow a different practice in each of the three nations, or should it adopt one, uniform policy? Why?
8. Assume that an employee has strong ethical and philosophic problems with a company's policies and practices. As a result, the employee refuses to carry out certain instructions from his or her supervisor. When questioned about the refusal to follow the instructions, the employee explains why they were not obeyed. What should the company do in this case in order to protect the integrity of the firm and to protect the values of the employee?
9. What is the difference between an "act utilitarian" and a "rule utilitarian"? How would an act utilitarian

view a rule that (in his or her opinion) did not provide the greatest good? How would a rule utilitarian view that same rule?

10. John Rawls proposes that universal rules can be developed provided that these rules are developed behind a "veil of ignorance." How would such a veil of ignorance enhance or hinder the development of a business code of ethics for an industry?

CASE PROBLEMS AND WRITING ASSIGNMENTS

1. The Commonwealth of Massachusetts had a statute that prohibited various public interest corporations, including banks, from making contributions or other expenditures "for the purpose of . . . influencing or affecting the vote on any questions submitted to the voters, other than one materially affecting any of the property, business or assets of the corporation." The state placed a proposed constitutional amendment on the ballot for 2 November 1976. This proposed amendment would have authorized the legislature to impose a graduated tax on the incomes of individuals. A number of banks opposed the proposed amendment, and wanted to spend money to publicize their views on it. The attorney general of Massachusetts informed the banks that if they attempted to spend funds to publicize their opposition to the amendment, he would enforce the statutory prohibition against such expenditures. The banks then filed an action to have the statutory restriction on their expenditures declared unconstitutional.

   Did the Massachusetts statute prohibiting the expenditure of funds by certain public interest corporations to influence voters violate the constitutional rights of those corporations? [See *First National Bank of Boston* v. *Bellotti*, 435 U.S. 765 (1978).]

2. Villanueva pulled a gun and threatened the life of Soldano at Happy Jack's Saloon. One of the other patrons in Happy Jack's slipped out the door, ran across the street to the Circle Inn, another saloon, and asked the Circle Inn's bartender either to call the police himself or to allow the customer to use the phone to call the police. The bartender refused both of the customer's requests. Shortly after this occurred, Villanueva shot and killed Soldano at Happy Jack's Saloon. Soldano's child sued the bartender at the Circle Inn and the owner of the Circle Inn, seeking damages in a wrongful death action. Evaluate the position of Soldano's child from both a legal and an ethical perspective, and explain any conclusions reached. [See *Soldano* v. *O'Daniels*, 190 Cal.Rptr. 310 (1983).]

3. Hennessey was employed as a lead pumper (a supervisory, but nonmanagerial position) by Coastal Eagle Point Oil Company. During his time working for Coastal Eagle, Hennessey's job performance was evaluated as "above average," and it was noted that his work "always got done well." After purchasing the facility from Texaco, Coastal Eagle conducted physical examinations of the employees, including a drug test. More than 19 percent of the employees tested positive for drug use, causing Coastal Eagle to establish a formal, written policy regarding drug use which included provision for subsequent random drug tests of any and all employees. The company also adopted a policy calling for the dismissal of any employees who failed these random drug tests, and notified the plant managers of this new policy. (Many of the plant managers did not relay this information to the nonmanagers at the company; Hennessey's supervisor was one of the managers who did not notify his employees.) When Hennessey was randomly selected for testing on 9 June, his drug urinalysis revealed positive results for marijuana and diazepam (the active ingredient in Valium). After verifying the results of the test, Coastal Eagle dismissed Hennessey. Hennessey then filed suit for wrongful discharge, alleging that the random drug test was an unwarranted invasion of his privacy and violated public policy. The company asserted that the position was "safety-sensitive," so that it had the need to conduct random drug tests, and that it was fully within its rights to dismiss a worker who tested positive for any of various controlled substances. Evaluate each party's arguments from an ethical perspective, and determine which argument is ethically superior. Justify your answer. [See *Hennessey* v. *Coastal Eagle Point Oil Co.*, 609 A.2d 11 (N.J. 1992).]

4. Combs worked for AT&T for 12½ years, working from 1979 through 1989 in the Phoenix area. With the exception of a back injury suffered in 1986, she never complained of any health problems due to her job. In 1990, Combs hurt her back again while lifting a heavy mail sack. Thereafter, the AT&T doctors restricted her to lifting no more than 10 or 15 pounds. Despite this restriction, her supervisor insisted that she do the same work as all other employees in the mailroom. Combs refused to lift more than 15 pounds, and her supervisor treated this refusal as a resignation by Combs. Combs was denied unemployment benefits

because she had "resigned" her job "voluntarily." Should Combs be entitled to unemployment benefits? Did she resign or was she fired? If she was fired, was the firing proper or improper? [See *Combs* v. *Board of Review*, 636 A.2d 122 (N.J.Super. 1994).]

5. In 1972 the Florida legislature enacted Chapter 373, the "Florida Water Resources Act of 1972." The dual purpose of the Act was to provide for conservation of the available water resources while maximizing beneficial use. The Department of Natural Resources and later the Department of Environmental Regulation (DER) was made responsible for administration of Chapter 373 on a statewide basis. The statute created the five water management districts of the state, including appellee. The legislature has stated its policy to be that, "to the greatest extent possible," the DER delegates its power to the governing boards of the water management districts. The department has authorized the district to administer and enforce certain laws and rules, including section 373.042.

   Concerned Citizens of Putnam County for Responsive Government, Inc., and Citizens for Water, Inc. (collectively, Citizens) sought injunctive relief against the St. Johns River Water Management District (District). The complaint requested that the District be required (1) to establish minimum water flows and levels; (2) to cease, until the flows and levels are established, issuance of consumptive water permits within certain areas of the District which have critical water shortage problems; and (3) to reduce the volume of water consumption in the critical areas until the water resources and ecology can recover. Citizens alleged that, because of the District's failure to establish and maintain minimum water flows and levels, it has allowed excessive water withdrawal. The excessive water withdrawal, Citizens alleged, has damaged water resources and ecology, has caused certain lakes to dry up, and has caused the flow rates of certain natural springs to diminish dramatically. The District objected to the suit, alleging that Citizens lacked standing. The District also asserted that the statute did not mandate the establishment of minimum water flows and levels, so that the complaint failed to state a cause of action. Did citizens have standing to sue, allowing them to seek the injunctive relief? Did the statute require the mandatory establishment of minimum water flows and levels? [See *Concerned Citizens* v. *St. Johns River Water*, 622 So.2d 520, 18 FLW D1643 (1993).]

6. **ETHICS APPLICATIONS CASE** The University of Texas law school is one of the most prestigious law schools in the country, consistently ranking in the top 20 listing of America's top law schools. Admission to the law school is extremely competitive, with many applicants being denied admission each year. In making its admission decision, the law school applied its "Texas Index" (TI), a numerical ranking system based on the applicant's undergraduate grade point average and Law School Admission Test score, to sort applicants into three categories: "presumptive admit," "presumptive deny," and "discretionary zone." The TI category of each applicant determined how extensive a review of the application would be applied by the admissions office.

   Candidates in the "presumptive admit" and the "presumptive deny" categories were subjected to little review, while the students in the "discretionary zone" category were subjected to extensive review. All students in this category except blacks and Mexican Americans were grouped and their files reviewed by a subcommittee from the admissions committee. These subcommittees could vote to extend an admission offer, place the student on the waiting list, or reject the application. Black and Mexican American candidates were reviewed differently. They were given a lower TI for initial classification (189 for blacks and Mexican Americans, 199 for other candidates in 1992), and had a much higher admission rate "on the margin" than did "nonminority" candidates. This was done, at least in part, to allow the University of Texas to attain its stated target of 10 percent Mexican Americans and 5 percent blacks in each law school class year. In addition, the law school maintained segregated waiting lists, using these lists to help ensure that the school met its stated targets for minority membership in the class.

   Four white applicants were denied admission to the law school in 1992, even though they had higher TI's than a number of black and/or Mexican American candidates who were admitted. These students sued the school, alleging a denial of due process and/or equal protection of the law under the Fourteenth Amendment to the U.S. Constitution. The law school relied on the precedent set in *Regents of the University of California* v. *Bakke*, a 1978 Supreme Court decision upholding this sort of admission program for public universities. Without regard to the legal issues involved, how should this case be resolved *ethically*? Would the resolution of this case by a utilitarian be different than its resolution under the theories of Kant or Rawls? [See *Hopwood* v. *State of Texas*, 78 F.3d 932 (1996).]

7. **BUSINESS APPLICATIONS CASE** Ibanez is a member of the Florida Bar Association. She is also a Certified Public Accountant (CPA), licensed by the Florida Board of Accountancy, and she is authorized by the Certified Financial Planner Board of Standards to use the designation "Certified Financial Planner" (CFP). Ibanez re-

ferred to these credentials in her advertising and other communications with the public concerning her law practice. She included the designations CPA and CFP on her business cards, her law office stationary, and in her yellow pages listing. Despite the fact that she had qualified for each of her designations and that there was no question raised as to the truthfulness of these communications, the Florida Department of Business and Professional Regulation, Board of Accountancy issued a reprimand to Ibanez for "false, deceptive, and misleading" advertising. Ibanez challenged this reprimand on the grounds that her advertising qualifies as "commercial speech," subject to constitutional protections. Commercial speech can be banned or regulated by the state if it is false, deceptive, or misleading. If it is not false deceptive or misleading, the state can only regulate such speech by showing that such regulation directly and materially advances a substantial state interest in a manner no more extensive than is necessary to serve that state interest.

Was the advertising by Ibanez "commercial speech," and therefore entitled to constitutional protections? Was the effort of the Florida Department of Professional and Business Regulation acting within its authority by reprimanding her for her advertisements? How far should a business (including a member of a profession) be allowed to go in advertising goods or services before that business should be subjected to state regulation affecting the right of the business to advertise? [See *Ibanez* v. *Florida Dep't of Business and Professional Regulation*, 114 S.Ct. 2084 (1994).]

8. **IDES CASE** Norris was hired as a mechanic by Hawaiian Airlines in 1987. The terms of Norris's employment were governed by a collective bargaining agreement between Hawaiian Airlines and the International Association of Machinists and Aerospace Workers. In 1987, during a routine preflight inspection of an airplane, Norris noticed that one of the tires on the plane was worn. After removing the wheel to replace the tire, Norris noticed that the axle sleeve was scarred and grooved (it should have been "mirror-smooth"), which could cause the landing gear to fail. He recommended that this axle sleeve be replaced, but his supervisor said that it should just be sanded smooth and returned to the plane. The sleeve was sanded and returned, and the plane flew as scheduled. At the end of the shift, Norris refused to sign the maintenance record indicating that the repairs had been performed satisfactorily and that the plane was fit to fly. When Norris refused to sign the maintenance record, he was suspended by his supervisor pending a termination hearing. Norris immediately went home and reported the problem with the sleeve to the Federal Aviation Administration (FAA). Norris then invoked the grievance procedure called for by the collective bargaining agreement. Following the grievance hearing, Norris was discharged for insubordination. Norris then sued the airline in Hawaii's circuit court for wrongful discharge, alleging that his discharge violated both the public policy of the Federal Aviation Act and the Hawaii Whistleblower Protection Act. The airline removed the case to the U.S. district court and asserted that Norris was not entitled to remedies due to the provisions of the Railway Labor Act (which has also covered airlines since 1936), which provides for mandatory arbitration proceedings to resolve such controversies.

   Apply the IDES model to determine how this case should be resolved, and state why you reached the conclusions at which you arrived. [See *Hawaiian Airlines, Inc.* v. *Norris*, 114 S.Ct. 2239 (1994).]

NOTES

1. *Merriam Webster's Collegiate Dictionary.* 10th ed. (Springfield, MA: Merriam-Webster, 1993), p. 398.
2. *Ibid.*
3. 410 U.S. 113, 93 S.Ct. 705 (1973).
4. William H. Shaw and Vincent Berry, *Moral Issues in Business,* 4th ed. (Belmont, CA: Wadsworth Publishing, 1989), p. 2.
5. *Ibid.*, p. 51
6. *Ibid.*, p. 55
7. *Ibid.*, p. 62.
8. John Rawls, *A Theory of Justice* (Cambridge, MA: Belknap Press of Harvard University Press, 1971).
9. *Ibid.*, pp. 195–201.
10. Vincent Berry, *Moral Issues in Business,* 2nd ed. (Belmont, CA: Wadsworth Publishing, 1983), pp. 44–45.
11. *Ibid.*, pp. 48–49.
12. *Ibid.*, pp. 54–55
13. *Ibid.*, pp. 8–85
14. Vincent Ryan Ruggerio, *The Moral Imperative* (Port Washington, NY: Alfred Publishers, 1973).
15. "Sorry about the car, but . . ."
16. A. Carr, "Is Business Bluffing Ethical?" *Harvard Business Review* (January–February, 1968).
17. *Payne* v. *Western & Atl. R.R. Co.*, 81 Tenn. 507, 519–20 (1884).
18. 417 A.2d 505 (N.J. Super. 1980).
19. Tom L. Beauchamp and Norman E. Bowie, *Ethical Theory and Business*, 2nd ed. (Englewood Cliffs, NJ: Prentice-Hall, 1983), p. 247.

AGENDA

The Kochanowskis need to understand how their business will operate in a global marketplace. CIT will be a regional business initially, so there is some question as to whether it should be concerned with international law and international business. What should a local or regional company know about the international business environment? How can international business and international law influence a local or regional business operation? Will the North American Free Trade Agreement affect the operation of CIT? If the firm expands its operations to include international sales, what must it know in order to export its product to other nations?

These and other questions need to be addressed in covering the material in this chapter. Be prepared! You never know when one of the Kochanowskis will need your advice.

International Law

OUTLINE

- Introduction
- Extraterritoriality: U.S. Laws, International Applications
- The "Rules of the Game"
- The European Union
- The North American Free Trade Agreement
- The General Agreement on Tariffs and Trade
- World Trade Organization
- Exports
- Imports
- Letters of Credit
- Information and Technology
- Nationalization
- Act of State Doctrine
- Sovereign Immunity
- Disputes
- Summary
- Discussion Questions
- Case Problems and Writing Assignments

INTRODUCTION

A mere generation ago, any business forecaster who had predicted the end of the Cold War, the political (and economic) collapse of the Soviet Union, the dismantling of apartheid in South Africa, or the possibility that Poland—or even Russia—would be considered for membership in the North Atlantic Treaty Organization (NATO), might have been told to sell his or her story to the supermarket tabloid newspapers. Many people would also have been very dubious about the prospects for a strong, unified European community. Yet each of these events has taken place over one generation. And these changes represent only some of the massive political and economic shifts that have occurred around the world in recent years. One can add to that list the destruction of the Berlin Wall and the reunification of Germany, the separatist referendum in Quebec, the split of Czechoslovakia into two countries, and the cruel civil wars in such countries as the former Yugoslavia and Somalia. In 1997, Hong Kong, the Asian economic powerhouse, reverts to the control of the Chinese government. The last quarter of our century is a time of unprecedented political and economic change; a businessperson must develop an international—even global—perspective in order to have the greatest chance for success.

Business in a Global Village

Each of these events has created both opportunities and risks for U.S. businesses. For example, the changes in the former Soviet Union have created new opportunities for companies such as Pepsico and McDonald's to develop substantial business activities in these newly independent nations. On the other hand, events such as the war in the former Yugoslavia have caused the destruction of many of the factories and offices of foreign businesses, the killing of employees, and the prevention of goods from entering and leaving the area. Viewed from a long-term perspective, however, opportunities for U.S. businesses to compete in global markets have never been better.

If U.S. businesses have learned one lesson in the past few years, it is, as Marshall McLuhan once said, that we all live in a "global village." Companies such as Coca-Cola and General Electric employ global advertising strategies. Other companies, including all of the major U.S. auto companies, have joint manufacturing and marketing agreements with their Japanese competitors. Numerous other firms and industries are also affected by the global market, some for the better and some for the worse. The textile firms of the American southeast find themselves competing with textiles imported from a number of other nations. Retail outlets across the country carry products manufactured in other nations. State governments are establishing departments to promote international trade by businesses located within the state. "Internationalization" is permeating society at virtually every level.

In 1994, the United States exported $696 billion in goods and services and imported $804.5 billion. When measured in goods and merchandise alone, U.S. imports have grown from $244 billion in 1980 to $669 billion in 1994. In that same time, U.S. exports have grown from $220.8 billion to $502.8 billion. In many cases, typically American companies such as McDonald's, General Motors, and Digital Equipment find most of their revenues or profits coming from overseas operations. Foreign investment in the United States doubled between 1985 and 1990. Marshall McLuhan was right: We are so economically interdependent on one another that we do live in a global village. To succeed in the business world of the next century, every businessperson must be familiar with the basic rules of international business.

Going "Global"

As communications and transportation have improved, buyers and sellers in different markets have been able to find one another more easily, which has made it easier for them to do business together. Technology has opened the global marketplace to businesses of all sizes, allowing them to sell their goods, services, and technology. Future advances in technology will make interactions between buyers and sellers in different markets even easier, increasing the potential for international trade and the likelihood—or even the need—for a business to "go global."

A business has many options once it decides to "go global." For example, as it develops its international customer base, the business may decide to change the way it organizes itself. The business may move from simple selling relationships toward direct investments in major foreign markets. Most businesses start their international operations simply by selling to foreign customers. They may exhibit their products at international trade fairs, or an international buyer may visit a potential seller on a buying trip or be referred to the seller by another satisfied international customer. Like any direct selling relationship, the parties govern their rights and obligations using a contract. Many of the concerns a seller or buyer would have in a local transaction will be the same in an international transaction. Others, however, are special to the international transaction.

Uniform Commercial Code
State statutory provisions covering various aspects of commercial law in the United States.

NAFTA
The North American Free Trade Agreement is a treaty between the United States, Canada, and Mexico designed to create a free-trade zone within North America.

European Union
The EU, formerly called the Common Market, creates a free-trade zone among the member nations of Europe.

Arbitration
The submission for determination of a disputed matter to private unofficial persons selected in a manner provided by law or agreement, with the substitution of their award or decision for the judgment of a court.

United Nations Convention on Contracts for the International Sale of Goods
A treaty developed by the United Nations and intended to provide uniform treatment for contracts involving the international sales of goods.

Suppose that Acme Novelties, Inc., a company based in Arizona, decides to expand its business from national to international. Acme may be selling a variety of items to its traditional buyers in the United States, another variety of items to a Mexican business, and still other items to a buyer in Ireland. Most sales in the United States will be governed by the **Uniform Commercial Code** (UCC); the sale to the Mexican customer will be influenced by the **North American Free Trade Agreement** (NAFTA) and its rules, and the sale to the Irish customer will be influenced by the **European Union** (EU) and its rules. What happens if the tendered goods are rejected by each of these buyers? Whose law will govern the rights and obligations of the parties? The UCC will govern the sales to the U.S. buyers, but may not govern the international sales. The domestic laws of each buyer may be controlling. Mexican law is likely to be very different from either Irish law or the UCC, which would normally be followed in Arizona. Similarly, Irish law is likely to be different from both Mexican law and the UCC. What is the seller to do?

Historically, experienced international traders would specify in their contracts which law would govern the transaction. Thus, the Arizona seller could have negotiated the contract so that the UCC was controlling in all three transactions from the example. Or the parties could have agreed to have any disputes settled by **arbitration.** International sales contracts would often call for any disputes to be arbitrated, rather than tried, so the parties could avoid using unfamiliar court systems and unfamiliar laws.

In 1988, the **United Nations Convention on Contracts for the International Sale of Goods** (CISG) went into effect. The CISG provides a law of sales contracts specifically for contracts between businesses in countries that have approved the convention. In the United States, the CISG replaces the Uniform Commercial Code in any sales transactions between a U.S. firm and a business from another CISG country. Fortunately, the CISG is much like Article 2 (the law of sales) of the Uniform Commercial Code, and follows many UCC provisions, so it should quickly become familiar to American managers. (Articles 2 and 2A of the UCC are covered in detail in Chapters 16 to 19; the CISG is covered in detail in Chapter 20.)

As of March 1997, fifty countries had ratified the CISG, including the United States and other important trading countries, such as China, France, Germany, and several republics of the former Soviet Union. (The complete list of member nations is shown in Exhibit 20.1.) Over the next several years, the CISG is likely to become the law in most of the Western European countries, most of the former socialist countries in Europe, and in several more Asian countries. This should reduce the concerns faced by companies like Acme Novelties in the example above.

Doing Business in a Global Market

As a business grows, it may decide that it needs a more systematic effort to find customers in foreign markets. Often, it will turn to individuals or businesses in other major markets to act as go-betweens in attracting foreign buyers to the company's products. The business may seek an agent or it may opt for a distributor. An *agent* is a person or company who finds buyers on behalf of the seller and usually is paid a commission for the resulting sales. The sales contract is still between the buyer and seller (although in a few cases the agent has the authority to accept orders on the seller's behalf). The buyer gets the goods directly from the seller and looks to the seller to solve any problems with the sale. A *distributor*, by contrast, buys goods from the seller and resells them directly to customers. The distributor bears the risk that the goods will not sell or that customers will fail to pay for the goods. Generally, customers look to the distributor for service after the sale. Businesses with intellectual property rights—such as patents, copyrights, and trademarks—sometimes find it best to sell to a foreign business the right to make, copy, or market the products covered by those rights. Generally, the buyer of the rights will pay a fee plus a royalty—that is, a percentage of the price or profit—on any products sold.

One very popular method for entering the international business environment is **franchising**. United States fast-food businesses have used franchising as the major method of entering foreign markets. In a franchise, a **license** is granted by the franchisor to allow the franchisee to conduct business under the name of the franchisor. This license covers primarily the trademarks, for example, brand names such as Big Mac, Whopper, or Century 21. In return for a fee and royalty paid to the franchisor, the franchisee earns the benefit of the reputation of the trademarks, national and international advertising, and a wide customer base. Many U.S.-based franchisors have identified their largest growth opportunities as coming from international franchising. (Franchising is covered in detail in Chapter 37.)

Franchising
Special privileges granted by a corporation that allow the franchisee to conduct business under the corporate name of the franchisor.

License
A permission granted by a competent authority to do some act that, without such authorization, would be illegal or a trespass or a tort.

Another method for entering the international marketplace is through a joint venture. Black's Law Dictionary defines a *joint venture* in the United States as "an association of two or more persons to carry out a single business enterprise for profit." In international business, joint ventures are viewed somewhat more broadly than that definition implies. The concept covers businesses such as General Motors and Toyota, who built a plant together in California to manufacture Chevrolets and Toyotas on the same production lines. It also covers groups of companies that cooperate in research and development activities and even those that jointly market products. The joint venture has proven itself a successful way for companies to enter new markets, because they get the benefit of local expertise from their joint venture partners.

In many instances, a growing international business will decide to incorporate an operation separately in another country. If the business controls the new corporation,

3.1

INTERNATIONAL BUSINESS

BENEFITS AND COSTS OF "GOING GLOBAL"

Lindsay has been using the Internet in her computer class at school, and she believes that CIT should take an international approach to its operation from the beginning. Dan is convinced that the best approach for the firm is to go slow at the start. He thinks that the firm will be best served by starting out with a regional perspective, with a relatively short-term goal of expanding into a national operation. Since Dan does not believe that CIT will be active in the international market for quite some time, he does not see any reason to adopt an international perspective now. The family agrees with Dan that the firm will initially be operating regionally, but Lindsay's argument intrigues them. They ask you which arguments support Lindsay's position and which support Dan's.

BUSINESS CONSIDERATIONS Should a newly created business operation be concerned with "going global," or should its emphasis be on survival for the short term in its natural regional location? When should a high-tech firm begin to think about global, or at least international, operations?

ETHICAL CONSIDERATIONS Should the firm take international considerations into account in setting up its business practices and internal code of ethics, or should it leave such considerations for the future? How might such international considerations affect how the firm conducts its business or establishes its code of ethics?

then it is the parent and the new corporation is the subsidiary. A subsidiary may be wholly owned by the parent company, or the parent company may have partial ownership. (In some countries, foreign businesses must involve local owners in the ownership and management of subsidiaries.)

Cross-cultural Negotiations

The United States is geographically isolated from most of its trading partners. When the U.S. economy was the benchmark for the rest of the world, such isolation was not much of a problem. In those halcyon days, the U.S. international business was frequently able to employ a "take it or leave it" attitude, knowing that the other party had little choice but to "take it," unless the other party was willing to do without. Why? Not many alternative sources existed for many goods beyond the United States.

Such a situation no longer exists. International competition has become heated, and the emergence of alternative sources of goods and services has produced the need for international traders to become aware of cultural differences in dealing with their customers. If a customer can receive satisfactory goods or services from several sources, other factors besides quality enter into the equation. The successful international businessperson needs to learn as much about his or her trading partners and their cultures as possible in order to present his or her goods and services in the best possible light.

While there are no universal characteristics of any given culture, there are certain guidelines that tend to hold true. Among these guidelines are the following: national negotiating styles; differences in decision-making techniques; proper protocol in the negotiations; the social aspects of negotiating; time, and how it is viewed by various cultures; the importance of developing personal relationships between the negotiators; and social mores and taboos.[1] For example, the American desire to get things done, and preferably to get them done quickly, is at odds with the Chinese approach, to proceed more slowly, operating at a pace that is personally satisfying. Americans frequently make decisions based on a cost-benefit analysis, with little consideration given to face saving. By contrast, the Japanese consider saving face crucial in their social interactions. Many gestures are deemed to be acceptable in some cultures, but may be considered obscene in others. The ability of a businessperson to successfully navigate through the cultural differences of his or her trading partners is instrumental to success in the international arena.

EXTRATERRITORIALITY: U.S. LAWS, INTERNATIONAL APPLICATIONS

Does the law of the United States (or of any other sovereign nation) end at its borders? You have probably seen movie scenes of automobile chases in which the sheriff of one county has to stop his "hot pursuit" of a criminal at the border of his county and depend on the cooperation of the sheriff of the adjoining county to take up the chase to apprehend the person he was chasing. Do nations work that way, too, or is there some way that *domestic* law can be applied internationally? This question is of major concern to international businesses. If domestic law applies internationally, businesses also need to know whether this means that *all* domestic laws apply or if application is limited to *some* laws.

Antitrust Law

The U.S. antitrust laws are intended to ensure that business in the United States is conducted on a level playing field by protecting competition. Various anticompetitive activities are prohibited by these statutes. For example, the Sherman Antitrust Act states in its first section that "every contract, combination . . . or conspiracy in restraint of trade or commerce among the several States, or with foreign nations, is declared to be illegal." Is this statute applicable internationally, or only domestically? While several courts have addressed this issue, the following landmark opinion is probably the best-known answer to this question.

3.1 TIMBERLANE LUMBER CO. v. BANK OF AMERICA N.T. & S.A. 549 F.2d 597 (9th Cir. 1976)

FACTS Timberlane is a lumber company with a long history in the lumber business. In looking for alternative sources of lumber for delivery to its distribution system on the east coast of the United States, Timberlane decided to expand its operation to Honduras. Accordingly, it formed a local company, acquired tracts of forest land, developed plans for a modern log-processing plant, and acquired equipment to transport to Honduras. Timberlane also learned that a plant once operated by Lima (another lumber company) might be available and began attempts to acquire this plant. According to Timberlane, Lamas and Casanova, both lumber companies, and the Bank of America, which had significant financial interests in Lamas and Casanova, conspired to prevent Timberlane from acquiring the Lima plant. In addition, Timberlane alleged that its operations were crippled and that its employees were harassed, defamed, and falsely imprisoned at various times in an effort to prevent Timberlane from gaining a position in the lumber industry in Honduras. Timberlane alleged that these actions constituted violations of the Sherman Act and the Wilson Tariff Act and sued the alleged conspirators, claiming more than $5 million in damages.

ISSUES Did the alleged conduct constitute a violation of the Sherman Act? Does the Sherman Act have extraterritorial application so that it applied in this case?

HOLDINGS Yes. The conduct alleged would constitute a violation of the Sherman Act. Yes, the Sherman Act has extraterritorial application, although if foreign interests outweigh American interests, the court should not exercise jurisdiction.

REASONING The defendants relied on the act of state doctrine, asserting that U.S. courts had no jurisdiction in this case because "Every sovereign state is bound to respect the independence of every other sovereign state, and the courts of one country will not sit in judgment on the acts of the government of another done within its territory." However, the court rejected this argument, pointing out that "there is no doubt that American antitrust laws extend over some conduct in other nations. . . . That American law covers some conduct beyond the nation's borders does not mean that it embraces all, however. . . . it is evident that at some point the interests of the United States

3.1 TIMBERLANE LUMBER CO. v. BANK OF AMERICA N.T. & S.A. *(cont.)* 549 F.2d 597 (9th Cir. 1976)

are too weak and the foreign harmony incentive for restraint too strong to justify an extraterritorial assertion of jurisdiction. . . . What that point is or how it is determined is not defined by international law." The court felt the test was whether the alleged restraint affected, or was intended to affect, the foreign commerce of the United States. Timberlane's complaint alleged a direct impact on the foreign commerce of the United States, which placed the case within the jurisdiction of the federal court under the Sherman Act. [The case was then **remanded** for a trial on the issues raised in the complaint.]

BUSINESS CONSIDERATIONS Why would Timberlane decide to form a local company rather than operate the Honduran facility under the Timberlane corporate name? What advantages and disadvantages do you see for operating a foreign location as a separate firm?

ETHICAL CONSIDERATIONS Suppose that a plant located in another nation would be subject to much less stringent regulations than a similar plant located in the United States. From an ethical perspective, should the U.S. firm conform to the local regulations or to the regulations it would face in the United States? Why?

Remanded
Sent back; sending a case back to the court from which it came for purposes of having some action taken on it there.

According to the precedent set in the *Timberlane* case, the United States does have antitrust laws with extraterritorial application. United States courts have not been in full agreement, however, on the meaning of those statutes with respect to international commerce. Among U.S. courts, there is no consensus on how far the jurisdiction should extend. Some courts use the "direct and substantial effect" test; it examines the effect on U.S. foreign commerce as a prerequisite for proper jurisdiction. Other courts have used a test that looks at whether a conspiracy exists that adversely affects American commerce.

In general, however, most courts prefer to evaluate and balance the relevant considerations in each case. The courts determine whether the contacts and interests of the United States are sufficient to support the exercise of extraterritorial jurisdiction. The U.S. Supreme Court even allowed an alleged violation of the Sherman Act to be decided by Japanese arbitration. In that case, *Mitsubishi Motors Corp.* v. *Soler Chrysler-Plymouth, Inc.*,[2] a firm in Puerto Rico entered into a contract with a Swiss firm and a Japanese firm. The contract specified that any disputes were to be resolved by submission of the case to the Japanese Arbitration Association. An antitrust issue arose in the case; and the Puerto Rican firm asserted that antitrust issues could not be resolved by arbitration, despite the contract's terms, but rather had to be settled by a U.S. federal court. The U.S. Supreme Court disagreed and compelled arbitration as provided for in the contract to settle the dispute.

The Foreign Corrupt Practices Act

Many businesses that are new to the international marketplace have some trouble understanding the different values of people from other cultures or the way business may be conducted in foreign nations. The differences may be relatively minor, or they may be substantial. One area that has been particularly troublesome involves payments to officials in other countries. If a business makes a payment to a foreign official, is the business giving that official a gift or is the official being bribed?

In an effort to address this problem and to provide guidelines for U.S. firms doing business in other nations, Congress passed the Foreign Corrupt Practices Act (FCPA) in 1977. This act, an amendment to the Securities Exchange Act of 1934, covers foreign corrupt practices and provides accounting standards that firms must follow in reporting payments made to foreign officials.

The FCPA only applies to firms that have their principal offices in the United States. The act prohibits giving money or anything else of value to foreign officials with the intent to corrupt. This is a very broad standard, but basically the act is intended to prevent the transfer of money or other items of value to any person who is in a position to exercise discretionary authority in order to have that person exercise his or her authority in a manner that gives an advantage to the donor of the "gift."

Interestingly, the act does *not* prohibit so-called grease payments to foreign officials, although these, too, may look like bribes. A *grease payment* is a payment to a person in order to have him or her perform a task or render a service that is part of the person's normal job. The "grease" is intended to get the person to do the job more quickly or more efficiently than he or she might have otherwise. By contrast, a payment that is made with the intent to corrupt is one that is designed to have the donee do something he or she might not have been obligated to do or to make a favorable choice among options.

Many businesspeople have claimed that the FCPA places American firms at a competitive disadvantage. These people argue that prohibiting American firms from making bribes means they are not able to compete with foreign firms, thus costing the American firms contracts, profits, and jobs. They argue that "everyone else is doing it, so why shouldn't we?" It is apparent that the U.S. Congress does not agree with them; and the FCPA will continue to regulate payments made or gifts given to foreign officials by representatives of American companies for the foreseeable future.

Employment

As pointed out previously U.S. antitrust law, at least in some cases, has extraterritorial application. Similar reasoning has led the courts to conclude that some U.S. employment laws also apply outside the domestic environment. Of particular concern are the nondiscrimination provisions of domestic employment law. In the following case, an American citizen sued his former employer under Title VII of the Civil Rights Act, alleging discrimination on the basis of his race, religion, and national origin. Note how the court treated the extraterritorial aspects of the case.

3.2 EQUAL EMPLOYMENT OPPORTUNITY COMMISSION v. ARABIAN AMERICAN OIL CO. 499 U.S. 244 (1991)

FACTS Boureslan was a naturalized U.S. citizen who was born in Lebanon. The two defendants were both Delaware corporations. In 1979, Boureslan went to work for Aramco Service Company (ASC), a subsidiary of Arabian American Oil Company (Aramco), in Houston, Texas. [Aramco's principal place of business was Dhahran, Saudi Arabia; ASC's principal place of business was Houston.] In 1980, Boureslan requested, and was granted, a transfer to Saudi Arabia to work for Aramco. He remained in Saudi Arabia until 1984, at which time he was discharged by Aramco. Boureslan filed a complaint of employment discrimination with the Equal Employment Opportunity Commission (EEOC) and also sought relief under both federal and state law, alleging that he was harassed and ultimately discharged because of his race, religion, and national origin in violation of law, including Title VII of the Civil Rights Act of 1964. The respondents filed a motion for summary judgment, alleging that the district court lacked subject matter jurisdiction in the case since Title VII protections do not extend to U.S. citizens working in other nations, even if working for an American company. The district court dismissed the suit, and this decision was upheld by the Fifth Circuit Court of Appeals. Boureslan and the EEOC petitioned for certiorari, and the Supreme Court granted their petitions in order to resolve the issue.

3.2 EQUAL EMPLOYMENT OPPORTUNITY COMMISSION v. ARABIAN AMERICAN OIL CO. *(cont.)* 499 U.S. 244 (1991)

ISSUE Did Congress intend for the protections of Title VII to apply to U.S. citizens employed by American employers outside the United States?

HOLDING No. No evidence was presented to substantiate the argument that Title VII applies outside the United States.

REASONING The court ruled that it was a long-standing principle of American law that "legislation of Congress, unless a contrary intent appears, is meant to apply only within the territorial jurisdiction of the United States." Such a principle serves to avoid unintended clashes between American law and the laws of other nations, preventing international discord. Unless Congress shows an intent to extend the coverage beyond the United States, it must be presumed that no such extension was planned or intended. For example, Congress addressed the subject of conflicts with foreign laws in amending the Age Discrimination in Employment Act in 1967. That act specifically addressed the issue, and the statute specified that it was to be applied abroad. There was no such treatment of Title VII by Congress. The court concluded that Congress did not intend for Title VII to be applied to foreign employment of U.S. citizens, even by firms that are authorized to do business within the United States. [The lower court judgments for Aramco and ASC were affirmed. After this ruling, the U.S. Congress amended Title VII of the Civil Rights Act of 1964 to extend protection against employment discrimination to Americans working for American companies even if the worker was working in another nation. While the statute did not help the plaintiff, his efforts will help other American workers facing similar situations in the future.]

BUSINESS CONSIDERATIONS Assume an American firm operating internationally decides to provide its employees abroad with the protections afforded by American law as well as those provided by local law, even though it will increase the cost of doing business. What benefits might the firm receive from such a decision? Should the firm provide these added protections or not?

ETHICAL CONSIDERATIONS What are the ethical implications when a multinational firm provides different protections and benefits to workers in two or more of its locations, based purely on the happenstance of geographic location and inconsistent national laws? What should the firm do in such a situation?

THE "RULES OF THE GAME"

At one time, it was necessary to know the laws of each of the countries involved in an international transaction. The complexity that entailed as well as the increased number of countries in the world since the end of World War II impeded international trade. In an effort to alleviate this problem, countries in common geographical areas have banded together to form economic unions to facilitate and expedite trade. The two most significant regional groupings are the European Union (EU), comprised of 15 Western European nations, and the North American Free Trade Area, which includes the United States, Canada, and Mexico. Other groups in Asia, Africa, and Latin America are now looking to the examples set by these major regional groups to create a legal foundation for their own free-trade areas.

THE EUROPEAN UNION

The European Union (EU) was created by the Treaty of Rome in 1957. Currently, the member states are Austria, Belgium, Denmark, Finland, France, Germany, Greece, Ireland, Italy, Luxembourg, the Netherlands, Portugal, Spain, Sweden, and the United Kingdom. Several other nations have applied to join the EU, and Switzerland is preparing for a referendum on joining the EU. Several former socialist nations of Eastern Europe and several republics of the former Soviet Union have also indicated their interest in joining the EU. The final composition of the EU, however, will not be known for several more years.

The purpose of the European Union is to establish a common customs tariff for outside nations importing goods into the community and to eliminate tariffs among EU members. In furtherance of this purpose, the EU has its own legislative, executive, and judicial branches. The treaty also covers the free movement of workers, goods, and capital within the community. It is aimed at accomplishing international cooperation. The EU is governed by the Council of Ministers, the European Commission, the European Parliament, and the Court of Justice. Exhibit 3.1 on page 68 depicts the governing structure of the European Union.

The Council of Ministers

The Council of Ministers is the legislative branch of the EU. Each country sends a cabinet-level official to the Council to represent its interests in the EU. While the Council includes a permanent representative from each member nation, its actual members change regularly, depending on the issue it is addressing at any given time. For example, when the Council is considering agricultural matters, the ministers of agriculture from each country attend. If the matter involves the environment, then the ministers for the environment from each country attend.

The Council issues both directives and regulations, depending on the circumstances it faces. Directives are instructions to each member country, generally asking it to bring its laws into harmony with overall EU policy. The EU has issued directives on such topics as insider trading, product liability, and television broadcasting, to name just a few examples. When directives are issued, the member countries may continue their own way of handling the issues, so long as their laws conform to the overall policy of the EU.

By contrast, council regulations are superior to each nation's law, and each nation must specifically comply with the terms of the regulation. If a nation's laws do not specifically comply with the regulation, that nation has to amend its laws so that the national law is in complete compliance with the EU regulation. The EU has a merger-control regulation requiring EU approval of mergers that might tend to restrict competition; this regulation extends to all countries in the EU, and each country's laws must reflect the need for EU approval of mergers that might tend to restrict competition within the EU.

3.2

INTERNATIONAL BUSINESS

INTERNATIONAL MARKETS

Tom is excited about the marketing opportunities presented to CIT by NAFTA. He feels that strong potential markets exist in both Canada and Mexico, as well as the United States, and that CIT will be in an excellent position to exploit all three national markets. Anna would prefer to have CIT plan its eventual international expansion into the European Union, arguing that there is a larger and wealthier market available and that there is more potential for growth and profits by dealing in the EU. They have asked you to prepare a position paper for them that addresses this question.

BUSINESS CONSIDERATIONS Should the firm be concerned with an "either–or" position in considering international growth and expansion, or should it be more willing to consider planned expansion into both trade zones? Should the firm look only at these two trade zones (NAFTA and EU), or should it be concerned with expanding to any global markets that seem interested in the product?

ETHICAL CONSIDERATIONS In considering expansion into new markets in other countries, what sorts of ethical issues might cause concern? Are there potential privacy and/or cultural issues the firm should consider?

EXHIBIT 3.1 The European Union

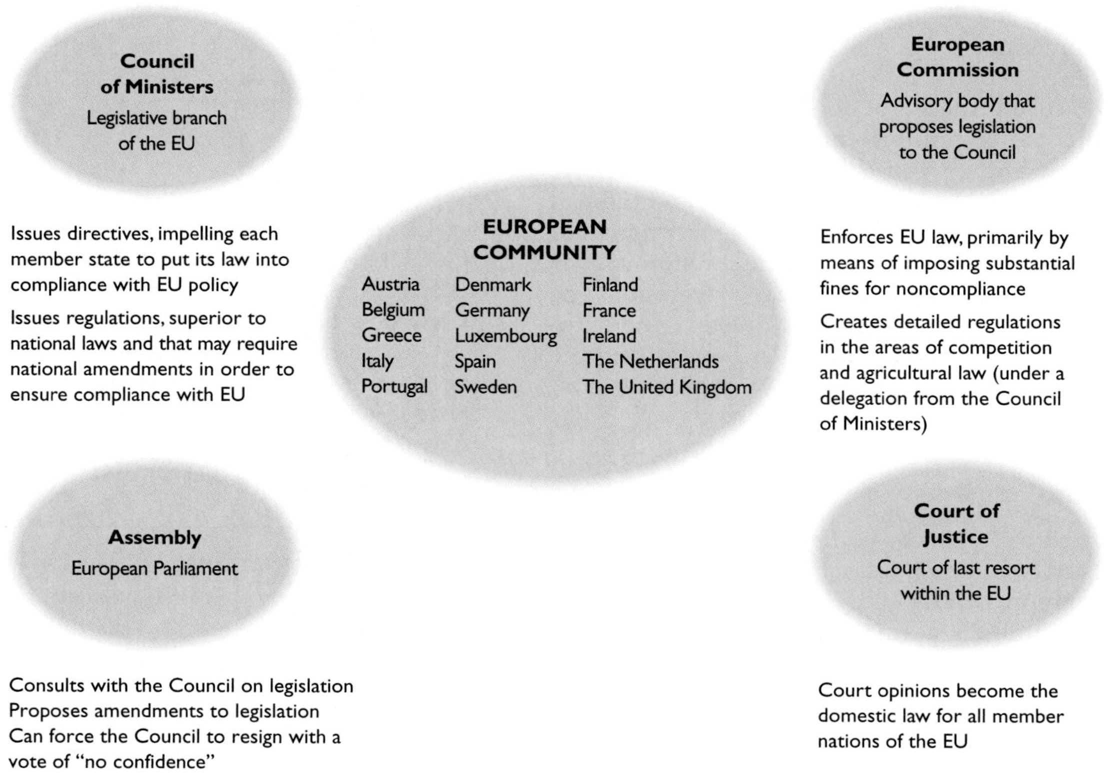

Council of Ministers
Legislative branch of the EU

Issues directives, impelling each member state to put its law into compliance with EU policy

Issues regulations, superior to national laws and that may require national amendments in order to ensure compliance with EU

European Commission
Advisory body that proposes legislation to the Council

Enforces EU law, primarily by means of imposing substantial fines for noncompliance

Creates detailed regulations in the areas of competition and agricultural law (under a delegation from the Council of Ministers)

EUROPEAN COMMUNITY

Austria	Denmark	Finland
Belgium	Germany	France
Greece	Luxembourg	Ireland
Italy	Spain	The Netherlands
Portugal	Sweden	The United Kingdom

Assembly
European Parliament

Consults with the Council on legislation
Proposes amendments to legislation
Can force the Council to resign with a vote of "no confidence"

Court of Justice
Court of last resort within the EU

Court opinions become the domestic law for all member nations of the EU

The European Commission

The European Commission is composed of 17 persons, with at least one from each member nation. However, members of the Commission do not represent their nations or national interests, as do the members of the Council of Ministers. Rather, they represent the EU as a whole. The Commission has two functions in the EU. First, it proposes legislation to the Council. (The council members cannot create directives or regulations by themselves, but must act only on matters coming to them from the Commission.) Second, the Commission enforces EU law. It has the power to impose substantial fines on businesses violating EU law. In the areas of agriculture and competition law (the EU's name for antitrust law), the Council has delegated to the Commission the powers to create detailed regulations. The Commission also has the power to issue exemptions from the competition law (see the discussion of negative clearance later in this section).

The European Parliament

The European Parliament has 518 members elected by voters in the member nations. While it is probably intended to be the European equivalent of the U.S. Congress, the Parliament has not yet found its role as a legislative body. It does have the right to consult with the Council on legislation and to propose amendments to legislation. It also approves parts of the EU budget. The Parliament can vote "no confidence" in the Council, which would then compel the Council as a group to resign.

The Court of Justice of the European Communities

The Court of Justice of the European Communities functions in much the same way as the United States Supreme Court does; it is the final arbiter of all disputes within the EU. Once the Court of Justice makes a ruling, that ruling becomes the domestic law of all the member nations. Convincing the member states to agree to this authority on the part of the court was a tremendous achievement. In order to accomplish this feat, all the member nations had to be convinced that it was in their best interests to give up some of their sovereignty in exchange for the uniformity necessary to maintain the union.

The Court of Justice issued an average of nearly 190 rulings per year from 1979 through 1993, and this caseload began to increase in 1991. From 1991 through 1993, the Court of Justice issued more than 200 judgments each year. In an effort to reduce the increasing workload of the Court of Justice and the backlog of cases awaiting argument before the court, the EU created an inferior court, the Court of First Instance (COFI) in 1989. Since its creation, the COFI has handled approximately 300 cases per year, cases that otherwise would have been heard by the Court of Justice. Even though the caseload for each of these courts is substantial, the load that the Court of Justice would have faced alone was truly daunting.

Objectives Within the EU

The Treaty of Rome established four main objectives for the freedom of movement within the EU: the movement of goods, people, services, and capital. Since the treaty, the EU has developed a large body of law designed to achieve these four objectives.

In 1986, the EU adopted the Single European Act, mandating the creation of a unified market by the end of 1992. In 1991, the heads of state of the EU member countries signed the Maastricht Treaty on European Political and Monetary Union, which strengthened the EU institutions and called for the establishment of a common currency, the European Currency Unit (ECU), by the close of the decade. The Maastricht Agreement has run into some trouble in the ratification process, but many of its objectives will most likely go forward.

Goods. The EU has a customs union that is designed to eliminate customs duties among all member nations. In addition, the union has a common tariff with respect to trade between member nations and nonmember nations. As a result, no burdens are placed on trade between member nations, but a burden is placed on trade with countries outside the EU.

Persons. One of the benefits of citizenship in an EU member country is the right to free movement anywhere within the union. EU nationals and their families may reside anywhere in the EU. Students may enroll in vocational programs anywhere in the EU. Workers may work anywhere in the EU without work permits, on the same terms as nationals of that country. One of the more controversial provisions of the Maastricht Agreement allows any EU national to vote in both municipal and European Parliament elections wherever they may live. Thus, an Irish citizen living in Rome could vote in Rome's city elections, as well as voting for Rome's representative to the European Parliament.

Services. As the world moves toward a more service-oriented economy, the free movement of services becomes an increasingly important benefit of EU membership. Banks, insurance companies, and financial services businesses are now entitled to provide their services equally across the EU. Similarly, many kinds of professionals may now practice their professions anywhere in the EU. For example, doctors, dentists, architects, travel agents, and hairdressers—once they meet minimum requirements—all may practice in countries other than their own. The EU also gives people the right to establish businesses anywhere in the EU on the same terms that apply to local entrepreneurs, thus allowing them to operate freely throughout the EU.

Capital. The European Monetary System (EMS) was created in 1979. Its purpose is to allow only limited fluctuations in the currencies of various member nations from preset parity prices. This is accomplished through a joint credit facility that lends support to an EMS currency when it needs an infusion of capital. To further stabilize the currencies of member countries, the EU created the European Currency Unit, or ECU. The ECU is actually a "basket" of currencies, based on the exchange rates of the member countries. In 1992, the Maastricht Agreement called for the creation of the ECU as a real currency, designed to replace the pounds, marks, pesos, and francs used in the various member nations. The estimated savings to business are very high. For example, if a business started today with an Irish pound, then exchanged that currency in each of the member countries, by the time it became an Irish pound again, more than half the value would be lost just to money-changing charges. Already, some businesses are accounting and issuing bonds in ECUs.

Competition (Antitrust) Law in the EU

To create a truly common market, the EU needs extensive rules on competition. The Treaty of Rome set up the basic structure of EU competition law, and the Council of Ministers has issued a large body of directives and regulations. Further, the European Commission, as the law's main enforcer, has issued regulations and decisions implementing the law. The main concerns under competition law are covered in Article 85, Article 86, the area of negative clearances, and extraterritoriality.

Article 85. In a manner similar to U.S. antitrust law, Article 85 of the Treaty of Rome prohibits agreements, contracts, cartels, and joint activities that intend to restrict or distort competition within the EU. For example, price fixing, limiting or allocating markets, tying arrangements, and price discrimination are all prohibited under Article 85. However, Article 85 recognizes that some contracts benefit consumers by improving the production or distribution of goods or by promoting product improvements. The European Commission, therefore, can exempt activities from Article 85, either by issuing an individual exemption for a particular situation or by a block exemption for similarly situated businesses. An example of a block exemption would be the Commission guidelines for franchises; these tell potential franchise businesses which contract provisions are acceptable and which will bring Commission action.

Article 86. The second major EU competition law is Article 86 of the Treaty of Rome. It bars one or more companies from using a dominant market position to restrict or distort trade. Prohibited abuses of dominant positions include tying arrangements, price fixing, price discrimination, and other conduct similar to that prohibited under U.S. antitrust law. Either buyers or sellers can have dominant positions. The Commission and the Court of Justice of the European Union have defined dominance by a practical test: a firm or firms having the power to "act without taking into account their competitors, purchasers or suppliers" possesses a dominant position. [See *Europemballage Corp.* v. *Commission,* E.C.R. 215 (1973).] Thus, no specific market share is required; instead, the Commission looks at the firm's power to control suppliers and customers and its ability to prevent competition.

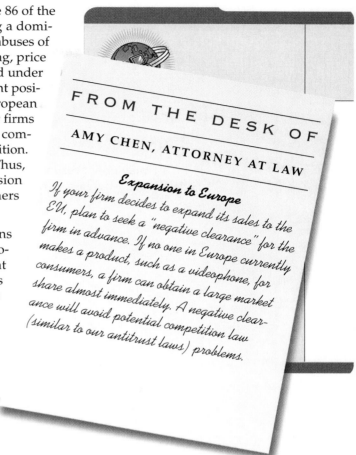

FROM THE DESK OF
AMY CHEN, ATTORNEY AT LAW

Expansion to Europe

If your firm decides to expand its sales to the EU, plan to seek a "negative clearance" for the firm in advance. If no one in Europe currently makes a product, such as a videophone, for consumers, a firm can obtain a large market share almost immediately. A negative clearance will avoid potential competition law (similar to our antitrust laws) problems.

Negative Clearance. A business concerned about its actions violating either Article 85 or Article 86 can apply to the European Commission for permission to engage in activities that appear to violate EU competition laws. This permission is known as a **negative clearance**. If a negative clearance is granted, this means that the commission has reviewed the proposed conduct, and—if the business does what it has indicated—the commission will not prosecute it under either Article 85 or Article 86.

Extraterritoriality. The EU position on the reach of its power to regulate competition has expanded considerably over the last twenty years. It now appears that conduct anywhere can be subject to EU competition rules if it is intended to affect and does affect the EU market. The European Court of Justice has ruled that Article 85 has extraterritorial application if the conduct in question is intended to affect parties or businesses located within the European Union.[3] This should serve as a warning to companies that engage in activities lawful in their home country but that also affect the European market.

Negative clearance
Permission given by the EU Commission to a firm or firms to act in a manner that appears to violate EU competition laws.

THE NORTH AMERICAN FREE TRADE AGREEMENT

One powerful alternative to the EU is the free-trade partnership recently formed in North America under the North American Free Trade Agreement (NAFTA). The first piece of NAFTA went into effect in 1989, with the ratification of the Canada–U.S. Free Trade Agreement. As with its counterpart, the EU, one major purpose of the Canada–U.S. Free Trade Agreement was the elimination of tariffs on sales of goods between the two countries. The agreement called for the elimination of all tariffs between the nations by 1998. (As a practical matter, most such tariffs were already gone.) Goods qualify for tariff-free treatment if they are 50 percent North American in content. Also like the EU, the Canada–U.S. Free Trade Agreement made it easier for Canadian and U.S. citizens to work in each other's countries and for investments to flow across the border. Unlike the EU, however, the Free Trade Agreement did not set up a host of new institutions or require the two countries to give up much of their

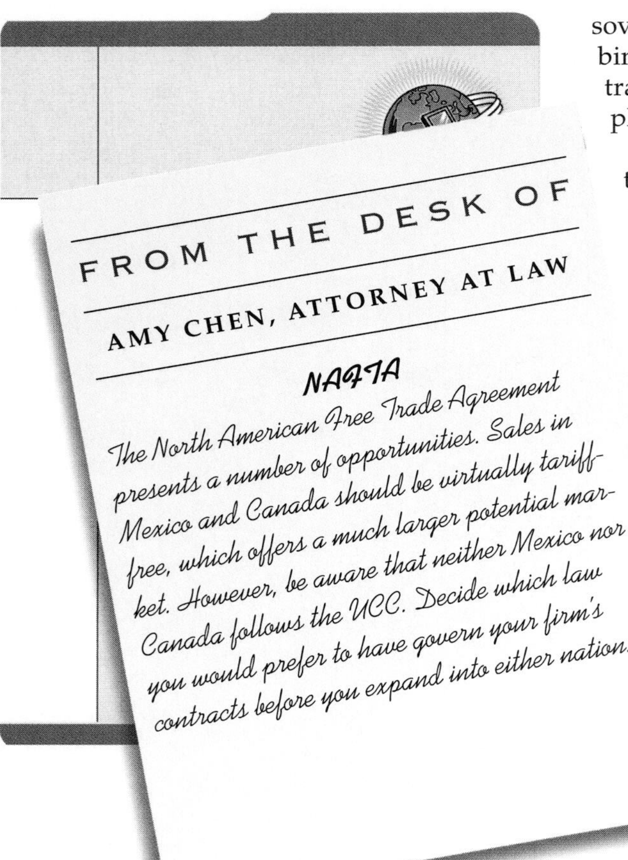

sovereignty. The only new institutions created by the agreement were binational panels of experts to be convened as needed to resolve trade disputes between the two countries. These expert panels replace the court systems for both countries in eligible cases.

In 1993, Mexico joined its Canadian and U.S. counterparts in the North American Free Trade Agreement. NAFTA creates a free trade area encompassing all of North America, a market large enough to compete successfully with Asian and European trade groups. The fate of the North American agreement is not yet certain, however. Free trade with Mexico presents different concerns than it did with Canada. United States environmental and labor groups object to Mexico's reputation for having a lax legal environment, and Canadians worry about more jobs moving south. Although there are still concerns to be addressed, and there is an "escape hatch" for either the United States or Canada to renounce the agreement, the future of NAFTA looks increasingly good. In addition, several South American and Central American nations have expressed interest in joining the agreement, presenting the potential for an even larger and more powerful Western Hemisphere Free Trade Agreement (WHFTA). [We feel that the American Free Trade Agreement (AFTA) provides a better acronym, but does not appear to be the name of choice at this point in time.] Already, businesses from several non-American nations, especially Japan, are looking into investment in South or Central America in preparation for the day when WHFTA is implemented.

THE GENERAL AGREEMENT ON TARIFFS AND TRADE

Following World War II, the Western Allies envisioned an international economic organization that would provide leadership and coordination for international trade in the same manner as the United Nations was to provide in the political environment. A charter was drafted for an International Trade Organization (ITO) in 1948, but the charter was not adopted by enough nations, effectively shelving the ITO.

Prior to the proposed ITO charter, U.S. negotiators proposed a general agreement on tariffs and trades as a stepping-stone to prepare the way for ITO ratification. The Western Allies accepted this American proposal in 1947, creating the first General Agreement on Tariffs and Trade (GATT). When the ITO failed to generate sufficient support for ratification, GATT became the accepted framework for regulating international trade.

The GATT promoted free trade by seeking to reduce tariffs and quotas between nations. It promoted fair trade by defining such trade practices as unfair government subsidies of exports and dumping (selling goods below fair value on a foreign market). It also provided panels to resolve trade disputes. The GATT worked through "rounds" of discussions, during which countries agreed to reduce tariffs for all GATT members. The most recent round, known as the Uruguay Round, also raised non-goods-related issues, such as trade-related intellectual property rights, investment protection, services, and agricultural subsidies.

The Uruguay Round was frustrating for many of the participants, and a number of the objectives that were expected were not achieved. One major achievement, however, was the establishment of the World Trade Organization, an international economic organization that is intended to provide leadership and coordination for international trade. Thus, 47 years after the ITO was defeated, a WTO has been created. The GATT did, indeed, provide an interim stepping-stone to the international organization, albeit for a much longer period than originally expected.

WORLD TRADE ORGANIZATION

The World Trade Organization (WTO) is intended to improve on the gains made by GATT in several ways. Where GATT was restricted to the international trade in goods, WTO will also cover services and intellectual property transactions. Since the WTO is an institution rather than an agreement, it will have the authority to establish trade rules that are binding on each of its 117 member nations. When controversies arise under the WTO, the dispute will be submitted to a panel of trade experts. This panel will then have the authority to rule for one or the other of the complainants. When the panel rules for one of the nations, that nation will be given permission to retaliate against the other nation unless or until the losing nation changes the trade practice that was the

YOU BE THE JUDGE

Is Kodak the Victim of Unfair Trade Practices?

The Eastman-Kodak Company has been trying, unsuccessfully, to gain a significant share of the film market in Japan for quite some time. Kodak alleges that it has been shut out of the Japanese market due to a conspiracy between Fuji Photo Film Company and the Japanese government, a conspiracy designed to create various anticompetitive barriers to prevent Kodak—or any other non-Japanese film company—from having its product widely distributed or available in Japan. Kodak complained to the U.S. government, which launched an eleven-month investigation into the allegations raised by Kodak. Following this investigation, the U.S. commerce secretary determined that, in his opinion, Kodak's allegations were accurate.

The United States has turned this matter over to the World Trade Organization for resolution, hoping that the WTO will be able to confront the Japanese system of *kereitsu* (the alleged interlocking arrangement between Japanese businesses and the Japanese government that effectively precludes non-Japanese firms from having full access to the Japanese market).[4]

Assume that you have been asked to chair the WTO panel of trade experts who will decide this case. How will you decide, and why? What additional information might you need before rendering your decision?

BUSINESS CONSIDERATIONS Presuming that the WTO rules in favor of Kodak, what implications should such a ruling have for non-Japanese businesses trying to export their goods to the Japanese market? How would your answer differ if the WTO ruled against Kodak in this situation?

ETHICAL CONSIDERATIONS What are the ethical arguments in favor of a government favoring its businesses over foreign competition? What are the ethical arguments against such a governmental policy?

SOURCE: *The Roanoke Times* (14 June 1996), pp. A7–A9.

MANUFACTURING/INTERNATIONAL BUSINESS

3.3

PRODUCTION AND LICENSE OF CALL-IMAGE INTERNATIONALLY

A European manufacturer has expressed serious interest in Call-Image and its product. This firm would like to manufacture Call-Image videophones at its European plant and sell them within the EU. The manufacturer has suggested a licensing agreement that would designate it as the sole and exclusive distributor of any CIT products or technology for Europe. He claims that by so doing he and CIT can control at least 85 percent of the interactive telephone market in Europe, cornering the market before any other firms develop the technology to provide any serious competition. Tom and Anna are worried about several potential legal issues raised by this proposal. They are especially concerned about the prospect of possibly violating EU competition rules, as well as possible problems with the U.S. government over the exportation of new technology. They have asked for your advice on these matters.

BUSINESS CONSIDERATIONS What are the potential drawbacks to allowing a firm to have an exclusive distributorship for Europe for the CIT product and other technology? Should the firm seek some other arrangement to better protect and position itself for sales in Europe?

ETHICAL CONSIDERATIONS Assume that the technology used by CIT has substantial national security implications, but that an export license can be acquired by the firm. Without regard to profits, should the firm export its products despite the potential for compromising national security? What argument(s) support your response?

subject of the dispute. In addition, the other member nations are expected to exert pressure on the losing nation to encourage a change in practice in order to ensure compliance. Since the 117 member nations encompass nearly 90 percent of world trade, such pressure and unofficial sanctions are expected to be very effective. However, given the novelty of the WTO, it remains to be seen how effective it will be in practice.

Exports

In order to have truly international trade, some countries must import goods and other countries must export goods. Many students have a simplistic view of importing and exporting, not realizing that there are a significant number of problems to resolve in moving goods from one nation to another. These problems frequently begin with getting goods out of their nation of origin.

All exports leaving the United States must be licensed. For most goods and technology, the licensing process simply involves stamping a general license statement on the export documents. Some goods and technology, however, require validated licenses issued by the Department of Commerce, which maintains a commodity control list that gives the licensing status of thousands of export items. Businesses that export in violation of the export-licensing policy face criminal prosecution and loss of export privileges.

United States exports are regulated for three purposes. The first is to protect the nation in time of short supply. For example, Alaskan crude oil may be exported only if it does not adversely affect domestic supply. The second purpose is to protect national security. For example, exporting nuclear material to Iraq is not permitted currently. The third purpose is to further U.S. foreign policy interests. For example, all exports to Libya were banned in 1986 as a response to Libya's support of terrorism.

Export controls have not always worked very well. Investigations after the Persian Gulf War in 1991 showed that several companies exported material to help Iraq build nuclear, chemical, and other weapons systems. Even more problematic is the fact that banned products are sometimes available from businesses in other countries. The Western powers have a Coordinating Committee (COCOM) to regulate the products that are most sensitive for security purposes. Since the collapse in 1989 of the Soviet Union and the Eastern European socialist governments export licenses have become significantly easier to obtain for products going to countries such as Poland, Hungary, and Russia.

IMPORTS

Getting the goods out of their home country is only half the battle. Next the goods must be moved into the nation of destination. All goods imported into a country must "pass" customs. Passing customs usually means paying a certain sum of money—known as a tariff or duty—at the port of entry, based on the type and value of the goods. For example, when Subaru imported the Brat motor vehicle into this country, the U.S. Customs Service had to determine whether the Brat was a truck or a sports car. This was an important determination, since the duty to be paid differed depending on the category to which it rightfully belonged. If the Brat was a truck, it would require a larger duty than if it was a sports car. Subaru successfully argued that the Brat—despite the fact that it was a two-seat vehicle with a cargo bed—was a sports car. To further this argument, Subaru sold the Brat with two rear-facing plastic seats bolted into the bed of the cargo deck.

Once the type of import is determined, the analysis turns to its valuation. Is the proper valuation its wholesale value at the point of origin or destination, its retail value at the point of origin or destination, or a combination of those factors? In general, the transaction value of the goods is used. The transaction value is the price the importer paid for the goods, plus certain other necessary and related expenses.

The U.S. Customs Court has exclusive jurisdiction over civil actions challenging administrative decisions of the U.S. Customs Service.

LETTERS OF CREDIT

International traders also face special problems when paying for goods, services, and technology. In a domestic transaction, a seller can easily check the buyer's creditworthiness. If the buyer wrongfully rejects the goods the seller is probably familiar enough with the market to know how to resell the goods or can have them returned fairly easily. In an international transaction, however, the seller will find it harder to check the buyer's financial status, harder to collect unpaid amounts from a foreign buyer, and more expensive or difficult to resell or reship rejected goods. To solve these problems posed by the international marketplace, buyers and sellers often use letters of credit to pay for goods, services, or technology.

When a letter of credit is used, the contract between buyer and seller will require the buyer to get a letter from its bank. The letter is the bank's promise that it will pay the contract price upon the seller's presentation of documents specified in the contract. To protect itself, the buyer will carefully specify which documents the seller must present to the bank to get payment. If the seller does not want to collect from a foreign bank, the contract can require the buyer to have a bank convenient to the seller that will confirm the letter of credit.

Suppose that Salesco, Inc., in California, contracts with Buyco, in Australia, for the sale of 5,000 electric motors at a total price of U.S. $5,000,000. The sales contract specifies that Buyco will pay by means of a letter of credit issued by First Australia Bank and confirmed by First San Diego Bank. The sales contract also specifies that payment will be made upon presentation of an invoice, packing list, export declaration, and negotiable on-board bill of lading (indicating the goods had been loaded on the ship). Buyco would go to its bank, First Australia, which would—for a fee—issue a letter stating the terms as specified in the contract. The bank would send that letter to First San Diego Bank, which would then write a letter to Salesco confirming the terms of the original letter of credit. Once Salesco obtained all the documents specified in the letter, it would go to its bank, First San Diego, which would compare the documents with the list in the letter of credit. If the documents were in order, First San Diego would pay Salesco, then forward the documents to First Australia, which would get payment from Buyco, then give Buyco the documents so it could take delivery of the motors. Exhibit 3.2 illustrates how the transaction would work.

As you can see, sellers are pleased to use letters of credit. They are paid for goods even before the buyer receives them, and they are paid even if the goods turn out to be defective. Buyers are less pleased to use letters of credit, but at least they know the goods are present, loaded, and ready for shipment before they pay for them. In order to further protect themselves, buyers can carefully specify which documents are required before the letter is to be paid. In some instances the buyer will also require a third party to inspect the goods as they are loaded for shipment. Buyers are also protected by the legal obligation that the documents the seller presents must strictly comply with the documents required in the letter of credit before the bank can pay the seller.

The following case addressed this issue.

3.3 BANQUE DE L'UNION HAITIENNE v. MANUFACTURERS HANOVER INTERNATIONAL BANKING CORP. 787 F. Supp. 1416 (S.D. Fla. 1991)

FACTS On 3 March 1989, Banque de L'Union Haitienne (Union Bank) issued a letter of credit in favor of its customer, Eleck S.A., in the amount of $1,400,000. On the same day, Union Bank contracted with Manufacturers Hanover to act as advising, confirming, and paying bank in the transaction. The parties all agreed that their relationship would be governed by the Uniform Customs and Practices (UCP) for documentary credit. After several amendments to the original document, the letter of credit was assigned an expiration date of 30 April 1989. The original letter was assigned to North American Trading, which subsequently changed its name to International Basic Economic Company (IBEC). On 19 April 1989, IBEC first presented the documents to Manufacturers Hanover, which rejected the initial request due to its (Manufacturers Hanover's) determination that the documents did not conform to the terms and conditions of the letter of credit. Eleck contacted Union Bank to notify them of the rejection. On 20 April, Union Bank telexed Manufacturers Hanover, inquiring as to the nature of the discrepancies that caused the rejection of the documents. On 21 April, Manufacturers Hanover telexed Union Bank, informing them that IBEC should resubmit the documents on 24 April. This telex did not reach Union Bank until 24 April, and it did not identify any particular discrepancies contained in the original documents submitted by IBEC. IBEC resubmitted its documents to Manufacturers Hanover without success twice, on 21 April and again on 24 April. On the afternoon of 24 April, IBEC finally made a successful presentation of the documents to an employee of Manufacturers Hanover who had not been involved in any of the earlier rejections of the documentation. As a result, Manufacturers Hanover transferred $1,473,189 to IBEC's account with Republic National Bank of Miami. The next day, IBEC wire-transferred the funds overseas, and the principals of IBEC disappeared shortly thereafter. Upon notification of the payment, Union Bank transferred the funds to Manufacturers Hanover. The documents presented to Manufacturers Hanover ultimately proved to be fraudulent, and Union Bank sued Manufacturers Hanover for reimbursement of the amount transferred under the letter of credit.

ISSUE Did the presentation of the documents satisfy the conditions as set out in the original letter of credit?

HOLDING Yes. The only defects initially pointed out by Union Bank were not in areas required to be covered by the letter of credit.

REASONING The documents presented to Manufacturers Hanover were sent to Union Bank on 26 April and were received either 26 April or 27 April. In either event, the IBEC principals and the money were gone before Union Bank received the documents. Union Bank claimed that it notified Manufacturers Hanover of discrepancies in the documentation on 5 May, although Manufacturers Hanover denied receiving any notification prior to 8 May. In the telex of 8 May, Union Bank pointed to two alleged

3.3 BANQUE DE L'UNION HAITIENNE v. MANUFACTURERS HANOVER INTERNATIONAL BANKING CORP. *(cont.)* 787 F. Supp. 1416 (S.D. Fla 1991)

discrepancies in the documents and based its demand for reimbursement on these two problems. However, neither alleged discrepancy was in an area required to be satisfied before the letter of credit was paid. Even if these discrepancies were sufficient to put Manufacturers Hanover on notice of a problem, however, Union Bank was required by UCP to give notice to Manufacturers Hanover within three days of receiving the documents that there was a problem. Union Bank did not meet its three-day limit, and thus it is precluded from raising these issues in this case. The suit for reimbursement is denied.

BUSINESS CONSIDERATIONS What could or should Union Bank have done differently in this case in order to maximize its protections and/or to minimize its risks? What, if anything, did Manufacturers Hanover do improperly in paying the questionable documents?

ETHICAL CONSIDERATIONS Given that the letter of the law protected Manufacturers Hanover from liability to Union Bank, is there an ethical reason why Manufacturers Hanover should pay even though it was not legally obligated to do so? Should a business use a strict literal interpretation of a statute or a contract to avoid making payments that it is ethically obligated to make?

EXHIBIT 3.2 Using a Letter of Credit in an International Sale of Goods

1. Buyco and Salesco enter a sales agreement, with Buyco agreeing to provide a letter of credit and Salesco agreeing to deliver 5,000 electric motors to Buyco.
2. Buyco goes to its bank, First Australia, to acquire a letter of credit to be paid at First San Diego Bank. The letter of credit specifies that payment is to be made on presentation at First San Diego Bank of an invoice, a packing list, an export declaration, and a negotiable on-board bill of lading.
3. First Australia produces the letter of credit and sends it to First San Diego Bank.
4. First San Diego Bank receives the letter of credit and contacts Salesco confirming the terms of the letter of credit and the documents required in order to receive payment.
5. Salesco arranges for the transportation of the goods, procures the necessary documents, and takes those documents to First San Diego Bank.
6. First San Diego Bank confirms that all required documents are present and in proper order and pays Salesco as per the letter of credit.
7. The paid letter of credit is returned to First Australia, which then pays First San Diego Bank for the letter of credit.
8. First Australia informs Buyco that the letter of credit has been paid and collects the amount of the letter, plus any fees, from Buyco.

INFORMATION AND TECHNOLOGY

Historically, patent, copyright, and trademark protection extended only within the boundaries of each country. An inventor who wanted to protect an invention in any other countries would have to obtain a patent in each country. To complicate matters, some countries did not recognize exclusive patent rights in some kinds of products, such as pharmaceuticals. These countries felt it more important to deliver life-saving drugs to their people than to protect the profits of the pharmaceutical companies. Today, although no worldwide intellectual property rights exist, a real trend has grown toward international protection of copyrights, patents, and trademarks. In 1988, for example, the United States became the eightieth member of the Berne Convention for the Protection of Literary and Artistic Works. A copyright holder who publishes a book in the United States will now receive the same protection in other member countries that local authors do.

The area of patent law is also moving toward international protection. The European Patent Convention allows only one filing and one patent examination to obtain protection in 18 countries. Similarly, the Patent Cooperation Treaty also allows only one patent application and examination to serve as a basis for patent filings in up to 47 countries, as of 1991.

Trademark law has also moved toward some international recognition, though not as quickly as the other areas of intellectual property protection. The Madrid Agreement—to which 42 countries (but not the United States) belonged as of 1996—allows one application to provide protection in all member countries. The EU has moved toward an EU-wide recognition of trademarks, but does not yet have uniformity. United States businesses have faced serious problems in recent years with counterfeit goods. Levi Strauss, Apple Computer, and other companies have reported large revenues lost due to imports that counterfeit company trademarks or patents. The United States has toughened its enforcement of the laws designed to oppose these counterfeiters. Section 337 of the Tariff Act of 1930 was amended in 1988 to allow any owner of a registered U.S. intellectual property right, who believes that an import infringes on that right, to apply to the U.S. International Trade Commission for an order banning the goods. This order can also fine the importer up to $100,000 per day or twice the domestic value of the goods. In addition, Congress amended the Trade Act of 1974 with a section called "Special 301," requiring the U.S. trade representative to identify countries that do not protect U.S. intellectual property rights. Once identified, the United States will negotiate improvements with those countries. If no improvements result, the United States must retaliate against those countries. Special 301 has been effective in getting many countries to improve their intellectual property laws.

NATIONALIZATION

Nationalization of privately owned business entities is a risk that exists primarily in developing countries. *Nationalization* is the act of converting privately owned businesses into governmentally owned businesses. In general, international trade can be carried on without fear of nationalization; the exporter merely ensures that payment is guaranteed before shipment of goods. However, international investment is not so simple a matter. To build and operate an aluminum plant or an oil refinery requires a large investment of capital. If, during the time the investment is paying for itself, it is nationalized, the result is usually a loss to the investor. It is for that reason, as well as for others, that international investment decisions usually require a shorter payback period than national investment decisions.

Is nationalization legal? It depends on your perspective. For the most part, from the viewpoint of the country that nationalizes a private property, some act of the legislature or head of state makes it legal within that country. From the viewpoint of international law, however, it may not be legal. If it does not comply with international law, it is termed a confiscation, not a nationalization. If it does comply with international law, it is called an expropriation. The key element is whether the state had a proper public purpose and, in addition, whether "just compensation" was paid for the property. No matter what it is called, there is little that can be done about it if it occurs. One means of insuring an investment against the risk of loss is by utilizing the facilities of the Overseas Private Investment Corporation (OPIC). OPIC furnishes low-cost insurance against nationalization; confiscation; lack of convertibility of foreign earnings; and general loss due to insurrection, revolution, or war. OPIC currently insures more than 400 projects in 50 countries.

ACT OF STATE DOCTRINE

One reason for the importance of seeking insurance protection for overseas investments is the act of state doctrine. The doctrine states that every sovereign state is bound to respect the independence of every other sovereign state and the courts of one country will not sit in judgment on the acts of the government of another performed within its own borders. The concept of the act of state doctrine is embedded in the notion of sovereign immunity. Certainly each sovereign state recognizes all other states' sovereignty. But the act of state doctrine is not a specific rule of international law. International law does not require that nations follow this rule; and in the United States, the Constitution does not require it. Judicial decisions of the United States, however, have recognized the doctrine. The doctrine is based on the theory that a nation is not qualified to question the actions of other nations taken on their own soil. In fact, denouncing the public decisions of other nations can have a decidedly adverse effect on the conduct of a nation's foreign policy.

But what about a situation in which a U.S. bank held promissory notes issued by a group of Costa Rican banks payable in the United States in U.S. dollars? Would there be a lack of jurisdiction if the Costa Rican government, after the notes were signed, refused to allow the payments in U.S. dollars? Does the act of state doctrine apply? The Second Circuit said an emphatic no when it held that the situs (location) of the debt was in the United States and not Costa Rica and, therefore, the doctrine did not apply. [See *Allied Bank* v. *Banco Credito,* 757 F.2d 516 (2d Cir. 1985).]

SOVEREIGN IMMUNITY

In the traditions of international law, all nations are equal and sovereign. Thus, a nation is immune from suit for its actions, either by individuals or by other countries. To be sued, a nation must agree to give up its sovereign immunity. For example, the United States passed the Federal Tort Claims Act to allow individuals to sue the U.S. government for negligent or wrongful acts. On an international level, the doctrine of sovereign immunity causes businesses some trouble, especially because many governments operate businesses such as airlines, banks, auto companies, and even computer firms. The United States has taken actions to limit the effect of sovereign immunity in its courts. In 1976, Congress enacted the Foreign Sovereign Immunities Act, which declared that U.S. courts would not recognize sovereign immunity when the sovereign engaged in commercial, rather than political, activities. So, for example, a state-owned bank could be subject to suit over its failure to pay a letter of credit. The United States has also negotiated many bilateral investment treaties, containing provisions for other governments to waive the right to claim sovereign immunity.

DISPUTES

The best method of resolving an international business dispute is by providing a means for handling that contingency at the time the international transaction is created. Three principal options for settling a dispute are available: the International Court of Justice, national courts, and arbitration.

The International Court of Justice

The International Court of Justice (ICJ) has limited value in solving international business disputes. The ICJ is an agency of the United Nations, and its procedures were established in the United Nations Charter. A private person has no standing before the ICJ. Only nations may appear before the court. A private person who has a grievance against a state not his or her own must first secure the agreement of his or her own state to present the claim. If his or her state asserts the claim, the issue then becomes whether the other state will allow the matter to appear before the ICJ for resolution. Each state must agree to be bound by the court's decision; if they do not, there is no jurisdiction to hear the claim. Exhibit 3.3 lists the authorities the ICJ uses in reaching its decisions.

EXHIBIT 3.3 The International Court of Justice

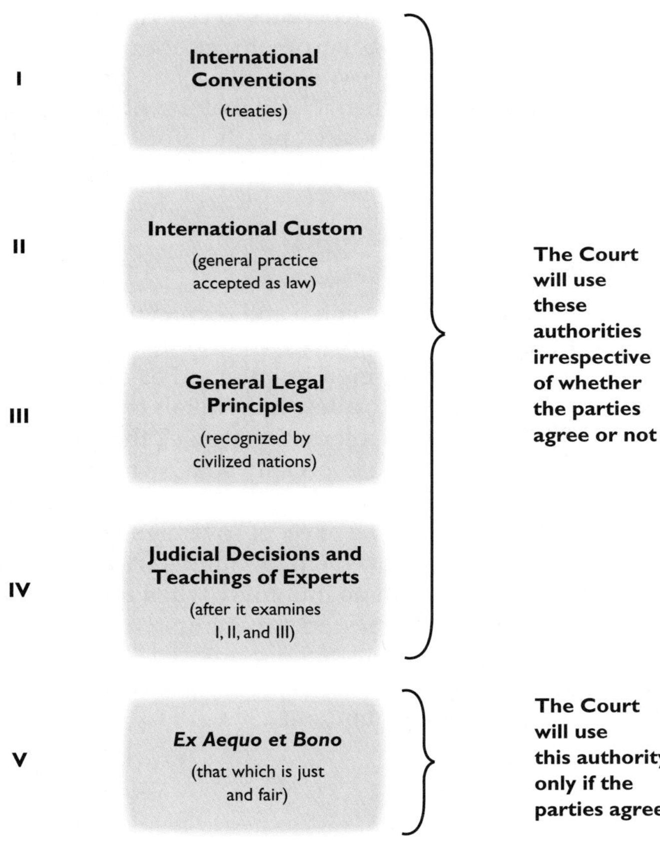

National Courts

A private person can usually resort to settlement of a dispute with a foreign nation by seeking redress through the courts of that state. Private persons can sometimes obtain adequate relief in their native state's judicial system. For example, a favorable judgment from a U.S. court may be filed in another country and, under certain conditions, can execute on assets in the foreign country on the basis of the other country's judicial decision. United States courts are likely to enforce a judgment obtained in another country following a full and fair trial, before an impartial court, with an opportunity for the defendant to be heard. A biased or corrupt court or a case that did not give a defendant an adequate chance to defend against the claims of the plaintiff would probably lead a U.S. court to require a plaintiff to retry the entire claim in a U.S. court, rather than enforce the prior judgment.

The recognition of foreign judgments is not a matter of international law, but rather a matter of comity. As the U.S. Supreme Court stated in the landmark case of *Hilton* v. *Guyot*, 159 U.S. 113 (1895), comity is "the recognition which one nation allows within its territory to the . . . acts of another nation, having due regard both to international duty and convenience, and to the rights of its own citizens, or other persons. . . ." Comity is a matter of respect, goodwill, and courtesy that one nation gives to another, at least partly with the hope that the other nation will return the favor.

http:// RESOURCES FOR BUSINESS LAW STUDENTS

NAME	RESOURCES	WEB ADDRESS
International Trade Law (ITL)	ITL, hosted by the University of Tromsö (Norway), provides international trade conventions and documents.	http://itl.irv.uit.no/trade_law/
The Multilaterals Project	The Multilaterals Project, maintained by Tufts University, provides texts of multilateral treaties, including GATT and NAFTA.	http://www.tufts.edu/fletcher/multilaterals.html
Pace University School of Law Institute of International Commercial Law (IICL)	IICL provides the full text of the United Nations Convention on Contracts for the International Sale of Goods (CISG), its legislative history, cases, and commentaries.	http://www.cisg.law.pace.edu/
Foreign Corrupt Practices Act—15 U.S.C. §78dd-2	LII provides a hypertext and searchable version of 15 U.S.C. §78dd-2, popularly known as the Foreign Corrupt Practices Act.	http://www.law.cornell.edu/uscode/15/78dd-2.html
Europa (European Union)	Europa, maintained by the European Commission, provides official documents, press releases, publications, and statistics on the European Union.	http://europa.eu.int/
World Trade Organization (WTO)	The WTO provides economic research and analysis, dispute settlement material, international trade policy, and publications.	http://www.wto.org/
United Nations (UN)	The UN provides material on the International Court of Justice, the report of the International Law Commission, materials from the UN Commission on International Trade Law (UNCITRAL), and access to the UN treaty database.	http://www.un.org/law/

The following case, while not dealing with business, does involve the issue of comity. Notice how the court addresses comity in its resolution of the case.

3.4 UNITED STATES v. CARO-QUINTERO

745 F. Supp. 599 (C.D. Cal. 1990)

FACTS Dr. Humberto Alvarez-Machain is a Mexican national. He was charged in connection with the torture/murder of U.S. Drug Enforcement Agency (DEA) Special Agent Enrique Camarena-Salazar. An indictment charged 22 people, including Dr. Machain, with crimes in connection with the torture/murder of Camarena. Since Machain resided in Mexico, and since his extradition was not deemed politically possible, the DEA and the Mexican Federal Judicial Police (MFJP) worked out an agreement under which the Mexican police would deliver Dr. Machain to the DEA, in exchange for the DEA's initiation of deportation proceedings against Isaac Naredo Moreno. [Moreno was suspected of the theft of a large sum of money in Mexico prior to his relocation to the United States.] The DEA also agreed to provide $50,000 in reward money for the delivery of Machain. On 2 April 1990, Machain was forcibly abducted from his office in Guadalajara at gunpoint, allegedly subjected to some corporal abuse, and then flown to El Paso, where he was turned over to the DEA. On 18 April 1990, the Embassy of Mexico presented a diplomatic note to the U.S. State Department, requesting information concerning the possible abduction of Machain. In a second diplomatic note on 16 May 1990, the Mexican government demanded that Machain be returned to Mexico. A third diplomatic note, dated 19 July 1990, requested the arrest and extradition of two DEA agents in conjunction with the abduction of Machain.

ISSUE Did the abduction and delivery of Machain to the DEA in El Paso, Texas, violate the U.S.–Mexico extradition treaty?

HOLDING Yes. As a result, the U.S. courts lacked jurisdiction over the defendant for the criminal prosecution.

REASONING The DEA failed to properly obtain the arrest and extradition of Machain in this case. Failing to obtain extradition through the proper channels, the DEA worked clandestinely with members of the MFJP in arranging to have him abducted at gunpoint and delivered into DEA custody on the American side of the border. In exchange, the DEA agreed to begin deportation proceedings against a suspected thief, and also agreed to pay $50,000 in "fees" and "reward" money to the abductors. This abduction and the subsequent surrender of custody to the DEA were not done properly under international law. The fact that the abducting parties were Mexican police officers did not properly establish that the operation was a joint U.S.–Mexico law enforcement operation, which would have negated the need for proper extradition. The court cannot permit itself to be made an "accomplice in willful disobedience of law." [The charges against Machain were discharged and he was repatriated to Mexico by the U.S. government.]

BUSINESS CONSIDERATIONS Assume that, instead of being a suspect in a criminal investigation, Dr. Machain was a defendant in a civil suit for breach of contract. Would an offer of a $50,000 reward by the plaintiff for the delivery of this defendant to a location within the jurisdiction of a U.S. court be a proper expenditure of funds? What issues would be raised by such an offer?

ETHICAL CONSIDERATIONS When is it appropriate to pay a military or police force for the delivery of a person to the control and jurisdiction of another nation? What approach to this problem might have allowed the U.S. to obtain jurisdiction over the defendant without violating any ethical principles?

Arbitration

For variety of reasons, a particular international dispute may not be appropriate for resolution in the ICJ or national courts. In that case, international arbitration might be the best course of action. Many international commercial contracts include provisions for using arbitration. More than 60 countries, including the United States, have signed the 1958 United Nations Convention on the Recognition and Enforcement of Foreign Arbitration Awards (T.I.A.S. No. 6997). The countries that have signed this convention have agreed to use their court systems to recognize and enforce arbitration decisions.

SUMMARY

We live in an interdependent world. Consequently, businesspersons should be aware of the international implications of their business dealings. In addition to being familiar with the laws and customs of the countries where they do business, managers must be aware that competition and employment laws, among others, may reach beyond national borders.

Global trade agreements (such as GATT and the WTO) and regional free-trade zones (such as the EU and NAFTA) are becoming much more important in the world economy. They provide businesses with frameworks for trade and, increasingly, with efficient access to large markets. These organizations have substantially changed the rules of the game in international business recently, and familiarity with them is essential if a businessperson desires success in the international arena. These organizations will serve as models for others all over the world in the years to come.

Changes in international trade, and in the emphasis placed on global development, have led to a number of "new" business concerns. Although imports and exports, labor, and information and technology have been recognized as important aspects of domestic trade for years, it is only recently that they have gained similar recognition in the international arena. Continuing development of regulation in these areas will shape the global market in the near future.

One risk to international business investment is nationalization. Nationalization is the taking of private property by a national government. If the nationalization complies with international law, it is called an expropriation. If it does not, it is called a confiscation. The act of state doctrine is used to justify the position that one country will not stand in judgment of the actions of other countries carried on within their own territories.

Sovereign immunity is a doctrine of law that a sovereign government cannot be sued unless it allows itself to be sued. International law provides three mechanisms for the resolution of international business disputes. The International Court of Justice (ICJ) is the appropriate forum when one nation sues another, provided that each nation agrees to the suit. Domestic courts are used for the resolution of disputes between citizens of different nations. Lastly, arbitration is used in international as well as domestic business disputes.

DISCUSSION QUESTIONS

1. Which recent agreements and enactments have increased the accuracy of the term "global village" in the area of international business? What, if anything, seems to be operating in a manner contrary to the concept of developing a global village?
2. What are the arguments in favor of restricting the application of a nation's laws to its territorial limits? What are the arguments in favor of expanding the application of a nation's laws beyond its territorial limits? Which set of arguments is more persuasive ethically?
3. What is the significance of the Treaty of Rome? How does the Treaty of Rome compare with the North American Free Trade Agreement (NAFTA)?

4. What are the main differences between Article 85 and Article 86 of the Treaty of Rome? Suppose that a business fears that conduct it is proposing may be subject to challenge under either of these articles. How can that business be sure in advance that its activities will not be found to violate either section?
5. Two corporations, one organized in Belgium and the other in Great Britain, seek to merge. They are both in the computer software business. The Belgian corporation has 15 percent of the EU market, and the British corporation has 30 percent. What problems do these facts raise with respect to the Treaty of Rome? If, instead, these two firms were located in the United States, with one in New York and the other in Illinois, would the same problems be raised by their prospective merger?
6. Assume that a letter of credit issued for the sale of goods internationally contains a simple typographical error. Is it more appropriate to penalize the seller or the buyer in such a situation? How substantial should an error be before either of the parties is penalized?
7. An American corporation wishes to export a new computer microchip outside the United States. Do you envision any problems in complying with U.S. law in exporting this computer microchip? Do you envision any problems in complying with European Union (EU) law in importing this computer microchip into the European market? Would problems exist in importing this computer microchip into nations outside the NAFTA or EU nations?
8. How do the United Nations Convention on Contracts for the International Sale of Goods (CISG), the General Agreement on Tariffs and Trade (GATT), and the World Trade Organization (WTO) affect international trade? To which types of international trade contracts do each of these (CISG, GATT, WTO) apply?
9. Three doctrines are often applied to international dealings: comity, act of state, and sovereign immunity. How do each of these doctrines affect international dealings and potential legal controversies?
10. You are a financial adviser to a multinational manufacturing corporation. You have been asked to evaluate a proposal for the firm to invest $500 million in a foreign country. The investment will involve building and staffing a factory in the foreign nation. What factors would influence your decision if the proposed location was in an underdeveloped nation with a relatively unstable government? Would your consideration be different if the proposed investment were to take place in a nation in the EU or in Russia? Why should the location of the investment affect the decision to invest?

Case Problems and Writing Assignments

1. Moosehead Breweries, a Canadian company, licensed its trademark rights and its secret brewing process to Whitbread, giving Whitbread the exclusive right to make and sell Moosehead beer in the United Kingdom. In exchange, Whitbread agreed not to brew or sell any other Canadian beer in the United Kingdom and also to purchase its brewer's yeast only from Moosehead. Once the agreement was made, the two companies applied to the European Commission for an individual exemption under Article 85. Should the commission grant an exemption under Article 85 in this case? Explain your reasoning. [See *Re the Agreement Between Moosehead Breweries, Ltd. and Whitbread and Co.*, (1990) O.J. L100/32; (1991) 4 C.M.L.R. 391.]

2. The Currency and Foreign Transactions Reporting Act requires that certain business transactions be reported to the government. The purpose of the act is to provide the government with information on certain types of transactions that are frequently connected with organized crime and its conduct. The American Civil Liberties Union sued on behalf of itself and other bank depositors to restrain the enforcement of the foreign transactions reporting requirements of the Currency and Foreign Transactions Reporting Act, claiming that compliance with the act was a violation of the Fourth Amendment right against unreasonable search and seizure. Is the reporting requirement a general search warrant in violation of the Constitution? Why or why not? [See *California Bankers Ass'n* v. *Shultz*, 416 U.S. 21 (1974).]

3. Stuth purchases ski boots from Artex, paying for them with a letter of credit issued by Bank One. The letter of credit was for 128,691,300 Italian lire. Sturgeon Bay Bank executed the letter of credit for Stuth. Eventually, the letter of credit was presented to Bank One, and the request for payment was denied by Bank One. When Artex sought to recover from Sturgeon Bay, Sturgeon Bay denied liability. According to Sturgeon Bay, it was only acting as a correspondent bank, so that its only obligations were to Bank One, the issuing bank. Is the fact that Sturgeon Bay served as an "advising bank" to Bank One in the handling of the letter of credit sufficient to make it liable on the dishonored letter? Explain your reasoning. [See *Artex, S.R.I.* v. *Bank One, Milwaukee, National Ass'n*, 801 F. Supp. 228 (E.D. Wis. 1991).]

4. Irwin invested in LeCheval, a Louisiana partnership in commendam. In payment for his interest in the partnership, Irwin executed a $45,000 promissory note, issued a $3,200 check to the firm, and secured a $10,000 letter of credit naming LeCheval as the beneficiary. The letter of credit had a one-year term, and a new letter of credit was procured annually upon the expiration of the prior letter. The general partner for LeCheval pledged the 1981 letter of credit to First National Bank (FNB) as security for a promissory note for another firm, LeCheval Esprit de Acadiens. The note was defaulted on, and the bank presented the letter of credit to the issuing bank, which paid the letter of credit. Irwin reimbursed the issuing bank and then sued FNB, alleging that the presentation of the letter was improper due to the different name for the maker of the promissory note. Was the name of the defaulting party on the promissory note sufficiently different from the name for which the letter of credit was issued to serve as notice to FNB? Explain your reasoning. [See *Irwin* v. *First National Bank of Lafayette,* 587 So.2d 203 (La. App. 1991).]

5. The European Commission charged 41 wood pulp producers with violations of Article 85 in that the producers were accused of taking concerted action to fix prices for the wood pulp sold to EU customers. Each of the wood pulp producers was operating outside the EU, although all of them imported products into the EU market. The producers claimed that the EU had no jurisdiction in this case, since all of the alleged price-fixing activity took place outside the EU and was therefore beyond the jurisdiction of the commission or its sanctions. The commission rejected this claim, and fined 36 of the producers. These 36 producers appealed to the Court of Justice of the European Communities. Does Article 85 have extraterritorial application beyond the borders of the EU in a case such as this? Which factors most influenced your decision? [See *Re Wood Pulp Cartel* v. *Commission,* 4 C.M.L.R. 901 (1988).]

6. **BUSINESS APPLICATION CASE** In 1981, Harry Carpenter, chairman and chief executive officer of W.S. Kirkpatrick & Co., learned that the Republic of Nigeria was interested in contracting for the construction and equipment of an aeromedical center at Kaduna Air Force Base in Nigeria. Carpenter made arrangements with Benson Akindele, a Nigerian citizen, under which Akindele agreed to secure the contract for W.S. Kirkpatrick. It was further agreed that, provided Akindele did secure the contract for W.S. Kirkpatrick, a "commission" equal to 20 percent of the total contract price would be paid to two Panamanian entities controlled by Akindele. It was understood that this "commission" would be paid to officials of the Nigerian government as a bribe once the contract was awarded to W.S. Kirkpatrick. The contract was awarded to W.S. Kirkpatrick, the "commission" was paid to the Panamanian entities, and was then distributed to various Nigerian officials. Environmental Tectronics, one of the unsuccessful bidders for the contract, learned of the arrangement between Carpenter and Akindele and brought the matter to the attention of both the Nigerian Air Force and the U.S. Embassy in Lagos, Nigeria. [All parties agreed that it is a violation of Nigerian law to pay or to receive a bribe in connection with the award of a government contract.] If the allegations made by Environmental Tectronics are proven, should Carpenter, Akindele, and W.S. Kirkpatrick be found guilty for violations of the Foreign Corrupt Practices Act? Should Environmental Tectronics be entitled to any remedies in a civil action against any or all of the parties accused of illegal conduct in this case? Explain your reasoning. [See *W.S. Kirkpatrick & Co.* v. *Environmental Tectronics Corp., Int'l,* 493 U.S. 400 (1990).]

7. **ETHICAL APPLICATION CASE** A number of celebrities have been embarrassed recently over adverse publicity concerning the construction of clothing that they endorse. Kathy Lee Gifford, Michael Jordan, and Jacqueline Smith, to name a few, have been criticized publicly because the clothing bearing their names and endorsements had been made in other nations, often by child laborers who were paid as little as 31 cents per hour. Even more embarrassing, at least for Kathy Lee Gifford, was the disclosure that some of the garments bearing her name were made in sweatshops in New York City in which immigrant workers were being paid—when they were paid—at less than the minimum wage. [It is generally agreed that the celebrities were not aware of the work environment of the factories in which the clothing was constructed.] Without regard to the legality of the situation, what are the ethical implications when a celebrity endorses a product, especially a "signature line" of clothing, at a substantial profit to the celebrity, but the apparel is constructed by child laborers earning a very low hourly wage? What should a celebrity be expected to do ethically or legally if or when such a situation is brought to the celebrity's attention? [See, for example, "Kathie Lee's Crisis Uncovered Sweatshop Tangle," *Denver Post,* 1 July 1996, p. 2E.]

8. **IDES CASE** The Kingdom of Saudi Arabia owns and operates King Faisal Specialist Hospital in Riyadh, Saudi Arabia, as well as Royspec Purchasing Services,

a corporate purchasing agent located in the United States. Hospital Corporation of America (HCA) is an independent corporation existing under the laws of the Cayman Islands. HCA recruits Americans for employment at the King Faisal Specialist Hospital. Nelson was recruited by HCA, eventually accepting an offer to work in the Hospital beginning in December 1983. His position required him to monitor all "facilities, equipment, utilities, and maintenance systems to insure the safety of patients, hospital staff, and others." Nelson performed his duties without incident until March 1984, when he discovered safety defects in the Hospital's oxygen and nitrous oxide lines that he felt posed fire hazards and otherwise endangered patients' lives. Over the next several months Nelson repeatedly reported these safety defects to various Hospital officials and to a Saudi government commission. Nelson was told to ignore the problem, but he refused to do so. Finally, in September 1984, Nelson was summoned to the Hospital security office, where he was arrested and transferred to a jail cell. Nelson claims that he was then shackled, tortured, beaten, and held without food for four days. He also was forced to sign a statement written in Arabic (which Nelson could not read), after which he was transferred to a prison to await trial on unknown charges. In November 1984, Nelson was released and allowed to leave the country, following the intercession on Nelson's behalf of a U.S. senator. In 1988, Nelson sued the Saudi Arabian government, the Hospital, and Royspec, seeking damages for personal injuries. The U.S. district court dismissed the case for lack of subject matter jurisdiction, citing the Foreign Sovereign Immunities Act. Did any of the defendants "carry on" business within the United States so that a U.S. court could assert subject matter jurisdiction over this case? Should an American citizen who is recruited in the United States for employment overseas be entitled to seek damages for injuries suffered on the job in the foreign nation? How should the courts resolve this case? Apply the IDES model to answer these questions. [See *Saudi Arabia* v. *Nelson*, 507 U.S. 349 (1993).]

NOTES

1. Paul A. Herbig and Hugh E. Kramer, "Do's and Don't's of Cross-Cultural Negotiations," *Industrial Marketing Management* 21 (1992): 287.
2. 473 U.S. 614 (1985).
3. *Re Wood Pulp Cartel et al.* v. *Commission*, 4 C.M.L.R. 901 (1988).
4. A.P., "U.S. Turns Kodak-Fuji Flap Over to World Trade Group," *The Roanoke Times*, 14 June 1996, pp. A7–A9.

P A R T

IDES PROBLEMS

Controversy has arisen over fund-raising activities of the Democratic party during the 1996 Presidential election. Did foreign interests, in making large contributions to the Democratic National Committee (DNC), attempt to influence Bill Clinton on foreign policy and/or trade policy issues? The DNC allegedly solicited contributions from foreign interests and accepted thousands of dollars from citizens of foreign nations, many of whom also regularly conduct business in the United States. Did Vice President Al Gore's telephone calls from the White House possibly imply that favorable treatment would follow for those who contributed? These calls were allegedly paid for by the DNC rather than the White House (and thus the taxpayers). However, federal law prohibits government employees from soliciting contributions while they are working, although Gore claimed not to be a "government employee" in the legal sense of the term. Despite congressional pressure, Attorney General Janet Reno, a Clinton appointee, refused to appoint an independent investigator to probe these fund-raising practices, citing a lack of "specific, credible evidence" of wrongdoing.

Federal campaign laws state that citizens and noncitizens legally admitted as permanent residents and who live in the United States at the time may donate to federal political campaigns. U.S. corporations and U.S. units of non-U.S. corporations may also donate, if those U.S. subsidiaries supply the money from their own revenues and do not act on foreign orders. These donations may not go to particular federal campaigns, but may be made to the party of the candidates (so-called soft money).

Given these controversies, use the IDES approach to evaluate the legal and ethical implications of the following hypothetical scenario. Dora, a Mexican citizen living permanently in the United States, is president of AirTex, Inc. (AirTex), the Texas-based subsidiary of AirMex, Inc. (AirMex), a Mexican corporation located in Mexico City. AirMex and AirTex produce military, commercial, and recreational airplanes. On the urging of Vice President Gore, Dora donated $500,000 of AirTex's money to the DNC. Dora also convinced other businesspeople to donate money, some of whom were Mexican citizens living in Mexico. Dora was unaware of the U.S. federal campaign financing laws. Dora agreed to donate the money without consulting AirMex officials, and neither AirTex nor AirMex had contact with Mexican authorities regarding these donations. Dora believed that these donations guaranteed that a pending federal military contract would be given to AirTex.

When this proved incorrect, Dora insisted on pursuing legal action against the White House. Frank, a manager at AirTex, worried that Dora's conduct was unethical and illegal and that AirTex and AirMex violated the U.S. Foreign Corrupt Practices Act (FCPA), the Act of State doctrine, and provisions of the North American Free Trade Agreement (NAFTA). Frieda, another manager, does not agree that the conduct was unethical in itself; however, she is worried that the donation may result in bad publicity. Dora has asked you to prepare a report addressing the following:

IDENTIFY What are the legal and ethical issues or problems surrounding AirTex's and Dora's actions?

DEFINE What are the meanings of the relevant legal terms associated with these issues?

ENUMERATE What are the legal and ethical principles relevant to these issues?

SHOW BOTH SIDES Consider all of the facts in light of the above questions. What are the legal and ethical positions of all the parties involved?

(To review the IDES approach refer to pages 29–30.)

THE AMERICAN LEGAL SYSTEM

To successfully handle (and avoid) legal problems in the workplace, businesspeople need to understand how the U.S. legal system operates. Chapter 4 describes the powers and limitations of the federal government as set forth in the U.S. Constitution. It also describes courts and jurisdiction, and introduces alternative forms of dispute resolution.

Chapter 5 describes torts and the body of civil law concerned with "private" wrongs that may arise in the workplace. In particular, this chapter discusses intentional torts, negligence, and strict liability. Chapter 6 provides a step-by-step example of a civil lawsuit, using Call-Image Technology as the basis for the example.

Chapter 7 describes crimes and the body of law concerned with public wrongs. This chapter concentrates on crimes that affect business—embezzlement, forgery, and fraud, for example. In particular, the chapter discusses the objectives of criminal law, the bases of criminal responsibility, and the nature of the offense. The chapter also contains a brief discussion of selected crimes.

I D E S

Albee, having been successful in his college investment courses, decided to begin his own "investment" business, investing in stocks for himself and, for a fee, his clients. Albee revealed to all of his clients that he possessed no license, no "real-world" business experience, no insurance, and that all investments were made at the client's "own risk." Albee insisted that his clients trust him and his natural ability to make money. When the business went sour, Albee's clients sought legal recourse.

What sort of liability—if any—might Albee face? Is there any evidence of illegal activities? Of civil wrongs? Of ethical errors? In what court and under what jurisdiction would these potential charges be brought? Do any alternative methods for resolving these disputes exist? Has Albee made any ethical errors? Consider these issues in the context of the chapter materials, and prepare to analyze these issues using the IDES model.

IDENTIFY the legal issues raised by the questions.

DEFINE all the relevant legal terms and issues involved.

ENUMERATE the legal principles associated with these issues.

SHOW BOTH SIDES by using the facts.

A G E N D A

The Kochanowskis never realized how important it is for owners and operators of a business to understand the complexities of the U.S. legal system. What, for example, does CIT need to know about state and federal court systems, or about the different types of jurisdiction? Tom and Anna obtained a U.S. patent on Call-Image, but they are not sure how well this patent will protect the technology behind the videophone. Can CIT test this claim in court before a challenge arises? Use care to distinguish the rules applicable to the federal government and those applicable to the states. Be prepared! You never know when one of the Kochanowskis will call on you for help or advice.

The American Legal System and Court Jurisdiction

O U T L I N E

THE FEDERAL CONSTITUTION

The Constitution of the United States is a unique document for two reasons: it is the oldest written national constitution, and it was the first to include a government based on the concept of a separation of powers. A copy of the Constitution is included as Appendix A of this book. The U.S. Constitution was created in reaction to the tyranny of English rule; it was intended to prevent many of the problems the founding fathers felt were present under the English government. England has an unwritten constitution and a system of government that tends to merge the legislative, executive, and judicial functions. In contrast, our written constitution established a governmental structure, which has three separate "compartments" and a series of checks and balances whereby the power of one "compartment" is offset, at least to some extent, by that of the others.

Because their study of history taught them that all tyrants had at least two powers—the power of the purse and the power of the sword—our founding fathers placed the power of the purse (fiscal and monetary) in the legislative branch of government and the power of the sword (armed forces) in the executive branch. The third branch of government, the judicial branch, does not have the formal, written power that exists in the other branches of government. It does, however, possess what may be the most important power, at least from a constitutional perspective. The judicial branch has the power to make the ultimate decision as to where and how the other two branches may properly exercise their powers. This power was "created" by the court itself in the landmark case, *Marbury* v. *Madison*,[1] and is called the power of *judicial review*. We shall discuss judicial review later in this chapter in greater detail.

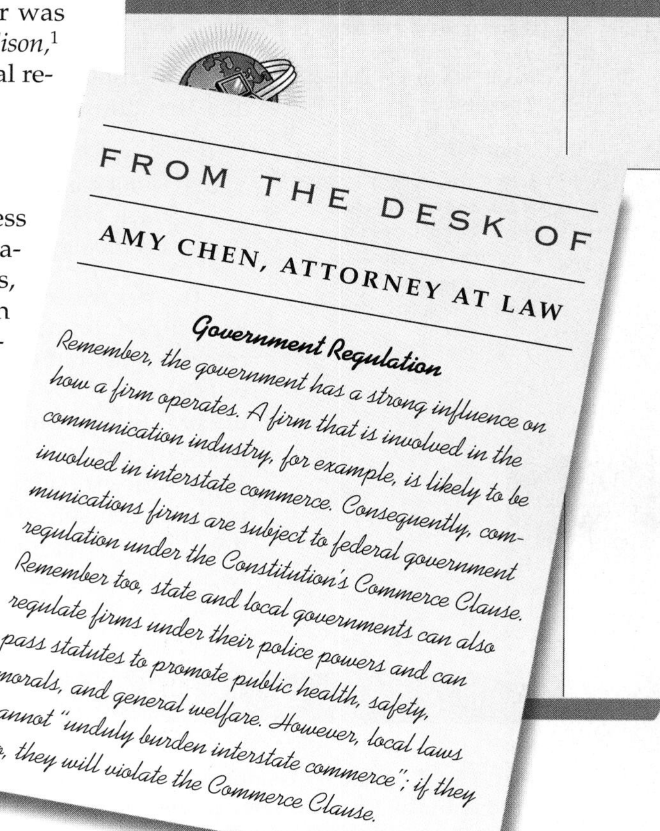

FROM THE DESK OF
AMY CHEN, ATTORNEY AT LAW
Government Regulation
Remember, the government has a strong influence on how a firm operates. A firm that is involved in the communication industry, for example, is likely to be involved in interstate commerce. Consequently, communications firms are subject to federal government regulation under the Constitution's Commerce Clause. Remember too, state and local governments can also regulate firms under their police powers and can pass statutes to promote public health, safety, morals, and general welfare. However, local laws cannot "unduly burden interstate commerce"; if they do, they will violate the Commerce Clause.

Allocation of Power

Legislative Power. Article I of the Constitution creates a Congress consisting of two houses: the Senate and the House of Representatives. Congress has the power to levy and collect taxes, pay debts, and pass all laws with respect to certain enumerated powers, such as providing for the common defense and general welfare, regulating commerce, borrowing and coining money, establishing post offices and building highways, promoting science and the arts, and creating courts inferior to the U.S. Supreme Court.

Executive Power. The U.S. Constitution, Article II, creates the executive branch of government by establishing the offices of president and vice president. The president is the commander-in-chief of the armed forces of the United States. In addition, the president has the power to make treaties and to nominate ambassadors, judges, and other officers of the United States. The Senate must confirm all presidential appointments. Without Senate confirmation, the appointee cannot take office. The vice president is the president of the Senate and also serves for the president when or if the president is unable to serve.

Administrative Agencies, an Additional Executive Power. Administrative agencies also wield power under the executive branch of government, even though they are not

Cases and controversies
Claims brought before the court in regular proceedings to protect or enforce rights or to prevent or punish wrongs.

Advisory opinion
A formal opinion by a judge, court, or law officer on a question of law submitted by a legislative body or a government official but not presented in an actual case.

Reversed
To overturn the lower court's decision.

Remanded
To return the case to the lower court for correction.

Certiorari
A writ used by a superior court to direct an inferior court to send it the records and proceedings in a case for review.

Moot case
A case not properly submitted to a court for resolution because it seeks to determine an abstract question that does not arise upon existing facts or rights

discussed in the U.S. Constitution. These agencies are sometimes called a fourth branch of government. They are generally created by statute at the request of the executive branch. The statute that creates the agency is called the *enabling statute* and it specifies the power and authority of the agency. Most federal agencies have the power, within their authority, to make rules that are similar to statutes and to decide cases involving these rules and regulations. (These cases take the form of administrative hearings; they are not cases in the literal sense of the word.) The exact authority and the organization of the agencies vary greatly. Administrative agencies exist on the federal, state, and local levels. See Chapter 39 for a more detailed discussion of administrative agencies.

Judicial Power. Article III of the Constitution vests federal judicial power in one Supreme Court and in such other inferior courts as Congress may create. All U.S. federal judges are nominated by the president; moreover, if they are confirmed by the Senate, they are permitted to serve in office for the rest of their lives, as long as their behavior is "good."

The actual wording of Article III limits rather than expands judicial power. Under Section 2 of Article III, generally the federal courts may only hear and decide **cases and controversies.** *Cases and controversies* can be defined as matters that are appropriate for judicial determination. For a matter to be appropriate for judicial determination, the matter must be: "definite and concrete, touching the legal relations of parties having adverse legal interests. It must be a real and substantial controversy admitting of specific relief through a decree of a conclusive character, as distinguished from an opinion advising what the law would be upon a hypothetical state of facts."[2] Constitutional law has evolved through precedents so that, today, the following are not considered to be a case or a controversy:

1. Advisory opinions
2. Moot cases
3. Lack of standing
4. Political questions

The doctrine of the separation of powers requires that federal courts deal only with judicial matters. An **advisory opinion** is one in which the executive branch refers a question to the judicial branch for a nonbinding opinion. However, that is not the purpose of the federal judicial system. Accordingly, whenever a member of the executive branch requires an advisory opinion, the question is referred to the justice department within the executive branch for an opinion of the attorney general. Under the U.S. federal system of government, the attorney general is the appropriate person to issue an advisory opinion. Some state courts are empowered to give advisory opinions. The following case illustrates that judicial power is limited to real controversies and does not encompass advisory opinions.

4.1 G.T.E. SYLVANIA, INC. v. CONSUMERS UNION — 445 U.S. 375 (1980)

FACTS Consumers Union brought an action under the Freedom of Information Act to obtain reports on television-related accidents from the Consumer Product Safety Commission (CPSC). The U.S. District Court dismissed the case. The U.S. Court of Appeals **reversed** and **remanded.** The U.S. Supreme Court granted **certiorari** and decided to remand. Then, the Court of Appeals remanded for a trial on the merits. *Certiorari* was again granted by the Supreme Court, resulting in this opinion.

4.1 G.T.E. SYLVANIA, INC. v. CONSUMERS UNION *(cont.)* 445 U.S. 375 (1980)

ISSUE Does this action present a sufficient case or controversy to establish proper jurisdiction, even though the CPSC agreed with the requester that the documents should be released?

HOLDING Yes.

REASONING There was a sufficient case or controversy. "The purpose of the case-or-controversy requirement is to limit the business of federal courts to questions presented in the adversary context and in a form historically viewed as capable of resolution through the judicial process. . . . The clash of adverse parties sharpens the presentation of issues upon which the court so largely depends for illumination of difficult questions." However, here the CPSC and Consumers Union do not want precisely the same result. Television manufacturers obtained an injunction to prevent the release of the information in question. Consequently, to allow the CPSC to release the information would subject it to attack for violating the injunction. Thus, the parties actually do not want precisely the same outcome.

BUSINESS CONSIDERATIONS What is the practical effect of the cases-and-controversy limitation on businesses? When might a business prefer to have an advisory opinion rather than an actual case?

ETHICAL CONSIDERATIONS Is it ethical for organizations, who are basically on the same side of an issue, to initiate litigation to obtain a legal ruling? Why or why not?

The federal courts will only hear cases that are appropriate for a judicial solution. **Moot cases** are those cases in which the matter has been resolved. In the case of *DeFunis* v. *Odegaard,*[3] the Supreme Court stated that the question of whether a student should be admitted to a law school was a moot case because by the time the Court could have issued its opinion, the student would have been on the brink of graduation. The law school informed the Supreme Court that regardless of the outcome of the suit, the law school would award DeFunis a degree if he passed his final quarter of coursework. Accordingly, as an example of judicial efficiency, it chose not to write an opinion on the merits of the suit.

Only persons who can assert that they have actually been harmed or injured have **standing** to sue. For example, if you saw a person punch someone in the nose, you would not have standing to sue the aggressor for **assault** or **battery**; only the person who was hit would have standing to sue because he or she was the one who was injured. The following classic case discusses one aspect of standing.

Standing
Legal involvement; the right to sue.

Assault
A threat to touch someone in an undesired manner.

Battery
Unauthorized touching of another person without legal justification or that person's consent.

4.2 FLAST v. COHEN 392 U.S. 83 (1968)

FACTS A federal taxpayer brought suit to prohibit the spending of federal monies to finance instructional materials in parochial schools. The spending was authorized under the Elementary and Secondary Education Act of 1965. The suit was based on the grounds that such expenditures were in violation of the First Amendment provisions guaranteeing freedom of religion.

ISSUE Does a taxpayer have standing to sue?

HOLDING Yes.

REASONING In such a case a taxpayer does have standing. "The fundamental aspect of standing is that it focuses on the party seeking to get his complaint before a federal court and not on the issues he wishes to have adjudicated." The party seeking relief must have a personal stake in the outcome of the controversy so as to ensure a real awareness. Under certain circumstances, a taxpayer may have a

4.2 FLAST v. COHEN *(cont.)* 392 U.S. 83 (1968)

personal stake in the outcome. Therefore, there is no absolute bar to a federal taxpayer suit. This case raised the sole question of the standing of individuals who rely only on their status as taxpayers. Because the taxpayer in this case successfully asserted that this legislation exceeds specific constitutional limits, he had standing to sue.

BUSINESS CONSIDERATIONS What is the practical purpose(s) behind the standing requirement? In a lawsuit, does standing operate for the benefit of businesses or does it harm them? Why?

ETHICAL CONSIDERATIONS Is it ethical for someone who does not have standing to initiate a lawsuit? Why or why not? Why might a business *want* a person who did not have standing to initiate a lawsuit against the firm?

Political questions
Questions that would encroach on executive or legislative powers, concerning government, the state, or politics.

Judicial questions
Questions that are proper for a court to decide.

Judicial restraint
A judicial policy of refusing to hear and decide certain types of cases.

Even though many **political questions** in our society involve real controversies, the doctrine of our courts is that courts will not hear them. Why? While a political question may be considered a very real controversy, it is not considered to be a **judicial question.** This rule is based on the concept of **judicial restraint.** For example, if a citizen asserts that a state is not based on a democratic form of government, that claim will not be heard in a U.S. federal court because it is a political question. Similarly, if a citizen thinks that our nation's foreign policy is incorrect, our courts cannot be used to debate the point because foreign policy is a political question. What constitutes a political question, however, is not always clear. For instance, is *legislative apportionment*—the ratio of legislative representation to constituents—a political question? Historically, the courts have said no. The following landmark case established a new precedent. The federal courts further clarified what legislative apportionment is acceptable in the cases that followed *Baker* v. *Carr*.

4.3 BAKER v. CARR 369 U.S. 186 (1962)

FACTS The plaintiffs alleged that the apportionment of the state legislature under Tennessee state law was unequal because rural voters had greater representation than urban voters.

ISSUE Is state legislative apportionment a political question and, therefore, **nonjusticiable**?

HOLDING No.

REASONING Legislative apportionment is a constitutional question under the Equal Protection Clause of the Fourteenth Amendment and is, therefore, a proper judicial question. The claim of the appellants that "they are being denied equal protection is justifiable, provided discrimination is sufficiently shown . . . [T]he right to relief under the equal protection clause is not diminished by the fact that the discrimination relates to political rights . . . [T]he nonjusticiability of a political question is primarily a function of the separation of powers . . . [T]he question here is the consistency of state action with the federal Constitution." This is not a question to be decided by a political branch of government equal with this court. When there are constitutional challenges to state action respecting matters of the administration of the affairs of the state and its officers that are amenable to judicial correction, this court should decide the claim.

[Note that the court itself is deciding whether an issue is a political question and nonjusticiable.]

BUSINESS CONSIDERATIONS Does the issue of whether a claim is a political question affect businesses? Suppose the legislature of a particular state decided to subsidize

4.3 BAKER v. CARR *(cont.)* **369 U.S. 186 (1962)**

its industries in order to allow them to "better compete" with other firms from other states. Would this decision be a political question, not subject to court review, or a legal question?

ETHICAL CONSIDERATIONS What ethical issues arise in political apportionment? What ethical issues arise when courts refuse to resolve an issue because the courts feel that the issue is a political question even though it may affect the lives of many people?

Now that you know the four limits that constrain judicial power, we will consider the one concept that has expanded judicial power. When you read the Constitution, you will not find the specific power of judicial review mentioned. That is because it is a court-created power. In 1803 the Chief Justice of the U.S. Supreme Court, John Marshall, created this doctrine of the law in the landmark case of *Marbury* v. *Madison*.[4] This power is based on an interpretation of the Constitution, which states that our courts may examine the actions of the legislative and executive branches of government to ascertain whether those actions conform to the Constitution. If they do not, the courts have the power to declare those actions unconstitutional and, therefore, unenforceable. Thus, the Supreme Court can declare an act of Congress invalid. This concept of judicial power does not exist in England, where the parliament is supreme. Therefore, the branch of government, which has neither the power of the purse nor the power of the sword, has significant power because it can say what is legally permissible by the other branches of the government. Since 1803, the power of U.S. courts to judicially review all actions of the legislative and executive branches of government has gone unchallenged. It has become the cornerstone of our doctrine of the separation of powers. Furthermore, this power of the Supreme Court to invalidate legislation also extends to all state legislation because of the supremacy clause in the federal Constitution.

The Watergate scandal, remembered by many as a low point in American history, may be viewed as a high point with respect to the doctrine of judicial review. In 1974, President Nixon was ordered to produce the now-famous Watergate tapes for use in a federal prosecution. Nixon claimed executive privilege and rejected the order to turn over the tapes to the federal prosecutor. The Supreme Court, in an unanimous opinion, denied Nixon's claim and ordered him to release

4.1 MANAGEMENT

PRODUCT SAFETY LAWS

Dan Kochanowski read an article in a business publication that predicted which states would pass the strictest product safety laws in the next 12 months. The author of the article thought that a number of the laws being proposed would be more consumer-oriented, and hence less "business-friendly" than the current statutes. The Kochanowskis believe that their products are not likely to be affected by such statutes at this point in time. However, Dan is still concerned about the long-term effect on the company that could be caused by the passage of additional consumer-friendly state legislation. He asks what you would advise the company to do. What will you tell him?

BUSINESS CONSIDERATIONS What practical steps can a business take to avoid the impact of a new product safety law proposed in a state? What legal steps can a business take to avoid a proposed product safety law? Can the firm avoid the jurisdiction of the state's courts?

ETHICAL CONSIDERATIONS Is it ethical for a business to attempt to avoid product safety laws? Since product safety laws are enacted to protect consumers, would it be ethical for a firm to be proactive and attempt to discourage state legislation that might harm the firm while helping consumers?

Nonjusticiable
Not subject to the jurisdiction of a court; not a proper question for a court.

the tapes. President Nixon complied with the order of the Supreme Court, thus ending a constitutional crisis. Subsequently, Nixon became the first—and so far, only—U.S. president to resign from office.

The following case contains the famous Supreme Court opinion that created the doctrine of judicial review.

4.4 MARBURY v. MADISON

1 Cranch 137, 2 L.Ed. 60 (1803)

FACTS John Adams, a Federalist president, was defeated by Thomas Jefferson, an Anti-Federalist or Republican, in the presidential election of 1800. Jefferson was scheduled to take office on March 4, 1801. Before Jefferson took office, the Federalist Congress passed the Circuit Court Act, which effectively doubled the number of federal judges and authorized the appointment of 42 justices-of-the-peace in the District of Columbia. Adams appointed people, primarily Federalists, to these judicial positions. Congress confirmed his last-minute appointments and their commissions were signed and sealed on March 3rd. However, several commissions, including William Marbury's, were not delivered on March 3rd. When Jefferson assumed the presidency on March 4th, he ordered James Madison, his Secretary of State, not to deliver the commissions that had yet to be delivered. [Following this, the Republican Congress repealed the Circuit Court Act and also eliminated the 1802 Supreme Court Term.]

ISSUES Does Marbury have a right to the commission? Do the U.S. laws give Marbury a remedy? Is Marbury entitled to a **writ** of **mandamus**? Can a writ of mandamus be issued from this court?

HOLDINGS Yes. Yes. Yes. No.

REASONING One of the first duties of government is to protect the rights of individuals. Consequently, it would surely provide a remedy for a vested legal right. "Questions in their nature political, or which are, by the Constitution and laws, submitted to the executive, can never be made in this Court." However, where a duty has been assigned by law and individual vested rights are involved, then that individual may resort to the courts for a remedy.

For mandamus to be a proper remedy, it must be directed to an officer to perform his duty and the person requesting it must be without any other specific and legal remedy. Here the claim is not based on executive discretion, but on particular acts of Congress and general principles of law. "This, then, is a plain case for a mandamus."

The Supreme Court is authorized to issue writs of mandamus under the Judiciary Act of 1789 (Act). Mandamus may be issued to any court or person holding office under the authority of the United States, including the Secretary of State. If the Supreme Court cannot issue mandamus in this case, it must be because the Act is unconstitutional.

Article III, Section 2 of the Constitution declares that the "Supreme Court shall have original jurisdiction in all cases affecting ambassadors, other public ministers and consuls, and those in which a state shall be a party. In all other cases, the Supreme Court shall have appellate jurisdiction." If Congress can change the Supreme Court's powers, then the Constitution would be without meaning. The language in the Act that "gives" the Supreme Court the authority to exercise original jurisdiction to issue writs of mandamus is not proper under the Constitution.

The Constitution was written to define and limit the powers of the legislature, and to ensure that those limits would not be misunderstood or forgotten. "[T]he Constitution controls any legislative act repugnant to it. . . ." It is a superior paramount law. An act that conflicts with the Constitution is void, and the courts are not bound by it. "It is emphatically the province and duty of the judicial department to say what the law is. Those who apply the rule to particular cases, must of necessity expound and interpret that rule. If two laws conflict with each other, the courts must decide on the operation of each."

BUSINESS CONSIDERATIONS How does the power of judicial review affect business decisions? Do businesses have a similar sort of review for conduct within the firm?

ETHICAL CONSIDERATIONS Was it ethical for the Federalists to appoint so many judicial officers right before losing political power? Was it ethical for President Jefferson to refuse to carry out the actions of his predecessor after assuming office?

Limitation of Power

The original Constitution, signed on 17 September 1787, contained a number of rights pertaining to individuals. Among these is the right of ***habeas corpus.*** The original act is the English statute of 31 Car. II, c.2; it has been amended in England and adopted throughout the United States.[5] In Latin, *habeas corpus* means "You have the body."[6] This right may be used by all persons who have been deprived of their liberty. There are special forms of the writ; however, when the words "writ of *habeas corpus*" are used alone, the writ is addressed to the person who detains an individual. The writ commands that person to produce the individual in a court and to comply with any order the court issuing the writ should make. This is probably the most common form of the writ. The following case, decided by a 5 to 4 vote, demonstrates how the modern court is narrowing this right.

Another right established by the Constitution is that Congress may pass no bills of attainder. A *bill of attainder* is a "legislative trial" whereby a person is judged a felon or worse by act of the legislature and not by a court of law.

Congress also may not enact ***ex post facto* laws.** For example, if a citizen entered into a perfectly legal transaction in January, then Congress cannot declare that transaction illegal in a statute passed after January. As used in the Constitution, the prohibition on *ex post facto* laws only applies to criminal law. This prohibition includes laws that make an act a crime; make a crime into a more serious crime; change the punishment for a crime; or alter the legal rules of evidence for proving a crime.[7]

4.2

MANAGEMENT

HOW TO PROTECT CIT'S PATENT

Tom is very concerned that another firm will "steal" the technology behind Call-Image, produce a copy, sell it, perhaps even at a price below what CIT can sell its Call-Image. Although CIT holds a patent on Call-Image, Tom knows that patents are not always upheld in court. Consequently, he would like to file a suit with the court to determine if the patent will be upheld *before* a competitor duplicates it. He asks you how he should proceed. What advice will you give Tom?

BUSINESS CONSIDERATIONS What effect does uncertainty about the validity of a patent cause for a business? What can a business do to reduce the risk? What technique or techniques would be most effective?

ETHICAL CONSIDERATIONS Analyze the ethical perspective of any business that would attempt to "steal" CIT's technology. Is commercial or industrial espionage an ethical method of doing business?

4.5 WOODARD v. HUTCHINS — 464 U.S. 377 (1984)

FACTS The state of North Carolina filed an application to vacate a circuit court judge's order, which granted a stay of execution. The application for the stay of execution included repetitious and novel claims as to why it should be granted. At no time did Hutchins deny that he deliberately murdered three police officers.

ISSUE Will the Supreme Court hear multiple *habeas corpus* petitions?

HOLDING No.

REASONING "This case is a clear example of the abuse of the writ. . . . All three of Hutchins' claims could and should have been raised in his first petition for federal *habeas corpus*. . . . A pattern seems to be developing in capital cases of multiple review in which claims are brought forward—often in piecemeal fashion—only after the execution date is set or becomes imminent. Federal courts should not continue to tolerate—even in capital cases—this type of abuse of the writ of *habeas corpus*."

4.5 WOODARD v. HUTCHINS (cont.) 464 U.S. 377 (1984)

BUSINESS CONSIDERATIONS Generally, writs of *habeas corpus* are filed against penal institutions and their officers. Can they be filed against businesses?

ETHICAL CONSIDERATIONS Is it ethical for criminal defendants and their attorneys to file multiple appeals, or writs, after being convicted? What ethical perspective is being advanced here?

YOU BE THE JUDGE

Deceased Citizens Allegedly Voted against Senate Candidate

A Republican Senate candidate, Michael Huffington, alleges that 17 deceased citizens "voted" in Fresno County in the 1994 election. Les Kimber, an ousted Fresno city council member, also charges that campaign workers for his opponent, Dan Ronquillo, used voter fraud. In one incident, election materials indicate D. Eddie Ronquillo, Dan Ronquillo's son, registered a 2-year-old boy and his 17-year-old mother. Absentee ballots were requested for these two minors. The absentee ballot requests indicated at the bottom "Paid for by the friends of Dan Ronquillo." (These two individuals did not vote, and the absentee ballots were discarded.) The mother contends that she never registered to vote.

Norma Logan, Fresno County elections manager, says that part of the problem is allowing political groups to pay a bounty for registering voters or getting the voters to use absentee ballots. She contends that it is an incentive for some people to file fraudulent documents. Norma would like California to ban bounty payments.

A lawsuit seeking the banning of "bounty payments" in elections has been brought before your court. How will you resolve this case?[8]

BUSINESS CONSIDERATIONS Consider the bounty for registering voters. What is the likely consequence of this practice? When bounties are paid in business situations, what are they called? What sometimes happens in businesses when "bounties" are offered to workers?

ETHICAL CONSIDERATIONS Analyze the ethics of individuals registering people who are not eligible to vote (e.g., minors and people who are deceased). Is whether the individuals are motivated by the bounty, or by political reasons, relevant?

SOURCES: Jim Boren and Angela Valdivia, *The Fresno Bee* (29 December 1994), pp. A1, A12; and Jim Boren, *The Fresno Bee* (5 January 1995), pp. A1, A14.

Writt

A writing issued by a court in the form of a letter ordering some designated activity.

These are some of the most notable constitutional rights. However, other individual rights, such as trial by jury in most criminal cases, were also written into the original Constitution.

Amendments to the Constitution

Four years after the U.S. Constitution was signed, the first 10 amendments were passed. These amendments, known as the Bill of Rights, were designed to ensure that certain individual rights were protected. (In all, 27 amendments to the Constitution have been passed—see Appendix A.) The amendments to the Constitution reflect the citizens' concerns about particular topics and reflect changes in the society. The Constitution itself serves as the supreme law over U.S. society.

The Courts and Jurisdiction

Jurisdiction, the power of a court to affect legal relationships, is a basic concept with respect to our courts. We will examine four aspects of jurisdiction:

1. **Subject matter jurisdiction**
2. Jurisdiction over the persons or property
3. Concurrent versus exclusive jurisdiction
4. Venue

Subject Matter Jurisdiction

In our discussion of the Constitution, we said that the Supreme Court was limited to deciding cases and controversies. In addition, Article III of the Constitution defines the Supreme Court's *subject matter jurisdiction* as including all cases in law and equity arising under the Constitution, the statutes of the United States, and all treaties. The subject matter jurisdiction granted to the Supreme Court is extensive. A state juvenile court, on the other hand, is limited solely to hearing matters concerning children, provided that the case or controversy also arose within that state and under its laws. If an adult were brought before a juvenile court, the court would lack subject matter jurisdiction. Because it may decide only matters concerning people under 18 years of age, a juvenile court is an inappropriate court for a case involving an adult. Likewise, a federal bankruptcy court may not decide a criminal matter because its jurisdiction is limited to bankruptcy matters. Subject matter jurisdiction determines which court is the "right" court to hear a particular type of case or controversy.

Jurisdiction over the Persons or Property

In addition to the appropriate subject matter jurisdiction, a court must also have jurisdiction over the persons or property whose rights, duties, or obligations the court will decide. Basically, three techniques exist for obtaining jurisdiction over persons or property—*in personam*, *in rem*, and *quasi in rem*. First we will discuss ***in personam* jurisdiction,** the authority of the court over the person.

In Personam *Jurisdiction.* Jurisdictional questions do not arise over the person of the **plaintiff.** The plaintiff chooses to file the suit in a particular court and so implicitly consents to the court's jurisdiction. It is inconsistent to allow the plaintiff to file the suit and then complain that the same court lacks jurisdiction over him or her.

The **defendant,** however, does not choose the court. Often, if the defendant were given a choice, he or she would choose not to have any trial. If a trial *must* take place, he or she might well prefer to have it held elsewhere. The question, then, is how to get jurisdiction over the person of the defendant. One technique is if the defendant consents to the court's jurisdiction. Consent can be in response to a lawsuit that has been filed, or it can occur either by express consent or by failure to raise the issue of jurisdiction and, instead, responding to the legal questions. Consent can also be given prior to the lawsuit. This is commonly accomplished by a contract clause or

Mandamus
A type of writ, which issues from a court of superior jurisdiction, commanding the performance of a particular act specified therein.

Habeas corpus
The name given to a variety of writs issued to bring a party before a court or judge.

***Ex post facto* law**
A law passed after an occurrence or act, which retrospectively changes the legal consequences of such act.

Subject matter jurisdiction
The power of a court to hear certain kinds of legal questions.

***In personam* jurisdiction**
Authority over a specific person or corporation within the control of the court.

Plaintiff
A person who files a lawsuit; the person who complains to the court.

Defendant
A person who answers a lawsuit; the person whose behavior is the subject of the complaint.

Service of process
Delivery of a writ or notice to the person named so as to inform that person of the nature of the legal dispute.

Foreign corporation
A corporation that received its articles of incorporation in another state.

by appointment of an agent to accept **service of process**. A corporation is considered to have given consent when it registers with a state as a **foreign corporation** and asks permission to conduct business in a state. Courts have concluded that a corporation that engages in business as a foreign corporation without the required registration has given implied consent.

A court will also have jurisdiction over a defendant who is physically present in the state when he or she is served with process. This would include a person who is on a trip to the state or even merely passing through the state on his or her way to another destination. A corporation is physically present in a state in which it is *doing business*. (Doing business is also used as the basis of implied consent by some states.) For example, a corporation is doing business in a state in which it has stores, offices, warehouses, and regular employees. The courts have decided numerous cases about what constitutes doing business and have devised various tests for recognizing doing business. Two of these tests are: (1) whether the corporation's activities were single, isolated transactions or continuous and substantial activities; or (2) whether the corporation's agents were only soliciting offers in the state or were engaged in additional activities.

In the landmark case, *International Shoe Co.* v. *Washington*, 326 U.S. 310 (1945), the U.S. Supreme Court concluded that before a defendant is required to appear in a state court, the defendant must have certain *minimum contacts* with the state. Otherwise, the suit would offend traditional concepts of fair play and substantial justice. This case created a constitutional test for *in personam* jurisdiction. The defendant in this case was a corporation, but the ruling appears to apply to individuals as well.

In personam jurisdiction also exists in the state of domicile. Domicile is a complicated legal doctrine (and most of its complexity is outside the scope of this text). Human beings have one and only one domicile. It may be chosen by the person or the law may assign a domicile. *Domicile* is usually a person's home, the place where he or she is physically present and where he or she intends to remain for the time being. Domicile does *not* require that a person live in a state for a certain minimum period of time. Consequently, domicile contrasts with residency statutes that require, for example, a person to live in a state for a set period of time before voting in the state or being eligible for in-state tuition at its colleges and universities.

Suppose that both the plaintiff and the defendant are residents of Alaska; Alaska has jurisdiction over them. On the other hand, if the plaintiff is a resident of Alaska but the defendant is a resident of Oregon, Alaska *may* not have proper jurisdiction over the defendant. If the plaintiff wants to sue the defendant in a state court, the plaintiff might need to go to Oregon and sue the defendant there, since a *defendant's* state of residence is almost always an appropriate forum. Potential jurisdiction in a federal court will be discussed later in this chapter.

Corporations are domiciled in the state in which they are incorporated. They are also considered to be domiciled in the state where they have their corporate headquarters, if this is a different state. A corporation may be sued where it is domiciled *and* in *all* states in which the corporation does business; therefore, it is subject to *in personam* jurisdiction in many states.

Most states have laws called *long-arm statutes*. The purpose of these statutes is to permit the state to exercise *in personam* jurisdiction when ordinarily this would not be possible. A common type of long-arm statute permits a state to exercise authority over a person who drives on its roads. This type of long-arm statute is also called a nonresident motorist statute. Suppose a resident of Nebraska drives a car on the roads of Kansas and injures a resident of Kansas. In that situation, the courts of

Kansas would have jurisdiction over the person of the resident of Nebraska, because it would be unfair to require the resident of Kansas to go to Nebraska to sue. Other states have enacted much broader long-arm statutes. For example, Illinois enacted a statute which listed certain acts that would confer jurisdiction, if done in the state. California, on the other hand, enacted a long-arm statute that provides for *in personam* jurisdiction whenever it complies with the U.S. Constitution. As with other matters under the control of the states, there is great variation among long-arm statutes.

***In rem* jurisdiction**
Authority over property or status within the control of the court.

***Quasi in rem* jurisdiction**
Authority obtained through property under the control of the court.

Attachment
Seizure of the defendant's property.

Garnishment
Procedure to obtain possession of the defendant's property when it is in the custody of another person.

In Rem *Jurisdiction.* If a state cannot obtain *in personam* jurisdiction on any of these grounds, another approach—called ***in rem* jurisdiction**—can be used. *In rem jurisdiction* allows the state to exercise its authority over something such as land or a marital domicile, within its boundaries. The court's judgment will affect everyone's rights in that "thing." It does not impose a personal obligation on the defendant. For example, if an individual or a corporation has real property in one state but resides in another, the state where the property is located can exercise *in rem* jurisdiction over the property in a condemnation proceeding.

Quasi in Rem *Jurisdiction.* In this type of jurisdiction, the court determines the rights of particular persons to specific property. (It is distinct from *in rem* jurisdiction, because a court with *in rem* jurisdiction will determine the rights of all persons in the thing. It differs from *in personam* jurisdiction because there is no authority over the person of the defendant.) The court obtains control of the property in ***quasi in rem* jurisdiction** through two methods. In one, the property is within the jurisdiction of the court and the plaintiff wishes to resolve issues of ownership, possession, or use of the property, for example, to foreclose a mortgage. In the second method, the dispute does not concern the property, but is personal to the plaintiff such as a breach of contract or the commission of a tort. Jurisdiction will exist if the plaintiff can locate the defendant's property within the state and bring it before the court by **attachment** or **garnishment**. Limitations exist on when attachment or garnishment is allowed. When the plaintiff's suit is successful, the recovery is limited to the value of the property. Exhibit 4.1 summarizes the techniques for obtaining jurisdiction over the defendant.

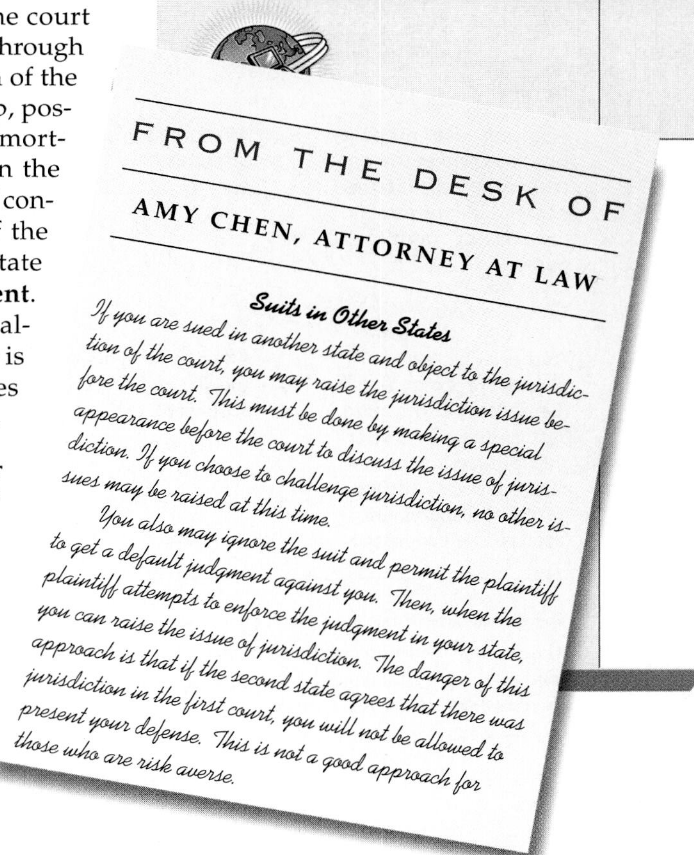

FROM THE DESK OF
AMY CHEN, ATTORNEY AT LAW
Suits in Other States
If you are sued in another state and object to the jurisdiction of the court, you may raise the jurisdiction issue before the court. This must be done by making a special appearance before the court to discuss the issue of jurisdiction. If you choose to challenge jurisdiction, no other issues may be raised at this time.
You also may ignore the suit and permit the plaintiff to get a default judgment against you. Then, when the plaintiff attempts to enforce the judgment in your state, you can raise the issue of jurisdiction. The danger of this approach is that if the second state agrees that there was jurisdiction in the first court, you will not be allowed to present your defense. This is not a good approach for those who are risk averse.

Service of Process. In cases of either *in personam, in rem,* or *quasi in rem* jurisdiction, there must be proper service of process on the defendant to inform him or her of the lawsuit. Proper service of process includes *actual notice,* in which one is personally served by an officer of the court; this can also include service by registered mail. If actual notice cannot be obtained after reasonable attempts to do so, notice may be served publicly by a posting on the property or in a newspaper. This is called *constructive service*. Proper notice may also include service at the office of the state's secretary of state. For example, when an out-of-state corporation registers in Delaware, the state may specify that process may be served on Delaware's secretary of state.

EXHIBIT 4.1 Methods to Obtain Jurisdiction over the Defendant

Type of Jurisdiction	Type of Judgment	Differences Between Individual and Corporate Defendants: *Individual*	*Corporation*
In personam		**Consent**	**Consent**
Authority over a specific person or corporation within the control of the state. Authority may derive from consent, domicile, physical presence, or long-arm statutes.	Affects the person	Defendant consents to personal jurisdiction; consent can occur before or after a suit has begun.	A corporation is registered as a foreign corporation within the state.[c]
		Domicile	**Domicile**
		Defendant has a residence—usually a home—at which he or she is/has been physically present and intends to remain for the time being; individuals have only one domicile.[a]	A corporation is incorporated (articles of incorporation) and/or has corporate headquarters in the state.
		Physical Presence	**Physical Presence**
		Defendant is served by hand while he or she is within the geographic boundaries of the state.[b]	A corporation is recognized as "doing business" in the state.
In rem			
Authority over property or status within the control of the state. Settles ownership interests in property or status for all persons.	Affects the property or status	The rules for individuals and corporations are basically the same.	
Quasi in rem			
Authority obtained through property under the control of the state. Settles issues of ownership, possession, or use of property; or settles personal disputes unrelated to the property.	Affects the rights of specific people to property[d]	The rules for individuals and corporations are basically the same.	

[a]Some people are not capable of selecting domiciles for themselves, thus, they have domiciles determined for them by legal rules (e.g., minors).

[b]Most states will decline to exercise jurisdiction if the defendant is brought into the state by force or enticed into the state by fraud.

[c]If the corporation failed to register, the court may imply consent from the act of doing business in the state. Generally, implied consent is limited to cases arising from the actual doing of business in the state.

[d]A successful plaintiff is limited to the value of the property.

Concurrent Versus Exclusive Jurisdiction

In certain cases, more than one court may exercise jurisdiction. If so, it is called *concurrent jurisdiction*. On the other hand, certain matters can be heard only by a particular court; this is called *exclusive jurisdiction*. Examples of exclusive jurisdiction in the federal courts are suits in which the United States is a party or that involve some areas of admiralty law, bankruptcy, copyright, federal crimes, and patent cases. Exhibit 4.2 illustrates the jurisdictional domains of federal and state courts.

Venue

Once a court establishes that it has proper jurisdiction over the subject matter and the person, it must then ascertain whether proper venue exists. *Venue* literally means "neighborhood." In a legal sense, however, it means the proper geographical area or district where a suit can be brought. In state practice, it is usually a question of which county is appropriate. In federal practice, venue is which federal judicial district is the proper one. For example, if both the plaintiff and the defendant are residents of the same state, *in personam* jurisdiction exists in that state's courts. But which state courts? Venue could be proper in the area where an incident, such as an automobile accident, occurred. The residence of the defendant also may be considered in determining the proper venue. More than one court may have proper venue. The laws of each state spell out in great detail the appropriate courts that would have venue.

Choice of Laws

Choice of laws is the legal doctrine that resolves any variance between the laws of two or more jurisdictions when applied to a particular set of parties; that is, the laws that should govern the subject matter before the court. Although it is also called "conflict

EXHIBIT 4.2 A Comparison of Federal and State Court Jurisdiction

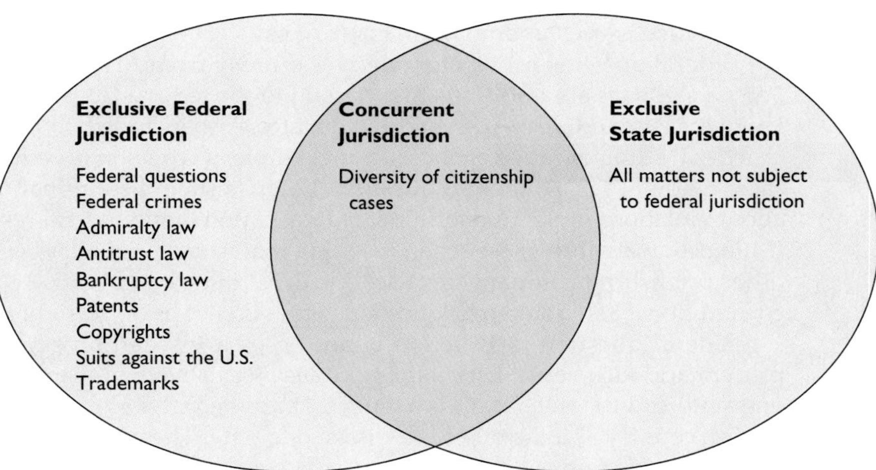

Substantive law

The law that creates, defines, and regulates rights.

Forum

The court conducting the trial.

Procedural law

The methods of enforcing rights or obtaining redress for the violation of rights.

of laws," legal scholars argue that choice of laws is the more appropriate title. Another complication in this area is that the court will use choice of laws rules to determine the **substantive laws** that should be applied to the dispute; however, the **forum** court will use its own **procedural laws.** The following example provides a hint of the difficulties that may arise when a choice of laws case arises.

> *Julia, a citizen of Massachusetts, entered into a contract with Karen, a citizen of Vermont, while they both were in Connecticut. The contract concerned goods that were located in Maine and were to be shipped to New York. While the goods were in transit, they were stopped and taken by Dawn, a citizen of New Hampshire, who was a creditor of Julia. This situation raises many legal questions. What should Karen do to get the goods? In which state should the lawsuit be filed? And, with reference to the choice of laws doctrine: What law should the court apply—the law of Massachusetts, Vermont, Connecticut, Maine, New York, or New Hampshire? It could be that Karen would win if the law of Massachusetts, Connecticut, or New York were applied but would lose if the law of Vermont, Maine, or New Hampshire were applied. Hence, choice of laws issues are quite important.*

Choice of laws issues might be resolved by a statute that indicates which law should be applied. In business transactions, it may also be resolved by the parties' specifying which state (or national) law should apply. The courts generally will use the parties' selection as long as there is a reasonable relationship between the state selected and the transaction.

We will not attempt to resolve this example's question in this text because it is clearly too complex for an undergraduate course in the law of business. You need only be aware of the complexity of this matter and the often quite simple solution to the problem—that is, stating in the written contract that if there should be any dispute concerning the contract, the laws of a particular state will apply. This is a form of *preventative law*.

Federal Courts

In addition to the general grounds discussed previously with respect to jurisdiction, two specific grounds exist for federal jurisdiction: (1) federal question and (2) diversity of citizenship *plus* amount in controversy.

Federal question jurisdiction derives directly from Article III of the Constitution. *Federal questions* are questions that pertain to the federal Constitution, statutes of the United States, and treaties of the United States. Also included, today, are all regulations of federal administrative agencies. For example, if a person is denied a job because of race, that will raise a federal question, because such discrimination raises concerns about violations of the Constitution, federal statutes, and federal regulations. If a publishing company brings an action asserting that its copyright has been infringed by another publishing company, it raises a federal question, because copyright is both a constitutional and a statutory question. States do not have the right to issue copyrights.

Federal question jurisdiction is not necessary when diversity of citizenship is present and vice versa. *Diversity of citizenship* exists when the plaintiff is a citizen of one state and the defendant is a citizen of another; it also exists when one party is a foreign country and the other is a citizen of a state. The primary reason underlying diversity jurisdiction is that if a citizen of Hawaii must file suit in Iowa in order to obtain jurisdiction over the defendant, it is possible that the court of Iowa might favor its citizen over the citizen of Hawaii. In that case, the plaintiff can file suit in federal court.

When federal jurisdiction is based on diversity of citizenship, a further requirement exists: a *minimum amount* in question. Title 28, §1332(a), of the United States Code now requires that the amount in question must exceed $75,000 in diversity cases. In contrast, cases in which the federal courts have exclusive jurisdiction generally do not require a minimum amount. The purpose behind the amount is to prevent federal courts from dealing with trifles. This rule complies with an ancient Latin legal maxim: *de minimis non curat lex,* which means "the law takes no account of trifles."

Most federal cases are highly complex, and the precise amount is a matter that is often unknown when the lawsuit is filed. Accordingly, the courts look to the amount the plaintiff, acting in good faith, has determined to be in dispute. This is called the *plaintiff viewpoint rule.*

Another aspect of diversity jurisdiction is called complete diversity. *Complete diversity* requires that no plaintiff be a citizen of the same state as any of the defendants. This rule, however, poses complex problems when there are multiple plaintiffs and/or defendants.

Exhibit 4.3 depicts the two grounds—federal questions and diversity of citizenship—for federal jurisdiction.

Specialized Courts

Congress has, from time to time, created courts of *limited* jurisdiction. At present, these courts include the claims court, the court of military appeals, the court of international trade, and the tax court.

Congress has created *federal district courts* in every state. Each state has at least one; some states have many. Rhode Island, for example, has one district court, and Texas has four. The courts contained in each district constitute the general trial courts of the federal system.

All of the district courts are grouped into circuits. Currently there are thirteen circuits. Each circuit has a court of appeals in which appeals from the trial courts are

EXHIBIT 4.3 The Two Grounds for Federal Jurisdiction

For Federal Jurisdiction the Case Must Involve

Either	*Or*
Federal Question	**Diversity of Citizenship**
The controlling law involves a federal statute, rule, or regulation; an issue of U.S. constitutional law; or a treaty.	Parties on one side of the controversy are citizens of a different state than the parties on the other side.
The case involves a consul or ambassador as a party.	*and*
The case involves maritime or admiralty law.	**A Minimum Amount in Controversy (Excluding Costs and Interest)**
The United States is a party to the action.	The minimum amount for which the plaintiff must sue currently exceeds $75,000.
The case is between two or more states.	

heard. Courts of appeal do not retry the case; rather, they review the record to determine whether the trial court made errors of law. Generally, a panel of three judges from the circuit hears appeals. For the most part, the decisions of these *circuit courts of appeals* are final. In a very few cases, further appeal may be made to the U.S. Supreme Court.

The thirteen federal judicial circuits and their seats are: First: Boston, Massachusetts; Second: New York, New York; Third: Philadelphia, Pennsylvania; Fourth: Richmond, Virginia; Fifth: New Orleans, Louisiana; Sixth: Cincinnati, Ohio; Seventh: Chicago, Illinois; Eighth: St. Louis, Missouri; Ninth: San Francisco, California; Tenth: Denver, Colorado; Eleventh: Atlanta, Georgia; Twelfth: District of Columbia, Washington, DC; Thirteenth: Federal Circuit, Washington, DC. For detail on the Thirteen Federal Judicial Circuits, see Exhibit 4.4.

The *Supreme Court* sits at the apex of the U.S. judicial system. It is the only court created by the Constitution. The Constitution does not specify the number of judges on the Supreme Court. It has nine judges, called Justices, by tradition. They are nominated by the President and confirmed by the Senate, and they serve for life, as do all federal judges—except those appointed to serve in the specialized courts.

As mentioned previously, certain cases may be appealed to the Supreme Court. However, the court may affirm a case routinely without permitting oral arguments or giving the case formal consideration. The court is more likely to hear a case under the following conditions:

1. Whenever the highest state court declares a federal law invalid
2. Whenever the highest state court validates a state law that is challenged based on a federal law
3. Whenever a federal court declares a federal statute unconstitutional and the government was a party to the suit
4. Whenever a federal appellate court declares a state statute invalid on the grounds that it violates federal law
5. Whenever a federal three-judge court has ruled in a civil case involving an equitable remedy

Certiorari, which means *"to be more fully informed,"* is used whenever the Supreme Court desires to hear a particular case even though there is no right of appeal. It is through this device that state court cases can be heard by the Supreme Court. No hard-and-fast rules exist in connection with this route other than that a minimum of four Justices must agree to hear the case. Nevertheless, there are certain situations in which *certiorari* is more likely:

1. Whenever two or more circuit courts of appeals have conflicting decisions with respect to the same legal issue
2. Whenever the highest state court has decided a question in such a manner that it is in conflict with prior decisions of the U.S. Supreme Court
3. Whenever the highest state court has decided a question that has not yet been determined by the U.S. Supreme Court
4. Whenever a circuit court of appeals has decided a state law question that appears to be in conflict with established state law
5. Whenever a circuit court of appeals has decided a federal question that has not yet been decided by the U.S. Supreme Court

As discussed earlier in this chapter, the Supreme Court also has original jurisdiction in a number of cases or controversies.

Exhibit 4.5 (page 108) describes how the federal courts are related to each other.

EXHIBIT 4.4 The Thirteen Federal Judicial Circuits

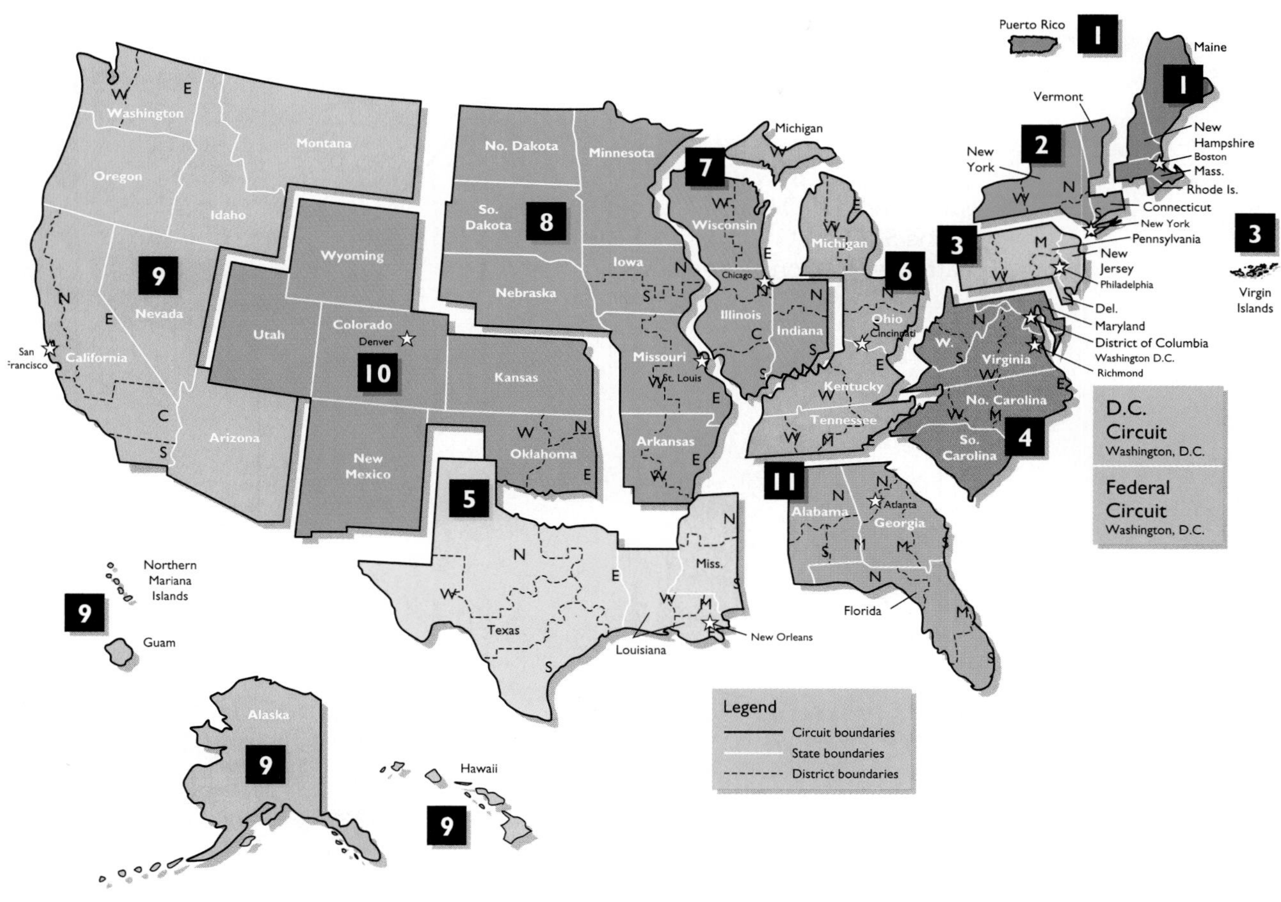

SOURCE: Administrative Office of the United States Courts, January 1983.

State Courts

All states have *inferior trial* courts. These may include municipal courts, juvenile courts, domestic relations courts, traffic courts, small claims courts, probate courts, and justice courts presided over by justices of the peace. (Historically, justices of the peace were not required to be lawyers. Many states have changed their rules and now require new justices of the peace to be lawyers.) For the most part, they are not *courts of record*—that is, there is no record or transcript made of the trial. In cases of appeals from their decisions, there is a *trial de novo,* "a new trial," in a court of general jurisdiction.

The more significant cases involving matters of state law originate in *courts of general jurisdiction* (courts having the judicial power to hear all matters with respect

EXHIBIT 4.5 The Federal Judicial System

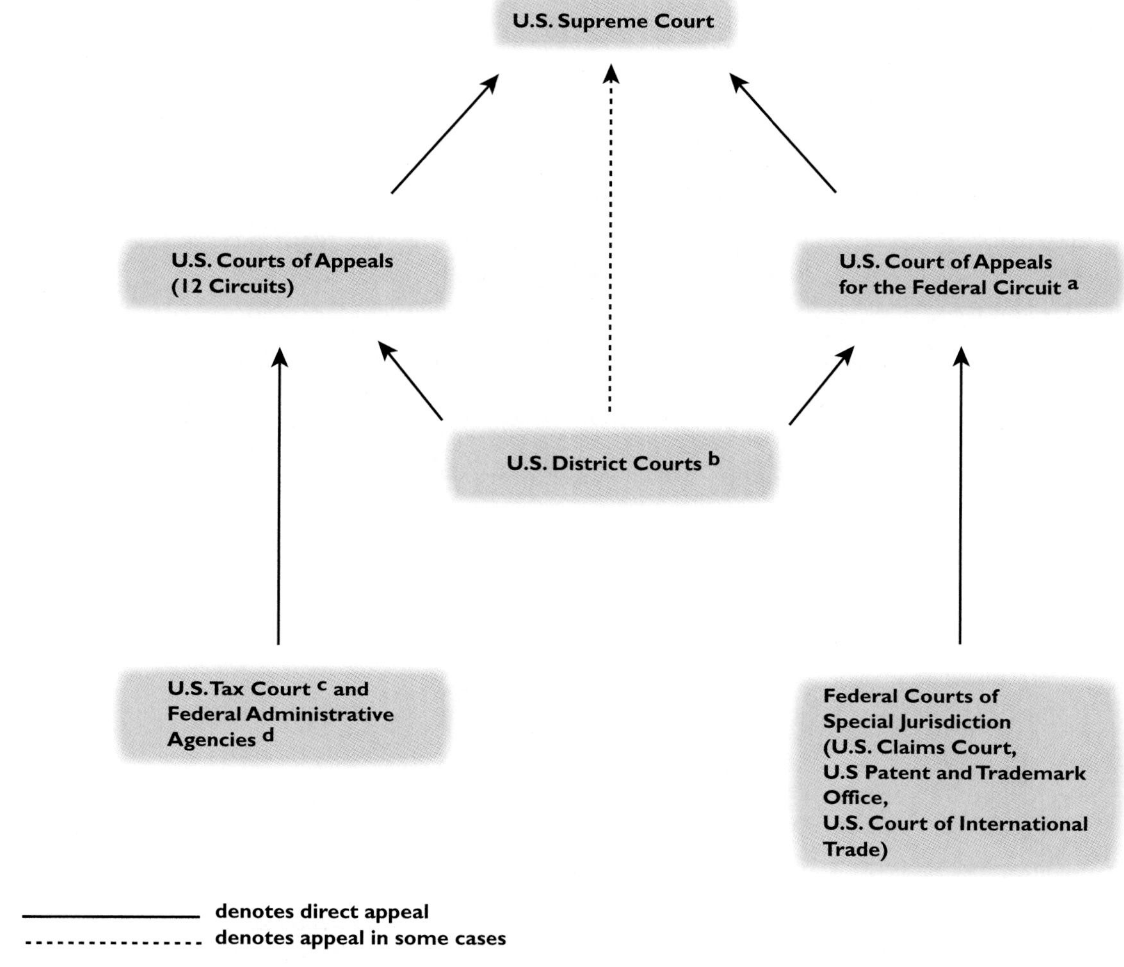

[a]Takes appeals from some specialized courts.

[b]Bankruptcy courts exist as units of the district courts.

[c]In some cases, there is direct Supreme Court review.

[d]Administrative agencies perform courtlike functions; however, they are *not* courts.

Injunction

A writ issued by the court of equity ordering a person to do or not do a specified act.

to state law). In some jurisdictions, two courts exist at this level. One court is charged with resolving all questions of law and the other with resolving all matters of equity. An example of a question of law is a suit seeking money damages. Most business law cases fall into this category. Equity suits, on the other hand, are those where the plaintiff is seeking a special remedy, such as an **injunction,** because monetary damages will not make the plaintiff "whole."

Each state has at least one *court of appeals*. It is usually, but not always, called the supreme court. In New York State, for example, the "supreme court" is a court of general trial jurisdiction, whereas the Court of Appeals is the highest court in the state. Sometimes intermediate courts of appeals also exist, as in the federal system. These appellate courts review the trial court record to determine whether there are any errors of law.

An example of this is *Bennis* v. *Michigan*, 134 L.Ed 2d 68 (1996). It was originally decided by the Wayne County Circuit Court, then appealed (in this order) to the Michigan Court of Appeals, the Michigan Supreme Court, and then the U.S. Supreme Court.

Exhibit 4.6 describes a typical state system and its interrelationship with the federal system.

HOW TO FIND THE LAW

We have already referred to some legal cases in this and previous chapters. Other cases will be cited in succeeding chapters. If you want to go to the library and read these or other cases in their entirety, you will need to know how to find the law.

Federal Court Cases

If you are looking for the case *Mitsubishi Motors Corporation* v. *Soler Chrysler-Plymouth, Inc.*, 473 U.S. 614, 87 L.Ed.2d 444, 105 S.Ct. 3346 (1985), for example, you will find it in any one of three sources. First, the U.S. Government Printing Office publishes the official *United States Reports*. The case will be found on page 614 of volume 473. Alternatively, you can find the case on page 444 of volume 87 of *Lawyers Edition, Second*, published by the Lawyers Cooperative Publishing Company. Finally, you can find the case in volume 105 of the *Supreme Court Reporter*, which is published by West Publishing Company, at page 3346.

All reported cases decided by the circuit courts of appeals are found in the *Federal Reporter.* If you are looking for the case of *Johnson Controls* v. *United Association of Journeymen*, you will find it at 39 F.3d 821 (7th Cir. 1994). In other words, go to volume 39 of the *Federal Reporter, Third Series*, and turn to page 821. The *(7th Cir. 1994)* means the case was decided by the Seventh Circuit Court of Appeals, which sits in Chicago, and hears cases from district courts in Illinois, Indiana, and Wisconsin. The case was decided in 1994.

U.S. district court cases are found in the *Federal Supplement Series*. If you are looking for the case of *Hoeflich* v. *William S. Merrell Co.*, you will find it at 288 F.Supp. 659 (E.D.Pa. 1968). Following the established format for legal references, look for volume 288 of the *Federal Supplement;* the case will be found on page 659. The *(E.D.Pa. 1968)* means the case was decided in the U.S. District Court for the Eastern District of Pennsylvania in 1968.

State Court Cases

The *National Reporter System* is published by West Publishing Company and includes the *Supreme Court Reporter*, the *Federal Reporter*, the *Federal Supplement*, *Federal Rules Decisions*, and the *Bankruptcy Reporter.* The reporter system also contains seven regional reporters for state cases. They are as follows:

EXHIBIT 4.6 The Typical State Judicial System[a]

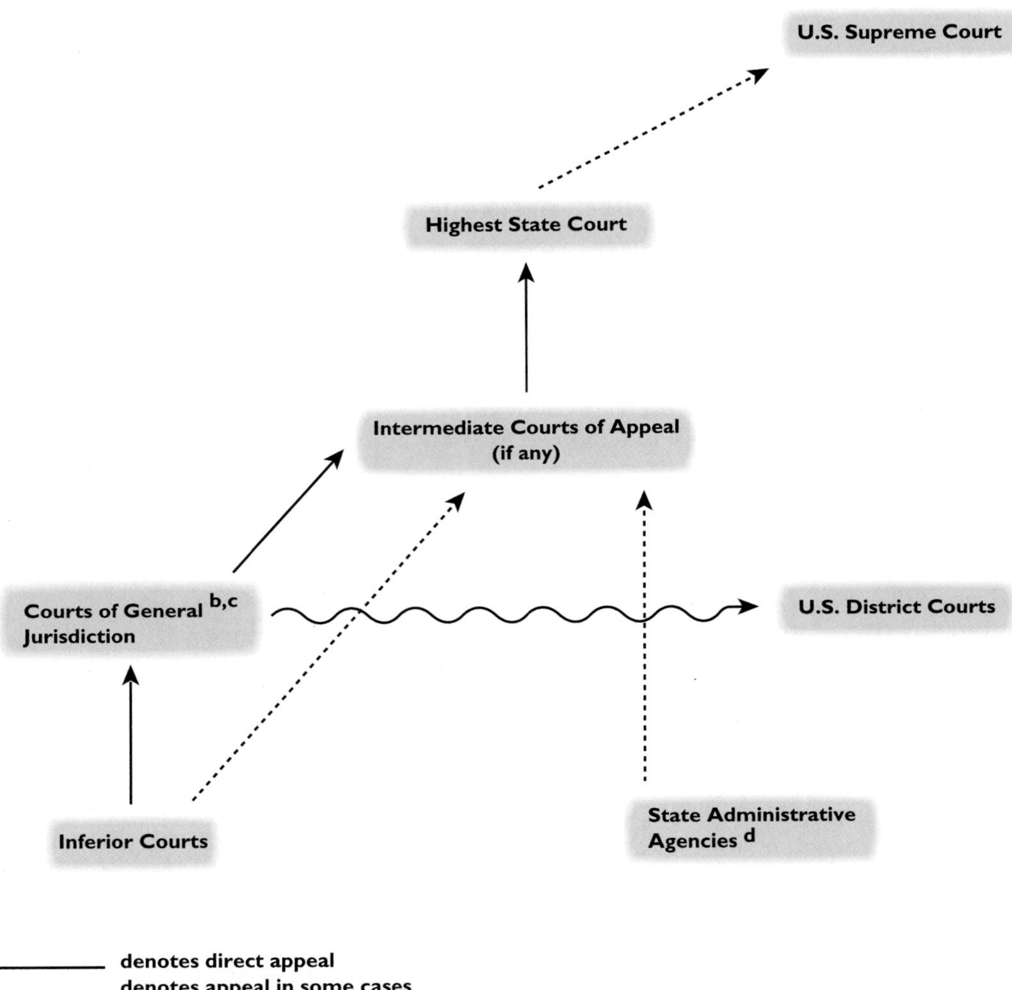

[a]As noted in the text, there is great variation among the states.

[b]The state trial courts may be divided into divisions, for example, the civil division, the criminal division.

[c]Removal jurisdiction generally is exercised when the defendant asks that the case filed in one court be moved to the other court.

[d]Administrative agencies perform some courtlike functions; however, they are *not* courts.

http:// RESOURCES FOR BUSINESS LAW STUDENTS

NAME	RESOURCES	WEB ADDRESS
U.S. Constitution	Emory Law School maintains a hypertext and searchable version of the U.S. Constitution.	http://www.law.emory.edu/FEDERAL/usconst.html
U.S. Federal Judiciary	The U.S. federal judiciary site, maintained by the Administrative Office of the U.S. Courts, provides a clearinghouse for information from and about the judicial branch of the U.S. government.	http://www. uscourts.gov/
U.S. Federal Courts Finder	Emory Law School maintains links to recent court decisions from the 13 U.S. circuit courts of appeals and the Supreme Court.	http://www.law.emory.edu/FEDCTS/
StateLaw	StateLaw, maintained by the Washburn School of Law, provides links for state and local legislative and governmental information—including court cases and statutes.	http://lawlib. wuacc.edu/washlaw/uslaw/statelaw.html
Local Government Home Page	The Local Government Home Page provides information for city, county, and state governments.	http://www.localgov.org/

1. *Atlantic Reporter*—Connecticut, Delaware, Maine, Maryland, New Hampshire, New Jersey, Pennsylvania, Rhode Island, Vermont, and the District of Columbia Municipal Court of Appeals
2. *Northeastern Reporter*—Illinois, Indiana, Massachusetts, New York, and Ohio
3. *Northwestern Reporter*—Iowa, Michigan, Minnesota, Nebraska, North Dakota, South Dakota, and Wisconsin
4. *Pacific Reporter*—Alaska, Arizona, California, Colorado, Hawaii, Idaho, Kansas, Montana, Nevada, New Mexico, Oklahoma, Oregon, Utah, Washington, and Wyoming
5. *Southeastern Reporter*—Georgia, North Carolina, South Carolina, Virginia, and West Virginia
6. *Southwestern Reporter*—Arkansas, Kentucky, Missouri, Tennessee, and Texas
7. *Southern Reporter*—Alabama, Florida, Louisiana, and Mississippi

These reporters contain most of the reported cases at the state supreme court and appellate court levels. Some significant trial court decisions are also included. Decisions of inferior courts are not included. The *National Reporter System* also includes the *Military Justice Reporter* and separate state reporters such as the *New York Supplement*, the *California Reporter*, and *Illinois Decisions.*

States generally also have their own system for publishing cases independent of the *National Reporter System.*

Computerized Legal Research

Legal research has entered the computer age. Two systems devoted to legal research are available—Lexis (part of Lexis/Nexis) and Westlaw. The techniques are similar although the particular computer commands vary. Both systems allow you to indicate what material you wish to search and to enter key words for search terms. If your search terms are not appropriate or are too broad, you may not locate the desired material. Historical cases may not have been added to the data banks, but recent cases and articles generally are available. Manuals and handbooks specify which material can be retrieved from the system, including the years that are in the database.

There are also a number of sites on the World Wide Web that contain articles on statutory law, court cases, and government activity. A few of these sites are highlighted at the end of each chapter. Web sites can be established without much restriction and some of the sites change addresses or stop operating. Consequently, the web addresses may become dated or the material may not be reliable.

SUMMARY

The federal Constitution is unique because it created the doctrine of separation of powers. As a result, our government is divided into three distinct branches: legislative, executive, and judicial. There is also an unofficial "fourth branch" of government, administrative agencies.

Judicial power has limits. For example, courts cannot issue advisory opinions or decide moot cases or political questions. In all cases, the plaintiff must have standing to sue. The doctrine of judicial review was created by Chief Justice John Marshall in the landmark case of *Marbury* v. *Madison*. The doctrine represents an expansion of judicial power, because it allows the Supreme Court to determine whether a statute passed by Congress is in compliance with the Constitution or whether the executive branch has acted in accordance with the Constitution.

Our court system is based on the concept of jurisdiction. Jurisdiction means the legal power to decide a case. It can be divided into subject matter jurisdiction, jurisdiction over the dollar amount (which is often considered an aspect of subject matter jurisdiction), and jurisdiction over the persons or property. There are basically three techniques for obtaining jurisdiction over the persons or property—*in personam*, *in rem*, and *quasi in rem*. The type of jurisdiction will affect the type of judgment the court can award.

Jurisdiction can be concurrent, in which more than one court can hear and decide a case, or it may be exclusive, in which case only one court can hear the matter. A federal district court's jurisdiction is based on either federal question or diversity of citizenship jurisdiction. In all diversity cases, the jurisdictional amount of over $75,000 must be met. The federal court system includes specialized courts, district courts, appellate courts, and the Supreme Court.

DISCUSSION QUESTIONS

1. Why is the U.S. Constitution considered unique?
2. What is the significance of the case of *Marbury* v. *Madison*?
3. Where is the constitutional protection of *habeas corpus* found? What does the term mean?
4. What is meant by the term *jurisdiction*?
5. Describe long-arm statutes. Do they serve a legitimate state purpose? Do they make it easier to sue businesses? Do they make it easier for businesses to file suit?
6. Why do some state courts have only one court of general jurisdiction, whereas others have two?
7. What is meant by this citation: 234 S.W. 358 (1946)?
8. In *Baker* v. *Carr* the issue of state legislative apportionment was determined to be a judicial question and not a political question. What arguments can you

make that it really was a political question and not a judicial question? Why do you think the Supreme Court decided as it did?

9. The highest court in a state determines that a state law violates the federal Constitution. Can that decision be reviewed by the U.S. Supreme Court, or is the decision of the state court final?
10. Go to the nearest law library, or Westlaw or Lexis terminal, and determine who was counsel for the plaintiff in *Flast* v. *Cohen*, 392 U.S. 83 (1968).

CASE PROBLEMS AND WRITING ASSIGNMENTS

1. Does a taxpayer have standing to sue the federal government challenging the creation of a Christmas postage stamp for the reason that it violates the establishment of religion clause of the First Amendment? [See *P.O.A.U.* v. *Watson*, 407 F.2d 1264 (D.C. Cir. 1968).]

2. Was the conducting of the Vietnam war by presidential authority, without a congressional declaration of war, in accordance with Article I, Section 8, Clause 11 of the Constitution, a "political question"? [See *Mora* v. *McNamara*, 389 U.S. 934 (1967).]

3. Federal courts apply the so-called American Rule that a party who prevails in litigation ordinarily is not entitled to collect attorneys' fees from the losing party. The Civil Rights Attorneys' Fees Awards Act, 42 U.S.C. 198, created an exception to this rule. Do you think that, under the statute, defendants who prevail should be awarded attorneys' fees in addition to any other award? Why? [See *Christiansburg Garment Co.* v. *EEOC*, 434 U.S. 412 (1978).]

4. International Shoe Co. was a Missouri corporation. The state of Washington wanted it to contribute to the state's unemployment compensation fund. International Shoe had local sales representatives in Washington who created a large volume of business. Was there sufficient contact between International Shoe and the state to justify this requirement or would it offend traditional notions of fair play and substantial justice? [See *International Shoe Co.* v. *Washington*, 326 U.S. 310, 66 S.Ct. 154, 90 L.Ed. 95 (1945).]

5. Does segregation of children in public schools on the basis of race, even though the physical facilities and other "tangible" factors may be equal, deprive the children of the minority group of equal educational opportunities? Discuss with respect to the Fourteenth Amendment. [See *Brown* v. *Board of Education*, 347 U.S. 483 (1954).]

6. **BUSINESS APPLICATION CASE** Viking Industries, Inc. (Viking) is an Oregon corporation that manufactures and sells windows to buyers in 30 different states. Viking brought a breach-of-contract action against Sierra Glass & Mirror (Sierra), a Nevada company, when Sierra refused to pay for windows delivered to it. At trial, Sierra claimed that Viking was not entitled to bring this action in a Nevada court because it was a foreign corporation doing business in Nevada without complying with Nevada law. A Nevada statute precluded foreign corporations doing business in Nevada from commencing an action in Nevada courts if the corporation had not filed qualifying documents with the secretary of state. Viking's total sales amounted to approximately $20 million in the 30 states in which it conducted business and approximately $3 million stemmed from sales in Nevada. Viking had one sales representative who worked in Nevada, resided in Las Vegas, and spent two weeks per month calling on customers and visiting sales prospects in Reno and Las Vegas. Viking maintained a listed telephone number in Las Vegas at the representative's home. Nevada customers placed orders through the representative who then phoned the orders and forwarded the checks to Portland. Viking contended that its contacts with Nevada were purely interstate, and that it was not required to qualify as a foreign corporation. Is Viking correct? Why? [See *Sierra Glass & Mirror* v. *Viking Industries, Inc.*, 808 P.2d 512 (Nev. 1991).]

7. **ETHICS APPLICATION CASE** The Pasadena Crematorium and other funeral service companies allegedly sold human body parts and organs to a biological supply company. The body parts were allegedly removed without permission from the decedents being prepared for cremations or funerals. In the class action lawsuit, the plaintiffs were suing for negligent infliction of emotional distress. The plaintiffs were relatives and friends of the deceased persons. Who has standing to sue in this situation? Would the alleged behavior of the crematorium and funeral homes be ethical? Why or why not? [See *Christensen* v. *Pasadena Crematorium of Altadena*, 2 Cal.Rptr.2d 79 (1991).]

8. **IDES CASE** Producers of chemicals used for pesticides sued the U.S. Administrator of the Environmental Protection Agency challenging Section 3(c)(1)(D) of the Federal Insecticide, Fungicide, and Rodenticide Act (FIFRA), alleging a denial of their rights. The challenged section of the law allowed parties to submit disputes to binding arbitration rather than submitting

the case to the courts for judicial resolution. The producers alleged that the law violated Article III of the U.S. Constitution by removing judicial functions from the court. The district court held that Congress acted unconstitutionally by assigning judicial power to arbitrators. The case was subsequently appealed to the U.S. Supreme Court. Apply the IDES principles to determine how this case should be resolved. [See *Thomas* v. *Union Carbide*, 473 U.S. 568, 105 S.Ct. 3325 (1985).]

NOTES

1. See 1 Cranch 137, 2 L.Ed. 60 (1803).
2. *Aetna Life Ins. Co.* v. *Haworth*, 300 U.S. 227 (1937).
3. See 416 U.S. 312 (1974).
4. See 1 Cranch 137, 2 L.Ed. 60 (1803).
5. *Black's Law Dictionary*, 3rd ed. (St. Paul, MN: West, 1933).
6. *Ibid.*
7. *Ibid.*
8. Jim Boren and Angela Valdivia, "Kimber Lawsuit Against Ronquillo Alleges Voter Fraud," *The Fresno Bee* (29 December 1994), pp. A1 and A12; and Jim Boren, "Huffington Says 17 Who Voted Were Dead," *The Fresno Bee* (5 January 1995), pp. A1 and A14.

Chapter 5

TORTS

OUTLINE

AGENDA

CIT recently has been victimized by some criminal activity. What steps can it legally pursue in the protection of its property interests? Huey, a former CIT employee, is applying for new positions; potential employers are calling Anna to inquire about Huey's employment with CIT. What should Anna tell them when they call? A videophone competitor has been advertising the merits of its product in comparison to another videophone that, although not named as such, appears to be a Call-Image unit in form if not in performance. Can Tom and Anna successfully sue the competitor to protect CIT's image? If so, on what basis? Also, a group of people have banded together to prevent the use of interactive videophones, and they have threatened to file invasion-of-privacy lawsuits. Should Tom and Anna worry about these legal threats? What legal defenses might be available to them? What would occur if an employee were negligent in operating a CIT vehicle on "official" business? Who would be liable for any damages? CIT? The employee? Or both? What can the Kochanowskis do to avoid liability?

These and other questions are discussed in this chapter. Be prepared! You never know when one of the Kochanowskis will need your help or advice.

OBJECTIVES OF TORT LAW

Tort law is concerned with a body of "private" wrongs, whereas *criminal law,* which we shall study in Chapter 8, is concerned with "public" wrongs. The laws, to support the protection of an individual's rights with respect to property and person, have evolved over hundreds of years. Tort law, therefore, reflects civilized society. It is a complicated body of law because of the long period of development and the various exceptions that have evolved in its application. In addition, tort law is based on common law; consequently, the rules vary from state to state. The discussion here, therefore, is fairly general.

Torts provide a mechanism for persons who have been wronged to seek remedies in our court system. In general, the remedy sought is money damages to compensate for the injury. People can avoid committing these wrongs by adhering to various "duties." For example, society recognizes a duty to refrain from physically injuring other persons or their property. Society also recognizes a duty to refrain from injuring the reputation of others.

Because tort law recognizes certain duties, it raises the policy question of exactly which rights society should protect through the imposition of duties. For example, should society recognize as a wrong only behavior *intended* to be a wrong? Should society recognize as a wrong not only intended wrong but also an unintended wrong due to someone's negligence? Should society also recognize as a wrong unintended behavior in which the person is not negligent? These are the questions discussed in this chapter.

Society has developed the body of tort law to resolve social and economic policy questions. The law has to take into consideration the social usefulness of the conduct of persons, the interests asserted by the plaintiff, the justification (if any) for the defendant's conduct, the economic burden placed on the defendant if liability is imposed, the question of spreading the cost of liability from one to many persons, and the unique problem of respecting past decisions while maintaining flexibility within the legal system by providing solutions to modern problems.

THEORIES OF TORT LIABILITY

This chapter discusses intentional torts, negligence, and strict liability. Exhibit 5.1 depicts the three theories of tort liability. *Intentional torts* are those wrongs in which the persons sued must have acted in a willful or intentional manner; they either wanted the act to occur or knew that the act would probably occur. Suppose that someone said something offensive to you, and you said, "If you don't apologize, I'll punch you in the nose." If that person did not apologize and you punched him in the nose, the law states that you were wrong. You committed the tort of *battery* on the other person. (Provocation is not an issue here, since generally the law does not recognize the privilege of striking someone for making offensive remarks.)

The law of *negligence* is based on a concept of fault in which morality and law have been intermingled. How should society apportion the costs of accidents? Often, society has to make a moral statement when an injury occurs. Suppose a child darts out from behind a parked car an instant before the driver's car reaches that point; the driver immediately brakes in an effort to avoid hitting the child but is unable to stop in time to avoid the accident. In all likelihood, this accident would be considered unavoidable—it occurred without any negligence on the part of the

EXHIBIT 5.1 The Three Theories of Tort Liability

TORT LIABILITY

Intentional Torts	Negligence	Strict Liability in Tort
The accused acts in a willful or intentional manner.	The conduct of the accused is compared to the "reasonable and prudent" person.	The accused is generally involved in conduct that is deemed abnormally dangerous.
Involves a simple duty to avoid the act or conduct.	Involves a reasonable duty to avoid the act or conduct.	Involves a strict duty to be responsible for harm caused, without regard to care.
There must be a showing of fault.	There must be a showing of fault.	There is no need to show fault.
The harm must be foreseeable.	The harm must be foreseeable.	The harm must be foreseeable.

driver. The child, even though injured, would be denied any compensation from the driver for the accident.

On the other hand, if a child walking across the street in a designated crosswalk is hit by an automobile because the driver is drunk or driving too fast, society says that the driver breached a duty to drive the car in a reasonable manner. Accordingly, the driver will have to pay for damages suffered by the child. The amount of injury is not a factor in determining liability: what is relevant is how the injury occurred.

Under *strict liability* persons are liable even if their conduct was unintentional or nonnegligent, that is, even if the damage was not their fault. Some activities are classified as either ultrahazardous or abnormally dangerous, and if injury results from either of those situations, the actor will be held liable. For example, suppose you have a pet rattlesnake in a sealed glass cage and you place the cage in your backyard with signs on the fence that say: Danger—Poisonous Snake, Beware. If the snake somehow gets out and bites someone, you will be held liable. The law prevents you from trying to prove how careful you were. Instead, if your rattlesnake caused injury, you will simply have to pay. Increasingly, legislatures are creating strict liability for parents when their children intentionally cause injury to others.[1]

Duty

We live in a legal system in which we all have a duty to protect other persons from harm. The question the courts must examine is what degree of duty exists under what specific circumstances. With respect to intentional torts, we all have a simple duty to avoid liability-causing behavior. However, with respect to negligence, we all have a "reasonable" duty to avoid this type of behavior. Generally, the law states that reasonable duty is a standard of ordinary skill and care, based on the facts of each individual case. In order to test for a duty in any particular situation, the law has constructed a person against whom the conduct of the defendant is to be compared. This purely hypothetical person is known as the *reasonable and prudent person*—not perfect, merely reasonable. The California Supreme Court analyzed the concept of duty in the following case.

5.1 RANDI W. v. MUROC JOINT UNIFIED SCHOOL DISTRICT

929 P.2d 582; 1997 Cal. LEXIS 10; 60 Cal.Rptr.2d 263 (Cal. 1997)

FACTS ". . . In May 1990, Gilbert Rossette, a Mendota official, provided to the placement office at Fresno Pacific College (where Gadams received his teaching credentials) a 'detailed recommendation' regarding Gadams, knowing that it would be passed on to prospective employers, although Rossette allegedly knew of Gadams's prior improper contacts with female students. These contacts included hugging some female junior high school students, giving them back massages, making 'sexual remarks' to them, and being involved in 'sexual situations' with them. Rossette's recommendation noted numerous positive aspects of Gadams's tenure in Mendota, including his 'genuine concern' for students and his 'outstanding rapport' with everyone, and concluded, 'I wouldn't hesitate to recommend Mr. Gadams for any position! . . .' Cole provided Fresno Pacific College's placement office with a 'detailed recommendation' of Gadams, although he knew of Gadams's prior inappropriate conduct while an employee of Golden Plains. Specifically, Cole knew that Gadams had been the subject of various parents' complaints, including charges that he 'led a panty raid, made sexual overtures to students, sexual remarks to students . . .' These complaints had allegedly led to Gadams's 'resigning under pressure from Golden Plains due to sexual misconduct charges.' Cole's recommendation listed Gadams's various favorable qualities as an instructor and administrator, and stated Cole 'would recommend him for almost any administrative position he wishes to pursue.' Gary Rice and David J. Malcolm, officials in the Muroc Joint Unified School District, also allegedly provided a 'detailed recommendation' to Fresno Pacific College's placement office in 1991, despite their knowledge of disciplinary actions taken against Gadams regarding sexual harassment allegations made during his employment with Muroc. The allegations included charges of 'sexual touching' of female students and induced Muroc to force Gadams to resign. The recommendation, signed by Malcolm, described Gadams as 'an upbeat, enthusiastic administrator who relates well to the students' and who was 'in a large part' responsible for making the campus of Boron Junior/Senior High School 'a safe, orderly and clean environment for students and staff.' Malcolm concluded by recommending Gadams 'for an assistant principalship or equivalent position without reservation.' Defendants made these recommendations on forms that Fresno Pacific College supplied, which clearly stated that the information provided 'will be sent to prospective employers.' . . . The plaintiff alleged that on February 1, 1992, while plaintiff was in Gadams's office, he 'negligently and offensively touched, molested, and engaged in sexual touching of 13-year old [plaintiff] proximately causing injury to her.'"

ISSUE Did Gadams's former employers owe a duty of care to plaintiff?

HOLDING Yes.

REASONING ". . . Our task . . . is to determine whether the complaint states a cause of action. . . . Section 311 of the *Restatement (Second) of Torts*, involving negligent conduct, provides that:

> *(1) One who negligently gives false information to another is subject to liability for physical harm caused by action taken by the other in reasonable reliance upon such information, where such harm results*
>
> *(a) to the other, or*
>
> *(b) to such third persons as the actor should expect to be put in peril by the action taken.*
>
> *(2) Such negligence may consist of failure to exercise reasonable care*
>
> *(a) in ascertaining the accuracy of the information, or*
>
> *(b) in the manner in which it is communicated.*

. . . Although ordinarily a duty of care analysis is unnecessary in determining liability for intentional misrepresentation or fraud . . . [h]ere we consider liability to a third person injured as a result of the alleged fraud, an extension of ordinary tort liability based on fraud. . . . We examine each element separately.

Did defendants owe plaintiff a duty of care? . . . Plaintiff acknowledges . . . that no California case has yet held that one who intentionally or negligently provides false information to another owes a duty of care to a third person who did not receive the information and who has no special relationship with the provider. Accordingly, the issue before us is one of first impression, and we apply the general analytical principles used to determine the existence of duty in particular cases. In this state, the general rule is that all persons have a duty to use ordinary care to prevent others from being injured as the result of their conduct. . . . [In citing precedents] 'the major [considerations] are the foreseeability of harm to the plaintiff, the degree of certainty that the plaintiff suffered injury, the closeness of the connection between the defendant's conduct and the injury suffered, the moral blame attached to the defendant's conduct, the policy of preventing future harm, the extent of the burden to the defendant and consequences to the community of imposing a duty to exercise care with resulting liability for breach, and the availability, cost, and prevalence of insurance

5.1 RANDI W. v. MUROC JOINT UNIFIED SCHOOL DISTRICT *(cont.)* 929 P.2d 582; 1997 Cal. LEXIS 10; 60 Cal.Rptr.2d 263 (Cal. 1997)

for the risk involved.' . . . The foreseeability of a particular kind of harm plays a very significant role in this calculus [citation], but a court's task—in determining 'duty'—is not to decide whether a particular plaintiff's injury was reasonably foreseeable in light of a particular defendant's conduct, but rather to evaluate more generally whether the category of negligent conduct at issue is sufficiently likely to result in the kind of harm experienced so that liability may appropriately be imposed on the negligent party.' . . .

[W]e first examine whether plaintiff's injuries were a foreseeable result of defendants' representations regarding Gadams's qualifications and character, coupled with their failure to disclose to the Fresno Pacific College placement office information regarding charges or complaints of Gadams's sexual misconduct. Could defendants reasonably have foreseen that the representations and omissions in their reference letters would result in physical injury to someone? Although the chain of causation leading from defendants' statements and omissions to Gadams's alleged assault on plaintiff is somewhat attenuated, we think the assault was reasonably foreseeable. Based on the facts alleged in the complaint, defendants could foresee that Livingston's officers would read and rely on defendants' letters in deciding to hire Gadams. Likewise, defendants could foresee that, had they not unqualifiedly recommended Gadams, Livingston would not have hired him. And, finally, defendants could foresee that Gadams, after being hired by Livingston, might molest or injure a Livingston student such as plaintiff. . . . [W]e may assume that standard business liability insurance is available to cover instances of negligent misrepresentation or nondisclosure. . . . Perhaps more significantly, defendants had alternative courses of conduct to avoid tort liability, namely, (1) writing a 'full disclosure' letter revealing all relevant facts regarding Gadams's background, or (2) writing a 'no comment' letter omitting any affirmative representations regarding Gadams's qualifications, or merely verifying basic employment dates and details. The parties cite no case or *Restatement* provision suggesting that a former employer has an affirmative duty of disclosure that would preclude such a no comment letter. . . . [L]iability may not be imposed for mere nondisclosure or other failure to act, at least in the absence of some special relationship not alleged here. . . .

As for public policy, the law certainly recognizes a policy of preventing future harm of the kind alleged here. One of society's highest priorities is to protect children from sexual or physical abuse. . . . [Defendants] observe that a rule imposing liability in these situations could greatly inhibit the preparation and distribution of reference letters, to the general detriment of employers and employees alike. We have recently stated that 'when deciding whether to expand a tort duty of care, courts must consider the potential social and economic consequences. . . .' Defendants argue that a rule imposing tort liability on writers of recommendation letters could have one very predictable consequence: Employers would seldom write such letters, even in praise of exceptionally qualified employees. . . . Defendants contend that the threat of potential tort liability will inhibit employers from freely providing reference information, restricting the flow of information prospective employers need and impeding job applicants in finding new employment. One writer recently explained that 'many employers have adopted policies, sometimes referred to as 'no comment' policies, under which they refuse to provide job references for former or departing employees. . . . These policies work to the detriment of both prospective employers and prospective employees.' . . . [P]laintiff asserts it is unlikely that employers will decline to write reference letters for fear of tort liability, at least in situations involving no foreseeable risks of physical injury to someone. Plaintiff observes that an employer would be protected from a defamation suit by the statutory qualified privilege for nonmalicious communications regarding a job applicant's qualifications (see [Ca.] *Civ. Code*, § 47, subd. (c)). This provision was amended in 1994 to provide that the qualified privilege available for communications to and by 'interested' persons 'applies to and includes a communication concerning the job performance or qualifications of an applicant for employment, based upon credible evidence, made without malice, by a current or former employer of the applicant to, and upon request of, the prospective employer.' . . . [T]he existence of this privilege may encourage more open disclosure of relevant information regarding former employees. . . .

In light of these factors and policy considerations, we hold, consistent with *Restatement (Second) of Torts*, §§ 310 and 311, that the writer of a letter of recommendation owes to prospective employers and third persons a duty not to misrepresent the facts in describing the qualifications and character of a former employee, if making these misrepresentations would present a substantial, foreseeable risk of physical injury to the prospective employer or third persons. In the absence, however, of resulting physical injury, or some special relationship between the parties, the writer of a letter of recommendation should have no duty of care extending to third persons for misrepresentations made concerning former employees. In those cases,

5.1 RANDI W. v. MUROC JOINT UNIFIED SCHOOL DISTRICT *(cont.)* 929 P.2d 582; 1997 Cal. LEXIS 10; 60 Cal.Rptr.2d 263 (Cal. 1997)

the policy favoring free and open communication with prospective employers should prevail.

Having concluded that defendants owed plaintiff a duty not to misrepresent Gadams's qualifications or character in their letters of recommendation, we next must determine whether defendants' letters indeed contained 'misrepresentations' or 'false information' within the meaning of *Restatement (Second) of Torts*, §§ 310 or 311. If defendants made no misrepresentations, then as a matter of law they could not be found liable under those provisions. . . . [W]e view this case as a 'misleading half-truths' situation in which defendants, having undertaken to provide some information regarding Gadams's teaching credentials and character, were obliged to disclose all other facts which 'materially qualify' the limited facts disclosed. . . . [D]efendants indeed made 'positive assertions' regarding Gadams's character, assertions deceptively incomplete because defendants knowingly concealed material facts regarding Gadams's sexual misconduct with students. . . . In a case involving false or fraudulent letters of recommendation sent to prospective employers regarding a potentially dangerous employee, it would be unusual for the person ultimately injured by the employee actually to 'rely' on such letters, much less even be aware of them. . . ."

BUSINESS CONSIDERATIONS What should an employer do when asked for a recommendation for a former employee? Why?

ETHICAL CONSIDERATIONS Are the defendants in this case morally blameworthy? Why or why not?

Foreseeability

Foreseeability
The knowledge or notice that a result is likely to occur if a certain act occurs.

Both intentional torts and negligence are based on the concept of fault. Strict liability, to the contrary, is not. All theories of liability, however, require **foreseeability.**

Foreseeability addresses the likelihood that something will happen in the future. It is easy to see that if you point a loaded gun at someone and pull the trigger, you will cause that person harm. But suppose you get in your car and drive down a dark street, within the speed limit and with your lights on. A child darts out from behind a parked car, and you hit the child. Were you negligent, or was it merely an unavoidable accident? This is a more difficult question. Foreseeability is determined by what a "reasonable and prudent person" would expect. Thus, the foreseeability of a child darting into the street in front of your car would depend on such factors as the degree of darkness, the lateness of the hour, how densely populated the area was (i.e., rural or urban, residential or business), other children observed in the area, signs regarding children at play, and so forth. Until these factors are considered, no determination of the foreseeability of the child's action, and thus of your negligence—or lack thereof—can be made.

INTENTIONAL TORTS

Assault

Assault is wrongful, intentional conduct that would put a reasonable person or victim in immediate apprehension *or* fear of offensive, nonconsensual touching. Verbal threats alone are not an assault. A verbal threat must be accompanied by some movement toward the person. The threats of harm must be immediate: Threats of future harm are not sufficient. The actor must have actual or apparent ability to harm the victim. Pointing an unloaded pistol at a person, for example, is an assault if the victim has no way of knowing whether the pistol is loaded. The victim must feel apprehension: Actual fear is not required.

Battery

Some legal authorities have defined *battery* as a consummated assault. It is the wrongful, intentional, offensive, and nonconsensual touching of the victim. Touching an extension of the victim's body, such as a purse or backpack, also constitutes a battery. For example, removing a chair from a person who briefly stood up and began to sit down again is a battery when the person hits the floor. The key element is that the actor intended the natural consequence of removing the chair: falling to the ground. As far as the law is concerned, it is the same as pushing the person to the ground. On the other hand, if the removal of the chair had been unintended, there is no battery.

Defamation

Defamation occurs when an actor intentionally makes an untrue statement concerning a victim, which injures the victim's reputation. The defamatory remark must be *published,* which is defined as read or heard by others. Consequently, a negative remark made directly to the victim and which is not overheard by anyone else is not "published." The statement need not name the victim; however, the statement must be reasonably interpreted as referring to the victim. The statements must reduce the victim's reputation among well-meaning individuals. If the actor curses at the victim, this will not reduce the victim's reputation. It is interpreted more as an indication that the actor is extremely angry and may not be controlling his or her temper. Some courts even apply the libel-proof plaintiff doctrine when the fact finder decides that the plaintiff's reputation for a trait is so poor that the statements could not further damage the plaintiff's reputation as to that particular trait.[2]

Two forms of defamation exist: slander and libel. The reason for the two forms, each of which has different elements, is that each was developed in a different English court. *Slander,* which is spoken defamation, developed in the English church courts (the ecclesiastical courts that had jurisdiction over spiritual matters). *Libel* (written defamation) developed in the Star Chamber (an English common law court that had jurisdiction over cases in which the ordinary course of justice was so obstructed by one party that no inferior court could have its process obeyed). The tort of defamation is an important exception to the First Amendment's guarantee of free speech. Accordingly, U.S. courts have modified some of the common law rules.

Slander is spoken communication that causes a person to suffer a loss of reputation. The common law rule distinguished between *slander per se* and *slander per quod. Slander per se* occurs when a person says that another person is seriously immoral, seriously criminal, has a social disease, or is unfit as a businessperson or professional. In those cases, there is no need to prove actual damages. *Slander per quod* is any other type of oral defamatory statement.

Slander
Any oral statement that tends to expose a person to public ridicule or injures a person's reputation.

Libel is written communication that causes a person to suffer a loss of reputation. There are also two kinds of libel. *Libel per se* is libelous without having to resort to the context in which the remark appeared. For example, if a newspaper printed a story that referred to a person as a "known assassin for hire," there is no need to show the context of the statement. On the other hand, *libel per quod* requires proof of

Libel
Any written or printed statement that tends to expose a person to public ridicule or injures a person's reputation.

the context. For example, suppose a television talk show host says that a particular woman just gave birth to a child. In order to prove that it was libel, the woman must prove that she is not married and that she has not made public knowledge of her cohabiting, but unmarried, private life. Recently, disgruntled employees, especially those who have been discharged, have been suing their ex-employers for libel and/or slander. These suits have been based on remarks made by the employer to co-workers or to potential new employers.

The following case describes how U.S. courts have tailored the English doctrine to our own situation with respect to public officials.

5.2 NEW YORK TIMES CO. v. SULLIVAN 376 U.S. 254; 84 S.Ct. 710; 1964 U.S. LEXIS 1655; 11 L.Ed.2d 686 (1964)

FACTS "... B. Sullivan is one of the three elected commissioners of the City of Montgomery, Alabama. He brought this civil libel action against the New York Times Company, a New York corporation that publishes the *New York Times*, a daily newspaper.... Respondent's complaint alleged that he had been libeled by statements in a full-page advertisement that was carried in the *New York Times* on March 29, 1960....The [advertisement] did not specifically name Sullivan.... [Sullivan] and six other Montgomery residents testified that they read some or all of the statements as referring to him in his capacity as Commissioner. It is uncontroverted that some of the statements contained in the two paragraphs were not accurate descriptions of events that occurred in Montgomery concerning student boycotts and the treatment of Dr. Martin Luther King, Jr....The [advertising] agency submitted the advertisement with a letter from A. Philip Randolph, Chairman of the Committee, certifying that the persons whose names appeared on the advertisement [as endorsers] had given their permission. Mr. Randolph was known to the *Times'* Advertising Acceptability Department as a responsible person, and in accepting the letter as sufficient proof of authorization it followed its established practice....The manager of the Advertising Acceptability Department testified that he had approved the advertisement for publication because he knew nothing to cause him to believe that anything in it was false, and because it bore the endorsement of 'a number of people who are well known and whose reputation' he 'had no reason to question.' Neither he nor anyone else at the *Times* made an effort to confirm the accuracy of the advertisement, either by checking it against recent *Times* news stories relating to some of the described events or by any other means."

ISSUE Does the Constitution limit a state's power to award damages in a libel action brought by a public official against critics of his official conduct?

HOLDING Yes.

REASONING When a libel suit involves a public official, *actual malice* must be demonstrated. "... Debate on public issues should be uninhibited, robust, and wide-open, and ... it may well include vehement, caustic, and sometimes unpleasantly sharp attacks on government and public officials....The constitutional guarantees require, we think, a federal rule [that] prohibits a public official from recovering damages for a defamatory falsehood relating to his official conduct unless he proves that the statement was made with 'actual malice'—that is, with knowledge that it was false or with reckless disregard of whether it was false or not.... [This is the definition of actual malice as it is used in defamation cases.] We hold that the Constitution delimits a state's power to award damages for libel in actions brought by public officials against critics of their official conduct."

BUSINESS CONSIDERATIONS If you were the manager of a newspaper or television news show, what steps would you take to reduce the likelihood of a successful defamation suit?

ETHICAL CONSIDERATIONS Does a newspaper have a moral duty to screen advertising printed in the paper? Why? Is it ethical for the news media to slant news coverage to influence an upcoming election (e.g., to withhold news stories until right after an election or to release information right before an election)? Does the media owe the public a *moral* duty in this regard?

The *New York Times* case is a landmark in U.S. jurisprudence. Since 1964, the U.S. Supreme Court, in a number of cases, has extended the holding to "public figures" as well as public officials. *A public figure* is a person who has a degree of prominence in society. Thus, a person who chooses to become active in society and who not only receives but actually solicits attention in the media will be classified as a public figure. Furthermore, the court has extended the definition of a *public official* to include candidates for public office as well as incumbents.

Disparagement

In most states *disparagement* occurs when a person makes a false statement about a business's products, services, reputation, honesty, or integrity; the actor publishes the remark to a third party; the actor knows the remark is false; and the actor makes the statement maliciously and with intent to injure the victim. It is also called *trade libel*, if the statements are written, or *slander of title*, if the statements are oral. It is also sometimes called *product disparagement*.

False Imprisonment

False imprisonment is the unlawful detention of one person by another against the former's will, and without just cause, for an appreciable amount of time. This tort protects a person from the loss of liberty and freedom of movement. For example, if after the end of a college class your professor locks the door and says that no one can leave the room, that action is false imprisonment. Sometimes standing in a doorway and refusing to let a person pass is also false imprisonment. On the other hand, when a suspected shoplifter is stopped by a store detective, this is not false imprisonment if the store detective has just cause. However, the store detective must exercise the privilege reasonably.

Mental Distress

A growing body of law concerns situations that, for public policy reasons, are being recognized by courts and legislatures as torts. The law protects an individual from suffering *serious indignity* that causes emotional distress. This right, however, is balanced against the interest of the state in not opening the courts to frivolous and trivial claims. In this context, an airline was liable when it unreasonably insulted a passenger on an aircraft. Liability has also been found where a mortician displayed a dead body without its having been embalmed. In that case, damages were recovered by near relatives who suffered the mental distress.

5.1

MARKETING

UNFAIR ADVERTISING

Another firm in the interactive videophone industry has been advertising that it has the best available videophone on the market. The firm's ads do not name any competitors, but they do show what appears to be a Call-Image phone next to their product. In the ads, the Call-Image phone has an unclear picture, and generally seems to be an inferior product. Dan wants to sue the other company for defamation, or disparagement, or something similar. Tom is not sure that CIT has grounds to sue, but he is concerned about what these ads will do to CIT's image. The family asks you what CIT's rights are in this situation, and what they would need to prove in court if they sue. What will you tell them?

BUSINESS CONSIDERATIONS What practical steps can a business take to bolster its reputation? What could a business do to counteract negative publicity by a competitor?

ETHICAL CONSIDERATIONS Is it ethical to use comparison advertising to create a false impression of a competitor's product? Is it ethical to intentionally create a negative impression of a competitor's product if you believe the impression to be reasonably accurate? What moral obligations do you owe to competitors?

Actionable
Furnishing legal grounds for an action.

Replevin
A personal action brought to recover possession of goods unlawfully taken.

Invasion of Privacy

Under common law, no tort of invasion of privacy existed. However, our courts have begun to recognize that unwarranted invasions of privacy are **actionable.** *Privacy* refers to an individual's right to be left alone. Originally, this tort began with someone's peering into a home without permission. A person's privacy is invaded if that person becomes subject to unwarranted intrusions into his or her right to be left alone. These unwarranted intrusions have led to lawsuits and to the awarding of damages to the person whose privacy was invaded. Liability has been found for the public disclosure of private matters, such as wiretapping a private citizen's telephone without permission or a valid search warrant. The use of a famous person's name, photograph, voice, song, or image without permission is an invasion of privacy when it is used in a commercial endeavor.

5.2

MANAGEMENT

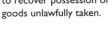

INVASION OF PRIVACY

Several people have complained that interactive videophones are overly intrusive and should be banned. A number of these people have banded together to form "SLAM" (Stop Looking At Me) and have threatened to file invasion-of-privacy lawsuits against every interactive videophone manufacturer and retailer in the United States. CIT is not yet on solid financial ground, and Tom is concerned that such a lawsuit could bankrupt the firm before it has a chance to succeed. Anna seems less concerned, but she is still worried. She has asked you if Tom's fears are valid. What will you tell her? Why?

BUSINESS CONSIDERATIONS Suppose that a business is facing the prospect of a number of lawsuits over its product. Should the business be proactive on the issue, or would it be better to wait and react to any suits that are filed?

ETHICAL CONSIDERATIONS Assume that a group is attempting to intimidate manufacturers and retailers in a given industry by threatening to file lawsuits unless the demands of the group are met. Is such behavior ethical? From an ethical perspective, how should the firms in the industry react to such threats?

Trespass

In common law, trespass was one of the most common torts. Today, the general tort of "trespass" has evolved into some of the specific torts already discussed. The traditional tort of *trespass* remains as the tort used to define actions that protect property interests against nonconsensual infringements. There are two types of trespass—trespass to land and trespass to personal property. A person who ventures onto the land of another without permission is a trespasser. If you return to the parking lot after class, and someone is sleeping in the back seat of your car, that person is trespassing on your car. The only question is one of damages. Even if the person trespassed through mistake and did no harm, there will be "nominal" damages of, say, one dollar. If, on the other hand, the person had trespassed before and had been warned, then higher damages likely would be assessed in order to compensate the owner for the unwarranted invasion of his or her land. Of course, the trespasser will be liable for any actual harm.

Conversion

Conversion occurs when a person intentionally exercises exclusive control over the personal property of another without permission. In such a case, the converter is liable for damages. If a person actually obtains possession of the property lawfully but is then told by the owner to return it and does not do so, that person is also a converter. If the owner seeks the return of the property, the proper action is one for **replevin**. Damages can also be obtained if the owner suffered harm during the conversion. Sometimes the owner does not desire the return of the property. This may be due to its current condition. In this case, the owner asks for reimbursement for his or her loss.

YOU BE THE JUDGE

Carjacker Sues for Victims' Property Left in Car

Todd Johnson has filed a suit demanding more than $2,000 in reimbursement for various items, all of which he previously stole from a couple. He stole their car and its contents at gunpoint outside a movie theater in San Bruno, California. Johnson contends that he should be reimbursed for the items that were still in the car when he was arrested for the carjacking. Todd is currently serving time in prison for the crime.[3] This case has been brought in *your* court. How will you rule?

BUSINESS CONSIDERATIONS What should a business do to protect its customers from carjackings and similar crimes? What responsibility should a business have for crimes committed against its customers at its business location?

ETHICAL CONSIDERATIONS Is it ethical for a business to deny any liability for crimes committed against its customers? Is it ethical for the customers to seek recovery from the business for crimes committed by individuals who do not work for the business?

SOURCE: *The Fresno Bee*, 29 January 1995.

Misappropriation of Trade Secrets

Misappropriation of trade secrets occurs when an actor unlawfully acquires and uses the trade secrets of another business enterprise. The victim must prove that a trade secret exists. The owner must have implemented reasonable steps to protect the trade secret. The actor must have acquired it by some unlawful means such as industrial espionage, theft, or bribery. Some states, like Texas, require that the actor acquire the secret as a result of a confidential relationship with the victim.[4] Texas also requires that the actor "use" the trade secret.[5] This tort is also called *theft of trade secrets*. Most states have adopted the Uniform Trade Secrets Act to codify their laws on trade secrets.

Fraud

Fraud is an extremely complex tort. It concerns the misrepresentation of a material fact made with the intent to deceive. If an innocent person reasonably relies on the misrepresentation and is damaged as a result, the injured person may successfully sue for fraud. Accordingly, there are five elements of fraud:

1. A material fact (not an opinion) was involved.
2. The fact was misrepresented (a falsehood).
3. The falsehood was made with the intent to deceive (scienter).
4. The falsehood was one on which another person justifiably relied (reliance).
5. That person was injured as a result (damage).

For example, if a jeweler sells a rhinestone as a diamond with the knowledge that it is a rhinestone, the action is fraud. If a bank customer knowingly obtains a loan on the basis of a false financial statement, it is fraud. If a landowner sells "one hundred" acres of land with the knowledge that it is only fifty acres, it is fraud. If a corporation solicits persons to buy stock for the purpose of building a new plant when in reality the corporation wanted the money to pay off existing liabilities, it is fraud. The list is virtually endless.

Exhibit 5.2 summarizes the intentional torts discussed in this chapter.

Civil RICO Violations

The Racketeer Influenced and Corrupt Organizations Act, commonly referred to by the acronym "RICO,"[6] is discussed in more detail in Chapter 8; however, it also deserves mention here. RICO is directed at a pattern of racketeering activity. A *pattern* means two or more racketeering acts within a 10-year period. Racketeering acts range from violent acts such as murder, to less violent acts, such as mail

EXHIBIT 5.2 Intentional Torts

Specific Tort	Definition	Defenses
Assault	Conduct that would put a reasonable person in apprehension of an immediate battery	Conditional privilege Consent Necessity/Justification Self-defense
Battery	Intentional offensive touching	Conditional privilege Consent Necessity/Justification Self-defense
Defamation	Slander (spoken), libel (written) Statements that harm a person's reputation	Truth Absolute privilege (legal or congressional proceeding) Conditional privilege
Disparagement	Defamation of a business product, service, or reputation	
False Imprisonment	The detention of one person by another against his or her will and without just cause	Privilege Consent
Mental Distress	Causing a serious indignity	
Invasion of Privacy	Unwarranted intrusions on the privacy of another	Privilege
Trespass	Subjecting real or personal property to harm or infringement	Privilege Consent Necessity
Conversion	Intentional exercise of exclusive control over the personal property of another without permission	Necessity Consent
Theft of trade secrets	Taking secret business data for unauthorized use	
Fraud	The misrepresentation of a material fact made with the intention to deceive	

fraud. The RICO statute includes a long list of racketeering acts. Individuals and businesses that are injured can sue those who are violating the statute. Successful plaintiffs in a civil action may recover **treble damages**, attorney's fees, and reasonable court costs. A criminal conviction is not a prerequisite to filing a RICO civil suit.

Treble damages
Three times the amount of actual damages.

Defenses to Intentional Torts

As is true with the torts themselves, there is a great deal of variation from state to state in how the defenses are actually defined and what constitutes a defense. The following sections contain a brief description of some of the common defenses.

Consent. Even though a tort has been committed, the law may not compensate the injured party if, in fact, that person consented to the tort. Most cases involve issues of **implied consent.** The law will not infer consent unless it is reasonable under the circumstances. For example, football players obviously batter each other throughout the course of a game. Therefore, even though the tort of battery may have been committed, it is not actionable because the law views each player as having consented to the touching. However, if a player intentionally exceeds the implied consent, he or she may be liable for the tort.

Implied consent
A concurrence of wills manifested by signs, actions, or facts, or by inaction or silence, which raises a presumption that agreement has been given.

Privilege. Permission is given voluntarily, whether it is expressed or implied. The law also recognizes a nonvoluntary defense beyond permission. Because the law seeks to protect certain social interests more than others, it developed the concept of **privilege.** Privilege may be recognized in a number of situations including:

1. If someone moves to strike you, you have the ancient privilege of self-defense. Most states also recognize the privilege to defend family members.
2. Retail businesspersons have a privilege to detain persons who they reasonably believe have committed theft.
3. Persons whose property is stolen have the privilege of going onto another person's property in order to retrieve it.
4. Judges and legislators have the privilege of saying things that might be slander under other circumstances in order to stimulate debate and encourage independence of thought and action.

Privilege
A particular benefit or advantage beyond the common advantages of other citizens; an exceptional right, power, franchise, or immunity held by a person, class, or company.

The court applies another privilege in the case that follows.

5.3 LEE v. CALHOUN — 948 F.2d 1162 (10th Cir. 1991)

FACTS Robert Wayne Lee filed a $38 million medical malpractice lawsuit against Dr. Scott Calhoun for surgery he performed. Lee claimed that Calhoun misdiagnosed his condition, failed to obtain his consent, and performed an unnecessary surgical procedure. When Lee arrived at the emergency room, two doctors diagnosed his condition as "possible acute appendicitis." Calhoun was called in to perform the surgery, and Lee signed a consent form to have his appendix removed. The surgery revealed a perforated bowel and Lee's bowel was removed instead. Lee tested positive for the HIV virus.

After the suit was filed, a reporter spoke with Dr. Calhoun about the suit. Calhoun responded that Lee's medical condition was initially diagnosed as appendicitis because they were unaware that Lee had HIV. If they had known about his AIDS exposure, other rarer ailments would have been

5.3 LEE v. CALHOUN (cont.) 948 F.2d 1162 (10th Cir. 1991)

considered. The *Daily Oklahoman* printed Calhoun's explanation. Lee is now also suing Calhoun for defamation, invasion of privacy, and breach of doctor–patient confidentiality.

ISSUE Could Dr. Calhoun be sued for invasion of privacy?

HOLDING No.

REASONING Dr. Calhoun's statements were privileged. Lee became a public figure by filing his lawsuit and attracting the attention of the media. The size of the claim and the fact that it deals with medical malpractice are reasons for legitimate public concern. One who has had his reputation attacked has a conditional privilege to defend himself. Dr. Calhoun's remarks to the media were an attempt to protect his own reputation and pertained to his defense in this lawsuit. His statements were sufficiently related to the news story to prevent them from being the basis of invasion of privacy. His remarks were conditionally privileged and he did not reveal more information than was necessary. No liability exists when the speaker further publicized information about Lee that Lee had already publicized. The defamation suit was dismissed because the statements that Lee was HIV positive were true. Under Oklahoma law, Lee waived his rights to the physician–patient privilege by filing his suit against the surgeon.

BUSINESS CONSIDERATIONS How do invasion-of-privacy and defamation laws affect the news media?

ETHICAL CONSIDERATIONS Was it ethical for Dr. Calhoun to discuss Lee's medical condition with the press? Why or why not?

Necessity. Whenever a person enters another's land for self-protection, the law recognizes that as necessity and disallows the nominal damages for the trespass. For example, if you are in a boat on a lake and a storm suddenly develops, you may enter a private cove, tie up to a private dock, and find shelter on the land in order to protect yourself. Due to the necessity, no trespass exists. However, the law permits the landowner to collect actual losses if, for example, you use his or her provisions while tied to his or her private dock.

Truth. Truth is the best defense with respect to the tort of defamation. If an individual accuses a businessperson of being a crook and is sued for defamation, the individual will win if it can be proven that the businessperson is a "fence" for stolen property. Exhibit 5.3 summarizes the defenses available against specific intentional torts.

Negligence

Negligence exists when four conditions are met. First, the defendant must have owed the plaintiff a duty. Second, the defendant must have breached the duty. Third, the breach of that duty must be the actual as well as the "legal" cause of the plaintiff's injury. Fourth, that injury must be one that the law recognizes and for which money damages may be recovered.

Duty

The reasonable-and-prudent-person rule has been established in negligence law in order to determine the "degree" of duty. With respect to negligence, everyone has a "reasonable" duty to avoid this type of behavior. This standard is more difficult to define, explain, and apply than is the standard of simple duty. Generally,

EXHIBIT 5.3 Effective Defenses Against Intentional Torts

Consent	Privilege	Necessity	Truth
Assault	Assault [in Self-defense]	Trespass	Defamation
Battery	Battery [in Self-defense]	Conversion	
False Imprisonment	False Imprisonment		
Trespass	Trespass		
Conversion	Defamation		
	Invasion of Privacy		

however, the law states that *reasonable duty* is a standard of ordinary skill and care, based on the facts of each individual case.

If, while you are quietly fishing on the shore of a lake, you see another fisherman who is 100 feet away fall out of his boat and begin to drown, does common law place on you a duty to help him? The answer is no, because you did not create the hazard in the first place. On the other hand, suppose you own a boatyard on the lake and the fisherman rents his boat from you. If the boat springs a leak because it was defective when rented, thereby causing the fisherman to drown, you will have breached your duty to rent safe boats. You created the harm in the second situation but not in the first.

Foreseeability, in negligence, addresses the likelihood that something will happen in the future. It is determined by what a "reasonable and prudent person" would expect.

To test for a duty in any particular situation, the law has constructed a person against whom the conduct of the defendant is to be compared. This purely hypothetical person is known as the *reasonable and prudent person*—not perfect, merely reasonable. Three areas help to define the reasonable and prudent person: knowledge, investigation, and judgment.

Knowledge. As the amount of knowledge existing in the world increases, so does the amount of knowledge that the reasonable and prudent person is expected to possess. In this sense, therefore, the law presumes that everyone has complete knowledge of the law. Without this rule, laws would be silly: If we have no knowledge of the law, how can we be expected to obey it?

Investigation. Investigation is closely related to knowledge. It is our obligation to find out. We assume that a reasonable person knows certain information. We also assume that the reasonable person will do research or tests to discover additional information. Before you drive a car, for example, the law presumes that you will have ascertained that the brakes are working properly. If you are a drug manufacturer, the law presumes that you will have discovered if your drug will cause any harmful side effects. If you have failed to do adequate testing, you will have violated the standard of care of a reasonable and prudent person. Note that a harmful side effect does not necessarily mean that the manufacturer is negligent. Some drugs do have harmful side effects for some or many patients; however, the drug is still beneficial for the majority

5.3

MANAGEMENT

JOB REFERENCES FOR FORMER EMPLOYEES

Recently CIT expanded by hiring three workers who are not family members. Unfortunately, Tom and Anna have not had much experience in selecting employees. Two of the workers are excellent and fit in well with the business and family members. The third, Huey, was not a good fit and was fired after the first three weeks. Tom and Anna also suspect Huey of falsifying company reports. Since his dismissal, Huey has been applying for other jobs. Although he did not list CIT as a reference, Huey did list CIT as his last place of employment. Consequently, potential employers have been calling CIT and leaving messages for Anna. They are understandably interested in why his employment there lasted only three weeks. Anna knows she cannot avoid the messages from four prospective employers much longer. She calls you to ask what she should do. What should she say and not say when she returns the calls?

BUSINESS CONSIDERATIONS Should a business adopt a policy regarding references for former employees? Is a business less likely to face liability if it only gives oral recommendations, or should it put everything in writing? Why?

ETHICAL CONSIDERATIONS Is it ethical to give a good recommendation for a "bad" employee to help that employee obtain other employment? Is it ethical to give a bad recommendation for a good employee to make his or her leaving more difficult?

to whom it is administered. In this case, distribution of the drug with proper warnings attached is permitted.

Judgment. You have heard some people say that one person has "good" judgment or another has "bad" judgment. The law measures both persons against the same standard. In a tort case, the defendant must have acted reasonably or else he or she will be found to have breached the duty of reasonable care. We have no hard-and-fast rules here. The outcome always depends on the facts of each case. A missing fact, once supplied, can change the outcome. Therefore, before beginning any activity, the law expects people to ask questions such as: What is the likelihood that this particular activity will harm someone else? If harm might occur, what is the likely extent of the harm? What must I give up to avoid risk to others?

Assume that you just got a new rifle and want to test it and adjust the sights (or scope) for maximum accuracy for the deer season. You find an isolated field in the country and set up a target at the base of a bald hill 300 yards away. No one else is present. After firing the first shot, however, you begin to attract a crowd. Assume that with each shot the crowd gets larger. At what point do you stop shooting to avoid injury to an innocent person? The decision to stop involves the exercise of reason. The exercise of reason is *judgment*.

Statutory Standard. In some cases, the law solves the problem of limits, like the ones just raised, by providing a standard contained in a statute. For example, most state traffic laws say that when it begins to get dark, all drivers are required to turn on their car lights. If, while traveling down a road at night without your lights on, you hit and injure a pedestrian, the law will conclude that you breached a standard of reasonableness no matter what your excuse. Most of these statutes provide a criminal penalty, but that penalty is irrelevant in a civil proceeding such as a tort case. In most states breaching the statutory standard is **negligence per se.** However, the states are not in agreement as to whether this should be treated as a conclusive presumption where evidence to the contrary is not permitted. Some states, such as California,[7] instead treat *negligence per se* as a rebuttable presumption. The person is allowed to present evidence that, under the circumstances, violating the statutory standard was the most careful behavior.

Negligence per se
Inherent negligence; negligence without a need for further proof.

Breach of Duty

In general, the plaintiff has to prove that the defendant caused injury by not adhering to the reasonable-and-prudent person standard. In some cases, however, that strict requirement of proof is relaxed; the law has developed the doctrine of *res ipsa loquitur,* which means "the thing speaks for itself." *Res ipsa loquitur* applies in situations where circumstantial proof is sufficient to shift the burden of proof. To apply *res ipsa loquitur* in a case, the injury must be such that it meets the following three tests: (1) it ordinarily does not occur in the absence of someone's negligence; (2) it must be caused by a device within the control of the defendant; and (3) the plaintiff in no way has contributed to his or her own injury. For example, if a patient submits to an operation to remove infected tonsils and leaves the operating room with a surgical instrument imbedded in her throat, there is no need to require direct testimony on the point. It speaks for itself; someone in the surgery room was negligent. The effect of *res ipsa loquitur* is to shift the burden of proof from the plaintiff to the defendants. In this situation, the hospital personnel and the surgeons will each need to show that they were careful.

FROM THE DESK OF

AMY CHEN, ATTORNEY AT LAW

People Who Enter Your Property with Consent

You have special duties of care when you allow others to enter your property with consent. Your duty is especially high for people you invite on your property. Business invitees include those who shop at retail establishments. Is the lighting adequate to deter crimes and reduce the likelihood of accident? Is there easy access to pay phones or security phones? Do you offer escorts for customers and employees after dark? Is there camera security? Is cash removed from safes frequently? Are there frequent security patrols by trained and competent personnel? Have you posted warning signs to remind customers and employees to be careful? Have you posted warning signs about any special risks (e.g., Do not swim at this beach—Strong undertow)?

Causation

The heart of the law of negligence is causation. Causation has two components: actual cause and proximate cause.

Actual Cause. The law determines whether X, an act by one party, is the actual cause of Y, a result affecting the other party, by examining the question of whether, "but for" the occurrence of act X, result Y would have happened. This is called the *but-for test*. For example, a defendant in an automobile accident case may have failed to signal a turn properly. But if the accident would have happened even if he had signaled properly, the failure to signal is not the actual cause of the accident. It fails the "but-for" test.

Proximate Cause. After actual cause has been established, the focus shifts to what the law calls *policy questions*. Such questions have nothing to do with whether the defendant actually did the act. What is decided here is whether the law should hold the defendant liable or not. At some point the law will say, "Enough." Beyond this point the defendant will not be held liable. To solve these policy questions, the law has developed a three-pronged test:

1. What is the likelihood that this particular conduct will injure other persons?
2. If injury should occur, what is the degree of seriousness of the injury?
3. What is the interest that the defendant must sacrifice to avoid the risk of causing the injury?

For example, if the defendant is negligent with respect to Tommy, and Bob tries to rescue Tommy and suffers some injury as a result, the defendant will be held liable for Bob's injuries as well as Tommy's because it is foreseeable that people will try to rescue someone in peril.

Harm

If the plaintiff is not injured, the defendant will not be held liable in damages. For example, a driver speeding down a road at 180 miles per hour is clearly breaching the duty to drive in a safe and reasonable manner; but if as a result no one is injured, no one can successfully sue for negligence.

Defenses to Negligence

Assumption of the Risk. Common law developed a doctrine in which the defendant will win if it can be proved that the plaintiff voluntarily assumed a known risk. For example, have you ever examined cigarette packages? They bear various warnings, some of which are "Surgeon General's Warning: Smoking by pregnant women may result in fetal injury, premature birth, and low birthweight," or "Quitting smoking now greatly reduces serious risks to your health," or "Cigarette smoke contains carbon monoxide." Historically, a longtime cigarette smoker who contracted lung cancer and sued the cigarette manufacturer has lost because the manufacturer defended on the basis of the plaintiff's voluntary assumption of the risk. (New scientific evidence is allowing the courts to reexamine tobacco company liability in this area.)

Contributory Negligence. If a plaintiff wears a black raincoat at night and, while jaywalking across a street, is hit by a car exceeding the speed limit, the defendant can assert that the plaintiff actually contributed to the injury. If the state in which the case is heard follows the rule of contributory negligence and if contributory negligence is successfully asserted, the plaintiff will lose because contributory negligence would **bar** recovery.

Bar

In the legal sense, to prevent or to stop.

Comparative Negligence. In a growing number of jurisdictions, the doctrine of contributory negligence has been replaced by the doctrine of *comparative negligence*, which has been adopted by the legislature or through judicial precedents. Here, the fact finder (usually the jury) determines to what degree the plaintiff contributed to his or her own injury. Comparative negligence is generally perceived to be more fair; however, it may be difficult for the trier of fact to determine the relative faults. For example, if Jason is injured to the extent of $100,000 in damages but contributed 35 percent to his injury, he will be awarded $65,000 instead of losing completely, as he would under the doctrine of contributory negligence.

Jurisdictions may select from three variations of comparative negligence. *Pure* comparative negligence would allow the plaintiff to recover no matter how negligent he or she was. [For example, the California Supreme Court adopted pure comparative negligence in *Li* v. *Yellow Cab Co.*, 119 Cal.Rptr. 858, 532 P.2d 1226 (1975).] However, some jurisdictions feel it would be unfair to allow the plaintiff to recover if he or she was the primary cause of the injury, for example, if the plaintiff was 95 percent responsible for causing the accident. Consequently, two other variations prevent recovery to the party who was mostly to blame. One version only permits recovery if the plaintiff contributed less than 50 percent to his or her injury. Another version allows recovery if the plaintiff contributed 50 percent or less to his or her injury. The differences may appear minimal, but they are significant to the parties of a lawsuit who may be denied recovery because the jury concluded that they were each 50 percent at fault. The effect of these laws may be minimal in automobile accidents in "no fault" states.

STRICT LIABILITY

Recall that with respect to intentional torts, everyone has a duty to avoid such behavior. With respect to negligence, we have a duty to use reasonable care. This section examines a situation in which the law states that our duty to avoid such behavior is absolute, regardless of whether we are at fault or not.

Whenever a person undertakes an extremely hazardous activity and it is foreseeable that injury may result, that person can be held "strictly liable" if injury does result whether or not the person was at fault. *Strict liability*, then, means without regard to fault. For example, if you use explosives on your property and by so doing cause windows to be blown out of an adjoining neighbor's house, you will be held liable no matter how careful you were in handling those explosives. Generally, the areas in which we have strict liability are set out in the applicable statutes and court precedents. *Rylands* v. *Fletcher*[8] is credited with creating this legal doctrine.

Through the development of the doctrine of strict liability, U.S. courts have shifted emphasis from ultrahazardous activity to dangerous activity, and the doctrine seems to be expanding in scope. Today, the following activities are considered strict liability activities in most states: the keeping of wild animals, the use of explosives, and dangerous activities. Some states have added strict liability for the owner of a motor vehicle if injury occurs when the vehicle is being driven by someone with the owner's permission.[9] Remember, though, strict liability does not automatically arise. Courts can create new precedents; generally, however, courts look to existing precedents and statutory law. This is another area in which the legal system is making policy decisions about who should justly bear the loss.

The following case illustrates a modern approach to strict liability.

Judgment proof
Unable to pay a legal judgment or award.

5.4 CURRY v. SUPERIOR COURT

24 Cal.Rptr.2d 495 (Cal.App. 4 Dist. 1993)

FACTS Latashia Washington was a student at Eisenhower High School operated by the Rialto Unified School District (RUSD). Due to cerebral palsy, Washington was confined to a wheelchair. She claimed that she was sexually molested at school by David Curry, a minor and a student at the school. She sued the school district for failing to provide adequate protection for her and sufficient supervision for Curry. RUSD wants to recover a portion of the judgment amount from Curry's parents.

ISSUE Are David Curry's parents liable for his conduct?

HOLDING Yes.

REASONING Under the common law, there is no parental liability for the torts of a minor. However, the California legislature amended the Civil Code to include § 1714.1. (California also enacted Penal Code § 272, which imposes criminal liability on parents or guardians who fail to make reasonable efforts to control a minor child.) Section 1714.1 imposes strict liability on the parents for the willful misconduct of minor children for up to $10,000. In personal injury cases, damages are limited to medical, dental, and hospital expenses. To recover under the statute, the parents' fault need not be proven. The child's acts are imputed to the parents. RUSD should be able to request payment from the parents: Washington could.

In enacting § 1714.1, the California legislature recognized that minor children are often **judgment proof** and cannot compensate victims of their acts. It is necessary then to impose liability on the parents so that the victims can be paid. One purpose of the law is to encourage responsibility in parents. Parents have the duty and opportunity to control, supervise, and train their children to behave responsibly.

BUSINESS CONSIDERATIONS Suppose that a business regularly hires employees who are viewed as "bad actors" by the general community. What affect does a concept like strict liability have on this business and its hiring practices? Should the business consider this in deciding whether to continue its hirings?

ETHICAL CONSIDERATIONS What ethical rights do handicapped individuals have? How would you analyze the moral perspective of Mr. and Mrs. Curry?

PRODUCT LIABILITY

Product liability is a growing concern of both distribution and manufacturing businesses. Manufacturers and distributors of products may be held liable based on these legal theories: (1) fraud in the marketing of the product, (2) express or implied warranties (warranties will not be discussed in this chapter, since they are based on contract theories), (3) negligence, and (4) strict liability.

Negligence in product liability can include negligence in design, construction, labeling, packaging, and assembly. When an injured person uses the negligence theory for product liability, there must be a close causal connection between the negligence and the injury. The lawsuit will be subject to the usual defenses for negligence, including contributory negligence, comparative negligence, and assumption of the risk.

Strict liability for products is clarified by § 402A of the *Restatement (Second) of Torts*, and has been adopted by most states. [*Restatement (Second) of Torts*, a publication of the American Law Institute (ALI), states the preferred version of the common law of torts. It is used by courts as an authoritative reference, but the *Restatement* is not binding on them. It becomes precedence in the court only after a judge has relied on a section and referred to it in his or her opinion.] Section 402A of the *Restatement (Second) of Torts* has long been considered the seminal document on product liability; however, now the ALI is drafting an entire volume on product liability, which is expected to be released in 1997.[10]

Section 402A of the *Restatement* establishes the strict liability rule: A seller will be held liable for a product that contains a defect or is unreasonably dangerous to use. ("Unreasonably dangerous" seems vague to both laypersons and lawyers; there have been many court decisions attempting to define and clarify the term.) The defect must be in the product when it leaves the control of the defendant. As with other forms of strict liability, the plaintiff does not need to prove negligence or fraud in order to recover. Generally, the plaintiff must show that strict liability applies to this situation, that the product had a defect when it left the defendant's possession or was unreasonably dangerous, and that the plaintiff was harmed. Since this is a tort cause of action, the seller cannot avoid liability by disclaiming it. Contributory negligence by the plaintiff cannot be a defense. The manufacturer may prove the following defenses depending on the situation—**obviousness of hazard,** product misuse by the plaintiff, and assumption of the risk.

Obviousness of hazard
The hazard in the product is obvious, such as a sharp knife.

The *Restatement (Second) of Torts* and the following landmark case are credited with initiating strict liability for products.

5.5 GREENMAN v. YUBA PRODUCTS, INC. — 59 Cal.2d 67, 377 P.2d 897 (1963)

FACTS Greenman's wife bought him a Shopsmith power tool for Christmas. While he was using the tool, it struck him and inflicted serious injuries. He sued the manufacturer for negligence.

ISSUE If the facts reflect that a product was defectively manufactured, must the plaintiff also prove negligence?

HOLDING No.

REASONING Liability will attach without any showing of negligence. "A manufacturer is strictly liable in tort when an article he places on the market, knowing that it is to be used without inspection for defects, proves to have a defect that causes injury to a human being. The purpose of such liability is to insure that the costs of injuries resulting from defective products are borne by the manufacturers that put such products on the market rather than by the injured persons

5.5 GREENMAN v. YUBA PRODUCTS, INC. *(cont.)* 59 Cal.2d 67, 377 P.2d 897 (1963)

who are powerless to protect themselves. . . . To establish the manufacturer's liability it was sufficient that plaintiff proved that he was injured while using the Shopsmith in a way it was intended to be used as a result of a defect in the design and manufacture of which plaintiff was not aware that made the Shopsmith unsafe for its intended use."

BUSINESS CONSIDERATIONS What are the business implications for manufacturers and retailers? What steps should they take to reduce the probability of lawsuits based on strict liability?

ETHICAL CONSIDERATIONS What is Yuba Products's ethical obligation to its customers? What is Yuba's ethical obligation to its other constituents? How can these obligations—if they exist—be balanced?

http: // RESOURCES FOR BUSINESS LAW STUDENTS

NAME	RESOURCES	WEB ADDRESS
Legal Information Institute (LII)—Tort law	LII, maintained by the Cornell Law School, provides an oveview of tort law, including the Federal Torts Claim Act (28 U.S.C. § 2671-80), recent Supreme Court tort decisions, and other information.	http://www.law.cornell.edu/topics/torts.html
The U.S. House of Representatives Internet Law Library—Tort law	The U.S. House of Representatives Internet Law Library for tort law provides links to cases, essays, statutes, and organizations concerned with tort law.	http://law.house.gov/110.html
American Bar Association's Tort and Insurance Practice Section (TIPS)	TIPS, a national professional group of plaintiff attorneys, defense attorneys, and insurance company counsel, provides information and links addressing tort law and insurance.	http://www.abanet.org/tips/home.html
American Tort Reform Association (ATRA)	ATRA provides information on tort reform issues, press releases, *The Reformer Newsletter,* "horror stories" about tort law abuse, and contact information.	http://www.atra.org/atra/

People who are injured by a product may claim and attempt to prove more than one theory of liability; that is, these theories are not mutually exclusive.

Tort Liability of Business Entities

Before leaving this introduction to tort law, we should mention that businesses *can* be held liable for the torts of their agents. Initially courts were reluctant to impose liability. Today, however, liability is more readily assessed. Liability is generally imposed through the doctrine of *respondeat superior. Respondeat superior* means that the superior should answer or pay for the torts of agents that occur in

5.4

MARKETING/MANAGEMENT

PRODUCT LIABILITY LAW

Anna just received disturbing news about a CIT customer, Ted Fredericson. Ted was so pleased with the CIT videophone that he bought one for himself and one for each of his adult sons. He installed his in the kitchen/dining area of his house. One Saturday, his eldest son called while Ted was washing the dishes. Ted reached for the phone with his right hand while his left hand was still in the dishwater. When he touched the phone, Ted received quite an electrical shock and was hospitalized for three days. Anna is concerned from both a legal and an ethical perspective. She has never perceived the videophone as being dangerous, but asks your advice about the firm's potential liability in cases like this. What will you advise her?

BUSINESS CONSIDERATIONS What should a business do to reduce the risks of accidents to users of its products? How can a firm minimize the risks of a product liability suit?

ETHICAL CONSIDERATIONS Does a business owe its purchasers and users an ethical obligation, or is it restricted to legal obligations? How *should* an ethical business behave in a situation in which its product causes an injury the firm never envisioned?

the course and scope of employment. *Respondeat superior* is discussed in detail in Chapter 33.

Summary

Tort law is designed to protect an individual's rights with respect to person and property. To do this, the law uses the concept of "duty." Tort law deals with "private" wrongs, whereas criminal law deals with "public" wrongs.

Three theories of tort liability exist: intentional torts, negligence, and strict liability. Intentional torts are those in which a person acted in a willful or intentional manner. Intentional torts to persons are assault, battery, defamation, false imprisonment, mental distress, and invasion of privacy. Intentional torts to property are trespass and conversion. The defenses of consent, privilege, necessity, and truth may apply in both categories.

Negligence is the unintentional causing of harm that could have been prevented if the defendant had acted as a reasonable and prudent person. Strict liability is a separate basis of tort liability because it is independent from intent or negligence. Our legal system has declared that if certain activities cause harm, the actor will be found liable.

Central to a discussion of all three theories of liability are the concepts of duty and foreseeability. Duty imposes a certain kind of conduct and therefore is action oriented. Intentional torts establish that one has a duty to avoid them. Negligence establishes that one has a "reasonable" duty to avoid it. Strict liability, on the other hand, establishes a strict duty so that no matter how reasonable the conduct, there is automatic liability if harm occurs. Foreseeability concerns thought rather than action. If the hypothetical reasonable and prudent person would have foreseen harm, liability exists.

Discussion Questions

1. A person decides to go shopping at the XYZ Department Store. While in the sportswear department, the store detective suspects the person of stealing a swimsuit. The detective approaches the person and says, "Excuse me, but would you mind if I asked you a few questions?" The person responds with, "Well, I'm really in quite a rush. I'm on my lunch hour and I have to get back to work." Nevertheless, the person submits to the questioning. The questioning lasts for 20 minutes. Has there been a false imprisonment? Would your answer be any different if the detective had said, "Excuse me, I suspect you of stealing a swimsuit. Would you mind if I asked you a few questions?"
2. A hotel waiter asks a male guest, "Is this woman your wife or your mistress?" Is the hotel liable for the waiter's insult? Would your answer be any different if the waiter had asked, "Is this woman your wife or your daughter?"

3. Someone knocks on your front door; after you have admitted him, he accuses you of having a "loathsome" disease and of being a rapist. Has he committed a tort against you? Would your answer be any different if he said the same things in the presence of another person?
4. When the legislature and the courts make parents civilly liable for their children's acts, what public policy is being advanced? Is this beneficial to society or not? Why?
5. Why is it that intentional torts, negligence, and strict liability all involve the issue of foreseeability?
6. We all have a duty to protect other persons from harm. How does tort law resolve the question of the extent of that duty?
7. A manufacturer of chemical products markets suntan oil without sufficiently investigating the fact that under certain circumstances the vapors of the product become flammable. Suppose a person uses the product, and as he rubs the oil on his chest, it ignites and burns him. Can he successfully sue the manufacturer for its negligence? Why?
8. It can be scientifically proven that pollution from the smokestacks of a steel plant in Beaumont, Texas, is carried in the clouds over the Gulf of Mexico and deposited on Orlando, Florida. It is also known that the pollutants carry cancer-causing chemicals. On what theory can a person who contracted cancer while living in Orlando successfully sue the steel plant? Discuss your answer with respect to proximate cause.
9. Because you love skydiving, you decide to open a parachute-jumping school. Before students can take the training and make a jump, you require that they sign a voluntary statement that frees you of all liability if they should be harmed. A student makes a jump, but the parachute fails to open. On the basis of these facts, can you be successfully sued for wrongful death? Would it make any difference if it develops that the student simply did not pull the ripcord?
10. A gorilla escapes from a traveling circus, enters a shopping center, and destroys $347,500 worth of property. Will the lawsuits succeed against the circus, or can the circus win if it proves it was not at fault?

CASE PROBLEMS AND WRITING ASSIGNMENTS

1. Teresa Penland and J. Ronnie Jackson were both employed as guards at the Buncombe county jail. A female inmate alleged that she was sexually assaulted by Jackson. Jackson and Penland were on duty the night of the alleged assault. Penland was the matron on the floor. Sheriff Long, who supervised the jail, fired both Jackson and Penland. In his press release and interviews, Sheriff Long implied that both Penland and Jackson were involved in an assault on an inmate. In the press release Sheriff Long mentioned that allegations had been made by an inmate, an investigation was being conducted, and two employees had been dismissed. WLOS-TV broadcast a story the same day. "Newscaster: Buncombe County Sheriff Charles Long today fired two detention officers at the Buncombe County Detention Center. Long ordered an investigation of Officers Ronnie Jackson and Teresa Penland after a female prisoner accused Jackson of assaulting her. Sheriff Long: Anytime we have an assault or anything that might be of an unlawful nature its [sic] a matter of concern . . . we have a high liability in the detention center and we have a lot of worry . . . we don't like for these things to happen." Penland and Jackson denied having anything to do with an assault on an inmate. [The investigation of the assault was later dropped when it was discovered that the inmate had a history of mental illness and a history of claiming sexual assault.] Are Penland and/or Jackson "public officials" who would have to show "malice" under *New York Times* v. *Sullivan*? [See *Penland* v. *Long*, 922 F.Supp. 1085 (W.D.N.C. 1996).]

2. The defendant published the following advertisement: "These progressive dealers listed here sell Armour's Star Bacon in the new window-top carton." If one of the dealers listed specialized in kosher meat exclusively (kosher meat dealers do not deal in bacon), has a defamation taken place? [See *Braun* v. *Armour & Co.*, 254 N.Y. 514, 173 N.E. 845 (1930).]

3. Helen Palsgraf was standing on a railroad platform waiting for her train. Another passenger attempted to board a train that was pulling out of the station. A railroad employee standing nearby attempted to give the passenger a "boost" to help him board the moving train. In the process, a package the passenger was carrying was dropped onto the tracks and exploded because it contained fireworks. The force of the explosion caused some scales standing at the opposite end of the railroad platform to fall on Palsgraf, causing severe injury. Palsgraf sued the railroad for her injuries, alleging negligence by the employee. Is the railroad liable for the injury to Palsgraf? Explain fully. [See *Palsgraf* v. *Long Island Railroad Co.*, 284 N.Y. 339, 162 N.E. 99 (1928).]

4. Michael Salima occasionally did repair work for Scherwood Country Club, which was operated by Marvin and Ron Hanson. He was not a licensed electrician. One

day Salima was at the Country Club doing other repairs when Marvin asked him to look at a parking lot light that was malfunctioning. The day prior to the accident, a Scherwood employee had examined the light but he was unable to determine the cause of the problem. Close to the light there were some electrical wires that were cut during some home construction in the vicinity. The wires had been spliced together and were clearly visible above ground. Salima decided that the problem was probably in some wiring that was on the pole about 18 feet above the ground. He climbed a ladder to investigate, touched the wires, was shocked, and fell to the ground suffering serious injuries. Salima contended that the Country Club, through the Hansons, owed him a duty to warn him about a dangerous condition. Did they violate a duty to Salima? [See *Salima* v. *Scherwood South, Inc.*, 38 F.3d 929 (7th Cir. 1994).]

5. On 19 December 1974, a bridge was damaged by the railroad, causing the rerouting of all vehicular traffic to a highway that normally took only westbound traffic, thus forcing that highway to take both eastbound and westbound traffic. Kopriva was seriously injured in an automobile accident on that stretch of highway on 21 May 1975. She brought an action against the railroad for negligence. The district court dismissed the action and the plaintiff appealed. Was the railroad's negligence a remote or a proximate cause of Kopriva's injuries? [See *Kopriva* v. *Union Pacific RR Co.*, 592 P.2d 711 (Wyo. 1979).]

6. **BUSINESS APPLICATION CASE** Betty Jane Stewart, a 70-year-old woman, entered a Wendy's restaurant on a rainy day in St. Louis, Missouri. Immediately after entering, Stewart slipped and fell in the entry area. As a result of the fall, Stewart sustained medical injuries. Stewart testified that she didn't see the water before she fell because she wasn't looking down when she entered. Stewart's husband, who entered the restaurant shortly after her fall, testified that he saw an eighth-inch of water on the floor. The Wendy's store manager testified that it was raining hard during the busy restaurant hour right before noon and that no mat was placed inside the door. The manager also testified that the floor was dry right before the fall. However, a wet floor sign had been put out about two hours before the fall due to the rainy conditions. Was Wendy's negligent in the care extended to its business invitees? Was there sufficient evidence of negligence on the part of Wendy's for the jury to deliberate on the issue? In a comparative negligence state, what should be the relative faults of the parties? What should a business do to avoid these types of accidents? [See *Stewart* v. *M.D.F., Inc.*, 83 F.3d 247 (8th Cir. 1996).]

7. **ETHICS APPLICATION CASE** Frank Ferlito and his wife, Susan, planned to attend a costume party for Halloween. They agreed to dress as "Mary had a little lamb." Frank was to be the lamb. Susan made him a costume from a suit of long underwear with cotton batting glued to it. Susan also made a headpiece with ears, which was also covered in cotton batting. The cotton batting was manufactured by Johnson and Johnson. The package said that the cotton batting was for cleansing, applying medications, and infant care. At the party, Frank tried to light a cigarette with a butane lighter. The flame got close to his costume setting the cotton batting on fire. Frank suffered substantial burns. Should Frank and Susan be able to recover against Johnson and Johnson? Why or why not? Is it ethical for the Ferlitos to sue Johnson and Johnson? Why or why not? [See *Ferlito* v. *Johnson & Johnson Products, Inc.*, 771 F.Supp. 196 (E.D. Mich. 1991).]

8. **IDES CASE** Professor Ortiz has established a listserver for her business law class. She posts procedural announcements on the listserver. She also uses the listserver to inform the class about interesting web sites, and to discuss journal articles and current events with the class. Students can post information to the listserver. Professor Ortiz also communicates with students individually via e-mail. She will often inform them about their grades and comment on student work.

   One day immediately after grading their second set of papers, she prepared an e-mail note to Nora Williamson. It said, "Nora, your last paper was extremely poorly written. It contained five sentence fragments, incorrect usages of words, and numerous misspelled words. In addition, you seem to have misunderstood the assignment. Consequently, your grade on this assignment is a D–. Sincerely, Professor Ortiz." Professor Ortiz intended to send this message only to Nora; however, she accidently hit the group reply function on her e-mail and sent the message to the entire class. There are two students named Nora in the class.

   Assume also that some of the students in Professor Ortiz's class begin discussing the Dean of Students, Dr. Watts, on the listserver. Many of the comments are critical since Dr. Watts has taken a strong stand against alcoholic beverages on campus. In addition, Dr. Watts is dating the President of the University. Some typical comments on the listserver include, "She is such a prude."; "Dr. Watts seems to believe in do as I say and not as I do."; and "The quality of student services has declined drastically since she was appointed as Dean of Students." Apply the IDES model in deciding whether any torts occurred.

NOTES

1. See *California Civil Code,* § 1714.1.
2. *Church of Scientology Int'l.* v. *Time Warner, Inc.,* 932 F.Supp. 589 (S.D.N.Y. 1996), at pp. 593–594.
3. "Carjacker Sues for $2,000 for Items Left Behind," *The Fresno Bee* (29 January 1995), p. A4.
4. *Texas Tanks, Inc.* v. *Owens-Corning Fiberglas Corp.,* 99 F.3d 734 (5th Cir. 1996).
5. Ibid.
6. See 18 U.S.C., §§ 1961 et seq.
7. See Jury Instructions for Negligence Per Se, BAJI 3.45 (1992 Revision), *California Jury Instructions, Civil,* 7th ed. (St. Paul: West Publishing Co., 1992). Drafted by the Committee of Standard Jury Instructions, Civil, of the Superior Court of Los Angeles County and used throughout the state of California.
8. L.R. 3 H.L. 330 (1868).
9. For example, *California Vehicle Code,* § 17150.
10. 64 LW 1177, May 28, 1996, *U.S. Law Week* 64(45), Section 1, p. 1.

AGENDA

While driving a CIT van, Dan Kochanowski is involved in an accident with another vehicle, causing property damage to both vehicles and physical injuries to the parties inside the other vehicle. The passengers in the other car are planning to file a lawsuit against Dan and against the firm. Is CIT liable for Dan's actions? How should CIT defend itself in this situation? What steps should the Kochanowskis take to minimize their involvement in future traffic accidents?

These and other questions need to be addressed in covering the material in this chapter of the text. Be prepared! You never know when one of the Kochanowskis will need your advice.

Anatomy of a Civil Suit

OUTLINE

Introduction
The Problem
Client's Interview with a Lawyer
Investigation of the Facts
Negotiation of Settlement
Filing the Suit
Pretrial Proceedings
The Trial
Post-Trial Proceedings
A Comment on Finality
Summary
Discussion Questions
Case Problems and Writing Assignments

INTRODUCTION

People in American society have a great many fears and concerns. Some of these fears may seem irrational to others, for example, a fear of the dark or a fear of heights. Others are viewed as much more rational to most members of our society, for example, a fear of catching certain diseases or a fear of losing one's job.

One area that causes fear and concern to the average person is becoming involved in the legal process. For example, someone might fear becoming involved in the legal process as a result of an automobile accident: They may fear either being sued or filing suit for the damages.

This chapter explores the stages of a hypothetical case arising from such a situation. While this material may not alleviate the concern or the fear that you may have, it should help to shed some light on *what* is done, *why* it is done, and *how* it all ties together within the workings of our judicial system in a civil suit. Exhibit 6.1 sets out the six stages a party is likely to encounter in a civil suit. Each of these stages is examined in more detail as we follow the progress of the suit through the legal system.

THE PROBLEM

Nic Grant, a college sophomore, saved some money earned from a part-time job to take his girlfriend, Nancy Griffin, to dinner at a very expensive and sophisticated

EXHIBIT 6.1 The Six Steps Involved in Most Civil Lawsuits

Pleadings	The case begins by filing documents identifying the parties (the person suing and the person being sued), explaining what the claim is about, and asking the court to do something—usually to award money.
Service	The person being sued must be formally notified. Service is usually obtained by preparing a summons and then having the summons and a copy of the complaint personally delivered to the defendant.
Discovery	Both sides have to gather facts and information to prepare for trial. Discovery can involve examining documents, records, and other pieces of physical evidence as well as taking the statements of witnesses or the parties themselves.
Pretrial **motions**	If the parties need the court to make procedural decisions or other rulings as the case moves along toward trial, they do so by filing the appropriate motions with the court.
Trial	The court hears the evidence offered by both sides and decides issues of both fact and law during this process.
Enforcing the judgment	If a party wins a judgment at trial, he or she still has to collect the money awarded. A judgment can be enforced by putting a lien on property, garnishing wages, or obtaining a court order for the turning over of bank accounts or other property.

Motions
Requests to a judge to take certain action. These requests are generally in writing.

6.1

MANAGEMENT

SHOULD AMY CHEN HANDLE THE LITIGATION?

After the accident, the Kochanowskis met to discuss the incident. They are concerned that a legal problem such as this, with its accompanying legal costs, may entirely consume their fledgling enterprise. They have two primary concerns at this point: how they can reduce the expenses related to this incident; and how they can reduce the risk that something like this will happen again. Since attorney's fees alone in a case like this can be extremely expensive, they are considering asking Amy Chen to handle the litigation. Although Amy is a very knowledgeable business lawyer, she does not normally handle civil litigation. The Kochanowskis ask your advice in this matter. What advice will you give them? Why?

BUSINESS CONSIDERATIONS What steps should a business take to minimize the risk of traffic accidents or other conduct that might involve the firm? Who should be authorized to drive company vehicles? What screening processes for drivers should a business utilize? How should the company insure itself against these types of risks?

ETHICAL CONSIDERATIONS Is it ethical for a business to attempt to deny liability for the conduct of its employees when that conduct occurs on the job and, at least presumably, in the furtherance of the firm's interests? Why or why not?

restaurant on Mount Washington, overlooking the Point in downtown Pittsburgh. Nic called for Nancy at her apartment in Cranberry Township about six o'clock on June 7 and was driving through Butler County toward the restaurant when his car was struck by a white van with the Call-Image logo on it. The accident happened at the intersection of Route 19 (Perry Highway) and Rowan Road in Cranberry Township, Butler County.

Nic spent the next five days in the hospital. As a result, he did not show up for work and consequently lost his job. He also failed to take his college final examinations and complete his research projects, forcing him to withdraw from college for the semester. Nancy, who did not have a job, also suffered injuries from the impact and sought medical treatment. Nic's roommate, who is taking a course in business law, advised Nic to consult a lawyer.

Dan Kochanowski, a full-time employee of Call-Image Technology, was in Pittsburgh to work at a trade show displaying electronic products. He worked at the booth in the Pittsburgh Convention Center from 8:30 A.M. until 5:30 P.M., with a half-hour lunch break. No one else could leave the Call-Image office for the trade show, so Dan had to work the booth by himself.

Dan packed the sample products in the CIT van and left the Convention Center parking lot at 5:45 P.M. Before heading home, he drove toward Butler, to a restaurant recommended by a friend, Trattoria Restaurant on Main Street. Dan had directions but was unfamiliar with the area. While he was trying to negotiate the streets and follow his friend's instructions, the CIT van hit the car owned and operated by Nic Grant. Call-Image is an Ohio corporation licensed as a foreign corporation doing business in Pennsylvania.

Client's Interview with a Lawyer

Nic recognized that he needed legal assistance, and consulted the local bar association. The local bar association referred Nic to an attorney, Lyn Carroll. Nic called her and scheduled an initial interview. At this initial interview, Nic recounted all the facts of that evening, to the best of his recollection. Nic then mentioned that he had not notified either the driver of the other vehicle or CIT. Ms. Carroll agreed to assist Nic in obtaining compensation and offered to help Nancy as well. Ms. Carroll recognized that it may be a conflict of interest for her to represent both Nic and Nancy, especially if Nic was also negligent in causing the accident. (In order for

Lyn Carroll to comply with the ethics rules for attorneys, she sent each prospective client a letter disclosing the possible conflict of interest.) The three met a few days later to discuss, read, and sign the client–attorney contract. This document appears as Exhibit 6.2 (page 144). As indicated in the contract, payment will be based on a **contingency fee.**

Other bases for attorney's fees are not dependent on results: for example, flat rate and hourly rate fees. Whatever the fee arrangement, it is specified in the contract between the client and the attorney.

The Kochanowskis decided that it is unwise to ask Amy Chen to defend them in this lawsuit because she is not familiar with personal injury litigation and with the Butler County courts. Instead, the Kochanowskis asked her for a recommendation; and she recommended the Pittsburgh law firm of Jones, Murphy, Sabbatino, and Schwartz, which specializes in defending against personal injury suits. The Kochanowskis scheduled an appointment to meet with Mr. Jones. (Chapter 1 contains additional information about hiring an attorney.)

Even though the accident occurred in Butler County, the defendants can hire an attorney from Pittsburgh, located in Allegheny County. Attorneys are licensed at the state level and not the county level. Once licensed, the attorney can practice law anywhere within the state's jurisdiction. Rules of court and court procedures may vary somewhat from county to county, and the attorney will need to know or learn the rules in Butler County for this trial, as well as knowing the Pennsylvania Rules of Civil Procedure. (Trials in federal court are controlled by the Federal Rules of Civil Procedure.)

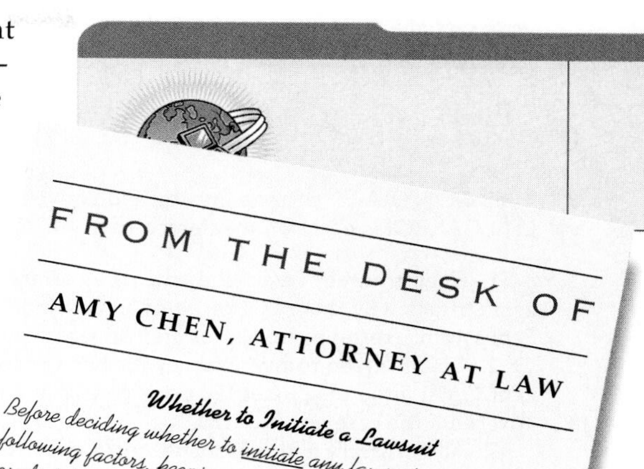

FROM THE DESK OF

AMY CHEN, ATTORNEY AT LAW

Whether to Initiate a Lawsuit

Before deciding whether to initiate any lawsuit, consider the following factors, keeping in mind that the legal system is unpredictable:

- *The likelihood of winning the suit*
- *The amount of money you might win or lose*
- *The ability of the other party to pay any judgment*
- *The amount that the lawyer(s) would charge and other expenses that would be incurred by litigating, such as expert witnesses and jury consultants and the amount of time that company employees would spend in preparing for the litigation*
- *The manner in which this lawsuit and/or additional publicity would affect the company's reputation*
- *The effect on the continuing relationship between parties to the suit*
- *The stress and emotional toll that the lawsuit will take on those involved.*

INVESTIGATION OF THE FACTS

In the interviews with her clients and in subsequent telephone conversations, Ms. Carroll gathered the information displayed in Exhibit 6.3 (page 146). On the basis of this preliminary information, she obtained medical releases from both clients in order to review the hospital and medical records—Exhibit 6.4 (page 147). Nic also gave her copies of the hospital bills and the estimate for the car repair. Finally, Ms. Carroll obtained a copy of the police report filed by José Gonzalez, the officer who responded to the accident scene—Exhibit 6.5 (pages 148–49).

Contingency fee
A fee stipulated to be paid to an attorney only if the case is settled or won, or is based on some other contingency or event.

After reviewing the file, Ms. Carroll wrote to the university that Nic and Nancy had been attending for proof that they had withdrawn from classes after 7 June 1996. She also wrote to Nic's former employer for information about Nic's wages, normal work week, and proof that he was fired on 10 June 1996. Once all the material requested was in the file, her preliminary investigation was finished. She concluded that Nic was driving with Nancy in his car on Rowan Road, Cranberry Township, Butler County, when the car was struck by a van operated by Dan Kochanowski. The van is owned by Call-Image Technology and is decorated with permanent signs on

EXHIBIT 6.2 Client–Attorney Contract

AGREEMENT

THIS CONTRACT entered into, by, and between NIC GRANT and NANCY GRIFFIN, hereinafter referred to as CLIENTS, and LYN CARROLL, hereinafter referred to as ATTORNEY, WITNESSETH:

1. Clients hereby retain and employ attorney to represent them in the prosecution of their claim and cause of action for damages sustained by them as a result of an automobile accident occurring June 7, 1996, on Route 19 and Rowan Road, Butler County, Pennsylvania, resulting in injuries and damages to clients.

2. Clients agree to pay attorney for her services rendered pursuant to this employment contract at the rate of twenty-five percent (25%) if the case is settled prior to trial and at the rate of thirty-three and one-third percent (33⅓ %) of the net amount recovered if the case goes to trial.

3. All necessary and reasonable costs, expenses, investigation, preparation for trial, and litigation expenses shall be initially paid for by attorney and then deducted from the amount of any settlement or recovery, and the division between the parties shall be made after deduction of said expenses. Furthermore, clients shall reimburse attorney for all such costs and expenses even if no recovery is made or, in the alternative, if the costs and expenses should exceed the amount of the recovery.

4. Attorney agrees to undertake the representation of clients in the prosecution of the above claims and causes of action, using her highest professional skill to further the interest of said clients in all matters in connection with their claims and causes of action, and to diligently pursue said claims and causes of action.

5. No settlement or other disposition of the matter shall be made by attorney without the written approval of clients.

IN WITNESS WHEREOF, the parties hereto have executed this instrument in triplicate originals this 20th day of June 1996.

CLIENT ____________________
NIC GRANT

CLIENT ____________________
NANCY GRIFFIN

ATTORNEY ____________________
LYN CARROLL

Suit
Lawsuit; the formal legal proceeding used to resolve a legal dispute.

Complaint
In civil practice, the plaintiff's first pleading. It informs the defendant that he or she is being sued.

Court of Common Pleas
Title used for some trial courts of general jurisdiction.

Prothonotary
Title used in some states to designate the chief clerk of courts.

both doors advertising Call-Image products. At this point, Ms. Carroll wrote a letter to an officer of Call-Image. It appears as Exhibit 6.6 (page 150).

NEGOTIATION OF SETTLEMENT

Upon receipt of the letter of notice, Anna Kochanowski contacted CIT's insurance company to inform them of its contents. The insurance carrier immediately assigned an adjuster to the case. The adjuster contacted Ms. Carroll to ascertain the nature of the injuries and learn the information shown in Exhibit 6.7 (page 151). On the basis of this information, the adjuster attempted to negotiate a settlement by offering $17,027 to Mr. Grant and $5,680 to Ms. Griffin. Since the offer covered only out-of-pocket expenses and did not include lost wages and pain and suffering, it was rejected; and Ms. Carroll filed **suit** on 15 November 1996. (Note that Nic Grant is claiming at least $16,000 and Nancy Griffin is claiming at least $8,000 in pain and suffering.)

There is some advantage to waiting to initiate suit. Plaintiffs will want to know that their injuries are completely healed and no new injuries are discovered. In this case, waiting might also be an advantage to CIT, since Nic may obtain replacement employment. In general, a plaintiff must be sure to initiate his or her suit by filing the **complaint** before the statute of limitations expires. The suit should also commence before the memories of the parties and witnesses begin to fade. At this time, the attorney should discuss alternatives to litigation (see Chapter 7).

6.2

PREPARING TO MEET WITH THE ATTORNEY

Anna and Dan are preparing for their first meeting with Mr. Jones, and they are understandably nervous. They would like to know what information they should collect and take to the meeting. They would also like to know what they should expect at the meeting. They ask you to make a list of the information that would be legally relevant to this lawsuit. They also ask you what they should expect at this first meeting. What will you tell them?

BUSINESS CONSIDERATIONS Frequently, a business will have certain items it wishes to treat in a confidential manner, but the business may need to reveal some or all of this information to its attorneys in a legal proceeding. What steps should the law firm take to protect the confidentiality of its clients? What procedures should the business follow to maximize its protection while still being as open and honest as necessary with its counsel?

ETHICAL CONSIDERATIONS Suppose that the facts as they are known to the parties make it relatively obvious that a business is liable for the wrongful conduct of one of its agents. Is it ethical for the business and its attorneys to use expensive and time-consuming delaying tactics in an effort to persuade the injured party to settle out of court? Would it be ethical to seek an alternate form of dispute resolution rather than going to trial?

MANAGEMENT

FILING THE SUIT

The complaint should be definite and contain sufficient information for the defendant to understand the nature of the litigation and begin his or her defense. Exhibit 6.8 (page 152) shows the plaintiffs' original complaint, which was filed in the **Court of Common Pleas.** After it was filed, the **prothonotary**'s office delivered a copy to the sheriff. (In many states, the clerk of court's office performs the same functions as the prothonotary's office.) The sheriff then serves copies of the complaint on the two defendants. Depending on the type of suit and the state, any responsible adult who is not a party to the suit may be able to serve the complaint. In some states, the complaint is accompanied by a **summons.**

Since Call-Image is registered as a foreign corporation, its complaint was delivered by mail to Anna at the principal office of the corporation. Many states permit service of process for registered foreign corporations on the secretary of state of that state. If Call-Image Technology or Dan Kochanowski had planned to claim that the court lacked jurisdiction over them or the lawsuit, they would have done it at this time instead of filing a general answer.

Sometimes the defendant does not answer the complaint. In these cases, the court will generally enter a *default judgment*, a judgment in default of the defendant's appearance. Since the court is only listening to one side, the judgment generally awards the plaintiff what he or she is requesting. Default judgments are valid in civil cases if the court has proper jurisdiction over the defendant and the defendant has been properly served in the case.

Summons

A writ requiring the sheriff to notify the person named that the person must appear in court to answer a complaint.

Exhibit 6.9 (page 153) displays a copy of the defendants' answer. Most complaints and answers will be more detailed than these examples and must include individual numbered items specifying the details that constitute the legal cause of action.

At this point in the proceedings, the plaintiffs have sued the defendants in a court of law and the defendants have filed an answer. Before trial, both attorneys may simplify the legal issues, amend their complaints and answers, and attempt to limit the number of expert witnesses, if any, with the purpose of reducing costs and the length of trial.

EXHIBIT 6.3 Preliminary Information

ACTIONS	INFORMATION	
	Nic Grant 4321 S. Medford, Apt. 32 Cranberry Township, PA 15203 (412) 555-2394 (Home) None (Work) DOB 21 May 1976	
	Nancy Griffin 1234 N. Mitford, Apt. 9B Cranberry Township, PA 15209 (412) 555-4932 (Home) None (Work) DOB 24 Dec 1977	
Get Copy of Police Report	Date of Injury	7 June 1996
	Place of Injury	Route 19 and Rowan Road Cranberry Township, Pennsylvania
	Other Driver	Dan Kochanowski
	Owner of Other Vehicle	Call-Image Technology, Inc. 9876 Appian Way Maineville, OH 44444
	Nature of Injury	Vehicular accident
Get Hospital and Doctor's Records	Treatment	Grant–Doctor's Hospital 7-11 June 1996
	Physician	Billy Lee, M.D., Professional Bldg. Butler, PA 15201
	Treatment	Griffin–Doctor's Hospital 7 June 1996
	Physician	Alfred Lowens, M.D. 8323 Farkleberry Ln. Butler, PA 15201

Write to the Commonwealth of Pennsylvania to verify that there is such a corporation, domestic or foreign, qualified to do business in Pennsylvania

Write to State of Ohio to verify the same information

PRETRIAL PROCEEDINGS

At this point, the discovery process begins. *Discovery* is a general term that applies to a group of specific methods used to narrow the issues to be decided by the trial. Lawyers use the process to shorten the actual trial, if there is one, or to eliminate the need for a trial if the case can be settled before trial. If one side sees that there is little hope they can win the suit, it is in their best interests to settle the case. The scope of discovery is very broad. Accordingly, one can discover all that is relevant even if the

EXHIBIT 6.4 Medical Release

MEDICAL AUTHORIZATION

TO: ______________________________

I hereby authorize and request you to allow my attorney, LYN CARROLL, free access to any and all hospital and/or medical records or reports in your possession or custody and, upon the request of LYN CARROLL, to furnish to her, at my expense, a full and complete report concerning your medical examination and treatment of

____

____
Date

____
Name

____
Address

evidence cannot be introduced at trial. The test is that the discovery request must be reasonably calculated to lead to admissible evidence. Exhibit 6.10 depicts the five common discovery devices.

Depositions

Traditionally, a *deposition* is the reducing to writing of a witness's sworn testimony taken outside of court. Increasingly, attorneys also video tape the deposition. This is permitted in a number of jurisdictions, including federal courts (Federal Rules of Civil Procedure § 30[b][2]) and California courts (California Civil Procedure § 2025[p]). If the deposition is later used at trial, the jury will view the film of the deposition instead of having the deposition read to them. Generally, this is more interesting and the jurors are more likely to pay close attention to the questions and answers. Depositions are used routinely today either to preserve testimony from someone who, for good cause, may not be able to attend the trial or to subsequently **impeach** the witness when the witness does appear at trial and gives evidence that conflicts with what he or she gave at the time the deposition was taken. A deposition may be obtained from *any* party *or* witness.

Impeach
To question the truthfulness of a witness by means of some evidence.

Interrogatories

Interrogatories are written questions from one side to the other. Like depositions, interrogatories produce a written record of answers to questions. However, because

EXHIBIT 6.5 Police Report (Front)

CRANBERRY TOWNSHIP SHERIFF DEPARTMENT

LOG

Code Section	Crime	Classification	
Location of Occurrence: Route 19 and Rowan Road			Date of Occurrence: 7 June 1996
Time of Occurrence: approx. 18:25		Report Date: 7 June 1996	Report TIme: 18:32

VICTIMS/WITNESSES

Code	Name	Occupation	Race	Sex	DOB
	Grant, Nic	Student/Cashier	W	M	21 May 1976

Residence Address	Apt.	City	State	Zip Code.	Res. Phone
4321 S. Medford	32	Cranberry Township	PA	15203	(412)555-2394

Business Address	Unit	City	State	Zip Code.	Bus. Phone
Discount Pharmacy		Butler	PA	15201	None

Code	Name	Occupation	Race	Sex	DOB

Residence Address	Apt.	City	State	Zip Code.	Res. Phone

Business Address	Unit	City	State	Zip Code.	Bus. Phone

Code	Name	Occupation	Race	Sex	DOB

Residence Address	Apt.	City	State	Zip Code.	Res. Phone

Business Address	Unit	City	State	Zip Code.	Bus. Phone

VEHICLE #1

License No.	State	Year	Make	Model	Colors
555 CAR 555	PA	1991	Chevrolet	Camaro	Silver

Reporting Officer	ID#	Date	
José Gonzalez	1234 mx 67	7 June 1996	
Reviewed by	ID#	Date	Case Status: Closed Pending Suspended Unfounded

both the questions and the answers are written, the answers are not as spontaneous as in a deposition. The answer is made under oath, but the respondent has the time to contemplate and carefully phrase the written answers to the questions posed. Interrogatories may be obtained from any party to the lawsuit but *not* from other witnesses. That is, if a witness is neither a plaintiff nor a defendant (the two groups that comprise the parties), an interrogatory may not be obtained.

Production of Documents and Things

In many lawsuits, testimony alone is insufficient to win the case. In Nic and Nancy's case, Ms. Carroll also must introduce the records of the two doctors, the hospital, and the police report. Because of the circumstances, Ms. Carroll may also request that CIT produce records it possesses reflecting when and where the van was bought and any internal communications used in tracking repair records and mechanical difficulties. The legal form used to obtain those documents is called a **subpoena duces tecum.**

Subpoena duces tecum
A court order to produce evidence at a trial.

EXHIBIT 6.5 Police Report (Back)

VEHICLE #2

CRANBERRY TOWNSHIP SHERIFF DEPARTMENT					
Complete the following information for vehicular accidents only Description of additional vehicles					
License No. 488 XZ 111	State Ohio	Year 1997	Make Plymouth	Model Van	Colors White

Draw a diagram of the accident scene below. Include trafffic lights, stop signs, buildings, road construction, and any obstructions.

MAP

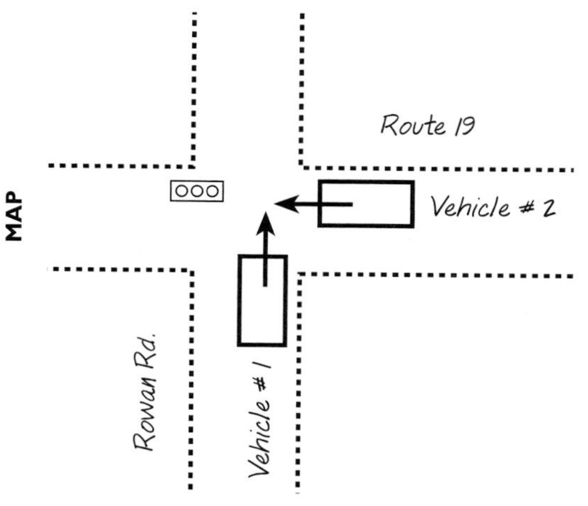

Narrative Officer arrived on scene shortly after the accident. Called tow trucks to remove both vehicles from intersection to allow rush hour traffic to pass. Ordered ambulance to take Nic Grant and Nancy Griffin to local hospital. No evidence of alcohol or drug use by either driver. Blood alcohol tests were not administered. Rush hour traffic was moving slowly and there was no evidence of excessive speed. No witnesses came forward during the on-scene investigation.

Initial finding of fault Officer did not assign fault.

Physical or Mental Examination

Whenever the physical or mental condition of a party to the suit is in question, the court may order that party to submit to an examination by a physician. Here both the present condition of the plaintiffs and their physical condition prior to the accident are in question, so a medical examination is necessary.

Request for Admission

One party can serve on the other party a written request for an *admission*, which takes the form of a question asked by one party to which the answer is either yes or no. If the party who is to respond fails to answer in a stated period of time (usually 30 days), the matter is deemed admitted.

The Result of Discovery

As a result of the discovery process, the attorneys for CIT and Dan Kochanowski informed their clients that it appears the accident was primarily caused by Dan's

EXHIBIT 6.6 Letter of Notice

LYN CARROLL, J.D.
Attorney at Law
Suite 654
Butler Savings Building
Butler, Pennsylvania 15205

28 June 1996

Ms. Anna Kochanowski
President
Call-Image Technology
9876 Appian Way
Maineville, OH 44444

Mr. Dan Kochanowski
c/o Call-Image Technology
9876 Appian Way
Maineville, OH 44444

RE: *Nic Grant and Nancy Griffin* v. *Call-Image Technology and Dan Kochanowski*

Dear Ms. Anna Kochanowski and Mr. Dan Kochanowski:

I have been retained by Mr. Nic Grant and Ms. Nancy Griffin to represent them in a cause of action arising from your van colliding into the car owned and operated by Mr. Grant on 7 June 1996. Ms. Griffin was a passenger in Mr. Grant's car at that time. My preliminary investigation indicates that the accident was caused by inattention and carelessness by your driver, Dan Kochanowski, and by improper maintenance of your van.

Should you or your liability carrier wish to discuss this matter with me in order to achieve a just and equitable settlement, please contact me within twelve days from the date of this letter. If I do not hear from you or your representative within that period, I shall file suit against you without further notice.

Sincerely,

Lyn Carroll

LC: rj
cc: Mr. Grant
Ms. Griffin

negligence and his unfamiliarity with the streets. Mr. Jones recommended a settlement offer of $23,000 and the Kochanowskis agreed. Ms. Carroll informed her clients of the offer and recommended rejection. Nic and Nancy agreed, and the case goes to trial.

Pretrial Conferences

Many courts now utilize pretrial conferences to encourage the parties to settle the dispute themselves. However, not all judicial systems and judges favor these conferences. Often the pretrial conferences result in a settlement. Even if they do not, they generally succeed in clarifying the legal and factual issues involved in the case. Depending on the situation, participation in settlement conferences may be mandatory or voluntary.

EXHIBIT 6.7 Summary of the Insurance Adjustor's Findings

DAMAGES

Mr. Grant	
1. Damage to car	$ 7,200.00
2. Transportation to hospital	250.00
3. Hospital bill	5,080.00
4. Doctor bill	3,137.00
5. Lost wages	unknown[a]
6. Tuition for one semester	1,125.00
7. Books	195.00
8. Computer lab fees	40.00
TOTAL	$17,027.00

Ms. Griffin	
1. Transportation to hospital	$ 250.00
2. Hospital bill	2,275.00
3. Doctor bill	1,800.00
4. Tuition for one semester	1,125.00
5. Books	190.00
6. Computer lab fees	40.00
TOTAL	$5,680.00
GRAND TOTAL	$22,707.00

[a]The amount of lost wages would be known, if Nic had obtained another position.

YOU BE THE JUDGE

Mounting Piles of Deposition Requests Disrupt Lives of CEOs

In a recent sexual harassment lawsuit against Monsanto, a chemical manufacturer, the plaintiff's attorney sought to depose Richard Mahoney, Monsanto's chief executive officer. Monsanto's attorney claimed that this deposition was harassment because Mr. Mahoney did not know the ex-employee; Mr. Mahoney's behavior was not involved; and Mr. Mahoney was not familiar with the circumstances. The plaintiff's attorney contended that Mr. Mahoney was being deposed because he should be familiar with company policies.

Should the court require Monsanto's chief executive to respond to this deposition? What limits, if any, would be proper on depositions of corporate executives? This matter has ended up in *your* court. How would *you* decide these issues?[1]

BUSINESS CONSIDERATIONS What steps, if any, can a CEO take to avoid becoming embroiled in litigation involving the firm, but not involving the CEO personally? How much is it realistic to expect the CEO or other officers of a firm to know of the day-to-day problems and operations of a large firm?

ETHICAL CONSIDERATIONS Is it ethical for a plaintiff's attorney to depose the officers or directors of a firm in an attempt to "persuade" the firm to settle a dispute? Is it ethical for the officers or directors of a firm to deny liability due to the "unauthorized" conduct of subordinates? Explain your reasoning.

SOURCE: Andrea Gerlin, *Wall Street Journal*, 7 November 1994.

EXHIBIT 6.8 | Plaintiffs' Original Complaint

Plaintiffs' Original Complaint
COURT OF COMMON PLEAS OF BUTLER COUNTY, PENNSYLVANIA

NIC GRANT and NANCY GRIFFIN, Plaintiffs	:	A.D. No. 23465 Civil Action Law
V.	:	A jury trial is demanded.
CALL-IMAGE TECHNOLOGY[a] and DAN KOCHANOWSKI[b], Defendants	:	

NOW COME NIC GRANT and NANCY GRIFFIN, hereinafter called PLAINTIFFS, complaining of CALL-IMAGE TECHNOLOGY, a foreign corporation doing business in the Commonwealth of Pennsylvania, and DAN KOCHANOWSKI, hereinafter called DEFENDANTS, who may be served with citation by service, upon Call-Image's statutory agent and Mr. Kochanowski's place of employment, ANNA KOCHANOWSKI, 9876 Appian Way, Maineville, Ohio, and for cause of action would respectfully show unto the court that:

On or about 7 June 1996, plaintiffs were driving on Rowan Road, Butler County, Pennsylvania. As a result of defendants' negligence, plaintiffs have incurred, and will continue to incur, various medical expenses; they have suffered, and will continue to suffer, pain; Mr. Grant has been unable to work and has already lost wages in the sum of $10,000.00; Mr. Grant's ability to earn wages in the immediate future has been temporarily impaired; and plaintiffs have suffered a loss of tuition incurred in the course of furthering their education by having to leave school and by having to postpone their graduation date by one semester.

WHEREFORE, plaintiffs demand judgment against defendants, individually, jointly, and/or severally in an amount in excess of $50,000.00[c], their costs, and all other proper relief.

LYN CARROLL
Attorney at Law
Suite 654
Butler Savings Building
Butler, PA 15205
(412) 555-1234

[a]If Call-Image Technology was not a corporation, but was the name under which the Kochanowski family did business, the complaint would name Anna and Tom Kochanowski, d.b.a. Call-Image Technology (d.b.a is an abbreviation for "doing business as" that is used when people operate a business under another name).

[b]Some states, including California, permit a plaintiff to include "John Doe(s)" as defendant(s), if the plaintiff does not know the true names of all the defendants. Then the plaintiff can add the defendant(s) later, if it would be just to do so.

[c]Many courts today require compulsory arbitration for smaller cases. For example, in Butler County, cases under $10,000 will be referred to compulsory arbitration. The arbitrators there consist of a panel of three attorneys who have agreed to serve as arbitrators. A party who is not satisfied with the arbitrators' award could appeal to the Court of Common Pleas.

EXHIBIT 6.9 Defendants' Answer

Defendants' Original Answer
COURT OF COMMON PLEAS OF BUTLER COUNTY, PENNSYLVANIA

NIC GRANT and NANCY GRIFFIN, Plaintiffs V. CALL-IMAGE TECHNOLOGY and DAN KOCHANOWSKI, Defendants	: : : : : : : : :	A.D. No. 23465 Civil Action Law

NOW COMES CALL-IMAGE TECHNOLOGY and DAN KOCHANOWSKI, defendants in the above styled and numbered cause, and for answer to Plaintiffs' Original Complaint would respectfully show unto the court:

Defendants deny each and every material allegation contained in Plaintiffs' Original Complaint. In addition, defendants allege that it was the negligent driving of Nic Grant that caused his injuries and the injuries of the defendants.

WHEREFORE, having fully answered, defendant prays that the complaint be dismissed, for their costs, and for all other proper relief, including damage to the Call-Image van.

JONES, MURPHY, SABBATINO, and SCHWARTZ
Suite 1010
First National Bank Building
Pittsburgh, PA 15205
(412) 555-9876

By ______________________________
ATTORNEYS FOR DEFENDANTS

On 14 December 1996 the original of this answer was filed in the Prothonotary's office. A copy of this answer was mailed to Ms. Lyn Carroll, attorney for plaintiffs, Suite 654, Butler Savings Building, Butler, Pennsylvania 15205.

By ______________________________
JEFFERSON JONES

Businesspeople need to be aware that *many* courts require the parties to participate in pretrial conferences. Some jurisdictions base the requirement on the amount of damages. In Butler County, for example, during pretrial conferences, the attorneys meet with the judge. The parties are requested to be available either outside the courtroom or by telephone. Then, if a settlement offer is made, the attorney can quickly inform his or her client and obtain a prompt response. This procedure is common in many courts. Depending on the jurisdiction and the judge's preferences, the judge *may* take a very active role in attempting to fashion a compromise that would be acceptable to both parties. Some judges may be harsh on parties who do not accept reasonable settlement offers or who do not participate in pretrial conferences in good

EXHIBIT 6.10 Discovery

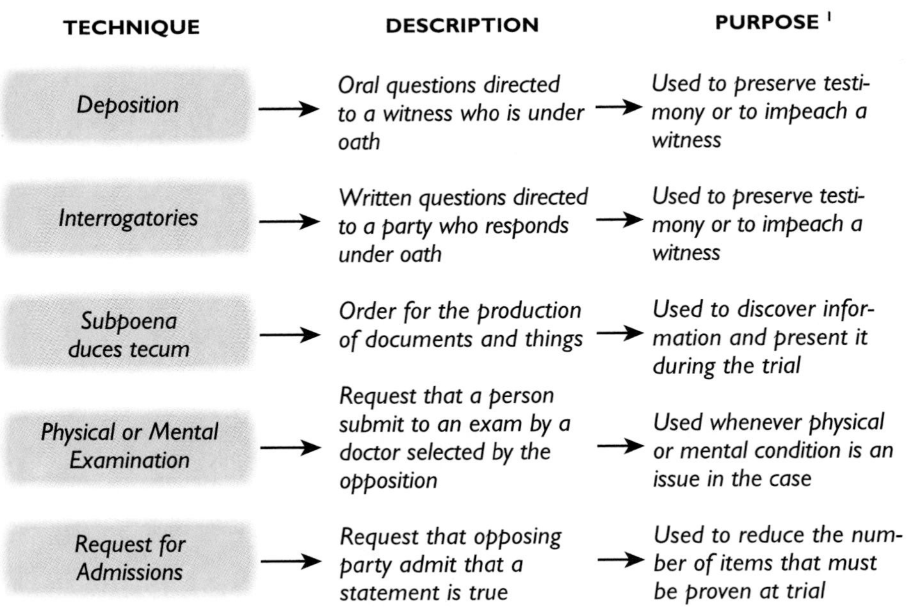

TECHNIQUE	DESCRIPTION	PURPOSE[1]
Deposition	*Oral questions directed to a witness who is under oath*	*Used to preserve testimony or to impeach a witness*
Interrogatories	*Written questions directed to a party who responds under oath*	*Used to preserve testimony or to impeach a witness*
Subpoena duces tecum	*Order for the production of documents and things*	*Used to discover information and present it during the trial*
Physical or Mental Examination	*Request that a person submit to an exam by a doctor selected by the opposition*	*Used whenever physical or mental condition is an issue in the case*
Request for Admissions	*Request that opposing party admit that a statement is true*	*Used to reduce the number of items that must be proven at trial*

[1]One of the purposes of all discovery techniques is to obtain information.

faith. In some jurisdictions, nonbinding arbitration (see detailed discussion in Chapter 7) may be required in addition to or instead of a settlement conference.

Demurrer

The purpose of a demurrer is to challenge the legal sufficiency of the other party's pleading as a pleading. For example, demurrers can be raised to the plaintiff's complaint; the defendant's answer; or the defendant's counterclaim. The grounds for a demurrer are usually limited by statute. Common grounds include failure to state facts sufficient to constitute a legal cause of action (general demurrer); lack of jurisdiction (special demurrer); lack of capacity to sue (special demurrer); and uncertainty or ambiguity (special demurrer).

A general demurrer only challenges defects that appear on the *face* of the pleading. At this point the parties cannot produce additional evidence or sworn statements. Each jurisdiction has different requirements as to what constitutes a sufficient pleading and the amount of detail required. In deciding whether to grant a demurrer, the court must accept as true all the facts that were in the pleading. The issue is whether, assuming all the facts that are pleaded are true, they would entitle the plaintiff to any judicial relief. If the demurrer is denied, the party requesting the demurrer will be given time to answer. If the demurrer is granted, generally the losing party will be given permission to amend the pleading to make it sufficient.

Demurrers have been abolished before federal courts. In federal courts, a party would use a motion to dismiss instead of a general demurrer. Motions to dismiss are discussed in the following section.

Motion to Dismiss

Depending on the jurisdiction, motions to dismiss can be raised on the same grounds as general or special demurrers. A motion to dismiss can be made after different pleadings. When a court considers a motion to dismiss, it *generally* accepts that the material facts alleged in the complaint are true. The pleading is construed in the light most favorable to the party who filed it. The pleading need only state a claim upon which relief can be granted. The purpose of a motion to dismiss is to avoid the expense of unnecessary trials.

If the motion to dismiss is granted, it may be with or without prejudice. If the motion is granted *without prejudice,* the plaintiff can amend and refile the complaint. The judge will often establish a deadline for amending the complaint. If the motion is granted *with prejudice,* the plaintiff cannot revise the complaint and the trial is terminated. In some jurisdictions, there is an absolute right to amend once. A motion to dismiss is a final decision in the case that can be appealed. Many of the cases in this text were decided on a demurrer or a motion to dismiss. In the *Skolnick* v. *Clinton* case, the court discusses whether the complaint should be dismissed.

Pro se

Appearing in his or her own behalf, in person.

6.1 SKOLNICK v. CLINTON

1996 U.S. Dist. LEXIS 19333 (N.D. Ill., E. Div., 1996)

FACTS Plaintiffs Sherman H. Skolnick and Joseph Andreucetti (together "Plaintiffs") filed this action against defendants Hillary Rodham Clinton, Amy Zisook, Mark Zisook, H. C. Valent, John E. Gierum, Gerald H. Parshall, Jr., Robert Alexovich, and ten John Does and Jane Roes (collectively "defendants"), claiming that the defendants, both individually and together, violated the plaintiffs' First, Fourth and Fifth Amendment rights. The defendants moved to dismiss plaintiffs' complaint pursuant to Fed. R. Civ. P. 41(b) for plaintiffs' failure in their complaint to meet the minimum standards of intelligibility and brevity required by the federal rules and/or to Fed. R. Civ. P. 12(b)(6) for failure to state a claim upon which relief can be granted.

ISSUE Should the plaintiffs' complaint be dismissed?

HOLDING Yes.

REASONING The plaintiff's complaint should be dismissed without prejudice. "Fed. R. Civ. P. 8(a)(2) requires that a complaint include 'a short and plain statement of the claim showing that the pleader is entitled to relief.' Rule 8(e)(1) commands that 'each averment of a pleading shall be simple, concise, and direct.' Taken together, these rules 'underscore the emphasis placed on clarity and brevity by the federal pleading rules. . . .' As aptly explained by Judge Grady, 'The primary purpose of these provisions is rooted in fair notice: a complaint must be presented with sufficient intelligibility that a court or opposing party can understand whether a valid claim is alleged and if so what it is. . . .'

The pleading requirements embodied in Fed. R. Civ. P. 8 are relaxed with respect to ***pro se*** plaintiffs . . . 'Allegations in *pro se* pleadings are to be construed liberally, applying substantially less stringent standards than those applied to pleadings drafted by professional counsel.' . . . '[E]ven where a plaintiff is suing *pro se*, a defendant is entitled to fair notice of the claim against it.' . . .

Here, even applying an extremely liberal standard, Plaintiffs' Complaint fails to comply with the minimal pleading requirements of Rules 8(a) and 8(e)(1). Initially, Plaintiffs' Complaint is neither clear nor concise; it is twenty-three pages of convoluted, confusing and often incomprehensible allegations of wrongdoing and/or malfeasance. The Complaint names seventeen defendants (only seven of which are known to Plaintiffs) and asserts that Defendants engaged in a scheme, among other things, (1) to obstruct public disclosure of—to 'cover-up'—the unlawful transfer of large sums of money from Household Bank and/or Madison Guaranty Savings & Loan; (2) to threaten, coerce, and terrorize Plaintiffs in order to stop Plaintiffs from investigating or publicizing the aforementioned 'cover-up'; (3) to place Plaintiffs on an official 'enemies of the state' list, so that they would be targeted by the IRS, the FBI and other federal and state

6.1 SKOLNICK v. CLINTON *(cont.)* 1996 U.S. Dist. LEXIS 19333 (N.D. ILL., E. Div., 1996)

agencies; (4) to steal Andreucetti's money and property for Defendants' own personal benefit; and (5) to file false papers and documents calling for the seizure of Andreuccetti's property.

Plaintiffs' Complaint is separated into three Counts, but each Count includes myriad rambling and/or unintelligible factual assertions. Further, nowhere in the Complaint do Plaintiffs plainly identify the nexus between Defendants' alleged misconduct and Plaintiffs' constitutional claims for relief. In short, Plaintiffs' Complaint neither 'identifie[s] the general nature of the claims involved [nor] afford[s] the opposing party fair notice of those claims. . . .'

Significantly, Plaintiffs, unlike most *pro se* litigants, are keenly aware of Federal Rules' pleading requirements and, indeed, repeatedly have been instructed by courts in this district as to the consequences of failing to heed those requirements: Although proceeding *pro se,* plaintiffs [including Skolnick and Andreuccetti] are not strangers to court proceedings. All have been involved in other lawsuits, with all having been warned about or having been found to have been involved in frivolous or vexatious litigation. . . . See, e.g., *Andreuccetti* v. *Steinberg*, . . . ('Andreuccetti is ordered to refrain from filing papers, issuing subpoenas or making any discovery requests in this case without prior leave of court'); *Vassilos* v. *Petersen* . . . ('admonishing Skolnick to take note of Fed. R. Civ. P. 11 before filing any future lawsuits'); *In re Andreuccetti* . . . (prohibiting Andreuccetti 'from any filings of any type in any court which relate to or pertain to any of the matters raised in this bankruptcy case.'). . . .

Thus, pursuant to Fed. R. Civ. P. 41(b), Plaintiffs' Complaint is dismissed for failure to comply with the requirements of Fed. R. Civ. P. 8. Plaintiffs will be given one, and only one, opportunity to replead their Complaint consistent with Rules 8(a) and 8(e)(1). As this Court presently is unable to ascertain the nature or the specific content of Plaintiffs' claims, the Court cannot, and, therefore, does not, address Defendants' various motions to dismiss pursuant to Fed. R. Civ. P. 12(b)(6). . . ."

BUSINESS CONSIDERATIONS There is a growing tendency to encourage the use of "plain language," whether in a complaint in federal court or in the prospectus of a security offering. Should a business adopt a policy of using "plain language" in its written communications and documents? If such a policy is adopted, how broadly should it be followed? For example, suppose that an industry normally uses certain technical or scientific language: should a firm in that industry abandon the use of such language in order to adhere to a plain language policy?

ETHICAL CONSIDERATIONS Is it ethical for the president and his/her spouse—or any high-ranking public or private officials—to place opponents on an "enemies" list based on the activities of those opponents? In this case it appears to many people that Skolnick and Andreucetti may have political motives for instituting their legal action. Is it ethical to harass the president and his or her family—or any other high-ranking public or private official—in this manner? Explain.

Motion for a Summary Judgment

A *motion for a summary judgment* is a request to have the judge declare one side the winner because there are no material issues of fact. It is a technique for *going beyond the allegations stated in the pleadings* and attacking the basic merits of the opponent's case. Traditionally, it was difficult to obtain summary judgment, because most courts believed that its use violated the other party's right to a trial. Other courts indicated that there was no *right* to a trial when there was no genuine dispute about the facts. The modern view is that there is no right to a trial, and courts today are thus more willing to grant summary judgments.

This technique permits the examination of evidentiary material, such as admissions and depositions, without a full-scale trial. The purpose of a motion for a summary judgment is to avoid the expense of unnecessary trials. Consequently, it is usually decided before trial. Either party can file a motion for summary judgment. The party filing the motion must make an initial showing to justify the court's review. The opposing parties are entitled to have time to present their own materials. The length of time depends on the jurisdiction. The standard for granting a summary judgment is that *no genuine issue or no triable issue exists as to any material fact*. If this standard is satisfied, the moving party is entitled to a judgment as a matter of law. In some jurisdictions the court will not consider the pleadings in making its decision. The court can grant a partial summary judgment on some issues or claims and not on others. In most courts, summary judgment is procedurally distinct from *judgment as a matter of law* even though they use essentially the same standard. It is also distinct from motions on the pleadings, which only permit the court to review the pleadings and do *not* permit review of evidence.

On Nic and Nancy's behalf, Ms. Carroll introduced a motion for a summary judgment claiming that no material facts appear to be in dispute; rather, the case is merely a matter of applying the law.

THE TRIAL

In Nic and Nancy's case, the judge denied the plaintiffs' pretrial motions; the legal process continues. The actual trial proceeding is governed by technical rules of trial practice. Generally, representation in court is best left to the attorneys. A good plaintiff or defendant, however, takes an active role in assisting the lawyer.

Jury Selection

A legal case can be resolved by a trial before a judge, without a jury. The judge then decides questions of fact *and* questions of law. Such a trial is often less expensive and less time-consuming. Nic Grant and Nancy Griffin agree with their attorney that a jury will generally favor the plaintiffs and their arguments and elect to have a jury trial. A request for a jury trial must be made in a timely manner. This was noted on the plaintiffs' original complaint (Exhibit 6.8).

Members of the jury are referred to as **petit jurors**. Traditionally, civil juries consisted of 12 jurors, although some jurisdictions have reduced this number in civil trials. Generally, the number of petit jurors is six to twelve. In federal court, a civil jury also consists of six to twelve trial members.[2]

Petit jurors
Ordinary jurors comprising the panel for the trial of a civil or criminal action.

Alternate jurors may also be selected. Alternate jurors sit with the regular jurors and hear the evidence. If a regular juror becomes ill or has to leave the jury for some reason, an alternate is selected for the regular jury and the jury continues to function. Without alternate jurors, the judge would have to select a new jury and begin the trial again. An alternate juror can substitute for a regular juror during deliberations in some jurisdictions: The jury will then start its deliberations from the beginning.

Most states select potential jurors from the voter registration list or the automobile registration list. The prospective jurors are required to complete a juror information form. The form elicits information on which the respective attorneys may base their questions to the jury in what is called the **voir dire** examination. This process is an important part of the trial. Questions need to be asked in the proper manner to obtain helpful, accurate answers, without offending potential jurors. The

Voir dire
The examination of potential jurors to determine their competence to serve on the jury.

information offered by the prospective jurors in response to the questions are used by the judge and counsel as the basis for challenging jurors as biased and, thus, ineligible for service. The attorneys for both parties and/or the judge can ask questions. For example, an attorney may request that the judge ask any potentially embarrassing questions so that the attorney can try to maintain good rapport with the potential jurors. Generally, the procedure is that the attorneys submit written questions to the judge prior to voir dire. In some jurisdictions, the judge may control voir dire by asking all the questions of the potential jurors. At the opposite extreme—New York, for example—voir dire is conducted by the attorneys outside the courtroom; the judge is called in only if problems arise. The procedure depends on the rules of court and the judge's preferences in courtroom procedure. In civil disputes in Butler County, the judge usually conducts voir dire of all the prospective jurors at one time. In Nic and Nancy's case, for example, if a potential juror happened to work for CIT, Ms. Carroll would challenge that person and request that the judge excuse the person. On the other hand, if one of the prospective jurors is a member of Nic's fraternity, Mr. Jones would examine the student very carefully to see whether he or she would favor a fellow member.

Businesses are available that specialize in assisting parties in selecting sympathetic jurors. These jury consultants come from varying backgrounds including psychology, sociology, and marketing. They investigate the backgrounds of potential jurors and collect statistics about the reactions of some socioeconomic groups to trials generally and to issues that are expected to arise in the particular trial on which they are consulting.

Jury consultants sometimes arrange a *shadow jury* consisting of "jurors" with demographic backgrounds similar to the impaneled jurors. The shadow jury sits in the public area of the courtroom and members report their impressions of the evidence. This can be particularly helpful in highly technical cases, where there is a concern that the jurors may be confused by the details. Through this technique, attorneys can have continuous feedback on how their presentation is being perceived.

Another technique is the *mock jury*—the lawyers practice their case before a group of mock jurors with demographic backgrounds similar to those of the actual jurors.

Two methods exist for dismissing prospective jurors. First, a potential juror can be removed *for cause.* When a juror is removed for cause, generally an attorney first suggests to the judge that the juror will probably be biased. Challenges for cause occur if (1) the juror has a financial stake in the case or similar litigation; (2) if members of the juror's family have such an interest; or (3) there is reason to believe the juror will be partial. The judge then decides whether he or she agrees; if so, the potential juror is dismissed. The judge can also make this decision on his or her own initiative. (When a judge raises an issue on his or her own, we say that the judge does it ***sua sponte.***) There is no limit on the number of potential jurors who can be removed for cause.

Sua sponte
Voluntarily, without prompting or suggestion, of his or her own will or motion.

A second technique is to remove a prospective juror by the use of a *peremptory challenge.* Unlike removal for cause, each side is allotted a limited number of peremptory challenges. In federal court, for example, each side receives three peremptory challenges.[3] With peremptory challenges, the attorney does not need to discuss his or her reasons for wanting to remove the juror. The purpose of peremptory challenges is to allow each side to act on hints of bias that may not be provable or even rationally explainable. Some attorneys act on their intuition in deciding whom to eliminate from the jury. The attorney intuitively decides which potential jurors he or she trusts and which he or she does not trust. The attorney then uses peremptory challenges to eliminate those potential jurors in whom there is the greatest distrust. The use of these challenges is discretionary with the attorney. Historically, there have been no limits on the use of this discretion. Recent court decisions, however, have determined that one side may not use peremptory challenges to remove jurors of one gender, religion, race, or color from the jury. The judge decides about the number of peremptory challenges prior to beginning the jury selection process. The court in *Di Donato* v. *Santini* discusses the appropriate use of peremptory challenges during voir dire.

Group bias
Presumption that jurors are biased merely because they belong to an identifiable group based on race, religion, ethnicity, or gender.

6.2 DI DONATO v. SANTINI

283 Cal.Rptr. 751 (Cal. App. 1991)

FACTS Adrienne Di Donato filed a civil suit against her former husband, claiming that he refused to share the profits from their joint business ventures. Her contention is that they both actively developed and marketed these enterprises. Steven Santini, through his attorney, used seven of his eight peremptory challenges to remove potential female jurors. Section 601 of the California Code of Civil Procedure, in effect at this time, allowed eight peremptory challenges per side when there are multiple parties on a side. Joshua Di Donato, Adrienne's son, was also a plaintiff; consequently, each side received eight peremptory challenges. After Di Donato complained about the jury selection process, Santini excused one potential male juror with a peremptory challenge. Orally and in writitng, Di Donato complained to the judge about the jury selection process. These complaints were summarily dismissed by the trial judge. At one point the trial judge asked Santini's counsel if he wanted to respond to Di Donato's claim. The counsel's response was simply that he did not intend to discriminate against women jurors. The jury that was selected made a decision in favor of Santini and the trial judge entered a judgment on that basis.

ISSUE Did the trial judge err in his handling of the jury selection process?

HOLDING Yes.

REASONING ". . . [W]e conclude that the trial court committed reversible error in (1) denying appellants' motion to dismiss the jury panel without first requiring respondent to demonstrate that his peremptory challenges were exercised on a neutral basis related to the particular case, and (2) refusing to hear the motion until after the jury had been sworn. . . .

We conclude, pursuant to the Fourteenth Amendment to the federal Constitution, and article I, sections 7 and 16, of the California Constitution . . . that a party to a civil lawsuit may not use peremptory challenges to exclude women from the jury panel on the basis of their gender. . . .

In criminal cases, the rule is well established that a party may not exclude potential jurors on the basis of **'group bias.'** . . . [T]he California Supreme Court held that a prosecutor's exercise of peremptory challenges to exclude prospective jurors solely on the basis of 'group bias' violates a defendant's right 'to trial by a jury drawn from a representative cross-section of the community under article I, section 16, of the California Constitution. This does not mean that the members of such a group are immune from peremptory challenges: individual members thereof may still be struck on grounds of specific bias, as defined herein.' . . . The court observed that neither side in a criminal case is permitted to exercise peremptory challenges on the basis of group bias. . . .

The California Supreme Court has since 'made it clear that the courts of this state cannot tolerate [such] abuse of peremptory challenges to strip from a jury, solely because of a presumed 'group bias,' all or most members of an identifiable group of citizens distinguished on racial, religious, ethnic, or similar grounds.' . . . 'Group bias' is defined as 'a presumption that certain jurors are biased merely because they are members of an identifiable group distinguished on racial, religious, ethnic or similar grounds. . . .

[T]he United States Supreme Court held, in the context of a challenge to the composition of a jury venire: 'We are . . . persuaded that the fair-cross-section requirement [of the federal Constitution] is violated by the systematic exclusion of women. . . . This conclusion necessarily entails the judgment that women are sufficiently numerous and distinct from men and that if they are systematically eliminated from jury panels, the Sixth Amendment's fair-cross-section requirement cannot be satisfied.' . . .

6.2 DI DONATO v. SANTINI *(cont.)* 283 Cal.Rptr. 751 (Cal. App. 1991)

We proceed to apply the procedural rules set forth in [precedents]. . . . First, we must determine whether appellants established a ***prima facie* case** of group bias. . . . Under the foregoing decisions, appellants initially were required to make as complete a record as possible of the circumstances affecting the fairness of the jury selection in progress. . . . [T]hey made as complete a record of the circumstances as then was feasible, by demonstrating the number and identities of women excluded.

Next, appellants were required to establish that peremptory challenges had been used against a 'cognizable group.' It is established that women constitute a 'cognizable group.' . . .

Finally, appellants were required to demonstrate 'a strong likelihood that such persons are being challenged because of their group association rather than because of any specific bias.' . . . To provide illustrations of the manner in which this third requirement might be satisfied, the court . . . set forth a number of alternatives, including a showing by counsel that the opposing attorney 'has struck most or all of the members of the identified group from the venire, or has used a disproportionate number of . . . peremptories against the group.' . . .

In view of the nature of the particular dispute underlying the present action, the information provided by the excluded female jurors, and the circumstance that defense counsel used all of his first six peremptory challenges to exclude females from the jury panel (prior to appellants' oral objection), and seven of his total of eight peremptory challenges to exclude females, we conclude that appellants met this third requirement and thus succeeded in establishing a *prima facie* case, . . . that respondent's use of peremptory challenges was motivated by group bias. . . .

'Once a *prima facie* case has been shown, the burden shifts to the other party to demonstrate that the peremptory challenges were exercised on a neutral basis related to the particular case to be tried. . . .

In the present case, appellants twice sought to approach the bench for the purpose of making their objection, and the trial court should have permitted them to do so. When appellants thereafter, at the time they made their oral objection, established a *prima facie* case, the court overruled that objection without first requiring a rebuttal from defense counsel. This action in and of itself requires reversal.

The court also erred in refusing to entertain appellants' written motion until after the jury was sworn. It is established that a *prima facie* case, in order to be timely, must be made prior to the time the jury is sworn. . . . The reason for this requirement is to enable the trial court to address the issues raised and thereby ensure that appropriate steps are taken to remedy the perceived discrimination during the selection process (rather than after the jury is sworn), presumably in order to avoid the necessity of repeating the entire jury-selection process. . . . Accordingly, the trial court may not delay its decision on a challenge to the selection process until after the panel has been sworn. . . .

Finally, even if we were to construe the trial court's comments as an implied finding that appellants had established a *prima facie* case, the statement made by respondent's counsel at the time of the hearing, that he 'had no intention of discriminating against women as opposed to men,' is inadequate to sustain his burden of 'demonstrat[ing] that the peremptory challenges were exercised on a neutral basis related to the particular case to be tried.' . . . [Quoting the California Supreme Court] 'The court . . . noted that the prosecutor may not rebut the defendant's *prima facie* case merely by denying that he had a discriminatory motive. . . .'"

[The approach of this court is consistent with that specified by the Supreme Court in *Edmonson* v. *Leesville Concrete Co., Inc.,* 500 U.S. 614 (1991).]

BUSINESS CONSIDERATIONS Di Donato was alleging an oral agreement/understanding with Santini in this case. She worked with Santini in the business enterprise. Is it prudent for any person to rely on an oral agreement in a situation such as this? What should a person do to provide the maximum protection in such a situation?

ETHICAL CONSIDERATIONS Is it ethical to systematically exclude certain groups from a jury panel? Is it ethical to systematically exclude certain groups from *any* social benefits or burdens? Why or why not? Why might exclusion from a jury be viewed differently than exclusion from other benefits or burdens?

The U.S. Supreme Court has also specifically ruled that peremptory challenges cannot be used to remove prospective jurors on the basis of their gender.[4]

The decision about whether to exclude a person from the petit jury is made one potential juror at a time until the jury is completed. Generally, after each one is considered, a decision is made about that person before questioning the next potential juror.

Removal of Judges

California has a unique procedure that allows each party one peremptory challenge against the judge assigned to the case. This peremptory challenge must be filed before any proceedings begin in front of the judge being challenged.[5]

Most jurisdictions do not permit peremptory challenges to a judge; however, they have other procedures to disqualify a judge. A judge is not permitted to preside over any action in which he or she has any bias, has a financial interest, is related to any of the parties or attorneys, or there are any facts that would impair the judge's impartiality. The judge may raise this issue *sua sponte* or it can be raised by one of the parties.[6]

6.3

SELECTING JURORS

Ms. Carroll and Mr. Jones are conducting the voir dire examination of a prospective juror, Andy Motz. Andy is a 23-year-old business student at the same university as Nic Grant and Nancy Griffin. His father, Ted Motz, is a senior claims supervisor at State-Wide Insurance Company. The Kochanowskis believe that Mr. Jones should exclude this person from the jury. The Kochanowskis ask you what additional questions should Mr. Jones ask Andy before making a decision about possibly removing him from the jury? What additional information would be helpful in making a rational decision? If cause for removal cannot be established, should Mr. Jones use a peremptory challenge to remove this potential juror in order to satisfy his clients?

BUSINESS CONSIDERATIONS Should the attorney for a business that sells high-tech, upscale products try to select jurors who have a relatively high income level and a higher than average educational level? Would such a firm be better served by waiving their right to a jury trial, letting the judge serve as finder of fact?

ETHICAL CONSIDERATIONS What ethical considerations enter into the jury selection process? Some wealthy parties to lawsuits are able to afford expensive jury consultants and profilers. Does this give them an unethical advantage over people who cannot afford such support?

MANAGEMENT

Opening Statements

After the jury is chosen, each side has an opportunity to tell the jury what it intends to prove during the trial. This serves as an introduction to the party's case and helps the jury integrate the evidence that follows. The attorney for the plaintiff makes an opening statement, followed by the defendant.

Direct Examination

An attorney questions his or her witnesses. The plaintiffs' attorney questions witnesses first. The rules of evidence include rules concerning what information an attorney may elicit from the witnesses as well as how an attorney may request information from them. (A detailed discussion of these rules, however, is beyond the scope of this book.)

Trial attorneys are reluctant to ask questions when they do not know how a witness will respond. This is the reason for pretrial preparation of witnesses. Failure to adequately prepare can be disastrous.

***Prima facie* case**
A case that is obvious on its face. It may be rebutted by evidence to the contrary.

Expert Witnesses

An expert witness is a witness possessing special knowledge who appears in a trial to offer an opinion from facts that have been produced as evidence. For example, Nic

Grant or CIT may call medical experts and accident-reconstruction engineers. Expert witnesses are permitted to testify concerning their opinions. They are allowed to state their own conclusions and to discuss hypothetical situations described by the attorneys. In this way, expert witnesses are distinguished from regular witnesses, who are not permitted to present opinions, conclusions, or respond to hypothetical questions. The *Sears* v. *Rutishauser* case discusses the propriety of cross-examining an expert witness regarding his or her status as a "professional witness."

6.3 SEARS v. RUTISHAUSER

102 Ill.2d 402, 466 N.E.2d 210 (1984)

FACTS Defense counsel wished to impeach a medical expert witness for the plaintiff by questioning him with respect to the number and frequency of patients referred to him by the plaintiff's attorney.

ISSUE Is this a proper question on cross-examination?

HOLDING Yes.

REASONING This inquiry is permissible. "The modern personal injury trial often becomes a battle between expert witnesses. . . . An expert medical witness is an important part of the technique of personal injury litigation. The principal safeguard against errant expert testimony is cross-examination. . . . Therefore, opposing counsel may probe bias, partisanship, or financial interest of an expert witness on cross-examination and that includes the number and frequency of referrals which he has received from an attorney."

BUSINESS CONSIDERATIONS Should a business establish a policy regarding activities of its officers as expert witnesses? What are the benefits to the firm if some of its officers testify as experts? What are the detriments?

ETHICAL CONSIDERATIONS Is it ethical for either or both sides to a lawsuit to be allowed to present their own expert witnesses? Would it be more ethical to have a court-certified list of experts who are randomly called in cases involving their area of expertise, without having them selected by the adversaries in the case? Explain.

Cross-examination

After Ms. Carroll questions each of her witnesses, Mr. Jones has an opportunity to question them. Skillful use of cross-examination by competent counsel is the best means to ascertain the truth of the matters brought up in direct examination. After the cross-examination, the party who called the witness (Ms. Carroll) *may* examine the witness again on redirect and the opposing party (Mr. Jones) *may* examine the witness on recross.

The process of examination and cross-examination continues until Ms. Carroll has no other witnesses to call. Next, Mr. Jones directly examines his witnesses one at a time, and Ms. Carroll cross-examines each one until the defense has no further witnesses to call. At this point, both sides "rest" their cases.

Motion for a Directed Verdict

A motion for a directed verdict is addressed to the judge. It is usually requested at the close of the opponent's case. The standard used by the judge is whether the plaintiff has made a *prima facie* case on which he or she is entitled to recover. If the plaintiff has *not* presented a *prima facie* case, the defendant is entitled to a directed verdict. In most jurisdictions, the judge cannot weigh the evidence—the judge must look solely at the evidence produced by the party against whom the motion is sought; accept any reasonable inference from that evidence; and disregard all challenges to the credibility of that evidence. (A minority of jurisdictions permit the weighing of evidence.) If the motion is granted, the court has found that the defendant must win as a matter of law.

If the motion is not granted, the trial will continue. After the presentation of the defendant's evidence, the plaintiff may request a directed verdict on the defendant's cross-complaint and/or the defendant can again request a directed verdict. In some states a motion for nonsuit is used in a similar manner.

Closing Arguments

After both sides rest, each has an opportunity to persuade the jury by reviewing the testimony, laying out all the facts presented in court, and then drawing conclusions from those facts that best support its position. Thus, each attorney takes the same body of evidence and attempts to reach a favorable conclusion by emphasizing the evidence favorable to his or her client and minimizing unfavorable evidence. This stage is called closing arguments or summation.

The Verdict

At the conclusion of closing arguments, the judge discusses the law with the jury and charges them to answer certain questions with respect to the evidence **adduced** at trial. As part of the charge, he or she instructs them in the applicable areas of law and defines any legal concepts. This is called the *charge to the jury* or *jury instructions.*

Adduced
Given as proof.

The jury may be requested to reach a general verdict and/or a special verdict. In a *general verdict,* the jury is asked who should win the lawsuit and how much damage was suffered, if any. In a *special verdict,* the jury is asked specific questions about the relevant factual issues in the case.

After the jury withdraws from the courtroom, they *deliberate* on the evidence and attempt to reach a verdict. In many jurisdictions, the jury *may* request that parts of the evidence be "read back" to them during the deliberation process. In a civil case, many rules of court do not require a unanimous decision; some even authorize a decision by a majority vote of the jurors. In Pennsylvania, the verdict is valid if at least five-sixths of the jurors agree to it.[7] In federal court, a civil case must be decided by a unanimous jury unless the parties agree to the contrary.[8] After the petit jurors reach a verdict, it is announced in open court. The verdict is the stated opinion of the jury. If the judge concurs in the verdict, he or she enters a judgment. This is the most common type of verdict.

In our case, the jury deliberated and held for the plaintiffs, Nic Grant and Nancy Griffin, for $21,026 and $5,498, respectively. The judgment is the court's official decision and appears as Exhibit 6.11 (page 164).

Judgment

In most cases, the judge will agree with the jury's verdict. The judge may disagree with the jury's verdict, however. In these situations, the judge may enter a *judgment notwithstanding the verdict*. Traditionally, this was called a judgment *non obstante veredicto,* hence the abbreviation judgment n.o.v. When a judge declares a judgment n.o.v., he or she substitutes his or her own decision for that of the jury. Either a plaintiff or a

EXHIBIT 6.11 | Court's Judgment

COURT'S JUDGMENT
COURT OF COMMON PLEAS OF BUTLER COUNTY, PENNSYLVANIA

NIC GRANT and NANCY GRIFFIN, Plaintiffs	:	A.D. No. 23465 Civil Action Law
V.	:	
CALL-IMAGE TECHNOLOGY and DAN KOCHANOWSKI, Defendants	:	

On the 7th day of November 1997 this cause came to be heard, plaintiffs appearing in person and by their attorney, LYN CARROLL, and defendants appearing in person and by their attorneys, JONES, MURPHY, SABBATINO, and SCHWARTZ. All parties announcing ready for trial, a jury composed of Mae Brown and eleven others of the regular panel of the petit jurors of this court was selected and impaneled and sworn according to law to try the issues of fact arising in this cause. After the introduction of all the evidence, the instructions of the court, and the arguments of counsel, said jury retired to consider its verdict, and after deliberating thereon returned unto court the following verdict:

We, the jury, find in favor of the plaintiffs, Nic Grant and Nancy Griffin, and assess their damages as $21,026 and $5,498, respectively.

____
MAE BROWN, FOREPERSON

IT IS, THEREFORE, BY THE COURT, CONSIDERED, ORDERED, AND ADJUDGED that the plaintiffs, NIC GRANT and NANCY GRIFFIN, are entitled to recover of and from the defendants, Call-Image Technology and/or Dan Kochanowski, the sums of $21,026 and $5,498, respectively, plus their court costs herein expended. Said judgment shall bear interest from this date until paid at the rate of SIX PERCENT PER ANNUM.[a]

ENTERED this 13th day of November 1997.[b]

____
JUDGE

APPROVED AS TO FORM:

____
Attorney for Plaintiffs

____
Attorneys[c] for Defendants

[a]The rate of interest allowed depends on the jurisdiction. Butler County allows 6 percent.

[b]Notice that this is approximately one year after the lawsuit was initiated.

[c]This is plural because the defendants are represented by a law firm—Jones, Murphy, Sabbatino, and Schwartz.

defendant may be awarded a judgment n.o.v. A judgment n.o.v. is appropriate only if the jury's verdict is incorrect as a matter of law, that is, there is no substantial evidence to support the jury verdict. Most courts use the same standard as that used for a directed verdict. The court disregards all conflicts in the evidence, does not consider whether the witnesses are credible, and gives face value to the evidence in favor of the party who received the verdict. The party who won the original verdict will likely appeal the judgment n.o.v.

POST-TRIAL PROCEEDINGS

Motion for a New Trial

A losing party may make a motion for a new trial. This motion is filed with the same judge who originally heard the case, unless that judge is disabled or disqualified. Often the party will request the court to either enter a judgment n.o.v. *or* grant a new trial. The party making the motion is requesting the court to order a new trial. The party must justify the request and explain why a new trial is proper.

Common grounds for a motion for a new trial include: the judge committed a **prejudicial** error in conducting the trial; irregularities in the jury's behavior; or the evidence was insufficient to support the verdict. In extremely rare cases, a new trial may be granted based on newly discovered evidence. To obtain a new trial on this basis, the moving party must show that the newly discovered evidence pertains to facts in existence at the time of trial; the evidence is material; and the moving party with reasonable diligence could not have obtained the information prior to trial. The latter requirement is to prevent a party from obtaining a new trial when the party was negligent in failing to obtain the evidence for the original trial. A new trial will *not* be granted because a party's attorney in the original trial was incompetent. A new trial can also be requested by a party who believes that the damage award is excessive *or* too small. When the motion for new trial is based on the amount of damages, a judge may, for example, grant a new trial unless a plaintiff agrees to accept a reduction in the amount of damages. This is called *remittitur*. Some states also permit granting a new trial unless a defendant agrees to accept an increase in the amount of the award. This is called *additur*. Obviously, conducting a new trial is expensive for the parties and the court system.

Prejudicial
Causing harm, injurious, disadvantageous, or detrimental.

Appeal

After losing the decision, the attorneys for CIT filed a notice of appeal to hear the case before a higher court. The rules of court specify the time limit for filing a notice of appeal. Appeals, however, are limited to questions of law. In other words, the appellate court will generally not reverse a lower court unless the lower court made an error of law. In this case, the decision is in accordance with the law; consequently, no appeal is granted. CIT now owes the plaintiffs $21,026 and $5,498.

If a case is appealed, the appellate court can *affirm* the decision, which indicates approval, or *reverse* the decision, which indicates an error of law. Appellate courts can affirm some parts of the decision and reverse others. Sometimes the appellate court reverses and *remands* the case because the lower court made a mistake of law and the case is returned to it for correction. Exhibit 6.12 depicts the stages of a trial (page 166).

EXHIBIT 6.12 Common Steps of a Trial

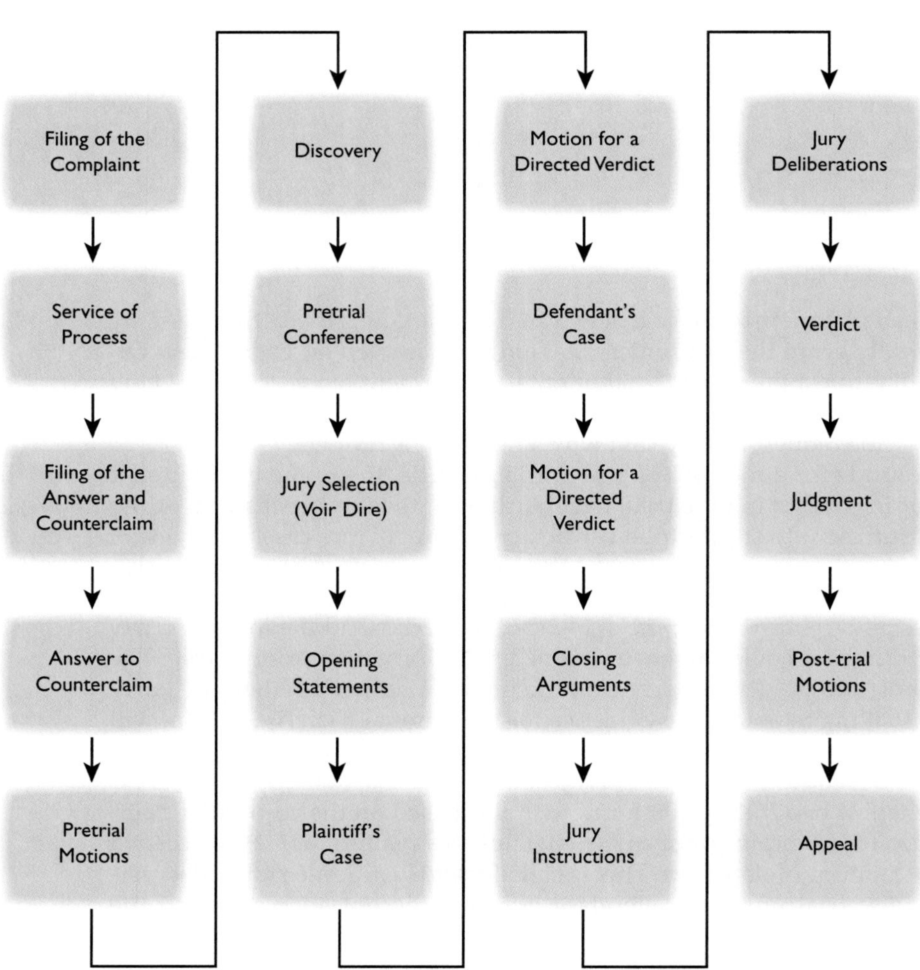

A Comment on Finality

One of the great virtues of the law is finality. When a cause of action has been litigated and reduced to a judgment and all appeals have been exhausted, the matter comes to an end. In this case, the doctrine of *res judicata* applies. *Res judicata* means that when a court issues a final judgment, the subject matter of that lawsuit is finally decided between the parties to the suit. This doctrine prevents further suits from being brought. In other words, the matter comes to rest. Remember, however, that *res judicata* does not prevent timely appeals nor does it prevent criminal proceedings based on the same behavior.

http:// RESOURCES FOR BUSINESS LAW STUDENTS

NAME	RESOURCES	WEB ADDRESS
Federal Rules of Civil Procedure (1996)	Legal Information Institute (LII), maintained by the Cornell Law School, provides the Federal Rules of Civil Procedure in a hypertext and searchable format.	http://www.law.cornell.edu/rules/frcp/overview.htm
The National Registry of Experts	The National Registry of Experts is a professional organization established to provide support, recognition, training, and continuing education to expert witnesses as well as those interested in becoming experts.	http://www.expert-registry.com/
Trial Behavior Consulting, Incorporated	Trial Behavior Consulting, Incorporated, provides mock trials, case strategy, voir dire questions, community surveys, focus groups, witness preparation, and jury selection, among other services.	http://www.lawinfo.com/biz/tbci/
American Bar Association's Center for Professional Responsibility	The American Bar Association's Center for Professional Responsibility provides standards and scholarly resources in legal ethics, professional regulation, professionalism, and client protection mechanisms.	http://www.abanet.org/cpr/home.html
West's Legal Directory	West's Legal Directory, updated daily, offers more than 800,000 profiles of lawyers and law firms in the United States and Canada, including international offices.	http://www.wld.com

SUMMARY

Lawsuits are based on factual circumstances. Therefore, it is the client's responsibility to reveal all the facts to his or her attorney. If all the facts are not known, the attorney might draw the wrong legal conclusion. If the facts warrant a lawsuit, the first thing the attorney should do is to apprise the potential defendant of liability and seek to settle the case without filing a lawsuit.

Attorney's fees are an important consideration in deciding whether the client should sue. Nic Grant and Nancy Griffin had contingency fee arrangements, whereby if the plaintiffs had lost the case, their attorney would have received no fees. Other bases for attorney's fees also exist, including a flat rate or an hourly rate. In these cases, the attorney receives compensation whether or not the attorney wins the case. The fee arrangement is specified in the oral or written contract that creates the attorney–client relationship.

Before a lawsuit is filed, the attorney has a duty to investigate the facts to determine whether sufficient evidence exists to justify litigation. Attorneys and clients who file frivolous lawsuits may be subject to penalties. Before filing suit an opportunity is usually provided for the parties to settle the matter, either through a settlement conference or arbitration.

After suit is filed, the discovery process takes place. Discovery is designed to narrow the legal issues, thus encouraging pretrial settlement or reducing the duration of the actual trial. During voir dire, the petit jury is selected for the trial. Potential jurors can be dismissed for cause or by use of a peremptory challenge. Consultants may be hired to assist the attorneys in selecting the jury and/or presenting an effective case before the jury.

The doctrine of *res judicata* means that when a court issues a final judgment, the subject matter of the case cannot be relitigated between the same parties. However, it does not prevent appeals from the final judgment.

Discussion Questions

1. The chapter discusses two methods for locating an attorney. What other techniques can a person (or business) use to locate competent counsel?
2. Is there any conflict of interest if Lyn Carroll represents both plaintiffs in this case? Why or why not? Is there any conflict of interest if Jefferson Jones represents both defendants in this case? Why or why not?
3. Refer to the attorney–client contract to answer this question: If Lyn Carroll spends 45 hours on this case but loses the lawsuit, will she be due the reasonable value of her services instead of the 33⅓ percent she would receive if she won? Explain your answer.
4. Are contingency fee contracts fair to clients? What are the advantages of contingency fee arrangements for clients? What are the disadvantages for clients?
5. What is a deposition? What is an interrogatory? How do they differ?
6. What is a subpoena duces tecum? What is its purpose? What is the reason for using a request for admission?
7. Why are interrogatories limited to a party to a lawsuit and yet depositions can be taken from any witness?
8. In the case of Nic Grant versus CIT, suppose a jury is made up almost solely of people on public assistance. In your opinion, is this providing the parties with a fair trial? Why?
9. What explanation can you provide for why the jury awarded $21,026 to Nic and $5,498 to Nancy. Should the defendants appeal the decision of the trial court? Why?
10. What is *res judicata*? How does the concept of *res judicata* affect lawsuits?

Case Problems and Writing Assignments

1. Zisook was an attorney, practicing law in a professional corporation. He was sued by one of his clients, who sought the production of certain documents in Zisook's possession to prove the client's case. When Zisook refused to provide the documents, the client asked the court to issue a subpoena duces tecum for these documents. Zisook failed to comply with the subpoena duces tecum, and the bar association instituted disciplinary proceedings against Zisook to decide whether his right to practice law should be suspended. Was Zisook obligated to comply with the subpoena duces tecum? Why? [See *Re Zisook*, 430 N.E.2d 1037 (Ill. 1981).]

2. The defendant objected to interrogatories that asked him to define a dishonest act in general and to state if certain acts were dishonest. Assuming that the state courts have previously ruled that interrogatories are to be "liberally construed," should these interrogatories be allowed? Why or why not? [See *Leumi Fin. Corp.* v. *Hartford Acc. & Indem. Co.*, 295 F.Supp. 539 (S.D.N.Y. 1969).]

3. Following a trial, one of the parties filed an appeal of the judgment entered by the trial court. The appeal contains an argument that was not raised during the trial. The other party objects to raising this argument for the first time at the appellate level, insisting that the argument had to be raised at the trial in order to be considered in the case. The moving party replies that the argument could not be raised during the trial because the case on which the argument is based had not yet been resolved at the time of the trial. Should the appellate court consider the argument that was raised for the first time on appeal if the argument is based on another case that was decided after the trial court decision in this case? What factors should the appellate court consider in reaching its decision in this situation? [See *Davis* v. *United States*, 413 F.2d 1226 (5th Cir. 1969).]

4. The Federal Rules of Civil Procedure provide that a motion for summary judgment "shall be served at least ten days before the time fixed for the hearing" on the motion. Suppose that one of the parties to a law-

suit makes an oral motion for summary judgment during the proceedings. Can the trial court grant this oral motion for summary judgment? Why or why not? [See *Hanson* v. *Polk County Land, Inc.*, 608 F.2d 129 (5th Cir. 1979).]

5. Thaddeus Donald Edmonson, a black man, was employed as a construction worker. He was injured at work and sued Leesville Concrete Company claiming that the company allowed one of its trucks to roll backwards, pinning him against some construction equipment. During voir dire, Leesville used two of its three peremptory challenges to remove potential black jurors. Edmonson asked the judge to require Leesville to provide a race-neutral explanation for its use of peremptory challenges. The judge refused the request on the basis that it was a civil trial, not a criminal trial. The jury found for Edmonson, however, it found that he was 80 percent responsible for his own injuries under comparative negligence. Consequently, his recovery was limited to 20 percent. Was the trial judge's decision on peremptory challenges proper? [See *Edmonson* v. *Leesville Concrete Co., Inc.*, 500 U.S. 614 (1991).]

6. **BUSINESS APPLICATION PROBLEM** On January 31, 1997, Judge Fujisaki instructed jurors in the civil trial of O. J. Simpson that they must "insulate themselves from all news media—watch no TV, listen to no radio and read no newspapers." He told them that he wanted to avoid sequestering the jury. A juror had just been removed from the trial for legal cause during deliberations; he was concerned that she might be giving interviews and did not want the jury tainted.

   Jurors were also instructed to "have someone screen their phone calls, mail and faxes." The judge was concerned about reports that two jurors in the Simpson criminal trial were contacting members of the civil jury panel. They were allegedly trying to promote a deal for public appearances after the trial. Brenda Moran and Gina Marie Rosborough, two criminal jurors, announced a book deal shortly after the verdict in the criminal trial. Moran acknowledged writing a letter to the civil jurors recommending Bud Stewart as an agent. Both women stated that it was supposed to be delivered *after* the verdict, not while deliberations were going on.

   Faxes were sent to news producers offering to arrange interviews with three civil trial jurors in the case. The faxes were signed Bud Stewart, the agent mentioned in the letter from Moran.

   Discuss the interrelationships between fair trials, the public's interest in obtaining information, and the media's business interests. It appears that Bud Stewart was attempting to get ahead of other agents. How could he have solicited business and clients without interfering with the legal process? [See Linda Deutsch and Michael Fleeman, "Simpson Juror Replaced; Talks Start Anew," *The Fresno Bee* (1 February 1997), pp. A1 and A11; and "Juror Dismissed in Simpson Case," *Merced Sun-Star* (1 February 1997), pp. A1 and A8.]

7. **ETHICS APPLICATION CASE** Dr. Gerald Zuk brought a suit for copyright infringement against the Eastern Pennsylvania Psychiatric Institute (EPPI). Dr. Zuk was a psychologist on the faculty of EPPI. In the 1970s, he had an EPPI technician film two of his family therapy sessions. As academic demand for the films developed, Zuk had EPPI duplicate the films and make them available for rental through their library. Zuk subsequently wrote a book which, among other things, contained transcripts of the therapy sessions. He registered the book in 1975 with the U.S. Copyright Office. In 1980, EPPI furloughed Zuk. In 1995, Lipman (Zuk's attorney) filed this suit, alleging that EPPI was renting out the films and thereby infringing on Zuk's copyright. The trial court, dismissing the claim, found that the copyright of the book afforded no protection to the films, that EPPI owned the copies of the films in its possession and that their use was not an infringement, and that Zuk's claims were barred by the statute of limitations. Should Lipman be sanctioned for filing this lawsuit? This was Lipman's first copyright-infringement case. Was it ethical for him to accept this case when he was unfamiliar with copyright law? As he told the court, a practitioner has to start somewhere. Is it lack of experience or was he merely unprepared? Does it make a difference? [See *Zuk* v. *Eastern Penn. Psychiatric Inst. of the Medical College of Penn.*, 1996 U.S. App. LEXIS 33917 (3d Cir. 1996).]

8. **IDES CASE** A lawsuit was originally filed in Alaska state court and was later removed to federal court. It is one of many lawsuits arising out of the 1989 grounding of the *Exxon Valdez* in Prince William Sound, Alaska, and the resulting massive oil spill. The complaint alleged a number of claims on behalf of a class of Alaska natives (the class) consisting of: "all Alaska Natives and Native organizations including but not limited to, individuals, Native villages, incorporated and unincorporated Native entities and associations and tribal entities, who engage in, rely upon, promote or preserve, wholly or in part, a subsistence way of life." The class definition was later modified to exclude all native villages and government entities. This left individual Alaska natives as plaintiffs in the

class action suit. "The 'subsistence way of life' allegedly harmed by the spill is: dependent upon the preservation of uncontaminated natural resources, marine life and wildlife, and reflects a personal, economic, psychological, social, cultural, communal and religious form of daily living." The class claims for harvest damages were settled, leaving only the claims for noneconomic injury. Use the IDES technique to analyze whether this group constitutes a proper class and whether the noneconomic claims should go forward or be dismissed by a summary judgment. [See *Alaska Native Class* v. *Exxon Corp.*, 1997 U.S. App. LEXIS 701 (9th Cir. 1997).]

NOTES

1. Andrea Gerlin, "Mounting Piles of Deposition Requests Disrupt Lives of Chief Executive Officers," *Wall Street Journal* (7 November 1994), p. B1.
2. *Federal Rules of Civil Procedure* § 48.
3. See 28 U.S.C. 1870.
4. See *J.E.B.* v. *T.B.*, 114 S. Ct. 1419 (1994).
5. California Code of Civil Procedure § 170.6.
6. See 28 U.S.C. 455 and California Code of Civil Procedure § 170.
7. See 42 Pa. C.S.A. § 5104.
8. Federal Rules of Civil Procedure § 48.

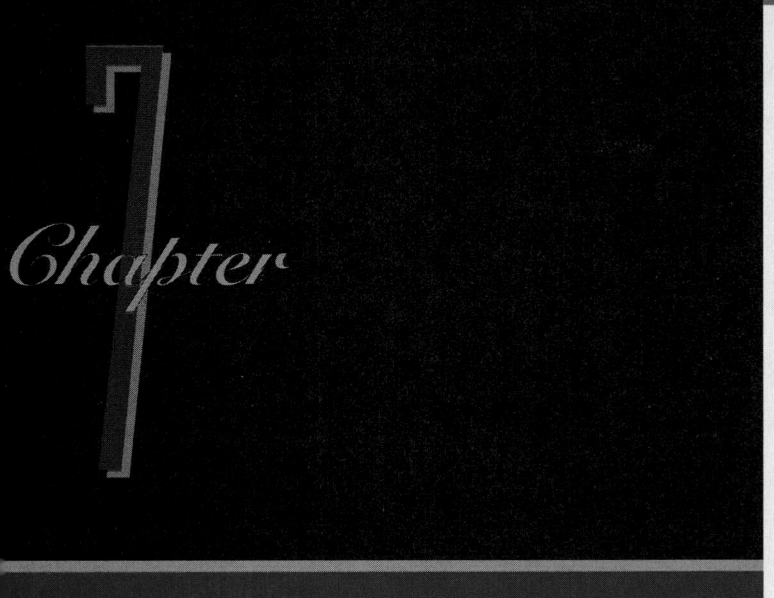

Alternate Dispute Resolution

OUTLINE

The Need for Alternatives
Negotiation
Mediation
Arbitration
Minitrial
Rent-a-Judge Trial
Small Claims Court
Summary
Discussion Questions
Case Problems and Writing Assignments

AGENDA

The Kochanowskis do not *plan* to be involved in any legal proceedings while conducting their business. They hope to select clients, customers, employees, and suppliers who will honor their contracts with CIT, so that CIT will not be forced to seek legal relief. The Kochanowskis recognize, however, that inevitably they and/or the firm are likely to have a legal controversy. From discussions with Amy Chen, and from their experience in the workplace, they realize that lawsuits can be time consuming and expensive. As a result, they would prefer to be able to settle any disputes or controversies in some alternative manner, if possible. Should they include mandatory arbitration provisions in their contracts with suppliers and retailers? Who should be specified as the arbitrator? Would it be better to include a provision for arbitration or a provision for mediation in their employment contracts? When might the firm want to "rent-a-judge" in settling a controversy? When is it better to negotiate than to litigate?

These and other questions need to be addressed in covering the material in this chapter of the text. Be prepared! You never know when one of the Kochanowskis will need your advice.

THE NEED FOR ALTERNATIVES

Regular lawsuits are often expensive, and they are frequently time-consuming. Refer to the stages of a civil lawsuit outlined in Chapter 6. There is normally a significant passage of time between the filing of a lawsuit and the resolution of the case by the court. Even if a plaintiff has what seems to be a good case, there is no guarantee that the plaintiff will prevail at trial. Product liability cases on average have a processing time of 530 days. Moreover, only 40 percent of the plaintiffs in these cases win. For a business defendant, the time spent in preparing for the trial and then having officers attend the pretrial and trial proceedings represents a significant cost factor even if the business wins the case. Many businesses prefer to settle the case—the earlier the better—by paying the plaintiff and saving all the time and trouble that a trial requires. If an alternative means of resolving the dispute was available, those businesses would be likely to use it.

Such alternatives *do* exist, and these *alternate* forms of *dispute resolution* are becoming increasingly popular. Alternate dispute resolution (ADR) provides a number of benefits:

1. The burden on the court system is reduced.
2. An injured party with a legitimate claim is likely to be compensated sooner. When one considers the time-value of money, this can be a significant factor.
3. Businesses (and other defendants) are less likely to settle specious claims merely for the sake of expediency and/or because the settlement is less expensive than the expenses of a trial.
4. ADR is less adversarial, allowing the parties to reach a more amicable resolution. This, in turn, permits the parties to continue to do business together or to coexist in harmony in the future.

As a result of these—and other—benefits, the use of ADR is becoming more common, especially in the resolution of disputes involving a business. Increasingly courts are *requiring* parties to attempt alternative methods of dispute resolution first, before allowing them to seek judicial remedies. Because these processes are usually less expensive and faster, they tend to create less tension in the relationship of the parties. This is particularly important in disputes between family members, such as child-custody cases, and in business situations where the parties may wish to continue to do business together.

Alternate dispute resolution has its limits, and it is not appropriate for resolving every form of legal dispute. ADR cannot be used in criminal matters, for example, and it does not establish legal precedence. In addition, some matters need to be debated in a public forum, which alternate dispute resolution does not provide. When used within its limits, however, it provides quick and sure resolutions for a number of problems in a manner that is mutually advantageous for all of the parties involved.

NEGOTIATION

Caucusing
Mediation technique in which the mediator meets with each party separately.

Perhaps the earliest, and simplest, form of ADR is *negotiation*. Negotiation involves the discussion and resolution of a controversy between two or more parties by the parties involved. Negotiation is so common that most people do not even consider it as a form of ADR. Instead, they think of it as merely a method for settling disputes or controversies. That is the gist of ADR, however—settling a dispute or a controversy without resorting to the courts.

If the parties to the dispute recognize the logic in handling the dispute themselves and are willing and able to negotiate a solution acceptable to the parties, negotiation is an excellent method of dispute resolution. If the parties are able to resolve the matter themselves, with or without consulting their attorneys, they can probably save time and money. However, the parties may not *think* of negotiation as a possible solution, or they may not be *willing* to negotiate a settlement. Since negotiation is handled strictly by the parties, all interested parties must be willing to negotiate before it can serve as an effective method for resolving the dispute.

7.1

SETTLING AN INSURANCE CLAIM

John was driving home from school during rush hour when he was involved in an accident. He had just glanced down at the car radio when the driver in front of him stopped. John did not look up in time to stop, and he rear-ended the other car. The driver of the other car submitted a claim to the Kochanowskis' insurance company for damages in the amount of $75,000, which is within the $200,000 liability coverage of the policy. The insurance company is willing to negotiate a settlement with the other driver. Although John admits he was at fault in the accident, he does not feel that the other driver suffered more than $30,000 in damages; and he wants the insurance company to refuse to settle. He asks you for your opinion. What will you tell him?

BUSINESS CONSIDERATIONS Why would an insurance company be willing to negotiate a settlement for what is probably more than the actual damages suffered by the victim in an accident but substantially less than the policy limit? Why might the insurer refuse to negotiate a settlement in this sort of situation?

ETHICAL CONSIDERATIONS Is it ethical for the victim in an accident to claim damages well in excess of those actually suffered in the hope that the insurer will settle, bestowing a windfall profit on the victim? Is it ethical for the insurer to lowball the victim if the victim is obviously in need of the cash from a quick settlement?

MANAGEMENT/PERSONAL LAW

MEDIATION

Mediation is similar to negotiation, although there is a significant difference. Mediation involves the use of an impartial third party, a *mediator,* who attempts to help the parties reach a mutually acceptable resolution to their dispute. Usually, just one mediator is used. The mediator does not act as a decision maker; however, he or she facilitates communication. The mediator listens to the parties and assists them in resolving their differences, or as many of the aspects of their dispute as possible. There are no formal procedures. The parties may choose to have a lawyer, a family member, or some other advisor present during the mediation. Generally, the mediator should not have any financial or personal interest in the result of the mediation without the written consent of all the parties. A prospective mediator should promptly disclose to the parties any circumstance likely to cause bias or the appearance of bias. The advantages of mediation are that it is less expensive than litigation, it is quicker, and generally the results are perceived as more satisfactory. Participants are generally more satisfied because they agreed to the result.

Generally, the mediator does not impose a solution on the parties. Some mediators, however, take a more forceful role in attempting to fashion an agreement; others believe a more passive role is appropriate.

More than one mediation technique can be used in an attempt to resolve the disagreement. One mediation technique is **caucusing**. In this technique, the mediator meets with each party separately. Another mediation technique is **shuttle mediation**, where the mediator physically separates the parties during the mediation session and then runs messages between them.

Shuttle mediation
Mediation technique in which the mediator physically separates the parties during the session and then runs messages between them.

Mediation sessions are private; usually only the parties, their representatives, and the mediator will be present. Other people generally may only attend with the permission of the parties and the mediator.

In most cases, mediation is successful; however, if it is not, the parties can utilize another ADR technique or submit their dispute for judicial resolution. Consequently, an important principle of mediation is confidentiality; otherwise the parties will not discuss the issues freely. The parties must be confident that what they say or admit in mediation will not be used against them in court. The parties should agree to maintain the confidentiality of the mediation and not to rely on or introduce into evidence at any arbitration, judicial, or other proceeding the views expressed by a party, suggestions made by a party, admissions made by a party, proposals made by the mediator, views expressed by the mediator, and/or the fact that a party was or was not willing to accept a proposal. The mediator should not be required to testify or divulge records in any adversarial proceeding. No stenographic record is prepared of the mediation process. See Exhibit 7.1 for typical steps in a mediation.

The proponents of mediator certification believe that standards would encourage the confidence of the courts and the disputing parties. It would also ease the backlog in civil courts. The opponents to certification feel that it would limit the diversity of mediators at a time when this diversity is in demand. Lawyers, judges, psychotherapists, and ministers have entered the field of mediation. In addition, they argue that the profession is still developing and it is too early for certification; there are no adequate standards for certification. Certification at this time would be unfair and misleading to the public. In addition, there have been relatively few complaints against mediators.

A mediator should have good problem-solving skills and be fair. Roberta Kerr Parrott, a professional mediator, explains:

> *The challenge is always, when there's conflict, to create a possibility for both sides, both parties, to win. To make sure that I'm quiet enough long enough to hear what the real issues are so that we're dealing with what people are feeling and thinking at the heart of the issue rather than dealing with the surface.*[1]

EXHIBIT 7.1 Steps in an American Arbitration Association (AAA) Mediation

1. When parties request mediation, a qualified mediator is appointed by the AAA. If the agreement of the parties names a mediator or specifies a method of appointing a mediator, that designation or method is followed.
2. After a mediator has been selected, the first meeting date is arranged.
3. The parties meet with the mediator, who guides their negotiations and helps them to reach a settlement.
4. Private caucuses may be held between the mediator and each party in an attempt to bring disputants closer together.

SOURCE: American Arbitration Association, *Resolving Your Disputes* (November 1995), pp. 8–9.

Knowledge of the law, while important in some cases, is only one possible competency a good mediator needs. Other necessary skills include:

1. Patience, persistence, concentration, and focus toward the goal.
2. The ability to distinguish between stated positions of the disputants and their real interests.
3. The ability to remain positive and constructive, even with difficult parties, while maintaining confidentiality.
4. The ability to remain unbiased in the search for the truth of the situation and the solutions that work best for all concerned under the circumstances.
5. The ability to secure a resolution that is truly satisfactory for the participants: substantively, procedurally, and psychologically.[2]

Standards of Conduct

A model standards of conduct for mediators has been drafted. The standards are nonbinding. The final draft has been available since September 1995 and has been endorsed by the American Bar Association (ABA) section on Dispute Resolution, the ABA section on Litigation, the American Arbitration Association (AAA), and the Society of Professionals in Dispute Resolution.[3] A summary appears as Exhibit 7.2.

The standards do not choose between the conflicting approaches to mediation; instead, they concentrate on the similarities between the approaches. One particularly difficult issue is how active a mediator should be. Some contend that a mediator should only *facilitate* the settlement of disputes. Others believe that mediators should *evaluate* the proposals and *comment* on the viability of an approach in court.

EXHIBIT 7.2 Model Standards of Conduct for Mediators

A mediator shall:

1. Recognize that mediation is based on principles of self-determination by the parties.
2. Conduct the mediation in an impartial manner.
3. Disclose actual and potential conflicts of interest.
4. Mediate only when he or she has the necessary qualifications.
5. Maintain the reasonable expectations of the parties with regard to confidentiality.
6. Conduct the mediation fairly and diligently.
7. Be truthful in advertising and solicitation for mediation.
8. Fully disclose and explain the basis of fees.
9. Have a duty to improve the practice of the profession.

SOURCE: Richard C. Reuben, "Model Ethics Rules Limit Mediator Role: Despite Controversy, Standards Expected to Improve Respect for Profession," *ABA Journal* (January 1996), p. 25.

7.2

MANAGEMENT

SERVING AS A MEDIATOR

Anna has been asked to serve as a mediator in a dispute between two local firms that are each active in telecommunication research. Both firms agreed that their controversy should be resolved without taking the issue to court; both agreed that they needed a person with experience and expertise in the field; and both agreed that Anna possessed the necessary qualifications to mediate their dispute. Anna is concerned about the request, and she has asked you whether she is qualified to serve as a mediator in this situation. What advice will you give her?

BUSINESS CONSIDERATIONS Should a business adopt a policy on its officers serving as mediators in disputes? What are the possible drawbacks—or benefits—to having officers mediate disputes between other firms?

ETHICAL CONSIDERATIONS Suppose a businessperson learned about certain new techniques or technical developments while serving as a mediator and this information would be of great use to the businessperson's firm. What ethical considerations would enter into any decision as to whether the information should be used? What legal considerations might enter into this situation?

A number of states, e.g., Florida, Texas, and Indiana, have adopted standards of conduct for mediators.[4]

Compensation

There is no hard-and-fast rule regarding the compensation of mediators. In fact, compensation among mediators can vary widely. Many mediators are volunteers who serve as mediators through various community organizations. Others are professional mediators who rely on mediation to provide much of their income. The parties should discuss the compensation issue and how the expenses will be shared before agreeing to submit their situation to mediation.

ARBITRATION

Arbitration is the process of submitting a dispute to the judgment of a person or group of persons called arbitrators for resolution. The final decision of the arbitrator or arbitrators is called an *award.* It is usually binding on the parties. *Advisory arbitration* is similar to traditional arbitration; however, it focuses on specific issues in the dispute and the award is not binding on the parties.

Arbitration begins with an agreement between the parties to arbitrate, usually in the initial agreement. The parties can agree to arbitrate after an actual dispute arises, however, if they are willing to do so. The terms in an arbitration agreement can vary widely. An agreement to arbitrate is basically a contract or a portion of a contract. Like all contracts, to be valid, it must be based on **mutual assent**. If a party agrees to an arbitration clause because of **fraud** or **duress**, the agreement will not be valid. (For a detailed discussion of what constitutes a valid contract, see Chapters 9–15.) Litigation may ensue if a party feels that the arbitration agreement was invalid. A judge would then determine the legality of the arbitration provision.

The Arizona Supreme Court considered that issue in the following case.

7.1 BROEMMER v. ABORTION SERVICES OF PHOENIX, LTD. — 840 P.2d 1013 (Ariz. 1992)

FACTS "Melinda Kay Broemmer, an Iowa resident, was 21 years old, unmarried, and 16 or 17 weeks pregnant. She was a high school graduate earning less than $100.00 a week and had no medical benefits. The father-to-be insisted that plaintiff have an abortion, but her parents advised against it. Plaintiff's uncontested affidavit describes the time as one of considerable confusion and emotional and physical turmoil for her. Plaintiff's mother contacted Abortion

7.1 BROEMMER v. ABORTION SERVICES OF PHOENIX, LTD. *(cont.)* **840 P.2d 1013 (Ariz. 1992)**

Services of Phoenix and made an appointment for her daughter for December 29, 1986. During their visit to the clinic that day, plaintiff and her mother expected, but did not receive, information and counseling on alternatives to abortion and the nature of the operation. When plaintiff and her mother arrived at the clinic, plaintiff was escorted into an adjoining room and asked to complete three forms, one of which is the agreement to arbitrate at issue in this case. The agreement to arbitrate included language that 'any dispute aris[ing] between the Parties as a result of the fees and/or services' would be settled by binding arbitration and that 'any arbitrators appointed by the American Arbitration Association (AAA) shall be licensed medical doctors who specialize in obstetrics/gynecology.' She completed all three forms in less than 5 minutes and returned them to the front desk. Clinic staff made no attempt to explain the agreement to plaintiff before or after she signed, and did not provide plaintiff with copies of the forms. After plaintiff returned the forms to the front desk, she was taken into an examination room where pre-operation procedures were performed. She was then instructed to return at 7:00 A.M. the next morning for the termination procedure. Plaintiff returned the following day and Doctor Otto performed the abortion. As a result of the procedure, plaintiff suffered a punctured uterus that required medical treatment."

ISSUE Was the arbitration provision binding on Broemmer?

HOLDING No.

REASONING "The printed form agreement signed by plaintiff in this case possesses all the characteristics of a contract of adhesion. The form is a standardized contract offered to plaintiff on a 'take it or leave it' basis. In addition to removing from the courts any potential dispute concerning fees or services, the drafter inserted additional terms potentially advantageous to itself requiring that any arbitrator appointed by the American Arbitration Association be a licensed medical doctor specializing in obstetrics/gynecology. The contract was not negotiated but was, instead, prepared by defendant and presented to plaintiff as a condition of treatment. Staff at the clinic neither explained its terms to plaintiff nor indicated that she was free to refuse to sign the form; they merely represented to plaintiff that she had to complete the three forms. The conditions under which the clinic offered plaintiff the services were on a 'take it or leave it' basis, and the terms of service were not negotiable. Applying general contract law to the undisputed facts, the court of appeals correctly held that the contract was one of adhesion. . . .

Our conclusion that the contract was one of adhesion is not, of itself, determinative of its enforceability. . . . To determine whether this contract of adhesion is enforceable, we look to two factors: the reasonable expectations of the adhering party and whether the contract is unconscionable. . . . [T]he clinic in this case did not show that it was the procedure of clinic staff to offer to explain the agreement to patients. The clinic did not explain the purpose of the form to plaintiff and did not show whether plaintiff was required to sign the form or forfeit treatment. . . . Clearly, the issues of knowing consent and reasonable expectations are closely related and intertwined. . . . The *Restatement [(Second) of Contracts* § 211] focuses our attention on whether it was beyond plaintiff's reasonable expectations to expect to arbitrate her medical malpractice claims, which includes waiving her right to a jury trial, as a part of the filling out of the three forms under the facts and circumstances of this case. Clearly, there was no conspicuous or explicit waiver of the fundamental right to a jury trial or any evidence that such rights were knowingly, voluntarily and intelligently waived. The only evidence presented compels a finding that waiver of such fundamental rights was beyond the reasonable expectations of plaintiff. . . . [We] conclude that the contract fell outside plaintiff's reasonable expectations and is, therefore, unenforceable. Because of this holding, it is unnecessary for us to determine whether the contract is also unconscionable."[5]

BUSINESS CONSIDERATIONS Assume that a business would prefer to resolve its disputes by arbitration rather than trial. What procedures should that business institute to increase the likelihood that its arbitration clauses will be upheld in court? What actions should the business avoid?

ETHICAL CONSIDERATIONS In this case, did the clinic owe Broemmer a duty? If so, what was it? Whose duty was it to see that Broemmer received adequate information about her alternatives? Why?

FROM THE DESK OF
AMY CHEN, ATTORNEY AT LAW
Binding Arbitration
A contract, such as a professional service contract or a health-care services contract, may require binding arbitration if a dispute arises. If you knowingly and willingly enter into such an agreement, you are agreeing to submit any claims to binding arbitration and relinquishing the right to a jury trial if a dispute arises. If you are willing to settle any disputes by binding arbitration, there is no problem. If you are not, however, do not sign the contract!

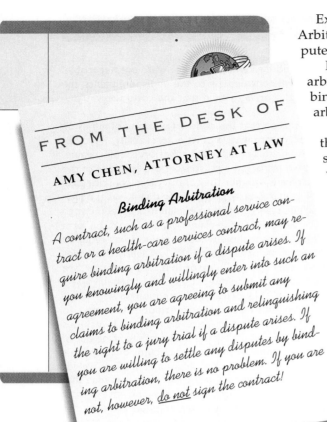

Exhibit 7.3 (page 181) illustrates the steps used in an American Arbitration Association arbitration. The form for submitting a dispute to the AAA appears as Exhibit 7.4 (page 182).

In arbitration, a hearing is held before an arbitrator or a panel of arbitrators. There are two types of arbitration—binding and nonbinding. Generally, a party *cannot* appeal the decision in binding arbitration.

Many states have statutes that provide for arbitration and the enforcement of the arbitrators' awards in the courts of the state. At one time, the law did not favor arbitration because it was considered an improper means of avoiding the judicial system. Today, that is no longer the case. In fact, former Chief Justice Warren Burger of the Supreme Court went on record as favoring the greater use of arbitration and other legitimate means of resolving disputes without expending the time and money required to move a case through the court system.

The judge in *Cole* v. *Burns International Security Services* evaluated many of the concerns about enforcing arbitration agreements against employees.

7.2 COLE v. BURNS INTERNATIONAL SECURITY SERVICES — 1997 U.S. App. LEXIS 2223 (D.C. Cir. 1997)

FACTS ". . . Clinton Cole used to work as a security guard at Union Station in Washington, D.C. for a company called LaSalle and Partners ('LaSalle'). In 1991, Burns Security took over LaSalle's contract to provide security at Union Station and required all LaSalle employees to sign a 'Pre-Dispute Resolution Agreement' in order to obtain employment with Burns. The Pre-Dispute Resolution Agreement ('agreement' or 'contract'), in relevant part, provides:

> *In consideration of the Company employing you, you and the Company each agrees that, in the event either party (or its representatives, successors or assigns) brings an action in a court of competent jurisdiction relating to your recruitment, employment with, or termination of employment from the Company, the plaintiff in such action agrees to waive his, her or its right to a trial by jury, and further agrees that no demand, request or motion will be made for trial by jury.*
>
> *In consideration of the Company employing you, you further agree that, in the event that you seek relief in a court of competent jurisdiction for a dispute covered by this Agreement, the Company may, at any time within 60 days of the service of your complaint upon the Company, at its option, require all or part of the dispute to be arbitrated by one arbitrator in accordance with the rules of the American Arbitration Association. You agree that the option to arbitrate any dispute is governed by the Federal Arbitration Act, and fully enforceable.*
>
> *You understand and agree that, if the Company exercises its option, any dispute arbitrated will be heard solely by the arbitrator, and not by a court.*

7.2 COLE v. BURNS INTERNATIONAL SECURITY SERVICES *(cont.)* 1997 U.S. App. LEXIS 2223 (D.C. Cir. 1997)

This pre-dispute resolution agreement will cover all matters directly or indirectly related to your recruitment, employment or termination of employment by the Company; including, but not limited to, claims involving laws against discrimination whether brought under federal and/or state law, and/or claims involving co-employees but excluding Worker's Compensation Claims.

The right to a trial, and to a trial by jury, is of value. YOU MAY WISH TO CONSULT AN ATTORNEY PRIOR TO SIGNING THIS AGREEMENT. IF SO, TAKE A COPY OF THIS FORM WITH YOU. HOWEVER, YOU WILL NOT BE OFFERED EMPLOYMENT UNTIL THIS FORM IS SIGNED AND RETURNED BY YOU.

. . . On August 5, 1991, Cole signed the agreement and began working for Burns. . . . In October 1993, Burns Security fired Cole. After filing charges with the Equal Employment Opportunity Commission, Cole filed the instant complaint in the United States District Court for the District of Columbia, alleging racial discrimination, harassment based on race, retaliation for his writing a letter of complaint regarding sexual harassment of a subordinate employee by another supervisor at Burns, and intentional infliction of emotional distress. Burns moved to compel arbitration of the dispute and to dismiss Cole's complaint pursuant to the terms of the contract. . . ."

ISSUE Is the pre-employment agreement that Cole signed enforceable in his Title VII action? Could he obtain judicial review of an arbitrator's award?

HOLDING Yes to both.

REASONING ". . .[T]his case involves a situation in which an employee has been required, as a condition of employment, to forego all access to jury trials and (at the employer's option) to use arbitration in place of judicial fora for the resolution of statutory as well as contractual claims. . . .American jurisprudence regarding the enforceability of arbitration agreements and the permissible scope of judicial review of arbitration awards has developed most fully in the context of collective bargaining. . . . In that context, strict enforcement of arbitration agreements and minimal review of arbitration awards are both logical and desirable. . . .

[M]any commentators have questioned the logic and desirability of extending arbitral jurisprudence developed in labor cases beyond the confines of the collective bargaining context. . . .The fundamental distinction between contractual rights, which are created, defined, and subject to modification by the same private parties participating in arbitration, and statutory rights, which are created, defined, and subject to modification only by Congress and the courts, suggests the need for a public, rather than private, mechanism of enforcement for statutory rights. . . .If the award purports to resolve a claim under external law (and hence preclude relitigation of that claim in any other forum), there is a public interest in the manner in which the external-law norms are articulated and applied in the arbitral forum. Thus, . . . when arbitrators sit to adjudicate a dispute governed by external law, there is a tension between the tradition of limited judicial review of arbitration awards and the presence of an independent public interest in ensuring that the law is correctly and consistently being applied, and that substantive policies reflected in the law are neither under-enforced nor over-enforced. . . .

Whereas an arbitrator serves as an agent or 'alter ego' for the parties to a collective bargaining agreement, an arbitrator who resolves statutory claims serves simply as a private judge. . . .

Arbitration of public law issues is also troubling, on a less abstract level, because the structural protections inherent in the collective bargaining context are not duplicated in cases involving mandatory arbitration of individual statutory claims. Unlike the labor case, in which both union and employer are regular participants in the arbitration process, only the employer is a repeat player in cases involving individual statutory claims. As a result, the employer gains some advantage in having superior knowledge with respect to selection of an arbitrator. . . .

Additionally, while a lack of public disclosure of arbitration awards is acceptable in the collective bargaining context, because both employers and unions monitor such decisions and the awards rarely involve issues of concern to persons other than the parties, in the context of individual statutory claims, a lack of public disclosure may systematically favor companies over individuals. Judicial decisions create binding precedent that prevents a recurrence of statutory violations; it is not clear that arbitral decisions have any such preventive effect. The unavailability of arbitral decisions also may prevent potential plaintiffs from locating the information necessary to build a case of intentional misconduct or to establish a pattern or practice of discrimination by particular companies. . . .

Finally, the competence of arbitrators to analyze and decide purely legal issues in connection with statutory claims has been questioned. Many arbitrators are not lawyers, and they have not traditionally engaged in the same kind of legal analysis performed by judges. For instance, arbitrators often cite to and rely extensively on treatises. . . .A court is unlikely to rely on a treatise—even . . . a widely respected one. Similarly, arbitrators frequently

7.2 COLE v. BURNS INTERNATIONAL SECURITY SERVICES *(cont.)* 1997 U.S. App. LEXIS 2223 (D.C. Cir. 1997)

rely on leading cases on the subject of employment discrimination. . . .This means that an arbitrator's decision may be based on broad stroke principles to the exclusion of cases more analogous to the claim being decided. Nor do arbitrators always analyze an intentional discrimination case within the judicially accepted three-prong framework articulated by the Supreme Court. . . .

Many of these concerns were raised by the Supreme Court to explain its initial hesitation to endorse the arbitration of statutory claims. The Court questioned, for example, arbitrators' competence to decide legal issues, noting that 'the resolution of statutory or constitutional issues is a primary responsibility of courts, and judicial construction has proved especially necessary with respect to Title VII, whose broad language frequently can be given meaning only by reference to public law concepts.' . . .The Court also worried that because the records of arbitration proceedings are incomplete, discovery is abbreviated, cross-examination and testimony under oath may be limited or unavailable, and arbitrators need not give the reasons for an award, arbitration could not appropriately substitute for the federal courts in resolving statutory issues under Title VII. . . .

Nonetheless, the Supreme Court now has made clear that, as a general rule, statutory claims are fully subject to binding arbitration, at least outside of the context of collective bargaining. . . .The Court has stressed that 'so long as the prospective litigant effectively may vindicate [his or her] statutory cause of action in the arbitral forum, the statute will continue to serve both its remedial and deterrent function.' . . .

[W]e turn to the arbitration agreement before us in this case. . . .We start with the assumption that . . .a person may agree to arbitrate statutory claims. We do not assume, however, that an employer has a free hand in requiring arbitration as a condition of employment. . . .

The beneficiaries of public statutes are entitled to the rights and protections provided by the law. Clearly, it would be unlawful for an employer to condition employment on an employee's agreement to give up the right to be free from racial or gender discrimination. . . .Any such condition of employment would violate Title VII, regardless of whether or not the agreement was viewed as a contract of adhesion. Thus, in a subsequent suit by the employee raising a viable claim of racial discrimination or sexual harassment, it would be no defense that the employee had signed a contract giving up her right to be free from discrimination.

Similarly, an employee cannot be required as a condition of employment to waive access to a neutral forum in which statutory employment discrimination claims may be heard. For example, an employee could not be required to sign an agreement waiving the right to bring Title VII claims in any forum. . . . At a minimum, statutory rights include both a substantive protection and access to a neutral forum in which to enforce those protections. . . .

Judicial review of arbitration awards covering statutory claims is necessarily focused, but that does not mean that meaningful review is unavailable. The FAA [Federal Arbitration Act] itself recognizes a number of grounds on which arbitration awards may be vacated. . . .The grounds listed in the FAA, however, are not exclusive. . . .The Supreme Court has also indicated that arbitration awards can be vacated if they are in 'manifest disregard of the law.'. . .Two assumptions have been central to the Court's decisions in this area. First, the Court has insisted that, ' 'by agreeing to arbitrate a statutory claim, a party does not forego the substantive rights afforded by the statute; it only submits to their resolution in an arbitral, rather than a judicial, forum.' . . . These twin assumptions regarding the arbitration of statutory claims are valid only if judicial review under the 'manifest disregard of the law' standard is sufficiently rigorous to ensure that arbitrators have properly interpreted and applied statutory law.

The value and finality of an employer's arbitration system will not be undermined by focused review of arbitral legal determinations. Most employment discrimination claims are entirely factual in nature and involve well-settled legal principles. . . .Nonetheless, there will be some cases in which novel or difficult legal issues are presented demanding judicial judgment. In such cases, the courts are empowered to review an arbitrator's award to ensure that its resolution of public law issues is correct. . . .Because meaningful judicial review of public law issues is available, Cole's agreement to arbitrate is not unconscionable or otherwise unenforceable. . . ."

BUSINESS CONSIDERATIONS Based on the reasoning of this court, how should you draft arbitration agreements with employees and perspective employees? What concerns would you have about their enforceability?

ETHICAL CONSIDERATIONS Is it ethical for an employer to require applicants to sign arbitration agreements before offering them a position? Why or why not?

Mutual assent

The parties must agree to be bound by exactly the same terms.

Fraud

When one party enters into a contract due to a false statement of material fact.

Duress

When one party enters into a contract due to a wrongful threat of force.

EXHIBIT 7.3 Steps in an AAA Arbitration

1. A party files a demand for arbitration with an AAA regional office, and a case administrator is assigned to follow the case through to its conclusion.
2. Other parties named in the demand are notified and replies are requested.
3. The case administrator reviews panel qualifications and lists individuals suitable for the particular case. Information on AAA panelists is maintained on a computer.
4. The list is sent to the parties, each of whom numbers in order of preference the names that it finds acceptable.
5. An arbitrator is selected by the administrator according to the mutual desires of the parties. If the parties are unable to agree, the AAA may appoint an arbitrator.
6. The administrator arranges a hearing date and location convenient to the parties and to the arbitrator.
7. At the hearing, testimony and documents are submitted to the arbitrator, and witnesses are questioned and cross-examined.
8. The arbitrator then issues a binding award, copies of which are sent to the parties by the case administrator.

SOURCE: American Arbitration Association, *Resolving Your Disputes* (November 1995), p. 8.

Various organizations offer panels of arbitrators. Parties may select their own arbitrator(s) or the arbitrator(s) may be selected by the organization. The AAA, for example, has a specific panel of arbitrators for commercial disputes. It also has panels for other types of disputes. The parties select their arbitrator from the panel members.

Arbitrators charge about $400 to $700 a day.[6] Fees vary depending on the region and the type of case. Despite the expense, one finance company reported a 66 percent reduction in legal expenses by using arbitration.[7]

If both parties comply willingly with the arbitration award, no further action is required. If one side does not, court action to "confirm" the decision is necessary.

Controls on Arbitration

The states have developed their own individual approaches and laws to address arbitration issues. Some state statutes are more pro-arbitration than others. Some attempted to restrict the scope of arbitration. For example, some states (such as Alabama), did not permit arbitration clauses in consumer contracts, although they permitted the use of arbitration and arbitration clauses in other types of contracts.[8] The U.S. Supreme Court addressed this issue in *Allied-Bruce Terminix Companies, Inc. v. Dobson*, 513 U.S. 265 (1995). The Alabama Supreme Court, relying on state law, had declared that a consumer did not have to go to arbitration as specified in the arbitration agreement signed by the parties. The U.S. Supreme Court heard the case on writ of certiorari to the Alabama Supreme Court and overturned that decision. It ruled that individual states could not regulate or prevent the use of arbitration by their statutes. This landmark case follows on page 183.

EXHIBIT 7.4 American Arbitration Association Submission to Dispute Resolution

American Arbitration Association

SUBMISSION TO DISPUTE RESOLUTION

Date: ____________

The named parties hereby submit the following dispute for resolution under the ____________ Rules* of the American Arbitration Association.

Procedure Selected: ☐ Arbitration ☐ Mediation Settlement
☐ Other ____________ (Describe.)

FOR INSURANCE CASES ONLY:

Policy Number ____________ Effective Dates ____________ to ____________ Applicable Policy Limits ____________

Date of Incident ____________ Location ____________

Insured: ____________ Claim Number: ____________

Names of Claimants	Check if a minor.	Amounts Claimed
	☐	
	☐	

Nature of Dispute and/or Injuries Alleged (Attach additional sheets if necessary.):

Place of Hearing: ____________

We agree that, if binding arbitration is selected, we will abide by and perform any award rendered hereunder and that a judgment may be entered on the award.

To Be Completed by the Parties

Name of Party	Name of Party
Address	Address
City, State, and ZIP Code	City, State, and ZIP Code
( ) Telephone Fax	( ) Telephone Fax
Name of the Party's Attorney or Representative	Name of the Party's Attorney or Representative
Name of Firm (if Applicable)	Name of Firm (if Applicable)
Address	Address
City, State, and ZIP Code	City, State, and ZIP Code
( ) Telephone Fax	( ) Telephone Fax
Signed† (may be signed by a representative) Title	Signed† (may be signed by a representative) Title

Please file three copies with the AAA.

• *If you have a question as to which rules apply, please contact the AAA.*
† *Signatures of all parties are required for arbitration.*

Form G1-9/95

SOURCE: Reprinted by permission of the American Arbitration Association, New York, NY.

7.3 ALLIED-BRUCE TERMINIX COMPANIES, INC. v. DOBSON 513 U.S. 265 (1995)

FACTS "In August 1987 Steven Gwin . . . who owned a house in Birmingham, Alabama, bought a lifetime 'Termite Protection Plan' (Plan) from the local office of Allied-Bruce Terminix Companies, a franchise of Terminix International Company. In the Plan, Allied-Bruce promised 'to protect' Gwin's house 'against the attack of subterranean termites,' to reinspect periodically, to provide any 'further treatment found necessary' and to repair, up to $100,000, damage caused by new termite infestations. . . . The Plan's contract document provided in writing that 'any controversy or claim . . . arising out of or relating to the interpretation, performance or breach of any provision of this agreement shall be settled exclusively by arbitration. . . .'

In the Spring of 1991 Mr. and Mrs. Gwin, wishing to sell their house to Mr. and Mrs. Dobson, had Allied-Bruce reinspect the house. They obtained a clean bill of health. But, no sooner had they sold the house and transferred the Termite Protection Plan to Mr. and Mrs. Dobson than the Dobsons found the house swarming with termites. Allied-Bruce attempted to treat and repair the house, but the Dobsons found Allied-Bruce's efforts inadequate. They therefore sued the Gwins, and . . . also sued Allied-Bruce and Terminix in Alabama state court. Allied-Bruce and Terminix, pointing to the Plan's arbitration clause . . . immediately asked the court for a stay, to allow arbitration to proceed. The court denied the stay. . . . The Supreme Court of Alabama upheld the denial of the stay on the basis of a state statute . . . making written, predispute arbitration agreements invalid and 'unenforceable.' To reach this conclusion, the court had to find that the Federal Arbitration Act, which pre-empts conflicting state law, did not apply to the termite contract."

ISSUE Was the arbitration clause enforceable against the Dobsons?

HOLDING Yes.

REASONING "Several state courts and federal district courts, like the Supreme Court of Alabama, have interpreted the Act's language as requiring the parties to a contract to have 'contemplated' an interstate commerce connection. . . . Several federal appellate courts, however, have interpreted the same language differently, as reaching to the limits of Congress' Commerce Clause power. . . . We granted certiorari to resolve this conflict. . . and, as we said, we conclude that the broader reading of the statute is the right one. . . .

First, the basic purpose of the Federal Arbitration Act is to overcome courts' refusals to enforce agreements to arbitrate. . . . The origins of those refusals lie in 'ancient times,' when the English courts fought 'for extension of jurisdiction—all of them being opposed to anything that would altogether deprive every one of them of jurisdiction.'. . . American courts initially followed English practice, perhaps just 'standing. . . upon the antiquity of the rule' prohibiting arbitration clause enforcement, rather than 'upon its excellence or reason'. . . . Regardless, when Congress passed the Arbitration Act in 1925, it was 'motivated, first and foremost, by a . . . desire' to change this anti-arbitration rule. . . . It intended courts to 'enforce [arbitration] agreements into which parties had entered,'. . . and to 'place such agreements upon the same footing as other contracts.'. . .

Third, . . . [d]id Congress intend the Act also to apply in state courts? Did the Federal Arbitration Act pre-empt conflicting state anti-arbitration law, or could state courts apply their arbitration rules in cases before them, thereby reaching results different from those reached in similar federal diversity cases?. . . [T]his Court decided that Congress would not have wanted state and federal courts to reach different outcomes about the validity of arbitration in similar cases. The court concluded that the Federal Arbitration Act pre-empts state law; and it held that state courts cannot apply state statutes that invalidate arbitration agreements. . . .

We therefore proceed to the basic interpretive questions aware that we are interpreting an Act that seeks broadly to overcome judicial hostility to arbitration agreements and that applies in both federal and state courts. We must decide in this case whether that Act used language about interstate commerce that nonetheless limits the Act's application, thereby carving out an important statutory niche in which a State remains free to apply its antiarbitration law or policy. We conclude that it does not. . . .

[Section] 2 [of the Federal Arbitration Act] gives States a method for protecting consumers against unfair pressure to agree to a contract with an unwanted arbitration provision. States may regulate contracts, including arbitration clauses, under general contract law principles and they may invalidate an arbitration clause 'upon such grounds as exist at law or in equity for the revocation of any contract.'. . . What States may not do is decide that a contract is fair enough to enforce all of its basic terms (price, service, credit), but not fair enough to enforce its arbitration clause. The Act makes any such State policy unlawful, for that kind of policy would place arbitration clauses on an unequal 'footing' directly contrary to the Act's language and Congress' intent. . . . For these reasons, we accept the 'commerce in fact' interpretation, reading the Act's language as insisting that the 'transaction' in fact 'involve' interstate commerce, even if the parties did not contemplate an interstate commerce connection. . . . Consequently, the

7.3 ALLIED-BRUCE TERMINIX COMPANIES, INC. v. DOBSON (cont.) 513 U.S. 265 (1995)

judgment of the Supreme Court of Alabama is reversed and the case is remanded for further proceedings consistent with this opinion."

BUSINESS CONSIDERATIONS Why would a business prefer to submit claims to arbitration rather than submitting the case to the court for review? Should a business have a policy of arbitrating every controversy? Why?

ETHICAL CONSIDERATIONS Is it ethical for a state government to attempt to "repeal" federal statutes through the enactment of state statutes that specifically negate the applicability of a federal law? Would it be ethical for a business to attempt to "repeal" a state statute by using contract language that negates rights provided to customers under state law?

The Federal Arbitration Act covers all transactions involving interstate commerce. For a more detailed discussion of what constitutes interstate commerce, see Chapters 39 and 40.

Exhibit 7.5 shows a sample arbitration clause.

As we have seen, arbitration is not exclusively applied to state-law issues. Arbitration is applicable at the state, national, and international levels. Arbitration is covered at the state level by state statutes, at the national level by federal statute, and at the international level by treaty. The statutory law is clarified by judicial interpretation at all levels.

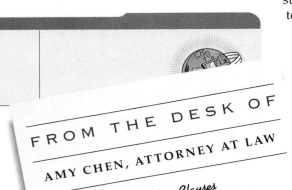

FROM THE DESK OF

AMY CHEN, ATTORNEY AT LAW

Arbitration Clauses

Expect to see an increase in the use of arbitration clauses when you buy consumer goods and services and when you purchase and sell business goods. Consider inserting an arbitration clause in your contracts, both to avoid litigation and to hasten the resolution of disputes! If so, you may want your clause to specify that you agree to arbitrate, the number of arbitrators, the identity of the arbitrator(s) or the selection procedure, the locale of the hearings, the substantive law that will apply, whether the arbitrator will write an opinion, and, in international agreements, the language of the proceedings and any written opinion and the citizenship of the arbitrator.

Statutory Coverage

Arbitration is subject to statutory coverage and provisions at the state, federal, and international levels. Parties seeking resolution of their disputes through arbitration should ascertain how arbitration is viewed and regulated at the level(s) in which they are involved.

At the state level, the Uniform Arbitration Act has been adopted in 46 states and the District of Columbia, Puerto Rico, and the Virgin Islands. Alabama, Georgia, Mississippi, and West Virginia have not adopted it; they each have their own methods for regulating arbitration.[9]

At the federal level, the Federal Arbitration Act (FAA), originally enacted in 1925, provides some federal guidelines to be followed in arbitration. It also attempts to ensure that arbitration clauses be given the same protection and enforceability as any other contract clauses. Section 2 of the Federal Arbitration Act provides that a "Written provision in any maritime transaction or a contract evidencing a transaction involving commerce to settle by arbitration a controversy thereafter arising out of such contract or transaction. . . shall be valid, irrevocable,

EXHIBIT 7.5 Standard AAA Contract Arbitration Clause

Any controversy or claim arising out of or relating to this contract, or the breach thereof, shall be settled by arbitration administered by the American Arbitration Association in accordance with its [applicable] rules and judgment on the award rendered by the arbitrator may be entered in any court having jurisdiction thereof.

SOURCE: American Arbitration Association, *Drafting Dispute Resolution Clauses—A Practical Guide* (June 1994), p. 5.

and enforceable, save upon such grounds as exist at law or in equity for the revocation of any contract."

At the international level, arbitration is most likely to be regulated by the 1958 UN Convention on Recognition and Enforcement of Arbitral Awards, an international treaty dealing with arbitration. This convention has been ratified by more than 80 nations.[10] In this hemisphere, international arbitration is also regulated by the Inter-American Convention on International Commercial Arbitration.[11] The International Chamber of Commerce also supports and encourages arbitration; and many firms involved in international business seek to resolve their disputes through its arbitration provisions.

The federal statute and the international treaties are designed to increase the acceptance and use of arbitration as an alternative method for resolving disputes. Not only has the Supreme Court ruled in a manner encouraging a wider use of arbitration (*Allied-Bruce Terminix Cos.* v. *Dobson, supra*) but an appellate court opinion interpreting the **CISG** also ruled in favor of the inclusion of an arbitration clause as a basic portion of the contract. In that case, *Filanto, S.P.A.* v. *Chilewich International Corp.*, 789 F.Supp. 1229 (S.D.N.Y. 1992), the appellate court upheld the enforcement of an arbitration clause that was included by reference in a contract that was never reduced to final written form. Since the arbitration clause was included in the documents to which the parties referred in their communications, the court ruled that the parties had agreed to submit any controversies to arbitration.

CISG
The United Nations Convention on Contracts for the International Sale of Goods.

Organizations

There are a number of organizations that actively support arbitration and provide both the forum in which an arbitration occurs and the arbitrator. Some of these organizations operate exclusively within the United States; others operate internationally.

Within the United States, arbitration is supported by the Judicial Arbitration and Mediation Services, Inc. (J.A.M.S.), which employs only former judges as arbitrators, the Federal Mediation and Conciliation Service, as well as the AAA. Internationally, arbitration is supported by the AAA (which operates both domestically and internationally); the International Chamber of Commerce, headquartered in Paris; and the London Court of Arbitration (which is *not* a court, despite the title of the organization).

The AAA administers more than 60,000 cases in an average year.[12] Its services include arbitration, mediation, minitrial, **fact-finding**, education, and training. When the AAA is involved in an arbitration, it can refer a list of potential arbitrators, serve as an *intermediator* between the parties and the arbitrator in negotiating the arbitrator's compensation, and collect a deposit for arbitrator compensation.

Fact-finding
A process where an arbitrator investigates a dispute and issues findings of fact and a nonbinding report.

The AAA administrator handles the administrative details so that the parties do not deal directly with the arbitrator. This helps ensure that the parties will not discuss the case privately with the arbitrator prior to the hearing. The AAA requires its arbitrators to issue awards within 30 days after the close of the hearings, unless the contract between the parties specifies another time limit.[13] Except in labor and international cases, the AAA does not encourage arbitrators to write lengthy opinions. Instead, it encourages them to write an itemized award.[14] It promulgates rules for specific types of arbitration and it also has special procedures for large, complex commercial cases. The slogan of the AAA is "Speed, Economy, and Justice."

In the *Lander Company* case, the court discusses enforceability of an arbitration award under the International Chamber of Commerce arbitration rules and the Federal Arbitration Act.

7.4 LANDER COMPANY, INC. v. MMP INVESTMENTS, INC. — 1997 U.S. App. LEXIS 2817 (7th Cir. 1997)

FACTS "This is a suit by the Lander Company against MMP Investments to enforce an arbitration award. . . . The parties are American firms that made a contract . . . for the distribution by MMP in Poland of shampoos and other products manufactured by Lander in the United States. The contract provides that disputes under it shall be settled by binding arbitration in New York City pursuant to the arbitration rules of the International Chamber of Commerce. The parties had a falling out, Lander notified MMP that it was terminating the contract, and . . . [MMP] filed a request for arbitration with the International Court of Arbitration, an organ of the International Chamber of Commerce. Lander did not contest the jurisdiction of the Court of Arbitration. The dispute proceeded to arbitration in New York City before a New York lawyer designated by the Court, who after five days of evidentiary hearings decided in favor of Lander, awarding it more than $500,000 plus interest.

The arbitration rules of the International Chamber of Commerce make arbitration awards final and deem the parties by submitting their dispute to arbitration 'to have waived their right to any form of appeal insofar as such waiver can validly be made.' . . . MMP refused to pay the award, so Lander brought this suit to enforce it in the federal district court in Chicago, which is MMP's home. The complaint (captioned 'petition to confirm') recites the diverse citizenship of the parties, notes that the United States is a party to the Convention on the Recognition and Enforcement of Foreign Arbitral Awards . . . (the 'New York Convention,' as it is known), claims that the suit arises under the Convention and its implementing legislation . . . and states that the district court 'has jurisdiction . . . and that the amount in controversy (exclusive of interest and costs) exceeds $50,000. When the complaint was filed this was the minimum amount in controversy . . . [necessary for diversity jurisdiction in] the federal courts. The amount has since been raised to $75,000. . . ."

ISSUE Does the Federal Arbitration Act apply to this contract? Does the New York Convention apply to this contract?

HOLDING Yes. Yes.

REASONING "The [trial] judge should not have dismissed Lander's suit, at least on jurisdictional grounds. The complaint sufficiently alleged jurisdiction under the Federal Arbitration Act as well as under the New York Convention. No other purpose than to allege jurisdiction under the Act can be assigned to the allegation of diversity jurisdiction and the citation of . . . the diversity statute, and . . . the provision of the Federal Arbitration Act that authorizes suits in federal court to enforce arbitration awards in cases arising out of maritime contracts or contracts evidencing a transaction involving interstate or foreign commerce. . . . [N]o one doubts that the contract between Lander and MMP falls into the second category. [T]he Federal Arbitration Act is limited to arbitration agreements or awards that arise out of disputes that could be litigated in federal court. . . . Chapter 2 of Title 9, the chapter that creates jurisdiction to enforce awards made under the New York Convention, is not so limited . . .and citation of the diversity statute would thus have been unnecessary had Lander thought that the district court had jurisdiction only by virtue of the Convention. . . .

The court either has jurisdiction or it does not. If it is pretty obvious that it has jurisdiction, the failure to cite the right statute is harmless and ought not lead to a forfeiture. . . . When a district judge sees a request to confirm an arbitration award coupled with an allegation of diversity juris-

7.4 LANDER COMPANY, INC. v. MMP INVESTMENTS, INC. *(cont.)* 1997 U.S. App. LEXIS 2817 (7th Cir. 1997)

diction, a light bulb labeled 'Federal Arbitration Act' ought to flash in his head. . . .

To agree to binding arbitration is to agree that if your opponent wins the arbitration he can obtain judicial relief if you refuse to comply with the arbitrator's award. . . .To invoke arbitration pursuant to such an agreement, as MMP also did, is further to agree to be bound, if necessary through court action, by the arbitrator's award, provided, of course, that the award does not have any infirmity of a sort that a court can use to invalidate an arbitration award. Imagine MMP's indignation if it had won the arbitration and Lander had denied that any court in the United States had jurisdiction to enforce the award. . . .

By assumption there is jurisdiction under the Federal Arbitration Act. . . .We have assumed rather than established that the district court had jurisdiction under the Federal Arbitration Act. . . .[I]f there are differences between that Act and the New York Convention that are material to the resolution of Lander's suit, we may have to decide whether the Convention applies. The Convention (including its implementing legislation) is more than a statute that confers jurisdiction; it contains procedural provisions besides. [If the Convention is not applicable,]. . . but the court has jurisdiction on some other basis, its inapplicability may still affect the course of the suit. It has, for example, a longer statute of limitations—three years rather than one. . . .That is not a factor here. But if a court . . . has less authority to turn down the request (in whole or part) under the Convention than under the Federal Arbitration Act, this could make a difference in this case. . . .[W]hether the Convention is applicable may make a difference even though jurisdiction is secure under the Federal Arbitration Act.

And it is secure. It is true that the provision of the Act that confers jurisdiction on the federal courts to confirm arbitration awards authorizes confirmation only in the court specified in the arbitration agreement (none was specified) or in the district in which the arbitration was conducted, which was the Southern District of New York rather than the Northern District of Illinois. . . . But this provision of section 9 merely creates alternatives to conventional venue . . . rather than exclusive venues for confirming arbitration awards. . . .The district in which the defendant resides is a conventional venue for civil cases. There is no reason to force Lander to go to another district that would be less convenient for both parties. . . .

It could also be argued that the New York Convention was intended to be exclusive within its domain. We would then have to consider its applicability to this case because if it were applicable there would be no jurisdiction under the Federal Arbitration Act. Nothing in the Convention or its history, or in the implementing legislation or its history, suggests exclusivity. . . . In fact, Article VII of the Convention provides that the Convention shall not 'deprive any interested party of any right he may have to avail himself of an arbitral award in the manner and to the extent allowed by the law or the treaties of the country where such award is sought to be relied upon.' . . .

So there is jurisdiction under the Act but we still have to consider whether the course of the suit may be affected if the New York Convention is also applicable. Although the Convention is not exclusive, the U.S. implementing legislation provides that in the event of a conflict between its terms and those of the Federal Arbitration Act the Convention's terms govern. . . .We noted earlier that the scope of judicial review under the two regimes may be different. The only substantive defense to the enforcement of the award that MMP claims to have, however, is a defense that part of the award was based on a matter that had not been submitted to the arbitrator; in other words, that the arbitrator had exceeded his terms of reference. And that is a defense under both the Federal Arbitration Act and the New York Convention. . . .The wording is slightly different but there is no reason to think the meaning different. . . . So we do not have to decide whether the Convention also applies to this case. But we think we should decide it. The possible difference in the scope of judicial review that we mentioned earlier could still make a difference in the outcome of this case, because the litigation is in an early stage and MMP may want and be permitted by the district court to interpose a defense of manifest disregard of law by the arbitrator. Moreover, the issue of the Convention's applicability has been fully and ably briefed and vigorously argued, and is bound to recur . . . with the expansion of foreign activities by U.S. firms.

Article I(1) provides that the Convention shall apply not only to arbitral awards made in a different country from the one in which enforcement is sought . . . but also to 'arbitral awards not considered as domestic awards' in the country in which enforcement is sought. . . .The United States will not enforce an arbitration award made in a country that, by failing to adopt the Convention, has not committed itself to enforce arbitration awards made in the United States. Granted, 'a Contracting State' would be clearer, but 'another Contracting State' is clear enough in context; it means 'another signatory of the Convention, like the United States, as opposed to nonsignatories.'

This reading of Article I . . . is supported by the U.S. implementing legislation: Chapter 2 of Title 9 authorizes the enforcement of arbitration awards in disputes wholly between U.S. citizens if, as here, the dispute arose out of a contract involving performance in a foreign country. 9 *U.S.C.* §202. . . . The section adopts the provisions of the Convention for any

7.4 LANDER COMPANY, INC. v. MMP INVESTMENTS, INC *(cont.)* 1997 U.S. App. LEXIS 2817 (7th Cir. 1997)

'arbitration agreement or arbitral award arising out of a legal relationship, whether contractual or not, which is considered as commercial, including a transaction, contract, or agreement described in section 2 of this title'—that is, either a 'maritime transaction or a contract evidencing a transaction involving commerce,' . . . provided only that if the relationship is entirely between U.S. citizens, it must involve performance abroad or have some other reasonable relation with a foreign country. There is no ambiguity; the relationship between Lander and MMP falls squarely within the inclusion. . . . Congress may have believed that confining enforcement under the Convention to awards rendered abroad would drive away international arbitration business from New York. Or it may have been seeking to secure the Convention's benefits, on the basis of reciprocity, to American businesses seeking judicial enforcement of foreign arbitration awards in the countries in which the award was made. Or it may simply have wanted to simplify the procedures governing the foreign activities of American firms, since American firms doing business abroad are bound to have contracts with foreign firms as well as other American firms. Whatever Congress's precise thinking on the matter, it spoke clearly. . . ."

BUSINESS CONSIDERATIONS What can a business do to assure that its arbitration awards are enforceable in court? Should a business specify the court(s) that will have jurisdiction and the body of law that will apply? Why or why not?

ETHICAL CONSIDERATIONS Is it ethical for a party to a contract to agree to arbitration and then subsequently refuse to pay an adverse award? Why or why not?

YOU BE THE JUDGE

Businesses Solve Disputes without Lawyers

A multimillion-dollar lawsuit was pending between Pacific Gas & Electric, Union Oil, and Thermal Power. The suit was expected to last at least one year and to cost each of the firms several million dollars in legal fees alone. The top executives for each of the three companies decided that there was a better and less expensive manner of fighting this battle. These executives met and resolved most of the issues among themselves, without their lawyers. They then called in a private arbitration and mediation service to help resolve the balance of the issues. The entire matter was settled within one month, at a total cost of less than one million dollars. If a stockholder of one of the parties filed a **class action lawsuit** in *your* court, alleging that the corporation was denied its day in court to the detriment of the stockholders and asking the court to nullify the settlement, how would *you* rule? Why?[15]

BUSINESS CONSIDERATIONS Did the top executives from the three firms make a wise business decision? Why or why not? What factors should a business person consider in deciding whether to use ADR rather than going to trial to resolve a controversy?

ETHICAL CONSIDERATIONS Was it ethical for the executives to resolve the dispute in this manner? Why or why not? Under these circumstances would it be ethical for a shareholder to file a class action lawsuit? Why or why not?

SOURCE: Jane Birnbaum with Morton D. Sosland, *Business Week*, 13 April 1992.

MINITRIAL

Class action lawsuit

A lawsuit involving a group of plaintiffs or defendants who are in substantially the same situation.

In alternative dispute resolution, the term *minitrial* describes a process in which the parties' attorneys present an abbreviated form of their case. The parties are permitted to use expert witnesses to support their case. A *neutral*, an unbiased person, chairs the case. Senior executives from the firms involved also attend the presentation. After the presentation, the senior executives meet in an attempt to resolve the dispute. Prior to the presentation, the parties usually specify what will happen if the senior executives are unable to settle the case. If the senior executives *are* unable to settle the case, the neutral may be empowered to mediate or to provide a nonbinding advisory opinion informing the parties of the probable outcome if litigation is pursued.

Note that in court matters, judges use the term *minitrial* to refer to an abbreviated judicial proceeding on a few issues, for example, a minitrial on damages.

RENT-A-JUDGE TRIAL

A "rent-a-judge" trial is another alternative method of dispute resolution. When the parties elect to use this method, they pay a fee to a "judge" to settle any disputes involving the parties. "Judges" in these cases are typically retired judges, people who are well-trained in presiding over dispute resolution and who bring the reputation and prestige of their former positions to their current role.

The major advantage of the rent-a-judge option is that it is much faster than regular civil litigation. In addition, the proceedings are relatively private and do not become part of the public record. Many time-consuming trial procedures are eliminated in rent-a-judge trials, providing an additional savings of time and money.[16] These "trials" are significantly less formal and are generally conducted in conference rooms.

It is not uncommon for the parties in a civil case to wait four to five years before they can get their case to trial. These same parties can get their case to "trial" with a rent-a-judge in a matter of weeks. As a result, the use of rent-a-judge trials is growing more popular. Because all states accept some form of private resolution of cases, rent-a-judge resolutions are likely to become more common in the future. A number of companies now exist to assist clients in locating a rent-a-judge. One company, Judicate, even has its own private courthouse in Los Angeles. Some degree of protection is afforded by virtue of the fact that the decisions in many of these private resolutions can be appealed to the public court of appeals.[17]

SMALL CLAIMS COURT

Another technique to reduce legal expenses is for a party to file the legal dispute in small claims court. Although this is still litigation, it significantly reduces the costs. This option permits a party to effectively represent him- or herself. Generally, the opponent can also appear without a lawyer. Small claims courts do not utilize legalese and standard rules of evidence. Quick resolution of disputes is usually available. The procedures in small claims courts vary from state to state. The jurisdictional amounts also vary—the upper limit may range from $1,000 (Mississippi and parts of Virginia) to $10,000 (parts of Tennessee).[18]

Some small claims courts publish booklets to assist parties in small claims actions. There may also be government employees who provide free or low-cost legal

http:// RESOURCES FOR BUSINESS LAW STUDENTS

NAME	RESOURCES	WEB ADDRESS
American Arbitration Association (AAA)	The American Arbitration Association provides membership information, rules and procedures, education and research, publications, a directory of its members, and information on ADR law.	http://www.adr.org/
International Academy of Mediators	International Academy of Mediators provides membership information and a directory of members, as well as other information on mediation.	http://www.iamed.org/
Society of Professionals in Dispute Resolution (SPIDR)	Society of Professionals in Dispute Resolution (SPIDR) provides membership information, publications, and current events in ADR.	http://www.igc.apc.org/spidr/
Federal Arbitration Act—9 USC § 1	Legal Information Institute, maintained by the Cornell Law School, provides a hypertext and searchable version of 9 USC § 1, popularly known as the Federal Arbitration Act.	http://www.law.cornell.edu/uscode/9/ch1.html
International Chamber of Commerce—Dispute Resolution	The International Chamber of Commerce provides an index of international arbitration and alternative dispute resolution services, including information on the International Court of Arbitration.	http://www.iccwbo.org/arb/index.htm

services to parties who are filing complaints in small claims courts. Participants do not need to be familiar with legal jargon; however, participants need to be organized and to bring their witnesses and any physical evidence with them to the hearing. Participants should prepare a brief, coherent presentation of the case. It is also helpful to observe a couple of small claims cases in advance.

Before filing the complaint, consider whether the defendant is likely to be able to pay a judgment. Generally, a successful plaintiff will have to conduct the collection process him- or herself. This is usually accomplished by discovering the defendant's assets and obtaining permission (in a written legal document called a writ) from the court to levy on them. The plaintiff then takes the writ to the court in the locality where the assets are located; completes a form requesting execution; pays a fee; and asks a sheriff, marshall, or constable to collect the described assets.

If the defendant does not show up on the trial date, the court hears only the plaintiff's side. This is called a *default judgment.* If the plaintiff does not appear on the trial date, the case is dismissed.

SUMMARY

The time, trouble, and expense associated with trials have led to an increasing emphasis on alternate dispute resolution (ADR) methods. There are five major ADR methods outside the judicial system, and one ADR method that involves a specialized court within the judicial system.

Negotiation is probably the oldest and most common form of alternate dispute resolution. The parties discuss their dispute and reach a mutually agreeable solution to the problem. Negotiation is only restricted by the willingness of the parties to compromise.

Mediation is slightly more formal than negotiation. In mediation, the parties turn to a mediator, a third person who helps the parties to find a mutually acceptable solution. Mediators do not provide a solution; they provide a procedure for helping the parties reach a solution. The mediator facilitates communication rather than acting as a decision maker.

Arbitration involves a third party, the arbitrator, who listens to the arguments of each party and then renders an award to resolve the controversy. The arbitrator is a decision maker. Arbitration is commonly *binding,* meaning that the parties agree to abide by the decision rather than going from arbitration to judicial review in a trial *de novo.*

Minitrials involve a neutral chairing a presentation of the evidence before the senior executives of the companies. After this presentation, the senior executives meet and attempt to settle the dispute.

Rent-a-judge trials are a variation on arbitration, using a person in the role of "judge" rather than arbitrator to resolve a controversy. Rent-a-judges, often retired judges, preside over informal "trials" in private "courtrooms" to resolve disputes. Rent-a-judge "cases" occasionally involve a "jury" of hired experts, particularly in technical cases.

Small claims courts provide relatively informal resolution for small civil claims. The rules and the jurisdictional limits of these specialized courts vary widely among the states.

DISCUSSION QUESTIONS

1. What is meant by *ADR*? How might ADR be more advantageous to a business than going to trial? How might it be less advantageous?
2. What are the distinctions between arbitration and mediation? What are the similarities?
3. The Los Angeles County Bar Association sued in federal court to obtain more local judges, primarily due to a backlog of cases in the civil courts.[19] What are the primary causes of the backlog in civil courts? What could be done to alleviate this backlog?
4. Parties who submit their claims to resolution with a rent-a-judge are generally allowed to appeal the result of their "case" to the court of appeals. Will wealthy parties, who can afford to use rent-a-judge ADR, lose interest in reforming the legal system if they can use private judging and still appeal to public appellate courts? Is that a concern? Why or why not?
5. In 1996, a bill was proposed in the California Senate (S.B. 1428) to require credentialing of mediators. In your opinion, should mediators be subject to some type of licensing or credentialing? Why or why not? Should there be some sort of licensing or credentialing required for arbitrators and rent-a-judges?
6. Arbitration clauses in contracts may effectively preclude class action lawsuits against lenders concerning Truth-In-Lending claims. Is this beneficial or disadvantageous to society? Why?
7. What ethical perspective(s) are reflected in the model standards of conduct for mediators?
8. Small claims courts are specialized civil courts within the state court system. Why is small claims court more like ADR than it is like a regular civil court? How is small claims court more like a regular civil court than a category of ADR?
9. How is binding arbitration different from nonbinding arbitration? Which type of arbitration is preferable? Why?
10. What are the advantages and disadvantages of including the following clause in an agreement to arbitrate: "Upon the request of a party, the arbitrator's award shall include findings of fact and conclusions of law"?[20]

CASE PROBLEMS AND WRITING ASSIGNMENTS

1. X agrees to arbitrate any disputes he might have with Y. In addition, X makes the same type of agreement with A, B, and C. If A, B, C, and Y all have disputes with X that raise common issues of fact and law, can a federal court consolidate all four arbitration proceedings so that they will be heard at one time and place? [See *Seguro de Servidio* v. *McAuto*, 878 F.2d 5 (1st Cir. Puerto Rico 1989).]

2. Tri-City Construction Company entered into a contract with Kansas City, Kansas. The contract called for Tri-City to perform certain improvements to the city's sewer system. In carrying out its duties, Tri-City signed a sub-contract with Alliett and Williams. A dispute arose between the contractor and the subcontractor, and the dispute was submitted to arbitration under the Missouri Uniform Arbitration Act. However, the arbitration award was not honored, and the case was taken to court. Should the court enforce an arbitration award, or should the court hear the case as if there had been no arbitration? [See *State ex rel. Tri-City Construction Co.* v. *Marsh*, 668 S.W.2d 148 (Mo.App. 1984).]

3. Andy Messersmith, a professional baseball player with the Kansas City Royals, claimed that he had "played out his option" with the Royals after the 1975 season. According to Messersmith, he had satisfied all the terms of his contract; owed no further duties to the Royals; and was a free agent, legally allowed to sign a new contract with any team that was interested in signing him. The Kansas City Royals alleged that they had the right to renew Messersmith's contract on a year-to-year basis for a reasonable number of years and that Messersmith was not free to negotiate with another team unless the Royals released him. The controversy was taken to arbitration, and the arbitration panel ruled in Messersmith's favor. The Royals, and other major league baseball team owners, attempted to have this decision overturned in the federal courts. How should the court resolve this case? [See *Kansas City Royals Baseball Corp.* v. *Major League Baseball Players Ass'n*, 532 F.2d 615 (8th Cir. 1976).]

4. AMF and Brunswick, rivals in the bowling industry, resolved a lawsuit alleging false advertising in 1983. Part of the resolution was an agreement to submit any future disputes concerning advertisements that claimed data-based superiority of one company's bowling products over similar products of the other company to an advisory third party, the National Advertising Division of the Better Business Bureau. In 1985, Brunswick began to advertise the alleged superiority of its new lane surfaces over the lanes surfaced by AMF. AMF asked for data from the research that supposedly supported this claim, but Brunswick refused. AMF then asked that the data be turned over to the National Advertising Division of the Better Business Bureau, as called for in their resolution. Again Brunswick refused. AMF then filed suit, asking the court to compel Brunswick to turn over the data for nonbinding arbitration. How should the court handle this request? Why? [See *AMF, Inc.* v. *Brunswick Corp.*, 621 F.Supp. 456 (1985).]

5. A number of customers of Shearson/American Express filed suit against Shearson, alleging violations of the Securities and Exchange Act of 1934 and the Racketeer Influenced and Corrupt Organizations Act (RICO) in the handling of their accounts. Shearson filed a motion with the court to compel arbitration in this matter. Assuming that the claims *can* properly be submitted to arbitration, should the court grant the motion? Why might Shearson prefer to have the case resolved in arbitration rather than in court? [See *Shearson/American Express, Inc.* v. *McMahon*, 107 S.Ct. 2332 (1987).]

6. **BUSINESS APPLICATION QUESTION** Keating owned and operated a 7-Eleven franchise in California. The franchise agreement between Keating and Southland Corporation specified that any claims or controversies relating to the franchising agreement were to be settled by arbitration in accordance with the rules and procedures of the AAA. Following a dispute between Keating and Southland, Keating filed suit against Southland in the state court system, alleging breach of contract, fraud, and violation of the California Franchise Investment Act. Southland filed a motion seeking compulsory arbitration of all issues, as called for in the franchise agreement. The trial court agreed that the fraud and the breach of contract issues should be submitted to arbitration, but ruled that the California Franchise Investment Act portion of the complaint should be resolved at trial. Southland appealed, and the California Court of Appeals ruled that all the issues should be submitted to arbitration. Keating appealed, and the California Supreme Court reinstated the trial court's ruling. Southland then appealed to the U.S. Supreme Court. How should the U.S. Supreme Court decide this case? Explain your reasoning. Why would a businessperson such as Keating prefer to have this issue tried by a court rather than settled by an arbitrator? [See *Southland Corp.* v. *Keating*, 465 U.S. 1 (1984).]

7. **ETHICAL APPLICATION CASE** Interstate Johnson Lane Corporation (Interstate) hired Gilmer as manager of financial services in 1981. At the time of the

hiring, Gilmer signed a "registration agreement" that provided, among other things, that Gilmer agreed to submit any disputes arising between him and Interstate to arbitration. In 1987, Interstate fired Gilmer. At the time of the firing, Gilmer was 62 years old. Gilmer filed suit in the U.S. District Court, alleging that he had been fired due to his age, in violation of the Age Discrimination in Employment Act (ADEA). Interstate filed a motion asking the court to compel Gilmer to submit his claim to arbitration as specified in the registration agreement. Should the court grant the motion, compelling resolution of the controversy through arbitration, or should the court deny the motion, permitting Gilmer to pursue his remedies in a trial? Why? Why might the business prefer arbitration rather than a trial in a situation such as this? What ethical considerations are raised by such a preference? [See *Gilmer* v. *Interstate Johnson Lane Corp.*, 111 S.Ct. 1647 (1991)].

8. **IDES CASE** Producers of chemicals used for pesticides sued the Environmental Protection Agency challenging § 3(c)(1)(D) of the Federal Insecticide, Fungicide, and Rodenticide Act (FIFRA). That section allowed parties to submit disputes to binding arbitration. The producers alleged that the law violated Article III of the Constitution by removing judicial functions. The district court held that Congress acted unconstitutionally by assigning judicial powers to arbitrators. On appeal, should the Supreme Court affirm or reverse? Use the IDES principles in reaching your decision. [See *Thomas* v. *Union Carbide*, 473 U.S. 568 (1985).]

NOTES

1. Quoted in Teresa V. Carey, "Credentialing for Mediators—To Be or Not To Be?," *University of San Francisco Law Review* 30 (Spring 1996), p. 640.
2. Ibid., p. 641.
3. Richard C. Reuben, "Model Ethics Rules Limit Mediator Role: Despite Controversy, Standards Expected to Improve Respect for Profession," *ABA Journal* (January 1996), p. 25.
4. Ibid.
5. Arizona expressly authorizes arbitration agreements in *A.R.S.* §§ 12-1501 to 1518. The same is true of California (9 Cal. Civ. Proc. Code §§ 1280 et seq., at § 1295), Michigan (Mich. Stat. Ann. §§ 27A.5040–27A.5065), and the Federal Arbitration Act (9 *U.S.C.* §§ 1 et. seq., at § 2).
6. "When You Need A Lawyer," *Consumer Reports* (February 1996), p. 39.
7. Curtis D. Brown, Esq., "New Law Lets Creditors Cut Court Costs," *Credit World* (July/August 1996), pp. 30–31.
8. Ibid.
9. Information on the current status of adoptions of Uniform State Laws provided by Katie Robinson, NCCUSL, in a telephone conversation on 24 February 1997.
10. American Arbitration Association, *Drafting Dispute Resolution Clauses—A Practical Guide* (June 1994), p. 37.
11. Ibid.
12. American Arbitration Association, *Resolving Your Disputes* (November 1995), p. 3.
13. American Arbitration Association, *Why Labor and Management Use the Services of the American Arbitration Association* (November 1993).
14. American Arbitration Association, *Drafting Dispute Resolution Clauses—A Practical Guide* (June 1994), p. 30.
15. Jane Birnbaum with Morton D. Sosland, "Coming to Terms—Without Bringing in the Lawyers," *Business Week* (13 April 1992), p. 63.
16. Deborah Shannon, "Rent-A-Judge," *American Way Magazine* (February 1991), pp. 33–36.
17. Ibid., at p. 34.
18. "Do-It-Yourself Justice—Small Claims Court," *Consumer Reports* (February 1996), p. 36.
19. Deborah Shannon, "Rent-A-Judge," *American Way Magazine* (February 1991), at p. 33.
20. American Arbitration Association, *Drafting Dispute Resolution Clauses—A Practical Guide* (June 1994), p. 30.

A G E N D A

CIT has recently been victimized by a series of minor crimes, including theft from its warehouses. This has led the family to a general discussion of crimes, and especially of victim's rights when crimes are committed. Throughout this chapter, we consider what CIT and other businesses can do to deter crime and to reduce the likelihood of becoming victims of criminal conduct.

Tom and Anna recognize that Call-Image may be used for purposes other than those they intend. For instance, another business may broadcast deceptive or false advertising or pornography through Call-Image units. What preventative measures should CIT take to avoid involvement in these illegal activities? In general, is CIT liable for criminal activity perpetrated by its employees on company time or on company property? For example, must CIT pay traffic tickets issued to its employees while driving company vehicles? What if its employees make unauthorized copies of computer software? Who will be criminally responsible in these situations—the employee, CIT, or both? Try to distinguish criminal law and civil law throughout this chapter.

These and other questions need to be addressed in this chapter. Be prepared! You never know when one of the Kochanowskis will need your advice.

Crimes and Business

O U T L I N E

WHY STUDY CRIMINAL LAW?

Why should a business law textbook contain a chapter on criminal law? The reason is that businesses are constantly confronted with the *effects* of crimes such as embezzlement, forgery, and fraud, to name only a few kinds of crimes we discuss in this chapter. In addition, there are a number of crimes with which a business can be charged. Therefore, to prevent a crime from happening, or to deal effectively with a crime once it has occurred, you need to know what the crime is and what the legal ramifications are for that crime.

The criminal law developed through a long history of precedents. However, most states have codified their criminal laws. As you should expect, the exact rules vary from state to state. Begin by referring to Exhibit 8.1, which summarizes the primary distinctions between civil law and criminal law. Try to distinguish between the two areas throughout this chapter. Remember that one action or series of actions may constitute both a civil wrong and a criminal wrong. It will also be helpful to look at Exhibit 8.2, which examines the six steps in a typical criminal proceeding.

OBJECTIVES OF CRIMINAL LAW

The objectives of criminal law are the protection of persons and property, the deterrence of criminal behavior, the punishment of criminal activity, and the rehabilitation of the criminal.

EXHIBIT 8.1 Distinctions Between Civil Law and Criminal Law

Question	Civil Law	Criminal Law
What type of action leads to the lawsuit or case?	Action against a private individual	Action against society
Who initiates the action?	Plaintiff	Government
Who is their attorney?	Private attorney	District Attorney (DA) or the U.S. Attorney General
What is the burden of proof in the case?	Preponderance of the evidence	Beyond a reasonable doubt
Who generally has the burden of proof?	Plaintiff	Government
Is there a jury trial?	Yes, except in actions in equity	Yes, except in cases involving certain misdemeanors
What jury vote is necessary to win the case?	Specific jury vote required by the jurisdiction or agreement. Often a simple majority or two-thirds vote	Unanimous jury vote needed for the government to win a conviction
What type(s) of punishment is imposed?	Monetary damages or equitable remedies	Capital punishment, prison, fines, and/or probation

EXHIBIT 8.2 The Six Steps in a Typical Criminal Proceeding

1. **Preliminary Hearing or a Grand Jury Hearing**
   A preliminary hearing is generally a public hearing where a magistrate considers the evidence against the accused and determines if there is probable cause to hold a criminal trial. The prosecutor need not present all the government's evidence at the preliminary hearing, just sufficient evidence to have the case go to trial. A grand jury, on the other hand, hears the evidence in secret: generally the witnesses appear before the grand jury one at a time. The district attorney appears before the grand jury and may lead the questioning of the witnesses. The grand jury determines if a crime has been committed and, if so, which individuals were involved in the crime. If a grand jury issues an indictment against an individual, there will be a trial.
2. **Arraignment**
   The suspect is informed of the criminal charges and asked how he or she pleads. Generally, the amount of bail is set at this stage.
3. **Discovery**
   Both sides have to gather facts and information to prepare for trial. Discovery can involve examining documents, records, and other pieces of physical evidence as well as taking the depositions (statements) of witnesses or the parties themselves. Discovery is more limited in criminal cases. One of the concerns is that if the defendant knows who will testify for the government, the defendant, defendant's relatives, and friends may intimidate the witnesses. Some discovery actually occurs at the preliminary hearing and arraignment.
4. **Pretrial Motions**
   If the parties need the court to make procedural decisions or other rulings as the case moves along toward trial, they do so by filing the appropriate motions with the court. In criminal cases, this may include a motion to suppress evidence that was illegally obtained by the police.
5. **Trial**
   The court hears the evidence offered by both sides and decides issues of both fact and law during this process.
6. **Sentencing**
   If the defendant is found guilty beyond a reasonable doubt, the defendant will be sentenced to jail, probation, parole, and/or a fine.

Protection of Persons and Property

Someone once said that a lock was designed to keep an honest person honest. It is for the same reason that the government declares certain conduct to be illegal. The government believes that all persons and their property should be protected from harm. In Chapter 5, however, you learned that tort law also protects persons and property. What is the difference? The primary difference between tort law and criminal law is that tort law results in money damages, whereas criminal law may result in loss of freedom by sending a person to jail or prison. Private interests are served through the awarding of damages. The public interest, on the other hand, is served by punishing criminal activity. If all persons respected everyone else's person or property, there would be very little reason for criminal law.

Deterrence of Criminal Behavior

Deterrent
A danger, difficulty, or other consideration that stops or prevents a person from acting.

One method to reduce criminal behavior is to present a sufficient **deterrent** to antisocial behavior. The presumption inherent in criminal law is that if we make the punishment sufficiently harsh, people and businesses who consider criminal behavior will avoid it because they fear punishment. If people fear the punishment, they will not commit a criminal act. If sufficient people fear the punishment, there will be a reduction in that crime. The severity of the punishment is often an issue with corporate defendants. What constitutes a substantial penalty for an individual would be a minimal penalty for a corporation such as General Motors or Merrill Lynch, Pierce, Fenner & Smith, Inc.

Criminologists have noted that severity alone is not a sufficient deterrent. Individuals considering criminal behavior must also believe that they are likely to be identified and punished. If criminals believe that they will not be identified and tried or that they will be found not guilty in court, the deterrent effect will be reduced.

In our society, the Constitution states that there shall be no cruel and unusual punishment. If our laws allowed the death penalty for even minor offenses, there would probably be fewer minor offenses. But is that just? To many people the loss of one's life for stealing a loaf of bread seems too high a price to pay for fewer loaves of bread being stolen. Similarly, many feel that caning a teenager for vandalism or graffiti or castrating a rapist is too extreme. The problem, therefore, is to decide how much punishment will deter criminal behavior without being excessive.

Punishment of Criminal Activity

Since we most likely cannot deter all criminal activity, our legal system accepts that a certain level of criminal activity will exist in society. Accordingly, we punish criminal activity for punishment's sake. There is no such thing as a free lunch: If a criminal takes something without paying for it, the criminal law makes that individual pay for it through deprivation of freedom for a period of time.

Rehabilitation of the Criminal

Our criminal justice system does not *end* with imprisonment, probation, or a fine. Our government has designed various programs to educate and train criminals in legitimate occupations during the period of incarceration. Theoretically, then, criminals should have no reason to return to a life of crime. Sometimes a sentence is suspended; that is, it is not put into effect. In such cases, the court supervises the individuals' activities to ensure that they have learned from their mistakes.

8.1

PROTECTING AGAINST CRIME

The Kochanowskis have become somewhat concerned about crimes in their community, and how those crimes may affect the business. They have read that the crime rate is rising in their community and across the country, and that crimes against business cause special hardships to family-owned operations. They are also worried because one of the students at Lindsay's high school was killed in a "random shooting" last weekend. The Kochanowskis wonder what they can do to protect their family and the business without violating legal rules. They ask you for advice. What will you suggest to them?

BUSINESS CONSIDERATIONS Suppose that a business decided to take aggressive steps to try to reduce crime in its community, especially crimes that affect the business enterprise. Would this be viewed favorably or unfavorably in the community? Why? From a business perspective, is public perception an important factor in making this decision? Why?

ETHICAL CONSIDERATIONS If a business *did* decide to take aggressive steps to try to reduce crime in its community, its conduct would have to be practical as well as legal. Is this feasible? Would such a decision be ethical? What ethical considerations should constrain the firm's decision?

MANAGEMENT

BASES OF CRIMINAL RESPONSIBILITIES

Generally, an individual is presumed innocent until proven guilty. The government has the burden of proving that the suspect is guilty beyond a reasonable doubt. The government must prove all the parts of the crime.

All crimes consist of two primary elements: a criminal *act* and a corresponding *mental state.* If only one element is present, no crime exists. For example, if you decide to embezzle from your employer and then take no steps to implement your decision, you have not committed a crime. Similarly, if a cigarette you are smoking in a motel ignites the draperies in your room and causes the motel to burn down, you have not committed a crime. In the latter case, you may be liable for negligence, but you have not committed the crime of arson.

The Act

The law generally imposes criminal liability only when an individual acts in a manner that is prohibited by law. Ordinarily, the prohibited act must be voluntarily committed by the person before criminal liability will attach. This means that a person who is forced to act illegally against his or her will does not act voluntarily, and may not be legally responsible for the act. However, the court *may* decide that the threat used to force the conduct was not sufficient to remove the free will of the actor, and will still impose liability. Also, some situations may require an individual to act (or react) to the circumstances. In these situations, a failure to act may be deemed a criminal "action" sufficient to justify prosecution by the government. This responsibility to act may be imposed by a statute or by judicial precedent.

Mental State

To be held criminally responsible for an illegal act, the actor must intend to do the act. Historically, various terms were used to describe this mental state: *consciously, intentionally, maliciously, unlawfully,* and *willfully.* Today our approach to the problem is more systematic. This current approach involves the use of one of five terms, depending on the specific requirements of the statute, and indicates more specifically the *degree* of intent than the older terms. The terms used are as follows:

1. *Purpose*—An actor acts with purpose if it is his or her conscious objective to perform the prohibited act.
2. *Knowledge*—An actor acts with knowledge if he or she is aware of what he or she is doing.
3. *Recklessness*—An actor acts with recklessness if he or she disregards a substantial and unjustifiable risk that criminal harm or injury may result from his or her action.
4. *Negligence*—An actor acts in a criminally negligent manner if he or she should have known that a substantial and unreasonable risk of harm would result from his or her action.
5. *Strict liability*—An actor will be held strictly liable if he or she acts in a manner that our law declares criminal even if none of the above four elements is present. This theory is used primarily for crimes that have a light punishment—for example, violating public health laws with respect to the sale of food. This theory is also used in statutory rape cases simply because our society has a vested interest in protecting our youth.

The parties in the following case argued about the type of intent that was required.

8.1 U.S. v. BARBER

39 F.3d 285 (10th Cir. 1994)

FACTS James Barber is an attorney charged with forgery. Barber accepted a $5,000 **retainer** to represent George Caine in a lawsuit Caine had already begun with another attorney. The lawsuit was dismissed for Barber's failure to prosecute (failure to continue forward with the matter). However, Barber lied to his client and stated that the matter was proceeding forward slowly. Eventually, Barber told Caine the dispute had been dismissed and sent Caine documents showing that the matter was dismissed in 1991. These documents included the forged signature. Caine called the judge's chambers to find out about appeals. He was told that the lawsuit had been dismissed three years earlier and that it was too late to file an appeal. Caine described his documents and the clerk asked Caine to fax the documents to the court and then the forgery was discovered. The jury concluded that Barber forged the signature of a judge in violation of the statute.

ISSUE Is there sufficient evidence to convict Barber of forgery?

HOLDING Yes.

REASONING The crime of forging a judge's signature does not require proof of intent to obtain financial gain. Section 505 of 18 **U.S.C.** defines the crime to "forge the signature of any judge . . . for the purpose of authenticating any proceeding or document . . . knowing such signature . . . to be false or counterfeit." The instruction given to the jury adequately described this crime of forgery. There is sufficient evidence for the jury to conclude that Barber intended to defraud his client by providing the false documents containing the judge's signature. [*Black's Law Dictionary* states "*Intent to defraud* means an intention to deceive another person, and to induce such other person, in reliance upon such deception, to assume, create, transfer, alter or terminate a right, obligation or power with reference to property."][1] Barber failed to show that financial gain was required under the statute defining forgery.

BUSINESS CONSIDERATIONS What can businesses or other organizations do to help prevent forgeries on checks and other documents? Should businesses adopt a policy for dealing with this problem, or should they address each problem individually as it arises?

ETHICAL CONSIDERATIONS Is forging a signature ever an ethical act? What might the forger do in order to attain his or her objective without resorting to forgery?

SERIOUSNESS OF THE OFFENSE

Criminal law classifies all offenses into three categories according to their level of seriousness. These categories are, from least to most serious, misdemeanors, felonies, and treason. Some states have an additional category called infractions or violations.

Retainer
Advance payment made to an attorney.

U.S.C.
Abbreviation for the United States Code (statutes).

Infractions or Violations

Some states have a separate category for petty offenses called *infractions* or *violations*. They are generally punishable only by fines. Some examples include illegal gaming and disturbing the peace.

Misdemeanors

Misdemeanors are minor offenses that are punishable by confinement of up to one year in a city or county jail, a small fine, or both. Public intoxication, speeding, and vandalism are examples of the types of conduct that are likely to be classified as misdemeanors.

8.2

CAN A BUSINESS COMMIT A CRIME?

The Kochanowskis have a large barn on their property. This barn has been vacant for quite some time, and Dan thinks that, with minor renovations, it would make an excellent warehouse from which to ship Call-Image videophones. Anna points out that the property is not zoned for commercial activities, and that such use might be criminal without the proper zoning. Dan counters that it cannot be criminal because CIT cannot *intend* to commit a crime (since businesses are inanimate creatures, they cannot have *any* intent), and criminal intent is an essential element in any criminal conviction. Anna doubts that this analysis is accurate, but she seeks your advice to be sure. What advice will you give her?

BUSINESS CONSIDERATIONS What can a business do to reduce the likelihood that it will commit a crime? Are there certain structures that reduce or increase the likelihood that a business or its agents will commit crimes?

ETHICAL CONSIDERATIONS Is it ethical for a business to knowingly violate a law, such as a zoning law? Would it be ethical for a business to engage in an act that would be criminal for an individual but that is not criminal for a business entity?

MANAGEMENT

Felonies

Felonies are major offenses punishable by confinement from one year to life in a state or federal prison, a large fine, or both. In some states special capital felony statutes provide for the sentence of death. Murder, arson, rape, burglary, and grand theft are examples of crimes that are normally classified as felonies.

Treason

Treason is the most serious offense against the government. It consists of waging war against the government or of giving aid and comfort to our enemies in time of war.

Crimes versus Torts

It is important to remember that one act can be the legal basis for both a criminal lawsuit and a civil lawsuit. The two separate suits will not be barred by the doctrine of *res judicata,* nor by the rule against double jeopardy. In many situations, a *criminal act* (an act against the rules of society) will also involve an infringement on the social rights and expectations of an individual. If one act is both a crime and a tort, it may be prosecuted by the criminal system and the harmed individual may be able to seek remedies in the civil system.

Selected Crimes

We are unable to list all of the common crimes in this text. We will, however, mention selected crimes that have applications for either detection or prevention in the marketplace. In many situations, it is the business that is the victim, not the perpetrator, of the crime. It is possible for a business to be the perpetrator of a crime, and there are a number of criminal statutes aimed primarily at business activities. Some of the federal statutes directed at business activities are discussed in other chapters of the text. In this chapter, we will discuss the federal Counterfeit Access Device and Computer Fraud and Abuse Act of 1984; Racketeer Influenced and Corrupt Organization Act (RICO); and the Currency and Foreign Transactions Reporting Act, among others.

Murder/Manslaughter

Homicide is the killing of one human being by another. It is not necessarily a criminal act. It will *not* be a criminal act if the killing was lawful; for example, if it was in self-defense. *Murder,* however, is the willful, unlawful killing of a human being by another with *malice aforethought* (deliberate purpose or design). *Manslaughter* occurs when the killing is unlawful, but without malice. Manslaughter is usually divided into two categories—voluntary (upon a sudden heat of passion) or involuntary (in the commission of an unlawful act or in the commission of a lawful act without due caution). It is common for the state to charge a defendant with both murder and manslaughter and to let the decider of fact determine which crime was actually committed.

Arson

Arson is the intentional or willful burning of property by fire or explosion. Originally, this crime was restricted to the burning of a house. Today, in most states, the crime has been expanded to include the burning of all types of real property and many types of personal property.

Burglary

Burglary is the breaking and entering of a structure with the intent to commit a felony. Originally, this crime was restricted to the breaking and entering of a house at night, but, like arson, it has been expanded to include more activities.

Embezzlement

Embezzlement is the taking of money or other property by an employee who has been entrusted with the money or property by his or her employer.

Forgery

Forgery is the making or altering of a negotiable instrument or credit card invoice in order to create or to shift legal liability for the instrument. It generally consists of signing another person's name to a check, promissory note, or credit card invoice or altering an amount on any of those documents. To win any such case, the government must generally prove that the accused acted with the intent to **defraud**.

Defraud

To deprive a person of property or of any interest, estate, or right by fraud, deceit, or artifice.

Credit Card and Check Legislation

Today customers make extensive use of credit cards and checks. This creates a number of difficulties, particularly for retailers and mail order companies. For instance, criminals may steal an individual's credit card or credit card number and use it to make substantial purchases. Credit card numbers may be obtained by accessing computer files where an owner has charged a purchase to his or her credit card. Carbon copies of credit slips are also used to obtain numbers. Some states have enacted separate legislation making it a crime to misuse someone else's credit card without permission. Other states treat this as a type of forgery.

Criminals may steal the checks of an individual or business and forge the signature on the checks. In addition, the owner of a bank account may write checks when there are insufficient funds in the account. Most states have enacted statutes that make it a crime to write or transfer (make, draw, or deliver) a check when there are insufficient funds in the account. These are commonly called *bad check statutes.* Some states require the *mens rea* that the suspect intended to defraud the recipient of the check.

FROM THE DESK OF
AMY CHEN, ATTORNEY AT LAW
Protect Your Checks
Establish safety procedures to protect your business's checks and signature stamps. If checks are printed by computer, prevent unauthorized access to the computer program, computer, and printer, as well. Occasionally, people steal payroll checks, complete them, and pass them on to stores and banks. This creates a risk for your business, which may also incur civil liability, if you do not take reasonable precautions. You should also initiate procedures to protect credit cards.

Criminal Fraud

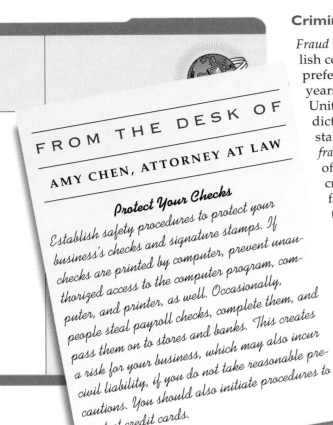

Fraud is a broad term that covers many specific situations. The English courts were very reluctant to criminalize fraudulent behavior, preferring to allow tort law to handle most situations. Over the years, however, legislation was passed in both England and the United States to overcome the historic view of "[we] are not to indict one for making a fool of another."[2] Today most states have statutes that cover variations of what is generally called *criminal fraud, false pretense,* or *theft by deception.* Most states require proof of the following elements in order to find a person guilty of criminal fraud: the speaker (or writer) made a false statement of fact; the statement was material, i.e., the statement would affect the listener's decision; the listener relied on the statement; and the speaker intended to mislead the listener. Note that the fraudulent party can be either the buyer or the seller. For example, suppose that a savings and loan creates the impression that certain real estate assets are worth $100,000 through the distribution of false appraisals in order to induce a person to invest in those assets. In fact, the assets are worth substantially less than the false appraisals show. The savings and loan and its officers could be found guilty of criminal fraud if an investor becomes a partner in those assets with the savings and loan.

Larceny

Larceny is the wrongful taking and carrying away of the personal property of another without the owner's consent and with the intent to permanently deprive the owner of the property. The most common forms of larceny are shoplifting and pickpocketing. The use of force is not needed. Larceny is a serious problem for retail businesses. Merchandise is often lost through shoplifting. If customers feel unsafe due to pickpocketing, they will avoid certain stores and shopping centers.

Robbery

Robbery is a form of aggravated theft. It is basically larceny plus the threat to use violence or force. To be classified as a robbery, the robber must use either violence or the threat of injury sufficient to place the victim in fear, and the robber then takes and carries away something either in the possession or the immediate presence of the victim. If the same property had been carried away without the use of violence or a threat of injury, the act would be a mere theft.

Computer Crime

Virus

A computer program that destroys, damages, rearranges, or replaces computer data.

"The only secure computer is one that's turned off, locked in a safe, and buried 20 feet down in a secret location—and I'm not completely confident of that one either" (quote from Bruce Schneier, author of a book entitled *E-mail Security*).[3] The legal aspects of computers will be discussed in detail in Chapter 47. However, advances in computer technology have led to the development of new activities, some positive and some negative. Some of these negative behaviors are now recognized as crimes.

With our increased dependence on computers, computer criminals can create extensive damage. According to a recent article on computer safety, "The going estimates for financial losses from computer crime reach as high as $10 billion a year. But the truth is that nobody really knows. Almost all attacks go undetected—as many as 95% says the FBI. . . ."[4] In addition to civil liability for improper use, many states now recognize the following activities as crimes:

1. *Unauthorized use of computers or computer-related equipment.* This may include the use of business computers for personal projects, including homework and personal e-mail. It also includes transferring software purchased by a business to a personal computer.
2. *Destruction of a computer or its records.* Computer viruses destroy or alter records, data, and programs. Annually there are numerous **virus** alerts—some are fakes and some are legitimate. Businesses expend significant resources to protect themselves from viruses and to correct the damage they cause. This includes a virus that "infects" the computers in a college computer lab and subsequently infects students' disks and home computers.
3. *Alteration of legitimate records.* This would include altering a student's grade record in the registrar's office.
4. *Accessing computer records to transfer funds, stocks, or other property.* This would include entering a bank's computer system and transferring funds without authorization. For example, in 1994 Citibank discovered that Russian **hackers** made $10 million in illegal transfers. Initially the bank called in a private security firm. When Citibank finally spoke to the FBI and the media, it lost some of its top customers. Competitors lured them away by promising them that the competitors' computer systems were more secure than those of Citibank.[5]

8.3

SALES/MANAGEMENT

PROTECTING AGAINST CHANGES IN TECHNOLOGY

CIT is involved in a business in which technology rapidly changes. Dan noticed an article in a trade journal that Virtual Images, an independent company, has developed the technology to send prerecorded video and audio messages on interactive videophones like those produced by CIT and its competitors. This would effectively enable businesses and individuals to play VCR tapes to people at remote locations. As such, it may be used to play advertisements on the phone lines, to show clients a product, and even to demonstrate its use.

This ability does not disturb CIT. However, the device may be used to defraud people by showing them products that do not exist or features that do not appear on the actual product. For example, people who are selling resort properties can show a false picture and entice someone to invest in the resort. Dan has even heard of companies that plan to send pornographic videos to their clients by way of this device. Dan has asked you what CIT should do about these potential uses of its product line, and also what preventative measures CIT should take to avoid involvement in fraud. What will you tell him?

BUSINESS CONSIDERATIONS Businesses are not restricted to any "moral minimum." Should a business take a proactive stand in a situation where it fears that its product might be used for an unethical or illegal purpose? (Remember that the law, including criminal law, often lags behind technological developments.)

ETHICAL CONSIDERATIONS Does a business have any moral responsibility for the manner in which its products are used? Suppose that a business has the opportunity to make a new product that will be very profitable, but that is likely to be used in an unethical manner by a number of its customers. From an ethical perspective, what should the firm do?

Congress enacted the Counterfeit Access Device and Computer Fraud and Abuse Act of 1984 to strengthen state attempts to deal with computer crime. The act criminalized the unauthorized, knowing use or access of computers in the following ways:

Hacker
An outsider who gains unauthorized access to a computer or computer network.

1. To obtain classified military or foreign policy information with the intent to injure the United States or to benefit a foreign country. This would include accessing classified Pentagon files. This constitutes a felony under the act.

2. To collect financial or credit information, which is protected under federal privacy law. This would include accessing credit card accounts to obtain credit card numbers and credit limits.
3. To use, modify, destroy, or disclose computer data and to prevent authorized individuals from using the data. This would include intentionally transferring a virus to a computer.
4. To alter or modify data in financial computers that causes a loss of $1,000 or more. (This would include the unlawful transfer of funds from Citibank.)
5. To modify data that impairs an individual's medical treatment.
6. To transfer computer data, including passwords, which could assist individuals in gaining unauthorized access that either affects interstate commerce or allows access to a government computer. This would include the use of a "sniffer" program, which can hide in a computer network and record passwords, and then transferring this information to others.

The first category constitutes a felony and the remaining five categories constitute misdemeanors.

In 1996, additional federal legislation was enacted to assist in prosecuting hackers. It provides for criminal forfeiture, fines of up to $10 million, and sentences of up to 15 years in cases involving stealing trade secrets. Stealing trade secrets is also called economic spying or espionage. The "victim" however must have taken reasonable safety precautions to protect its trade secrets.[6] FBI director Louis Freeh told a Senate panel that 23 countries are engaged in economic spying against U.S. businesses.[7] Companies like the Gap, Hitachi America, PeopleSoft, Playboy Enterprises, and Twentieth Century Fox each attract from 1 to 30 hacker attempts per day.[8]

Computer users may engage in some of these new crimes. In addition, computer technology has enabled some individuals to commit more traditional crimes. For example, Mark Johnson is being investigated for a number of computer-linked activities—computer fraud, computer "stalking" under the computer nickname "Vito," harassing and threatening computer users on-line, transporting a minor for sexual purposes, and sexual molestation.[9]

Corporate Liability for Crimes

Originally courts held that a corporation was not answerable for crimes because the corporation was not authorized to commit crimes and, therefore, lacked the power to commit them. However, there is a growing trend in many states to hold corporations criminally responsible when their officers and agents commit criminal actions in the execution of their office. Corporate directors, officers, and employees are also *personally* liable for crimes they commit while acting for the corporation. This trend is evidenced by court decisions and statutory law and the Model Penal Code.[10] Another specific example is the California Corporate Criminal Liability Act, which enlarged the criminal liability of corporate managers.[11]

Mala prohibita
Wrong because it is prohibited.

Corporate liability is more common when the corporation is accused of violating a statute that is ***mala prohibita***. However, when the criminal act is one requiring a specific mental state, such as battery with intent to kill, the courts generally refuse to hold the corporation liable unless the corporation itself participated in the acts or a high-ranking official participated in the acts with the intent to benefit the corporation.

Corporate liability is sometimes limited to *white-collar crime*. Although this term does not have a precise meaning, it generally means crimes committed in a commercial context by professionals and managers. The officers and agents are generally tried separately and convicted for their behavior. When liability *is* imposed against the corporation, punishment is usually in the form of a fine.

There is an active debate over whether, as a matter of policy, corporations *should* be held criminally liable. The following arguments are generally advanced in support of corporate criminal liability:

1. Financial sanctions against the corporation will reduce dividends for the shareholders. The shareholders will then take a more active role to ensure that the corporation will behave legally; express concern to management when acts or policies appear to be unethical or illegal; and elect directors who will carefully monitor corporate behavior.
2. The shareholders are the ones who benefit when the corporation commits crimes. They receive higher dividends when the crime increases revenue or lowers the cost of doing business. If the corporation does not pay the fine, the shareholders benefit from the criminal activity. For example, past violation of criminal statutes controlling the disposal of hazardous wastes may have benefitted the company and the stockholders by reducing expenses and increasing profits.
3. There are a large number of potential individual suspects in a corporation. Governments lack the resources to build cases against specific individuals; it is less expensive and time consuming to build a case against the corporation as a whole.
4. Many corporate decisions are committee decisions or are decisions that are approved at a number of managerial levels. The responsibility for making decisions and implementing them is often divided between individuals or divisions. In these cases it is difficult to identify the culpable individuals, so the entire corporation should be held responsible for the decision.
5. When individual wrongdoers can be identified, it is unfair to single them out for punishment. Their actions are probably consistent with the general pattern of conduct throughout the corporation.
6. Corporations are not really harmed by the loss of an individual manager. The manager can take the blame and act as a scapegoat; and the corporation can continue to thrive. The corporation benefits from the illegal act and does not suffer the costs of the crime. The public may forgive the corporation for the crime if an individual wrongdoer is identified and punished.
7. When the sanction is based on a crime of omission (i.e., failure to act), the failure often occurs because the duty to perform was not clearly delegated to any specific person or office. If no specific person is held liable and the corporation is not held liable, there is no incentive to comply with the law.
8. When the government takes action against the corporation, the public then identifies the crime with the corporation. Disclosure of full information about businesses is essential in market-oriented societies. Consumers can then make informed decisions about which firms they want to transact business with. [See for example, Mark Whitacre as told to Ronald Henkoff, "My Life as a Corporate Mole for the FBI," *Fortune* (4 September 1995), pp. 52–62, about Archer Daniels Midland's alleged price fixing.]

The following arguments are advanced by those opposed to corporate criminal liability:

1. Imposing fines against corporations are a waste of time and effort because the fines are not substantial and do not act as a deterrent. The firm will respond by increasing prices and passing the costs on to consumers. In reality, consumers would be punished and not the corporation.
2. Fines themselves are paid from profits and, therefore, reduce shareholders' dividends. It is unjust to pass the costs on to the shareholders because they lack the power to control corporate decision making in most corporations.
3. Commonly, criminal prosecutions of corporations are not well publicized. Consequently, they do not harm the corporation's public image. Corporations will use their public relations expertise to overcome any negative publicity.

Currency transaction report (CTR)
A report businesses must file if a customer brings $10,000 or more in cash to the business.

In the following case, the corporation was charged with criminal conduct.

8.2 U.S. v. LBS BANK—NEW YORK, INC. 757 F.Supp. 496 (E.D.Pa. 1990)

FACTS A jury convicted LBS Bank—New York, Inc. (LBS) of conspiring to defraud the United States by filing false and fraudulent **currency transaction reports (CTRs)** and/or failing to file reports of apparent crimes. On appeal, LBS argued that the jury should have acquitted it because insufficient evidence had existed to establish that a single agent of LBS had had the specific intent to defraud the government, as required for conviction under 18 U.S.C. § 371. It argued that Vinko Mir, the bank's chairman, was the only agent of LBS about whom the government had presented any evidence of specific criminal intent that could have been imputed to the bank and that the government could not rely on this evidence to sustain LBS's conviction because the jury, in acquitting Mir, had found that Mir had not possessed this requisite intent.

ISSUE Could the government successfully prosecute a bank for conspiracy to defraud the United States in circumstances in which the jury had acquitted the bank's chairman of the same charge?

HOLDING Yes.

REASONING A court could use evidence of the officer's conduct to sustain a verdict against the corporate defendant, despite the fact that the jury had acquitted the officer. In determining whether sufficient evidence supports the jury verdict, the court must decide whether the verdict can be sustained on evidence of Mir's specific intent or whether the evidence necessarily must be disregarded owing to Mir's acquittal. LBS claimed that evidence of Mir's intent cannot be used to sustain the verdict against the bank; that is, the guilt of a corporate defendant cannot be based on the acts of an agent acquitted by the jury of the same charge. The bank's position, however, runs contrary to the rulings of the vast majority of the courts of appeals. More important, it is contrary to the rulings of the Supreme Court in several recent cases in which the Court held that the acquittal does not necessarily indicate that the jury had found insufficient evidence on that count; rather, the acquittal simply could be a result of juror's mercy. The Supreme Court has instructed, therefore, that an acquittal should not mandate a reversal of a finding of guilt on another count that is dependent on the same factual finding.

Under this rationale, a court, in attempting to determine whether sufficient evidence supports the conviction of a corporate defendant, remains free to consider all the evidence presented at trial, including evidence that concerns the acts of corporate agents whom the jury had acquitted. For this reason, the court concluded that evidence of Mir's conduct could be used to sustain a verdict against LBS, despite the fact that Mir himself was acquitted. A review of the evidence presented at trial relating to Mir's activities revealed that there was sufficient evidence relating to Mir on which the jury reasonably could have convicted LBS. There was also sufficient evidence presented from which a jury could reasonably conclude that Mir had known that the bank had filed false CTRs. The government additionally presented sufficient evidence from which a jury could conclude that Mir had known that two different individuals had attempted to defraud the United States through the filing of false CTR forms and that Mir had intended to help achieve at least one of their objectives.

BUSINESS CONSIDERATIONS Is it in a business's best interest to comply with government reporting re-

8.2 U.S. v. LBS BANK—NEW YORK, INC. *(cont.)* 757 F.Supp. 496 (E.D.Pa. 1990)

quirements? What steps should a business take to encourage compliance by its employees and agents?

ETHICAL CONSIDERATIONS What moral responsibility does a business have to comply with government-reporting and information-collecting activities? What should a business do if complying with government reporting requirements would involve revealing confidential information about stakeholders who desire to maintain the confidentiality of that information?

RICO: Racketeer Influenced and Corrupt Organizations Act

The RICO statute[12] became law in 1970. It was included as part of the Organized Crime Control Act. According to the law's legislative history, it was the intent of Congress to remedy a serious problem: the infiltration of criminals into legitimate businesses as both a "cover" for their criminal activity and as a means of "laundering" profits derived from their crimes. RICO makes it a federal crime to obtain or maintain an interest in, use income from, or conduct or participate in the affairs of an enterprise through a pattern of racketeering activity.

Use of the statute in commercial enterprises soon became apparent to criminal prosecutors and plaintiffs' attorneys. Plaintiffs' attorneys are involved because the statute permits individuals whose business or property is injured by a violation of the statute to file a civil action. Successful plaintiffs in a civil action may recover treble damages, attorney's fees, and reasonable court costs. This is an example of the overlap between criminal and civil law systems. A prior conviction in a criminal suit is not required in order to file a civil RICO suit. Some observers contend that this is leading to unfounded lawsuits and out-of-court settlements by intimidated firms. The government can also file civil RICO actions. When the federal government proceeds with a civil suit, the burden of proof is reduced. High civil penalties can provide a lucrative law enforcement technique.

Since 1970, Congress has amended the law, which is incorporated in 18 U.S.C. §§ 1961–1968, and the courts have interpreted a number of its sections. The definitions of terms used in the statute are found in § 1961. Section 1962 lists the activities that are prohibited. Persons employed or associated with any enterprise are prohibited from engaging in a pattern of racketeering activity. A *pattern* constitutes committing at least two racketeering acts in a 10-year period. These racketeering acts are called *predicate acts* under RICO. Racketeering activity has been broadly defined and includes most criminal actions, such as bribery, antitrust violations, securities violations, fraud, acts of violence, and providing illegal goods or services. Michael Milken was convicted under RICO of scheming to manipulate stock prices and of defrauding customers. Racketeering acts also include acts relating to the Currency and Foreign Transactions Reporting Act, which is an act passed to prevent money-laundering and requires the filing of CTRs. RICO violations are added to other criminal charges when there is a pattern of corrupt behavior, such as bribery.

Criminal and civil penalties are described in U.S.C. § 1963, and §§ 1965 to 1968 cover procedural rules. Individuals convicted of criminal RICO violations can be fined up to $25,000 per violation, imprisoned for up to 20 years, or both. RICO also provides for the forfeiture of any property, including business interests obtained through RICO violations. The property will be forfeited even if the property or business is itself legitimate. The defendant's assets can be temporarily seized before the trial begins to prevent further crimes. Some states have enacted their own RICO laws.

Since the federal RICO law is applied to legitimate business activities, it presents a potential concern for all business organizations, public and private. Recently, businesses have been lobbying for legislative amendments to limit the application of RICO. In the following case, the court heard pretrial motions in a RICO case of an alleged organized crime family.

8.3 U.S. v. BELLOMO

1997 U.S.Dist. LEXIS 434 (S.Dist.N.Y. 1997)

FACTS "The original indictment in this case contains 60 counts against a total of 19 defendants. . . .The core of the indictments are charges under the Racketeer Influenced and Corrupt Organizations Act (RICO). The enterprise is the alleged Genovese organized crime family, said to be one of the five 'families' that reportedly dominate organized crime in the New York area. Twelve of the defendants . . . are said to be members or associates of the family. They are charged in counts one and two with conspiring to conduct and conducting the affairs of the enterprise through a pattern of racketeering activity including murder, conspiracy to murder, solicitation to murder, extortion, attempted labor racketeering, operation of illegal bookmaking and gambling businesses, loansharking, money laundering, mail and wire fraud, obstruction of justice, and interstate transportation of stolen property. . . . Other counts of the indictments charge these defendants with a wide variety of substantive offenses, all or most of which are alleged as RICO predicate acts in the first two counts. . . .

Count one of the indictments alleges a conspiracy to conduct the affairs of the alleged enterprise through a pattern of racketeering activity in violation of 18 U.S.C. § 1962(d). Count two alleges that specified defendants actually conducted the affairs of the alleged enterprise through a pattern of racketeering in violation of 18 U.S.C. § 1962(c). . . . It was a part of the pattern of racketeering activity that from on or about November 1, 1994, through on or about April 1995, in the Southern district of New York and elsewhere, James Ida, . . . and John Schenone, . . . and others known and unknown, unlawfully, willfully, and knowingly did transport in interstate and foreign commerce a good, namely, a Caterpillar 950B Front End Loader, having a value in excess of $5,000, knowing the same to have been stolen and converted. . . .

In May 1995, Schenone was arrested and charged in the Eastern District of New York with conspiring to transport stolen property during the period beginning in October 1994 and continuing until May 11, 1995. . . . Insofar as is relevant here, the overt act with which he was charged involved the theft of a front end loader on December 15, 1994. Schenone pleaded guilty on July 14, 1995. . . . [The guilty plea that Schenone signed indicated 'this agreement does not bar the use of such conduct as a predicate act . . . in a subsequent prosecution including, but not limited to, a prosecution pursuant to the RICO statute.']"

ISSUE Is Schenone's RICO count barred by double jeopardy?

HOLDING No.

REASONING Double Jeopardy—"The RICO conspiracy with which Schenone is charged in this case allegedly commenced in 1980 and continued to the date of the present indictments. . . . The racketeering act in these indictments to which Schenone objects involved the same front end loader that was a subject of the Eastern District case. The last predicate act with which Schenone is charged in this case is said to have occurred in March 1995.

Schenone . . . argues that he is entitled to dismissal of this racketeering act. . . . In considering whether the Double Jeopardy Clause bars a subsequent RICO indictment to the extent it alleges prior convicted conduct as a predicate act, it is useful to bear in mind that the . . . [precedents] cases together stand for the proposition that RICO offenses are crimes separate and distinct from the predicate acts of racketeering. . . . '[T]he language, structure and legislative history of RICO . . . make Congress' intent . . . unmistakably clear. . . . This is critical in analysis of the double jeopardy issue.

The Supreme Court wrote in . . . [precedents], that the Double Jeopardy Clause protects against 'a second prosecution for the same offense' after either an acquittal or a conviction and prevents multiple punishment 'for the same offense.' . . . As a RICO violation is an offense separate and apart from the predicate acts, it cannot be said that prosecution on RICO charges based on a predicate act which resulted in a prior substantive conviction is a second prosecution, or that a RICO conviction results in multiple punish-

8.3 U.S. v. BELLOMO *(cont.)* **1997 U.S.Dist. LEXIS 434 (S.Dist.N.Y. 1997)**

ment, 'for the same offense' as the predicate act. That is true irrespective of whether the RICO prosecution, although relying on conduct that resulted in a prior conviction, alleges additional post-conviction conduct. Any different view would be inconsistent with the premise that the RICO offense is an offense distinct from the underlying predicate acts. . . .

[T]he Double Jeopardy Clause does not preclude successive prosecutions for different offenses even where conduct constituting an offense for which the defendant already has been convicted is an essential element of the second alleged crime. Hence, the fact that Schenone already has been convicted of an offense involving the transport of the stolen front end loader does not alone preclude a RICO charge which also rests in part on the transport of the front end loader. . . .

Here . . . Schenone is charged with racketeering acts including participation in a murder conspiracy, solicitation to commit another murder, loansharking, mail and wire fraud in connection with the San Gennaro street festival, and obstruction of justice as well as the unlawful transportation of the stolen front end loader. To suggest that Schenone now is being prosecuted although he is not alleged to have done anything unlawful other than that for which he pleaded guilty previously would be ridiculous. . . .

This view is buttressed by the serious issues for law enforcement that would be created were Schenone's argument accepted. If a law enforcement agency conducting complex, lengthy investigations of organized crime were to learn of unlawful conduct by a low or middle ranking figure before the investigation had borne the fruit ultimately hoped for, it would be put to a hard choice in determining whether to prosecute. Prompt prosecution on non-RICO charges would entail the risk that the government would not learn of another predicate act, post-conviction, that would enable it to charge the defendant with the RICO offense that otherwise would be chargeable if the investigation reached a successful conclusion. If the government, on the other hand, were to defer prosecution in order to preserve the RICO option in the event the investigation were successful, however, it would be risking the possibility that the passage of time ultimately would prevent prosecution of the defendant at all should the broader investigation fail. . . .[T]he Double Jeopardy Clause is not intended to "force the Government's hand in this manner." . . . Accordingly, the Court holds that Schenone's double jeopardy challenge to the front end loader racketeering act is without merit. . . .

Nor need the Court rest at this point with respect to the RICO conspiracy charged in count one. The conspiracy count alleges that Schenone conspired to violate RICO from on or about 1980 until the date of the indictment, June 1996 in the case of the original indictment and December 1996 in the case of the superseder. The essence of the offense of conspiracy is an unlawful agreement, and a conspirator's adherence to a conspiracy continues for its entire duration absent withdrawal. . . ."

BUSINESS CONSIDERATIONS Should a "legitimate" business that is charged with a criminal act be less likely to enter a guilty plea knowing that such a plea might subsequently help to support a RICO charge against that same business?

ETHICAL CONSIDERATIONS Is it ethical for the government to use the RICO statute to seek a second prosecution of a business that has already been convicted of the prior crimes that constitute the RICO charges?

SELECTED DEFENSES

The four classic defenses to criminal liability are duress, insanity, intoxication, and justification.

Duress

Duress exists when the accused is coerced into criminal conduct by threat or use of force that any person of reasonable firmness could not resist. Not all governments permit this defense. Those governments that recognize the defense vary with respect to the crimes to which it is applicable. Generally, the three essential elements of the defense are:

YOU BE THE JUDGE

RICO—The "Trials" of General Motors and Volkswagen

José Ignacio Lopez de Arriortua (Lopez) was a high-level General Motors (GM) executive when Volkswagen AG of Germany (VW) hired him as president after a "public and bitter" contest between GM and VW. [VW in this "You Be the Judge" refers to VW of Germany only.] Much of the bidding war for Lopez's services was reported in newspapers like the *Wall Street Journal*. When Lopez eventually left GM for VW, he took other GM managers with him. Subsequently, GM documents were found in "possession" of these executives and in apartments frequented by them in Germany. GM contends that its proprietary information was taken, including designs for "Plant X," a new factory design that is supposed to improve flexibility.

GM has accused Lopez and VW of conspiring to steal company secrets when Lopez left GM in 1993. The VW board has been trying unsuccessfully to extricate itself from this conflict. German prosecutors filed criminal charges of industrial spying against Lopez in December 1996. In addition, U.S. federal judge Nancy Edmonds in Detroit has ruled that GM can proceed with a civil suit against Lopez and all of VW's top management.

Lopez resigned his position with VW on 29 November 1996. This occurred shortly after a federal judge decided that GM was permitted to file RICO charges against VW. Consequently, if GM wins the lawsuit they will be eligible for treble damages.[13]

A number of issues have been raised in this case. Among them are the following: Is it likely that VW violated RICO? Is it likely that Lopez and his colleagues who "relocated" to VW violated RICO? What critical evidence must be proven by GM? Suppose that this case is brought in *your* court. How would *you* resolve the issues presented?

BUSINESS CONSIDERATIONS What should a business do to reduce the risk of losing a key executive, and of having that executive "confiscate" confidential information when he or she leaves? If a business *really* wants to hire a key executive away from one of its rivals, how can the hiring firm protect itself from these types of charges by the rival firm?

ETHICAL CONSIDERATIONS Is it ethical for an employee to take material and information with him to a new position when that material or information has been treated as confidential by the former employer? Suppose that the former employer had decided *not* to follow through with a planned development (such as "Plant X" in this case). Would that decision influence the ethics of the conduct by the former employer?

1. An immediate threat of death or serious bodily harm
2. A well-grounded fear that the threat will be implemented, *and*
3. No reasonable opportunity to escape the threatened harm

Insanity

Insanity exists when, as a result of a mental disease or defect, the accused either did not know that what he or she was doing was wrong or could not prevent himself or herself from doing what he or she knew to be wrong. The exact definition varies from state to state. This defense has been attacked for a variety of reasons, but chiefly because the definition is still ambiguous. Although it is raised often, the insanity defense is rejected in many of the cases in which this defense is used.

Intoxication

Intoxication may be either voluntary or involuntary. Voluntary intoxication is not a defense unless it negates the specific intent required by a statute. For example, the crime of rape is said to require a general intent. Intoxication, therefore, would not be a valid defense. On the other hand, assault with the intent to commit rape is said to require specific intent. In that case, intoxication may be a valid defense. Generally, involuntary intoxication is a good defense. *Involuntary* intoxication, for instance, can occur if one is forced to drink an alcoholic beverage against one's will or without one's knowledge.

Justification

Justification exists when a person believes an act is necessary in order to avoid harm to himself or herself or to another person. The key to this defense is that whatever the person does to avoid harm must be lesser than the harm to be avoided. For example, sometimes property has to be destroyed to prevent the spread of fire or disease. Also, a pharmacist may dispense a drug without a prescription if to do so would save a person's life.

THE LAW OF CRIMINAL PROCEDURE

Criminal procedure is the area of law that addresses the judicial process in a criminal case. It is concerned with ensuring criminal justice without unduly infringing on individual rights. The drafters of the U.S. Constitution were determined to avoid the excesses and abuses that had occurred under English rule. As a result, the area of criminal procedure was very important. There was a desire to protect the rights of the individual to the greatest extent possible without making law enforcement impossible.

The Constitution contains numerous criminal procedure provisions and protections, among them the guarantees of **due process** and **equal protection.** The defendant must be informed of the charges against him or her, must be tried before an impartial tribunal, must be permitted to confront witnesses against him or her, and cannot be compelled to testify against himself or herself. The defendant is entitled to a speedy trial, may not be held subject to excessive **bail**, and may not be subjected to cruel and unusual punishment if convicted. No citizen may be subjected to unreasonable searches and seizures, and the only evidence that may be admitted at trial is evidence properly and lawfully obtained. Exhibit 8.3 depicts the stages of criminal procedure. Note that a criminal trial is similar to a civil trial in many respects. The stages of a civil trial are discussed in Chapter 6. Many of the motions discussed in Chapter 6 can also be used in criminal trials.

The law carries a *presumption* of innocence until the defendant is proved guilty, and the burden of proof that must be satisfied in a criminal trial is the heaviest such burden in U.S. jurisprudence. The government must convince the jury of the defendant's guilt **beyond a reasonable doubt**, or the defendant must be acquitted.

Legal disputes may arise between a suspect and the police who search the suspect's business, home, car, or person. Under the Fourth Amendment to the Constitution, people are protected from unreasonable searches and seizures. When is a search and possible seizure legal? A search will be valid if any *one* of the following occurs:

Due process
The proper exercise of judicial authority as established by general concepts of law and morality.

Equal protection
The assurance that any person before the court will be treated the same as every other person before the court.

Bail
Technique for the release of a person charged with a crime while ensuring his or her presence in the court at future hearings by the posting of money or property.

Beyond a reasonable doubt
The degree of proof required in a criminal trial, which is proof to a moral certainty; there is no other reasonable interpretation.

EXHIBIT 8.3 The Common Stages of Criminal Procedure*

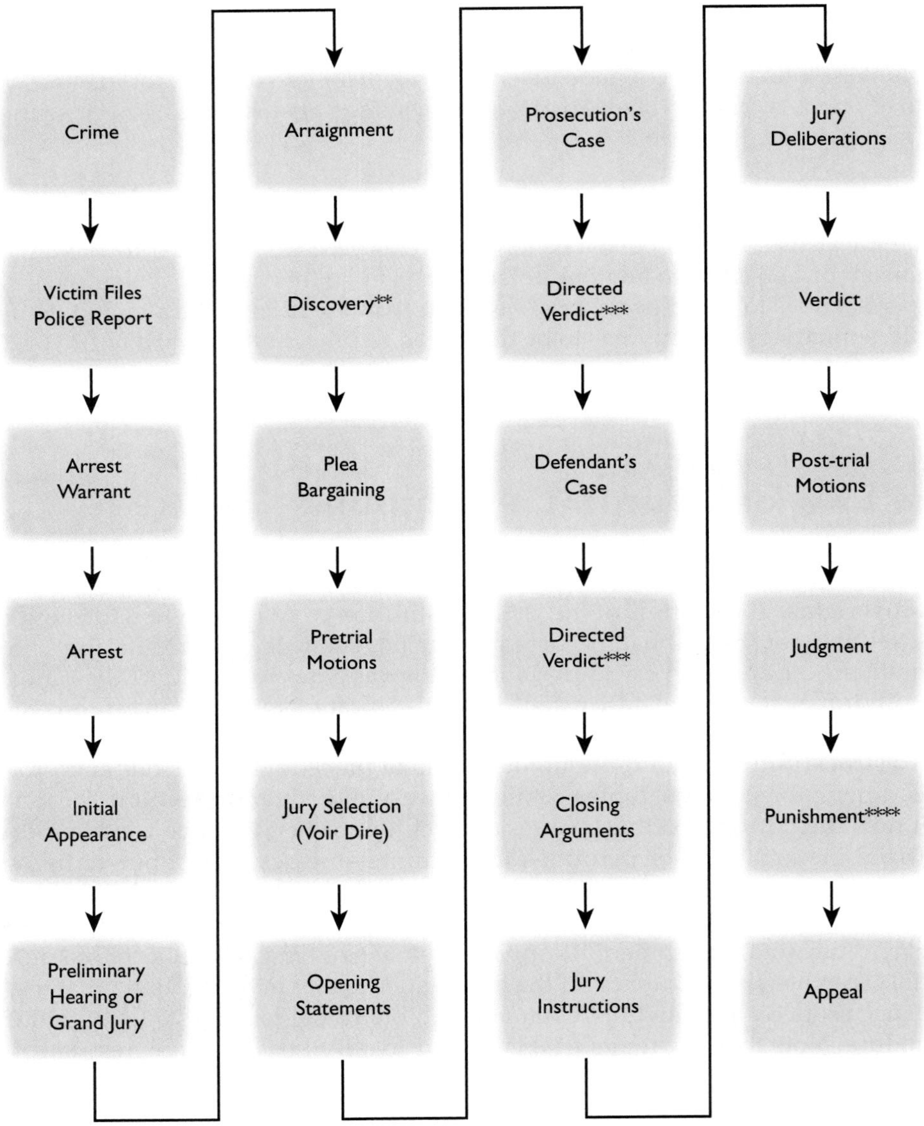

Crime → Victim Files Police Report → Arrest Warrant → Arrest → Initial Appearance → Preliminary Hearing or Grand Jury → Arraignment → Discovery** → Plea Bargaining → Pretrial Motions → Jury Selection (Voir Dire) → Opening Statements → Prosecution's Case → Directed Verdict*** → Defendant's Case → Directed Verdict*** → Closing Arguments → Jury Instructions → Jury Deliberations → Verdict → Post-trial Motions → Judgment → Punishment**** → Appeal

*The exact order may vary.

**Discovery is more limited in criminal cases than in civil cases.

***Directed verdicts are not generally used *against* a criminal defendant.

****A criminal defendant may be imprisoned beginning at the time of the arrest, if the court determines that bail is not appropriate or if the defendant cannot raise the amount of bail.

1. It is properly conducted under a legal search warrant based on probable cause.
2. It is conducted without a warrant by officers acting with probable cause. In some situations courts use a more reduced standard than probable cause. Most common examples of the reduced standards are when an officer "pats down" a suspect because the officer is concerned that the suspect has a concealed weapon or the evidence is in a motor vehicle that could be driven away.
3. It is conducted with the permission of the owner of the property or a person with proper possession of the property, such as a tenant who rents an apartment.
4. An emergency or exigent circumstance exists that requires police to enter onto the premises.

Once police are legally on the property, they may observe and act on any criminal behavior they see. In the following case, a husband and wife are complaining about the police and animal control officers' entry into their home.

Nolo contendere

A plea in a criminal proceeding that has the same effect as a plea of guilty but that cannot be used as evidence of guilt.

8.4 CONWAY v. PASADENA HUMANE SOCIETY — 52 Cal.Rptr.2d 777 (Cal.App. 2 Dist. 1996)

FACTS Pasadena entered into a contract with the Humane Society, under which the Humane Society provided animal control services for the city. "On February 4, 1993, Sergeant Endel Jurman of the Humane Society observed a dog running at large. . . . Based on his previous experience, Sergeant Jurman identified the dog as Toby, a beagle belonging to Nicholas and Virginia Conway. Over a 4½-year period Toby had been impounded or a citation had been issued to the Conways on 14 prior occasions. Jurman lost track of Toby and radioed for assistance. Officer Barry Blair responded that he had seen Toby 'run home' to the Conway residence. Jurman met Blair at that location. Blair told Jurman that Toby had run up the driveway and into the backyard. Jurman knocked on the front door of the house and received no response. . . . While the officers looked for Toby in the backyard, they noticed that one of the rear doors to the house was open approximately two feet.

The officers wanted to enter the house; however, the officers wanted to comply with departmental policy and also they were afraid that a burglar might be in the home. They requested the assistance of the Pasadena Police Department. Two police officers arrived and searched the home thoroughly while the animal control officers waited outside. The police officers did not see any sign of an intruder or burglar. Toby was in one of the bedrooms. The police officers closed him in the bedroom during their search. Jurman and Blair indicated that they wanted to enter the home to remove Toby. They led the police officers to believe that Toby was a stray and did not belong in the home. One of the police officers testified that he would not have entered the home again if he had known that Toby belonged there. All four officers entered again and Toby was removed. Sergeant Jurman posted a notice of impoundment on the front door of the Conway home and took Toby to the pound. . . . Four months later, the Conways entered a plea of ***nolo contendere.*** They were placed on probation for two years and fined $500. Toby was returned to them at that time."

ISSUE Was the search of the Conway's property and the seizure of their dog unconstitutional?

HOLDING Perhaps. A trial should be held on this issue.

REASONING "The Fourth Amendment to the U.S. Constitution, made applicable to the states by the Fourteenth Amendment . . . provides: 'The right of the people to be secure in their persons, houses, papers, and effects, against unreasonable searches and seizures, shall not be violated, and no Warrants shall issue, but upon probable cause, supported by Oath or affirmation, and particularly describing the place to be searched, and the persons or things to be seized.'. . .

It is axiomatic that the 'physical entry of the home is the chief evil against which the wording of the Fourth Amendment is directed.'. . . And a principal protection against unnecessary intrusions into private dwellings is the warrant requirement imposed by the Fourth Amendment on agents of the government who seek to enter the home for purposes of search or arrest.'. . . 'It is settled doctrine that probable cause for belief that certain articles subject to seizure are in a dwelling cannot of itself justify a search

8.4 CONWAY v. PASADENA HUMANE SOCIETY *(cont.)* 52 Cal.Rptr.2d 777 (Cal.App. 2 Dist. 1996)

without a warrant.'. . .Thus, a warrantless entry into a residence is presumptively unreasonable and therefore unlawful . . . Government officials 'bear a heavy burden when attempting to demonstrate an urgent need that might justify warrantless searches or arrests.'. . .

Absent consent, exigent circumstances must exist for a warrantless entry into a home, despite probable cause to believe that a crime has been committed or that incriminating evidence may be found inside. . . .Such circumstances are 'few in number and carefully delineated.' . . .'Exigent circumstances' means 'an emergency situation requiring swift action to prevent imminent danger to life or serious damage to property, or to forestall the imminent escape of a suspect or destruction of evidence.'. . .

There is no litmus test for determining whether exigent circumstances exist, and each case must be decided on the facts known to the officers at the time of the search or seizure. . . . However, two primary considerations in making this determination are the gravity of the underlying offense and whether the delay in seeking a warrant would pose a threat to police or public safety. . . .

Finally, even where exigent circumstances exist, '[t]he search must be strictly circumscribed by the exigencies which justify its initiation.' . . .'An exigent circumstance may justify a search without a warrant. However, after the emergency has passed, the [homeowner] regains his right to privacy, and . . . a second entry [is unlawful].' . . .

In sum, '[t]he presence of a search warrant serves a high function. Absent some grave emergency, the Fourth Amendment has interposed a magistrate between the citizen and the police. This was done not to shield criminals nor to make the home a safe haven for illegal activities. It was done so that an objective mind might weigh the need to invade that privacy in order to enforce the law. . . . We cannot be true to that constitutional requirement and excuse the absence of a search warrant without a showing by those who seek exemption from the constitutional mandate that the exigencies of the situation made that course imperative.' . . .Without exigent circumstances or consent, the Fourth Amendment precluded the animal control officers from making a warrantless entry into the Conway residence to enforce the leash law."

[The trial court had awarded the defendants a summary judgment and the Conways had filed a timely appeal from that decision. Consequently, this appellate court was determining whether there is a triable issue on the Conways' claim.]

BUSINESS CONSIDERATIONS Officers must comply with search and seizure law when searching a business premise. How are these searches similar and distinct from a search of a person's home? Should a business establish a policy for its employees to follow if a government official arrives at the business asking for permission to conduct a search?

ETHICAL CONSIDERATIONS Is it ethical for a business to refuse to allow a search if the police do not have a warrant, and to then attempt to correct any problems before the officer returns with a warrant?

In England, police who conduct illegal searches are punished by the police force for violating the rules. In the United States, we generally use a different approach. Evidence obtained through an illegal search may not be used in court; this is called *suppression of evidence.* Many of the disputes involving searches of businesses are based on the validity of searches by the Occupational Safety and Health Administration (OSHA).

A police officer acting with probable cause may arrest and accuse an individual of committing a crime, or the arrest may occur under a warrant issued by a judge. A police officer who has probable cause to believe that a crime has been committed, or is being committed, may take the suspect into custody without obtaining a warrant. If an arrest warrant is used, it must be issued by a judge based on probable cause. The judge *may* find probable cause to believe that a crime has been committed solely on the basis of a sworn, written complaint that names the person to be arrested or adequately describes him or her.

Once arrested and charged with criminal conduct, the accused should be given a preliminary hearing. Preliminary hearings are not required in most jurisdictions if there has been a **grand jury** hearing. At the preliminary hearing, a magistrate determines whether there is probable cause to proceed to a trial. The charges against the accused will be dropped if the magistrate decides that there is no probable cause, or that there is not enough evidence to proceed to trial, or that there is virtually no chance to obtain a conviction. Then the accused will be released from custody.

Grand jury
A jury whose duty it is to receive complaints of criminal conduct and to return a bill of indictment if convinced a trial should be held.

A grand jury may also be involved in the pretrial stages of criminal proceedings. A *grand jury* is a panel charged with determining whether there is reason to believe that a person has committed a crime. After hearing the evidence presented by the prosecutor, the grand jury will issue an **indictment** if it believes that the accused has committed a crime. The government will then proceed to trial on the basis of this indictment, and a preliminary hearing is not required.

Indictment
A written accusation of criminal conduct issued to a court by a grand jury.

Once the grand jury has issued an indictment or the magistrate at a preliminary hearing has determined that probable cause exists, the accused is **arraigned**. At the arraignment, the accused is informed of the charges against him or her, and, if necessary, the court appoints an attorney to represent the defendant.

Arraigned
Called before a court to enter a plea on an indictment or criminal complaint.

A common pretrial motion at this point is a motion for *change of venue.* In criminal cases this motion is made if defense counsel believes that pretrial publicity was negative to the defendant and that the trial should be moved to ensure the defendant a fair trial.

The defendant enters a plea to the charges. If the plea that is entered is guilty or *nolo contendere*, the court moves to the sentencing stage. If the plea is not guilty, a trial date is set and bail is determined, if appropriate.

At the trial, the government has the burden of proving its case beyond a reasonable doubt, and it must satisfy this burden within the established rules of evidence. Any violation of the rules of evidence will result in the exclusion of the improper evidence, and often the exclusion of the evidence will effectively destroy the government's case. When this happens, the defendant will be acquitted.

In the following case, the court analyzed the admissibility of scientific evidence.

8.5 PEOPLE v. SOTO

35 Cal.Rptr.2d 846 (Cal.App. 4 Dist. 1994)

FACTS Frank Soto was arrested and tried for the rape and/or attempted rape of a 78-year-old woman. About a year later, the woman suffered a severe and totally debilitating stroke. The criminal case was based on the composition of the semen stain on her bedspread and statements made by the victim the day of the attack. [Because of the stroke the woman was unable to testify at the trial. Statements that she made the day of the incident were admitted under the spontaneous statement exception to the hearsay rule. The admission of this evidence was also upheld by the appellate court.]

The trial court admitted evidence that there was a match between the deoxyribonucleic acid (DNA) of a semen stain on the victim's bedspread and Soto's blood. [In DNA analysis, a sample of body fluid is taken and the laboratory isolates the DNA, which is a particular type of long molecule. Some parts of the DNA are the same for all human beings and some parts are different. DNA research indicates that all humans have different DNA with the exception of identical twins. The analysis then focuses on four parts that are different and the pattern, location, and response of these chromosomes to stimuli. The results are compared by laboratory technicians and computer programs. Since only four parts are analyzed, instead of the entire DNA sample, the lab results are followed by a statistical analysis. DNA samples are analyzed and matched; once a match is found, the scientist does an analysis of the probability of a random match of this DNA. The matching evidence is based on the "product rule," a mathematical formula based on probability theory.] In this analysis, Soto's

8.5 PEOPLE v. SOTO (cont.) 35 Cal.Rptr.2d 846 (Cal.App. 4 Dist. 1994)

DNA was compared to every DNA sample in the county database and there was no other matching DNA, except the semen stain. The jury found Soto guilty of attempted rape and a judgment was entered based on the jury verdict.

ISSUE Should the trial court have admitted evidence of the DNA matching of the semen stain to a sample of Soto's blood?

HOLDING Yes.

REASONING It was not an error to admit this evidence. Soto contended that since disagreement exists about the probability theory used, all the DNA evidence should be excluded. He relied on a theoretical paper by two scientists who did not testify. The legal rule is that if an advocate wishes to use any scientific testimony, the advocate must show (1) the technique is sufficiently established to have gained general acceptance in its field, (2) the testimony about the technique and its application is offered by a properly qualified expert, and (3) correct scientific procedures are used in the case. The trial court correctly concluded that these three requirements were met. Soto did not establish that the scientific community had shifted away from the use of this particular probability factor in DNA testing. Just because there are two sides to a scientific discussion does not mean that all evidence about DNA must be excluded from the trial. When a scientific technique is being presented as evidence, the technique must have gained *general acceptance*. A technique has gained general acceptance when there is a consensus from a typical cross section of the relevant, qualified scientific community. Most of Soto's witnesses were from other scientific disciplines. The trial court should not examine the number of experts on each side, but should qualitatively weigh the testimony. Dispute and some uncertainty is inherent in scientific inquiry. Rules of evidence do not require certainty or unanimity. There is a consensus within the scientific community on the application of probability calculations to the results of DNA analysis. [Twenty-eight state supreme courts have admitted DNA testing; four state supreme courts refuse to allow DNA evidence in criminal court cases.][14]

BUSINESS CONSIDERATIONS What should be the role or attitude of a business that provides scientific data and/or testimony in criminal trials? Should such a firm refuse to provide scientific data or testimony on behalf of people charged with particularly heinous crimes?

ETHICAL CONSIDERATIONS Is it *ethical* to convict a criminal defendant purely on the basis of prior statements made by the victim, coupled with scientific evidence? What is the government's duty in cases such as this one? What is the ethical obligation of the firm that provides the scientific expertise?

In criminal cases we still use 12 jurors plus alternates. The purpose of alternates is in a situation where a regular juror is not able to continue on the jury, the alternate can replace him or her and the trial can continue. A jury may be sequestered. When a jury is *sequestered,* jurors are not permitted to return home during the evenings and weekends. The jurors are kept separate from the rest of society so that others will not influence their views. Jurors are generally not sequestered in civil cases. For example, in the O.J. Simpson civil trial, Judge Fujisaki rejected the plaintiffs' request that the jury be sequestered stating that "there was no precedent for sequestering jurors at public expense in a civil trial. . ."[15]

If the jurors are deadlocked and are unable to reach a decision, it is called a *hung jury.* In 1994 Erik and Lyle Menendez were accused of the murder of their parents. The Menendez brothers admitted to the killing but defended themselves based on self-defense. The jury(ies) that heard the case were unable to reach a verdict. The Los Angeles County District Attorney had the Menendez brothers retried.

If the defendant is found guilty, the court moves to the sentencing stage. Sentencing is governed by legislative guidelines to some extent, but the guidelines are nor-

http:// RESOURCES FOR BUSINESS LAW STUDENTS

NAME	RESOURCES	WEB ADDRESS
Legal Information Institute (LII)—Criminal Law	The LII, maintained by the Cornell Law School, provides links to federal and state criminal statutes, organizations, journals, and other resources.	http://www.law.cornell.edu/topics/criminal.html
U.S. Department of Justice	The U.S. Department of Justice provides links to its agencies, including the Federal Bureau of Investigation and the Bureau of Justice Statistics, as well as to cases and statutes.	http://www.usdoj.gov/
U.S. Sentencing Commission	The U.S. Sentencing Commission provides publications and guidelines, statistics, reports to Congress, and links to state sentencing commissions.	http://www.ussc.gov/
Racketeer Influenced and Corrupt Organizations (RICO) Act, 18 U.S.C. § 1961	The LII provides a hypertext and searchable version of 18 U.S.C. § 1961, popularly known as the Racketeer Influenced and Corrupt Organizations (RICO) Act.	http://www.law.cornell.edu/uscode/18/1961.html

mally very broad and somewhat vague, and a great deal of judicial discretion is usually involved in sentencing. Under current federal law, federal judges have much less discretion in sentencing for federal crimes than most state court judges. Federal judges rely heavily on the federal sentencing guidelines.

SUMMARY

Criminal law is designed to protect persons and property from harm. In addition, it should deter criminal behavior. Of course, the best protection is the absence of criminal activity; however, some criminal activity will always exist. Many believe that the law should punish criminals for their wrongful acts and/or try to rehabilitate them while they are incarcerated.

Criminal responsibility is based on two essential elements—a physical act and a mental state. The physical act must be overt. The mental state actually consists of one of the following: purpose, knowledge, recklessness, negligence, or strict liability. A similarity to civil law exists, but the interests protected are different: Civil law protects private interests, whereas criminal law protects public interests. Accordingly, one can be held liable twice for the same act, once in civil law and once in criminal law. This is not double jeopardy because there are two distinct bases of liability.

All crimes can be classified as misdemeanors, felonies, or treason. Misdemeanors constitute the least serious crimes; felonies are more serious. Treason, the most serious, involves acts to overthrow the government or provide aid or information to another government.

The selected crimes discussed in the chapter are murder/manslaughter, arson, burglary, embezzlement, forgery, credit card and check crimes, fraud, larceny, robbery, computer crimes, and violations of the RICO statute. Courts may hold a corporation liable for crimes committed on its behalf. A public policy debate is occurring over the appropriateness of this trend. The defenses mentioned are duress, insanity, intoxication, and justification.

The law of criminal procedure is very technical. An individual suspected of committing a crime can be arrested only upon probable cause. Probable cause is initially determined either by the arresting officer or by a judge issuing an arrest warrant. Once arrested, the accused is entitled to a preliminary hearing, which requires finding that there is sufficient evidence to proceed to a trial. A grand jury can also be used, issuing an indictment if it believes that the accused has committed a crime.

If there should be a trial, the government must prove its case beyond a reasonable doubt, and it must abide by numerous constitutional guarantees, such as due process, equal protection, and the rules of evidence. Only on conviction can an accused person be sentenced to a fine or imprisonment. However, temporary forfeiture is permitted for certain crimes. In addition, a criminal defendant can be imprisoned pending trial because the magistrate determines that bail is not appropriate or the defendant is not able to post bail.

Discussion Questions

1. Some states have enacted "Son of Sam" laws, which prevent criminal defendants from receiving financial gain by publishing books about their crimes. These laws are not applicable to attorneys, the victims, or the victims' families. Are these laws just? Why or why not? Should these laws be applied to defendants who wish to use profits from books for their legal defense? Why or why not?
2. A house is on fire during a drought, and there is not enough water available to put out the fire. A volunteer firefighter dynamites the houses immediately surrounding the house that is on fire to prevent the spread of the fire. Will this firefighter face any criminal responsibility? Explain your reasoning.
3. What crimes are associated with the computer age? What steps can a company take to protect itself from falling victim to these crimes?
4. In 1951, 21 corporations were convicted on criminal price-fixing charges in violation of federal antitrust laws and were fined a total of $822,500. The judge who sentenced them said, "The real blame is to be laid at the doorstep of corporate defendants and those who guide and direct their policy." What is to be gained by society when fines are levied on corporations in addition to punishing those officers and agents who actually committed the criminal activity?
5. Elizabeth's business is losing money. She decides to burn down her place of business, collect the proceeds of her insurance, and start over again. The building burns down, but a homeless person sleeping in the building at the time is burned to death. What is Elizabeth's criminal liability? Is she liable for arson, homicide, criminal fraud? Why?
6. If an individual is observed entering an alleyway next to a retail store at night and carrying a ladder and a bag of tools, can that person be convicted of attempted burglary? Why?
7. Crimes are either *mala in se* (morally wrong) or *mala prohibita* (wrong because the law says they are wrong). To which category do arson, income tax evasion, and the activities covered under the RICO statute belong? Why?
8. The Model Penal Code is a proposed criminal code that many states have used to revise and modernize their criminal laws. It consolidates larceny, embezzlement, false pretense, extortion, blackmail, fraudulent conversion, receiving stolen property, and all other similar offenses into the one general offense of theft. What advantages and/or disadvantages can you find to this approach?
9. Should a criminal defendant and his or her attorney have access to the personnel files of a police officer who played a significant role in investigating the crime and identifying the individual as the suspect? Why or why not?
10. Explain the criteria for a lawful search of a building.

CASE PROBLEMS AND WRITING ASSIGNMENTS

1. Michael Generoso and John Schenone asked the trial judge to dismiss the RICO forfeiture allegations. They argue that the forfeiture allegations fail "to provide notice of the government's claim . . ." and that they are improper because they do not allege that any of their property "was derived, directly or indirectly, from the racketeering activity alleged or that any such property is subject to forfeiture." "The indictment states that Generoso and Schenone have property which constitutes proceeds from racketeering activity and that the government will seek its forfeiture. The indictment further states that the government will seek substitute assets, if necessary, in the amount subject to forfeiture." Paragraph 139 alleges that: "through the aforesaid pattern of racketeering activity . . . Michael Generoso . . . [and the other RICO defendants] have property constituting, and derived from, proceeds which they obtained, directly and indirectly, from racketeering activity in violation of [18 U.S.C. § 1962], thereby making such property, or the amount of cash equivalent thereto, forfeitable to the United States of America." Should the forfeiture allegations of Generoso and Schenone be stricken? Why? [Other issues involved in this case are included in this chapter.] [See *U.S.* v. *Bellomo,* 1997 U.S.Dist. LEXIS 434 (S.Dist.N.Y. 1997).]

2. Film Recovery Systems, Inc. was engaged in the business of extracting, for resale, silver from used x-ray and photographic film. Metallic Marketing Systems, Inc., operated out of the same premises and owned 50 percent of the stock of Film Recovery. The recovery process involved "chipping" the film product and soaking the granulated pieces in large open bubbling vats containing a solution of water and sodium cyanide. The cyanide solution caused the release of silver contained in the film. A continuous flow system pumped the silver-laden solution into polyurethane tanks that contained electrically charged stainless steel plates to which the separated silver adhered. Workers removed the plates from the tanks to another room where the accumulated silver was scraped off. On the morning of 10 February 1983, shortly after Stefan Golab had disconnected a pump on one of the tanks and had begun to stir the contents of the tank with a rake, he became dizzy and felt faint. He left the production area to rest in the lunchroom area of the plant. Golab eventually lost consciousness and he was pronounced dead on arrival at the hospital. The Cook County medical examiner, after receiving the toxicological report, determined at the autopsy that Golab had died from acute cyanide poisoning through the inhalation of cyanide fumes in the plant air. Those who testified as to the working conditions in the plant had established that the firms had not told the employees they were working with cyanide or that the compound put into the vats could be harmful when inhaled. Should Film Recovery and/or its high ranking officers be criminally liable for Golab's death? Why? [See *People* v. *O'Neil,* 550 N.E.2d 1090 (Ill.App. 1990).]

3. Carolyn Grant-Campbell admitted that she stole more than $220,000 from Light Line United Mission, a homeless shelter founded by her adoptive mother 36 years ago. According to the indictment, Grant-Campbell embezzled and misapplied funds between February 4, 1994, and January 10, 1995, while she was the director of the mission. According to the indictment she obtained the funds by writing checks to herself from mission bank accounts. Grant-Campbell pled guilty to 10 counts of embezzlement of money given to the mission by the federal government. The mission was receiving funds from the Federal Emergency Management Agency to help homeless and dispossessed families obtain shelter. She has agreed to make restitution of $146,310 and to cooperate with the federal government in the "investigation and prosecution of other individuals." The federal government stopped funding the mission when the thefts were discovered. Now, the mission is falling behind on its payments and owes a number of creditors. Is theft morally wrong? Is some theft worse than others? Is it more wrong when the theft is against those in need? Is it worse to steal from the government (and the people)? If an officer or employee steals from his or her organization, what is his or her moral perspective? Explain your reasons. [See Jerry Bier, "Shelter's Former Director Admits Embezzling Money," *The Fresno Bee* (5 February 1997), pp. B1 and B2.]

4. Robert J. Riggs, a.k.a. Prophet, and Craig Neidorf, a.k.a. Knight Lightning, collaborated on a scheme to defraud Bell South Telephone Company. They agreed to steal Bell South's computer text file containing information on its enhanced 911 emergency calling system. Using his home computer in Decatur, Georgia, Riggs accessed Bell South's computer system, retrieved the file, and concealed his unauthorized access by using account codes of persons with legitimate access. Riggs transferred the file to Neidorf, a university student at the University of Missouri, via a bulletin board system and the interstate computer network. Subsequently, Neidorf altered the file so that people could not identify its source and published it in his *Phrack* newsletter. Can Riggs and Neidorf be successfully prosecuted for

any crimes? If so, which ones? [See *U.S.* v. *Riggs*, 967 F.2d 561 (11th Cir. 1992); *U.S.* v. *Riggs*, 743 F.Supp. 556 (N.Dist.Ill., E.Div. 1990); and *U.S.* v. *Riggs*, 739 F.Supp. 414 (N.Dist.Ill., E.Div. 1990).]

5. Frances Lagana contends that she was wrongfully evicted from her home in Brooklyn, New York, by unspecified persons, and that a court-appointed receiver committed fraud when he sold her house and denied her any of the proceeds from the sale. The court-appointed receiver was not sued in this lawsuit. Lagana also claims that she contacted the district attorneys (DAs) to secure a share of the proceeds from the sale of her home. "Lagana's only claim against the three DAs is that they failed to prosecute the court-appointed receiver for the fraudulent eviction and/or sale of her home, even after Lagana allegedly complained." Does Lagana have a viable claim against the DAs or should her suit be dismissed? [See *Lagana* v. *Dillon*, 1996 U.S.App. LEXIS 33243 (2d Cir. 1996) (Unpublished Opinion).]

6. **BUSINESS CONSIDERATION CASE** Michael Lasch has been arrested and charged with theft by deception, criminal attempt, unlawful use of a computer, criminal trespass, and impersonating an employee. Lasch is a plumber in the Philadelphia area and he called Bell Atlantic and ordered an "ultra call-forwarding" service for telephones of at least five of his competitors. [Call-forwarding can be used to transfer phone calls from one phone number to another, and is activated by entering code numbers from any phone.] Through this technique Lasch was able to intercept calls placed to his competitors. Moreover, Lasch knew most of the plumbers whose calls he intercepted.

   One competitor, Lucas Ltd., claimed that Lasch only took the better customers and told others that he would not take their service calls. Lucas says he is getting phone calls from angry customers who were not served. The scheme was discovered when a customer called Lucas to compliment him on work that was done over the Christmas holiday. Lucas told her that his plumbers had not been to her home during the holidays. How would you decide this case? Why? What could Lasch's competitors have done to protect their telephone calls and customers? Can you suggest any business practices that would have helped the plumbers discover the scheme more quickly? What steps could Bell Atlantic have taken to prevent this from occurring or to discover it more quickly? [See Dinah Wisenberg Brin, "Plumber Flushes His Competitors by Using Call-Forwarding," *The Fresno Bee* (29 January 1995), p. A10.

7. **ETHICS CONSIDERATION CASE** *Fortune* magazine published an article about security on company computers. They hired WheelGroup Corp., a computer security firm, to "break into" the computer system of a *Fortune* 500 company. The company agreed to have its security tested as long as its identity was kept secret. A computer expert from Coopers & Lybrand was hired to protect the company, its data, and systems during the experiment. In a companion article, *Fortune* published the steps used by WheelGroup to gain access to the computer system, including the names and functions of software commonly used by hackers to gain access. There are also periodicals, such as *Phrack* and *2600: The Hacker Quarterly*, which specialize in hacker information. Is it ethical to publish detailed information about how to break into others' computers? Why or why not? [See "How We Invaded a *Fortune* 500 Company," *Fortune* (3 February 1997), pp. 58–61; and Richard Behar, "Who's Reading Your E-mail?" *Fortune* (3 February 1997), pp. 57–70.]

8. **IDES CASE** At 2:30 A.M. three bounty hunters came to the home of Linda Childs in Kansas City. They were searching for Virgil McCubbins, her son. The bounty hunters had received a tip that morning that Virgil was there and they had a certified copy of his bond with them, as required by state law. Virgil had apparently "skipped bail." During the search, the bounty hunters broke Childs's front door, hurt her husband, and sprayed her grandsons, ages 5 and 10, with mace. According to Childs, her son had moved out three years ago. The law allows bondsmen and bounty hunters a lot of latitude in capturing people who have skipped bail. Often they have more authority than police officers do in making arrests. Apply the IDES model to analyze this situation in terms of the objectives of the criminal justice system. [See Paula Barr, "Old Law Upholds Leeway Given to Bounty Hunters," *The Fresno Bee* (29 January 1995), p. A9.]

NOTES

1. See *Black's Law Dictionary*, 6th ed. (St. Paul: West Publishing Co., 1990), at p. 381.
2. See *Regina* v. *Jones*, 91 Eng. Rep. 330 (1703).
3. Richard Behar, "Who's Reading Your E-mail?" *Fortune* (3 February 1997), pp. 57–70, at pp. 58 and 59.

4. Ibid. at p. 59.
5. Ibid. at p. 64.
6. Ibid. at p. 59.
7. Richard Behar, "Who's Reading Your E-mail?" *Fortune* (3 February 1997), pp. 57–70, at p. 64.
8. Richard Behar, "Who's Reading Your E-mail?" *Fortune* (3 February 1997), pp. 57–70, at p. 70.
9. Jerry Bier, "Computer Stalker Trial Is Delayed," *The Fresno Bee* (5 June 1996), pp. B1 and B3.
10. See Model Penal Code (1985) § 2.07.
11. See California Penal Code § 387.
12. See 18 U.S.C. §§ 1961 et seq.
13. On 9 January 1997, GM and VW voluntarily settled their legal differences, thus avoiding costly and highly publicized litigation. Both sides officially apologized. The agreement specified that GM would get $100 million in cash and VW promised to purchase $1 billion of GM parts over a seven-year period.
14. See *People* v. *Soto*, 35 Cal.Rptr.2d 846, 857 (Cal.App. 4 Dist. 1994), footnote 23, which contains a listing of the states and references to the cases.
15. Linda Deutsch and Michael Fleeman, "Simpson Juror Replaced; Talks Start Anew," *The Fresno Bee* (1 February 1997), pp. A1 and A11.

PART 2

IDES PROBLEMS

Albee, while a business student enrolled in a college finance course, performed better than all of his classmates in an investment game created by his professor. In the game, students, using hypothetical money, would invest in and track a portfolio of stocks. Emboldened by his success, Albee decided to begin his own business, investing in stocks for himself and, for a fee, his clients. Albee revealed to all of his clients that he possessed no license to trade securities, no "real-world" business experience, no insurance, and that all investments were made at the client's "own risk." All client transactions and communications were handled verbally; no paperwork was created and no contracts were signed. Albee insisted that his clients trust him and his natural ability to make money.

Despite these disclaimers, within a few months Albee had 50 clients, each of whom gave Albee $500 to invest. Albee used the $25,000, along with $5000 of his own money, to create an investment fund for stocks and bonds.

Initially, Albee's investments were sound, and the fund grew at a steady but unspectacular rate. However, Albee's returns were not as spectacular as those he generated in his finance course. To compensate, Albee began to seek riskier—and potentially more profitable—investments for the fund. This effort initially met with success, and Albee began to take even more risks. However, with more than 95% of his money invested in speculative technology stocks, a downturn in the technology market decimated Albee's fund. Albee lost everything.

Sadder but wiser, Albee called a meeting with his clients and explained the situation. He apologized for the failed investments but reminded his clients that the investments were not guaranteed, citing "bad luck" as the cause of the failure. Albee's clients refused to accept his excuse, and they insisted on their money back "or else." Albee, broke himself, could not repay his clients; moreover, he believed he had no legal reason to do so.

In search of a remedy, the clients contacted the local prosecutor and the U.S. Attorney's office to investigate if a crime had been commited; the Securities and Exchange Commission (SEC) to investigate whether or not they had been the victims of fraud; and a civil attorney to investigate whether civil or other action could be taken to recover their loses.

When Albee learned of these investigations, he decided to seek legal help as well. In preparation for this, Albee needs to answer the following questions:

IDENTIFY What are the legal and ethical issues surrounding Albee's actions? Can Albee be charged with a crime? Is he liable for civil damages? Can Albee settle the differences by some means other than the legal system? Given these answers, does Albee need an attorney? If yes, what type of attorney?

DEFINE What are the meanings of the revelant legal terms associated with these issues?

ENUMERATE What are the legal and ethical principles relevant to these issues? What sanctions and penalties might Albee face under the potential charges? Under what jurisdiction would these potential charges be adjudicated? What is the relationship between any potential criminal and civil charges Albee may face?

SHOW BOTH SIDES Consider all of the facts in light of the above questions. Do Albee's former clients have legitimate complaints under criminal and/or civil law? Do Albee's former clients have any motivation to settle out of court?

[To review the IDES approach refer to pages 29–30.]

CONTRACTS

The law of contracts forms the foundation of business law. Virtually every aspect of business involves contracts, as does much of a person's everyday life. When you rent an apartment, you sign—or orally agree to—a contract known as a lease. When you take a job, you enter into a contract of employment. Any purchase of goods, services, or real estate involves some form of contract. Even marriage is a type of contract.

This part of the book will examine the traditional elements of contract law—the common law of contracts. Later parts will consider various special types of contracts, among them sales, commercial paper, and secured transactions. Keep in mind, however, that all of these specialized forms are merely variations on the basic form. Thus, to understand these specialized forms of contracts, you first need to understand well the common law of contracts presented here.

I D E S

Sean, a gifted engineering graduate student, has decided to open CompConsult, a computer consulting business, in his hours outside the classroom. While CompConsult has so far met with success, Sean is troubled over a few legal problems that have arisen. A pharmaceutical company, citing an "ironclad money-back guarantee" CompConsult promised in its advertising, has refused to pay for work Sean has performed. In another project for a bank, the job required three times more work than Sean originally estimated in his bid. The bank, however, refused to pay more than the original bid. Finally, while working with a database for a realty company, Sean accidentally introduced a virus into the firm's systems, causing quite a bit of damage. The realty company has sued Sean for damages.

Consider these issues in the context of the chapter materials, and prepare to analyze them using the IDES model:

IDENTIFY the legal issues raised by the questions.

DEFINE all the relevant legal terms and issues involved.

ENUMERATE the legal principles associated with these issues.

SHOW BOTH SIDES by using the facts.

A G E N D A

CIT will enter into a large number of contracts as the business develops. CIT will have contracts with suppliers, customers, and employees. CIT is likely to have contracts with its insurer and may well have to enter into leases for rented space. Tom and Anna Kochanowski will need to know how a contract is formed, what type of contract to enter, and what their rights and liabilities are in the contracts they make. It is quite likely they will turn to you for help and assistance at many steps along the way. Be prepared! You never know when one of the Kochanowskis will need your help or advice.

Introduction to Contract Law and Contract Theory

O U T L I N E

THE IMPORTANCE OF CONTRACT LAW

Of all the aspects of law examined in this text, probably none is as significant or pervasive in our lives as the law of contracts. Virtually every personal or business activity involves contract law: Charging a birthday gift on a credit card, buying and insuring a car, leasing an apartment, writing a check, paying for college, and working at an establishment covered by an employment agreement are some examples. Even filling up our gasoline tanks involves contract law. Not only are we making a contract with the gasoline retailer, but the gasoline companies themselves receive much of their oil as a result of international contracts.

The law of contracts affects our most mundane activities, as well as some rather sensational ones, such as surrogacy contracts (whereby women agree contractually to have babies for infertile couples) or lawsuits between famous "live-in" couples involving *palimony* (requests by one member of an unmarried couple that the other pay alimony or a similar form of financial support after the couple's breakup). This chapter discusses the broad categories of contracts and contractual situations.

Commercial Law Contracts

When most of us think of the word *contract,* we envision the **mercantile** world. Indeed, our system of **free enterprise** historically has stressed the importance of freedom of contract and a corresponding protection of contractual rights. This was not always so, however. Blackstone's *Commentaries on the Laws of England,* first published in 1756, devoted 380 pages to real property law but only 28 pages to contracts. Thus, the law of contracts apparently constituted a subdivision of the law of property rather than the independent branch of law as we know it today.[1]

Mercantile
Having to do with business, commerce, or trade.

Free enterprise
The carrying on of free, legitimate business for profit.

Part of the reason for the eighteenth century's de-emphasis of contract law stems from the historical roots of this substantive part of the law. Although always broadly a part of the common law, mercantile traditions grew out of the *law merchant,* which represented the accumulation of commercial customs from as early as Phoenician times. The mercantile courts were separate from courts of law, and the merchants (or guilds) administered their own rules and customs. Hence, the evolution of commercial law remained outside the mainstream of legal development until fairly late in English history, the end of the seventeenth century. In the late 1800s, after the assimilation of the law merchant into the common law, several acts of parliament addressed commercial law subjects.

Not surprisingly, then, various legal bodies in the United States, influenced by these English precedents, penned a wide variety of statutes, such as the Uniform Negotiable Instruments Law and the Uniform Sales Act, covering American commercial law. By the 1930s, several such model acts existed. Because each state had not completely adopted these acts, however, commercial remedies differed from state to state. Moreover, these acts rather quickly became outmoded and thus not reflective of modern commercial practices. For these reasons, and especially to effect an integration of inconsistent statutes, the American Law Institute (ALI) and the National Conference of Commissioners on Uniform State Laws (NCCUSL) in the 1940s began working on what we call today the Uniform Commercial Code.[2]

By viewing commercial transactions as a single subject of the law, the UCC, as the Uniform Commercial Code is commonly known, revolutionized prior approaches to commercial transactions. The drafters saw, for example, that a sale of **goods** may constitute one facet of such a transaction. They also realized that a buyer may use a check for payment of the purchase price of the goods or that, alternatively,

Goods
Movable, identifiable items of personal property.

Security interest
An interest in personal property or fixtures that secures payment or performance of an obligation.

the seller may retain a **security interest** in the goods to ensure payment of the balance of the debt. An examination of the Uniform Commercial Code reveals articles on sales, **negotiable instruments**, bank deposits and collections, and **secured transactions**—these subdivisions correspond roughly to the scenarios described above. The UCC has fulfilled its original goals of simplifying, clarifying, and modernizing the law governing commercial transactions; permitting the continued expansion of commercial practices through custom, usage, and agreement of the parties; and making uniform the law among the various jurisdictions [§ 1-102(2) and Comment 1]. Most states' commercial statutes, with minor variations, have reproduced the UCC articles in their entirety. Louisiana, while it has incorporated some of the articles of the UCC into its commercial laws, remains unique in that it has not wholly adopted the UCC. The Code appears in the back of the text as Appendix B.

In addition to the Uniform Commercial Code, the National Conference of Commissioners on Uniform State Laws has drafted other statutes for possible adoption by the states. Examples include the Uniform Partnership Act and the Uniform Consumer Credit Code, among others. These laws have regularized commercial transactions so that transactions from state to state will remain more consistent. Such uniformity fosters predictability of result without necessarily sacrificing the law's capacity to change when commercial practices dictate such adjustments. You should check whether your state has adopted these uniform acts and codes or whether it instead relies on its own statutes to cover these areas of the law.

9.1

SALES/MANAGEMENT

CALL-IMAGE TECHNOLOGY

WHAT TYPE OF LAW WILL GOVERN CIT'S CONTRACTS

CIT will sell its interactive videophones directly to a number of its initial customers, and the firm also will install many of the systems purchased. The sale of the product involves the sale of *goods* and thus is governed by the Uniform Commercial Code. However, the installation of the product is a *service* and as such is governed by common law principles. Tom and Anna want to know whether the contracts the firm enters will be governed in part by one type of law (the UCC) and in part by another type of law (common law of contracts) or is the court more likely to determine that one aspect of the transaction "controls," so that the entire contract will be governed by this type of law. What will you tell them?

BUSINESS CONSIDERATIONS If a business provides both goods and services, should it price one higher than the other in order to imply which aspect of law—the UCC or common law—controls? Should the firm specify which aspect controls in the contract? Why?

ETHICAL CONSIDERATIONS The sale of goods carries certain *warranties* if the seller is a merchant. Is it ethical to try to designate the contract as being primarily for services in order to avoid giving these warranty protections to the customers?

Common Law Contracts

The existence of statutes concerned with commercial contract law should not overshadow the importance of common law contracts. Many doctrines regarding modern-day contracts stem from "judge-made" law, or court decisions growing out of contractual disputes from earlier times. Contract disputes decided on a daily basis in jurisdictions around the country significantly add to this body of precedents. The UCC states that common law supplements the UCC in those areas where the Code is silent. It is appropriate, then, that most of the discussion in Chapters 9–15 centers on common law contract principles—that is, principles derived from the judgments and decrees of courts.

Definition of a Contract

As you may expect, many definitions exist for the word *contract*. In general, a contract is a legally binding and legally enforceable promise, or set of promises, between two or more competent parties. Put another way, a contract is "a promise or set of promises for the breach of which the law gives a remedy, or the performance of which the law in some way recognizes as a duty."[3] Most of us intuitively understand what a contract is. Still, situations exist that at first glance may appear to be contracts but are not.

> Assume that you are a Rolling Stones fan. The Stones are in the United States for a concert tour. You are extremely eager to attend a concert by these vintage rock-and-rollers. A friend promises you tickets to the show, and you of course are elated. Two days later, your friend calls to tell you he is taking an old flame instead of you. As you hang up, your anger and disappointment cause you to think about suing your friend. After all, you had an agreement; and he has broken a promise to you. You think you deserve to collect money damages for the harm you have suffered.

Negotiable instruments
Checks, drafts, notes, and certificates of deposit; governed by Article 3 of the UCC, instruments are used for credit and/or as substitutes for money.

Secured transactions
Credit arrangements, covered by Article 9 of the UCC, in which the creditor retains a security interest in certain assets of the debtor.

Does your agreement give rise to a legally enforceable contract? Will a court protect your expectations and award you damages? The short answer is probably no. Most courts will view this situation as a breached social obligation, not a breached contractual promise. You occasionally may read of people suing in small claims courts for the expenses incurred in making plans for dates that never occurred because they were "stood up." If the plaintiffs win these "contract" actions (and sometimes they do), higher courts generally overturn these results on appeal because the more settled rule calls such situations broken social obligations, not breached contracts. Stated differently, you should be aware that a court will not deem all agreements "contracts."

Contrast the earlier situation involving the Rolling Stones with this scenario:

> You call a ticket outlet and order two tickets for the Rolling Stones concert, and give your credit card number. When you arrive at the box office days before the concert to pick up your tickets, you learn the outlet has sold them to someone else.

Can you successfully sue this time? Perhaps you can, because this situation seems to involve more than a mere social obligation and to have created binding economic obligations on both sides. Thus, to protect your economic expectations, a court may call this a contract and award you *damages* (that is, the amount of money it will take to put you back in the position you would have enjoyed had the contract been performed). Hence, the part of the definition that alludes to a "legally enforceable" or "legally binding" agreement takes on significance because it means that not every promise, agreement, or expectation ripens into a contract. In essence, a contract is any agreement between two or more parties that a court will recognize as one that creates legally binding duties and obligations between the parties.

Elements of a Contract

Given the law's emphasis on promises or mutual assent, it is not surprising that the first requirement for a valid contract is an *agreement.* Basically, an agreement consists of an offer and an acceptance of that offer. The law necessarily looks at the agreement from the viewpoint of a reasonable person and asks whether such a person would believe that an offer and an acceptance, respectively, actually had occurred.

Second, the parties must support their agreement with *consideration,* that is, something bargained for and given in exchange for a promise.

Third, the parties must have *capacity,* or the legal ability to contract.

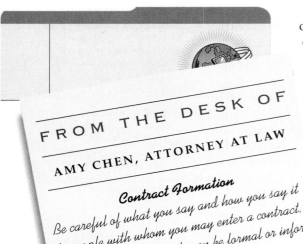

FROM THE DESK OF

AMY CHEN, ATTORNEY AT LAW

Contract Formation

Be careful of what you say and how you say it to people with whom you may enter a contract. Remember that contracts can be formal or informal, written or oral. If you agree to certain terms, there may be enough detail for a court to find that a contract was formed, without regard to your personal intent. This is especially important in discussions with people from other countries, since oral contracts are valid and enforceable in much of the world without regard to the size of the contract.

Fourth, the contract must reflect the *genuine assent* of each party. If one party has procured the assent of the other person by fraud or duress, for example, courts may set the contract aside owing to the disadvantaged party's lack of genuine assent to the agreement.

Fifth, the subject matter of the contract must be *legal.* The legality of the bargain is questionable, for instance, if the parties have agreed to do something that violates a statute or **public policy**.

Sixth, in some cases, the law requires that a contract evince certain *formalities.* Despite the fact that courts ordinarily will enforce oral contracts (even though it is risky to make an oral contract because of the difficulties in trying to prove exactly what each party said), some categories of contracts must be in writing to be legally effective.

In summary, to be valid, a contract must be (1) founded on an agreement (that is, an offer and an acceptance), (2) supported by consideration, (3) made by parties having the capacity to contract, (4) based on these parties' genuine assent, (5) grounded in a legal undertaking, and (6) expressed in proper form, if applicable. Each of these requirements is discussed in detail in Chapters 10–13. Exhibit 9.1 shows the elements of a contract.

In *Rogus* v. *Lords*, the court, in reaching its decision, considered many of these same concepts. As you read the case, consider the ethics of both parties.

9.1 ROGUS v. LORDS — 804 P.2d 133 (Ariz.App. 1991)

FACTS David Lords, Marge Rogus, and Sylvia Waters were licensed real estate salespersons or brokers. All were members of the Mesa-Chandler-Tempe Board of Realtors (the board). In 1985, Lords, representing landowners, solicited offers to purchase a certain parcel of real property from Sylvia Waters. Although Lords did not have a written listing agreement, he did have a verbal listing agreement from the owners. Waters later obtained a written offer to purchase the property from Walter Bush. The offer contained Bush's name, address, and phone number and provided for payment of a real estate commission of 6 percent. Rogus and Waters would receive one-half of the commission and Lords the other one-half. Waters gave the written offer to Lords, who submitted it to the owners. The owners then contacted Bush directly and negotiated a sale of the property to Bush on terms virtually identical to those contained in the original offer, except for the deletion of the commission provision. No real estate commission ever was paid in connection with Bush's purchase of the property. Rogus and Waters subsequently brought this breach of contract action against Lords to recover $66,000, the commission they would have received from Bush's original offer to purchase the property. Rogus and Waters based their lawsuit on the board's Code of Ethics, which, in their interpretation, created a contractual relationship between real estate agents and therefore would allow them to sue Lords, the listing agent, for the real estate commission they allegedly had earned.

ISSUE Did the obligations set forth in the board's code of ethics give rise to a contractual relationship that entitled Rogus and Waters to recover for breach of contract from a fellow member of the board?

9.1 ROGUS v. LORDS *(cont.)* 804 P.2d 133 (Ariz.App. 1991)

HOLDING No. The realtor members intended the board's code of ethics to constitute a noncontractual pledge of moral conduct rather than a contract that would give rise to enforceable rights between members.

REASONING For an enforceable contract to exist, there must be an offer, acceptance, consideration, and sufficient specification of terms so that a court can ascertain the obligations involved in the transaction. The requirement of certainty is relevant to the ultimate element of contract formation; that is, whether the parties have manifested assent or an intent to be bound. The language of the code of ethics—for example, "The term REALTOR has come to connote competency, fairness, and high integrity resulting from adherence to a lofty ideal of moral conduct in business relations . . . "—constitutes evidence that the board members intended to impose upon themselves a moral, not a contractual, obligation with respect to their relations with the public and one another. Moreover, in order to be binding, an agreement must be definite and certain so that a court can exactly fix the liability of the parties. Not only were the obligations set forth in the code of ethics generally aspirational in nature, but the code also failed to include any terms providing for specific enforcement of ethical violations by an individual member against another member. Furthermore, the code makes no reference to the obligations assumed by the members. Therefore, this lack of specificity in the terms of the code indicated that the parties never had intended it to bind them contractually. Hence, in the absence of other evidence, the code of ethics did not constitute a contract between the parties that would enable Rogus and Waters to bring an action for damages against Lords.

BUSINESS CONSIDERATIONS What could the realtors have done to protect themselves against the owners' dealing directly with Bush? Should the realtors sue the owners for fraud or misrepresentation?

ETHICAL CONSIDERATIONS What, if anything, can a business do to ensure that its clientele behaves ethically? Would you ever be inclined to behave as the owners did? If so, how would you justify your actions?

From Status to Freedom of Contract and Back Again

The development of contract law occurred relatively late in English legal history. Why? In part, because of feudalism. Feudal society set social hierarchies that prevailed throughout Europe between the eleventh and thirteenth centuries. In such a rigid, stratified society, each person occupied a special status or social position. Consequently, one's social circumstances determined the rights owed to that person and the conduct expected of that person. For example, feudal lords owed few duties to lowly serfs; but serfs owed their lives to their lords.

Imagine the disruptive effect contract law, which calls for the performance of mutual duties and obligations, would have had on such a social order. It is not surprising, then, that property law assumed foremost importance during these times and that status was more important than contract rights. If a serf was the property of the lord, courts did not need to bother with protecting what the state considered the serf's rather trivial expectations. Accordingly, the development of contract law was unnecessary.

Yet, as England became a commercial center, the law merchant and contracts became more important than status. Furthermore, during the social and political reforms of the late eighteenth and nineteenth centuries, the rise of capitalism brought with it demands for freedom of contract. This political emphasis on the importance of the individual and of private property accelerated the growth of what we now call contract law. To a largely agrarian society dedicated to self-reliance and

EXHIBIT 9.1 The Elements of a Contract

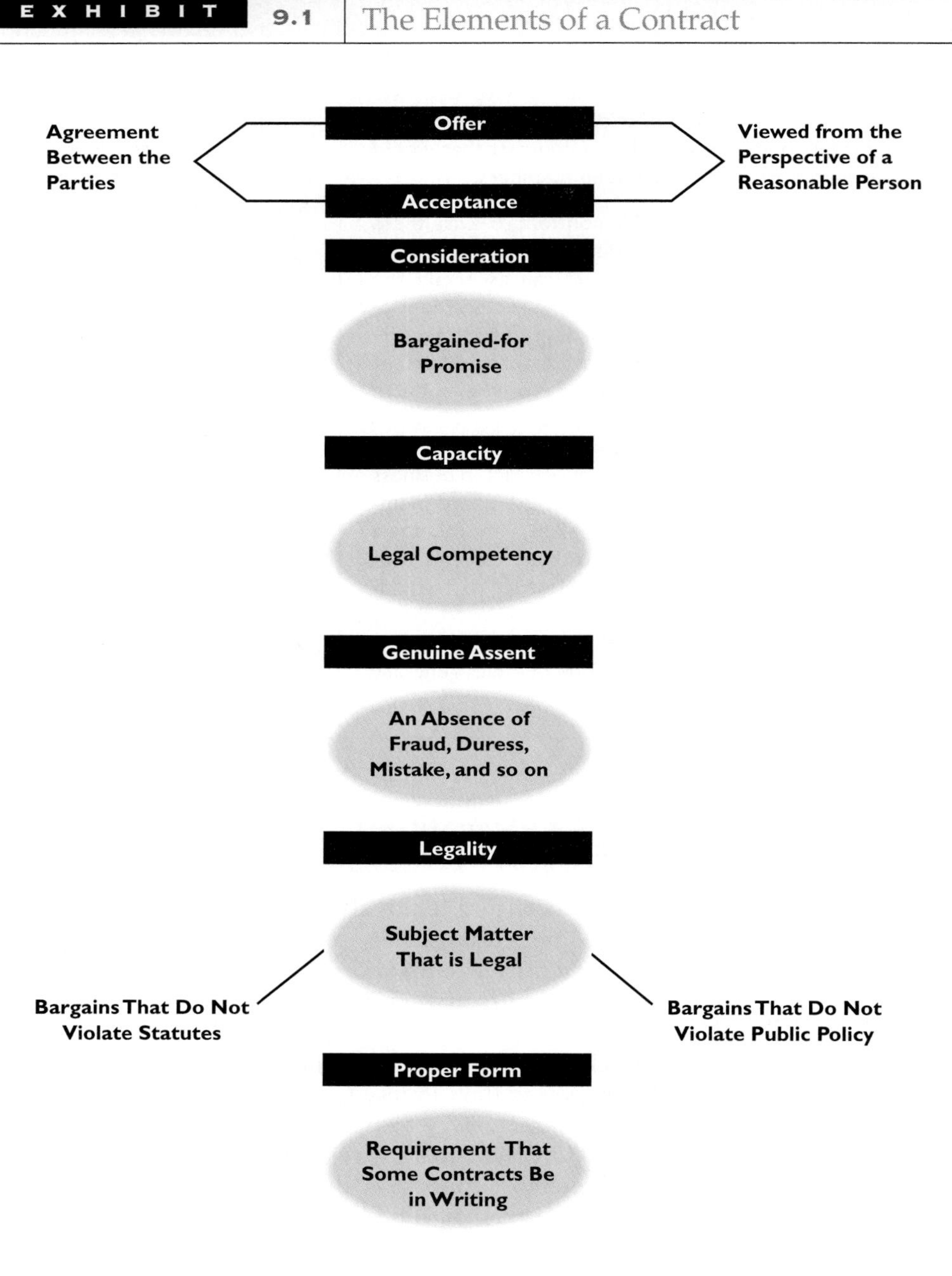
Agreement Between the Parties
Offer
Acceptance
Viewed from the Perspective of a Reasonable Person
Consideration
Bargained-for Promise
Capacity
Legal Competency
Genuine Assent
An Absence of Fraud, Duress, Mistake, and so on
Legality
Subject Matter That is Legal
Bargains That Do Not Violate Statutes
Bargains That Do Not Violate Public Policy
Proper Form
Requirement That Some Contracts Be in Writing

individualism, protection of expectations and enforcement of obligations took on added importance. The demise of a status-oriented society thus ushered in a contractually oriented social order.

Ironically, as an aftermath of the Industrial Revolution, the twentieth century has witnessed numerous restrictions on the nineteenth century's adoption of virtually unrestricted freedom of contract. Legislatures and courts have curtailed this freedom of contract and have reinstated—to a limited extent—a tilt toward status once again. Labor laws, environmental protection statutes, and consumer enactments represent a few examples of how lawmakers lately have restricted freedom of contract. Similarly, through common law decisions, courts, by protecting individuals who have little bargaining power even after these persons have consummated a contract, have hampered the continued development of freedom of contract.

The doctrine of unconscionability, mentioned in Chapter 1 and explored in Chapters 11 and 12, provides a perfect example of this protection. Suppose two parties have bargained. If, in the court's opinion, one of them (usually a corporation or business entity) had grossly superior bargaining power, or leverage, over the other (especially a consumer), the court sometimes will set such contracts aside on the grounds of unconscionability—that is, because the contract is shockingly oppressive or grossly unfair to one of the parties. (Do not, however, make the mistake of believing you can rely on this remedy to get out of each and every contract for which you belatedly wish to avoid responsibility!) Such developments have convinced some commentators that this progression shows an interesting circularity: that is, a movement from status to freedom of contract and back to status again.

CLASSIFICATIONS OF CONTRACTS

The law categorizes or distinguishes contracts in various ways. These categories are not always mutually exclusive, so several different terms may apply to the same contract. For example, suppose a restaurant orders produce and meat from its supplier at set prices; and the supplier promises to deliver on a predetermined schedule. The understanding between these parties invokes several categories of contracts simultaneously: In short, this agreement is an informal, bilateral, valid, express contract.

Formal versus Informal Contracts

The distinction between formal and informal contracts derives from the method used in creating the contract. In early common law times, the contracting parties generally engaged in certain formalities (hence, the term *formal*). To be valid, for example, a contract had to be under seal; that is, the document had to be closed with wax and imprinted with one's insignia, or distinctive mark. Very few contracts are under seal today; because most jurisdictions have abolished the need for certain classes of private contracts or instruments to be under seal, very few are. A seal, if used, does not affect the legal validity of most contracts. This trend toward eliminating sealed, or formal, contracts demonstrates that the need for ceremonies and formalities to ensure validity largely has passed.

Informal (or simple) contracts are a more common category of contracts today. In these, the emphasis is not on the form or mode of expression but instead on giving effect to the promises of the parties. Informal contracts do not require a seal. Such contracts may be either oral or written and, in fact, may even be implied from the conduct of the parties.

Unilateral versus Bilateral Contracts

Every contract has at least two contracting parties. The person who makes an offer (called the *offeror*) generally promises to do something or to pay a certain amount if the person to whom the offer has been made (called the *offeree*) will comply with the offeror's request. Usually, then, in return for this promise, the offeror demands a certain act or a certain promise of the offeree as acceptance. The form of the acceptance demanded determines whether the contract is a *unilateral* contract (a promise on one side only) or a *bilateral* contract (promises on both sides).

If the offeror promises to pay the offeree $50 for raking the offeror's yard, this contract is unilateral. Only one person, the offeror, has promised to do anything. The offeree accepts the offer by performing the requested act (that is, raking).

In contrast, if one party (the promisor) makes a promise and the other party (the promisee) accepts the offer by promising to do the requested act, a bilateral contract results because promises exist on both sides of the agreement. To use the same example, assume the offeror promises to pay the offeree $50 if the offeree will promise to rake the offeror's yard. When the offeree accepts by so promising, an exchange of promises has occurred; and a bilateral contract has derived from the parties' bargaining. Try to apply these concepts to *Kuhnhoffer* v. *Naperville Community School District 203.*

9.2 KUHNHOFFER v. NAPERVILLE COMMUNITY SCHOOL DISTRICT 203

758 F.Supp. 468 (N.D. Ill. 1991)

FACTS From 1979 to 1988, Naperville Community School District 203 (the school district) employed Larry Kuhnhoffer as a school bus driver. At the end of each school year, Kuhnhoffer received a letter from the school district thanking him for his work during the year and inviting him to return as a bus driver for the following year. On 27 May 1988, Kuhnhoffer received the following letter from the school district:

> *Dear Mr. Kuhnhoffer:*
>
> *Thank you for your work for Naperville students during the 1987–88 school year. We appreciate your efforts and recognize the important role which you play in the District's educational program.*
>
> *Based on your performance this year and the staff needs which we anticipate at this time, we are looking forward to your return to your position for the 1988–89 school year.*
>
> *I hope that you will find your summer to be enjoyable and rewarding. If I can be of any assistance, please do not hesitate to call me.*
>
> *Sincerely,*
> *(signed) Dr. Michael L. Kiser*
> *Assistant Superintendent for Personnel*

On 26 July 1988, the Naperville police department arrested Kuhnhoffer for driving under the influence of alcohol. Upon his arrest, Kuhnhoffer refused to submit to a Breathalyzer test. Shortly after Kuhnhoffer's arrest, the Office of the Illinois Secretary of State notified the Illinois State Board of Education that Kuhnhoffer would begin serving a six-month summary suspension of his driving privileges on 10 September 1988. The Board of Education, in turn, notified the DuPage County Educational Service Region that Kuhnhoffer's bus driver's permit would be suspended as of 10 September and that he would not be eligible to reapply for his permit until 11 March 1992. Dr. Kiser, the assistant superintendent of the school district, received the same notification from the board of education. Approximately two weeks before the school year began, Kiser informed Kuhnhoffer that, owing to Kuhnhoffer's DUI arrest, the school district could not hire him as a school bus driver. Kuhnhoffer subsequently sued the school district for breach of contract.

ISSUE Did the 27 May letter sent by Kiser to Kuhnhoffer, coupled with the parties' course of dealing over the previous nine years, create an implied contract of employment?

HOLDING No. The school district's offer contemplated the formation of a unilateral contract. Because an offer for a

9.2 KUHNHOFFER v. NAPERVILLE COMMUNITY SCHOOL DISTRICT 203 *(cont.)* 758 F.Supp. 468 (N.D. Ill. 1991)

unilateral contract is accepted by performance, no contract could result between Kuhnhoffer and the school district until he commenced performance. Without a valid license, Kuhnhoffer would be unable to perform fully his end of the bargain; hence, no contract ever came into existence.

REASONING According to Kuhnhoffer, the 27 May letter, coupled with the parties' course of dealing over the previous nine years, was sufficient to create an implied contract of employment. While Kuhnhoffer was correct in asserting that express or implied contracts may create property interests, Kuhnhoffer's argument presupposed that the parties had an existing employment agreement. The school district denied that the parties ever had formed a contract, however. The school district contended that the 27 May letter had constituted not an offer but an "invitation" for possible future employment. This distinction, though merely a semantic one, in these circumstances became irrelevant because even if the letter had constituted an offer of employment, the school district had properly revoked its offer prior to acceptance. This case involves the principles associated with unilateral contracts. A unilateral contract arises from a promise made by one party in exchange for the other party's act or performance. Here, the school district offered to employ Kuhnhoffer in exchange for Kuhnhoffer's performance; the offer did not solicit a return promise from Kuhnhoffer (and Kuhnhoffer refrained from giving one). Because Kuhnhoffer could accept the offer for a unilateral contract only by performance, the school district was not contractually bound until Kuhnhoffer commenced performance. Accordingly, the school district remained free to revoke the offer any time prior to acceptance. After learning of the six-months' suspension of Kuhnhoffer's license, the school district promptly notified Kuhnhoffer that he would not be hired as a bus driver for the 1988–1989 school year and thus revoked the offer.

BUSINESS CONSIDERATIONS Should the school district have promulgated a policy that sets out certain grounds (for example, arrests or convictions for drunken driving, child molestation, and so on) that would preclude a driver's becoming (or remaining) an employee? Why or why not?

ETHICAL CONSIDERATIONS Did the school district have an ethical obligation to try to retain Kuhnhoffer (for example, by placing him in a nondriving position for which he might have been qualified)? Did the school district have an ethical obligation to offer an employee assistance plan (EAP) for employees like Kuhnhoffer who may have a substance abuse problem?

Valid, Voidable, Void, and Unenforceable Contracts

A valid contract is one that is legally binding and enforceable. In contrast, a voidable contract is one that may be either affirmed or rejected at the option of one or more of the contracting parties. The agreement is nonetheless valid until it is rejected or disaffirmed. For example, if a person buys a car in the belief that it was driven only 50,000 miles when in actuality it was driven 250,000 miles, that contract may be voidable on the basis of fraud or misrepresentation. However, the contract remains valid and fully enforceable until the buyer disaffirms the agreement.

Void agreements, though they outwardly may appear to be contracts, can never have any legal effect. They are unenforceable and in actuality never become contracts because they lack one of the essential elements of a contract. An agreement to murder someone is void; hence, a court will not enforce this agreement because it lacks the element of legality.

On the other hand, it is possible to have a seemingly binding contract that will not be given effect in a court of law. Suppose, for example, that the contract involved

YOU BE THE JUDGE

"Drink Pepsi—Get Stuff?"

As part of a promotional campaign, PepsiCo, Inc. ran a television advertisement showing a computerized simulation of a $33.8 million Harrier jet, a military aircraft that can take off and land vertically. Under the picture of the jet was the caption "Drink Pepsi—Get Stuff." The Pepsi promotion enticed customers to rack up points on beverage containers and claim prizes. The advertisement indicated that one could redeem the jet for seven million beverage points. John Leonard, a 21-year-old business student, calculated that in order to earn the Harrier, he would have to drink 16.8 million cans of Pepsi. Leonard later claimed that he had called the company and was told he had the option of buying "Pepsi Points" at ten cents each. Therefore, he rounded up five investors and in March delivered to Pepsi 15 original "Pepsi Points" and a check for $700,008.50 (the remaining 6,999,985 "Pepsi Points" and a sum for shipping and handling). At this point, Leonard argued, a contract existed between him and Pepsi. Assume that this case has been brought in *your* court. Would *you* agree with Leonard's contention?[4]

BUSINESS CONSIDERATIONS What can a business do to protect itself from situations like this one when it attempts to use humor in its commercial advertisements? Should a business be responsible for its commercials if those commercials are misinterpreted by the audience?

ETHICAL CONSIDERATIONS Is it ethical for a business to run an advertisement that makes certain claims, and then attempt to avoid honoring those claims? Is it ethical for a customer to attempt to hold a firm liable for commercial statements that are obviously not meant to be taken seriously?

SOURCE: *The National Law Journal* (2 September 1996), p. A20.

is one that must be in writing (such as a contract for a sale of goods priced at $500 or more); if this contract is oral, it will be unenforceable. Note that the contract otherwise appears to meet all the criteria of a valid contract.

Express versus Implied Contracts

An *express contract* is one in which the parties set forth their intentions specifically and definitely, either in writing or orally. Most contracts are of this type.

An *implied contract* is one that must be discerned or inferred from the actions or conduct of the parties. Even though the parties should have expressed their intentions more clearly, it still is possible to conclude that a true contract exists. These agreements are often called contracts implied in fact because based on the facts it is possible to say, despite the absence of explicit language to this effect, that the parties intended to create a contract.

Assume, for example, that two parties have had a well-known, years-long understanding that grain will be accepted when delivered. If one party takes grain to the elevator and the elevator refuses to accept it, the facts of the parties' prior, longstanding relationship and their previous conduct may allow a court to enforce this agreement as a contract implied in fact.

Practically speaking, many agreements have express provisions and also include terms that must be discerned from the actions of the parties. In short, a given contract may not fall neatly into one or the other of these categories. In *Fletcher, Barnhardt & White, Inc.* v. *Matthews*, the judge refused to find either an express contract or a contract implied in fact.

9.3 FLETCHER, BARNHARDT & WHITE, INC. v. MATTHEWS 397 S.E.2d 81 (N.C.App. 1990)

FACTS Fletcher, Barnhardt & White, Inc. (the firm) sells individualized promotional materials to businesses throughout the Southeast. In October 1984, the firm hired Jeffrey Matthews as a sales representative. The firm paid Matthews a base salary during his first year of employment plus commissions that he earned. After his first year of employment, the firm compensated Matthews solely on the basis of the commissions earned. After being on straight commission for approximately six months, Matthews approached the firm and requested permission to draw against his commissions. A *draw* is an arrangement in which a sales representative receives a predetermined amount of money each pay period. Thus, in a month when Matthews earned few commissions, he would receive a set amount of pay; in a month when commissions exceeded the draw, the firm would retain the excess to repay any deficits incurred during months in which the draw exceeded the earned commissions. The firm initially set Matthews's draw at $1,750 per two-week pay period and increased this amount in May 1986 to $1,950 per pay period. Along with his paycheck, Matthews received a monthly statement that advised him of his commissions for that month versus the draw he was receiving. In months when his commissions exceeded his draw, the firm applied the excess to any deficits that had accrued. In October 1987, Matthews began the initial steps to form a business to compete with the firm. On 7 February 1988, Matthews went to the home of Mr. Fletcher, the president of the firm, and informed Fletcher of his (Matthews's) intention to leave the firm's employ and begin operating his own company. Matthews, after that exchange, indicated that he would pay back the money that Fletcher, on behalf of the firm, demanded. After receiving no payments from Matthews, on 18 May 1989 the firm sued him to recover the deficit in his draw account.

ISSUE Had the firm and Matthews entered into a contract that made Matthews personally liable for the deficit in his draw account?

HOLDING No. The parties had not entered into any agreement concerning the consequences of a salesperson's terminating his or her employment with a deficit owed to the firm.

REASONING When a material term of a contract is absent, the agreement is not legally binding on the parties. The failure of the parties to consider whether Matthews might be personally liable for the excess advances over commissions indicated the absence of an express contract. Furthermore, Matthews's statements that he would repay the money to the firm occurred after he had terminated his employment; thus, the statements were unenforceable because they were not supported by consideration. Finally, the parties' failure to agree at any point that Matthews would be personally liable for the deficits in the draw account, besides indicating the lack of an express contract, also showed that no implied contract in fact ever had come into existence. Hence, in the absence of either an express contract or a contract implied in fact concerning Matthews's personal liability, the firm could not recover the deficits in the draw account.

BUSINESS CONSIDERATIONS Assume you are the personnel director of the firm involved in this litigation. What modifications in company policies should the firm undertake to avoid similar problems in the future?

ETHICAL CONSIDERATIONS Was Matthews ethically obligated (1) to repay the deficits in the draw account and (2) to refrain from starting a competing business? Explain.

Executory versus Executed Contracts

An *executory contract* is one in which some condition or promise remains unfulfilled by one or more of the parties. For instance, if a person agrees to buy a king-sized mattress set from Honest John's, the contract is executory: The firm still must deliver the mattresses, and the buyer must pay for the set. If the buyer pays for the mattresses prior to delivery, the contract is also executory, although technically the buyer has executed his or her part of the contract.

An *executed contract* is one in which the parties have fully completed or performed all the conditions or promises set out in the agreement. In the last example, when Honest John's delivers the mattress set, the contract will be executed. Neither party has anything further to do.

Quasi Contracts versus Contracts Implied in Fact

One type of implied contract deserves special attention. This is a contract implied in law, or a *quasi contract.* Lawsuits alleging quasi contract as the basis for recovery also may be called suits for *unjust enrichment.* Under certain circumstances, the law will create a contract between the parties, despite their wishes and intentions, in order to prevent the unjust enrichment of one party. In these circumstances, even though it may be clear that the parties did not actually contract with each other, the law will treat the parties as if they had.

A contract implied in fact also is an implied contract. It differs from a contract implied in law in that sufficient facts or evidence of conduct exist for a court to find on equitable grounds that the parties actually meant to contract with each other. Their transaction perhaps was a bit sloppy; that is, the language should have been more explicit. But a court can conclude with some certainty that the parties intended a binding agreement between themselves. Thus, a contract implied in fact is a true contract. In contrast, a contract implied in law is a fiction engineered by a court so as to effect justice between two parties. Unlike a contract implied in fact, this is not a true contract, hence the name quasi contract.

To clarify further the difference between a contract implied in fact and a contract implied in law, consider this example: Mattie is sitting on her front porch when a painting crew arrives. The painting crew has the wrong address (111 Riverside Drive instead of 1111 Riverside Drive). Mattie nevertheless allows the crew to paint her house and later tries to argue that since she had not asked for the services, she owes zero for them. To prevent Mattie's unjust enrichment at the painters' expense, most courts will force Mattie to pay the painters, on a **restitutionary** basis, for the benefit she has received (a newly painted house) or, put another way, for the detriment suffered by the painters (the cost of their supplies, services, and so on). Mattie will be liable in quasi contract or a contract implied in law only for the reasonable value of the services rendered; the painters cannot "gouge" her by charging, after the fact, an exorbitant price. A contract implied in fact does not exist here because of the lack of any facts suggesting that Mattie and the painting company had dealt with each other before the crew arrived at Mattie's house. Evidence of an intention to contract, however sloppy the execution of the contract, would have made this a true contract, or a contract implied in fact. Given the absence of any such evidence, the court instead creates a contract—a quasi contract or contract implied in law—to prevent Mattie's unjust enrichment.

Restitutionary

An equitable basis by which the law restores an injured party to the position he or she would have enjoyed had a loss not occurred.

Do not be misled into believing that every time one person receives a benefit, a quasi-contractual recovery will be possible. Remember that the policy underlying such recoveries is the avoidance of injustice. Mattie has to pay because she knowingly allowed the painters to proceed. Had she not been present, however, the painters probably would be unable to hold Mattie liable because they had conferred the services on her as a result of their negligence or mistake; they had come to the wrong house. In these circumstances, it is not inequitable to allow Mattie to retain the benefits bestowed on her. By the same token, a person who confers a gift (for example, assume Mattie's brother contracts with a painting company to redo Mattie's dilapidated house as a surprise for her) or one who volunteers a service (a neighbor who decides to paint Mattie's house while Mattie is away for the weekend) will not be able to recover later from Mattie in quasi contract, either. The same result will apply to a person who buys supplies in a mistaken belief that a contract exists, or who incurs foreseeable difficulties and later tries to make the recipients of the services pay for these extra costs or services on a quasi-contractual basis. Still, remember that courts can, in a given circumstance, create a contract in order to avoid injustice.

Analyze *Ellis* v. *City of Birmingham* in light of these principles of contract law.

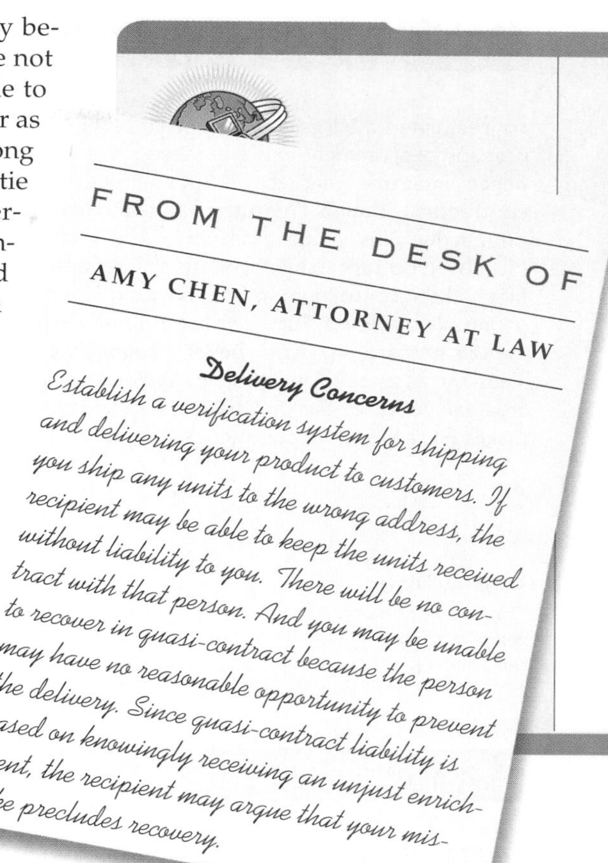

FROM THE DESK OF
AMY CHEN, ATTORNEY AT LAW
Delivery Concerns
Establish a verification system for shipping and delivering your product to customers. If you ship any units to the wrong address, the recipient may be able to keep the units received without liability to you. There will be no contract with that person. And you may be unable to recover in quasi-contract because the person may have no reasonable opportunity to prevent the delivery. Since quasi-contract liability is based on knowingly receiving an unjust enrichment, the recipient may argue that your mistake precludes recovery.

9.4 ELLIS v. CITY OF BIRMINGHAM

576 So.2d 156 (Ala. 1991)

FACTS Paul Ellis sat as a volunteer member on the Birmingham City Council's Horse Racing Job Retraining Committee. The city council had formed the committee to determine the types of jobs the advent of horse racing in Birmingham would create and the sources of training needed to supply these jobs. The committee further was to report its recommendations to the Birmingham–Jefferson County Job Training Consortium, an agency established to approve such recommendations and to distribute to approved facilities the funds received from a federal job training program. The committee subsequently recommended Ellis's Equestrian College to the consortium as one such job training facility. According to Ellis, owing to this recommendation and the alleged encouragement of various city officials, he believed he would receive federal funding if he submitted a training proposal. Ellis thus claimed that he had spent considerable time and money in formulating various proposals that the consortium rejected on ten different occasions. Ellis later argued that the city and the city council, by encouraging him to develop a job training program, had created an implied contract and they had breached it by failing to provide him with the promised funding.

ISSUE Did an implied contract exist between Ellis and the city?

HOLDING No. In the absence of either an agreement or a bargained-for exchange, no contract ever existed between Ellis and the city.

REASONING A contract implied in fact requires the same elements as an express contract and differs only in the method of expressing mutual assent. Implied contracts normally arise in situations in which the parties have

9.4 ELLIS v. CITY OF BIRMINGHAM *(cont.)* 576 So.2d 156 (Ala. 1991)

contemplated a bargained-for exchange, but no overt expression of agreement exists. In these circumstances, no evidence indicates that the parties intended to become contractually bound. The retraining committee simply recommended Ellis's Equestrian College as a training facility. Moreover, no successful negotiations ever ensued between Ellis and the consortium; in fact, the consortium rejected his proposals ten times. Furthermore, no one ever authorized him to prepare any work beyond submitting a proposal. Thus, the absence of any evidence showing an agreement or a bargained-for exchange between Ellis and the defendants makes Ellis's breach of contract claim untenable.

BUSINESS CONSIDERATIONS The city council would use taxpayers' money in funding the successful proposals. Should more stringent standards apply to those seeking public works contracts than would operate in connection with those forging everyday private contractual agreements? Explain your reasoning.

ETHICAL CONSIDERATIONS Was Ellis, as a volunteer committee member, ethically bound to refrain from submitting proposals to the city council? Put differently, did he have a conflict of interest that would exempt him from becoming a training site applicant?

Counterclaimed
Presented a cause of action in opposition to the plaintiff's.

Contrast the results in *Ellis* v. *City of Birmingham* with the results in *George* v. *Custer.* Why did the courts reach such different conclusions?

9.5 GEORGE v. CUSTER 862 P.2d 176 (Alaska 1993)

FACTS In 1974, Spiro George bought a meatpacking plant site that included a house and approximately 40 acres of land. In 1981, George leased the property to the Heatons, who, in turn, hired Custer, an experienced butcher, who occupied the house as part of his financial arrangements with the Heatons. In 1984, when the Heatons decided to leave the meatpacking business, Custer continued to reside in the house at a rental rate of $400 per month. At this time, George, by offering Custer free rent the first year and a monthly rate of $1,500 the second year, coupled with Custer's continuing to rent the house for $400 a month, encouraged Custer to reopen the meatpacking plant. George and Custer agreed it would take a substantial investment of both time and money to make the plant operational. The parties understood that Custer was to have an option to buy the plant, house, and eight acres of land. But, during the exchanges relating to this agreement, the parties had not discussed a time frame for exercising the option, a definite purchase price, or either payment or security terms. Custer made improvements on the plant, and expended time, labor, and $8,600 in equipment to make the plant operational and to meet certain certification requirements. During this initial three-month period, George indicated to Custer that he would sell Custer the facility for $150,000. Custer eventually decided to bring the plant up to federal standards so that he could sell meat to third parties. The acquisition of the necessary equipment and renovations for this upgrade took place over a period of two years. In June 1987, George informed Custer that the rent was being raised to $2,500 per month. Custer responded that, because he could not afford this rent increase, he would either have to leave or purchase the premises. George indicated that he would now sell the plant to Custer for $300,000. Custer did not attempt to negotiate the price with George and refrained from making any effort to obtain the money to purchase the property until 1988. When George sued Custer for $11,500 owed in back rent, George **counterclaimed** for damages allegedly resulting from George's breach of the alleged option agreement to purchase the property.

ISSUES Had George and Custer entered into an option contract? In the absence of a binding contract, could Custer nonetheless sue on a restitutionary (that is, quasi-contractual) basis as opposed to a contractual one?

HOLDING No. The uncertainty regarding many of the essential terms of the purported agreement precluded its being an enforceable contract. Yes. Custer could be entitled to restitution, even in the absence of a binding contract.

9.5 GEORGE v. CUSTER *(cont.)* 862 P.2d 176 (Alaska 1993)

REASONING George's conversations with Custer concerning the sale of the property remained inconclusive and thus precluded a finding that an option contract had existed. A court cannot enforce a contract unless it can determine what it is. It is not enough that the parties think that they have made a contract; they must have expressed their intentions in a manner that a reasonable person can understand. It is not enough that they have actually agreed, if their expressions, when interpreted in the light of the accompanying factors and circumstances, are such that the court remains unable to determine what the terms of that agreement are. Courts often have used vagueness of expression, indefiniteness, and uncertainty as to any of the essential terms as reasons for preventing the creation of an enforceable contract. While the parties threw out a purchase price figure of $150,000, the lack of discussion of such items as financing or the amount of the down payment indicates that a valid option contract never arose. Yet even in the absence of a binding contract, the improvements made by Custer to the property could entitle him to a restitutionary remedy for unjust enrichment in an action based on quasi contract. Custer's numerous improvements to the plant and equipment brought the plant considerably closer to obtaining federal inspection status, a resultant benefit George obviously desired and appreciated. Indeed, George, the would-be seller, encouraged Custer to proceed with the improvements. Unjust enrichment does not depend on any actual contract, or any agreement between the parties, objective or subjective. Rather, it is a prerequisite for the enforcement of restitution; that is, in the absence of any unjust enrichment, no basis for restitution exists.

BUSINESS CONSIDERATIONS If you had been either Custer or George, what would you have done differently to minimize the chances of subsequent litigation?

ETHICAL CONSIDERATIONS Was George's raising the purchase price from $150,000 to $300,000 *prima facie* unethical? To answer this question, would you need additional information? If so, what?

http:// RESOURCES FOR BUSINESS LAW STUDENTS

NAME	RESOURCES	WEB ADDRESS
Uniform Commercial Code (UCC)	The Legal Information Institute (LII), maintained by the Cornell Law School, provides a hypertext and searchable version of Articles 1–9 of the Uniform Commercial Code. LII also maintains links to the UCC as adopted by particular states, as well as proposed revisions.	http://www.law.cornell.edu/ucc/ucc.table.html
Legal Information Institute—Contract Law Materials	LII provides an overview of contract law; links to federal government statutes, treaties, and regulations; federal and state judicial decisions regarding contract law (including Supreme Court decisions); state statutes; and other materials.	http://www.law/cornell.edu/topics/contracts.html
The American Law Institute	The American Law Institute, publisher of restatements of the law, model codes, and other proposals for law reform, provides press releases, its newsletter, and other publications.	http://www.ali.org/
The National Conference of Commissioners on Uniform State Laws	The National Conference of Commissioners on Uniform State Laws (NCCUSL), the drafters of the UCC, provides drafts and revisions of its uniform and model acts.	http://www.law.upenn.edu/library/ulc/ulc.htm

EXHIBIT 9.2 Classification of Contracts

Type of Contract	Definition	Example
Formal	One created by certain rituals, ceremonies, or formalities.	A contract that requires notarization, such as the transfer of an automobile title to another person.
Informal	One created through oral or written statements or through the parties' conduct; needs no special rituals.	An oral contract to buy a used compact disk player costing $400.
Unilateral	One created by a promise given in exchange for an act.	A contract in which the borrower agrees to pay back the $400 consumer loan obtained from a bank.
Bilateral	One created by a promise given in exchange for another promise.	A contract in which one person promises to sell her dental equipment and another promises to buy the equipment.
Valid	One that manifests all the essential elements of a contract.	A contract to buy a car from a dealership.
Voidable	One that manifests all the essential elements of a contract and is legally binding unless disaffirmed by one or more of the contracting parties.	A contract to sell a termite-ridden house when the seller has knowledge of the extensive termite damage.
Void	One that lacks the essential elements of a contract.	A contract in which a lender charges the borrower a 40 percent rate of interest on a loan.
Unenforceable	One that manifests the essential elements of a contract but will not be given effect by a court of law.	An oral contract to guarantee the payment of another person's debts if that person fails to pay.
Express	One created by the parties' setting out their intentions specifically and definitely.	A contract that lists the price, the terms of the sale, the delivery date, and other details regarding the purchase of a car.
Implied	One discerned or inferred from the actions or conduct of the parties.	A person walking into a hair salon and asking for a hair cut without discussing price.
Implied in fact	Despite the absence of explicit language, the parties intended to contract with each other; a true contract.	A contract in which a person receives medical care without discussing the terms. The person will be obligated to pay for the treatment.
Implied in law	Contract created by a court for the parties, despite their wishes and intentions, in order to avoid injustice and/or the unjust enrichment of one party.	A contract to provide landscaping around a home in a development. When the homeowner fails to pay, a court orders the owner of the development to pay the landscaper because of the enhanced value of the development.
Executory	One in which some promise or obligation remains unfulfilled.	A contract to sell a horse, saddle, and bridle. The seller forgets to bring the saddle on the date of delivery.
Executed	One in which all parties have completed their promises or obligations under the terms of the agreement.	A contract to buy a computer for $2,000 with delivery effected by the seller in exchange for the buyer's giving a certified check for $2,000 at the time of delivery.

Exhibit 9.2 shows the different classifications of contracts.

SUMMARY

The law of contracts affects us more often than any other area of law. Commercial law, especially the Uniform Commercial Code's integration of older statutes and common law rules, has become increasingly important in the United States. For the first time, many statutes that attempt to harmonize areas of the law that previously varied from state to state now exist. Besides statutes, the common law has also spawned numerous contract principles that affect the legal environment of business. Although the word *contract* has many definitions, it commonly means a legally binding and legally enforceable promise or set of promises between two or more competent parties.

Historically, contracts were of minor importance because a feudal society had little interest in protecting the parties' expectations. With the advent of freedom of contract and rising industrialism, by the nineteenth century contract law had outstripped property law in significance. Ironically, today the law appears to be swinging back to a concern with status, as evidenced by protective statutes and common law decisions.

Six requirements must be met for a contract to be valid: (1) an agreement (that is, an offer and an acceptance), (2) supported by consideration, (3) made by parties having the capacity to contract, (4) based on these parties' genuine assent, (5) grounded in a legal undertaking, and (6) expressed in proper form, if applicable. Contracts may be classified as formal or informal; unilateral or bilateral; valid, voidable, void, or unenforceable; express or implied; and executed or executory. These categories are not necessarily mutually exclusive.

A contract implied in fact consists of evidence of sufficient facts or conduct from which a court can conclude that the parties intended a binding agreement between themselves. A contract implied in fact thus is a true contract. A quasi contract, or contract implied in law, is not a true contract. It is a different type of implied contract in which a court will create a contract for the parties, despite their wishes and intentions, in order that justice may be served. Not every situation in which a benefit has been conferred, however, gives rise to this equitable, restitutionary remedy called a quasi contract.

9.2

COLLECTING DAMAGES FROM A FRIEND

One of Dan's friends recently purchased a car stereo and a set of speakers for his new car. As a favor for his friend, Dan installed the stereo and the speakers. In order to complete the installation, Dan had to purchase some installation hardware and had to cut larger openings in the dash and the rear deck. By the time Dan had obtained the installation hardware, cut the holes, and installed the stereo system, he had spent about four hours working on his friend's car. Once the installation was complete, the friend complained that Dan had taken too long to complete the job, causing the friend to miss an appointment. He also complained about the holes Dan had cut, alleging that they were not needed and that they hurt the aesthetic look of the interior. Dan was offended by this response to his "good deed" and decided that he should be compensated for his efforts. (He also would like an apology, but realizes that there *are* limits to his legal options.) He asks you whether he can recover for his time and expenses in either contract law or under quasi-contract. What will you tell him?

BUSINESS CONSIDERATIONS If a service business needs to modify or alter the customer's property in order to render the service, should the business obtain permission before making the modification or alteration, or should the business just complete the job? What legal issues might doing the alteration without prior permission raise?

ETHICAL CONSIDERATIONS Is it ethical for an employee to use his or her employer's tools and equipment to do favors for friends? What ethical issues are raised when an employee does so?

PERSONAL LAW

DISCUSSION QUESTIONS

1. Define the term *contract.*
2. Distinguish between a contractual obligation and a social obligation.
3. Name and define the six requirements for a valid contract.
4. Why do some commentators claim that the history of contract law has swung from status to freedom of contract and back again?
5. Explain the following categories of contracts: (a) formal, (b) informal, (c) unilateral, (d) bilateral, (e) valid, (f) voidable, (g) void, (h) unenforceable, (i) express, (j) implied, (k) executory, and (l) executed.
6. What are the legal requirements for showing a quasi contract?
7. What is the Uniform Commercial Code, and why is it important?
8. Suppose Joan asks the bank for a loan. What kind of a contract will result from the bank's granting her this loan?
9. A contract involving an interest in land (such as a contract for the sale of a house) must be in writing. What is the legal effect of an oral contract in this situation?
10. What is the difference between a contract implied in fact and a contract implied in law?

CASE PROBLEMS AND WRITING ASSIGNMENTS

1. Wallace Brown went to a 7-Eleven store to purchase two California lottery tickets. The store clerk informed him that the terminal was not functioning properly and that he could purchase only tickets with terminal-generated number selections. The clerk suggested Brown travel to another store nearby, but he was unable to get there in time to purchase tickets. Brown later sued the California State Lottery Commission (the state), the Southland Corporation (which was doing business as 7-Eleven Stores), and the 7-Eleven clerk for breach of contract. Brown alleged that the state's advertisements soliciting participation in the lottery enticed him to accept this offer of a "shortcut to millions." He claimed that his acceptance of this offer—the tendering of his play slips and sufficient money to the 7-Eleven clerk—created an enforceable unilateral contract. Hence, Brown argued that the failure of the clerk to sell him the lottery tickets resulted in a loss to him of approximately $7.25 million because he would have picked the winning numbers. Should Brown prevail in this breach of contract action? [See *Brown* v. *California State Lottery Comm'n,* 284 Cal.Rptr. 108 (Cal.App. 1991).]

2. Carole B. Tindal, the former wife of deceased policyholder Thomas Badners, sued Prudential Life Insurance Company (Prudential) and First Alabama Bank of South Baldwin (FAB) for breach of contract. While still married, the Badners had taken out a Prudential life insurance policy that named Thomas as the insured and Carole as his beneficiary. An agreement between Thomas and FAB required FAB to pay the monthly premium ($28.62) by drawing a "Prumatic" draft each month on account number 21-076-50, owned by Thomas. In March 1984, when Thomas and Carole were divorced, Thomas closed his checking account (21-076-50) and opened a new one. Thereafter, whenever Prudential sent the draft on the closed account, FAB personnel manually would change the account number of the draft to the number of a funded account (either Thomas's personal or business account). This was all done with Thomas's knowledge. Eventually, Thomas requested that the draft be deducted from his personal account. However, he never formally changed his account number with Prudential on the "Prumatic" draft. This procedure continued for more than 25 months, until June 1986. For reasons that are unclear, FAB did not pay the June premium draft but returned it to Prudential on 12 June 1986. The statement closing date for both of Thomas's active checking accounts with FAB was 17 June 1986. Thomas received the statements issued on that date; but they were not opened until after his death, which had occurred on 18 July 1986. Prudential subsequently paid Carole greatly reduced benefits, using the facts that FAB returned the June 1986 premium draft unpaid and Thomas died outside the 31-day policy grace period as justifications. Carole, seeking the entire insurance proceeds, claimed that FAB personnel's actions in manually charging the monthly draft to an open account for more than 25 consecutive months (with Thomas's knowledge and approval) had created a contract implied in fact between FAB and Thomas by which FAB was to continue paying the Prudential drafts out of this new account. Did FAB's failure to honor the June 1986 draft constitute a breach of contract? [See *First Alabama Bank* v. *Prudential Life Ins.,* 619 So.2d 1313 (Ala. 1993).]

3. Participants in American Airlines's (American's) frequent flyer program challenged American's retroactive changes in the program's terms and conditions that would limit the seats subject to frequent flyer credits and restrict the dates on which one could use

such credits. The plaintiffs claimed that the application of these changes to previously accumulated mileage credits violated the Illinois consumer fraud and deceptive business practices act and constituted a breach of contract. American maintained that the Airline Deregulation Act of 1978 (ADA), which prohibits states from enacting or enforcing any law having the force and effect of law relating to airlines' rates, routes, or services, preempted (that is, precluded) the plaintiffs' claims. The plaintiffs answered that contention by arguing that the terms and conditions offered by airlines and accepted by consumers are privately ordered obligations and therefore do not amount to a state's enforcing any law relating to airlines' rates, routes, or services. Rather, according to the plaintiffs, the common law remedy for a contractual commitment voluntarily undertaken and confined to the contract's terms simply holds parties to their agreements—in this case to business judgments an airline has made public about its rates and services. Would the ADA permit state-law-based court adjudications of routine breach of contract claims? [See *American Airlines, Inc.* v. *Wolens*, 513 U.S. 219 (1995).]

4. Leo Sonnenburg and Gerald Hartnett, Indiana state mental hospital patients, filed a class action lawsuit against the governor of the state and the commissioner of the state department of mental health. The plaintiffs sought compensation for labor they performed—fixing meals, scrubbing dishes, cutting grass, styling hair, washing laundry, typing administrative reports, and the like—during their hospital stays. What theory could the plaintiffs use, and would they win their case? [See *Bayh* v. *Sonnenburg*, 573 N.E.2d 398 (Ind. 1991).]

5. Ed Hoon, an architect, asked Pate Construction Co., Inc. (Pate) and five other prequalified contractors to submit a bid on the Stuart construction project that Hoon's firm was developing. The written instructions accompanying the requests for bids stated that Hoon intended to award the bid to the lowest bidder and that he reserved the right to reject any and all bids for any reason. Although Pate was the lowest bidder, Hoon awarded the bid to the second lowest bidder. While agreeing that ordinarily no contract results from the mere making of a bid pursuant to an invitation to bid, Pate nonetheless sued Hoon for breach of an implied contract in which Hoon allegedly had promised to give Pate's bid "fair consideration." Should a court find Pate's contentions persuasive? [See *Hoon* v. *Pate Construction Co., Inc.*, 607 So.2d 423 (Fla.App. 1992).]

6. **BUSINESS APPLICATION CASE** Charles Koehler, the owner of Gateway Exteriors, Inc. (Gateway), claimed that in the spring or summer of 1990 a concrete contractor recommended Gateway to Joseph Knapp, one of Suntide Homes's (Suntide's) employees. According to Koehler, Knapp stopped by Gateway's office and told Koehler about Suntide and the Tiffany Square subdivision for which Suntide anticipated building 60 homes. Knapp said that Suntide had a couple of siding contractors doing its work, but Suntide was not happy with them. Koehler then told Knapp about Gateway's operations. Thereupon, Knapp said he would give Koehler preliminary plans to bid. Koehler thought that Knapp, like most builders, also would get bids from other subcontractors. Knapp subsequently sent Koehler plans for four different home styles. On 26 July 1990, Gateway gave Knapp a proposal for (and some samples of) Dutch-lap vinyl siding for these four home styles. Knapp said the proposal and prices looked good and asked how much more Triple 3 siding would cost. Koehler told him it would be 9 percent more, and Knapp indicated that this price would be fine. At that point, Knapp told Koehler that Suntide had not as yet broken the ground for the subdivision. Knapp subsequently gave Koehler the names of other subdivisions, however, and asked Koehler to look at the siding installation and tell him what Gateway would do differently to avoid some of the problems that had arisen in those subdivisions. Koehler thereafter told Knapp what he (Koehler) had observed and how Gateway would do the job. Knapp later informed Koehler that Suntide still was waiting for the final plans for the Tiffany Square subdivision. In August 1990, after Koehler had met with Knapp about colors and styles, Gateway ordered Triple 3 and Dutch-lap siding in the most popular colors for approximately 12 homes at a cost of $32,640.25. Suntide had not yet built any homes in the subdivision, and Knapp had not asked Koehler to order ahead of time; nonetheless, Koehler had ordered the materials because he understood that Knapp wanted him to be prepared. Koehler furthermore testified that he did not know how many homeowners would order vinyl siding or what colors, styles, or amounts they would choose. On 5 September 1990, Gateway received what Koehler termed a "start sheet" for lot 44, a display house. This document, entitled "Tiffany Square Color Selection," indicated the outside selections for a display house on Lot #44. In October 1990, after Koehler had shown Knapp the siding Koehler had ordered, Koehler submitted a second proposal for Tiffany Square. At the end of October or the beginning of November, Koehler went to the Tiffany Square development, where he noticed display homes had been started and that a siding crew was working on one house. Koehler testified

Knapp apologized and said that the office mistakenly had sent out the old contractors and that Suntide would let Koehler construct houses in another subdivision. On about 5 November 1990, Gateway received a payment schedule addressed "to whom it may concern" and which showed the payment schedules for six of Suntide's subdivision developments, including Tiffany Square. Ultimately, Gateway never supplied or installed siding on any of the Tiffany Square homes. On 20 January 1991, Gateway filed a breach of contract action against Suntide. Had Koehler provided sufficient evidence of the existence of a valid and enforceable contract with Suntide? (See *Gateway Exteriors, Inc.* v. *Suntide Homes, Inc.*, 882 S.W. 2d 275 [Mo.App. 1994].)

7. **ETHICAL APPLICATION CASE** Celeste Ahern found that her air conditioner was failing to cool her home. She picked a service person, James M. Knecht, because of his Yellow Pages advertisement, which stressed honesty. Knecht gave Ahern the following quotation for the work he needed to do: making the service call of $69 combined with the $85 charge for diagnosing problems in the system ($154); raising and leveling the condenser and slab ($210); wet washing the condenser and coils ($138); checking, cleaning, and tightening all electrical connections ($69); leak checking eight service connections and stopping the obvious leak at the condenser with a suction nut and seal cap ($72); and installing instruments for monitoring the coolant and adding all required freon to bring the unit back up to service ($119). The total amount quoted to Ahern (to her amazement) was $762. When Ahern told Knecht that she needed to leave the house to attend to other business, he told her that he required payment at the time he did the work. Therefore, Ahern prepared a check in the amount of $762, which she left with Knecht. After she departed, Knecht raised and leveled the condenser and slab merely by shoveling several inches of landscaping gravel (taken from Ahern's patio) under the slab. Moreover, during the process of adding the freon, Knecht, by mistakenly switching the compressor's wires, apparently further disabled the unit. Consequently, Ahern hired another service person who fixed the unit properly for $72. Ahern and her husband sued to recover the $762 paid to Knecht. What grounds could a court use to set aside the agreement with Knecht? If the facts were different and Knecht were your employee, how would you, as the manager, handle this situation from an ethical point of view? Would you fire Knecht, make complete restitution to the Aherns, or do something completely different? [See *Ahern* v. *Knecht*, 563 N.E.2d 787 (Ill.App. 1990).]

8. **IDES CASE** Cecil Perkins, in partnership with Kindred Homes, Inc. (Kindred), began developing Crosswoods Subdivision. Bill Daugherty, a licensed engineer, was retained to do the engineering and contracting work for the subdivision. There was no written contract between Daugherty and the developers; rather, he worked by verbal agreement. Perkins and Kindred, each taking a portion of the property, later dissolved their partnership. Daugherty, however, continued to work on Kindred's portion of the property and planned to complete his work on Perkins's property as well, after finishing Kindred's. Daugherty still had no written contract with either Perkins or Kindred. Daugherty subsequently worked on Perkins's property until it became apparent that Perkins had obtained the help of another engineer for the project. At that time, Daugherty sent Perkins a bill for $18,256.52. When Perkins did not pay the amount due, Daugherty filed an engineer's lien against Perkins's property. This action, in turn, led Perkins to sue Daugherty for damages allegedly incurred by the wrongful filing of the lien. Daugherty counterclaimed for the amount of the bill, plus interest on the lien. Should Daugherty receive compensation for the work done for Perkins on the basis of either a contract implied in fact or a contract implied in law? [See *Perkins* v. *Daugherty*, 722 S.W.2d 907 (Ky.App. 1987).]

NOTES

1. A. G. Guest, *Anson's Law of Contracts*, 26th ed. (Oxford: Clarendon Press, 1984), p. 1.
2. Bradford Stone, *Uniform Commercial Code in a Nutshell*, 2e (St. Paul, MN: West, 1995), pp. ix–x.
3. *Restatement (Second) of Contracts*, §1 (St. Paul, MN: American Law Institute Publishers, 1981).
4. Associated Press, "High Flying Scheme to Buy Jump-Jet from Pepsi Shot Down," *The National Law Journal* (2 September 1996), p. A20.

Chapter 10

Contractual Agreement: Mutual Assent

O U T L I N E

The First Step in Contract Formation
Mutual Assent
The Objective Theory of Contracts
Offer
Acceptance
Summary
Discussion Questions
Case Problems and Writing Assignments

A G E N D A

As the Kochanowskis work to get CIT "up and running," they will be entering into quite a few contracts. They will be buying goods and services from a number of businesses. They need to know *how* to enter contracts, and they will need to know what legal effect different types of communications have on the existence—or lack thereof—of contracts. They will also want to know whether any advertising they use constitutes a potential contract offer.

These are just a few of the areas where they might have questions. Be prepared! You never know when one of the Kochanowskis will ask for your help or advice.

THE FIRST STEP IN CONTRACT FORMATION

Agreement is the essence of a contract. Once there has been a valid offer by the *offeror* (the person making the offer) and a valid acceptance by the *offeree* (the person to whom the offer is made), we are well on our way to having a legally binding contract because, generally, few problems with consideration, capacity, genuine assent, legality, and proper form (the remaining requirements for a contract) exist. On the other hand, precisely because these two aspects of contract formation (offer and acceptance) are so important, courts closely examine the words and conduct of the parties to determine whether a **bona fide** offer and acceptance indeed are present.

Bona fide
In good faith; honest; without deceit; innocent.

From common law times, numerous rules have developed for checking the authenticity of the offer and the acceptance. Broadly speaking, under these rules, the threshold for contract formation remains high because courts require rather clear-cut statements that the parties are freely and voluntarily entering into a particular agreement. Conversely, under the Uniform Commercial Code (UCC), a court can more easily infer a bona fide offer and acceptance from the *conduct* of the parties, even if the parties have omitted terms such as price, mode of payment, or mode of delivery. In this chapter, we discuss the reasons for these developments.

MUTUAL ASSENT

The assent of both parties to the agreement is a requirement of the initial phase of contract formation. This assent must be mutual, and the parties must agree to exactly the same terms. In short, both parties must actually intend to bind themselves to the terms embodied in the offer and acceptance. Without mutual assent, no agreement ever comes into existence.

THE OBJECTIVE THEORY OF CONTRACTS

Given the necessity for mutual assent, the question of how to judge whether the parties have mutually consented to the transaction naturally arises. If you are in a particularly mischievous mood, you may say to a friend, "Tom, I'll let you buy my mountain bike for $300; that's the offer." Since Tom knows the frame itself sells for $500, Tom quickly says, "I'll take it." Does this exchange constitute a valid offer and acceptance? Will you have to sell the bike, or will the law permit you to say that you were kidding and did not intend to make an offer?

Common law rules tell us that the offeror has the right to set the terms of the offer (and to control the method by which the offeree accepts the offer). In so doing, the offeror must exhibit a clear and present intent to offer. You fairly straightforwardly enumerated the terms of the offer, it seems. Is it nevertheless apparent from your statement that you were only kidding?

To determine whether a valid offer exists, the law applies an **objective** standard. Under common law, to decide whether an offer has been made, a court or a jury puts itself in the offeree's place (i.e., in Tom's shoes) to ascertain if a reasonable offeree would believe that you, in offering the bike at this price, were serious. Since your words and conduct are judged by an objective (instead of a **subjective**) test, your secret intent (i.e., you were joking and did not really want to sell the bike) cannot be shown. Hence, in this example, a court may find that you have made a valid offer to Tom.

Objective
Capable of being observed and verified without being distorted by personal feelings and prejudices.

Subjective
Capable of being observed and verified through individual feelings and emotions.

Obviously, this result depends heavily on the facts. If you clearly are jesting, are excited, or are even visibly angry, details supporting the existence of these facts may lead to a different result. Thus, a word to the wise: Beware of making "offers" you do not mean, since both common law and UCC principles may hold you to these statements.

The following case illustrates these important concepts.

Employment at will
An employment relationship in which, owing to the absence of any contractual obligation to remain in the relationship, either party can terminate the relationship at any time and for any reason not prohibited by law.

10.1 BARBER v. SMH (U.S.), INC.

509 N.W.2d 791 (Mich.App. 1993)

FACTS In May 1989, SMH (U.S.), Inc. (SMH) employed Jon Barber as a sales representative to sell Tissot watches to independent jewelry stores in certain Midwest states. Barber claimed that during the course of his discussions with company executives, he had negotiated the specific terms and conditions under which the company could terminate him. Barber thus argued that SMH's vice president of sales had promised Barber that "as long as [Barber] was profitable and doing the job for [SMH], [Barber] would be [SMH's] exclusive representative in . . . Michigan, Ohio, and Indiana." Barber likewise maintained that the company's executives had reiterated this promise during his tenure as a sales representative. In 1991, upon SMH's termination of his employment, Barber filed a breach of contract lawsuit based on his contention that this alleged verbal promise had created an employment relationship that SMH could not terminate in the absence of just cause.

ISSUE Had SMH's executives orally promised that Barber's employment could not be terminated in the absence of just cause?

HOLDING No. The application of the "reasonable person"/objective test would lead to the conclusion that Barber's employment was at will and that the company therefore could terminate him even in the absence of just cause.

REASONING The court noted that the law presumes that employment contracts of indefinite duration provide for **employment at will**. However, the court emphasized that one may rebut this presumption if one shows the existence of an express contract, oral or written, forbidding discharge in the absence of just cause. The court moreover stressed that contractual liability is consensual and will not arise unless the parties mutually assent to be bound. Put differently, when analyzing oral statements for contractual implications, a court must determine the meaning that reasonable persons might have attached to the language. In order to determine whether there was mutual assent to a contract, the court applies an objective test that looks "to the expressed words of the parties and their visible acts." In other words, a court must consider the relevant circumstances surrounding the transaction, including all writings, oral statements, and other conduct by which the parties have manifested their intent. According to the court, oral contracts for just-cause employment will be recognized only where the circumstances suggest that both parties intended to be bound. In short, to overcome the presumption of employment at will, oral statements of job security must be clear and unequivocal. Here, the court found an absence of evidence to prove the existence of terminations for just cause only.

As to Barber's assertion that SMH had promised it would employ him "as long as he was profitable and doing the job," the court commented that Barber had not asserted that SMH had made this promise in response to Barber's articulated concerns that he be terminated only for just cause. The court also viewed as dispositive a written document purporting to constitute an agreement between Barber and the company (Barber acknowledged receiving a copy of this "agreement" but denied signing it). Specifically, the court construed the language allowing for the termination of the agreement by either party as the only objective evidence presented, indicative in itself of an intent and understanding—at least on the part of SMH—that the relationship between it and Barber was one of employment at will. Accordingly, the court held that the oral statements were insufficient to rise to the level of an agreement for just-cause employment.

BUSINESS CONSIDERATIONS Although a majority of states follow the employment-at-will doctrine, some states have carved out public policy exceptions to this rule. In other words, in some cases courts will disregard the rule if it believes the employer has asked the employee to engage in activities that are detrimental to the welfare and mores of the public. (Usually the employee refuses to accede to the employer's wishes, and when fired,

10.1 BARBER v. SMH (U.S.), INC. *(cont.)* 509 N.W.2d 791 (Mich.App. 1993)

subsequently uses the employer's request as a basis for a wrongful discharge suit against the employer.) Give some examples of activities that you believe may constitute such public policy exceptions.

ETHICAL CONSIDERATIONS Some employment-at-will jurisdictions prohibit firings based on whistleblowing. Discuss the ethics of whistleblowing, especially when, how, and why an employee should (or should not) engage in whistleblowing.

OFFER

Let us look more closely at this first phase of reaching agreement: the offer. An *offer* generally involves an indication (by a promise or another commitment) of one's willingness to do or refrain from doing something in the future. An offer implicitly invites another person, in order to seal the bargain, to assent to the promise or commitment.

Clear Intention to Contract and Definiteness of the Offer

If it is to fulfill the common law's requirements, an offer must show a clear intention to contract and be definite in all respects. An agreement to agree at some future time, for example, lacks these prerequisites of a common law offer. Similarly, statements of opinion, statements of intention, and preliminary negotiations do not result in bona fide offers because they lack definiteness. But reasonable people will differ as to what constitutes a clear, definite offer and what instead involves only preliminary negotiations or dickering.

Since these are questions of fact that a judge or jury can later decide, caution of course is desirable. If you want to make an offer, be specific in all particulars. On the other hand, haggling or dickering lacks this definiteness regarding the details of the transaction and your intentions. Such preliminary negotiations ordinarily are too vague to constitute a valid offer. Winning or losing a lawsuit can turn on such minute distinctions as how a court interprets the words expressed by the parties. For example, are the words, "I can send you two trademark logos at $5,000 per logo" identical in intent to "I offer to sell you two trademark logos at $5,000 per logo"? Many people would view these statements as virtually identical, but a strict common law interpretation treats only the second statement as a bona fide offer. The law views the other statement as an indication of a willingness to negotiate that does not rise to the level of a bona fide offer.

Output contract
A contract that calls for the buyer to purchase all the seller's production during the term of the contract.

Requirements contract
A contract in which the seller agrees to provide as much of a product or service as the buyer needs during the contract term.

Despite the common law requirement that an offer be definite in all its material (or essential) terms, you should be aware that the UCC relaxes this common law prerequisite in several significant ways. For instance, UCC § 2-204 states that a contract for sale under the Code will not fail for indefiniteness as long as the parties have intended to form a contract and a reasonably certain basis for giving an appropriate remedy exists even though one or more of the terms of the agreement may have been left open. In addition, the UCC contains several so-called gap-filling provisions whereby the court can supply the terms—including price, place of delivery, mode of payment—omitted by the parties.[1] The Code also validates **output** and **requirements**

contracts, both of which would be too indefinite for common law courts to enforce.[2] Because the Code is predicated on the idea that commercial people (particularly merchants) want to deal with each other, it has eliminated some of the ticklish technicalities that impede contract formation under common law. You will learn more about these and other revolutionary changes in common law brought about by the Uniform Commercial Code when you read Chapters 16 through 20.

Advertisements and Auctions

The law in general does not treat advertisements as valid offers but rather as invitations to deal, or statements of intention to sell certain merchandise. Advertisements are characterized in this fashion because they usually lack sufficient specificity to become offers. Instead, the law views advertisements as invitations for persons to come in and make offers for the types of goods and at the prices indicated in the advertisements. Notice that this rule demonstrates yet another "pro-offeror" tilt of the common law. A contrary perspective that advertisements constitute offers would presuppose that a merchant has an unlimited supply of merchandise. Thus, the principle that advertisements ordinarily are not offers protects merchants from the hardships such a contrary rule might produce. On occasion, however, an advertisement, catalog, circular, price list, or price quotation shows sufficient detail for a court to say that a valid offer exists. Such a result, however exceptional, sometimes occurs, as the following case demonstrates.

10.2 JACKSON v. INVESTMENT CORP. OF PALM BEACH — 585 So.2d 949 (Fla.App. 1991)

FACTS John Jackson read a *Miami Herald* ad that stated that the Pic-6 Jackpot for the last evening of the dog track racing season would be $825,000. Jackson attended the races on that date, picked the winners in the six designated races, and won the jackpot. However, Investment Corporation of Palm Beach (ICPB), the owner of the track that had placed the ad, contended that the ad should have stated the amount of the jackpot as $25,000. ICPB had submitted to the *Miami Herald* a prior ad on the face of which ICPB had written "Guaranteed Jackpot $25,000 Must Go." The confusion had resulted from the newspaper employee's mistaking the dollar sign with one slash through it for the number eight, thus causing the $800,000 error that had appeared in the final draft of the ad. On the night of the races, ICPB paid Jackson only $25,000. When Jackson later sued for the balance, he claimed that the ad constituted an offer and that he had accepted this offer. He therefore argued that he should recover the remaining $800,000.

ISSUE Did the advertisement in these circumstances constitute a valid offer?

HOLDING Yes. In these circumstances, an offer existed; and Jackson, by winning the Pic-6 bet, had accepted the offer.

REASONING ICPB contended that no valid offer ever existed because of an absence of any intention on ICPB's part to make the offer included in the published ad. Furthermore, ICPB argued, even if the circumstances had given rise to an offer, ICPB had revoked the offer prior to Jackson's acceptance. Finally, ICPB submitted, the ad simply constituted an "invitation to bargain," which does not, upon acceptance by the other party, create a completed contract. Jackson himself conceded that ICPB never intended the jackpot to amount to $825,000. However, in determining what the contract between the parties involved, ICPB's subjective intent was not material. The making of a contract depends not on the agreement of two minds in one intention, but on the agreement of two sets of external signs—not on the parties' having *meant* the same thing but on their having *said* the same thing. Professor Williston, in his work on *Contracts*, similarly states: "[T]he test of the true interpretation of an offer or acceptance is not what the party making it thought it meant or intended it to mean, but what a reasonable person in the position of the parties would have thought it meant." Here, all a member of the public had to do to accept the offer was to buy a winning ticket on six races. Jackson did so and thus enjoyed an enforceable contract against ICPB.

10.2 JACKSON v. INVESTMENT CORP. OF PALM BEACH *(cont.)* 585 So.2d 949 (Fla.App. 1991)

BUSINESS CONSIDERATIONS In hindsight, what—if anything—could ICPB have done to protect itself against being held liable for the printing error made by the *Miami Herald*? What might ICPB do in the future to avoid such litigation? The court presumably could have followed the usual rule that an advertisement is not an offer. Why did the court view this situation as an exception to that general rule?

ETHICAL CONSIDERATIONS Assess ICBP, Jackson, and the *Miami Herald*'s conduct from an ethical standpoint. Among other things, discuss who—if any of the three—in these circumstances has a rightful claim to the moral high ground.

Normally, courts require a showing that the merchant has placed some limitation on the advertised goods before courts will find that the advertisement constitutes an offer. For example, the merchant may have specified a time limit, such as "for one day only," on the advertisement. Or the merchant may have designated a quantity limit, such as "while they last" or "to the first 10 customers," in the advertisement. In such a situation, the courts are somewhat more likely to find that the advertisement is an offer and not an invitation to deal or to negotiate. Again, as the *Jackson* case shows, courts utilize as the deciding factor the objective standard of what a reasonable person would have thought.

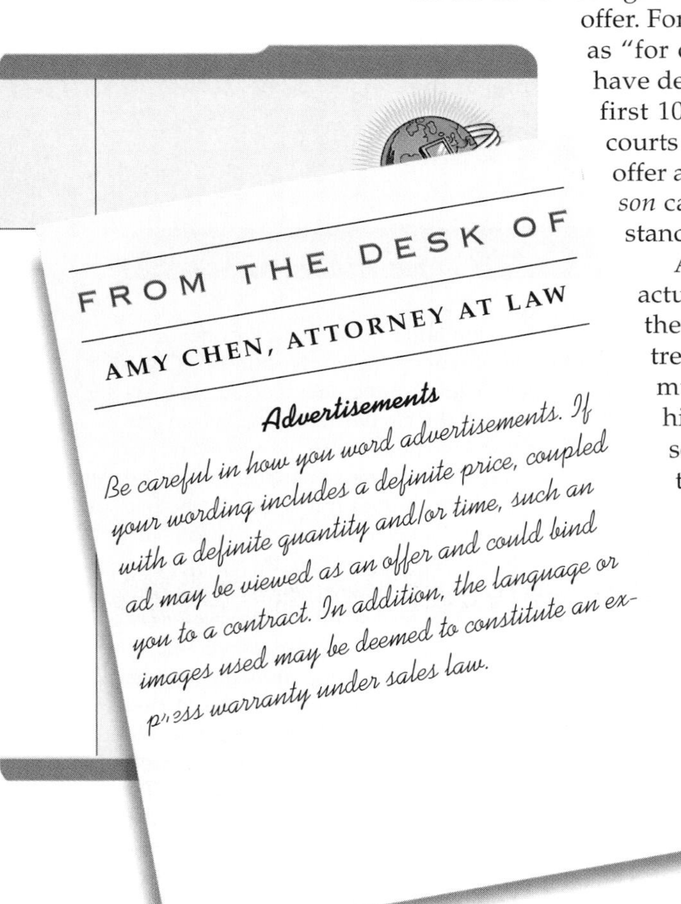

FROM THE DESK OF
AMY CHEN, ATTORNEY AT LAW
Advertisements
Be careful in how you word advertisements. If your wording includes a definite price, coupled with a definite quantity and/or time, such an ad may be viewed as an offer and could bind you to a contract. In addition, the language or images used may be deemed to constitute an express warranty under sales law.

Auctions are similar to advertisements in that the seller is not actually the offeror, although he or she may appear to be offering the goods for sale through the auctioneer. In reality, the law treats the bidder as the offeror. For a sale to occur, the seller must accept the bid. The seller can even refuse to sell to the highest bidder unless the auction is publicized as "without reserve." In this type of auction, the seller must let the goods go to the highest bidder; he or she cannot withdraw the goods if the price bid is too low. Once the auctioneer lets the hammer fall, the seller has accepted the bid. But until this point, the bidder can withdraw the offer and thus avoid the formation of a contract of sale. Section 2-328 of the UCC covers these points, which are discussed again in Chapter 17.

Communication of the Offer to the Offeree

Another requirement for a bona fide offer is that the offeror (or his or her agent) must communicate the offer to the offeree. At first glance this rule may seem nonsensical. How, you may ask, can a person accept an offer if he or she is ignorant of the existence of the offer! Believe it or not, that sometimes happens. For example, assume that two parties have been haggling over the terms of a real estate transaction. After much correspondence, the would-be buyer (offeree) writes, "Okay, you win. I will pay $80,000 for the land," and mails the letter to the offeror. A day later, before the arrival of the mail, the would-be seller (offeror) coincidentally arrives at the same figure, and writes, "This is my final offer. I will sell you the land for $80,000. Take it or leave it," and mails this letter to the offeree. Later, the offeror wants to sell this land to a third person who is interested in purchasing it; but the original offeree claims that he and the offeror now have a contract for $80,000. Despite the claims of the original offeree, the offeror probably can sell the land to the third party because most courts will hold that the first party (the original offeree) has not validly accepted the offer. This is true because at the time of the would-be buyer's purported acceptance, no offer to sell the land at a price of $80,000 had been communicated to the original offeree. And, as mentioned previously, an offer has no legal effect until the offeror (or his or her agent) communicates it to the offeree. Courts liken the correspondences in this example to identical offers crossing in the mail, each asking for and necessitating an acceptance before any valid contract ensues, and neither receiving the required acceptance. Note that this result once again underscores the common law offeror's iron-fisted control over the terms of the offer (and the method of acceptance).

This requirement of communicating the offer to the offeree sometimes arises in the context of *general offers.* Although most offers are made by one person to another, offers made to the general public or a similar class of large numbers of persons are perfectly legal, as the *Jackson* case discussed earlier indicates. A reward, such as money for the arrest and conviction of the persons who vandalized an office complex, represents the best example of a general offer. Even though some case results to the contrary exist, most courts require that the party who performs the act contemplated by the reward (here, the identification of the vandals so as to lead to their prosecution and conviction) must have known of the reward and must have intended the act as acceptance of that offer. Under this view, in order for a valid acceptance to occur, a general offer must be communicated to the offeree. Under the rule followed in a majority of jurisdictions, then, a person who coincidentally identifies the vandals without knowledge of the reward is ineligible to receive the reward.

As you will see, in the following case, the court used these common law principles to determine the identity of the person to whom the offeror had intended to communicate the offer.

10.3 LUCAS v. GODFREY

467 N.W.2d 180 (Wis.App. 1991)

FACTS Robyn Warren Godfrey had been George Lucas's secretary for several years. She performed various office duties, including picking up the mail. From time to time, Godfrey received personal mail at the office address, a post office box. This controversy centers around a contest entry form sent to that address. The *Reader's Digest* sweepstakes is a promotional effort on the part of the magazine, designed among other things to increase subscription sales. The magazine sends contest "eligibility cards" to people around the country, who then return the card to the magazine and thereby enter the sweepstakes.

The magazine obtains lists of subscribers to various other publications and mails promotional materials and contest eligibility cards to persons whose names appear on these lists. Each card contains a number code indicating the particular magazine subscriber list from which the *Reader's Digest* takes the recipient's name and address. *Reader's Digest* sent one such eligibility card, addressed by a computer, to "Robyn W. Lucas" at the office post office box address. Godfrey crossed out the initial and the name "Lucas," inserted her surname in its place, and returned the card. The magazine eventually selected this card as the

10.3 LUCAS v. GODFREY *(cont.)* 467 N.W.2d 180 (Wis.App. 1991)

winner of a $150,000 prize. The code number on the card indicated that the name and mailing address had been taken from a list of subscribers to *Ellery Queen's Mystery Magazine* (*Ellery Queen*). Godfrey was an *Ellery Queen* subscriber, but Lucas was not. The circulation director of *Ellery Queen* testified that, for a period of time, Godfrey's subscription was listed in the name "Robyn W. Lucas." The magazine had corrected this error and at some point Godfrey began receiving the magazine in her own name. When Godfrey's receipt of the sweepstakes prize became known, Lucas, claiming that he was entitled to the money, sued Godfrey and *Reader's Digest.* Godfrey answered and cross-claimed, seeking a judgment that the money was hers. In light of these competing claims, *Reader's Digest* deposited the $150,000 with the court and asked the court to decide whether Lucas or Godfrey was entitled to claim the prize.

ISSUE Was there a contract between *Reader's Digest* and either Godfrey or Lucas?

HOLDING Yes. The contract was between the magazine and Godfrey, the intended offeree, who, by returning the sweepstakes card, had accepted the offer.

REASONING Lucas submitted that because *Reader's Digest* had addressed the card to "Robyn W. Lucas," and because Robyn Warren Godfrey is not "Robyn W. Lucas," she would be unable to recover. (Under that reasoning, of course, neither could Lucas.) Contract law, however, holds that the manifested intention of the offeror determines the person or persons in whom is created a power of acceptance. According to the *Reader's Digest* general counsel, the magazine sent the contest eligibility card to the Lucas post office box to get the contest materials and the magazine's promotional messages to prospective customers—in this particular case, active subscribers to *Ellery Queen.* Hence, these facts admit of a single reasonable inference, that *Reader's Digest* intended to offer entry in its sweepstakes to a person whose name appeared on the list of active subscribers to *Ellery Queen* and who would receive mail at the address taken from that magazine's subscriber list—Post Office Box 579, Wisconsin Rapids, Wisconsin. The fact that the card was addressed to Robyn W. Lucas, rather than Robyn Godfrey, is explained by the manner in which Godfrey's name was originally—and mistakenly—listed in the *Ellery Queen* subscriber files. The evidence indicated that any error in listing Godfrey's name that appeared in the *Ellery Queen* files, and thus on the *Reader's Digest* sweepstakes computer-generated contest mailing label, was indeed inadvertent and therefore would not detract from the validity of the *Reader's Digest* sweepstakes offer. An entrant or contestant who performed the act requested—returning the card—would accept the offer to enter the contest and thereby form a valid and binding contract with the promoter. Consequently, by accepting the offer *Reader's Digest* had made to her, Godfrey became eligible for the prize. When *Reader's Digest* selected her number as the winner, she, not Lucas, was entitled to receive the $150,000 prize.

BUSINESS CONSIDERATIONS As noted in the case, magazines use sweepstakes as a promotional tool for increasing subscription sales. Yet, given the vast number of pieces of "junk mail" people receive each day, many recipients may well toss the sweepstakes letter into the wastebasket. If you were the head of marketing for *Reader's Digest,* how would you go about assessing the success of this particular marketing mechanism?

ETHICAL CONSIDERATIONS Many sweepstakes letters say on the outside of the envelope, "We have $100,000 waiting for you"—or something to that effect. In actuality, of course, you are not an instant winner. Documented stories and cases, though, show that some people actually believe the caption on the envelope. Is this advertising arguably deceptive as well as unethical? Explain.

Exhibit 10.1 summarizes the steps needed for reaching an agreement.

Lapse
The expiration or the loss of an opportunity because of the passage of a time limit within which the opportunity had to be exercised.

Duration of the Offer

Usually, offers satisfy these common law rules and will be legally effective. The next question that often arises concerns the duration of the offer; that is, how long will it remain open? Basically, four methods for terminating an offer exist: (1) lapse, (2) revocation, (3) rejection, and (4) acceptance.

It is quite possible that the offeror will state in the offer when it will terminate and thus set the life span for the offer. This brings about the potential **lapse** of the offer. For instance, an offer may state, among other things, "This offer will remain open for 30 days." If after 30 days the offeree has not responded, the offer automatically lapses. The offeror is under no legal duty to communicate the fact that the offer has lapsed to the offeree. After 30 days, the offeror can, without worrying about facing a lawsuit from the first offeree, make the same offer to anyone else.

In many cases, the offeror neglects to state any time period in the offer. In these situations, how long does the offeree have before he or she must respond? To avoid lapse, the offeree must accept within a *reasonable time*. Determination of what constitutes a reasonable time becomes a question of fact that a judge or jury decides. The trier of fact will consider such things as industry conditions, customs, and usages of trade. In volatile commodities markets, an offer may lapse in a matter of seconds. On the other hand, given a downturn in the real estate market, a period of days or weeks may constitute a reasonable time if the offer involves a sale of real property. To avoid such uncertainties, the offeror should state specifically when the offer lapses.

Lapse also may occur by operation of law. That is, regardless of the wishes of the parties, an offer automatically lapses upon the following occurrences: (1) the death or insanity of the offeror or offeree, (2) the **supervening** illegality of the subject matter of the offer, or (3) the destruction of the subject matter involved in the offer. In other words, if Joe Olivetti offers to sell his car to Joan Hays but dies before she accepts, the offer automatically lapses. Joe's estate does not have to inform Joan of his death. Similarly, if two days after Joe makes the offer, his city passes an ordinance stating that sales of private cars without safety stickers are illegal, Joe's offer will lapse if the car does not have a sticker. If lightning strikes the car and destroys it, the offer also lapses. No communication to Joan is necessary in these last instances either.

Another method of terminating an offer, besides lapse, is **revocation**. Under common law, the offeror possesses virtually unlimited rights to revoke at any time before acceptance. This is true whether or not the offeror uses the word revoke, as long as an intention to terminate the offer is clear. In general, revocation does not become effective until it is communicated to (or received by) the offeree. Interestingly, such communication may be effective whether communicated directly or

10.1

SALES/MANAGEMENT

UNDERSTANDING CONTRACT FORMATION

John has been studying contract law in his Legal Environment of Business class. He explains to the family that, based on what he has been told in class, contracts are fairly technical and difficult to create, due in part to such things as the "mirror image" rule. He believes that this gives CIT a great deal of latitude in discussing its product with potential customers because much of the conversation can be classified as mere "sales talk," and no contract offer will result. Tom is not sure that John has a thorough knowledge of contract law. Tom remembers that service contracts and employment contracts are often technical and that courts are likely to examine them very carefully. However, he has also heard that courts are much more likely to "find" contracts in the area of sales even if the courts discern that the traditional common law requirements are lacking. Tom asks you for your advice. What will you tell him?

BUSINESS CONSIDERATIONS What can a business do to protect itself from the exuberance of its sales force when the sales representatives are trying to make contracts with customers?

ETHICAL CONSIDERATIONS Suppose a business found itself with a questionable deal and there was a possible escape from that deal due to a technicality in contract law. Is it ethical for the firm to use this technicality to get out of the deal? Would it be ethical to hold another party to a contract he or she did not realize was being formed?

Supervening
Coming or happening as something additional or unexpected.

Revocation
The cancellation, rescission, or annulment of something previously done or offered.

EXHIBIT 10.1 Offer: The First Phase of Reaching an Agreement

A *bona fide* offer by the offeror must:

- Show a *clear intention* to enter into a contract.
- Be *definite* in all respects.
- Be *communicated* to the offeree or to his or her agent.

Communications by the offeror that do *not* reflect a *bona fide* offer include:

- Any *undisclosed secret* intentions.
- Statements made in *jest* or in *strong excitement*.
- Preliminary negotiations.
- Price quotations, dickering, advertisements, invitations to deal.

indirectly. Using our earlier example, Joe may state bluntly, "Joan, I revoke my offer to you." Alternatively, Joan may hear that Joe has sold the car to Len Hill. In either case an effective revocation has occurred.

Usually, Joe will be dealing only with Joan or, at most, with a few parties. This is not the case with a general offer to the public. If Joe has lost his prize Dalmatian, Jake, and has offered a reward for the return of or information about the dog, Joe need only revoke his offer in the same manner (or medium) in which he made the original offer. Because it is too burdensome to require Joe to communicate with every possible "taker" of his offer, public revocation suffices. It is even effective against a person who has not seen the advertisement and who later comes forward with information about Jake.

Option
A contract to keep an offer open for some agreed-on time period.

Methods do exist for taming this seemingly unlimited power of revocation by the Joes of the world. For example, by forcing Joe to promise to keep the offer open for a stated time, Joan can prohibit Joe's power of revocation. The promise itself does not protect Joan from revocation. But if she takes an **option** on the car, Joe is legally bound to hold the offer open for the agreed-on period of time. Joan will have to pay Joe for the option; but once she does so, he cannot sell the car to anyone else during the option period without breaching this option contract. Usually, Joan is under no obligation to exercise the option. If she does not, Joe can keep the money or other consideration paid to him for the option. If Joan does exercise the option, normally the money paid for the option will be subtracted from the purchase price. Depending on the bargaining position of the parties, however, this is not always the case.

Another exception to the rule that an offeror can revoke an offer at any time before acceptance comes from UCC § 2-205:

> *An offer by a* merchant [emphasis added] *to buy or sell goods which by its terms gives assurance that it will be held open is not revocable, for lack of consideration, during the time stated, or if no time is stated, for a reasonable time, but in no event may such period of irrevocability exceed three months.*

The Code demands that merchants, as professionals, keep their word even if they have been given no consideration for their assurances. Simply put, the Code dramatically changes the common law doctrine regarding the offeror's right to revoke when the offeror is a **merchant** and the other provisions of § 2-205 have been met.

Finally, the equitable doctrine of **promissory estoppel** prohibits offerors from revoking their offers. Under this theory, offerors are prevented (estopped) from asserting a defense otherwise available to them (generally that they as common law offerors have the right to revoke the offer). For Joan, the offeree in our earlier example, to assert this doctrine, she must show that (1) Joe, the offeror, promised or represented to her that he would hold the offer open; (2) she relied on these promises or representations; (3) she consequently suffered a detriment (maybe she passed up another car because she thought she would get Joe's); and (4) injustice can be avoided only by forcing the offeror to leave the offer open. In several cases, successful plaintiffs have used this doctrine to cut off the offeror's power of revocation.

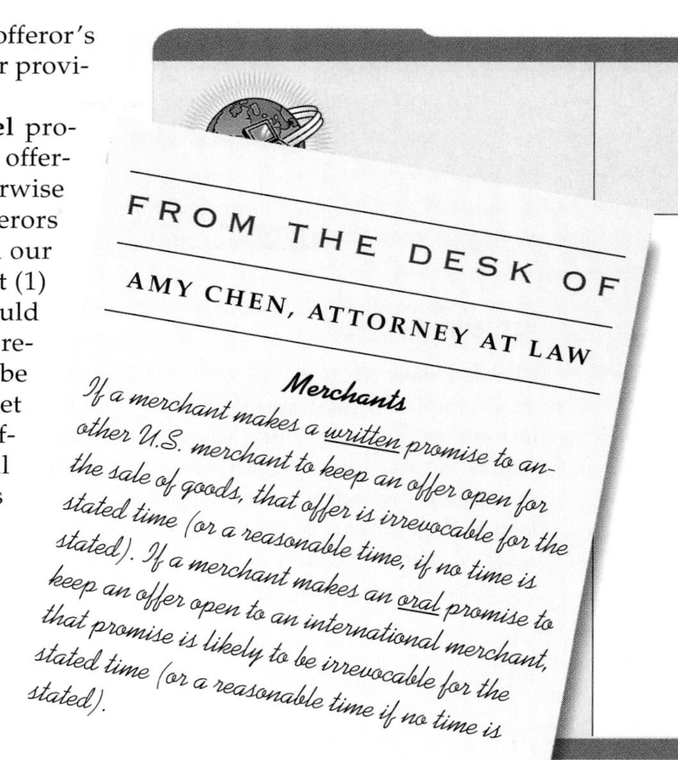

FROM THE DESK OF
AMY CHEN, ATTORNEY AT LAW
Merchants
If a merchant makes a written promise to another U.S. merchant to keep an offer open for the sale of goods, that offer is irrevocable for the stated time (or a reasonable time, if no time is stated). If a merchant makes an oral promise to keep an offer open to an international merchant, that promise is likely to be irrevocable for the stated time (or a reasonable time if no time is stated).

Thus far, we have dwelt on the offeror's power to terminate the offer. The offeree, of course, can refuse the offer and thereby terminate it. The law calls the offeree's power of termination **rejection**. Like revocations, rejections are not effective until communicated to (or received by) the offeror. Hence, as the offeree, Joan can tell Joe that she no longer is interested in the car and thereby reject Joe's offer.

The usual rule holds that an offer cannot later be accepted after lapse, revocation, or rejection, because after these events the offer has expired. Yet, if the parties nonetheless still are willing to deal, there may be a valid agreement subsequent to one of these events. However, the parties generally are not obligated to continue the transaction unless they find it advantageous to do so.

Exhibit 10.2 summarizes the various methods for terminating an offer.

ACCEPTANCE

Acceptance is the usual mode of terminating an offer. As noted earlier, this represents a significant moment for the offeror and offeree because they have arrived at an agreement at that time. Barring problems with consideration, capacity, genuineness of assent, legality, or proper form, a binding contract now exists.

Acceptance involves the offeree's assent to all the terms of the offer. Because this is so, the offeree's intention to be bound to the total offer must be clear. Thus, the offeree's uncommunicated mental reservations will not be binding on the offeror. As with offers, courts apply the objective test to see whether the acceptance is valid. That the acceptance is oral, written, or implied (e.g., through an act such as cashing a check) generally does not affect its validity, as long as the offer has been communicated to the offeree (or the offeree's agent), and it is the offeree (or the offeree's agent) who accepts.

Merchant
A person who regularly deals in goods of the kind or has the knowledge or skill peculiar to the practices or goods involved in the transaction.

Promissory estoppel
A doctrine that prohibits a promisor from denying the making of a promise or from escaping the liability for that promise because of the justifiable reliance of the promisee that the promise would be kept.

Rejection
A refusal to accept what is offered.

10.2

SALES/MANUFACTURING

REVOKING AN OFFER

CIT made a written offer to Joe Daily, one of its suppliers, in which the firm offered to buy Joe's entire supply of diagram boards and fiber optics at list price. CIT's letter promised to keep the offer open for four weeks. Two weeks after mailing the letter, CIT received an offer from another firm to sell diagram boards and fiber optics to CIT for 20% less than Joe's list price. Tom would like to accept this offer and has asked you whether he can revoke the offer to Joe. What will you tell him?

BUSINESS CONSIDERATIONS What factors should a business consider when it makes a written promise to keep an offer for goods open for a specific time? Would the business consider different factors if the offer were for the purchase of services?

ETHICAL CONSIDERATIONS Is the common law rule that generally permits revocation of an offer at any time prior to acceptance an ethical rule? Is the UCC rule regarding merchants and the sale of goods more ethical?

Mirror-Image Rule

Under common law rules, an acceptance must not only be clear but also unconditional. This concept, called the *mirror-image* or *matching-ribbons rule* of common law, means that the acceptance must match, term by term, the provisions in the offer. Any deviation from these terms, whether by alteration, addition, or omission, makes the acceptance invalid and tantamount to a rejection of the offer originally made. This result follows from the common law offeror's power to set the terms of the offer and the acceptance.

Any deviation from the terms of the offer brings about a qualified acceptance, known as a *counteroffer.* Counteroffers terminate offers unless the original offeror remains willing to accept the terms of the counteroffer. As you have seen in other contexts, such offerors are not obligated to do so unless they still want to deal. Therefore, if you desire to enter into a contract with the offeror, you should pay close attention to the language of the acceptance. Mere inquiries, requests, and terms implied by law, if part of the acceptance, do not invalidate it. Thus, if Joan says, "I'll take the car at $2,000 as you offered, but I'd like you to throw in the snow tires," a valid acceptance probably exists (Joan's added statement is a request). Contrast this with Joan's saying, "I accept if you throw in the snow tires." The latter statement sounds more like a proviso or a condition and may make the purported acceptance legally ineffective unless Joe is prepared to let Joan have the snow tires as part of the deal.

In the following case, the court concluded that the writings reflected a counteroffer and thus the lack of any mutual assent to the terms of the purported agreement. Note that in reaching this conclusion, the court applied the mirror-image rule.

10.4 D'AGOSTINO v. BANK OF RAVENSWOOD — 563 N.E.2d 886 (Ill.App. 1990)

FACTS Steve Spanos, the owner of the building located at 3928-32 N. Broadway in Chicago, was three years behind in property tax payments. Spanos listed the property for sale with a real estate broker, William Vranas. On 8 May 1986, Vranas presented Spanos with a written offer from Vincenzo D'Agostino to purchase the property for $230,000. An earnest money check in the amount of $1,000 was submitted with the offer. Spanos testified that when he received the offer on 13 May 1986, he drew a line through the $230,000 figure, raised the price to $235,000, initialed the price change, and signed the offer at the bottom. Later that day, Vranas informed Spanos that D'Agostino would not accept the offer at $235,000. Spanos then orally agreed with Vranas during a subsequent telephone conversation that he (Spanos) would reduce the price to the original $230,000. D'Agostino later drew a line through the $235,000 figure that Spanos had inserted in the offer, reduced the price to $230,000, and initialed the change. But Spanos never initialed

10.4 D'AGOSTINO v. BANK OF RAVENSWOOD *(cont.)* 563 N.E.2d 886 (Ill.App. 1990)

the document after D'Agostino had changed the written price back to $230,000. The parties continued, without success, to draft a contract that manifested a price acceptable to both. On 29 May, D'Agostino made another offer that included mortgage and inspection contingencies as well as certain seller's warranties. Shortly thereafter, Spanos rejected this offer; and on 10 June, Spanos sold the property to another buyer. Upon learning of this sale, D'Agostino sued the Bank of Ravenswood, the trustee for Spanos, for **specific performance** of the contract.

ISSUE Did the agreement dated 8 May 1986 represent an enforceable contract between Spanos and D'Agostino?

HOLDING No. Spanos's response was a counteroffer that rejected the original offer. In the absence of a valid contract, D'Agostino had no grounds for requesting specific performance.

REASONING An acceptance requiring any modification or change of terms constitutes a rejection of the original offer and becomes a counteroffer that the original offeror must accept before a valid contract is formed. In the present case, Spanos had rejected D'Agostino's original offer of 8 May when he (Spanos) drew a line through the $230,000 figure, raised the price to $235,000, initialed the price change, and signed the offer at the bottom. Spanos's actions thus created a counteroffer rather than an acceptance. Spanos's oral acquiescence to the previously offered price constituted merely an acceptance of a rejected offer. Because later acceptance ordinarily fails to revive a rejected offer, the evidence showed that a valid contract never came into existence. Accordingly, D'Agostino was not entitled to specific performance.

The court also held that Spanos's failure to sign the document after the alleged oral agreement to reduce the price to the original $230,000 made the contract unenforceable because of noncompliance with the Statute of Frauds. (You will learn in Chapter 13 that the Statute of Frauds requires that the defendant sign any contract involving a sale of land; otherwise, a court generally will refuse to give effect to the contractual terms.)

BUSINESS CONSIDERATIONS Spanos and D'Agostino probably were using a standard Offer to Purchase form prepared by the local board of real estate agents and brokers. What provisions would you expect to find on such a form? Why?

ETHICAL CONSIDERATIONS Does the existence of a standard realty form give an inherent advantage to the seller? If so, does this fact make the use of such forms unethical? Does the arguably excessive verbiage employed in such forms confuse—or enlighten—the would-be purchaser? Would the adoption of a "plain-English" approach to the drafting of these forms affect your assessment of the underlying ethical issues? Why or why not?

Uniform Commercial Code § 2-207, by permitting a contract to arise between the parties even if the offeree adds terms or includes different terms in the purported acceptance, continues its relaxation of common law rules. This provision of the UCC reflects the drafters' knowledge of commercial realities, specifically the fact that buyers and sellers in commercial settings generally exchange their respective forms (e.g., purchase order forms or order acknowledgment forms), which may contain contradictory terms. Rather than hamper commercial dealings by judging the inconsistent terms under the common law rule that any variance in the material terms of the offer and acceptance constitutes a counteroffer and hence a rejection of the original offer, the UCC drafters permit a contract to arise between the parties unless the offeree expressly has indicated that his or her acceptance of the offer is conditioned on the offeror's assent to these additional or different terms.

Specific performance
An equitable remedy granted when monetary damages would be insufficient and the object of the contract is unique and in which the court orders performance of the contract exactly as agreed.

Section 2-207 of the Code, furthermore, sets out a scheme for determining the operative terms of the contract in these circumstances. For instance, between merchants, the additional terms automatically become part of the contract without the

EXHIBIT 10.2 Termination of the Offer

Method of Terminating the Offer	General Rule	Exceptions to the General Rule
1. Lapse—the termination of an offer through the passage of time or the occurrence of some condition	1. The offer ends at the time stated in the offer if a time is stated. 2. If no time is stated, the offer lapses after a reasonable time has passed. 3. The offeror does not need to communicate to the offeree the fact that the offer has lapsed. 4. Lapse may occur by operation of law upon: (1) the death or insanity of any of the contracting parties; (2) the supervening illegality of the subject matter; or (3) the destruction of the subject matter when neither party is at fault.	
2. Revocation—the termination of an offer by the offeror	1. Under common law, the offeror has a virtually unlimited right to revoke at any time before acceptance.	1. Options—contracts for which a person has paid money and that allow the person to buy or sell property at an agreed-on price or time period—make an offer irrevocable. 2. The "firm offer" provision of the UCC (§ 2-205) makes an offer irrevocable. 3. Promissory estoppel, whereby an offeror will be prevented from asserting a defense otherwise available to him or her in order to serve justice, can be applied to cut off the power of revocation.
	2. Revocation is not effective until it is communicated to (or received by) the offeree or the offeree's agent (i.e., the mailbox rule is inapplicable to revocations).	1. In public offers, public revocation is effective even against a person who does not know about it. The offeror need not communicate directly with every possible offeree.
3. Rejection—the termination of an offer by the offeree	1. The offeree rejects the offer by indicating directly or indirectly that he or she will not accept the offer.	
	2. A counteroffer is tantamount to a rejection of the offer.	1. Inquiries, requests, and terms implied by law that avoid making the acceptance conditional are not counteroffers. 2. The original offeror can deal with the new "offeror" on the new terms if he or she so desires.
	3. Rejection is not effective until it is communicated to (or received by) the offeror or the offeror's agent (i.e., the mailbox rule is inapplicable to rejections).	

EXHIBIT 10.2 Termination of the Offer *(cont.)*

Method of Terminating the Offer	General Rule	Exceptions to the General Rule
4. Acceptance—the termination of an offer by the offeree's assenting to all the terms of the offer	1. Acceptance must be clear and unconditional.	
	2. Silence generally is not tantamount to acceptance.	1. The prior dealings of the parties may validate acceptance based on silence.
	3. Acceptance must match, term by term, the provisions of the original offer.	1. Inquiries, requests, and terms implied by law that avoid making the acceptance conditional have no effect on the validity of the acceptance. 2. Under UCC § 2-207, an acceptance containing additional or different terms may still constitute a valid acceptance unless acceptance is expressly made conditional on assent to such terms.
	4. Qualified, or conditional, acceptances are counteroffers.	1. The original offeror can accept these new terms if he or she wishes.
	5. Acceptance may be oral, written, or implied.	1. Under the UCC, the conduct of the parties alone may establish a contract (see UCC § 2-207).
	6. Acceptance must be accomplished by the offeree or the offeree's agent.	
	7. Acceptance is not effective until it is communicated to (or received by) the offeror or the offeror's agent.	1. In the absence of a stipulated mode, acceptance is effective upon dispatch to the implied agent in jurisdictions that recognize the mailbox rule. 2. The UCC sanctions acceptances in any manner and by any medium reasonable in the circumstances (UCC § 2-206).

offeror's consent unless the original offer expressly requires the offeree to accept the terms of the offer; the additional terms materially alter the contract (i.e., they would unfairly surprise or be unduly oppressive to the offeror); or the offeror has notified the offeree that he or she will not accept the new terms. This same section of the Code also states that conduct by both parties that recognizes the existence of a contract is sufficient to establish a contract for sale even though the writings of the parties otherwise do not establish a contract. You will learn more about these concepts in succeeding chapters, but for now appreciate the alterations of common law rules embodied in the UCC and the underlying rationales for these changes.

Manner and Time of Acceptance

Besides accepting unconditionally, in order to effect a valid acceptance, the offeree must avoid one other pitfall: The offeree must accept in exactly the mode specified, or *stipulated*, by the offeror in the offer. Thus, should the offeror say that acceptance must occur by a telegram, a letter will not constitute an effective acceptance. Similarly, if the offer says, "Acceptance required by return mail," an acceptance placed in the mail two days later is invalid. Finally, when the offer says, "Acceptance effective only when received at our home office," a contract will not arise until the offeror receives the acceptance.

Although the offeror enjoys the right to set out exactly the terms of acceptance, the offeror may not care to stipulate the mode necessary for a valid acceptance. In such cases, the offeree can use any *reasonable* medium of communication, as long as he or she acts within a reasonable time. Usually, the offeree will choose the same medium used by the offeror. By implication, this medium is a reasonable and therefore an *authorized* mode of communication. Hence, in the absence of a stipulated method of acceptance, if the offeror makes the offer via the mail, the offeree's mailing of an acceptance represents a reasonable (or authorized) mode of acceptance and thus a valid response. Another medium, such as the telephone, may be reasonable, and therefore authorized as well, if the parties have used this medium in their prior dealings or if local or industry custom sanctions it.

Use of an authorized mode of communication in such circumstances takes on particular significance because, in most states, these acceptances become legally effective *at the time of dispatch* (mailing, wiring, etc.). This is called the *mailbox rule,* or *implied-agency rule,* because the post office or telegraph office is deemed to be the agent of the offeror. To illustrate, assume that the offeror has not stipulated the mode of acceptance for an offer that was mailed to the offeree on 28 September. The offeror subsequently attempts to revoke the offer on 1 October and then learns that the offeree had mailed an acceptance to the offeror on 30 September. A contract exists as of 30 September, and thus there is no "mere offer" that the offeror can revoke. The fact that the offeror had not received the acceptance until after he or she attempted to revoke the offer is irrelevant. The law treats the post office as the offeror's agent and thus concludes that the offeror "received" the acceptance on 30 September, the date the offeree deposited the letter with the post office. Because some letters never arrive, it is advisable, of course, for the offeree to secure postal or telegraphic receipts in order to prove after the fact the date on which he or she actually dispatched the acceptance.

In contrast, where the offeree has used an *unauthorized* mode of communication, the strict rule states that the acceptance is ineffective until the offeror actually receives it; the mailbox rule is not applicable. Even so, some courts will enforce the agreement if the acceptance, even though communicated via an unauthorized mode, is timely, especially if the courts can construe the offeror's language about the proper mode as a suggestion rather than a stipulation or condition. The UCC, § 2-206(1)(a), by sanctioning acceptances "in any manner and by any medium reasonable in the circumstances," lends credence to such decisions.

As you can see, the time of contract formation is crucial. The mailbox rule allows acceptance, and hence a contract, to occur even before the offeror knows of the acceptance. Such acceptances cut off the offeror's otherwise almost unlimited right to revoke, because in order for an attempted revocation to be effective, it must occur prior to acceptance. Offerors can curtail the effect of the mailbox rule if they stipulate that acceptances will not be effective until received by them. Note, too, that in any event, the mailbox rule applies only to acceptances: Revocations and rejections do not take effect until they are communicated to (i.e., are received by) the offeree and offeror, respectively. Moreover, revocations and rejections do not become legally binding upon dispatch, as acceptances sometimes do.

Silence

As the foregoing discussion implies, some overt act necessarily accompanies acceptance. For this reason, acceptance requires a clear intent to accept. Thus, the settled weight of authority holds that mere silence by the offeree cannot constitute acceptance. However, in some isolated cases, the prior dealings of the parties may permit acceptance based on silence. The following case illustrates the necessity of an overt act to denote an acceptance.

Declaratory judgment
A decision by a court that merely sets out the rights of the parties without ordering either party to perform any actions.

10.5 KARSCH v. CARR — 807 S.W.2d 96 (Mo.App. 1990)

FACTS In the spring of 1987, John M. Karsch informed Robert C. Carr that he (Karsch) was interested in buying property consisting of approximately 1,364 acres in Washington County. At the time, Karsch viewed the land and told Carr that he (Karsch) wanted to construct a large lake on the property. Thereafter, Carr and Karsch continued negotiations toward the purchase of the property. Neither party signed this draft form of the contract. On 8 January 1988, Karsch told Carr that he (Karsch) was willing to pay $240,000 for the property; but Carr rejected that offer. The next day, Karsch offered to pay $265,200 for the property. After further negotiations, on 14 January 1988, Carr informed Karsch that he and the other sellers would sell the property to Karsch for $265,200. On that same day, Carr received from Karsch an original memorandum prepared by Karsch, as well as a $5,000 check. On 3 February 1988, Carr personally delivered the following items to Karsch: a general warranty deed for the property and all the sellers' signatures, the promissory note, the deed of trust, the title insurance commitment, and Karsch's original memorandum of terms. Karsch kept the documents and expressed no dissatisfaction with them. On 10 February, Karsch learned from an engineer who had inspected the property that it would not be "economically practical" to build a 100-acre lake on the property. On 17 February 1988, Karsch informed Carr that he (Karsch) did not intend to purchase the property and cited as his reason the fact that he would be unable to construct a lake as large as he wanted on the property. Carr, however, refused to release Karsch from the alleged contract. Karsch then returned the documents to Carr and filed a **declaratory judgment** action against Carr to determine if an enforceable contract existed here.

ISSUE Had Carr and Karsch entered into a contract for the sale of the property?

HOLDING No. Karsch's actions in taking the documents without objection and retaining them from 3 February until 17 February did not evince an acceptance of Carr's proposed terms.

REASONING As a general rule, silence or inaction cannot constitute acceptance of an offer. In the absence of any duty on the part of the offeree to speak, the offeror may not translate the offeree's silence into an acceptance merely because the offeror attaches that effect to it. Karsch did not at any time communicate his acceptance of Carr's terms to Carr. In fact, within two weeks of receiving the documents, Karsch clearly rejected Carr's offer. Hence, because Karsch's acts failed to manifest an acceptance, no enforceable contract ever came into existence.

BUSINESS CONSIDERATIONS Why does it make sense for the law to require some overt action on the offeree's part if the offeree intends to accept? What difficulties would a contrary rule cause?

ETHICAL CONSIDERATIONS Karsch kept the documents related to the sale of the property for two weeks. Ethically, then, was he bound to proceed with the sale? Would your answer differ if, during that two-week period, Carr had refused another prospective buyer?

Bilateral versus Unilateral Contracts

The last major issue regarding acceptance concerns whether the contract, if formed, will be bilateral or unilateral. The weight of authority holds that an offer that contemplates the making of a *bilateral* contract may be accepted by either a direct communication of a promise to the offeror or a counterpromise inferred from the offeree's conduct or other circumstances.

When the offer instead contemplates the formation of a *unilateral* contract, it usually is unnecessary for the offeree to communicate acceptance. The offeree accepts the offer merely by completing the act called for in the offer. Subsequent notice to the offeror is not required. Besides, such notice is redundant because the offeror eventually will learn of the acceptance when the offeree requests payment for the services rendered.

Nevertheless, disputes may arise between the parties as to how much time an offeree has for completing the performance mentioned in the purported unilateral contract. If the offeror says, "I'll pay you $50 to chop firewood for me" and the offeree says, "Okay," the offeree may think chopping wood at any time within the next two months will constitute a binding acceptance. On the other hand, the offeror may get nervous when the firewood is not in the wood rack within two weeks and therefore may make the same offer to someone else who completes the job sooner. In such circumstances, the offeror may not want to pay the first offeree for the wood delivered two months later; enough wood already has been supplied.

Because of such timing problems, courts remain somewhat hostile to unilateral contracts and, if possible, construe such alleged contracts as bilateral. More important, the contracting parties can avoid such timing problems by writing down all the pertinent details (delivery date, price, etc.) in advance, whether the offeror proposes a bilateral or a unilateral contract. Good business planning, even in everyday affairs, helps avoid potential legal difficulties.

Section 2-206(1)(b) of the Uniform Commercial Code, by specifying that unless the parties unambiguously indicate otherwise "an order or other offer to buy goods for prompt or current shipment shall be construed as inviting acceptance either by a prompt promise to ship or by the prompt or current shipment of conforming or nonconforming goods . . .," eliminates many of the distinctions made in the common law between bilateral and unilateral contracts. In the first instance, a bilateral contract is formed; in the second, a unilateral contract. Acceptance is effective in either case.

10.3

SALES/MANUFACTURING

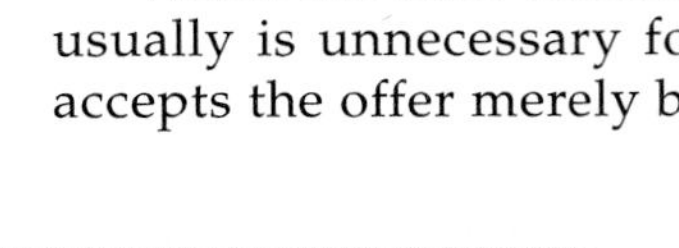

ACCEPTING OFFERS

CIT decided not to try to revoke the offer it had made to Joe Daily, reasoning that even if the offer could be revoked, such an action might make it difficult to deal with Joe in the future. The four weeks elapsed without any reply from Joe, and CIT quickly contacted the other firm to accept the offer it had made. A few days later Joe called to ask when and how CIT wanted the diagram boards and fiber optics delivered. When asked what he was talking about, Joe replied that he had accepted the CIT offer, and that his acceptance had been mailed two weeks ago. Tom said that no letter had been received. He promised to "check things out" and to "get back" to Joe as soon as possible. He then promptly called you and asked you what this information might mean for CIT. What will you tell him?

BUSINESS CONSIDERATIONS The mailbox rule imposes the risk of nondelivery on the offeror. What can a business do to reduce or eliminate bearing this risk in its communications with potential customers?

ETHICAL CONSIDERATIONS How can the risk of nondelivery of a reply be allocated in a manner that is fair and equitable to both parties? Is the current rule ethical? Explain your reasoning.

YOU BE THE JUDGE

Time Is Money

The old truism—"time is money"—still holds sway; hence, businesspeople across the world have championed facsimile ("fax," or telecopy) machines, electronic mail (e-mail), electronic data interchanges (EDIs), and video-texts as harbingers of the speed and efficiency that will revolutionize the modes of communication on which business has relied in past centuries. Given the labor-intensive nature and the costs (storage, processing, transportation) associated with "paper," it is no wonder that electronic communications increasingly are replacing paper ones. EDIs, or communications solely between computers in which computer-generated purchase orders generally beget computer-generated order acknowledgments, can even bring about the total displacement of the human aspects of contracting. Hence, contract law is moving toward a regime that will be largely faceless as well as paperless. Whereas communication nowadays can occur instantaneously, the evolution of common law in contrast moves at glacial speeds. This contradiction has led to an absence of clear-cut rules as to the applicability of the common law to situations involving these new technologies. Indeed, the few courts that have considered some of the situations that involve the intersection of the old and the new have done so in a summary fashion and have come to inconsistent results. It also may be the case that businesspeople have blithely assumed that the law will treat faxes, e-mail, and EDIs in the same fashion as it historically has treated paper communications. Hence, the present dearth of precedents may be misleading (and short-lived), once questions over such issues become more public and widespread. Moreover, given this unsettled state of the law, business firms' reluctance to eschew totally the older, slower technologies (mail, telegraph, and delivery services) arguably impedes the further development of the newer technologies and erodes the potential future efficiencies represented by these breakthrough modes of communication.

Assume that this case has been filed in *your* court asking you to rule on when acceptance occurs if the mode of communication is by fax or e-mail. How will *you* rule?

BUSINESS CONSIDERATIONS Should the mailbox rule apply to electronic means of communication, or should acceptance be effective only when received by the offeror when electronic means are used?

ETHICAL CONSIDERATIONS What ethical issues are raised by the continuing advent of technology in the formation of contracts? What should businesspeople do to protect their interests, both ethically and legally?[3]

SOURCE: *The National Law Journal* (9 September 1996), p. B3.

http:// RESOURCES FOR BUSINESS LAW STUDENTS

NAME	RESOURCE	WEB ADDRESS
Uniform Commercial Code (UCC)	The Legal Information Institute (LII), maintained by the Cornell Law School, provides a hypertext and searchable version of Articles 1–9 of the Uniform Commercial Code.	http://www.law.cornell.edu/ucc/ucc.table.html
The American Law Institute	The American Law Institute, publisher of Restatements of the law, model codes, and other proposals for law reform, provides press releases, its newsletter, and other publications.	http://www.ali.org

SUMMARY

Agreement represents perhaps the most important aspect of contract formation. To have agreement, there must be an offer and an acceptance. Assent to a contract must be mutual, and the common law offeror can set the terms of both the offer and the acceptance. An offer is an indication (by a promise or another commitment) of one's willingness to do or to refrain from doing something in the future. Courts employ an objective test to assess whether the parties have mutually assented to the terms of the agreement. Such a test asks whether a reasonable offeree would believe that the offeror has made an offer. No secret intent on the offeror's part can be shown.

To be a genuine offer under the common law, the offer must manifest a clear and present intent to contract and be definite in all respects. Statements of opinion, statements of intention, and preliminary negotiations are too indefinite to constitute offers. The same is true of most advertisements: The law usually construes advertisements as invitations for persons to come in and make offers for the types of goods and at the prices indicated in the advertisements. An offer has no legal effect until the offeror communicates it to the offeree. General offers are perfectly legal; but many jurisdictions require that they, too, be communicated to the offeree in order for a valid acceptance to occur.

The four methods of terminating an offer include (1) lapse, (2) revocation, (3) rejection, and (4) acceptance. Generally, neither a revocation nor a rejection takes legal effect until communicated to or received by the other party. However, if an offeree uses an authorized (or reasonable) mode of communication, an acceptance may be effective on dispatch. The offeror's power of revocation may be limited by options, by the "firm offer" provision of the Code, or by promissory estoppel. All three doctrines have certain elements that the offeree must prove before the offeree can cut off the offeror's right to revoke. Acceptance is the usual mode of terminating an offer. A bona fide offer and acceptance bring about an agreement, which in most cases will be tantamount to a contract. Acceptance involves the offeree's assent to all the terms of the offer. The acceptance must be clear and must be communicated to the offeror. Under the mirror-image rule of common law, an acceptance has to match, term by term, the provisions in the offer. A qualified acceptance—one that deviates from the original terms—is called a counteroffer. A counteroffer terminates the original offer and in effect brings about the rejection of the offer unless the original offeror is willing to deal on the new terms. If the offeror has not stipulated the mode necessary for a valid acceptance, use of any reasonable (or authorized) mode of communication will make the acceptance effective on dispatch. This is called the mailbox rule. If, in contrast, the offeree has used an unauthorized mode, acceptance actually must be received to be effective; the mailbox rule will be inapplicable. The mailbox rule does not apply to revocations or rejections. Silence by the offeree ordinarily does not constitute acceptance.

In bilateral contracts, communication of the acceptance usually is necessary; but this is not true for unilateral contracts. In unilateral contracts, the offeree accepts the offer merely by completing the act called for in the offer. Because of the problems that can arise from disputes concerning how much time the offeree in unilateral contracts has to accept, courts are hostile to this category of contract. The Uniform Commercial Code eliminates many of the common law distinctions between bilateral and unilateral contracts.

DISCUSSION QUESTIONS

1. What does a court mean by "mutual assent"?
2. Explain the phrase "objective theory of contracts."
3. Briefly state the common law rules surrounding a valid offer.
4. Name and define the ways in which an offer can terminate.
5. Is an advertisement a bona fide offer? Why or why not?
6. In what situations will "lapse" occur by operation of law?
7. Discuss the common law rules of revocation.
8. Name and list the elements for each of the methods available for terminating the offeror's power of revocation.
9. What are "counteroffers," and how do they arise?
10. Explain the term "mailbox rule" and its significance.

CASE PROBLEMS AND WRITING ASSIGNMENTS

1. The City of St. George, Utah (the City), invited contractors to bid on an airport terminal expansion project. The proposal provided by the City specified that, even after the execution of the contract, the City could order changes in the work covered under the agreement. On 19 January 1991, the City Council awarded to Wadsworth Construction Company the contract, subject to the condition that the price be negotiated to a level that would allow the City to meet its budget. The City Council indicated to Wadsworth that if such negotiations failed, the City would solicit other bids for the project. On 29 January 1991, city officials personally informed Wadsworth that a $100,000 reduction in the price of the project would be necessary to bring it within the City's budget. The next day, Wadsworth returned with a proposal; but the parties never reached a formal agreement regarding a reduction in the project's cost. Shortly thereafter, the City announced its intention to reject all bids and rebid the project, at which time Wadsworth sued the City for breach of contract. Had the parties' actions given rise to an enforceable contract? Why or why not? [See *Wadsworth Construction* v. *City of St. George*, 865 P.2d 1373 (Utah App. 1993).]

2. Globe Life and Accident Insurance Company (Globe) issued a life insurance policy to Mrs. Reddick, which policy insured the life of Alexis D. Reddick, her son. This coverage extended from 1 December 1987 through 1 December 1988. Mrs. Reddick did not pay the premium due on 1 December 1988. Accordingly, after the expiration of the 31-day grace period, the coverage, pursuant to the terms of the policy, automatically lapsed as of the due date. On 5 January 1989, Globe sent the following letter to Mrs. Reddick:

   Dear Policyholder: We're sorry, but at this time your Globe Life Insurance Policy is in danger of lapsing. Our records show that we have not received the premium that was due on 1 December 1988 . . . . PLEASE ACT NOW! Send in your payment, along with the attached notice, and the benefits of your policy will remain in full force. We must receive your payment by 20 January 1989.

   The final notice that accompanied this letter stated, "PAYMENT IS NEEDED SO YOUR INSURANCE WILL NOT LAPSE." Alexis D. Reddick died on 17 January 1989. On 20 January 1989, Mrs. Reddick notified Globe of the death and mailed in the requested premium. Globe did not receive the premium until after 20 January. When Globe did not pay under the life insurance policy for Alexis's death, Mrs. Reddick sued for breach of contract. She argued that the 5 January 1989 letter had extended the grace period and that, pursuant to the mailbox rule, she had accepted in a timely fashion Globe's offer to extend the insurance coverage to 20 January. How should a court rule in this case? [See *Reddick* v. *Globe Life and Accident Ins. Co.*, 596 So.2d 435 (Fla.App. 1992).]

3. Greene put up for sale several pieces of antique furniture from her mother's estate. After seeing the furniture, Keener inquired about the price of an antique secretary. Greene actually wanted $6,000 and was unsure whether she genuinely wanted to sell it, but in conversation with Keener she agreed to sell it for $4,200. Keener said he was very interested but wanted to be sure it blended with the rest of his furniture. After some discussion, Greene permitted Keener to take the secretary home to see if it matched. The night after Keener had the secretary taken to his home, Greene called and informed him that she no longer wanted to sell the secretary and asked that he return it. Keener said, "Hold on a minute," and went to speak with his wife, who indicated that she liked the piece. When Keener refused to return the secretary, Greene sued for rescission (cancellation) of the sale. Should she prevail? [See *Greene* v. *Keener*, 402 S.E.2d 284 (Ga.App. 1991).]

4. Sewell Coal Company operated a coal mining facility in Nicholas County, West Virginia. In early 1982, a severe downturn in the coal market forced Sewell to

shut down some of its facilities and to lay off certain of its supervisory and clerical employees. Through March and April 1982, Sewell paid, in conformity with its normal severance plan, such laid-off employees two weeks' severance. In May 1982, when it became apparent that the layoffs would be permanent, the company sent a letter to all laid-off salaried personnel informing them that a special severance procedure would be used for that layoff and would apply retroactively to salaried employees laid off since 1 January 1982. A memorandum attached to the letter explained the special procedure: The laid-off employee would receive one week's severance pay for each year of service, with a minimum of two weeks, not to exceed 20 weeks' severance pay. The letter and accompanying memorandum went only to those salaried employees who were laid off. The company neither distributed these materials to the workforce in general, nor posted or circulated them among the remaining workforce. Further layoffs occurred in August and October 1982. On each occasion, the laid-off employee received a letter similar to that of May 1982, which letter set forth the special severance procedure. On each occasion, the company sent the letter and accompanying memorandum to those salaried employees only who were being laid off.

In November 1982, the company promulgated guidelines stating that the special severance procedure henceforth would be discontinued and would not apply to future layoffs. Rather, for future layoffs, employees would receive the normal two weeks' severance pay. The company distributed these guidelines to the managers who were to implement them, but the company did not provide the information to the general workforce to whom the guidelines were inapplicable. The company treated the layoffs that occurred through 1987 according to these written guidelines. Mark Bailey, a salaried employee laid off after the discontinuation of the special severance procedure, subsequently filed suit. He contended that the adoption of the special severance plan constituted an offer that he had accepted by continuing to work for the company and that, as a consequence, upon the termination of his employment, he was entitled to the special severance pay. Should a court agree with Bailey's reasoning? [See *Bailey* v. *Sewell Coal Co.*, 437 S.E.2d 448 (W.Va. 1993).]

5. Dr. John J. Eufemio had practiced orthopedic and hand surgery at Kodiak Island Hospital (KIH) from 1966 to 1980. However, in 1979, KIH had revoked his privileges and had suspended him from his practice at the facility. After concluding that it had used flawed procedures in suspending him, in 1980 KIH revoked the suspension. Although Dr. Eufemio had left Kodiak in the fall of 1980 to attend law school, he reapplied for renewal of his staff privileges in 1981 and 1982. In denying these requests, the hearing committee that had considered Dr. Eufemio's arguments in 1982 wrote him a letter that said in part,

   None of the problems which resulted in the denial of [Dr. Eufemio's] medical staff privileges appear [sic] to be irreparable, but they provided sufficient cause for the medical staff's decision. We support that decision, but we also encourage Dr. Eufemio to pursue his stated goal of obtaining additional residency training and his surgical board certification. We speculate that a year's additional training in a structured setting, surrounded by examples of current medical and surgical practice, would substantially improve his qualifications for medical staff membership.

   Between 1984 and 1985, Dr. Eufemio sought further medical training in New York and received his surgical board certification. On his return to Kodiak in 1985, Dr. Eufemio again applied for appointment to KIH's staff. When the hospital's hiring committee yet again denied his application, Dr. Eufemio claimed that the hearing committee's 1982 letter had estopped the hospital from denying him staff membership privileges. Should a court apply promissory estoppel to the hospital's decision? [See *Eufemio* v. *Kodiak Island Hospital*, 837 P.2d 95 (Alaska 1992).]

6. **BUSINESS APPLICATION CASE** Rollins Environmental Services (NJ), Inc. (Rollins) operates a waste disposal facility in Bridgeport, New Jersey, where it disposes of hazardous waste materials through incineration and other chemical and biological processes for customers throughout the country. During the 1970s, Polaroid Corporation (Polaroid) and Hooker Chemical Corporation (Hooker) were customers of Rollins, which disposed of their hazardous wastes. Between 1971 and 1976, 13 of the 14 purchase orders issued by Hooker contained an indemnity (reimbursement) clause and instructions that stated, among other things, that Rollins was to return to Hooker the acknowledgment orders containing this language regarding indemnification. Hooker used this language until 6 January 1977, when Rollins objected to the typed indemnity request for the first time. At Rollins's behest, the parties thereafter adopted an indemnification clause that provided indemnification only for negligent acts by Rollins. When the Environmental Protection Agency (EPA) notified Polaroid and Hooker that, as waste generators, they faced possible liability under the Comprehensive Environmental Response Compensation and Liability Act (CERCLA) for cleanup costs

incurred by the government in Bridgeport, both companies requested that Rollins indemnify them with regard to the Bridgeport site spills. In refusing these requests, Rollins argued that, by failing to return the acknowledgment copy of the purchase agreement as requested, it had rejected the indemnification language. Polaroid and Hooker dismissed Rollins's failure either to return the acknowledgment or to object to the indemnification clause until 1977 as irrelevant. In their view, Rollins's routinely completing performance under the various purchase orders showed that Rollins had accepted all the purchase orders' terms. Should a court agree with Polaroid and Hooker's reasoning, or could a court use other aspects of contract law to find in favor of Rollins? What should each party have done differently so as to minimize the probability of this litigation occurring? [See *Polaroid Corp.* v. *Rollins Environmental Services (NJ), Inc.*, 624 N.E.2d 959 (Mass. 1993).]

7. **ETHICS APPLICATION CASE** In August 1986, Oakie Ford responded to an advertisement run by Tandy Transportation, Inc. (Tandy), which was attempting to solicit trailer loads for its Dallas, Texas, route. Ford told Hartman, Tandy's sales representative, of a potential customer, Republic, with whom Ford no longer had an employment relationship but who had paid Ford $1,450 per load during the duration of his contract with Republic. In this conversation, Ford also advised Hartman that Republic at this time probably would want to pay a lower per-load figure. On 12 September 1986, Hartman sent Ford the following letter:

    > *Thank you for taking time to respond to our ad in* Transportation Topics. *During our conversation, you stated that you had a customer requiring weekly service from Ironton, OH to Dallas, TX. . . . We would be able to perform [such services] for the gross amount you quoted of $1,450. We will pay you $200 per load as your fee. As discussed, we would move this on our Authority. Freight charges would be collected and we would bill the consignee in Dallas, TX. Again, we would like to thank you for calling and we look forward to working with you.*

    Following his receipt of this letter, Ford had further conversations with both Hartman and Republic's Dallas site manager, Adams. Ford understood that Tandy wanted him merely to set up the relationship between Tandy and Republic, but not to act as either a broker or a sales agent. In his further conversations with Hartman, Ford agreed to a deal with Tandy of $200 per load, a figure not contingent on Tandy's securing the $1,450 fee, which Ford viewed as merely a starting point for negotiations between Tandy and Republic.

    For the next few months, Ford acted as an intermediary between Hartman and Adams. Ford ultimately informed Tandy that it could have the Dallas route for $1,100. In January 1987, Tandy bid $1,100 for the job and successfully acquired the route. Tandy did not advise Ford of its successful bid, but Ford subsequently discovered that Tandy had acquired the Republic route. Ford therefore requested compensation pursuant to the parties' agreement. Tandy eventually transported 204 loads but refused to pay Ford anything. When Ford sued Tandy for breach of contract, Tandy maintained that the absence of any meeting of the minds and the lack of an acceptance on Ford's part precluded the existence of an enforceable contract. In whose favor—Ford or Tandy's—should the court rule? The legalities aside, assess the ethics of Tandy's conduct toward Ford. When it behaves unethically, what does a company put at risk? [See *Ford* v. *Tandy Transportation, Inc.*, 620 N.E.2d 996 (Ohio App. 1993).]

8. **IDES CASE** Cyberchron Corporation (Cyberchron) produces customized computer hardware for military and civilian use. During 1989 and 1990, Grumman Data Systems Corp. (Grumman) and its subsidiary, Calldata Systems Development, Inc., engaged in extensive negotiations with Cyberchron aimed at producing "ruggedized" computer equipment. Grumman had contracted with the U.S. Marine Corps to build a combat command control system that included a "rugged computer workstation" designed to operate under combat conditions in a command center. Grumman planned to use this "ruggedized" computer equipment, consisting of a video processor, a workstation, and a color monitor, in a Marine Corps defense program known as Advanced Tactical Air Command Central (ATACC). From the outset, the weight of the three units became critical, because the Marine Corps needed lightweight, compact, easily deployable equipment. By 1 March 1990, the parties had agreed on a total price of $1,383,879. But the question of the weight of the units and the penalties (i.e., deductions in the per-unit price) that Grumman would impose for units that exceeded a combined weight of 175 pounds remained unsettled. In a 24 May 1990 letter to Grumman, Cyberchron took exception to both the weight specifications and the penalties set by Grumman. Grumman responded on 15 June 1990 that the weight of the units and the weight penalties were nonnegotiable elements of the order it had given to Cyberchron. On 22 June 1990, Cyberchron answered that it was suspending all its testing and manufacturing activities with regard to this hardware until both companies could arrive at mutually acceptable terms.

Over the next two months, through a series of exchanged memos, the sparring between the two companies continued. Verbally, off the record, Grumman apparently was insisting that Cyberchron perform; but in writing, on the record, Grumman refrained from authorizing the initiation of any work. While orally pressuring Cyberchron to do the work, Grumman assured Cyberchron that if it did, the negotiation problems could be resolved. Even after the delivery date of 22 August 1990 had passed, Grumman officials pushed Cyberchron to keep performing and told Cyberchron officials to ignore Grumman's written notice that indicated Grumman was considering terminating the order owing to Cyberchron's default. In fact, as late as 7 September 1990, Cyberchron still was proposing a detailed delivery schedule. On 25 September 1990, Grumman terminated its relationship with Cyberchron and, on 26 September 1990, entered into a contract with another company to produce the "ruggedized" equipment. When Grumman refused to pay the $495,207.58 that Cyberchron had billed for its work, Cyberchron sued for breach of contract. Would Cyberchron prevail on this theory? Could Cyberchron argue other theories for imposing liability on Grumman? Apply the IDES model to resolve these questions. [See *Cyberchron Corp.* v. *Calldata Systems Development, Inc.*, 831 F.Supp. 94 (E.D.N.Y. 1993).]

NOTES

1. See Uniform Commercial Code, §§ 2-305, 2-309, and 2-310.
2. Ibid., § 2-306.
3. "Fax Notice by Union Not Enough for Offer, *The National Law Journal* (9 September 1996), p. B3.

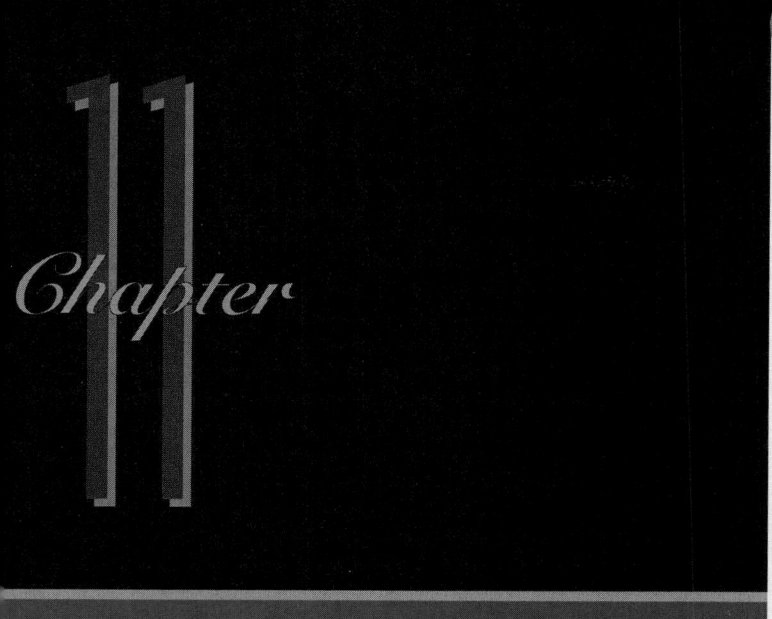

Chapter 11

Consideration (The Basis of the Bargain) and Contractual Capacity (The Ability to Agree)

Outline

Introduction
The Bargain as a Contract Theory
Definition of Consideration
Consideration in Special Contexts
Absence of Consideration
Exceptions to the Bargaining Theory of Consideration
Legal Capacity
Minors
Insane Persons
Intoxicated Persons
Aliens
Convicts
Married Women
Summary
Discussion Questions
Case Problems and Writing Assignments

Agenda

The Kochanowskis want to be certain CIT is entering into legally binding contracts. One of their concerns is whether they are truly giving and/or receiving consideration in their contracts. They are also concerned with avoiding illusory promises in their contracts.

Tom has heard about voidable contracts but is unclear as to what this means. He definitely wants to refrain from entering into any contracts that are voidable at the option of the other party. Lindsay thinks that there could be a large market for the videophones among well-to-do teenagers. She thinks the firm should investigate this market. From both a professional and a legal perspective, Dan does not think the firm should be seeking the youth market.

These and other contractual issues face CIT. Be prepared! You never know when one of the Kochanowskis will ask for your help or advice.

INTRODUCTION

As discussed in Chapter 10, contract law addresses the importance of the parties' reaching an agreement. In addition, the law requires some evidence that the parties' agreement is mutual and that the parties actually have the legal ability to bind themselves to the agreement and to enforce any promises made to them. The law fulfills this first obligation by requiring that the parties support the agreement with consideration and the second requisite by mandating that all parties to the agreement have the legal capacity to contract. This chapter concentrates on these two requirements for contract formation.

THE BARGAIN AS A CONTRACT THEORY

Despite the rather checkered history that surrounds its principles, no doctrine of common law is as firmly entrenched today as the concept of consideration. Although the meaning of the concept is shrouded in historical traditions, familiarity with the doctrine's tenets is fundamental to an understanding of modern contract law.

Remember that early in the history of contracts the parties underwent elaborate rituals, such as sealing their contracts with wax and placing their insignia in the wax, in order to demonstrate their willingness to be bound to the terms embodied in the agreement. Although few contracts are under seal nowadays, the idea that the parties actually ought to bargain and exchange something of value rather than merely make empty promises has lingered. Today, this emphasis is evident in the notion that the presence of consideration indicates the parties' exchange of something of value that results in an agreement between the parties. Thus, consideration shows that some obligation or duty worthy of a court's protection genuinely exists. It also establishes that the parties are acting deliberately and intend to bind themselves to the terms of the agreement.

Because it rids contracts of excessive formality while encouraging exchanges between people, the doctrine of consideration initially appears well suited to commercial and economic activity and hence to the study of business law. Nevertheless, some of the legal results under this doctrine seem quite harsh. For this reason, theories have emerged that permit an agreement to be binding in some cases despite a lack of consideration.

DEFINITION OF CONSIDERATION

Waiver

The voluntary surrender of a legal right; the intentional surrender of a right.

Among the many definitions of the term *consideration,* one of the most common states that consideration is a **waiver**, or promised waiver, of rights bargained for in exchange for a promise. Consideration always consists of either a benefit to the promisor or a detriment to the promisee, bargained for and given in exchange for a promise. In view of the previous discussion, it is no surprise to see that the words *bargain, promise,* and *exchange* play such a prominent role in this definition. Consideration usually takes the form of money; but it may consist of an intangible, noneconomic benefit (or detriment) or anything of value to the parties.

Consideration as an Act or a Forbearance to Act

Implicit in this doctrine is the necessity of the parties' bargaining over some present event or object and exchanging something of value in order to bind themselves to do (or to refrain from doing) something. It is important, then, to check the parties' language closely. Words that sound like promises actually may be **illusory** because the parties really have not committed themselves in any manner to the bargain. If one party never actually agrees to do anything (for example, if someone says, "I will sell you my car for $8,000 if I feel like it"), the promise is illusory and unenforceable because consideration is absent.

Illusory
Fallacious; nominal as opposed to substantial; of false appearance.

In unilateral contracts, consideration manifests itself in an act or a forbearance to act. In the latter situation, the consideration comes from refraining from engaging in a legal act. For example, suppose your parents promise you a new car if you will earn straight A's in school. If you do, the agreement is supported by consideration and will be enforceable in a court of law, assuming you live in a state where family members can sue each other if they breach (that is, fail to perform) this agreement.

Now apply the definition of consideration to see why this agreement is enforceable. You waived your right to unlimited leisure time in exchange for your parents' promise. You and your parents bargained about the straight A's, so the car is not a gift to you. You must do something (study more than you would like) or refrain from doing something (watching television and engaging in other leisure activities) to earn it. Furthermore, your parents, the **promisors**, received a benefit (the satisfaction of knowing you are an honor student) while you, the **promisee**, suffered a detriment (studying hard all year) as a result of this bargain. Your act of making perfect grades therefore has been given in exchange for your parents' promise to buy you a car. Note that the benefit they receive has no dollars-and-cents economic value, yet the law views the benefit as sufficient consideration to support their side of the bargain. They will receive what they asked of you.

Promisors
Those who make a promise or commitment.

Promisee
One to whom a promise or commitment has been made.

Think about these principles as you consider *Taylor* v. *Bonilla*.

11.1 TAYLOR v. BONILLA

801 S.W.2d 553 (Tex.App. 1990)

FACTS In December 1985, Scott Taylor met with Tony Bonilla to discuss surrendering Taylor's whole-life insurance policy and obtaining its accumulated cash surrender value. Although the parties disagreed about whether Taylor intended to replace the policy when he first contacted Bonilla, they did not dispute the fact that during the meeting the two men discussed Taylor's obtaining a $100,000 term-life policy as a replacement of the surrendered whole-life policy. During the same meeting, Bonilla completed and Taylor signed a number of forms drafted by New York Life Insurance Company. These forms included an application for the term policy and a form requesting the surrender of the whole-life policy and the return of its accumulated cash value. On the term policy application, Bonilla, New York Life's agent, noted that the whole-life policy would terminate upon the issuance of the new term policy. In addition, Taylor signed a sheet entitled "Important Notice Regarding Replacement," which included the following warning:

If after studying the information made available to you, you do decide to replace the existing life insurance with our company with a new life insurance policy issued by our company, you are urged not to take action to terminate or alter your existing life insurance coverage until after you have been issued the new policy, examined it, and have found it acceptable to you. If you should terminate or otherwise materially alter your existing coverage and fail to qualify for the life insurance for which you have applied, you may find yourself unable to purchase other life insurance or able to purchase it only at substantially higher rates.

Taylor never gave Bonilla a check for the first premium on the term policy. In addition, he failed to complete a policy loan form or a dividend withdrawal form, either of which would have allowed him to use the accumulated cash value of the whole-life policy to pay the first premium on the

11.1 TAYLOR v. BONILLA (cont.) 801 S.W.2d 553 (Tex.App. 1990)

term policy. Approximately two weeks before his death, Taylor received a New York Life check in "full settlement of all claims" under the whole-life policy. Taylor negotiated the check. During the same two-week period, Bonilla received the newly issued term policy. Before Bonilla could deliver the policy to Taylor, however, Taylor was killed in a car wreck. When Mrs. Taylor called Bonilla to inform him of her husband's death and to ask about her spouse's coverage with New York Life, Bonilla told her that the new term policy was not yet in force because Taylor had failed to pay any premium on it. Mrs. Taylor sued for breach of contract.

ISSUE Did Taylor's surrender of the whole-life policy serve as consideration for the issuance of the new (that is, the term-life) policy?

HOLDING Yes. The surrender of valid contract rights, which one is not bound to surrender, would constitute valuable consideration for a return promise.

REASONING Fundamental contract principles support the proposition that, when no other consideration is shown, mutual obligations by the parties to an agreement will furnish sufficient consideration to constitute a binding agreement. In addition, the general rule is that a promisee's surrender of valid contractual rights, which one is not bound to surrender, constitutes valuable consideration for a return promise. New York Life's contention that Taylor had paid no consideration is correct only in the sense that he neither had remitted a check or cash with the application nor completed a dividend withdrawal or policy loan form to pay the premium out of the cash value of the whole-life policy. Taylor, however, had surrendered his right for the whole-life policy to continue in force under the policy's automatic premium protection clause (that is, the accumulated cash value of the policy would cover any premium payments Taylor had failed to make). Therefore, upon the surrender of the policy, Taylor gave up his valuable contractual right to have the insurance company pay the face amount of the policy to the beneficiary of his choice. Taylor relinquished this right in return for a promise from the company to provide him with term insurance, conditioned only on his meeting underwriting guidelines. Sufficient evidence also existed to show that the parties intended that, upon Taylor's surrender of the whole-life policy, the company in fact would issue him a new term policy. Thus, Taylor's surrender of the first policy constituted legally valuable consideration for the issuance of the new policy.

BUSINESS CONSIDERATIONS Assume New York Life Insurance Company has asked you to modify its contractual language so that in the future it can avoid litigation of the type it had with Taylor. What additions, deletions, or modifications will you make?

ETHICAL CONSIDERATIONS Ethically speaking, should the company have denied coverage in these circumstances? Why or why not?

Consideration as a Promise to Act or to Forbear

Both the *Taylor* case and the earlier hypothetical bargain evince the formation of a unilateral contract. The analysis will be the same, however, if you *promise* to earn straight A's in exchange for your parents' *promise* to buy the car. In this situation, a bilateral contract is created, with the respective promises constituting the consideration to support the agreement, as long as the promises are genuine and not illusory.

Take this example one step further. For instance, if your parents breach this contract and you want to sue them, they may bargain with you about dropping the lawsuit. If they promise to pay you $1,000 if you do not sue, in exchange for your promise to forgo legal action, you will have made another enforceable contract. Why? A promise to act or to forbear from a certain action, bargained for and given in exchange for another promise, is consideration. Therefore, you should be able to convince a court to force your parents to pay, should they refuse to do so.

Adequacy of Consideration

Will your parents win in the earlier example if they argue that $8,000 for a new car is too much, or that you really are doing nothing—because becoming an honor student is insufficient to constitute a detriment to you—to secure your side of the bargain? Usually not, because courts generally are unreceptive to such arguments. The classic rule states courts will not inquire into the adequacy of the consideration. Courts instead will assume that the parties themselves remain the best judges of how much their bargain is worth and whether their performances are substantially equivalent. In other words, courts ordinarily will not second-guess the parties after the fact. *Apfel* v. *Prudential-Bache Securities, Inc.* illustrates this important principle.

11.2 APFEL v. PRUDENTIAL-BACHE SECURITIES, INC. 600 N.Y.S.2d 433 (NY App. 1993)

FACTS Robert C. Apfel had sold a computerized system of trading municipal securities (the Apfel system) to Prudential-Bache Securities, Inc., an investment bank. The Apfel system permitted bonds to be sold, traded, and held exclusively through computerized "book entries." Under the sale agreement, Apfel conveyed its rights to the techniques involved in the system in exchange for a stipulated rate based on actual usage from October 1982 to January 1988. The contract obligated Prudential-Bache to pay even if the techniques became public knowledge or standard industry practice and even if Apfel's patent and trademark applications were denied. Apfel agreed to keep the techniques, which it had disclosed only to Prudential-Bache, confidential until the information became public. From 1982 until 1985, Prudential-Bache implemented the contract, although the parties disputed whether Prudential-Bache had fully paid the amounts due. Prudential-Bache actively encouraged bond issuers to use the computerized "book entry" system and, for at least the first year, served as the sole underwriter in the industry employing such a system. In 1985, however, following a change in personnel, Prudential-Bache refused to make any further payments because of its belief that the ideas conveyed by Apfel had been in the public domain at the time of the sale agreement and that what Apfel had sold Prudential-Bache never actually had been its to sell. Moreover, by 1990 computerized systems handled 60 percent of the dollar volume of all new issues of municipal securities. Apfel sued, seeking $45 million in damages. As one of its numerous defenses, Prudential-Bache asserted that no contract ever existed between the parties because the sale agreement lacked consideration.

ISSUE Did the agreement lack consideration?

HOLDING No. Consideration was present because the system had value for Apfel.

REASONING Under traditional principles of contract law, the parties to a contract are free to make their bargain, even if the consideration exchanged is grossly unequal or of dubious value. In the absence of fraud or unconscionability, the adequacy of consideration is not a proper subject for judicial scrutiny. It is enough that something of real value in the eyes of the law was exchanged. The fact that the sellers may not have had a property right in what they sold does not, by itself, render the contract void for lack of consideration. As its own conduct indicated, Prudential-Bache received something of value. After signing the confidentiality agreement, Prudential-Bache thoroughly reviewed Apfel's system before buying it. Having done so, Prudential-Bache was in the best position to know whether the idea had value. It decided to enter into the sale agreement and aggressively marketed the system. Indeed, Prudential-Bache became the only underwriter to use Apfel's "book entry" system for municipal bonds; and the firm handled millions of such bond transactions during that time. Having obtained full disclosure of the system, used it in advance of competitors, and received the associated benefits of precluding its disclosure to others, Prudential-Bache hardly could claim now that the idea had no value to its municipal securities business. Indeed, Prudential-Bache acknowledged that it had made payments to Apfel under the sale agreement for more than two years, conduct that would belie any claim that the idea lacked value or that Prudential-Bache actually had obtained it from some other source before Apfel's disclosure. Thus, Prudential-Bache had failed to demonstrate that the agreement was void because of lack of consideration.

11.2 APFEL v. PRUDENTIAL-BACHE SECURITIES, INC. *(cont.)* 600 N.Y.S.2d 433 (NY App. 1993)

BUSINESS CONSIDERATIONS This litigation involved computer technology. Do contracts concerning such intellectual property pose special challenges for the parties? Why or why not?

ETHICAL CONSIDERATIONS Did the contract language to which Prudential-Bache had agreed ethically preclude the firm from arguing that the Apfel system had been in the public domain at the time of the sale agreement? Justify your response.

There are, however, exceptions to the general rule that courts will not inquire into the adequacy of the consideration. If a court finds evidence of fraud, duress, undue influence, mistake, or other similar situations at the time of contract formation, adequacy of consideration becomes a much more significant issue. Courts in these situations may permit one or more of the litigants to back out of the deal. The doctrine of unconscionability under either the common law or the Uniform Commercial Code (see § 2-302 of the UCC, which holds that a court may refuse to enforce a contract if it is shockingly unfair or oppressive) in some circumstances also can form a further basis for overturning bargains when the consideration appears to be grossly inadequate. But remember that courts do not routinely use this rationale to overturn bargaining between parties.

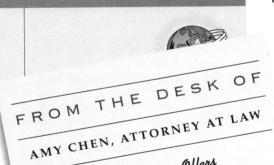

FROM THE DESK OF

AMY CHEN, ATTORNEY AT LAW

Time Limits on Offers

Be very specific regarding time limits on any offers you make, especially to other merchants. If you promise in writing to leave an offer open for a specified time, you may not revoke the offer until the stated time has expired. If no time is mentioned, the offer cannot be revoked for a "reasonable" time, to be determined by the court. You should also remember that contracts to sell goods must be in writing if the amount is $500 or more and that contracts to lease goods must be in writing if the amount is $1000 or more.

CONSIDERATION IN SPECIAL CONTEXTS

Contracts for the Sale of Goods

As explained in Chapter 10, the "firm offer" provision of the Uniform Commercial Code (§ 2-205) states that an offer to buy or sell goods by a merchant who gives assurance in writing that the offer will be held open may be irrevocable for a period of up to three months even if no consideration has been paid to the offeror. Intended to encourage commercial activity that is free from hagglings about "options," this provision dramatically changes the common law rules concerning consideration. Thus, even in the absence of consideration, courts will enforce a UCC firm offer. The same is true of modifications under the UCC: They, too, are enforceable without consideration (§ 2-209(1)). In contrast, the common law would require consideration in both situations.

In this context, let's turn again to output and requirements contracts, two types of sales contracts mentioned earlier in Chapter 10. Unless the language of these contracts indicates otherwise, courts ordinarily enforce output and requirements contracts as contracts supported by consideration. These courts reason that consideration is present in the form of the respective detriments suffered by the buyer and seller when they obligate themselves to deal exclusively with the other party in these circumstances. The promises undergirding such contracts, then, are nonillusory and make the bargains enforceable.

Suretyship Contracts

Default
A failure to do what should be done, especially in the performance of a contractual obligation, without legal excuse or justification for the nonperformance.

Although the UCC has relaxed the requirement of consideration in some situations, the common law definitely requires consideration in suretyship contracts. Such contracts always involve three parties: a principal debtor, a creditor, and a surety. The surety agrees to be liable to the creditor in the event of the principal debtor's **default**. This occurs in a typical commercial transaction. To illustrate, let us assume that Chan Wai (the principal debtor) wishes to buy a new car. She may seek financing from a credit union (the creditor), which in turn may require that she bolster her credit (and decrease its risk) by having another person (such as her father or mother) sign the note as a surety.

If the principal debtor and surety simultaneously promise to pay the promissory note, a single consideration (the loan of money to Chan Wai by the credit union) will support these promises. Both promises will be supported by consideration and hence will be enforceable. If, in contrast, the credit union lends the money for the car to Chan Wai and later asks a surety to promise to pay in the event of her default, this second promise must be supported by new consideration before the surety's promise is legally binding. As discussed in the Past Consideration section of this chapter, Chan Wai's preexisting obligation to the credit union (because the loan already has been made) does not constitute consideration for enforcing the surety's subsequent promise to pay the credit union.

11.1

FINANCE

ACQUIRING FINANCING FOR CIT

The Kochanowskis are considering a number of options to acquire financing for the firm as it grows. Tom recently discussed acquiring a line of credit for CIT from a local commercial bank. The bank officer with whom Tom dealt informed him that CIT at this point in time did not have an adequate history to justify a significant line of credit. The officer did point out, however, that the bank might be willing to grant the firm a line of credit if the firm had a *surety* who would be willing to join the firm in its application. Tom is not sure exactly what a suretyship arrangement entails. He has asked you what a surety is and whether the firm should seek such an arrangement. What will you tell him?

BUSINESS CONSIDERATIONS When should a business be willing to enter into a suretyship arrangement? When should an officer of a business be willing to serve as a surety for the firm?

ETHICAL CONSIDERATIONS Is it ethical for a lender to require the officers of a small business to serve as sureties for the firm? Would your answer be different if the business were a partnership or proprietorship rather than a corporation? Why?

Liquidated Debts

If one owes a debt to another person, partial payment of that debt is not consideration for full discharge of the debt. For instance, assume Jim Hays has his dentist perform a root canal treatment on him. At the outset, the dentist tells Jim the treatment will cost $190; and Jim agrees that this is a fair price. If Jim pays $150, he cannot successfully argue that this part payment is consideration for full discharge of the debt. Put in legal terms, the dentist will be able to argue that Jim is under a preexisting duty to pay the entire $190. Since neither party has waived any rights nor has either engaged in any bargaining in exchange for this promise to pay $150, there is, by definition, an absence of consideration here. Hence, by the settled rule, Jim is liable for the entire bill, or $190. It is crucial to note that the debt is *liquidated;* that is, the amount owed is not disputed. Jim has agreed to pay $190, and he should not, after the fact, be allowed to escape this obligation. Such a legal result would throw commercial dealings into shambles!

Unliquidated Debts

Now let us assume that the debt is not liquidated. Suppose that Jim initially has agreed to pay $190 for the root canal treatment. However, after the dentist treats him, Jim continues to have soreness around the gums; and the treated tooth still is sensitive to thermal changes. Although Jim wants to live up to his obligation to pay his debt, he does not believe he should pay the dentist the entire amount because he remains dissatisfied with the results of the treatment. At the point Jim expresses these objections to the dentist, the debt is unliquidated; that is, the precise amount owed is in dispute. If Jim in these circumstances sends the dentist a check for $150—particularly if he in some fashion indicates that this amount represents full payment for his entire indebtedness—the dentist should understand that cashing Jim's check permits Jim to argue that he owes her nothing more. Her act of cashing the check shows that she impliedly has agreed to accept $150 as full payment of the debt. Hence, she is subject to the common law rule that payment toward an unliquidated debt that is intended as and accepted as full payment is consideration for full discharge of the debt.

Instead, if the dentist wishes both to collect the entire $190 she alleges Jim owes and to protect her rights fully, she should not cash Jim's check for $150. Rather, she should return it to Jim with a note stating that she is not agreeing to accept the tendered amount as full payment of the debt. If she is strapped for cash, she may be able to cash the check and try to preserve her rights against Jim by endorsing it "with full reservation of all rights." Ideally, to avoid the application of the rule that partial payment of an unliquidated debt that is accepted (expressly or impliedly) as full payment of the debt is consideration for a full discharge of that debt, she should refrain from cashing the check.

Alternatively, Jim and the dentist may negotiate and ultimately agree that $150 is the amount owed. In this case, each receives a benefit—Jim, by paying $40 less than he thought he would have to pay; the dentist, by getting most of the $190—and each suffers a detriment—Jim, by believing $150 is still too much; the dentist, by thinking she has lost $40—as a result of the bargained-for promise to pay. This notion of an exchange of rights is a hallmark of consideration.

One last note is appropriate. When Jim and the dentist agree on the $150 sum, technically there is a compromise (of the unliquidated debt) that subsequently has led to a satisfaction and an accord. A *compromise* is the settlement of a disputed claim by the mutual agreement of the parties. The agreement as to the amount is an *accord,* and the fulfillment of the agreement (the actual payment of the agreed-upon amount) is a *satisfaction.*

Composition Agreements

Unliquidated debt situations form the basis for a court's enforcement of a composition agreement, or an agreement between a debtor and a group of creditors to accept a smaller percentage of the debt owed in full satisfaction of the claim, as consideration for full discharge of the debt. Even though you will not study **bankruptcy** until Chapters 29 and 30, you probably are aware that the bankruptcy of the debtor poses grave financial risks for the creditor, because in bankruptcy proceedings a creditor ordinarily realizes only a few cents on every dollar owed. Consequently, it often is in the creditor's best interest to give the debtor more time to pay (before the creditor

Bankruptcy
An area of law designed to give an "honest debtor" a fresh start; the proceedings undertaken against a person or a firm under the bankruptcy laws.

forces the debtor into bankruptcy) or to agree with other creditors to accept smaller sums in full cancellation of larger claims through a composition agreement.

Cancellation
Any action shown on the face of a contract that indicates an intent to destroy the obligation of the contract.

For example, suppose Doug (the debtor) owes Ann, Bill, and Cara (the creditors) $6,000, $4,000, and $2,000, respectively. The creditors each may agree to accept 50 percent of the respective debts as full satisfaction of their claims against Doug. Thus, if Doug pays Ann $3,000, Bill $2,000, and Cara $1,000, none of the three will be able to sue for the remaining amount. Courts analogize the result here to a settlement of an unliquidated debt situation, in which the resultant compromise between the debtor and a creditor represents a satisfaction and accord for the debts. Similarly, in *composition agreements,* those agreed to by the debtor and a group of creditors, payments accepted by the creditors are supported by consideration and thus constitute full discharge of the debts.

Some courts instead will characterize the sums owed to Ann, Bill, and Cara as liquidated debts and will find insufficient consideration in the subsequent agreement to justify full discharge of the debts. Ironically, these same courts in the next breath may sanction such agreements on public policy grounds (the debtor's avoidance of bankruptcy and the creditors' realization of partial payment). Whatever the rationale, courts clearly favor composition agreements and therefore enforce them.

11.2

ARRANGING CREDIT TERMS

CIT recently made a large sale to a retail establishment. The purchaser arranged credit terms with CIT and was scheduled to pay for the purchase over the next twenty-four months. Shortly after making this purchase, the customer encountered some serious short-term financial difficulties. As a result, it is behind in its payments to CIT and is facing the possibility of being forced into bankruptcy. The customer is convinced that it can weather these problems and shortly can become a profitable and viable business entity again, *if* it can find a way to meet its short-term financial problems without resorting to bankruptcy. The customer has asked CIT to agree to accept smaller monthly payments spread over the next thirty-six months. The company's president states that his company has proposed similar arrangements with several of its other creditors. The family asks you what they should do under these circumstances. What will you say? What is the legal significance of agreeing to the proposal of the customer?

BUSINESS CONSIDERATIONS Should a business that regularly sells on credit to its customers establish a policy for handling situations in which its customers encounter financial problems, or should it handle each case individually as the situation arises? What are the benefits and the drawbacks to each approach?

ETHICAL CONSIDERATIONS Is it ethical for a firm that has granted credit to its customers to adopt a hard-line approach when any of the customers encounters difficulties? Is it ethical for a credit customer to threaten bankruptcy relief if it is not allowed to refinance its credit arrangement?

FINANCE/MANAGEMENT

ABSENCE OF CONSIDERATION

Under certain circumstances, courts will find a total absence of consideration and will not enforce the agreement that the parties have shaped.

Illusory Promises

Promises that do not bind the promisor to a commitment are illusory promises, as mentioned earlier. Such promises can be performed without any benefit to the promisor or without any detriment to the promisee and hence are not supported by consideration. A promise "to order such goods as we may wish" or "as we may want from time to time" is not a genuine promise at all; it only appears to set up a binding commitment. Instead, it actually allows the promisor to order nothing. Such "will, wish, or want contracts," as they often are called, are void because they lack consideration.

Contracts that purport to reserve an immediate right of arbitrary **cancellation** fall into this category of contracts as well. Because of the potential unfairness of allowing one side, by merely giving notice of cancellation, to free itself from an agreement to which the other side considers itself bound, courts are hostile to attempted exercises of a right of arbitrary cancellation. Courts therefore try to find some actual or implied limitations on the purported immediate right of arbitrary cancellation so as to make it a nonillusory, or binding, promise. Since consideration will exist for such promises, the agreement will be enforceable.

Preexisting Duty

If one performs or refrains from performing an act that one has a preexisting obligation to do or to refrain from doing, settled law holds that such a person has suffered no detriment. Consequently, no consideration is present to support the underlying promise or performance.

We often see this principle explicit in cases involving law enforcement officers. Assume you live next door to a policewoman, and she approaches you with this proposition: For $50 she will patrol around your house when you are gone on a trip. Since this sounds like a good deal to you, you agree. But you have second thoughts later and do not pay her. When she sues you in small claims court, she probably will lose because she has a preexisting duty (imposed by law) to try to keep your home free from burglaries. In patrolling around your house, she has suffered no detriment; so consideration to support her promise to you is lacking.

Besides obligations or duties imposed by law, preexisting duties may stem from contractual agreements. There are numerous cases that address these situations. For example, suppose G & H Painting Service has contracted with you to paint your basement for $900. Halfway through the job, the crew boss tells you he will dismiss the crew unless you agree to pay him $200 more (he has just seen the latest consumer price index and knows inflation is winning against him). Because you are having a party in two days, you grudgingly say yes. On completion of the job, do you have to pay $900 or $1,100? Based on the doctrine of preexisting obligations, you generally will have to pay only $900, since the firm already owes you the duty of finishing the basement. But if you subsequently want G & H to lay a concrete patio for you, your promise to pay $500 in return for G & H's work on the patio is supported by new consideration—G & H has not obligated itself to construct the patio as part of the original agreement—and you must pay $500 more for this additional work.

To return to the earlier example, assume now that in the middle of winter a freakish humid spell causes a paint-resistant fungus to grow in your basement. As a result, G & H has to paint the walls three times to cover them. If this blight arises after the firm begins the work, most courts will characterize it as an unforeseen or unforeseeable difficulty and will order you to pay the higher price. The same will hold true if you and the firm had canceled the original contract and had started anew with different promises and obligations. In both situations, consideration will support the new promises. Under the common law, strikes, inflation in the prices of raw materials, and lack of access to raw materials do not meet the test of "unforeseen or unforeseeable difficulties." Accordingly, new promises extracted on these bases ordinarily will lack consideration and thus be unenforceable.

Moral Consideration

We have noted that harsh outcomes sometimes result from the application of the doctrine of consideration. Promises made from a so-called moral obligation embody one such subcategory of consideration and ordinarily are not enforced. In general, courts adhere strictly to the requirement of consideration in these contexts.

YOU BE THE JUDGE

Foreseeability[1]

Not surprisingly, courts have had trouble determining the existence of "unforeseen or unforeseeable difficulties" subsequent to the parties' agreement. If the following issues arose before *your* court, how would *you* rule? Which of these should—or should not—constitute an "unforeseen or unforeseeable difficulty"?

- Contract modifications due to labor difficulties, loss of unexpected sources of materials, historical conflicts, or recurrent weather patterns that have affected the parties previously.
- An outside event that is truly exceptional and one of first impression between the parties.

BUSINESS CONSIDERATIONS Does a rule of thumb that limits the extra payment to an amount no greater than the actual, additional, out-of-pocket costs and expenses incurred in completing the contract or that assesses objective reasonableness in terms of whether one party is taking unfair advantage of the other make sense?

ETHICAL CONSIDERATIONS Is it ethical to hold merchants (as opposed to nonmerchants) to a higher standard for anticipating business risks and transactional conduct?

SOURCE: Martin E. Segal, *The ABA Journal* (November 1996), p. 86.

For example, suppose your child has been saved without injury from the jaws of a snarling Doberman pinscher because of the efforts of a passerby. The person who saved your child unfortunately suffers deep cuts that eventually require cosmetic surgery. Faced with such generosity, who among us will not promise this person the world? You are only human, so you offer to pay this Good Samaritan's lost wages while she is in the hospital. As time passes, however, you grow less willing to pay; and finally you cease paying her altogether. If she sues you, you usually will win because a court will conclude that she has bestowed a gift on you—that is, saving your child. Consequently, no consideration was present. Note, too, that prior to the humanitarian gesture, no bargaining in exchange for your promise to pay occurred. You may not think this particular result under this doctrine is harsh. Another disinterested party might, however, and may question your ethics here as well. Therefore, in a few jurisdictions, courts will reject the settled rule and hold that the passerby is entitled to win. Remember, though, that this is a position taken by a minority of courts.

Past Consideration

Related to this doctrine of moral consideration is the doctrine of past consideration. This issue typically arises when a person retires and the company offers the former employee a small **stipend** "in consideration of 25 years of faithful service." Since the old services are executed (completed or finished), they cannot form the basis for a new promise. The same is true of a promise to pay a relative based on the promisor's "love and affection" for the promisee. Notice that, in both cases, neither bargaining nor an exchange of anything of value has occurred. Neither of the promises is supported by consideration, and neither will be enforceable. In short, as traditional legal authority holds, "Past consideration is no consideration."

Stipend
A fixed sum of money paid periodically for services or to defray costs.

Exceptions to the Bargaining Theory of Consideration

As should now be apparent, whether or not the parties have bargained with a resulting exchange of value appears crucially important under the common law rules surrounding consideration. Still, in the following four situations courts will enforce agreements despite a lack of consideration: (1) promissory estoppel, (2) charitable subscriptions, (3) promises made after the statute of limitations has expired, and (4) promises to repay debts after a discharge in bankruptcy.

Promissory Estoppel

Promissory estoppel was discussed in Chapter 10 in the context of preventing an offeror's revocation of an offer. To recapitulate, courts apply this equitable doctrine in order to avoid injustice. Essentially, the elements are the same for consideration as for offers. In both, the promisor makes a definite promise that he or she expects, or should reasonably expect, will induce the plaintiff/promisee to act (or refrain from acting) in a manner that may be detrimental to the latter person. Accordingly, the law, to avoid injustice, holds the promisor to his or her promise. Simply put, the promisor is prevented from asserting a defense (here, that there is no consideration) normally available to the promisor.

In the case of the employer who offered to pay its employee "in consideration of 25 years of faithful service," promissory estoppel might be used as a substitute for consideration to enable the employee to win. In other words, if the employer in fact has paid the former employee $100 a month for 10 years, and the employee, owing to an expectation of continued stipends, has given up opportunities for part-time employment, some courts will conclude that the employer must continue the payments despite the absence of bargaining or of an exchange of anything of value.

Charitable Subscriptions

Likewise, promissory estoppel may help promisees win in the category of charitable subscriptions, which is another exception to the requirement of consideration. You probably can guess how this legal issue—the written promise to pay a certain sum to a nonprofit charity—arises.

Typically, a generous person wishes to donate a sizable amount to a worthy charity and promises to do so. Later, this humanitarian zeal wanes, and the person no longer wishes to live up to the written agreement. If you are the donor, what do you argue? In all likelihood, you will try to argue that you intended to bestow a gift. Since consideration by definition is lacking in a gift (there is neither bargaining nor an exchange of value), you can avoid liability for this promise.

Ordinarily, though, a would-be donor will have to live up to the agreement because charitable institutions rely on the belief that the amount pledged in written subscriptions will be forthcoming and because people make pledges based on the knowledge that other people will be making similar pledges. Courts, of course, believe that charitable institutions (like universities, hospitals, or churches) serve noble purposes. Thus, in addition to resorting to promissory estoppel as a substitute for consideration, courts alternatively may enforce the promise on public policy grounds. Again, the would-be donor needs to examine the ethical dimensions of his or her decision to renege on the promised charitable subscription.

Promises Made After the Expiration of the Statute of Limitations

State statutes of limitations set time limits on when creditors can bring suit against debtors for the sums owed to the creditors. Ordinarily, this period is from two to six years, after which the creditor cannot maintain suit against the debtor. Sometimes the debtor wants to repay the debt even if this time limit has passed. As we already have learned, there seems to be no consideration present in such a circumstance; there is an absence of any bargaining, and the debtor's promise arguably represents moral consideration at best.

Yet under most state statutes and decisions, the law will enforce the debtor's new promise to pay if it is in writing. The public policy of encouraging people to pay their debts generally forms the basis for this exception to the bargaining theory of consideration.

Promises to Pay Debts Covered by Bankruptcy Discharges

The same policy applies and the result is similar when a debtor promises to pay a debt covered by a discharge in bankruptcy. Again, no consideration underlies this new promise; but most states will allow the enforcement of the promise, provided that the debtor makes the promise to pay with full compliance with the reaffirmation provisions of the Bankruptcy Act and a full understanding of its significance, as required by the Bankruptcy Code.

Exhibit 11.1 offers a summary of many of the principles associated with consideration.

LEGAL CAPACITY

Capacity, the fourth requirement for a valid contract, mandates that the parties to the contract have the legal ability to bind themselves to the agreement and to enforce any promises made to them. However, incapacity, or the lack of such capacity, is the exception, not the rule. Hence, the burden of proof regarding incapacity falls on the party raising it as a defense to the enforcement of the contract or as a basis for **rescission** of the contract.

Rescission

An annulment or cancellation; a termination of the contract through the restoration of the parties to the status quo.

To determine contractual capacity, the law looks at the relative bargaining power of the parties involved. Historically, older persons have taken care of the younger members of society. By allowing children under a certain age to disaffirm (or withdraw from) the contract, the law attempts to protect children, who remain less adept at bargaining, from overreaching by these more experienced bargainers. The same is true of persons who lack mental capacity, such as insane persons: Contracts made by these persons may be absolutely void, voidable (the insane person can disaffirm the contract), or even valid (if, for example, contract formation occurs during a period of lucidity). Thus, the existence or absence of legal capacity and the consequences of proving incapacity depend heavily on the facts and on a given person's status.

Indeed, the law often uses the status of a person as a basis for making legal distinctions and in fact may **circumscribe** the legal rights of any persons falling within these classifications. For this reason, many jurisdictions limit the contractual rights of minors, insane persons, intoxicated persons, aliens, and convicts. In earlier times, the common law, through statutes called Married Women's Property Acts, curtailed the contractual rights of married women. Most states have eliminated these legislative

Circumscribe

Limit the range of activity associated with something.

EXHIBIT 11.1 Consideration: A Summary

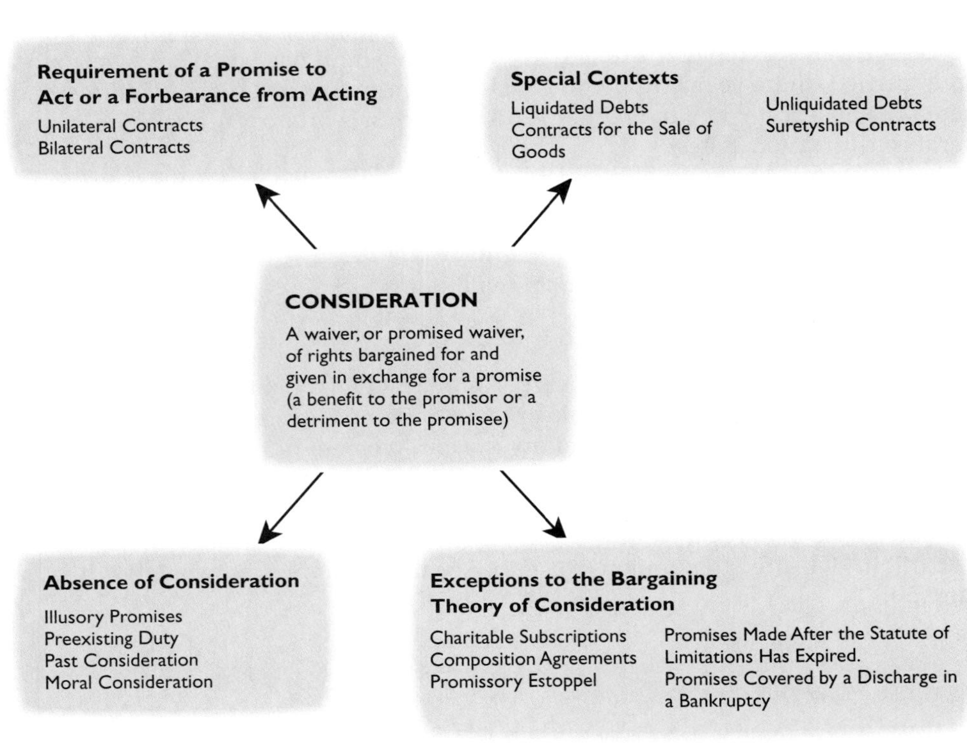

restrictions, but some vestiges of these acts remain in a few states. The extent of the legal disability placed on such classes of individuals comprises the focus of this section of the chapter.

MINORS

Most jurisdictions no longer follow the earlier common law rule that any person of either sex under 21 years of age is a minor (or an infant). Most states by statute have changed this rule to allow for achievement of majority status (that is, adult status) as early as age 18 for almost all purposes. (A common exception involves the purchase or consumption of alcoholic beverages.) Other states allow for termination of infancy status upon marriage or **emancipation**.

Emancipation
Freedom from the control or power of another; release from parental care; or the attainment of legal independence.

Disaffirmance/Rescission

To protect minors in their dealings with adults, the law allows minors to *disaffirm* (or avoid) their contracts with adults except in certain specialized cases, such as contracts involving necessaries (things that directly foster the minor's well-being). When the minor decides not to perform the legal obligations contemplated in the agreement and thus *disaffirms* the contract, this action results in a voidable contract. Stated differently, the minor has the option either of performing the contract or avoiding it. The converse is untrue: The adult who has contracted with a minor ordinarily will not be able to use the infancy of the minor to avoid the contract unless the minor allows the adult to disaffirm the contract. Simply put, do not contract with minors! Or, if you do, realize that the minor's powers in a given instance may be quite pervasive. Practically speaking, besides refusing to deal with minors, you can curtail their powers of avoidance by insisting that a parent or other adult cosign the contract as well. In this fashion, you effectively will limit the minor's power of *rescission,* the ability to have the contract set aside. This is true because even if the minor disaffirms the contract, the adult cosigner still will remain liable on it.

Analyze *Smoky, Inc.* v. *McCray* in light of these principles.

11.3 SMOKY, INC. v. McCRAY

396 S.E.2d 794 (Ga.App. 1990)

FACTS Fourteen-year-old Julie Ann McCray was taking a riding lesson from Deirdre Dunn in a riding ring at the Rocky Pine Ranch. McCray was circling Dunn on a horse controlled by a longe line rein held by Dunn. Because the longe line regulated the direction of the horse's movement, McCray could ride the horse and work on leg strength and balance without touching the reins, although her feet were in the stirrups. Terry Meier, the son of the president of the ranch, and two other boys entered the ring with three ponies, which were on halters, and moved to the far end of the ring. At trial, the parties disputed whether one of the ponies escaped from Terry's control as he was adjusting the saddle stirrups; or whether Terry, at the behest of his sister, Karen Meier, released the pony in order to play a trick on another equestrienne also working in the far end of the ring. At any rate, the pony ran to the other end of the ring and startled McCray's mount. As a result, Julie fell and broke her arm. Her parents later brought suit against Smoky, Inc., d.b.a. Rocky Pine Ranch, to recover damages for the injuries incurred by their daughter when she fell off this horse. At trial, the judge refused to admit an agreement that Julie had signed when she was 14 years old and that waived all claims against Smoky, Inc.

ISSUE Was this agreement voidable under Georgia law owing to infancy?

HOLDING Yes. Julie could disaffirm this agreement, signed when she was an infant, because it did not involve a necessary and thus represented a voidable contract.

REASONING The trial court properly refused to admit at trial the agreement signed by Julie Ann McCray, which Smoky, Inc., had tendered for the sole purpose of enabling the jury to determine whether McCray had waived all claims against it. The trial court found that at the time of the execution of the agreement, McCray had been 14 years old and unaccompanied by any parent or guardian. Moreover, as a contract by a minor for an item not a "necessary" under Georgia law, the agreement was voidable as a matter of law. Furthermore, according to Georgia precedents, "A contract by which an infant [waives] a claim which he [or she] may have for damages against another for personal injuries received by the infant is voidable, and may be disaffirmed by the infant. The institution or maintenance by the infant of a suit against the other contracting party [here, Smoky, Inc.] to recover damages for the injuries sustained by the infant amounts to a disaffirmance by the infant of the contract."

BUSINESS CONSIDERATIONS What policies should Smoky, Inc., establish and enforce as a consequence of this litigation?

ETHICAL CONSIDERATIONS Was Smoky, Inc., behaving ethically when it asked youngsters like Julie to sign waivers of all claims against the ranch? Given the existence of this agreement, was Julie's family, in bringing this lawsuit, acting ethically?

Summary judgment
Owing to an absence of any genuine issue of fact, a judgment rendered in favor of one party before trial and on the basis of the pleadings.

Upon disaffirmance, the minor, if possible, must return to the adult the property or other consideration that was the object of the contract. Strong policy reasons exist for this rule, called the *duty of restoration.* It clearly seems unfair to let the minor "have it both ways"—that is, get out of the contract and yet retain the consideration. The law therefore says that if the minor wants to avoid a contract, he or she must *totally* avoid it.

Sometimes, however, the minor cannot return the property or other consideration because it has been damaged or destroyed. For example, Ace Used Cars will be very upset if, eighteen months into the agreement, Marcie, the 17-year-old with whom Ace has dealt, asks for the money that she already has paid on the car as well as total release from the contract and in exchange presents Ace with a demolished car. In most states, minors like Marcie will get exactly what they wish because merely giving the car back fulfills the minor's duty of restoration. In some states, however, Ace will be able to set off any payments received from Marcie due to the damaged condition of the car. Courts in other jurisdictions will impose liability on minors like Marcie for the reasonable value of the benefit the minor received by virtue of Marcie's having use of the car for the period prior to the wreck.

FROM THE DESK OF
AMY CHEN, ATTORNEY AT LAW

Minors

You should make every effort not to deal with minors (people under the age of 18) in the sale or leasing of your product. A minor has a right to disaffirm the contract and recover his or her money. Although the minor also has a duty to return the consideration received, this duty is tempered somewhat due to the youth of the minor. You may find yourself returning money but not recovering your product, with virtually no legal recourse.

Misrepresentation of Age

What if the minor intentionally misrepresents his or her age? For example, suppose 17-year-old Marcie tells the salesperson at Ace Used Cars that she is 21 and, to "prove it," pulls out a falsified driver's license. If Marcie later tries to avoid the contract with Ace, can Ace argue that this intentional misrepresentation (fraud) prevents rescission? Under the law of most jurisdictions, the minor still can disaffirm the contract. But some states by statute hold that such a misrepresentation completely cuts off the minor's power of disaffirmance. Alternatively, some states allow rescission but force the minor to put the adult back in the position he or she would have been in but for the contract. In other words, in such age-misrepresentation cases, some states will allow Marcie to disaffirm the contract but either will force her to return the car or hold her liable in quasi contract for the reasonable value of the benefit Ace has conferred on her by furnishing her with the car. Also, Marcie probably will have to pay for any damage done to the car while she has had custody of it. Courts may employ some of these alternatives in situations involving minors who have not misrepresented their ages; but when age misrepresentation is present, courts increasingly will hold the minor to a heightened duty of restoration (or even restitution). Given the lack of uniformity among the states, you should check your own jurisdiction's precedents in this regard.

Scott Eden Management v. *Kavovit* does not involve age misrepresentation, but it does illustrate many of the points discussed.

11.4 SCOTT EDEN MANAGEMENT v. KAVOVIT

563 N.Y.S.2d 1001 (Sup. 1990)

FACTS In 1984, when defendant Andrew M. Kavovit was 12 years of age, he and his parents entered into a contract with Scott Eden Management (Scott Eden) whereby Scott Eden became the exclusive personal manager to supervise and promote Andrew's career in the entertainment industry. This agreement ran from 8 February 1984 to 8 February 1986, with an extension for another three years to 8 February 1989. It entitled Scott Eden to a 15 percent commission on Andrew's gross compensation, including residuals or royalties from such contracts, notwithstanding any earlier termination of the agreement. In 1986, Andrew signed an agency contract with the Andreadis Agency, a licensed agent selected by Scott Eden pursuant to industry requirements. This agreement involved an additional 10 percent commission. Thereafter, Andrew signed several contracts for his services. The most important contract, from a financial and career point of view, secured a role for Andrew on *As the World Turns,* a long-running television soap opera. Income from this employment contract appears to have commenced on 28 December 1987 and continued through 28 December 1990, with a strong possibility for renewal. One week before the expiration of the contract with Scott Eden, Andrew's attorney notified Scott Eden of Andrew's disaffirmance on the basis of infancy. Until then, the Andreadis Agency had been forwarding Scott Eden its commissions; but by letter of 4 February 1989, Andrew's father, David Kavovit, advised Andreadis that Andrew's salary should go directly to Andrew and that he would send Andreadis its 10 percent. Because Scott Eden received no additional commissions thereafter, it sued, seeking money damages for the commissions owed it.

ISSUE Does a 15-year-old child actor have the right to disaffirm his contract with his exclusive personal manager?

HOLDING Yes. To avoid the unjust enrichment of the infant, however, the infant must pay the fees and commissions due under the managerial contract.

REASONING An infant's contract is voidable, and the infant has an absolute right to disaffirm. This aspect of the law of contracts became well entrenched in the common law by the early fifteenth century. In bringing this action and defending against the **summary judgment** motion, Scott Eden fully acknowledged the principle of law involved here and in no way challenged the infant's right to disaffirm. Rather, Scott Eden relied on a corollary to the main rule, which also evolved early in the common law: "After disaffirmance, the infant is not entitled to be put in a position superior to such a one as he would have occupied if he had never entered into his voidable agreement. He is not entitled to retain an advantage from a transaction which he repudiates. The privilege of infancy is to be used as a shield and not as a sword." The restoration of consideration requirement also finds voice in New York statutes, one of which states that the infant need not tender restoration of benefits received prior to disaffirmance, "but the court may make a tender of restoration a condition of its judgment, and may otherwise in its judgment so adjust the equities between the parties that unjust enrichment is avoided." The restoration of consideration principle, as interpreted by the courts, has, for example, resulted in the infant's being responsible for wear-and-tear on the goods returned by him. In other such cases, the minor's inability to return the benefits obtained effectively precludes the minor from disaffirming the contract in order to get back the consideration given. Once a performance contract has been signed, the personal manager is entitled to his percentage fee, subject only to the condition subsequent that the client perform and earn his fee. When the client signs a performance contract, it is with the understanding that the gross amount to be paid is not solely for him. It is the expectation of all parties—the agent, the performer, and, in this case, the soap opera production company—that 15 percent of that gross amount belongs to the personal manager. To the extent that the performer obtains that 15 percent for himself, he is unjustly enriched. Here, the infant consumed the fruits of the contract and refused to pay for that fruit, to the clear prejudice of the other party. If a court adopts the argument asserted by the Kavovits, the infant would be put in a position superior to that which he would have occupied had he never entered into the contract with Scott Eden. He would be retaining an advantage from the repudiated transaction, that is, using the privilege of infancy as a sword rather than a shield. Not only is this manifestly unfair, but it would undermine the policy underlying the rule allowing disaffirmance. In this case, adjustment of the equities so as to prevent unjust enrichment, as suggested by New York statutory provisions, leads to the conclusion that Andrew and his parents must continue to pay to Scott Eden, as they become due, all commissions owed to Scott Eden under its contract.

BUSINESS CONSIDERATIONS Fortunately for Scott Eden, New York case law and statutes supported its recovering the commissions. In the absence of these protections, could Scott Eden have done anything to prevent this litigation?

11.4 SCOTT EDEN MANAGEMENT v. KAVOVIT *(cont.)* **563 N.Y.S.2d 1001 (Sup. 1990)**

ETHICAL CONSIDERATIONS Although Mr. Kavovit promised the Andreadis Agency that he would continue to send it the 10 percent commission owed to it, he failed to do so. Do parents have a duty to serve as role models of exemplary ethical behavior for their children? If you answer yes to this question, does this obligation expire upon a child's attaining a certain age, say 16?

Bona fide purchaser
A person who purchases in good faith, for value, and without notice of any defects or defenses affecting the sale or transaction.

Changing the circumstances of our previous example in which Marcie had not misrepresented her age, let us assume that Marcie had traded in another car when she had purchased the now-demolished car from Ace. When she avoids the contract, Ace has to return the trade-in to the minor as well in order to fulfill the adult's corresponding duty of restoration. If Ace already has sold this car to a **bona fide purchaser**, the minor cannot get the car back (as would be the usual result under the common law) but can recover the price paid to Ace by the third party. This result follows from the fact that the UCC (in § 2-403) covers this transaction. Thus, the UCC, by cutting off the minor's power of disaffirmance in some circumstances, has changed the common law.

When minors like Marcie attempt to disaffirm transactions with adults, no special words or acts are required to effect an avoidance. Disaffirmances may be made orally or in writing, formally (by a lawsuit) or informally, directly or indirectly (the minor's conveying the car to someone else when the minor reaches majority age is an avoidance of the contract with Ace Used Cars).

The minor's power of disaffirmance, whether the contract is executory or executed, ordinarily extends through his or her minority and for a reasonable time after achieving majority. How long is reasonable is a question of fact for a judge or jury to decide in light of all the circumstances.

Ratification

Ratification means that the minor in some fashion has indicated (1) approval of the contract made while he or she is an infant and (2) an intention to be bound to the provisions of that contract. Ratification, then, represents the opposite of disaffirmance and cuts off any right to disaffirm. Ratification takes two separate forms: express and implied. Even with express ratifications, or those situations in which the minor explicitly and definitely agrees to accept the obligations of the contract, the policy of protecting minors is so strong that many states require express ratifications to be in writing.

The more common type of ratification occurs through indirect means, such as conduct that shows approval of the contract, even though the minor has said nothing specifically about agreeing to be bound to it. To illustrate, failure to make a timely disaffirmance constitutes an implied ratification of an executed contract. Thus, a minor who is not diligent in disaffirming within a reasonable time after attaining majority will have impliedly ratified the contract. Such inaction does not ordinarily bring about ratification of an executory contract, however. Some courts will hold that, by itself, partial payment of a debt usually is not tantamount to ratification, unless payment is coupled to the minor's express intention to be bound to the contract. In any event, ratification cannot occur until the minor achieves majority status. If ratification were possible beforehand, the law's protection of minors would be meaningless. *Fletcher* v. *Marshall* provides a good illustration of these principles.

11.5 FLETCHER v. MARSHALL

632 N.E.2d 1105 (Ill.App. 1994)

FACTS Kristin Fletcher and John E. Marshall III dated while in high school. When Marshall's parents ejected him from their home shortly after his graduation from high school, he and Fletcher decided to rent an apartment and share the expenses. The parties disputed when Marshall signed the lease: He said he signed it on 29 April 1991, when he was only 17 years old and a minor; Fletcher maintained that, although the apartment complex manager had typed the lease on 29 April 1991, Marshall had signed it on 30 June 1991, the day preceding the commencement of the lease. All the parties agreed that Marshall turned eighteen on 30 May 1991. Marshall also admitted that he had paid part of the security deposit (although the date on which he had done so remained unclear) and that he had made rent payments. Marshall moved out of the apartment in August (he said on the second, while Fletcher said the fifteenth) because he and Fletcher were not getting along and because he planned to attend college. When Fletcher sued Marshall for $2,500 in rent, he argued his lack of capacity permitted him to disaffirm the lease. Fletcher disputed Marshall's statement that he had signed the lease while a minor but argued in the alternative that Marshall had ratified the contract after turning eighteen.

ISSUE Had Marshall ratified the contract and thereby become liable for his part of the rent?

HOLDING Yes. By taking possession of the premises and paying rent, Marshall had ratified the lease after attaining majority.

REASONING A contract of a minor is not void from the beginning but merely voidable at the election of the minor upon attaining majority. After attaining majority, a person either may disaffirm or ratify a contract one had entered into while still a minor. Ratification of a contract occurs when a minor fails to disaffirm it within a reasonable time after attaining majority. A minor also ratifies a contract if, after becoming of age, one does any distinct and decisive act clearly showing an intention to affirm the contract. Once a person ratifies such a contract, one cannot thereafter avoid one's obligations under it. Moreover, it is well established that whether a minor has disaffirmed a contract within a reasonable time after attaining majority is a question of fact dependent on the circumstances of the case. In the context of ratification, the trier of fact often will have to infer from a person's actions that he or she intended to ratify a contract. Therefore, whether a ratification has occurred depends largely on the facts of a particular case. Here, it is undisputed that about two weeks after becoming 18 years of age, Marshall moved into the apartment and paid rent. Marshall's living in the apartment for about one and one-half months and his failure before moving out to take any action that would evince an intention to disaffirm the lease constituted an unequivocal ratification of the lease. Because he already had ratified the lease, his later attempt to disaffirm it by moving out of the apartment and refusing to make further payments had no legal effect on his liability for the rent.

BUSINESS CONSIDERATIONS Among other things, this situation illustrates graphically the old adage that it is unwise to mix business and romance. In hindsight, what, respectively, should Kristin, John, and the apartment complex manager have done so as to minimize the probability of litigation?

ETHICAL CONSIDERATIONS Assume John had few resources (and few prospects) when he signed the lease. In those circumstances, would a person who adheres to the ethical precept known as the Golden Rule have signed the lease? Which classical ethical theory did John apparently follow? Did the apartment complex, in accepting John as colessee, ethically exploit John and Kristin?

Necessaries

Even in the absence of ratification, minors will be liable for transactions whereby they have been furnished "necessaries." *Necessaries* formerly encompassed only food, clothing, and shelter; but the law has broadened the doctrine to cover other things that directly foster the minor's well-being. The basis for the minor's liability is quasi contract, which you learned about in Chapter 9. (Remember that there can be no liability in *contract* law because of a lack of capacity.) If an adult has supplied necessaries to the minor, the law will imply liability for the reasonable value of those necessaries. Often, though, the law will not impose liability on the minor for the cost of necessaries unless the minor's parents are unable to discharge their obligation to support their child and pay for such essentials.

The definition of necessaries depends on the minor's circumstances, or social and economic situation in life. In this sense, the rule is applied somewhat subjectively. Although food, clothing, and shelter are covered, is a fur coat a necessary for which the minor is liable? It may be, depending on the minor's social station. Similarly, loans for medical or dental services or education also may comprise necessaries in some situations. Numerous cases involve cars; and many courts hold that a car, especially if the minor uses it for coming and going to work, is a necessary for which the minor remains liable. The definition of what constitutes a necessary changes as community values and mores change.

Special Statutes

Legislatures in many states have passed special statutes making minors liable in a variety of circumstances. Under such laws, minors may be responsible for educational loans, medical or dental expenses, insurance policies, bank account contracts, transportation by common carrier (for example, airline tickets), and other expenses. These statutes protect the interests of those persons who deal with minors who, despite their age, exhibit the skills and maturity of adults.

Torts and Crimes

The law similarly protects the interests of adults when an adult has suffered losses owing to a minor's torts and crimes. Minors, therefore, generally cannot disaffirm liability for torts and crimes unless the minor is of *tender years,* or too young to understand the consequences of his or her acts. Minors sometimes may escape liability in these areas if the imposition of tort liability will bring about the enforcement of a contract the minor previously has disaffirmed. Note how, in this latter context, the law once again has chosen to protect minors at the expense of adults.

INSANE PERSONS

Like minors, insane persons may lack the capacity to make a binding contract. However, the law in this area is somewhat more complicated.

To be insane, a person must be so mentally infirm or deranged as to be unable to understand what he or she is agreeing to or the consequences attendant upon that agreement. The causes of such disability—lunacy, mental retardation, senility, or alcohol or drug abuse—are irrelevant.

Effects of Transactions by Insane Persons

The contract of a person whom a court has adjudged insane through court proceedings is absolutely void. Only his or her **guardian** has the legal capacity to contract on the person's behalf. The contracts of other insane persons are voidable, however. To disaffirm a contract, the person using insanity as a defense must prove that he or she actually was insane at the time of contracting. If the person instead was lucid and understood the nature and consequences of the contract, that person is bound by the contract.

Guardian
A person legally responsible for taking care of another who lacks the legal capacity to do so.

This power of an insane person to avoid contracts also extends to the heirs or personal representative of a deceased insane person. A living insane person's guardian possesses similar powers. Upon regaining sanity, a formerly insane person nonetheless may ratify a contract made during the period of insanity.

Determining whether a transaction by an insane person is void, voidable, or enforceable depends heavily on the facts.

Necessaries

By analogy to the rules covering minors, the law makes insane persons liable for necessaries in quasi contract. The categories of goods and services deemed necessaries for minors generally extend to insane persons. In the context of insanity, fewer controversies should arise regarding whether medical or legal services are necessaries—they probably constitute necessaries for which the insane person remains liable.

Intoxicated Persons

If a person is so thoroughly intoxicated that he or she does not understand the nature or consequences of the agreement being made, the person's mental disability approaches that of an insane person. Hence, under certain circumstances, such a person can disaffirm a given agreement. This power of possible disaffirmance depends, however, on the degree of intoxication involved, which in turn involves a question of fact. Slight degrees of intoxication do not constitute cause for disaffirmance of a contract.

Whether the intoxication was involuntary or voluntary may bear on the result, too. If a plaintiff has plied the defendant with liquor, any resulting intoxication may factor into a court's finding of incapacity, fraud, or overreaching that will release the defendant from the agreement. Even voluntary intoxication sometimes can result in a voidable contract if the facts support this conclusion.

Upon regaining sobriety, the formerly intoxicated person either may avoid or ratify the contract. The rules about acting within a reasonable time apply here as well; if the person does not quickly disaffirm the contract, an implied ratification will result. Courts generally are hostile to avoiding contracts on the basis of intoxication except in unusual circumstances.

Aliens

An *alien* is a citizen of a foreign country. Most of the disabilities to which the law formerly subjected an alien have been removed, usually through treaties. Thus, a *legal* alien ordinarily can enter into contracts and pursue gainful employment without legal disabilities, just as any U.S. citizen can. Some states make distinctions based on

http:// RESOURCES FOR BUSINESS LAW STUDENTS

NAME	RESOURCES	WEB ADDRESS
Legal Information Institute—Contract Law Materials	LII provides an overview of contract law; links to federal government statutes, treaties, and regulations; federal and state judicial decisions regarding contract law (including Supreme Court decisions); state statutes; and other materials.	http://www.law.cornell.edu/topics/contracts.html
The American Law Institute	The American Law Institute, publisher of restatements of the law, model codes, and other proposals for law reform, provides press releases, its newsletter, and other publications.	http://www.ali.org

the alien's right to hold or convey personal property (generally authorized under such statutes) and the right to hold, convey, or inherit real property (some restrictions potentially are applicable here). *Enemy* aliens, or those who are residents of countries with whom we officially are at war, cannot enforce contracts during the period of hostility but sometimes can after the war ends. Given the large numbers of illegal aliens in the United States, this area of the law, with its attendant ethical questions, promises to be ripe for future developments.

Convicts

In many states, conviction of a felony or treason carries with it certain contractual disabilities. For instance, laws may prohibit convicts from conveying property during their periods of incarceration. Such disabilities, if applicable, exist only during imprisonment. Upon release from prison, these persons have full rights to contract.

Married Women

Under early common law, married women's contracts were void. The law viewed women as their husbands' property and as otherwise lacking in capacity to make contracts. This common law disability, reflected in Married Women's Property Acts, has been eliminated by statute or by judicial decision in almost all states.

Exhibit 11.2 summarizes the contractual capacities of minors, insane persons, intoxicated persons, aliens, convicts, and married women.

Summary

Consideration is a firmly entrenched doctrine in modern law. Consideration consists of any waiver or promised waiver of rights bargained for in exchange for a promise. Consideration exists when there is a benefit to the promisor or a detriment to the promisee bargained for and given in exchange for a promise. In unilateral contracts,

EXHIBIT 11.2 Contractual Capacity

Class of Person		Classification of Contract	Exceptions
Minors		Voidable (upon return of consideration to seller)	1. Misrepresentation of age, which eliminates power of rescission in some jurisdictions. 2. Failure to rescind within a reasonable time after achieving majority (implied ratification). 3. Express ratification after achieving majority (necessity of a writing in some jurisdictions). 4. Necessaries (liability in quasi contract in some cases if parents unable to pay). 5. Special statutes making minors liable.
Insane persons	Those adjudged insane	Void	1. Capacity by guardians to contract on these insane persons' behalf.
	Those insane but not adjudged so by a court	Voidable	1. Ratification possible during periods of lucidity. 2. Necessaries (liability in quasi contract in some circumstances).
Intoxicated persons	Slightly intoxicated persons	Valid	
	Seriously intoxicated persons	Voidable	1. Subsequent ratification upon regaining sobriety possible. 2. Failure to rescind within a reasonable time after achieving sobriety in involuntary intoxication circumstances (implied ratification).
Aliens	Legal aliens	Valid	1. Some restrictions sometimes regarding ownership of real property and workers' compensation claims.
	Enemy aliens during hostilities	Void	
	Enemy aliens after hostilities end	Valid	
	Illegal aliens	Valid	
Convicts	Convicts during incarceration	Void	
	Convicts after release	Valid	
Married women		Valid	1. Some anachronistic restrictions remaining in a few states.

consideration may take the form of an act or a forbearance to act. In bilateral contracts, the respective promises constitute consideration. In the absence of fraud, duress, undue influence, or unconscionability, courts generally will not inquire into the adequacy of the consideration. Although no consideration is necessary under the UCC provisions relating to firm offers and modifications of sales contracts, consideration is necessary to hold a surety liable.

The doctrine of preexisting obligations mandates that one pay a liquidated debt in full; part payment is not consideration for full discharge of the debt. In contrast, part payment of an unliquidated debt, if accepted as full payment, represents a compromise of the debt and is supported by consideration. Such satisfaction and accord completely cancel the debt. The same rationale validates composition agreements between the debtor and a group of creditors.

Agreements based on illusory promises or promises grounded in either preexisting legal duties or preexisting contractual relationships lack consideration. The same is true of promises founded on moral obligations and on past consideration. The four exceptions to the bargaining theory of consideration are (1) promissory estoppel, (2) charitable subscriptions, (3) promises to repay made after the statute of limitations has expired, and (4) promises to repay debts covered by discharges in bankruptcy. Courts will give effect to agreements without consideration in these situations.

Certain classes of people may lack capacity, or the legal ability to bind themselves to an agreement and to enforce any promises made to them. For example, the contracts of a minor, usually defined as a person under age 18, often are voidable at the option of the minor, even when the minor has misrepresented his or her age. This power of disaffirmance ordinarily extends through the person's minority and for a reasonable time after attaining majority. After reaching majority, however, a minor may ratify, or approve, the contract. Ratification may be express or implied. Even in the absence of ratification, a minor may be liable for necessaries in quasi contract. The definition of necessaries depends on the minor's station in life and the parents' ability to provide for the minor. Sometimes special statutes broaden a minor's areas of liability. A minor almost always will be liable for any tort or crime unless the minor is very young or the imposition of tort liability will bring about the enforcement of a contract previously disaffirmed by the minor.

The contracts of insane persons may be void, voidable, or valid. To be insane, a person must demonstrate sufficient mental derangement to be unable to understand that to which he or she is agreeing or the consequences attendant upon that agreement. Such agreements are void, but contracts entered into during periods of lucidity are enforceable. Upon regaining sanity, a person either may ratify the contract or avoid it. Insane persons are liable for necessaries, just as minors are.

Total intoxication may render a person incapable of entering into a binding contract, but slight intoxication will not. Upon regaining sobriety, the person either may disaffirm or ratify the contract. However, courts generally are hostile to avoiding contracts on the basis of intoxication, except in unusual circumstances.

Aliens, or persons who are citizens of foreign countries, may face legal disabilities with regard to contractual capacity. This is especially true of enemy aliens, that is, residents of countries with whom the United States officially is at war. Convicts and even married women may have limited rights to contract as well. To determine the degree of disability, if any, that exists for these persons, one should consult the relevant state statutes.

DISCUSSION QUESTIONS

1. Define *consideration.*
2. Can "doing nothing" ever suffice as consideration to support a promise?
3. Why do courts refuse to inquire into the adequacy of consideration?
4. Explain why part payment of a liquidated debt is not consideration for full discharge of the debt, but part payment accepted as full payment for an unliquidated debt is.
5. Explain the four situations in which courts will enforce agreements despite a lack of bargaining (and hence consideration).
6. Why do smart business people say, "Don't deal with minors"? Can minors disaffirm contracts if they have misrepresented their ages at the time of contracting?
7. How long does an infant's power to rescind a contract last?
8. What is *ratification,* and how can it occur?
9. Define *necessaries.*
10. Can an insane or intoxicated person's contracts ever be enforceable? Why or why not?

CASE PROBLEMS AND WRITING ASSIGNMENTS

1. Jackie Mohr worked as a secretary for Arachnid, Inc. On 13 February 1989, Mohr and Arachnid entered into a written agreement for the payment of six months' severance pay if Mohr's employment should cease as a result of a significant change in the ownership of the firm's stock. The agreement was to be effective only if such termination occurred within one year of the date of the agreement. On 24 February 1989, owing to a shareholder buyout, the ownership of the company changed significantly. Mohr was notified on 12 April 1989 that her employment would terminate. At that time, Arachnid paid Mohr two weeks' severance pay. When Mohr sued for breach of contract, Arachnid argued that the agreement was void and unenforceable because Mohr had provided no consideration. Did Mohr's continuing to work for Arachnid constitute consideration sufficient to support an express agreement to pay severance wages? [See *Mohr* v. *Arachnid, Inc.,* 559 N.E.2d 1098 (Ill.App. 1990).]

2. National Super Markets, Inc.'s (National's) security personnel caught Y.W., an 11-year-old girl, shoplifting candy. While National's security personnel still detained her, Y.W.'s mother signed a release whereby National agreed to decline to prosecute the minor as consideration for the minor's agreement not to bring civil charges against National. Y.W. and her mother later disputed whether Y.W. actually had signed the agreement or whether her mother, in a representative capacity, had signed both names. Y.W. subsequently filed a civil suit for assault and battery against National. Y.W. asserted, as a defense to the enforcement of the release, her infancy as well as a Missouri statute requiring that a representative who purports to act in behalf of a minor be duly appointed by a judge. Y.W. therefore argued that her mother, acting only as Y.W.'s natural guardian, lacked the authority to enter into a binding settlement of Y.W.'s claim. Should a court accept Y.W.'s arguments? [See *Y.W. By and Through Smith* v. *Nat'l Super Mkts., Inc.,* 876 S.W.2d 785 (Mo.App. 1994).]

3. James "Buster" Douglas and his manager, John P. Johnson, signed a boxing promotional agreement with Don King Productions, Inc. (DKP) for $25,000 on 31 December 1988. The agreement provided DKP with the "sole and exclusive right to secure and arrange all professional boxing bouts" for Douglas for the term of the agreement. The promotional agreement also set forth DKP's intention to promote a heavyweight championship bout involving Douglas and provided that the three-year term of the agreement automatically would be extended in the event that Douglas were recognized as world champion "to cover the entire period [Douglas was] world champion and a period of two years following." Pursuant to this promotional agreement, Douglas participated in three bouts arranged by DKP during the first year (ending 26 February 1990). The last of these involved the heavyweight championship bout held on 10 February 1990, in Tokyo, Japan, between Douglas and then-heavyweight champion Michael Tyson. Douglas won the bout and became the undisputed heavyweight champion of the world. Relations between Don King and the Douglas camp soured, however, when King, who also was Tyson's promoter, objected to the alleged "long count" that had occurred during the eighth round of the fight. Shortly after this championship bout, Douglas and Johnson executed a contract for Douglas, now the heavyweight champion, to

fight two bouts at the Mirage Hotel for a minimum of $50 million. But the Mirage Hotel contracts would not become binding until Douglas and Johnson obtained a release from DKP of its allegedly exclusive promotional rights or, alternatively, a judicial declaration that the promotional and bout agreements (whereby Douglas would receive at least $1 million for each of the three bouts following the Tokyo bout) were void and unenforceable. In filing suit, Douglas and Johnson argued that the contractually specified million-dollar purse represented inadequate consideration because this figure amounted to a "mere token" of Douglas's value as the world heavyweight champion. Should a court accept these arguments in these circumstances? [See *Don King Productions., Inc.* v. *Douglas*, 742 F.Supp. 741 (S.D. N.Y. 1990).]

4. When Sean T. Power was 17 years old, he bought an automobile insurance policy from Allstate Insurance Company (Allstate). At that time, Power rejected the underinsured motorist portion of the coverage. Three months after the issuance of the policy, Power suffered injuries in an automobile accident. Power thereafter filed a declaratory judgment action in which he sought to repudiate his rejection of Allstate's offer and to add the underinsured motorist coverage to his policy. Could Power, as an adult, disaffirm a portion of the agreement he, as a minor, had made with Allstate and ratify the remainder of the contract? [See *Power* v. *Allstate Ins. Co.*, 440 S.E.2d 406 (S.C.App. 1994).]

5. Kate Michaelis, a 17-year-old who lived with her parents, signed a binding arbitration agreement with Dr. Janet Schori, whom Michaelis had consulted for medical treatment related to Michaelis's pregnancy. Schori also signed this agreement. California, by statute, makes unemancipated minors liable for medical care relating to the prevention or treatment of pregnancy even without the consent of the minor's parents. The relevant statutes expressly limit the minor's power to disaffirm such contracts. Section 1295 of California's code of civil procedure, however, allows disaffirmance if a minor's parents have not signed the medical contract whenever the contract for medical services contains a provision for the arbitration of any dispute relating to the professional negligence of a health-care provider. After the stillborn death of her baby, Michaelis disaffirmed the arbitration agreement she had signed and sued the hospital, its staff, and Schori for medical malpractice. Could Michaelis disaffirm the arbitration agreement? [See *Michaelis* v. *Schori*, 24 Cal.Rptr.2d 380 (Cal.App. 1993).]

6. **BUSINESS APPLICATION CASE** Kenneth W. Morris and Mack S. Love were employees of Milner Airco, Inc. After working for the company for several years, both Morris and Love were asked to sign employment contracts that contained a noncompete clause. Morris signed the contract on 21 January 1990, so he could become an account manager "when the economy improved." (Morris actually became an account manager on 1 April 1991, some 15 months later). Love signed the agreement on 1 May 1991, shortly after he had received a demotion. Indeed, Love was told either to sign the document or leave the company. Milner explained that it was asking the employees to sign the documents in order to increase the employees' job security and to protect the company's investment in job training for its employees and thereby to prevent future competition from former employees. When Morris and Love began working for a competing company in October 1991, Milner petitioned the court to enforce the covenant not to compete provisions of the two men's employment contracts. Morris and Love argued that no consideration supported their signing of the covenants. How should the court rule in this case? Could the company have taken any steps that would have minimized Morris and Love's chances of prevailing in this litigation? Explain. [See *Milner Airco, Inc.* v. *Morris*, 433 S.E.2d 811 (N.C.App. 1993).]

7. **ETHICS APPLICATION CASE** In a lawsuit filed against Shoals Ford, Inc. (Shoals Ford), Maxine Clardy sought to have a transaction entered into between Shoals Ford and her husband Bobby Joe for the purchase of a 1989 Ford pickup truck set aside and to recover the monies paid by Bobby Joe to Shoals Ford. Maxine claimed Bobby Joe had suffered from a manic-depressive disorder for more than 15 years and that, while in a manic state, he had purchased the pickup. In the five days' period before Bobby Joe picked up the truck, both Maxine and her daughter had talked to representatives of Shoals Ford concerning Bobby Joe's condition and had asked that the dealership not allow him to take the truck. Indeed, Bobby Joe's conduct on the day he took possession—his refusal to resume taking his medicine, his threatening his daughter's family's lives, and his forcing her to write him a check for $500—had caused Maxine to call 911 and to ask her attorney to prepare a petition requesting Bobby Joe's involuntary commitment. Calling to notify Shoals Ford of Bobby Joe's mental condition, she told a representative that Bobby Joe would be coming in to purchase a truck; specifically described the particular truck; stressed to the representative that Bobby Joe was not healthy; and informed the representative that she had filed a petition to have Bobby Joe involuntarily committed. She also asked Shoals Ford to call the Lauderdale County sheriff, a family member, her attorney, Riverbend Center for Mental

Health, or the probate office for verification in the event Bobby Joe did appear at the dealership. She further explained to the representative that "buying sprees" constituted a symptom of Bobby Joe's illness, that he would be unable to make the payments, and that he was not insurable. Shoals Ford responded that if Bobby Joe had the money to purchase the truck, it was "none of her concern." Around 10 a.m. on 5 April 1989, she drove by Shoals Ford and, noticing that the truck was still there, she once again telephoned to plead with Shoals Ford to notify her when Bobby Joe arrived. At this time, the representative reiterated that "it was really not of concern to Shoals Ford." A jury returned a verdict in favor of Maxine, who was acting as Bobby Joe's personal representative, in the amount of $6,715.02 in compensatory damages and $18,000 in punitive damages. On appeal, could Shoals Ford win? The legalities aside, how would a dealership bent on maintaining high ethical standards have handled this situation? [See *Shoals Ford, Inc.* v. *Clardy,* 588 So.2d 879 (Ala. 1991).]

8. **IDES CASE** Carter, at age 20, paid $500 down and bought a car from A-1 Motors for $5,000. In the bill of sale, Carter certified that he was "21 years of age or older" (and thus of majority in this jurisdiction). In fact, he told the salesperson he was 22. Carter took the car home but brought it back the next day for repairs. When A-1 failed to correct the problems, Carter had his attorney write the company to repudiate the contract and to demand the return of the down payment. Should Carter prevail? What if Carter had kept the car for 18 months before he had tried to repudiate the contract? Would your answer differ?

   Assume further that the owner of A-1 Motors (A-1) had hired a painter to paint the showroom for an agreed-on rate of $15 per hour plus materials. The painter finished the job and presented A-1 with a bill for $2,000. The owner of A-1 contended that the job was worth only $1,000. After protracted negotiations, the painter agreed to settle for $1,700. The owner then wrote a $1,700 check, on the back of which he wrote "payment in full." The painter cashed the check but subsequently sued A-1 in small claims court for $300. Who would win and why? [Case derived from materials developed for in-class discussions and hypothetical questions.]

NOTE

1. Martin E. Segal, "Foreseeability in a Fog," *The ABA Journal* (November 1996), p. 86.

A G E N D A

The Kochanowskis will have to decide how to advertise and market the CIT videophones. Should they use slick advertising that possibly portrays the product as capable of doing more than it actually does? If they adopt this strategy, will it have any effect on the contracts they enter? Can a firm be held responsible for misleading ads that may constitute misrepresentation and fraud?

Many people have questioned the legality of videophones. These people assert, among other things, that videophones invade the privacy of the user and thus violate public policy. Should the firm concern itself with controversies such as this? Could these issues affect the legality of contracts the firm enters? What other legal considerations might arise?

These and other questions are likely to surface in this chapter. Be prepared! You never know when one of the Kochanowskis will ask you for help or advice.

Legality of Subject Matter and Reality of Consent

O U T L I N E

THE REQUIREMENTS OF LEGALITY OF SUBJECT MATTER AND REALITY OF CONSENT

By this time, you undoubtedly noted the emphasis U.S. contract law places on bargaining and contract formation through the agreement of the parties. Yet, as with most human activities, the permissible boundaries of such conduct remain limited. Society at large may have a stake in the agreement the parties have forged. An agreement to bribe public officials or to murder someone, for instance, has definite repercussions for society that extend beyond the parties who initiated the bargain. The law, then, imposes a requirement that in order for the bargain to be recognized as a valid contract, the subject matter and purpose of the bargain must be legal. In this sense, the term *illegal contract* constitutes a misnomer; in general, a bargain cannot attain the status of "contract" unless it is legal. Hence, illegal "contracts" are void.

A bargain, however innocent it seems, nevertheless may involve a violation of a statute, common law, or public policy and hence is void. Similarly, the law will not recognize as a contract any agreement in which there is an absence of the parties' genuine assent. Put another way, we have to ascertain whether the consent given by the parties is real or whether the facts actually differ from those to which they have outwardly agreed. The existence of fraud, misrepresentation, mistake, duress, undue influence, or unconscionability precludes genuine mutual assent.

Components of Illegality

A widely accepted definition of *illegality*, taken from the *Restatement (First) of Contracts*, § 512, and augmented by the *Restatement (Second) of Contracts* § 178, states that a bargain is illegal if its performance is criminal, tortious, or otherwise opposed to public policy.[1] Both the subject matter of the bargain and the realization of its objectives must be permissible under state and federal statutes. Sometimes these statutes impose criminal penalties for their violation (for example, an agreement to engage in arson for money). Other statutes, however, may prohibit certain kinds of bargains (for example, a contract with an improperly licensed electrician) without imposing criminal penalties on those who violate these statutes.

The desire to protect the public also underlies the prohibition of bargains involving **tortious** conduct (for example, an agreement between two parties for the purpose of defrauding a third person).

Tortious
Relating to private or civil wrongs or injuries.

Similarly, even in the absence of an agreement that violates a statute or requires the commission of a tort, courts may declare as illegal on public policy grounds any bargain that will be detrimental to the public at large. Although the concept of *public policy* may fluctuate as different courts apply different standards, courts increasingly have used this rationale in a variety of contexts in which there appears to be no other basis for protecting the peace, health, or morals of the community. For instance, a bank may offer a rather one-sided night depository agreement in which it refuses to accept liability for a deposit placed in its after-hours slot, even if the loss stems from the negligence of its own employee and the depositor can prove that he or she actually deposited the amount in question with the bank. The concept of public policy—here the protection of depositors' expectations that the bank will take proper care of their deposits and the protection of consumers against one-sided agreements—will permit a court to invalidate such agreements on the grounds of illegality.

Exculpatory clauses
Parts of agreements in which a prospective plaintiff agrees in advance not to seek to hold the prospective defendant liable for certain losses for which the prospective defendant otherwise would be liable.

Contracts of adhesion
Contracts in which the terms are not open to negotiation; so-called take-it-or-leave-it contracts.

A court may characterize such agreements as **exculpatory clauses** or **contracts of adhesion** (in these circumstances, depositors may have had no choice but to accept the bank's terms). In general, an illegal bargain is void and hence unenforceable. This ordinarily is true whether the agreement is executory or fully executed. Usually a court merely leaves the parties where it finds them. Neither party, then, can sue the other. Exceptions to the general rule that courts will not give relief to parties who have created an illegal bargain do exist, however.

Mala in Se and *Mala Prohibita* Bargains

Early on, many courts became dissatisfied with the rule that illegal contracts are absolutely void. Some of these courts therefore distinguished between bargains that violate statutes because they are evil *in themselves (mala in se)* and bargains that have been *merely forbidden by statute (mala prohibita).* The first type (for example, an agreement to murder someone) fell within the general rule and was void. Some courts, however, depending on the nature and effect of the act prohibited by the statute, were prepared to view bargains included within the second type as voidable rather than void.

To illustrate, one case involved the sale of cattle in violation of a law stating that all cattle sold must be tested for brucellosis (a serious disease in cattle) within the 30-day period preceding the sale. The court clearly could have used this statutory violation as a basis for holding the agreement void. Yet the court concluded that this bargain was *mala prohibita,* rather than *mala in se,* because the contract was neither in bad faith nor contrary to public policy, and therefore enforced the contract. [See *First National Bank of Shreveport* v. *Williams,* 346 So.2d 257, 264 (La.App. 1977).]

More recent commentators have criticized the distinction between *mala in se* and *mala prohibita* bargains as invalid because any bargain that violates a statute is absolutely void no matter what underlying rationale the prohibition involves. This conclusion represents the position most widely accepted today. Nevertheless, the continued use of these terms demonstrates the tendency of courts to weigh differences in the degree of evil and accordingly determine the availability of judicial relief.

Courts, however, almost universally recognize two types of agreements as *mala in se* bargains: agreements to commit a crime and agreements to commit a tort. The agreement mentioned earlier involving arson could be called a *mala in se* bargain because the subject matter of the agreement itself, the commission of a crime, is morally unacceptable. The same would be true of an agreement to kill someone, a so-called murder "contract." Neither party can enforce such agreements; they are absolutely void. Likewise, an agreement that involves the commission of a tort is void. Besides fraud, such bargains may involve agreements to damage the good name of a competitor, to inflict mental distress on a third party, or to trespass against another's **chattels** or real property in order to cause injury to the property.

Chattels
Articles of personal (as opposed to real) property.

Determining whether a particular activity violates a statute (assuming the activity is not *mala in se*) is more difficult and requires that courts resort first to the words of the underlying statute. Courts then must assess the legislative intent and, finally, examine the social effects of giving or refusing a remedy in the particular situation. The *Stampco Construction Co., Inc.* v. *Guffey* case is instructive in regard to how courts use public policy rationales for deciding cases involving *mala prohibita* bargains.

12.1 STAMPCO CONSTRUCTION CO., INC. v. GUFFEY — 572 N.E.2d 510 (Ind.App. 1991)

FACTS Stampco Construction Co., Inc. (Stampco) performed work under contracts for the construction of public works. W. Keith Guffey and Wendell Guffey both were employees of Stampco between July 1984 and October 1985. At that time, Indiana statutes and the federal Davis Bacon Act mandated payment of prevailing wages for workers employed on public works projects. Keith worked on the Muncie Sanitary District and Community Development project for $13 per hour. He also worked on the Blair's Green Acres project (the Blair's project) for $350 per week from June to October 1985. Stampco employed Wendell on the Blair's project and paid him $8 per hour for regular hours and $12 per hour for overtime. On 30 October 1985, Keith signed an affidavit of release in exchange for $500 cash and a $1,500 IOU. That affidavit released Stampco from the payment of minimum wages and prevailing wages for work performed on public works projects. After Stampco terminated Keith and Wendell's employment, both filed suit seeking compensation for the difference between the wages paid and those to which they had been entitled under the prevailing scale of wages. The trial court awarded Keith $8,146.74 and Wendell $2,502.11 and then, pursuant to Indiana statutory provisions, trebled these awards. Stampco argued that Keith's and Wendell's agreeing to accept lower wages and Keith's signing the release concerning any claim he might have had for unpaid wages against Stampco constituted a waiver of such statutory benefits.

ISSUE Owing to their agreements with Stampco, were Keith and Wendell precluded from bringing lawsuits under the prevailing wage statutes?

HOLDING No. They could sue under these statutes because the agreements with Stampco violated public policy and hence were illegal.

REASONING In determining the question of law of whether an agreement violates public policy, a court must look at all the circumstances of a particular case. A court should keep in mind that refraining from unnecessarily restricting freedom of contract furthers the public's best interests. Moreover, a court should not hold agreements void as against public policy unless such contracts clearly contravene what the legislature has declared to be public policy or unless they clearly tend to injure the public in some fashion. A 1983 case held that Indiana's prevailing wage statute does not infringe on the liberty to contract and thus is constitutional. Prevailing wage statutes on both the state and federal levels protect public works employees from substandard wages. Hence, Stampco's employment agreements with Keith and Wendell violated both Indiana's statute and the federal Davis Bacon Act that require paying wages at the prevailing rate. As a general rule, courts characterize as void any contracts made in violation of a statute. Thus, condoning Stampco's failure to follow the law would violate public policy. Moreover, allowing agreements, settlements, or releases of claims in such circumstances would permit unscrupulous contractors to force employees to submit to economic pressures and accept lower wages. Such employment agreements are void as against public policy, illegal, and unenforceable because these agreements would subvert the federal and state legislatures' intentions to protect public works employees.

BUSINESS CONSIDERATIONS Prevailing wage statutes reflect a pro-labor bias. Muster arguments both for and against such statutes.

ETHICAL CONSIDERATIONS Keith and Wendell used prevailing wage statutes as a sword to force Stampco to pay them the wages mandated by these laws. Explain who should have won the case if the court had used ethics (rather than the law) as the basis for its decision.

Agreements Violative of Statutes

Courts ordinarily find certain categories of activities, among which are price-fixing agreements, performances of services without a license, Sunday laws, and wagering and usury statutes, in violation of statutes.

Monopoly
The power of a firm to carry on a business or a trade to the exclusion of all competitors.

Oligopoly
An economic condition in which a small number of firms dominates a market but no one firm controls it.

Price-fixing Agreements

The purpose of price-fixing agreements generally is to restrain competition so as to create a **monopoly** or **oligopoly** in order to control price fluctuations. The Sherman

Antitrust Act, the Clayton Act, and the Federal Trade Commission Act comprise the major federal legislative enactments that make such bargains illegal. Price-fixing agreements also may violate state statutes; or, alternatively, courts may invalidate these arrangements on public policy grounds.

Performances of Services Without a License

Agreements relating to the performances of services without a license may constitute another type of statutory violation. To protect the public from unqualified persons, state statutes often require (or regulate) the licensing of professions such as law, medicine, and public accountancy and trades such as electrical work, contracting, and plumbing. Before the state grants a license, the would-be practitioner, after achieving the required educational qualifications, usually must demonstrate minimal competency by successfully passing an examination. In such cases, the absence of a license prevents the professional or tradesperson from enforcing the bargain.

In contrast to such a regulatory licensing scheme, some states require licensing primarily as a revenue-producing mechanism rather than as a device for protecting the health and welfare of its citizens. If the primary intent of the licensing requirement is to produce revenue, the lack of a license will not affect the contract between the parties.

It pays to remember that courts have fairly wide discretion in these matters and may take into account such factors as the absence of harm resulting from failure to obtain the license, the extent of the knowledge of the persons involved, and the relative "guilt" of the respective parties. If, for example, a court deems the amount forfeited by the unlicensed professional sufficiently large to constitute a penalty, the professional ordinarily will be able to sue for the fee, despite the lack of a license. As mentioned earlier, even in statutes assigning criminal sanctions, courts will look closely at the legislative intent of the statute in deciding whether to give or to withhold remedies.

Sunday Closing Laws

Sunday closing laws, (also called "blue laws") are so named because they prohibit the formation or performance of contracts on Sundays. These laws are troublesome because the terms of such statutes vary widely from state to state. The most common type of statute prohibits the conducting of secular business, or one's "ordinary calling" (such as selling merchandise), on Sunday. You may be familiar with Sunday laws that forbid the sale of certain alcoholic beverages. Exceptions usually involve works of charity or necessity, which one can undertake on Sunday without fear of sanctions.

In some jurisdictions, a violation of a Sunday statute voids the contract, unless the party asking for recovery can show, for instance, that he or she had no knowledge that the execution of the contract occurred on Sunday. He or she also can argue that the agreement, though initiated on Sunday, was not accepted until later in the week and thus actually ripened into a contract at that time.

Litigants in some jurisdictions have challenged the constitutionality of such statutes. These laws, by singling out Sunday as a "day of rest" from mercantile activity, may violate the First Amendment's prohibition against a governmentally established religion. State governments' enactments of such laws, therefore, arguably put the interests of one religious group ahead of the interests of others and thus raise constitutional questions.

YOU BE THE JUDGE

Is a Manager an Agent?

The California Talent Agencies Act provides that "[n]o person shall engage in or carry on the occupation of a talent agency without first procuring a license therefor from the Labor Commissioner." The act defines a "talent agency" as "a person or corporation who engages in the occupation of procuring, offering, promising, or attempting to procure employment or engagement for an artist or artists, except that the activities of procuring, offering, or promising to procure or offer recording contracts for an artist or artists shall not of itself subject a person or corporation to regulation and licensing under this chapter." Although it does not define the words *occupation* or *procure*, the act sets forth a comprehensive licensing and regulatory scheme. A person who procures employment for artists in violation of the act risks having his or her contract with those artists declared void and unenforceable. In addition, one found to have violated the act may be ordered to forfeit all commissions earned for services rendered in behalf of the artist. The act is administered by the California Labor Commissioner, who has jurisdiction to decide disputes between artists and agents, including whether a manager should have been licensed as an agent.

In California, personal managers generally perform the traditional functions of a manager—advising, counseling, directing, and coordinating the artist as to the development of the artist's career. While a manager occasionally may book a performance or appearance for an artist, the manager typically leaves that function to the artist's booking agent. Instead, personal managers ordinarily involve themselves only incidentally in efforts directed at seeking and/or procuring employment for their clients. Suppose that the state challenged the legality of personal managers performing their obligations without a license as required for a talent agency. The case is brought before *your* court. How will *you* rule in this situation?

BUSINESS CONSIDERATIONS Why might a business want to procure a license allowing it to provide services that it would not ordinarily provide for its clients or customers? Why would the business prefer to wait until the situation arises before applying for a license?

ETHICAL CONSIDERATIONS Is it ethical for the state to require a license before allowing a business to provide a service for which there is no recognized educational or experiential preparation? Is it ethical for a business to provide services without a license when the state has enacted a license requirement?[2]

SOURCE: David A. Steinberg and Yakub Hazzard, *The National Law Journal* (26 November 1996), pp. B7–8.

Wagering Statutes

Wagering contracts and lotteries are illegal in certain states because of statutes prohibiting gambling, betting, and other games of chance. The underlying rationale for these laws focuses on the protection of the public from the crime and familial discord often associated with gambling. To constitute illegal wagering, the activity must involve a person's paying consideration or value in the hope of receiving a prize or other property by chance. Wagering in the legal sense always consists of a scheme involving the artificial creation of risk; hence, insurance contracts or stock transactions in which risk is an inherent feature do not comprise situations that implicate illegal wagering. On the other hand, courts may view raffles as unlawful wagering. For instance, because of the relatively soft demand in the housing market, some enterprising couples in various parts of the country recently have attempted to raffle off their homes. The conduct of these people has violated the wagering statutes of some of these jurisdictions. Note, however, that public lotteries are perfectly legal in many

Acceleration clauses
Clauses in contracts that advance the date for payment based on the occurrence of a condition or the breach of a duty.

Prepayment clauses
Contract clauses that allow the debtor to pay the debt before it is due without penalty.

Conditional sales contracts
Sales contracts in which the transfer of title is subject to a condition, most commonly the payment of the full purchase price by the buyer.

states. Additionally, in the absence of a requirement that the participant give something of value in order to take part in the activity, the activity probably is not a lottery and consequently probably is legal.

Usury Statutes

Usurious contracts occur when a lender loans money at a greater profit (or rate of interest) than state law permits. For usury to exist, there must be a loan of money (or an agreement to extend the maturity of a monetary debt) for which the debtor agrees to repay the principal at a rate that exceeds the legal rate of interest. In addition, the lender must intend to violate the usury laws. If these elements are present, the resultant contract is illegal. In most states, a usurious lender will be unable to collect any interest and also may be subject to criminal or other statutory penalties. In some states, courts deny only the amount of excess interest; the lender can recover the remaining interest and principal. In a few states, the agreement is void; the lender receives no interest or principal.

Because such wide variations exist among state usury laws, it is difficult to generalize one set of rules. Loans to corporations may be exempt from a jurisdiction's usury statutes, for example, as may short-term loans, especially if the lender will be incurring large risks in making the loans.

Acceleration clauses and **prepayment clauses** generally are not usurious. The same is true of service fees that reflect the incidental costs of making a loan—filing and recording fees, for example. Sales under revolving charge accounts (open-ended credit accounts) or **conditional sales contracts** ordinarily are not usurious even if the seller charges a higher-than-lawful rate. Two reasons have been forwarded in justification of this position: (1) A bona fide conditional sale on a deferred-payment basis is not a loan of money, and (2) the finance charge is merely a part of an increased purchase price reflective of the seller's risk in giving up possession of personal property (clothes, refrigerators, compact disk players, and the like) that depreciates quickly in value.

Time–price differential sales contracts may or may not be usurious, depending on applicable state law and/or special consumer protection statutes. Time–price differential sales contracts involve an offer to sell at a designated price for cash (say $6,000 for an entertainment center) or at a higher price on credit (say $7,500). Even though the maximum legal rate of interest in this state may be 18 percent, the 25 percent actual rate represented by the credit price does not involve usury as long as the final price reflects the credit nature of the sale rather than an intent to evade the usury laws.

The trend today is to raise the maximum interest rate and to increase the exceptions to the usury laws. Moreover, federally guaranteed loans allow interest rates that otherwise would violate state law. These fac-

12.1

FINANCE

MALA PROHIBITA CONTRACT SITUATIONS

CIT has obtained a guaranteed offer to provide a $100,000 line of credit, which will be very helpful in any upcoming expansion or growth for the firm. However, the prospective lender insists on receiving 3% simple interest on any balance each month. Tom is concerned that this interest rate amounts to a usurious loan, and he asks your advice. What will you tell him?

BUSINESS CONSIDERATIONS Should lenders gouge their customers who are in desperate need of money by charging these customers the highest possible interest? What factors should a lender (or a borrower) consider in deciding how much interest is appropriate in a credit transaction?

ETHICAL CONSIDERATIONS Is it ethical for a lender to take advantage of its customers by charging the highest interest rate the market will permit? Is it ethical for a borrower to agree to credit terms and then later object because the terms are too high?

tors have seriously eroded the original purpose of usury laws—the protection of debtors from excessive rates of interest. But, as mentioned earlier, little uniformity exists in the various states' usury statutes; it is wise, therefore, to consult these statutes if you have doubts about the legality of a particular transaction.

Time–price differential sales contracts
Contracts with a difference in price based on the date of payment, with one price for an immediate payment and another for a payment at a later date.

AGREEMENTS VIOLATIVE OF PUBLIC POLICY

As evident in the *Stampco Construction Co., Inc.* case, judges more and more frequently resort to public policy as a basis for invalidating agreements. In holding that a contract is void on public policy grounds, the court is deciding the legality of the agreement in light of the public interests involved. Hence, public policy frequently becomes an alternative ground for finding illegality. To illustrate, a court may strike down a contract to fix prices because the agreement violates statutes (for example, the Sherman Act) or because the agreement will damage the public. The *Stampco Construction Co., Inc.* decision also illustrates the law's use of this double-edged sword, since one basis for the statute at issue in that case focused on public policy: the prevention of injury to the public interest that otherwise may result from a public works employee's succumbing to the employer's unscrupulous offer to pay wages lower than those mandated by prevailing wage statutes. However, because *public policy* is such a wide-ranging term, courts, in judging the legality of certain types of bargains, often have to juggle competing interests.

Covenants Not to Compete

Covenants not to compete, also called *restrictive covenants,* are express promises that a seller of a business or an employee who leaves a company will not engage in the same or similar business or occupation for a period of time in a certain geographic area. Such bargains may or may not be legal. If the purpose of these "noncompete clauses" is to protect the recent buyer of a business from the possibility that the seller will set up shop two blocks from the original business establishment or the former employer from the possibility that the ex-employee will sign on with a competitor, the restrictions on the seller or former employee, if *reasonable* in *time* and in *geographic scope,* ordinarily are legal. But, as mentioned earlier, competing policies complicate these situations. It clearly is unfair to shackle unduly the employment opportunities of the seller (or former employee) who must make a living. Similarly, to curtail this person's business activities or occupational activities in effect insulates the buyer (or former employer) from competition and thereby may result in higher prices. For this reason, when examining these covenants, many courts use public policy considerations.

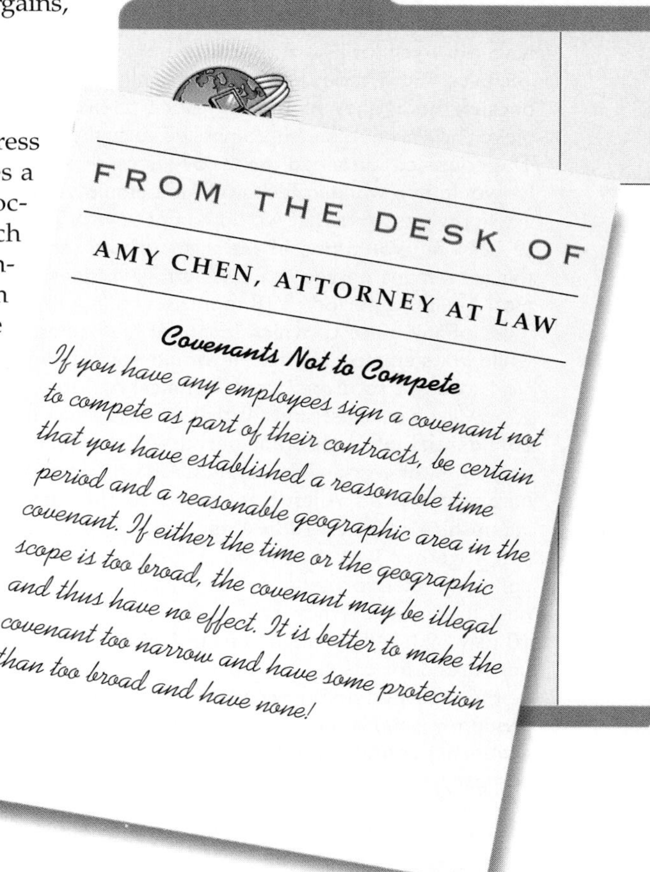

FROM THE DESK OF
AMY CHEN, ATTORNEY AT LAW
Covenants Not to Compete
If you have any employees sign a covenant not to compete as part of their contracts, be certain that you have established a reasonable time period and a reasonable geographic area in the covenant. If either the time or the geographic scope is too broad, the covenant may be illegal and thus have no effect. It is better to make the covenant too narrow and have some protection than too broad and have none!

Usually such covenants are incidental to the sale of a business or to an employment contract and are legal. (Agreements not to compete that have as their sole purpose the curtailing of competition are illegal as restraints on trade—they violate the antitrust laws.) If, however, under the facts and circumstances, a particular covenant not to compete is unreasonably restrictive in time or geographic scope, a court has the power to rewrite the covenant so that it is less restrictive—a process called *blue-penciling*—and hence reasonable. Bargainers should not expect courts to save them from bad, or illegal, bargains, however. Blue-penciling is relatively rare. In fact, most courts reject this approach and will void the restrictive covenant and construe the agreement without any reference to the covenant not to compete.

The *Technical Aid Corp.* v. *Allen* case shows how the question of the legality of a restrictive covenant can become the basis for a lawsuit.

12.2 TECHNICAL AID CORPORATION v. ALLEN

591 A.2d 262 (N.H. 1991)

FACTS Technical Aid Corporation provides temporary and contract professionals to industry. Technical Aid hired Allen on or about 20 April 1981. When he first reported for work on 27 April 1981, a company employee told Allen that the company expected him to sign an employment contract containing a number of restrictive covenants. Allen had not known about the contract until then, and he wanted to have a lawyer look at it. Because he could not work for Technical Aid without immediately signing the contract and because he already had given notice to his previous employer, however, Allen felt compelled to sign the agreement. The contract contained the following restrictions: (1) that he would not, while in Technical Aid's employ, engage in any activity whatsoever that would compete with Technical Aid; (2) that he would not, in the event of the termination of this agreement, engage in a competitive business with Technical Aid, for a period of 18 months, within a radius of 100 miles of any office to which Technical Aid had assigned him while in its employ; (3) that he would not, for the same period, attempt to divert from Technical Aid any personnel, goodwill, or business; and (4) that he would not divulge any confidential information acquired while in Technical Aid's employ. After working in Technical Aid's national office for a number of years, Allen transferred to the Nashua, New Hampshire, office. In 1985, Allen decided to leave Technical Aid. Together with Redmond, a former employee of the company, Allen formed E & S, a temporary personnel business. In April 1986, they leased office space for E & S; and on 10 May 1986, Allen resigned from Technical Aid. Thereafter, he worked for E & S, participating only in management; he neither solicited nor serviced customers. Technical Aid subsequently sued Allen for violations of various restrictive covenants contained in his employment contract with the company.

ISSUE Were these restrictive covenants enforceable?

HOLDING Yes. The restrictive covenants overall were enforceable despite the unenforceability of one provision, because this unenforceable term was not essential to the agreed-on exchange and because Technical Aid had avoided engaging in any serious misconduct.

REASONING The law does not look with favor on contracts in restraint of trade or competition; courts therefore construe such contracts narrowly. Nonetheless, restrictive covenants are valid and enforceable if the restraint is reasonable given the particular circumstances of the case. To determine the reasonableness of a restrictive covenant ancillary to an employment contract, New Hampshire courts employ a three-pronged test: First, is the restriction greater than necessary to protect the legitimate interests of the employer? Second, does the restriction impose an undue hardship on the employee? And third, is the restriction injurious to the public interest? If the courts answer any of these questions in the affirmative, the restriction in question is unreasonable and unenforceable.

The contract in question here contains a number of restrictive covenants. Judging the validity of these involves identifying the legitimate interests of the employer and determining whether the restraint is narrowly tailored to protect those interests. Here, Technical Aid's interest derives from Allen's contact with its customers. The employer has a legitimate interest in preventing its employees from appropriating its goodwill to the employer's detriment. For a restrictive covenant based on an employee's client contact to protect narrowly the legitimate interests of the employer, the geographic scope of the restriction generally must be limited to that area in which the employee has client contact, that is, the area in which the employer's goodwill is subject to appropriation by the employee. For salespersons, this area often corresponds to their assigned sales territory.

As a salesperson in Technical Aid's Nashua sales office, Allen's territory included the entire state of New Hampshire and possibly Vermont and part of Massachusetts. However, the covenant against competition prohibits Allen from engaging in competition anywhere within a 100 mile

12.2 TECHNICAL AID CORPORATION v. ALLEN *(cont.)* 591 A.2d 262 (N.H. 1991)

radius of the Nashua office (that is, large portions of Maine, Massachusetts, Rhode Island, and Connecticut). The geographic limitation is greater than necessary to protect the legitimate interests of Technical Aid. In addition, this covenant seriously limits Allen's employment opportunities without providing any legitimate benefit to Technical Aid and thus imposes an undue hardship on Allen. Finally, although the covenant against competition does not seem injurious to the public interest, the covenant against competition is unreasonable and unenforceable as written because it violates two prongs of the reasonableness test.

The second restrictive covenant of the contract (the covenant against servicing customers) encompasses far less activity than that covered by the covenant against competition. Yet, Technical Aid has clients far outside Allen's allotted territory; indeed, it purports to be not only a national but an international organization. Accordingly, Technical Aid has no legitimate interest in protecting its entire client base from Allen. As with the previous covenant, the lack of a legitimate interest underlying this covenant means that this restriction imposes an undue hardship on Allen and therefore is unenforceable as written.

The third restriction—in which Allen agreed to refrain from diverting personnel, goodwill, or business from Technical Aid—is no greater than necessary to protect the firm's business. As to these restrictions regarding its own staff, Technical Aid certainly has a legitimate interest in retaining the services of its current employees about whom an ex-employee has become knowledgeable. To hold otherwise would be to encourage employers to limit the contacts between its employees, thereby reducing the employers' vulnerability to former employees' recruiting away current employees. Moreover, the 18-month duration for the restrictions appears reasonable. Technical Aid, in effect, seeks a time period for the goodwill owed it—but directed to Allen—to dissipate. As such, this period does not seem excessive.

Finally, the restriction prohibiting Allen, while in Technical Aid's employ, from engaging in activity competitive to Technical Aid bears examination. The legitimate interests of an employer in enforcing a restrictive covenant remain considerably stronger during the employee's term of employment than subsequent to it. Employers are entitled to undivided loyalty from their present employees. Therefore, this restriction is reasonable and enforceable.

Courts can give the enforceable terms of a contract effect if the unenforceable terms are unessential to the agreed-on exchange and if the party seeking enforcement has not engaged in serious misconduct. Therefore, Allen's violations of the enforceable provisions of the contract entitled Technical Aid to recover actual damages.

BUSINESS CONSIDERATIONS Assume you are on a student-consultants' team as part of one of your management courses and that your team has been assigned for the entire semester to Technical Aid. Would you expect Technical Aid to ask everyone on the team to sign a nondisclosure clause as well as a noncompete clause? Why or why not?

ETHICAL CONSIDERATIONS Did Technical Aid behave unethically in not telling Allen about the noncompete agreement before he resigned from his previous job, thereby precluding him from seeking an attorney's advice before he signed it? Did Technical Aid's conduct justify Allen's subsequent misconduct? Why or why not?

Exculpatory Clauses

Agreements to commit torts are illegal. Indeed, little justification exists for a court to validate an agreement that stipulates an intentional breach of the duty of reasonable care to others. On the other hand, is anything illegal about a bargain in which one party tries in advance to limit its liability in a particular set of circumstances? Unfortunately, no clear-cut answer exists to this question. Courts judge the legality of such *exculpatory clauses,* or bargains in which one person agrees *in advance* to exonerate another person's activities from liability, on a case-by-case basis.

For example, a dry cleaner may always write on his customers' tickets, "Not responsible for elastic and buttons." When customers sign the tickets, the dry cleaner can argue that the customers agree to hold him harmless for any damages to elastic and buttons. Similarly, restaurants that have signs saying "Not responsible for belongings left in booths" attempt to achieve the same end. In general, these and other agreements in which one party promises not to hold the other liable for tortious or wrongful conduct are legal.

In many jurisdictions, statutes covering workers' compensation, innkeepers, and landlord–tenant relationships make the issue of liability for these particular areas moot. In the absence of statutes or clear precedents, however, courts look closely to see whether the party who agrees to assume the risk of tortious conduct without any recovery has done so voluntarily. In other words, the courts consider whether the party who has initiated the exculpatory clause has vastly superior bargaining power (or superior knowledge) over the other person. (Recall the bank deposit example earlier in this chapter.) If so, courts may strike down the exculpatory clause as contrary to public policy.

If the court believes an *adhesion contract* exists—that is, a contract drafted by the stronger party in order to force unfavorable terms on the weaker party—the court probably will find the clause contrary to public policy and thus illegal. This finding by no means is an easy task, though. Courts necessarily will weigh a variety of factors, such as the age of the parties, their respective degrees of expertise, their mental condition at the time they signed the clause (was the injured party drunk when he signed the exculpatory clause just before climbing onto the mechanical bull in Joe's Pub?), and whether the language of the clause was in fine print. After analyzing these and other facts and policies, the court decides the legality of such clauses.

The *Topp Copy Products, Inc.* v. *Singletary* case that follows illustrates the disposition of a lawsuit involving exculpatory clause issues.

12.3 TOPP COPY PRODUCTS, INC. v. SINGLETARY

626 A.2d 98 (Pa. 1993)

FACTS Topp Copy Products, Inc., entered into a commercial lease for the first floor of a multistoried building. Singletary was the owner of the building and the landlord on the commercial lease. A toilet in an apartment located above the premises leased by Topp Copy developed a leak, resulting in substantial water damage to Topp Copy's inventory stored in the leased unit. Alleging negligence, Topp Copy (the lessee) sued Ernest Singletary (the lessor). Singletary, in turn, contended that an exculpatory clause in the parties' lease agreement barred Topp Copy's suit for the water damage caused by the broken plumbing fixture. This clause, in paragraph 19, released Singletary "from any and all liability for damages that may result from the bursting, stoppage and leakage of any water pipe . . . watercloset . . . and drain, and from all liability for any and all damage caused by the water . . . and contents of said water pipes, . . . waterclosets and drains." Topp Copy argued that this exculpatory clause did not apply to its damage because the clause explicitly failed to relieve the landlord of liability for his own negligence and because the clause was ambiguous when read in context with another clause in the agreement. Specifically, Topp Copy asserted that the language of paragraph 15 of the lease—"[a]ll damages or injuries done to the said premises other than those caused by fire and by ordinary wear and tear or by the acts or omission of the landlord shall be repaired by the lessee herein. . . ."—made the exculpatory clause in paragraph 19 ambiguous.

ISSUES Was the exculpatory clause in paragraph 19 of the lease enforceable? Did that clause relieve Singletary of liability for his own negligent conduct?

HOLDING Yes to both questions. The exculpatory clause was enforceable and determinative of the rights of the parties. The precision and clarity of the language used by the parties showed that they had intended the clause to immunize Singletary from liability for his own negligent acts.

REASONING In Pennsylvania, an exculpatory clause generally is valid whenever it satisfies three conditions: (1) The clause does not contravene any policy of law (that is, there is an absence of any matter of interest to the public or state); (2) the contract relates entirely to the parties' own private affairs; and (3) each party is a free bargaining agent, in that the agreement is not in effect a mere contract of adhesion. Once the clause fulfills these conditions and thus becomes a valid contract, the contract must meet four

12.3 TOPP COPY PRODUCTS, INC. v. SINGLETARY *(cont.)* 626 A.2d 98 (Pa. 1993)

additional standards for a court to interpret it as relieving a person of liability for his or her own acts of negligence. These four standards hold that (1) a court must construe the contract immunizing a party from liability for negligence strictly, since the law does not favor such a party; (2) the contract must state the intentions of the parties with the greatest particularity, beyond doubt by express stipulation, and no inference from words of general import can establish it; (3) a court must construe the contract against the party seeking immunity from liability; and (4) the burden of establishing this immunity rests on the party seeking the protection of the clause. Here, the parties meant something by what they said in their agreement; and, because they used language so definite and precise, there can be no doubt of their meaning. It necessarily follows that their intention was to release the landlord "from all liability for any and all damage caused by water" resulting from negligence. The covenant of this lease fully complies with that requirement. Because there was only one purpose for the clause, it was sufficiently precise to protect the landlord from all liability, including the landlord's own negligence. All the law requires in the case of a tenant's waiver of his or her landlord's responsibility for losses resulting from the landlord's negligence is that the parties plainly express the waiver. Thus, the trial court's grant of a summary judgment in favor of Singletary was proper.

BUSINESS CONSIDERATIONS The court upheld a Pennsylvania commercial lease containing an exculpatory clause that exonerated a landlord from liability for his own negligence. If you were a member of the Pennsylvania legislature, would you support the enactment of legislation that would make such an exculpatory clause void as against public policy? Why or why not? Would you make distinctions between commercial (that is, both parties are businesspeople) and noncommercial (for example, a lease of an apartment by a consumer) leases? Does the existence of an exculpatory clause give the landlord an incentive to maintain the premises in a less than ship-shape fashion? Why or why not?

ETHICAL CONSIDERATIONS Is it ethical for a business like a restaurant to refrain from staffing a coatcheck room and to rely instead on a large sign that says "NOT RESPONSIBLE FOR ARTICLES LEFT IN THE COATCHECK ROOM WHEN THE ROOM IS UNATTENDED"?

EXCEPTIONS: UPHOLDING ILLEGAL AGREEMENTS

The general rule, as mentioned earlier, holds that an illegal bargain is void; and courts will leave the parties to such agreements where they are as a result of the bargain. Despite this general rule, some situations exist in which a party may bring a successful suit based on an illegal agreement. Put differently, one usually cannot sue for enforcement of an illegal executory agreement; but in certain circumstances one may sue if the performance called for in the bargain has been rendered.

Parties Not *in Pari Delicto*

When one of the parties is less guilty than the other, the law states that the parties are not *in pari delicto* (they are not equally at fault or equally wrong). This allows the less-guilty person to recover if recovery serves the public interest in some way. For instance, the less-guilty party may belong to the class of persons a regulatory statute was designed to protect. Such results consequently focus on the conduct of the less-guilty party rather than on the illegality of the subject matter of the contract. For example, if Joanne works for a photographer who does not have a license as required by a local ordinance, she still can recover the wages due her if she is unaware of her boss's noncompliance. The law terms the illegality here incidental or collateral to Joanne's bargain.

12.2

MANAGEMENT

EMPLOYEE AGREEMENTS AND RELEASES

Tom and Anna would like to have any employees hired by CIT (including family members) sign a covenant not to compete with the firm anywhere in the U.S. for at least three years after leaving employment with CIT. Both Lindsay and Dan consider such a covenant an insult and refuse to sign an employment contract unless the clause is removed. Tom and Anna have asked you for your advice. What will you tell them?

BUSINESS CONSIDERATIONS What sort of policy regarding covenants not to compete should a business adopt? When would such a covenant be a good idea? When would such a covenant be a bad idea? Explain.

ETHICAL CONSIDERATIONS Is it ethical for a firm to routinely require employees to sign covenants not to compete, even if the employee would not have access to any confidential business information? What ethical issues are raised by the use of such covenants?

Repentance

Even if the parties are in pari delicto, the law allows recovery by the person who shows repentance by rescinding the illegal bargain before its consummation. For example, let us assume that a partnership attempts to bribe a state senator to enact favorable legislation. This agreement would be illegal because it harms the public. If one of the partners attempts to rescind the transaction before delivery of the money to the senator, he or she can do so. The law calls this action *repentance.* Courts justify the partner's recovery of the money he or she earlier directed to the senator because such a result furthers the public interest of deterring illegal schemes.

Partial Illegality

Agreements, as you may recall, may consist of several different promises supported by different considerations. While refusing to enforce those parts of the bargain that are illegal, courts enforce the parts of the bargain that involve legal promises and legal considerations if the courts can sever these legal promises. If, instead, either the illegal promise or the illegal consideration (or both) wholly taints the agreement, courts declare the entire agreement void. The *Technical Aid Corporation* decision and others like it that involve a restrictive covenant provide good examples of partial illegality. If a court finds the restrictive covenant unreasonable in scope, the judge may, owing to the clause's illegality, sever it from the rest of the agreement. The court, however, ordinarily enforces the remainder of the contract (the sale of a business, for example), because the balance of the contract is perfectly legal; it is divisible from the illegal portion. In short, after severing the illegal portions, courts will give effect to those provisions that constitute a legal contract.

Exhibit 12.1 summarizes the key components of legality as an element of contract formation and enforcement.

The Requirement of Reality (or Genuineness) of Consent

Appearances often are deceptive. The same is true of contract formation; what seems to be a valid agreement in actuality may lack the parties' genuine assent.

EXHIBIT 12.1 The Requirement of Legality as an Element of Contract Formation and Enforcement

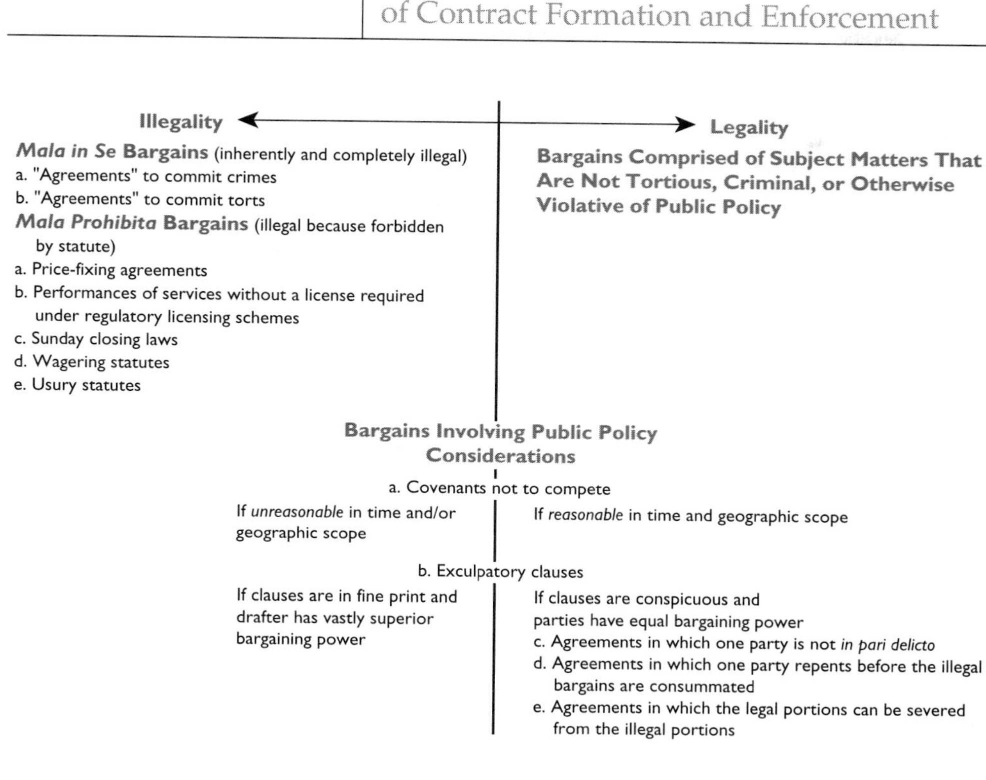

Illegality
Legality
Mala in Se Bargains (inherently and completely illegal)
a. "Agreements" to commit crimes
b. "Agreements" to commit torts
Mala Prohibita Bargains (illegal because forbidden by statute)
a. Price-fixing agreements
b. Performances of services without a license required under regulatory licensing schemes
c. Sunday closing laws
d. Wagering statutes
e. Usury statutes
Bargains Comprised of Subject Matters That Are Not Tortious, Criminal, or Otherwise Violative of Public Policy
Bargains Involving Public Policy Considerations
a. Covenants not to compete
If *unreasonable* in time and/or geographic scope
If *reasonable* in time and geographic scope
b. Exculpatory clauses
If clauses are in fine print and drafter has vastly superior bargaining power
If clauses are conspicuous and parties have equal bargaining power
c. Agreements in which one party is not *in pari delicto*
d. Agreements in which one party repents before the illegal bargains are consummated
e. Agreements in which the legal portions can be severed from the illegal portions

FRAUD

Fraud is a word we all use fairly loosely, mainly because it lends itself to many definitions. At base, it consists of deception or hoodwinking; and it seems to involve a communication of some sort. But as one ancient case notes, "[a] nod or a wink, or a shake of the head or a smile" will do. [See *Walters* v. *Morgan*, 3 Def., F. & J. 718, 724 (1861).] Sometimes even silence will suffice. The essence of fraud is hard to pin down. One common definition states that fraud is a deliberate misrepresentation of a material fact with the intent to induce another person to enter into a contract that will be injurious to that person.[3] If we break this definition down into smaller components, we can see that fraud consists of six elements.

Elements of Fraud

To constitute fraud, the misrepresentation or misstatement first must concern a fact. A *fact* is something reasonably subject to exact knowledge. Thus, statements about the size of a car engine or the dimensions of a real estate parcel involve facts.

To show this first element of fraud, then, the plaintiff will have to prove that the defendant misstated a fact. Predictions, statements of value, and expressions of opinions generally do not equate with misrepresentations of fact. Neither do misstatements of law.

Actually, in any given situation, it may be difficult to distinguish a fact from an opinion. Suppose a car salesperson says to you, "This little dandy will get you down the road at a pretty good clip. It has a great engine. It's a V-6, and those engines have been very serviceable." The first two remarks probably are opinions, also known as "puffs" or "dealer's talk." The statement about the type of engine probably constitutes a fact. You may be unhappy, for instance, if you find a V-8 engine in the car after you purchase it, or if you find out V-6 engines have many problems and the salesperson knows this. You may want to argue that you have been a victim of intentional misrepresentation. On the other hand, courts tend to discount statements of value because of genuine differences in the way people assess things. When Joe says, "That ring is worth a thousand dollars," unless Joe is a jewelry dealer or an expert and the other person is not, most courts will refuse to call Joe's statement a fact. Such nonfactual statements of value ordinarily do not constitute this first element of a showing of fraud.

The second element of fraud a plaintiff must prove involves the *materiality* of the fact that the defendant allegedly misstated. A fact is not material unless the plaintiff, when making the decision to enter the contract, considers it a substantial factor. To use our earlier example, if you do not care if the engine is a V-6, the lack of a V-6 in the car you buy makes the fact immaterial. A court will enforce the bargain despite your protestations. The mileage of the car, the number of previous owners, and the extent of any **warranties** given, however, all ordinarily are material. Misstatements about these facts therefore may lead to liability if you prove the other elements of fraud.

Warranties

Representations that become part of the contract and that are made by a seller of goods at the time of the sale and that concern the character, quality, or nature of the goods.

Scienter

Guilty knowledge; specifically, one party's prior knowledge of the cause of a subsequent injury to another person.

The most distasteful element of fraud, as well as the most difficult to prove, is the defendant's knowledge of the falsity of his or her statements. This sometimes is called **scienter**. In other words, at the time of making the statement, the defendant knew, or should have known, that he or she was misstating an important fact. Outright lies, of course, would meet this third requirement. Interestingly, the defendant also may be liable for reckless use of the truth or for a statement made without verifying its accuracy when verification is possible. To illustrate, assume that a prospective buyer says to the homeowner, "I guess the property line extends to the fence, doesn't it?" The homeowner nods yes, even though the line actually does not extend that far. If the buyer purchases in reliance on this statement, a cause of action in fraud may result.

Closely related to the requirement of knowledge of the falsity of the statement is an *intent to deceive.* As noted earlier, deception is the hallmark of fraud. This element is difficult to disprove if the first three elements have been established, because courts usually can find no satisfactory reason for a defendant's misstatements except as an intent to induce the plaintiff into accepting a "sharp" bargain.

The plaintiff also must prove that he or she *relied* on the deception. Assuming the plaintiff's reliance is reasonable, this showing will not be particularly burdensome. For example, if Tom inspects a lakefront cottage with a front porch that is on the verge of caving into the lake, a court will not allow him to cry "foul" (or "fraud") if the porch crumbles into the water one month after Tom buys the cottage. The same will be true even if the owner has said the cottage is structurally sound. Clearly, Tom should have been aware of such a *patent* (obvious) defect. If we assume the damage derives from a *latent* (hidden/unobservable by the human eye) defect, such as carpenter ant infestation, Tom may win unless the court thinks Tom's refraining from ordering a pest inspection in itself is unreasonable.

The final element of a plaintiff's proof—*injury*, or *detriment*—normally is not difficult to show. In our last example, Tom can argue that his damages amount to the sum needed to rid the cottage of carpenter ants and to repair the substructure of the dwelling. Alternatively, Tom may ask for rescission of the contract. When a court grants rescission, Tom will turn the cottage over to the original owner; and the owner will make restitution of the price Tom has paid for the property.

Scott v. *Bodor, Inc.* illustrates what happens when a plaintiff is unsuccessful in proving all the elements of fraud.

12.4 SCOTT v. BODOR, INC. 571 N.E.2d 313 (Ind.App. 1991)

FACTS Bodor, Inc., is a closely held Indiana corporation wholly owned by Robert and Stephen Kesler. In 1983, John Scott contacted Bodor and offered his services as a financial planner. Scott told Robert Kesler that he could provide Bodor with a variety of plans that would result in income tax advantages to Bodor. Eventually, Scott became Bodor's general financial advisor, with unfettered access to Bodor's offices and financial information. Bodor's officers trusted Scott and never consulted third parties for advice concerning any financial arrangements that Scott had made on behalf of Bodor. In 1985, when Bodor's officers met with Scott to discuss the company's tax situation for the year, Scott recommended that Bodor's officers meet with Thomas J. Brown, a person Scott proclaimed to be an expert in "supplemental income" plans. In November 1985, Brown flew to Indiana and explained the supplemental income plan to the Bodor officers. According to Brown, the supplemental income plan had two features that were extremely important to Bodor: The corporation could take an immediate tax deduction for any funds it contributed to the program and could retrieve any funds paid in if it needed to do so. When Steve Kesler asked if the plan were a life insurance vehicle, Brown replied that it primarily was an investment vehicle with a small life insurance component. Robert Kesler then told Scott that he did not want the program if it were only a life insurance policy, but Scott assured him that it was an investment program. Neither Brown nor Scott mentioned that the program in actuality consisted exclusively of a whole-life insurance policy, and the plan brochure prepared by Brown failed to mention that the funding of the plan would occur exclusively through life insurance. Within a month after the meeting, Robert Kesler decided to implement the plan. When the Bodor officers signed the policy applications, the documents specified neither the cost nor the amount of insurance to be procured; Scott filled in that information after he had obtained the signatures on the applications. In March 1986, three months after the implementation of the plan, Scott presented amended insurance applications to Robert for his signature. These applications, while stating the face value of the insurance policy, did not set out the nature or the cost of the insurance to be procured. Robert, as was his custom with regard to documents prepared for Bodor by Scott, signed the applications without reading them. Moreover, despite Robert Kesler's requests for such documentation, Scott never presented Bodor's officers with copies of the insurance policies or any other documents concerning the supplemental income plan. In April 1987, Bodor's officers discovered that the $370,000 that Bodor had put into the plan was not tax-deductible. When Robert Kesler met with Scott, Scott confirmed that the contributions to the plan were not deductible. Robert demanded the immediate withdrawal of Bodor's funds from the plan and asked for the return of these funds. In fact, Bodor managed to recover only $117,000 of its $370,000 investment. When Bodor sued Scott for fraud, Scott moved for a summary judgment on this issue.

ISSUE Had Scott and Brown's statements concerning the alleged supplemental income plan amounted to fraud?

HOLDING Yes. The lack of evidence establishing that Bodor knew that the funding of the plan would derive exclusively from the purchase of life insurance, coupled with Scott (and Brown's) express assurances that it would not, constituted sufficient evidence of fraud to withstand a motion for summary judgment.

REASONING Actionable fraud consists of six elements: (1) the one accused of fraud (the defendant) must have made at least one representation of a past or existing fact, (2) which was false, (3) which was material, (4) which the defendant knew to be false or made with reckless disregard as to its truth or falsity, (5) on which the plaintiff reasonably relied, and (6) which harmed the plaintiff.

Scott and Brown argued that Bodor had failed to produce evidence tending to show that they had made any misrepresentations of material fact. They denied that their statements concerning the tax-deductibility of the funds involved misrepresentations of past or existing fact. According

12.4 SCOTT v. BODOR, INC. (cont.) 571 N.E.2d 313 (Ind.App. 1991)

to Scott and Brown, even assuming they had made misstatements, the misstatements at most were misstatements of law. They further argued that, in Indiana, misstatements of law never can form the basis of fraud since everyone is presumed to know the law. Consequently, they argued, the allegedly defrauded party cannot justifiably have relied on the misstatements.

While this assertion correctly states the law in Indiana, exceptions to this general rule exist. Here, for example, Bodor introduced evidence tending to show that the defendants had made misrepresentations of law and fact. The factual misrepresentations dealt with the form and structure of the proposed plan, and the legal misrepresentations concerned the tax-deductible status of the plan. To the extent that the legal misrepresentations were premised on the factual misrepresentations, thereby impairing the plaintiffs' ability to discover the law applicable to the true facts, the legal misrepresentations constituted a sufficient basis for an action in fraud.

The defendants next submitted that their misrepresentations concerning Bodor's ability to retrieve funds from the plan at will represented predictions of future events and hence were not actionable fraud under Indiana law. However, Scott and Brown's representations concerning Bodor's ability to retrieve funds from the plan consisted of representations concerning past or existing facts—the present features or terms of the proposed plan—and not mere statements of opinion or promises of future action.

Scott and Brown also pointed out that, under Indiana law, a party has no right to rely on a statement if he or she has failed to exercise ordinary care in guarding against fraud. Nonetheless, there was evidence supporting the inference that Bodor had relied on Scott and Brown, self-proclaimed experts in the field, for tax-planning advice. In short, genuine issues of material fact as to the making of the misrepresentations and reliance upon them and as to whether the misrepresentations, if made, would support recovery for actual fraud existed in this case. Accordingly, the trial court's denial of the defendants' motion for partial summary judgment merited affirmance.

BUSINESS CONSIDERATIONS Identify the miscues management made with regard to its dealings with Scott. Armed with hindsight, what steps should future Bodor managers take so as to avoid the losses represented by the funds contributed to the plan and the costs of the ensuing litigation?

ETHICAL CONSIDERATIONS Is it ethical for corporate managers to go outside the corporation for such services as financial planning? Put differently, is a company employee subject to stricter ethical standards than an independent contractor like Scott would be? If the applicable standards do differ, should they?

Successful proof of a cause of action in fraud usually justifies *rescission,* or the setting aside of the contract. Hence, such contracts are voidable at the option of the injured party. As mentioned, an alternative to rescission is the recovery of damages sufficient to restore the injured party to the status quo, or the position he or she would have enjoyed had the facts of the transaction mirrored his or her conception of them at the time of acceptance. The facts of each case normally will dictate which remedy a plaintiff will elect to pursue. The injured party, as plaintiff, faces a final pitfall: He or she must act as quickly as possible or, as will be discussed later in this chapter, possibly waive the cause of action.

Silence

No discussion of fraud is complete without a reference to *silence* and its effect on whether a court will grant relief. The common law steadfastly held that "mere silence is not fraud." This conclusion rests on the belief that fraud necessitates some sort of overt communication. Because, by definition, silence denotes the total absence of any statement, the rule arose that one cannot be liable for fraud unless one had said or done something. (Remember our first element requiring a misstatement or misrepresentation of a fact.)

Many jurisdictions, in order to encourage nonconcealment and honesty in business transactions, now reject this rule and hold, for instance, that defects in a house must be made known to the buyer. Similarly, if the buyer asks a question, the seller must answer truthfully and correct any wrong assumptions that the buyer believes. A seller's silence in such instances today may not prevent legal liability. Still, the strict rule is that there generally is no duty to speak (that is, to disclose such facts).

Even the common law, however, deemed some situations so fraught with the possibility of injury or detriment that it placed a duty to speak on the party possessing the information. One of these situations, latent defects, has already been examined.

There also is a duty to speak in situations in which the parties owe each other **fiduciary** duties, or duties that arise from a relationship of trust. For example, an investment advisor should inform all clients of her part ownership in ABC Corporation before she suggests that clients purchase ABC stock. Similarly, if you are applying for insurance coverage, you cannot be silent if you are asked questions about your medical history. To avoid fraud, you must, for example, disclose the existence of a heart condition. Finally, a statement made in preliminary negotiations that no longer is true at the time of the execution of the contract must be disclosed in order for one to escape a possible lawsuit based on fraud.

Fiduciary
One who holds a special position of trust or confidence and who thereby is expected to act with the utmost good faith and loyalty.

MISREPRESENTATION

In general, everything we previously discussed about the elements of fraud is true of a cause of action involving misrepresentation, with one notable exception: Misrepresentation lacks the elements of *scienter* and intent to deceive. Nevertheless, misrepresentation (often called *innocent misrepresentation* to differentiate it from fraud) can lead to the imposition of legal remedies. The property owner's statement about the property boundaries may amount to innocent misrepresentation if the plaintiff cannot prove *scienter. Misrepresentation,* or the innocent misstatement of a material fact that is relied on with resultant injury, makes the contract voidable at the option of the injured party. Rescission thus remains a possible (and, in many jurisdictions, the exclusive) remedy. Again, the plaintiff must act in a timely manner so as not to waive the cause of action.

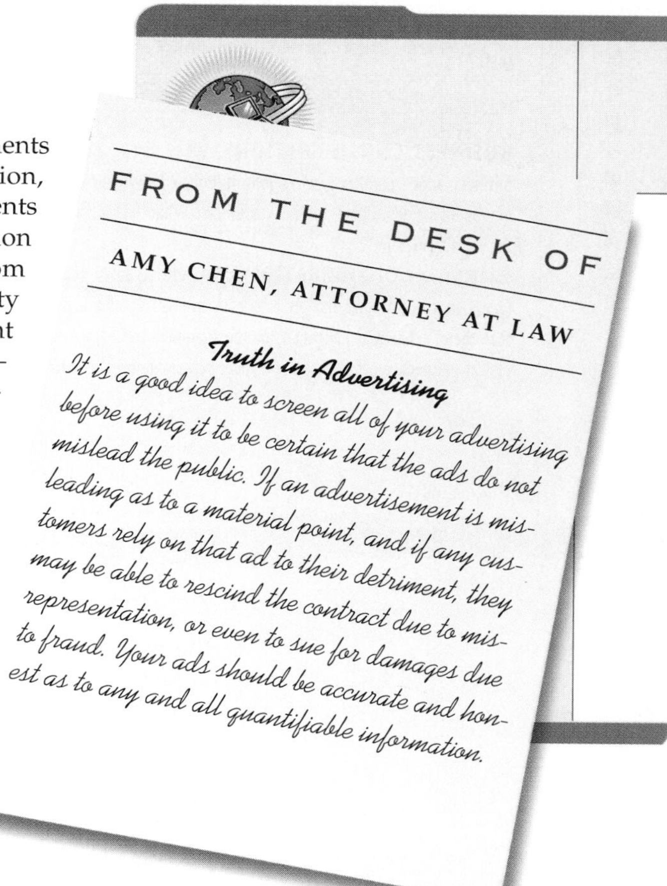

FROM THE DESK OF
AMY CHEN, ATTORNEY AT LAW
Truth in Advertising
It is a good idea to screen all of your advertising before using it to be certain that the ads do not mislead the public. If an advertisement is misleading as to a material point, and if any customers rely on that ad to their detriment, they may be able to rescind the contract due to misrepresentation, or even to sue for damages due to fraud. Your ads should be accurate and honest as to any and all quantifiable information.

Practically speaking, most plaintiffs allege both fraud and misrepresentation in the same lawsuit. Fraud is harder to prove but more desirable from the plaintiff's point of view; successful proof of fraud brings with it the possibility of recovery of damages under the tort of deceit. The elements of deceit are identical to those of fraud. Upon a showing of deceit, a court may award *punitive* damages (damages beyond the actual losses suffered) in addition to the actual (or compensatory) damages normally recoverable for fraud. But even if the plaintiff fails to prove fraud (and its twin, deceit), recovery on grounds of misrepresentation is possible. At the very least, a

12.3

SALES/MARKETING

MARKETING AND SALES STRATEGIES

CIT needs to generate revenues very quickly at the outset of its business life if it hopes to survive. As a result, Dan favors a very aggressive approach to the marketing of the videophones. Tom prefers to be a bit more cautious in marketing the product. Tom believes that sales representatives who answer questions honestly and completely will build a loyal customer base and that a few lost sales early on is preferable to a number of lost customers in the future. Dan argues that, without a lot of sales early, there will be *no* future in which customer concerns need to be addressed. They have asked for your advice. What will you tell them?

BUSINESS CONSIDERATIONS What sort of policy should a business adopt regarding what information a sales representative can or should communicate to the customers? What factors will influence the firm's decision?

ETHICAL CONSIDERATIONS Suppose a sales representative knows that a customer has an erroneous impression of the product, but that there is no legal obligation for the representative to speak. From an ethical perspective, what should the sales representative do? Why?

showing of fraud or misrepresentation will be the basis for rescission.

Exhibit 12.2 describes the elements of misrepresentation and fraud; it shows the analysis a court may follow in determining the presence of either as a defense to a contract.

MISTAKE

Human nature is such that people often try to unravel transactions because they have made an error about some facet of the deal. Imagine the chaos, however, if courts readily accepted these hindsight arguments. The result would be a decrease in contracts, since people would be wary of dealing with each other. As you recognize, such unpredictability would unduly hamper commercial pacts. On the other hand, we have repeatedly stressed the importance of mutual assent in contract law. Thus, the law, on policy grounds, wishes to set the contract aside if the error is so great that it has tainted the parties' consent to the agreement.

The legal doctrine of mistake tries to balance these competing interests. *Mistake* occurs when the parties are wrong about the existence or absence of a past or present fact that is material to their transaction. Note that the parties must be wrong about *material* facts. Thus, legal mistake is not synonymous with ignorance, inability, or inaccurate judgments relating to value or quality. Courts will rescind contracts on the ground of mistake only if the error is so fundamental that it cannot be said that the parties' states of mind were in agreement about the essential facts of the transaction. Mistakes as to law, in contrast, oftentimes will not form grounds for rescission of the contract. Two kinds of mistakes exist: unilateral and bilateral (or mutual) mistakes.

Unilateral Mistake

As the term implies, in a unilateral mistake, only one party is mistaken about a material fact. The general rule, with some exceptions, is that the courts will not rescind such contracts.

Unilateral mistakes often occur because of misplaced expectations of value. Let us suppose that Jacques goes to an antique store to look for a Duncan Phyfe table. He finds a table that he believes to be a Duncan Phyfe and, without mentioning his belief to the store owner, pays a hefty price for it. Later that evening, a friend informs him the table is not a Duncan Phyfe. If Jacques tries to avoid the contract, he will not be successful because only he was mistaken about a material fact—that is, that the table was a Duncan Phyfe. He also was mistaken as to value. In such uni-

EXHIBIT 12.2 The Elements of Fraud and Misrepresentation

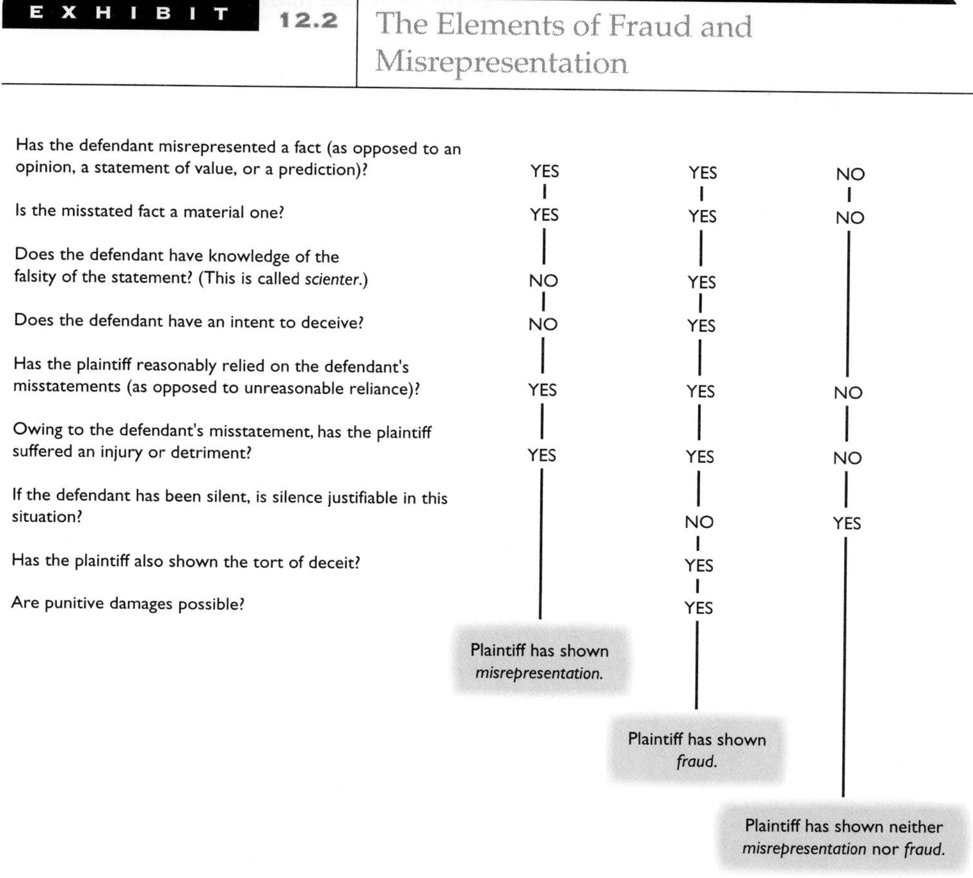

lateral mistake situations, courts take a hands-off approach and leave the parties with the bargains they have made. Rescission of the contract ordinarily is not granted.

Has the defendant misrepresented a fact (as opposed to an opinion, a statement of value, or a prediction)?
Is the misstated fact a material one?
Does the defendant have knowledge of the falsity of the statement? (This is called *scienter.*)
Does the defendant have an intent to deceive?
Has the plaintiff reasonably relied on the defendant's misstatements (as opposed to unreasonable reliance)?
Owing to the defendant's misstatement, has the plaintiff suffered an injury or detriment?
If the defendant has been silent, is silence justifiable in this situation?
Has the plaintiff also shown the tort of deceit?
Are punitive damages possible?
YES
YES
NO
NO
YES
YES
Plaintiff has shown *misrepresentation.*
YES
YES
YES
YES
YES
YES
NO
YES
YES
Plaintiff has shown *fraud.*
NO
NO
NO
NO
YES
Plaintiff has shown neither *misrepresentation* nor *fraud.*

The result here can be different if the store owner knows (or should know) of Jacques's error or in some other fashion acts fraudulently or unconscionably. But the facts in this example do not support such a conclusion; if they did, courts might allow rescission of the contract, despite the unilateral mistake.

Similarly, in situations in which the mistake is a result of business computations, courts will suspend the general rule of refusing to grant relief for unilateral mistakes. Such situations may arise if a contractor makes an addition error (say $100,000) in computing a bid. The person soliciting the bid generally will choose the lowest bidder. Once the successful contractor/bidder recognizes its mistake, it will wish to rescind the contract. Even though these circumstances involve a unilateral mistake on the bidder's part, it can attempt to show that a court should grant the equitable remedy of rescission (or **reformation**) because (1) the mistake was of such magnitude that enforcement would be unconscionable, (2) the mistake related to a material aspect of

Reformation
Equitable remedy whereby a court corrects a written instrument in order to remove a mistake and to make the agreement conform to the terms to which the parties originally had agreed.

the agreement, (3) the mistake occurred in good faith and in the absence of clear negligence, (4) it would be possible to return the other party to the status quo without causing injury to third parties, and (5) no other circumstances exist that would make the granting of relief inequitable.

Bilateral Mistake

If both parties are in error about the essence of the agreement, bilateral (or mutual) mistake exists. Courts will rescind such agreements on the rationale that, owing to a mistake about the existence, identity, or nature of the subject matter of the contract, a valid agreement has not occurred. If a mutual mistake of fact is present, either party may disaffirm this voidable contract unless rescission will cause injuries to innocent third parties. Why? The parties' minds have not met on the salient facts of the transaction. For example, assume an American company contracts with a foreign company (headquartered in New York) for hand-loomed rugs. The firms contract in April; but, unknown to both parties, a warehouse fire had destroyed the rugs in March. The destruction of the subject matter makes the contract voidable on the grounds of bilateral mistake: The parties have made an error regarding a significant fact—that the rugs existed at the time of contract formation.

Ambiguities
Uncertainties regarding the meanings of expressions used in contractual agreements.

Ambiguities are another cause of mutual mistake. If the American buyer believes that the term *rugs* means room-sized carpets, but, because of language difficulties, the international seller envisions rugs as smaller, that is, more comparable in size to wall hangings, this ambiguity may constitute mutual mistake. If so, rescission is justifiable. *Harding* v. *Willie* involves a simple example of bilateral (or mutual) mistake.

12.5 HARDING v. WILLIE

458 N.W.2d 612 (Iowa App. 1990)

FACTS Dale Harding is the owner of a home in Eagle Grove. Prior to 10 January 1987, Harding listed the real estate for sale. On 3 January 1987, B.V. Willie and his wife inspected the home for possible purchase or rental. Willie, an attorney, and Harding, a doctor, had been friends for many years. Willie noticed a crack in the ceiling and inquired about it; Harding informed Willie that a water leakage problem had existed in that area but since it was repaired in 1985, it had not leaked again. On 12 January 1987, Willie made an offer on the house; Harding accepted it the next day. Willie paid earnest money in the amount of $5,000, with the contract balance of $85,000 due on 1 March 1987. On 1 March 1987, when Willie went to the residence to make a final inspection before the closing on 2 March 1987, Willie observed water leaking through a crack in the ceiling and in the garage. At the closing, Willie informed the real estate agent that he was rescinding the contract because of the leaks. Although Harding subsequently rented the property to another party, in August 1987, Harding filed a petition at law seeking specific performance of the contract or money damages for breach of contract. Willie argued that the contract was void owing either to a mutual mistake of fact or fraud. Following a trial, the district court entered judgment against Willie for $29,155.79, plus interest and court costs.

ISSUE Was the contract void owing to a mutual mistake of fact or fraud?

HOLDING Yes. Owing to Harding and Willie's mutual mistake of a material fact as to whether the roof leaked, there was no meeting of the parties' minds. Hence, no contract ever existed between the parties.

REASONING Willie contended the contract is void owing to a mutual mistake of fact or to fraud on the part of Harding. A mistake of fact is one of the fundamental grounds of equitable relief, and an agreement based on a mutual mistake between two parties as to their relative and respective rights entitles either party to have the agreement set aside. When a material mutual mistake made by the parties in respect to the subject matter of a contract exists, in contemplation of law there is an absence of a contract, because the minds of the parties do not meet. Yet under the doctrine of mutual mistake, the mistake must be both mutual and material. Here, unquestionably either a

12.5 HARDING v. WILLIE *(cont.)* 458 N.W.2d 612 (Iowa App. 1990)

mutual mistake occurred or Harding committed fraud. Upon his examination of the home, Willie noticed the crack in the ceiling and inquired about it. Harding, at the very least, stated that while there had been a leak in the past, there was "absolutely no problem" with the roof. Regardless of how he said it, Harding either knew the roof still leaked, which would constitute fraud, or thought the roof was repaired and did not leak, which would lead to a mutual mistake of fact. No evidence of fraud on Harding's part was apparent here: The roof had been fixed; the parties were friends; and Harding had the roof fixed again as quickly as possible. However, both parties acted under the assumption that the roof would not leak. Harding was mistaken because he had had the roof repaired and expected those repairs to last. Willie was mistaken because of the representations made by the seller, Harding. Willie also reasonably relied on Harding's representations. They were friends; and although there was no evidence that a fiduciary relationship existed (as claimed by Willie), enough of a relationship existed to make trusting the other's statements a reasonable action. The contract in this instance involved the purchase of a home. Because the parties often consider a home a necessity, a leak in the roof certainly would constitute a material consideration. Therefore, a mutual mistake of a material fact existed; and, as a result, the minds of the parties had not met. Accordingly, no contract ever was made. Hence, the trial court should have granted judgment in favor of Willie for the amount of the earnest money paid, plus interest.

BUSINESS CONSIDERATIONS Did Willie and Harding's friendship displace the behavior each might have shown in a more arms-length transaction? What might each have done differently if the person on the other side of the transaction had been a stranger? Can one ever effectively mix business and friendship?

ETHICAL CONSIDERATIONS The court used the existence of a friendship between Willie and Harding as the underpinnings for some of its findings of fact. Do friends owe each other higher standards of ethical behavior? If so, should Willie and Harding each have behaved differently here? Both Willie and Harding were professionals, each subject to his respective profession's canons of ethics. Is society justified in expecting overall higher standards of ethics (even in areas outside their areas of expertise) from professionals owing to their presumed heightened ethical sensitivities?

Reformation

If a court easily can remedy the mistake, a court may *reform* the contract, or rewrite it to reflect the parties' actual intentions. In the ambiguity example, assuming the rugs were obtainable, once the ambiguity comes to light, reformation would permit a court to make room-sized rugs the subject matter of the contract. After the parties resort to a court's equitable powers of reformation, the contract will be fully enforceable. Be aware, though, that large backlogs of court cases form a substantial impediment to the availability of reformation as a practical remedy. Therefore, take pains when making a deal to ascertain exactly what your agreement means: You will avoid a great many frustrations (and expenses).

DURESS

There can be no genuine assent to the terms of an agreement in which one person has assented while under duress. The person who has so assented, then, can ask for rescission of the contract on the ground of duress.

To assert the defense of *duress* means to allege that one has been forced into the contract against one's will. To constitute duress, the coercion must be so extreme that the victim has lost all ability to assent freely and voluntarily to the transaction. Given this definition, courts look for evidence of physical threats or threats that, if carried out, will cause intense mental anguish. Forcing a person to sign a contract at gunpoint, of course, will represent duress. To most courts, so will a spouse's threat to tell the parties' children that the other spouse has committed adultery: If, as a result of this intimidation, the spouse signs over a disproportionate share of the marital property, courts can rescind this agreement on the basis of duress. Similarly, courts generally view threats to initiate criminal actions (even if there is a basis for these) in order to extract a contractual agreement as duress. Courts, however, ordinarily do not see threats of civil suits as constituting duress.

The discussion to this point has focused on *personal duress.* Recently, the doctrine of economic duress has arisen. *Economic duress* occurs when one party is forced to agree to a further, wrongful, and coercive demand (usually a price increase) as a consequence of receiving the commodities or services to which he or she is entitled under the original contract. In most instances, the injured party cannot obtain the goods or services elsewhere.

The earlier example of the hand-loomed rugs illustrates this concept. Assume that the New York–based rug company has the only available hand-loomed rugs, and the American buyer has agreed to pay $2,500 per rug. Economic duress exists if the seller subsequently tells the American buyer (who wants to fill his orders for the rugs) that he can have the rugs only if he is willing to pay $4,000 apiece for them. Basing its decision on the concept of economic duress, a court may force the seller to sell the rugs at the original price of $2,500 or allow the American buyer after the fact to recover any difference in price.

Whether a court will grant a recovery to a plaintiff who alleges economic duress (or *business compulsion*) depends heavily on the particular facts of a given situation. For a good example of this proposition, read *Brock* v. *Entre Computer Centers.*

12.6 BROCK v. ENTRE COMPUTER CENTERS

933 F.2d 1253 (4th Cir. 1991)

FACTS Entre Computer Centers, Inc. (Entre), a Delaware corporation with its headquarters and principal place of business in McLean, Virginia, is a franchisor of approximately 150 retail computer stores located across the United States. Jerry Brock became interested in starting an Entre franchise after reading an ad in the *Wall Street Journal.* Brock subsequently traveled to Vienna, Virginia, for a franchise "visitation day," during which Entre made prepared presentations regarding its formula for success. Brock later alleged that Entre made untrue representations at that time. On 20 March 1984, Brock entered into a franchise agreement with Entre for the establishment of an Entre Computer Center store in Beaumont, Texas, and ten days later entered into a second franchise agreement for a store in Baton Rouge, Louisiana. These franchise agreements, among other things, stated that Entre would not consent to a transfer of ownership by the franchisee to a third party unless the franchisee signed a general release of all claims against Entre. In early 1986, Brock decided to sell the Beaumont and Baton Rouge centers. Entre would not consent to Brock's transfers of the centers to third parties unless Brock first signed the releases called for in the franchise agreements. Brock thereupon entered into two general releases with Entre. Each release was virtually identical to the first release that Brock had signed when he had become an Entre franchisee. After the execution of these releases, Brock sold the Beaumont and Baton Rouge stores to third parties. Brock later sued Entre for fraud and asserted in addition that Entre's procurement of the releases through economic duress had made the releases legally invalid.

ISSUE Were the releases invalid owing to economic duress?

HOLDING No. Entre's promise to enforce its rights under the original agreement unless Brock executed the re-

12.6 BROCK v. ENTRE COMPUTER CENTERS *(cont.)* 933 F.2d 1253 (4th Cir. 1991)

quested releases did not constitute a wrongful threat that had destroyed his freedom to act. Hence, Entre's conduct had not amounted to economic duress.

REASONING Brock asserted that he had entered into the releases owing to economic duress; and, as a result, the releases were invalid. There are three elements to a claim of economic duress: (1) wrongful acts or threats, (2) financial distress caused by the wrongful acts or threats, and (3) the absence of any reasonable alternative to the terms presented by the wrongdoer. Furthermore, to prove economic duress, a plaintiff such as Brock must establish that Entre had made a wrongful threat that was of such character as to destroy the free agency of the party to whom the threat was directed (here, Brock). The evidence in this case failed to show these elements. Even assuming that Brock's portrayal of the dire financial condition of the centers was correct, Brock, the franchisee, at a time when he was under no financial distress whatsoever, had expressly agreed in the franchise agreements that he would refrain from transferring the businesses without Entre's consent and that Entre had the right to condition its consent on the execution of a general release in Entre's favor. Thus, Entre had made no wrongful threat that had destroyed Brock's free agency; rather, Entre had required the franchisee to do only what he already had agreed to do. Brock was under no obligation to enter into that agreement and was free to negotiate if he did not want to be bound by the release provision. As a result, the releases Entre provided Brock pursuant to the original agreement had not been procured through economic duress.

BUSINESS CONSIDERATIONS The court apparently believed that Brock and Entre had enjoyed relatively equal bargaining power at the time Brock signed the franchise agreements. What factors should a court use in assessing the bargaining power held by each party?

ETHICAL CONSIDERATIONS Should franchisees who sign franchise agreements have a cooling-off period of seven days in which they can rescind the agreements if they wish? Is the bargaining power between the franchisor and franchisee so great that it permits the franchisor to engage in unethical behavior if the franchisor wishes to do so? Explain.

As with most of the reality-of-consent situations discussed in this chapter, contracts made under duress ordinarily are voidable. Hence, rescission may be effected at the option of the injured party *unless* the injured party, by acquiescing in the coercive conduct for an unreasonably long time, ratifies the contract. Sometimes in such cases, however, the conduct exemplifying duress is so extreme that a court will find the contract void. Threats directed at third parties (such as a relative) may give rise to duress of this sort if one party enters into the contract to protect the innocent third party from these threats.

UNDUE INFLUENCE

Closely related to duress is the concept of undue influence. Indeed, many courts view it as a subcategory of duress. Like duress, its existence depends heavily on the facts.

Undue influence is the use of a relationship of trust and confidence to extract contractual advantages. Newspapers are full of examples of such situations. Recall the allegations of undue influence involving nurses who have been named beneficiaries of their patients' sizable estates or lawyers who have benefited enormously from their clients' **testamentary** dispositions. Since the favored nurse or lawyer by virtue of the relationship enjoyed with the other party has the ability to dominate or overreach the other party, the law often allows the rescission of such contracts. Because

Testamentary
Pertaining to a will.

http:// RESOURCES FOR BUSINESS LAW STUDENTS

NAME	RESOURCES	WEB ADDRESS
Uniform Commercial Code § 2-302	The Legal Information Institute (LII), maintained by the Cornell Law School, provides a hypertext and searchable version of UCC § 2-302, Unconscionable Contract or Clause.	http://www.law.cornell.edu/ucc/2/2-302.html
Sherman Antitrust Act—15 U.S.C. §§ 1–7	LII provides a hypertext and searchable version of 15 U.S.C. §§ 1–7, popularly known as the Sherman Antitrust Act.	http://www.law.cornell.edu/uscode/15/1.html
Clayton Act—15 U.S.C. §§ 12–27	LII provides a hypertext and searchable version of 15 U.S.C. §§ 12–27, popularly known as the Clayton Antitrust Act.	http://www.law.cornell.edu/uscode/15/12.html
Federal Trade Commission Act, 15 U.S.C. §§ 41–58	LII provides a hypertext and searchable version of 15 U.S.C. §§ 41–58, popularly known as the Federal Trade Commission Act.	http://www.law.cornell.edu/uscode/15/41.html
National Fraud Information Center	National Fraud Information Center, a project of the National Consumers League, provides a daily report and other information on fraud, as well as the opportunity to report fraud.	http://www.fraud.org/

of the domination by another, the contracting party actually has not exercised his or her free will in entering into the contract, but instead has given effect to the will or wishes of the other party.

The law will presume undue influence in certain circumstances, notably in fiduciary relationships. In the lawyer example just cited, the mere existence of the relationship will require the lawyer to prove that the client made the disposition free from the lawyer's coercion. The law will demand that the lawyer, as a fiduciary, act with utmost good faith in dealing with persons who will be predisposed to follow whatever the lawyer advises. Like lawyers, parents may enjoy fiduciary relationships with their children, doctors with their patients, accountants with their clients, and so on. Sometimes it is difficult for courts to determine when the persuasiveness of the fiduciary has become so intense that the other party has lost all vestiges of free will. But when they are convinced that this has occurred, they permit rescission of the challenged contract.

UNCONSCIONABILITY

You may note similarities between the concept of unconscionability, which we address in Chapters 9 and 11, and the ideas we discuss in this chapter. Especially in the context of consumer law, some courts have set contracts aside when these courts have found the bargaining power of the parties so unequal as to be commercially shocking or unreasonably oppressive. In this chapter, we learned that some courts call such agreements contracts of adhesion, meaning that one party to the contract, through overreaching, is able to impose its will on the other party. The Uniform Commercial Code validates this approach in § 2-302, but not all states have adopted this section of the UCC. Nevertheless, unconscionability may signal a lack of meaningful assent to a contract and may justify a court's subsequent intervention on behalf of the injured party.

SUMMARY

In order for the bargain to be recognized as a valid contract, the law imposes a requirement that the subject matter and purpose of a bargain must be legal. A bargain is illegal if its performance is criminal, tortious, or otherwise opposed to public policy. Some courts distinguish between bargains that violate statutes because they are evil in themselves *(mala in se)* and bargains that are merely forbidden by statute *(mala prohibita)*. Many types of bargains (such as price-fixing agreements, bargains in contravention of Sunday laws, wagering agreements, and usurious transactions) violate statutes. Performances of services without a license may make the agreement void if the statute is regulatory. In contrast, if the statute requires licensing as a revenue-enhancing measure, lack of a license will not void the bargain. When deciding cases, judges today look increasingly to public policy factors. Covenants not to compete (promises to refrain from engaging in the same or a similar business for a period of time in a certain geographic area) and exculpatory clauses (agreements in advance to exonerate another from negligence or other torts), if too restrictive or one-sided, may be struck down on public policy grounds. Some exceptions to the rule that illegal bargains are void exist. These exceptions include agreements in which the parties are not *in pari delicto*, or of equal guilt; agreements in which one party repents before it consummates the illegal bargain; and agreements in which courts can sever the legal portions from the illegal segments.

To have a valid contract, one must prove that the assent of the parties is genuine. The existence of fraud, misrepresentation, mistake, duress, undue influence, or unconscionability precludes the reality of consent that serves as the foundation of modern contract law. Fraud is a deliberate misrepresentation of a material fact with the intent to induce another person to enter a contract that will be injurious to that person. Predictions, statements of value, opinions, and misstatements of law do not constitute fraud. Probably the most difficult element to prove is the defendant's knowledge of the falsity of the statement, or scienter. The plaintiff's reliance on the deception must be reasonable, or the plaintiff will be precluded from recovering. Successful proof of fraud makes the contract voidable and justifies rescission. Although the common law held that mere silence is not fraud, exceptions to this doctrine existed even in early common law times. Today, the judicial trend is to force disclosure of material facts if their concealment may injure the other party. Innocent misrepresentation also may result in legal liability. Mistake occurs when the parties are wrong about the existence or absence of a past or present fact that is material to their transactions. There are two types of mistakes: unilateral (one person is in error) and bilateral/mutual (both parties are in error). Courts generally will not rescind unilateral mistakes unless the other party knows, or should have known, of the mistaken party's error or uses it to take unconscionable advantage of the injured party. In these cases, as in situations involving errors in business computations, courts will allow rescission. If a mutual or bilateral mistake of fact is present, either party can disaffirm the contract. Ambiguity, for example, may lead to rescission. The equitable remedy of reformation allows a court to rewrite a contract to reflect the parties' actual intentions, but courts will not always permit reformation. Duress exists when a person's will has been overridden as a result of another person's threats. Duress may be either personal or economic, the latter occurring when a seller, in order to extract a higher contract price, wrongfully or coercively withholds scarce commodities or services. Undue influence is the use of a relationship of trust and confidence to gain contractual advantages. In certain relationships, the law will presume undue influence. The existence of unconscionability may signal a lack of meaningful assent to a contract and thus constitute grounds for a court's setting aside the contract.

Discussion Questions

1. What is the difference between a *mala in se* and a *mala prohibita* bargain?
2. What is an exculpatory clause? Is it always legal? Why or why not?
3. What are covenants not to compete? What standards do courts use to judge their legality?
4. Why are wagering and lotteries illegal in various jurisdictions?
5. What is a usurious contract? What kinds of common financing devices would not violate the usury laws?
6. Describe the three most important exceptions to the general rule that an illegal bargain is void.
7. Set out, respectively, the legal requirements of fraud and misrepresentation.
8. How does silence relate to the legal theory of fraud? In what situations is there a legal duty to speak?
9. Name, define, and explain the remedies for the two types of mistake.
10. Define *duress, economic duress,* and *undue influence.*

Case Problems and Writing Assignments

1. In 1988, Ogelean Riddick sold the Suncoast Beauty School of Florida, Inc., to Suncoast Beauty College, Inc., a Florida corporation, and JoAnn Phillips. Riddick, in exchange for a payment of $20,000 from Suncoast Beauty College, Inc., and Phillips, executed a covenant not to compete, which stated:

   For a period of five (5) years from date of closing and transfer of the business interest and assets, SUNCOAST BEAUTY SCHOOL OF FLORIDA, INC. and OGELEAN RIDDICK, as an individual, will not directly or indirectly for themselves or on behalf of any person, persons, partnership or corporation engage or attempt to engage in the ownership or operation of a beauty school in Pinellas County, Florida; nor aid or assist anyone else, except the Buyer, to do so within these limits; nor solicit in any manner any past accounts of the business; nor have any interest, directly or indirectly, in such a business; except that Ogelean Riddick, individually, may perform inspections for National Accrediting Commission of Cosmetology Arts and Sciences (NACCAS), and may be a free-lance conductor of seminars and a teacher of instructors and students in the beauty school environment.

   Riddick, however, subsequently opened a hair salon within one mile of the location of the beauty school. Suncoast Beauty College, Inc., and Phillips filed suit against Riddick for breach of the covenant not to compete. Would their lawsuit succeed? [See *Riddick* v. *Suncoast Beauty College, Inc.*, 579 So.2d 855 (Fla.App. 1991).]

2. In January and February 1987, Doye Baker, with four advances of funds that ended on 18 February, lent Daymon Howard $55,000. Baker agreed to finance the loan over a period of seven years, at 15 percent interest per annum, with monthly payments of $1,061.32 beginning 1 March 1987. The loan agreement between the parties was oral, and it was completed on 18 February. Baker testified that on that day, "When we were discussing it, [Howard] asked me what his payments would be on the $55,000 at the 15 percent interest, and I did have an amortization book, and that is where we came up with a figure of $1,061.00, whatever it is." Howard did not execute a promissory note or any other instrument evidencing the loan. Between 18 February and 1 March, however, after the parties had agreed on the terms of the loan, Baker gave Howard a printed amortization schedule setting forth the amount of the loan, the rate of interest, and the eighty-four monthly payments of $1,061.32 required under the original agreement. After Howard had made eight payments and a part of the ninth, he quit paying on the loan. Texas statutes stated that the maximum legal rate of interest for oral agreements is 10 percent; for a written contract, Texas law allowed interest rates higher than 10 percent before requiring the lender to forfeit, as a penalty, three times the amount of usurious interest charged. Was this a usurious contract under Texas law because it was an oral agreement, or did the unsigned amortization schedule make it a written contract? [See *Baker* v. *Howard*, 799 S.W.2d 450 (Tex.App. 1990).]

3. Portable Embryonics, Inc. (Portable) was in the business of performing nonsurgical bovine embryo transfers for clients in Montana and other states. Dr. Albert

C. Mills III and his wife are the sole shareholders of Portable. Portable employed Gary Porter and Alton James from 1977 until 1988. Technicians (such as Mills, Porter, and James) removed fertilized eggs from donor cows and then implanted the embryos into recipient cows, which served as surrogate mothers; alternatively, the technicians froze the embryos for later use. In the spring of 1980, Portable prepared an employment contract that contained provisions for the protection of trade secrets and restrictions concerning employees who left the company. James signed the contract on 17 April 1980, and Porter signed on 6 May 1980. Porter and James terminated their employment with Portable in February 1988, and, within a few days, formed J. P. Genetics, Inc., a Montana corporation. J. P. Genetics, Inc., also performed nonsurgical bovine embryo transfers. When Mills learned that J. P. Genetics, Inc., had successfully lured away many of Portable's clients, Mills, citing the employment agreement, sued Porter and James for breach of contract, breach of loyalty, fraud, and bad faith. Porter and James, in turn, cited Montana statutes that characterized ova or embryo transfers on animals as the practice of veterinary medicine and that made the practice of veterinary medicine without a license a misdemeanor. Using these statutes, Porter and James argued that the purported employment contracts were illegal and unenforceable. Given these facts, should a court find in favor of Portable or Porter and James? [See *Portable Embryonics, Inc.* v. *J. P. Genetics, Inc.*, 810 P.2d 1197 (Mont. 1991).]

4. In 1984, Dorothy L. Bird, in contemplation of selling her home in Buckhead, Georgia, ordered a termite inspection of the property. That inspection revealed prior termite infestation and the need for termite treatment, which was performed. In 1986, Bird listed her property for sale with Madison Realty and gave the real estate agent a document she had received from the company that had performed the termite treatment in 1984. The undisputed evidence showed that both the real estate agent and Bird thought that document was a "termite bond." A friend of Debra E. and Jess C. Lester told them that Bird was going to auction her property. During their three visits to the property before the auction, the Lesters performed walk-through inspections of the property, but did not attempt to examine the crawl space area underneath the house, because it either was boarded or bricked closed. The Lesters further claimed that they had not examined the crawl space area of the house because the real estate agent had assured them that owing to the absence of any termite damage, there was no reason to examine that area. The Lesters furthermore did not employ a professional termite inspector either before the purchase or at any time during the 40-day period before the closing. The sales contract the Lesters had signed on the day of the auction warranted only that the seller would transfer good and marketable title to the purchaser. The sales contract did not contain any provision or contingency relating to termite inspection and treatment that would allow the Lesters to cancel the sales agreement. At the closing, Bird made available to the Lesters an official Georgia wood-infestation inspection report prepared by the company that had inspected and treated the property in 1984. Among other things, the report noted the existence of previous termite infestation and that the property had been treated for termites six days before the closing. The Lesters thereupon became concerned about the purchase and, before proceeding with the closing, unsuccessfully attempted to contact their attorney. When the agent informed them that the contract did not contain a provision that would allow them to refuse to close based on the termite inspection report they had received, the Lesters decided to close on the property. Shortly thereafter, a contractor hired to remodel the kitchen discovered substantial termite damage and that portions of the house were propped up with wood, stacks of stones and bricks, and railroad ties. The Lesters' 1989 suit against Bird, Madison Realty, and Crown Auctions asserted fraud, conspiracy to defraud, and negligent misrepresentation. How should a court rule on these claims? [See *Lester* v. *Bird*, 408 S.E.2d 147 (Ga.App. 1991).]

5. Quest Exploration and Development Company (Quest) owned an interest in mineral production fields situated in southwest Louisiana. The wells in which Quest owned interests produced gas for resale to purchasers. In 1980, Quest and several other producers entered into a gas purchase agreement (GPA) with Transco Energy Company (Transco), which purchased gas and transported it by pipeline to sell in interstate markets. Required to take or pay for 85 percent of Quest's delivery capacity of the covered well or wells, Transco, in September 1984, requested a suspension of certain portions of the GPA and the implementation of a Transco-imposed "market maintenance plan" (MMP) that would modify other terms of the GPA during the period of suspension. Quest acceded to a modification of the GPA and agreed to participate in the MMP as an accommodation to Transco from 1 November 1984 to 31 October 1985. Upon expiration of the MMP on 31 October 1985, the parties again renegotiated the terms of the GPA—this time apparently at Quest's insistence. Under the terms of the settlement, Quest was to receive a cash payment

of $2,000,000 and Transco was to reduce its take-or-pay obligations by one-half. Quest later asserted that, during the period of negotiations, Transco unilaterally reduced the volume of its monthly take from Quest from the 85 percent of Quest's delivery capacity as required under the GPA to no more than 5 percent and refused to pay for the untaken difference. Quest claimed that by October 1985—before negotiation of the settlement agreement and before Transco had reduced the amount of gas it would take—Quest had lost $4 million, in part as a result of Transco's refusal to fulfill its obligations under the GPA and the MMP. Quest also asserted that the precipitous drop in its gas sales revenue, which Quest alleged had resulted from its participation in the MMP (that is, the GPA's temporary modification), had forced it to settle the dispute. Quest thus submitted that, as it was facing imminent bankruptcy because of Transco's unlawful conduct, Quest's "forced" settlement was the result of economic duress on Transco's part. Should a court agree with Quest's reasoning? [See *Quest Exploration and Dev. Co.* v. *Transco Energy Co.,* 24 F.3d 738 (5th Cir. 1994).]

6. **BUSINESS APPLICATION CASE** On 7 April 1980, President Carter severed diplomatic relations with Iran and issued Executive Order 12205. The order proscribed, among other things, "[t]he sale, supply or other transfer, by any person subject to the jurisdiction of the United States, of any items, commodities or products . . . from the United States . . . either to or destined for Iran." In June 1980, National Petrochemical Company of Iran (NPC) sought to purchase supplies of certain urgently needed chemicals for delivery to Iran. Because of the trade embargoes facing Iran, NPC was not able to procure these chemicals from any of its normal sources. Seeking new sources of supplies, NPC therefore approached numerous new traders and brokers. Consequently, Monnris Enterprises, of Dubai, United Arab Emirates, agreed to serve as an intermediary for NPC's purchase of the chemicals from Rotex, a West German firm. Rotex agreed to make the sale through a Swiss affiliate, Formula S.A. (West Germany was part of the embargo against trade with Iran). The documents involved called for shipment of the chemicals from "any Western European and UAE ports," but the chemicals actually were shipped from Houston, Texas, aboard the *Stolt Sheaf.* The original shipping document called for delivery from Texas to Spain, but a subsequent addendum specified Iran as the ultimate destination of the cargo. War broke out between Iran and Iraq before the *Stolt Sheaf* reached Iran; and Rotex ordered the ship to sail to Taiwan, where Rotex successfully resold the cargo. None of the proceeds from this resale ever reached NPC, although the sale in Taiwan allegedly was made for NPC's account. NPC sued the *Stolt Sheaf* in the New York federal court for negligently and conspiratorially allowing Rotex's sale of the cargo in Taiwan. The *Stolt Sheaf* defended by arguing that NPC, because of the underlying illegality of the contract, could not recover. Bakhtiari, head of NPC's procurement department, indicated that he knew the bills of lading would not reflect the true destination of the cargo and that he also knew this was done to avoid the effects of the trade embargo. Were the agreements that NPC was attempting to enforce illegal? If so, was NPC nevertheless entitled to recover because it was not *in pari delicto* with those who had intentionally violated the trade embargoes? What policies could the management of NPC have adopted so as to avoid the situation in which it found itself? [See *Nat'l Petrochemical Co. of Iran* v. *M/T Stolt Sheaf,* 930 F.2d 240 (2d Cir. 1991).]

7. **ETHICAL APPLICATION CASE** On 25 August 1987, Helen Turner was involved in an automobile accident with Sheila A. Lucas, who was operating an automobile owned by Donnie M. Lucas. Both Turner and the Lucases were insured by State Farm Mutual Automobile Insurance Company. After the accident, Turner was directed by her State Farm agent to the State Farm claims office. She met with Debra Pendergrass on 26 August 1987, the day after the accident. At the meeting, Turner assumed Pendergrass was acting as her adjuster and not that of Mrs. Lucas; and, in fact, because only the Lucas file was present, Pendergrass initially was unaware that Turner was insured by State Farm. After some discussion, Pendergrass presented to Turner an agreement and release providing $500 for "pain and suffering and inconvenience" and for the payment of medical expenses up to $5,000. Although Turner told Pendergrass she had injured her foot, neck, and back and had an appointment with a doctor that afternoon, Turner signed this release. After consulting with her attorney, however, Turner did not cash the $500 draft and returned it to State Farm. At trial, Turner testified that she thought the agreement was for inconvenience and payment of medical bills. When asked if she had considered the agreement to be a complete release of the Lucases, she replied: "No, I did not consider this a release at all." She testified that she had attempted to read the agreement but could not because she had forgotten her glasses. The cross-examination of Pendergrass at trial showed that Pendergrass had not checked Turner's policy and file on the computer and thus had failed to advise Turner

of her rights under the policy until after Turner had signed the release. Moreover, Pendergrass admitted that, during her conversation with Turner, she (Pendergrass) had never revealed she was serving in a dual capacity (that is, representing both the Lucases and Turner) on this claim. When State Farm sued for a declaratory judgment (a court judgment that merely sets out the rights of the parties in a given situation without the court's ordering any performance by either party) sustaining the validity of the release, Turner sought rescission of the release. Assuming Turner's signing of the release had constituted a unilateral mistake, should a court nonetheless grant this request for rescission? What affirmative steps can the company take to ensure that employees like Pendergrass manifest a more heightened sense of ethics when they deal with the firm's customers? [See *State Farm Mut. Auto. Ins. Co.* v. *Turner,* 399 S.E.2d 22 (S.C.App. 1990).]

8. **IDES CASE** Hallen was a farmer who worked on clocks during the non–growing seasons. He had gained some local notoriety as a clock collector. Thus, he often dealt with potential buyers. Although most of his clocks were antiques, he had a sizable number of Japanese wooden clocks that had been manufactured around 1945. One afternoon, Parker, who was interested in collecting antique American ogee clocks, stopped by Hallen's farm. Parker looked over all of Hallen's collection, but Parker's interest soon fastened on an ogee that sported brightly varnished wood overall and a newly painted glass door on the front. After Parker expressed interest in the clock, Hallen said, "It's a dandy, all right, and an 'oldie'." When Parker at one point said, "This ogee looks too new to be an antique; I want an antique," Hallen merely stroked his chin. But shortly thereafter, Hallen said, "You can trust me." Parker paid $1,200 for the clock. Two days later, he found out it was a Japanese reproduction worth $150. Use the IDES model to analyze this case. What theory (theories) could Parker use to sue Hallen? How could Parker maximize his potential recovery?

NOTES

1. *Restatement (Second) of Contracts* (St. Paul: American Law Institute Publishers), § 178.
2. David A. Steinberg and Yukub Hazzard, "'Employment Services' May Trigger Act," *The National Law Journal* (26 November 1996), pp. B7–8.
3. Guest, A. G., *Anson's Law of Contracts,* 26 ed. (Oxford: Clarendon Press, 1984), pp. 209–210.

A G E N D A

The Kochanowskis recognize that CIT will enter into a number of contracts in the near future. They plan to put most of their contracts in writing, but they may need to know which of their contracts *have* to be in writing in order to be enforceable, and which contracts merely *should* be in writing, although they do not have to be. They also will need to know how detailed their writings need to be, and whether any of CIT's written agreements are subject to amendment or alteration by oral testimony.

They are likely to look to you for help as they work through this area. Be prepared! You never know when one of the Kochanowskis will ask for your help or advice.

Proper Form and Interpretation of Contracts

O U T L I N E

The Importance of Form
Statute of Frauds
Parol Evidence Rule
Exceptions to the Parol Evidence Rule
Judicial Interpretation
Summary
Discussion Questions
Case Problems and Writing Assignments

THE IMPORTANCE OF FORM

In the preceding chapters, we discussed the requirements for a contract in detail: agreement (offer and acceptance), consideration, capacity, legality, and reality of consent. In addition, according to the Statute of Frauds, to be enforceable, certain categories of contracts must be in writing. Contracts to answer for the debt of another if the debtor defaults, contracts involving interests in land, contracts not to be performed within one year from the date of their making, promises of executors and administrators to pay a claim against the estate of the deceased out of their own personal funds, contracts made in consideration of marriage, and contracts involving a sale of goods priced at $500 or more, or the lease of goods for $1,000 or more represent the classifications of contracts that must be in proper form—that is, in writing—in order for the law to give them effect. The *writing* in these situations provides evidence that the parties did contract about the matters in dispute, and it avoids the **perjuries** traditionally and historically associated with these categories of contracts. In most other situations, the parties are free to contract orally even though it is unwise to do so.

Perjuries
False statements made under oath during court proceedings.

Moreover, once the parties reduce their agreement to writing, judges necessarily are wary of tampering with the contract. For this reason, the parol evidence rule states that oral testimony ordinarily is not admissible to add to, alter, or vary the terms of a written agreement. In certain situations, parol evidence will be admissible to clear up ambiguities. Reference to the trade usages and customs of a particular industry may dispose of these types of ambiguities.

Unfortunately, even though the parties may have tried to be as precise as possible, questions about what the contract "really says" and whether certain conditions have been met may crop up as the parties begin their performance. One classic case involved a dispute over the word "chicken." A Swiss buyer thought chicken meant broilers and fryers, or tender, juicy chicken. The New York seller, however, shipped stewing chicken (older, tougher fowl) to fulfill part of the contract. The Swiss buyer was not amused (see Case 20.1 in Chapter 20). As these parties found out, contract **interpretation** often becomes an extremely important matter.

Interpretation
The process of discovering the meaning of a contract; the defining, discoveri and explaining of uncl language.

If the parties cannot resolve their differences, they often will call on a court to decide what the disputed terms mean. As aids for this task, courts have certain standards they can apply to unravel even the most ambiguous terms and phrases. Simply put, writing a contract does not guarantee that the subsequent performance of the contract will remain free of semantic wranglings or disputes. But the alternative of contracting orally makes little sense because oral transactions multiply the potential interpretive problems.

Since the previous chapters presented the most significant transactional aspects of contract formation, we now turn to an examination of the interplay among the Statute of Frauds, the parol evidence rule, and contract interpretation.

STATUTE OF FRAUDS

The historical ancestor of the present-day **Statute of Frauds** was called "An Act for the Prevention of Frauds and Perjuries,"passed by the English Parliament in 1677. Because perjury was so widespread in lawsuits involving oral contracts, Parliament decreed that, to be enforceable, certain classes of contracts must be in writing. Thus, the term Statute of Frauds is somewhat misleading, because such statutes deal with the requirement of a writing rather than with reality-of-consent situations like fraud.

Statute of Frauds
A statute requiring that specified types of contracts be in writing in order to be enforceable.

(In the Statute of Frauds, the term *frauds* refers to the wholesale misrepresentations or perjured statements made to early English courts.) Almost every state has a Statute of Frauds modeled on this original statute.

The Statute of Frauds requires that certain types of contracts be in writing before courts will enforce them. Thus, if the subject matter of the contract involves a type of contract enumerated in the Statute of Frauds, the agreement generally cannot be oral but instead must be in writing before a court will give it effect. The Statute of Frauds never is a legal issue unless a valid contract exists; hence, it becomes an issue only after all the stages of contract formation are present.

Affirmative defense
A defense to a cause of action that the defendant must raise.

The Statute of Frauds also is an **affirmative defense**, one used by a person who wants to avoid the enforcement of a contract. A defendant who wishes to utilize this defense must expressly plead it, or it will be waived; if a waiver is found, an oral contract that otherwise would have been unenforceable because of a violation of the Statute of Frauds will be enforced against the defendant. Courts have been somewhat hostile to Statute of Frauds claims because of the injustice such statutes can cause. Consequently, some courts construe these statutes broadly and find various rationales for removing the contract at issue from the coverage of the statute, which construction allows the court to give effect to oral contracts that otherwise would not be enforceable.

Types of Contracts Covered

The following sections examine six categories of contracts covered by the Statute of Frauds:

- Contracts to answer for the debt of another if the person so defaults
- Contracts for interests in land
- Contracts not to be performed within one year of the date of their making
- Contracts of executors and administrators of estates
- Contracts made in consideration of marriage
- Contracts for the sale of goods priced at $500 or more, and contracts for the lease of goods where the total lease price is $1,000 or more.

Guarantor
One who promises to answer for the payment of a debt or the performance of an obligation if the person liable in the first instance fails to make payment or to perform.

Surety
A person who promises to pay or to perform in the event the principal debtor fails to do so.

Novations
By mutual agreement, substitutions of new contracts in place of preexisting ones, whether between the same parties or with new parties replacing one or more of the original parties.

Contracts to Answer for the Debt of Another If the Person So Defaults. Ordinarily, oral promises between two persons are perfectly valid and enforceable in court. When Linda orally promises to pay George $200 for a used cash register and he orally promises to sell it to her, a contract exists between the two parties. We call such promises original promises because both parties have promised to be *primarily* liable (i.e., liable in all events) if something in the transaction should go awry.

Sometimes people agree to be *secondarily* liable—that is, only in the event someone else (i.e., the debtor) defaults. Such agreements, called *collateral contracts,* are promises to answer for the debt or default of another. Collateral contracts typically involve three persons: the debtor (the original promisor), the creditor (the promisee), and the third party, who generally is called a **guarantor** or **surety**. Notice that a collateral contract exhibits definite characteristics:

1. There are three parties (but not all three-party transactions are collateral contracts; **novations**, for example, are not collateral contracts).
2. There are two promises, one original (debtor to creditor) and the other collateral (third party to creditor).
3. The second promise is a promise to accept only collateral, or secondary, liability resulting from the default of another.

Since such collateral promises are somewhat unusual (we generally assume people will be responsible for their own debts but not for another person's), the purpose of this provision of the Statute of Frauds is to require evidence—through a writing—of this undertaking of possible secondary liability.

The *intent of the parties* determines whether a three-party transaction involves a collateral contract, which must be in writing to be enforceable, or an original contract, which may be enforceable even if oral. For example, if Stein wants his grandson to have a car, he may cosign the note his grandson has signed with a bank. This is a three-party situation (Stein, his grandson, and the bank), but it is not a collateral contract. Stein and his grandson are joint, original promisors to the bank. As such, Stein is accepting liability in all events. If the grandson defaults on the car payment, the bank can sue *either* Stein or his grandson. If, however, Stein wishes to be only secondarily liable and the note is phrased accordingly, the contract is a collateral one. In the event of the grandson's default, the bank must sue the grandson *without success before* it can attempt to hold Stein liable. Note that the intent of the parties is crucial in determining the type of contract—original or collateral—that is involved. By requiring any transaction deemed a collateral contract to be in writing, the bank is protecting itself from a defense based on the Statute of Frauds.

Because courts generally are hostile to the Statute of Frauds, they sometimes allow an exception to the rule that a collateral contract must be in writing to be enforceable. This is called the *leading-object* or *main-purpose* exception: When the third party agrees to be liable chiefly for the purpose of obtaining an economic benefit for himself or herself personally, the second promise, even if oral, will be enforceable. Let us change our earlier example to one in which Stein orally tells the bank he will pay if his grandson defaults. When the grandson fails to pay and the bank sues Stein, Stein will use the Statute of Frauds as his defense: No writing exists, and the contract appears to be a collateral one. If the bank nonetheless can prove that before Stein agreed to be liable, Stein knew that the institution was about to force the grandson into bankruptcy, which, in turn, meant that Stein might lose sizable loans he had made to his grandson, the bank may be able to show that Stein's "leading object" in making the promise principally involved preventing economic loss to himself rather than displaying grandfatherly love and generosity. Proving this, the bank can argue that the "main purpose" of Stein's conduct focused on protecting his own economic position vis-à-vis his grandson's impending bankruptcy. Owing to the personal, immediate, pecuniary benefits Stein himself may have realized from the bank's loan, courts will cast aside their usual skepticism concerning such oral promises and impose liability on Stein.

By requiring all promises to be in writing, the wise businessperson or firm avoids such potential legal problems. The following case illustrates a number of these concepts.

13.1 BILLER v. ZIEGLER 593 A.2d 436 (Pa.Super. 1991)

FACTS Mr. and Mrs. James Wright had engaged the architectural firm of Willergerod and MacAvoy, P.C., to oversee the construction of a house. Monroe Construction Company (Monroe), owned by Edward Ziegler and Rich Marchi, served as the general contractor. Since Mr. Biller's custom was to work on a "handshake basis," the architectural firm and the general contractor orally had hired Gilbert B. Biller to do the masonry work on the house. In November 1985,

13.1 BILLER v. ZIEGLER *(cont.)* 593 A.2d 436 (Pa.Super. 1991)

Biller became concerned that Monroe was about to declare bankruptcy while owing him approximately $9,000 for work done on other jobs. Therefore, Biller met with William MacAvoy, one of the architects employed by the Wrights, and explained that he would cease working on the Wrights' house, as he could not take the risk of losing payment for the work. MacAvoy assured Biller that Biller would receive payment by Thanksgiving. When the funds were not forthcoming, Biller pulled his crew off the Wrights' job site; and a different masonry subcontractor ultimately completed the project. In 1986, Biller sued the architectural firm, Monroe, and Mr. MacAvoy individually for the unpaid work. In 1989, a jury found the architectural firm liable and awarded Biller $16,000 in damages. On appeal, the firm asserted the Statute of Frauds as a defense and argued that the jury had erred in finding the firm liable for the personal guarantee of payment made orally by MacAvoy to Biller.

ISSUE Was MacAvoy's oral promise enforceable under the Pennsylvania Statute of Frauds?

HOLDING Yes. The Statute of Frauds's requirement of a writing for promises to answer for the debt of another would not apply here, since MacAvoy's promise fell within the "leading-object/main-purpose" rule.

REASONING Pennsylvania by statute sets out the usual rule that a promise to answer for the debt or default of another must be in writing and signed by the party to be charged therewith. However, the Statute of Frauds's rule that a promise to answer for the debt of another must be in writing does not apply if the main object of the promisor is to serve his own pecuniary or business purpose. The law calls this exception the "leading object" or "main purpose" rule. The "leading object" rule applies whenever a promisor, in order to advance some pecuniary or business purpose of his or her own, purports to enter into an oral agreement even though that agreement may take the form of a provision to pay the debt of another. In short, where the surety-promisor's main purpose is his or her own primary or business advantage, the law sees a lesser need for cautionary or evidentiary formality in this context. Moreover, the determination as to whether a promisor's main purpose for making a guarantee was to serve his or her own pecuniary or business ends is for the trier of fact; and such a determination will not be reversed in the absence of abuse of discretion. However, the defendants contended that neither William MacAvoy nor the firm had had any pecuniary interest in seeing that Biller performed the masonry work on the Wright project. The defendants predicated their claim on the fact that their agreement with the Wrights had not conditioned payment of the architect's fee on the completion of any particular portion of the work by any particular contractor or subcontractor. But since the firm would receive full payment only on the completion of the project, the firm certainly had an interest in facilitating the completion of the masonry work as rapidly as possible. Thus, it was logical and reasonable for the jury to determine that this pecuniary interest was advanced by the firm's encouraging Biller to remain on the job rather than by suspending progress while the firm sought a different subcontractor to take over the work. Hence, in concluding that Mr. MacAvoy's oral promise also advanced a business purpose for Willergerod and MacAvoy, P.C., the fact finder had not abused its discretion. Mr. MacAvoy admitted that at the time he had made the oral promise to Biller, the Wrights had been concerned that the project was moving too slowly and that they wanted the masonry and brickwork completed before "deep winter" set in. The Wrights also wanted the job to be completed as quickly as possible in order to reduce the amount of interest due on their construction loan. Therefore, this testimony made it reasonable for the jury to conclude that the architectural firm had a business purpose for the oral promise, that is, to enhance the firm's reputation by finishing the brickwork before winter made completion of the project impossible.

BUSINESS CONSIDERATIONS Why do you think Mr. Biller insists on doing business "on a handshake basis"? Explain to him the disadvantages associated with conducting work on this basis.

ETHICAL CONSIDERATIONS Discuss MacAvoy's ethics in assuring Biller that Monroe would pay Biller. Although the jury found the architectural firm legally liable for MacAvoy's statement to Biller, is the firm ethically responsible for MacAvoy's comments? If it is, what kinds of policies can the firm devise to apprise its employees of the parameters of the ethical behavior the firm wishes to foster?

Contracts for Interests in Land. Any agreement that involves buying, selling, or transferring interests in land must be in writing to be enforceable. **Mortgages, leases, easements,** and sales agreements about standing timber and buildings attached to the land also should be in writing to satisfy the Statute of Frauds. Thus, if you orally offer to buy someone's house and the seller accepts your offer, this contract will be unenforceable because it does not comply with the Statute of Frauds.

Mortgages
Conditional transfers of property as security for a debt.

Leases
Contracts that grant the right to use and occupy realty.

Easements
Limited rights to use and enjoy the land of another.

Courts nevertheless will enforce oral contracts for the sale of land if the purchaser has paid part of the purchase price and, with the seller's consent, takes possession of the land and makes valuable improvements on it. This equitable remedy is called the *doctrine of part performance.* For example, assume Green moves onto Berry's land and, with Berry's oral permission, tears down an old garage, repaints the entire house, and rebuilds a barn, all at Green's expense. Before undertaking these actions, Green also has paid $5,000 to Berry. When Berry later tries to claim an absence of any enforceable contract of sale between the two, a court nonetheless can order specific performance of the contract despite noncompliance with the Statute of Frauds. Courts justify such an exception to the requirement of a writing on the ground that the *conduct* of the parties prior to litigation shows the existence of a contract. Courts in such cases conclude that the parties' actions can be explained only by the actuality of such a contract. To avoid the unjust enrichment of the seller, equity also will give remedies in such situations.

Contracts Not to Be Performed Within One Year of the Date of Their Making. According to the Statute of Frauds, a promise in a contract that cannot be performed within one year from the date of the making of the agreement must be in writing to be enforceable. To illustrate, an oral promise to haul milk for a dairy producer during a one-year period is invalid under the Statute of Frauds if the milk cannot be hauled in less than one year. This is the case when the parties enter into a contract on 15 December, with the term of the contract stated as running from 1 January to 31 December of the next year. Such a contract is one not to be performed within one year of the date of its making (15 December). Therefore, under the Statute of Frauds, to be enforceable, this agreement must be in writing.

Courts have reacted hostilely to this section of the statute because, when applied, it may harshly affect the parties to the contract. Thus, courts often have limited the coverage of this proviso to situations in which *performance cannot possibly occur within one year's time* (as in our example above). This limitation has led to rather strained results. For example, a bilateral contract in which an employee promises to work for an employer "for the employer's lifetime" in exchange for the employer's promise to pay a monthly salary sounds as if it invariably cannot be performed within one year. Some courts, however, interpret such language to mean that since it is *possible*—though not *probable*—that the employer might die within a year, an oral contract is enforceable despite the Statute of Frauds. Under this approach, if the contract in our earlier example obligated the hauler to transport the milk for "as long as the dairy farmer produces milk," such courts would reason that the dairy farmer possibly could cease operations within one year, thereby making the contract capable of being performed within one year from the date of the making of the contract. Although a remote possibility, the fact that such a contingency *could* happen makes the oral contract enforceable and this section of the Statute of Frauds inapplicable. Other courts, nevertheless, will adopt the stricter approach and hold that the contracts at issue in both cases must be in writing to be enforceable.

For one court's view of this matter, see the following case.

13.2 ARGONAUT INS. COMPANIES v. MEDICAL LIABILITY MUTUAL INS. CO.

760 F.Supp. 1078 (S.D.N.Y. 1991)

FACTS Since the mid-1960s, physicians who are members of the Medical Society of the State of New York (MSSNY) have received medical malpractice liability insurance coverage from three successive insurance companies. The initial coverage, furnished by Wausau Insurance Company (Wausau), ran from the inception of the coverage to 30 June 1974. Argonaut Insurance Companies (Argonaut) succeeded it and wrote medical liability insurance for MSSNY members from 1 July 1974 to 30 June 1975. Argonaut was succeeded by Medical Liability Mutual Insurance Company (MLMIC), which commenced its coverage on 1 July 1975. The insurance industry calls this type of nonoverlapping coverage "end-to-end" coverage.

A claim for medical malpractice may arise from a single diagnosis or treatment or from a physician's allegedly negligent treatment of a patient over a number of years (e.g., negligent failure to diagnose cancer). This latter situation represents a "continuous treatment" medical malpractice claim. Within the parlance of medical malpractice insurance, a "continuous-treatment case" involves allegations of malpractice spanning more than one policy period when a single insurer is involved. An "end-to-end case" involves allegations of malpractice spanning more than one policy period when two or more insurers are involved. Because of Argonaut's relatively brief appearance as the malpractice insurer for MSSNY physicians, it found itself involved in continuous treatment cases in which the plaintiff alleged malpractice beginning during the period of Wausau's coverage, extending through Argonaut's period of coverage, and continuing into MLMIC's coverage. This led to Argonaut's relationship with the other two insurance companies regarding, among other things, the costs of defending against the action (e.g., attorneys' fees, investigation expenses, etc.). A continuous-treatment case alleging malpractice beginning during the policy year 1 July 1974 through 30 June 1975 and extending thereafter concerned only Argonaut and MLMIC, since Wausau had dropped out of the picture.

A question of obvious mutual concern, then, centered on the allocation of defense costs among insurers in end-to-end cases. Until February 1987, Argonaut shared end-to-end defense costs equally with Wausau and MLMIC (or with MLMIC only, if the malpractice claim did not arise until after Wausau's coverage had ceased). However, during that month, Argonaut put both Wausau and MLMIC on notice that it no longer would allocate end-to-end defense costs equally when the policy periods of the respective insurers were unequal. Both MLMIC and Wausau maintained that the prior agreement to allocate defense costs equally had bound Argonaut; and the two companies therefore instructed defense attorneys handling such cases to bill the fees and expenses on an equal basis among the insurance companies concerned. Since February 1987, Argonaut had continued to pay on that basis, under protest and with all rights reserved. Argonaut argued that the alleged agreement that bound it to share end-to-end defense costs equally was unenforceable under the Statute of Frauds.

ISSUE Did an exchange of memoranda that had given rise to an alleged agreement between Argonaut and MLMIC to share equally the expenses of defending overlapping coverage claims fall within the Statute of Frauds because it involved an agreement that could not be performed within one year from the date of the making thereof?

HOLDING No. Because the companies could have disposed of each malpractice claim falling within their coverage by motion, settlement, or trial within one year, the Statute of Frauds did not cover the alleged agreement. Hence, the agreement was enforceable against Argonaut.

REASONING Argonaut contended that its purported agreement to share defense costs equally with MLMIC falls within the Statute of Frauds of New York, which provides in part that

> *a. Every agreement, promise or undertaking is void, unless it or some note or memorandum thereof be in writing, and subscribed by the party to be charged therewith, or by his lawful agent, if such agreement, promise or undertaking:*
>
> *1. By its terms is not to be performed within one year from the making thereof. . . .*

Argonaut further maintained that the exchange of correspondence quoted earlier is not sufficient to satisfy the statute. In this case, however, the alleged agreement did not fall within the Statute of Frauds. The provision on which Argonaut relied applies to an agreement that "by its terms" could not be performed within one year. Unless the wording of the agreement requires that construction, the agreement does not fall within the statute. In the case at bar, the parties could have disposed of each malpractice claim falling within Argonaut's coverage by motion, settlement, or trial within one year. Such a result remained unlikely, but likelihood was not the issue.

Application of the Statute of Frauds depends on the explicit terms of the agreement. To fall outside the Statute of Frauds in New York, the contract must be one that by its terms can be performed within a year—even if, as a practical

13.2 ARGONAUT INS. COMPANIES v. MEDICAL LIABILITY MUTUAL INS. CO. (cont.) 760 F.Supp. 1078 (S.D.N.Y. 1991)

matter, it were well nigh impossible of performance within a year. Therefore, the agreement to share expenses, which Argonaut allegedly entered into with MLMIC, would not fall within the Statute of Frauds. But that does not end the inquiry: It still must appear that the exchange of correspondence has given rise to a binding contract. The malpractice cases forming the basis for this action involved only those cases in which the malpractice plaintiff alleged negligence during Argonaut's one-year policy and also continued treatment and negligence during the period of two or more of the successive annual policies issued by MLMIC. Malpractice during the year of Argonaut's coverage and only during the first succeeding year of MLMIC's coverage would, even on Argonaut's theory, result in an even allocation of the costs of defense.

Although Argonaut based its claim primarily on its perception of fairness, MLMIC resisted anything other than the equal division of the costs of defense. Consequently, MLMIC contended that in an exchange of correspondence beginning in 1977, Argonaut had agreed to the equal division of defense costs among the insurance companies concerned. In determining whether an exchange of memoranda between the parties will give rise to a binding and enforceable contract, courts must examine (1) the language of the agreement; (2) the context of the negotiations; (3) the existence of open terms; (4) partial performance; and (5) the necessity of putting the agreement in final form, as indicated by the customary form of such transactions. Of those factors, the first, "the language of the agreement," remains the most important. In the case at bar, Argonaut's exchange of correspondence with MLMIC clearly expressed an intent by Argonaut to be bound by the procedures its staff had suggested. Argonaut's subsequent correspondence, including the drafting of the form letter to be used in processing claims, implemented its staff's proposal, to which MLMIC had agreed. Thus, "partial performance" of the agreement by Argonaut was evident.

A number of factors favored the conclusion that Argonaut and MLMIC had entered into a binding agreement for the division of defense costs. And because this agreement could be performed within one year from the date of its making, the contract fell outside the Statute of Frauds and remained enforceable against Argonaut.

BUSINESS CONSIDERATIONS What steps could the insurers in this lawsuit have taken so as to avoid the occurrence of this litigation? What policies aimed at avoiding interpretive problems should each have had in place?

ETHICAL CONSIDERATIONS The insurers in this case provided medical malpractice insurance for physicians. Some jurisdictions "cap" the amount of total damages a patient can receive for malpractice claims. Are such statutes unethical? Why or why not?

Some jurisdictions allow recovery for oral contracts that fall under this provision of the Statute of Frauds—that is, because they extend for periods longer than one year—when one party to the contract will be able to complete its performance within one year, even though the other party will be unable to do so. Courts also may apply promissory estoppel, which we learned about in Chapter 10, to allow recovery for otherwise unenforceable contracts.

Promises by Executors and Administrators of Estates. Promises by **executors** and **administrators** of estates to pay estate claims out of their own personal funds must be in writing to be enforceable. Since such promises are relatively unusual, the courts require a writing as evidence that the parties actually reached such an agreement.

Executors

The persons named and appointed in a will by the testator to carry out the administration of the estate as established by the will.

Administrators

The persons who have been empowered by an appropriate court to handle the estate of a deceased person.

Contracts Made in Consideration of Marriage. Like the previous category, unilateral promises to pay money or to transfer property in consideration of a promise to marry are so uncommon that the law will enforce such promises only if they are in writing. If the Benson family promises to pay $20,000 and to transfer the ownership of their condominium in Florida to Pat Lloyd—if Pat promises to marry their child—the Statute of Frauds will require the Bensons' promise to be in writing. By analogy, antenuptial (or prenuptial) agreements, into which couples enter before marriage and which typically spell out the disposition of the marital property should the marriage end in divorce, also ordinarily must be in writing to be enforceable.

Contracts for the Sale of Goods Priced at $500 or More, or the Lease of Goods for $1,000 or More. In addition to the five common law categories of contracts that need to be in writing to be enforceable under the Statute of Frauds, the Uniform Commercial Code (UCC) also has several provisions that implicate the Statute of Frauds. The most important of these are UCC Sections 2-201 and 2A-201. Section 2-201 states that contracts for the sale of goods priced at $500 or more are not enforceable unless there is a writing sufficient to indicate that a contract for sale has been made between the parties and the writing is signed by the person against whom enforcement of the contract is sought. Section 2A-201 states that contracts for the leasing of goods calling for total payments of $1,000 or more, excluding payments for an option to renew or to buy, are not enforceable unless there is a writing sufficient to indicate that a contract for the lease has been made between the parties, and the writing has been signed by the party against whom enforcement is sought. Therefore, according to the Statute of Frauds, a contract for a sale of produce—since the Code would classify produce as goods (i.e., identifiable, movable, personal property)—priced at $500 or more must be in writing. (The contract involving chicken, which we mentioned earlier, would involve goods too.) The Code further states that a writing is not insufficient if it omits or incorrectly states a term agreed on, but courts will refuse to enforce the agreement beyond the *quantity* of goods mentioned in such a writing. Similarly, a contract for the leasing of a computer—which is also classified as goods under the UCC—with lease payments of $1,000 or more must be in writing.

Merchant

A person who deals in goods of this kind, or otherwise, through his or her occupation, holds himself or herself out as having knowledge or skill peculiar to the practice or goods involved in the transaction.

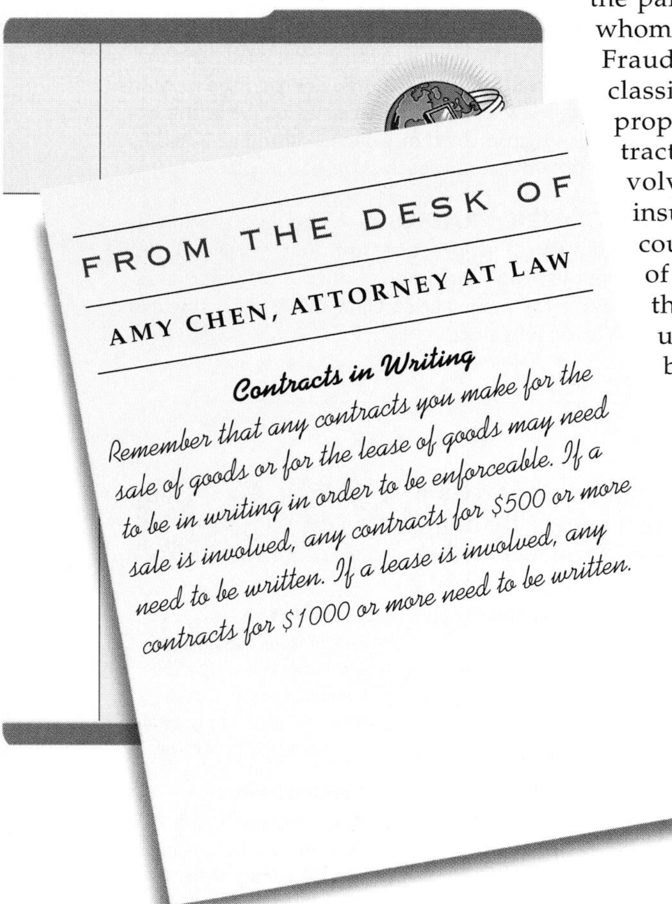

FROM THE DESK OF
AMY CHEN, ATTORNEY AT LAW
Contracts in Writing
Remember that any contracts you make for the sale of goods or for the lease of goods may need to be in writing in order to be enforceable. If a sale is involved, any contracts for $500 or more need to be written. If a lease is involved, any contracts for $1000 or more need to be written.

Under § 2-201, however, courts will enforce *oral* contracts if (1) the goods are to be specially manufactured for the buyer and are not suitable for sale to others in the ordinary course of the seller's business; (2) the buyer makes a partial payment or a partial acceptance, although the contract will be enforced only for the portion of goods paid for or accepted; or (3) the party being sued admits in court, or in court documents, that a contract was made for a certain quantity of goods. These same exceptions also apply to lease contracts that would otherwise require a writing.

UCC § 2-201 also contains a novel provision that may trap the unaware merchant. A **merchant** who receives a signed written confirmation (e.g., "This is to confirm our sale to you of 2,000 bushels of apples, #6 grade, at $1.25/bushel, delivery Tuesday /s/ Seller") from another merchant and does not object to the confirmation in writing within 10 days is bound to the contract. The policy underlying this result is a familiar one: A valid oral contract on the terms stated must exist if the other party (who, as a merchant, is considered a "pro") does not object to the confirmation. The moral of this section of the UCC is: Answer your mail, merchants!

Writing

As we have seen in other contexts, the writing required to satisfy the Statute of Frauds may be rather negligible; it may take the form of letters, telegrams, receipts, or memoranda. The writing must, at a minimum, identify the parties to the agreement, the subject matter of the agreement, and all material terms and conditions. Several writings may be pieced together as long as they all refer to the same transaction.

Signature

Similarly, anything intended by the parties as a signature will suffice to satisfy the Statute of Frauds. This, of course, would include written signatures; but courts even have held stamped signatures or stationery letterheads to be sufficient. The memorandum need not be signed by both parties as long as the party against whom enforcement is sought, or the party's authorized agent, has signed.

Note how the court in deciding the following case uses these principles.

13.1

MANAGEMENT

CHECKING THE MAIL

The Kochanowskis traditionally take a two-week family vacation during the summer. Anna is concerned that, if the family takes such a vacation, mail sent to the firm will go unanswered. She suggests that they select an employee to check the mail daily during their absence. Tom does not like the idea of having an employee reading CIT's mail. He asserts that two weeks is not such a long time, and that he and Anna can catch up with the mail on their return. Anna continues to insist that the firm cannot afford to ignore its mail for two weeks. They have asked for your advice. What will you tell them? Does the time involved affect your answer?

BUSINESS CONSIDERATIONS Why is it important for a businessperson to read and react to his or her mail in a timely manner?

ETHICAL CONSIDERATIONS Is it ethical to hold a merchant responsible for mail received but not answered (or even read), when the same rules do not apply to a nonmerchant? Why does the distinction between merchants and nonmerchants matter?

13.3 BARBER & ROSS CO. v. LIFETIME DOORS, INC.

810 F.2d 1276 (4th Cir. 1987), CERT. DENIED 484 U.S. 823 (1987)

FACTS Barber & Ross (B & R) purchases millwork products, including doors, from manufacturers, prepares them for installation in new homes, and sells them to new home builders. Lifetime Doors, Inc. (Lifetime) is a large manufacturer of doors. In 1982, B & R began to buy various types of doors from Lifetime. In early 1983, Lifetime supplied B & R with sales literature that promised new purchasers "continuous production availability . . . in full proportion to monthly needs" that would ensure that purchasers could "order flexible quantities" in shipments of a "desired number" if they joined Lifetime's VIP Club. B & R's president entered into an oral agreement with Lifetime whereby Lifetime promised to supply B & R's requirements of four truckloads of six-panel doors each month, in return for which B & R would purchase doors exclusively from Lifetime.

From the middle of March to the middle of May that year, B & R purchased both flush and six-panel doors exclusively from Lifetime under this agreement. However, in May, owing to its shortages of these types of doors, Lifetime suggested that B & R should purchase the six-panel doors from other manufacturers.

In July, Lifetime instituted an "allocation system" that tied purchases of the more popular six-panel doors to sales of the less desirable flush doors. This system caused B & R

13.3 BARBER & ROSS CO. v. LIFETIME DOORS, INC. *(cont.)* 810 F.2d 1276 (4th Cir. 1987), CERT. DENIED 484 U.S. 823 (1987)

to buy more flush doors than it needed and simultaneously resulted in B & R's receiving fewer six-panel doors. In September, citing the negative effects on B & R's business caused by Lifetime's policy, B & R terminated its contractual relationship with Lifetime. B & R then sued Lifetime, claiming that Lifetime's allocation system had violated the antitrust laws and that Lifetime had breached the requirements contract between the parties.

The trial court awarded B & R $2.1 million on these claims. On appeal, Lifetime argued that there could be no breach of contract because the alleged requirements contract was unenforceable under the Statute of Frauds.

ISSUE Was the alleged contract unenforceable under the Statute of Frauds?

HOLDING No. There was a sufficient writing to indicate that the parties had formed a contract for the sale of goods; and the party against whom enforcement was sought had signed this writing.

REASONING The written sales brochures Lifetime had given to B & R met the requirements of the Statute of Frauds's signature requirement because the Lifetime Doors trademark that appeared on the documents was sufficient to authenticate the brochures. The writings also stated a sufficiently definite quantity for purposes of the statute because they referred to meeting the purchaser's needs.

To be enforceable under this category of the Statute of Frauds, a writing must provide a basis for believing that the proffered oral evidence rests on a real transaction. To fulfill the requirements of the Statute of Frauds, the writing need not, however, conclusively establish the existence of a contract. Because the writings in this case had promised that Lifetime would meet the monthly needs of B & R, they were sufficient to support B & R's claim that the parties had reached an oral agreement to form a requirements contract.

BUSINESS CONSIDERATIONS What is a requirements contract? Why should Lifetime undertake an exhaustive examination of its sales brochures? After so doing, should it modify any of the language in the brochures? Why or why not? Should Lifetime have adopted the "allocation system" described here? Why or why not?

ETHICAL CONSIDERATIONS Lifetime's "allocation system" forced B & R to buy more flush doors and to receive fewer of the doors (i.e., the six-panel ones) B & R really wanted. Had Lifetime acted unethically toward B & R? Why or why not?

Exhibit 13.1 explains the scope of the Statute of Frauds, the elements required to find coverage, and the exceptions to the general rules.

PAROL EVIDENCE RULE

Parol evidence
Oral statements.

So far we have explored some of the concepts and rules concerning the application of the Statute of Frauds. We now turn to another important facet of contract law, the **parol evidence** rule. This rule is predicated on the belief that oral evidence should not be admissible to alter, add to, or vary the terms of an integrated, written contract. If the parties appear to have intended the writing as the final expression of their agreement, a court's allowing later oral or written evidence which contradicts that writing will call into question the whole process of reducing one's agreement to writing. For instance, assume that Larry and Ahmed sign a contract for the sale of a used car. They both agree, in writing, that the price of the car is $6,000. If Larry or Ahmed later tries to argue that the price is higher or lower and litigation ensues, the parol evidence rule will preclude oral testimony to this effect. Imagine the havoc a contrary rule would cause. By applying the parol evidence rule, courts therefore uphold the sanctity of totally integrated written contracts.

EXHIBIT 13.1 The Statute of Frauds

Types of Contracts Covered (and Which Must Be in Writing)	Elements	Exceptions
1. Contracts to answer for the debt of another if that person so defaults.	1. There are three parties.	1. Novations and other three-party transactions are not guaranty contracts but joint, original contracts.
	2. There are two promises, one original (debtor to creditor) and the other collateral (third-party guarantor to creditor).	
	3. The second promise is a promise to accept only secondary liability resulting from the default of another.	
	4. The intent of the parties determines whether a three-party transaction involves a collateral contract (which must be in writing) or an original contract (which can be oral yet still enforceable).	1. The "leading object" or "main purpose" doctrine may apply.
2. Contracts for interests in land.	1. The agreement involves buying, selling, or transferring interests in land.	1. The doctrine of part performance may take the contract out of the statute.
	2. Leases, easements, and sale agreements about standing timber and buildings attached to the land also are covered.	
3. Contracts not to be performed within one year of the date of their making.	1. Contracts in which it is impossible to perform the contract completely within one year of the date of the creation of the contract are involved.	1. Courts may circumvent the application of the statute by resorting to the fiction that it is possible (albeit not probable) for the contracts to be performed within one year.
		2. Part performance by one party has occurred.
		3. Circumstances that justify the application of promissory estoppel exist.
4. Promises by executors and administrators of estates.	1. The executors or administrators have promised to pay estate claims out of their own personal funds.	
5. Contracts made in contemplation of marriage.	1. One person has promised another person to pay a given amount or otherwise to perform a contractual duty in order to induce that person to enter a marriage.	

(continued)

EXHIBIT 13.1 The Statute of Frauds *(cont.)*

Types of Contracts Covered (and Which Must Be in Writing)	Elements	Exceptions
6. Contracts for a sale of goods priced at $500 or more (UCC § 2-201), or contracts for the lease of goods costing $1,000 or more (UCC § 2A-201).	1. The contract involves a sale or lease of goods. 2. The price of the goods must be at least $500, or the lease is for at least $1,000. 3. The writing is not insufficient if it omits or incorrectly states an agreed-on term, but the contract will be unenforceable beyond the quantity of goods shown in the writing. 4. The writing must be signed by the person (or by his or her authorized agent or broker) against whom enforcement is sought.	1. Between merchants, a written confirmation sent by one party to another must be objected to by the other within 10 days or the Statute of Frauds will be satisfied. 2. Oral contracts that are enforceable consist of those involving (a) specially manufactured goods not readily resellable in the ordinary course of the seller's business, (b) goods for which payment has been received, (c) goods for which acceptance has been made, or (d) an admission in a court proceeding by the person against whom enforcement is sought that a contract for sale was made.

Substantive law
The portion of the law that regulates rights, in contrast to law that grants remedies or enforces rights.

Because the parol evidence rule is designed to further a policy of protecting writings—those instruments representing the final intentions and terms of the parties—it actually is a rule of **substantive law** rather than a rule of evidence.

For a good example of how the parol evidence rule can become an issue, read the following case.

13.4 MAGNETIC COPY SERVICES, INC. v. SEISMIC SPECIALISTS, INC. 805 P.2d 1161 (Colo.App. 1990)

FACTS Magnetic Copy Services, Inc. (MCS) is a Colorado corporation that engages in the business of copying magnetic tapes. Seismic Specialists, Inc. (SSI) is a Colorado corporation that, by generating sound waves through a dynamite blast or other vibration equipment, conducts seismic surveys in areas of potential oil and gas exploration. SSI then records sound waves on magnetic tapes, which companies such as MCS duplicate for sale to SSI customers. On 22 October 1986, MCS and SSI signed a contract, prepared by MCS, involving MCS's copying of SSI's field tapes. The contract stated: "SSI agrees to provide MCS 3,000 field tapes to be copied for its clients within one year of this agreement. . . . MCS will pay SSI a commission of $10.00 per tape. . . ."

A year after the execution of the contract, SSI had provided only 1,399 tapes to MCS for copying. Nevertheless, SSI continued to provide tapes to MCS for copying during the fall of 1987.

During this one-year period, several events pertinent to the parties' agreement occurred. For instance, SSI lost one or two of its primary customers, which loss reduced the number of tapes SSI could produce to provide for copying to MCS. In addition, SSI had several hundred tapes copied by companies other than MCS because SSI's customers wanted either a shorter turnaround time on the copying than MCS could provide or wanted a different copying method. Moreover, during this one-year contract period, MCS had cash-flow difficulties; and, at times, it delayed making payments to SSI after it (MCS) had received payment from these customers. At those times, SSI allowed MCS significant flexibility in making its payments.

MCS claimed that SSI's failure to produce 3,000 tapes within one year of the contract constituted a breach of the contract and that SSI therefore was not entitled to its commission on certain tapes, including the last 43 tapes provided before 22 October 1987, the anniversary date of the

13.4 MAGNETIC COPY SERVICES, INC. v. SEISMIC SPECIALISTS, INC. 805 P.2d 1161 (Colo.App. 1990)

signing of the contract. Furthermore, MCS argued that it need not pay a commission to SSI for the 538 tapes copied during the months of November and December 1987.

At trial, the court allowed SSI and MCS's employees to testify about the provision specifying that SSI would provide 3,000 tapes to MCS. SSI's employees testified that the reference in the contract to 3,000 tapes constituted a goal, not a guarantee. These employees, however, also testified that SSI always had intended to provide 3,000 tapes but was not able to do so within the year. MCS's employees testified that they had construed SSI's statement as a promise or commitment to provide 3,000 tapes within one year. MCS, moreover, viewed the terms of the contract as clear and unambiguous and thus asserted that the trial court improperly had used parol evidence to vary the terms of the contract.

ISSUE Did the trial court, in admitting parol evidence concerning this contract provision, commit reversible error?

HOLDING Yes. Because the contract provision in dispute here is unambiguous, the trial court, in admitting parol evidence regarding the terms of the provision in question, erred.

REASONING In the absence of an ambiguity, extrinsic evidence cannot vary the terms of a written agreement. Moreover, courts must enforce an unambiguous agreement according to its express terms. The determination of whether a contract is ambiguous remains a question of law for the court, and the trial court's conclusion will not necessarily bind an appellate court. Settled law holds that the mere disagreement between the parties regarding the proper interpretation of a contract, in itself, does not create an ambiguity.

Here, SSI argued that (1) the contract is ambiguous because of the omission of the term "guarantee" and that (2) the testimony that SSI's promise to provide 3,000 tapes merely connoted a goal therefore is admissible to confirm the ambiguity and to explain the intent of the parties. However, the phrase "agrees to provide" constituted an unambiguous promise by SSI to provide MCS with 3,000 tapes within a year of the contract. Furthermore, the contract neither conditioned SSI's performance on any set of circumstances nor stated or implied that providing 3,000 tapes within a year represented merely a goal or objective. Yet the trial court had admitted without objection SSI's testimony regarding the 3,000-tape "goal," and SSI implicitly had argued that MCS's failure to object to this parol evidence would mandate the affirmance of the trial court's determination.

The parol evidence rule is one of substantive law, not merely one of evidence. Therefore, if, as here, a contract is unambiguous, the trial court, even if it has received parol evidence without objection, must ignore it. As S. Williston states in *Contracts,* § 631: "[Because the parol evidence rule] is one of substantive law, and not a mere rule of evidence, testimony introduced in violation of the rule, even in the absence of objection thereto, can be given no legal effect." Although the trial court could consider parol evidence to determine if a contract is ambiguous, if, as here, after hearing the evidence the court concludes that the contract is unambiguous, the court should strike the parol evidence. Thus, the trial court erred in using parol evidence to vary the terms of an unambiguous contract; and its interpretation of the contract premised thereon accordingly could not stand.

BUSINESS CONSIDERATIONS What preventive steps could MCS and SSI have taken to avoid this litigation? If you were the CEO of each corporation, what corporate policies—or changes—would you institute as a result of this lawsuit?

ETHICAL CONSIDERATIONS Was it unethical for SSI to remain in a contract, the terms of which it was failing to fulfill? What actions—if any—should MCI have taken early on vis-à-vis SSI and vice versa?

EXCEPTIONS TO THE PAROL EVIDENCE RULE

The preceding notwithstanding, courts will disregard the parol evidence rule and will admit parol evidence in certain circumstances. The following sections describe common circumstances in which the parol evidence rule is not applied.

13.2

SALES/MANUFACTURING

MUST AN ORDER BE IN WRITING?

Tom recently placed an order for a $5,000 custom-designed piece of equipment to be used in the production of the videophones. The order was placed over a CIT videophone (of course), with no writings exchanged between the parties. Soon after placing the order, Tom discovered that it would be cheaper for CIT to subcontract this aspect of the production process, and he decided to try to cancel his order. Unfortunately, when he called the seller, he was informed that the equipment was already en route. Tom remembers that the Statute of Frauds requires a writing for any contract for the sale of goods for $500 or more. He asks you if this means he can refuse to accept the equipment without liability. What will you tell him?

BUSINESS CONSIDERATIONS What should a business do to protect itself when it regularly takes telephone orders for the sale of goods and those goods regularly cost $500 or more? How can the business protect itself from buyers who change their minds after placing their orders?

ETHICAL CONSIDERATIONS Is it ethical for a buyer to take advantage of a "loophole" in the law to escape a contract that he or she *did*, in fact, enter, even though there is no writing to prove that he or she agreed to the contract? Is enforcement of the Statute of Frauds provisions unethical?

Partially Integrated Contracts

The policy base that underlies the parol evidence rule is not as compelling in situations in which the contract is partially integrated (i.e., incomplete). In such cases, although the writing may not be contradicted by evidence of earlier terms, it may be supplemented by evidence of additional, consistent terms.

Mistake, Fraud, and Other "Reality-of-Consent" Situations

Parol evidence similarly is admissible to show mistake, fraud, duress, and failure of consideration—the kinds of situations covered in Chapter 12. Since the existence of these circumstances casts doubt on the validity of the integrated writing, there is no overwhelmingly persuasive policy reason to justify the exclusion of contradictory oral statements.

Ambiguities and Conditions Precedent

Courts also will allow parol evidence in order to clear up ambiguities (remember the "chicken" example) and to show that the agreement was not to become binding on the parties until a *condition precedent* (i.e., a certain act or event that must occur before the other party has a duty to perform or before a contract exists) was met, such as reduction of the agreement to writing or approval of the contract by a party's attorney. However, courts may allow evidence about a condition precedent only if this evidence does not contradict the written terms of the contract at issue.

Uniform Commercial Code

Sections 2-202 and 2-208 of the UCC concern the parol evidence rule. Basically, the Code recognizes the rule but then reduces its impact by stating that evidence of course of dealing (the parties' previous conduct), usage of trade (a regularly observed practice in a trade), and course of performance (a contract that contemplates repeated occasions of performance) is admissible. Courts also can admit evidence of consistent, additional terms unless they find that the parties intended the writing as a complete and exclusive statement of the terms of the agreement. Moreover, the Code sets up priorities among these types of evidence: The express terms of the agreement control course of performance, course of dealing, and usage of trade. Evidence relating to course of performance, in turn, controls admissions about course of dealing and usage of trade.

Section 2A-201 of the UCC covers the Statute of Frauds' provisions concerning contracts for the lease of goods. Section 2A-201 requires a writing when the total payments under the lease contract total $1,000 or more, excluding any payments for an option to renew the lease or any payments for an option to buy.

JUDICIAL INTERPRETATION

In previous chapters, we stressed the importance of a *meeting of the minds* of the parties to the contract. Imprecise though this phrase is, it highlights one of the essential elements of a contract: The parties of necessity must have indicated, by their words or conduct, an intention to agree about some matter. Yet because language is an imprecise vehicle of expression, it subsequently may become apparent that the parties were not binding themselves to identical terms and courses of action (witness the "chicken" controversy). When this variance in expectations surfaces, disputes arise. If the parties cannot resolve these disputes, courts must interpret what the contract "really says." This last aspect of contract formation focuses on issues that arise from the wording chosen by the contracting parties.

Interpretation is the process used to determine the meaning of the words and other manifestations of intent that the parties used to forge their agreement when the language of the agreement is unclear. Ascertaining the parties' intent in order to enforce the contract as the parties wished, however, is not easy. Problems arise primarily because words are symbols of expression and can take on an almost infinite number of meanings. Moreover, words do not exist in a vacuum. Determining how a certain party intended to use words or actions therefore becomes a factual issue. A court must examine one party's understanding and conduct in the situation, but it also must be conscious of how other reasonable persons would have understood these same words and actions under similar circumstances. In deciding between two competing views, courts often must consider the intentions of the parties through a frame of reference known as the "reasonable person," or objective, approach. This perspective allows the court to choose the interpretation that would be most consonant with the expectations of a reasonable person in the same circumstances. Although an imperfect method, it at least ensures that the interpretation the court chooses is not so divergent from normality that it becomes nonsensical.

13.3

MANAGEMENT

MERGER CLAUSES

The Kochanowskis have recently reviewed the standard form contracts the firm uses, and they have decided to revise some of these forms. As a part of this revision, Dan suggests that the firm include a so-called "merger clause" stating that the written contract represents the parties' agreement, and that the written terms supersede any previous oral communications. They have asked you whether such a "merger clause" is a good idea for CIT. What advice will you give them on this matter?

BUSINESS CONSIDERATIONS Should a business develop a policy that all its written agreements be designed and treated as fully integrated contracts? Why might this be a good policy? What potential drawbacks would such a policy present?

ETHICAL CONSIDERATIONS Is it ethical for a salesperson to orally imply that the item he or she is selling is better than it really is, knowing that the firm uses a fully integrated written contract that tempers the sales presentation and its language? What ethical issues does this present?

Standards

Because interpretation involves comparing the parties' words and conduct from some other perspective, certain standards of interpretation have evolved over the years. Probably the most common is the standard of *general usage,* or the meaning that a reasonable person who was aware of all operative uses and who was acquainted with the circumstances involved prior to and during the making of the agreement would attach to the agreement. For example, Paul signs an agreement in which he gives $10,000 as a life membership fee for admission to a nursing home. The agreement states that for a trial period of two months, either Paul or the nursing home can suspend the agreement. Upon the occurrence of that event, the $10,000 (minus $200 per month) will be returned. What if Paul unfortunately dies after one month in the home? Can his estate recover the $9,800, or has the life membership fee been paid irrevocably? By resorting to the standard of general usage, a court in a similar case decided that a reasonable person in Paul's "shoes" at the time of the execution of the contract would have understood the provision to mean that unless and until life membership status were obtained, the nursing home should return the money (less the amounts specified) to him. The court also asserted that if the nursing home had intended to retain the money in the event of a probationary member's death, it should have expressly stated this fact in the contract. Had the facts been different, the court might have applied the standard of *limited usage* (the meaning given to language in a particular locale) instead of the standard of general usage.

Total Integration

The standards employed in contract interpretation, moreover, can turn on whether the contract is totally integrated. A *totally integrated* contract is one that represents the parties' final and complete statement of their agreement. Such a contract can neither be contradicted nor supplemented by evidence of prior agreements or expressions. The law assumes that the writing supersedes the terms set out earlier in preliminary negotiations.

Partial Integration

If a writing is intended to be the final statement of the parties' agreement but is incomplete, it is a *partially integrated* contract. Such a writing cannot be contradicted by evidence of earlier agreements or expressions, but it can be supplemented by evidence of additional, consistent terms. Perhaps Paul and the nursing home orally agreed that his personal physician (rather than the nursing home's) will provide needed medical care. If the parties leave out this provision, the contract represents a partially integrated writing. Since this provision does not appear to contradict the original agreement, some courts may allow the parties to add it to the agreement later.

Rules of Integration

In general, the more formal and complete the instrument, the more likely a court will find it to be a totally integrated agreement. According to the *rules of integration,* exchanges of letters, telegrams, and memoranda may indicate the formation of a contract; but they cannot represent the final intentions of the parties. Rather, these communications may show only tentative and preliminary agreement. Some judges employ different standards of interpretation, depending on whether there has been integration. When no integration has occurred, judges may use the standard of reasonable expectations—that is, the meaning one party reasonably expects the other to attribute to a term, given what the first party has said or done. If John is trying to buy a "fully equipped" car and a dispute later arises as to whether an air conditioner is included, a court will need to scrutinize the car salesperson's representations. If the agreement is integrated, a judge may instead apply the standard of limited usage—the meaning of the term as understood locally and in the trade—to see whether "fully equipped" cars ordinarily include air conditioners.

Rules of Interpretation

To supplement the appropriate standard of interpretation, courts also use *rules of interpretation*. Although authorities disagree as to the relative importance of these rules, you should be aware of the following common ones:

1. Courts should attempt to give effect to the manifested intentions of the parties.
2. Courts should examine the contract as a whole in order to ascertain the intentions of the parties.
3. Courts should give ordinary words their ordinary meanings and technical words their technical meanings, unless the circumstances indicate otherwise.
4. Subject to the requirements of the parol evidence rule, courts should take into account all the circumstances surrounding the transaction.

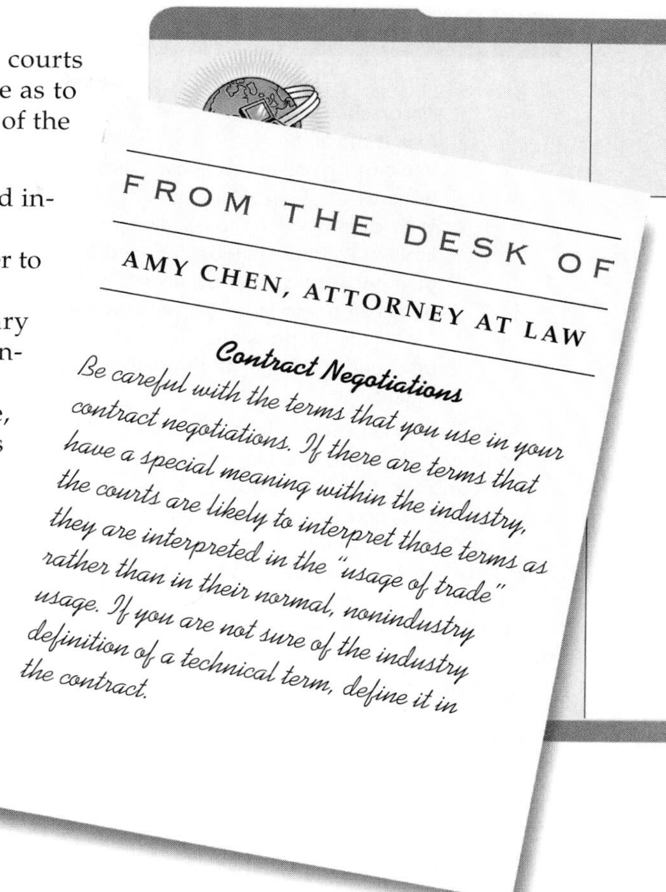

FROM THE DESK OF
AMY CHEN, ATTORNEY AT LAW
Contract Negotiations
Be careful with the terms that you use in your contract negotiations. If there are terms that have a special meaning within the industry, the courts are likely to interpret those terms as they are interpreted in the "usage of trade" rather than in their normal, nonindustry usage. If you are not sure of the industry definition of a technical term, define it in the contract.

Other rules state that reasonable constructions are favored when unreasonable alternative constructions are possible, that the main purpose of the agreement and all parts of the instrument will be given effect if possible, that special and specific words or provisions control general ones, that written words control printed ones, that words will be construed most strictly against the party who drafts the agreement, and that contracts affecting the public interest will be construed in favor of the public.

The following case demonstrates how vital interpretation is in determining what the wording of a contract means when disagreements subsequently develop. Note that in disposing of this case, the court used some of the concepts just discussed.

13.5 RODRIGUEZ v. GENERAL ACCIDENT INS. CO. OF AMERICA — 808 S.W.2d 379 (Mo. 1991)

FACTS On 11 September 1987, Gail Rodriguez received injuries when the vehicle she was driving collided with a vehicle operated by John Fruehwirth. Fruehwirth's insurance company paid Rodriguez $50,000, the limits of liability under Fruehwirth's insurance policy. Rodriguez sought the balance of her damages from her insurance carrier, General Accident Insurance Company of America (General Accident), pursuant to the policy's "underinsured motorist coverage." The face sheet of the policy in question showed various coverages for two automobiles, including underinsured motorist coverage, with a limit of $50,000 on each vehicle. The salient portions of the Underinsured Motorist Coverage Endorsement provided the following:

Underinsured Motorist Coverage

INSURING AGREEMENT

A. *We will pay damages which an "insured" is legally entitled to recover from the owner or operator of an "underinsured motor vehicle" because of "bodily injury," 1. Sustained by an "insured."...*

LIMIT OF LIABILITY

A. *The limit of liability shown in the schedule for this coverage is our maximum limit of liability for all damages resulting from any one accident.* This is the most we will pay regardless of the number of:

13.5 RODRIGUEZ v. GENERAL ACCIDENT INS. CO. OF AMERICA *(cont.)* 808 S.W.2d 379 (Mo. 1991)

1. *"Insureds";*
2. *Claims made;*
3. Vehicles or premiums shown in the Declarations; *or*
4. *Vehicles involved in the accident.* However, the limit of liability shall be reduced by all sums paid because of the "bodily injury" by or on behalf of persons or organizations who may be legally responsible. *This includes all sums paid under part A of this policy.* [emphases added]

Citing this contractual language, General Accident declined to pay. Owing to the alleged ambiguity of the wording of the contract, the Rodriguezes, in bringing this action, sought both to recover under the uninsured motorist coverage and to have their underinsured motorist coverage "stacked," thereby realizing a total of $100,000 in underinsured motorist coverage. Holding that under the insurance contract, Fruehwirth was not an "underinsured motorist," the trial court sustained General Accident's motion for summary judgment. The Rodriguezes appealed this decision.

ISSUE Was the Rodriguezes' insurance contract sufficiently ambiguous to warrant the application of the objective reasonable expectations test to resolve this alleged ambiguity?

HOLDING No. In the absence of statutes or public policies requiring the construction advocated by the Rodriguezes, the law mandated the enforcement of insurance policies as written when such policies are unambiguous.

REASONING The Rodriguezes argued that the ambiguity of their insurance contract with General Accident entitles them to a resolution of this ambiguity consistent with their objective reasonable expectations. They further submitted that application of the objective reasonable expectations doctrine renders their underinsured motorist coverage as excess coverage entitling them to $50,000 in coverage beyond that previously paid by Fruehwirth's insurer.

The law holds that an ambiguity arises when there is duplicity, indistinctness, or uncertainty in the meaning of the words used in the contract. If there is a conflict between a technical definition within a contract and the meaning that the average layperson reasonably would understand, a court will apply the layperson's definition unless it plainly appears that the parties intended the technical meaning. The law will not permit a court to create an ambiguity in order to distort the language of an unambiguous policy or in order to enforce a particular construction it believes more appropriate. Thus, where insurance policies are unambiguous, in the absence of a statute or public policy requiring coverage, courts will enforce such agreements as written.

The contract between General Accident and the Rodriguezes clearly states that an underinsured motor vehicle is a vehicle whose limits for bodily injury liability are "less than the limit of liability for this coverage." By their own admission, the Rodriguezes acknowledged that Fruehwirth's liability insurance coverage was $50,000. Since Fruehwirth's coverage equals the limit of liability under the Rodriguezes' policy, Fruehwirth would not qualify as an underinsured motorist as defined by the Rodriguezes' policy. Moreover, a setoff provision of the Rodriguezes' policy, which provides that "the limit of liability shall be reduced by all sums paid because of the 'bodily injury' by or on behalf of persons or organizations who may be legally responsible . . ." reinforces this definition of underinsured motorist. Indeed, this provision sets off the $50,000 paid by Fruehwirth's insurer against the $50,000 coverage provided by General Accident.

The underinsured motorist coverage, therefore, does not, as the Rodriguezes argued, equate with excess coverage. Instead, that coverage provides a total amount of protection General Accident will pay to the Rodriguezes if the other persons legally responsible for Mrs. Rodriguez's injuries have lesser liability limits than those provided under the Rodriguezes' underinsured motorist coverage.

The Rodriguezes also contended that the court should permit them to "stack" the underinsured motorist coverage of each of their two vehicles insured by the General Accident policy, thereby yielding a combined limit of $100,000. The contract language applicable to this issue—"The limit of liability shown in the schedule for this coverage is the maximum limit of liability for all damages resulting from any one accident. This is the most we will pay regardless of the number of . . . vehicles or premiums shown in the Declarations"—clearly and unambiguously constitutes an antistacking provision. In the absence of ambiguity and any public policy violations, courts will enforce the clear language of the contract. Hence, the trial court in these circumstances properly granted summary judgment in favor of General Accident.

BUSINESS CONSIDERATIONS Should Congress pass a federal "truth-in-insurance" law mandating that all insurance agents go over each policy line-by-line with each insured person? What would be the advantages and disadvantages of such a law?

13.5 RODRIGUEZ v. GENERAL ACCIDENT INS. CO. OF AMERICA *(cont.)* 808 S.W.2d 379 (Mo. 1991)

ETHICAL CONSIDERATIONS Most states require proof of insurance as a condition of receiving a license for a vehicle. Is such a law, assuming it has an adverse impact on poorer persons who seek vehicle tags, ethical? In a related vein, it is common knowledge that in order to get a license, some people take out a policy and then let the policy lapse after one month. Does a state have an ethical issue to oversee those who receive licenses so that these kinds of circumventions of the law become impossible?

YOU BE THE JUDGE

What Is Considered a Valid Insurance Claim?

While sitting on the passenger side of his parked truck, which had the ignition key in the "off" position, Jeffrey W. Peterson's shotgun discharged, shooting Peterson in the foot. When the shotgun discharged, Peterson apparently was about to alight from his truck to go deer hunting. Peterson filed a claim with his auto insurance company, State Farm Mutual Automobile Insurance Co. State Farm denied Peterson's request for benefits because State Farm determined that his injury had not arisen from "the use or operation of the vehicle." If this case were brought in *your* court, how would *you* rule?[1]

BUSINESS CONSIDERATIONS Why might an insurance company decide to deny a claim filed by one of its customers? Is it a better business practice to honor as many claims as possible, or to deny any claims that are questionable unless ordered to pay by the court?

ETHICAL CONSIDERATIONS Is it ethical for an insured to file a questionable claim with his or her insurance company when an incident arises that costs the insured money? What ethical issues are raised by such conduct?

SOURCE: *The National Law Journal* (14 October 1996), p. A27.

Conduct and Usage of Trade

The *conduct* of the parties often aids in contract interpretation. If the court is in doubt, it will follow the interpretation placed on the agreement by the parties themselves. For example, when one party for years has accepted a grade of wool inferior to the contract specifications, evidence of this conduct will be admissible in determining how to interpret the specifications. Uniform Commercial Code § 2-208, which covers course of performance, course of dealing, usage of trade, and contract construction, incorporates this rule of interpretation. Therefore, note its importance to the concept of contract interpretation and the courts' increasing reliance on it in Code transactions.

http:// RESOURCES FOR BUSINESS LAW STUDENTS

NAME	RESOURCE	WEB ADDRESS
Uniform Commercial Code (UCC) § 2-201	The Legal Information Institute (LII), maintained by the Cornell Law School, provides a hypertext and searchable version of UCC § 2-201, Formal Requirements; Statute of Frauds.	http://www.law.cornell.edu/ucc/2/2-201.html
Uniform Commercial Code § 2-202	LII provides a hypertext and searchable version of UCC § 2-202, Final Written Expression: Parol or Extrinsic Evidence.	http://www.law.cornell.edu/ucc/2/2-202.html
The American Law Institute	The American Law Institute, publisher of Restatements of the Law, Model Codes, and other proposals for law reform, provides press releases, its newsletter, and other publications.	http://www.ali.org

SUMMARY

In accordance with the Statute of Frauds, certain types of contracts must be in writing to be enforceable. These include collateral contracts, contracts for sale or transfer of interests in land, contracts not to be performed within one year from the date of their making, promises of executors and administrators of estates, promises made in consideration of marriage, and contracts for the sale of goods priced at $500 or more, or the lease of goods with payments of $1,000 or more. Nevertheless, very little in the way of a memorandum or signature is necessary to satisfy the Statute of Frauds. The parol evidence rule states that oral evidence is not admissible to alter, add to, or vary the terms of an integrated, written contract. However, the parol evidence rule will not be applied in some circumstances: partially integrated contracts; agreements involving mistake, duress, fraud, ambiguity, or conditions precedent; or in some commercial contexts. Interpretation is the process of determining the meaning of words and other manifestations of intent that the parties have used in forging their agreement. Over the years, certain standards and rules of interpretation, based on whether the contract is totally integrated or partially integrated, have evolved. A totally integrated contract represents the parties' final and complete statement of their agreement and cannot be contradicted. Similarly, a partially integrated contract is intended to be the parties' final statement; but it is incomplete. It may be supplemented with consistent, additional terms. The conduct of the parties and usage of trade may aid in contract interpretation as well.

DISCUSSION QUESTIONS

1. Explain both the historical and the current basis for the Statute of Frauds.
2. What are the most important characteristics of a collateral contract, or a contract to guarantee the debt of another if a person so defaults? Also, explain the exception to the rule that collateral contracts must be in writing.
3. Describe the exceptions to the rule that a contract for a sale of goods priced at $500 or more or the lease of goods with payments of $1,000 or more must be in writing.
4. What is the parol evidence rule?
5. Name and discuss the exceptions to the parol evidence rule.

6. What is the process of contract interpretation?
7. What is the legal difference between a totally integrated contract and a partially integrated contract?
8. Name and define any three rules of interpretation.
9. How are conduct and usage of trade important in contract interpretation?
10. Give an original example of a contract interpretation problem.

CASE PROBLEMS AND WRITING ASSIGNMENTS

1. John Parkos and Sheila Searcy had signed a lease–purchase agreement in which Searcy agreed to operate a restaurant on commercial premises owned by Parkos. When Parkos subsequently tried to evict Searcy, Searcy argued that the written lease–purchase agreement entitled her to remain in possession. Parkos, in turn, asserted that the agreement was invalid under the Statute of Frauds because the agreement incorrectly had identified the lessor and lessee and had omitted the exhibit that would have described the real property in detail, as well as the price and the terms of payment. Who had the better argument here, Parkos or Searcy? [See *Parkos* v. *Searcy,* 589 A.2d 1197 (R.I. 1991).]

2. National Microsales Corporation (NMC) is a Connecticut corporation engaged in the business of buying and selling computer output microfilming (COM) equipment. In 1988, Chase Manhattan Bank, N.A. (Chase), a national bank, entered into negotiations with NMC to sell some of its used COM equipment to NMC for resale. When Chase subsequently sold the equipment to a third party, NMC filed a breach of contract action against Chase. In June 1989, Chase moved for summary judgment on the basis of the Statute of Frauds. Striking Chase's affirmative defense of the Statute of Frauds on the ground that the "merchant's exception" (i.e., § 2-201[2]) to the statute covered these contracts, NMC cross-moved for summary judgment. Although a factual dispute as to whether Chase was a "merchant" for UCC purposes existed, the evidence showed that Chase had disposed of COM equipment worth $6.5 million. NMC also pointed out Chase's adoption of uniform procedures for purchasing new equipment and disposing of used equipment and other "surplus fixed assets," including procedures for soliciting bids from prospective purchasers of surplus property. However, George J. Stehle, Chase's vice president in charge of office purchasing and contracts administration, testified that Chase never purchases goods for resale and that Chase has no specialized knowledge concerning the goods that it buys for its own use. He also stated that Chase is unfamiliar with the market for the equipment that it purchases and that, when it disposes of surplus goods, it generally sells them to resellers, rather than end users, and usually sells the equipment for less than fair market value. Did Chase's status as a merchant preclude it from relying on the Statute of Frauds as an affirmative defense to the buyer's action for breach of contract? [See *National Microsales Corp.* v. *Chase Manhattan Bank, N.A.,* 761 F.Supp. 304 (S.D.N.Y. 1991).]

3. Gilbert M. Aust agreed to purchase a residence from Billy R. Webster at 2400 Whitesburg Drive, Huntsville, Alabama. Aust specifically wished to use the property for commercial purposes. According to Aust, Webster informed him that there were no restrictions on the property and that the property could be used for commercial purposes if Aust obtained a variance. Aust stated that he gave Webster a $5,000 check as "earnest money" but that the parties never executed a written contract for the sale of the land. Aust claimed that, after discovering restrictions limiting the property's use only to residential purposes, he demanded the return of his money and never took possession of the property. When Aust sued for fraud and the return of the $5,000 check, Webster counterclaimed for specific performance of the contract. At that point, Aust defended with the Statute of Frauds. Webster contended that the agreement fulfilled the Statute of Frauds, because the check Aust had tendered constituted a sufficient writing to satisfy the statute. On its face, the check contained some identifying information, including the names of the parties, the date, the check amount, Aust's signature, and some words describing its purpose. Who had the stronger argument here, Aust or Webster? [See *Webster* v. *Aust,* 628 So.2d 846 (Ala.Civ.App. 1993).]

4. Monica Guzman's friend, Barbara Graves, rented a car from AAA Auto Rental (AAA) in Bloomington, Indiana, and listed Guzman as an authorized driver. Guzman telephoned AAA to inform it that she would be driving the rental car to Chicago. At dusk on 8 November 1993, about 25 miles from her destination, the battery light went on in the car. About 10 minutes later, the temperature light came on. Skipping a couple of exits from the interstate, Guzman continued to drive the car toward her destination. The car eventually broke down on the interstate. Owing to Guzman's

failure to stop the car immediately after the warning lights had come on, the car's engine sustained damage from overheating. AAA had the car towed back to Bloomington where substantial repairs to the car's engine—including the resurfacing of the cylinder heads, a valve job, and the replacement of the fan relay switch—were made. Indeed, the towing and repair bills totaled nearly $1,000.00. Although Guzman testified that she had been afraid to pull off the highway earlier, the trial court found that Guzman willfully had failed to stop because she was anxious to reach her destination. Viewing Guzman's explanation of her actions as not credible, the trial court determined that Guzman had breached the car rental contract when she had failed to return the car in good and safe mechanical condition. The trial court also found Guzman liable for the damages because she had "committed vandalism by the willful infliction of damage to this car by continuing to drive it after knowing it was not operating properly."

In making this finding, the court relied on an Indiana statute governing motor vehicle rental companies and their contracts with customers, which statute permits rental companies to hold renters responsible "for physical or mechanical damage to the rented vehicle. . ., resulting from collision" and for "physical damage to the rented vehicle. . ., resulting from vandalism unrelated to the theft of the rented vehicle." On the basis of the second provision, the trial court entered judgment in favor of AAA in the amount of $1,437.00, which represented the sum of the towing and repair bills and AAA's attorneys' fees. Guzman on appeal argued that the trial court's judgment was contrary to law because the car had sustained mechanical, as opposed to physical, damages. Hence, she claimed, the rental company could recover for mechanical/engine damage only in the event of a collision. Whose interpretation—Guzman or AAA's—would seem more logical? Why? [See *Guzman* v. *AAA Auto Rental,* 654 N.E.2d 838 (Ind.App. 1995).]

5. In 1981, Dorasco Scarber and Jacqueline McLemore sued James and Frances Kelsoe for the amount due on a mortgage note executed by them in February 1983. The Kelsoes then counterclaimed, requesting that the court reform the mortgage note to reflect an annual interest rate of 10 percent. In 1981, Scarber and McLemore had entered into a contract to purchase a parcel of land owned by the Kelsoes. At that time, or shortly thereafter, in contemplation of closing the sale, Bishop Walker, an attorney, had prepared a note, a mortgage, and a closing statement. These documents contained provisions for the payment of 10 percent interest yearly. However, owing to Scarber's lack of funds, the parties did not consummate the sale. In 1982, the parties again entered into discussions concerning the sale of the Kelsoes' property; and, in February 1983, Scarber and McLemore purchased approximately 63 acres from the Kelsoes for $50,000. The Kelsoes themselves, taking a note and a second mortgage from Scarber and McLemore, financed over half of the sale.

   Russell, the attorney for the bank that had financed the remainder of the sales price, prepared the closing documents for the bank. Because of James Kelsoe's poor health, Russell took the deed that conveyed the property to the purchasers to the Kelsoes' home for the Kelsoes' signatures. After executing the deed, James Kelsoe informed Russell that it would be necessary to prepare a second mortgage and a note in the Kelsoes' favor. Russell did not take notes during this meeting at the Kelsoes' home. Because the Kelsoes had executed the deed earlier in the day, the Kelsoes did not attend the closing that afternoon at Russell's office, where Scarber and McLemore signed the note and the mortgage. Russell testified that it was his custom to return the original documents to the persons entitled to them and that he assumed that the Kelsoes had received the original note and the mortgage after Scarber and McLemore had signed them. James Kelsoe testified that he and his wife neither received the signed note prepared by Russell nor saw a copy of the note until the commencement of this action in 1990. The note that Russell intended to send to the Kelsoes apparently was sent, along with other documents, to First State Bank.

   The dispute in this case began when, in 1990, Scarber and McLemore requested a letter from the Kelsoes stating that the payoff balance to satisfy the Kelsoes' mortgage on the property amounted to $23,240.18. The Kelsoes refused to issue the requested letter. They argued that 10 percent interest was due on the principal amount from the date of the execution of the mortgage.

   Although the note signed by McLemore and Scarber contained no provision for the payment of interest, the trial court ruled that the parties actually had intended to enter into an agreement whereby Scarber and McLemore would pay interest in the amount of 10 percent per year. The trial court then reformed the note so that the payoff balance, including principal and interest, totaled $42,710.99. On appeal, Scarber and McLemore contended that the trial court had erroneously admitted parol evidence, documents, and correspondence relating to the unconsummated 1981 contract for the purchase of the Kelsoes' property. On appeal, how should the court rule? [See *Scarber* v. *Kelsoe,* 594 So.2d 68 (Ala. 1992).]

6. **BUSINESS APPLICATION CASE** Albert Vajda, a former manager with Arthur Andersen & Company (Andersen), sued Andersen for damages based on wrongful termination of his employment. Vajda, who had worked at Andersen for over 21 years, claimed that Andersen's employee manual precluded dismissal from employment except for just cause and through procedures that accorded with the company's three-warning policy. Andersen, while contesting the claim that the employee manual had set up enforceable contractual rights, also argued that, in any event, such a contract would be unenforceable under the Statute of Frauds. Discuss the specific provision of the Statute of Frauds on which Andersen had grounded this portion of its contentions and whether a court should agree with Andersen's reasoning. In addition, discuss the steps Andersen could have taken to avoid this litigation. [See *Vajda* v. *Arthur Andersen & Co.*, 624 N.E.2d 1343 (Ill.App. 1993).]

7. **ETHICS APPLICATION CASE** Alleging breach of an employment contract, Earl Maddox brought an action against his former employer, Corbett Plywood Company, and its parent company, Baxley Veneer and Clete Company (Baxley). Maddox asserted that when the lumber mill's owner, Horace Corbett, recruited him to work as general manager of the mill, Corbett had promised him that he could stay on the job until age 65. Maddox had left other lucrative employment to accept the job at the mill and had worked at the mill for two years without taking a vacation. Sometimes he had worked long hours. However, no written employment contract existed between the parties.

   When Corbett died in 1981, one month later, the mill fired Maddox. Maddox then sued for breach of contract. At trial, the employer, arguing that Georgia's Statute of Frauds makes oral contracts for employment longer than one year unenforceable, moved for a directed verdict. Maddox responded that the contract was enforceable because he had partially performed the contract within the meaning of a Georgia statute stating that oral contracts of employment for longer than one year are unenforceable unless "there has been part performance of the contract as would render it a fraud on the party refusing to comply if the court did not compel a performance."

   The trial court denied Baxley's motion for a directed verdict and refused to grant Baxley's requested instruction regarding what conduct would constitute part performance too insufficient to remove the contract from the coverage of the Statute of Frauds. The jury returned a verdict in favor of Maddox for $87,000. Baxley subsequently appealed this verdict. Should the appellate court reverse the jury's verdict? Many managers maintain that the "Golden Rule" represents the ethical standard they follow. Did the mill's treatment of Maddox comport with this precept? Why or why not? [See *Baxley Veneer and Clete Co.* v. *Maddox*, 404 S.E.2d 554 (Ga. 1991).]

8. **IDES CASE** Bakers Equipment/Wholesalers, Inc. (BE/W) is a New York corporation with its principal place of business in Bergen, New Jersey. Eugene Stoller owned 100 percent of the voting stock of BE/W and also served as the president and chief executive officer of the company. In June 1986, BE/W retained Sebaly, Shillito, & Dyer, a law firm, to investigate contemplated legal actions against certain individuals who allegedly had conspired to appropriate the business of and compete against the Mixer Division of BE/W located in Sidney, Ohio. The agreement between the firm and BE/W never was reduced to writing, but in July 1986 the firm filed a lawsuit alleging unfair competition. The law firm continued to represent BE/W from the initial investigation of the matter through the eventual settlement and dismissal of the case, which included the sale of the Mixer Division to the defendants in the lawsuit.

   According to the undisputed testimony of James Dyer, the partner in the law firm who had primary responsibility for litigating the unfair competition case, Stoller had, throughout the firm's representation of BE/W, without specifically making any personal commitment, given Dyer repeated assurances that the firm would be paid the delinquent fees and costs that had accrued. However, Dyer testified that, given the insolvent condition of BE/W, he viewed Stoller's assurances of payment as a personal commitment.

   When settlement negotiations began, other members of the firm expressed their misgivings about proceeding with these extensive negotiations in the absence of Stoller's personal guarantee for payment of legal fees and costs. To this end, in March 1987, Dyer telephoned Stoller and advised him that Stoller's personal commitment with respect to the account would be a prerequisite to the firm's continued representation of Stoller in the settlement negotiations. In the course of that telephone conversation with Dyer, Stoller agreed to pay the legal fees incurred by BE/W. The firm subsequently continued its representation of BE/W throughout the settlement negotiations and the sale of the business. The additional legal services and expenses incurred after the March conversation amounted to $9,650.66. When the trial court found in favor of the law firm, Stoller argued that he had not personally guaranteed BE/W's obligations; in the alternative, he claimed that the Statute of Frauds would render such a promise to answer for BE/W's debts unenforceable. How should the appellate court rule in this case? [See *Sebaly, Shillito, & Dyer* v. *Baker's Equipment/Wholesalers, Inc.*, 597 N.E.2d 1144 (Ohio App. 1991).]

NOTE

1. "Insurer Must Toe the Line," *The National Law Journal* (14 October 1996), p. A27.

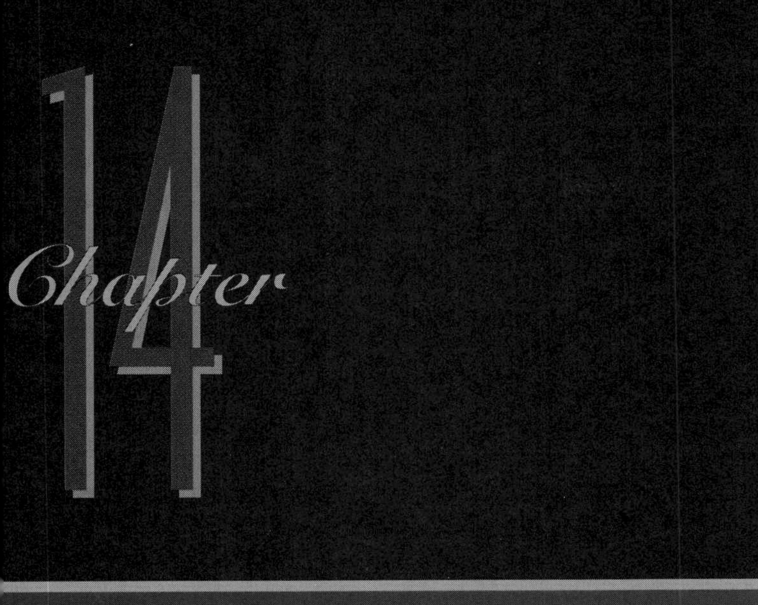

Chapter 14

The Rights of Third Persons

Outline

- Addition of Third Parties to the Relationship
- Third-Party Beneficiary Contracts
- Defining Assignments and Delegations
- Assignments
- Delegations
- Uniform Commercial Code Provisions
- Summary
- Discussion Questions
- Case Problems and Writing Assignments

Agenda

Third-party contracts are common in business situations. What happens when an intermediary contracts for parts and supplies to be shipped to CIT? What occurs when supplies are lost or destroyed in the possession of a trucking company? What if a loyal customer orders a videophone to be shipped to his or her mother for Mother's Day? What is the legal effect of CIT's purchasing liability insurance?

A retail distributor for CIT is having financial difficulties and owes CIT $65,000 for inventory CIT has already delivered. The distributor would like to transfer its accounts receivable—$40,000 worth, most of which are not past due—to CIT to discharge the distributor's obligation. Should CIT accept this arrangement? CIT is considering hiring other companies to serve as official repair centers for its videophones. What constraints should be evaluated by CIT before entering into these arrangements with other firms?

These and other questions will arise about the involvement of third parties. Be prepared! You never know when one of the Kochanowskis will ask you for help or advice.

ADDITION OF THIRD PARTIES TO THE RELATIONSHIP

A contract affects the legal rights of the two parties who enter into it. It may also influence the rights of other people. In some situations, these other people are so significant in the contract that they have legal rights under the contract and can file a lawsuit to enforce these contractual rights. The two types of situations are those in which the third person is significant when the contract is initially formed and those in which the third person is added later. This chapter discusses what enforceable legal rights, if any, these third persons have.

THIRD-PARTY BENEFICIARY CONTRACTS

Persons and corporations who immediately receive rights in a contract to which they are not a party are called *beneficiaries.* It is really more appropriate to call this kind of beneficiary a *third person* because the additional person is not a party to the contract. However, we shall use the common terminology and refer to this person as a *third party.*

The two people who enter into the contract are commonly called the promisor and the promisee. The *promisor* is the party who promises to perform; the *promisee* is the party to whom that promise is made. Often, in third-party beneficiary contracts, the promise is to deliver goods to or perform a service directly for a third party. For example, Jane is very busy; to save time in shopping for a Father's Day present and mailing it to her father in St. Cloud, Minnesota, she orders an expensive shirt from the Neiman-Marcus catalog to be gift wrapped and delivered to her father. This arrangement is a third-party beneficiary contract; her father is the third-party beneficiary. A beneficiary does not need to know about the contract for it to be valid.

Many businesses rely primarily on these contracts to achieve financial success. Examples include florist shops, singing telegram companies, mail-order companies that send fruit baskets, and life insurance companies.

Because these third parties are called beneficiaries, it is generally assumed that they receive something beneficial and good, but this is not always the case. The legal requirement for an intended beneficiary is that at least one of the contracting parties, usually the promisee, intended to have goods delivered to or services performed for the third party. The third party may not necessarily desire these goods or services. The beneficiary may, in fact, be displeased on receipt of the goods or services. An example is a singing telegram that embarrasses the recipient or is in poor taste.

An Incidental Beneficiary

Probably the most important factor in determining the rights of a third party is whether the third party is an intended or an incidental beneficiary. When the original parties to the contract, or at least one of them, *meant* to affect a noncontracting person by establishing the contract, the noncontracting person is an *intended beneficiary.* Intended beneficiaries have legal rights in the contract. If the benefit or action to the noncontracting party was *accidental,* or *not intended,* this party is an *incidental beneficiary.*

For example, suppose an owner of a vacant city lot decides to build a high-rise garage on it. The owner enters into a contract with a builder to construct the garage. The neighboring lot has a high-rise office building on it, so the owner of the office building will benefit financially by the construction of the garage. This person is an incidental beneficiary, because neither the builder nor the lot owner intended to benefit that person.

An Intended Beneficiary

An intended beneficiary does not have to be mentioned by name in the contract. It is sufficient for the parties to *clearly intend* to provide the beneficiary with rights under the agreement. In the absence of a clear expression of such an intent, the contracting parties are presumed to act for themselves. Sometimes the intended beneficiary may be one person from a group of people for whose benefit the contract was established. Automobile insurance, for example, is a contract between an insurance company and an automobile owner, but insurance is also partially for the benefit of drivers and pedestrians who share the road.

Suppose a legal environment professor signs a teaching contract with the university president. Do the students benefit from the employment contract? Of course. Are the students intended or incidental beneficiaries? They are one of the primary reasons for soliciting the faculty member's promise to teach, so the students are intended beneficiaries; they do not need to be listed in the contract. In fact, students may not even be specifically mentioned. However, both the faculty member and the university president know that students are one of the primary reasons for the employment contract. The legal relationships in this example are diagrammed in Exhibit 14.1 (page 354).

The distinction between intended and incidental beneficiaries is discussed in the following case.

14.1 THE GATEWAY COMPANY v. DiNOIA — 1994 Conn.Super. LEXIS 176 (Conn.Super. 1994)

FACTS W.T. Grant Company (Grant) was a tenant renting commercial property known as No. 41 Main Street, New Milford, Connecticut, from The Gateway Company (Gateway). Under the terms of an approximately thirty-year lease, Grant was obligated to keep the premises in good repair. DiNoia was the owner of a shopping center. Grant wanted to vacate the property owned by Gateway and move to the property owned by DiNoia. Grant signed a lease with DiNoia, which provided "in order to induce the tenant, Grant, to execute this lease, landlord, DiNoia, hereby assumes all of tenant's obligations under that certain lease and lease agreement dated June 17, 1954, between The Gateway Company . . . and Tenant Grant . . . [covering] premises known as No. 41 Main Street in the Town of New Milford. . . ." Gateway was not a party to this lease.

ISSUE Did Grant intend to benefit Gateway by entering into the lease provision with DiNoia?

HOLDING No.

REASONING An entity claiming to be a third-party beneficiary must claim and prove that the parties to the contract intended to benefit the entity. The language of the lease does not indicate an intention to benefit Gateway. No relationship was shown between Grant and Gateway that would make Grant desire to protect Gateway. Grant was merely trying to reduce its liability as much as possible. Gateway offered no supporting evidence on this crucial issue of intent.

The parties responsible for failure to maintain the property are Grant and/or Village Green, which was the tenant during the previous 9 years. [Village Green was originally named as a defendant in this case. It failed to appear before the trial court and a default judgment was entered against it. Note that Grant declared bankruptcy and was not a party to this lawsuit.]

BUSINESS CONSIDERATIONS What can a business do to help protect itself from entering into contracts

14.1 THE GATEWAY COMPANY v. DiNOIA *(cont.)* 1994 Conn.Super. LEXIS 176 (Conn.Super. 1994)

with firms that may become bankrupt? Is the potential bankruptcy of other businesses a serious risk? Why or why not?

ETHICAL CONSIDERATIONS Did DiNoia owe the landlord a duty to maintain the property in good repair? Why? Was the landlord behaving ethically in suing DiNoia? Why?

EXHIBIT 14.1 Intended Beneficiary

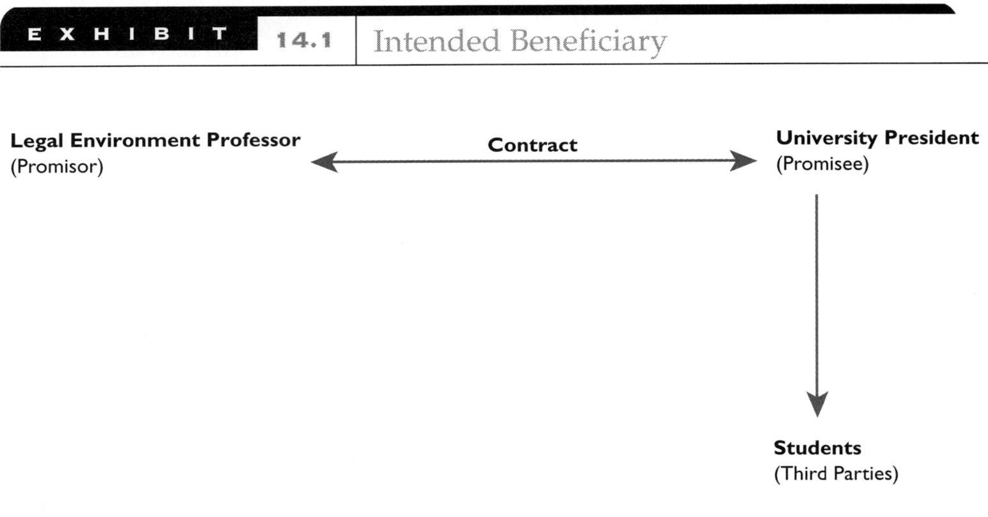

A Donee Beneficiary

The rights of an intended third-party beneficiary in a contract *may* be affected by the relationship between the promisee and the third party. If the promisee means to make a gift to the third party, the third party is a *donee beneficiary.* Life insurance policies are excellent examples of third-party beneficiary contracts. If a husband purchases a $100,000 life insurance policy from Prudential Insurance Company of America and names his wife as the beneficiary, she is a donee beneficiary. The husband has no legal obligation to purchase this insurance. (He might be under a legal obligation to purchase life insurance under some marital contracts or divorce decrees, but this is uncommon.) He is, in effect, planning a gift to his wife that will take effect at his death. She is a donee beneficiary. A donee beneficiary example is shown in Exhibit 14.2.

Prudential Insurance Company, the promisor, promises to deliver $100,000 to the promisee's wife if the promisee dies under situations covered by the policy. If Prudential refuses to pay, the wife may sue the company directly as an intended third party. Prudential (the promisor) can use the same legal defenses against the wife (the third party) as it can against the husband (the promisee). These defenses might include lack of capacity to enter into a contract, lack of mutual assent, illegality in the

EXHIBIT 14.2 Donee Beneficiary

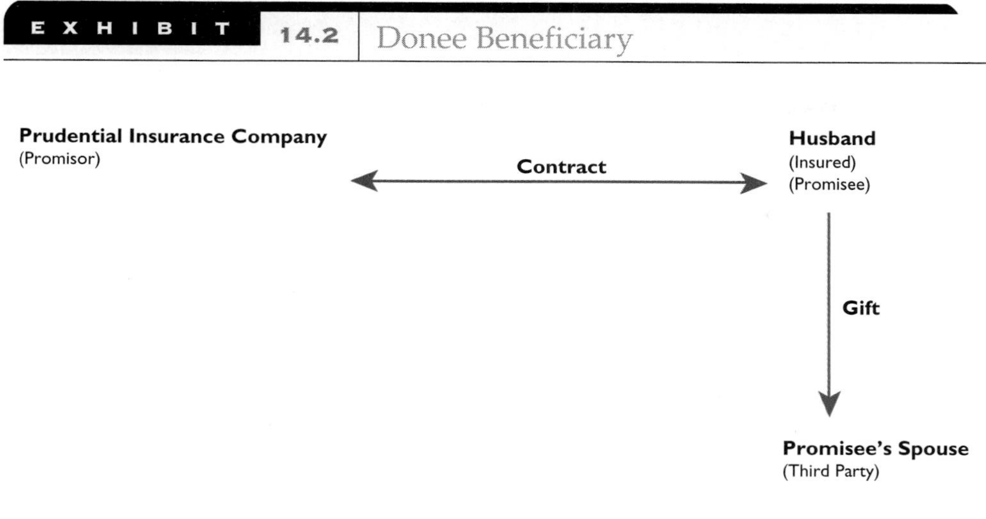

contract, mistake in contract formation, fraudulent statements about the promisee's health, an improperly formed contract, or cancellation of the policy. The promisor would not be obligated to make a payment if the cause of death is excluded by the terms of the contract. In addition, the courts usually disallow recovery by the beneficiary if the promisee failed to perform his or her duty under the contract.[1]

According to the law in some states, the donee beneficiary's rights cannot be terminated after the contract is made. However, the promisee can still defeat the rights of the donee by not performing his or her contractual obligations.[2] In other states, the beneficiary's rights are limited to situations in which the beneficiary knows about the contract and has accepted it verbally or by reliance on its terms. If the beneficiary has accepted the contract, the beneficiary has a **vested interest** in it. In these states, a beneficiary with a vested interest must consent before there can be an effective rescission of the contract. This rule applies to both donee and **creditor beneficiaries**. Even so, a donee beneficiary cannot prevent the promisee from taking some action that will defeat the rights of the donee beneficiary; for example, breaching the contract by refusing to pay for the goods or services.

In the following case, the court considered the legal rights of a donee beneficiary who was promised a gift of a house.

Vested interest
A fixed interest or right to something, even though actual possession may be postponed until later.

Creditor beneficiary
A third party who is entitled to performance because the promisee has a contractual obligation with him or her.

14.2 OMAN v. YATES — 422 P.2d 489 (Wash. 1967)

FACTS Noelene and John Sunday agreed to sell a house to Annette Suppa Oman. Oman signed the contract, but under the agreement she was not going to pay for the property; instead, George Rheims was going to pay the *complete* purchase price to the Sundays, in cash. Rheims wrote a check for the down payment, but his bank account lacked sufficient funds to cover the check. The Sundays did not receive any payment on the contract. Shortly thereafter, Rheims died and Yates was named the executor of Rheims's estate.

ISSUE Is Oman entitled to the house?

14.2 OMAN v. YATES (cont.) 422 P.2d 489 (Wash. 1967)

HOLDING No.

REASONING The Sundays did not receive payment. Oman is not entitled to specific performance. She was a donee beneficiary and could not require Rheims or his estate to complete the gift. Delivery is necessary to complete the gift, and the property was never delivered to Oman. Promises to make gifts in the future are not enforceable. Rheims had no contractual obligation to deliver the property to Oman. In a suit against the promisor, third-party beneficiaries have the same rights as the promisee. Oman could not require the Sundays to transfer the property to her, because they were not paid. Defenses which are valid against the promisee are valid against the third-party beneficiary. The Sundays could have requested specific performance, but they requested monetary damages instead. A settlement was worked out and they received monetary damages from Rheims's estate.

BUSINESS CONSIDERATIONS Should a business be concerned when it is dealing with a donee beneficiary in a contract? Is this the sort of situation for which the firm should develop a policy?

ETHICAL CONSIDERATIONS Is it ethical for a donee beneficiary to expect to receive the benefits of the contract when his or her donor fails to perform the contract as agreed? What ethical issues are raised in this sort of situation?

A Creditor Beneficiary

If the promisee owes a legal duty to the third party, the third party is a *creditor beneficiary.* In a contract between a university president and a professor for teaching services, the third-party beneficiaries are students. The students are creditor beneficiaries. This is true even at state-supported universities where tuition payments only constitute a portion of the cost of offering classes.

Another excellent example involves a life insurance policy. A working couple wishes to purchase a house with a $100,000 mortgage. The bank is willing to lend them $100,000 based on the value of the home and both of their salaries. Since the bank feels that the husband cannot afford the monthly payments without his wife's salary, the bank makes the loan contingent on the purchase of **mortgage insurance** on her life. She agrees to purchase a $100,000 mortgage insurance policy from Metropolitan Life Insurance Company. The bank is a creditor beneficiary. This arrangement is diagrammed in Exhibit 14.3.

Mortgage insurance
Insurance that will provide funds to pay the mortgage balance on a home if the insured dies.

If the wife dies during the term of the mortgage, the bank is entitled to sue Metropolitan directly on the insurance contract if Metropolitan refuses to pay. Metropolitan can use any defenses that it had against the wife as defenses against the bank.

If the wife tries to cancel the policy, the bank can successfully sue the wife, because to cancel the insurance policy and not replace it is a breach of the contract. The bank, however, will probably allow her to substitute another policy from a different insurance company if the coverage is essentially the same. In reality, if the bank does not trust the wife to make the premium payments, the bank will require her to make the payments through the bank; then, it will be assured that the premium payments are made in a timely manner.

The differences between donee and creditor beneficiaries are not significant. They both have basically the same rights against the promisor. Although many states say that the rights of a creditor beneficiary are directly derived from the promisee,

EXHIBIT 14.3 Creditor Beneficiary

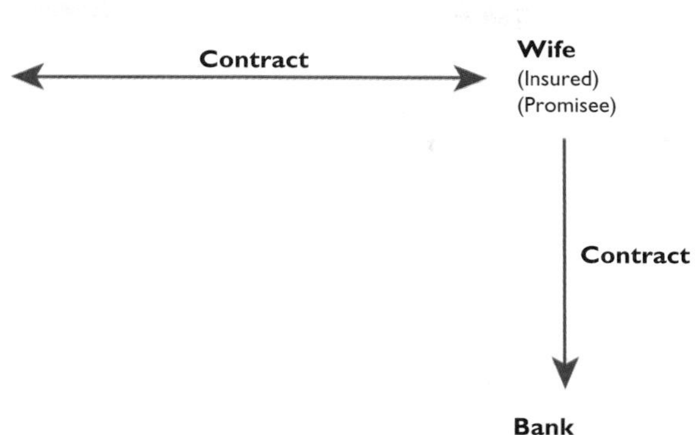

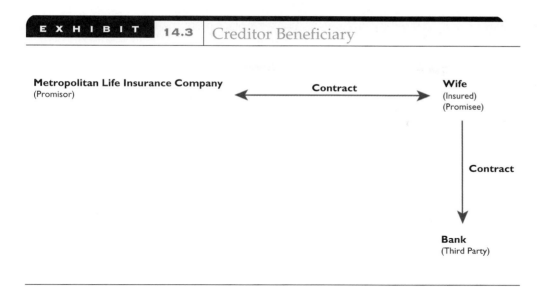

courts usually provide the same type of protection for the donee beneficiary as they do for the creditor beneficiary. The only real differences are their rights against the promisee, and even these differences are becoming less pronounced. The distinction between creditor and donee beneficiaries is excluded from the *Restatement (Second) of Contracts*,[3] which relies solely on the distinction between intended and incidental beneficiaries. The donee/creditor distinction is also beginning to disappear in some states, such as California.[4]

A third party cannot successfully claim any better rights than those provided in the contract. The following case examines the importance of the underlying legal rights.

Arbitration
Submission of claim to people (arbitrators) who will determine the rights of the parties.

14.3 HARRIS v. SUPERIOR COURT (MIRSAIDI) 233 Cal.Rptr. 186 (Cal.App. 1986)

FACTS The Harrises claimed that Dr. Mirsaidi was negligent in the birth of their daughter. They wished to have the dispute settled by **arbitration**. However, Dr. Mirsaidi wished to have the dispute settled by a court. The Harrises received medical care from Dr. Mirsaidi and Hawthorne Community Medical Group, Inc., under a prepaid health services program provided through Mr. Harris's employer. The enrollment form signed by Mr. Harris stated, "I agree that any claim asserted by a Member . . . against Maxicare, Hawthorne Community Medical Group, Inc. [three other entities], their employees or other contracting health professionals, pharmacies, or their employees for bodily injury to or death of a member, is subject to binding arbitration."

ISSUE Does Dr. Mirsaidi have the right to choose either arbitration or litigation?

HOLDING No.

REASONING The contract clause clearly provided that Hawthorne Community Medical Group was a party to the agreement. Hawthorne Community Medical Group could only provide medical care through its employees, such as Dr. Mirsaidi. Dr. Mirsaidi could not accept patients and payments under the terms of the contract *and* deny the arbitration clause. He knew or should have known of the existence of the clause. Dr. Mirsaidi is a third-party beneficiary of the contract entered into by Mr. Harris and Hawthorne Community Medical Group. Third parties cannot gain greater rights under the contract than the contracting parties already have. If Dr. Mirsaidi had been allowed to choose litigation, he would have been given greater rights.

14.3 HARRIS v. SUPERIOR COURT (MIRSAIDI) *(cont.)* 233 Cal.Rptr. 186 (Cal.App. 1986)

BUSINESS CONSIDERATIONS Why might a business prefer to have its disputes submitted to arbitration rather than to a court? Why might the business prefer *not* to have the controversy decided by arbitration?

ETHICAL CONSIDERATIONS Is it ethical for a business to include a mandatory arbitration clause in its contracts if arbitration reduces the potential rights of employees of the business who are *also* likely to be defendants in any dispute? Explain your reasoning.

14.1

MANAGEMENT/MANUFACTURING

LIABILITY FOR DAMAGES IN SHIPPING

CIT placed an order for 100 videoscreens from BG, a manufacturer in Palo Alto, California. CIT was a bit concerned because this was the first time CIT had ordered screens from this supplier, and the videoscreens are the most delicate component of the CIT videophones. BG packed the screens in sturdy cardboard boxes, 20 screens to a box, with foam pellets to cushion them. BG then contracted with Joe's Trucking to deliver the five boxes to CIT. When the boxes were delivered three weeks later, there was substantial damage to three of the boxes and their contents. CIT believes that the screens were in good condition when BG sent them, and that the damages occurred during the transportation of the screens. They have asked you who is responsible for the damaged goods. What will you tell them?

BUSINESS CONSIDERATIONS What steps could BG have taken to further reduce the risk of loss? How might Joe's Trucking and CIT have reduced the risk of loss? How could/should CIT protect its interests in future situations like this one?

ETHICAL CONSIDERATIONS Do BG and Joe's Trucking owe CIT moral obligations in addition to their legal obligations? Why or why not?

In this case, the mother and daughter were also third-party beneficiaries under the insurance contract the father signed.

Analysis of Third-Party Beneficiary Contracts

In analyzing a situation involving a potential third party, the following questions should be addressed:

1. Was the additional person involved from the beginning, or was that person added later?
2. Did the promisee intend to benefit the third party, or was it an accident?
3. Was the promisee making a gift to the third party, or was the promisee fulfilling a contract obligation to the third party?

DEFINING ASSIGNMENTS AND DELEGATIONS

If the third person becomes involved after the initial contract formation, that person is *not* a third-party beneficiary. Instead, the relationship may be either an assignment or a delegation. To understand the distinction between assignments and delegations, remember the distinction between rights and duties. *Contractual rights* are the parts of the contract a person is entitled to *receive.* Examples include delivery of goods, payment for goods, payment for work completed, and discounts for early payment. Payments owed to car dealers, mortgage companies, finance companies, and collection agencies are rights that are commonly assigned.

Contractual duties are the parts of the contract a person is obligated to *give.* These could include working an eight-hour day, paying 17 percent interest on credit card charges, and providing repair services. A common example is a general contractor who subcontracts certain aspects of a construction job such as installing the roof.

Rights can be assigned, and duties can be delegated. This may be confusing because judges and lawyers are sometimes careless in their use of terminology; however, duties *cannot* be assigned. A common example of contractual duties is a document that states "I assign all my rights and duties in the 8 April note with Tom Anderson." The rules of law dealing with delegation always will be applied to duties.

ASSIGNMENTS

An *assignment* occurs when a person transfers a contractual right to someone else. The transferor is called the *assignor,* and the recipient is called the *assignee.* The assignor loses the contractual right when the right is transferred to another party. The assignor's right has been **extinguished**, and now it belongs exclusively to the assignee. The other party to the original contract, the promisor, now has to deliver the promised goods or services to the assignee. The assignee is the only party entitled to them.

Extinguished
Destroyed, wiped out.

For example, Mira (a tenant) rents a house from Susan (a landlord). Under the terms of the lease, Mira must pay $400 per month for rent. Susan is in default on a small business loan obtained from the bank and assigns the $400 per month rent payment to the bank. Therefore, Susan (the assignor) has relinquished the legal right to the money—that right now belongs exclusively to the assignee, the bank. This situation is diagrammed in Exhibit 14.4.

Formalities Required for Assignments

Generally, an assignment does not have to follow any particular format. Assignors must use words that indicate an intent to vest a present right in the contract to the assignee. This means that the assignor intends to transfer the right immediately, not at some time in the future. However, this does not mean that the word *assignment* must be used. A writing is not required unless the state Statute of Frauds applies. This includes the Statute of Frauds' provisions in the Uniform Commercial Code (UCC) as adopted by the individual state. As with other contractual provisions, it is

EXHIBIT 14.4 Assignment

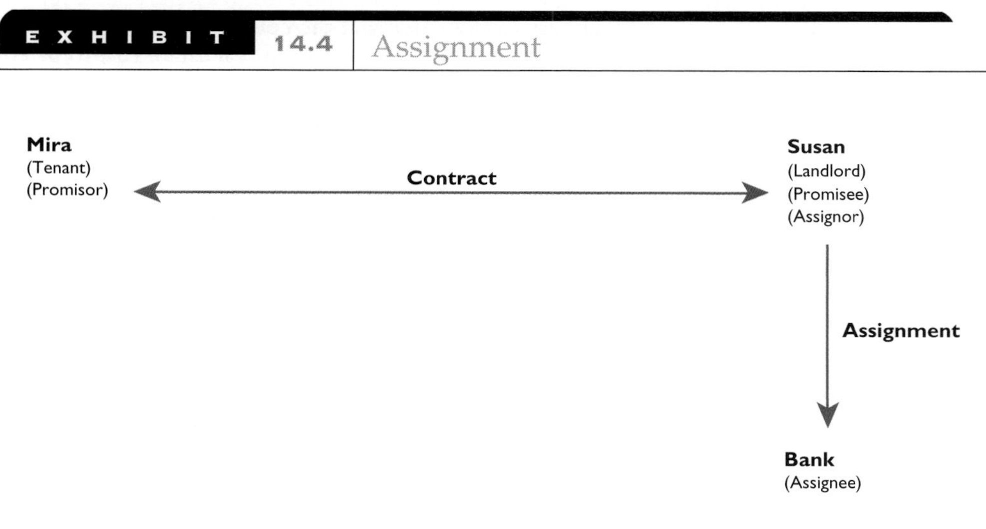

preferable to reduce the assignment to writing. The assignment must contain an adequate description of the rights being assigned.

Consideration, consisting of a bargained-for exchange and a legal detriment (or benefit) for both parties, is not required in order to have a valid assignment. (Consideration is discussed in detail in Chapter 11.) Although the assignee need not give up consideration in exchange for the contract right, consideration is generally present. This factor affects the legal relationship between the assignor and the assignee—that relationship can be either a contract or a gift. However, the relationship is generally a contract, especially in business settings. In our earlier example, Susan (the landlord) assigns the payments to the bank so that the bank will not sue her or take other action to collect. People in business are not in the habit of making gifts to other businesspeople. A gift assignment occurs, for example, when a sales representative for a concrete company assigns the 10 percent Christmas bonus he earns to his eldest daughter for her college education fund.

In the following case, the judge analyzed some of the requirements for an assignment.

14.4 KELLER v. BASS PRO SHOPS, INC.

15 F.3d 122, 1994 U.S.App. LEXIS 1524 (8th Cir. 1994)

FACTS Ron Keller, his brother, and Richard Bleam developed the Tornado lure at the request of Bass Pro Shops. The manufacturing process was developed through Kel-Lure, a company owned by Keller and his brother. Kel-Lure was sold at auction, its assets were purchased by Keller and his brother, and it was reincorporated as Sports Products. Sports Products manufactured the Tornado lures almost exclusively for Bass Pro Shops. In August 1989, the three developers signed a patent assignment on the process for making the Tornado lure in favor of Bass Pro Shops. It read in part that it was made for "good and valuable consideration, the receipt and sufficiency of which are hereby acknowledged." The assignment conformed to 35 U.S.C. 261 (1988), which governs patent assignments.

This assignment occurred just before Sports Products moved to Costa Rica and reincorporated as Productos Deportivos, which continued to manufacture the lures. Keller was surprised to learn that he would not become a shareholder in Productos Deportivos and he terminated his employment with the company in 1990. He claimed that his brother forced him out of the business. Keller contended that the assignment was not valid because he did not receive consideration and, consequently, he sued. Keller originally initiated this lawsuit in Arkansas; Bass Pro Shops had the case removed to federal court based on diversity jurisdiction and federal question jurisdiction.

ISSUE Was the assignment to Bass Pro Shops valid without consideration?

HOLDING Yes.

REASONING It is appropriate to follow the same rule for patent assignments as for real estate deeds. If an assignment recites that consideration has been paid, that precludes further investigation into the matter. This rule enables people to rely on the written document.

In addition, consideration is not a requirement for a valid assignment. What is necessary is delivery of the property (if any) with intent to make an immediate and complete transfer of all rights, title, and interest from the assignor to the assignee. This case was before the court on diversity jurisdiction and the court believed the Arkansas Supreme Court would apply the real estate rule to patent assignments. The court construed U.S. Supreme Court cases as also supporting this approach.

BUSINESS CONSIDERATIONS What could Ron Keller have done to help ensure that he would have a role in Productos Deportivos? Could he have taken any steps to protect himself?

ETHICAL CONSIDERATIONS Did Ron Keller's brother treat him ethically? Why or why not? Did Ron Keller have any moral rights?

Notice of the Assignment

Because an assignment extinguishes the assignor's rights and creates rights only for the assignee, one would assume that the person obligated to perform must be informed about the assignment. Surprisingly, this is not a legal requirement; an assignment is perfectly valid even though the person obligated to perform is never informed. An assignee may want to give notice to the promisor for a number of reasons, particularly if the assignor is potentially unethical or dishonest.

If the person obligated to perform *has* received notice of the assignment and then pays the assignor or delivers performance to the assignor, the person will still be obligated to pay or deliver performance to the assignee. In many instances, the promisor is not told about the assignment, and the assignor receives the performance and transfers it to the assignee. If the promisor, who is obligated to perform, has not been given notice and the assignor receives performance and does not transfer it to the assignee, the assignee will be limited to taking action against the assignor even if the assignor has absconded with the funds.

In some cases, assignors have "benefitted" by selling the *same* contract right to more than one assignee through mistake, negligence, or fraud. Of course, if the second assignee has notice or knowledge of the prior assignment, that person will receive the assignment *subject* to the rights of the first assignee. In many cases, however, the second assignee lacks notice. The problem is also relatively simple if the first assignment is revocable. The second assignment merely revokes the first.

Dishonest assignors generally disappear with the funds and leave the innocent assignees to resolve their conflicting claims. Three theories are widely used by the courts to resolve these problems. One theory is based on the belief that the first assignee to receive the assignment receives all the rights; the assignor has nothing to assign to later assignees. This theory, known as the *New York Rule,* is one version of the *first-in-time approach* and is applied in some states. If Anita, the promisee, assigns her right to Joel for value on January 1 and then assigns her right to Larry for value on January 15, Joel will receive the right according to this rule. Under the New York Rule, there are two primary exceptions: (1) if the first assignment is revocable, like an undelivered gift; or (2) if the first assignee fails to obtain documents evidencing the assignment, thus enabling the assignor to "transfer" the rights to a second assignee.

Closely related to the New York Rule is the *Massachusetts Rule,* which is a slightly different first-in-time approach. Under this rule, the first assignee also has priority if the first assignment is not revocable. However, the second assignee will have the priority if the second assignee acquires the assignment in *good faith, for value,* and does any *one* of the following:

1. obtains payment from the promisor,
2. recovers a judgment against the promisor,
3. obtains the promisor's promise to pay the assignee instead of the assignor, or
4. receives delivery of tangible evidence representing the claim.

Still other states apply the rule that the first assignee to actually give notice to the promisor receives the better right. This is called the *first-to-give-notice approach* or the *English Rule,* which is followed in California, Florida, and a few other states. In the prior example, if Larry gives notice to the promisor first, he will prevail under the English Rule, provided he takes for value without notice of the prior assignment to Joel. One of the policies underlying this rule is that a prudent assignee, who is about to pay value for the assignment, will check with the person obligated to perform. The promisor, who has notice of earlier assignments, will tell the prospective purchaser, and this information will prevent additional assignments. The advantage of giving notice should be obvious, especially under the English Rule.

Under all three of these rules of law, the assignor is liable for fraud and injured parties can collect from the assignor if the assignor can be located with assets. (Similar policy problems arise when multiple security interests are created in the same property or there are multiple transfers of the same property.) However, there is nothing inappropriate if a promisee (assignor) divides up the contract rights and assigns *different* contract rights to different assignees.

FROM THE DESK OF

AMY CHEN, ATTORNEY AT LAW

Assignments and Notice

Notice is not legally required. However, the assignee should give notice to the promisor. The assignee should check with the promisee prior to parting with consideration. Immediately after the assignment, the assignee should notify the promisor that an assignment has been made and that future performance should be delivered directly to the assignee. The address for performance should be included in this notice. Note that an assignee can be seriously injured by failure to give notice. An injured assignee is permitted to sue the assignor under breach of warranty or fraud. Generally, however, the assignor does not have funds or has left the area.

Nonassignable Rights

Assignments have become an important aspect of our business and financial structure. They are important techniques for selling goods and obtaining cash. A common business practice among retail outlets is to sell expensive items on time. The retailer assigns the monthly payments to a credit corporation in exchange for cash, then uses the cash to buy more merchandise. A simple example of this practice occurs when a buyer purchases an automobile financed through a car dealership. Because of the importance of assignments in commercial transactions, courts are generally predisposed to allow assignments. This favorable perspective is obvious in the courts' treatment of contract assignments. Assignments do not require the approval of the promisor. Even when the promisor objects to the assignment in court, the court will still generally allow it.

To prevent the assignment, the promisor must prove to the court that at least one of the following conditions exists:

1. The assignment will materially change the duty of the promisor.
2. The assignment will materially impair the chance of return performance or reduce its value.
3. The assignment will materially increase the burden or risk imposed by the contract.

Basically, the promisor must convince the court that he or she will be in a substantially worse position if the assignment is allowed. These requirements are discussed in the *Restatement (Second) of Contracts* in § 317(2) (1981) and are also included in § 2-210(2) of the UCC. These provisions are applicable unless the language of the contract provides otherwise or the assignment is forbidden by statute or is against public policy.

When the assignment materially changes the promisor's duty, the promisor must perform a substantially different type or degree of work. Many assignments involve assigning monthly payments. Because this simply requires that the promisor change the address on the monthly envelopes, the promisor's duty is not substantially different. As an example of a substantially different duty, Thad (a promisor) agrees to paint the exterior of any one house and he makes this promise to Lynda, who owns a 1,000-

square-foot single-level house. Lynda assigns the right to Joanne, who owns a 2,500-square-foot two-story house. Thad might convince the court that this assignment materially affects his duty. However, it is unwise for a promisor to enter into a contract that is ambiguous. Generally, a house painter like Thad will provide a bid for a house specifying a particular address.

If the assignment impairs the risk of return performance, it increases the chance that the promisor will not receive consideration from the promisee. For example, Chris wants to have her portrait painted; she locates a talented but struggling artist, John, to paint the portrait for $200. John explains that he needs the money to buy canvas and quality oil paint. Chris agrees to pay him the money on the first of the month, and John is to start the portrait on the fifteenth. Later, however, John wants to assign that payment to his landlord for unpaid rent. Consequently, Chris may convince the court that this assignment will impair her chance of receiving the portrait.

An assignment will not be allowed if it increases the risk or burden of the contract. If John, the artist, tries to assign only $150 of the payment to his landlord, Chris might be able to convince the court that this assignment increases the burden or risk imposed by their contract, because John might purchase inferior materials.

Not all types of assignments are favored. Some types of assignments are considered less desirable and are limited by state law. Common examples are prohibitions or limitations on the assignment of wages. Statutes in Alabama, California, Connecticut, the District of Columbia, Missouri, and Ohio generally prohibit the assignment of future wages. In addition, California, Connecticut, and many other states have special rules that apply to assignments of wages as security for small loans.[5] Recently assignments of **post-loss** insurance payments also are being scrutinized more closely by the legislature and the courts.

14.2

FINANCE

ACCEPTING ACCOUNTS RECEIVABLE AS PAYMENT OF DEBT

All Electronics, Inc. (AEI) is one of CIT's major retail distributors in Chicago. AEI has been suffering financial difficulties for over a year, and currently owes CIT $65,000 for inventory that it has already received. This $65,000 is 90 days past due, which causes Anna some anxiety. AEI has $40,000 in accounts receivable, most of which are current (not past due). AEI has suggested that it transfer its own accounts receivable to CIT. AEI would prefer to do this to discharge its entire obligation. If that is not acceptable to CIT, then AEI would like to transfer the accounts as partial payment on the obligation. Anna and John have never before accepted another firm's accounts receivable. They ask you for advice. What will you advise them?

BUSINESS CONSIDERATIONS What information should CIT obtain in order to decide if this is a sound business decision? What are the legal and business consequences of such an arrangement? Why? What would be CIT's position if it accepted the assignments?

ETHICAL CONSIDERATIONS Evaluate AEI's ethical perspective as it relates to this series of transactions.

Contract Clauses Restricting Assignments

Another example of court behavior that favors assignments is their interpretation of the language in the original promisor/promisee contract. Even if the contract states that "no assignment shall be made" or that "there shall be no assignment without the prior consent of the promisor," many courts will still allow the assignment. Courts *may* interpret these clauses as promises or covenants not to assign the rights. The assignor is then held legally responsible for making the assignment and must pay the promisor for any loss caused by the assignment. Often the promisor cannot prove any loss in court, so this is a rather hollow right. These clauses can also be interpreted by courts as preventing the transfer of the contract duties. This latter

Post-loss
Obligations of insurance companies after a covered loss has actually occurred.

approach is followed by § 2-210(3) of the UCC. If the contracting parties really want to prevent assignments, they must use clauses such as "all assignments shall be void" or "any attempt at assignment shall be null and void." Most courts will interpret this language as actually removing the power to make assignments. The following case addresses the issue of whether the assignment should be permitted.

14.5 PARRISH CHIROPRACTIC CENTERS v. PROGRESSIVE CASUALTY INS. CO. 1994 Colo. LEXIS 465, 18 BTR 877 (Colo. 1994)

FACTS Colorado has no-fault auto insurance and Progressive Casualty Ins. Co. (Progressive) issues personal injury protection (PIP) policies under the state statute. The PIP policies include the following clause: "Interest in this policy may not be assigned without our written consent." Parrish Chiropractic Centers (Parrish) provides treatment to insureds under these PIP policies. When treatment begins, the insureds are required to sign assignment forms provided by Parrish. This dispute arose when Progressive refused Parrish's requests for payment and paid the **insureds** directly. The insureds did not apply the payments to their chiropractic bills.

ISSUE Should the assignments by the insureds to Parrish be permitted?

HOLDING No.

REASONING Attempts to assign contract rights may be disallowed based on the language of the contract. The language of these policies clearly stated that interests under the policies may not be assigned. Assignments may also be prohibited if they materially change Progressive's obligations under the policies. Progressive argued that assignments would increase administrative costs and reduce its ability to control the costs of treatment. The insurer has a right to deal only with the parties with whom it has contracted. The court in the Parrish case discussed the recent trend to disallow assignments of proceeds of health insurance policies. [This case has limited precedential value in Colorado due to a revision in the no-fault statute, which became effective 1 January 1994. Section 10-4-708.4(1) (a), 4A C.R.S. (1993 Supp.) specifically allows an insured to assign payments from an insurance policy to a health-care provider.]

BUSINESS CONSIDERATIONS What could Progressive do to reduce the likelihood of these and similar disputes? Why doesn't Progressive want to pay Parrish and similar assignees? Why doesn't Parrish seek payment from the insureds, after all, they have been paid by Progressive? What considerations may have influenced the Colorado legislature to change the statute?

ETHICAL CONSIDERATIONS Is it ethical for Parrish to require patients to sign the assignment forms? Is it likely that the patients are in pain? Is it probable that the patients correctly understand the documents? Is it ethical for health-care providers to solicit patients based on promises that the insurance company will be billed? Why or why not?

Insureds
Persons or entities covered under an insurance policy.

Warranties Implied by the Assignor

An assignor who makes an assignment for value implies that certain things are true about the assigned rights. These implied warranties exist without any action by the assignor, or even his or her knowledge. The warranties include (1) the right is a valid legal right and actually exists; (2) there are no valid defenses or limitations to the assigned right that are not specifically stated or apparent; and (3) the assignor will not do anything to defeat or impair the value of the assignment. These warranties need not be expressly stated but, instead, can be implied. If the assignor breaches the warranties, the assignee can successfully sue. The assignor and assignee may expressly agree to limit or exclude warranties.

Rights Created by the Assignment

An assignee obtains the same legal rights in the contract that the assignor had. If the assignee sues the promisor, the promisor generally may use the same defenses against the assignee as were available against the assignor. Examples of these defenses would include fraud, duress, undue influence, and breach of contract by the assignor. The promisor will not, however, be able to use every conceivable defense against an assignee.

Waiver of Defenses Clause

A waiver of defenses clause in a contract attempts to give the assignee better legal rights than the assignor had. Often such a clause is part of a standard printed contract prepared by the assignee or assignor and signed by the promisor. Generally the promisor (buyer) is not aware that the contract contains a waiver of defenses clause or does not understand what it means. In the clause, the promisor promises to give up legal defenses in any later lawsuit by the assignee. In other words, the promisor agrees not to exert defenses, such as fraud in the inducement or breach of warranty against any subsequent assignees. Exhibit 14.5 shows the effect on the promisor/assignee relationship of a valid waiver of defenses clause.

If the waiver of defenses clause is effective, it reduces the promisor's bargaining power. For example, if a purchaser buys a product on time and the product is defective, a common reaction is to stop making payments. A waiver of defenses clause means that the buyer must continue to make the payments.

Consumer groups and government agencies have often opposed waiver of defenses clauses because they reduce a consumer's bargaining power. Such a clause is

EXHIBIT 14.5 Comparison of the Contract Rights of the Assignor and Assignee

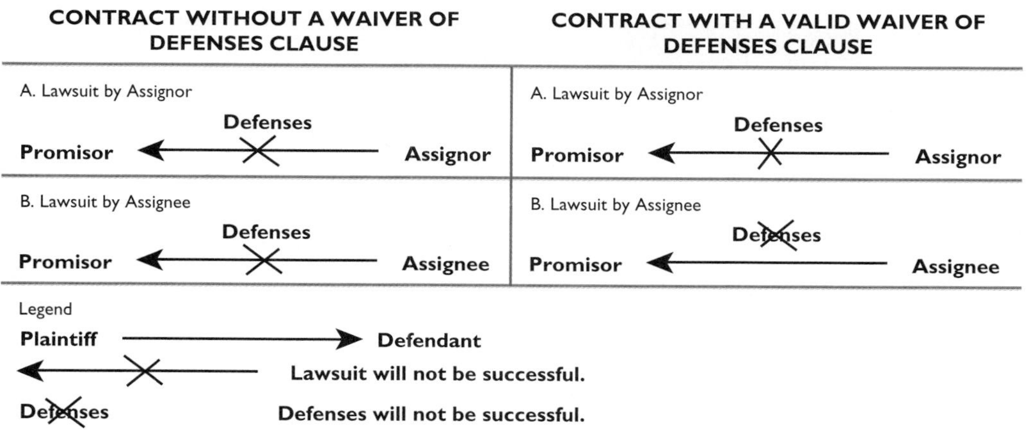

(This exhibit assumes that the promisor has valid defenses that can be proven in court.)

generally enforceable under § 9-206(1) of the UCC, unless there is a different rule under statutes or court decisions for buyers or lessees of consumer goods. Under the UCC, the assignee is subject to the same defenses as a holder in due course of a negotiable instrument. Some states, including Alaska, Missouri, Ohio, and Washington, and the District of Columbia, have statutes that forbid or limit these clauses.[6] The Federal Trade Commission enacted a regulation barring these agreements in contracts by consumers.[7]

Delegations

Assignments and delegations may occur simultaneously. However, it will be easier to understand delegations if they are analyzed as independent transfers. In fact, they are completely separate concepts that can and do occur independently. In a *delegation,* the promisor locates a new promisor to perform the duties under the contract. The original promisor is called the delegator, and the new promisor is called the delegatee. For example, suppose Jeff buys a new automobile from a Hyundai dealer. One of the terms of that contract is a promise by the dealer to provide certain warranty work on the car for three years. Later, Carmen, the mechanic employed by the Hyundai dealer, quits, and the dealer contracts with a garage to do the warranty work. This particular delegation is illustrated in Exhibit 14.6. As with assignments, there may be consideration for the delegation, but it is not necessary. If no consideration exists, the delegation is really a gift from the new promisor to the old promisor.

The purchaser of the car (Jeff) can sue the car dealer who made the promise if the warranty work is not performed. The purchaser can also generally sue the garage for failure to perform. In many states, the purchaser can sue both the dealer (delegator) and the garage (delegatee) at the same time, but the courts will not permit the purchaser to collect twice.

The relationship between the delegator and the delegatee may be that of a contract or of a gift. If a contract relationship is present, the delegator has the right to

EXHIBIT 14.6 Delegation

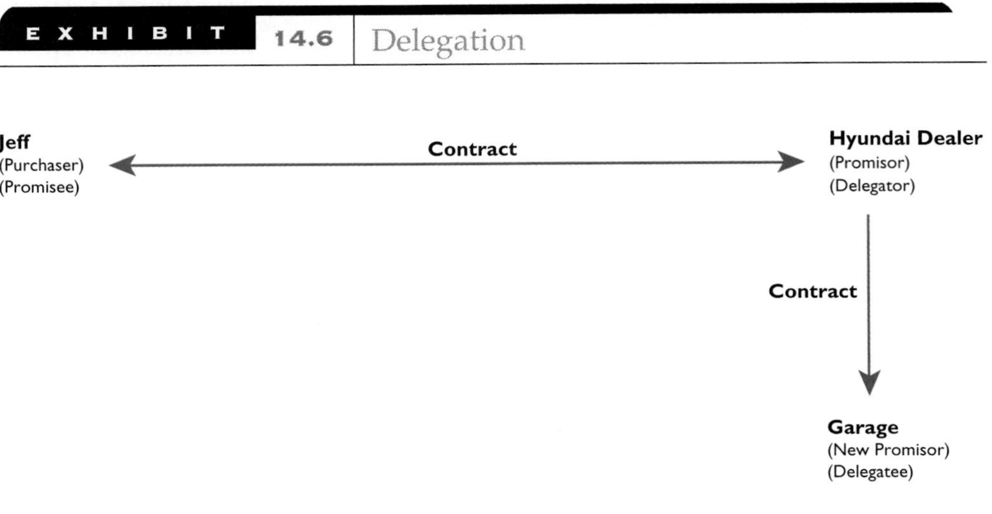

sue the delegatee for nonperformance. If a gift relationship is present, the court would hold that the delegatee promised to make a gift in the future but failed to deliver it. Generally, promises to make gifts in the future are not enforceable without **promissory estoppel**.

Promissory estoppel
Doctrine used to enforce a gift promise because of the justifiable reliance of the promisee.

Delegations do not occur unless the delegatee assumes the contract duties. This assumption can be either expressly stated or implied. The modern trend in court decisions is to imply the assumption of the duties, especially when there is an assignment and a delegation. Implied assumption of duties is also supported by the *Restatement (Second) of Contracts* and the Uniform Commercial Code. An example of this occurs when the parties state that there is an "assignment of the contract" or an "assignment of all my rights under the contract." Such statements are generally interpreted as indicating (1) an assignment, (2) a delegation of the duties by the delegator, and (3) an acceptance of the duties by the delegatee unless there is a clear indication of a contrary intention. This position is followed by the UCC § 2-210(4) and the *Restatement (Second) of Contracts* § 328.

Delegations do not have the favored legal status that assignments do. Courts are more inclined to deny a delegation. If the contract between the promisor and the promisee states that "there shall be no delegations," the courts will prevent delegations. The same is true if the contract requires personal performance. Courts are also more likely to decide that a delegation is unfair to the promisee. Under the UCC § 2-210(1), duties cannot be delegated if the agreement states that there will be no delegation or the promisor has a substantial interest in having the delegator perform the contract. The *Restatement (Second) of Contracts* § 318(2) states that delegations should not be allowed if the promisee has a substantial interest in having the delegator control or perform the acts promised. Consequently, personal service contracts generally cannot be delegated. Section 2-210(3) of the UCC indicates that a contract

YOU BE THE JUDGE

Should Leases Be Interpreted Literally?

The owners of Clark's Restaurant in Boston tried to negotiate a sale of the business. The restaurant's lease stated that the landlord was granted the right to approve all future subtenants of the property. The restaurant argued that the lease really required good faith and fair dealing in the approval of subtenants. The landlord argued that the lease should be interpreted literally; that is, a lease that requires the landlord's consent means the landlord's actual consent.

If you were the judge deciding this case, how would you interpret the contract clause? Why?

BUSINESS CONSIDERATIONS How can a business tenant best protect itself from the risks associated with leasing business property? What problems could arise if the business decides to move to a new location?[8]

ETHICAL CONSIDERATIONS Does the owner of the real estate owe Clark's Restaurant a duty to accept subtenants? Why or why not?

SOURCE: Jonathan M. Moses and Junda Woo, *Wall Street Journal* (17 March 1992), p. B12.

http:// **RESOURCES FOR BUSINESS LAW STUDENTS**

NAME	RESOURCES	WEB ADDRESS
Preservation of Consumers' Claims and Defenses—16 C.F.R. 433	The law firm of Arent Fox Kintner Plotkin & Kahn maintains a collection of advertising law resources, including waiver of defense clauses, under the U.S. Code of Federal Regulations (C.F.R.).	http://www.webcom.com/~lewrose/trr/holder.html

14.3

MARKETING/FINANCE

CREATING AUTHORIZED REPAIR CENTERS

Call-Image videophones are sold to consumers with a one-year warranty, which has become the standard in the industry. Currently, consumers must send the videophones back to CIT for any necessary warranty work. Anna and Tom are thinking about identifying certain retailers who are selling CIT videophones in large cities and designating them as "authorized CIT repair centers." John feels this arrangement will improve the marketability of CIT videophones. However, they are concerned about how this might change their relationships with their distributors. They ask you about the legal and business effects of this decision. What do you tell them and why?

BUSINESS CONSIDERATIONS What are the business advantages of such an arrangement? What are the disadvantages? What types of legal arrangements could CIT have with authorized repair centers? What will be CIT's obligations under these arrangements? If you were assisting Amy Chen in drafting these contracts, what provisions would you include and why?

ETHICAL CONSIDERATIONS Is it ethical to require an authorized repair center to also sell CIT products? Why or why not?

clause that prohibits the assignment of "the contract" is to be construed as preventing only a delegation of the contract duties to the assignee.

Analysis of Assignments and Delegations

To characterize an assignment or a delegation situation, one should answer the following questions:

1. Was the additional person involved from the beginning or added later?
2. Did the additional person undertake to perform a contract duty or become entitled to a contract right? Or both?
3. Did the language of the original contract prevent this transfer to an additional person?
4. Did the type of rights or duties prevent this transfer to an additional person?

Uniform Commercial Code Provisions

When the Uniform Commercial Code is applicable, businesspeople need to review its assignment and delegation provisions. Certain types of assignments are excluded from Article 9 by UCC § 9-104—for example, claims for wages, interests under an insurance policy, claims arising from the commission of a tort, and deposits in banks. Under § 9-201 and § 9-203 of the UCC, provisions of Article 9 may be subordinated to state statutes regulating installment sales to consumers. Section 2-210 of the code covers assignments and delegations under contracts for the sale of goods. However, some questions concerning assignments are not resolved in either Article 2 or Article 9 of the UCC. (This is only a brief overview of the code's provisions.)

SUMMARY

An additional person who is involved in a contract from the beginning may be a third-party beneficiary. If the promisor or promisee meant to affect the third person under the contract, that person will be an intended beneficiary and will have enforceable rights. Intended beneficiaries can file lawsuits to protect their own legal rights. If they sue the promisor, the promisor can use the same defenses that would be valid against the promisee. Creditor beneficiaries can sue a promisee who tries to cancel the contract. Donee beneficiaries generally will not be successful in a suit against the promisee because legally the donee beneficiary did not receive the promised gift.

An additional party who becomes involved after the contract is formed may be an assignee or a delegatee. An assignee receives a contract right from the transferor. An assignment extinguishes the contract right of the assignor and sets up this contract right exclusively in the assignee. The assignee is now entitled to performance under the contract. Legally, the assignee does not have to notify the promisor of the assignment. The assignee is better protected if he or she *does* give notice. This is especially important if the assignor makes multiple assignments of the same contract right.

In a delegation, a delegatee assumes the transferor's obligation to perform under the contract. The delegator will still be obligated to perform if the delegatee does not. Generally, courts will respect contract clauses that state that there shall be no delegation.

DISCUSSION QUESTIONS

1. Julia promises to buy her son, Jonathan, a car from Ted McNare's Volkswagen dealership if Jonathan graduates from college. Does Ted McNare have any rights in the contract? Why or why not?
2. Legal Hit employees throw cream pies in the face of any target designated by the promisee. If you hired Legal Hit to deliver a cream pie greeting to your boss, what are the legal rights of Legal Hit, you, and your boss?
3. Some states have statutes prohibiting or limiting assignment of wages. What public policies might state legislatures be trying to promote with these statutes?
4. Should waiver of defenses clauses be enforced? What are the advantages and disadvantages of these clauses?
5. Andrew owes Clairise $100. Clairise assigns $25 of this amount to Diane. With knowledge of the assignment, Andrew pays the entire $100 to Clairise. Has Andrew discharged his duty to pay?[9]
6. What are the differences between assignees and third-party beneficiaries? In what ways are they similar?
7. States sometimes distinguish between before-loss and after-loss assignments of insurance policies. What public policies might be advanced by separate rules for the two types of assignments?
8. When will an assignment be allowed if the contract does not mention assignments?
9. What happens if the assignor assigns the identical contract right to three assignees? Who should recover from whom? Why?
10. How do assignments and delegations differ from each other?

CASE PROBLEMS AND WRITING ASSIGNMENTS

1. Stevens Air Systems contracted with Health Care Services Corporation (HCS) to provide health care to its employees. HCS contracted with Omaha Indemnity to cover the catastrophic illnesses of these employees. The insurer signed the contract with the knowledge that HCS intended to benefit the Stevens employees who participated in the health plan. Were these employees intended third-party beneficiaries who could sue Omaha? Should contrary language in the HCS/Omaha contract influence this decision? [See *Gilmore* v. *Omaha Indemnity,* 158 Cal.Rptr. 229 (Cal.App. 1979).]

2. Jed Allan was the announcer and master of ceremonies of a television series called *Celebrity Bowling.* He also had a partnership interest in the show, which was produced from 1970 to 1976. The producer of the show entered into a contract with Bekins Archival Service to store, inventory, and ship the videotapes of the series to distributors and tape-duplicating firms when authorized by the producer. Bekins was to receive a monthly fee for this service. Bekins's inventory mistakenly indicated that tapes 1 through 26 had been returned. The duplicates of these tapes were destroyed in reliance on the Bekins' inventory. Was Allan an intended third-party beneficiary of the storage contract? Why or why not? [See *Allan* v. *Bekins Archival Service, Inc.,* 154 Cal.Rptr. 458 (Cal.App. 1979).]

3. Raymond Robson, Sr., and Raymond Robson, Jr., entered into a contract in which the father was to receive all of his son's shares in their company when the son died. In addition, the father was to pay $500 per month from the company proceeds to his son's wife for five years following the son's death or until she remarried, whichever occurred first. Two days before Robson, Jr.'s death, the two men modified the contract. This modification removed the father's obligation to make payments to the widow from the company proceeds. Birthe Robson and Robson, Jr., were separated at the time of his death and a divorce action was pending. Was Birthe Robson a third-party beneficiary of the contract between her husband and her father-in-law? Did she have any enforceable rights? [See *Robson* v. *Robson,* 514 F.Supp. 99 (N.D. Ill. 1981).]

4. Zelmo Beaty, a professional basketball player, signed a contract to play for James Kirst. General Insurance Company posted a security bond for his salary. Beaty's "contract" was sold to Daniels, then to the Stars, and then to the Spirits of St. Louis. Under the last contract, the Spirits were supposed to pay Beaty, but they have not been doing so. Could Beaty enforce the Stars/Spirits contract? Could Kirst or General Insurance Company enforce the Stars/Spirits contract? Why or why not? [See *Kirst* v. *Silna,* 163 Cal.Rptr. 230 (Cal.App. 1980).]

5. J. D. Williams was injured while working on a drilling rig at Amchitka Island, Alaska. He was working for Parco, Inc. Parco had contracted with the Atomic Energy Commission (AEC) to drill certain test holes on Amchitka Island. Fenix & Scisson had a contract with the AEC to furnish engineering services in conjunction with drilling and mining operations there. Under this contract, Fenix & Scisson was required to inspect drilling operations and to recommend any improvements to the AEC. The firm also was required to take reasonable safety precautions in the performance of its work. This contract was supplemented by provisions that Fenix & Scisson had responsibility for the overall industrial safety at the site. At the time of the accident, there were seven Parco employees and one Fenix & Scisson employee on the job. Did Fenix & Scisson have a contractual duty to Williams? Was he an intended third-party beneficiary of their contract with the AEC? [See *Williams* v. *Fenix & Scisson, Inc.,* 608 F.2d 1205 (9th Cir. 1979).]

6. **BUSINESS APPLICATIONS CASE** The county tax collector arranged for seven parcels of land to be sold at a public tax sale. Under applicable California law, the owners could file a claim to receive any excess proceeds received by the tax collector for one year after the sale. (Excess proceeds are the amounts the tax collector receives minus the taxes owed and the tax collector's costs.) Neal, the attorney for Mission Valley East, Inc., wrote the owners and offered them $100 each for their remaining interests in the parcels. He led them to believe that their interests were almost worthless and that his client had purchased the property at the tax sale and needed a quitclaim deed and an assignment to obtain title insurance. Mission Valley East, Inc., had not purchased the parcels. After buying the quitclaim deeds and assignments, Mission Valley East filed a claim for the excess proceeds. The assignors were not aware that they had the right to excess proceeds. Did the assignments transfer the right to the excess proceeds? Why or why not? [See *Mission Valley East, Inc.* v. *County of Kern,* 174 Cal.Rptr. 300 (Cal.App. 1981).]

7. **ETHICAL APPLICATIONS CASE** An automobile driven by Tracy Smith hit the rear end of an auto driven by George Romstadt. Smith's liability was admitted; however, Romstadt's damages were not. Shortly before trial, Romstadt offered to settle the case against Smith for $125,000 if Smith would assign all her claims against Allstate (the insurer) to Romstadt. Romstadt would release Smith from any unpaid amounts. After receiving independent counsel, Smith agreed. The amount of the settlement was irrelevant since Smith would not have to pay it. Romstadt then sued Allstate for failure to settle the claim against Smith in good faith, which resulted in a claim in excess of the limits of the insurance policy. Should Romstadt recover under the assignment? [See *Romstadt* v. *Allstate Insurance Co.,* 844 F.Supp. 361, 1994, U.S.Dist. LEXIS 1923 (N.D. Ohio, West. Div. 1994).]

8. **IDES CASE** Robert T. Phillips signed six equipment leases with First Interstate Credit (FIC), which contained valid security interest provisions in the equip-

ment. Security interests are protected rights in the property of another. FIC entered into an agreement with Textron, which also held security interests in some of Phillips's assets. FIC and Textron entered into an agreement to subordinate FIC's security interests to those of Textron. This subordination agreement provides that FIC's interests will be paid after those of Textron. The letter from FIC setting forth the agreement provided:

> *In the event that at any time, or for any reason, you cease to have your above-mentioned security interest in said specific items, our subordination of lien as provided herein shall thereupon immediately cease and be terminated and any security interest which you may have in the above-captioned's goods, other than those described in Schedule A, shall be subordinate to our security interest. No person other than you and us shall have any right, benefit, priority or interest under or because of the existence of this Letter Agreement.*

Textron tried to assign all its interests, including the subordination, to Miller and Miller Auctioneers. FIC refused to consent to the assignment and claimed a security interest in the proceeds of the auction. Should the assignment be valid? Why or why not? Use the IDES principles to analyze this case and to answer the questions. [See *First Interstate Credit* v. *Phillips*, 1994 Tenn.App. LEXIS 97 (Tenn.App. 1994).]

NOTES

1. See Walter H. E. Jaeger, ed., *Williston on Contracts*, 3rd ed. (Mount Kisco, N.Y.: Baker Voorhis, 1957), § 395, p. 1066.
2. See *Ibid.*, § 396, pp. 1067–1070.
3. See *Restatement (Second) of Contracts*, 302 and Introductory Note to Chapter 14 at pp. 438–439.
4. See *Allan* v. *Bekins Archival Service, Inc.*, 154 Cal.Rptr. 458, 463 fn 8.
5. See *Restatement (Second) of Contracts*, Statutory Note to Chapter 15 at pp. 7–9.
6. See *Restatement (Second) of Contracts*, Statutory Note to Chapter 15 at p. 10.
7. See 16 C.F.R. 433.1-.3 (1975, as amended in 1977).
8. Jonathan M. Moses and Junda Woo, "Law," *Wall Street Journal* (17 March 1992), p. B12.
9. See *Restatement (Second) of Contracts*, 326, Comment b, Ill. 1.

A G E N D A

The Kochanowskis realize that CIT is likely, from time to time, to have customers who do not pay their bills as they come due. They would like to know what rights they will have in such a situation. They will be ordering component parts that need to be produced to certain fairly exact standards. They wonder how they can word their contracts so that the parts meet these specifications, and what they can do if the specifications are not satisfied. They are also concerned with the time element in their contracts, both as sellers and as buyers. How important is the time for performance?

These and other questions are likely to arise during this chapter. Be prepared! You never know when one of the Kochanowskis will ask for your help or advice.

Contractual Discharge and Remedies

O U T L I N E

- Termination of the Contract
- Discharge by Performance
- Discharge by Agreement of the Parties
- Discharge by Operation of Law
- Discharge by Nonperformance
- Types of Remedies
- Damages
- Equitable Remedies
- Limitations on Remedies
- Waiver of Breach
- Summary
- Discussion Questions
- Case Problems and Writing Assignments

TERMINATION OF THE CONTRACT

When parties contract with one another, each party naturally assumes that the other party will faithfully and satisfactorily perform according to the terms of the agreement. Consequently, whenever the parties do what the contract calls for, we say that they have discharged their duties under the contract. *Discharge* of a contract involves the legally valid termination of a contractual duty. Upon discharge, the parties have fulfilled their agreement; at this time, the parties' duties and obligations to one another end. The law groups the numerous methods for discharging contracts into four main categories: discharge by performance, discharge by agreement of the parties, discharge by operation of law, and discharge by nonperformance. Exhibit 15.1 shows various methods for discharging a contract and details both the methods of discharge as well as the general rules applied to each method.

EXHIBIT 15.1 Methods of Discharging Contracts

Type of Discharge	General Rules
1. Discharge by performance	
a. Complete performance: the parties' exact fulfillment of the terms of the contract.	1. Completion of the contract on tender of delivery or payment.
b. Substantial performance: less-than-perfect performance that complies with the essential portions of the contract.	1. Applicable only to nonmaterial and nonwillful breaches. 2. The injured party's suit for damages resulting from the minor deviations that have led to substantial performance.
2. Discharge by agreement of the parties	
a. Release: the surrender of a legal claim.	1. Necessitates a writing, consideration, and an immediate relinquishment of rights or claims owed to another.
b. Rescission: the voluntary, mutual surrender and discharge of contractual rights and duties whereby the parties are returned to the original status quo.	1. May be either written or oral (subject to the Statute of Frauds), formal or informal, express, or implied.
c. Accord and satisfaction: an agreement whereby the parties decide to accept performance different from that required by their original bargain and the parties' later compliance with this new agreement.	1. Actual agreement and subsequent performance necessary.
d. Novation: a contract that effects an immediate discharge of a previously existing contractual duty, creates a new contractual obligation or duty, and includes as a party to this new agreement one who neither was owed a duty nor obligated to perform in the original contract.	1. Assent of creditor and new obligor required. 2. Different from an accord and satisfaction in that it effects an immediate discharge of an obligation rather than a discharge predicated on a subsequent performance.
3. Discharge by operation of law	
a. Bankruptcy: a court decree/discharge of the debtor's contractual obligations.	1. Revival of the obligation possible if done in compliance with applicable statutory provisions.
b. Statute of limitations: a definite statutory time period during which a lawsuit must be commenced or be barred forever.	1. Applicable time periods different from state to state.

continued

EXHIBIT 15.1 Methods of Discharging Contracts *(cont.)*

Type of Discharge	General Rules
c. Material alteration of the contract: a serious change in the contract effected by a party to the contract.	1. Must be done intentionally and without the consent of the other party.
4. Discharge by nonperformance	
a. Impossibility: an unforeseen event or condition that precludes the possibility of the party's performing as promised.	1. Discharge stemming from only objective (as opposed to subjective) impossibility. 2. Includes such events as the destruction of the contract's subject matter without the fault of either party, supervening illegality, the death or disability of either party whose performance is essential to the performance of the contract, and conduct by one party that makes performance by the other party impossible.
b. Commercial frustration: the destruction of the essential purpose and value of the contract.	1. Destruction of the value of the contract brought about by a supervening event not reasonably anticipated at the contract's formation. 2. Term *commercially impracticable* used in the UCC.
c. Breach: the nonperformance of the obligations set up by the contract.	
1. Complete (or actual) breach.	1. A party's failure to perform a duty material and essential to the agreement; the other party justified in treating the agreement as at an end.
2. Anticipatory breach: an indication in advance by one of the contracting parties that he or she does not intend to abide by the terms of the contract.	1. Covered by both the common law and the UCC.
d. Conditions: limitations or qualifications placed on a promise.	
1. Express conditions: those in which the parties explicitly or impliedly in fact set out the limitations to which their promises will be subject.	1. Strict compliance with express conditions necessary to avoid a breach.
2. Constructive conditions: those read into the contract or implied in law in order to serve justice.	1. Substantial compliance with constructive conditions necessary to avoid a breach.
3. Condition precedent: performance contingent on the happening of a future event; resultant discharge of both parties stemming from the failure of the condition precedent.	
4. Condition subsequent: the occurrence of a particular event that cuts off all ongoing contractual duties and discharges the obligations of both parties.	

Despite the parties' original intentions, the possibility exists that one party will fail to live up to the contractual obligations. As you will learn, such nonperformance constitutes a breach of the contract and entitles the injured party to certain remedies, assuming the injured party does not wish to *waive* (or ignore) the breach. A *remedy* is a cause of action resulting from the breach of a contract. After the occurrence of a breach, remedies attempt to satisfy the parties' expectations as of the time of the contract's formation. Remedies fall into two main categories: those resulting from a court's exercise of its powers "at law" (*legal* remedies) and those arising from a court's use of its powers of equity (**equitable** remedies). Although you have probably always used the term *legal remedies* to encompass both types of relief, in this chapter you will learn to identify the sorts of situations in which it is appropriate for a court to order one kind of relief or the other. You also will become aware that these types of remedies usually are mutually exclusive.

Equitable
Arising from the branch of the legal system designed to provide a remedy where no remedy existed at common law; a system designed to provide fairness when there was no suitable remedy "at law."

DISCHARGE BY PERFORMANCE

Complete Performance

The simplest, most common, and most satisfactory method of discharge consists of *complete performance.* (Yet, as we will see later in this chapter, rendering complete performance may be easier said than done.) If Johnson has agreed to deliver five carloads of grain, and Kreczewski has promised to pay $2,000 per carload, complete performance will occur when Johnson makes the deliveries to Kreczewski and Kreczewski pays Johnson. The parties' exact fulfillment of the terms of the contract satisfies the intent of their agreement and their reason for contracting. Complete performance also extinguishes all the legal duties and rights that the contract originally set up. Note, too, that performance will be complete if one of the parties *tenders* either the grain or the payment—that is, unconditionally offers to perform his contractual obligation and can so perform. That person will have completely performed the contract even if the other person does not accept the grain or the payment.

As long as Johnson is fulfilling Kreczewski's reasonable expectations under the contract, discharge by complete performance will ensue once the parties have met their respective obligations under the agreement. If during the course of the deliveries, however, Johnson does not live up to the letter of the agreement as to the quality of the grain sent to Kreczewski, Kreczewski should give Johnson prompt notice of these defects and should state formally that he (Kreczewski) expects complete performance. Kreczewski's failure to take such actions may allow Johnson to argue after the fact that Kreczewski has waived his right to expect complete performance.

Substantial Performance

In some circumstances, one party's performance does not mirror precisely the rights and obligations enumerated in the agreement. In such cases, the other party may question whether this degree of performance adequately fulfills the requisites of the contract. The issue raised by such a question involves the legal sufficiency of less-than-complete performance.

The law does not always require exact performance of a contract. Hence, minor deviations from the performance contemplated in the contract may not preclude the discharge of the contract. This type of performance is called *substantial performance.* Construction of a new house in which the contractor still needs to finish the woodwork or touch up the painting in certain rooms—assuming the contractor has completed everything else—probably constitutes substantial performance. A party who has substantially performed may receive the payment to which the parties have agreed. Because substantial performance represents a type of contract breach, since the performance is not perfect and instead is a notch below the parties' reasonable expectations under the contract, the other party can sue for the damages occasioned by substantial, as opposed to complete, performance.

Two criteria must be met before the doctrine of substantial performance is available to discharge the responsibilities of a performing party. First, the breach must not have been material. In other words, the defective performance must not destroy the value or purpose of the contract.[1] Second, the breach must be nonwillful and devoid of bad faith conduct.

Courts usually are more willing to apply the concept of substantial performance to construction contracts than to sales contracts. Why? A disgruntled buyer has a duty to return or to reject a defective suit, whereas a dissatisfied occupier of land necessarily must keep the defective house or garage. The possibility of the unjust enrichment of the landowner in construction situations makes the doctrine of substantial performance more attractive to courts in these circumstances than in most other commercial contexts.

15.1

MANUFACTURING/SALES

SECURING REPLACEMENT MANUFACTURERS

Anna has recently negotiated a preliminary agreement with a television manufacturer—TeleVision, Inc. (TVI)—that calls for TVI to produce the glass screens to be used in Call-Image videophones. Anna realizes that these screens are difficult to manufacture. She also realizes, however, that CIT will need the screens to be produced to very exact specifications if they are to be useful in production of the videophones. She has asked for your advice as to how to word the final written contract between CIT and TVI so that CIT is protected and so that the screens will meet CIT's specifications. What advice will you give her?

BUSINESS CONSIDERATIONS Suppose a business is offered a very lucrative contract if it will produce a product to very specific standards. What factors should the firm consider in deciding whether to accept the offer?

ETHICAL CONSIDERATIONS Is it ethical for a person to enter a contract that requires personal satisfaction in the performance of the other party? What, if anything, would make such a measure unethical

Discharge by Agreement of the Parties

The parties themselves can specifically agree to discharge the contract. Provisions to that effect may be part of the original contract between the parties or part of a new contract drafted expressly to discharge the initial contract.

Release

Release represents a common method of discharging the legal rights one party has against another. To be valid, a *release* should be in *writing,* should be supported by *consideration,* and should effect an *immediate relinquishment* of rights or claims owed to another. For example, a landowner may sign a release in which he or she agrees, usually in exchange for money, to discharge the builder from the original contractual obligations. Insurance companies commonly execute similar releases that the insured parties must sign before the insurers will pay for the insured parties' injuries.

Rescission

Sometimes the parties may find it advantageous to call off their deal. The law calls this process *rescission.* A contract of rescission is a voluntary, mutual surrender and discharge of contractual rights and duties whereby the law returns the parties to the original status quo. A valid rescission is legally binding. In general, rescission may be either in writing or oral (subject, you will recall, to the Statute of Frauds's requirements under § 2-209 of the UCC; moreover, rescissions of realty contracts often must be written), formal or informal, and express or implied.

The simplest method of rescission involves the termination of executory bilateral contracts. If Johnson and Kreczewski in our earlier example *mutually agree to cancel* their transaction, *express rescission* has occurred. On the other hand, they may subsequently agree that Johnson will deliver seven carloads of grain instead of five. Substituting this later agreement for the old one brings about an *implied rescission* of the earlier agreement. However, problems often ensue if the parties attempt rescission of a unilateral contract (or a bilateral contract where one party has fully executed his or her duties). In these situations, some courts, before they will grant rescission, will infer a promise to pay for the performance rendered or require that consideration be paid to the party who has performed. Courts ordinarily resolve these issues by trying to ascertain the intent of the parties; but as we have learned, this task often is difficult.

Note how the court applies these concepts in *Mor-Wood Contractors, Inc.* v. *Ottinger.*

15.1 MOR-WOOD CONTRACTORS, INC. v. OTTINGER — 562 N.E.2d 1247 (Ill.App. 1990)

FACTS In June 1987, the Ottingers purchased an undeveloped parcel of property in the Village of Hawthorn Woods. On 30 June 1987, J. & W. Trenching Service, Inc. (J&W) filed with the Lake County Health Department an application for a permit to build a septic system for the property on the Ottingers' behalf. The site plan accompanying the application showed a proposed septic field to the west of the planned home with a proposed drainage swale to be cut on the southwest portion of the lot. Based on J & W's application, the health department issued the Ottingers a septic permit. In July 1987, the Ottingers retained an architect to draw up plans for the construction of a single-family home on the property. The architect's site plan showed that the house was to be set slightly counterclockwise on the lot instead of being perfectly square within it. The site plan also indicated that the lot was to be graded to create a valley or swale sloping away from the southwest corner of the home. The Ottingers and Mor-Wood Contractors, Inc. (Mor-Wood) entered into a contract under which Mor-Wood, by 1 February 1988, was to grade the property and construct the home pursuant to the architect's plans and specifications. Two of the contract's provisions, relevant here, stated:

> *1) If the Contractor fails to correct defective Work or persistently fails to carry out the Work in accordance with the Contract Documents, the Owner, by a written order, may order the Contractor to stop the Work, or any portion thereof, until the cause for such order has been eliminated.*
>
> *2) If the Contractor defaults or persistently fails or neglects to carry out the Work in accordance with the Contract Documents or fails to perform any provision of the Contract, the Owner, after seven days' written notice to the Contractor . . . may make good such deficiencies and may deduct the cost thereof . . . from the payment then or thereafter due the Contractor or, at his option . . . may terminate the contract and take possession of the site and of all materials, equipment, tools, and construction equipment and machinery thereon owned by the Contractor and may finish the work by whatever method he may deem expedient. . . .*

Mor-Wood retained Lake-Cook Trenching (Lake-Cook) as a subcontractor for the project; and on 21 September 1987, Lake-Cook applied to the health department for a new septic permit. Accompanying the application was a site plan showing the septic field to the south of the home instead of to its west and without the swale indicated on the architect's plans. This site plan also depicted the planned home as sitting squarely within the lot rather than being turned slightly counterclockwise. After the issuance of the permit on 21 October 1987, Tim Morvay of Mor-Wood testified that while the lot was being graded, Craig Ottinger insisted that the swale be cut even though Morvay indicated that it would traverse the septic area. At Morvay's request, a health department inspector visited the job site and, owing to the swale's interference with septic lines and its reduction of the available septic absorption area, this

15.1 MOR-WOOD CONTRACTORS, INC. v. OTTINGER *(cont.)* 562 N.E.2d 1247 (Ill.App. 1990)

inspector subsequently revoked the septic permits as of that day. On 17 November, Morvay met with Ottinger and picked up a check for partial payment under the contract. That day, because of the revoked septic permits, the village posted a stop-work order on the Ottingers' property. After discovering the stop-work order on the property, Ottinger stopped payment on the check the same day. Morvay denied that when he had collected the check from Ottinger, he (Morvay) had known that the stop-work order had been posted. On 18 November, Ottinger's attorney, Lawrence Rochell, sent a letter to Mor-Wood's attorney. The letter restated Ottinger's concern that the Morvays had attempted to secure a check from Ottinger despite their alleged knowledge that a stop-work order had been posted. The letter also indicated that Mor-Wood had failed to give the Ottingers copies of subcontractor affidavits as requested and that Mor-Wood's negligence had led to the stop-work order's being issued after the revocation of the septic permit. The letter stated that the Ottingers, by demanding that Mor-Wood "stop any further work at the project site," were exercising their rights under the contract. Mor-Wood's workers left the job site on or about 19 November and at that time removed all of Mor-Wood's equipment. The Ottingers subsequently completed construction of the home without Mor-Wood's involvement. In the litigation that followed, Mor-Wood sued the Ottingers for the reasonable value of the services rendered in partially constructing the Ottingers' home, which partial construction, Mor-Wood claimed, had resulted from the Ottingers' alleged rescission of the construction contract. The Ottingers, in turn, argued that Mor-Wood, by abandoning the job site, had breached the contract.

ISSUE Had the letter from the Ottingers' attorney effected a rescission of the contract?

HOLDING Yes. The phrasing of the letter, in conjunction with Mor-Wood's later evacuation of the job site, had constituted a rescission of the contract.

REASONING The Ottingers claimed that the 18 November 1987 letter sent by their attorney, Rochell, to Mor-Wood's attorney had not constituted either a termination of Mor-Wood or a rescission of the contract. The trial court apparently had focused on Rochell's demand that Mor-Wood "stop any further work at the project site" and the statement that "recission [sic] of the contract would be in [Mor-Wood's] best interests." The Ottingers, on the other hand, stressed the closing line of the letter, which had stated that Rochell would be "happy to discuss this further." The Ottingers contended that the plain language of the letter indicated that they had not intended to terminate Mor-Wood or to rescind the contract. The letter made it clear that the Ottingers' demand that Mor-Wood cease work on the project grew out of the second contractual provision. The Ottingers argued, however, that although this section does deal with termination, it also separately empowered the Ottingers to "make good" any deficiencies in Mor-Wood's work. Thus, the Ottingers contended, Rochell's letter merely had notified Mor-Wood that the Ottingers would exercise this right under the contract. However, this interpretation of Rochell's letter was untenable for two reasons. First, some of the defects noted in Rochell's letter pertained to Mor-Wood's failure to provide the Ottingers with the subcontractor affidavits, a deficiency the Ottingers could not "make good" themselves. Second, the letter never expressed the Ottingers' intention to "make good" any deficiencies in Mor-Wood's performance. Instead, the letter demanded that Mor-Wood stop work completely, a demand more consistent with outright termination. Hence, the trial court correctly determined that Rochell's letter had constituted an attempt to terminate the contract (or rescind it) on behalf of the Ottingers. Generally, rescission means the cancellation of a contract so as to restore the parties to their initial status. Rescission can arise in two settings: First, rescission of a contract can occur by the mutual agreement of the parties; and second, rescission also comprises an equitable remedy that a court can afford to one party under a contract because of the one party's fraud, substantial nonperformance, or breach. A party seeking rescission must restore the other party to the status quo existing at the time of the making of the contract. Although the law sometimes uses the terms "abandonment" and "rescission" interchangeably, authorities urge the drawing of a distinction: "Where, upon a material breach by one party, the other party treats the breach as total by refusing to perform further and by maintaining an action for damages for such total breach, he is said to abandon further performance, but such abandonment is not technically a rescission of the contract, but a mere acceptance of a situation created by the wrongdoing of the adverse party."[2] In the instant case, the Ottingers' use of the word "abandonment" appeared to mean unilateral abandonment or, in other words, a breach of Mor-Wood's obligation to perform under the contract. The Ottingers argued that Mor-Wood's removal of equipment from the job site and the failure to return constituted "abandonment," or a breach of the contract. The trial court, on the other hand, had found that the Ottingers' termination of Mor-Wood by the 18 November letter, combined with Mor-Wood's evacuation of the job site, effected a rescission of the contract. The evidence presented at trial amply supported the trial court's conclusion that Mor-Wood's decision to leave the job site after Mor-Wood had received the termination letter from the

15.1 MOR-WOOD CONTRACTORS, INC. v. OTTINGER (cont.) 562 N.E.2d 1247 (Ill.App. 1990)

Ottingers' attorney constituted an effective rescission of the contract. Mor-Wood elected to treat the contract as rescinded and to seek recovery under **quantum meruit** for the reasonable value of the services it had performed and for the materials furnished to the Ottingers before the rescission of the contract. Where one party repudiates a contract and refuses to be bound by it, the injured party may treat the contract as rescinded and recover under quantum meruit so far as he or she has performed. Thus, the trial court correctly determined that Mor-Wood could recover under quantum meruit.

BUSINESS CONSIDERATIONS What could Morvay, Mor-Wood's representative, have done differently when he spoke to Mr. Ottinger shortly after the 21 October 1987 issuance of the permit? Would a different approach possibly have avoided this litigation? Why or why not?

ETHICAL CONSIDERATIONS Assess the respective ethics of Ottinger's stopping payment on the check and Mor-Wood's leaving the job site in November. Had one party behaved relatively more ethically than the other?

Accord and Satisfaction

Parties may agree to accept performance different from that required by their original bargain (as discussed in Chapter 11 concerning consideration in unliquidated debt situations). The law calls such an agreement an *accord*. When the parties comply with the accord, *satisfaction* occurs; and discharge of the original claim by *accord and satisfaction* (that is, substituted performance) has resulted. The process of accord and satisfaction requires evidence of assent. Moreover, an accord will not be legally binding unless and until the performance required in the accord (that is, the satisfaction) is rendered.

Novation

Just as the parties may agree to substituted performances, so they may agree to substituted parties. A *novation* is a contract that effects an immediate discharge of a previously existing contractual obligation, creates a new contractual obligation or duty, and includes as a party to this new agreement one who in the original contract neither was owed a duty nor obligated to perform. A novation, then, is a contract in which a new party is substituted for one of the parties in the previous contract. The novation immediately discharges an obligation, whereas in contrast an accord is not executed until performance occurs. As you might expect, both the assent of the person to whom the obligation is owed (usually the creditor) and the assent of the new obligor (third party) are required for a valid novation. The assent of the previous debtor usually is not required, although that party can, if it wishes, disclaim the benefit of the discharge. The novation, in addition, must be supported by valid consideration.

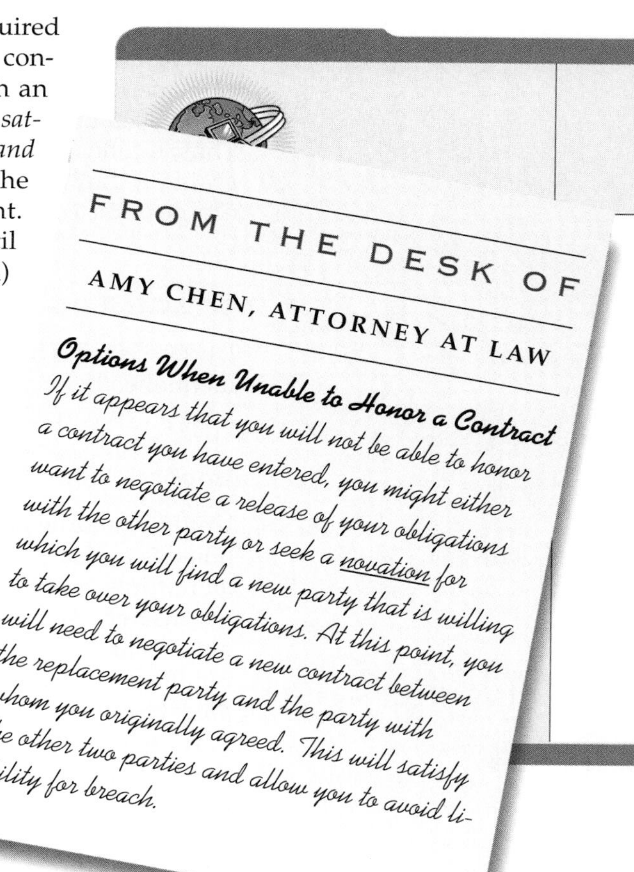

FROM THE DESK OF
AMY CHEN, ATTORNEY AT LAW
Options When Unable to Honor a Contract
If it appears that you will not be able to honor a contract you have entered, you might either want to negotiate a release of your obligations with the other party or seek a novation for which you will find a new party that is willing to take over your obligations. At this point, you will need to negotiate a new contract between the replacement party and the party with whom you originally agreed. This will satisfy the other two parties and allow you to avoid liability for breach.

Quantum meruit
An equitable remedy allowing one to recover the reasonable value of the services rendered.

DISCHARGE BY OPERATION OF LAW

We have seen in other contexts that the law itself can mandate the discharge of certain contracts. As you will learn in Chapter 29, bankruptcy decrees may grant to honest debtors a discharge of contractual obligations by operation of law. Most of the time a creditor will not receive the total owed, and yet the discharge in bankruptcy prevents the creditor from later suing the debtor for nonperformance (usually nonpayment). Most states, however, pursuant to the Bankruptcy Act's provisions, allow the debtor to revive the obligation by a later promise to pay the creditor. This reaffirmation of the debt involves several stringent new requirements under the Bankruptcy Act.

Statutes of limitations in all jurisdictions establish time periods within which, depending on the nature of the claims, litigants must initiate lawsuits. Noncompliance with these statutory time limits may discharge contractual claims by operation of law. For example, one typically must bring claims for breach of common law contracts within six years of the date of the alleged breach. Filing a lawsuit after this time limit makes the claim unenforceable. When the transaction involves a sale of goods, § 2-725 of the UCC states that the injured party ordinarily must file suit within four years of the occurrence of the breach. The underlying claim is discharged by operation of law if the injured party fails to file a lawsuit within this period. These periods of limitations differ from jurisdiction to jurisdiction, so each state's statutes should be checked.

The law also may grant a discharge of any contract that one of the parties to the agreement has materially altered. Before this rule will be applied, it must be shown that the alteration was done intentionally and without the consent of the other party. Thus, if Johnson, without Kreczewski's permission, changes the carload price of the grain on the written contract from $2,000 to $5,000, Kreczewski can obtain a discharge of the contract through operation of law.

DISCHARGE BY NONPERFORMANCE

Under certain circumstances, nonperformance may discharge a contract. Still, as mentioned before, do not expect courts to apply these doctrines in order to save you from a bad bargain.

Impossibility

Until the middle of the last century, courts rejected outright the doctrine of impossibility as a method of discharging contracts. *Impossibility* as a legal concept refers to an unforeseen event or condition that precludes a party's performing as promised. For instance, such events as the destruction of the subject matter of the contract without the fault of either party (Johnson's wheat burns before being loaded), supervening illegality (after the contract's formation, the legislature passes a law making it illegal for trains to carry agricultural products into certain states), or conduct by one party that makes performance by the other party impossible (in carrying out other deals, Kreczewski contracts for every possible car so that Johnson cannot procure the necessary cars for their transaction) generally discharge contracts. These examples denote *objective impossibility* (nonperformance of the contract is unavoidable; *no one* could perform the contract in these circumstances).

Another instance of objective impossibility involves the death or disability of either party to a personal services contract (Johnson hires Pollock to paint his portrait, and Pollock has a debilitating heart attack). This contingency forms an exception to the general rule that a contract will be binding and thus not dischargeable except through performance despite the death or disability of either party, unless the parties have agreed otherwise. The contract will not be discharged, however, if another painter is acceptable to Johnson.

On the other hand, courts have held that circumstances involving subjective impossibility (as opposed to objective impossibility) will not discharge contractual obligations. *Subjective impossibility* consists of nonperformance owing to personal, as contrasted to external, impossibility. In such cases, the contract can be performed, but *this particular person* is unable to fulfill the obligations contemplated in the contract. For this reason, nonperformance owing to insolvency, shortages of materials, strikes, riots, droughts, and price increases ordinarily will not discharge contracts. However, some courts temporarily will suspend the duty to perform until the conditions causing the inability to perform have passed. More liberal courts even may discharge the contract if later performance will place an appreciably greater burden on the one obligated to perform. Given this division of opinion, the parties often will try to protect their rights by including express provisions covering the types of contingencies just described. Still, it is up to the courts to decide the validity of any such clauses.

Commercial Frustration

Because of the harshness of the general rule that impossibility ordinarily will not discharge the performance called for in a contract, the doctrine of *commercial frustration* (or *frustration of purpose*) has recently emerged as a basis for justifiable nonperformance. Courts will not invoke this doctrine to excuse performance, however, unless the essential purpose and value of the contract have been frustrated. If the parties reasonably could (or should) have foreseen the resultant frustration, courts will hold the nonperforming party to the terms of the bargain. Hence, courts will not utilize this doctrine to release parties from bad bargains. It is important to understand that in these cases performance is possible; but the value of the contract has been frustrated or destroyed by a supervening event that was not reasonably anticipated at the contract's formation. The Uniform Commercial Code uses the term *commercially impracticable* (§ 2-615) in like fashion to excuse nonperformance in cases of severe shortages of raw materials owing to war, embargo, local crop failure, and other similar reasons. Before courts will allow discharge, these factors must have caused a marked increase in price or must have totally precluded the seller from obtaining the supplies necessary for performance.

In the *Chase Precast* case, the court accepted the doctrine of commercial frustration as a defense.

15.2

MANAGEMENT

DEFENSES TO CONTRACT ENFORCEMENT

One of John's professors mentioned in class last week that a number of subcontractors who encounter difficulties in meeting their contractual obligations often try to use the defenses of impossibility, impracticability, or commercial frustration to escape liability when they fail to satisfy their contracts. Call-Image jobs out much of its work to subcontractors, and John is concerned that these sorts of situations might arise with the firm. He asks you what the firm should do to protect itself. What will you tell him?

BUSINESS CONSIDERATIONS Should a business enter into contracts that it is not sure it can perform, hoping to use impracticability as an excuse if it cannot perform as promised? What legal risk is the firm assuming if it uses such an approach to its obligations?

ETHICAL CONSIDERATIONS Is it ethical for a firm to avoid liability by asserting that its promised performance was made impossible or impracticable by some external factor? Is it ethical for a firm to try to collect damages when an external factor made the performance by the other firm impossible or impracticable?

15.2 CHASE PRECAST CORPORATION v. JOHN J. PAONESSA COMPANY, INC.

566 N.E.2d 603 (Mass. 1991)

FACTS In 1982, the commonwealth of Massachusetts, through the Department of Public Works, entered into two contracts with the John J. Paonessa Company, Inc. (Paonessa) for resurfacing and improvements to two stretches of Route 128. Part of each contract called for replacing a grass median strip between the north- and southbound lanes with concrete surfacing and precast-concrete median barriers. Paonessa entered into two contracts with Chase Precast Corporation (Chase) under which Chase was to supply, in the aggregate, 25,800 linear feet of concrete median barriers according to the specifications of the department for highway construction. After this highway construction began in the spring of 1983, the department began receiving protests from angry residents who objected to the use of the concrete median barriers and the removal of the grass median strip. Paonessa and Chase became aware of the protest around 1 June. On 6 June, a group of about 100 citizens filed an action in superior court to stop the installation of the concrete median barriers and other aspects of the work. On 7 June, anticipating modification by the department, Paonessa notified Chase by letter to stop producing concrete barriers for the projects. Upon receipt of the letter the following day, Chase did so. On 17 June, the department and the citizens' group entered into a settlement providing, in part, for the banning of the installation of any additional concrete median barriers. On 23 June, the Department deleted the permanent concrete median barriers item from its contracts with Paonessa. Before stopping production on 8 June, Chase had produced approximately one-half of the concrete median barriers called for by its contracts with Paonessa and had delivered most of them to the construction sites. Paonessa paid Chase at the contract price for all that Chase had produced. Although Chase had suffered no out-of-pocket expenses as a result of the cancellation of the remaining portion of the barriers, it sued Paonessa to recover the profits it allegedly had lost owing to the cancellation of the contracts to supply the median barriers. Paonessa defended on the grounds of impossibility and frustration of purpose.

ISSUE Did either the doctrine of impossibility or the doctrine of frustration of purpose serve as a defense to immunize Paonessa from liability?

HOLDING The doctrine of frustration of purpose immunized Paonessa from liability because, at the time of contract formation, the parties had not contemplated the cancellation of the items and thus in the contract had not allocated the risk of such cancellation to either party.

REASONING Massachusetts courts have long recognized and applied the doctrine of impossibility as a defense to an action for breach of contract. Under Massachusetts courts' construction of that doctrine

> *where from the nature of the contract it appears that the parties must from the beginning have contemplated the continued existence of some particular specified thing as the foundation of what was to be done, then, in the absence of any warranty that the thing shall exist . . . the parties shall be excused . . . [when] performance becomes impossible from the accidental perishing of the thing without the fault of either party.*

On the other hand, although Massachusetts courts have referred to the doctrine of frustration of purpose in a few decisions, they never have clearly defined it. Other jurisdictions, however, have explained the doctrine as follows: When an event neither anticipated nor caused by either party, the risk of which was not allocated by the contract, destroys the object or purpose of the contract, thus destroying the value of performance, the parties are excused from further performance.

At least one Massachusetts precedent has called frustration of purpose a "companion rule" to the doctrine of impossibility. Both doctrines concern the effect of supervening circumstances on the rights and duties of the parties. The difference lies in the effect of the supervening event. Under frustration of purpose, performance remains possible; but the fortuitous event has destroyed the expected value of the performance to the party seeking to be excused. Clearly, frustration of purpose represents a more accurate label for the defense argued in this case than impossibility of performance, since performance was not literally impossible. Paonessa still could have honored its contract to purchase the remaining sections of median barrier, whether or not the department approved their use in the road construction. The principal question in both kinds of cases remains whether an unanticipated circumstance, the risk of which should not fairly be thrown on the promisor, has made performance vitally different from what was reasonably to be expected.

In the present case, Paonessa bore no responsibility for the department's elimination of the median barriers from the projects. Therefore, whether Paonessa can rely on the defense of frustration of purpose turns on whether elimination of the barriers was a risk allocated by the contracts to Paonessa. Simply put, given the commercial circumstances in which the parties dealt, was the contingency that developed one that the parties could reasonably have foreseen as a real possibility that could affect performance? Or, alternatively, was it one of that variety of risks that the par-

15.2 CHASE PRECAST CORPORATION v. JOHN J. PAONESSA COMPANY, INC. *(cont.)* 566 N.E.2d 603 (Mass. 1991)

ties, by their failure to provide for it explicitly, were tacitly assigning to the promisor? If it was, performance will be required. If it cannot be so considered, performance is excused. This becomes a question for the trier of fact. Paonessa's contracts with the department contain a standard provision allowing the department to eliminate items or portions of work found unnecessary. The purchase order agreements between Chase and Paonessa do not contain a similar provision. Yet this difference in the contracts does not mandate the conclusion that Paonessa assumed the risk of reduction in the quantity of barriers. Chase was aware of the department's power to decrease the quantities of contract items, since Chase had supplied median barriers to the department in the past; and the provision giving the department the power to eliminate items was a standard one. In this case, even if the parties were aware generally of the department's power to eliminate contract items, the judge could reasonably have concluded that they had not contemplated the cancellation for a major portion of the project of such a widely used item as concrete median barriers and had failed to allocate the risk of such a cancellation. Hence, the doctrine of frustration of purpose would discharge Paonessa's remaining duties to render performance and would immunize it from liability to Chase for lost profits.

BUSINESS CONSIDERATIONS The citizens' group's lawsuit led to Paonessa's canceling the contracts with Chase concerning the median barriers. Should the law allow citizens' protests to interfere with the contractual rights of private parties like Paonessa and Chase? Why or why not? Would the fact that these were state-initiated contracts affect your viewpoint?

ETHICAL CONSIDERATIONS Paonessa paid Chase for all the concrete median barriers Chase had produced before the cancellation of the contract occurred. Was Chase's suit for lost profits unethical?

Actual Breach

Breach of contract occurs when one or more of the contracting parties fails to perform the obligations set up by the contract. That degrees of breach exist complicates the issue somewhat. A *complete or actual* breach of contract involves the nonperformance of a duty that is so material and essential to the agreement that the other party is justified in treating the agreement as at an end. The Uniform Commercial Code in §§ 2-703 and 2-711 embraces this common law principle. Actual breach generally discharges the other party's obligation to perform under the terms of the contract. However, rather than canceling the contract upon breach, the injured (or nonbreaching) party may elect instead to hold the nonperforming party to the contract through various types of remedies, which we will discuss later in this chapter.

The following case deals with a situation in which each party to the contract accused the other party of breach. Note how the court resolved these issues.

15.3 MARSHALL CONSTRUCTION, LTD. v. COASTAL SHEET METAL & ROOFING, INC. 569 So.2d 845 (Fla.App. 1990)

FACTS On 20 February 1988, Marshall Construction, Ltd. (Marshall) entered into a general contract with the state of Florida for the repair and replacement of the roofs of buildings 51, 52, and 53 at the Florida State Hospital in Chattahoochee, Florida, for the sum of $239,095. The contract called for substantial completion within 120 days after the date of the notice to proceed and final completion within 30 days after the date of substantial completion. In

15.3 MARSHALL CONSTRUCTION, LTD. v. COASTAL SHEET METAL & ROOFING, INC. *(cont.)* 569 So.2d 845 (Fla.App. 1990)

the event that Marshall failed to complete the contract within the time specifications, the contract required Marshall to pay liquidated damages. In March 1988, Marshall and Coastal Sheet Metal & Roofing, Inc. (Coastal) entered into an oral contract to replace the roofs of buildings 51, 52, and 53. Coastal was to perform the work; Marshall was to receive $7,265 for its bond premium and for its fee; and Coastal was to receive the balance of Marshall's contract with the state. Coastal agreed to replace the roof according to the specifications of the architect. Coastal received notice to proceed on 28 March 1988, and Coastal was given 120 days for substantial completion and an additional 30 days for final completion. A problem subsequently developed with the roofing system installed in building 51 because water had penetrated the roof insulation. Both parties agreed that, because of these defects, the new roof on the east wing of building 51 needed replacing. Coastal admitted that it could not afford to proceed with the work—including the repair of the defective roof—unless Marshall paid it for the work already completed. On 15 June 1988, Coastal stopped work on the project. Marshall requested several times that Coastal continue the work, but Coastal refused to work until it received payment. On 24 June 1988, Marshall ordered Coastal off the job and hired someone else to complete the work. Coastal subsequently filed a complaint against Marshall seeking damages for breach of an oral contract and alleging that Marshall had wrongfully discharged Coastal from the contract prior to the completion of the construction. Coastal also claimed it was entitled to the performance bond issued to Marshall by Continental Insurance Company relating to the roofing project. Marshall filed a counterclaim seeking damages for Coastal's breach of contract and negligent workmanship.

ISSUE Did Coastal's failure to replace the roofing system amount to a material breach of its contract with Marshall?

HOLDING Yes. Coastal's refusal to repair the roof without further payment represented a material breach of the contract that would discharge Marshall's duty to pay Coastal.

REASONING A well-settled contract principle states that unexpected difficulty, expense, or hardship does not excuse a party from the performance of its obligations under a contract. In addition, in order to maintain an action for breach of contract, the claimant first must establish its own performance of the contractual obligations imposed in the contract. Here, Coastal failed to install the roofing system on the east wing as required under the contract. When Coastal refused to repair the work without further payment, it committed a material breach that entitled Marshall to treat the breach as a discharge of its duty to pay Coastal until Coastal repaired the defective roof and fulfilled its contractual duties. The terms of the contract had required substantial completion by 25 July 1988, and Coastal had refused to return to work without being paid. These facts completely justified Marshall's concluding that a material breach had occurred and then ordering Coastal off the job. No substantial, competent evidence surfaced to support a finding that Marshall had breached the contract. Rather, the undisputed evidence demonstrated that Coastal had committed a material breach of the contract. This breach, in turn, excused Marshall's obligation to pay Coastal until Coastal had completed the repairs to the roof.

BUSINESS CONSIDERATIONS Should Marshall and Coastal's contract have spelled out with more particularity what would constitute substantial performance and/or material breach? Is it feasible (or indeed possible) to set out such specifications in construction contracts?

ETHICAL CONSIDERATIONS Should the fact that the contract here involved a state hospital (and thus presumably sick people) have entered into the ethics of Coastal's decision to stop work at the job site or into Marshall's decision to withhold payment? Why or why not?

Anticipatory Breach

Sometimes one of the contracting parties will indicate in advance, through words or conduct, that he or she does not intend to abide by the terms of the contract. To illustrate, if Johnson unequivocally tells Kreczewski before the time performance is due that he will not send the grain as scheduled, Johnson will have wrongfully repudiated the contract. In legal terms, Johnson's action is called *anticipatory breach,* or *anticipatory repudiation.* In this situation, as in actual breaches, the injured party need not limit its potential responses to discharge of the contract.

The Uniform Commercial Code sanctions a kind of anticipatory repudiation in circumstances less definite than those allowable under the common law. Section 2-609 of the Code states that when reasonable grounds for insecurity arise with respect to one party's performance, the other party may demand adequate assurances of due performance and suspend performance until such assurances are forthcoming. If 30 days pass without reply, the party who has demanded the assurances can deem the contract repudiated. Kreczewski's actual or apparent **insolvency**, for example, may cause Johnson to invoke the provisions of § 2-609. If Kreczewski does not respond within 30 days, Johnson then may treat the contract as repudiated (see § 2-610).

Insolvency
Inability to pay one's debts as they become due.

Conditions

The presence of conditions may result in nonperformance that will justify discharge of a contract as well. A *promise* is a vow or a covenant that places on the promisor a duty to do something or to refrain from doing something. A *condition,* in contrast, is an act or event that limits or qualifies a promise. The condition must occur before the promisor has a duty to perform or to refrain from performing.

Courts classify conditions in two ways. The first category emphasizes the *timing* of the qualifying occurrence (the condition) in relation to the promised performance. Three subsets of this category include *conditions precedent, concurrent conditions,* and *conditions subsequent.* The second category stems from the *manner* in which the conditions arise. Conditions created by law are deemed *constructive* (or *implied*) *conditions.* In contrast, conditions created by the agreement of the parties themselves are called *express conditions.*

Under the first category (timing), an agreement may explicitly state that a certain act or event must occur before the other party has a duty to perform or before a contract results. If so, a *condition precedent* exists. For example, a person may promise (for consideration) to buy a car if the seller can deliver the car within 10 days. A duty to buy the car does not arise unless and until the seller fulfills the condition. Thus, the timing of the condition and any later duty to perform go together.

To be a condition precedent rather than a mere promise, the parties must indicate that the condition is an essential, vital aspect of the transaction. If the buyer in our example later wishes to sue for rescission of the contract or for damages on the ground that the seller has not delivered the car on time, the buyer will have to prove that delivery within 10 days is essential to the transaction. A common condition precedent involves a buyer's signing a contract for the purchase of a new house subject to the sale of the buyer's current residence. The buyer views this provision as an important consideration regarding his or her willingness to enter into the contract.

Concurrent conditions, related to conditions precedent in regard to the timing of the condition and the promised performance, obligate the parties *to perform at the same time.* Concurrent conditions (for example, the transfer of goods in exchange for payment) underlie most commercial sales.

A *condition subsequent* is any occurrence that the parties have agreed will cut off an existing legal duty. It also may be a contingency, the happening or performance of which will defeat a contract already in effect. When a sales contract involving grain storage states that the contract will be of no effect if fire destroys the grain, a condition subsequent exists.

Genuine conditions subsequent are rare. What may sound like a condition subsequent—for example, "Acme Insurance will not pay for casualty losses if the premises are unoccupied"—will be construed by many courts as a condition precedent. Courts that characterize such a provision as a condition subsequent will interpret the clause as stating that the occurrence of the condition (vacant premises) will cut off an existing legal duty (payment of the casualty loss). Other courts will say that it is a condition precedent (the premises must be kept occupied) that merely sounds like a condition subsequent because of the phrasing. This distinction can be procedurally significant. If it is a condition precedent, the insured has the burden of proof; if it is a condition subsequent, the insurer has the burden of proof. And when the evidence is conflicting, the party who has the burden of proof often loses.

Express conditions (for example, "This sale can be consummated only by payment of cash") are those spelled out by the parties explicitly or impliedly in fact. A *constructive condition* is one not expressed by the parties, but rather read into the contract in order to serve justice (that is, the condition is implied in law). Differentiating between an express condition implied in fact and a constructive condition can be difficult. For example, a provision regarding place of delivery normally is a condition precedent in a contract involving grain; but if such a condition is lacking, and in the absence of clear intent, a court may imply that the place for delivery is the seller's place of business (see UCC § 2-308).

Nonperformance of an express condition precedent (such as posting a performance bond) causes a failure of the condition that nullifies the other party's duty to perform and discharges the contract. Similarly, the presence of an express condition subsequent (meaning that the occurrence of a particular event cuts off all ongoing contractual duties) discharges the obligations of both parties. For example, the buyer's returning goods before payment is due under the terms of a contract in which the buyer has reserved this right would constitute discharge of the contract. But to avoid a breach of an express condition, courts ordinarily require strict compliance. In contrast, substantial compliance generally avoids a breach of a constructive condition.

It should be noted that a condition may require one party to perform "to the satisfaction" of the other party. In fact, in certain cases, such as those involving custom tailoring, some courts hold that in order to discharge the contract, the performing party must meet the personal, subjective expectations of the dissatisfied party. Other courts hold that performance is substantial if the performance rendered will satisfy our old friend, a reasonable person. Courts generally will apply this latter test when the parties base performance not on personal tastes or aesthetic preferences (as may be involved in our custom tailoring example) but rather on satisfaction as to merchantability or mechanical utility (as in the purchase of a car).

TYPES OF REMEDIES

Upon breach of contract, in order to satisfy his or her expectations as of the time of contract formation, the injured party can choose among various remedies.

The most common legal remedy sought consists of *damages.* The injured party must *mitigate,* or minimize, these damages; but having fulfilled this legal duty, the injured party at the very least should be able to receive *compensatory damages,* those

YOU BE THE JUDGE

Confidentiality and Nondisparagement Clauses

In this era of corporate downsizing, severance agreements that contain confidentiality and nondisparagement clauses—which prohibit departing employees from saying anything negative about the company to persons who may be suing the company under various state and federal laws—have become commonplace. Indeed, severance agreements long have included provisions in which the employee agrees to waive a panoply of claims against a company and to refrain from saying anything negative about the employer to other employees, a competitor, or the media. Simply put, such broadly-worded settlement agreements and releases nowadays represent the *quid pro quo* that employers expect in return for settlement payments. Critics of such agreements have charged that the resultant veil of contractual secrecy unfairly hinders remaining employees from making informed decisions about such things as whether they, too, are victims of illegal discrimination. These critics therefore focus on the tension between society's interest in promoting settlements and these agreements' potential suppression of information regarding alleged injuries.

Suppose that a departing employee wanted to talk to the Equal Opportunity Commission (the EEOC) about allegations of discrimination—say sexual harassment—within the firm, and that the former employer was attempting to enforce this sort of clause to prevent such a discussion. If this case were brought before *your* court, how would *you* rule? Would you strike down a settlement agreement that prohibits a departing employee from talking to the EEOC, or would you uphold such a settlement agreement?[3]

BUSINESS CONSIDERATIONS Why would a company want to have a nondisparagement clause in a severance agreement? Why would an employee sign such an agreement?

ETHICAL CONSIDERATIONS Is it ethical for an employer to ask a departing employee to surrender his or her right to free speech in exchange for a settlement package upon termination of the employment? What sorts of ethical issues are raised by such a contract clause?

SOURCE: Darryl Van Duch, *The National Law Journal* (28 October 1996), pp. B1 and B3.

that will put the party in the same economic position that he or she would have occupied had the other party performed. If the facts permit, the injured party moreover may receive *consequential damages,* those indirect or special damages springing from the effects or aftermath of the breach itself; *punitive damages,* those damages over and above the actual damages that a court may award in order to deter the defendant from future malicious conduct; and *liquidated damages,* those agreed on in advance by the parties in the event breach occurs. A court also may award *nominal damages* (a small amount of compensation) for minor, technical contractual breaches that cause no actual losses.

In some situations, money damages will represent inadequate compensation for the loss of the bargain occasioned by the breach. Injured persons in these cases ordinarily resort to *equitable* remedies. These possible modes of relief include *rescission,* the cancellation or termination of the contract through the restoration of the parties to the status quo. Restoration is accomplished by *restitution*—the return of the goods, money, or property involved in the contract or the recovery of the reasonable value of the services rendered. *Specific performance,* that is, the court-ordered enforcement of the contract according to its exact terms, is an alternative type of equitable remedy, as is quasi contract. *Quasi contract,* you may remember, refers to the situation in which a court creates a contract for the parties, despite their wishes and intentions, in order to prevent the unjust enrichment of one party. The remedy available in quasi contract is restitution-based, allowing the injured party to recover the reasonable value of the services rendered. *Reformation,* the court's rewriting of a contract in order to remove a mistake and to make the agreement conform to the terms to which the parties originally agreed, and *injunctions,* court-ordered writs directing a person to do or to refrain from doing some specified act, constitute two other equitable remedies.

It has been said that for every legal wrong the law attempts to provide a legal remedy. This chapter explores some of the contractual remedies that are obtainable. Exhibit 15.2 classifies various common types of contractual remedies.

EXHIBIT 15.2 Types of Contractual Remedies

Type of Remedy	Definition
Legal remedies (money damages)	Those damages resulting from a court's exercise of its power "at law."
Compensatory damages	Damages awarded to a nonbreaching party in order to compensate him or her for the actual, foreseeable harm or loss caused by the breach.
Consequential damages	Indirect or special damages springing from the effects or aftermath (that is, the consequences) of the breach itself; not recoverable unless the breaching party knew, or should have known, at the time of contract formation of the potential effect of a breach on the nonbreaching party.
Punitive damages	Unusual damages awarded to punish for willful, wanton, malicious harm caused to a nonbreaching party.
Nominal damages	Inconsequential sums that establish that the plaintiff had a cause of action but suffered no measurable pecuniary loss.
Liquidated damages	A provision in a contract that a stated sum of money or property will be paid, or forfeited if previously deposited, if one of the parties fails to perform in accordance with the contract; enforceable unless unreasonable.
Mitigation of damages	Nonbreaching party's duty to reduce the actual losses, if he or she is able to do so.
Equitable remedies	Remedies arising from a court's use of its powers of equity.
Rescission and restitution	The cancellation or abrogation of a contract and the return of the previously rendered consideration or its value; may be mutually agreed to by the parties to a contract or awarded as a remedy by a court.
Specific performance	An order by a court to render a contractually promised performance.
Quasi contract	A court's requiring that one who has received a benefit pay for the benefit conferred in order to prevent the unjust enrichment of that party.
Reformation	A court's correction of an agreement to conform to the intentions of the parties.
Injunction	An order requiring a person to act or restraining a person from doing some act.
Waiver of breach	A party's relinquishment, repudiation, or surrender of a right that he or she has to seek a remedy for breach of contract.

DAMAGES

When one party breaches a contract, the other party is entitled to payment for lost expectations. The injured party therefore can bring an action for damages. It is not necessary that the injured party have the ability to compute exactly what the damages are, as long as the losses represent the natural and proximate consequences of the breach. In computing damages, courts ask whether the breaching party, as a reasonable person, at the time of contracting should have foreseen that these injuries would result from breach. If the nonperforming party should have foreseen the losses, courts will award damages to the injured party. The amount of damages awarded of course will depend heavily on the facts of the case.

Compensatory Damages

The most common type of damages is *compensatory damages,* or those sums of money that will place the injured party in the same economic position that would have been attained had the contract been performed. Such damages also are called *actual* damages. Injured parties may recover only the damages that the parties reasonably can foresee.

The 1854 English case, *Hadley* v. *Baxendale,* enunciated this doctrine, which courts still widely accept as a limitation on the damages recoverable for breach of contract. Under the *Hadley* v. *Baxendale* rule, courts ordinarily will confine compensatory damages awards to those losses naturally arising from the breach, or those the parties may have reasonably contemplated or foreseen, at the time of contract formation, as the probable result of a breach of the contract. Compensatory damages include all damages directly attributable to the loss of the bargain previously agreed on by the parties, including lost profits and any incidental expenses incurred as a result of the breach. In a sale of goods, courts, in formulating the actual damages, usually compute the difference between the contract price and the market price. The same ordinarily is true of land contracts. Thus, if Miranda Construction Company, a developer of real estate for its own particular purposes, orders three bulldozers from Welling Machinery Company and, unfortunately, none of the bulldozers functions properly, Miranda should be able to recover the general or *direct damages* or losses occasioned by the defective equipment. Miranda's costs of repairing the machines constitute one type of direct loss. Alternatively, if Miranda has to buy new bulldozers at higher prices, Miranda will be able to recover the costs associated with obtaining this substitute performance.

Assuming that Miranda's bad luck continues and a seller with whom Miranda has contracted to buy land for investment purposes fails to go through with this realty contract, Miranda can sue the reneging seller for the difference between the price of this piece of land and the one Miranda eventually purchases. Miranda also can sue for such expenses as the additional brokers' fees or commissions involved in obtaining the second parcel of real estate, since these losses flow directly and foreseeably from the seller's breach as well. However, Miranda in both cases must deduct any expenses saved as a result of the breaches.

Consequential Damages

Besides compensatory damages, it also is possible for plaintiffs like Miranda to receive *consequential damages.* Consequential damages are those indirect or special

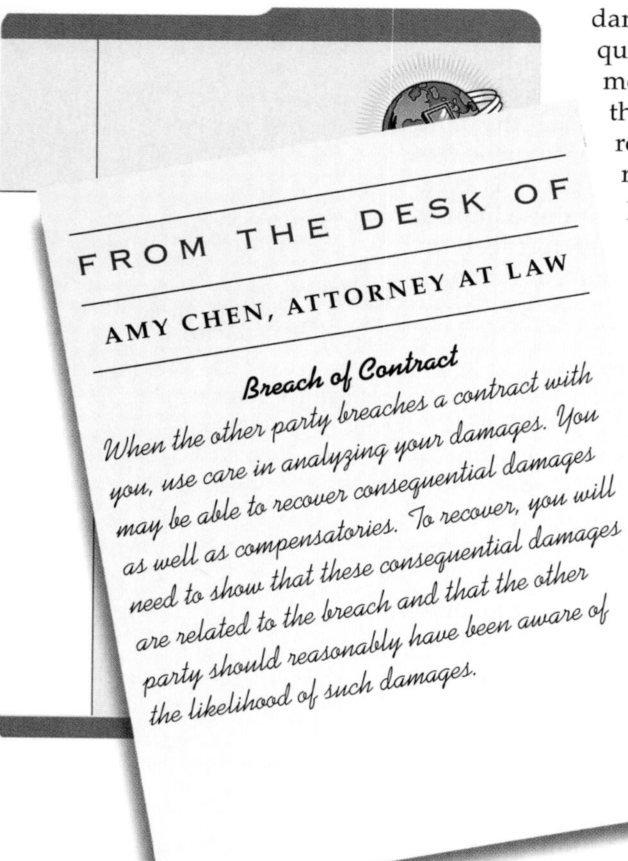

damages springing from the effects or aftermath (that is, the consequences) of the breach itself. Assume that in addition to the contracts mentioned, Miranda loses a grading contract with the city because the bulldozers will not work and, as a result, also loses several rental contracts from retailers who wished to be part of a mall Miranda was planning to develop on the real estate he had tried to purchase. Can Miranda sue Welling and the seller for the losses accruing from these special circumstances and not just from the direct breach? To determine liability or the lack thereof, a court will apply the reasonable person test to see whether such lost contracts were a foreseeable result of Welling and the seller's breaches. A judge will not award purely speculative or conjectural damages; but if a court finds Welling and the seller knew, or should have known, at the time of contract formation, of Miranda's circumstances and the potential effect of their breaches on Miranda, it may award incidental or consequential damages. The Uniform Commercial Code in §§ 2-715 and 2-710 also recognizes this doctrine.

FROM THE DESK OF
AMY CHEN, ATTORNEY AT LAW
Breach of Contract
When the other party breaches a contract with you, use care in analyzing your damages. You may be able to recover consequential damages as well as compensatories. To recover, you will need to show that these consequential damages are related to the breach and that the other party should reasonably have been aware of the likelihood of such damages.

Duty to Mitigate

In determining whether to award damages and, if so, how to measure them, courts place on the injured party the duty to *mitigate* (or minimize) these damages if possible. In other words, the injured party must take affirmative steps to prevent the escalation of the losses brought about by the breaching party.

In our bulldozer example, courts will expect Miranda to attempt to procure substitute bulldozers, assuming this is possible without undue risk or expense. If Miranda does not undertake such reasonable steps, his failure to mitigate damages will preclude his receiving consequential damages. Rather, the court will limit his losses to those accruing directly from the breach. But if Miranda can prove it was impossible to obtain substitute bulldozers, most courts will excuse his failure to mitigate. The duty of mitigation does not require the injured party to go to superhuman lengths. If the risks or expenses in mitigation attempts are unreasonably great, no duty to mitigate arises.

Punitive Damages

In contrast to their willingness to make compensatory and consequential damages available to injured parties, courts generally will not allow the recovery of *punitive* damages in breach of contract situations. *Punitive,* or exemplary, damages are imposed not to compensate the injured party but to punish the wrongdoer in order to deter future conduct of this sort. The old common law rule was that punitive damages never were appropriate for breaches of contract. Though still rare, some statutes now permit the imposition of punitive damages in contractual situations (such as **treble damages** under the antitrust laws). Furthermore, some courts have been willing to grant punitive damages in situations in which one party has acted willfully. An insurance company that unduly delays paying off legitimate contractual claims against it may be subject to punitive damages in order to discourage this

Treble damages
A statutory remedy that allows the successful plaintiff to recover three times the damages suffered as a result of the injury.

type of conduct. If the circumstances so warrant, consumer transactions also may form the basis for an award of punitive damages.

In the *Haslip* case, the Supreme Court upheld a punitive damages award in a contract action involving an insurance company. On appeal, the insurance company challenged as unconstitutional the jury's discretion to award such damages under the common law. Note how the Court handled this contention.

Respondeat superior
Doctrine asserting that an employer is liable for the tortious acts of employees while they are acting within the scope of their employment.

15.4 PACIFIC MUTUAL LIFE INSURANCE COMPANY v. HASLIP 499 U.S. 1 (1991)

FACTS Beginning in August 1981, Cleopatra Haslip and other employees of Roosevelt City, Alabama, had paid premiums to Lemmie L. Ruffin, Jr., a Pacific Mutual Life Insurance Company (Pacific Mutual) agent, for health and life insurance. After her hospitalization in January 1982, Haslip discovered that she had no insurance coverage. Apparently, Ruffin had failed to remit the premiums he had collected to the appropriate insurers, with the result that Haslip's policies had lapsed without her knowledge. Owing to Ruffin's misappropriation of these premiums, Haslip sued Pacific Mutual for damages in fraud and sought to hold the company liable on a theory of **respondeat superior**. Following the court's charge instructing the jury that it could award punitive damages if it determined liability for fraud existed, the jury, among other things, returned a verdict for Haslip of more than one million dollars against Pacific Mutual and Ruffin. This sum included a punitive damages award representing more than four times the amount of compensatory damages Haslip had claimed. The Supreme Court of Alabama affirmed and specifically upheld the punitive damages award. On appeal to the U.S. Supreme Court, Pacific Mutual argued that the punitive damages award assessed against it violated the due process clause of the Fourteenth Amendment.

ISSUE Would the due process clause of the Fourteenth Amendment, which requires fundamental fairness, act as a check on undue jury discretion to award punitive damages and, in the absence of any express statutory limits, thus place outer limits on the size of such civil damages awards?

HOLDING No. The common law method for assessing punitive damages, consistently upheld by state and federal courts for many years, would not demonstrate such inherent unfairness as to deny defendants due process.

REASONING Punitive damages long have been a part of traditional state tort law in the United States. And as early as the 1700s in England, Blackstone appeared to note their use. Moreover, the early American cases (in the 1780s and 1790s) that used the traditional common law approach allowed the jury, after a court's instructing it to consider the gravity of the wrong and the need to deter similar wrongful conduct, initially to determine the amount of the punitive damages award. Trial and appellate courts then reviewed the jury's determination to ensure its reasonableness. Furthermore, it appears that every state and federal court that has considered the question has ruled that the common law method for assessing punitive damages is not so inherently unfair as to be per se unconstitutional and violative of due process.

On the other hand, it is inappropriate to say that, because courts have recognized punitive damages for so long, the imposition of such damages never is unconstitutional. One must concede that unlimited jury discretion (or unlimited judicial discretion) in the fixing of punitive damages might invite extreme results that jar one's constitutional sensibilities. In fact, concerns about punitive damages that "run wild" abound. Yet one need not, and indeed one cannot, draw mathematically precise lines between the constitutionally acceptable and the constitutionally unacceptable that will fit every case. Nonetheless, general concerns of reasonableness and adequate guidance for the court when the case is tried to a jury properly enter into this constitutional calculus.

In this case, the punitive damages assessed by the jury against Pacific Mutual did not violate the due process clause of the Fourteenth Amendment for the following reasons: First, the trial court's punitive damages instruction, which stated (1) that the purpose of punitive damages is to punish the defendant and to protect the public by deterring future wrongdoing and (2) that the jury had to consider the character and degree of wrong shown and the necessity of preventing similar wrong, reasonably accommodated Pacific Mutual's interest in rational decision making and the state's interest in meaningful individual assessment of appropriate deterrence and retribution without giving the jury undue discretion. Hence, no violation of the due process clause resulted from this instruction. Second, Alabama's post-trial procedures for scrutinizing punitive damages awards, which required trial courts to reflect in the record their reasons for interfering with the verdict or their refusing to do so owing to the excessiveness of the damages, included such

15.4 PACIFIC MUTUAL LIFE INSURANCE COMPANY v. HASLIP (cont.) 499 U.S. 1 (1991)

factors as a consideration of the culpability of the defendant's conduct, the desirability of discouraging others from similar conduct, and the impact on the parties or innocent third parties. Such post-trial procedures ensured meaningful and adequate review of punitive damages awards. Similarly, in this case, under Alabama law, the Alabama Supreme Court's review of this punitive damages award, by first undertaking a comparative analysis and then applying detailed substantive standards for evaluating the award to ensure that the award did not exceed the amount that would accomplish society's goals of punishment and deterrence, constituted an appropriate method to help assure the reasonableness of the amount of punitive damages and the rationality of the award in furthering the purposes of deterrence and punishment.

In short, such procedural safeguards imposed a sufficiently definite and meaningful constraint on the discretion of Alabama factfinders in awarding punitive damages to ensure that such awards were not grossly disproportionate to the severity of the offense and were adequate to protect the due process rights of an insurer whose agent had defrauded the insureds. In sum, the standard of proof requiring the jury to be "reasonably satisfied from the evidence" before it could impose punitive damages under Alabama law, when buttressed by other existing procedural and substantive protections, was constitutionally sufficient, notwithstanding the desirability of requiring a higher standard of proof. Hence, a punitive damages award of more than $800,000 against an insurer whose agent had defrauded an insured was reasonable and did not violate the insurer's due process rights, even though the award exceeded by more than four times the amount of compensatory damages, was more than 200 times the out-of-pocket expenses incurred by the insured, and greatly exceeded the fine that Alabama law imposed for insurance fraud.

BUSINESS CONSIDERATIONS What policies does the doctrine of *respondeat superior* further? Do you agree that these policies justify the imposition of strict (vicarious) liability on the employer? Why or why not?

ETHICAL CONSIDERATIONS What—if anything—could the company have done to ensure more ethical conduct on the part of its agent, Ruffin? Is the imposition of punitive damages on the employer (as opposed to Ruffin) in this case inherently unethical?

Notice how the *Haslip* Court emphasized the policy underpinnings for a jury's award of punitive damages. There must exist various procedural and substantive protections that act as a curb on the jury's otherwise unfettered discretion to award any amount of damages, no matter how gargantuan the award might be.

Indeed, relying on *Haslip,* the Court in the 1996 case, *BMW of North America, Inc.* v. *Gore,* 116 S.Ct. 1589 (1996), for the first time voided a state court's award of punitive damages as unconstitutional under the Fourteenth Amendment's due process clause. The Court held that a $2 million punitive damages award against BMW of North America, Inc. (BMW) for BMW's fraudulent failure to disclose that it had repainted a new $40,000 car, thereby reducing the vehicle's value by $4,000, was "grossly excessive."The jury apparently had arrived at the $4 million punitive damages figure it had awarded (the state supreme court had remitted—that is, lowered—-the damages to $2 million) by multiplying the $4,000 compensatory damages award by the 1,000 nationwide instances of BMW's similar nondisclosures of minor repairs. The Court stressed that while Alabama had the right to protect its own citizens through the punishment of firms that engage in deceptive trade practices, such a state would not have the right, by the imposition of a punitive damages award or a legislatively authorized fine, to punish out-of-state activity that was lawful where it had occurred. Hence, the Court viewed this $2 million award as excessive in light of the interest of Alabama consumers and BMW's conduct in Alabama. And while the Court quoted *Haslip* for the proposition that the Court cannot "draw a mathematically bright line" with regard to when the ratio between the compensatory and the punitive damages awarded would become unconstitutional, the Court concluded that when, as here, the ratio was "a breathtaking 500–1," any such award must surely "raise a suspicious judicial eyebrow." The Court then held that the grossly excessive award imposed in this case would transcend the constitutional limit.

Liquidated Damages

The parties may agree in advance that, upon breach of contract, a certain sum of money will be paid to the injured party. This remedy is called *liquidated damages.* The amount to which the parties have agreed in advance fully satisfies any liability attendant upon the breach that has occurred. Courts will enforce such provisions if (1) the agreed-on amount is reasonable and not out of proportion to the apparent injury resulting from the breach and (2) calculation of the resulting damages in advance and with any accuracy will be difficult, if not impossible. In the context of sales contracts, UCC § 2-718 takes a similar approach.

The contractor mentioned earlier, Miranda, may well find himself subject to such a clause. Construction contracts typically have clauses assessing a per-day charge for delays in completing a building on time. Because it is difficult to ascertain the amount of damages that breach of such a contract will cause, as long as the per-day charge is reasonable, courts generally uphold these clauses.

Courts will not enforce *penalties,* however. Penalties consist of amounts unrelated to the possible damages that may occur and usually are excessively large. Such an arbitrary lump sum, even if the parties have agreed to it as satisfaction of a breach, will be void.

Nominal Damages

We have noted that for most breaches of contract, an action for damages may be possible. However, in certain cases, especially those involving a minor, or technical, breach, the injured party sustains no actual losses or damages. A court nevertheless may award a *small amount of compensation* (say $1) for the breach. This type of remedy is called *nominal damages.* Sometimes a court or jury awards nominal damages because the injured party has not been able to prove the substantial damages that he or she claims to have suffered. Upon proof of a breach, the injured party therefore is entitled only to nominal damages, the token sum that a court will require the defendant to pay as an acknowledgment of the wrongful conduct in which he or she has engaged.

15.3

MANAGEMENT

LIQUIDATED DAMAGES CLAUSES

Amy Chen recently suggested that CIT should begin to include liquidated damages clauses in its contracts with subcontractors. As she pointed out, damages are often difficult to calculate in these cases, and using a liquidated damages clause will eliminate that problem. Dan pointed out that these clauses also could be used to set damages high enough to encourage subcontractors to make *every* effort to perform since they will not be able to afford the effects of a breach. The family has asked for your advice. What will you tell them?

BUSINESS CONSIDERATIONS Why would a business prefer to use a liquidated damages clause instead of trying to compute its actual damages in the event of a breach? What factors should be used in deciding what liquidated damages should be?

ETHICAL CONSIDERATIONS Is it ethical to set liquidated damages so high that the other party cannot afford to breach its contract? What ethical issues would be raised by such an action?

EQUITABLE REMEDIES

When the "at law" remedy of damages is unavailable, indeterminable, or inadequate, courts in the exercise of their powers of equity may award certain remedies. The plaintiff's eligibility to receive such fairness-oriented relief will depend on the absence of bad faith on the plaintiff's part and similar factors. Simply put, a plaintiff will not necessarily receive equitable remedies just because he or she asks for them. When they are available, the most significant types of equitable relief include rescission and restitution, specific performance, quasi contract, reformation, and injunction.

A court's power to award equitable remedies is **discretionary**; hence, courts normally will not give equitable remedies if the injured party has "unclean hands" (that is, has shown bad faith or dishonesty); if the injured party has unduly delayed bringing the lawsuit; if a **forfeiture** of property will result from the conferring of an equitable decree; if the court itself necessarily will have to supervise the implementation of the remedy granted; or if the remedy at law (ordinarily money damages, as you will recall) is available, determinable, and adequate.

Discretionary

Having the freedom to make certain decisions.

Forfeiture

The loss of a right or privilege as a penalty for certain conduct.

Rescission and Restitution

As we learned earlier in this chapter, the parties may voluntarily agree to rescind, or set aside, their contract before rendering performance. This type of rescission discharges the contract. But rescission also may occur as a result of a material breach of the agreement. Rescission in this context refers to the cancellation or termination of the contract through the restoration of the parties to the status quo. Upon such rescission, the injured party may ask for restitution.

Restitution, or the return of the goods, money, or property involved in the contract or the recovery of the reasonable value of the services rendered, is the legal term that describes the process by which the parties are returned to their original positions at the time of contract formation. In essence, then, restitution relies on quasi-contractual principles rather than on the original agreement, because once rescission has occurred, the original contract no longer exists.

To avoid the unjust enrichment of the breaching party, the law permits restitution by allowing the plaintiff to sue in quasi contract in order to recover. For this reason, in most jurisdictions, one cannot sue for both damages and restitution; damages and restitution constitute *mutually exclusive* remedies. The injured party must *elect* (that is, choose) to pursue one remedy or the other. If Miranda has paid Welling for the bulldozers, upon Welling's breach, Miranda can treat the contract as at an end (that is, rescind it) and then recover the money (consideration) already paid to Welling in order to avoid the unjust enrichment of Welling. Or, alternatively, Miranda can sue for damages. The common law *election of remedies* doctrine prevents Miranda from recovering twice.

Specific Performance

Whenever the remedy represented by damages or restitution is inadequate or unjust, the injured party may ask a court to order *specific performance.* In these cases, a court compels the breaching party to perform according to the exact terms of the agreement.

Courts rely on uniqueness as one factor in deciding whether to grant specific performance. Since land by definition is unique, courts ordinarily grant specific performance for breaches of land contracts. For example, should you try to buy a prairie-style home on the river, money damages for breach of that contract are unfulfilling: Money can buy a house similar to the one in the contract, but not that particular house. The inherent uniqueness of real estate therefore may convince a court to order the breaching party to convey the house to you—that is, give you specific performance—in order that justice may be done.

The same may be said of contracts involving unique goods or *chattels* (articles of movable personal property). If Bogan breaches a contract to sell a Rembrandt painting, in the absence of fraud or illegality, a court can compel Bogan to convey the painting to the buyer. But when the injured party easily can obtain the personal property or chattels, specific performance is an inappropriate remedy: Money damages will be adequate in these cases. Just as damages and restitution generally are mutually exclusive remedies, so too are damages and specific performance.

Money damages ordinarily will not satisfy the parties in situations involving personal services contracts. If these contracts are at issue, courts are reluctant to force the parties into a relationship in which at least one of the parties will be unhappy. For example, when Reggie Jackson wanted to break his contract with the Oakland A's and play for the Yankees, how could the A's be sure Jackson would give his best efforts if he really wanted to play for the Yankees? For this reason, and because courts are reluctant to force a party into what one party may characterize as involuntary servitude, courts ordinarily do not grant specific performance in contracts that consist of personal services. The A's instead could sue Reggie and the Yankees for money damages once he became a Yankee.

The court wrangled with the issue of specific performance in the following case.

Indemnify
To reimburse a party for a loss suffered by that party for the benefit of another.

15.5 CONNECTICUT NATIONAL BANK v. TRANS WORLD AIRLINES, INC.

762 F.Supp. 76 (S.D.N.Y. 1991)

FACTS In February 1986, Trans World Airlines, Inc. (TWA) entered into an equipment trust agreement with the Connecticut National Bank (CNB). The agreement, commonly known as a sale/leaseback, provided that CNB would purchase 10 aircraft and approximately 96 jet engines from TWA and then would lease them back to TWA until 1 February 1996. In connection with the lease/purchase, CNB received senior secured trust notes, some of which matured on 1 February 1991 and others of which were scheduled to mature on 1 February 1996. The aggregate original principal of these notes amounted to approximately $312 million, with the principal on the 1991 notes being worth $100 million and the balance being covered by the 1996 notes. The agreement stipulated that TWA would pay all the necessary interest and principal on the notes directly to CNB, as trustee, which, in turn, would pay the noteholders, or the trust beneficiaries. TWA also guaranteed payment to the beneficiaries and agreed to **indemnify** CNB. Finally, the agreement stated that once the lease had expired and TWA had paid off the loss suffered by that party under the notes, the equipment reverted to TWA. TWA met its obligations in a satisfactory fashion until 31 January 1991. At that time, TWA failed to make the required payments of approximately $57 million, $9 million of which represented interest on the 1991 and 1996 notes and the other $48 million of which represented the remaining principal on the then-matured 1991 notes. Consequently, CNB failed to pay the beneficiaries, since the agreement specifically obligated CNB to pay the beneficiaries only to the extent that TWA had paid CNB. CNB then demanded the return of its property and the immediate payment of the approximately $81 million presently due as principal on the 1996 notes. Although the agreement specifically afforded CNB these remedies, TWA failed to make any payments and did not return any of CNB's property. Therefore, on 26 March 1991, CNB filed a lawsuit seeking specific performance of the agreement's default remedies, including the return of the equipment located inside and outside the United States, delivery of various records relating to the property, and a permanent injunction preventing TWA from removing any of the property from the United States. TWA argued that a court's requiring specific performance of the agreement's default provisions would be inappropriate because CNB had a remedy at law. In addition, TWA asserted that requiring it to return the property in light of the tremendous ramifications such an order might have on both TWA and the public at large would be inequitable.

15.5 CONNECTICUT NATIONAL BANK v. TRANS WORLD AIRLINES, INC. *(cont.)*

762 F.Supp. 76 (S.D.N.Y. 1991)

ISSUE Should the court grant CNB's motion for summary judgment and order specific performance of the agreement?

HOLDING Yes. Specific performance represents the most appropriate and fairest remedy. Granting CNB an "at law" remedy (that is, money damages) in essence would leave CNB remediless; if TWA possessed the cash to pay CNB, TWA presumably would not have defaulted in the first place.

REASONING This case did not involve the ordinary situation in which a party demands specific performance of a contractual obligation, although CNB's complaint denominated its demands as such. The contractual obligation placed on TWA consisted of its paying money in exchange for the use of CNB's property. Technically, if CNB were demanding specific performance of TWA's obligations, CNB would be demanding that TWA pay the money it owes pursuant to the agreement. Such a demand, of course, would be futile, since TWA already had failed to pay. Instead, CNB sought to have the property returned—the precise remedy to which the parties previously had agreed. Thus, CNB really did not seek specific performance of TWA's obligations; rather, CNB sought to enforce an agreed-on contractual remedy in the event of a default. Under this rationale, CNB clearly was entitled to the return of the property. Moreover, even if one considered CNB's demands traditional claims for specific performance of a contractual obligation, CNB merited a summary judgment.

Yet, according to TWA, CNB would be adequately protected if it secured a money judgment against TWA for the amount due on the notes. In TWA's view, since the agreement required CNB to make payments to the beneficiaries solely from the funds it actually had received from TWA, CNB allegedly would suffer no loss or risk because of TWA's failure to pay or return the property. TWA's suggestion, however, that by obtaining a money judgment CNB would be adequately protected was nothing short of specious. Because TWA had been teetering on the brink of bankruptcy for years, its possession of cash in its coffers to satisfy such a judgment remained very unlikely. Indeed, if TWA had had the money, it presumably would not have defaulted in the first place. Therefore, the likely scenario under TWA's view would be that after obtaining such a judgment, CNB would attach TWA's property (the planes and engines) to satisfy the judgment. This result would return the parties precisely to the position in which they find themselves today. Requiring such actions would be extremely unfair to CNB in light of the fact that the agreement itself provided such a remedy in the event of a default.

In addition, with respect to the balance of equities, it would be difficult to imagine a more grievous wrong than permitting TWA to continue to use CNB's property without bothering to pay for it. Of course, a judgment that forced TWA to turn over the property might well diminish TWA's ability to serve consumers and also might represent a threat to the jobs of TWA employees. TWA itself had attributed its failure to meet its obligations under the agreement to a lack of customers, however. Moreover, TWA recently had received permission to sell certain of its international routes to another carrier. This fact suggested that TWA possessed more planes and engines than it actually needed. Furthermore, TWA's fleet included 207 planes; and only 10 planes were completely involved in the repossession. As to the 62 engines involved in the agreement, TWA failed to explain how many planes would be affected by their return. Finally, TWA asserted that the recent Persian Gulf War, which had resulted in decreased air travel, owing to fears of terrorism and increased oil prices, had curtailed its cash flow. Without a doubt, all airlines had experienced certain financial difficulties because of events in the Middle East. But none of these factors excused TWA from its obligations. Moreover, all the alleged factors having an impact upon TWA's profits constituted clearly foreseeable risks of doing business in an international forum. In short, TWA had not demonstrated its entitlement to relief from meeting its obligations, since all the factors it had mentioned fell well within the foreseeable at the time of its entering into the agreement.

BUSINESS CONSIDERATIONS The secured transaction involved here, though outwardly complicated, represents a typical credit-financing device by which the lender (here, CNB) tried to hedge its financial risks. Assume you are a lending officer with CNB and that the rest of the class is TWA. Parse out the various points of the equipment trust agreement and explain them so that the debtor here (TWA) will have an informed understanding of the credit arrangement to which it has bound itself.

ETHICAL CONSIDERATIONS Did CNB behave unethically when it tried to gain possession of the planes and engines? Did TWA act unethically when it tried to resist complying with the equipment trust agreement's default provisions? Why or why not?

Quasi Contract/Reformation/Injunction

Two concepts that we have discussed on several occasions in the contracts section, quasi contract and reformation, bear mentioning again before we leave the topic of equitable remedies. *Quasi contract* involves the situation in which a court creates a contract for the parties, despite their wishes and intentions, in order to prevent the unjust enrichment of one party. When the parties have not entered into a contract, but one party knowingly has received a benefit to which he or she is not entitled, an unjust enrichment has occurred. Given the absence of a valid contract, the injured party cannot seek contract-related remedies. In the interests of equity and fairness, however, the injured party may receive a restitution-based remedy, the reasonable value of the services rendered. *Reformation,* on the other hand, concerns a court's rewriting a contract in order to remove a mistake and to make the agreement conform to the terms to which the parties originally agreed. (See the discussion of reformation in Chapter 12.)

An injunction is another type of equitable remedy. An *injunction* is a writ issued by a court of equity ordering a person to do or refrain from doing some specified act. It does not arise often in the context of contracts, however.

LIMITATIONS ON REMEDIES

The parties may attempt in advance to limit the remedies available to the injured party. Chapter 12 discussed such efforts in the context of exculpatory clauses. The UCC also permits the parties to limit remedies. However, if an exclusive remedy—as defined in the contract—fails in its essential purpose, UCC § 2-719 permits the injured party to seek any remedies available under the Code. This same section, § 271-9, also forbids contractual limitations of consequential damages for *personal* injuries resulting from the use of *consumer* goods. The UCC dubs limitations on these sorts of damages **prima facie unconscionable** but notes that limitations of damages in purely *commercial* settings are not.

Prima facie

At first sight; on its face; something presumed to be true because of its appearance unless disproved by evidence to the contrary.

Unconscionable

Blatantly unfair and one-sided; so unfair as to shock the conscience.

WAIVER OF BREACH

Even though we have spent a great deal of this chapter studying the various remedies available to an injured party when the other party breaches the contract, we noted in the beginning of the chapter that the injured party may be willing to accept less-than-complete performance. The law terms an injured party's giving up the right to receive the performance set out in the contract a *waiver of breach.* Once a waiver of breach occurs, the waiver in effect eliminates the breach; the performance required under the contract continues as if the breach never happened. In essence, waiver of breach precludes the termination or rescission of the contract; it serves as a method of keeping the contract operative between the parties. As usual, the non-breaching party later can recover damages for anything that constitutes less-than-complete performance. Thus, if only one of the bulldozers delivered to Miranda is slightly defective or if Welling is only slightly late in making what otherwise is a satisfactory delivery, Miranda, in order to receive Welling's performance under the rest of the contract, may choose to waive such breaches.

A waiver of breach ordinarily applies only to the matter waived and not inevitably to the rest of the contract. The same is true of subsequent breaches of the

http:// RESOURCES FOR BUSINESS LAW STUDENTS

NAME	RESOURCE	WEB ADDRESS
Uniform Commercial Code (UCC)	The Legal Information Institute (LII), maintained by the Cornell Law School, provides a hypertext and searchable version of Articles 1–9 of the Uniform Commercial Code.	http://www.law.cornell.edu/ucc/ucc.table.html
The American Law Institute	The American Law Institute, publisher of Restatements of the Law, Model Codes, and other proposals for law reform, provides press releases, its newsletter, and other publications.	http://www.ali.org

contract: The first waiver normally will not cover additional, later breaches, especially when the later breaches bear no relation to the first one. However, the waiving party may want to stand on his or her rights after the first waiver and indicate unambiguously that he or she will not tolerate future breaches. This action will eliminate the possibility of the breaching party's arguing that the waivers were so numerous and systematic that the breaching party believed less-than-complete performance was acceptable for the duration of the contract. Still, waiver remains a common business response in those circumstances in which the continuation of the contract will further the interests of the injured party.

SUMMARY

Discharge of a contract refers to the legally valid termination of a contractual duty. Performance may be either complete or substantial. Both degrees of performance ordinarily discharge the contract. The parties themselves may agree to discharge the contract. Release, rescission, accord and satisfaction, and novation are examples of this method of discharging contracts. Bankruptcy decrees, the running of statutes of limitations, and material alterations of the contract will justify discharge of a contract by operation of law. In some circumstances, the nonperformance of one of the parties will discharge a contract. Courts that find evidence of destruction of the subject matter, intervening illegality, or conduct by one party that makes performance by the other party objectively impossible will excuse the resultant nonperformance. This is the doctrine of impossibility. In many other situations, however, impossibility will not justify discharge of the contract. The doctrine of commercial frustration consequently has arisen to mitigate the harshness of the common law's rejection of impossibility as a defense to nonperformance. Breach, whether actual or anticipatory, also may bring about discharge of the contract. The nonoccurrence of express conditions precedent and the occurrence of express conditions subsequent, in addition to constructive conditions, may cause discharge of a contract as well.

Upon one party's breach of a contract, the other party is free to pursue several kinds of remedies unless the injured party waives the breach. Remedies fall into two main categories: legal ("at law") and equitable remedies.

Damages are the "at law" remedy. Usually a party sues for compensatory damages, or the amount of money that will place the party in the same economic position that he or she would have enjoyed had the contract been performed. Because the breaching party is liable for the foreseeable consequences of the breach, courts may award these actual losses and may even grant consequential, or special, damages if the facts so warrant. The injured party must mitigate the damages unless doing so will cause unreasonable expense or unreasonable risk. Failure to mitigate will limit the injured party to the recovery of direct losses. Courts impose punitive damages to punish the wrongdoer and to deter future malicious conduct. Some modern courts and statutes reject the old common law rule that punitive damages never can constitute appropriate remedies for breaches of contract. The parties may agree in advance on the sum of money to be paid for breaches of certain types. Such liquidated damages clauses are enforceable unless a court construes them as penalties. If the party sustains no actual damages, nominal damages may be awarded.

When the "at law" remedy of damages is unavailable, indeterminable, or inadequate, courts may order equitable remedies. Rescission and restitution constitute one such remedy and involve the termination of the contract through the restoration of the parties to the status quo. Damages and restitution are mutually exclusive remedies, so the injured party must elect (or choose) one remedy or the other. If either damages or restitution will be inadequate, a court may order specific performance. This is an equitable remedy that compels the breaching party to perform according to the terms of the agreement. Courts usually grant specific performance when the subject matter of the contract is unique, but they are reluctant to grant specific performance in suits involving nonunique goods or personal services contracts. Quasi contract; reformation; and injunctions (writs ordering a person to do or refrain from doing some specified act) represent other types of equitable relief.

The injured party may choose to waive the breach in order to keep the contract going between the parties. Waiver of breach, or the injured party's giving up the right to receive the performance set out in the contract, does not preclude the injured party's seeking recovery for damages resulting from the breach, however.

Discussion Questions

1. What are the four main methods of contract discharge?
2. What is rescission?
3. Explain fully the doctrine of impossibility and the doctrine of commercial frustration as they relate to contract discharge.
4. What sorts of situations will discharge a contract by operation of law?
5. What is a complete, or material, breach of contract? What are the injured party's options when a complete breach occurs?
6. Name and define the two main types of remedies.
7. Define the duty of mitigation.
8. Why does the remedy of restitution differ from an action in damages?
9. Under what circumstances is specific performance an appropriate remedy?
10. What is the legal consequence of waiving a breach of contract?

Case Problems and Writing Assignments

1. Central Garage, Inc., d.b.a. Gulfcoast Auto and Automotive Accessories (Gulfcoast), is a Florida corporation engaged in the installation, repair, and maintenance of auto air conditioners and related auto accessories. It has facilities in Tampa, St. Petersburg, Sarasota, and Fort Myers and draws customers from other surrounding areas. In 1988, David Hapney, an experienced installer and repairer of auto and truck air-conditioning systems, began to work for Gulfcoast. As a condition of his employment, Hapney entered into an "Employee Confidentiality Agreement and Covenant Not to Compete," which

provided that for three years following the termination of his employment, Hapney would not offer, as an agent, employee, owner, or distributor, similar products or services on behalf of a competitor of Gulfcoast on the west coast of Florida from Crystal River to Naples or inland 100 miles. On 14 July 1989, Hapney voluntarily terminated his employment and began working for a direct competitor of Gulfcoast. On 1 August 1989, Gulfcoast instituted a court action to enforce the covenant not to compete against Hapney and his new employer. The evidence showed that while employed by Gulfcoast, Hapney had received no significant training in the installation and repair of automobile air-conditioning systems, beyond the knowledge and skill that he already possessed; but he had received significant training in the installation of cruise controls and cellular telephones in automobiles. Hapney moreover had failed to develop any significant relationships with Gulfcoast's customers; and he had acquired no trade secrets or confidential business information from Gulfcoast. Hapney argued that in determining the legality of a covenant not to compete, in addition to evaluating the reasonableness of the covenant as to time and geographical scope, a court also must consider, as a condition precedent, whether the covenant reasonably relates to protecting a legitimate interest of the employer. Was the existence of a legitimate, protectible interest on the employer's part a condition precedent for a court's finding a valid restrictive covenant? [See *Hapney* v. *Central Garage, Inc.*, 579 So.2d 127 (Fla.App. 1991).]

2. In early 1984, Carter Hawley Hale Stores, Inc. (Carter Hawley) hired David Dworkin as president of its Neiman-Marcus division. His five-year employment contract included an "evergreen" provision: At the end of each year, another year was added to the back of the contract, thus giving Dworkin, in effect, a new five-year contract. The contract provided for a base salary and a number of other benefits, including stock options, annual bonus potential, and various executive perquisites. After Carter Hawley had spun off its Neiman-Marcus division to a newly formed company, NMG, Dworkin's relationship with Richard Marcus, the Neiman-Marcus chairman, deteriorated; by late October 1987, Dworkin was fired as president of Neiman-Marcus. For five months after Dworkin's departure, NMG continued to pay the amount of Dworkin's monthly base salary, $37,500. Dworkin then assumed the presidency of Bonwit Teller and sued NMG for breach of his employment contract and for wrongful discharge. In the litigation that followed, NMG asserted that Dworkin had resigned pursuant to a resignation agreement. A jury subsequently awarded Dworkin $790,000 in damages, however. On appeal, NMG argued that Dworkin's Bonwit Teller salary, which was higher than that he would have received from Neiman-Marcus, barred his recovering damages from NMG. How should the appellate court rule in this case? [See *Neiman-Marcus Groups, Inc.* v. *Dworkin*, 919 F.2d 368 (5th Cir. 1990).]

3. Bart Schuman, a real estate syndicator in Los Angeles, asked Frank Short to act as a banker for the proposed syndication of Eastwind Village, an apartment complex in Indianapolis, Indiana. The property was to be purchased from Eden United, Inc. (Eden). Short left a May 1981 meeting confident that he and Eden had reached an agreement on the deal. After an inspection of the property, the parties amended the agreement to require Eden to obtain from Chatlee, the current owner, warranties that Chatlee would maintain the property in the condition found by Short during the inspection and would close with Short under the terms of the Short–Eden agreement should Eden default and not close on the property. During the months that followed, Eden delayed ordering the title work and postponed the closing. At a 17 August 1981 meeting, Eden proposed a mortgage containing provisions more stringent than the mortgages reviewed by Short in May and that, in fact, made the deal unworkable for Short. After negotiations, Eden ultimately agreed to make the changes requested by Short. The closing documents, however, were presented exactly as they had been prior to the 17 August meeting. Short still assumed these matters would be resolved with additional drafting at the closing. He arrived at the closing financially ready to complete the deal. Nonetheless, the closing ended abruptly with the Eden people walking out. When Eden failed to meet the terms of its escrow arrangement with Chatlee and defaulted on that deal, Chatlee began working with Short to close on Eastwind. However, when Chatlee and Short tried to close under the terms of the Short–Eden agreement, Eden blocked the escrowed Eden–Chatlee closing documents without justification, demanded compensation if Chatlee sold directly to Short, offered to allow Chatlee to sell to any purchaser except Short without interference, and proposed alternative purchasers for brokerage fees far less than the sums demanded from the proposed Short–Chatlee closing. Ultimately, Eden's actions forced both Chatlee and Short to abandon the transaction. Short later sued Eden for tortious interference with contract. Did the evidence support an award of punitive damages against Eden? Why? [See *Eden United, Inc.* v. *Short*, 573 N.E.2d 920 (Ind.App. 1991).]

4. George Halas, Sr., was the founder of the Chicago Bears (the Bears) and the club's president until his death on 31 October 1983. The Chicago Bears originally was incorporated as an Illinois corporation on 1 April 1922. George Halas, Sr.'s children, George Halas, Jr., and Virginia McCaskey, had acquired stock in the team through prior gifts and sales. At the time of his son's death, George Halas, Sr., owned 76.5 shares, or a 49.35 percent interest, in the Bears. The estate of George Halas, Jr., owned 30.5 shares, representing a 19.68 percent interest in the Bears. Virginia McCaskey and others owned the remaining outstanding shares. In his will, George Halas, Jr., directed that his 30.5 shares be held in separate trusts for the benefit of his children, Stephen and Christine. In addition to naming his father executor of his estate, George Halas, Jr., also appointed his father trustee of his children's trusts. In July 1980, Thomas Chuhak was appointed guardian ad litem (a guardian appointed by a court to prosecute or defend the rights of a child who is involved in a lawsuit) to represent Stephen and Christine Halas. In October 1981, Mr. Chuhak obtained a court order requiring that the executor of the estate give Chuhak "30 days advance notice in writing in the event the Executor decides to sell, convey, mortgage, encumber . . . or effect a redemption of any of the shares of stock issued by the Chicago Bears Club, Inc., ..." In July 1981, at a special meeting of the shareholders, a proposal to reorganize the Bears was discussed. The purpose of the reorganization was to (1) freeze the value of stock owned by Halas, Sr., and shift future appreciation to the grandchildren in order to save estate taxes, (2) maintain control of the Bears within the family, and (3) reduce the income taxes on the rental income derived from the skyboxes that were to be built at the stadium. The Chicago Bears Football Club subsequently was incorporated in Delaware. On 7 December 1981, George Halas, Sr., executed a stock exchange agreement on behalf of the testamentary trusts, which received 183 shares of Class C common stock in the Delaware corporation in exchange for their 30.5 shares of common stock in the Illinois corporation. George Halas, Sr., gave no notice of the reorganization to either the guardian ad litem or the beneficiaries. The successor executor filed suit, alleging injury to the estate of George Halas, Jr., by virtue of the restrictions that the reorganization had imposed on the transfer of stock under the Delaware corporation's certificate of incorporation. These restrictions, among other things, limited the transfer of stock and gave the corporation the right of first refusal for 60 days should a shareholder wish to transfer any shares. Following a bench trial, the trial court held that George Halas, Sr.—by failing to protect the interests of Stephen and Christine in the reorganization and failing to give notice of the reorganization to the guardian ad litem—breached his fiduciary duties. Yet because there were sufficient votes to bring about the reorganization without the votes of the shares held in trust for the benefit of Stephen and Christine, the trial court declined to rescind the reorganization or declare it void. Despite evidence that the restrictions on the transfer of the stock and the right of first approval with its 60-day waiting period—two significant aspects of the reorganization—had reduced the value of the stock, the trial court awarded only nominal damages of one dollar. Should the appellate court uphold this result? Why? [See *In re Estate of Halas,* 568 N.E.2d 170 (Ill.App. 1991).]

5. On 22 February 1984, Kvassay, who had been an independent insurance adjuster, contracted to sell 24,000 cases of baklava to Great American Supermarket at $19 per case. Under the contract, the sales were to occur over a one-year period with Great American as Kvassay's only customer. The contract included a clause that provided: "If Buyer refuses to accept or repudiates delivery of the goods sold to him, under this Agreement, Seller shall be entitled to damages, at the rate of $5.00 per case, for each case remaining to be delivered under this Contract." Early in this contractual relationship, checks issued by Great American were dishonored for insufficient funds. Frequently, one of the Murrays (the controlling shareholders of Great American) issued a personal check for the amount due. After producing approximately 3,000 cases, Kvassay stopped manufacturing the baklava because the Murrays had refused to purchase any more of the product. In April 1985, Kvassay filed suit for damages arising from the collapse of his baklava-baking business. The trial court deemed the liquidated damages provision unreasonable (and hence unenforceable) because of the great disparity between Kvassay's previous yearly income (about $20,000) and the liquidated damages claim ($105,000). The court also refused to permit Kvassay to recover damages for lost profits. Kvassay appealed these findings by the trial court. Should an appellate court find the liquidated damages clause in the contract unreasonable? Why? [See *Kvassay* v. *Murray,* 808 P.2d 896 (Kan.App. 1991).]

6. **BUSINESS CONSIDERATION CASE** In November 1980, Paul L. Gould individually and as president of Paul L. Gould, Inc., entered into a contract with P. A. Argentinis for the construction of a custom-designed house. The agreement incorporated the house plans and specifications prepared for Argentinis by professional architects. The contract contained Gould's various express warranties, including a warranty against

water leakage into the premises for one year after closing. The house was to be ready for occupancy by 1 May 1981. The closing took place in April 1981. Gould took from Argentinis a purchase money mortgage for the final $50,000 of the total sale price of $334,000. Although a certificate of occupancy had been issued, the Argentinis family was unable to occupy the house as scheduled because 40 to 50 items of construction remained unfinished. The parties thereupon reached a supplemental agreement modifying the terms of the mortgage. The parties agreed to a modified promissory note and mortgage for $43,000 and a cash payment of $3,000, which was to be released upon the completion of those construction items deemed unsatisfactory. The Argentinis family moved into the house in early July 1981, and the cash payment and documents were released to Gould from escrow. Some items due for completion later that month or "within a reasonable period of time" had not yet been performed. Of principal concern to Argentinis were the lack of water pressure in the house and the contaminated well water. In addition, the basement remained vulnerable to flooding during rains. Storm flooding occurred within the warranty period, again in June 1982, and twice more in April 1983, causing substantial damage to personal and real property. Argentinis, within the warranty period, made repeated demands on Gould to rectify the problems of the improperly sited well, the flood-prone basement, and numerous other significant deficiencies. Gould refused to repair the defects unless given an unconditional release concerning all such defects and the right to determine those defects for which he had borne responsibility. Argentinis refused to give this release, refused to make payments on the outstanding debt, and brought suit against Gould for breach of contract and breach of express warranties. When Gould sought to foreclose the $43,000 mortgage, a trial referee ruled that Gould, owing to his failure to substantially complete construction, should not receive the final contract payment. On appeal, Gould claimed that the referee's conclusion that the company had not substantially completed the construction had been against the weight of the evidence. Gould argued that Argentinis's architects had performed inspections as the work progressed and had approved the materials and workmanship. Moreover, Gould submitted, the town building inspector had found that the project met all but one minor code requirement and thus had issued a valid certificate of occupancy. Had Gould substantially performed this contract? What should Argentinis have done differently at the outset so as to ease his burden of proof regarding breach of contract and breach of express warranties? Similarly, what should Gould have done early on to minimize the probabilities that he would face legal liability in this contract? [See *Argentinis* v. *Gould,* 579 A.2d 1078 (Conn.App. 1990).]

7. **ETHICS APPLICATION CASE** When he retired in July 1983, John R. Hunt, M.D., purchased a "claims-made" professional liability insurance policy from St. Paul Fire and Marine Insurance Company (St. Paul). The policy provided coverage for claims made from 1983 through 29 July 1986, regardless of when the acts or omissions giving rise to any such claim had occurred. The policy specifically and unambiguously stated that in order to be covered, a claim must "be made while this agreement is in effect." Additionally, the policy answered the question "When is a claim made?" as follows: "A claim is made on the date you first report an incident or injury to us or our agent." A former patient of Dr. Hunt's filed a medical malpractice claim against him on 29 August 1985. Dr. Hunt failed to answer the complaint, and a default judgment of $250,000 was entered against him on 17 April 1987. The patient's claim was not reported to St. Paul until July 1987; the company therefore denied coverage because notice of the claim had occurred after the expiration of the policy. Dr. Hunt died on 28 February 1988. On 23 August 1988, through a declaratory judgment action, St. Paul requested that the court declare that no coverage had existed as to the medical malpractice claim here at issue. Lenore Hunt, the personal representative of Dr. Hunt's estate, answered the complaint by alleging that Dr. Hunt's failure to provide notice had been "excused as a result of [his] infirmity and incapacity." Although Dr. Hunt never had been adjudicated an incompetent or an incapacitated person, the jury had determined that Dr. Hunt, because of mental impairment, was unable to give notice of the claim in question to St. Paul during the period of August 1985 to 29 July 1986. The jury also found that his inability to give notice of the claim had not been reasonably foreseeable to Dr. Hunt at the time he had purchased the policy. Based on these findings, the trial court declared that coverage by St. Paul did exist for the patient's claim to the policy limits. On appeal, St. Paul contended that Dr. Hunt's mental impairment did not excuse noncompliance with the notice provisions of the policy. Specifically, it alleged that, under a claims-made policy, the insured's duty to provide notice of a claim is a material condition precedent to coverage and that impossibility or impracticability of performance does not excuse the failure to comply with such a condition. Should a court accept St. Paul's reasoning in these circumstances? Why? The legalities aside, was it ethical for

the company to deny coverage for an insured who was mentally impaired at the time the insured was required to give notice of a claimed incident of malpractice? In other words, should the company—on ethical grounds—have accepted liability here, particularly since Dr. Hunt presumably paid hefty premiums for the insurance? [See *St. Paul Fire and Marine Ins. Co.* v. *Estate of John R. Hunt, M.D.*, 811 P.2d 432 (Colo.App. 1991).]

8. **IDES CASE** Riverbend Products, Inc. (Riverbend) processes and sells tomato paste and frozen citrus products. On 14 July 1988, Cliffstar Corporation (Cliffstar) ordered 3.2 million pounds of tomato paste from Riverbend. In the same purchase order, Cliffstar attempted to purchase an option on an additional 500,000 pounds of paste. Delivery of the paste was to be spread over the following year, until 30 June 1989. Riverbend accepted the order in writing on 25 July 1988 but rejected Cliffstar's requested option "due to the uncertainty of the incoming tonnage." Between October and December 1987, Riverbend forecast sales for the 1988 tomato crop of approximately 53 million pounds of tomato paste. By combining firm contracts with spot buys, Riverbend planned to acquire sufficient numbers of raw tomatoes to support its sales forecast. Thereafter, Riverbend received oral and written orders for approximately 78 million pounds of tomato paste. It remained disputed, however, whether Riverbend accepted these orders and thus entered into contracts to supply this amount. About the time of the formation of the Cliffstar–Riverbend contract and extending into the early fall, a shortage developed in the tomato crop in Arizona and California. Riverbend's contract growers delivered only 56–58 percent of the 170,000 tons of tomatoes for which Riverbend had contracted. Because of these shortages, Riverbend failed to deliver the 3.2 million pounds of paste to Cliffstar. Instead, Riverbend allocated its available supply among its customers. Riverbend first notified Cliffstar by letter on 27 September 1988 that all contracts were to be reevaluated. Riverbend then notified Cliffstar by letter on 21 November 1988 that Cliffstar would be allocated one million pounds of paste. When Cliffstar demanded its full contract amount, this lawsuit ensued. Riverbend defended its failure to deliver by citing the UCC doctrine of commercial impracticability. Apply the IDES model. Was this a valid defense given the circumstances? Why? Would it be a valid defense under the common law? If it is not, what damages could Cliffstar recover? Explain. [See *Cliffstar Corp.* v. *Riverbend Prod., Inc.*, 750 F.Supp. 81 (W.D.N.Y. 1990).]

NOTES

1. A material breach, as we will see in later sections of this chapter, occurs when the performance rendered falls appreciably below the level of performance the parties reasonably expected under the terms of the contract. Such a breach discharges the other party from the contract.
2. 17 American Jurisprudence 2d, *Contracts*, § 484 (1964).
3. Darryl Van Duch, "Keeping Employees Quiet May Exact a Public Price," *The National Law Journal* (28 October 1996), pp. B1 and B3.

P A R T 3

IDES PROBLEMS

Sean, a gifted engineering graduate student, specializing in information systems, has decided to open CompConsult, a computer consulting business, in his hours outside the classroom. Sean intends to help businesses design, install, or upgrade their computer operations. To announce his business to the public, Sean advertised in the local newspaper and on the radio. The advertisements state his qualifications and that Sean provides an "ironclad money-back guarantee" should customers not be satisfied with his work. While CompConsult has so far met with success, Sean is troubled over a few legal problems that have arisen.

One of Sean's first projects for a business involved the setup of an accounting system for Triste, a local pharmaceutical company, for which Sean submitted a $650 bill for the work performed. Triste however, was dissatisfied with the work and refused to pay, based on CompConsult's money-back guarantee. Triste did offer to pay $200, indicating that this was all that the job was worth.

Shortly after this project, Sean decided to be more careful about clarifying what he thought his work on any particular project was worth. When CompConsult was hired to network the computers for a local branch of National Bank, Sean submitted a bid for $500 (10 hours @ $50 per hour). National accepted the bid and offered the work to Sean. When Sean began the work, he realized, among other problems, that many of the computers were not working properly and the equipment National had purchased was wrong for the job. Sean corrected these problems but, as a result, spent almost 30 hours on the project. Consequently, he submitted a bill for $1500. National, however, has refused to pay more than the $500 originally bid.

A large commercial real estate firm, Realty, Inc., hired CompConsult, for a fee of $5000, to merge its disparate project management database files into one system. Sean successfully completed the work, but in the process he inadvertently introduced a virus into Realty's computers. The virus destroyed the data for over half of Realty's projects, and it took Realty's systems off-line for more than a month while the virus was being removed. Sean offered to fix the problem for free, but Realty, questioning Sean's abilities given the virus, hired a large information systems company to fix the mess. Eventually, the virus was removed and the lost electronic data were replaced, albeit painstakingly by hand. Realty paid $4000 to have the virus removed and the data replaced. In addition, Realty estimated that the firm lost another $10,000 in lost business and productivity. Realty has sued CompConsult for the $14,000 it claims in economic losses. Sean denies any liability and has billed Realty for $1000 (his $5000 fee minus the $4000 it cost to fix the damage). However, Sean still feels he is owed $5000, since he offered to fix the problem for free and Realty declined his offer.

One of his teachers has arranged for Sean to meet with a lawyer to discuss these issues. In preparation for this meeting, Sean needs to answer the following questions:

IDENTIFY What are the legal and ethical issues surrounding CompConsult's actions with Triste, National Bank, and Realty, Inc.?

DEFINE What are the meanings of the relevant legal terms associated with these issues?

ENUMERATE What are the legal and ethical principles relevant to these issues?

SHOW BOTH SIDES Consider all of the facts in light of the above questions. Do Triste, National Bank, and Realty, Inc., have legitimate complaints under the law? What facts support their positions?

[To review the IDES approach refer to pages 29–30.]

Part 4

SALES AND LEASES

The early common law of contracts was inappropriate—if not inadequate—for the commercial society that took form in the nineteenth century. As a result, the law merchant was developed. The sociological and technological advances of the twentieth century made the law merchant as outmoded for this era as the common law had been for the Industrial Revolution. Once again, new rules were developed and codified in the Uniform Commercial Code (UCC), including the sale of goods (Article 2) and the leasing of goods (Article 2A).

Firms involved in international trade also need to be aware of their rights and obligations, but contracts between firms in different nations make such awareness difficult. One potential solution to this problem can be found in the United Nations Convention on Contracts for the International Sale of Goods, the CISG.

The next five chapters discuss how contracts involving the sale or lease of goods are formed; the rules that govern performance, title, and risk of loss; how warranties and liabilities operate in these transactions; what remedies are available for a breach in a sales contract; and how international laws may affect the sales of goods outside the borders of the United States.

I D E S

Mildred has a woodworking hobby. Over time she has made a number of items as gifts for friends, and her friends have told their friends about her talent. Eventually, some people approached Mildred to ask her to build some items for them, for a fee. She accepted these offers, and her hobby became a source of income for her. Despite Mildred's good intentions, a few customers were dissatisfied with her work and sought remedies. These customers allege that Mildred is a merchant in wooden goods and that Mildred has breached a contract or a warranty.

The law of sales makes a distinction between merchants and nonmerchants. Is Mildred a merchant or a nonmerchant? For either designation under the law, what legal obligations does this entail? Consider these issues in the context of the chapter materials, and prepare to analyze these issues using the IDES model.

IDENTIFY the legal issues raised by the questions.

DEFINE all the relevant legal terms and issues involved.

ENUMERATE the legal principles associated with these issues.

SHOW BOTH SIDES by using the facts.

AGENDA

The Kochanowskis will enter the electronic communications market as merchants. What added responsibilities will such a status entail? What can or should Tom do differently in his marketing approach because the firm will be treated as a merchant in the industry?

If Tom and Anna are correct, the firm should experience some success soon after entering the market. Should CIT plan to negotiate each sales contract differently, or should Tom and Anna ask Amy Chen to draft a standard form contract for CIT to use in most Call-Image sales? Should Amy develop a standard purchase order to be used in ordering parts prior to the final construction of a Call-Image videophone? What are the advantages and disadvantages of developing such forms?

These and other questions need to be addressed in covering the material in this chapter. Be prepared! You never know when one of the Kochanowskis will need your advice.

Formation of the Sales Contract: Contracts for Leasing Goods

OUTLINE

INTRODUCTION

The common law coverage of contracts provides a good *framework* for studying agreements between people. As society has progressed and developed in England and in the United States, however, some elements of the common law have become outdated. When this occurs, the law-making bodies often step in to try to resolve the problems presented by a changing society. One early result of this legislative intervention is the *Statute of Frauds* (the original statute was enacted by the English Parliament in 1677), which requires that certain types of contracts be in writing in order to be enforceable. Another—and more contemporary—example of legislative intervention to help the law keep pace with society is the Uniform Commercial Code (the first UCC was adopted in the United States in 1954). The UCC was developed by the National Conference of Commissioners on Uniform State Laws. It is designed to update and modernize the law of commerce in code form and to reflect modern commercial reality.

Under the early common law, contract law developed primarily to reflect the importance of land in the economy of England. The common law treatment of contracts involving the sale of land was quite extensive, whereas the treatment of contracts for the sale of goods was sparse. As a merchant class began to develop in England, the merchants realized that the common law did not adequately treat their contracts or their contractual concerns. As a result, the merchants developed their own law, the **law merchant** (*lex mercatoria*). Eventually, the law merchant was adopted by parliament as an official part of English law, giving official status to the merchants and their transactions under the law.

Law merchant
The system of rules, customs, and usages generally recognized and adopted by merchants and traders, and that constituted the law for their transactions.

This same legal tradition was followed in the United States after its formation. Since the United States had been a part of England, and since the courts in existence were based on English law, it was natural for the United States to follow English laws initially. By the early twentieth century, the law merchant was still in effect, but it was substantially out of date. As a result, the Uniform Sales Act (USA) was enacted to update and modernize the law merchant in the United States. While the USA was significantly more modern than the law merchant, it too was quickly out of date.

The Uniform Commercial Code (UCC) was adopted in 1954 to reflect contemporary commercial practices. The UCC replaced the USA and the NIL (the Uniform Negotiable Instrument Law), among other areas. The Code is organized into sections, with each section covering a different aspect of commercial law. For example, the UCC replaced the USA with Article 2, which governs the sale of goods. Other sections of the Code include Article 2A, which deals with the leasing of goods (many modern transactions involve leasing goods rather than buying them); Article 3, which deals with negotiable instruments (checks, a form of negotiable instrument, are often used to pay for goods); Article 4, which deals with banks and customers; Article 4A, which deals with fund transfers; Article 5, which deals with letters of credit (a standard method of payment, especially when the parties are separated geographically); Article 7, which deals with documents of title (often used in sales of goods between merchants); and Article 9, which deals with secured transactions (goods are often used as collateral when goods are sold on credit).

The UCC has been adopted, in whole or in part, in all 50 states. (Louisiana, with its French heritage and its tradition of following the Napoleonic Code, has not adopted all sections of the Code.) Thus, the coverage and the principles of the Code are applicable nationally, even though the Code itself is state law. This uniformity allows widespread understanding of the rules, and the reasonable expectations that the rules followed in one state are likely to be followed in other states as well.

Money
A legally recognized medium of exchange authorized or adopted by a government.

While the UCC has basically been adopted throughout the United States, it is not applicable internationally unless the parties to an international contract specify that the UCC will control, or unless the contract is entered into in the United States. As international trade increases, the need for a uniform set of legal rules and guidelines will increase. The closest thing to a uniform set of international laws governing such trade that we have at present is the United Nations Convention on Contracts for the International Sale of Goods (CISG). The CISG is similar in many respects to Article 2 of the UCC.

16.1

MANAGEMENT

WHAT TYPE OF LAW WILL MOST AFFECT CIT?

The Kochanowskis disagree as to what type of law will be most important in governing their business. Anna has done a great deal of work involving patents over the years, and she has filed for several patents involving the "Call-Image" telephone. She also recognizes that the company's product is likely to be subjected to Federal Communication Commission recognition. As a result, she insists that federal regulation, especially in the areas of patent and administrative regulations, will be most important. Tom, recalling his background in marketing, insists that the firm is providing a service, and he also is cognizant of the fact that the firm is organized under state law. He insists that traditional common law rules will be most important to the firm. Dan disagrees with both Anna and Tom. He points out that the Call-Image telephone is a *good* and that the firm will be most involved in *sales* of that good, so that Article 2 of the UCC is most important to them. They have asked you to help them settle this dispute. What will you tell them?

BUSINESS CONSIDERATIONS A new business, especially one in a relatively high-tech industry, is likely to be subjected to numerous types of legal and administrative regulations. Is any one type of regulation more important than the others? Should a business try to deduce which areas of law or administrative regulation will affect it before it begins doing business?

ETHICAL CONSIDERATIONS Should a business be more concerned with evading regulations, avoiding regulations, or complying with regulations? Explain your reasoning.

THE SCOPE OF ARTICLE 2

Article 2 of the UCC (Sales) deals with the sale of goods. This is a somewhat limited topic when compared to all the types of contracts that a party might enter. However, most of us will enter into more contracts for the sale of goods than any other types of contracts.

To understand the scope of Article 2, we need to know what is covered. Thus, we must begin by defining a *sale* and then by defining *goods*. According to § 2-106(1), a sale is the passing of title from the seller to the buyer for a price. This is the only definition of a sale in Article 2, but there are several related and similar terms that also need to be examined. For example, the words *contract* and *agreement*, when used in Article 2, refer to either the present or the future sale of goods. Contract for sale covers both a present sale and a contract to sell goods in the future. A present sale is a sale made at the time the contract is made. Goods are defined in § 2-105(1) of the Code. According to that section, *goods* mean "all things that are movable at the time they are identified to the contract." The Code lists several things that are specifically included as goods, such as specially manufactured items, the unborn young of animals, growing crops, and things attached to land, if they are to be separated from the land for their sale. The Code also specifically excludes some things, declaring them not to be goods. Examples are **money** when used as a payment for sale, **investment securities**, and **things in action**, such as rights under a contract yet to be performed. (Things in action are also sometimes referred to as **choses in action**.)

Transactions under Article 2 must involve two persons. One is the buyer—the person who purchases, or agrees to purchase, the goods. The other person is the seller—the person who provides, or agrees to provide, the goods covered by the contract.

The law of sales is very broad. It covers every sale of goods, whether made by a seller who is a merchant or by one who is a nonmerchant, and whether made to a buyer who is a merchant or to one who is a nonmerchant. Regardless of the status of the parties, Article 2 controls the sale. However, the status of the parties may affect how strictly the sale is regulated by the Code; the key factor here is the status of the parties as merchants or nonmerchants.

A *merchant* is defined as a person who deals in the type of goods involved in the sale, or a person who claims to be (or is recognized as) an **expert** in the type of goods involved in the sale, or a person who employs an expert in the type of goods involved in the sale (§ 2-104). A person who is represented by an agent or a broker or any other intermediary who, by his occupation, holds himself out as an expert is deemed to be a merchant. Any other person is viewed as a nonmerchant.

A merchant is required by the terms of the Code to act in good faith, to cooperate with the other party in the performance of the contract, and to act in a commercially reasonable manner in the performance of the contract. (A *commercially reasonable manner* means that the conduct must comply with the normal fair dealings and practices of the trade.) A nonmerchant is required to act in good faith and cooperate in the performance of the contract. However, a nonmerchant is not required to act in a commercially reasonable manner. Thus, a merchant is held to a higher standard of conduct than is expected of a nonmerchant. Further, merchants are presumed to give an implied warranty of merchantability in their contracts, whereas a nonmerchant does not give such an implied warranty. Obviously, the

Investment securities
Bonds, notes, certificates, and other instruments or contracts from which one expects to receive a return primarily from the efforts of others.

Things in action
A personal right; an intangible claim not yet reduced to possession, but recoverable in a suit at law.

Choses in action
A personal right not reduced to possession, but recoverable in a suit at law.

Expert
A person with a high degree of skill or with a specialized knowledge.

YOU BE THE JUDGE

Is Apple Computer, Inc., a Merchant in the Software Industry?

A recent advertisement for the Apple Internet Server made the following claims concerning its product:

> *the server is designed to support over 200,000 hits per day; because it is cross-platform, even people running Windows and Unix can access your site; because security is built in, you never have to worry about break-ins.*

Suppose that a customer purchased this software, basing his or her purchasing decision on the advertisement, and was dissatisfied with the results obtained. This customer files suit against Apple for its losses. Obviously Apple Computer, Inc. is a merchant in the computer industry. But is Apple also a merchant in the software industry? Is the sale of the Apple Internet Server a sale of goods governed under Article 2? If it is, does this advertisement provide warranties to purchasers of the software, or is this just "sales talk" and therefore beyond the scope of warranty protection?

The customer has brought this case in *your* court. How will you rule on these issues?

BUSINESS CONSIDERATIONS The Internet seems to offer a huge potential for marketing and sales. How can a firm take advantage of this potential without compromising its primary business objective? How much attention should a business pay to the Internet and its potential?

ETHICAL CONSIDERATIONS Advertisers want to make claims for their products that will help to sell the product to potential customers. In attempting to attract customers, advertisers frequently puff the product. Is such conduct ethical? What should an advertiser do in order to attract potential customers while still operating in an ethical manner?

SOURCE: Advertisement for Apple Premium Server Reseller, *Entrepreneur* (August 1996), pp. 1 and 3.

status of a party as a merchant or as a nonmerchant is an important consideration in determining rights and duties under the sales contract.

The following case shows how one court decided whether a party to a sales contract was a merchant. Notice what impact that decision had on the liability of the buyer in the case. Similar reasoning is likely to be followed by other courts facing the question of whether a party in a transaction is a merchant.

16.1 TRI-CIRCLE, INC. v. BRUGGER CORP.

829 P.2d 540 (Idaho App. 1992)

FACTS Weimer leased and operated a farm from Brugger/Western Ag (hereafter Western Ag). In 1987, Weimer met with McQueen, the manager of Western Ag, to discuss Weimer's proposal for a new lease agreement on the farm. One of the terms of this discussion called for Western Ag to repair the farm's irrigation system, which had fallen into a state of dysfunction. McQueen stated that the new terms looked good, but that they could not be approved until Brugger reviewed them. One week later, Weimer called McQueen and informed him that Weimer could no longer operate the farm unless the irrigation system was repaired. Weimer alleged that McQueen approved the repairs at that point and promised that Western Ag would pay for them. Weimer contacted Tri-Circle relative to providing labor and materials for the repair of the irrigation system on the farm, asking Tri-Circle to set up an account separate from Weimer's personal account, to which material and labor expended on specified components of the irrigation system would be charged to Western Ag. Tri-Circle was to send bills to Weimer, who would verify their accuracy before submitting them to Western Ag. By June 1987, Tri-Circle had charged $9,769.33 to the Western Ag account and had sent the bills to Weimer. Weimer, in turn, had forwarded these bills to Western Ag. On 30 June 1987, Western Ag paid the entire balance by check. Subsequent charges totaling $11,540.71 were billed to the Western Ag account in 1987, with the bills sent to Weimer. Weimer testified that he forwarded these bills to Western Ag as before. However, Tri-Circle received no further payments nor had any communications with Western Ag. In December 1987, Tri-Circle sent a letter to Western Ag demanding payment, and in January 1988, Tri-Circle's attorney sent a letter demanding payment for the services billed to the account. Western Ag asserted that the January letter was the first notice it received of any bills for work on the irrigation system and denied any knowledge of the arrangement between Weimer and Tri-Circle. Western Ag denied liability, claiming that Weimer had no authority to set up the account. Tri-Circle then sued Western Ag and Weimer to recover the account balance plus service charges and attorney's fees. [There was a provision for finance charges and service charges in the invoice form Tri-Circle initially sent to Weimer and which Weimer allegedly forwarded to Western Ag.] The trial court found that Weimer had acted as an authorized agent for Western Ag, a disclosed principal, and found Western Ag liable for the claims of Tri-Circle. Western Ag appealed.

ISSUES Was Weimer an authorized agent for Western Ag in this situation? Was the contract between Tri-Circle and Western Ag a contract between "merchants" so that the finance and service charges were properly assessed?

HOLDINGS Yes. Weimer was an authorized agent for Western Ag, possessing apparent authority to enter into the contract with Tri-Circle. Yes. This contract was between merchants, permitting Tri-Circle to assess the finance and service charges.

REASONING The court found substantial evidence to establish that an agency relationship had been entered into between Weimer and Western Ag. Weimer testified that he received express authority to purchase repairs to the irrigation system from McQueen, the manager of Western Ag. Western Ag did not rebut this testimony. Further, Weimer forwarded the first bill to Western Ag and that bill was paid by Western Ag in a timely manner and without any objections to either Weimer or Tri-Circle. [There was a substantial discussion of other aspects that dealt with the court's ruling that an agency existed and that Weimer had apparent authority to bind Western Ag to the contract. However, that discussion is not relevant to the sales issue involved herein.]

Because this action involved the sale of goods as defined in [UCC Section 2-205], it is governed by the provisions of the Uniform Commercial Code. Under the Code, contracts which contain additional terms in the acceptance are governed by Section 2-207, which reads:

> *Additional terms in acceptance or confirmation—(1) A definite and seasonable expression of acceptance or a written confirmation which is sent within a reasonable*

16.1 TRI-CIRCLE, INC. v. BRUGGER CORP. *(cont.)* **829 P.2d 540 (Idaho App. 1992)**

time operates as an acceptance even though it states terms additional to or different from those offered or agreed upon, unless acceptance is expressly made conditional on assent to the additional or different terms.

(2) The additional terms are to be construed as proposals for addition to the contract. Between merchants such terms become part of the contract unless:

a) the offer expressly limits acceptance to the terms of the offer;
b) they materially alter it; or
c) notification of objection to them has already been given or is given within a reasonable time after notice of them is received.

Pursuant to the district court's findings . . . a contract had been formed between Tri-Circle and Western Ag. The finance charges contained in the invoices sent by Tri-Circle to Weimer and from Weimer to Western Ag were additional terms to the contract under section 2-207.

The question for us to decide, then, is whether these additional terms became part of the contract. Initially we must determine whether this contract was "between merchants." The Idaho Code defines the words "merchant" and "between merchants."

(1) "Merchant" means a person who deals in goods of the kind or otherwise by his occupation holds himself out as having knowledge or skill peculiar to the practices or goods involved in the transaction. . . .

(3) "Between merchants" means in any transaction with respect to which both parties are chargeable with the knowledge or skill of merchants.

The district court correctly applied these definitions to the transaction between Tri-Circle and Weimer/Western Ag. Since all the parties were merchants with respect to this contract, they all had "knowledge or skill peculiar to the practices or goods involved in this transaction. . . ."

Clearly, under these provisions, Tri-Circle, Weimer, and Western Ag are all merchants with respect to this transaction for material and repairs for a farm irrigation system. Therefore, the additional terms regarding finance charges became part of the contract unless one of the enumerated exceptions is present. . . . In this case, there is no evidence that the contract offer expressly limited acceptance to the terms of the offer or that Weimer or Western Ag objected to the finance charges within a reasonable time after notice of these charges were received. The district court specifically found that "sufficient notice was sent directly to Brugger and its agent Weimer to justify imposing financial charges in this matter. Further, the fact that Brugger paid the first bill or [sic] is proof that they received these billings and knew of the financial charges being assessed."

The judgment of the district court is affirmed.

BUSINESS CONSIDERATIONS What steps can a firm take to prevent being held to different or additional terms included in an acceptance or an invoice from another merchant? How could Western Ag have protected itself in this case when it received the first invoice from Tri-Circle?

ETHICAL CONSIDERATIONS Why would a merchant *not* include additional terms favorable to that merchant in an acceptance form being sent to another merchant? What ethical and practical considerations would affect the decision of whether to add additional or different terms?

FORMING THE CONTRACT

A contract for the sale of goods under Article 2 is formed in basically the same manner as a contract is formed under the rules of common law. A sales contract can be formed with much less formality or rigidity than is required by common law, however. While the common law requires an exact agreement, a "mirror image" between the offer and the acceptance, the Code recognizes that a contract exists whenever the parties act as if they have an agreement. The common law requires that the acceptance has to comply exactly with all the terms of the offer.

Any variation is treated as a counteroffer (an attempt to vary the terms of the original offer) rather than as an acceptance. In an effort to reflect commercial reality, the Code will sometimes recognize a contract that would not be considered binding under the common law.

For example, in § 2-204(2), the Code recognizes that a contract exists even though the time of the agreement is uncertain. Further, in § 2-204(3), the Code permits a contract to stand even though some other terms (such as price or quantity) are omitted from the agreement. Under the common law, the omission of any of these terms would negate the existence of a contract. The courts would rule that the attempt to form a contract failed due to the "indefiniteness of the terms." Under the UCC, if the parties intend to have a contract and if remedies can be found in case there is a breach, the mere lack of some terms can be held to be unimportant. A contract will be found to exist, and the missing terms will be supplied under other provisions of the Code.

As in regular common contract law, a contract for the sale of goods needs both an offer and an acceptance. These technical requirements are covered by UCC § 2-206, which states that, unless an offer obviously requires otherwise, it can be accepted in any manner reasonable under the circumstances. Suppose the seller received an offer that included the following clause: "Acceptance must be made by sending a white pigeon carrying your note of acceptance tied to its left leg." Under the common law, a seller could accept this offer only by tying a note to the left leg of a white pigeon. If the message was tied to the right leg or if the pigeon was gray, the seller would be deemed to have made a counteroffer. Under the Code, the seller can accept by complying exactly with the terms of the offer (tying a message to the left leg of a white pigeon), by nearly complying (tying a message to either leg of a pigeon, or using a gray pigeon rather than a white one), or by using any other method of accepting that is reasonable under the circumstances. Thus, under some circumstances, the Code even permits the acceptance of an offer by performing rather than by communicating.

For example, an offer to buy goods may call for prompt shipment of the goods. Under the common law, the seller could accept this offer only by making a prompt shipment of the goods. However, under the UCC, the seller can accept in any of the following manners:

1. The seller can promptly ship conforming goods to the buyer.
2. The seller can notify the buyer that the goods will be shipped promptly.
3. The seller can promptly ship nonconforming goods to the buyer.

Accommodation

Something supplied for a convenience or to satisfy a need.

Seasonably

Timely; something occurring in a prompt or timely manner.

Option

A privilege existing in one person, for the giving of consideration, which allows him or her to accept an offer at any time during a specified period.

Thus, the UCC permits acceptance in at least three different ways, while the common law only permitted acceptance in one exact manner. However, in the last acceptance under the UCC, the seller would not only have accepted the offer but would also (possibly) have breached the contract that was entered into by shipment-as-acceptance. According to § 2-206(1)(b), a seller who receives an order or other offer, with the offer calling for acceptance by prompt shipment, may ship nonconforming goods as an **accommodation** to the buyer, and the shipment will not be treated as an acceptance of the offer. In order to qualify as an accommodation shipment, however, the seller must **seasonably** notify the buyer that nonconforming goods have been shipped and that the buyer has the **option** of accepting these (counteroffered) goods or rejecting them and returning them to the seller at the seller's expense. If the seller fails to give the required seasonable notification, the buyer may treat the goods shipped as an acceptance of the offer—and as a breach of the contract, since the goods do not conform to the terms specified in the offer.

The seller who accepts an offer by means of a prompt or current shipment must be careful for another reason. Assume the seller accepts by promptly shipping the goods but does not notify the buyer that the goods have been shipped. If the buyer neither receives the goods nor hears from the seller within a reasonable time, the buyer may treat the offer as lapsed before acceptance. When this happens, the buyer has no duty to pay for the goods when they finally arrive (if they finally arrive). This leaves the seller with unsold goods at some distant point and no contract remedies to fall back on.

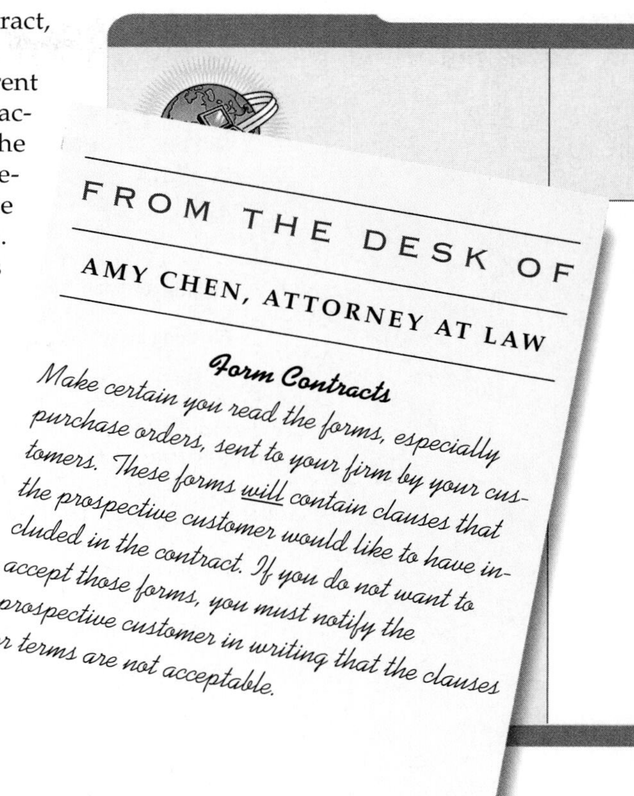

FROM THE DESK OF
AMY CHEN, ATTORNEY AT LAW
Form Contracts
Make certain you read the forms, especially purchase orders, sent to your firm by your customers. These forms will contain clauses that the prospective customer would like to have included in the contract. If you do not want to accept those forms, you must notify the prospective customer in writing that the clauses or terms are not acceptable.

Standard Form Contracts

Very often both parties to the contract are merchants, and they are transacting business over a substantial distance. When this situation occurs, it is common to have the offer made on a standard form prepared by the offeror and the acceptance made on another standard form, this one prepared by the offeree who is accepting the offer. (A *standard form* is a preprinted contract form, often with blanks left in certain key places for later completion as the final contract terms are agreed on by the parties.) Use of a standard form contract would normally have negated the contract under the common law, but the Code makes allowance for it. Under § 2-207(1), an acceptance that is made within a reasonable time is effective, even if it includes terms that add to or differ from the terms of the original offer. The only exception is when the acceptance is expressly made subject to an agreement with the new or different terms.

If the purported acceptance includes new or different terms, the Code provides a solution. The new terms are treated as proposed additions to the contract. If the contract is between merchants, the new terms become a part of the contract unless one of the following conditions exists:

1. The offer explicitly limits acceptance to the terms of the offer.
2. The new terms materially alter the contract.
3. The offeror objects to the new terms within a reasonable time.

If the contract is not between merchants, the courts will not normally uphold the new terms unless it can be shown that both parties accepted them. If the offeree proposes different terms, § 2-207(3) controls. This section states that when the parties act as if they have a contract, they have a contract. And if they have writings, the writings will be construed consistently, so that an agreement exists. The written contract will consist of the terms on which the parties agree, as well as the terms included by one party without any objection by the other party. But it will not include any terms that contradict other terms, have been objected to by one of the parties, or materially alter the basic agreement. Exhibit 16.1 shows how a "conflict of forms" problem would be resolved.

EXHIBIT 16.1 A "Conflict of Forms" Resolution

IF THE OFFER SAYS "..."	and	IF THE ACCEPTANCE SAYS "..."	THE CONTRACT WILL SAY "..."
Include "A"		Nothing about "A" is mentioned	Include "A"
Include "A"		Include "A"	Include "A"
Nothing about "A"		Include "A"	Include "A" (maybe)[a]
Nothing about "A"		Exclude "A"	Exclude "A" (maybe)[b]
Include "A"		Exclude "A"	Nothing on "A" (maybe)[c]
Exclude "A"		Include "A"	Nothing on "A" (maybe)[d]
Exclude "A"		Exclude "A"	Exclude "A"
Exclude "A"		Nothing about "A" is mentioned	Exclude "A"

[a] The contract will include "A" unless including "A" will materially alter the duties of the parties, or the offeror objects to the inclusion of "A," or the offer specifically limits acceptance to the offer's original terms.

[b] The contract will exclude "A" unless excluding "A" will materially alter the duties of the parties, or the offeror objects to the exclusion of "A," or the offer specifically limits acceptance to the offer's original terms.

[c] The contract will not mention "A" unless the exclusion of "A" will materially alter the duties of the parties, or the offeror objects to the exclusion of "A," or the offer specifically limits acceptance to the offer's original terms.

[d] The contract will not mention "A" unless the inclusion of "A" will materially alter the duties of the parties, or the offeror objects to the inclusion of "A," or the offer specifically limits acceptance to the offer's original terms.

The following case is the current benchmark under which the courts resolve a conflict of forms between merchants. Compare the court's results with Exhibit 16.1.

16.2 WESTECH ENGINEERING, INC. v. CLEARWATER CONSTRUCTORS, INC.

835 S.W.2d 190 (Tex.App.-Austin 1992)

FACTS Clearwater Constructors was one of the bidders for the city of Austin's expansion of the Walnut Creek wastewater treatment facility. WesTech Engineering submitted a bid for certain equipment to Clearwater. Clearwater used the WesTech bid in preparing its own bid on the project. Clearwater was awarded the general contract, and notified WesTech that its (WesTech's) bid had been accepted by Clearwater. A Clearwater purchase agreement was sent to WesTech in December. WesTech signed the agreement and returned it with an attached letter. The attached letter indicated that the purchase agreement contained different terms from the original WesTech proposal and that WesTech intended for the terms of its original proposal to be "made a part of the [purchase] agreement." Clearwater subsequently signed the purchase agreement. As work progressed on the project, the city's engineering firm decided that the WesTech equipment did not meet the particular specifications for the job as set out in the city's contract. Despite efforts to resolve this disagreement, the engineers refused to approve the WesTech equipment, and Clearwater eventually informed WesTech (1) that it was seeking another source for the equipment, and (2) that it planned to hold WesTech liable

16.2 WESTECH ENGINEERING, INC. v. CLEARWATER CONSTRUCTORS, INC. *(cont.)* 835 S.W.2d 190 (Tex.App.-Austin 1992)

for any increased procurement costs. Clearwater eventually purchased the equipment elsewhere, but at a much higher cost. Clearwater sued WesTech for the difference in cost ($123,495). WesTech argued that its agreement with Clearwater was governed by the original bid proposal, as specified by its letter attached to the purchase agreement, which would preclude the liability sought by Clearwater.

ISSUE Was the contract between the parties governed by the WesTech letter, or was it governed by both the purchase agreement and the letter?

HOLDING The court ruled that the contract was formed by merging the two writings to arrive at the agreement for the parties.

REASONING The court applied UCC § 2-207 as the mechanism for ascertaining the intent of the parties in forming this contract. The court granted greater weight to the "filled in" terms of the writings than it did to the preprinted terms, stating that: "Not being part of the preprinted verbiage, the filled-in terms reflect not only a high degree of importance attached to them by the offeree, but also the term's particular applicability to the specific agreement." However, attaching a typed letter did not nullify the acceptance of the printed form WesTech signed and, by signing, accepted. WesTech agreed to provide acceptable equipment for Clearwater's bid; it failed to do so; as a result, Clearwater had to pay more to procure the equipment elsewhere, and suffered damages for its failure to complete the job in a timely manner. WesTech was liable, its typed addendum to the agreement notwithstanding.

BUSINESS CONSIDERATIONS Given the court's preference for "filled in" terms in a contract over preprinted terms, should a business bother to prepare standard form contracts, or would the business be better served to prepare each contract as it is negotiated?

ETHICAL CONSIDERATIONS Is it fair for a party to append favorable additional terms to a standard form that it submits as a bid for a contract, knowing that the other party is not likely to read the appended additional terms carefully? Should a party who appends additional terms take any action to draw the attention of the other party to those additional terms?

Firm Offers

Another area that gets special treatment for merchants under the Code is that of firm offers. Under common law, an offer could be freely revoked by the offeror at any time before its acceptance. This right to revoke existed even though the offeror might have "promised" to keep the offer open for some given time period. (If the offeree wanted a guarantee that the offer would remain open, the offeree had to enter into an *option*, giving consideration for the benefit of having a guaranteed time period to decide.) Such a situation makes it very difficult for the offeree to make detailed plans based on the offer.

The Code recognizes that the offeree may have to make plans and explore options before accepting an offer, but may still need to be able to rely on the offer being available if and when the decision to accept is reached. The offeree may be harmed if an offer that is supposed to be "open" is revoked. To eliminate this potential problem, the Code guarantees that firm offers cannot be freely revoked before acceptance. Firm offers are only given by merchants. But if a merchant promises in writing to keep an offer open and unmodified for some specified time and signs the writing, a firm offer exists. The offer cannot be revoked by the offeror during the time the offeror agreed to keep the offer open. And if no time was specified, the offer cannot be revoked for a "reasonable time." To place some limit on this, the reasonable time cannot exceed three months.

The following case involved a question of whether a firm offer had been made, or whether the parties were still in the negotiations stage. Notice how the court resolved this issue, and hence the case.

16.3 CITY UNIVERSITY OF NEW YORK v. FINALCO, INC. 514 N.Y.S.2d 244 (A.D.1 Dept. 1987)

FACTS City University of New York (CUNY) solicited "firm" bids for the sale of a used IBM computer system. Finalco submitted the highest bid, and CUNY officially awarded the sale of the computer to Finalco. During the bidding process, the parties discussed the need for signing a formal written document as evidence of the contract; however, no written contract was ever prepared. Finalco decided to withdraw its offer to purchase the computer, stating that its prospective lessee for the system had decided not to proceed with the lease, so Finalco no longer had a reason to purchase the computer system. CUNY made repeated demands for performance by Finalco, to no avail. Finally, CUNY sold the system to a substitute buyer for substantially less money. CUNY then sued Finalco for the difference between the price received from the substitute buyer and the bid Finalco had submitted. Finalco denied liability, claiming that no binding contract was ever entered.

ISSUES Was a written contract necessary in this case before an agreement existed? Had Finalco made a firm offer to CUNY in submitting its bid to purchase the computer system?

HOLDINGS No. A formal written contract was not necessary. Yes. Finalco had made a firm offer to CUNY, and CUNY accepted this firm offer before it expired.

REASONING The court noted that both CUNY and Finalco considered the bid by Finalco to be an offer, as evidenced by the use of the word *offer* in all correspondence between them regarding the bid on the computer system. In addition, Finalco stated at one point in the bidding process: "this offer is valid through the close of business, December 18, 1978." The UCC specifically states that a written offer by a merchant to buy or sell goods that gives assurance that it is open for a specified period is not revocable during the time stated. CUNY sent Finalco a written confirmation on 18 December 1978 that Finalco's bid had been accepted. This was deemed to be a valid acceptance, establishing Finalco's obligation to buy, and CUNY's obligation to sell, the computer system. The fact that some terms were still in dispute does not change this conclusion. There was a contract; Finalco breached that contract; CUNY acted properly in reselling the computer in a commercially reasonable manner; CUNY was entitled to the damages it sought.

BUSINESS CONSIDERATIONS What should a business do in order to ensure that a final written document *must* exist before there is a binding contract? Why would a business want or need to operate in this manner?

ETHICAL CONSIDERATIONS Suppose that a business agreed to all of the terms of a contract and the contract turned out to be disadvantageous for the firm. Suppose further that the business could escape liability for the contract on a technicality. What should the business do, from an ethical perspective?

Statute of Frauds

So far, the discussion has focused on the intent to have a contract and the Code's recognition that a contract exists in such a situation. However, some technical rules still exist that will override intent. One of these involves the Statute of Frauds, which requires that a contract for the sale of goods for $500 or more must be in writing to be enforceable. According to § 2-201 of the Code,

> *. . . a contract for the sale of goods for the price of $500 or more is not enforceable by way of action or defense unless there is some writing sufficient to indicate that a*

contract for sale has been made between the parties and signed by the party against whom enforcement is sought or by his authorized agent or broker. A writing is not insufficient because it omits or incorrectly states a term agreed upon but the contract is not enforceable under this paragraph beyond the quantity of goods shown in such writing.

The Official Comments state that there are only three definite and invariable requirements for the writing:

1. The writing must evidence a contract for the sale of goods;
2. The writing must be "signed," which includes any authentication; and,
3. It must specify a quantity of goods covered by the contract.

An oral agreement that falls within the coverage of the Statute of Frauds is normally unenforceable. However, the Code attempts to recognize modern commercial practices in this area as well. If the parties have any writing (a note, a memorandum, or "other writing") signed by the party being sued, that writing is sufficient to satisfy the statute. (This is the common law rule.) Terms that are omitted or incorrectly stated in the writing will not defeat the proof of the contract's existence. When both parties are merchants, however, a slightly different rule applies. Suppose one merchant sends a written **confirmation** that would be binding on the sender. Under common law rules, the sender would be bound by the writing, but the other party would not be since he or she did not sign it. Under the UCC, the other merchant will also be bound by this written confirmation unless he or she objects to its contents in writing within 10 days after receiving it. This rule forces merchants to read their forms and to cooperate with other merchants.

Finally, § 2-201(3) of the Code lists three exceptions to the general provisions of the Statute of Frauds:

16.2

STANDARD FORM SALES CONTRACTS

CIT will be making most of its sales to retailers or wholesalers, parties who will also be recognized as merchants under the provisions of Article 2. Since most of their sales will be similar, Donna has recommended that the firm asks Amy to prepare a standard form contract that will be easy for the firm to use in filling its orders. This standard form will contain blanks for the name of the buyer, the quantity of Call-Image telephones being purchased, shipping terms, and any other items that Amy believes should be included. Tom would prefer to have the firm negotiate each contract individually and to wait until a contract is made before setting out the terms in writing. They have asked you for your opinion. What will you tell them?

BUSINESS CONSIDERATIONS What are the drawbacks to preparing a standard form to use as you contract in dealing with other merchants? What are the advantages to using a standard form contract?

ETHICAL CONSIDERATIONS If a business uses a standard form contract, should that standard form include "fine print" clauses that are advantageous to the firm, or should it avoid using such language? Why?

SALES

1. No writing is needed when the goods are to be specially manufactured for the buyer and are of such a nature that they cannot be resold by the seller in the ordinary course of his or her business, and when the seller has made a substantial start in performing the contract.
2. No writing is needed if the party being sued admits in court or in the legal proceedings that the contract existed.
3. No writing is needed for any portion of the goods already delivered and accepted or already paid for.

When the parties have a written agreement, the **parol evidence rule** applies; that is, the writing is meant to be the final agreement, and the writing cannot be

Confirmation

A written memorandum of the agreement; a notation that provides written evidence that an agreement was made.

Parol evidence rule

A rule stating that when contracts are in writing, only the writing can be used to show the terms of the contract.

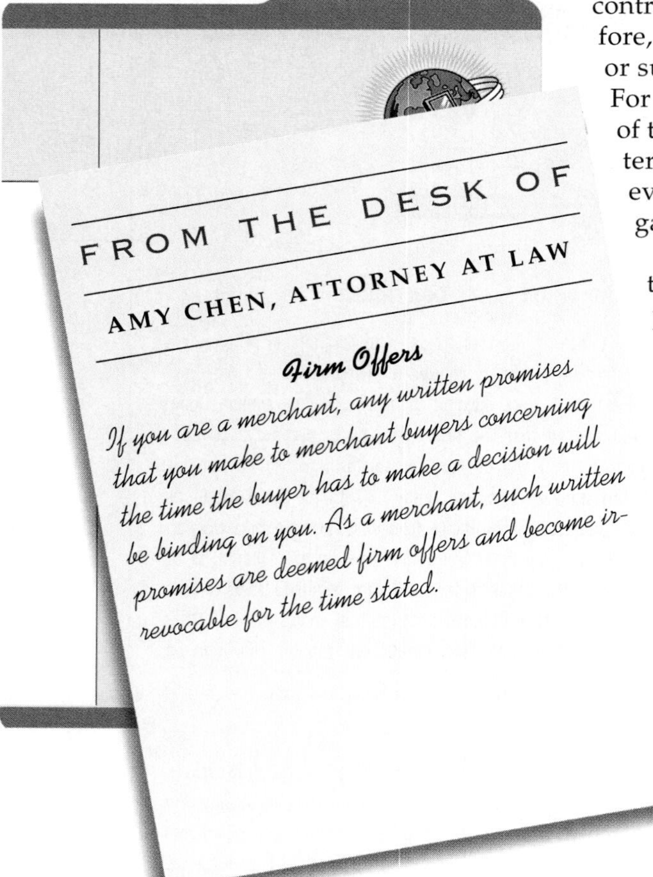

contradicted by any oral agreements made at the same time as, or before, the written document. However, the writing can be explained or supplemented by additional evidence, including oral evidence. For example, either party may show that course of dealings, usage of trade, or course of performance gives special meaning to certain terms contained in the writing. And either party may introduce evidence of additional consistent terms to fill out any apparent gaps in the written agreement.

FROM THE DESK OF
AMY CHEN, ATTORNEY AT LAW
Firm Offers
If you are a merchant, any written promises that you make to merchant buyers concerning the time the buyer has to make a decision will be binding on you. As a merchant, such written promises are deemed firm offers and become irrevocable for the time stated.

Course of dealings refers to any prior conduct or contracts between the parties. Prior conduct between the parties sets up a pattern that either party may reasonably expect will be followed in the present setting. *Course of performance* involves repeated performances between the parties in their present contract. If neither party objects to the performance, it is considered appropriate to continue such performance. *Usage of trade* refers to a widely recognized and accepted industry practice. When usage of trade is proven, it is expected to be followed by the parties.

In interpreting a contract, the court will first look to the express language used by the parties. Whenever possible, the court will read the express language of the agreement and then consider the course of performance, any course of dealings, and any usages of trade in a consistent manner. If a consistent interpretation is not possible, however, express terms control any other interpretation. Course of performance controls either course of dealings or usage of trade, and course of dealings controls usage of trade.

In the following case, the court had to decide whether a contract existed and also determine whether the parties had established a course of performance or a course of dealings. (There was also a "conflict of forms" issue involved.) Note that one party in this case asserted that the parties had entered into a lease, while the other party asserted that the contract was a sale. Although the decision was pre–Article 2A, it is likely that the same result would occur whether the case had been decided under Article 2A rather than under Article 2.

16.4 ESSEX CRANE RENTAL v. WEYHER/LIVSEY CONSTRUCTORS

713 F.Supp. 1350 (D. Idaho 1989)

FACTS In May 1986, defendant Weyher/Livsey Constructors, Inc., leased a crane from plaintiff Essex Crane Rental Corp. for a minimum term of one year. On 26 January 1987, a cable that supported the boom of the crane failed, causing the death of a Weyher/Livsey employee and property damage. Essex was sued, along with others, for damages arising from the death of the Weyher/Livsey employee. Essex brought this suit against Weyher/Livsey, seeking a declaration of rights and duties regarding (1) indemnity for the death of the Weyher/Livsey employee, (2) Weyher/Livsey's duty to obtain insurance covering Essex, and (3) Weyher/Livsey's duty to maintain and repair the damaged crane. Weyher/Livsey counterclaimed on seven theories: (1) failure to provide a crane serviceable for twelve months, (2) breach of an implied warranty of fitness for a particular purpose, (3) breach of an implied warranty of merchantability, (4) restitution of lease overpayments, (5) breach of express contract terms and war-

16.4 ESSEX CRANE RENTAL v. WEYHER/LIVSEY CONSTRUCTORS (cont.)

713 F.Supp. 1350 (D. Idaho 1989)

ranties, (6) negligent failure to inspect and maintain the crane, and (7) strict product liability. At the root of most of the issues in this case is the determination of which document, if any, embodies the agreement between the parties. Weyher/Livsey contends that the controlling document is one of two purchase orders Weyher/Livsey prepared. Essex claims that its form lease agreement controls. Weyher/Livsey did not sign the lease agreement, and Essex claims that it never agreed to either of the alleged purchase orders. Essex began transporting the crane to the Weyher/Livsey job site in May 1986 and forwarded the lease agreement to Weyher/Livsey. The lease agreement was never signed by Weyher/Livsey. After using the crane for about two weeks, Weyher/Livsey sent a letter to Essex advising it that Weyher/Livsey would not sign the lease agreement and stating that the terms of the agreement were contained in purchase order number 3039-PO2400. [It is not controverted that Essex never received this purchase order.] Weyher/Livsey refused to pay the agreed rent, alleging that its policy prohibited any payments without a signed purchase order. After Weyher/Livsey had used the crane for about two months, purchase order number 3039-R00100 was forwarded to Essex. This purchase order had been signed by a Weyher/Livsey agent and by an Essex agent. The Essex agent's signature, however, included the notation "subject to our lease #03190." When the cause of action arose, Essex argued that the case should be decided under the common law of contracts since the contract was a lease and not a sale. Weyher/Livsey argued for the application of Article 2 of the UCC, alleging that the crane had been sold to them. [The cause of action arose prior to the adoption of Article 2A in Idaho.]

ISSUES Should this case be decided under the provisions of the UCC or under the provisions of the common law? Had the parties established a course of performance or course of dealings that would resolve the liability issues between the parties?

HOLDINGS This case should be decided under the provisions of the UCC [the UCC provides a contract, and therefore a remedy, while common law denies the existence of a contract between the parties], using the provisions of Article 2 by analogy. The parties had established a course of performance in which the terms of the lease were controlling.

REASONING Prior to the enactment of Article 2, the mirror image rule applied to sales of goods. Under that rule, a document that purported to accept an offer would be construed as a rejection and counteroffer if the terms of the acceptance differed in any way from the terms of the offer. This created problems in commercial transactions, where merchants on either side of a deal would send to the other parties forms containing boilerplate slanted in their favor. By operation of the mirror image rule, the net result of a battle of forms would often be that no contract was formed.

Article 2 addresses this and similar problems in several ways, two of which are at issue here. First, the Code does away with the need for a formal offer and acceptance. Rather, a contract can be found to exist even where it is impossible to determine when the contract was made. Also "[a] contract for sale of goods may be made in any manner sufficient to show agreement, including conduct by both parties which recognized the existence of such a contract." Second, the Code does away with the mirror image rule, providing that an acceptance which varies from an offer may nonetheless operate as an acceptance.

The battle of forms is not a situation unique to sales of goods. It can occur in any commercial transaction. In fact, this case is an example of the phenomenon in a lease of goods. When the policies that gave rise to a Code provision apply in a transaction other than a sale of goods, Idaho courts look at those provisions in determining the applicable law. Because this case presents the very situation covered by the rules on formation of contracts in the Code, this court will look to the Code to find applicable rules of law.

The lease was an offer. The terms of this offer were never expressly rejected by Weyher/Livsey. Rather, they proposed additional terms by reference to their purchase order. In summary, this court believes that the offer embodied in the lease agreement was accepted, despite the fact that it was not signed, by virtue of Weyher/Livsey's acceptance of benefits under the agreement . . . .

Under Idaho law, when a contract calls for repeated occasions for performance on either side (such as monthly lease payments, in this case), a course of performance that is accepted or not objected to is relevant in interpreting the contract. Also, as stated above, when the terms of an acceptance vary from the terms of offer, the conflicting terms cancel out, and the court refers to other sources, such as trade usage and the parties' course of dealing. . . . The course of performance here clearly established that the terms of the lease are controlling.

Paragraph 8 of the lease agreement provides that Essex would supply parts and labor during normal working hours to repair damage resulting from normal wear and tear. The purchase order relied upon by Weyher/Livsey makes no reference to repairs on the crane.

16.4 ESSEX CRANE RENTAL v. WEYHER/LIVSEY CONSTRUCTORS *(cont.)* 713 F.Supp. 1350 (D. Idaho 1989)

In late July 1986, Essex billed Weyher/Livsey for overtime work on the crane that was performed in early July. . . . even more telling, Essex made minor repairs to the crane in early December 1986. Essex billed Weyher/Livsey for the costs of this repair. Weyher/Livsey responded that it should not have been billed, in part because the repairs were necessitated by normal wear and tear. . . . This course of performance entirely supports the preceding analysis showing that the lease agreement is controlling. Thus, if there were any questions as to which document controls, the course of performance shows as a matter of law that the lease agreement is controlling.

[The court went on to rule that Essex was a merchant, that Essex had a legal duty to provide an implied warranty of merchantability for leased goods under Idaho law, and that the crane was not merchantable due to several defects in the crane. The court also ruled that Essex was entitled to indemnification and to further rent from 20 February 1987 through the end of the lease.]

BUSINESS CONSIDERATIONS If a business regularly leases rather than sells equipment, should that business insist on a signed lease agreement before it delivers the equipment or otherwise provides services to a potential customer? What risks does a business face when it enters into performance without having its lease agreement signed and on file?

ETHICAL CONSIDERATIONS A strict interpretation of common law's mirror image rule in this case would have resulted in a finding that no contract had been entered between the parties. Is it ethical for a firm that leased a nonmerchantable piece of equipment to avoid liability due to the lack of a contract?

Course of dealings and course of performance are normally based on current or prior conduct of the parties with one another. As such, both are readily apparent and difficult to deny. Some trade usage patterns are less obvious, especially since the usage of trade may be applicable to situations in which one (or even both) of the parties are not merchants. For example, in California it is a standard usage of trade to use a formal bill of sale to transfer an automobile, truck, or boat by contract (see Exhibit 16.2). It is generally the obligation of the parties to acquaint themselves with the usages of trade that apply and to comply with them if necessary.

Special Rules Under Article 2

The basic assumption under Article 2 is that both parties will be acting in good faith, with the seller selling and the buyer buying. And, of course, all is done according to the terms of the contract. If that was all that Article 2 said, the rules of contracts from common law would be more than adequate to cover sales. The true value of the Code's coverage of sales is what it provides if, or when, the contract is defective, incomplete, or unclear in some area.

For example, § 2-302 makes provisions for unconscionable contracts or contract clauses. *Unconscionability* means so unfair or one-sided as to shock the conscience. Unlike the common law, which presumed that equal bargaining power existed, the Code realized that some parties can "force a bargain" on the other party, and such forced bargains may be unconscionable to the party who was forced into the bargain. If the court feels that a contract is unconscionable, it may refuse to enforce the

EXHIBIT 16.2 Bill of Sale

BILL OF SALE

VEHICLE LICENSE NO OR VESSEL CF NO

VEHICLE OR HULL IDENTIFICATION NO	MAKE	BODY TYPE	MODEL	YEAR

FOR MOTOR CYCLE ONLY:

ENGINE NO. ________________

For the sum of ________________ Dollars ($ ________________) and/or other valuable consideration in the amount of $ ________________ , the receipt of which is hereby acknowledged, I/we did sell, transfer and deliver to ________________
(BUYER)

ADDRESS CITY STATE ZIP CODE

on the ________ day of ________ 19 ____ my/our right, title and interest in and to the above described vehicle or vessel.

I/WE certify under penalty of perjury that: (1) I/WE are the lawful owner(s) of the vehicle/vessel and (2) I/WE have the right to sell it, and (3) I/WE guarantee and will defend the title to the vehicle/vessel against the claims and demands of any and all persons arising prior to this date and (4) the vehicle/vessel is free of all liens and encumbrances.

Signature of seller X ________________ Date ________

ADDRESS CITY STATE ZIP CODE

SOURCE: Courtesy of Bingham Toyota, Clovis, California.

contract. If the court feels that only a clause of the contract is unconscionable, it normally will enforce all of the contract except the challenged clause.

Open Terms

The Code also recognizes that the parties may intend to have a contract even though the contract may omit some elements. In an effort to give the parties the "benefit of their bargain," the Code allows the omitted terms to be filled in by the court. (Remember from Chapter 13, the court may complete a contract for the parties, but it will not write or make a contract for the parties.)

What happens when, for example, the parties intend to create a contract but fail to set a price? In such a case, § 2-305 controls. Under this section, the price can be set by either of the parties or by some external factor. If nothing is said about price, the price is a reasonable price at the time of delivery of the goods. If the price is to be set by one of the parties, that party must set the price in good faith. A bad faith price may be treated by the other party as a cancellation of the contract, or the other party may set a reasonable price and perform the contract.

Sometimes the parties set a price and otherwise agree to contract terms, but fail to provide for delivery. Again, the Code provides a method to save the contract and to resolve the problem. Three different delivery sections may be utilized.

First, under § 2-307, the seller can make a complete delivery in one shipment unless the contract allows for several shipments. However, if the seller tenders a partial delivery and the buyer does not object, the seller can continue to make partial shipments until the buyer objects.

Second, § 2-308 covers the place for delivery. If the contract is silent as to the place of delivery, delivery is at the seller's place of business. (Law students often miss this point. At first glance, it seems illogical. In reality, it is very logical. When a person buys a toaster or a can of beans, that person takes delivery at the store—the seller's place of business.) If the seller has no place of business, delivery is at the seller's residence. If the goods are known by both parties to be at some other place, that place is the proper place for the delivery.

Third, § 2-309 covers the time for delivery. If the contract is silent about when delivery is to occur, delivery is to be within a reasonable time. Reasonable time here means reasonable in both clock time and in calendar time. The seller is to make delivery during normal business hours (clock time), and the seller is not allowed to delay unduly the number of days before delivery (calendar time).

In addition to these rules, the Code resolves several other potential problems. Under § 2-306, the Code specifically allows requirement contracts and output contracts. In a *requirement contract,* the seller provides all of a certain good that the buyer needs. In an *output contract,* the buyer purchases all of a certain good that the seller produces. Both types of contracts were often declared unenforceable at common law since they were too indefinite in terms. Exhibit 16.3 summarizes the treatment of open terms in a sales contract.

Options

The Code also deals with options. If a contract calls for an unspecified product mix, the assortment of goods is at the buyer's option. If the contract is silent as to how the goods are to be shipped, the shipping arrangements are at the seller's option. However, if a party having an option delays unduly, the other party may act. A party may elect to wait until he or she hears what is being done by the other party or may pro-

EXHIBIT 16.3 Open Terms in Sales Contracts

Open Term	Treatment	Code Section
Price	The buyer or the seller sets the price *in good faith*, if the contract so provides.	2-305(2)
	The price is a *reasonable price* at the time and place of delivery.	2-305(1)
Delivery	If no place for delivery is mentioned, delivery is at the seller's place of business (or the seller's home if the seller has no place of business).	2-308(a)
	If the goods to the contract are identified, and if both parties know the goods are at a place other than the seller's location, delivery is presumed to occur at the location of the goods.	2-308(b)
	If the time for delivery is not mentioned, delivery is to occur within a reasonable time considering the nature of the goods (calendar time) and the nature of the buyer's business (clock time).	2-309
Payment	Payment is expected at the time and place of delivery unless some other payment terms are specified; payment is to be made in any commercially reasonable manner.	2-310, 2-511(1)
	If the seller insists on payment in cash, but did not specify cash payment in the contract, the buyer must be given a reasonable time to procure cash for the payment.	2-511(2)

ceed on his or her own. Thus, if the buyer does not notify the seller as to the product mix desired, the seller may delay shipping any goods, and the delay is excused. Or, the seller may select his or her own assortment and ship it, providing the act is in good faith. Or, the seller may treat the delay as a breach of contract by the buyer and seek remedies for the breach.

Cooperation

As a final and overriding obligation, the parties are required to cooperate with one another in the performance of their duties. Any failure to cooperate or any interference with the performance of the other party can be treated as a breach of contract or as an excuse for a delayed performance.

Contracts for Leasing Goods

When the National Conference of Commissioners on Uniform State Laws decided to codify the coverage of leases, the drafting committee looked for comparable areas for guidance. Eventually they decided that Article 2 of the UCC was most analogous to leases, and they used this article for guidance in their efforts. The coverage of leases was originally embodied in the Uniform Personal Property Leasing Act, which was approved by the National Conference of Commissioners on Uniform State Laws in 1985. It was decided, however, that this coverage would be better suited for inclusion in the UCC, and the Uniform Personal Property Leasing Act was reworked into its present form as Article 2A. In August 1986, the conference approved Article 2A for promulgation as an amendment to the UCC. The Council of the American Law Institute approved and recommended the article in December 1986; and the Permanent

16.3

CHANGES TO THE TERMS OF A SALES CONTRACT

A regional electronics store ordered 200 Call-Image telephones for delivery the first of the month, with payment to be made 30 days after delivery. The manager of the store called Tom yesterday, asking whether the firm would be willing to delay delivery until the 15th of the month so that the receiving dock foreperson could take medical leave without worrying about receiving and stocking the units. (The foreperson needed minor surgery and did not want to delay the operation if such a delay could be avoided.) When Tom asked the family what they thought, John replied that business is a "dog-eat-dog" world and that the problems of the receiving dock foreperson were of no concern to CIT. John, Dan, and Lindsay all believe that the firm should hold the store to the original contract terms. Tom has asked for your help in this matter. What advice will you give him?

BUSINESS CONSIDERATIONS What factors should a business consider when another party to a contract asks for changes to the terms of the contract that has already been entered? When should a firm be willing to permit changes to a contract? When should it object to making changes in a contract?

ETHICAL CONSIDERATIONS Article 2 of the UCC requires the parties to act in good faith and to cooperate with one another. Do these requirements impose a duty on one party to alter its performance—or allow the other party to alter its performance—based on nonbusiness events or circumstances that change the expectations of the other party? How far should a person in a sales contract be expected to go in cooperating with the other party?

SALES/MANAGEMENT

Editorial Board of the Uniform Commercial Code approved the article in March 1987.

Much of the coverage from Article 2 was carried into Article 2A, with changes to reflect the differences between a sale and a lease. Amendments were also made to Articles 1 and 9 to make these areas consistent with the new coverage of Article 2A. The article is designed to help protect the basic tenets of freedom of contract by permitting the parties to vary certain terms of their lease agreements. At the same time, the parties cannot vary such staples of the UCC as the requirements that the parties act in good faith and in a reasonable manner and that they exercise due diligence and due care.

Article 2A has five parts, as opposed to the seven parts in Article 2. Part 1 contains general provisions. Part 2 covers the formation and construction of lease contracts. Part 3 covers the effect of lease contracts, including enforceability. Part 4 deals with the performance of lease contracts. Part 5 concerns defaults and remedies.

The scope of Article 2A is restricted to leases of goods. It does not include "security leases," which are already provided for in Article 9. Similarly, there is no need for a lessor to file any financing statement or other document in order to protect his or her interest in the leased property. Lessees are entitled to warranty protections similar in scope and coverage to those protections given to buyers of goods under Article 2. Thus, there are both express and implied warranties given to lessees.

Article 2A defines a lease as "a transfer of the right to possession and use of goods, for a term in return for consideration" [§ 2A-103(j)]. Subleases are specifically included under the definition of a lease. Parties to a lease, the same as parties to a sale, are classified as merchants or nonmerchants. Protections are provided for a *lessee in the ordinary course of business,* a person who leases goods in the ordinary course of business and in good faith and without knowledge that the lease is a violation of the rights of a third person.

Article 2A recognizes two basic types of leases, consumer leases and finance leases. A *consumer lease* is defined as a lease made by a lessor who regularly engages in the business of making leases and which is made to a lessee (excluding an organization) for personal, family, or household usage. In order to qualify as a consumer lease, the total payments called for, excluding renewals or options to buy, may not exceed $25,000. A *finance lease* is a lease in which the lessor (1) does not select, manufacture, or supply the leased goods, (2) the lessor

http:// RESOURCES FOR BUSINESS LAW STUDENTS

NAME	RESOURCES	WEB ADDRESS
Uniform Commercial Code (UCC) Article 2, Sales	The Legal Information Institute (LII), maintained by the Cornell Law School, provides a hypertext and searchable version of Article 2, Sales. LII also maintains links to the UCC as adopted by particular states and to proposed revisions.	http://www.law.cornell.edu/ucc/2/overview.html
UCC Article 3, Negotiable Instruments	LII provides a hypertext and searchable version of UCC Article 3, Negotiable Instruments. LII also provides links to Article 3 as enacted by a particular state and to proposed revisions.	http://www.law.cornell.edu/ucc/3/overview.html
UCC Article 2A, Leases	LII provides a hypertext and searchable version of UCC Article 2A, Leases. LII also provides links to Article 2A as enacted by a particular state and to proposed revisions.	http://www.law.cornell.edu/ucc/2A/overview.html
The National Conference of Commissioners on Uniform State Laws	The National Conference of Commissioners on Uniform State Laws (NCCUSL), the drafters of the UCC, provides drafts and revisions of its uniform and model acts.	http://www.law.upenn.edu/library/ulc/ulc.htm
The American Law Institute	The American Law Institute, publisher of restatements of the law, model codes, and other proposals for law reform, provides press releases, its newsletter, and other publications.	http://www.ali.org

acquires the goods in connection with the lease, and (3) the lessee either receives a copy of the contract under which the lessor acquired rights to the goods before the lease is signed or the lessee's approval of the contract under which the lessor acquires rights to the goods is a condition to the effectiveness of the lease contract.

A lease contract may be made in any manner sufficient to show agreement between the parties, including the conduct of the parties. Similarly, a lease contract can be entered even though some of the terms of the contract are omitted, provided that the parties intended to make a lease and there is a reasonably certain basis for giving appropriate remedies in the event of a breach.

Leases may also be subject to the rules providing for *firm offers.* A merchant who makes a written offer to lease goods to or from another party in a signed writing is deemed to have made an irrevocable offer when that writing gives assurance that the offer will be held open. The offer may not be revoked for the time stated in the writing. If no time period is stated, the offer is irrevocable for a reasonable time. In no event may the period during which the offer is irrevocable exceed three months. Further, if the offeree is the party who makes the firm offer on a form prepared by the offeree, the offeror must sign the form before the offer is considered "firm," and therefore irrevocable.

The Statute of Frauds for leases requires a writing for any lease that calls for total payments, excluding options for renewals or options to buy, of $1,000 or more. If the total payments are less than $1,000 an oral contract is valid and enforceable. Article 2A also recognizes the same three exceptions to the Statute of Frauds as are recognized under Article 2 if there is no writing and the lease has total payments of $1,000 or more (specially manufactured goods, admission in a legal proceeding by the party against whom enforcement is sought, or to the extent the goods have been received and accepted).

SUMMARY

This chapter introduces the law of sales, Article 2 of the Uniform Commercial Code, and the law of leases, Article 2A of the Uniform Commercial Code. It is important to distinguish sales contracts from other types of contracts. Article 2 attempts to deal with "commercial reality" in the sale of goods, whereas common law developed strict and rigid rules for the treatment of contracts. Article 2 also recognizes the difference between a merchant—a person who "specializes" in dealing with a particular type of goods—and a nonmerchant—a "casual dealer" in the goods. The Code provides built-in flexibility in the formation of sales contracts. Intent, rather than form, is the key element in sales. Offers and acceptances are likely to be found if the parties act as if they have an agreement. The Code even provides methods to supply missing terms, if it seems appropriate to do so in order to carry out the wishes and intentions of the parties. The Statute of Frauds remains operative under Article 2, but its provisions are less restrictive than they are under common law. Three exceptions to the Statute of Frauds are built into the Code, and the past dealings of the parties may also be taken into consideration in deciding what the parties have agreed to do. Some general obligations are imposed on the parties to prevent or minimize abuses of the less rigid rules of Article 2. The parties are required to act in good faith, they may not act unconscionably, and they must cooperate with one another. Performance options are available to either party if the other party fails to cooperate fully or properly.

Article 2A was enacted because of the growing importance of leases in our society. Many people today lease goods rather than purchase them. Historically, leases were governed by common law, whereas sales of goods have been governed by the UCC since 1954. Despite the similarity between a sale of goods and a lease of goods, there was likely to be a different outcome in a lawsuit. For quite some time courts have drawn analogies between leases and sales and then applied Article 2 provisions to leases. This will no longer be necessary with the enactment of Article 2A.

DISCUSSION QUESTIONS

1. What does Article 2 of the UCC govern, and how are these terms defined? What does Article 2A of the UCC govern? How is it different from Article 2?
2. What are the three conditions that the UCC uses to determine whether a person in a sales contract is a merchant? How are merchants treated differently from nonmerchants under Article 2? Why do you think this difference in treatment exists?
3. What is a firm offer under Article 2, and how is a firm offer treated differently from a similar offer at common law?
4. Generally speaking, how can an offer be accepted under the law of sales? How is this different from the mirror image requirement for acceptance at common law?
5. Assume that a seller sends the buyer a form offering to sell certain goods. The buyer returns a form accepting the offer. When these two forms are compared, it is discovered that they do not agree on every point. Do the parties have a contract under Article 2? If so, what are its terms? If not, why?
6. There is a special Statute of Frauds provision for contracts involving the sale of goods. According to this provision, when does the Statute of Frauds apply to a sale of goods contract? What are the exceptions to the Statute of Frauds under Article 2 on the law of sales?
7. Assuming that a contract for the sale of goods is governed by the Statute of Frauds, what constitutes a sufficient writing between merchants to satisfy the

Statute of Frauds? What special rules apply to writings between merchants under Article 2?

8. If the sales contract is silent as to the place of delivery, where should delivery occur? If the sales contract is silent as to when delivery is to occur, when should delivery be tendered? Explain fully.
9. Prior to the enactment of Article 2A, many courts applied the rules of Article 2 to cases involving the lease of goods by analogy rather than resolving these cases under common law rules. Why would the courts apply the provisions of Article 2 to a lease case by analogy?
10. In interpreting a written sales contract, the court will permit merchants to use parol evidence to establish course of dealings, course of performance, and usage of trade. What do each of these terms mean, and what is the hierarchy among them if there is a conflict between them?

CASE PROBLEMS AND WRITING ASSIGNMENTS

1. Musil and Hendrich were both hog farmers, raising hogs for sale and slaughter. Both raised pigs and both also purchased hogs and pigs. Hendrich had been in the business for more than 30 years, and Musil for 13 years. In September, Hendrich approached Musil at a sale barn in Colorado and told him that he had some feeder pigs for sale. Musil subsequently visited Hendrich's farm, looked at the feeder pigs, and bought 60 of them. At the time of the sale, the pigs appeared to be healthy, although a few had dysentery. After two weeks, some of the feeder pigs appeared wobbly, and soon several of them died. Over the next month, Musil lost nearly 60 pigs, some from the feeder pigs purchased from Hendrich and the rest from his general hog population. A postmortem examination revealed that the pigs were infected with swine dysentery, pneumonia, atrophic rhinitis, and whipworm parasitism, all fairly common ailments in swine. (If properly treated, none of the infections would affect the merchantability of the hogs.) Musil contacted Hendrich seeking reparations. When Hendrich refused, Musil sued for breach of the implied warranty of merchantability of the pigs. Hendrich denied that he was a merchant and denied liability. Is Hendrich a merchant in this case? Were the pigs sold to Musil merchantable, so that the warranty of merchantability was not breached? [See *Musil* v. *Hendrich,* 627 P.2d 367 (Kan.App. 1981).]

2. S&B and Tree Top had done business together numerous times over the years, with each transaction being more or less similar and each involving the same type of contract. S&B would order dehydrated apple powder from Tree Top, and would use the powder in making strawberry and blueberry "toastettes," which it would then sell to Nabisco. On 27 April, S&B telephoned Tree Top and ordered 40,000 pounds of the apple powder. At that time, S&B informed Tree Top that, as usual, the sale was subject to an S&B purchase order. However, no copy of the purchase order was ever sent to Tree Top. Soon after, Tree Top sent a written confirmation form to S&B. This confirmation form included an arbitration clause in bold print on its face. S&B did not object to this confirmation form, nor had it objected to the confirmation form in any previous dealings. S&B subsequently filed suit against Tree Top, asserting that the powder was so full of apple stems and splinters that it clogged S&B's equipment, constituting a breach of contract. Tree Top filed a motion to stay the proceedings pending arbitration as provided for in the confirmation form. Should this case be removed to arbitration, or should it be resolved in court? Explain. [See *Schulze and Burch Biscuit Co.* v. *Tree Top, Inc.,* 831 F.2d 709 (7th Cir. 1987).]

3. Bunge Corp. was a major purchaser of corn. Bunge signed three contracts with Toppert, each calling for the delivery of 10,000 bushels of corn to Bunge. Bunge was to pay for each contract as it was performed. Before the first three contracts were performed, Bunge offered Toppert a fourth contract with the same terms as the original contracts, but Toppert did not accept this offer. Toppert delivered the corn for the first contract and began delivery on the second. At that time, Bunge announced that it would not pay for the first contract. Bunge's sole reason for refusing to pay was that it wanted to force Toppert and Toppert's family to sign additional contracts at the same terms. Is this a valid reason not to pay? Explain fully. [See *Toppert* v. *Bunge Corp.,* 377 N.E.2d 324 (Ill. 1978).]

4. Kemper, a retailer, had been doing business with Celebrity, a wholesaler, for five years. Whenever Kemper received any defective goods from Celebrity, Kemper would set those goods aside. Later, assuming that the Celebrity salesman verified that the goods were defective, Kemper's account would be adjusted to reflect the defective merchandise and the goods set aside would be removed by Celebrity. In the case in question, Kemper set aside allegedly defective goods for subsequent inspection by the Celebrity salesman. The salesman refused to verify that the goods were

defective or to adjust the account, claiming that the invoice required written objection regarding any nonconformity and also required a return of such defective goods by the buyer within five days of delivery. Did Kemper properly reject the goods in this case, or was the rejection improper? Explain. [See *Celebrity, Inc.* v. *Kemper*, 632 P.2d 743 (N.M. 1981).]

5. Schinmann grew peppermint and spearmint for oil since 1946. In 1981, Schinmann wished to purchase spearmint roots and sought a seller. Eventually, Schinmann went to Moore to make the purchase. Although Moore had been raising spearmint for 20 years, this was his first sale of roots. Prior to entering the sales contract, Schinmann walked the root field with Moore. The ground was frosted over, and it was difficult to determine the root type by visual examination. Schinmann later claimed that Moore had asserted that some of the "odd-looking" roots were hybrid or nuclear spearmint and that all of the roots were spearmint. Moore claimed that Schinmann was informed that there were "some peppermint" roots scattered in the field and was advised to check the previous year's assay to determine the proportion. In fact, the roots from the field contained nearly 50 percent peppermint. (The industry recognized that 10 percent "contamination" was acceptable, but more than that amount was not acceptable.) Schinmann claimed that Moore was a merchant in the sale of roots and that his sale had breached the warranty of merchantability. Moore denied that he was a merchant and, therefore, denied that he had even given a warranty of merchantability. Who should prevail in this case? Why? [See *Fred J. Moore, Inc.* v. *Schinmann*, 700 P.2d 754 (Wash.App. 1985).]

6. **BUSINESS APPLICATION CASE** Jo-Ann, a corporation formed under the laws of Iceland, solicited Alfin, a New Jersey corporation, for permission to sell Glycel products (a line of beauty care products) in Iceland. Jo-Ann also asked for information about other Alfin products. Alfin sent samples of the Glycel products to Jo-Ann, and Jo-Ann then contacted Alfin by telex, stating in part: "We are very excited to be the exclusive distributors for these products in Iceland. We have not received any prices yet. Please send us your net prices on each item as soon as possible." Alfin replied with its own telex, stating prices in terms of a percentage of American retail, and asking for opening orders for the products as soon as convenient. At no time did the parties agree as to: (1) the duration of the agreement; (2) the quantity of products to be purchased; (3) the timing of payments; (4) inventory levels; or (5) the method for termination. Several months later, a representative of Alfin met with Jo-Ann's representatives. Following this meeting, he recommended that Alfin not deal with Jo-Ann, but rather seek another exclusive distributor in Iceland. Alfin eventually agreed to terms with another Iceland firm, GASA, and Jo-Ann sued for breach of contract. Alfin denied that a contract existed between the parties. Did the parties have an agreement under the UCC, or was the alleged agreement void due to its vagueness and indefiniteness? [See *Jo-Ann, Inc.* v. *Alfin Fragrances, Inc.*, 731 F.Supp. 149 (D. N.J. 1989).]

7. **ETHICS APPLICATION CASE** In 1978, Earl and Linda Miller purchased a 44-foot fiberglass sailboat from Miller Marine, Inc. Earl Miller was the president and principal stockholder of Miller Marine, a company specializing in making custom-built sailboats. Earl was also a well-known boat builder, sailor, and racer. In 1981, Badgley saw an advertisement for a Miller 44 sailboat and contacted Earl regarding purchase of the boat. Badgley informed Earl that she planned to live on the boat and to use it for ocean cruising. Earl replied that the boat was suitable and safe for these uses, and added that the boat was "beefier" (stronger and more durable) than normal because he and his family had used the boat personally; it was not merely a boat that Earl was selling. Earl did not tell Badgley that he had modified the original plans of the boat, including a modification in the tuck (the hull-to-keel connection, an area subject to substantial stress when a sailboat heels over). This modification of Earl's was never structurally analyzed, and he himself was not an engineer. On 16 April 1981, the sale was completed, with a total sales price of $135,200, to be paid in installments. Over the next four years, Badgley raced the boat some thirty-five times. During this period, she discovered a minor but persistent leak. She finally had a naval architect and engineer examine the boat. He discovered a weakness in the tuck, and he recommended reinforcing the area to correct the problem. (These reinforcements cost approximately $6,000.) Badgley eventually paid off all of the purchase price except for $6,000, which she withheld to cover the cost of the reinforcement and repairs she had made to the boat. When she refused to pay the last $6,000, Miller sued for the balance due. Badgley counterclaimed, alleging that Miller had breached the warranty of merchantability by selling her the boat with a defect in the tuck. Was Miller a merchant, so that he gave the implied warranty of merchantability to Badgley in this sale? [See *Miller* v. *Badgley*, 753 P.2d 530 (Wash.App. 1988).]

8. **IDES CASE** Smith-Scharff was a distributor of paper products. One of its customers was P. N. Hirsch, which purchased paper bags imprinted with the P. N.

Hirsch logo from Smith-Scharff. The two companies had been doing business almost continuously since 1947. Smith-Scharff kept a supply of Hirsch paper bags in stock so that purchase orders could be filled in a timely manner. Hirsch was aware of this practice and kept Smith-Scharff up to date on its (Hirsch's) business forecasts. When P. N. Hirsch was liquidated and its stores sold to Dollar General, the president of Smith-Scharff promptly called the president of P. N. Hirsch, seeking assurances that the bags Smith-Scharff had in stock would be purchased. He was told that Hirsch would honor all of its commitments. Subsequently, Smith-Scharff sent Hirsch a bill for $65,000, representing the amount of all Hirsch bags in stock. Over the next six months, Hirsch ordered and paid for $45,000 worth of bags, leaving Smith-Scharff with an inventory of just over $20,000 in Hirsch bags. When no additional orders from Hirsch were forthcoming, Smith-Scharff sued for the $20,000 balance. Apply the IDES model. Was there an enforceable contract between Smith-Scharff and P. N. Hirsch for the sale of these bags? If so, what were the terms of the contract? [See *Smith-Scharff Paper Co.* v. *P. N. Hirsch & Co. Stores, Inc.*, 754 S.W.2d 928 (Mo.App. 1988).]

AGENDA

Once Call-Image catches on and demand for the videophone grows, what type of delivery terms should CIT seek in its contracts? How much inventory should be stored, and how should this storage be arranged? What sort of payment terms can CIT give its customers? Should the goods be paid for on delivery, or should credit be extended for some time period?

Furthermore, there are a number of problems the family will need to resolve as they begin selling their product. The Kochanowskis are offering a new product, and CIT is not (yet) a household name. How should Tom plan CIT's entry into the market? Will the Call-Image videophone be sold to wholesalers and/or retailers, or will it be marketed directly to consumers? If the target market involves merchants, should Call-Image be sold by traditional sale of goods contracts, or should the product be sold through a "sale or return" arrangement? Be prepared! You never know when the Kochanowskis will call on you for help and advice.

Performance, Title, and Risk of Loss

OUTLINE

PERFORMANCE OF A SALES CONTRACT

General Obligations

The parties to a sales contract are required by the Uniform Commercial Code to act in good faith. In addition, any merchant who is a party to a sales contract is obligated to act in a commercially reasonable manner. These two standards are broad enough that they could adequately regulate the basic sales contract. The drafters of the Code decided, however, that more specific provisions were needed to supplement these rules and standards.

The most basic and obvious obligation is spelled out in § 2-301. Under that section, the seller is to transfer and deliver conforming goods to the buyer. The buyer is then to accept and pay for the goods so delivered. Both parties are to perform in accordance with the terms of the contract.

Conforming goods are goods that are within the description of the goods as set out in the contract. Payment by the buyer will normally be made at the time and place of delivery and will be made in money. However, § 2-304 permits payment in money, goods, realty, or "other." The manner of payment, whatever the form, will normally be spelled out in the contract.

The Code presumes that both parties will be acting in good faith, with the seller selling and the buyer buying. And, of course, everything is being done according to the terms of the contract. If that was all that Article 2 said, the rules of contracts from common law would be more than adequate to cover sales. The true value of the Code's coverage of sales is what it provides if, or when, the contract is defective, incomplete, or unclear in some area.

Cooperation

As a final and overriding obligation, the parties are required to cooperate with one another in the performance of their respective duties. Any failure to cooperate or any interference with the performance of the other party can be treated as a breach of contract or as an excuse for a delayed performance.

SELLER'S DUTIES

The seller in a contract for the sale of goods has a very simple basic duty: the seller is to **tender** delivery of conforming goods according to the terms of the contract. The parties can agree to make delivery in any manner they desire. If they do not agree, or if they simply fail to consider how delivery is to occur, the Uniform Commercial Code covers the topic for them. Section 2-503 explains tender of delivery. The seller has properly tendered delivery by putting and holding conforming goods at the buyer's disposition and then notifying the buyer that the goods are available. Normally, the contract will tell the seller when and where to make the goods "available." When it does not, the seller must make his or her tender at a reasonable time and place, and the buyer must provide facilities suitable for receiving the goods. This all sounds technical and confusing, but in practice delivery is fairly simple. There are five possible ways delivery can occur:

Tender
An offer to perform; an offer to satisfy an obligation.

1. The buyer personally takes the goods *from* the seller.
2. The seller personally takes the goods *to* the buyer.
3. The seller *ships* the goods to the buyer by means of a **common carrier.**

Common carrier
A company in the business of transporting goods or people for a fee and holding itself out as serving the general public.

Bailee
One to whom goods are delivered with the understanding that they will be returned at a future time.

Document of title
Written evidence of ownership or of rights to something.

4. The goods are in the hands of a third person (**bailee**), and no documents of title are involved.
5. The goods are in the hands of a third person (bailee), and the seller is to deliver some **document of title** to the buyer.

If the seller properly tenders delivery under any of these situations and the goods are conforming, the seller has performed his or her duty under the contract.

The following case involved a tender-of-delivery question. The buyer, a subcontractor, sued to recover damages it incurred in its contract with the general contractor.

17.1 H. SAND & CO. INC. v. AIRTEMP CORP. 934 F.2d 450 2d Cir. 1991

FACTS H. Sand & Co. accepted a subcontract from Carlin-Atlas Joint Venture to install the heating and air conditioning in the reconstruction and expansion of the New York Port Authority Bus Terminal in Manhattan. On 6 June 1977, Sand ordered four chillers from Airtemp Corp., to be used in the air conditioning system Sand was installing. All four chillers were shipped to Sand by Associated Rigging and Hauling, the agent of Sand. The shipments were made between January and March 1978. One of the chillers (chiller #4) was not tested prior to shipping, allegedly because Airtemp was in the process of relocating its testing facility at the time this chiller was ready for transportation. In November 1978, chiller #4 was sent to the new Airtemp testing center for a test run. This was authorized and paid for by Airtemp. After testing the chiller, Airtemp shipped it back to Associated Rigging and Hauling in January 1979. Sand installed the four chillers in the renovated building as per its contract with Carlin-Atlas.

The chillers were started up for the first time in mid-1980. Sand states that shortly after being started the chillers exhibited defects. Airtemp was contacted regarding these problems, but Airtemp refused to perform any repair work without additional payment. As a result, Sand made the repairs itself and withheld $10,000 of the purchase price. The Port Authority officially accepted the equipment on 23 May 1981. On 16 December 1982, Sand sued Airtemp's parent corporation, Fedders, in the Supreme Court of New York County for damages arising from the defects in the chillers. The parties agreed to dismiss the action without prejudice to allow Sand to bring its suit in federal court, and further stipulated that the action be deemed to have commenced on 16 December 1982 for statute-of-limitations purposes. After Sand brought its suit in federal court, Airtemp asserted the statute of limitations as a bar to the case and filed a counterclaim for the withheld $10,000.

After a number of other legal maneuverings, including a claim by the Port Authority of New York against Carlin-Atlas for $650,000 for expenses incurred due to the defective chillers, Airtemp filed a motion for summary judgment. The district court granted the motion and dismissed Sand's action as time-barred under the New York Uniform Commercial Code. Sand appealed from this order.

ISSUE When did tender of delivery of the chillers occur? (If the chillers were tendered between January and March 1978, the action would be barred by the statute of limitations. If tender of delivery was made in January 1979, the suit was filed within the statutory time limit.)

HOLDING There was a genuine issue of fact as to when delivery was tendered, resulting in a reversal of the motion for summary judgment and a remand of the case for further proceedings.

REASONING Tender of delivery takes place under the UCC when the seller puts and holds "conforming goods at the buyer's disposition." Sand argues that the chiller in question was shipped to Associated in March 1978 for the convenience of Airtemp, so that it could be stored in a safe place while Airtemp was relocating its testing facilities. Sand asserts that this was not an actual delivery and that chiller #4 was not at its disposal until January 1979, so that tender of delivery could not have occurred until that date.

Sand points to three documents to support its argument. The first is a letter from Sand to Airtemp dated 27 July 1978 stating that chiller #4 was shipped without being tested "due to the moving of your plant. . . . Arrangements were made at that time . . . that the machine would be shipped from our rigger's yard at your expense to your plant for testing." Second is a letter dated 30 October 1987 from Airtemp's Northeast Manager to Associated stating that "You [Associated] are currently holding this Chiller for Sand to be eventually delivered to Port of New York Bus Terminal" and that Airtemp's letter is to be used "as Authorization for the Return of the Airtemp Centrifugal Chiller . . . to Airtemp." Third Sand points to a memo from Airtemp's Northeast Manager dated 23 February 1979 stating that when the Port Authority asked that the chiller be

17.1 H. SAND & CO. INC. v. AIRTEMP CORP. *(cont.)* 934 F.2d 450 2d Cir. 1991

shipped to Airtemp's new facility to be tested after being informed that testing could not be done immediately in which he stated that he directed the delivery of the chiller to the Rigger's Yard for security reasons.

These three documents would allow a reasonable jury to conclude that Associated was holding the chiller for Airtemp's convenience and at Airtemp's disposition, not Sand's. We of course intimate no view as to how this issue should be decided at trial where all relevant evidence will be considered.

Airtemp argues that testing is not, as a matter of law, a precondition to tender of delivery, even when contractually required. Yet, whether testing was or was not a precondition to the delivery of the chillers is not the issue upon which this case hinges. Rather, it is whether Airtemp, when it originally shipped the chiller in March 1978 intended to and in fact did place chiller #4 at Sand's disposition.

Further, Airtemp asserts that delivery of nonconforming goods may constitute a tender of delivery. . . . Airtemp correctly recites the law regarding tender of nonconforming goods, but the recitation is irrelevant because it begs the question of whether the March 1978 shipment—whether of conforming or nonconforming goods—was a tender of delivery.

The district court improperly granted summary judgment on the basis that the action is barred by the statute of limitations since there exists a genuine issue of material fact as to whether tender of delivery of chiller #4 occurred in March 1978 or in January 1979. We therefore reverse the dismissal of Sand's amended complaint and remand the case to the district court for further proceedings.

BUSINESS CONSIDERATIONS When a buyer of goods is to have those goods delivered to its agent, does tender of delivery occur when the goods are placed at the disposition of the *buyer* or when the goods are placed at the disposition of the *agent?* What concerns might the buyer have if the tender occurs when the agent has the goods placed at its disposition?

ETHICAL CONSIDERATIONS Suppose that Airtemp prevailed in this case purely because the filing date of the federal court complaint fell outside the statute of limitations, while the filing date in the state court complaint fell within the time limits. Would it be ethical for the defendant to win a case under such circumstances? Would it be ethical for a defendant in a lawsuit to stipulate certain facts in order to have the case moved from state to federal court and then to assert different facts than those that were stipulated in order to win the case without ever getting to the merits?

Tender entitles the seller to have the buyer accept the goods and entitles the seller to receive payment for the goods. If the buyer and seller make the delivery personally and directly (possibilities 1 and 2), proper tender is obvious. The seller will provide properly packaged goods to the buyer. The buyer will accept the goods and pay for them. Very neat and very simple. If the goods are in the hands of a third person, referred to as a bailee, delivery becomes somewhat more complicated. The seller in these cases must either provide the buyer with a **negotiable** document of title covering the goods (possibility 5) or get some acknowledgment from the bailee that the goods now belong to the buyer (possibility 4). If the buyer objects to anything less than a negotiable document of title, the seller must provide a negotiable document in order to prove that a proper tender of delivery was made. The UCC treats the topic of documents of title in Article 7. This article, entitled "Warehouse Receipts, Bills of Lading, and Other Documents of Title," specifies the rights and duties of all relevant parties in the handling of documents of title, whether those documents are negotiable or nonnegotiable. In addition to the coverage of a document of title by Parts 1 and 2 (for a warehouse receipt) or Parts 1 and 3 (for a bill of lading), both Parts 4 and 5 of this article deal with warehouse receipts and bills of lading if the document of title is negotiable. In order to reduce the amount of statutory coverage involved, and

Negotiable

A document that is transferable either by endorsement and delivery or by delivery alone.

Warehouseman
A person engaged in the business of receiving and storing the goods of others for a fee.

to avoid the problems of determining whether there has been "due negotiation" of the document making the holder a "holder by due negotiation" (a favored position under the law), most commercial **warehousemen** and common carriers simply issue nonnegotiable documents of title to protect themselves. Exhibit 17.1 shows the first page of such a document. Exhibit 17.2 (page 436) shows the provisions listed on the back of the same document. Note provision 8 and the nine boldface lines at the bottom of Exhibit 17.2. These two areas limit and control how a seller of stored goods may tender delivery to a buyer.

None of the methods of delivery that have been described is very troublesome. The problems in understanding delivery normally arise when a common carrier enters the picture (possibility 3). Now the seller must give the goods to the carrier, the carrier must transport the goods to the buyer, and the buyer must accept the transported goods and make payment for them. As one might expect, the more parties involved in a transaction, the more likely that problems and confusion will enter the picture.

Carriage
The transportation of goods or people from one location to another.

The seller must provide for reasonable **carriage** of the goods, taking into account the nature of the goods, the need for speed, and any other factors that will affect delivery. The seller must then obtain and deliver to the buyer any necessary documents concerning the carriage, and the seller must promptly notify the buyer of the shipment. Again, all these steps seem obvious, and none should cause any undue problems or hardships. The problems arise when the parties use technical and/or legal terms without understanding their meaning.

Exhibit 17.3 (page 437) illustrates one type of contract a seller may have to use in order to send the goods by means of a common carrier.

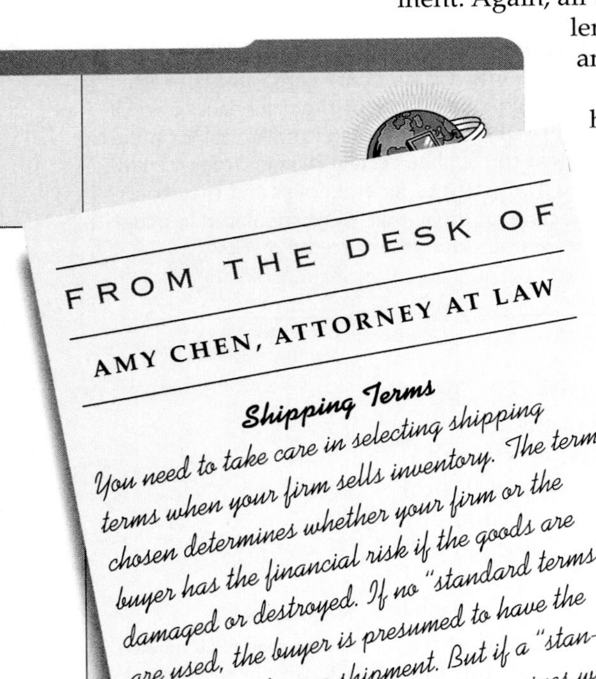

FROM THE DESK OF
AMY CHEN, ATTORNEY AT LAW
Shipping Terms
You need to take care in selecting shipping terms when your firm sells inventory. The term chosen determines whether your firm or the buyer has the financial risk if the goods are damaged or destroyed. If no "standard terms" are used, the buyer is presumed to have the risk of loss during shipment. But if a "standard term" is used, that term determines who has the risk of loss.

STANDARD SHIPPING TERMS

Every shipping contract must take one of two positions: It is either a *shipment* contract or it is a *destination* contract. In a shipment contract, once the seller makes a proper contract for the carriage of the goods and surrenders them to the care of the carrier, the goods belong to the buyer. The buyer has title and risk of loss. The seller has performed his or her part of the contract. In contrast, in a destination contract, the seller retains title and all risk of loss until the carrier gets the goods to the buyer or wherever the goods are supposed to go under the contract. The seller has not performed until the goods reach their destination.

Under § 2-303, the parties can agree to allocate or share the risk of loss during transit. This sort of arrangement seems to be the exception rather than the rule, however. Most parties seem to ignore the problem of loss during shipment until a loss occurs. And, at that point, it is too late to begin negotiating about what to do if one occurs. Because of this normal oversight, and because so many shipments use standard terms, the UCC allocates risk of loss when the parties to a contract use any of these standard shipping terms. If the parties do not designate how loss is to be allocated, and if the contract does not specify whether it is a shipment contract or a

EXHIBIT 17.1 | A Nonnegotiable Warehouse Receipt (Front)

Warehouse Receipt

Non-Negotiable

Lot No. ....

WAREHOUSE RULES
PLEASE READ

Present this Warehouse receipt and a written order when any goods are to be withdrawn.

Reasonable notice is required for access to or delivery of goods.

Access to goods by appointment only.

A labor charge will be made for handling of and access to goods in the Warehouse.

This Warehouse Receipt must be returned when all goods enumerated in the Schedule are to be withdrawn.

A platform charge will be made when goods are delivered to outside truckmen.

The final settlement of this account must be made in CASH, at this office. No checks will be accepted upon withdrawal of goods unless certified.

Courtesy of Clinton Transfer and Storage, Blacksburg, Virginia.

EXHIBIT 17.2 A Nonnegotiable Warehouse Receipt (Back)

TERMS AND CONDITIONS

1. **OWNERSHIP OF PROPERTY:** The customer has represented and warranted to the company that he is the legal owner or in lawful possession of the property and has the legal right and authority to contract for services for all of the property tendered, upon provisions, limitations, terms and conditions herein set forth and that there are no existing liens, mortgages or encumbrances on said property. If there be any litigation as a result of the breach of this clause, customer agrees to pay all charges that may be due together with such costs and expenses including attorneys fees which this company may reasonably incur or become liable to pay in connection therewith and this company shall have a lien on said property for all charges that may be due them as well as for such costs and expenses.

2. **PAYMENT:** (a) It is agreed that the company shall have a general lien upon any and all property deposited with it or hereafter deposited with it. All goods deposited upon which storage and all other charges are not paid when due, will be sold at public auction to pay said accrued charges and expenses of the sale, after due notice to the depositor, and publication of the time and place of said sale, according to law.

   (b) The company shall have a further lien for all monies advanced to any third parties for account of the depositor.

   (c) Accounts are due and payable monthly in advance. Interest will be charged on all accounts unpaid for a period of three months after they become due. All charges must be paid in cash, money order, or certified check before the delivery or transfer of goods deposited under this contract and no transfer will be recognized unless entered on the books of the company.

3. **LIABILITY OF THE COMPANY:** (a) The company when transporting to or from the warehouse for permanent storage acts as a private carrier only, reserving the right to refuse any order for transporting and in no event is a common carrier.

   (b) This contract is accepted subject to delays or damages caused by war, insurrection, labor troubles, strikes, Acts of God or the public enemy, riots, the elements, street traffic, elevator service or other causes beyond the control of the company.

   (c) The company is not responsible for any fragile articles injured or broken, unless packed by its employees and unpacked by them at the time of delivery. The company will not be responsible for mechanical or electrical functioning of any article such as but not limited to, pianos, radios, phonographs, television sets, clocks, barometers, mechanical refrigerators or air conditioners or other instruments or appliances whether or not such articles are packed or unpacked by the company.

   (d) No liability of any kind shall attach to this company for any damage caused to the goods by inherent vice, moths, vermin or other insects, rust, fire, water, changes of temperature, fumigation or deterioration.

   (e) Unless a greater valuation is stated herein, the depositor or owner declared that the value in case of loss or damage arising out of storage, transportation, packing, unpacking, fumigation, cleaning or handling of the goods and the liability of the company for any cause for which it may be liable for each or any piece or package and the contents thereof does not exceed and is limited to 60¢ per lb. per article, or for the entire contents of the entire storage lot does not exceed and is limited to $2,000, upon which declared or agreed value the rates are based, the depositor or owner having been given the opportunity to declare a higher valuation without limitation in case of loss or damage from any cause which would make the company liable and to pay the higher rate based thereon.

   (f) In no event shall the company be responsible for loss or damage to documents, stamps, securities, specie or jewelry or other articles of high and unusual value unless a special agreement in writing is made between the customer and the company with respect to such articles.

4. **MINIMUM PERIOD FOR STORAGE:** On storage accounts three months storage will be charged for any fraction of the first three months period. Thereafter one months storage rate will be charged for thirty days or less.

5. **TERMINATION OF STORAGE:** The company reserves the right to terminate storage of the goods at any time by giving the depositor 30 days written notice of its intention to do so and unless the depositor removes such goods within that period the company is hereby empowered to have the same removed at the cost and expense of the depositor. And upon so doing the company shall be relieved of any liability with respect to such goods therefore or thereafter incurred.

6. **ADDRESS AND CHANGE:** It is agreed that the address of the depositor of goods for storage is as given on the front side of this contract and shall be relied upon by the company as the address of the depositor until change of address is given in writing by the company and acknowledged in writing by the company and notice of any change of address will not be valid or binding upon the company if given or acknowledged in any other manner.

7. **FILING OF CLAIM-NOTICE:** (a) As a condition precedent to recovery, claim must be in writing, supported by a paid freight bill and filed with the company within sixty (60) days after delivery of the goods. No action may be maintained by the depositor against the company either by suit or arbitration to recover for claimed loss or damage, unless commenced within twelve (12) months next after the date of delivery by the company.

   (b) The company shall have the right to inspect and repair alleged damaged articles.

8. **CORRECTION OF ERRORS:** The depositor agrees that unless notice is given in writing to the company within ten days after the receipt of the inventory list accompanying the warehouse receipt and made a part thereof including any exceptions noted thereon as to the condition of the property when received for storage, the inventory list shall be deemed to be correct and complete.

9. **ARBITRATION:** Any controversy or claim arising out of or relating to this contract, the breach thereof, or the goods affected thereby, whether such claims be found in tort or contract shall be settled by arbitration law of the Company's State and under the rules of the American Arbitration Association, provided however, that upon any such arbitration the arbitrator or arbitrators may not vary or modify any of the foregoing provisions.

10. **AGREEMENT:** The contract represents the entire agreement between the parties hereto and cannot be modified except in writing and shall be deemed to apply to all the property whether household goods or goods of any other nature or description which the company may now or any time in the future store, pack, transport or ship for the owner's account.

11. **GENERAL CONDITIONS:** (a) If goods cannot be delivered in the ordinary way by stairs or elevator, the owner agrees to pay an additional charge for hoisting or lowering or other necessary labor to affect delivery. Customer shall arrange in advance for all necessary elevator and other services and any charges for same shall be met by the customer. Customer agrees to pay the hourly charge in this contract for waiting time caused by lack of sufficient elevator service.

    (b) Packing or moving charges do not include the taking or putting up of curtains, mirrors, fixtures, pictures, electric or other fittings, or the relaying of floor coverings of similar services but if such services are ordered a charge will be made therefor.

Courtesy of Clinton's Transfer and Storage, Inc., Blacksburg, Virginia.

EXHIBIT 17.3 A Nonnegotiable Bill of Lading (Back)

Contract Terms and Conditions

Sec. 1. (a) The carrier or party in possession of any of the property herein described shall be liable as at common law for any loss thereof or damage thereto, except as hereinafter provided.

(b) No carrier or party in possession of all or any of the property herein described shall be liable for any loss thereof or damage thereto or delay caused by the act of God, the public enemy, the acts of public authority, quarantine, riots, strikes, perils of navigation, the act or default of the shipper or owner, the nature of the property or defect or inherent vice therein. Except in case of negligence of the carrier or party in possession, no carrier or party in possession of all or any of the property herein described shall be liable for the loss or damage thereto or responsible for its condition, operation or functioning, whether or not such property or any part of it is packed, unpacked, or packed and unpacked by the shipper or its agent or the carrier or its agent. Except in case of negligence of the carrier or party in possession, no carrier or party in possession of all or any of the property herein described shall be liable for damage to or loss of contents of pieces of furniture, crates, bundles, cartons, boxes, barrels or other containers unless such contents are open for the carrier's inspection and then only for such articles as are specifically listed by the shipper and receipted for by the carrier or its agent.

(c) Except in case of negligence of the carrier or party in possession, the carrier or party in possession of any of the property herein described shall not be liable for delay caused by highway obstruction, or faulty or impassable highway, or lack of capacity of any highway, bridge, or ferry, or caused by breakdown or mechanical defect of vehicles or equipment.

(d) Except in case of negligence of the carrier or party in possession the carrier or party in possession shall not be liable for loss, damage, or delay occurring while the property is stopped and held or stored in transit upon request of the shipper, owner, or party entitled to make such request, whether such request was made before or after the carrier comes into possession of the property.

(e) In case of quarantine the property may be discharged at the risk and expense of the owners into quarantine depot or elsewhere, as required by quarantine regulations, or authorities, and in such case, carrier's responsibility shall cease when the property is so discharged, or property may be returned by carrier at owner's expense to shipping point earning charges both ways. Quarantine expenses of whatever nature or kind upon or in respect to property shall be borne by the owners of the property or be a lien thereon. The carrier shall not be liable for loss or damage occasioned by fumigation or disinfection or other acts done or required by quarantine regulations or authorities even though the same may have been done by carrier's officers, agents, or employees, nor for detention, loss, or damage of any kind occasioned by quarantine or the enforcement thereof. No carrier shall be liable, except in case of negligence, for any mistake or inaccuracy in any information furnished by the carrier, its agents, or officers, as to quarantine laws or regulations. The shipper shall hold the carriers harmless from any expense they may incur, or damages they may be required to pay, by reason of the introduction of the property covered by this contract into any place against the quarantine laws or regulations in effect at such place.

Sec. 2. (a) No carrier is bound to transport said property by any particular schedule, vehicle, train or vessel or otherwise than with reasonable dispatch. Every carrier shall have the right in case of physical necessity to forward said property by any carrier or route between the point of shipment and the point of destination. In all cases not prohibited by law, where a lower value than actual value has been represented in writing by the shipper or has been agreed upon in writing as the released value of the property as determined by the classification or tariffs upon which the rate is based, such lower value shall be the maximum amount to be recovered, whether or not such loss or damage occurs from negligence.

(b) As a condition precedent to recovery, claims must be filed in writing with the receiving or delivering carrier, or carrier issuing this bill of lading, or carrier in possession of the property when the loss, damage, injury or delay occurred, within nine months after delivery of the property (or in case of export traffic, within nine months after delivery at port of export) or, in case of failure to make delivery, then within nine months after a reasonable time, for delivery has elapsed; and suits shall be instituted against any carrier only within two years and one day from the day when notice in writing is given by the carrier to the claimant that the carrier has disallowed the claim or any part or parts thereof specified in the notice. Where claims are not filed or suits are not instituted thereon in accordance with the foregoing provisions, no carrier hereunder shall be liable, and such claims will not be paid.

(c) Any carrier or party liable on account of loss or damage to any of said property shall have the full benefit of any insurance that may have been effected upon or on account of said property so far as this shall not avoid the policies or contracts of insurance; provided that the carrier reimburse the claimant for the premium paid thereon.

Sec. 3. Except where such service is required as the result of carrier's negligence, all property shall be subject to necessary cooperage, packing and repacking at owner's cost.

Sec. 4. (a) Property not received by the party entitled to receive it within the free time (if any) allowed by tariffs lawfully on file (such free time to be computed as therein provided) after notice of the arrival of the property at destination or at the port of export (if intended for export) has been duly sent or given, and after placement of the property for delivery at destination, or at the time tender of delivery of the property to the party entitled to receive it or at the address given for delivery has been made, may be kept in vehicle, warehouse or place of business of the carrier, subject to the tariff charge for storage and to carrier's responsibility as warehouseman, only, or at the option of the carrier, may be removed to and stored in a warehouse at the point of delivery or at other available points, at the cost of the owner, and there held without liability on the part of the carrier, and subject to a lien for all transportation and other lawful charges, including a reasonable charge for storage. In the event the consignee can not be found at the address given for delivery, then in that event, notice of the placing of such goods in warehouse shall be left at the address given for delivery and mailed to any other address given on the bill of lading for notification, showing the warehouse in which such property has been placed, subject to the provisions of this paragraph.

(b) Where nonperishable property which has been transported to destination hereunder is refused by consignee or the party entitled to receive it upon tender of delivery or said consignee or party entitled to receive it fails to receive it or claim within 15 days after notice of arrival of the property at destination shall have been duly sent or given, the carrier may sell the same at public auction to the highest bidder, at such place as may be designated by the carrier; provided, that the carrier shall have first mailed, sent, or given to the consignor notice that the property has been refused or remains unclaimed, as the case may be, and that it will be subject to sale under the terms of the bill of lading if disposition be not arranged for, and shall have published notice containing a description of the property, the name of the party to whom consigned, and the time and place of sale, once a week for two successive weeks, in a newspaper of general circulation at the place of sale or nearest place where such newspaper is published; provided, that 30 days shall have elapsed before publication of notice of sale after said notice that the property was refused or remains unclaimed was mailed, sent, or given.

(c) Where perishable property which has been transported hereunder to destination is refused by consignee or party entitled to receive it, or consignee or party entitled to receive it shall fail to receive it promptly, the carrier may, in its discretion, to prevent deterioration or further deterioration, sell the same to the best advantage at private or public sale: provided, that if there be time for service of notification to the consignor or owner of the refusal of the property or the failure to receive it and request for disposition of the property, such notification shall be given, in such manner as the exercise of due diligence requires, before the property is sold.

(d) Where the procedure provided for in the two paragraphs last preceding is not possible, it is agreed that nothing contained in said paragraphs shall be construed to abridge the right of the carrier at its option to sell the property under such circumstances and in such manner as may be authorized by law.

(e) The proceeds of any sale made under this section shall be applied by the carrier to the payment of advances, tariff charges, packing, storage, and any other lawful charges and the expense of notice, advertisement, sale, and other necessary expense and of caring for and maintaining the property, if proper care of the same requires special expense; and should there be a balance, it shall be paid to the owner of the property sold hereunder.

(f) Where the carrier is directed to load property from (or render any services at) a place or places at which the consignor or his agent is not present, the property shall be at the risk of the owner before loading.

Where the carrier is directed to unload or deliver property (or render any services) at the place or places at which the consignee or its agent is not present, the property shall be at the risk of the owner after unloading or delivery.

Sec. 5. No Carrier hereunder will carry or be liable in any way for any documents, specie, or for any articles of extraordinary value not specifically rated in the published classifications or tariffs unless a special agreement to do so and a stipulated value of the articles are endorsed hereon.

Sec. 6. Explosives or dangerous goods will not be accepted for shipment. Every party whether principal or agent shipping such goods shall be liable for and indemnify the carrier against all loss or damage caused by such goods and carrier will not be liable for safe delivery of the shipment.

Sec. 7. The owner or consignee shall pay the advances, tariff charges, packing and storage, if any, and all other lawful charges accruing on said property: but, except in those instances where it may lawfully be authorized to do so, no carrier shall deliver or relinquish possession at destination of the property covered by this bill of lading until all tariff rates and charges thereon have been paid. The consignor shall be liable for the advances, tariff charges, packing, storage and all other lawful charges, except that if the consignor stipulates, by signature, in the space provided for that purpose on the face of this bill of lading that the carrier shall not make delivery without requiring payment of such charges and the carrier, contrary to such stipulation, shall make delivery without requiring such payment, the consignor (except as hereinafter provided) shall not be liable for such charges; Provided, that, where the carrier has been instructed by the shipper or consignor to deliver said property to a consignee other than the shipper or consignor, such consignee shall not be legally liable for transportation charges in respect of the transportation of said property (beyond those billed against him at the time of delivery for which he is otherwise liable) which may be found to be due after the property has been delivered to him, if the consignee (a) is an agent only and has no beneficial title in said property, and, (b) prior to delivery of said property has notified the delivering carrier in writing of the fact of such agency and absence of beneficial title, and, in the case of a shipment reconsigned or diverted to a point other than that specified in the original bill of lading, has also notified the delivering carrier in writing of the name and address of the beneficial owner of said property; and in such cases the shipper or consignor, or in the case of a shipment so reconsigned or diverted, the beneficial owner, shall be liable for such additional charges. If the consignee has given to the carrier erroneous information as to who the beneficial owner is, such consignee shall himself be liable for such additional charges. Nothing herein shall limit the right of the carrier to require at time of shipment, the prepayment of the charges. If upon inspection it is ascertained that the articles shipped are not those described in this bill of lading, the advances or tariff charges must be paid upon the articles actually shipped.

Sec. 8. If this bill of lading is issued on the order of the shipper, or his agent, in exchange or in substitution for another bill of lading, the shipper's signature to the prior bill of lading as to the statement of value or otherwise, or election for common law or bill of lading liability, in or in connection with such prior bill of lading shall be considered a part of this bill of lading as fully as if the same were written or made in or in connection with this bill of lading.

Sec. 9. Any alteration, addition or erasure in this bill of lading which shall be made without the special notation hereon of the agent of the carrier issuing this bill of lading shall be without effect and this bill of lading shall be enforceable according to its original tenor.

Courtesy of Clinton Transfer and Storage, Blacksburg, Virginia.

destination contract, the law presumes that the contract is a shipment contract. Thus, once the seller properly transfers the goods to the carrier and makes arrangements for the transportation of the goods, the title and the risk of loss pass to the buyer.

FOB

FOB means "free on board." A seller frequently quotes a price for the goods to the buyer "FOB." This quoted price represents the total cost to the buyer for the goods (including any transportation or loading expenses incurred) at the place named as the FOB point. The buyer is responsible for any costs incurred beyond the FOB point named in the contract. Free on board may be either a shipment contract term or a destination contract term, depending on the place named. If the contract terms are FOB and the named place is the place of shipment (the seller's location), the contract is a shipment contract. Once the seller has the goods loaded by the carrier, the seller has performed fully. If the contract terms are FOB and the named place is the destination (the buyer's location), the contract is a destination contract. The seller has not performed until the goods arrive at the final point, and thus the seller faces the risk of damages during transit.

FAS

FAS means "free along side" and is a standard shipping term for seagoing transportation. This term is normally followed by the name of a vessel and the name of a port. When a seller quotes the price to the buyer "FAS," the seller is telling the buyer that this is the total cost of the goods, including any expenses incurred, to get the goods to the named location. Again, the buyer is responsible for any costs incurred (loading, transportation, insurance, and so on) beyond the FAS point named in the contract. The seller is required only to get the goods to the named vessel and port. Having done so, the seller has performed. The buyer then has all the risks of loading, transporting, and unloading the goods. The buyer is responsible from the dock of shipment to the buyer's location. There is a recent trend to treat FAS as a seagoing FOB term, with the term being either a shipment contract or a destination contract, depending on the named port. This current usage is gradually replacing the more traditional and more correct treatment of FAS as a shipment contract term, with ex-ship being the more traditional and more correct term for a destination contract.

Ex-Ship

The term ex-ship always involves a destination contract. The seller quotes the buyer an "ex-ship" price, which means the price the buyer is to pay to receive tender of the goods from the named ship at the named dock. Like FAS, ex-ship indicates that the transportation is by sea. However, now the seller is responsible for getting the goods both to the named vessel and port and unloaded from the vessel. Here the seller shoulders the risks of loading, transportation, and unloading the goods. Until the goods reach the destination dock, they are the seller's responsibility.

CIF and C & F

CIF means cost, insurance, freight. C & F means cost and freight. When either of these terms is used, the seller quotes a lump-sum price to the buyer. That single price will include the cost of the goods, the freight to get the goods to the buyer, and possibly the cost of the insurance to cover the goods during the carriage. Both terms are deemed to be shipment contracts, with the buyer assuming all the risks associated with the transportation. Under both terms, the seller pays the carrier for the transportation and then includes these freight charges as part of the price quoted to the buyer. The buyer repays the seller for the expenses of the carriage.

No Arrival, No Sale

Under a no arrival, no sale contract, the seller faces the risk of loss if the goods are damaged or destroyed during transit. However, even if the goods are damaged or destroyed, the seller may not be responsible to the buyer to perform the contract. If it can be shown that the seller shipped conforming goods and if it is not shown that the seller caused the loss or damage, the seller is released from the duty to perform. If the goods shipped were not conforming or if the seller caused the loss, however, the seller is still obligated to ship conforming goods.

COD

COD means collect on delivery. COD is a destination contract with a special feature: The buyer is required to pay for the goods on tender by the carrier, but is not permitted to inspect the goods until payment has been made. If the buyer is unable or unwilling to pay on tender, the goods are returned to the seller, and the buyer is likely to be sued and found liable for breach of contract.

INTERVENING RIGHTS

Once the seller's single duty has been performed, the focus of the sales contract shifts. The seller has performed, but it is not yet time for the buyer to perform. First, the buyer has an intervening right, the right to inspect the goods. If this inspection results in a discovery of some nonconformity, the seller may have a right to cure the defective performance to avoid a breach. Only after these intervening rights have been exercised or waived does the duty of the buyer to perform arise.

Inspection

The right of the buyer to inspect the goods is covered in § 2-513. This section empowers the buyer to inspect the goods in any reasonable manner and at any reasonable time and place. This includes inspection after the goods arrive at their destination, if the seller ships the goods. The buyer bears the expense of inspection. This serves two functions: (1) It encourages the buyer to use a more reasonable method of inspection (since the buyer must pay for it), and (2) it eliminates "phantom" inspections, with the expenses billed to the other person. If the inspection reveals that the goods do not conform to the contract, the buyer is entitled to recover the expenses of the inspection from the seller, along with any other damages the buyer may be entitled to recover.

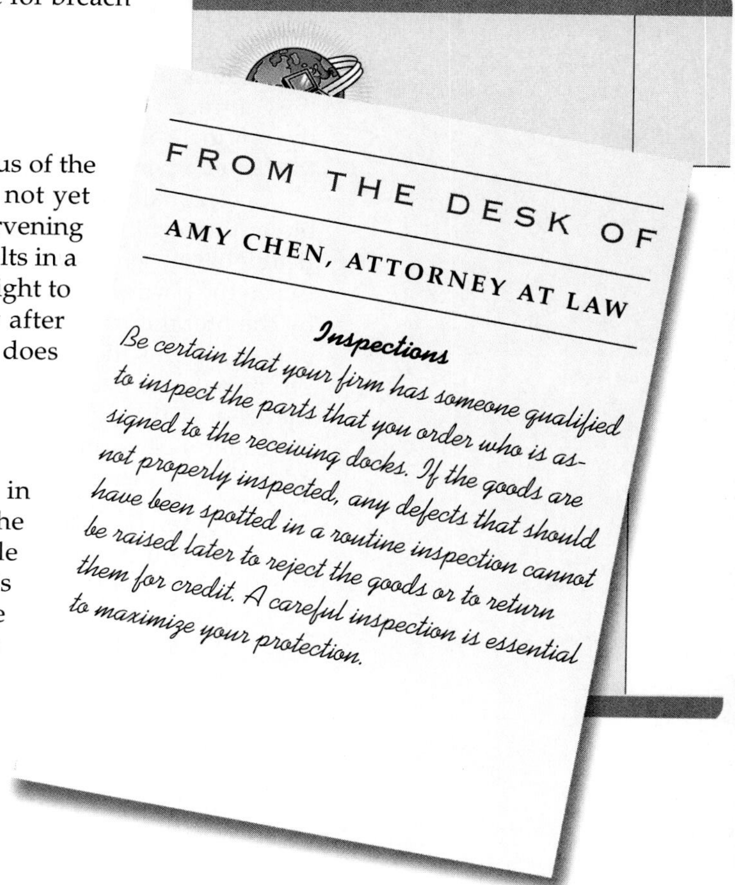

FROM THE DESK OF
AMY CHEN, ATTORNEY AT LAW
Inspections
Be certain that your firm has someone qualified to inspect the parts that you order who is assigned to the receiving docks. If the goods are not properly inspected, any defects that should have been spotted in a routine inspection cannot be raised later to reject the goods or to return them for credit. A careful inspection is essential to maximize your protection.

There are two circumstances in which the buyer is required to pay for the goods before being allowed to inspect them. If the contract calls for payment against documents or if it is COD, inspection before payment is not allowed. However, such a pre-inspection payment is not treated as an acceptance under the Code.

In contrast, if the right to inspect the goods before payment exists, a pre-inspection payment is treated as an acceptance. If the buyer fails to inspect, or refuses to inspect, or inspects poorly, the buyer may waive some rights. Any defects that should be noticed or discovered by a reasonable inspection may not be argued after an unreasonable inspection. The one exception is when the seller promises to correct, or cure, the problem and then fails to do so. In other words, unless the defect is hidden (so that a reasonable inspection would not reveal it), the buyer must "speak now or forever hold his peace."

Cure

Often the buyer will discover, on inspection, that the goods do not conform exactly to the description in the contract. When this happens, the buyer must make a decision. Either (1) the nonconformity is minor, or of little or no consequence, in which case the buyer will normally accept the goods despite the nonconformity; or (2) the goods are too different from those described in the contract to be acceptable. When this happens, the buyer must promptly notify the seller, specifying in detail the problems with the goods that result in nonconformity. If the time for performance has not yet expired, the Code gives the seller a chance to avoid being held in breach. The seller may cure the defect in the goods, putting the goods into conformity with the contract. However, the cure must be completed within the time period in which the original contract was to be performed. No extension of time is permitted without the buyer's permission.

Occasionally, a seller ships nonconforming goods and reasonably expects the buyer to accept them despite the nonconformity. Such an expectation may be realistically based on typical past dealings between the parties, prior performances between the parties, or industry standards. In such a case, if the buyer decides to stand by the literal terms of the contract and refuses to accept the nonconforming goods and so informs the seller, the UCC gives the seller a right to cure even if the time for performance is past. If the seller informs the buyer of an intention to cure the defect, the seller is given a reasonable time to cure by substituting conforming goods so that the seller's performance is in compliance with the contract. The following example addresses this issue.

> A merchant seller and a merchant buyer have done business together over several previous contracts, each of which involved the sale of a particular component part the seller uses in its manufacturing process. Each of these previous contracts called for the seller to deliver the component part Brand A. On at least one prior occasion, the seller did not have an adequate supply of Brand A to satisfy the contract, so the seller substituted Brand B (a competing brand with similar characteristics and price), and the buyer accepted the substituted component without objection. In the current contract, the seller once again had an inadequate supply of Brand A and decided to fill the contract by shipping Brand B instead. When the delivery was tendered, the buyer rejected the goods because the component was not Brand A, as called for in the contract. Since the seller reasonably believed that the substitution would be acceptable (based on their prior dealings), the seller will have a reasonable

YOU BE THE JUDGE

Intel Corporation and the Flawed Chips

The Intel Corporation has encountered some problems with its chips of late. First there was the problem with the Pentium microprocessor chip, a problem that Intel initially denied before finally agreeing to correct the problem (to the tune of more than $475 million). Now it appears that there is a bug in a PCI controller chip that is installed on its motherboards. This flawed chip apparently produces data errors because the chip inadvertently shifts data from one part of the hard drive to another when more than one device is being used. For example, a person using both a modem and a floppy disk drive at the same time might have his or her data shifted to another part of the hard drive.

This case was brought before *your* court. What would you order Intel to do?

BUSINESS CONSIDERATIONS Should a computer company that sells a defective chip only be expected to replace the defective chip, or should they also be liable for any and all damages its customers suffered due to the defect in the chip? What should the customer reasonably expect when it purchases a new model computer?

ETHICAL CONSIDERATIONS In any high-tech industry, there seems to be a constant rush to get the next generation of a product into the marketplace as soon as possible. Should a firm in such an industry take more time in testing and validating the "next generation" before placing it on the market? What ethical issues are raised by these questions?

SOURCE: Dean Takahaski, *The Fresno Bee* (15 August 1995), p. E1.

time to ship conforming goods in order to satisfy the contract. If this had been the first time the seller had shipped substitute parts, there would not be a reasonable belief that they would be accepted (unless such a belief was based on industry standards), and there would not be an extension of time to allow the seller to perform.

While a seller who reasonably believes that the substitute goods will be accepted is given an extension of time to satisfy the contract, the seller will *not* be given unlimited time or opportunity to cure the defect. This has often been a problem in automobile cases. In the following case, the seller claimed a willingness to cure defective performance, but the attempt to cure was inadequate, allowing the buyer to seek other alternatives. Notice how the court treats the purported cure and the consequences of that action.

17.2 BERNING v. DRUMWRIGHT

832 P.2d 1138 (Idaho App. 1992)

FACTS The Bernings owned a Chevrolet van that was in good condition and had only been driven 40,000 miles. In 1988, the Bernings discovered that the van had water in the oil and would not start. They had it towed to Drumwright, a mechanic, for repairs. Drumwright told them he would need to remove the engine to determine the problem. He then gave them three alternatives: rebuild the engine at a cost of $1,200; have Drumwright work on the engine at an hourly rate, without a price estimate; or have a secondhand engine installed. He also informed them that he had a secondhand

17.2 BERNING v. DRUMWRIGHT (cont.) 832 P.2d 1138 (Idaho App. 1992)

engine "with good compression" that he could install for about $800. The Bernings elected to go with the secondhand engine. Five weeks later, the engine was installed, but there were a few problems: The engine that was installed was not a van engine and did not fit properly in the van; in order to check the engine oil, the firewall, radio, and other equipment had to be removed; the engine tended to overheat and to consume about one quart of oil every 50 miles; and the engine frequently stopped and would not restart. The Bernings then took the van to another mechanic, where they purchased a newly rebuilt engine and a new manifold for $2,000. They then sued Drumwright for his alleged "grossly incompetent auto repair," seeking to revoke their acceptance of the engine and to recover their costs for his work. Drumwright claimed that he had not been paid for his labor, nor had he been paid for the engine. He sought the return of the engine, rental for the miles the secondhand engine had been used to propel the van, and payment for his labor.

ISSUES Did the Bernings rightfully revoke their acceptance of the engine provided by Drumwright? Did Drumwright have a right to cure the alleged defects in the engine, a right that was denied him by the buyers?

HOLDINGS Yes. When a defect substantially impairs the value of the contract, the buyer has a right to revoke an acceptance of the goods. No. Drumwright's opportunity to cure had already passed.

REASONING The court ruled that the secondhand engine provided by Drumwright was not merchantable. When goods are not merchantable, the Code allows the buyer to revoke his or her acceptance (§ 2711). Upon revocation, the buyer is entitled to cancel the purchase and to recover as much of the purchase price as had been paid. Here the Bernings revoked the "whole contract," which included the cost of the engine, the cost of removing the old engine, and the cost of installing the engine. Once a buyer accepts goods, the right of the seller to cure defects is cut off. When the Bernings accepted the secondhand engine, any right to cure by Drumwright was terminated. Despite this, the Bernings allowed Drumwright two more opportunities to cure. Neither was effective. The Bernings were under no obligation to give Drumwright unlimited opportunities to fix the problem.

BUSINESS CONSIDERATIONS Automobile sales and services provide a wealth of problems, and most of us are familiar with stories about problems in this area. What protection does a business have against unreasonable complaints by customers after goods (for example, a car stereo) have been installed for the customer? What protection does a customer have against improper installation of parts (for example, an air conditioner) by a business?

ETHICAL CONSIDERATIONS Should special protections or special damages be available when a merchant obviously takes advantage of his or her expertise and/or bargaining position to "rip off" an unprotected consumer? What ethical theory or theories would support such special sanctions?

Buyer's Duties

The buyer's duties with respect to the sales contract arise after the seller's duties have been completed and the intervening rights of the parties have been exercised, if these intervening rights in fact exist in the contract. Since the buyer is not required to inspect the goods, a failure to inspect operates as a waiver, and the buyer's duty to perform arises. If the buyer inspects and discovers a defect, the seller may have a right to cure. If the seller does in fact cure, the duty of the buyer arises. The buyer has a duty to accept the goods and to pay for the goods.

Acceptance

When delivery of the goods is tendered, the buyer has three options:

1. He or she can accept the entire shipment, without regard to the conformity of the goods.

2. He or she can reject the entire shipment, without regard to the conformity of the goods.
3. He or she can accept some of the goods and reject the rest of the shipment.

If the buyer accepts the entire shipment, the seller may view the contract as properly performed, and is entitled to payment for the goods as called for in the contract. If the buyer rejects the entire shipment, either the seller is in breach for tendering delivery of nonconforming goods or the buyer is in breach for rejecting a proper tender of delivery. One of the parties will be entitled to damages due to the breach of the contract by the other party. If the buyer decides to accept some of the goods and to reject the rest, there is a limitation imposed by the Code. The buyer must accept all conforming goods and may then also accept as many nonconforming goods as he or she desires. This means that the seller breached the contract, at least in part, and that the buyer will be entitled to some remedies.

Obviously, the decision of the buyer to accept—or to reject—the goods is of paramount importance. The UCC states that the buyer accepts the goods, and thus is obligated to pay for them, in a number of ways. After having had a reasonable time to inspect the goods, the buyer is deemed to have accepted them in one of the following ways:

1. By signifying that the goods conform to the contract
2. By signifying that the goods do not conform, but that they will be retained and accepted despite the nonconformity
3. By failing to make a proper rejection of the goods if they are nonconforming
4. By doing anything that is not consistent with the seller's ownership of the goods (Since the buyer is attempting to reject the goods, he or she must treat the goods as if they still belong to the seller. Any conduct by the buyer that is not consistent with this hypothetical ownership of the seller is taken as proof that the buyer owned the goods, and had therefore accepted them!)

The following case deals with the issues of timely rejection by the buyer and the adequacy of a purported cure by the seller.

17.3 LATHAM & ASSOC. v. RAVEIS REAL ESTATE

589 A.2d 337 (Conn. 1991)

FACTS Raveis is a real estate company that sought computerized capacity to provide efficient interconnections between its multiple offices and the various banks with which it dealt. Latham & Associates, aware of Raveis's needs and of its reliance on Latham's expertise to satisfy these needs, undertook to provide two computer systems that would meet those needs. (Latham misrepresented the extent of its expertise in creating functioning computer systems in order to persuade Raveis to enter into the contracts.)

The parties entered into two contracts for the delivery of computer systems. The first contract, dated 15 October 1982, called for Latham to deliver hardware and software for a so-called real estate system. Raveis made all scheduled payments under this contract. The second contract, dated 25 March 1984, called for Latham to develop and install a second computer system, the so-called mortgage system. Because of dissatisfaction with the performance of the software tendered under both contracts, Raveis did not fully pay license fees or software support charges for the mortgage system.

Latham sued to recover the amounts unpaid on the mortgage system, while Raveis counterclaimed to recover the payments it had made and the damages it had incurred with respect to the software on both systems. Raveis contended that the software it received did not conform to the express warranties given by Latham in the sale and that it had properly rejected the software in a reasonable and timely manner. Raveis presented no expert testimony in support of its claims that the software did not conform to the warranties allegedly given by Latham. Despite the lack of any expert testimony, the trial court ruled for Raveis, awarding damages of $81,500, and Latham appealed. Latham's appeal focused on (1) the lack of expert testimony at trial, (2) the fact that Raveis delayed too long in attempting to reject the computer systems, thus "accepting" due to an improper rejection of the goods, and (3) the fact that there were no express warranties given to Raveis in the contract.

ISSUES Did Raveis have to present expert testimony in order to establish the breach of any express warranties? Did Raveis reject the goods in a timely and reasonable manner? Was Raveis entitled to damages, or was it restricted to the recovery of monies paid?

HOLDINGS No. There was no need to present expert testimony to establish the existence of an express warranty or to show that the warranty had been breached. Yes. The computer systems were properly rejected in a timely and reasonable manner. No. Raveis did not present sufficient evidence to justify the damages asserted, and it was only entitled to recover the monies paid for the systems.

REASONING The need for expert testimony to establish a breach of warranty for computer systems is a question of first impression in this state and elsewhere. As a rule, expert testimony is required "when the question involved goes beyond the field of the ordinary knowledge and experience of judges or jurors."... On the present record, we are not persuaded that we should adopt a hard-and-fast requirement for expert evidence in every case of dissatisfaction with the output produced by computer systems. Significant facts support the trial court's conclusion that expert testimony was not required in this case. First, the purchaser's burden of proof in this case was attenuated by virtue of the trial court's finding that the purchaser's right to return of the software purchase price was grounded in the purchaser's exercise of its right of rejection under Article 2 of the Uniform Commercial Code.... [A] rejecting buyer need only demonstrate that "the tender of delivery fail[s] in any respect to conform to the contract...." The trial court found that the vendor had not sustained its burden of proving that malfunctioning of the computer systems was caused by personnel failures attributable to the purchaser. [And], at least with respect to the real estate computer system, the purchaser relied on representations by the vendor that included the promise of support services that inferentially encompassed some vendor responsibility for the work product of the purchaser's employees. In these circumstances, given the trial court's unchallenged finding that the computer software did not perform in accordance with the expectations of the parties, the court could reasonably conclude that the purchaser had produced sufficient evidence to sustain its recovery of the purchase price without expert testimony detailing the cause of the software failure.

The vendor has raised ... other issues concerning the purchaser's recovery of the software purchase price on its counterclaim with respect to the real estate computer system. The vendor's appeal alleges the running of the statute of limitations and accord and satisfaction arising out of the subsequent negotiation of the mortgage system contract.

To sustain its affirmative defense that the purchaser's counterclaim was time-barred, the vendor had to establish the purchaser's noncompliance with the Code requirements. For this purpose, the vendor had the burden of proving that the date on which "tender of delivery [was] made," because delivery is what starts the running of Article 2's statute of limitations. The record shows that the vendor did not satisfy this burden. It asserted that the statute began to run on 15 October 1982, but that was the date when the real estate system contract was negotiated. Delivery of the hardware was not completed until 1983, and delivery of the software was arguably never completed. On this factual record, the vendor has not established its affirmative defense.

The vendor's affirmative defense of accord and satisfaction arises out of its claim that the mortgage system contract was intended to encompass and replace its obligations under the real estate system contract. The trial court made a factual finding to the contrary.

The court's further finding of the vendor's misrepresentation about the extent of its expertise in the development of comparable computer systems negates the vendor's assertion that the mortgage system contract, as a complete and exclusive integration of the agreement, excluded parol evidence about express warranties. A misrepresentation undermines the intentional adoption of an integrated writing that is an essential prerequisite to invocation of the parol evidence rule.

The judgment is affirmed.

BUSINESS CONSIDERATIONS There is an obvious danger for a business that claims to possess expertise or experience that it does not, in fact, possess. What should a business do in selling its goods and/or services to put itself in the best possible light without assuming the sort of liabil-

17.3 LATHAM & ASSOC. v. RAVEIS REAL ESTATE *(cont.)* 589 A.2d 337 (Conn. 1991)

ity that Latham faced in this case? How would you advise Latham to promote its hardware and software systems?

ETHICAL CONSIDERATIONS The game theory of business permits—if not encourages—bluffing as a method of doing business. Exaggerated sales talk is often referred to as puffing. Can a business promote itself and its image ethically without resort to bluffing or puffing? How should a business promote itself in an ethical manner while maximizing its potential business opportunities?

As mentioned earlier, acceptance obligates the buyer to pay for the goods at the contract price. It also prevents rejection of the accepted goods unless the defect was hidden or the seller promised to cure the defect and then failed to do so. Also, the acceptance of any part of a commercial unit is treated as an acceptance of the entire commercial unit.

Payment

Once the seller tenders delivery and the buyer accepts (or fails to reject properly), the buyer has a duty to tender payment. Likewise, in the case of a COD contract or a payment against documents, the buyer has a duty to tender payment. The buyer is allowed to tender payment in any manner that is normal in the ordinary course of business, typically by check or draft. A seller who is not satisfied with this can demand cash. But in so doing, the seller must allow the buyer a reasonable extension of time to obtain cash. This would normally be viewed as one banking day. Once the buyer tenders payment, the normal contract for the sale of goods is fully performed. Each of the parties received what it wanted, and nothing further is required. However, some contracts present special problems, some of which will be discussed next.

SPECIAL PROBLEMS

The commercial world is crowded with businesses trying to get, or trying to keep, "a foot in the door;" or just looking for a new gimmick that will provide an edge. As a result, some special forms of business dealings have arisen. The UCC has attempted to deal with two of these special areas: "sale on approval" and "sale or return." Both these forms of business dealings resemble yet another: consignments. The Code deals with these special areas in §§ 2-326 and 2-327.

Sale on Approval

A sale on approval exists if the buyer "purchases" goods primarily for personal use with the understanding that the goods can be returned, even if they conform to the contract. The buyer is given a reasonable time to examine, inspect, and try the goods at the seller's risk. Neither title nor risk of loss passes to the buyer until and unless the buyer accepts the goods. The seller retains both title and risk of loss during the buyer's "approval" period even though the buyer has possession of the goods. The buyer is deemed to have accepted the goods if one of the following occurs:

1. The buyer signifies acceptance.
2. The buyer does not return the goods.
3. The buyer subjects the goods to unreasonable usage.

The following example involves a contract for sale on approval.

> Sam "purchases" a new lawn mower with a thirty-day "free home trial." He uses the mower six times in three weeks, cutting his lawn and in no way abusing the product. After the third week, Sam returns the mower and refuses to pay the purchase price. Since this was a sale on approval and Sam never approved, he is not responsible for payment.

Sale or Return

A sale or return exists if the buyer "purchases" goods primarily for resale with the understanding that the unsold goods may be returned to the seller even if they conform to the contract. In this situation, both title and risk of loss lie with the goods. Goods stolen from the buyer cannot be returned, so they are "sold" to the buyer. The seller must be paid for them. The following example indicates how the purpose of a sale or return differs from the purpose of a sale on approval.

> Sam "purchases" some automobile stereo systems from Smooth Sounds, Inc., on a sale-or-return contract. Sam displays one of the stereos in his service station. If a customer wants an auto stereo system, Sam will sell it and install it. Sam can return any unsold units to Smooth Sounds for a refund or for credit on future goods. However, a thief breaks into Sam's station and steals the stereos. Sam must pay Smooth Sounds for the stereos since he cannot return them.

Consignment

In a consignment, the owner of the goods allows a consignee to display and sell the goods for the owner/consignor. The UCC treats such an arrangement as a sale or return unless one of the following occurs:

1. The consignor ensures that signs are posted specifying that the goods on display are consigned goods.
2. The consignor proves that the creditors of the consignee were generally aware of the consignments.
3. The consignor complies with the rules for secured transactions under Article 9 of the UCC.

Obviously, the Code has limited, if not eliminated, consignment in the modern business world. Most such arrangements today are treated merely as sale-or-return contracts.

Auctions

Knocking down
The acceptance of a bid by an auctioneer, signified by the falling of the gavel after the announcement that the goods are "Going, going, gone."

Auctions receive special mention in § 2-328. In an auction, the auctioneer, on behalf of the seller, sells the goods to the highest bidder. The auctioneer does not normally give the same warranties to a buyer that other sellers of goods give. A sale at auction is not complete until the auctioneer accepts a bid. Even then, if a bid is made while the auctioneer is in the process of **knocking down**, the auctioneer may elect to reopen bidding. The goods at an auction are presumed to be put up "with reserve." An auction will be deemed "without reserve" only if, by its terms, it is specifically and expressly stated to be "without reserve." *With reserve* means that the auctioneer may declare all the bids to be too low and may refuse to accept any bids or to make any sale. In contrast, if the auction is *without reserve,* the highest bid made must be accepted and a sale made.

What if the seller enters a bid, directly or indirectly, in an effort to drive up the bidding? The winning bidder in such a case may choose to renounce his or her bidding and to avoid the sale or may elect to take the goods at the last good-faith bid before the seller entered the bidding.

17.1

METHODS OF SELLING

CIT is having some difficulty gaining adequate shelf space in a number of retail outlets, and this is causing Tom some concern. Lindsay is interested in music, and she knows that many musical instruments are sold by stores that carry a wide range of brand names and cover a large price range. She asked the manager of one such store how he manages to carry so many brands at such diverse prices and was told that many of the instruments were on consignment. She has suggested to the family that they might want to offer a consignment arrangement to the retail store in order to acquire shelf space. John would prefer to use some other method of selling, perhaps a sale or return or a sale on approval. Anna asks what you recommend they do. What will you tell her?

BUSINESS CONSIDERATIONS A firm trying to break into an established industry might have to decide between trying to gain a market share through price competition or using a nonstandard marketing method, such as a sale or return arrangement. What are the benefits to using sale or return rather than reduced price to gain market recognition and share? What are the potential drawbacks to this approach?

ETHICAL CONSIDERATIONS The rights of the creditors of a retail merchant are different in regard to the merchant's inventory if the merchant has goods through a consignment or a sale or return. If the merchant carries inventory under both bases, what are the ethical obligations of that merchant to provide its creditors with adequate information regarding the inventory?

TITLE TO GOODS

When the term *title* is used, it refers to legal ownership. The legal owner of goods is said to have title. When goods are sold, title passes from the seller to the buyer. Title is a very important concept.

Historic Importance

Under common law, title was of paramount importance. Nearly all aspects of the contract hinged on title and its location. Risk of loss was placed on the party holding title. The outcome of many lawsuits depended on who had title, so the courts spent a great deal of time and energy on this issue. In some respects it is not as important today as it was in the past, at least under Article 2 of the UCC.

Modern Rule

The UCC specifically states that all the rights, duties, and remedies of any party apply without regard to title unless title is specifically required. However, in recognition of the importance of title, some provisions have been made to help in locating title in the sale of goods. Under the Code, title passes from the seller to the buyer when the seller completes performance of delivery. Thus, the type of delivery contract becomes important in determining which party has title. If the delivery contract is a shipment contract, title passes to the buyer at the time and place of shipment. If the contract is a destination contract, title passes to the buyer when delivery is tendered at the destination. These rules apply even though the seller may claim to have "reserved title." The Code states that a **reservation of title** is, in reality, only the reservation of a security interest.

Reservation of title
An attempt by the seller to retain title until the buyer has fully performed the contract.

In some sales contracts, the goods are not to be delivered physically. Again, the Code specifies how title is to pass. If the goods are not to be moved and the seller is to deliver a document of title, title passes when and where the document is given to the buyer. If no documents are to be delivered, title passes at the time and place the contract is made. Of course, under any set of circumstances, title cannot pass unless the goods are in existence and identified to the contract. The existence of the goods presents no problem: either the goods exist or they do not exist. However, identification can present a problem. Goods are identified to a contract when they are shipped, marked, or otherwise designated by the seller as the goods that will satisfy the contract. (Determining what qualifies as "otherwise designated" is a question of fact.)

Revests
Vests again; is acquired a second time.

Occasionally, title will pass from the buyer back to the seller. If the buyer rejects the goods or refuses to accept, receive, or retain them, title **revests** in the seller. This is true even if the buyer is acting improperly by refusing the goods. Likewise, if the buyer properly revokes an acceptance, title revests in the seller.

Unsecured creditor
A general creditor; a creditor whose claim is not secured by collateral.

The location of title is still important in the area of creditor rights. A creditor of one of the parties may be able to attach any goods that belong to that party. Thus, creditors are very anxious to know where title lies. This also helps to explain the UCC's treatment of consignments. The Code is very careful in spelling out the rights of each party when creditors are involved. Section 2-402 deals with the rights of creditors of the seller when goods are sold. The rights of an **unsecured creditor** of the seller are limited by the rights of the buyer to recover the goods once the goods are identified to the contract. In a legal tug-of-war between the buyer and a creditor of the seller, the buyer normally will win if the goods have been identified as the goods covered by the sales contract.

Fraudulent Retention

Another problem arises when, as sometimes happens, the seller "sells" goods but retains possession. In such a case, the seller's creditors can treat the sale as void *if* the retention by the seller is fraudulent under state law. Historically, the seller's only defense was to show that he or she was a merchant who retained the goods in good faith in the ordinary course of business, and then only if the goods were retained only for a commercially reasonable time. Thus, a seller who holds identified goods in "layaway" would have a valid defense to a fraudulent retention charge. But a seller who holds the goods without a valid reason could be in trouble. The following hypothetical case illustrates a fraudulent retention by the seller.

> John, a blacksmith deeply in debt, feared his creditors would sue him and take his equipment to pay the debts. To prevent this, he "sold" his equipment to Lil, who let John retain possession of "her" equipment. When John's creditors tried to attach the equipment to satisfy the debts, John denied he owned it. He produced the bill of sale as proof.

The sale in this example would be fraudulent since John retained the goods after the sale in bad faith. The creditors thus could treat the sale as void and attach the equipment.

Conclusive presumption
An inference of the truth or falsity of a fact from which a result must follow as a matter of law.

Different states treat the issue of fraudulent retention differently. Three possible rules exist for a state to follow. In some states, a fraudulent retention by the seller is treated as a **conclusive presumption** of fraud; if a seller sells goods and then retains possession of those goods for any reason other than a commercial reason, the seller is deemed guilty of fraud. Other states view a retention of the goods by the seller after the sale as prima facie proof of fraud; the seller is presumed to be guilty of fraud unless the seller is able to show good cause for the retention. In other states, the retention of the goods by the seller is viewed merely as one bit of evidence, to be viewed together with all the other evidence, in determining whether a fraud has occurred.

The enactment of Article 2A, Leases, has further complicated this issue. Article 2A specifically recognizes the validity of a sale and leaseback arrangement, provided that the buyer in the sale portion of the deals acts in good faith and gives value for the goods purchased. Sale and leaseback arrangements have become very popular in a number of industries, especially construction, and the increase has presented numerous problems with the former attitude toward sellers who retained possession of the goods following the sale. The specific authorization of this sort of dealing under Article 2A should reduce the problems and help to clarify this area of law.

Entrustment

As a general rule, any person who sells goods can transfer to the buyer only those rights that are equal to or less than the rights the seller possesses in those goods. Thus, the person who has valid title (that is, the owner of the goods) can sell the goods and pass valid title to the buyer. A person who has void title (that is, a thief) has no true title to the goods and passes void title to the buyer. The true owner of the goods may legally reclaim the goods from the person who bought the goods from the thief, if and when the true owner discovers the location of the goods.

A person who has voidable title, however, may legally transfer rights that are better than he or she possesses in the goods. A person with voidable title may legally pass full and valid title to a buyer if that buyer is a good-faith purchaser for value. For example, a person who acquires goods through fraud or misrepresentation has voidable title to those goods. The person who was defrauded or who was the victim of the misrepresentation may avoid the transaction and recover title to the goods if the avoidance occurs while the defrauding or misrepresenting party still has possession of the goods. However, if the defrauding or misrepresenting party sells the goods before any attempt to avoid the transaction occurs, the buyer may have full and valid title to the goods.

The issue of **entrustment** addresses these problems regarding voidable title and the passage of valid title. An entrustment occurs when there is "any delivery and acquiescence in retention of possession regardless of any conditions expressed between the parties to the delivery or acquiescence and regardless of whether the procurement of the entrusting or the possessor's disposition of the goods has been such as to be larcenous under the criminal law" [UCC 2-403(3)]. Commonly, an entrustment involves a situation in which possession of the goods is given to a merchant who regularly deals in goods of that kind (often for repairs). The entruster, the person who delivers possession of the goods to the merchant, gives the merchant voidable title, which gives the merchant the legal power to transfer all of the entruster's rights to a buyer who in the ordinary course of business purchases the entrusted goods from the merchant. Thus, an owner who takes his or her goods to a merchant for repairs entrusts those goods to the merchant. If the merchant happens to sell the entrusted goods to a customer in the ordinary course of business, and if the customer acted in good faith, the customer takes valid title to the goods. Of course, the entruster does have rights and remedies against the merchant to whom the goods were entrusted. If the entrustment involves a party who obtains the goods but who is not a merchant in goods of that kind, the entrusted party can transfer

Entrustment

The delivery of goods to a merchant who regularly deals in goods of the type delivered.

good title to any good faith purchaser for value. The following two examples show the difference between an entrustment to a merchant and an entrustment to a nonmerchant.

> Betty took her watch to Roger's Jewelry to have it repaired. Roger's sells new and used watches in its normal business dealings. If a customer comes into the store and "purchases" Betty's watch, that customer will own the watch. Betty's only recourse will be to sue Roger's for her loss. By entrusting the watch to Roger's, she gave Roger's the legal power to transfer good title to any buyer in the ordinary course of business who purchases the watch from Roger's.
>
> Roger took his watch to Betty's Radio Shop to have it repaired. Although Betty's does not deal in watches, Betty sometimes repairs watches for her friends, and she agrees to do this for Roger. If a customer comes into Betty's and purchases Roger's watch, Roger may be able to recover the watch from the customer. Since Betty does not deal in watches, the transaction with Roger was not an entrustment to a merchant. However, if the person who bought the watch bought it as a good faith purchaser for value, the buyer would still acquire good title due to the entrustment of the watch to Betty by Roger.

The following case concerns the issues of entrustment of goods to a merchant, whether the entrusted goods were stolen prior to their sale, and whether the buyers acquired good title to the goods.

17.4 HEINRICH v. TITUS-WILL SALES, INC. 868 P.2d 169 (Wash.App. 1994)

FACTS In 1989, Michael Heinrich wished to buy a particular model new Ford pickup truck. James Wilson held himself out as a dealer/broker, licensed to buy and sell vehicles. Heinrich retained Wilson to make the purchase, but did not direct Wilson to any particular automobile dealer. Unbeknownst to Heinrich, Wilson had lost his Washington vehicle dealer license the previous year.

Wilson negotiated with Titus-Will for the purchase of a Ford pickup truck with Heinrich's desired options. Titus-Will had been involved in hundreds of transactions with Wilson over the years and also was unaware that Wilson was no longer licensed to act as a vehicle dealer.

Heinrich made two initial payments to Wilson: an $1,800 down payment and a $3,000 payment when Titus-Will ordered the truck. Wilson gave Heinrich a receipt using a "Used Car Wholesale Purchase Order" that displayed Wilson's alleged vehicle dealer license number. Wilson then ordered the truck from Titus-Will, using his own check to make a $7,000 down payment. The purchase order indicated the truck was being sold to Wilson. "Dealer" was written in the space on the form for tax. Wilson told the Titus-Will salesman handling the sale that he was ordering the truck for resale.

On 13 October 1989, Wilson told Heinrich the truck was ready for delivery. Heinrich paid Wilson $15,549.55 as final payment, including tax and license fees. Wilson gave Heinrich a copy of the purchase order and of an options checklist with corresponding prices. These documents indicated that Wilson was buying the truck from Titus-Will. The Titus-Will salesman had signed off on the options list; Wilson marked it "paid in full" and signed it after Heinrich paid him. On the same day, at Wilson's behest, Heinrich signed a Washington application for motor vehicle title.

Wilson agreed to deliver the truck to Heinrich at Titus-Will on Saturday, 21 October 1989. He arranged with a Titus-Will salesman to deliver a check on the morning of 21 October to a clerk in the Titus-Will office and, in return, to receive the truck keys and paperwork. The clerk accepted Wilson's check for $11,288, postdated to Monday, 23 October 1989, and delivered to Wilson a packet containing the keys to the truck, the owner's manual, an odometer disclosure statement, and a warranty card. The odometer statement . . . showed Wilson as the transferor. Titus-Will did not fill out the warranty card with the name and address of the purchaser because the sale appeared to be dealer to dealer, with the warranty to benefit the ultimate purchaser.

Titus-Will retained the manufacturer's certificate of origin. The certificate of origin is apparently a "pre-title" document used to obtain state title documents when a car is sold to a nondealer. Titus-Will, believing this to be a

17.4 HEINRICH v. TITUS-WILL SALES, INC. *(cont.)* **868 P.2d 169 (Wash.App. 1994)**

dealer-to-dealer transaction, planned to give the certificate to Wilson when his check cleared.

Wilson immediately taped Heinrich's application for title in the rear window of the truck that was parked on the Titus-Will lot. When Heinrich arrived, Wilson gave him the keys and the documents and Heinrich drove off.

Wilson's check did not clear. Titus-Will demanded return of the truck. On 6 November, Wilson picked up the truck from Heinrich, telling him he would have Titus-Will make certain repairs under the warranty. Wilson returned the truck to Titus-Will.

On 9 November 1989, Wilson admitted to Heinrich that he did not have funds to cover the check to Titus-Will and that Titus-Will would not release the truck without payment. Heinrich sued Titus-Will and Wilson, seeking replevin of the truck and damages of his loss of use. Heinrich obtained a default judgment against Wilson. He also won title to the truck and $3,500 in damages in his trial against Titus-Will, which appealed.

ISSUE Did Titus-Will entrust the truck to Wilson, giving him voidable title and permitting him to pass valid title to Heinrich, a buyer in the ordinary course of business?

HOLDING Yes. The truck was entrusted to Wilson, who sold it to a buyer in the ordinary course of business who received good title from Wilson.

REASONING The entrustment provisions of the UCC provide as follows:

> *(2) Any entrusting of possession of goods to a merchant who deals in goods of that kind gives him power to transfer all rights to a buyer in ordinary course of business.*
>
> *(3) "Entrusting" includes any delivery and any acquiescence in retention of possession regardless of any condition expressed between the parties to the delivery or acquiescence and regardless of whether the procurement of the entrusting or the possessor's disposition of the goods have been such as to be larcenous under the criminal law.*

To prevail under this statute, Heinrich must show 1) Titus-Will "entrusted" the truck to Wilson, and thus empowered Wilson subsequently to transfer all rights of Titus-Will in the truck to Heinrich; 2) Wilson was a merchant dealing in automobiles; and 3) Heinrich bought the truck from Wilson as a "buyer in the ordinary course of business."

Wilson was a merchant who dealt in automobiles; he held himself out as a dealer and appeared to be a dealer in automobiles. Both parties treated him as a dealer in automobiles. Titus-Will argues that he was not a dealer because he did not have a valid state license. However, the UCC does not require proper state licensing for merchant status. Wilson's apparent violation of state licensing statutes may subject him to penalties, but it does not void an otherwise valid UCC commercial transaction. Indeed, the exclusion of an unlicensed dealer from merchant status under the UCC would be contrary to the statutory purpose of protecting innocent purchasers from illegal (or even larcenous) conduct of the entrustee.

We affirm the trial court's judgment.

BUSINESS CONSIDERATIONS This case illustrates what can happen when an honest business and an honest consumer are involved with a dishonest third party who is allegedly brokering a deal. How can the businessperson protect his or her interests in such a situation? What alternatives are available to the businessperson in such circumstances?

ETHICAL CONSIDERATIONS What are the ethical obligations of each of the parties in this case to the other two parties who were also involved? Between the dealer and the buyer, who has the better ethical claim to the truck? Why?

Insurable Interest

The term insurable interest refers to the right to purchase insurance on goods to protect one's property rights and interests in the goods. The buyer gains an insurable interest when existing goods are identified to the contract, even if the goods are nonconforming. If the goods are not identified, the buyer gains an insurable interest once identification occurs. Likewise, if the goods are not yet in existence, the buyer gains an insurable interest as soon as the goods come into existence.

The seller has an insurable interest in the goods for as long as the seller retains title to or any security interest in the goods; and either party has an insurable interest if that party also has a risk of loss. Notice that title is not necessary for an insurable interest to exist.

Exhibit 17.4 outlines the circumstances in which title and risk of loss are transferred from the seller to the buyer in the different types of sales contracts we have discussed. We will take up the subject of risk of loss in the next section.

Risk of Loss

The term *risk of loss* refers to the financial responsibility between the parties if the goods are lost, damaged, or destroyed before the buyer has accepted them. Notice that risk of loss refers to the relationship between the buyer and the seller. It does not refer to the possibility that an independent carrier of the goods may be liable. Nor does it refer to the possible liability of any insurer of the goods or of their delivery. The allocation of risk of loss often depends on the method of performance.

A buyer who has risk of loss must pay the seller for the goods if the goods were properly shipped. This situation arises most commonly in a shipment contract: if the seller shipped conforming goods, but during the journey the goods were damaged, destroyed, or lost, the buyer is liable and must perform the contract as agreed. Of course, the buyer may have recourse against the carrier or against an insurer for the loss, but such recourse involves a separate contract or relationship and does not affect the buyer's liability to the seller.

EXHIBIT 17.4 The Movement of Title and Risk of Loss

Form of Delivery	Circumstances in Which Title Passes to Buyer, §2-401	Circumstances in Which Risk of Loss Shifts to Buyer, §2-509
Delivery by carrier		
• with a shipment contract	At the time and place of shipment	When carrier receives goods
• with a destination contract	Upon tender of delivery	When delivery is tendered at the destination
Delivery by warehouseman		
• via negotiable document of title	Upon delivery of documents to the buyer	When buyer receives the document
• via nonnegotiable document of title	Upon delivery of documents to the buyer	After the buyer has a reasonable time to notify the bailee
• with no document of title	At the time and place of the contract	Upon the bailee's acknowledgment of the buyer's rights to the goods
Personal delivery		
• by merchant seller	At the time and place of the contract	Upon delivery of the goods to the buyer
• by nonmerchant seller	At the time and place of the contract	Upon tender of delivery of the goods

If the contract involved is a destination contract, the seller bears the risk of loss. In this situation, any lost, damaged, or destroyed goods are the responsibility of the seller. The seller will be required to ship more goods or to make up the loss to the buyer in some other manner. And the seller will then have to proceed against the carrier or the insurer for any remedies that may be available.

In contracts that do not involve the use of an independent carrier, the risk of loss will frequently depend on how adequately the parties have performed. Several possibilities are explored next.

Breach of Contract

If the seller breaches the contract by sending nonconforming goods, risk of loss remains with the seller until either the seller cures the defect or the buyer accepts the goods despite the nonconformity. In order for this provision to apply, the goods must be so nonconforming that the buyer may properly reject the tender of delivery. Sometimes the buyer accepts the goods that the seller sends but later finds them to be nonconforming. When this occurs, the buyer often has the right to revoke acceptance. When accepting the goods, the buyer assumes risk of loss. When the nonconformity is discovered and the acceptance is revoked, what happens? The buyer retains risk of loss, but only to the extent of the buyer's insurance coverage. Any loss in excess of the insurance rests on the seller.

Sometimes the buyer breaches a contract, usually by **repudiation**, after the goods are identified but before they are delivered. In such a case, risk of loss has not yet shifted from the seller to the buyer. As a result, the risk still rests on the seller. However, since the buyer is in breach, any loss in excess of the seller's insurance coverage rests on the buyer. Of course, the buyer will face this possible loss only for a commercially reasonable time.

Repudiation
Rejection of an offered or available right or privilege, or of a duty or relation.

In the following case, a buyer was seeking damages due to the breach of a contract involving ostriches. Note how the court treated the buyer's argument concerning the damages he allegedly suffered.

17.5 DONER v. SNAPP — 649 N.E.2d 42 (OhioApp. 1994)

FACTS In an attempt to feather their nest, as it were, the Doners decided to invest in the burgeoning, albeit risky, ostrich breeding and production industry. Ostriches are promoted as an alternative food source, and coupled with the demand for their feathers and leather, are completely consumable. The potential rewards of the investment are great: Mr. Doner stated that the hen he purchased from the Snapps for $3,000 was worth at least $20,000 three years later, although she had yet to lay a fertile egg. The risks of the business include ostrich infertility and mortality.

The appellants purchased a "trio" of ostrich chicks by oral agreement from the appellees in 1990 for $9,000. In breeders' parlance, a "trio" means two hens and one male. One male may mate with as many as three hens. The appellants' bid to build a nest egg suffered a bad break in early 1991, when they discovered that their "trio" consisted of two males and one hen. Mr. Doner testified that his first knowledge of the error came when the darker features and feathers of the males appeared. Mr. Snapp testified that it can be difficult to determine an ostrich's sex, and that he had advised Mr. Doner to have the birds' sex confirmed within ninety days of the sale. Mr. Doner denied that he had been so counseled.

There also was disputed testimony as to whether the appellees agreed to exchange a hen for one of the males upon learning of the alleged breach. In any event, no agreement was reached between the parties. Rather than bury their heads in the sand, the appellants traded both of their male ostriches in 1992, one to a Michigan breeder for another male of equal value, and the other to an Indiana supplier for two female chicks. Since ostrich hens do not mature sexually for three years, the younger hens have not

17.5 DONER v. SNAPP *(cont.)* 649 N.E.2d 42 (OhioApp. 1994)

been bred. The hen purchased from the appellants has not produced any offspring. The record indicates that the appellants also acquired another hen, now of breeding age, from the Michigan breeder. This particular hen has produced offspring.

The appellants filed suit against appellees for breach of contract on 15 June 1993. The appellants requested compensatory damages of $15,000 plus lost profits. The appellees filed a motion for summary judgment, asserting that appellants had not raised a genuine issue of material fact on the issue of liability, specifically that the appellants had suffered damage from the alleged breach. The trial judge granted appellees' motion and the appellants appealed.

ISSUE Did the buyers establish that they had suffered any damages in this case?

HOLDING No. Despite the apparent breach of contract by the sellers, there was no showing of any damages suffered by the buyers.

REASONING The Doners based their appeal on the one lone assignment of error, stating that "the judgment in favor of the appellee[s] is against the manifest weight of the evidence because the common pleas court erred in ruling that no genuine issue of material fact existed regarding the difference in value between the male ostrich delivered and the female ostrich appellee[s] was bound by the contract to deliver, and failed to do so, causing summary judgment to be entered against appellant[s]."

The Ohio Supreme Court has interpreted the summary judgment standard to say:

> *The appositeness of rendering a summary judgment hinges upon the tripartite demonstration: (1) that there is no genuine issue as to any material fact; (2) that the moving party is entitled to judgment as a matter of law; and (3) that reasonable minds can come to but one conclusion, and that conclusion is adverse to the party against whom the motion for summary judgment is made, who is entitled to have the evidence construed most strongly in his favor.*

We initially point out that the appellants' assignment is poorly cast. It is axiomatic that we may not determine the propriety of a trial court's grant of summary judgment by looking at the manifest weight of the evidence. "As it is not the province of a trial court in ruling on a motion for summary judgment to weigh evidence, a claim that the court's ruling could be 'against the manifest weight of the evidence' is a legal chimera incompatible with the concept of summary judgment."

Appellants seek to recover lost profits from their transaction. Therefore, appellants must show with "reasonable certainty" the difference in value between the ostriches bargained for and those received or their lost profits to raise a genuine issue of material fact on the basis of damages and survive summary judgment. The Doners thought they had purchased one male and two female ostriches. The following spring they discovered that they had one female and two males. They subsequently traded one of the males for another male and the other male for two hen chicks.

Two avenues were available to the appellants once they discovered that one of the birds was nonconforming. First, "where a tender has been accepted . . . the buyer must within a reasonable time after he discovers or should have discovered any breach notify the seller of the breach or be barred from any remedy. . . ." Once a buyer satisfies this provision, "he may recover as damages for any nonconformity of tender the loss resulting in the ordinary course of events from the seller's breach as determined in any manner which is reasonable."

Second, the appellants may revoke their acceptance of the goods if they accepted them "without discovery of such non-conformity if . . . acceptance was reasonably induced either by the difficulty of discovery before acceptance or by the seller's assurances."

Following either approach, it is still essential that the nonbreaching party show damages. We hold that the appellants have failed to do so.

We hold that the appellants did not establish a genuine issue of material fact on the issue of damages. Therefore, the trial court properly granted the appellees' motion for summary judgment. Thus, we affirm the decision of the trial court.

BUSINESS CONSIDERATIONS The buyers in this case received nonconforming goods from the seller. What could or should the buyers have done differently in order to establish their right to damages? Should a seller in a speculative industry assume the risk that an investor will not make the profits the investor anticipates?

ETHICAL CONSIDERATIONS Did the sellers in this case act in an ethical manner? What should the sellers have done differently, if anything, to have been more ethical than they were?

No Breach of Contract

If the contract is not breached, risk of loss is much more technical. It is difficult to determine where risk of loss resides until the entire contract is reviewed. The UCC recognizes four distinct contract possibilities to allocate risk of loss when the contract has not been breached. In addition, the parties can agree by contract to allocate the risk.

The first situation arises in a contract whereby the seller sends the goods by means of a carrier. If the goods are sent by means of a shipment contract, risk of loss passes to the buyer when the goods are delivered to the carrier. This is true even if the seller reserves rights in the goods pending payment. In contrast, the seller may enter into a destination contract with the carrier. Risk of loss then does not pass to the buyer until the goods are properly tendered at the point of destination. Once the goods are made available to the buyer, the buyer has risk of loss.

The second situation arises when the goods are in the hands of a bailee and they are not to be physically delivered. When the bailee is holding the goods, the contract must be very carefully analyzed. The contract may call for the seller to deliver a negotiable document of title to the buyer. If so, risk of loss passes when the buyer receives the document from the seller. If the seller is not to use a negotiable document of title but does use a nonnegotiable document, risk of loss passes only after the buyer has a reasonable opportunity to present the document to the bailee. And sometimes no document at all is used. In such cases, risk of loss passes to the buyer only after the bailee acknowledges the rights of the buyer in the goods.

The third situation arises when the goods are in the possession of the seller and a carrier is not to be used. Under these circumstances, the status of the seller is the key. If the seller is a merchant, risk of loss does not pass to the buyer until the buyer takes possession of the goods. If the seller is not a merchant, risk of loss passes on tender of delivery to the buyer. The following two examples show how risk of loss varies with the status of the seller.

> Joan is a used-car dealer. She enters a contract with Bob to sell him a car. She tells Bob that the keys are in the car and to go pick it up at any time. Before Bob gets there, the car is destroyed by a fire. Since Joan is a merchant, she still has risk of loss. She will have to provide Bob with another car or refund his money.
>
> Jack is not a car dealer of any sort. He enters a contract to sell his car to Marie. He tells her the keys are in the car and she can pick it up at any time. This is a tender of delivery. Before Marie gets the car, it is destroyed by a fire. She must bear the loss since Jack was a nonmerchant.

The fourth set of circumstances applies to a sale on approval. Here risk of loss remains with the seller until the buyer accepts the goods by approval of the sale. Of course, the various ways the buyer can accept should be kept in mind.

Finally, the parties can agree to allocate risk of loss in any way they wish. Risk of loss can be divided in any manner the parties feel is proper. Such an agreement must be very explicit or the Code provisions just discussed will be applied.

LEASES

In much the same manner as under Article 2, Article 2A is not overly concerned with the concept of title. Article 2A specifically separates title and possession. It states that

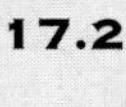

SALES/MANAGEMENT

LEASE ARRANGEMENTS FOR CALL-IMAGE

A regional corporation has expressed interest in acquiring Call-Image telephones for each of its offices in the region, a total of 200 units. However, this firm does not want to purchase the equipment, proposing instead that they enter into a lease arrangement with CIT. Anna thinks that the firm should make the contract, believing that the exposure to customers of the other firm will help to increase sales. Tom is concerned that such an arrangement will present more problems for the firms than benefits. They have asked you for your advice. What will you tell them?

BUSINESS CONSIDERATIONS What burdens does a business face in leasing its equipment that it would not face in selling the equipment? What benefits accrue to a firm through a lease that might not accrue through a sale?

ETHICAL CONSIDERATIONS Assume that a large business is about to make a contract with a small supplier and that both parties know this contract will make or break the small firm. Should the business use its size to "persuade" a small supplier to make a lease rather than a sale when the small supplier would prefer to sell goods than to lease them? Should the business use its size to "persuade" a small supplier to sell it goods when the small supplier would prefer to lease them?

the provisions governing leases apply whether the lessor or a third party has title to the leased goods, and whether the lessor, the lessee, or a third party has possession of the leased goods.

Risk of loss with respect to the leased goods varies depending upon the type of lease involved. In a finance lease, risk of loss passes to the lessor. If the lease is other than a finance lease, risk of loss is retained by the lessor. If the leased goods are in the hands of a bailee *and* risk of loss is to pass to the lessee, rules similar to those under Article 2 are followed in allocating risk of loss:

- If the goods are in the possession of a bailee and delivery is to occur without movement of the goods, risk of loss passes to the lessee upon the bailee's acknowledgment of the lessee's right to possession of the goods. (Since there is not a sale, there will not be a document of title involved in such a situation.)
- If the goods are to be delivered to the lessee by a carrier, the carriage contract is presumed to be a shipment contract, passing risk of loss to the lessee when the goods are duly delivered to the carrier. If a destination contract is specified, risk of loss passes to the lessee when the goods are duly tendered at the destination.
- If the goods are to be delivered to the lessee by the lessor, passage of risk of loss depends upon the status of the lessor. If the lessor (or the supplier, in the case of a finance lease) is a merchant, risk of loss passes to the lessee when the goods are actually delivered to the lessee. If the lessor is not a merchant, risk of loss passes to the lessee upon tender of delivery.

http:// RESOURCES FOR BUSINESS LAW STUDENTS

NAME	RESOURCES	WEB ADDRESS
Uniform Commercial Code (UCC) Article 2, Sales	The Legal Information Institute (LII), maintained by the Cornell Law School, provides a hypertext and searchable version of the UCC's Article 2, Sales. LII also provides links to Article 2 as enacted by states and to proposed revisions.	http://www.law.cornell.edu/ucc/2/overview.html
Uniform Commercial Code Article 2A, Leases	LII provides a hypertext and searchable version of the UCC's Article 2A, Leases. LII also provides links to Article 2A as enacted by states and to proposed revisions.	http://www.law.cornell.edu/ucc/2A/overview.html
Uniform Commercial Code Article 7, Warehouse Receipts, Bills of Lading, and Other Documents of Title	LII provides a hypertext and searchable version of the UCC's Article 7, Warehouse Receipts, Bills of Lading, and Other Documents of Title. LII also provides links to Article 7 as enacted by a particular state and to proposed revisions.	http://www.law.cornell.edu/ucc/7/overview.html

SUMMARY

In this chapter, we examine the concept and importance of title to goods. Under the UCC, title passes at any time the parties agree. If the parties do not agree, title passes when the seller completes his or her performance. Title can revest in the seller if the buyer refuses to accept the goods, rejects them, or revokes the acceptance. The primary area in which title is important today is that of creditor rights.

The concept of risk of loss is much more important under the Code than it is under common law. Risk of loss refers to the party—buyer or seller—who must bear the burden of lost, damaged, or destroyed goods when the loss occurs during the performance stage of the contract. Risk of loss is allocated in a similar manner in both a sale of goods and in the leasing of goods under a finance lease. In a non–finance lease, risk of loss remains with the lessor throughout the lease.

In the performance of a sales contract, each party has some duty or duties to perform, and each has some rights that may be asserted. The seller is to tender delivery of conforming goods as per the contract. The buyer is to accept and pay for the goods so tendered. The buyer normally has the right to inspect the goods before accepting or paying. If the inspection discloses any defects, the seller frequently has the right to cure, or correct, the defect in the goods or in the performance.

The parties to a sale often use standard shipping terms. These terms have been defined by the UCC as forming either a shipment contract or a destination contract. In a shipment contract, the buyer bears the risks of loss or damage during transportation. In a destination contract, the seller bears the risks of loss or damage during transportation.

Some special problems have developed from modern business practices. Before the adoption of the UCC, consignments were frequently used to sell goods. Today, consignments have virtually been replaced by sale-on-approval and sale-or-return contracts. Each of these areas is specifically treated under Article 2. Special treatment is also provided for consignments and for auctions under Article 2.

DISCUSSION QUESTIONS

1. According to the UCC, what constitutes a proper tender of delivery by the seller in a sales contract? Does the type of delivery vary the concept of "tender"?
2. What is the legal effect of a shipment contract as compared with that of a destination contract when the seller hires a common carrier to deliver the goods to the buyer?
3. What would an owner/consignor need to show in order to establish that goods in the hands of a merchant were *consigned* goods rather than goods that had been sold under a sale-or-return (or other sales) contract? Why might the owner/consignor want or need to establish that a consignment exists?
4. Biltless Mfg. sends goods to Smart Set Co. under a "no arrival, no sale" contract. After the goods are sent but before they arrive, Biltless learns it can double its profit by selling the goods to another buyer in another market. Assume that Biltless is able to recover the goods from the carrier before the goods are tendered to Smart Set. What rights can Smart Set assert against Biltless in this situation? Explain.
5. Chen, a merchant, sends Roy some goods under a contract. Roy is to receive the goods by 18 December. On 12 December, Roy receives nonconforming goods from Chen, and Roy promptly calls Chen to inform her of the nonconformity. What are Chen's rights and the duties under these circumstances? What can Chen do to avoid being sued for breach of the contract?
6. Under Article 2 of the Uniform Commercial Code, when does title pass from the seller to the buyer? When does risk of loss pass from the seller to the buyer? Under Article 2A, when does risk of loss pass from the lessor or supplier to the lessee?
7. What does a seller mean when he or she attempts to "reserve title" to the goods being sold? What is the legal effect of such a reservation of title under Article 2?
8. Ralph operates a repair shop in the local community. While Ralph repairs all sorts of things, he does not sell anything on a regular basis. Harvey takes his watch to Ralph's Repair Shop and asks Ralph to fix it. After the watch is repaired, but before Harvey returns to pay for the repairs, one of Ralph's employees sells Harvey's watch to another customer. Who has title to the watch? What should Harvey do in this situation?
9. Marge, a merchant, sold goods to Dennis, receiving payment in full at the time the contract was made. Dennis is to pick up the goods from Marge's store later in the day. When Dennis arrives to pick up the goods, he discovers that the goods were damaged when they were removed from the showroom floor and taken to the loading dock. Marge insists that, since Dennis has already paid for the goods, he owns them and he is therefore responsible for the loss due to the damage. Is Marge correct or not? Explain your reasoning.
10. George sold some goods to Dana, but George retained possession of the goods. Several of George's creditors discover the location of the goods, and they attempt to attach the goods to cover the debts George owes them. These creditors allege that the sale to Dana is void as to the creditors since George retained possession of the goods after the sale. George and Dana both insist that the transaction is perfectly valid and that the creditors should not be able to assert any rights to the goods. What must George and/or Dana prove in order to avoid the claims of George's creditors? Has the enactment of Article 2A changed the potential rights of George and Dana?

CASE PROBLEMS AND WRITING ASSIGNMENTS

1. Sacks wanted to purchase a particular type of television. He called several stores until he located a store that carried the type of television he desired. Sacks then arranged for Smith, who had a history of purchasing items with bad checks, to go to the store and purchase the television for him. Sacks then purchased the television from Smith after Smith had purchased the television from the merchant, paying for it with a bad check. Sacks claims that Smith had voidable title and that his (Sacks's) purchase gave Sacks good title, superior to the title of the merchant. Does Sacks have good title to the television? Explain fully. [See *Sacks* v. *State*, 360 N.E.2d 21 (Ind.App. 1977).]
2. In July, the Stephensons purchased a modular home from Frazier. The contract price of $22,500 included the installation of a septic system and the construction of a foundation for the home, both on property owned by the Stephensons. During the installation of the modular home, the Stephensons complained to Frazier about a number of alleged defects in the home and in the foundation that was being constructed. The Stephensons also asserted that the foundation was being built improperly. Frazier replied that the foundation was "100 percent" and that if they did not like the work, they could take him to court. At that point, the Stephensons ordered Frazier and his crew off of their

property and told them the property was "off limits" to them. The Stephensons then notified Frazier that they intended to rescind the contract. Were the Stephensons entitled to rescind the contract and recover their purchase price? Explain. [See *Stephenson* v. *Frazier*, 399 N.E.2d 794 (Ind. App. 1980).]

3. B&B was a supplier of stereo equipment. B&B entered into a contract with Collier that called for B&B to deliver stereo equipment to Collier. The contract also called for the equipment to be picked up by B&B if it had not been sold within 90 days. After the goods were delivered, but before the 90 days had expired, Collier's store was burglarized and the stereo equipment was stolen. B&B demanded payment from Collier for the equipment. Collier argued that the goods were "on consignment" from B&B, so that B&B had risk of loss. Was this a consignment, giving B&B risk of loss, or a sale or return, making Collier liable? Explain. [See *Collier* v. *B&B Sales, Inc.*, 471 S.W.2d 151 (Tex. 1971).]

4. SWEPCO owned the Pirkey Power Plant, a plant that produced electricity by burning lignite, a soft coal. Lignite has a relatively high sulfur content, which meant that SWEPCO had to install a sulfur-scrubbing system to reduce the gaseous and particulate emissions generated by burning lignite. UOP was hired by SWEPCO to design, manufacture, and install a scrubbing system at the plant. RM Engineering submitted a bid to UOP to provide a spray-on lining in the scrubber that was corrosion-resistant. UOP investigated numerous plants that were using the RM spray-on lining and then orally granted the subcontract to RM. RM claimed that it provided testing during the application and that the lining was within the specifications for the job. Subsequently, there were some problems at the plant involving the lining. RM agreed to replace the lining, provided that RM and UOP would investigate the problem to determine the cause and to decide who was at fault. According to RM, there was also an agreement that whoever was at fault for the problem would pay for the replacement of the lining. RM subsequently had independent tests run by two laboratories. Both labs reported that the lining failure was not the result of the type of acid attack normally expected in such a scrubber. Despite this, UOP claimed that the lining failed upon its initial application and was never accepted by them. UOP denied liability under the contract based on (1) a lack of a writing as required by the Statute of Frauds, and (2) a lack of acceptance of the goods even if there was a contract. Was there a contract despite the lack of a writing? Did UOP ever accept the goods? [See *RM Engineered Products, Inc.* v. *UOP, Inc.*, 793 F. Supp. 1373 (W.D. La. 1991).]

5. In March 1975, Nahim Amar B., a resident of Mexico, entered into a contract with Karinol, an exporting company operating out of Miami. The terms of the contract, contained in a one-page invoice written in Spanish, called for Amar to purchase 64 electronic watches for $6,006. A notation at the bottom of the contract read: "Please send the merchandise in cardboard boxes duly strapped with metal bands via air parcel post to Chetumal. Documents to Banco de Commercio de Quintano Roo, S.A." There were no provisions in the contract specifically allocating the risk of loss while the goods were in the possession of the carrier, nor were any standard shipping terms used. The evidence established that on 11 April 1975 Karinol properly packaged and shipped the watches to Belize, Central America, to an agent of Amar. The cartons arrived in Belize on 15 April and were stored in the air freight cargo room. On 2 May, Amar's agent opened the boxes and discovered that there were no watches in the boxes. Mr. Pestana, as the representative of Amar (who died in the interim), sued Karinol and its insurer, alleging that the watches were lost or stolen while under the care and control of Karinol and while Karinol had risk of loss. Karinol filed a cross-complaint alleging that Amar had risk of loss and that Karinol was thus not liable. Which party had risk of loss in this case? Why? [See *Pestana* v. *Karinol Corp.*, 367 So.2d 1096 (Fla.App. 1979)].

6. **BUSINESS APPLICATION CASE** Kingston House is a restaurant in Kingston, New Hampshire. Law Warehouse stores wine for the state of New Hampshire. B.S.P. is a common carrier. Kingston House ordered forty cases of wine from Law Warehouse, asking that a carrier be used to deliver the wine. Law Warehouse, in turn, hired B.S.P. as a carrier. B.S.P. attempted to deliver the wine the following Monday, a day on which the restaurant was normally closed. The only employee on the premises that Monday was an elderly vice president of the restaurant. The driver informed this employee that he would need help in unloading the wine. The employee refused to help, and B.S.P. had the wine returned to its warehouse for storage. Thereafter, B.S.P. refused to deliver the wine unless the restaurant agreed to pay the original delivery charges, storage charges, and a redelivery charge. The restaurant refused to pay any charges beyond the original delivery charges, and sued B.S.P. for conversion. B.S.P. countered that it had made a proper tender of delivery, delivery had been refused, and it was entitled to all of the charges for which it sought payment. Should the attempted delivery of goods by a carrier to a consignee at a time when the consignee's business is normally closed be considered a proper

tender of delivery? Should the carrier be allowed to refuse to deliver the goods until the consignee paid extra delivery and storage charges? [See *Kingston 1686 House, Inc.* v. *B.S.P. Transportation, Inc.* 427 A.2d 9 (N.H. 1981).]

7. **ETHICAL APPLICATION CASE** In late 1981, Mitchell Energy entrusted oil field pipe to Port Pipe Terminal for storage. Two high-ranking officials of Port Pipe fraudulently transferred the pipe to Pharaoh, Inc., a dummy corporation created by them in order to facilitate their fraudulent sales of merchandise stored with Port Pipe. Pharaoh sold the pipe to Nickel Supply Co. in March 1982. During the remainder of March, Nickel sold the pipe to Yamin Oil Supply, which, in turn, sold the pipe to NorthStar, which sold the pipe to Western Drilling, which sold the pipe to Canterra Petroleum. In all of these transactions, the pipe remained in the physical possession of Port Pipe. After Canterra purchased the pipe, it was moved to Getter Trucking, where it was stored until Canterra returned the pipe to Mitchell in December 1983. Canterra returned the pipe to Mitchell after being informed by law enforcement officials that the pipe was owned by Mitchell. There followed a chain reaction of lawsuits as each buyer sued its seller for breach of the warranty of title in the sales of the pipe by the various parties. Was Port Pipe a merchant in oil field pipe? If so, was this a situation in which the entrustment doctrine can be applied to the sales of the pipe? What ethical considerations does this fact situation present? [See *Canterra Petroleum, Inc.* v. *Western Drilling and Mining Supply*, 418 N.W.2d 267 (N.D. 1987).]

8. **IDES CASE** In 1986, Kummer entered into a dealer agreement with Suzuki giving Kummer the right to sell and service Suzuki motorcycles. In 1987 and again in 1988, Kummer sold only 26 Suzuki motorcycles. Suzuki was not satisfied with this performance and on 13 December 1988 sent Kummer notice that it was terminating the dealer agreement in 60 days. Upon receiving notice of the termination, Kummer filed a complaint with the Office of the Commissioner of Transportation (OCT) of Wisconsin. Under Wisconsin law, the filing of this complaint served as an automatic stay of the termination, leaving the original dealer agreement in effect until the OCT reached a final decision on the complaint. As could be expected, Kummer and Suzuki did not get along well during the automatic stay period. Kummer stopped ordering Suzuki motorcycles, and Suzuki stopped visiting Kummer's dealership. The strain between Kummer and Suzuki was exacerbated by the OCT's delay in resolving the complaint. While the original complaint was filed 7 February 1989, no hearing was held until October 1991, and the final decision was not filed until 8 June 1993. The OCT ruled in Kummer's favor. By that time, however, Kummer no longer had any Suzuki motorcycles in stock, having sold his last one August 1990. When Suzuki received the OCT decision in June 1993, it sent a *new* notice of termination to Kummer, citing his failure to stock and sell Suzuki products. Suzuki also filed suit against Kummer, alleging that (1) Kummer breached the dealer agreement, (2) violated the Wisconsin Motor Vehicle Dealer law, and (3) tortiously interfered with Suzuki's prospective contractual relations. Kummer countersued, claiming that Suzuki had violated the Wisconsin Motor Vehicle Dealer law and had wrongfully terminated the dealership. Apply the IDES principles to analyze this case and reach a decision on its merits. [See *American Suzuki Motor Corp.* v. *Bill Kummer, Inc.*, 65 F.3d 1381 (7th Cir. 1995).]

Warranties and Product Liability

Outline

Agenda

While most consumers likely will be pleased with Call-Image, some customers will encounter problems. CIT, therefore, must establish a warranty strategy for Call-Image. Should the firm attempt to exclude as many warranty provisions as possible, or should it offer wide warranty protections? Assuming that warranties will be given, should the firm offer a full or a limited warranty under the Magnuson-Moss Act? What should be printed on the box used to package the Call-Image videophone? What warranty information should be packaged with the product?

These and other questions may arise in covering the material in this chapter. Be prepared! You never know when one of the Kochanowskis will call on you for advice.

INTRODUCTION

A warranty is defined as "a promise that a proposition of fact is true."[1] Since a warranty involves a promise, it becomes a part of the contract. This is especially important in the sale of goods. Warranty protection is very often the best protection that a buyer can have in a sale. There are two types of warranties in sales: **express** and **implied**. (There are also **statutory** warranty provisions, but these tend to be informational rather than coverage-based.) The fact that one type of warranty is present does not mean that the other type is absent. In fact, both types will frequently be present in one contract.

Express
Actually stated; communicated from one party to another.

Implied
Presumed to be present under the circumstances; tacit.

Statutory
Created by statute; imposed by law.

At common law, the courts presume that the parties to a contract have equal bargaining power. The courts also strongly believe in "freedom of contract." Thus, they are reluctant to interfere in the contractual relationship. Historically, the rule of *caveat emptor*—let the buyer beware—was regularly followed. As the commercial world matured, the relative positions of the parties to a sales contract began to change. Businesses grew larger, and the location of the business became more likely to be removed from the location of the individual buyer. It became less likely that the parties would truly have equal bargaining power. It also became less likely that the seller of the goods had also manufactured them. The courts and legislatures began to seek means of protecting consumers. Implied warranties (and statutory warranty provisions) and product liability provided those means. The consumer has thus now become so protected that many people feel the modern rule of commerce is *caveat venditor*—let the seller beware!

FROM THE DESK OF
AMY CHEN, ATTORNEY AT LAW

Advertising

Make certain that your firm's advertising does not make any claims about your products that are not true. It is quite likely that an advertisement may be interpreted as an express warranty, especially if your products are new and unique.

EXPRESS WARRANTIES

An express warranty can only be given by the seller; it is not present until such time as the seller gives it. However, once given, such a warranty is said by the UCC to be a part of "the basis of the bargain." Section 2-313 mentions three different ways in which the seller creates an express warranty.

1. Any affirmation of a fact or a promise that relates to the goods creates an express warranty that the goods will match the fact or the promise.
2. Any description of the goods creates an express warranty that the goods will match the description.
3. Any sample or model of the goods creates an express warranty that the goods will conform to the sample or the model.

Any of these three methods creates an express warranty if it is a part of "the basis of the bargain." It is not necessary for the seller to use words such as "warrant" or "guarantee." It is not even necessary for the seller to intend to create an express warranty. All that is necessary is that the seller employ one of these methods in a manner that causes the buyer to reasonably believe that a warranty covering the goods has been given.

The Uniform Sales Act, which preceded the UCC, required the buyer to show *reliance* before an express warranty was found. The UCC seems to have removed the requirement of proving reliance. Instead, reliance appears to be presumed. The rule under the Code is that the seller must disprove the existence of an express warranty. In other words, if the buyer can prove the seller affirmed a fact, described the goods, or used a model or a sample, an express warranty is presumed. To disprove the existence of the warranty, the seller must show proof that the conduct described by the buyer was not the basis of the bargain. If such proof cannot be shown, the express warranty is included in the contract.

Express warranties focus on facts. Mere opinions of the seller are not taken to be warranties. The seller is also allowed a certain amount of puffing. However, there is often a fine line between opinion and fact, and the seller should be extremely careful. If a statement is **quantifiable**, it is likely to be treated as a fact. If the statement is **relative**, it normally will be treated as opinion. Thus, the statement "this car gets 30 miles per gallon" likely would be treated as a warranty. But the statement "this is a good car" likely would not be a warranty. The problem lies with comments that fall between these two extremes.

Quantifiable
Capable of exact statement; measurable, normally in numbers.

Relative
Not capable of exact statement or measurable; comparative.

Exhibit 18.1 illustrates the difficulty faced by the court in deciding whether something is a matter of fact or a matter of opinion. There is a great deal of gray area between things that are obvious facts and those that are obviously opinion, and the court has the task of deciding whether something within this gray area is a fact or an opinion.

If a statement that falls between an obvious fact and an obvious opinion was made by the seller, the court must decide how to interpret this statement in terms of warranty protections. To do so, the court must weigh the relative knowledge of the parties, the reliance (if any) the buyer placed on the seller, the likelihood that the seller was aware of any reliance, and any other pertinent facts that influence the balancing of interests of the two parties. Thus, if the seller conveyed an impression that seemed to be based on facts to the buyer, the court may decide that there was an assertion of facts and therefore may find an express warranty exists, despite the intent of the seller.

The seller also needs to be careful in advertising. Advertisements that claim certain characteristics for a product may also be treated by the courts as affirmations of fact and thus as express warranties. The following example shows how an advertisement may be viewed by the court in an express warranty case.

EXHIBIT 18.1 Finding an Express Warranty

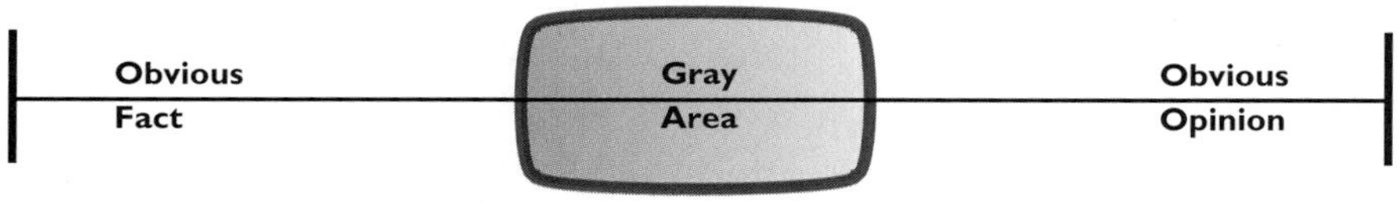

Obvious Fact — Gray Area — Obvious Opinion

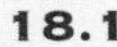

18.1

MARKETING/SALES

ADVERTISING CALL-IMAGE

Tom wants to advertise the Call-Image videophones extensively on television, preferably with the ads showing the product in use. Dan and John agree with Tom in principle, but they suggest that the ads should be enhanced somewhat to show the product in the best possible light. They have suggested using a larger viewing screen on the unit used in the commercial, so that the images being transmitted are more striking, and that the images be enhanced if possible. Anna objects to this. She believes that any ads should show only what the product is currently capable of performing. She has, however, agreed to defer to the family in this decision. Tom recognizes the marketing strength of the suggestion by Dan and John, but he also respects Anna's insights and integrity. He has asked you what the firm should do in this situation. What advice will you give?

BUSINESS CONSIDERATIONS Visual ads can be very effective, especially with the technological devices available today. Computer enhancements can place famous people in contemporary settings, and "morphing" can allow the advertiser to transform products from or to something else. While such ads can be effective, they can also be misleading. How much care should an advertiser take to ensure that an ad does not create express warranties that the advertiser will then have to honor? What should the advertiser tell the advertising agency in an effort to protect the advertiser's interests?

ETHICAL CONSIDERATIONS Many fast-food video commercials use mock-ups of the food being advertised because the lights and the time that a commercial can require often cause the food being advertised to become dry and visually unappetizing. From an ethical perspective, should these commercials include some disclaiming language informing the viewers that the "food" in the commercial is not an actual product? Explain.

A television advertisement for the Pick Pen Company, manufacturers of disposable ballpoint pens, shows a couple on a picnic. The couple removes a can of fruit juice from the picnic hamper, only to discover that they forgot to bring a can opener. One of them reaches into a pocket, removes a Pick Pen, and uses the uncapped pen to punch a hole in the top of the can. The couple smiles, the camera pulls back, and a voice solemnly intones, "Pick Pens! For 79¢, it's not just a great writing instrument."

A customer who has seen this commercial decides to use his or her Pick Pen to open a can. Unfortunately for the customer—and for the Pick Pen Company—the pen shatters and plastic shards enter the customer's wrist and hand, causing serious injury to the customer during this attempted use. A good argument could be made that the commercial had created a belief in the mind of the customer that this use was expressly warranted by the commercial. If, however, the Pick Pen Company used a disclaimer in the commercial—normally by scrolling script across the bottom of the screen—the courts might be less likely to find that the commercial created an express warranty.

Finally, the Code considers the timing of the statement or conduct from the buyer's perspective. Under § 2-209(1), a modification of a sales contract is valid without *consideration*. This means that the seller can create an express warranty before the contract is formed (through sales talk, negotiations, or even commercials); while forming the contract (in the language used in the agreement or in oral commitments made while forming the writing); or even after the contract is formed (through continued reassurances to the buyer that he or she has made a "good deal"). As a result, sellers should remember two things:

1. If they know a fact, they should state it honestly.
2. If they do not know a fact, they should not speculate! It is too easy to give an express warranty without realizing it.

The following case is one of the landmark cases in express warranty law. Many of the principles of express warranty law included in the Code seem to be based, at least indirectly, on the court's language from this case. Notice how the court viewed the relative knowledge of the parties and the special circumstances of the case in reaching its finding of fact.

18.1 WAT HENRY PONTIAC CO. v. BRADLEY 210 P.2d 348 (Supp.Ct. Okla. 1949)

FACTS On 22 October 1944, Mrs. Bradley went to the Wat Henry Pontiac Company to purchase a used car. She dealt with the used-car sales manager throughout the transaction. Mrs. Bradley testified that she asked many questions and the seller assured her that the car in question was in good condition. When Mrs. Bradley stated that she had to drive to Camp Shelby, Mississippi, with her seven-month-old child to see her husband, the salesman allegedly said: "This is a car I can recommend" and "It is in A-1 shape." When Mrs. Bradley asked for a test drive in the car, the sales manager replied that because of wartime gas rationing she could not go. He did state, however, that the car was mechanically perfect. Eventually, Mrs. Bradley bought the car and drove it home. Several days later, after she set out for Camp Shelby, the car broke down and required extensive repairs. Mrs. Bradley sued for breach of express warranties concerning the car. The sales manager, a former mechanic, testified that he gave no warranties in the sale and that he had explained to Mrs. Bradley at the time of the sale that there were no warranties covering the car.

ISSUE Did the seller give express warranties on the car in this sale?

HOLDING Yes. Under the circumstances in this case, the seller gave express warranties to the buyer.

REASONING Mrs. Bradley was not generally knowledgeable concerning automobiles, and she was ignorant of all of the facts concerning this car in this case. The defects in the car were hidden, and the buyer was denied the opportunity to take a test drive during which the defects might have been discovered. The seller was an expert in automobiles. He had worked for a long time as a mechanic and had so informed the buyer. He repeatedly reassured her as to the quality of the car (albeit in general and nonquantifiable terms) throughout the sale. His statements concerning the condition of the car, when viewed with her inability to personally examine the car prior to the sale, created express warranties and not mere opinion.

BUSINESS CONSIDERATIONS It is very difficult to make sales by criticizing your products, but it is also very dangerous to make sales by exaggerating the good features of your product. How should a firm train its sales force so that they can make the maximum positive statements concerning the product without giving warranties the firm does not want to give?

ETHICAL CONSIDERATIONS The game theory once put forward for business ethics permits lying or exaggeration in making sales, assuming that buyers are aware that sales personnel will lie or exaggerate to close the deal. Why is such a practice not considered ethical in the modern business environment?

IMPLIED WARRANTIES

As pointed out in the preceding section, express warranties are a part of the contract. They are not present until given by the seller. The court will not find an express warranty unless it is created by the seller as a part of the "basis of the bargain." Thus, a careful seller will not give any express warranties until—and unless—so desired.

In contrast, implied warranties are imposed by operation of law (subject to certain limitations involving the status of the seller). Implied warranties are automatically present in the contract unless they are voluntarily surrendered by the buyer or properly excluded by the seller.

The UCC recognizes four types of implied warranties: the warranty of title, the warranty against infringement, the warranty of merchantability, and the warranty of fitness for a particular purpose. Some, all, or none of these warranties may be present in any given sales contract, depending on the circumstances surrounding the transaction and on the status of the seller of the goods.

Warranty of Title

Every contract for the sale of goods carries a warranty of title by the seller unless such a warranty is excluded by specific language warning the buyer that title is not guaranteed or unless the sale is made under circumstances that put the buyer on notice that title is not guaranteed. Absent one of these two conditions, a warranty of title exists to protect the buyer. A warranty of title ensures the buyer of the following:

1. The transfer of the goods by the seller is proper.
2. The buyer is receiving good title.
3. The goods are free of hidden security interests, encumbrances, or liens.

In other words, the buyer is assured that no one may assert a hidden claim to the goods that is superior to the claim of the buyer.

In the following case, a merchant buyer who purchased an automobile at auction sued for an alleged breach of the warranty of title. Notice how the court dealt with the auctioneer's position regarding the language the auctioneer used in its warranty of title.

18.2 GORDON v. NORTHWEST AUTO AUCTION, INC. 387 S.E.2d 227 (N.C.App. 1990)

FACTS In February 1985, plaintiff (Gordon), a Richmond County automobile dealer, for $3,420 bought what was represented to be a 1977 Cadillac automobile at an automobile auction conducted by the defendant (Northwest Auto Auctions, Inc.). He received an executed document on defendant's printed form entitled "Bill of Sale and Title Warranty," which carried the notation that it was issued at Northwest Auto Auction and stated "THIS SALE IS SOLELY A TRANSACTION BETWEEN THE BUYING AND SELLING DEALERS." *Inter alia,* the document identified plaintiff as purchaser and Archie's Auto Sales of Rock Hill, South Carolina as seller, and stated that:

> *The seller covenants with the purchaser that he is the true and lawful owner of the said described automobile; that the same is free and clear from all incumbrances; that he has good right and full power to sell the same as aforesaid; and that he will warrant and defend the same against the lawful claims and demands of all persons whosoever. The purchaser agrees that he has examined the above vehicle and accepts it in its present condition.*
>
> *We, NORTHWEST AUTO AUCTION of Charlotte, N.C., guarantee title to the above car to be free and clear of all liens and encumbrances at the time of execution of this instrument. . . .*

In the transaction, the plaintiff paid the defendant auction company the sale price of $3,420 plus a $20 buyer's fee and received the car and purported title to it. Several months later, after plaintiff had cleaned up the car and sold it for $3,900, the North Carolina Department of Motor Vehicles discovered that it was a 1976 Cadillac that had been stolen in Atlanta in 1984 and returned it to its true owner; and the plaintiff gave its customer another car of equal value. Gordon sued Northwest Auto Auction for breach of the warranty of title. The trial court ruled for the auction company, ruling that the guarantee that "title to be free and clear of all encumbrances" was not a warranty of title. According to the judge, the fact that the automobile was stolen was neither a lien nor an encumbrance on the title. Gordon appealed this ruling.

ISSUE Did the language of the contract in question state that the *title* was free of liens and encumbrances, or that the *automobile* was free of liens and encumbrances?

HOLDING The language stated that *title* to the automobile was free of liens and encumbrances, and this warranty was breached by the auctioneer/seller.

REASONING According to the Appellate Court, the trial court's findings were factually erroneous since defendant's warranty was not "that the *automobile* is free from liens and encumbrances," or even that the certificate on hand was without encumbrances, but that "*title* to the *car*" [emphasis supplied], a different matter altogether, was free and clear; and those words can only be construed to mean a valid title, not a sham, spurious or non-existent title. Since the execution of the document is admitted and its terms are without ambiguity, their meaning is a question of law for us, . . . and they plainly mean that defendant warranted that the seller of the automobile had *title* to it. Defendant's argument that it only warranted that there was no lien on the

18.2 GORDON v. NORTHWEST AUTO AUCTION, INC. *(cont.)* 387 S.E.2d 227 (N.C.App. 1990)

title *if* the seller happened to have one is absurd; for there can be no lien on a non-existent or fictitious title or a need for a warranty against them.

Though it is true, as defendant maintains, that as auctioneer it acted as agent for a disclosed principal, Archie's Auto Sales, and ordinarily an agent is not liable on the principal's warranties, an agent may nevertheless make a personal contract of warranty whenever it sees fit, and the evidence establishes without contradiction that this agent did so. For the obvious and profitable purpose of inducing dealers to buy cars at its automobile auction sales business, defendant regularly delivered an executed warranty form to each buyer, and the consideration that supported the warranty was the $20 fee it collected from each buyer. That the language is not as explicit as it might be is immaterial. . . . An express warranty may arise by implication. It need not be expressly stated, provided that what is stated reasonably conveys the warranty.

Vacated and remanded.

[There was also a dissent to this opinion in which two judges felt that Gordon should have pursued remedies against Archie's Auto rather than the auctioneer.]

BUSINESS CONSIDERATIONS The court in this case ruled that the auctioneer—who does not normally give the implied warranty of title—gave an express warranty of title. The court also stated that there was consideration to support this warranty, the $20 fee charged to purchasers at the auction. If there were no fee connected to the sale, would the written "Bill of Sale and Title Warranty" form suffice to establish a warranty of title from the auctioneer to the buyer? Explain.

ETHICAL CONSIDERATIONS The appellate court implied that the auctioneer in this case was attempting to use semantics to avoid liability. Is it ethical for a merchant to use semantics to avoid what appears to be an express guarantee or warranty to a customer? Does it matter if the customer is a merchant or a nonmerchant? Why?

Section 2-312 of the UCC specifies that every seller of goods gives an implied warranty of title unless the contract contains specific language that the warranty is being excluded or the circumstances of the sale are such that the buyer should realize that the seller does not warrant title. Thus, a merchant who is entrusted with goods gives a warranty of title if the merchant sells the entrusted goods to a good-faith purchaser. If the merchant has *voidable* title to the entrusted goods, the buyer receives good title, and there is no breach of the warranty. However, if the goods entrusted to the merchant have been stolen, the person who purchases the goods from the merchant would receive *void* title, and the merchant would be liable for breach of the implied warranty of title.

Warranty Against Infringement

The implied warranty against infringement is unique in that it can be given by either the buyer or the seller, although it is normally given by the seller. (None of the other implied warranties can be given by the buyer.) The infringement protected against is the rightful claim of any third person concerning the goods.

Patent infringement is probably the most common type of problem dealt with under this warranty, but another area that is becoming increasingly important is copyright infringement. Videotapes, audiotapes, and computer software normally are copyrighted, and all are easy to copy without a great deal of equipment, expertise, or expense. Experts estimate that pirated copies of copyright-protected materials cost each of these industries millions of dollars per year. As a result, more attention is being paid to the protection and enforcement of copyrights. As this trend continues, an increase in the number of cases involving the warranty against infringement will likely occur.

In order for a seller to give this warranty, the seller must be a merchant who regularly deals in the type of goods involved. A buyer who gives the warranty against infringement need not be a merchant. Any buyer who furnishes specifications to the seller in order to have the seller specially manufacture the goods described warrants against infringement if the seller complies with the specifications.

Warranty of Merchantability

Probably the most commonly breached, and the most commonly asserted, implied warranty is the warranty of merchantability. A warranty of merchantability is given whenever a merchant of goods, including a merchant of food or drink, makes a sale. It is a very broad warranty, designed to assure buyers that the goods they purchase from a merchant will be suitable for the normal and intended use of goods of that kind. Failure to satisfy any of the following six criteria means that the goods are not merchantable and that the warranty has been breached.

Fungible
Virtually identical and interchangeable; not different from other goods of the same description.

1. The goods must be able to pass without objection in the trade, under the description in the contract.
2. If the goods are **fungible**, they must be of fair average quality within the description.
3. The goods must be suitable for their ordinary purpose and use.
4. The goods must be of even kind, quality, and quantity.
5. The goods must be adequately contained, packaged, and labeled as required under the agreement.
6. The goods must conform to the promises and facts contained on the label, if any.

Merchant sellers have been found liable for breaching this warranty because of such things as bobby pins in soft-drink containers, worms in canned peas, a decomposing mouse in a soda bottle, and a hair dye that caused the buyer's hair to fall out.

Because many merchantability cases involve disputes over food and drink, the courts have developed special tests to determine merchantability in these cases. These tests are the foreign–natural test and the reasonable expectations test. Under the *foreign–natural test,* "foreign" objects found in the food does constitute a breach of warranty, whereas "natural" objects found in the food do not constitute a breach. Thus, a chicken bone found in a chicken salad sandwich does not involve a breach since chicken bones are "natural" to chicken. But a cherry pit found in a chicken salad sandwich is "foreign" and thus establishes a breach. Under the *reasonable expectations test,* the court attempts to establish what a reasonable person expects to find in the food. A reasonable person does not expect to find a "foreign" object in the food, so any foreign object found constitutes a breach. However, a reasonable person may not expect to find a "natural" object in the food either, so that finding such a natural object can also constitute a breach. Thus, a chicken bone in a chicken salad sandwich might show a breach if it is unreasonable to expect to find a bone in such a sandwich. The reasonable expectations in any given case is a question of fact.

The following case is considered a classic in the law. This opinion illustrates one approach a court might take in deciding a merchantability-of-food case.

18.3 WEBSTER v. BLUE SHIP TEA ROOM

347 Mass. 421, 198 N.E.2d 309 (1964)

FACTS One Saturday in 1959, Mrs. Webster, her sister, and her aunt entered the Blue Ship Tea Room, a restaurant on the waterfront in Boston. Webster, who was born and raised in New England, initially ordered clam chowder and a crabmeat salad. When she was informed that there was no clam chowder, she ordered a cup of fish chowder. After she ate three or four spoonfuls of the chowder, she became aware that something was lodged in her throat. She could not swallow or clear her throat by gulping, and she was taken to the hospital. She underwent two esophagoscopies, in the second of which a fish bone was found in her throat and removed. She sued the Blue Ship Tea Room for damages, alleging breach of the warranty of merchantability in the sale of the fish chowder.

ISSUE "Whether a fish bone in a fish chowder, about the ingredients of which there is no other complaint, constitutes a breach of implied warranty under applicable provisions of the Uniform Commercial Code?"

HOLDING No. The fish chowder, as served, was fit to be eaten and was merchantable.

REASONING At trial, the judge charged the jury with the following: "Was the fish chowder fit to be eaten and wholesome? . . . [N]obody is claiming that the fish itself wasn't wholesome. . . . But the bone of contention here—I don't mean that for a pun—but was this fish bone a foreign substance that made the fish chowder unwholesome or not fit to be eaten?" Webster emphasized the high standard to which the sale of food is held by the courts. But the Blue Ship Tea Room urged the court to remember that Webster was a native New Englander who had eaten fish chowder before and that "fish chowder, as it is served and enjoyed by New Englanders, is a hearty dish, originally designed to satisfy the appetites of our seamen and fishermen." In reaching its conclusion, the court examined (among others) *The American Woman's Cookbook, A New English Dictionary, The House of Seven Gables, Fannie Farmer* [cookbook], and *The Boston Cooking-School Cook Book*. Based on its research, the court concluded: "It is not too much to say that a person sitting down in New England to consume a good New England fish chowder embarks on a gustatory adventure which may entail the removal of some fish bones from the bowl as he proceeds. We are not inclined to tamper with age-old recipes by any amendment reflecting the plaintiff's view of the affect [sic] of the Uniform Commercial Code upon them. . . . We should be prepared to cope with the hazards of fish bones, the occasional presence of which, in the light of hallowed tradition, do not impair their fitness or merchantability."

BUSINESS CONSIDERATIONS Reasonable expectations is a logical test for determining the merchantability of food, but can the same test be applied to goods that are not to be eaten by the consumer? For example, should the manufacturer of hair care products be held to a reasonable expectations test if the product manufactured causes some customers to lose their hair? How far should this test be extended?

ETHICAL CONSIDERATIONS A number of courts have ruled that hospitals and blood banks provide *services* rather than *goods*, thereby removing the implied warranty of merchantability from their transactions. Should a hospital or blood bank that gives a patient tainted blood in a transfusion be held to have breached the warranty of merchantability, or should they be exempted from this warranty's liability for public policy reasons? Would their argument be stronger if they gave the blood to patients rather than selling it to them?

Warranty of Fitness for a Particular Purpose

Any seller, whether a merchant or a nonmerchant, may give the implied warranty of fitness for a particular purpose. In order for this warranty to come into existence, all of the following conditions must be present:

1. The seller must know that the buyer is contemplating a particular use for the goods.
2. The seller must know that the buyer is relying on the seller's skill, judgment, or knowledge in selecting the proper goods for the purpose.

3. The buyer must not restrict the seller's range of choices to a particular brand or price range or otherwise limit the scope of the seller's expert judgment.

STATUTORY WARRANTY PROVISIONS

Before 1975, consumers faced certain problems in the area of warranty law: many manufacturers disclaimed warranty protection, leaving the consumer with little or no protection; and most manufacturers put the warranty terms inside a sealed package, so the consumer did not even know what warranty provisions were being offered until after the sale was completed. The warranty terms inside the package frequently were in the form of a warranty card. The instructions told the buyer to complete the card and return it to the manufacturer in order to obtain his or her warranties. In fact, these cards often specified that the buyer was agreeing to accept the express warranties the manufacturer was offering as the exclusive warranties in the contract. By completing and returning the card, the buyer was surrendering any implied warranties he or she possessed in exchange for a very restricted (frequently sixty- or ninety-day) express warranty coverage proposed by the merchant.

As a result of these problems, the Magnuson-Moss Act–Consumer Product Warranty Act was passed and took effect in 1975. This law covers any consumer good manufactured after 3 January 1975. The manufacturer must provide the consumer with presale warranty information. The manufacturer also should set up informal settlement procedures to benefit the consumer. The manufacturer does not have to give any express warranties under the statute. However, according to the law, a manufacturer who does give an express warranty must designate it as either full or limited. To qualify as a full warranty, the warranty must meet at least four requirements:

1. It must warrant that defects in the goods will be remedied within a reasonable time.
2. It must conspicuously display any exclusions or limitations of consequential damages.
3. Any implied warranty must not be limited in time.
4. It must warrant that if the seller's attempts to remedy defects in the goods fail, the consumer will be allowed to select either a refund or a replacement.

Any warranty that is not full is limited. In a limited warranty, implied warranties may be limited to a reasonable time, frequently the same time as the express warranties given in the contract by the seller. There may also be limits on when the buyer can select a refund or a replacement.

Note that Magnuson-Moss does *not* provide warranty protection. All that this law requires is for the manufacturer or seller who deals in consumer goods to *inform* the consumer of his or her warranty protections. The Magnuson-Moss Act–Consumer Product Warranty Act is a *disclosure* law, designed to ensure that consumers are made aware of the warranty protections available with different products so that the consumer can make an informed and intelligent choice between products based on all of the available information, including warranty coverage.

WARRANTY EXCLUSIONS

The seller can modify or exclude warranties. The simplest way to exclude an express warranty is not to give one. If the seller is careful, no express warranties will exist. Sometimes a seller will create an express warranty orally but will attempt to exclude any express warranties in writing. In this case, the court will turn to UCC § 2-316(1). The court will take the warranty and the exclusion as consistent with one another if possible; otherwise, the warranty will override the exclusion. Excluding or modifying implied warranties is not so easy. To exclude or modify a warranty of merchantability, either orally or in writing, the word merchantability must be used. If the exclusion is written, the exclusion must be **conspicuous**. To exclude or modify a warranty of fitness for a particular purpose, the exclusion must be written, and it must be conspicuous; no oral exclusions of fitness are allowed. Under § 2-316(3), it is possible to exclude all implied warranties of quality (which normally do not exclude title or infringement protections) under three sets of circumstances:

1. Language such as "as is" or "with all faults" must be used properly so that the buyer is duly informed that no implied warranties are given.
2. If the buyer has thoroughly examined the goods or has refused to examine them before the sale, no implied warranty is given for defects that the examination should have revealed.
3. Under course of dealings, course of performance, or usage of trade, implied warranties are not given as a matter of common practice.

18.2

WARRANTIES

The professor in John's legal environment of business course recently explained warranty law, its scope, the potential for liability, and the methods for disclaiming or excluding warranties. After the class discussion, John became concerned that warranty liability could be very costly to the family business. Accordingly, he is urging the family to consider excluding any and all warranties that they can possibly exclude from their sales. Donna is concerned that, by excluding warranties, CIT will cause potential customers to doubt the quality and reliability of the product, thus hurting sales. They have asked you what they should do in this area. What will you tell them?

BUSINESS CONSIDERATIONS A firm produces a product that it sells to both consumers and to merchants. The Magnuson-Moss Act requires disclosure of warranty information prior to the sale, if the buyer is a consumer. No such requirement exists, however, if the buyer is a merchant. Should the firm put the warranty information on the product package, thus giving the same warranties to all customers, whether consumer or merchant, or should they use some other method of disclosure, thus being in a position to exclude some or all of the warranties in sales to other merchants?

ETHICAL CONSIDERATIONS Suppose that a company that sells primarily to consumers decided to use its excellent warranty coverage as a selling device. In order to emphasize its warranty coverage, the firm's advertising carries the message that the firm offers "a FULL four-year limited warranty." Although this ad is, technically, honest, it misleads many consumers who, upon hearing the emphasis on the word "full," believe that they are getting a full warranty. In fact, they are getting a full four years of warranty coverage, with a limited warranty in effect for that time. Is such an ad ethical?

SCOPE OF WARRANTY PROTECTION

If warranties do exist, the next question is, whom do they protect? At common law, the answer is simple but unsatisfactory. Since the warranty is a part of the contract, it extends only to a party to the contract. Thus, the buyer is covered, but no one else is protected. The UCC has changed this. Section 2-318 contains the following three alternative provisions, and each state has selected one of the alternatives:

1. Warranties extend to any member of the buyer's family or household or any guest in the buyer's home if it is reasonable to expect that person to use or consume the goods.
2. Warranties extend to any natural person (human being) who could reasonably be expected to use or consume the goods.
3. Warranties extend to any person (remember, a corporation is a legal person) who could reasonably be expected to use or consume the goods.

Conspicuous
Easy to see or perceive; obvious.

The seller may not exclude or modify the extension of the warranties to those third-party beneficiaries.

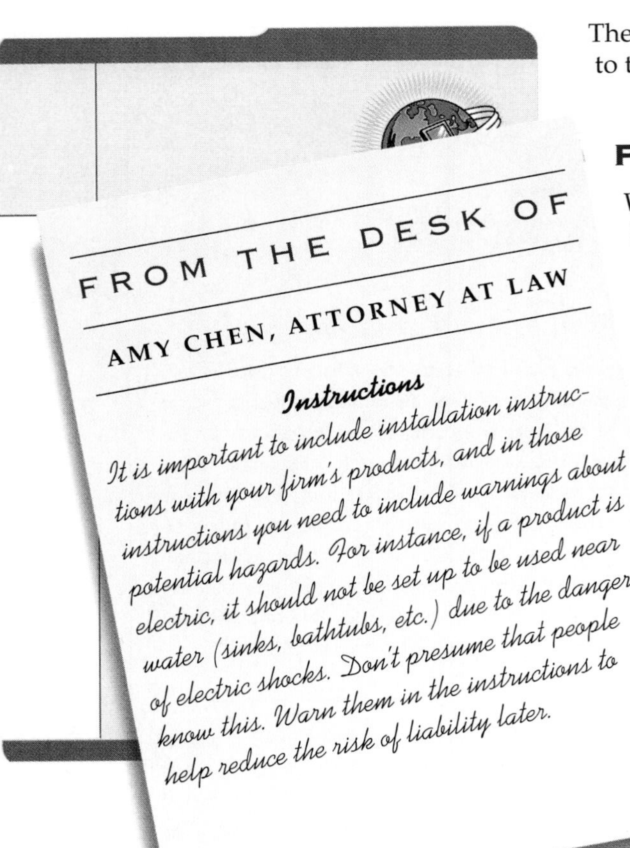

FROM THE DESK OF
AMY CHEN, ATTORNEY AT LAW
Instructions
It is important to include installation instructions with your firm's products, and in those instructions you need to include warnings about potential hazards. For instance, if a product is electric, it should not be set up to be used near water (sinks, bathtubs, etc.) due to the danger of electric shocks. Don't presume that people know this. Warn them in the instructions to help reduce the risk of liability later.

PRODUCT LIABILITY

While a great deal of energy and emphasis is placed on warranty law and warranty protections, this is not the only area in which buyers and consumers are protected from injuries caused by goods they have purchased and/or are using. Because they are a part of the contract, warranty protections are obvious to the buyer and the seller. Less obvious to the buyer, and to many sellers, are the other sources of remedies to which the buyer may be entitled. These other remedies may well be broader, they often last longer, and they frequently lead to larger judgments for injured parties. Sellers, in particular, need to be aware of the potential liability they face for injuries caused by the goods they sell beyond the liabilities imposed under warranty law.

Assume that a person is injured while using goods he or she has purchased, and he or she decides to seek remedies for the injury suffered. The first alternative many people consider is a breach of warranty claim. However, in many cases the warranty protections do not extend to the injury suffered, or the warranty protections have expired. When such a situation occurs, the injured party is not necessarily left without remedies. He or she may discover that, although warranty protections are lacking, potential remedies are still available under tort law. The injured party may be able to assert *negligence* against the manufacturer, or may even be able to establish *strict tort liability* against the manufacturer or the seller of the goods.

Negligence

Privity of contract
Direct contractual relationship with another party.

Innately dangerous
Dangerous as an existing characteristic; dangerous from the beginning.

Proximate cause
An act that naturally and foreseeably leads to harm or injury to another.

At common law, negligence can be used in only two circumstances: The buyer can argue breach of duties established by the **privity of contract** between the parties; or the buyer can argue that the goods are **innately dangerous**, so that privity of contract is not necessary in order to establish the liability of the seller or the manufacturer.

An injured party trying to establish that the tort of negligence occurred has to show the requisite elements of negligence: duty, breach of duty, harm, and **proximate cause**. Duty, the first element, is often the most difficult to establish. The injured party has to show that he or she is in privity of contract with the negligent party in order to establish that the seller owes a duty to the buyer. If there is privity, the contractual relationship establishes a duty by the seller to provide reasonably safe goods. The buyer next has to establish that the duty is breached, normally by showing that the goods provided are not reasonably safe for their intended use. The injured party then has to show that he or she was injured while using the goods and that the injury was proximately caused by the seller's breach of duty. This presents a relatively difficult task for the buyer. Even if the buyer can establish that the goods are not reasonably safe, that an injury did occur, and that there is a proximate causative link between the defect and the injury, establishing a duty owed by the manufacturer to the buyer is hard to show. In most instances, the injured party is in contact only with an innocent intermediate party and not with the negligent manufacturer. The manufacturer would argue that it only owes a duty to its buyer, the intermediate party. The intermediate party would assert that it has not breached any duty owed to the injured party. The lack of privity thus negates the duty element, effectively removing the possibility of suing the manufacturer for negligence.

Historically, an injured user who was able to argue that the goods were innately dangerous had an easier time establishing his or her case, if the innate danger of the goods could be shown. If the goods were found to be imminently or inherently dangerous, privity was not required. However, establishing the imminent or inherent danger of the product is more difficult. A product is deemed to be imminently dangerous if it is reasonably certain to threaten death or severe bodily harm as produced and/or sold. An item is considered to be inherently dangerous if it is dangerous by its nature. Imminent danger is most commonly found in negligent production; inherent danger is most commonly found in negligent use.

The difficulty of establishing either of these bases for proving that the manufacturer is liable for injuries serves as an effective shield from product liability at common law. However, times change, and so did the law's approach to product liability. In 1916, U.S. courts effectively laid the privity defense to rest in product liability cases. In the landmark case of *MacPherson* v. *Buick Motor Co.*, the owner of a Buick automobile was injured when the wooden spoke wheel of his automobile broke while he was driving the car. MacPherson sued Buick for his injuries. Buick denied liability for two reasons. It had not produced the wheel, but rather it had purchased the wheel from a supplier; so if liability attached to the defect in the wheel, the supplier should be the liable party. Buick also claimed lack of privity in that MacPherson had purchased his car from a dealer, not from the Buick Motor Company. The court rejected both arguments made by Buick, allowing the injured plaintiff to recover damages from Buick despite a lack of privity. Other courts quickly adopted the *MacPherson* rule, and, as a result, privity of contract is seldom asserted as a negligence defense today.

The following case shows how the theories of negligence and of strict tort liability are currently being applied. Notice that the plaintiffs in this case are asserting a defect in design and are also asserting a "crashworthiness doctrine" in seeking damages from the manufacturer. Such rulings apparently will continue to be the thrust of strict tort liability for some time to come.

18.3

MANAGEMENT

WARNING NOTICES FOR CALL-IMAGE

There has been some concern expressed about the effect of radiation from exposure to certain electronic displays (computer monitors, televisions, and so on). Julio is concerned that, although there is currently no evidence that the CIT display causes harm to users, there could be some basis for claims later. He feels that the firm should take affirmative steps, placing a warning label on the monitor urging users to be certain that they maintain "a safe distance" from the screen during use. Donna disagrees with Julio. She feels that such a label would discourage some people from buying the product while encouraging others to file suit. They have asked you for your thoughts on this topic. What will you tell them?

BUSINESS CONSIDERATIONS Should a business include warnings on its products concerning any potential risk the firm can think of in an effort to protect its customers from harm while simultaneously protecting itself from lawsuits, or should it only give warnings for obvious misuses of the goods?

ETHICAL CONSIDERATIONS What is the ethical obligation of a company to warn potential customers of dangers in those areas where the firm knows that a number of customers are likely to misuse a product? Does such a warning plant the idea of the misuse in the minds of some customers, possibly placing them at risk in areas where they would not have been at risk without the warning?

18.4 VOLKSWAGEN OF AMERICA, INC. v. MARINELLI — 628 So.2d 378 (Ala. 1993)

FACTS Nicholas Marinelli was driving a 1973 Volkswagen Thing, a convertible utility vehicle with a detachable hardtop roof. He testified that he was returning to the Marinelli residence after giving driving lessons to his sister when he saw an animal approaching from the right side. He further testified that he steered to the right, tried to slow and/or stop by using his brakes, which were defective and did not work, and then applied his emergency brake in an effort to avoid hitting the animal; but this caused the vehicle to skid, and the vehicle flipped over. All three passengers (Nicholas, his sister, and her boyfriend) were thrown from the vehicle in the accident. Nicholas suffered minor injuries. His sister and her boyfriend were killed. None of the three were wearing their seatbelts at the time of the accident. Nicholas knew that his brakes were defective, but this was not the basis for the lawsuit against Volkswagen. The parents of the deceased passengers each filed wrongful death actions against Volkswagen, alleging negligence and strict liability by the defendant in the design and construction of the vehicle. Volkswagen denied liability, asserting (among other things) that the decedents were contributorily negligent, that they had assumed the risk by failing to use their seatbelts, and that the driver was guilty of product misuse. Volkswagen also objected to the admission of "crashworthiness" testimony, alleging that the proper test was the Alabama Extended Manufacturers' Liability Doctrine.

ISSUE Was Volkswagen negligent and/or strictly liable for this crash due to a defective design of the product that made it unreasonably dangerous in its normal and intended use?

HOLDING Yes. The court did not err in using the crashworthiness doctrine, and the jury determined under this doctrine that the vehicle was unreasonably dangerous.

REASONING Volkswagen based its defense primarily on an opposition to the crashworthiness doctrine, alleging that such a doctrine was *contra* to Alabama law. The crashworthiness doctrine, as explained to the jury, required the plaintiff to prove each of the following:

1. That there was an automobile accident
2. That Volkswagen manufactured the automobile involved in the accident
3. That the automobile was in substantially the same condition at the time of the accident as when it was manufactured
4. That the automobile was defective—that it did not meet the reasonable expectations of an ordinary consumer—as to its safety in its ordinary purpose
5. That the injuries suffered were proximately caused by the defect.

In order to show that the vehicle was defective, the plaintiff had to prove that a safer, practical, or alternative design was available, and that such a design would have prevented the injuries suffered. Evidence was presented that showed the vehicle to have an unreasonably low track width relative to the height of its center of gravity. The jury apparently believed this evidence, as it found for the plaintiffs. The lower court's opinion is affirmed.

BUSINESS CONSIDERATIONS Assume that a business manufactures products that are relatively dangerous, even when used properly. The business is aware that technological advances over the next few years are likely to make their current products obsolete even though the product should still be in good operating condition. Should the firm design the product with the idea of *planned obsolescence,* designing the product to have a relatively short life in order to avoid potential liability to users in the future, or should the firm make as durable a product as possible, taking its chances on liability issues in the future?

ETHICAL CONSIDERATIONS Is it ethical to hold a manufacturer liable for strict product liability based on contemporary standards years after the product for which they are sued was manufactured? Is it ethical for a firm to deny liability simply based on the passage of time? How can these conflicting interests be balanced to protect the ethical and financial interests of both parties?

Strict Liability in Tort

The other basis for recovery frequently asserted by an injured party is *strict liability* in tort (also referred to frequently as strict liability or strict tort liability). Strict liability in tort appears to be a public policy area. It is possible for a manufacturer to disclaim warranty provisions, leaving a purchaser without the protections envisioned by warranty law. Similarly, an injured consumer may not be able to establish the necessary elements for a successful negligence suit. Nonetheless, there seems to be a general feeling that an injured consumer should be able to recover from *someone*, and the manufacturer is seen as the best available source for recovery. Not only is the manufacturer normally better able to absorb the loss than the injured consumer, but the manufacturer is also in a position to pass the cost on to society in the form of higher prices for the goods.

The basis for this theory of recovery is found in *Restatement (Second) of Torts*, § 402A. Section 402A is widely followed by the courts of the United States. The section states:

> (1) *One who sells any product in a defective condition unreasonably dangerous to the user or consumer or to his property is subject to liability for physical harm thereby caused to the ultimate user or consumer, or to his property, if*
> *(a) the seller is engaged in the business of selling such a product, and*
> *(b) it is expected to and does reach the user or consumer without substantial change in the condition in which it is sold.*
>
> (2) *The rule stated in subsection (1) applies although*
> *(a) the seller has exercised all possible care in the preparation and sale of his product, and*
> *(b) the user or consumer has not bought the product from or entered into any contractual relation with the seller.*

Note that this provision applies only to a merchant, that the goods must sell a "defective" product that is "unreasonably" dangerous to the consumer, and that the product must reach the consumer without any substantial change in its condition. If these three criteria are satisfied, and if the consumer is injured using the product, the manufacturer can be held liable even though it used all possible care in the production of the product and even though there is no allegation of negligence.

This basis for liability imposes a substantial potential burden on the manufacturer. The "defective condition unreasonably dangerous to the user or consumer" referred to in part 1 is often measured at the time the injury occurs and not at the time the product was produced. Thus, a manufacturer who produces a product with a long useful life may face liability in the future, due to technological advances in the industry after production of the product but before the product is removed from service. The manufacturer can be found liable under this section for defects in design, defects in construction, or for failing to warn the consumer of a known danger commonly faced when using the product. This is one of the reasons for the warning on the blade platform on power lawn mowers ("Keep hands and feet from under mower while in operation."), the warning label on the power cords of electric hair driers ("Keep away from water—Danger"), and other labels or tags on consumer goods. This could also be an argument for planned obsolescence of products. A product whose useful life is supposed to end before too many technological advances can be made is less likely to lead to liability for the manufacturer.

The following case involves a claim for damages based on negligence, strict liability, and breach of contract. The choice of law rules of the forum court also had an impact, since the case would seemingly have a different result under one state's laws than under the other's. The court's opinion dealt only with the adequacy of the complaint to withstand a motion for summary judgment, but it raises some interesting points.

18.5 BIG RIVERS ELECTRIC CORPORATION v. GENERAL ELECTRIC COMPANY

820 F.Supp. 1123 (S.D. Ind. 1992)

FACTS Big Rivers Electric Corporation is a public utility in Kentucky. General Electric Company is a New York corporation that does business in every state in the United States except Kentucky and Massachusetts. Big Rivers purchased several transformers from General Electric. These transformers were all delivered and installed during the year 1984 (no more accurate date was provided by either party). On 2 September 1989, one of the transformers failed, spraying boiling oil from a pressure-relief valve over a large area of property owned by Big Rivers and surrounding the transformer's location. As a result of this failure and the resulting oil spill, Big Rivers filed suit against General Electric, claiming damages to the transformer and to the soil. Its complaint was based on three theories of liability: strict liability, negligence, and breach of contract. General Electric denied liability and filed a motion for summary judgment on all counts.

ISSUES Which state's laws should be applied in this case? Was there a sufficient question of fact on any of the allegations to deny the Motion for Summary Judgment filed by General Electric?

HOLDINGS The court applied Indiana's choice-of-laws rules to determine that the laws of Kentucky should be applied to this case since Kentucky had the most significant contacts with the cause of action. There was a sufficient question of fact on the allegations for product liability and for negligence to deny the Motion for Summary Judgment.

REASONING General Electric argues that summary judgment should be granted on the strict liability issue because purely economic damages associated with an allegedly defective product are not recoverable in a strict liability case. Though captioned "Strict Liability," the Product Liability Act of Kentucky applies to Big Rivers' claim in Count One [the strict liability claim]. "A 'product liability action' shall include any action brought for or on account of personal injury, death or property damage caused by or resulting from the manufacture, construction, design, formulation, development of standards, preparation, processing, assembly, testing, listing, certifying, warning, instructing, marketing, advertising, packaging or labeling of any product." It is clear from reading the Product Liability Act of Kentucky that it does not, and was not intended to, create a cause of action for product liability actions. Rather, as the Kentucky Supreme Court has recognized, "it was enacted 'to codify certain existing legal precedents and to establish certain guidelines which shall govern the rights of all participants in products liability litigation.'"

Kentucky's law follows Section 402A of the Restatement, Second, of Torts: Did the defendant manufacture, sell or distribute the product "in a defective condition, unreasonably dangerous to the user"? This Court declines to extend Kentucky law to include a product liability claim under strict liability for damages to the product giving rise to the strict liability cause of action even though there is a cause of action for damages to other property damaged by the product. Therefore, summary judgment will be granted on Count One to the extent that it seeks recovery for damage to the transformer.

General Electric argues that summary judgment should be granted on all of Count One and that Big Rivers' claim for damage to the soil should also be denied. Nevertheless, there is a material issue of fact concerning the nature of the damaged soil, and this part of the motion is therefore denied.

General Electric argues that summary judgment should be granted on Count Two [the negligence claim] because purely economic damages associated with an allegedly defective product are not recoverable in a negligence action. Though captioned "Negligence," the Product Liability Act of Kentucky applies to Big Rivers' claim in Count Two. As with Count One, the Product Liability Act of Kentucky does not create a cause of action. Rather it codifies some aspects of a common law products liability cause of action. An examination of the common law of Kentucky reveals that Kentucky recognizes a negligence claim where recovery is only obtainable for damage to the product itself. Thus, the motion for summary judgment on Count Two is denied.

General Electric argues that summary judgment should be granted on Count Three [the breach-of-contract claim] because the contract is predominately one for goods, and the UCC provides for a four-year statute of limitations, which expired in November 1986. While General Electric is incorrect on when the statute of limitations expired, it is correct that the statute had expired prior to this event. Thus, the motion for summary judgment on Count Three is granted.

BUSINESS CONSIDERATIONS What can a firm in a position similar to Big Rivers do to protect itself when product liability law will not allow it to collect damages for harm done to the defective product itself, especially when that product is the most expensive part of the damaged property?

18.5 BIG RIVERS ELECTRIC CORPORATION v. GENERAL ELECTRIC COMPANY *(cont.)* 820 F.Supp. 1123 (S.D. Ind. 1992)

ETHICAL CONSIDERATIONS Big Rivers claimed that the oil spill damaged soil around the transformer, while the transformer itself was damaged, causing the oil to spill. Should a business be allowed to claim injury to soil in order to force a case to fit within the coverage of product liability, when, in reality, the damages being sued for occurred to the product rather than to the soil? Was this an unethical attempt to force the case within the definition of a strict liability action by "finding" harm beyond that done to the allegedly defective and dangerous product?

YOU BE THE JUDGE

Has DuPont Produced a Dangerous Insecticide?

In November 1989, Donna Castillo was taking her daily "health walk" near some tomato and strawberry fields when she was drenched with Benlate DF, an insecticide produced by DuPont, that was being sprayed on the crops. At the time of this incident, Ms. Castillo, a Miami-area school teacher, was pregnant. The child Ms. Castillo was carrying was subsequently born without eyes. She sued DuPont, alleging that the company knew that the product was likely to cause birth defects if pregnant women were exposed to the insecticide. DuPont denied that the product had any effect on Ms. Castillo or that it caused any birth defects. However, their insecticide was pulled from the market in 1991, following widespread reports of crop damage caused by its use, and DuPont paid more than $500 million to settle claims from growers.

This case has been brought before *your* court. How will you rule?

BUSINESS CONSIDERATIONS Suppose that a company produces a product that has recently been alleged to cause injury to people, animals, or plants. There is no proof yet that the product does, in fact, cause this alleged harm, but the rumors of its danger are spreading. What obligation does the company have to issue warnings in this situation? If there is an obligation to issue warnings, how should the warnings be given?

ETHICAL CONSIDERATIONS While DuPont denies that the insecticide in question causes birth defects, there have been a significant number of children born in England with no eyes or with eyes that are not fully developed. Most of these children were born in regions where Benlate DF was widely used during their gestation period. While there has not yet been any conclusive scientific proof that Benlate DF is the cause of these birth defects, does DuPont have an ethical duty in this situation, pending conclusive scientific evidence? If so, what should DuPont do ethically?

SOURCE: Milo Geyelin, *Wall Street Journal*, (10 July 1996), p. B10.

LEASES

When goods are leased, the lessee receives certain warranties. These warranties are analogous to the warranties given to the buyer in a sale of goods, although there are some differences due to the difference in the reason the contract is entered. The lessee receives express warranties on the same basis as a buyer of goods does.

http:// RESOURCES FOR BUSINESS LAW STUDENTS

NAME	RESOURCES	WEB ADDRESS
Uniform Commercial Code (UCC) Article 2, Sales	The Legal Information Institute (LII), maintained by the Cornell Law School, provides a hypertext and searchable version of Article 2, Sales. LII also maintains links to the UCC as adopted by particular states and to proposed revisions.	http://www.law.cornell.edu/ucc/2/overview.html
UCC Article 3, Negotiable Instruments	LII provides a hypertext and searchable version of UCC Article 3, Negotiable Instruments. LII also maintains links to Article 3 as adopted by particular states and to proposed revisions.	http://www.law.cornell.edu/ucc/3/overview.html
Magnuson-Moss Warranty Act—15 USC §§ 2301–2312	LII provides a hypertext version of 15 USC §§ 2301–2312, popularly known as the Magnuson-Moss Warranty Act.	http://www.law.cornell.edu/uscode/15/ch50.html
UCC Article 2A, Leases	LII provides a hypertext and searchable version of the UCC Article 2A, Leases. LII also provides links to Article 2A as enacted by particular states and to proposed revisions.	http://www.law.cornell.edu/ucc/2A/overview.html

Express warranties are created when the lessor makes any affirmation of fact or promise that relates to the character, quality, or nature of the goods. These express warranties become part of the basis of the bargain. The lessor also provides express warranties based on descriptions of the goods or by providing any sample or model of the goods being leased. Article 2A of the UCC specifically excludes any statements as to the value of the goods, as well as any statement purporting to be merely the lessor's opinion or commendation of the goods, from attaining the status of an express warranty.

Lessees also receive four implied warranties in their lease contracts. These implied warranties are: the warranty against interference, the warranty against infringement, the warranty of merchantability, and the warranty of fitness for a particular purpose. The warranty against interference is similar to the warranty of title under Article 2. It warrants that, during the term of the lease, no person holds a claim to or interest in the goods that will interfere with the lessee's use and enjoyment of the goods. The other three implied warranties are the same for lessees as they are for buyers. Warranties under Article 2A can be excluded in the same manner as they are excludable under Article 2.

SUMMARY

Warranty law and product liability are two major areas of consumer protection—a subject that has been receiving an increasing amount of attention for some years. Warranty protection comes in two broad forms: express warranties, which are given by the seller; and implied warranties, which are imposed by law. There are also statutory warranty provisions, which are primarily concerned with disclosures to consumer-purchasers. Warranties are considered a part of the contract covering the sale of goods. Warranties may be excluded by the seller or surrendered by the buyer. The method of exclusion depends on the type of warranty involved.

Under product liability, the manufacturer or the seller may be held liable because of negligence in making, designing, or packaging the product. The manufacturer may also be held strictly liable, despite any lack of due care. This is true if the product, in its normal use, is imminently or inherently dangerous.

Leases also carry protections for the lessee in the area of warranty law. Lessees can receive express warranties when the lessor creates a belief in the mind of the lessee as to the character, quality, or nature of the goods being leased. Lessees also enjoy the protection of four implied warranties. These warranties are analogous to the implied warranties of Article 2.

Discussion Questions

1. According to Article 2 of the UCC, what is necessary before a seller is deemed to give a buyer express warranties in a sales contract? What is necessary to give a lessee express warranties in a lease contract under Article 2A?
2. What does a seller warrant to the buyer in the implied warranty of title? What does the lessor warrant to the lessee in the implied warranty against interference?
3. When does a buyer of goods receive an implied warranty of merchantability? When does the lessee of goods receive an implied warranty of merchantability? What assurances does the buyer or lessee receive with this warranty?
4. What is the purpose of the Magnuson-Moss Act–Consumer Warranty Act? What is the difference between a full warranty and a limited warranty under the Magnuson-Moss Act?
5. What are the requirements that must be satisfied before a seller will be found liable for strict tort liability under § 402A of the *Restatement (Second) of Torts*?
6. George was negotiating with Steve for the sale of a boat. (Neither of the parties is a merchant.) During the negotiations, Steve mentioned that he frequently takes three of this friends water-skiing, and George told Steve the boat would easily pull three water-skiers. Steve bought the boat and discovered that if there are three skiers, the boat would not move fast enough to allow them to get up on their skis. Steve decided to sue George for breach of warranty in the sale of the boat. What warranty or warranties should Steve claim to have received? How, if at all, were they breached? Explain.
7. Carl saw an advertisement on television in which a driver drove his new four- wheel-drive Macho up the side of a building to the garage on the roof. (Carl did not pay attention to the disclaimer scrolling across the bottom of the screen.) Carl had recently purchased a new Macho, and he decided to drive it up the side of his apartment building. The Macho and Carl both were injured in Carl's efforts, and Carl has filed suit against Macho Motors, alleging breach of an express warranty. What result should occur? Explain.
8. Bob is buying a stereo from Earl. Bob asks Earl about the distortion figures for the stereo. Earl does not know the correct answer, but he does not want Bob to realize his lack of knowledge. What will happen if Earl answers, and his answer is incorrect? How should Earl answer?
9. A manufacturer negligently built a door so that the lock would not hold properly. Debbie bought the door for her home. The lock did not hold, and a burglar robbed Debbie because of the improperly functioning lock. Can Debbie sue the manufacturer for negligence?
10. Rayex sold sunglasses advertised as safe for baseball. A high school athlete was using the baseball sunglasses when he misplayed a fly ball. The ball hit the glasses and they shattered, blinding the athlete in one eye. It was subsequently discovered that the lenses of the sunglasses were unreasonably thin and not impact-resistant. How should the athlete argue to establish strict tort liability?

Case Problems and Writing Assignments

1. Klages was employed as a night auditor at Conley's Motel. While working, Klages was the victim of an armed robbery at the motel. In order to protect himself in the event of another robbery, Klages purchased a mace pen from General Ordnance. The pen was advertised as a device that would cause "instantaneous incapacitation" of an attacker. The pen was also advertised to be as effective as a gun without

the permanent injury from using a gun. Shortly after purchasing the pen, Klages was again held up by an armed robber. He squirted the robber with the mace, hitting him in the face with the mace discharge. The robber was not instantaneously incapacitated, however, and he shot Klages in the head. As a result of the gunshot wound, Klages lost all sight in his right eye. Klages has sued the manufacturer of the mace pen for misrepresentation. What should be the result in this case? [See *Klages* v. *General Ordnance Equipment Corp.,* 367 A.2d 207 (Pa. 1976).]

2. Jones did business as Sunbelt Auctions in Forest, Mississippi. On 9 January 1988, Jones offered a used John Deere backhoe for sale at a public auction. Jones had recently received the backhoe under a consignment agreement with Luckey. This agreement authorized Jones to sell the backhoe for an 8 percent commission. (The facts concerning the consignment were not disclosed in the auction.) Ballard purchased the backhoe at the auction for $10,500, delivered a check to Jones as payment in full, and took possession of the backhoe. Ballard subsequently spent approximately $1,000 in repairs on the backhoe and then resold it to Black, a third party, for $15,000. In April, Black was contacted by the Mississippi Department of Public Safety and informed that the backhoe had been stolen. The backhoe was then taken from Black and returned to its rightful owner. Black contacted Ballard, explained what had happened, and demanded his money back. Ballard refunded Black's purchase price and then contacted Jones seeking to recover his purchase price plus the money he spent on repairs ($11,500). Jones refused, and Ballard sued for breach of the implied warranty of title. Jones denied liability and also filed a third-party complaint against Luckey, demanding indemnity from Luckey if Ballard prevailed in his action. Did Jones, an auctioneer, give the implied warranty of title to Ballard in the sale of the used backhoe? [See *Jones* v. *Ballard,* 573 So.2d 783 (Miss. 1990).]

3. Falcon purchased a front-end loader from Clark in February 1973. In October 1973, after some 2,800 hours of use, the loader caught fire and was destroyed. Falcon claimed that the loader caught fire due to a manufacturing defect and sued Clark to recover the value of the equipment. Clark denied liability, alleging that § 402A applied only if a defective product caused harm to other property of the buyer, not when the only item injured was the allegedly defective product. Can a buyer recover from a manufacturer in a product liability tort action based on the doctrine of strict liability where the subject damage is limited to the product itself? [See *Falcon Coal Co.* v. *Clark Equipment Co.,* 802 S.W.2d 947 (Ky.App. 1990).]

4. Camacho purchased a new motorcycle from Honda. Some time later, Camacho was involved in an accident while riding his motorcycle, causing serious injuries to both of his legs. As a result, Camacho and his wife sued Honda, seeking recovery for the injuries and also for loss of consortium. The basis of the lawsuit was strict liability, but there were no allegations of any problems or defects in the motorcycle that in any way contributed to the accident. Rather, the Camachos argued that Honda failed to adequately warn them of the dangers of riding a motorcycle at the time of the sale. Honda denied any liability. How should this case be resolved? Should there be any ethical issues raised in this situation concerning *any* of the parties involved in filing or arguing this case? [See *Camacho* v. *Honda Motor Co., Ltd.,* 701 P.2d 628 (Colo.App. 1985).]

5. Gryka was seriously burned when her five-year-old brother used a disposable cigarette lighter to set her shirt on fire. Gryka suffered second- and third-degree burns over a significant part of her body, which led to multiple surgical procedures and skin grafts. She has suffered a great deal of pain, has permanent disabilities from the burns, and is disfigured. As a result, Gryka sued BIC, the manufacturer of the lighter, on strict liability grounds, alleging that the lighter was negligently designed and that BIC failed to provide adequate warnings regarding the dangers posed by its product. BIC has filed a motion for summary judgment, asserting that the dangers from a butane cigarette lighter are generally known, so that no warning was required. How should the court resolve this case? Is the argument advanced by BIC persuasive? [See *Gryka* v. *BIC Corp.,* 771 F.Supp. 856 (E.D. Mich. 1991).]

6. **BUSINESS APPLICATION CASE** On 17 January 1987, Riley purchased a new 1986 Yugo automobile from Ken Wilson Ford for a total of $7,762.56, including license, title, registration fees, credit life insurance, and credit disability insurance. Pursuant to the installment sales contract, Riley maintained liability and collision insurance at a cost of $154 per six months. At the time of the purchase, the salesman informed Riley that the car carried a standard 12 month/12,000 mile warranty. However, the salesman never explained that this was a warranty from the manufacturer and that Ken Wilson Ford did not give any warranties. Riley also never received any written copy of the warranty provisions in the sale. Riley had problems with the car from the first day, when the oil light came on during the drive home. The car suffered from oil and coolant leaks, problems with the rear window washer, squeaky brakes, trouble with the speedometer cable, and peeling paint. Throughout

these problems, Ken Wilson Ford made the necessary repairs and adjustments under the warranty provisions of the contract. Finally, when Riley had the Yugo towed in for repairs, he was informed that no work was needed. On the drive home, the car overheated and lost its compression. Riley had the car towed to a mechanic who disassembled the engine and determined that the engine had a blown head gasket, a warped cylinder head, and piston rings unsuitable for use. According to Riley's mechanic and the mechanic for Ken Wilson Ford, the engine needs to be rebuilt.

Riley sued Ken Wilson Ford for breach of express warranties, and Ken Wilson Ford denied that it was the party who gave warranties in this sale. Ken Wilson Ford insisted that the warranties were from Yugo America and that Riley should be suing Yugo rather than his dealership. How should this case be resolved? What should a business do if it intends to deny warranty liability on its own part, insisting that any warranties come from the manufacturer? [See *Riley* v. *Ken Wilson Ford, Inc.*, 426 S.E.2d 717 (N.C.App. 1993).]

7. **ETHICS APPLICATION CASE** Goodman went to Wendy's restaurant for lunch. He purchased a double hamburger "with everything." While eating the hamburger, he bit a hard substance, which turned out to be a bone of approximately one and one half inches in length and one quarter inch in thickness. As a result of biting into the bone, Goodman broke three teeth. The broken teeth, in turn, caused Goodman to undergo substantial dental treatment, including tooth extractions, a root canal, and the installation of permanent crowns. Goodman sued Wendy's for damages, alleging that the hamburger he purchased did not satisfy the implied warranty of merchantability in that it was not suitable for human consumption. Wendy's defended by pointing out that the bone of contention was a beef bone and thus a natural object. Wendy's argued because the bone was not a foreign material, there was no breach of warranty and no liability should attach. Assuming that the state courts have not yet decided whether the state should follow the foreign–natural test or the reasonable expectations test with respect to food, which side has the better argument in this case? How would you decide the case from an ethical perspective? [See *Goodman* v. *Wendy's Foods, Inc.*, 423 S.E.2d 444 (N.C. 1992).]

8. **IDES CASE** U.S. Roofing is a roofing contractor specializing in government roofing jobs. In 1983, U.S. Roofing was awarded a contract for the Alameda Naval Air Station in Oakland. U.S. Roofing determined that it would need a crane to complete the work and began contacting dealers about purchasing a crane. After some investigation, U.S. Roofing was persuaded to enter into a lease arrangement, with an option to purchase the crane at the end of the lease. Eventually, a lease was entered between U.S. Roofing and Leasing Service Corporation (LSC). The terms of the lease required U.S. Roofing to make lease payments for 57 months, with an option to purchase the crane at the end of the lease for an additional payment of $8,049. Included in the lease agreement, in all capital letters in red print just above the signature line was a disclaimer that read: "THE EQUIPMENT IS LEASED HEREUNDER AS-IS, AND LESSOR MAKES NO EXPRESS NOR IMPLIED NOR STATUTORY WARRANTIES AS TO ANY MATTER WHATSOEVER, INCLUDING WITHOUT LIMITATION THE CONDITION OF THE EQUIPMENT, ITS MERCHANTABILITY OR ITS FITNESS FOR ANY PURPOSE."

The crane was delivered to U.S. Roofing on 24 August 1983, and the company immediately began to encounter problems with the crane. It was unstable, would not lift to its listed full capacity, leaked fluids, and was generally unsatisfactory. After attempts to have the crane repaired proved futile, U.S. Roofing stopped using the crane or making lease payments for it, sending a letter to LSC in which it attempted to revoke the lease. Instead, LSC treated the nonpayment of lease payments as a breach, repossessed the crane, and sold it at a public auction for $60,000.

U.S. Roofing filed suit against LSC for breach of warranties on the crane. LSC filed a cross-complaint for breach of contract, and also sought a deficiency judgment for the monies it lost on the lease and in selling the crane. (The deficiency amount sought was $125,354.60, which was determined by computing the balance due under the terms of the lease and subtracting the net proceeds from the sale.)

Apply IDES principles in analyzing this case and determining how it should be resolved. [See *U.S. Roofing* v. *Credit Alliance Corporation*, 279 Cal.Rptr. 533 (Cal.App. 1991).]

NOTE

1. *Black's Law Dictionary*, rev. 4th ed. (1968).

Remedies

A G E N D A

Although the Kochanowskis have devoted a great deal of time and effort to making the best possible product, they realize that some of the units they sell will be defective and a customer who purchases such a defective unit may well sue them for damages. They also realize that, no matter how carefully they select the people or firms with whom they do business, there are likely to be times when contracts are breached. They are concerned about the types of remedies they may have to honor and the types of remedies they may have to seek, and they are likely to ask for your advice in these areas. Be prepared! You never know when one of the Kochanowskis will be asking you for advice or guidance.

O U T L I N E

THE REASON FOR REMEDIES

The overwhelming majority of sales contracts are performed by the parties as expected. The seller tenders conforming goods to the buyer at the time and place of delivery. The buyer then inspects the goods, accepts them, and pays the seller the price agreed to in the contract. Of course, not every tender is letter-perfect; but when the tender of delivery is flawed, the seller normally cures the defect. Again, the parties are left with their bargain as agreed.

In some cases, however, the tender is never made or it is made in so insubstantial a manner that it is treated as a breach of contract. Furthermore, some sellers refuse to cure a defective performance or lack the time to do so, and some buyers refuse to pay the agreed price or are unable to do so. Under these circumstances, the other party must look to **remedies** to minimize the effect of the breach.

This chapter examines remedies first from the seller's viewpoint and then from the buyer's. In either case, certain remedies will be available at some times and other remedies will be available at other times. The last part of the chapter explores some technical rules that affect how and when remedies may be sought or established.

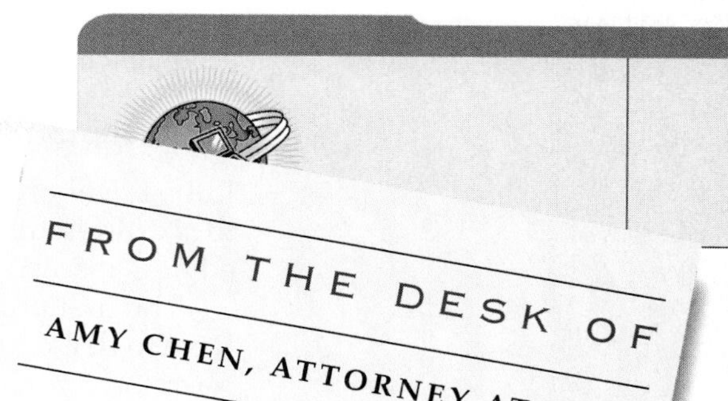

Remedies

Be aware of the various remedies available to sellers of goods under the UCC. The Code permits an innocent party to select from a "laundry list" of possible remedies when a breach occurs, and these remedies are not mutually exclusive. Being aware of the available remedies makes it easier to decide on a course of conduct and may also help in negotiating with any parties who breach their relevant contracts.

SELLER'S REMEDIES

If the buyer wrongfully **rejects** goods, refuses to pay for the goods, or otherwise breaches the contract, the seller is entitled to remedies. The remedies available to the seller depend on when the buyer breaches. The seller has six possible remedies if the breach occurs before acceptance. If the breach happens after acceptance, the seller has two possible remedies. Exhibit 19.1

Remedies
Methods for enforcing rights or preventing the violation of rights.

Rejects
Refuses to accept something when it is offered.

EXHIBIT 19.1 Seller's Remedies

PREACCEPTANCE REMEDIES

1. Withhold delivery of goods still in the seller's possession.
2. Stop delivery of goods in transit to the buyer.
3. Sue for the contract, which includes the right to identify goods to the contract and the right to complete work-in-process.
4. Resell any goods (or raw materials or work-in-process).
5. Sue for damages suffered due to the breach, whether based on the resale or based on lost profits.
6. Cancel any future performance obligations.

POSTACCEPTANCE REMEDIES

1. Sue for the amount still due under the contract.
2. Reclaim the goods (provided that the buyer is insolvent and the seller asserts the claim within 10 days of delivery *or* that the buyer made a written misrepresentation of solvency, which waives the 10-day limit).

summarizes the types of preacceptance and postacceptance remedies available to the seller. Each of these is discussed in turn.

Preacceptance Remedies of the Seller

If the buyer breaches the contract before accepting the goods, the seller may seek up to six different remedies. The seller does not have to choose just one possible remedy: As many of the six can be used as are needed in the particular case.

The first possible remedy is to *withhold delivery* of the goods. The seller does not have to deliver or to continue delivering goods to a buyer who is not willing to perform the contract properly. In addition, if the seller discovers that the buyer is insolvent, the seller may withhold delivery unless the buyer pays in cash all prior charges and the cost of the current shipment.

The second possible seller's remedy is a little more complicated. It is known as *stoppage of delivery in transit.* To use this remedy, the goods must be in the possession of a third person—a **carrier** or a bailee. If the seller discovers that the buyer is insolvent, the seller may stop delivery of any goods in the possession of a third person. If the buyer breaches the contract, the seller may also be able to stop the delivery; however, before the seller can stop delivery because of a breach, the delivery must be of a planeload, carload, truckload, or larger shipment. The seller also must make provisions to protect the carrier or the bailee before a stoppage is permitted. The seller must notify the carrier or bailee in enough time to reasonably allow a stoppage and must indemnify that carrier or bailee for any charges or damages suffered because of the stoppage.

Carrier
A third party hired to deliver the goods from the seller to the buyer.

The third remedy allows the seller to *sue for the contract.* This remedy does provide a potential burden to the seller, however. If or when the buyer pays the contract price, the seller must tender delivery of the goods. Thus, a seller who sues for the contract must be prepared to perform the contract upon the buyer's performance.

The fourth seller's remedy gives the seller the right to *resell* those goods that are still in the seller's possession. A seller who does resell the goods, and who does so in good faith in a commercially reasonable manner, may also be able to collect damages from the buyer. The seller may elect to resell in a public sale or in a private sale and may resell the entire lot of goods as a unit or make the resale by individual units. All the seller has to do is establish that the resale was conducted in a commercially reasonable fashion. This means that the method, time, place, and terms all must be shown to be reasonable. And the seller must give the breaching buyer notice of the sale, if possible. Normally, the issue of reasonableness will be raised in a private sale, but if he or she is given notice, the buyer has little opportunity to defeat the resale. In a public resale, reasonableness is well defined. Except for recognized futures, the resale can be made only on identified goods. It must occur at a normal place for a public sale unless the goods are perishable. The breaching buyer must be given notice of the time and place of the resale. Notice must be given as to where the goods are located so prospective bidders can inspect them. If the seller fails to meet any of these criteria, the resale is not commercially reasonable, and therefore the seller cannot recover any damages. If the seller resells the goods for more than the contract price, an interesting situation arises. If the buyer breached, the seller may keep the excess. If the buyer rightfully rejected the goods, the seller may still keep the excess, but now the excess is defined as anything above the buyer's **security interest.**

Security interest
An interest in the personal property of another as a means of securing payment or performance of a contractual obligation.

The fifth option available to the seller is to *sue the buyer, either for damages or for lost profits.* If the seller has not yet completed the goods or has not yet identified the goods to the contract, the seller normally will be content to sue for damages. In such a situation, damages are determined by taking the difference between the contract price and the market price at the time and place of breach, adding any incidental damages incurred, and then subtracting any expenses avoided. The seller may discover that the damages computed in this manner do not put him or her in as good a position as performance of the contract would have. If so, the seller may instead elect to sue for lost profits. The seller will show the profits that full performance would have netted and sue for this amount plus the recovery of any expenses reasonably incurred due to the breach. The seller may decide to resell the goods and then to sue for any losses or damages not recovered in the resale. If so, the damages are figured by deducting the resale price from the original contract price, adding **consequential damages** incurred due to the buyer's breach, and then subtracting any expenses saved by not having to deliver the goods to the original buyer.

Consequential damages
Damages or losses that occur as a result of the initial wrong but that are not direct and immediate.

Remedies 3, 4, and 5 allow the seller to exercise some discretion in the treatment of unidentified goods. If the buyer breaches the contract, the seller may identify goods to the contract that were unidentified before the breach, thus helping to establish damages. Also, the seller may decide either to complete goods that were incomplete or to stop production and resell the goods for scrap. Either of these options may be used, provided that the seller is exercising reasonable business judgment.

The seller's final preacceptance remedy is the right to *cancel*. On giving notice to the buyer, the seller can cancel all future performance due to the buyer under the contract. Cancellation does not discharge the buyer or hinder the seller in collecting or enforcing any other rights or remedies resulting from the breach; it merely terminates the duties of the seller under the contract due to the breach by the buyer.

The following case involves a seller's preacceptance remedies. In reading the case, ask yourself: How should the seller have proceeded in order to collect damages, and should other remedies have been sought as well?

19.1 LAKEWOOD PIPE OF TEXAS, INC. v. CONVEYING TECHNIQUES, INC.

814 S.W.2d 553(Tex.App. Houston [1st Dist.] 1991)

FACTS Conveying Techniques manufactures and fabricates conveying and material-processing equipment. Lakewood Pipe processes and sells steel pipe for the oil industry and for agricultural irrigation. In 1979, Conveying sold Lakewood a manual hydrostatic testing system. In 1984, Conveying gave Lakewood a written proposal for the construction and installation of an automatic system. The two corporate presidents met soon thereafter and Conveying demonstrated a prototype automatic system. According to Conveying's president (Lee), the president of Lakewood (Tybus) orally agreed to buy the system for $240,000. Tybus denied that he agreed, orally or otherwise. Conveying began construction of the automatic system in late 1984. In December 1984, Lee wrote to Lakewood, summarizing his understanding of the agreement, and reminding Lakewood that all of Lakewood's outstanding accounts receivable must be paid before the system would be installed. [Lee noted that the system had been delayed because Lakewood failed to pay, and Lee was concerned that Lakewood would not pay for the system prior to installation.] In February 1985, Lakewood informed Conveying that it was not in the market for the automatic system. In March, Conveying billed Lakewood for $80,000, determined by taking 30 percent of the contract price as "cancellation charges" on the contract.

ISSUES Did Lakewood breach a contract with Conveying in this case? If so, were the damages properly computed by Conveying?

HOLDINGS Yes. Lakewood breached the contract. No. Damages were not properly computed.

REASONING Lakewood and Conveying customarily entered into oral agreements with one another, so the order

19.1 LAKEWOOD PIPE OF TEXAS, INC. v. CONVEYING TECHNIQUES, INC. *(cont.)* 814 S.W.2d 553(Tex.App. Houston [1st Dist.] 1991)

for the automatic hydrostatic testing system was a valid contract even absent a writing, based on two factors: course of dealings between the parties and the fact that the system was being specially manufactured for Lakewood and would not be suitable for resale to any other buyers. Given that there was a contract, Tybus breached the contract by repudiation when the contract was approximately three-fourths complete, providing a reason for Conveying to recover damages. However, Conveying did not properly establish what its damages were in this case. Lee testified that he calculated the "cancellation charge" by estimation. He believed that Conveying had spent more than $80,000, but he was not sure. He stated that Conveying would "normally" have spent between $125,000 and $135,000 in direct equipment costs, not counting overhead, but he did not know if this was accurate or not. There was no **liquidated damages** clause in this contract, so Conveying had the burden of proving its damages before it could collect. Since there was insufficient evidence to support Conveying's damages, the case was remanded for a new trial on the issue of damages.

BUSINESS CONSIDERATIONS Should a business rely on alleged oral agreements in a contract that will entail hundreds of hours of work and thousands of dollars, or should the firm wait until the agreement is reduced to writing before recognizing the existence of a contract? How much reliance should a firm place in a "handshake" agreement with another firm?

ETHICAL CONSIDERATIONS Is it ethical to tie the performance of a current contract with another firm on that other firm's payment of any and all other accounts and arrearages? Should each contract be treated as a separate and distinct agreement, or should there be some linkage?

Liquidated damages
An amount expressly stipulated by the parties as the proper measure of damages if a breach occurs; cannot be a penalty.

Postacceptance Remedies of the Seller

Once the goods have been accepted by the buyer and the buyer has breached the contract, the seller may seek either or both of two remedies.

The first of these remedies is by far the more common. The seller may *sue the buyer for the price of the goods.* Since the buyer has accepted, the buyer's duty to pay is established. Thus, winning the case is almost a certainty. Many buyers who do not pay, however, are unable to pay. They are insolvent. In such a situation, winning the case is a Pyrrhic victory—the winner suffers nearly as much as the loser.

If the buyer has accepted goods and the buyer is insolvent, the seller will possibly seek the second available postacceptance remedy: The seller will attempt to *reclaim the goods.* To do so, the seller must prove that the following two conditions have been satisfied:

1. The buyer received the goods on credit while insolvent.
2. The seller demanded the return of the goods within 10 days of delivery to the buyer.

This remedy is obviously of limited value, since many businesses operate on credit terms providing for payment after 30 days (or longer) and the seller has only 10 days in which to act. But there is one exception. If the buyer misrepresented his or her solvency in writing to the seller within three months before delivery, the 10-day limit does not apply. In practice, many sellers extend credit in conjunction with a security interest (as provided for in Article 9 of the UCC) to protect themselves from the drawbacks presented by the "reclaim the goods" postacceptance remedy. Otherwise, if the seller discovers that the buyer is unable to pay after the goods have been accepted, the seller may find himself or herself with little hope of ever collecting the full contract price.

It is possible, at least in theory, for a seller to use all eight potential remedies in a single contract upon a breach by the buyer. In order to use all eight possible remedies, the circumstances would have to be unusual (to say the least), and the conduct of the buyer would have to fit within certain guidelines. Although such a confluence of circumstances is highly unlikely, it could happen, as is shown in the following example.

> Tara entered into a contract with Jaime that called for Jaime to produce and deliver 1,000 video games to Tara each month for the next 12 months. Tara was to make payments for each shipment within 30 days of receipt. Jaime did not ordinarily allow deferred or delayed payment, but Tara had provided a written financial statement that presented a picture of a very profitable business. (As it turned out, the financial statement was fraudulent; Tara was, in fact, insolvent at the time of the contract.) Jaime purchased sufficient raw materials to produce 8 months' worth of goods and began the manufacturing process. The performance of the contract can be summarized as follows:
>
> 1. The first two monthly shipments were sent to Tara.
> 2. The third monthly shipment had been turned over to a common carrier for delivery.
> 3. The fourth monthly shipment was ready for pickup by the common carrier when Jaime learned that Tara was insolvent.
> 4. The goods for monthly shipments 5 through 8 were, at that time, in various stages of "work in process."
> 5. The balance of the raw materials to complete the contract had been ordered by Jaime.

19.1

SALES/FINANCE

SHOULD CIT MAXIMIZE SALES THROUGH CREDIT OR CASH FLOW?

Tom would like to see the firm get off to a quick start by making a large number of sales early in the firm's existence. He is convinced that the best way for the company to grow and to meet its potential is to have many units in the market before anyone else can duplicate its efforts. He believes that the best way to do this is by selling the units on credit to a number of retail outlets. Donna and Julio are concerned about the cash flow of the firm and would prefer to have the early sales be made for cash, or at the very worst to have a short payment term. They both feel that 30 days is about as much credit as the firm should extend. Anna agrees, to some extent, with Tom, but she is worried about what will happen if one of the stores to whom CIT has extended credit defaults or goes bankrupt. Tom does not think this is a problem since, according to Tom, CIT could just go in and repossess the units not yet paid for. The family asks what you think. What advice will you give them?

BUSINESS CONSIDERATIONS A new company in an industry may have trouble getting its product into stores unless it is willing to take some chances, including making credit sales. What should a company do to maximize its protection if it decides to sell goods on credit? Are the Article 2 postacceptance remedies adequate for the firm's protection?

ETHICAL CONSIDERATIONS Suppose that a credit customer is having a temporary cash flow problem, but will probably be able to meet its debt obligation to your company in the near future. Should your company play "hardball" and demand payment when due, be caring creditors who allow the debtor a bit of leeway, or take a position somewhere between these extremes? How can the position you choose be justified ethically?

Jaime decided to seek any and all remedies that might be available under Article 2. Jaime first looked at the preacceptance remedies. He decided to withhold delivery of the fourth shipment to the carrier and to notify the carrier to stop the goods that were already in transit (the third shipment). The goods in shipments 3 and 4 had been identified to the contract, as was the work in process. Jaime decided to stop the work in process and to sell the partially completed goods for scrap. He also decided to resell the completed goods that were stopped in transit and the goods withheld from delivery. Jaime also called Tara and canceled all future performance on the contract due to Tara's insolvency. Jaime sued for damages on shipments 3 through 8 and for lost profits on shipments 9 through 12. Jaime then decided to exercise the postacceptance remedies. He reclaimed all the unsold goods still in Tara's possession from shipments 1 and 2 and sued for the amount due under the contract for all goods that Tara had disposed of before Jaime was able to assert his right to reclaim the goods from Tara.

The seller is seeking postacceptance remedies in the following case. Note the conflict between the seller and the creditors of the buyer, who was seeking relief in bankruptcy, a not uncommon situation when the buyer is unable to pay for goods that have already been accepted under the contract.

19.2 IN RE PESTER REFINING CO. — 964 F.2d 842 (8th Cir. 1992)

FACTS On 19 and 22 February 1985, Ethyl Corporation delivered 6,000 gallons of gasoline additive in a railroad tank car, together with twelve 55-gallon drums of an antioxidant, to Pester's refinery in Kansas. Ethyl invoiced Pester for almost $127,000 for this credit sale. On 25 February 1985, Pester filed for protection under Chapter 11 of the Bankruptcy Code. On 27 February 1985, Pester received a written demand from Ethyl, which was seeking to reclaim the chemicals. Although the chemicals were still on hand at the refinery and were still identifiable, Pester refused to return them to Ethyl. [The chemicals were also subject to the perfected security interests of various of Pester's creditors, and these creditors had claims in excess of the value of Pester's assets.] While Ethyl's claim was still pending, the bankruptcy court approved Pester's reorganization plan, declared that reclamation creditors were an impaired creditor class, and allowed these creditors the option of settling or continuing their reclamation efforts. Only Ethyl continued its reclamation efforts. Pester objected to this ruling.

ISSUE Does a seller who is otherwise entitled to reclaim accepted goods retain the right to reclaim the goods in the face of superior competing claims by secured creditors of the buyer?

HOLDING Yes. The seller's rights in this situation are superior to the rights of the debtor's secured creditors.

REASONING Reclamation is the right of a seller to recover goods delivered to an insolvent buyer. It is a rescissional remedy, based on the theory that the seller has been defrauded. (At common law and under the Uniform Sales Act, the seller could only recover goods if it could prove that the buyer had fraudulently induced delivery by misrepresenting its solvency!) The UCC allows reclamation without proof of misrepresentation of solvency, but only under very narrow circumstances. The seller must reclaim the goods within 10 days of delivery, provided the buyer was insolvent at the time of the delivery of the goods on credit. This right to reclaim is subject to the claim of any good faith purchasers who buy the goods from the buyer in the ordinary course of business before the seller can reclaim them. Since most secured creditors are good faith purchasers under the UCC, they would normally move ahead of the reclaiming seller. Unless the secured creditors released their claims, they had positions superior to that of Ethyl, effectively cutting off any rights Ethyl could assert against the chemicals it sought to reclaim. The court then examined the reorganization plan, and found that the secured creditors each released their security interest under the plan, leaving Ethyl with the right to reclaim unimpaired by the security interests of the creditors. Accordingly, Ethyl was entitled to reclaim the chemicals or to collect the full invoice price if the chemicals could not be reclaimed.

BUSINESS CONSIDERATIONS The right of the seller to reclaim goods that have been accepted by the buyer is very narrow. The seller must initiate the reclamation effort within 10 days of delivery unless the buyer misrepresented its solvency in order to acquire the goods. Given that normal payment terms are likely to call for payment in 30 days, this remedy seems almost worthless. What can/should the seller do in sales contracts where payment is to be made later in order for the seller to protect its interest in the goods sold?

19.2 IN RE PESTER REFINING CO. *(cont.)* 964 F.2d 842 (8th Cir. 1992)

ETHICAL CONSIDERATIONS Is it ethical for creditors of an insolvent debtor-buyer to assert claims against recently purchased goods, often at the expense of the seller who also extended credit to the debtor-buyer? Which of these parties (prior creditors or current seller-creditor) is in the best position to prevent this conflict of interests?

BUYER'S REMEDIES

The buyer also has a range of possible remedies. Like the seller, the buyer's remedy options depend on the timing of the breach. The buyer has six preacceptance and three postacceptance remedies available. These remedies are summarized in Exhibit 19.2. We will discuss each of them in turn.

Preacceptance Remedies of the Buyer

Before the buyer accepts, the seller may breach by nondelivery or by delivery of nonconforming goods. Under either circumstance, the buyer may elect any or all of the following remedies.

The buyer's first remedy is to *sue for damages.* The buyer is allowed to recover the excess of market price over contract price at the time of breach and at the place of delivery. Any additional damages are added to this amount. The amount is then reduced by any expenses the buyer saved because of the breach.

The second remedy available to the buyer is that of *cover.* The buyer covers by buying substitute goods from another source within a reasonable time of the

EXHIBIT 19.2 | Buyer's Remedies

PREACCEPTANCE REMEDIES

1. Sue for damages for breach of the contract.
2. Cover, and sue for damages resulting from the cost of covering.
3. Seek specific performance (unique goods) or replevin (common goods, temporary short supply in the market).
4. Claim any identified goods still in the seller's possession, provided the seller has become insolvent within 10 days of receiving payment from the buyer.
5. Resell any nonconforming goods shipped by the seller.
6. Cancel any future duties under the contract.

POSTACCEPTANCE REMEDIES

1. Revoke the acceptance (if the hidden defect substantially impairs the value of the contract) and then seek any appropriate preacceptance remedies.
2. Sue for damages due to the nonconformity of the goods shipped.
3. Recoup by deducting the damages suffered from the total contract price still owed to the seller (recoupment may only be used with the agreement of the seller).

Specific performance
A court order that the breaching party perform the contract as agreed; the object of the contract must be unique.

breach. If the goods obtained through cover cost more than the contract price, the buyer can collect the excess costs from the breaching seller, plus other expenses incurred in effecting cover.

The third remedy is available if the goods cannot be obtained by cover. The buyer may seek **specific performance** or **replevin.** If the goods are unique, the court may order specific performance; and the seller will have to deliver the goods in accordance with the contract. If the goods are not unique but are unavailable from other sources at the time, replevin is available. Once the buyer shows an inability to cover, the court will order replevin.

19.2

MANUFACTURING/MANAGEMENT

ADDRESSING DELIVERY PROBLEMS WITH A SUPPLIER

One of the firms that supplies component parts to CIT has recently been troubled by labor problems. Its employees were out on strike for several weeks, and the company has virtually exhausted its inventory of component parts. The strike ended last week, and the president of the company called Dan to let him know that the company planned to be back up to full production very shortly. Since the strike depleted their inventory, however, they might be a few days late with their next shipment to CIT. Dan reported this to the family and asked what the family planned to do. Dan would prefer to cancel the contract with this supplier, buy the components from another source, and sue for any damages. Anna would prefer to take a wait-and-see position, giving the firm time to get its production back up to normal. Tom is worried that the delay in receiving component parts may put CIT behind its production schedule, but is unsure of the best alternative for the firm. He asks you what you think they should do. What advice will you give him?

BUSINESS CONSIDERATIONS Does the fact that one or more remedies are available mean that a business should *use* those remedies? Should a business base its decisions on the fact that remedies are available, or should it view remedies as a last resort after all else has failed?

ETHICAL CONSIDERATIONS Is it a better business practice to work problems out in an equitable manner or to hold the other person to the literal terms of the bargain? Is it a better ethical practice to work problems out in an equitable manner, or to hold the other person to the literal terms of the bargain?

The fourth remedy is probably rare in actual practice. If the seller has identified the goods to the contract, and if the buyer has paid some or all of the contract price, and if the seller becomes insolvent within 10 days of receipt of the payment, the buyer can *claim the identified goods.* The likelihood of this chain of events occurring is not very high. But if it does occur, the buyer is protected.

The fifth remedy available to the buyer frequently baffles and amazes students: Under appropriate circumstances, the buyer may *resell the goods.* (Students frequently ask: "How can someone resell goods that were never accepted and thus never sold in the first place?") This remedy becomes available when the seller ships nonconforming goods to the buyer. On receipt of the nonconforming goods, the buyer must notify the seller of the nonconformity. Furthermore, if the buyer is a merchant, the buyer must request instructions from the seller as to disposal of the goods. If no instructions are given (or if the seller asks the buyer to resell the goods on the seller's behalf), the buyer must attempt to resell the goods for the seller. The resale must be reasonable under the circumstances. A buyer who does resell the goods will be allowed to deduct an appropriate amount from the sale amount for expenses and commissions, and may then apply the balance of the sale proceeds to the damages resulting from the breach. Any excess must be returned to the seller.

The final preacceptance remedy available to the buyer is the right to *cancel.* On discovery of a breach by the seller, the buyer may notify the seller that all future obligations of the buyer are canceled. Cancellation will not affect any other rights or remedies of the buyer under contract.

The following case involved a buyer's preacceptance remedies. Notice the court's efforts to determine *when* the breach occurred so that it could properly measure damages.

19.3 TRINIDAD BEAN AND ELEVATOR COMPANY v. FROSH 494 N.W.2d 347 (Neb.App. 1992)

FACTS Trinidad is a Colorado corporation that owns and operates an elevator in Imperial, Nebraska. Elmo Frosh is an individual engaged in the business of farming. On or about 26 April 1988, Frosh entered into a written contract with Trinidad whereby Trinidad agreed to buy and Frosh agreed to sell 1,875 hundredweight of dried, edible navy beans, which were to be delivered to Trinidad at Imperial upon completion of the harvest of the 1988 crop. The written contract entered into by the parties on 26 April, at paragraph 7, provided for two options with respect to payment to Frosh. Option 1 provided for payment of $16.25 per hundredweight on 15 January 1989, and option 2 provided for 50 percent payment at $16 per hundredweight upon the completion of the harvest and for 50 percent payment at $16 per hundredweight on 1 December 1988. Option 1 would be accepted if the grower wished to defer income for tax purposes, and option 2 would be used if the grower wished immediate payment. Buffington, who had been employed with Trinidad for only one month when he prepared the Frosh agreement, inadvertently filled out both payment options. The error was first noticed by James Peterson, a commodity trader, when the contract was received in Trinidad's Denver office. Peterson contacted the Imperial office and asked that someone ascertain which option Frosh intended to exercise so that Trinidad's accounting department could process the contract. Peterson spoke with Roberta Frosh, Trinidad's secretary at the Imperial elevator, and alerted her to the problem. Roberta Frosh had been the bookkeeper and secretary at the Imperial offices for 10 years. She was also the wife of Elmo Frosh. Buffington testified that Roberta Frosh alerted him to the error and told him to prepare a second page, limiting the payment provision to option 2. Buffington testified that he gave the second page to Roberta Frosh to obtain Elmo's signature. Roberta Frosh admitted that she knew about the second page of the contract, but denied that anyone from Trinidad had requested that she obtain Elmo's signature. Elmo Frosh never signed a contract with only one payment option. He insisted that the contract was void since no payment option was ever agreed on and sent a letter to that effect to the Denver offices on 8 September. Harvest was completed in mid-October; no beans were delivered as promised in the contract. Because of drought conditions, the price of navy beans rose during the 1988 growing season from $16 per hundredweight in April to $32 per hundredweight in late August–early September and to $36 per hundredweight in late September, when Trinidad purchased beans from other sources. Trinidad sued Frosh for damages. The court instructed the jury that a contract existed and how to compute damages. The jury returned a verdict for Frosh, and Trinidad filed a motion for a judgment NOV, which was overruled. Trinidad then appealed.

ISSUE What was the proper measure of damages in this contract between the parties?

HOLDING The proper measure of damages is the difference between the cover price and the contract price *on the date of repudiation.*

REASONING [The court was required] to determine the measure of a buyer's damages under the Nebraska UCC upon anticipatory repudiation, a question which "presented one of the most impenetrable interpretive problems in the entire Code." Specifically, the question is whether the language "at the time when the buyer learned of the breach" refers to the time when the seller repudiated or the time when the performance came due.

The Code provides that an aggrieved party may

> *a) for a commercially reasonable time await performance by the repudiating party; or*
> *b) resort to any remedy for breach, even though he has notified the repudiating party that he would await the latter's performance and has urged retraction; and*
> *c) in either case suspend his own performance.*

In this case, Trinidad chose not to cover and sought damages for the contract–market differential under § 2-713(1), which provides:

> *Subject to the provisions of this article with respect to proof of market price, the measure of damages for non-delivery or repudiation by the seller is the difference between the market price* at the time when the buyer learned of the breach *and the contract price. . . .*

The key question this court must determine on appeal is whether "learned of the breach" refers to time of repudiation or time of performance. The trial court found that damages were to be measured at the time of performance and so instructed the jury; however, the court also instructed the jury to consider whether Trinidad awaited performance unreasonably after Frosh's anticipatory repudiation.

The most common interpretation, accepted by a majority of courts, is that the Code refers to the time of repudiation. . . . The performance date measurement . . . was followed before the adoption of the Code and is still followed by a number of courts. . . . Since the Code's vocabulary is not consistent, both of these interpretations appear equally plausible. However, . . . we conclude that the repudiation date interpretation gives the provisions their best combined effect.

Having determined that date of repudiation is the correct date for measurement of damages, we must determine when repudiation took place in the case at bar. Frosh

19.3 TRINIDAD BEAN AND ELEVATOR COMPANY v. FROSH *(cont.)* **494 N.W.2d 347 (Neb.App. 1992)**

repudiated the contract in May when he first instructed Peterson to "tear up the contract." Since, at the repudiation date, the market price and the contract price for the beans were identical, there were no damages. The jury's finding in favor of Frosh was not clearly erroneous. The judgment of the district court is affirmed.

BUSINESS CONSIDERATIONS The court's opinion seems to put the risk of increased prices on the buyer when the seller repudiates well before the performance date. A buyer seemingly must cover in order to maximize its protection. In a case of early anticipatory repudiation, should the buyer guess at the likely price at the performance date, waiting to cover if it expects the price to go down, and covering now if it expects the price to rise? How might such an expectation affect the business?

ETHICAL CONSIDERATIONS Is it ethical to permit a party to repudiate its contract obligation and then to avoid having to pay damages because he happened to repudiate before the price made a drastic rise? Should a person in Frosh's position be allowed to retain double the amount called for in his first contract without any liability, merely because of the timing of his repudiation?

Replevin
Similar to specific performance, but the object of the contract is not unique; it must be currently unavailable.

Substantially impairs
Makes worth a great deal less, seriously harms or injures, or reduces in value.

Postacceptance Remedies of the Buyer

Once the buyer has accepted the goods, the focus shifts. A buyer who accepts cannot reject the goods, since accepting and rejecting are mutually exclusive. However, the buyer may be able to *revoke the acceptance.* Revocation is permitted only if the following criteria are met:

1. The defect must have been hidden; or the seller must have promised to cure the defect, but no cure occurred.
2. The defect must **substantially impair** the value of the contract.

While a hidden defect is not necessarily rare, a hidden defect that also substantially impairs the value of the contract may well be rare. If something is so wrong with the goods that the buyer's rights are substantially harmed, that problem would seem to be one that a reasonable inspection should reveal. A substantially impairing defect that is not cured when cure is promised is probably more common.

If the buyer properly revokes acceptance, the buyer is treated as if he or she rejected the initial delivery, and the buyer is then permitted to assert any or all of the available preacceptance remedies that apply to the case.

The buyer may accept the goods and later discover a defect or other breach that is not sufficient to permit a revocation. When this happens, the buyer will select the second possible remedy, *suing the seller for damages.* Damages are likely to be measured by comparing the value of the goods as delivered with the value that the buyer would have received if the goods that were delivered had conformed to the contract. Damages can also be established as the expense the buyer incurs in having the defects in the goods repaired by a third person.

The third remedy available to the buyer is *recoupment.* Normally, this third remedy will be used together with the second. The buyer will notify the seller that the buyer is recouping by deducting damages from the contract price owed to the seller. If the seller does not object, recoupment is used. If the seller objects, the buyer may not recoup but can still sue for damages.

The following case deals with a buyer who used the postacceptance remedy of recoupment. The buyer was then sued for the offset balance due on the contract by a secured creditor of the breaching seller. Observe how the court treats these conflicting issues.

19.4 PAGE v. DOBBS MOBILE BAY, INC. 599 So.2d 38 (Ala.Civ. App. 1992)

FACTS On 17 September 1987, Ance and Alice Page purchased a new van from the Treadwell Ford automobile dealership, trading in their old car and financing the remainder of the van's $24,500 purchase price through Treadwell. At the time of the purchase, the Pages received warranties from Ford Motor Company, which had manufactured the basic vehicle, and the Zimmer Corporation, which had installed various modifications transforming the vehicle into a conversion van. Treadwell, however, disclaimed all express or implied warranties. Soon after their purchase, the Pages discovered numerous problems with the van, finding a steady stream of leaks around the van's windshield and top and around its side and back doors. There was water damage to the interior. The Pages also discovered that, among other things, the motors controlling the passenger- and driver-side windows malfunctioned, rubber sealing around the back door had come loose, wall panels and a cabinet were broken, the television set and the interior lights would not work at the same time, the stereo speakers often did not work, molding around the television set was loose, the van rattled badly, the paint on the roof had faded, the gas gauge and the cruise control did not work, the front end was misaligned, and the van used three to five quarts of oil per month. On a regular basis the Pages began taking the van for repairs by Treadwell, the authorized agent for warranty work, traveling some 80 miles round trip with another vehicle to drive home each time. Eventually, many of the defects were repaired; but a number were not, with Treadwell indicating that there were certain problems that could not be corrected. The Pages attempted and failed to receive satisfaction through numerous letters and telephone conversations with Treadwell and Ford. In late 1987, the Pages gave notice to Treadwell of their desire to revoke acceptance of their purchase. Treadwell, however, refused to recognize the Pages' attempt at revocation. On 21 February 1989, the Pages filed suit against Treadwell, Ford, and Zimmer. The jury returned verdicts in favor of Ford and Zimmer, but found that the requisite elements of the revocation claim had been met. The court then permitted the revocation and assessed $7,500 in damages against Treadwell. The Pages and Treadwell appealed.

ISSUES Were the Pages entitled to revoke their acceptance after ten months without a showing of fraud or breach of warranty by the seller? If they were entitled to revoke, were they also entitled to any damages in this case?

HOLDINGS Yes. They were entitled to revoke their acceptance. Yes. They were entitled to damages.

REASONING A buyer has a reasonable time to "revoke his acceptance of a lot or commercial unit whose nonconformity substantially impairs its value to him." Treadwell contends . . . that the UCC confers upon a buyer a right to revoke acceptance only in instances where there has been fraud or breach of warranty on the part of the seller. . . . This court, however, does not read the Code that narrowly. This court . . . concludes that § 2-608 should properly be viewed as affording a remedy in situations where a seller has successfully disclaimed its own warranties. To hold otherwise would be to place the risk of loss on the buyer and to find little meaningful obligation on the part of the seller, who receives substantial benefits from the sale of its goods. . . . Our interpretation is also consistent with the principle that, when a buyer's remedy fails of its essential purpose, the buyer may resort to further remedies provided by the Code in order to gain the substantial value of the bargain.

We find that in order to revoke their acceptance, the Pages—once they had otherwise met the requirements of § 2-608—were obligated to show only that the van's nonconformity substantially impaired its value to them and that it was not necessary that they prove fraud or breach of warranty on the part of Treadwell.

The trial court erroneously awarded damages based on a difference-in-value formula, comparing the difference in value between the van as delivered and the van as warranted. A buyer who revokes acceptance of nonconforming goods may recover, in addition to any consideration paid on the contract, incidental and consequential damages. We hold as a matter of law that such damages are available and remand to the trial court for consideration of whether the Pages have sufficient proof of these damages.

Affirmed in part, reversed in part, and remanded with instructions.

19.4 PAGE v. DOBBS MOBILE BAY, INC. *(cont.)* 599 So.2d 38 (Ala.Civ. App. 1992)

BUSINESS CONSIDERATIONS As is seen in this case, the fact that the merchant disclaimed any and all warranties does not provide complete protection, since the dealer ended up with an unacceptable van that had been worked on by a van customizing company. How can a merchant protect its interests when it subcontracts for special additions to goods that it sells and the subcontracting party fails to properly install those special additions?

ETHICAL CONSIDERATIONS Is it ethical for the merchant to disclaim any responsibility for the custom work that is done on the merchant's goods when the merchant is the party paying the customizer and then collecting the full purchase price from the ultimate buyer? Is it ethical to expect the merchant to pay for problems caused by a third person, such as the customizing firm in this case, when the buyer knows that the merchant did not perform or inspect the work that was done? How can these interests be balanced?

Modifications

The parties to the contract are allowed to tailor their remedies to fit their particular contract and their particular circumstances. For example, the parties may, by expressly including it in the contract, provide for remedies in addition to the remedies provided by the Uniform Commercial Code. Or, they may provide for remedies in lieu of those provided by the Code. Or, they may place a limit on the remedies that may be used. If the parties so desire, they can select one remedy that is to be used as the exclusive remedy for their particular contract. (When an exclusive remedy is selected, it must be followed unless circumstances change so that the remedy no longer adequately covers the damages.)

Consequential damages may be excluded or limited by the parties in the contract. Such an agreement will be enforced unless the court finds it to be unconscionable. The parties may also provide for liquidated damages if the provision is reasonable, the difficulty of setting the loss is substantial, and establishing actual loss would be inconvenient, if not impossible. Of course, if the amount designated as liquidated damages is found unreasonable or unconscionable or is deemed to be a penalty, the clause is void.

Sometimes the seller justifiably withholds delivery from the buyer when the buyer has paid part of the contract price. In such a case, the buyer, even though in breach, can recover any payments made in excess of any liquidated damages called for in the contract, or, if there is no liquidated damages amount, the lesser of 20 percent of the total contract value or $500.

Special Problems

In determining when remedies may be obtained and what remedies to seek, several special problems may arise. The court may be asked to determine whether a breach has occurred or whether the contractual performance was excused. If there has been a breach, the courts may need to determine when it occurred. There may be a problem with the expectations of the parties or a question as to whether a party is capable of performing as scheduled. And sometimes there is just a special circumstance involved that requires special treatment.

(Anticipatory) Repudiation

Occasionally, one of the parties to a contract will repudiate his or her obligations before performance is due. If such a repudiation will substantially reduce the value expected to be received by the other party, the other party may choose one of three courses of conduct:

1. He or she may await performance for a commercially reasonable time despite the repudiation.
2. The nonrepudiating party may treat the repudiation as an immediate breach and seek any available remedies.
3. The nonrepudiating party may suspend his or her own performance under the contract until there is a resolution of the problem.

A repudiating party is allowed to retract the repudiation at any time up to and including the date performance is due, if the other party permits a retraction. No retraction is allowed if the nonrepudiating party has canceled the contract or has materially changed his or her position in reliance on the repudiation. A retraction re-establishes the contract rights and duties of each party.

Excused Performance

Sometimes a seller may be forced into a delay in making delivery, may not be able to make delivery, or may have to make only a partial delivery. Normally, this would be treated as a breach. Some of these situations fall into the area of excused performance, however, and hence are not treated as a breach. Performance is excused, in whole or in part, if performance has become impracticable because of the occurrence of some event whose nonoccurrence was a basic assumption of the contract. Also, performance is excused if the seller's delay or lack of performance is based on compliance with a governmental order or regulation.

If the seller has an excuse for less than full performance, the seller must notify the buyer seasonably. If performance will be reduced but not eliminated, the seller is allowed to allocate deliveries among customers in a reasonable manner. On receiving notice of a planned allocation due to some excuse, the buyer must elect whether to terminate the contract or to modify it. Modifying it means accepting the partial delivery as a substitute performance. A failure to modify within 30 days will be treated as a termination.

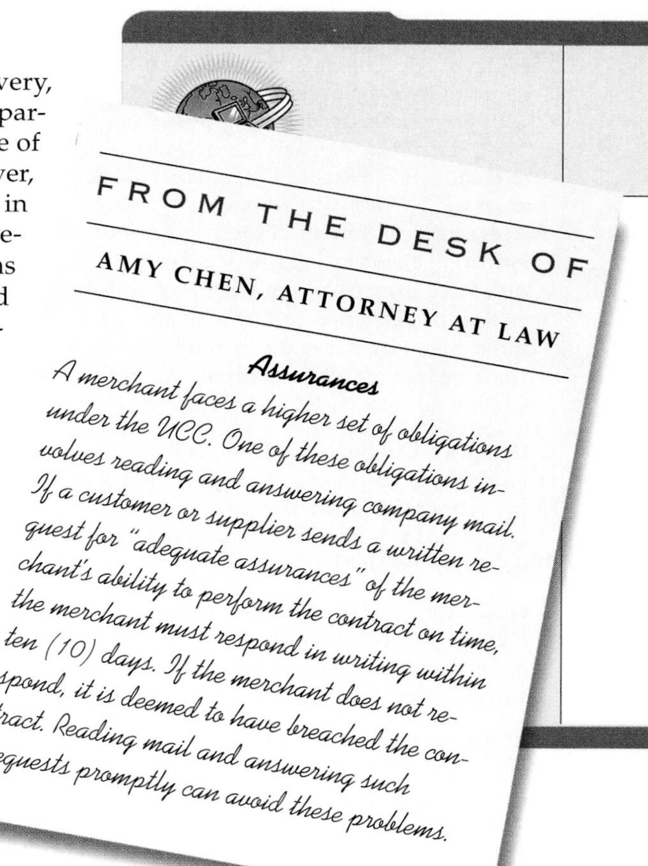

FROM THE DESK OF
AMY CHEN, ATTORNEY AT LAW
Assurances
A merchant faces a higher set of obligations under the UCC. One of these obligations involves reading and answering company mail. If a customer or supplier sends a written request for "adequate assurances" of the merchant's ability to perform the contract on time, the merchant must respond in writing within ten (10) days. If the merchant does not respond, it is deemed to have breached the contract. Reading mail and answering such requests promptly can avoid these problems.

Adequate Assurances

When the parties enter a contract for the sale of goods, each expects to receive the benefit of the bargain made. If, before performance is due, either party feels insecure in expecting performance, the insecure party may demand assurances of performance. The insecure party must make a written demand for assurance that

Suspend
To cause to cease for a time; to become inoperative for a time; to stop temporarily.

performance will be tendered when due. Until the assurances are given, the requesting party may **suspend** performance. If no assurance is given within thirty days of request, it is treated as repudiation of the contract.

The following case involved an "adequate assurances" issue, as well as an issue as to whether a proper demand for adequate assurances was made.

19.5 S & S, INC. v. MEYER

478 N.W.2d 857 (Iowa App. 1991)

FACTS Star Grain had been a licensed Iowa grain dealer, but lost its license on 1 July 1988 when its principal officers and owners were indicted by an Illinois grand jury for defrauding customers and defaulting on certain checks. The defendants in this case were all farmers who had, prior to 1 July 1988, entered into contracts with Star Grain calling for them to deliver various amounts of grain in October and November 1988. When Star Grain had its license suspended, it sought relief under Chapter 11 of the Bankruptcy Code. The defendants objected to Star Grain's attempt to have the bankruptcy court enforce their contracts with Star Grain as debtor-in-possession. On 7 October 1988, Star Grain assigned its contracts with the defendants to Duffe Grain, a licensed grain dealer. Duffe then contacted all of the parties with whom Star Grain had futures contracts, informing them of the assignment and providing information on when and where delivery was to be tendered. All of the farmers except the three defendants ultimately delivered their grain to Duffe as per the assignment. The three defendants eventually sold their grain elsewhere; Duffe reassigned their contracts to Star Grain, and Star Grain sued each for breach of contract.

ISSUES Did the letter from Duffe to the farmers constitute proper notice of a change in delivery to be binding on the farmers? Did the farmers properly demand adequate assurances that the contracts would be performed, as required by the UCC?

HOLDINGS No. Iowa law mandates that a change in delivery is valid only if made "without fault of either party." Here, Star Grain was at fault, so the change was improper. Yes. The demanded assurances were properly made.

REASONING The contracts in question here were valid when made and could have been valid when performed, either through the reinstatement of the license of Star Grain or through a valid assignment of the contracts to another licensed grain dealer. Thus, the simplest solution—declaring the contracts void upon the suspension of Star Grain's license—was not a viable solution to the problem. However, when Star Grain had its license revoked, it became at fault in the proposed changes to the delivery terms for the farmers. This constituted an anticipatory repudiation, and the farmers were free to treat their contracts as breached at that point in time. The court also determined that the farmers had reason to feel insecure—the bankruptcy of the buyer, the criminal proceedings against the officers of the buyer, and the license suspension of the buyer—in their contracts and to seek adequate assurances. It was stated that assurances were demanded in writing (although no such written demands were introduced into evidence), but that no assurances were given. When a party does not provide the assurances demanded, the insecure party is allowed to treat this as a repudiation. Thus, on two different grounds, the farmers were entitled to view the contract as repudiated.

BUSINESS CONSIDERATIONS A party that demands adequate assurances in a sales contract is likely to find out well in advance of the performance date whether it can properly expect performance as agreed. This permits the requesting party to protect itself. What are the arguments for and against requesting adequate assurance in *every* contract with a performance date six months or more in the future? When should a firm seek adequate assurances from the other party?

ETHICAL CONSIDERATIONS Suppose that a party to a sales contract realizes after the contract is made, but well in advance of the performance date, that the contract will result in a financial loss. From an ethical perspective, should that firm request adequate assurance, hoping that the other party will not respond, thus excusing itself from the duty to perform? Explain your reasoning.

Duty to Particularize

When the buyer rightfully rejects goods, the buyer must do so properly. If the goods are rejected owing to a curable defect, the buyer may reject only by stating exactly what the defect is. A failure to do so will preclude the use of that defect to prove breach in court. And if the buyer cannot prove breach, the seller will be deemed to have performed properly. Thus, a failure to particularize can result in the buyer's being required to pay for nonconforming goods or in other liability to the seller.

STATUTE OF LIMITATIONS

Any lawsuit for breach of a sales contract must be started within four years of the breach, unless the contract itself sets a shorter time period. (The time period cannot be less than one year.) The fact that a breach is not discovered when it occurs is not material. The time limitation begins at breach, not at discovery. This reemphasizes the need for a buyer to inspect goods carefully and completely in order to protect his or her interests.

LEASES

Article 2A provides for remedies in the event a lease contract is breached. As under Article 2, the remedies available depend to a significant extent on when the breach occurs. A brief synopsis of the remedies is set out below.

Lessor's Remedies

If a lessee wrongfully rejects goods tendered under the lease, wrongfully revokes acceptance, fails to make payments when due, or repudiates the lease, the lessor may:

1. cancel the lease contract
2. proceed respecting goods not identified to the lease contract
3. withhold delivery of the goods and take possession of goods previously delivered
4. stop delivery of the goods by any bailee
5. dispose of the goods and recover damages, or retain the goods and recover damages, or, in a property case, recover rent

If a lessee is otherwise in default, the lessor may exercise the rights and remedies provided in the lease, as well as those listed in Article 2A.

19.3

HANDLING COMPLAINTS FROM RETAILERS

One of the retail outlets that purchased a number of Call-Image videophones has been very difficult to please. The sales manager of the store recently wrote a letter to the firm in which he alleged that the videophones were "unacceptable as delivered" and demanded that CIT send a truck to pick up the shipment because his store was not going to carry them or sell them any longer. Tom immediately called the sales manager to find out why the units were "unacceptable as delivered," but he could not get any more concrete information from the sales manager as to what the alleged problem was. Dan and Anna want to rent a truck and go recover the units. They are willing to accept the fact that this one store does not want to carry the product, cancel their contract, and go on. Lindsay and John believe that the sales manager is acting improperly, and they want the firm to refuse to go get the units or to cancel the contract. They would prefer to sue, if need be, to get the money called for in the contract. They have asked for your opinion. What advice will you give them?

BUSINESS CONSIDERATIONS What are the contractual rights of a merchant who is notified by one of its customers that a product delivered under a contract is unacceptable as delivered? Does it make any difference whether the customer is a merchant or a nonmerchant? What sort of policy should a firm have to handle situations such as this?

ETHICAL CONSIDERATIONS A number of retail establishments have a "money-back guarantee," under which they allow customers to return merchandise for a refund with "no questions asked." Suppose that an employee of the store knows that a customer has purchased a product with the intention of only using it one time and then returning it for a refund. Could that employee refuse to give the customer a refund on ethical grounds? How should such a situation be handled, from an ethical perspective?

SALES/MANAGEMENT

Lessee's Remedies

If a lessor fails to deliver goods in conformity with the lease contract or repudiates the lease contract, or the lessee rightfully rejects the goods or justifiably revokes acceptance of the goods, then the lessee may:

1. cancel the lease contract
2. recover as much of the rent and security as has been paid; but in the case of an installment lease contract, the recovery is that which is just under the circumstances
3. cover and recover damages as to all goods affected, whether or not they have been identified to the lease contract, or recover damages for nondelivery

If the lessor fails to deliver the goods or repudiates the contract, the lessee may also:

1. recover any goods that have been identified to the contract
2. obtain specific performance or replevin

If the lessor is otherwise in default under a lease contract, the lessee may exercise the rights and remedies provided in the lease contract and/or those included in Article 2A.

YOU BE THE JUDGE

Bennett Funding Group Sued for More than One Billion Dollars

The Bennett Funding Group, Inc., attracted thousands of investors by seemingly offering tremendous returns on investments. Bennett sold leases on equipment. Unfortunately, the equipment that was supposedly covered by the leases did not exist. In addition, Bennett inflated its financial statements to attract investors. The Securities and Exchange Commission (SEC) filed a civil suit against the firm in which it alleged that Bennett sold $570 million in fraudulent securities. Because of the civil suit, Bennett filed a voluntary petition for relief under the provisions of the Bankrupty Act. Now the trustee in bankruptcy has filed suit against the owner of Bennett Funding seeking more than one billion dollars in damages.

This case is being argued in *your* court. How will you decide the case?

BUSINESS CONSIDERATIONS Selling leases is no longer regulated purely by common law provisions. Businesses that deal with leases now need to become familiar with Article 2A of the UCC. How does Article 2A affect this area of law? What provisions of Article 2A are of special importance in this case?

ETHICAL CONSIDERATIONS It appears that the investors were attracted to the Bennett Fund with promises of very large returns on their investments. While the reason for investing is to receive a return on the investment, there are two old adages that seem to apply to situations like this: (1) when something seems too good to be true, it probably is; and (2) *caveat emptor.* How much of the blame for the situation in these cases should be placed on the investors?

SOURCE: *Wall Street Journal* (10 July 1996), p. B10.

http:// RESOURCES FOR BUSINESS LAW STUDENTS

NAME	RESOURCES	WEB ADDRESS
Uniform Commercial Code (UCC) Articles 7, Warehouse Receipts, Bills of Lading, and other Documents of Title	The Legal Information Institute (LII), maintained by the Cornell Law School, provides a hypertext and searchable version of Article 7, Warehouse Receipts, Bills of Lading, and other Documents of Title. LII also maintains links to Article 7 as adopted by particular states and to proposed revisions.	http://www.law.cornell.edu/ucc/7/overview.html
UCC Article 2A, Leases	LII provides a hypertext and searchable version of the UCC Article 2A, Leases. LII also provides links to Article 2A as enacted by particular states and to proposed revisions.	http://www.law.cornell.edu/ucc/2A/overview.html

Summary

Although most sales contracts are fully performed and the performance is normally satisfactory, sometimes a nonperformance occurs. When nonperformance is found, the innocent party usually seeks remedies for breach of contract.

When the buyer fails to perform, the seller will seek remedies. The available remedies depend on when the buyer breached. If the buyer breached before acceptance, the seller will seek one or more of six preacceptance remedies. If the buyer accepts the goods and then breaches, the seller will seek one or both of two postacceptance remedies. By the same token, if the seller breaches, the buyer will seek remedies. Again, the buyer's available remedies will depend on when the seller breached. If the seller breached before the buyer accepted the goods, the buyer may seek one or more of six preacceptance remedies. If the seller breaches after the buyer accepts, the buyer has up to three available postacceptance remedies.

Occasionally, a nonperformance turns out not to be a breach. It may involve a special problem that excuses performance or affects the rights of the innocent party. Great care must be exercised by both parties in these special problem areas.

Leases are also normally performed properly by both parties. Again, however, sometimes breaches occur. When they do, the breaching party is held liable for those damages that the nonbreaching party suffers. Article 2A lists specific remedies that are available, and also specifically states that the parties are entitled to those damages called for in the lease contract as well as any of the remedies listed in the article. These Code remedies are very similar in nature and application to the remedies provided by Article 2.

Injunction *pendente lite*
A preliminary injunction pending a suit.

Discussion Questions

1. What remedies can a seller seek if the buyer breaches a sales contract before the buyer has accepted the goods? Are these remedies mutually exclusive?
2. What are the seller's two potential postacceptance remedies, and when may the seller utilize either or both of them?

3. What are the three possible postacceptance remedies available to the buyer, and when may the buyer utilize each of them? Are these remedies mutually exclusive?
4. What is an anticipatory repudiation, and how does it affect contracts formed under the law of sales? Does a repudiation have the same meaning and impact under the law of leases?
5. What is meant by a duty to particularize, and how does this duty affect the rights of the parties to a sales contract?
6. Ace Manufacturing agreed to produce and sell some goods to Sampson. The contract called for 10 shipments of 25 units each. After satisfactorily completing 5 shipments, Ace sent the sixth shipment. Order 7 was then "in process." Sampson wrongfully rejected shipment 6. Ace decided to complete the work on order 7 and to sue Sampson for the contract price on shipments 6 and 7 and for lost profits on the remaining three shipments. Sampson argued that Ace could not complete order 7 at his (Sampson's) expense. Who is correct? Explain.
7. Tom shipped goods to Martin via Allied Parcel Service. After the goods were shipped, Tom discovered that Martin was insolvent. What can Tom do in this situation to prevent Martin from receiving the goods? What obligation does Tom have to Allied? Suppose that Tom discovered that Martin had repudiated the contract. Would Tom have the same rights in that situation?
8. Roberto, the seller, was in possession of goods that Suzanne had wrongfully rejected. Roberto sold the goods to Brenda for one-half the contract price without telling anyone about the sale. Can Roberto collect the unpaid balance of the contract price from Suzanne? Does Suzanne have a claim against Roberto for damages even though Suzanne had initially breached the contract? Explain.
9. Bob and Sam entered into a contract that called for Sam to deliver goods to Bob and for Bob to pay $1,500 for the goods. Bob gave Sam a $500 deposit on the goods. During the contract period, Sam discovered that Bob was insolvent and decided to withhold delivery of the goods to Bob. While Bob admits that he is in breach, he also asserts that he is entitled to restitution for his deposit on the goods. Is Bob entitled to restitution, and, if so, how much can he recover from Sam? Explain.
10. Martha entered into a contract with Amy that called for Amy to manufacture and deliver goods to Martha, with delivery to occur in six months. Three months later, Martha phoned Amy and repudiated the contract. At the time, Martha thought she could obtain the goods from another source at a substantially lower price. When Martha realized that her repudiation would operate as a breach, she immediately called Amy, apologized for her conduct, and attempted to retract her repudiation. What are Amy's rights in this case? What are Martha's rights in this case?

CASE PROBLEMS AND WRITING ASSIGNMENTS

1. In January, Stridiron purchased a new Renault automobile from Island Motors. Less than two weeks later, Stridiron returned the car to Island Motors for repairs due to an oil leak. Island kept the car for five days while making the necessary repairs. Two months later, Stridiron again returned the car to Island, this time for replacement of the roller gears in the electric sun roof of the car. These repairs took two days. In May, Stridiron returned the car because the engine stalled every time the car was shifted into third gear. The alternator, regulator, and battery had to be replaced to solve this problem. Stridiron received his car back on 11 June. Three days later, it had to be towed back to Island because it would not start. Finally, in September, all needed repairs were completed on the automobile. At that time, Stridiron returned the keys to the Renault to Island Motors and informed Island Motors that he was revoking his acceptance. Island refused to take possession of the car. Stridiron then sued, seeking to revoke his acceptance and to recover his money. He claimed that hidden defects in the automobile substantially impaired its value to him. Island Motors objected, claiming that it had not been given a reasonable opportunity to cure the defects, and that revocation was not appropriate in this case. Should Stridiron be allowed to revoke his acceptance of the automobile under these circumstances? Explain your answer. [See *Stridiron* v. *I.M., Inc.*, 578 F.Supp. 997 (1984).]

2. Hurd Lock is a manufacturer of locks for motor vehicles. In February 1984, Hurd Lock entered into a contract with Ford Motor Company to manufacture and provide certain locks for Ford vehicles. To carry out its duties, Hurd Lock entered into a contract to purchase certain manufacturing equipment from Oak Ridge Precision Instruments, Inc. Oak Ridge delivered equipment, but the equipment did not conform to the contract specifications. Hurd Lock elected to set off its damages from the breach against the balance it still

owed Oak Ridge on the original contract. First Tennessee Bank, a secured creditor of Oak Ridge, objected to the setoff and sued to recover the balance owed on the original contract between Hurd Lock and Oak Ridge. Did the court err in allowing Hurd Lock to use lost profits in reaching the amount it recouped in the contract? [See *First Tennessee Bank Nat'l Ass'n* v. *Hurd Lock & Mfg.*, 816 S.W.2d 38 (Tenn.App. 1991).]

3. Banque Arabe et Internationale d'Investissement (BAII) financed an agreement involving the buying and selling of petroleum. Will Petroleum was a small oil trading company that specialized in "blending." Will would purchase unfinished oil, add a component to boost octane, and then sell the oil to petroleum companies. In order to finance its operations, Will borrowed money from various banks, including BAII. When Will sold the oil after blending, the buyer would send a check to BAII, which would credit its account to repay Will's loan and then credit Will's account with the balance of the check, reflecting Will's profit on the deal. BAII had been involved in more than 50 such transactions between Will and UPG over the years. Will and UPG entered another such agreement in December 1985, with BAII providing the financing. However, UPG became concerned that Will would be unable to perform as agreed and requested assurances from Will as to its ability to meet its obligations. When Will did not provide the necessary assurances, UPG covered by purchasing its oil needs from another firm. As a result, BAII never received payment from UPG as expected. Will Petroleum filed for bankruptcy in February 1986 and assigned its rights under the contracts to BAII. When UPG refused to honor the contracts assigned to BAII, BAII sold the oil to other buyers for approximately $5.5 million less than the agreement between Will and UPG specified. BAII then filed suit against UPG for the difference. Did UPG breach its contract with Will, providing the assignee under that contract with rights against UPG? Explain your answer. [See *BAII Banking Corp.* v. *UPG, Inc.*, 985 F.2d 685 (2d Cir. 1993).]

4. Young had been cutting evergreen boughs on Michigan farms and selling them in the Toledo area since 1971. After he had built up a customer base of 25 to 30, he began selling boughs to Frank's Nursery in 1975. From 1976 through 1987, Young dealt exclusively with Frank's. Young's sales grew from $10,224 in 1976 to an order from Frank's totaling $238,332.85 in 1988. After receiving the order, Young began to prepare to fill it. He obtained cutting rights for enough boughs to fill the 360-ton order, repaired his machinery, and made 75 new hand tyers with which to tie the bundles. Then, on 30 June 1987, Frank's mailed Young a new purchase order in which it reduced its order to about 70 tons, cutting the price from more than $328,000 to less than $60,000. Young attempted to find other buyers, but was unable to do so. Young filed suit 7 October 1987, seeking damages for breach of contract. Did Frank's breach the contract with Young? If so, what damages is Young entitled to receive? How should damages be calculated in a case such as this? [See *Young* v. *Frank's Nursery & Crafts, Inc.*, 569 N.E.2d 1034 (Ohio 1991).]

5. Mancini was hired as a subcontractor to perform improvements on a building owned by Cornell University. After obtaining the job, Mancini entered into an agreement with Milligan under which Milligan was to furnish to Mancini all the materials required to finish the job. Although Milligan agreed to furnish all field measurements that were required, these measurements were, in fact, provided by Mancini. Milligan used these measurements to determine the quantities of tackable wall panels to be shipped to Mancini. The first shipment of panels was delivered in August 1988. Mancini notified Milligan that the panels were the wrong size and that they had inadequate Velcro adhesive attached to them. Despite these complaints, Mancini paid the invoice for these panels when he received it. Two more shipments of panels were sent, invoiced, and paid in October. The final shipment was sent in January 1989, with the invoice sent soon thereafter. Mancini held this invoice for six weeks, then sent a letter of protest to Milligan. This letter stated that the square footage of the panels did not match the square footage listed on the invoices. As a result, Mancini requested a refund for alleged overpayments as well as payment for labor allegedly performed to re-install panels with adequate Velcro. Milligan refused to make these payments; and when Mancini did not pay, Milligan filed suit for the balance due. Mancini counterclaimed for damages. How should the court resolve this case? What could either (or both) of the parties have done to simplify this matter and avoid resorting to a court to settle their claims? [See *B. Milligan Contracting, Inc.* v. *Andrew R. Mancini Assoc., Inc.*, 578 N.Y.S.2d 931 (A.D. 3 Dept 1992).]

6. **BUSINESS APPLICATION CASE** Gradall manufactured and sold a small four-wheel drive vehicle known as the 534B, primarily used in construction, where its maneuverability makes it ideal for delivering materials to workers on construction sites. The 534B requires a four-cylinder, turbocharged diesel engine. From 1982 to 1985, Gradall purchased its engines from Dresser. Each time Gradall ordered engines, it sent Dresser a purchase order containing its (Gradall's) terms on

price, delivery date and location, quantity, and warranty coverage. The purchase orders stated that acceptance of the order constituted an acceptance of all of Gradall's terms. Dresser would then respond with an order acknowledgment form that stated it would accept the offer, but only on its (Dresser's) terms, as set forth on the form. Needless to say, the terms on the two forms were quite different. Dresser's form disclaimed all implied warranties and limited its express warranties to one year. Gradall's form included all implied warranties and called for a 15-month express warranty. Without attempting to resolve this discrepancy, the parties acted as if a contract existed. Dresser shipped engines and Gradall paid for them. Beginning in 1983, many of Gradall's customers began to experience problems with the Dresser engines. Dresser and Gradall met to discuss how to handle the problem and reached an agreement. Gradall would repair any problems unrelated to the engines, and Dresser would sell Gradall new oil pump kits to repair defective oil pumps that appeared to be the root of the problem. However, Dresser stopped delivering the oil pump kits in an effort to force Gradall to agree to additional terms. Gradall then decided to purchase its engines from another company. At that point, Dresser sued Gradall for any unpaid balances and sought a declaratory judgment as to the contract rights of the two parties. What were the warranty terms of the contracts between the parties? Which of the parties was entitled to damages? How should these damages be figured? [See *Dresser Industries, Inc., Waukesha Engine Div.* v. *The Gradall Co.*, 965 F.2d 1442 (1992).]

7. **ETHICS APPLICATION CASE** Burberrys had an agreement with Abraham Zion Corp. under which Zion was to manufacture 30,000 Burberry raincoats for Burberrys. Burberrys raincoats are of a unique design and style, and their trademarks are registered in the United States. Burberrys provided the distinctive material, patterns, styles, data, labels, tags, and documents necessary for making the raincoats; and 22,000 of the raincoats were produced by Zion. Then, a dispute arose between the parties, and their relationship ceased. Burberrys now alleges that Zion plans to produce the remaining 8,000 raincoats and sell them to After Six. Burberrys sued, seeking an **injunction *pendente lite*** (preliminary injunction pending the suit) to prevent the manufacture and/or sale of the remaining 8,000 raincoats. Should Zion be allowed to complete manufacture of the remaining goods called for under the contract and then resell them as a seller's preacceptance remedy? What ethical considerations enter into your resolution of this case? [See *Burberrys (Wholesale) Ltd.* v. *After Six, Inc.*, 471 N.Y.S.2d 235 (Sup. 1984).]

8. **IDES CASE** Mass Cash is a Massachusetts corporation that sells, installs, and services electronic cash registers. In 1990, Mass Cash was a dealer for various companies that produced point-of-sale (POS) equipment and cash registers. Comtrex is a New Jersey corporation with its principal place of business in Moorestown, New Jersey. Formed in 1981, Comtrex originally serviced cash registers, but expanded its business to include the manufacturing, marketing, and distribution of electronic cash registers used in the fast-food industry. In 1993, Comtrex sold approximately 3500 electronic cash registers. Beginning in 1978, Mass Cash sold cash registers and POS machines to Dunkin' Donuts, selling some 2500 registers to Dunkin' Donuts from 1985 to 1990. Dunkin' Donuts was Mass Cash's largest major account. In 1988, Dunkin' Donuts informed Mass Cash that it needed a new POS terminal with certain characteristics. Mass Cash began to search for a manufacturer who could produce the type of POS terminal needed by Dunkin' Donuts, finally finding one in Comtrex. Mass Cash then proceeded to negotiate with Comtrex as to the viability of having Comtrex produce the POS terminals, selling them to Mass Cash, which would then sell them to Dunkin' Donuts. Comtrex assured Mass Cash that it (Comtrex) did not sell directly to the customers. Then, in 1990, Comtrex met directly with Dunkin' Donuts—without Mass Cash. Following this meeting, Comtrex prepared a proposal for meeting the POS needs of Dunkin' Donuts. Eventually Comtrex entered into a contract with Dunkin' Donuts under which Comtrex agreed to sell and service the POS terminals. Mass Cash was excluded from the contract. Mass Cash then sued Comtrex, alleging breach of contract, tortious interference with contract relations, fraud, and unjust enrichment. How should this case be resolved? Apply the IDES principles to analyze this case and render your verdict. [See *Mass Cash Register, Inc.* v. *Comtrex Systems Corp.*, 901 F.Supp. 404 (1995).]

International Sale of Goods

O U T L I N E

- Introduction
- The United Nations Convention on Contracts for the International Sale of Goods
- Obligations Under the CISG
- Remedies Under the CISG
- ISO 9000
- Ethical Issues in the International Sale of Goods
- Standard Shipping Terms in International Trade (Incoterms)
- Proposed International Coverage
- Summary
- Discussion Questions
- Case Problems and Writing Assignments

A G E N D A

Suppose that CIT solves its initial problems and achieves success locally and regionally. How can the firm place the invention in the international market? What statute(s) will regulate the sale of Call-Image internationally? When will the sales be governed by the UCC? The CISG?

These and other questions will arise during our discussion of sales contracts. Be prepared! You never know when one of the Kochanowskis will call on you for advice or guidance.

INTRODUCTION

Business is rapidly "going global," with international trade increasing each year. A significant portion of international trade involves the sale of goods, with the balance comprised of services. Whether goods or services are involved, the trade entails contracts between the parties. Most of these contracts will be performed with little or no problems—at least legally. However, some of these contracts will not be performed or will not be performed satisfactorily, and legal issues will arise due to the inadequate performance. These legal issues may well present legal problems beyond the "mere" problem of the alleged breach of contract.

There are more than 100 separate nations today, each with its own (somewhat) unique legal system. Familiarity with each of these legal systems would be impractical at best. Yet a person who does business with a person in another nation may be subject to the laws of that other nation in a contract action.

To reduce the complexity somewhat, there are a few overriding legal theories that provide the basis for most—if not all—of the legal systems in the world. A number of countries base their legal systems on a common law tradition in which the law is provided by court cases and statutes used in combination. Legislation is enacted by the government, but that legislation is subject to interpretation by the courts. In addition, areas that are not specifically covered by legislation are interpreted by the courts, and the gaps in the law are filled by court opinions. Common law originated in England and is the basis for the legal systems in Australia, Canada, England, the United States, and a number of other nations that are—or were—closely allied with England in the past.

A second basis for law is found in civil law nations. A civil law nation bases its law and its legal theory on the codes of the nation. The legislation is meant to provide exclusive coverage of a topic. Judicial interpretation is not a major factor in civil law nations, and the courts are not concerned with precedents from prior judicial opinions. Most of Europe follows the civil law tradition, with their systems based on the Napoleonic Code.

Islamic law forms a third basis for law. Islamic law is based on the religious beliefs and doctrines of Islam. Many Middle East nations base their legal systems on Islamic law, and this legal theory has influenced the development of legal systems in a number of developing nations.

A significant part of Eastern Europe and Asia is still influenced by communist or socialist philosophies. These philosophies form an important component of the legal systems in some nations.

In addition, there are many different languages used in the world. Communication between people who speak different languages can make international trade more difficult than national trade between people who share a common language and a culture.

The following case is a classic in the area of international sales. The case involves parties from three different nations, and each party used a different language for the formation of the contract. Ironically, the central controversy involved the definition of a seemingly simple term: *chicken.*

As the *Frigaliment* case indicates, the potential for confusion or misunderstanding as to what meaning is in effect in a given contract is present with any international sales contract. Determining which laws are in effect and need to be followed also provides for potential confusion or misunderstanding to a much greater extent in international trade than in domestic trade. This potential for confusion, in turn, has had a negative impact on the growth and development of international trade. Something new was needed to reflect the increasingly international nature of business as the twentieth century progressed. This "something new" became the United Nations Convention on Contracts for the International Sale of Goods, the CISG.

20.1 FRIGALIMENT IMPORTING CO. v. B.N.S. INT'L SALES CORP. 190 F.Supp. 116 (S.D.N.Y. 1960)

FACTS Stovicek, a representative of the Czechoslovak government, was in New York at the World Trade Fair, where he met Bauer, the secretary of B.N.S. Several days later, Stovicek contacted Bauer to see if B.N.S. would be interested in exporting chicken to Switzerland. Frigaliment, a . . . Swiss firm represented by Stovicek, offered to purchase "25,000 lbs. of chicken 2½–3 lbs. weight, Cryovac packed, grade A government-inspected, at a price up to 33 cents per pound," and stated an interest in further offerings. B.N.S. accepted the offer, and Frigaliment sent a confirmation the following morning. The cables exchanged by the parties were predominantly in German, although the English word "chicken" was used to avoid confusion. (The German word "huhn" includes both broilers and stewing chickens.) B.N.S. sent a total of 175,000 pounds of chicken to Frigaliment under the two contracts the parties entered. Frigaliment objected to the tendered delivery, alleging that the "heavier" chickens (125,000 pounds of 2½–3-pound chickens) were not young chickens suitable for broiling or frying, but were older, stewing chickens, or "fowl." Frigaliment sued for breach of warranty, alleging that the goods delivered did not correspond to the description of the goods as established by trade usage. B.N.S. denied a breach, asserting that it delivered goods that corresponded to the contract term "chicken."

ISSUE The issue is, what is chicken? Or, more specifically, did the goods tendered by B.N.S. satisfy the description of the term *chicken* as used in the contract?

HOLDING Yes. Frigaliment failed to persuade the court that the word *chicken* meant only young chickens suitable for broiling and frying.

REASONING The issue is, what is chicken? Plaintiff says "chicken" means a young chicken, suitable for broiling and frying. Defendant says "chicken" means any bird of that genus that meets contract specifications on weight and quality, including what it calls "stewing chicken" and plaintiff pejoratively terms "fowl." Dictionaries give both meanings, as well as some others not relevant here. To support its claim, plaintiff sends a number of volleys over the Internet; defendant essays to return them and adds a few serves of its own. Assuming that both parties were acting in good faith, the case nicely illustrates Holmes's remark "that the making of a contract depends not on the agreement of two minds in one intention, but on the agreement of two sets of external signs—not on the parties' having *meant* the same thing but on their having *said* the same thing. . . ." I have concluded that the plaintiff has not sustained its burden of persuasion that the contract used "chicken" in the narrow sense.

The action is for breach of the warranty that goods sold shall correspond to the description. Two contracts are in suit. In the first, dated 2 May 1957, defendant, a New York sales corporation, confirmed the sale to plaintiff, a Swiss corporation, of

> *US Fresh Frozen Chicken, Grade A, Government Inspected, Eviscerated 2 ½ - 3 lbs. And 1 ½ - 2 lbs. Each*
>
> *all chicken individually wrapped in Cryovac, packed in secured fiber cartons or wooden boxes, suitable for export*
>
> *75,000 lbs 2 ½ - 3 lbs @ $33.00*
>
> *25,000 lbs 1 ½ - 2 lbs @ $36.50*
>
> *per 100 lbs FAS New York*
>
> *Scheduled May 10, 1957, pursuant to instructions from Penson & Co., New York.*

The second contract, also dated 2 May 1957, was identical save that only 50,000 lbs. of the heavier "chicken" were called for, the price of the smaller birds was $37 per 100 lbs., and shipment was scheduled for 30 May. The initial shipment under the first contract was short but the balance was shipped on 17 May. When the initial shipment arrived in Switzerland, plaintiff found, on 28 May, that the 2½–3-lb. birds were not young chicken suitable for broiling and frying but stewing chicken or "fowl"; indeed many of the cartons and bags plainly so indicated. Protests ensued. Nevertheless, shipment under the second contract was made on 29 May, the 2½–3-lb. birds again being stewing chicken. Defendant stopped the transportation of these at Rotterdam.

This action followed. Plaintiff says that, notwithstanding that its acceptance was in Switzerland, New York law controls. Defendant does not dispute this, and relies on New York decisions. I shall follow the apparent agreement of the

20.1 FRIGALIMENT IMPORTING CO. v. B.N.S. INT'L SALES CORP. *(cont.)* 190 F.Supp. 116 (S.D.N.Y. 1960)

parties as to the applicable law. Since the word "chicken" standing alone is ambiguous, I turn first to see whether the contract itself offers any aid to its interpretation. Plaintiff says that 1½–2-lb. birds necessarily had to be young chickens since the older birds do not come in that size, hence the 2½–3-lb. birds must likewise be young. This is unpersuasive—a contract for "apples" of two different sizes could be filled with different kinds of apples even though only one species came in both sizes. Defendant notes that the contract called not simply for "chickens" but for "US Fresh Frozen Chicken, Grade A, Government Inspected." It says the contract thereby incorporated by reference the Department of Agriculture's regulations, which favor its interpretation. . . .

When all the evidence is reviewed, it is clear that defendant believed it could comply with the contracts by delivering stewing chicken in the 2½–3-lb. size. Defendant's subjective intent would not be significant if this did not coincide with an objective meaning of "chicken." Here it did coincide with one of the dictionary meanings, with the definition in the Department of Agriculture's regulations to which the contract made at least oblique reference, with at least some usage in the trade, with the realities of the market, and with what plaintiff's spokesman had said. Plaintiff asserts it to be equally plain that plaintiff's own subjective intent was to obtain broilers and fryers; the only evidence against this is the material as to market prices and this may not have been sufficiently brought home. In any event, it is unnecessary to determine that issue. For plaintiff has the burden of showing that "chicken" was used in the narrower rather than in the broader sense, and this it has not sustained.

This opinion constitutes the Court's findings of fact and conclusions of law. Judgment shall be entered dismissing the complaint with costs.

BUSINESS CONSIDERATIONS One of the potential problems in international trade is the likelihood of misunderstandings when the parties to a contract speak different languages. What should a business do to minimize the risk of misunderstandings due to the fact that the other party to a contract speaks a different language?

ETHICAL CONSIDERATIONS Is it ethical for a U.S. business to insist that any contracts it enters into with firms from other nations be written in English rather than in the language of the other nation? Should the contract be drafted in both languages to ensure that each party is dealing with a contract written in its native tongue?

THE UNITED NATIONS CONVENTION ON CONTRACTS FOR THE INTERNATIONAL SALE OF GOODS

The CISG was drafted at the behest of the United Nations to provide for international sales what Article 2 of the Uniform Commercial Code (UCC) provides in the United States for domestic sales, a uniform set of rules governing sales contracts. There had been earlier attempts to provide regulations for international sales, most notably the efforts arising from the international diplomatic conference in The Hague in 1964. In fact, beginning in 1930, the International Institute for the Unification of Private Law (UNIDROIT) began work on a uniform law regulating the international sale of goods. Following World War II, the draft prepared by UNIDROIT was submitted to the diplomatic conference at The Hague. This conference drafted two conventions, one dealing with the international sale of goods (ULIS) and one dealing with the formation of contracts for the international sale of goods (ULF). Both conventions eventually were ratified by several nations, and each went into effect in 1972. However, neither ever received widespread acceptance, being limited almost exclusively to European ratifiers.

Even before either of these conventions went into effect, the United Nations instituted the Conference on International Trade (UNCITRAL) in 1968, charging this conference with the task of unifying the international law governing sales. To help ensure broader acceptance of its actions, the conference was composed of representatives from numerous countries, with broad diversity in the legal traditions and the economic status of the represented states. Initially, UNCITRAL tried to modify ULIS to make it more widely acceptable. However, this effort soon proved hopeless, and UNCITRAL began work on two new conventions to replace the ULIS and the ULF.

Meeting once a year, UNCITRAL took nine years to prepare draft conventions dealing with the international sale of goods and with the formation of international sales contracts. These two drafts were combined into one draft **convention** in 1978, and that combined convention was submitted to an official diplomatic convention convened in Vienna in 1980 by the United Nations General Assembly.

The final language of the CISG was approved at the Vienna Conference in 1980. Sixty-two nations participated in the Vienna conference, and these nations helped in the drafting of the Convention. By having such broad participation (one commentator characterized the participants as 22 Western nations, 11 socialist nations, and 29 third-world nations[1]), the Convention provides compromise standards that should eventually prove acceptable to most of the world. There were 20 signatory nations, including the United States. (The U.S. Senate unanimously ratified the CISG in 1986.) The CISG became effective 1 January 1988 for all of the ratifying nations.

As of March 1997, 50 nations had signed and/or ratified the Convention. These nations are listed in Exhibit 20.1.[2]

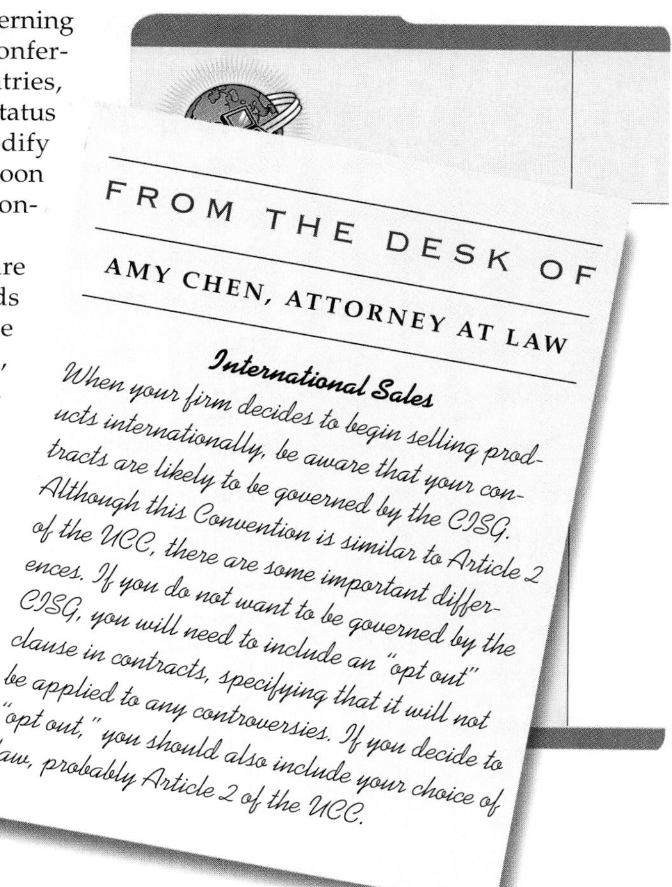

FROM THE DESK OF
AMY CHEN, ATTORNEY AT LAW
International Sales
When your firm decides to begin selling products internationally, be aware that your contracts are likely to be governed by the CISG. Although this Convention is similar to Article 2 of the UCC, there are some important differences. If you do not want to be governed by the CISG, you will need to include an "opt out" clause in contracts, specifying that it will not be applied to any controversies. If you decide to "opt out," you should also include your choice of law, probably Article 2 of the UCC.

Convention
An agreement between nations; a treaty.

Domestically, there are numerous legal traditions that various nations follow, and there are various levels of economic development among the member nations of the United Nations. Both of these differences present problems in deriving a uniform set of laws to govern the international sale of goods. Common law nations, such as England, the United States, and the numerous nations that are—or have been—heavily influenced by England, traditionally follow a less rigid system in forming and performing sales contracts. Civil law nations, including most of Europe except for England, follow a more rigid system in which statutes provide the entire framework of the sales contract. Nations that follow Islamic law, including most of the Middle East, have different expectations regarding contract law. Socialist nations prefer much more controlled terms and allow much less flexibility in forming contracts, establishing prices, and dealing with remedies. Industrialized nations have different expectations than developing—or "third-world"—nations. All of these differences have made the creation and ratification of the CISG very difficult.

Despite these differences, and despite the difficulties, a Convention was agreed on and ratified by 44 nations. This Convention holds out the hope for a truly uniform international law governing the sale of goods. In the interim, the CISG may provide the controlling law for international sale-of-goods contracts under two different sets of circumstances:

EXHIBIT 20.1 CISG Signatory Nations

Nation	Ratification Date	Signature Date
Argentina	19 July 1983	
Australia	17 March 1988	
Austria	29 December 1987	11 April 1980
Belarus	9 October 1989	
Belgium	31 October 1996	
Bosnia and Herzegovina	12 January 1994	
Bulgaria	9 July 1990	
Canada	23 April 1991	
Chile	7 February 1990	11 April 1980
China	11 December 1986	30 September 1981
Cuba	2 November 1994	
Czech Republic[a]	5 March 1990	1 September 1981
Denmark	14 February 1989	26 May 1981
Ecuador	27 January 1992	
Egypt	6 December 1982	
Estonia	20 September 1993	
Finland	15 December 1987	26 May 1981
France	6 August 1982	27 August 1981
Georgia	16 August 1994	
Germany	21 December 1989	26 May 1981
Ghana		11 April 1980
Guinea	23 January 1991	
Hungary	16 June 1983	11 April 1980
Iraq	5 March 1990	
Italy	11 December 1986	30 September 1981
Lesotho	18 June 1981	18 June 1981
Lithuania	18 January 1995	
Luxembourg	30 January 1997	
Mexico	29 December 1987	
Netherlands	11 December 1990	29 May 1981
New Zealand	22 September 1994	
Norway	20 July 1988	26 May 1981
Poland		28 September 1981
Republic of Moldavia	13 October 1994	
Romania	22 May 1991	
Russian Federation[b]	16 August 1990	
Singapore		11 April 1980
Slovakia	28 May 1993	
Slovenia	7 January 1994	
Spain	24 July 1990	
Sweden	15 December 1987	26 May 1981
Switzerland	21 February 1990	
Syrian Arab Republic	19 October 1982	
Uganda	12 February 1992	
Ukraine	3 January 1990	
United States of America	11 December 1986	31 August 1981
Uzbekistan	27 November 1996	
Venezuela		28 September 1981
Yugoslavia[c]	27 March 1985	11 April 1980
Zambia	6 June 1986	

[a] Slovakia, by succession, 28 May 1993; Czech Republic, by succession, 30 September 1993.

[b] Estonia, by accession, 20 September 1993.

[c] Slovenia, by succession, 7 January 1994; Bosnia and Herzegovina, by succession, 12 January 1994.

1. The contract for the sale of goods is made between firms from different countries, if both countries have ratified the Convention.
2. The contract for the sale of goods designates that the law of a particular country will be the applicable law governing the contract, provided that the country whose laws will be applicable has ratified the Convention.

OBLIGATIONS UNDER THE CISG

The CISG provides the framework for the international sale of goods in much the same way that Article 2 of the UCC provides the framework for the domestic sale of goods in the United States. However, students should avoid drawing too strict a comparison between the UCC and the CISG. Not all the subjects covered by the UCC are also covered by the CISG, nor does the CISG extend to as many sales as does Article 2. For example, the CISG does not apply to the sale of goods intended for personal or household use unless the seller neither knew or should have known that the goods were being purchased for personal or household use.[3] By contrast, Article 2 does apply to such purchases by a consumer, even providing warranty protection to the consumer in many such situations.

There are some other significant differences between the UCC and the CISG, and some of these differences may prove troublesome for U.S. businesses (as well as businesses from other common law nations) new to the international marketplace. For example, under common law, in order to have a contract there must be (1) an offer, (2) an acceptance, and (3) consideration. The CISG does not mention "consideration"—a basic element of contract formation in common law countries. Instead, the CISG view is that since consideration is part of the formation of the contract, it relates to the "validity" of the contract. Validity-of-the-contract issues are to be determined by applicable national law, not by the CISG.

Another formation-of-the-contract issue involves acceptance. Unlike consideration, which is a matter to be resolved under applicable national law, the CISG does address the issue of acceptance. Under common law, an acceptance is effective when sent by the offeree (the "mailbox rule"), placing the risk of misdelivery or nondelivery on the offeror. Under civil law, an acceptance is not effective until it is received by the offeror, placing the risk of misdelivery or nondelivery on the offeree. These two positions are diametrically opposed. This means that in a civil law nation an offer can be revoked by the offeror at any time

20.1

EXPANDING SALES INTO THE INTERNATIONAL MARKETPLACE

Amy Chen still represents the firm in its legal matters, but she has expressed some concerns about the firm's recent interest in expanding its sales into the international marketplace. As Amy points out, she has no experience in international law and she has little knowledge of, and no experience with, the CISG. She is quite comfortable with the UCC, and she is very comfortable representing the firm in court so long as the case involves U.S. law. Tom wonders if there is any way for the firm to conduct business internationally without having its contracts subject to the provisions of the CISG. He would like to know what options are available for the firm, and has asked you for advice. What will you tell him?

BUSINESS CONSIDERATIONS When a firm enters into a contract with a business located in another country, should the firm include dispute resolution as part of the contract? For example, should the contract include a choice of applicable law and/or a designation as to which nation's courts will hear disputes? Should provisions be made for some alternative dispute-resolution method, such as arbitration?

ETHICAL CONSIDERATIONS Is it ethical to designate a nation's courts and/or laws as the sole means for resolving disputes in an international sale of goods contract? Does this provide the party who selects the courts and/or laws with an unfair "home-court advantage," to the detriment of the other firm? How should this issue be resolved in a manner that is fair and equitable to all parties?

prior to his or her receipt of an acceptance. In a common law nation, the offer cannot be revoked once an acceptance has been sent by the offeree.

In Article 18(2), the CISG states that an acceptance is effective when it reaches the offeror—the civil law rule. However, it also states, in Article 16(1), that an offer may not be revoked after an acceptance has been sent (even though it may not yet have been received)—a variation on the common law rule. Finally, Article 18(3) says that an acceptance is effective as soon as the offeree shows acceptance by beginning to perform—another concession to common law traditions.

Another difference involves the need for a written agreement for some contracts. Many U.S. firms are used to the applicability of the Statute of Frauds, requiring that a contract for the sale of goods (subject to numerous exceptions) must be in writing if the contract is for $500 or more. These parties may be shocked to learn that the CISG specifically states that oral contracts for the sale of goods are enforceable.[4] Since there is no need for any writing, U.S. firms may believe that they are still in the negotiations (prewriting) stage while their non-U.S. counterparts (especially if those counterparts are from civil law nations) will believe that an oral agreement has been reached and will be expecting performance. If the CISG is the statute governing the sale, a contract will exist, and the U.S. firm will have to perform despite the lack of a writing.

Even if a writing exists, it is possible that some confusion and uncertainty may arise about the contract and its terms. In the following case, a writing was prepared by one party, then signed and returned by the other party. Despite this, the seller—the party who signed the agreement—contended that the writing did not mean what it said. Notice how the court resolved the controversy. (Even though this case was in the United States under the provisions of the UCC, the same result would probably have followed under the CISG.)

20.2 INTERSHOE, INC. v. BANKERS TRUST CO. 571 N.E.2d 641 (N.Y. 1991)

FACTS Intershoe, Inc., a shoe importer, uses various foreign currencies in its business, including the Italian lira. It frequently entered into foreign currency futures transactions with various banks, including Bankers Trust Company. On 13 March 1985, Intershoe telephoned Bankers Trust and entered into several foreign currency transactions, including one for a futures transaction involving lire. Bankers Trust sent a confirmation of these transactions to Intershoe on 13 March 1985, including a confirmation that the bank had purchased from Intershoe 537,750,000 Italian lire, and that the bank had sold 250,000 U.S. dollars to Intershoe. The treasurer for Intershoe signed this confirmation and returned it to the bank on 18 March 1985. In a letter dated 11 October 1985, the bank notified Intershoe that it was awaiting instructions as to Intershoe's delivery of the lire. Intershoe responded by a letter dated 25 October 1985 that the transaction was a mistake and that it would not go through with the deal. Subsequently, on 19 December 1985, Intershoe filed suit against Bankers Trust, alleging that Intershoe had suffered a loss of $55,019.85 from Bankers Trust's failure to deliver the lire as per the contract. Bankers Trust counterclaimed for its damages under the same contract.

ISSUE Was Intershoe permitted to introduce parol evidence to contradict the contract as represented by the confirmation prepared by Bankers Trust and signed by the treasurer of Intershoe?

HOLDING No. Under the UCC, parol evidence is not permitted to contradict the terms of a writing signed by or agreed to by the parties.

REASONING The sole basis for Intershoe's objection was the affidavit of its treasurer in which he stated that: "I unequivocally know that it is simply not the case that [Intershoe] agreed to sell Italian lire. While I cannot recall each conversation I had with [Bankers Trust] in 1985 concerning lira transactions, I know I never placed an order to sell lira at any time that year." The treasurer also pointed out that Intershoe had only sold foreign currency to Bankers Trust in one of nearly 1,000 transactions over the course of their relation-

20.2 INTERSHOE, INC. v. BANKERS TRUST CO. *(cont.)* 571 N.E.2d 641 (N.Y. 1991)

ship. Despite this affidavit and despite the alleged course of dealings, the court ruled for Bankers Trust. Here the parties had communicated by telephone, following which there was a written confirmation prepared by Bankers Trust and sent to Intershoe, then signed and returned by Intershoe without any alteration to the writing and without any objections to its terms. Intershoe cannot now be permitted to testify that when it signed an agreement saying it would sell Italian lire, it meant that it would buy Italian lire. Verdict for Bankers Trust.

BUSINESS CONSIDERATIONS Suppose that a party to an international sale of goods contract wants the contract reduced to a writing before it is obligated, and also wants that writing to be the entire agreement, not subject to any changes or amendments. What can that person do to ensure, as much as possible, that it will not have an enforceable contract until there is a writing, and that the writing will be the entire agreement?

ETHICAL CONSIDERATIONS Is it ethical to sign a written agreement and then to argue in court that the words used in the writing were not representative of what the parties truly agreed? Should a party to a written agreement be allowed to introduce evidence contradicting what the writing says?

U.S. sellers expect their buyers to inspect the goods tendered for delivery and to give specific reasons for any rejection. A failure to properly reject is deemed to be an acceptance of the goods as tendered, making the buyer liable for the purchase price. Under the CISG, a buyer may not rely on any lack of conformity as a reason to reject the goods unless notice of the nonconformity is given to the seller within a reasonable time. This sounds like the UCC rule, but there is a difference—the CISG states that there is a time limit of two years for the giving of notice, unless the contract includes an agreement setting a different time.[5] To further confuse U.S. firms, even if the buyer fails to give the required notice, Article 44 of the CISG allows the buyer to "reduce the price . . . or claim damages, except for the loss of profit, if he has a reasonable excuse for his failure to give the required notice."[6]

Common law nations treat offers as freely revocable at any time prior to acceptance, unless the offeree has an option or unless the parties are governed by the UCC and a merchant has made a firm offer. Civil law countries generally treat an offer that states a time limit as irrevocable. Thus, there is a basic difference between common law and civil law in this area. The CISG generally adopts the common law approach, making the offer freely revocable at any time prior to acceptance. However, there are, based on civil law, two important exceptions:

1. The offer is irrevocable where the offer states that an acceptance must be made within a stated time.
2. The offer is irrevocable if it was reasonable for the offeree to rely on the offer remaining open, and the offeree did, in fact, rely on the offer remaining open.[7]

Thus, an offer that says the offeree has 20 days to accept is deemed to be irrevocable for the 20-day period even though the offer does not take the form of a firm offer as provided for in the UCC. In addition, the CISG applies a **promissory estoppel**-like exception when the facts of the case make it appear that the offeree relied on the fact that the offer would remain open and will be harmed if the offer is not held open for the time indicated in the offer. (Note that the CISG does not require the offeror to reasonably expect the offeree to reply, to his or her detriment, as the common law would.)

Promissory estoppel
A legal doctrine that prohibits a promisor from denying that a promise was made due to the justifiable reliance of the promisee that the promise will be kept.

The following case is the first instance where a U.S. court decided a case based on the CISG principles. Think of the similarities between the decision the court reached in applying the CISG and the decision the court would have reached under Article 2 of the UCC.

20.3 FILANTO, S.P.A. v. CHILEWICH INT'L CORP. 789 F.Supp. 1229 (S.D.N.Y. 1992)

FACTS By motion fully submitted on 11 December 1991, defendant Chilewich International Corp. moves to stay this action pending arbitration in Moscow. Plaintiff Filanto has moved to enjoin arbitration or to order arbitration in this federal district.

This case is a striking example of how a lawsuit involving a relatively straightforward international commercial transaction can raise an array of complex questions. . . . Plaintiff Filanto is an Italian corporation engaged in the manufacture and sale of footwear. Defendant Chilewich is an export–import firm incorporated in the state of New York. . . . On 28 February 1989, Chilewich's agent in the United Kingdom signed a contract with Raznoexport, the Soviet Foreign Economic Association, which obligated it to supply footwear to Raznoexport. Section 10 of this contract—the "Russian Contract"—is an arbitration clause, which reads in pertinent part as follows:

> *All disputes or differences which may arise out of or in connection with the present Contract are to be settled, jurisdiction of ordinary courts being excluded, by the Arbitration at the USSR Chamber of Commerce and Industry, Moscow, in accordance with the Regulations of the said Arbitration. [sic]*

The first exchange of correspondence between the parties to this lawsuit is a letter dated 27 July 1989 from . . . Chilewich to . . . Filanto, as part of the negotiations to fulfill the Russian Contract. This letter states as follows:

> *Attached please find our contract to cover our purchases from you. Same is governed by the conditions which are enumerated in the standard contract in effect with the Soviet buyers [the Russian Contract], copy of which is also enclosed.*

Following an exchange of correspondence, Filanto accepted the contract with Chilewich, but attempted to exclude the arbitration provision found in the Russian Contract, and which was also included in the original communication to Filanto from Chilewich. . . . The next document in this case, and the focal point of the parties' dispute regarding whether an arbitration agreement exists, is a Memorandum Agreement dated 13 March 1990. This Agreement . . . is a standard merchant's memo prepared by Chilewich for signature by both parties confirming that Filanto will deliver 100,000 pairs of boots to Chilewich at the Italian/Yugoslav border on 15 September 1990, with the balance of 150,000 pairs to be delivered on 1 November 1990. . . . This Memorandum includes the following provision:

> *It is understood between Buyer and Seller that [the Russian Contract] is hereby incorporated in this contract as far as practicable, and specifically that any arbitration shall be in accordance with that Contract.*

Chilewich signed this Memorandum and sent it to Filanto. Filanto at that time did not sign or return the document. . . . Then, on 7 August 1990, Filanto returned the Memorandum Agreement, sued on here, that Chilewich had signed and sent to it in March; although Filanto had signed it, Filanto had also appended a cover letter purporting to exclude the arbitration provisions. . . .

It appears that the parties performed as agreed on 15 September 1990, but that problems arose with the scheduled 1 November 1990 performance. According to the complaint, what ultimately happened was that Chilewich bought and paid for 60,000 pairs of boots in January 1991, but never purchased the 90,000 pairs of boots that comprise the balance of Chilewich's original order. It is Chilewich's failure to do so that forms the basis of this lawsuit, commenced by Filanto on 14 May 1991.

ISSUES Did the contract require that the parties submit any claims to arbitration, or had Filanto excluded arbitration? If arbitration was to be used, where was the arbitration to occur?

HOLDINGS The parties were bound to submit their claims to arbitration. The proper place for the arbitration was in Moscow, as per the contract terms.

REASONING There is in the record one document that post-dates the filing of the Complaint: a letter from Filanto to Chilewich dated 21 June 1991. The letter is in response to claims by Chilewich that some of the boots that had been supplied by Filanto were defective. The letter expressly relies on a section of the Russian Contract which Filanto had earlier purported to exclude—Section 9 regarding claims procedures. . . . This letter must be regarded as an admission

20.3 FILANTO, S.P.A. v. CHILEWICH INT'L CORP. *(cont.)* 789 F.Supp. 1229 (S.D.N.Y. 1992)

in law by Filanto, the party to be charged. A litigant may not blow hot and cold in a lawsuit. The letter of 21 June 1991 clearly shows that when Filanto thought it desirable to do so, it recognized that it was bound by the incorporation by reference of portions of the Russian Contract. . . . This position is entirely inconsistent with the position which Filanto had earlier professed, and is inconsistent with its present position. Consistent with the position of the defendant in this action, Filanto admits that the other relevant clauses of the Russian Contract were incorporated by agreement of the parties, and made a part of the bargain. Of necessity, this must include the agreement to arbitrate in Moscow. . . .

As plaintiff correctly notes, the "general principles of contract law" relevant to this action, do *not* include the Uniform Commercial Code; rather, the "federal law of contracts" to be applied in this case is found in the United Nations Convention on Contracts for the International Sale of Goods. . . . Although there is as yet virtually no U.S. case law interpreting the Sale of Goods Convention . . . it may safely be predicted that this will change: absent a choice-of-law provision, and with certain exclusions not here relevant, the Convention governs *all* contracts between parties with places of business in different nations, so long as both nations are signatories to the Convention. . . . Since the contract alleged in this case was most certainly formed, if at all, after 1 January 1988, and since both the United States and Italy are signatories of the Convention, the Court will interpret the [contract] in light of, and with reference to, the substantive international law of contracts embodied in the Sale of Goods Convention. . . . Chilewich signed the Memorandum Agreement and forwarded it to Filanto; Filanto signed the Memorandum and returned it to Chilewich. . . . The chosen forum in this case does have a reasonable relation to the contract at issue, as the ultimate purchasers of the boots was a Russian concern and the Russian Contract was incorporated by reference into Filanto's Memorandum Agreement with Chilewich. Furthermore, though conditions in the Republic of Russia are unsettled, they continue to improve and there is no reason to believe that the Chamber of Commerce in Moscow cannot provide fair and impartial justice to these litigants.

BUSINESS CONSIDERATIONS Why might two businesses, each from a different nation, want to have any conflicts submitted to arbitration in a third nation? Why might two businesses prefer to submit a case to arbitration rather than taking the case to court?

ETHICAL CONSIDERATIONS Is it ethical to agree to submit a claim to arbitration, and then to file a lawsuit attempting to either avoid the arbitration option or to change the location in which the case will be arbitrated?

Obligations of the Seller

Chapter II of the CISG covers the obligations of the seller of goods under the Convention, and Chapter III covers the obligations of the buyer. These chapters include remedies for breach of the contract among the obligations, which reflects the basic implication of the Convention that a contract for the sale of goods is expected to be performed by both parties to the contract.

The obligations of the seller under the CISG can be found in Articles 30 through 44 of the Convention; these articles are broken down into three sections. The first section is general, calling for the seller to deliver goods, turn over any relevant documents, and surrender any property in the goods as provided in the contract. The second section deals with the conformity of the goods and with any claims by third parties. The third section deals with remedies that are available upon breach by the seller (see Remedies Under the CISG).

Section I. Articles 31 through 34 describe the obligations of the seller in a contract under the CISG. Under the provisions of Article 31, if the seller is not specifically obligated to deliver the goods at a particular place, then he or she is expected to follow these guidelines:

1. If the contract involves carriage of the goods, the seller is to hand the goods over to the first carrier for transmission to the buyer.
2. If the goods are not to be carried, the seller is to place the goods at the buyer's disposition either where the goods are known by both parties to be located or at the seller's place of business.

Article 32 deals with contracts involving carriage of the goods by independent carrier. It specifies that the seller must notify the buyer of the consignment of the goods to the carrier, must make the reasonable and necessary contracts for carriage of the goods, and must either procure insurance on the goods or give the buyer sufficient information regarding the goods and the carriage to permit the buyer to procure insurance.

Articles 33 and 34 deal with the proper time for delivery and with the handing over of any necessary documents relating to the goods as a part of the performance duty.

Section II. Made up of Articles 35 through 44, Section II deals with conformity of the goods and possible claims by third parties. This section specifies that the goods must be fit for their normal and intended purpose, fit for any particular purpose of which the seller was aware at the time of the contract, and are properly packaged in order to be deemed conforming. Conformity is measured at the time when the risk of loss passes to the buyer, although the seller may cure any nonconformity if the goods are delivered prior to the delivery date as set out in the contract. The buyer is expected to examine the goods as promptly as practical and to notify the seller of any nonconformity in a timely manner, or the buyer loses his or her right to object to any nonconformity in the goods delivered. This section was hotly debated at the conference, and a compromise was reached on this topic. The buyer is given special rights here in that the buyer has up to two years to assert that the goods contain a hidden defect. In addition, a buyer who fails to give timely notice of a defect can still deduct the "value" of the defect from the contract price, provided that the buyer has a "reasonable excuse" for a failure to give timely notice.[8]

The seller is also expected to deliver goods to the buyer that are free of any rights or claims of any third parties, and can be held liable to the buyer and to the third party for any violations of this obligation.

Obligations of the Buyer

Chapter III of the CISG covers the obligations of the buyer under the contract, which consists of the duty to accept the goods and to pay for them. This chapter is also broken down into three sections. Section I, comprised of Articles 54 through 59, discusses the duty of the buyer with respect to payment of the contract price for the goods. Section II, which consists solely of Article 60, explains taking delivery. Section III, made up of Articles 61 through 65, discusses remedies upon a breach by the buyer (description follows).

Section I. This section specifies the payment obligation of the buyer under a number of different sets of circumstances. If the contract is silent as to payment, the buyer is to pay the price generally charged for such goods at the time and place of the conclusion of the contract. If the price is to be based on weight and the method for determining weight is not specified, it is presumed to be net weight. If no place for payment is specified, the buyer is to pay the seller at the seller's place of business or at the place where any documents are handed over, if payment is to be "against documents." In addition, unless the contract specifies a different time, the buyer is to pay for the goods when the goods or the documents are made available by the seller.

Section II. Article 60 is the only article included in this section. This article specifies that the buyer is to take delivery by doing all the acts that are necessary and could reasonably be expected in order to allow the seller to deliver the goods, and in actually taking delivery of the goods.

REMEDIES UNDER THE CISG

Remedies for Breach by the Seller

Section III of Chapter II specifies remedies that are available to the buyer upon a breach of the sales contract by the seller. In addition, Articles 74 through 77 provide damages that may be available to either the buyer or the seller upon a breach by the other party. The CISG also specifically states that a party is not deprived of any rights to claim damages if that party seeks other remedies under the Convention as well. If the seller fails to deliver conforming goods or fails to meet any other aspect of the agreement, the buyer may seek any or all of the appropriate remedies from the alternatives shown in Exhibit 20.2.

Remedies for Breach by the Buyer

Section III of Chapter III specifies the remedies that are available to the seller upon a breach of the sales contract by the buyer. Again, Articles 74 through 77 provide damages that may be available as well. Recall also that the CISG specifically states that a party is not deprived of any rights to claim damages if that party seeks other remedies under the Convention as well. If the buyer fails to accept delivery of the goods or fails to pay for the goods as agreed, the seller may seek any or all of the appropriate remedies from the alternatives shown in Exhibit 20.3.

EXHIBIT 20.2 Buyer's Remedies

1. The buyer may require the seller to perform, unless the buyer has chosen another remedy that is inconsistent with performance by the seller. Additionally, the buyer may require the seller to deliver conforming substitute goods or to cure any nonconformity, if the seller has delivered nonconforming goods.
2. The buyer may set an additional time for the seller to perform, provided that the seller is notified. During this additional time, the buyer will be precluded from seeking other remedies.
3. The buyer can declare the contract avoided if the seller does not deliver the goods within the time permitted under the contract (including any additional time allowed) or within a reasonable time after learning that the seller has breached the agreement.
4. If the seller delivers nonconforming goods, the buyer may reduce the price paid so that payment reflects the actual value of the performance.
5. If the seller tenders delivery prior to the agreed delivery date, the buyer may accept or refuse the delivery; if the seller tenders delivery of a larger shipment than called for in the contract, the buyer may accept any or all of the excess quantity, paying for any accepted goods at the contract rate.

EXHIBIT 20.3 Seller's Remedies

1. The seller may require the buyer to pay the contract price, to take delivery, or to perform any other obligations, unless he or she has resorted to any other remedies that are inconsistent with this remedy.
2. The seller may fix an additional reasonable period of time during which the buyer can perform, provided that the buyer is notified of this extension. During this additional time period, the seller cannot seek any other remedies.
3. The seller can declare the contract avoided as to any unperformed portion of the contract.
4. If the contract calls for the buyer to specify any form, measurement, or other feature of the goods and he fails to do so, the seller may supply such specifications, if he or she does so within a reasonable time.

Damages

Section II of Chapter IV specifies damages that may be available to either party under the Convention following a breach of the contract by the other party. These damages may be available even if other remedies are also sought by the nonbreaching party.

The basic measure of damages under the CISG is "a sum equal to the loss, including loss of profit, suffered by the other party as a consequence of the breach. Such damages cannot exceed the loss which the party in breach foresaw or ought to have foreseen at the time of the conclusion of the contract."

If the contract is avoided and the buyer then purchases replacement goods, the buyer is entitled to the difference between the price of the replacement goods and the original contract price, plus any other damages computed under the prior damage provisions. If the contract is avoided and the seller then resells the goods, the seller is entitled to the difference between the resale price and the original contract price, plus any other damages computed under the prior damage provisions.

If the contract is avoided and there is a current price for the goods covered by the contract, the nonbreaching party can recover the difference between the current price and the contract price, plus any other damages allowed under Article 74, without the need to purchase (by the buyer) or resell (by the seller). In any case, the party seeking damages must take any and all reasonable steps to mitigate damages, or the other party can use the failure to mitigate as grounds for reducing the damages assessed to the level that would have been attained with mitigation.

The international sale and movement of goods should continue to expand over the foreseeable future. This means the CISG will become increasingly important to the U.S. domestic business environment in the future, although it will not replace the UCC in its importance. Business will need to be aware of the differences between the CISG in international agreements and the UCC domestically, because conduct that is merely a preliminary negotiation under the UCC may well be a binding contract under the Convention.

Value-added taxes are also likely to be used with greater frequency; this may affect intracompany transfers and result in tax assessments even though no money changes hands in the transaction. Firms will have to pay a tax on the value added to the goods they receive while those goods were in the hands of the transferor, even if that transferor is a subsidiary of the transferee. This could lead to accounting problems and/or some "creative" bookkeeping, and it could serve to discourage moving manufacturing or processing facilities to other nations.

Many international transactions call for payment by means of a *letter of credit,* a document issued by the buyer and sent to the seller. The seller presents the letter of credit to the bank—together with the required documentary evidence that the seller has the goods and is ready to ship them—and receives payment for the goods. By using a letter of credit, numerous worries are removed or alleviated. The seller receives a document providing for payment before the goods are shipped, easing the seller's concerns about receiving payment for goods to be shipped to another nation. The buyer knows that no payments will be made unless the bank is assured that the seller is ready, willing, and able to ship the goods called for in the contract. Letters of credit are regulated, at least in the United States, by UCP 500, the Uniform Customs and Practices for Documentary Credit, enacted on 1 January 1994.

Business is becoming truly global, which ultimately should result in a lessening of cultural isolation and increased awareness of the needs, demands, and expectations of the people of other nations. This, in turn, will increase the access to these other nations and—at least under economic theory—should result in the growth of the world economy as each nation strives to maximize its relative competitive advantage and, in so doing, to increase its sales and its purchases in the global marketplace.

20.2

INTERNATIONAL BUSINESS/SALES

LETTERS OF CREDIT

The firm recently received an order from a prospective customer in Europe who is interested in placing an initial order for 500 Call-Image units, provided that acceptable terms can be worked out. This buyer has offered to pay for the videophones with a letter of credit payable at the Kochanowskis's bank. The family has never done business with a letter of credit before, and they are unsure how to proceed. They ask you whether they should accept the letter of credit as a means for receiving payment or if they should use a method for payment more familiar to them. What advice will you give them?

BUSINESS CONSIDERATIONS Letters of credit are a fairly common payment method for long-distance business transactions, especially internationally. Should a newly organized business consider having a policy on letters of credit in advance, or wait until the need arises before developing a policy? What protections are afforded by a letter of credit that might not be available under other methods for arranging payment when goods are sold internationally?

ETHICAL CONSIDERATIONS What ethical concerns might a company have about using a letter of credit, making payments on the basis of documents that are examined by a banker rather than on the basis of an inspection of the goods by the buyer? How can these concerns be alleviated?

ISO 9000

The CISG is not the only major international agreement involving business and the sale of goods. Numerous free-trade zones have been established in the recent past, greatly affecting trade both within and outside of these zones. (See Chapter 3 for a brief discussion of free-trade zones.) A number of other initiatives that will have an impact on international trade have also been adopted or proposed. It appears that international business will be a focal point for uniform law for the foreseeable future.

Product quality and quality control are topics which have attracted a substantial amount of attention in the global marketplace. The concerns with these topics led to the promulgation and eventual adoption of an international quality-control standard, ISO 9000.

The International Standards Organization (ISO) is an international agency headquartered in Geneva, Switzerland. The ISO was established to develop uniform international standards in certain specified areas. The ISO is comprised of representatives from the national standards organizations of a number of countries; they have joined their efforts in an attempt to create certain uniform international standards. The first major success was in the area of quality control—ISO 9000.

ISO 9000 is *not* a standard. Rather, it is a mechanism providing a comprehensive review process and guidelines. By following this review process and the guidelines, companies can ensure that their products comply with the quality standards established for their industry. ISO 9000 is a set of five international standards concerning quality management and quality assurance in the production process. Firms that decide to participate in the program register with the national standards body and acquire an ISO number. As the number of registered firms increases, the importance of participation also increases. Many firms that are active in international trade require ISO 9000 participation as a condition to entering a contract. Quality standards may have a significant impact on international sales over the next few years.

Ethical Issues in the International Sale of Goods

Some U.S. commentators have argued that business operates under a game theory of ethics, and that honesty and good faith cannot reasonably be expected in such a situation. To these commentators, the purpose of business is to generate profits, and so long as those profits are generated in a manner that does not break the law, the business has not acted unethically. These people also feel that business is an amoral institution so that normal societal mores do not—and cannot—apply.

Contemporary social values in the United States do not reflect this approach, nor does the UCC. Our society expects—and demands—more from business than a mere showing of net profits. The "bottom line" is not a justification for acting in an improper manner. For example, the Uniform Commercial Code mandates that all parties to a sales contract are to act in good faith and to cooperate with one another. In addition, the Code requires all merchants in a sales contract to act in a commercially reasonable manner.

Although business ethics is not discussed per se in the CISG, good faith is. The issue of "good faith" provides an interesting example of the problem of ethics in an international setting. Common law nations tend to require good faith in the performance and the enforcement of contracts. Civil law nations expand the good-faith requirement, requiring good faith in the negotiation of a contract, as well as in its performance, enforcement, and interpretation. Since the Convention did not determine a uniform meaning for good faith, and since there was strong disagreement as to the scope of good faith if it were to be included, a compromise was reached. Article 7(1) of the CISG requires that the Convention must be interpreted in a manner that observes good faith in international trade. This compromise reinforces the difficulty of determining what conduct is deemed ethical in various cultures.

The common law nations were vehemently opposed to including a good-faith requirement in the formation of the contract, a standard practice in civil law nations. The civil law nations were concerned that common law nations do not require good faith in the formation of a contract, although they do require good faith in the performance of the contract. The representative from France expressed a fear that including good faith as a requirement would lead to divergent and arbitrary interpretations by national courts, negating uniformity in applying the CISG.

The following case involved a good-faith issue that was resolved under UCC principles rather than under the principles espoused in the CISG.

20.4 TARBERT TRADING, LTD. v. COMETALS, INC. 663 F.Supp. 561 (S.D.N.Y. 1987)

FACTS A South African agent of Tarbert sold 2,000 metric tons of Kenyan red haricot beans warehoused in Rotterdam, Holland, to Cometals. The contract specified that the seller had to supply a certificate of origin for the goods, stating that the goods originated within the European Community (EC) even though both parties were aware that it was impossible to honestly provide such a certificate. The beans were to be "sound, loyal and merchantable, max. 1 pct impurities, free from live and practically free from dead weevils," and the quality would be certified by an independent surveyor. Cometals subsequently inspected the beans in the warehouse and informed Tarbert that the goods were extensively damaged by weevils, so Cometals rejected the goods. Tarbert sued Cometals for breach of contract, alleging that the goods conformed to the contract so that the rejection was improper. Cometals denied it had breached, and also asserted that the contract was void because the certificate of origin could only be obtained through fraud or forgery.

ISSUE Was Tarbert entitled to damages for the alleged breach of contract by Cometals?

HOLDING No. The contract was void, so no remedies were available for any alleged breach.

REASONING The court found that the beans conformed to the contract. Only a small amount (0.8 percent) of the beans were "holed" (infested with weevils), and the overall quality of the beans conformed to the contract specifications. However, the necessity for the parties to commit fraud or forgery to satisfy a condition of the contract made the contract violative of public policy, illegal, and therefore void. There was no possible way for the parties to procure an EC certificate of origin for beans grown in Kenya, and both parties were aware of this at the time the contract was entered. Since neither party acted with good faith, and both parties were *in pari delicto,* the contract was void. No damages were granted.

BUSINESS CONSIDERATIONS What should a businessperson do when another party proposes forming a contract which contains terms and/or conditions that are not legally possible to satisfy? What should that businessperson do if another party states that a very attractive contract can be entered, but that there will be certain payoffs required in order to get the benefits of the contract?

ETHICAL CONSIDERATIONS Is it ethical for a party to enter a contract knowing the other party has committed an illegal act, and that the illegal act will allow the first party to elect whether to perform the contract or escape it due to the illegality?

Concerns with the CISG were also expressed along the lines that separate developed—or industrialized—nations from developing nations, a "north/south" division. The developing nations (frequently joined by the socialist nations) feared they would be placed at a disadvantage by the nature of the goods they sell, as opposed to the goods they import. Generally speaking, developing nations export raw materials and agricultural products; they import finished goods and technological equipment. The compromises reached in this area reflect a recognition of economic differences that mandated a legal—and an ethical—difference in treatment. Included in these compromises were the extended time given for a buyer to discover hidden defects and the ability of the buyer to deduct the "value" of a defect even if there was not a timely notice of the defect, provided that the buyer has a "reasonable excuse" for not giving timely notice. Given the lack of technological expertise, the difficulty of transportation, and the other problems faced by so-called third world nations, the compromises reached reflect a concern that they be assured of fair treatment in their dealings with industrialized nations.

YOU BE THE JUDGE

Kentucky Fried Chicken® in Bangalore

There was nothing remarkable about the two men who kept coming back for fried chicken at the Kentucky Fried Chicken® (KFC) outlet in Bangalore. Nothing, that is, until they proved to be undercover agents for city officials, who charged that the chicken they had bought was adulterated, misbranded, unfit for consumption and laced with dangerously high levels of monosodium glutamate—a seasoning that authorities claim could cause cancer when consumed in large amounts. (Studies conducted by the U.S. Food and Drug Administration have found no link between MSG and cancer.) Shaken KFC managers, who denied the charges and pointed out that the company serves the same chicken in 9,400 restaurants in 78 countries, were given several weeks to prepare their case for why the store should not be shut down permanently.

This case has been brought before *your* court. How will you decide the case?

BUSINESS CONSIDERATIONS India has recently become a less-than-friendly location for non-Indian businesses. There have been numerous demonstrations against PepsiCo and its subsidiaries, including KFC. What should PepsiCo do in this situation? How should KFC handle this case?

ETHICAL CONSIDERATIONS Suppose that a business is accused of selling a product that is harmful to the health of its customers. Even if the ingredients used in the product have been tested and used in a number of other locations without any evidence that customers are harmed, the accusation raises ethical issues and concerns. What are the ethical obligations of the firm in such a situation? Suppose that the accusations are made purely as a means of procuring bribes for local "health inspectors." Does this fact change the ethical obligations of the firm?[9]

SOURCE: *Time*, September 18, 1995, pp. 91–92.

STANDARD SHIPPING TERMS IN INTERNATIONAL TRADE (INCOTERMS)

When goods are sold in international trade, they do not just magically appear at their ultimate destination. They must be transported, frequently by third parties—common carriers. This transportation is governed to a significant extent by the use of standard shipping terms. Just as the UCC provides for the interpretation of standard shipping terms within the United States, there are provisions for standard shipping terms in international trade. However, these provisions are not found in the CISG.

In 1936, the International Chamber of Commerce developed the "International Rules for the Interpretation of Trade Terms," which provides for one uniform meaning for international commercial terms, or *incoterms*. These incoterms became widely known and followed and are encouraged by trade councils, courts, and international experts. However, these terms have no automatic legal standing and are only applied if the parties agree to accept them and so state in their contract.

There are four broad categories of incoterms, with each category placing different burdens and responsibilities on the buyer and the seller. These categories are designated by letters—"E" terms, "F" terms, "C" terms, and "D" terms.

"E" Terms

There is only one "E" term, EXW, which stands for "ex-works." Under this term, the seller fulfills its obligation when the goods are made available to the buyer at the seller's premises. The seller is not responsible for loading the goods or for clearing the goods for export. The buyer bears all risks and responsibilities. The "E" term represents the minimum obligation the seller can face.

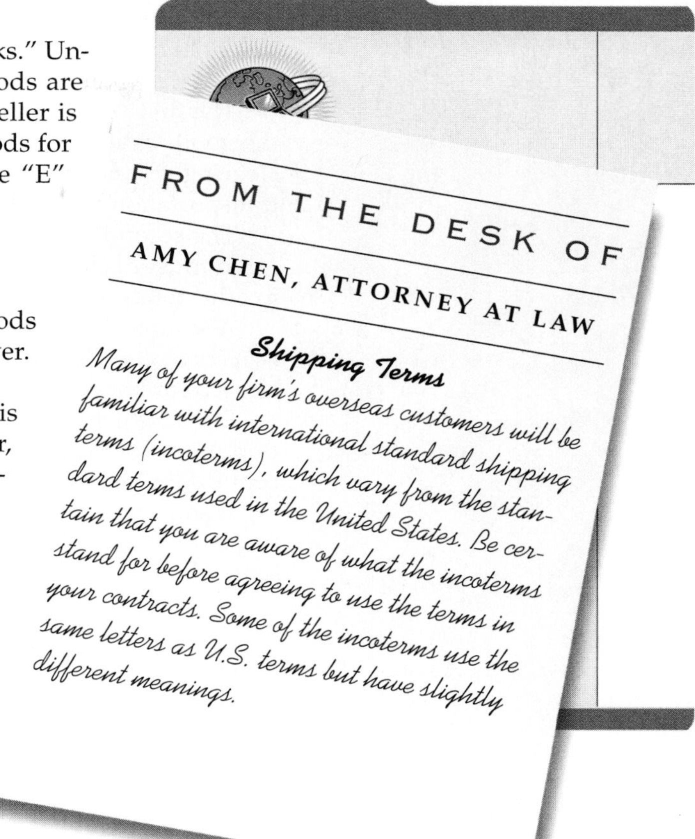

FROM THE DESK OF
AMY CHEN, ATTORNEY AT LAW
Shipping Terms
Many of your firm's overseas customers will be familiar with international standard shipping terms (incoterms), which vary from the standard terms used in the United States. Be certain that you are aware of what the incoterms stand for before agreeing to use the terms in your contracts. Some of the incoterms use the same letters as U.S. terms but have slightly different meanings.

"F" Terms

"F" terms require the seller to hand over the designated goods to a nominated carrier free of any risk or expense to the buyer. There are three basic "F" terms.

The first is FCA, which means *free carrier.* To satisfy this term, the seller must hand over goods to a named carrier, cleared for export, at the named location. The name of the location will follow the term, as in "FCA London."

The second is FAS, which means *free along side.* The seller must place goods alongside a named vessel at a named port with all fees and risks covered to that point. The buyer assumes responsibility and risk once the goods reach the docks alongside the named vessel.

The final "F" term is FOB, which means *free on board.* As an incoterm, FOB transfers risk and responsibility to the buyer as soon as the goods "pass over the ship's rail" at the named destination port. The seller must clear the goods for export under this term, which is only used for sea or inland waterway transportation internationally.

"C" Terms

"C" terms imply that the seller must bear certain costs under the contract. There are four "C" terms.

The first "C" term is CFR, which stands for *cost and freight,* and is normally followed by a named location such as Lisbon. The seller must clear the goods for export and bears all risks until the goods pass over the ship's rail at the port of shipment. CFR is only used for sea or inland waterway transportation.

The second "C" term is CIF, which is the same as CFR except that the seller must also insure the goods during the carriage. The insurance to be carried need only be a minimum (contract price plus 10 percent) unless the agreement sets a different rate.

The third "C" term is CPT, which means *carriage paid to* (named location). The seller makes arrangements for shipping the goods to a named location, pays the freight or carriage charges, and delivers the goods to the carrier. At that point, the risk transfers to the buyer.

The final "C" term is CIP, which means *cost and insurance paid to* (named location). The seller has the same obligations as under CPT, plus the obligation to procure insurance (again at minimum coverage) to protect the buyer's potential risk of loss.

"D" Terms

The final type of incoterm is the "D" term, which refers to a named destination; the duty of the seller depends on the particular "D" term used.

The first "D" term is DAF, which means *delivered at frontier.* The seller must make the goods available and clear the goods for export at a named place, but prior to the clearing of customs at the next country. This term is most common with overland transportation of the goods, normally by rail or by truck.

The second term is DES, which means *delivered ex-ship* at some named port. The seller must make the goods available to the buyer on board the ship, prior to clearing the goods for import, at the named port. This is a seagoing transportation term.

A similar term, again used with seagoing transportation, is DEQ, which means *delivery ex-quay.* The seller in a DEQ contract is to place the goods on the quay (dock) cleared for importation before the risk passes to the buyer.

DDU, which stands for *delivered duty unpaid,* may be used for any type of transportation. The seller is to get the goods to a named destination with all fees paid except for import fees and costs, which are to be borne by the buyer.

A similar term, again valid with any type of transport, is DDP, which means *delivered duty paid.* With this term, the seller is to get the goods to the named destination with all costs paid, including import duties and taxes, and cleared for importation.

Proposed International Coverage

United Nations Convention on International Bills of Exchange and Promissory Notes

The CISG has already been fairly successful, establishing a widely adopted uniform coverage of contracts for the international sale of goods. Following this success, the United Nations was encouraged to continue to propose conventions designed to regulate various aspects of international business. In late 1988, the United Nations General Assembly approved the Convention on International Bills of Exchange and Promissory Notes. This Convention, which is now available for ratification by any member nations, has two primary purposes:

1. To create a new type of international negotiable instrument, an international *bill of exchange,* which will be the standard negotiable instrument for payments in international trade.
2. To provide the same sort of uniform treatment for international negotiable instruments as is provided for interstate transactions in the United States by Article 3 of the UCC.

This Convention needs to be studied so that international businesspeople can be ready to comply with its terms if or when it acquires widespread ratification.

ISO 14000

In a similar vein, the International Standards Organization has been so pleased with the widespread adoption of ISO 9000 in the area of quality control and quality assurance that it has proposed another set of standards to treat the issue of environmental standards and protections. This new set of basic standards is ISO 14000. Firms that decide to follow the standards will adopt an Environmental Management System

http:// RESOURCES FOR BUSINESS LAW STUDENTS

NAME	RESOURCES	WEB ADDRESS
Pace University School of Law Institute of International Commercial Law (IICL)	Pace University School of Law's IICL provides the full text of the United Nations Convention on Contracts for the International Sale of Goods (CISG), as well as legislative history, cases, commentaries, and a bibliography.	http://www.cisg.law.pace.edu/
United Nations Commission on International Trade Law (UNCITRAL)	UNCITRAL, drafter of the CISG, provides background information, texts and recent documents, case law, and the current status of conventions and model laws.	http://www.un.or.at/uncitral/index.html
ISO Online	ISO, drafter of international standards guidelines, such as the ISO 9000 and ISO 14000, provides more on the structure of the organization, as well as a catalog of publications.	http://www.iso.ch/
International Chamber of Commerce (ICC) World Business Organization	The ICC, developer of the International Rules for the Interpretation of Trade Terms (incoterms), provides current news, publications, and information on the ICC International Court of Arbitration.	http://www.iccwbo.org/
International Centre for Commercial Law	The International Centre for Commercial Law offers current updates on European commercial law, as well as listings for commercial law firms in over 40 European countries.	http://www.link.org/

(EMS) under the guidelines of ISO 14001. Following this, the firm will establish an Eco Management and Auditing System (EMAS) to assess its performance.

The International Standards Organization hopes that ISO 14000 will lead to the development of international environmental standards and to more firms registering as being environmentally aware and friendly. Ideally, this effort will help customers select firms with whom they deal on bases other than merely price.

Summary

Work on an international law of sales began in 1930, prior to World War II, when the International Institute for the Unification of Private Law tried to develop uniform coverage in this area. The initial work was submitted to an international conference at The Hague following World War II and resulted in the creation of two conventions, one dealing with the formation of sales contracts and one dealing with the performance of sales contracts. Unfortunately, neither convention has been widely adopted. The United Nations created an International Conference on International Trade and charged it with creating an international law governing sales. This led to the United Nations Convention on the International Sale of Goods (CISG), which was approved at the Vienna Conference in 1980 and became effective 1 January 1988 for all ratifying nations.

The CISG was created by compromises among the various factions that make up the United Nations. There were disagreements among common law, civil law, and Islamic law nations; between developed and developing nations; and between capitalist and socialist nations. Despite these differences, a Convention was created and has been ratified or adopted by 50 nations as of March 1997. The CISG covers formation-of-contracts issues; seller obligations and rights; buyer obligations and rights; and remedies for both sellers and buyers. Ratifying nations have the option of not ratifying all sections of the CISG, but most have opted to follow the entire Convention.

The International Standards Organization, a standards agency headquartered in Geneva, has developed guidelines for firms in an effort to establish international standards for quality and for environmental protection. ISO 9000 deals with quality issues. ISO 14000 deals with environmental issues.

The International Chamber of Commerce developed the "International Rules for the Interpretation of Trade Terms," which provides uniform meanings for these incoterms. Incoterms are broken down into four broad categories, with each category imposing different burdens and responsibilities on the parties to contracts when they use standard shipping terms. The categories are "E" terms, "F" terms, "C" terms, and "D" terms.

The United Nations General Assembly has approved a new Convention dealing with International Bills of Exchange and Promissory Notes. This Convention is intended to provide a new type of negotiable instrument for use in international trade, and also to provide for a uniform international treatment of negotiable instruments.

As international trade grows, U.S. businesses need to be familiar with the CISG and with incoterms; these will become as important to them as their knowledge of the UCC and its provisions for standard shipping terms.

Discussion Questions

1. What is a United Nations "Convention"? Where does such a Convention fall within the hierarchy of laws in the United States, presuming that the United States has joined in the Convention?
2. What is the primary difference between a "common law" nation and a "civil law" nation? How do the courts of each type of nation view previous court opinions? How did this difference affect the development of the CISG?
3. When is an acceptance considered valid under the provisions of the CISG? How does this compare to the time when an acceptance becomes valid under the UCC?
4. Which contracts for the sale of goods must be in writing under the CISG? How does this compare to contracts that must be in writing under the UCC?
5. Suppose a seller makes an offer to a buyer and states that the offer will remain open for three weeks. Can the seller revoke this offer before the three weeks have elapsed under the CISG? How does this compare to the ability of an offeror to revoke an offer under the UCC?
6. How long does a buyer of goods have to inspect the goods and to inform the seller of any nonconformities under the CISG? How does this compare to the time for inspection and notification under the UCC?
7. What must a buyer do to properly take delivery of goods under a contract governed by the CISG? Does the buyer have similar duties under the UCC?
8. When can a buyer require the seller to deliver goods when the seller breaches due to nondelivery under the CISG? How does this compare to the specific performance or replevin remedy available under the UCC?
9. What options are available to a buyer under the CISG when the seller tenders delivery of nonconforming goods? What options are available to a buyer in similar circumstances under the UCC?
10. When does the CISG require good faith in the contract? When does the UCC require good faith in the contract?

Case Problems and Writing Assignments

1. Florence Beef agreed to buy four loads of Australian boneless beef from Cunningham. The contract stated that the beef was to be "85% chemically lean." When the beef was tendered for delivery, Florence rejected the goods, claiming that the beef did not meet the requirements specified in the contract. Florence based

its rejection on the fact that the beef was not "visually lean," although this test was not a recognized scientific standard for judging the meat. Cunningham claimed that the rejection was based on the declining price for beef just before the shipping date. How should the court resolve this case? Why? [See *A.J. Cunningham Packing Corp.* v. *The Florence Beef Co.*, 785 F.2d 348 (1st Cir. 1986).]

2. Schlunk's parents were killed in an automobile accident while driving a Volkswagen. Schlunk filed suit in the United States against both Volkswagen AG (the German parent company) and Volkswagen of America (a wholly owned subsidiary). Schlunk never attempted to serve process on Volkswagen AG, arguing that service on Volkswagen of America was sufficient to bring both parties before the court. Volkswagen AG refused to recognize the lawsuit, alleging that it had never been properly served with process. Should Volkswagen AG be subject to the jurisdiction of the court when process was only served on its U.S. subsidiary? Why? [See *Volkswagenwerk Aktiengesellschaft* v. *Schlunk*, 108 S.Ct. 2104 (1988).]

3. The U.S. Customs Service imposes certain duties on goods imported into the United States. In 1984, the United States amended the law governing customs duties, permitting "drawback" (a refund of customs duties) for the exportation of merchandise which was not the same merchandise originally imported and on which import duties had been paid. Guess? Inc. produces and sells cotton denim clothing. Many of its products are exported from the United States for sale in other nations. All items exported by Guess? are manufactured in the United States and bear the label "Made in the U.S.A." Many of the items sold in the United States are made in other nations and then imported into the United States for sale. Guess? argued that the imported clothing and the exported clothing were fungible so that it was entitled to "drawbacks" for the goods it exported. The U.S. Customs Service asserted that the items were not fungible since the labeling of the products was different. How should this case be resolved by the U.S. Court of International Trade? Why? [See *Guess? Incorporated* v. *United States*, 752 F.Supp. 463 (CIT 1990).]

4. Mebco Bank, a Swiss firm, did a substantial amount of business with Refco F/X Associates, mostly in the area of foreign currency exchanges and dealings. Mebco encountered financial difficulties and was being liquidated under the insolvency laws of Switzerland. One of Mebco's creditors at the time of the liquidation proceeding was Refco. Fearing that it would not recover the debt owed it by Mebco, Refco attached the Mebco bank accounts in New York. Under Swiss law, funds "in account" are considered part of the debtor's estate. Refco argued that the funds "in account" were, in reality, goods, since the transactions underlying the debt were foreign currency exchanges. If the funds were goods, Refco prevails under the provisions of Article 2 of the UCC. However, if the funds were not goods, the Swiss liquidator prevails. How should this case be resolved? Why? [See *In re Koreag, Controle et Revision, S.A.*, 961 F.2d 341 (2d Cir. 1992).]

5. Gestetner was the U.S. distributor of a line of office equipment, including stencil duplicators (mimeograph machines). Case was experimenting with stencil duplicators in an effort to develop a method for producing full-color heat transfers to garments. Case discovered that, with some minor modifications, the Gestetner stencil duplicators were suitable for this heat-transfer process. Case contacted Gestetner to see if Gestetner would be willing to modify its stencil duplicators and then sell them to Case. Gestetner agreed and began to sell the machines to Case. Several months later, problems arose. Case was allegedly in arrears on its account, and Gestetner refused to make any additional shipments until Case brought its account up to date. Case denied liability, asserting that a number of the machines had been defective and could not be sold. Gestetner filed suit for breach of contract. Case filed a motion to dismiss the suit due to the lack of any writing, asserting the Statute of Frauds as an affirmative defense. (The parties never entered into any written agreement in this case.) How would this case be resolved under the UCC? Would a different result occur under the CISG? Explain your answer(s). [See *Gestetner Corp.* v. *Case Equipment Co.*, 815 F.2d 806 (1987).]

6. **BUSINESS APPLICATION CASE** A hay baler was manufactured in 1978 for Massey-Ferguson (a Maryland corporation) by Vermeer Manufacturing (an Iowa corporation), and was then shipped to a Canadian dealership of Massey-Ferguson Industries, Ltd., a Canadian corporation. Kozoway purchased the hay baler from the Canadian dealer. (The Kozoway family operated a farm in Alberta, Canada.) In July 1987, Kozoway lost both of his arms above the elbows in the compression rollers of a Massey-Ferguson hay baler while operating the machine on the family farm. Kozoway sued Massey-Ferguson and Vermeer in Colorado, alleging strict liability in tort for a failure to warn of known dangers, negligence, and willful and wanton conduct. The defendants did not object to the choice of Colorado as the forum court, but they argued that Canadian law should control in this case. Kozoway asserted that U.S. law should control.

Which jurisdiction had the most significant contacts with this contract so that its law should control?

Should a plaintiff be allowed to choose a forum that gives it an opportunity to receive a much larger settlement than it could receive in its home nation? [See *Kozoway* v. *Massey-Ferguson, Inc.*, 722 F.Supp. 641 (D.Colo. 1989).]

7. **ETHICS APPLICATION CASE** Monte Carlo, a New York corporation, contracted with Daewoo, a South Korean corporation, to purchase 2,400 dozen men's shirts, to be manufactured to Monte Carlo's specifications and to bear its label. Daewoo manufactured the shirts, but when the shirts were delivered, the documents were delayed by one day. As a result of this delay, Monte Carlo alleged that the shirts were not available in time for Christmas sales, and it rejected the shipment. Daewoo then sold the shirts to Daewoo International, which, in turn, sold them to numerous discount retailers. The resold shirts contained the Monte Carlo label, and Daewoo International did not have permission to sell the shirts with the labels intact. Monte Carlo sued both Daewoo and Daewoo International for breach of contract and for trademark infringement. Both defendants denied liability.

   Did Daewoo infringe the trademark of Monte Carlo by reselling these shirts to the discount retailers? What ethical issues are raised in this case? [See *Monte Carlo Shirt, Inc.* v. *Daewoo Int'l (America) Corp.*, 707 F.2d 1054 (9th Cir. 1983).]

8. **IDES CASE** Union Carbide India Limited, a subsidiary of Union Carbide Corporation, a New York company, operated a plant in Bhopal, India. The plant manufactured pesticides. Methyl isocyanate (MIC), a highly toxic gas, is an ingredient in the production of these pesticides. One December night in 1984, MIC leaked from the plant in substantial quantities. The wind blew this deadly gas into a heavily populated part of Bhopal, causing more than 3,000 human deaths, with more than 200,000 people suffering injuries of one sort or another. In addition, there was substantial damage to livestock and to crops in the region. Soon thereafter a class action lawsuit was filed against Union Carbide in the United States. Union Carbide objected to having the case heard in the United States, arguing that a U.S. court was a *forum non conveniens.* The plaintiffs' attorneys argued that the Indian courts were not sufficiently mature to handle the cases, and that the United States was the most appropriate forum for the cases.

   Should the case be decided by U.S. courts, or should the case be decided by Indian courts? Apply IDES principles to decide this issue. Presuming that the victims would not be able to recover, or would have their recoveries restricted under Indian law, is it ethical to sue in a nation that has very little contact with the cause of action simply to receive a larger verdict in the event of a favorable judgment? [See *In re Union Carbide Corp. and Gas Plant Disaster at Bhopal, India, in December, 1984* v. *Union Carbide Corp.*, 809 F.2d 195 (2d Cir. 1987).]

NOTES

1. Alejandro M. Garro, "Reconciliation of Legal Traditions in the U.N. Convention on Contracts for the International Sales of Goods," *The International Lawyer* 23 (Summer 1989), p. 443, at 444.
2. United Nations, Treaty Section, March 1994.
3. United Nations. *Convention on Contracts for the International Sales of Goods,* Article 2.
4. Ibid., Article 11.
5. Ibid., Article 39.
6. Ibid., Article 50.
7. Ibid., Article 16.
8. Ibid., Article 44.
9. John Greenwald, "No Passage to India," *Time,* September 18, 1995, pp. 91–92.

PART 4

IDES PROBLEMS

Mildred, an advertising copywriter, has a talent for woodworking, especially for building and carving wooden curios. For several years, Mildred has made wooden gifts for her closest friends for special occasions, always to the delight of her friends. In the past, several friends urged Mildred to open a store to sell her work, but she always refused to "mix business with pleasure." One friend, however, suggested that if Mildred did not wish to start a full-fledged business, she could, during her free time, make a little money by building a few custom pieces. Eventually, Mildred was spending nearly 20 hours per week of her "free" time making wooden objects for other people. In fact, income from her woodworking was beginning to rival her advertising salary.

However, Mildred has recently encountered a number of problems. One customer, Alfred, ordered a $200 cigar humidor with a carved lid, and Mildred spent nearly six months working on the project. Mildred was particularly proud of her work, and she had several pictures of the finished humidor on display in her workshop as evidence of the box's quality and beauty. Alfred, however, was not as happy with the work as was Mildred. He alleged that the humidor was not designed to his specifications and that it did not properly protect his cigars. In addition, Alfred complained that the box had a rough finish on the sides, rough enough to give him splinters when he handled it. Alfred claimed that the splinters led to an infection needing medical treatment. Citing that the box was not merchantable and that Mildred breached her warranty to him, Alfred has threatened to sue Mildred for the cost of the humidor plus his medical expenses.

Another customer, Beatrice, agreed over the phone to pay Mildred $800 for a dining table. When Mildred finished the work to the agreed-upon specifications, Beatrice refused to accept the table or pay the $800. Mildred objected, but Beatrice raised the Statute of Frauds as a defense and denied any liability on the alleged oral contract.

A third customer, Cleo, is a Canadian merchant who operates a store in Manitoba. Cleo claims that Mildred promised to sell her several thousand dollars worth of merchandise over a two-year period but that Mildred has yet to send Cleo any of these items or even to explain her failure to send the promised items. Mildred remembers a series of phone calls with Cleo, the contents of which Mildred is uncertain about, but Mildred contends that no written agreements were created.

Because of these problems, Mildred has retained an attorney. In preparation for her first meeting, Mildred needs to answer the following questions:

IDENTIFY What are the legal and ethical issues surrounding Mildred's actions with Alfred, Beatrice, and Cleo? Is she a merchant in the sale of wooden curios? Are Mildred's transactions covered under the UCC or common law? Are her customers entitled to a warranty?

DEFINE What are the meanings of the relevant legal terms associated with these issues?

ENUMERATE What are the legal and ethical principles relevant to these issues? What are the legal ramifications if Mildred is a merchant or if she is a nonmerchant? What warranty protections, if any, does Mildred owe her customers?

SHOW BOTH SIDES Consider all of the facts in light of the above questions. Do Alfred, Beatrice, and Cleo have legitimate complaints under the law?

[To review the IDES approach refer to pages 29–30.]

NEGOTIABLES

"Negotiables" take many forms. Negotiable instruments consist of checks, notes, drafts, and certificates of deposit. All of these forms are governed by (Revised) Article 3 of the Uniform Commercial Code (UCC). "Negotiables" can also take the form of negotiable documents of title. Documents of title are governed by Article 7 of the UCC.

In general, negotiable instruments are short-term instruments that arise out of commercial transactions. Millions of such instruments are signed each day, not only because they are a safe and convenient means of doing business, but also because they are acceptable in the commercial world as credit instruments and/or as substitutes for money. Documents of title are not as widely used, but they also have an important place in our commercial law.

This part of the text explains how and why negotiables are widely used and accepted in the modern commercial world. In addition, the topics of electronic funds transfers and bank–customer relations will be discussed.

I D E S

Amir works for National Bank as vice president of customer service and relations. In this position, Amir formulates strategies for addressing common (and not so common) customer complaints, many of which have legal dimensions. He must communicate these legal issues to National's corporate lawyers and then implement the legal advice he receives. Lately, Amir has encountered the following problems. A number of customers who issued stop payment orders for their checks have complained that National paid the checks regardless of the order. Is National liable to these customers for the amounts of these checks? Also, National occasionally finds that, for checks their customers deposit into their checking accounts, the drawee bank will dishonor these checks. Under what circumstances is National liable to customers who complain that National has taken too long to notify them about the dishonored checks? Recently, a rash of stolen ATM cards has led to a fair amount of illegal withdrawals. Under what circumstances must National reimburse these customers for the illegal transactions?

Consider these issues in the context of the chapter materials, and prepare to analyze them using the IDES model:

IDENTIFY the legal issues raised by the questions.

DEFINE all the relevant legal terms and issues involved.

ENUMERATE the legal principles associated with these issues.

SHOW BOTH SIDES by using the facts.

A G E N D A

In establishing CIT, the Kochanowskis may need to obtain loans. CIT will also need a checking account to pay its bills. What legal issues are associated with these processes?

CIT will have customers who wish to pay by personal check. These checks create a risk, albeit small, for CIT. Should CIT, because of the risk, refuse to accept payment by personal check?

As CIT grows, the company will need to deal with an increasingly large geographic market area. This entails sales to distant buyers. To avoid the problem of dishonored checks and/or the need to travel to remote locations to seek remedies, CIT may want to consider alternative payment forms. Should CIT use sight drafts? Should it use some other form of draft? Should CIT use letters of credit?

Be prepared! You never know when one of the Kochanowskis will ask you for advice or guidance.

Introduction to Negotiables: UCC (Revised) Article 3 and Article 7

O U T L I N E

HISTORIC OVERVIEW

An industrial or a commercial society needs some form of negotiable documents or negotiable instruments. When goods are transported or stored, some document is needed to reflect their transportation or their storage. When goods are sold and paid for, some instrument is needed to reflect the payment while providing some safety for the parties involved, since sending cash payment is somewhat risky.

Commercial paper of various types has been present in nearly every society that has developed a substantial commercial system. Documents very similar to the contemporary promissory note date back to about 2100 B.C. The merchants of Europe were using negotiable documents on a broad scale by the thirteenth century. In fact, the use of drafts was so widespread that a substantial portion of the Law Merchant was devoted to their proper treatment.

Commercial paper had become so pervasive by the late nineteenth century that the English Parliament began to enact special statutes to govern its use. Following the example of the English, the National Conference of Commissioners on Uniform State Laws drafted the Uniform Negotiable Instruments Law (NIL) for the United States in 1896. Each of these statutes merely attempted to cover the common law rules that had been developed over the years. The NIL was designed to unify and codify the rules and laws of each jurisdiction regarding all negotiable commercial documents. However, the breadth of the topical coverage made the NIL unwieldy and difficult to apply to the commercial world of the twentieth century.

The Uniform Commercial Code (UCC) was written to comply more readily with the demands of the modern business world. The topical coverage contained in the NIL was updated, divided into different articles, and included in the UCC. The Code has been adopted by every state in the union except Louisiana, and Louisiana has adopted some portions, including Articles 3 and 4, which deal with negotiable instruments and with bank–customer relations. Changes in banking law and the increased use of instruments that were not covered by the original Article 3 led to a revision of Article 3 to more accurately reflect modern practices and usage of instruments. As of July 1996, the Revised Article 3 has been adopted in 47 states and the District of Columbia (Massachusetts, New York, and South Carolina had not adopted, but all were expected to do so by 1997). As a result, our coverage here will only discuss Revised Article 3, which will henceforth be referred to simply as Article 3. (The cases included in Chapters 21 to 25, interpreting Article 3, are based on Article 3 *before* the revision, but the same results would follow under the revised version of the Article.)

The UCC, or "the Code" as it is frequently called, has standardized and clarified the rules of negotiable instruments while retaining most of the traditional rules and views of the topic. This codification of negotiable instruments is located in Article 3 of the Code. The UCC has also standardized and clarified the rules governing documents of title. Both warehouse receipts and bills of lading are covered in Article 7 of the Code. Article 7 retains many of the traditional rules and views of documents of title, while also codifying the contemporary use of these documents in the U.S. legal system. Each of these articles will be discussed in some detail in the remainder of this chapter.

THE SCOPE OF ARTICLE 3

Article 3 of the Uniform Commercial Code covers negotiable instruments. A *negotiable instrument* is a written promise or order to pay money to the order of a named person or to bearer. (Prior to its revision, Article 3 covered "commercial paper"). Although

Article 3 provides most of the coverage of negotiable instruments, there are also provisions in other articles of the UCC that affect negotiable instruments. For example, a number of definitions from Article 1 apply in Article 3. Article 4, Bank Deposits and Collections, and Article 9, Secured Transactions, also affect the coverage of negotiable instruments. In fact, Article 3 specifies that its (Article 3's) provisions are "subject to" the coverage in Articles 4 and 9. The scope of Article 3 is somewhat narrow, being restricted solely to negotiable instruments, as defined in § 3-104. Further, Section 3-102(a) states that Article 3 does not apply to money, to payment orders governed by Article 4A, or to securities governed by Article 8. Thus, one finds that Article 3 covers negotiable instruments but not other types of commercial or negotiable documents, and that two other articles of the Code may supplement, complement, or override the provisions of Article 3. To fall within the coverage of Article 3, an instrument must qualify as a "negotiable instrument." If an instrument does not qualify, it is likely to be governed by common law provisions, primarily in the area of contract law.

The following case dealt with the issue of whether a document was a negotiable instrument, governed by Article 3, or a contract, governed by common law.

21.1 STATE v. FAMILY BANK OF HALLANDALE

623 So.2d 474 (Fla. 1993)

FACTS The Department of Transportation awarded a contract to Ted's Sheds, Inc., for several metal buildings to be used at various service plazas on the Florida Turnpike. Ted's Sheds provided a Ft. Lauderdale address during the bidding process. When the buildings were delivered, the State received an invoice from Ted's Sheds listings its address as Bonita Springs, Florida. The State approved the invoices for payment, and, on 5 February 1987, the comptroller issued a warrant for $16,932 payable to the order of Ted's Sheds and sent it to the Ft. Lauderdale address listed on the original bid. On 12 February 1987, Ted's Shed of Broward, Inc., presented the original warrant to Seminole National Bank. The warrant was endorsed "Ted's Sheds of Broward, Inc.," and was credited to that account by the bank. Sometime thereafter, the agents of Ted's Sheds, Inc., in Bonita Springs stated that they had not received the warrant and requested a duplicate warrant.

It was then discovered that there were two Ted's Sheds, one in Ft. Lauderdale known as "Ted's Sheds of Broward, Inc.," and one in Bonita Springs, known as "Ted's Sheds, Inc." These separate legal entities shared common corporate officers. On 19 February 1987, the comptroller placed a stop payment order on the original warrant, issued a duplicate warrant to Ted's Sheds, and mailed it to Ted's Sheds, Inc., in Bonita Springs. Subsequently, the Federal Reserve Bank of Miami returned the original warrant to the bank indicating that payment had been stopped by the state treasurer.

The bank initiated this action some 14 months after the original warrant was returned. In the intervening time, Ted's Sheds of Broward, Inc., was involuntarily dissolved. The bank argued that it had no knowledge of the stop payment order and asserted that it was a "holder in due course" entitled to reimbursement by the State of Florida on the theory that state warrants are negotiable instruments. The State maintained that state warrants are not negotiable instruments under the UCC, and thus the bank was not entitled to repayment of these funds. The trial court entered summary judgment for the bank, and the State appealed.

ISSUES Are state warrants negotiable instruments under Article 3 of the UCC? Is a holder of a state warrant entitled to prejudgment interest on the amount of the warrant?

HOLDINGS No, state warrants are not negotiable instruments under Article 3 of the UCC. No, the holder is not entitled to prejudgment interest on the warrant.

REASONING A brief examination of the meaning and use of warrants is desirable before addressing the issues in this case. In connection with state funds, the term warrant has a well-defined meaning. *Warrants* are devices, prescribed by law, for drawing money from the state treasury. They are orders issued by the official whose duty it is to pass on claims to the treasurer to pay a specified sum from the treasury for the persons and purposes specified. A warrant is not an order to pay absolutely, rather it is generally prima facie evidence of indebtedness payable out of a particular fund or appropriation. . . . Thus, warrants drawn for ordinary governmental expenses are licenses authorizing pay-

21.1 STATE v. FAMILY BANK OF HALLANDALE *(cont.)* 623 So.2d 474 (Fla. 1993)

ment and are not intended to have all the qualities of commercial paper. . . .A warrant is best characterized as a chose in action, payable when funds are available for its purpose. . . . Prior to the adoption of the Uniform Commercial Code in Florida, warrants issued by sovereign governmental entities were expressly declared non-negotiable for public policy reasons. . . . Thus, under Florida law warrants have always been non-negotiable. The Family Bank of Hallandale is not a holder in due course because the state treasury warrant involved is not a negotiable instrument to which the UCC applies. As a result, the Family Bank took the warrant subject to the State's defense that it had issued a valid stop payment order.

We do not know the ultimate outcome of the case. Should the bank prevail, the issue of prejudgment interest would be involved. We also hold that the assessment of prejudgment interest against the State is improper because, under the doctrine of sovereign immunity, governmental entities are not liable for interest on their debts unless a statute or contract calls for it. . . . In the instant case we hold that, because the facts fail to establish the conditions precedent for an implied waiver of sovereign immunity, it is inappropriate to assess interest against the State.

Therefore, we quash the decision under review and direct the district court to remand for further proceedings consistent with this opinion.

BUSINESS CONSIDERATIONS Should a firm doing business with a governmental entity negotiate in its contract that payment *must* be made by check or draft, rather than by warrant, in order to avail itself of the potential benefits of Article 3? What protections are available to a business that receives its payment in the form of a state warrant?

ETHICAL CONSIDERATIONS Ted's Sheds and Ted's Sheds of Broward both operated from the same office and had the same officers. Does it seem likely that a warrant sent to Ted's Sheds of Broward instead of being sent to Ted's Sheds could be cashed without the management of Ted's Sheds knowing about it? Does the apparent interrelationship of the two firms raise any ethical issues?

Section 3-104 defines a negotiable instrument as

> *an unconditional promise or order to pay a fixed amount of money, with or without interest or other charges described in the promise or order, if it:*
>
> *1) is payable to bearer or order . . . ;*
> *2) is payable on demand or at a definite time . . . ; and*
> *3) does not state any other undertaking or undertaking by the person promising or ordering payment . . .*

The Article then states that any instrument that meets these criteria and falls within the definition of a *check* is a negotiable instrument and a check. Any instrument other than a check that satisfies these criteria is a negotiable instrument *unless*:

> **3-104(d)** *A promise or order other than a check is not an instrument if, at the time it is issued or first comes into possession of a* ***holder****, it contains a conspicuous statement, however expressed, to the effect that the promise or order is not negotiable or is not an instrument governed by this article.*

Holder
A person who receives possession of a negotiable instrument by means of a negotiation.

This means that a person who issues a check must abide by the provisions of Article 3, but a person who issues any other type of instrument that appears to be negotiable many *opt out* of Article 3's coverage by placing a conspicuous term on the face of the instrument excluding it from treatment as a negotiable instrument.

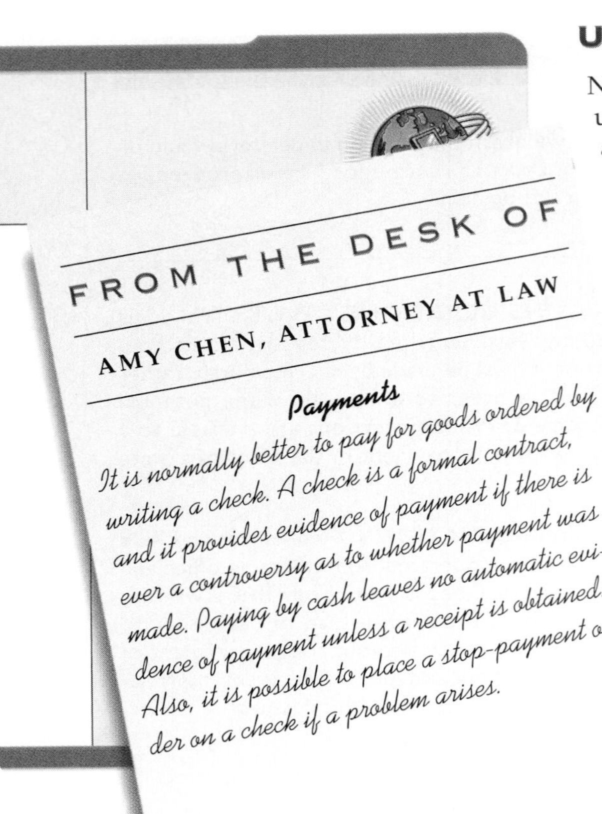

FROM THE DESK OF
AMY CHEN, ATTORNEY AT LAW
Payments
It is normally better to pay for goods ordered by writing a check. A check is a formal contract, and it provides evidence of payment if there is ever a controversy as to whether payment was made. Paying by cash leaves no automatic evidence of payment unless a receipt is obtained. Also, it is possible to place a stop-payment order on a check if a problem arises.

Uses of Negotiable Instruments

Negotiable instruments are widely used in our economy. They are used as a substitute for money. They are used for convenience. They are used as credit instruments. They are used to pay bills, to buy things, and to borrow. Some of the most important uses of each type are set out in the following sections.

Checks

The most commonly used type of negotiable instrument is a check. Many people use checks rather than cash for daily purchases. Checks are regularly written to the supermarket for groceries, to the utility companies to pay bills, to the landlord to pay the rent, and to the bank to make loan payments. In addition, many working people receive their salaries or wages in periodic paychecks from their employers.

Checks are widely used because they are easily written, easily carried, and widely accepted. Carrying and using checks is safer than carrying and using cash. If a person loses a blank, unsigned check, no harm is done. All that was lost was a piece of paper. If a person loses cash, the money is gone. The bank will not take an unsigned check, but it will take lost money. Great care should be taken with checks, particularly signed ones. A signed check, otherwise blank, is nearly as good as cash. Anyone finding such a check can complete the blanks and possibly receive cash for it as completed, to the detriment of the depositor/"drawer."

The revision to Article 3 recognizes a number of specialized drafts as "checks" within the coverage of Section 3-104. Each of these specialized checks have the primary use of serving as a substitute for money. However, they also have some aspect that distinguishes them from "regular" checks. For example, a *cashier's check* is a check drawn *by* a bank *against* that same bank and then issued to the person who purchased it. Cashier's checks are commonly used by a purchaser who wants to guarantee payment to the payee. (The payee knows that there are sufficient funds on deposit since the bank is holding those funds already, and knows that the cashier's check cannot have payment stopped.)

These are *preaccepted* checks (acceptance is discussed in a later chapter), which ensure the payee that he or she will be paid upon presentment. A *teller's check* is similar to a cashier's check, being a check that is drawn *by* one bank *against* another bank. Again, the act of issuing the teller's check shows *preacceptance,* ensuring the payee that he or she will be paid upon proper presentment. A *traveler's check* is a special type of check used by people who are away from home and want the security of having checks that will be accepted. A traveler's check is signed once by the drawer upon purchase, but it requires a second signing by that same drawer (a countersigning) before it can be negotiated. The payee knows that a bank is holding the funds used to purchase the traveler's check, so there is no danger of insufficient funds; and the payee can compare the countersignature to the "authenticating" original signature, minimizing the risk of a forgery. A *credit union check* (formerly called a "share draft") is simply a check drawn against a credit union. As banks become more and more specialized, many individuals are turning to credit unions to handle their personal banking needs simply because the credit union specializes in individual accounts, and the fees imposed are normally substantially less.

Drafts

Businesses often use drafts to pay for merchandise ordered, especially when the buyer and the seller are in different states. Drafts may be payable "at sight" (i.e., on demand), or they may be "time drafts" (i.e., they are payable at a future date). Often a seller of goods will send a draft to the buyer for acceptance. If the buyer accepts, he or she has agreed to pay any holder who makes proper **presentment**. Such a draft is called a *trade* ***acceptance***.

With the recent liberalization of federal and state banking laws and regulations, a number of changes have occurred in the area of negotiable instruments. One of these changes has been in the area of drafts. Today some financial institutions offer accounts similar to the checking accounts offered by banks and savings and loan institutions. These drafting accounts offer the same privileges for these depositors as are available to depositors of banks. Technically, however, these are not checking accounts; there are some minor differences.

Presentment
A demand by a holder for the maker or the drawee of a negotiable instrument to accept and/or pay the instrument.

Acceptance
The agreement by the maker or the drawee to accept and/or pay a negotiable instrument upon presentment.

Promissory note
A written promise to pay a sum certain in money without conditions, either at a preset time in the future or "on demand."

Promissory Notes

Promissory notes are most often used as instruments of credit. They are also used as evidence to show a pre-existing debt. Any time a customer borrows money from a

YOU BE THE JUDGE

Who Is at Fault for a Late Payment?

A person recently received his monthly statement for one of his credit cards, and he discovered that the credit card issuer had imposed a late payment service charge on his bill. He was more than a little upset, since he distinctly remembers mailing his payment at least a week before the payment deadline specified on the bill. He would like to know how he can be assessed a service charge for a late payment when he made his payment prior to the deadline. He has filed a suit against the credit card firm seeking recovery of the fees, alleging that he made the payment before the due date, and that it is not his fault that the credit card company did not receive the payment in a timely manner.[1]

The case has been filed in *your* court. How will you resolve this case?

BUSINESS CONSIDERATIONS Which party is, or should be, responsible for any delays or nondeliveries by the postal service of payments on the credit card account? What sort of policies should the credit card company establish to handle this sort of situation?

ETHICAL CONSIDERATIONS Is it ethical for a creditor to send a bill with a preaddressed envelope, thereby implying that the mails should be used to remit payment, and to then hold the debtor responsible for the timeliness of the postal delivery? How should the rights of the parties be balanced in this sort of situation?

SOURCE: *Independent Banker*, May 1996, pp. 7–8.

21.1

FINANCE

CO-MAKERS FOR COMPANY LOANS

When the family first formed CIT, they needed to borrow money from their bank. The bank's lending officer was more than willing to make the loan, but *not* if the borrower was going to be CIT. She insisted that Tom and Anna had to be co-makers of the note along with Call-Image before she was willing to make the loan. Since they needed the money—and they viewed the family and the business as an entity—they agreed to be co-makers of the note along with CIT. They recently were discussing their various loans and this issue arose again. They ask you if the bank was acting improperly in requiring them to sign as co-makers. What will you tell them?

BUSINESS CONSIDERATIONS It is very common in a number of business classes to discuss the advantages and disadvantages of the various forms a business may take. Limited liability is often mentioned as an advantage of a corporation. However, when a corporation is newly formed, it has no credit history and no "track record" of being profitable. What should a potential creditor insist on when considering the extension of credit to a newly formed corporation? Why?

ETHICAL CONSIDERATIONS Is it ethical for an entrepreneur to form a corporation or a limited liability partnership or a limited liability corporation to avoid potential liability if his or her entrepreneurial skills do not flourish, and the business enterprise fails? How can this be justified—or criticized—from an ethical perspective?

bank, the borrower must sign a *promissory note;* this signed note proves the existence of the debt, the amount owed, the manner of repayment, and any other terms important to the loan agreement. Notes are so widely used that special types of notes have developed. Real estate loans normally involve a mortgage note. Automobile loans usually involve an installment note. Many banks also use a device called a commercial loan note or a signature note for short-term unsecured loans (loans made without collateral).

Certificates of Deposit

A *certificate of deposit* (CD) is an instrument issued by a bank evidencing a debt owed to a depositor. These instruments commonly call for the bank to pay to a proper presenter the amount deposited plus interest at a stated future date. Although regularly thought of as a type of special savings account, CDs are really credit instruments. They recognize money "borrowed" by the bank from its depositor.

Functions and Forms

Negotiable instruments have two major functions: They are designed to serve as a substitute for money, and they are designed to serve as credit instruments. In satisfying either use, they carry certain contract rights, certain property rights, and some special rights due exclusively to their nature as negotiable instruments. Every negotiable instrument is presumed to be a contract, but not every contract is a negotiable instrument. The difference between a contract and a negotiable instrument is one of form. To be negotiable, an instrument must be (1) current in trade and (2) payable in money. These criteria are obviously too broad and too vague to be of much practical significance. Accordingly, Article 3 has more fully defined the requirements an instrument must meet in order to be negotiable.

As mentioned earlier, UCC § 3-104 defines the various types of negotiable instruments. These definitions include the following, by subsection of 3-104:

- *(e) lists the only forms a negotiable instrument may take:*
  An instrument is a "note" if it is a promise and it is a "draft" if it is an order. If an instrument falls within the definition of both "note" and "draft," a person entitled to enforce the instrument may treat it as either.
- *(f) defines a "check":*
  "Check" means (i) a draft, other than a documentary draft, payable on demand and drawn on a bank or (ii) a cashier's check or teller's check. An instrument

may be a check even though it is described on its face by another term, such as "money order."

- *(g) defines a "Cashier's check":*
  "Cashier's check" means a draft with respect to which a drawer and drawee are the same bank or branches of the same bank.
- *(h) defines a "Teller's check":*
  "Teller's check" means a draft drawn by a bank (i) on another bank, or (ii) payable at or through a bank.
- *(i) defines a "Traveler's check":*
  "Traveler's check" means an instrument that (i) is payable on demand, (ii) is drawn on or payable at or through a bank, (iii) is designated by the term "traveler's check" or by a substantially similar term, and (iv) requires, as a condition to payment, a countersignature by a person whose specimen signature appears on the instrument.
- *(j) defines a "Certificate of deposit":*
  "Certificate of deposit" means an instrument containing an acknowledgment by a bank that a sum of money has been received by the bank and a promise by the bank to repay the sum of money. A certificate of deposit is a note of the bank.

Drafts, including checks, are one form of negotiable instrument and are known as *order paper.* Notes, including certificates of deposit, are the other form of negotiable instrument and are known as *promise paper.* Order paper is most commonly used as a substitute for money. Promise paper is most commonly used as a credit instrument, providing proof that credit has been extended and showing evidence of the terms of payment for that credit.

PAPER PAYABLE "TO ORDER" ("THREE-PARTY" PAPER)

The distinctive features of paper payable "to order," or three-party paper, are that each instrument contains an *order* to pay money and that at least *three parties* are necessary to fill the legal roles involved. The order element will be pointed out in the following sections, while the rules governing this class of negotiable instrument will be explained later. The three parties involved on "to order" paper are: the *drawer,* the *drawee,* and the *payee.* As noted, this class consists of drafts, including checks in the various forms checks can take.

Drafts

A **draft** is an instrument in which one party, the drawer, issues an instrument to a second party, the payee. The draft is accepted by the payee as a substitute for money. The payee expects to receive money at some time from the third party, the drawee. The reason the payee expects to receive money from the drawee is contained in the basic form of the instrument. As will be pointed out, the drawer issues an order to the drawee to pay a sum of money. This order, coupled with the three roles involved, distinguishes drafts from promise paper. The components of a draft are shown in Exhibit 21.1.

Draft
An order for a third person to pay a sum certain in money without conditions, either at a preset time in the future or "on demand."

EXHIBIT 21.1 A Bank Draft

42764

UNITED VIRGINIA BANK

(6)

DATE ____________ 19____

(1) (2)
PAY TO THE
ORDER OF ____________ (3) ____________ $ ______ (4)

______________________ (5) ______________________ DOLLARS

(7)
______________ TELLER

MANUFACTURERS HANOVER TRUST COMPANY (8)
NEW YORK, NEW YORK

VOID VOID VOID VOID VOID VOID VOID

AUTHORIZED
SIGNATURE

"042764" '0210'"0030' :0144 7""36834"'

Courtesy of Crestar Bank (formerly United Virginia Bank), Radford, Virginia. (1) The order. (2) Words of negotiability. (3) The payee. (4) The amount, in numbers. (5) The amount, in words. (6) The date of issue. (7) The drawer's signature. (8) The drawee.

Checks

The most common type of paper payable "to order" is a check. A check is a special type of draft. Like a draft, a check necessitates the involvement of three parties, but there are two differences. A check is, by definition, a demand instrument; in contrast, a draft may be a demand instrument or a time instrument. Furthermore, a check must be drawn on a bank or payable at or through a bank; in contrast, anyone may be the drawee on a draft. The revision to Article 3 specifically includes cashier's checks, teller's checks, traveler's checks, and checks drawn against credit unions (formerly referred to as *share drafts*) within the definition of "checks" to better reflect contemporary usage of that term. Exhibit 21.2 shows the various elements of a check.

In the case of both a check and a draft, the drawee is obligated to the drawer. This obligation is normally a debt or contractual obligation owed to the drawer by the drawee. When the drawer orders the drawee to pay, the drawer is directing the drawee as to how the debt or contractual obligation should be discharged or partially discharged. The order to the drawee to pay, coupled with the obligation to pay, assures the payee that payment will (normally) be made by the drawee at the appropriate time.

The Order. All drafts (including checks) contain an order. The drawer *orders* the drawee to pay the instrument. The language used is not a request. The drawer does not "ask," or "hope," or even "expect" the drawee to pay. The drawer demands that payment be made. If you look at Exhibit 21.1 or Exhibit 21.2, you will see that the

EXHIBIT 21.2 A Check

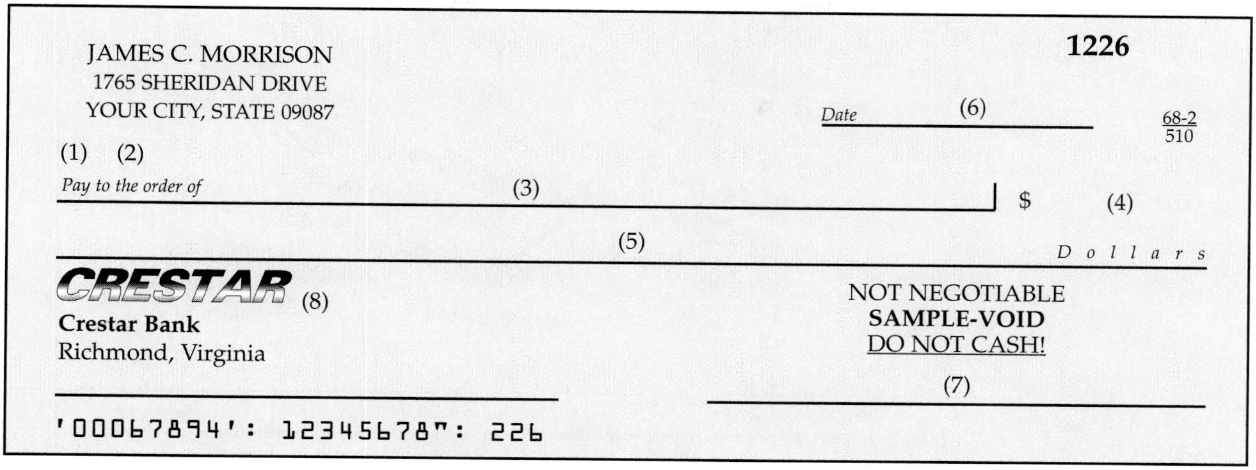

JAMES C. MORRISON
1765 SHERIDAN DRIVE
YOUR CITY, STATE 09087

1226

Date (6)

68-2/510

(1) (2)
Pay to the order of (3) $ (4)

(5) Dollars

CRESTAR (8)
Crestar Bank
Richmond, Virginia

NOT NEGOTIABLE
SAMPLE-VOID
DO NOT CASH!

(7)

'00067894': 12345678": 226

Courtesy of Crestar Bank, Radford, Virginia. (1) The order. (2) Words of negotiability. (3) The payee. (4) The amount, in numbers. (5) The amount, in words. (6) The date of issue. (7) The drawer's signature. (8) The drawee.

drawer tells the drawee to "*Pay* to the order of (Payee)." It should also be noted that the order is the word *pay*; the phrase "to the order of" is not the order. This phrase is a term of negotiability; its meaning will be explained later, when negotiability is discussed.

The Drawer. The person who draws an order instrument, who gives the order to the drawee, and who issues the instrument to the payee is known as the drawer. This person originates the check or the draft. The drawer does not pay the payee directly. The drawee is expected to pay the payee or the holder, upon proper presentment. That is why the drawer gives the drawee the order. The drawer expects the order to be obeyed because of a prior agreement or relationship between the drawer and the drawee. If the order is obeyed, the drawee pays the payee or holder, and both the drawer and the drawee have performed.

The Drawee. The party to whom the order on the draft is directed is the drawee. The drawee is told by the drawer to "Pay to the order of" the payee. It is the drawee who is expected to make payment to the presenting party. However, the drawee has no duty to the payee or to the holder to pay, despite the order. The only duty the drawee has is a duty owed to the drawer. The duty of the drawee is to accept the instrument. Before acceptance, there is only the prospect that the drawee will pay when the time for payment arrives. Once the drawee accepts, the drawee has a contractual obligation to pay the presenter. This relationship is shown in Exhibit 21.3.

EXHIBIT 21.3 The Parties on Order Paper

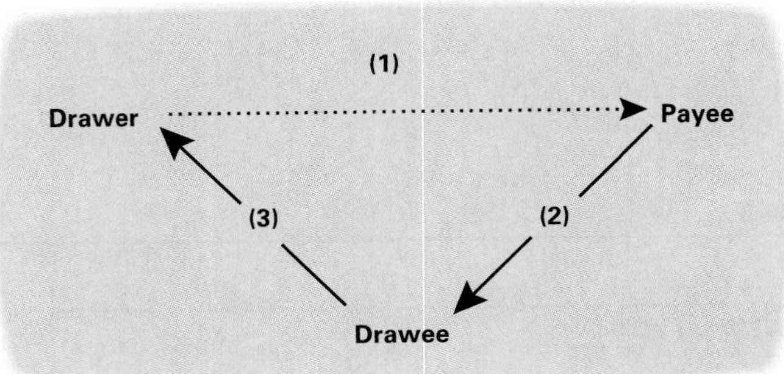

(1) The drawer issues the order instrument to the payee. The instrument contains an order directed to the drawee.

(2) The payee (or an endorsee or holder) presents the order instrument to the drawee in order to collect. The drawee is expected to obey the order directed to it by the drawer.

(3) Assuming that the drawee obeyed the order, the drawer is charged (or his or her account is debited) for the amount of the order instrument.

In the following case, a question arose as to whether the drawee had obeyed the order of the drawer.

21.2 STATE v. BARCLAY'S BANK OF NEW YORK, N.A. 563 N.E. 2d 11 (N.Y. 1990)

FACTS The case stems from the activities of Richard Caliento, an accountant. He prepared tax returns for various clients. To satisfy their tax liability, the clients issued checks payable to various State taxing entities, and gave them to Caliento. Between 1977 and 1979, he forged endorsements on these checks, deposited them in his own account with defendant, and subsequently withdrew the proceeds. In November 1980—shortly after the scheme was uncovered—Caliento died when the plane he was piloting crashed. The State never received the checks. In 1983, after learning of these events, the State commenced this action seeking to recover the aggregate amount of the checks.

The Supreme Court denied defendant's motion to dismiss the complaint and its subsequent motion for summary judgment, concluding that the payee's possession of the checks was not essential to its action against the depository bank. On appeal, the Appellate Division reversed and dismissed the complaint. It held that requiring "delivery, either actual or constructive, [as] an indispensable prerequisite for" a conversion action . . . is consistent with the view of most authorities and supported by practical considerations. . . . We agree.

ISSUE In the absence of actual or constructive possession of a check, does the payee have rights against the drawee for honoring a forged endorsement of the payee?

HOLDING No. Delivery is an indispensable prerequisite for a conversion action under Article 3 of the UCC.

REASONING It has long been held that a check has no valid inception until delivery. Further, a payee must have actual or constructive possession of a negotiable instrument in order to attain the status of a holder and to have an interest in it. These are established principles of negotiable in-

21.2 STATE v. BARCLAY'S BANK OF NEW YORK, N.A. *(cont.)* **563 N.E. 2d 11 (N.Y. 1990)**

strument law. . . . Permitting a payee who has never had possession to maintain an action would be inconsistent with these principles. It would have the effect of enforcing rights that do not exist. For this reason, most courts and commentators have concluded that either actual or constructive delivery to the payee is a necessary prerequisite to a conversion action. . . . Significant practical considerations support this conclusion. Where a payee has never possessed the check, it is more likely that the forged indorsement resulted from the drawer's negligence, an issue which could not be readily contested in an action between the payee and the depository bank. . . . Moreover, as noted by the Appellate Division, the payee is not left without a remedy, inasmuch as it can sue on the underlying obligation. [The State] never acquired a property interest in the checks and cannot be said to have suffered a loss.

The order of the Appellate Division should, accordingly, be affirmed, with costs.

BUSINESS CONSIDERATIONS Businesses very commonly trust their attorneys and their accountants to a degree that they do not necessarily trust others with whom they work or do business. When an attorney or an accountant violates that trust, the business is sometimes left in a serious dilemma. In this case, Caliento's clients may have up to three years of unpaid taxes, plus interest and costs. What can/should a business do to protect itself in such a situation?

ETHICAL CONSIDERATIONS An accountant who embezzles or steals from his clients not only hurts the clients, that accountant also hurts the image of the profession, at least to some extent. What should the profession do to help ensure that its practitioners are honest and reputable? Does a code of ethics adequately address this situation?

The Payee. The payee is the person to whom the instrument is originally issued. The payee may be specifically designated, as in "Pay to the order of Jane Doe"; the payee may be an office or title, as in "Pay to the order of Treasurer of Truro County"; or the particular payee may be unspecified, as in "Pay to the order of bearer." The payee may decide to seek payment personally, or the payee may decide to further negotiate the instrument. The words "to the order of" allow the payee to order the drawee to make payment to some other party. (*To the order of* means to whomever the payee orders, literally allowing the negotiation of the instrument.)

Promise Paper ("Two-Party" Paper)

The distinctive features of promise paper, or *two-party* paper, are that each such instrument contains a promise, and that only two parties are necessary to fulfill the legal roles involved on the instrument. This class of negotiable instruments involves notes, including certificates of deposit. These two parties are known as the *maker* and the *payee.*

The term "two-party" is confusing to many people. Many stores have signs prominently posted stating that they do not accept "two-party checks." These so-called two-party checks are, in reality, checks that have been negotiated by the payee to a later holder. The store does not want to accept a check unless it receives it directly from the drawer. But there is no such legal creature as a check that is "two-party paper."

The promise element of promise paper will be pointed out in the following sections, and the rules governing this class of negotiable instrument will be explained later.

(Promissory) Notes

The promissory note is the oldest known form of negotiable instrument. It is normally used as a credit instrument, executed either at the time credit is extended or as evidence of a pre-existing debt not yet repaid.

In a note, one party (the maker) promises to pay the other party (the payee) a sum of money at some future time. The promise may call for a lump-sum payment, or it may call for installment payments over time. The note may specify the payment of interest in addition to the principal; it may have the interest included in the principal; or it may be interest free. The note may recite details about collateral. Despite any or all of these possibilities, the basic form is constant. Such an instrument is shown in Exhibit 21.4 (pages 546–547).

The following case involved an interesting approach to the enforcement of a "promissory note," and emphasizes the importance of being certain that one's instruments are, indeed, negotiable.

21.3 ALMOND v. RHYNE — 424 S.E.2d 231 (N.C.App. 1993)

FACTS On 1 May 1984, Rhyne executed an agreement whereby Rhyne agreed to purchase fifty (50) shares of stock in A & H Millworks, Inc., from Jesse Almond (the deceased). In addition, this agreement gave Rhyne an option to purchase an additional fifty (50) shares of stock. To secure the purchase price of $35,000, Rhyne also executed a document entitled "Promissory Note and Security Agreement."

In either June or September of 1988, after the deceased was diagnosed with cancer, Rhyne visited the deceased. During this visit, Rhyne obtained possession of the promissory note and a stock certificate representing the original fifty (50) shares of stock. Only Rhyne and the decedent were present during this time.

Margaret Almond filed suit on 9 April 1990 to collect the balance owing on the promissory note. No payment has been made on the promissory note since 10 May 1988. On 12 September 1991 the trail court granted Almond's motion for summary judgment for the balance due on the note plus interest.

ISSUE Did Almond deliver the "promissory note" to Rhyne with the intent to cancel the note and discharge the debt?

HOLDING No. Rhyne failed to present admissible evidence sufficient to persuade the court of any intent to discharge the obligation.

REASONING Rhyne argued that his possession of the note and the stock certificate was evidence that Almond intended to cancel the note and discharge the debt as a matter of law. In support of his argument, Rhyne quoted the UCC, § 3-605. However, the court rejected this argument, stating that the UCC did not govern this case since the "promissory note" was not negotiable under Article 3. The note in question contained language stating that "the terms of the May 1984 Agreement are incorporated herein by reference as though fully written herein." Because of this language, the instrument is conditional, and therefore not a negotiable instrument. Thus, § 3-605 was inapplicable, and the case had to be resolved under common law.

Under the laws of this state, a debtor's obligation under a note can be discharged when the note is surrendered to the debtor and there is ample evidence that the party surrendering the note *intended* to discharge the debtor. Here, the operation of Rule 601 (c) (Deadman's Statute) precludes evidence that the deceased intended to discharge defendant's obligation. [The "Deadman's Statute" provides that no person with an interest in an event can be examined as a witness in his own behalf against the executor of the estate of a decedent concerning any oral communication between the witness and the deceased.]

Several jurisdictions have recognized that surrender of a note to the debtor will discharge the debtor's obligation if it is done with the intent to discharge. . . . Also, other authorities recognize that surrender of an instrument must be accompanied by an intent to discharge the debtor's obligation. . . . We find the approach advocated by these authorities is well-reasoned and applicable to the present situation. Accordingly, having reviewed defendant's pleadings, depositions, and affidavits, and since he has presented no admissible evidence in regards to the deceased's intent when surrendering the documents, we cannot say, as a matter of law, that the debt has been extinguished.

21.3 ALMOND v. RHYNE *(cont.)* 424 S.E.2d 231 (N.C.App. 1993)

Defendant further contends that at a minimum, surrender of the note created a presumption of discharge. We first observe that cancellation or discharge of an obligation is an affirmative defense and defendant, as payor, bears the burden of proving a valid discharge. Since defendant must prove not only surrender of the note but also an intent to discharge the debt on the part of the deceased, we cannot say that a finding of one element raises a presumption that the other exists. Accordingly, defendant's argument has no merit.

BUSINESS CONSIDERATIONS What precautions should an individual take when he or she is dealing with a terminally ill person in an investment setting? What should Rhyne have done in his circumstances to prove that Jesse Almond intended to cancel the note and release Rhyne from liability?

ETHICAL CONSIDERATIONS The maker of a $35,000 note acquires possession of the note *and* a certificate for stock that the note was purportedly issued to purchase. Both the note and the stock certificate are acquired from a terminally ill person. The maker then claims that the payee canceled the note and delivered the stock as an "accord and satisfaction." How credible is the witness in this situation? What ethical issues does such testimony raise? Does the "Deadman Statute" seem to provide an adequate solution to this problem?

Certificates of Deposit

A certificate of deposit (or a CD, as it is frequently called) is a special type of note issued by a bank as an acknowledgment of money received, with a promise to repay the money at some future date. Many people think of a CD as a "time savings account," in contrast to a passbook savings account. In reality, though, a CD is not a savings account at all. It is most commonly a time deposit of money with a bank.

A CD normally pays higher interest than a savings account, with the interest varying according to the amount of time the certificate is to run. Most certificates run for some multiple of six months, and they are available in some multiple of $1,000. However, a number of banks offer CDs for shorter time periods such as 90 days. Some banks are beginning to offer CDs for multiples of $100. One type of CD is shown in Exhibit 21.5. Today, many banks offer some variation of a "saver's certificate," which is nonnegotiable, rather than a negotiable certificate of deposit. It appears that the CD is becoming extinct, although some CDs still exist. However, the widespread replacement of CDs with other forms of certificates makes this an area of primarily historic interest.

The Promise. *Promise paper* is so called because it contains a promise. The maker of the instrument promises to pay an amount of money to the payee or to a holder. The instrument does not say that the maker "might" pay, or will "probably" pay, or will "agree" to pay. The instrument says that the maker promises to pay an amount of money to the payee or to the order of the payee.

The Maker. The duties performed by the drawer and the drawee on order paper are effectively combined in promise paper: Both duties fall to the maker. The maker makes the promise—"I promise to pay to the order of (the payee)"; the maker issues the instrument to the payee; and the maker pays the instrument upon proper presentment. However, there is one important difference from order paper. While the drawee is not obligated to any holder until acceptance, the maker is liable to a holder from the date of original issue. This obligation is shown in Exhibit 21.6.

21.2

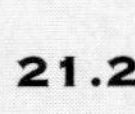

FINANCE

SHOULD CIT PLACE ITS ACCOUNT IN A CREDIT UNION?

Dan has his personal checking account with a credit union, and he is very pleased with the service he receives. He is strongly urging the family to place the CIT account with the credit union. Julio disagrees. He believes the family and the business will be better served by having a commercial account with a commercial bank. The family asks what you would recommend for them. What advice will you give them. (Before answering, you might want to contact a local bank and a local credit union for information, suggestions, and guidance.)

BUSINESS CONSIDERATIONS What services would a business want and/or reasonably expect from a bank? How are these services different from those that an individual would want and/or reasonably expect on his or her account?

ETHICAL CONSIDERATIONS Many banks today are beginning to charge customers fees and service charges for using an automated teller machine (ATM). Some banks are also imposing fees when a customer enters the bank and uses a human teller when the transaction could have been handled by an ATM. Is the imposition of a fee or a service charge for normal and expected banking services ethical?

The Payee. As in order paper, the *payee* is the party to whom the instrument is originally issued. Again, the payee may be specifically designated by name, or designated by title or office, or unspecified. The payee on promise paper is the person to whom the promise is made by the maker. By contrast, the payee on order paper is the person to whom the drawee is directed (ordered) to make payment.

THE SCOPE OF ARTICLE 7

The UCC treats the topic of documents of title in Article 7. This article, entitled "Warehouse Receipts, Bills of Lading, and Other Documents of Title," specifies the rights and the duties of all relevant parties in the handling of documents of title, whether those documents are negotiable or nonnegotiable. Part 2 of Article 7 deals with warehouse receipts; Part 3 deals with bills of lading; Part 5 deals with the negotiation and transfer of a document of title.

FUNCTIONS AND FORMS

The essential function of a *document of title* is to reflect the rights of the owner when the goods are turned over to the custody and care of a bailee, whether for storage or for carriage. A secondary function of a document of title, especially if the document is negotiable, is to enable the owner to transfer title to the goods without having to reclaim possession of the goods in order to make the sale. The owner can negotiate the document of title, and in so doing the owner also transfers title to the goods to the person receiving the negotiation. The importance of the negotiability of a document of title is shown in the following case.

21.4 BANK OF NEW YORK v. AMOCO OIL CO. 831 F.Supp. 254 (S.D.N.Y. 1993)

FACTS Amoco uses platinum to prepare catalysts that are used in reactors at Amoco's six refineries around the country. These catalysts accelerate the refining process in the manufacture of gasoline. During the refining process, some platinum is lost—between 2,000 and 4,000 ounces each year. Although Amoco owns 280,000 ounces of platinum, it must occasionally lease platinum from other sources. Sloss, who was Amoco's Senior Supply Negotiator until 1992, testified that he leased from metal trading companies that delivered platinum to Amoco's catalyst manufacturers. A particular shipment of platinum, once it is used to prepare catalysts for use in the refining process, can no longer be traced. . . . When leasing, Amoco would issue a holding certificate to the precious metal company from whom the platinum had been obtained. . . .

21.4 BANK OF NEW YORK v. AMOCO OIL CO. *(cont.)* 831 F.Supp. 254 (S.D.N.Y. 1993)

DBL Trading leased metals to companies such as Amoco in order to improve profitability on its precious metals inventory. Metal was also used as collateral by DBL Trading in lending transactions with various banks, including Bank of New York (BNY). . . . The amount of the loans made available by BNY were limited to 95% of the daily value of the pledged collateral. BNY would receive a telex from the depository where the collateral was being held, a warehouse receipt, or a holding certificate. The banks' rights in the collateral were reflected in a General Loan and Security Agreement between BNY and DBL Trading, which had been signed in 1982. . . . Three of the four holding certificates at issue in this litigation were accepted by BNY in December of 1989. They conform to previous certificates that BNY had accepted. . . . The fourth certificate is identical in wording to the other three, but is dated 2 January 1990. . . . On 13 February 1990, DBL Trading defaulted on an overnight loan that it had obtained from BNY. BNY immediately began liquidating collateral; after an exchange of communications discussed in detail below, Amoco returned platinum to BNY. It did not do so, however, until 4 April 1990, after this action had been brought. Sloss instructed UOP, Inc., a platinum reclaimer that held platinum in a pool account for Amoco, to transfer 22,230 troy ounces of platinum from Amoco's account to BNY's account. BNY sued Amoco for conversion, alleging that Amoco had refused to turn over the platinum upon the bank's proper demand based on its possession of the holding certificates.

ISSUE Were the holding certificates negotiable documents of title under Article 7, granting the bank the right to immediate transfer upon demand?

HOLDING Yes. The holding certificates fell within Article 7's definition of a negotiable document of title, which gave the bank the right to an immediate transfer of the platinum upon demand.

REASONING BNY bases its conversion claim on the alleged superior rights that it had to the platinum under Article 7 of the UCC. If the holding certificates were negotiable documents of title that DBL Trading duly negotiated to BNY, then BNY obtained title to the platinum, and Amoco was under an obligation to "hold or deliver the goods according to the terms of the document free of any defense or claim by [it] except those arising under the terms of the document . . ." The holding certificates come under the purview of Article 7 only if they fall within the definition of a document of title. The UCC states that the following are documents of title: Bill of lading, dock warrant, dock receipt, warehouse receipt or order for the delivery of goods and also any other document which in the regular course of business or financing is treated as adequately evidencing that the person in possession of it is entitled to receive, hold and dispose of the document and the goods it covers. . . . BNY contends that [the documents] fall within the broad language describing "other documents" that constitute documents of title, and the court agrees. . . . The court finds that BNY did treat the holding certificates as "adequately evidencing that [BNY] is entitled to receive, hold and dispose of the document and the goods it covers." Moreover, industry practice was to accept holding certificates as well, at least in some circumstances, as documents of title. . . . Notwithstanding Amoco's objections, . . . the holding certificates here did constitute documents of title and fall within the purview of Article 7. . . .

In order to be negotiable, a document of title must state "by its terms [that] the goods are to be delivered to bearer or to the order of a named person. . . ." Although the holding certificates did not literally comply with [the Code's requirements for negotiability], they represented title to the goods on their face, stating that their are no liens or encumbrances and that the metal was being held for DBL Trading's account or order. They were signed by Amoco's representative, and stated that the goods would be delivered when the certificates were properly endorsed. . . .

The court finds that the holding certificates issued by Amoco constituted negotiable documents of title that were duly negotiated to BNY by DBL Trading. Plaintiff is to be awarded $550,000, as the agreed-on limit, and prejudgment interest thereupon from 4 April 1990.

BUSINESS CONSIDERATIONS Amoco's representatives had a very lackadaisical attitude in this case. The Senior Supply Negotiator testified that he did not pay too much attention to the language of the holding certificates, and he merely drew a line diagonally across the face of the certificates when they were redeemed. What sort of policies and practices should a business have in place when it is dealing with negotiable documents of title representing goods of substantial value?

ETHICAL CONSIDERATIONS Amoco testified that the individual sources of the platinum were no longer distinguishable once the platinum was used in one of the catalysts. When is it ethical for a firm to commingle fungible goods it is leasing? What precautions should the lessee take to protect the interests of the lessor?

EXHIBIT 21.4 A Promissory Note

FEDERAL BANK

PROMISSORY NOTE

Loan No.

Borrower(s)
Name(s) ______ first middle last and ______ first middle last

______ Address

(1) (2) (3) (2)

Borrower (jointly and severally if more than one) promises to pay to Federal Savings Bank ("Lender"), or order, in U.S. money, at its office in San Diego, California, or elsewhere Lender designates, principal and interest on unpaid principal from the date advanced until paid, in amount, annual rate and consecutive monthly installments as follows:

Principal	$ (4)	Annual Interest Rate	%
Installments	$	on the same day of month beginning	
Minimum Interest	$ 100.00		

Interest will be computed on the basis of a 12 month year and 30 day month. The date of payment, whether early or late, will be disregarded for purposes of allocating the payment between principal and interest: each payment will be treated for this purpose as though made on its due date.

PREPAYMENT: Full or partial prepayment may be made without penalty except Borrower will pay any minimum interest amount specified. Borrower will tell Lender in writing that Borrower is making a prepayment. Lender will use all prepayments to reduce the principal subject to its right to first apply payments received to any past due interest or other charges. Partial prepayments will not delay the due dates nor change the amount of monthly payments unless Lender agrees in writing to those delays or changes. Full prepayment may be made at any time. Lender may require that partial prepayment be made on the same day as monthly payments are due. Lender may also require that the amount of any partial prepayment be equal to the amount of principal that would have been part of the next one or more monthly payments.

LATE CHARGE: Borrower will pay a late charge of 5% of each installment not paid within 15 days of its due date, or $5.00, whichever is greater.

DEFAULT AND ACCELERATION: If Borrower fails to timely pay any installment when due or to perform any provision contained in any document securing this Note, Lender may, at Lender's option, declare all sums owed hereunder immediately due and payable. Borrower will pay all reasonable expenses and attorney's fees of Lender in any action relating to Borrower's obligations.

SELLER, IF ANY: Borrower intends to use some or all of the loan proceeds to pay ______, as Seller, amounts due Seller under a contract between Seller and Borrower, dated ______, Borrower represents that a true and correct copy of the contract has been furnished to Lender and that it contains the entire agreement between Seller and Borrower. The following notice applies only to the named Seller, if any, and to the proceeds hereof paid to said Seller under the described contract.

NOTICE: ANY HOLDER OF THIS CONSUMER CREDIT CONTRACT IS SUBJECT TO ALL CLAIMS AND DEFENSES WHICH THE DEBTOR COULD ASSERT AGAINST THE SELLER OF GOODS OR SERVICES OBTAINED WITH THE PROCEEDS HEREOF. RECOVERY HEREUNDER BY THE DEBTOR SHALL NOT EXCEED AMOUNTS PAID BY THE DEBTOR HEREUNDER.

EXHIBIT 21.4 A Promissory Note *(cont.)*

NON-WAIVER: By accepting payment after its due date or after notice of default, Lender will not waive its right to prompt payment when due of other sums, or to declare a default, or to proceed with any remedy it has. Without affecting the liability of anyone else, Lender may release anyone liable, may change payment terms, and add, alter, substitute, or release security.

❒ This Note is secured by a Security Agreement.
❒ This Note is unsecured.

BEFORE SIGNING ORIGINAL, WE RECEIVED AND READ A COMPLETED COPY HEREOF.

(5)

Borrower's Signature Date Borrower's Signature Date

Borrower's Signature Date Borrower's Signature Date

C-1-424 (REV 6/83) *(Sign Original Only)*

Courtesy of Great American Federal Savings Bank of San Diego and Fresno, California. (1) The promise. (2) Words of negotiability. (3) The payee. (4) The amount borrowed. (5) The signature of the maker.

http:// RESOURCES FOR BUSINESS LAW STUDENTS

NAME	RESOURCES	WEB ADDRESS
Uniform Commercial Code (UCC) Article 3, Negotiable Instruments	The Legal Information Institute (LII), maintained by the Cornell Law School, provides a hypertext and searchable version of UCC Article 3, Negotiable Instruments. LII also maintains links to Article 3 as adopted by particular states and to proposed revisions.	http://www.law.cornell.edu/ucc/3/overview.html
UCC Article 7, Warehouse Receipts, Bills of Lading and Other Documents of Title	LII provides a hypertext and searchable version of UCC Article 7, Warehouse Receipts, Bills of Lading and Other Documents of Title.	http://www.law.cornell.edu/ucc/7/overview.html
Legal Information Institute—Negotiable Instrument Law Materials	LII provides an overview of negotiable instruments law, federal and state statutes and regulations, and federal and state court decisions.	http://www.law.cornell.edu/topics/negotiable.html
The National Conference of Commissioners on Uniform State Laws	The National Conference of Commissioners on Uniform State Laws (NCCUSL), the drafters of the UCC, provides drafts and revisions of its uniform and model acts.	http://www.law.upenn.edu/library/ulc/ulc.htm

EXHIBIT 21.5 A Certificate of Deposit

NEGOTIABLE CERTIFICATE OF DEPOSIT

FEDERAL BANK
SAVINGS AND LOAN ASSOCIATION
600 B Street, San Diego, California 92183

NO. 5014

DATE (1)

THIS CERTIFIES THAT THERE HAS BEEN DEPOSITED IN FEDERAL SAVINGS AND LOAN ASSOCIATION

THE SUM OF (2) DOLLARS (3) ($) VOIDED

PAYABLE TO THE ORDER OF (4) VOIDED

UPON PRESENTATION AND SURRENDER OF THIS CERTIFICATE PROPERLY ENDORSED AT OFFICE	INTEREST RATE % PER ANNUM	INTEREST AMOUNT	MATURITY DATE	TOTAL AMOUNT PAYABLE
			(5)	(6)

This deposit bears interest from the date hereof to the maturity date at the stated rate computed for the actual number of days elapsed on the basis of a 360-day year payable on the maturity date. This certificate is not payable before maturity and bears no interest after maturity.

(FIXED RATE/ FIXED TERM)

SAN DIEGO FEDERAL SAVINGS AND LOAN ASSOCIATION

(7)

Authorized Signature

Courtesy of Great American Federal Savings Bank (formerly San Diego Federal) of San Diego and Fresno, California. (1) The date of issue. (2) The amount of the "deposit," in words. (3) The amount of the "deposit," in numbers. (4) The payee. (5) The maturity date. (6) The amount to be paid. (7) The signature of the maker.

EXHIBIT 21.6 The Parties on Promise Paper

Maker ——(1)——> Payee

Maker ——(2)——> Payee or holder

(1) The maker issues the promise paper to the payee, promising to pay the payee (or a subsequent holder) upon presentment.
(2) The payee (or a subsequent holder) presents the promise paper to the maker, expecting to receive payment as per the promise.

Field warehousing
A method of perfection in a secured transaction in which the creditor takes "possession" of a portion of the debtor's storage area.

Warehouse Receipts

A *warehouse receipt* is a document issued by a person who takes goods for storage. There is no particular form that a warehouse receipt needs to take, but most will contain at least the following provisions:

1. The location of the warehouse
2. The date the receipt for the goods is issued
3. The number of the receipt (receipts are numbered consecutively)
4. A statement as to whether the stored goods will be delivered to the bailor (nonnegotiable) or either to the bearer or to a named person or that person's order (negotiable)
5. The fees and expenses for the storage (unless the goods are stored in a **field warehousing** arrangement)
6. A description of the goods or the packages stored
7. The signature of the warehouseman or his or her agent

The warehouseman assumes a duty to exercise due care in the handling of the goods and a duty to deliver the goods as agreed in the receipt at the close of the storage period.

The warehouseman assumes liability for any damages to the goods stored with him or her if the damages are caused by a failure to exercise reasonable care. The warehouseman also acquires a warehouseman's lien on the goods for the storage and transportation charges, insurance, and expenses reasonably necessary to preserve the goods.

21.3

FINANCE/SALES

NEGOTIABLE BILLS OF LADING

A wholesaler in the next state has inquired about purchasing several hundred Call-Image units. She thought the price quoted to her was fair, and she was very pleased with the prospective delivery date the firm offered. She asked if it would be possible to have the goods shipped to her by common carrier with a negotiable bill of lading, and to have payment terms of "2/10, net 60." Dan and Tom each expressed concern about the use of a negotiable bill of lading when payment will not be made for up to two months. They have asked you what you think of this proposal. What will you tell them?

BUSINESS CONSIDERATIONS The granting of some sort of payment terms is fairly common in business. The use of a negotiable bill of lading is fairly common in business. What possible concerns should a business have with using/granting both to a distant firm the first time they do business together?

ETHICAL CONSIDERATIONS Documents of title are much less strictly interpreted than are negotiable instruments. Among other things, the issue of whether the document is negotiable is often subject to interpretation. Does this "lax" attitude present any potential ethical problems or concerns for a shipper? For the carrier? Explain.

Bills of Lading

A *bill of lading* is issued by a carrier who is taking possession and custody of the goods for the purpose of transporting the goods, normally from a seller to a buyer. The person who arranges the transportation is the **consignor**; the person to whom the goods are to be delivered is the **consignee**; the carrier is the **issuer** of the bill of lading. The bill must adequately describe the goods covered by the bill, and must designate whether the goods were consigned to a particular consignee (nonnegotiable) or to a named consignee or order or to the consignee or bearer (negotiable). The carrier is liable for any misdescription or irregularity unless the document is properly qualified by words such as "contents of package unknown," "shipper's weight and count," or comparable language. Even then, the alleged qualification may not be sufficient to protect the carrier, as the following case illustrates.

Consignor
A person who ships goods to another party.

Consignee
A person to whom goods are shipped by another party.

Issuer
One who officially distributes an item or document.

21.5 IN RE SIENA PUBLISHERS ASSOCIATES 149 B.R. 359 (1993)

FACTS On 16 October 1989, Harris Trust and Savings Bank sold to Siena Publishers the book inventory and accounts receivables of Bookthrift Marketing following a foreclosure on Bookthrift by the bank. Siena agreed to pay $2,250,000 for the assets on an "as is, where is" basis, without any representations, recourse, or warranty, including title or description. The sale was financed by the bank, as evidenced by a demand note signed by the president of Siena dated 19 October 1989. In this demand note, Siena promised to pay to the bank on demand the sum of $2,250,000, representing the purchase price of the Bookthrift assets. Siena also agreed to grant the bank a purchase money security interest in all of Siena's accounts receivable, general intangibles, inventory, and equipment. The bank properly perfected its security interest, filing its UCC-1 with the Rockland County clerk on 10 November 1989; with the New York Secretary of State on 13 November 1989; and with the New York County Register on 21 November 1989.

At some time prior to 31 August 1989, Metro Services, Inc., provided fulfillment and warehousing services for Bookthrift. (Fulfillment services include the receipt and unloading of books from delivering carriers, storage of the books, picking, counting, packing, loading, and shipping books pursuant to instructions, preparation and maintenance of inventory records, and obtaining and arranging transportation for outgoing shipments.) Metro was also indebted to Harris Trust and Savings Bank, and Metro also defaulted on its loans. The bank arranged for NCI to purchase Metro's assets. This sale was consummated 31 August 1989, with the bank receiving full payment for Metro's debt and NCI purchasing Metro's assets, although NCI did not acquire Metro's accounts receivables, which means that NCI did not purchase the fulfillment services claim against Bookthrift.

On 29 August 1990, MSI (a limited partnership of which NCI was a corporate partner) and Siena entered into a Fulfillment Services Agreement, with MSI agreeing to act on behalf of Siena as Metro had acted on behalf of Bookthrift. On 18 March 1992, Siena filed for relief under Chapter 11 of the Bankruptcy Act, continuing as a debtor-in-possession until the case was transferred to Chapter 7 for a liquidation proceeding on 14 December 1992. MSI claimed that it possessed a warehouseman's lien on the inventory of Siena and that its lien was superior to the perfected security interest filed by the bank. The bank asserted that its perfected security agreement preceded any warehouseman's liens, and that it should have priority.

ISSUES Does a warehouseman's lien take priority over a pre-existing perfected security interest? Did MSI have a warehouse receipt as described in Article 7 of the UCC?

HOLDING No. Since the perfected security interest preceded any claimed warehouseman's lien, the security agreement had priority. No. MSI did not have a warehouse receipt as described in Article 7 of the UCC.

REASONING Under New York law, a warehouse lien is a statutory lien, and can only exist upon goods for which a warehouse receipt has been issued. The New York UCC provides that a warehouse receipt need not be in any particular form, but should embody certain essential information, including:

a) the location of the warehouse where the goods are stored;
b) the date of issue of the receipt;
c) the consecutive number of the receipt;
d) a statement whether the goods received will be delivered to the bearer, to a specified person, or to a specified person or his order;
e) the rate of storage and handling charges . . .
g) the signature of the warehouseman, which may be made by his authorized agent. . . .

The Fulfillment Services Agreement between these parties lacked "a statement whether the goods received will be delivered to the bearer, to a specified person, or to a specified person or to his order, . . . a rate of storage . . . and the signature of the warehouseman. . . ." A warehouse receipt is a condition precedent to establishing a lien on the goods in the possession of the warehouseman.

Thus, the documents claimed by MSI to constitute a warehouse receipt do not contain the necessary information required by the Code to qualify as a warehouse receipt; MSI does not have a valid warehouseman's lien against the liquidated inventory; MSI does not have priority over the bank's perfected security interest; and the bank is entitled to the proceeds from the liquidation sale.

BUSINESS CONSIDERATIONS What could or should MSI have done to protect its interests in this situation? Why would a company place itself in an inferior position with respect to the assets of a creditor in a situation such as this?

21.5 IN RE SIENA PUBLISHERS ASSOCIATES *(cont.)* **149 B.R. 359 (1993)**

ETHICAL CONSIDERATIONS Is it ethical for the bank to arrange for the sale of the assets of two different debtors who had defaulted on their loans from the bank, and then to retain an interest in the assets superior to the position occupied by one of the firms that purchased the assets through the bank-arranged sale? Should the bank have removed itself from the situation to avoid any apparent conflicts of interest?

SUMMARY

"Negotiables" are an important part of the modern commercial world. Negotiable documents cover goods that are placed in the hands of a bailee, either for storage or for transportation. Negotiable instruments are used as a substitute for money or as a credit instrument. Both are governed by the UCC.

Article 3 of the Uniform Commercial Code involves negotiable instruments. These negotiable instruments are "current in trade" and are payable in money. There are two major classes of negotiable instruments, and each major class contains two types of instruments. The first class, paper payable "to order," is comprised of checks and drafts. Checks and drafts are used primarily as a substitute for money. There are three legal roles involved on "to order" paper: the drawer, who "draws" (*drafts*) the instrument and issues the order; the payee, to whom the instrument is issued; and the drawee, the party who is ordered to pay the instrument upon presentment.

The second class of negotiable instruments, promise paper, is comprised of promissory notes and certificates of deposit. Promise paper is used principally as a credit instrument. There are two legal roles involved on promise paper: the maker, who makes the promise to pay and who issues the instrument; and the payee, to whom the instrument is issued.

The recent revision to Article 3 has greatly expanded the concept of "checks," making the article more closely reflect contemporary business practices. The revision also removed some of the older, more technical aspects of negotiable instrument law.

Documents of title, including negotiable documents, are governed by Article 7 of the UCC. The two primary types of documents of title are warehouse receipts, issued by a bailee who accepts goods for storage, and bills of lading, issued by a carrier who accepts possession of goods for transportation. However, Article 7 is much more flexible than Article 3. Any other document which in the regular course of business or financing is treated as a document of title is recognized as falling within the coverage of Article 7.

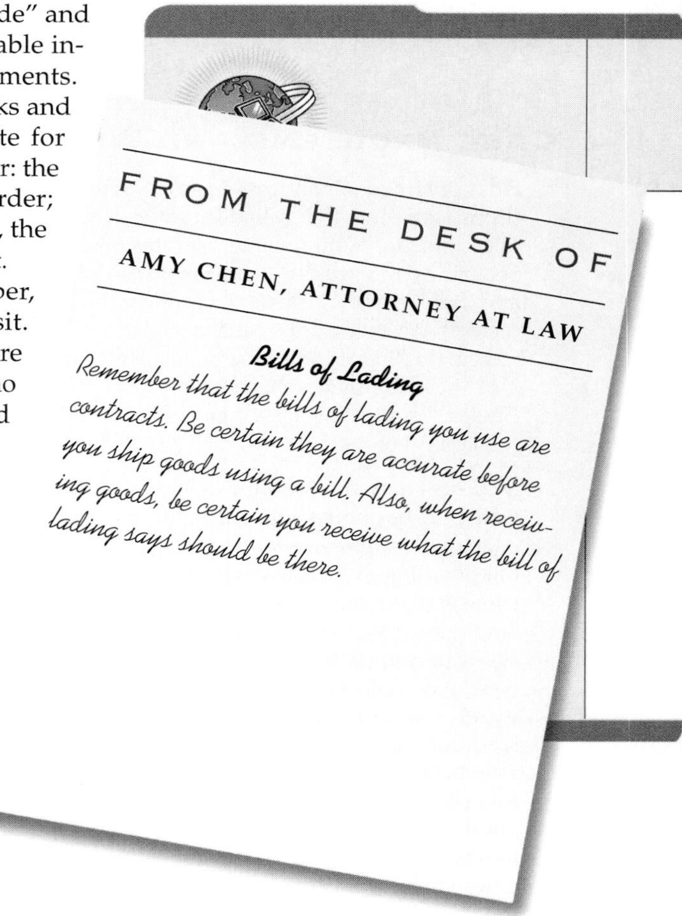

FROM THE DESK OF
AMY CHEN, ATTORNEY AT LAW
Bills of Lading
Remember that the bills of lading you use are contracts. Be certain they are accurate before you ship goods using a bill. Also, when receiving goods, be certain you receive what the bill of lading says should be there.

Discussion Questions

1. Who is expected to make payment on negotiable instruments that are designated as paper payable "to order"? Who is expected to make payment on negotiable instruments that are designated as "promise paper"? Why are different parties expected to pay on these different instruments?
2. What characteristics distinguish a check from other types of drafts? What characteristics distinguish a promissory note from a certificate of deposit?
3. A check or a draft contains a specific type of communication from the drawer to the drawee. What form does this communication take? Why does this communication obligate the drawee to pay the instrument issued by the drawer?
4. Who may serve as a drawee on a check? Who may serve as a drawee on a draft? Is the difference as to who may serve as drawee significant?
5. What duty or duties is/are performed by the "maker" on promise paper? What do we call the party or parties who perform comparable duties on order paper?
6. What are the two major functions of negotiable instruments? Which function is most likely to be involved with the use of a draft or a check? Which function is most likely to be involved with the use of a note or a certificate of deposit?
7. How does Article 3 define a "check"? Why is this definition important in negotiable instrument law?
8. What is a document of title under the provisions of Article 7? How is a negotiable document of title different from a nonnegotiable document of title?
9. When do the parties to a contract use a warehouse receipt? When do the parties to a contract use a bill of lading? Why do the parties need two different documents of title?
10. What sort of limitation or qualification can a carrier use on a bill of lading to protect itself from liability if the goods delivered are mislabeled or improperly identified?

Case Problems and Writing Assignments

1. Goss obtained a loan from Trinity Savings, signing a promissory note that called for interest to be adjusted in conjunction with the interest rates on U.S. Treasury Securities. Eventually, a dispute arose between Goss and Trinity, and Goss sued to cancel the note and to recover the excess interest charges that he alleged to have paid. Should this case be resolved under Article 3 of the UCC or under common law? Explain. [See *Goss* v. *Trinity Savings & Loan Ass'n,* 813 P.2d 492 (Okla. 1991).]

2. McCausland hired Mayflower Moving and Storage to transport her household furnishings from Florida to Alabama. Mayflower loaded the goods and issued a bill of lading to McCausland for the goods. When the truck arrived at the destination in Alabama, McCausland was unable to pay for the carriage. Mayflower refused to unload the goods until the carriage charges were paid, and subsequently stored the goods in its warehouse pending resolution of the matter. McCausland then moved to Kentucky to live with her mother. Eventually, Mayflower decided to sell the furnishings to recover for its expenses in hauling and storing the goods. A letter was sent to McCausland at her mother's home, and legal notices were run in the newspaper for the jurisdiction in Alabama. Mayflower then sold the furnishings. McCausland filed suit against Mayflower for conversion, fraud, and breach of contract. Did Mayflower have the right to sell the furnishings? What could—or should—Mayflower have done differently? [See *McCausland* v. *Tide-Mayflower Moving and Storage,* 499 So.2d 1378 (Ala. 1986).]

3. Hoesch issued a check payable to the order of Farr and drawn on the account of Gasco-Osage Realty, in the amount of $5,672. In exchange, Farr gave $4,000 in cash to Hoesch (Hoesch already owed Farr $1,672 from an earlier deal). One month later, Farr deposited the check with his bank, but the check was dishonored upon presentment. As a result, Farr sued Hoesch for fraud, alleging that the issuance of a bad check was fraudulent. Hoesch asserted that issuing a "bad" check was not fraudulent, since a check merely needs to be negotiable, and that "good" is not the same as negotiable. Is this argument persuasive? Is the fact that a check is "bad" enough to make it nonnegotiable? Explain your reasoning. [See *Farr* v. *Hoesch,* 745 S.W.2d 830 (Mo.App. 1988).]

4. The Banque de Depots, a Swiss bank, alleged that Ferroligas had fraudulently misused and/or misapplied bank funds. In seeking a monetary judgment, the bank sought and received a non-resident writ of at-

tachment against Ferroligas. Under this writ, 1,300 metric tons of calcium silicon, which Ferroligas had shipped to New Orleans for distribution to three purchasers, were seized. Ferroligas filed a motion to dissolve the writ, asserting that the bank's petition was deficient, that Ferroligas was not the owner of the goods, and that the goods were covered by a negotiable bill of lading, making them exempt from seizure by creditors of Ferroligas under Louisiana law. Can the Banque de Depots seize the goods covered by a negotiable bill of lading for debts allegedly owed by the shipper of the goods? Explain your reasoning. [See *Banque de Depots* v. *Ferroligas*, 569 So.2d 40 (La.App. 4th Cir. 1990).]

5. Arizona enacted a statute which purported to regulate home solicitations and sales. The statute provided, in part, that any notes signed by a buyer in a home solicitation are not negotiable. The Direct Sellers Association challenged the statute as unconstitutional, and also challenged the right of the state to expressly declare certain types of notes nonnegotiable even though the notes in question satisfy all elements of negotiability under Article 3 of the UCC. May a state declare certain specific types of notes to be nonnegotiable despite the compliance of those notes with Article 3 negotiability requirements? Explain your answer. [See *State* v. *Direct Sellers Ass'n*, 494 P.2d 361 (1972).]

6. **BUSINESS APPLICATION CASE** The state of Alaska is a tenant in an office building owned by Univentures. On 24 November 1987, Alaska made a lease payment to LeViege, the managing partner of Univentures, using a state treasury warrant. LeViege assigned the treasury warrant to Garcia, an individual to whom LeViege owed money. The Univentures partners had a falling-out in November, and the state was notified on 25 November 1987 that no further payments should be made to LeViege. The state placed a stop-payment order on the warrant issued to LeViege on 27 November 1987. Garcia presented the warrant to NBA on 30 November, and NBA paid Garcia the face amount of the warrant. However, the bank did not debit the state's account due to the stop-payment order. In January 1988, NBA sued the state, LeViege, and Garcia to recover the amount paid to Garcia on the warrant. NBA alleged that it was a holder in due course (HDC) on the warrant and, as such, not subject to any defenses available to the state. (If NBA was a holder in due course, it was entitled to recover; if it was not an HDC, it would not recover.) Was the state treasury warrant a negotiable instrument? What factors will influence your decision in this case? [See *Nat'l Bank of Alaska* v. *Univentures 1231*, 824 P.2d 1377 (Alaska 1992).]

7. **ETHICS APPLICATION CASE** Westway Coffee, a New York firm, placed an order for 1,710 cartons of instant coffee with Dominium, S.A. of São Paulo, Brazil. Dominium agreed to the sale and acquired six containers from Netumar, the owner of the M.V. Netuno in which to ship the coffee. These containers were delivered to Dominium where they were loaded with the coffee under the supervision of the Brazilian Coffee Institute, the government agency in charge of coffee exports. The institute certified that each container was loaded with 285 cartons of instant coffee, then sealed the containers and padlocked them. The containers were shipped to the Eud Marco warehouse at Netumar's direction, weighed, and stored for 10 days. The containers were then taken to the ship and loaded for carriage to New York. The bills of lading for the containers included the legends "STC" (said to contain), "SLAC" (shipper's load and count), and "Contents of packages are shipper's declaration." When the goods arrived in New York, two of the containers were short of the quantity of coffee expected, with a total shortage of 419 cartons ($138,000 value). Westway sued the carrier for the shortage, and the carrier denied liability.

   Did the carrier show "due care" in its handling of the goods? Should the carrier be held liable for the shortage in the goods shipped to the consignee in New York? What ethical issues are raised by this case? [See *Westway Coffee Corp.* v. *M.V. Netuno*, 528 F.Supp. 113 (1981).]

8. **IDES CASE** Haygood Contracting, Inc., entered into a contract that called for Haygood to provide paving for a real estate subdivision. The subdivision was being developed by CFI, whose president was Crolley. The initial contract specified a price of $29,500 for the work, and was in written form on a standardized form prepared and signed by Crolley. During the course of performing the contract, it became obvious that some additional work would need to be done, so Haygood prepared a handwritten estimate of $7,275 for this additional work. Crolley initialed the estimate, approving the work. However, below Crolley's initials there appeared two additional charges: one for $500 for "equipment time" and the other for $7,560 for "extra stone." Subsequently, both CFI and Crolley refused to pay for the work, and Haygood sued both CFI and Crolley. Haygood argued that Crolley had approved the charges when he initialed the estimate. Crolley denied that he approved the additional expenses, and

also denied that he was liable for any of the amount since he signed as a representative of CFI and not as an individual. Under Article 3, Crolley would not be liable since he signed a document containing the name of the principal (CFI), and his signature was in a representative capacity. Under common law principles, Crolley and CFI would both face potential liability, although Haygood would have to elect which party to sue. Apply the IDES principals to analyze this case. [See *Crolley* v. *Haygood Contracting, Inc.*, 411 S.E.2d 907 (Ga.App. 1991).]

NOTE

1. "Postmark Bill Misses Mark," *Independent Banker*, May 1996, pp. 7–8.

Chapter 22

NEGOTIABILITY

OUTLINE

AGENDA

The Kochanowskis will be receiving most of their payments in the form of instruments issued by their customers. They will need to know if these instruments are negotiable, and therefore governed by Article 3, or non-negotiable, and therefore governed under the provisions of common law. They will also be issuing a number of instruments to purchase supplies, pay bills, and generally operate the business. The need to be certain that the instruments they issue are negotiable.

They will be shipping finished goods by means of common carriers, and they will be receiving shipments of component parts by means of common carriers, so they will need to be familiar with documents of title, especially bills of lading. Since they are relatively new to operating their own business, they are quite likely to have a number of questions for you.

Be prepared! You never know when one of the Kochanowskis will come to you for advice or guidance.

Formal Requirements for Negotiability: Article 3

Negotiable instruments have a special place in business law. Every negotiable instrument is a contract, and carries with it the rights that a person would enjoy under contract law. As you remember from contract law, a person possessing rights under a contract can *assign* those rights to another person. The person who assigns his or her rights—the assignor—is expected to give notice to the party who will be conferring the benefits—the obligor—that an assignment has been made, and the assignor will identify the person to whom the rights were transferred—the assignee. You should also remember that the assignee takes the rights assigned under the contract *subject to* any and every defense the obligor could assert against the assignor. These two things, taking the benefits subject to any defenses and the need for the assignor to give notice, make assignments a less-than-popular method for transferring benefits under a contract.

A negotiable instrument is also a contract. In fact, a negotiable instrument is a *formal* contract, one of the few formal contracts still in use in the U.S. legal system. Since it is a contract, the benefits called for in the instrument can be assigned, the same as the benefits under other types of contracts can be assigned. But, as we just discussed, assignments are not a very good method for ensuring that the assignee will receive the benefits the assignor is trying to transfer. Unless there is more to it than that, negotiable instruments would just be a specialized type of contract with no particular benefits beyond those of other contracts. However, under certain circumstances the *holder* (think of the holder as roughly analogous to an assignee for now) of a negotiable instrument is permitted to collect the money (receive the benefits under the contract), *despite* any defenses the maker or drawer can assert. *This* is the primary reason that negotiable instrument law is so important! A person having the right to enforce a "mere" contract through an assignment would not have this same benefit. The holder of a negotiable instrument has all of the rights of an assignee under contract law, *plus* any additional rights conferred on him or her by Article 3 of the Uniform Commercial Code (UCC). Not only that, but the instrument, if correctly made or drawn, will move easily through the commercial world as a substitute for money and/or as a credit instrument.

The benefits derived from holding a negotiable instrument should already be obvious. However, the law is very jealous of these benefits. To carry the benefits of negotiability, an instrument must meet all the formal requirements of negotiability. It is not enough for it to meet "some" of the requirements, or even for it to meet "most" of the requirements. It must meet each and every one of the requirements in order to fall within the coverage of Article 3. Any missing element removes the instrument from Article 3 and places it under the coverage of common law contracts. The requirements for negotiability are set out in § 3-104 (a) of the UCC:

Section 3-104. Negotiable Instrument

(a) Except as provided in subsections (c) and (d), "negotiable instrument" means an unconditional promise or order to pay a fixed amount of money, with or without interest or other charges described in the promise or order, if it:

(1) is payable to bearer or to order at the time it is issued or first comes into possession of a holder;

(2) is payable on demand or at a definite time; and,

> *(3) does not state any other undertaking or instruction by the person promising or ordering payment to do any act in addition to the payment of money, but the promise or order may contain (i) an undertaking or power to give, maintain, or protect collateral to secure payment; (ii) an authorization or power to the holder to confess judgment or realize on or dispose of collateral; or (iii) a waiver of the benefit of any law intended for the advantage or protection of an obligor.*

Two other important definitions must also be reviewed before the discussion of *negotiability* can commence:

> ***Section 3-103. Definitions***
>
> *(a) In this Article:*
>
> *(6) "Order" means a* written *instruction to pay money signed by the person giving the instruction. The instruction may be addressed to any person, including the person giving the instruction, or to one or more persons jointly or in the alternative but not in succession. An authorization to pay is not an order unless the person authorized to pay is also instructed to pay.* [Emphasis added]
>
> *(9) "Promise" means a* written *undertaking to pay money signed by the person undertaking to pay. An acknowledgment of an obligation by the obligor is not a promise unless the obligor also undertakes to pay the obligation.* [Emphasis added]

Thus, to qualify as a negotiable instrument, the instrument in question must:

1. be written; *and*
2. be signed by the maker (promise paper) or by the drawer (order paper); *and*
3. contain an unconditional promise or order to pay a fixed amount of money and no other instruction or undertaking by the person who promises or orders payment; *and*
4. be payable on demand or at a definite time; *and*
5. be payable to order or to bearer.

These elements are shown in Exhibit 22.1. Notice that every element must be present. The absence of any element negates negotiability. This does not make the paper worthless, but it is no longer negotiable under the law; this means that no holder would have the protections afforded by the UCC. The person holding the paper would only have his or her (potential) contract rights under the common law.

It should be emphasized that negotiability has *nothing* to do with validity or enforceability. If an instrument is negotiable, this merely means that the instrument is governed by the provisions of Article 3. The enforceability of the instrument or the collection of money called for in the instrument has nothing to do with whether the instrument is negotiable. We will examine each of the six elements of negotiability in the following sections.

Writing Requirement

Commercial paper represents an intangible right, the right to collect money at some time. However, to satisfy the requirements of Article 3, the proof of this right must be tangible. The simplest way to prove that the right exists is to put it in writing, as defined in § 1-201(46), which states that: "'written' or 'writing' includes printing, typewriting, or any other intentional reduction to tangible form."

EXHIBIT 22.1 The Elements of Negotiability

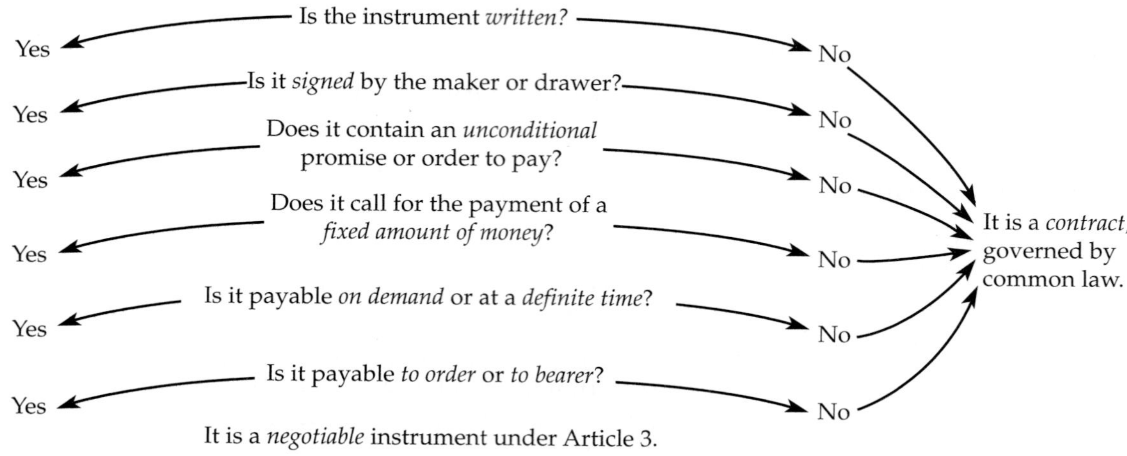
Is the instrument *written?*
Yes
No
Is it *signed* by the maker or drawer?
Yes
No
Does it contain an *unconditional* promise or order to pay?
Yes
No
Does it call for the payment of a *fixed amount of money*?
Yes
No
Is it payable *on demand* or at a *definite time*?
Yes
No
Is it payable *to order* or *to bearer*?
Yes
No
It is a *negotiable* instrument under Article 3.
It is a *contract*, governed by common law.

For many people the type of negotiable instrument most frequently encountered is a check. Most checks are in a standard form, preprinted on paper, with magnetic ink to designate the drawee bank and the drawer's account number. Similarly, many drafts are preprinted, in standard form, on paper, with magnetic ink encoding; most certificates of deposit (CDs) are preprinted on paper, with magnetic ink encoding; and many notes are preprinted in a form readily adaptable to the needs of the lender/preparer. These preprinted, standardized forms are familiar, they contain blanks at all the appropriate places to streamline their completion, and they are pre-encoded with magnetic ink to make computerized processing readily available. However, such convenience is just that—a convenience, but it is not a necessity.

Commercial paper is equally valid when prepared by handwriting on a scratch pad, or on a blank sheet of paper, or on virtually any other relatively permanent thing. For example, several years ago, on a television series entitled *Love American Style*, a couple was marooned on a desert island. The only thing they had for entertainment was a deck of cards. According to the plot, they spent their time playing gin. When they were rescued, the young woman had won $1 million. As evidence, she had a check . . . written on her stomach! Despite the comedic implications, such a check would (theoretically) be valid.

In another (possible apocryphal) example, a disgruntled taxpayer completed his tax return on 15 April. When he mailed his return, he included a check for the taxes due and a note. The note said: "You've been trying to get it for years, and you've finally succeeded. Here's the shirt off my back." The note was pinned to his check, which was written on his undershirt. However, the joke was on him. The IRS cashed it!

Although the definition of a "writing" was not changed with the revision to Article 3, the Official Comments to the revised article do reflect a change of sorts. According to the Official Comments, in order to qualify as a writing the "reduction to tangible form" must be on something capable or being readily transferred and easily

YOU BE THE JUDGE

Is the Check Valid?

Frances-Rose Straith, a resident of Falls City, Nebraska, received a plain manila envelope in her mail. There was no return address on the envelope, and it only contained one piece of paper. That piece of paper appeared to be a check in the amount of $95,093, payable to the order of F.R. Straith. The document also stated that it was from "The Office of the Treasurer," although there was no notation as to whom or for what entity the person allegedly served as Treasurer. There was also a notation that the instrument was "non-negotiable for cash." Ms. Straith held the instrument for a week before deciding to take it to her bank to deposit it into her checking account. Accordingly, she endorsed the instrument and took it to the bank for deposit. The bank teller accepted the instrument without question.

Ms. Straith then went out and purchased a used car, a used pickup truck, some clothing, and some diapers for her daughter. In fact, she wrote six checks, totaling $8,331, that first day. In the interim, the bank had discovered that the instrument had no value. According to the bank, this was a non-negotiable instrument worth nothing, and they so informed Ms. Straith. When the six checks were dishonored by the bank, the used car and the used pickup truck were repossessed, and the county began discussing whether criminal charges should be brought against Ms. Straith for passing bad checks. Ms. Straith insists that she did nothing wrong, and that any errors were made by the bank.[1]

Presume that criminal charges are brought against Ms. Straith, and that the case is brought in *your* court. How will you resolve this case?

BUSINESS CONSIDERATIONS What responsibility does a business have for attempting to validate a check before allowing a customer to take purchased items home? Should the auto dealers have called the bank before accepting the checks for the car and the truck, or should they have waited to see what the bank did once the checks were presented for payment?

ETHICAL CONSIDERATIONS Is it ethical for a business to mail what appear to be checks—often with a "notification" that the recipient has "won" some amount of money—to thousands of people, many of whom are unaware of the requirements for negotiability? What ethical concerns are raised by such a practice?

SOURCE: T. L. Henion, *Omaha World Herald*, p. 1.

borne by the payee or holder. Even though no cases have been seen on this topic yet, it appears that at least one of the examples above would run afoul of the Official Comments to Revised Article 3 and might not qualify as a writing under the revisions. (*Hint:* It would not involve the disgruntled taxpayer.)

Signature Requirement

On a check or a draft, an order is given by the drawer. On a note or a CD, a promise is given by the maker. Given the widespread use of preprinted forms as negotiable instruments, some protection is needed from fraud or trickery. The UCC tries to minimize the potential for fakery by requiring a signature by the maker or the drawer. Most people think of a signature as a **manual subscription,** an autograph. Although a manual subscription *is,* obviously, a signature, it is not the only possible type of signature.

Manual subscription
Autograph; the act of physically writing one's name in longhand.

A corporation, being an inanimate object, cannot sign its own name. Yet corporations need to "sign" negotiable instruments, particularly checks. The instruments can, of course, be signed by agents of the corporation. But even this is impractical.

22.1

FINANCE/MANAGEMENT

SIGNING COMPANY CHECKS

It has been agreed that CIT checks will need the signatures of two officers (Tom, Anna, and Dan will all be authorized signers), and that the monthly statements will be reconciled by Donna or Julio. Initially the firm does not expect to be issuing many checks, so the signing function should not take too much time. However, if the company grows as expected, the signing of checks could become a time-intensive activity.

Lindsay thinks the firm should investigate alternate methods for writing and signing checks. The family has asked you what you think. Should the firm plan to write checks manually, or should they obtain a software package, such as Quicken, to prepare checks and simultaneously update the check register? What advice will you give them?

BUSINESS CONSIDERATIONS There have been myriad instances in which a business has lost substantial sums of money because the firm had poor internal auditing practices and/or controls, especially with the company's checking account. What sort of safeguards should a firm have in place to minimize the risk of employee malfeasance with business checks?

ETHICAL CONSIDERATIONS People have been known to "play games" with their checks, especially when paying bills. Is it ethical to "play the float" by writing checks before deposits are made in the hope (or expectation) that a deposit will be made in time to cover the checks? Is it ethical to send out unsigned checks to creditors so that the check arrives in a timely manner but then must be returned for a signature before it can be sent to the bank?

Some corporations issue thousands of checks each month. An "authorized signer" could spend an entire career "autographing" checks for the corporation.

Fortunately, the UCC solved this problem. The solution is found in § 1-201(39), which states that: "'signed' includes any symbol executed or adopted by a party with present intention to authenticate a writing." Thus, a corporation can use a stamp to sign checks. Likewise, a negotiable instrument can be signed by affixing an X, or a thumbprint, or any other intentionally affixed symbol.

There are practical problems with unusual types of signatures, but these problems deal more with the acceptability of the instrument than with the negotiability of it. An unusual signature may be so strange that people will be hesitant to accept it or the instrument containing it. The unusual signature also must be proved by the person trying to claim the instrument.

It makes no difference where the instrument is signed. Although it is normal to sign in the lower right-hand corner of the face of the instrument, the signature can be anywhere. For example, in a note beginning "I, Mary Smith, promise to pay," Mary Smith's signature following the word "I" would be sufficient.

Unconditional Promise or Order Requirement

Negotiable instruments are designed to move easily through the commercial world. To serve effectively as a substitute for money, a negotiable instrument must be freely transferable. It also needs to be in a form that people can accept. These needs are met by the requirement that the promise made, or the order given, be unconditional. A person taking possession of a negotiable instrument wants to know that payment can reasonably be expected under *every* circumstance. A prospective holder would not be eager to accept an instrument that says payment might be made or will be made only if something happens. The holder wants an unconditional promise that the money will be paid.

The Code has gone to great lengths to define "unconditional." Section 3-106 lists the requirements that must be met to make the promise or order conditional. (This requirement has been substantially simplified by the revisions to Article 3.) These requirements will be set out here, with a brief explanation inserted between each of the four subsections of the Code section. According to this Code section:

> *(a) Except as provided in this section [3-106], for the purposes of [negotiable instruments], a promise or order is unconditional unless it states (i) an express condition to payment, (ii) that the promise or order is subject to or governed by another writing,*

or (iii) that rights or obligations with respect to the promise or order are stated in another writing. A reference to another writing does not of itself make the promise or order conditional.

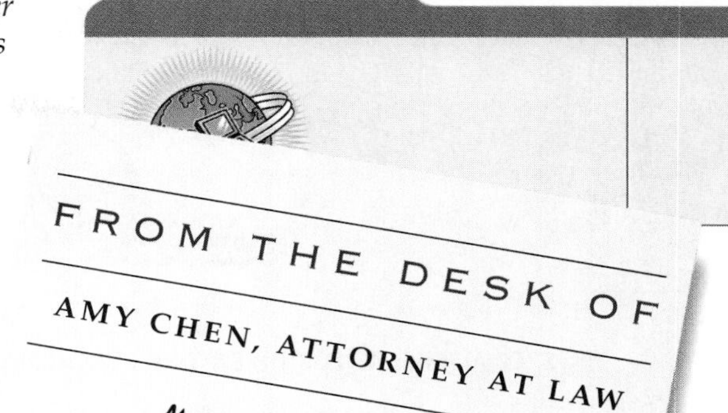

FROM THE DESK OF
AMY CHEN, ATTORNEY AT LAW
Negotiable Instruments
Remember to inspect and verify orders before issuing any negotiable instruments as payment for goods received. A negotiable instrument is an unconditional promise or order to pay, and any shortages or nonconformities in the goods may not be available as a defense if the instrument is negotiated by the payee. Better to be safe than sorry!

There appears to be a presumption that every promise or order is unconditional *unless* a condition is obvious from reading the instrument. For example, if an instrument says "payment to be made *only if* [statement of condition] that instrument would contain an express condition and would not be negotiable." Similarly, if an instrument contained a clause stating that the payment of the instrument is *governed by* a separate document or writing, the instrument would be conditional and, therefore, nonnegotiable.

(b) A promise or order is not made conditional (i) by a reference to another writing for a statement of rights with respect to collateral, prepayment, or acceleration, or (ii) because payment is limited to resort to a particular source of funds.

This subsection makes a significant change in the law of negotiable instruments, again emphasizing the effort to remove conditions from written promises or orders unless they are very explicit. Before the revision to Article 3, the "particular fund" doctrine made an instrument conditional, hence negating negotiability, any time the instrument required payment from a particular fund, *unless* the drawer or maker was a governmental entity. Many students have wondered why a check drawn against their account was not drawn against a "particular fund." The (technically accurate) explanation that the check was *not* drawn against the student's deposited funds, but rather against any or all of the funds in the bank, with the student's account being merely a bookkeeping notation, seemed to be an evasive answer at best, and begged the question at worst. This particular rule was confusing at best, and its demise was long overdue.

(c) If a promise or order requires, as a condition to payment, a countersignature by a person whose specimen signature appears on the promise or order, the condition does not make the promise or order conditional. If the person whose specimen signature appears on an instrument fails to countersign the instrument, the failure to countersign is a defense to the obligation of the issuer, but the failure does not prevent a transferee of the instrument from becoming a holder of the instrument.

This subsection appears to be intended specifically to permit the inclusion of traveler's checks within the revised coverage of Article 3.

(d) If a promise or order at the time it is issued or first comes into possession of a holder contains a statement, required by applicable statutory or administrative law, to the effect that the rights of a holder or transferee are subject to claims or ***defenses*** *that the issuer could assert against the original payee, the promise or order is not thereby made conditional . . . ; but if the promise or order is an instrument, there cannot be a holder in due course on the instrument.*

Defenses
A legal reason, excuse, or justification for the conduct of the party.

22.2

FINANCE

SPECIAL CHECKS FOR INVENTORY PURCHASES

John is concerned that the firm will, on occasion, pay for component parts by check only to discover that the parts are nonconforming to the contract. He reasons that if this happens the firm will have spent the funds already, but will not yet have the parts it needs. As a result, he has suggested that the firm order special checks for its inventory purchases, and that these checks should contain a line instructing the bank not to honor the checks until CIT informs the bank that the parts the check is to pay for have been deemed acceptable by the firm. Donna thinks that this could cause some problems with the bank and with the suppliers. They have asked you for your advice. What will you tell them?

BUSINESS CONSIDERATIONS Many businesses order goods or parts, pay for them by check shortly after they are received, and then do not use or sell them until some time later. It is quite likely that at least some of these goods or parts will be nonconforming. Is there any way the firm can restrict payment of the checks issued to pay for their orders until the goods are determined to conform to the contract? What alternatives are available to the firm?

ETHICAL CONSIDERATIONS Should a business allow the person responsible for receiving inventory orders to issue the checks to pay for the inventory, or should the checks be written by some other person within the organization? What ethical and practical considerations affected your answer the most?

This subsection reflects the Code's recognition of the "Federal Trade Commission Holder in Due Course Rule" as it affects consumer credit transactions (explained in the next chapter), while also recognizing that other statutory or regulatory enactments may also occur in the future. By addressing this issue in general terms, the Code greatly simplifies the task facing courts that would otherwise have to interpret the effect of these enactments on (1) whether they created a condition and (2) whether it would be possible to attain holder in due course (HDC) status under the enactment.

In determining whether an instrument is conditional, the courts have frequently relied on the so-called four-corner rule. The *four-corner rule* requires that every necessary bit of information to determine rights on an instrument must be contained within its four corners; that is, the information must be found on the face of the instrument itself. If the holder must look to some source of information other than the instrument in order to determine rights, the instrument is conditional, and therefore it is not negotiable. (The four-corner rule also applies to the "time of payment" and, to a lesser extent, the "fixed amount of money" requirements.)

Fixed Amount of Money Requirement

A holder of a negotiable instrument must know how much money is to be received when the instrument is paid. The amount is commonly specified exactly, which makes the determination simple, but this is not necessary to satisfy the fixed amount of money requirement. (This requirement was referred to as the *sum certain* requirement prior to the revision of Article 3.) The revised Article 3 does not address this requirement to any significant degree, except for a statement in § 1-201(24) defining money and in § 3-107 explaining how to handle an instrument that is payable in foreign money. According to these sections:

1-201(24) *"Money" means a medium of exchange authorized or adopted by a domestic or foreign government and includes a monetary unit of account established by intergovernmental organization or by agreement between two or more nations . . .*

3-107. Instrument Payable in Foreign Money

Unless the instrument otherwise provides, an instrument that states that it is payable in foreign money may be paid in the foreign money or in an equivalent amount in dollars calculated by using the current bank-offered spot rate at the place of payment for the purchase of dollars on the day on which the instrument is paid.

Historically, to meet the requirement that the instrument calls for the payment of a fixed amount of money, the total amount to be paid must be calculable from the face of the instrument. This requirement once again raises the four-corner rule. All the necessary information for the calculation of the amount to be paid had to be on the instrument, even if the calculation has not yet been done. This requirement no longer applies under the new standards, at least with regard to interest.

Many instruments call for the payment of interest as well as the payment of the principal. The old rules regarding interest were somewhat confusing and substantially out of date. As a result, the rules for the treatment of interest have been changed significantly. The provisions for interest are set out in § 3-112. An instrument is presumed to be issued without interest unless interest is specifically called for in the instrument. However, if interest is called for in the instrument, the interest will run from the date of the instrument. The significant change in the treatment of interest is found in § 3-112(b), which states:

> *Interest may be stated in an instrument as a fixed or variable rate or rates. The amount or rate of interest may be stated or described in the instrument in any manner and may require reference to information not contained in the instrument. If an instrument provides for interest, but the amount cannot be ascertained from the description, interest is payable at the judgment rate in effect at the place of payment of the instrument and at the time interest first accrues.*

This means that an instrument can call for the payment of interest at "the prime rate," and it still satisfies the fixed amount of money requirement.

The following case involved the interpretation of whether a commitment contained in a note to pay taxes on the collateral negates the (former) sum certain requirement.

22.3

NEGOTIABILITY AND PROMISSORY NOTES

The firm has been buying circuit boards from one supplier from the beginning of its operations. This supplier has been very supportive of the CIT enterprise, willingly extending credit to the firm from the start. Tom recently called the supplier to discuss placing a large order, asking that the firm be given credit terms. Because of the size of the order, the supplier sent a promissory note to the firm. The note included a statement that interest would be at "the normal rate" between the firms. Donna, recalling her business law class of a few years ago, stated that this interest term made the note nonnegotiable. John, who is currently enrolled in a legal environment class, says that the law has been changed so that this clause will not affect negotiability. They ask you for your advice. What will you tell them?

BUSINESS CONSIDERATIONS The revisions to Article 3 greatly expanded the permissible language regarding interest while allowing an instrument to retain negotiability. Is this change better or worse for businesses that make notes in the course of their operations? Are firms better served if their notes are governed under Article 3 or under common law?

ETHICAL CONSIDERATIONS What ethical considerations arise when a maker inserts a condition into a promissory note negating negotiability? How important should a condition be before a firm inserts that condition into a note as a method of restricting or limiting its payment obligation?

FINANCE

22.1 BURNS v. RESOLUTION TRUST CORP. 880 S.W.2d 149 (Tex.App.—Houston [14th Dist.] 1994)

FACTS In 1981, Whistler Village Partnership executed nine promissory notes, each in the original amount of $44,595, payable to Alpine Federal Savings & Loan in connection with Whistler's purchase of nine units of Phase II of the Whistler Village Townhomes in Steamboat Springs, Colorado. Each of the notes was secured by a deed of trust covering one of the nine units. In 1982, Burns and McEncroe purchased the nine condominiums and assumed the loans, executing assumption agreements, which released the original borrowers from liability on the notes.

22.1 BURNS v. RESOLUTION TRUST CORP. *(cont.)* 880 S.W.2d 149 (Tex.App.—Houston [14th Dist.] 1994)

After a disagreement about the management of the property, Burns conveyed his interest in the property to McEncroe by deed dated 11 May 1983. In 1987, Burns and McEncroe executed loan modification agreements, which reduced the interest rates on the loans.

Burns and McEncroe defaulted on the notes in 1988, and Alpine began foreclosure proceedings. Alpine obtained an Order Authorizing Sale from the district court in Colorado, and on 11 April 1989, the Public Trustee conducted a foreclosure sale. Alpine purchased the nine units at the sale. Burns did not exercise his right of redemption provided under Colorado law. . . . Alpine later sold the units to third parties, and it instituted this litigation to recover alleged deficiencies on the notes. After Alpine was declared insolvent, Resolution Trust Corporation (RTC) was appointed receiver. The RTC, as receiver, was substituted on each case. . . . After trial in September 1991, the jury returned a verdict in favor of Burns. . . . Over 15 months later the trial court granted the RTC's motion for judgment notwithstanding the verdict (JNOV). On 15 March 1993, it entered deficiency judgments against Burns in the amount of $44,038.68 and $62,208.68 in the two suits and awarded attorney's fees to the RTC.

ISSUES Were the notes in question negotiable instruments? Did RTC qualify as a holder in due course on the notes?

HOLDINGS Yes, the notes were negotiable instruments despite their statements that the maker was responsible for paying taxes on the collateral. Yes, RTC qualified as a holder in due course on the notes under the federal holder in due course doctrine.

REASONING Burns's contractual claims are based on his contention that Alpine and RTC did not comply with the express terms of the notes and deeds of trust in sending the required notice of acceleration before foreclosure. The notes and deeds of trust provided that the holder must give at least 30 days' notice of its intent to accelerate the balance due on the note after default. That notice must be sent, by certified mail, to the property address or such other address as the borrower designates by proper written notice to the lender. . . . This notice of acceleration was mailed to Burns and McEncroe at P.O. Box 774485, Steamboat Springs, Colorado, which is neither the property's address nor an address designated by Burns. [This alleged lack of notice provided Burns with a defense on the instruments.]

Burns argues that the court erred in basing its JNOV on the federal holder-in-due-course doctrine. This doctrine allows the FDIC and RTC, as receivers for failed financial institutions, to acquire holder in due course status under federal common law even though they cannot meet the technical requirements under state law. A holder in due course takes a note free of all claims against it or any personal defenses. . . . Burns contends the RTC only urged this doctrine in its motion for JNOV against his wrongful foreclosure claim, and it was not raised against and cannot defeat his other defenses of claims. . . . We disagree with Burns's strict interpretation of this requirement under these facts. Because the RTC's motions specifically urged the federal holder in due course doctrine as one of the grounds for JNOV and quoted case law holding that the holder in due course doctrine bars a claim of lack of notice, the doctrine's application to all of Burns's notice contentions, including his breach of contract, was apparent. . . .

Burns argues that the notes are not negotiable because they contain an obligation to pay taxes on the property, which amount is estimated in the assumption agreement, and may vary each year. Burns argues this estimated payment makes the documents non-negotiable because they no longer contain an obligation to pay a sum certain. We disagree.

First, the obligation to pay taxes is not a *new* promise; it already existed by virtue of provisions in paragraph two of each deed of trust. Moreover, it is to the terms of the *note* that we look for satisfaction of the negotiability requirements. "A separate agreement does not affect the negotiability of an instrument." In addition, the negotiability of an instrument is not affected by "a promise or power to maintain or protect collateral or to give additional collateral. . . ." We consider the obligation to pay taxes a promise to maintain or protect the collateral, for failure to pay taxes could cause the note holder to lose the collateral through foreclosure of a tax lien on the property. . . . This court has previously rejected a lack of notice defense in a deficiency suit by applying this holder in due course doctrine. . . . We hold that Burns's claims of lack of notice, including his breach of contract claims, are barred by the federal holder in due course doctrine.

BUSINESS CONSIDERATIONS Alpine sent the notice of its intent to accelerate the loan to the wrong address, allegedly failing to provide Burns with notice of its intent. The improper notice from Alpine would probably have been sufficient to allow Burns to prevail if Alpine had continued in the suit. What precautions should a business take to ensure that, when it gives notice of a problem un-

22.1 BURNS v. RESOLUTION TRUST CORP. *(cont.)* 880 S.W.2d 149 (Tex.App.—Houston [14th Dist.] 1994)

der a contract, that notice is properly sent, including having it sent to the *right* person at the *right* address?

ETHICAL CONSIDERATIONS Is it ethical to allow the Resolution Trust Corporation to assert HDC status, thus overcoming the defenses of Burns, when Alpine could not have done so? What public policy considerations might enter in to allow special provisions for the Resolution Trust Corporation?

Determinable Time Requirement

A holder wants to know not only how much money will be paid (fixed amount in money), but *when* payment can be expected. The question of when will depend on the terms of the instrument, but in order to be negotiable the instrument must be payable either on demand or at a definite time. This element of negotiability is discussed in § 3-108 of Article 3. This section provides that:

> *(a) A promise or order is "payable on demand" if it (i) states that it is payable on demand or at sight, or otherwise indicates that it is payable at the will of the holder; or (ii) does not state any time for payment.*
> *(b) A promise or order is "payable at a definite time" if it is payable on elapse of a definite period of time after sight or acceptance or at a fixed date or dates or at a time or times readily ascertainable at the time the promise or order is issued, subject to rights of (i) prepayment, (ii) acceleration, (iii) extension at the option of the holder, or (iv) extension to a further definite time at the option of the maker or acceptor or automatically upon or after a specified act or event.*
> *(c) If an instrument, payable at a fixed date, is also payable upon demand made before the fixed date, the instrument is payable on demand until the fixed date and, if demand for payment is not made before that date, becomes payable at a definite time on the fixed date.*

The payee or holder must be able to tell when the instrument is payable by looking at the face of the instrument. Unless the instrument specifies that it is to be paid at some future date (payable at a definite time), it is payable on demand. An instrument is payable on demand when payment is to be made on sight, or at presentment, or when no time for payment is stated. Any form of instrument may be payable on demand, but promise paper (notes and CDs) normally is not payable on demand. A check must be payable on demand, by definition.

An instrument is payable at a definite time if, by its terms, it is payable at a time that can be determined from its face. This definite time frequently will be some stated future date such as "24 September 19XX." Or it may be at some time after a stated date such as "90 days after 3 March 19XX." Either of these dates would be definite even if some provision were made for accelerating the payment date. They also would be definite with a provision for extending the time if the holder has the option of extension, or even if the maker or acceptor has the option of extending the time. However, in this last situation the extension must be a predetermined definite period, not to exceed the original term.

The UCC also stipulates that payment is at a definite time if payment is a stated period after sight (i.e., after presentment). Thus, an instrument calling for payment "60 days after sight" is payable at a definite time. Although the holder must act (present the instrument to the drawee to establish the date of sight), once the act is done, the date for payment is definite.

However, one must be careful in this area. Payment is *not* at a definite time if it is to occur only upon an act or occurrence that is of uncertain date. For example, an instrument payable "30 days after Uncle Charlie dies" is probably not negotiable, since the holder would have to go outside the instrument to determine the time of occurrence before the time to pay the instrument could be set. [The language of the revised Article that a definite time exists if the time or times are "readily ascertainable at the time the promise or order is issued" may change this area. We will have to wait for judicial interpretations to see how broadly or how narrowly this provision will now be construed.]

Words of Negotiability Requirement

To be negotiable, even if every other element is present, an instrument must contain words of negotiability. The words of negotiability are "Pay to order" or "Pay to bearer." The reason these words are so important is that the law reads them as authorizing the free transfer of the instrument. Failing to use one of these terms is a denial of free transferability and therefore a denial of negotiability.

If an instrument that is otherwise negotiable calls for payment by stating "Pay to Pete Jones" (rather than "Pay to the order of Pete Jones"), it is not negotiable. By its terms, only Pete Jones is authorized to receive payment; he cannot transfer payment. However, an endorsement that says "Pay to Pete Jones" would not affect negotiability. Endorsements cannot negate negotiability once it exists. To be payable to order, the terms of the instrument must state that it is payable to the order or assigns of a specified individual or to a specified individual or to the individual's order. The designated individual may be a person, as in "Pay to Paula Lopez or order"; an office, as in "Pay to the order of the Treasurer of Washington County"; an estate or trust, as in "Pay to the order of the Johnson Estate"; or an unincorporated association, as in "Pay to the XYZ Partnership or order." An instrument payable to order requires an endorsement to be negotiated.

If no particular individual is designated, the instrument must be payable to bearer to be negotiable. An instrument is payable to bearer when, by its terms, it is payable to bearer or to the order of bearer; or to "cash" or the order of "cash"; or to a named person or bearer, as in "Pay to Joe Jakes or bearer" or "Pay to the order of Joe Jakes or bearer" (§ 3-111). An instrument is also considered payable to bearer if no payee is stated. No endorsement is legally needed to negotiate an instrument payable to bearer, although most holders will request (or demand) an endorsement for added protection.

The following case involves "words of negotiability" and how they may restrict the rights of a bank to make payment on an instrument, even if that instrument is not negotiable. [This case was decided under the old Article 3. Section 3-110(c)(2) of the revised Article would give the same result if the case were tried under it.]

22.2 HOLLOWAY v. WACHOVIA BANK & TRUST CO. 423 S.E.2d 752 (N.C. 1992)

FACTS On 13 October 1975, Wachovia Bank issued a $20,000 certificate of deposit to "Timmy S. Holloway, Jr., by Rountree Crisp, Sr., Agent." At the time Timmy was a six-year-old minor. Crisp died on 5 April 1978. At Crisp's death, the certificate of deposit in Timmy's name with Crisp as agent was found in Crisp's safe deposit box. . . . As to the certificate of deposit in Timmy's name, on 11 April 1980 Wachovia paid to Marcia Coleman, Timmy's mother, and Louise Crisp, Crisp's widow and Timmy's grandmother, the sum of $26,294.92, purportedly the proceeds then due on the certificate of deposit, upon an endorsement reading "Timothy S. Holloway, Jr., by Estate of George R. Crisp, Sr., Marcia Coleman, Adminx." On the same date and on a second occasion, Coleman rolled over the proceeds of the certificate of deposit into new certificates. . . . On 23 October 1981, Coleman presented the [most recent] certificate to Wachovia for payment. Wachovia paid the certificate with a check in the amount of $26,294.92 payable to "Timmy S. Holloway, Jr., by Marcia Coleman."

Coleman stated that she did not remember what she did with the $26,294.92 proceeds of the 23 October 1981 check. At this time, Timmy was still a minor. No court had appointed Coleman as Timmy's guardian with authority to receive the funds for him. In June 1986, Coleman was appointed Timmy's guardian for purposes of holding real property inherited by Timmy from his grandmother. . . . Timmy attained his majority on 5 September 1987. Shortly before his eighteenth birthday, Timmy's relationship with his mother had deteriorated to the point that he had moved away from her house and to an aunt's house. In the summer of 1988, Timmy was in need of money and his aunt told him about the certificate of deposit left by his grandfather. . . . On 12 May 1989, Timmy brought this action against Wachovia seeking to recover the original value of the certificate ($20,000) plus interest. Both parties moved for summary judgment. The trial court denied Timmy's motion and granted Wachovia's motion. The Court of Appeals affirmed. . . . On 4 March 1992, we allowed plaintiff's petition for discretionary review. On appeal, the parties agree that no triable issue of fact exists; neither party has disputed that the case is appropriate for summary judgment.

ISSUE Did the bank breach its contract with Crisp when it paid the certificate to Coleman?

HOLDING Yes, the bank breached its contract by paying the certificate to Coleman in contravention of the terms of the certificate.

REASONING We first note that the certificate of deposit in question does not qualify as a negotiable instrument under the UCC. While the UCC explicitly recognizes that certificates of deposit can be negotiable instruments, . . . the certificate at issue fails to meet two elements of negotiability . . . first, it is not payable "to order" or "to bearer." Rather, the certificate is "payable to the Registered Holder, or to the duly registered assignee hereof." While the UCC states that "assigns" language may satisfy the requirements of being payable to order . . . , this Court has held that language similar to that contained in the certificate lacks the essential words of negotiability. . . . If the certificate of deposit merely lacked "order" or "bearer" language and met all of the other requirements of negotiability under the UCC, the UCC would still govern, except there could be no holder in due course of the certificate. . . . There is a second aspect of the certificate, however, which places it in a class of certificates of deposit which are not negotiable by either means under the UCC because they contain terms precluding transfer. . . . These instruments are non-negotiable because they do not contain the unconditional promise to pay required by [the Code].

The terms of the contract between Crisp and Wachovia are contained in the certificate of deposit. "[A] certificate of deposit is a bank's promissory note, payable only according to its terms. . . ." Those terms are that the sum of $20,000 "shall be payable to the Registered Holder, or to the duly registered assignee hereof." "Timmy S. Holloway, Jr., by Rountree Crisp, Sr., Agent" is listed in the blank for "registered holder." In order to pay the certificate according to its terms, therefore, at the time Coleman presented it, Wachovia had to pay the certificate to Timmy or to someone authorized to accept payment on his behalf. Because Timmy was a minor at the time Wachovia paid the certificate, Wachovia's only legally permissible option was to pay the funds to a legally appointed guardian for Timmy. . . . Rather than following the only legally authorized procedure—i.e., ascertaining whether Coleman was in fact Timmy's legally appointed guardian, "deriving [her] authority from the action of a competent court, evidenced by a proper record," . . . Wachovia improperly paid the certificate of deposit to Coleman, who was not Timmy's legally appointed guardian at the time.

The result would be the same under the UCC had the certificate been negotiable. As explained here, in order to pay this certificate according to its tenor, Wachovia would have had to pay the proceeds to Timmy or his guardian. . . . For the reasons stated, we hold that the Court of Appeals erred in affirming the trial court's denial of Timmy's motion for summary judgment and granting Wachovia's motion for summary judgment. The decision of the Court of Appeals is therefore reversed, and the cause is remanded to that

22.2 HOLLOWAY v. WACHOVIA BANK & TRUST CO. *(cont.)* 423 S.E.2d 752 (N.C. 1992)

court for further remand to the Superior Court for entry of summary judgment for plaintiff.

BUSINESS CONSIDERATIONS In this case the bank paid the certificate of deposit upon presentment and demand for payment from the administratrix of the estate of Crisp and the mother of the named payee. What more should the bank have done to ascertain the right of Timmy's mother to act as his "legal guardian" in the handling of this nonnegotiable certificate of deposit?

ETHICAL CONSIDERATIONS Does it seem ethical for Timmy to sue the bank in this case to recover his money? Why is the bank the proper defendant rather than his mother? Should the bank be able to recover its losses from Coleman?

CONSTRUCTION AND INTERPRETATION: ARTICLE 3

The revised Article 3 takes a very short-and-simple approach to construction and interpretation. Basically, Section 3-114, which covers contradictory terms, provides the coverage in this area. According to this section: "If an instrument contains contradictory terms, typewritten terms prevail over printed terms, handwritten terms prevail over both, and words prevail over numbers."

The following case involved the issue of interpretation under the old Article 3. The case involved the placement of numbers on a check in the location where words normally go.

22.3 GALATIA COMMUNITY STATE BANK v. KINDY 821 S.W.2d 765 (Ark. 1991)

FACTS Kindy agreed to purchase four diesel engines from Hicks, with Hicks agreeing to deliver the engines to Kindy. The purchase price was $13,000. Kindy agreed to wire transfer $6,500 and to pay the remainder by check. The check was not to be cashed until the engines had been delivered. Kindy wrote and mailed a post-dated check to Hicks in June of 1989. This check had two different amounts on its face: $6,500 in numbers on the number line, and $5,500 imprinted with a check imprinting machine on the line where words normally appear. Kindy stated that he had intentionally put two amounts on the check, reasoning that the bank would call him to find out which amount was to be paid, allowing him to tell the bank whether to honor the check (if the engines had been delivered) or to dishonor the check (if the engines had not been delivered). Hicks presented the check to the Galatia Bank 10 June 1989, and the bank honored the check for $5,500. A bank employee altered the amount in the normal "number" location, changing the "6" in $6,500 to a "5" so that the amounts in each area were in agreement. The check was subsequently presented to the drawee bank, which refused it. Galatia sued Kindy for the amount of the check. Kindy denied liability, asserting that he had a defense (nondelivery) and that the bank was a mere holder.

ISSUES Was Galatia Bank a holder in due course and thus entitled to recover from Kindy on the check? Do imprinted numbers, located where the words are normally located, take precedence over figures placed where the figures are normally placed on a check?

HOLDINGS Yes, Galatia was an HDC on the check. Yes, the imprinted numbers in the word location should take precedence over the figures in the figure location.

REASONING The bank employee did not make a "fraudulent and material" alteration of the check. Rather, the alteration by the employee was done in good faith and with no intent to harm anyone. The alteration was done to place the amounts in harmony and to make the controlling amount the amount reflected on the check.

22.3 GALATIA COMMUNITY STATE BANK v. KINDY (cont.) 821 S.W.2d 765 (Ark. 1991)

Words take precedence over numbers because words are harder to alter than numbers. A person uses a check imprinting machine because its imprint is more difficult to alter than words are. Thus, the purposes of the UCC are best served by considering an amount imprinted by a check writing machine to be "words," at least for the purpose of resolving an ambiguity between that amount and an amount entered on the line usually used to express the amount in figures. Since the imprinted amount is in "words" and the figures are in numbers, and since "words" take precedence over numbers, the imprinted amount is the amount to be used in resolving the ambiguity.

BUSINESS CONSIDERATIONS Suppose that your business receives a check from a customer, and that the check has different amounts in words and in numbers. What should you do? Why?

ETHICAL CONSIDERATIONS Should a bank employee take it upon himself or herself to "correct" a mistake made by a customer in drafting a check? Is it ethical for a bank employee to change negotiable instruments issued by its customers, even if it does so in good faith?

REQUIREMENTS FOR NEGOTIABILITY: ARTICLE 7

Where Article 3 is very strict in determining the negotiability of commercial paper, Article 7 is much more relaxed in determining whether a document of title is negotiable. Section 7-104 states that a document of title is negotiable if:

1. By its terms the goods are to be delivered to bearer or to the order of a named person.
2. Where recognized in international trade, if it runs to a named person or assigns.

Every other document of title is deemed to be nonnegotiable. In fact, a bill of lading that is consigned to a named person is not made negotiable by a provision which specifies that the goods are only to be delivered against an order signed by a named person.

Obviously, Article 7 is more concerned with the rights of the parties to the goods than it is concerned with the rights of the parties in the documents covering the goods, as is shown in the following case.

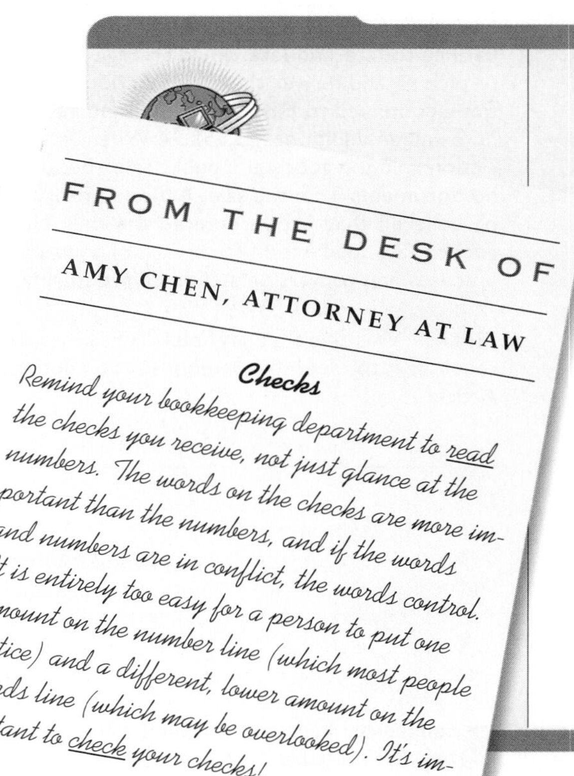
FROM THE DESK OF

AMY CHEN, ATTORNEY AT LAW

Checks

Remind your bookkeeping department to read the checks you receive, not just glance at the numbers. The words on the checks are more important than the numbers, and if the words and numbers are in conflict, the words control. It is entirely too easy for a person to put one amount on the number line (which most people notice) and a different, lower amount on the words line (which may be overlooked). It's important to check your checks!

22.4 TATE v. ACTION MOVING & STORAGE, INC.

383 S.E.2d 229 (N.C.App. 1989)

FACTS Tate contacted Action Moving & Storage to ship his household belongings from his home in Charlotte, North Carolina, to Monrovia, Liberia. Action inspected the items and gave Tate a written estimate, quoting a price of $4,281.60 to package, store, and then ship the items. Tate accepted the price offered and paid Action $1,000 down with the balance to be paid prior to shipment. (The contract also stated that if the goods were left in Action's possession for six months, they became the property of Action.) On 26 March 1984, Action loaded the goods. On 29 March 1984, Tate left for Liberia. At that point Action stored the goods since it had not been paid the balance due. Tate wrote to Action on 26 September asking for the final weight of the shipment, enclosed a check for $3,800, and asked for information as to when he could expect to receive his goods. Receiving no answer, Tate again wrote to Action on 24 October 1984. In this letter he instructed Action to deduct $2,708.20 from the $4,800 he had paid for its charges and expenses, send the balance to Tate, and Tate would arrange for another carrier to pick up and deliver the goods. Action ignored the directions, continued to hold the $4,800, and informed Tate that he owed an additional $3,652.24. When Tate did not reply, Action sold the goods at a public sale. (Because there were no documents from the sale, Action's president stated that he believed that Action entered the only bid, $1, for the goods.) Tate sued Action for breach of contract, unfair trade practices, and conversion. Action denied liability.

ISSUE Was there a warehouse receipt issued by Action, requiring it to meet the warehouseman's duties imposed by Article 7?

HOLDING Yes. The inventory document prepared by Action was a warehouse receipt under Article 7, imposing a warehouseman's duties on Action.

REASONING Article 7 is vague as to what constitutes a warehouse receipt. Basically, a warehouse receipt is treated as "a receipt issued by a person engaged in the business of storing goods for hire." Here Action agreed to store the goods for up to six months, and issued a Household Goods Descriptive Inventory on those goods. Under Article 7, this was sufficient to constitute a warehouse receipt. Once a warehouse receipt is issued, the issuer must conform to the duties imposed on a warehouseman under Article 7; Action failed to do so. Tate offered a reasonable settlement, but Action refused it. Action then made a questionable sale of the goods. Action acted in bad faith, violated its duties, and converted Tate's goods. Action is liable for the damages suffered by Tate.

BUSINESS CONSIDERATIONS How cooperative should a warehouseman be in a situation like the one facing Action Moving & Storage? Do the good-faith and duty-to-cooperate provisions of Article 2 carry over to Article 7 transactions?

ETHICAL CONSIDERATIONS Is it ethical for the warehouseman to enter the only bid at an auction, and thus to acquire the goods for a nominal amount while retaining its claim for the unpaid balance of the storage fees? What protections should be provided for the bailor in this sort of situation?

http:// RESOURCES FOR BUSINESS LAW STUDENTS

NAME	RESOURCES	WEB ADDRESS
Uniform Commercial Code (UCC), Article 3, Negotiable Instruments	The Legal Information Institute (LII), maintained by the Cornell Law School, provides a hypertext and searchable version of UCC, Article 3, Negotiable Instruments. LII has links to Article 3 as adopted by particular states and to proposed revisions.	http://www.law.cornell.edu/ucc/3/overview.html
UCC, Article 7, Warehouse Receipts, Bills of Lading and Other Documents of Title	LII provides a hypertext and searchable version of UCC, Article 7, Warehouse Receipts, Bills of Lading and Other Documents of Title.	http://www.law.cornell.edu/ucc/7/overview.html

Even though Article 7 is more concerned with rights in the goods, there are certain rights to be gained if the document of title is negotiable, especially if the party qualifies as a holder by due negotiation. In addition, a holder by due negotiation can exist only if the document of title is negotiable. (This topic will be covered in more detail in Chapter 23.)

SUMMARY

This chapter examines the technical requirements for negotiability of an instrument under Article 3. The first requirement is that the instrument be written or reduced to tangible form. Next, the instrument must be signed by the maker or the drawer. The promise (for notes or CDs) or the order (for checks or drafts) must be unconditional. The instrument must call for the payment of a fixed amount in money—a recognized governmental currency. In addition, the time of payment must be determinable from the face of the instrument, or it must be payable on demand. Finally, the instrument must contain "words of negotiability." This means it must be payable "to order" or "to bearer."

In case the instrument contains ambiguities, the Code provides a method of interpretation. Handwriting takes precedence over typing and over printing. Typing takes precedence over printing. Words take precedence over numbers if the words make sense. If the words do not make sense, the numbers control.

Article 7 of the UCC governs documents of title. Documents of title may be negotiable or nonnegotiable. The requirements for negotiable documents under Article 7 are much less stringent than the requirements under Article 3. Article 7 is more concerned with the goods than it is with the documents covering the goods, but it does provide some special protections if the document is negotiable and the holder qualifies as a holder by due negotiation.

DISCUSSION QUESTIONS

1. What is meant by "signing" under Article 3 of the UCC? Why is this requirement so important in determining whether an instrument is negotiable?
2. In order to qualify as a negotiable instrument, the promise or the order must be "written." How does the UCC define "written," and how is that definition modified for negotiable instruments?
3. What is meant by a "fixed amount of money" under Article 3 of the UCC? How does the Code define "fixed amount"? What is meant by "money"?
4. Why is an instrument that is payable "30 days after sight" payable at a determinable time, but an instrument payable "30 days after my anniversary" not payable at a determinable time? How is the date of "sight" determined?
5. The courts have consistently held that an "IOU is not a negotiable instrument." Below is a typical IOU. Why would such an instrument be deemed nonnegotiable? Be specific.

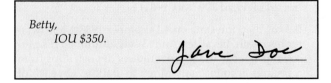

Betty,
IOU $350.

Jane Doe

6. A promissory note was issued by Larry to Darryl. The note had the following terms included in the body of the instrument:

   Interest to be paid at 14 percent per annum. [This term was preprinted on the promissory note form.] Interest at 14.5 percent per annum. [This term was typewritten above the preprinted term.] Plus interest. [This term was handwritten in the margin and initialed by both Larry and Darryl.]

   How will interest be computed on this note, and why will that method for computing interest be used?
7. Marvella issued what appeared to be a time draft payable to the order of Herman. The terms of the instrument called for payment "90 days after our marriage." Marvella and Herman were married on 4 January of this year. Subsequently, they got a divorce on 15 March. Herman presented the instrument to the drawee 90 days after the wedding date, demanding payment. The drawee refused to pay, and Herman has sued Marvella on the instrument. Will this case be resolved under the provisions of Article 3, or will it be resolved under the provisions of common law? Why?
8. What is required by Article 7 in order for a document of title to be deemed negotiable? Is this more or less rigorous than the requirements for negotiability under Article 3? Why is there a difference in the requirements of negotiability under the two articles?
9. A bill of lading called for the delivery of the goods to Acme, Inc. It went on to specify that delivery was only to take place on receipt of a written order signed by Mr. Aziz. Is this document of title negotiable? Explain.
10. An international shipment of goods is being made. The bill of lading states that the goods are consigned to "Mr. Smythe-Harrington of London, England, or to his assigns." What information would be required to determine whether this bill of lading is negotiable? Explain.

CASE PROBLEMS AND WRITING ASSIGNMENTS

1. The Smiths were the officers and the directors of Fastwich, Inc. As officers of the corporation, they were authorized to borrow money on behalf of the firm. Fastwich needed funds, and the Smiths approached First Bank for a loan. First Bank agreed to lend the firm $10,000 and prepared a promissory note as evidence of the debt. In the upper left-hand corner of the note was typed "Fastwich, Inc." In the lower right-hand corner of the note, "Fastwich, Inc." was typed, and immediately below that were the signatures of the Smiths. Subsequently, the firm defaulted on the note. When First Bank sought to recover, the firm denied that it was liable since its name was only typed on the instrument. According to the firm, it had never signed the note, so it could not be liable. Was Fastwich's signature on the note? If so, was the signature valid? [See *First Security Bank of Brookfield* v. *Fastwich, Inc.*, 612 S.W.2d 799 (Mo. 1981).]

2. Balkus died intestate on 4 December 1983. Shortly after his death, his sister, Ann Vesely, examined his personal property and discovered six deposit slips from a savings account maintained by Balkus. On each of these six slips was the following notation: "Payable to Ann Vesely on proof of my death, the full amount of this and any other deposits." There were also two promissory notes, each payable to her order. Vesely filed suit against the estate for the amounts represented by the six deposit slips and the two promissory notes. The court considered this case to involve two issues: Were these negotiable instruments? Was Vesely a holder of these instruments? How should these issues have been resolved? [See *Matter of Estate of Balkus*, 381 N.W.2d 593 (Wis.App. 1985).]

3. Wall borrowed money from the East Texas Credit Union, signing a promissory note with the following provisions for payment:

Nineteen hundred and eight hundred and ninety-six and 01/100 dollars ($19,896.01)

   Wall insisted that he only owed two thousand seven hundred ninety-six and 01/100 dollars (1,900 + 800 + 96 + 01/100), since words take precedence over numbers in an ambiguous instrument. The credit union insisted that it was entitled to nineteen thousand eight hundred and ninety-six dollars and one cent. How should the court resolve this case? Explain your reasoning. [See *Wall* v. *East Texas Teachers Credit Union*, 533 S.W.2d 918 (Tex. 1976).]

4. The Campbells issued a note payable to the order of Strand. The note called for payment of $12,500 plus interest, and was issued to purchase shares in a limited partnership Strand was allegedly forming. Strand subsequently endorsed the note and delivered it to the Centerre Bank for value. Strand never completed the formation of the limited partnership, so the Campbells never acquired their anticipated interest in the venture. Since no limited partnership was formed, the Campbells defaulted on the note. Centerre Bank

sued the Campbells for the note, and the Campbells asserted two defenses that they felt excused their default: There was a failure of consideration because the limited partnership was never formed; and a clause in the note stated that interest could vary with changes in the interest rate the banks charged to Strand, which made the instrument nonnegotiable. How should the court treat the two defenses raised by the Campbells? Does it make any difference in which order the defenses are addressed? Explain your answer. [See *Centerre Bank of Branson* v. *Campbell*, 744 S.W.2d 490 (Mo.App. 1988).]

5. McDonald stole numerous money orders from the U.S. Postal Service, along with an imprinting machine. McDonald used the machine to prepare a number of money orders for the maximum amount of $100, endorsed the money orders, and cashed them at First Bank. First Bank then presented the money orders to the government and received payment for them. The government discovered that the money orders were stolen, and sued First Bank to recover the money given to First Bank by them. The bank denied any liability to the government, arguing that the money orders were negotiable instruments, so the bank was protected by Article 3 of the UCC. The government denied that the money orders were negotiable instruments, so Article 3 should not apply, and the bank should be liable for the money received. Which party should prevail in this case? Why? [See *U.S.* v. *The First Nat'l Bank of Boston,* 263 F.Supp. 298 (D.C.Mass. 1967).]

6. **BUSINESS APPLICATION CASE** Williams (d.b.a. Howard R. Williams, Inc.) invested with Prasad (d.b.a. P.S. Investment Co.) from time to time. In December 1980, Prasad assigned to Williams a promissory note for $75,000, payable in unconditional payments of $991.14 per month. On 11 April 1983, R & D Development issued a $200,000 promissory note payable to the order of Prasad. In August 1983, Williams assigned the $75,000 note to Prasad in exchange for a partial interest in the $200,000 note from R & D. This assignment was governed by a written document, which specified that Prasad had the right to reacquire the partial interest in the $200,000 note from Williams by issuing another promissory note, which would pay Williams $991.14 per month. On 30 December 1984, Prasad issued a note to Williams in order to reacquire this partial interest. This new note stated that "payments under this note will be paid on and when payments are received from the [R & D] note." R & D filed for bankruptcy in 1987 and stopped making payments at that time. Accordingly, Prasad stopped making payments to Williams at that time. Williams sued Prasad to collect the accrued payments and the balance of the note. Was the note from Prasad to Williams a negotiable instrument, allowing Williams to collect despite the bankruptcy of R & D? [See *Williams* v. *P.S. Investment Co., Inc.,* 401 S.E.2d 79 (N.C.App. 1991).]

7. **ETHICS APPLICATION CASE** The Oaks Apartments Joint Venture and its five partners executed a promissory note payable to the order of Meridian Service Corporation, a wholly owned subsidiary of Meridian Savings Association. The note read, in pertinent part:

> FOR VALUE RECEIVED, THE OAKS APARTMENTS JOINT VENTURE, a Texas Joint Venture . . . promises to pay to the order of MERIDIAN SERVICE CORPORATION, a Texas Corporation . . . the sum of TWO MILLION AND NO/100 DOLLARS ($2,000,000.00) or so much thereof as may be advanced in accordance with the terms of a certain Loan Agreement executed on even date herewith, with interest thereon at the rate provided below.

The five partners also executed an unconditional personal guaranty of the note, obligating each partner for 20 percent of the total debt. The Oaks Apartments was subsequently sold to Veigel, who assumed the loan obligation in 1985. Veigel then entered into an agreement with Meridian which modified the time and manner of payment. Veigel subsequently defaulted on the note, and Meridian began attempting to collect from Veigel, the partnership, and each of the partners in 1986. In 1987, Meridian foreclosed on the apartment complex and sold it, leaving a deficit of $755,249.06 on the note. Meridian then sued to recover this deficit. (Resolution Trust replaced Meridian as conservator when Meridian failed.) Resolution Trust argued that it was an HDC of the note and the guaranty, not subject to any defenses. The partners objected, alleging that the note was not negotiable, so RTC could not be an HDC.

Was the note originally signed by Oaks Apartments a negotiable instrument? Is it ethical to try to avoid liability by denying that a note issued by the defendant is negotiable? [See *Resolution Trust Corp.* v. *Oaks Apartments Joint Venture,* 966 F.2d 995 (5th Cir. 1992).]

8. **IDES CASE** O'Mara, a West Virginia corporation with its principal place of business in Steubenville, Ohio, operated 15 Bonanza restaurants. O'Mara hired GSD, an accounting firm, to manage its accounting and other financial matters. Included in GSD's services were the computation of O'Mara's weekly federal withholding taxes, preparation of checks for

deposit of these taxes, and reconciliation of bank statements. Smith was the sole owner of GSD, and also owned 20 percent of O'Mara. Thompson was the comptroller for both O'Mara and GSD. Smith encountered financial difficulties beginning in 1979, and Smith and Thompson devised a plan whereby Smith would embezzle O'Mara's withholding taxes. This scheme involved endorsing the withholding checks, which were payable to the order of the Heritage Bank, as follows:

> Pay to the order of The First National Bank & Trust Company in Steubenville, Ohio FOR DEPOSIT ONLY GAIL SMITH DEVELOPMENT #009-215, W. Gail Smith.

Heritage Bank accepted each of these checks with this endorsement and without question. When O'Mara discovered what had happened, it sued Heritage Bank (along with two other banks similarly involved) to recover the funds. The banks denied liability, asserting that the checks as issued were "bearer" instruments, not "order" instruments. Were these checks "bearer paper" so that Heritage Bank acted properly in accepting them? Apply the IDES principles in analyzing and resolving this case. [See *O'Mara Enterprises, Inc.* v. *People's Bank of Weirton,* 420 S.E.2d 727 (W.Va. 1992).]

Note

1. T. L. Henion, "Fake Check for $95,093 Fools Recipient, Bank," *Omaha World Herald,* p. 1.

Negotiation and Holders in Due Course/Holders by Due Negotiation

A G E N D A

CIT will be receiving a number of checks from their customers. How should these checks be indorsed? Does the type of indorsement *really* make a difference? Suppose that some of the checks are dishonored by the bank. What rights will the firm be able to assert on those checks? Should the firm take any special steps or plan any special precautions for handling the checks they receive?

Be prepared! You never know when one of the Kochanowskis will ask for your advice and guidance.

O U T L I N E

TRANSFER

Negotiable instruments are intended to "flow" through the commercial world. In order to "flow," the instrument needs to be *transferred* from person to person. The form these transfers take determines the rights that can be asserted by each person gaining possession of the instrument.

The Uniform Commercial Code (UCC) defines a *transfer* as a delivery by any person other than the issuer for the purpose of giving the person receiving the instrument the right to enforce the instrument. A transfer, whether by negotiation or not, confers on the transferee the rights possessed by the transferor, including the rights of a holder in due course (HDC) if the transferor has those rights. Thus, as was discussed in the previous chapter, a transfer of a negotiable instrument is treated like an assignment of a contract right. The transferee receives any and all rights of the transferor. However, this is, in effect, the same as an assignment. As was discussed earlier, this is not an ideal position, and if negotiable instruments could only be transferred—treated the same as an assignment—they would not be as readily acceptable as they are in the modern commercial world.

Indorsed

Signature placed on the back of a negotiable instrument in order to properly negotiate to the next holder.

Nonetheless, the transfer of a negotiable instrument does give the transferee some rights in the instrument, although these rights are fewer than the rights that a holder or a holder in due course possesses, as the following case shows.

23.1 BREMEN BANK AND TRUST CO. v. MUSKOPF — 817 S.W.2d 602 (Mo.App. 1991)

FACTS On 30 November 1984, the Fergusons executed and delivered a promissory note for $230,000 and a deed of trust on real estate to Muskopf. The deed of trust named Donavan as trustee and Muskopf as the beneficiary. It was on a standard preprinted form, with the blanks filled in and slightly modified by both typewritten and handwritten terms. Both the note and the deed of trust were properly filed and recorded. On 11 December 1985, Muskopf applied for and received a loan from Bremen Bank and Trust, executing a promissory note and assigning the note and deed of trust from the Fergusons as security for this loan. Muskopf delivered physical possession of the note and the deed of trust to Bremen, neither **indorsed** by Muskopf. Bremen retained possession of both documents, but did not record its interest in either until 15 May 1989. Bremen also did not file a statutory request for notice of any foreclosure sales, as was permitted under Missouri law.

The Fergusons defaulted on their loan in July 1987, and Muskopf initiated steps to foreclose on the note and the deed of trust. Bremen was not consulted concerning this proposed foreclosure, nor was it ever contacted prior to the foreclosure sale. Muskopf was the high bidder at the foreclosure sale, and he subsequently sold the property to the Hoffmans in May 1988. The Hoffmans, in turn, sold the land to Faix in December 1988. Both the Hoffmans and Faix's recorded the deeds upon their respective purchases. Muskopf filed for bankruptcy relief in January 1989, and Bremen sought to acquire its rights to the property covered by the original deed of trust, as assigned to it by Muskopf.

ISSUE Was Bremen a holder of the original note and deed of trust so that the foreclosure sale was not valid without its permission?

HOLDING No. The promissory note from the Fergusons was payable to the order of a named person. As such, it requires an indorsement and a delivery to be negotiated, and this note was never indorsed.

REASONING Since Muskopf never indorsed the note, he never negotiated it to the bank. He did, however, transfer it to the bank, giving the bank rights as an assignee. Further, he transferred rights to a $230,000 note to secure an $80,000 loan, thus making only a partial transfer to the bank, and giving the bank fewer rights than it would possess if there had been a total transfer of rights. Further, since Bremen did not record the documents, they were only valid between Bremen and Muskopf. Bremen did not have the right to object to the foreclosure sale. It must seek its remedies against Muskopf and not against the collateral pledged to secure the loan made to him.

23.1 BREMEN BANK AND TRUST CO. v. MUSKOPF *(cont.)* 817 S.W.2d 602 (Mo.App. 1991)

BUSINESS CONSIDERATIONS The borrower in this case transferred his rights in the note to the bank when he delivered the note to it, but he never negotiated the note since he never indorsed it. Should a lender have procedures established to ensure that it only receives notes to be used as collateral through a negotiation? How important is it for the transferee to receive a negotiation rather than a mere transfer?

ETHICAL CONSIDERATIONS Is it ethical for a borrower who has made a partial assignment of his rights in collateral to dispose of that collateral without permission of the assignee? What should the borrower do in this situation to ensure that he or she is acting ethically?

NEGOTIATION

Obviously, something more is needed to protect the possessor of the commercial paper and to facilitate the free flow of commercial paper through commercial channels. That "something more" is provided by the UCC, and it is known as negotiation. Section 3-201(a) defines a *negotiation* as "a transfer of possession, whether voluntary or involuntary, of an instrument by a person other than the issuer to a person who becomes a holder thereby." Section 3-201(b) adds that: "Except for negotiation by a remitter, if an instrument is payable to an identified person, negotiation requires transfer of possession of the instrument and its indorsement by the holder. If an instrument is payable to bearer, it may be negotiated by transfer of possession alone."

For example, a check that says "Pay to the order of Ollie Oliver" must be indorsed by Ollie Oliver before it can be negotiated. If Ollie simply transfers possession of the check to another person without indorsing it, the transfer would be an assignment. The terms imposed by the drawer—pay to the order of Ollie Oliver—require that Ollie *prove* he is transferring his rights. His indorsement provides that proof.

In contrast, a check that says "Pay to the order of bearer" does not need to be indorsed to be negotiated. Transfer of possession alone is enough to show negotiation. The terms imposed by the drawer at the time of issue—pay to the order of bearer—tell the drawee that anyone in possession is entitled to payment.

If the instrument requires an indorsement, the indorsement must be written on the instrument itself or on an *allonge*—a paper so firmly affixed to the instrument as to become a part of the instrument. Also, to be a negotiation, the indorsement must transfer the entire instrument or the entire unpaid balance. Any attempt to transfer less than the entire balance of the instrument is treated as a partial assignment, not as a negotiation.

INDORSEMENTS

Section 3-204 defines an indorsement. According to the Code, "*indorsement*" means a signature, other than that of a signer as maker, drawer, or acceptor, that alone or accompanied by other words is made on an instrument for the purpose of (i) negotiating the instrument, (ii) restricting payment of the instrument, or (iii) incurring indorser's liability on the instrument." This section goes on to add that "regardless of the intent of the signer, a signature and its accompanying words is an indorsement unless the accompanying words, terms of the instrument, or other circumstances unambiguously indicate that the signature was made for a purpose other than indorsement."

This means that a signature on a negotiable instrument is *presumed* to be an indorsement unless some other purpose is unambiguously shown as the purpose for the signature's placement on the instrument. There are two reasons that this is important. First, any instrument payable "to order" requires an indorsement before it can be further negotiated. Second, and perhaps more important, each and every indorsement is a separate contract added to the contract that the instrument itself represents, and to any other indorsement contracts already present on the instrument. Indorsers are assuming contractual liability to the person to whom they transfer the instrument and to every subsequent holder or transferee of that instrument. For this reason, many people will not accept the negotiation of a bearer instrument unless the holder indorses it. Even though bearer paper may legally be negotiated by delivery alone, the transferee usually demands the added security of an indorsement, thereby adding the indorsement contract and its rights to the rights represented by the instrument itself.

There are two reasons for indorsing an instrument. One reason is to affect negotiation. The other is to affect liability. The indorsements that affect negotiation will tell the holder (1) that another indorsement is needed to negotiate the instrument further (a special indorsement); (2) that no further indorsements are needed in order to negotiate the instrument further (a blank indorsement); or (3) that the instrument has been restricted to some special channel of commerce such as banking (a restrictive indorsement). The indorsements that affect liability either (1) admit and/or agree to honor the contract of indorsement (an unqualified indorsement) or (2) expressly deny any liability on the indorsement contract (a qualified indorsement). Every indorsement must affect negotiation as well as liability. Thus, each indorsement must fit one of the boxes in the matrix shown in Exhibit 23.1.

Notice that each box is numbered. We will use these numbers to refer back to the matrix as we discuss some examples of the various types of indorsements. Throughout the examples, we will be using the check shown in Exhibit 23.2.

EXHIBIT 23.1 The Indorsement Matrix

	Unqualified	**Qualified**
Special	(1) Designates the next holder, so an additional indorsement is required; does not deny liability for the indorsement contract.	(2) Designates the next holder, so an additional indorsement is required; denies contract liability for the indorsement.
Blank	(3) Does not designate the next holder, making the instrument "bearer paper"; does not deny liability for the indorsement contract.	(4) Does not designate the next holder, making the instrument "bearer paper"; denies contract liability for the indorsement.
Restrictive	(5) Attempts to restrict or limit future negotiation of the instrument, as in "for deposit only"; does not deny liability for the indorsement contract.	(6) Attempts to restrict or limit future negotiation of the instrument, as in "for deposit only"; denies contract liability for the indorsement.

Special Indorsements

A special indorsement specifies the party to whom the instrument is to be paid or to whose order it is to be paid. This means that a special indorsement makes (or leaves) the instrument payable "to order." Even if the instrument was issued as bearer paper, a special indorsement will make it payable "to order." The party specified will have to indorse it before it can be negotiated further. Exhibit 23.3 shows an example of a special indorsement.

EXHIBIT 23.2 The Check as Issued

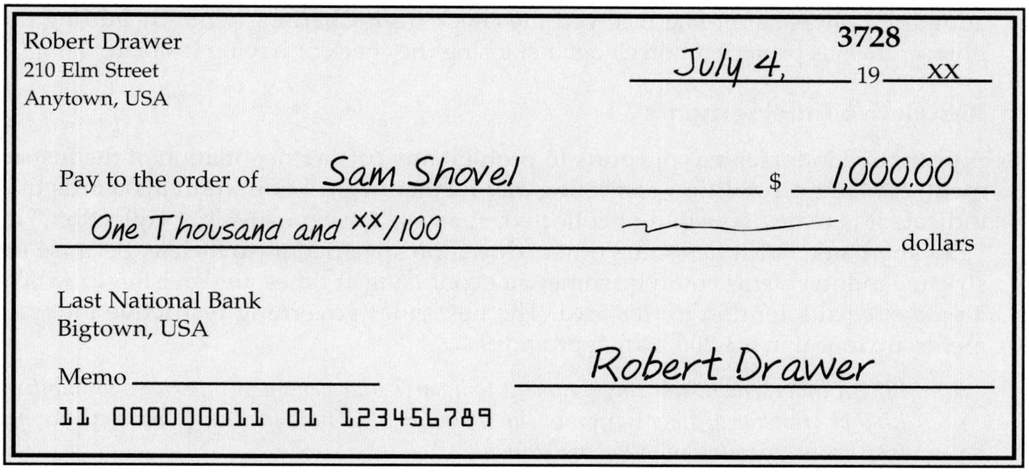

Robert Drawer
210 Elm Street
Anytown, USA
3728
July 4, 19 XX
Pay to the order of Sam Shovel $ 1,000.00
One Thousand and XX/100 dollars
Last National Bank
Bigtown, USA
Memo
Robert Drawer
11 000000011 01 123456789

EXHIBIT 23.3 A Special Indorsement

Pay to Charlie Chenn
Sam Shovel
(1)

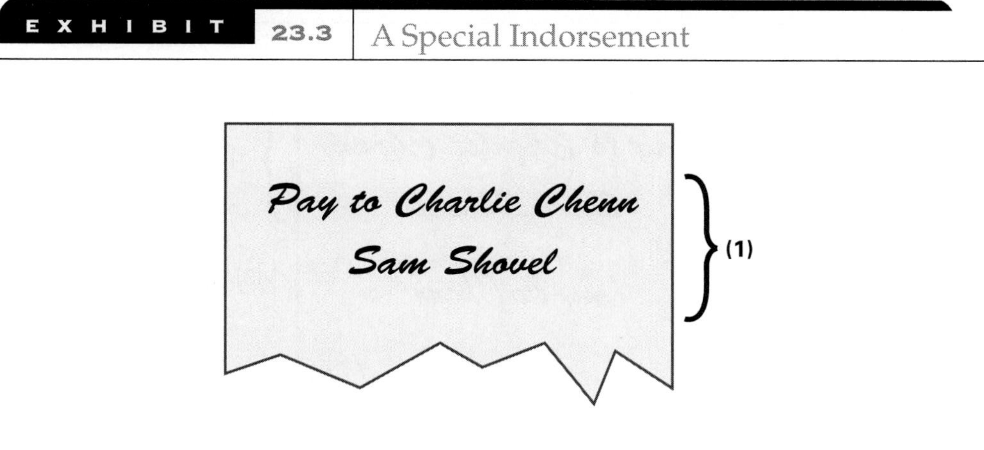

Blank Indorsements

A blank indorsement does not specify the party to whom the instrument is to be paid. The normal form of a blank indorsement is a mere signature by the holder. Such an indorsement makes the instrument bearer paper. As such, it is negotiable by transfer of possession alone, without any need for further indorsements. In Exhibit 23.4, a blank indorsement has been added to the previous special indorsement. Note that at this point the check has every indorsement that is necessary for negotiation. Should the check now be lost or stolen, the finder or the thief could effectively negotiate it. To protect against such an occurrence, § 3-205(c) empowers the holder to **convert** a blank indorsement into a special indorsement by writing, above the signature of the indorser, words identifying the person to whom the instrument is now made payable. This is shown in Exhibit 23.5. Here a holder added the words "Pay to Mata Harry, or order" above Charlie Chenn's indorsement. This phrase could have been added by Charlie Chenn when he negotiated the check to Mata Harry. More likely, Mata Harry added the phrase after she received the check from Charlie Chenn. By adding the phrase, she has protected herself against losing the check or having it stolen.

Convert
Change

Restrictive Indorsements

A restrictive indorsement purports to prohibit any further negotiation of the instrument, contains a condition restricting any further negotiation, contains words that indicate it is to be deposited or collected, such as "for deposit," "for collection," or "pay any bank," or it has some other restriction specified as to its use. Because restrictive indorsements could be somewhat confusing at times, the revision to Article 3 paid special attention to this area. The new rules governing restrictive indorsements are found in § 3-206, which provides:

> *(a) An indorsement limiting payment to a particular person or otherwise prohibiting further transfer or negotiation of the instrument is not effective to prevent further transfer or negotiation of the instrument.*

EXHIBIT 23.4 A Blank Indorsement

EXHIBIT 23.5 Conversion of a Blank Indorsement to a Special Indorsement

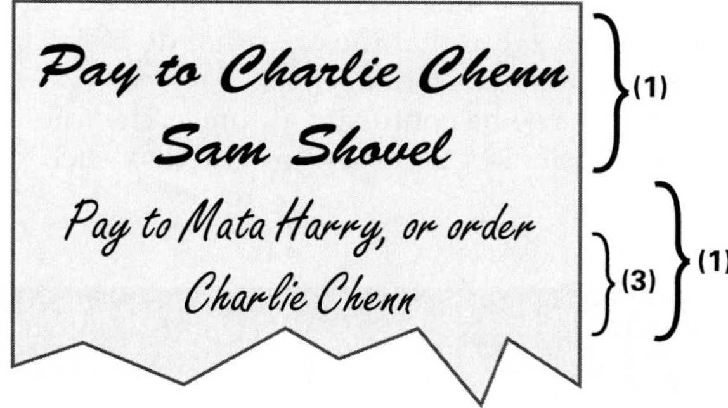

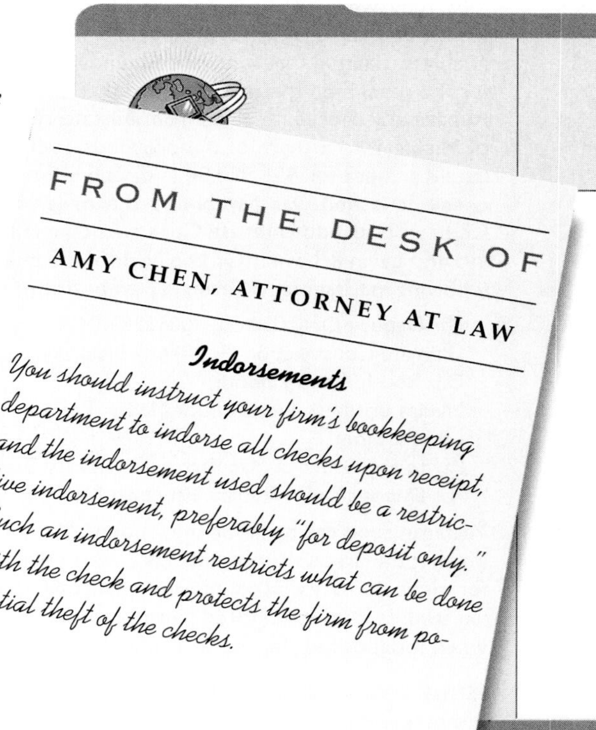

FROM THE DESK OF
AMY CHEN, ATTORNEY AT LAW
Indorsements
You should instruct your firm's bookkeeping department to indorse all checks upon receipt, and the indorsement used should be a restrictive indorsement, preferably "for deposit only." Such an indorsement restricts what can be done with the check and protects the firm from potential theft of the checks.

(b) An indorsement stating a condition to the right of the indorsee to receive payment does not affect the right of the indorsee to enforce the instrument. A person paying the instrument or taking it for value or collection may disregard the condition, and the rights and liabilities of that person are not affected by whether the condition has been fulfilled.
(c) If an instrument bears a indorsement . . . using the words "for deposit," "for collection," or other words indicating a purpose of having the instrument collected by a bank for the indorser or for a particular amount, the following rules apply:

(1) A person, other than a bank, who purchases the instrument when so indorsed converts the instrument unless the amount paid for the instrument is received by the indorser or applied consistently with the indorsement.
(2) A depository bank that purchases the instrument or takes it for collection when so indorsed converts the instrument unless the amount paid by the bank with respect to the instrument is received by the indorser or applied consistently with the indorsement.
(3) A payor bank that is also the depositary bank or that takes the instrument for immediate payment over the counter from a person other than a collecting bank converts the instrument unless the proceeds of the instrument are received by the indorser or applied consistently with the indorsement.

Thus, under the new rules, a restrictive indorsement that purports to restrict payment or negotiation may be disregarded by the indorsee, with no affect on the rights or liabilities of the indorsee. However, a restrictive indorsement that restricts the instrument to banking channels ("for deposit" or "for collection") is a valid restriction, and any person who subsequently deals with that instrument without ensuring that the funds are applied consistently with the indorsement is deemed guilty of *conversion*. This seems to imply that only those restrictive indorsements that restrict the instrument to banking have any meaning or effect, but that the ones that do restrict the instrument to banking have a very serious and substantial effect.

Restrictive indorsements can be confusing at times. The following case adds an interesting twist to the confusion occasionally presented by such an indorsement.

23.2 MICHIGAN INSURANCE REPAIR CO., INC. v. MANUFACTURERS NAT'L BANK OF DETROIT

487 N.W.2d 517 (Mich.App. 1992)

FACTS Michigan Insurance Repair Co. (Michigan) entered into a joint venture with Ultimate Construction for the purpose of doing fire damage repair work. One of the jobs they were to perform was on property owned by Booth and the Madias Brothers, and insured by Allstate. Michigan claimed that it advanced funds to Ultimate to pay for the repairs on this property, and that Ultimate promised to have any checks received from Allstate reflect the rights of Michigan to a share of the proceeds. Eventually, Allstate issued a check for $28,964.94 in payment for the work. The check as issued was payable to the order of "Nella and Chutry Booth and Ultimate Construction and Madias Bros., Inc. and Levin & Levin." On the back of the check were the following indorsements (from top to bottom):

For Deposit Only to Acct. #0051255-04
Ultimate Construction Co., Randy Bidlofsky
C.L. Booth, Chutry Booth
Madias Brothers, Inc. (by Nick Madias, President)
Levin & Levin
Pay to the Order of Manufacturers National Bank of Detroit,
For Deposit Only, Ultimate Insurance Repair or Construction

Michigan sued the bank for the amount of the check, claiming that the first indorsement was a restrictive indorsement for deposit to its account, and asserting that the bank violated its duty as imposed by this restrictive indorsement when it deposited the check to the Ultimate account.

ISSUE Was the bank obligated to honor the first restrictive indorsement on this check?

HOLDING No. The first indorsement did not identify the party or the account to which it was to be deposited, nor was it the indorsement of any of the payees on the check.

REASONING The court determined that Michigan had no rights on the check as issued. It was not named as one of the joint payees, and at the time the instrument was issued, Michigan was a nonparty on this check. The rights of a nonparty are subordinate to the rights of parties on an instrument. The purported restrictive indorsement by (or on behalf of) Michigan preceded the necessary indorsements of the named payees, so it could have no effect until those other indorsements were appended to the instrument. Since Michigan had no apparent rights on the check, its restrictive indorsement was of no effect. The bank was within its rights in ignoring the first indorsement.

BUSINESS CONSIDERATIONS Revised Article 3 takes a much harsher attitude toward restrictive indorsements than the prior law. Banks will be much more hesitant to ignore a restrictive indorsement under the revisions. What should a business do to protect itself when it receives a check that has been endorsed restrictively?

ETHICAL CONSIDERATIONS The bank in this case ignored Michigan Insurance Repair's restrictive indorsement on the check. Presuming that Michigan had a valid claim for the amount of the check, should the bank be ethically obligated to ensure that Michigan received the funds, or should the bank's ethical concern only be the proper handling of the check?

Remember that negotiability is determined by the information contained on the *face* of the instrument, and that indorsements are normally placed on the *back* of the instrument. Once an instrument as issued satisfies all the tests of negotiability, the instrument is deemed to be negotiable and no indorsement can remove its negotiable status.

In Exhibit 23.6, item (5) shows a restrictive indorsement.

It should be noted that each of these sample indorsements refers to the unqualified indorsement column of the matrix set out in Exhibit 23.1. The reason for this is contained in UCC § 3-415, Obligation of Indorser, which provides:

> *(a) . . . If an instrument is dishonored, an indorser is obliged to pay the amount due on the instrument (i) according to the terms of the instrument at the time it was indorsed; or (ii) if the indorser indorsed an incomplete instrument, according to its terms when completed [presuming that the completion was authorized]. The obligation of the indorser is owed to a person entitled to enforce the instrument or to a subsequent indorser who paid the instrument under this section.*
>
> *(b) If an indorsement states that it is made "without recourse" or otherwise disclaims liability of the indorser, the indorser is not liable under subsection (a) to pay the instrument.*

Under this section, an indorsement is presumed to be unqualified. To be qualified, the indorsement must contain specific words of qualification. An unqualified indorsement carries with it a contractual commitment to pay the amount due on the instrument if there is a dishonor. The indorser is committed to the *indorsee* (the person to whom the instrument is transferred by indorsement) or to any later holder if the instrument is dishonored and proper notice of the dishonor is given. The normal order of payment among the indorsers is the reverse of the order in which they indorsed the instrument. Thus, on a dishonored check, which had four indorsers, indorser four would collect from indorser three, who in turn would collect from indorser two, who in turn would collect from indorser one. (This is known as the *secondary chain of liability,* and will be discussed in detail in the next chapter.)

A qualified indorsement is one that denies contract liability. The indorser includes words such as "without recourse" in the indorsement. These words have the legal effect of telling later holders that the qualifying indorser will not repay them if the instrument is dishonored. By accepting a qualified indorsement in a negotiation, the later holders also agree to the contract terms of the qualified indorsement. In Exhibit 23.7,

23.1

PROCEDURE FOR DEPOSITING COMPANY CHECKS

As part of his job with the firm, John is responsible for depositing checks the company receives into the firm's account. John has been stamping the backs of the checks on the day they are received, using a rubber stamp that reads "Call-Image Technology." John then places the checks in his "out" basket until he makes his regular trip to the bank each Friday afternoon. Lindsay complained to the family that, in her opinion, John was not being careful enough with the checks. Tom and Anna agree with Lindsay. They ask you to talk with John and to help him to develop a better procedure for handling the checks. What advice will you give John in your discussion?

BUSINESS CONSIDERATIONS How should a business handle checks it receives to (a) minimize its risk of losing funds through embezzlement or theft, and (b) maximize its cash position? If a firm indorses checks with a stamp, what sort of indorsement should the stamp have?

ETHICAL CONSIDERATIONS Trusting people is an admirable character trait, but it is not always the best business practice. Is it ethical for a firm to have checks indorsed in blank and sitting on a desk, thus placing temptation before customers and employees? Should the firm share at least part of the blame if it handles checks in this manner and suffers losses as a result?

FINANCE

EXHIBIT 23.6 A Restrictive Indorsement

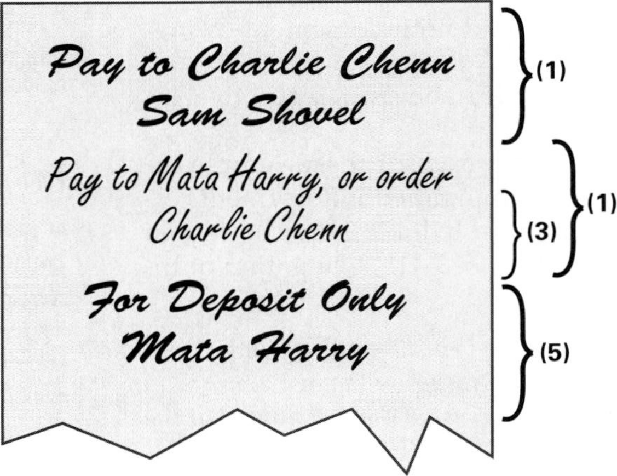

EXHIBIT 23.7 Unqualified Indorsements

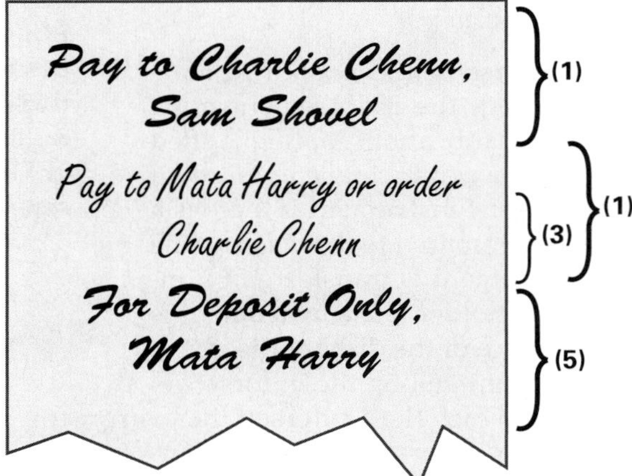

each of the earlier indorsements is shown as unqualified; in Exhibit 23.8, the same indorsements are shown as qualified. Note the specific language necessary to change an indorsement from the presumed unqualified indorsement to a qualified indorsement.

EXHIBIT 23.8 Qualified Indorsements

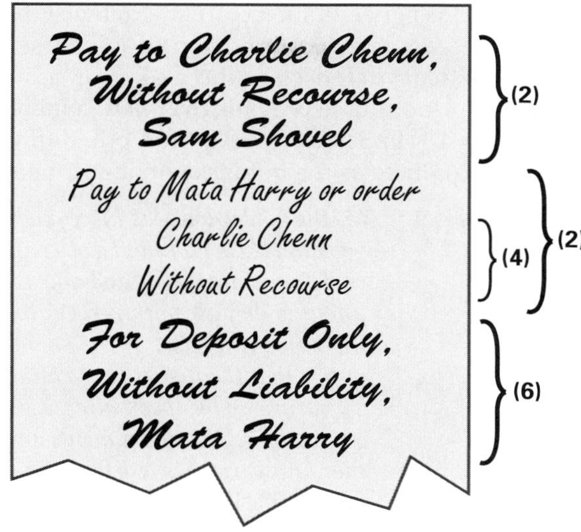

HOLDER

At the beginning of this chapter, we examined the transfer of negotiable instruments. It was pointed out that a transfer leaves the transferee in the role of an assignee. It also was stated that a negotiation leaves the transferee in the role of a holder. The role of a holder is important in negotiable instruments. A holder takes an instrument by *transfer,* giving the holder all of the rights that his or her transferor possessed. However, a holder also acquires personal rights above and beyond those conferred by the transfer. Thus a holder can have better rights than the person from whom the holder received the negotiation. A holder normally acquires *contractual* rights against several parties involved with the instrument. A holder also normally acquires *warranty* rights against some parties involved with the instrument. Also, being a holder is an essential element before the party can become a holder in due course, perhaps the most favored position in the law of negotiable instruments.

A *holder* is a person in possession of a negotiable instrument drawn, issued, or indorsed to him or her, to his or her order, to bearer, or in blank. Thus, the holder either receives the original issue from the maker or drawer or receives a negotiation through indorsement and/or delivery. A holder has the right to transfer, negotiate, discharge, or enforce the instrument in the holder's own name. However, a holder is subject to any defenses on the instrument that a maker or drawer can assert.

HOLDER IN DUE COURSE

To overcome even one of the defenses on the instrument that may be available to the maker or drawer, the holder needs to acquire holder in due course status. Great care

23.2

FINANCE

QUALIFIED INDORSEMENT

One of the firm's customers recently sent a check to CIT as a payment on its account. The check had been drawn payable to the order of the customer, and the customer then indorsed it over to CIT. Dan is afraid the check may be dishonored upon presentment, and he thinks that John should use a qualified indorsement when he indorses the check for deposit to the company account. John does not believe that such an indorsement would help the firm in this situation. They have asked you for advice. What will you tell them?

BUSINESS CONSIDERATIONS The use of a qualified indorsement helps to minimize risks in negotiable instruments by denying the contract liability that an indorsement normally carries. Should a firm have a policy of always using a qualified indorsement? Should a firm have a policy of never using a qualified indorsement? Why?

ETHICAL CONSIDERATIONS Is it ethical to qualify an indorsement if the indorser has any doubts about the validity of the instrument? Would it be ethical to adopt a company policy of never accepting a qualified indorsement on the theory that the indorsement would not have been qualified unless there was a problem with the instrument?

needs to be exercised here. The burden of proof for establishing HDC status lies with the person claiming the status. A holder must prove he or she is a holder in due course; such status is not presumed. A holder or an assignee is subject to any defense the drawer or maker can assert. A holder in due course is subject only to *some* defenses of the maker or drawer. The holder in due course prevails over *most* available defenses.

In Section 3-302, the Code defines a holder in due course as the holder of an instrument, if:

> *(2) the holder took the instrument (i) for value, (ii) in good faith, (iii) without notice that the instrument is overdue or has been dishonored or that there is an uncured default with respect to payment of another instrument as part of the same series, (iv) without notice that the instrument contains an unauthorized signature or has been altered, (v) without notice of any claim to the instrument, and (vi) without notice that any party has a defense or claim in recoupment against the instrument.*

The issues of value and good faith are relatively simple to establish. However, the various notice issues can be difficult to prove at times. Each of these three elements of holder in due course status is discussed in the following sections.

For Value

Under Article 3, *value* is more than consideration. Section 3-303 sets out five methods of giving value for an instrument. Notice that each method involves actual performance by the holder, not just a commitment to perform in the future. The first method involves an instrument issued or transferred for a promise of performance, to the extent the promise has been performed. The second method arises when the transferee acquires a security interest or other lien in the instrument, other than a lien obtained in a judicial proceeding. Third, the instrument is issued or transferred as payment of, or as security for, an antecedent claim against any person, whether or not the claim is due. Fourth, the instrument is issued or transferred in exchange for another negotiable instrument. Fifth, the instrument is issued or transferred in exchange for an irrevocable obligation to a third person by the person taking the instrument. Once the holder can prove that value was given, the holder goes on to the next test.

In Good Faith

The next requirement is that the holder take the instrument in good faith. *Good faith* is defined as honesty in fact in the transaction. This requirement is actually measured by a negative test. The holder acted with good faith if bad faith is not present. To show a lack of good faith, it must be proved that the holder either had actual knowledge of a defect in the instrument or ignored facts that would have shown the defect. Usually, all the holder needs to do is to allege good faith. The burden of proof then shifts to the maker or drawer. It is up to the maker or drawer to prove bad faith, or actual knowledge of some defect, by the holder. Very few cases involve bad faith.

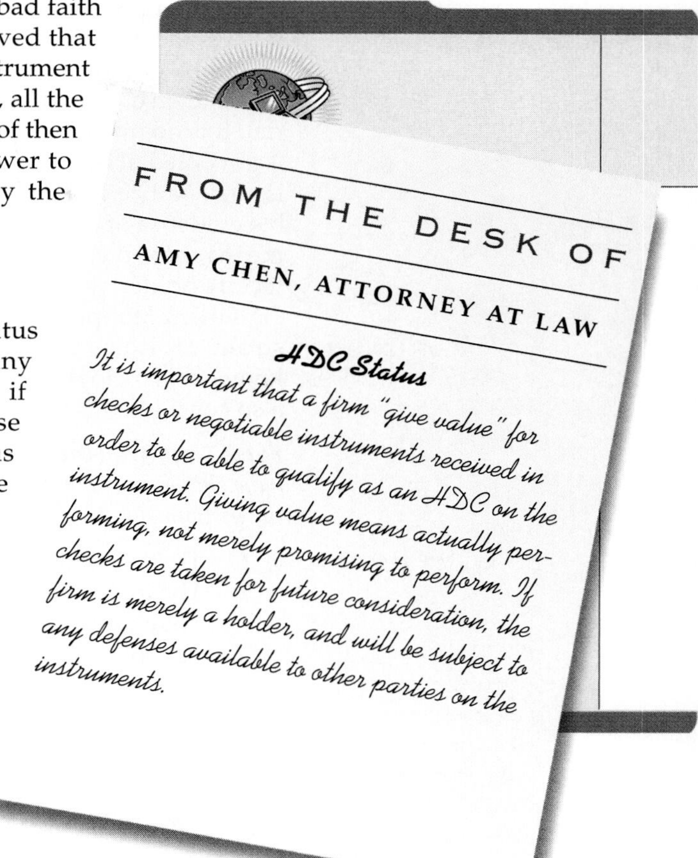

FROM THE DESK OF
AMY CHEN, ATTORNEY AT LAW
HDC Status
It is important that a firm "give value" for checks or negotiable instruments received in order to be able to qualify as an HDC on the instrument. Giving value means actually performing, not merely promising to perform. If checks are taken for future consideration, the firm is merely a holder, and will be subject to any defenses available to other parties on the instruments.

Without Notice of Defenses or Defects

The final requirement to establish holder-in-due-course status is that the holder take the instrument without notice of any defenses or defects on the instrument. *Notice* is present if a reasonable person would know that there was a defense or a defect, or if a reasonable person would be suspicious and would make further inquiry before accepting the instrument.

Revised Article 3 has deleted the specific sections that spelled out what facts constituted notice and what facts did not constitute notice, leaving this area for judicial interpretation to a much greater extent. There are the four provisions of § 3-302 detailing the requirement for acquiring holder in due course status to provide some guidance. The Code now provides only that notice must be received at a time and in a manner that gives a reasonable opportunity to act on it.

In § 3-304, overdue instruments are defined. According to this section, an instrument payable on demand becomes overdue at the earliest of the following times:

> *(1) on the day after the day demand for payment is duly made;*
> *(2) if the instrument is a check, 90 days after its date; or*
> *(3) if the instrument is not a check, when the instrument has been outstanding for a period of time after its date which is unreasonably long under the circumstances of the particular case in light of the nature of the instrument and usage of the trade.*

With respect to an instrument payable at a definite time the following rules apply:

> *(1) if the principal is payable in installments and a due date has not been accelerated, the instrument becomes overdue upon default under the instrument for nonpayment of an installment, and the instrument remains overdue until the default is cured;*
> *(2) if the principal is not payable in installments and the due date has not been accelerated, the instrument becomes overdue on the day after the due date;*
> *(3) if a due date with respect to principal has been accelerated, the instrument becomes overdue on the date after the accelerated due date.*

Facts That Are Considered Notice. Although the specific provisions contained in the original Article 3 are not included in Revised Article 3, some of the things that have traditionally served as notice of a defect or a defense affecting an instrument are set out here. A purchaser of a negotiable instrument has notice of a defect if the instrument is incomplete in some material respect. Thus, a missing signature or a missing amount would be notice. So would a missing date on a time instrument. But a missing date on a demand instrument, such as a check, is not notice since it is not material. It is not material because a demand instrument is payable at issue, and even if it is not dated, it has been issued. The simple fact of its existence proves that it has been issued. Notice of a defect also exists if the instrument is visibly altered or bears visible evidence of a forgery. Notice exists if the instrument is irregular on its face. This means that an erasure of an obligation of a party or of an amount is notice of a defect. A holder who takes an instrument stamped "NSF" (not sufficient funds), or "Payment Stopped," or "Paid" would have notice of a defense or defect on the instrument. It has been presented, and it has been dishonored or paid. The holder knows this by looking at the face of the instrument. Taking an overdue instrument is also considered notice.

Facts That Are Not Considered Notice. *Again, traditional interpretations of Article 3 have shown that the following facts, standing alone, are not notice of a defense or defect on the instrument, even if the holder has knowledge of the fact:*

1. The instrument was antedated or post-dated.
2. The instrument was issued or negotiated for an executory promise, unless the holder has notice of defenses to the promise.
3. Any party has signed as an accommodation party.
4. A formerly incomplete instrument was completed.
5. Any person negotiating the instrument is or was a fiduciary.
6. There was a default on an interest payment on the instrument.

In addition, it is not treated as notice if any party has filed or recorded a document, if the holder would otherwise qualify as an HDC. In addition, before notice is effective, it must be received in a time and a manner that give a reasonable opportunity to act on the information. Notice must be received before the holder receives the instrument. Once the holder has received the instrument, later notice is irrelevant.

The following case hinged on the issue of whether a holder had notice of a misappropriation of funds by an employee of the drawer.

23.3 ADMASTER, INC. v. MERRILL LYNCH, PIERCE, FENNER, & SMITH, INC.

583 N.Y.S.2d 408 (A.D. 1 Dept. 1992)

FACTS An Admaster employee prepared a number of Admaster checks payable to the order of Merrill Lynch, signed the checks without authorization, and deposited the checks in the employee's account with Merrill Lynch. The Admaster employee then used the funds so deposited for his personal transactions with Merrill Lynch. Eventually, Admaster learned that its employee had embezzled these funds, and sued Merrill Lynch to recover the funds taken by the employee.

ISSUE Did Merrill Lynch have notice of the unauthorized signature, thus negating its HDC status?

HOLDING No. The signatures on the checks were not irregular, nor were they obvious forgeries. They did not present Merrill Lynch with notice that any defenses were good against the checks.

REASONING The court cited the UCC § 3-304(7), which says that notice of a defense or defect only exists if

23.3 ADMASTER, INC. v. MERRILL LYNCH, PIERCE, FENNER, & SMITH, INC. *(cont)* 583 N.Y.S.2d 408 (A.D. I Dept. 1992)

the purchaser of the instrument has knowledge of a claim or defense of knowledge of such facts that taking the instrument amounts to bad faith. Holders in due course are determined by what they knew, not by speculation about what they might have been suspicious about. There was nothing about the checks that should have put a reasonable person on notice as to the fraud of the Admaster bookkeeper. Merrill Lynch was an HDC and was entitled to the money as against Admaster.

BUSINESS CONSIDERATIONS Should Merrill Lynch have been suspicious of the checks it received from the Admaster employee? Does it seem like a normal business practice for a business to draw checks payable to an investment firm when those checks are being placed in the account of one of the drawer's employees?

ETHICAL CONSIDERATIONS Should a business that handles investments and receives large amounts of money be more aware of the likelihood of thefts and embezzlements? Does an investment firm have a higher ethical duty in handling the funds of customers than other types of businesses? Why did you answer as you did?

Effect of Holder in Due Course Status

The status of holder in due course is a preferred legal position. The HDC takes an instrument free of personal defenses. Although the holder in due course is subject to real defenses, he or she will be able to enforce the instrument against any other defense or defect. This position is far superior to that of a mere holder or an assignee. A holder or an assignee is subject to any and every defense or defect in the instrument, real or personal. A mere holder, an assignee, or a transferee takes possession of a negotiable instrument subject to every available defense. In contrast, an HDC takes the instrument subject only to real defenses. The HDC is not subject to personal (sometimes referred to as limited) defenses.

A personal defense is one that affects the agreement for which the instrument was issued. It does not affect the validity of the instrument. The validity of the instrument is not in question; it is acknowledged to be valid. The underlying agreement is the point of contention. A real defense, on the other hand, questions the legal validity of the instrument.

Personal Defenses

The most common types of personal defenses are those available on a simple contract. The most common of these contract defenses are failure of consideration, fraud, duress, and breach of warranty. In addition, the holder frequently may be faced with the personal defenses of nondelivery, theft, payment, or any other cancellation.

Most of the simple contract defenses were covered in Part 3, "Contracts," and need no further review here. However, fraud does need some added coverage because negotiable instrument law recognizes two types of fraud. One type, fraud in the inducement, is a personal defense. The other type, fraud in the execution, is a real defense.

Fraud in the inducement is a personal defense because the fraud committed is a fraud related to the agreement. The maker or drawer intentionally and knowingly issues a negotiable instrument to the payee. However, this issue is made to support an underlying agreement, and the agreement is based on fraudulent representations. The underlying contract is voidable because of the fraud, but the instrument is valid, subject only to a personal defense. (Fraud in the execution is discussed in the following section.)

Of the other personal defenses not based on simple contract defenses, only one will be covered here. Nondelivery of the instrument needs special treatment. To issue an instrument, the maker or drawer must deliver the instrument to the payee or to an authorized representative of the payee. If the payee gains possession of the instrument without the knowledge or consent of the maker or drawer, the defense of nondelivery is available against a mere holder. Another type of nondelivery occurs when the maker or drawer gives the payee possession, but with a condition attached before delivery is effective. The condition may be that the payee perform some act, which is then not performed. Technically, delivery never occurred because the condition was never satisfied, and the defense of nondelivery can be raised as a personal defense.

Real Defenses

A real defense, sometimes referred to as a universal defense, challenges the *validity* of the instrument itself. If a real defense can be established, the negotiable instrument is voided by operation of law, and no one can enforce the instrument. Thus, even an HDC will lose to a real defense. It should be kept in mind that if a maker or drawer alleges a real defense, the maker or drawer must establish the defense as real. A failure to do so will normally still leave a valid personal defense, but such a defense will not prevail against a holder in due course. Section 3-305(a)(1) of the UCC lists the four defenses that are valid against an HDC. These defenses are covered in the following sections. There are two additional *potential* real defenses, found in § 3-403 and § 3-407, which are also discussed here.

Infancy. The first real defense is infancy (or minority), but only "to the extent that it is a defense to a simple contract." *Infancy* refers to the period before a person attains majority status and gains complete contractual capacity. Thus, anyone who is not yet 18 years of age is still, legally, an infant, or a minor. To determine whether infancy is a real defense, state law must be examined. If the statutes or cases in the state where the instrument is issued allow infancy to be asserted as a defense to the underlying contract, the infancy may also be raised as a real defense on the instrument. Even if state law does not give such a broad defense, it is still useful as a personal defense; however, a holder in due course can override that defense.

Duress, Lack of Legal Capacity, or Illegality. The second real defense is "*duress,* lack of legal capacity, or illegality of the transactions which, under other law, nullifies the obligation." Again, the relevant state law will be controlling. If the state statutes or prior cases void the transaction, the instrument also is voided. If not, the defense is merely personal in nature. An example would be the issuance of a check to pay a gambling debt. If gambling agreements are illegal in the state, a defense exists on the instrument, but it is probably only a personal defense. However, if the check contains a notation that it is meant as payment for a gambling debt, the defense becomes real. The instrument itself now reflects the illegality.

Other types of illegality that might affect a negotiable instrument, and hence operate as a real defense on the instrument, include *usury*—agreements that violate public policy—and attempting to do business in a state when not licensed to do so.

Fraud. The third real defense is "fraud that induced the obligor to sign the instrument with neither knowledge nor reasonable opportunity to learn of its character or its essential terms." In this defense, the maker or drawer must prove two things: (1) lack of knowledge of the instrument signed and (2) no reasonable opportunity to discover the nature or terms of the instrument. To establish this defense, the maker or drawer must prove that discovering the nature of the signed instrument was not reasonable at the time of signing. Such proof will be virtually impossible unless the signing person is either illiterate or is involved in a strange set of circumstances. The following hypothetical case illustrates such a setting.

> Freddy Hornet, a famous rock musician, was signing autographs outside a theater after a performance. Sonya Smith, among others, shoved a paper in front of Freddy for him to sign. However, the paper she shoved was a promissory note, payable to her order, for $50,000. Freddy signed it without reading it, and Sonya left the theater area. Sonya later sued Freddy to collect the money called for in the note. If Freddy can prove these facts, he may have a real defense and will not have to pay the note.

Discharge in Insolvency. The fourth real defense is a "discharge of the obligor in insolvency proceedings." This area basically refers to a discharge in bankruptcy proceedings. Bankruptcy is a federally guaranteed privilege, and federal law prevails over conflicting state law. The federal bankruptcy law discharges the enforceability of the instrument, creating a statutory real defense on the instrument.

Forgery. Section 3-403 of the Code treats a forgery—or any unauthorized signature—as ineffective against any one except the person who signed. Thus, a forgery of the signature of the drawer or a draft or the maker of a note is ineffective against the person whose signature was forged. However, if the drawer or maker *ratifies* the signature, the signature become authorized, and thus effective against that person. In addition, if the drawer or maker contributed to the forgery, the defense is "reduced" to a personal defense, it is no longer valid against a holder in due course.

Material Alteration. Section 3-407 provides that an unauthorized material alteration is a real defense to the *extent of the alteration.* An HDC can still enforce the instrument as issued, but would have to seek recovery for the altered terms from the person who altered the instrument without authorization. Again, if the drawer or maker *contributed* to the alteration, the defense becomes merely personal, and is not effective against a holder in due course.

Section 3-406 provides the standards for determining whether an unauthorized signature or an unauthorized alteration becomes merely a personal defense. According to this section, "a person whose failure to exercise reasonable care substantially contributes to an alteration of an instrument or to the making of a forged signature on an instrument is precluding from asserting the alteration or the forgery against a person who, in good faith, pays the instrument or takes it for value or for collection."

In addition to the real defenses, a maker or drawer can avoid liability on an instrument against an HDC under two other circumstances. One circumstance may afford total avoidance: Section 3-403 states that an unauthorized signature is wholly inoperative against the person whose name is signed unless that person ratifies the signing or

YOU BE THE JUDGE

Embezzlement and Forged Checks

An employee of the Museum of African American Culture was responsible for issuing checks for the museum and also for reconciling the bank statement. The employee became disgruntled—to say the least—because she felt that the museum's officers did not appreciate her work or her long hours of service. To remedy this situation, she decided to give herself a "raise," which she did—in the form of more than $40,000 in forged checks over a two-year period. For two years the employee forged 36 checks payable to her order. Her scheme came to light only after she had drained the account of the museum, causing a number of checks to bounce.

The forger/embezzler was convicted of her crimes and sentenced to six months in jail. USF&G, the bonding company, which covered the museum employees, paid the $40,000 to the museum as required by its coverage; then, USF&G decided to try to recover the money from the bank. In its lawsuit against the bank USF&G argued that the bank should have detected the forgery and embezzlement scheme, and that it had not exercised ordinary care in its handling of the checks. At least one of the checks the bank honored for the embezzler was not signed, which was ignored by the bank. The bank countered by claiming that the ultimate responsibility rested with the museum, which failed to exercise reasonable care in reconciling its statements. The bank also claimed to be an HDC and asserted that the museum was negligent in handling the checks at the time of issue.

This case has been brought before *your* court. How will you decide this case?[1]

BUSINESS CONSIDERATIONS What sorts of policies and procedures should a business have in order to prevent this type of embezzlement scheme from occurring? How important is it for a business to have an indemnity bond covering its employees?

ETHICAL CONSIDERATIONS Should the bonding company try to recover its pay-out in this type of case when the bonding company's customer was a significant contributor to the losses it suffered? In such a situation, is it ethical to try to pass the blame to another party?

SOURCE: Laurence Hammack, *Roanoke Times*, 19 March 1996, p. A1.

is not allowed to deny its validity. Thus, a forgery is a possible defense against even a holder in due course. The other circumstance may afford partial avoidance: Section 4-407 states that if an instrument is materially altered through no fault of the maker or drawer, an HDC may enforce it as originally issued (the alteration is a real defense to the extent altered). If the alteration is due to the fault of the maker or drawer, the defense is merely personal and cannot be asserted against a holder in due course.

Statutory Limitations

The protected status given to holders in due course makes abuses possible. If a payee obtains an instrument by wrongful means and then negotiates it to an HDC, the maker or drawer will nearly always be obliged to pay the instrument. As will be seen in the next chapter, the maker or drawer can sue the payee to recover the money paid. However, the payee must be found to be sued; and, the finding may not be easy. If the payee and the HDC are working together, the maker or drawer is easily taken, usually with no chance of recovering.

Because of this potential, the Federal Trade Commission (FTC) passed a regulation in 1976 designed to protect consumers. This regulation modifies the holder in due course rules in some circumstances. If a consumer credit transaction is involved, the instrument used must contain the following notice, printed prominently:

> ANY HOLDER OF THIS CONSUMER CREDIT CONTRACT IS SUBJECT TO ALL CLAIMS AND DEFENSES WHICH THE DEBTOR COULD ASSERT AGAINST THE SELLER OF GOODS OR SERVICES OBTAINED HERETO OR WITH THE PROCEEDS HEREOF. RECOVERY HEREUNDER BY THE DEBTOR SHALL NOT EXCEED AMOUNTS PAID BY THE DEBTOR HEREUNDER.

The effect of the rule is to make even an HDC subject to any defenses available against the payee, which is a tremendous protection for the consumer. This rule may have a great impact on the use of consumer credit contracts in the future.

If the notice is present in a consumer credit transaction, any holder of the instrument has agreed by the terms of the instrument to remain subject to any defenses of the maker or drawer. This means that a consumer could avoid payment to any HDC in possession of the instrument if the consumer could avoid payment to the payee. This is true even if the notice is included in a credit contract with a nonconsumer, as is pointed out in the following case. [This case is still viewed as *the* definitive case in this area. The new restriction on HDC status included in the revision to Article 3 is based, at least in part, on this opinion.]

Unconscionable
So one-sided as to shock the conscience; blatantly unfair.

23.4 JEFFERSON BANK & TRUST CO. v. STAMATIOU — 384 So.2d 388 (La. 1980)

FACTS Stamatiou purchased a truck from Key Dodge, signing a chattel mortgage and a sale agreement. The agreement included a promissory note and the FTC clause that preserves the consumer debtor's rights against subsequent holders in due course. The agreement also specified that the note was to be assigned to Jefferson Bank & Trust Co. Shortly after the sale, Stamatiou alleged that the truck had become inoperable. As a result, he notified Key Dodge and Jefferson Bank that he wanted to rescind the contract. Jefferson Bank eventually instituted this lawsuit against Stamatiou for the unpaid loan amount, alleging that Stamatiou used the truck as a business asset and not as a consumer good, so the FTC clause was not applicable to the loan.

ISSUE Is the FTC clause preserving defenses against a holder in due course in a consumer credit contract valid in a nonconsumer credit transaction?

HOLDING Yes. If the clause is included in the agreement, it is a part of the contract despite the debtor's status as a consumer or a nonconsumer.

REASONING Freedom of contract is a basic right of the parties under U.S. law. The parties can include any contractual clauses they choose, subject to the limitation of **unconscionability**. In this contract, the parties included the FTC consumer credit protection clause. The fact that Jefferson Bank later asserted that such a clause was not meant to apply because the debtor was not a consumer is immaterial. Jefferson Bank included the clause in the contract, and it must honor the clause. With this clause included, the defenses that could be asserted against Key Dodge can also be asserted against Jefferson Bank. The bank was put on notice by the terms of the contract it provided that any defenses good against Key Dodge were also good against the bank. It cannot now deny its own contractual agreement.

BUSINESS CONSIDERATIONS When a business deals with merchants and with consumers, and when the legal protections provided for consumers is different from the protections provided for merchants, should the

23.4 JEFFERSON BANK & TRUST CO. v. STAMATIOU (cont.) 384 So.2d 388 (La. 1980)

business have different forms and/or agreements that it uses, based on the status of the customer? How should the business decide which form to use?

ETHICAL CONSIDERATIONS Is it ethical for a business to take advantage of an apparent mistake made by the other party to a contract? Should Stamatiou have pointed out to the bank that it had prepared a consumer credit form rather than a commercial credit form, or should the bank be expected to protect its own interests?

23.3

CONSUMER CREDIT TRANSACTIONS

CIT is considering the viability of making direct sales to consumers on a mail-order basis. As part of this plan, they are considering financing the sales by means of a short-term consumer note. Dan points out that such notes must have the Federal Trade Commission holder in due course notice or the firm will be deemed to have committed an unfair trade practice. He is concerned that, if the firm uses two different note forms, the firm may inadvertently use the wrong form, causing problems for them in their collections. He has asked you what the firm should do. What advice will you give him?

BUSINESS CONSIDERATIONS What should a business do in order to ensure that it complies with the law on consumer credit transactions without extending special treatment to nonconsumer creditors? How important is the FTC/HDC provision on the note if the firm does not sell the note after the loan is made?

ETHICAL CONSIDERATIONS Is it ethical to refuse to extend credit to consumers in order to avoid special consumer protection statutes, even if credit sales are a major source of revenue with nonconsumer customers?

FINANCE/SALES

Delivered
Intentional transfer of physical possession of some thing or right to another person.

If the notice is not included in a consumer credit transaction, an unfair trade practice is involved. The consumer can file suit against any holders who are deemed to have committed an unfair trade practice for all damages involved.

Holder by Due Negotiation

When a negotiable warehouse receipt is issued calling for delivery of the goods to the order of a named individual, or to bearer, the document is negotiable. As such, it can be negotiated by indorsement and delivery (if the goods are to be delivered "to order") or by delivery alone (if the goods are to be **delivered** "to bearer"). When a document is negotiated to a person who purchases the instrument in good faith and the purchaser takes the document without notice of any defense against or claim to the goods or the document, the instrument has been duly negotiated. This makes the recipient of the document a holder by due negotiation (HDN), a preferred and protected status in the area of documents of title.

A holder by due negotiation is assured of the following rights:

1. Title to the document
2. Title to the goods the document represents

3. All rights accruing under the laws of agency or estoppel, including the right to goods delivered to the bailee after the document was issued
4. The direct obligation of the issuer of the document to hold or to deliver the goods according to the terms of the document and free of any claims or defenses of the issuer except those specified in the document or specified in Article 7

In contrast, if the document is not negotiable or was not negotiated despite its negotiability, the recipient only acquires the rights and the title the transferor possesses or has the authority to convey. Further, if the document is nonnegotiable, the rights of the recipient may be defeated by any claims or defenses that arise after the transfer but before the bailee receives notice of the transfer.

The following case involved a holder by due negotiation, and the rights of the HDN in a bankruptcy proceeding.

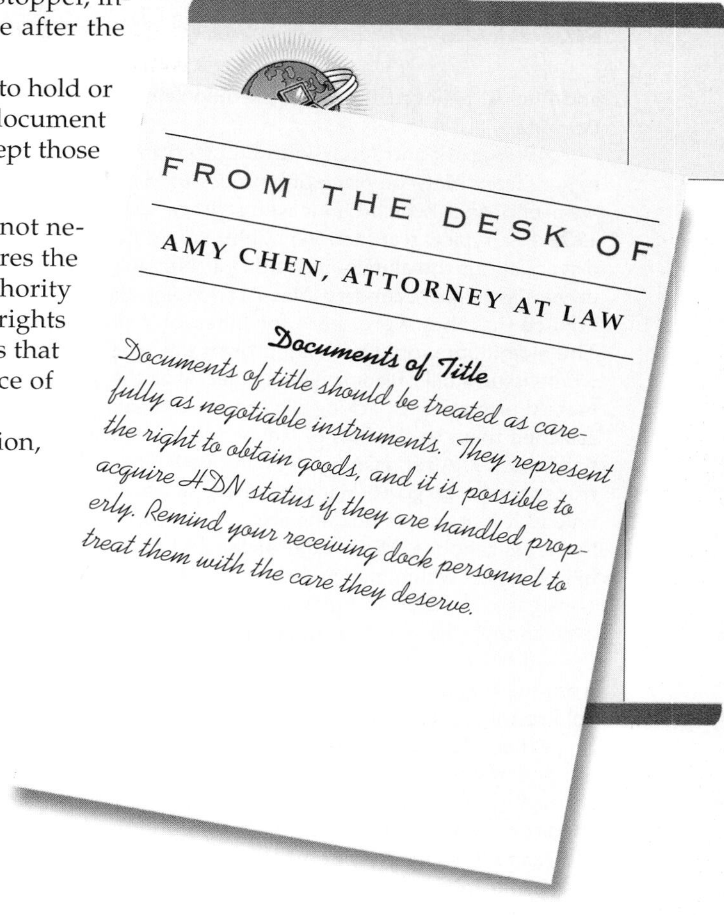

FROM THE DESK OF
AMY CHEN, ATTORNEY AT LAW
Documents of Title
Documents of title should be treated as carefully as negotiable instruments. They represent the right to obtain goods, and it is possible to acquire HDN status if they are handled properly. Remind your receiving dock personnel to treat them with the care they deserve.

23.5 MET-AL, INC. v. HANSEN STORAGE CO.

828 F.Supp. 1369 (1993)

FACTS The plaintiff in this adversary proceeding lost over $4 million when an unscrupulous aluminum broker set up phony transactions, diverted aluminum from the plaintiff's intended customers, and failed to pay for goods delivered. The plaintiff now claims that the carrier of the aluminum and the warehouse in which it was stored should be held liable for the loss based on their failure to honor the original bills of lading.

Met-Al produces ingots from aluminum scrap. Metal Brokers International, Inc. (MBI) brokers aluminum, matching producers with purchasers and facilitating their transactions. Distribution Express, Inc. (DEI) and Hansen Storage Company, respectively, are a trucking company and warehouse owned by the same family. Green, the president of MBI, convinced Met-Al that he was an authorized broker for Emerson Electronics and General Electric (GE) when, in fact, it was not true. As a result, he convinced Met-Al to ship substantial quantities of aluminum to these two companies. After the aluminum left Met-Al's place of business, ostensibly for Emerson and GE, it was cross-docked at Hansen's warehouse. Once the aluminum arrived at Hansen's, Green persuaded DEI to change the original bills of lading issued to Met-Al. Once the bills were changed, MBI diverted the aluminum to other buyers, using the proceeds from these sales to pay Met-Al. Met-Al believed it was receiving payments from Emerson or GE, albeit on terms of extended credit. Before the scheme collapsed, MBI had transferred in excess of $13 million of aluminum, but had paid Met-Al only slightly more than $8 million.

Shipments of the aluminum began in December of 1991. . . . The aluminum was shipped free on board (FOB) Met-Al's place of business. . . . MBI paid the freight charges

23.5 MET-AL, INC. v. HANSEN STORAGE CO. *(cont.)* 828 F.Supp. 1369 (1993)

and Met-Al believed the buyers would reimburse MBI on delivery.

MBI began contracting with DEI to transport the aluminum from Met-Al's place of business to Hansen Storage, a warehouse in which DEI leased storage space, in May of 1992. In a typical transaction . . . MBI would notify the DEI drivers about the aluminum waiting at Met-Al's facility. The drivers would proceed to Met-Al's loading dock and announce that they were there for Emerson's aluminum. . . . The aluminum would be loaded onto the trucks, and DEI would issue a bill of lading naming Met-Al as the shipper. . . . Met-Al printed out packing slips to record each shipment, attached them to the bills of lading, and gave them to DEI's truckers. . . . After issuing the bills of lading, DEI would transport its cargo to Hansen, where it leased space, and unload it in its cross-docking area. . . . Once the cargo was in the warehouse, MBI would order DEI to issue another bill of lading, which changed the name and address of the consignee. . . . DEI, as MBI's client, would always comply, even though the new bills of lading were inconsistent with the old ones. . . . In this manner, the aluminum was diverted from the original consignees in St. Louis or Fort Wayne and sold to third parties pursuant to Green's orders.

When Met-Al discovered what Green was doing, it suspended any further sales to "Emerson" or to "GE" made through Green and/or MBI. Met-Al was unable to meet its creditors' obligations, filed for bankruptcy in August of 1992, and it is currently reorganizing under Chapter 11 of the Bankruptcy Code. MBI was forced into involuntary bankruptcy by its creditors, and a federal indictment has been issued against . . . Green. Met-Al sued DEI and Hansen to recover its losses under Green's scam.

ISSUE Was DEI guilty of conversion due to its conduct in changing the original bills of lading?

HOLDING Yes. DEI had a duty to Met-Al, and it breached that duty when it issued replacement bills of lading without permission, thereby converting the goods.

REASONING A bill of lading is an instrument by which goods may be transferred from seller to buyer when a direct transfer is impossible and the goods must be shipped by carrier. . . . A negotiable bill of lading calls for the freight to be delivered to the bearer of the bill; one who has possession of a negotiable bill of lading is deemed to have title to the shipped goods. . . . Bills of lading are thus contracts between shippers and carriers that spell out the carrier's obligation to deliver specific goods to specific people. . . . As contracts of adhesion, they are strictly construed against the carrier. . . .

The Federal Bills of Lading Act (FBLA) governs bills of lading for goods in interstate commerce. . . . If a carrier operating under the FBLA disregards the bill of lading and delivers the goods to a person not entitled to their possession, it will be liable to anyone with a property right in the goods. . . .

DEI argues that Met-Al sold the aluminum to "imposters," giving MBI and Green voidable title to the goods. Under this theory, MBI had the right to change the bills of lading because MBI was the buyer—as an imposter—so that the originally named consignees had no rights or expectations in the goods shipped. . . .

Whether the defendants should be held liable for Met-Al's loss depends on whether Met-Al retained a possessory interest in the aluminum once shipped, and whether MBI obtained title, and of what kind, to the aluminum. . . . The UCC makes a substantial distinction between one who unlawfully converts goods by theft and one who unlawfully converts goods by deceit. The first is a mere thief, condemned to hold no title (or void title) to the goods and unable to convey good title, even to a good faith purchaser for value. The deceiver, on the other hand, is the holder of voidable title and has good title against anyone other than the original owner of the goods. The holder of voidable title, moreover, may transfer good title as against the original owner to a good faith purchaser for value.

"Voidable title," undefined by the Code, passes when the underlying contract between the seller and the defrauder is subject to avoidance at common law. . . . To argue that MBI and Met-Al intended to enter into a contract, and that good title as against the world passed when DEI's carriers took the aluminum from Met-Al's place of business, simply defies the record. . . .

If MBI held voidable title to the aluminum, it was entitled to immediate possession and had authority to divert the aluminum, regardless of the bills of lading. . . . In this case, DEI was apparently told that MBI owned the aluminum. If this had been true, MBI would have been justified in issuing new bills of lading. Because swindlers who fraudulently claim to be acting on behalf of unwitting third parties cannot obtain even voidable title, however, MBI had no lawful interest in the aluminum, and thus, no authority to modify the bills of lading. . . .

The defendants, though arguing about imposters, voidable title, and indicia of ownership, fail to address why the bills of lading were altered when MBI, at least from the face of the bills, had no interest in the aluminum. . . . The court finds DEI liable to Met-Al for amending the bills of lading at MBI's direction and thus enabling MBI to divert the freight to its warehouses in Florida.

23.5 MET-AL, INC. v. HANSEN STORAGE CO. *(cont.)* 828 F.Supp. 1369 (1993)

BUSINESS CONSIDERATIONS Met-Al assumed that Green and MBI were authorized brokers acting on behalf of Emerson and General Electric purely based on representations made by Green. What should Met-Al have done to prevent this conversion from ever occurring? What sorts of policies and practices should a business have to ensure that it is, in fact, dealing with an authorized representative of some purported third person?

ETHICAL CONSIDERATIONS Both Met-Al and DEI acted in a careless manner in this case. Which party was better able to have prevented the losses suffered by Met-Al from occurring? From an ethical perspective, which company acted less properly? Why?

http:// **RESOURCES FOR BUSINESS LAW STUDENTS**

NAME	RESOURCES	WEB ADDRESS
Uniform Commercial Code (UCC), Article 3, Negotiable Instruments	The Legal Information Institute (LII), maintained by the Cornell Law School, provides a hypertext and searchable version of UCC, Article 3, Negotiable Instruments. LII has links to Article 3 as adopted by particular states and to proposed revisions.	http://www.law.cornell.edu/ucc/3/overview.html
Uniform Commercial Code, Article 7, Warehouse Receipts, Bills of Lading and Other Documents of Title	LII provides a hypertext and searchable version of UCC, Article 7, Warehouse Receipts, Bills of Lading and Other Documents of Title.	http://www.law.cornell.edu/ucc/7/overview.html

SUMMARY

A negotiable instrument can be transferred in a number of ways. The original transfer from the maker or the drawer is an issue. Once issued, it can be further transferred by assignment or by negotiation. An assignment gives the assignee no special rights or protections. In contrast, a negotiation may confer some individual rights on the recipient. When a negotiation occurs, the transferee becomes a holder.

Most negotiations involve the use of an indorsement. Indorsements may affect further negotiation, and they may affect liability of the parties. Special, blank, and restrictive indorsements affect negotiations. Qualified and unqualified indorsements affect liability.

Once a negotiation occurs, the holder has the opportunity to achieve the most favored status in commercial paper: He or she may become a holder in due course. An HDC is a holder who takes an instrument in good faith, for value, and without notice of any defenses or defects on the instrument. A holder in due course can defeat a personal defense. A real defense will defeat a holder in due course.

The Federal Trade Commission enacted a special rule in 1976 to protect consumers. The rule denies any protection against any defenses, even for an HDC, on a consumer credit instrument.

Article 7 provides for special protections in handling negotiable documents of title. A person who acquires a negotiable document of title who purchases the document in good faith without notice of any defenses or defects qualifies as a holder by due negotiation. This status confers benefits beyond the benefits acquired in the document itself.

Discussion Questions

1. Why is the distinction between a mere transfer and a negotiation so important in determining the rights of a party in possession of a negotiable instrument?
2. How can a holder indorse an instrument to minimize his or her potential secondary liability on the instrument in the event of a dishonor upon presentment? What, if anything, will such an indorsement tell the indorsee?
3. Amita issued Carol a check payable to the order of Carol. Carol sold the check to Lynn, but neglected to indorse it at the time of the sale. At that point, what legal status would Lynn possess? What duty, if any, would Carol owe to Lynn?
4. Terry issued a check to Phil. Phil indorsed the check and delivered it to Irene. The name on the payee line of the check had originally read "Ben," but Terry had crossed out Ben's name and replaced it with Phil's name. To show what he had done, Terry initialed the change on the payee line. Under these circumstances, can Irene qualify as a holder in due course on the check? Explain your reasoning.
5. Ann is in possession of a check that Dan issued to her. She would like to mail the check to her bank to be deposited to her checking account. How should she indorse the check to give herself the maximum possible legal protection, and why does such an indorsement give her this maximum protection?
6. Lloyd had a promissory note originally issued by Brandy. However, Lloyd is afraid Brandy might default on the note when it comes due. Jim is willing to buy the note from Lloyd. Is there a way for Lloyd to indorse the note to minimize his potential loss if Brandy dishonors the note upon maturity? What should Lloyd do in this case?
7. Charles had a note issued by David. Charles discovered that David was about to go through a bankruptcy, so he negotiated the note to Richard. Richard qualified as a holder in due course. David filed for bankruptcy, and Richard sued David to collect on the note. What are Richard's rights against David? Why?
8. Denise issued the following check to Bill:

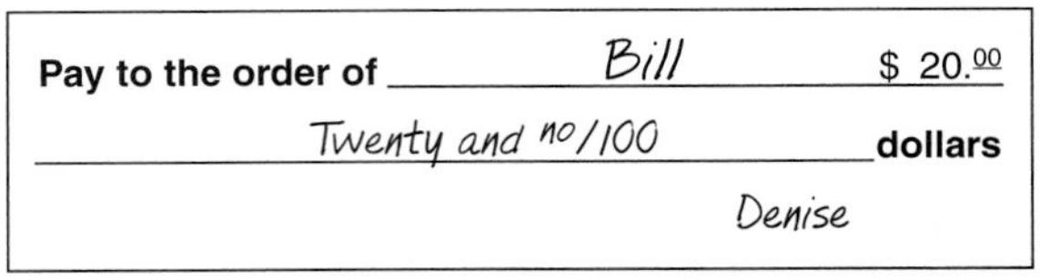

   Pay to the order of ______ *Bill* ______ $ 20.00
   ______ *Twenty and no/100* ______ dollars
   Denise

   Bill adds the number 2 before the "20.00" and adds the words Two Hundred before the "Twenty." He then negotiates the check to Sarah, an HDC. How much will Denise have to pay Sarah, and why?
9. John's Television Sales and Service offered credit terms to its customers who desired credit. To obtain credit, the customer signed a promissory note for the amount of the credit, and after the customer took the television, John sold the signed note to his bank. The notes John provided did not contain the FTC consumer credit language. If a customer has a personal defense on his or her purchase from John, may the customer raise that defense against the bank as well? Why?
10. What rights are acquired by a holder by due negotiation, and how are these rights superior to the rights of a person who merely possesses a nonnegotiable document of title?

Case Problems and Writing Assignments

1. Jerry Waters and his ex-wife, Patsy Waters, entered a property settlement as part of their divorce. Part of the property settlement agreement was that a note Jerry had issued to Patsy's father should be paid to Patsy. The note, payable to Jim Still, was delivered to Patsy, but it was not indorsed by the payee. Sometime later Jim Still died. When the note came due, Patsy demanded payment, but Jerry refused to honor the note. When Patsy sued, Jerry denied that Patsy was entitled to enforce the note since she was not a holder. Was Patsy entitled to enforce the note? Explain. [See *Waters* v. *Waters*, 498 S.W.2d 236 (Tex.App. 1973).]

2. On 30 November 1979, Ms. Minix executed a promissory note payable to the order of First Federal Savings and Loan Association. The note called for monthly payments, and it was secured by a mortgage on property located in Pulaski County. On 27 April 1987, Ms. Minix married Larry Tackett, and they executed a second mortgage on the property to Mr. and Mrs. Charles Tackett. By December 1987, Ms. Tackett was in default on the loan from First Federal, which had changed its name to First Savings of Arkansas in 1983; the S&L filed a foreclosure suit on the note and mortgage. The Charles Tacketts were notified of the suit, and they subsequently filed a cross-complaint to foreclose their second mortgage. During the pendency of the suit, First Federal became insolvent and was placed under conservatorship, with the Resolution Trust Company (RTC) appointed as receiver. RTC sold most of the assets of First Federal, including the mortgage note from Ms. Tackett. First Savings of Arkansas purchased the note and requested permission to be substituted as the plaintiff in the lawsuit. Ms. Tackett objected to this substitution, alleging that there was no evidence of a proper assignment or indorsement of the note to First Savings.

   Did First Savings have the right to prosecute this suit without evidence of a negotiation of the note to it? [See *Tackett* v. *First Savings of Arkansas*, F.A., 810 S.W.2d 927 (Ark. 1991).]

3. The Aiklens issued a note payable to the order of Schulingkamp in the amount of $10,500, and dated 15 November 1984. The note was given to the payee in conjunction with an offer to purchase real estate. The payee had not accepted the offer by 21 December 1984, at which time the Aiklens sent a telegram withdrawing their offer. On 28 December 1984, Schulingkamp notified the Aiklens that she was accepting the original offer. When Schulingkamp sought to collect the note, the Aiklens refused to pay. Schulingkamp sued, alleging that she had given value for the note, and that she was entitled to collect. Had Schulingkamp given value for the note in this case? Explain. [See *Schulingkamp* v. *Aiklen*, 534 So.2d 1327 (La.App. 4th Cir. 1988).]

4. Murphy issued a check payable to the order of Brownsworth. Brownsworth took the check to Manufacturers Bank seeking a cashier's check to replace the check given to him by Murphy. A Manufacturers Bank employee called the drawee bank to ascertain that the check issued by Murphy was good, received a positive reply, and took the check issued by Murphy as payment for the cashier's check requested by Brownsworth. Murphy subsequently issued a stop-payment order on the check. When Manufacturers Bank sued to collect the amount of the check, Murphy asserted that Manufacturers could not be a holder in due course since it lacked good faith in the transaction. As evidence of this lack of good faith, Murphy asserted that Brownsworth was not a regular customer of the bank, so the bank should not have issued a cashier's check in this situation. Does the argument advanced by Murphy establish a lack of good faith? Explain. [See *Manufacturers & Traders Trust Co.* v. *Murphy*, 369 F.Supp. 11 (Penn. 1974).]

5. Tibbs had a long-standing course of dealings with Virginia Capital Bank and with Mathews Insurance. Tibbs purchased business insurance from Mathews, borrowing money from the bank to finance the premiums. Tibbs normally signed a blank promissory note on one of the bank's loan forms and then delivered the signed note to Mathews. Mathews would figure the premiums and interest, complete the note, and deliver the note to the bank. The bank would then give Mathews the premium amount, and Tibbs would pay the bank the principal and the interest. The parties had done business in this manner for 22 years. In March 1980, Tibbs signed a blank note and delivered it to Mathews, who told Tibbs the note would be for approximately $960. However, Mathews completed the note for $9,600 in principal and $696 in interest, indorsed the note in his business name, and presented the check to the bank. The bank paid Mathews the $9,600 and took possession of the note. Tibbs refused to honor the note, alleging that it had been completed improperly, and denying liability. Could the bank enforce this note against Tibbs as completed? Explain. [See *Virginia Capital Bank* v. *Aetna Casualty & Surety Co.*, 343 S.E.2d 81 (Va. 1986).]

6. **BUSINESS APPLICATION CASE** Gilliam loaned Westhampton $345,200. As security for this loan, Westhampton assigned three deed of trust notes to Gilliam. These deed of trust notes were apparently issued by White. White refused to pay the notes when they came due, and Gilliam filed suit to collect the notes. Gilliam asserted that he was a holder in due course on the notes and was, therefore, entitled to receive payment even if White had a defense. White asserted that either he never executed the notes or that, if he executed them, the execution was the result of fraud and constituted a real defense against enforcement of the notes. According to White, the only document he was aware of signing was purported to be a "disclosure statement." White did admit that he had not read the "disclosure statement" very carefully, but that he did not know that the papers he was signing were, in fact, deed of trust notes.

How should the court resolve this case? How much influence would White's experience—or lack of same—in real estate loans and financing have on your decision? Assume that White had substantial experience in real estate transactions. What should White have done to protect his interests in a situation like this? [See *White* v. *Gilliam,* 419 S.E.2d 247 (Va. 1992).]

7. **ETHICS APPLICATION CASE** Doyle borrowed money from Trinity Savings & Loan, signing a promissory note that included an adjustable interest rate. The interest rate typed on the appropriate blank on the loan form provided for interest in the amount of 11.375% per annum. After Doyle signed the note, Trinity "whited out" the interest rate, typed in a new interest rate of 15.875% per annum, and appended what were purportedly Doyle's initials to the change. Trinity subsequently sold the note to the Federal National Mortgage Association (FNMA). When the note came due, Doyle refused to pay. He cited the material alteration as a defense to his obligation to Trinity, and asserted that the FNMA could not qualify as a holder in due course because the note contained an obvious alteration.

   How should this case be decided? What ethical issues are raised when any negotiable instrument has some essential element "whited out," new terms inserted, and initials appended? [See *Doyle* v. *Resolution Trust Corp.,* 999 F.2d 469 (10th Cir. 1993).]

8. **IDES CASE** Naef owned a snowmobile repair facility in Wyoming. In early 1988, he purchased Weeks Motor Sports, a snowmobile dealership. As part of the contract for sale, Weeks agreed to help Naef acquire the franchise rights to sell Polaris and Yamaha snowmobiles. Naef arranged to purchase 100 snowmobiles from Polaris, financing the purchase by arranging for a loan from Transamerica. When Naef met with the Transamerica representative to sign the loan documents, he was informed that Transamerica would not make the loan unless Naef's wife also signed the note as co-borrower and guarantor. The terms of the loan agreement called for Naef to remit to Transamerica the portion of any sale of any snowmobile that covered the financing of that snowmobile. In carrying out this obligation, Naef set up an account into which the portion of each sale that represented the financing of the snowmobile was deposited, and then a check was drawn against that account and mailed to Transamerica.

   While Naef was on vacation, his employee made several snowmobile sales but did not set aside in the separate account the portion of the sale proceeds needed to cover the financing. As a result, when Naef wrote the check to Transamerica, it was returned for insufficient funds. As a result, Transamerica sought to foreclose on the loan. Naef filed for bankruptcy protection, and Transamerica then filed suit against Naef's wife. Ms. Naef denied liability, asserting that she never received any consideration in exchange for her signature on the note, and that she was, therefore, not liable to the payee on that note.

   Apply the IDES principles to determine whether: Ms. Naef was liable as a guarantor; Ms. Naef was liable as an accommodation party; Ms. Naef was liable as a co-maker of the note. Explain your reasoning. [See *Transamerica Commercial Finance Corp.* v. *Naef,* 842 P.2d 539 (Wyo. 1992).]

NOTE

1. Laurence Hammack, "Bank held liable for bad checks," *Roanoke Times,* 19 March 1996, p. A1.

Liability and Discharge

O U T L I N E

A G E N D A

CIT is likely to receive a few "bad" checks in its course of its business, and the family will need to know what CIT's rights are in those situations. They will also be granting the bank rights in some of their assets as collateral on several loans. What happens to their collateral if the bank decides to sell the loan? If business goes well, the firm may want to pay off some of its loans early. What are its rights if these loans are paid before their due dates. These are just some of the questions that may arise in this chapter.

Be prepared! You never know when one of the Kochanowskis will ask for your advice and guidance.

Basic Concepts

Commercial paper is used as a substitute for money. However, at some point, the holder of the paper is going to want the money for which the paper has been substituted. Normally, this desire will lead to a *presentment* to the maker or drawee. In most cases, the maker or drawee then will pay the money as called for by the instrument, the instrument will be canceled, and its commercial life will terminate. Unfortunately, such a series of events does not happen every time. Some makers or drawees refuse to pay the presented instrument—they **dishonor** it. When this occurs, the issue of secondary liability arises. Some holders inadvertently fail to make a proper presentment. When this occurs, the issue of discharge arises. These possibilities are shown in Exhibit 24.1. You may want to refer back to this exhibit as you move through this chapter, keeping the roles and responsibilities of the various parties in mind.

Dishonor

A refusal to accept or to pay a negotiable instrument upon proper presentment.

The Chains of Liability

The term *liability,* when used with commercial paper, refers to an obligation to pay the negotiable instrument involved. There are several possible types of liability in commercial paper. The obligation to pay may be based either on *primary* liability or on *secondary* liability. The liability also may be based on contract principles, warranty principles, or the admissions of one of the parties.

Primary Liability

Every negotiable instrument has a primary party, and every negotiable instrument has secondary parties. The primary party is the party who is expected to pay the instrument upon proper presentment. The secondary parties are the parties who face conditional liability if or when the primary party refuses to pay the instrument upon proper presentment.

EXHIBIT 24.1 The Movement of a Negotiable Instrument

Issue ---> **Negotiation(s)** ---> **Presentment** ---> **Acceptance & Payment (Primary Liability Accepted)**
---> **Dishonor & Secondary Liability Claims**

Issue	The initial negotiation of an instrument. Normal delivery is to the payee, although it may also be delivered to a remitter.
Negotiation(s)	The transfer of an instrument by indorsement and delivery or by delivery alone, in which the transferee becomes a holder.
Presentment	Demand made to the primary party for the acceptance and/or payment of the instrument.
Acceptance	Commitment by the primary party to pay the instrument as presented.
Dishonor	Refusal by the primary party to accept the instrument; activates secondary liability of the prior parties on the instrument.
Payment	

The *maker* of a note is the primary party on that note. It is the maker to whom the holder will look for payment, and it is the maker who is normally expected to pay the note on its due date. Similarly, the *drawee* is the primary party on a check or a draft. It is the drawee to whom the holder will first look for payment of the order instrument, and it is the drawee who is normally expected to pay the order instrument, either on demand or on its due date.

A substantial difference exists between the position of the primary party on a note and that of a primary party on a check or a draft. On a note, the maker is primarily liable as soon as the note is issued. This is because the primary party, the maker, is also the person who gives the promise to pay. The maker is in a contractual relationship with the payee from the time he or she issues the instrument. By contrast, the drawee is normally not primarily liable on a check or a draft until a holder presents the instrument and the drawee accepts the instrument as presented. (This is not true if the instrument is a cashier's check, certified check, or teller's check.)

The reason the drawee is not normally liable on an order instrument upon issue is that there are usually *two* contractual relationships involved in order paper: the first contract is the contract between the drawer and the payee, the reason for the issuance of the instrument; the second contract is between the drawer and the drawee, the reason the drawee is expected to obey the drawer's order upon proper presentment. No contractual relationship exists between the drawee and the payee on the negotiable instrument issued by the drawer unless or until the drawee *accepts* the instrument, thereby agreeing to honor the order given by the drawer. Thus, a note has a commitment of primary liability from the time of its issue (the maker is legally obligated to the payee or any subsequent holders), but a check or a draft has a mere expectation that primary liability will exist at a future time. (The drawee has not yet made a commitment to the payee or any subsequent holders; its commitment is to the drawer.) On most negotiable instruments the primary party does, in fact, pay the instrument, honoring the primary liability of the instrument. Occasionally, however, the primary party does not honor his or her primary liability. When this happens, the holder of the dishonored instrument may seek recovery from one of the secondary parties on that instrument.

Secondary Liability

The *drawer* of a check or a draft, as well as the *payee* and any *indorsers* of any negotiable instrument are secondary parties on that instrument. Secondary parties face potential **secondary liability** on the instrument. A secondary party agrees, by acting either as the drawer, the payee, or as an indorser, to pay the instrument if certain conditions are met. Remember, though, that secondary liability is *conditional* liability. The secondary parties can only be held liable if the conditions are satisfied or if the secondary party waives the need for the conditions to be met. To hold a secondary party liable on his or her contract (represented by the indorsement or signing of the instrument), a person holding the instrument must prove all three of the following actions:

Secondary liability
Conditional responsibility; liability following denial of primary liability.

1. Presentment of the instrument was properly made.
2. The primary party dishonored the instrument upon proper presentment.
3. Notice of the dishonor was properly given to the secondary party.

It should also be recalled that there are two types of potential secondary liability: contractual liability and warranty liability. Any indorsement that is unqualified (indorsements are presumed to be unqualified) gives a contract to the indorsee and to every subsequent holder that, upon proper presentment and dishonor, the indorser will "buy" the instrument back. However, indorsers who use a qualified indorsement deny this contractual liability. Nonetheless, they, too, face potential secondary liability. (This warranty liability will be discussed later in the chapter.)

ESTABLISHING LIABILITY

Presentment

Presentment is a demand for acceptance or for payment of a negotiable instrument. The demand is made to the maker, the drawee, or the acceptor of the instrument by the presenter. The rules governing presentment have been changed somewhat in Revised Article 3. According to the revised Code section:

Clearinghouse
An association of banks and financial institutions that "clear" items between banks.

Section 3-501. Presentment

(a) "Presentment" means a demand made by or on behalf of a person entitled to enforce an instrument (i) to pay the instrument made to the drawee or a party obliged to pay the instrument or, in the case of a note or accepted draft payable at a bank, to the bank, or (ii) to accept a draft made to the drawee.

(b) The following rules are subject to Article 4, agreement of the parties, and clearing-house rules and the like:

(1) Presentment may be made at the place of payment of the instrument and must be made at the place of payment if the instrument is payable at a bank in the United States; may be made by any commercially reasonable means, including an oral, written, or electronic communication; is effective when received by the person to whom presentment is made; and is effective if made to any two or more makers, acceptors, drawees, or other payees.

(2) Upon demand of the person to whom presentment is made, the person making presentment must (i) exhibit the instrument; (ii) give reasonable identification and, if presentment is made on behalf of another person, reasonable evidence of authority to do so, and . . . sign a receipt on the instrument for any payment made or surrender the instrument if full payment is made.

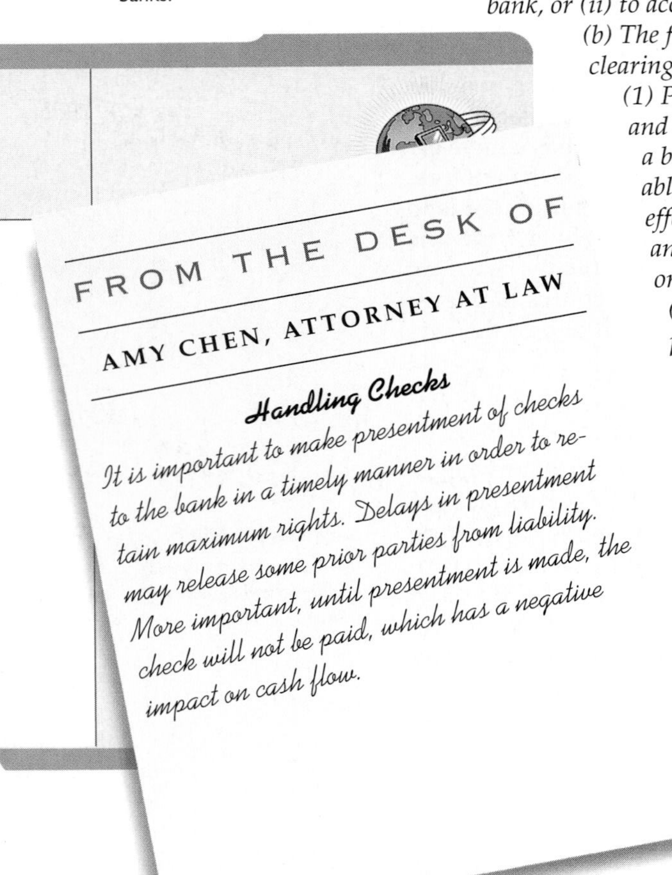

FROM THE DESK OF
AMY CHEN, ATTORNEY AT LAW
Handling Checks
It is important to make presentment of checks to the bank in a timely manner in order to retain maximum rights. Delays in presentment may release some prior parties from liability. More important, until presentment is made, the check will not be paid, which has a negative impact on cash flow.

The Code also says that an instrument is not dishonored if the party to whom presentment is made returns the instrument due to the lack of any necessary indorsements, or for the presenter to comply with the terms of the agreement, the instrument, or any applicable rules of law. Further, as a concession to banks, if presentment is made after the close of business for the day (presuming that the cut-off for the business day is no earlier than 2 P.M.), the party to whom presentment is made may treat presentment as occurring on the next business day. [Prior law required that presentment be made through a **clearinghouse** or at a place specified in the instrument. It did not permit presentment by either oral or electronic communication.]

If the presentment is made through the mail, presentment occurs when the mail is received. (This places the danger of postal delay on the presenting party.) If the presentment is to be made at a specified place and if the person who is to receive it is not there at the proper time, presentment is excused. This makes the drawee or the maker responsible for being at the proper place at the proper time. It also removes a possible worry from the presenting party—that the drawee or the maker will be absent when presentment is due, and will then deny that a presentment was ever made to that drawee or maker. If a note is payable at a bank in the United States or a draft is to be accepted at such a bank, the note or draft must be presented at that bank.

The rules of presentment are very important because presentment must be properly made before a dishonor can be shown. Dishonor also must be shown before any secondary party (except the drawer) can be held on his or her liability. The only exception to this rule is if presentment is excused.

The rules that govern presentment are fairly straightforward. The holder must make presentment within a reasonable time, or the presentment is improper. The reasonable time concept has two components: The time must be reasonable in both a clock sense (time of day) and a calendar sense (day of the week). In every case, presentment must be made at a reasonable time of day—that is, during normal working hours. An alleged presentment made at a bank or business address at 3 A.M. would be improper and would not be effective to prove a dishonor. Article 3 as revised has no time requirements for presentment, leaving the determination of whether presentment was made in a timely manner for interpretation based on the terms of the instrument and on other provisions of the Code.

Instruments that are payable at a definite time must be presented on or before the due date in order to establish that proper presentment was made. Demand instruments are treated differently. The holder of a check must present the check to the drawee bank within 90 days of its date or its issue, whichever is later, to hold the drawer liable on that check. A delay beyond this 90-day period will *not* excuse the drawer from liability on the underlying obligation, but it *will* excuse the drawer (and any secondary parties) from liability on that particular check. The drawer may be forced to redeem the check by paying cash or by issuing a new negotiable instrument to replace the original check. [The requirement that a check had to be presented within seven days of an indorsement in order to hold the indorser liable for the indorsement contract is no longer included in Article 3. Thus, it appears that the indorsement contract now extends from the time of indorsement until presentment *or* until 90 days from the date of the check or from the issue of the check.]

Once presentment is made, the focus shifts to the maker, drawee, or acceptor. If the presentment is made for acceptance alone (as when a presenter asks a bank to certify a check), the drawee (the bank in this example) has until the close of business the next business day to accept the instrument. (If the holder agrees—in good faith—another business day may be granted to the drawee to decide whether to accept the instrument.) If the presentment is made for acceptance and payment (or for payment alone, if acceptance occurred previously), payment must be made before the close of the business day on which the presentment was made. (Some short delay in paying the instrument is permitted if the drawee, acceptor, or maker needs to investigate whether payment would be proper.) Any delay beyond these time limits is treated as a dishonor of the instrument presented.

Persons receiving a presentment do have some protection. They can require some proof from the presenter of the presenter's right to have the check; requesting this proof is not treated as a dishonor. They can require the presenter to show them the instrument. They can demand reasonable identification of the presenter. They can require a showing of authority to make the presentment. They can demand the surrender of the instrument upon payment in full. If the presenter fails or refuses to comply with any of these requests, the presentment is considered improper. However, the presenter is allowed a reasonable time to comply with any of the requests.

The following case is one of two older cases that is still frequently cited in showing the importance of proper presentment. After reading this case, try to decide whether the new rules regarding presentment would change the outcome of the case.

24.1 KIRBY v. BERGFELD — 182 N.W.2d 205 (Neb. 1970)

FACTS Kirby agreed to purchase some land from the Bergfelds, giving them $10,000 as a down payment at the time of the contract, and agreeing to pay the remaining $342,560 by (1) assuming a $172,000 mortgage, (2) paying $20,000 in cash to the Bergfelds by 1 November, and (3) paying the balance of $150,560 in 10 years. The closing took place on 1 November, and Kirby delivered a $20,000 check to the Bergfelds to cover the cash payment called for in the contract. The next morning the Bergfelds took the $20,000 check to their bank and asked the cashier to telephone Kirby's bank to determine if sufficient funds were on deposit to cover the check. The bookkeeper at Kirby's bank informed the cashier that sufficient funds to cover the check were not on deposit in Kirby's account. Despite this, the Bergfelds continued to hold the check, which was never presented to Kirby's bank. Some time later they ordered their attorney to tear their signatures off the bottom of the contract. When Kirby called and told the Bergfelds to "send the check through," they refused to do so. When they continued to refuse to deal with Kirby in any manner, he sued them for specific performance of the contract. The Bergfelds contended that Kirby was in breach, so specific performance was not appropriate.

ISSUE Had the Bergfelds made a proper presentment of the check, establishing a dishonor, and thus a breach by Kirby?

HOLDING No. An inquiry by telephone is not a proper presentment. Since the check was never properly presented, it was never dishonored.

REASONING Under the UCC, presentment may be made by mail, through a clearinghouse, or in person. Presentment by telephone is not authorized or contemplated. The ability of the sellers to terminate the contract and to recover damages was suspended until the check was properly presented and dishonored. Since there was never a proper presentment of the check, there was never a dishonor of the check. Accordingly, Kirby was never in breach of the contract. Given this, specific performance was an appropriate remedy for Kirby.

BUSINESS CONSIDERATIONS The revised rules regarding presentment state that presentment can be made in any commercially reasonable manner, including written, oral, or electronic communication. Under the revised guidelines, did the Bergfelds make a proper presentment in this situation? What sort of policy should a business have to ensure that any instruments the business receives are properly presented?

ETHICAL CONSIDERATIONS Did Kirby act ethically in giving the Bergfelds a check that was not covered by sufficient funds at the time the check was issued? Is it ethical to knowingly issue a "bad" check, hoping that the check can be redeemed after it is dishonored by the bank?

Acceptance

When the drawee decides to accept an instrument, the drawee must sign the instrument. By signing the draft or check, the drawee agrees to honor the instrument as presented. This act of acceptance fixes the primary liability of the drawee. (Remember: An order instrument has no primary liability until it has been accepted by the drawee.)

The acceptance can be made even if the instrument is incomplete, but it must be made for the instrument as presented. Suppose the drawee tries to change the terms of the draft in the acceptance. The presenter can treat this as a dishonor or can agree to the changed terms. However, if this draft-varying acceptance is agreed to by the presenter, the drawer and every indorser are discharged from secondary liability.

24.1

SEEKING RECOVERY FOR A BAD CHECK

Last week one of the checks received by CIT and deposited into the business account was returned by the bank, stamped "Account Closed" across the face of the check. The check was originally issued by James Smitts, payable to the order of Helen Rudzinski. Ms. Rudzinski had indorsed the check "Pay to CIT" and forwarded it to the firm as payment in full for the Call-Image videophone she had ordered. Dan has asked you what the firm can do to recover the amount of this check, and from whom he should seek recovery. What advice will you give him?

BUSINESS CONSIDERATIONS Many businesses have a policy of not accepting what they call "two-party checks," checks that were drawn to the order to a payee who now wants to indorse the check over to the business. What reasons might a business have for this policy? Do the protections afforded by Article 3 make such a policy unnecessary?

ETHICAL CONSIDERATIONS Is there an ethical issue raised when a person indorses a check over to a creditor rather than depositing the check into his or her own account and then writing a check to the creditor?

FINANCE

Dishonor

An instrument is *dishonored* when proper presentment is made and acceptance or payment is refused. A dishonor also occurs when presentment is excused and the instrument is not accepted or paid. [Under UCC § 3-501(b)(3)(i), the return of an instrument for lack of a proper indorsement is not a dishonor.] The failure of the primary party to accept the instrument within the proper time is also a dishonor. A check returned because of insufficient funds or because of a stop-payment order is dishonored. A refusal by the primary party to accept the instrument is a dishonor, subject to the limitations in 3-501(b)(3). Dishonor is a denial of primary liability, and it activates the secondary liability of indorsers and of the drawer (see Exhibit 24.2). Remember that before dishonor, the secondary parties faced only potential secondary liability. The act of dishonor may, and usually will, move this liability from potential to actual.

Notice

The holder of a dishonored instrument has an obligation to give *notice* to prior parties in order to establish their secondary liability. The notice may be given to any or all persons who may be secondarily liable on the instrument, and it may be given by any person who has received notice. Thus, if the presenter/holder gives notice of dishonor to Indorser 2, Indorser 2 may then give notice to Indorser 1, and so on. The notice may be given in any commercially reasonable manner, including an oral, a written, or an electronic communication. It may be given in any terms or in any form, as long as it reasonably identifies the instrument and states that it has been dishonored or has not been paid or accepted.

The UCC is primarily concerned with the rights of the holder of a dishonored instrument. Allowance is made for an error in the description of the instrument in the notice. A misdescription will not affect the validity of the notice unless it misleads the person being notified. The notice must be given in a timely manner. Again, there

EXHIBIT 24.2 The Chains of Liability on Commercial Paper

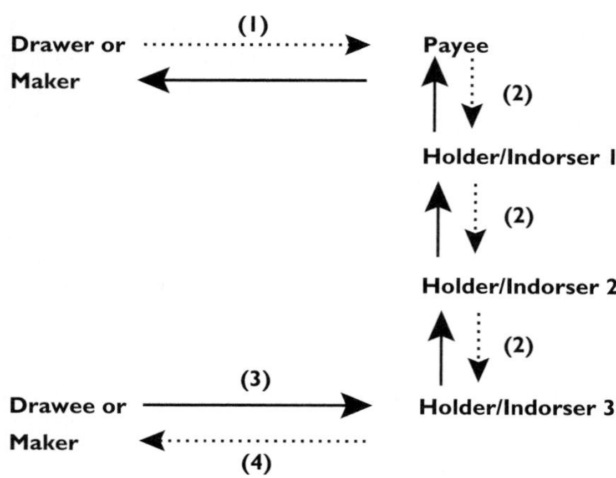

The (potential) primary liability moves in a clockwise manner, following the dashed lines: (1) is the issue, (2) is a negotiation, and (3) is a presentment. If the drawee or maker accepts the instrument, it is paid and discharged. If the drawee or maker dishonors the instrument on presentment (4), secondary liability is activated. Secondary liability moves counterclockwise, following the solid lines. (The number of holder/indorsers may be larger or smaller than the number shown in this exhibit.)

has been a significant change in the time limit for notice under the revised Article 3. This new provision is found in Section 3-503, which provides that:

> *(c) Subject to Section 3-504(c), with respect to an instrument taken for collection by a collecting bank, notice of dishonor must be given (i) by the bank before midnight of the next banking day following the banking day on which the bank receives notice of dishonor of the instrument, or (ii) by any other person within 30 days following the day on which the person receives notice of dishonor. With respect to any other instrument, notice of dishonor must be given with 30 days following the date on which dishonor occurs.*

Midnight deadline
Midnight of the next business day after the day on which an item is received.

Section 3-504(c) excuses giving notice of the dishonor within these time limits, *if* the delay is caused by circumstances beyond the control of the person giving notice, and *if* that person acts with reasonable diligence once the reason for the delay is removed. [Prior to the revision, the time limit for a bank was the same—its **midnight deadline** on the next banking day. However, other parties only had *three* days after they learned of the dishonor to give notice, or they lost their secondary liability contract claim. The new rules are obviously much more favorable for secondary parties.]

The following case contains an example of what can happen to a bank that fails to act within its time limits. Notice in this case that the controversy was between two banks over a dishonored check.

24.2 FIRST UNION NAT'L BANK OF FLORIDA v. FIRST FLORIDA BANK

616 So.2d 1168 (Fla.App. 2d Dist. 1993)

FACTS Elias had a bank account with First Florida Bank. On 13 August 1986, he wrote a $10,000 check payable to National Computer Consultants, Inc. National Computer endorsed the check and deposited the check in its account with Union Bank. Union Bank posted the check to National Computer's account on Thursday, 14 August.

Union Bank presented the check to First Florida on the following day at the local clearinghouse. At the clearinghouse, Union Bank was credited $10,000 and First Florida was debited $10,000. The clearinghouse forwarded the check to First Florida.

On 14 August, Elias gave a verbal stop-payment order to First Florida. Under statutory provisions, First Florida had until midnight Monday, 18 August, to notify Union Bank of its intention to dishonor this check. As a result, First Florida took steps on Monday, 18 August, to return the check to Union Bank via the clearinghouse. Unfortunately, First Florida misrouted the check when it returned the item to the clearinghouse by addressing it to the wrong bank. That bank received the misrouted check and returned it to First Florida through the clearinghouse on 20 August. First Florida did not return the check to the clearinghouse for Union Bank until 21 August.

In addition to returning the check, First Florida tried to give Union Bank notice of the dishonor. In August 1986, First Florida was a member of a service offered by Security Pacific to give notice of dishonor on checks over $2,500. Security Pacific provided notice through a computer system to banks participating in its service. It telephonically informed nonmember banks of dishonored checks. Union Bank was not a member of the Security Pacific system. First Florida did not request Security Pacific to give notice of dishonor to Union Bank until 5:54 P.M. on 18 August 1986. Security Pacific gave that notice by telephone at 11:40 A.M. on 19 August 1986. The trial court ruled for First Florida, stating that a "rule of reasonableness" should control, and that First Florida had acted reasonably. Union Bank appealed.

ISSUE Did First Florida give proper notice of dishonor to Union Bank by its midnight deadline?

HOLDING No. First Florida did not give proper notice of dishonor in a timely manner, failing to meet the midnight deadline imposed on banks.

REASONING [The applicable] statutes are complex, but generally make a payor bank accountable to a presenting bank if a check is not returned or notice of dishonor is not provided before the "midnight deadline." In this case, First Florida is the payor bank and Union Bank is the presenting bank. It is undisputed that the midnight deadline in this case, due to a weekend, expired at midnight on Monday, 18 August 1986.

By the midnight deadline, First Florida had delivered the check to the clearinghouse, but had routed this item to the wrong bank. It had notified Security Pacific of its intention to dishonor the check, but Security Pacific had not notified Union Bank. These efforts were insufficient to negate the payor bank's responsibility for the check.

The payor bank must bear the responsibility of its errors in misrouting this item. . . . First Florida argues that it returned the check to the clearinghouse, and that its erroneous instructions to deliver the check to the wrong bank are irrelevant. The trial court rejected this argument and we agree with the trial court. . . . The purpose of these statutes can be fulfilled only if they are interpreted to require delivery to the clearinghouse in a manner reasonably designed to result in an item's return to the presenting or last collecting bank. . . . In light of the substantial violation of the procedures established by the local clearinghouse, First Florida did not effectively return the item by the midnight deadline.

First Florida's telephonic notification was also deficient because Union Bank did not receive it prior to the midnight deadline. First Florida argues that it provided notice of dishonor when it notified Security Pacific. We recognize that notice of dishonor may be given in any reasonable manner. . . . Nevertheless, Security Pacific was clearly the agent of First Florida, not Union Bank. Union Bank was not a member of the Security Pacific system of notification. Thus, Union Bank did not receive oral notice of dishonor until it received the telephone call on Tuesday, after the midnight deadline. . . . Because First Florida presented no evidence in the trial court which might justify another basis for recovery from Union Bank, we reverse the judgment with instructions to enter judgment in favor of Union Bank.

BUSINESS CONSIDERATIONS Why should a bank have to adhere to a "midnight deadline" when non-banks have 30 days to give notice of a dishonor? What public policy reasons might exist for imposing such high standards

24.2 FIRST UNION NAT'L BANK OF FLORIDA v. FIRST FLORIDA BANK (cont.) 616 So.2d 1168 (Fla.App. 2d Dist. 1993)

and requirements on a bank in the area of returned and dishonored checks?

ETHICAL CONSIDERATIONS Is it ethical to argue for a "rule of reasonableness" when one's own negligence was the reason for failing to meet a statutory deadline? How could it be reasonable for First Florida to have misaddressed the envelope with a returned check in the amount of $10,000?

24.2

FINANCE

DISHONORED CHECKS

One of the checks received as a payment on account from a CIT customer was returned by the bank for insufficient funds. Dan has redeposited the check twice, and both times is was returned dishonored. He recently heard Donna saying something about the need to give notice of a dishonor within three days in order to preserve your rights on a dishonored instrument, and he fears that by redepositing the check he has waived the firm's right to collect from the drawer. He asks you for advice. What will you tell him?

BUSINESS CONSIDERATIONS A number of businesses will hold a dishonored check for a short time and then "re-run" the check through the bank in the hope that the drawer has made a deposit and that the check will be honored the second time through banking channels. Is this a good practice or a bad practice? Why?

ETHICAL CONSIDERATIONS Most banks impose a service charge on their customers for every check presented against the customer's account and dishonored. Is it ethical to present a check more than once, thus increasing the service charges imposed on the customer by the bank, and to also impose a service charge as the payee for a check that is dishonored? When does submission of a check stop being good business and start being an attempt to punish the drawer for writing a bad check?

It is normal for each party to give notice to the party who transferred the instrument to him or her. However, sometimes this transferor cannot be found or, when found, cannot pay. For that reason, a holder should give notice to every prior party who can be located. This increases the chances that the holder eventually will recover on the dishonored instrument.

A failure to give proper or timely notice will operate as a release from the conditional secondary liability for all the secondary parties except the drawer, unless the need to give notice is either excused or the need to receive notice is waived. Failure to give notice, or giving improper notice, may release other secondary parties, but it does not release the drawer or maker.

Frequently, the duty to make presentment or to give notice is waived or excused. When these situations arise, § 3-504 of the Code governs the situation. Under subsection (a), a delay in making presentment is excused if *any* of the following are true:

1. The person entitled to make presentment cannot with reasonable diligence make presentment.
2. The maker or acceptor has repudiated an obligation to pay the instrument, or has died, or is involved in an insolvency proceeding.
3. The terms of the instrument state that presentment is not necessary in order to enforce the obligation of the indorsers or the drawer.
4. The drawer or indorser whose obligation is being enforced has waived presentment or otherwise has no reason to expect or right to require that the instrument be paid or accepted.
5. The drawer instructed the drawee not to pay or accept the instrument or accept the draft or the drawee was not obligated to the drawer to pay the draft.

Under subsection (b), notice of dishonor is excused if *any* of the following are true:

1. By the terms of the instrument, notice is not necessary to enforce the obligation of a party to pay the instrument.
2. The party whose obligation is being enforced waived notice of dishonor.
3. Presentment was waived, which also constitutes a waiver of notice.

Impress on the bookkeeping department the importance of giving notice to all prior parties on any negotiable instruments that are returned unpaid by the bank. By giving notice, the firm increases its chances of collecting the amount from one of the prior parties. Not giving notice may release these same people from their liability to the firm.

LIABILITY

A negotiable instrument is a contract with special treatment under the law. One recognition of contract law principles is found in UCC § 3-401. This section states that "a person is not liable on an instrument unless (i) the person signed the instrument, or (ii) the person is represented by an agent or representative who signed the instrument and the signature is binding on the represented person . . ." However, once such a signature is found, the signing—or represented—party faces potential liability. The type of liability depends on the capacity in which it was signed. Again, the Code helps. As was pointed out earlier, § 3-204 states that every signature is presumed to be an indorsement unless the instrument clearly indicates some other capacity.

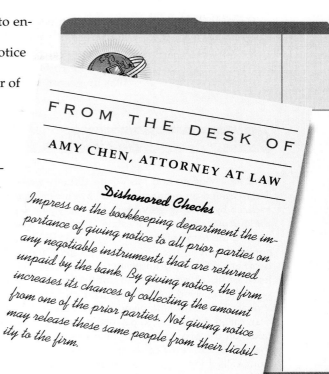

It is important to remember that there are two types of contracts involved with negotiable instruments. The first type of contract is represented by the instrument itself. The maker of promise paper and the acceptor of order paper give a contract. Each agrees to pay the instrument according to the terms of the instrument at the time of his or her engagement, or as completed if it was incomplete. The drawer of order paper promises to pay any holder or any indorser the amount of the instrument if it is dishonored. The second type of contract is the contract encompassed in the indorsement.

Indorsement Liability

The indorsers of commercial paper also give a contract by the act of indorsing, unless the indorsement is qualified. By the act of indorsing, the indorser promises that upon dishonor, and proper notice, he or she will pay the instrument as indorsed to any subsequent holder. The indorsers are presumed to be liable to one another on a dishonored instrument in the order indorsed, moving from bottom to top.

Two other parties may be involved in contractual liability on commercial paper: the accommodation party and the guarantor. Each of these parties has special potential contract liability. An *accommodation party* is a person who signs an instrument to "lend his name," or his credit, to another party. He signs as a favor, usually without getting anything out of the transaction. The accommodation party is liable to subsequent parties in the capacity in which he signed. If required to pay because of his secondary liability, he is entitled to recover from the party for whom he signed as an accommodator. A person signing an instrument is presumed to be an accommodation party and there is notice to all subsequent holders that the instrument was signed for accommodation if the signature is an *anomalous* indorsement (any indorsement made by a person who is not a holder of the instrument is considered anomalous), or if the signature is accompanied by words indicating that the indorser is acting as a surety or as a guarantor with respect to the obligations of another party to the instrument.

In the following case, a party attempted to avoid liability by asserting that he was an accommodation party. Notice how the court treated this defense.

24.3 CATANIA v. CATANIA

601 A.2d 543 (Conn.App. 1992)

FACTS Vincent and Mary Jane Catania were married. They resided on property owned by Vincent's mother and secured by a mortgage. Vincent and Mary Jane were to pay the mortgage and the real estate taxes, but title was to remain in the name of Vincent's mother. In 1977, the mother conveyed title to the property to Joseph Catania, Vincent's brother, without his knowledge or consent. (He did not learn of his title to the land until some time after 1980, when he received a tax notice from the town of Enfield.) Vincent and Mary Jane divorced in 1980. The divorce decree called for Vincent to pay the mortgage, insurance, and taxes on the property until their youngest child reached the age of 18. The decree also contained certain conditions calling for the sale of the property and the division of the proceeds between Vincent and Mary Jane. In 1982, Vincent arranged for a second mortgage on the property, and Joseph—the owner of record of the property—also signed the loan agreement. Eventually, Vincent defaulted on the mortgage, and Mary Jane paid the bank, receiving an assignment of the mortgage in exchange. Since Vincent had procured relief through bankruptcy, Mary Jane sued Joseph on the note. Joseph asserted that he was merely an accommodation party on the mortgage, and was not liable to Mary Jane.

ISSUE Was Joseph an accommodation party on the note, or was he a co-maker on the note?

HOLDING Joseph was a co-maker of the note, and as such he was liable to Mary Jane.

REASONING Joseph signed the note on a line labeled "borrower's signature." There was no showing that he signed as an accommodation party. The fact that he received no personal benefit was not considered material to the case. The court felt that since Joseph was the owner of record of the land, and since he signed the note on the line for the borrower's signature, and since there was no evidence that the bank agreed to treat Joseph as an accommodation party, he is to be viewed as a co-maker. Since Joseph was a co-maker, he could not avail himself of the defenses normally available to a surety under Connecticut law. He was liable to Mary Jane for the note as a co-maker.

BUSINESS CONSIDERATIONS Why would a person indorse a negotiable instrument as an accommodation party? What rights and liabilities are incurred when a person signs as an accommodation party? What policies or procedures should a business have with respect to accommodating another person on a negotiable instrument?

ETHICAL CONSIDERATIONS Are any ethical concerns raised in this case by the fact that the owner/mortgagee of property agreed to have one son pay the mortgage and taxes, and then deeded the property over to another son without telling either son what was being done? What should the son (and daughter-in-law) who occupied the property and paid the mortgage and taxes have done to prevent such a situation from arising?

If the signature of a party to an instrument is accompanied by words indicating unambiguously that he or she is guaranteeing collection, rather than guaranteeing the payment of the obligation of another party to the instrument that party is endorsing as a *guarantor.* Revised Article 3 has reduced the obligation of a guarantor somewhat. A guarantor is obliged to pay the amount due on the instrument to any person entitled to enforce the instrument, but only if:

1. An execution of judgment against the party whose obligation was guaranteed has been returned unsatisfied, or

2. The party whose obligation was guaranteed is insolvent or involved in an insolvency proceeding, or
3. The party whose obligation was guaranteed cannot be served with process, or
4. It is otherwise apparent payment cannot be obtained from the party whose obligation was guaranteed.

Warranty Liability

In addition to the basic contract liabilities just discussed, persons who present or transfer negotiable instruments make certain warranties. These warranties also carry with them the possibility of liabilities, and warranty liabilities cannot be disclaimed as easily as contract liabilities. An indorser may deny contract liability by the use of a qualified indorsement, but warranty liability is still present even if the indorsement is qualified, unless the qualified indorsement also specifically excludes warranties. An indorser could qualify the indorsement so that warranties are also excluded, even though endorsing with such a qualification to later holders makes the indorsement highly unusual. The indorser who would use such an indorsement would be well protected, but the instrument would be very difficult to transfer since few subsequent holders would be willing to accept such a negotiation.

The warranties involved in negotiable instruments are set out in § 3-416 and § 3-417 of the UCC. Section 3-416 provides for *transfer* warranties, while § 3-417 provides for *presentment* warranties. Any person who transfers an instrument for consideration gives transfer warranties to his or her transferee. In addition, if the transfer is by indorsement the transferee gives the transfer warranties to every subsequent transferee. Notice that the instrument does *not* need to be negotiated, and the transferee does *not* have to give value in order to have transfer warranties arise.

The transfer warranties provide protection to the transferee(s) in the following five areas:

1. The warrantor (transferor) is a person entitled to enforce the instrument.
2. All signatures on the instrument are authentic and authorized.
3. The instrument has not been materially altered.
4. The instrument is not subject to a defense or claim in recoupment of any party which can be asserted against the warrantor.
5. The warrantor has no knowledge of any insolvency proceedings commenced with respect to the maker or acceptor or, in the case of an unaccepted draft, the drawer.

Transfer warranties cannot be disclaimed on checks. Notice of any breach of the transfer warranties must be given to the warrantor within 30 days after the claimant has reason to know of the breach of warranty in order to have maximum protection. After 30 days the liability of the warrantor is reduced by any amount the warrantor can show was lost due to the delay.

If an unaccepted draft is presented to the drawee for payment or acceptance and the drawee pays or accepts the draft, the person making presentment and *any previous transferees* of the draft give presentment warranties to the drawee. The presentment warranties provide the following three protections to the drawee:

1. The warrantor is, or was, at the time the warrantor transferred the draft, a person entitled to enforce the draft or authorized to obtain payment or acceptance of the draft on behalf of a person entitled to enforce the draft.

2. The draft has not been altered.
3. The warrantor has no knowledge that the signature of the drawer is unauthorized.

Again, these warranties cannot be disclaimed on a check, and again notice of a claim for breach of the warranty must be given within 30 days of the time the drawee has reason to know of the breach. Any losses suffered by the warrantor as a result of a delay beyond the 30 days reduces the liability of the warrantor.

The new provisions of Article 3 have removed presentment warranty protections from promise paper, have removed the added protections that were formerly available with a qualified indorsement, and have added a time limit within which the person claiming damages based on a breach of warranty must give notice in order to have maximum protection.

Exhibit 24.3 summarizes the order of liability on a negotiable instrument.

The following case involved an alleged breach of warranty by an indorser of a check.

24.4 PUGET SOUND NAT'L BANK v. BURT

786 P.2d 300 (Wash.App. 1990)

FACTS Roberta Ward married Lee Adams in 1951. In 1967, Adams executed a general power of attorney authorizing his wife to sign his name and to transact business on his behalf. In 1981, the parties divorced, with Adams awarded life insurance policies on his life as his separate property in the divorce decree. In May 1981, Ward received two checks from the insurance company—one a dividend, the other representing a portion of the cash surrender value of the policy. Since the 1967 power of attorney was still valid, Ward signed both checks for Adams. She then signed both checks for Burt (her second husband) and deposited them in Burt's account. In 1983, Adams filed an affidavit of forgery and recovered the amount of both checks from the depository bank, PSNB. PSNB then sued Burt for breach of warranty, alleging that the signatures on the checks were not valid or authorized. Burt denied liability.

ISSUE Were the signatures of Adams's name by Ward on the checks valid or authorized?

HOLDING Yes. Ward still possessed a valid power of attorney which authorized her to sign Adams's name on the checks payable to his order.

REASONING Adams executed and recorded a general power of attorney which designated Ward as his attorney in fact, and which authorized her to sign checks on his behalf. He never revoked this power of attorney, and the divorce did not automatically revoke the power of attorney under Washington law. While it is true that Ward breached her fiduciary duty to Adams, this had no bearing on the issue raised by PSNB. The signatures were authorized by the power of attorney, so Burt did not breach his warranty to the bank, and Burt is not liable to the bank for the checks.

BUSINESS CONSIDERATIONS What policies and procedures should a business establish as to who is authorized to sign checks issued by the business? Should a business require two signatures on its checks to protect itself from the potential problem of employee embezzlement?

ETHICAL CONSIDERATIONS What, if anything, did Burt do in this case that was unethical? What should Burt have done when he discovered his wife was depositing checks into his account?

SPECIAL PROBLEMS

As was pointed out earlier, a person's signature or the signature of a person authorized to represent him or her, must appear on an instrument before that person can be held liable on the instrument. Thus, a forgery or an unauthorized signature is normally of no legal effect. However, an unauthorized signature can be ratified by the named person, and it then becomes fully effective. There are also some special rules in effect for situations involving *imposters* and for situations involving *fictitious payees.* These two similar areas each require attention.

An *imposter* is a person who pretends to be the person to whom an instrument is payable in order to induce the issuer of the instrument to issue the instrument to the imposter. Situations involving imposters arise when there is a legitimate reason for issuing the instrument and the person named as payee has a legitimate claim to the instrument, but the issuer is tricked into issuing the instrument to a person claiming to be the payee. A *fictitious payee* is a person who obtains an instrument that either (a) is made payable to the order of a legitimate person, but one who has no legitimate claim to the particular instrument, or (b) is made payable to a nonexistent person, a "fictitious" payee.

Section 3-404 provides the coverage for these two topics. According to subsection (a) of that section, when an imposter acquired a negotiable instrument, "an indorsement of the instrument by any person in the name of the payee is effective as the indorsement of the payee in favor of a person who, in good faith, pays the instrument or takes it for value or for collection." Subsection (b) applies when a fictitious payee acquires the instrument until the instrument is negotiated by a special indorsement. Under this subsection: (1) any person in possession of the instrument is its holder, (2) an indorsement by any person in the name of the payee stated in the instrument is effective as the indorsement of the payee in favor of a person who, in good faith, pays the instrument or takes it for value or for collection." However, the provisions of each of these subsections is limited to some extent. If the person who pays the instrument or who takes it for value or for collection does not exercise ordinary care in acquiring the instrument, and if the failure to exercise ordinary care substantially contributes to the loss resulting from paying the instrument, the person suffering that loss can recover the portion of the loss suffered because ordinary care was not exercised.

The following hypothetical cases illustrate these two special problem areas.

> Fred stole a radio from Herb. Fred then approached Thelma, told her that he was Herb, and offered to sell the radio to her. Thelma wrote a check payable to the order of Herb to pay for the radio. Under the impostor rule, Fred may effectively indorse the check by writing Herb's name, UCC § 3-403 on unauthorized signatures notwithstanding.

24.3

FORGED SIGNATURES

The firm received a check as payment for a new videophone system recently. Dan was concerned when the check was received because he thought there was something unusual about the signature. Despite his misgivings, however, he passed the check on to John, who deposited the check to the business account in normal fashion. The check was returned by the bank with the notation that the signature of the drawer was a forgery. Dan and John want to know if they have done anything wrong, or if the firm faces any possible liability in this case. What will you tell them?

BUSINESS CONSIDERATIONS Many firms "sign" checks by means of a stamp. What should the firm do to minimize the risk that someone who is not authorized to issue checks for the firm will manage to acquire some business checks and the stamp?

ETHICAL CONSIDERATIONS How should a business handle a situation in which the signature on a check looks suspicious to the business? What ethical issues are raised by presenting a check on which the signature raises questions?

FINANCE

EXHIBIT 24.3 Liability on a Negotiable Instrument

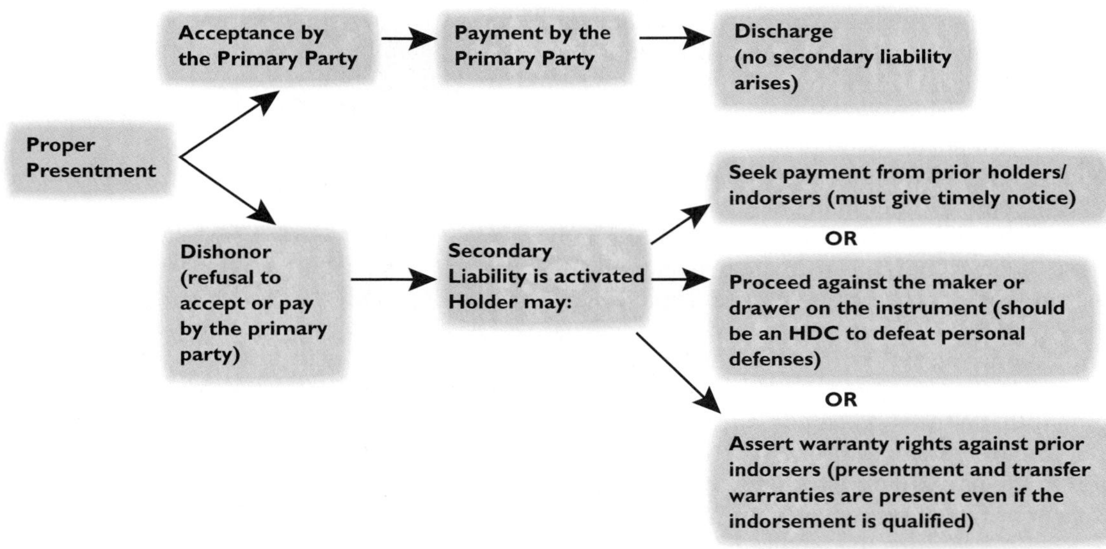

> Steve works for Acme. Part of his job is preparing checks to be used in paying bills and then taking those checks to Mr. Burton to be signed for the company. Steve slipped a check payable to Hall and Associates in among the other checks for Mr. Burton to sign. In fact, no money was owed to Hall and Associates. If Steve later removes the phony check and indorses it "Hall and Associates," the indorsement is valid under the fictitious-payee rule, UCC § 3-403 notwithstanding.

In the following case, the court was faced with an impostor-indorsed check and had to use the impostor rule to resolve the issues. To complicate matters, this was a case of first impression for the state court.

24.5 MINSTER STATE BANK v. BAYBANK MIDDLESEX — 611 N.E.2d 200 (Mass. 1993)

FACTS Edward Bauerband (Bauerband) and his wife (Michelle Bauerband) had been customers of Minster State Bank, an Ohio bank, for many years prior to the events in this case. Bauerband applied for a loan from Minster purportedly for himself and his wife. The loan officer knew both Bauerband and his wife. Minster mailed loan documents to Bauerband in Massachusetts, including a promissory note to be executed by Bauerband and his wife. Bauerband forged his wife's name on these documents. The signed note acknowledged falsely that Michelle had received a copy of the note. On return of these documents, Minster issued a bank customer's check payable to the order of both Bauerband and his wife and mailed it to their home in Massachusetts. Bauerband endorsed the check for himself, forged his wife's name on the check, and deposited the check into a business account which he maintained at BayBank Middlesex. Bauerband's wife had no knowledge of the loan transaction, the note, or the check.

24.5 MINSTER STATE BANK v. BAYBANK MIDDLESEX *(cont.)* **611 N.E.2d 200 (Mass. 1993)**

Minster claims that BayBank violated the warranty provisions of [the Code]. . . . In response, BayBank urges that Bauerband was an imposter, which exculpates BayBank under the provisions of [the Code]. . . . Apart from the "imposter" statute, in the face of Bauerband's forgery of his wife's name on the check, BayBank would be liable for warranting to Minster that "all signatures are genuine or authorized" under [the Code].

The trial court ruled on a motion for summary judgment that Bauerband was an imposter and ordered judgment for BayBank. Minster requested a report to the Appellate Division of the District Court Department which affirmed the judge's ruling and dismissed the report. Minster appealed and we transferred the case to this court on our own motion.

ISSUE The narrow issue in this case is whether the forged endorsement by Bauerband of his wife's name makes him an imposter within the sweep of Article 3.

HOLDING Yes. Bauerband was holding himself out as Michelle for purposes of acquiring the loan and the check, which makes him an imposter under the provisions of Article 3.

REASONING [A party] may be an imposter whether he acts face to face, by mail, or "otherwise." We do not get much help from the UCC as to the meaning of "imposter" in its commercial law context except that the official comment . . . provides that "imposter" refers to "impersonation. . . ." We have not previously considered this question of who qualifies as an imposter, and there is precious little case law under the UCC to help us. "Questions about who is and who is not an 'imposter' remain unanswered. . . ." What cases exist fall on both sides of the question. Two New York opinions support the proposition that an imposter was involved in the case before us. . . . Cases to the contrary are not particularly persuasive for our purposes. . . . The impersonation by forgery that is crucial to the imposter defense is one that is made to the drawer bank that issued the check and not any impersonation inherent in the forged endorsement presented to the collecting bank. . . .

The only inquiry is whether Bauerband, as an imposter, by the use of the mails or otherwise induced Minster to issue the check to him in the name of the payees. By his conduct in signing his wife's name to the promissory note and submitting it to Minster, he was holding himself out as Michelle Bauerband in writing. In acknowledging that she will pay the note and that she had received a copy of it, Bauerband was purporting to be Michelle when he forged her name and sent the note to Minster. He was impersonating her, not in the literal "in person" sense, but "by use of the mails or otherwise. . . ." By signing Michelle's name to the note, Bauerband implicitly was indicating that he was Michelle. The fact that Bauerband also signed the note on his own behalf does not make him any less an imposter. Therefore, we affirm the order of the Appellate Division dismissing the report.

BUSINESS CONSIDERATIONS Do the new provisions for defining an imposter under the Revised Article 3 help or hinder in this area? How can a business protect itself from imposters when it issues negotiable instruments?

ETHICAL CONSIDERATIONS Why did the court seem to have so much difficulty deciding if Bauerband was an imposter? Does it seem like the court was more concerned (tacitly) with determining which bank was more responsible for Bauerband's acquisition of the money than it was with whether Bauerband was truly an imposter?

Discharge

The term *discharge* means to remove liability or potential liability on a negotiable instrument. A **discharge** can take place in a number of ways. Some methods discharge all the parties, and others discharge only a few. The most important and most common types of discharge are explained in the following sections.

Discharge
Release from obligation or liability.

Payment

The most common type of discharge is the payment or other satisfaction of the instrument. In the vast majority of cases, the primary party pays the instrument on presentment and cancels it (or otherwise marks it as paid). If this were not so, negotiable instruments would not be so readily accepted in the commercial world. There are only two exceptions to payment operating as a discharge. A payment will not operate as a discharge when it is made in bad faith to a thief or to a person holding through (receiving the instrument from) or after (receiving the instrument from a party who received it from) a thief. Also, it will not operate as a discharge if the paying party makes a payment that violates a restrictive indorsement. (*Note:* An intermediary bank or a nondepository bank may be discharged even though it ignores the restrictive indorsement, provided it acts in good faith.) In these examples, the bad faith of the payer does not remove liability. The *proper party,* the person who should have received payment, is still entitled to payment, and the liability of the wrongfully paying party remains.

Tender of Payment

If a party tenders payment in full to a holder when an instrument is due, or later, and the holder refuses the payment, a discharge occurs. The party tendering payment is discharged to a limited extent. No additional interest can be added to the instrument after the date of the tender, nor can any other costs or attorney's fees be added to the instrument. Any other parties on the instrument (indorsers, drawers, and the like)

YOU BE THE JUDGE

Reservation of Rights

A customer of a business received his bill from the business and objected that he had been overcharged. The business replied that the bill was accurate, and that payment was expected within a reasonable time. When the customer continued to object to the amount of the bill, the business threatened to turn the matter over to a collection agency. Finally, the customer sent a check to the business. The check was written for the amount the customer claimed was the proper amount, although significantly less than the amount the business had billed the customer. On the face of the check, on the memo line, the customer wrote "Payment in full." The business indorsed the check, added the phrase "without prejudice, under protest," and deposited the check into its account. It then billed the customer for what the business asserted was the balance due. The customer argued that when he wrote "payment in full" on the face of the check he was proposing an accord, and that by cashing the check, the business was agreeing to his term, effecting a satisfaction. The business is now suing the customer for the balance allegedly due.

This case has been brought in *your* court. How will you resolve the case?

BUSINESS CONSIDERATIONS What sort of policy should a business establish to deal with customers who disagree with the amount for which they are billed? How should a business handle negotiable instruments sent to them with statements, such as "payment in full," on the face of the instrument?

ETHICAL CONSIDERATIONS Is it ethical to attempt to avoid paying a portion of a legitimate debt by writing "payment in full" on the face of the instrument sent in as a payment? Is it ethical for a creditor to refuse to accept a bona fide offer of settlement from a debtor?

SOURCE: UCC, Revised Sections 1-207 and 3-311.

are totally discharged if, to collect on the instrument, they could theoretically have sued the party who made the tender of payment.

Cancellation and Renunciation

A holder may discharge a party by canceling that party's signature on the instrument or by canceling the instrument itself. Cancellation may be shown either by striking out a portion, such as one signature, or by striking out the entire instrument. It can also be shown by destroying or mutilating a signature or the entire instrument. To be effective, the cancellation must be done intentionally.

Renunciation operates as a discharge whenever the holder delivers a written and signed statement to the discharged party that renounces (gives up) any rights against that person. Such a discharge is good against the renouncing party but not against any later holders, unless they were aware of the renunciation.

Impairment

Under the UCC section on impairment, a holder may elect to release some party from liability on the instrument. Or a holder may decide to release some collateral that is being used to secure payment of the instrument. However, in so doing, the holder also will discharge some or even all of the secondary parties on the instrument. When the holder releases a particular prior party, the holder also releases any other prior party who might have had recourse against the originally released party. In addition, when a holder releases collateral, the holder releases every prior party, since each prior party might have had recourse against the collateral. The following are the only two exceptions to these rules:

1. If a prior party agrees to the release of another party or to a release of the collateral, this prior party is not discharged by the release.
2. If the holder expressly reserves rights against a party, that party is not released or discharged. However, the releases by the holder are also not effective as far as the nondischarged party is concerned. In other words, the party who was expressly not discharged does not have any change in his or her position.

Other Discharges

If a party is a former holder of an instrument and later reacquires it, a partial discharge occurs. Any person who held the note between the two holdings of the reacquiring party is discharged from liability to the reacquiring party. Also, if the reacquiring party strikes out the indorsements of the intervening persons, they are totally discharged on the instrument. For example, if George holds a note, indorses it to Betty, and then buys it back from Betty, Betty is discharged from liability to George.

A fraudulent material alteration also acts as a discharge. If the alteration is fraudulent and material, any party who does not consent to the alteration is totally discharged from liability under most circumstances. A holder in due course may still enforce the instrument as it was originally issued, even though it has been materially altered.

Finally, an undue delay in making presentment operates as a discharge for all prior indorsers. An undue delay in giving notice of a dishonor will also operate as a discharge of all prior indorsers, and may even discharge a drawer or maker.

http:// RESOURCES FOR BUSINESS LAW STUDENTS

NAME	RESOURCES	WEB ADDRESS
Uniform Commercial Code (UCC) § 1-207	The Legal Information Institute (LII), maintained by the Cornell Law School, provides a hypertext and searchable version of § 1-207, Performance or Acceptance Under Reservation of Rights.	http://www.law.cornell.edu/ucc/3/1-207.html
UCC, Article 3, Negotiable Instruments	LII provides a hypertext and searchable version of UCC, Article 3, Negotiable Instruments. LII has links to Article 3 as adopted by particular states and to proposed revisions.	http://www.law.cornell.edu/ucc/3/overview.html
UCC, Article 7, Warehouse Receipts, Bills of Lading and Other Documents of Title	LII provides a hypertext and searchable version of UCC, Article 7, Warehouse Receipts, Bills of Lading and Other Documents of Title.	http://www.law.cornell.edu/ucc/7/overview.html

Summary

As formal contracts, negotiable instruments carry certain contract responsibilities and liabilities. The maker of promise paper has primary liability on the instrument from its issue date. The drawee of order paper faces potential primary liability. However, once the drawee accepts the instrument, the drawee has primary liability. If the primary liability is denied or refused, every prior holder is secondarily liable. In addition, the drawer of order paper is secondarily liable on a dishonored instrument.

For the holder to enforce the primary liability of the instrument, proper presentment must be made to the maker or drawee. At that point, the primary party will either accept the instrument or dishonor it. If dishonor occurs, the holder will give notice to prior parties to establish their secondary liability.

Negotiable instruments carry both contract liability and warranty liability. The warranty liability may be transfer warranty liability or presentment warranty liability. Transfer warranties exist on all negotiable instruments that are transferred for consideration. Presentment warranties only apply to order paper that is presented to the drawee for acceptance or payment.

The final stage for most instruments is discharge. Discharge can be, and normally is, based on payment or satisfaction. Some discharges are partial, discharging either a portion of the liability or a few of the parties. Tender of payment is a partial discharge. Cancellation, renunciation, and impairment are all discharges of some of the secondary parties.

Discussion Questions

1. What is "primary liability," and when does it exist on a negotiable instrument? What is "secondary liability," and when does it exist on a negotiable instrument? Is it possible for a party to be both primarily and secondarily liable on the same instrument at the same time?
2. In order to show proper presentment, what must the presenting party establish? What are the rights of the primary party when a presentment is made?
3. There are five transfer warranties involved with negotiable instruments? Who gives transfer warranties, and to whom are they given?

4. What is an "impairment" as it relates to discharge of liability on a negotiable instrument? Why is a discharge granted to some of the parties on an instrument when an impairment occurs?
5. What are the presentment warranties associated with negotiable instruments? Who receives the benefit of these warranties? Who gives these warranties?
6. Who or what is an "imposter" under Article 3? How is an indorsement by an imposter treated?
7. Presume that a holder makes proper presentment of a negotiable instrument and that the instrument is dishonored upon presentment. The holder now has three options. What are the three options available to the holder of an instrument that has been dishonored after proper presentment? Under what circumstances should the holder pursue any or all of the options available? Explain your reasoning.
8. When a person indorses a check, that person gives an additional contract to the indorsee. How long is that indorsement contract valid? What must the indorsee (or a subsequent transferee) do in order to hold the indorser to the indorsement contract?
9. Amy transferred a note to Jim by delivery alone. At the time of the transfer, the maker of the note was involved in an insolvency proceeding. Because of the insolvency proceeding, Jim was unable to collect the note from the maker. What are Jim's rights against Amy? Would it alter his rights if Amy had indorsed and delivered the note to him initially? Why?
10. Joe issued an interest-bearing demand note to Jane. Jane negotiated the note to Larry. Larry, in turn, negotiated it to Tom. Joe offered to pay Tom, but Tom refused the payment. What effect does Tom's refusal to accept the tender of payment have on each of the other parties?

CASE PROBLEMS AND WRITING ASSIGNMENTS

1. The Shumways borrowed money from Horizon Credit, signing a promissory note payable in monthly installments over a 15-year period. The money was used to purchase a sailboat. During the life of the loan, the sailboat was damaged in an accident. The Shumways considered the boat to be damaged beyond repair, although their insurance company felt that repairs were possible. The Shumways then stopped making the payments called for on their loan, and Horizon accelerated the note, suing the Shumways for the entire balance due on the loan, plus interest and fees. The Shumways argued that Horizon should have contacted the insurance company for the money. They also asserted that Horizon had not made presentment nor given notice of any dishonor, so acceleration of the note was not allowed. Did Horizon have a duty to make presentment and then to give notice of the dishonor to the makers of the note? Explain. [See *Shumway* v. *Horizon Credit Corp.*, 801 S.W.2d 890 (Tex. 1991).]

2. Myles and Theresa Bryant issued a promissory note payable to the order of Thomas, with monthly installments to begin 1 April 1989. The note recited that payment in full was due if the note were to become two months past due. In November 1989, Thomas sued Myles Bryant for the full amount of the note, alleging that no payments had ever been made. Bryant denied liability, asserting that he and his wife had separated earlier, and that he never received any consideration for the note. He also alleged that Thomas was guilty of fraud in procuring the note and that Thomas had failed to meet several conditions orally agreed to with regard to the note. Would a failure by Thomas to satisfy the conditions to which he agreed when he accepted the note preclude his ability to recover on the note? Would this same failure to satisfy conditions affect a third person taking the note by negotiation from Thomas? Explain your reasoning. [See *Thomas* v. *Bryant*, 597 So.2d 1065 (La.App. 2d Cir. 1992).]

3. Cotton issued a negotiable promissory note to Jones in 1955. Over the next 12 years, until the death of Jones in 1967, Cotton made regular payments on the note. After Jones died, a paper was found among his personal effects. The paper called for the cancellation of any unpaid balance on the note Cotton had issued if Jones died before Cotton. Cotton alleged that this paper was a valid renunciation. Jones's estate argued that it was not a valid renunciation and that Cotton still owed the balance of the note. What should be the result of this case? Explain. [See *Greene* v. *Cotton*, 457 S.W.2d 493 (Ky. 1970).]

4. Ridley issued a check payable to the order of Clements and drawn on his bank in Tennessee. Clements indorsed the check to Continental, and Continental deposited the check to its account at Central Bank. Central Bank, in turn, mailed the check to the drawee bank in Tennessee, asking the drawee to "Check for collection—Return if not paid in three days." Several days later, Central Bank called the bank in Tennessee

and inquired about the check. On being informed that the check was not good, Central Bank asked the drawee to continue to try to collect on the check. One month later, when the amount of the check remained uncollected, the drawee returned it to Central Bank. Central Bank sued Clements for the amount of the check, based on his indorsement. Clements alleged that his liability was discharged by the bank's failure to give him timely notice of the dishonor. What result should occur in this case? Explain your answer. [See *Clements* v. *Central Bank of Georgia,* 270 S.E.2d 194 (Ga.App. 1980).]

5. Penn Mutual issued a check payable to the order of Morris, and drawn against Penn Mutual's account at Girard Bank. Eventually, the check was deposited by Payung at the Mount Holly Bank. The check as deposited contained a forgery (possibly by Payung) of the Morris indorsement and an indorsement by Payung. Mount Holly Bank transferred the check through normal banking channels to Penn Central (which paid Mount Holly the full amount of the check) and on to Girard Bank. Girard paid Penn Central for the check on presentment. Eventually, Penn Central notified Girard Bank that Morris's indorsement had been forged and requested that its account be recredited for the amount of the check. Girard Bank returned the money to Penn Central, and then sued Mount Holly to recover its money. Girard Bank alleged that Mount Holly breached the presentment warranties on the check, based on the presence of the forged indorsement. Mount Holly defended by arguing that the drawer was negligent in its handling of the check, and thus Mount Holly was relieved of liability. How should this case be resolved? Explain your reasoning. [See *Girard Bank* v. *Mount Holly Bank,* 474 F.Supp 1225 (1979).]

6. **BUSINESS APPLICATION CASE** Quality Kitchens delivered a $10,000 check drawn on its account with First Wyoming Bank to Cabinet Craft as payment on its account. Cabinet Craft deposited the check with Security Bank in Billings, Montana. Security Bank placed the check into the bank collection system, and it was then presented to First Wyoming. First Wyoming sent the check by courier to its computer center for processing. The courier delivered a batch of checks, including the check from Quality Kitchens, to the computer center, but decided not to wait for the checks to be processed. (He was concerned about travel due to possible flooding of the main roads back to the First Wyoming location.) Three days later the Quality Kitchens check was returned to First Wyoming from the computer center, and First Wyoming dishonored the check due to insufficient funds in the Quality Kitchens account. Cabinet Craft sued the bank for the value of the check, citing an undue delay in deciding to dishonor the instrument, and arguing that this meant that the bank had accepted the check. Did First Wyoming dishonor the check in a timely manner? If it did not, was its delay in dishonoring the check excused? [See *First Wyoming Bank* v. *Cabinet Craft Distributors, Inc.,* 624 P.2d 227 (Wyo. 1981).]

7. **ETHICS APPLICATION CASE** Erb was a financial consultant at Shearson Lehman in Provo, Utah, rising to the rank of vice president by 1987. In 1987, Erb was contacted by Matthews, the controller for WordPerfect Corporation and its sister firm, Utah Softcopy, concerning the establishment of several accounts for the firms and for the principals of WordPerfect. Erb established the three accounts and assumed responsibility for managing all three. Shortly thereafter, Matthews delivered a check to Erb for $460,150.23. The check was payable to the order of ABP Investments, and was to be used for the WordPerfect principals. At the time there was no "ABP Investments" account with Shearson, although the WordPerfect principals did business elsewhere under this name. Matthews offered to replace the check with another, payable to the name on the account used at Shearson. However, Erb assured Matthews that there would be no problem with the check as drawn. Erb then opened an account at Shearson in the name ABP Investments and forged the signature of one of the principals. Over the next 11 months, Erb procured and negotiated 37 checks drawn by Shearson Lehman and payable to the order of ABP Investments. The checks, totaling $504,295.30, were all deposited to Erb's personal account at Wasatch Bank, with forged indorsements for ABP Investments. None of the checks contained Erb's indorsement. Eventually, an audit of Erb's handling of the various WordPerfect accounts revealed the extent of his misappropriations. Shearson settled with WordPerfect for $1,208,903, and then sued Wasatch Bank for negligence, breach of warranty, and conversion. Wasatch denied liability.

   Is a depository bank liable to the drawer of a check when the drawer's faithless employee induces the drawer to issue checks, fraudulently indorses them in the name of the specified payee, and absconds with the funds? What ethical considerations are raised by the facts in this case? [See *Shearson Lehman Brothers, Inc.* v. *Wasatch Bank,* 788 F.Supp. 1184 (D.Utah 1992).]

8. **IDES CASE** Pauline Pagani was an employee of Maryland Industrial Finishing Company, Inc. (MIFCO) from 13 April 1989 through 23 February 1990. In June of 1989, Pagani began embezzling funds

by depositing some of MIFCO's checks into her own account at Citizens Bank of Maryland, rather than depositing the checks into MIFCO's account at Citizens. She continued this practice until February of 1990, when Brenda Alexander discovered the embezzlement. MIFCO later sued Citizens to recover the funds that were deposited into Pagani's personal account. MIFCO alleged, among other things, that Citizens converted the checks under the UCC, and that Citizens was negligent.

At trial, Brenda Alexander testified that MIFCO is a small company with seven employees and that it has had an account with Citizens since 1976. Alexander also testified that she instructed Pagani that when MIFCO received a check from a customer, she should retrieve the invoice from the file, mark it paid, and write on it the check information, and to then place the invoice in the "paid" file. Pagani was also instructed to indorse the check by stamping the back with two stamps—one with the name and address of MIFCO and the other containing the words, "For deposit only." Pagani was then directed to deposit the indorsed checks into MIFCO's account at Citizens Bank and to file a copy of the deposit slip in MIFCO's files.

Were the indorsements made by Pagani "unauthorized" since she did not make the indorsements restrictive, as she had been instructed to do? Was the bank liable under conversion, negligence, or breach of warranty theories? Use the IDES principles to resolve this case. [See *Citizens Bank of Maryland* v. *Maryland Industrial Finishing Co., Inc.*, 659 A.2d 313 (Md. 1995).]

A G E N D A

The Kochanowskis will need to open a checking account for the firm, and they will need to know what sort of account they should get and what sort of financial institution they should deal with. Various family members also need checking accounts, and they will need to know the same things on an individual basis. Most of the banks in their community offer ATM cards. Should they get an ATM card, a debit card, both, or neither? What are their rights and responsibilities when dealing with banks? You may be asked these and other questions during the coverage of this chapter.

Be prepared! You never know when one of the Kochanowskis will ask for your advice or guidance.

Bank–Customer Relations/ Electronic Fund Transfers

O U T L I N E

Basic Concepts
The Customer: Rights and Duties
The Bank: Rights and Duties
Special Problems
Funds Transfers
Summary
Discussion Questions
Case Problems and Writing Assignments

BASIC CONCEPTS

In the United States today, nearly every business organization has a checking account. In addition, many, if not most, of the adults in this country have checking accounts. Workers receive their pay by check. Checking account information is normally required on credit and loan applications, and increasingly, is asked for on job applications. Millions of checks move through the economic system each day. Yet few people actually understand the checking system they are using.

A new customer walking into a bank follows the signs that lead to the "New Accounts" desk. Upon sitting down at this desk, the novice depositor is inundated with seemingly trivial information and details. Several different types of accounts—interest plus checking, free checking, ready-reserve checking, and so on—are briefly mentioned in passing; multiple colors and styles of checks are displayed; a "signature card" is handed to the customer with instructions to "sign at the X"; a deposit ticket is prepared; and a deposit is made in the customer's name in a new account. Before really knowing what has happened, the new customer is back on the street, the proud possessor of a personal checking account. More likely than not, the customer has no idea of what all this means legally.

By signing a signature card, the customer has entered a multirole legal relationship with the bank. The signature card represents a contract with the bank that the customer accepts on signing the card, even though he or she probably is unaware of any of its terms or conditions. In addition, the customer is now governed by Part 4 of Article 4 of the Uniform Commercial Code (UCC), which governs the bank–customer relationship. (Article 4 has been revised, although most of the changes in this article are in Part 2, Collection of Items: Depository and Collecting Banks. A few changes that affect the bank–customer relationship are also covered in Part 4.) The customer has entered into an agency relationship and has agreed to a debtor–creditor relationship, as well.

The contract that the customer entered into is relatively simple. It covers things like service charges that can be imposed by the bank for various services, minimum balance requirements for the customer's account, and technical terms and conditions. Likewise, the coverage afforded by Article 4 of the Code is fairly simple; basically, it spells out the mandatory rights and duties of each of the parties. These will be dealt with later in this chapter.

The agency portion of the agreement is a complete surprise to most depositors. To put it simply, the bank is the agent and the depositor is the principal. An agent is required to obey any lawful orders of the principal that deal with the agency. This explains, in part, the language used on a check. The depositor (principal) is ordering the bank (agent) to "Pay to the order of" someone. The check does not say, "Please pay" or "I would appreciate it if you would pay." It says, "PAY!" This language is an order, and the order is usually lawful. Therefore, the bank must obey that order or face possible liability to the depositor for the disobedience.

The final relationship is variable. Normally, the customer will have a positive balance in the checking account. As a result, the customer is a creditor of the bank, and the bank is a debtor of the customer. Occasionally, the bank will pay an **overdraft** on the customer's account. When this happens, the customer has a negative balance in the account, and the roles reverse. Now the bank is a creditor of the customer, and the customer is a debtor to the bank.

Overdraft
A check or draft written by the drawer for an amount in excess of the amount on account, and accepted by the drawee.

25.1

FINANCE

CIT OPENS A CHECKING ACCOUNT

CIT will need to open a checking account for the business. Tom and Anna are not sure what sort of account they should open, or what sort of financial institution they should prefer, if any. They have asked for your advice. What will you tell them?

BUSINESS CONSIDERATIONS Banks offer a number of different types of checking accounts. A firm that "shops" carefully is likely to be able to find an account that is ideal for the particular needs of that business. What sort of things should be considered in seeking a checking account for a newly formed business?

ETHICAL CONSIDERATIONS An old adage states that ignorance of the law is "no excuse." Does this adage—presuming that it is still true—justify the failure of many banks to fully inform new customers of the rights and responsibilities of both parties to a checking account? Should banks make more of an effort to convey all information to their new customers, or should the banks rely on the customers to read the brochures and learn what they need to know on their own?

THE CUSTOMER: RIGHTS AND DUTIES

The first and main duty of a customer is to act with due care and diligence. Whether writing a check, inspecting a monthly statement, or indorsing a check, or whether making a deposit or cashing a check, the customer is required to act in a careful and reasonable manner. If customers remember that it is their money being handled, and that carelessness could cause them to lose that money, they are more likely to be careful.

Customers have several rights they may exercise. They may stop payment on a previously issued check, and they may collect damages from the bank if the bank errs in the handling of the account to the customer's financial detriment. But before they can exercise these rights, customers must show that they have acted properly and/or that the bank has acted improperly. For example, suppose that Louis issues a check to pay for some merchandise. The merchant presents the check to the bank for payment, and the bank dishonors the check. Louis is now likely to have some problems with the merchant. He may have to pay the merchant a "handling fee" or a "service charge" for the returned check. He may face a lawsuit filed by the merchant to collect the amount of the check plus costs and interest. In many states a person may face a criminal charge for passing "hot" (bad) checks. But what if the dishonor was due to an error by the bank, not to any carelessness or wrongdoing on Louis's part? Louis will still have to settle his own problems with the merchant, but the criminal action will be dropped. And, Louis will be able to proceed against the bank for recovery of the damages he might have suffered in this ordeal.

According to UCC § 4-402, the bank is liable to its customer for any damages proximately caused by a wrongful dishonor of the customer's check, although damages are limited to actual damages proved by the customer. The damages expressly covered in the section include the following:

1. Damages due to an arrest
2. Damages due to a prosecution
3. Any other consequential damages that can actually be proved

From this language, it sounds as if the customer will end up in a reasonably good position: The customer will recover the "handling fees," the interest, and any other costs paid to the merchant; the customer will recover any damages related to the arrest; and the bank will end up taking all the losses on this case. In seeking damages from the bank, however, the customer must prove that the bank's conduct was the proximate cause of the losses suffered by the customer. Such proof is often difficult. If the bank can show that the customer contributed to the loss, the bank probably will owe nothing, and the customer will collect nothing. The following hypothetical case represents the type of problem that might prevent the customer's victory.

> Bob had a balance of $120.15 in his checking account. He made a deposit of $900 on Friday, using a blank deposit slip provided by the bank. When completing the deposit slip, Bob accidentally wrote his account number incorrectly. The following Tuesday, Bob wrote a $500 check to Sam's Stereo to purchase a CD player. Sam's took the check to the bank on Wednesday, and the bank returned it unpaid due to insufficient funds. Sam's assessed Bob a $10 service charge and demanded that Bob "repurchase" the check, along with a 10 percent "collection fee." Sam's also filed criminal charges against Bob for the "hot check," and Bob was arrested. Bob paid $100 bail to get out of jail after his arrest, and he paid Sam's the $560 in cash to get the proceedings dropped. If Bob now sues the bank, he may learn a shocking lesson. Bob's negligence may have caused the loss, so the bank will not be liable. If Bob had used his own personalized, pre-encoded deposit slips, he probably would have won. Since he did not, he will possibly lose.

Sometimes the customer not only recovers for the damages proximately caused, but also recovers **exemplary damages** when it is determined that the bank wrongfully handled the customer's account, and did so either with malice or with reckless disregard for the rights of its depositor. The following case involves just such a situation.

Exemplary damages
Punitive damages; damages imposed in a case to punish the defendant.

25.1 AMERICAN BANK OF WACO v. WACO AIRMOTIVE, INC. 818 S.W.2d 163 (Tex.App.-Waco 1991)

FACTS Waco Airmotive was established in 1976, chiefly to repair aircraft components. By 1979, its main areas of operations were maintenance on airframes, flight instruction, and fuel sales. In 1979, Waco Airmotive obtained a $295,000 SBA loan from American Bank. Waco Airmotive also obtained other loans from American in 1979. These other loans were eventually combined into a single note for $18,036, due 22 May 1980. On 8 July 1980, Waco Airmotive paid the accrued interest and renewed the smaller note. The terms of the renewal allowed the bank to declare all of the company's notes due under certain specified conditions, and also provided for a waiver of notice or demand for payment prior to such an acceleration. At the time of the renewal, the bank knew that Waco Airmotive was several hundred dollars overdrawn on its checking account and also knew that the firm was seven months delinquent on its SBA loan payments, totaling $24,584. On 22 July 1980, the bank offset Waco Airmotive's checking account balance of $31,752.68 to pay the entire balance of the 8 July note, with the balance of the account being applied to the SBA loan delinquency. This led to the dishonoring of more than $15,000 in checks written by Waco Airmotive. The checking balance was subsequently applied totally to the SBA loan, and American reinstated the smaller loan balance. In December, Waco Airmotive gave the bank a new note covering the balance from the 8 July note. The bank eventually sued Waco Airmotive on the December note, and Waco Airmotive counterclaimed against the bank for wrongful offset and for malicious conduct by the bank.

ISSUES Did the bank act improperly when it offset the checking account balance of the depositor to cover the loan delinquencies? Was the conduct of the bank malicious toward its customer, and did that entitle the customer to exemplary damages?

HOLDINGS Yes to both issues, although the case was remanded for additional consideration on the amount of the exemplary damages awarded to the depositor.

REASONING American Bank received the $15,132.50 in checks issued by Waco Airmotive on Monday, 21 July 1980, and had tentatively posted these checks to the customer's account on 22 July. At that time, the bank decided to use its ability to offset to apply the checking account proceeds to the delinquent loans. Accordingly, it reversed the postings of the checks and returned them stamped "Account Closed," and then offset the entire checking account balance of Waco Airmotive against the loan balances. While

25.1 AMERICAN BANK OF WACO v. WACO AIRMOTIVE, INC. *(cont.)* 818 S.W.2d 163 (Tex.App.-Waco 1991)

a bank has the right to offset customer accounts against mature or past-due debts, it must do so in good faith. Here the bank had granted Waco Airmotive a new loan on 8 July, and then two weeks later used its power to offset to effectively close the customer's account, and in so doing it dishonored more than $15,000 in checks issued by the customer. The jury at trial felt that the bank had not acted in good faith in accelerating the loans and using the offset provision a mere two weeks later, thus the dishonored checks were wrongfully dishonored. The dishonored checks had been posted, and these postings were then reversed by the bank. This conduct caused Waco Airmotive to lose credit, and the jury awarded $25,000 in damages for this loss. The jury also found that the bank acted in a "willful, wanton, or malicious" manner in its handling of the account, and awarded exemplary damages of $500,000 to Waco Airmotive. [This amount was challenged as excessive and unconstitutional, and the case was remanded for a review of the amount of exemplary damages.]

BUSINESS CONSIDERATIONS Banks very commonly retain a right of set-off with a customer's checking account when that customer also has a loan with the bank. How should such a right be negotiated in the loan agreement so that the interests of both parties are adequately protected?

ETHICAL CONSIDERATIONS Is it ethical for a bank to use its right of set-off to force a customer to make up arrearages for payments that have been missed or that are late? What should be the responsibility of the bank as far as notifying the customer prior to exercising the right of set-off?

The customer also has a right to issue stop-payment orders to the bank. If done properly, the bank must obey this order to stop payment, or it will face liability to the customer for any damages caused by disobeying the order. To be effective and to be properly made, the order must be given to the bank in a reasonable manner. In other words, the bank must receive a complete description of the check (number, payee, amount, date, reason) with enough "lead time" to allow the bank to react to the order. A minimum of a few hours is normally required, but it may take as long as a full banking day to get the word out to the bank's various branch offices.

The customer can give either an oral or a written stop-payment order. If made orally, the order is valid for 14 calendar days. After 14 days, the stop-payment order expires unless it has been put in writing. A written order is good for six months, and it can be renewed for additional six-month periods. Of course, every renewal will entail another service charge.

If the customer properly gives the bank a stop-payment order, and the bank pays the check despite the order, the customer may be able to collect damages from the bank. To do so, the customer will have to prove that he or she suffered damages because the check was paid. To prove this, he or she will have to show that the presenter could not have collected from him or her (the customer) if payment had been stopped as ordered. If the customer would have lost a case to the presenter, he or she will not be able to collect any damages from the bank for paying the check despite the stop-payment order. If payment is stopped by the bank, the drawer may be sued by the holder in an effort to recover his or her money.

In the following case, a payee bank sued a drawer bank for wrongful dishonor of a cashier's check. Although not technically involving a stop-payment order, some of the principles from stop-payment orders as they relate to cashier's checks were applied by the court in reaching its decision.

25.2 BANK ONE, MERRILLVILLE v. NORTHERN TRUST BANK/DUPAGE

775 F.Supp. 266 (N.D.Ill 1991)

FACTS On or before 7 June 1990, Sakoff wrote a check for $98,581.40 (the Sakoff check) on its account at Northern, payable to the order of Zaragoza. Zaragoza deposited the Sakoff check in its account at Bank One on 7 June 1990. Bank One sent the Sakoff check to Northern for payment. On 13 June 1990, it was returned to Bank One, because the funds in Sakoff's account were insufficient to cover the amount of the Sakoff check.

Dykstra, a Bank One employee, telephoned Northern upon receiving the returned Sakoff check on 13 June, and was told that Sakoff's account did contain sufficient funds to cover the check. On the same day, Dykstra drove to Northern's offices and exchanged the Sakoff check for a Northern cashier's check for $98,581.40. When Bank One sent the cashier's check through the Federal Reserve Bank to Northern for payment, however, Northern refused to honor the check.

The reasons for Northern's refusal to pay relate to another check (the Zaragoza check), drawn on Zaragoza's account at Bank One, for $103,200, which Zaragoza presumably transferred to Sakoff at about the same time Zaragoza received the Sakoff check for $98,581.40. At some point before 12 June 1990, Sakoff deposited Zaragoza's check into Sakoff's account at Northern. Northern then sent the Zaragoza check to Bank One for collection. Bank One received the check on 12 June but, on 13 June, issued notice to Northern, through the Federal Reserve Bank, that it was dishonoring the Zaragoza check, because of insufficient funds in Zaragoza's account. This notice did not reach Northern until after Dykstra had obtained the cashier's check. As a result of Bank One's rejection of the Sakoff check, the funds in Sakoff's account were insufficient to cover the Sakoff check for which Northern had issued its cashier's check.

ISSUE Could Northern dishonor the cashier's check that it had issued to Bank One?

HOLDING No. A bank cannot dishonor a cashier's check it has issued, even if the cashier's check is obtained by fraud.

REASONING According to Bank One, Illinois law forbids a bank from dishonoring its cashier's checks for any reason. On the basis of this understanding of the law, Bank One contends that it is entitled to summary judgment, since any arguments Northern might raise are immaterial to the issue of wrongful dishonor. In response, Northern asserts bad faith on the part of Bank One. Northern contends that when Dykstra drove to Northern to obtain the cashier's check, he was aware that his bank was in the process of dishonoring the Zaragoza check. According to Northern, Bank One feared that its dishonor of the Zaragoza check would result in there being insufficient funds to cover the Sakoff check. This fear allegedly prompted Dykstra to hurry to Northern in order to obtain a cashier's check before Northern received notice of Bank One's dishonor. Northern contends that bad faith such as that alleged justifies a refusal to honor a cashier's check, and that the factual issue of Bank One's bad faith precludes summary judgment.

Although the Illinois [Uniform Commercial] Code does not specifically address the subject of a bank's cashier's checks, the Illinois Appellate Court interpreted the Code's application to this issue. . . . The court employed a line of analysis under the Code which led it to indorse "a rule which prohibits a bank from refusing to honor its cashier's checks." Characterizing the bank's issuance of a cashier's check as acceptance of the item, the court applied Section 4-303, which provides that a stop order on a check is ineffective after acceptance.

In the face of . . . case law which holds that a bank has no right to dishonor its cashier's check, but must instead assert its reason for nonpayment as part of its own action to recover the funds, Northern essentially argues for a "bad faith" or "fraud" exception to the general principle. Northern reasons that, while Illinois courts have held that failure of consideration is no excuse for dishonoring a cashier's check, they have never ruled that the procurer's bad faith does not provide a defense.

As previously discussed, Illinois courts view an issued cashier's check as accepted . . . and as the equivalent of cash. . . . As a consequence of the application of Illinois law to the subject of cashier's checks, Northern . . . can raise no excuse "whether or not effective under other rules of law" justifying its refusal to pay. The proper context for Northern's arguments regarding Bank One's alleged bad faith is its counterclaim rather than as a defense to Bank One's action for wrongful dishonor. Unfortunately for Northern in this case, its claim concerning the underlying transaction is not yet ripe for judgment.

Northern must therefore honor its cashier's check and seek to recover the funds in the hands of Bank One, just as it would have to do if it had paid cash. Under Illinois law, Northern assumed the risk of having to pursue litigation to recover improperly paid funds when it issued the cashier's check.

[The Illinois court and Northern cited several New York cases which held that a bank *could* issue a stop-payment order on a cashier's check if that cashier's check was obtained by fraud. The Illinois court, however, applied the majority rule to the case.]

25.2 BANK ONE, MERRILLVILLE v. NORTHERN TRUST BANK/DUPAGE (cont.) 775 F.Supp. 266 (N.D.Ill 1991)

BUSINESS CONSIDERATIONS Suppose that a business is entering into a contract with a distant buyer, and that this is the first contract between the two parties. Should the seller insist on being paid by means of a cashier's check, teller's check, or certified check? Why would this matter to the seller? Why would it matter to the buyer?

ETHICAL CONSIDERATIONS Presuming that Northern's allegations are all true, did Dykstra and Bank One act unethically by having Northern issue a cashier's check before notifying Northern that the Zaragoza check was being dishonored by Bank One? Does the exchange of large checks between Zaragoza and Sakoff raise any ethical issues?

The bank periodically must send statements to its customers. One of the changes under Revised Article 4 involves the requirements for what the bank must provide in the statement sent to the customer. The prior law required the bank to send the actual canceled checks and other items to the customer for the customer's examination and reconciliation. The revised rules allow the bank to "either return or make available to the customer the items paid or provide information in the statement of account sufficient to allow the customer reasonably to identify the items paid. The statement of account provides sufficient information if the item is described by item number, amount, and date of presentment." This change does increase the burden on the bank to some extent since the bank now must retain the actual items or maintain the capacity to produce legible copies of the items for at least seven years. It also increases the burden on the customer, and to a much greater extent. The customer now must reconcile the statement, verify signature, and notice alterations, all without actually seeing the canceled items. This means the customer *must* keep adequate and accurate records, especially his or her check register, or face the probability that he or she will not notice any unauthorized signings or material alterations in a timely manner.

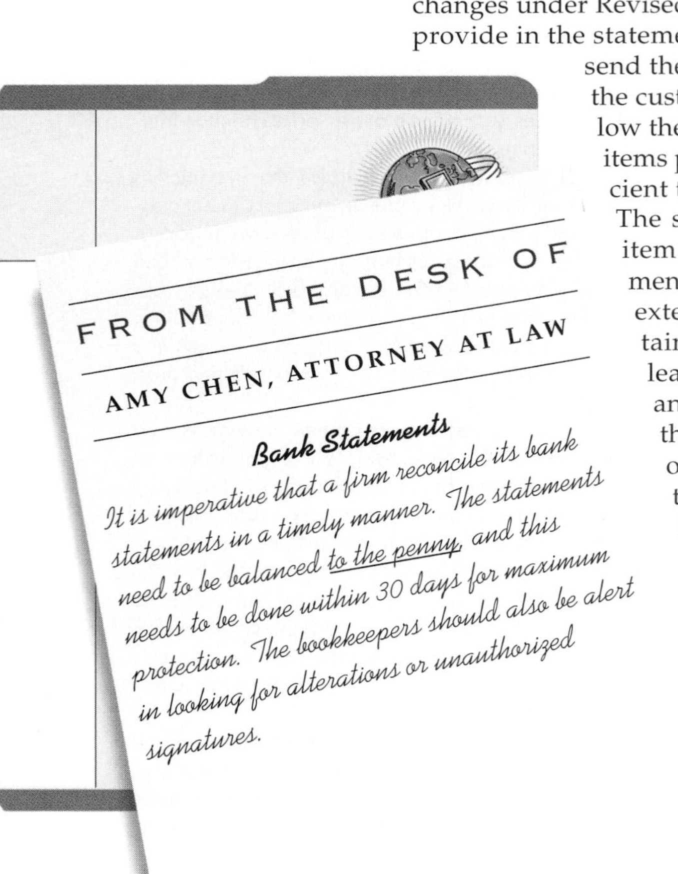

FROM THE DESK OF
AMY CHEN, ATTORNEY AT LAW
Bank Statements
It is imperative that a firm reconcile its bank statements in a timely manner. The statements need to be balanced to the penny, and this needs to be done within 30 days for maximum protection. The bookkeepers should also be alert in looking for alterations or unauthorized signatures.

The customer has a duty to examine and to reconcile the statements of account received from the bank with reasonable promptness, and must notify the bank of any unauthorized signings or alterations promptly in order to retain his or her maximum rights. A failure to act with reasonable promptness may well result in a waiver of the customer's rights in favor of the bank. The bank satisfies its duty to provide a statement to the customer by mailing it or by holding it available for the customer, if the customer so requests. The customer satisfies his or her duty by promptly and carefully examining and balancing the statement when it is received. By failing to make a reasonably prompt investigation and/or failing to notify the bank promptly of any errors or inconsistencies in the statement, the customer will lose the right to assert against the bank:

1. Any unauthorized customer signatures
2. Any material alterations of any of the checks
3. Any other unauthorized signatures or alterations made by the same person, provided that the customer had a reasonable time to examine the statement and to notify the bank of any problems or irregularities

The revision to Article 4 did extend the time period somewhat. Now the "reasonable time" available to the customer may not exceed 30 calendar days. (Under the previous rules, the customer only had 14 days to reconcile the statement and to give the bank notice.)

To complete the statement inspection duty, the customer must report any unauthorized signatures and/or any material alterations within one year of the statement date or lose the right to raise these issues. If the customer notifies the bank within 30 days of receiving the statement, he or she gets all the money back on the unauthorized signatures, and the alteration amounts back on the alterations. If notice is given to the bank after 30 days but within one year, the customer recovers the amount of the first signature or the first alteration by each signer or alterer; and the customer puts the bank on notice for any future signings or alterations. However, the customer cannot recover on any of the checks containing forgeries or alterations received by the bank between the first one and the date of notice. If notice is over one year after the statement date, the customer cannot recover anything from the bank.

25.2

RECONCILING BANK STATEMENTS

Donna and Julio reconcile the bank statements received by the firm, normally, within a day or two of receipt. However, when the next statement arrives, both Donna and Julio will be out of town. They are scheduled to attend a professional conference in Orlando, and they plan to spend an additional week "seeing the sights" while they are there. Dan is concerned that their absence will cause an undue delay in reconciling the statement, but he does not want to interfere with their plans if there is no cause for concern. He asks your advice. What will you tell him?

BUSINESS CONSIDERATIONS Reconciling bank statements is not always an enjoyable task. How should a business view the task of statement reconciliation? Should statements be reconciled immediately? Should they balance "to the penny," or is close good enough? Who should have the responsibility for this job?

ETHICAL CONSIDERATIONS Suppose the bank has made an error on a statement of account, posting a check for $19 when it should have been posted for $91. Should the customer tell the bank, or should the customer keep the $72 "profit" from this transaction? Would your answer be different if the error was made the other way? If so, how can this be reconciled ethically? When does an error become significant enough that the bank should be notified of the error?

FINANCE/MANAGEMENT

THE BANK: RIGHTS AND DUTIES

Since the bank is the agent of the customer, it must obey any lawful orders of the customer. This duty to obey gives the bank a very important right: It can charge to the customer's account any item that is properly payable from the customer's account. The bank can pay the check even if payment creates an overdraft. The bank can also pay a check that was incomplete when issued and then completed by some later holder. The bank may even know that a holder completed the check and still pay it as completed. The only exception is when the bank has notice that the completion was improper or was done in bad faith.

In accordance with the rules that govern timely presentment, the bank may refuse to honor any **stale checks**. A *stale check* is one that is more than six months old

Stale checks
Checks a bank may dishonor due to their age (over six months old) without regard to the drawer's account balance.

and has not been certified. If the bank dishonors a stale check, it is not liable to the customer for any damages. Alternatively, the bank may, at its option, honor a stale check. Again, the bank will not be liable for any damages suffered by the customer if it honors the check in good faith. It should be remembered that a written stop-payment is good for six months, the period after which a check becomes stale. Suppose a customer issues a written stop-payment order. Six months elapse without the check ever being presented, and the customer does not renew the stop-payment order. The payee now presents the check to the bank. The check is stale. A stop-payment order had been in effect on that check. The bank honors the check. If the bank can prove it acted in good faith, it will face no liability for its payment of the stale check the customer once tried to stop.

Under normal agency rules, if the principal dies or becomes incompetent, the agency terminates by operation of law. After this termination, if the agent continues to perform its agency duties, the agent becomes personally liable, and the principal has no liability. This rule would be impractical with negotiable instruments, so the UCC expressly changed it. As applied to the bank–customer relationship, agencies do not automatically end at the instant of the principal's death or incompetence. Under § 4-405(1), the bank is fully authorized to perform its banking functions on the account of a customer who has died or has become incompetent until the bank knows of the occurrence and has had adequate time to react to the news. Even if the bank knows of the customer's death, its power to act is not terminated. Section 4-405(2) permits the bank to continue to honor checks drawn on the account for 10 days after the date of a death unless a stop-payment is placed on the account by an interested party.

The following case involves the right of a bank to pay checks drawn on an account after the customer died, even though the signature of the deceased did not appear on the signature card of the account in question.

25.3 LIETZMAN v. RUIDOSO STATE BANK — 827 P.2d 1294 (N.M. 1992)

FACTS Robert Lietzman and his wife Carolyn were the owners of the O-Bar-O ranch, where they lived. The Lietzmans planned to develop some of their land, and formed the O-Bar-O Property Development Company for this reason. Heckman, a business associate of Robert Lietzman, was hired by the O-Bar-O ranch to manage the property development deal. Heckman was the only person whose signature appeared on the signature card of the O-Bar-O Property Development Company. When Robert Lietzman died, Heckman wrote checks transferring the funds on deposit in the O-Bar-O Property Development account to one of his other accounts. Carolyn Lietzman objected to this transfer, arguing that the funds on deposit belonged to her and to her husband, and also alleging that the bank had a fiduciary duty to the Lietzmans not to allow the transfer of the funds. She and the representative of her husband's estate sued the bank to recover the funds so transferred, and the bank denied liability.

ISSUE Did the bank owe a duty to Ms. Lietzman on this account, notwithstanding the fact that neither her name nor her husband's name appeared on the account in question?

HOLDING Yes. There was sufficient evidence to show that the Lietzmans were customers of the account, broadly speaking, despite the lack of either of their signatures on the account's signature card.

REASONING There was a controversy as to the type of account involved in this case. It was not a corporate account, nor was it a partnership account, nor was it a regular individual business account. Under such circumstances, the court felt that a variety of factors had to be examined to determine who the customer was on the account. These factors included not only the name on the account, but also the circumstances surrounding the opening of the

25.3 LIETZMAN v. RUIDOSO STATE BANK *(cont.)* **827 P.2d 1294 (N.M. 1992)**

account, who controlled the account, and the beneficial interests of any persons affected by the account. In this case, while neither Robert nor Carolyn Lietzman was a signatory on the account, the bank was aware of the interest of the Lietzmans in the account (based to a significant extent on the similarity in name between the ranch and the development company), so the bank was aware of at least the beneficial rights of the Lietzmans in the account. As such, there was evidence that the Lietzmans were customers of the bank with regard to the account, so the bank owed a duty to Carolyn Lietzman regarding the funds in the account following the death of her husband. As such, the bank had a duty not to honor checks drawn on the account after the bank learned of the death of the customer.

BUSINESS CONSIDERATIONS What business reasons exist for allowing a bank to continue to honor checks drawn by one of its customers following the bank's notice of the death of the customer? Does it make more sense, from a business perspective, to allow the bank to continue to honor such checks or to force the bank to dishonor any checks on the death of a customer?

ETHICAL CONSIDERATIONS From an ethical perspective, is it better to allow a bank to honor checks drawn by a customer for a reasonable time after the bank learns of the death, or would it be better to "freeze" the account on the death of the customer, forcing the estate to take care of any checks or obligations dishonored due to the "freezing" of the account at the death of the customer?

Sometimes banks make mistakes. A bank may honor an instrument that had a stop-payment order covering it, or it may do something else that allows the customer to recover damages from the bank. When this happens, the bank has some protection: It is entitled to subrogation. *Subrogation* means the bank is given the rights that some other parties could have raised if the bank had not made improper payment. UCC § 4-407 gives the bank three different sets of rights to assert through subrogation:

1. The rights of a holder in due course against the maker or drawer
2. The rights of the payee or any other holder against the maker or drawer
3. The rights of the drawer or maker against the payee or any other holders

Thus, the bank holds the rights of both sides and of every interested party. From this buffet of rights, the bank can select the set of rights that gives it the greatest likelihood of winning the case.

The bank has the right to enforce the terms of its contract with the customer. Among other things, this right allows the bank to impose certain service charges and fees against many of its customers each month. The bank may be able to collect a specific amount every month, it may be able to collect a specific amount in any month the customer's account balance falls below a certain amount, or it may be able to charge a specific amount for every check written by the customer. The bank will impose a service charge for handling a stop-payment order. Likewise, it may charge a customer when it pays an overdraft or when it dishonors a check, if honoring it would have created an overdraft. These service charges are specified in the contract the customer agreed to when the signature card was signed.

The duties of the bank are simple. The bank is required to honor the terms and conditions of its contract. It is required to obey the rules of agency and to act in good faith in a commercially reasonable manner.

In the following case, the bank's duty to act in good faith and to obey reasonable commercial standards was challenged by a customer. Note the court's deference to the bank and its literal interpretation of the bank's duties.

25.4 M.G. SALES, INC. v. CHEMICAL BANK

554 N.Y.S.2d 863 (A.D. Dept. 1990)

FACTS In November 1991, Marc Gardner, the president of the plaintiff corporation, M.G. Sales, Inc., made out two checks on its account at Chemical Bank. The checks were both in the amount of $6,000 and were payable to, signed and indorsed by Gardner. Gardner did not remember whether or not he dated the checks. Apparently, he lost both checks. Consequently, on 16 November 1981, he went to defendant Chemical Bank and obtained two stop-payment orders, which gave 10 November 1981 as the date of the checks. The stop-payment orders were by their terms valid for a period of six months. Gardner did not obtain renewals of the stop-payment orders.

In January and February 1983, Leon Fried, the third-party defendant, deposited the checks in his account at another branch of Chemical Bank, and Chemical paid the proceeds of the checks to him.

Plaintiff commenced this action against Chemical Bank, one of its officers, and the bank tellers who accepted the checks. The first two causes of action allege that Chemical Bank violated the stop-payment orders, in derogation of its fiduciary obligation, and failed to comply with the Uniform Commercial Code and the applicable banking laws and rules. . . . The IAS court denied various motions by the parties seeking summary judgment. It found that Gardner signed and endorsed the undated checks, then lost them, and failed to renew the stop-payment order. It found, further, that the fact that the checks were torn and tattered, and that the date on one of them appeared to be altered, did not . . . impair the acceptability of an otherwise valid check. However, the court concluded that there was a question of fact, the allegation that the bank did not accept double-indorsed checks for deposit.

ISSUES Did the bank act improperly in failing to stop payment on the two checks? Did the bank act in good faith, and consistently with its commercial practices, in accepting the two checks indorsed by Fried?

HOLDINGS No. The stop-payment orders had expired at the time the checks were presented. Yes. The bank acted in good faith and in a manner consistent with its internal commercial practices and the provisions of the UCC in its handling of the two checks.

REASONING Plaintiff's complaint alleges essentially that the defendant bank failed to comply with the written stop-payment orders signed by Gardner on 16 November 1981, and failed to follow the bank's own directive not to accept double-indorsed checks. However, the complaint should have been dismissed insofar as it alleged that the bank violated or failed to honor the stop-payment orders. The record conclusively establishes that both stop-payment orders were signed on 16 November 1981, and that by their terms they were effective for six months unless renewed in writing. Further, Gardner failed to renew the stop-payment orders and the checks were presented to the bank after the expiration of the stop-payment orders. Since no stop-payment directive was in effect when the checks were presented to the bank, no violation of these orders occurred. Any claim by plaintiff that a normal representation was made that no renewal was necessary is completely negated by the contrary provisions of the written stop-payment orders. . . .

[The] UCC provides "An indorsement in blank specifies no particular indorsee and may consist of a mere signature. An instrument payable to order and indorsed in blank becomes payable to bearer and may be negotiated by delivery alone until specially indorsed." Thus the two checks were bearer paper when lost by Mr. Gardner, as they were signed, payable to, and indorsed in blank by him. Gardner stated also that the checks were undated when he lost them. . . . While the IAS court noted that the checks were torn and it appeared that the date on one check was altered, since it was admitted by the plaintiff that the checks were undated, the date could properly have been assumed to have been correct. Moreover, if those dates were viewed as correct, neither check would have appeared stale when presented. . . . The IAS court found a question of fact existed as to whether the bank paid the checks in violation of its own directive against acceptance of double-indorsed checks. However, the only evidence presented that such a policy existed was a sign from an unidentified Chemical Bank branch stating that the bank did not accept double-indorsed checks, without any indication as to when the sign was posted or obtained. Chemical, however, submitted the affidavit of an officer responsible for the branch that accepted the checks. He stated that the bank's policy limiting the acceptance of double-indorsed checks for deposit commenced in 1984, and that signs to that effect were put up in August 1984. . . . Further, as the UCC contains no prohibition against the acceptance of double-indorsed checks, it was no error for the bank to accept the checks here in question.

BUSINESS CONSIDERATIONS The checks deposited by Fried in this case were described as "torn and tattered," and the date on at least one of the checks appeared to have been altered. Should *any* business—particularly a bank—accept such checks without taking some

25.4 M.G. SALES, INC. v. CHEMICAL BANK *(cont.)* 554 N.Y.S.2d 863 (A.D. Dept. 1990)

positive steps to verify the checks with the drawer? Is it a good business practice to accept "torn and tattered" checks from an apparent holder through a blank indorsement?

ETHICAL CONSIDERATIONS Why should a stop-payment order expire at the end of six months? Is there some ethical reason for expecting the bank to stop payment on a check, without regard to time, after a written order is placed (especially since the customer is likely to be assessed a significant service charge)?

SPECIAL PROBLEMS

Two areas deserve further mention: certified checks and unauthorized signatures.

Certified Checks

A *certified check* is one that has already been accepted by the drawee bank. In other words, the bank has assumed primary liability and agreed to pay the check on a later presentment. Certification can be done at the request of the drawer or of any holder. A refusal by the bank to certify the check is not a dishonor. How does certification occur? Either the drawer or a holder presents the check to the bank and requests certification. If the bank agrees to certify, it follows certain steps. First, it charges the account of the customer and credits its own "Certified Check Account." Thus, the money is held by the bank in the bank's own account, and the customer has already "paid" the amount of the check. Second, the bank punches a hole in the encoded account number of the check to ensure that the check will not be paid a second time on a later presentment. Third, a stamp is made on the face of the check, and the terms of the certification are written into the stamped form.

If the drawer seeks and receives the certification, the drawer remains secondarily liable until final payment. However, if a holder seeks and receives the certification, the drawer and all prior endorsers are discharged from liability.

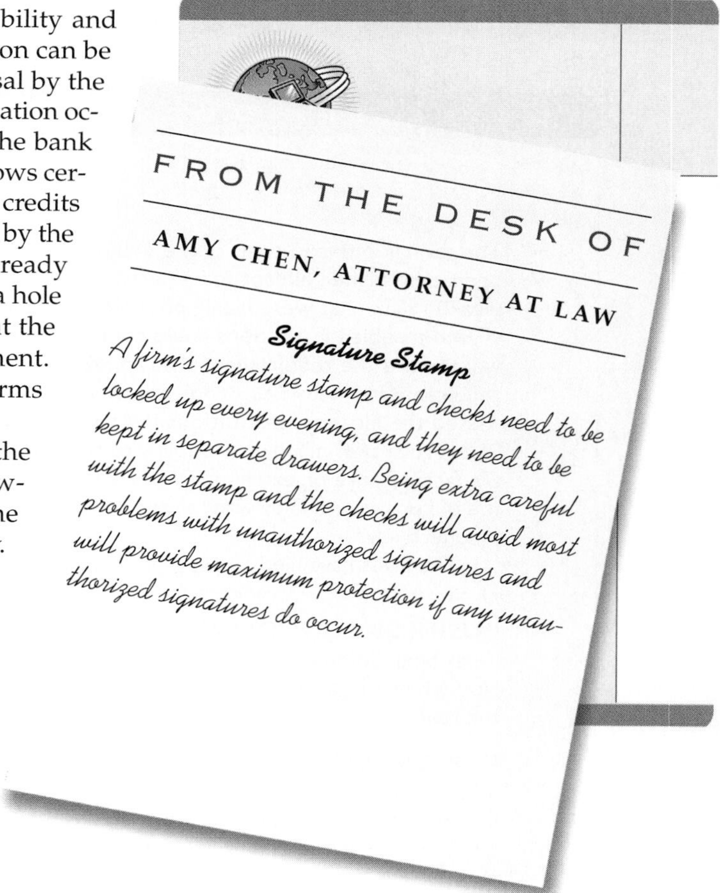

FROM THE DESK OF
AMY CHEN, ATTORNEY AT LAW
Signature Stamp
A firm's signature stamp and checks need to be locked up every evening, and they need to be kept in separate drawers. Being extra careful with the stamp and the checks will avoid most problems with unauthorized signatures and will provide maximum protection if any unauthorized signatures do occur.

Unauthorized Signatures

Under UCC § 1-201(43), an *unauthorized signature* is one made without any authority, express or implied, and it includes a forgery. An unauthorized signature is wholly inoperative against the person whose name was signed unless that person later ratifies the signing. It cannot be used to impose liability on the purported signer. However, in some circumstances, an unauthorized and unratified signature is still binding on the purported signer. According to § 3-406, if a person contributes to the unauthorized signing through negligence, he or she will be held liable to any good faith holder of the instrument.

Many businesses "sign" checks by means of a stamp. The business may leave the stamp and its checks in a place where they are easily reached by a nonauthorized person (most likely a thief). Such conduct on the part of the business is negligent, and the negligence may lead to the unauthorized "signing." In such circumstances, the business may not later assert the defense that the signing was unauthorized if the holder is a holder in good faith. Notice that the holder does not have to be a holder in due course; the fact that the holder is in good faith is sufficient. The negligence of the wronged party is the key: The wronged party must be negligent, and the negligence must cause the loss. Otherwise, the unauthorized signature cannot be used against the person whose name was signed.

FUNDS TRANSFERS

Changes in banking laws, the growth of international business, and technology have affected the banking industry to a significant extent over the last quarter of the twentieth century. The savings and loan industry crisis of the 1980s led to numerous changes in banking regulations. International trade frequently requires that large

YOU BE THE JUDGE

The Savings and Loan Crisis

The savings and loan crisis of the 1980s cost U.S. taxpayers an estimated $130 billion. The bill would have been even higher, except for a decision by the government intended to allow strong S&Ls to purchase weaker S&Ls that were facing possible failure. In the 1980s the government decided that S&Ls that purchased troubled institutions could count the losses of insolvent S&Ls as goodwill and to count that goodwill toward the requirement that an S&L keep a certain amount of capital on hand to meet its reserve requirements. Many S&Ls took advantage of this rule to purchase other S&Ls. Then, in 1989, Congress passed the Financial Institutions Reform, Recovery, and Enforcement Act (FIRREA). FIRREA overhauled S&L regulations, including the ability to treat the paper losses as goodwill. As a result, many S&Ls claim they are facing failure or extremely high costs under the new provisions, when they were turning profits under the old provisions. They want to see the old rules stay in place, and ask that FIRREA should only be applied prospectively.[1]

The S&Ls have filed suit in *your* court. How will you decide this case?

BUSINESS CONSIDERATIONS Should a business be granted some sort of special exemption when it has been complying with a law in good faith, and then the law changes? Should there be a "phase-in" period when a legal change is likely to have significant impact on businesses that have been complying with the law?

ETHICAL CONSIDERATIONS Is it ethical for the government to grant special rights to an industry in order to further governmental interests or to avoid a crisis, and then to change those rights once the interest has been satisfied or the crisis has passed?

SOURCE: Aaron Zitner (*The Boston Globe*), *The Denver Post*, 2 July 1996, p. C1.

amounts of money be transferred from one nation to another quickly. Technology has reduced the need for personnel, and made automated banking much simpler. Each of these changes has moved banking ahead, while many of the banking regulations have lagged behind. However, the distance between banking practice and banking regulation is narrowing.

Electronic Funds Transfers

Recent technological advances have provided banking with a new method of doing business and with a new type of service. This new method of doing business is the electronic funds transfer (EFT), which allows for computerization of checking accounts and for faster (theoretically), more accurate banking transactions.

The Electronic Funds Transfer Act, which became effective in 1980, provides the basic legal framework for this method of doing business. This method of financial dealing eventually may make the current checking or drafting account obsolete, or nearly so, due to the delays and expenses of handling checks or drafts when compared to electronic banking.

Four methods of EFTs have become widely used. One method is the point-of-sale (POS) terminal and the "debit" card. In a POS transaction, the customer presents the merchant with a debit card, the merchant imprints the card and has the customer sign, and the funds are transferred from the customer's account to the merchant's account. The transaction is similar in format to the use of a credit card, but there should be no delay in receiving the money from the sale for the merchant. Unfortunately, the use of a POS transaction is often no faster or safer for the merchant than the use of a check. In most parts of the country, the POS transaction must be processed through a clearinghouse in the same manner as a check, making the transfer of funds to the merchant no faster than it would be with a check. In addition, the cost is slightly higher for a POS transaction than for a check when a clearinghouse is involved.

A second, and more familiar, method is the use of automated teller machine (ATM) transfers. The bank customer inserts his or her card in the machine, enters his or her personal identification number (PIN), and selects a transaction. The customer can make a deposit, a withdrawal, a transfer from one account to another, a payment, or a number of other banking transactions.

If the bank is a participant in a network, the customer may be able to authorize payments to predetermined accounts by phone. Here, the customer calls the bank and, using the buttons on a touch-tone phone, can designate preselected "payees" who will be paid an amount determined by punching in the amount of the "electronic check" so that the funds are automatically transferred.

Finally, there are preauthorized automatic payments and preauthorized direct deposits. In both cases, regular amounts are deducted from, or added to, the customer's account balance on designated dates to ensure that payment (or credit) is received without any worries about forgetting to send in the check or drive to the bank to make the deposit.

In general, a consumer who uses EFTs has the same type of rights and duties as a consumer who has a checking or drafting account with a financial institution. For example, a customer can place a stop-payment order on a preauthorized payment by notifying the bank orally or in writing at least three days prior to the date for preauthorized payment. A consumer can recover damages from a financial institution for failure to make EFT payments as instructed, provided the consumer has sufficient funds on deposit.

Numerous protections also exist for the consumer who is using EFTs. For example, consumer liability is limited in case of unauthorized use of an account, provided the consumer gives proper and timely notice to the bank. The bank has the burden of proof to establish either that the use was in fact authorized or that the customer did not give proper and/or timely notice.

As the public becomes more familiar and more comfortable with EFTs, the use of this form of money management will grow and develop. As that happens, the use of checks will begin to decline. The decline will be gradual at first, but by the turn of the century, we may do virtually all our banking electronically.

Article 4A: Funds Transfers

Bank customers have long had a need for a particular type of funds transfer, the wire transfer. However, this type of funds transfer has not been uniformly regulated until very recently. Now the UCC has proposed Article 4A to provide uniform coverage in the area of funds transfers within the United States. As of 1993, Article 4A had been adopted by 43 states and the District of Columbia. The remaining seven states are expected to adopt the article shortly.

To avoid confusion, Article 4A specifically excludes coverage in any area already governed by the Electronic Funds Transfer Act. Thus, the UCC will provide state coverage for funds transfers, but will defer to federal regulation of EFTs.

The following case provides an interpretation of the provisions of Article 4A. This was a case of first impression in Wisconsin, and relied heavily on a prior Article 4A case from New York. Notice how the court justifies its decision to follow the New York precedent.

25.5 GENERAL ELECTRIC CAPITAL CORP. v. CENTRAL BANK — 49 F.3d280 (7th Cir. 1995)

FACTS Duchow's Marine, Inc., financed its inventory of boats with a loan from General Electric Capital Corporation (GECC), which took a security interest in the boats and the proceeds from their sale. The security interest was perfected under Wisconsin law. Duchow's Marine and its owner Roger Duchow (collectively Duchow) promised to deposit proceeds into an account from which they could be disbursed only on GECC's signature. The name on this account at Central Bank was "Duchow Marine, Inc. GE Escrow Account." Following the parties' convention, we call this the blocked account. Duchow maintained a separate account at Central Bank for revenues from other sources; we call this the regular account. In November 1990, Duchow sold a yacht to Gray Eagle, Inc., and directed the customer to remit $215,370 of the purchase price to the regular account. By issuing this instruction, Duchow set out to defraud GECC.

Gray Eagle instructed its bank to make a wire transfer, giving it the number of Duchow's regular account. Gray Eagle's bank, which we call the "originator's bank" following the convention of . . . Article 4A, asked Banker's Bank of Madison, Wisconsin, to make the transfer on its behalf. The originator's bank performed correctly. As an intermediary bank, Banker's Bank should have relayed the payment order exactly. It didn't. Banker's Bank made the transfer by crediting Central Bank's account at Banker's Bank, but it bobtailed the instructions. Banker's Bank told Central Bank (which the UCC calls the "beneficiary's bank") that the credit was for Duchow's benefit. That's all: the payment order omitted account identification. A clerk at Central Bank routed the funds to the first account she found bearing Duchow's name: the blocked account. This credit was made on 23 November 1990. Entirely by chance, Duchow's fraudulent scheme had been foiled. But not for long. Duchow, thinking the funds were in the regular account, promptly wrote a check in an effort to spirit them away. The check appeared on the overdrawn-accounts list of 29 November. When contacted, Roger Duchow asserted that the money belonged in the regular account. Central Bank inquired of Banker's Bank, which on 30 November relayed the full payment order, including the number of Duchow's regular account. Without notifying GECC, Central Bank then

25.5 GENERAL ELECTRIC CAPITAL CORP. v. CENTRAL BANK *(cont.)* **49 F.3d280 (7th Cir. 1995)**

reversed the credit to the blocked account, credited Duchow's regular account, and paid the check. When it discovered what had happened, GECC filed this diversity action seeking to hold Central Bank liable for conversion of its funds. Central Bank impleaded Duchow, but no one believes that he or his firm is good for the money; Duchow has not participated in this case. The parties agree that Wisconsin supplies the applicable law.

ISSUE Did Central Bank convert funds that properly should have been subject to the control of GECC?

HOLDING Yes. Once Central Bank had deposited the funds into the "blocked account" GECC acquired rights to those funds, and the subsequent release of the funds without GECC's permission was a conversion.

REASONING That the money removed from the blocked account belonged to GECC there can be no doubt. . . . Central Bank does not deny that GECC has established the ordinary elements of conversion so much as it asserts a bankers' privilege: a beneficiary's bank following the payment order of an intermediary bank in a funds transfer should be free from liability, Central Bank insists. We may assume that this is so if the beneficiary's bank follows the original payment order. GECC does not contend that it could recover from any of the three banks if all three had slavishly followed a set of instructions that Gray Eagle gave its bank, even though Duchow devised these instructions to cheat GECC. Central Bank could not be thought to "convert" funds over which it never had a right of control. . . . Once the funds landed in the blocked account, however, Central Bank had to make a nonclerical decision. Must it move them? *Could* it move them? By accepting the payment order, Central Bank incurred an obligation to credit the funds to Duchow. As it had done exactly that, crediting an account where they discharged one of Duchow's debts, Duchow had no legitimate complaint—certainly not given GECC's security interest in the proceeds. No rule of law obliged Central Bank to change the credit. Banker's Bank fouled up and may have been liable to Gray Eagle; Central Bank was in the clear. . . . Seven days had passed, and credits in the banking system often become irrevocable in less time. Think of the "midnight deadline" for checks. . . . Removing funds from an account bearing the title "escrow" calls for the exercise of considerable discretion.

Some alterations in credits to accounts are essentially risk-free no matter what the rules of banking law say. . . . If Central Bank had credited the Duchow–GECC blocked account with $500,000 meant for Acme Widget Corp., the bank could have reversed the bookkeeping blunder without GECC's consent. . . . Things are dicier when the bank credits the account of someone who has a legitimate claim to the funds. If GECC had withdrawn the money on the fifth day, Central Bank could not have compelled it to make restitution, because GECC's security interest gave it the legal rights to the funds. . . . If GECC's interest is strong enough to resist a suit for restitution if it gets to the money first, is it not strong enough to support a suit for conversion if the bank drains the account?

During 1990, when the events of this case took place, the right way to approach the last question we have posed was obscure. . . . The new Article 4A was enacted in Wisconsin in 1991, after these events. Yet because the highest court of New York has used the provisions of Article 4A to illuminate the law preceding its enactment . . . , the parties agree that the Supreme Court of Wisconsin would do likewise. We accept this understanding and turn to Article 4A. . . . Whether a credit properly made after acceptance by the beneficiary's bank may be reversed is a subject addressed almost in passing by Section 4A-303, which principally concerns a receiving bank's obligation, to the sender, to execute a payment order. . . . By issuing a revised payment order with the number of Duchow's regular account, Banker's Bank attempted to recoup from GECC and make the funds available to Duchow personally. . . . If the law permitted this step, Central Bank is off the hook without needing its own shelter in Article 4A. If it did not, Central Bank is liable for conversion. . . . The New York courts have followed the "discharge for value" rule found in the *Restatement of Restitution*. . . . One of Wisconsin's options is to follow New York law in order to promote national uniformity in the treatment of funds transfers. Wisconsin enacted Article 4A of the UCC for this very reason. . . . Funds transfers cross state and national borders, and because New York is the nation's (and the world's) largest financial center, many transfers go through banks in New York. Uniform, known law governing these transactions . . . enables banks to tailor their practices accordingly, and it produces lower costs for all customers. . . . We believe that Wisconsin would adopt the discharge for value rule. . . .

On reading this, the president of Central Bank may be tempted to tear out his hair in exasperation. In exchange for the few dollars it collects for a wire transfer, how can the bank have accepted such a risk? he may well wonder. . . . The answer is that it ought not lead to liability for the beneficiary's bank—and it would not have left Central Bank holding the bag had it taken precautions after learning of the error. . . . Before reversing the credit in response to Duchow's request, Central Bank could have sought an indemnity agreement from Banker's Bank, and perhaps from

25.5 GENERAL ELECTRIC CAPITAL CORP. v. CENTRAL BANK *(cont.)* 49 F.3d280 (7th Cir. 1995)

Duchow as well. This is what happened in *Banque Worms*, where a chain of indemnities brought the costs of the error home to the responsible party. . . . Even the absence of an indemnity does not necessarily leave Central Bank with the loss. On paying GECC, Central Bank will be **subrogated** to all of GECC's rights against Duchow. . . . It is, after all, Central Bank's customer Duchow who devised this scam and made off with the money, and it was Banker's Bank's error that put Central Bank in this pickle. Central Bank must pay GECC; whether Central Bank may be made whole remains to be seen.

BUSINESS CONSIDERATIONS What steps should a beneficiary's bank take in a wire transfer when there is a report that the funds were erroneously credited to the wrong account, and that report is more than one week after the funds were originally received by the beneficiary's bank?

ETHICAL CONSIDERATIONS Is it fair to let the intermediary bank off the hook when its error (failing to relay the entire wire transfer order) was a significant factor in the resulting misallocation of the funds? Should there be some allocation of the loss to the intermediary on ethical grounds?

http: // **RESOURCES FOR BUSINESS LAW STUDENTS**

NAME	RESOURCES	WEB ADDRESS
Uniform Commercial Code (UCC), Article 4, Bank Deposits and Collections	The Legal Information Institute (LII), maintained by the Cornell Law School, provides a hypertext and searchable version of UCC Article 4, Bank Deposits and Collections. LII also maintains links to Article 4 as adopted by particular states and to proposed revisions.	http://www.law.cornell.edu/ucc/4/overview.html
Electronic Funds Transfer Act—15 USC § 1693	LII provides a hypertext and searchable version of 15 USC § 1693, popularly known as the Electronic Funds Transfer Act.	http://www.law.cornell.edu/uscode/15/78dd-2.html
Uniform Commercial Code Article 4A, Funds Transfer	LII provides a hypertext and searchable version of Article 4A, Funds Transfer.	http://www.law.cornell.edu/ucc/4A/overview.html

Subrogated
Placed in the position of another; given the rights that another person previously held.

SUMMARY

The most frequently used negotiable instrument is the check. As a result, special attention must be paid to the bank–customer relationship. When a customer opens a checking account, a multirole relationship is created. The bank and the customer have a contract, they are involved in an agency, they have a debtor–creditor relationship, and they are controlled by Article 4 of the UCC.

Customers have a duty to exercise due care in their dealings with their accounts. They are required to inspect their statements carefully and promptly for any irregularities, alterations, or unauthorized signings. They may also issue stop-payment orders to the bank. Since the bank is the agent of its customers, it is obligated to obey such orders.

The bank is required to abide by the terms of its contract with the customer. It must pay properly drawn checks if the customer has sufficient funds, and it must act in good faith.

Certified checks and unauthorized signatures can present special problems. A certified check is one that has been accepted by the bank and then circulated through the normal channels of commerce. Unauthorized signings are sometimes caused by the negligence of the customer; in such a case, the bank is not liable for honoring the unauthorized signing.

Credit unions have become actively involved in the business of providing accounts to customers. Credit union checking accounts have become a common alternative to the traditional checking accounts offered by banks. The credit unions tend to have lower minimum balance requirements and lower fees and charges for their credit union members who elect to open checking accounts.

Funds transfers are the "wave of the future" for banking and for businesses. There are two major areas of funds transfers: electronic funds transfers, governed by the Electronic Funds Transfer Act; and funds (wire) transfers, governed by Article 4A of the UCC. By using the capacity and the speed of computers and by eliminating the paper required for traditional checking accounts, funds can be moved more quickly, more accurately, and more efficiently than is possible with checking accounts. This developmental area will continue to grow and to spread over the next several years.

Discussion Questions

1. Where do the terms and conditions of the contract between the bank and the customer originate? How many different sources are likely to affect this contract?
2. What is a "stop-payment" order? Why must a bank obey a customer's order to "stop payment" on a check? What should a stop-payment order include?
3. What is the bank customer's duty with respect to the bank statement sent to the customer each month? How has the customer's duty changed under revised Article 4? What should the customer do to maximize his or her protection in meeting this duty? Explain.
4. How does the duty and authority of a bank as an agent for the customer differ from the duty and authority of an agent in other circumstances when the principal dies or becomes incompetent? Why do you think this difference exists?
5. What is the bank's liability to a customer when the bank wrongfully dishonors one of the customer's instruments? What limitations are imposed on this liability?
6. Denise made a deposit at her bank on a personalized deposit slip provided by the bank. Despite the fact that she used a personalized deposit slip, her deposit was mistakenly credited to the account of another customer. She wrote a check that would have been good if the deposit had been properly credited to her account, but was not good without the deposit. As a result, the check was dishonored due to insufficient funds. What are her rights in this situation? Would your answer differ if the deposit was made on a blank deposit slip provided in the bank lobby? Why?
7. James received his bank statement 1 August. He examined the statement and discovered a forgery on 14 August. He notified the bank of the forgery on 3 September. A second forgery by the same person had been presented to the bank and honored by the bank on 2 September. What are James's rights against the bank on the second forged check? Explain fully.
8. Bob issued a check to Carl. Carl negotiated it to Dave. Dave negotiated it to Edna. Edna went to the bank seeking certification of the check. The bank refused to certify the check for Edna. Has the bank dishonored the check? What are Edna's rights against each of the parties? Why?
9. What is an electronic funds transfer? What current methods can a customer use to transfer funds electronically? What advantages, if any, are provided by EFTs over payment by negotiable instrument?
10. What is a wire transfer? How are wire transfers regulated under current U.S. law?

CASE PROBLEMS AND WRITING ASSIGNMENTS

1. Brown was the bookkeeper for Reynolds Lumber. Part of Brown's job involved the depositing of checks received by the company into the corporate account. The checks were all indorsed "For Deposit Only." However, the bank permitted the customers to make a "Less Cash" notation on the deposit slip and receive a portion of the check total back in cash. Over the years between 1962 and 1974, Brown expropriated $75,000 by use of the "Less Cash" notation on the deposit slips she took to the bank. When these expropriations were discovered, Reynolds Lumber sued the bank to recover the funds Brown had embezzled. According to Reynolds Lumber, the bank had no authority to permit the bookkeeper to take cash back on checks indorsed "For Deposit Only," so the bank had breached its duty to the customer by allowing this practice. The bank countered that it allowed all its customers this right and that it was a standard banking practice. Which side had the more persuasive argument? Who should have prevailed in this case? [See *J.W. Reynolds Lumber Co.* v. *Smackover State Bank*, 836 S.W.2d 853 (Ark. 1992).]

2. Begg issued a check payable to the order of Newwall, a subcontractor who was performing work for Begg in November, in the amount of $32,000. Subsequently, in January Begg issued a second check to Newwall, the second check allegedly being for the entire amount Begg owed Newwall, including the $32,000 from the first check. Begg also issued a stop-payment order to the drawee bank covering the first ($32,000) check. The bank honored the $32,000 check despite the stop-payment order, paying the check in November of 1988. Begg did not notice that the check had been paid until February of 1989, at which point he demanded that the bank recredit his account for the $32,000. The bank refused to do so, and Begg instituted a suit for damages. The bank moved for summary judgment, alleging that the customer breached his duty by failing to inspect his statement, and that had he done so he would not have issued the second check to the payee. Should the failure of the customer to inspect his statement, and to discover that the check had been cashed, protect the bank in this case? [See *Begg & Daigle, Inc.* v. *Chemical Bank*, 575 N.Y.S.2d 638 (Sup. 1991).]

3. Bank of America erroneously transmitted the principal of an account as well as the accrued interest on the account to Sanati by means of a wire transfer. When Bank of America realized its error, it attempted to recover the principal from Sanati, but Sanati refused to return the funds. Bank of America sued for restitution, and Sanati denied liability, asserting that since Bank of America was negligent when it transferred the money, it was not entitled to restitution. Is this argument persuasive? How should the court resolve this case under Article 4A of the UCC? [See *Bank of America* v. *Sanati*, 14 Cal.Rptr.2d 615 (Cal.App. 2d, 1992).]

4. Unbank operated a number of check-cashing facilities in the area. Dolphin operated a temporary help service for casual laborers in the region. On 5 December 1991, Dolphin issued a payroll check to Ricky Smith. Smith reported the check as lost, and Dolphin issued a replacement check to him. Dolphin also placed a stop-payment order on the "lost" check. On 15 December 1991, someone (both parties believed the person was Ricky Smith) brought the "lost" check to Unbank for cashing. Unbank checked the signature on the check against its list of signatures and then cashed the check. The check was subsequently presented to Dolphin's bank, which returned the check to Unbank stamped "Payment Stopped." Unbank then sued Dolphin for the amount of the check, alleging that it was entitled to recover since it was a holder in due course. Was Unbank an HDC and thus entitled to recover from Dolphin? [See *The Unbank Co.* v. *Dolphin Temporary Help Services, Inc.*, 485 N.W.2d 332 (Minn.App. 1992).]

5. Prior to 1976, Phariss operated a business known as Railroad Salvage Company. Phariss entered into several contracts with the Chicago, Rock Island, and Pacific Railroad to perform salvage jobs. In 1975, Phariss learned that the railroad had been placed in involuntary bankruptcy, and he filed a claim with the trustee in bankruptcy in the name of his salvage company for over $18,000. In 1976, Phariss closed his account with Security State Bank and moved out of Iowa. In 1984, Phariss contacted the railroad company in regard to his claim and was informed that the claim had been paid by check the previous year. The check, payable to the order of Railroad Salvage Company, had been endorsed "Railroad Salvage Co., Carl Eddy," and had been accepted by Security State Bank. Eddy had done business in the past under the name Independence Salvage Company. He also had a history of overdrawn checks. Phariss sued the bank and Eddy to recover the money paid by the railroad. Eddy filed for bankruptcy, and Phariss proceeded against the bank alone. Did the bank breach its duty to Phariss, a former customer, by accepting the check in question from Eddy? [See *Phariss* v. *Eddy*, 478 N.W.2d 848 (Iowa App. 1991).]

6. **BUSINESS APPLICATION CASE** The checking account Saboya maintained with Banco Santander reflected a zero balance on 18 November 1985, when Saboya simultaneously deposited $100 cash and a counterfeit cashier's check for $26,250. Two days later,

Sainz presented a check in the amount of $16,100, payable to Sainz and drawn by Saboya. Sainz was informed that the check was good and could be cashed, but Sainz requested a cashier's check instead. Sainz was then given a cashier's check by Banco Santander in exchange for the check drawn by Saboya. Sainz deposited the cashier's check in the Banco Guipuzconao, in Spain, receiving credit for 2,558,870 pesetas. On the same day, Sainz used the proceeds of the cashier's check and some other funds to purchase a 4 million peseta certificate of deposit.

When Banco Santander learned that the cashier's check deposited by Saboya was counterfeit, it stopped payment on the cashier's check it had issued to Sainz. As a result, Banco Guipuzcoano canceled the CD it had issued to Sainz, seized the original amount of the cashier's check (2,558,870 pesetas) from Sainz, and issued a new certificate of deposit for the 1,441,130 peseta difference. Sainz then sued Banco Santander for the losses he suffered due to the alleged wrongful dishonor of the cashier's check he had purchased from the bank. Who should prevail in this case? If Sainz prevails, should he be entitled to compensatory and consequential damages? [See *Sainz Gonzalez* v. *Banco de Santander-Puerto Rico,* 932 F.2d 999 (1st Cir. 1991).]

7. **ETHICS CASE** Maria Johnson was a depositor at Republic National Bank. In March 1989, she opened a checking account with the bank by depositing $59,000. From May through July she made a series of cash withdrawals from her account at the bank, eventually depleting the account balance. Unbeknownst to the bank, during this same time period Ms. Johnson's landlord was attempting to have the Department of Health and Rehabilitative Services take action to determine her competency. No action was accomplished during that period, but Ms. Johnson was adjudged incompetent by reason of organic mental syndrome in September 1989. She was 76 years of age at the time of the hearing. The guardian appointed for Ms. Johnson attempted to locate the money she had withdrawn, but was unable to ascertain what had happened to it. The guardian then filed suit against the bank to recover the money, alleging that there were "red flags" that should have alerted the bank to the condition of its customer, and that the bank should have taken steps to protect Ms. Johnson. Does a bank have an obligation—legally or ethically—to "protect" its customers even though those customers have not been declared incompetent at the time of the transactions in question? Discuss. [See *Republic Nat'l Bank of Miami* v. *Johnson,* 622 So.2d 1015 (Fla.App. 1993).]

8. **IDES CASE** On 10 April 1989, Spedley Securities, an Australian firm, instructed Security Pacific International Bank by telex to wire $1,974,267.97 into the account of Banque Worms, a French bank, at the New York office of BankAmerica. The transfer was a mistake, which Spedley realized several hours later. As a result, Spedley telexed instructions to Security Pacific to stop the initial transfer, and instead to make the payment to National Westminster Bank (NatWest). At the time Security Pacific received the telexes, Spedley had a balance of $84,500 remaining with Security Pacific, although sufficient funds for the transfer were received later that morning. Security Pacific mistakenly disregarded the cancellation of the transfer to Banque Worms, and made the transfer later, on 10 April. Banque Worms was notified of the transfer through the Clearing House Interbank Payment System (CHIPS). The wire transfer to NatWest was also made, creating an overdraft in the Spedley account. Security Pacific realized that it had made an error, and it contacted BankAmerica to have the funds returned to Security Pacific. BankAmerica agreed to return the funds, but only if Security Pacific would furnish a Council on International Banking, Inc., indemnity. The indemnity was furnished, and BankAmerica returned the funds the following day. However, Banque Worms refused to consent to having its account debited to reflect the return of the funds, and BankAmerica called on Security Pacific to perform as per its indemnity. Security Pacific was unable to cover the indemnity because Spedley had entered into involuntary liquidation. Banque Worms sued BankAmerica to recover the amount of the wire transfer, BankAmerica instituted a third-party action against Security Pacific for return of the funds, and Security Pacific counterclaimed against Banque Worms seeking a declaration that Banque Worms was not entitled to the funds in question. Was Banque Worms able to show either discharge for value or detrimental reliance so that it was entitled to keep the funds transferred initially? Apply the IDES principles to resolve this case. [See *Banque Worms* v. *BankAmerica Int'l,* 570 N.E.2d 189 (N.Y. 1991).]

NOTE

1. Aaron Zitner (*The Boston Globe*), "S&Ls Win in Big Case." *The Denver Post,* Tuesday, 2 July 1996, p. C1.

PART 

IDES PROBLEMS

Amir works for National Bank as vice president of customer service and relations. In this position, Amir develops strategies for finding, enlisting, and retaining customers for the bank. Part of this responsibility involves formulating strategies for addressing common (and not so common) customer complaints, many of which have legal dimensions.

Recently, a number of customers who issued stop payment orders for their checks have complained that National paid the checks regardless of the order. As far as Amir can tell, this is due to a processing error by National, but he cannot tell for sure. A number of these customers have demanded reimbursement for the amount of the check plus all service charges imposed to institute the order. One customer, Enrique, who had written a check to satisfy a contract, stopped payment when she realized the payee had committed fraud. Another customer, Linus, stopped payment on a tuition check to his local college when he decided not to enroll. A third customer, John, had out of generosity written a $100 check to his friend and, when the two later had an argument, John changed his mind and wished to stop payment.

Also, National occasionally finds that drawee banks will dishonor checks National customers deposit into their checking accounts. National will notify these customers within three days that their checks were dishonored. Still, one customer, Louis, insists that National took too long to notify him that his $5000 check was dishonored and asserts that he is entitled to the funds because of this undue delay. Louis claims that the payer of the check, in the time between the writing of the check and National's notification of its being dishonored, left town. National did notify Louis within three days via mail and by phone; Louis, however, was out of town and did not receive the message until a week later.

National has a large number of ATMs, and many of National's customers enjoy this option. Recently, though, a rash of stolen ATM cards has led to a fair amount of illegal withdrawals. One such thief, using a stolen card from a National customer, Kate, withdrew $1000 over a one-week period before National learned of the theft and stopped the card. The thief held the card for ten days before Kate reported the theft. National admits that it is liable for the first $50 but denies any liability beyond that amount. Kate is demanding the return of the entire $1000.

Amir is not a lawyer. Hence, he must be able to avoid legal problems, communicate efficiently to National's corporate legal department when problems arise, and implement solutions based on this advice. The better Amir understands the legal issues and principles and the legal positions of all parties to the complaint, the better prepared he is to talk with the lawyers. In preparation for his meeting, Amir needs to answer the following questions:

IDENTIFY What are the legal and ethical issues surrounding each of National's problems? What rules govern National's responsibilities in these situations?

DEFINE What are the meanings of the relevant legal terms associated with these issues?

ENUMERATE What are the legal and ethical principles relevant to these issues?

SHOW BOTH SIDES Consider all of the facts in light of the preceding questions. Do the customers discussed above have legitimate complaints under the law? What is the position of National in relation to each of the customers? When does it make sense for National to pursue legal remedies?

[To review the IDES approach, refer to pages 29–30.]

DEBTOR-CREDITOR RELATIONS

The use of credit is integral to the U.S. economy. People purchase homes on credit, they purchase automobiles on credit, and they purchase major appliances on credit. In addition, businesses use credit to obtain equipment and inventory.

Secured transactions are used to protect creditors by providing a hedge against losses if or when the debtor defaults. Secured transactions provide the creditor with collateral that can be used to minimize potential losses when the credit extended is not repaid in a timely manner. The law of secured transactions establishes priorities among creditor claims and provides a structured method for enforcing the rights of competing creditors in the collateral of the debtor. Bankruptcy law provides a protection for debtors who encounter financial problems beyond their control or their ability to repay. The law of bankruptcy provides for a *fresh start* for *honest debtors*. This section examines the law of secured transactions and bankruptcy.

I D E S

Donna opened Suds 'n Duds, a combination laundromat and tavern, purchasing most of her equipment and materials on credit. Initial success gave way to disaster, however, when spoiled shrimp sickened dozens of customers. Despite her efforts, the business never recovered and Donna has decided to seek legal help to discuss relief in bankruptcy. What should Donna do from a business perspective? Is bankruptcy the only alternative? If so, what are Donna's legal obligations? Who are Donna's creditors, and what are their positions relative to Donna's financial problems? What, if anything, does she owe her creditors and employees? What, if any, are the priorities among her creditors?

Consider these issues in the context of the chapter materials, and prepare to analyze them using the IDES model:

IDENTIFY the legal issues raised by the questions.

DEFINE all the relevant legal terms and issues involved.

ENUMERATE the legal principles associated with these issues.

SHOW BOTH SIDES by using the facts.

A G E N D A

The Kochanowskis will need to borrow money at times in order to expand the business and to take advantage of opportunities that consequently arise. They need to know how they can borrow money on the most favorable terms available and what sorts of collateral they can use to obtain those terms. They also want to know what, exactly, granting a security interest in assets they own means to them and to their other creditors. Furthermore, it is likely that some customers will want to finance CIT videophones when purchases are made. How can CIT best protect its interests in this property when it grants claims while still granting credit to these customers?

These and similar questions will arise as you study this chapter. Be prepared! You never know when one of the Kochanowskis will seek your help or advice.

Secured Transactions: Security Interests and Perfection

O U T L I N E

- Credit Financing and Article 9
- Scope of Article 9
- Security Interest
- Creation and Enforceability of the Security Interest
- Perfection
- Related Topics
- Summary
- Discussion Questions
- Case Problems and Writing Assignments

CREDIT FINANCING AND ARTICLE 9

Credit is an extremely important aspect of current American business practices. Without it, many successful firms might never have gotten started. Yet the person who extends credit (the creditor) undertakes the risk that the person to whom he or she has given credit (the debtor) will not be able to repay the debt in full. Understandably, the creditor wishes to be protected against such losses before they occur. The Uniform Commercial Code's methods of creating protection for the creditor form the basis of this chapter's discussion.

We already have seen that a commercial transaction in one of its simplest forms may involve a sale of goods in which the buyer pays cash. Alternatively, the buyer may use a check or draft to pay for all (or a portion of) the goods. In this chapter, we examine a third method of closing a commercial transaction: The buyer gives the owner of the goods a *security interest.* The portion of the Uniform Commercial Code that deals with these matters is Article 9, "Secured Transactions; Sales of **Accounts** and **Chattel Paper**."

Accounts

Rights to payments for goods sold or leased or for services rendered that are not evidenced by an instrument or chattel paper.

Chattel paper

A writing that evidences both a monetary obligation and a security interest in specific goods.

Despite the availability of several methods of structuring a commercial transaction, use of secured transactions is very common in business today; hence, an understanding of Article 9 is crucial. To illustrate, assume that Bart Brown wishes to buy a meat freezer and a cash register for his new restaurant business. He may pay for part of the sale in cash and receive possession of the items in exchange for giving the seller of the goods a security interest in this equipment. Such a security interest secures (or ensures) payment by the buyer so that if Bart does not pay the seller, the latter can repossess the goods. Thus, a secured transaction allows buyers to receive goods sooner than if they had been forced to pay cash; and, at the same time, it permits sellers who retain the right of repossession in the event of a buyer's nonpayment to protect themselves. As we shall see, to ensure that they will have first rights to the equipment in the event of Bart's **default**, sellers must comply with several additional Article 9 rules relating to perfection and priorities. These concepts are developed further in this chapter and in Chapter 27.

Default

A failure to do what should be done, especially in the performance of a contractual obligation, without legal excuse or justification for the nonperformance.

Using the terminology adopted by the Code, the seller is characterized as the *secured party* ("a lender, seller, or other person in whose favor there is a security interest, including a person to whom accounts or chattel paper have been sold").[1] Bart, of course, is the *debtor* ("the person who owes payment or other performance of the obligation secured, whether or not he owns or has rights in the collateral, and includes the seller of accounts or chattel paper").[2] Bart and the seller presumably have entered into a *security agreement* ("the agreement which creates or provides for a security interest").[3] The freezer and cash register constitute *collateral* ("the property subject to a security interest").[4] Article 9's application is very broad: It may cover relatively simple business transactions like the one we have described; or it may extend to highly complex forms of business financing, such as accounts receivable financing.[5]

The 1972 Official Text of Article 9 differs substantially from the 1962 official text. Most states have adopted the 1972 version; but since some states still follow the 1962 rules, check your jurisdiction to see which version applies. In Chapters 26 through 28, we use the 1972 Official Text of Article 9. You also should be aware that in the mid-1990s the American Law Institute and the National Conference of Commissioners on Uniform State Laws began to reexamine Article 9 in order to suggest revisions. These efforts, which will continue over the next few years, bear watching.

Part of the richness of Article 9 stems from its unified approach to secured financing. Before the UCC was drafted, a wide variety of security devices existed;

they had arisen rather haphazardly as a result of 100 years' worth of common law and statutory developments in response to perceived security financing needs. These devices—known by such strange names as "pledges," "chattel mortgages," "conditional sales," "trust receipts," and "factor's liens"—were very technical. Hence, a seller who mistakenly had chosen the wrong device or who had failed to comply with the ticklish requirements of a particular device later might find that he or she had no valid security interest. Moreover, these devices remained limited in scope; they could not reach **general intangibles**, such as television or motion picture rights or the goodwill of a business or service, which most of us today would recognize as important sources of commercial collateral. Finally, these devices placed great emphasis on who had held title during the course of the parties' dealings.

General intangibles
Personal property other than goods, accounts, chattel paper, instruments, documents, or money; for example, goodwill, literary rights, patents, or copyrights.

The Code's creation of a *single* device, the Article 9 security interest, was welcome indeed. Article 9's rejection of the older devices' distinctions based on form (and concepts of title)[6] has led to a simplified structure. This format more accurately reflects the wide variety of present-day secured financing transactions and allows for commercial recognition of new forms of financing without requiring state legislatures to pass new statutes or change old ones. This chapter focuses on some of the provisions of Article 9 that illustrate the Code's breadth and flexibility.

Scope of Article 9

In general, § 9-102 of Article 9:

> *applies (a) to any transaction (regardless of its form) which is intended to create a security interest in personal property or fixtures including goods, documents, instruments, general intangibles, chattel paper or accounts and also (b) to any sale of accounts or chattel paper.*

By a *security interest,* Article 9 means "an interest in personal property or fixtures which secures payment or performance of an obligation."[7] The personal property or collateral that will be subject to a security interest takes many forms. Moreover, the Code categorizes collateral according to either (1) the *nature* of the collateral or (2) its *use.* Thus, *documents* (warehouse receipts, bills of lading, and other documents of title); *instruments* (drafts, certificates of deposit, stocks, and bonds); *proceeds* (whatever is received upon the sale, exchange, collection, or other disposition of collateral or proceeds); and the three kinds of collateral defined earlier—*accounts, chattel paper,* and *general intangibles*—represent the types of collateral the Code classifies primarily on the basis of their *nature.*

Goods, the most common type of collateral, are categorized on the basis of their *use* by the debtor. According to the Code, *goods* include all things that are movable at the time the security interest attaches or that are fixtures.[8] *Consumer goods* consist of those goods used or bought for use primarily for personal, family, or household purposes. Thus, a debtor may give a security interest in his or her furniture or car to a secured party. *Equipment* includes goods used or bought for use primarily in business. Bart's freezer and cash register are equipment collateral, as a truck would be for the electric company. Farm products also constitute a type of goods. The Code defines *farm products* as crops, livestock, or supplies used or produced in farming operations. Interestingly, then, a farmer may give a security interest in wheat, corn, cows, or even milk, since the Code covers the products of crops or livestock in their unmanufactured states as well.[9] *Inventory,* defined as goods held by a person for sale or lease or raw materials used or consumed in a business, is another type of goods. Inventory differs from consumer goods and equipment because inventory is held for sale rather than use.[10] Such things as coal or the packaging for goods are inventory, as is a dealer's supply of cars or a merchant's supply of tires, paint, clothing, or toys. The last type of goods that the Code delineates is *fixtures.* Goods are fixtures when they become so related to particular real estate that an interest in them arises under real estate law.[11] Furnaces and central air-conditioning units are fixtures.

Given these differences in definition, it is not surprising that the Code makes these classes of goods *mutually exclusive.* In other words, the same property cannot at the same time and to the same person be both equipment and inventory. In borderline cases—for example, a social worker's car or a farmer's pickup—the principal use to which the debtor has put the property determines the type of collateral involved.[12] Because the Code's rules regarding perfection, priorities, and default often turn on the type of collateral involved (as we shall see in Chapters 27 and 28), it is important to know which category of collateral is present in a given transaction.

Whatever the kind of collateral that is subject to the security interest, the Code drafters apparently meant Article 9 to apply to all *consensual* security interests in personal property and fixtures as well as to certain sales of accounts and chattel paper (often called *assignments*).[13] In our earlier example, we can say that Bart Brown and the seller of the meat freezer and the cash register each has consented to enter into this commercial transaction. Since personal property is involved (the freezer and register are goods), Bart has agreed to let the seller retain an interest in the goods until Bart pays for them (a method of ensuring the performance of Bart's obligations); and the seller, in turn, has agreed to give the goods to Bart now (even though the seller has not received the total price for them) in exchange for the right to repossess the freezer and register if Bart fails to pay. This transaction therefore fulfills all the requirements of an enforceable security interest.

Given the need for consent between the parties, Article 9 accordingly does not apply to a security interest that arises by **operation of law** rather than through the agreement of the parties. Examples of such situations include a **mechanic's lien** on Bart's restaurant that an unpaid contractor obtains as a result of renovating Bart's place of business. The lien represents the money Bart owes for the labor and materials involved in the remodeling of the restaurant. Since Bart and the contractor have not agreed in advance that the contractor will have an interest in Bart's restaurant, this is a nonconsensual arrangement that arises as a consequence of the parties' *status* (the contractor is a creditor who now is using the restaurant as security for the debt Bart owes) rather than as a result of *mutual consent.* It therefore is not an Article 9 security interest.

Operation of law
Certain automatic results that must occur following certain actions or facts because of established legal principles and not as the result of any voluntary choice by the parties involved.

Mechanic's lien
Given to certain builders, artisans, and providers of material, a statutory protection that grants a lien on the building and the land improved by such persons.

This result also stems from the fact that Article 9 in general does not apply to real property or real estate. Instead, as mentioned, it applies only to security interests in *personal property.* Hence, Article 9 has no bearing on land mortgages or on landlords' liens. And although it specifically includes within its scope the old methods of creating security interests (for example, pledges, chattel mortgages, and factor's liens),[14] Article 9 specifically exempts from its coverage security interests that are subject to any federal statute and certain other categories of transactions, including wage and salary claims and claims resulting from court judgments.[15]

In some cases, a transaction, although covered by Article 9, also may be subject to any local statutes governing usury, retail installment sales, and the like (for example, the Uniform Consumer Credit Code). In those situations, in the event of a conflict, the provisions of any such statute, and not Article 9, are controlling.[16]

26.1

MANAGEMENT/FINANCE

SOURCES OF FINANCING

Tom and Anna would like to borrow money for the operation of the business, but they would prefer not to use their personal assets as security for any credit they receive. They ask you what assets CIT has that might be useful as collateral for any loans they seek. What will you tell them?

BUSINESS CONSIDERATIONS How can businesspersons who are starting a closely held business acquire financing without using their personal assets as collateral? Is it a good idea for the owner/managers of small businesses to have their personal and their professional assets so closely entwined in the business venture?
ETHICAL CONSIDERATIONS Is it ethical for a lender to insist that the owners of a start-up business use their personal assets as security for loans extended to the business? What ethical principles does this situation involve?

One test a person can use in deciding whether Article 9 applies is to ask whether the transaction *is intended* to have effect as security. If the answer is *yes*, Article 9 probably covers the transaction.

Security Interest

As we have just noted, Article 9 broadly defines the term *security interest* as an interest in personal property or fixtures that secures payment or performance of an obligation. One of the assets of the Code derives from the flexibility of such a sweeping definition. In fact, courts have had few problems in recognizing a security interest. Despite this seeming simplicity of definition, one area—that of leases "intended as security" in contrast to "true" leases—has caused businesspeople and courts some difficulties.

The Code states definitively that Article 9 applies to "a lease intended as security."[17] It also notes that the facts of each case determine whether a lease is intended as security and that the inclusion of an option to purchase does not in and of itself make the lease one intended for security. On the other hand, a provision that upon the expiration of the lease the person who is leasing (called the *lessee*) becomes the owner, or has the option of buying the property for very little money, makes the lease one intended as security.[18] In this latter situation, the transaction more closely resembles an installment sales contract, especially when, as is often the case, the "rental" payments equal the selling price of the property subject to the "lease." In such circumstances, the *lessor* (the person leasing the personal property to another) actually is a secured party who is using the monthly leasing payments as monthly installments on a conditional sales agreement. This transaction *is* subject to the Code's provisions because it is a lease intended as security, not a true lease.

Why is this an important distinction anyway? The answer will become clear when we discuss the process of perfection. If such a lease is intended as security, it will be subject to Article 9's filing requirements. A true lease will not require an Article 9 filing because Article 9 in general does not apply to situations in which one merely pays for the right to use the goods for a specified period of time without ever becoming the owner of the leased property. Debtors in Article 9 transactions are trying to buy the property that is the object of the security interest. At the same time, secured parties are retaining an interest in the property until this transfer of ownership is accomplished by the debtor's paying all that is owed. In a true lease, the parties never contemplate such an eventual transfer of ownership.

Thus, if we change the facts of our earlier hypothetical case and have Bart lease the freezer and cash register, assuming this is a true lease, Article 9 does not govern the transaction. If the owner of the freezer and register in effect is retaining *title* to the goods to ensure that Bart will pay for the goods, however, we have *a lease intended as security;* and the parties must follow Article 9's rules. As we shall see later, this means that if Bart becomes bankrupt, the **trustee in bankruptcy** will be able to get the equipment because the law will deem Bart the owner of the equipment. He in essence has been paying for the items on an installment sales basis, even though the parties have called the transaction a lease. By failing to file, the original owner of the equipment has not perfected his or her interest in the equipment and will be unable to repossess the equipment (or any other type of collateral). Since the law in these circumstances treats the bankruptcy trustee as a **lien creditor**, the trustee will have superior rights to those of our unperfected original owner.

Walton v. *Howard* does not involve the trustee in bankruptcy, but it illustrates the necessity of following the Code's rules if a court later characterizes the transaction at issue as a lease intended as security.

Trustee in bankruptcy
The person appointed by the bankruptcy court to act as trustee of the debtor's property for the benefit and protection of the creditors.

Lien creditor
One whose debt is secured by a claim on specific property.

26.1 WALTON v. HOWARD

403 S.E.2d 90 (Ga.App. 1991)

FACTS Ronnie Howard entered into a contract entitled a "Lease/Purchase Agreement" with Donnie Walton regarding a John Deere tractor. Walton agreed to "sell" the equipment to Howard in exchange for Howard's promise to pay off the amount in arrears that Walton owed to John Deere Finance Plans, Inc. (John Deere) and to take over the future monthly installment payments owed on the equipment until all the debts owed under the financing agreement between Walton and John Deere had been paid. The agreement granted Howard the right to a bill of sale for the equipment when he had paid $1 and other consideration once the lien in favor of John Deere had terminated. In the interim, the parties considered the monthly payments as lease payments between Walton and Howard. The agreement imposed on Howard the duty to pay taxes and to provide insurance on the equipment. Howard furthermore paid Walton $4,000 for Walton's equity in the equipment and then made six monthly payments of more than $1,000 to John Deere before he (Howard) fell into arrears. When Howard was three months behind in payments, Walton repossessed the equipment and retained it in his possession without notice of intent either to retain the collateral in satisfaction of the debt or to dispose of it to satisfy the debt. Howard subsequently brought suit against Walton for breach of contract or, in the alternative, for a judgment ordering Walton to return the equipment. The trial judge found the written agreement a security agreement subject to Georgia's Commercial Code and granted Howard the right to redeem the collateral when he had paid the remaining debt plus $400 for interest on the sum paid by Walton to John Deere to extinguish the lien. Walton appealed this decision.

ISSUE Was the lease a true lease? Or was it a lease intended as security and hence covered under Georgia's Commercial Code?

HOLDING The lease was subject to Georgia's Commercial Code because the lease agreement had created a security interest; as such, it did not constitute a true lease but rather a conditional sale.

REASONING The trial court rightly concluded that Howard and Walton had entered into a secured transaction. The agreement granted Howard the right to purchase the equipment for a nominal sum after John Deere had received the final monthly installment payment. Pursuant to the definition of *security interest* in Georgia's Commercial Code, "an agreement that upon compliance with the terms of the lease, the lessee shall become or has the option to become the owner of the property for no additional consideration or for a nominal consideration does make the lease one intended for security." Additional factors that tend to establish that a transaction is a conditional sale instead of a true lease include an initial down payment and the placing of responsibility for payment of taxes and insurance on the lessee. In this case, the evidence showed that Howard, referred to in the agreement as "Lessee/Buyer," had made a down payment of $4,000 to compensate Walton, the "Lessor/Seller," for Walton's equity interest in the equipment. The agreement also required Howard to pay taxes and insurance. Hence, ample evidence existed to support the finding that the agreement had created a security interest. Having determined that the agreement had created a security interest, the trial court had not erred in finding that the Commercial Code covered the agreement. Moreover, the court had not erred, pursuant to such statute, in awarding Howard the right to redeem the equipment upon Howard's payment of the amount due under the agreement ($6,954) plus $400 for interest to Walton to reimburse Walton for paying off the prior lien on the equipment.

26.1 WALTON v. HOWARD *(cont.)* 403 S.E.2d 90 (Ga.App. 1991)

BUSINESS CONSIDERATIONS Why would a seller prefer to characterize a lease as a true lease rather than as a lease intended as security? Why would competing creditors prefer to characterize a lease as a lease intended as security rather than as a true lease?

ETHICAL CONSIDERATIONS Has a seller who recognizes the legal distinctions between a true lease and a lease intended as security acted unethically toward the lessee/debtor if the seller couches the arrangement as a true lease but asks for monthly payments that in effect mean the lessee will pay twice the fair market value of the item leased?

Creation and Enforceability of the Security Interest

A security interest is of negligible value unless it is valid and enforceable. It therefore behooves the owner of the freezer and the register in our earlier hypothetical case to attain the status of a *secured creditor* (or secured party). In this way, if Bart, the debtor, later cannot or will not pay for the equipment, the secured party will be able to repossess the goods and, if perfected, enjoy priority over the claims that other third parties, such as the bankruptcy trustee, may assert regarding the property.

However, before the secured party has an enforceable security interest in the collateral, the security interest must attach.[19] *Attachment* is the process by which the secured party and the debtor create the security interest and thereby confer on the secured party certain enforceable rights to the collateral vis-à-vis the debtor. Attachment does not give the secured party rights necessarily superior to those obtained by other creditors (an additional step called perfection is necessary to accomplish this). Nevertheless, as the first step in the creation and enforceability of a security interest, attachment remains extremely important.

According to the UCC, attachment occurs when a prospective secured party does all of the following:

1. enters into a *security agreement* whereby the prospective secured party and the debtor agree that a security interest will attach
2. possesses a security agreement signed by the debtor or, alternatively, pursuant to agreement, retains possession of the collateral
3. ascertains that the debtor has rights in the collateral
4. gives value

The omission of any of the requirements just listed invalidates the security interest. Such an argument underlies the *Wawak* v. *Affiliated Food Stores, Inc.* case.

26.2 WAWAK v. AFFILIATED FOOD STORES, INC. 812 S.W.2d 679 (Ark. 1991)

FACTS Billy J. Wawak and Earlene Wawak began operating the Oak Grove Supermarket in 1978. The Wawaks acquired their stock from Affiliated Food Stores, Inc., which, by a security agreement and a UCC financing statement covering the inventory of the supermarket, secured its account with them. In 1986, the Wawaks made arrangements to sell the supermarket to Robert S. Davis, operating under the names Bob's Thriftway and Bob's Supermarket of Arkansas.

26.2 WAWAK v. AFFILIATED FOOD STORES, INC. *(cont.)* 812 S.W.2d 679 (Ark. 1991)

Davis and the Wawaks signed an agreement under which Davis began operating the supermarket on 28 January 1986 while the documents of sale were being prepared. Davis made immediate arrangements with Affiliated Food Stores, Inc. (Affiliated) to purchase inventory for the Oak Grove Supermarket and executed with Affiliated a security agreement and financing statement covering the inventory of the supermarket. The financing statement and security agreement were properly recorded in February. In April, Davis and the Wawaks completed their transaction; Davis executed a security agreement and financing statement covering the inventory to secure the indebtedness due the Wawaks; and Davis properly recorded these instruments on 8 April 1986. After 18 months, Davis declared bankruptcy; and, on 15 January 1988, the Wawaks took possession of the supermarket and inventory from the trustee in bankruptcy. The Wawaks sought a declaratory judgment that their security interest was prior and superior to the security interest of Affiliated because no attachment had occurred owing to Davis's lack of any rights in the collateral. When the court ruled that the security interest of Affiliated was prior to that of the Wawaks, the Wawaks appealed.

ISSUE Did Davis have sufficient rights in the collateral for attachment to have occurred?

HOLDING Yes. Davis, as the buyer in possession of the supermarket, had sufficient rights in the collateral to satisfy this requirement of attachment.

REASONING The Wawaks maintained that under Arkansas statutes a security interest does not attach until the debtor has "rights in the collateral." They contended that Davis had no rights in the inventory of the supermarket (the collateral) until 7 April 1986, when the sale was completed. They submitted that, prior to 7 April, Davis merely functioned as a manager or bailee. However, Davis was effectively the buyer in possession of a going concern and as such fully empowered to convey title to the collateral to purchasers in the ordinary course of business. The profits, as well as the losses, were his from and after 28 January 1986, when he took possession and began operating the supermarket. Moreover, the final purchase documents reflect that the sale to Davis became effective on 27 January 1986. The fact that the sale still was in process on 7 February 1986 does not mean that, within the context of the law, he was without rights in the collateral. Although the Code fails to define "rights in the collateral" and Arkansas courts have not had occasion to construe the term, other states have done so in precedents stating, for example, that "possession of the collateral, accompanied by a contingent right of ownership, has been held sufficient for a security interest to attach. . . . An interest greater than naked possession has been deemed a sufficient right in the collateral to satisfy the requirements of statutes similar [to the one in issue]. . . ." According to these authorities, Davis had rights in the collateral. Moreover, Arkansas law provides that when all the applicable steps to perfect a security interest are taken before the interest attaches, it is perfected as of the time it attaches. In the words of one commentator, "Perfection [the completion of all the steps of attachment, plus filing] . . . does not require a particular sequence of events. Thus, a security interest [can be] perfected even though the financing statement was filed prior to the time the security interest attached. . . ." Here, even if Davis's rights in the collateral had not matured until 7 April, that is, upon the conclusion of the sale, the Wawaks had failed to perfect their security interest by filing until 8 April, whereas the security interest of Affiliated became perfected on 7 April at the instant Davis's rights in the collateral attached.

BUSINESS CONSIDERATIONS Armed with hindsight, how should the Wawaks' conduct have differed with regard to the contract they made with Davis?

ETHICAL CONSIDERATIONS Some 18 months after purchasing the supermarket, Davis declared bankruptcy. Is a debtor's use of the bankruptcy laws unethical vis-à-vis the debtor's creditors?

Note that the judge in the *Wawak* case took into account the fact that Davis was in possession of the supermarket. Attachment by possession, though, more appropriately centers on the creditor's *physically* retaining the goods used as collateral. For example, a simple **pledge** of a coin collection in which, by agreement, the owner of the collection insists on keeping it until the debtor pays for it ordinarily will be enforceable because attachment will have occurred. In most cases, however, as in our

Pledge
A debtor's delivery of collateral to a creditor, who will possess the collateral until the debt is paid.

situation involving Bart, the debtor will not agree to the secured party's retaining possession of the collateral (without his meat freezer on site, Bart will have few customers!). Thus, in lieu of possession and evidence of an oral security agreement, a *signed security agreement* will be necessary to make the security interest valid.

To comply with the Code,[20] this latter type of security agreement must

1. be in writing
2. create or provide for a security interest
3. reasonably identify the collateral
4. be signed by the debtor

Although these requirements seem simple, a great deal of litigation has resulted from a creditor's failure to use forms that include this minimal information or from a failure to fill out these forms correctly. A security agreement may contain many other terms as well, such as the amount of the indebtedness and the terms of payment; liability in the event of risk of loss or damage to the collateral; a requirement of insurance on and the maintenance and repair of the collateral; a warranty by the debtor that he or she owns the collateral free from liens or security interests; a statement of the debtor's rights (if any) regarding removal of the collateral to another location; and a description of events that constitute default by the debtor. The security agreement in Exhibit 26.1 includes some of these terms.

A security agreement also may extend the security interest of the secured party to all collateral of the kind that is the subject of the agreement and that the debtor may acquire *after* entering into this agreement. Thus, if Bart, after entering into a security agreement with the seller of the freezer, obtains an industrial-grade bread-making machine, inclusion of an *after-acquired property clause* in the original security agreement means that the seller also may get the bread-making machine if Bart ultimately fails to pay for the freezer and the cash register. Or, alternatively, assume Bart is a seller of radios and that he gives a security interest to a creditor who has provided him with an inventory of radios. Every time Bart sells one of the original radios and uses the money from this sale to purchase another radio to replenish his inventory, the creditor's security interest in the original inventory of radios leaves the first radio, affixes to the proceeds, follows the proceeds through Bart's bank account, and affixes to the radio purchased to restock the inventory. Such after-acquired property clauses are common in secured transactions.

In the *In re Orix* case, one party disputed whether the financing statement had adequately described the property in question. Financing statements, which we discuss in some detail shortly, consist of forms placed in the public records that indicate a secured party's retention of a security interest in certain collateral.

26.3 ORIX CREDIT ALLIANCE v. OMNIBANK, N.A. — 858 S.W.2d 586 (Tex.App. 1993)

FACTS Orix Credit Alliance, Inc. (Orix) and Omnibank, NA (Omnibank), two creditors of W. T. Stephens, respectively contended that each held superior security interests in funds payable to Stephens under an agreement between him and BFI Special Services, Inc. (BFI). On 4 March 1988, Stephens had executed a promissory note to Orix in which he promised to pay Orix approximately $202,140. On the same date, Stephens executed a written security agreement in which he granted Orix a security interest in three specific pieces of equipment and "all other goods, chattels, machinery, equipment, inventory, accounts, chattel paper, notes receivable, accounts receivable, furniture, fixtures, and property of every kind and nature, wherever located, now or hereafter belonging to Mortgagor." On 14

26.3 ORIX CREDIT ALLIANCE v. OMNIBANK, N.A. *(cont.)* 858 S.W.2d 586 (Tex.App. 1993)

March 1988, Orix filed as a financing statement with the Texas secretary of state a copy of the security agreement. Stephens made some payments to Orix under the 4 March note, but never paid it off. On 27 March 1991, Stephens executed a second note to Orix for $344,452.73, plus interest—an amount that purportedly represented Stephens's total indebtedness to Orix. Stephens also failed to pay the second note when it became due. During this same period, Stephens and his partner, Cody Birdwell, sold all the stock of their company, W. T. Stephens Contracting, Inc., to BFI, a subsidiary of Browning Ferris Industries, Inc. In consideration of the restrictive covenants that both Birdwell and Stephens had signed with BFI, in which they agreed not to compete with BFI for five years in the asbestos business, BFI agreed to pay them one-half of 1 percent of BFI's gross revenues from its asbestos-abatement business for the next five years. Under the terms of the agreement, Birdwell and Stephens would split this amount. Earlier, on 28 February 1990, Stephens had borrowed $300,000 from Omnibank. As security, Stephens had granted Omnibank a security interest in those same proceeds he was to receive from the BFI noncompetition agreement. The security agreement and financing statement later filed by Omnibank specifically identified and covered the BFI agreement. When Stephens subsequently became insolvent and filed for bankruptcy, both Orix and Omnibank claimed a superior security interest in the amounts payable to Stephens under the BFI agreement. When both parties filed motions for summary judgment, the trial court entered a summary judgment in favor of Omnibank. Orix in appealing that determination, argued, among other things, that its security agreement covered all W. T. Stephens's personal property, including the amounts payable to Stephens under the BFI agreement.

ISSUE Did the description "and property . . . wherever located, now or hereafter belonging to the Mortgagor [Stephens]" sufficiently identify the right of Stephens to receive payments under the covenant not to compete so as to give Orix a valid security interest?

HOLDING No. The description at issue in the security agreement was insufficient as a matter of law to cover the right to receive payments under the restrictive covenant.

REASONING The phrase used in the security agreement "property of every kind and nature, wherever located" plainly refers to tangible property. If an item of property is located somewhere, it has a physical form. *Black's Law Dictionary* defines *tangible* as: "Having or possessing physical form. Capable of being touched or seen; perceptible to the touch; tactile; palpable; capable of being possessed or realized; readily apprehensible by the mind; real; substantial." A right to receive payments under a covenant not to compete has no physical form; it cannot be seen or touched. Thus, such a right is intangible. This interpretation follows the definition in *Black's* for *intangibles:* "Property that is a 'right' such as a patent, copyright, trademark, etc., or one which is lacking physical existence; such as goodwill." What Stephens had was a right to receive payments under a covenant not to compete. Therefore, the description contained in the security agreement, clearly referring to tangible property, did not describe or identify the collateral at issue here, intangible property. Hence, even though the filing of Orix's security interest predated Omnibank's filing, Omnibank's interest would have priority owing to the invalidity of Orix's purported security interest.

BUSINESS CONSIDERATIONS At the time of the execution of the second note between Orix and Stephens, what additional steps might Orix have taken so as to protect itself more completely against the adverse effects of Stephens's later actions?

ETHICAL CONSIDERATIONS Given the state of Stephens's finances, assess Orix, Omnibank, and Stephens's ethics, respectively, from a utilitarian perspective. Would your analysis differ if you applied the Golden Rule to each's conduct?

The need for evidence of the parties' intentions forms the basis for requiring such information on the security agreement. If the parties have spelled out their respective rights and duties in advance, fewer disputes over the terms of the agreement and over the property that represents the collateral for the obligation secured should ensue.

EXHIBIT 26.1 Security Agreement Form

SECURITY AGREEMENT USED WITH
LOAN ON
GOODS, FIXTURES, OR EQUIPMENT

________________________, 19 ______

____
(NAME)
____
(NO. AND STREET) (CITY) (COUNTY) (STATE)

(Hereinafter called "Debtor") hereby grants to KeyBank National Association, South Bend, Indiana (Hereinafter called "Bank"), a security interest in the following property together with all tools, accessories, parts, equipment and accessions now attached to or which may hereafter at any time be placed or added to the property; also any replacements of such property herein described (hereinafter called "Collateral"):

____
____
____
____

The security interest granted hereby is to secure payment and performance of the liabilities and obligations of debtor to Bank of every kind and description, direct or indirect, absolute or contingent, due or to become due, now existing or hereafter arising (hereinafter called Obligations").

Debtor hereby warrants and covenants:

1. The collateral is being acquired for the following primary uses: _____ personal, or family use, _____business use, or _____farming operations.

2. The Collateral _____will _____will not be acquired with the proceeds of the loan provided for in this Agreement. (In the event the Collateral will be acquired with the proceeds of the loan, the Bank may disburse such proceeds to the seller of the Collateral.)

3. In the event the Collateral will be attached to real estate, the description of such real estate and the known owner of record of such real estate are set forth hereafter. If the Collateral is attached to such real estate prior to the perfection of the security interest granted herein, the Debtor will, on demand, furnish the Bank with a disclaimer or disclaimers executed by persons having an interest in such real estate. Real estate described:

____
____
____

4. The Collateral will be kept at the address of the Debtor set out below, which in the case of a business is the address of the principal office of such business within this state. Debtor will not remove the Collateral from the state without the prior written consent of the Bank. If the Collateral is being acquired for farming use and the Debtor is not a resident of Indiana, the Collateral will be kept at the address set forth in the description of the Collateral. Debtor will immediately give written notice to the Bank of any change of address and in the case of a business any change in its principal place of business and if the Collateral consists of equipment normally

EXHIBIT 26.1 Security Agreement Form *(cont.)*

used in more than one state, any use of the Collateral in any jurisdiction other than a state in which the Debtor shall have previously advised the Bank such Collateral will be used.

5. Debtor has, or will acquire, full and clear title to the Collateral and except for the security interest granted herein, will at all times keep the Collateral free from any adverse lien, security interest or encumbrance.

6. No financing statement covering all or any portion of the Collateral is on file in any public office.

7. Debtor authorizes the Bank at the expense of the Debtor to execute and file on its behalf a financing statement or statements in those public offices deemed necessary by the Bank to protect its security interest in the Collateral. Debtor will deliver or cause to be delivered to the Bank any certificates of title to the Collateral with the security interest of the Bank noted thereon.

8. Debtor will not sell or offer to sell or otherwise transfer the Collateral or any interest therein without the prior written consent of the Bank.

9. Debtor will at all times keep the Collateral insured against loss, damage, theft and other risks in such amounts, under such policies and with such companies as shall be satisfactory to the Bank, which policies shall provide that any loss thereunder shall be payable to the Bank as its interest may appear and the Bank may apply the proceeds of the insurance against the outstanding indebtedness of the Debtor, regardless of whether all or any portion of such indebtedness is due or owing. All policies of insurance so required shall be placed in the possession of the Bank.

Upon failure of the Debtor to procure such insurance or to remove any encumbrance upon the Collateral or if such insurance is cancelled, the indebtedness secured hereby shall become immediately due and payable at the option of the Bank, without notice or demand, or the Bank may procure such insurance or remove any encumbrance on the Collateral and the amount so paid by the Bank shall be immediately repayable and shall be added to and become a part of the indebtedness secured hereby and shall bear interest at the same note rate as the indebtedness secured hereby until paid.

10. Debtor will keep the Collateral in good order and repair and will not waste or destroy the Collateral or any portion thereof. Debtor will not use the Collateral in violation of any statute or ordinance or any policy of insurance thereon and the Bank may examine and inspect such Collateral at any reasonable time or times wherever located.

11. Debtor will pay promptly when due all taxes and assessments upon the Collateral or for its use or operation.

12. The occurrence of any one of the following events shall constitute default under this Security Agreement: (a) nonpayment when due of any installment of the indebtedness hereby secured or failure to perform any agreement contained herein; (b) any statement, representation, or warranty at any time furnished the Bank is untrue in any material respect as of the date made; (c) Debtor becomes insolvent or unable to pay debts as they mature; (d) entry of judgment against the Debtor; (e) loss, theft, substantial damage, destruction, sale or encumbrance to or of all or any portion of the Collateral, or the making of any levy, seizure or attachment, thereof, or thereon; (f) death of the Debtor who is a natural person or of any partner of the Debtor which is a partnership; (g) dissolution, merger or consolidation or transfer of a substantial portion of the property of the

EXHIBIT 26.1 Security Agreement Form *(cont.)*

Debtor which is a corporation or partnership; or (h) the Bank deems itself insecure for any other reason whatsoever.

When an event of default shall be existing, the note or notes and any other liabilities may at the option of the Bank and without notice or demand be declared and thereupon immediately shall become due and payable and the Bank may exercise from time to time any rights and remedies of a secured party under the Uniform Commercial Code or other applicable law. Debtor agrees in the event of default to make the Collateral available to the Bank at a place acceptable to the Bank which is convenient to the Debtor. If any notification or disposition of all or any portion of the Collateral is required by law, such notification shall be deemed reasonable and properly given if mailed at least ten (10) days prior to such disposition, postage prepaid to the Debtor at its latest address appearing on the records of the Bank. Expenses of retaking, holding, repairing, preparing for sale and selling shall include the Bank's reasonable attorneys' fees and expenses. Any proceeds of the disposition of the Collateral will be applied by the Bank to the payment of expenses of retaking, holding, repairing, preparing for sale and selling the Collateral, including reasonable attorneys' fees and legal expenses and any balance of such proceeds will be applied by the Bank to the payment of the indebtedness then owing the Bank.

No delay on the part of the Bank in the exercise of any right or remedy shall operate as a waiver thereof, and no single or partial exercise by the Bank of any right or remedy shall preclude other or further exercise thereof or the exercise of any other right or remedy. If more than one party shall execute this Agreement, the term "Debtor" shall mean all parties signing this Agreement and each of them, and such parties shall be jointly and severally obligated hereunder. The neuter pronoun, when used herein, shall include the masculine and the feminine and also the plural. If this agreement is not dated when executed by the Debtor, the Bank is authorized, without notice to the Debtor, to date this Agreement.

This Agreement has been delivered at South Bend, Indiana, and shall be construed in accordance with the laws of the State of Indiana. Wherever possible each provision of this Agreement shall be interpreted in such manner as to be effective and valid under applicable law, but if any provision of this Agreement shall be prohibited by or invalid under applicable law, such provision shall be ineffective to the extent of such prohibition or invalidity, without invalidating the remainder of such provision or the remaining provisions of this Agreement.

This Agreement shall be binding upon the heirs, administrators and executors of the Debtor and the rights and privileges of the Bank hereunder so insured to the benefit of its successors and assigns.

Address: ____________________

____________________ ____________________

____

Courtesy of KeyBank National Association, Indiana, South Bend, Indiana.

PERFECTION

Thus far, we have focused primarily on the relationship between the creditor and the debtor and how the creditor, by becoming a secured party, may protect his or her interest in the collateral. Yet, in that earlier discussion, we noted that the processes leading to the creation and enforceability of a secured interest only give the secured party rights greater than those of the debtor; they do not necessarily confer on the secured party superior rights to the collateral vis-à-vis other creditors and the bankruptcy trustee.

Now we turn to a discussion of how secured parties can protect themselves against such third parties who also may be claiming rights in the collateral. In other words, how can the seller/secured party in our earlier example protect the freezer and register from Bart's other business creditors (for example, produce suppliers) if Bart's financial situation deteriorates to the point that either the other creditors or—if Bart is on the verge of insolvency—the trustee in bankruptcy is trying to get all of Bart's equipment so as to satisfy Bart's creditors' claims against him?

Perfection is the process by which secured parties protect their collateral from the clutches of later creditors who also have given value when the debtor has used the same pieces of equipment as collateral for loans from them. The date of perfection, in turn, represents the date from which the law measures priorities whenever competing claims among other perfected creditors exist. The topic of priorities among secured parties is addressed in Chapter 27.

26.2

SALES/MANAGEMENT

SHOULD CIT SELL OR LEASE CALL-IMAGE?

Assume that CIT agrees to provide 100 Call-Image videophones to a local telemarketing firm and that CIT is willing to provide them on credit. Tom is willing to lease the units to the telemarketing firm. Dan insists that the units should be sold and that CIT should retain a security interest in them. Tom and Dan have asked for your advice. What will you tell them?

BUSINESS CONSIDERATIONS If a business leases equipment to a customer, should the lessor comply with the Article 9 filing requirement even though the transaction is a lease? Why or why not? If a business sells equipment to a customer on credit, what broad language should the seller include in the security agreement so as to maximize its protection?

ETHICAL CONSIDERATIONS Is it ethical for a creditor who is entering into a secured transaction to use an after-acquired property clause, thus increasing its collateral to substantially more than the total debt secured? Why or why not?

In general, perfection occurs in one of three ways: by the creditor's filing a financing statement, by the creditor's taking possession of the collateral, or by the creditor's refraining from doing anything beyond attachment. This last type is called *automatic perfection* (or perfection by attachment), and it is the method that sellers of high-volume, relatively inexpensive items like televisions or compact disk players ordinarily choose. Rather than file a financing statement or take possession of the collateral, such creditors instead rely solely on their security agreement with the debtor as the means for perfecting their interests in the collateral.

The policy underlying the first two methods involves giving public notice of the existence of the security interest. In other words, the drafters of the Code believed that, to deserve the status of a perfected secured creditor, the would-be secured party ought to undertake some affirmative action. And by either filing or possessing, the secured party is doing something that will give anyone looking for a security interest in the collateral notice of the secured party's claim. In the third situation, the nature of the collateral makes the costs of providing public notice arguably higher than the benefits one might gain from filing; for this reason, the Code does not place any affirmative duties on the secured creditor in these situations beyond attachment. Exhibit 26.2 summarizes the methods of perfecting a security interest in various types of collateral.

Filing

Whether filing is necessary in order to perfect a security interest depends on the type of collateral involved. If the collateral consists of accounts or general intangibles, filing ordinarily is the only method of perfection.[21] For goods (including fixtures), chattel paper, and negotiable documents, the secured party may file but is not obligated to do so. Because of their negotiability, interests in money, instruments, and **letters of credit** never can be perfected by filing (possession is the usual method).[22]

Letters of credit

Agreements made at the request of a customer that, upon another party's compliance with the conditions specified in the documents, the bank will honor drafts or other demands for payment.

If filing is necessary, § 9-403 of the UCC states that the presentation of a financing statement and the required fees to the appropriate state or local filing officer and that officer's acceptance of the statement constitute filing. Hence, the device that the Code uses to give notice of the security interest is a *financing statement.* An alternative method of filing, which is not discussed in detail here, involves registering the security interest according to the requirements of statutes other than the UCC, such as state acts covering the certification of title for automobiles, trailers, mobile homes, and boats.

According to § 9-402, to be legally effective, a financing statement must contain certain information: the names of the debtor and secured party; their addresses; a statement indicating the types, or describing the items, of collateral; and the signature of the debtor. Exhibit 26.3 represents a typical financing statement. The filing of such a document allows third parties to obtain information about the security interest from either the secured party or the debtor. Thus, if Bart wants credit from a wholesaler and the latter wants to take a security interest in Bart's equipment, the wholesaler will check the public records for financing statements before extending credit to see which of Bart's equipment already is subject to security interests held by other creditors. This information will help the wholesaler make its decision about whether to extend credit to Bart.

This question arises repeatedly: Does a copy of the security agreement, if filed, constitute the legal equivalent of a financing statement? The Code notes that filing the security agreement will constitute an effective filing if it contains the information required for a financing statement and if the debtor has signed it.[23] But because the description of the collateral in the security agreement serves to create enforceable rights in the collateral for the secured party, it necessarily must be more detailed than the information set out in the financing statement, which only provides public notice of a claimed interest in the collateral. Given these differing rationales, it probably is wise not to treat security agreements and financing statements interchangeably for filing purposes.

On the other hand, a financing statement that substantially complies with the Code's requirements will be effective even though it contains *minor* errors that are not seriously misleading.[24] This provision of the Code is indicative of one policy of Article 9, which is to simplify the filing requirements and "to discourage the fanatical and impossibly refined reading of such statutory requirements in which courts have occasionally indulged themselves."[25] Nevertheless, failure to provide an address, an omission that seems rather negligible, may preclude perfection of the security interest.

EXHIBIT 26.2 Methods of Perfecting a Security Interest

Type of Collateral	Perfection Method (Generally)
Consumer goods (excluding motor vehicles and fixtures)	Automatic (if a purchase money security interest) Possession Filing
Equipment	Filing Possession
Farm products	Filing Possession
Inventory (including motor vehicles)	Filing Possession
Fixtures	Filing Automatic (if a purchase money security interest) Possession (in theory)
Proceeds	Filing Automatic (if security interest in original collateral perfected)
Documents (negotiable)	Filing Possession Automatic (for 21 days)
Instruments	Possession Automatic (for 21 days)
Chattel paper	Filing Possession
Accounts	Filing Automatic (in some instances)
General intangibles	Filing
Letters of credit	Possession
Motor vehicles	Filing Compliance with state certificate of title statutes
Aircraft, copyrights, and the like	Filing (under applicable federal statutes, not under the UCC)

The financing statement ordinarily will be effective if it contains enough information to cause the party searching the records to look further; this so-called inquiry notice will enable that party to discover the perfected security interest. Note, in the *In re Nowling* case, however, that the court believed the defect in the financing statement was so seriously misleading that it invalidated the creditor's attempted perfection of the security interest.

26.4 IN RE NOWLING

124 B.R. 858 (N.D. Fla. 1991)

FACTS Prior to filing for bankruptcy under Chapter 7 of the Bankruptcy Code in August 1987, the debtors, Billy and Brenda Nowling, operated a lawnmower shop. The Nowlings did business as B&B Equipment. All their business stationery, invoices, and business cards used that name. On 26 June 1986, the Nowlings executed a security agreement in the name of B&B Equipment with Roberts Supply, Inc. (Roberts), along with a financing statement that Roberts filed centrally with the secretary of state. This financing statement listed B&B Equipment as the debtor. Roberts sold various merchandise to the Nowlings on credit; the Nowlings ultimately returned the merchandise to Roberts for credit, prior to the bankruptcy filing. Venn, as trustee, sought to avoid this transfer as a preference under § 547 of the Bankruptcy Code, which allows the trustee to avoid transfers to unsecured creditors. [If Roberts were a secured creditor of the debtors, the return of items for credit would not represent a voidable preference under § 547.]

ISSUE Was the financing statement filed by Roberts solely in the trade name of the debtors (and not in their individual names) sufficient to perfect a security interest in the merchandise returned by the Nowlings?

HOLDING No. The financing statement filed by Roberts solely in the trade name of the debtors inadequately identified the debtors and, as such, under Florida law was insufficient to perfect a security interest in the merchandise at issue.

REASONING A determination of the adequacy of the notice provided by the financing statement necessitates consideration of Article 9 of the Uniform Commercial Code, which provides: "A financing statement is sufficient if it gives the names of the debtor and the secured party, is signed by the debtor, gives an address of the secured party from which information concerning the security interest may be obtained, gives a mailing address of the debtor, and contains a statement indicating the types, or describing the items, of collateral." Regarding the identification of the debtor, the UCC provides in pertinent part: "A financing statement sufficiently shows the name of the debtor if it gives the individual, partnership, or corporate name of the debtor, whether or not it adds other trade names or names of partners." A third subsection also provides generally: "A financing statement substantially complying with the requirements of this section is effective even though it contains minor errors which are not seriously misleading." The bankruptcy judge correctly noted in his order that the purpose of the UCC filing system involves giving notice to interested parties that a security interest exists in the property of the debtor. A financing statement is effective as long as it puts any searcher on inquiry notice. The law also considers the trustee to be in the position of a hypothetical but prudent creditor. The judge concluded that any reasonably prudent creditor conducting a search with the secretary of state would have discovered Roberts's financing statement because the statement consisted of a technical defect that was "not seriously misleading." Yet the commentary underlying another Florida amendment notes that since the secured party or other person searching the record likely may be unaware of trade names, filing a financing statement under trade names will not suffice to perfect a security interest in collateral, because such filings may seriously mislead the searcher. The other basis for the bankruptcy judge's decision stemmed from his conclusion that the debtors' filing their bankruptcy petition as "Billy and Brenda Nowling, d.b.a. B&B Equipment" had put the trustee on notice to search for a financing statement under both the trade and individual names. However, as the trustee pointed out, § 544 of the Bankruptcy Code permits a trustee to avoid a transfer of property to an unsecured creditor "without regard to any knowledge of the trustee or of any creditor." Thus, even actual knowledge on the part of the trustee will not suffice if the financing statement is defective. Further, in 1979 the Florida legislature amended the law so that creditors with knowledge would have priority over unperfected security interests. This section would apply to Venn. Roberts acknowledged that the trustee's knowledge of the encumbrance is irrelevant to the question of the perfection of the security interest. But Roberts asserted that the trustee's knowledge of the fact that the Nowlings were doing business under a trade name different from their individual names had placed on the trustee the duty to inquire into recordings under both names. Roberts, however, cited no authority for this untenable proposition. If *actual knowledge* of the encumbrance itself is insufficient to defeat a lien creditor's priority over an unperfected security interest, constructive notice of the fact that a debtor goes by two different names should be **a fortiori** insufficient. Hence, neither of the grounds relied on by the trial court was persuasive. Moreover, a form filed in only a trade name (and not in the individual names of the debtors) remained insufficient to perfect a security interest in the subject property. Consequently, a remand of the case to the Bankruptcy Division for further proceedings was warranted.

26.4 IN RE NOWLING *(cont.)* 124 B.R. 858 (N.D. Fla. 1991)

BUSINESS CONSIDERATIONS As an aftermath of this litigation, what office procedures should Roberts put in place so as to minimize the probabilities of such litigation in the future?

ETHICAL CONSIDERATIONS If the court could have applied an ethical—as opposed to a legal—perspective here, would the court have reached a contrary result? Why or why not?

Numerous other courts have held that the creditor's filing of a financing statement that lists the debtor's trade or business name rather than its legal name constitutes an insufficient filing to perfect a security interest under § 9-402. Because the law differs among the various jurisdictions on this point, however, the creditor's precision in filing the appropriate information often determines whether the courts deem the security interest at issue perfected or unperfected.

A fortiori
All the more; said of a conclusion that follows with even greater logical necessity than another already accepted in the argument.

Sometimes a creditor files a financing statement even before the security agreement is completed or a security interest attaches;[26] but filing before attachment does not constitute perfection.[27] Without attachment at some later time, no perfection ever occurs.

The Code's flexibility nowhere is more apparent than in its handling of the *proper place for filing* the financing statement. The Code does not take a stand on whether filings should be local or statewide, an issue that had caused a great many pre-Code problems. Instead, in § 9-401(1), the UCC provides three different options that depend on the type of collateral involved, thus allowing the respective states to choose the method they believe is most conducive to giving notice of claims.

A financing statement generally is effective for a period of five years from the date of filing, after which the security interest lapses (or becomes unperfected) unless the secured party files a *continuation statement* before this lapse.[28] The secured party may file such a statement within six months prior to the expiration of the financing statement. The secured party must sign the continuation statement, identify the original statement by file number, and state that the original statement still remains in effect.[29] The filing of a continuation statement prolongs the effectiveness of the original financing statement for five years, and the Code does not limit the number of such statements that a secured party can file.

Assuming that the secured party neither has released all or part of the collateral described in the financing statements[30] nor assigned its security interest to another,[31] the Code imposes certain additional duties on the secured party. For example, the secured party must comply within two weeks whenever the debtor *requests a statement of account or a list of collateral* from the secured party. (Presumably, the debtor will request such information because of a lack of certainty about the total amount owed.) Failure to comply may make the secured party liable for losses to the debtor caused by the noncompliance and, in rare cases, even may cost the secured party its security interest. This will be true regarding any security interests reflected in the lists written up by the debtor should any persons be misled by the secured party's failure to comply (as, for instance, by failing to correct the list).[32] On the other hand, the Code, by limiting the debtor to one such list or statement every six months, protects the secured party from burdensome requests. The secured party can charge 10 dollars for each additional request within this time period.[33]

EXHIBIT 26.3 Financing Statement Form

UNIFORM COMMERCIAL CODE INSTRUCTIONS

STATE OF INDIANA
FINANCING STATEMENT

FORM UCC-1
BANKERS SYSTEMS, INC., ST. CLOUD, MINN.

1. Please type this form. Fold only along perforation for mailing.
2. Remove Secured Party and Debtor copies and send other three copies with interleaved carbon paper to the filing officer. Enclose filing fee of $2.00 (plus $.50 if collateral is or is to become a fixture).
3. When filing is to be with more than one office, Form UCC-2 may be placed over this set to avoid double typing.
4. If the space provided for any item(s) is inadequate, the item(s) may be continued on additional sheets, preferably 5" × 8" or sizes convenient to secured party in case of long schedules, indentures, etc. Only one sheet is required. Extra names of debtors may be continued below box "1" in space for description of property.
5. If the collateral is crops or goods which are or are to become fixtures, describe the goods and also the real estate with the name of the record owner if he is other than the debtor.
6. Persons filing a security agreement (as distinguished from a financing statement) are urged to complete this form with or without signature and send with security agreement. An extra charge of $2.00 is imposed for an irregular form.
7. If collateral is goods which are or are to become fixtures, use Form UCC-1a over this Form to avoid double typing, and enclose regular fee plus $.50.
8. The filing officer will return the third page of this Form as an acknowledgment. Secured party at a later time may use third page as a Termination Statement by dating and signing the termination legend on that page.

This Financing Statement is presented to Filing Officer for filing pursuant to the UCC:

3 Maturity Date (if any):

1 Debtor(s) (Last Name First) and Address(es)

2 Secured Party(ies) and Address(es)

KeyBank National Association
202 South Michigan Street
South Bend, Indiana 46601

For Filing Officer (Date, Time, Number, and Filing Office)

4 This financing statement covers the following types (or items) of property (also describe realty where collateral is crops or fixtures):

Assignee of Secured Party

This statement is filed without the debtor's signature to perfect a security interest in collateral check ☒ if so

☐ under a security agreement signed by debtor authorizing secured party to file this statement, or
☐ already subject to a security interest in another jurisdiction when it was brought into this state, or
☐ which is proceeds of the following described original collateral which was perfected:

Check ☒ if covered: ☐ Proceeds of Collateral are also covered. ☐ Products of Collateral are also covered. No. of additional Sheets presented:

Filed with: ☐ Secretary of State ☐ Recorder of ______ County

By: ______
Signature(s) of Debtor(s)

KeyBank National Association
By: ______
Signature(s) of Secured Party(ies)

(1) Filing Officer Copy–Alphabetical
FORM UCC–1 INDIANA UNIFORM COMMERCIAL CODE

Approved by:

Secretary of State

Courtesy of KeyBank National Association, South Bend, Indiana.

Once no outstanding obligations remain under the financing statement, the Code sets out a procedure that may require the secured party to file a *termination statement* noting the discharge of the obligations and/or the termination of the financing agreement. Where consumer goods are concerned, the Code places an affirmative duty on the secured party to file a termination statement within one month or within ten days following written demand by the debtor once the debtor has completely paid for the goods. In all other cases, however, the secured party need not file a termination statement unless the debtor requests such a filing.[34] But when compliance is necessary, the Code subjects noncomplying secured parties to certain penalties. Termination statements, which refer to the appropriate financing statement by file number, clear the public records so that the presence of old, irrelevant financing statements will not leave a would-be creditor with an unrealistic picture of a credit applicant's creditworthiness and reliability.

Possession

In some cases the secured party's possession of the collateral is the method used for perfecting the security interest,[35] as mentioned earlier. Historically, when financing arrangements were more primitive, possession of the personal property was the surest sign of ownership; hence, perfection by possession evolved as the most popular method. Even today, secured parties ordinarily must perfect security interests in letters of credit, money, and instruments in this manner and may perfect goods, negotiable documents, or chattel paper in this fashion as well. For instance, a bank may require a debtor to give it possession of the debtor's stocks and bonds as collateral for securing a loan. In such circumstances, the secured creditor has accepted a pledge of these instruments as collateral.

YOU BE THE JUDGE

Liens

In order to guarantee that its client will pay, a law firm doing personal injury work on behalf of its clients has each client sign an agreement in which the client gives the firm a lien on the client's potential damages recovery. The firm's lien has been challenged by a client and one of the client's other creditors, who allege that this is not the sort of asset on which a lien can be established in advance. Suppose this case has been brought before *your* court. How will *you* rule on this issue?[36]

BUSINESS CONSIDERATIONS To protect its interests, should the law firm file an Article 9 financing statement describing its claim against each client? What else might the firm want to do to protect its claim against each client?

ETHICAL CONSIDERATIONS Is it ethical for a law firm—or any other business—to seek a lien on future earnings of clients or customers in an effort to assure that payment for the benefits conferred will occur? What public policy and/or ethical concerns do such agreements raise?

SOURCE: *UCC Bulletin* (Deerfield: Clark Boardman Callaghan) (July 1996), p. 12.

As we discuss in more detail later, the type of collateral involved is relevant in determining whether perfection can occur by possession. If the creditor's possession of collateral (and the debtor's resultant lack of possession) is to serve to other parties as public notice of the security interest, the collateral must be tangible; that is, one must be able to see, touch, or move it. All the types of collateral perfectible by possession share this attribute. On the other hand, contract rights, accounts that constitute a significant portion of the debtor's business, and general intangibles merely *represent* rights and have no physical embodiment. Thus, one never can perfect these categories of personal property by possession; filing is necessary.

Automatic Perfection

Automatic perfection is the method ordinarily used for perfecting purchase money security interests in consumer goods.[37] In these situations, as mentioned earlier, perfection occurs upon attachment alone. A look at the nature of these transactions shows why filing is unnecessary. The Code defines a *purchase money security interest* as one retained by the seller of the collateral to secure all or part of its price or taken by a person who by making advances or incurring an obligation gives value to enable the debtor to acquire rights in the collateral.[38]

Typically, a seller retains a purchase money security interest in the collateral, whether it is a stove, refrigerator, washing machine, or compact disk player. This means that the seller usually sells to the buyer, on an installment basis, goods that the buyer will use for personal purposes. The seller, in turn, retains a security interest in the consumer goods—for instance, the compact disk player—to secure the unpaid purchase price. If the buyer misses any installment payments, the seller can repossess the collateral. The secured party's purchase money security interest is perfectible the moment the transaction has occurred because a written security agreement signed by the debtor exists; the secured party has given value; and the debtor has rights in the collateral (that is, attachment has occurred). All this has happened (thanks to the modern wonder of "form contracts") a short time before the debtor, with the compact disk player in hand, walks out of the store.

Given the type of collateral involved (consumer goods) and the frequency with which such transactions occur, the UCC has followed pre-Code law in eliminating the filing requirement for these types of commercial deals. It makes little sense to require a merchant to pay the filing fees and other administrative costs associated with filing for every $100 item sold. Moreover, in such situations, few benefits result from filing, since consumer goods—already low in price and prone to rapid deterioration—are not the types of property later secured parties will want as collateral anyway. Therefore, public notice to such creditors afforded by filing has little value and will only clutter the filing offices. The same rationale underlies the availability of automatic perfection as a method for perfecting certain transfers of accounts, documents, and instruments as well. Note in the *In re Lockovich* case the court addressed many of these concepts.

26.5 IN RE LOCKOVICH

124 B.R. 660 (W.D. Pa. 1991)

FACTS On about 20 August 1986, John J. and Clara Lockovich purchased a 22-foot 1986 Chapparel Villian III boat from the Greene County Yacht Club (club) for $32,500. The Lockoviches (debtors) paid $6,000 to the club and executed a security agreement/lien contract that set forth the purchase and finance terms. In the contract, the Lockoviches granted a security interest in the boat to the holder of the contract. When Gallatin National Bank (Gallatin) paid the

26.5 IN RE LOCKOVICH (cont.) 124 B.R. 660 (W.D. Pa. 1991)

club $26,757.14 on the Lockoviches' behalf, the club assigned the contract to Gallatin. Gallatin then filed financing statements in the appropriate Greene County office and with the secretary of the Commonwealth of Pennsylvania. Greene County was the county in which Gallatin was located, but the Lockoviches resided in Allegheny County. The filing of the financing statements therefore was ineffective to perfect the security interest in the boat. The Lockoviches, by failing to remit payments as required, subsequently defaulted under the terms of the security agreement they had signed with Gallatin. Before Gallatin could take action, the Lockoviches filed for relief under Chapter 11 of the Bankruptcy Code. Gallatin then sought, pursuant to the security agreement, to enforce its rights. On 2 October 1989, the Bankruptcy Court, in denying Gallatin's motion, held that because Gallatin had failed to perfect its security interest in the boat by filing, it was an unsecured creditor. Pursuant to the bankruptcy laws, as a holder of an unperfected security interest, Gallatin's right to the boat remained inferior to that of the debtor-in-possession, a hypothetical lienholder.

ISSUE In order to perfect its purchase money security interest in the boat, did Gallatin need to file a financing statement?

HOLDING No. Gallatin held a purchase money security interest in a consumer good (the boat) and hence did not need to file a financing statement in order to achieve secured party status.

REASONING To perfect a security interest in collateral under the Code, a secured party must file a financing statement in the office of the secretary of the commonwealth and in the appropriate office of the county in which the debtor resides. Yet, depending on the type of collateral, the Pennsylvania UCC permits several exceptions to this general rule: "(a) General Rule—A financing statement must be filed to perfect all security interests except the following . . . (4) a purchase money security interest in consumer goods; but filing is required for a motor vehicle required to be registered." Three significant problems exist in determining the automatic perfection of purchase money interests in consumer goods. First, what is a "purchase money security interest"? Second, what are "consumer goods"? Third, can massive and expensive items qualify as consumer goods? As to the first question, a purchase money security interest consists of one "(1) taken or retained by the seller of the collateral to secure all or part of its price; or (2) taken by a person who by making advances or incurring an obligation gives value to enable the debtor to acquire rights in or the use of collateral if such value is in fact so used." The parties did not dispute the fact that the security interest held by Gallatin amounts to a purchase money security interest. As to the remaining questions—which involve issues of first impression in this state—a court's analysis must focus on whether a $32,500 watercraft is a consumer good under Pennsylvania law. In Pennsylvania, "consumer goods" include those used or bought for use primarily for personal, family, or household purposes. Such goods are not classified according to design or intrinsic nature, but according to the use to which the owner puts them. The Lockoviches never maintained that they utilized the boat for anything other than for their personal use. Under the clear mandate of the Code, a consumer good subject to exception from the filing of financing statements is determined by the use or intended use of the good; design, size, weight, shape, and cost remain irrelevant. In fact, if a millionaire decides to purchase the *Queen Mary* for his or her personal or family luxury on the high seas, under the Code, the great *Queen* is nothing but a common consumer good. There need be no debate as to cost, size, or life expectancy. In short, creditors must be confident that when they enter into a commercial transaction, they will play by the rules as written in the Code. Those who do not believe Pennsylvania law should permit an expensive boat to fall within the classification of consumer goods have two legislative solutions available. One is to require explicitly the filing of security interests in motorboats. The other approach, adopted in some states, involves limiting the value to which the consumer goods exemption applies. But, for the present analysis, the boat is a consumer good; and, pursuant to Pennsylvania law, Gallatin did not have to file a financing statement in order to perfect its security interest in the boat. Since Gallatin had a valid security interest in the boat, it could enforce its security interest under the bankruptcy laws.

BUSINESS CONSIDERATIONS Would you favor Gallatin's lobbying the legislature for a statute limiting the value of consumer goods to which the exemption from filing would apply? Why or why not? What advantages and disadvantages would inhere in such a state UCC enactment?

ETHICAL CONSIDERATIONS The Lockoviches here were seeking to retain the boat despite their filing for protection under Chapter 11 of the Bankruptcy Code and despite Gallatin's filing a financing statement (albeit in the wrong place). Would you characterize the Lockoviches' actions as unethical? Why or why not?

RELATED TOPICS

Two other topics deserve consideration before we leave the issues covered in this chapter: multistate transactions and proceeds.

Multistate Transactions

A related aspect of perfection involves the problem of collateral, such as equipment, that the debtor can move across state or county lines. For example, a debtor in Indiana may take threshing equipment subject to an Indiana security interest to Illinois or Iowa and keep this equipment in the new state for several months (that is, until the harvesting season ends). The Code's rules for such situations, expressed in § 9-103, are very complex. In general, the Code says that, with respect to ordinary goods, the secured party should perfect its interest by filing (or by some other method) in the state where the collateral is originally located. Upon the debtor's removal of the collateral, the secured party should file in the new jurisdiction.

If a purchase money security interest is involved and both parties at the time of the creation of the security interest understand that the debtor will move the collateral to another jurisdiction, the law of the new jurisdiction controls perfection for 30 days after the debtor receives possession, assuming the collateral is moved in that time. To avoid losing priority of perfection, the secured party ought to file in both jurisdictions. If collateral previously has been perfected in one jurisdiction and then is moved to another, it remains perfected for its period of original perfection or for four months, whichever expires first. Thus, the secured party should file in the new jurisdiction before this four-month period expires.

The removal of motor vehicles from one jurisdiction to another is covered by state certificate of title laws and by the Code.[39] Because these laws are very complicated, a wise secured creditor, in order to do everything possible to retain a perfected security interest in them, will keep abreast of the debtor's removal of these vehicles. Generally speaking, if the new jurisdiction is a non–certificate of title state, a secured party will need to reperfect (usually by filing) within four months of the collateral's removal to the new jurisdiction. If, in contrast, the jurisdiction to which the debtor has removed the motor vehicle requires perfection by notation of the security inter-

http:// RESOURCES FOR BUSINESS LAW STUDENTS

NAME	RESOURCES	WEB ADDRESS
Uniform Commercial Code (UCC) Article 9, Secured Transactions; Sales of Accounts and Chattel Paper	The Legal Information Institute (LII), maintained by the Cornell Law School, provides a hypertext and searchable version of UCC Article 9, Secured Transactions; Sales of Accounts and Chattel Paper. LII also maintains links to Article 9 as adopted by particular states and to proposed revisions.	http://www.law.cornell.edu/ucc/9/overview.html
The National Conference of Commissioners on Uniform State Laws	The National Conference of Commissioners on Uniform State Laws (NCCUSL), the drafter of the UCC, provides drafts and revisions of its uniform and model acts.	http://www.law.upenn.edu/library/ulc/ulc.htm

est on the vehicle's title, in this situation reperfection will not occur by filing in the new jurisdiction but rather by the secured party's noting its interest on the motor vehicle's certificate of title. In such circumstances, the secured party may have longer than four months in which to reperfect, since reperfection will be necessary only when the debtor, in order to receive valid registration papers in the new state, requests the surrender of the vehicle's title. At that time, the prudent secured party will note its interest again on the new certificate of title and thus remain perfected.

Proceeds

The final point we should make about security interests and perfection is that the Code allows a secured party's interest to reach the proceeds of the debtor's disposition of the collateral.[40] In other words, the secured party has a "lien" (similar to that which we discussed in the context of multistate transactions) that "floats" over the collateral and includes as "proceeds" whatever is received on the sale, exchange, collection, or other disposition of the collateral.[41] If Bart sells the freezer and cash register to another person, the secured party's interest in the collateral will extend even to the cash proceeds realized from this sale. Thus, the issue of proceeds, and the Code's treatment of it, implicates not only perfection rules but also priority rules (especially when, as often is the case, the trustee in bankruptcy is involved as well).

26.3

FINANCE

MOVING COLLATERAL

CIT has enjoyed quite a bit of success selling the videophones in California, and the firm decides to establish a major warehouse facility in California to provide better service to CIT's West Coast customers. The firm already has arranged a lease of warehouse space, and CIT is planning to send several of the firm's trucks and several thousand completed videophones to the new warehouse. Lindsay and John believe that CIT should not do this without CIT's bank's permission since the trucks and the videophones are collateral for CIT's line of credit with the bank. Tom and Dan do not think that this will cause the bank any problems. They are seeking your advice, however, before they finalize the decision. What will you tell them?

BUSINESS CONSIDERATIONS Should a debtor in a secured transaction adhere to a policy of informing the creditor any time the collateral will be removed from the jurisdiction? Why or why not? What can the creditor in this situation do to maximize its protections in the event the collateral is removed from the jurisdiction without notice?

ETHICAL CONSIDERATIONS Is it ethical for a debtor to remove collateral from the jurisdiction without notifying the creditor? Is it ethical for the creditor to demand notice from the debtor in advance before the collateral can be moved?

SUMMARY

A secured transaction assures payment by the buyer: If the buyer does not pay the seller, the seller's security interest will allow the seller to repossess the property. A secured transaction typically involves a secured party, a debtor, a security agreement, and collateral. The Code categorizes collateral according to its nature or its use. One type of collateral is goods; the different classes of goods are mutually exclusive. Collateral also may consist of documents, instruments, letters of credit, proceeds, accounts, chattel paper, and general intangibles. Article 9 applies to consensual security interests in personal property or fixtures but not to those arising by operation of law. It covers leases meant as security but not "true" leases. Attachment is the process by which the secured party creates an enforceable security interest in the collateral. A signed security agreement, in conjunction with the occurrence of other events, provides evidence that attachment has occurred. Perfection refers to the method by which secured parties protect themselves against later creditors of the debtor. Perfection can take place in one of three ways: (1) by the creditor's filing a valid financing statement, (2) by the creditor's possession of the collateral, and (3) by automatic perfection. The method of perfection that the secured party should use often depends on the type of collateral involved. If filing is the applicable method, the creditor must use a legally effective financing statement. The Code's rules regarding multistate transactions are very complex; but, in order to ensure continuation of perfection, the secured party should check them whenever the debtor moves the collateral from one jurisdiction to another. The secured party, if he or she has met certain requirements under the Code, generally can reach the proceeds of the debtor's later disposition of the collateral.

Discussion Questions

1. What is a secured transaction?
2. Define a security interest.
3. Name and define the various types of property the Code recognizes as collateral.
4. If Will does not pay Carla, the mechanic who fixes his car, and she obtains a judgment against him, does Carla have an Article 9 security interest in Will's car? Why or why not?
5. What is the difference between a true lease and a lease intended as security?
6. What is attachment, and what are the requirements for it?
7. Give the criteria necessary for a valid security agreement.
8. Define perfection, and discuss in detail the three methods by which perfection occurs.
9. What kinds of defects cause a financing statement to be ineffective?
10. What problems can arise if Debbie Dunn has given her bank a security interest in bulldozers and she moves the bulldozers from Indiana to Michigan?

Case Problems and Writing Assignments

1. William Owens made a loan of $25,000 to Howard. Two promissory notes signed by Howard, each containing the words "SECURITY: 1956 GMC bus," evidenced the loan. As security for payment of the notes, Howard endorsed the certificate of title for the bus and delivered the certificate to Owens. Five months later, Howard sold the bus to Don Simplot for $45,000, to be paid in installments. After Simplot had paid the last installment, he took possession of the bus and received from Howard a bill of sale stating that the bus was free of all liens and encumbrances. When Simplot asked for the certificate of title, Howard told him it was lost. Simplot requested that the Idaho Department of Transportation conduct a title search; at the same time, he also applied for a transfer of title. Meanwhile, after Owens had approached Howard and unsuccessfully demanded payment of the loan, Owens applied for a certificate of title showing Howard as the owner and Owens as the lienholder. Despite Simplot's pending application, the Department of Transportation issued Owens the requested title. The Department also issued a certificate of title to Simplot. The certificate designated him as the owner and showed no liens or encumbrances. Some time later, Howard notified Simplot that Owens was claiming a security interest in the bus. At Simplot's request, the Idaho Department of Transportation held a hearing to determine the parties' respective interests. The Department concluded that Simplot owned the bus, but that the title remained encumbered by Owens's lien. Simplot, claiming ownership free of all liens and seeking an award of damages against Howard, then filed this action. Simplot based his claim on the fact that the promissory notes bearing the notation "SECURITY: 1956 GMC bus," in conjunction with Howard's execution and delivery of the certificate of title to the bus to Owens, constituted actions legally inadequate to create a security interest and to effect attachment of such an interest. Would you agree with Simplot? Why or why not? [See *Simplot* v. *William C. Owens, M.D., P.A.*, 805 P.2d 449 (Idaho 1990).]

2. In December 1983, Silverline Building and Maintenance Company (Silverline) contracted with the District of Columbia to perform janitorial services in two office buildings occupied by the district. At approximately the same time, Silverline entered into a factoring arrangement with Thomas Funding Corporation (Thomas) in which Silverline assigned its right to pay-

ment pursuant to its contracts with the district to Thomas in exchange for money Silverline received from Thomas to use as working capital. By letter, Silverline notified the district of the assignment and directed the district, upon receipt of Silverline's invoices, to make payments to Thomas. In addition, Thomas filed with the recorder of deeds a financing statement covering "all now owned and hereafter acquired accounts, contract rights . . . [and] general intangibles of the debtor." The financing statement, however, inadvertently identified the debtor as "Silvermine Building and Maintenance Co.," mistakenly substituting the letter *m* for the second letter *l* in the word *Silverline.* Until October 1984, the district paid Thomas the amount due Silverline under the janitorial services contracts. In April and May 1984, the Internal Revenue Service (IRS) had made assessments against Silverline for unpaid federal income taxes totaling $22,370.19. On 5 October 1984, the IRS filed a notice of tax lien against Silverline with the recorder of deeds and served the district with a notice of tax levy against any property or rights to property belonging to Silverline. At the time, the district owed $18,747 on the janitorial services contracts for work performed during September 1984. Instead of paying the amount owed under the contracts to Thomas, on 1 January 1985, the district paid this amount to the IRS. Thomas then brought suit against the district for $18,747, the amount due under the Silverline contracts. Thomas, as a perfected secured party, had full rights to the $18,747. If Thomas had failed to perfect its interest in the assignment of the accounts, however, Silverline retained a property interest on which a third-party lien creditor, such as the IRS, could attach a lien. The IRS argued that the misspelling of Silverline's name on the financing statement had made the filing by Thomas invalid. Was the misspelling of Silverline's name as "Silvermine" an error so seriously misleading as to render the financing statement ineffective for the purposes of putting a third party on notice that Silverline had given Thomas a security interest in the accounts? Why? [See *District of Columbia* v. *Thomas Funding Corp.,* 593 A.2d 1030 (D.C. App. 1991).]

3. Rollins Cotton Company (Rollins) was the owner and possessor of certain certificated cotton (that is, cotton classified by the government as being of sufficiently high quality for delivery under New York Cotton Exchange futures contracts), some of which it sold to The Julien Company (Julien). After paying for this cotton, Julien, in turn, sold the certificated cotton to third parties. Rollins subsequently agreed with Julien to enter into a financing agreement under which Rollins paid for the repurchase of some of the certificated cotton as Rollins received the warehouse receipts, and Rollins held these certificated cotton warehouse receipts while Julien marketed the cotton for other sales. At this stage, having advanced funds to or for Julien for the repurchases, Rollins was a secured creditor; and Rollins held a possessory security interest pursuant to an oral agreement with Julien. At this same time, Julien also had a financing arrangement with Bankers Trust Company (BTCo) under which a line of credit was established in exchange for BTCo's holding other cotton collateral, including uncertificated cotton warehouse receipts, through its subdepository L & S Cotton Systems (L & S). Under this arrangement, L & S maintained an inventory of that portion of Julien's collateral held by L & S for BTCo. Julien determined that, in order to pursue a federal decertification and recertification process, it needed the certificated cotton warehouse receipts held by Rollins. In an attempt to remain a secured creditor, Rollins agreed to relinquish its possession of the certificated cotton warehouse receipts before being paid, but it conditioned this relinquishment upon receiving substitute collateral in the form of the uncertificated cotton warehouse receipts being held by L & S. Julien obtained the certificated cotton warehouse receipts; L & S signed two trust receipts; and L & S, by carrying them in Rollins's trust receipt accounts, simultaneously blocked the required number of uncertificated cotton warehouse receipts. Rollins asserted that this blocking preserved its security, as L & S's actions amounted to an acknowledgment of possession by the bailee, L & S. Subsequently, Julien paid Rollins its debt of $22,028,569.52; and L & S released its collateral block. Later, when Julien was in Chapter 11 bankruptcy, the trustee sought to avoid, as a preferential transfer, the $22,028,569.52 paid to Rollins. To rebut the trustee's claim, Rollins argued that it was a secured creditor pursuant to an oral security agreement. Rollins further contended that it had maintained possession of the collateral pursuant to this agreement, that the other requirements for attachment had occurred, and that its claimed security interest therefore was valid and enforceable. The trustee submitted that, because L & S, a bailee, had had possession of the collateral, Rollins's security interest never had attached to the collateral. Given these circumstances, had Rollins effected attachment of a security interest even though the bailee (L & S) had had possession of the collateral? Why? [See *In re The Julien Co.,* 168 B.R. 647 (Bankr. W.D. Tenn. 1994).]

4. In August 1988, seeking to recover on a debt secured by a Caterpillar D9H tractor, Laurel Explosives, Inc. (Laurel) filed an action against H & P Coal Company (H & P). A default judgment granted against H & P upheld the validity of Laurel's security interest in the

Caterpillar D9H tractor. Subsequently, Laurel filed a lawsuit against First National Bank & Trust Company of Corbin (First National), which had possession of the Caterpillar D9H tractor, because First National had claimed that it possessed a security interest in the tractor that was superior to Laurel's. First National maintained that its security interest, which was perfected more than two years after Laurel's, nonetheless was superior because the financing statement it had filed correctly listed the serial number of the tractor, whereas the security agreement Laurel had filed as a financing statement contained an error. The evidence showed that Laurel's security agreement described the tractor as a "CATERPILLAR D9H #9OV04695 (TRACTOR)" instead of #9OV4695. First National subsequently filed two financing statements that listed the tractor as secured collateral. The first described the tractor as "One (1) Caterpillar Tractor D8H, Serial No. 9OV4695." But First National's second financing statement correctly described the tractor as "CAT D9H TRACTOR S/N 9OV4695." Laurel argued that the serial number in its security agreement, which erroneously included a zero before the last four digits, was not seriously misleading and that this description gave adequate notice of Laurel's claimed security interest in this particular tractor. Thus, Laurel asserted that its security interest should enjoy priority over First National's. Was Laurel correct? Why? [See *Laurel Explosives, Inc.* v. *First Nat'l Bank & Trust Co. of Corbin,* 801 S.W.2d 336 ([Ky. App. 1990).]

5. Trans Canada Credit Corporation, Ltd. (Trans Canada), a Canadian corporation, lent money to DiCicco and secured its interest in the loan proceeds with a chattel mortgage. By the terms of the chattel mortgage, Trans Canada could take immediate possession of the vehicle DiCicco purchased upon either DiCicco's removal of the vehicle from Canada or DiCicco's sale or transfer of the vehicle. DiCicco later removed the vehicle from Canada and obtained a Pennsylvania certificate of title on or about 14 April 1987. The certificate of title did not have an endorsement indicating Trans Canada's lien as an encumbrance on the vehicle, but it did bear a notation indicating that the vehicle was an out-of-state vehicle. On 16 May 1987, DiCicco sold the secured vehicle to Kosack, an automobile broker and dealer. Kosack subsequently resold the vehicle at an interstate auto auction. In January 1988, Trans Canada made application in Pennsylvania to perfect its security interest. This statute allows the perfection of a security interest in Pennsylvania before or after the expiration of a four-month period within which an out-of-state lien might otherwise be perfected under the laws of the jurisdiction where the motor vehicle had been located when the secured interest had attached. Thus, Trans Canada subsequently characterized this filing in January 1988 as a "reperfection" of the security interest. Trans Canada, after making several unsuccessful demands on Richard Kosack, d.b.a. Family Motors, filed this lawsuit for $4,875, the uncontested fair market value of the automobile at the time Kosack had resold it at the auto auction. A nonjury trial resulted in a verdict in favor of Kosack. Upon consideration of posttrial motions, the trial court, owing to its belief that Trans Canada, as a validly perfected creditor, had enjoyed priority regarding the sold automobile, granted a judgment non obstante veredicto (judgment n.o.v.) in favor of Trans Canada. Did the perfection of Trans Canada's security interest in Canada cover the removal of the automobile to Pennsylvania and thus give Trans Canada priority regarding the automobile? [See *Trans Canada Credit Corp., Ltd.* v. *Kosack,* 590 A.2d 1295 (Pa.Super. 1991).]

6. **BUSINESS APPLICATION CASE** Heritage House Interiors, Inc. (Heritage House) is in the business of selling and installing furniture and accessories. In August 1988, Heritage House entered into a security agreement with Pennsylvania House (a division of Chicago Pacific Corp.). The terms of the agreement called for Pennsylvania House to sell furniture and accessories to Heritage House on credit, with Pennsylvania House receiving a security interest in all the furniture purchased by Heritage House from Pennsylvania House and any proceeds from the collateral. The security agreement noted that the agreements were "for the benefit of [Pennsylvania House], its successors and assigns." In connection with this agreement, Heritage House then filed a financing statement with the Florida secretary of state. This statement identified the secured party as "Pennsylvania House, a division of Chicago Pacific Corporation." In January 1989, Chicago Pacific merged with Maytag Corporation (Maytag), with Maytag as the surviving corporation. While continuing to operate in the same manner from the same location, Pennsylvania House thus became a division of Maytag. In June 1989, LADD Furniture, Inc. (LADD) agreed to purchase the assets of Pennsylvania House–Maytag, excluding "any of [Maytag's] claims or causes of action against third parties relating to the assets, properties, business, or operations . . . arising out of transactions occurring prior to the closing date." In July 1989, LADD made Pennsylvania House, Inc., a wholly owned independent subsidiary and assigned to it the interests LADD had acquired in Pennsylvania House–Maytag. On that same day, Maytag assigned to Pennsylvania House, Inc., the assets previously held by Pennsylvania House–Maytag. Throughout this period Pennsyl-

vania House, Inc. continued to do business with Heritage House under the original agreements and documents involving Pennsylvania House and Pennsylvania House–Maytag. In June 1990, Heritage House filed a voluntary petition for relief under Chapter 11 of the Bankruptcy Code. At that time, Heritage House owed Pennsylvania House, Inc., $426,505.78; and its inventory (all purchased from Pennsylvania House, Pennsylvania House–Maytag, or Pennsylvania House, Inc.) included furniture and accessories valued at approximately $195,000. In September 1990, Maytag and LADD each assigned "any and all security interests and causes of action" they held against Heritage House to Pennsylvania House, Inc. Arguing that the original agreement never had been amended to reflect Pennsylvania House, Inc.'s security interest and that Heritage House never had entered into a security agreement with Pennsylvania House–Maytag or Pennsylvania House, Inc., Heritage House challenged the perfection of the security interest in the inventory held by Pennsylvania House, Inc. How should a judge decide this issue? What steps should the respective parties have taken so as to avoid this litigation? [See *In re Heritage House Interiors, Inc.*, 122 B.R. 605 (Bankr. M.D. Fla. 1990).]

7. **ETHICS APPLICATION CASE** On 29 September 1989 and 7 and 9 July 1990, Keith Alan Powers rented used household goods from Royce, Inc. The three rental agreements provided for an initial two-week rental period with a series of optional two-week rental periods thereafter. No obligation to rent property beyond the initial two-week rental period existed. A renter exercised the option to rent the property for an additional two-week period upon the renter's paying a designated rental payment to Royce. The agreements were terminable at any time by the lessee/debtor without penalty or further obligation. With two exceptions, Powers rented used (as opposed to new) property from Royce. Under the agreements he signed, Powers could purchase the used household goods: (1) immediately for cash, (2) for the cash price at any time within ninety days of taking possession ("90 days same as cash"), (3) for a sliding-scale price that could be exercised after 90 days ("the early buy-out option price"), or (4) by making the total number of rental payments to acquire ownership with no additional consideration. On 22 May 1991, Powers filed a Chapter 13 bankruptcy proceeding. At the time of this filing, he had possession of the property covered in the agreements and had been making rental payments. In the Chapter 13 proceedings, Powers listed Royce as a secured creditor for $3,041—$1,000 of which was secured by the goods and $2,041 of which was unsecured. Under the debtor's plan, Royce would receive $1,000, with the unsecured creditors receiving approximately 30 percent of the remaining unsecured balance. Royce filed an objection to the confirmation of the plan and sought the return of the property it had leased to Powers. Royce took the position that its agreements constituted true leases rather than disguised security agreements. Royce asserted that, in order to retain possession of the property, the debtor (here, Powers) must assume the leases pursuant to § 365 of the Bankruptcy Code, cure any existing rental defaults, and thereafter make the rental payments stated in the agreements or exercise one of the purchase options. Because no such assumption had occurred, Royce claimed that, under § 365, the debtor had rejected the leases, that the debtor's right to possession therefore had terminated, and that Royce was entitled to the return of property. In contrast, Powers characterized the agreements as disguised installment sales that gave Royce a security interest in the goods. Hence, Powers argued, as a debtor, he could keep the property without assuming the leases under § 365 or without paying Royce the amounts necessary to purchase the property under the options provided in the agreements. Who had the better argument here, Powers or Royce? Why? The legalities aside, assess Powers's ethics in these circumstances. Would you like to do business with him? Explain. [See *In re Powers*, 983 F.2d 88 (7th Cir. 1993).]

8. **IDES CASE** The 1981 collapse of the skywalks surrounding the atrium of the Hyatt Regency Hotel in Kansas City, Missouri, crushed Joseph Hayes III's legs and compressed the vertebrae in his back. For a year, Hayes could not walk. In 1982, in exchange for an annuity contract purchased by Hyatt's insurers for Hayes's benefit, Hayes settled with Hyatt. The annuity provided for scheduled cash contract payments over a 20-year period. In 1991, Hayes became interested in going into business for himself. United Missouri Bank (UMB) ultimately loaned Hayes the money to buy a radiator and auto repair shop and used Hayes's pledge of the annuity as collateral for this loan. When Hayes later filed for bankruptcy, he challenged UMB's status as a secured creditor on the basis that he was not the owner of the annuity contract but only the beneficiary of it. As such, Hayes argued, he had been unable to grant UMB an interest in something he did not own. In short, Hayes claimed that attachment of UMB's security interest was lacking because he, the debtor, had had no rights in the collateral. Had UMB complied with the Code's requisites for attachment so as to enjoy a security interest in the stream of payments guaranteed to Hayes in the annuity contract? Why? Apply the IDES model. [See *In re Hayes*, 168 B.R. 717 (Bankr. D. Kan. 1994).]

NOTES

1. Uniform Commercial Code, § 9-105(m).
2. Ibid., § 9-105(d). This section further states that "[w]here the debtor and the owner of the collateral are not the same person, the term 'debtor' means the owner of the collateral in any provision of the Article dealing with the collateral, the obligor in any provision dealing with the obligation, and may include both where the context so requires. . . ."
3. Ibid., § 9-105(1).
4. Ibid., § 9-105(c). Collateral also includes accounts and chattel paper that have been sold.
5. Ibid., § 9-106.
6. Section 9-202 makes the concept of title—that is, whether the secured party or the debtor has title to the collateral—immaterial under the Code.
7. Uniform Commercial Code, § 1-201(37).
8. Ibid., § 9-105(h). Goods also may include such things as standing timber, growing crops, and the unborn young of animals.
9. Ibid., § 9-109(1)–(3).
10. Ibid., § 9-109(4), Official Comment 3.
11. Ibid., § 9-313(1)(a).
12. Ibid., § 9-109, Official Comment 2.
13. Ibid., § 9-104(c).
14. Ibid., § 9-102(2).
15. Ibid., § 9-104.
16. Ibid., §§ 9-201, 9-203(4).
17. Ibid., § 9-102(2).
18. Ibid., § 1-201(37).
19. Ibid., § 9-203.
20. Ibid., §§ 9-203(1), 9-110.
21. Ibid., §§ 9-302, 9-401.
22. Ibid., § 9-304(l).
23. Ibid., § 9-402(l).
24. Ibid., § 9-402(8).
25. Ibid., § 9-402, Official Comment 9.
26. Ibid., § 9-402(1).
27. Ibid., § 9-303(1).
28. Ibid., § 9-403(2),(3).
29. Ibid.
30. Ibid., § 9-406.
31. Ibid., § 9-405(2).
32. Ibid., § 9-208(2).
33. Ibid., § 9-208(3).
34. Ibid., § 9-404(1).
35. Ibid., § 9-305.
36. "Law Firm's Lien in Client's Tort Recovery," *UCC Bulletin* (Deerfield: Clark Boardman Callahan) (July 1996), p. 12.
37. Uniform Commercial Code, § 9-302(1)(d).
38. Ibid., § 9-107.
39. Ibid., §§ 9-103(1)(a), (2); 9-302(3)(b), (4).
40. Ibid., § 9-204.
41. Ibid., § 9-306.

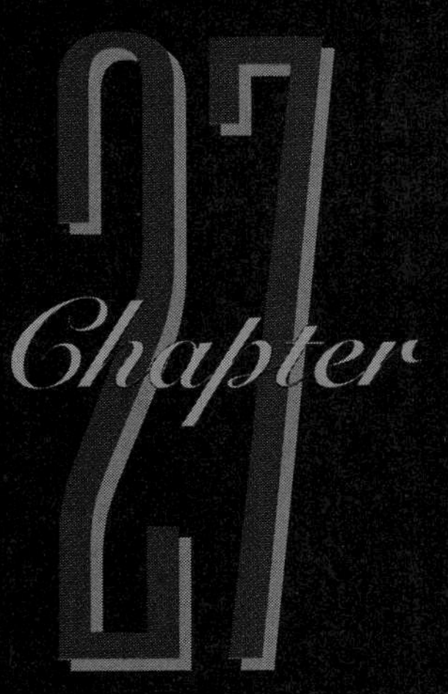

Secured Transactions: Priorities

O U T L I N E

A G E N D A

The Kochanowskis will need to borrow money at times in order to help CIT grow and prosper. They need to know whether they can use any assets as collateral for more than one loan and what effect this may have on their creditors. They also will be selling a number of Call-Image videophones on credit, and they want to hold the best possible security interests in those videophones. In order to maximize their protections what methods of perfection should the Kochanowskis use? What rights might they be able to assert against competing creditors?

These and other questions are likely to arise during your study of this chapter. Be prepared! You never know when one of the Kochanowskis will need your help or advice.

THE CODE AND COMPETING CLAIMS FOR THE SAME COLLATERAL

In Chapter 26, we examined the processes of attachment and perfection, the methods by which secured parties protect their respective interests in the collateral against the debtor and against later creditors of the debtor, especially the trustee in bankruptcy, who occupies the status of a lien creditor under the bankruptcy laws. As discussed, the date of perfection becomes particularly significant when, as sometimes is the case, upon the debtor's default, several secured parties claim a perfected security interest in the same collateral. The Uniform Commercial Code's system for deciding which competing claim is superior—that is, which claim has *priority*—is the focus of this chapter.

PRIORITIES

A secured party's priority over other creditors is of enormous practical importance. The one catastrophe every creditor fears most is the bankruptcy of the debtor. The reason is simple: In the event of bankruptcy, each creditor runs the risk of receiving only a few cents on every dollar loaned to the debtor. Yet, as we have previously discussed, a creditor can maximize the chances of recovering the money owed by attaining the status of a perfected secured party. This status gives the creditor first claim to the collateral and thus the best chance (generally by selling the collateral) of realizing most, if not all, of the debt. A perfected secured party, then, will have priority over general (or unsecured) creditors and lien creditors, including the trustee in bankruptcy. After the secured party has disposed of the collateral, any money in excess of that owed to the secured party may be applied to the claims of these other creditors. In many instances, however, no money remains to satisfy these latter claims. Thus, we cannot overemphasize the importance of becoming a secured party.

CONFLICTING INTERESTS IN THE SAME COLLATERAL

Given the advantages attendant on being a secured party, most creditors strive to achieve this status. This fact, in turn, leads to the possibility that several secured parties will claim a security interest in the same collateral. How, then, can we determine who among this class of favored parties has priority? Or, in other words, who has "first dibs" on the collateral?

The UCC's rules on priorities, set out in § 9-312, are difficult to unravel and understand. In general, the Code validates a *first-in-time, first-in-right approach* whereby those who have perfected their claims first have priority. For example, if two competing security interests have been perfected by filing, the first to be filed has priority, whether the security interest attached before or after filing.[1] For this reason, it makes sense for a creditor/lender to file a financing statement covering the transaction even *before* all the requirements for attachment have been met, because the date of filing will control who has priority in the collateral. Thus, the time of attachment often takes on less importance than the time of perfection (here, by filing), even though there can be no perfection without attachment.

For example, suppose that on 10 December 1996, Third Bank files a financing statement covering CIT's inventory and Fourth Bank files such a statement on the same inventory on 1 February 1997. Third Bank will have priority over Fourth Bank, even though Fourth Bank may have given value first and thus have attached its interest before Third Bank did. However, note that neither Third Bank nor Fourth Bank can have a perfected interest until attachment occurs. Simply put, Third Bank's earlier filing gives it a superior interest in the inventory under the UCC's first-to-file rules. Because the Code determines priorities from the time of filing—if all secured parties have filed—a would-be secured party should file as early as possible.

The Code's drafters have justified this "race to the recording office" as a necessary protection of the public filing system. In the drafters' view, Fourth Bank, though it has attached its interest first, cannot complain, because before taking its security interest, it could have checked the public records and thus learned of Third Bank's claimed interest. According to the drafters, lenders like Third Bank who plan to make a series of subsequent advances and who have filed first should be able to make those later advances without having, as a condition of protection, to check each time for filings *later* than theirs.[2]

27.1

PRIORITY POSITION

John overheard a conversation in which secured creditors of CIT and their priority positions were being discussed. Tom stated that Third Bank has the first priority on the firm's inventory, with Fourth Bank having the next claim on the inventory. John remembers that CIT borrowed money from Fourth Bank before CIT received any funds from Third Bank, and he is confused as to how Third Bank could make the second loan and yet occupy the first priority position. John asks you if Tom's interpretation sounds correct to you. What will you tell him?

BUSINESS CONSIDERATIONS Should a business that regularly extends credit to its customers have a policy of checking the records for prior security interests? Why would such a policy be a good business practice? When would such a policy not be necessary?

ETHICAL CONSIDERATIONS Is it ethical for a borrower or credit purchaser to use assets as collateral when he or she knows that the assets are already being used as collateral for another loan or debt? What can/should the borrower do in order to ensure that he or she has acted as ethically as possible in such a situation?

FINANCE

Order of Perfection

As we learned in Chapter 26, filing represents one of three alternative methods of perfection. With purchase money security interests in consumer goods, for instance, one may rely on automatic perfection or one may perfect by taking possession of the collateral. In all such cases (that is, where none of the parties has filed), the first to perfect takes priority.

Order of Attachment

If for some reason none of the parties has perfected its security interest, the first interest to attach enjoys priority. Relying on attachment alone as a vehicle for attaining priority, however, generally makes little sense because an *unperfected* secured creditor will not enjoy a preferred status in bankruptcy proceedings. Simply stated, to gain priority over other secured parties and over the trustee in bankruptcy, it is imperative to file as soon as possible if filing is an acceptable mode for perfecting a security interest in the type of collateral involved or, if filing is not appropriate, to perfect one's interest as soon as possible in the appropriate manner. The seller in *Crystal Bar* v. *Cosmic, Inc.*, unfortunately learned this rule the hard way.

27.1 CRYSTAL BAR, INC. v. COSMIC, INC.

758 F.Supp. 543 (D.S.D. 1991)

FACTS In March 1984, Crystal Bar, Inc. (Crystal Bar), Reese M. Williams individually, and the Reese Williams Trust sold 200 shares of capital stock (a minority interest); a liquor license; and the business assets, inventory, and stock in trade of Crystal Bar to Cosmic, Inc. (Cosmic) under a written "Purchase Agreement." The total purchase price was $225,000, with a down payment of $50,000 and the balance financed by the assumption of $40,468.58 of the sellers' debts and $164,531.42 amortized monthly at 12 percent per annum for ten years. The parties characterized the purchase agreement as an option to purchase and never perfected it as a security agreement under the South Dakota statutory provisions dealing with secured transactions. In December 1984, Cosmic, as assignor, with codefendant Virgil Hauff, as assignee, entered into an assignment covering the property subject to the prior purchase agreement. In this assignment, Hauff agreed to assume all the obligations of Cosmic under the original purchase agreement ($159,174.41). In a similar manner to the original purchase agreement, the assignment reserved title pending final payment. Again, Cosmic failed to perfect the assignment as a security agreement. By failing to make his monthly payments in August and September 1989, Hauff subsequently defaulted. In September, Crystal Bar mailed a notice of default regarding the total delinquency of $110,545.15 to Hauff. The Internal Revenue Service (IRS) also claimed a lien on the property described in the two agreements for income, withholding, and social security taxes due to the government by Hauff and his wife. Because the liquor license, estimated to be worth $75,000 to $100,000, represented Hauff's major asset, the IRS, through its levy on this property, sought to satisfy a portion or all of its lien. The IRS argued that because the seller had failed to perfect its security interest in the property, the IRS's interest was superior to that of Crystal Bar.

ISSUE Would the holder of a tax lien enjoy priority over the holder of an unperfected security interest in the liquor license?

HOLDING Yes. Article 9 would cover the liquor license; and since the secured party, which had sold its business to the debtor, failed to perfect its interest in the liquor license in accordance with Article 9, the IRS as a lien holder would enjoy priority.

REASONING The Federal Tax Lien Act provides that a federal tax lien attaches to all property, real or personal, belonging to a taxpayer whenever he or she fails to pay taxes. The IRS had filed tax liens against Virgil D. Hauff and Karen M. Hauff on 27 June 1988, 26 December 1988, and 13 October 1989. Regarding the priority of a lien creditor over an unperfected security interest, the South Dakota UCC states, "(1) Except as provided in subsection (2), an unperfected security interest is subordinate to the rights of: (b) A person who becomes a lien creditor before the security interest is perfected; . . . (3) A 'lien creditor' means a creditor who has acquired a lien on the property involved by attachment, levy, or the like and includes an assignee for [the] benefit of creditors from the time of [the] assignment, and a trustee in bankruptcy from the date of the filing of the petition or a receiver in equity from the time of appointment." In South Dakota, a liquor license is considered property. Under the UCC, therefore, it represents a general intangible subject to a security interest in favor of a creditor. Under South Dakota UCC statutes, a security interest in a general intangible must be filed in order to protect it from the claims of third parties. Accordingly, since Crystal Bar had failed to file properly the security interest created by the purchase agreement, Crystal Bar enjoyed only an unperfected interest in the license. Since an unperfected security interest is subordinate to the rights of a third party (in this case, the IRS) that becomes a lien creditor before the security interest is perfected, the IRS liens deserved first priority. All Crystal Bar needed to do to protect itself was to perfect its security interest. In its final argument, Crystal Bar maintained that since the parties had labeled the purchase agreement an option, the agreement did not give rise to a "security interest." Calling a security agreement an option does not make it an option, however; the location of the title is immaterial. Moreover, according to South Dakota statutes, "Each provision of this chapter with regard to rights, obligations and remedies applies whether title to collateral is in the secured party or in the debtor." Hence, the clear intent of the law of South Dakota is to bring contracts of the type being considered here under the umbrella of a "security interest."

BUSINESS CONSIDERATIONS As a result of this litigation, what office procedures should Cosmic implement so as to ensure that, in the future, it will have taken all the steps necessary to protect completely its Article 9 interests? Explain fully.

ETHICAL CONSIDERATIONS In this case, the Hauffs failed to pay their income taxes when due. Muster arguments for and against the proposition that the current U.S. income tax system unethically benefits certain interests at the expense of others. If you agree that inequities do result, are these differentials justifiable from a utilitarian perspective?

EXCEPTIONS

We now turn our attention to some very important exceptions to the general rules of priority. The first of these concerns a purchase money security interest that is held by a purchase money secured party.

Purchase Money Security Interests

For reasons that soon will be clear, a purchase money secured party enjoys priority over interests that precede his or her interest in time, provided the party complies with certain provisions of the Code. In other words, a purchase money security interest contradicts our previously described first-to-file-or-to-perfect rules on priorities. An analysis of the types of commercial situations that involve purchase money security interests and purchase money secured parties will explain why the Code sanctions a special status for these interests.

As we learned in Chapter 26, a security interest is a purchase money security interest to the extent that it is "(a) taken or retained by the seller of the collateral to secure all or part of its price; or (b) taken by a person who by making advances or incurring an obligation gives value to enable the debtor to acquire rights in or the use of collateral if such value is in fact so used."[3] As should be apparent from this definition, purchase money secured parties typically are sellers or lenders who, by their extensions of credit, permit the debtor to acquire rights in the collateral. But not all sellers or lenders qualify for purchase money secured party status. Let's reexamine our earlier example involving Third Bank and CIT to understand how purchase money secured parties differ from other secured parties.

This time assume that Third Bank has agreed to finance CIT's inventory. As CIT's inventory financier, Third Bank agrees to give CIT a *line of credit* on which CIT can draw at irregular intervals and from which the bank can issue *future advances* of funds to CIT if CIT needs them. To protect itself, Third Bank creates and perfects a security interest in all present and after-acquired property of CIT's and all proceeds thereof. In such situations, Third Bank has a so-called *floating lien* over CIT's inventory, since the lien covers the items of inventory as they stand on the shelf and even "floats" over other inventory and property that CIT acquires through subsequent advances or loans from Third Bank. Third Bank's lien also covers the *proceeds* of any items that CIT sells. Generally speaking, Third Bank will compel CIT to maintain a certain ratio of inventory and will gauge CIT's repayment of the loans and the bank's later advances with reference to this ratio. Typically, Third Bank will ask CIT to promise to refrain from *double financing,* or using this same inventory as collateral for a subsequent loan from another creditor, say Fourth Bank.

Third Bank's reasons for protecting its security interest in the inventory are understandable: The bank knows that, should CIT become bankrupt, the bank will need to have priority if it hopes to realize any money from its extension of credit. Hence, on the one hand, the law wants to protect secured parties like Third Bank so that they will be willing to extend credit to businesspeople or firms like CIT. One way to accomplish this policy objective is to give such lenders priority if they are the first to file or to perfect.

On the other hand, it seems unfair for Third Bank to have the ability to restrict unduly CIT's access to credit. Potential subsequent creditors may see Third Bank's previously filed financing statement on the inventory and may refuse to extend CIT credit because of Third Bank's seeming priority based on its compliance with the first-to-file-or-to-perfect rules. Where will the firm get credit if, for some reason, Third Bank refuses to give CIT additional loans or advances?

The UCC, by giving priority to purchase money security interests, attempts to balance both CIT and Third Bank's interests. In other words, if Fourth Bank advances money (say $10,000) to enable CIT to acquire additional inventory, Fourth Bank has priority over Third Bank to the extent of the value given—here, $10,000—because the law characterizes Fourth Bank in these circumstances as a purchase money secured party; that is, the money advanced by Fourth Bank relates directly to CIT's acquisition of specific, identifiable collateral. (Third Bank, as the inventory financier and the holder of after-acquired property and future advances clauses, is a non-purchase money secured party here.) To earn this priority, however, Fourth Bank has to fulfill certain requirements, depending on the type of collateral involved.

If the collateral consists of inventory, Fourth Bank enjoys priority over Third Bank's conflicting security interest in the same inventory (and in identifiable cash proceeds) received on or before the delivery of the inventory to a buyer (here, CIT). This is true provided that the purchase money security interest has been perfected by filing at the time the debtor receives possession of the inventory and the purchase money secured party notifies *in writing* any persons who previously have filed financing statements covering inventory of the same types that it (the purchase money secured party) has or expects to acquire a purchase money security interest in the inventory of the debtor. The purchase money secured party also must describe the inventory by item or type. To acquire priority over Third Bank, Fourth Bank must meet these requirements.[4]

To those who see this "super priority" for purchase money secured parties as unfair to inventory financiers like Third Bank, the drafters of the Code offer the following policy justifications. The notification procedures required by the Code will tip off Third Bank that CIT is double financing. At this point, if it believes itself vulnerable, Third Bank may curtail future advances to CIT. And, assuming that the security agreement so provides and that it (the bank) gives notice, it may argue that such double financing constitutes a condition of default and may demand payment from CIT. Third Bank thus has ways of protecting itself if it so desires, and in the meantime CIT has acquired new avenues of credit. Third Bank also has the added protection of knowing that it still will have priority with regard to the inventory if Fourth Bank does not comply with the Code's requirements.

If the security interest covers noninventory collateral (such as equipment or consumer goods), Fourth Bank, as a purchase money secured party, has priority over Third Bank, as a holder of a conflicting security interest in the same collateral or its proceeds, if the purchase money security interest is perfected at the time the debtor receives possession of the collateral or within 10 days thereafter.[5] Hence, it is clear that the type of collateral involved dictates what a creditor must do to achieve purchase money secured party status.

Why is less required (a ten-day grace period for filing and no need to give notice to holders of previously filed security interests) of one who wishes to attain priority in noninventory collateral? Apparently, the drafters of the Code believed that arrangements for periodic advances against incoming property are unusual outside the inventory field; thus, they did not think there was a need to notify noninventory secured parties because, in fact, only in rare instances would such a previous financier even exist. Simply put, equipment and consumer goods usually are not valuable enough for several creditors to have taken security interests in them. To illustrate, if CIT buys a new lathe for use in cutting out the housing for the Call-Image videophones, the lathe is equipment because CIT uses it in its business. If Fourth Bank lends CIT the money to buy the lathe, the bank becomes a purchase money secured party if the bank files a financing statement within 10 days of CIT's receipt of the lathe. Fourth Bank enjoys priority over Third Bank, despite lack of notice to the latter, even if Third Bank has filed a financing statement indicating an interest in "all inventory, equipment, and after-acquired property of Call-Image Technology, Inc." If Fourth Bank does not file within 10 days, Third Bank, under the usual first-to-file-or-to-perfect rules, has a priority claim to the lathe.

If there are two or more competing purchase money security interests in the same type of collateral, the Code, in determining priority in this situation, applies the usual first-to-file-or-to-perfect rules. Thus, the purchase money secured party who files first has superior rights.

YOU BE THE JUDGE

Is a Charge Agreement a Security Agreement?

When Mrs. Oszajca went into bankruptcy, she owed a debt of slightly more than $2,000 on her Sears credit card. The department store, in filing proof of a claim against her bankruptcy estate, asserted a purchase-money security interest in certain household merchandise that she had charged to her Sears credit card. Sears argued that it had a valid purchase money security interest in the merchandise held by the bankruptcy estate because the woman had signed a Sears retail charge agreement ("SearsCharge Agreement") granting Sears a security interest in any merchandise purchased with the credit card. Sears argued that the customer's signature on this document gave it an enforceable purchase money security interest in the merchandise. The trustee in bankruptcy argued that Sears did not have a properly perfected security interest, thus giving the trustee a superior claim to the merchandise. Assume that this case is brought before *your* court. How will *you* decide this case?[6]

BUSINESS CONSIDERATIONS Should a business that regularly extends credit to its customers have a policy regarding the acquisition and perfection of its security interests? What should the business do to maximize its protection under Article 9?

ETHICAL CONSIDERATIONS Is it ethical for a retail store to have customers sign a charge slip that the store intends to use as a security agreement, thus giving the store a purchase money security interest in the goods sold, often without the knowledge of the customer? What should the retail store do in order to ensure that its conduct is ethical?

SOURCE: *UCC Bulletin* (Deerfield: Clark Boardman Callaghan) (October 1996), pp. 7–8.

The two cases that follow illustrate how courts dispose of lawsuits involving assertions of purchase money security interests.

27.2 TOWNSHIP OF STAMBAUGH v. AH-NE-PEE DIMENSIONAL HARDWOOD, INC.

841 F.Supp. 803 (W.D. Mich. 1993)

FACTS Ah-Ne-Pee Dimensional Hardwood, Inc. (Hardwood) manufactures wood products. In the late 1970s, Hardwood began operating from a facility in Ogema, Wisconsin. In the late 1980s, Hardwood financed a new Michigan facility with a $200,000 loan from Miners State Bank, a $625,000 loan from the local township, and $125,000 of owner equity. On 20 January 1989, Miners State Bank loaned Hardwood $200,000 in exchange for a promissory note secured by a mortgage on real property, the equipment and personal property located at the Michigan facility, an after-acquired property clause, and a future advances clause. On 26 January 1989, the bank recorded the mortgage. That security interest was perfected by Hardwood's filing financing statements with the Michigan secretary of state on 6 February 1989, 7 March 1989, and 25 September 1989. (The township later contended that Hardwood had used the loan proceeds for building renovations and as a down payment on equipment.) On 22 September 1989, the township, pursuant to a U.S. Department of Housing and Urban Development (HUD) economic development implementation grant, loaned Hardwood $625,000 in exchange for a promissory note. The promissory note was secured by a mortgage on the same real property as the promissory note given to Miners State Bank, but Miners State Bank agreed to subordinate its interest in the real property to the township's interest. In addition, this promissory note was secured by an interest in all tangible and intangible personal property and fixtures located at the Michigan facility. The township, however, did not obtain a subordination of Miners State Bank's security interest in the personal property as the township had done with the earlier real property mortgage. Like the Miners State Bank's security interest, the township's security interest also contained after-acquired property and future advances clauses. By filing a financing statement with the Michigan secretary of state on 12 October 1989—after Miners State Bank had filed its financing statements—the township perfected its security interest. [The township later contended that Hardwood purchased a majority of its equipment shortly after Hardwood received the $625,000 loan from the township.] After June 1991, Hardwood stopped making payments on the $625,000 township promissory note. Consequently, claiming that Hardwood was in default on the note, the township filed a lawsuit seeking a judicial determination that it, as a purchase money secured party in the equipment purchased by Hardwood shortly after the township extended the loan to Hardwood, should enjoy priority in this personal property.

ISSUE Did the township have a purchase money security interest in the equipment?

HOLDING No. Given the absence of any evidence showing that it had loaned the money for the purchase of specific, identifiable personal property, the township was not a purchase money secured party regarding the disputed equipment.

REASONING The order in which the creditor perfects its security interest ordinarily defines a creditor's right to recover from a debtor. However, the holder of a purchase money security interest is excepted from the general rule. Moreover, the holder of a purchase money security interest takes priority over an interest acquired under an after-acquired property clause (UCC § 9-107, Official Comment). This exception allows a creditor to extend money to a debtor to purchase collateral without the creditor's being concerned with the debtor's prior debts. As the Michigan UCC states:

> *A security interest is a "purchase money security interest" to the extent that it is (a) taken or retained by the seller of the collateral to secure all or part of its price; or (b) taken by a person who by making advances or incurring an obligation gives value to enable the debtor to acquire rights in or the use of collateral if such value is in fact so used.*

Subsection (b) is disputed in this case, but subsection (a) is inapplicable because the township is not the seller of the collateral. In short, a purchase money security interest requires that the person claiming the purchase money security interest intended to loan money for the purchase of the exact items in which one claims the purchase money security interest. The lender must demonstrate that the money given was "intended, and actually used, for the purchase of *identifiable* [emphasis added] collateral." Hence, the township did not have a purchase money security interest in the equipment acquired with the money it had loaned to Hardwood because the township had failed to loan the money for the purchase of specific, *identifiable* property. The

27.2 TOWNSHIP OF STAMBAUGH v. AH-NE-PEE DIMENSIONAL HARDWOOD, INC. *(cont.)* 841 F.Supp. 803 (W.D. Mich. 1993)

economic development implementation grant agreement between the Michigan Department of Commerce and the township stated that the grant funds "shall be used to make a $625,000 loan to Ah-Ne-Pee Dimensional Hardwood, Inc., for the purchase of equipment and working capital." This agreement defined the security interest as "a first position on the building and real estate and a second position on the new equipment." However, the loan agreement never mentioned specific equipment that Hardwood would buy with the loaned money. And, according to Michigan precedents, a purchase money security interest exists only if the creditor makes that loan for the purpose of the debtor's purchasing specific property. Otherwise, all loans that result in the debtor's purchasing collateral would have a purchase money security interest aspect; however, the purchase money security interest exception was not designed for such a purpose. This interpretation of the purchase money security interest would prevent the township from claiming a purchase money security interest because its loan agreement did not identify specific collateral to be purchased with the loan money. Instead, the loan agreement stated generally that the loan money would be used to purchase equipment. As such, the township did not have a purchase money security interest in the equipment purchased.

BUSINESS CONSIDERATIONS Assume you are the township clerk. Your boss has asked you to redraft the instruments connected with this case to ensure that in future cases the township will enjoy the status of a purchase money secured party. Although the township attorney will write the final draft, what language will you use in this first draft?

ETHICAL CONSIDERATIONS Is the township under an ethical obligation to disclose to its constituents (that is, the taxpayers) the facts surrounding its failure to attain a preferred priority status? Why or why not?

27.3 VALLEY BANK v. ESTATE OF RAINSDON 793 P.2d 1257 (Idaho App. 1990)

FACTS Prior to 1981, Burton and Thelma Rainsdon ran a cattle-raising operation. In the spring of 1982, Burton became ill and asked his son, Robert Rainsdon, to care for approximately 150 head of cattle. Robert thereupon moved the cattle to Hamer, Idaho, and placed them with cattle that he and his wife, Janice, owned. In the spring of 1982, Burton and Thelma Rainsdon signed a short "memorandum agreement" with Robert and Janice Rainsdon to the effect that Robert and Janice would purchase 100 head of Burton's best cows and their calves, the rest to be culled from the herd and sold on the market by Burton and Thelma. The agreement also recited that the sellers, Burton and Thelma, would "retain a [purchase money] security interest in the cows only. . . ." Robert and Janice, in addition, signed a promissory note dated 23 March 1982 for $37,500, payable in four annual installments. Burton and Thelma did not file a financing statement on this transaction until 30 April 1982. In the meantime, on 26 March 1982, Robert and Janice contacted Valley Bank to discuss renewal of their annual operating line of credit. That same day, Valley Bank agreed to advance the funds to feed and maintain Robert and Janice's cattle as well as the 100 cows and calves to be purchased from Burton and Thelma pursuant to the memorandum agreement. A security agreement executed between Valley Bank and Robert and Janice on 26 March 1982 granted the bank a security interest in "all debtors' livestock, increase thereof, additions and replacements thereto, now owned or hereafter acquired." Valley Bank previously had filed financing statements on 8 March 1978 and 22 January 1980 covering "all livestock now owned or hereafter acquired"; consequently, Valley Bank filed no new financing statement to cover this most recent security agreement. When Robert and Janice failed to make the first payment on Burton's cattle, Valley Bank agreed to advance $12,346, the amount of the installment due. In 1984, Robert and Janice's default as to the payments owed to Valley Bank and to Burton and Thelma caused the liquidation by sale of all cattle in the possession of Robert and Janice. The proceeds from the sale of the cows purchased from Burton then became the subject of litigation. Based on their alleged, respective statuses as purchase money secured parties, both the Rainsdons (Burton and Thelma) and Valley Bank claimed priority as to the proceeds of the sale.

27.3 VALLEY BANK v. ESTATE OF RAINSDON *(cont.)* 793 P.2d 1257 (Idaho App. 1990)

ISSUE Who should enjoy priority as to the proceeds?

HOLDING Valley Bank, although it had not attained the status of purchase money secured party, enjoyed priority over the Rainsdons, who, though they were purchase money secured parties, had failed to perfect their interest within the 10-day period required by the UCC.

REASONING Valley Bank contended that because it had advanced $12,346 for the first installment, it had acquired the status of a lender with a purchase money security interest, at least with regard to the amount of this advancement. But a security interest cannot become a purchase money security interest unless it is taken by a person who by making advances or incurring an obligation gives value to enable the debtor to acquire rights in or the use of collateral if such value is in fact so used. Here, the debtor (Robert) had not used the money advanced by the bank to acquire any rights in the cows or the use of them because he already had all the possible rights in the cows he could have. Nevertheless, because Valley Bank had perfected its general security interest prior to Burton's security interest, Burton could not prevail unless he had the super priority of a purchase money security interest. Had Burton filed under I.C. 28-9-312(4), he could have perfected his purchase money security interest. Alternatively, he might prevail if Valley Bank had subordinated its security interest to Burton's interest. The trial court held that Burton and Thelma enjoyed a super priority under I.C. 28-9-312(4), which states:

> *A purchase money security interest in collateral other than inventory has priority over a conflicting security interest in the same collateral or its proceeds* if the purchase money security interest is perfected at the time the debtor receives possession of the collateral or within ten (10) days thereafter *[emphasis added]*.

The trial court found that although Robert had retained possession of his parents' cattle for a long period of time, Robert was a mere caretaker without rights in the cattle until the signing of the purchase agreement; during this time he was not a "debtor." While Burton's cattle were mixed with Robert's cattle, Burton's cattle continued to bear his (Burton's) brand; therefore, according to the trial judge, Robert functioned as a mere bailee with no rights in the "collateral" to which a security interest could attach. In contrast, Valley Bank contended that once Robert and Janice had signed the memorandum agreement dated 23 March 1982, Robert became a "debtor receiv[ing] possession of the collateral" within the meaning of I.C. 28-9-312(4). Yet, according to affidavits and the deposition testimony of Robert and Thelma, Robert had the right to select 100 of the best cows and calves from Burton's herd. Because the cows were calving during the spring, he was unable to accomplish this task until the completion of calving. Hence, the Rainsdons submitted that, until the 100 cows and calves were identified or selected by Robert, he was not a debtor in possession of collateral within the meaning of I.C. 28-9-312(4). After admitting this parol evidence, the court found that "possession" of the cattle as contemplated by I.C. 28-9-312(4) did not occur until the 100 cows and calves were identified or "delivered" to Robert. Because Burton Rainsdon had filed a financing statement four to ten days before such "delivery," the trial court viewed Rainsdon's purchase money security interest as timely perfected within the 10-day filing period. However, under this view, a seller can delay indefinitely the filing of a financing statement showing his security interest in cattle in possession of the buyer and thereby await such time as the buyer makes a final selection of the last animal. The UCC, in most cases, requires secured parties to file a financing statement in order to perfect their security interest. To define "possession" as requiring completion of tender of delivery terms will permit a secured creditor to delay performance of a tender of delivery term and avoid the filing requirement indefinitely. Even if a debtor has use of the collateral, under the trial court's analysis, he is not deemed to have "possession"; and purchase money security interest holders who file after complying with a tender of delivery term, at any future date, still will be entitled to the 9-312(4) priority. Such a result frustrates the purpose of Article 9 and cannot have been intended by the drafters. To summarize, possession under 9-312(4) is not dependent on completion of tender of delivery terms that affect only the buyer and seller of the goods. Accordingly, "possession" for the purpose of I.C. 28-9-312(4) should not be construed to mean the time when Robert completed the selection of 100 cows from Burton's herd. The Rainsdons' 10-day grace period for filing a financing statement commenced on 6 April 1982 when the security agreement was executed and the Rainsdons were in possession of all the cows. Thus, the Rainsdons had not perfected their purchase money security interest in a timely fashion. This holding is consistent with the purposes of the Uniform Commercial Code to provide a readily ascertainable date from which the parties' rights can be determined.

BUSINESS CONSIDERATIONS Defend or refute—in detail—the proposition that this case illustrates the old truism that one should not mix "blood" and business. In

27.3 VALLEY BANK v. ESTATE OF RAINSDON (*cont.*) 793 P.2d 1257 (Idaho App. 1990)

other words, consider whether Burton and Thelma might have behaved differently had they not been dealing with close relatives.

ETHICAL CONSIDERATIONS Valley Bank's foreclosure on the cattle followed from Robert and Janice's default. Should the other ranchers in the area have boycotted—on ethical grounds—the sale of their neighbors' property? Why or why not?

Bona Fide Purchasers of Consumer Goods

Besides purchase money secured parties, another class of persons who may have priority over a previously perfected security interest is the *bona fide purchaser* of consumer goods.[7] Recall from Chapter 26 that *consumer goods* are goods that have been used or bought for use primarily for personal, family, or household purposes.[8] Thus, this section of the Code limits priority to the purchase of this type of collateral. Examination of this Code provision shows further limitations, since to enjoy priority over a previously perfected security interest, a buyer must be ignorant of the security interest, must pay value, and must use the goods for personal, family, or household purposes.

To illustrate, assume that Henry Smith wishes to sell his refrigerator to Margaret Hernandez. Margaret does not know it, but Handley, the owner of the appliance store where Henry bought the refrigerator, has a perfected security interest in this consumer good. (Handley is relying on automatic perfection—that is, the mere attachment of the security interest.) If Margaret pays value and uses the refrigerator in her home, she will have priority; in other words, should Henry default in his payments, she will retain the refrigerator even if Handley tries to repossess it from her. If Margaret plans to use the refrigerator in her dental office for the purpose of keeping anesthetics cold, however, Handley will win because Margaret does not fit § 9-307(2)'s definition of a bona fide purchaser.

So far, we have been assuming that Handley will rely on automatic perfection, which, as discussed in Chapter 26, is the mode generally preferred by the Handleys of the world because they thereby can avoid the expense and inconvenience of filing. Under § 9-307(2), however, if Handley files a financing statement covering a consumer good before a buyer like Margaret purchases it, Handley, not the bona fide purchaser, will have a priority claim to it. Handley, then, must decide whether the possibility that a refrigerator will be sold to a bona fide purchaser outweighs the inconvenience of filing. If he thinks it does, in order to attain priority, he should file; if not, he can rely on automatic perfection to keep him secure from the claims of everyone except this specialized type of bona fide purchaser.

Buyers in the Ordinary Course of Business

According to § 9-307(1), buyers in the ordinary course of business may have priority over a perfected security interest. To use our earlier example, when Henry Smith buys the refrigerator from Handley's Appliance Store, he is a buyer in the ordinary

27.2

FINANCE

SECURITY INTEREST

The firm sold 50 Call-Image videophones on credit to a local retail store. CIT retained a security interest in the videophones and properly perfected its interest by filing in the appropriate office in a timely manner. The Kochanowskis have learned that this retail store is having serious financial problems and may be forced to go out of business. They ask you if they can assert their security interest against the units still in the store's possession and against any customers who have purchased units from the store if the retailer ultimately should default on the contract. What will you tell them?

BUSINESS CONSIDERATIONS What should a business creditor that holds a perfected security interest do if or when it hears that one of its debtors is having financial difficulties? How can the business creditor protect its interests without jeopardizing the future of the debtor?

ETHICAL CONSIDERATIONS Assuming that it would be legal to do so, would it be ethical for a secured creditor to seek enforcement of its security interest against buyers in the ordinary course of business who purchased collateral from a retail seller that was also a debtor of the secured creditor?

course of business. Anyone who buys goods from a merchant seller in a standard (as opposed to an extraordinary) transaction is a *buyer in the ordinary course of business.* As such, Henry will take the refrigerator free of a security interest created by his seller (Handley may have given a security interest in his inventory of appliances to Third Bank), even though the security interest is perfected and even if Henry knows of Third Bank's perfected security interest. The policy reasons for such a result are clear: Purchasers will not buy refrigerators or compact disk players or garden tractors out of a seller's stock of trade or inventory if lenders like Third Bank can repossess these items. Therefore, buyers in the ordinary course of business—by definition those who may know of the existence of a perfected security interest in the goods but who buy in good faith and without knowledge that the sale of the goods is in violation of the ownership rights or security interest of a third party—have priority in such competing claims situations.

Although many people use the terms *bona fide purchaser* and *buyer in the ordinary course of business* interchangeably, they are distinct concepts. We more appropriately term a consumer who has bought goods from another consumer in an occasional sale a bona fide purchaser. Buyers in the ordinary course of business, in contrast, are purchasers who are buying from a seller who routinely sells from inventory or otherwise regularly engages in such transactions.

Note how the court's disposition of *GMAC* v. *Third National Bank in Nashville* hinges on the purchaser's status as a buyer in the ordinary course of business.

27.4 GENERAL MOTORS ACCEPTANCE CORPORATION v. THIRD NATIONAL BANK IN NASHVILLE

812 S.W.2d 593 (Tenn.App. 1991)

FACTS General Motors Acceptance Corporation (GMAC) held a security interest in the inventory of Richard Smith, Inc. (Richard Smith), a Dickson County GMC dealer. On 1 December 1989, Karen Russell signed a retail installment sales contract in which she agreed to purchase a 1989 GMC pickup truck from Richard Smith. She had driven the truck for a few days' trial period. The contract called for a $4,000 down payment that Russell proposed to borrow from her father. In lieu of the down payment, the dealer took her promissory note for $4,000 payable on 5 December 1989. As part of the same transaction, Russell also signed the usual and customary documents required to

27.4 GENERAL MOTORS ACCEPTANCE CORPORATION v. THIRD NATIONAL BANK IN NASHVILLE (*cont.*) 812 S.W.2d 593 (Tenn.App. 1991)

finance the purchase of the truck over a period of five years. Russell said the dealer promised to hold the papers until she came back with the down payment. On 4 December 1989, the dealer assigned the contract to Third National Bank in Nashville (TNBN) and filed an application for title with the county clerk of Dickson County. The application contained a manufacturer's statement of origin that was to be forwarded to the Motor Vehicle Division of the Tennessee Department of Revenue. Approximately two weeks later, Russell decided she could not come up with the $4,000 down payment. She returned the truck to the dealer and obtained a promise that Richard Smith would void the transaction if she could retrieve the manufacturer's statement of origin from the county clerk. Russell, with the aid of the county clerk, managed to recall the documents from the Department of Revenue. Someone at Richard Smith also wrote "Void" on the face of the dealer's copy of the retail installment sales contract. However, the transfer of the original document to TNBN already had occurred because TNBN had purchased the chattel paper covering the pickup. Shortly after the dealer's transaction with Russell, GMAC discovered that the dealer had made other sales out of inventory without making the required payments to GMAC. Accordingly, GMAC took possession of the dealer's inventory, including the vehicle formerly possessed by Russell. At trial, the court held that TNBN's lien had failed to attach because title to the pickup never had rested in the purchaser. On appeal, TNBN argued that, since a sale had taken place, Russell had become a buyer in the ordinary course of business. As a consequence, TNBN submitted, GMAC had lost its security interest; and TNBN, as the purchaser of chattel paper covering the pickup, enjoyed priority over GMAC, the inventory financier.

ISSUES Was Russell a buyer in the ordinary course of business? Did TNBN's interest have priority over GMAC's interest in the pickup?

HOLDINGS Yes to each issue. Russell was a buyer in the ordinary course of business; and, as a consequence of the sale, GMAC lost its original security interest in the vehicle. Moreover, when goods have been returned to the dealer, Tennessee law would grant priority to the transferee of chattel paper covering the goods sold out of the inventory rather than to the inventory financier of the goods.

REASONING The result in this case hinges on the answer to the question, "Did the dealer sell the truck to a buyer in the ordinary course of business?" If the answer to that question is yes, the applicable provisions of the Uniform Commercial Code dictate a result favorable to the bank. A buyer in the ordinary course of business means "a person who in good faith and without knowledge that the sale to him is in violation of the ownership rights or security interest of the third party in the goods buys in ordinary course from a person in the business of selling goods of that kind but does not include a pawnbroker. . . . 'Buying' may be for cash or by exchange of other property or on secured or unsecured credit and includes receiving goods or documents of title under a pre-existing contract for sale. . . ." If Russell in fact were a buyer, she is a perfect example of a buyer in the ordinary course of business. Pursuant to an ordinary transaction of purchase and sale, she bought the truck out of the dealer's inventory and paid the purchase price by secured and unsecured credit. Hence, the trial court erred in holding that Russell had not purchased the truck. Rather, the facts showed that she had signed a contract agreeing to purchase and to pay for it in installments; she had signed a power of attorney allowing the dealer to secure for her the certificate of title from the state; and she had signed a promissory note for the down payment and had taken possession of the truck. GMAC nevertheless argued that the contract was subject to a condition precedent, that is, the ability of Russell to obtain the down payment. Cases in Tennessee and elsewhere recognize that noncompliance with a condition precedent will prevent the formation of a contract. Moreover, courts, in order to show such a condition, may admit parol evidence. But the record had not established that the ability to raise the $4,000 down payment was a condition precedent to the contract between Russell and the dealer. Indeed, the written agreement did not contain any language to that effect. It merely reflected her obligation to make a $4,000 down payment. In addition, Russell testified that after she had signed the contract and, because of her concerns about securing the required down payment, had expressed the desire to postpone the financing for a few days, Richard Smith's salesperson asked her to sign a promissory note for the down payment; and she had done so. At that point, the sale was complete. The additional testimony about the dealer's agreeing to hold the papers for a few days at most showed an agreement to rescind the sale if Russell were unable to pay the note. By the time the attempted rescission took place, however, other interests had intervened. Simply put, as a consequence of the sale to Russell, GMAC lost its original security interest in the vehicle. A buyer in the ordinary course of business "takes free of a security interest created by his seller even though the security interest is perfected and even though the buyer knows of its existence" [Tenn. Code Ann. 47-9-307(1)]. A dealer selling his inventory to a buyer in the ordinary course of business

27.4 GENERAL MOTORS ACCEPTANCE CORPORATION v. THIRD NATIONAL BANK IN NASHVILLE *(cont.)* 812 S.W.2d 593 (Tenn.App. 1991)

has the power to pass good title to the buyer. If this were not true, any plan of inventory financing would clog the exchange of goods between the seller and the buyer. As to the question of who has priority—the inventory financier or the transferee of chattel paper covering the goods sold out of inventory—when the goods are returned to the dealer, the Uniform Commercial Code resolves this question in favor of TNBN. The retail installment sales contract signed by Russell was "chattel paper" as defined in the Code. Since GMAC had a perfected security interest in the proceeds of the sales from the dealer's inventory, the security interest continued in the chattel paper. The bank, however, as the purchaser of the chattel paper, took priority over a security interest in the chattel paper "which [was] claimed merely as proceeds of inventory subject to a security interest" [Tenn. Code Ann. 47-9-308(b)]. Thus, where an unpaid transferee of chattel paper meets the requirements of Tenn. Code Ann. 47-9-308(b), the Code gives the transferee priority over an inventory financier when the goods are returned to the dealer after the sale. To the extent that perfection of TNBN's interest in the vehicle was important, TNBN had perfected its interest when the county clerk of Dickson County received the application for a title showing the bank's lien. That event occurred on or before 8 December 1989. Hence, TNBN, not GMAC, enjoyed the right to possession of the vehicle in question.

BUSINESS CONSIDERATIONS Assuming Russell's testimony was correct, should the dealership have allowed its personnel to promise that it would hold the papers until she came back with the down payment? What are the positive and negative aspects of such a policy on the firm's part? If you were the owner of a dealership, would you adopt this policy?

ETHICAL CONSIDERATIONS Again, assuming Russell told the truth, was it unethical for the dealership to promise to hold the papers until she returned with the down payment and then not fulfill this promise? Did Russell behave unethically here? Explain in detail.

Common Law and Statutory Liens

Under § 9-310 of the UCC, certain liens that arise by operation of law have priority over a perfected security interest in the collateral. For example, if Monty Moore takes his car to Harry's Auto Repair and does not pay Harry, the owner (Harry) will have a common law or statutory lien on the car to the extent of the money owed him for his services or materials. Harry can retain possession of the car; and, in the event of Monty's default, Harry can force Westside Savings and Loan, the secured party for Monty's car, to pay him (Harry) for his repairs before Westside realizes any proceeds from the sale of Monty's car.

ITT v. *Madisonville Recapping* involves a contest between a statutory lien holder and a purchase-money secured party.

27.5 ITT COMMERCIAL FINANCE CORPORATION v. MADISONVILLE RECAPPING COMPANY, INC. 793 S.W.2d 849 (Ky.App. 1990)

FACTS Coal Exchange of Kentucky, Inc. (Coal Exchange) operated a strip mine in Webster County, Kentucky; and all its equipment was in that county. However, Coal Exchange's registered office was located in Jefferson County, Kentucky. In September 1985, Madisonville Recapping Company, Inc. (Madisonville Recapping) performed repairs on and supplied tires for a Michigan loader owned by Coal Exchange. The bill for the repairs and tires

27.5 ITT COMMERCIAL FINANCE CORPORATION v. MADISONVILLE RECAPPING COMPANY, INC. *(cont.)* 793 S.W.2d 849 (Ky.App. 1990)

amounted to $10,260.62. At about that same time, Watson Brothers Industries, Inc. (Watson Brothers) provided $5,616 in repair services and parts for Coal Exchange's loader. Because of the size of the loader, all repairs took place at the mining site in Webster County. Because it never received any payment, Madisonville Recapping filed a mechanic's lien against Coal Exchange on 4 December 1985. On 20 December 1985, Watson Brothers asserted its mechanic's lien against Coal Exchange. On 30 December 1985, Coal Exchange filed for bankruptcy. During those proceedings, ITT Commercial Finance Corporation (ITT) claimed a purchase money security interest in the loader. Accordingly, ITT subsequently repossessed and sold the loader. After Madisonville Recapping had filed a complaint against Coal Exchange, Watson Brothers, and ITT, a special commissioner concluded that Madisonville Recapping and Watson Brothers had properly perfected their liens and that these statutory liens took priority over ITT's alleged security interest. On 24 August 1988, the trial court sustained the special commissioner's findings. On appeal, ITT argued that its purchase money security interest was superior to Madisonville Recapping's interest because the latter had not validly perfected its statutory lien.

ISSUE Whose lien should enjoy priority—ITT or Madisonville Recapping's?

HOLDING Since Madisonville Recapping had failed to perfect its lien, ITT's lien had priority, even though Madisonville Recapping as a statutory lienholder ordinarily would enjoy priority.

REASONING Madisonville Recapping had filed its lien in Webster County rather than in Coal Exchange's county of residence (that is, the location of Coal Exchange's registered office—here, Jefferson County) as required by the pertinent Kentucky statute. Consequently, Madisonville Recapping had not perfected its lien properly. ITT furthermore argued that a purchase money security interest should take priority over a nonpossessory statutory lien. The relevant Kentucky statute provides:

> *When a person in the ordinary course of his business furnishes services or materials with respect to goods subject to a security interest, a lien upon goods in the possession of such person given by statute or rule of law for such materials or services takes priority over a perfected security interest unless the lien is statutory and the statute expressly provides otherwise.*

In holding that such liens prevail over purchase money security interests, the trial court relied on Kentucky precedents. In these precedents, however, the lienholders had possession of the vehicles at issue and had removed them pursuant to court order. Hence, these precedents did not cover the present case. Moreover, the plain language of the statute justified the interpretation of the statute urged by ITT—that is, that the statute grants priority only to lienholders who retain possession—since that statute refers to "goods in possession" of a lienholder. In addition, when the words of a statute are clear and unambiguous and express the legislative intent, no need for judicial construction will arise; courts must accept the statute as written. Simply put, KRS 355.9-310 is clear and unambiguous in its requirement of possession by the lienholder. On the other hand, Watson Brothers argued that courts should not require possession in cases such as this where the size of the machinery necessitated repairs being done on the owner's premises. Watson Brothers maintained that if the statutory provision at issue requires possession, then those who repair large mining or construction equipment will not enjoy the same protection as others. Even though Watson Brothers's argument might have merit, courts should not disregard the plain meaning of a statute simply because they believe a different interpretation states a better policy. Yet, because the special commissioner referred to ITT's "alleged" security interest, on remand, in order to prevail, ITT would need to produce sufficient evidence of its claimed security interest.

BUSINESS CONSIDERATIONS Assume you are the attorney for Madisonville Recapping and Watson Brothers. Write a brief memo explaining the law of priorities as it relates to statutory lienholders. In your discussion, be sure to explain what the firms could have done to maximize their chances of prevailing in this litigation and what they should do in such situations in the future.

ETHICAL CONSIDERATIONS Compose a position paper in which you set out the ethical arguments that support the law's priority rules concerning statutory lienholders.

27.3

FINANCE

PURCHASE-MONEY SECURITY INTEREST

CIT sold two Call-Image videophones to a customer, retaining a purchase money security interest in the videophones. The customer defaulted on the debt, and CIT now wants to enforce its interest in the units. Tom learned that the videophones are in the possession of a repairperson whom the customer had hired to work on the videophones. Tom wants to know what rights due to the default of the customer CIT has in this situation and whether the firm can insist that the repairperson turn over the videophones. What will you tell him?

BUSINESS CONSIDERATIONS Why might a secured creditor, in order to obtain possession of the collateral itself, want to pay a person who has a possessory lien from repairing collateral? What can the creditor do if it decides not to redeem the collateral from the possessory lien holder?

ETHICAL CONSIDERATIONS Is there an ethical reason for allowing a possessory lien holder to gain priority over a properly perfected security interest? What ethical considerations justify such a rule?

Fixtures

As discussed in Chapter 26, Article 9 ordinarily does not cover security interests in real estate. As you may remember, however, in addition to covering personal property, Article 9 also encompasses *fixtures*—goods that have become so related to real estate that an interest in them arises under real estate law. Many factories, schools, and homes have a fixture called a furnace. In most cases, a mortgagee (the party who loaned the money for the purchase of the land) has a security interest in the real property, while a secured party may have retained an interest in the furnace. If the seller of the furnace wishes to repossess the furnace but confronts the mortgagee of the land, who claims the furnace as part of his or her real estate security interest, knock-down, drag-out fights over priority sometimes occur as a result of this dovetailing of real property and personal property interests.

Section 9-313 of the Code sets out rules for settling these problems. According to the Code, a perfected security interest in fixtures has priority over the conflicting interest of an **encumbrancer** or owner of real estate when (1) the security interest is a purchase money security interest; (2) the security interest is perfected by a fixture filing—that is, filing in the office where real estate mortgages are filed or recorded—before the goods become fixtures (or within 10 days thereafter); and (3) the debtor has an interest of record in the real estate or is in possession of it. Thus, if Fire Power Furnace Company sells Earl LePage, the lessee of Port-Hole Pub, a furnace on an installment basis and retains a security interest in the furnace until Earl pays for it, Fire Power will have priority over Earl's lessor (or the mortgagee of the Pub) if (1) it is a purchase money secured party and (2) it perfects its security interest before the furnace is installed (or within 10 days of that time).[9]

Encumbrancer
The holder of a claim relating to real or personal property.

Similarly, a perfected security interest in fixtures will have priority if (1) the fixtures are readily removable factory or office machines or readily removable replacements of domestic appliances that are consumer goods and (2) before the goods become fixtures, the security interest is perfected by any method permitted under Article 9.[10] Therefore, if Don Dunn's garbage disposal disintegrates and he buys one from Hosinski's Appliance Store through a conditional sales contract, Hosinski's will have priority over Don's mortgagee (whose mortgage covers not only the real property but the plumbing and appliances) if Hosinski's perfects its security interest before it installs the disposal in Don's home. As you no doubt recall, perfection of such consumer goods may occur through attachment; thus, Hosinski's will have priority as of the moment Don signs the security agreement.

It may, however, be in Hosinski's best interests to perfect by resorting to a fixture filing: Such a filing will ensure its priority over subsequent encumbrancers or purchasers whose interests arise after Hosinski's.

http:// RESOURCES FOR BUSINESS LAW STUDENTS

NAME	RESOURCES	WEB ADDRESS
Uniform Commercial Code (UCC) Article 9, Secured Transactions; Sales of Accounts and Chattel Paper	The Legal Information Institute (LII), maintained by the Cornell Law School, provides a hypertext and searchable version of UCC Article 9, Secured Transactions; Sales of Accounts and Chattel Paper. LII also maintains links to Article 9 as adopted by particular states and to proposed revisions.	http://www.law.cornell.edu/ucc/9/overview.html
The National Conference of Commissioners on Uniform State Laws	The National Conference of Commissioners on Uniform State Laws (NCCUSL), the drafter of the UCC, provides drafts and revisions of its uniform and model acts.	http://www.law.upenn.edu/library/ulc/ulc.htm

When the secured party has priority over all owners and encumbrancers of the real estate, that party, upon the debtor's default, may sever and remove the collateral (such as the furnace) from the real estate. A secured party who elects to do this has a duty to reimburse any encumbrancer or owner of the real estate who is not the debtor for any physical injury caused to the property by the removal. Correspondingly, a person entitled to reimbursement may refuse permission concerning the removal of the fixtures until the secured party gives adequate security for the performance of this obligation.[11]

Exhibit 27.1 illustrates the attachment and the perfection of a security interest. It also examines the order of priorities in the event of a conflict among the creditors seeking to enforce their rights in the same collateral.

SUMMARY

The rules on priorities represent the Code's attempt to decide who, among validly perfected secured parties, has superior rights to the collateral. In general, the Code validates a first-in-time, first-in-right approach. Thus, if competing security interests have been perfected by filing, the first to be filed has priority, whether the security interest attached before or after filing. If neither party has filed, the first party to perfect has priority. And if no one has perfected, the first interest to attach has superior rights to the collateral.

There are some exceptions to these priority rules. For instance, if a purchase money secured party follows certain Code provisions that make distinctions according to the type of collateral involved, such a party may prevail over earlier, perfected creditors. Similarly, in some situations, bona fide purchasers of consumer goods and buyers in the ordinary course of business may defeat prior perfected interests. Likewise, certain liens that arise by operation of law have priority over perfected security interests in the collateral. Moreover, a secured party holding a security interest in fixtures will defeat a real property claimant if, for example, the secured party follows the requirements of the Code for a "fixture filing," or a filing in an office where real property interests are recorded.

EXHIBIT 27.1 Anatomy of a Security Interest: Attachment, Perfection, and Priorities

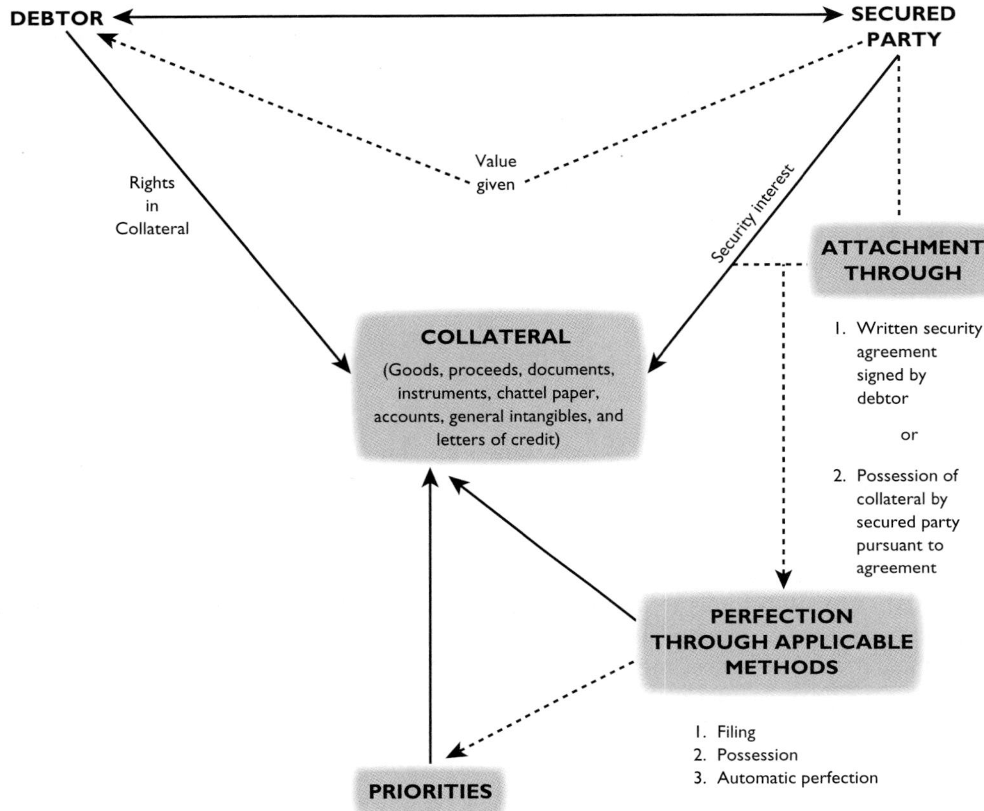

1. Holders of certain common law or statutory liens arising by operation of law.
2. Among perfected secured parties in the same collateral, first in time to file or otherwise perfect. Yet such priorities may be upset by
   a. Purchase money security interests in which applicable U.C.C. rules have been followed.
   b. Bona fide purchasers (BFPs) of consumer goods where secured party has filed beforehand and where BFPs have given value and are ignorant of the security interest.
   c. Buyers in the ordinary course of business.
3. Lien creditors (including trustees in bankruptcy).
4. Unperfected secured parties.
5. General creditors (i.e., sellers on account).

Discussion Questions

1. Why is the issue of priority important?
2. Why should a lender file a financing statement even before the completion of the deal?
3. Enumerate the rules regarding priorities in the absence of filing.
4. Explain the importance of purchase money secured parties and why they merit priority.
5. List the rules for becoming a purchase money secured party in inventory collateral.

6. List the rules for becoming a purchase money secured party in noninventory collateral.
7. What is a bona fide purchaser? Does such a purchaser always have priority? How does this person differ from a buyer in the ordinary course of business?
8. Does a secured party have priority over the holder of a common law lien? Explain why or why not.
9. What steps should a secured party in fixtures take to protect his or her interest?
10. Why does a secured party in fixtures have to reimburse the owner of the land (when that person is not the debtor) if the secured party has removed the collateral from the real property?

CASE PROBLEMS AND WRITING ASSIGNMENTS

1. James Freeman purchased tools for $1,261.40 from Bobby Majors, a dealer for Snap-On Tools Corporation. Because he already had a significant balance on his revolving account, Freeman agreed to consolidate his new purchase with the outstanding balance of his revolving account and enter into a security agreement with Majors. This agreement provided for a "purchase money security interest" and listed as "property" the $1,261.40 in new purchases and $826.07 in tools transferred from the revolving account. Thus, the agreement attached $2,087.47 in tools to secure Freeman's obligation of $1,643.00 (Freeman made a cash down payment of $412.06). Majors subsequently assigned his interest to Snap-On, which transformed the agreement into an "extended credit account." The account became interest bearing and required payments of $85.60 for 24 months. Snap-On's agreement with Freeman additionally allowed for a first-in, first-out method of payment allocation to the time balance. Furthermore, it provided that when the prior purchase money time balance had been paid, the secured party would retain a non-purchase money security interest in the property described in prior agreements as security for the net balance due and the performance of any other obligations under the agreement. This is the only language in the agreement that made reference to the release of the "purchase money" security status as Freeman forwarded payments on the account. After the establishment of the extended credit account, Freeman continued to purchase tools on credit from Majors; and the charges were posted to the revolving account. When Freeman made another significant credit purchase, a consolidation followed. This time the outstanding balance of the extended credit account was consolidated with the balance of the new revolving account and the new purchase. This consolidated security agreement also provided for a "purchase money security interest." After three such consolidations, a UCC financing statement was filed. This perfection of the security agreement occurred before Freeman voluntarily petitioned for bankruptcy. The Bankruptcy Code, however, allows a debtor such as Freeman to avoid a lien that consists of a nonpossessory, non-purchase money security interest. Freeman, in attempting to avoid Snap-On's lien on the tools purchased, argued that a purchase money security interest used to secure the purchase price of goods sold in a particular transaction is transformed into a non-purchase money security interest when antecedent or after-acquired debt is consolidated with the new purchase under one contract. Given the UCC's definition of a purchase money security interest, should a court find Freeman's argument persuasive? Why? [See *In re Freeman*, 956 F.2d 252 (11th Cir. 1992).]

2. On 2 December 1981, Dupont Feed Mill Corporation executed and delivered a $300,000 promissory note to Wells Fargo Bank. On 12 April 1982, Dupont Feed executed a security agreement that granted to Wells Fargo a security interest in Dupont Feed's present and after-acquired inventory wherever located and all proceeds therefrom. Wells Fargo filed a financing statement on this security agreement with the county recorder of Jefferson County on 17 June 1982 and with the Indiana secretary of state on 28 June 1982. In August 1983, William Wildman, the president of Dupont Feed, contacted Rushville National Bank (Rushville) to inquire about a $100,000 loan to purchase the Arlington Ag-Center in his individual capacity. In the course of requesting the loan, Wildman issued a personal financial statement to Rushville. On 26 September 1983, Rushville agreed to loan Wildman $100,000 for the mortgage on the property and to extend a line of credit for $150,000 to William and Sandra Wildman, d.b.a. Arlington Ag-Center. Wildman testified that he orally informed Wells Fargo that Rushville would be financing his acquisition of Arlington. On 27 October 1983, Wildman received title to the Arlington property and personally executed a mortgage note for $100,000 payable to Rushville. Subsequently, Wildman released the Arlington property to Dupont Feed, and Dupont Feed operated it as a branch location. On 9 February 1984, Rushville filed a financing statement with the county recorder of Rush County, Indiana. The financing statement listed "Arlington Ag-Center"

as the debtor and further stated that it covered "all inventory, accounts receivable, equipment, furniture, and fixtures located at Arlington Ag-Center." On 10 September 1984, Dupont Feed filed a Chapter 11 bankruptcy petition listing Arlington as an asset and Wells Fargo and Rushville as creditors. Thereafter, on or about 17 December 1984, Rushville filed with the Indiana secretary of state's office a financing statement covering the inventory of Dupont Feed. In December 1984 and January 1985, Rushville took possession of and sold Arlington's fertilizer for the sum of $95,000 and credited Dupont Feed's account with that amount. On 8 April 1985, Wells Fargo sued Rushville for conversion of the proceeds of the sale of the fertilizer. During this litigation, Rushville argued that its perfected purchase money security interest in inventory took priority over Wells Fargo's conflicting security interest in the same collateral. Did Rushville, as a perfected purchase money secured party, enjoy priority in the proceeds of the sale of the fertilizer? Why or why not? [See *In re Dupont Feed Mill Corp.*, 121 B.R. 555 (S.D. Ind. 1990).]

3. In January 1988, the secured creditor, Kit Car World, Inc., and other corporations owned by Robert and Eileen Tietz, transferred to the debtor, Richard Skolnick, molds, equipment, inventory, and other assets necessary to manufacture and secure replica car kits of a 1953 Corvette. In consideration, the debtor executed a promissory note for $185,000, with the debt secured by all assets related to the replica car kits, including inventory and all after-acquired property. The promissory note and security agreement obligated the debtor to pay $500 on the note each time he collected full payment for a kit and to sell a minimum of 50 car kits the first 15 months and every 12 months thereafter or be deemed in default. The debtor also promised to provide monthly financial reports. In April 1989, the debtor, by failing to make payments when due and to provide the required monthly financial reports, defaulted on the note and the security agreement. The secured creditors then accelerated the balance due under the note and filed suit seeking damages for the unpaid balance and seeking possession of the property covered by the security agreement. On 2 November 1989, the secured creditors served the debtor with a prejudgment writ of replevin directing seizure of the assets under the security agreement. Among the items seized were steel frames, fiberglass bodies, molds, and other component parts and inventory used in the assemblage of replica car kits. After the execution of the writ of replevin, the debtor ceased to conduct business. The trial court allowed seven customers of the debtor to file complaints in intervention alleging that they each owned a replica car kit that the secured creditors wrongfully had seized. Although the customers individually had paid the full price for each car kit, the debtor's assets were seized before he could assemble and deliver them. In fact, the debtor never had identified any of the goods to the particular contracts in dispute. After a nonjury trial, the trial court entered final judgment in favor of the seven customers for money damages. The court found that the secured creditors had converted the customers' car kits and that, since the car kits constituted consumer goods, the secured creditors had not enjoyed an interest in the car kits under the after-acquired property clause of the security agreement. On appeal, the secured creditors claimed that under Florida's Uniform Commercial Code, their interest in the debtor's inventory was superior to any interest claimed by the customers. However, the customers claimed a superior interest as "buyers in the ordinary course of business." If you were the appellate judge, how would you decide this case? Why? [See *Kit Car World, Inc.* v. *Skolnick*, 616 So.2d 1051 (Fla.App. 1993).]

4. On 30 April 1987, Contractor's Glass Co., Inc., the debtor, owed City National Bank (CNB) $185,000, as evidenced by a promissory note executed on the same date. To secure the note, the debtor executed and delivered to CNB a corporate real estate mortgage and a security agreement. The security agreement granted CNB a security interest in all the debtor's inventory, accounts receivable, equipment, furniture, and fixtures then owned or thereafter acquired by the debtor. The security agreement also contained a future advances clause to secure any future loans made to the debtor by CNB. CNB filed properly executed financing statements and thereby perfected its security interest as of 6 May 1987. On 30 April 1987, the debtor also borrowed from J. Faulkner $50,000, as evidenced by a promissory note executed on the same date. By granting a security interest in the same personal property that secured CNB's indebtedness, the debtor secured the note to Faulkner. Faulkner's security agreement acknowledged his security interest as second and inferior to the bank's security interest. Faulkner validly perfected his security interest as of 15 May 1987. On 23 June 1988, the debtor borrowed from CNB an additional sum of $33,700. To secure the promissory note made on that same date, the debtor executed an additional security agreement granting CNB a security interest in the debtor's inventory, equipment, accounts receivable, furniture, and fixtures. CNB did not file a new financing statement covering this new security agreement. After the debtor

had filed for bankruptcy, the trustee liquidated the debtor's real and personal property. The trustee determined that CNB had a first priority lien in the real and personal property and accordingly disbursed the sale proceeds to CNB. Faulkner did not dispute CNB's entitlement to the proceeds from the sale of the real property; however, he argued that because the proceeds of the sale satisfied the debtor's initial indebtedness of $185,000 to CNB in full, his (Faulkner's) security interest in the personal property was superior to CNB's security interest. CNB contended that, although the $185,000 indebtedness of the first promissory note had been paid in full, by virtue of the $33,700 advance, the debtor remained indebted to CNB. CNB therefore claimed that its security interest remained perfected because of the financing statements filed on 5 and 6 May 1987, notwithstanding the fact that CNB had advanced the $33,700 on 23 June 1988. Who should enjoy priority as to the net proceeds of the sale of the debtor's personal property, CNB or Faulkner? Why? [See *In re Contractor's Glass Co., Inc.*, 152 B.R. 270 (Bankr. W.D. Ark. 1992).]

5. Donald L. Pippin, Jr., purchased about $40,000 worth of jewelry from Osterman, Inc. Pippin paid Osterman $30,000 by check and agreed to pay the balance in installments. In actuality, Pippin had drawn the check on a closed account. During the next six days, Pippin pawned the jewelry with two different pawnbrokers, who each entered into a security agreement with Pippin. Pursuant to a criminal complaint issued against Pippin, police seized the jewelry from the pawnbrokers, who thereupon petitioned for the return of the jewelry. A month after that, Osterman also petitioned for the return of the jewelry and filed a financing statement covering the jewelry. Osterman argued that the pawnbrokers had no security interest in the jewelry owing to their failure to attach their security interest. Osterman alternatively argued that the police's seizure of the jewelry made the pawnbrokers' reliance on possession as their mode of perfection ineffective. Given these circumstances, who had the superior right to the jewelry, the pawnbrokers or Osterman? Why? [See *National Pawn Brokers Unlimited* v. *Osterman, Inc.*, 500 N.W.2d 407 (Wis.App. 1993).]

6. **BUSINESS APPLICATION CASE** On 11 September 1978, Kubota Tractor Corporation filed a financing statement giving notice of an alleged security interest between itself, as secured party, and Harvey's, Inc., a dealer in farm and related equipment, as debtor. On 27 September 1978, Citizens & Southern National Bank (C & S) entered into a security agreement with Harvey's and took a security interest in certain of Harvey's property. The next day, C & S filed a financing statement giving notice of its security interest. On 30 July 1979, Kubota entered into a dealership agreement with Harvey's, whereby Kubota appointed Harvey's as an authorized dealer of Kubota products. This agreement created and provided for a certain security interest between the secured party Kubota and Harvey's. In 1981, 1982, 1983, and 1984, C & S also executed certain other security agreements with Harvey's. On 12 May 1983, C & S filed a timely continuation of its 28 September 1978 financing statement. On 25 June 1983, Kubota entered into a supplemental agreement with Harvey's whereby Kubota amended the description of the property secured by the original dealership agreement. On 12 August 1983, before the expiration of its 11 September 1978 financing statement, Kubota filed a document that on its face purported to amend its original financing statement. This document bore the handwritten caption of an "Amendment" and contained an apparent modification of Kubota's financing statement's description of the secured property, so as to conform that description to the language of the amended dealership agreement and include an expressly stated, broad after-acquired property clause. The expiration date of the filing of Kubota's original financing statement was 10 September 1983. On 2 March 1984, Kubota filed a document expressly identified as a "Continuation" to its original financing statement of 11 September 1978; the document did not include any reference either to the 25 June 1983 amendment to the dealership agreement or to the captioned "Amendment" document of 12 August 1983. Ultimately, when Harvey's defaulted on its obligations to Kubota and C & S, a controversy over the priority of the security interests arose. Specifically, C & S argued that, owing to Kubota's failure to file a timely continuation statement, Kubota's security interest against Harvey's had lapsed and C & S therefore enjoyed priority as to the collateral. How should a court rule on C & S's claims? As a result of this litigation, what intra-office policies would you expect Kubota to develop? [See *Kubota Tractor Corp.* v. *Citizens & Southern Nat'l Bank*, 403 S.E.2d 218 [Ga.App.1991).]

7. **ETHICS APPLICATION CASE** In 1985, Arkansas Valley State Bank (AVSB) had perfected a security interest in all the present and future inventory of LaSelle's Bicycle World. AVSB's financing statement named "LASELLES, INCORPORATED" (one word, no possessive) as the debtor. In 1987, General Bicycle and Moped, Inc., after extending credit to LaSelle's, asked the county clerk whether any outstanding liens against LaSelle's inventory existed. When the county

clerk mistakenly advised General that no such liens existed, General properly perfected a purchase money security interest in all LaSelle's inventory thereafter sold to LaSelle's. General did not notify AVSB of its purchase money security interest because of its (General's) reliance on the county clerk's statement concerning the absence of any liens. When LaSelle's filed for bankruptcy in 1989, General argued that its interest took priority over AVSB's floating lien. AVSB maintained that General's failure to notify AVSB of General's purported purchase money secured interest nullified General's attempt to attain purchase money secured party status. Who should enjoy priority? Why? The legalities aside, if you were deciding this case solely on ethical grounds, who would win and why? [See *In re LaSelle's Bicycle World,* 120 B.R. 579 (Bankr. N.D. Okla. 1990).]

8. **IDES CASE** United Bank of Littleton and Davis Bros., Inc., were creditors of Drug Fair, a retail drug store and pharmacy. On 14 November 1995, the bank filed a financing statement covering all the debtor's inventory, furniture, fixtures, equipment, accounts receivable, and all after-acquired property. On 27 September 1996, Davis Bros. filed a financing statement to secure payment of a $62,822.28 note. The statement listed as collateral Drug Fair's inventory, prescription records, and all "drug and sundry inventory of debtor which debtor has purchased or may purchase from secured party and in which secured party has taken or will take a purchase money security interest." Davis Bros. subsequently supplied Drug Fair with merchandise on a weekly credit basis. As the result of a lien search, the bank learned of Davis Bros.'s financing statement on 16 February 1997. During April 1997, the bank took possession of and sold Drug Fair's inventory and prescription records without giving Davis Bros. notice of the sale. At the time of the sale, Drug Fair owed Davis Bros, $7,951.84 on an open account for drugs and sundries purchased from Davis Bros. after the filing of Davis Bros's financing statement. This amount was over and above the amount due on the note. Davis Bros. then brought suit for an accounting of the proceeds of the sale and for damages for conversion of the items in which it had priority. The trial court granted summary judgment as to Davis Bros.'s claim for conversion of the debtor's prescription records and the drugs and sundries for which Davis Bros. had a purchase money security interest. Following trial on the issue of damages, the court entered judgment for $25,000 for conversion of the prescription records and $7,951.84 plus interest at the rate of 18 percent per annum for conversion of the drugs and sundries. Was the court correct in holding that Davis Bros. enjoyed priority as to these items? If the security interest instead involved noninventory collateral, what steps would Davis Bros. have had to take to enjoy priority? Apply the IDES model to these questions. [Based on *Davis Bros., Inc.* v. *United Bank of Littleton,* 701 P.2d 642 (Colo.App. 1985).]

NOTES

1. Uniform Commercial Code, § 9-312(5)(a).
2. Ibid., § 9-312, Official Comment 5.
3. Ibid., § 9-107.
4. Ibid., § 9-312(3).
5. Ibid., § 9-312(4).
6. "Dep't Store Charge Agreement Not Valid as 'Security Agreement,'" *UCC Bulletin* (Deerfield: Clark Boardman Callaghan) (October 1996), pp. 7–8.
7. Uniform Commercial Code, § 9-307(2).
8. Ibid., § 9-109(1).
9. Ibid., § 9-313(4)(a).
10. Ibid., § 9-313(4)(c).
11. Ibid., § 9-313(8).

Secured Transactions: Default

O U T L I N E

A G E N D A

CIT will need to use some of its equipment, most of its inventory, and its patents as collateral. The Kochanowskis want to know what actions the firm's creditors can take against the collateral, the firm, and the family members in the event that CIT is unable to pay its bills as they come due. In addition, the firm hopes to sell and lease a significant number of videophones. Some of these sales will be made on credit, and the family plans to retain a security interest in the videophones as collateral for these extensions of credit. The family, therefore, wants to know what rights CIT will have against any customers who default on their obligations to the firm.

These and other questions will arise in the course of this chapter. Be prepared! You never know when one of the Kochanowskis will need your help or advice.

THE CODE AND DEFAULT

Chapters 26 and 27 considered the methods by which secured parties can protect their interests in the collateral. Neither the debtor nor the secured party, however, wants to consider the possibility that the debtor will *default,* or fail to meet the obligations set out in the security agreement. Still, this contingency sometimes occurs.

The default of the debtor represents a bittersweet moment for the secured party. On the one hand, default distresses the secured party because it reveals that the debtor may be unable or unwilling to pay the debt to the secured party. But, on the other hand, the secured party has worked hard to preserve his or her status as one superior to an unsecured lender and as one who, upon the debtor's default, thus has rights to the collateral. In brief, Part 5 of Article 9 of the UCC allows the secured party, upon the debtor's default, to take possession of the collateral and to dispose of it in satisfaction of the secured party's claim. Yet the Code provides the debtor with certain protections once the secured party seeks to enforce its rights in the collateral and makes the secured party liable for any noncompliance with applicable Code provisions.

Interestingly, the Code does not define the term *default*. Basically, the parties decide what events constitute default, and the security agreement embodies these conclusions. Simply put, *default* means whatever the security agreement says it means. Nonpayment by the debtor perhaps constitutes the easiest definition of default. But default clauses often are broad and lengthy (see Exhibit 26.1). Security agreements also typically include *acceleration clauses* by which the secured party demands that all obligations be paid immediately. In the absence of bad faith and unconscionability, courts routinely uphold these clauses whenever the secured party can show the default of the debtor.

Upon default, the secured party may resort to various alternative remedies. Using non-Code remedies, the secured party may become a judgment creditor, may **garnish** the debtor's wages, or may **replevy** the goods. Code remedies include strict foreclosure (retention of the collateral in satisfaction of the debt) and resale of the collateral. In § 9-501(l), the UCC further provides that non-Code and Code rights and remedies are cumulative. Yet it is clear that before secured parties can utilize another method against the debtor, they must be unsuccessful in enforcing their rights by the first method. Neither the Code nor case law sanctions an approach whereby a secured creditor may employ non-Code and Code remedies simultaneously against the debtor.

Garnish
Receive the debtor's assets that are in the hands of a third party; a remedy given to satisfy a debt owed.

Replevy
Acquire possession of goods unlawfully held by another.

Foreclose
Cut off an existing ownership right in property.

Exhibit 28.1 describes the rights and duties of the parties in a secured transaction upon default.

The *Grocers Supply* v. *Intercity Investment Properties, Inc.,* case illustrates some of the principles and concepts that arise from a debtor's default.

28.1 GROCERS SUPPLY CO., INC. v. INTERCITY INVESTMENT PROPERTIES, INC.

795 S.W.2d 225 (Tex.App. 1990)

FACTS On 2 February 1989, Grocers Supply Co., Inc. (Grocers Supply) perfected a security interest exceeding $600,000 to secure its inventory financing of The Grocery Store, Inc., and Cedric Wise. On 6 March 1989, Intercity Investment Properties, Inc. (Intercity) obtained a judgment in the county court against The Grocery Store, Inc., and Cedric Wise for approximately $36,000; and on 22 June 1989, the county court issued an order to allow Intercity to

28.1 GROCERS SUPPLY CO., INC. v. INTERCITY INVESTMENT PROPERTIES, INC. *(cont.)* 795 S.W.2d 225 (Tex.App. 1990)

levy on the collateral covered by the judgment. Grocers Supply was not a party to that suit. On 12 July 1989, the constable, accompanied by three attorneys for Intercity, levied writs of execution obtained by Intercity on The Grocery Store and took possession of the inventory of groceries, equipment, and other items described in the writ of execution. The attorneys for Intercity knew of the prior recorded security interest of Grocers Supply but had not contacted Grocers Supply. Upon learning of the execution on The Grocery Store inventory, Grocers Supply filed a lawsuit to determine its rights in the property and argued that it, as a prior secured party, enjoyed a superior right to repossess the collateral than that enjoyed by a judgment creditor.

ISSUE Would a secured party, upon the debtor's default, have the right to repossess the collateral; and was this right superior to the right of a judgment creditor to repossess?

HOLDING Yes to both. Grocers Supply, as a prior secured creditor, had superior rights to repossess the collateral; and the rights of the judgment creditor (Intercity) therefore were subordinate to Grocers Supply's rights.

REASONING Texas's version of UCC § 9-503 provides that "unless otherwise agreed a secured party has on default the right to take possession of the collateral." With the exception of Wisconsin, other states considering the issue consistently have held that the right of a prior perfected creditor to take possession of its collateral is superior to any right of a mere judgment creditor and that the prior perfected secured creditor may regain possession of the collateral from an officer who has levied on the property at the direction of a judgment creditor. The interpretation followed by these precedents makes sense because to hold otherwise will take away from the perfected security interest holder the important right of repossession of the collateral. Here, the security agreement between Grocers Supply and The Grocery Store clearly provides that a judgment against the debtor or the levy, seizure, or attachment of the collateral constitutes a default and that, upon the occurrence of any of those events, "the entire obligation [will become] immediately due and payable at secured party's option without notice to debtor." Hence, the right of Grocers Supply, as a prior secured creditor, to take possession of its collateral would be superior to the right of Intercity, a mere judgment creditor. Grocers Supply accordingly could regain possession of the collateral from the constable who had levied on the property.

BUSINESS CONSIDERATIONS Note that the court grounded its decision in part on language found in Grocers Supply's security agreement with The Grocery Store. What other provisions relating to default, especially the specific grounds that will constitute default, would you expect to find in the security agreement? Explain fully.

ETHICAL CONSIDERATIONS Were the attorneys for Intercity under an ethical duty to inform Grocers Supply that Intercity had obtained a writ of execution? Why or why not?

NON-CODE REMEDIES

The Code says that, upon default, secured parties may seek a court judgment, may **foreclose**, or may otherwise enforce the security agreement by any available judicial procedure.[1] Accordingly, secured parties can use their Code remedies of repossession and resale with the possibility of a deficiency judgment for which the debtor is liable, or they can follow the non-Code remedy of becoming judgment creditors whereby they file suit, obtain a judgment, and have the sheriff use a **writ of execution** to levy on the goods and then sell the goods at a public sale. The proceeds of this sale are paid to the secured party. Another non-Code alternative to levying on the goods involves **garnishment** of a set percentage of the debtor's wages. Although there are certain advantages to following these non-Code remedies in cases where the value of the collateral has decreased so far that the possibility of reaching assets

Writ of execution
A court-issued writing that enforces a judgment or decree.

Garnishment
A legal proceeding in which assets of a debtor that are in the hands of a third person are ordered held by the third person or turned over to the creditor in full or partial satisfaction of the debt.

EXHIBIT 28.1 Rights and Duties Upon the Debtor's Default

SECURED PARTIES' RIGHTS

Cumulative Rights and Remedies

UCC Remedies

[Right of repossession on default; "self-help" repossession by secured party possible, provided no breach of peace occurs]

Foreclosure by Sale

Public or Private Sale

REQUIREMENTS:

A. Notice:

1. For consumer goods and all other types of collateral, written notice of time and place of sale sent by secured party to debtor (in absence of written waiver by debtor of right to receive notice).
2. For all collateral except consumer goods, written notice of time and place of sale sent by foreclosing secured party to all other secured parties who previously in writing notified foreclosing secured party of claimed interests in the collateral.

B. Exception:

1. No notice necessary if collateral is perishable, threatens to decline speedily in value, or is of a type customarily sold on a recognized market.

C. Other considerations:

1. Sale commercially reasonable in all respects: notice, time, place, and manner.
2. Secured party's application of proceeds of sale in order specified in UCC.
3. For secured party's failure to foreclose by sale within 90 days when mandatory, liability in damages for conversion or from UCC statutory provisions.

STRICT FORECLOSURE IMPOSSIBLE:

a. Objections given in writing by junior secured parties within 21 days after receiving foreclosing secured party's notice of intention to retain collateral.
b. Debtor's previous payment of 60% of the cash price of a purchase money security interest in consumer goods or 60 percent of the loan in another security interest in consumer goods in conjunction with debtor's failure (after default) to renounce in writing the right to require foreclosure by sale.
c. If (a) or (b) applicable, foreclosure by sale mandatory.

Strict Foreclosure

[Retention of collateral in complete satisfaction of debt]

RATIONALE:

Attractive to secured parties because:

1. value of collateral equal to debt.
2. expenses of court actions thereby avoided.
3. absence of subsequent controversies about fairness of resale price.
4. requirements for effecting strict foreclosure in compliance with UCC set out matter-of-factly in UCC.

REQUIREMENTS:

A. Notice:

1. For consumer goods and all other types of collateral, written notice of intention to retain collateral sent by secured party to debtor unless debtor—after default—has signed a statement renouncing his or her rights regarding strict foreclosure.
2. For all collateral except consumer goods, written notice of intention to retain collateral sent by foreclosing secured party to all other secured parties who previously in writing notified foreclosing secured party of claimed interests in the collateral.
3. Waiting period of 21 days after secured party sends notice in order to receive written objections to proposed retention of the collateral (and no objections received by secured party).

STRICT FORECLOSURE POSSIBLE
(but no deficiency judgment possible)

Non-UCC Remedies

1. Become a judgment creditor
   a. Writ of execution obtained
   b. Goods levied on by appropriate officials
   c. Foreclosure sale conducted
2. Obtain garnishment of debtor's wages
3. Replevy the goods

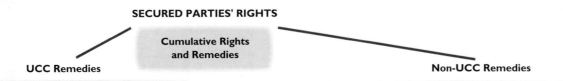

SECURED PARTIES' DUTIES

1. Take reasonable care of the collateral in secured party's possession after debtor's default.
2. Keep the collateral identifiable (exception: fungible collateral).
3. Repledge the collateral (if need be).
4. Turn over any remaining proceeds after sale to debtor.

DEBTORS' RIGHTS

Redemption

[Unless waived after default, debtor's right to extinguish secured party's security interest by tendering all expenses due—including secured party's expenses for repossession, etc. Cuts off both UCC and non-UCC remedies]

Right to Force Sale of Collateral

(As outlined under "Strict Foreclosure" above)

beyond the collateral will be desirable, most creditors, in practice, elect the tidier and speedier remedies of repossession and resale that the UCC allows.

RIGHT OF REPOSSESSION

Unless already in possession of the collateral, a secured party, upon the debtor's default, has the right to take possession of the collateral. In so doing, that party may employ "self-help" measures; that is, secured parties can repossess the collateral themselves without judicial procedures if they can do so without breaching the peace.[2] Repossession carries with it inherent dangers, however. Besides risking possible tort liability if the repossession involves a breach of the peace, the secured party also risks UCC liability[3] and the loss of the right to a deficiency judgment.

Needless to say, this aspect of the Code has spawned numerous lawsuits. In general, courts assess such factors as whether the secured party entered the debtor's home or driveway without permission and whether the debtor agreed to the repossession. Although it is difficult to make generalizations in this area, if the creditor repossesses an automobile from a public street and the debtor fails to object to this procedure, most courts will hold that there has been no breach of the peace. Nevertheless, in recent years, some questions have arisen as to the constitutionality of this "self-help" provision of the Code. Specifically, some have argued that repossession without notice to the debtor may deprive the debtor of due process rights.[4] Statutes authorizing replevin may be subject to the same constitutional argument.

The *Ivy* v. *GMAC* case illustrates one court's disposition of a case involving a "self-help" repossession.

28.1

FINANCE/MANAGEMENT

REPOSSESSION

CIT has been suffering because of lagging collections for a while and has fallen behind on its payments to one of its secured creditors. The creditor has made several requests for payments, but the firm has been unable to catch up. As a result, last week the creditor seized a CIT truck (containing 400 Call-Image videophones) from the CIT parking lot. The family asks you if this was a lawful repossession or a conversion by the creditor. What will you tell the family members?

BUSINESS CONSIDERATIONS Should a business that regularly extends credit to its customers rely on self-help measures when it takes possession of collateral? What legal problems might the business face if it does rely on the use of self-help repossession?

ETHICAL CONSIDERATIONS Without regard to the legality of a self-help repossession, is such conduct ethical? What ethical concerns does the use of self-help repossession raise?

28.2 IVY v. GENERAL MOTORS ACCEPTANCE CORPORATION

612 So.2d 1108 (Miss. 1992)

FACTS Lester Ivy defaulted on his van loan. As a result, General Motors Acceptance Corporation (GMAC) hired American Lenders Service Company of Jackson (American Lenders) to repossess Ivy's van. On 14 March 1988, around 6:30 A.M., Dax Freeman and Jonathan Baker of American Lenders drove to Ivy's home. They drove on Ivy's gravel driveway, which is about a quarter-mile long, past a chicken house and the van parked near Ivy's mobile home. They quietly attempted to start the van, but their attempt failed. They then hitched the van to their tow truck and began towing it away. When Freeman and Baker reached the end of Ivy's driveway, Freeman stopped the tow truck and checked on the van. At that point, Freeman noticed Ivy running from the chicken house toward the mobile home. Freeman jumped into the tow truck, drove off Ivy's property onto adjacent Chain Road, and approached the intersection of Chain Road and Highway 35. Ivy had decided to chase after Freeman and Baker because Ivy thought they were stealing his van. At that point, a pickup truck driven by Ivy passed Freeman and Baker. Ivy pulled in front of the tow

28.2 IVY v. GENERAL MOTORS ACCEPTANCE CORPORATION *(cont.)* 612 So.2d 1108 (Miss. 1992)

truck and allegedly slammed on his brakes. Freeman hit his brakes but was unable to stop before a slight collision with the rear bumper of Ivy's truck occurred. Ivy exited his truck, and Freeman informed Ivy that he and Baker worked for American Lenders and at GMAC's request were repossessing Ivy's van. According to Freeman, Ivy responded that he would have given Freeman the keys to the van if Freeman simply had asked; but Ivy denied making that statement. After Freeman showed Ivy some "official-looking" documents that seemed to validate the repossession, Ivy retrieved his personal belongings from the van. According to Freeman, he asked Ivy if Ivy wanted to call the sheriff's department to report the accident; but Ivy said no. Freeman then provided Ivy with a telephone number to call if Ivy wanted to get the van back. At that point, they all departed. On 20 October 1988, Ivy sued GMAC. Ivy claimed that GMAC's alleged breach of the peace had led to an invalid repossession. At trial, the jury awarded Ivy $5,000 in actual damages and $100,000 in punitive damages. The circuit court judge granted GMAC's motion for a judgment n.o.v. [judgment notwithstanding the verdict] with regard to the punitive damages award and set that part of the verdict aside.

ISSUE Had GMAC's agents accomplished this self-help repossession without breaching the peace?

HOLDING No. Since GMAC's agents had breached the peace during the execution of this self-help repossession, GMAC's attempted repossession was legally improper.

REASONING Mississippi law authorizes a creditor or secured party to repossess collateral without judicial process if he or she can do so without breaching the peace. The legislature has not defined "breach of peace," but Mississippi Supreme Court precedents provide some guidance. For example, entering a private driveway to repossess collateral without use of force does not constitute a breach of peace. Moreover, a creditor who repossesses collateral, despite the fact that the debtor has withheld his or her consent or has strongly objected, does not breach the peace under Mississippi law, either. Courts in other jurisdictions generally have held that the use of trickery or deceit to peaceably repossess collateral does not constitute a breach of peace. However, a Florida court of appeals has opined that a debtor's "physical objection"—"even from a public street"—bars repossession. Furthermore, a Georgia court of appeals has found a breach of peace in a case in which: (1) the creditor repossessed the debtor's automobile by blocking it with another automobile; (2) the creditor informed the debtor that he could just "walk his a__ home"; and (3) the debtor "unequivocally protested" the manner of repossession. In similar fashion, the Ohio Supreme Court has concluded that the use of intimidation or acts "fraught with the likelihood of violence" constitutes a breach of peace. In sum, much of the litigation relating to self-help repossession statutes involves the issue of whether a breach of peace has occurred. Moreover, the disposition of this issue is not a simple task, as one noted authority has stated:

> *Since physical violence will ordinarily result in a breach of peace, the secured party's right to repossession will end if repossession evokes physical violence, either on the part of the debtor or the secured party. At the other extreme from physical violence, a secured party may peaceably persuade the debtor to give up the collateral so that no breach of peace occurs. Between those two extreme situations—one in which violence occurs and the other in which the debtor peaceably gives up the collateral—lies the line which divides those cases in which the secured party may exercise self-help repossession and those in which he must resort to the courts. As with most dividing lines, the line between those two extremes is sometimes hard to locate and, even if it is located, it sometimes moves.*

The application of the foregoing principles would lead to the conclusion that a breach of peace had occurred. The lower court's decision therefore should be affirmed.

BUSINESS CONSIDERATIONS Assume that you are going to file a friend of the court brief with the Supreme Court because it once again is planning to take up the issue of whether the self-help provision of the Code is unconstitutional. What arguments would you muster against this proposition? What arguments would you expect consumer advocates to use in support of this proposition?

ETHICAL CONSIDERATIONS Does the leeway given to secured creditors under the "self-help" provision implicitly condone unethical behavior on their part? Explain fully.

YOU BE THE JUDGE

Was the Repossession a Breach of Peace?

The debtor, James Koontz, was behind in his payments; and the secured party, Chrysler Credit Corp. (Chrysler), had warned him that it would repossess the car if he did not catch up those payments. In response, Koontz said he would make every effort to become current and that, in the meantime, Chrysler was not to enter onto his private property. Koontz then parked the car in his front yard where he could see the car by the light of his front porch. When the repossession began, Koontz was not watching the car; but he heard the repossessor at work and ran out. Koontz, in his underwear, hollered at the repossessor, "Don't take it." The repossessor ignored the protest and took the car. Koontz has filed suit against Chrysler Credit Corp., claiming that the repossession was a breach of the peace. Koontz is seeking damages and/or the return of his car. This case has been brought before *your* court. How will *you* decide this controversy?[5]

BUSINESS CONSIDERATIONS What sort of policy should a business creditor establish for dealing with debtors who have fallen behind in their payments? What sort of policy should a business creditor have for using self-help in the repossession of collateral?

ETHICAL CONSIDERATIONS Is it ethical for a creditor to repossess collateral after the debtor has assured the creditor that he or she will make every effort to catch up on any arrearages? What is the ethical obligation of a creditor when a debtor falls behind on a secured loan?

SOURCE: *UCC Bulletin* (Deerfield: Clark Boardman Callaghan) (June 1996), p. 9.

Besides repossession by self-help, if the security agreement so provides, the Code also sanctions the secured party's requiring the debtor to assemble the collateral at a reasonably convenient place to be designated by the secured party.[6] Moreover, when the collateral consists of heavy equipment that makes physical removal burdensome or expensive, the Code permits the secured party to render the equipment unusable and to dispose of the collateral on the debtor's premises, thus eliminating the need for physically removing the collateral.

These rules do not cover accounts and general intangibles, because one cannot possess purely intangible collateral. When the debtor is in default with regard to these types of collateral, the secured party may notify the person who is obligated on the intangibles to make payments directly to the secured party. The secured party also may take control of any proceeds to which he or she is entitled under the UCC.[7]

STRICT FORECLOSURE

After default and repossession, the secured party may decide to retain the collateral in complete satisfaction of the debt.[8] This remedy, called the secured party's right of *strict foreclosure*, may be attractive to the secured party for several reasons: (1) The value of the collateral may be approximately equal to the debt; (2) the expenses of court actions are avoided; (3) there can be no subsequent controversies about whether the resale price was fair; and (4) the UCC sets out matter-of-factly the requirements for effecting strict foreclosure.

However, to effect strict foreclosure, the secured party must comply with certain requirements, which include the following:

1. The secured party must send written notice of his or her intention to retain the collateral to:
   a. the debtor, unless the debtor after default has signed a statement renouncing his or her right to force a sale of the collateral (in the case of consumer goods, no other notice need be sent);
   b. any other secured parties who in writing have notified the secured party who is foreclosing that they claim an interest in the collateral.
2. After sending notice, the secured party must wait twenty-one days so as to receive objections in writing concerning this proposed retention of the collateral.[9]

Conversion
The unauthorized and wrongful exercise of dominion and control over the personal property of another to the detriment of that other person.

If the secured party receives no such objections, he or she can utilize the remedy of strict foreclosure; but the secured party thereby will give up any claims to a deficiency judgment.

In contrast, strict foreclosure is not permissible in certain situations:

1. Whenever the secured party actually receives written objections from those entitled to notification within twenty-one days, the secured party must sell the collateral.
2. If the collateral consists of consumer goods and the debtor has paid 60 percent of the cash price of a purchase money security interest or 60 percent of the loan in all other security interests in these goods, the secured party must sell the collateral unless the debtor, after default, has renounced in writing the right to require a sale of the collateral.[10]

The policy behind this UCC provision recognizes the debtor's substantial equity in the collateral and the fact that resale may result in a surplus that by right should belong to the debtor. Therefore, in the absence of the debtor's renunciation of the right to demand resale, the secured party cannot retain the collateral. This section also contains penalties for noncompliance. Once the secured party becomes obligated to sell the collateral, failure to do so within 90 days makes the secured party liable in either **conversion** or damages (under a statutory formula enumerated in the Code).[11]

Apply the principles just discussed to *Oliver v. Bledsoe.*

28.2

FINANCE/MANAGEMENT

CALL-IMAGE TECHNOLOGY

STRICT FORECLOSURE

One of the customers to whom CIT sold numerous videophones on credit has defaulted on its account. Having perfected a security interest in the videophones, CIT, upon its customer's default, has regained possession of them following the default. Dan wants to use strict foreclosure in this situation. He plans to sell the units to other customers, and expects to receive more money from such sales if they can be made at CIT's option, rather than being made quickly. He asks you what CIT needs to do in order to take advantage of this UCC option as to remedies. What advice will you give him?

BUSINESS CONSIDERATIONS What advantages can a business realize if it uses strict foreclosure? What risks does a business face if it elects to use this remedy?

ETHICAL CONSIDERATIONS Is it ethical for a creditor to use strict foreclosure when the collateral has a higher market value than the balance owed by the debtor? What protections are available to the debtor in such a situation?

28.3 OLIVER v. BLEDSOE

7 Cal. Rptr.2d 382 (Cal.App. 1992)

FACTS In February 1988, James F. Bledsoe pledged a $500,000 promissory note secured by a deed of trust on real property (the Chang note) to Burlingame Bank & Trust Co. as collateral for a $250,000 line of credit, at which time the bank took possession of the note. In early July 1988, Matthew A. Oliver obtained a judgment against Bledsoe in the amount of $102,000, pursuant to which a writ of execution was issued. On 21 July 1988, at Oliver's direction, the sheriff served on the bank a notice of levy under a writ of execution. In a memorandum of garnishee served on the sheriff, the bank described the note as an "obligation owed to the judgment debtor that is not levied upon." At the time of the levy, Bledsoe apparently owed the bank not only the $250,000 secured by the Chang note, but also certain unsecured debts. After receiving Oliver's notice of levy, the bank—by obtaining Bledsoe's signature on a secondary promissory note and a pledge agreement for $75,000—created a second security interest in the Chang note. The new security interest arose after Oliver's execution lien, and the bank did not contest the trial court's finding that this interest was subordinate to the lien. On 27 December 1988, the bank's counsel wrote to Bledsoe and declared both the $250,000 and the $75,000 loans in default. This letter, in effect, also represented a proposal by the bank to keep the Chang note in exchange for a discharge of the debts that the note secured. Bledsoe apparently received the letter and failed to object to the proposal within the statutorily prescribed 21 days. On this basis, the bank took the position that, as of 17 January 1989 (twenty-one days after notice to Bledsoe), it had acquired Bledsoe's interest in the note. In April 1989, Bledsoe filed a lawsuit contesting the bank's claim. The bank did not send Oliver a copy of its 27 December 1988 Bledsoe letter or otherwise notify him that it had invoked § 9-505(2). Oliver apparently first learned of these matters on or about 14 July 1989, when the bank's counsel wrote Oliver and enclosed copies of the pleadings from the Bledsoe suit. The bank's cover letter did not discuss the suit, except to suggest that attempts were underway to resolve the dispute by agreement. The letter, however, repeated the bank's argument in its earlier memorandum of garnishee that Oliver's 1988 notice of levy had failed to reach the Chang note. On 25 July, counsel for Oliver wrote back disputing this assertion, reasserting Oliver's claim of an execution lien, and objecting to any disposition of the Chang note that did not properly recognize Oliver's lien. On 26 July 1989, Oliver's attorney had the sheriff serve a second notice of levy on the bank, which responded with a second memorandum of garnishee asserting that the levy had not reached the Chang note. About a year later, the bank filed a third-party claim in the Oliver/Bledsoe litigation and argued that, owing to its strict foreclosure on the collateral, it was the sole owner of the Chang note. Oliver asserted that his execution lien had priority over the bank's purported strict foreclosure.

ISSUE Did Oliver's execution lien survive the bank's purported retention, pursuant to § 9-505(2), of the Chang note?

HOLDING Yes. Where, as here, the would-be foreclosing creditor had received written notice of the execution lien, strict foreclosure did not extinguish the execution lienholder's rights in the absence of notice to that lienholder.

REASONING Professor Gilmore, one of the major participants in the drafting of the Code, wrote that "lienors" should possess the same right to object to a strict foreclosure under § 9-505(2) as is afforded to "secured parties." Although Professor Gilmore did not address the precise question at issue here—the lienholder's entitlement to notice of a proposed strict foreclosure—the basic principle is clear: To the end that their rights in the collateral as third parties can be respected equally with those of secured parties without prejudice to the secured creditor in possession, lien creditors should be granted equivalent procedural rights so far as is practicable. And that is the case whenever, as here, the creditor receives a notice of levy sufficient to create an execution lien in the collateral. Such a creditor thereafter is on written notice of the lien and, in the absence of giving the lienholder notice and an opportunity to object, cannot hope to extinguish it by strict foreclosure. To hold otherwise will encourage mischief. A secured creditor who receives notice of levy will be tempted promptly to serve a § 9-505(2) notice of strict foreclosure on the debtor, hoping that the statutory period will elapse without the lienholder's learning of the impending extinction. Assuming there is surplus value in the collateral (for otherwise survival of the lien will be academic), the creditor in possession, the debtor, and any junior secured parties all will have a financial incentive to deprive the lienholder of the surplus value to which he or she is entitled pursuant to § 9-504. A rule that encourages the deliberate disregard of a lienholder's perfected rights will operate in derogation of the central guiding principles of commercial reasonableness and good faith. Consequently, strict foreclosure in the absence of notice to the lienholder cannot operate to extinguish the rights of an execution lienholder where, as here, the would-be foreclosing creditor has received written notice of the execution lien. The bank also asserted that it had given notice of the proposed foreclosure in July 1989, when its attorney had sent

28.3 OLIVER v. BLEDSOE (cont.) 7 Cal. Rptr.2d 382 (Cal.App. 1992)

Oliver's attorney copies of pleadings from Bledsoe's action against the bank. Even assuming the 14 July letter had constituted a notice of foreclosure, Oliver's response of 25 July was a sufficient written objection to prevent any then-pending foreclosure under § 9-505(2) as against his rights. Certainly the response was timely, coming well within the 21-day statutory period. The letter also adequately communicated Oliver's opposition to any disposition that failed to take full account of his lien. Thus, the bank erroneously had asserted that the letter was deficient for lacking a "demand that a foreclosure sale under 9-504 be conducted." Section 9-505(2) does not require such a demand or any other form of words; it requires only an "objection in writing" to the proposed retention of collateral. Assuming, therefore, that Oliver had received notice of the bank's intention to retain the note under § 9-505(2) and had been required to object, he sufficiently did so. Hence, the bank's retention of the note under § 9-505(2) did not extinguish Oliver's lien.

BUSINESS CONSIDERATIONS As a result of this litigation, what changes would you expect the bank to make in its intra-office procedures?

ETHICAL CONSIDERATIONS Provide justifications for the argument that the court would have found in favor of Oliver if it had based its decision on ethical (as opposed to legal) grounds.

Resale of Repossessed Collateral

The secured party initially may choose to satisfy the debtor's obligation by reselling, leasing, or otherwise disposing of the collateral.[12] In fact, secured parties use this remedy of *foreclosure by sale* much more frequently than strict foreclosure. The liberality of the Code's provision for resale allows the secured party to realize the highest resale price possible and, at the same time, to reduce the possibility of a *deficiency judgment* (the debtor's liability for the difference between the amount realized at resale and the amount owed to the secured party). In this way, both the secured party and the debtor benefit.

The sale may be either public or private, subject always to the requirement that the method, manner, time, place, and terms of such sale be commercially reasonable.[13] A public sale, or auction, is the more ordinary occurrence; but the Code encourages private sales when, as often is the case, a private sale through commercial channels will increase the chances for a higher resale price.

Notice

Secured parties usually must notify debtors of the time and place of any public or private sale. When the collateral consists of nonconsumer goods, foreclosing secured parties in addition must notify any other secured party who has notified them in writing of a claimed interest in the collateral. A secured party who claims an interest must notify the foreclosing secured party before the latter sends notification to the debtor or before the debtor renounces his or her rights. Thus, the burden is on the so-called **junior secured parties** to notify the foreclosing secured party of their interest before a corresponding duty to notify them of sale ever arises. In certain circumstances, the secured party nonetheless may dispense with notification if the collateral is perishable, threatens to decline speedily in value, or is of a type customarily sold on a recognized market.[14] The policy reason for notification stems from a belief

Junior secured parties
Any secured parties whose security interests are subordinate to that of the foreclosing secured party.

that those who have an interest in the collateral—the debtor and junior secured parties—may want to bid on the collateral or send their friends to do so.

A debtor may agree contractually to waive this required notice. Since courts generally enforce the terms set out in security agreements, such waivers ordinarily give secured parties, upon the debtor's default, the right to take possession of the collateral without any notification to the debtor.

Commercially Reasonable Sale

A great deal of litigation has arisen from the Code provision stating that the sale itself must be commercially reasonable. According to the UCC, the fact that the secured party might have obtained a better price at a different time or by a different method in itself does not make the sale commercially unreasonable. Similarly, sales in conformity with the commercial practices of dealers in the type of collateral sold or sales made in the usual manner on recognized markets demonstrate commercial reasonableness as well. Likewise, a court's approval of a sale or the sanctioning of a sale by a creditors' committee makes the sale commercially reasonable.[15] In these cases, the debtor's argument that the resale price is insufficient will not constitute grounds for a court's denying the secured party a deficiency judgment. Moreover, if the secured party has conducted the sale in full compliance with the requirements of § 9-504(3), the law views the sale price as reflecting the true value of the collateral; and courts automatically award any deficiency to the creditor.

But given the secured party's noncompliance with § 9-504(3), courts approach the issue of whether the creditor nonetheless retains the right to a deficiency judgment in three different ways. Some jurisdictions absolutely bar the secured party from recovering the deficiency regardless of whether the noncompliance stems from a failure to give notice or to conduct the sale in a commercially reasonable manner. A second line of cases permits the secured party to recover the deficiency but reduces (or *sets off*) from this amount the debtor's damages, that is, the difference between the *fair market value* (the price obtained if the secured party had sold the collateral in a commercially reasonable way) and the sale price actually realized. The third line of authorities opts for a compromise between the other two views. Under this so-called rebuttable presumption approach, courts will allow the secured party to sue; but these courts impose a presumption that the actual value of the collateral at the time of the wrongful sale equals the amount of indebtedness owed to the secured party. The secured party therefore merits a deficiency judgment only upon the secured party's successfully rebutting this presumption.

Bank of Chapmanville v. *Workman* illustrates how one court grappled with the concept of commercial reasonableness and related issues.

28.4 BANK OF CHAPMANVILLE v. WORKMAN — 406 S.E.2d 58 (W.Va. 1991)

FACTS On 26 July 1982, the Workmans bought a 1982 Duke mobile home and entered into an installment loan contract with the Bank of Chapmanville whereby the Workmans promised to pay $38,703.60 in 120 monthly payments over a period of 10 years in exchange for the bank's retaining a security interest in the mobile home. Five years later, the Workmans failed to make two consecutive payments; and, on 19 August 1987, the bank sent them a written "notice of right to cure default." On 24 August 1987, Ms. Workman met with the bank's loan officer, Charles Dale. The bank claimed that Ms. Workman told Dale that she and her husband no longer could afford the mobile home and that the

28.4 BANK OF CHAPMANVILLE v. WORKMAN *(cont.)* 406 S.E.2d 58 (W.Va. 1991)

bank could repossess it. The Workmans, on the other hand, contended that they attempted to negotiate a schedule for catching up on their payments, but the bank insisted on repossession. On 2 September 1987, the bank sent the Workmans a "final demand letter." At the bank's request, the Workmans vacated the mobile home. They later moved to North Carolina. Whether Ms. Workman provided the bank with their address and telephone number in North Carolina remained unclear. On 26 September 1987, the bank, by certified mail, sent to the Workmans a "notice of public sale" dated 25 September 1987. The bank sent the notice to the same address to which it had sent the "notice of right to cure default" and the "final demand letter," both of which communications the Workmans had received. The "notice of public sale" was returned unclaimed around 15 October 1987. The bank placed a single "notice of public sale" in the legal notices section of the 1 October 1987 issue of the *Logan Banner* and posted a copy of the notice in the courthouse. This notice, among other things, stated that the Bank of Chapmanville would, on Friday, 23 October 1987, at the hour of 11:00 A.M., sell at public auction on the front step of the mobile home in Garretts Fork, Logan County, West Virginia, a certain mobile home described in the security agreement as a 1982 Duke 14-by-70-foot mobile home, serial number 10068. The public auction took place on 23 October 1987. No bidders attended, and the bank sold the mobile home to itself for $10,614. The bank did not have the home appraised before the public sale but did realize that the sale price was lower than the NADA reference value set out in the industry guidebook. The bank applied the sale price to the balance owed by the Workmans, leaving a deficiency of $7,873.25 as of the date of sale. Four and a half months after the repossession, the bank sold the mobile home to a private person, Michael Mays, for $13,000 but did not credit its net profit from that sale to the Workmans' deficiency debt. The Workmans therefore argued that because the bank had engaged in a commercially unreasonable sale, it should be barred from seeking a deficiency judgment and should be made to pay the statutory damages the UCC sets out for these kinds of omissions.

ISSUE Had the secured creditor conducted a commercially reasonable sale of the mobile home?

HOLDING Maybe yes, maybe no. The notice of sale might have been so general as to make the sale of the mobile home commercially unreasonable. Because the evidence was in conflict on this issue, however, only a jury could decide this question. The case therefore should be remanded to the trial court for a determination of this issue.

REASONING The Workmans' first point—that the bank improperly had failed to credit its net profit from the sale—was not correct. If a secured creditor buys a repossessed good from itself at a public sale conducted in a commercially reasonable manner and then resells it for a higher price, such conduct by the secured creditor legally is permissible, provided the creditor's purchase price is not unreasonably low. If a secured creditor buys low at its own commercially unreasonable "public sale" and only after this sale earnestly attempts to sell the good in a commercially reasonable manner, however, its behavior is at least as bad as that which the statutory damage provisions of the UCC are designed to discourage. The Workmans alleged that the bank had engaged in this kind of misconduct and thus should be barred from seeking a deficiency judgment and be made to pay statutory damages. West Virginia has adopted UCC § 9-504, which mandates a sale that is commercially reasonable in every aspect of the disposition of the collateral. Here, even if the bank had attempted to provide the Workmans with adequate public notice of the public sale, the evidence revealed three aspects of the published notice that a jury could find disturbing: (1) the notice lacks a specific address; (2) no telephone number is given for inquiries about the mobile home; and (3) no mention is made of an opportunity to inspect before sale. Although such deficiencies would not render every public sale commercially unreasonable, they did illustrate that the trial court had erred in directing a verdict for the bank. Moreover, because no other advertisement of the "public sale" occurred, this legal notice had to serve as an effective advertisement to potential buyers as well as notice to the debtors. Hence, the sufficiency of the notice's description of the location of the public sale went to the issue of the commercial reasonableness of the sale. The bank pointed out that Garretts Fork is a rural community without road names and numbers; thus, it might be awkward to give the address, or rather directions, in the notice. The bank did not even place a "For Sale" sign on the mobile home, however, and the record suggested that there are many mobile homes in Garretts Fork. The only way a potential buyer would know where to look for the mobile home would be to call the bank; and the notice, by lacking a telephone number, did not encourage such inquiries. After selling the mobile home to itself at the repossession sale, the bank placed an advertisement in the *Logan Banner* that described the mobile home and listed the bank's telephone number. The trial court did not allow the Workmans to present evidence concerning the later advertisement. The Workmans wanted to show that the bank had utilized one standard of what was commercially reasonable when it had been selling for the Workmans' account and

28.4 BANK OF CHAPMANVILLE v. WORKMAN *(cont.)* 406 S.E.2d 58 (W.Va. 1991)

another when it had been selling for its own account. Hence, the court should have allowed the newspaper advertisement into evidence because its probative value far outweighed the possible unfair prejudice to the bank. In addition, an instruction to the jury that a secured creditor is not required to use the same selling method when the secured creditor resells goods for its own account as it uses at a repossession sale could have cured any potential unfair prejudice. Thus, whether the bank's sale of the mobile home has been commercially reasonable remained unclear. Because of the conflicting evidence, the issue became a question only a jury could decide. If, on remand, the jury were to find that the bank's sale of the mobile home was commercially unreasonable, the court would need to address the question of whether a secured creditor's commercially unreasonable disposition of collateral bars it from seeking a deficiency judgment, an issue of first impression in West Virginia.

BUSINESS CONSIDERATIONS Besides the omissions that the court mentions, what other actions might the bank have taken to ensure that the ensuing sale was commercially reasonable under the Code? Alternatively, would you disagree with the court's finding that the bank had done too little?

ETHICAL CONSIDERATIONS Using an ethical viewpoint, assess the bank's presale and postsale actions. Had the bank acted unethically here?

Proceeds

The Code even sets out the order for applying the proceeds of the sale.[16] According to the Code, the secured party must apply the proceeds realized from the disposition of the collateral in this order:

1. Payment of the reasonable expenses of retaking and disposing of the collateral, including reasonable attorneys' fees
2. Satisfaction of the debt owed to the secured party
3. Payment of the remaining proceeds to eligible junior secured parties in the same collateral
4. Payment to the debtor of any surplus and corresponding liability on the debtor's part for any deficiency, unless the parties otherwise have agreed.

DEBTORS' RIGHTS

Because the debtor has the right to redeem the collateral at any time before the secured party has disposed of it, it is possible that no sale ever will occur. *Redemption* consists of the debtor's tendering payment of all obligations due, including the expenses incurred by the secured party in retaking and preparing the collateral for disposition (usually resale) and in arranging for the resale, and thereby extinguishing the secured party's security interest in the collateral. Such expenses also may include attorneys' fees and legal expenses. A debtor who can accomplish redemption before sale or strict foreclosure can retain the collateral. On the other hand, a debtor, after default, may agree to waive the right to redeem.[17] The debtor presumably cannot waive such rights in the original security agreement; rather, default must precede such waivers.

In *Friendly Credit Union* v. *Campbell*, the secured party's disregard of the debtor's rights in the collateral left the secured party vulnerable to a punitive damages award in favor of the debtor.

28.5 FRIENDLY CREDIT UNION v. CAMPBELL

579 So.2d 1288 (Ala. 1991)

FACTS In February 1986, Freddie B. Campbell, an employee of International Paper Company (International Paper), borrowed approximately $12,000 from Friendly Credit Union so that he could purchase a truck. Campbell signed a security agreement with the credit union and, to secure the loan, gave the credit union a security interest in the vehicle. Monthly payments of $337.50 were regularly deducted from Campbell's paychecks until 21 March 1987, when a lockout occurred at International Paper. As a result of the lockout, the credit union posted in the union hall a notice stating that monthly payments on all loans were waived after 31 March 1987. Apparently, the credit union was proceeding under paragraph 15 of its security agreement, which provided, "in the event that . . . there is a strike . . . failure to make any payments hereunder for a period not to exceed ninety days, during the continuation of such a strike shall not constitute a default hereunder. . . ." When the lockout continued after the 90-day period had expired, the credit union issued another notice allowing the payment of interest only on all loans. In July 1987, Campbell contacted the credit union about the payment of interest on his loan. In order to make the interest payments, Campbell turned over to the credit union $465.29 from his Christmas savings account and approximately $900 from a personal and holiday vacation fund. In December 1987, in response to pressure from regulatory agencies, the credit union notified Campbell that his interest-only payments no longer satisfied his obligation under the original purchase agreement. The National Credit Union Administration (NCUA) had directed the credit union to require that loan payments, including all amounts in arrears, would become due no later than 31 July 1987. As a result of the NCUA's advice, the credit union gave Campbell three options: (1) catch up the payments on his loan—that is, pay the amount in arrears and make the $337.50 monthly payments called for by his original loan obligation, (2) pay off the total balance of the loan, or (3) refinance the loan. Campbell, still unemployed, could choose only the refinancing option. He tried to refinance by applying for a loan with another institution, but it denied Campbell's application because of the insufficiency of his income. Friendly Credit Union denied his request for refinancing for the same reason. Owing to Campbell's inability to meet the credit union's demands, which had been increased from those on which the parties originally had agreed, the credit union peaceably repossessed Campbell's vehicle. On 14 March 1988, the credit union notified Campbell that he had 14 days in which to pay the balance of his loan ($10,650.38 plus interest). Still unemployed, Campbell could not redeem his truck under the terms of this notice. The credit union sold his truck for $6,417 on 24 March 1988—before the end of the period in which Campbell had been told he could redeem his truck. That sale resulted in a deficiency of $4,277.04. Campbell's subsequent lawsuit alleged that he had not been in default according to the modified interest-only agreement he had made with Friendly Credit Union. Campbell also asserted that this modified agreement had estopped the credit union from requiring the payment of the total amount or the amount in arrears plus the current monthly payments. Campbell supported this estoppel theory by noting his alleged reliance on the contract modifications he had made with Friendly Credit Union. Campbell asserted that the repossession therefore was invalid and amounted to a conversion of his vehicle. Campbell's complaint also stated that: (1) the sale of the truck was commercially unreasonable, and (2) the credit union's notice concerning his period of redemption had indicated that he would have until 28 March 1988 to redeem his truck. The credit union had cut short the period in which he had been told he could redeem his truck, since the truck was sold on 24 March 1988. Because the sale of the truck had left Campbell with a deficiency of $4,277.04, he claimed he had suffered injury.

ISSUE Was Campbell in default when the credit union had sold his truck on 24 March 1988?

HOLDING No. At the time of the sale of the truck, Campbell was not in default under the modified contract.

REASONING Campbell was not in default under the terms of the modified July 1987 contract. The credit union's written notice allowing interest-only payments amounted to a written public offer satisfying Alabama statutory law. Campbell's payment of the interest with money taken from his vacation and Christmas funds signaled his acceptance of the credit union's modified offer. As

28.5 FRIENDLY CREDIT UNION v. CAMPBELL *(cont.)* 579 So.2d 1288 (Ala. 1991)

this evidence showed, Campbell also relied on the modified interest-only arrangement. Thus, the jury could have found that Friendly Credit Union, owing to Campbell's reliance on the credit union's past actions, was estopped from changing Campbell's payment terms. Consequently, Friendly Credit Union's repossession of the truck, when Campbell had not been in default, constituted conversion, for a creditor may validly repossess only the property of a defaulting party.

BUSINESS CONSIDERATIONS Note that the credit union's administrator (the NCUA) had directed the credit union to clear up all arrearages by 31 July 1987. In judging the credit union's actions, did the court give too little weight to the effect this regulatory pressure would have on a local credit union like Friendly? Explain your reasoning.

ETHICAL CONSIDERATIONS Does a firm have an ethical duty to work with a debtor who is having difficulty making the required payments? If so, would Friendly Credit Union's dealings with Campbell prior to the sale of the vehicle satisfy its duties in this regard?

Secured Parties' Duties

Besides having to observe the previously mentioned duties regarding disposition of the collateral, secured parties also have the duty of taking reasonable care of the collateral while it is in their possession, either before or after default. They are liable for any losses caused by their failure to meet this obligation, but they do not lose their security interests if such a loss occurs.[18] Unless the parties otherwise have agreed, the secured party can charge to the debtor the payment of reasonable expenses, such as insurance and taxes, incurred in the custody, preservation, or use of the collateral. Moreover, the Code places the risk of accidental loss or damage on the debtor to the extent of any deficiency in insurance coverage. The secured party also may hold as additional security any increase in the value of or any profits (except money) received from the collateral, but the secured party either should turn over any money so received to the debtor or apply it to reduce the secured obligation. There is a duty to keep the collateral identifiable except for **fungible** collateral that may be commingled. The secured party either may repledge the collateral on terms that do not violate the debtor's right to redeem it or use the collateral (for example, in an ongoing business, the continued operation of equipment that has been given as security) if this will help to preserve it or its value.[19]

Fungible
Virtually identical; interchangeable; descriptive of things that belong to a class and that are not identifiable individually.

Once the secured party defrays the expenses of holding the collateral, as mentioned earlier, the secured party must turn over any remaining proceeds to the debtor. On the other hand, the debtor remains liable for any deficiency—the difference between the available proceeds and the amount of outstanding indebtedness and expenses—unless the parties otherwise have agreed or state law eliminates this obligation.[20]

Debtors sometimes try to argue that the amount received from the sale of the collateral (the usual basis for computing deficiencies or surpluses), if lower than the collateral's market value, makes the sale commercially unreasonable. But courts

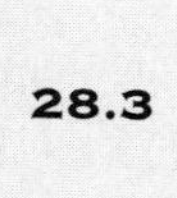

28.3

FINANCE

DEFAULT

Third Bank holds a perfected security interest in some of CIT's inventory, and the perfection is by possession (through a field warehousing arrangement). Third Bank is asserting that CIT has defaulted on its obligations and that it (Third Bank) is going to seek recovery under the provisions of Article 9. Tom and Anna ask you what obligations or liabilities Third Bank may owe to CIT and what obligations or liabilities CIT may owe to Third Bank in this situation. What will you tell them?

BUSINESS CONSIDERATIONS What factors should a secured creditor consider before it decides whether to seek a recovery under Article 9 or under common law? Why might a business decide to forego its Article 9 protections and seek a recovery under common law?

ETHICAL CONSIDERATIONS Is it ethical for a secured creditor to elect *not* to enforce its security interest upon default by the debtor? What impact might such a decision have on the other creditors of the defaulting debtor?

ordinarily respond unfavorably to such arguments as long as fraud is not present and the secured party has attempted in good faith to attract buyers. Similarly, these arguments generally will not affect the rights of the purchaser at the sale: The purchaser takes the collateral free and clear of such claims if the purchase is made in good faith.[21]

A secured party's failure to comply with the duties regarding disposition of the collateral, however, may subject the secured party to statutory liability under § 9-507 for losses by debtors or junior secured parties and, if consumer goods are involved, to a damages formula that sets up a statutory penalty. As we learned earlier, some courts, as a consequence of creditor noncompliance or misbehavior, also will deny the secured party the right to a deficiency judgment.

The *Biglari Import Export* case involved allegations that the secured party had failed to live up to its duty to take reasonable care of the collateral.

28.6 IN RE BIGLARI IMPORT EXPORT, INC.

130 B.R. 43 (Bankr. W.D. Tex. 1991)

FACTS Biglari Import Export, Inc. (Biglari) the debtor, operates The Ritz Oriental Rug Gallery. In 1986, Biglari borrowed operating capital from the International Bank of Commerce (IBOC) and granted IBOC a lien on its inventory of rugs. Later in the lending relationship, IBOC became concerned about Biglari's business and loan performance and asked that some of the rugs be pledged to the bank. Biglari complied and ultimately delivered 40 rugs into IBOC's possession. IBOC stored the rugs in a storage room in its bank building. The room, though not designed as a collateral storage vault, is the same room in which the bank stores its own records. It has a concrete floor, no windows, and no public access. The room is located toward the rear of the building, on an upper level, and is the only room on that level. A winding stairway leads to a vestibule area, which has one door opening out to a fenced courtyard and one door into the employee-only area of the bank. The bank keeps this back door locked, and only bank officers have a key to this door. According to the witnesses, the rugs were removed from this room on two occasions only, once in July 1988 and again in March 1990. On both occasions, Biglari took out the rugs and brought them back. In March 1990, Biglari removed all 40 rugs so they could be aired out in the sun and mothballed

28.6 IN RE BIGLARI IMPORT EXPORT, INC. *(cont.)* 130 B.R. 43 (Bankr. W.D. Tex. 1991)

(the standard procedure for maintaining the quality of the rugs). During the lunch hour one day, while the bank officer in charge of this loan was away from the office, one of Biglari's employees (along with an assistant) picked up the rugs. The employees told bank personnel that the loan officer had approved their coming by to pick up the rugs, and someone from the bank let them into the storage room. No one had the employees sign any paperwork relative to checking out the rugs. Three days later, after the mothballing process, two Biglari employees brought the rugs back to the bank. No one from the bank checked the bundles to be sure that all 40 rugs were there. The rugs were returned to the storage room, where they remained undisturbed. During an inventory of the rugs taken at the bank in December 1990, the bank came up 10 rugs short. Later, during its bankruptcy proceedings, Biglari argued that the judge should reduce IBOC's secured claim by the value of the 10 rugs because of IBOC's alleged failure to take reasonable care of the collateral in its possession.

ISSUE Had IBOC used reasonable care in the custody and preservation of Biglari's rugs?

HOLDING Yes. The basic manner in which IBOC had stored the rugs and the bank's conduct in releasing the rugs on two occasions to Biglari's employees satisfied the reasonable care standard.

REASONING The law applicable to this matter is Texas's adoption of the Uniform Commercial Code, which in applicable part says, "[A] secured party must use reasonable care in the custody and preservation of collateral in its possession. . . ." The question is whether, under the facts of this case, IBOC had used reasonable care in the custody and preservation of Biglari's rugs. If it had not, it ". . . [would be] liable for any loss caused by its failure to meet any obligation imposed by the preceding subsections but [would] not lose its security interest." However, Biglari had the burden of establishing IBOC's breach of the duty to use reasonable care. The evidence indicated that the basic manner in which IBOC had stored the rugs satisfied the reasonable care standard. The room, while not expressly designed for the purpose of storing rugs, was adequately secure, confirmed by the fact that the same room housed the bank's own records. In addition, the bank limited access to bank employees, and only officers had keys to the back door. The reasonable care standard would impose no greater obligations than these for storing and preserving these rugs. Biglari highlighted the "mothballing" incident, however, in which the bank had released the rugs to two employees of Biglari merely on their oral representation of authority and the bank had failed to confirm the return of all 40 rugs three days later. Biglari argued that this laxity in the bank's procedures for handling the collateral violated the reasonable care standard. According to the debtor, the bank, before it permitted anyone into the collateral storage area or permitted the removal of any of the collateral, should have required proper express authorization from a bank officer. Furthermore, in Biglari's opinion, if the bank had counted the rugs when they were returned after the mothballing, it would have caught the shortfall immediately (assuming that this is when the shortfall occurred) and could have contacted Biglari immediately, presumably so Biglari could have taken prompt steps to intercept the dishonest employees involved. Nevertheless, Biglari's argument overlooked the fact that IBOC had released the rugs to Biglari's own employees; and it had been Biglari's own employees who had brought the rugs back to the bank three days later. The bank could not bear responsibility for the conduct of Biglari's employees to a greater degree than Biglari's own responsibility. Given that there was just as much evidence to suggest wrongdoing on the part of Biglari or its employees (for example, refusals by Biglari's insurance companies to honor claims made by the firm), a court should not hold IBOC liable under the reasonable care standard simply because the rugs ended up missing.

BUSINESS CONSIDERATIONS As an aftermath of this case, the bank presumably will revamp its procedures relating to situations like the one that occurred here. Assume you have been asked to draft such a policy. What provisions will you include in it?

ETHICAL CONSIDERATIONS Do you think the facts here indicate unethical conduct on the part of the Biglari employees? Explain your reasoning.

http:// RESOURCES FOR BUSINESS LAW STUDENTS

NAME	RESOURCES	WEB ADDRESS
Uniform Commercial Code (UCC) Article 9, Secured Transactions; Sales of Accounts and Chattel Paper	The Legal Information Institute (LII), maintained by the Cornell Law School, provides a hypertext and searchable version of UCC Article 9, Secured Transactions; Sales of Accounts and Chattel Paper. LII also maintains links to Article 9 as adopted by particular states and to proposed revisions.	http://www.law.cornell.edu/ucc/9/overview.html
The National Conference of Commissioners on Uniform State Laws	The National Conference of Commissioners on Uniform State Laws (NCCUSL), the drafter of the UCC, provides drafts and revisions of its uniform and model acts.	http://www.law.upenn.edu/library/ulc/ulc.htm

SUMMARY

When a debtor defaults, the secured party may pursue either non-Code or Code remedies. Under the Code, the secured party may take possession of the collateral and either retain it in complete satisfaction of the debt (strict foreclosure) or dispose of it by public or private sale (foreclosure by sale). In either case, if the secured party is to escape Code liability, notification of the debtor and perhaps other parties must take place. The secured party's right of strict foreclosure may be limited by such things as the debtor's paying 60 percent of the price of collateral consisting of consumer goods. If a sale is undertaken, it must be conducted in a commercially reasonable manner. Assuming a sale has occurred, the Code also enumerates the order in which the proceeds of a sale should be applied. The debtor's redeeming the collateral prior to foreclosure may cut off the secured party's right to foreclosure by sale or strict foreclosure, however. When the secured party is in possession of the collateral either before or after default, the party must take reasonable care of the collateral. Failure to live up to this and other duties subjects the secured party to liability for any losses caused thereby, to possible damages under a statutory formula, and to the possible denial of the right to a deficiency judgment. Debtors ordinarily are liable for any deficiency that remains after the sale or other disposition of the collateral.

DISCUSSION QUESTIONS

1. What is default?
2. What kinds of non-Code remedies can the secured party pursue?
3. Describe fully the UCC's treatment of the right of repossession.
4. Explain the requirements necessary for effecting strict foreclosure.
5. Name the situations in which strict foreclosure is not permissible.
6. Discuss the rules relating to foreclosure by sale or resale of the repossessed collateral.
7. How can one tell whether a sale has been conducted in a commercially reasonable manner?
8. Enumerate the order in which the proceeds are applied after a sale.
9. What is redemption?
10. List the secured party's duties of reasonable care of the collateral and the liabilities that may result from a secured party's failure to observe any applicable duties.

CASE PROBLEMS AND WRITING ASSIGNMENTS

1. In 1985, Commercial Credit Equipment Corporation (CCEC) repossessed a tractor from Paul Parsons, who had defaulted on his loan with CCEC. CCEC arranged with Selby Implement Company (Selby) to recover the tractor from the Parsons farm and to store the tractor until the sale. To help establish a sale price, on 13 May 1985, Selby furnished CCEC with a condition report. CCEC then advertised the tractor for sale in *Farmers Hot Line* for two consecutive weeks. CCEC also sent bid letters to 16 area farm-equipment dealers. CCEC mailed to Parsons a copy of the list and a certification that letters of invitation to bid on the tractor had been mailed on 7 June 1985 to the listed dealers. Two bids were returned, one from Selby for $5,100 and the other from Mid-South Tractor (Mid-South) for $6,600. The tractor was sold to Mid-South for $6,600 on 18 September 1985. CCEC notified Parsons of the sale and of the fact that a deficiency of $18,791.37 remained. On 29 April 1985, before CCEC's repossession of the tractor, Parsons had purchased from Selby another Steiger Tiger II tractor for a price of $21,500. At trial, Parsons used the price of this second tractor, in conjunction with CCEC's failure to repair the windshield and back glass of the repossessed tractor, to support his contention that CCEC had conducted its private sale in a commercially unreasonable manner. The trial court had found that the $6,600 bid CCEC had accepted for the sale of the tractor represented its salvage, or junk, value. The court, moreover, accepted as fact the evidence of Parsons's expert that the tractor's fair market value at the time of repossession had been $27,000. The court noted that in 1981 Parson had installed a nearly new engine in the tractor at a cost of $8,000. This engine was capable of 10,000 hours of service and only 3,220 hours had been used. The court also mentioned that the replacement tractor Parsons had purchased from Selby for $21,500 was virtually identical to the tractor repossessed and sold by CCEC for $6,600. (The replacement tractor sold five years later, in the spring of 1990, for $18,000.) The court applied § 9-504 of the Uniform Commercial Code to the transaction at issue and determined that CCEC had failed to dispose of the repossessed tractor in a commercially reasonable manner. The court nevertheless awarded CCEC a judgment of $18,944.37 for the deficiency and Parsons a separate judgment of $10,000 as damages. Both parties appealed this verdict. How should the appellate court rule? [See *Commercial Credit Equipment Corporation* v. *Parsons*, 820 S.W.2d 315 (Mo.App. 1991).]

2. In January 1987, Chittenden Trust Company (CTC) filed suit and secured a writ of attachment on the inventory, accounts receivable, fixtures, and equipment of Andre Noel Sports (ANS). Pursuant to the writ, CTC repossessed some outdated, high-fashion sports and ski apparel; but, after months of intermittent discussion, the parties failed to agree on how to liquidate the merchandise. On 4 November 1987, CTC informed ANS that CTC would pursue the sale of the goods beginning the week of 2 November 1987 and that notification of the specific sale times and places would follow as soon as practicable. On 23 December 1987, CTC informed ANS that it had advertised the sale of the collateral and was conducting the sale at a certain location. The sale had begun approximately one month earlier, and an enclosed advertisement indicated that the sale would continue through Christmas. CTC netted about $35,000 from the sale of the merchandise. Claiming that CTC had failed to provide it with proper notice of the sale, ANS eventually moved for summary judgment. The trial court, concluding that CTC's improper notice would absolutely bar CTC from obtaining a deficiency judgment, granted the motion. On appeal, CTC argued that it could dispense with notice to the debtor because the collateral in this case "threatened to decline speedily in value" and/or was of "a type customarily sold on a recognized market." Should a court agree with CTC's contentions? Why? [See *Chittenden Trust Company* v. *Andre Noel Sports*, 621 A.2d 215 (Vt. 1992).]

3. Guaranty Bank & Trust Company (Guaranty Bank) and the Small Business Administration (SBA) originally litigated their lien priority dispute concerning the debtors' farm equipment before a bankruptcy court judge. That judge held that the lien of Guaranty Bank enjoyed priority over that of the SBA. The U.S. District Court for the Northern District of Mississippi affirmed that decision, but the Fifth Circuit Court of Appeals reversed the decision. In the meantime, Guaranty Bank, in preparing for a foreclosure sale, posted public notices and sent copies of the notice to local equipment dealers, the debtors' attorney, and the attorney representing the SBA. Guaranty Bank's attorney conducted the foreclosure sale during legal hours on 10 September 1987. Prior to the sale, Guaranty Bank had the farm equipment appraised by Jerry Mitchell, a Yokley and Lundy Auction Company (Yokley and Lundy) employee, who had valued the equipment at $40,000 to $55,000. His appraisal worksheet, which reflected his evaluation of the individual items, noted a total value of between $41,312.50 and $42,000. After receiving the appraisal, Guaranty Bank calculated its foreclosure bid as $25,000. Mitchell testified, without contradiction, that he had thought this

bid was reasonable under the circumstances. At the foreclosure sale, Guaranty Bank was the only bidder and purchased the equipment for the $25,000 price. Pursuant to the provisions of the earlier court order, Guaranty Bank deposited this amount in an interest-bearing account. The following day, Guaranty Bank put the equipment in an auction sale being conducted by Yokley and Lundy. According to Mitchell, the equipment had been sold "without reservation"; that is, Guaranty Bank would take whatever price the equipment brought. At this auction, Guaranty Bank received net proceeds of $39,748.29. Following the Fifth Circuit's reversal of the two earlier decisions, Guaranty Bank paid the SBA the $25,000 price that it bid at the foreclosure sale plus accrued interest of $2,848.11, for a total payment of $27,848.11. The legal question on remand centered on whether the court should permit Guaranty Bank to retain the difference in the price that it paid at the foreclosure sale and the amount that it received at the auction sale, an alleged "profit" totaling $14,748.29 ($39,748.29 less $25,000). The three underlying issues that the court faced were (1) whether Guaranty Bank, in disposing of the farm equipment, owed a fiduciary duty to the SBA; (2) whether Guaranty Bank's foreclosure sale of the equipment met the UCC commercial reasonableness standard; and (3) whether equity dictated that Guaranty Bank pay over the excess proceeds received at the auction sale to the SBA. Assume you are the judge. How will you decide these issues? [See *In re Whatley*, 126 B.R. 231 (Bankr. N.D. Miss. 1991).]

4. In 1985, Commonwealth Federal Savings Association (Commonwealth) loaned Craig Hall $7.2 million, evidenced by a promissory note and a security agreement pledge. Commonwealth accepted common stock in Resource Savings & Loan Association (Resource Savings) as collateral for the loan, and Hall later pledged additional security in the form of his interest in certain collateral notes. This latter security agreement provided as follows: "If Secured Party [Commonwealth] should at any time be reasonably of the opinion that the Collateral is not sufficient or has declined or may decline in value . . . then Secured Party may call for additional collateral." In March 1988, the parties modified the loan agreement by a document that had a retroactive effective date of 1 October 1987. Among other provisions, this master amendment modified the security agreement in two critical respects: First, it provided that Commonwealth would permit Hall to substitute $5 million in debenture notes for the collateral notes he originally had furnished. Second, it deleted the default provision in the security agreement concerning unsatisfactory or insufficient collateral. Thus, the master amendment did not modify the collateral call provision. By a letter dated 13 December 1988, Hall offered to substitute a $6.45 million debenture note for the collateral notes. Although the master amendment only required that Hall substitute debenture promissory notes in the aggregate amount of $5 million, Hall offered $6.45 million, the principal and interest then owing on the Hall note. But, in exchange, Hall requested the return of the Resource Savings stock that comprised part of the collateral held by Commonwealth. The master amendment omitted any reference to the stock; thus, the master amendment did not require Commonwealth to relinquish that collateral as part of a proposed substitution. At the time of the proposed substitution, Hall was current on all the payments due to Commonwealth. By a 28 March 1989 letter, Commonwealth rejected Hall's proposal. In doing so, Commonwealth indicated that it viewed the $6.45 million debenture note proffered by Hall as unsatisfactory because Commonwealth had information that the debenture was delinquent. Commonwealth also expressed concern about its collateral position in view of the declining value of the Resource Savings stock and the deteriorating financial condition of the makers of the promissory notes originally pledged by Hall under the collateral agreement. Specifically, Hall had provided information to Commonwealth that showed that during the calendar year 1988, Resource Savings's regulatory capital had declined dramatically, from a positive balance of some $4 million in January 1988 to a deficit balance of some $25 million in January 1989, and that Resource Savings's net income had declined by more than $16 million between March 1988 and December 1988. Accordingly, Commonwealth exercised its right under the security agreement to call for additional collateral. In response to Commonwealth's 28 March letter, Hall stopped making the loan payments. Hall later argued that Commonwealth, by unreasonably refusing to accept Hall's offer of substitute collateral, had breached the loan agreement. Commonwealth counterclaimed and asserted that it had had the right to accelerate all the loan payments then due and owing. When Commonwealth won in the lower court, Hall, on appeal, argued that Commonwealth had not acted reasonably in calling for additional collateral and in accelerating the note. Was Hall correct? Why or why not? [See *Hall v. Resolution Trust Corporation*, 958 F.2d 75 (5th Cir. 1992).]

5. Ford Motor Credit Company (FMCC) hired Badgerland Auto Recovery, Inc. (Badgerland) to repossess a Ford Bronco II from Florence Hollibush, who was behind in her payments and who had had a poor record of making the required payments under her install-

ment contract with FMCC. Badgerland's employee testified that at about midnight on 18 January 1990, he arrived at Hollibush's tavern. Her vehicle was parked in front of the tavern, and the employee hooked the Bronco up to his tow truck. He saw a man looking out of the tavern window at him and entered the tavern to tell the man who he was. He spoke with Hollibush and with William Finn, Hollibush's fiancé. Finn called an attorney and then stated that he would call the sheriff's office. Hollibush observed Finn's conversation and occasionally would say something. Finn told Badgerland's employee: "You are not going to take the Bronco"; but shortly after that, the employee left with Hollibush's automobile. Although Hollibush and Finn's description of the repossession differed considerably from the description given by Badgerland's employee, both testified that Finn had told the employee not to take the automobile. Did the Badgerland employee's subsequent repossession in disregard of the statement not to repossess the car constitute a breach of the peace under § 9-503? Why or why not? [See *Hollibush* v. *Ford Motor Credit Company,* 508 N.W. 2d 449 (Wis.App. 1993).]

6. **BUSINESS APPLICATION CASE** Pursuant to a court-issued replevin order, State Bank of Hallsville took possession of certain pieces of the debtor's farm equipment and vehicles that represented the collateral the debtor had given to the bank as security for a loan. The bank ultimately repossessed the equipment and sold it at a public auction that the debtor had attended. When the bank sued for a deficiency judgment, the debtor argued that the bank's failure to give the debtor formal notice of sale had precluded the bank's receiving a deficiency judgment. Did the bank's noncompliance with the UCC notice provisions in circumstances in which the debtor had had actual notice of the sale and actually attended the sale bar the bank's recovering a deficiency judgment? Why? What intrafirm policies should the bank institute so as to avoid future litigation of this type? If the bank had had procedures in place and an employee had failed to follow them, should the bank levy sanctions against this employee? [See *In re Furlong,* 155 B.R. 517 (Bankr. W.D. Mo. 1993).]

7. **ETHICS APPLICATION CASE** On 8 February 1985, Clyde Parrish, Jr., in order to purchase a 1985 Honda Accord, obtained a loan from the McChord Credit Union (McChord). The debt owed to McChord ($10,014) was guaranteed by Clyde, Sr. Clyde, Jr., made the required monthly payments of $225.75 until October 1986, when he sold the car to Stephanie Irons. Irons made the monthly payments to McChord until April 1988, when she ceased payments. On 5 January 1989, McChord filed an action for the entire balance due on the note. McChord named as defendants Clyde, Jr., and his wife; Clyde, Sr., and his wife; and Stephanie Irons and her husband. McChord took possession of the Honda automobile and advertised it for sale in the Pierce County Credit Union's newsletter and on signs posted in the Credit Union lobby. On 20 March 1989, McChord sold the car for $3,500. None of the Parrishes received notice of the sale until May 1989. Clyde, Sr., acknowledged, however, that in April 1989 he had been aware of McChord's possession of the car. Clyde, Sr., nonetheless contended that both he and his son had been entitled to proper notification of McChord's sale of the car. He claimed that McChord's failure to provide such notice violated the UCC and precluded McChord from recovering a deficiency judgment. Was a guarantor, such as Clyde, Sr., a "debtor" and thus entitled to statutory notice of the creditor's proposed sale of the collateral? Explain your answer. In attempting to avoid legal liability, had Clyde, Sr., behaved ethically? Why or why not? [See *McChord Credit Union* v. *Parrish,* 809 P.2d 759 (Wash.App. 1991).]

8. **IDES CASE** Between October 1983 and August 1985, George P. Selvais operated a diesel-repair business but was unable to make his payment obligations to Carlton Fritts. On 30 August 1985, Fritts declared Selvais to be in default, and pursuant to Fritts's rights under a security agreement, repossessed the collateral. At that time, the parties executed a repossession agreement. In this agreement, Selvais and the corporation under which Selvais conducted his business, Beltech Enterprises, Inc., admitted default, tendered the collateral for repossession, and waived any right to notice of a public or private sale of the collateral and of any proposal by Fritts to retain the collateral in satisfaction of the debt. The agreement further provided that Fritts would release Selvais from any liability for any deficiency in excess of $75,000. Upon repossession, Fritts reentered the premises and operated the business in his own name for a period of two to five weeks, after which time Fritts incorporated the business under the name of Tarheel Diesel Service, Inc. (Tarheel). Fritts was the only shareholder in the corporation, and Fritts and his wife were the officers of the corporation. Fritts then transferred the repossessed collateral to Tarheel in exchange for a promissory note in the amount of $26,415 made to Fritts by Tarheel. Fritts signed this note in his capacity as president of Tarheel. In February 1988, Fritts filed this action seeking a deficiency judgment in the amount of $75,000. At trial, Selvais argued that Fritts, after repos-

session, had retained the collateral and thereby had discharged any claim for a deficiency against Selvais. Specifically, Selvais claimed that Tarheel was Fritts's "alter ego" and should not be considered as a separate entity. If a court disregarded the corporate entity, Fritts would be deemed to have retained the collateral himself in satisfaction of Selvais's obligation and thereby would be precluded from seeking any deficiency under North Carolina law. Should a court find Selvais's argument persuasive? Why or why not? Assume that Fritts actually had strictly foreclosed. What statutory requirements would he need to fulfill if the collateral were equipment and other junior secured parties existed? Would Fritts be able to use strict foreclosure if the collateral were consumer goods and Selvais had paid 75 percent of the purchase price that Fritts had loaned to Selvais? Apply the IDES model to answer these questions. [Based on *Fritts* v. *Selvais*, 404 S.E.2d 505 (N.C.App. 1991).]

NOTES

1. Uniform Commercial Code, § 9-501(1).
2. Ibid., § 9-503.
3. Ibid., § 9-507.
4. *Fuentes* v. *Shevin*, 407 U.S. 67 (1972); *Mitchell* v. *W. T. Grant Co.*, 416 U.S. 600 (1974).
5. "Repossession from Debtor's Yard over His Oral Protest Did Not 'Breach Peace,'" *UCC Bulletin* (Deerfield: Clark Boardman Callaghan) (June 1996), p. 9.
6. Uniform Commercial Code, § 9-503.
7. Ibid., § 9-502.
8. Ibid., § 9-505(2).
9. Ibid.
10. Ibid., § 9-505(1).
11. Ibid.
12. Ibid., § 9-504.
13. Ibid., § 9-504(3).
14. Ibid.
15. Ibid., § 9-507(2).
16. Ibid., § 9-504(1), (2).
17. Ibid., §§ 9-501(3), 9-506.
18. Ibid., § 9-207(3).
19. Ibid., § 9-207(2).
20. Ibid., § 9-504(2).
21. Ibid., § 9-504(4).

Straight Bankruptcy

O U T L I N E

Historical Background
The Bankruptcy Reform Act
Bankruptcy Amendments and Federal Judgeship Act of 1984
The Bankruptcy Reform Act of 1994
Straight Bankruptcy: A Chapter 7 Liquidation Proceeding
The Bankruptcy Proceeding
Summary
Discussion Questions
Case Problems and Writing Assignments

A G E N D A

The Kochanowskis have invested virtually everything they own in CIT, and they are very aware of how risky a business venture can be. While they are making every effort to operate their businesses as safely as possible, they recognize the risks inherent in their position. They also realize that they cannot control the business practices of their customers or their suppliers. It is possible that some of CIT's customers may encounter severe financial problems and be forced to resort to bankruptcy. What legal and financial ramifications will this have on CIT? It is also possible that, despite their best efforts, CIT might encounter financial troubles and face bankruptcy. What remedies and/or relief might be available in bankruptcy? What alternatives does CIT have to a straight bankruptcy? These are just some of the questions that might arise. Be prepared! You never know when one of the Kochanowskis may call on you for help, advice, or guidance.

Historical Background

When the colonists broke away from England to set up the United States of America, they had a strong desire to avoid the problems they had encountered under the English system of government. The U.S. Constitution and the Bill of Rights were drafted specifically to prevent some of these problems. One problem area the Constitution addresses is the treatment of debtors. Included in this treatment is the area of bankruptcy.

In England, persons unable or unwilling to pay their debts were very commonly thrown into debtors' prison. A debtor might remain in prison for years waiting for friends or family to raise the funds necessary to repay the debt, or for the creditors to agree to the debtor's release. Less commonly, the debtor might agree to some form of indentured servitude, agreeing to work for a preset number of years at little or no salary to repay the debt.

To prevent such treatment of debtors in this country, the founding fathers made provisions in the Constitution to allow "honest debtors" to make a "fresh start" by providing for relief in the form of bankruptcy. Article I, Section 8, of the U.S. Constitution says: "The Congress shall have the Power . . . to establish . . . uniform Laws on the subject of Bankruptcies throughout the United States."

It should be noted that the Constitution only *allows* Congress to establish uniform laws on bankruptcy. There is no constitutional *requirement* that Congress provide bankruptcy laws or relief. Nonetheless, for much of the history of the United States, some form of federal bankruptcy regulation has existed. Specifically, Congress has passed five bankruptcy acts. The first federal bankruptcy statute was enacted in 1800. This was followed by the bankruptcy acts of 1841, 1867, 1898, and, most recently, the Bankruptcy Reform Act of 1978, as amended by the Bankruptcy Amendments and Federal Judgeship Act of 1984 and the Bankruptcy Reform Act of 1994.

Although the Constitution seemingly calls for exclusive federal control of this area, the bankruptcy laws tend to coexist with state law in many areas. In fact, state law often is used to define problems or to provide solutions to bankruptcy problems. For example, each state has its own *exemption* provisions, a listing of the assets that an honest debtor can retain following a bankruptcy. There are also federal exemptions that might be available to the debtor. State law determines whether the debtor can choose between the state and the federal exemptions or whether the debtor must choose the state's exemption provisions.

For most of the twentieth century, bankruptcy was governed by the federal Bankruptcy Act, enacted in 1898. This act was quite technical, and many people found it confusing. In 1978, Congress passed a new law, the Bankruptcy Reform Act, which took effect 1 October 1979. The Bankruptcy Reform Act had two major purposes. It was designed to provide for fair and equitable treatment of the creditors in the distribution of the debtor's property, and, more importantly, it was designed to give an "honest debtor" a "fresh start." The Reform Act attempted to modernize the bankruptcy coverage, providing treatment for both the debtor and the creditors that was consistent with the credit-intensive, consumer-oriented society of the late twentieth century.

Unfortunately, the Bankruptcy Reform Act had some technical problems that resulted in its being declared unconstitutional. As a result, the Bankruptcy Amendments and Federal Judgeship Act of 1984 was enacted. This act was intended to clarify the jurisdictional authority of the bankruptcy courts and to resolve the constitutional problems discovered in the Bankruptcy Reform Act. At the same time, Congress made the amended bankruptcy coverage more sensitive to the needs of the creditors and made some effort to reduce or eliminate the problem of debtor abuses that had occurred under the former bankruptcy laws. Additional changes were made to the act with the Bankruptcy Reform Act of 1994, again with the aim of balancing protections while ensuring that the basic purpose of bankruptcy was maintained. While far from perfect, the Bankruptcy Reform Act and the accompanying Bankruptcy Amendments and Federal Judgeship Act and the Bankruptcy Reform Act of 1994 are a vast improvement over the 1898 act they replaced.

The Bankruptcy Reform Act has (from a business law perspective) three major operative sections, called chapters. These chapters are Chapter 7, Liquidation; Chapter 11, Reorganization; and Chapter 13, Adjustments of Debts of an Individual with Regular Income. A fourth important operative section, Chapter 12, Adjustment of Debts of a Family Farmer with Regular Annual Income, was added under the Bankruptcy Amendments in 1984.

In a Chapter 7 proceeding, the debtor's nonexempt assets are sold, the proceeds are distributed to the creditors, and a discharge is (normally) granted. Under Chapters 11, 12, and 13, the debtor restructures and rearranges finances and (possibly) organization so that the creditors will be paid, hopefully in full, but at least more than in a liquidation proceeding. This chapter examines a straight bankruptcy proceeding—that is, a Chapter 7 liquidation. The next chapter looks at other bankruptcy proceedings available under Chapters 11, 12, and 13 and at alternatives to bankruptcy.

The Bankruptcy Reform Act

The Bankruptcy Reform Act called for a whole new adjudicative system of bankruptcies. Under the act, each U.S. district court was to contain a separate, adjunct bankruptcy court. These bankruptcy courts were to be staffed by bankruptcy judges, each of whom was to serve a 14-year term, with their salaries to be determined annually by Congress. The bankruptcy judges were to be appointed by the president, subject to approval by the Senate. It was hoped that this new system, which replaced "referees" acting through the district courts, would simplify and speed up bankruptcy proceedings.

The new bankruptcy court/bankruptcy judge system encountered a major roadblock when, on 28 June 1982, the U.S. Supreme Court declared the Bankruptcy Reform Act unconstitutional. As a result of this ruling, the entire area of bankruptcy law was placed in doubt. The case that raised the challenge to the Bankruptcy Reform Act involved the Northern Pipeline Company.

Northern Pipeline filed a petition in bankruptcy in January 1980. As a part of its petition, Northern Pipeline sued Marathon Pipe Line Company in the bankruptcy court, alleging that Marathon Pipe Line had breached a contract. (Under the Bankruptcy Reform Act, the bankruptcy court had jurisdiction over all issues relating to the bankruptcy.) Marathon sought dismissal of the suit on the grounds that the bankruptcy courts established by the Bankruptcy Reform Act lacked jurisdiction over the alleged contract action and that the restrictions placed on the appointment of the bankruptcy judges were unconstitutional. The U.S. Supreme Court handed down its opinion in *Northern Pipeline Construction Co.* v. *Marathon Pipe Line Co.*[1] on 28 June 1982. This opinion upheld the position of Marathon Pipe Line, declaring that the Reform Act violated the Constitution in the manner it provided for appointing judges and in the extensive authority given to the bankruptcy judges. This ruling challenged the validity of any further bankruptcy coverage under the Bankruptcy Reform Act.

Congress did nothing to resolve the constitutional problems raised in Northern Pipeline for nearly two years. During this period, the bankruptcy courts continued to operate under an "emergency rule" suggested by the Judicial Conference of the United States and accepted by the U.S. Courts of Appeals.

Bankruptcy Amendments and Federal Judgeship Act of 1984

The Bankruptcy Amendments and Federal Judgeship Act of 1984 went into effect on 10 July 1984. This act addresses the problems presented by the Northern Pipeline opinion by restructuring and redefining the bankruptcy court system and its jurisdiction. In addition, it makes a number of substantive changes to the Bankruptcy Reform Act and its coverage.

Under the new law, bankruptcy judges are still appointed for a term of 14 years, and their salary is still established by Congress. Since the tenure and the salary both are established by statute and are subject to changes by the legislature, the bankruptcy judges are still not Article III judges, the original problem addressed by the court in *Northern Pipeline.* The appointments are made by the U.S. court of appeals in which the district court is located from a slate of nominees recommended by the judicial councils of each circuit. Only persons who apply to the judicial council for a judgeship may be considered for recommendation by the court of appeals. The judicial council is to submit a list of three nominees for each judgeship. The court of appeals will then either select one of the nominees or reject all of them and request a new submission.

Since these bankruptcy judges are not Article III judges, the bankruptcy courts have only limited jurisdiction under the law. The 1984 Bankruptcy Amendments grant exclusive and original jurisdiction in all bankruptcy matters to the U.S. district court. The district court may then refer any or all such cases to the bankruptcy court for adjudication. After referral to the bankruptcy court, however, the case may be withdrawn by the district court, either on its own motion or on the motion of any party to the proceedings, "for cause shown."

The Bankruptcy Reform Act of 1994

The Bankruptcy Reform Act of 1994 makes several substantial changes in the bankruptcy law. It also creates a National Bankruptcy Review Commission charged with studying issues and problems related to bankruptcy.

The National Bankruptcy Review Commission is composed of nine members and it is designed to be as nonpartisan as possible. Three of the members, including the chair of the commission, are appointed by the president. The speaker of the house, the president pro tempore of the Senate, the minority leader of the House, and the minority leader of the Senate each name one member. The Chief Justice of the Supreme Court names the remaining two members. It has an initial term of two years and seven months, with the initial appointments to be made within 60 days after enactment of the bill. The initial commission's term will expire in July of 1997.

There were numerous substantive changes to the Bankruptcy Code included in the Bankruptcy Reform Act of 1994. Among the more important of these changes are the following:

- Compensation for trustees is now set at "25 percent of the first $5,000 or less, 10 percent of any amount in excess of $5,000 but not in excess of $50,000, 5 percent on any amount in excess of $50,000 but not in excess of $1,000,000, and reasonable compensation not to exceed 3 percent of such moneys in excess of $1,000,000."[2]
- The debt limits for Chapter 13 debtors is increased from $450,000 to $1,000,000, and the dollar amounts for involuntary petitions, priorities, and exemptions are doubled.[3]
- Future adjustments for these dollar amounts for the future are included in the act on a three-year cycle, beginning 1 April 1998. These adjustments will be based on the Consumer Price Index for All Urban Consumers published by the Department of Labor, rounded to the nearest $25 amount.
- Purchase money security interests are given a 20-day grace period for perfection to reflect the majority state law provisions now in effect, an increase from the 10-day grace period previously allowed.
- Independent sales representatives are classified as employees and are entitled to the same priority status as employees, for purposes of claims against the debtor.
- Limited liability partnerships are treated in bankruptcy as they would be treated in a nonbankruptcy proceeding (limited liability partnerships are discussed in Business Organizations in Chapters 34 to 36), reflecting the growing recognition of this relatively new form of business.
- Debtors who are represented by an attorney may reaffirm debts without the need for a separate reaffirmation hearing as required under the provisions of the original Bankruptcy Reform Act.
- The nondischargeability of "loading up" debts is triggered at $1,000 rather than $500.
- Bankruptcy fraud is now recognized as a crime. This crime involves filing a petition or a document or making a false representation with the intent to devise a scheme to defraud under Chapter 11.
- A streamlined treatment is provided for small businesses (businesses involved in commercial or business activities other than solely real estate and with liquidated debts of $2,000,000 or less) seeking relief under Chapter 11.
- Small business investment companies are not eligible for relief in bankruptcy.

Given the relative novelty of the Bankruptcy Reform Act of 1994, its impact will not be known for some time. The initial application of its provisions seems to balance the interests of the debtor and the creditors, however.

STRAIGHT BANKRUPTCY: A CHAPTER 7 LIQUIDATION PROCEEDING

To many people, the term *bankruptcy* means just one thing—a liquidation of the debtor's assets in order to obtain a discharge from debts. This form of bankruptcy carries negative connotations to many people. These people view a straight bankruptcy, or a Chapter 7 proceeding, as an admission of failure. Rather than viewing this as a "fresh start" for an "honest debtor," they feel that it is a "cop-out" by a "deadbeat." Times are changing, however. More and more people are beginning to realize that a liquidation is a financial and legal option designed to help a person who has been flooded by debt. The stigma of failure is being removed, and the number of Chapter 7 proceedings increases annually.

There are two types of Chapter 7 bankruptcies: voluntary and involuntary. Voluntary bankruptcies are bankruptcies initiated by the debtor. Involuntary bankruptcies are bankruptcies initiated by some combination of creditors of a debtor. Any person, firm, or corporation may file a voluntary bankruptcy petition under Chapter 7, with five exceptions:

1. Railroads
2. Government units
3. Banks
4. Savings and loan associations
5. Insurance companies

In addition, any person, firm, or corporation may be subjected to an involuntary petition under Chapter 7, with seven exceptions:

1. Railroads
2. Government units
3. Banks
4. Savings and loan associations
5. Insurance companies
6. Farmers (a *farmer* is defined as an individual who received more than 80 percent of gross income in the prior year from the operation of a farm that he or she owns and operates)
7. Charitable corporations

Voluntary Bankruptcy Petition

The debtor who files a voluntary petition does not need to be insolvent. If a debtor desires to eliminate his or her debts, the debtor can file the petition, consent to the court's jurisdiction, and receive a discharge. In theory, a debtor with $1 million in cash and total debts of $250 can file for bankruptcy. In practice, such an event is extremely unlikely.

The 1984 Bankruptcy Amendments made a major substantive change in this area. Prior to the 1984 act, bankruptcy was viewed as a right of the debtor, and the needs of the debtor or the creditors were not considered by the court. As a result, some creditors alleged that some debtors were abusing the bankruptcy system, using Chapter 7 proceedings to eliminate unsecured debts they could have repaid in full. The law now permits the bankruptcy judge to hold a hearing designed to determine the need of the debtor for the relief being sought. If the judge feels that granting the relief will be a substantial abuse of Chapter 7, the petition can be dismissed.

In addition, the law requires that all debtors be made aware of the alternative provisions of Chapter 13 repayment plans before they are allowed to file a Chapter 7 petition. By so doing, it is hoped that more debtors will elect a repayment plan rather than a liquidation procedure. This will work to the benefit of the creditors and may also help a number of debtors by allowing them to retain more of their assets than they would under a Chapter 7 liquidation.

YOU BE THE JUDGE

Kim Basinger Files for Bankruptcy

Actress Kim Basinger entered into a contract with Main Line Pictures to play the title character in the movie "Boxing Helena." When she subsequently backed out of the performance, Main Line sued her for breach of contract, winning the case and receiving a judgment of $8.1 million. Following the judgment, Basinger filed a petition for relief under Chapter 11 of the Bankruptcy Act. In the plan she submitted to the court under the Chapter 11 proceedings, she offered to pay three years of future earnings to the court for distribution to her creditors. Main Line objected to the plan, asserting that she might choose not to work during the three-year period for any of a number of reasons, including the possibility that she might choose to get pregnant rather than work, since her earnings would be going to her creditors. Following this objection by Main Line, Basinger asked the court to allow her to remove her petition from a Chapter 11 proceeding to a Chapter 7 proceeding. At the time of the request, she had between $2 and $3 million in assets, with liabilities of more than $10 million. The request to remove the proceedings from Chapter 11 to Chapter 7 has been submitted to *your* court. How would *you* decide this matter?[4]

BUSINESS CONSIDERATIONS Should a creditor in a bankruptcy petition be more concerned with resolving the issue, or should the creditor be more concerned with receiving the greatest amount of money possible under the circumstances?

ETHICAL CONSIDERATIONS Is it ethical for a creditor in a bankruptcy proceeding to assert that the debtor is likely to act in bad faith, or should the creditor wait until such bad faith is shown? Should a creditor raise an issue such as "she might get pregnant" or that she might choose not to work during the period covered by the debtor's plan?

SOURCE: Dan Cox, *Daily Variety*, 29 December 1993, p. 3.

Involuntary Bankruptcy Petition

Often a debtor will get deeply in debt and try to avoid bankruptcy. When this happens, the creditors frequently will decide to petition the debtor into bankruptcy against his or her will. They do so by initiating an involuntary bankruptcy proceeding.

If a debtor does not fall within one of the groups exempted from involuntary petitions, the debtor is potentially subject to an involuntary petition. The vast majority of debtors in this country do not fit into one of these exceptions. That does not make most debtors subject to an involuntary petition automatically, however. The creditors who file the petition must show that three criteria—one related to the conduct of the debtor, one to the number of creditors of the debtor, and one to the unsecured debt of the debtor—are satisfied before they may file an involuntary petition against the debtor.

Debtor Conduct. The petitioning creditors must establish that the debtor is "guilty" of one of two acts: either the debtor is not paying debts as they become due, or the debtor appointed a receiver or made a general assignment for the benefit of the creditors within the 120 days that preceded the filing of the petition. (Under the latter test, the receiver or assignee must have taken possession of the debtor's property.)

Number of Petitioning Creditors. The petition filed with the court must be signed by the "proper number" of creditors. The proper number of creditors for a particular debtor is determined by the total number of creditors the debtor has. If the debtor has a total of twelve creditors or more, at least three creditors must sign the petition. If the debtor has fewer than twelve creditors, only one creditor must sign the petition, although more may choose to sign the petition.

Debt Requirement. The creditors who file the petition must have an aggregate claim against the debtor of at least $10,000 that is neither secured nor contingent. This means that a debtor with less than $10,000 in general unsecured debts may not be involuntarily petitioned into bankruptcy. It also explains why more than the minimum number of creditors (from the "number of petitioning creditors" requirement) will often need to sign the petition.

The following example shows one problem that petitioning creditors may face.

> Bob has seven creditors. He has made no payments to any of them for four months. He owes Ralph, one of the creditors, $6,000, of which $2,000 is secured by collateral. Ralph wants to file an involuntary petition against Bob. Since Bob is not paying his debts as they come due, the conduct requirement is satisfied. Since Ralph has less than twelve creditors, only one must sign the petition to satisfy the number requirement. However, unless another creditor with at least $6,000 in unsecured debt will join Ralph on a petition, Ralph cannot institute an involuntary petition. His unsecured claim of $4,000 does not satisfy the debt requirement.

In this example, Ralph also needs to exercise care prior to filing the petition. If a debtor is involuntarily petitioned into bankruptcy, the debtor may deny that he is bankrupt and request a trial. A debtor who wins such a trial can collect damages from the creditors who signed the petition.

THE BANKRUPTCY PROCEEDING

Once a petition is filed, the judge will issue an order for relief (unless the debtor files an answer denying bankruptcy and demands a trial). At this point, the proceeding is in motion, and it will continue until the final orders are entered. Upon entering the order for relief, the judge promptly appoints a trustee from a panel of private trustees. This trustee takes possession of—and legal title to—the debtor's property and begins the administration of the debtor's estate. (At the first creditors' meeting, a new trustee may be selected. If creditors having collective claims of at least 20 percent of the unsecured claims against the debtor request an election, the creditors can select a "permanent" trustee. If no such request is made, the court-appointed trustee serves throughout the proceedings.)

The Trustee

The trustee is the key figure in the bankruptcy proceeding. The trustee is the representative of the debtor's estate, and the trustee will attempt to preserve this estate to protect the interests of the unsecured creditors. The estate that the trustee preserves is made up of all the property the debtor has when the case is begun and any property the debtor acquires within the 180 days following the petition-filing date, reduced by any collateral removed from the estate and by the exempt assets of the debtor. The trustee must gather all of these assets, liquidate them, and generally handle the creditors' claims. The trustee also raises objections to the granting of a discharge if the debtor gives cause to do so. The trustee may be helped by a creditors' committee, a group of at least three and at most eleven unsecured creditors who consult with the trustee as needed.

The trustee is responsible for representing the interests of the general unsecured creditors in the bankruptcy petition. While the trustee takes legal title to the debtor's estate, the creditors have equitable title—the trustee possesses the estate for the benefit of the creditors. The trustee's job is difficult and demanding. Under the Bankruptcy Act, both individuals and corporations may serve as trustees, although corporations need to be authorized to perform this function in their corporate charter. In order for an individual to serve as trustee, he or she must be "competent to perform the duties of a trustee." The trustee must also satisfy a residency requirement by residing or having an office in the district where the case is pending or in an adjacent district. Under current bankruptcy law, the U.S. attorney general prescribes qualifications for appointment to a panel of trustees. The U.S. trustee sets up such a panel for the bankruptcy court; the bankruptcy judge appoints the trustee in each bankruptcy case from this panel. The appointment of a trustee is basically a mechanical chore, with the trustees appointed on a rotational basis. This method of appointment has virtually eliminated a common complaint under the prior law—that the trustees were appointed by friendly judges, were too close to the judges in too many instances, and were not always qualified for the role.

Interestingly, the 1994 bankruptcy bill restored the former method for appointing trustees in Chapter 11 proceedings, to an extent. In a Chapter 11 proceeding, any interested party may call for a meeting of the creditors in order to elect a trustee, provided the meeting is called within 30 days of the court's appointment of an operating trustee. There is some expectation that similar provisions will be enacted regarding Chapter 7 trustees in the near future.

29.1

FINANCE/MANUFACTURING

A CIT SUPPLIER FILES FOR CHAPTER 7 BANKRUPTCY

One of the firms that supplies component parts to CIT missed a delivery deadline recently, causing CIT to fall behind in its production schedule. After several phone calls to the supplier, repeated promises to deliver the component, and repeated failures by the supplier to keep these promises or to honor the terms of the contract, CIT decided that it needed to sue the supplier. Accordingly, Amy Chen filed the complaint with the appropriate state court, seeking damages from the supplier for breach of the contract. This morning, Tom received a fax from Amy informing him that the supplier has filed a voluntary petition for relief under Chapter 7 of the Bankruptcy Act. Tom asks you what effect this will have on the lawsuit. What will you tell him?

BUSINESS CONSIDERATIONS Suppose the trustee in bankruptcy offers CIT a settlement to their lawsuit, admitting that the debtor did, in fact, breach and agreeing to pay 50 percent of the amount sought in damages. What should the firm do in this situation? What other alternatives does the firm have?

ETHICAL CONSIDERATIONS Assume a business knows it has breached a contract and that it will be held liable for damages in a lawsuit. Assume further that the business is aware of the automatic stay provisions of bankruptcy law. Should the business file a bankruptcy petition in order to halt the lawsuit and then attempt to settle the suit for a substantially lesser amount of money than it would have lost had the case been heard?

Automatic Stay Provision

The filing of a petition in bankruptcy operates as an automatic stay against creditors who are involved in any legal actions against the debtor. The creditors must suspend any legal actions already commenced and must delay filing any new actions, pending the outcome of the bankruptcy proceedings. Similarly, the creditors may not initiate any repossession actions against the assets of the debtor. This automatic stay provision is designed to ensure that all the creditors are afforded equitable treatment under the bankruptcy proceedings by preventing any one creditor from gaining an advantage through his or her actions at the expense of the other creditors.

The Creditors' Meeting

The court will call for a meeting of the creditors within a reasonable time of the order for relief. The debtor, the trustee, and the creditors—but not the judge—will all attend this meeting. The debtor is expected to provide schedules of anticipated income, assets and their locations, and debts and liabilities at that time and to submit to an examination by the creditors concerning the debtor's assets, liabilities, and anything else the creditors feel is important. Although the debtor may not like it, it is best to cooperate fully: A refusal to cooperate may result in a denial of discharge. At this first creditors' meeting, the trustee is required to orally advise the debtor as to the possible repercussion from filing for bankruptcy relief and to explain to the debtor about other bankruptcy chapters that the debtor might want to utilize in lieu of a Chapter 7 liquidation proceeding.

The Debtor

The debtor also has certain duties to perform. The debtor must file a relatively detailed series of schedules that are intended to reveal his or her financial position so that (1) the bankruptcy court can properly evaluate the need for relief and (2) the interests of the various creditors can be protected. The debtor must provide a list of creditors, both secured and unsecured, the address of each creditor, and the amount of debt owed to each. The debtor also must provide a schedule of his or her financial affairs and a listing of all property owned, even if that property will be claimed as an exempt asset. Finally, the debtor must provide a list of current income and expenses. This list may show that the debtor should be in a Chapter 13 repayment plan rather than a Chapter 7 liquidation proceeding. If it does, the court may, on its own motion, dismiss the Chapter 7 proceeding following a hearing and encourage the debtor to refile under Chapter 13. However, the law also carries with it a presumption in favor of the debtor. The debtor is presumed to be entitled to receive the order of relief for whatever chapter was chosen by the debtor. The schedules are prepared by the debtor under oath and signed. Knowingly submitting false information in these schedules is a crime under the bankruptcy law.

The issue in *Matter of Holt* involved a falsified schedule of assets.

29.1 MATTER OF HOLT

190 B.R. 935 (Bkrtcy.N.D.Ala. 1996)

FACTS Holt purchased a 1988 Ford Aerostar, signing a promissory note and security agreement with Dana Federal Credit Union to finance the purchase. This loan was executed in connection with an open line of credit extended by Dana to Holt on 22 March 1988. On 22 May 1995, Holt filed a voluntary petition for relief under Chapter 7 of the Bankruptcy Code. In his schedule of debts, Holt listed Dana as an unsecured creditor with a claim of $6,012.87. (There were only four other unsecured creditors listed, each with a claim of less than $300.) Dana asserted it was owed $7,926.88. [The Aerostar was not listed among Holt's assets, and the court presumed that the van had either already been repossessed or that it had no value as of the petition date.] Holt proposed to discharge in full his debt to Dana through the

29.1 MATTER OF HOLT (cont.)

190 B.R. 935 (Bkrtcy.N.D.Ala. 1996)

Chapter 7 proceeding; Dana objected to the discharge by asserting that Holt had knowingly and fraudulently made numerous false oaths and that the debtor failed to explain the loss of assets that occurred immediately preceding the petition. According to Holt's schedule of assets, he had $7 in cash, $400 in his checking account, and $25 in his savings account on the petition date. However, three days prior to the petition date Holt had a checking account balance of more than $2,350, and a savings account balance of more than $4,500. Holt also denied depositing any of his severance pay of $9,162 in either his checking or savings accounts, although bank records indicated that he had deposited $4,500 in each of the accounts on the day that he received the severance pay check.

ISSUE Should the court deny a discharge to a debtor who cannot satisfactorily explain the dissipation of his assets immediately preceding his petition for relief under the Bankruptcy Code?

HOLDING Yes. A debtor who cannot satisfactorily explain the dissipation of assets is presumed to be acting in bad faith and will not be entitled to a discharge or a fresh start.

REASONING In order for a creditor to prevail on its objection to a discharge based on false oaths or accounts, the creditor must establish that:

1. the debtor made a false statement under oath;
2. the debtor made such false statements knowingly and with fraudulent intent; and,
3. the false statement was material to the bankruptcy case.

False oaths include false statements or omissions in a debtor's schedules, false statements made by the debtor during the creditors' meeting, and false statements in the debtor's deposition. In this case, Holt denied depositing any of his severance pay in either of his bank accounts in his schedules. At his deposition, he admitted depositing $4,500 in his checking account, but claimed to have forgotten that deposit because he was nervous. The bank's records, however, reflect that he deposited $4,500 each to his checking and his savings accounts. The bank's records also reflect that Holt had substantial balances in both accounts three days prior to the petition, funds that Holt claimed to spend on various bills and investments, but for which he cannot present receipts or other evidence.

Debtors are expected to make full and accurate disclosures of all assets and liabilities. Holt's false oaths and his refusal and/or inability to explain the uses to which he put the funds did not meet this expectation. The court found that Holt knowingly and fraudulently made numerous omissions from his statements with the intent to delay or defraud his creditors, and his petition for discharge is denied.

BUSINESS CONSIDERATIONS What can/should a business do to protect itself from potentially dishonest debtors to whom the business has extended credit? Why did the credit union not have to explain what had happened to the Aerostar van on which it had a security interest in this case?

ETHICAL CONSIDERATIONS Bankruptcy relief is available in the United States, to a significant extent, because of the abuses to which debtors were subjected under English law in the eighteenth century. Why should this relief only be available to "honest debtors"? Should a debtor who is less than honest be entitled to a fresh start?

The debtor also must cooperate fully with the trustee and surrender all property to the trustee. Finally, the debtor must attend any and all hearings and comply with all orders of the court. If this is done, a discharge will normally result.

Secured Creditors

Once the debtor has selected those assets to be exempted for a "fresh start," the trustee must communicate with the secured creditors concerning their status. Each

29.2

FINANCE

PERFECTED SECURITY INTEREST

One of CIT's early customers has recently been experiencing financial difficulties. As a result, this firm has not been paying all of its bills as they come due, although the business has been making its regularly scheduled payments to CIT in a generally timely manner. CIT has learned that the unsecured creditors of this business are planning to file an involuntary bankruptcy petition against the business, throwing it into a Chapter 7 proceeding. CIT has a perfected security interest in the Call-Image inventory in the possession of this debtor. Dan asks you what options are available to CIT if the unsecured creditors decide to proceed with the involuntary petition. What will you tell him?

BUSINESS CONSIDERATIONS Suppose one of the credit customers of a business faces a bankruptcy proceeding. What factors should the business consider when deciding whether to retain its security interest and opt out of the bankruptcy proceeding or to release its security interest and participate in the bankruptcy proceeding as an unsecured general creditor?

ETHICAL CONSIDERATIONS Assume that a secured creditor of a firm undergoing a Chapter 7 bankruptcy has a security interest in the majority of the debtor's nonexempt assets. Is it unethical to retain the security interest, thereby reducing the amount paid to each of the unsecured creditors while maximizing its own recovery when the proceedings are completed? Would it be more ethical to release the security interest, thus increasing the payment to each of the other unsecured creditors but reducing the amount realized by the formerly secured creditor?

secured creditor must make a selection. Secured creditors may elect to take their collateral in full satisfaction of their claims; dispose of the collateral and surrender any surplus to the trustee to be included in the bankruptcy estate; dispose of the collateral and participate as unsecured creditors to the extent they are not satisfied by the collateral; or have the trustee dispose of the collateral, paying the secured creditor the proceeds realized (up to the debt amount) and allowing the creditor to participate as an unsecured creditor for any balance owed.

Exemptions

The debtor can exempt some assets from the trustee's liquidation. The exempted assets are what provide a fresh start for those honest debtors who successfully complete the bankruptcy proceeding. This exemption is, surprisingly, governed by state statutes. If state law permits, the debtor may elect to take either the state exemptions or the federal exemptions. If no such choice is allowed by state law, the debtor must take the state exemptions. Under no circumstances may the debtor take both sets of exemptions.

More than 30 states have elected the override provision, requiring the debtor to take the state exemptions. In addition, even if the debtor is in a state that allows the choice of either the federal or the state exemptions, another limitation has been imposed by the 1984 Bankruptcy Amendments. In a joint filing, both the husband and the wife must select the same exemptions, either state or federal. They no longer will be allowed to select the exemptions individually, allowing one spouse to take the federal exemptions and the other to select the state exemptions.

Certain types of property are exempt under most state statutes. Typically, a debtor who elects (or is required) to take the state exemptions will be able to retain the following types of assets for his or her fresh start:

- Some cash (the amount varies from state to state)
- Residence or homestead
- Clothing
- Tools of the trade
- Insurance

In *In re Mayer,* a debtor claimed a special exception to the state's homestead exemption. Notice how the court treated this issue.

29.2 IN RE MAYER

156 B.R. 54 (Bkrtcy.S.D.Cal. 1993)

FACTS On 6 November 1989, Nadel obtained a judgment against Mayer in the amount of $40,052.62. On 19 December 1989, Nadel recorded the abstract of judgment against real property owned by Mayer located at 1597 Casa Real Lane, San Marcos, California. At the time the judicial lien attached, Mayer used the property as a rental. The property did not become Mayer's principal residence until sometime in July 1992, when he re-occupied the house. On 3 March 1993, Mayer filed for protection under Chapter 7 and claimed an automatic homestead exemption of $100,000 for the property under California law. Mayer claims that he is entitled to the $100,000 exemption because he is older than 55 with a gross annual income of less than $20,000. Nadel timely objected to Mayer's homestead exemption. In the alternative, Nadel claims the homestead exemption amount should be the amount in effect in 1989, when the judgment lien attached, not the amount permitted as of the petition-filing date.

ISSUES Without considering the bankruptcy laws, would the debtor be entitled to the automatic homestead exemption under state law? Does the avoidance provision of the Bankruptcy Code affect the operation of state exemption laws and/or alter the substantive rights they provide? Is the homestead exemption amount fixed at the time a judicial lien attaches or at the time of the bankruptcy petition?

HOLDINGS No. The debtors are not entitled to the automatic homestead exemption under state law since they did not reside in the home on the date the lien attached. Yes. Bankruptcy laws permit a debtor to transfer assets from nonexempt to exempt prior to the bankruptcy in order to obtain a fresh start, even if this overrides the state's limitations. The homestead exemption amount is fixed at the time the judicial lien attaches.

REASONING California allows a homeowner to select from two types of homestead exemptions, the automatic and the declared homestead. The automatic homestead attaches to the principal dwelling of each homeowner in the state, with no need for any filing. The declared homestead requires the homeowner to record a declaration in the office of the county recorder where the property is located. Once filed, a declared homestead replaces the automatic homestead for exemption purposes. In this case, Mayer did not file a declared homestead declaration, so that the automatic homestead exemption is the only one potentially applicable in this case. California law requires the debtor to actually be in residence on the date the judgment lien attaches to the property in order to assert the automatic homestead exemption, however. Mayer did not reside in the house on the date that the judicial lien attached, thus making his assertion of an automatic homestead exemption invalid in this case.

Bankruptcy law permits a debtor to avoid certain liens if those liens impair the debtor's full exemptions. California's homestead exemption can be read as helping to protect a debtor and to insure that debtor of a fresh start. Since California has opted out of the federal exemptions, the debtor is forced to rely on the state exemptions in a bankruptcy proceeding. A debtor is permitted to avoid a judicial lien on any property to the extent that the property could have been exempted in the absence of the lien. Since California provides for a homestead exemption if there is no lien on the property, the bankruptcy code permits the debtor to overturn that lien in order to take advantage of the exemption in a bankruptcy proceeding.

It is well established that every statute will be construed to operate prospectively unless legislative intent to the contrary is clearly expressed. This rule is especially applicable to cases where retroactive operation of the statute would impair the obligations of contracts or interfere with vested rights. Laws impairing the obligations of contracts are forbidden.

In this case, when Nadel's judicial lien attached in 1989, it created a vested right. An increase in the statutory exemption amount cannot be applied retroactively to impair Nadel's vested right. Thus, the proper amount of the homestead exemption is the amount to which Mayer would have been entitled when Nadel's lien attached in 1989.

BUSINESS CONSIDERATIONS Why should a debtor be permitted to exchange nonexempt assets for exempt assets prior to filing a petition for relief in bankruptcy? What impact is this likely to have on a business that extends credit to an individual who later seeks relief under Chapter 7?

ETHICAL CONSIDERATIONS Why does the Bankruptcy Code provide for a discharge for individual debtors under Chapter 7, but not for corporate debtors? Is such a restriction fair to individuals who incorporate a business?

In some state exemption provisions, the debtor also may exempt one automobile (there is likely to be a value limit imposed on the automobile, and this amount varies from state to state). In addition, the debtor is allowed to exempt some benefits for public policy reasons:

- Veteran's benefits
- Social security benefits
- Unemployment compensation benefits
- Disability benefits
- Alimony

The federal exemptions, as provided for under the Bankruptcy Reform Act, allow the debtor to exempt the following property from the proceeding if state law allows the debtor to select the federal exemptions:

1. Equity in the debtor's home, up to $15,000.
2. If there is no equity in the home or if the equity is less than $15,000, the unused portion of the $15,000 in a joint petition or $7,500 in an individual petition may be used as a "wild card," exempting anything the debtor desires.
3. Equity in one automobile, up to $2,400.
4. Household goods and clothing, up to $200 per item and up to $8,000 aggregate.
5. Jewelry up to $1,000.
6. Tools of the debtor's trade, including books, up to $1,500.
7. Any unmatured life insurance policies owned by the debtor.

The Bankruptcy Reform Act also permits a debtor to convert goods from nonexempt classes to exempt classes before filing the bankruptcy petition. In addition, if there is a lien on, or security interest attached to, otherwise exempt property, the debtor can redeem it—which automatically exempts it—by paying off the lien-holding creditor.

FROM THE DESK OF

AMY CHEN, ATTORNEY AT LAW

Bankruptcies

Inevitably, some of your firm's customers will file for bankruptcy. Always keep good records of your credit accounts and pay attention to the legal notices in the local papers. If a customer files for bankruptcy, you must file your claim with the bankruptcy court to participate in the proceedings. To retain a security interest in the customer's inventory, you must decide whether to retain your security interest and opt out of the bankruptcy proceeding or to release your security interest and participate in the bankruptcy proceeding.

Allowable Claims

Once the permanent trustee has assumed control of the estate and the exempt property has been removed from the estate, the serious business of bankruptcy begins. Those claims of creditors that are allowable must be filed. Only allowable debts may participate in the distribution of the estate. Allowable claims may be filed by the debtor, a creditor, or even the trustee. But they must be filed within six months of the first creditors' meeting.

Nearly every debt that existed before the order for relief will be allowed in the bankruptcy. There are four major exceptions to this statement. Two of these four debts are not allowable:

1. Claims that would be unenforceable against the debtor, such as contracts based on fraud or duress
2. Claims for interest that are figured beyond the petition date, since interest may no longer accrue once a petition is filed

The other two of these four debts are not fully allowable, but are partially allowable:

3. Damages based on a lease violation or termination, to some extent [the landlord can claim a debt only up to the greater of one year's rent or 15 percent of the balance of the lease (with a three-year maximum) plus any unpaid rent already due and payable]
4. Damages based on breach of an employment contract, if those damages exceed one year's compensation, plus unpaid wages due and payable

In *In re Whitten,* there was a question as to whether certain claims were allowable under the Bankruptcy Code and also a challenge to the granting of a discharge to the debtor.

29.3 IN RE WHITTEN

192 B.R. 10 (Bkrtcy.D.Mass. 1996)

FACTS The Governor's Park condominium was created by master deed on 10 July 1986. The Governor's Park Condominium Trust (Trust) was also established in order to represent the organization of condominium owners. On 22 October 1986, Whitten and another person purchased two units that were then rented to tenants. Both units were encumbered by mortgages held by BoWest. Whitten fell into arrears with respect to his common area fee obligations in late 1991 and early 1992, and the Trust attempted, unsuccessfully, to collect rents from Whitten's tenants. Whitten filed a voluntary bankruptcy petition under Chapter 7 on 3 June 1992, stating an intention to surrender both units to BoWest. The Trust was not originally listed as a creditor. However, on 17 July 1992, Whitten amended his schedule to include the Trust's claim for condo fees, which were estimated to be $4,505. Whitten received a discharge and his case was closed 10 November 1992, and the condominium units reverted to him at that time. Fifteen months later, BoWest foreclosed its mortgages on both units. At that time, unpaid common area fees for the two units for the period from December 1992 through March 1994 totaled $7,921.17. The Trust collected $2,889 from the mortgagee, leaving an unsecured balance of $5,032.17. On 31 March 1994, the Trust filed suit against Whitten to collect the unpaid post-petition common area fees. Whitten denied liability on the grounds that the debt had been discharged by his bankruptcy. The District Court entered judgment for the Trust in the amount of $6,356.37 (including attorney's fees and costs) and Whitten filed a petition to reopen his bankruptcy case to determine whether the debt to the Trust had been discharged.

ISSUE Are the post-petition fees assessed against the debtor discharged by the original bankruptcy proceeding in which Whitten was granted a discharge?

HOLDING No. The obligation to pay condominium fees is a covenant that runs with the land, so that a debtor is obligated to pay any and all such fees except for those assessed during the time that the property constituted property of the bankruptcy estate.

REASONING There are two approaches to this issue. One line of cases holds that a condominium declaration is a contract and that, although the amount of future fees is contingent and unmatured until assessed, these fees constitute a debt under the broad definition of debt under the Bankruptcy Code. Thus, when a bankruptcy court issues a discharge order, the unmatured, contingent condominium debts are discharged. The other line of cases holds that an obligation to pay condominium fees derive, not from contract, but from a covenant that runs with the land. Thus, any obligations to pay assessments arise from continued post-petition ownership of the property, and not from any pre-petition contractual obligations. These cases hold that a debtor's liability for the assessments cannot be discharged in bankruptcy because the obligation to pay the fees ends only upon the termination of the debtor's ownership of the property.

A discharge in bankruptcy does not discharge a debtor for any debts that arise *after* the filing of the petition for relief. If the fees assessed by the Trust are contractual in nature, then the assessment is discharged. However, if the claims are based on covenants that run with the land, the debtor is liable for them if they accrue post-petition. In Massachusetts the courts have ruled that condominium fees assessed for common areas are covenants that run with the land. Accordingly, the court finds that the debtor's obligation to pay the fees arose post-petition following reversion of the units to him, and thus, were not included in his bankruptcy discharge. The debtor is held personally liable for the balance of the common fees for the period between December 1992 and March 1994.

29.3 IN RE WHITTEN (cont.) 192 B.R. 10 (Bkrtcy.D.Mass. 1996)

BUSINESS CONSIDERATIONS How should a condominium word its contracts and deeds with purchasers in order to ensure that any fees are covenants that run with the land rather than contractual obligations that are contingent and unmatured?

ETHICAL CONSIDERATIONS Is it ethical for an owner of a condominium unit to avoid paying common area fees due to the protections afforded by bankruptcy, even though that owner continues to be able to take advantage of the benefits of the assessment in using the common areas? What arguments could you make for denying a discharge for these fees, from an ethical perspective?

Recovery of Property

While administering a debtor's estate, a trustee may discover that the debtor committed certain improper actions. A trustee who discovers such conduct is obligated to recover the transferred property for the benefit of the unsecured creditor. These improper acts fall into two major categories: voidable preferences and fraudulent conveyances.

Voidable Preferences. A *voidable preference* is a payment made by a debtor to one or a few creditors at the expense of the other creditors in that particular creditor class. This is not as complicated as it may seem at first glance. A transfer is deemed a preference and therefore voidable if all the following five conditions are met:

1. The transfer benefits a creditor.
2. The transfer covers a preexisting debt.
3. The debtor is insolvent at the time of the transfer. (A debtor is presumed to be insolvent during the 90 days preceding the date of the petition; this presumption is rebuttable by the debtor.)
4. The transfer is made during the 90 days preceding the petition date.
5. The transfer gives the creditor who receives it a greater percentage of the creditor's claim than fellow creditors will receive as a result of the transfer.

A transfer is not deemed a preference if it fits any one of the following tests:

1. The transfer is for a new obligation, as opposed to a preexisting debt.
2. The transfer is made in the ordinary course of business.
3. The transfer involves a purchase-money security interest.
4. The transfer is a payment on a fully secured claim.
5. The transfer is for normal payments made to creditors within 90 days prior to the petition, if the payments total less than $600 per creditor.

Fraudulent Conveyance. A *fraudulent conveyance* is a transfer by a debtor that involves actual or constructive fraud. Actual fraud is involved if the debtor intended to hinder or delay a creditor in recovering a debt. Such a transfer will occur if the debtor transfers assets to a friend or a relative—or hides assets—to prevent any creditors from foreclosing on the assets. Constructive fraud is involved when the debtor sells an asset for inadequate consideration and as a result of the sale becomes insolvent or if the debtor is already insolvent at the time of the unreasonable sale. It is also deemed constructive fraud to engage in a business that is undercapitalized.

Any fraudulent conveyance made during the year preceding the petition may be set aside by the trustee under federal law. In addition, some state statutes permit the avoidance of such conveyances during the preceding two to five years. The trustee uses the time period that most strongly favors the creditors.

Union Bank v. *Wolas* involved an allegedly voidable preference. The debtor made three payments to one of its creditors during the 90 days preceding the petition date. Note how the court treated these payments.

29.4 UNION BANK v. WOLAS 502 U.S. 151 (1991)

FACTS Section 547 of the Bankruptcy Code authorizes a trustee to avoid certain property transfers made by a debtor within 90 days before bankruptcy. The Code makes an exception, however, for transfers made in the ordinary course of business. On 17 December 1986, the debtor, ZZZZ Best Co., Inc., borrowed $7 million from Union Bank. On 8 July 1987, the debtor filed a voluntary petition under Chapter 7 of the Bankruptcy Code. During the preceding 90-day period, the debtor had made two interest payments totaling approximately $100,000 and had paid a loan commitment fee of about $2,500 to the bank. After his appointment as trustee of the debtor's estate, Wolas filed a complaint against the bank to recover these payments, pursuant to § 547(b). The bankruptcy court found that the loans had been made "in the ordinary course of business or financial affairs" of both the debtor and the bank, and that both interest payments as well as the payment of the loan commitment fee had been made according to ordinary business terms and in the ordinary course of business. Shortly thereafter, in another case, the court of appeals held that the avoidance of preferential transfers was not available to long-term creditors. The importance of this question of law, coupled with the fact that the Sixth and Ninth Circuits had reached differing opinions, persuaded the Court to grant certiorari.

ISSUE Can payments made on long-term debts qualify as payments in the ordinary course of business and thus not be treated as voidable preferences?

HOLDING Yes. Payments made on long-term debts, as well as payments for short-term debts, may qualify for the ordinary course of business exception to the trustee's power to avoid preferential transfers.

REASONING The Bankruptcy Reform Act of 1978 originally provided that the ordinary course of business exception did not apply unless the payments in question were made within 45 days of the date the debt was incurred. This provision apparently excluded payments on long-term debts from the ordinary course of business exception. However, the Bankruptcy Amendments of 1984 repealed this 45-day limit and did not substitute any time limitations for § 547.

The policy of preventing preferential treatment is intended to assure, so far as possible, that creditors are treated equally. It also deters the race of diligence of creditors by permitting the trustee to recover pre-bankruptcy transfers that occur shortly before the petition, thus discouraging creditors from racing to the courthouse to dismember the debtor during his slide into bankruptcy. The protection thus afforded often allows the debtor to work his way out of a difficult financial situation through cooperation with all of his creditors. On the other hand, the ordinary course of business exception may benefit all creditors by deterring the race to the courthouse and enabling the struggling debtor to continue operating its business.

While the trustee argues that the ordinary course of business exception should be limited to short-term debts only, the statutory language makes no such distinction. If payments in the ordinary course of business fall within an exception, it should not matter whether the debt for which the payments are made are short-term or long-term in nature. The Court expressed no opinion, however, on the question of whether this loan was made in the ordinary course of business, nor whether the payments made were made in the ordinary course of business, nor whether the payments were made according to ordinary business terms. These questions remained open for decision by the court of appeals on remand.

BUSINESS CONSIDERATIONS Does the exception to the voidable preference rule for payments made in the

29.4 UNION BANK v. WOLAS (cont.) 502 U.S. 151 (1991)

ordinary course of business help a struggling business to acquire loans in an effort to salvage the business? Why?

ETHICAL CONSIDERATIONS If the Bankruptcy Code grants an exception to the voidable preference rule for payments made in the ordinary course of business, what difference should it make when the loan was made or how long the loan's term is? Is there an ethical reason for favoring a short-term creditor over a long-term debtor? For favoring a long-term debtor over a short-term debtor?

Distribution of Assets

Once the trustee has gathered and liquidated all available assets and admitted all allowable claims, the estate is distributed to the creditors. The Bankruptcy Reform Act contains a mandatory priority list of debts. Each class of creditors takes its turn, and no class may receive any payments until all higher-priority classes are paid in full. All creditors within a given class will be paid on a pro rata basis until either the claims are paid in full or the estate is exhausted.

The highest priority of claims is the expense of handling the estate. All the costs incurred by the trustee in preserving and administering the bankruptcy must be paid first.

The next class of claims involves debts that arise in the ordinary course of business between the date the petition is filed and the date the trustee is appointed.

The third and fourth priorities are interrelated. Priority 3 is wages earned by employees of the debtor during the 90 days preceding the petition, up to a maximum of $4,000 per employee. Priority 4 is unpaid contributions by an employer to employee benefit plans, if they arise during the 180 days before the petition, up to $4,000 per employee. However, these claims are reduced by any claims paid in Priority 3. Thus, the maximum priority for each employee is a total of $4,000. Any claims in excess of this amount go to the bottom of the list.

The fifth priority is given to grain farmers who have a claim against the owner or operator of a grain storage facility and to U.S. fishermen who have a claim against individuals who operate a fish storage or fish-processing facility. In either case, the priority is limited to $4,000 per individual creditor.

The sixth priority is claims by consumers for goods or services paid for but not received. The maximum here is $1,800 per person as a priority, with any surplus claim going to the bottom of the list.

As of 1994, alimony, maintenance agreements or obligations, and child support were granted the next priority, being inserted into the list above obligations owed to the government. This placement reflects the increasing public policy position of "family values" and a desire to help protect spouses or ex-spouses, especially those with children. To further emphasize this change, the payment of alimony, maintenance, or child support is specifically not a voidable preference, nor are such payments subject to the automatic stay provisions of other debts and obligations of the debtor.

The final priority claim is in favor of debts owed to government units. This class consists basically of taxes due during the three years preceding the petition.

After all priority claims are paid, the balance of the estate is used to pay general unsecured creditors. When all unsecured creditors have been paid in full, any monies left are paid to the debtor. Normally, the funds will not cover the general creditor claims, and a pro rata distribution is necessary. This leaves the creditors with less money than they were owed. The debtor must hope for a discharge to make the balance of the claims uncollectible.

Exhibit 29.1 summarizes the distribution of proceeds in a Chapter 7 bankruptcy proceeding.

The Discharge Decision

A discharge can be granted only to an individual and only if he or she is an honest debtor. A discharge will be denied if the debtor made a fraudulent conveyance or

EXHIBIT 29.1 Distribution of Proceeds in a Chapter 7 Bankruptcy Proceeding

Priority 1—Expenses of the bankruptcy.

If any funds remain,

Priority 2—Debts arising in the ordinary course of business between the petition date and the date a trustee is appointed (pro rata if necessary).

If any funds remain,

Priority 3—Wages earned during the 90 days preceding the petition by employees of the debtor but not yet paid, to a maximum of $4,000 per employee (pro rata if necessary).

If any funds remain,

Priority 4—Fringe benefits earned during the 180 days preceding the petition by employees of the debtor but not yet paid, to a maximum of $4,000 per employee (pro rata if necessary). Priorities 3 and 4 combined cannot exceed $4,000 per employee.

If any funds remain,

Priority 5—Claims of grain farmers against grain storage facilities, and/or of U.S. fishermen against fish storage or fish-processing facilities, limited to $4,000 per creditor (pro rata if necessary).

If any funds remain,

Priority 6—Claims by consumers for goods or services paid for but not received, up to $1,800 per consumer (pro rata if necessary).

If any funds remain,

Priority 7—Claims against the debtor for alimony payments, separate maintenance payments, or child support.

If any funds remain,

Priority 8—Debts owed to the government, especially for taxes owed for the previous three years.

If any funds remain,

General unsecured creditors—pro rata, together with any excess over the priority claims set out above.

When no funds remain, or when all eight levels have been treated, the court makes a *discharge decision.*

does not have adequate books and records. In addition, a debtor will be denied a discharge if he or she refuses to cooperate with the court during the proceedings. Furthermore, a discharge will not be granted if a discharge was received during the previous six years. A denial of discharge means that the unpaid portions of any debts continue and are fully enforceable after the proceedings end.

In *Hibernia National Bank* v. *Perez,* a debtor was denied a discharge when he failed to properly account for assets or to properly and accurately complete his required schedules.

29.5 HIBERNIA NATIONAL BANK v. PEREZ

124 B.R. 704 (E.D.La. 1991)

FACTS On a financial statement dated 31 December 1985, Perez listed the following assets, among others: furnishings with a cash basis of $26,403.06 and a market basis of $21,122; jewelry and furs with a cash basis of $47,883.63 and a market basis of $62,248.72. On a financial statement dated 31 December 1986, these items were not listed, nor were they listed on his schedule of assets in support of his petition for bankruptcy. When asked to explain their absence, Perez stated that the assets belonged to his wife and should not have been included in his 1985 financial statement. The court refused to accept this explanation without evidence in support of it. It would be just as easy to state that the items were erroneously left off the 1986 statement as to state that they were erroneously included on the 1985 statement. Without some evidence, Perez failed to satisfy the court as to why these items should not be included in the bankruptcy estate. During the year prior to the bankruptcy proceeding, Perez received a $290,000 tax refund, which he split equally with his wife. The bankruptcy judge enlarged the pleadings to include this tax refund, even though Hibernia had not listed it. Perez argued that the court acted improperly in enlarging the pleadings in such a manner. Perez filed a petition for relief under Chapter 7 of the Bankruptcy Code. He was denied a discharge for allegedly failing to properly explain the absence of certain items in his bankruptcy schedules that had been included in previous financial statements he had prepared. In addition, the court felt that he had acted in a manner intended to hinder, delay, or defraud his creditors. Perez appealed the findings of the bankruptcy court.

ISSUES Did Perez give a satisfactory explanation for certain items included on his financial statement of 1985, but not included in his bankruptcy schedules in support of his petition? Did Perez's conduct show an intent to hinder, delay, or defraud his creditors?

HOLDINGS No. Perez did not satisfactorily explain the discrepancies between his financial statement and his bankruptcy schedule of assets. Yes. The conduct did show an intent to hinder, delay, and/or defraud his creditors.

REASONING The Bankruptcy Code states that a court shall not grant a debtor a discharge if the debtor has failed to explain satisfactorily any loss of assets. Hibernia carried its burden of proof by showing that assets "disappeared"; the financial statements clearly included assets in Perez's estate in 1985 that were no longer included in 1986. Perez explained the loss of the listed assets by stating that they belonged to his wife and that they never belonged to him. This explanation does not satisfy the court. The court is unwilling to allow a debtor to explain away the loss of assets from his estate by simply disclaiming ownership as such a practice could too easily be abused.

A list of jewelry and furs compiled for insurance purposes did not indicate the source of acquisition of the items. Neither was the source or acquisition given for the furniture in response to a request for this information from Hibernia.

During the year prior to the filing of Perez's petition, the Perez's, who file a joint tax return despite being separate in property, received approximately $290,000 in tax refunds. Perez and his wife split the refund equally. The court is allowed to enlarge the pleadings to take this asset into account unless such an action is shown to be an abuse of discretion. Since Perez did not establish an abuse of discretion, this enlargement of the pleadings is proper.

Since Perez filed his petition within one year after receiving this refund, the court held that he made a fraudulent conveyance with the intent to hinder, delay, or defraud his creditors. The court was correct in denying Perez a discharge, and its judgment was affirmed in this trial.

BUSINESS CONSIDERATIONS What sorts of records should Perez have maintained in order to support his position that the assets in question belonged to his wife?

29.5 HIBERNIA NATIONAL BANK v. PEREZ *(cont.)* **124 B.R. 704 (E.D.La. 1991)**

How complete and how detailed should the records of an individual be in order to show adequate records in a bankruptcy proceeding?

ETHICAL CONSIDERATIONS What protections are available to a creditor when it deals with a "dishonest" debtor? Should some sort of penalty be applicable to a debtor who is found to be dishonest after credit has been extended to that debtor?

Even if a discharge is granted, some claims are not affected. Under the Bankruptcy Reform Act, certain debts continue to be fully enforceable against the debtor even though the debtor received a discharge. The following 11 major classes of debts are not affected by a discharge:

1. Taxes due to any government unit
2. Loans where the proceeds were used to pay federal taxes
3. Debts that arose because of fraud by the debtor concerning his financial condition
4. Claims not listed by the creditors or by the debtor in time for treatment in the proceedings
5. Debts incurred through embezzlement or theft
6. Alimony
7. Child support
8. Liabilities due to malicious torts of the debtor
9. Fines imposed by a government unit
10. Claims that were raised in a previous case in which the debtor did not receive a discharge
11. Student loans, unless the loan is at least five years in arrears

In addition to these 11 classes of debts, the 1984 Bankruptcy Amendments addressed the problem of debtors who "load up" with debts just prior to filing a petition, expecting to use the bankruptcy proceeding to discharge these recently incurred debts. Under the law, any debtor purchases from one creditor of $1,000 or more in luxury goods or services that are incurred within 40 days of the petition are presumed to be nondischargeable. Similarly, any cash advances of $1,000 or more that are received from one creditor within the 20 days prior to the petition are presumed to be nondischargeable. The debtor will have the burden of proof and will have to convince the court that these debts were not fraudulently incurred with the intent of receiving a discharge in order to have these debts discharged. Notice that a discharge is possible but that the debtor has the burden of proof!

Exhibit 29.2 summarizes the steps in a Chapter 7 bankruptcy proceeding.

Finally, even if a discharge is granted, it may be revoked. If the trustee or a creditor requests a revocation of the discharge, the request may be granted. The request must be made within one year of the discharge, and the debtor must have committed

EXHIBIT 29.2 The Steps in a Chapter 7 Bankruptcy Proceeding

Petition is filed	By the debtor (voluntary), five exceptions exist; by the creditors (involuntary), seven exceptions exist.
Order for relief	Automatic stay on any legal proceedings involving the debtor.
Interim trustee appointed	Takes immediate control of the debtor's estate.
Creditor meeting	Debtor examined, debtor schedules submitted, permanent trustee elected.
Marshaling of assets	Trustee gathers the debtor's estate.
Exemptions taken	Debtor selects exempt assets (federal or state exemptions, if the state law allows such a choice).
Claims allowed	Some claims will not be allowed (interest figured after petition date, wages owed for more than one year in the future, rent due for future periods).
Recovery of assets	Trustee may challenge certain actions of the debtor (voidable preferences and fraudulent conveyances); debtor's insolvency is required.
Distribution of assets	Mandatory provisions (eight priority categories, balance is allocated pro rata).
Discharge decision	Trustee recommends, judge decides.

some wrongful act, such as fraud during the proceedings. The possibility of revocation encourages the debtor to remain honest.

On some occasions, a debtor who has been granted a discharge in bankruptcy may decide that he wants to repay the creditor despite the discharge. If the debtor truly wants to repay the debt, he may voluntarily reaffirm the debt and then repay it. However, the requirements for a reaffirmation were substantially increased by the 1984 Bankruptcy Amendments. Prior to the 1984 amendments, a debtor could reaffirm any debts at virtually any time. Too often this led to a debtor reaffirming debts out of a sense of guilt following the discharge and putting himself in the same sort of financial position as had originally led to the petition. As a result, the 1984 amendments require that any reaffirmations be made in writing and filed with the court. In addition, the written agreement must be filed before the debtor is granted a discharge. If the debtor has an attorney, the attorney must file a declaration that the debtor was fully informed of his rights, voluntarily agreed to the reaffirmation, and that the agreement will not impose an undue hardship on the debtor or his dependents. If the debtor does not have an attorney, the court must approve the reaffirmation, and the court will not grant approval unless the repayment is in the best interests of the debtor.

http:// RESOURCES FOR BUSINESS LAW STUDENTS

NAME	RESOURCES	WEB ADDRESS
Legal Information Institute (LII)—Bankruptcy Law Materials	The Legal Information Institute (LII), maintained by the Cornell Law School, provides an overview of bankruptcy law, including the Federal Bankruptcy Code; rules in the Code of Federal Regulations (C.F.R.); state and federal court decisions; and state civil codes.	http://www.law.cornell.edu/topics/bankruptcy.html
11 U.S.C. Chapter 7—Liquidation	LII provides a hypertext and searchable version of Chapter 7, Liquidation, of the U.S. Code.	http://www.law.cornell.edu/uscode/11/ch7.html
11 U.S.C. Chapter 11—Reorganization	LII provides a hypertext and searchable version of Chapter 11, Reorganization, of the U.S. Code.	http://www.law.cornell.edu/uscode/11/ch11.html
11 U.S.C. Chapter 12—Adjustment of Debts of a Family Farmer with Regular Annual Income	LII provides a hypertext and searchable version of Chapter 12, Adjustment of Debts of a Family Farmer with Regular Annual Income	http://www.law.cornell.edu/uscode/11/ch12.html
11 U.S.C. Chapter 13—Adjustment of Debts of an Individual with Regular Income	LII provides a hypertext and searchable version of Chapter 13, Adjustment of Debts of an Individual with Regular Income	http://www.law.cornell.edu/uscode/11/ch13.html
Bankruptcy Reform Act of 1994	The U.S. Congress provides the Bankruptcy Reform Act of 1994.	http://thomas.loc.gov/cgi-bin/query/z?c103:H.R.5116:
ABI World (American Bankruptcy Institute)	American Bankruptcy Institute provides daily bankruptcy headlines, legislative news, and materials from the National Bankruptcy Review Commission (NBRC).	http://www.abiworld.org/

SUMMARY

Federal law governs the topic of bankruptcy, which is designed to give an honest debtor a fresh start. The Bankruptcy Reform Act, which took effect in October 1979, provided for the establishment of bankruptcy courts as a separate branch of the U.S. district court system. These courts were to be presided over by bankruptcy judges who specialized in handling bankruptcy petitions. Following a constitutional challenge to the bankruptcy courts established by the Bankruptcy Reform Act, the Bankruptcy Amendments and Federal Judgeship Act of 1984 modified these bankruptcy courts and severely restricted the authority of the courts and judges. The Bankruptcy Reform Act of 1994 added a number of additional provisions designed to close loopholes and to further balance the rights of the parties in a bankruptcy proceeding. This act also includes a built-in adapter in an effort to keep the dollar amounts involved in bankruptcy current without the need to amend the Code every few years.

Under Chapter 7 (Liquidation), bankruptcy can be initiated voluntarily by the debtor or involuntarily by the creditors. The debtor initiates the proceedings by filing a voluntary petition. The creditors initiate the proceedings by filing an involuntary petition against the debtor. Five types of "public interest" corporations are prohibited from filing a voluntary petition; any other debtor may file such a petition, even if solvent. Creditors may file an involuntary petition against most debtors, although there are seven classes of debtors who are exempt from an involuntary petition filed against them. Even for those debtors who are legally subject to an involuntary petition, there are safeguards. An involuntary petition can be filed only if the debtor is "guilty" of specified conduct, the proper number of creditors join the petition, and the proper amount of unsecured debts is involved.

Once the petition is filed, a judge appoints a trustee to administer the bankrupt's estate. The trustee is to preserve the estate for the protection of the unsecured creditors. The debtor is allowed some exemptions so that a fresh start is possible. The rest of the estate is available for settling debts. Secured creditors must choose between removing themselves and their collateral from the bankruptcy or surrendering their security interest and participating in the proceedings. Once the exempt property and the collateral securing certain loans is removed, the balance of the estate is liquidated and the proceeds are applied to the allowable claims of the creditors.

The proceeds are applied first to priority classes set up by the Bankruptcy Reform Act. After all priority classes are paid in full, the remaining proceeds are applied to the claims of the unsecured creditors. The debtor will then seek a discharge. If the debtor has been honest and has cooperated, a discharge will probably be granted. If not, the debts will continue.

Discussion Questions

1. What are the two major purposes of the Bankruptcy Reform Act? What public policy considerations support these two purposes? What public policy considerations oppose these two purposes?
2. What are the five classes of debtors who cannot file a *voluntary* petition for a Chapter 7 bankruptcy? What are the seven classes of debtors who cannot be *involuntarily* petitioned into Chapter 7 bankruptcy? What are the public policy considerations for excluding these debtors from a Chapter 7 bankruptcy proceeding?
3. Before a debtor can be involuntarily petitioned into bankruptcy, that petitioning creditors must satisfy three tests. What are the three tests the petitioning creditors must satisfy? Why must these tests be satisfied prior to the imposition of an involuntary bankruptcy proceeding?
4. Ronald is involved in a Chapter 7 bankruptcy. The state in which he lives allows the debtor to select either the federal or the state exemptions. The state exemptions completely exempt the debtor's homestead, one automobile, and personal articles of clothing. However, Ronald does not own a home. What should he do? Would your answer be different if Ronald did own a home? Why?
5. On 1 August of last year, Martha filed a voluntary bankruptcy petition, seeking relief under Chapter 7 of the Bankruptcy Code. Included among the debts she listed on her schedule of assets and liabilities were: a $30,000 loan with 18 percent interest per annum from Last Bank and Trust dated 1 June of last year; an employment contract with her housekeeper for the next three years; and a lease on her apartment that runs for five more years. She has not paid her housekeeper for the past two months, nor has she paid her rent for the past three months. What portion of each of these debts will be allowable in the bankruptcy proceeding?
6. What does it mean when a debtor *loads up* with debts prior to filing a bankruptcy petition? How does bankruptcy law deal with this problem? Is this treatment an appropriate solution to the problem of debtors who load up with debts in anticipation of bankruptcy?
7. What was the basis for the challenge to the Bankruptcy Reform Act in the *Northern Pipeline* case? Does such a challenge to a statute on procedural grounds make sense from a substantive perspective?
8. Suppose a father gave his daughter a new car when she graduated from college last spring, and that the father then filed a petition in bankruptcy seven months after the date of the graduation ceremonies. Can the trustee challenge this gift to the daughter as a fraudulent conveyance? If a challenge is made, what will need to be shown in order for the daughter to be allowed to keep the car?

9. What is meant by a *voidable preference* in bankruptcy law? Why is the trustee allowed to recover payments made if those payments fit the definition of a voidable preference?
10. Why are alimony and child support obligations not discharged in a bankruptcy proceeding? Is such a rule good or bad, from a public policy perspective? Do the same justifications apply to not permitting the discharge of taxes or student loans?

CASE PROBLEMS AND WRITING ASSIGNMENTS

1. Duffy entered into a long-term lease agreement with Avis Rent-a-Car. He failed to make numerous payments due under the lease, and Avis threatened to repossess the leased car. On 30 July 1979, Duffy mailed Avis a check for $400 (the check was postdated 3 August 1979). Avis presented the check and received payment from Duffy's bank on 6 August 1979. Duffy eventually filed a petition for relief under Chapter 7. The petition was filed 94 days after Duffy mailed the check to Avis, but only 88 days after the check was paid by the bank. The trustee in bankruptcy challenged the payment as a voidable preference, alleging that Avis was paid within 90 days of the petition. Avis argued that it received the check more than 90 days before the petition, so the payment was not a preference. Which party has the better argument? Explain your reasoning. [See *Matter of Duffy*, 3 B.R. 263 (1980).]

2. BH & P, Inc., filed a voluntary petition for relief under Chapter 7, as did its principals. Maggio was appointed as trustee for the firm, as well as trustee for each of the principals. Several claims of the firm involved claims against the principals. When Maggio filed an application to recover interim fees for his work as trustee, several creditors of the business objected. These creditors asserted that Maggio had a personal conflict of interest between his role as trustee for the firm and his role as trustee for the principals and that Maggio should be removed as trustee and not be awarded any fees for his work to date. Should Maggio be removed as a trustee in the case? Should Maggio be entitled to recover interim expenses and fees even if he is removed? [See *In re BH & P, Inc.*, 949 F.2d 1300 (3rd Cir. 1991).]

3. Stephen and Deborah Cox were married in 1973. Mrs. Cox taught school until 1980, when she quit working after the birth of their first child. Mr. Cox provided the family's sole support thereafter. Over the years of the marriage, Mrs. Cox signed various documents, in which she became the co-owner of at least 14 parcels of real estate, a partner in at least two partnerships, and an officer or director in at least four corporations. Mrs. Cox did not actively participate in any of these ventures, and she did not question Stephen about any of these matters. In September 1984, the Cox family left Oregon for San Francisco to "escape some angry creditors," and then flew on to Hawaii, where they lived as fugitives for several months. On 29 October 1984, an involuntary petition in bankruptcy was filed against Mrs. Cox, and she eventually met with government agents and the trustee in bankruptcy to try to resolve the matter. (Mr. Cox remained a fugitive, and his whereabouts were unknown to the parties.) The trustee in bankruptcy objected to a discharge for Deborah Cox, alleging that she failed to keep proper books and records of her financial dealings, as required by bankruptcy law. She replied that her husband kept the records, so she did not feel a need to duplicate his efforts. Should the court grant Mrs. Cox a discharge in this case if the only objection was her inadequate books and records? Explain. [See *In re Cox*, 904 F.2d 1399 (9th Cir. 1990).]

4. New Concept Housing filed a petition for relief under Chapter 7 on 22 April 1988. On 24 July 1989, Poindexter filed a proof of claim for $185,436.16, the deficiency remaining after Poindexter foreclosed on two separate properties owned by the debtor and on which Poindexter held deeds of trust. The trustee examined the situation and settled the claims with Poindexter. The debtor objected to the settlement reached by the trustee and asked the court to review the matter. Should the trustee be allowed to settle the claims against the debtor without the debtor's permission in a case such as this? Explain. [See *In re New Concept Housing, Inc.*, 951 F.2d 932 (8th Cir. 1991).]

5. Ruth Herman owned and resided on real property located in San Bernardino, California. The property was encumbered by first and second trust deeds in the approximate amounts of $30,000 and $60,000, respectively. Harris obtained default judgments against Herman in two cases and recorded abstracts of these two judgments against Herman's property. As of August 1989, Herman owed approximately $43,000 on these two judgments, which constituted liens on her real property. On 18 May 1989, Herman filed a Chapter

7 petition in which she claimed an exemption in the residence in the amount of $75,000 under the homestead exemption provided in California law. The next day, Herman entered a contract to sell her residence for $149,500. Prior to the close of the sale, Herman moved to avoid Harris's judgment liens since the sale was voluntary, so that the homestead exemption should not apply. Should Harris's liens be avoided as liens that impair an otherwise available exemption for the debtor? [See *In re Herman,* 120 B.R. 127 (9th Cir. BAP 1990).]

6. **BUSINESS APPLICATION PROBLEM** The Rostecks purchased a condominium unit from Old Willow Falls Condominium Association in July 1981. They were obligated to pay assessments to the association monthly. In March 1983, the Rostecks purchased a new home and moved out of the condominium. Once they moved, the Rostecks stopped making any assessment payments to the association. In September 1983, the Rostecks filed a petition seeking relief under Chapter 7 of the Bankruptcy Code. In their schedules, they listed Old Willow Falls as a creditor, describing their debt as a "possible liability for condo assessments." The trustee abandoned his interest in the condominium unit and proceeded to handle the estate. The Rostecks were granted a discharge in December 1983. Two weeks after the discharge, Glenview State Bank filed a foreclosure action on the condominium unit. Eventually, the state court entered a foreclosure judgment in favor of Glenview State Bank and also allowed a lien to Old Willow Falls for the assessments levied against the condo after the bankruptcy petition was filed by the Rostecks. When Old Willow Falls attempted to collect this amount from the Rostecks, they filed a petition seeking relief from the claim with the bankruptcy court. Did the bankruptcy discharge the Rostecks's obligation to pay condominium assessments levied after they filed their bankruptcy petition? Should these fees be treated as contractual obligations or as covenants that run with the land? Explain you reasoning. [See *Matter of Rosteck,* 899 F.2d 684 (7th Cir. 1990).]

7. **ETHICAL APPLICATION PROBLEM** On 13 November 1987, Swicegood filed for relief under Chapter 7 of the U.S. Bankruptcy Code. His debts totaled $861,778.19, with $179,418 of this amount owed to Ginn from a default judgment on promissory notes. In his Statement of Financial Affairs and Schedule of Assets and Liabilities, Swicegood indicated that his assets totaled $12,700. On 12 February 1988, Ginn filed a complaint in bankruptcy court objecting to the discharge of Swicegood's debts on several grounds not relevant to this appeal. Ginn amended his complaint to add as a ground for objection that Swicegood had omitted from his bankruptcy schedule a Rolex watch, a set of silver flatware, two shares of AT&T stock, golf clubs, and two demitasse sterling silver cups. Swicegood learned from his former wife that she had reviewed his bankruptcy schedules with Ginn's counsel and had informed him that the items were omitted. As a result, Swicegood amended his schedule to include the items he had previously omitted. Did Swicegood intend to defraud his creditors by intentionally omitting certain assets in his schedules? Should Swicegood be denied a discharge in this case? What ethical issues are raised by a situation in which the debtor acts in the same manner as Swicegood is alleged to have acted? [See *Swicegood* v. *Ginn,* 924 F.2d 230 (11th Cir. 1991).]

8. **IDES PROBLEM** In 1975, Ingersoll and his wife acquired a one-half interest in two real estate lots in the Crystal Downs development, located in Benzie County, Michigan. In 1982, they acquired a one-half interest in a third lot in the same development. In 1980, Ingersoll, his father, and two others purchased Modern Wholesale Hardware, Inc. In 1982, the debtor's father formed a real estate investment and development corporation known as Hinchcliff Corporation. Eighty of the 920 shares in this firm were issued to Ingersoll. The debtor's father loaned Ingersoll and/or Modern Wholesale Hardware a total of $725,000 from 1983 through 1985. On 1 January 1984, Ingersoll agreed to transfer his interest in the first two lots in Crystal Downs and his 80 shares back to his father. Despite this transfer, Ingersoll continued to reside on the property and to pay the mortgage, maintenance, and taxes on the property. That same day, Ingersoll applied for a mortgage, using his alleged ownership of the Crystal Downs property and house as collateral for the loan. Also in 1984, Ingersoll received a 1979 Lincoln Towncar as a gift from his father. He owned and operated this car from 1984 through the date of his bankruptcy petition. Ingersoll breached—directly or indirectly—several contracts related to Modern Wholesale Hardware, which went bankrupt in August 1985. One creditor, in particular, sued Ingersoll, receiving a judgment in the amount of $668,872.12 on 23 April 1987. On 1 November 1985, Ingersoll gave his father a quitclaim deed on the Crystal Downs property. (This deed was not recorded until 29 January 1988.) Ingersoll filed a petition for relief under Chapter 7 of the Bankruptcy Code on 28 February 1988. In his schedule of assets, Ingersoll listed a 1976 Buick station wagon as his only automobile, he listed his homestead as his only real property, and he

denied any interest in any businesses, incorporated or unincorporated. The bankruptcy court ruled that Ingersoll was guilty of a fraudulent conveyance and of knowingly making a false oath in preparing his statements. Ingersoll appealed. Did the debtor make a fraudulent conveyance within one year of the date of his petition? Did he knowingly and fraudulently make a material false oath by failing to reveal his interest in the Lincoln Towncar? Explain your answers using the IDES legal analysis framework. [See *In re Ingersoll*, 124 B.R. 116 (M.D.Fla. 1991).]

NOTES

1. 458 U.S. 50 (1982).
2. Bankruptcy Reform Act of 1994, 11 U.S.C. § 326.
3. Ibid., 11 U.S.C. § 109(e).
4. Dan Cox, "Main Line Strikes Back; Basinger's Ch. 7 Filing Angers 'Boxing Helena' Producers," *Daily Variety* (29 December 1993), p. 3.

ALTERNATIVES TO STRAIGHT BANKRUPTCY

A G E N D A

The Kochanowskis sell Call-Image videophones to a number of businesses (the CIT technology is *very* popular for business conference calls), many of which are corporations. Although a lot of the sales are made on a cash basis, some customers purchase the units on credit. Tom and Anna are concerned that some of these credit customers may become insolvent and seek relief in bankruptcy. They want to know what can happen to their accounts in a Chapter 11 or a Chapter 13 bankruptcy proceeding. They are also concerned about their alternatives outside of bankruptcy if any customers are unable or unwilling to meet their payment schedules.

These and other questions may arise in the course of this chapter. Be prepared! You never know if or when the Kochanowskis will call on you for suggestions, guidance, or advice.

O U T L I N E

OTHER BANKRUPTCY PLANS

In the previous chapter, we examined a Chapter 7 liquidation proceeding, commonly referred to as a straight bankruptcy. Many people have the mistaken idea that Chapter 7 proceedings are all the Bankruptcy Reform Act covers. In reality, several other types of proceedings are also available under the Bankruptcy Reform Act. The first sections of this chapter discuss three of the Bankruptcy Reform Act proceedings: a reorganization under Chapter 11, a repayment plan for family farmers under Chapter 12, and a wage earner's repayment plan under Chapter 13. None of these plans calls for a liquidation of the debtor's assets in order to cover the debts; and under these plans, the creditors can reasonably expect to be paid more than would be received under a liquidation proceeding. In fact, many times the creditors will be paid in full by the debtor. In the last sections of the chapter, we discuss alternatives to bankruptcy. These nonbankruptcy alternatives are available under state statutes or through the application of common law principles, in contrast to the federal statutes that provide for bankruptcy. Ironically, a number of these nonbankruptcy alternatives may provide the necessary "action" by the debtor to permit the creditors to file an involuntary petition against the debtor.

Reorganizations: Chapter 11

Chapter 11 bankruptcy proceedings, known as *reorganizations,* are designed to allow the debtor to adjust his or her financial situation, restructuring the business financially in order to save the enterprise. Chapter 11 is used by debtors to avoid liquidations. Although reorganizations are designed primarily for use by corporate debtors, individuals are also allowed to use the reorganization format. The following case examined whether an individual is allowed to use Chapter 11 rather than Chapter 7.

30.1 TOIBB v. RADLOFF 111 S.Ct. 22197 (1991)

FACTS Toibb filed a voluntary petition for relief under Chapter 7 of the Bankruptcy Code. The Schedule of Assets and Liabilities accompanying this petition disclosed that Toibb had no secured debts, a disputed federal tax claim of $11,000, and various other unsecured debts totaling $170,605. He only listed two nonexempt assets; 24% of the stock of Independence Electric Corporation (IEC) and a possible claim against his former business associates. The Schedule stated that the value of each of these assets was unknown. During the course of the Chapter 7 proceedings, the trustee informed the creditors that IEC had offered to purchase Toibb's shares in the firm for $25,000. When Toibb discovered that the stock had such a substantial value, he decided to avoid liquidation by converting to a Chapter 11 proceeding. The bankruptcy court initially approved his petition, and Toibb filed his reorganization plan. At that point, the court dismissed his petition, finding that he did not qualify for relief under Chapter 11 because he was not engaged in an ongoing business. Toibb appealed.

ISSUE Was Toibb entitled to seek relief under Chapter 11 of the Bankruptcy Code despite the fact that he was not engaged in operating an ongoing business?

HOLDING Yes. Chapter 11 is not restricted to business debtors, although they are the debtors most likely to take advantage of its provisions.

REASONING The court took a literal view of the provisions of the Bankruptcy Code, which provides that "a person who may be a debtor under Chapter 7 . . . except a stockbroker or a commodity broker, and a railroad may be a debtor under Chapter 11." Toibb was entitled to file as a debtor under Chapter 7 (as, indeed, he originally did); he was not a stockbroker or a commodity broker, so there was no valid reason for dismissing his petition for relief under Chapter 11. From the legislative history, it is apparent that Chapter 11 was intended primarily for ongoing businesses; there is no ongoing business requirement in the Code, and the court found no reason for imposing one.

30.1 TOIBB v. RADLOFF *(cont.)* 111 S.Ct. 22197 (1991)

BUSINESS CONSIDERATIONS Why would the value of a debtor's nonexempt assets affect the debtor's decision to seek relief under Chapter 11 rather than under Chapter 7? What other factors should a debtor consider before deciding which bankruptcy chapter offers the best "fresh start"?

ETHICAL CONSIDERATIONS Is it fair to allow a debtor to select the bankruptcy chapter under which he or she will seek relief? Can an argument be made that it is more ethical to allow the *creditors* to make this decision?

The major advantages of a reorganization are that it allows a business to continue, and it forces creditors who object to go along with the plan despite their objections. In addition, the creditors normally will receive more than they would have in a liquidation under Chapter 7.

Any debtor who can use Chapter 7, except stockbrokers and commodity brokers, can also use Chapter 11. Moreover, railroads, which are prohibited from using Chapter 7, can take advantage of the provisions of Chapter 11. Like a liquidation proceeding, a reorganization may be either voluntary or involuntary. In addition, the same limitations apply here as apply to a liquidation petition (refer to pages 724–726 for a description of how petitions may be initiated).

The Proceedings. Once the petition has been filed, the court will do three things:

1. It will enter an order for relief.
2. It will appoint a trustee, if requested to do so by any interested party.
3. It will appoint creditor committees to represent the creditors. (Equity security holders will be represented by a separate committee.)

If no interested party asks for the appointment of a trustee, the debtor is permitted to retain possession and control of the assets and/or the business (such a debtor is referred to as a *debtor-in-possession*). The committees appointed by the court will meet with the trustee, if one is appointed, or with the debtor-in-possession, if no trustee is appointed, to discuss the treatment of the proceedings. The committees also will investigate the debtor's finances and financial potential, and they will help prepare a plan for reorganizing the enterprise that will benefit all the interested parties.

In the event that no one asks for the appointment of a trustee, the court may appoint an examiner. The examiner or the trustee will investigate the debtor, the debtor's business activities, and the debtor's business potential. On the basis of this investigation, a recommendation will be made to the court. The recommendation may be a reorganization plan, or it may be a suggestion that the proceedings be transferred from Chapter 11 to Chapter 7 (liquidation) or to Chapter 13 (wage earner plan). The court normally will follow such a recommendation unless a good reason not to follow it is presented.

The debtor-in-possession is deemed to have the same basic duties as a trustee, including the fiduciary duty owed to the creditors. In the following case one creditor objected to the conduct of the debtor-in-possession and attempted to assume those duties itself. Note how the court addressed the competing claims and interests of the two creditors.

30.2 IN RE SRJ ENTERPRISES, INC. 151 B.R. 189 (Bkrtcy.N.D.Ill. 1993)

FACTS SRJ Enterprises, Inc. (SRJ) owned and operated a Nissan automobile dealership. NBD Park Ridge Bank (NBD) financed SRJ's new vehicle inventory with a loan of approximately $1,400,000 in March 1991. NBD took and perfected a security interest that purportedly covered all the debtor's assets. As additional security, the president of SRJ guaranteed the loan. Later SRJ borrowed an additional $900,000 from Success National Bank. Success claims to hold a perfected lien on assets of SRJ already subject to NBD's lien. The NBD loan agreement required that SRJ receive and hold all its inventory, and the proceeds from its inventory sales, in trust. NBD also required SRJ to keep a separate account of each item of inventory, to segregate the sales proceeds held in trust, and to pay these proceeds to NBD. Using the jargon of the automobile financing industry, NBD provided "floor planning" financing and employed a "trust receipt" repayment device. According to Success, however, NBD failed to enforce its agreement with SRJ, and as a result SRJ withheld approximately $600,000 of trust proceeds from NBD. Success argues that NBD allowed SRJ to become "out of trust" in an effort to salvage the loan and the business relationship between SRJ and NBD.

At the date of the bankruptcy petition, SRJ owed NBD more than $1,400,000, an amount that Success argues would have been less had NBD enforced its loan agreement with SRJ. SRJ, as debtor-in-possession, sold its assets and franchise rights free and clear of all liens for an amount less than $1,400,000. To the extent they were valid, the lien rights of NBD and of Success attached to the proceeds of this sale. In connection with the sale NBD filed an adversary proceeding against SRJ and Success to determine the validity and the priority of NBD's liens. SRJ and Success filed counterclaims against NBD. (SRJ subsequently dropped its counterclaim.) In its counterclaim, Success alleged that NBD had received a voidable preference and sought to recover the property transferred preferentially. Success also sought to subordinate the claims of NBD. NBD objected to the motion by Success and filed its own motion to dismiss the counterclaim of Success due to Success's lack of standing.

ISSUES Did Success have standing to challenge the alleged preferential transfers from SRJ to NBD, to the detriment of Success?

HOLDINGS No. Success lacked standing to bring this case, and its motion must be dismissed.

REASONING The Bankruptcy Code provides that "the *trustee* may avoid any transfer of an interest of the debtor in property" that constitutes a preferential transfer, and that a debtor-in-possession shall have the powers, rights and duties of a trustee. Therefore, a trustee or a debtor-in-possession can avoid a preference. Success argues that it, too, has standing to avoid a preference because the debtor-in-possession failed to bring suit to avoid the transfer. Such an interpretation is clearly inconsistent with the clear and unequivocal language of the Bankruptcy Code. Success could have petitioned the court to have a trustee appointed or to have an examiner appointed if the debtor-in-possession breaches his duty or fails to act as a fiduciary for the creditors.

Success asserts that it should be able to stand in the shoes of the debtor to pursue a voidable preference against NBD because the debtor voluntarily dismissed its preference action against NBD. Success does not allege that SRJ breached its fiduciary duty in doing so. In fact, Success admits that "it is impossible for creditors to determine whether the debtor's abandonment of its own adversary proceeding is justified where the debtor fails to comply with discovery." Success feels that *maybe* there is a cause of action out there that could be asserted for its benefit. So, in order to "see if a fire rages," Success filed its motions. To Success, it may appear as though it is caught in a procedural catch-22. It has no standing because it cannot show that SRJ unjustifiably refused to bring a voidable preference action—but it cannot seek discovery to prove such unjustified refusal if it has no standing. Success has a remedy, however. Success is entitled to file a motion for the appointment of an examiner. Therefore, Success lacks standing to pursue these remedies. As a result, NBD's Motion to Dismiss is granted and Success's Motion to Prosecute Countercomplainant is denied.

BUSINESS CONSIDERATIONS What steps should Success have taken as a junior secured creditor to protect its interests in this situation? What should Success have done differently in an effort to protect itself from a bankruptcy by SRJ?

ETHICAL CONSIDERATIONS The auto dealer in this case was bankrupt and had sold the business. The proceeds of the sale were not sufficient to cover the claims of both creditors. Should the debtor have prosecuted the alleged preferential transfer claim in order to either provide some payment to the junior creditor, or at least to show the junior creditor that the debtor had done everything possible to protect the interests of the junior creditor? What duties are owed to the creditors by a debtor who is seeking relief in bankruptcy?

The Plan. The purpose of a reorganization is to develop a plan under which the debtor can avoid liquidation while somehow managing to satisfy the claims of the creditors. Obviously, the right to propose a plan can be very important. If the debtor remains in possession (i.e., no trustee is appointed), only the debtor may propose a plan during the first 120 days after the order for relief. Any interested party (debtor, creditor, stockholder, or trustee) can propose a plan under any of three conditions:

1. If a trustee is appointed, any interested party can propose a plan at any time until a plan is approved by the court.
2. If the debtor fails to propose a plan within the 120-day period, any interested party can propose a plan.
3. If the debtor proposes a plan within 120 days, but it is not accepted by all affected classes of creditors within 180 days of the order for relief, any interested party can propose a plan to the court.

The 1994 Bankruptcy Reform Act includes provisions for a "fast track" reorganization for small-business debtors. To be eligible, the business must have less than $2 million in liabilities, and it cannot have as its primary activity the owning or managing of real estate. The debtor must file a plan within 100 days, rather than the 120 days granted under a "regular" Chapter 11. All plans must be filed within 160 days, as opposed to the 180 days granted under a "regular" Chapter 11.

For a plan to be confirmed, it must designate all claims by class as well as specify which classes will be impaired and which will not be impaired. It must also show how the plan can be implemented successfully. Among the factors that the court will examine are the following:

1. Plans to sell any assets
2. Plans to merge, consolidate, or divest
3. Plans to satisfy, or modify, any liens or claims
4. Plans to issue new stock to generate funds

If new stock is to be issued, it must have voting rights. No new nonvoting stock may be issued under a reorganization plan. Each class of creditors that is impaired is allowed to vote on the plan.

A class is deemed to have accepted the plan if creditors having at least two-thirds of the dollar amount involved and more than one-half of the total number of creditors vote in favor of the plan. If a creditor class is not impaired by the plan, it does not need to approve the plan.

Despite the vote, no plan can be accepted or rejected by the creditors. The final word is left to the court. The court will hold a hearing on the plan, and the court can confirm or reject it. The court can confirm a plan if it is accepted by at least one class of creditors. If all the creditor classes approve the plan, the court normally will confirm it. Similarly, if all the creditor classes reject the plan, the court normally will reject it. Still the final word is with the court alone. The vote of the creditor classes simply provides the court with guidance.

Once the court approves a plan, it becomes binding on everyone affected by it. The court also will look at the plan's fairness to each interested group, especially those creditors impaired by the plan. The court also will look at the viability of the plan. Finally, if the court feels the plan will not work or is not fair, the court can order the proceedings converted to a Chapter 7 liquidation. This last-ditch power encourages everyone involved to act in good faith, since Chapter 11 usually is better than Chapter 7 for all concerned.

Chapter 11 as a Corporate Strategy. Reorganizations have recently taken on an interesting twist. A number of corporations, some of which are very large and successful, have availed themselves of Chapter 11 to escape or avoid potentially onerous debts or obligations. Johns-Manville was, at one time, a giant in the asbestos industry. When the effect of asbestos on health became known, Johns-Manville was faced with potential liability to its customers and employees that could have literally reached billions of dollars. Despite the size and success of the firm, such liability would have destroyed Johns-Manville. Rather than await the imposition of such a liability, Johns-Manville went to court seeking a reorganization under Chapter 11. The firm proposed the establishment of a trust fund to be used for victims entitled to compensation due to asbestos-related health problems.[1] The court approved the reorganization plan, and the firm endowed the trust with millions of dollars and continued to operate the business. The firm recently paid its first dividends in several years and has once again assumed its position on the *Fortune* 500 list.

Similar strategies have been used to escape other potentially disastrous liabilities. Several firms have recently used Chapter 11 to avoid burdensome labor contracts. The following case shows how one bankruptcy case involving such a labor contract was resolved. Notice how the court justified approval of the plan despite the objection of the union.

30.3 IN RE APPLETREE MARKETS, INC.

155 B.R. 431 (S.D.Tex. 1993)

FACTS AppleTree Markets, Inc., filed a petition for relief under Chapter 11 of the Bankruptcy Act. As part of its reorganization plan, AppleTree proposed rejecting the collective bargaining agreement (CBA) it had with the United Food and Commercial Workers (UFCW) Local Unions. AppleTree argues that the UFCW participated in the drafting of AppleTree's First Amended Disclosure Statement in connection with its Second Amended Plan of Reorganization under Chapter 11. According to AppleTree, the disclosure statement was premised in part on the benefits that the bankruptcy estate would receive from the rejection of the collective bargaining agreements. The Bankruptcy Court approved the plan on 29 September 1992. Because the UFCW did not appeal the plan, it became final and nonappealable in October of 1992. The collective bargaining agreements expired by their own terms early in 1993. The UFCW then appealed the decision of the Bankruptcy Court to reject the collective bargaining agreement. AppleTree argues that the appeal by the UFCW is moot because the substantial consummation of the plan has so changed the circumstances as to render appellate relief both ineffective and inequitable to the parties to the plan.

ISSUE Should the UFCW be allowed to appeal the Bankruptcy Court's rejection of the collective bargaining agreement after the debtor's reorganization plan, including the rejection of the collective bargaining agreement, has been approved and implemented?

HOLDING While the court held that the UFCW's appeal was not moot, it ruled that the plan as approved was valid and upheld the rejection of the collective bargaining agreement.

REASONING Dismissal of appeals from confirmation orders on mootness grounds may be warranted because of one or more equitable considerations: (1) substantial consummation of a plan may preclude a reviewing court from granting effective relief if the confirmation order is set aside, (2) innocent parties may have acted in reliance upon the confirmation order, and (3) the relief sought on appeal may jeopardize the entire plan. . . . The test for mootness reflects a court's concern for striking the proper balance between the equitable considerations of finality and good faith reliance on a judgment and the competing interests that underlie the right of a party to seek review of a bankruptcy court order adversely affecting him. . . . This court has evaluated all of the arguments urged by AppleTree in support of its motion to dismiss. In attempting to strike a proper balance between these considerations the court is not persuaded that the confirmation and substantial consummation of the plan have so changed the circumstances

30.3 IN RE APPLETREE MARKETS, INC. *(cont.)* 155 B.R. 431 (S.D.Tex. 1993)

as to render appellate relief ineffective or inequitable. AppleTree's Amended Motion to Dismiss Appeal as Moot will therefore be denied . . .

To reject a collective bargaining agreement the bankruptcy court must find

> *(1) that before the hearing on the motion for rejection the trustee has made a proposal to modify the agreement that fulfills the requirements of the Code,*
> *(2) that the Union refused to accept the proposal without good cause, and*
> *(3) that "the balance of the equities clearly favors rejection of such agreement.". . . .*

The Bankruptcy Court found that AppleTree's proposed modifications to the CBAs were fair and equitable to all affected parties. The UFCW argues, as it did to the Bankruptcy Court, that AppleTree's proposed modifications were unfair because they did not require reductions in compensation for management and did not include any "snap-back" or other incentives to allow employees to recoup the reductions included in AppleTree's proposed modifications.

The Bankruptcy Court found, and the record corroborates, that AppleTree's costs under the CBAs were above prevailing competitive wage levels, while management salaries at AppleTree had already decreased from prior levels and were at or below prevailing levels among AppleTree's competitors. The evidence also showed that management had shared other burdens caused by AppleTree's bad financial condition. As AppleTree closed almost half of its stores, managers and assistant managers lost their jobs, with no opportunity to 'bump" other managers and with no seniority to bump nonmanagerial employees for jobs at the stores that remained open. Management benefits had declined so that AppleTree was barely competitive, was experiencing difficulty in attracting people to entry-level management positions, and salary reductions among managers would result in losses of good people at this level. . . .

The UFCW's snap-back argument consists of two sentences: "the Company did not offer any snap-back or incentives to allow the employees to recover any of the sacrifices it was demanding. . . . This is not fair and is not equitable." . . . Neither the absence of a snap-back provision nor the failure to reduce further the salary and benefits paid to management makes AppleTree's proposed modifications unfair or inequitable. . . . Taken as a whole, AppleTree's proposed modifications were necessary.

Because this court concludes that the Bankruptcy Court's legal determinations are correct and its factual findings are not clearly erroneous, the order of the Bankruptcy Court rejecting the UFCW's CBAs with AppleTree is affirmed.

BUSINESS CONSIDERATIONS Presume that a business proposes a reorganization plan that includes rejection of a collective bargaining agreement. Should management show its willingness to make sacrifices in its salary and benefits package before asking the court the allow the firm to reject the collective bargaining agreement? How much should management have to sacrifice before it can properly ask nonmanagement workers to make sacrifices to save the firm?

ETHICAL CONSIDERATIONS Is it ethical for management to negotiate a collective bargaining agreement with a union knowing that the business can possibly escape the agreement in Chapter 11? Should negotiators for the firm tell union representatives that an overly generous agreement may lead to bankruptcy and a rejection of the agreement as a method of saving the business?

Repayment Plans for Farmers: Chapter 12

Historically, U.S. public policy has provided special protections for farmers. For the most part, this has benefited farmers, but in some instances it has not proved to be such a benefit. One area in which the public policy considerations that urged protection of farmers turned out to be less than ideal was bankruptcy. Under Chapter 7, a farmer cannot be involuntarily petitioned into bankruptcy. While this protects the farmer from an involuntary liquidation, it might leave that farmer unable to forestall creditors who might otherwise have resorted to a bankruptcy proceeding.

Admittedly, the farmer can file a voluntary petition, but that will lead to a liquidation—and probably the loss of the farm.

To further complicate the dilemma, farmers who operate large farms are likely to have debts in excess of the ceilings imposed by Chapter 13, which precludes the use of a repayment plan. This left farmers with two options: avoid bankruptcy, using nonbankruptcy alternatives to resolve the financial problems; or make use of Chapter 11, reorganizing the financial condition and position of the operation in an effort to salvage the farm. In many cases, neither alternative was particularly attractive to the debtor–farmer.

As a result, in 1986, Chapter 12, "Adjustment of Debts for Family Farmers," was added to the Bankruptcy Code. Chapter 12 seems to be a hybrid chapter, combining elements of Chapter 11 and Chapter 13 to produce a specialized, custom-tailored method for granting relief to family farmers.

Under Chapter 12 of the Bankruptcy Code, family farmers who have debts of no more than $1.5 million are allowed to use a special reorganization/repayment plan designed for this one special type of debtor. Chapter 12 allows a family farmer to develop a repayment plan despite a total debt in excess of that allowed under Chapter 13 for other individual debtors and to reorganize the farm and its financial structure to a significant extent in the development of that plan.

The Proceedings. A family farmer can file a voluntary petition for relief under the provisions of Chapter 12 but cannot be involuntarily petitioned into court. Upon the filing of the petition, the court enters an order for relief and the automatic stay provision of bankruptcy law takes effect. The petitioning farmer will be allowed to continue to operate the farm as a debtor-in-possession unless there is an objection and a showing of cause for removal of the debtor and the appointment of a trustee. If the debtor remains in possession, the debtor can exercise all powers that would be available to a trustee under a Chapter 11 proceeding.

The Plan. The debtor must either present a plan for the adjustment of debts within 90 days of the petition or must request an extension of time for the preparation of such a plan. The court can also unilaterally extend the time period if it feels that there were circumstances beyond the control of the debtor that made it unduly difficult to meet the 90-day deadline.

The plan must provide for the payment in full in deferred payments of the debts of the farmer. The plan

30.1

FINANCE/SALES

CHAPTER 11 BANKRUPTCY

Mail-Mart, a mail-order retail business, purchased 4,000 Call-Image videophones from CIT on credit. Mail-Mart gave CIT a security interest in all its electronic inventory to secure the credit, and CIT properly perfected its interest prior to delivering the phones. Mail-Mart has filed a petition for relief under Chapter 11 of the Bankruptcy Act and has submitted a reorganization plan to the court. This plan calls for the release of all current security interests on its inventory, thus allowing Mail-Mart to use its inventory as collateral to obtain new financing from a bank. Mail-Mart has also proposed that its payments to the former secured creditors be maintained at the same interest rates, but with an extension in the number of payments to be made to each creditor.

Dan thinks the plan proposed by Mail-Mart will cost CIT a great deal of money and he opposes the plan. Tom is also concerned, but thinks the firm can handle this situation, provided all the payments still owed are, in fact, made by Mail-Mart. However, the firm would be better served either receiving its scheduled payments or enforcing its security interest. They have asked you how they should proceed. What are CIT's rights in this situation? How should the firm proceed?

BUSINESS CONSIDERATIONS Any time a business extends credit to a customer that business assumes the risk of default or bankruptcy affecting the account. What can a business like CIT do to protect itself short of refusing to make credit sales? Why would a business *not* decide to deal strictly on a cash-and-carry basis?

ETHICAL CONSIDERATIONS Suppose that a customer is encountering financial difficulties and facing the possibility of failure. That customer asks for an extension of the time for making its payments. What considerations would cause a creditor to agree to the extension? When should the creditor take a hard-line stance and refuse to vary the payment terms?

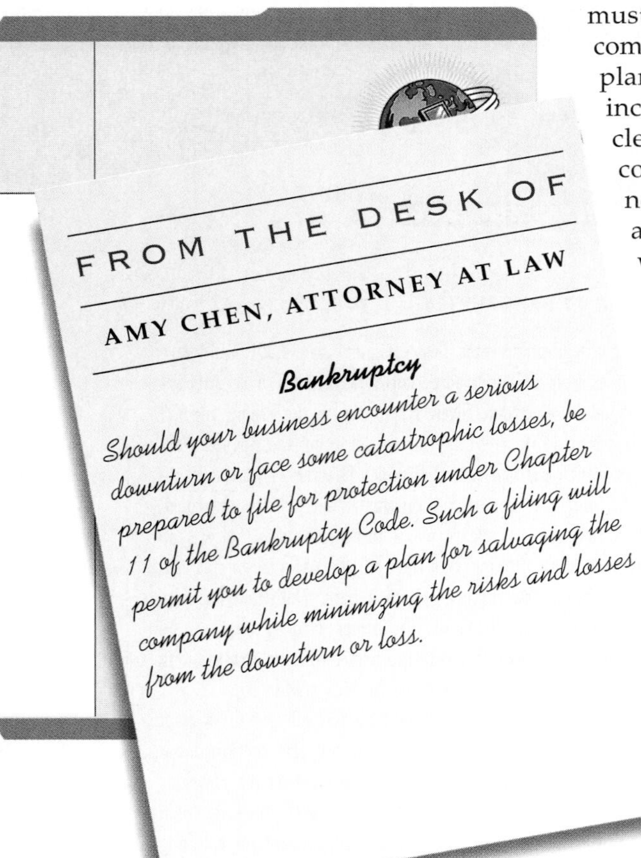

must also provide for the submission of a portion of the future income of the farmer into the plan for distribution to the creditors. The plan can call for the sale of any or all of the property of the debtor, including farm land and equipment, and such sales are free and clear of any claims of the creditors. Once a plan is submitted, the court will call for a confirmation hearing. This hearing is to occur no later than 45 days after the plan is submitted. Any party with an interest may object to the plan at this hearing, and the court will consider the objections before ruling on the plan. However, if the court feels that the plan conforms to the provisions of Chapter 12, that it has been proposed in good faith, and that it is capable of performance by the debtor, the plan will be approved.

FROM THE DESK OF
AMY CHEN, ATTORNEY AT LAW
Bankruptcy
Should your business encounter a serious downturn or face some catastrophic losses, be prepared to file for protection under Chapter 11 of the Bankruptcy Code. Such a filing will permit you to develop a plan for salvaging the company while minimizing the risks and losses from the downturn or loss.

A Chapter 12 proceeding can be converted to a Chapter 7 proceeding at the request of the debtor at any time. In addition, the proceeding can be converted to a Chapter 7 proceeding upon the request of any interested party, provided that the requesting party can present evidence of fraud in connection with the case. Thus, if the farmer commits a fraud in the case and then seeks relief under Chapter 12, his or her creditors can request a removal to Chapter 7, in effect involuntarily petitioning the farmer into a liquidation proceeding.

The following case dealt with a debt adjustment plan under Chapter 12 of the Bankruptcy Code and its removal to Chapter 7.

30.4 IN RE PLATA

958 F.2d 918 (9th Cir. 1992)

FACTS The Platas filed a petition for relief under Chapter 12 of the Bankruptcy Code in 1987. They submitted a plan early the following year, and the plan as submitted was confirmed by the court. Under the terms of the plan, $29,000 was to be paid to the trustee during 1988, and the trustee would then distribute this money to the creditors. When it became apparent during 1988 that the crops for the year would not generate sufficient income to meet the payment required under the plan, the Platas converted their case from Chapter 12 to Chapter 7. At the time of the conversion, the trustee held $14,000 which had not been distributed.

Upon conversion to Chapter 7, the Platas claimed $8,300 of those undistributed dollars as exempt assets under the provisions of the Code. The trustee objected to the return of this money to the debtors.

ISSUE Did the creditors obtain a vested right in the proceeds paid to the trustee prior to distribution?

HOLDING No. Until the proceeds were distributed the creditors had no vested rights in the money.

REASONING The court began its opinion by explaining what it meant for the debtors to file for relief under Chapter 12. According to the court, the "debtors created an estate consisting not only of all existing legal and equitable interests in their property, . . . but also of all property and earnings acquired 'after the commencement of the case but before the case [was] closed, dismissed, or converted to . . . Chapter 7.'" Since this issue had not previously been addressed under Chapter 12, the court then looked to similar cases under Chapter 13. Using these earlier opinions as a

30.4 IN RE PLATA *(cont.)* 958 F.2d 918 (9th Cir. 1992)

foundation, the court ruled that the conversion of a case from Chapter 12 to Chapter 7 causes an automatic reversion of any monies paid to the trustee under the plan but not yet distributed to the creditors. The debtors were entitled to the return of their funds, and were then entitled to take from those funds any exemptions permitted under the applicable exemption statute.

BUSINESS CONSIDERATIONS Why are special protections given to "family farmers" that are not made equally available to corporate farming operations? What public policy considerations exist for excluding corporate farms from using Chapter 12 of the Bankruptcy Code?

ETHICAL CONSIDERATIONS Is it ethical for a debtor who has already initiated a bankruptcy proceeding to change Chapters when he or she discovers that a different chapter will provide the debtor with a better financial position at the end of the proceedings?

YOU BE THE JUDGE

Quibell Files for Chapter 11 Bankruptcy

Quibell, a local producer of bottled water, has encountered serious financial difficulties. When Quibell was unable to pay for the bottles it ordered for its water, the bottle manufacturer stopped delivering bottles. Without bottles, Quibell was unable to "package" its product and get it into stores, causing an even worse cash flow problem. Finally, Quibell was forced to shut down its operation, laying off all its workers. When the plant shut down, the creditors filed suit for the amounts that they were owed. Quibell then filed for relief under Chapter 11 of the Bankruptcy Code, forestalling the claims of the creditors. Quibell has proposed the sale of its entire operation to another bottled water company as its Chapter 11 Reorganization Plan. The bottle manufacturer, Quibell's largest creditor, objects to the sale unless it is given some assurance that it will be paid.[2]

This case has been brought before *your* court. How will you decide this case?

BUSINESS CONSIDERATIONS Should the owner of a regional business that is facing failure unless it is able to reorganize under Chapter 11 be most concerned with the rights of the employees, the customers, the creditors, or the community? How optimistic should a firm be when it files its plan for reorganization?

ETHICAL CONSIDERATIONS Presume that a relatively small, family-owned and operated corporation is facing financial problems. Should that business file a Chapter 11 petition to forestall the creditors, or should it "face the music" and face numerous lawsuits for breach of contract? Is it ethical to use the provisions of the Bankruptcy Code to minimize personal losses, even though that results in larger losses for creditors who helped the family to get the business operating in the first place?

SOURCE: *The Roanoke Times*, June 14, 1996, p. A7.

Repayment Plans: Chapter 13

Chapter 13 of the Bankruptcy Reform Act is designed to allow a debtor with a regular source of income to adjust his or her debts in a manner that (hopefully) will repay all creditors. Chapter 13 plans are available only to individual debtors; they cannot be used by corporations. As a further restriction, they are available only to debtors who have less than $1 million of debt, with a maximum of $750,000 in secured debts and a maximum of $250,000 in unsecured debts. (Prior to the 1994 Bankruptcy Bill, the debt ceilings for a Chapter 13 repayment plan limited the debtor to no more than $100,000 in unsecured debts and no more than $350,000 in secured debts.) There is also a cost-of-living adjustment (COLA) provision in the 1994 Bankruptcy Bill. The debt ceiling for Chapter 13 proceedings will be adjusted to inflation every three years, thus (hopefully) allowing this relief to keep up with inflation and negating the need for periodic adjustments. The debt ceilings in effect prior to 6 October 1994 made Chapter 13 unavailable to many farmers, which led to the creation of Chapter 12. The increase in consumer debt, coupled with inflation from 1978 through 1994, made the debt ceiling an impediment to the public policy objectives of Chapter 13 proceedings, and led to the upward revision on allowable debt and to the inflation adjustment mechanism now in effect.

Debtors who exceed the debt ceiling will have to use Chapter 7, Chapter 11, or some nonbankruptcy alternative. Chapter 13 is only available by means of a voluntary petition. The debtor can seek relief under this option, but the creditors cannot force a debtor to enter a repayment plan. (However, the threat of forcing a debtor into Chapter 7 may persuade the debtor that Chapter 13 is in his or her best interests.)

The Proceedings. In many respects, a repayment plan is the simplest bankruptcy proceeding for an individual debtor. The debtor files a voluntary petition seeking relief. The court will issue an order for relief, an automatic stay takes effect, and a trustee will be appointed. The trustee will perform the investigation duties normally followed under a reorganization, but only if the debtor operates a business. In addition, the trustee will carry out the plan proposed by the debtor, if the plan is approved by the court.

The Plan. The debtor must file a proposed repayment plan with the court. The plan must provide equal treatment to each creditor claim within any given class of creditors. This does not mean that each class must be treated equally—only that within each class, every creditor must be treated equally. The plan also must make some provisions for clearing up any defaulted debts or defaulted payments on debts. The plan must not call for payments beyond a three-year period, unless the court feels that a longer period is necessary. Even then, the plan must be carried out within five years.

The court will approve the plan if the following conditions are met:

1. The plan appears to be fair to all parties.
2. The plan is in the best interests of the creditors.
3. It appears that the debtor can conform to the plan.
4. The plan proposes to pay at least as much as would have been paid under Chapter 7.

Once approved, the plan is binding on all parties, with or without their consent. At that point, the debtor must turn over to the trustee enough of the debtor's income to make the payments called for under the plan.

If the debtor performs the plan as approved, the court will grant a discharge. The discharge terminates all debts provided for in the plan—if they are dischargeable in a liquidation—that received their full share under the plan. In addition, the court can intercede and grant a discharge during the plan, even though the plan has not been completely carried out. The court will do so only if the following three factors are present:

1. The debtor cannot complete the plan owing to circumstances beyond the debtor's control.
2. The general (lowest-priority) creditors have received at least as much as they would have received in a liquidation.
3. The court does not feel it is practical to alter the plan.

The likelihood of such a court intervention during the plan is not very high, but the option is there. And, once again, the desire to provide a fresh start for an honest debtor is obvious.

The following case deals with the right of an "oversecured" mortgagee to recover interest on his debt even if the plan does not provide for interest. Note how the court attempts to balance the interests and rights of the parties in its opinion.

30.5 RAKE v. WADE

113 S.Ct. 2187 (1993)

FACTS At the time they initiated their bankruptcy petitions the Rakes (and two other couples, each of whom filed separate petitions) were in arrears on long-term promissory notes held by Wade, the trustee, which were secured by home mortgages. The notes in question did not provide for the payment of interest on any arrearages, although they did provide for a $5 charge for each missed payment. The value of the residence owned by each of the debtors exceeded each note's outstanding balance, making Wade an oversecured creditor. In their repayment plans the debtors proposed to make all future payments due on the notes and to cure the default on the mortgages by paying off the arrearages without interest. Wade objected to each plan on the ground that he was entitled to interest and attorney's fees. The Bankruptcy Court overruled the objections, and the District Court affirmed. The Court of Appeals reversed, ruling that Wade was entitled to postpetition interest on the arrearages and any other charges, even if the mortgage notes were silent on the subject and state law would not require the payment of interest.

ISSUE Must Chapter 13 debtors who cure a default on an oversecured home mortgage pay postpetition interest on the arrearages?

HOLDING Yes. An oversecured creditor is entitled to recover both preconfirmation and postconfirmation interest on the arrearages that were paid off under the debtor's plan.

REASONING The mortgage instruments in question provided that in the event of a default by the debtors, the holder of the note had the right to declare the remainder of indebtedness due and payable and to foreclose on the property. Because the value of the residence owned by each of the debtors exceeded the balance on the corresponding notes, Wade was an oversecured creditor.

Petitioners' Chapter 13 plans proposed to "cure" the defaults on the oversecured home mortgages by establishing repayment schedules for the arrearages. Three interrelated provisions of the Bankruptcy Code determine whether respondent is entitled to interest on those arrearages: Sections 506(b), 1322(b), and 1325(a)(5).

Section 506(b) provides that holders of oversecured claims are "allowed" postpetition interest on their claims. The Court had previously held that the right to postpetition interest is "unqualified" and exists regardless of whether the agreement giving rise to the claim provides for interest. It is generally recognized that the interest allowed will accrue until payment of the secured claim or until the effective date of the plan.

Section 1322(b) authorizes debtors to modify the rights of secured creditors, but it provides protection for home mortgage lenders by creating a specific "no modification" exception for holders of claims secured only by a line on the debtor's principal residence. This section expressly authorizes debtors to cure any defaults on long-term debt, such as a mortgage.

30.5 RAKE v. WADE (cont.) 113 S.Ct. 2187 (1993)

The final provision bearing on this case—Section 1325(a)(5)—states that "with respect to each allowed secured claim provided for by the plan," one of three requirements must be satisfied before the plan can be confirmed: (1) the holder of the claim has accepted the plan; (2) the debtor surrenders the property securing such claims to the secured creditor; or (3) the holder of the secured claim retains the lien securing such claim. Thus, unless the creditor accepts the plan or the debtor surrenders the property, the payments made must equal the present dollar value of the claim as of the confirmation date. When a creditor must be paid the present value, this implies the payment of interest. Further, Section 506(b) "directs that postpetition interest be paid on *all* oversecured claims." The arrearages on the debts are clearly part of the oversecured claims, and the debtors must pay interest on these arrearages, as well as on the debts themselves.

BUSINESS CONSIDERATIONS What benefits accrue to the debtor who is allowed to redeem oversecured collateral sufficient to justify the payment of interest on arrearages as a part of the plan? Do these same benefits exist to call for the imposition of interest on "undersecured" collateral?

ETHICAL CONSIDERATIONS Why should special considerations that are not applied to other types of secured debts apply to a home mortgage debt in a bankruptcy proceeding? Are there ethical concerns involved with the possible loss of the debtor's home in a bankruptcy proceeding?

Congress did not like the court's opinion in *Rake* v. *Wade.* The Bankruptcy Reform Act of 1994 contains a section intended to overrule the court's opinion. The 1994 act provides:

> Interest on Interest. *This provision is applicable in Chapter 11, 12 and 13 cases, and provides that if a plan cures a default, the liability for interest is to be determined in accordance with the agreement and nonbankruptcy law. The purpose is to overrule* Rake *v.* Wade *. . . , which required the payment of interest on mortgage arrearages when the chapter 13 debtor attempted to cure the default and reinstate the mortgage even if not contained in the agreement and not required by State law.*[3]

1984 Bankruptcy Amendments. The Bankruptcy Amendments of 1984 have tightened the requirements for a Chapter 13 repayment plan. The new standards also reduce the burden on the courts, since the good faith of the debtor is not an issue. Rather, a more tangible standard than the apparent good faith of the debtor has been substituted.

The more recent law allows any unsecured creditor to block the debtor's proposed repayment plan if the plan does not meet one of two criteria:

1. The plan calls for the payment of 100 percent of the creditor's claim;
2. The plan calls for the debtor to pay 100 percent of all income not necessary to support the debtor's immediate family for at least three years.

Unless the debtor shows that the plan satisfies one of these two criteria, the Chapter 13 repayment plan will be rejected by the court. The debtor will then have to file a new plan, change over to a Chapter 7 proceeding, or withdraw the petition.

Under the 1978 Bankruptcy Reform Act, debtor payments under a repayment plan did not begin until the plan was confirmed by the court. This gave many debtors a four- to six-month "grace period" in which the debtor retained all of his or her assets but made no payments, to the detriment of the creditors. The 1984 Bankruptcy Amendments call for payments to begin within 30 days of the filing of the plan, subject to confirmation of the plan by the court. The debtor makes these payments to the trustee, who holds the monies paid until confirmation of the plan by the court and then distributes them to the various creditors. If the debtor fails to make payments to the trustee in a timely manner, the plan can be dismissed by the court.

Finally, the 1984 Bankruptcy Amendments provide for the possible modification of the plan after it is confirmed. The trustee, the debtor, or any creditor can petition the court to increase or decrease the debtor's payments whenever the debtor's circumstances or income warrant such a modification. Prior to the 1984 Amendments, decreases were possible, but increases were not permitted.

The four bankruptcy alternatives discussed in this chapter and Chapter 29 are designed to give an honest debtor a fresh start. An individual may use any of the four alternatives. Most businesses can use two of the alternatives. Exhibit 30.1, at the end of this chapter, compares these four bankruptcy alternatives.

30.2

FINANCE/MANAGEMENT

CHAPTER 13 BANKRUPTCY

One of John's friends has been working for CIT since the firm first began operations. This friend recently encountered some financial difficulties and asked for an advance on his pay. While the firm has no formal policy regarding advances, the family generally agrees that advances on pay should not be given. However, since the employee is a friend of John's, Tom agreed to advance the young man $3,000. (Donna was opposed to the idea, and advised Tom that it was a bad idea in the strongest possible terms.) Several weeks after receiving this advance, the employee filed for relief under Chapter 13 of the Bankruptcy Act. Among the creditors he listed was CIT, listing them for the amount of the advance. He listed total debts of $22,500, all unsecured except for a car loan from his bank. His only assets are his car, his stereo, and his job. He currently takes home $175 per week. In his repayment plan, the employee proposes that he make weekly payments of $37.50 for the next three years. (CIT would receive $5 per week, or a total of $780 under this plan.) The employee is single, and his monthly share for his apartment is $150. Tom has asked you if this repayment plan is likely to be approved by the Bankruptcy Court. What would you tell him? Why?

BUSINESS CONSIDERATIONS Should a business have a formal policy regarding employee salary advances? What can a business do to protect itself from situations such as this if the business does, in fact, allow employees to receive advances on their pay?

ETHICAL CONSIDERATIONS Suppose that an employee "takes advantage" of his employer by getting an advance on his or her pay, and then lists that advance as a creditor's claim in bankruptcy. Should the firm retaliate against the employee through a firing or a reassignment? How should the employee be treated following his or her seeming mistreatment of the employer?

NONBANKRUPTCY ALTERNATIVES

In many cases, a debtor or creditor will object to undergoing a bankruptcy, perhaps because of a distaste for the stigma of bankruptcy, or for any number of other reasons. But a wish to avoid bankruptcy does not remove the financial problems of the debtor. Often the debtor or creditor will select a nonbankruptcy alternative to allow—or to force—the debtor to "get out from under." Whether such a decision will work depends on a number of factors, including the attitudes of the creditors who did not select or agree to the nonbankruptcy alternative chosen.

Prejudgment Alternatives

The creditors of a troubled debtor frequently will use some prejudgment procedure in an effort either to get paid or to force the debtor into acting before a judicial solution is sought. Three major prejudgment procedures are available to creditors.

Attachment. The first remedy is *attachment.* A creditor can go to the clerk of the court and obtain a writ of attachment on the basis of the creditor's word that the debtor has not satisfied some claim. Usually, the creditor must post a bond to cover any potential

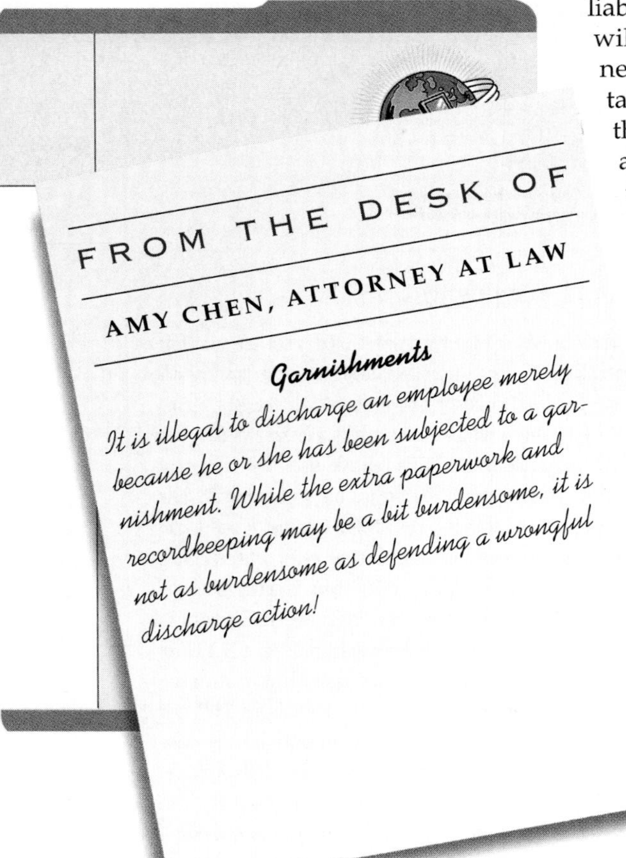

liability in case the attachment is not made in good faith. The creditor will then have the sheriff levy on as much of the debtor's estate as is needed to satisfy the claim of the attaching creditor. The sheriff will take control over these assets until the proceedings terminate. Once the attachment occurs, the creditor must proceed to get a judgment against the debtor. If a judgment is obtained, the assets may be sold to cover the judgment unless the debtor pays outright in order to have the assets released. If the creditor fails to get a judgment within some preset time period, the attachment and lien will expire and the attached assets will be returned to the debtor.

Attachments frequently lead to bankruptcy petitions. The creditors who did not seek an attachment can file an involuntary petition, alleging that the attaching creditor has received a preference. If they petition within four months of the attachment, the courts normally will overturn the attachment.

Garnishment. The second major prejudgment remedy is a *garnishment*. (A garnishment can also be used as a postjudgment remedy under some circumstances.) In a garnishment, the targeted assets are in the hands of some third person and not in the hands of the debtor. However, the assets that the third person controls belong to the debtor or are owed to the debtor. For example, a checking account balance belongs to the debtor but is "held" by the bank. The debtor's wages are owed to the debtor but are "held" by the employer.

The creditor will again go to court, this time seeking a writ of garnishment. When the writ is issued, the creditor will officially notify the third person to hold, or retain, the assets pending a judgment. A third person who ignores this notification will become personally liable to the creditor if and when a judgment is entered. Normally, the freezing of the debtor's checking account or paycheck will "encourage" the debtor to resolve the dispute rapidly. Again, if the creditor does not receive cooperation and does not reduce the claim to a judgment within a preset time period, the writ will be dissolved and the garnished assets will be released to the debtor.

Receivership. The third major prejudgment remedy is *receivership*. This remedy is not a favored prejudgment choice today, unless it is initiated by the debtor, because of the ready availability of bankruptcy relief. In a receivership, the court appoints a disinterested third person to manage the affairs of the debtor. This receiver is responsible for preserving the debtor's estate until a judgment is reached. Liens on the property of the debtor continue under a receivership, but the property affected cannot be bothered without permission of the court. Unless the debtor pays the debt or the creditor cancels it, the parties eventually must resolve the case by some other means. This normally is done by the entry of a judgment by the court.

Postjudgment Alternatives

A creditor who wins the case and receives a judgment probably will seek one of three major postjudgment remedies—execution, supplementary proceeding, garnishment—to satisfy his or her claim.

Execution. The first of these is an *execution.* In an execution, the creditor will attempt to seize and sell as many of the debtor's assets as are needed to cover the judgment. This is done by procuring a writ of execution from the court and then having the sheriff levy on the debtor's assets. After the sheriff levies, the assets seized are appraised, a notice of sale is made, and the goods are sold. (The sale is usually at a public auction, commonly referred to as a judicial sale.) The proceeds of the sale or a predetermined percentage of the appraised value, whichever is higher, will be applied to the debts owed to the creditor. (The percentage varies from state to state, since this is a state remedy.)

The debtor is usually allowed to redeem any real property and some personal property within a fixed period after the sale by paying the purchaser the necessary amount. A purchaser should also be aware that only the debtor's interest in the asset has been purchased. There may very well be other liens or claims or other problems to be confronted later. Thus, the selling price usually is fairly low.

Supplementary Proceeding. The second major postjudgment remedy is a *supplementary proceeding.* A supplementary proceeding can be used only if the writ of execution is unsatisfied. In a supplementary proceeding, the creditors attempt to discover any assets of the debtor by examining and questioning any interested parties. If assets are discovered, the creditors can have a receiver appointed to preserve the assets or they can have the court order a sale of the assets.

Garnishment. The third major postjudgment remedy is a *garnishment.* Garnishments were already discussed as a prejudgment remedy, but there is a slight difference here. Before a judgment is entered, the third person is instructed to hold the assets. After a judgment is entered, the third person is told to turn the assets over to cover the debts owed. If wages are garnished, some amount must be left to allow the debtor to subsist until the debt is paid.

30.3

SALES/FINANCE

COLLECTING ON UNPAID DEBTS

One of CIT's customers has not yet paid for 100 Call-Image videophones that were delivered to it several months ago. Neither Tom nor Anna wants to sue the firm unless it is absolutely necessary. However, the customer refuses to accept their phone calls or to talk with them concerning the past due bill. Lindsay recently learned that this business is storing quite a large quantity of inventory in a warehouse owned by the family of one of her classmates. She tells you that this inventory is stored in the warehouse and asks you if there is any way for CIT to get possession of the inventory, either to force the business to pay their bill or to sell the inventory to cover the debt owed to CIT. What do you tell her?

BUSINESS CONSIDERATIONS When a debtor refuses to talk with a creditor concerning the debt, the creditor is forced to take action. What should a debtor do if or when it finds itself unable to make payments as they come due to one or more of its creditors?

ETHICAL CONSIDERATIONS Suppose that there is a legitimate disagreement as to the amount due on an account between two parties. Suppose, also, that the creditor learns that the debtor's inventory is in the hands of a warehouseman and is therefore susceptible to garnishment. If the creditor garnishes the inventory the debtor can be forced to agree to pay the amount the creditor asserts is owed, even though the debtor honestly believes that a lesser amount is owed. How should the parties act in this situation? Explain your reasoning.

Debtor-Initiated Remedies

Debtors often decide to get out from under on their own by initiating remedies under state law rather than seeking a discharge in bankruptcy. A debtor who so decides usually will choose one of three options—assignment for the benefit of creditors, composition agreement, extension agreement.

Assignment for the Benefit of Creditors. The first option is an *assignment for the benefit of creditors.* Here the debtor freely and voluntarily transfers property to a third person, in trust, to use in order to pay the creditors. Creditor consent is not needed, and once the transfer is made, the property is beyond the reach of the creditors. Unfortunately for the debtor, such a transfer does not result in an automatic discharge. Not only that, it may result in the filing of a bankruptcy petition by the creditors.

To avoid these problems, many debtors prefer to reach a contractual agreement with the creditors. Such an agreement does require creditor consent, but it will also result in discharge. The debtor may seek either a composition, or an extension, or both.

Composition Agreement. In a *composition agreement,* each creditor who is involved agrees to take less money than is owed, if the money is paid immediately, as full satisfaction of the debt. Such an arrangement is a contract between the debtor and the creditors as well as among the creditors. Thus, at least two creditors must join before the composition is valid. Otherwise, it would be invalid because of lack of consideration.

Extension Agreement. In an *extension agreement,* the creditors agree to a longer repayment period in order to receive full payment. Again, the courts view it as a dual contract between the debtor and the creditors and among the creditors.

In either a composition or an extension, the contract among the creditors is based on their acceptance of a change in performance in exchange for an agreement by each not to file suit to collect the original contract. Thus, both a composition and an extension are supported by consideration. Each is a contract, and the court will enforce either as it would enforce any other contract.

http:// RESOURCES FOR BUSINESS LAW STUDENTS

NAME	RESOURCES	WEB ADDRESS
11 U.S.C. Chapter 11—Reorganization	The Legal Information Institute (LII), maintained by Cornell Law School, provides a hypertext and searchable version of Chapter 7, Liquidation, of the U.S. Code.	http://www.law.cornell.edu/uscode/11/ch11.html
11 U.S.C. Chapter 12—Adjustment of Debts of a Family Farmer with Regular Annual Income	LII provides a hypertext and searchable version of Chapter 12, Adjustment of Debts of a Family Farmer with Regular Annual Income.	http://ww.law.cornell.edu/uscode/11/ch12.html
11 U.S.C. Chapter 13—Adjustment of Debts of an Individual with Regular Income	LII provides a hypertext and searchable version of Chapter 13, Adjustment of Debts of an Individual with Regular Income.	http://www.law.cornell.edu/uscode/11/ch13.html
Bankruptcy Alternatives	Bankruptcy Alternatives, maintained by Mory Brenner, Attorney at Law, provides questions and answers about alternatives to bankruptcy.	http://www.debtworkout.com/

EXHIBIT 30.1 A Comparison of the Bankruptcy Alternatives

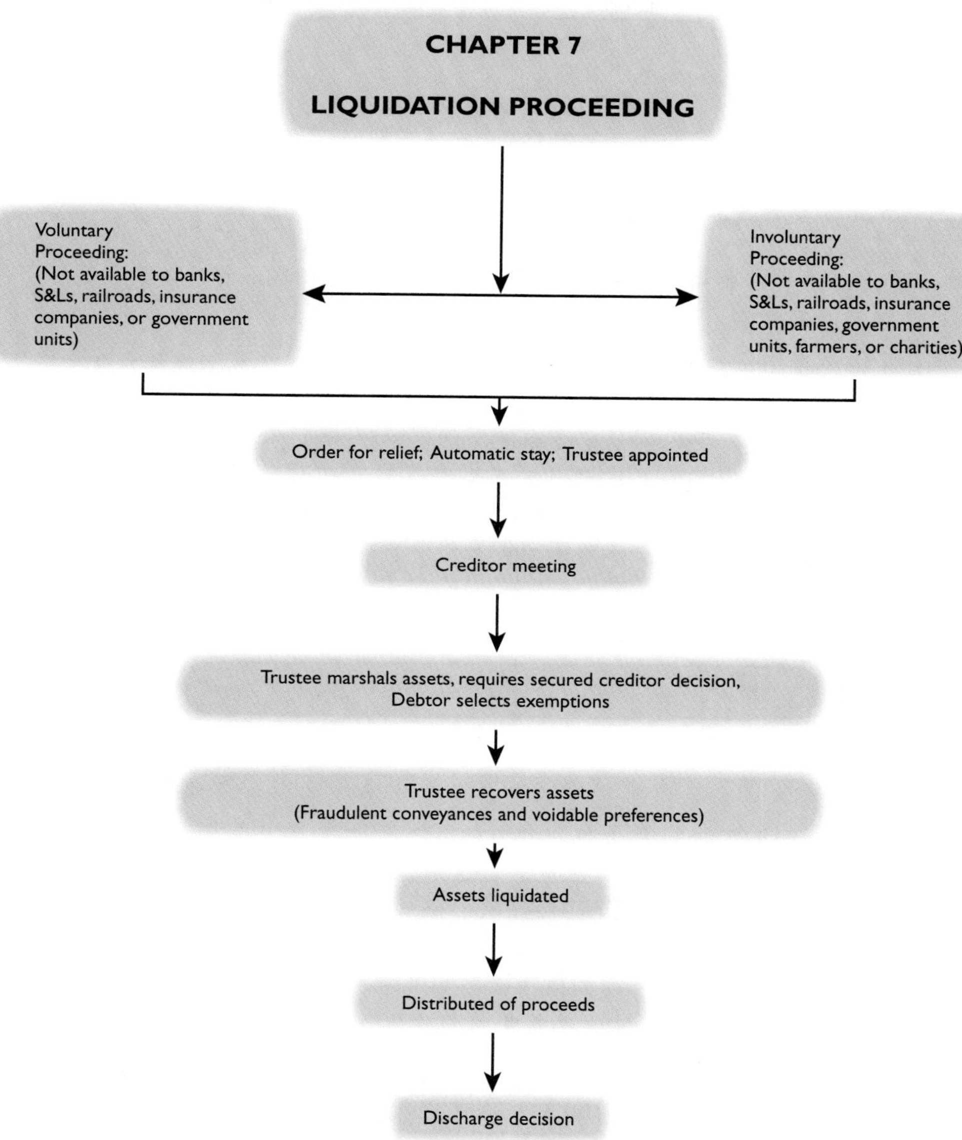

EXHIBIT 30.1 A Comparison of the Bankruptcy Alternatives *(cont.)*

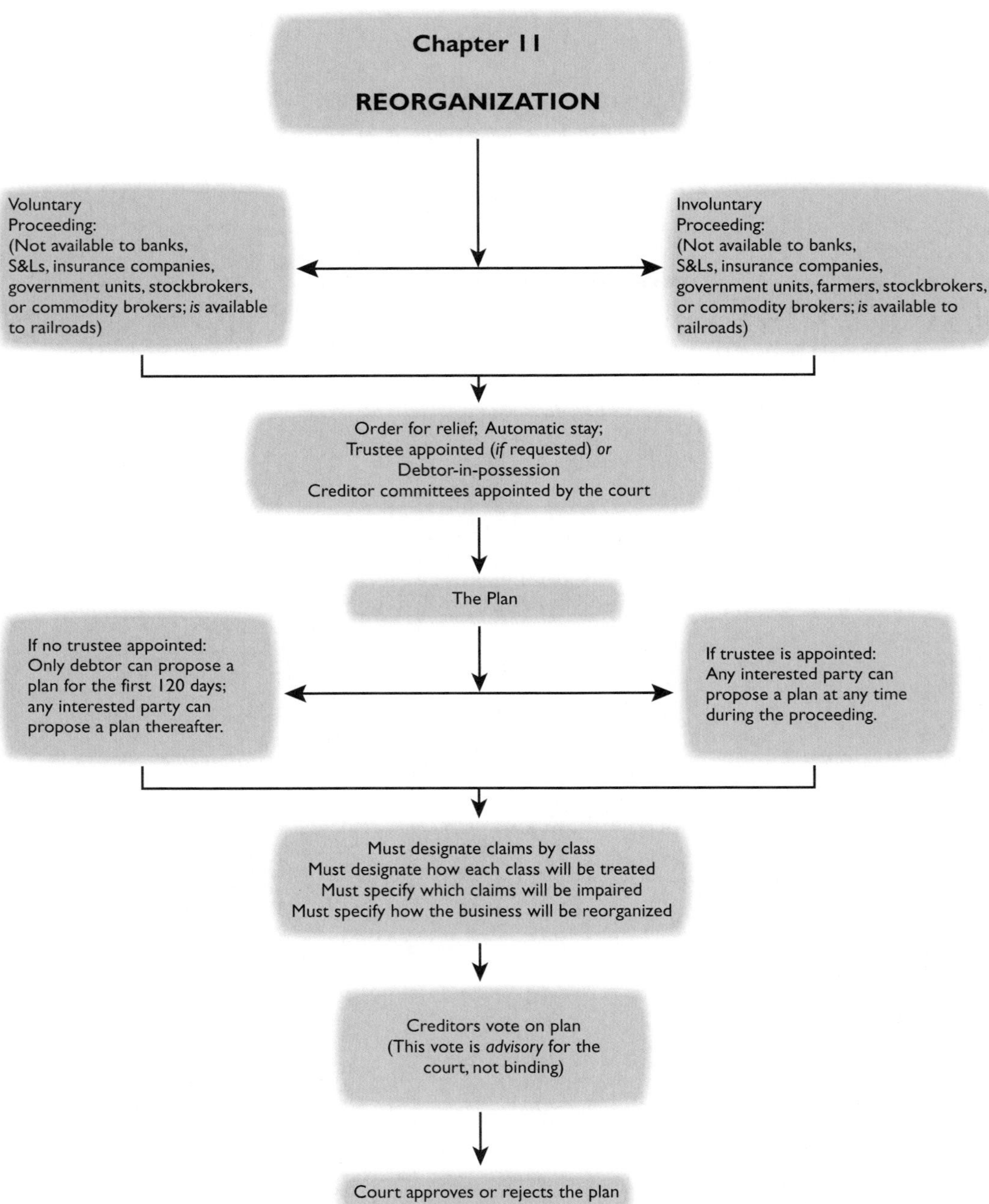

EXHIBIT 30.1 A Comparison of the Bankruptcy Alternatives *(cont.)*

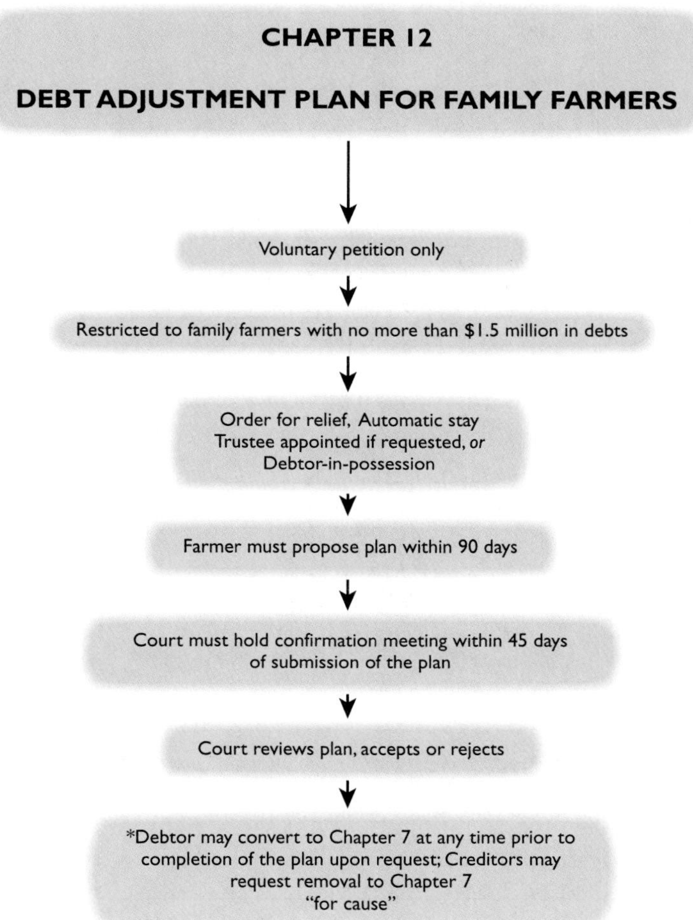

CHAPTER 12
DEBT ADJUSTMENT PLAN FOR FAMILY FARMERS
Voluntary petition only
Restricted to family farmers with no more than $1.5 million in debts
Order for relief, Automatic stay
Trustee appointed if requested, or
Debtor-in-possession
Farmer must propose plan within 90 days
Court must hold confirmation meeting within 45 days
of submission of the plan
Court reviews plan, accepts or rejects
*Debtor may convert to Chapter 7 at any time prior to
completion of the plan upon request; Creditors may
request removal to Chapter 7
"for cause"

SUMMARY

An embattled debtor need not always go through liquidation in order to make a fresh start. Other bankruptcy and nonbankruptcy remedies may work equally well.

Under bankruptcy, the debtor may seek a reorganization under Chapter 11 or a repayment plan under Chapter 13. A farmer may seek a repayment plan under Chapter 12. Each of these requires court approval of a plan, and each requires the debtor to propose the plan in good faith. In a reorganization, the debtor adjusts his or her financial position to allow a business to continue. In a repayment plan, the

EXHIBIT 30.1 | A Comparison of the Bankruptcy Alternatives *(cont.)*

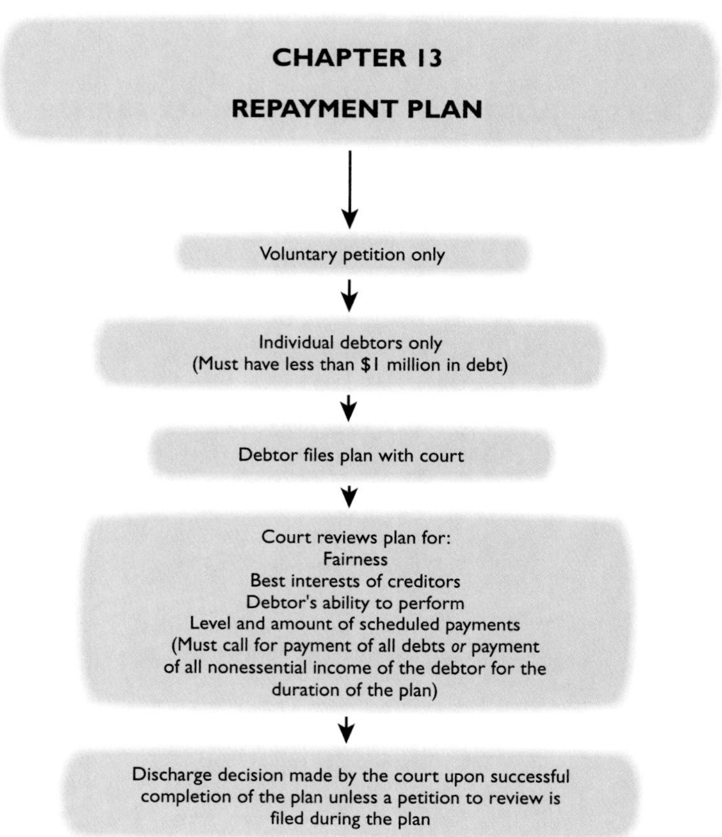
CHAPTER 13
REPAYMENT PLAN
Voluntary petition only
Individual debtors only
(Must have less than $1 million in debt)
Debtor files plan with court
Court reviews plan for:
Fairness
Best interests of creditors
Debtor's ability to perform
Level and amount of scheduled payments
(Must call for payment of all debts or payment
of all nonessential income of the debtor for the
duration of the plan)
Discharge decision made by the court upon successful
completion of the plan unless a petition to review is
filed during the plan

debtor proposes a method of repaying debts over a three-to-five-year period. Good faith and fairness are essential in any plans before they will be approved by the courts. Recently, Chapter 11 has been used as a corporate strategy, allowing corporations to escape liabilities or obligations that the firm feels are blatantly unfair or may lead to the demise of the organization.

Some creditors seek nonbankruptcy remedies under state law. The creditor may seek either prejudgment remedies to force the debtor to act or postjudgment remedies in order to collect. Either type of action may result in a bankruptcy proceeding. The debtor may also seek a nonbankruptcy remedy under state law. This normally will involve a contract with the creditors and frequently will result in a bankruptcy proceeding.

DISCUSSION QUESTIONS

1. What role does the examiner play in a reorganization under Chapter 11? How is this different from the role that a trustee plays in a Chapter 11 reorganization?
2. The 1984 Bankruptcy Amendments provide some rather specific guidelines for a repayment plan under Chapter 13. What does the court look at in deciding whether to approve a repayment plan under these guidelines? How does this differ from the requirements for a repayment plan under the original Bankruptcy Reform Act?
3. What can the court do under a repayment plan if, owing to a change in circumstances, the debtor cannot complete the plan as approved by the court? Who may ask the court to intercede and to change the repayment plan?
4. What public policy considerations might lead a court to prefer a Chapter 11 reorganization over a Chapter 7 liquidation for a corporation seeking relief in bankruptcy? What considerations will lead the court to order a removal from Chapter 11 to Chapter 7 when a corporation files its petition for reorganization under Chapter 11?
5. Chapter 12 provides relief for individual farmers by allowing them to establish repayment plans. Why did the Bankruptcy Code require a special chapter for farmers when there is already a repayment plan for individual debtors available in Chapter 13 and a reorganization plan available primarily for businesses under Chapter 11?
6. What substantive changes were included in the Bankruptcy Reform Act of 1994? Why do you think Congress felt these changes were necessary?
7. Why does the law specify that a minimum percentage of appraised value must be applied to debts in an execution, even if the assets sold in the execution bring less at sale than their appraised value? Does this rule reflect more of a public policy concern for the debtor or for the creditor?
8. What are the nonbankruptcy prejudgment alternatives available to a creditor when the debtor cannot or will not make the payments owed to the creditor? What are the nonbankruptcy postjudgment remedies available to the creditor?
9. In a composition agreement, the creditors agree to accept less than the debtor owes and to treat this lesser payment as payment in full. Why is a creditor willing to agree to a composition agreement? Why will a composition agreement occasionally be better for the creditor than a bankruptcy proceeding?
10. How are extension plans and composition agreements similar to a Chapter 13 repayment plan? How are they different from a Chapter 13 repayment plan? Which seems to be better for the debtor? Which seems better for the creditors?

CASE PROBLEMS AND WRITING ASSIGNMENTS

1. Bustop Shelters entered into several contracts with Classic. These contracts called for Classic to install 400 shelters from kits provided by Bustop, to perform periodic maintenance, and to clean Bustop's shelters weekly. Bustop and Classic subsequently filed suits against one another, each alleging breach by the other. Classic prevailed, receiving a damage award in the amount of $440,000. Bustop filed for relief under Chapter 11, availing itself of the automatic stay provision before Classic could enforce its judgment. In its plan, Bustop listed three classes of creditors: Class 1, Citizens Bank, based on a fully secured loan; Class 2, unsecured creditors owed between $201 and $20,000; and Class 3, unsecured creditors owed more than $20,000. (The only creditor in Class 3 was Classic.) Creditors in Classes 1 and 2 approved the plan, while Classic rejected it. The court refused to approve the plan, however. According to the court, Class 1 was not impaired, and Classes 2 and 3 should have been combined into just one class. Had they been combined, no impaired creditor class would have approved the plan, so the court was precluded from approving the plan. Should Bustop be allowed to distinguish the unsecured creditors as it did, validating its plan, or should all of its unsecured creditors be placed in one class, invalidating its plan? Explain your reasoning. [See *Bustop Shelters of Louisville* v. *Classic Homes,* 914 F.2d 810 (6th Cir. 1990).]

2. The Internal Revenue Service (IRS) filed liens for employment taxes due but unpaid against Dade Helicopters, Inc., Dade Helicopters Service, Inc., and Tropical Helicopters, Inc. When the taxes remained unpaid, the IRS seized virtually all the assets of three companies—Dade Helicopter Jet Service, Inc., Brickell Investment Corp., and Tropical Helicopter Airways, Inc.—asserting that these companies were "alter-egos" of the taxpayers who were delinquent with their taxes. In fact, despite the similarities in names, these firms were totally separate and distinct from the delinquent taxpayers. Due to these seizures, the three companies were forced to shut down their

entire operations immediately, and all three were forced to file for relief under Chapter 11 of the Bankruptcy Code. The debtors petitioned the Bankruptcy Court to order release of the assets in the possession of the IRS and to grant the debtors' costs and attorney's fees. The IRS objected to the award of costs and attorney's fees, although it did not object to the order to release the assets. Should the debtors be granted costs and attorney's fees in this case? Explain your reasoning. [See *In re Brickell Investment Corp.*, 922 F.2d 696 (11th Cir. 1991).]

3. Graven filed for relief under Chapter 12 of the Bankruptcy Code. During the period from 1984 through 1986, prior to the petition date, Graven had transferred certain real estate to a corporation owned by the Graven family. In January 1988, Graven petitioned for relief. Several creditors objected to the petition, alleging that Graven was guilty of fraud in the treatment of the real estate. The court ordered an investigation into these allegations by the trustee. The investigation by the trustee led to his determination that some fraudulent conveyances had, in fact, occurred, and he recommended further proceedings consistent with this finding. Graven then moved to dismiss the Chapter 12 proceeding in order to treat the creditors out of bankruptcy. The trustee objected and filed a motion to transfer the proceedings from Chapter 12 to Chapter 7 due to the fraudulent conduct of Graven. Should the debtor be allowed to dismiss the petition prior to any showing—but following an allegation—of fraud in order to avoid a transfer to Chapter 7, or must the proceeding be transferred and carried through once the allegation of fraud has been made? Discuss your reasoning. [See *In re Graven*, 936 F.2d 378 (8th Cir. 1991).]

4. BFP took title to a California home subject to a deed of trust in favor of Imperial Savings Association. After Imperial entered a notice of default because the loan was not being serviced, the home was purchased by Osborne for $433,000 at a properly noticed foreclosure sale. Shortly thereafter, BFP filed for bankruptcy relief and, acting as a debtor-in-possession, filed a complaint to set aside the sale to Osborne as a fraudulent conveyance, claiming that the home was worth more than $725,000 when sold, and thus not exchanged for "reasonably equivalent value" as required by the Bankruptcy Code. Does the consideration received in a noncollusive, regularly conducted, nonjudicial foreclosure sale amount to "reasonably equivalent value" as a matter of law? Explain your answer. [See *BFP* v. *Resolution Trust Corp.*, 114 S.Ct. 1757 (1994).]

5. On 30 November 1988, Francisco Pacana filed a petition seeking relief under Chapter 13 of the Bankruptcy Code. At the same time, he filed a repayment plan with the court. His schedules showed a total unsecured debt of $34,500, which included a $13,900 debt to his ex-wife for child support arrearages. Pacana's plan classified the debt to his ex-wife as a "priority" and provided for payment to her, but did not state the timing or the amount of the payments she was to receive. The overall plan called for payment of 14 percent to unsecured creditors, which would include the child support arrearages owed to Ms. Pacana-Siler. The court approved the plan without modification on 13 February 1989. On that date there was outstanding an unresolved application filed by Ms. Pacana-Siler on 20 January 1989 seeking relief from the automatic stay in order to allow her to enforce the child support debt. The court held a hearing on the application 3 March 1989 and granted her relief from the stay.
   The court ordered that:

   > to the extent that in addition to what is paid to [Ms. Pacana-Siler] on her priority claim in the Chapter 13 she may collect an additional $250 per month from the debtor to be applied against the arrearages. This additional $250 may be collected upon immediately by agreement with or by levy upon the debtor's wages or other monies due him.

   Mr. Pacana appealed, arguing that this order rendered his plan infeasible, because he could not afford to carry out his plan and to pay an additional $250 to his ex-wife. He also argued that his plan implied that he intended to pay his ex-wife 100 percent of her claim since he had designated her as a "priority claimant." Can the court grant relief from the automatic stay provisions in a bankruptcy proceeding to provide for collection by a priority creditor? [See *In re Pacana*, 125 B.R. 19 (9th Cir. BAP 1991).]

6. **BUSINESS APPLICATIONS CASE** Carey Transportation filed, in April 1985, a voluntary petition for relief under Chapter 11 of the Bankruptcy Code. Both before and after the petition date, Carey was in the business of providing commuter bus service between New York City and Kennedy and LaGuardia Airports. Truck Drivers Local 807 had been the exclusive bargaining representative for Carey's bus drivers and station employees. Local 807 and Carey entered into collective bargaining agreements covering these two groups of employees on 20 August 1982, thereby settling a 64-day strike by the union members. Both of these collective bargaining agreements were scheduled to expire on 28 February 1986. Carey blamed the strike for its declining ridership and annual revenue losses, and reported net losses in 1983, 1984, and 1985.

In September 1983, Carey terminated 50 station workers (although 10 were later rehired, with back pay, following arbitration on the firings), with an annual cost savings of approximately $1 million. In 1984 and 1985, Carey sought and obtained concessions from a union representing Carey's mechanics and repair-shop workers, with an annual savings of $144,000. On 31 January 1985, Carey contacted Local 807 representatives and asked for additional modifications of the agreements. The union was also told that, without these modifications, Carey would probably be forced to seek relief in bankruptcy, where Carey would attempt to reject the existing contract. The proposed modifications were expected to save Carey $750,000 annually. Union representatives agreed to present the proposed modifications to the union membership. However, before the proposal was taken to the union membership, on 27 March 1985 Carey added several other modifications to the package and described this resultant package as its final offer. These last modifications extended the union contracts two years, freezing both wages and fringe benefits until 1 April 1987, at which point negotiations regarding wages and benefits would be possible. The union rejected this "final offer" on 29 March 1985, and Carey filed for relief six days later. Carey then proposed a postpetition meeting with the union to renegotiate the contracts. This meeting produced no viable solutions, and Carey presented as a portion of its reorganization plan that it be allowed to reject the collective bargaining agreement with Local 807. The court agreed with Carey, and the union appealed. Should Carey be allowed to reject the collective bargaining agreement with the union as the foundation of its Chapter 11 reorganization plan? [See *Truck Drivers Local 807* v. *Carey Transportation, Inc.*, 816 F.2d 82 (2nd Cir. 1987).]

7. **ETHICAL APPLICATIONS CASE** Pioneer filed for relief under Chapter 11 of the Bankruptcy Code. Brunswick Associates, one of Pioneer's unsecured creditors failed to file its proof of claim by the deadline—the bar date—established by the Bankruptcy Court and included in the Notice of Meeting of Creditors sent to an official of Brunswick. Four weeks after the bar date, Brunswick asked the court for permission to file its proof of claim. The Bankruptcy Code permits late filings where the creditor's failure to comply with the deadline was the result of excusable neglect. The court refused the request, ruling that a late filing will only be permitted if the failure to meet the deadline is due to circumstances beyond the reasonable control of the creditor. Should the creditor be allowed to file its proof of claim after the bar date if the failure to meet the deadline was due to a simple oversight, or excuseable neglect, or should the creditor be barred from filing unless it can show that its failure to meet the deadline was due to circumstances beyond its reasonable control? What ethical arguments can be made to support each of these criteria? [See *Pioneer Inv. Services* v. *Brunswick Associates*, 113 S.Ct. 1489 (1993).]

8. **IDES CASE** Roppollo was involuntarily petitioned into bankruptcy under the provisions of Chapter 11 of the Bankruptcy Code. The petitioning creditors also asked the court to appoint an examiner with special powers rather than a trustee. Following a full adversarial hearing, the court appointed an examiner with expanded powers. Williamson et al. appealed this decision, arguing that the Bankruptcy Court had improperly expanded the powers of the examiner, in effect giving this examiner the powers normally reserved for a trustee. They asserted that an examiner may only exercise those powers specified by the Bankruptcy Code. Apply the IDES model in analyzing this case. Can the Bankruptcy Court grant "expanded powers" to an examiner beyond the powers specified in the Code? Why would the court want to grant such extended powers? [See *Williamson* v. *Roppollo*, 114 B.R. 127 (W.D.La. 1990).]

NOTES

1. See, for example, "Reshaping Corporate America," *Management Accountant*, 71(9) (March 1990), p. 21; "Court Reverses Own Ruling: Negotiations Over Revised Manville Payout Plan to Continue," *Business Insurance*, 27(21) (May 1993), p. 2; or Kevin J. Delaney, *Strategic Bankruptcy* (Berkeley: University of California Press, 1992).
2. "Va. Firm to Buy Quibell," *The Roanoke Times*, June 14, 1996, p. A7.
3. H.R. 5116, Sec. 306.

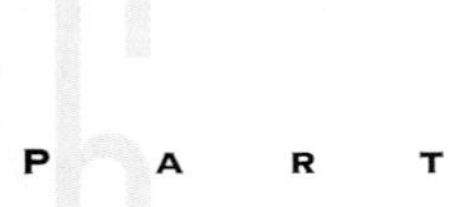

PART 6

IDES PROBLEMS

Donna started her own establishment, Suds 'n Duds, a combination laundromat and tavern. Donna purchased restaurant equipment, paying part of the price with money she had received from an inheritance and borrowing the rest from National Bank. National did insist on obtaining a security interest in the equipment as collateral for the loan, along with an after-acquired property clause on any additional equipment obtained during the life of the loan. Donna also signed a five-year lease, with an option to renew the lease for an additional five years.

Next, Donna hired a contractor to remodel the interior to her specifications and rework the plumbing and electrical wiring. Donna paid the contractor 25 percent of the agreed fee up front and signed a contract to pay the balance on completion of the work. Donna purchased washers and dryers on credit from Wally's Washers and Dryers, paying 20 percent of the price as a down payment and granting Wally's a security interest in the washers and dryers. Donna also purchased restaurant supplies from Rick's Restaurant Supplies, again paying 20 percent down, financing the rest, and agreeing to a security interest in the purchased supplies as security on the loan. Donna arranged for the purchase of food, beer, wine, soft drinks, and related items from Farmer's Cooperative, a local wholesale outlet and supplier for several restaurants in the community. Donna purchased these items on credit, with payment due 30 days after each delivery and with deliveries scheduled for Monday morning of each week. Donna also activated the utilities and telephone and arranged for cable service.

All of Donna's hard work paid off with the opening of Suds 'n Duds. People enjoyed the relaxed atmosphere of the restaurant while doing their laundry. By all accounts, Suds 'n Duds was a success. Then, six months after the opening, disaster struck. Donna designated Tuesday nights as "shrimp" night, and it quickly became a favorite for customers. One Monday night, though, the refrigeration unit in which the shrimp was stored malfunctioned and the shrimp spoiled. The cooks on Tuesday failed to notice and served the spoiled shrimp to dozens of customers. Every customer who ate shrimp suffered food poisoning, and several needed hospitalization.

Understandably, business thereafter suffered. For three months, Donna made a herculean effort to save her business, but to no avail. She laid off a few of her workers and convinced others to accept less than full pay for now, promising to pay them any deficits in the future when business rebounded. Donna fell behind in her bills, being at least one month in arrears on every account. Then, when Donna thought the worst was over, she learned that her insurance would not cover all of the costs she faced from her shrimp night. Creditors began to dun her for payment.

Seeing no other alternative, Donna has decided to seek relief in bankruptcy and has arranged for a meeting with a lawyer. Before this meeting, Donna needs to understand better her situation vis-à-vis her creditors and former employees.

IDENTIFY What are the legal and ethical issues surrounding the failure of Suds 'n Duds?

DEFINE What are the meanings of the relevant legal terms associated with these issues?

ENUMERATE What are the legal and ethical principles relevant to these issues?

SHOW BOTH SIDES Consider all of the facts in light of the preceding questions. Who are Donna's creditors, and what are their positions relative to Donna's financial problems?

[To review the IDES approach, refer to pages 29–30.]

Part 7

AGENCY

One of our fondest dreams is to have the ability to be in more than one place at the same time. Obviously, this is a physical impossibility. Fortunately, however, the law has found a way to do legally what cannot be done physically. By using an agent, a person can legally be in more than one place at a time.

An *agent* is a person empowered to "be you" within the scope of the agency. Whatever the agent hears, you "heard." Whatever the agent says, you "said." Whatever an agent does, you "did." In other words, you are legally responsible for your agent's conduct—within the scope of the agency.

A businessperson derives obvious benefits from "being" in many places at the same time; however, if the agent does not act properly, many problems may arise. Part 7 explores these benefits and problems of agency.

I D E S

Koolin'-Aid, which manufactures and sells air conditioning equipment, has recently encountered legal trouble. A freelance jobber and salesperson terminated by Koolin'-Aid has been misrepresenting himself as an agent of Koolin'-Aid, profiting by this misrepresentation. Also, a truck driver for Koolin'-Aid is a primary actor in a $100,000 tort liability lawsuit. Is Koolin'-Aid legally and/or financially responsible for these actions? What steps should Koolin'-Aid take to avoid future problems?

Consider these issues in the context of the chapter materials, and prepare to analyze them using the IDES model:

IDENTIFY the legal issues raised by the questions.

DEFINE all the relevant legal terms and issues involved.

ENUMERATE the legal principles associated with these issues.

SHOW BOTH SIDES by using the facts.

A G E N D A

As CIT grows, the Kochanowskis will need to hire more and more workers. As a consequence, Anna and Tom need to fully understand the duties and responsibilities associated with the relationship between the employer and employee, as well as their relationships with the public at large. What types of work relationships are possible?

CIT does not make its own deliveries to retailers. What is the relationship of CIT to the people who drive the trucks and make the deliveries to the retailers? CIT is considering hiring other companies to serve as official repair centers for the videophones. What constraints should be evaluated by CIT before entering into these arrangements with other firms?

Tom is concerned that salespersons hired to sell Call-Image videophones will copy the technology and start their own competing businesses. Is this a valid concern?

These and other questions will arise during our discussion of agency law. Be prepared! You never know when one of the Kochanowskis will call on you for help or advice.

The Creation and Termination of an Agency

O U T L I N E

AGENCY LAW AND AGENCY RELATIONSHIPS

Agency law concerns the relationships between workers and the people who hire workers. It includes their duties and responsibilities both to each other and to the public at large. No one can really avoid agency law; almost everyone at some time works as an employee or hires an employee. Moreover, agency relationships arise not only in business situations but also in nonbusiness situations; for example, when a person returns books to the university library for a friend.

Most agency relationships do not require litigation because they function smoothly. To resolve the legal problems that do arise, one must look to agency law, contract law, and tort law. In most of these subject areas, the court will place significant reliance on state law. Much of the law of agency has been studied by the American Law Institute and is discussed in its publication, *Restatement (Second) of Agency*. *Restatements* are treatises that summarize detailed recommendations of what the law should be on a particular subject. Although *Restatements* are not legislature- or court-made law, they become part of the legal precedents when courts rely on them and incorporate them into court decisions. (See Chapter 4 for a more detailed discussion of precedents.) The three agency chapters in this book rely on the *Restatement*.

You should note that the position of your state may vary from that in the *Restatement*. The *Restatement (Second) of Agency* states some key terms:

1. Agency *is the fiduciary relation which results from the manifestation of consent by one person to another that the other shall act on his* [sic] *behalf and subject to his control, and consent by the other so to act.*
2. *The one for whom action is to be taken is the* principal.
3. *The one who is to act is the* agent.[1]

An *agency relationship* is consensual in nature. It is based on the concept that the parties mutually agree that (1) the agent will act on behalf of the principal and (2) the agent will be subject to the principal's direction and control. The agreement can be expressed or implied. In addition, the parties must be competent to act as principal and agent.

Analysis of Agency Relationships

To analyze a situation involving an agency relationship, ask these questions:

1. Was the dispute between the principal and the agent?
2. Was an agency formed voluntarily by the principal and the agent, or is there some other relationship?
3. Did the parties have the capacity to perform their roles as the principal and the agent?
4. What authority did the principal vest in the agent?
5. Did the agent enter into a contract or commit a tort?

RESTRICTIONS ON CREATING AN AGENCY RELATIONSHIP

Agency law affects a broad range of situations, from a small partnership with two partners to a corporation with thousands of employees, and from a highly skilled developer of computer peripherals to a 16-year-old babysitter. In fact, everything a corporation does, it does through agents. There are few restrictions on who can form agency relationships and what can be done through agency relationships. One restriction is that the agreement must require the agent to perform acts that are legal in order to form a lawful agency relationship. An agreement to distribute "crank," for example, would not be a lawful agency relationship.

Capacity to Be a Principal

With the exception of minors and incompetents, any person can appoint an agent. It is generally true that any person having capacity to *contract* has capacity to employ a servant agent or a nonservant agent. (The distinction between these two agents is that a principal has more control over the actions of the former than over those of the latter.) Since agency is a consensual relationship, the principal must have capacity to confer a legally operative consent.[2]

Some states have determined that a minor lacks capacity to be a principal. In other states, a minor has the capacity to enter into an agency relationship, but the agency relationship is voidable. The *Restatement (Second) of Agency,* § 20, takes the second position. In this second group of states, the agreements entered into by the minor's agent will also be voidable to the same extent that the minor's own contracts will be voidable. The key to understanding this concept is to remember that the contract is really entered into by the principal.

Capacity to Be an Agent

Generally, anyone can be an agent. Strange as it seems, even persons who do not have the capacity to act for themselves—for example, minors or insane persons—can act as agents for someone else. It is the capacity of the *principal,* not that of the agent, that controls. Obviously, however, principals should exercise care to appoint agents who are able to make sound decisions.

Duties an Agent Can Perform

A principal "appoints" an agent to deal with the public. Generally, an agent can be assigned to do almost any legal task. There are, however, some nondelegable duties such as the following:

1. An employer's duty to provide safe working conditions[3]
2. A person's duty under some contract terms
3. A landlord's duty to tenants
4. A **common carrier**'s duty to passengers
5. A person's duty under a license issued to that person
6. The duty of a person engaged in inherently dangerous work to take adequate precautions to avoid harm

Common carrier

A company in the business of transporting people or goods for a fee and serving the general public.

Other nondelegable duties are defined by various state statutes. These may consist of many different types of duties. If the duty is nondelegable and the principal attempts to delegate the duty to someone else, the principal will be personally liable if the task is not properly completed. *Nondelegable duties* really means that the *tasks* can be delegated, but the responsibility for their proper completion cannot.

A person who hires another to engage in ultrahazardous activities is liable for any injury that results. This rule applies whether the person hired is a servant or an **independent contractor**.

Independent contractor

A person hired to perform a task but not subject to the specific control of the hiring party.

TYPES OF AGENCY RELATIONSHIPS

General and Special Agents

The distinction between general and special agents is a matter of degree. A *special agent* is employed to complete one transaction or a simple series of transactions. The relationship covers a relatively limited period and is not continuous. A *general agent* is hired to conduct a series of transactions over time. The amount of **discretion** the agent has is immaterial in making the distinction between general and special agents, as is the expertise of the agent.

In deciding whether an agent is a general agent or a special agent, courts should examine all of the following factors:

1. The number of acts that will need to be completed to achieve the authorized result
2. The number of people who will need to be dealt with before achieving the desired result
3. The length of time that will be necessary to achieve the desired result[4]

The manager of an electronics store is a general agent. In contrast, a person who delivers a package to a customer of the store on a one-time basis is a special agent. Categorizing an agent who is between these two extremes can be difficult. As Exhibit 31.1 shows, a continuum of relationships exists between the roles of special agents and those of general agents.

31.1

MANAGEMENT

ARE FAMILY MEMBERS AGENTS OF CIT?

John is concerned that various family members each may be viewed as agents of CIT, and that their conduct, therefore, could be financially detrimental to the firm. Dan contends that there is virtually no danger of this happening, and that John is overreacting. According to Dan, only adults can be agents, so Lindsay and John cannot represent the firm. In addition, Dan says that agents must be full-time employees of the firm, so Donna and Julio are excluded as potential agents. According to Dan, this only leaves Tom, Anna, Dan, and those full-time employees hired by the firm as possible agents of CIT. John asks you if Dan's analysis is correct. What will you tell him?

BUSINESS CONSIDERATIONS What are the business implications of having people represent themselves as working for or on behalf of a firm? When does the firm have a legal obligation for the actions of these people? What are the public relations implications of successfully denying that an alleged agent was, in fact, not working on behalf of the firm?

ETHICAL CONSIDERATIONS What ethical obligations does CIT owe to its agents? What ethical obligations does CIT owe to members of the public who deal in good faith with agents of CIT?

Gratuitous Agents

Payment is not necessary in a principal–agent relationship. If a person volunteers services without an agreement or an expectation of payment, that person may still be an agent. The requirements for a *gratuitous agency* are that one person volunteered to help another and that the person being served accepted this assistance. For example, Susie offers to help Joel with his yard work. While she is pruning a tree, she carelessly saws off a limb, which falls on a car belonging to Joel's neighbor. The courts *can* find that Susie is Joel's agent, in which case Joel is liable for the damage Susie causes.

Discretion
The right to use one's own judgment in selecting between alternatives.

SERVANTS AND INDEPENDENT CONTRACTORS

Most workers are either servants or independent contractors. The distinction among the terms *agent, servant,* and *independent contractor* is confusing, partly because authors and judges apply differing definitions to these terms and partly because common usage differs from legal usage. This text uses the definitions of the *Restatement*

EXHIBIT 31.1 Distinction Between Special Agents and General Agents

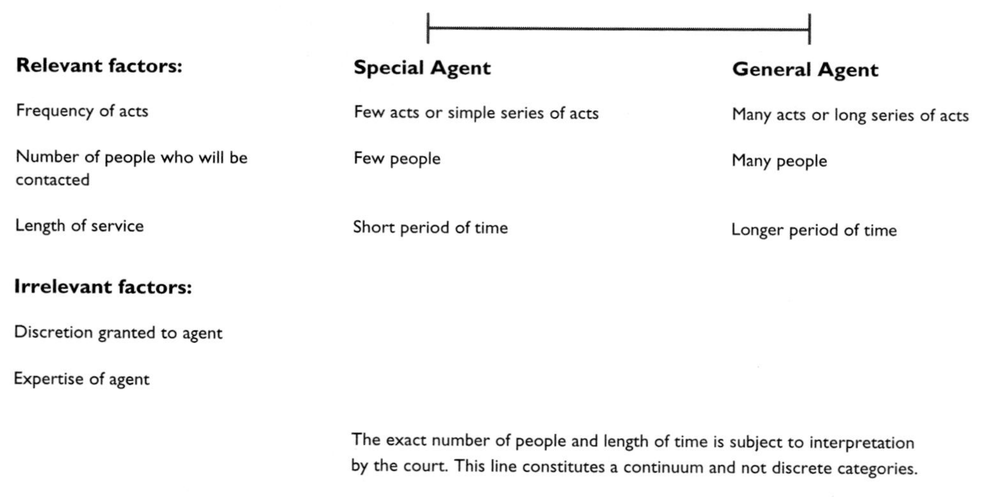

Relevant factors:	Special Agent	General Agent
Frequency of acts	Few acts or simple series of acts	Many acts or long series of acts
Number of people who will be contacted	Few people	Many people
Length of service	Short period of time	Longer period of time
Irrelevant factors:		
Discretion granted to agent		
Expertise of agent		

The exact number of people and length of time is subject to interpretation by the court. This line constitutes a continuum and not discrete categories.

(Second) of Agency. Using legal definitions, servants and employees are synonymous. We generally use the term *servant* to describe someone who is subject to the control of his or her *master.*

Servants

A master is a special type of principal who has the right to tell his or her worker both what to do and how to do it. The worker then is included in a special class of workers called *servants* or *employees.* (The more modern term is *employee.*) A *servant* is one who works physically for the hiring party. A *master* (employer) has a right to control how the task is accomplished by the servant (employee). The actual exercise of this control is not necessary; it is sufficient that the master has the *right* to control. Thus, interns in hospitals, airline pilots, sales clerks, and officers of corporations are servants.

The distinction between servants and independent contractors is important, because a principal is rarely liable for the unauthorized *physical* acts of an agent who is not a servant. Consequently, a principal generally is not liable for the torts of an independent contractor. Principals sometimes label a worker as an independent contractor in an attempt to escape liability, but the courts will look behind the designation and make a judgment about the true nature of the relationship. The distinction between servants and independent contractors is also important in determining rights and benefits under unemployment insurance laws, workers' compensation laws, and similar statutes.

The distinction between an independent contractor and a servant is represented in Exhibit 31.2. Remember that this distinction is material only when there is a question about who is responsible for the physical acts of the worker. When the worker

EXHIBIT 31.2 Distinction Between Servants and Independent Contractors

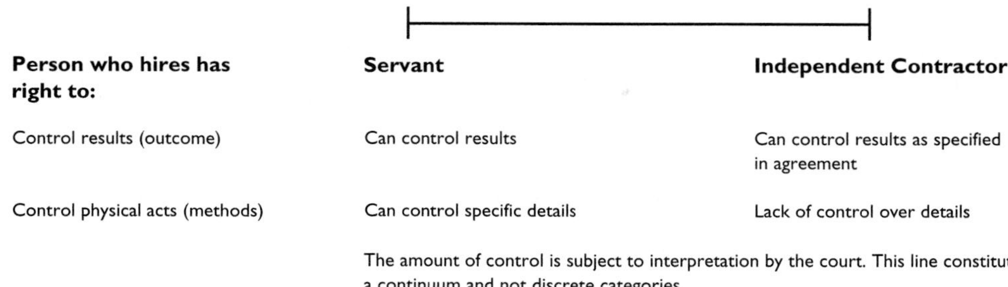

Person who hires has right to:	Servant	Independent Contractor
Control results (outcome)	Can control results	Can control results as specified in agreement
Control physical acts (methods)	Can control specific details	Lack of control over details

The amount of control is subject to interpretation by the court. This line constitutes a continuum and not discrete categories.

has entered into a contract for his or her employer, it is irrelevant whether the worker is a servant or an independent contractor.

Independent Contractors

An *independent contractor* is hired to complete a task for someone else. The physical acts of the independent contractor are not controlled or subject to the control of the hiring party. Instead, the independent contractor relies on his or her own expertise to determine the best way to complete the job. Anyone who contracts to do work for another does so as either a servant or an independent contractor. Courts look at many factors in distinguishing between the two.

In addition to considering the *right* to control, courts commonly consider the following factors:

1. Whether the worker hires assistants
2. What the method of payment is; for example, by the number of hours worked or by the job completed
3. Who supplies the tools and equipment to be used
4. Whether the worker is engaged in a distinct occupation or independent business, and how long the relationship is intended to last

The court examined the working relationship of the parties in the following case to determine the status of a worker, and hence his or her ability to recover from the hiring party for injuries suffered on the job.

31.1 TORRES v. REARDON 5 Cal.Rptr.2d 52 (Cal.App. 2 Dist. 1992)

FACTS José Torres was a self-employed gardener doing business as José Torres Gardening Service from 1980 to 1988. He performed weekly gardening services at a number of homes in Torrance, California, including the home of Michael and Ona Reardon. In 1988, the Reardons began discussing the possibility of having Torres trim a 65- to 70-foot tree in their front yard. An agreement was reached in mid-June that Torres would trim the tree for $350. David Boice,

31.1 TORRES v. REARDON (cont.) 5 Cal.Rptr.2d 52 (Cal.App. 2 Dist. 1992)

the Reardons' neighbor, was present during the final discussion. Boice indicated that he was concerned about a large branch of the tree that overhung his house. He feared that the branch would fall onto his roof. Torres and one helper arrived at 11:00 A.M. on 20 June to do the job. The Reardons were not at home. Boice was at home working in his garage-workshop and he reminded Torres about the branch. Periodically, Boice came out to watch the progress. He mentioned that Torres was not using safety lines and Torres responded that he did not need them. Torres used a chain saw to cut the larger branches. When Torres was ready to cut the branch that overhung Boice's house, Boice came out to hold a rope tied to the branch. He was going to pull on it so the branch would not fall on his roof. Torres was wearing a safety belt, but it was not attached to the tree. He did not have enough line to reach a branch that could support his weight. Torres claims that Boice pulled on "Boice's rope" when Torres did not expect it, causing Torres to lose control of the chain saw and fall. Torres became a paraplegic due to the fall and sued the Reardons.

ISSUE Was Torres a servant of the Reardons and, therefore, entitled to workers' compensation?

HOLDING No.

REASONING Under the California Workers' Compensation statute, employees can collect even though they are contributorily negligent or they assume the risk. The statute expressly excludes independent contractors. The principal test of the nature of an employment relationship is whether the person to whom the service is rendered has the right to control the manner and means of accomplishing the objective. "In addition, several secondary criteria are used to determine the nature of a service relationship. Such secondary criteria include, among others, (1) whether or not the worker is engaged in a distinct occupation or an independently established business; (2) whether the worker or the principal supplies the tools or instrumentalities used in the work, other than tools and instrumentalities customarily supplied by employees; (3) the method of payment, whether by time or by the job; (4) whether the work is part of the regular business of the principal; (5) whether the worker has a substantial investment in the business other than personal services; and (6) whether the worker hires employees to assist him."[5] Torres was employed as an independent contractor. The Reardons discussed with Torres the desired result, not the methods Torres was to use. The Reardons reasonably relied on Torres' representations that he had experience trimming trees. There is no evidence whatever that Boice was acting as the Reardons' agent or at their request.

BUSINESS CONSIDERATIONS What should Torres have done to reduce the likelihood of injuries and/or losses? Why? What if Torres's assistant had been injured instead?

ETHICAL CONSIDERATIONS Do the Reardons owe Torres a moral duty to pay for his injuries and/or lost wages? Why or why not? Does Boice owe Torres a moral duty to reimburse him for his losses? Why or why not?

Fiduciary duty

The legal duty to exercise the highest degree of loyalty and good faith in handling the affairs of the person to whom the duty is owed.

Independent contractors may be agents, but that is not a necessary condition for being an independent contractor. This is shown in Exhibit 31.3. If the independent contractor does not represent the hiring party or act for the hiring party in relation to third parties, the independent contractor is not the hiring party's agent. For example, a nonagent independent contractor who is building a house on an owner's lot cannot bind the owner to a contract. In these situations, the independent contractor does not owe the hiring party any **fiduciary duties**. A *fiduciary* is a person who owes a special duty of good faith and loyalty due to his or her status. Fiduciary relationships include attorney–client, priest–confessor, husband–wife, and agent–principal. Ordinary business transactions, such as contracts, do *not* create fiduciary relationships. Special relationships, such as agency relationships where the agent will represent the principal in contract negotiations, compel the exercise of utmost fairness and good faith by the agent. Agents *do* have fiduciary duties to their principals.

EXHIBIT 31.3 Independent Contractors May Also Be Agents

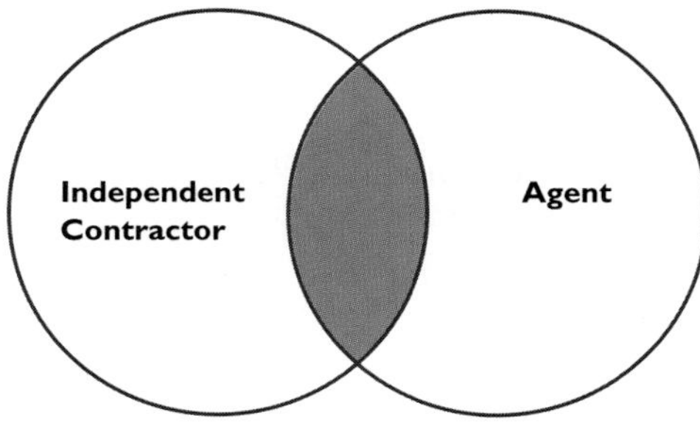

The shaded area indicates independent contractors who are also agents.

Independent contractors who are agents (1) have fiduciary duties and (2) can bind their principals to contracts. For example, attorneys owe their clients fiduciary duties when they negotiate settlements and then agree to them on the clients' behalf. On the other hand, attorneys are not the clients' employees. Legal clients have no control over when their attorneys come to work in the morning or when they leave work at the end of the day. These relationships are represented in Exhibit 31.4.

The following case addressed the issue of whether an independent contractor was an agent.

31.2 CANTON LUTHERAN CHURCH v. SOVIK, MATHRE, SATHRUM & QUANBECK

507 F.Supp. 873 (D.S.D. 1981)

FACTS Canton Lutheran Church wanted to build an addition to its principal structure. It entered into a contract with Sovik, Mathre, Sathrum & Quanbeck for professional services as an architect. Later, the church entered into a contract with a builder to construct the building the architect had designed. The architect agreed to be responsible for supervision of the work. The architect signed a certificate that the addition was substantially completed in accordance with the specifications. However, the building addition cracked because the concrete contained calcium chloride. The building specifications did not call for the use of calcium chloride, and its use was not authorized.

ISSUES Did the architect have a fiduciary duty to the church?

HOLDING Yes.

REASONING The architect was an agent and, as such, owed a fiduciary duty to the principal. An architect preparing a plan for a landowner generally acts as an independent contractor. With respect to the architect's duty to supervise the builder, the architect generally acts as an agent, thus serving as a representative of the party for whom the job is being completed. In such a case, there is a fiduciary duty. This is especially true when the architect has agreed to

31.2 CANTON LUTHERAN CHURCH v. SOVIK, MATHRE, SATHRUM & QUANBECK *(cont.)* 507 F.Supp. 873 (D.S.D. 1981)

guard against deficiencies in the work of the builder by supervising the builder's work. The relationship, then, is one of trust and confidence. South Dakota law defines a fiduciary, in part, as an agent. In this case, there was sufficient evidence that the architectural firm breached its fiduciary duty. It appeared that the architect had fraudulently concealed the builder's breach of contract. This issue was returned to the trial court.

BUSINESS CONSIDERATIONS What could or should the architect have done to avoid this dispute? Could the church have better protected its interests? How?

ETHICAL CONSIDERATIONS What moral obligation did the architect owe to the church? Why?

EXHIBIT 31.4 Is the Independent Contractor an Agent?

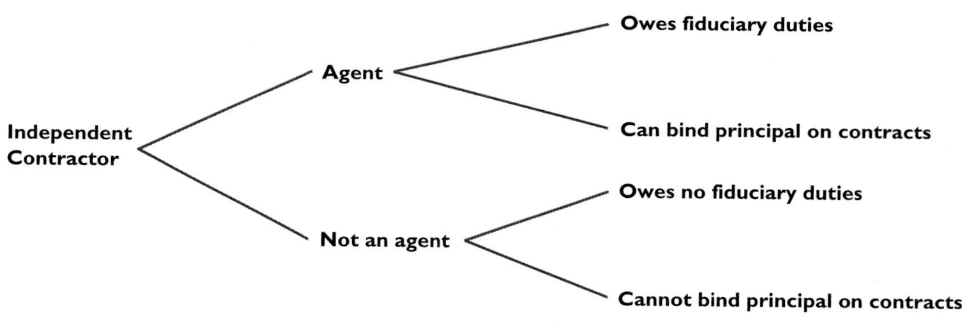

When legal questions concern fiduciary duties or contracts, the worker will simply be identified as an agent, rather than applying the cumbersome term "independent contractor agent."

Responsibility for Independent Contractors

Contract Liability. Principals who engage independent contractors as agents will be liable on the contract *if* the contract was authorized. Authorization is discussed in detail in Chapter 32. This liability complies with the general rule for agents.

Tort Liability. As was pointed out in *Torres* v. *Reardon,* the independent contractor generally cannot recover from the hiring party if he or she is injured while working. Employees of the independent contractor, however, have been permitted to recover from an independent contractor.

In addition, a person who hires an independent contractor usually is not responsible to third parties for the independent contractor's physical wrongdoings. Courts do make exceptions when the independent contractor is hired to engage in ultrahazardous activities or to commit a crime. The hiring party is also responsible if the hiring party actually directs the independent contractor to do something careless or wrong or if the hiring party sees the independent contractor do something wrong and does not stop it. In addition, courts have recently begun to hold hiring parties liable for their failure to adequately supervise independent contractors and for carelessly selecting them.

In many states, the trend has been to increase the number of situations in which a person who hires an independent contractor can be held liable. One method courts use is to reduce the standard from ultrahazardous activities to hazardous activities. In other words, a person is liable when he or she hires an independent contractor to engage in hazardous activities. The court applied the hazardous activities standard in the following case.

31.3 HENDERSON BROTHERS STORES, INC. v. SMILEY

174 Cal.Rptr. 875 (Cal.App. 1981)

FACTS Charles R. Smiley, a licensed roofing contractor, was hired to reroof L. A. MacDonald's building with asphalt. The asphalt must be heated to the melting point in a large tar kettle. Smiley was using such a kettle. He had placed it in a passageway between MacDonald's building and Henderson's warehouse. The kettle suddenly erupted and shot flames 10 to 20 feet into the air, setting fire to the Henderson building. This type of eruption is very common in the use of a tar kettle. The normal operation of tar kettles in roofing work presents a significant, recognizable danger of fire. Setting the thermostat too high, allowing the tar level in the kettle to be too low, and allowing carbon to build up increases the risk. There is evidence that all three occurred in this case.

ISSUE Did the hot roofing operation involve a special danger of fire so that MacDonald should be liable for the acts of its independent contractor, Smiley?

HOLDING Yes.

REASONING The general rule is that there is no vicarious liability for the person who hires an independent contractor. U.S. courts recognize a number of exceptions to this rule. One such exception to the general rule of nonliability is where the contractor is engaged in the performance of "inherently dangerous" work. This is also called the "peculiar risk" doctrine. Under the *Restatement (Second) of Torts*, the hiring party is directly liable for failing to provide in the agreement with the independent contractor for the independent contractor to take appropriate precautions in cases of "peculiar risk." It is not required that the work be of the type that cannot be done without a risk of harm to others. The rule is based on the negligent failure of the hiring party or the contractor to take appropriate special precautions. MacDonald should be liable for the acts of its independent contractor.

BUSINESS CONSIDERATIONS What could MacDonald do to reduce the risk of injury due to the reroofing operation? What could Smiley do to reduce the risks associated with this procedure?

ETHICAL CONSIDERATIONS Does MacDonald owe a duty to its neighbor, Henderson Brothers Stores? Why or why not?

The independent contractor is also liable for his or her wrongdoings. In fact, in the previous case Henderson was suing Smiley, the roofing contractor, *and* MacDonald, the owner who hired Smiley.

Duties of the Agent to the Principal

The agent must protect the interests of the principal, as the duties discussed in the following sections show. Some of the duties overlap. In fact, when an agent breaches one duty, most likely others will be breached as well.

Duty of Good Faith

The duty of good faith is also called the fiduciary duty, and the rule is that every agent owes the principal the obligation of faithful service. The most common violations of this duty include concealing essential facts that are relevant to the agency, obtaining secret profits, and self-dealing. Suppose the principal is looking for a parcel of agricultural land, and the agent locates a suitable parcel. The agent arranges for its sale to the principal without first informing the principal that the agent owns a one-third interest in the parcel. In this case, the agent has violated his or her fiduciary duty to the principal.

Duty of Loyalty

An agent has a duty to be loyal to the principal and to protect the principal's best interests. Thus, an agent must not compete with the principal, work for someone who is competing with the principal, or act to further the agent's own interests.

The following case addresses breach of the duty of loyalty. In this case, the agent did not provide loyal service because he concealed essential facts and did not perform the purpose of the agency.

31.4 BLACK v. DAHL 625 P.2d 876 (Alaska 1981)

FACTS Frank Dahl rented and operated Illiamna Lake Lodge on a long-term lease. Dahl was behind in his rent and was in danger of losing his entire investment. He contacted Richard D. Black, a real estate salesperson, about finding a purchaser for Dahl's interest. They entered into an agreement under which Black would receive a 10 percent commission if he located a buyer. Black located two partners who were interested in the premises. These partners wanted to see the financial records and to make a physical inspection. Dahl was not informed of these requests. Black also told the partners that if they delayed 10 to 15 days, they could acquire the lease for $10,000 less. When Dahl asked Black about the progress on the negotiations, Black indicated that he guessed the partners were not interested. Dahl lost his financial interest because he defaulted on the lease. After the default, the partners purchased the lease from others. Dahl did not share in these proceeds.

ISSUE Did Black violate his duty of loyalty as an agent?

HOLDING Yes.

REASONING Black owed Dahl a duty to try to find a buyer for Dahl's interest in the premises. Once a buyer was located, Black had a duty to use due diligence to close the transaction. Black violated his duty. In fact, he discouraged the buyers from completing the purchase until after Dahl had lost his interest by default. Black did not protect Dahl's interest.

BUSINESS CONSIDERATIONS What procedures should Black have followed? Why? How could Dahl have better protected his financial interests?

ETHICAL CONSIDERATIONS Analyze Black's ethical perspective. What moral duty did Black have?

An agent may not use his or her agency position for personal benefits at the expense of the principal. Such self-dealings involve a breach of the duty of loyalty. The following example shows a variation on a common problem many businesses must confront—employee conversion of firm assets.

> André works in the marketing division of a large company. One of his responsibilities is to purchase supplies for the division. He tells Katie, the division chief, that the division has 5¼-inch computer diskettes no one is using. André indicates that this is not a problem because he will take them home.
>
> Allowing André to take the diskettes home will be a breach of fiduciary duties and a poor business practice. He will be setting a bad example for the other employees and he will be unlikely to search for alternatives that would be more beneficial to the division and the company. There are a number of options available to the division: trade the diskettes for supplies with the other divisions; return the diskettes to the vendor (seller) for a credit; or keep the diskettes for future use. Perhaps the employees who use this size diskette already have a supply at their workstations and they will come to the supply room when their supply runs out.
>
> If André is permitted to take unused supplies home, this might encourage him to order supplies that he wanted at home with the hope that he would be able to use them himself. Katie should resolve this conflict of interest as soon as possible.

Duty to Obey All Lawful Instructions

Agents must follow all *lawful* instructions as long as doing so does not subject them to an unreasonable risk of injury. This is true even if agents think the instructions are capricious or unwise. Agents need not follow instructions that are outside the course and scope of the agency relationship. They must repay their principals for damages suffered because they failed to follow instructions that are in the course and scope of their employment.

Duty to Act with Reasonable Care

An agent has a duty to act as a reasonably careful agent would under the same circumstances. Again, if the agent fails to live up to this obligation and it causes the principal a loss, the agent will be obliged to reimburse the principal.

Duty to Segregate Funds

The agent has a duty to keep personal funds separate from the principal's funds. If the agent wrongfully uses the principal's funds to purchase something, the court can impose a **trust** and treat the situation as though the purchase were originally made for the benefit of the principal. Such a trust—that is, a trust imposed by a court for the purpose of preventing unjust enrichment—is called a *constructive trust*. Constructive trusts are discussed in Chapter 46.

Trust

An arrangement in which legal title, indicated on the deed or other evidence of ownership, is separated from the equitable or beneficial ownership.

Duty to Account for Funds

An agent has a duty to account for money received. This is really a combined function of delivery of the funds and recordkeeping. The funds usually must be delivered

31.2

SALES/MANAGEMENT

THE RISKS OF HIRING SALESPEOPLE

CIT needs to expand its geographic market area in order to succeed as an entity. To do so, the firm will need to make sales in other regions. Neither Tom nor Anna want to spend the necessary time away from home, nor do they want to send any of their children out for such extended periods of time. However, they are also hesitant to hire sales representatives for the Call-Image product line. Among other things, they fear that such representatives may copy the product and start a competing firm based on the customers they have cultivated. Dan does not feel that this is a valid concern. He believes there are protections available to the firm, but is not sure that he is fully informed. He has asked for your input about the potential problem. What will you tell the family?

BUSINESS CONSIDERATIONS What policies should a firm establish to maximize its protection in the event an agent violates his or her duty? What are the legal rights of a principal whose agent attempts to utilize technological information obtained in the course of employment for the personal benefit of that agent?

ETHICAL CONSIDERATIONS What are the ethical implications of acting as a sales agent for a firm that produces a highly technical product? What ethical principles would preclude an agent from attempting to establish a business in competition with his or her former principal based on either the knowledge or the customers he or she developed as an agent?

to the principal (or an authorized third party). If the money was received while the agent was not in the course and scope of the employment, the agent has a duty to return the proceeds to the third party. Compare the agent's duty in each of the two examples that follow for an illustration of how this duty is applied.

> Bhudi is a sales representative for Finch, Inc. He takes a potential client to dinner to discuss possible orders the client might place with Finch. The client, impressed with the presentation Bhudi makes during the meal, places an order for $10,000 worth of goods, writing a check as payment in full for the goods ordered. Although Bhudi is technically "off the clock," this sale would be considered to have occurred in the course and scope of Bhudi's employment, and he would be expected to account to Finch for the proceeds from the sale.

> Bhudi is a sales representative for Finch, Inc., but he is not authorized to accept payments for goods he sells for the principal. He takes his wife to dinner to celebrate their anniversary. While they are eating, a client of Finch recognizes Bhudi as an employee of Finch. The client approaches Bhudi's table and hands Bhudi a check for $10,000 as payment for goods ordered from Finch the previous week. Bhudi is technically "off the clock," *and* he is not authorized to receive payments for his principal. In this situation, Bhudi would be expected to return the check to the client and to explain to the client that the check should be sent directly to Finch, the principal.

Duty to Give Notice

The *duty to give notice* requires that an agent will inform the principal about material facts that are discovered within the scope of the agent's employment. For example, if a tenant gives an apartment manager notice that the tenant will move out at the end of the month, it is assumed that the manager will inform the owner. In fact, the principal may be bound by this notice even though the agent failed to inform the principal. It is said that the notice is "imputed" to the principal.

Duties of the Principal to the Agent

Many of the duties of the principal may be specified in the contract between the principal and the agent. In general, the principal has the following obligations to the agent:

YOU BE THE JUDGE

No More Computer Games on the Job for Virginia Employees

Industry specialists contend that employees playing games on company computers has significant costs for businesses. A 1993 survey of 1,000 corporations by a software company found that workers spend an average of 5.1 hours a week doing non-job-related tasks on their company computers. This includes playing games. It is estimated that this costs the nation $10 billion annually in lost productivity.

Governor George Allen of Virginia has ordered that games be *deleted* from *all* state-owned computers, including those of university faculty members. To quote an administrative memo, "[T]ime spent by employees playing such games should be considered an improper use of taxpayer funds." The ban, which eliminates playing games during breaks and lunch time, is raising questions among Virginia employees. If an employee challenged this in *your* court, how would *you* rule?[6]

BUSINESS CONSIDERATIONS Assume you are a high-level corporate manager. What approach would you take and why? What are the advantages of this approach?

ETHICAL CONSIDERATIONS Is Virginia taking an ethical approach to this problem? Why or why not? If an individual feels that playing games is acceptable, is it moral for that individual to play? Why or why not?

SOURCE: Rajiv Chandrasekaran, *The Fresno Bee,* 10 January 1995, p. D10.

1. To pay the agent per the agreement
2. To maintain proper accounts so that compensation and reimbursement will be correct
3. To provide the agent with the means to do the job
4. To continue the employment for the time period specified in the agreement

With the exception of gratuitous agents, agents are entitled to be paid under the terms of their agreements with the principal. Some types of agents are entitled to compensation under special arrangements such as commission sales. Also, these unique situations are usually mentioned in the written contract. For example, in some states real estate agents are entitled to their commissions if they find a buyer who is ready, willing, and able to buy the parcel. This is true even if the transfer does not occur because of destruction of the building, the buyer's inability to obtain a loan, or some other circumstance. Some states follow a different rule, whereby a sale must close before a commission is earned.

In addition if the worker is a servant, his or her master has an obligation to provide the servant with a reasonably safe place to work and safe equipment to use. This obligation is based on common law *and* state and federal safety statutes, such as the federal Occupational Safety and Health Act (OSHA). Under OSHA, the secretary of labor *may* pass regulations permitting workers to refuse to work under hazardous conditions.[7] A master also owes a servant an obligation to compensate him or her for injuries under state workers' compensation laws. Workers' compensation laws are discussed in Chapters 33 and 43.

31.3

PROTECTING AGAINST WORKPLACE VIOLENCE

John has become very concerned about workplace violence. This topic has been discussed in several of his classes as one of the fastest-growing problem areas in the 1990s. One example cited in one class involved a manager who fired an employee for using drugs while on the job. The dismissed employee became verbally abusive, and he had to be physically removed from the workplace. At that point he went home to get his hunting rifle, returned to the plant with the rifle, and proceeded to shoot the manager and four of his former co-workers.

Although John is unsure as to exactly how to best protect the family members at work, he believes they should at least keep a gun in the office suite for protection. He asks you for any suggestions you have. What will you tell him?

BUSINESS CONSIDERATIONS Workplace violence is not just a legal problem. It also presents serious business implications. What policies should a business establish to protect its employees and its business operation from workplace violence? Should a business establish policies for some sort of intervention and/or counseling prior to the dismissal of an employee?

ETHICAL CONSIDERATIONS What should a firm do, from an ethical perspective, before it fires an employee? Is having a gun in the office area an ethical solution to the potential threat of violence in the workplace?

MANAGEMENT

TERMINATION OF THE AGENCY RELATIONSHIP

Agreement of the Parties

An agency relationship is governed in the first instance by the agreement between the principal and the agent. Commonly the contract will be established for a set period. For example, if a real estate agent has a listing to sell a house according to certain terms, one of the terms may specify the period for which the contract is going to run, say 90 days; that agreement, therefore, will terminate at the end of 90 days.

The parties can consent to amend the agency agreement to terminate the agency relationship early or to extend it. For example, if the house we just referred to is not sold within 90 days, the owner and agent may specifically extend the agency agreement for another 60 days.

If the parties consent to the continuation of the agency relationship beyond the period originally stated, this consent may be implied as a renewal of the original contract for the same period and under the same conditions. This is true only if they have not specifically altered the terms and conditions of the original agreement.

Agency at Will

If the agency agreement does not specify a set date, a set period, or a set occurrence that will terminate it, the relationship is an *agency at will.* Either party can terminate the relationship by giving notice to the other. The principal or agent does not need cause or justification to terminate the relationship. This is consistent with the theory that agency is a voluntary relationship between the parties. Traditionally, it was perceived that the two parties were relatively equal in their bargaining position and that, consequently, this rule was fair.

The traditional concept of an agency at will is being eroded rapidly. In addition, courts are recognizing various theories for recovery by the discharged agent. Adoption of these theories of recovery vary depending on the situation and state law.[8] Three common examples follow:

1. The courts are recognizing a breach of employment contract, that is, an express or implied agreement that the employment will not be terminated *or* will not be terminated without following a specific set of procedures. For example, union–management contracts generally prevent the dismissal of union employees without a showing of cause and the following of specific procedures. Implied contracts often are based on procedures and policies in personnel manuals.

2. Courts are also recognizing a tort of bad faith discharge, where the employee has a right of continued employment and has developed a relationship of trust, reliance, and dependency on the employer. Bad faith is usually evidenced by fraud, malice, or oppression.
3. Some states are holding an employer liable for a tortious discharge if the termination violates public policy. This is based on the theory that employees should not have to forfeit their positions because they acted in a manner that supports some *important* public policy. This basis is commonly used to protect whistle-blowers, for example, employees who report safety violations to OSHA. Antiretaliation statutes provide statutory protection to whistle-blowers in *some* situations at both the federal and state levels.

States may not recognize any of these theories or they may recognize some combination of them. Most of the court cases involve servants instead of independent contractors. The courts generally use the terms "employer" and "employee" when discussing both agency at will and wrongful discharge. In the following case, the court addressed an agency at will.

Precedents

Prior court cases that control the decision in court.

31.5 SAVODNIK v. KORVETTES, INC. 488 F.Supp. 822 (E.D.N.Y. 1980)

FACTS Morton Savodnik was employed by Korvettes from 7 October 1963 to 26 January 1977, when he received his termination notice. During that period, he received frequent promotions and annual increases in pay. He was never fined, demoted, or warned about his job performance. Savodnik claimed that he suffered a heart attack because of his termination. He had participated in Korvettes' retirement plan and would have been entitled to the money Korvettes contributed to the plan in his name after 15 years of employment. Savodnik alleged that Korvettes fired him to prevent him from receiving its contribution. Korvettes did not deny this.

ISSUE Did Korvettes lawfully fire Savodnik?

HOLDING No.

REASONING Under the traditional doctrine of employment at will, the employer or the employee can terminate the contract at will and without reason. However, this doctrine is undergoing dynamic development. In many states, the courts are rewriting the traditional doctrine based on careful assessments of the public good and what will benefit the economic system. Courts are allowing an employee to recover when the firing is based on retaliation, bad faith, or an attempt to avoid paying an employee's commissions. Since this is an issue governed by state law, the court in this case was bound by New York law. New York courts have not yet recognized a cause of action for wrongful firing or abusive discharge. New York **precedents** indicate a willingness to recognize this tort cause of action.

The court found that Mr. Savodnik was a model employee for more than 13 years and that Korvettes had no justification for firing him; in addition, Korvettes had a pattern of firing employees to avoid granting them rights in the company retirement plan. Consequently, Korvettes needs a valid reason to fire Savodnik. [These parties were also involved in a trial on related issues, which is reported at 489 F.Supp. 1010 (E.D.N.Y. 1980).]

BUSINESS CONSIDERATIONS What procedures should Korvettes have followed in firing employees? What would be valid considerations in selecting whom to fire?

ETHICAL CONSIDERATIONS Does Korvettes owe Savodnik a moral obligation? What duties do employers owe to employees?

Other public policy prohibitions exist on firing agents at will. If the agent was fired on the basis of gender, race, religion, or national origin, or some other violation of civil rights, the courts may decide that the principal cannot terminate the relationship. Notice that wrongful discharge has been used to prevent employers from firing employees, but employees in employment-at-will relationships are still free to quit at any time and for any reason. (Wrongful discharge is discussed more fully in Chapters 2 and 43.)

Fulfillment of the Agency Purpose

Logically, an agency relationship terminates when the purpose for which it was created has been fulfilled. It does not make sense to continue the relationship beyond that point.

Revocation

Principals can revoke or terminate the authority of their agents to act on their behalf. They should directly notify their agents of the termination. The notice that the agency relationship is being terminated, moreover, should be clear and unequivocal. Indirect notice will *sometimes* be sufficient—for example, hiring a second agent to complete all the duties of the first agent. Due to the agent's obligation to obey, the principal can terminate the agency at any time. This is true even though there was an agreement that the agency relationship should continue longer. Even a statement in the agreement that the agency cannot be terminated does not affect the principal's ability to terminate it. Although the principal may have the *ability* to terminate the agency, he or she may not have the legal *right* to do so; in such a case, the agency can be terminated, but the principal may be liable for damages if this termination is a breach of contract.

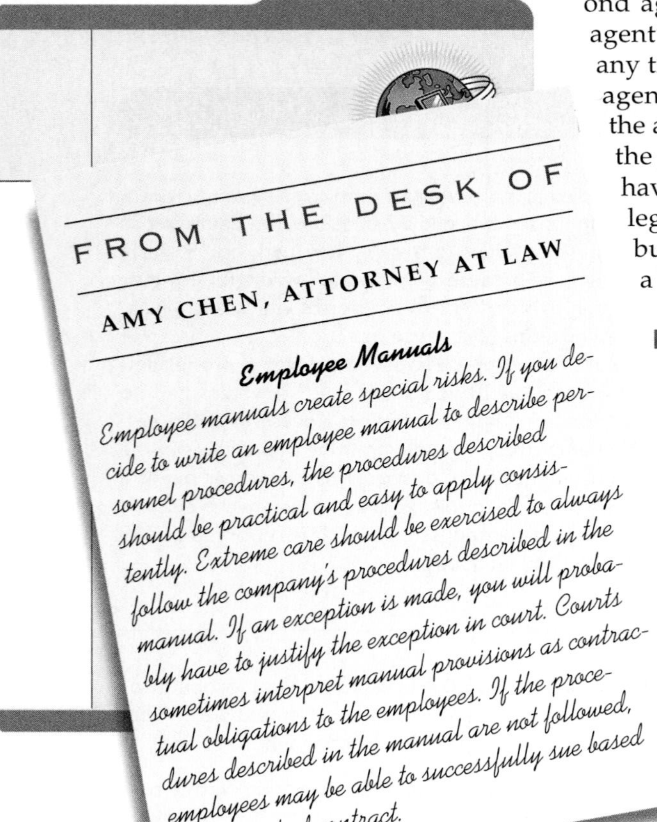

FROM THE DESK OF
AMY CHEN, ATTORNEY AT LAW
Employee Manuals
Employee manuals create special risks. If you decide to write an employee manual to describe personnel procedures, the procedures described should be practical and easy to apply consistently. Extreme care should be exercised to always follow the company's procedures described in the manual. If an exception is made, you will probably have to justify the exception in court. Courts sometimes interpret manual provisions as contractual obligations to the employees. If the procedures described in the manual are not followed, employees may be able to successfully sue based on an implied contract.

Renunciation

Renunciation occurs when the agent notifies the principal that he or she will no longer serve as an agent. In other words, the agent resigns. Since an agency relationship is voluntary, an agent can renounce. However, the agent may be liable to the principal if the renunciation is a breach of their contract.

Operation of Law

In the legal system, operation of law "expresses the manner in which rights, and sometimes liabilities, devolve upon a person by the mere application to the particular transaction of the established rules of law, without the act or co-operation of the party. . . ."[9] There are some occurrences that automatically terminate an agency relationship without any additional action. These occurrences include:

1. When the agent dies
2. When either party becomes insane

3. When the principal becomes bankrupt
4. When his or her agent becomes bankrupt, if the bankruptcy affects the agency
5. When the agency cannot possibly be performed (e.g., when the subject matter of the agency is destroyed)
6. When an unusual and unanticipated change in circumstances occurs that destroys the purpose of the agency relationship
7. When a change in law makes completion of the agency relationship illegal

The traditional rule is that the death of the principal also terminates the agency relationship immediately. Because this rule can cause hardship, many states modified their laws to take a more liberal approach. Under this more liberal rule, the death of the principal does not immediately terminate the agency relationship *if* immediate termination will cause a hardship.

When the relationship is terminated by the operation of law, usually it is unnecessary to give notice to the other party or to the public at large. This rule is discretionary, and a court may decide to require notice if its absence causes a great hardship.

Importance of Notice

When an agent or a principal terminates the agency relationship early, the agent or principal has a duty to notify the other party so that the other party does not waste effort on a relationship that no longer exists. If the principal revokes the agency relationship and does not notify the agent, the principal is obligated to indemnify the agent for liabilities which the agent incurs in the proper performance of his or her duties.[10]

It may be crucial to notify third parties even if it is not legally required, such as in termination by operation of law. The agent may find it advantageous to provide notice, but the principal will find notice even more important. If the principal fails to notify a third party, the third party can transfer money, such as a rent payment, to the agent with the expectation that the agent will forward the funds to the principal. If the agent is unhappy with the termination, the agent may unlawfully abscond with the money.

The notice can take various forms. The preferred method is to personally notify the third person by mail, electronically transmitted facsimile copy, telephone, or telegram. Personal notice is generally required for all third parties who have had dealings with the agent. The advantage of using an electronically transmitted facsimile copy is that it is fast, and there is written proof of the notification. Without written proof, the third party may deny receiving the notice. Notice should be given promptly, since one of its purposes is to prevent losses caused by a disgruntled agent who feels that the termination is unjust.

In addition, the law accepts notice by publication (also called constructive notice). Usually, such notice is published in the legal notices in the newspaper. This is the only type of notice that is practical for members of the public who are aware of the agency but who have not had previous dealings with the agent.

The principal will be protected if the third party actually knows that the agency relationship has been terminated, even if the third party did not receive notice from the principal (i.e., the third party may have heard about the termination from the agent or from someone else).

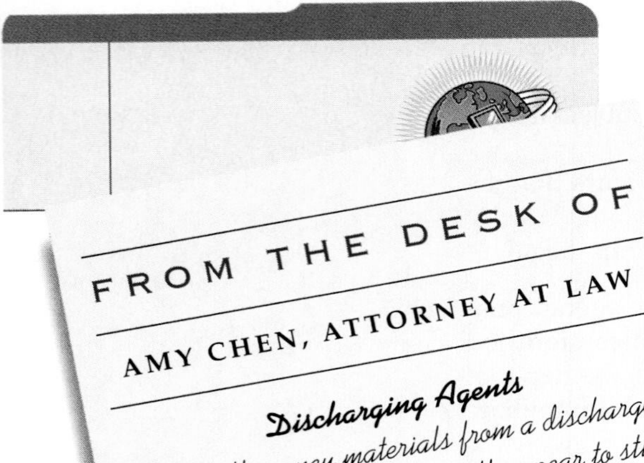

Discharging Agents

Recover all agency materials from a discharged agent. Otherwise the agent will appear to still work for you. A third party who is aware of the agency with your firm but has not received actual notice of the termination may continue to deal with the "agent." To the third party, the "agent" will appear to still act for the firm. You can be liable for the "agent's" acts under apparent authority. Since the "agent" has been terminated, the agent may be displeased and may maliciously attempt to cause the loss of finances and good reputation.

Breach of Agency Agreement

Generally the principal has the power to terminate the agency, even if the principal does not have the right. If the principal wrongfully revokes the agent's authority, the agent can sue for breach of express or implied contract. Many principal–agent contracts contain provisions for arbitrating disputes between them. Arbitration is discussed in Chapter 7. If there is an anticipatory breach and the principal notifies the agent in advance of the breach, the agent can sue the principal immediately for the anticipated damages. The agent, at his or her election, may decide to wait until after the contract period and then sue for actual damages. In either case, the agent has an obligation to *mitigate damages* or to keep them as low as possible by searching for another similar position with another principal in the same locality. Mitigating damages are discussed more fully in Chapter 15.

SPECIAL SITUATIONS

Most agency relationships are formed for the benefit of the principal, but some are formed for the protection and benefit of the agent. The latter most commonly occur when the agent has loaned money to the principal, and the principal is securing the loan with collateral.

The mere statement in a contract that an agency is irrevocable will not make it true. Courts analyze the facts to make sure the agent has an *interest* in the collateral itself. Many of these legal disputes arise because the principal wishes to terminate the agency relationship and the agent wishes to prevent the termination. Two special situations do restrict the principal's *ability* to terminate the agency relationship: (1) agency coupled with an obligation and (2) power coupled with an interest.

Agency Coupled with an Obligation

Suppose Paula needs cash for an investment. Since the banks will not lend Paula the money, she decides to borrow the $50,000 from Angela for two years. Angela insists on having collateral, so Paula gives Angela the right to sell her building if Paula does not repay the loan within two years. Angela is entitled to take her $50,000 and her expenses out of the sale, but she has to give the rest of the money to Paula. In this situation, Paula, the principal, has an *obligation* to repay the $50,000 to her agent, Angela. Angela can, if necessary, sell the property to obtain payment. Although a principal cannot terminate such an arrangement at will, the death of a party or a bankruptcy that affects the agency can terminate it.

Power Coupled with an Interest

Power coupled with an interest is similar to an agency coupled with an obligation, but it is more formal and the "agent's" rights are better protected. As the name implies, it is not actually an agency relationship. The parties have a power coupled with an interest if the "agent's" interest is taken through some formal document—for ex-

http:// RESOURCES FOR BUSINESS LAW STUDENTS

NAME	RESOURCES	WEB ADDRESS
American Law Institute	The American Law Institute, publisher of *Restatements* of the law, model codes, and other proposals for law reform, provides press releases, its newsletter, and other publications.	http://www.ali.org
Independent Contractor Report	The *Independent Contractor Report,* a monthly newsletter, has materials on employment tax cases, rulings, and other issues for users of independent contractors.	http://www.webcom.com/ic_rep
DB Basics, Inc., Company Policy Manual	DB Basics, Inc., a software development company, maintains its employee handbook on-line.	http://www.dbbasics.com/Web_Employment_Manual.html

ample, if Angela's interest is arranged through a mortgage on Paula's property. It also differs from an agency coupled with an obligation in that the death or bankruptcy of a party will not terminate it.

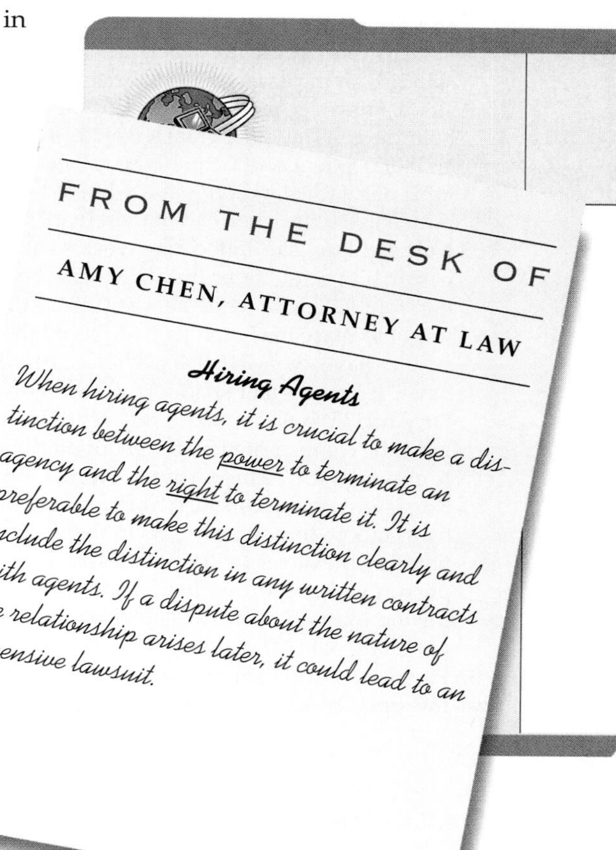

FROM THE DESK OF
AMY CHEN, ATTORNEY AT LAW
Hiring Agents
When hiring agents, it is crucial to make a distinction between the power to terminate an agency and the right to terminate it. It is preferable to make this distinction clearly and include the distinction in any written contracts with agents. If a dispute about the nature of the relationship arises later, it could lead to an expensive lawsuit.

SUMMARY

Agency relationships center on the agreement between a principal and an agent that the agent will act for the benefit of the principal. The principal must have the capacity to consent to the relationship. The agent need not have contractual capacity. Most agents are compensated. An agent who does not receive compensation is called a gratuitous agent.

In analyzing the legal rights of the parties, one must determine whether the worker is a servant or an independent contractor. An independent contractor is hired to complete a job. The hiring party does not direct how the independent contractor does the task. In contrast, a principal can exert a great deal of control over a servant and how the servant performs assigned duties. Because the principal can control the servant, the principal is more likely to be held financially responsible for the servant's physical acts.

An agent has a duty to act in good faith, to act loyally, to obey all lawful instructions, to act with reasonable care, to segregate funds, to account for all funds, and to give notice.

An agency relationship may terminate at a specified time agreed on by the parties, at the will of the parties, or after the purpose of the agency has been fulfilled. It can be revoked or renounced by one of the parties or terminated by operation of law. Even in an agent at will situation, the employer can be successfully sued for breach of an expressed or implied employment contract; bad faith discharge; or tortious discharge in violation of public policy.

A principal generally has the power to terminate an agency relationship even if the termination is wrongful. The principal does not have the power to terminate either an agency coupled with an obligation or a power coupled with an interest without the agent's consent.

Discussion Questions

1. Jesse purchases a new home through Gary, his realtor. The house needs a lot of work, so Jesse arranges for Joyce to paint the interior, for Harry to repair the furnace, for his own daughters to plant grass in the backyard, and for Martha to clean the interior. Based on normal hiring relationships, who are agents, servants, or independent contractors, and why? Are the agents special agents or general agents, and why?
2. Juan hires Jack to deliver one cord of pine wood for the fireplace in the house Juan rents. Jack usually just dumps the wood in the driveway—a practice known as a driveway delivery. However, this time he decides to help Juan stack the wood in the garage. Juan is standing in the garage as Jack backs the truck into position. However, Jack backs the truck too far, damaging both the truck and the garage wall. Is Jack a servant or an independent contractor? Who is liable to the injured third party (the landlord), and why? Who would have been liable if the truck had injured Juan? Why?
3. Kurt went to Lake Tahoe for a week's vacation. Before he left, his friend, Karen, gave him $5 to bet on a particular football game while he was there. Kurt, however, forgot to place the bet. If he had placed the bet, Karen would have won $15,000. What rights does Karen have? If Karen's team had lost, what rights would she have had? Would it make a difference if Kurt was going to be compensated by Karen for placing the bet?
4. Ron works for Acme Grocery Store. One day while Ron is unloading produce from a truck, Jimmy stops by to talk to him. Jimmy gets in the truck, and, while handing the boxes to Ron, carelessly drops a box on a person walking down the alley. Who is responsible for the injury, and why? Is it relevant that Jimmy is not being paid? If so, why?
5. Peter hires Andy to purchase some goods for him on the open market. While Andy is obtaining prices from vendors, Ted offers Andy a $100 rebate if Andy purchases the goods from Ted; Andy does and keeps the $100 for himself. What are the rights of the parties? Why?
6. Elaine works as a travel agent for Travel Enterprises, Inc. As an incentive, a cruise ship line offers travel agents one free passage on a cruise for every 25 paying passengers they book on the line. The cruise ship line feels that this practice is good public relations. Elaine has earned two free passages. Who is entitled to these passages, and why? Should Elaine's customers be concerned about this practice? Why or why not?
7. After nine years of marriage, Jill and Jon decide to get a divorce. Their neighbor Charlie, who is an attorney, will do the legal work for both parties and handle the property settlement. Are there any problems with this arrangement? Why or why not?
8. Brad calls Marty, his stockbroker, to tell him that Ellen, Brad's friend, will purchase some stock from Marty. Brad directs Marty to charge the purchases against the brokerage account of Brad and his wife, Sue. What is Marty's responsibility to Brad and his wife? What advice will you give Marty?
9. Steve manages a 200-unit apartment complex. The owners want to convert the apartments to condominiums. The city council will have a hearing on the issue. Instead of sending the notice to the owners, the council sends the notice to Steve. What are the rights and obligations of the parties? Why?
10. Sarah signs a written contract stating that her agency relationship will last for four years and that she will have the irrevocable right to take orders from parents for children's educational software for her principal. In an attempt to downsize and economize, however, her principal fires her. What rights does Sarah have?

Case Problems and Writing Assignments

1. Harold Frankel incorporated as a one-person corporation in order to obtain some pension benefits under the federal tax code. He then entered into a contract with Bally, Inc., to serve as a sales repre-

sentative. When Bally terminated the arrangement, Frankel, age 61, filed a suit against Bally under the federal Age Discrimination in Employment Act (Act). Only employees are covered by the Act. Can a person who incorporates himself be an employee under the Act? [See *Frankel* v. *Bally, Inc.*, 987 F.2d 86 (2d Cir. 1993).]

2. Jeffrey Paul Russell was an employee of Uniq'wood. As such he received health-care coverage provided by Uniq'wood, pursuant to a group health insurance contract issued by Blue Cross. Uniq'wood was specified as the group agent. One of its duties was to notify employees of changes in their coverage. Uniq'wood notified Blue Cross to terminate Russell's coverage and notified Russell that it had been canceled. Does Blue Cross owe Russell a fiduciary duty? Why or why not? [See *Russell* v. *Uniq'wood Furniture Galleries, Inc.*, 1994 U.S.Dist. LEXIS 9620 (S.D.Ala., S.Div., 1994).]

3. The attendant at a service station fatally shot Mrs. Giles's son. Under the lease agreement and the dealer contract, the oil company did not have the right to control the day-to-day operations of the service station and its employees. It was not its custom to exercise such control. Was the attendant an employee of the oil company? Should the oil company be held liable? [See *Giles* v. *Shell Oil Corp.*, 487 A.2d 610 (D.C.App. 1985).]

4. Robert T. Darden was an insurance "agent" who worked for Nationwide Mutual Insurance Co. Under their written contract Darden was enrolled in a Nationwide "insurance agents retirement plan," which provided that Darden would forfeit his retirement benefits if he sold insurance for a competitor within one year of retirement and within 25 miles from his prior business location. Darden began selling for a competitor and Nationwide implemented the forfeiture provision. Darden sued under the federal Employee Retirement Income Security Act of 1974 (ERISA). Only employees have rights under ERISA. Was Darden an employee or an independent contractor when he worked for Nationwide? Was the Nationwide "insurance agents retirement plan" subject to ERISA? [See *Nationwide Mutual Insurance Co.* v. *Darden*, 503 U.S. 318 (1992).]

5. Personnel employed by an independent security agency committed intentional torts. The security agency had been hired by the owners of the property for the purpose of protecting their premises and their invitees. Under these circumstances, should the owner be liable for the acts of the security personnel? Why or why not? [See *Peachtree-Cain Co.* v. *McBee*, 327 S.E.2d 188 (Ga. 1985).]

6. **BUSINESS APPLICATIONS PROBLEM** Richard and Marian Silva wanted to sell a parcel of real estate, and they listed it for sale with Bernice Bisbee, who worked for Midkiff Realty. A joint venture was formed for the purpose of purchasing this property. Bisbee was to manage this joint venture and in exchange was to receive 10 percent of the profits. The buyers and sellers agreed on a purchase price of $100,000 and terms. The Silvas were never informed that the purchaser was part of a joint venture or that Bisbee had an interest in the joint venture. There was substantial evidence that Bisbee believed that the property was worth more than $100,000 at the time of the sale. Did Bisbee breach her fiduciary duty to the Silvas? Why or why not? [See *Silva* v. *Bisbee*, 628 P.2d 214 (Hawaii App. 1981).]

7. **ETHICS APPLICATION CASE** Robert Jones worked for Western States operating heavy equipment. When the equipment broke down, he was assigned a position in the cyanide leach pit. Previously Jones had attended one of his employer's safety courses, where he had learned about the dangers of absorption of cyanide and the need to avoid contact with open wounds. Since Jones had an open wound from surgery, he asked to be assigned an alternate position. He was then fired for insubordination. Was Robert Jones wrongfully discharged? Why or why not? Analyze the ethical perspective of Western States. Compare this case to *Geary* v. *U.S. Steel Corp.*, 319 A.2d 174 (Pa. 1974), Case Problem 8. [See *Western States Minerals Corp.* v. *Jones*, 819 P.2d 206 (Nev. 1991).]

8. **IDES CASE** From 1953 until July 1967, Geary worked as a sales representative for United States Steel Corporation (USS). Geary, an agent at will, sold tubular products to the oil and gas industry. USS designed a new product for use under high pressure. Geary believed that this new product had not been adequately tested and posed a serious danger to users. He voiced his concerns to his supervisors and was told to sell the product. He then contacted the vice president in charge of the product to get action. The product was withdrawn from the market. Geary was fired. Under the circumstances, was Geary entitled to protection from being discharged? Should he be protected from being fired? Use the IDES model to analyze this case. Based on your analysis, could USS have better handled the situation? [See *Geary* v. *United States Steel Corporation*, 319 A.2d 174 (Pa. 1974).]

NOTES

1. *Restatement (Second) of Agency* (Philadelphia: American Law Institute, 1958), § 1.
2. Ibid., § 20, Comment b.
3. Ibid., § 492, Comment a.
4. Ibid., § 3, Comment a.
5. *Torres* v. *Reardon*, 5 Cal.Rptr.2d 52, 55 (Cal.App. 2 Dist. 1992), citing other precedents.
6. Rajiv Chandrasekaran, "No More Games for Virginia Employees," *The Fresno Bee* (10 January 1995), p. D10.
7. *Whirlpool Corp.* v. *Marshall*, 445 U.S. 1 (1980).
8. On 8 August 1991, the National Conference of Commissioners on Uniform State Laws approved the Model Employment Termination Act 2 (Proposed Official Draft, 1991), which addresses these issues. To date, no states have adopted this model act. [Information on the current status of adoptions of Uniform State Laws provided during a telephone conversation with Katie Robinson, NCCUSL, 1 April 1997.]
9. *Black's Law Dictionary*, West Publishing Co. (St. Paul, MN 1933), p. 1241.
10. Harold Gill Reuschlein and William A. Gregory, *Hornbook on the Law of Agency and Partnership*, 2nd ed. (St. Paul: West Publishing Co., 1990), § 89(b), pp. 151–152.

Chapter 32

Agency: Liability for Contracts

Outline

Agenda

Will CIT appoint agents? If so, will CIT be a disclosed, undisclosed, or partially disclosed principal? What authority should CIT expressly grant to agents? What additional authority will the agents have?

Tom is concerned that salespersons will negotiate contracts with buyers and distributors that Tom and Anna have not authorized and find unacceptable. What can Tom do to alleviate this concern? In general, what steps should CIT take with its sales force to reduce the risk of this type of problem?

What steps should CIT agents take to minimize their personal liability on contracts they negotiate for CIT?

CIT will deal with the agents of suppliers and retailers. In these relationships, CIT will be the third party. What rights will CIT have against these agents and their principals?

These and similar questions arise when agents enter into contracts with third parties. Be prepared! You never know when one of the Kochanowskis will ask you for help or advice.

A Framework for Contractual Liability

An agent may have many and varied duties, which may include negotiating contracts for the principal. This chapter addresses the liability of the agent, the principal, and the third party for the proper performance of these contracts. In applying rules of law, the court often is influenced by the reasonable expectations of the third party; that is, how the third party perceives the situation. The distinction between servants and nonservants is not significant when the agent has entered into a contract; the courts will treat both types of agents the same. The distinction *is* significant if the agent commits a tort. Because the distinction is irrelevant in contract cases, it is logical to use the term *agent* in this chapter. The prime issue for consideration is whether the principal authorized the agent to enter into the contract. Another important factor is whether the principal's identity is to be revealed to the third party. The principal then will be classified as a disclosed, an undisclosed, or a partially disclosed principal. The status of the principal in this regard is determined when the agent and the third party enter the contract; the legal relationships are fixed at that time.

Imposing Liability on the Principal

Regardless of the principal's classification, the principal will not be liable for every act committed by his or her agent or for every contract signed by the agent. To determine whether the principal should be held liable, the court will examine whether the agent was authorized to enter into this type of contract. Authority can be established in a number of different ways, normally referred to as *types of authority,* and often they overlap in a given situation. The types of authority are listed in Exhibit 32.1. A full discussion follows.

For the third party to recover a judgment against the principal, all that needs to be shown is that *one* type of authority exists. Authority to act as an agent usually includes authority to act only for the benefit, not the detriment, of the principal.

Express Authority

Express authority occurs when the principal informs the agent that the agent has authority to engage in a specific act or to perform a particular task. Generally, express authority need not be in writing; and, in most cases, it is not. For example, a principal may say to her secretary, "Please order more stationery." Courts often strictly construe the words the principal uses when giving the authority. If the principal says to the agent, "Locate premises for another card shop," usually the court will interpret this to mean that the agent is authorized only to *find* the premises and not actually to purchase the store. Therefore, an agent should interpret the instructions narrowly or ask for clarification of the scope of authority.

Ratification Authority

Ratification authority occurs when the agent does something that was unauthorized at the time, and the principal approves it later. It requires approval by the principal after the contract was formed by the agent and after the principal has knowledge of the material facts.

When a principal ratifies a contract, the principal must ratify the whole agreement. The principal cannot elect to ratify parts of the contract and disregard the less advantageous parts.

EXHIBIT 32.1 Rights of a Third Party to Sue a Principal

Principal ---- (Appointment) -----› Agent	[Agent is the *representative* of the principal. Legally the agent's actions are treated as *if* done by the principal.]
Agent ---- (Interacts) -----› Third Person	[Third person can treat the agent's conduct as equivalent to the principal performing the action, *provided* the agent possesses apparent authority.]
Third Person ------ (Sues) -----› Principal	[The third person can sue the principal for conduct of the agent, provided that the conduct was authorized *or* within the course and scope of employment.]

Types of Authority an Agent may possess:

- Express
- Ratification
- Incidental
- Implied
- Emergency
- Apparent
- Estoppel

Furthermore, the principal does not need to communicate the ratification verbally to anyone.[1] Generally, ratification may occur by an express statement or may be implied by the principal's clear indication through his or her conduct of an intent to affirm. An example of implied ratification occurs when the principal retains and uses goods delivered under an agreement *after* learning of the contract and its terms. Another example occurs when a principal initiates a lawsuit to enforce the agreement. The ratification needs to follow the same format required of the original authorization. In a limited number of situations, the ratification will have to be in writing. If the agent/third-party contract must be in writing under the Statute of Frauds, then the ratification must be written, too.

Courts have imposed additional limitations on the doctrine of ratification. Both the principal and the agent must have been capable of forming a contract when the original contract occurred *and* when it was ratified. The relation back doctrine is applied to ratified contracts. It states that *if* the contract is properly ratified, it is as if the contract were valid the whole time. Modern courts will not apply this doctrine if it will injure an innocent party who obtains rights in the contract between the time of the original contract formation and the ratification.

Ratification cannot occur if important contract terms are concealed from the principal. Ratification will be effective only if the principal knows all the relevant facts. Also, the agent must have **purported** to act for the principal when the agent entered into the contract. If the agent did not reveal his or her agency capacity or if the agent was working for an undisclosed principal, there can be no ratification.

Purported
Gave the impression authority was present. Often this is a false impression.

Incidental Authority

In most cases, the principal does not discuss the grant of power in detail, if at all. Generally, the agent is given a brief explanation of his or her authority or he or she is given an objective. This brief grant of authority includes the power to do all acts that are incidental to the specific authority that is discussed. *Incidental authority* reasonably and necessarily arises in order to enable the agent to complete his or her assigned duties. Suppose an agent is provided with merchandise that is to be sold door to door. The agent will reasonably and necessarily have incidental authority to deliver the merchandise and to collect the purchase price. Incidental authority is also referred to as incidental powers.

In *St. Ann's Home for the Aged* v. *Daniels*, although the court in its reasoning refers to authority, which may be implied from the facts, the case really centers on the issue of incidental authority.

32.1 ST. ANN'S HOME FOR THE AGED v. DANIELS 420 N.E.2d 478 (Ill.App. 1981)

FACTS Daniels arranged to have his mother hospitalized in 1977. When she was ready to be released, Dr. Smith, the physician in charge of the case, told Daniels that his mother should not return to her own apartment. Dr. Smith suggested that she be placed in St. Ann's and said that he could arrange this. Daniels agreed. Dr. Smith was a neighbor of Daniels as well as his family physician. When Daniels returned from a business trip, he found that his mother had been admitted to St. Ann's, and he indicated that this arrangement was satisfactory.

ISSUE Did Dr. Smith have authority to bind Daniels to pay for his mother's care?

HOLDING Yes.

REASONING Dr. Smith was acting as Daniels's agent. An agency relationship does not depend only on an express statement, it may also be implied from the facts. It may be shown by reference to the situation of the parties, their acts, and other relevant circumstances. Daniels admitted that he had told Dr. Smith to go ahead and make the arrangements to have his mother placed in St. Ann's. Daniels did not have to expressly say that he would be responsible for the costs. A principal is bound by the acts he or she expressly authorizes the agent to perform. A principal is also bound by the agent's normal acts that are necessary to complete performance.

BUSINESS CONSIDERATIONS What procedures should St. Ann's Home implement to avoid similar problems in the future? What process should Dr. Smith use the next time this occurs?

ETHICAL CONSIDERATIONS What ethical perspective is evidenced by Daniels's behavior? Why did Daniels object to the bill? Did he really anticipate that his mother's care would be free?

Implied Authority

Implied authority is based on the agent's position or on past dealings between the agent and the third party. One type of implied authority arises when an agent is given a title and a position. It is to be implied that the agent can enter into the same types of contracts that people with this title normally can. A vice president of sales and marketing, for example, will have implied authority to purchase advertising in newspapers and on radio and to contract with an advertising agency for a new ad campaign. Why? The agent will have this authority because *most* vice presidents of sales and marketing have such authority. In other words, it is customary. When the principal confers the title on the agent, the agent acquires the implied power that accompanies it.

Implied authority may exist because of a series of similar dealings in the past between the agent and the third party. If the principal did not object to the past transactions, it is assumed that the principal authorized the earlier contracts and that this type of transaction is within the agent's power. For example, if a secretary customarily orders office supplies for a business on a monthly basis, the secretary has implied authority to continue to order office supplies in this manner.

Implied authority may exceed actual expressed authority. The third party can recover a judgment in court on the basis of this implied authority if 1) the third party reasonably *believed* that the agent had some particular authority, and 2) the third party was unaware that the authority was lacking. Both elements are required.

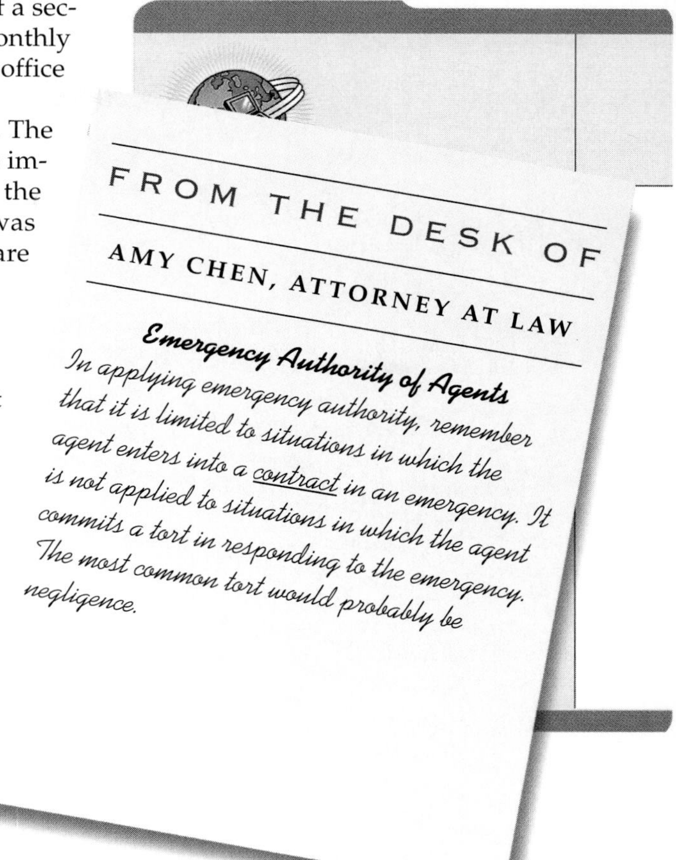

FROM THE DESK OF
AMY CHEN, ATTORNEY AT LAW
Emergency Authority of Agents
In applying emergency authority, remember that it is limited to situations in which the agent enters into a contract in an emergency. It is not applied to situations in which the agent commits a tort in responding to the emergency. The most common tort would probably be negligence.

Emergency Authority

Emergency authority is inherent in all agency relationships. It need not be expressed. It provides the agent with authority to respond to emergencies, even though the principal and agent never discussed the type of emergency or how to respond to it. Suppose the owner of a jewelry shop leaves his manager in charge and goes out for supper. While the owner is absent, a fire starts in the stock room. In an effort to contain the fire, the manager rushes to the hardware store next door and buys four fire extinguishers on credit. The principal—the owner—must pay for the fire extinguishers because the manager had emergency authority to purchase them.

Emergency authority will be found when all the following circumstances exist:

1. An emergency or unexpected situation occurs that requires prompt action.
2. The principal cannot be reached in sufficient time for a response or advice.
3. The action taken by the agent is reasonable in the situation and it is *expected* to benefit the principal.

Apparent Authority

Apparent authority occurs when the principal creates the appearance that an agency exists or that the agent has broader powers than he or she actually has. Here, the representation of authority is made to the third party rather than to the agent.[2] Apparent authority is based on the conduct of the principal; the conduct must cause a reasonable third party to believe that a particular person has authority to act as the principal's agent. An agent with apparent authority may or may not have actual authority.

Apparent authority may be created by intentional or careless acts of the principal and reasonable reliance by the third party. Obviously, if the third party knows the agent does not have this authority, the reliance will not be reasonable.

In some cases, apparent authority exists even though there is no real agent. The person acting in the agent's role may be considered a "purported agent" (that is, one who claims to be an agent). Sometimes this purported agent is an agent who has been terminated, and sometimes the person never was an agent. For example, suppose a company fires a sales representative but neglects to collect its samples, displays, and order forms from the representative. The ex-representative then takes a number of

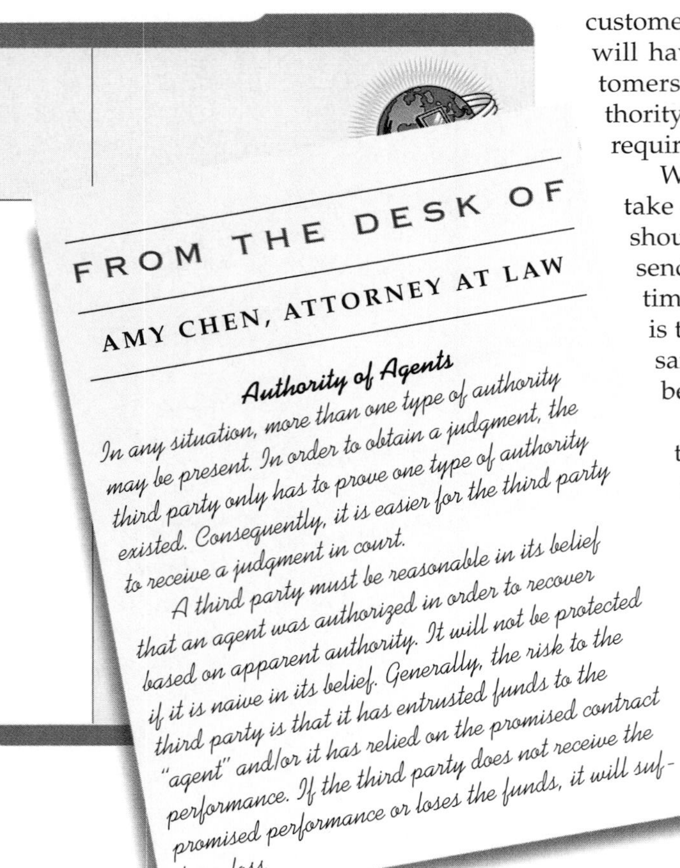

customer orders and disappears with the cash deposits. The company will have to return the deposits or credit the deposits to the customers' orders, because the ex-representative still has apparent authority to take orders. To prevent this situation, the company should require the ex-representative to return all its sales materials.

FROM THE DESK OF
AMY CHEN, ATTORNEY AT LAW
Authority of Agents
In any situation, more than one type of authority may be present. In order to obtain a judgment, the third party only has to prove one type of authority existed. Consequently, it is easier for the third party to receive a judgment in court.
A third party must be reasonable in its belief that an agent was authorized in order to recover based on apparent authority. It will not be protected if it is naive in its belief. Generally, the risk to the third party is that it has entrusted funds to the "agent" and/or it has relied on the promised contract performance. If the third party does not receive the promised performance or loses the funds, it will suffer a loss.

When an agency relationship is terminated, a principal should take certain steps to terminate apparent authority. The principal should inform the agent that the relationship is terminated, call or send notices to people who have dealt with that agent, and sometimes advertise in newspapers and journals that the relationship is terminated. The principal should collect all identification tags, samples, displays, order forms, and any other materials that can be used as evidence of the agency relationship.

Sometimes the purported agent never was employed by the principal, and yet the principal's conduct may cause the principal to be liable for the "agent's" actions. For example, a department store may not require its clerks to wear identifying jackets, vests, or even name tags. Suppose a customer selects some merchandise and walks toward a cash register. In place of a clerk, another customer steps behind the cash register, rings up the sale, puts the merchandise in the bag, and pockets the payment. In this case, the store cannot charge the customer again for the merchandise; it is bound by the acts of the purported agent.

Before applying apparent authority, some courts require that the principal's actions give rise to a reasonable belief in the agent's authority and that there be detrimental reliance on the part of the third party.[3] A number of factors need to be considered: The existence of apparent authority is a factual issue to be determined in each case.

A third party must act reasonably or the court will not apply the concept of apparent authority. The third party must take into consideration the facts and circumstances surrounding the transaction and the type of action involved. Sometimes, based on the information available, the third party must investigate further before reasonably relying on apparent authority.

Apparent authority may be used to hold a principal liable on contracts entered into by the agent. It *ordinarily* will not be used to make a principal accountable for physical harm caused by the agent through negligence, assault, trespass, and similar torts.

The court grappled with the concept of authority in deciding the following case.

32.2 FIRST INTERSTATE BANK OF TEXAS, N.A. v. FIRST NATIONAL BANK OF JEFFERSON — 928 F.2d 153 (5th Cir. 1991)

FACTS In 1982, the Louisiana Public Facilities Authority (the Authority) agreed to issue $3 million worth of bonds and to lend the proceeds to New Orleans Property Development (NOPD). In February, NOPD submitted a loan application to First National Bank of Jefferson (FNJ) for the full $3 million in bonds. On 12 March, FNJ, through Stratton Orr, sent to NOPD a commitment letter agreeing to purchase the *entire* $3 million bond issue. NOPD accepted

32.2 FIRST INTERSTATE BANK OF TEXAS, N.A. v. FIRST NATIONAL BANK OF JEFFERSON *(cont.)* 928 F.2d 153 (5th Cir. 1991)

FNJ's offer. Before FNJ sent the commitment letter to NOPD, First Interstate Bank of Texas notified FNJ that it was willing to purchase only $1 million of the bond issue. First Interstate later agreed to purchase $2 million of the bond issue. First Interstate claimed that it conditioned its agreement to purchase the *additional* $1 million in bonds on FNJ's commitment to buy all First Interstate's NOPD bonds if First Interstate ever desired to sell them.

One of the parties had instructed Butler & Binion, the law firm representing FNJ and First Interstate, to reduce to writing the oral agreement that FNJ would buy, on First Interstate's demand, the entire $2 million of NOPD bonds held by First Interstate. The attorneys sent a draft of the agreement, called a Bond Purchase Agreement (BPA), to FNJ senior vice president John Boyd. Boyd, who was Orr's supervisor, assumed this responsibility when Orr left FNJ. According to Boyd, he discussed the agreement with FNJ president Arceneaux, who gave Boyd the impression that execution of the BPA was an "acceptable approach."

On 4 May, First Interstate and FNJ signed an agreement with NOPD and the Authority in which First Interstate agreed to purchase $2 million worth of bonds and FNJ $1 million. The parties closed the NOPD transaction on 29 July. The bank sent Boyd to the closing with a certification that Boyd, as a senior vice president, was acting on behalf of the FNJ board of directors. At the meeting, FNJ, through Boyd, and First Interstate, through vice president Robert LaRue, signed the BPA, whereby FNJ agreed to purchase all of First Interstate's NOPD bonds on First Interstate's demand. In August 1988, First Interstate demanded that FNJ buy its bonds pursuant to the 29 July 1982 BPA. FNJ refused and claimed that Boyd did not have the authority to sign the agreement for FNJ.

ISSUE Had FNJ given Boyd, a senior vice president of the bank, authority to execute this BPA?

HOLDING Yes.

REASONING Louisiana law governs the transactions here. Actual authority can be express or implied. A principal can confer actual authority orally. For instance, Boyd testified that FNJ had authorized him to sign the BPA. Boyd said that he discussed the NOPD transaction, including the BPA, with Arceneaux and other FNJ officers. Boyd's position in the FNJ hierarchy would lend credibility to his claim that the bank had authorized him to sign the BPA. A jury could infer that if Arceneaux had participated in negotiating the buyback agreement, FNJ must have authorized Boyd to consummate the transaction.

The record also demonstrated that the BPA had not obligated FNJ any further than its 12 March commitment letter to NOPD, in which FNJ had agreed to buy the entire $3 million bond issue. The 29 July BPA had not extended FNJ's obligation on the bonds beyond its 12 March commitment. Both agreements had made FNJ the principal lender on a $3 million loan. The evidence had presented a jury question as to whether FNJ had given Boyd express authority to execute the BPA. The issue of implied authority should also be examined. Implied authority is inferred from the circumstances and the nature of the agency. Implied authority connotes permission from the principal for the agent to act, though that permission is not expressly set forth orally or in writing.

The Louisiana Civil Code provides, in part, that "the power [of agency] must be *express* for the following purposes: . . . To contract a loan or acknowledge a debt." The Code would prevent First Interstate from recovering under an implied authority theory. First Interstate's final argument centered on apparent authority. A corporation will be liable to a third party even for the unauthorized acts of its agent under the doctrine of apparent authority if the following occur: (1) the corporation manifests the agent's authority to the third party; and (2) the third party reasonably relies on the agent's purported authority as a result of the manifestation. Indeed, First Interstate had also introduced sufficient evidence to create a jury question regarding Boyd's apparent authority to bind FNJ. When FNJ had hired Boyd as a senior vice president, it had manifested to the public that Boyd had the authority to bind the bank in agreements necessary to conduct the bank's business. On the day of the NOPD closing, FNJ specifically had manifested to First Interstate that Boyd had authority to execute the necessary closing papers on behalf of FNJ, since FNJ had sent Boyd and one of its trust officers to the closing with a certification that Boyd was its senior vice president acting on behalf of FNJ's board of directors.

The jury was entitled to conclude that when FNJ had sent Boyd to the closing with a certificate of his authority, the bank also was manifesting Boyd's authority to sign the BPA, without which First Interstate would not have agreed to buy the NOPD bonds. FNJ maintained that Louisiana imposes an absolute duty on a third party to inquire about an agent's authority. However, a third party can rely on the apparent authority of an agent until something occurs that would cause a reasonable person to inquire further into the circumstances. Here, a jury could conclude that First Interstate need not have made further inquiry.

[Note how the court analyzed various types of authority in its reasoning in this case.]

32.2 FIRST INTERSTATE BANK OF TEXAS, N.A. v. FIRST NATIONAL BANK OF JEFFERSON *(cont.)* 928 F.2d 153 (5th Cir. 1991)

BUSINESS CONSIDERATIONS If FNJ wanted to effectively limit Boyd's authority at the closing, what should FNJ have done? What occurrence probably caused this legal dispute?

ETHICAL CONSIDERATIONS Is FNJ trying to use Boyd as a scapegoat since he is no longer a senior vice president at the bank? Is this ethical or not? Why?

Authority by Estoppel

Authority by estoppel prevents a principal who has misled a third party from denying the agent's authority. This is also called ostensible authority. It occurs when the principal *allows* the purported agent to pass himself or herself off as an agent and does not take steps to prevent the purported agent's representation.

Estoppel authority may occur by itself or in conjunction with other types of authority. When there is only estoppel authority and no other authority, estoppel authority will be used solely for the protection of the third party. It will not constitute the basis of a successful lawsuit by the principal against the third party. It creates rights for the third party and liabilities for the principal. It protects the third party and allows the third party reimbursement for injuries. As with other doctrines of agency law, the courts are weighing the respective rights of two relatively innocent people—the third party and the principal. The purported agent can be sued for fraud, but generally that person cannot be located or has insufficient funds to cover the resulting losses.

Authority by estoppel is illustrated in Exhibit 32.2 and in the example that follows.

EXHIBIT 32.2 Authority by Estoppel

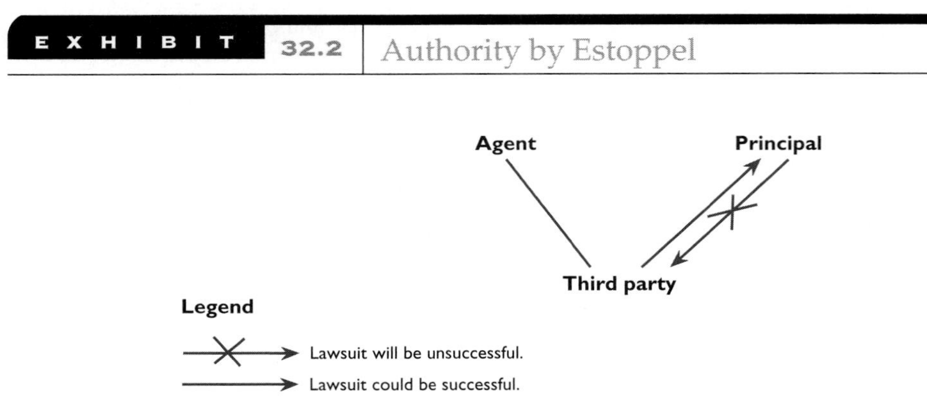

Roy was walking to class one Wednesday when he passed Grace and David, who were standing next to Roy's car. He overheard Grace pointing out all the car's features to David. It was evident that Grace was trying to sell the car to David on Roy's behalf. Roy thought this amusing and did not stop to explain the truth. He went to class instead. He later learned that David made a $200 down payment on the car and that Grace disappeared with the money.

In a lawsuit between David and Roy, David will prevail. The court can apply agency by estoppel and decide that Roy is estopped (prevented) from denying that Grace was his agent. Roy knew that Grace was pretending to be Roy's agent, and Roy easily could have denied this. Roy's failure to speak helped to cause David's loss. The court will protect David from a loss by allowing him to recover.

32.1

SALES/MANAGEMENT

HONORING SALES AGENT'S CONTRACTS

CIT appointed several sales agents. Each agent was assigned a territory, and each was provided with an "order book" containing standard order forms. These order forms contain the list price for Call-Image videophones, including any quantity discounts that can be given. One of the sales agents called on a large retail outlet in another state. The retailer expressed an interest in buying a large number of the Call-Image videophones, but only if the firm would give the retailer an additional 10% discount above the quantity discount normally given by CIT. The sales agent agreed to these terms and completed the order form, including an indication of the additional 10 percent discount. Once the form was completed and signed by the sales agent and the store's representative, a copy was faxed to CIT. When Tom received the copy of the order, he was livid. He knows that the additional discount will take virtually all the profit from the sale, but he fears that the firm is bound by the signed order. He asks you whether the firm must honor this contract. What will you tell him?

BUSINESS CONSIDERATIONS What can a firm do to protect itself from overly zealous sales agents? Should a firm have a policy in place for handling situations such as this, or should each case be handled on an individual basis? How should the business communicate with the buyer in this sort of situation in order to (a) avoid the contract, and (b) retain the buyer as a customer?

ETHICAL CONSIDERATIONS Is it ethical for a firm to refuse to honor a commitment made by one of its agents, even if the agent exceeded his or her authority? Is it ethical for a buyer to utilize its size to force special concessions from a sales agent beyond those normally granted by the firm?

Imputing the Agent's Knowledge to the Principal

In addition to being liable for contracts entered into by an agent, a principal may be legally responsible for information known to the agent but not actually known by the principal. This concept is called *imputing knowledge.* Because an agent has a duty to inform the principal about important facts that relate to the agency, it will be assumed that the agent has performed this duty. If the agent fails to perform this duty and the failure causes a loss, the principal—not the third party—should suffer the loss. Courts justify this result because the principal selected the agent, placed the agent in a position of authority, and had (legal) control over the agent.

The agent's knowledge is not always imputed to the principal. Before a principal will be bound by knowledge received by the agent, generally the agent must have actual or apparent authority to receive this type of knowledge. In addition, the information received by the agent must relate to the subject matter of the agency. For example, if the principal owns a real estate firm, a movie theater, and a hardware store, and the agent works in the hardware store, knowledge that the agent obtains about the real estate firm will not be imputed to the principal. The knowledge must be within the scope of the agency. The court examined this issue in the following case.

32.3 FORD MOTOR CREDIT CO. v. WEAVER 680 F.2d 451 (6th Cir. 1982)

FACTS Weaver Farms purchased two Ford tractors and other pieces of farm equipment from Cleveland Ford Tractor, Inc. (CFT) on an installment sale. One provision of the installment sales contract was that the contract would be assigned to Ford Motor Credit Company (FMCC), and it was. CFT and FMCC have the same parent corporation. FMCC frequently purchases commercial paper from CFT. FMCC has the right of first refusal on commercial paper that CFT creates, and customers leave contracts and payments at CFT for FMCC. Weaver Farms filed a petition for a Chapter 11 bankruptcy. FMCC was listed as a creditor, but its bankruptcy notice was delivered to CFT.

ISSUE Should notice delivered to CFT be imputed to FMCC?

HOLDING No.

REASONING Notice or knowledge of an agent may be imputed to the principal in certain situations. It is imputed when the agent acquires the notice or knowledge while acting within the scope of his or her authority and when the knowledge concerns matters within the scope of that authority. Just because an agent can collect payments for another, it does not follow that the agent can accept legal notice. This general rule is applicable in bankruptcy cases. CFT did not have actual or implied authority to collect the outstanding balance, receive legal notices for FMCC, or represent FMCC in any bankruptcy proceeding. CFT can act as a repository and accept individual payments, but that is a different type of authority. There was no apparent authority to accept legal notice in this case.

BUSINESS CONSIDERATIONS What should Weaver Farms have done to assure that the notices were properly filed on its creditors? What steps should a principal take to protect himself or herself from losses caused by agents who "forget" to inform the principal?

ETHICAL CONSIDERATIONS *If* FMCC had actual notice of the bankruptcy proceeding, would it be ethical to object to notice delivered to CFT? Is it ethical for Weaver Farms to file bankruptcy proceedings? Why or why not?

Disclosed Principal

When an agent clearly discloses that he or she is representing a principal and identifies the principal, the principal is *disclosed.* In these situations, the principal may be bound to the contract by any of the types of authority that have been discussed. Exhibit 32.3 illustrates a disclosed principal.

Liability of the Agent

Normally, when an agent indicates that he or she is entering into a contract on behalf of the disclosed principal, the agent will not be liable for the contract. It is clearly understood that the third party should look to the principal alone for performance. As with most legal rules, there are exceptions. For example, if the agent fails to represent his or her capacity as such, the agent will be personally bound. In addition, the agent will be bound if he or she intends to be bound. For example, the agent may say, "You can rely on me," or "You have my word on it."

Why would an agent want to be liable on the principal's contract? Why would an agent want to undertake additional liability? An agent might do this if it is necessary to make a sale. The prospective buyer may be unsure about the principal and his or her reputation or financial backing. Perhaps the prospect has a long working relationship with the agent, so the agent's guarantee of performance persuades the prospect. The agent does not really have valid grounds to complain if he or she is ac-

EXHIBIT 32.3 Disclosed Principal

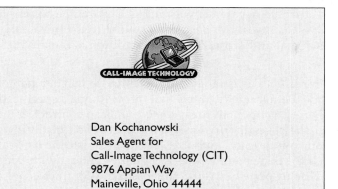

Dan Kochanowski
Sales Agent for
Call-Image Technology (CIT)
9876 Appian Way
Maineville, Ohio 44444

cepted at his or her word. The third party generally will prefer to sue the principal on the contract instead of the agent since the principal often has more assets.

The third party, then, has legal rights against both the agent and the disclosed principal. This does not mean that the third party can collect twice. The third party must make an *election* to sue either the agent *or* the principal. Obviously, an important factor in this decision is who has the funds to pay a judgment. If the third party sues the principal and loses, he or she will be barred from then suing the agent. The reverse is also true. The more modern approach permits the third party to sue both the principal and the agent together. However, either defendant can require the third party to make an election prior to judgment.

Warranty of Authority

Whenever an agent of a disclosed principal enters into a contract, the agent makes all of the following implied warranties. These warranties are not stated by the agent; they are implied by the situation.

1. The disclosed principal exists and is competent.
2. The agent is an agent for the principal.
3. The agent is authorized to enter into this type of contract for the principal.

The third party can sue the agent to recover for losses that are caused by the breach of warranty of authority. Perhaps the third party has losses because he or she did not receive the goods that are covered by the contract.

FROM THE DESK OF
AMY CHEN, ATTORNEY AT LAW

Signatures!

Instruct agents that when they sign contracts to be sure to indicate they are signing as agents and to name their principal. The preferred format for signatures would indicate (name of principal) by (name of agent), (title of agent). Otherwise, the agents can be held personally liable on the contracts. Agents often mistakenly believe that they are not liable. Liability can have a disastrous effect on the personal finances of an agent.

Further, suppose the principal is not responsible for the losses because the agent is not authorized to enter into this type of contract. The third party can sue the agent.

If the agent fears that he or she does not have the authority to enter into this type of contract, the agent may be concerned about the warranties of authority. He or she would be wise, then, to negate the warranties. This can be accomplished by stating that there is no warranty or by specifically stating to the third party the limitations on the agent's actual authority. The latter condition is illustrated in the following example.

> Rhoda hires Beth as an agent and tells her to locate a parcel of agricultural real estate. Beth locates a parcel that meets Rhoda's specifications. The owner of the parcel wants Beth to sign the purchase contract, but Beth is not sure whether she has authority to sign. If she fully and truthfully discloses the situation surrounding her authority, Beth will negate the *implied* warranty of authority. If the owner still wishes to sign the contract with Beth, the owner will assume the responsibility and the loss if the contract is not authorized. The owner would be relying on his own judgment.

The agent may be liable for fraud if the agent intentionally misrepresents his or her authority. Exhibit 32.4 illustrates the agent's liability.

Liability of the Third Party

Lawsuit by the Principal. When a principal has been disclosed from the beginning, the third party realizes, or should realize, that the principal has an interest in the contract. The principal can successfully sue the third party on the contract if the agent was authorized to enter into this type of contract for the principal. In other words, the third party will be liable if there is express, implied, incidental, emergency, apparent, or ratification authority. The third party will not be liable if the only type of authority is estoppel authority.

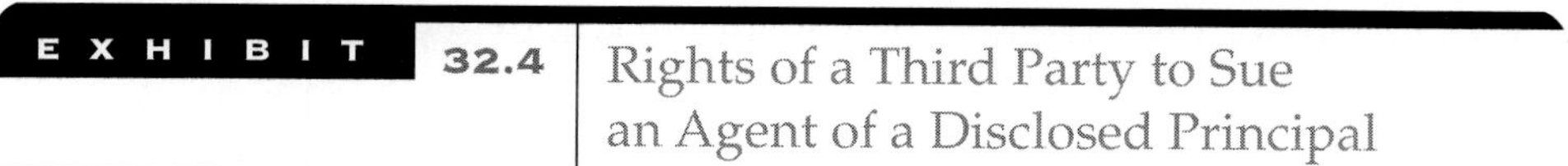

Rights of a Third Party to Sue an Agent of a Disclosed Principal

Exceptions:

- agent fails to represent capacity
- agent intends to be bound
- agent breaches warranties of authority
- agent commits fraud

Agent

Disclosed principal

Third party

Legend

—X→ Lawsuit will be unsuccessful.

Lawsuit by the Agent. Normally, the agent has no right to sue the third party on a contract. An agent *may* successfully sue the third party if the agent can show that he or she has an interest in the contract. The most common type of interest is one in which the agent is entitled to a commission on a sale. For example, a real estate broker (the agent) enters into a contract on behalf of a homeowner (the principal). The agent is entitled to a 6 percent commission payable from the proceeds of the sale. If the buyer (the third party) breaches the contract, the agent can sue to recover the lost commission. (In this type of case, the principal may decide that it is not worth suing, but the agent may feel that it is.)

An agent may successfully sue the third party when the agent intends to be bound. This rule is based on equitable principles. If the agent is liable to the third party, the third party should be liable to the agent, too. In some cases, a principal may transfer to the agent the right to file the lawsuit. In these cases, also, the agent can sue on the contract. These relationships are illustrated in Exhibit 32.5.

32.2

SALES/MANAGEMENT

HOW MUCH LEGAL AUTHORITY DOES AN AGENT HAVE?

When one of the firm's sales agents was discussing the Call-Image videophones with a potential customer, the customer demanded a quantity discount greater than the quantity discount authorized by the firm as stated on the order form. The agent told the customer that he doubted that any of the firm's agents had the authority to grant such a discount. However, the customer insisted that the agent commit to the discount immediately or there would be no sale. Despite his misgivings, the agent wrote the order with the additional discount. After leaving the customer's office, the agent called Dan and told him what had happened. Dan has asked you what the legal implications of this situation are. What will you tell him?

BUSINESS CONSIDERATIONS How can an agent handle a situation in which a customer makes demands that the agent believes would require the agent to exceed his or her authority? Is an agent legally liable to the customer if the agent knowingly exceeds the authority granted by the principal?

ETHICAL CONSIDERATIONS Does an agent have an ethical obligation to disclose to the third person any conduct that exceeds the authority given to the agent? Does the agent have an ethical obligation to inform the principal if or when the agent exceeds his or her authority?

UNDISCLOSED PRINCIPAL

An *undisclosed* principal is one whose existence and identity are unknown to the third party. There are many valid reasons why a principal might want to be undisclosed—to be able to negotiate a deal, to negotiate a better deal, or to conceal an investment in a project or a donation to a charity.

There may be situations where the third party would have refused to contract with the principal. If the agent and principal agree that the principal should remain undisclosed for the purpose of defrauding the third party, the third party can have the contract set aside by proving fraud in the court. Exhibit 32.6 illustrates an undisclosed principal.

Liability of the Agent

When the principal is completely undisclosed, the third party believes that he or she is contracting with the agent and that the agent is dealing for himself or herself. Based on the third party's knowledge, that assumption is rational. If there is a default on the contract, the third party can sue the agent. As far as the third party is concerned, at the time of contracting there are only two parties to the contract: the third party and the agent. The court addresses such an issue in the following case.

32.4 MURPHY v. DELL CORPORATION

440 A.2d 223 (Conn. 1981)

FACTS DeLisa, an agent for Dell Corporation, entered into a contract with Murphy. There was conflicting testimony over whether DeLisa indicated his role as an agent for Dell Corporation. The lawsuit originally was filed against Dell Corporation and DeLisa. Murphy withdrew the complaint against Dell Corporation.

ISSUE Is DeLisa personally liable for the balance due on the contract?

HOLDING Yes.

REASONING The trial court concluded that Murphy did not "notice" that the contract was with Dell Corporation and that DeLisa failed to disclose his representative capacity. "The law is settled that where an agent contracts in his own name, without disclosing his representative capacity, the agent is personally liable on the contract." The trial court decided the questions of fact in favor of Murphy. Their decision must be upheld unless it is clearly erroneous.

BUSINESS CONSIDERATIONS Why would Murphy withdraw the complaint against Dell Corporation? What should DeLisa do in the future in order to avoid liability? Should Dell Corporation have handled their agency relationship with DeLisa differently?

ETHICAL CONSIDERATIONS Is it ethical to hold DeLisa financially liable in this situation? Why or why not? Would it have been ethical to hold Dell Corporation liable in this situation? Why or why not?

EXHIBIT 32.5 Rights of an Agent of a Disclosed Principal to Sue a Third Party

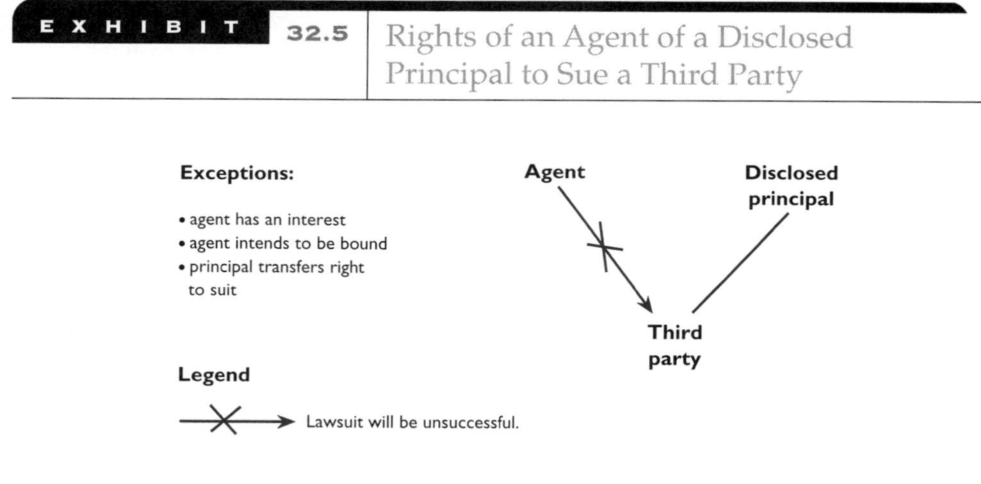

Liability of the Principal

If the third party later discovers the identity of the principal, the third party can sue the principal. The principal will be held liable if the agent was authorized to enter into this type of contract for the principal. The third party must make an *election* to sue either the agent *or* the principal. There is one important exception, however: if the third party sues the agent and loses *before* discovering the principal. In that case, the third party is not considered to have made an election and will be permitted to sue the principal later.

Liability of the Third Party

The third party may not be the one who suffers damages because of a breach of contract but may, in fact, be the one who committed the breach. Since the third party thought he or she was liable to the agent, it is reasonable to allow the agent to sue the third party. The law allows this action.

Under some circumstances, the undisclosed principal may, in his or her own name, also be able to sue the third party. There are some limitations, however. Generally, the principal can file a lawsuit by himself or herself, only if the contract is **assignable**. (See Chapter 14 for a discussion of assignable contracts.) If it is assignable, the position of the third party will not be jeopardized by either an assignment or the suit by the principal. Since the agent can assign the contract to anyone else, the principal should be able to enforce the contract rights. Either way, the third party will be in the same position. This relationship is shown in Exhibit 32.7. The third party will have to pay any damages only once.

The principal may not be able to sue in his or her own name because the contract is not assignable, or the principal may still wish to keep his or her identity secret. Then the principal can arrange for the agent to file the lawsuit in the agent's name.

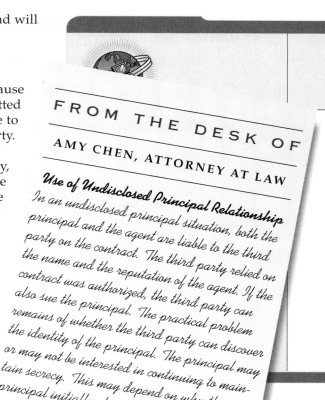

FROM THE DESK OF

AMY CHEN, ATTORNEY AT LAW

Use of Undisclosed Principal Relationship

In an undisclosed principal situation, both the principal and the agent are liable to the third party on the contract. The third party relied on the name and the reputation of the agent. If the contract was authorized, the third party can also sue the principal. The practical problem remains of whether the third party can discover the identity of the principal. The principal may or may not be interested in continuing to maintain secrecy. This may depend on why the principal initially chose to be undisclosed.

Assignable
Legally capable of being transferred from one person to another.

EXHIBIT 32.6 Undisclosed Principal

Personal Communications for the 21st Century

Dan Kochanowski
9876 Appian Way
Maineville, Ohio 44444

EXHIBIT 32.7 Rights of an Undisclosed Principal

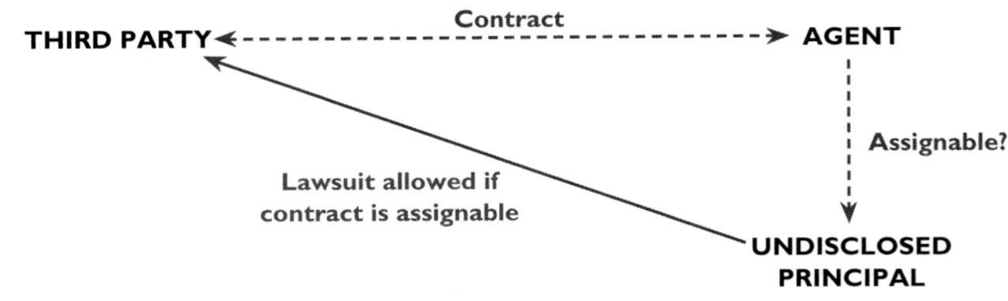

Partially Disclosed Principal

A *partially disclosed principal* is one whose existence is known to the third party but whose identity is not. In other words, the agency is disclosed, but the principal is undisclosed. An example is Robert Smith's signing a contract as "Robert Smith, agent." The rules that are applied to partially disclosed principals are similar to those applied to undisclosed principals. The principal may be sued if the contract is breached, and the suit will be successful if the principal authorized the actions of the agent. Once again, the third party must make an election whether to sue the principal or the agent. If the principal suffers damages, he or she can sue the third party. The contract need not be assignable, because the third party knew that another party in interest was involved. Exhibit 32.8 illustrates a partially disclosed principal.

The general rule is that when an agent is working for a partially disclosed principal, the agent will be personally liable for the contract. The third party is probably relying on the agent's reputation and credit. It is unlikely that the third party is relying on the reputation and credit of the unrevealed principal. An exception arises if the contracting parties agree that the agent will not be held liable. This may occur if the agent indicates that he or she will not be bound and the third party does not object to this limitation.

Analysis of Agent's Contracts with Third Parties

To characterize a contract situation involving any type of principal, one should answer the following questions:

1. Was the person acting as an agent for the hiring party?
2. Did the agent enter a contract on behalf of the hiring party or make contractual promises?
3. Was the agent acting within the scope of his or her contractual authority? What type or types of authority are present?

EXHIBIT 32.8 Partially Disclosed Principal

Dan Kochanowski
Sales Agent
9876 Appian Way
Maineville, Ohio 44444

4. Was the hiring party a disclosed, undisclosed, or partially disclosed principal?
5. Did the third party make an election to sue the agent or principal?
6. Is the agent liable for the contractual promises?

CONTRACT BETWEEN THE PRINCIPAL AND THE AGENT

The Need for a Writing

The agency relationship is consensual in nature. It actually will be a contract if the principal and agent both give up consideration, which is generally the case. As with other contracts, the Statute of Frauds may apply and require written evidence of the contract. The provisions of the Statute of Frauds that are most likely to be applicable are those relating to contracts that cannot possibly be performed within one year and contracts involving the sale of real estate. Even if the Statute of Frauds does not apply, it is wise to write out the contractual provisions.

The equal dignities rule also requires that some agency agreements be in writing. This rule states that the agent/principal contract deserves (requires) the same dignity as the agent/third-party contract, as shown in Exhibit 32.9: If contract A must be written, then contract B must be written. For example, if the agent is hired to locate and purchase goods costing more than $500, the UCC Statute of Frauds requires that the agent/third-party contract be in writing, so the principal/agent contract must also be in writing.

Covenants Not to Compete

Some employment contracts contain *covenants* (promises) that the agent will not work for a competing firm. The contract may provide that (1) the agent will not

EXHIBIT 32.9 Equal Dignities Rule

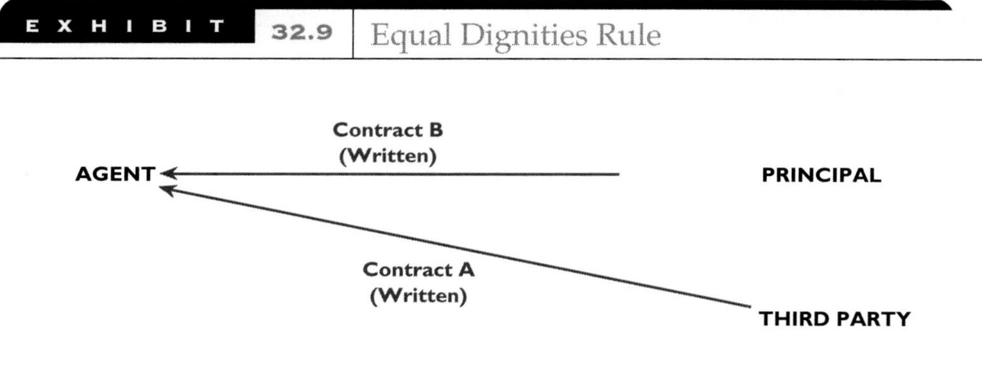

moonlight with the competition, or (2) the agent will not compete with the principal after this employment relationship is terminated. Some contracts contain both prohibitions. The second provision is usually applicable if the agent either quits or is fired.

Competing legal considerations arise in disputes about these covenants. On the one hand, the agent agrees not to compete. Perhaps the agent desperately wants the position and feels that he or she will not be hired unless he or she signs the covenant. The agent may not have equal bargaining power with the principal. Generally, parties *are* bound by their contract provisions. On the other hand, it may be a hardship on the agent to unduly restrict his or her ability to locate another position. In addi-

http:// RESOURCES FOR BUSINESS LAW STUDENTS

NAME	RESOURCES	WEB ADDRESS
"Getting Around Barriers to Non-Compete Pacts"	"Getting Around Barriers to Non-Compete Pacts," by James A. Diboise and David J. Berger and originally published in *The National Law Journal*, discusses whether courts will consider trade secret confidentiality as covenants not to compete.	http://wsgrgate.wsgr.com/Resources/IntProp/Pubs/Articles/barriers.htm
"Non-Compete Agreements"	"Non-Compete Agreements," by Mindy G. Farber and published in *Women Today*, discusses the merits of having an attorney review any covenant not to compete before signing.	http://www.womenconnect.com/bu93051.htm
The Patent Examiner	The Patent Examiner, maintained by the firm of Arent, Fox, Kintner, Plotkin, and Kahn, discusses the basic issues surrounding patent protection and the formation of employment contracts.	http://www.patentexaminer.com/patent/corpsurviv.html

tion, it will be detrimental to society if people are not allowed to seek the occupations for which they are most highly qualified. For these reasons, courts scrutinize covenants not to compete to determine whether the covenant is legal. As a rule, courts do not favor covenants not to compete. The covenant will be illegal if the court concludes that it is against public policy.

To determine whether the covenant is against public policy, the court will examine its reasonableness. The court will look at the situation surrounding the employment to see whether the principal has a legitimate interest in preventing the competition.

Covenants not to compete are also prevalent in contracts in which the owner of a business sells the business to a buyer and the buyer obtains a promise that the previous owner will not compete with him or her. In such cases, the buyer has an interest in not having competition from the seller. Generally, the buyer pays a larger purchase price so that the seller will sell the **goodwill** of the business *and* sign a covenant not to compete with the buyer. Courts are more inclined to enforce covenants not to compete in these situations.

Additional requirements exist for a valid covenant not to compete. The time and area specifications of the covenant must be reasonable. What is reasonable, moreover, depends on the type of employment. Covenants containing time periods of two to five years are generally acceptable to the courts. The limitation is really the time period during which the agent is able to draw contacts away from the principal or the time period in which these contacts still have value.

The covenant also must be reasonable in the area or distance specified. Another way to consider this is to ask the following question: How far will customers or clients travel to do business with the agent? The answer depends on the field of the agent's expertise. For example, a patient might travel halfway across the country to see a world-famous heart transplant specialist, but many patients will not even go across town to see a general practitioner.

32.3

MANUFACTURING/MANAGEMENT

CREATING EMPLOYMENT CONTRACTS TO PROTECT TECHNOLOGY

The firm has been more successful than anticipated, and it is producing videophones at nearly full capacity. In order to keep up with demand, the firm will need to expand its production capacity, including the hiring of new employees. There have also been several suggestions for improvements in the product from a number of customers, and the family would like to hire some engineers to help implement these suggested changes. However, the family is concerned that some of the new employees might reveal (or "borrow") the technology the firm has developed, to the detriment of CIT. They ask you what protections they have or could build into their employment contracts to help protect them. What advice will you give them?

BUSINESS CONSIDERATIONS How can a firm prevent employees from revealing confidential business information or technology? What practical protections are available to a firm that is trying to protect a trade secret?

ETHICAL CONSIDERATIONS Is it ethical for an employee to utilize information gained in a previous position to benefit a competitor of the former employer? Is it ethical to restrict a former employee from using knowledge or information gained in a job when that knowledge or information makes the former employee a more productive or valuable individual? How can these competing interests be balanced?

If the principal has a legitimate business interest and the covenant is reasonable, the principal can sue the breaching agent or former agent for an injunction or contract damages. However, a principal may structure a covenant not to compete that is too broad. The courts apply one of two approaches in such cases. First, the court declares the covenant void and ignores it. The agent then can do whatever he or she wishes with impunity. A less common approach is for the court to reform (modify) the contract to make its restrictions reasonable.

Goodwill

The good name and reputation of a business and the resulting ability to attract clients.

Courts may examine the following criteria in determining whether to enforce a covenant not to compete in an employment contract:

1. Is the restraint reasonable in the amount of protection it affords, or is it excessive?
2. Is the restraint unreasonable because it is unduly harsh on the agent?
3. If the agent works for a competitor, will that threaten irreparable injury to the principal?
4. Is the agency relationship of a unique and unusual type?

Some state statutes hold that a principal cannot prevent an ordinary employee from engaging in competition once the employment is over.[4]

A covenant not to compete is not required in order to prevent an agent from divulging trade secrets or customer lists after the employment is terminated. Under common law, this behavior is a violation of the agent's duties of loyalty.

The following case addressed the issue of a covenant not to compete.

32.5 HOLIDAY FOOD CO., INC. v. MUNROE — 426 A.2d 814 (Conn.Super. 1981)

FACTS Munroe worked as a salesperson for Holiday Food, a company that sold and delivered frozen foods. Munroe never examined or used the customer list that the company made available to its sales staff. His supervisor provided him with the names and addresses of contacts, which he kept in a personal notebook. During his employment with Holiday Food, Munroe expressly refused to sign a covenant not to compete. When he left to start a competing frozen-food business, Munroe took his notebook with him and started to call on his old contacts.

ISSUE Did Munroe violate his duties to Holiday Food when he solicited orders from his old customers?

HOLDING No.

REASONING Unless the name of a customer is a trade secret, former employees can contact customers who used to order from them. A trade secret may include any formula, device, pattern, or compilation of information that people use to get an edge over their competitors. Unless there is a covenant not to compete, agents may compete with principals after the agency is terminated. They may not use trade secrets revealed to them or surreptitiously discovered by them. Customer lists may or may not be trade secrets, depending on the facts of a particular case. Courts may examine the extent to which the employee/employer relationship was a confidential one, how the employee acquired the information, the former employee's personal relationship with the customers, and any unfair advantage obtained by the former employee. An appellate court should not overturn a trial court's decision unless it is clearly erroneous. The trial court's decision that the customer list was not a trade secret was upheld in this case.

BUSINESS CONSIDERATIONS What practical steps, if any, could the business have taken to better protect its customer lists in this situation?

ETHICAL CONSIDERATIONS Was it ethical for Munroe to start a competing business? Why or why not? Was it ethical for Munroe to call on the customers listed in his notebook? Why or why not?

Summary

A disclosed principal is one whose identity and existence are known to the third party. A partially disclosed principal is one whose existence is known but whose identity is not. When the principal is undisclosed, the third party thinks he or she is dealing only with the agent. The agent will be bound on the contract because the third party believes that the agent is a party to the contract. The type of principal affects the rights and obligations of the agent, the principal, and the third party.

When the principal has been disclosed, the principal can sue and be sued on the contract if there is express, implied, incidental, emergency, apparent, or ratification authority. These types of authority often overlap. If only authority by estoppel exists, it will be applied to protect a third party but not to protect the principal. Information received by the agent within the course and scope of the job generally will be imputed to the principal. Usually, the agent of a disclosed principal will not be bound on the contract itself, but the agent may be responsible for breach of warranty of authority. The third party will be liable to the principal on the contract and to the agent if the agent has an interest or intends to be bound. In situations of undisclosed or partially disclosed principals, the agent will be held liable.

The agency agreement must be in writing, if this is required by either the Statute of Frauds or the equal dignities rule. Covenants not to compete may be valid if the principal has a legitimate interest in preventing the competition, provided that the limitation is reasonable in the length of time and the area specified.

DISCUSSION PROBLEMS

1. What is a partially disclosed principal? How might partial disclosure occur?
2. Ted farms 200 acres planted with grape vines. His neighbor has an additional 100 acres planted with grapes, which are for sale. Since Ted and his neighbor have been feuding for 12 years, the neighbor will not sell the land to Ted. Therefore, Ted hires Rose to act as his agent without revealing Ted's identity. Rose buys the land and starts to transfer it to Ted. Upon discovering this, the neighbor tries to stop the transfer. What are the legal rights of the parties in this situation?
3. How do the rights and liabilities of an agent for a partially disclosed principal differ from those of an agent for an undisclosed principal?
4. Sally, a secretary, often orders office supplies, such as photocopy paper, tablets, and pens, for her employer. One day, Sally orders a personal computer and has it delivered to her home. Sally has the bill sent to her employer. Based on the information provided, does Sally have authority to do this? Why or why not? What additional information would be helpful? Why?
5. What is the difference between implied authority and implied ratification?
6. Besides collecting samples, displays, and order forms, what else should a principal do to terminate the apparent authority of an agent?
7. Bonnie buys a house through Angie, who is a real estate agent. Before the sale is completed, Angie recommends that they have an appliance inspector examine the house. Angie makes the arrangements. Joe, the inspector, says that all the major appliances are in proper working order. Bonnie completes the sale and is now living in the house. Joe, however, has not been paid yet. Who is obligated to pay Joe? Why?
8. Why are warranties of authority applicable only when there is a disclosed principal?
9. Is it reasonable for a fast-food chain to require all new employees to sign an agreement that they will not work for another fast-food restaurant for six months after leaving the chain? Is it legal? Can an ex-employee legally reveal the recipe for a chain's special blend of 11 herbs and spices? Why or why not?
10. Lisa has charges on her telephone bill that she does not understand. The bill states that billing inquiries should be made by calling (800) 555-2941. She calls the number and speaks with Janet. Janet says that she will remove the charges; the charges, however, are not removed. Is Lisa entitled to have them removed? Do you think Janet had authority for her statement? Why or why not?

CASE PROBLEMS AND WRITING ASSIGNMENTS

1. Jason Weimer leased and operated a farm owned by Brugger Corporation. When a new lease was negotiated in 1987, Grant McQueen, a manager for Brugger, agreed Brugger would pay for some necessary repairs to the irrigation system. Weimer negotiated with Tri-Circle to make the repairs. Weimer indicated that he

had authority from Brugger to arrange for this work. Tri-Circle was directed to set up a separate billing for Brugger for this work, and to send the bill to Weimer. When Weimer received the first bill for $9,769, he verified the amount and forwarded the bill to Brugger. Brugger sent Tri-Circle a check for this amount. A second billing for $11,540 was sent to Weimer, approved by him, and forwarded to Brugger. This second bill was not paid and Tri-Circle sued. Who is liable for this second bill and why? [*Tri-Circle, Inc.* v. *Brugger Corp.*, 829 P.2d 540 (IdahoApp. 1992).]

2. Partners in a California law firm agreed that partners who withdrew from the firm would forfeit their withdrawal benefits under the partnership agreement *if* they competed with the firm. Assuming that the provision specified a reasonable length of time and geographic area, should the provision be upheld? Why or why not? [*Howard* v. *Babcock*, 863 P.2d 150 (Cal. 1993).]

3. Horowytz opened a checking account with Bank of America. The account documents indicated that Horowytz was doing business under the trade name of E.D.S. The signature card indicated that J. Pearl, Horowytz's father, had power of attorney. The card stated that Pearl had authority to sign and endorse checks, notes, and drafts and transact all business with the bank. It did not specifically state that Pearl had authority to borrow money on Horowytz's credit. Does Pearl have authority to borrow money that Horowytz will have to repay? Why? [See *Bank of America, National Trust and Savings Association* v. *Horowytz*, 248 A.2d 446 (N.J. County Ct. 1968).]

4. Morrow was planning a business trip to Honduras in a private plane and wanted flight insurance. He discussed the matter with Bennett, who was the attendant at the insurance counter in the airport and who sold insurance from a number of different companies. Bennett selected an insurance policy for Morrow and completed the application. In the space provided for flight information, Bennett wrote "private air." The printed policy stated that it covered only travel on an aircraft operated by a scheduled air carrier. It also stated that the insurance agent could not vary the terms of the policy. Morrow died when the private plane crashed. Did Bennett have implied or apparent authority to issue insurance coverage to Morrow? Why or why not? [See *Travelers Ins. Co.* v. *Morrow*, 645 F.2d 41 (10th Cir. 1981).]

5. Snelling and Snelling, Inc., licensed PPS to operate an employment agency in Pittsburgh. The contract between them stated, in part, that it was a license agreement; that the licensee was not authorized to act for or on behalf of Snelling in any matter whatsoever; that the licensee could not change location without Snelling's written approval; that the licensee could not use any name or service mark other than that of Snelling and Snelling; that the licensee had to use Snelling's training manuals and procedures; that the licensee had to advertise in the Yellow Pages following a form required by Snelling; that the licensee had to obtain insurance naming Snelling as an additional insured; and that the licensee had to promptly notify Snelling of any claims under the insurance. When a dispute arose over PPS's placement practices, the plaintiff filed suit against PPS and Snelling and Snelling. Process for both defendants was served at the PPS office. Was this adequate service of process on Snelling and Snelling, or should the lawsuit against Snelling and Snelling be dismissed? Did PPS have the authority to act as Snelling's agent in accepting service of process? Why? [See *Sauers* v. *Pancoast Personnel, Inc.*, 439 A.2d 1214 (Pa.Super. 1982).]

6. **BUSINESS APPLICATION CASE** Taylor, a district manager for Pargas, Inc., diverted checks into his personal account at Rapides Bank. The payee on these checks was his employer. He endorsed the checks with a rubber stamp that had Pargas's name and address on it. Rapides Bank never obtained a corporation resolution authorizing Taylor to endorse the checks. There was no authorization for Taylor to deposit these checks to his personal account. Should Rapides Bank or Pargas suffer the loss? Why? What business practices should Pargas and Rapides Bank establish to prevent this type of problem in the future? [See *Pargas, Inc.* v. *Estate of Taylor*, 416 So.2d 1358 (La.App. 1982).]

7. **ETHICAL APPLICATIONS CASE** At the suggestion of Petrich, a real estate broker, Chapple decided to build a movie theater on an unimproved lot that she owned and to rent the theater to Rodriques. When the construction bids were in, Chapple felt the lowest bid was still too high, and she asked Petrich to negotiate with Big Bear (the lowest bidder) to obtain a lower price. Big Bear prepared a list of modifications and presented them at a meeting attended by Petrich, Rodriques, and the architect. Those present at the meeting agreed to reduce the capacity of the air conditioner from twenty tons to eight tons. Chapple was not informed of this agreement. She signed a written contract to have Big Bear construct a movie theater and to install a twenty-ton-capacity air-conditioning unit. Rodriques signed an addendum to the contract calling for a reduction to an eight-ton air conditioner. No one asked Chapple to sign the addendum. An eight-ton unit was used. Can Chapple successfully sue for breach of contract, or did someone, acting as her

agent, authorize the change of plans? What type of authority did the agent have? Should knowledge about this change be imputed to Chapple? Discuss the ethical perspective of Petrich, Rodriques, and the architect. [See *Chapple* v. *Big Bear Super Market No. 3,* 167 Cal.Rptr. 103 (Cal.App. 1980).]

8. **IDES CASE** Continental sued Grovijohn and his new employer, Amoco Chemicals, to enforce a covenant not to compete. Grovijohn was a plant manager in the plastic beverage bottle division of Continental. He was never employed there as an engineer or a technician. Grovijohn had agreed not to disclose, "directly or indirectly," or "use outside of the Continental organization during or after [his] employment, any confidential information" without Continental's consent. Amoco hired Grovijohn as a plant manager. There was no evidence that Grovijohn intended to reveal confidential information or that Amoco intended to use confidential information. Should Amoco be prevented from employing Grovijohn in this capacity? Why or why not? Continental has many employees who are exposed to confidential information. What could Continental have done to better protect itself? Use the IDES principles to analyze this case and to develop your answers to the questions posed. [See *Continental Group, Inc.* v. *Amoco Chemicals Corp.,* 614 F.2d 351 (3d Cir. 1980).]

NOTES

1. *Restatement (Second) of Agency* (Philadelphia: American Law Institute, 1958), § 97.
2. Warren A. Seavey, *Handbook of the Law of Agency* (St. Paul: West, 1964), § 8D, p. 19.
3. *General Overseas Films, Ltd.* v. *Robin International, Inc.,* 542 F.Supp. 684 (S.D. N.Y. 1982), p. 688, fn. 2.
4. See, for example, California Business and Professions Code, § 16600.

Agency: Liability for Torts and Crimes

A G E N D A

CIT hires a number of delivery people to deliver Call-Image units to retailers. Is CIT liable for the tortious conduct of these delivery people when they are acting for CIT? What financial risk is involved with hiring delivery people, and how can CIT best minimize this risk?

Tom and Anna have given all the family members sweatshirts with the Call-Image videophone and company logo printed on the back. Lindsay likes to wear her shirt during her high school field hockey games. One day, while wearing her shirt, Lindsay gets into a fight with a teammate and hits the player with her stick. The other girl suffers moderately serious injury. Can the parents of the injured player successfully sue CIT for damages, saying that Lindsay is advertising for CIT and, as a result, this makes her conduct "job-related?"

What duties does CIT owe its employees? What if an employee is injured at work? These and related questions will arise during our discussion of agency law. Be prepared! You never know when one of the Kochanowskis will call on you for help or advice.

O U T L I N E

AGENT'S LIABILITY

Agents often engage in physical activities or labor on behalf of the principal. These activities bring the agent into close contact with the general public. When the agent is careless or overly aggressive, there is a good chance that members of the public will be injured. This chapter discusses the agent's and the principal's responsibility to the public for these types of injuries. These relationships can occur in business and nonbusiness settings.

Vicarious liability for torts involves different policy considerations from those surrounding an agent's ability to bind the principal in business dealings with third persons. In contract matters, there is generally a conscious desire to interact with the public and a conscious decision to enter into business arrangements with the public by means of the agent. In most tort situations, however, neither the master nor the servant desires that the tort occur. But once the tort has occurred, someone has to suffer the financial burden, even if that someone is the innocent victim. Who should pay? The master? The servant? Or the third person?

Vicarious liability
Legal responsibility for the wrong committed by another person.

The general rule of tort law is that everyone is liable for his or her own torts. Furthermore, this general rule is followed in agency law. Since the agent committed the tort, the agent is liable for the harm that occurs. The fact that the agent is working for the principal at the time of the tort does not alter the general rule. Refer to Chapter 5 for a more complete discussion of specific torts.

MASTER'S LIABILITY: *RESPONDEAT SUPERIOR*

When the agent commits a tort that harms a third person, the agent should be responsible for the harm. However, in agency law, some circumstances exist in which the principal is also held liable for the torts committed by the agent. Notice that in these situations the *principal* is being held liable for the conduct of the *agent*. Since the agent is also liable for the tortious conduct, the liability is said to be *joint and several*. This means that either party may be held liable individually (several liability) or that both parties may be held liable (joint liability).

The theory under which principals are held liable for the torts of their agents even though the principals are not personally at fault is known as *respondeat superior*. Literally, it means "let the master answer." It is also referred to as a "deep-pockets" theory, based on the belief that the principal's pockets are deeper (that is, they hold more money) than those of the agent. The law generally involves an attempt to balance competing interests, clearly seen in the application of the *respondeat superior* doctrine. For example, if a victim has suffered $175,000 in injuries from an automobile accident caused by the negligence of an agent, and the agent has a total net worth of only $50,000, the agent cannot fully compensate the victim. However, if the principal is a multimillion-dollar corporation, the principal can fully compensate the victim. In these circumstances, the court must evaluate all the facts and determine whether *respondeat superior* should be applied in this particular case. This chapter generally uses the traditional terms *master* and *servant* because *respondeat superior* is limited to master–servant relationships.

Respondeat superior has been justified on numerous grounds in court opinions and in legal treatises. The justifications for holding the master liable for wrongful acts of the servant include the following:

1. The master will be more careful in choosing servants in order to avoid liability.
2. The master will be more careful in supervising servants in order to avoid liability.
3. The liability for servants is a cost of conducting business.
4. The master is the person benefiting from the servant's actions.
5. The master can purchase liability insurance.
6. The person with the power to control the conduct should be the person to bear financial responsibility.
7. The master can better afford the costs, especially when compared to an innocent third person who is injured by the servant's conduct, and so the master should pay.

Strict liability
Liability for an action simply because it occurred and caused damage, and not because it is the fault of the person who must pay.

Respondeat superior is not based on the idea that the master did anything wrong. Rather, it involves a special application of the doctrine of **strict liability**. Simply put, the master hired the servant; the servant did something wrong; the master should pay. "But for" the existence of the master–servant relationship, no harm would have resulted. In other words, someone should pay, and the master is best able to pay and afford the loss; therefore, the master must pay. However, *respondeat superior* does require a *wrongful act* by a servant for which the master can be held liable.

Judgment proof
Inability to pay a civil judgment if ordered to do so by the court.

In *Mary M.* v. *City of Los Angeles*, the court considered whether the master could be held civilly liable for a rape committed by a police officer. This case evidences a new trend toward increasing the liability of a master for rape. Note that the police officer was also sued; however, he was effectively **judgment proof** and did not appeal the decision against him. He was serving a criminal sentence for the rape at the time of this appeal.

33.1 MARY M. v. CITY OF LOS ANGELES

285 Cal.Rptr. 99, 814 P.2d 1341 (1991)

FACTS Sergeant Schroyer was on duty as a field supervisor at about 2:30 A.M. in Los Angeles. He was responsible for supervising and training police officers who were patrolling the streets. He was wearing his uniform and he was driving a marked police car by himself. He stopped a vehicle Mary was operating; she was alone in her vehicle. He administered a field sobriety test to Mary. She had difficulty performing the specified tasks. She began to cry and asked him not to take her to jail. Schroyer ordered her into his patrol car, and then drove her to her home. He said she owed him a "payment" for not arresting her and he began to rape her. She stopped screaming and struggling with him when he threatened to take her to jail.

ISSUE Should the City of Los Angeles be held responsible for Sergeant Schroyer's acts under *respondeat superior?*

HOLDING Yes.

REASONING Police officers have a unique position in our society. They are responsible for protecting us from criminal acts. They have authority to arrest, detain, and use deadly force, if necessary. Officers have visible signs of their authority and power in their marked cars, uniforms, badges, and guns. People who challenge police officers are subject to their use of force and criminal prosecution. When police officers abuse their authority, they violate the public trust. *Respondeat superior* applies to public masters as well as private masters.

Respondeat superior is a rule of policy. It is based on the belief that it would be unjust to allow an enterprise to disclaim responsibility for losses that occur in the course and scope of its activities. There are three underlying rationales for applying the doctrine: "(1) to prevent recurrence of the tortious conduct; (2) to give greater assurance of compensation for the victim; and (3) to ensure that the victim's losses will be equitably borne by those who benefit from the enterprise that gave rise to the injury." The court concluded that these rationales would be achieved by applying *respondeat superior* in this case. By imposing liability here, it would encourage police departments to exercise care and take preventative measures. It would also assure that the victim is compensated and that the compensation is paid by the community that benefits from the police service.

33.1 MARY M. v. CITY OF LOS ANGELES *(cont.)* 285 Cal.Rptr. 99, 814 P.2d 1341 (1991)

To recover based on *respondeat superior*, the plaintiff must show that the tortious conduct occurred in the scope of the employment. "[T]he inquiry should be whether the risk was one 'that may fairly be regarded as typical of or broadly incidental' to the enterprise undertaken by the employer." Considering the amount of force used by officers on the job, Schroyer's behavior was broadly incidental to his job. The evidence supported the jury's finding that the officer was in the course and scope of employment when he raped Mary. Schroyer used his authority to commit the sexual assault.

Note that since the city was held liable, the expenses will be borne by city taxpayers.

BUSINESS CONSIDERATIONS If you operated a business that hired police, prison wardens, or security personnel, what steps should you take to avoid rapes and serious assaults? Which step(s) would be most effective?

ETHICAL CONSIDERATIONS Analyze the ethical perspectives of Sergeant Schroyer, the city officials, and Mary M.

Respondeat superior does not make the master an insurer for every act of the servant. The master is only liable for those actions that are within the *course* and *scope* of the employment. Therefore, the issue in most cases in which the servant committed the tort, but in which the suit is against the master, involves a decision as to whether the servant was acting within the course and scope of his or her employment when the tort was committed. To resolve this question, it is important to know the servant's duties, working hours, state of mind, deviation from route, assigned location, and the master's right to control the worker. It is immaterial if the principal fails to exert actual control over how the worker completes the tasks as long as the master has the right to use this control. The principal's *right to control* is really what distinguishes servants from nonservants. A principal who has the right to control may be called a *master*, and the worker may be called a *servant*. *Respondeat superior* applies only to servants. It does not apply to nonservants because the principal lacks control and, thus, is not a master. *Respondeat superior* has been criticized by "masters" on the grounds that it is unconstitutional, but the Supreme Court recently affirmed that *respondeat superior* is not fundamentally unfair or unconstitutional.[1]

In *Bowers* v. *Potts*, the court examined the course and scope of a servant's employment.

Personal representative
Person who handles the financial affairs of someone who has died.

33.2 BOWERS v. POTTS 617 S.W.2d 149 (Tenn.App. 1981)

FACTS Potts was employed as foreman for J. W. Petty Construction Company (Petty), which was laying an underground conduit for South Central Bell. The job required the extraction of dirt, which was stored at two locations so that it could later be replaced in the trenches. Petty had promised any excess dirt to South Central Bell and to Smyrna Hardware and Lumber Company. Terrell knew that Potts was supplying dirt and contacted Potts about hauling some to Terrell's property. Potts agreed to perform this service in his spare time for $10 or $15 per load. Potts was hauling the dirt to Terrell's on a Saturday, his day off, using his own truck to do so, when he had an accident with another vehicle. Weatherly, the driver of the other vehicle, died at the scene. Bowers, Weatherly's **personal representative**, filed this suit for wrongful death, naming Potts and Petty as defendants.

33.2 BOWERS v. POTTS *(cont.)* 617 S.W.2d 149 (Tenn.App. 1981)

ISSUE Was Potts acting within the course and scope of his employment for Petty?

HOLDING No.

REASONING Potts was being paid by Terrell and not by Petty. Potts worked for Petty on weekdays and not on Saturdays. Potts was not at the location where he conducted work for Petty. There is no evidence that this activity helped Petty or was strongly motivated by an intent to help Petty. Potts did it to help himself and Terrell. There is no competent testimony to support the idea that Potts's activities were authorized, permitted, known, or ratified by Petty, nor did Potts's actions benefit Petty. When the conduit was finished, Petty had to correct the dirt stockpile deficiency. The deficiency was caused, at least in part, by Potts's activities. Potts was held liable for his negligence, but Petty was not. Potts was acting for himself, not for Petty.

BUSINESS CONSIDERATIONS Could Petty have taken any steps to prevent servants from taking the dirt? If so, what steps would have been effective and practical?

ETHICAL CONSIDERATIONS Was it ethical for Potts to agree to sell the dirt to Terrell? Analyze Potts's ethical perspective.

Factors Listed in the Restatement of Agency

The *Restatement (Second) of Agency* indicates the factors that should affect the determination of whether an agent is within the scope of his or her employment. The factors include the following:

General Statement

(1) *Conduct of a servant is within the scope of employment if, but only if:*
- (a) *it is of the kind he is employed to perform;*
- (b) *it occurs substantially within the authorized time and space limits;*
- (c) *it is actuated, at least in part, by a purpose to serve the master; and*
- (d) *if force is intentionally used by the servant against another, the use of force is not unexpectable by the master. . . .*[2]

(2) *In determining whether or not the conduct, although not authorized, is nevertheless so similar to or incidental to the conduct authorized as to be within the scope of employment, the following matters of fact are to be considered:*
- (a) *whether or not the act is one commonly done by such servants;*
- (b) *the time, place, and purpose of the act;*
- (c) *the previous relations between the master and the servant;*
- (d) *the extent to which the business of the master is apportioned between different servants;*
- (e) *whether or not the act is outside the enterprise of the master or, if within the enterprise, has not been entrusted to any servant;*
- (f) *whether or not the master has reason to expect that such an act will be done;*
- (g) *the similarity in quality of the act done to the act authorized;*

(h) *whether or not the instrumentality by which the harm is done has been furnished by the master to the servant;*
(i) *the extent of departure from the normal method of accomplishing an authorized result; and*
(j) *whether or not the act is seriously criminal.*[3]

In many cases, certain factors may indicate that the servant is within the scope of employment and other factors may indicate the contrary. For example, the master furnishes the truck (the instrumentality), but he or she has no reason to suspect that the servant will drive under the influence of alcohol (engage in this conduct). No one factor controls this decision; the judge or jury weighs all the factors involved to reach a decision. Since the triers of fact exercise a lot of discretion in these cases, fact situations that seem very similar may result in different decisions by different courts.

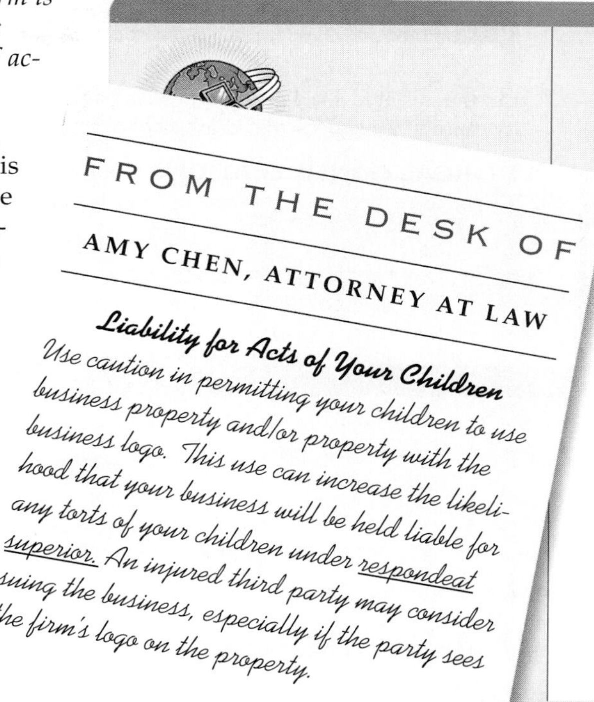

FROM THE DESK OF
AMY CHEN, ATTORNEY AT LAW
Liability for Acts of Your Children
Use caution in permitting your children to use business property and/or property with the business logo. This use can increase the likelihood that your business will be held liable for any torts of your children under respondeat superior. An injured third party may consider suing the business, especially if the party sees the firm's logo on the property.

Time and Place of Occurrence

Two of the factors that courts analyze in determining the course and scope of employment are the time and place of the act[4]—whether the tort occurred on the work premises and whether it occurred during work hours. These factors were influential in *Chastain* v. *Litton Systems, Inc.*

33.3 CHASTAIN v. LITTON SYSTEMS, INC.

694 F.2d 957 (4th Cir. 1982), Cert. Den., 462 U.S. 1106 (1983)

FACTS Beck was an employee of Litton Systems, Inc. On the day in question, Litton Systems was having its annual pre-Christmas party. Employees were to clock in and out that day in order to be paid for a full day of work, but they did not have to perform any actual work. Litton provided music, food, and beverages. Beck became intoxicated at the party. About one hour and twenty minutes after he left, while driving his van, Beck ran through a red light and hit another car. He killed the occupants of that car, and their husbands filed this suit.

ISSUES Was Litton responsible for the accident based on *respondeat superior?*

HOLDING Perhaps. The case is remanded to the trial court for a decision on the facts.

REASONING Litton is responsible for the negligent or willful acts of its employees within the scope of their employment. North Carolina courts have not decided whether an employer who provides alcoholic beverages is liable to innocent victims who are injured. State law imposes liability on businesses that serve and charge for alcoholic beverages, but not on social hosts. This situation is similar to that of a business that serves drinks. Whether Litton was advancing a business purpose is a question of fact to be decided by a jury. Beck's activities may have been within the course and scope of his employment. The time that should be examined is the time during which he became intoxicated.

BUSINESS CONSIDERATIONS Why do businesses have holiday parties? What purpose(s) do they serve? How

33.3 CHASTAIN v. LITTON SYSTEMS, INC. *(cont.)* 694 F.2d 957 (4th Cir. 1982), Cert. Den., 462 U.S. 1106 (1983)

can the business avoid negative publicity and potential liability caused by servants who drink alcohol at these functions?

ETHICAL CONSIDERATIONS Does a business have a right to restrict how servants celebrate and/or relax during nonwork hours? Why or why not? Does it have the right to place restrictions on parties at work and/or lunchtime activities? Why or why not?

33.1

LIABILITY FOR DRIVERS MAKING DELIVERIES

As CIT's business has expanded, the firm has begun to hire drivers to make deliveries of the product to customers, especially retail outlets. John recently read an article in the local newspaper about a case in which the driver of a delivery van was at fault in an accident. The local court entered a judgment against the employer of the driver for $1.5 million dollars. John is concerned that a similar case would destroy CIT if the firm was the employer of a driver who caused an accident. John has asked you if there is any way for the firm to be able to avoid liability while still hiring drivers to make deliveries for the firm. What will you tell him?

BUSINESS CONSIDERATIONS How can a business minimize its potential financial risk when one of its employees is guilty of negligence? What policies should a business institute to provide the best possible protection when hiring drivers who will be driving company-owned vehicles?

ETHICAL CONSIDERATIONS Would it be ethical for a firm to state that its delivery personnel are independent contractors and to require all of its drivers to drive their (the drivers') personal vehicles and provide proof of adequate insurance coverage?

MANAGEMENT

Failure to Follow Instructions

A master can be held liable for a servant's acts even though the master instructed the servant not to perform a specific act or commit torts. The disobedience of the servant does not necessarily exempt the master from liability.

Failure to Act

A master can also be held liable under *respondeat superior* when the servant fails to act as directed, as shown in the following example.

> A railroad switch operator is supposed to throw a switch on the track at the same time every day. One day, he carelessly fails to do so, a train derails as a result, and passengers on the train are injured. The master (the railroad) is liable for the servant's negligence in failing to act as instructed.

Respondeat superior does not decrease the servant's liability for wrongdoing, but it makes an additional party, the master, also liable. In many legal situations, such as the one just described, multiple parties are liable for a single occurrence.

Two Masters

Another problem that may arise is deciding *who* the master is. Who controls the manner in which the servant will do the work? The master, or employer, is the one who not only can order the work done, but also can order how it will be done.

Identifying the master would seem to be a simple question. However, the question is complex in cases of borrowed servants. In these cases, who is the master? Is it the lending master, the borrowing master, or both? Again, the important factors are the course of the employment and the ability to control the servant. Consider the following example:

Jerry works for Computer, Inc., which is having its office remodeled by Interiors Redone. Since the contractors doing the work are understaffed, Jerry's supervisor tells Jerry to help them. In this situation, Computer, Inc., is referred to as the general master and Interiors Redone as Jerry's special master. (The meanings of general master and special master here are similar to those used to define general and special agents in Chapter 31.) Jerry is classified as a borrowed servant. After painting the walls in the main lobby, Jerry negligently fails to put up Wet Paint signs. A customer brushes against the wall and ruins his clothes. Who is Jerry's master at the time of his negligent act?

Some courts will decide that both Computer, Inc., and Interiors Redone are liable. Jerry was subject to the control of both, and his actions benefitted both. Other courts will conclude that Interiors Redone is liable because Jerry was working primarily for Interiors Redone at the time of the negligence. Still other courts will hold Computer, Inc., liable because ultimately Jerry was subject to its control and it supplied his paycheck.

Liability in *Krzywicki* v. *Tidewater Equipment Co., Inc.* was decided on the basis of which of the two masters employed a worker who negligently caused an injury to another person.

33.4 KRZYWICKI v. TIDEWATER EQUIPMENT CO., INC. 600 F.Supp. 629 (D. Md. 1985)

FACTS A longshoreman, Krzywicki, suffered extensive injuries when a crane operator dropped a 2½-ton load of cargo directly on him. Krzywicki was a member of a gang of longshoremen supplied to Prudential Lines by Atlantic and Gulf Stevedores, Inc. The barge was owned by Prudential Lines, Inc. The crane was owned by Tidewater and was furnished to Prudential under a written lease. The crane operator, George Eberling, was loading the barge at the time. Jocelyn Taylor, the signalman, was employed as a longshoreman by Atlantic and Gulf. Eberling and Taylor were working under a system in which Eberling moved a load of cargo over the barge and lowered it, unless he observed a signal to stop. In this case, he did not observe a signal to stop, since Taylor temporarily left his station to go to the bathroom. Taylor was determined not to have been negligent in causing the accident. Krzywicki was determined not to have been negligent in moving across the barge when he knew that a signalman was on duty to alert the crane operator if men were under the load. Krzywicki had a right to reasonably assume that a warning would be given if he were in a danger zone and that the load would not be lowered. Krzywicki is now permanently disabled and unable to return to work. [Exhibit 33.1 illustrates these relationships.]

ISSUE Who was the master of Eberling, the crane operator?

HOLDING Tidewater, the crane owner.

REASONING Eberling knew that there were longshoremen working in the barge whom he could not see. It was negligent to load the barge unless there was a negative signal that it was unsafe to lower the load. The court concluded that this was true whether this was the practice in this port. Affirmative signals should have been used. Standard crane signal procedures called for affirmative signals if it was okay to lower the load. If Eberling had been paying attention, he would have noticed that the signalman was not in position. He had a duty to find out who was acting as signalman. Taylor was not in position. Eberling wrongly assumed that some other longshoremen standing on the pier were acting as signalmen even though neither one of them had given him a signal. Under the borrowed servant doctrine, the parties may allocate between themselves the risk of any loss caused by the employee's negligent acts. One of the factors to be considered was whether there was a meeting of the minds between the parties as to the status of the employee in question. One factor that is important is whose work was being performed. This is usually decided by who had the power to direct and control the servant. Another factor to be considered is whether one or both parties carried liability insurance that covered the risk of loss. Eberling was the servant of his general employer, Tidewater. He was paid by Tidewater; Tidewater had the right to discharge him; Tidewater selected him for this job; Tidewater had employed him for a considerable period of time; Tidewater owned the crane; and the benefit to Prudential

33.4 KRYZWICKI v. TIDEWATER EQUIPMENT CO., INC. *(cont.)* 600 F.Supp. 629 (D. Md. 1985)

was for only a short period of time. The work was for the benefit of Prudential, but Prudential did not have control over the crane operations. Eberling, a skilled crane operator, was free to operate the crane in accordance with his own judgment. Both Prudential and Tidewater had liability insurance; they agreed that Eberling should remain the servant of Tidewater. Eberling was not a borrowed servant of the barge owner at the time of the accident.

A ship owner has no duty to be present during the complete loading operation or to inspect the equipment. It is reasonable for him to rely on the harbor workers to avoid unreasonable risks.

BUSINESS CONSIDERATIONS What effect does it have when a worker is following standard industry procedures? What about failing to follow the standard industry procedures? What effect *should* either of these have?

ETHICAL CONSIDERATIONS What ethical duties did Krzywicki and/or Taylor owe to the longshoremen working in the barge? Why?

When analyzing a complicated fact pattern such as the one in *Krzywicki,* drawing a diagram of the relationships is helpful. Exhibit 33.1 provides an example. As you can see from the exhibit, this case contains at least three instances of potential borrowed servants.

To avoid the uncertainties caused by borrowed servants, prudent employers enter into agreements about which master will be liable and/or obtain liability insurance for the servants' acts.

EXHIBIT 33.1 Legal Relationships in *Krzywicki* v. *Tidewater Equipment Co., Inc.*

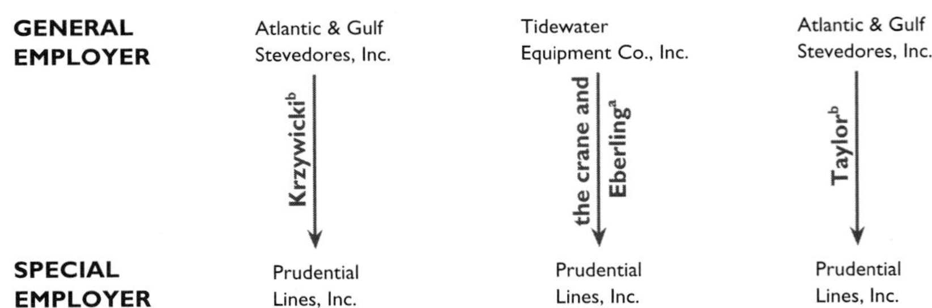

[a]According to the court, the crane and Eberling were loaned to Prudential Lines, Inc. under a written contract. The parties had agreed that Eberling would remain the servant of Tidewater Equipment.

[b]The court focused on the status of Eberling, because he was the one who was found to be negligent. However, Krzywicki and Taylor also were potential borrowed servants.

A closely related problem occurs when one servant appoints another servant (a subservant) to complete his or her tasks. Under *respondeat superior,* who is responsible for the torts of the subservant? If the servant had authority to appoint the subservant, the master will be held liable for the subservant. However, if the servant lacked authority, generally the servant will be liable as the "master" under *respondeat superior.* The primary justification for this rule is that the servant is the one with the right to control the subservant.

Crimes and Intentional Torts

Courts are more reluctant to hold a master liable under *respondeat superior* for intentional wrongs such as **assault** and **battery** than they are for negligence on the part of the servant. In fact, some courts still follow the traditional rule that a master is not responsible for the intentional acts of his or her servant. The modern view, however, is that a master is liable if the servant advanced the master's interests or the servant believed that his or her conduct was advancing the master's interests. Consequently, masters can be held liable under *respondeat superior* for intentional torts such as slander, libel, invasion of privacy, and assault and battery. Many criminal acts are also torts, and the master may be held civilly liable under *respondeat superior* for the financial losses suffered by the victim of the servant's criminal act. *Respondeat superior* is not used to impose criminal liability on the master.

Assault

A threat to touch someone in an undesired manner.

Battery

Unauthorized touching of another person without legal justification or that person's consent.

Manning v. *Grimsley* addressed whether the master can be held civilly liable for an intentional act by a servant (a professional baseball player). In this case, the servant was also being sued.

33.5 MANNING v. GRIMSLEY

643 F.2d 20 (1st Cir. 1981)

FACTS Manning attended a professional baseball game at Fenway Park in Boston. As Grimsley, a pitcher for the visiting Baltimore Orioles, was warming up in the right-field bullpen, the spectators in the nearby stands continuously heckled him. Grimsley periodically turned to stare at them. His catcher left and walked over to the bench. Grimsley wound up and threw the ball, which went toward the stands, through the fence, and hit Manning.

ISSUE Can the Baltimore Orioles be held liable for Grimsley's conduct?

HOLDING Yes.

REASONING Under Massachusetts law, an employer can be liable for damages resulting from an assault by an employee. It must be proved that the employee's assault was in response to the plaintiff's conduct, which at the time was interfering with the employee's ability to perform his or her duties successfully. In this case, there was sufficient evidence that Grimsley was responding to the heckling, which might have annoyed him and interfered with his ability to perform his duties successfully. The court held that Manning was entitled to a jury trial on the factual issue and returned the case to the trial court for a decision on the facts. The Baltimore Orioles could be held financially liable for Grimsley's conduct.

BUSINESS CONSIDERATIONS What could the Baltimore Orioles and other professional teams do to reduce the risk of intentional torts committed by their players? Remember that assaults on customers may reduce ticket sales and attendance at games. Are these types of assaults more likely in some sports than others? If so, how does this affect the liability of the owners?

ETHICAL CONSIDERATIONS Do the Baltimore Orioles owe a moral duty to the customers in the stands? Why or why not? Remember that the Baltimore Orioles were playing an away game. Does that affect the duty owed to customers?

33.2

IS LINDSAY AN AGENT OF CIT?

One of Lindsay's extracurricular activities is playing field hockey for her school team. She was at a field hockey practice last week when she and one of her teammates had an altercation. The other girl pushed Lindsay, Lindsay pushed the other girl back, and tempers flared out of control. In the heat of anger, Lindsay hit the other girl with her stick, causing a moderately serious injury, which required stitches to close the cut caused by the edge of Lindsay's stick. During that practice, Lindsay had been wearing a sweatshirt with the CIT logo imprinted on its back. The parents of the other girl are now threatening to sue the firm for damages. They base their claim on the fact that, in their opinion, Lindsay was acting as an agent for CIT when she was wearing the sweatshirt with the CIT logo, thus making her conduct "job-related." Tom and Anna have asked you whether the family should be concerned about this claim. What advice will you give them?

BUSINESS CONSIDERATIONS Should a business expect to be held liable whenever any person acts negligently or in a tortious manner while wearing a shirt (or other item of apparel) that advertises the firm? Should it matter if the person wearing the logo is related to a manager of the "advertised" firm?

ETHICAL CONSIDERATIONS Is it ethical for the plaintiff in a tort case to sue the wealthiest possible defendant, regardless of the degree of fault that may attach to that defendant? Is it ethical for a business to derive the benefits of "free advertising" when people wear its logo on their apparel and yet for the business to deny liability when those same people act in a tortious manner?

MANAGEMENT

Courts will hold a master liable for some of a servant's serious wrongdoings, but not for others. The question is often one of degree. How serious was the tort or crime? Should the master have expected it? Is there much variance between the assigned tasks and the wrongdoing? Courts frequently examine the underlying policies for *respondeat superior* (see Case 33.1, *Mary M.*, discussed earlier).

Direct Liability of the Principal

The agent must be a servant before *respondeat superior* will be applied. However, principals may be held *directly* responsible for some of the wrongs committed by their agents, even if the agents are not servants. For example, the principal is liable if the principal *instructed* the agent to commit the wrong, did not properly supervise the agent, ratified or approved the agent's tort, or was negligent in the selection of the agent.

The rules of agency are not the only rules of law that may be involved when an agent commits a crime. Often a principal will be criminally liable based on his or her own fault. If a principal directs or encourages an agent to engage in criminal activity, the principal will probably be held personally liable for such acts as **conspiracy, solicitation,** or **accessory to the crime**. In addition, some criminal statutes create liability for the principal even though the principal does not intend to violate the statute or does not know of the illegal act or condition. For example, state liquor laws often specify that tavern or restaurant owners are liable if minors are served alcohol in their bars. In most states, this is true whether or not the owner approves of such action or even knows that it has occurred. Other examples include statutes that prohibit the sale of impure food or beverages no matter who is at fault. The purpose of these statutes is to stimulate the principals' concern so that they are *interested* in whether these activities occur in their establishments.

Indemnification

When a master pays a third person under *respondeat superior* for injuries caused by the servant's unauthorized acts, the master is entitled to *indemnification* (the right to be repaid) from the servant. Unlike most other theories, *respondeat superior* is not based on the fault of the master; it only creates legal liability for the master. The master should be entitled to recover from the person who caused the loss—the servant—so the law allows the master to recover. As a practical matter, the master generally will have insurance to cover the payment. Furthermore, the servant normally will not have sufficient funds to make the payment. If the servant is still employed by the master, the master may be able to withhold part of the reimbursement from each paycheck until the master is completely repaid. Continuing to employ the servant, however, may increase the likelihood that the master will be liable for any future similar wrongs by the servant.

Sometimes an agent may be entitled to indemnification from the principal if the agent paid the third person who was injured by the agent's tort. It will depend on the particular facts of the case. Such cases are based either on contract law or on the law of restitution.[5] Courts are influenced by what they believe to be just, considering the business and the nature of the particular relationship.[6] Under the *Restatement (Second) of Agency,* an agent is entitled to indemnification if the agent, at the direction of the principal, commits an act that constitutes a tort but the agent believes that it is not tortious.[7] Obviously, if an agent completes a task that he or she knows to be illegal or tortious, the agent is not entitled to indemnification.[8]

Exhibit 33.2 illustrates the relationships among the primary parties when the agent commits a tort. The agent's right to indemnification is questionable because the courts require that the agent follow the principal's instructions in good faith before receiving indemnification. The principal's *right* to indemnification is established by law. The principal's ability to collect, however, is questionable because, realistically, many agents cannot afford to reimburse the principal.

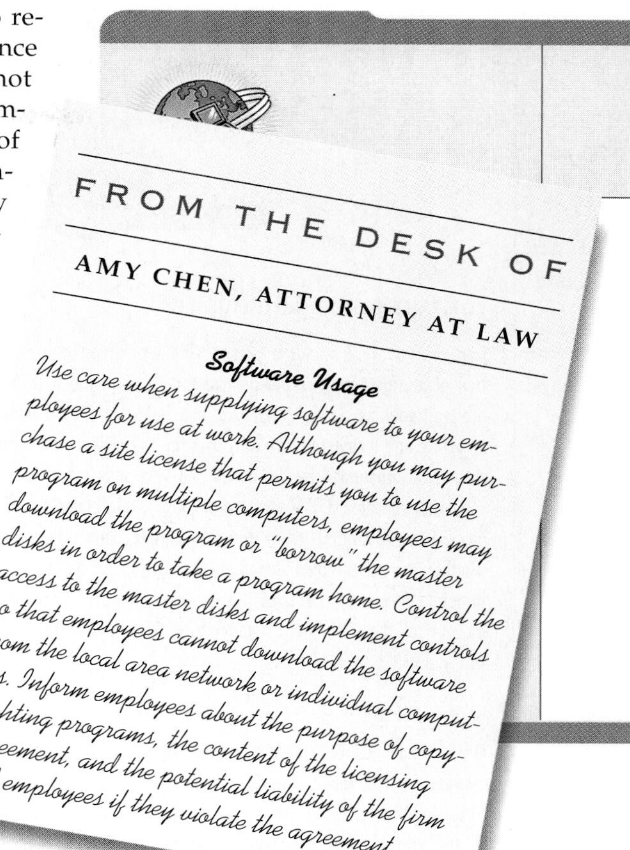

FROM THE DESK OF
AMY CHEN, ATTORNEY AT LAW
Software Usage
Use care when supplying software to your employees for use at work. Although you may purchase a site license that permits you to use the program on multiple computers, employees may download the program or "borrow" the master disks in order to take a program home. Control the access to the master disks and implement controls so that employees cannot download the software from the local area network or individual computers. Inform employees about the purpose of copyrighting programs, the content of the licensing agreement, and the potential liability of the firm and employees if they violate the agreement.

EXHIBIT 33.2 Liability for Tortious Injury to a Third Person

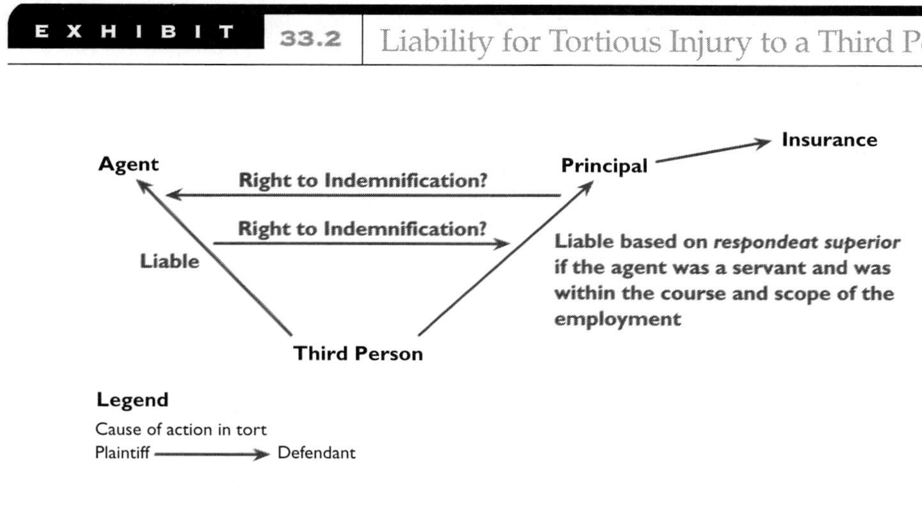

Conspiracy
An unlawful situation in which two or more people plan to engage in an illegal act or to use illegal means to achieve a lawful objective.

Solicitation
A situation in which one person convinces another to engage in criminal activity.

Accessory to the crime
A situation in which one person assists another in the commission of a crime, without being the primary actor.

33.3

COMPANY-OWNED AUTOMOBILES

Dan recently read about a person who was arrested for solicitation of a prostitute. The person had his car impounded by the police and sold at auction. Dan has also heard of people who were arrested and convicted for narcotics in their cars and who had their cars impounded by the police and sold at auction. He is quite concerned because CIT is now employing several sales agents who have been provided with company-owned cars. He asks you whether the police could impound and auction off a CIT-owned automobile if one of the sales agents would happen to be arrested for one of these crimes, or under any other circumstances. What will you tell him?

BUSINESS CONSIDERATIONS What can a business do to minimize its risk when it provides employees with company-owned automobiles? If a company car should happen to be impounded and sold by the police in such a situation, what rights could the company assert, and against whom could it assert those rights?

ETHICAL CONSIDERATIONS Suppose that a husband and wife are co-owners of an automobile, and that the husband is arrested for solicitation of a prostitute while driving that automobile. Under the local law, the police are allowed to take the automobile after his conviction and to sell it at auction since it was used in the commission of a crime. Is it ethical for the government to be allowed to take property used in the commission of this sort of crime and to sell that property without regard to who owns the property?

MANAGEMENT/SALES

Analysis of an Agent's Torts

To characterize a tort situation, one should answer the following questions:

1. Was the person acting as a servant for the hiring party?
2. Did the servant commit a tort?
3. Was the servant acting within the course and scope of the job?
4. Is the servant entitled to indemnification from the master? Is the master entitled to indemnification from the servant?

Remember that the servant is ultimately the one who is liable for the tort, unless he or she is entitled to indemnification from the master. The master may also be liable in his or her own right.

Injury on the Job

Courts generally use the terms *employer* and *employee* when discussing injuries on the job. Consequently, the same terminology is used here. An employer has a duty to provide employees with a reasonably safe place to work and reasonably safe equipment to use at work, both of them appropriate to the nature of the employment. If this is not possible, the employer should warn employees about unsafe conditions that they may not discover even if they are reasonably careful.[9]

Although courts *sometimes* apply similar rules to employees and independent contractors, there are distinct differences in their legal relationships. Nevertheless, courts have, on occasion, allowed independent contractors to recover for injuries sustained on the job.[10]

Under the common law, if an employee is hurt at work, the employer can utilize a number of defenses to avoid reimbursing the employee for the injury and for any medical bills. Negligence by the employee and the employee's assumption of the known risk are two such defenses. For example, the employee might have been driving a truck too fast for icy road conditions, or the employee might not have been wearing safety goggles provided by the employer. Assumption of the risk, contributory negligence, and its modern counterpart—comparative negligence—are discussed in detail in Chapter 5.

At common law, the *fellow employee doctrine* also acts to bar recovery by the employee. Traditionally, this concept was called the fellow servant doctrine. More recent

YOU BE THE JUDGE

Use of Company Voice Mail

Fred Remillard operates 12 McDonald's franchises in western New York state. Two of his employees, Michael Huffcut and Rose Hasset, who worked at separate restaurants 60 miles apart, had an affair. When they were not able to meet, they left "lovey-dovey" messages for each other on their voice mail boxes at work. It is alleged that Fred listened to the messages, tape-recorded them, and even played them back to Michael's wife, Lisa Huffcut. The affair is over and the Huffcuts have reconciled. Michael and Lisa are suing McDonald's Corporation and Fred Remillard for $1 million each. They claim their rights to privacy were violated and that they suffered from intentionally inflicted emotional distress, embarrassment, loss of reputation, and loss of income. If this case were brought to *your* court, how would *you* decide?[11]

BUSINESS CONSIDERATIONS What arguments can employers make that they should be able to monitor and record messages on company voice mail systems and electronic mail systems? Was Fred Remillard's behavior reasonable in this situation? What reasonable limitations and procedures can a business implement?

ETHICAL CONSIDERATIONS Some ethical theories are based on rights. Discuss the right to privacy in this context. Should voice mail recordings be protected? Is there anything special about the employment situation?

SOURCE: Ben Dubbin, *The Fresno Bee* (23 January 1995), p. A6.

court cases and treatises call it the fellow employee doctrine. Under this theory, an employee cannot recover damages for work-related injuries if they are caused by another employee of the same employer. Like assumption of the risk, this doctrine acts as a complete bar to recovery. This rule is applicable to many worksite accidents. Most of the time, when an employee is injured on the job, the injury is caused not by the employer, but by another employee at the job site. One justification suggested for this doctrine is that the employer is often remote from the worksite. The employee, on the other hand, is likely to know of hazards at work and to know of careless fellow employees. Another justification used to support the doctrine is that an employee "assumes the risk" of being injured by co-workers. The existence of the fellow employee doctrine encouraged the spread of state **workers' compensation** statutes.

Workers' compensation
Payments to injured workers based on the provisions in the state workers' compensation statute.

In some cases, the injured employee will be covered by workers' compensation. In some states, however, particular types of workers are not covered under the workers' compensation statutes. For example, in New Mexico agricultural workers are not covered under the state statute.

These statutes may seem to be the opposite extreme of the fellow employee doctrine. They are not based on the fault of the employer, and the employer's negligence need not be shown in court. The worker needs only to show that his or her injury was caused in the course and scope of the job. In many states, the policies underlying these statutes are to "provide prompt and limited compensation benefits for job-related injuries and to facilitate the employee's speedy return to employment

http:// RESOURCES FOR BUSINESS LAW STUDENTS

NAME	RESOURCES	WEB ADDRESS
EFF Legal Issues and Policy: Cyberspace and the Law Archive	The Electronic Frontier Foundation, a nonprofit civil liberties organization, provides articles and links to information regarding the use of technology and workplace privacy.	http://www.eff.org/pub/Legal/
Legal Information Institute (LII)—Workers' Compensation Law Materials	LII, maintained by the Cornell Law School, provides an overview of and resources addressing workers' compensation law.	http://www.law.cornell.edu/topics/workers_compensation.html

without regard to fault."[12] In other words, these statutes are intended to be "economic insurance" for workers. These statutes exist in most states and provide for a fixed schedule of compensation for listed injuries. Moreover, workers can easily determine how much they are entitled to receive. Therefore, this procedure allows for the quick settlement of claims and discourages many lawsuits. When workers' compensation statutes are applied, legal action against the employer based on common law theories generally is prohibited.

State statutes vary in format. Some states have organized a fund to which the employers contribute; and injured employees collect from the fund. Some states allow employers to purchase insurance or to establish their own funds. In most states, the employee is allowed to recover even if he or she was negligent in causing the injury, assumed the risk, or was injured by a fellow employee. The injured employee generally receives compensation according to a schedule of payments, depending on the type of disability and how long the employee is unable to work.

Workers' compensation statutes vary in the following respects:

1. Some cover only major industrial occupations.
2. Some exclude small shops with few employees.
3. Some exclude injuries caused intentionally by the employer or other workers.

Because of the variations, it is important to examine the particular statute at issue.

If the workers' compensation statute does not apply, generally the employee will be permitted to sue based on common law theories. (Workers' compensation is also discussed in Chapter 43.)

SUMMARY

An agent is liable for his or her own tortious and criminal acts. The fact that the agent was working at the time is immaterial. The fact that the principal may also be liable to the third party is irrelevant as well.

A principal may be liable for the acts of his or her agents. Much of this liability is based on the doctrine of *respondeat superior.* A master is liable for the torts committed by a servant if the servant was acting within the course and scope of the employment. The courts have discussed many policy reasons for enforcing *respondeat superior.* These include: encouraging masters to be careful in selecting servants; encouraging masters to be careful in supervising servants; this is a necessary expense of conducting business; the master is benefiting from the servant's acts; the master can purchase liability insurance; the master has control and so should pay; and the master can better afford these costs.

Numerous factors are used in analyzing what activity is "within the course and scope of the employment." There is no formula, however. Courts look at the factors and determine if *respondeat superior* should be applied. Even though a court holds a master liable to the third party under *respondeat superior,* this does not mean that the master necessarily will bear the ultimate loss. The master generally will be entitled to indemnification from the servant, although such indemnification may not be practical. The master may also have purchased insurance for this risk. In rare cases, the master may owe the servant the duty to reimburse the servant for tort compensation paid to third parties.

A principal may also be held directly liable if he or she commits a tort or a crime; this liability is not based on *respondeat superior.* It includes situations in which a principal is negligent in selecting an agent or directs an agent to commit a crime or a tort.

The employer owes the employee various duties, such as the duty to compensate the employee according to the terms of the agreement. These duties were discussed in Chapter 31. As discussed in this chapter, the employer has a duty to provide a reasonably safe place to work. This includes furnishing appropriate tools and equipment, adherence to safety regulations, and proper supervision, at a minimum. Injuries to employees on the job are normally covered by workers' compensation statutes. The amount of coverage and how payment is funded varies by state.

DISCUSSION QUESTIONS

1. David hires Annabelle as a housekeeper. Her main duties are to remain in the house and clean, prepare meals, and do the laundry. One afternoon, Annabelle receives a call from One-Day Drycleaners. David's suit is ready to be picked up. Annabelle decides to go and get the suit in her car. On the way home, she runs a red light and hits Julie's car. The police officer at the scene says that Annabelle's intoxication is the main cause of the accident. Annabelle had a few drinks with her lunch. David knew that Annabelle had a drinking problem when he hired her and that she is trying to stop drinking. Who is responsible for the damage to Julie's car, and why?
2. Cindy has just started working as an accountant for Big Six Accounting Firm. On her first audit, Cindy's supervisor sends her to get the coffee and doughnuts every morning. One morning, on the way to get the doughnuts, Cindy does not notice that the traffic has stopped in front of her, and she collides with Claudia's car. Who is responsible for the damage to Claudia's car, and why?
3. Cindy prepares a joint tax return for Sammy and Lenora Johnson during her first year at Big Six. However, she does not prepare the return correctly, and the IRS assesses $4,000 more in taxes and penalties. What rights do the Johnsons have? Why?
4. The employees at an Atlantic City casino "assist" a compulsive gambler in losing millions of dollars that the gambler had embezzled from his employer. This is in violation of the state gambling regulations pertaining to credit and cash procedures. Should the casino be held liable for the acts of its employees? Why or why not? Should the employees be held liable? Why or why not?
5. After class in the afternoon, Jim has a job delivering floral arrangements for Flowers by Flo. Flo often instructs Jim not to give his friends rides in the truck when he makes deliveries. One day, Jim sees Nanci, a

classmate, waiting for the bus. He is going toward her home, so he gives her a ride. On the way, Jim carelessly drives off the side of the road, and Nanci is injured. Who is liable to Nanci for her injuries, and why?

6. Janet works as Bill's secretary at Waincoat, Inc. Bill forgot to buy his wife a birthday present, so he sends Janet out to buy a gift at lunch. While Janet is looking in the discount store for a present, she carelessly runs into another customer with her shopping cart. Who is liable for the injuries to the other customer, and why?
7. Randy works as a stocker in the produce department of May Fair Market. The store prides itself on having the best produce in town. Caroline, a customer, comes into the grocery store and starts to complain about the generally poor quality of the produce and, specifically, of the lettuce. When Randy cannot stand her ranting and raving any more, he pushes Caroline, who falls and breaks her ankle. Who is liable to Caroline, and why?
8. Saul works for Central Cable Co. installing the cable for cable television in residential areas. The company needs water to repave the street after the cable is installed. Without permission, Saul uses water from Rosemary's tap. When Rosemary arrives home from work and sees this, she is furious. Her water bill is based on usage, and Saul has been using her water all day. Who is liable to Rosemary, and why?
9. Jeff makes deliveries for Superior Meat Packing Company. On Wednesday, he complains to the company mechanic that his truck is not braking correctly. The mechanic says he will check it out immediately. On Thursday afternoon, the brakes fail, and Jeff is unable to stop the truck. He collides with a telephone pole and suffers neck and back injuries. Who is liable? Why?
10. Neal is stationed on the aircraft carrier *USS Archer.* One night in August, the carrier is having night maneuvers so the pilots and crew can practice night takeoffs and landings. During these maneuvers, one of the planes crashes on the deck, injuring a number of people and killing Neal. The investigation reveals that some of the crew were suffering from fatigue and some were under the influence of narcotics. Can Neal's wife and children recover? From whom and why?

Case Problems and Writing Assignments

1. Elizabeth Paraiso was employed as a fitness instructor at a health spa. She received a telephone call from the spa manager, who asked Elizabeth to go to a supermarket on her way to work to get a birthday cake. They were giving the assistant manager a birthday party. Elizabeth left for work early and drove five blocks out of her way to get the cake at a supermarket. While driving back toward her usual route, Elizabeth reached over to protect the cake so that it would not slide off the car seat. She lost control of her car and struck William Sussman, as he was sitting on the bench at the bus stop. Should William Sussman be permitted to collect from Elizabeth's employer under *respondeat superior?* Why or why not? [See *Sussman* v. *Florida East Coast Properties, Inc.,* 557 So.2d 74 (Fla.App. 1990).]

2. Klauschie worked as a meat trimmer in a meatpacking plant owned and operated by Union Packing Company. Meat trimmers spend most of the day standing at their work stations. Union Packing required its employees in the plant, including the meat trimmers, to wear rubber boots while at work. In March, Klauschie noticed a small blister on his foot. The blister did not heal, nor did it cause any problem other than discomfort for quite some time. Finally, in June the blister began to darken and Klauschie's foot began to swell. Klauschie consulted a doctor, who diagnosed the problem as a severe infection of the foot. Klauschie was admitted to the hospital for treatment, but the infection did not respond to the medical attention. Finally, in August, Klauschie had part of his foot amputated. He then filed a workers' compensation claim with the state, alleging that the injury and the resulting amputation were work-related. Union Packing denied that the injury was work-related and denied that Klauschie was entitled to workers' compensation. How should the court rule in this case? Explain your reasoning. [See *Union Packing Co. of Omaha* v. *Klauschie,* 314 N.W.2d 25 (Neb. 1982).]

3. A car driven by Appling, a lawyer employed by Richman and Garrett, collided with the car in which the Wanks were riding. Appling had gone to lunch with a representative of one of the firm's clients and a number of other business contacts. At the lunch, Appling had consumed several alcoholic drinks. Between 3:30 and 4:00 that afternoon, Appling called the office and spoke to one of the partners to tell him that he would not be coming back to the office. The partner advised Appling to stay where he was and someone would

come to get him. Appling rejected that suggestion and drove himself in his own automobile. The accident occurred between 6:30 and 6:45 P.M. Appling does not remember where he was going at the time of the accident. There was evidence at the time of trial that Appling had had another accident earlier that afternoon in the parking lot of another restaurant. Is the law firm liable for the alleged negligent driving of Appling? Why? [See *Wank* v. *Richman and Garrett,* 211 Cal.Rptr. 919 (Cal.App. 1985).]

4. Sams was a pastor of a church and Calhoun was a member of his congregation. Calhoun often mowed the lawns of Sams's rental properties without charge as a favor to Sams. Calhoun's lawnmower was defective because it was missing a protective guard. One day when Calhoun was operating the lawnmower on Sams's rental property, it threw up a projectile into Michael Burns's eye. Michael, a six-year-old, had been playing on the sidewalk. Is Sams liable for the injury caused to Michael Burns? Why or why not? [See *Burns* v. *Sams,* 458 So.2d 359 (Fla.App. 1984).]

5. Wallace drowned in a swimming pond located on the premises of Sunnyside Beach and Campground. The campground was operated by Wilgus. Wallace was employed by Consolidated Cigar Corporation as a summer worker at a youth farm work camp called Camp Clark. Camp Clark was leased by Consolidated from Clark Brothers and was operated by the Shade Tobacco Growers Agricultural Association in connection with Consolidated and others. Wallace's employer had a verbal agreement with Wilgus to allow its workers to use the swimming pond. Wallace was not being paid for work at the time of the drowning. Wallace and two other boys were at the swimming pond under the supervision of two Camp Clark employees at the time. The employer provided supervisors, transportation, and equipment for its employees to use the swimming pond. The purpose was to improve the morale of its workers and to increase productivity. Did the drowning occur during the course of Wallace's employment within the meaning of the Massachusetts Workmen's Compensation Act? [See *Wallace* v. *Shade Tobacco Growers, Etc.,* 642 F.2d 17 (1st Cir. 1981).]

6. **BUSINESS APPLICATIONS CASE** Maria Marino drove a cab for Yellow Cab. One day, she parked her cab at the taxicab stand outside the Sundance Hotel and Casino in Las Vegas. She was the first cab in line; she would get the next fare. She was standing next to her cab talking to another taxi driver. James Edwards was the driver of the third cab, owned by Desert Cab. While seated in his cab, James began to verbally harass Maria. Maria approached James's cab, to find out why he was yelling at her. James jumped out of the cab and grabbed Maria, choked her, and threw her in front of his cab. An observer pulled them apart and walked Maria back to her cab. Maria missed work due to her injuries. Should Desert Cab be liable for James's acts under *respondeat superior?* Why or why not? [See *Desert Cab, Inc.* v. *Marino,* 823 P.2d 898 (Nev. 1992).]

7. **ETHICAL APPLICATIONS CASE** Nealey was instructed to haul a load of furniture from North Carolina to Texas. Nealey stopped in Mobile, Alabama, and picked up Bryant, a hitchhiker. Bryant and Nealey struck up a friendship and Nealey bought meals for Bryant and let Bryant sleep in the cab of the truck in exchange for Bryant's help in unloading the furniture. Nealey stated that he might be able to find work for Bryant in North Carolina, so Bryant returned with Nealey instead of getting off at his original destination. One tire blew out on the truck and Nealey elected to drive on to a larger town with only one tire on that axle. Bryant realized that this was dangerous. Bryant was injured when the second tire blew out and the truck rolled over. Under Mississippi law, the assumption-of-risk defense cannot be used in employment relationships. Did an employment relationship exist between Nealey and Bryant? Why? What are the ethical implications if the employer is permitted to avoid liability due to the status of the injured party? What are the ethical implications of holding the employer liable for injuries to a worker the employer never hired? [See *Bryant* v. *Nealey,* 599 F.Supp. 248 (N.D. Miss. 1984).]

8. **IDES CASE** On 15 January 1992, Johnny Carson said on the *Tonight Show* that Mr. Blackwell called Mother Teresa a "nerdy nun." Mr. Blackwell, as he is known, is a fashion critic who has become famous by bashing celebrities in his annual ten worst-dressed women list. Johnny said, "Did you see what he said about Mother Teresa? 'Miss nerdy nun is a fashion no-no.' Come on now, that's just too much. That's right, that's Mr. Blackwell, that's the guy I'm talking about." Mr. Blackwell filed an $11 million lawsuit against Johnny Carson and NBC. According to the suit, "Mr. Blackwell did not make any statement about Mother Teresa." Mr. Blackwell "holds Mother Teresa in high regard and has never maligned her or her saintly work." How should this case against Johnny Carson and NBC be decided, and why? Use the IDES principles to analyze this case and to answer the question. [See "Mr. Blackwell Isn't Amused, Johnny Sued," *The Fresno Bee* (19 March 1992), p. A2.]

NOTES

1. *Pacific Mut. Life Ins. Co.* v. *Haslip,* 111 S.Ct. 1032 (1991).
2. *Restatement (Second) of Agency* (Philadelphia: American Law Institute, 1958), § 228(1).
3. Ibid., § 229(2).
4. Ibid., § 229(2)(b).
5. Warren A. Seavey, *Handbook of the Law of Agency* (St. Paul: West, 1964), § 168, p. 265.
6. *Restatement (Second) of Agency,* § 438(2)(b).
7. Ibid., § 439(c) and Comment on Clause (c).
8. Harold Gill Reuschlein and William A. Gregory, *Hornbook on the Law of Agency and Partnership,* 2nd ed. (St. Paul: West, 1990), § 89(B), pp. 151–52.
9. Ibid., § 492.
10. *Rodney* v. *U.S.,* 77-4028 (9th Cir. 1980); *Cioll* v. *Bechtel Corp.,* No. 733794 (San Francisco City Super.Ct., 23 April 1981).
11. Ben Dubbin, "Voice Mail Love Affair Turns Privacy Issue Public," *The Fresno Bee* (23 January 1995), p. A6.
12. *Sussman* v. *Florida East Coast Properties,* 557 So.2d 74 (Fla. App. 3 Dist. 1990) at 75.

P A R T 7

I D E S P R O B L E M S

Koolin'-Aid manufactures and sells air conditioning equipment. Koolin'-Aid started operations a year ago and, with all of the work in the startup, has not thought much of the legal ramifications of the business. However, two recent legal problems have forced Koolin'-Aid's owners to seek legal help.

First, Jimmy Smith, a freelance jobber and salesperson, sold $20,000 worth of Koolin'-Aid equipment to Castleman Apartments. Koolin'-Aid had retained Smith previously to sell certain products for the firm. The relationship had deteriorated, however, and for more than six months Jimmy had not been commissioned to make such sales. Nevertheless, Jimmy, representing himself as the sales agent for Koolin'-Aid, made the sale to Castleman. On receiving the Castleman order from Smith, Koolin'-Aid notified Castleman that it would accept the order and would ship within 10 days. Prior to delivery, however, Castleman, on learning of Jimmy's lack of authority and realizing that it had made a bad bargain, promptly repudiated its order by notifying Koolin'-Aid that it was not bound on the purchase contract because of Jimmy's lack of authority.

Second, Shelia Adams, one of Koolin'-Aid's truck drivers, decided that instead of making deliveries she would watch the Olympic Games on television. Fearing detection, she drove to another part of town. Shelia parked the truck on a side street and went to a nearby tavern. While in the tavern, Shelia became embroiled in a heated argument with another customer, Tony, and pushed him off of his bar stool, causing Tony to break his hip. Tony later initiated a tort liability claim against Koolin'-Aid for $100,000.

Koolin'-Aid thereupon dismissed Shelia and thereafter published in appropriate trade journals the following notice: "This is to notify all parties concerned that Jimmy Smith and Shelia Adams are no longer employed by Koolin'-Aid, and the firm assumes no further responsibility for their acts." Jimmy, however, continued to call on several of Koolin'-Aid's suppliers with whom he had previously dealt. Most sent him away, but one supplier, Parts, Inc., was unaware of the dismissal. Jimmy purchased $10,000 worth of parts to be delivered to a warehouse in which Koolin'-Aid rented space when its storage facilities were crowded. Jimmy also called on several suppliers with whom Koolin'-Aid had never dealt and made purchases (about $5000 each on average) from them on an open account in the name of Koolin'-Aid. The merchandise purchased by Jimmy was also delivered to the warehouse. Jimmy then sold all of the merchandise and absconded with the money.

Shelia voluntarily agreed to leave Koolin'-Aid, although she continues to wear her favorite Koolin'-Aid driver's jacket. Another Koolin'-Aid driver, Hector, mentioned to his manager that he occasionally sees Shelia in local bars boasting of her "job" with Koolin'-Aid, "the toughest company in the world," wearing the jacket, and picking fights with the other customers.

Before Koolin'-Aid's owners meet with their lawyers, they need to clarify a few issues.

IDENTIFY What are the legal and ethical issues surrounding Jimmy and Shelia's actions?

DEFINE What are the meanings of the relevant legal terms associated with these issues?

ENUMERATE What are the legal and ethical principles relevant to these issues?

SHOW BOTH SIDES Consider all of the facts in light of the above questions. What legal steps are Castleman Apartments and the other suppliers Jimmy dealt with likely to take with Koolin'-Aid? How will Tony likely present his tort liability claim?

[To review the IDES approach refer to pages 29–30.]

Part 8

BUSINESS ORGANIZATIONS

Should the entrepreneur "go it alone" in a proprietorship? If so, the entrepreneur will have both absolute authority and total responsibility. Should a partnership be formed? For many businesses, the simplicity of a partnership makes it an ideal form, but the entrepreneur should be aware that a partnership entails the sharing of management powers and duties. Should a corporation be formed? The corporate form offers a number of advantages, including limited personal liability and the ability to franchise, but corporations are subject to heavy federal regulation and taxation.

Part 8 compares and contrasts these three main forms of business—proprietorship, partnership, and corporation—by showing the legal steps taken in their formation, operation, and termination. In addition, this part discusses several variations of these forms, such as limited liability partnerships and corporations. Finally, franchising and securities regulation are addressed.

I D E S

InterActive is a small, private multimedia software developer specializing in consumer CD-ROMs, especially games. InterActive is a corporation, with three majority and two minority owners, five managers, and twenty employees. InterActive maintains an office and retail store in San Francisco to sell the software the firm develops. InterActive also maintains a "storefront" on the Internet. Despite InterActive's small size and informal atmosphere, it has recently encountered a number of legal problems.

Can InterActive seek legal recourse against a former manager who, when presented with a business opportunity, started her own business rather than pursue the opportunity through InterActive? Can a minority owner who wishes for InterActive to expand either through franchising or through the issuance of debt securities sue to have these steps taken if the majority owners refuse to entertain these ideas?

Consider these issues in the context of the chapter materials, and prepare to analyze them using the IDES model:

IDENTIFY the legal issues raised by the questions.

DEFINE all the relevant legal terms and issues involved.

ENUMERATE the legal principles associated with these issues.

SHOW BOTH SIDES by using the facts.

A G E N D A

Anna and Tom realize they have created a product—Call-Image videophones—that will have broad public appeal. Hence, they need to consider what form of business—proprietorship, partnership, or corporation—is best for producing, marketing, and distributing this product. Should the firm incorporate and "go public," selling stock to investors to help acquire badly needed capital? Would such a sale open the possibility that the Kochanowskis may lose control of the business to an outsider? Is there a business form that will allow for outside investment without the fear that investors might take control of management?

These and other questions will arise as you read this chapter. Be prepared! You never know when one of the Kochanowskis will seek your help or advice.

Formation of a Business

O U T L I N E

HISTORIC OVERVIEW OF PARTNERSHIPS

The partnership as a form of business organization is very old. It can be traced back to ancient Babylon, and perhaps came into existence even earlier. It was widely used by the Romans during the height of the Roman Empire. In fact, Roman merchants introduced the partnership throughout Europe as they conducted trade with the peoples conquered by the Roman legions.

England was one of the nations that "discovered" the Roman partnership. Later, English common law modified this form of organization somewhat and utilized it in the development of the British Empire, including the colonies in North America that later became the United States.

The United States followed the English common law of partnerships for quite some time. Partnership law in the United States, however, has now been codified. The controlling law today is found in the Uniform Partnership Act (UPA)[1] or the Revised Uniform Partnership Act (RUPA)[2] for general partnerships. The RUPA (1994) has been adopted in Alabama, Arizona, California, Connecticut, Washington, D.C., Florida, Iowa, Montana, New Mexico, North Dakota, Virginia, West Virginia, and Wyoming.[3] The UPA (1914) has been adopted by every other state except Louisiana. The UPA is also followed in the Virgin Islands.[4] We will refer to the 1914 version as UPA, and the 1994 version as RUPA.

Professional

In the sense used here, a member of a "learned profession," such as a doctor, a lawyer, or an accountant.

Corporation

An artificial person or legal entity created by or under the authority of a state or nation, composed of a group of persons known as stockholders or shareholders.

Proprietorship

A business with legal rights or exclusive title vested in one individual; a solely owned business.

Rules for limited partnerships are codified in either the Uniform Limited Partnership Act (ULPA) or the Revised Uniform Limited Partnership Act (RULPA). The RULPA has been adopted by every state except Louisiana and Vermont. The ULPA is followed only in Vermont; the ULPA, consequently, has little effect. Louisiana does not follow either act.[5]

Partnerships are formed for a variety of reasons. Many **professionals**, for example, enter partnerships because they are not allowed to incorporate under some state laws. Some people enter partnerships to avoid the technical steps and expense required to form a **corporation**. And some people form partnerships because it seems appropriate, without giving the matter serious consideration.

A partnership has many of the best features of the other major types of business organizations—**proprietorships**, limited partnerships, and corporations—but also some of the worst features. A partnership is relatively easy to form, and the formation is normally informal—as is the case with a proprietorship. Like a corporation, a partnership has a wider potential financial base than a proprietorship. And like a corporation, the partnership has more expertise from which to draw.

A partnership is not perpetual, however, as a corporation may be. A partnership will dissolve eventually. Also, the partners face unlimited liability for business-related conduct, as does a proprietor. Shareholders in a corporation, in contrast, have limited liability.

FROM THE DESK OF
AMY CHEN, ATTORNEY AT LAW
Forming a Partnership
Although oral partnerships are legal, if you decide to form a partnership, you should have a written partnership agreement. It provides a written record of the parties' agreement and helps to avoid—or at least simplify—litigation between the partners.
A partnership must have a profit motive. It must also be a voluntary association. You cannot be forced to accept a person or business entity as a partner against your will.

No one form of business organization is perfect. Each has some advantages that the others lack; and each has some drawbacks the others avoid. The decision to choose a type of business organization should

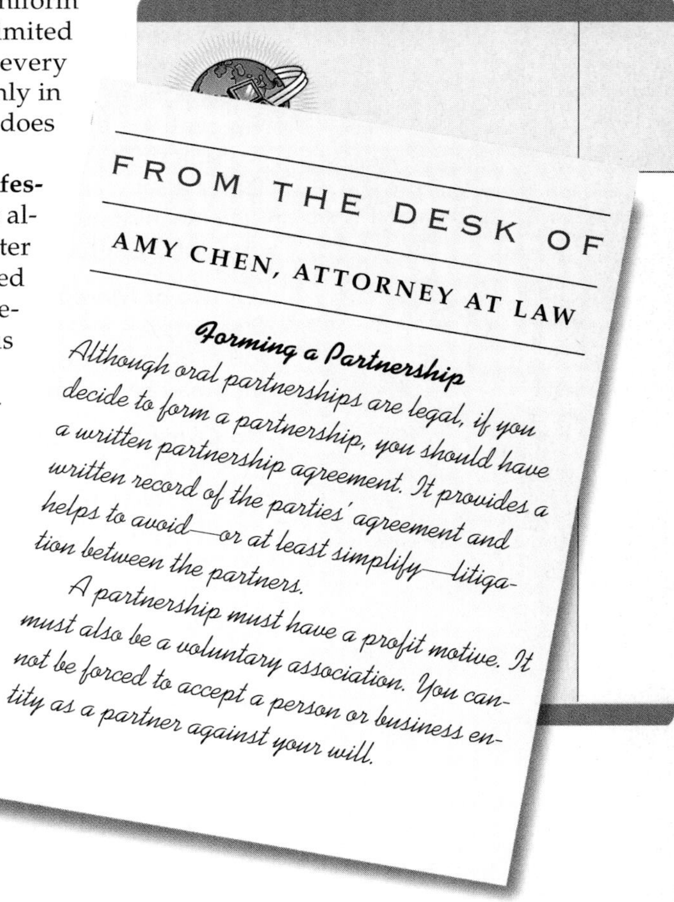

never be made lightly or automatically. All "pros" and "cons" for each available alternative should be weighed carefully before a decision is made. A comparison of the various business organizations appears in Exhibit 34.1 (pp. 844–845).

PARTNERSHIPS DEFINED

Uniform Partnership Act

Section 6(1) of the Uniform Partnership Act defines a partnership. According to this section, a partnership has five characteristics. It is

1. an association
2. of two or more persons
3. to carry on a business
4. as co-owners
5. for profit.

The 16 words in the definition are deceptively simple. In fact, a tremendous amount of interpretation often is involved in fitting an organization into the definition of a partnership. To illustrate the potential problem, we will discuss the terms in the order listed.

An Association. The courts have consistently held that a partnership must be entered voluntarily; that is, no one can be forced to be a partner against his or her will. Thus, *an association* has been interpreted as being "a voluntarily entered association." Being realistic, the courts also realize that people occasionally disagree. The measure of voluntariness is the willingness to associate at the time of *creation* of the relationship. Later disagreements will not automatically destroy the partnership. Thus, *an association* means a mutual and unanimous assent to be partners jointly and severally at the time of the agreement.

Of Two or More Persons. *Persons* here is interpreted broadly. It means persons in the biological sense, or persons in the legal sense, or persons in any other sense—in other words, two or more identifiable entities that elect to associate. Thus, each partner may be a human being, a corporation, a partnership, or even a joint venture.

To Carry on a Business. The third element of the definition has two separate segments. First, it must be determined whether there is a business. A *business* is defined as any trade, occupation, or profession; so most associations meet this test. Next, it must be determined whether the business is being carried on. *Carrying on* implies some *continuity.* A business must be fairly permanent and lasting in order to be carried on. If a business appears to be short term, it is quite possible that the court will rule that no partnership exists. If the other elements of a partnership are present, however, the short-term business may qualify as a joint venture instead.

As Co-Owners. The fourth element is probably the most important and the most confusing. Co-ownership is like pornography: It is hard to define, but you know it when you see it.

Co-ownership does not refer to a sharing of title on the assets used in the business. Instead, it refers to a sharing of ownership of the *business itself.* The business is an intangible asset. A business often uses assets of a tangible nature, but it need not own any tangible assets. For example, several accountants may enter a partnership.

The partnership owns a business that provides services, and services are intangible. The accountants may lease an office; they may rent furniture; they may not own a single tangible asset, and yet they co-own a business.

How, then, is one to know if people involved in a business are co-owners? The simplest way is to look at the agreement the people made when the business began. If the agreement states that they are partners, or co-owners, of the business, they are co-owners of the business. But all too often the agreement is ambiguous, unclear, or oral. In such a situation, the agreement is of no help in resolving the co-ownership question. Then the courts must look beyond the agreement.

The courts normally will look at how the parties treat **profits.** If the parties share profits, or net returns, there is prima facie evidence that a partnership exists—that is, the partnership is presumed to exist unless disproved by evidence to the contrary. The sharing of profits creates a **rebuttable presumption** that a partnership was formed. The burden then shifts to the parties to *disprove,* or to rebut, the presumption.

Profits

The gain made in the enterprise, after deducting the costs incurred for labor, materials, rents, and all other expenses.

Rebuttable presumption

A legal assumption that will be followed until a stronger proof or presumption is presented.

The UPA recognizes five rebuttals.[6] If one of the parties can prove that profits were shared for one of the reasons listed below, no partnership exists. If such proof is not made, the sharing of profits establishes that a partnership did exist. The rebuttal is valid if profits are shared for one of the following purposes:

1. As payment of a debt, by installments or otherwise (a promissory note or a judgment note should be produced as evidence)
2. As payment of wages to an employee or of rent to a landlord
3. As payment of an annuity to the representatives of a deceased partner
4. As payment of interest on a loan (again, some document probably will be necessary)
5. As payment of consideration in the sale of goodwill or other property, whether by installment payments or otherwise

For Profit. The fifth and final element of the definition of a partnership is probably the easiest to show. A partnership must operate *for profit.* To be specific, all that is needed is a *profit motive.* If the business was created to generate profits and to return these profits to the owners of the business, this test for the existence of a partnership is satisfied. Thus, nonprofit associations cannot, by definition, be partnerships. However, an unprofitable business can be a partnership, provided that profits are the goal of the business. In short, the court is looking at the motive of the organization, not the financial bottom line.

Limited Partnership

A limited partnership is set up in accordance with the controlling state laws governing limited partnerships—either the Uniform Limited Partnership Act, which is followed in Vermont, or the Revised Uniform Limited Partnership Act, which is followed in all the other states, except Louisiana. Louisiana follows its own statutes. Our discussion will center on the RULPA, since it has been adopted by 48 states. Any parties who plan to establish a limited partnership, however, need to check the applicable statute for the jurisdiction in which the limited partnership will be created.

A limited partnership can be created by two or more persons, as long as at least one person is designated a **limited partner.** With this one exception—the classification of partners—a limited partnership has the same characteristics as a general partnership set up under the UPA. A limited partnership is more formal than a general

Limited partner

A limited-partnership member who furnishes certain funds to the partnership and whose liability is restricted to the funds furnished.

EXHIBIT 34.1 A Comparison of Different Types of Business Organizations

	Proprietorship	Partnership	Limited Partnership[a]
Creation:	Proprietor opens the business, subject to state and local licensing laws, and so on.	Partners enter into an agreement, either orally or in writing; no formalities are required.	Partners enter into a partnership agreement and file a written form designating the limited partners and the general partners.
Termination:	Proprietor closes the business; death, insanity, or bankruptcy of the owner also terminates the business.	Partners agree to dissolve the partnership; death, bankruptcy, or withdrawal of any partner also dissolves the partnership. The terms of the agreement or a court order may dissolve the partnership. Liquidation of the assets after a dissolution winds up the business.	Partners follow same procedure as for a partnership, but with a difference in the order of distributing assets in case of a dissolution and liquidation of the business.
Taxation:[b]	All business profits are taxed as regular income of the owner; there are no federal income taxes on the business, per se.	The business must file a federal tax return, but it is for information only. The income of the business is taxed as regular income to the partners.	The same tax procedure is followed as for a regular, general partnership.
Liability:	Proprietor is liable for all business assets and then all personal assets of the owner (unlimited personal liability).	Partners are liable for all business assets and then all personal assets of the partners, jointly and severally (unlimited personal liability).	Partners are liable for all business assets and then all personal assets of the *general* partners, jointly and severally; limited partners have limited liability (they are liable only to the extent of their contribution).
Advantages:	Simplicity of creation; complete ownership and control of the firm.	Informality of creation; greater potential for expertise and capital in management (because there is more than one manager).	Somewhat greater flexibility than a general partnership; much greater potential access to capital.
Disadvantages:	Limited capital; limited expertise; limited existence (when the owner dies, the business terminates).	Limited existence; lack of flexibility; potential liability.	Some rigidity in ownership and decision making; personal liability of general partners; limited existence.

[a] This applies to limited partnerships under the Revised Uniform Limited Partnership Act.

[b] There may be significant tax consequences of changing from one business form to another.

[c] This may also be an advantage.

EXHIBIT 34.1 A Comparison of Different Types of Business Organizations *(cont.)*

Limited Liability Partnership	Corporation	Limited Liability Company
Partners enter into a partnership agreement and the partnership files a copy or some other notice with the state.	Parties prepare and file *formal* legal documents known as articles of incorporation with the state of incorporation; they must comply with any relevant state or federal security statutes or regulations.	LLCs may be formed by two or more members, who enter into an agreement. Generally LLCs must file articles of organization with the state government.
Partners follow same procedure as for a general partnership.	Parties close the business, liquidate all business assets, surrender the corporate charter, and distribute the assets as per state law; termination may also be due to state action revoking the charter.	Statute and/or agreement will probably limit the term of the LLC: state laws vary on whether the association can be renewed for an additional period.
The same procedure is followed as for a regular, general partnership.	A normal corporation is taxed as a separate taxable entity; any dividends are taxed to the stockholders. A Subchapter S corporation, regulated by the IRS, is taxed as if it were a general partnership despite its corporate status. A Subchapter S corporation is treated differently only for federal tax purposes.	LLC is taxed as a partnership or a corporation depending on its characteristics and tax law. Characteristics are determined by the agreement and the state statute. The LLC may have different taxation for state and federal purposes.
Partner is liable without limit for his/her own wrongs and wrongs of people the partner directly supervises; the partner's liability is limited to the partner's contribution for the wrongs of others.	Parties are liable for all business assets; stockholders are *not* personally liable for debts of the corporation (limited liability).	All members are liable for association debts only to the extent of their capital contribution(s).
Limited liability except for a partner's own wrongs and the wrongs of people the partner directly supervises.	Longevity—potential for perpetual existence; potentially unlimited access to capital and to expertise; freely transferable ownership; limited personal liability of the owners.	Limited liability for all the members.
Unlimited liability for partner's own wrongs; only permitted in some states.	"Double taxation" (except for Subchapter S); much more federal regulation; considerably more state regulation; formality and rigidity of the organization.	LLCs cannot be formed in all states. LLC statutes vary greatly from state to state. Professionals may not be permitted to form an LLC, depending on the state. There may be limitations on the transferability of shares.[c] Selling interests in an LLC may be subject to state and federal securities regulations. There is uncertainty about how the LLC and its members will be taxed. LLCs may have a limited term of existence.[c]

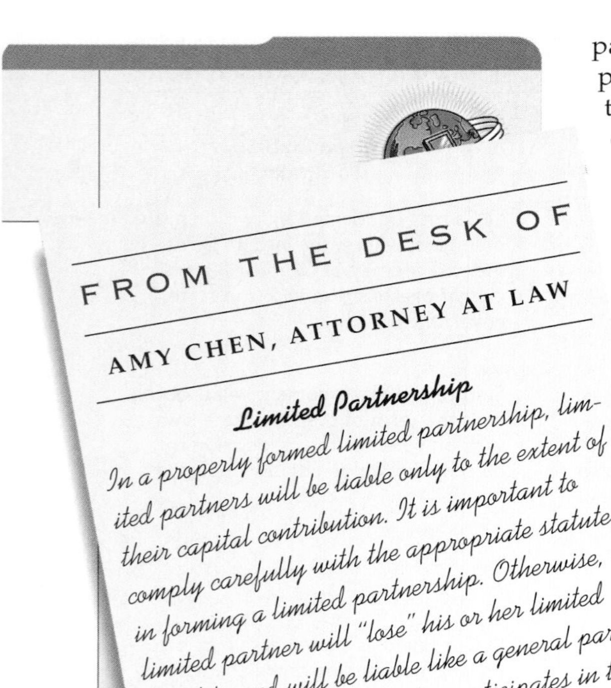

partnership, however. In order to set up a limited partnership, the partners must sign and swear to a written certificate that details all the important elements of the partnership agreement. This certificate must be filed with the correct public official, as specified in the statutes of the state where the limited partnership is created.

FROM THE DESK OF
AMY CHEN, ATTORNEY AT LAW
Limited Partnership
In a properly formed limited partnership, limited partners will be liable only to the extent of their capital contribution. It is important to comply carefully with the appropriate statute in forming a limited partnership. Otherwise, a limited partner will "lose" his or her limited liability and will be liable like a general partner. A limited partner who participates in the management and control of the enterprise will also "lose" his or her limited liability.

A limited partner is so called because the limited partners have *limited liability*. In other words, a limited partner is not personally liable for any obligations of the partnership. However, there is a price to pay for this protection: A limited partner is precluded from management of the business. A limited partner who takes part in management loses the limited status[7] and may be treated as a general partner, subject to unlimited personal liability—but only in dealings with third persons who actually know of the limited partner's participation in the management of the business. Limited partners who act as agents or employees of a general partner or of the firm or who advise the general partners about business are not considered to be involved in management.

Revised Uniform Limited Partnership Act

In 1976, the National Conference of Commissioners on Uniform State Laws (NCCUSL) approved a Revised Uniform Limited Partnership Act (RULPA). It became available to the states in 1977 and by the end of 1994 had been adopted by forty-eight states. Although most of the topical coverage is essentially the same, there are some technical differences between the ULPA and the RULPA. Under the RULPA, for example, the certificate of agreement forming the limited partnership must be filed with the secretary of state for the state in which the limited partnership is formed. The revised act calls for profits and losses to be shared on the basis of capital contributions unless the agreement specifies some other distribution. The distribution of assets upon termination of the entity and the liquidation of its assets is treated differently under the revised act than under the ULPA. One of the interesting aspects of the RULPA is § 1105, which specifies that any cases not provided for in the revised act are to be governed by the provisions of the ULPA.

Throughout this chapter and Chapters 35 and 36, we will discuss the majority rule contained in the RULPA.

Checkers Eight Limited Partnership v. *La-Van Hawkins* addresses the liability of a limited partner. Carefully note the legal basis for liability.

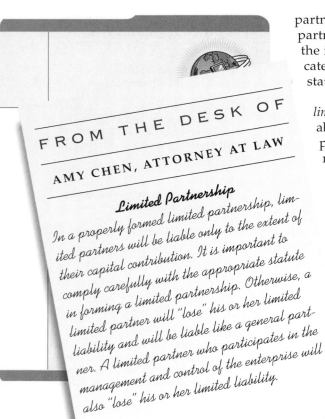

34.1 CHECKERS EIGHT LIMITED PARTNERSHIP v. LA-VAN HAWKINS

1996 U.S. Dist. LEXIS 19597 (N.D. Ill., E. Div., 1997)

FACTS On November 10, 1992, defendant La-Van Hawkins (La-Van) entered into a partnership agreement with plaintiffs Thomas W. Lonergan and James T. Lonergan (Lonergans) to develop and operate a Checkers restaurant in the Philadelphia metropolitan area. The partnership was known as the Hawkins-Tower L.P.: Hawkins Two, Inc. [with La-Van Hawkins as president] was the general partner, holding a 1 percent interest, and La-Van was a limited partner,

34.1 CHECKERS EIGHT LIMITED PARTNERSHIP v. LA-VAN HAWKINS 1996 U.S. Dist. LEXIS 19597 (N.D. Ill., E. Div., 1997)

holding a 33 percent interest. James T. Lonergan and Thomas W. Lonergan, Trustee of Thomas W. Lonergan Trust No. 1, were also limited partners, holding a combined interest of 66 percent. The Hawkins-Tower, L.P. restaurant was opened in the Philadelphia area in January 1993. Later that year, negotiations began to sell the Checkers restaurants, including the one held by the Hawkins-Tower, L.P. The restaurants were sold to Checkers Drive-In in exchange for unregistered Checkers Drive-In stock on September 7, 1993. The stock was to be registered within 120 days of closing. Due to an error in the closing documents, the registration of the stock was delayed. During the delay, the stock value dropped significantly. In January 1994, a document, stating that the parties had entered into various limited partnerships that held interests in nine Checkers restaurants, was executed. The Agreement states that those partnerships sold their interests in the restaurants to Checkers Drive-In Restaurants, Inc., pursuant to a July 22, 1993, purchase agreement and related closing documents. . . . Hawkins-Tower, L.P. was dissolved on or about December 31, 1994.

ISSUE Is La-Van Hawkins personally liable on the agreement?

HOLDING Yes.

REASONING ". . . Although La-Van was only a limited partner in the Hawkins-Tower, L.P., the Agreement was not solely based on that partnership: it covered various limited partnerships which held interests in the Checkers restaurants. There is nothing indicating that La-Van signed the Agreement in his capacity as a limited partner of the Hawkins-Tower, L.P. Rather, the face of the document unequivocally shows that he signed the Agreement separately in his individual capacity and as president of four Hawkins corporations. Thus, we do not find any **ambiguity** creating a factual question as to the meaning of the contract. . . . Mutual promises are ordinarily sufficient consideration to support mutual obligations. The Agreement states that 'in consideration of the mutual agreements contained herein, and other good and valuable consideration, the receipt and sufficiency which is hereby mutually acknowledged. . . .' . . . The Agreement provides for an exchange of amounts owed and, in several attachments, specifies the various expenditures on which the amounts are based.

Furthermore, the complaint alleges consideration that went beyond mere promises. It states: 'The amount due from the defendants for the Checkers Eight Limited Partnership is based on the distributions made pursuant to the directions of the defendant, La-Van Hawkins.' Thus, we reject La-Van's argument that there is no allegation of any consideration that would support his promise to assume personal liability for debt owed. . . ."

BUSINESS CONSIDERATIONS La-Van Hawkins testified that he did not intend to assume personal liability. Since the agreement dealt with a number of partnerships and La-Van had various roles, what should he have done to protect himself from personal liability? What should limited partners do to protect their personal assets?

ETHICAL CONSIDERATIONS What ethical duties does a limited partner owe to the partnership? Why?

PARTNERSHIP PROPERTY

Although no partnership is *required* to own property, most partnerships do, in fact, own some property. Even if the partnership chooses not to own property, it must have access to possession and use of some physical assets. And this access and use may lead to ownership, at least under the UPA and in the eyes of the court.

Section 8 of the UPA defines partnership property for general partnerships. Under this section, the following kinds of property are deemed to be *partnership property* (property owned by the partnership rather than the partners as individuals):

1. all property originally contributed to the partnership as a partner's capital contribution(s)
2. all property acquired on account of the partnership

Ambiguity
Subject to two or more reasonable interpretations.

3. all property acquired with partnership funds, unless a contrary intention is shown
4. any interest in real property that is acquired in the partnership name
5. any conveyance to a partnership in the partnership name, unless a contrary intention is shown

If an individual partner wants to retain personal ownership but allow the partnership to use property, he or she should be extremely cautious. Unless the intention is made obvious, the property the partner thought he or she still owned may legally belong to the partnership. (The reason this is so important is discussed in detail in Chapter 36, which covers dissolution.)

The Partnership Agreement

A partnership is created by agreement of the partners. The agreement is a contract. This contract may be oral, unless it falls within the Statute of Frauds. In other words, no formality is required in setting up a general partnership. (Note, however, the formal requirements for creating a limited partnership, which we have already discussed.)

A reasonably prudent, cautious person is expected to take great care in negotiating the basic partnership agreement and then reducing the agreement to written form. Yet all too often a partnership is begun with little or no detailed negotiation. And even if the parties are very careful, situations may arise that were never considered and, therefore, are not covered by the agreement. To minimize the harm such situations can create, the UPA imposes certain rules, which apply unless the agreement provides otherwise, and specifies certain areas that the agreement must cover.

Imposed Rules

Unless the agreement between the parties states otherwise, the following rules are imposed by operation of law:

1. Each partner is entitled to an equal voice in the management of the business. (Limited partners are obviously exceptions to this rule.)
2. Each partner is entitled to an equal share of profits, without regard to capital contributions. (The RULPA takes the totally opposite approach for limited partnerships.)
3. Each partner is expected to share any losses suffered by the business in the same proportion as profits are to be shared.
4. The books of the partnership are to be kept at the central office of the business.

In addition, some rules are imposed and must be followed by the *general* partners, no matter what the agreement says. Any attempt to modify these rules in the agreement is contrary to public policy; so any modification will be deemed void. Some of the rules are:

1. Each partner is deemed to be an agent for the partnership and for each partner, as long as the partner is acting in a business-related matter.
2. Each partner is personally liable, without limit, for torts or contracts for which the partnership has too few assets to cover the debt or liability.
3. Each partner is expected to devote service to the partnership only and not to any competing business ventures.

In some states, Arizona[8] for example, general partners are *jointly and severally* liable for partnership debts. As a result, a partner may be sued severally and his or her assets reached even though the partnership assets are not exhausted and the other partners are not sued.

Express Terms

In addition to those terms imposed by law, the partnership agreement should cover some other areas. For instance, the agreement should designate the name of the business. This name cannot be deceptively similar to the name of any other company or business, and it cannot mislead the public as to the nature of the business. (If a limited partnership is involved, the name should reflect that fact.)

The agreement should cover the duration of the business—how long the partnership will last. Such an understanding in the beginning can avoid serious disagreements later. It also should cover the purpose of the business. Knowing what you are trying to do not only makes it easier to operate a business but also helps to avoid any controversies later.

Finally, the agreement should discuss in detail how, or if, a partner can withdraw from the business. In this area, the rights of a withdrawing partner should be very carefully spelled out so that no one, including a court, will misconstrue the agreement's terms.

Of course, any other items the partners feel should be included can be discussed, agreed on, and included. In fact, the more detailed the original agreement, the better. A carefully drawn, well-thought-out agreement will always benefit honest partners.

In the *Altman* case, violations of the partnership agreement led to a lawsuit and a court-ordered dissolution of the partnership.

34.2 ALTMAN v. ALTMAN — 653 F.2d 755 (1981)

FACTS From 1952 to 1973, Sydney and Ashley Altman operated a number of partnerships engaged in real estate construction and management in southeast Pennsylvania. The brothers shared equally in the management and control of the business. They received equal salaries and equal reimbursement for certain personal expenses. In January 1973, Sydney moved to Florida to establish residence in order to obtain a divorce. The brothers agreed that Sydney should commute to Pennsylvania to continue working until he established his residency. For the first six months, Sydney returned to Pennsylvania every week to work for two or three days. In July, the brothers agreed that Sydney needed to return only once a month, and subsequently Sydney was advised by counsel to remain in Florida until the divorce was final. In November 1973, Sydney told Ashley that he was considering retiring from the business and remaining in Florida permanently. Ashley agreed to consult with the firm's accountant to develop a mutually acceptable retirement agreement. At that point, their stories diverged. Ashley claimed that Sydney accepted the accountant's recommendations and retired, effective 31 December 1973. Sydney claimed that the brothers never agreed and that in the fall of 1974, Ashley presented Sydney with a one-sided retirement proposal prepared at Ashley's direction by the firm's attorney. At that point, Sydney sued for a court-ordered dissolution, alleging that Ashley had violated the partnership agreements, misappropriated partnership assets, and excluded Sydney from the business. Ashley denied all of the allegations, insisting that Sydney had retired as of 31 December 1973, thus dissolving the partnerships and ending the agreements.

ISSUE Had the partnerships been dissolved as of 31 December 1973; or were the partnerships, and the agreements of the partners, still in effect?

HOLDING The partnerships had not been dissolved; the agreements were still in effect, and therefore Ashley had violated the agreements.

REASONING Ashley argued that Sydney had retired, as shown by his absence from the firm's office from October 1973 to September 1975, the time of the filing of this suit.

34.2 ALTMAN v. ALTMAN (*cont.*) 653 F.2d 755 (1981)

His absence meant that Ashley had been left to manage the business alone for nearly two years and served as evidence that Sydney had retired. However, the trial court felt that Sydney's denial of his retirement was more credible than was Ashley's testimony to the contrary. In addition, a document prepared by the firm's attorney in September 1974, which proposed a "plan to clarify the [retirement] situation," casts doubt on Sydney's retirement. Further, Ashley made no attempt to buy Sydney out or to settle business matters with Sydney. Thus, proof of a retirement and dissolution prior to the institution of these proceedings was inadequate. Turning to the alleged violations of the agreements, the court found that Ashley had paid himself a salary well in excess of that agreed to by the partners. His argument that he was doing more work and, therefore, deserved more money is not justified under Pennsylvania law. Similarly, Ashley violated the agreement in the matter of reimbursing himself for his personal expenses to a greater degree than Sydney was reimbursed. As a result, Sydney's request for a judicial dissolution was granted. In addition, Ashley had to account for and return the excess compensation and the excess reimbursements for distribution in the final settlement of the partnership estate.

BUSINESS CONSIDERATIONS Why would a partner want a continuation clause in the partnership agreement? Why would a partner want a clause prohibiting continuation of the business upon his or her withdrawal?

ETHICAL CONSIDERATIONS Is it ethical for a partner to withdraw from a partnership, and then to object to an attempt by his or her remaining partners to continue operating the business? Why might a continuation be deemed unethical?

LIMITED LIABILITY PARTNERSHIPS

A new form of business organization, limited liability partnerships (LLPs), has recently attracted great attention. LLPs are currently permitted only in some states; however, the numbers are growing rapidly—both of states permitting this form of business and of enterprises adopting this form once it is permitted. Sometimes the enabling legislation is passed as amendments to the state's partnership act or as part of the state's limited liability company act.

The advantage of an LLP over a general partnership is, as the name implies, the limit on the liability of the partners. In an LLP, a partner's personal assets are protected from liability claims against the partnership. Generally, the protection is from liability arising from negligence, wrongful acts, or misconduct committed in the ordinary course of business by any *other* partner, employee, agent, or representative. The exception to this is liability created by the partner himself or herself. In other words, a partner has unlimited liability for his or her own wrongdoings and limited liability for the wrongdoings of others. Generally, the statutes broadly interpret the partner's own wrongs to include the wrongs of persons under that partner's direct supervision and control. As in other general partnerships, the partners are jointly liable for contracts and jointly and severally liable for the normal business debts of the partnership.

In most other respects an LLP will be treated as a partnership. Some states, however, will not permit professionals to use LLPs. Other states permit professionals to form LLPs, but may require the professional LLPs to purchase liability insurance. For example, South Carolina requires professional LLPs to carry a minimum of $100,000 of insurance. Many enterprises that were general partnerships are becoming LLPs. Examples include Coopers & Lybrand, Ernst & Young, and Price Waterhouse.[9] The National Conference of Commissioners on Uniform State Laws (NCCUSL) includes Limited Liability Partnership Act provisions as part of the 1996 amendments to the RUPA (1994).[10]

YOU BE THE JUDGE

Three Accounting Firms Now Limited Liability Partnerships

Coopers & Lybrand, Ernst & Young, and Price Waterhouse have changed the form of their enterprise to that of a limited liability partnership (LLP). Arthur Andersen & Co. and Deloitte & Touche intend to file for LLP status shortly. KPMG Peat Marwick is also considering making the switch. These recent changes occurred because New York amended its law during the summer of 1994: It now permits accounting firms to form LLPs. Assume that the change in the form of these firms has been challenged in *your* court due to its potential impact on parties who may sue these firms at a later date. How will *you* address these issues, and how will you resolve the case?[11]

BUSINESS CONSIDERATIONS Why is this new form of business so popular with the Big Six accounting firms? Will it be this popular with smaller firms? What should a business consider before deciding to adopt this form of organization?

ETHICAL CONSIDERATIONS Is it ethical for an existing business to change its structure so that it faces less potential liability for its owners? Would it be ethical to deny a firm the right to change to a form approved by the legislature because of the *potential* for claims in the future?

SOURCE: *Wall Street Journal* (2 August 1994), p. A8.

TAXATION OF PARTNERSHIPS

For taxation purposes, the partnership form of business is neither an advantage nor a disadvantage. Basically, the partnership is not taxed, but the individual partners are taxed on the receipts of the firm. Why? Federal income tax rules and regulations do not recognize the partnership as a taxable entity. The firm must file an annual federal tax return, but the return is for information purposes only. Each partner is taxed on his or her share of the firm's profits for the year, whether these profits are distributed to the partners or not. Each partner is also taxed on the capital gains—or may take the deductions for capital losses—the firm experiences during the tax year.

Many states also treat the partnership as a mere conduit for the transfer of income to the partners. In these states, the partnership is not taxed, but the partners are taxed on the firm's income whether it is distributed or retained by the firm for reinvestment or expansion.

HISTORIC OVERVIEW OF CORPORATIONS

No exact moment of recorded history pinpoints the existence of the first corporation. But some evidence suggests that people recognized the concept of corporate personality to some extent as early as the time of Hammurabi (about 1750 B.C.). Certainly by Roman times, vestiges of corporateness had appeared through imperial **fiat.** From its very origins, then, the concept of corporateness depended on legislative grant. Canon law, borrowing from the Romans, distinguished between the *corporation sole* (composed of a single person, usually a high-ranking church officeholder) and the *corporation aggregate* (composed of several persons). The *fiction theory*—that a

Fiat
An order issued by legal authority.

corporation is an artificial legal person separate from its shareholders—probably developed from the papacy's desire to accommodate priests who had taken vows of poverty forbidding them to hold property. Since controlling the activities and finances of these clergymen was very lucrative, the church devised ways (the corporation) to allow church officers to own property. This separation of the artificial person from the natural person associated with it spawned the modern view that the corporation, not the shareholders, owns the corporate property and that shareholders ordinarily are not liable for debts incurred by the corporation. The development of the law merchant, the forerunner of modern commercial law, mirrored these and similar views of corporateness.

By the seventeenth century, English monarchs had tightened control over corporations, which were deemed to exist by virtue of *concessionary grants* of power from the state. Not surprisingly, the concession theory was part of the common law heritage that remained with American colonists after they gained independence from Britain. At first, Americans viewed corporations with suspicion because several well-known, unsavory schemes had been perpetrated through use of the corporate form. But such suspicions gradually relaxed as the advantages of corporations, such as the potential to raise **capital,** became apparent. As the corporate form developed, however, each state jealously guarded its power over these artificial creatures. This careful regulation of corporations, augmented now by federal securities statutes, remains an essential characteristic of the law of corporations.

Capital
Business assets or property of a permanent nature used in carrying on a business.

Corporate Nature

We define a *corporation* as an artificial person created under the statutes of a state or nation, organized for the purpose set out in the application for corporate existence. A corporation is an invisible, intangible, artificial person. Therefore, because it is considered a person, the corporation ordinarily enjoys most of the rights that natural (flesh-and-blood) persons possess. For example, it is a citizen and a resident of the state in which it has been incorporated. Thus, under the Fourth Amendment, it cannot be the object of unreasonable searches or seizures. Similarly, under the Fourteenth Amendment, it must be afforded its rights of due process and equal protection. In addition, a corporation assumes the nationality of either the nationality and/or the residence of the persons controlling it (called the *aggregate test*), or the nation in which it was incorporated or where it has its principal place of business (dubbed the *entity test*).

A landmark case follows that illustrates a number of these concepts.

34.3 PETROGRADSKY MEJDUNARODNY KOMMERCHESKY BANK v. NATIONAL CITY BANK OF NEW YORK

170 N.E. 479 (N.Y. 1930), Cert. Den. 282 U.S. 878 (1930)

FACTS Petrogradsky, a Russian bank, sued a New York bank for a $66,749.45 balance standing to its credit. In 1917, as a result of the Bolshevik Revolution, the Russian bank's assets had been confiscated and its stock canceled. On this basis, the New York bank argued that the Russian bank, as a corporation, had been dissolved and no longer was a juristic (legal) person. Therefore, the New York bank had refused to pay the credit balance.

34.3 PETROGRADSKY MEJDUNARODNY KOMMERCHESKY BANK v. NATIONAL CITY BANK OF NEW YORK *(cont.)* 170 N.E. 479 (N.Y. 1930), Cert. Den. 282 U.S. 878 (1930)

ISSUE Had the Russian bank ceased to exist as a legal person?

HOLDING No. It continued to exist. Hence, the American bank was obligated to pay the Russian bank the amount in dispute.

REASONING The Russian bank had not ceased to exist as a legal person. Indeed, the law presumes that a corporation continues perpetually. If assets remain either in the domicile or elsewhere, there is no dissolution, either virtual or legal. Since there is no indication that pre-Bolshevik Russian law regarding juristic personality differs from American law, the presumption of continuance of corporate personality must tilt the balanced scales. Therefore, the corporation survives in such a sense and to such a degree that it can still be dealt with as a person in countries that do not recognize the decrees of the Bolsheviks.

BUSINESS CONSIDERATIONS Suppose that a corporate debtor *has* ceased to exist. How would the creditors of that corporation seek satisfaction of their claims? What protections might they have?

ETHICAL CONSIDERATIONS Is it ethical to form a corporation in order to have limited liability, and then to dissolve that corporation if or when its debts become too heavy? Would it be ethical to permit creditors of the dissolved firm to proceed against the stockholders of the dissolved firm?

Advantages of the Corporate Form

The popularity of the corporation as a business form results from its comparative advantages over other types of business organizations. These advantages include:

1. *Insulation from liability.* Corporate debts are the responsibility of the corporation. The shareholders' liability ordinarily is limited to the amount of their investment; creditors of the corporation normally cannot reach the shareholders' personal assets to pay for corporate debts.
2. *Centralization of management functions.* Centralizing the management functions in a small group of persons possessing management expertise avoids some of the friction that may plague partnerships.
3. *Continuity of existence.* The corporation continues to exist in the eyes of the law even after the deaths of the officers, directors, or shareholders, or the withdrawal of their shares. This potential for perpetual existence provides stability. A corporation exists in perpetuity unless a specific length of time is stated in its articles of incorporation.
4. *Free transferability of shares.* This creates opportunities for access to outside capital (as well as allowing investors to sell their interests without the need for unanimous approval) or the dissolution of the firm.

These attributes unquestionably convince many large and small businesses to employ the corporate form. In a given situation, however, another form may better suit the business's needs. This is a decision that requires careful thought and the advice of knowledgeable experts, such as a lawyer, accountant, or investment adviser. There are also distinct disadvantages that may result from choosing the corporate form.

FORMATION OF A CORPORATION

The process of forming a corporation involves complicated issues that demand the attention of well-versed professionals. One of these considerations consists of choosing the most desirable type of corporation for the particular circumstances.

Types of Corporations

The *public-issue private corporation* is the best-known type of private corporation. We are all familiar with American Telephone & Telegraph (AT&T), General Motors (GM), International Business Machines (IBM), General Electric (GE), and other large public-issue corporations. The central advantage of public-issue corporations is their access to capital in the form of new shares. The shareholder, however, has very little say in the management of such giant concerns.

For this reason, there is another type of private corporation, the *close corporation.* This form limits the management of the firm to a select few shareholders and restricts the transferability of shares in order to consolidate control. Close corporations allow a firm to enjoy many of the advantages of the corporate form (such as favorable tax treatment) without giving up the day-to-day control more commonly associated with sole proprietorships or partnerships. An inherent disadvantage of close corporations, on the other hand, stems from a lack of free transferability of shares; these shares are often not as liquid or saleable as those of public-issue corporations.

Private corporations may also include *professional corporations,* those organized for conducting a particular occupation or profession. Doctors, lawyers, dentists, and accountants may find it advantageous financially (because of tax and pension benefits, for example) to form such corporations. Most states have special statutes regulating professional corporations. Typically, these statutes limit share ownership in such corporations to duly licensed professional persons. Despite the limited liability offered by the corporate form, under these statutes the professional is ordinarily personally liable for his or her own malpractice or similar torts as well as for any such acts performed by others who are under the professional's supervision.

A city is an example of a *public* or *municipal corporation.* We often call some public utilities *quasi-public corporations* because they are private corporations that, nevertheless, furnish public services such as electricity, gas, or water.

Corporations are generally for-profit. But *nonprofit corporations,* or those organized for charitable purposes, also exist. Special statutes in some jurisdictions regulate educational institutions, charities, private hospitals, fraternal orders, religious organizations, and other types of nonprofit corporations.

Promoters

Despite the negative connotation of the word, promoters may be vital to the formation of the corporation, practically speaking. Although the law does not require the services of promoters as a precondition to incorporating, *promoters* begin the process of forming a corporation by procuring subscribers for the stock or by taking other affirmative steps toward incorporating. Thus, promoters facilitate the creation of the corporation by bringing interested parties together and by encouraging the venture until the corporation is formed. We can also label promoters *preincorporators.*

Promoters' activities bring up a host of legal issues. Since the promoter is working on behalf of an entity not yet created, questions arise as to who is liable on contracts made on the corporation's behalf before its inception: the promoter or the corporation? The general rule is that the promoter will be liable for goods and services rendered to him or her before the corporation's formation. However, the corporation may become liable for the promoter's contracts (and possibly torts) after formation by novation, release, or by adoption or **ratification** of the promoter's contracts. In most cases, this liability is joint and does not (except for novations and express releases of liability) eliminate the promoter's personal liability.

Ratification

Accepting an act that was unauthorized when committed and becoming bound to that act upon its acceptance.

The possibility of double-dealing is inherent in the process of promotion. For this reason, the law treats promoters as owing fiduciary duties to the corporation. Therefore, the promoter must act in good faith, deal fairly, and make full disclosure to the corporation. The liability of promoters as fiduciaries is not as pervasive a problem today as in the past because of the disclosures mandated by the Securities Act of 1933. In a few cases, however, the promoter has had to give back to the corporation secret profits, embezzled funds, and other damages. Therefore, anyone desiring to act as a promoter should seek professional advice beforehand.

Articles of Incorporation

The document that signals the official existence of the corporation is the *articles of incorporation.* State statutes prescribe the contents of the articles; but typically the articles include the name of the corporation, its purpose, its duration, the location of its principal office or **registered agent** (also called resident agent), its powers, its capital structure (that is, the number of shares and minimum **stated capital**), its directors and their names (these people are usually the incorporators), and the signatures of the incorporators (in most jurisdictions they do not have to be shareholders). Once the incorporators file the articles with the appropriate state official (ordinarily, the secretary of state) and pay all the required filing fees, the state issues a formal *certificate of incorporation,* or license.

Registered agent

Person designated by a corporation to receive service of process within the state.

Stated capital

The amount of consideration received by the corporation for all shares of the corporation.

Corporate Charter/Certificate of Incorporation

In most states, corporate existence begins with the issuance of the certificate of incorporation by the secretary of state in the state of incorporation. After it issues such a certificate, the state normally will not interfere with this grant of power. Unless the corporation by its conduct poses a definite and serious danger to the welfare of the state's citizens (for example, by engaging in wholesale fraud), the state will honor the certificate and allow the corporation to conduct its usual business without impediment. Exhibit 34.2 represents a typical certificate of incorporation.

Organizational Meeting

In some jurisdictions, official corporate existence begins not on the issuance of the certificate of incorporation, but after the first organizational meeting of the corporation. The organizational meeting is important because it is during the meeting that (1) bylaws are adopted, (2) the preincorporation agreements are approved, and (3) officers are elected.

Bylaws

Bylaws are the rules and regulations adopted by a corporation for the purpose of self-regulation, especially of day-to-day matters not covered by other documents. These ordinarily are not filed in a public place as the articles of incorporation are. Rather, they constitute the corporation's internal rules for the governance of its own affairs. They

EXHIBIT 34.2 Certificate of Incorporation

STATE OF INDIANA
OFFICE OF THE SECRETARY OF STATE

CERTIFICATE OF INCORPORATION

OF

. . . ., INC. . . . .

. . . .

I, EDWIN J. SIMCOX, *Secretary of State of Indiana, hereby certify that Articles of Incorporation of the above Corporation, in the form prescribed by my office, prepared and signed in duplicate by the incorporator(s), and acknowledged and verified by the same, have been presented to me at my office accompanied by the fees prescribed by law; that I have found such Articles conform to law; that I have endorsed my approval upon the duplicate copies of such Articles; that all fees have been paid as required by law; that one copy of such Articles has been filed in my office; and that the remaining copy of such Articles bearing the endorsement of my approval and filing has been returned by me to the incorporator(s) or his(their) representatives; all as prescribed by the provisions of the*
INDIANA GENERAL CORPORATION ACT . . . .

. . . ., *as amended.*
NOW, THEREFORE, *I hereby issue to such Corporation this Certificate of Incorporation, and further certify that its corporate existence has begun.*

In Witness Whereof, I have hereunto set my hand and affixed the seal of the State of Indiana, at the City of Indianapolis, this...*day of* ...., *19*.........

....
EDWIN J. SIMCOX, *Secretary of State*

By..
Deputy

SOURCE: Courtesy of Douglas D. Germann, Sr., Attorney-at-Law, Mishawaka, Indiana.

must, however, be consistent with the jurisdiction's corporate statute and the corporation's articles. Bylaws typically cover the location of the corporation's offices and records; describe the meetings of the shareholders and the directors; set out the powers and duties of the board of directors, officers, and executive committee; establish the capitalization of the corporation; and fix the methods for conducting the corporation's business, such as execution of contracts, signatures on deeds, and notices of meetings.

DE JURE VERSUS DE FACTO CORPORATIONS

As we have seen, it is relatively easy to obtain corporate status if one carefully follows the required statutory procedures. Nevertheless, because it is not a perfect world, it is still necessary to examine the consequences of failure to comply with such statutory requirements. *Defective incorporation,* as this concept is called, may be a matter of degree. If the defect in formation (or noncompliance with the incorporation statute) is slight, the law characterizes the corporation as *de jure* (valid by law). The general rule is that where substantial compliance with all steps necessary for incorporation has occurred, the resultant entity is a de jure corporation. If an address is wrong in a provision mandating an address or a relatively insignificant provision has been overlooked, courts will not invalidate corporate status. Such minor flaws ordinarily will not cause the loss of de jure status.

Sometimes, however, the defect involved is so serious that the law cannot consider the corporation as de jure. Corporateness and all its attributes may still be retained, however, if certain conditions are met: (1) A law under which the business could have been incorporated exists; (2) there was a good faith effort to comply with the statute; and (3) there was some use or exercise of corporate powers. Such entities are called *de facto* corporations (corporations in fact, if not in law). Only the state can attack the existence of a de facto corporation. Hence, if the state does not bring an action to dissolve its certificate (or its charter), the firm will enjoy all the powers and privileges that exist in the corporate form.

This result is probably fair. Even if the defects in compliance are serious, if both the entity and third parties have previously dealt with each other in the belief that corporateness exists, fulfilling the expectations of the parties seems justifiable. Yet the law should scrutinize the parties' nonfulfillment of statutory dictates in order to avoid the frustration of legislative intent. In recent years, statutory provisions have increasingly reflected the view that the issuance of a certificate of incorporation will create a presumption that the corporation has been validly formed (that is, it has attained de jure status) except in actions brought by the state. If the state has taken no action and has issued no certificate, the presumption is that corporate status is as yet unrealized. In this case, third parties can hold individual shareholders personally liable. These developments have greatly eroded the importance of the de facto doctrine; but, some courts have continued to make distinctions between de jure and de facto corporations. It is, therefore, important to understand both the historical backdrop and the modern trends in this area of the law.

CORPORATE POWERS

The articles of incorporation may set forth the powers of the corporation, as we learned earlier. Such provisions actually may be redundant because state statutes normally specify what corporations can permissibly do. These express powers include

34.1

MANAGEMENT

DE JURE VERSUS DE FACTO CORPORATIONS

Tom and Anna Kochanowski have just about decided that the benefits of incorporating CIT outweigh the disadvantages of the corporate form. They are unsure, however, about the legal steps involved in incorporation and ask your advice as to what CIT must do to incorporate. What will you advise them to do?

BUSINESS CONSIDERATIONS What advice and guidelines can you suggest to an enterprise to ensure that it forms a de jure corporation rather than a de facto corporation?

ETHICAL CONSIDERATIONS Is it ethical to grant a business that does not comply fully with the state's incorporation statute the benefits of limited liability and perpetual existence? Would it be more ethical, due to some minor flaw in formation of the enterprise, to treat the stockholders as partners?

the ability to conduct business, to exist perpetually (unless the articles define a shorter period or the state dissolves the corporation), to sue and be sued, to use the corporate name or seal, and to make bylaws.

In addition, corporations possess implied powers to do everything reasonably necessary for the conduct of the business. Typical implied powers consist of holding or transferring property, acquiring stock from other corporations, borrowing money, executing commercial paper, issuing bonds, effecting loans, reacquiring the corporation's own shares, and contributing to charity. Statutes may enumerate these and other implied powers.

Ultra Vires Acts

As noted earlier, the powers of corporations were more heavily circumscribed years ago than they are today. Since the strict application of the concession theory had held that corporate status was a privilege (in contrast to a right), acts outside the boundaries established by law for the corporation were ultra vires and therefore void. *Ultra vires* means beyond the scope or legal power of a corporation as established by the corporation's charter or by state statute.) When sued, corporations could use ultra vires as a defense to enforcement of a contract. With the advent of implied powers, and a consequent relaxation of the concession theory and a widening of permissible corporate purposes, a corporation's use of this doctrine for avoidance of contractual duties has become largely outmoded. Thus, the modern trend is to curtail application of the ultra vires doctrine as a defense and in general to uphold the validity of actions taken by the corporation unless the action is a public wrong or forbidden by statute. Sometimes, however, the result depends on whether the transaction is executory or executed.

State statutes have abolished the defense of ultra vires in most jurisdictions. The statutes usually continue to permit suits only in three situations:

Injunctive actions
Lawsuits asking a court of equity to order a person to do or to refrain from doing some specified act.

1. shareholder **injunctive actions** against the corporation
2. shareholder suits on behalf of the corporation to recover damages caused by an impermissible act
3. proceedings by the state to dissolve the corporation because of repeated violations of applicable law

These situations constitute practically the only areas that remain for application of the ultra vires doctrine.

The court in *Goebel* v. *Blocks and Marbles Brand Toys, Inc.* considered the ultra vires defense in reaching its conclusions of law.

34.4 GOEBEL v. BLOCKS AND MARBLES BRAND TOYS, INC. 568 N.E.2d 552 (Ind.App. 1991)

FACTS Mark Launer incorporated Blocks and Marbles Brand Toys, Inc., in 1985, operated it, and served as its sole director and president until March or April 1986. On 20 May 1986, he executed an agreement with Lawrence E. Goebel to employ Goebel as president and chief operating officer. The term of the agreement commenced 1 April 1986 and was to terminate on 31 December 1991. Goebel began his duties in April 1986. On 3 February 1987, the corporation amended its bylaws and expanded the board of directors from one person to not less than three nor more than five persons. Launer resigned as director and sold his stock in Blocks and Marbles. The new board elected Goebel president for a one-year term. The directors remaining after Launer's resignation apparently did not become aware of Goebel's employment agreement of 20 May 1986 until sometime in 1988. Although the 20 May 1986 employment agreement provided for Goebel to receive a salary of $5,000 per month plus 25 percent of the annual pretax profits in excess of $150,000, Goebel received substantially less than the agreed salary in 1986 and 1987. Nevertheless, he told an accountant and outside auditors preparing financial statements for each year not to show any accrued salary as a liability of the corporation. In February 1989, four members of the five-member board of directors resigned and a new board was elected. On 14 March 1989, this new board voted to terminate Goebel's employment effective 31 March 1989. Contending he was owed additional salary for 1986 and 1987, Goebel, on 12 July 1989, filed a notice of intention to hold a corporate employee's lien on Blocks and Marbles' corporate property. In addition, relying on an arbitration provision in the 20 May 1986 contract, Goebel filed a request for arbitration of his dispute with Blocks and Marbles. The company argued that Goebel's employment contract was ultra vires because it had violated both the corporation's own bylaws and an Indiana statute mandating that the president be chosen from the corporation's directors.

ISSUE Was the Blocks and Marbles contract with Goebel ultra vires and hence unenforceable?

HOLDING No.

REASONING Blocks and Marbles could have sued Launer for causing or authorizing an ultra vires act. Goebel, however, probably did not know of the contract's invalidity; consequently, the corporation could not use the ultra vires defense against Goebel. Blocks and Marbles argued that the corporation could not legally enter into the agreement to employ a president because the contract directly violated both the statute under which the corporation had been created and the corporation's own bylaws. Blocks and Marbles made the following arguments: (1) The directors' minutes did not show a resolution authorizing the contract to make Goebel president or the creation of the additional office of chief operating officer; (2) the directors' minutes did not show approval of the employment contract; (3) the secretary had not attested to the execution of the employment agreement, as required by the bylaws; and (4) any blanket ratification of action by shareholders could not be considered ratification of the employment agreement because the shareholders had been unaware of the material fact of the existence of the agreement. Blocks and Marbles contended that Indiana law permitted the company to challenge the employment agreement as an ultra vires act of the corporation and an insider transaction by Goebel. The pertinent Indiana statute states that a corporation in a proceeding against a former director, officer, employee, or agent may challenge its own power to act. The Official Comment to this statute notes that the suit against the director or other agent is for "authorizing or causing the corporation to engage in an *ultra vires* act. . . ." Otherwise, "the validity of corporate action may not be challenged on the ground that the corporation lacks or lacked power to act." Thus, although Blocks and Marbles could have sued Launer for causing or authorizing ultra vires acts, Blocks and Marbles could not defend against Goebel or sue him for authorizing or causing the corporation to enter into an employment agreement with himself. Although the record indicates that not all the stockholders knew of the contract, Launer had had apparent authority to enter into the contract. And Goebel could not have been presumed to know of the agreement's invalidity. Thus, Blocks and Marbles could not rely on the ultra vires defense here.

BUSINESS CONSIDERATIONS Should the owners and/or managers of an allegedly incorporated business check periodically to ensure that the business is still in good standing with the state and that its corporate status has not changed? Why might this be a matter of concern?

ETHICAL CONSIDERATIONS Is it ethical for a person who dealt with another business as if it were a corporation to seek unlimited liability from its owners due to an error in the organization of the other business? Is it ethical for owners to hide behind the limited liability provisions of corporate status when the firm cannot pay its obligations?

Taxation of Corporations

The tax treatment of corporations stems from the law's recognition of corporations as separate entities for federal income tax purposes. This is a disadvantage of the corporate form. The corporation pays taxes on all its income as earned; and this income, when distributed to shareholders in the form of dividends, produces taxable income for the shareholders. This structure in effect brings about so-called double taxation. Moreover, because corporate losses are not passed on to the shareholders, shareholders do not receive the tax advantages that otherwise accompany such losses.

The creation of what the Internal Revenue Code terms an *S corporation* (regular corporations are dubbed *C corporations*) may offset these tax drawbacks and, thereby, provide tax relief. Subchapter S of the Internal Revenue Code permits certain corporations to avoid corporate income taxes and, at the same time, to pass operating losses on to their shareholders. In this sense, federal tax laws covering S corporations are analogous to the laws covering partnerships, but are uniquely corporate at the same time. Attaining S corporation status involves an elective procedure and the necessity for strict compliance with statutory requirements.

Federal tax laws limit eligibility for Subchapter S election to domestic small-business corporations having 35 or fewer shareholders (individuals, estates, and certain trusts qualify as shareholders, but partnerships, corporations, and nonqualifying trusts do not) and only one class of stock issued and outstanding. Moreover, the presence of even one nonresident-alien shareholder or passive investment income in excess of statutory limitations makes the corporation ineligible for S status. In order to make a proper election, all shareholders must consent to the election, and the filing must be timely and proper. Once an election occurs, renewals are unnecessary; S status remains in effect as long as none of the events that can trigger loss of the election occurs.

Limited Liability Companies

Limited liability companies (LLCs) and limited liability partnerships are hybrid forms of business organizations. The state enabling statute that allows LLPs is often the same state statute that authorizes LLCs. In addition to the usual concerns about whether the enterprise will be financially successful, additional uncertainties arise with the LLC form of business organization. There are concerns about both federal and state tax structures. Will the LLC be taxed in the manner expected and desired by the investor? The conclusion depends on the state statute, the articles of organization, and any Revenue Rulings or private letter rulings of the Internal Revenue Service. In general, businesspeople need to remember that state statutes vary and what is true of New York LLCs may not be true of Florida LLCs. Some states allow for much flexibility while others are more restrictive.

History of Limited Liability Companies

The first LLC statute was enacted in Wyoming in 1977. After enacting the statute, however, a number of questions arose about the federal income-tax treatment of an LLC and how sister states would treat Wyoming LLCs. Florida adopted the next LLC statute in 1982, primarily to attract foreign capital to the state.[12] Colorado and Kansas followed in 1990. Now approximately 40 states have adopted LLC acts, ten of these in 1993.[13] In addition, some states recognize out-of-state LLCs or permit registration of foreign LLCs.[14] For example, the California Franchise Tax Board recognizes out-of-state LLCs; and Mississippi allows the registration of foreign LLCs.

The purpose of limited liability companies is to provide limited liability for all investors, who are called members. (Limited liability connotes that investors may lose their investments in the enterprise, but not their personal assets.) No need exists for a general partner. LLCs have an advantage over limited partnerships in this regard: A limited partnership must have at least one general partner who is personally liable for the partnership's debts. With an LLC, each member's liability is limited to his or her capital investment. Many state statutes require LLCs to file articles of organization with the state similar to the articles of incorporation filed by corporations. There are generally no limitations on who may become a member of an LLC, as opposed to Subchapter S corporations, which have a number of restrictions on who may be a shareholder.

LLCs are based on state statutes, so the provisions vary from state to state. Generally, the statutes dictate the following characteristics:

1. The LLC must be formed by two or more members.
2. The LLC must have a stated term of duration not to exceed 30 years.
3. All members of the LLC must have limited liability to the extent of their invested capital plus any additional capital contribution contractually promised by the members.
4. The LLC members' shares are not freely transferable. (Due to this requirement, LLCs are not appropriate where a large number of investors are anticipated.)
5. The central management must be elected by the members.

The statutes also require that the entity indicate in its name that it is an LLC. Most states require the use of "limited liability company," "limited company," "L.L.C." or "L.C." in the title.

Taxation of Limited Liability Companies

LLCs are not automatically treated as partnerships. Federal tax law is not controlled by the label the parties attach to the enterprise. Rather, the Internal Revenue Service (IRS) examines whether the enterprise has the characteristics of a corporation or not. Section 301.7701-1(b) of the IRS Procedure and Administration Regulations divides organizations into categories for purposes of taxation; these categories include corporations, partnerships, and trusts.

Under the federal tax law, there is no question that an LLC is an association, which is a nontechnical term. An association must bear a resemblance to a corporation in order to be taxed as a corporation under federal tax law.[15] The law then prescribes the characteristics of a corporation; it must have the following:

1. associates
2. an intent to conduct a business for profit and to divide those profits
3. continuity of life
4. centralization of management functions
5. liability for business debts limited to business assets
6. free transferability of investors' interests[16]

The IRS Regulations (in § 301.7701-2(a)(2)) provide that characteristics common to both corporations and partnerships are not material in making the distinction. Since the first two characteristics exist in all business organizations, attention focuses on the latter four. "[I]f an unincorporated organization possesses more corporate characteristics than noncorporate characteristics, it constitutes an association taxable as a corporation."[17]

The exact interpretation is left to the courts, the Department of the Treasury, and the Internal Revenue Service. In determining the characteristics of the LLC, reliance is placed on the LLC's articles of organization and the applicable state's statute. Generally, most members hope that the LLC has the income pass-through characteristics of partnerships. The desire for partnership tax treatment may not be universal. Individual and corporate tax rates are progressive at the federal level and under most state laws. In some instances, less taxation is owed if the entity is taxed at the corporate rates. This is especially true if the entity is retaining net profits and not distributing them. This aspect of tax planning should not be overlooked.

Obviously, states are not empowered to enact federal tax laws. It is likely that the Internal Revenue Service and the courts will decide that partnership taxation is appropriate if the LLC lacks two of the following: continuity of life, centralized management, and/or transferability of shares. Always remember that an LLC will not automatically qualify for partnership taxation.

Flexibility and Variance

LLC statutes vary from state to state. One characteristic on which LLC statutes vary is whether businesses providing professional services can form an LLC.[18] Many states will not permit an LLC to continue in perpetuity in the way that a corporation can. Most LLC statutes or the LLC articles greatly restrict the transferability of shares.[19] Some states, including Idaho, Missouri, Montana, Arkansas, North Carolina, Colorado, and Texas,[20] allow one person to form an LLC.[21] Another unresolved issue is whether the selling of LLC interests falls under the applicable state and/or federal securities laws. The SEC's position appears to be that LLCs consisting of a large number of members are required to file under the 1933 and 1934 securities statutes. One factor in the determination is whether the members actually manage the enterprise or whether the entity uses centralized managers.

Since most states have already enacted their own particular version of an LLC enabling statute,[22] it seems doubtful that uniform legislation will take hold. The National Conference of Commissioners on Uniform State Laws (NCCUSL) has drafted a Uniform Limited Liability Company Act, which was approved by the Commissioners on 4 August 1994. Hawaii, South Carolina, Vermont, and West Virginia have adopted it.[23] In addition, there is a Prototype Limited Liability Company Act issued by a committee of the American Bar Association Section on Business Law. Both of these documents appear to be a little too late to create much consistency.

Estoppel
A legal bar (or impediment) that prevents a person from claiming or denying certain facts as a result of the person's previous conduct.

Other Types of Business Organizations

Three other types of business organizations exist that are very similar to partnerships, yet qualify as their own business forms: partnerships by estoppel, joint ventures, and mining partnerships.

Partnerships by Estoppel

Technically, no partnership can exist without an agreement. A third person who is dealing with someone who *claims* to be a partner but is not, however, may be able to proceed against the partnership and/or the alleged partner. Such a situation may lead to a partnership by **estoppel.**

To use estoppel, three facts must be shown:

1. someone who is not a partner was held out to be a partner by the firm
2. the third person justifiably relied on the holding out
3. the person will be harmed if no liability is imposed

Joint Ventures

A **joint venture** has all the characteristics of a partnership except one. It is not set up to "carry on a business." A joint venture, by definition, is set up to carry out a limited number of transactions, very commonly a single deal. As soon as that deal (or those transactions) is completed, the joint venture terminates. Why is this form important? The agency power in a joint venture is limited; thus, a member of the venture is not as likely to be held responsible for the conduct of the other members of the venture. Also, the death of a joint venturer does not automatically dissolve the joint venture. In all other respects, partnership law is applicable.

34.2

FINANCE

LIMITED LIABILITY WITHOUT DOUBLE TAXATION

Tom and Anna Kochanowski have decided to incorporate CIT in order to take advantage of the protections of limited liability that incorporation provides, among other reasons. John, however, is concerned that the firm will face "double taxation" if it incorporates. He knows that other methods of organization exist whereby CIT can gain limited liability but not be subject to double taxation. He is unsure what those methods are, however, or how CIT could organize under one of them. John asks you what methods are available for organizing the business with limited liability for the family but without double taxation. What will you tell him?

BUSINESS CONSIDERATIONS What factors need to be considered by a group of people who have decided to form a business before they decide on the appropriate form of organization? Is there a single best form for businesses?

ETHICAL CONSIDERATIONS What is the ethical duty of a business in regard to the tax code? Is it ethical to select a particular form of organization to avoid or reduce taxation?

Mining Partnerships

A **mining partnership** is a uniquely American creation. It is a partnership, but it has special characteristics not found in a nonmining partnership. In a regular partnership, a partner cannot sell his or her interest or leave the interest to his or her heirs in a will. In a mining partnership, however, the selling of an interest or the bequeathing of an interest by will is permitted.

One theory about how this special treatment evolved is that during the California gold rush, after partners discovered gold, one partner would suddenly and "mysteriously" have a fatal accident that left the mine to the surviving partner. In an effort to extend the life span of successful miners, mining partnership laws were developed. The death of a partner merely brought another partner, the deceased partner's heir, into the business. Thus, no advantage was gained by the death of a partner.

Joint venture
A commercial or maritime enterprise undertaken by several persons jointly; an association of two or more persons to carry out a single business enterprise for profit.

Mining partnership
An association of several owners of a mine for cooperation in working the mine.

DISREGARDING THE CORPORATE ENTITY

We have seen that the law sometimes will recognize corporateness when incorporation has been defective. Now we will examine situations that call for disregarding the corporate entity even when compliance with the incorporation statute has occurred.

http:// RESOURCES FOR BUSINESS LAW STUDENTS

NAME	RESOURCES	WEB ADDRESS
U.S. Small Business Administration (SBA)	The SBA provides information and materials, such as forms, software, and publications, to help start, finance, and expand a business.	http://www.sba.gov/
Internal Revenue Service	The Internal Revenue Service and its publication the "Digital Daily" provide tax advice and information on a variety of issues, including business formation issues.	http://www.irs.ustreas.gov/
Code of Hammurabi	The Yale Law School maintains a hypertext version of the legal code of Hammurabi.	http://www.yale.edu/lawweb/avalon/hamframe.htm

The usual rule is that the shareholders in a corporation enjoy limited liability. Because the corporation is a separate entity from the shareholders, the law normally will not be interested in who owns or runs the corporation. Sometimes, though, it will be necessary to *pierce the corporate veil* in order to serve justice. In other words, the law will ignore the shield that keeps the corporation and its shareholders' identities separate. For example, the corporate veil will be "pierced" when the corporate form is being used to defraud others or for similar illegitimate purposes. Courts may pierce the corporate veil to place liability on the shareholder who is using the corporate form without permission.

The law may create personal liability on a shareholder, despite the fact that these are corporate liabilities: (1) if the shareholder is the sole shareholder in an association that is so thinly capitalized initially that it cannot reasonably meet its obligations; or (2) if the shareholder is draining off the corporation's assets for his or her own personal use. If the shareholder instead can reasonably meet his or her obligations and does not drain off corporate assets, he or she will achieve limited liability. In this case, there will be no personal liability.

Courts examine the facts closely to see if a particular situation justifies disregard of corporateness. Put another way, if the corporation is a mere "shell" or "instrumentality," or in reality is the "alter ego" of the shareholder, courts can use their powers of equity to impose liability on the controlling shareholders.

This is not to say that "one-person" corporations are always candidates for disregarding corporate entity—quite the contrary. The usual rule is that the law will not disregard corporateness if there has been no domination by the shareholder for an improper purpose (such as fraud or evasion of obligations) with resultant injury to the corporation (such as mismanagement), third parties, or the public at large. Courts will uphold corporateness as long as the controlling shareholder keeps corporate affairs and transactions separate from personal transactions; adequately capitalizes the business initially and forgoes the draining off of corporate assets; incorporates for legitimate reasons (tax savings, limitation of liability, and so on); and directs the policies of the corporation toward its own interests, not personal ones. These same principles, in general, apply to situations involving parent/subsidiary (that is, affiliated) companies, another potentially troublesome area for courts deciding whether corporateness should be retained or disregarded. Exhibit 34.3 illustrates these points.

Note how the court applied these concepts in *Evans* v. *Multicon Construction Corporation*.

EXHIBIT 34.3 Piercing the Corporate Veil

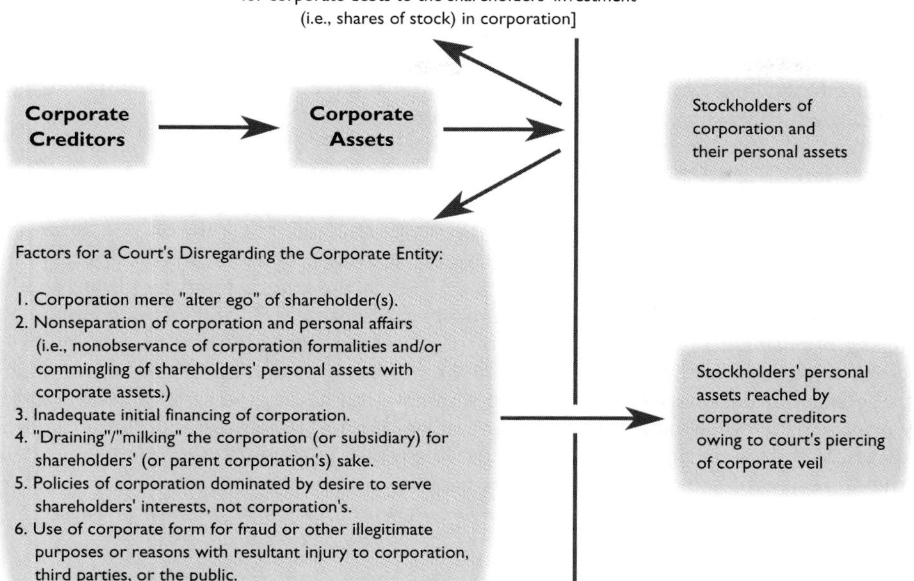
CORPORATE VEIL
[Represents limitation of liability of corporate shareholders for corporate debts to the shareholders' investment (i.e., shares of stock) in corporation]
Corporate Creditors
Corporate Assets
Stockholders of corporation and their personal assets
Factors for a Court's Disregarding the Corporate Entity:
1. Corporation mere "alter ego" of shareholder(s).
2. Nonseparation of corporation and personal affairs (i.e., nonobservance of corporation formalities and/or commingling of shareholders' personal assets with corporate assets.)
3. Inadequate initial financing of corporation.
4. "Draining"/"milking" the corporation (or subsidiary) for shareholders' (or parent corporation's) sake.
5. Policies of corporation dominated by desire to serve shareholders' interests, not corporation's.
6. Use of corporate form for fraud or other illegitimate purposes or reasons with resultant injury to corporation, third parties, or the public.
Stockholders' personal assets reached by corporate creditors owing to court's piercing of corporate veil

34.5 EVANS v. MULTICON CONSTRUCTION CORPORATION 574 N.E.2d 395 (Mass.App. 1991)

FACTS More than a decade after initiating action, Robert Evans, a subcontractor, on 9 August 1978 won a judgment of $124,176.45 against Multicon Construction Corporation (MCC). By that time, MCC, an Ohio corporation, had ceased doing business in Massachusetts and, if it existed at all, was an empty shell. Evans, therefore, sought alternative sources of recovery by invoking Rule 69 of the Massachusetts Rules of Civil Procedure, which makes available post-judgment discovery and equips the court with "all the traditional flexibility of a court of equity," including enforcement of orders of the court against persons who may not originally have been parties. Under Rule 69, Evans argued that MCC had been a sham corporation functioning as a front for John W. Kessler and Peter H. Edwards, the individuals who had organized MCC. Evans claimed that the factors typically utilized in piercing the corporate veil justified a court's holding Edwards and Kessler personally liable for the judgment that Evans had won against MCC.

ISSUE Should a court pierce the corporate veil to hold the officers of MCC personally liable?

HOLDING No.

REASONING The evidence showed that the bases in law for so holding were insufficient to permit a court to disregard corporateness. The court noted that rare, particular situations may warrant disregard of separate corporate entities; that is, allow a court to pierce the corporate veil. Occasion for doing so arises when (1) related business entities are actively and pervasively controlled by the same controlling persons, with fraudulent or injurious consequences by reason of the relationships among those business entities; or (2) confused intermingling of activity exists between two or more corporations engaged in a common enterprise, resulting in substantial disregard of the separate nature of the corporate entities or serious ambiguity about the manner and capacity in which the various corporations

34.5 EVANS v. MULTICON CONSTRUCTION CORPORATION *(cont.)* 574 N.E.2d 395 (Mass.App. 1991)

and their respective representatives are acting. In the present case, a court must consider the factors of MCC's operations in view of these criteria. For example, common ownership existed among MCC and its related companies—Georgetown, Multicon, and MPI (MCC's parent company)—in the sense that Edwards and Kessler were a significant presence in all of them. But Edwards and Kessler had partners in Multicon and Georgetown to whom they owed a fiduciary duty. Edwards and Kessler could not, and did not, run MCC as their own enterprise; MCC had to deliver value to the various limited partnerships for which it had served as a construction company. Moreover, the several entities in the Multicon complex were operated on an arm's length basis from one another. Edwards and Kessler maintained pervasive control from 1966 through 1970. There was no confused intermingling of business activity, assets, or management. MCC did not engage in identifying and acquiring project locations, the formation of local partnerships, advertising, or property management. While initial capital was unquestionably thin (that is, $500), the pertinent question is whether it was too thin. A review of activities showed that, during its corporate life, MCC did not ever want for assets. The observance of corporate formalities occurred. Furthermore, separate tax returns for each company were meticulously filed. Throughout its years of activity in Massachusetts, MCC also filed the appropriate corporate certificates with the secretary of the commonwealth. At the time of the litigated transaction, MCC was not insolvent. MCC's cash position at the end of 1966 was $121,762.67 and at the end of 1967, $275,731.43. There was no suggestion that MCC during that period, or at any time while it was active, had experienced difficulty in paying debts as they became due, a test of insolvency. For the years in question, assets and liabilities were in close balance, but those assets remained sufficient to pay existing debts as they matured. At the end of its active period, in December 1973, MCC showed assets in excess of liabilities and retained earnings of $1,109. In the cases in which courts have penetrated the corporate veil, finagling, an element of dubious manipulation and contrivance that confuses corporate identities and causes third parties uncertainty, exists. Here, no one suggested that Evans thought he was doing excavation work for Multicon, Georgetown, Edwards, or Kessler. He entered into a conventional subcontracting arrangement with MCC and did not rely on the interests of Georgetown (the owner) or Multicon (Georgetown's general partner). Hence, the contract between Evans and MCC and the manner in which MCC had functioned in the Multicon enterprise did not justify looking beyond MCC to its parent MPI or to Edwards and Kessler, who had been the sole stockholders of MCC at the time of contracting. The risk that a defendant may become unable to pay a judgment is inherent in any civil litigation. But that in itself can never form the basis for piercing the corporate veil in the absence of evidence supporting such a result, such as fraud.

BUSINESS CONSIDERATIONS What steps should the officers of a corporation take to prevent a court from piercing the corporate veil if the corporation loses a lawsuit?

ETHICAL CONSIDERATIONS Is it ethical for a corporation to leave the corporation thinly financed, relying on limited liability provisions to protect their interests in the event of a lawsuit?

SUMMARY

Every business enterprise must have an organizational form, choosing among a proprietorship, a partnership, a limited partnership, a LLP, a LLC, and a corporate form. Partnerships fall between the two extremes of organizational form—that is, proprietorships and corporations. A partnership has the advantages of being easily formed and of having multiple contributors, whose different opinions and expertise are always available. A partnership also has the disadvantages of somewhat limited existence and unlimited personal liability for each general partner.

A partnership is defined in the Uniform Partnership Act as an association of two or more persons carrying on a business as co-owners for profit. This definition requires that the partners voluntarily agree to enter the business and that the business be somewhat permanent in nature. Co-ownership is the key element of the definition. This element is so important that a sharing of profits by the people involved creates a presumption of co-ownership, which, in turn, creates a presumption that a partnership exists.

A limited partnership is similar to a regular, or general, partnership with two major exceptions: There must be at least one limited partner who may not participate in the management of the business, and somewhat formal documents must be prepared and correctly filed in order to establish the limited partnership.

A corporation is an artificial entity created by the state and endowed with certain powers by the state. The historical development of corporations illustrates an acceptance of the "fiction" (or "entity" theory) of corporations—that is, that the corporation is an entity separate and distinct from its shareholders. As a business form, corporations have the advantages of limited liability, centralization of management functions, continuity of existence, free transferability of shares, and sometimes favorable tax treatment. There are various types of for-profit corporations: public-issue private corporations, close corporations, professional corporations, public corporations, and quasi-public corporations. Nonprofit corporations exist in all jurisdictions as well.

The filing of the articles of incorporation signals the corporation's official beginning, but some jurisdictions require the issuance of a certificate of incorporation or an organizational meeting before the corporation can attain corporate status. In general, corporate status will not be lost if substantial compliance with incorporation statutes occurs; courts will view the entity as a *de jure* (legal) corporation. Courts will even grant *de facto* (in fact, but not in law) corporations corporate status on the fulfillment of certain requirements. The issuance of a certificate of incorporation by the state eliminates the need to resort to the de facto doctrine in some jurisdictions. This development actually represents the modern trend: to presume de jure status in such circumstances, except in actions brought by the state.

Corporations enjoy certain express and implied powers. Years ago courts held that corporations were not responsible for ultra vires acts (those beyond the power of the corporation), but the law now limits the application of this doctrine to a few specialized situations.

Limited liability corporations (LLCs) have a number of advantages over the older forms of business. The LLC can be a hybrid of the generally favorable features of partnerships and corporations, providing for tax consequences only in the hands of the ultimate recipient, including both income and active losses; and insulating personal income from the LLC's debts. Many state statutes restrict the transferability of LLC shares and limit the life of the organization.

Extreme care must be used in establishing an LLC. Members must conform to the applicable state statute. In order to be entitled to partnership tax treatment, it is necessary to comply with the state law. Many states seem to follow the federal tax rules, which look to the entity's characteristics, while some have not specifically addressed the issue. For federal tax purposes, it is important to structure the LLC so that it complies with the Internal Revenue Service Regulations and Revenue Rulings.

There are three additional forms of business operation. The first is partnership by estoppel, where there is no partnership agreement, but the parties act as if there were an agreement, to the detriment of some third party. The other two types of organizations are joint ventures and mining partnerships. Both have special rules that separate them from ordinary general partnerships.

At times courts will disregard corporate status even when complete compliance with the state statute has taken place. "Piercing the corporate veil" in order to impose personal liability on a shareholder will occur when the corporation becomes the means for furthering illegitimate ends.

DISCUSSION QUESTIONS

1. Under § 6 of the UPA, what are the five characteristics of a partnership?
2. Bob, Carol, and Ted set up a partnership. Later, Bob and Ted want to bring in Alice as a fourth partner. Carol, however, objects to allowing Alice to enter. A vote is taken, and Alice receives two votes of approval and one of disapproval. Will Alice be admitted as a fourth partner? Explain your answer.
3. Ed, Tim, and Dennis have a business concept they are sure will succeed if they can establish it properly. Unfortunately, they are short of capital and cannot afford to begin the business without financial support. Marge is willing to put up the necessary capital, but she is unwilling to face the liability of a general partner. Therefore, Marge agrees to be a limited partner in the business. What must the parties do to establish a limited partnership under the RULPA?
4. Larry and Darrin form a partnership. Darrin contributes $10,000. Larry, on the other hand, lets the partnership use an office building he owns, rent free. Three years later, the business dissolves. Darrin claims the building is partnership property. Larry claims he still owns the building personally. Who is correct, and why?
5. Sam and Ruth enter a partnership, but Sam does not want Ruth to be his agent or to participate in managing the business. What should he do to see that his wishes are carried out?
6. Tim and Margie are partners. In order to get a loan, they tell the bank that Denise is also a partner. Relying on Denise's credit, the bank makes the loan. Tim and Margie default, and the bank sues Denise. What must the bank prove in order to hold Denise liable for the loan?
7. Name five advantages of corporations as business associations.
8. How does a de jure corporation differ from a de facto corporation? What requirements are necessary for a corporation to acquire de facto status?
9. Under what circumstances will a court or the state pierce the corporate veil?
10. Discuss the express and implied powers of corporations. What is the ultra vires doctrine, and what are the circumstances in which it may be applied?

CASE PROBLEMS AND WRITING ASSIGNMENTS

1. Three sisters, Louise W. Veal, LaWanda W. Davis, and Lynn W. Martin, agreed to purchase and operate a farm together. The sisters had other jobs, so they did not operate the farm themselves. None of them lived on the farm. The sisters agreed to split the profits from the farm. There is no partnership agreement. Did the three sisters form a partnership? Why or why not? [*In re LLL Farms*, 111 B.R. 1016 (Bankr. M.D. Ga. 1990).]

2. Robert Edward Pitman was a limited partner in Ramsey Homebuilders. Michael C. Ramsey was the sole general partner; however, he had a poor credit history. Consequently, Ramsey was unable to borrow the money or obtain the credit needed to sustain the partnership's business. Pitman secured a partnership account with Flanagan Lumber Company through Flanagan's credit manager. When the partnership failed to pay its debts, Flanagan sued Pitman. Pitman claimed that he was a limited partner and was not liable for partnership debts. Should Pitman be held liable? Why or why not? [See *Pitman* v. *Flanagan Lumber Co.*, 567 So.2d 1335 (Ala. 1990).]

3. Acruem was a partnership formed in 1967. The partnership certificate filed with the county clerk's office listed three partners: Ackman, Rubin, and Emil. Emil immediately assigned each of his two children one-half of his 25 percent interest in the partnership. Emil remained as nominal partner, making all business decisions with respect to the business. (Ackman and Rubin had been informed of this arrangement prior to the formal execution of the partnership agreement, and neither had objected to the arrangement.) Emil's children made all contributions and payments to the business through their father and received their shares of partnership income directly from the business. One of Emil's children, Judy Tenney, had a per-

sonal liability insurance policy from Insurance Company of North America (INA) that covered any losses for which the policyholder became personally liable due to personal injury. A fire at Acruem in 1969 resulted in numerous lawsuits against the partners for liability. Tenney paid $141,000 as her share of the personal liability claims of the firm and submitted a claim to INA for indemnification. INA refused to pay the claim, alleging that Tenney was not a partner and, therefore, not legally liable for the claims. Is INA correct; or is Tenney a partner and, therefore, personally liable? Explain your answer. [See *Tenney* v. *Insurance Co. of North America,* 409 F.Supp. 746 (N.Y. 1975).]

4. Lincoln M. Polan formed a corporation entitled Industrial Realty Company. Polan was the sole shareholder. The state issued a certificate of incorporation. The corporation never held an organizational meeting, however; no officers were elected, no stocks were issued, and no payments were made to the corporation for stock. The corporation failed to observe other corporate formalities as well. Polan, acting for the corporation, signed a lease for commercial space in a building controlled by Kinney Shoe Corp. The first rental payment was made by Polan from his personal funds. No further rental payments were made. Kinney obtained a court judgment against the corporation for $66,400 in unpaid rent. When the corporation did not pay, Kinney filed suit against Polan individually. Should the court pierce the corporate veil? Why or why not? [See *Kinney Shoe Corp.* v. *Polan,* 939 F.2d 209 (4th Cir. 1991).]

5. Civil penalties of $90,350 were assessed against WRW Corporation (WRW) for violating safety standards under the Federal Mine Safety and Health Act. The violations had resulted in the deaths of two miners. WRW then liquidated its assets and went out of business. Roger Richardson, Noah Woolum, and William Woolum were the sole shareholders, officers, and directors of WRW. The three were later indicted and convicted of willful violations under the act and were sentenced to prison and paid criminal fines. The United States brought a lawsuit against WRW and the three men to recover the civil penalties previously assessed. Should the corporate veil be pierced and the three individuals held liable for the civil penalty? Why or why not? [See *United States* v. *WRW Corporation,* 986 F.2d 138 (6th Cir. 1993).]

6. **BUSINESS APPLICATION CASE** Samuel Shaw took a Delta flight to Salt Lake City and then connected with a SkyWest flight from Salt Lake City to Elko, Nevada. The SkyWest flight crashed just before landing in Elko, seriously injuring Shaw. Shaw sued Delta, claiming that Delta was SkyWest's partner. Delta had a contract with SkyWest, under which Delta served as SkyWest's ticketing and marketing agent. Was there a partnership between Delta and SkyWest? Why or why not? What could Delta do to avoid these claims in the future? [See *Shaw* v. *Delta Airlines, Inc.,* 798 F.Supp. 1453 (D. Nev. 1992).]

7. **ETHICS APPLICATION CASE** McElfish was the president and a primary stockholder of Gags Enterprises, Inc. Gags owned the Sandspur Bar in Melbourne, Florida. The bar had a studio apartment attached to the back, which was occupied at various times by McElfish, who acted as the bar's manager. As he had done on other occasions, McElfish invited Schroeder to go with him to a party at another lounge in Melbourne to assist him in entertaining business clients. After the party, they returned to the apartment at the Sandspur. An argument arose between them that resulted in McElfish's inflicting numerous personal injuries on Schroeder. McElfish explained that he had been trying to remove Schroeder from the premises because she was rowdy and intoxicated and that he had wanted to lock up the bar for the evening. Should Gags be liable for the $31,500 in compensatory damages and $30,000 in punitive damages awarded by the jury to Schroeder? Why? What ethical issues are raised by this lawsuit? Explain. [See *Kent Ins. Co.* v. *Schroeder,* 469 So.2d 209 (Fla.App. 1985).]

8. **IDES CASE** William Ruszkowski and his wife own A-l Contracting, Inc. Mr. Ruszkowski claims that he was injured while using a circular saw in connection with his employment at A-l. In his complaint, he sets forth causes of action in negligence and breach of warranty against the defendant, Sears, Roebuck and Company, for the manufacture, sale, and distribution of a defectively designed product. Sears's answer contains general denials and several affirmative defenses, one of which calls for reducing any recovery received by Ruszkowski owing to Ruszkowski's culpable fault. New York law allows a manufacturer/seller of a product that has allegedly injured an employee at his or her place of employment to implead (that is, to bring a new party into the lawsuit on the ground that this new party ultimately may be liable to the impleading party) the employer in order to receive indemnification from the employer in the event the manufacturer/seller is found liable to the employee. Ruszkowski contends that if the court allows this third-party action to stand, the result may be inequitable because whatever allocation of fault the court or the jury makes in the main action will then

carry over to the third-party action. According to Ruszkowski, if, for example, the decision maker finds that the plaintiffs are 30 percent negligent and are awarded $10,000, this award will be reduced to $7,000, to be paid by Sears. Sears, in turn, may then recover $3,000 from A-l; so the net final effect is that the plaintiffs will recover $4,000, owing to the doubling of the allocation of fault, once as plaintiff/employee and once as impleaded employer. In essence, then, in requesting a dismissal of the third-party action, Ruszkowski is asking the court to disregard the corporate status of A-l for Ruszkowski's own benefit. Apply the IDES model in analyzing this case. Will a court accept Ruszkowski's argument in this case? Why? [See *Ruszkowski* v. *Sears, Roebuck and Co.*, 571 N.Y.S.2d 187 (Sup. 1991).]

NOTES

1. Uniform acts are drafted by the National Conference of Commissioners on Uniform State Laws (NCCUSL) and made available for adoption by the state legislatures. Officially, this is the UPA (1914).
2. The NCCUSL made the Revised Uniform Partnership Act available in 1992. It is not officially called the Revised Uniform Partnership Act or RUPA; officially, it is the Uniform Partnership Act or UPA (1992). Unofficially, it is called RUPA, even by the NCCUSL. We will use the standard nomenclature and call it RUPA. It was further amended by the commissioners in 1993 and 1994; and in 1994 they released UPA (1994), which is basically the 1992 version with the 1993 and 1994 amendments. It was further amended in 1996.
3. Both states adopted the 1992 version, without the 1993 and 1994 amendments.
4. Information on the current status of adoptions of Uniform State Laws was provided by Katie Robinson, Public Affairs Coordinator, NCCUSL, during a telephone conversation on 22 May 1997.
5. Information on the current status of adoptions of Uniform State Laws was provided by Katie Robinson, Public Affairs Coordinator, NCCUSL, during a telephone conversation on 22 May 1997.
6. Uniform Partnership Act, § 7(4).
7. Uniform Partnership Act, § 303.
8. Arizona statutes §§ 29-215 and 44-141.
9. "Three Accounting Firms Now Limited Partnerships," *Wall Street Journal* (2 August 1994), p. A8.
10. Per Katie Robinson, Public Affairs Coordinator, NCCUSL, during a telephone conversation on 22 May 1997.
11. "Three Accounting Firms Now Limited Partnerships," *Wall Street Journal* (2 August 1994), p. A8.
12. Carol J. Miller and Radie Bunn, "Limited Liability Companies—A Taxing Alternative." (Paper presented at the annual meeting of the Academy of Legal Studies in Business, 11 August 1994.)
13. G. Kent Renegar and David Kunz, "The Growth of the Limited Liability Company: Is It Warranted?" (Paper presented at the annual meeting of the Academy of Legal Studies in Business, 11 August 1994) and published in the *Proceedings of the Meeting*.
14. Ibid. The authors provide an interesting analysis of the number of LLC filings.
15. An association is broadly defined under the Internal Revenue Code. It includes any organization formed to transact specified affairs or to seek some objective. It has a representative individual or group that makes decisions for the whole and it does not terminate with a change of membership (I.R.S. Regs. 39.3797-2).
16. Treas. Reg. § 301.7701-2(a)(1)–301.7701-4.
17. Rev. Rul. 88-76, 1988-2 C.B. 360, 1988 IRB LEXIS 3773, *4.
18. California specifically forbids LLCs from providing professional services, Cal. Corp. Code § 17000 (1996). An earlier draft, however, allowed professional limited liability companies in Chapter 9. The Uniform Limited Liability Company Act, drafted by the NCCUSL, expressly permits professional LLCs (in § 101(3)).
19. Transferability of shares is also greatly restricted in Subchapter S corporations. The Internal Revenue Code limits who may own stock in a Subchapter S corporation. The corporation, desiring to maintain Subchapter S status, will generally also have ownership restrictions, because all shareholders must agree to be treated as a Subchapter S corporation.
20. Miller and Bunn, "Limited Liability Companies."
21. Renegar and Kunz, "The Growth of the Limited Liability Company."
22. For an analysis of the three general forms for LLCs, see Miller and Bunn, "Limited Liability Companies."
23. Information on the current status of adoptions of Uniform State Laws was provided by Katie Robinson, Public Affairs Coordinator, NCCUSL, during a telephone conversation on 22 May 1997.

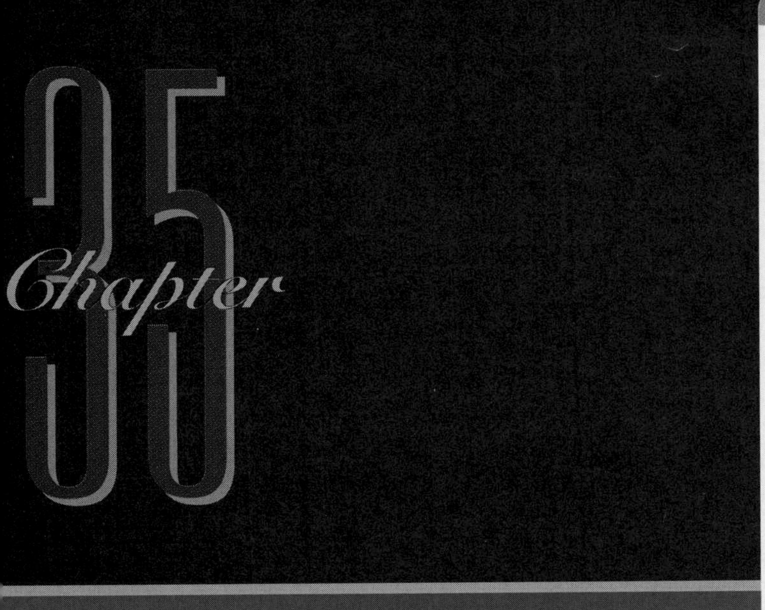

Operation of a Business Organization

O U T L I N E

Operation of a Partnership
Rights of the Partners
Duties of the Partners
Rights of Third Persons Who Deal with Partnerships
Operation of a Corporation
Rights of the Shareholders of a Corporation
Liabilities of Shareholders
Rights and Duties of the Managers of a Corporation
Summary
Discussion Questions
Case Problems and Writing Assignments

A G E N D A

The Kochanowskis are still unsure as to what form of business they should select for CIT. If they choose to form a partnership, who would have authority and responsibility for decisions? How much—if any—ownership should they give to their children? If they decide to incorporate, how should the corporation be structured? Obviously, it will be a for-profit enterprise, but should it be publicly owned or closely held? Should the children be given stock and titles; and, if so, what will this mean to and for them legally? If Tom and Anna decide to incorporate the business, what legal steps must they follow in managing and operating the firm? How do these steps compare to those followed in a proprietorship or a partnership? Can they be compelled to distribute profits, or can they retain the firm's earnings to help it grow?

These and other questions will arise as you read this chapter. Be prepared! You never know when one of the Kochanowskis will seek your help or advice.

Operation of a Partnership

A partner has certain rights by virtue of his or her status as a partner. These rights *may* be limited or defined by the partnership agreement, the type of partnership formed, and any statutory restrictions. If there is no agreement to limit the rights, each partner is a manager for the enterprise, an agent for every other partner, and a principal of every other partner. As a result, all the regular rules of agency apply. Each partner is a fiduciary of the other partners. When a partner deals with some third party, the firm is bound by the conduct if it was apparently or actually authorized.

Rights of the Partners

A person who enters a partnership acquires certain rights. Some of these rights are gained through the agreement, and some are gained through the terms of the Uniform Partnership Act (UPA).[1] This book cannot cover all the rights that the partners might include in the agreement, but it can examine those rights imposed by operation of law.

Management

By virtue of his or her status as a partner, each partner is entitled to an equal voice in management. In conducting the ordinary business of the partnership, a majority vote controls. In order to conduct any extraordinary business, a unanimous vote is required.[2] A matter is considered extraordinary if it changes the basic nature or the basic risk of the business.

While the UPA requires that each partner be given an equal voice in managing the business, the partners are allowed to agree on the definition of "equal." Such an agreement can be beneficial to a dynamic business. If the partnership is forced to conduct its business by majority vote, opportunities may be lost because a vote cannot occur quickly enough.

To avoid this problem, many partnership agreements *define* the management voice of each partner. Remember that the agreement must include such a definition to be valid. For instance, a partnership composed of A, B, C, and D might provide the following management divisions:

1. A is in charge of purchasing.
2. B is in charge of marketing.
3. C is in charge of accounting and personnel.
4. D is in charge of paper clips and office neatness.
5. Any other areas are governed by a vote.

Under such an agreement, B can make marketing decisions immediately, without needing to meet with the partners to vote on the issue. Likewise, A can decide matters concerning purchasing; C can make personnel decisions; and D can dust the furniture without first consulting the other partners. Absent such an agreement, each partner has a truly equal voice in management, with decisions made by majority vote.

Reimbursement

Each partner is entitled to repayment by the partnership for any money spent to further the interests of the partnership. In addition, each partner is entitled to interest on the advances or payments made, unless the agreement says otherwise. Each partner is also entitled to a return of his or her **capital contribution** at the close of the partnership, provided enough money is present to repay each partner after all liabilities have been satisfied.[3]

Capital contribution
Money or assets invested by the business owners for commencing and/or promoting an enterprise.

Profits and Losses

Unless the agreement states otherwise, each partner is entitled to an equal share of the profits of the business. The profits are not automatically divided in the same percentage as capital was contributed, nor are they automatically divided in any other unequal manner. This is the *only* remuneration to which any partner is always entitled.[4] No partner is automatically permitted to draw a salary from the business even if that partner devotes extra time to running the business. However, the agreement can be worded in such a manner that a partner receives a salary from the business, with the remaining profits then divided in some predetermined manner. Any salary provision for partners must be expressly set out in the agreement. Losses are divided among the partners in the same ratio as profits are shared.

Books and Records

Each partner is entitled to free access to the books and records of the business. This includes the right to inspect the records and to copy them as the partner sees fit. Similarly, each partner is expected to give, and entitled to receive, detailed information on any matter that affects the partnership.[5]

Partnership Property

Each partner is a co-owner of partnership property with the other partners. The ownership is defined as **tenancy in partnership.**[6] This tenancy entitles the partner to possess the property for partnership purposes, but not to possess it for nonpartnership purposes. If all the partners agree to a nonpartnership usage, however, such a usage is allowed.

Tenancy in partnership
A special form of ownership of property, found only in partnerships, in which each partner has an equal right to possess and to use partnership assets for partnership purposes and that carries a right of survivorship.

This tenancy also carries with it a right of survivorship. This means that if a partner dies, the other *partners* own the property. It is *not* inherited by the heirs of the deceased partner if any other partners are still surviving. Thus, the last surviving partner will own the partnership individually. The heirs of the last partner may not possess the property except for partnership purposes.

Right to an Account

Any partner is entitled to a formal *account*—that is, a statement or record of business transactions or dealings—if he or she feels mistreated in the partnership.[7] Specifically, any partner who is excluded from the business or from use of business properties is entitled to an account. And the UPA provides for an account in any other circumstances that render it just and reasonable. In effect, any time an internal argument or disagreement arises about the business operation, the courts will say an account is just and reasonable.

Each partner is a fiduciary for every other partner and is expected to account to the other partners and to the partnership for any benefits received or any profits derived without the knowledge and consent of the other partners.[8]

Duties of the Partners

Agency Duties

Each partner is an *agent* of the partnership and of every other partner. Thus, any conduct by a partner that is *apparently* authorized is binding on the partnership. And because each partner is *personally* liable for partnership debts, such an act makes each partner at least *potentially* personally liable.

This obviously creates a possible financial hazard to the partners. To reduce somewhat the danger that a reckless partner can present, the UPA restricts some agency power. Under § 9(3), there is no apparent authority to do any of five specific acts unless *unanimously approved.* These five acts are as follows:

Assignment for the benefit of creditors
An assignment in trust made by debtors for the payment of their debts.

Goodwill
The fixed and favorable consideration of customers arising from established and well-conducted business.

Arbitrator
An independent person chosen by the parties or appointed by statute and to whom the issues are submitted for settlement outside of court.

1. making an **assignment for the benefit of creditors** by transferring partnership property to a trust for the creditors of the business
2. selling or otherwise disposing of the **goodwill** of the business
3. performing any act that makes it impossible to carry on the business
4. confessing a judgment against the partnership (In this situation, *confessing a judgment* is an acknowledgment in court that the partnership is legally to blame. Standard-form contracts may provide that the party contracting with the partnership has authority to confess judgment against it.)
5. submitting a partnership claim or liability to an **arbitrator**

Notice the scope of these acts. The first three frustrate business, and the last two remove the partners' rights to their "day in court." With these five exceptions, any other act of a partner within the scope of apparent authority is binding.

For example, a partner may sell and convey real property owned in the partnership name.[9] The conveyance may be made in the business name *or in the name of the partner.* In either case, the conveyance is valid, even if unauthorized, if the grantee has passed title on to an innocent third party in a subsequent sale. If the grantee is still in possession of the property, the other partners can recover the property, provided the sale was not authorized.

Admission
A statement acknowledging the truth of an allegation, and accepted in court as evidence against the party making the admission.

Also, if a partner makes an **admission** about partnership affairs, and the admission is within the partner's authority, the partnership is bound.[10] The firm must honor the admission and uphold it if it was within the admitting partner's authority, even if it harms the business.

Since each partner is an agent, *notice* given to any partner on a partnership matter is as valid as notice given to each of the partners.[11] This is simply the application of basic agency law to a partnership/agency situation. Similarly, knowledge gained, or *remembered,* while one is a partner is imputed to each partner.

If a partner acts, or fails to act, within the course and scope of the business, and the act or omission causes harm to a third person, each partner is as liable to the third person as the partner who committed the tort.[12] The partners face joint and several liability. In other words, they can be sued together or separately for the harm. Thus, the injured party might be harmed by partner A but sue only partners B and C and win the suit. In such a case, B and C must pay for the harm caused by A even though A was not named as a defendant. Again, this is merely an application of agency law principles to the partnership setting.

Likewise, if a partner *misapplies* money or property of a third person that is in the possession of the partnership, the partnership is liable. All the partners, or each of them, may need to answer for the breach of trust of one partner.[13] Again, the liability is joint and several.

Obviously, being a partner *may* be hazardous to your financial health. Even if you are a careful, cautious person, you face potential financial liability, maybe even disaster, from the conduct of your partners. What rights do you have that protect you? What rights are available for the protection of any partner from the excesses of another member of the partnership?

One such right protects the other partners and the partnership from a creditor of a partner. For example, assume that Al, Bill, and Cindi are partners. The business is very profitable, and Bill and Cindi are solvent. However, Al is in deep financial trouble. Several of Al's creditors sue Al to collect their claims. They win the suit, only to discover that Al cannot pay the judgment from his personal assets.

Can these creditors foreclose on Al's share of the partnership assets? No. All the creditors can do is to get a **charging order** from a court.[14] Under a charging order, the debtor/partner's *profits* are paid to the creditors until the claims are fully paid. Thus, the partnership can continue, and Bill and Cindi are protected. Only Al, the debtor, suffers.

On the other hand, suppose that the partnership is in financial difficulty, but that some of the partners are solvent. Can the partnership's creditors proceed directly against the individual partners, bypassing or ignoring the assets of the firm? No. The creditors of the firm must first proceed against the assets of the firm.

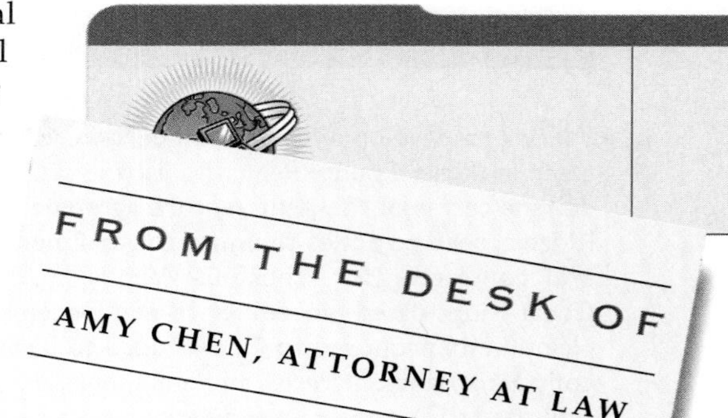

Duty of Loyalty

Partners owe the partnership a duty of loyalty. Consequently, partners must: avoid self-dealing unless they obtain the partnership's permission in advance, not compete with the partnership without permission, not seize a partnership opportunity for themselves, not make a secret profit from the partnership, not misuse partnership assets, not disclose trade secrets and other confidential partnership information, and not breach any fiduciary duty.

Like other agency relationships, partners also owe a duty to exercise due care.

Fiduciary Duties

Another protection given to the partners is the legal status assigned to each partner. Each member of a partnership is a *fiduciary* of the other partners and of the business itself.[15] The fiduciary position carries with it certain responsibilities and certain duties. Each partner is required to account for, and to surrender to the firm, any profits derived from the business or from the use of business assets. No partner is allowed to have a conflict of interest with the partnership. And each partner is entitled to indemnification from a partner who causes a loss or liability from misconduct in the course and scope of employment.

Charging order
A court order permitting a creditor to receive profits from the operation of a business; especially common in partnership situations.

In *Henkels & McCoy, Inc.* v. *Adochio*, the court discusses whether the general and managing partner made the correct decision.

35.1 HENKELS & MCCOY, INC. v. ADOCHIO

1997 U.S. Dist. LEXIS 26 (E.D. Pa. 1997)

FACTS "Plaintiff Henkels & McCoy (HM) is a Pennsylvania corporation. . . . Defendants [including Robert Adochio] are the limited partners of Red Hawk North Associates, L.P. (Red Hawk), a New Jersey limited partnership. G&A Development Corporation (G&A) is the general partner of Red Hawk. . . . In 1987, Red Hawk and Cedar Ridge Development Corporation (Cedar Ridge), a New Jersey corporation, entered into a joint venture agreement in order to form a partnership under the name of Chestnut Woods Partnership (Chestnut Woods), whereby Red Hawk and Cedar Ridge were both general partners of Chestnut Woods. . . . Red Hawk and Cedar Ridge created Chestnut

35.1 HENKELS & MCCOY, INC. v. ADOCHIO *(cont.)* 1997 U.S. Dist. LEXIS 26 (E.D. Pa. 1997)

Woods to develop and then sell certain real property located in Bucks County, Pennsylvania (the property).... Under the terms of the joint venture agreement, ... Cedar Ridge agreed to act as the managing partner and the general contractor for Chestnut Woods.... By letters to Cedar Ridge dated November 18 and December 13, 1988, plaintiff HM proposed to Cedar Ridge to furnish, as a subcontractor, labor, material, and equipment necessary to install the storm sewer and sanitary sewer systems for the Chestnut Woods project. On December 29, 1988, ... Cedar Ridge entered in a subcontract agreement with plaintiff, ... and under the terms of the agreement Cedar Ridge promised to pay HM a fixed price of $300,270.... The subcontract agreement identified Cedar Ridge solely as the general contractor for the project and failed to mention the partnership connection between Cedar Ridge and Chestnut Woods. HM was unaware that Cedar Ridge was a partner in Chestnut Woods at the time HM entered into the subcontract agreement.... [Cedar Ridge and Red Hawk entered into another joint venture agreement called the Timber Knoll Partnership. When that project failed to materialize, Cedar Ridge signed a promissory note to pay $2.1 million to Red Hawk. This is the amount of Red Hawk's capital contribution for the failed project.] On January 6, 1989, Cedar Ridge made a payment to Red Hawk, against the promissory note in the amount of $78,750, and on January 11, 1989, Red Hawk made a distribution to its general and limited partners in the amount of $76,923, leaving a balance of $1,904 in the checking account of Red Hawk.... HM began work on the sewer systems at Chestnut Woods on January 16, 1989.... On April 4, 1989, Cedar Ridge made payment to Red Hawk against the promissory note in the amount of $215,000, and on April 4, 1989, Red Hawk made distributions to its general and limited partners in the amount of $210,000, leaving a balance of $5,782 in the checking account of Red Hawk.... On July 6, 1989, Cedar Ridge made a payment to Red Hawk against the promissory note in the amount of $215,000. On July 10, 1989, Red Hawk made distributions to its general and limited partners in the amount of $210,000, leaving a balance of $8,779 in the checking account of Red Hawk.... On or about October 1, 1989, Cedar Ridge defaulted on one or more obligations to Red Hawk, including the promissory note to Red Hawk. On March 16, 1990, Cedar Ridge sold its remaining assets to Red Hawk.... [HM sent the first two invoices to Cedar Ridge: Cedar Ridge paid these invoices. HM sent an invoice on August 14, 1989 and this invoice was not paid in full. Later invoices were not paid at all.] The total unpaid balance of the invoices from August, September and November amounts to $237,943.50.... In March 1990, G&A Development Corporation, the general partner of Red Hawk, contacted plaintiff to attempt to resolve the indebtedness of Cedar Ridge to HM.... [This debt was not paid.] During 1989, Red Hawk received cash receipts of at least $508,750.... G&A, and thus Red Hawk, did not establish reserves from cash receipts of the limited partnership in 1989."

ISSUE Must the limited partners return funds dispersed by the general partner?

HOLDING Yes.

REASONING "[T]he general partner was plainly obligated to follow the terms [the partnership agreement], which require the general partner to use the cash receipts to establish reasonable reserves prior to distributing those cash receipts to limited partners.... The Red Hawk Agreement of Limited Partnership fails to define the term 'reasonable reserves.' Counsel for the parties have not directed this Court to any case law or treatise defining reasonable reserves nor has this Court found any [appropriate definitions].... I find that the term 'reasonable reserves' amounts to sufficient funds, neither excessive [n]or immoderate, to cover expenses and contingent obligations known to Red Hawk or those which should have been known to Red Hawk.... Kemp specifically notes in the December 19 letter to Scutellaro that these financial burdens are worrisome given the decline already experienced by the housing market.... The tax return of Chestnut Woods shows that at the end of 1988, the assets of the project approximated $1.8 million and the liabilities approximated $1.7 million, revealing scant resources to cover the site improvements planned for the winter.... Notably, the figure calculated for the assets of Chestnut Woods is based upon the value of the unimproved land, which Red Hawk could not reasonably consider, in light of information known by Red Hawk at the time, to be a liquid source of assets for the purpose of financing the expected improvements.... I find that ... Red Hawk knew or, at the very least, should have known and should have considered in determining its contingent liabilities that the Chestnut Woods project continued to incur the ... expenses for site improvements.... [U]nder the law of partnerships, knowledge and actions of one partner are imputed to all others. Accordingly, I find that as the general partner of the Chestnut Woods project, Red Hawk is imputed to have had the knowledge that Chestnut Woods must make interest payments on its loan, in addition to the current expenses to fund the site improvements, prior to making its second distribution to limited partners.... With the unimproved land as its most significant asset, I find that

35.1 HENKELS & MCCOY, INC. v. ADOCHIO *(cont.)* 1997 U.S. Dist. LEXIS 26 (E.D. Pa. 1997)

Chestnut Woods did not have sufficient cash flow to cover expenses attributed to site improvements performed by plaintiff HM. Having found that Red Hawk had notice of the delays experienced by the Chestnut Woods project, the continued site improvements on the project by HM, and the high value and non-liquid nature of the most valued asset of Chestnut Woods, I find that Red Hawk had ample information indicating the inability of Chestnut Woods to cover its expenses. . . . [A] reasonable level of reserves from cash receipts . . . would have been at least that amount necessary to cover the expenses that Red Hawk knew would be the subject of invoices of HM and, therefore, would have prevented, under the plain terms of the partnership agreement, the distribution of money to the limited partners. . . . [T]he general partner was obligated to follow the mandate of paragraph 12(a)(iv), which required the establishment of reasonable reserves prior to distributing cash receipts to limited partners. Having found that Cedar Ridge and Red Hawk allied themselves as general partners in the Chestnut Woods project, that Cedar Ridge acted within its actual authority under the Chestnut Woods partnership agreement and that Chestnut Woods was liable on the costs incurred by Cedar Ridge in its capacity as general contractor, . . . and pursuant to the principles of agency law, Red Hawk is imputed to have had knowledge of the subcontract agreement between Cedar Ridge and HM for the benefit of Chestnut Woods, the nature and chronological progress of the work performed by HM, the amount agreed upon as payment to HM for services rendered, the timing of invoices sent by HM, and the inability of Cedar Ridge to complete payment. . . ."

BUSINESS CONSIDERATIONS What would constitute adequate reserves for a partnership developing residential property? How could a general partner develop guidelines for establishing adequate reserves?

ETHICAL CONSIDERATIONS Was it ethical for the general partner of Red Hawk to pay the funds to the general and limited partners maintaining a very small reserve? Why or why not? Is there a conflict of interest between the Chestnut Woods Partnership and the failed Timber Knoll Partnership? Why?

Rights of Third Persons Who Deal with Partnerships

When partners are dealing internally, each is aware of the rights and duties of the other partner(s). Each general partner should know the terms of the basic agreement and the limits of his or her authority. A third person who deals with the partnership, however, has no such advantage. Any nonpartner who deals with the firm must rely on *appearances*. As a result, a third person who deals with the partnership may be given certain rights by the court that are specifically denied by the basic partnership agreement.

Contracts

As noted earlier, each partner is an agent of the partnership. Thus, if a partner negotiates a contract on behalf of the partnership, that partner is negotiating as an agent. From agency law, we know that if the agent has the *apparent authority* to perform an act, the principal is bound by the act. The same rule applies here. If the partner has the apparent authority to enter the contract, the partnership is bound to honor the contract.

In many instances, the partner has the actual authority to enter the contract. If so, the partnership is obviously bound, and the partner who negotiated the contract is no more liable than the other partners.

35.1

FINANCE/MANAGEMENT

LIABILITY IN A GENERAL PARTNERSHIP

Assume that CIT is continuing to operate as a general partnership. Tom, a partner, signed a contract with a marketing consulting firm to develop a new marketing plan at a cost of $20,000. He entered this contract without consulting with the other partners in the firm, believing that the consultants he was hiring would provide a better opportunity for CIT to establish its niche in the industry. Unfortunately, when the plan is implemented, it is a disaster. Dan thinks that his father should have consulted with the family before signing the contract and asks you whether CIT and/or the other partners are liable for this contract action. What will you tell him? What is Tom's personal liability in this situation to the consulting firm and/or CIT?

BUSINESS CONSIDERATIONS Assume that a partnership does not want an individual partner to unilaterally enter into specialized service contracts for the firm. What should the partnership do to prevent such conduct?

ETHICAL CONSIDERATIONS Suppose that an individual partner *does* enter into a contract without consulting with his or her partners. Is it ethical for the firm to refuse to honor the contract because it was not discussed by the partners? Why or why not?

In some cases, the partner has the apparent authority to enter the contract but lacks the actual authority. (Recall, for example, the division of duties discussion earlier in this chapter.) Under these circumstances, the partnership must still honor the contract with the third person. But the partner who negotiated the contract will be liable to the partnership for any losses that arise because the partner exceeded his or her authority.

In still other cases, the partner does not have even apparent authority; if a contract is negotiated, the negotiating partner is personally obligated to perform, but the firm is *not* liable on the agreement.

When the court examines these agreements, the apparent authority of the partner is of overriding importance. To help in deciding the scope of authority, courts often look at the type of business the firm is conducting. If the partnership buys and sells as its primary business purpose, the court views the partnership (unofficially) as a *trading* partnership. If the primary business purpose is to provide services, the court views it (unofficially) as a *nontrading* partnership. In a trading partnership, the partners are presumed to have broad powers. In a nontrading partnership, partners are deemed to have much narrower powers. A partner in a trading partnership is presumably authorized to perform *any* management-related duties. In contrast, a partner in a nontrading business is apparently authorized to do only those things reasonably necessary to further the main business purpose of the partnership.

A third person who is dealing with a partnership for the first time needs to exercise care. The partner with whom the third person is dealing may exceed his or her authority, and the third person will find that the resulting contract is not binding on the partnership.

Borrowing in the Partnership Name

Perhaps the most important area in which the court applies the trading-versus-nontrading distinction is in the borrowing of money. In a trading partnership, the firm deals from inventory. Inventory must be purchased. Purchases require money. Thus, a partner has the apparent authority to borrow money in the firm's name.

In a nontrading partnership, the need for money is less obvious. As a result, the courts are less apt to impose liability on the firm for a loan that was made to a single partner even though that partner borrowed the money in the partnership name.

Torts and Crimes

Tortfeasor
A wrongdoer; one who commits a tort.

Again, remember that each partner is an agent for every other partner. Under agency law, when a *tort* is committed by an agent, the agent is liable as the **tortfeasor.** And the principal may also be liable, jointly and severally with the agent, under the theory of *respondeat superior.* If the injured person can establish that the partner was performing in "the course and scope of employment," the firm and each of the partners are liable for the tort. For example, assume Mary, Ned, and Oscar are partners. Ned is driving to a business meeting to represent the firm in some negotiations. On the way to the meeting, Ned runs a stop sign and hits Sam. Since Ned was on a job-related errand, all three partners are liable to Sam, as is the partnership itself.

If the tort is willful and malicious, however, the firm is normally not liable. From our previous example, assume Oscar is driving to a business meeting to represent the firm. On the way, Oscar sees Tom crossing the street. Oscar is still angry at Tom for an insult from long ago. Oscar accelerates the car and *intentionally* runs over Tom. Since the tort was willful and malicious, neither Mary nor Ned nor the firm is liable to Tom.

If the willful and malicious tort is one that furthers any business interests of the firm, the other partners may be liable. If the intentional tort is not related to the business purpose, the other partners can still be held liable, provided that they assent to or ratify the conduct. Otherwise, the other partners face no liability for intentional torts.

If a partner commits a crime, what liability do the noncriminal partners face? For most crimes, the other partners are not liable. Most crimes require a specific criminal intent. To be convicted of such a crime, a person must commit it or **aid and abet** in its commission. Unless evidence of involvement is shown, only the partner who committed the crime will be liable.

Aid and abet
To help, assist, or facilitate the commission of a crime; to promote the accomplishment of a crime.

However, some crimes can be committed *without* a specific criminal intent. Such crimes are normally *regulatory* in nature; in other words, these crimes involve violations of administrative areas rather than violations in traditional criminal areas. If one of these crimes is committed, all the partners are criminally liable.

Operation of a Corporation

The officers and the board of directors bear the responsibilities for both the day-to-day operations and the overall policies of a corporation. The management of the entity is centralized. The managers are ultimately answerable to the shareholders, the owners. Stock certificates signify the ownership interests of the shareholders. Shareholders exert only indirect control, generally through the election of directors.

Rights of the Shareholders of a Corporation

Types of Stock Owned

Shareholders exert indirect control over the corporation by virtue of their ownership of shares; the more they own, the more power they wield. Ownership is generally evidenced by a stock certificate. See Exhibits 35.1 and 35.2. A shareholder may own *common stock,* which allows the shareholder to receive dividends, to vote on corporate issues, and to receive property upon the corporation's liquidation. Or, the shareholder may own *preferred stock,* which, as its name suggests, confers priority with regard to dividends, voting, or liquidation rights. Furthermore, within the preferred stock, several classes, or series, may exist that set out different gradations of priority for each class. Under most state statutes, the articles of incorporation must spell out the preferences; such preferences generally will not be implied.

EXHIBIT 35.1 Stock Certificate (Front)

NUMBER

SHARES

ORGANIZED UNDER THE LAWS OF THE STATE OF

Authorized Capital ______________ Shares of ____________ Par Value Each

This Certifies that ____________________________ *is the owner of* ____________________________ *fully paid and non-assessable Shares of the Capital Stock of the above named Corporation transferable only on the books of the Corporation by the holder hereof in person or by duly authorized Attorney upon surrender of this Certificate properly endorsed.*

In Witness Whereof *the said Corporation has caused this Certificate to be signed by its duly authorized officer and its Corporate Seal to be hereonto affixed this* ____________ *Day of* ______________ *19* ____

SECRETARY

PRESIDENT

THOUSANDS 0 1 2 3 4 5 HUNDS TENS CENTS 1 1 1 2 2 2 3 3 3 4 4 4 5 5 5 6 6 6 7 7 7 8 8 8 9 9 9 0 0 0 SHARES

SOURCE: Courtesy of Charles Roener, Roener & Mintz, Attorneys-at-Law, South Bend, IN.

Par value
The face value assigned to a stock and printed on the stock certificate.

The most common preference right involves priority with regard to *dividends* (cash, property, or other shares that the board of directors declares as payment to shareholders). For example, preferred stockholders may receive dividends paid at a specified rate (for example, 7 percent) before any other classes of stock receive dividends. If any dividends remain after payment to the various classes of preferred and common stockholders, preferred shareholders often have *participation* rights; that is, they can take part in this further distribution of dividends rather than have their dividend rights restricted to the preferred stock dividend. In addition to dividend and participation rights, preferred shareholders receive corporate assets before any other stockholder does if the corporation is liquidated. After the debts of the corporation are paid, preferred shareholders are the first to receive the **par value** of their stocks (plus any outstanding dividends); common stockholders receive corporate assets only if sufficient assets remain to pay their stocks' par values. If there are any addi-

EXHIBIT 35.2 Stock Certificate (Back)

CERTIFICATE

FOR

SHARES

OF

Issued to

Dated

NOTICE THE SIGNATURE OF THIS ASSIGNMENT MUST CORRESPOND WITH THE NAME AS WRITTEN UPON THE FACE OF THE CERTIFICATE IN EVERY PARTICULAR, WITHOUT ALTERATION OR ENLARGEMENT OR ANY CHANGE WHATEVER.

For Value Received, ______ hereby sell, assign and transfer unto ______

______ Shares represented by the within Certificate, and do hereby irrevocably constitute and appoint

______ Attorney to transfer the said Shares on the books of the within named Corporation with full power of substitution in the premises.

Dated ______ 19__

In presence of

______

SOURCE: Courtesy of Charles Roener, Roener & Mintz, Attorneys-at-Law, South Bend, IN.

tional assets after payment to the common stockholders, the preferred and common shareholders normally share this balance in proportion to the shares that each holds individually. Preferred shareholders also may enjoy *conversion* rights (the option to change preferred stock into common stock or corporate bonds) and/or *redemption* rights (the enforced repurchase of shares by the corporation in certain authorized circumstances). These features are summarized in Exhibit 35.3.

Shareholders' Meetings

Notice. In general, shareholders' meetings may not occur unless the corporation has sent written notice of the meeting to all shareholders of record. Statutory and bylaw provisions often spell out the procedures for giving notice. Such notice ordinarily contains the time, date, and place of the meeting, as well as a statement of the purpose of the meeting. Most statutes require at least ten days' notice before a meeting can legitimately be conducted, but shareholders can expressly waive this requirement in writing before or after the meeting, or they can impliedly waive it by not protesting the lack of notice.

EXHIBIT 35.3 Stock Characteristics

Type of stock	Characteristics
Common	Basic shares issued by a corporation; they generally have a lower priority for dividends and distribution of assets upon dissolution
Preferred	Shares that include special rights to dividends and/or distribution of assets upon dissolution
Cumulative Preferred	Shares that include the right to a specified dividend; any unpaid dividends to these shareholders must be paid before dividends can be paid on the common stock
Convertible Preferred	Shares that include the shareholder's right to convert them into another type of stock; generally they are convertible into common stock or corporate bonds
Redeemable Preferred	Shares that the corporation can repurchase according to the terms of the redemption agreement

Quorum. Shareholder meetings cannot take place in the absence of a quorum. State statutes and corporate bylaws or articles usually state the percentage of *outstanding shares,* or shares entitled to vote, that constitutes a quorum. A majority of such votes is usually necessary; yet the Model Business Corporation Act sanctions articles that set the quorum requirement at a mere one-third of all outstanding shares.[16] *Dissident shareholders* (those who disagree with the actions of management) may prevent a quorum by not attending meetings; but the law remains unsettled as to whether a subsequent walkout of dissident shareholders, once a quorum is present, invalidates the meeting.

Election and Removal of Directors. One of the foremost powers held by shareholders is their capacity to elect and remove directors. Although the articles of incorporation usually designate the people who are to serve as the initial directors, these directors may serve only until the first annual meeting. At that time, the shareholders may elect some (or all) of them to the board of directors. If vacancies occur on the board because of deaths or resignations, the shareholders normally vote to fill these vacancies. The articles of incorporation or bylaws, however, may permit the directors to fill these posts. Directors usually serve staggered terms. This means that only a certain proportion of directors (for example, one-third) will be up for reelection at any given meeting. Such staggered terms ensure continuity of leadership on the board. In recent years, there has been a trend toward adding **outsiders** to the board of directors.

Outsiders
Directors who are not shareholders or officers.

Shareholders have *inherent* power (that is, power regardless of the articles or bylaws) to remove a director for cause. Previous cases have upheld the exercise of such rights when directors have engaged in embezzlement or other misconduct, failed to live up to their duties to the corporation, or undertaken unauthorized acts. The director, of course, may appeal his or her removal to a court of law. Statutes, articles of incorporation, and bylaws may also allow removal without cause.

Amendment of the Bylaws. Bylaws are provisions intended to regulate the corporation and its management. To be valid, bylaws must comply with state incorporation statutes and the articles of incorporation. Shareholders retain inherent power to amend (or repeal) bylaws. State law generally mandates the proportion of outstanding shares needed to approve an amendment.

Voting. The voting rights exercised by shareholders at meetings allow them *indirect control* of the corporation and the board of directors. All shareholders of record as of the date of the shareholders' meeting ordinarily appear on the voting list and can vote. Shareholders can either be present at the meeting and vote in person, or they can assign their voting rights to others, who then vote their shares for them by **proxy.** (Proxy can be used to designate both the person or the document used to appoint someone to act in a representative capacity as a proxy.) If a distant shareholder in a public-issue corporation does not want to participate personally in the meeting, he or she can sign a document called a proxy, giving the proxy holder authority to act as his or her agent. Exhibit 35.4 shows the front of a proxy and Exhibit 35.5 shows the back.

Proxy
A person appointed and designated to act for another, especially at a public meeting.

Whoever controls large blocs of proxies in a public-issue corporation may, in effect, dictate the outcome of the election. For this reason, management (and sometimes dissident stockholders) in such corporations may solicit proxy votes in order to consolidate voting power. Not surprisingly, then, vicious proxy fights have

EXHIBIT 35.4 Proxy (Front)

ST. JOSEPH BANCORPORATION, INC.
COMMON STOCK PROXY SOLICITED ON BEHALF OF THE BOARD OF DIRECTORS

The undersigned Shareholder of ST. JOSEPH BANCORPORATION, INC., South Bend, Indiana, does hereby nominate, constitute and appoint Richard A. Rosenthal, Arthur H. McElwee, Jr., or either of them (with full power to act alone), my true and lawful attorney(s) and proxy(ies), with full power of substitution, for me and my name, place and stead to vote all of the shares of common stock of said Bancorporation, standing in my name on its books, at the annual meeting of its shareholders to be held in the Center for Continuing Education at the University of Notre Dame, on April 19, 1983 at 7:30 o'clock p.m., and at any adjournment thereof, upon all subjects that may properly come before the meeting including the matter described in the proxy statement furnished herewith, subject to any directions indicated below, with all powers the undersigned would possess if personally present.

ELECTION OF DIRECTORS—Frederick K. Baer, Roy L. Beck, Edwin S. Ehlers, Jack E. Ellis, James W. Frick, Gerald Hammes, V. Robert Helper, Gerald A. Hickey, William P. Johnson, Jr., Gerald A. Kamm, Edward A. Mangone, Donald A. Manion, Arthur H. McElwee, Jr., Godfrey V. Miholich, Joseph C. Miller, Joseph H. Nash, Robert W. O'Connor, Samuel Raitzin, Richard A. Rosenthal, Frank E. Sullivan and Phillip A. Traub.

☐ VOTE FOR all nominees listed above, except vote withheld from (to withhold authority to vote for any individual nominee, write in the name on the line below):

____

☐ VOTE WITHHELD from all nominees.

(continued on reverse side)

SOURCE: Courtesy of KeyBank, National Association, South Bend, IN.

EXHIBIT 35.5 Proxy (Back)

IF NO DIRECTIONS ARE GIVEN, THE PROXIES WILL VOTE FOR THE ELECTION OF ALL LISTED NOMINEES. THE BOARD OF DIRECTORS RECOMMENDS A VOTE "FOR" ALL NOMINEES LISTED ON THE REVERSE SIDE. THE UNDERSIGNED HEREBY REVOKES ANY PROXY HERETOFORE GIVEN IN RESPECT OF THE SAME SHARES OF STOCK.

Dated: ______________________________ ,1983 ______________________________ (L.S.)

______________________________ (L.S.)

Please sign your name in the same manner as it appears on your stock certificate. When signing for a corporation or partnership or as agent, attorney or fiduciary, please state your full title as such. If your stock stands in the names of two or more persons, it is necessary that each sign this Proxy.

PLEASE DATE, SIGN AND MAIL THIS PROXY PROMPTLY IN THE ENCLOSED ENVELOPE.

SOURCE: Courtesy of KeyBank, National Association, South Bend, IN.

occurred at various times in U.S. corporate history. Because of these high stakes and the accompanying possibilities for abuse, federal law now ensures that proxy solicitations are carried out fairly. Within the corporation, impartial parties called inspectors, judges, or tellers oversee the election to ensure fairness (see Chapter 38).

In most corporate matters, a shareholder can cast one vote for each share held. This is called *straight voting.* Unless the voting involves an extraordinary corporate matter (such as dissolution, merger, amendment of the articles of incorporation, or sale of substantially all the assets), the decision made by a majority generally controls. Thus, votes of more than 50 percent for any ordinary corporate matter usually become binding on the corporation. In extraordinary matters, statutes may require a higher proportion (for example, two-thirds) of votes for the action taken to be legally binding.

To offset shareholders who own large blocs of votes and who may therefore be able to control appreciably the outcomes of elections, most state statutes today either permit or require *cumulative voting.* Cumulative voting applies only to the election of directors and is a method for ensuring some minority representation on the board.

The following example illustrates the difference between straight and cumulative voting. Assume that at the annual shareholders' meeting, three directors will be elected from a field of six candidates—U, V, W, X, Y, and Z. Under straight voting, shareholder A, who owns 100 shares, can cast 100 votes for each of three directors, say U, V, and W. If, instead, cumulative voting is used, A can cast 300 votes for U or can divide 300 votes among any three candidates in any proportion he or she wishes (e.g., 150 for U, 100 for V, and 50 for Y). In this fashion, A's votes accumulate—hence, the term cumulative voting. The ability of a minority shareholder to have an impact on the election of directors thus becomes more formidable under cumulative voting than under straight voting.

To dilute any advantage that the minority might gain through cumulative voting, management may stagger the terms of directors, reduce or enlarge the size of the board, or remove directors elected by the minority. To counter such steps, lawmakers in many jurisdictions have passed statutory provisions that protect cumulative voting rights by making such steps illegal or by using statutorily enacted formulas that safeguard the beneficial effects of cumulative voting.

Voting trusts, like proxies and cumulative voting, represent devices used to consolidate votes for control. A shareholder can create a voting trust by transferring to **trustees** the shares he or she owns. Once the shareholder has entered into such a trust, the shareholder has no right to vote the shares until the trust terminates. The trustees issue a *voting trust certificate* to the shareholder to indicate that the shareholder retains all rights incidental to share ownership except voting. In contrast to proxies, which are generally revocable, voting trusts are normally irrevocable. State statutes, however, usually limit the duration of voting trusts to a specified time period, such as ten years (with possible extensions).

Trustees
Persons in whom a power is vested under an express or implied agreement in order to exercise the power for the benefit of another.

Pooling agreements are similar to voting trusts. In such agreements, shareholders agree to vote the shares each owns in a specified way. Both voting trusts and pooling agreements remain valid and enforceable as long as they do not, in effect, preempt the directors' managerial functions. This could happen if the shareholders who enter into these arrangements are also directors. For example, it is legal for the shareholders to agree through voting trusts or pooling agreements to vote for director A at the annual meeting's election of directors (even if director A is also one of the shareholders who enters into the arrangement). If the shareholders' agreements involve their pledging to bring about the dismissal of the current chief executive officer of the corporation, however, voting trusts or pooling arrangements to this effect normally will be unenforceable. Why? Selection of officers is ordinarily a function of the directors.

Shareholders of close corporations probably utilize voting trusts and pooling arrangements more than their counterparts in publicly held corporations. Modern statutes recognize that close corporations are more similar to partnerships than are most other corporate entities. Consequently, some states will enforce agreements that treat shareholders as if they were directors, when all the shareholders are parties to the agreement. Such statutory developments illustrate the law's ability to change whenever reality dictates such modifications.

Dividends

Most shareholders buy shares in for-profit, public-issue corporations primarily to receive dividends. Such shareholders normally care less about the control functions than about the financial aspects of their shares—namely, dividends. Thus far, we have spoken of a *right* to receive dividends, but that constitutes a very loose use of the term. Actually, there is no absolute right to receive dividends. The power to declare dividends resides with the board of directors. In the absence of demonstrated bad faith on the directors' part, shareholders cannot compel the directors to declare dividends. The directors alone decide, first, *if* dividends will be distributed. If so, they also determine the timing, type, and amount of the dividend.

Of course, shareholders hope to receive the financial profits represented by dividends. *Cash dividends* are the most common type. However, the dividend may also take the form of *property* or *stocks.*

If cash dividends are involved, the directors must make certain that the dividends will be paid from a *lawful source.* In general, statutes limit the sources of dividends to *current net profits* (those earned in the preceding accounting period) or *earned surplus* (the sum of the net profits retained by the corporation during all previous years of existence). Any declaration of dividends that will impair the corporation's *original capital structure* (the number of shares originally issued times their stated value) is illegal and may subject the directors and shareholders to personal liability. Similarly, payment of dividends during the corporation's insolvency or any payment that will bring about insolvency or financial difficulties is illegal.

As noted earlier, preferred stockholders enjoy priority with regard to the distribution of dividends. They also receive protection from the rules that limit the source of dividends because directors normally cannot declare dividends if the declaration will thereby jeopardize the **liquidation preferences** of the preferred shareholders. Once a dividend is lawfully declared, preferred stockholders receive their dividends first. Common stockholders receive dividends only if adequate funds remain after the preferred stockholders have been paid. Sometimes preferred stockholders have *participating* preferred stock. This means they not only receive their original dividend but also share (or participate) with the common stockholders in any dividends that are paid after the preferred stockholders have received their original dividends. In other words, participating preferred stockholders may be able to dip into the dividend fund twice. Usually, however, preferred stock is nonparticipating.

Liquidation preferences
Priorities given to creditors and owners when the enterprise is terminated and the assets are distributed.

We should note one last complexity in declaring preferred dividends. Preferred dividends may be *cumulative,* which means that the sum (or accumulation) of all preferred dividends that were not paid in a given year must be paid before common shareholders receive any dividends. In contrast, in *noncumulative* preferred dividends, the preferred stockholder receives only the dividend preferences for the *current accounting period;* and the common stockholders then receive their dividends should any funds remain. Under this type of preference, the preferred shareholders lose all dividends for any years in which the directors have chosen not to declare a dividend.

Preemptive Stock Rights

Sometimes it is necessary for a corporation to increase its capital by issuing new shares. Since this is an extraordinary matter involving amendment of the articles of incorporation (the original number of shares and their par value will change with this new capitalization), shareholders must vote on the issuance of these new shares. A shareholder's interest in this matter extends beyond voting rights. For example, assume Bonnie owns 10 shares of Samp Corporation. Samp's original capitalization involved 100 shares sold at $100 each ($10,000 stated capital). At that time, Bonnie owned 10 percent of Samp Corporation (10 shares/100 total shares). If Samp issues another 100 shares as a result of the amending of the articles, Bonnie then will own 5 percent of the corporation (10 shares/200 total shares). As a result of this new capitalization, her voting power will decrease proportionately; and so will her right to receive a higher amount of dividends and a higher proportion of corporate assets in the event of liquidation.

Early on, common law courts, realizing the inherent unfairness of this sequence of events, began to protect the Bonnies of the corporate world by a doctrine called *preemptive rights.* These courts promoted the notion that the right of first refusal inheres in stock ownership; hence, before the corporation can sell to anyone else, it must offer to sell to Bonnie the number of shares that will restore her total share of ownership to the proportion she held before this new issuance. Bonnie, in effect, can preempt the rights of other would-be purchasers of the stock because she can purchase before they have the chance to do so. Nevertheless, once the corporation notifies Bonnie of her preemptive rights, she has a limited time to exercise them. If she does not take advantage of the offer, she waives her rights of preemption.

Preemptive rights normally apply only to shares issued for cash and will not apply to shares issued in exchange for property (such as a commercial building) or services (such as shares issued to lure a chief executive officer to Samp), or to shares issued as share dividends, or to treasury stock (stock originally issued but subsequently reacquired by the corporation). In this last situation, there is no new issue and, hence, no reduction in Bonnie's proportionate interest in Samp Corporation. In the two prior situations, preemptive rights may cripple the corporation's financing efforts and obstruct the corporation's legitimate, profit-maximizing activities, such as acquiring property and recruiting top-flight executives. Because of the possible frustration of these worthwhile aims, courts and statutes alike deny Bonnie's preemptive rights, despite the dilution of her proportional ownership interests. In addition, judicial and statutory treatment of Bonnie's preemptive rights might be different if Samp is a publicly held (as opposed to a close) corporation.

Inspection of Corporate Books and Records

The rights of shareholders to inspect corporate records arise from both common law doctrines and express statutory provisions. In general, shareholders have access to such corporate materials as stockholder lists; minutes of shareholders' meetings; board or officers' meetings; financial records, such as books of account or other periodic summaries; and business documents, including tax returns, contracts, and office correspondence or memoranda.

At common law, inspection rights were qualified (rather than absolute) because shareholders needed to demonstrate that the reason for inspection involved a "proper purpose"; that is, the motivation for the inspection related to his or her status as a shareholder. Requests that seek shareholder lists to communicate with shareholders about corporate matters or attempt to examine corporate financial records to determine the value of shares, the propriety of dividends, or possible mismanagement ordinarily qualify as proper purposes. On the other hand, shareholder requests that ask for information to learn trade secrets for the benefit of the corporation's competitors or to bring *strike suits* (those without any real merit) in order to impede the management of the corporation normally will constitute improper purposes. Assuming the inspection is for a proper purpose, the shareholder generally can employ attorneys, accountants, and other personnel to aid in examining records, making copies or summaries, and the like.

Most statutes similarly require a showing of proper purpose; but once the shareholder has alleged a proper purpose, the burden of proof shifts to the corporation to show an improper purpose on the shareholder's part. Sometimes statutes change the burden of proof or the party who has the burden, depending on the type of record being requested. Statutes may also restrict inspection rights only to certain shareholders (for example, those who have held their shares for at least six months or who own at least 5 percent of the outstanding shares). These statutory restrictions, however, do not eliminate the shareholder's common law inspection rights. But, as mentioned, the shareholder, not the corporation, has the burden of proving proper purpose under these common law doctrines.

Federal securities law and state statutes that mandate annual disclosure of profits and losses, officer compensation, and so on have made inspection rights somewhat

Beneficial owner
One who does not have title to the property but who has rights in the property; the equitable, as opposed to the legal, owner of the property.

less important. The information made available to the shareholder under these statutes encompasses the type of information that shareholders in the past could obtain only by exercising their rights of inspection.

Sadler v. *NCR Corporation* illustrates a number of these concepts involving the right of inspection. As you read it, consider whether you think the agreement between the Sadlers and AT&T is ethical.

35.2 SADLER v. NCR CORPORATION

928 F.2d 48 (2d Cir. 1991)

FACTS NCR Corporation, a large computer company, maintains at least eight offices in New York and conducts substantial business there. NCR has 75,000 shareholders. AT&T is a New York corporation. AT&T became a **beneficial owner** of 100 shares of NCR stock on 21 November 1990. The Sadlers are New York residents who own more than 6,000 shares of NCR stock and were record holders of NCR stock for more than six months prior to this lawsuit. On 6 December 1990, AT&T began a tender offer for the shares of NCR, offering to purchase all the common stock of NCR for $90 per share. In compliance with Rule 14(d)-5 of the Securities and Exchange Act, NCR mailed the offer to purchase to all NCR stockholders. The NCR board rejected the tender offer and refused to remove a **poison pill** shareholders' rights plan, which presented and continues to present an obstacle to a hostile tender offer. AT&T solicited NCR shareholders to convene a special meeting of stockholders to replace a majority of the NCR directors, so that this barrier to the tender offer could be removed. NCR subsequently scheduled a special meeting for 28 March 1991, the date selected for its annual meeting. AT&T and the Sadlers, acting at AT&T's request, sought from NCR a stockholder list and related materials to facilitate communication with owners of NCR shares because it needed 80 percent of all outstanding shares in order to replace the board at the special meeting. AT&T also sought a magnetic computer tape of the list and daily transfer sheets showing changes in shareholders from the date of demand to the date of the meeting. Finally, AT&T sought two other lists, a CEDE list and a NOBO list. A *CEDE list* identifies the brokerage firms and other record owners who have bought shares in a street name for their customers and who have placed those shares in the custody of depository firms, such as Depository Trust Co.; these shares are reflected in the corporation's records only under the names of the nominees used by such depository firms. A *NOBO list* (nonobjecting beneficial owners) contains the names of those owning beneficial interests in the shares of a corporation who have given consent to the disclosure of their identities. The Securities and Exchange Commission requires brokers and other record holders of stock in a street name to compile a NOBO list at a corporation's request. NCR refused to produce the requested materials. The Sadlers and AT&T sued, relying on § 1315 of the New York Business Corporation Law. NCR argued that the Sadlers were not qualified under § 1315 to obtain NCR's shareholder list and that the NOBO list was not producible under § 1315 because it was not then in existence and required compilation.

ISSUES Do the Sadlers qualify to inspect NCR's shareholder list? Can a court require NCR to compile a NOBO list?

HOLDINGS Yes, to both questions.

REASONING The Sadler's agreement with AT&T was proper, particularly since nothing in the agreement created the risk of using the statute for an improper purpose or in bad faith. The Sadlers are residents of New York and have owned NCR stock for six months prior to their demand. The corporation whose stockholder list they seek does business in New York. Moreover, the fact that the Sadlers had entered into an agreement with AT&T would not disqualify the Sadlers from invoking § 1315. Though that arrangement gave AT&T considerable control over the demand, particularly the right reasonably to refuse settlement of the demand or any litigation arising from it, the Sadlers had agreed to that control in exchange for AT&T's assurance that they would incur no financial exposure. Since New York wishes to accord its residents the rights specified in § 1315, it is not likely to impose any restrictions on their exercise of that right. The only restrictions are those specified in the statute and those necessary to prevent the statute from being used in bad faith. Nothing in the arrangement between the Sadlers and AT&T creates a risk of using the statute for an improper purpose or in bad faith. The demanding stockholder is entitled to turn the list over to others involved in a proxy contest, and he or she may make reasonable arrangements to avoid his or her own financial exposure. Whether New York law entitled the Sadlers to require NCR to assemble a NOBO list presented a more substantial question. The parties agreed that § 1315 applied to NOBO lists in a corporation's possession; but at the

35.2 SADLER v. NCR CORPORATION *(cont.)* 928 F.2d 48 (2d Cir. 1991)

time of the demand, NCR did not have a NOBO list in its possession. A corporation can obtain a NOBO list, however, normally within ten days, by requesting compilation of the list by firms that offer data-processing services for this task. As to both lists, the underlying data exists in discrete records readily available to be compiled into an aggregate list. Both lists facilitate direct communication with stockholders. In the case of the NOBO list, those beneficial owners have indicated no objection to disclosure of their names and addresses. Hence, New York law applies § 1315 to permit a qualifying shareholder to require the compilation and production of such a list. Even if the statute might not require compilation of NOBO lists routinely, compilation was properly ordered in this case.

BUSINESS CONSIDERATIONS Why would a business object to having stockholders inspect corporate books and records? What public policy considerations favor allowing stockholders to inspect the books and records of the corporation?

ETHICAL CONSIDERATIONS Is it ethical for a business considering a hostile takeover action to use stockholders of the target company in order to gain access to records and/or data that the firm would not otherwise be able to obtain? Is it ethical for the target company to deny information to a firm planning a takeover effort?

Transfer of Shares

Poison pill
Any strategy adopted by the directors of a target firm in order to decrease their firm's attractiveness to an acquiring firm during an attempted hostile takeover.

As discussed earlier, ownership of share (stock) certificates signifies ownership of a portion of the corporate entity. Thus, these shares are the shareholder's property. Shareholders, like other owners of property, generally can transfer their shares to someone else (by gift or sale). A transfer of shares generally occurs through endorsement and delivery of the stock certificate in conjunction with a surrender of the certificate for subsequent reissue to the new owner by the corporation's secretary or, in a large corporation, by its transfer agent, as Exhibit 35.6 illustrates. Stock exchange rules regulate the conduct of transfer agents, who are professionals who help the corporate secretary with the myriad details attendant on large-scale transfers of stocks.

Transfers of stock in these situations, including the cumbersomeness of actual physical transfers of stock certificates, cause numerous administrative headaches. As a result, present-day techniques, such as a brokerage firm's holding title to stock through bookkeeping entries rather than actual transfers of certificates, will likely lead to the abolition of stock certificates and their replacement by computer printouts.

Generally, the right to transfer stock remains unfettered. Restrictions placed on the stock itself, however, may limit this right of transferability. It is easy to understand why these restrictions may be advisable. Such restrictions commonly occur in close corporations. We have already discussed the fact that close corporations are like partnerships in that the controlling shareholders actively take part in the day-to-day management of the corporation. Consequently, shareholders in close corporations often attempt to preserve their control over the affairs of the corporation through voting trusts and pooling arrangements. Such attempts at consolidation of power will be meaningless without restrictions on the stock's transferability.

Courts try to balance the legitimate interests of the shareholders in limiting the corporation to a few congenial shareholders and the right of a shareholder to transfer his or her property. In our legal system, this right of **alienation** is considered to be inherent in the ownership of property. A right of first refusal, where the shareholder who wishes to sell must first offer his or her shares to the corporation or to the other

Alienation
The transfer of ownership to another.

EXHIBIT **35.6** Stock Certificate Record of Transfer

PASTE CANCELLED CERTIFICATE IN THIS SPACE

Certificate No. ____________ *For* ____________ *Shares*

Dated ____________ 19__

Issued to ____________

IF NOT AN ORIGINAL ISSUE SHOW DETAILS OF TRANFER BELOW

Transferred from	Original Certificate No.	Certificate Date	No. of Origl. Shares	No. of Shrs. Transf'd.

IF THIS CERTIFICATE IS SURRENDERED FOR TRANFER SHOW DETAILS

New Certificate Issued to	No. of New Certificate		No. of Shares Tranferred	

Received this Certificate ____________ 19__

Surrendered this Certificate ____________ 19__

SOURCE: Courtesy of Charles Roener, Roener & Mintz, Attorneys-at-Law, South Bend, IN.

shareholders, is enforceable as a valid restriction on transfer because it is a reasonable restraint on alienation. In contrast, a restriction that states that "these shares are non-transferable" will probably be unreasonable and, therefore, unenforceable.

It follows that even a reasonable restriction, such as "future sale or disposition of these shares shall take place in accordance with the shareholder agreement that controls them; and sale of them cannot take place until the holder of them offers them to the corporation or to each other shareholder, on the same terms" must appear conspicuously on the stock certificate for the restriction to be valid. Such conspicuous notice is meant to protect any subsequent purchaser of the shares by informing him or her of the restricted nature of the stock. If this notice of restriction on transfer is missing, the purchaser will not have to abide by the restriction unless he or she otherwise has notice of the restriction. If the restriction is reasonable and appears on the face of the stock certificate, however, the corporation can refuse to transfer the shares to the purchaser. The purchaser's remedy involves forcing the seller to return the money paid to the seller for the shares.

If the transfer satisfies all legal requirements, including the applicable provisions of Article 8 of the UCC and state securities laws, the purchaser (transferee) pays the price asked and the shareholder (transferor) then endorses and delivers the stock to the purchaser. The corporation, when notified, must register the transfer and change corporate records to denote the new ownership in order to guarantee the new owner the rights incidental to stock ownership in the corporation.

LIABILITIES OF SHAREHOLDERS

As we learned in Chapter 34, one of the most significant advantages of the corporation as a type of business association is the limited liability afforded to shareholders. In other words, the shareholders risk only their investment. Except for situations in which courts can disregard the corporate entity, shareholders normally do not become personally liable for corporate debts. In this section, we will look at some other circumstances that may cause a shareholder to be personally liable for obligations of the corporation.

Watered Stock

At the time of the formation of the corporation, the articles of incorporation spell out the *capital structure* of the corporation. In brief, the money to operate the corporation initially results from the issuance of securities to investors. The authorization for such securities ordinarily occurs early in the process of the corporation's formation, probably by board action at the organizational meeting.

The consideration the corporation receives for these shares constitutes the stated capital of the corporation. The board of directors establishes a fixed value of each share of such capital stock (for example, $10 per share). This is called *par value stock.* The corporation may also issue *no–par value stock,* which has no fixed value but may be sold at whatever price the directors deem reasonable (called *stated value*). No–par value shares permit a corporation to issue stock in return for corporate assets that currently are worth little but have the possibility of high, though speculative, returns (such as corporate assets in the form of high-technology developments).

If no statutory provisions to the contrary exist, the corporation may issue shares in exchange for any lawful consideration, including cash received, property received, or services actually rendered. Just as the board of directors generally sets the price of the shares, it also normally fixes the value of the property received or services rendered. As long as the board makes these decisions in good faith and in the absence of fraud, courts will not impose legal liability on the directors for these decisions.

However, the shareholder who receives shares of a corporation that are issued as fully paid when, in fact, the full par value has not been paid by the purchaser owns *watered stock.* The shareholder is personally liable for the deficiency, that is, "the water." For example, if a shareholder pays $8 per share and the par value or stated value is $10 per share, the shareholder is liable to the corporation for $2 per share.

Watered-stock problems normally arise in situations in which services have been rendered in exchange for stock. For example, if CIT incorporates and issues $4,000 worth of its shares in exchange for Ted making a high-technology videophone and the videophone is later found to be worth $2,000, Ted will be liable for $2,000 worth of watered stock. Usually Ted's liability is to the corporation, but some states will allow corporate creditors to impose liability on Ted if CIT becomes insolvent and unable to meet its obligations as they come due. In some jurisdictions, such creditors can hold shareholders liable for the amounts by which their shares are watered. A later purchaser from Ted normally will not be liable for watered stock, however, because the rule regarding watered stock applies only to initial corporate issuances and purchases of stock, rather than to later transfers of the stock.

The use of no–par value stock and the impact of federal and state securities regulation have greatly reduced the incidence of suits alleging liability for watered stock. Still, shareholders should be aware of this legal doctrine.

Stock Subscriptions

Stock subscriptions are agreements by investors ("subscribers") to purchase shares in a corporation. The law views a subscription as an offer, and most state statutes make subscriptions irrevocable for a certain period unless the subscription itself provides otherwise. A subscriber may enter into such agreements either before or after the corporation's formation. If the stock subscription occurs before the corporation's formation (usually as a result of promoters' activities), some states treat the subscription as an offer that is automatically accepted by the corporation upon its formation, creating a valid contract. Other states, however, require formal acceptance of the subscription/offer before a valid contract between the subscriber and the corporation arises.

Because an accepted stock subscription constitutes a contract, various types of liabilities arise on the breach of the subscription contract. Thus, the corporation can sue the subscriber for the subscription price if the subscriber refuses to pay the agreed price. In some cases, creditors of a corporation that has become insolvent may force the subscriber to pay the amount owed on the subscription. By the same token, the subscriber can sue the corporation if the corporation refuses to issue the shares that are the object of the subscription. As in the case of watered stock, securities laws have reduced the incidence of shareholder liability for stock subscriptions.

Illegal Dividends

We noted earlier that cash dividends must be paid from a lawful source. Any declaration of dividends that will impair the original capital structure of the corporation is illegal and may subject both the directors and the shareholders to personal liability. Shareholders who receive an illegal dividend are absolutely liable for its return if the corporation is insolvent at the time the dividend is paid. In such cases, the corporation's creditors can sue the shareholders directly for the amount of the illegal dividend. If the corporation is solvent when an illegal distribution takes place and remains solvent even after it, however, only shareholders who knew the dividend was illegal (from an improper source, for example) must repay the dividend to the corporation. Innocent shareholders can retain the dividends. Directors who have been held liable for distributing illegal dividends can force shareholders who knew of the illegal dividends to pay the amounts received back to the directors. The shareholders and directors thus share liability in such circumstances.

Dissolution

Dissolution signals the legal termination of the corporation's existence. It may occur voluntarily (by actions of the incorporators or shareholders), or involuntarily (by court actions initiated by the state or a shareholder). It is important to note that majority (or controlling) shareholders may incur liability if the purpose of the dissolution is to freeze out minority stockholders and to strip them of rights or profits they would otherwise enjoy. The basis of this liability is that controlling shareholders owe fiduciary duties to minority shareholders. Generally speaking, controlling shareholders must exert control for the benefit of all shareholders, not just for themselves. Dissolutions that prejudice minority shareholders' interests while greatly enhancing majority shareholders' interests may subject the latter to personal liability if minority shareholders sue.

In the *Peñasquitos* v. *Superior Court (Barbee)* case, the court imposed liability for claims that arose after the dissolution of the two corporations involved, despite the disadvantage to the former shareholders who must pay any judgment.

35.3 PEÑASQUITOS v. SUPERIOR COURT (BARBEE) — 812 P.2d 154 (Cal. 1991)

FACTS Several owners of single-family homes in San Diego County brought suit on a variety of legal theories against Peñasquitos, Inc., and Crow Pacific Development Corporation to recover damages for construction defects. Crow Pacific had built the homes on lots graded and prepared by Peñasquitos; the homes were all located within a subdivision commonly known as Peñasquitos Bluffs, Unit No. 4. Unfortunately, both corporations had dissolved before the homeowners discovered the construction defects. When the homeowners brought suit against the corporations, each corporation argued that it could not be sued because it had dissolved.

ISSUE Can parties sue dissolved corporations on claims that arose after the dissolutions?

HOLDING Yes.

REASONING California's statutory scheme reveals a legislative intent to permit suits against dissolved corporations for damages that occur or are discovered after dissolution. The common law treated the dissolution of a corporation like the death of a natural person: Once it had dissolved, a corporation ceased to exist and could not sue or be sued. However, California abandoned the common law rule and replaced it with a statute in 1929. This statutory scheme has endured with relatively few changes. Section 1905 (b) now provides that when the certificate of dissolution is filed, "the corporate existence shall *cease, except for the purpose of further winding up if needed*" (emphasis added). Section 2010 (a) further explains the purposes for which the corporate existence continues after dissolution: "A corporation which is dissolved nevertheless continues to exist for the purpose of winding up its affairs, prosecuting and defending actions by or against it and enabling it to collect and *discharge obligations,* dispose of and convey its property and collect and divide its assets, but not for the purpose of continuing business except so far as necessary for the winding up thereof" (emphasis added). Section 2010 permits parties to sue dissolved corporations. A court must determine whether these postdissolution actions are limited to those brought on predissolution claims, that is, claims that arose before the corporation filed its notice of dissolution. On its face, § 2010 draws no distinction between pre- and postdissolution claims. This is particularly significant in view of the language of § 2011 (9a), which limits postdissolution actions against the dissolved corporation's shareholders to those on causes of action "arising prior to [the corporation's] dissolution." The legislature's use of this restrictive language in the provision governing suits against shareholders, while omitting it from the provision governing suits against the dissolved corporations themselves, strongly implies that the legislature did not intend to restrict suits against dissolved corporations to those on predissolution claims.

In addition, the drafters of the 1984 Revised Model Business Corporation Act have abandoned the distinction drawn in earlier versions between pre- and postdissolution causes of action. However, the plaintiff must file the action within five years after the date of publication of the notice of dissolution.

BUSINESS CONSIDERATIONS What can the stockholders of a corporation do to protect themselves from lawsuits filed against them as individuals if the corporation in which they invested ceases to exist?

ETHICAL CONSIDERATIONS Is it ethical for a creditor who extended credit to a corporation to sue the individual stockholders personally upon dissolution of the corporation, knowing that the loan was made to the corporate entity and that the stockholders are generally entitled to limited liability?

RIGHTS AND DUTIES OF THE MANAGERS OF A CORPORATION

Board of Directors

The right to manage the affairs of the corporation falls squarely on the board of directors. Although shareholders, the ultimate owners of the corporation, retain the power to elect and remove directors, this prerogative does not give shareholders a direct voice in management. Nor can shareholders compel the board to take any action. The directors are not agents of the shareholders; they owe loyalty primarily to the corporation. As we discussed, however, different rules may apply if the corporation is a close corporation.

Number and Qualifications. The articles of incorporation usually name the initial directors. Older statutes required at least three directors, but the modern trend—due, no doubt, in part to the increased numbers of close corporations—is to permit as few as one or two directors. To avoid deadlocks, the articles or bylaws usually authorize an uneven number of directors.

Unless otherwise provided in the relevant statutes, articles, or bylaws, directors need not be either shareholders in the corporation or residents of the state where the corporation has its principal place of business. Where qualifications are necessary, the election of unqualified persons is voidable, not void. In other words, until the corporation employs proper proceedings to displace the unqualified directors, the law considers them de facto directors (that is, directors in fact if not in law). Consequently, most of their acts as directors are effective; and de facto directors must live up to the same corporate duties and standards as do qualified directors. Directors generally have the right to appoint interim replacements on the board when vacancies arise owing to the death, resignation, or incapacity of a director.

Term of Office. Directors serve for the time specified in state statutes, unless the articles or bylaws limit the term to a shorter period. Directors usually serve for one year unless the corporation has set up a *classified board* (a board divided into classes of directors with staggered election dates). Directors continue to hold office until the shareholders elect their successors and the latter take office. Thus, sitting directors do not automatically drop off the board at the end of their terms.

Sometimes shareholders remove directors before their terms on the board end. Shareholders may remove directors for cause (which was the only basis for removal at common law). Modern statutes relax this standard by permitting a majority of shareholders to remove directors at any time during their terms without cause. In those jurisdictions that require cumulative voting, however, directors cannot be removed if the number of votes cast against the removal would have been sufficient to elect those directors to the board. In most jurisdictions, directors who have been removed can seek court review of such dismissals to determine if the proper procedures were followed.

Meetings. Traditionally, the board could validly exercise its powers only when acting collectively, not individually. The law emphasized the value of decision making arrived at through collective debate, deliberation, and judgment. For this reason, statutes set out rules permitting the board to act only when it was formally convened. Moreover, directors traditionally had to be present to vote (they could not vote by proxy or send substitutes to deliberate for them) and could do so only at a duly announced and formalized meeting.

Today, most modern statutes dispense with the formalities previously required of directors' meetings. Thus, even though the bylaws usually fix the times for regular or special board meetings, statutes today allow meetings to occur even without prior notice. To be a valid meeting, however, either before or after the meeting, each absent director—in writing—must waive the right to prior notice, consent to the meeting, or approve the minutes of the meeting.

Similarly, some states even allow the board to act without a meeting, assuming the articles or bylaws permit informal action, as long as all directors consent and file their consents in the corporate minute book. In fact, telephone conference calls suffice in several states. Given this decided trend toward informality, the board can hold its meetings anywhere unless the articles or bylaws declare otherwise. Meetings outside the corporation's state of incorporation or principal place of business are, in general, perfectly legal.

Unless the articles or bylaws set a higher or lower percentage, a simple majority of the directors ordinarily constitutes a quorum. Actions taken by a quorum of directors are binding on the corporation. Yet two questions may still arise in any discussion about quorums. First, can directors who intentionally miss a meeting to prevent a quorum later question the validity of the action taken at the meeting? Since different cases have produced different results, you should check the law on this matter in your particular jurisdiction. Second, can directors count toward the quorum (or vote) if the board will be voting on matters in which they are personally interested? Modern statutes generally allow directors to participate as long as there has been compliance with statutory provisions meant to ensure fairness to the corporation (such as disclosure of the interest). If there is no such statute, the case results vary from jurisdiction to jurisdiction. Some cases have allowed interested directors to be counted; other cases have not.

Directors usually cannot agree in advance about how they will vote on corporate matters. Such a formal agreement is not binding because it is void on public policy grounds; directors owe fiduciary duties to the corporation and must be free to exercise their judgment in a totally unrestricted fashion. Such agreements may be valid, however, among directors in a close corporation if all the shareholders/directors agree to the plan.

Delegation of Duties. Most statutes authorize the board of directors to delegate managerial authority to officers and executive (or other) committees. Such delegations of duties ensure the smooth running of the day-to-day affairs of the corporation and promote efficiency by utilizing the expertise of the various committee members (as in a salary committee).

If no statutory provisions specifically allow the delegation of duties, courts will interpret any attempts at delegation very strictly. Moreover, if the delegation becomes too broad and pervasive, such actions will probably be void because it is too great a relinquishment of the board's management functions. Similarly, attempts to place control of the corporation in fewer persons than the entire board of directors will be illegal (even in close corporations), because the corporation deserves the best efforts of all its directors, who, in turn, owe fiduciary duties to the corporation. Delegation of authority to persons outside the directorial ranks (except for officers), such as arbitrators or management consultants, therefore, becomes extremely difficult to justify legally.

Compensation. In times past, the corporation had no duty to compensate directors for their services. Older cases ruled that directors were not to be paid for their services unless the articles or bylaws authorized the compensation before the directors had rendered the services. Even under these circumstances, however, directors could receive payment for extraordinary services taken at the board's request (such as recruitment of executive officers), despite the lack of a prearranged, specific agreement. The payment is based on quasi-contractual grounds. Today, although many corporations still pay their directors little or no compensation for their services, an increasing number of corporations do pay rather hefty sums. Since directors often are not substantial shareholders and are subject to ever-expanding duties and potential liability, compensation seems more justifiable.

The directors normally determine the salaries of the officers of the corporation. Possible conflict of interest concerns may arise when directors also serve as officers because, in effect, the directors will be participating in setting their own salaries. As noted earlier in the discussion of quorum requirements, statutes may empower interested directors to vote on these issues as long as disclosure of the interest has been made and the transaction is otherwise fair to the corporation. The board can hire officers to serve for periods longer than the board's tenure as long as the period involved is reasonable in length. Likewise, the amount of compensation paid to officers also must be reasonable. Otherwise, the compensation package (fixed salary, bonuses, share options, profit sharing, annuities, deferred-compensation plans, etc.) may be attacked as a "waste" of corporate assets by the directors.

Corporate salaries in the millions of dollars are not uncommon today. Moreover, it has become a relatively common strategy for the board to give *golden parachutes*—hefty, guaranteed salary packages—to their chief executive officers when the board's corporation is the target of a hostile takeover attempt. Since the acquirer will be obligated to pay these inflated salaries after the acquisition, golden parachutes become a strategy for fending off a takeover attempt. Golden parachutes, which allow officers to receive money after their severance from the corporation for doing no work, raise controversial questions about possible conflicts of interest and waste of corporate assets.

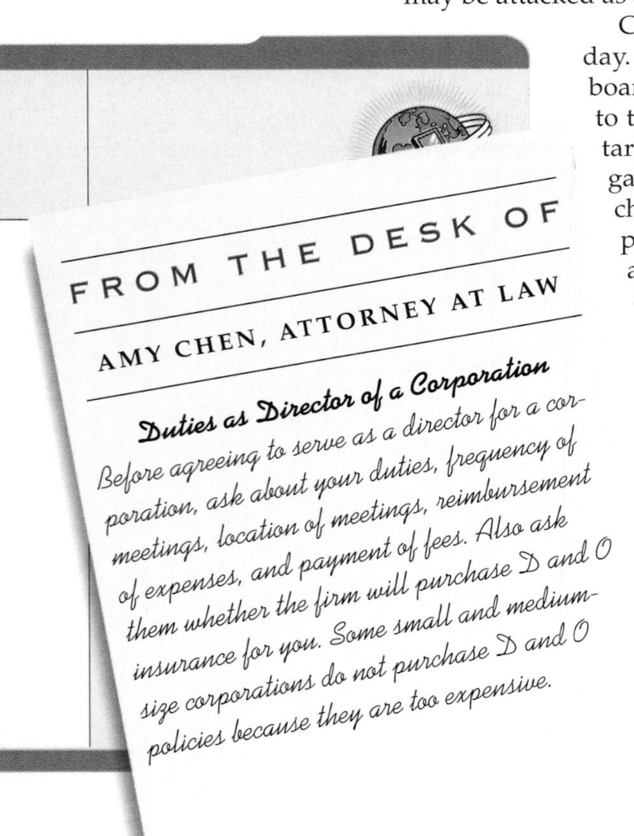

FROM THE DESK OF
AMY CHEN, ATTORNEY AT LAW
Duties as Director of a Corporation
Before agreeing to serve as a director for a corporation, ask about your duties, frequency of meetings, location of meetings, reimbursement of expenses, and payment of fees. Also ask them whether the firm will purchase D and O insurance for you. Some small and medium-size corporations do not purchase D and O policies because they are too expensive.

Liabilities. State corporation statutes, common law doctrines, and federal securities and antitrust laws may impose liability on a director for noncompliance with the duties or requirements set out in those doctrines and statutes. Directors, by the very nature of their positions, make numerous decisions, collectively and individually. Increasingly, the performance of these duties subjects directors to possible personal liability, either individually or with the other members of the board who have approved or engaged in the forbidden conduct. Directors must use great caution in order to avoid liability in the form of civil damages or criminal fines.

Although not always the case, today it is legal—indeed, common—for corporations to indemnify (pay back or reimburse) their directors for liabilities accruing from their corporate positions. Through indemnification, directors receive from the corporation the losses and expenses incurred from litigation brought against them personally for actions undertaken on behalf of the corporation in the directors' corporate capacities.

YOU BE THE JUDGE

Firms Rethink Lucrative Severance Pacts for Top Executives

Charles Zwick served as Southeast Banking Corp.'s chairman and chief executive officer. He was ousted from his $500,000 a year job in January 1991 and signed a severance agreement of $1.25 million, consisting of monthly payments of $41,667 spread over two-and-a-half years. Although once the leading corporate lender in Florida, Southeast's banks were failing. Due to pressure from regulatory entities, such as the comptroller of the currency, and from shareholders, Southeast stopped paying Zwick the agreed-upon sum after only a few months. Zwick then sued Southeast for breach of contract. The comptroller of the currency argued that regulators had not exceeded their lawful powers by cracking down on golden parachutes extended to departing executives at failing institutions. Zwick's attorney, however, maintained that regulators, in these circumstances, unlawfully interfered with valid and legal contracts when they brought pressure to bear on companies to cease payments under these severance arrangements. This case has been brought before *your* court. How will *you* decide it?[17]

BUSINESS CONSIDERATIONS Why might a business decide to provide golden parachutes to its key executives? How does such a decision affect the duty of the board of directors to its other constituents?

ETHICAL CONSIDERATIONS Golden parachutes and poison pills are frequently used as antitakeover devices by a corporation. Is it ethical for a business to establish antitakeover devices? What should the board of directors be concerned with when a takeover appears imminent?

SOURCE: Joann S. Lublin, *Wall Street Journal*, 11 November 1991, p. B1.

Statutes may limit the right of indemnification in certain circumstances. For instance, indemnification for criminal fines may be unavailable when directors have engaged in unlawful activities that they knew at the time were illegal. Statutes often empower corporations to purchase liability insurance for their directors, officers, and other employees to cover nonindemnifiable liabilities. These policies are commonly called *D and O liability insurance*—for directors and officers' liability and reimbursement policies.

Other Rights. Because directors alone have the right to declare dividends, they (as well as the shareholders) may be personally liable for improper dividends.

Directors, like shareholders, may enter into agreements about how they will vote as directors. But if such agreements unduly hamper the board's managerial functions, the agreements will be void on public policy grounds. These agreements ordinarily will be valid, however, in close corporations in which all the shareholders/directors have assented to the terms.

The rights of directors to inspect corporate records are even more compelling than shareholders' rights. Why? Access to corporate records is essential if directors are to discharge their fiduciary duties and decision-making functions. Unlike shareholders' rights, many states characterize the directors' right of inspection as absolute. Yet this right is likely to be lost if directors abuse the right by using it for an improper purpose that damages the corporation, such as misappropriation of trade secrets or confidential trade information.

Officers

The selection or removal of officers represents an important managerial function of the board of directors. While directors are responsible for the overall policies of the corporation, officers conduct the day-to-day operations of the firm and execute the policies established by the board. These lines of authority are well established in American law. The directors should manage, and the officers should carry out the management goals delegated to them by the directors.

Qualifications. Officers are agents of the corporation and, therefore, must live up to the fiduciary duties placed on agents. Statutes often name the officers that a corporation must have, and usually either these statutes or the corporate bylaws spell out the respective officers' authority. Typical officers include president, vice president, secretary, and treasurer (or comptroller). The top executive may also be called the chairman of the board, the chief executive officer, or the general manager. The same person ordinarily can serve as more than one officer, but some statutes prohibit the same person from serving as both president and secretary.

Term of Office. The board ordinarily appoints the officers, who serve at the will of the directors. Some modern statutes, on the other hand, allow the shareholders to elect the officers. Either the board or the president can appoint junior or senior officers.

Officers usually serve at the pleasure of the board because the board in most jurisdictions can remove officers with or without cause, even when the officer has a valid employment contract. But after such removal without cause, the corporation may be liable in damages to the former officer for breach of the employment contract. As we shall see later in this chapter, the directors normally escape personal liability if they have removed the officer in accordance with the business judgment rule; that is, they have exercised due care while making corporate decisions. In rare instances, the state, the courts, or the shareholders can remove officers. These instances nearly always involve a removal with cause.

Compensation. In earlier times, officers, like directors, traditionally served without pay because they usually were shareholders who expected their investment in the corporation to multiply by virtue of their work on the corporation's behalf. Thus, there was no need to supplement these corporate profits with a salary. Today, since neither directors nor officers are required to be shareholders, the corporation usually pays a prearranged, fixed salary (recall in this context the possibility of golden parachutes as well). In addition, the corporation commonly adds to this salary, profit-sharing plans, bonuses, share options, deferred-compensation plans, pensions, annuities, and other fringe benefits like health care and expense accounts. Such compensation packages often turn out to be substantial indeed.

Compensation, to be lawful, should be reasonable and not represent waste of corporate assets. If waste is present, both directors and officers may be liable to the corporation for this waste. Courts have even ordered officers to return amounts deemed excessive compensation to the corporation.

Agency Law. Because officers are agents of the corporation, they have authority to bind the corporation. To help with this section, you should review the material on agency in Chapters 31 through 33. Briefly, an officer's authority may be actual (either express or implied) or apparent.

Express authority derives from state statutes, the articles, or the bylaws. Any of these three sources may spell out the duties, responsibilities, and authority of the respective officers, although the bylaws are the most common source. Under express authority, the corporation has determined the boundaries within which the officer shall act on behalf of the corporation.

Implied authority, on the other hand, also known as inherent authority, derives from the virtue of the office or title of the person. Presidents have inherent authority to direct corporate meetings and to act on behalf of the corporation with regard to transactions occurring in the ordinary and regular course of business. For example, a president normally has authority to hire real estate brokers for the purpose of selling corporate property. Yet the president cannot validly sell or mortgage corporate assets without the approval of the board (and sometimes that of the shareholders). The president can have authority, however, to bind the corporation to sale or services contracts arising in the usual course of business; for instance, the president of a grain elevator can authorize purchases of wheat from local farmers. Courts sometimes uphold expansions of authority for presidents who are chief executive officers or general managers.

Vice presidents normally possess no authority by virtue of their office. Similarly, neither the treasurer nor the secretary can normally bind the corporation. The law ordinarily limits them to fairly ministerial intracorporate functions. Some jurisdictions, however, do give the treasurer authority to write, accept, endorse, and negotiate corporate checks and promissory notes.

Corporate officers may have *apparent authority* to bind the corporation. Apparent authority arises when the corporation, by its actions, indicates to a third party that an officer or agent is empowered to engage in certain transactions on behalf of the corporation. For example, if the corporation has customarily allowed its president to buy property on the corporation's behalf without prior board approval, he or she has apparent authority to bind the corporation to such a real estate transaction. The corporation cannot later allege lack of actual authority as a defense to consummation of the sale.

Likewise, the seller of the property may use the theory of estoppel to counter a defense of lack of actual authority. Estoppel may be used when the third party has been damaged because of the third party's good faith in and reasonable reliance on the corporation's creation of circumstances that appear to clothe the officer with apparent authority. In fact, estoppel may bind the corporation to transactions that result from unauthorized acts of the officer.

Subsequent ratification (approval) of previously unauthorized acts will also bind the corporation. Even if the president had no authority to buy real estate, a later board resolution that approves the purchase constitutes a ratification and binds the corporation to the completion of the transaction.

Liabilities. Officers who attempt to contract on behalf of the corporation without authority to do so may be personally liable to the other contracting party. Similarly, nondisclosure of the fact that the officer is acting on behalf of the corporation, even when the officer's actions are authorized, will lead to the personal liability of the officer. Officers who commit torts may be personally liable to the injured party, although, as you may recall from Chapter 33, the corporation may also be liable for torts committed by the officer during the scope of his or her employment under the doctrine of *respondeat superior.* Thus, a bank president who converts funds to his or her own use may be liable to the depositor, as may the bank under *respondeat superior*.

Fiduciary Duties Owed to the Corporation

Directors, officers, and controlling shareholders owe duties to the corporation and sometimes to shareholders and creditors. These are called fiduciary duties because the directors, officers, and controlling shareholders occupy a position of trust and faith with regard to the corporation and other constituencies. Generally speaking, these obligations fall into three broad categories: the duty of obedience, the duty of diligence (or due care), and the duty of loyalty. These duties may arise from statute but, more often, they issue from case law.

Obedience. Directors, officers, controlling shareholders, and other corporate managers must restrict their actions and those of the corporation to lawful pursuits. Any action taken beyond the scope of the corporation's power is an illegal, *ultra vires* act. By definition, violation of a positive rule of law or statute constitutes an illegal act. Any such actions by managers violate the duty of obedience and may subject them to personal liability.

Diligence. Because corporate managers act on behalf of the corporation, they are obligated to perform their duties with the amount of diligence or due care that a reasonably prudent person would exercise in the conduct of his or her own personal affairs or in the same or similar circumstances. You probably notice the familiar ring of this language. We discussed this kind of standard when we addressed negligence (see Chapter 5). Basically, the duty of due care obliges a corporate manager to perform his or her duties in a nonnegligent fashion. Note that the law does not expect a director, officer, or controlling shareholder to be perfect or all-knowing. Honest errors of judgment will not lead to liability for breach of the duty of diligence. If liability were imposed in such situations, who would ever consent to be a director or officer?

Instead, the law excuses the conduct if the manager has made the error in good faith and without being clearly and grossly negligent. This is the *business judgment rule.* A jury must decide whether the manager's decision satisfies the business judgment rule or is grossly negligent and, hence, unacceptable. A manager who fails to attend corporate meetings or pays no attention to corporate affairs and is consequently ill-prepared may incur liability for breach of the duty of diligence or due care. Similarly, failure to fire an obviously unworthy employee, failure to obtain casualty insurance, failure to heed warning signs suggesting illegal conduct (such as embezzlement), or reliance on unreasonable statements by attorneys or accountants may lead to liability.

Nonetheless, the manager will incur liability only for such losses as his or her own negligent conduct causes. Consequently, if a director formally dissents about a matter that is later held to be negligent, that director will avoid liability. If the director does not dissent, it is usually no defense that the director was a figurehead or served without pay; but a manager's reasonable reliance on expert reports, such as those by accountants or attorneys, usually exonerates the manager from liability unless violations of securities acts are involved.

NCR v. *American Telephone and Telegraph* centered on the possible application of the business judgment rule to a decision made by the directors. Note that it is part of the same disagreement between NCR and AT&T addressed earlier in this chapter in *Sadler* v. *NCR Corporation,* 928 F.2d 48 (2d Cir. 1991) (Case 35.2).

35.4 NCR CORPORATION v. AMERICAN TELEPHONE AND TELEGRAPH COMPANY

761 F.Supp. 475 (S.D. Ohio 1991)

FACTS American Telephone and Telegraph Company (AT&T) is a New York corporation with its principal place of business in New York City. NCR Corporation, a leader in the computer field, develops, manufactures, markets, installs, and services business information-processing systems for worldwide markets from its principal place of business in Dayton, Ohio. NCR first began considering the implementation of an employee stock ownership plan (ESOP) in 1986, when management mentioned the idea as one of several possible defenses that the firm could raise in case of a hostile takeover attempt. In mid-1989, the board discontinued its investigation into the advisability of an ESOP. NCR began reconsidering the concept of establishing an ESOP as a takeover defense, not as an employee benefit option, because it was concerned that AT&T could obtain sufficient shareholder votes to approve its takeover bid. ESOPs were discussed at the January board meeting. At the 20 February 1991 board meeting, there was a presentation on the proposed ESOP and the directors received "board books." These sources did not contain a great deal of substantive information regarding the specifics of the proposed ESOP. Nonetheless, following this presentation, the board voted unanimously to adopt the proposal. No benefits personnel made a presentation at either the January or February board meeting. At both meetings, the board discussed the usefulness of the ESOP as a reaction to AT&T's takeover attempt. In the period between mid-1989, when the board had tabled the ESOP idea, and the adoption of the ESOP in 1991, changes in tax laws and accounting rules had caused ESOPs to become less attractive financing options. Yet the board was apparently unaware or only vaguely aware of these developments. Nine days before the record date of 1 March, NCR authorized the issue of 5,509,641,873 shares of preferred stock for an aggregate price of $500 million. Since the ESOP in question was a leveraged ESOP, all shares were issued at once. The 5.5 million share block (more than 20 times larger than the ESOP originally considered in 1986 and 1989) put about 8 percent of the outstanding NCR voting stock into employee hands while diluting outstanding common stock shares by approximately 6 percent. Unleveraged ESOPs enjoyed substantial tax advantages not available to leveraged ESOPs. If NCR's stock rose in the manner predicted by NCR's financial advisors, NCR would forego potentially hundreds of millions of dollars in tax savings by leveraging its ESOP. The size of the ESOP was apparently not related to benefits objectives but, rather, was an attempt to place as large a number of shares into friendly hands as possible.

ISSUE Can the decision of the directors be upheld based on the business judgment rule?

HOLDING No.

REASONING The business judgment rule will not protect the transaction because the directors failed to act in an informed fashion. Bad faith is not a requirement. Under Maryland precedents, it is a well-settled rule that "in all cases, the business judgment rule creates the presumption that directors act in good faith." This presumption is heightened where, as here, the majority of the board members are independent outside directors. The party challenging the validity of a board's actions must produce evidence sufficient to rebut the presumption that the directors have acted in accordance with their fiduciary duties. The heart of the fiduciary duty imposed on directors of publicly held corporations is the obligation to act in a manner they reasonably believe to be in the best interests of the corporation. This duty is plainly composed of two separate elements, one subjective and the other objective. A director may take no action on behalf of a corporation unless he or she is of the belief that such action is in the corporation's best interests. However, the second condition implicit in the director's fiduciary duty is that his or her belief must be reasonable. Applying the first prong of this test to the facts of this case, it was clear that NCR's outside directors, accomplished and respected in their various fields and independent of NCR's management, had little to gain by acting improperly.

The board sought no fairness opinion; a legal opinion regarding the validity of the offer was quickly negotiated; the benefits people were not consulted to any significant degree; there was a general unfamiliarity with the changes in tax laws and accounting rules and no conception of how the plan would be received by employees; and the features of the preferred stock—that is, the heavy voting provision, the reset provision that negated the risk of market fluctuations, the higher dividend—were all dilutive of the common stock. These features also created a potential conflict of interest between the two classes of stock.

The ESOP was similarly unfair to NCR itself, for the corporation, not the beneficiaries of the stock issue, would foot the bill. Given the plan's internal leveraging, no new capital would flow into the company. NCR had locked itself into a large ESOP that NCR could not adjust to meet actual needs. The firm, in deciding to leverage the plan, had also lost significant tax advantages. Hence, AT&T had met its burden of proof demonstrating that the primary purpose of the

35.4 NCR CORPORATION v. AMERICAN TELEPHONE AND TELEGRAPH COMPANY *(cont.)* 761 F.Supp. 475 (S.D. Ohio 1991)

NCR ESOP was not benefits-related but, rather, an attempt by NCR management to impede corporate democracy and to perpetuate its control of the company. Therefore, AT&T merited a permanent injunction invalidating NCR's ESOP and enjoining the preferred shares issued thereunder from voting at the 28 March 1991 special meeting.

BUSINESS CONSIDERATIONS The business judgment rule provides a wide umbrella of protection for the officers and directors of a corporation. What types of decisions should be protected by the business judgment rule, and what types of decisions should fall beyond its protections?

ETHICAL CONSIDERATIONS Is it ethical for an officer or director to be protected from liability for poor decisions due to the provisions of the business judgment rule? Would it be ethical to hold people liable after the fact for decisions they made that turned out to be less profitable than originally expected?

35.2 MANAGEMENT/FINANCE

AVOIDING LIABILITY

Tom, as you recall, contracted for a unique marketing plan that he fully expected would be a great success. Unfortunately, the plan was a disaster, and the firm lost a significant amount of money on the plan. While the firm will weather this financial storm, the setback made Tom consider what might have happened if the firm was publicly owned. He is afraid that such a result in a publicly held firm might have resulted in his dismissal and/or liability for the losses. Tom has asked you what liabilities he would have faced if CIT had been publicly owned at the time he made the decision to enter the marketing plan. What will you tell him?

BUSINESS CONSIDERATIONS What must a manager be able to show in order to avoid liability for a decision gone bad? Is this a difficult defense to establish? Why or why not?

ETHICAL CONSIDERATIONS What ethical duties do managers owe to the firm and/or the shareholders? To whom do managers owe the greatest duty?

Loyalty. Because directors, officers, and controlling shareholders enjoy positions of trust with the corporation, they must act in good faith and with loyalty toward the corporation and its shareholders. The undivided loyalty expected of fiduciaries means that managers must place the interests of the corporation above their own personal interests. Sometimes these corporate interests and personal interests collide, and it becomes necessary to resort to applicable statutes and case law. Usually such collisions involve (1) corporate opportunities or (2) conflicts of interest.

The *corporate opportunity doctrine* forbids directors, officers, and controlling shareholders from diverting to themselves business deals or potential deals that in fairness or in justice belong to the corporation. For the sake of simplicity, we will call these persons "managers." Personal gains at the expense of the corporation represent a breach of the managers' fiduciary duties. A corporate opportunity is commonly found (1) if the manager discovers the opportunity in his or her capacity as director, and (2) it is reasonably foreseeable that the corporation will be interested in the opportunity because it relates closely to the corporation's line of business. For example, if Wanda is a director in a real estate development corporation (Real Property Corporation) and Ray offers to sell property to Wanda because he knows she is a director of Real Property, Wanda should not buy the property for herself. To do so will violate her duty of loyalty. If the corporation might reasonably be interested in the land for its corporate development program, Wanda must disclose this opportunity to the corporation. Once she has given the corporation this right of first refusal, Wanda ordinarily can purchase the property if the corporation refuses the opportunity or is financially unable to implement the purchase.

If Wanda breaches the duty of loyalty and purchases the land for herself, corporate remedies will include damages (the profits Wanda makes as a result of the sale) or the imposition of a **constructive trust** (a court will treat Wanda as a trustee who is holding the property for the benefit of the corporation). A court then can force Wanda to convey the property to Real Property Corporation and to pay Real Property any profits she realized on the transaction.

Constructive trust
A trust imposed by law to prevent the unjust enrichment of the person in possession of the property (the purported owner).

The *Steelvest* v. *Scansteel* case concerns an alleged violation of the fiduciary duty of loyalty.

35.5 STEELVEST, INC. v. SCANSTEEL SERVICE CENTER, INC. 807 S.W.2d 476 (Ky. 1991)

FACTS Scanlon had been employed by Steel Suppliers, Inc., a company engaged in warehousing and distributing structural steel, for 30 years. He had served as president and a director. On 21 November 1984, Steelvest, Inc., a corporation owned by Lucas, purchased the assets of Steel Suppliers for approximately $5 million. After this purchase, Steelvest continued Steel Suppliers, as a separate, unincorporated division under the same name. At Lucas's request, Scanlon agreed to stay on as president and general manager of Steel Suppliers. He also subsequently became a director of Steelvest and a member of its executive committee. Scanlon's employment with Steel Suppliers continued for 11 months after the purchase by Steelvest. During these eleven months, Scanlon began to formulate a plan to start and incorporate his own steel business, which would compete directly with Steelvest. Toward this end, he sought the advice of counsel, contacted potential investors, and sought financing. He disclosed none of these activities to any representative of Steelvest. Furthermore, he recruited two chief executive officers of major clients of Steelvest to invest in his new company. Scanlon resigned from his employment with Steel Suppliers and Steelvest on 15 October 1985. One day prior to this, on 14 October, Scanlon had completed most of the necessary arrangements for setting up his new business, including the signing of documents for the purchase of property to be used as the site for the business. Immediately after Scanlon's resignation from Steelvest, he, along with the other investors, incorporated Scansteel Service Center, Inc., which began actual operations soon thereafter. Nine office and supervisory employees of Steelvest resigned to take employment with Scansteel. On 2 June 1986, Steelvest instituted this action against Scansteel and Scanlon, alleging a breach of fiduciary duties by Scanlon and a conspiracy on the part of the investors and the bank that had provided the financing for the formation of Scansteel.

ISSUE Had Scanlon breached his fiduciary duties to Steelvest by planning and organizing a directly competitive business?

HOLDING Perhaps. A complete trial should occur, because genuine issues of fact exist as to this question.

REASONING Generally, in the absence of a contractual provision to the contrary, corporate fiduciaries, such as directors or officers, remain free to resign and form an enterprise that competes with the corporation after they sever their connection with it. However, Kentucky law has recognized that directors and officers of a corporation may not set up, or attempt to set up, an enterprise that competes with the business in which the corporation is engaged while they are still serving as directors and officers. Thus, they should terminate their position/status as directors or officers when they first make arrangements or begin preparations to compete directly with the employer corporation. In this case, Scanlon was not a mere employee; he served the corporation as both a director and an officer. This relationship provides a fiduciary relationship. Scanlon, therefore, owed a duty of loyalty and faithfulness to the corporation and a duty not to act against the employer's interest. A direct corollary of this general principle of loyalty is that a corporation officer or other high-level employee is barred from actively competing with his or her employer during the tenure of the employment, even without an express covenant prohibiting competition. Before employment is terminated, an employee must not solicit for himself or herself business that he or she is required to obtain for the employer. The employee must refrain from actively and directly competing with the employer for customers and employees, and must continue to exert his or her best efforts on behalf of the employer. Genuine issues of material fact respecting Scanlon's alleged

35.5 STEELVEST, INC. v. SCANSTEEL SERVICE CENTER, INC. *(cont.)* 807 S.W.2d 476 (Ky. 1991)

breach of fiduciary duty exist and a trial should be held to resolve these issues.

BUSINESS CONSIDERATIONS What contract terms or clauses could a firm include in its contracts with key employees to prevent this sort of situation from arising? Should a business have a policy regarding contractual restrictions to be included in any contracts with upper-level management?

ETHICAL CONSIDERATIONS Is it ethical for a key executive to plan the organization of a competing firm while still holding his or her executive position? What ethical concerns would such a situation present?

35.3

FINANCE

SUBCHAPTER S CORPORATIONS

The Kochanowskis have decided either to incorporate CIT as a Subchapter S corporation or to remain a general partnership. They are concerned, however, about the need to satisfy several of the more burdensome and/or time-consuming aspects of corporate existence. They need to know what requirements they will face as a Subchapter S corporation in such matters as annual meetings, distribution of authority, tax returns, and rights of shareholders. They also need to know how these requirements might vary if they were just to remain a partnership. What advice will you give them?

BUSINESS CONSIDERATIONS What business criteria are important in making the decision to adopt any particular business organization? What personal factors should a businessperson consider?

ETHICAL CONSIDERATIONS Will the businesspersons have different ethical duties if they operate the business as a partnership as compared to a corporation? Why or why not?

The most common example of a possible conflict of interest occurs when a director, officer, or controlling shareholder personally contracts with the corporation. For example, Wanda, a director of Real Property Corporation, is willing to sell a piece of her own property to the corporation. Because of her personal interests, Wanda will undoubtedly hope to make as much money as possible on the transaction. Yet her position as a director of Real Property obligates her to accept as low a price as possible in order to benefit the company. Wanda obviously faces a difficult dilemma. Most states will allow the transaction (1) if Wanda makes a full disclosure of her interest to the board of directors of Real Property before the board begins its deliberations on the proposed contract, and (2) if the resultant contract is fair and reasonable to the corporation. If Wanda does not fully disclose her interest or if the terms of the contract are unfair or unreasonable, however, the contract will be voidable by the corporation.

An additional concern in these situations stems from whether Wanda (who is called an interested director) should be allowed to vote on the contract. At common law, Wanda could not vote—or even be counted toward the quorum—at the meeting where the matter was to be discussed. Although modern statutes (and articles or bylaws) vary, in general, Wanda can vote and be counted toward the quorum if, as noted earlier, she discloses her interest and the resultant contract is fair to the corporation.

As previously discussed, the duty of loyalty also prohibits directors, officers, or controlling shareholders from prejudicing minority shareholders' rights by freezing out minority shareholders through such actions as forcing dissolution of the corporation or modifying the distribution of assets if the firm is liquidated.

http:// RESOURCES FOR BUSINESS LAW STUDENTS

NAME	RESOURCES	WEB ADDRESS
American Success Institute	American Success Institute promises a "free business education on the web," providing tips on operating small businesses.	http://www.success.org/
Educom, Inc., articles of incorporation	Educom (Interuniversity Communications Council, Inc.), a not-for-profit corporation specializing in education information, maintains its articles of incorporation, bylaws, trustees' terms of office, and trustees' names and addresses, online.	http://educom.edu/web/admin.html
Limited liability companies	Attorney Steven E. Davidson provides basic information on limited liability companies, including a state-by-state comparison chart.	http://www.hia.com/llcweb/ll-home.html

In the context of corporate takeovers, allegations of breach of fiduciary duties commonly arise. As the sophistication of both the "raider" and the target corporation has increased, directors of the latter have responded creatively to mount a host of defensive moves meant to blunt the would-be acquiring firm's appetite for the target corporation. The development of exotic (but apt) terms such as **greenmail** and poison pill to describe these thrusts and countermeasures masks the more important issue of whether the law will approve of these deterrent efforts.

Greenmail
The process by which a firm threatens a corporate takeover by buying a significant portion of a corporation's stock and then selling it back to the corporation at a premium when the corporation's directors and executives, fearing for their positions, agree to buy the firm out.

SUMMARY

Each partner has certain rights in the business by virtue of his or her status as a partner. These rights may be limited or defined by the agreement. If no agreement exists, each partner has an equal voice in management, a right to an equal share of profits or losses, equal access to books and records of the firm, and an equal right to use partnership property for partnership purposes. Each one also has a right to be reimbursed for expenditures and a right to an account.

Each partner is an agent for every other partner and is a principal of every other partner. As a result, all the rules of agency apply. Each partner is a fiduciary of the other partners. When a partner deals with some third party, the firm is bound by the conduct if it was apparently or actually authorized. Agency principles also apply to the torts of a partner. If the tort is in the course and scope of employment, the partners are jointly and severally liable. If it is beyond the scope of employment, only the tortfeasor is liable, unless the other partners ratify the conduct. Any liability for crimes committed by a partner is not imposed on the nonacting partners unless they ratify the conduct.

Ownership of corporate shares carries with it certain rights. The types of rights shareholders enjoy may vary depending on the type of stock involved. Ownership of common stock permits the shareholder to receive dividends (without priority) and to vote on corporate issues. In contrast, ownership of preferred stock confers priority as to dividends, voting, and/or liquidation rights. In addition, preferred stock may have participation rights, conversion rights, and/or redemption rights.

Shareholders' meetings provide the vehicle by which both common and preferred stockholders exercise their most significant control over the corporation. Corporate bylaws usually require an annual meeting (primarily for election of directors) and may authorize special meetings in appropriate circumstances. Such meetings ordinarily cannot occur in the absence of either prior notice or a quorum. One of the shareholders' foremost powers involves the election and removal of directors. Shareholders have inherent power to remove a director for cause and may have power to remove a director without cause. Shareholders may also amend or repeal bylaws.

Shareholders can cast their votes either in person or by proxy. For most corporate matters, straight voting is used. However, for the election of directors, many state statutes either permit or require cumulative voting. Cumulative voting protects the interests of minority shareholders but may be countered by such strategies as staggered terms for directors. Other devices used to consolidate voting power include voting trusts and pooling arrangements. These devices are especially useful in close corporations.

Dividends represent financial returns on shareholders' investments. Yet shareholders cannot compel directors to declare dividends; the directors alone have this power. The board also must make certain that dividends, if declared, have been paid from a lawful source. Dividends may be cumulative or noncumulative.

When a corporation increases its capital by issuing new shares, shareholder approval is necessary. To protect a shareholder's proportionate interest in the corporation when recapitalization occurs, the doctrine of preemptive rights is ordinarily applicable.

Shareholders' rights to inspect corporate records arise from both common law doctrines and express statutory provisions. Ordinarily, if a shareholder can demonstrate a proper purpose for requesting access to the records, the shareholder will be able to examine certain corporate documents.

Shareholders may be liable to the corporation or creditors for watered stock, and a subscriber may be liable to the corporation or to creditors if the subscriber breaches a stock subscription. Declaration and distribution of illegal dividends may subject both directors and shareholders to personal liability. Controlling shareholders also may incur liability if the purpose of the corporation's dissolution is to freeze out minority stockholders and to strip these stockholders of rights or profits they would otherwise enjoy.

The right to manage the corporation falls squarely on the board of directors. Shareholders cannot compel directors to take any action, because the directors are not the agents of the shareholders but, rather, owe loyalty primarily to the corporation. The modern trend is to lower the number of directors and to lessen the traditionally stringent rules concerning directors' qualifications. Directors generally are qualified to appoint replacements on the board when vacancies arise due to death, resignation, or incapacity. In many jurisdictions, shareholders can remove a director with or without cause.

Most statutes authorize the board of directors to delegate managerial authority to officers and executive committees. Broad delegations of authority to persons outside the directorial ranks are usually invalid.

Directors may or may not receive compensation from the corporation. The directors normally determine officers' compensation. Such compensation packages are usually legal if reasonable in amount. Otherwise, a shareholder can attack the compensation as a waste of corporate assets.

Performance of directorial duties may lead to personal liability for directors. Occasionally, the corporation will indemnify the directors for liabilities accruing from their corporate positions. Directors have the right to declare dividends, enter into agreements, and inspect corporate records.

Officers are agents of the corporation and, thus, must live up to the fiduciary duties placed on agents. The board ordinarily appoints the officers, who serve at the will of the directors. Officers may bind the corporation by express, implied, or apparent authority. But the unauthorized acts of officers may make them personally liable to the other contracting party.

Directors, officers, and controlling shareholders owe fiduciary duties to the corporation. Broadly speaking, these duties fall into three categories: the duty of obedience, the duty of diligence (or due care), and the duty of loyalty. The duty of obedience forbids ultra vires acts. The business judgment rule constitutes a defense to liability for violation of the duty of diligence. Under this rule, the manager will not be liable if he or she makes an erroneous decision in good faith and without clear and gross negligence. The duty of loyalty, among other things, precludes directors, officers, and controlling shareholders from usurping corporate opportunities or prejudicing the corporation because of undisclosed conflicts of interest.

DISCUSSION QUESTIONS

1. Explain what the following have to do with shareholders' meetings: (a) proxies, (b) straight voting, (c) cumulative voting, (d) voting trusts, and (e) pooling agreements.
2. Explain how a shareholder secures the right to inspect corporate documents.
3. How can liability arise for watered stock, stock subscriptions, illegal dividends, and dissolution?
4. What are the limitations on directors' delegations of authority to officers and corporate committees?
5. Briefly enumerate the rights and liabilities of directors. How do officers' rights and liabilities differ from those of directors?
6. In what ways can corporate managers prevent charges of conflicts of interest from being levied against them?
7. Tim and Ed are partners. Tim, however, is tired of the business and sells it to Dan. Ed objects to the sale and sues to have it declared void. Dan claims Tim has the apparent authority to sell. How should the court rule, and why?
8. Margaret and Barbara are partners. Barbara calls a customer and says the firm will not be able to deliver certain goods on time. The customer immediately sues for anticipatory breach. Margaret objects to the suit, saying the customer has no grounds to expect a breach. Do you agree? Explain.
9. April, Jim, and Dan are partners in a retail business. Dan borrows $10,000 from the bank to "buy more goods." The loan is made in the partnership name. Dan, however, takes the money to Las Vegas and loses it all at the roulette table. If the bank sues April and Jim on the loan, what should be the result? Explain.
10. Judge Benjamin Cardozo wrote, "Many forms of conduct permissible in a workaday world, for those acting at arm's length, are forbidden to those bound by fiduciary ties. A . . . [fiduciary] is held to something stricter than the morals of the market place. Not honesty alone, but the punctilio of an honor the most sensitive, is the standard of behavior. As to this there has developed a tradition that is unbending and inveterate." Is his description of fiduciary duty helpful? Why or why not? How do you define fiduciary duty? [See *Meinhard* v. *Salmon,* 164 N.E. 545 (N.Y. 1928).]

CASE PROBLEMS AND WRITING ASSIGNMENTS

1. Hodge entered into a contract with Voeller to purchase land owned by a partnership. Voeller was the managing general partner of the partnership, which owned and operated a drive-in movie theater. Voeller signed the contract in the partnership's name and on behalf of the partnership and his partners. One of the partners objected to the sale, and the deed was not transferred to Hodge. Hodge has sued for specific performance of

the contract. How will the court resolve this case? What factors will the court examine in reaching its decision? [See *Hodge* v. *Garrett,* 614 P.2d 420 (1980).]

2. Kaneco was a limited partnership involved in the oil and gas industry. Kaneco hired Winterhawk to operate its business, agreeing to pay a management and administration fee based on a percentage of drilling and completion costs. In order to acquire funding for its projects, Kaneco obtained a loan from the bank, secured with letters of credit. The loan proceeds were paid directly to Winterhawk by the bank, as per Kaneco's instruction. Winterhawk misappropriated substantial amounts of the loan proceeds, and Kaneco was placed in a poor financial position. Eventually, Kaneco had difficulty making its payments on the loan, and the bank informed the general partners that the loan was being called since the loan balance exceeded the value of the letters of credit. Kaneco sought an injunction to prevent the bank from calling the loan or calling the letters of credit. Kaneco argued that the general partners were not jointly and severally liable for the loan balance. How should the court resolve this case? Why? [See *Kaneco Oil & Gas, Ltd., II* v. *University Nat'l Bank,* 732 P.2d 247 (Colo.App. 1986).]

3. At the opening of the 2 November 1989 annual meeting of the Center for Communications and Development/KMOJ Radio (CCD/KMOJ), a nonprofit corporation, the president of the board of directors announced the suspension of the right to vote of two directors. Several directors protested the suspension as a violation of the bylaws. When the president refused to reconsider this matter, seven of the thirteen directors left the meeting. The seventh departing director requested that the record of the meeting reflect that she had not been part of the decision and that she had "challenged the quorum of those remaining." The president continued the meeting, and the board added four new directors and reelected the president for another term. The seven directors who had left the meeting brought a lawsuit to enjoin the president and new directors from acting on behalf of the corporation until a procedurally correct annual meeting could be held. They also sought a temporary injunction to prohibit the president from decreasing community programming on the radio station or significantly altering the station's operations or policies. Minnesota corporate statutes provided for enactment of bylaws "for the purpose of administering and regulating the affairs of the corporation" if the bylaws were "not inconsistent with law or the articles of incorporation." Section 5.5 of CCD/KMOJ's bylaws stated: "Once established, a quorum remains established until the adjournment of the meeting or until a member calls for a quorum count and one is found lacking." The trial court granted summary judgment against the departing directors. Was the case against the directors so clear that a trial was unnecessary? Why or why not? [See *Johnson* v. *Edwards,* 467 N.W.2d 333 (Minn.App. 1991).]

4. Southwest Breeders, Inc., an Oklahoma corporation, had offered to sell shares of its stock to Jack Agosta. At the time, Southwest Breeders' articles of incorporation allowed the corporation, through its officers and directors, to issue no more than 50,000 shares of its stock at $1 per share. On 31 March 1986, Agosta purchased 15,000 shares of the stock. Agosta later discovered that the officers and directors had, on 27 December 1985, issued to themselves 1,370,000 shares at below par value, clearly in excess of the amount allowed by the articles of incorporation. Southwest Breeders subsequently filed an amendment of its articles of incorporation with the secretary of state that authorized it to increase the number of shares of its stock from 50,000 to 50,000,000. Agosta filed suit to rescind his contract, seeking $6,000 in damages for his purchase of the overissued stock. Agosta then filed a motion for summary judgment, which the trial court sustained on the ground that the sale of the overissued stock to Agosta constituted a sale of nonexistent stock for which the officers and directors remained personally liable. On appeal, Southwest Breeders alleged that the trial court had erred in characterizing the sale of stock to Agosta as unauthorized and, therefore, void. How should the appellate court rule? [See *Agosta* v. *Southwest Breeders, Inc.,* 810 P.2d 377 (Okla.App. 1991).]

5. Doemling incorporated Specialty Plastics, Inc. (Specialty) in 1975 to manufacture and sell plastic containers to another business he owned, Imaging Systems Corp. Doemling was the sole shareholder of Specialty and served on its board of directors. When Specialty declared bankruptcy in December 1982, Doemling was serving as its president. In early 1981, Doemling personally purchased a B75 and a B100 blow molder and related equipment and leased both machines to Specialty. During the lease term, Specialty was responsible for the equipment's installation, maintenance, and repair. In June 1982, Doemling personally purchased a Uniloy 300 blow molder and related equipment and leased it to Specialty. Doemling purchased all of this equipment in his personal capacity; Specialty's board of directors had approved none of the leases. In December 1982, Doemling unilaterally terminated Specialty's leases on the B100 blow molder and the Uniloy 300 blow molder. He sold the B100 molder to a third party for $65,000 and the Uniloy 300 for $72,500. These sales resulted in sub-

stantial personal profits ($38,000) for Doemling. On 1 May 1984, Doemling unilaterally terminated Specialty's remaining lease on the B75 blow molder. He sold the B75 to a third party for $85,000 and, thus, realized an additional profit of $50,500. During the course of the three leases, Specialty had paid Doemling a total of $24,300 in rental payments. Specialty also had expended an additional $23,331 for the installation, maintenance, and repair of the three blow molders and related equipment. When Specialty filed for bankruptcy under Chapter 11, the bankruptcy court concluded that Doemling had usurped a corporate opportunity that had properly belonged to Specialty. It, therefore, ordered Doemling to give up any profits he had made through this opportunity and to pay Specialty all the money he had received in rent; all the profits he had realized as a result of the sale of the three blow molders; and all the money Specialty had spent for the installation, repair, and maintenance of the machines. The bankruptcy court further found that Doemling's actions with regard to the purchase and leasing of these machines constituted *defalcation* (misconduct, moral dereliction) and, therefore, held that Doemling's obligation to repay these monies was nondischargeable in bankruptcy. Should the appellate court uphold the bankruptcy court's decision? Why? [See *Committee of Unsecured Creditors of Specialty Plastics, Inc.* v. *Doemling,* 127 Bankr. 945 (W.D. Pa. 1991).]

6. **BUSINESS APPLICATION CASE** When Pantry Pride, Inc., made a hostile tender offer for Revlon, Inc., Revlon adopted a poison pill Note Purchase Rights Plan in order to thwart the takeover and the allegedly grossly inadequate offer ($45 per share). The Note Purchase Rights Plan consisted of a self-tender for 10 million shares on 29 August 1985, each share paid for with one subordinated note worth $47.50 plus 1/10 of a $9 cumulative convertible preferred share valued at $100 per share. Revlon shareholders thereupon tendered 87 percent of the approximately 33 million outstanding shares. The notes contained covenants limiting Revlon from incurring additional debt, selling assets, or paying dividends without the independent board members' approval. For the next two months, while Revlon continued to search for a "white knight," Pantry Pride increased its offer, culminating in a price of $56.25 on 7 October. Forstmann Little & Co. (Forstmann) offered to pay $57.25 per share on 12 October in exchange for Revlon's waiving the loan covenants, Revlon's giving it a lock-up option on two divisions (which would allow Forstmann to buy these for $100 to $175 million below their appraised value), and Revlon's promising not to shop for a more attractive offer (called a *no-shop provision*). Forstmann, in turn, promised to support the notes' par value because the announcement of the covenant waiver had resulted in a sagging market price owing to threatened litigation by the holders of the notes. The directors argued that they had fulfilled their duties of care and loyalty by entering into negotiations with a white knight in order to protect the noteholders. Pantry Pride, however, in seeking injunctive relief from the Note Purchase Rights Plan, argued that the lock-up/no-shop provisions authorized by the Revlon board did not satisfy either the board's duty of care or the business judgment rule because, once the board had authorized the sale of the company to a third party, its legal responsibilities had changed. Pantry Pride reasoned that the original threat posed by Pantry Pride—the breakup of the company—had become a reality that even the directors had accepted. Selective dealing to fend off a hostile, but determined, bidder was no longer a proper objective. Instead, obtaining the highest price for the benefit of the stockholders should have been the central theme guiding director action. According to Pantry Pride, the noteholders required no further protection, and when the Revlon board entered into an auction-ending lock-up agreement with Forstmann on the basis of impermissible considerations at the expense of the shareholders, the directors had breached their primary duty of loyalty. Favoritism for a white knight to the total exclusion of a hostile bidder might be justifiable when the latter's offer adversely affected shareholder interests; but when bidders had made relatively similar offers or dissolution of the company had become inevitable, the directors could not fulfill their enhanced duties by playing favorites with the contending factions. Rather, the directors must allow market forces to operate freely to bring the target's shareholders the best price available for their equity. Should a court uphold Pantry Pride's contentions? Why? [See *Revlon, Inc.* v. *MacAndrew & Forbes Holdings, Inc.,* 506 A.2d 173 (Del. 1986).]

7. **ETHICS APPLICATION CASE** Danny Hill was an officer and general manager of Southeastern Floor Covering Co. (Southeastern), which completed ceiling and floor-covering work for general contractors. Southeastern often subcontracted its asbestos-removal work to Southern Interiors. Southeastern bid on construction work on the Chata project. Hill arranged with Southern Interiors for it to bid on the Chata project directly without involving Southeastern. Southern Interiors was awarded the bid and Hill earned $90,000 according to their arrangement. When Southeastern discovered the arrangement, it sued Hill. Should Southeastern be awarded the $90,000 payment Hill received? What ethical issues are raised? [See *Hill* v. *Southeastern Floor Covering Co., Inc.,* 596 So.2d 874 (Miss. 1992).]

8. **IDES CASE** In the mid-1960s, James Covington, the owner of Mexico Feed and Seed Company (Mexico), entered into an oral lease agreement with Jack Pierce, the president of Pierce Oil Waste Service, Inc. (Pierce), for the placement by Pierce of waste oil tanks on a parcel of land owned by Covington and used as the site for Mexico storage. From 1967–1976, Pierce employees hauled various types of oils, including transformer oils. During that period, many transformers contained PCBs (polychlorinated byphenyls). One of Pierce's customers was Mid-Mo Electric Company (Mid-Mo), a rebuilder of transformers. A Pierce driver pumped waste oil directly out of transformers at Mid-Mo and hauled the oil to the Mexico site. In 1985, PCBs were found at the Mid-Mo location, later designated as a PCB Superfund site. During that time, Pierce drivers also hauled oil from Findett, a company that reclaimed fluids from Monsanto Company. Until about 1979, Monsanto was the major manufacturer of PCBs in the United States. Pierce drivers also regularly collected oil from other companies using products showing the presence of PCBs and, in fact, never rejected any customers' oil because of its contents. Mexico never used the Pierce tanks for its own purposes, never agreed to accept ownership of the tanks in lieu of rental payments, and never listed the tanks as an asset of Mexico Feed and Seed Company or of James and Mary Covington. In June and July 1984, a representative of the U.S. Environmental Protection Agency inspected the Mexico site for the presence of PCBs, which federal regulations list as hazardous substances. At the time of the inspection, waste oil sludge, which can contain PCBs, was present in all four tanks and water dripped from the valve of one of the tanks. The inspection revealed that two of the tanks contained high concentrations of PCBs (80 percent and 74 percent) and that the other two tanks contained traces of PCBs. A chemist with the EPA, who had conducted tests on the samples taken from the site, testified that an area becomes a cleanup site when the soil contains 50 parts per million of PCBs. Samples of soil from the tank area revealed 330 parts per million of PCBs. The chemist concluded that the Mexico site was contaminated and that the contamination area radiated out from the tanks for about 100 feet. Moreover, the incorporation of the PCBs into the environment over a period of time (weathering) had occurred, indicating that the initial point of contamination had begun as much as twenty years before. The United States cleaned up the site and incurred costs of more than $1,024,321.79 under the Comprehensive Environmental Response, Compensation and Liability Act (CERCLA). [Congress had enacted CERCLA in 1980 as a response to hazardous waste problems.] According to 42 U.S.C. § 9607(a), the United States is authorized to sue to recover for damage to natural resources and for "all costs of removal or remedial action." A liable person is "any person who at the time of the disposal of any hazardous substance owned or operated any facility at which such hazardous substances were disposed of."

   Use the IDES model to evaluate this case from a legal and an ethical perspective. Was Jack Pierce, the president of Pierce, liable under CERCLA? Why or why not? [See *United States* v. *Mexico Feed and Seed Co.*, 764 F.Supp. 565 (E.D. Mo. 1991).]

NOTES

1. Uniform Partnership Act (UPA) refers to the 1914 act drafted by the National Conference of Commissioners on Uniform State Laws (NCCUSL). The UPA is the majority rule in the United States today.
2. Uniform Partnership Act, § 18(h).
3. Ibid., § 18(a), (b), (c).
4. Ibid., § 18(f).
5. Ibid., §§ 19 and 20.
6. Ibid., § 25.
7. Ibid., § 22.
8. Ibid., § 21.
9. Ibid., § 10.
10. Ibid., § 11.
11. Ibid., § 12.
12. Ibid., § 13.
13. Ibid., § 14.
14. Ibid., § 28.
15. Ibid., § 21.
16. The Model Business Corporation Act (1969) began as a drafting effort in 1943 by the American Bar Association's Section on Corporation, Banking, and Business Law; its intent was to modernize corporate law and to achieve greater uniformity among jurisdictions by creating a statute that balances the interests of the state, the corporation, the shareholders, and management. Most of the states follow either the older Model Business Corporation Act (MBCA) or the 1984 version, the Revised Model Business Corporation Act (RMBCA).
17. Joann S. Lublin, "Firms Rethink Lucrative Severance Pacts for Top Executives as Criticism Swells," *Wall Street Journal* (11 November 1991), p. B1.

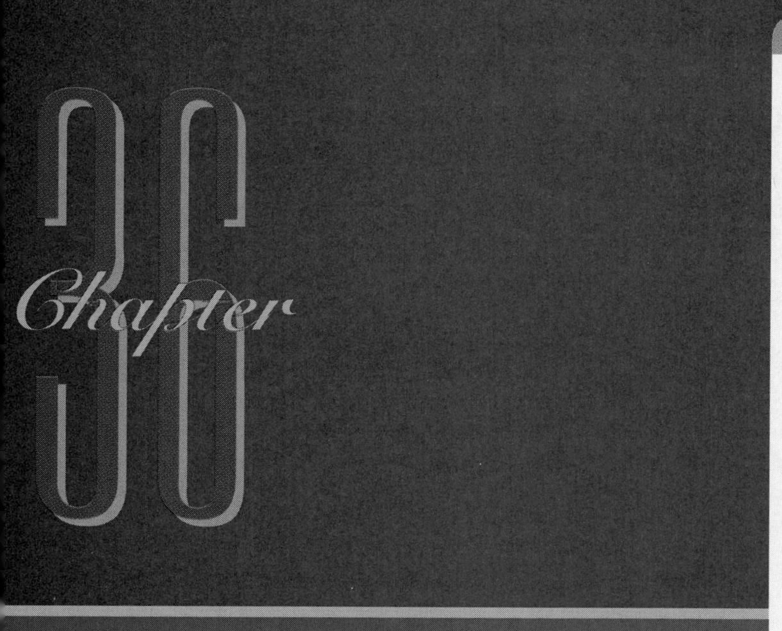

Business Terminations and Other Extraordinary Events

Outline

Agenda

CIT may be a big success in developing and marketing Call-Image. On the other hand, the enterprise may fail miserably. If the firm is a success, it is likely that a large corporation may wish to acquire CIT. The Kochanowskis do not wish to give up ownership of the company, and they would resist any takeover efforts. If the other firm persists in its efforts to acquire CIT, how can the Kochanowskis prevent a takeover? What legal or ethical restrictions may limit its actions? If the enterprise is a failure, the Kochanowskis are afraid that they will lose everything they have acquired over the years. How can they protect their assets while providing adequate support to the firm to give it a chance to succeed?

These and other questions will arise as you read this chapter. Be prepared! You never know when one of the Kochanowskis will ask for your help or advice.

Termination of a Sole Proprietorship

The termination of a sole proprietorship is a relatively simple matter. The owner simply pays the business debts and then the remaining assets belong to him or her. As an alternative, the owner might sell the business to someone else. Care must be used to assure that business liabilities are handled correctly, however. Often, but not always, this is an obligation undertaken by the buyer.

Partnership Terminations

The ending of a partnership is different from what most people expect. The partnership may end while the business enterprise continues; if so, a dissolution occurs. Or the partnership and the business enterprise may both end. If so, a dissolution and a **winding up** occur. These variations in the termination of a partnership are the focus of this section.

Winding up

Paying the accounts and liquidating the assets of a business for the purpose of making distributions and dissolving the concern.

Partnership Dissolution

Technically, a *dissolution* is "the change in the relation of the partners caused by any partner ceasing to be associated in the carrying on as distinguished from the winding up of the business."[1] This means that any time a partner leaves the business, the partnership is dissolved. The change in the relations of the partners changes the partnership.

The fact that a partner leaves the business does not mean that the *business* must cease to exist. The remaining partners may continue the business, or they may need to terminate the business. What they may or may not do depends on the method and manner of dissolution.

Section 31 of the Uniform Partnership Act (UPA) lists several different causes of dissolution. [Note that references in this chapter to the Uniform Partnership Act (UPA) are to the UPA (1914), which is the majority rule.] Any of these events will cause a dissolution of the partnership, but they may not require a winding up of the business. We shall examine these causes of dissolution next.

Without Violation of the Agreement

A dissolution may be caused by the terms of the partnership agreement. For example, the time period established in the agreement may expire, or the original purpose of the partnership may be fulfilled. If a partnership was established to operate for two years, and two years have elapsed, the partnership is dissolved. If a partnership was established to sell 100 parcels of land, and all the land has been sold, the partnership is dissolved. Of course, a new agreement may be made to extend the time or to modify the purpose, if the partners so desire.

If the agreement does not specify a particular time period or a particular, limited purpose, a partner may simply decide to quit. Unless the agreement denies this right to withdraw, such a decision operates as a dissolution without violation of the agreement.

All the partners may decide to terminate the partnership. If so, the partnership is dissolved without violating the agreement. This is true even *if* a definite time period was specified and that time has not yet expired. And it is true even if a particular purpose was declared and the purpose has not yet been achieved.

Finally, a partnership is dissolved without violation of the agreement if any partner is expelled from the partnership by the other partners, *provided* that the expulsion is permitted by the agreement. Thus, if X, Y, and Z vote to remove Q from the firm, and the agreement permits such a vote, the partnership is dissolved without violation of the agreement.

Normally, a dissolution that does not violate the agreement will lead to a winding up *unless* the agreement itself provides for a continuation of the business. If the agreement does not specify that a continuation is permitted, the partner who causes the dissolution may demand that a winding up take place. Such a demand must be obeyed, even though it normally will harm the remaining partners who may wish to continue the business. Thus, every partnership agreement should contain some provisions for continuing the business. (Of course, an *expelled* partner cannot demand a winding up of the business if the expulsion was done in good faith by the other partners.)

In Violation of the Agreement

No one can be forced to be a partner against his or her will. Thus, any partner has the *power* to withdraw from any partnership at any time—but a partner does not have the *right* to withdraw at any time. A withdrawing partner may violate the terms of the partnership agreement by withdrawing. If so, the remaining partners may continue the business if they desire, even though the partnership has been (technically) dissolved. The partner who withdrew in violation of the agreement has no right to demand or require a winding up.

Similarly, the partner who withdraws in violation of the agreement does not have the right to demand that the business be continued. Once a partner withdraws in violation of the agreement, the remaining innocent partners may decide to do whatever they believe is most appropriate. In *Ohlendorf* v. *Feinstein,* a partner who withdrew in violation of the agreement learned on his withdrawal that all the options belonged to the remaining partners.

36.1 OHLENDORF v. FEINSTEIN

636 S.W.2d 687 (Mo. 1982)

FACTS The Missouri State Highway Commission was accepting bids on seven tracts of land. Feinstein's bid of just over $568,000 was accepted by the commission. When he learned that his bid had been accepted, Feinstein entered into a partnership with Ohlendorf and Whaley to sell the land. Several months later, Ohlendorf notified the other partners that he was withdrawing from the partnership due to differences of opinion. Ohlendorf also informed the commission that the partnership did not intend to close the sale of the seven tracts of land. After this, Ohlendorf sued the other two partners to recover his capital contributions. The other partners refused to return his capital and countersued Ohlendorf for damages and for lost profits from the aborted purchase in order to wind up the partnership affairs.

ISSUE Did the remaining partners have a duty to continue the business so as to mitigate (reduce) the damages faced by Ohlendorf?

HOLDING No.

REASONING Ohlendorf's withdrawal in violation of the agreement permitted the remaining partners at their option to either continue the business or wind it up. The UPA specifically allows the remaining partners to elect their remedies when a partner withdraws in violation of the partnership agreement. They may continue the business if they so desire and seek damages from the withdrawing partner. Or they may elect to wind up the business and sue the withdrawing partner for damages caused by the wrongful withdrawal. The mere fact that continuing the business

36.1 OHLENDORF v. FEINSTEIN *(cont.)* 636 S.W.2d 687 (Mo. 1982)

will likely result in profits to the remaining partners is irrelevant. When Ohlendorf withdrew, he placed the other partners in a position to decide how to proceed. They chose to sue for damages, as was their right under the law. Their selection must be enforced under the provisions of the UPA.

BUSINESS CONSIDERATIONS What factors should the remaining partners in a dissolved partnership consider in deciding whether to continue the business? How important is the partnership agreement in this decision?

ETHICAL CONSIDERATIONS What ethical obligations are owed to a withdrawing partner by the partners who did not withdraw from the agreement? Should personal feelings be a factor in the decision to continue or wind up the enterprise?

By Operation of Law

A partnership may also be dissolved by operation of law, if any one of the following three events occurs:

1. Something happens that makes it unlawful for the business to continue or for the partners to continue the business. (Thus, a law that prohibits anyone from selling elephant tusks will terminate a partnership in the tusk-selling business. And a partnership that loses its import license will be dissolved even though importing itself is still legal.)
2. A partner dies.
3. A partner or the partnership becomes bankrupt.

By Court Order

The final method for dissolving a partnership is by court order. As explained in § 32 of the UPA, a court will order a dissolution only if *asked* to do so. The person who wants to dissolve the partnership must petition the court; the court will not go searching for partnerships that should be dissolved.

Most commonly, the petitioning person is one of the partners or a representative of one of the partners. Even if a petition is filed, dissolution is not automatic. The court must have *grounds* to grant the request. The following grounds will justify a dissolution by court decree:

1. insanity of any partner
2. incapacity, other than insanity, of a partner that prevents that partner from performing the contractual duties called for in the agreement
3. misconduct by any partner that makes continued operation of the business difficult
4. intentional or repeated breach of the agreement by a partner, or any behavior that makes the continuation of the business impossible or impractical
5. evidence that the business can be continued only at a loss with no prospect of a profit turnaround in the near future
6. any other circumstances that, in the court's opinion, justify dissolution as the equitable response

Note that insanity does *not* automatically dissolve the partnership; a petition must be filed seeking dissolution. If the remaining partners wish to continue the business with an insane partner, they have the right to do so.

It is also possible that some person may purchase the interest of a partner and then decide to seek a court-ordered dissolution.[2] Such a court order may be granted only if one of two sets of circumstances can be shown:

1. The agreement had a specific term or a particular purpose that has been fulfilled or satisfied.
2. The partnership was a partnership **at will** at the time of the purchase.

At will
Having no specific date or circumstance to bring about a dissolution.

CONTINUATION OF THE PARTNERSHIP BUSINESS

Once a dissolution occurs, an important decision must be made. Will the business terminate through a winding up, or will the business continue? In most cases, an ongoing business is more valuable than the assets that make up the business; the sum is greater than its parts. Thus, the remaining partners normally want to continue operating the business if they can possibly do so. This may not be satisfactory to a withdrawing partner, however. For this reason, the partners should consider the problem of a continuation when they draw up the original agreement, and they should make provisions for the problem at that time.

The remaining partners have the *right* to elect to continue the business under any one of the following circumstances:

1. The withdrawing partner withdraws in violation of the agreement.
2. The withdrawing partner consents to the continuation when he or she could have demanded a termination and winding up.
3. The agreement permits a continuation following a dissolution.

Unless one of these circumstances occurs, a dissolution will be followed by a winding up.

Withdrawing Partners

Any time the business is continued following a withdrawal, the continuing partners have a duty to the withdrawing partner. The withdrawing partner must be both indemnified (that is, secured against anticipated losses) and bought out. The purpose of the indemnification is to protect the withdrawing partner from any claims of creditors of the partnership. The withdrawing partner is still liable for any debts owed that arose during membership in the partnership and association with the business. Without an indemnification agreement, a withdrawing partner might be tempted to force a winding up in order to minimize potential liability. But the indemnification agreement is assurance that the continuing partners will repay any losses the withdrawing partner may suffer on account of partnership obligations.

Withdrawing partners are also entitled to payment for their interest in the business, including any undistributed profits, at the time of withdrawal. However, if a withdrawal is in violation of the partnership agreement, the continuing partners may first deduct *damages,* based on breach of contract theories. The amount of these damages should adequately cover the harm caused by the breach.

The continuing partners may pay former partners in a lump sum and settle the matter. If they do not, or cannot, make a lump-sum payment, the withdrawing partners are allowed to elect how payment will be made. They can either: (1) receive interest on the unpaid portion until they receive payment in full; or (2) elect to receive a portion of profits that corresponds to their unpaid portion of their share until they are paid in full. This election must be made at the time of withdrawal, however, and once made, it cannot be changed unless the continuing partners agree to the change.

Entering Partners

Occasionally, a new partner is brought into the business. When this happens, a continuation obviously occurs. No one wants to enter a business in order to see it go through a winding up. The continuation is treated slightly differently, however, when a new partner enters the firm. As a partner, the new entrant is liable for the debts of the partnership. But existing creditors did not rely on the new partner's credit when they decided to extend credit. As a result, it seems unfair to impose unlimited liability on the new partner. UPA § 41(7) resolves this problem by specifying that the new partner is liable to preexisting creditors only up to the amount of his or her capital contribution. In other words, an entering partner has limited liability to preexisting creditors but faces unlimited personal liability with respect to future creditors.

WINDING UP THE PARTNERSHIP

Winding up is the termination of the business enterprise. In winding up, one must **marshal** and **liquidate** the assets of the business and then distribute the proceeds of this process to the proper parties.

Marshal

To arrange assets or claims in such a way as to secure the proper application of the assets to the claims.

Liquidate

To settle with creditors and debtors and apportion any remaining assets.

General Partnerships

The priority for distributing the proceeds is set out in the UPA § 40. The first priority is the claims owed to creditors who are not partners. If the proceeds are sufficient to pay this class entirely, they will be so paid. Any surplus carries over to the next priority class. Any deficit will cause two things to happen: (1) a pro rata distribution of the proceeds within the class; and (2) a collection of the balance from the personal assets of the partners, jointly and severally.

The second priority in receiving the proceeds is claims owed to the partners as *creditors* of the business. Again, any surplus will be applied to the next priority class, and any deficit will be made up from the personal assets of the partners. Note that a partner who wishes to be treated as a creditor of the firm will need to present clear and convincing evidence of the debt. It is normally presumed that any monies advanced to the firm were advanced as a capital contribution, not as a loan. The court probably will demand some written proof, such as a promissory note, that the funds were meant as a loan. Without such proof, the partner is likely to find that what he or she viewed as a loan was, in the eyes of the court, a capital contribution.

The third priority is the return of the capital contributions of the partners. Any surplus will be carried over to the fourth and final priority. Any deficit will be allocated among the partners pro rata.

The fourth and final priority category is profits. Any monies left over after all the other classes have been satisfied will be distributed as profits, according to the terms of the partnership agreement. There can be no deficit here.

The creditors of the partnership have first claim on any partnership assets, as well as a secondary claim on the partnership assets that reflect the interest of the indebted partner in the business. However, the claims by individual creditors against partnership shares are limited by the UPA § 28. Usually, the individual creditor is given a **charging order** by the court while the business is in operation in order to minimize the disruption of normal business operations.

Charging order
A court order permitting a creditor to receive profits from the operation of a business; especially common in partnership situations.

The three examples that follow illustrate how the various interested parties may be treated in a dissolution of a partnership and a winding up of the business. In each example, there are three partners—Jerrod, Carmen, and Eric—whose net worths are shown in the first example. In addition, each partner has made the capital contributions specified, and Jerrod has made a loan to the firm. Notice the effect the different asset positions of the partners have on the partners individually.

Partners	Personal Assets	Personal Liabilities	Net Worth
Carmen	$ 80,000	$ 40,000	$ 40,000
Eric	40,000	100,000	(60,000)
Jerrod	100,000	20,000	80,000

Each partner has already contributed $50,000 to the partnership; moreover, profits and losses are to be shared equally. Jerrod has already loaned the firm $30,000 (there is a signed promissory note for this loan).

Example I

Further assume that the partnership has $200,000 in proceeds and $290,000 in liabilities to regular creditors, plus the $30,000 owed to Jerrod.

Step 1. Partnership proceeds are distributed to regular creditors (priority 1), leaving a deficit of $90,000.

Step 2. Each partner owes an additional $30,000 to priority 1 creditors. However, Eric has no money, and so Jerrod and Carmen must pay the full $90,000 between them (Jerrod will pay $50,000 and Carmen will pay $40,000) and hold claims against Eric (Jerrod for $20,000, and Carmen for $10,000). Both Carmen and Eric are now insolvent.

Step 3. Under priority 3, Jerrod, Carmen, and Eric each owe Jerrod $10,000. Jerrod "pays" himself, and Carmen and Eric each owe Jerrod $10,000.

Consequently, Jerrod had a net worth of $80,000, which has decreased to $30,000 plus $40,000 in debts owed by Carmen and Eric. Carmen had a net worth of $40,000, which has decreased to ($10,000), including the amount that Carmen owes Jerrod. Carmen also has a claim of $10,000 against Eric. Eric had a net worth of ($60,000), which has technically decreased to ($100,000).

Example 2

Assume instead that the partnership has $309,000 in proceeds and $300,000 in liabilities to regular creditors, plus the $30,000 owed to Jerrod.

Step 1. The priority 1 debts are paid in full, and the $9,000 surplus is carried over.

Step 2. Priority 2 debts are paid until the money runs out. Thus, Jerrod receives the $9,000 carried over from priority 1 and is still owed $21,000. Jerrod "pays" himself $7,000; Carmen pays Jerrod $7,000; Eric owes $7,000. Eric is insolvent, and Jerrod probably will not collect from Eric.

Consequently, Jerrod, who had a net worth of $80,000, now has increased it to $96,000 plus a $7,000 debt owed by Eric. Carmen had a net worth of $40,000, which has decreased to $33,000. Eric had a net worth of ($60,000), which has technically decreased to ($67,000).

Example 3

Assume instead that the partnership has $500,000 in proceeds, $200,000 in liabilities to regular creditors, and the $30,000 owed to Jerrod.

Step 1. Priority 1 debts are paid in full, leaving a surplus of $300,000.

Step 2. Priority 2 debts are paid in full (Jerrod gets his $30,000), leaving a $270,000 surplus.

Step 3. Priority 3 is taken care of next. Each partner receives a full return of his or her capital contribution, leaving a surplus of $120,000.

Step 4. The final priority is satisfied; the $120,000 is distributed as profits, with $40,000 going to each of the partners.

In addition, the partners will also be paid in full in this case. Jerrod receives:

$ 30,000 loan payment
50,000 return of capital
40,000 profits
80,000 prior net worth
$200,000 new net worth

Carmen and Eric each receive:

$ 50,000 return of capital
40,000 profits
$ 90,000 distribution

Consequently, Carmen had a net worth of $40,000, which has increased to $130,000. Eric had a net worth of ($60,000), which has increased to $30,000.

Limited Partnerships

The distribution of assets in a limited partnership is substantially different from that in a normal, general partnership. Also, the ULPA and the RULPA differ in their treatment of distributions, and we will discuss the latter since the vast majority of states follow the RULPA. The Revised Act calls for distribution in the following order:

1. claims of nonpartner creditors and claims of partners as creditors
2. any amounts owed to former partners prior to their withdrawal from the firm
3. return of capital contributions of all partners
4. the remainder distributed as profits to all of the partners

The two examples that follow illustrate how various interested parties may be treated in a dissolution of a limited partnership and a winding up of the business under the RULPA. In each example, there are two general partners—Alice and

Bob—and two limited partners—Chuck and Diane. The financial positions and contributions of each of the four are set out in the first example.

Partners	Personal Assets	Personal Liabilities	Net Worth
Alice	$150,000	$ 75,000	$ 75,000
Bob	375,000	135,000	240,000
Chuck	100,000	150,000	(50,000)
Diane	200,000	185,000	15,000

Each partner has already contributed $75,000 to the firm. The general partners are to receive 30 percent of the profits each, and the limited partners are to receive 20 percent of the profits each. Chuck has already loaned the firm an additional $50,000 and has a signed promissory note.

Example 1

Further assume the partnership has $400,000 in proceeds and $500,000 in liabilities to nonpartner creditors. Under the RULPA, the distribution is as follows:

Step 1. Claims of creditors, both partner and nonpartner, are first priority. Here, the $400,000 in proceeds are allocated to the $550,000 in debt owed to nonpartners and to Chuck. These debtors are paid at the rate of approximately 73 percent each, which is calculated by dividing $400,000 by $550,000. The balance of $150,000 in debt is owed by the general partners individually. Since Alice and Bob have the funds, they share this liability equally.

Step 2. Amounts owed to former partners are paid next; however, there are no former partners in this example.

Step 3. Capital contributions of all partners are returned. Since the firm has no money left, the general partners are personally liable for this $300,000 ($75,000 times 4) claim. Bob "pays" himself, and he pays Chuck and Diane $75,000 each. Since Alice already owes Bob, she does not collect $75,000 from him. (Alice owes Bob on his loan to the firm in Step 1 as well as her share of the payments to Chuck and Diane in Step 3.)

Step 4. Remaining funds are distributed as profits; however, no funds remain in this example.

Example 2

Assume instead that the partnership has $500,000 in proceeds and $100,000 in liabilities to nonpartner creditors. Under the RULPA, the distribution is as follows:

Step 1. Claims of creditors, both partner and nonpartner, are satisfied first. The entire $150,000 owed is paid, leaving $350,000.

Step 2. Any amounts owed to former partners are paid; however, there are none in this example.

Step 3. Capital contributions of all partners are returned. The entire $300,000 is paid, leaving a balance of $50,000.

Step 4. The balance is distributed as profits. Each general partner gets $15,000 (30 percent each), and each limited partner gets $10,000 (20 percent each).

CHANGES IN CORPORATE STRUCTURE

In Chapter 35, we briefly touched on the subject of dissolution when we discussed shareholders' rights in the event of the liquidation of the corporation. So far, though, we have paid scant attention to fundamental changes in the corporate structure that may endanger the rights of shareholders and creditors. We will now focus on actions bringing about some of these fundamental changes—dissolution, merger and consolidation, sale of substantially all the corporate assets, and stock acquisition. Exhibit 36.1 illustrates these four major changes in corporate structure.

LIQUIDATION OF THE CORPORATION

The process of *liquidation* consists of the winding up of the affairs of a business in order to go out of business, that is, the marshaling of assets and the subsequent conversion of those assets to cash in order to pay the claims of creditors. During this winding up, the corporation pays all debts and creditors from the corporate assets and then distributes any remaining assets to the shareholders. The process of dissolution, which denotes the end of the corporation's legal existence, may immediately precede or follow liquidation. Although the terms *dissolution* and *liquidation* are often used together, they are not synonymous.

Receiver
An unbiased person appointed by a court to receive, preserve, and manage the funds and property of a party.

Throughout the liquidation period, the corporation has all the rights and powers reasonably necessary to effect liquidation. Moreover, during this period, the corporation can sue and be sued. Under most statutes, the board of directors continues the management of the corporation unless a court has ordered the dissolution and liquidation. In the latter case, the court may appoint a **receiver** to oversee the liquidation. If the directors unlawfully continue the business of the corporation after dissolution and beyond the time reasonably necessary to wind up the corporation's affairs, they may become personally liable for the corporation's debts. Caution among the directors (and controlling shareholders) is therefore in order during the liquidation process.

State statutes normally protect creditors during liquidation because the creditors have rights superior to those of the stockholders in liquidations. The statutes require the corporation to notify creditors of dissolution and liquidation so that these creditors can file their claims against the corporation during this time period. A creditor who receives notice but does not file a claim may lose the right to sue later on this claim. Retention of this right, on the other hand, allows the creditor to recoup from shareholders any distributions of corporate assets that have occurred before payment of creditors' claims. To protect creditors, the law characterizes the illegal distributions as held "in trust" for the benefit of the creditors. The directors also may incur liability for distributions illegally declared up to the amount of claims that remain unpaid.

After the corporation has satisfied its debts to its creditors, the shareholders ordinarily receive the proportion of the remaining net assets represented by their respective share ownership. As discussed earlier, however, the articles of incorporation may set out one or more classes of shares as meriting liquidation preferences over

EXHIBIT 36.1 Fundamental Changes in Corporate Structure

MERGER OR CONSOLIDATION

Rationales:
- Economies of scale
- Knowledge (i.e., acquisition of "know- how")
- Diversification
- Securing of competitive advantages
- Tax savings
- Utilization of assets
- Preservation of management prerogatives

Formalities:
- Both boards' adoption of merger plan
- Both corporations' shareholder approval (usually 2/3 of outstanding shares or more needed) unless short-form merger involved
- Filing of plan with state
- Issuance of certificate of merger
- Provision of appraisal rights to dissenting shareholders and compliance with statutory procedures covering such rights, including:
  (a) Dissenting shareholders' written notice of objection to merger
  (b) Dissenting shareholders' written demand on corporation for fair value/fair market value of shares
  (c) On failure to agree, either corporation or dissenting shareholders petition court for an appraisal proceeding

Effect:
- Assets, rights, and liabilities of acquired firm assumed by surviving firm by operation of law
- Dissolution of acquired firm

SALE OF SUBSTANTIALLY ALL THE ASSETS

Formalities:
- Simpler than merger procedures
- Approval only by seller's shareholders (i.e., approval of buyer's shareholders unnecessary)
- Provision of appraisal rights to seller's dissenting shareholders and compliance with applicable statutory procedures
- Compliance with statutory provisions protecting creditors' rights
- These formalities not applicable to sale, in the regular course of business, of substantially all the assets created by the corporation

Effect:
- Liabilities of seller ordinarily not assumed by purchaser by operation of law

STOCK ACQUISITION

Formalities:
- Simpler than procedures for merger or sale of substantially all the assets
- Compliance with all applicable state statutes and federal securities laws
- Neither board action nor shareholder approval by either corporation needed; necessary only for shareholders of target firm to decide to sell to would-be acquirer or refrain from selling
- Transactions may be deemed de facto mergers and set aside by courts

DISSOLUTION

Voluntary (Initiated by shareholders)

Formalities:
- Board recommendation
- Shareholder approval (usually 2/3 of outstanding shares or more needed)
- Filing of notice to creditors
- Filing of certificate of dissolution
- Liquidation of corporation[a]

Involuntary (Initiated by shareholders or other entities)

Types:
- At request of state, owing to
  (a) Securities fraud; or
  (b) Noncompliance with state statutory procedures (e.g., failure to pay taxes or file annual reports)
- At request of shareholders, owing to
  (a) Mismanagement; or
  (b) Deadlock among directors or controlling shareholders so serious as to warrant dissolution
- At request of creditors, owing to the need to preserve creditors' rights

[a]This may occur before or after dissolution.

another class or classes of shares. For instance, preferred stockholders usually receive their shares of the net assets before holders of common stock do. (Note, however, that preferred shareholders *never* receive payment before creditors do.) But if the preferred shareholders do not enjoy liquidation preferences, they will participate with the common shareholders on a share-for-share basis. Sometimes the articles give the preferred shareholders both liquidation preferences and participation rights with the common shareholders. Because cash is the usual method for satisfying liquidation preferences, the corporation may need to sell its assets to raise the amount required to take care of these preferences. Under most statutes, the corporation can distribute property instead of cash in satisfying liquidation preferences; but it will be illegal to favor some shareholders through grants of property (as when a corporation gives controlling shareholders valuable patents or trademarks) while doling out cash to minority shareholders.

Dissolution of the Corporation

Dissolution involves termination of the corporation as a *legal entity,* or juristic person. The term *dissolution* is not synonymous with *liquidation,* which refers to the winding up or termination of the corporation's business or affairs. Corporate existence remains impervious to most events, including such unusual occurrences as bankruptcy or the cessation of business activities. Dissolution, then, because it represents an extraordinary circumstance, or an organic change in corporate structure, must occur formally in order to have legal effect. Dissolutions are of two types: voluntary and involuntary.

Voluntary Dissolution

As we learned in Chapter 34, corporations theoretically can exist perpetually. On the other hand, a corporation's articles may limit the period of corporate life to, say, 10 years. Alternatively, the incorporators may decide at some point to end the corporation's existence, even though the articles specify the perpetual duration of the corporation. In both cases, such voluntary dissolutions must be carried out through formal procedures.

Statutes ordinarily set out the requirements for these nonjudicial, voluntary dissolutions. Typically, these statutes mandate (1) board action recommending dissolution, (2) shareholder voting to approve the dissolution (usually by the holders of two-thirds of the outstanding shares), and/or (3) filing of a notice to creditors prior to dissolution.

On compliance with these and any other necessary procedures, a certificate of dissolution is filed with the secretary of state or other designated state officer. At this time, the dissolution is legally effective. Remember, though, that liquidation may follow or precede dissolution; so it is possible that some limited corporate activity may occur after dissolution. In voluntary liquidation, the shareholders share proportionately—subject, of course, to any liquidation preferences—in the net assets of the corporation that remain after satisfaction of creditors' claims. As discussed in earlier chapters, courts prohibit dissolutions that freeze out minority shareholders, especially if a controlling shareholder initiated the dissolution. Also, be aware that the rules regarding dissolutions may vary when a close corporation, instead of a publicly held corporation, is involved.

Involuntary Dissolution

Occasionally, the state, the shareholders, or the corporation's creditors may request the dissolution of the corporation because of wrongdoing or prejudice to shareholders or creditors. Such judicial proceedings are involuntary because the corporation itself is not asking for dissolution. Involuntary dissolutions by their very nature occur less frequently than voluntary ones.

Dissolution at the Request of the State. Because the corporation is a creation of the state, the state retains the power to rescind the corporation's certificate when the corporation's actions present a clear danger to the public. For instance, the state may ask for involuntary dissolution of a corporation that has engaged in systematic securities fraud. More often, however, grounds for involuntary dissolution involve noncompliance with state requirements, such as failure to pay taxes or to file annual reports.

Rather than seek dissolution, the state may seek suspension of the corporation. Suspension works as a deprivation of the corporation's right to conduct its business and certain other powers, but is not as drastic or as permanent a remedy as dissolution. When the firm is in compliance with the corporate statutes, the state can order a reinstatement of the corporation.

Dissolution at the Request of Shareholders. Shareholders can petition the courts for dissolution of the corporation. Statutes generally authorize shareholder actions based on freeze-outs (or oppression) of minority shareholders' interests, allegations of corporate waste of assets, and other examples of corporate mismanagement. Courts sometimes order dissolutions in similar circumstances even in the absence of express statutory provisions. Deadlock among directors or shareholders constitutes an additional ground for involuntary dissolution. For example, courts intervene when a shareholder shows that the deadlock among directors or controlling shareholders has so paralyzed the corporation that it can no longer conduct its business advantageously.

As a less severe alternative, some state statutes permit the appointment of a provisional (or temporary) director who breaks the deadlock and thus allows the corporation to continue functioning. Statutes also may allow holders of a majority of the corporation's outstanding shares to purchase the shares owned by the shareholders who are requesting dissolution. Statutes may contain provisions setting out a minimum number of shareholders (for example, one-third of the corporate shareholders) who must join in the petition for involuntary dissolution before it can be presented to a court.

In contrast to these potential actions, shareholders in close corporations frequently agree in advance that upon the occurrence of a certain event, such as deadlock, each shareholder will be able to request dissolution. Courts ordinarily enforce such agreements.

Dissolution at the Request of Creditors. The theory of corporate personality normally prevents creditors from compelling the involuntary dissolution of the corporation. But in order to protect creditors' rights during dissolution and liquidation, statutes require prior notice to creditors. Statutes also allow the appointment of a receiver who takes over the corporation's business and conducts it for the benefit of the creditors. In some circumstances, creditors can petition for the involuntary bankruptcy of the corporation to preserve their rights. Neither the appointment of a receiver nor the institution of involuntary bankruptcy proceedings results in the dissolution of the corporation, however. As we have seen, formal statutory procedures spell out the necessary steps for effecting this fundamental change in corporate structure. Courts are reluctant to force dissolution and generally do so only if they have no other alternative.

Corporate Merger and Consolidation

Like dissolutions, mergers and consolidations bring about fundamental, or organic, changes in the corporation's structure. Dissolution is also related to these two concepts because dissolution of a corporation (or corporations) occurs automatically when either a merger or a consolidation occurs, and the procedures for carrying out a merger or consolidation are similar to dissolution procedures.

Technically, a merger differs from a consolidation. In a *merger,* one corporation (called the "acquirer" or "acquiring firm") purchases another firm (called the "acquired" or "disappearing firm") and absorbs it into itself. This new entity is called the *survivor corporation;* the acquired firm no longer exists.

A *consolidation* is similar, except that in a consolidation two or more existing corporations combine to form a wholly new corporate entity. Since most statutes treat the procedures for mergers and consolidations as if the two were identical transactions, this part of our discussion focuses only on mergers. But, as noted, they are analytically different ways of bringing about major changes in corporate structure.

Rationales for Merger

For various reasons, the last three decades have witnessed a phenomenal upsurge in the number of mergers. We will review some more common motivations.

Economies of Scale. *Economies of scale* refer to reductions in per-unit costs resulting from larger plant size. A merger may permit a firm to achieve economies of scale and thus to compete much more efficiently: The larger the firm, the easier it is for the firm to receive discounts on sales and advertising and thereby to achieve lower costs. Accumulation of resources resulting from merged firms also facilitates access to financing. Two beer producers that merge generally present a more attractive credit risk for lending institutions than a wine business operating from someone's basement. Bigness may also spawn more research and development. A merged firm, for example, ordinarily is able to allocate more funds to these activities. The capital in the struggling wine business, in contrast, typically goes for electricity, rent, and other overhead costs. The vintner may want to invest in research on capping methods or grape hybrids, but economies of scale make such research and development much more feasible in large firms. Mergers between manufacturers and customers (called *vertical mergers*) may lessen transaction costs and bring about economies of scale in this fashion also.

As you will learn in Chapter 40, a firm can use economies of scale to drive out smaller, less efficient firms because of the dominance it may achieve because of its size and wealth ("deep pockets"). Antitrust laws generally protect the competitive environment from any retaliatory, abusive conduct in which large firms may engage. In the absence of antitrust concerns, mergers to effect economies of scale are legal and customary.

Knowledge. Often a larger company will merge with a smaller company because the latter possesses valuable technological information or know-how. An established computer firm, for example, may find a merger with a software firm valuable if the software firm has made technological breakthroughs deemed valuable by the computer firm. Thinking back to economies of scale, it may well be cheaper for the computer firm to purchase the software firm and its patents, trademarks, and trade secrets than to expend research and development funds necessary to create similar software. Furthermore, the merged firm may be able to retain the staff of the smaller firm and thereby realize further future gains from these persons' collective expertise and inventive capacities.

Diversification. The 1970s marked a large increase in the number of mergers undertaken for the purpose of diversification. Many firms jumped into areas previously unrelated to their principal lines of business through **conglomerate mergers**. Diversification minimizes the risks that are inherent in a firm's restricting itself to one industry and the risks caused by economic cycles. Critics of diversification have argued, however, that diversification dilutes capital markets by making it easier for a diversified company to hide its actual profits and losses. These authorities maintain that lending institutions' abilities to assess credit-worthiness are impaired by corporate diversification resulting from mergers. This concern, coupled with some experts' fears about the implications of the excessive concentrations of economic power represented by diversified companies, argue for limiting conglomerate mergers. At this time, governmental regulators are not enforcing a strict policy against conglomerate mergers. (Antitrust enforcement policies often change with the political and economic climate of the country.)

Conglomerate mergers
Mergers between noncompeting firms in different industries.

Competition. Inherent in much of what we have discussed so far is an underlying desire to control, if not curtail, competition. One firm clearly does not want to be at the mercy of another firm in times of scarcity. Therefore, a merger between a supplier of aluminum and a fabricator of aluminum, for instance, seems a viable strategy for cutting down on some of the supply-side uncertainties. Naturally, though, antitrust concerns may also lurk in mergers designed to control the competitive process, so caution is warranted.

One example of such a problem involved the planned merger between Microsoft and Intuit in 1996. When the proposed merger was announced, the Justice Department objected on the grounds that competition in the software market would be harmed. Eventually, Microsoft withdrew its offer rather than enter a prolonged and expensive legal battle over the competitive effect of the proposed merger.

Other Rationales. Other rationales for mergers include tax savings, utilization of cash-rich assets to infuse businesses that need such assets for expansion and growth, and preservation of rights of management. Critics of the last rationale have argued that many mergers occur because of the egos of important management officials who want to become the executive officers of even bigger companies. Such "power trips," these critics assert, lead to the possible sacrifice of shareholders' interests, personnel displacement, and the uprooting of smaller corporations from the local community of which they were an integral part. The previously mentioned controversies over hostile takeovers, "golden parachutes," "poison pills," and defensive mergers (that is, mergers in which corporation A merges with corporation C to avoid A's being taken over by corporation B) often surface in such criticisms as well.

YOU BE THE JUDGE

Cadbury's Bid for Dr Pepper

Cadbury Schweppes PLC, a London group, and Dr Pepper–Seven-Up Cos., Inc., are competitors in the soft-drink market. Cadbury is offering to purchase all the shares of Dr Pepper that it does not currently own, which is about 75 percent of the company. After an eighteen-month negotiation period, Cadbury increased its initial offer to a cash price of $33 per share. [A few days prior to the offer, the closing price of Dr Pepper on the New York Stock Exchange was $30.50.] Dr Pepper shareholders are urged to accept the offer.

After Cadbury had acquired about one-quarter of Dr Pepper, Dr Pepper began taking steps to make a takeover more difficult. During the negotiation, John Albers, Dr Pepper chairman, kept forcing the price up until the price seemed about right. Observers noted that Dr Pepper got about all it could from Cadbury. Cadbury will finance the deal by a variety of techniques, including asking shareholders to accept extra stock in lieu of cash dividends, borrowing funds, and offering preferred stock for purchase. Cadbury will also assume Dr Pepper's $828.4 million debt.

According to the deal, Cadbury will be entitled to sell Dr Pepper worldwide; however, it will receive only the U.S. rights to sell Seven-Up brands. [Pepsi owns the international rights to Seven-Up brands.] As Cadbury's group finance director, David Kappler, stated, "What we are really buying is brands." Cadbury expects to assume third place in the U.S. soft drink market with this acquisition.

Assume that a number of Dr. Pepper shareholders object to this takeover, and they have filed suit in *your* court to prevent it. How will *you* decide this case? What factors will you consider?[3]

BUSINESS CONSIDERATIONS Should Dr Pepper shareholders accept the offer? Is it beneficial to them? Is it beneficial to Cadbury and/or Cadbury's shareholders?

ETHICAL CONSIDERATIONS What ethical considerations are raised by takeover bids? Are there different ethical considerations with hostile takeovers compared to relatively friendly takeovers?

SOURCE: Dirk Beveridge, *The Fresno Bee,* 27 January 1995.

Procedure

Board of Directors. Whatever the rationale for the merger, once the firms have decided to merge, state statutes set out the steps that must be followed in bringing about the merger. Such statutes generally require that each corporation's board of directors adopt a merger plan that includes (1) the names of each corporation and the surviving corporation, (2) the appropriate terms and conditions of the merger, (3) the method for converting the acquired firm's securities into the securities of the acquiring firm (stock for cash, stock for stock, and the like), and (4) any amendments to the articles of the acquiring corporation that have resulted from the merger. Thorny problems can arise from these procedures.

Shareholders. After each of the boards of directors has adopted a merger plan, the shareholders of both corporations ordinarily must approve the merger. As with dissolutions, normally the holders of two-thirds of the outstanding shares must approve this fundamental change, although in a few states approval by a bare majority of the holders of the outstanding stock suffices.

In some states, statutory provisions dispense with the necessity for shareholder approval in *short-form mergers* (those involving a merger between a subsidiary and a parent company that owns 90 to 100 percent of the subsidiary's stock). Because the parent's ownership interest is so high, a vote of approval is a mere formality; requiring such a vote thus makes little practical sense.

Once all the required steps have been followed, the directors file the plan with the appropriate state office. After the state approves this plan, the surviving corporation receives a certificate of merger and can begin conducting business.

Effect of Merger

Once the state issues the certificate of merger, the acquired corporation ceases to exist; only one corporation survives. The survivor takes on all the assets, rights, and liabilities of the disappearing (acquired) corporation by operation of law. This means, among other things, that creditors of the acquired corporation are now the creditors of the survivor corporation. Similarly, pending damages suits (such as products liability cases) against the acquired corporation, if successful, will be paid by the survivor corporation.

Appraisal Rights

Thus far, we have discussed the positive qualities of a merger from the point of view of those who want it. In any given merger, however, persons will object to, or dissent from, the merger. Many people believe it is unfair to require someone to become a shareholder in a new corporation that may be totally different from the one in which he or she originally invested. Therefore, statutes in most states give dissenting shareholders appraisal rights. *Appraisal rights* allow dissenters to sell their shares back to the corporation for cash for the **market value** or **fair market value** of the shares. In this way, a dissenting shareholder can avoid becoming a shareholder in the survivor corporation and still protect his or her original investment.

To be eligible for appraisal rights, a shareholder ordinarily must follow a set statutory procedure. Although the respective state statutes vary regarding the steps with which a dissenting shareholder must comply; in general, such statutes require the following steps:

1. The dissenter must send a written notice of his or her objection to the merger before the meeting at which the merger will be considered.
2. The shareholder must make a written demand on the corporation for the fair value of the shares after the merger has been approved.

FINANCE/MANAGEMENT 36.1

SHOULD CIT DIVERSIFY?

During a field trip with her high school class, Lindsay saw a for-sale sign on a local fast-food restaurant. Lindsay has suggested that CIT might want to purchase this business to provide a steady source of cash until CIT establishes its reputation and builds a regular market. She feels that the restaurant does a steady business and that the funds generated from this enterprise should carry the firm for the first year or two. The other members of the Kochanowski family, however, are unsure about this suggestion and ask for your opinion. What legal complications might arise if CIT tries to expand into the operation of a fast-food restaurant?

BUSINESS CONSIDERATIONS What are the advantages and disadvantages of diversification by a newly formed business? What information should a firm acquire in order to make an informed decision in this instance?

ETHICAL CONSIDERATIONS Does a business have any duties to expand or not expand when an opportunity presents itself? Do these duties vary depending on the business form of the enterprise—limited liability company, corporation, partnership, sole proprietorship?

Market value

The current price the stock will sell for on a stock exchange.

Fair market value

The current price for selling an asset between informed willing buyers and informed willing sellers.

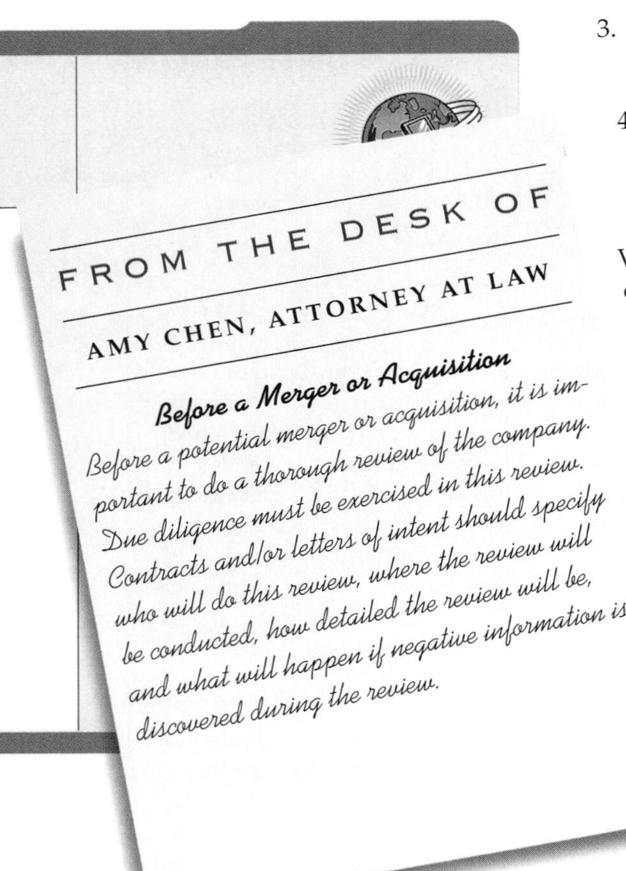

FROM THE DESK OF
AMY CHEN, ATTORNEY AT LAW
Before a Merger or Acquisition
Before a potential merger or acquisition, it is important to do a thorough review of the company. Due diligence must be exercised in this review. Contracts and/or letters of intent should specify who will do this review, where the review will be conducted, how detailed the review will be, and what will happen if negative information is discovered during the review.

3. The corporation must then make a written offer to purchase at a price it believes represents the fair value (or the fair market value) of the shares.
4. If the corporation and the dissenting shareholder disagree about the fair value of the shares, either party may petition a court to determine the fair value of the shares in an appraisal proceeding.

Valuation of shares is quite complicated and requires a sophisticated understanding of valuation issues. This task becomes somewhat easier if the stock is traded on the New York, American, Tokyo, or other stock exchanges; in such cases, a court will place great importance on the market price of the stock when assigning a fair value to the stock. Otherwise, a court usually will arrive at its valuation determination by weighing a number of factors, including market price, investment value, net asset value, and dividends.

Some jurisdictions deny appraisal rights for certain types of mergers (for example, shareholders of the parent company in a short-form merger may have no appraisal rights) and certain types of corporations (those with stock listed on a national securities exchange or those with more than 2,000 shareholders). Since appraisal rights generally represent the *exclusive* remedy for a dissenting shareholder who opposes a merger, the shareholder must use vigilance in complying with the strict statutory provisions and short time periods involved.

In determining the value of shares in a statutory appraisal proceeding, a court retains broad discretionary powers, as *Alabama By-Products Corporation* v. *Neal* illustrates.

36.2 ALABAMA BY-PRODUCTS CORPORATION v. NEAL — 588 A.2d 255 (Del. 1991)

FACTS Minority shareholders, including Neal, challenged an appraisal, pursuant to Delaware statutes, of approximately 120,000 shares of the stock of Alabama By-Products Corporation (ABC). Following a short-form merger between ABC and Drummond Holding Corporation, effective 13 August 1985, Drummond absorbed ABC. The ABC minority shareholders were cashed out, pursuant to the merger, and received $75.60 per share. That consideration reflected the $75.00 per share paid to ABC shareholders pursuant to a tender offer less than six months earlier, plus a $0.60 quarterly dividend omitted in 1985. After a six-day trial, the court of chancery [also called the court of equity] concluded that the fair value of ABC stock on 13 August 1985 was $180.67 per share and that Neal and the other minority shareholders were entitled to that amount plus interest. ABC, however, contended that the court of chancery committed an error of law when determining value in a statutory appraisal proceeding.

ISSUE Had the court of chancery inappropriately considered the majority shareholders' wrongdoing when determining the value of the dissenting shareholders' stock in a statutory appraisal hearing?

HOLDING No.

REASONING A court can admit evidence of unfair dealing by majority shareholders in a statutory appraisal

36.2 ALABAMA BY-PRODUCTS CORPORATION v. NEAL (cont.) 588 A.2d 255 (Del. 1991)

action for the purpose of impeaching the majority shareholders' credibility. According to Delaware precedents, an appraisal action is "entirely a creature of statute." It is a limited remedy created by the legislature to provide dissenting shareholders with an independent judicial determination of the fair value of their shares. The statute provides that "the Court shall appraise the shares, determining their fair value exclusive of any element of value arising from the accomplishment or expectation of the merger or consolidation. . . ." The value of the dissenting shareholders' shares on the date of the merger is the only litigable issue in a statutory appraisal.[4] The court acknowledged that an appraisal may be an inadequate remedy in certain cases, "particularly where fraud, misrepresentation, self-dealing, deliberate waste of corporate assets, or gross and palpable overreaching are involved." Nevertheless, this court has consistently held that a "*statutory appraisal is limited* to 'the payment of the fair value of the shares . . . by the surviving or resulting corporation. . . .'" Thus, claims for unfair dealing cannot be litigated in the context of a statutory appraisal.

The court of chancery properly dismissed Neal's claim for unfair dealing by noting that it was inappropriate to join an appraisal action and an unfair dealing action. The court then stated that "if corporate fiduciaries engage in self-dealing and fix the merger price by procedures not calculated to yield a fair price, these facts should, and will, be considered in assessing the credibility of the corporations' valuation contentions." ABC submitted that this statement is incorrect and maintained that any acts of unfair dealing in the merger process cannot be considered in an appraisal proceeding.

The court of chancery was entitled to consider the evidence of unfair dealing only to impeach ABC's credibility. The statute specifically provides that the court of chancery must consider "all relevant factors" when it determines the fair value of shares that are subject to appraisal. Nothing in the appraisal statute or in prior holdings suggests that the court of chancery may not consider ABC's conduct at the time of the merger in assessing the credibility of ABC's testimony in support of its valuation contentions in an appraisal proceeding. Indeed, the weight ascribed to expert valuations necessarily depends on the validity of the assumptions underlying them.

Where factual determinations turn on a question of credibility and the acceptance or rejection of testimony by the trier of fact, a court will accept them, since it is well settled under Delaware precedents that the trier of fact is the sole judge of the credibility of witnesses and the weight to be accorded their testimony and is responsible for resolving conflicts in the evidence. The court of chancery's decision in this appraisal proceeding was not arbitrary, and its valuation of ABC's shares was the product of an orderly and logical deductive process, and its decision is affirmed.

BUSINESS CONSIDERATIONS What factors should a shareholder consider in deciding whether to assert appraisal rights or retain his or her interest following a merger decision? Why would the firm be opposed to the exercise of appraisal rights?

ETHICAL CONSIDERATIONS What ethical violations were committed by the majority shareholders in this case? What should they have done in order to act in an ethical manner?

Sale of Substantially All the Assets

Rather than acquiring another firm through a merger, a corporation can instead buy all, or substantially all, of another firm's assets. For example, a shipping company may buy the ships of a rival company as an alternative to merging with it. This method of acquisition enjoys favor because it is procedurally simpler than a merger. Approval by the shareholders of the acquired firm ordinarily is necessary, but approval by the acquiring firm's shareholders is not. Even then, a sale of substantially

36.2

FINANCE/MANAGEMENT

HOW TO DISCOURAGE A TAKEOVER

CIT has had success in developing and marketing the Call-Image videophone. The videophones have been featured in articles in business journals and in the news. As a result of this success and the publicity, Person-to-Person, a long-distance telephone service, wishes to acquire CIT. The Kochanowskis have a family meeting (which you attend) and decide they are not ready to sell the firm. They ask for your advice about resisting this takeover attempt. [Assume that CIT is a regular (Subchapter C) corporation.] What can the Kochanowskis legally do to discourage or prevent a takeover? What legal limitations may restrict their options? Why is this problem less likely with a Subchapter S corporation?

BUSINESS CONSIDERATIONS From a practical perspective, what can a business do to discourage or prevent a takeover? Which techniques are most effective? Why?

ETHICAL CONSIDERATIONS From an ethical perspective, what can a business do to discourage or prevent a takeover? What ethical limitations may restrict their options?

all the assets made in the regular course of the corporation's business (as when a corporation is formed to build a tanker, and the tanker is then sold to an oil company) would not normally require shareholder approval. Shareholder approval thus becomes necessary only in the event of a fundamental change in the corporate structure (that is, the disposal of operating assets in order to terminate the business activities of the corporation). Most states provide appraisal rights for dissenting shareholders in these circumstances as well. In addition, various methods of protecting creditors find expression in the statutes governing sales of substantially all the assets. In a merger, the acquiring firm takes on all the liabilities of the acquired firm by operation of law; but because this is not ordinarily the case when all or substantially all the assets are sold, corporate statutory provisions, the provisions on bulk transfers in UCC Article 6, and decisional law have been developed to give creditors remedies if such sales prejudice their rights.

Conrad v. *Rofin-Sinar, Inc.* focuses on the purchaser's potential liability for the alleged contracts of the selling corporation.

36.3 CONRAD v. ROFIN-SINAR, INC.

762 F.Supp. 167 (E.D. Mich. 1991)

FACTS In early 1985, Conrad applied for a job as a laser systems salesperson with the Industrial Laser Division (ILD) of Spectra Physics, Inc. During the application process, Conrad asked about job security. Herbert Dwight, the president of Spectra, told Conrad that he would remain employed as long as he did a good job selling laser systems. Shortly after beginning his employment, Conrad received a personnel manual describing Spectra's policies and practices. It listed specific grounds for discipline and provided for formal yearly performance reviews. A separate manual for ILD listed the same reasons for discipline as the Spectra manual itself and provided for progressive discipline before termination. In March 1988, Spectra sold all its ILD assets to Siemens Capital Corporation, which, in turn, incorporated Rofin-Sinar, Inc., specifically to continue the business of ILD. Rofin-Sinar informed Spectra's customers that ILD "has been sold and is now Rofin-Sinar." Rofin-Sinar did not issue policy statements that it would adopt any "just cause" employment contracts allegedly in effect prior to the sale. The asset purchase agreement stated that Rofin-Sinar reserved the right to terminate Spectra employees and that Rofin-Sinar retained Spectra employees under the "terms and conditions of employment as it may determine in its discretion."

36.3 CONRAD v. ROFIN-SINAR, INC. *(cont.)* 762 F.Supp. 167 (E.D. Mich. 1991)

After the asset sale, Conrad continued to work without interruption at the same salary; under the same commission plan; and with the same reporting requirements, vacation plan, hire date, employee number, personnel file, supervisor, office, car, and insurance deductions. Rofin-Sinar never had him file an employment application or a W-4 income tax form for the new firm. Rofin-Sinar retained and relied on Spectra's personnel manual; and it also used the personnel codes, personnel forms, and expenses reports contained in it. In terminating Conrad on 27 January 1989, Rofin-Sinar followed the termination and exit interview procedures contained in the personnel manual. Rofin-Sinar had not developed any additional or different personnel practices before Conrad's termination and had not notified employees of any changes in personnel policies. The precipitating factor in Conrad's discharge was that he allegedly withheld information concerning Ford Motor Company's plans to purchase a competitor's laser system; Conrad testified that he had notified Rofin-Sinar. Rofin-Sinar had not given Conrad any written notice of performance problems between 11 May 1988 and his termination. His sales performance had met the goals established by his supervisors. At the time of his termination, Conrad had been negotiating the sale of two large laser systems; after his termination, Rofin-Sinar had received the purchase orders for these two systems, and Conrad received no commissions on these sales. Conrad sued for wrongful discharge.

ISSUE Had Rofin-Sinar implicitly agreed to assume liability under an alleged "just cause" employment contract between Spectra and Conrad?

HOLDING Maybe yes, maybe no. This is an issue for the finder of fact.

REASONING The fact finder may reasonably conclude that Rofin-Sinar had consented to most, if not all, of the seller's personnel practices, including honoring any "just cause" employment contracts. The Michigan Supreme Court has held that an employee can enforce an employer's promise not to terminate employment except for just cause. Such an enforceable agreement can result from either: (1) an employer's "express agreement, oral or written" or (2) "an employee's legitimate expectations grounded in an employer's policy statements." Applying this standard, a reasonable trier of fact might conclude that an implied "just cause" employment contract had existed between Spectra and Conrad. The record contained undisputed evidence that Dwight, the president of Spectra, had promised Conrad he would remain employed as long as he did a good job. This fact alone would support a verdict that Conrad had had a "just cause" employment contract with Spectra. Furthermore, Spectra had adopted other policies that might have given Conrad a "legitimate expectation" that he had a "just cause" employment contract. In particular, its personnel manual had listed grounds for discipline, which would enhance an employee's legitimate expectation that he or she would be terminated only for just cause. The personnel manual also had provided for annual performance reviews. Spectra had provided in the personnel manual for progressive discipline prior to termination. Michigan precedents hold that a policy of terminating employees only after a graduated series of disciplinary measures contributes to the legitimate expectation that the employee will be terminated only for cause.

Ordinarily, a purchaser of assets does not assume the liabilities of the selling corporation. However, under Michigan law, a purchaser of assets assumes the selling corporation's liabilities where: (1) there is an express or implied assumption of liability; (2) the transaction amounts to a consolidation or merger; (3) the transaction is fraudulent; (4) some of the elements of a good faith purchase are lacking, or where the transfer is without consideration and the creditors of the transferor are not provided for; or (5) the transferee corporation is a mere continuation or reincarnation of the old corporation. The issue of whether the purchasing corporation agrees to assume the predecessor corporation's liabilities is a question of fact for the jury; the presence of such an intention moreover depends on the facts and circumstances of each case. Here, a material fact as to whether Rofin-Sinar impliedly agreed to assume liability under the alleged "just cause" employment contract between Conrad and Spectra existed.

Nevertheless, a reasonable trier of fact could conclude from the undisputed facts that Rofin-Sinar impliedly agreed to assume liability under the contract. For instance, the period of transition after the sale of the ILD assets represented one of continuity in which Rofin-Sinar availed itself of many of Spectra's practices, policies, and workforce. Rofin-Sinar failed to promulgate new personnel policies, and it never disclaimed liability under any "just cause" employment contracts that may have existed. Furthermore, it used Spectra's personnel manual, which fact ordinarily indicates the existence of a "just cause" contract. When all these undisputed facts are considered together, the finder of fact could reasonably conclude that Rofin-Sinar approved most, if not all, of Spectra's personnel practices, including honoring any alleged "just cause" employment contracts.

36.3 CONRAD v. ROFIN-SINAR, INC. *(cont.)* 762 F.Supp. 167 (E.D. Mich. 1991)

BUSINESS CONSIDERATIONS Why would a business agree to assume liability under a "just cause" provision in a contract? What public policy considerations enter into this decision?

ETHICAL CONSIDERATIONS Is it ethical for the management of a business to agree to assume liabilities that the business would not otherwise face?

Stock Acquisition

An alternative method for acquiring the business of another corporation involves stock acquisitions. Instead of buying substantially all the assets of a corporation, the acquiring corporation's directors may decide to buy the stock of the acquired corporation. Because the acquisition implicates only the latter corporation's individual shareholders, who can decide for themselves whether to sell at the price offered for the stock, the directors of the acquired corporation have no right to approve or disapprove the stock acquisition. Similarly, no requirements usually exist for shareholder approval or appraisal rights. However, federal securities laws may apply to such corporate takeovers, as we will see in Chapter 38.

Because sales of substantially all the assets and stock acquisitions may have the ultimate effect of mergers, some companies have characterized their acquisitions in one of these fashions in order to avoid the strict statutory procedures required of mergers. Transactions that take the *form* of sales of assets or stocks but nevertheless have the *effect* of mergers are called *de facto mergers.* Because shareholders and creditors can be injured through de facto mergers, courts in jurisdictions that recognize the doctrine can set the transactions aside and require compliance with the relevant merger statutes (shareholder approval, appraisal rights, and so on).

A famous case involving a de facto merger, *Farris* v. *Glen Alden Corporation,* follows.

36.3

FINANCE/MANAGEMENT

MERGERS AND ACQUISITIONS

A business that provides a key component for the production of Call-Image videophones is experiencing financial difficulties. If this firm fails, CIT will need to find another source for this component, probably at a substantially higher cost per unit. The owner of the business has proposed either selling his firm to CIT or merging with CIT. If CIT buys the firm, it will need to expend a substantial amount of cash. If CIT agrees to merge, the seller of the component part wants 20 percent of the common stock in CIT. The Kochanowskis have asked your advice as to their best course of conduct. What do you recommend?

BUSINESS CONSIDERATIONS Should a business have a policy regarding potential mergers, or should it analyze and decide on each opportunity separately as it arises?

ETHICAL CONSIDERATIONS What duties does a business owe to its supplier in a situation like the one confronting CIT? What duties does it owe its owners and other constituents?

36.4 FARRIS v. GLEN ALDEN CORPORATION

143 A.2d 25 (Pa. 1958)

FACTS The officers of Glen Alden Corp. entered into a reorganization agreement with the officers of List Industries Corp. Glen Alden was a coal company, and List was a more diversified company owning interests in textiles, theaters, real estate, and gas and oil. Glen Alden's shareholders approved the transaction. As a result of the reorganization agreement, Glen Alden acquired most of the assets and all the liabilities of List, and List was dissolved. Farris, a shareholder in Glen Alden, sought an injunction against the reorganization, stating that it was actually a merger and that it had not given appraisal rights to dissenting shareholders. Glen Alden argued that the transaction was a purchase of corporate assets with respect to which shareholders had no rights of dissent or appraisal.

ISSUE Was the transaction a purchase of assets or instead a de facto merger?

HOLDING The transaction was a de facto merger that should have followed the statutory procedures required of mergers in order to be legal.

REASONING Farris will be a shareholder in a much different type of corporation once the transaction is consummated. The new company will be twice as large but will have seven times the long-term debt held by Glen Alden before the reorganization. Control of Glen Alden will also pass to the List directors, who will have a majority of the directorships on the new board of directors. Farris's proportionate interest in Glen Alden will be reduced to only two-fifths of what it was before the reorganization, and the value of his shares will be substantially reduced. In reality, the transaction was a merger, and Glen Alden should have accorded Farris his statutorily required appraisal rights.

BUSINESS CONSIDERATIONS Why would a business prefer to have a transaction viewed as a purchase of assets rather than a merger? What legal considerations might affect their attitude?

ETHICAL CONSIDERATIONS Is it ethical to attempt to classify a de facto merger as something else in order to avoid seeking shareholder approval?

http:// RESOURCES FOR BUSINESS LAW STUDENTS

NAME	RESOURCES	WEB ADDRESS
General Business Forms	The 'Lectric Law Library's™ business forms include a variety of sample partnership and corporation documents.	http://www.lectlaw.com/formb.htm
U.S. Chamber of Commerce	U.S. Chamber of Commerce provides news, information, services, and products to assist small-business owners.	http://www.uschamber.org/
Law Journal EXTRA! (LJX!)—Corporate Law	LJX!, sponsored by the New York Law Publishing Company, provides daily corporate law news, case law, and legal analysis.	http://www.ljx.com/practice/corporate/index.html
CNNfn: The Financial Network	CNNfn, Turner Broadcasting's financial news complement to CNN, provides reports on mergers and takeovers. CNNfn is interactive, allowing visitors to "ask the experts" or respond to the day's programs.	http://www.cnnfn.com/

SUMMARY

When a partnership undergoes a change in the relationship among the partners, a dissolution occurs. Thus, a withdrawal by any partner is a dissolution, whether the agreement allows such conduct or not. Likewise, a dissolution will occur when the purpose of the agreement has been carried out or when its time has expired. A dissolution will happen by operation of law if a partner dies; if any partner goes bankrupt; or if the purpose becomes illegal, or the partners cannot legally continue in the business. A dissolution can also happen by court order. When a dissolution occurs because a partner withdraws, the remaining partners may be allowed to continue the business. If they do, the withdrawing partner must be bought out and indemnified.

Often the partnership must be wound up if a dissolution occurs. In a winding up, the assets of the firm are marshaled and liquidated, and the proceeds are distributed according to law. In a general partnership under the UPA, the proceeds must be used first to pay debts that the partners owe to nonpartner creditors. Next, the creditors who are also partners must be paid. After that, the partners recover their capital contributions. Anything left is distributed as profits.

The process of liquidation (or winding up) of a corporation occurs when it pays all debts and creditors from the corporate assets and then distributes any remaining assets to the shareholders. Directors may incur personal liability if they continue the business of the corporation beyond the time reasonably necessary to wind up the corporation's affairs. Creditors who have preserved their claims against the corporation can recoup from shareholders any distributions of assets that happened prior to payment of creditors. Directors may also incur liability for the remaining unpaid claims. After creditors' claims have been satisfied, the shareholders normally receive the proportion of the remaining net assets represented by their respective share ownership, subject to any liquidation preferences that the corporation has authorized.

Dissolution of a corporation involves the termination of the corporation as a legal person. It is not synonymous with the term *liquidation,* which refers to the winding up of the corporation's business. Dissolutions may be either voluntary or involuntary. Statutes set out the formal requirements for a voluntary dissolution. Typically, voluntary dissolution involves board action, shareholder approval, and notice to creditors. Upon voluntary dissolution, the shareholders share proportionately in the net assets of the corporation that remain after satisfaction of creditors' claims. Involuntary dissolutions—those effected by judicial proceedings—occur less frequently than voluntary dissolutions.

The state can rescind or suspend the corporation's certificate when the corporation's actions present a clear danger to the public. Upon compliance with corporate statutes, the state often orders the corporation's reinstatement. Shareholders also can petition the courts for dissolution of the corporation. Statutes sometimes limit the conditions under which shareholders can petition for involuntary dissolution. Creditors normally cannot compel involuntary dissolution of the corporation. Neither the appointment of a receiver nor the institution of involuntary bankruptcy proceedings results in the dissolution of the corporation.

Mergers and consolidations can bring about fundamental changes in the corporation's structure. Technically, mergers and consolidations differ, because in a merger one firm absorbs another, whereas in a consolidation both firms combine to produce a wholly new entity. The upsurge in mergers stems from a desire to effect economies of scale, to gain technical knowledge, to diversify, to control competition, and to avoid taxes. The negative aspects of mergers include the possible sacrifice of shareholders' interests, personnel displacement, and the uprooting of firms from the local community.

State statutes set out the procedures necessary for bringing about a merger. The directors ordinarily adopt a merger plan, which the shareholders of both firms must approve. Shareholder approval is not necessary in short-form mergers. After the state approves the filed merger plan, the surviving corporation receives a certificate of merger and can begin conducting business. At this time, the acquired corporation ceases to exist. The surviving corporation takes on all the assets, rights, and liabilities of the transferor (that is, acquired) corporation by operation of law.

Most state statutes permit appraisal rights for stockholders who object to the merger. Appraisal rights allow dissenters to sell their shares back to the corporation for cash equal to the shares' fair market value. To be eligible for appraisal rights, shareholders usually must follow a set statutory procedure. If the corporation and dissenting shareholders cannot agree about the fair market value of the shares, either party may petition a court to determine their value in an appraisal proceeding.

Rather than merging, a corporation instead can buy all or substantially all the assets of another firm. This method of acquisition entails far fewer procedures than a merger. Nevertheless, most statutes in this area try to protect creditors' rights when such sales take place. Stock acquisitions are also simpler than mergers but may be subject to federal securities laws.

Care must be taken to avoid de facto mergers, transactions taking either the form of a sale of substantially all the assets or a stock acquisition but nevertheless having the effect of a merger. Because noncompliance with merger statutes can prejudice the rights of shareholders and creditors, courts may set such sales aside and order compliance with the procedures mandated by the merger statute.

DISCUSSION QUESTIONS

1. Abner, Bert, and Lois are partners in a bakery. Abner, however, suffers a nervous breakdown and is placed in a mental institution. Abner's wife demands Abner's share of the business, alleging that his insanity has dissolved the partnership. Discuss her allegation.
2. Scott is in a partnership, but is also heavily in debt. One of his creditors has gone to court and obtained a charging order against Scott's share of the business. Under what circumstances can this creditor seek a court-ordered dissolution of the business?
3. Maria entered an existing partnership as a new partner in 1995. She contributed $20,000 at that time. By 1997, her share had grown to $50,000. How much can creditors who had claims predating Maria's entry into the firm collect from Maria's share of the business? From her personal assets?
4. Given the following figures, work out the final financial position of each of the partners (net worth, cash, amounts owed, amounts receivable) following a winding up of their general partnership business:

	Bill	Charles	Larry	BCL Partnership
Assets	$70,000	$50,000	$50,000	$200,000
Liabilities	20,000	45,000	85,000	190,000
Capital contribution	50,000	25,000	25,000	
Profits	50%	25%	25%	

5. Given the following figures, work out the final financial position of each of the partners (net worth, cash, amounts owed, amounts receivable) following a winding up of their business under the RULPA.

	Beth	Cheryl	Linda	B & C
	(General Partners)		(Limited Partner)	(The Firm)
Assets	$67,500	$123,250	$87,900	$350,000
Liabilities	24,000	101,000	86,400	200,000
Capital contribution	50,000	50,000	100,000	
Loans to firm	0	5,000	7,000	
Share of profit	35%	35%	30%	

6. Who can bring about an involuntary corporate dissolution, and how is this done?
7. How does a corporate merger differ from a consolidation?
8. What procedures must a corporation generally follow to merge with another company?
9. Explain the meaning and importance of appraisal rights.
10. Why in a given case will a sale of substantially all the corporate assets be preferable to a merger?

CASE PROBLEMS AND WRITING ASSIGNMENTS

1. Nestle and Ellis formed a partnership, Red Rocks Meat and Deli, which they operated from a building leased from Wester. In 1978, Nestle withdrew from the business, selling his interest to Herline. Ellis and Herline agreed that Nestle should be released from any and all liabilities of the firm. Subsequently, Herline also withdrew, and Ellis continued the business as a proprietorship. In 1980, Ellis and Wester renegotiated the lease, giving the firm additional space and increasing the total rent due under the lease agreement. When Ellis fell behind in his rent payments under the new lease, Wester filed suit against Nestle, arguing that he was liable for the lease jointly and severally with Ellis due to their partnership. Nestle denied that he was liable for the rent because he had withdrawn from the firm two years earlier. How should the court resolve this case? What factors will be decisive? Why? [See *Wester & Co.* v. *Nestle,* 669 P.2d 1046 (Colo.App. 1983).]

2. C. L. Barnhouse Co. was a limited partnership with two general partners and three limited partners. One of the limited partners was a trust created by Kilpatrick and represented by the trustee, Kilpatrick's son. The Kilpatrick trust stated that, on the death of Kilpatrick, the trust was to terminate and all trust assets were to be distributed to the beneficiaries. The partnership agreement provided that the partnership was to terminate on the death of any of the partners, limited or general. It also specified that, on the termination of the partnership, the capital contributions of each partner were to be returned, and then all other assets were to be distributed as per the agreement. Kilpatrick died, and the general partners notified the limited partners that Kilpatrick's death terminated the limited partnership. The trustee argued that the death of Kilpatrick did not terminate the limited partnership. Did the death of Kilpatrick, which terminated her trust, serve to dissolve the limited partnership as well? Why? [See *Porter* v. *Barnhouse,* 354 N.W.2d 227 (Iowa 1984).]

3. Clyde and Graydon Bohn formed a partnership to operate a farm. The partnership agreement included a buy-out provision that was to be based on "the capital amount" of the partnership. Clyde died, and Graydon offered the estate $135,000 to buy out the interest of Clyde. The estate refused the offer, asserting that the buy-out price should be one-half the fair market value of the partnership. The net fair market value of the farm as of the date of Clyde's death was $1,500,000. An accountant testified that the phrase used in the partnership agreement, "the capital amount," has no known definition in the accounting profession. What should the court decide is the proper amount to be paid in order to allow Graydon Bohn to buy out the interest of his deceased partner and continue to operate the business? Why? [See *Bohn* v. *Bohn Implement Co.,* 325 N.W.2d 281 (N.D. 1982).]

4. Roberta Hesek, the surviving spouse of David Hesek, a shareholder in 245 South Main Street, Inc., petitioned the court for judicial dissolution of the corporation. The remaining shareholders, in turn, sought a court order compelling Roberta to resell her husband's shares pursuant to a stock-redemption agreement her husband had executed in 1973. The corporation's shareholders had entered into agreements in 1970 and 1973 providing for the redemption of corporate stock on the death of a shareholder. Accordingly, on the death of Roberta's husband, the corporation had given timely notice of its intent to redeem the husband's shares of stock and had tendered the agreed-on price. In these circumstances, did Roberta, as the surviving spouse of a shareholder, have standing to petition for judicial dissolution of the corporation? Why or why not? [See *Hesek* v. *245 South Main Street, Inc.,* 566 N.Y.S.2d 127 (1991).]

5. Keenan, the corporate president of Superior Grain Company, Inc., had executed a broker contract with American River Transportation Company on 5 November 1987, which provided for the shipment of soybeans on two barges. The barge freight totaled $21,447.24. At the time of the contract's execution, Superior had merged into Keenan Cotton Gin & Grain Elevator, Inc. No one was aware of the merger other than Keenan and his CPA. The broker contract listed

American as the seller and Superior/Robert Keenan as the buyer. Keenan stated in his deposition that he had read the broker's contract, known what it contained, and signed it. He further stated by deposition that he had continued to do business under the name of Superior until July 1988, and had never notified Marine Freight Exchange, Inc. (the broker) or American that Superior had merged into another corporation. The barge freight was never paid, and Keenan admitted there was no reason to doubt the accuracy of the charges. American contended the above facts were sufficient for the trial court to rule as a matter of law that Keenan was personally liable for the debt incurred on behalf of Superior. According to American, upon Superior's merger with Keenan Cotton Gin & Grain Elevator, Inc., Superior had ceased to exist and any contracts entered into by or on behalf of Superior involved contracts with a nonexistent entity. The Arkansas statute under which the merger had occurred provided as follows: "The separate existence of all corporations parties to the plan of merger or consolidation, except the surviving or new corporation, shall cease." In these circumstances, should the court hold Keenan personally liable to American for the nonpayment of the barge freight charges? Why? [See *Keenan* v. *American River Trans. Co.*, 799 S.W.2d 801 (Ark. 1990).]

6. **BUSINESS APPLICATION CASE** Don Tyson, chairman of Tyson Foods, met with Jim Keeler, the president of WLR Foods. They discussed Tyson's acquiring WLR. Keeler presented Tyson's offer to WLR's board of directors, which rejected the offer. Tyson made a tender offer to acquire WLR stock for $30 per share—the market price was only $19.25. The WLR board met on 28 January 1994 to obtain legal and investment advice. The board met again on 4 February 1994 and rejected Tyson's tender offer. At that time the board approved lucrative severance packages for some of the officers and employees. They adopted a poison pill that would issue shares to existing shareholders if the tender offer was successful. The purpose of the poison pill was to make the tender offer less attractive to Tyson and to dilute Tyson's interest in WLR if the tender offer was successful. Did the WLR board behave properly? Why did they consult with their advisers on 28 January 1994? WLR is a Virginia corporation and Virginia has an antitakeover statute. Is the Virginia statute or federal law controlling in this situation? Why? [See *WLR Foods, Inc.* v. *Tyson Foods, Inc.*, 869 F. Supp. 419 (W.D. Va. 1994); 65 F.3d 1172 (4th Cir. 1995).]

7. **ETHICS APPLICATION CASE** Davis and Levy were the sole shareholders of Shayne-Levy Associates, Inc., which functioned as a sales representative in the knit-goods industry. Davis, who held 18.36 percent of the stock, handled the foreign business, consisting primarily of an account with Kowa Trading Corp. Levy, who owned the balance of the stock, handled the domestic business, primarily the Star Knitwear, Inc., account, which provided 50 percent of Shayne-Levy's gross income. Each individual earned his own commissions and did not have to account to the other. Levy also held one-third of the stock in Star. When Levy suggested in 1983 that Shayne-Levy should drop the foreign business as unprofitable, Davis left the corporation's employ and joined Kowa. Levy, with the aid of a new corporate accountant, began to alter the corporate structure to increase the benefits to him and his family and to shelter the income he derived from it. These actions in actuality amounted to a siphoning away and wasting of a substantial portion of the firm's assets. The benefits shared by Davis and Levy in the past in no way resembled the wholesale dissipation that took place at Levy's behest, for the benefit of himself and his family, after Davis's departure. Although the corporation had the right, under a 1970 shareholders' agreement, to buy out Davis's interest within 60 days of termination of his employment at the book value of the firm as of the last day of the month preceding such termination, it failed to exercise this right in a timely manner, thereby forgoing its rights under the agreement. The parties nevertheless entered into negotiations for a buy-out. When the corporate accountant offered him only $4,000, however, Davis sought judicial relief. After lengthy hearings, the referee reached an adjusted valuation 20 times greater than the amount Shayne-Levy had offered. The lower court confirmed this finding and entered judgment against the corporation in that amount. In light of the referee's confirmed findings, namely that Levy had looted the corporate defendant by completely controlling the corporation and that his actions might have rendered it unable to pay this judgment, the appeals court added Levy to the lawsuit. The court did this in order to afford complete relief to Davis by making Levy jointly and severally liable with the corporation. In these circumstances, was the court's reasoning persuasive? Why? What ethical considerations are raised by this case? [See *Matter of Davis*, 571 N.Y.S.2d 234 (1991).]

8. **IDES CASE** When Cameron Crew Boats, Inc., was incorporated, the company issued 100 shares of stock. Claude V. McCall, Sr., the father of the plaintiffs, later acquired ownership of some shares. He owned 7.54 shares at his death, which were inherited by his relatives, the plaintiffs in this suit. In December 1984,

McCall Enterprises, Inc., began acquiring shares of stock in Cameron and, by June 1988, owned more than 90 percent of the firm's shares. On 8 June 1988, McCall Enterprises merged with Cameron, with McCall Enterprises becoming the successor corporation. On 9 June 1988, McCall Enterprises filed the necessary documentation with the secretary of state and at the same time mailed a copy of the documentation to each shareholder. The articles of merger set the fair cash value of the shares of Cameron at $7,406.75 per share. The plaintiffs decided to dissent from the merger and filed a demand for the fair cash value of their shares with the corporation on 28 June 1988 and filed the bank acknowledgment, required by law, on 30 June 1988. On 1 July 1988, McCall Enterprises disagreed with the value demanded by the plaintiffs. The plaintiffs filed suit for the fair cash value of their shares on 29 August 1988. Apply the IDES model in analyzing this case. Did the 20-day statutory period begin when the certificate of merger was delivered to the secretary of state or from the time when the secretary of state acknowledged the document? In other words, was the lawsuit filed timely? Why or why not? [See *McCall* v. *McCall Enterprises, Inc.*, 578 So.2d 260 (La.App. 1991).]

NOTES

1. Uniform Partnership Act § 29.
2. Ibid., §§ 27 and 28.
3. Dirk Beveridge, "Cadbury Hits on Right Bid for Dr Pepper," *The Fresno Bee* (27 January 1995), p. C1.
4. Delaware Corporation Code § 262.

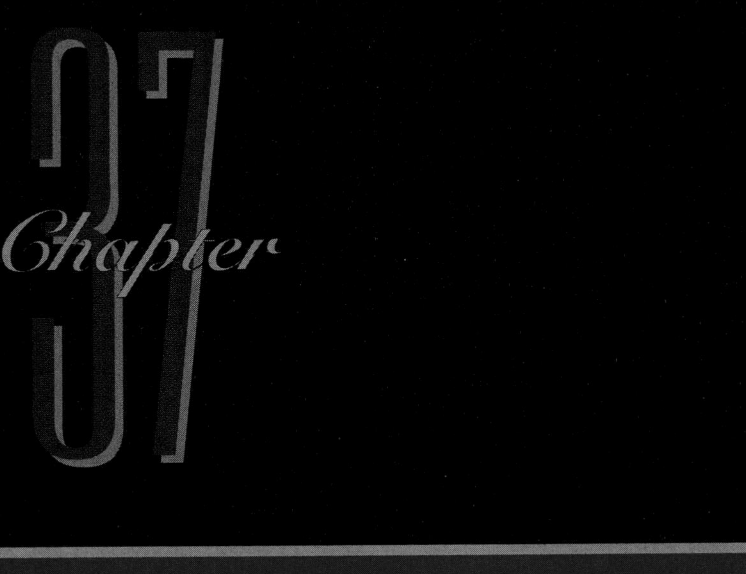

Chapter 37

Franchising

O U T L I N E

A G E N D A

The Kochanowskis have been informed by several of their friends that they should consider franchising CIT. Such a distributional system could give the firm access to new financing and allow it to expand its market. CIT would like to know what establishing a franchising system for the production and sale of Call-Image videophones would involve. CIT also would like to know the potential risks and/or benefits franchising might provide. These and other questions are likely to arise in the course of this chapter.

Be prepared! You never know when one of the Kochanowskis will need your help or advice.

The Significance of Franchising as a Business Method

Although franchising began in the United States over a century ago when breweries licensed beer gardens as a means of distributing their products, franchising did not become recognized as a distinct method of doing business until after World War II.[1] Since then, and especially in the last 20 years, franchising has significantly helped the United States achieve its position as the world's largest market.

Presently more than 2,000 U.S. companies encompassing over 40 different economic sectors use the franchise method for distributing their goods or services both domestically and internationally.[2] Among the types of businesses that use franchise systems are the following: automobile dealerships; gasoline stations; restaurants; convenience stores; soft drink bottlers; nonfood merchandising businesses (such as drug, electronics, cosmetics, and home furnishings companies); travel agencies; hotels, motels, and campgrounds; automobile and truck rental services; printing and copying services; tax preparation firms; real estate businesses; accounting firms; cleaning services; lawn and garden services; laundry services; equipment rental businesses; early childhood education and daycare centers; and beauty salons.

Overall, franchising has developed into an important and popular method of marketing and distribution. This chapter examines why this phenomenon has occurred.

Definition

No universally accepted definition of the word *franchise* exists. The following definition, taken from the Washington Franchise Investment Protection Act, § 19.100.010(4), is typical:

> *"Franchise" means an oral or written contract or agreement, either expressed or implied, in which a person grants to another person a license to use a trade name, service mark, trade mark, logotype or related characteristic in which there is a community of interest in the business of offering, selling, distributing goods or services at wholesale or retail, leasing or otherwise and in which the franchisee is required to pay, directly or indirectly, a franchise fee.*[3]

Service marks
Distinctive symbols designating the services offered by a particular business or individual.

Trademarks
Distinctive marks or symbols used to identify a particular company as the source of its products.

Logotypes
Identifying symbols.

Service marks, **trademarks**, and **logotypes** are symbols that identify the origin of goods and services. The person or firm that grants a franchise to another is called the *franchisor.* The person receiving the franchise is known as the *franchisee.* Franchises, or retail businesses involving sales of products or services to consumers, fall into two general categories:

1. *Distributorships* (also called product or trade name franchises), in which a manufacturer/franchisor licenses a franchisee to sell its product either exclusively or with other products. The franchisee often has the exclusive right to sell the product in a designated area or territory.
2. *Chain-style businesses* (also called business format franchises), in which a franchisee operates a business under the franchisor's trade name and is identified as a member of a select group of persons who deal in this particular business. In exchange for the franchise, the franchisee ordinarily must follow a standardized or prescribed format as to methods of operation and may be subject to the franchisor's control with regard to the materials used in making the

product, site selection, the design of the facility, the hours of the business, the qualifications of personnel, and the like.[4]

As a result of the closings of gasoline stations and automobile and truck dealerships, the overall number of distributorships has decreased since 1972.[5] In contrast to this decrease in distributorships, chain-style franchises have increased in number. Large franchisors (those with 1,000 or more units each) should continue to dominate this category of franchising; most of these large franchisors engage either in restaurant businesses or in the retailing of automotive products and services.[6]

BENEFITS OF FRANCHISING

Whatever form the particular franchise takes, the advantages of a franchise system as a method of doing business make it attractive to both potential franchisees and franchisors. The benefits to franchisees include the following:

1. The opportunity to start a business despite limited capital and experience
2. The goodwill that results from marketing a nationally known, high-quality trademark or service mark, which not only benefits the individual franchisees but also raises customer acceptance throughout the system
3. The availability of the franchisor's business expertise in such areas as inventory control, warehousing, advertising, market research, and product innovation
4. An assured supply of materials, the use of bulk buying techniques, and access to training and supervision

The benefits to franchisors include:

1. The franchisee's investment of capital
2. The goodwill and other advantages flowing from the franchisee's entrepreneurial abilities, including the enhanced value of the trademark or service mark
3. The availability of an assured distribution network, which brings about economies of scale in labor costs, produces a more certain demand curve, and reduces wide fluctuations in sales
4. A larger asset base, which makes the franchisor better able to secure credit, enhance profits, avoid financial risks, attract the best talent, lobby for favorable legislation, and defray litigation costs.[7]

Simply put, the franchisor and the franchisee are able to accomplish more together than they can through individual effort. In an era of increasing vertical integration, some observers view franchising as the last bastion for the independent businessperson. Franchising provides independent businesspersons with the means of opening and operating their own businesses, and it allows small businesses to compete with mammoth corporations. In addition, franchising fosters the expansion of an established product or service. It also may bring about the rescue of an otherwise failing business.

By lowering barriers to entry, franchising as a type of business system furthers many of the antitrust policies you will learn about in Chapter 40. It thus provides social and economic benefits to the public at large as well as to individual consumers. On the other hand, the franchisor's often extensive control over the franchisee's conduct of the business, together with other aspects of the franchisor/franchisee relationship, has spawned complicated legal questions. The remainder of this chapter considers some of these issues.

37.1

MANAGEMENT

FRANCHISING CIT

During a recent family dinner, Donna suggested that Tom and Anna should consider franchising CIT. Donna stated that, by franchising, CIT could rapidly expand into a number of states that the firm will not be able to reach for quite some time under its current operating system. The next day Tom and Anna ask you for your advice concerning the benefits and the risks of franchising. What will you tell them?

BUSINESS CONSIDERATIONS Why might a relatively small but dynamic business want to consider franchising? Why might this same firm prefer to avoid franchising or otherwise letting outsiders have access to its products or ideas?

ETHICAL CONSIDERATIONS Is franchising ethical? Is it ethical for a franchisor to be able to control the conduct of its franchisees as completely as many franchisors do? Explain your reasoning.

FRANCHISING COMPARED WITH OTHER BUSINESS RELATIONSHIPS

A franchise generally involves a form of marketing or distribution in which one party grants to another the right or privilege to do business in a specified manner in a particular place over a certain period of time. It sometimes has been difficult to distinguish franchising from other types of business relationships. The distinction nonetheless may be legally important, since in recent years about one third of the states have passed laws dealing specifically with franchising; and the Federal Trade Commission (FTC) has established regulations covering franchising. Until trouble develops, the two parties may view the holder of the right to do business in a prescribed manner as an independent contractor. But when the grantor terminates its business relationship with the holder, the holder, in order to fall under the protection of such statutes, may try to characterize the relationship as a franchise. Even before the relationship between the two parties sours, governmental agencies tend to see the relationship as one of employment, not of independent contracting. If the holder of the privilege is an employee or agent rather than an independent contractor, the law requires the grantor to pay withholding and social security taxes, federal minimum wages, and workers' compensation. In addition, in such circumstances, the grantor may be subject to the provisions of other labor laws and private antitrust suits.

It is especially difficult to classify the relationship if the holder of the privilege is a distributor. As we already have noted, a distributor may be a franchisee. Yet, depending on the details surrounding the distributor's relationship with its supplier, it also is possible that a distributor instead is an employee, a **consignee**, or an independent contractor. As you might expect, courts, in making such determinations, delve deeply into the particular facts at issue (most notably evidence of the grantor's degree of control over the distributor).

Consignee
A person to whom goods are shipped for sale and who generally can return all unsold goods to the consignor.

Cooperatives
Groups of individuals, commonly laborers or farmers, who unite in a common enterprise and share the profits proportionately.

Concessionaires
Operators of refreshment centers.

Still, the law is fairly well settled with regard to certain issues: **Cooperatives**, **concessionaires**, joint ventures, general partnerships (although a partnership can act either as a franchisor or a franchisee), and sales agencies ordinarily are not deemed franchises. In addition, as you will learn in Chapter 38, a franchise agreement usually does not amount to a security under federal or state law because the distributors/franchisees invest their own efforts in the franchise and do not expect to obtain benefits solely from the efforts of others. In other words, the typical franchising arrangement lacks the "passive investment" component generally associated with certain types of securities.

In the following case, the court needed to decide whether the business relationship at issue involved a franchise arrangement.

37.1 BLANKENSHIP v. DIALIST INTERNATIONAL CORP. 568 N.E.2d 503 (Ill.App. 1991)

FACTS Clyde E. Blankenship and James Cronin, vice president and national sales manager of Dialist International Corporation (Dialist International), entered into a distributor's agreement naming Blankenship as the sales representative of Dialist International for a specified territory. In return, Blankenship paid Dialist International $15,000. Thereafter, Blankenship met with Cronin and received a detailed explanation of the Dialist system and instruction on how to market the product, a list-finder device designed for attachment to telephones. Cronin also provided Blankenship with a binder that contained promotional materials; letters from proposed customers; and samples of Dialist International's advertising, cost sheets, and purchase orders. Upon attempting to market the Dialist, Blankenship encountered difficulties regarding the credibility of the company. Herman L. Smith, president of Dialist International, provided Blankenship with a letter vouching for the credibility of the firm. In March 1987, Blankenship sued Dialist International, Smith, and Cronin for rescission of the distributorship agreement and for damages under § 21 of the Franchise Disclosure Act (the Act). Blankenship asserted that the agreement had constituted a sale of the franchise and because the sale had violated § 4 of the Act, he was entitled to the return, with interest, of the full amount paid by him for the franchise, plus attorneys' fees and costs. On 13 April 1989, the trial court granted summary judgment for Blankenship for the $15,000, plus interest.

ISSUE Had Blankenship and Dialist International entered into a franchise agreement?

HOLDING Yes. The agreement between the parties had satisfied the statutory requirements for the creation of a franchise under Illinois law.

REASONING The defendants argued that the affidavit and supporting documents submitted by Blankenship had failed to establish that, under Illinois law, a franchise agreement had existed between the parties. The definition of "franchise" set forth in § 3 of the Act reads:

> *(1) "Franchise" means a contract or agreement, either expressed or implied, whether oral or written, between two or more persons by which: (a) a franchisee is granted the right to engage in the business of offering, selling or distributing goods or services, under a marketing plan or system prescribed or suggested in substantial part by a franchisor; and (b) the operation of the franchisee's business pursuant to such plan or system is substantially associated with the franchisor's trademark, service mark, trade name, logo-type, advertising, or other commercial symbol designating the franchisor or its affiliate; and (c) the person granted the right to engage in such business is required to pay a fee of $100 or more.*

Thus, by statutory definition, a franchise exists where an agreement meets these three objective criteria. Section 3 of the Act defines a marketing plan as "[a] plan relating to some aspect of the conduct of a party to a contract in conducting business, including but not limited to (a) specification of price, or special pricing systems or discount plans, (b) use of particular sales or display equipment or merchandising devices, (c) use of specific sales techniques, (d) use of advertising or promotional materials or cooperation in advertising efforts."

When Blankenship encountered difficulty regarding the credibility of Dialist International, its president, Smith, had furnished Blankenship with a letter asserting the company's integrity and financial responsibility. Hence, these representations amply satisfied the statutory requirement of the existence of a marketing plan or system. The second statutory criterion concerns the use of a trade name or other commercial symbol designating the franchise or its affiliate. The "Dialist Agreement" granted to Blankenship "the distributorship and authority to sell Cooperative Dialists." Moreover, all the promotional materials provided to Blankenship referred to the product as the Dialist. Furthermore, as to the marketing of the product, Blankenship had been instructed to rely on the purported good name of the Dialist and the company of the same name. Given the strong association between the Dialist name and the nature of the product to be distributed and the promised benefits to be derived from being identified with Dialist International, Blankenship's business had been substantially associated with the trade name Dialist such as to satisfy the second statutory requirement. The final statutory requirement is that, to be granted the right to engage in the business, Blankenship must have paid a fee of $100 or more. Blankenship claimed, and the defendants did not dispute, that he had paid $15,000 for the right to engage in his business. Thus, inasmuch as Blankenship had asserted facts sufficient to satisfy each criterion in the statutory definition, no genuine issue of material fact existed as to the applicability of the Act. Therefore, the trial court had not erred when it granted summary judgment to Blankenship.

37.1 BLANKENSHIP v. DIALIST INTERNATIONAL CORP. *(cont.)* 568 N.E.2d 503 (Ill.App. 1991)

BUSINESS CONSIDERATIONS Assume the CEO of Dialist has asked you to prepare a memo in which you explain how the company could have avoided the liability ultimately imposed on it. What ideas would you stress most heavily?

ETHICAL CONSIDERATIONS Once Blankenship encountered sales resistance to the product, was the company ethically bound to buy out Blankenship's distributorship agreement? Why or why not?

SETTING UP THE FRANCHISING RELATIONSHIP

To recruit franchisees, franchisors usually use advertising. The franchisor typically sends "franchise kits" to those who answer the advertisements. Ordinarily, this franchise kit, in glowing terms, points out the potential for success in this particular business. To the uninitiated layperson or the businessperson with little previous experience and limited capital—those who may be most inclined to enter a franchising arrangement—the franchisor's promotional documents, market studies, and statistics seem highly persuasive. Even at the outset, then, the franchisee relies heavily on the franchisor for guidance. But, as we will see, the pervasiveness of the franchisor's control often leads to subsequent legal difficulties.

Although many variables are involved, the details of a franchising arrangement usually follow a set pattern. Once the parties have established initial contact and have decided to enter into a franchising relationship, first, the parties typically sign a detailed agreement. In this agreement, the franchisor grants to the franchisee the right to use the mark or standardized product or service in exchange for a franchise fee. The franchisor then uses its real estate expertise to designate a specific franchise location, designs and arranges for the standardized construction of the facility, and installs fixtures and equipment therein. In exchange for an advertising fee (usually a percentage of gross sales) paid by the franchisee, the franchisor intensively advertises the product. In addition, the franchisor creates training programs, prepares training manuals, and sets out stringent guidelines—even for the hiring of personnel, the personnel's dress and grooming standards, and the like—for the day-to-day operation of the business.

Once the franchise becomes operative, the franchisee must follow the procedures set out in the franchisor's confidential operating manual or risk termination of the franchise. This manual usually man-

37.2 MANAGEMENT

POTENTIAL PROBLEMS WHEN FRANCHISING

Anna seems to be convinced that franchising CIT is an excellent idea and that the firm should proceed with all due speed to establish franchises in the neighboring states. Dan and John are both hesitant to proceed without further investigation. They ask you what potential problems CIT might encounter in establishing franchises, especially from an agency and a liability perspective. What will you tell them?

BUSINESS CONSIDERATIONS If it establishes franchises, what steps should a business take to ensure that the franchisees are not viewed as employees or agents of the franchisor? Why should such steps be taken?

ETHICAL CONSIDERATIONS Is it ethical to use franchising to expand a business venture while simultaneously trying to avoid the traditional liability areas facing businesses as they expand? How does franchising affect the ethical duties a business owes to its constituents?

dates strict accounting procedures and authorizes the franchisor to inspect the books and records at any time. The franchisee customarily pays to the franchisor a set **royalty fee** (usually based on a certain percentage of the gross sales) on a monthly or semimonthly basis. The franchise agreement normally obligates the franchisee to secure liability insurance to protect the franchisee and franchisor against casualty losses and tort suits. Usually, the franchisee has the responsibility of meeting state requirements regarding workers' compensation as well.

Royalty fee
Payment made in exchange for the granting of a right or a license.

The last two areas customarily covered in the franchise agreement—quality control and termination—pose most of the potential legal problems. It is easy to understand the franchisor's desire for quality control: Only by maintaining uniform standards of quality and appearance can the franchisor preserve its reputation and foster the public's acceptance of its product. For this reason, franchisors typically obligate the franchisee to buy products and supplies from them at set prices or from suppliers who can meet the franchisors' exacting specifications and standards.

Forcing franchisees to buy only from their own franchisors probably constitutes antitrust violations—a topic we shall discuss later in this chapter. As the law currently stands, the same is true if the franchisor sets resale prices for the franchisee; nevertheless, within the law, the franchisor can suggest resale prices. Critics of franchising have argued that, practically speaking, the franchisee will have a difficult, if not impossible, time finding a supplier who will meet the franchisor's specifications, with the result that under the guise of quality control franchisees often must pay inflated prices for supplies.

The termination provisions of a franchising agreement also constitute legal pitfalls for the unwary. The franchise agreement ordinarily sets out the duration of the franchise (say 10 years) and usually contains provisions for renewals after this time period has passed. As part of the covenants, or promises, made about the term of the agreement, the franchisee usually agrees to a covenant not to compete for a set time period after the termination of the franchise. The conditions of default, such as a franchisee's insolvency or failure to pay monthly or semimonthly fees when due, that lead to termination are reproduced in the franchise agreement. In these and other "for cause" situations, the agreement normally calls for the franchisor to give the franchisee time (for example, 10 days) to cure these instances of default. Most agreements provide for notice of termination, and the existing state laws on franchising generally set out a required notice period (say 90 days) before the franchisor can effect a termination.

When prospective franchisees lack business acumen, they are likely to accept without question the 30- to 50-page agreement that the franchisor typically offers. This disparity in bargaining power has led to the passage of state and federal laws and the promulgation of administrative regulations designed to protect franchisees when they enter their agreements (through

37.3

MANAGEMENT

QUALITY CONTROL OVER FRANCHISES

The Kochanowskis have decided to franchise CIT, and they plan to offer franchises to investors in each of the neighboring states. They are concerned, however, with quality control and preservation of the image and the name the firm has established. They ask for your advice as to how they can make provisions for these areas in the franchise agreement. What advice will you give them?

BUSINESS CONSIDERATIONS Why might a franchisor want to control the material used by the franchisees in operating their franchises? How much freedom should the franchisor grant to the franchisees, and how much control should the franchisor exert for the sake of company image and consistency?

ETHICAL CONSIDERATIONS Is it ethical for a franchisor to require the franchisee to purchase materials and supplies from the franchisor? Would it be more ethical for the franchisor to allow the franchisee to act as he or she desires, but to make termination of the franchise easier if the franchisee did not meet certain quality standards?

mandated disclosures) and upon termination (through notice provisions). By closely scrutinizing franchise agreements, courts, too, increasingly have tried to protect franchisees. In the following case, the court addressed the issue of whether the franchisor had breached its alleged promise to select a suitable site for its franchisee's ice cream store.

37.2 BRENNAN v. CARVEL CORP.

929 F.2d 801 (1st Cir. 1991)

FACTS In 1977, Robert and Joanne Brennan responded to a newspaper advertisement describing Carvel Corporation (Carvel) franchise opportunities. On 24 April 1977, the Brennans met with Richard Monaco, an assistant to Carvel's vice president and sales manager, who gave the Brennans a Carvel informational brochure and a Carvel disclosure statement. The brochure stated that "Carvel employs its own Real Estate location experts [who are] . . . dedicated to helping its owner–operators succeed in their stores." The disclosure statement stated in paragraph 11: "Carvel will assume responsibility for selecting, obtaining and negotiating a suitable location for the Carvel Store. When a location has been approved, Carvel will negotiate a rental arrangement, prepare and approve lease documents, and handle the closing and signing of the lease. A one-time real estate fee of $2,500.00 is paid by the Licensee." Paragraph 23 of the disclosure statement provided, "Earnings and/or profits, if any, of a Carvel Store are the responsibility of the Licensee and no representations or statements of projected earnings or profits are made to Licensees with respect to Carvel retail manufacturing stores."

On 21 May 1977, the Brennans again met with Monaco and gave him a $1,000 deposit on a Carvel franchise. The Brennans and Carvel entered into a deposit agreement, which was attached to the Carvel disclosure statement. The agreement stated that "the Applicant understands that, in reliance upon this application, a substantial amount of time and effort shall be exerted in seeking, surveying and showing a location suitable for a Carvel Store." At this meeting, the Brennans told Monaco that they knew of available retail space at 195 State Street in Boston, Massachusetts. Monaco stated that he would not approve a location for the Carvel franchise until the proposed site was "studied, evaluated, and approved" by Carvel; hence, the Brennans continued to look at other possible locations for their Carvel store.

On 16 July 1977, the Brennans met at the 195 State Street location with Monaco, Urezzio (Carvel's vice president), and the Brennans' attorney. At the meeting, Urezzio approved the 195 State Street location and, according to the testimony of the Brennans, stated that "everything [checked] out" and that "he had never approved a site which had failed." But the evidence indicated that, at the time that Urezzio had approved the site, he had not believed that the store could succeed on foot traffic alone; rather, he had thought that the Brennans would have to generate additional business in the form of office and institutional (O and I) sales. Carvel had located most of its stores in suburban locations where 70 percent of the sales of a typical Carvel franchise consisted of take-home sales. The 195 State Street site, located in downtown Boston, was not conducive to such take-home sales.

On 28 October 1977, the Brennans and Carvel entered into a franchise agreement. The franchise agreement in paragraph 27 contained a merger clause stating,

> *This Agreement contains all oral and written agreements, representations and arrangements between the parties hereto, and any rights which the respective parties hereto may have had under any other previous contracts are hereby canceled and terminated, and no representations or warranties are made or implied, except as specifically set forth herein. This Agreement cannot be changed or terminated orally.*

The franchise agreement, in paragraph 34, also contained a statement repeating Carvel's disclaimer of any guarantee of success. At the closing, the Brennans in addition signed several sales contracts, one of which assessed a $2,500 real estate services fee. Yet neither the franchise agreement nor the sales contracts contained any description of the real estate services so provided. The Brennans had testified that they worked very hard at making the business a success. They pursued O and I sales and, by the time of the store's closing, had obtained over 30 O and I accounts. While these efforts helped their business, the promotions and other efforts did not generate enough income to make the Carvel store successful.

In 1980, the Brennans closed their store; and in 1981 they brought suit against Carvel and Urezzio for, among other things, breach of contract and promissory estoppel. At the close of the nonjury trial, the district court entered judgment in favor of the Brennans on the breach of contract claim and awarded the Brennans $780,406.70. Carvel appealed this result.

ISSUE Had Carvel breached its contract to select, evaluate, and approve a suitable site for the Brennans' franchise?

37.2 BRENNAN v. CARVEL CORP. *(cont.)* 929 F.2d 801 (1st Cir. 1991)

HOLDING Yes. The insufficient foot traffic—which Carvel's representatives had recognized—made the site chosen unsuitable for the Brennans' ice cream store. Thus, Carvel had breached its contract with the Brennans.

REASONING Carvel asserted that the franchise agreement entered into between the Brennans and Carvel was an integrated contract into which all prior agreements between the parties had merged and, therefore, as a matter of law, had discharged any prior contractual duty that Carvel had had to find the Brennans a suitable site. Under the parol evidence rule, "a binding integrated agreement discharges prior agreements to the extent that it is inconsistent with them" [*Restatement (Second) of Contracts,* § 213(l)]. Nevertheless, the parol evidence rule does not apply to a collateral agreement (that is, a separate contract between the parties). The deposit agreement entered into by the Brennans and Carvel and Carvel's promise to select, evaluate, and approve a suitable site for the Brennans' ice cream store constituted a separate contract, or an agreement collateral to the franchise agreement. Moreover, the disclosure statement specifically stated that Carvel would "assume responsibility for selecting, obtaining and negotiating a suitable location for the Carvel Store." In addition, the sales contract required the Brennans to pay a $2,500 fee for real estate services, but did not describe the services provided. Thus, notwithstanding the existence of the merger clause, the finding of the district court—that the Brennans and Carvel had entered into a separate contract collateral to the franchise agreement in which Carvel had promised to select, evaluate, and approve a suitable location for the Brennans' ice cream store—was not clearly erroneous.

Carvel next contended that, even if the Brennans and Carvel had entered into a separate and enforceable contract for the selection, evaluation, and approval of a suitable site, Carvel had not breached that contract. Carvel asserted that a suitable location or site is one that "is properly zoned, has the necessary electrical and mechanical facilities to operate a Carvel ice cream store, and . . . has enough space to house both the factory facility and retail sales." The evidence presented at trial indicated that, under the circumstances, a "suitable site" means one that is in a location with adequate traffic or population, or other appropriate characteristics, and in which a Carvel franchise may succeed. Hence, the district court had not erred in concluding that Carvel had breached the contract to select, evaluate, and approve a suitable location for the Brennans' ice cream store, since the 195 State Street site was an unsuitable location for a Carvel store; there was insufficient foot traffic at the 195 State Street site; and, to succeed, the Brennans would have had to make the majority of their business O and I sales even though Carvel's operations were primarily directed toward take-home sales.

Finally, the district court had credited the Brennans' testimony that they had worked hard at their ice cream store and that the store's failure had not been attributable to any lack of effort or mismanagement. Carvel, however, contended that the principles of waiver and estoppel would bar the Brennans' claims against Carvel because the Brennans, who initially had mentioned the 195 State Street site, had recognized beforehand many of the shortcomings of the site. The party asserting a waiver must show clear, decisive, and unequivocal conduct indicating that the opposing party would not insist that the contractual provision at issue be performed. Moreover, estoppel precludes a party who makes a representation of fact from later denying that fact, if the opposing party justifiably has relied on the representation. Thus, the Brennans had neither waived their right to assert, nor were they estopped from asserting, that Carvel had failed to select, evaluate, and approve a "suitable site" for the Brennans' ice cream store.

BUSINESS CONSIDERATIONS What intra-office policies—if any—can a business like Carvel institute so as to weed out employees like Urezzio?

ETHICAL CONSIDERATIONS In approving the site, did Urezzio act unethically toward Carvel and the Brennans? Why or why not?

Most litigation involving franchises has centered on the termination provisions in the franchising agreement. Because termination can leave the franchisee with little to show after years of effort and expense, courts, whenever possible, try to find a basis of relief so the franchisee is not without a remedy. However, courts will not force franchisors to stick with obviously inept franchisees. The following case illustrates this point.

37.3 FOREIGN MOTORS, INC. v. AUDI OF AMERICA, INC. 755 F.Supp. 30 (D.Mass. 1991)

FACTS Foreign Motors, Inc. (FMI), the plaintiff, commenced this action in response to an attempt by the defendants, Audi of America, Inc. and Volkswagen of America, Inc. (hereinafter collectively referred to as "Audi"), to terminate FMI's franchise to sell, lease, and service Audi automobiles as of 15 January 1991. The plaintiff's complaint alleged that Audi had terminated FMI's franchise arbitrarily and without good cause in violation of the Massachusetts regulatory statute. In addition, according to the plaintiff, Audi had breached the contract and the duty of good faith and fair dealing. FMI sought an injunction to **stay** this termination, pending final resolution of its dispute with Audi. FMI had operated in Boston, Massachusetts, for many years as an authorized dealer of certain imported luxury cars. Under individual dealer agreements, FMI sold, leased, and serviced automobiles for BMW, Mercedes-Benz, Porsche, and Audi. FMI earlier had rejected the purchase offer of Bahig F. Bishay; but on 6 November 1987, Herbert G. Chambers became the sole owner of FMI. Chambers had agreed to purchase FMI, subject to the constraints FMI's agreements with Bishay had imposed. In December 1986, Bishay commenced litigation aimed at effecting a transfer of the FMI franchise from Chambers to Bishay. At the time Chambers had purchased FMI and entered into a new dealer agreement with Audi, both parties also were aware that the franchise consistently had experienced financial and operational difficulties, including massive operating losses, high employee turnover, and poor customer satisfaction ratings. Since acquiring ownership of FMI, Chambers apparently had invested $6.4 million to recapitalize FMI and to fund the accrued losses. To improve the quality of customer service, he moreover had replaced sales and service employees. Nevertheless, the franchise continued to fall below Audi's established capital requirements, sales objectives, and performance standards, and continuously failed to achieve compliance with the terms of the Audi dealer agreement. FMI contended that Audi should not penalize FMI for failing to attain certain rigid objectives that FMI could not reasonably attain under the constraints imposed by the Bishay litigation, particularly when Audi had had full knowledge of FMI's peculiar situation. According to FMI, the resolution of the Bishay litigation would provide Chambers with the opportunity to implement more dramatic changes in the business. Hence, FMI submitted that Audi should not terminate FMI's franchise at this time. Moreover, FMI alleged that Audi's decision to terminate stemmed from improper motives—Audi's learning that Chambers might seek to sell FMI. In FMI's view, Audi wanted to reap the benefits accruing from FMI's current marketability. Audi responded that, despite the steadfast assistance of Audi and its executives, FMI never had satisfied the requirements of its dealer agreement with Audi. Even though Audi had taken into account the constraints imposed on FMI as a result of the Bishay litigation, FMI's deficiencies had persisted. FMI's poor performance and unprofitability therefore had led Audi to terminate FMI's franchise.

ISSUE Should the court, owing to the absence of good cause to support such a termination, issue an injunction to stay Audi's termination of FMI's franchise?

HOLDING No. FMI would not suffer irreparable injury, as it would still have a franchise from three other manufacturers; and money damages would suffice to compensate for any loss of revenue owing to the termination of the franchise. Moreover, Audi had demonstrated good cause when it had noted that Chambers's equity in the dealership had represented only 26.3 percent of Audi's working capital; FMI's working capital had stood at only 15.4 percent of Audi's requirements; and FMI had attained only 23.2 percent of its projected sales.

REASONING Given FMI's poor customer service ratings vis-à-vis its Audi customers, the extent of harm to the dealership's reputation or goodwill as a result of the termination of its Audi franchise remained speculative. Hence, FMI could not demonstrate that it would suffer irreparable harm in the absence of a stay of termination necessary to support the granting of an injunction. Massachusetts statute Chapter 93B prevents a manufacturer from terminating a franchise agreement with an automobile dealer "without good cause," but the statute does not define specifically what the term "good cause" means. The legislature, in directing the court to consider "all pertinent circumstances," including, but not limited to, the amount of business transacted by the dealer, the level of investment made, the adequacy of the services provided, and the existence of any breach of the terms of the franchise agreement, has provided some guidance. In addition, Massachusetts courts have taken into account both the business judgment of the decision maker and the economic realities confronting the business. Audi insisted that it had had legitimate and compelling business reasons for terminating the FMI franchise. In particular, Audi stressed that the most recent statistics showed that FMI had attained only 23.2 percent of its projected sales while dealers in the Boston metropolitan area and the Atlantic Zone had reached 85.3 percent and 77.8 percent of their objectives, respectively. FMI's customer satisfaction ratings and its service record similarly remained deficient. Moreover, Chambers's equity in FMI was

37.3 FOREIGN MOTORS, INC. v. AUDI OF AMERICA, INC. *(cont.)* 755 F.Supp. 30 (D.Mass. 1991)

$638,544, only 26.3 percent of Audi's capital requirements, while FMI's working capital stood at only 15.4 percent of Audi's requirements.

In sum, FMI had experienced, and continued to experience, serious operational difficulties; and the franchise had continually failed to comply with the performance standards set out in the Audi dealer agreement. Repeated correspondence with and assistance from Audi executives had been unsuccessful in bringing about any change. In light of the overwhelming evidence of FMI's deficiencies, Audi had had sound business reasons and sufficient "good cause" to terminate FMI. Although Chapter 93B unquestionably seeks to protect automobile dealers from the "inequitable consequences of [the] overweening economic power wielded by manufacturers," it does not purport to shield them entirely from adverse decisions formulated on legitimate business and economic grounds. Hence, a court should not force Audi to continue the franchise where FMI's chronically and irremediably poor performance justifiably caused Audi substantial concern. Moreover, whatever harm FMI might suffer by having its franchise terminated would not constitute irreparable injury. The loss of the Audi franchise might result in reduced revenue, but FMI would not go out of business altogether; FMI still would be able to deal in BMW, Mercedes-Benz, and Porsche automobiles; and money damages would suffice to compensate for any loss of additional revenue attributable to Audi sales. Given FMI's failure to demonstrate both irreparable injury and a likelihood of success on the claim, a court should not order the relief sought by FMI.

BUSINESS CONSIDERATIONS Audi apparently had worked with FMI for five years before Audi attempted to terminate the franchise. Should Audi have taken more summary action against FMI? Why or why not?

ETHICAL CONSIDERATIONS If the court had grounded its decision on ethical grounds as opposed to legal ones, would its decision have been different? Explain fully.

DECISIONAL LAW AND STATUTES AFFECTING FRANCHISING

Stay
Suspend.

As the *Foreign Motors, Inc.*, case illustrates, courts have been sensitive to the issue of damages in the franchising context. This is particularly true in circumstances involving terminations, because upon termination the franchisee may be left with nothing. Termination provisions, especially when coupled with transferability terms that allow the franchisor to reject potential buyers, may clothe the franchisor with an inordinate amount of power vis-à-vis the franchisee.

In shaping relief, as we have seen, courts can turn to common law, their own powers of equity, and/or applicable statutes. Some of the statutes mentioned earlier were designed by their drafters to correct perceived abuses and overreaching by franchisors; indeed, few regulations pertain to the conduct of franchisees. Clearly, such statutes have improved the bargaining position of franchisees; but some critics have argued that they also make franchise systems more rigid and encourage litigation. Some state legislatures have passed special laws to protect automobile dealers from excessive competition. These statutes typically require that a franchisor who wishes to establish a new dealership or to relocate an existing one must give notice to established automobile dealers and to the state motor vehicle

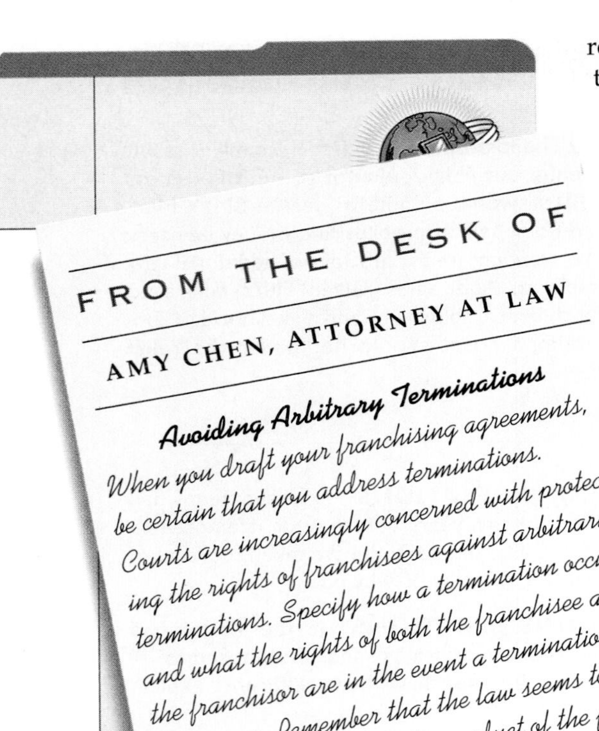

regulatory agency. This notice provision allows established dealers to object to the granting of any additional dealership licenses and thereby to protect their economic stakes in a particular territory. In *New Motor Vehicle Board of California* v. *Orrin W. Fox Co.*,[8] the Supreme Court upheld a California statute of this type even though Fox had argued that the statute violated antitrust laws and was unconstitutional on grounds of due process.

FROM THE DESK OF
AMY CHEN, ATTORNEY AT LAW
Avoiding Arbitrary Terminations
When you draft your franchising agreements, be certain that you address terminations. Courts are increasingly concerned with protecting the rights of franchisees against arbitrary terminations. Specify how a termination occurs and what the rights of both the franchisee and the franchisor are in the event a termination does occur. Remember that the law seems to pay particular attention to the conduct of the franchisor, so be certain that your agreement provides adequate protection for the parties.

On the federal level, the Automobile Dealers' Franchise Act, also known as the Automobile Dealers' Day in Court Act (15 U.S.C. § 1221), in a similar fashion allows a terminated dealer to bring a federal court action seeking retention of the franchise if the dealer can prove that the franchisor has conducted the termination in bad faith and coercively. The federal Petroleum Marketing Practices Act (15 U.S.C. § 2801) protects motor fuel distributors and dealers from arbitrary terminations as well. However, even with these statutes, courts have allowed franchisors to terminate franchisees for such reasons as misconduct, or alternatively, failure to meet sales quotas, to observe quality standards, to maintain appropriate investment levels, and the like. Nevertheless, the presence of these laws helps to ensure that the bargaining power between franchisors and franchisees will be more commensurate and balanced. The following case illustrates these points.

37.4 UNION OIL COMPANY OF CALIFORNIA v. O'RILEY — 276 Cal.Rptr. 483 (Cal.App. 1991)

FACTS On 22 June 1981, Patrick M. O'Riley entered into a franchise lease with Union Oil Company of California (Union Oil) wherein he agreed to operate a Union Oil full-service station. Andre Van der Valk, the Union Oil area manager in charge of the service stations in O'Riley's area, met with him often and suggested that the station become a self-service station. O'Riley, however, had no intention of becoming self-service and told Van der Valk so. When O'Riley next placed an order for the delivery of gasoline, it was not delivered. He was informed that a credit hold had been placed on his order and that he would have to speak to Van der Valk. Unable to contact Van der Valk, O'Riley finally spoke to Bill Thomas, the Union Oil retail representative. Thomas later informed O'Riley that Van der Valk was on vacation and that the terminal would not release O'Riley's order without Van der Valk's authorization. Meanwhile, O'Riley ran out of fuel and was forced to close the station. Van der Valk thereafter lifted the hold and apologized for the mistake. Some time later, 48 hours before the Fourth of July, O'Riley placed an order for gas. He prepared the payment for the previous load, but the load was not delivered during the three-day holiday weekend. Afterward, O'Riley was told the load mistakenly had been delivered to another station, which had not ordered gas—an explanation O'Riley found unbelievable. Van der Valk once more had recommended that O'Riley's station become self-service. When O'Riley again had declined, Van der Valk had been unhappy.

In September 1981, O'Riley agreed to convert the station to self-service. Van der Valk told him that when he stopped servicing cars and selling tires and other accessories, Union Oil would reduce his rent by $500 per month

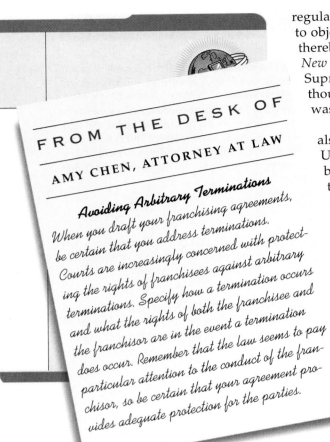

37.4 UNION OIL COMPANY OF CALIFORNIA v. O'RILEY *(cont.)* 276 Cal.Rptr. 483 (Cal.App. 1991)

and within 30 days would install automated pumps, increase the fuel capacity, install freeway signs and other self-service signs around the station, and give O'Riley credit for, or purchase, his inventory. The two men shook hands on the deal. When O'Riley ceased selling tires and other accessories and closed his mechanical bays, Union Oil lowered his rent but did nothing else.

In November 1981, having concluded that Union Oil was not going to live up to its end of the bargain, O'Riley informed Van der Valk that he would place his franchise up for sale and would seek legal advice. In December 1981, while in the hospital, O'Riley received several calls in which Union Oil demanded payment for a load that Union Oil said had been delivered between 1 and 6 December. O'Riley asked who had ordered the gas and why it had been delivered without payment for the previous load. Union Oil responded that the delivery was related to a tank test it had performed, although no one from Union Oil had given O'Riley notice about performing any such test. Union Oil claimed O'Riley owed between $24,000 and $34,000. In the meantime, the station was running low on gas; therefore, O'Riley attempted to place an order. Union Oil refused to deliver until he had paid for the gas that had been delivered.

O'Riley left the hospital on 15 December and stayed in bed until 20 December. His mail that day included three notices of default (the last of which was dated 16 December 1981 and which terminated his lease as of 21 December 1981). Union Oil had sent all the notices to the service station rather than to O'Riley personally. Union Oil filed a complaint alleging that O'Riley owed $23,466.41. O'Riley cross-complained that Union Oil had violated the provisions of the federal Petroleum Marketing Practices Act (PMPA) when it had terminated his franchise, that Union Oil had breached certain of its contractual obligations, and that Union Oil had made promises it had not intended to keep. At trial, the jury returned a special verdict in favor of Union Oil in the amount of $15,869.68, against O'Riley for breach of contract and fraud, and in favor of O'Riley on his PMPA claims. The court awarded O'Riley attorneys' fees of $40,000, punitive damages of $40,500, and expert witness fees of $2,625. Union Oil moved for judgment notwithstanding the verdict or, in the alternative, for a new trial.

ISSUE When it attempted to terminate O'Riley's franchise, had Union Oil violated the PMPA?

HOLDING Yes. In failing to give O'Riley 90 days' notice before termination, Union Oil had violated the act.

REASONING By a special verdict the jury had found (1) that O'Riley owed Union Oil $15,869.68 for the gas that had been delivered to effectuate the tank tests and (2) that Union Oil deliberately had created this indebtedness and had used it as the basis for its decision to terminate the franchise. Thus, the jury apparently had believed the testimony of O'Riley regarding the various disagreeable incidents that had occurred between O'Riley and Union Oil. The fact that Union Oil had arranged for the testing of the tanks and the related delivery of the unordered gasoline when O'Riley was hospitalized constituted further evidence that Union Oil had not been treating O'Riley in a fair manner. Hence, in coming to the conclusion that Union Oil had "deliberately created" this indebtedness, the jury had not erred. In its special verdict, the jury had found that Union Oil had not given O'Riley 90 days' notice, had not personally delivered notice to O'Riley, and had not been excused from personal delivery of the notice to him. The jury had found that Union Oil had violated the PMPA when it gave O'Riley, at the most, five days' notice of its intention to terminate the franchise and, without excuse, had failed to serve O'Riley personally with the notice. Union Oil asserted that the shortened notice afforded to O'Riley stemmed from a "drafting error" but offered no explanation of how this error had occurred. Finally, Union Oil objected to the $40,500 punitive damages award stemming from the jury's finding that Union Oil deliberately had created the indebtedness on which it had based its termination of O'Riley's franchise or that it willfully had disregarded the requirements of the PMPA. Yet the evidence indicated that Union Oil had ignored the 90 days' notice requirement. In addition, Union Oil apparently had terminated O'Riley's franchise in retaliation for his complaints—the very sort of conduct that Congress had enacted the PMPA to prevent.

BUSINESS CONSIDERATIONS Enumerate all the managerial mistakes that Union Oil personnel made in this case. Should the company terminate the employees in question?

ETHICAL CONSIDERATIONS Using the facts, support—or rebut—the proposition that a corporate climate of "win-at-any-cost" contributed to the unethical conduct in which the Union employees had engaged.

The FTC has promulgated a trade regulation rule on franchise disclosure meant to satisfy the same aims. This 1979 rule, and state laws that mandate similar disclosure provisions, have helped to do away with the abuses associated with the sale of franchises. Continuing investigations of the franchise industry under the power to prohibit deceptive and unfair trade practices granted to the FTC by the Federal Trade Commission Act should effectively reinforce these other regulatory measures.

In addition, antitrust laws, such as the Sherman Antitrust Act and the Clayton Act, may apply to various aspects of the franchising relationship. We learned earlier that, as a condition of using their trademark or service mark, franchisors often attempt to impose on franchisees territorial restrictions and restrictions on supplies or prices that may run afoul of the antitrust laws. Consumer protection statutes also may affect the franchising relationship: Franchises that extend credit on installments or through charge accounts may be subject to various truth-in-lending statutes. In addition to its requirement of good faith, the UCC's warranty provisions and its section on unconscionability may be applicable to franchising. Since the law on franchising at this time appears to be unsettled yet proliferating, a thoughtful examination of such laws by franchisors and franchisees alike seems warranted.

YOU BE THE JUDGE

Class Action Suit Against Meineke Muffler

Some 2,500 franchisees of Meineke Muffler Discount Shops (Meineke) brought a class action lawsuit against Meineke in which they alleged that over a 10-year period beginning in 1986, Meineke siphoned off about $31 million from the firm's common advertising fund. The evidence presented at trial showed that Meineke officials invariably told potential franchisees that the company made no money on the franchisees' contributions, which amounted to 10 percent of their weekly revenues. Rather, the officials asserted, the advertising monies represented a trust fund. The franchisees, however, claimed that Meineke's siphoning off of the money violated North Carolina's unfair and deceptive business practices laws. When sued, Meineke argued that the $31 million sum was a proper allocation of commissions to an in-house advertising agency the firm had created and that the franchise contract had authorized these disbursements. To this contention, the franchisees responded that had the firm actually spent the money on advertising, the $31 million would have generated many times more in revenue. Pursuant to the state statute, the judge trebled the $197 million jury verdict in favor of the franchisees, which sum—after interest—totaled $601 million.[9]

Assume that this case has been appealed to *your* court. How will *you* resolve these issues?

BUSINESS CONSIDERATIONS Did Meineke misuse the franchisees' advertising contributions? Why or why not? Do you think future class action suits, such as this one, may affect the present balance of power between franchisors and franchisees? Explain your response.

ETHICAL CONSIDERATIONS What ethical obligations are owed to franchisees by the franchisor? Does the fact that, for many franchisees, the franchise arrangement provides an opportunity to "be one's own boss" increase or decrease the ethical obligations of the franchisor?

SOURCE: Rex Bossert, *The National Law Journal*, 24 March 1997, p. A11.

The following case involved an alleged violation of state antitrust laws.

37.5 YAMAHA STORE OF BEND, OREGON, INC. v. YAMAHA MOTOR CORP., U.S.A.

798 P.2d 656 (Or. 1990)

FACTS Yamaha Motor Corporation (Yamaha), the U.S. distributor for Yamaha motorcycles, published a list of the prices that it charged its dealers for motorcycles. Yamaha Store of Bend, Oregon, Inc. (Yamaha/Bend), a retail Yamaha motorcycle dealer from 1978 to 1983, purchased motorcycles, parts, and accessories from Yamaha for resale in Bend, Oregon, and the surrounding area. After the largest Portland-area Yamaha dealer went out of business, Yamaha sold 550 of the motorcycles it had repossessed to Beaverton Honda (Beaverton) at prices substantially below Yamaha's regular dealer list prices. Yamaha did not offer to sell any of the repossessed motorcycles at the lower prices to Yamaha/Bend or to any of its other dealers. Yamaha also provided Beaverton with advantageous credit terms and advertising support. Beaverton then changed its name to Beaverton Honda-Yamaha and became metropolitan Portland's largest Yamaha dealer. Beaverton subsequently sold the repossessed motorcycles at retail prices close to other dealers' wholesale costs for the same models. Beaverton advertised its low prices extensively in Portland newspapers and on Portland television stations. Since Yamaha/Bend's customers were aware of Beaverton's lower prices, Yamaha/Bend reduced its own prices and, in some cases, sold motorcycles at or below actual costs. Beaverton sold at least two motorcycles to customers with Bend addresses and several others to customers residing in Yamaha/Bend's central Oregon market area. When Yamaha/Bend sued Yamaha for price discrimination allegedly violative of the Oregon Anti-Price Discrimination Law, the jury awarded Yamaha/Bend a verdict on both the price discrimination and breach of contract claims. At trial, Yamaha, moving for a directed verdict on Yamaha/Bend's price discrimination claim, argued that as a matter of law Yamaha/Bend and Beaverton were not "competitors," a necessary element of an Oregon statutory price discrimination claim. When the court of appeals affirmed the trial court's denial of that motion, Yamaha argued that the court of appeals had erred in holding that actual competition between Yamaha/Bend and Beaverton had existed.

ISSUE Had the plaintiff presented sufficient evidence of actual competition between it and the other Yamaha dealer to whom Yamaha had granted more favorable prices so as to support a price discrimination claim?

HOLDING Yes. For the purposes of the Oregon Anti-Price Discrimination Law, the two dealers were in actual competition; hence, the trial court properly had directed a verdict in the plaintiff's favor on this issue.

REASONING Yamaha argued that the question of whether Beaverton's competitive market had included the Bend area hinged on how many actual sales Beaverton had made to Bend-area residents. Yamaha claimed that the evidence showing that, out of more than 800 sales, Beaverton had sold only two motorcycles to Bend residents, as a matter of law had established that Yamaha/Bend and Beaverton were not competitors. Yamaha also alleged that it was not sufficient for the plaintiff to show the effects of Beaverton's advertising campaign on the plaintiff's competitive position (for example, that Bend-area residents would shop in the Portland area or that they knew about Beaverton's lower prices and expected the plaintiff to meet them), since the relevant federal precedents had held that the existence of a few "crossover" sales would fail to prove actual competition. These federal cases were inapposite, however, because they were concerned with exclusive geographic market areas having defined boundaries. No such clearly defined market areas were involved here.

The rationale behind the requirement for actual competition in the same market area was that if the favored and disfavored buyers, here Beaverton and the plaintiff, did not in fact compete for the same customers, a reasonable probability of harm to competition would be absent. Yamaha clearly had sold 1980, 1981, and 1982 motorcycles to Beaverton at prices significantly lower than the prices Yamaha had charged Yamaha/Bend for the same models. Furthermore, Yamaha also had given Beaverton advantageous credit terms not given to the plaintiff. Beaverton then had advertised the sale of its lower-priced motorcycles extensively in Portland newspapers and on Portland television stations, media that Yamaha acknowledged had "statewide" coverage. One of Yamaha/Bend's owners had testified that Beaverton's advertising of its lower prices actually forced the plaintiff to lower its own prices. Of 12 Yamaha dealers in northwestern Oregon before the challenged sale to Beaverton, some started closing up within a few months after the sale; and all 12 were out of business by the time this case had come to trial.

37.5 YAMAHA STORE OF BEND, OREGON, INC. v. YAMAHA MOTOR CORP., U.S.A. *(cont.)* 798 P.2d 656 (Or. 1990)

Yamaha/Bend's expert witness, an economist, had testified that the relevant competitive market was wherever the impacts of a price differential are felt; that Beaverton's extensive advertising of its low prices would have an impact on the plaintiff; that competition in the Bend area definitely would be lessened; and that the effect was a foreseeable, natural, and necessary consequence of Beaverton's extensive advertising of its low prices. The witness also had testified that the foreseeable consequences to the plaintiff would include diversion of sales, negative customer relations, and the depressed value of the plaintiff's new and used motorcycle inventory because the Bend area reasonably is in the Portland market area. Hence, the trial court and the court of appeals correctly had found that evidence in the record existed from which a jury could find that the Bend area was part of Beaverton's market, that Beaverton competed with the plaintiff for customers from the Bend area, that Yamaha discriminated in the prices it had charged Beaverton and the plaintiff for 1982 motorcycles, and that such discrimination had the proscribed effect on competition delineated in the Oregon Anti-Price Discrimination Law. The trial court, in denying Yamaha's motion for a directed verdict, therefore had not erred.

BUSINESS CONSIDERATIONS The franchisees' lack of control over the placement of additional—and potentially competing—franchise outlets and alternative means of distributing products promises to be one of the most important issues in future litigation involving the franchising relationship. Enumerate the franchisor's reasons for wanting to control the placement of other franchisees and why franchisees desire to have some say in such situations.

ETHICAL CONSIDERATIONS Analyze the plaintiff and the defendant's conduct from the following ethical viewpoints: egoism, utiltarianism, and the Golden Rule.

Challenges to Franchising Regulatory Statutes

Some franchisors have bridled at the passage of such franchising statutes because they view these laws as serious limitations on their freedom to contract and to manage their businesses. Consequently, franchisors have raised constitutional arguments against these laws. The parts of the Constitution relied on in these challenges include the following:

1. *Impairment of the obligation of contracts.* The Constitution prohibits a state from passing a law that makes substantive changes in contractual rights.
2. *Due process.* The Fourteenth Amendment bans vague, standardless laws.
3. *Federal supremacy.* Article VI of the Constitution makes federal law the supreme law of the land. Thus, a state franchising law that conflicts with a federal law (say the Lanham Act's regulation of trademarks) will be unconstitutional.
4. *Interstate commerce.* Article I, § 8 of the Constitution prohibits the states from placing undue burdens on interstate commerce.

A landmark case involving one such constitutional challenge follows.

Forum shopping
Choosing the court or place of jurisdiction that will be most favorable to the litigant.

37.6 SOUTHLAND CORP. v. KEATING 465 U.S. 1 (1984)

FACTS The Southland Corporation is the owner and franchisor of 7-Eleven convenience stores. Southland's standard franchise agreement provides each franchisee with a license to use certain registered trademarks, a lease or sublease of a convenience store owned or leased by Southland, inventory financing, and assistance in advertising and merchandising. The franchisees operate the stores, supply bookkeeping data, and pay Southland a fixed percentage of gross profits. The franchise agreement also contains the following provision requiring arbitration: "Any controversy or claim arising out of or relating to this Agreement or the breach thereof shall be settled by arbitration in accordance with the rules of the American Arbitration Association . . . and judgment upon any award rendered by the arbitrator may be entered in any court having jurisdiction thereof."

Keating was a 7-Eleven franchisee. In May 1977, he filed a class action against Southland on behalf of a class of 800 California franchisees and alleged, among other things, fraud, oral misrepresentation, breach of contract, breach of fiduciary duty, and violation of the disclosure requirements of the California Franchise Investment Law. Southland asserted as an affirmative defense to this suit the franchisees' failure to arbitrate and moved to compel arbitration. The trial court granted Southland's motion to compel arbitration of all claims except those based on the California Franchise Investment Law. This statute provides: "Any condition, stipulation or provision purporting to bind any person acquiring any franchise to waive compliance with any provision of this law or any rule or order hereunder is void." After a trial and appeals, the California Supreme Court interpreted this statute to require judicial consideration of claims brought under the state statute and accordingly refused to enforce the parties' contract to arbitrate such claims. In so doing, California's highest court rejected the state appellate court's holding that the California Franchise Investment Law did not invalidate arbitration agreements and that if it had rendered such agreements involving commerce unenforceable, such a result would conflict with § 2 of the Federal Arbitration Act.

ISSUE Was the California Franchise Investment Law in conflict with federal law and thus unconstitutional?

HOLDING Yes. This state law directly conflicted with the Federal Arbitration Act and thereby violated the Supremacy Clause.

REASONING Congress's enactment of § 2 of the Federal Arbitration Act represented a declaration of a national policy favoring arbitration and a withdrawal of the power of the states to require a judicial forum for the resolution of claims that the contracting parties had agreed to resolve by arbitration. A portion of § 2's language—"an agreement in writing to submit to arbitration an existing controversy arising out of such a contract, transaction, or refusal, shall be valid, irrevocable, and enforceable, save upon such grounds as exist at law or in equity for the revocation of any contract"—stood as clear evidence that Congress had mandated the enforcement of arbitration agreements and that courts should revoke such clauses only on "grounds as exist at law or in equity for the revocation of any contract." Nothing in the act indicated that this broad principle of enforceability had been subject to any additional limitations under state law. Indeed, the legislative history revealed that Congress, in enacting the Federal Arbitration Act, had meant to remedy two problems: the old common law hostility toward arbitration and the failure of state arbitration statutes to mandate enforcement of arbitration agreements. To confine the scope of the act to arbitrations sought to be enforced in federal courts would frustrate what Congress had intended as a broad enactment appropriate in scope to meet the large problems Congress was addressing.

Accordingly, Justice O'Connor's interpretation of the Federal Arbitration Act as a procedural statute applicable only in federal courts was erroneous. Under her interpretation, claims brought under the California Franchise Investment Law would not be arbitrable when they had been raised in state court. But it was clear beyond question that if this suit had been brought as a diversity action in a federal district court, the arbitration clause would have been enforceable. Because the interpretation given to the Federal Arbitration Act by the California Supreme Court therefore would encourage and reward **forum shopping,** to attribute to Congress the intent, in drawing on the comprehensive powers of the Commerce Clause, to create a right to enforce an arbitration contract and yet make the right dependent for its enforcement on the particular forum in which it is asserted would be inappropriate. And since the overwhelming proportion of all civil litigation in this country is in state courts, Congress apparently had not intended to limit the Arbitration Act to disputes subject only to federal court jurisdiction, since such an interpretation would frustrate congressional intent to place "[a]n arbitration agreement . . . upon the same footing as other contracts, where it belongs." Rather, Congress, in creating a substantive rule applicable in state as well as federal courts, had intended to foreclose state legislative attempts to undercut the enforceability of arbitration agreements. Therefore, for these reasons, the California Franchise Investment Law violated the Supremacy Clause of the Constitution.

37.6 SOUTHLAND CORP. v. KEATING (cont.) 465 U.S. 1 (1984)

BUSINESS CONSIDERATIONS The Court alluded to the Federal Arbitration Act's embodiment of a national policy favoring arbitration. What are the advantages of arbitration? What are the disadvantages? Explain fully.

ETHICAL CONSIDERATIONS The Court mentions that the California Supreme Court's interpretation in this case would encourage forum shopping. Is forum shopping inherently unethical? Why or why not?

THE FRANCHISING ENVIRONMENT

Ownership Trends

Since 1975, there has been a demonstrated increase in conversions of company-owned franchise units to franchisee-owned ones. According to industry sources, this increase probably has occurred because most of the units that companies have repurchased have represented temporary buybacks for legitimate business reasons rather than the companies' desire to withdraw from the franchise system or to operate these units permanently themselves. Recent industry statistics show a renewal rate of 90 percent.[10] Approximately 16 percent of the nonrenewals resulted from franchisors' objections; the remainder stemmed from franchisees' decisions not to renew or from mutual agreement between the franchisor and franchisee.[11] Recent statistics also indicate that franchisees initiated approximately 57 percent of the terminations, compared with approximately 43 percent initiated by franchisors.[12] Taken together, these statistics indicate overall stability in the field of franchising.

http: // RESOURCES FOR BUSINESS LAW STUDENTS

NAME	RESOURCES	WEB ADDRESS
Franchising Online	The American Bar Association's (ABA's) forum on franchising, a Forum Committee of the ABA, provides publications and information on laws affecting franchising.	http://www.abanet.org/forums/franchising.html
FranInfo	FranInfo provides tips and materials on buying a franchise or making a business into a franchise. FranInfo also provides a detailed directory of franchises.	http://www.frannet.com/
Federal Trade Commission (FTC) Act, 15 U.S.C. § 41-58	LII provides a hypertext and searchable version of 15 U.S.C. § 41-58, popularly known as the Federal Trade Commission Act.	http://www.law.cornell.edu/uscode/15/41.html
FTC	The FTC provides information on proposed franchising rules, as well as news and press releases, speeches and articles, and facts for consumers and businesses.	http://www.ftc.gov/

International Markets

Government studies suggest that U.S. franchisors will continue to pierce international markets, despite the numerous problems inherent in complying with the local laws of other nations. Canada remains the most important market for U.S. franchisors. As recent statistics show, Canada represented about one-third of all U.S. international outlets; Japan constituted the second-largest foreign outlet; and Australia ranked third. Interestingly, in a similar fashion, Canada, Mexico, Japan, the United Kingdom, and the continental European countries are setting up an increasing number of franchises in the United States. The international ramifications of franchising thus should become even more significant as the growth of communication and transportation systems continues to narrow the gap among consumer preferences around the world and as the advantages of franchising become more apparent to our international neighbors. This is a development that promises to be well worth watching.

SUMMARY

Franchising has become a significant method of doing business both in the United States and abroad. A franchise is an agreement in which one person pays a fee in exchange for a license to use a trademark, service mark, or logotype while one engages in the distribution of goods or services. The person or firm granting the franchise is called the franchisor; the person receiving the franchise is known as the franchisee. Franchises fall into two general categories: distributorships or chain-style businesses. For both franchisees and franchisors, the advantages of franchising make it an attractive method of doing business. Courts have had some problems in distinguishing franchise relationships from other types of business relationships, such as independent contracting. Yet such a distinction may be important under state and federal franchising laws, tax laws, labor laws, and antitrust laws. Some areas of the law are settled: Cooperatives, concessionaires, joint ventures, general partnerships, and sales agencies generally are not deemed the legal equivalent of a franchise. A franchise is not considered a security, either.

To ensure product uniformity and protect the goodwill associated with its trademark or service mark, the franchisor strictly controls the franchise relationship. Two areas ordinarily covered in the franchise agreement—quality control and termination—pose the most legal problems. State and federal laws may cover these two aspects of the agreement, and a wise franchisor should take care not to run afoul of these laws by pressing for unreasonable provisions or terms. Special industry laws at both the federal and state levels also may protect franchisees. The Federal Trade Commission's franchise disclosure regulations, antitrust laws, consumer protection statutes, and the Uniform Commercial Code constitute further bases for controlling abusive behavior by franchisors. Franchisors have challenged such statutes on constitutional grounds, sometimes successfully.

In the last few years, the franchising industry has witnessed an increase in conversions of company-owned units to franchisee-owned ones. This and other industry statistics indicate overall stability in the franchising field; for example, nonrenewals usually are franchisee-initiated. The international aspects of franchising should continue to gain in significance in the coming decades as more sophisticated communication and transportation systems allow for global dissemination of goods and services.

DISCUSSION QUESTIONS

1. Name eight different types of businesses that use franchising as their distributional method. Then list and describe the two main classifications of franchises.
2. Define the term "franchise."
3. Describe four benefits of franchising for the franchisee and franchisor, respectively.
4. For what purposes does the law make distinctions between franchising and other types of business relationships such as independent contracting?
5. Briefly explain the steps involved in setting up a franchising arrangement, and describe what areas the franchising agreement normally covers.
6. Discuss why quality-control and termination clauses are important to franchisors and how these same provisions nevertheless pose legal pitfalls for franchisors.
7. Enumerate the types of statutes that franchisees can use to curb the power of franchisors.
8. What four constitutional bases have franchisors used to challenge franchising statutes?
9. List some of the current trends in franchising regarding renewal and termination decisions.
10. Name the three most important international markets for U.S. franchisors.

CASE PROBLEMS AND WRITING ASSIGNMENTS

1. On 19 November 1984, Yamaha Motor Corporation, U.S.A. (Yamaha) and Northshore Cycles, Inc. (Northshore) entered into a dealer agreement. The dealer agreement contains no provision specifying its term or duration but, to the contrary, provides that it "shall continue until terminated as provided herein." The dealer agreement provides for "Termination for Cause (Immediate Effect)" upon any one of several enumerated occurrences; for "Termination—General Non-Performance" on the failure of either party to fulfill the responsibilities and obligations of the dealer agreement (at least 60 days' prior written notice is required); and for "Termination—Death, Incapacity," which allows Yamaha to terminate the agreement on at least 15 days' prior written notice in the event of the death, physical or mental incapacity, or disassociation of certain individuals affiliated with Northshore. The dealer agreement also permits termination whenever Yamaha offers a new or modified form of agreement to all its dealers if Yamaha gives the dealers at least 60 days' prior notice. Notably, the dealer agreement fails to provide for unilateral termination without cause. Because the agreement is "open ended," having no term specified, it lacks any express provisions for extension or renewal, whether automatic or otherwise. The dealer agreement contains a provision for repurchase of products by Yamaha on the termination of the arrangement with a franchise such as Northshore; but the provision clearly gives Yamaha the "option, but not the obligation, to repurchase" products from the dealer.

   While this dealer agreement was in full force and effect, the Louisiana legislature adopted a statute obligating manufacturers of motorcycles, on the termination of a dealership, to repurchase inventories. The statute became effective on 1 September 1988. On 5 April 1989, a letter to Yamaha from Northshore advised Yamaha of Northshore's decision to terminate its operations as a new motorcycle dealer 30 days following the date of the letter. On 30 May 1989, a follow-up letter to Yamaha from Northshore purported to comply with the notification provision of the statute, including mail delivery of Northshore's final parts inventory. Yamaha accepted Northshore's request to terminate the dealer agreement but declined to repurchase Northshore's inventory.

   In November 1989, in a suit against Yamaha, Northshore sought to compel Yamaha to repurchase the parts listed on the final inventory submitted by Northshore and, in addition, to pay certain penalties prescribed in the statute plus additional damages. Article I, Section 10, Clause 1 of the U.S. Constitution prohibits the several states from passing any "Law Impairing the Obligation of Contracts." The substantive provision of the Louisiana statute, requiring the manufacturer to repurchase inventory from the dealer, appears to violate this constitutional prohibition if such repurchase obligation were enforced against a manufacturer whose contract with the dealer had predated the effective date of the statute. When the district court dismissed the case on this constitutional basis, the dealer appealed. How should the circuit court of appeals rule in this case? [See *Northshore Cycles, Inc.* v. *Yamaha Motor Corp., U.S.A.*, 919 F.2d 1041 (5th Cir. 1990).]

2. Lawrence F. Tynan was the sole owner of Towne Chevrolet, a former General Motors (GM) franchisee that had sold all its assets in July 1985. In December 1985, Tynan had entered into a conditional purchase agreement with another GM franchisee, J & B Chevrolet and Olds, Inc. (J & B). To purchase that

dealership, Tynan had formed L. T. Chevrolet and Olds, Inc. The sale was contingent on GM's issuance and execution of a franchise agreement with Tynan. Citing its past relationship with him, GM ultimately refused the franchise proposal offered by Tynan. J & B, which the parties agreed had standing to sue GM under the New Jersey Franchise Practices Act (the Act), had not challenged GM's decision. Rather, J & B had exercised its right to terminate the agreement with Tynan and had sold its business to a third party whom GM had accepted as a franchisee. Tynan sued; the trial court found that since "Tynan was not a GM franchisee" on 21 January 1986, having sold the Towne franchise, he lacked standing under the Act to challenge GM's decision. Nonetheless, Tynan argued that his status as a contract purchaser of a franchise entitled him to the protections of a franchisee. He claimed that the legislature had intended to protect the persons who would suffer from the arbitrary conduct of franchisors with respect to the transfer of a franchise, particularly since only the transferor and transferee can be hurt by the wrongful denial of consent. GM maintained, however, that only a franchisor can offer a franchise and therefore Tynan was not a franchisee with respect to the J & B transaction. GM pointed to a New Jersey statute that distinguishes between a franchisee and a "proposed transferee" or "prospective transferee." According to GM, a purchaser does not become a franchisee within the meaning of the Act until offered a franchise by the franchisor.

The trial court found that, given the ordinary and well-understood implication of the word "offer," only the one who holds the ownership rights to a franchise can offer it to a third party. Hence, it concluded that Tynan was not a franchisee within the definition of the relevant New Jersey statute. The court also cited the language in another statute to support the proposition that a franchisee is in a different class from a prospective transferee. The judge further reasoned that a court's entertaining suits by prospective purchasers would be contrary to the purpose of the legislation; that is, the protection of the public welfare brought about by the legislation's defining the relationship and responsibilities between franchisors and franchisees, not hopeful third parties. The judge also suggested that a franchisee should not be required to litigate with the franchisor over the lack of consent to a transfer and noted that the Act allows a franchisee to elect between litigation and the less burdensome transfer to a third party acceptable to the franchisor. Given these arguments, for whom should the appellate judge rule in this case? Why? [See *Tynan* v. *General Motors Corp.*, 591 A.2d 1024 (N.J. Super. A.D. 1991).]

3. Snydergeneral Corporation (Snyder), a manufacturer of air-conditioning systems for industrial use, purchased the Climate Control Division of the Singer Company in 1982. Cassidy Podell Lynch, Inc. (Cassidy) had functioned as the exclusive manufacturer's sales representative in Northern New Jersey and Rockland County, New York, for the Singer Company's air-conditioning and heating products. Cassidy continued to act for Snyder in the same capacity. The service vehicles and uniforms of Cassidy's employees bore the Snyder logo, but Cassidy managed its own salesforce, made its own decisions about hiring and firing, and solicited new customers on its own. Cassidy derived most of its income from the sales and servicing of Snyder's product; but Cassidy could, and did, sell other lines of products not directly competitive with Snyder's products. Cassidy had no office or place of business in New Jersey. Rather, it ran its distributorship from a New York City location. Cassidy used the New York address on correspondence relating to its New Jersey business and processed all its orders through the New York City office. Cassidy's New Jersey salespersons operated out of their own New Jersey residences. Cassidy used a Clifton, New Jersey, repair facility to repair Snyder products; but there were no secretaries or office personnel at that location, and Cassidy refrained from processing any orders there. In April 1984, Snyder and Cassidy executed a distributorship agreement renewing Cassidy's exclusive distributorship in parts of New Jersey and New York for a term of one year but subject to earlier termination at Snyder's option upon 30 days' notice.

On 27 August 1984, Cassidy contracted to supply New Jersey Bell with Snyder air-conditioning equipment to replace the existing climate control system at New Jersey Bell's main place of business in Newark, New Jersey. To meet this contract, Cassidy needed to purchase $350,000 worth of Snyder equipment for delivery in installments beginning in February 1985. New Jersey Bell was to pay Cassidy $680,371.60 for the equipment. On 2 November 1984, Snyder acquired McQuay Incorporated (McQuay), another manufacturer of industrial-size heating and air-conditioning equipment. Snyder then advised 36 current representatives (including Cassidy) that Snyder was replacing them with other sales representatives, most of whom were part of the McQuay marketing organization. The 2 November 1984 letter to Cassidy served as notice that Snyder intended to terminate the distributorship agreement 30 days thereafter. After Cassidy received the termination letter, Snyder agreed to sell it the equipment Cassidy needed to fulfill the New Jersey Bell contract. Snyder began the installment deliveries as Cassidy required them. Although Cassidy did not pay for them in the 30 days called for by the purchase order and sales manual, Snyder continued timely deliveries of all but the last six orders. After a flurry of correspondence relating to late payment, Snyder refused to ship the six remaining orders Cassidy needed to fulfill its contract with New Jersey Bell on any payment terms other than cash on delivery despite the fact that Cassidy had made payments of $250,000 for products delivered by Snyder during 1985. Cassidy objected strenuously to the payment terms; demanded delivery on what it considered its customary credit arrangements of a 90-day open term; and, when Snyder refused, filed a lawsuit alleging the wrongful termination of its alleged franchise and breach of contract based on Snyder's failure to deliver the equipment Cassidy needed to perform its contract with New Jersey Bell. Did the distributorship agreement between Snyder and Cassidy create a franchisor/franchisee relationship? Why or why not? [See *Cassidy Podell Lynch, Inc.* v. *Snydergeneral Corp.*, 944 F.2d 1131 (3rd Cir. 1991).]

4. Shell Oil Company (Shell), pursuant to the PMPA statutory provision that provides that proper grounds for nonrenewal exist upon the "conviction of the franchisee of any felony involving moral turpitude," terminated the franchise of Camina Services, Inc. (Camina Services). The president of Camina Services, Jorge Camina, had been convicted of such a felony—possession of cocaine with the intent to distribute. Yet Camina Services contended that, despite Jorge Camina's conviction, Shell's termination of the franchise was improper. In order to insulate Camina Services from the repercussions of Jorge Camina's conviction, Camina Services attempted to distinguish Camina Services, the party to the agreements, from Jorge Camina. Jorge Camina was the president, director, and 50 percent owner of Camina Services and executed all the relevant documents and attended the relevant meetings on behalf of Camina Services. Camina Services further argued that Shell had promised the firm that Mrs. Camina could act on behalf of Camina Services, despite her husband's conviction. The PMPA defines a "franchisee" as a retailer or distributor who under a franchise is permitted to use a trademark in connection with the sale, consignment, or distribution of motor fuel. The PMPA then defines a "distributor" to include "any affiliate," that is, "any person who (other than by means of a franchise) controls, is controlled by, or is under common control with any other person," who purchases motor fuel for sale. The Act leaves the term "control" undefined. How should a judge rule on Camina Services's claims? [See *Camina Services, Inc.* v. *Shell Oil Co.*, 816 F.Supp. 1533 (S.D. Fla. 1992).]

5. In 1975, Carolina Truck & Body Company, Inc. (Carolina), and General Motors Corporation (GMC) entered into a renewal contract entitling Carolina to sell heavy-duty trucks manufactured by GMC. From 1950 until that time, Carolina had been a franchisee, selling light- and medium-duty GMC trucks. On 1 November 1985, the two firms entered into a renewal of the heavy-duty franchise agreement (the heavy-duty addendum), which had a term of five years to and including 31 October 1990. This heavy-duty addendum gave Carolina the nonexclusive right to purchase and sell new heavy-duty truck motor vehicles marketed by the GMC Truck & Coach Operation of General Motors Corporation. The addendum also stated that it would remain in effect unless canceled.

   In August 1985, owing to an economic decline in its share of the heavy-duty truck market during the 1980s, GMC and Volvo Truck Corporation (Volvo) met to consider forming a joint venture in the area of heavy-duty truck manufacturing. GMC notified Carolina and its other heavy-duty franchise dealers as early as 7 November 1986 that the heavy-duty addendum would be canceled no later than 31 December 1987 because of GMC's plans to cease manufacturing heavy-duty trucks. GMC conclusively notified Carolina of such cancellation on 23 December 1986. When Carolina subsequently sought a joint venture franchise from Volvo GM (the new joint venture) for heavy-duty trucks, Carolina learned that it would not receive such a franchise. GMC had no role in the daily operation of Volvo GM and lacked any control over any of Volvo GM's decisions relating to its dealers. On 31 December 1987, GMC stopped marketing all its heavy-duty truck models, no longer shipped these models to any of its dealers nationwide, and canceled all heavy-duty addenda as of that date. Carolina later sued GMC for wrongful termination of Carolina's franchise. Carolina asserted that GMC's actions in discontinuing its heavy-duty truck models and canceling Carolina's heavy-duty truck addendum had failed to comply with the relevant North Carolina statutes because neither good cause nor good faith had underlain GMC's actions. In these circumstances, would a franchisor's cancellation of a franchise for the sale of heavy-duty trucks, owing to the discontinuance of a product line, satisfy the "good cause" and "good faith" standard mandated by North Carolina statutes? Why? [See *Carolina Truck & Body Co., Inc.* v. *General Motors Corp.*, 402 S.E.2d 135 (N.C.App. 1991).]

6. **BUSINESS APPLICATION CASE** Burger King Corporation (BKC) had terminated several franchisees for failure to pay over $1,000,000 in monthly financial obligations under their franchise and lease agreements. When these franchisees refused to vacate their premises and continued to hold themselves out to the public as authorized Burger King restaurants and to use the BKC marks, BKC sued the franchisees under the federal Lanham Act, which protects trademarks from infringement. In opposing BKC's motion for injunctive relief, the franchisees argued that they had the right to continue the operation of their franchises on a royalty- and rent-free basis until the disposition of their wrongful termination lawsuits against BKC. Who had the better argument, BKC or the franchisees? Why? What steps could the franchisor at the outset of the parties' relationship have taken so as to minimize the possibility of such litigation? [See *Burger King Corp.* v. *Majeed,* 805 F.Supp. 994 (E.D. Fla. 1992).]

7. **ETHICS APPLICATION CASE** In 1976, Katherine Apostoleres became the sole shareholder of Minerva, Inc., which owned the rights to a Dunkin' Donuts of America, Inc. (Dunkin') franchise in Brandon, Florida. In 1978, Apostoleres became the sole shareholder of Rosebud, Inc., which owned the rights to a Dunkin' Donuts franchise in Temple Terrace, Florida. Apostoleres and her family (the franchisees) operated both stores. In early 1982, Dunkin' offered to all its franchisees the right to renew the term of the franchisees' existing franchise agreements for an additional 10 years at a fixed cost of $5,000 each. In return, Dunkin' required the franchise owners to participate in a program to abide by advertising decisions favored by at least two-thirds of the local franchise owners in a given television market. Apostoleres refused to accept the offer because she did not want to be bound by the "two-thirds" clause. In August 1982, Dunkin' employees audited Apostoleres's Temple Terrace and Brandon stores and during this audit employed the "yield-and-usage" method, which, by taking the weights of a small number of donuts and extrapolating how many donuts should have been produced based on those weights, projects a store's gross sales. The franchisees' agreements with Dunkin' did not authorize Dunkin' to conduct an audit based on such methodology. In late 1982, the audits revealed that reported sales generally agreed with the sales run through the cash registers, bank deposits, and tax returns for the audited period; however, the yield-and-usage analysis indicated an underreporting of gross sales at both stores. The franchisees denied such underreporting and asserted that the yield-and-usage analysis provided inherently unreliable results.

In September 1985, Dunkin' again audited the two stores. The audit of the Temple Terrace store disclosed no underreporting, but the audit of the Brandon store reflected an underreporting of gross sales based on the yield-and-usage analysis. The audit also detected a substantial difference between the total sales rung into the registers at the Brandon store and the total sales actually reported to Dunkin'. In a 17 June 1986 letter, Dunkin' gave the franchisees notice of immediate termination of the franchises. Despite the notice of termination and the ensuing litigation, the franchisees continued to operate profitably the two stores as Dunkin' franchises. When Dunkin' sued for damages accruing from the allegedly unreported sales, the franchisees counterclaimed that Dunkin' had breached the obligations of good faith and fair dealing implied in the franchise agreements. The franchisees argued that Dunkin's predicating the audit on Mrs. Apostoleres's refusal to subscribe to the franchise renewal option offered by Dunkin' and Dunkin's failure to disclose in the franchise agreement the yield-and-usage test as a measure for enforcing Dunkin's contractual rights evinced Dunkin's lack of good faith. Would you agree with the franchisees' assertions? Why or why not? The legalities aside, how would you assess the ethics of the franchisor here? [See *Dunkin' Donuts of America, Inc.* v. *Minerva, Inc.,* 956 F.2d 1566 (11th Cir. 1992).]

8. **IDES CASE** Lois H. and Howard L. Gruver and E. Patrick Halpin purchased new Midas International Corporation (Midas) muffler shop franchises in 1983 and 1984, respectively. Midas previously had done market studies indicating that both franchisees' franchise locations would be unprofitable. However, Midas represented to both franchisees that its studies had indicated that the franchises would be profitable. The franchises nonetheless lost money. The franchise agreements gave the franchisees the right to terminate the franchises upon 30 days' notice. Upon termination, however, accrued liabilities remained; and Midas was entitled to the prompt repayment of all money due. Midas could require that the franchisees sell all Midas parts in their inventory back to Midas, with the right to set off the repurchase price against the money due from the franchisees. The franchisees individually approached Midas concerning terminating their franchises. In the Gruvers' case, Midas did not draw up a termination agreement until three-and-one-half months later. In the meantime, Midas refused to extend further credit to the Gruvers and required them to pay cash for all items purchased from Midas. In Halpin's case, Midas also cut off credit; but Midas drew up a termination agreement

within approximately one month. After brief discussions with their lawyers, the franchisees executed the termination agreements, which provided that Midas would buy back the Gruver franchise for $95,160.60 and the Halpin franchise for $87,756.15. Midas also agreed to employ Halpin as a manager at another muffler shop.

Under the termination agreements, all the money that the franchisees received, however, would be paid back to Midas to satisfy their debts or would be paid to a bank to release liens on the property Midas owned. The agreements further provided that the franchisees would release all claims they had against Midas. The Gruvers at that point knew that, as to Midas, they had potentially successful fraud claims arising out of their purchases of the Midas franchises. Halpin did not have specific evidence to support such claims at that time, although Halpin suspected that evidence supporting some such claims existed and, prior to signing his termination agreement, had discussed with his attorney the viability of such claims. Both the Gruvers and Halpin subsequently sued Midas for fraud, breach of contract, and related claims stemming from their purchases of the Midas franchises. Midas moved for summary judgment on the ground that the franchisees in their termination agreements had released these claims. The franchisees claimed that the termination agreements were invalid because they had entered into the agreements under economic duress, defined as: (1) wrongful acts or threats, (2) financial distress caused by those acts, and (3) the absence of any reasonable alternative to the terms presented by the wrongdoer. How should the appellate court rule in this case? Apply the IDES model in reaching your answer. [See *Gruver* v. *Midas International Corp.*, 925 F.2d 280 (9th Cir. 1991).]

NOTES

1. Harold Brown, *Franchising—Realities and Remedies*, 2nd ed. (New York: Law Journal Press, 1978), p. 1.
2. International Franchise Association Educational Foundation, Inc. and Horwath International, *Franchising in the Economy 1988–1990* (Washington, D.C., 1990), p. 13.
3. Ibid., p. 11.
4. Gladys Glickman, *Franchising*, vol. 15 of *Business Organizations* (New York: Matthew Bender, 1983), § 2.02.
5. International Franchise Association Educational Foundation, Inc. and Horwath International, *Franchising in the Economy 1988–1990*, p. 94.
6. Ibid., p. 13.
7. Brown, *Franchising*, pp. 6–12.
8. 439 U.S. 96 (1978).
9. Rex Bossert, "Meineke Judgment May Spawn Similar Litigation," *The National Law Journal* (24 March 1997), p. A11.
10. International Franchise Association Educational Foundation, Inc. and Horwath International, *Franchising in the Economy 1988–1990*, p. 108.
11. Ibid.
12. Ibid., p. 109.

Chapter 38

Securities Regulation

Outline

Federal Laws
State Regulation
The Foreign Corrupt Practices Act
Summary
Discussion Questions
Case Problems and Writing Assignments

Agenda

The Kochanowskis have incorporated CIT, and they are now considering taking the firm public in order to raise money for needed expansion and growth. They will consider issuing stock, bonds, and debentures to the public. They will need to know how these offerings may affect their liability and what they will need to do to comply with federal securities laws. They also will need to know what is expected of them under state security regulations. In addition, the firm is considering an expansion into the international marketplace. If the expansion occurs, the family members are likely to have questions about the Foreign Corrupt Practices Act and its impact on their dealings. These and other questions may arise as you study this chapter.

Be prepared! You never know when one of the Kochanowskis will seek your help or advice.

FEDERAL LAWS

In Chapters 34 and 35, we briefly examined some provisions of the 1933 and 1934 Securities Acts. It is not possible in one chapter to discuss fully the complex interplay of federal and state securities laws, but we will attempt to understand the broad outlines of this complicated area of the regulation of business.

Securities regulation has come to be known as "federal corporate law." This label in large measure stems from the extensive federal laws and the rules set forth by the Securities and Exchange Commission (SEC), the federal agency charged with primary responsibility for the enforcement and administration of federal laws covering securities, public utility holding companies, trust indentures, investment companies, and investment advisers. The SEC consists of five members appointed by the president for five-year terms. To ensure impartiality, securities law requires that no more than three of the commissioners be members of the same political party. The SEC and its staff generally have enjoyed a high-quality reputation among securities professionals.

The Securities Act of 1933

The Securities Act of 1933 (the '33 Act) defines a *security* as "any note, stock, treasury stock, bond, debenture, evidence of indebtedness, . . . or participation in any profit-sharing agreement, . . . investment contract, . . . fractional undivided interest in oil, gas, or other mineral rights, or, in general, any interest or instrument commonly known as a 'security.'" The Supreme Court in *Gould* v. *Ruefenacht*, 471 U.S. 701 (1985), held that where an instrument bears the label "stock" and possesses all the characteristics typically associated with stock, the instrument is a "security"; in such cases, a court need not look beyond the character of the instrument to the economic substance of the transaction.

But in other situations in which the instrument bears no such label, courts oftentimes must construe what the statutory term "investment contract" means. Subsequent case decisions interpreting this phrase have made it clear that, in this sense, a security involves an investment in a common enterprise whereby the investor has no managerial functions but instead expects to profit solely from the efforts of others. For this reason, court determinations of what constitutes a security based on this so-called "economic reality" test have been broad and far-reaching. Courts have construed investments in condominiums, citrus groves, and cattle, when others have been employed to manage such assets, as securities subject to the federal securities laws.

The '33 Act basically is a disclosure statute meant to protect the unsophisticated investing public. By requiring the registration of most securities when they initially are offered and by enforcing various antifraud provisions, the '33 Act ensures such protection.

Uncollateralized
Having no underlying security to guarantee performance.

In *Reves* v. *Ernst & Young*, the Court in its threshold analysis needed to decide whether certain promissory notes constituted "securities" under federal law. If so, the '34 Act's antifraud provisions were applicable. Note the detailed analysis the Court, in reaching its conclusion, followed.

38.1 REVES v. ERNST & YOUNG 494 U.S. 56 (1990)

FACTS The Farmers Co-operative of Arkansas and Oklahoma (the Co-Op) is an agricultural cooperative that, at the time relevant here, had approximately 23,000 members. In order to raise money to support its general business operations, the Co-Op sold promissory notes payable on demand by the holder. Although the notes were **uncollateralized** and uninsured, they paid a variable rate of interest that the Co-Op adjusted monthly to keep the rate higher than the rate paid by local financial institutions. The Co-Op, marketing the scheme as an "Investment Program," advertised the notes as safe, secure investments. Despite these assurances, in 1984, the Co-Op filed for bankruptcy. At the time of the filing, over 1,600 people held notes worth a total of $10 million. Reves and others, a class of holders of the notes, filed suit against Arthur Young & Co. (Arthur Young), Ernst & Young's predecessor, the firm that had audited the Co-Op's financial statements. Alleging violations of the '34 Act's antifraud provisions and Arkansas's security laws, Reves asserted that in order to inflate the assets and net worth of the Co-Op, Arthur Young, in its audit, had intentionally failed to follow generally accepted accounting principles. Reves maintained that if Arthur Young had properly treated the assets in the audits, he (Reves) would not have purchased the demand notes because the Co-Op's insolvency would have been apparent. At trial, Reves and the others prevailed on both their federal and state law claims and received a $6.1 million judgment. Arthur Young appealed on the grounds that the demand notes did not constitute "securities" under either federal law or Arkansas law and that the statutes' antifraud provisions therefore were inapplicable. Agreeing with Arthur Young on both the state and federal issues, a panel of the Eighth Circuit Court of Appeals reversed.

ISSUE Were the notes issued by the Co-Op "securities" within the meaning of the '34 Act?

HOLDING Yes. The demand notes issued by the Co-Op fell under the "note" category of instruments that are "securities."

REASONING Section 3(a)(10) of the '34 Act, the starting point for analysis, states, as does the '33 Act, that

> *the term "security" means any note, stock, treasury stock, bond, debenture, certificate of interest or participation in any profit-sharing agreement or in any oil, gas, or other mineral royalty or lease, any collateral-trust certificate, preorganization certificate or subscription, transferable share, investment contract, voting-trust certificate, certificate of deposit . . . or in general, any instrument commonly known as a "security," or any certificate of interest or participation in, temporary or interim certificate for, receipt for, or warrant or right to subscribe to or purchase, any of the foregoing; but shall not include currency or any note, draft, bill of exchange, or banker's acceptance which has a maturity at the time of issuance of not exceeding nine months. . . .*

Congress, in enacting the securities laws, meant to regulate investments, in whatever form they are made and by whatever name they are called. A commitment to an examination of the economic realities of a transaction does not necessarily entail a case-by-case analysis of every instrument, however.

Some instruments obviously fall within the class Congress intended to regulate because they by their nature are investments. For example, in *Landreth Timber Co. v. Landreth,* 471 U.S. 681 (1985), the Supreme Court held that an instrument bearing the name "stock" that, among other things, is negotiable, offers the possibility of capital appreciation, and carries the right to dividends contingent on the profits of a business enterprise plainly is within the class of instruments Congress intended the securities laws to cover. *Landreth Timber* does not signify a lack of concern with economic reality; rather, it signals a recognition that stock, as a practical matter, always is an investment if it has the economic characteristics traditionally associated with stock. Unlike "stock," the term "note" ". . . encompasses instruments with widely varying characteristics, depending on whether issued in a consumer context, as commercial paper, or in some other investment context." Thus, notes are not securities per se but must be defined using the "family resemblance" test. Under that test, a note is presumed to be a security unless it bears a strong resemblance, determined by a court's examining four specified factors, to one of a judicially crafted list of categories of instruments that are not securities.

Applying this approach, one can conclude that the notes at issue here constitute "securities." Given the facts of this case, an examination of the four relevant factors provides few reasons to treat the notes as nonsecurities: (1) The Co-Op sold them to raise capital, and purchasers bought them to earn a profit in the form of interest, so that the notes most naturally are conceived of as investments in a business enterprise; (2) there was "common trading" of the notes, which were offered and sold to a broad segment of the public; (3) the public reasonably perceived from the advertisements that the notes were investments; and (4) the application of the securities acts was necessary, since the notes were uncollateralized and uninsured and would escape federal regulation entirely if a court held the acts inapplicable.

38.1 REVES v. ERNST & YOUNG *(cont.)* **494 U.S. 56 (1990)**

BUSINESS CONSIDERATIONS The Court determined that Arthur Young's auditors had not followed generally accepted accounting principles when they had audited the Co-Op's financial statements. Should the firm fire the staff members responsible for these audits? How could a firm minimize the risk that it would face such litigation?

ETHICAL CONSIDERATIONS Should educational institutions and firms be expected to instill a sense of ethics into students and employees, respectively, or is the development of an admirable ethical perspective solely an individualized, personal endeavor?

Procedures. Section 5 is the heart of the '33 Act. It provides that any security that is not exempt must be registered with the SEC before a firm can sell it through the mails or through any facility of interstate commerce, such as **securities exchanges**. All U.S. issuers now are required to utilize EDGAR, the SEC's electronic data-gathering system, when the firms engage in any initial public offering (IPO). The corporation issuing the security must file a *registration statement* with the SEC and provide investors and would-be investors with a *prospectus*—a document presented by a corporation or its agents, which document announces the issue of corporate securities, states the nature of the securities and the financial status of the issuing firm, and asks the general public to purchase the securities covered. The registration statement contains detailed information about the plan for offering and distributing the security, the names and salaries of managers and others who control the corporation, a description of the security, and information about the issuer and its business, including detailed financial reports. The prospectus must contain similar information in summary form.

Securities exchanges
Organized secondary markets in which investors buy and sell securities at central locations.

The underlying purpose of both the registration statement and the prospectus is the protection of the unsophisticated investor. These documents purport to inform a prospective investor of everything he or she should know before a purchase of a security occurs. Some critics argue, however, that the SEC requires so much information that an unsophisticated investor can make little sense of the myriad details that appear in the registration statement and the prospectus. These commentators believe the SEC's "overregulation" actually has undercut the worthy purposes of the '33 Act.

Although the '33 Act prohibits all offers to buy or sell prior to the filing of a registration statement, some activities can take place before this filing. For example, the issuer (the corporation selling the stock) typically enlists the services of third parties, such as **underwriters**, who agree to help the issuer finance the stock offering. During this prefiling period, then, the issuer can enter into preliminary negotiations with such underwriters. Next, during the registration process's so-called "waiting period," the SEC has 20 days in which to examine the registration statement. If the registration statement is complete and accurate, it becomes effective at the end of this 20-day waiting period.

Underwriters
Persons or institutions that, by agreeing to sell securities to the public and to buy those not sold, insure the sale of corporate securities.

During this period, the issuer or underwriter can accept oral purchase orders; but the SEC limits written advertisements to "tombstone ads," so designated because they are boxed in the shape of a tombstone, and written information to preliminary "red herring" prospectuses, so dubbed because of the red lettering on them, to the effect that a registration statement has been filed but is not yet effective.

After the registration statement becomes effective but before any sale can occur—this is the so-called "posteffective period"—the issuer or underwriter must provide virtually every would-be investor with a prospectus (the so-called "statutory prospectus") that sets out the information required by the statute. The issuer must make sure the information contained in the prospectus remains accurate during the posteffective period as well; otherwise, the sale of the securities will not be legal. These rules reinforce the '33 Act's "truth-in-securities" policies.

Exemptions. The '33 Act exempts from the registration and prospectus requirements discussed above certain *classes* of securities. Note, however, that there are no exemptions from the antifraud provisions, which we will examine in the next section of this chapter. The exempted classes include securities issued by federal and state governments and banks; short-term commercial paper; issues by nonprofit organizations; issues by savings and loan associations subject to state or federal regulation; issues by common carriers subject to the jurisdiction of the Surface Transportation Board; certain qualifying employee pension plans; insurance policies and certain annuities subject to regulation by state and federal authorities; and intrastate issues of securities.

In addition, the '33 Act exempts certain *transactions:* private offerings (those that do not involve public offerings of securities, as is the usual case); transactions by persons other than issuers, underwriters, or dealers; certain brokers' and dealers' transactions; and small public issues (defined generally as transactions up to $5 million and that involve sales only to "accredited investors"). As the latter exemption shows, SEC rules oftentimes may limit the issuers who qualify, the aggregate offering price, the number and qualifications of investors, the manner in which the issuer conducts the offering, the resale of the shares, and the like. In short, the SEC has established prerequisites and complex rules that firms must follow if they hope to secure an exemption from the registration process for this and certain other transactions.

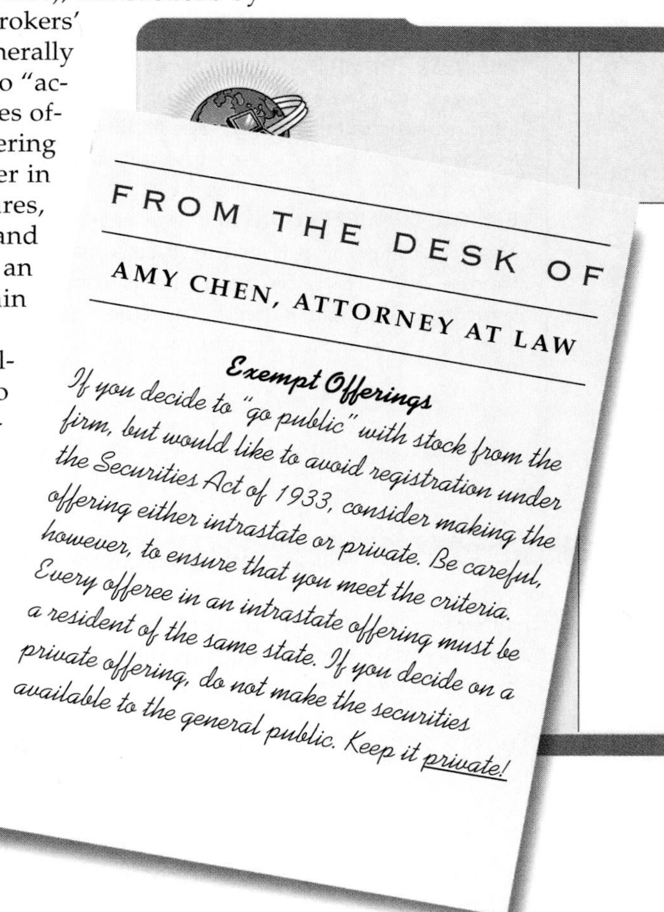

FROM THE DESK OF
AMY CHEN, ATTORNEY AT LAW
Exempt Offerings
If you decide to "go public" with stock from the firm, but would like to avoid registration under the Securities Act of 1933, consider making the offering either intrastate or private. Be careful, however, to ensure that you meet the criteria. Every offeree in an intrastate offering must be a resident of the same state. If you decide on a private offering, do not make the securities available to the general public. Keep it private!

For instance, in one famous case, Ralston Purina Co. (Ralston Purina) had sold nearly $2 million of unregistered stock to its "key employees." The "key employees" who had purchased the stock included shop and dock foremen, stenographers, copywriters, clerical assistants, and veterinarians. Because it had made offers to only a few of its employees, Ralston Purina construed its actions as falling under the "private offering" exemption. Asserting that the aim of the '33 Act is to protect investors by promoting full disclosure of the information thought necessary for informed investment decisions, the Supreme Court concluded that Ralston Purina had not shown that the employees involved here had enjoyed access to the kind of information that registration would disclose. Thus, the Court held that this attempted private offering (or "private placement") was not a bona fide exempt transaction and that registration under the 1933 Act should have occurred.[1]

Antifraud Provisions. In addition to registration requirements, the '33 Act contains several antifraud

38.1

ISSUING STOCK IN CIT

Tom and Anna want to issue stock in CIT. To generate funds for the expansion of the firm, they believe that, if successful, their IPO will result in a huge inflow of cash for the firm. However, they also know that their IPO is likely to be subject to regulation under the Securities Act of 1933. They ask you what they will need to do in order to qualify for an exemption from registration under the '33 Act, or, in the alternative, what they will need to do to comply with the registration requirements. What advice will you give them?

BUSINESS CONSIDERATIONS Why might a business prefer a potentially smaller inflow of funds if it meant that the firm qualified for an exemption from registering under the '33 Act? What factors should a firm consider in deciding whether the registration requirements justify a larger public offering?

ETHICAL CONSIDERATIONS Is it ethical for a firm to tailor its securities offerings so as to avoid registration of the securities under the '33 Act? Are the directors of a business acting ethically toward their constituents if they fail to consider a security-issuing plan that legally avoids registration?

FINANCE/MANAGEMENT

provisions. Section 12 prohibits oral or written misstatements of material facts or omissions of material facts necessary to keep the statements from being misleading in the circumstances in which they were made. Section 17 is a general antifraud provision that makes it unlawful for any person to use the mails or interstate commerce to employ any device or scheme that will defraud another person or to engage in any transaction, practice, or course of business that defrauds or deceives the purchaser. Basically, § 17 makes illegal any form of fraud, untrue statement of a material fact, or omission of a material fact involving the sale of any securities in interstate commerce or through the mail.

Section 27A of the 1995 Private Securities Litigation Reform Act (PSLRA) redefines when liability exists for certain misleading "forward-looking" statements. The PSRLA represents the most sweeping and comprehensive reform of the nation's securities laws in the last two decades. Designed to reassert legislative control over securities fraud litigation, the PSLRA sets out specific procedural and substantive rules with regard to these and other sections of the '33 Act. To encourage corporate executives to offer investors more meaningful information, § 27A, the so-called "safe harbor" provision, exempts from liability filed registration documents containing certain types of forward-looking statements (including projections of revenues, income, earnings per share, and company plans or objectives relating to certain products or services) by certain issuers and underwriters. (Significantly, this "safe harbor" is not applicable to IPOs.) To fall within the available safe harbor, a forward-looking statement (either oral or written) should be accompanied by meaningful cautionary statements identifying important factors that would cause actual results to differ materially from those projected in the forward-looking statements. Registration statements consisting of traditional "boilerplate" language in which the issuer's purported cautionary statements mention "lack of demand," "an increase in competition," etc., presumably would not suffice. But information relating to the issuer's business that discusses the possible loss of a major customer or a serious glitch in the development of technology for a product in the prototype stage would fulfill the statutory requirements for a "meaningful cautionary statement."

Besides providing encouragement for executives to offer investors more meaningful information, other central aims of the PSLRA include the discouragement of class action suits brought for frivolous—or purely entrepreneurial—reasons (so-called "strike suits") and the preservation of such suits in situations in which shareholders in fact have been the victims of securities fraud. The act accomplishes these goals by codifying stringent pleading requirements for certain private actions under the '34 Act (but not the '33 Act) and by awarding sanctions (e.g., costs and attorneys' fees) for a party's failing to fulfill these pleading requirements. Given the PSLRA's complexities as well as those that generally inhere in the issuance of securities, anyone who contemplates issuing securities should seek the counsel of professionals who specialize in the securities field.

Liabilities and Remedies. The potential liabilities spawned by the '33 Act also pose a significant reason for seeking competent advice. Section 11 imposes civil liability for any registration statement that contains untrue statements of a material fact or omissions of material facts that would make the registration statement misleading in the circumstances in which a purchaser buys the securities. Such a purchaser can receive as damages an amount not exceeding the price paid for the securities.

Section 11 places liability on every person who signed the registration statement; on every person who was a director or was named in the registration statement as about to become a director; on every accountant, engineer, appraiser, or any other professional expert whose statement or report appears in the registration statement; and on every underwriter. By showing that they acted with "due diligence," all such persons, except the issuer, may escape liability.

This statutory defense of "due diligence" varies as to the type of defendant involved and whether the misrepresentations or omissions are found in the "expertised" or "nonexpertised" portions of the registration statement. The defense generally is available to anyone who, after reasonable investigation, had reasonable grounds to believe, and did believe, that the registration statement was accurate and did not omit material facts that either were required or necessary to make the statement not misleading. In this context, note that the PSLRA changes § 11's longstanding joint and several liability rules, in which each defendant potentially was liable for all the damages awarded to the plaintiff, to a standard that embraces proportionate liability. The PSLRA grounds this change on the rationale that the imposition of joint and several liability in the past had led to the plaintiff's joining "deep pocket" defendants (lawyers, accountants, underwriters, and directors) in the lawsuit, even though these persons bore little responsibility for the plaintiff's injuries.

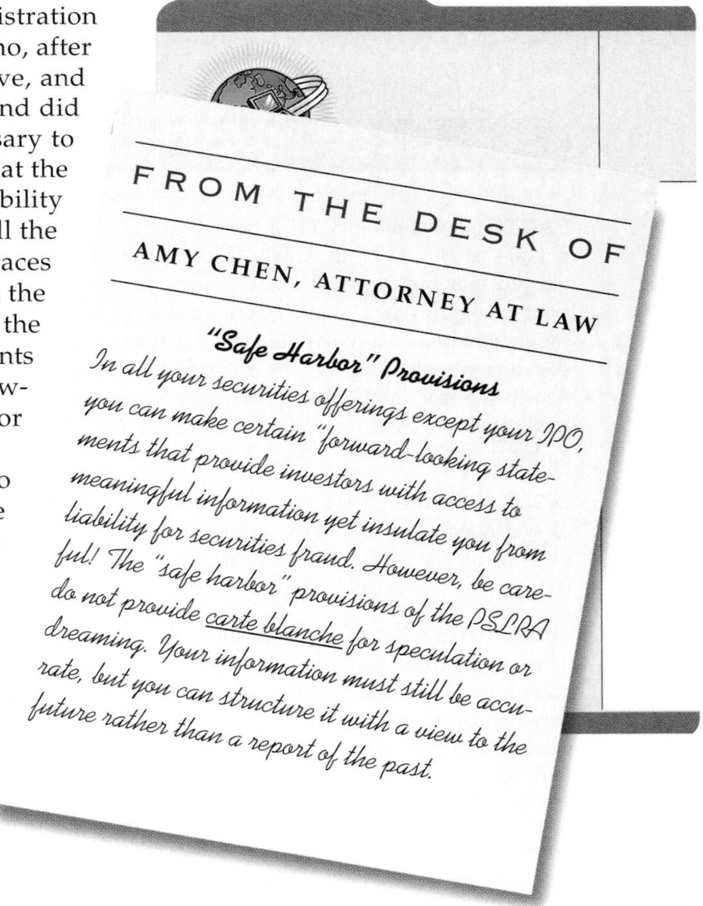

FROM THE DESK OF
AMY CHEN, ATTORNEY AT LAW
"Safe Harbor" Provisions
In all your securities offerings except your IPO, you can make certain "forward-looking statements that provide investors with access to meaningful information yet insulate you from liability for securities fraud. However, be careful! The "safe harbor" provisions of the PSLRA do not provide carte blanche for speculation or dreaming. Your information must still be accurate, but you can structure it with a view to the future rather than a report of the past.

These defendants often felt overwhelming pressures to settle—even if the suits were meritless—so as to avoid the enormous damage awards recoverable by plaintiffs in huge class action suits. Hence, the PSLRA adopts a "fair share" rule approach to liability in general and applies this rule in specific to outside directors who have refrained from "knowingly" violating the securities laws. These outside directors ordinarily will be liable only for the portion of damages attributable to their percentage of responsibility. In enacting this legislation, Congress hoped to give qualified persons an incentive to sit on the boards of start-up and high-technology companies without these persons becoming apprehensive about their possible exposure to grossly disproportionate liability. It is important to note that the PSLRA applies solely to the allocation of damages; the PSLRA otherwise preserves the plaintiff's Section 11 claims against all other defendants as well as the rights of contribution and settlement set out in the '33 Act. Nor does the PSLRA change the state-of-mind requirements of § 12 and § 17; reckless conduct, for example, would not violate the '33 Act.

Additionally, § 12 exacts civil liability from any person who sells securities through the mails or in interstate commerce by means of a prospectus or oral communication that includes misrepresentations or omissions of necessary material facts. Such persons can avoid liability if they can show that they did not know, and in the exercise of reasonable care could not have known, about the untruths or omissions. The injured party can sue only the person who actually sold the security but can recover the price paid for the security. The PSLRA amends § 12 to allow a defendant to escape liability if he or she can prove that the depreciation in the value of the security resulted from factors unrelated to the alleged misstatement or omission (e.g., from a general market decline). Thus, purchasers suing under the '33 Act's civil liability provision must prove that the alleged misstatements or omissions actually *caused* their losses. In addition to § 12's civil liabilities, § 17's antifraud provisions may be used as a basis for criminal liability. Moreover, § 24 sets up criminal sanctions for willful violations of the '33 Act.

Escott v. *Barchris Construction Corp.*, a landmark, pre-PSLRA case, illustrates many of the principles just discussed.

38.2 ESCOTT v. BARCHRIS CONSTRUCTION CORP. 283 F.Supp. 643 (S.D.N.Y. 1968)

FACTS Suing under § 11 of the '33 Act, the purchasers of certain securities of BarChris Construction Corporation alleged that the registration statement filed with the SEC concerning this stock had contained materially false statements and material omissions. The defendants included the persons who had signed the registration statement (primarily directors and officers), the underwriters (investment bankers), and Peat, Marwick, Mitchell & Co. (BarChris's auditors).

ISSUES Had the registration statement included materially false statements and material omissions? If so, had the defendants successfully shown the statutory defense—that is, that they had acted with due diligence?

HOLDINGS Yes to the first question, no to the second. The registration statement had included materially false statements and material omissions. Only the outside directors had been able to sustain even a part of their "due diligence" defense (and they could show due diligence only with respect to the "expertised" portion of the registration statement).

REASONING A material fact is a fact that, had it been correctly stated or disclosed, would have deterred the average prudent investor from purchasing the securities in question. Therefore, BarChris's overstatement of its sales and gross profits and its understatement of its liabilities in 1961 constituted material facts. But the prospectus statements about BarChris's status in December 1960 consisted of rather minor and hence nonmaterial errors. However, the prospectus's 1961 balance sheet had contained material errors. Nonetheless, although the due diligence statutory defense had been available to all the defendants except the issuer, BarChris, none of the inside directors and officers had sustained the due diligence defense with respect to either the "expertised" (i.e., the financial reports prepared by accountants) or the "unexpertised" portions of the registration statement. The outside directors similarly had not sustained their due diligence defense as to the unexpertised part of the registration statement, primarily because they had neither familiarized themselves with its contents nor questioned its major points. On the other hand, the outside directors, because of their confidence in the auditors, Peat, Marwick, Mitchell & Co., had shown due diligence regarding the expertised portion of the statement. Like the inside directors and officers, the underwriters and the auditors had failed to establish the due diligence defense with respect to either portion of the registration statement.

38.2 ESCOTT v. BARCHRIS CONSTRUCTION CORP. (*cont.*) 283 F.Supp. 643 (S.D.N.Y. 1968)

BUSINESS CONSIDERATIONS Does it make sense to hinge potential liability on whether one is relying on the expertise of another for information? In other words, does the distinction set out by the court give an incentive to a nonexpert "insider" to "play dumb"?

ETHICAL CONSIDERATIONS What are the ethical (as opposed to the legal) obligations that one undertakes when one agrees to serve on a corporate board of directors?

The Securities Exchange Act of 1934

While the 1933 Act deals with the initial issuance of securities, the Securities Exchange Act of 1934 (the '34 Act) regulates the secondary distribution of securities. As such, the '34 Act's jurisdiction extends to the registration and distribution of securities through national stock exchanges, national securities associations, brokers, and dealers. The '34 Act also covers proxy solicitations of registered securities, regulates tender offers, limits insider trading, forbids short-swing profits, and in general tries to eliminate fraud and manipulative conduct with respect to the sale or purchase of securities. Thus, in many ways the '33 and '34 Acts are similar and supplement each other. But the reach of the '34 Act, with its supervision of national exchanges and over-the-counter sales of securities, is even broader than that of the '33 Act.

Registration and Reporting. The '34 Act requires any issuer who trades securities on a national stock exchange to register with the SEC. In addition, any firm engaged in interstate commerce with total assets of over $5 million and at least 500 shareholders must comply with the registration provisions of § 12. For violations of § 12, the SEC can revoke or suspend the registration of the security involved.

Like the '33 Act, the '34 Act tries to ensure that the investing public will have sufficient information about publicly traded securities when these investors make their decisions about whether to buy stocks. Hence, the '34 Act mandates certain disclosures by firms covered by the act when the securities are listed with national exchanges or traded over the counter. Basically, these obligatory disclosures include detailed registration statements similar to the information required under the '33 Act as well as annual and quarterly reports. SEC Forms 8-A, 8-K, 10-K, and 10-Q, which companies use for compiling this information, are complex and contain substantial numbers of facts and figures relating to the companies' businesses. Other SEC provisions impose liability on the company for damages resulting from an investor's reliance on misleading statements contained in any such documents.

Proxy Solicitations. A *proxy* is an assignment by the shareholder of the right to vote the shares held by the shareholder. Since proxies become a device for consolidating corporate power and control, one cannot underestimate their importance both to management and to those "dissident" shareholders who wish to oust the present management. Because of the high stakes involved for both competing factions, it is vitally important that the information provided to shareholders be accurate. If shareholders receive misleading information, they will make their decision regarding who should be given their proxies—management or dissidents—in ignorance of the true facts. To prevent such abuses, § 14 of the '34 Act makes it illegal for a company registered under § 12 to solicit proxies in a manner that violates the SEC rules and regulations that protect the investing public. Section 14 also sets out rules mandating disclosure of pertinent information to shareholders at corporate meetings even when no solicitation of proxies will occur.

The disclosure required of proxy solicitations includes a proxy statement, which contains detailed information, and a proxy form, on which the shareholder can note his or her approval or disapproval of each proposal that will be decided at the corporation's meeting. Before either the corporation or the dissidents send proxies to shareholders, the SEC must approve the statement and the form. These preliminary proxies must be filed with the SEC at least 10 days before they are sent to shareholders. If the meeting involves the election of directors, any proxy statement also must include an annual report detailing, among other things, the financial aspects of the company (including a graph that analyzes the company's performance) and the company's executive compensation plans and arrangements (including "golden parachutes"). Similarly, as mentioned earlier, any proxy contest requires full disclosure of all pertinent facts regarding the matters under consideration, such as the identity of all participants in the proxy contest and the reasons for the proxy solicitation.

Section 14 furthermore authorizes the inclusion of shareholder proposals of no more than 500 words in any management-backed proxy solicitation. This SEC rule allows any eligible shareholder to express an opinion regarding the recommendations management has made without incurring the significant costs involved in an independent proxy solicitation. This aspect of § 14 thus attempts to preserve the balance of power between management and the insurgents so as to safeguard the democratic aspects of the corporation.

As you may expect, management usually opposes the inclusion of such proposals. SEC rules authorize the exclusion of proposals that are not "proper subjects" for action by shareholders, proposals that center on personal claims or grievances, proposals that are not significantly related to the corporation's business or are beyond the corporation's power to effectuate (e.g., proposals that primarily promote economic, political, racial, religious, or social causes), and proposals that are substantially similar to a proposal submitted but not approved within the past five years. In disputes over whether the corporation can exclude the proposal, the SEC normally decides who is correct. Management bears the burden of proof regarding why it properly excluded the proposal. Shareholder proposals have dealt with management compensation, company policies allegedly leading to discrimination or pollution, and even opposition to the Vietnam War. Shareholder proposals, however, usually are unsuccessful.

The corporation ordinarily pays for the expenses incurred in proxy contests if either management or the insurgents win. The law is unsettled as to whether the corporation should pay the costs of a contest if management loses, but the trend is to make the corporation (not the managers themselves) pay even in those circumstances.

Liability for misleading proxy statements or those that omit a material fact necessary to make the statement true and not misleading is absolute. Any person who sells or buys securities in reliance on such statements can recover from the corporation.

Tender Offers. In addition to regulating proxies, since 1968 the Williams Act, codified in § 13 and § 14, also has regulated tender offers or takeover bids, whether hostile or friendly, wherein one publicly held corporation (the "tender offeror") attempts to acquire control of another publicly held company (the "target"). Section 14, in conjunction with § 13, sets forth filing and registration requirements for any person who becomes the owner of more than 5 percent of any class of securities registered under § 12. In general, these provisions force the offeror to provide the target company's shareholders with the names of the offerors and their interests, the purpose of the takeover, the method of disposing of the target firm's stocks and assets, and so forth. Additionally, any statements the management of the target firm makes in opposition to the merger also must be filed with the SEC. Provisions for liability under this aspect of the '34 Act are similar to those instituted for violations of the proxy rules.

Insider Trading. Directors, officers, and controlling shareholders may violate the federal securities laws if they engage in "insider trading." We noted that the '34 Act makes such activities illegal and sets out possibilities of far-ranging liability. Section 10(b) of the '34 Act makes unlawful any manipulative or deceptive device used through the mails or in interstate commerce in connection with the purchase or sale of any security. By providing for liability for any fraudulent or deceitful activity that involves misleading material facts or omissions of material facts that would make a statement misleading in the circumstances in which it was made, SEC Rule 10(b)-5 augments § 10(b).

When material inside information is involved, the insider *either* must publicly disclose the information so as to ensure that the investing public that does not have access to the information will remain free from prejudice *or* abstain from trading in the securities. Nevertheless, it is difficult to judge when information is important enough to be considered "material." *Basic Incorporated* v. *Levinson* provides guidelines in this important area.

38.3 BASIC INCORPORATED v. LEVINSON

485 U.S. 224 (1988)

FACTS Basic Incorporated (Basic) was a public-issue corporation that provided materials for the manufacture of steel. In 1976, Basic held meetings with representatives of Combustion Engineering Co. (Combustion) regarding the possibility of a merger. During 1977 and 1978, Basic made three public statements denying that it was engaged in merger negotiations. Yet, on 18 December 1978, Basic asked the New York Stock Exchange to suspend trading in its shares and issued a release stating that it had been "approached" by another company concerning a merger. On 19 December, Basic's board endorsed Combustion's offer of $46 per share for its common stock and on the following day publicly announced the company's approval of Combustion's tender offer for all the outstanding shares of Basic. Levinson and other Basic shareholders who had sold their stock after Basic's final public statement on 21 October 1977, and before the suspension of trading in December 1978, sued Basic and its board of directors for violations of § 10(b) of the 1934 Act and Rule 10(b)-5 allegedly stemming from Basic's denials of the merger negotiations prior to the official announcement.

ISSUE Did Basic's denials about the preliminary merger negotiations constitute material misrepresentations under § 10(b) and Rule 10(b)-5?

HOLDING Yes. Information concerning the existence and the status of preliminary merger discussions is significant to a reasonable investor's trading decision. Consequently, Basic's inaccurate and incomplete statements were material and thus violative of § 10(b) and Rule 10(b)-5.

REASONING As the *SEC* v. *Texas Gulf Sulphur* case had shown, the materiality requirement of Rule 10(b)-5 with respect to contingent or speculative information or events depends on the facts. Whether merger discussions in a particular case are material therefore is similarly fact-specific.

38.3 BASIC INCORPORATED v. LEVINSON *(cont.)* 485 U.S. 224 (1988)

Generally, in order to assess the probability that the event will occur, a fact finder will need to look to indicia of interest in the transaction at the highest corporate levels. Board resolutions, instructions to investment bankers, and actual negotiations between the principals or their intermediaries may serve as indicia of such interest. To assess the magnitude of the transaction to the issuer of the securities allegedly manipulated, a fact finder will need to consider such facts as the size of the two corporate entities and the stocks' potential premium over market value. No particular event or factor short of closing the transaction need be either necessary or sufficient by itself to render merger discussions material. Rather, materiality depends on the significance the reasonable investor would place on the withheld or misrepresented information. If, as noted in the *TSC Industries, Inc.* v. *Northway, Inc.* case, there is a substantial likelihood that the disclosure of the omitted fact would have been viewed as significant by a reasonable investor, the information is material. Hence, there is no valid justification for artificially excluding from the definition of materiality information concerning merger discussions, which otherwise would be considered significant to the trading decision of a reasonable investor, merely because the parties (or their representatives) had failed to reach an agreement-in-principle as to price and structure. The lower courts in this case had accepted a presumption, created by the fraud-on-the-market theory and subject to rebuttal by Basic, that persons who had traded Basic shares had done so in reliance on the integrity of the price set by the market; but that because of Basic's material misrepresentations, that price had been fraudulently depressed. Requiring plaintiffs to show a speculative state of facts—that is, how they would have acted if omitted material information had been disclosed or if the misrepresentations had not been made—would place an unnecessarily unrealistic evidentiary burden on the Rule 10(b)-5 plaintiff who had traded on an impersonal market. Because most publicly available information is reflected in the market price, an investor's reliance on any public material misrepresentations, therefore, may be presumed for purposes of a Rule 10(b)-5 action. Nevertheless, any showing that severs the link between the alleged misrepresentation and either the price received (or paid) by plaintiffs, or their decision to trade at a fair market price, will be sufficient to rebut the presumption of reliance. In summary, the standard of materiality set forth in *TSC Industries, Inc.* v. *Northway* will govern future § 10(b) and Rule 10(b)-5 cases. Thus, materiality in the merger context depends on the probability that the transaction will be consummated and its significance to the issuer of the securities. Hence, materiality depends on the facts and must be determined on a case-by-case basis. Courts may apply a presumption of reliance supported by the fraud-on-the-market theory; that presumption, however, is rebuttable.

BUSINESS CONSIDERATIONS Why did Basic make three public denials that it was engaged in merger negotiations? What could the firm have included in its press release that would have withstood the subsequent litigation brought against the firm?

ETHICAL CONSIDERATIONS Assume the Court had grounded its decision on ethics rather than the law. What ethical perspectives could form the basis for the Court's decision?

Although § 10(b) does not expressly provide for civil liability, it, as a broad antifraud provision, applies to any manipulative or deceptive device used in connection with any purchase or sale of any security by any person; there are no exemptions from coverage. Similarly, Rule 10(b)-5 has been applied to the activities of corporate insiders—directors, officers, controlling shareholders, employees, lawyers, accountants, bankers, consultants, and anyone else who has access to material inside information that may affect the price of the stock. Prior to 1980, persons considered insiders included even those who purchased or sold stock based on tips provided directly or indirectly by directors, officers, and the like. Hence, the SEC considered, for example, a barber who overheard a director's discussion of an upcoming business trip and bought stock based on this market information an insider as well. But the *Chiarella* v. *United States* [445 U.S. 222, (1980)] case has cast some doubt on whether such remote "tippees" should be liable.

Chiarella was a printer who worked for a firm that printed takeover bids. Although the identities of the firms had been left blank, Chiarella—using the information contained in the documents he was preparing for printing—was able to deduce the names of the target companies. Without disclosing his knowledge, Chiarella purchased stock in the target companies and sold the stock when the takeover attempts became public knowledge. Chiarella thereby gained $30,000 in 14 months. The SEC indicted him on 17 counts of violating § 10(b) and Rule 10(b)-5 of the '34 Act.

However, the Supreme Court held that neither Section 10(b) nor Rule 10(b)-5 would apply to Chiarella. According to the Court, he was not a corporate insider, a fiduciary, or a tippee. Rather, he was a complete stranger who had dealt with the sellers only through impersonal market transactions. The Court therefore believed that affirming Chiarella's conviction would recognize a general duty between all participants in market transactions to forgo actions based on material, nonpublic information. In the Court's opinion, the imposition of such a broad duty, departing as it would from the established doctrine that duty arises from a specific relationship between two parties, would be ill-advised.

According to the *Chiarella* case, then, the mere possession of inside information does not create a legal duty owed to faceless market participants. The Supreme Court's decision in *Dirks* v. *Securities and Exchange Commission* [463 U.S. 646, (1983)], by emphasizing the basic principle that only some persons, under some circumstances, will be barred from trading while they are in possession of material, nonpublic information, appears to reinforce *Chiarella*'s holding.

In 1973, Raymond Dirks was an officer of a New York broker/dealer firm that specialized in providing investment analyses of insurance company securities to institutional investors. On 6 March, Ronald Secrist, a former officer of Equity Funding of America (Equity Funding), told Dirks that the assets of Equity Funding, a diversified corporation primarily engaged in selling life insurance and mutual funds, had been vastly overstated as the result of fraudulent corporate practices. Stressing that various regulatory agencies had failed to act on similar charges made by Equity Funding employees, Secrist urged Dirks to verify the fraud and to disclose it publicly. Although neither Dirks nor his firm owned or traded any Equity Funding stock, some of Equity Funding's clients and investors ultimately sold their holdings in Equity Funding as a result of information that Dirks had shared with them during his investigation. The SEC also subsequently investigated Dirks's involvement and found that his repeating of confidential corporate information had violated securities rules. However, since he had played an important role in bringing Equity Funding's massive fraud to light, the SEC merely **censured** him.

Censured
Formally reprimanded for specific conduct.

The Supreme Court found that Dirks, as a tippee of material nonpublic information received from the insiders of a corporation with which Dirks was unaffiliated, in these circumstances had no duty to abstain from the use of such inside information. The Court based its holding on the following grounds: The tippers had been motivated by a desire to expose fraud rather than from a desire either to receive personal benefits or to bestow valuable information on him so that he

38.2

FINANCE/MANAGEMENT

INSIDER TRADING RULES UNDER THE '34 ACT

CIT stock is being sold on a national exchange, which subjects the firm to regulation under the '34 Act. The initial public reaction to the firm and its prospects has been good, and the stock has had steady increases in its market price. CIT is currently negotiating with a small technology firm that has a new video imaging process. This new process will greatly increase the sharpness of the images shown on the Call-Image videophones. No one outside the immediate family is aware of these negotiations. Dan, Donna, and Amy want to purchase a significant number of CIT shares before the news "leaks out" about the negotiations. However, they are concerned that if they do so, they will be guilty of insider trading. They ask you what they should do to avoid liability under the '34 Act in this situation. What will you tell them?

BUSINESS CONSIDERATIONS What should the officers, directors, and controlling shareholders of a firm whose stock is publicly traded be concerned about when they trade in their firm's securities? What can the firm do to minimize its potential liability when an insider trading scandal erupts?

ETHICAL CONSIDERATIONS Is it ethical for an insider to trade in securities when he or she has information that is not yet available to the general public? Is it ethical to prevent people from using the knowledge or information they have acquired through their jobs from making a profit based on that knowledge or information? Can these two areas be reconciled ethically?

could derive monetary benefits from what they had told him.

Hence, in the absence of personal gain to the insider, there was no breach of duty to the stockholders. Similarly, in the absence of such a breach by the insider, there could be no derivative breach by someone like Dirks. In short, tippees in Dirks's position would inherit no duty to disclose or abstain until a breach of the insider's fiduciary duty had occurred. Dirks's conduct, therefore, had not violated the antifraud provisions of the '33 or '34 Acts.

The *Chiarella* and *Dirks* cases thus appear to limit significantly the concept of who an "insider" is for § 10(b) purposes. According to *Chiarella,* "outsiders"—those who are not in positions of trust or confidence within the companies involved in the litigation—can escape the duty to abstain from trading on nonpublic material information, unless they are actual tippees of insiders. Reinforcing *Chiarella, Dirks* holds that tippees of insiders who have divulged material inside information out of motives other than personal gain may avoid liability as well. Because the tippees' potential liability derives from the insiders' fiduciary duties to the corporation, the absence of any breach of those duties by the insiders leads to a finding of no breach on the tippees' part, either. The SEC, however, is continuing to prosecute outsiders and their tippees on the theory that outsiders' misappropriation of nonpublic material information works a fraud on the securities market or constitutes fraud as to the outsiders' employers, owing to the outsiders' breach of a fiduciary's duty or similar relationship of trust and confidence. As such, the SEC reasons, this fraudulent conduct violates the securities laws' insider-trading prohibitions.

The SEC's aggressive posture in this context is particularly noteworthy, given the absence of authoritative Supreme Court rulings or legislation (even though Congress has considered legislation to amend the securities laws to reflect the SEC's position) regarding the legal validity of the so-called "misappropriation" (or "fraud-on-the-market") theory. The doctrinal development of these insider-trading precedents and the role of the Supreme Court, Congress, and the SEC in addressing this issue serve as further illustrations of the complexities inherent in our legal system.

In *United States* v. *Chestman,* note how the court disposes of the issues (the SEC's rule-making authority and the possible application of the misappropriation theory) before it.

38.4 UNITED STATES v. CHESTMAN

947 F.2d 551 (2d Cir. 1991), *cert. denied* 503 U.S. 1004 (1992)

FACTS Keith Loeb's wife, Susan, was the niece of the president and controlling shareholder of the target corporation. The government presented evidence that Susan's mother, Shirley Witkin (the sister of the target's president), had told Susan of the impending favorable sale of the target but had added that Susan should tell no one except her husband. The next day, Susan told Loeb of the sale and admonished him not to tell anyone because "it could possibly ruin the sale." Loeb testified that he telephoned broker Robert Chestman the next day and told Chestman that he (Loeb) "had some definite, some accurate information" that the target was being sold at a "substantially higher" price than the market value of its stock. That day, Chestman purchased shares of the target for himself and for Loeb. A jury later convicted Chestman of 10 counts of fraudulent trading in connection with the tender offer in violation of Rule 14(e)-3(a), 10 counts of securities fraud in violation of '34 Act Rule 10(b)-5, and other offenses. The government based its Rule 10(b)-5 case against Chestman on the misappropriation theory, which holds that one who misappropriates nonpublic information in breach of a fiduciary duty and trades on that information to his or her own advantage violates § 10(b) and Rule 10(b)-5. Chestman, challenging his convictions for fraudulent trading in connection with a tender offer, claimed that the SEC had exceeded its rule-making authority under § 14(e) when it had adopted Rule 14(e)-3 in its present form. Specifically, Chestman asserted that the rule improperly imposes liability in three ways: (1) in the absence of either a duty to disclose or a fiduciary duty; (2) for trading while in the possession of material nonpublic information, whether or not such information is used in effecting the transaction; and (3) on the basis of a "quasi-negligence standard."

ISSUE Was the 1934 Securities Exchange Act Rule 14(e)-3(a), which bars trading on the basis of material nonpublic information concerning a tender offer that the trader knows or has reason to know has been acquired from an insider of the offeror or issuer or the insider's agent, within the Securities and Exchange Commission's rule-making authority under §§ 14(e) and 23(a)(1) of the '34 Act, even though it dispenses with the common law fraud element of breach of fiduciary duty?

HOLDING Yes. Nothing in the legislative history of § 14(e) indicated that the SEC, by enacting Rule 14(e)-3(a), had frustrated congressional intent. On the contrary, the legislative history suggested that Congress had intended to grant the SEC broad rule-making authority.

REASONING Section 14(e) of the '34 Act prohibits the making of material misstatements or omissions of fact in connection with tender offers. It further provides: "The Commission shall . . . by rules and regulations define, and prescribe means reasonably designed to prevent such acts and practices as are fraudulent, deceptive, or manipulative." Section 23(a)(1) of the '34 Act authorizes the SEC "to make such rules and regulations as may be necessary or appropriate to implement the provisions of this chapter for which [it is] responsible or for the execution of the functions invested in [it] by this chapter." One violates Rule 14(e)-3(a) if one trades on the basis of material nonpublic information concerning a pending tender offer that one knows or has reason to know has been acquired "directly or indirectly" from an insider of the offeror or issuer or someone working on the insider's behalf. Rule 14(e)-3(a) is a disclosure provision. It therefore creates a duty in traders within its ambit to abstain or disclose, without regard to whether the trader owes a preexisting fiduciary duty to respect the confidentiality of the information. Chestman claimed that the SEC, in drafting Rule 14(e)-3(a) so as to dispense with one of the common law elements of fraud (i.e., breach of fiduciary duty), had exceeded its authority. However, the plain language of § 14(e) represents a broad delegation of rule-making authority that would represent a hollow gesture if Congress had meant to confine the SEC's rule-making authority to common law definitions of fraud. Moreover, the SEC's power to "prescribe means reasonably designed to prevent" fraud extends the agency's rule-making authority further and necessarily encompasses the power to proscribe conduct outside the purview of fraud, be it common law or SEC-defined fraud. Because the operative words of the statute, "define" and "prevent," have clear connotations, the language of the statute is sufficiently clear to be dispositive.

In short, nothing in the legislative history of § 14(e) indicates that the SEC, by enacting Rule 14(e)-3(a), frustrated congressional intent. It is clear that the government based its Rule 10(b)-5 case against Chestman on the misappropriation theory, which provides that one who misappropriates nonpublic information in breach of a fiduciary duty and trades on that information to his or her own advantage violates § 10(b) and Rule 10(b)-5. Although Chestman is the defendant here, the alleged misappropriator was Loeb. The application of the misappropriation theory—and its predicate requirement of fiduciary breach—in the context of family relationships represents a case of first impression in this circuit. Under the misappropriation theory of liability, a person violates Rule 10(b)-5 when he or she misappropriates material nonpublic information in breach of a fiduciary

38.4 UNITED STATES v. CHESTMAN *(cont.)* 947 F.2d 551 (2d Cir. 1991), *cert. denied* 503 U.S. 1004 (1992)

duty or similar relationship of trust and confidence and uses that information in a securities transaction. Cases in this circuit previously have held that the predicate act of fraud may be perpetrated on the source of the nonpublic information, even though the source may be unaffiliated with the buyer or seller of securities. To date, the application of this theory has occurred only in the context of employment relationships.

Regarding the central inquiry here—what constitutes a fiduciary or similar relationship of trust and confidence in the context of Rule 10(b)-5 criminal liability—it is clear that the relationships involved here—those between Loeb and his wife and between Loeb and his wife's family—were not traditional fiduciary relationships. However, the misappropriation theory requires a court to consider not only whether a fiduciary relationship exists but also whether a "similar relationship of trust and confidence" exists. Obviously, kinship alone does not create the necessary relationship in either case. Moreover, Loeb was not an employee of the family; and there was an absence of any showing that he had participated in confidential communications regarding the business. Rather, the critical information was gratuitously communicated to him. And this disclosure did not serve the interests of the patriarch, his children, or the company. Nor was there any evidence that the alleged relationship was characterized by any influence or reliance. Furthermore, Loeb's status as his wife's husband could not in itself establish a fiduciary status. In short, Loeb owed neither his wife nor her family a fiduciary duty or its functional equivalent. Hence, he had not defrauded them when he disclosed to Chestman the news of the pending tender offer. In the absence of a predicate act of fraud by Loeb, the alleged misappropriator, Chestman, could not be derivatively liable as Loeb's tippee or as an aider and abettor.

BUSINESS CONSIDERATIONS Would it have served the underlying purposes of the '34 Act for the court to have found Chestman liable under the "misappropriation" theory? Why or why not? If familial relationships do not represent the functional equivalents of fiduciary relationships, how can a firm protect itself from this sort of "tipping"?

ETHICAL CONSIDERATIONS What ethical considerations are raised by the conduct of Loeb and Chestman? Should the family "disown" Loeb?

In pari delicto
Equally at fault or equally wrong.

Bateman Eichler, Hill Richards, Inc. v. *Berner*, which owes a large analytical debt to both *Chiarella* and *Dirks*, employs in the context of insider trading the common law doctrine of ***in pari delicto***, a concept discussed in Chapter 12. It also shows that, *Chiarella* and *Dirks* notwithstanding, tippees of corporate insiders who have provided tips containing false and incomplete information may sue these insiders for losses.

38.5 BATEMAN EICHLER, HILL RICHARDS, INC. v. BERNER 472 U.S. 299 (1985)

FACTS Berner and other investors sued Bateman Eichler, Hill Richards, Inc. (Bateman Eichler) for trading losses resulting from an alleged conspiracy between Charles Lazzara, a broker employed by Bateman Eichler, and Leslie Neadeau, the president of T.O.N.M. Oil & Gas Exploration Corporation (T.O.N.M.). Berner contended that Lazzara and Neadeau had divulged false and incomplete information on the pretext that it was accurate inside information about a gold strike that T.O.N.M. soon would announce. Berner and the others, relying on this information, had bought T.O.N.M. stock, which, when the mining venture had fallen through, had decreased substantially below the purchase price. The district court dismissed Berner's suit and absolutely barred him and the others from any recovery because they had been *in pari delicto* with Lazzaro and Neadeau. However, the court of appeals refused to allow the *in pari delicto* doctrine to be used as a defense to shield the violators from the reach of the securities laws' sanctions.

ISSUE Would the common law *in pari delicto* defense bar a private damages action under the federal securities laws against corporate insiders and broker–dealers who, by mis-

38.5 BATEMAN EICHLER, HILL RICHARDS, INC. v. BERNER *(cont.)* 472 U.S. 299 (1985)

representing that they have been conveying material nonpublic information about the issuer, fraudulently induced investors to purchase securities?

HOLDING No. A private action for damages on the grounds of Berner's own culpability would be barred only where, as a direct result of his own actions, Berner bore at least substantially equal responsibility for the violations he had sought to redress and where preclusion of the suit would not significantly interfere with the effective enforcement of the securities laws and the protection of the investing public.

REASONING The common law defense at issue in this case is grounded on two premises: first, that courts should not lend their good offices to mediating disputes among wrongdoers; and, second, that denying judicial relief to an admitted wrongdoer is an effective means of deterring illegality. Traditionally, courts narrowly limited the *in pari delicto* defense to situations in which the plaintiff truly bore at least substantially equal responsibility for his or her injury, because in such cases it did not always follow that the wrongdoers stood *in pari delicto,* for there might be, and often were, very different degrees of guilt. Notwithstanding these traditional limitations, many judges had given the *in pari delicto* defense a broad application to bar actions where the plaintiffs simply had been involved generally in the same sort of wrongdoing as the defendants.

Using this latter rationale, Bateman Eichler had argued that Berner was an ordinary tippee who had acted voluntarily in choosing to trade on inside information and that § 10(b) and Rule 10(b)-5 would apply to any violations. However, such precedents as *Chiarella* and *Dirks* mandate the rejection of this contention in the context of insider-trading cases because a person whose liability is solely derivative cannot be said to be as culpable as one whose breach of duty gives rise to that liability in the first place. Moreover, insiders and broker–dealers who selectively disclose material nonpublic information commit a potentially broader range of violations than do tippees who trade on the basis of that information. Although a tippee trading on insider information in many circumstances will be guilty of fraud against individual shareholders, the insider, in disclosing such information, also frequently violates fiduciary duties toward the issuer itself. And in cases in which the tipper additionally intentionally conveys false or materially incomplete information to the tippee, the tipper commits fraud against the tippee. Such conduct is particularly egregious when committed by a securities professional, who owes a duty of loyalty and fair dealing to his or her client. In the absence of other culpable actions by a tippee that fairly can be said to outweigh these violations by such insiders and broker–dealers, the tippee properly cannot be characterized as being of substantially equal culpability as his or her tippers. Nothing in the facts of this case shows anything to the contrary, either.

Finally, denying the *in pari delicto* defense in such circumstances will best promote the primary objective of the federal securities laws—the protection of the investing public and the national economy through the promotion of a high standard of business ethics in every facet of the securities industry. The deterrence of insider trading most frequently will be maximized by litigants' bringing enforcement pressures to bear on the sources of such information: corporate insiders and broker–dealers. Allowing defrauded tippees to sue broker–dealers without making the *in pari delicto* defense available to the latter will "nip in the bud" the first step in the chain of dissemination of material inside information, will expose illegal practices by corporate insiders and broker–dealers, and will advance appreciably the public interest.

BUSINESS CONSIDERATIONS On what policy grounds did the Court base its conclusion that defrauded tippees can sue their tipper–broker–dealers for securities violations? Did you agree with the Court's decision? Why or why not?

ETHICAL CONSIDERATIONS Had the Court grounded its decision on ethics rather than law, would the Court have come to a different conclusion? Explain fully.

Short-Swing Profits. Section 16(b) also is aimed at gains by corporate insiders. This provision of the '34 Act requires everyone who is directly or indirectly the owner of more than 10 percent of any security registered under § 12 or who is a director or officer in a so-called § 12 corporation to make periodic filings with the SEC. In these SEC filings, they must disclose the number of shares owned and any changes in the amount of shares held.

Disorge

This section, designed to prevent unfair use of information obtained by virtue of an inside position in the corporation, forces insiders to **disgorge**, or return to the corporation, any profits they realize from the purchase or sale of any security that takes place in any time period of less than six months—that is, *short-swing profits.* Section 16(b) does not apply to any transaction in which the beneficial owner was not an owner at both the time of purchasing and the time of selling; on the other hand, directors and officers face liability if they held their positions at the time either of sale or of purchase. Interestingly, though, § 16(b) covers transactions that fit the enumerated criteria even when the transactions were not actually based on inside information. In essence, then, it is a preventive section. Thus, if director Wallis sells stock in Continuing Corp. for $5,000 and five months later buys an equal number of shares for $3,000, Wallis will have to pay back to the corporation the $2,000 in profits so realized.

Note that in a merger case involving § 16(b), *Gollust* v. *Mendell,* 501 U.S. 115 (1991), the Supreme Court held that a plaintiff who had properly instituted a § 16(b) action as the owner of a security of the issuer had standing to continue to prosecute the action even after a merger involving the issuer had resulted in exchanging the stockholder's interest in the issuer for stock in the issuer's new corporate parent.

Liabilities and Remedies. The '34 Act creates a private right of action for those who have dealt in securities on the basis of misleading registration statements (liability pursuant to §§ 12 and 18), tender offers (§ 13), and proxy solicitations (§ 14). Under § 16(b), the corporation or a shareholder suing in a derivative action for the benefit of the corporation may recover short-swing profits realized by officers, directors, and shareholders controlling at least 10 percent of the securities involved. Private actions under § 10(b) and Rule 10(b)-5, the catchall antifraud provision, may be brought by any purchasers or sellers of any securities against any person who has engaged in fraudulent conduct, including a corporation that has bought or sold its own shares. Recall that the PSLRA of 1995 preserves the state-of-mind requirements set out in the '34 Act and interpreted in subsequent Supreme Court and other court holdings.

The early § 10(b) cases, such as the *Texas Gulf Sulphur* case cited in the *Basic Incorporated* decision, had expansively imposed liability under § 10(b) and Rule 10(b)-5. However, in *Ernst & Ernst* v. *Hochfelder,* 425 U.S. 185 (1976), *reh'g. denied,* 425 U.S. 986 (1976), the Supreme Court has limited the reach of § 10(b) in that the Court has required a private person to prove that the securities law violator intended to deceive, manipulate, or defraud the injured party. After *Hochfelder,* proof of negligent conduct alone will not constitute a violation of § 10(b). Similarly, *Santa Fe Industries, Inc.* v. *Green,* 430 U.S. 462 (1977), which held that the term "fraud" in § 10(b) and Rule 10(b)-5 would not cover management's breach of fiduciary duties in connection with a securities transaction, signals somewhat of a retreat from the Court's prior, expanding view of possible liability under § 10(b).

Yet the SEC's ability (under the Insider Trading Sanctions Act of 1984) to penalize insider traders up to three times the amount of the profit gained or the loss avoided as a result of the unlawful purchase or sale suggests the availability of potent remedies aimed at discouraging securities laws' violations. Such penalties are payable to the U.S. Treasury; *private parties* cannot seek relief based on this act. This act also increases the criminal penalties that can be levied against individual violators from $10,000 to $100,000.

In addition, the Insider Trading and Securities Fraud Enforcement Act of 1988, which creates an express private right of action in favor of market participants who traded contemporaneously with those who violated the '34 Act or SEC rules by trading while in possession of material, nonpublic information, supplements all other existing express and implied remedies and does not limit either the SEC or the Attorney General's authority to assess penalties for illegal use of material, nonpublic information. However, the 1988 legislation limits the damages one can receive in such private actions to the profits gained or losses avoided by the illegal trading (less any disgorgement ordered in an SEC action brought under the 1984 Act). The 1988 Act also allows private individuals who provide information that leads to the imposition of penalties to receive a bounty of up to 10 percent of any penalty.

Although the 1988 legislation considerably bolsters the remedies provided under the 1984 Act, Congress in 1988—as it had done in 1984 as well—declined to expand the definition of what constitutes illegal insider trading under the misappropriation theory to include trading by anyone who merely is in possession of material, nonpublic information. Some legislators rejected the "possession" test as unduly broad, and others thought the law should prohibit only the improper use of such information. In short, Congress in the 1988 amendments ultimately declined to add any express definition of insider trading to the '34 Act.

Nonetheless, the legislative history of the 1988 Act reflects a clear endorsement of the misappropriation theory as articulated by lower federal courts. Indeed, both the 1984 and the 1988 Acts seem to represent a congressional backlash directed at the perceived leniency of the Supreme Court's holdings in the *Chiarella* and *Dirks* cases.

Those who advocate more potent remedies for violations of the securities laws and who disagree with the *Chiarella* and *Dirks* holdings recently were dealt a harsh blow by the Supreme Court—see *Central Bank of Denver* v. *First Interstate Bank of Denver, NA,* 511 U.S. 164 (1994). By further limiting the scope of the implied remedies available to litigants under the '34 Act, this case built on these earlier precedents. Prior to 1994, plaintiffs often sued not only the person who violated a specific provision of the securities acts but also those who "aided and abetted" the wrongdoer. By bringing "aiding" and "abetting" cases under § 10(b) and Rule 10(b)-5, a plaintiff could expand the number of persons from whom he or she could seek damages (several courts had held that "aiders" and "abettors," along with the primary violator, were jointly and severally liable). Simply put, the plaintiff was assured of a "deep pocket" because the plaintiff could recover from the most solvent defendant. Alternatively, the court, by requiring each defendant to contribute to the overall monetary award granted to the successful plaintiff, could distribute the damages among all the defendants. Because the '34 Act was silent as to a defendant's potential liability for aiding and abetting and as to the right of contribution, it was only a matter of time before the issue reached the Supreme Court.

Interestingly, in enacting the PSLRA, Congress refused to give an express private right of action for aiding and abetting; hence, the *Central Bank of Denver* ruling survives the PSLRA. The 1995 Act, however, does give the SEC enforcement authority to bring actions against aiders and abettors.

Recall that the PSLRA sets out a "fair share" rule of proportionate liability for those who have engaged in "non-knowing" violations. Joint liability will befall only those who knowingly violate the securities law. As in the '33 Act, the plaintiffs who sue for damages will have to prove the alleged misstatements actually caused their losses. The PSLRA further requires the calculation of damages based on the mean trading price of the stock (i.e., the average daily trading price of the stock determined as of the close of the market each day during the 90-day period after the dissemination of any information that corrects the misleading statement or omission).

Experts have posited that the PSLRA will have a dramatic impact on private actions brought under Rule 10(b)-5. Since the representations that form the basis of such actions often involve forward-looking statements, the "safe harbor" rule probably will lessen the incidence of such actions. Presumably, the PSLRA's pleading rules that require that scienter be pleaded with particularity in lawsuits involving the '34 Act (as opposed to the '33 Act) similarly will dampen the ardor of class action lawyers and plaintiffs who used to rush to the courthouse to file class action suits whenever a major company announced a sharp decline in the company's stock. The legal developments spawned by this newest securities law therefore bear watching.

Besides the remedies allowable under the '33 and '34 Acts, the Supreme Court's opinion in *Sedima S.P.R.L.* v. *Imrex Co., Inc.,* 473 U.S. 479 (1985), that apparently allowed securities cases to be brought under the Racketeer Influenced and Corrupt Organizations Act (RICO) for a time represented a significant remedial vehicle as well. To illustrate, some commentators argued that then-Drexel, Burnham, Lambert Inc.'s much-ballyhooed decision to plead guilty to six criminal counts and to pay a record-breaking $650 million in fines and restitution for securities violations stemmed from its desire to avoid further indictments under RICO. However, the PSLRA brings to an end this chapter in the history of securities litigation. By removing fraud as a predicate act for the purposes of a private civil action based on RICO except in certain rare instances, the PSLRA has turned this past remedy for securities violations into little more than a legal artifact.

Yet since the late 1980s, the Supreme Court has validated, under the provisions of the Federal Arbitration Act, arbitration of both RICO and securities act claims. In a related vein, then, in *First Options of Chicago, Inc.* v. *Kaplan,* 514 U.S. 398 (1995), the Supreme Court recently held that whenever it is clear that the opposing sides have agreed to submit the question to arbitration, a court should defer to the arbitrator's decision. In all other circumstances, federal courts have wide latitude to review the arbitrator's determination and to come to an independent conclusion regarding this issue. In giving courts authority to "second-guess" arbitrators on this procedural issue, the Supreme Court disappointed securities industry organizations that had urged the Court to restrict such judicial authority so as to make the arbitration process more streamlined and speedier. Nonetheless, particularly with regard to disputes between investors and their brokers, arbitration represents an increasingly significant possible remedy for investors.

Securities and Exchange Commission Actions

The '34 Act empowers the SEC to conduct investigations of possible violations of the securities laws. Many times such investigations lead to censure or, alternatively, culminate in a consent decree signed by the alleged wrongdoer in exchange for less stringent sanctions. But the SEC also can order an administrative hearing conducted by an administrative law judge to determine if penalties are in order with respect to any security, person, or firm registered with the SEC. As mentioned earlier, revocation of registration or suspension of the distribution of the security (or the activities of the person or firm) are two of the enforcement powers that the SEC possesses. The SEC itself may review the hearing officer's decision and, if necessary, modify the sanctions originally levied. A party adversely affected by a final SEC order can seek review of such an order in a circuit court of appeals.

Besides administrative proceedings, the SEC can, on a "proper showing" of a reasonable likelihood of further violations, bring court actions to enjoin violations of the securities laws. The SEC also can refer cases to the Justice Department, which then mounts criminal actions against willful violators of securities laws and rules. A crackdown on Wall Street insider-trading abuses in recent years led to successful criminal cases against well-known traders such as Ivan Boesky, Dennis Levine, and Michael Milken.

STATE REGULATION

Because the assorted federal statutes preserve the states' power to regulate securities activities, any transactions involving securities may be subject to state law as well as federal law. Such state laws, often called "blue sky" laws, though varied, normally include three types of provisions: (1) antifraud stipulations, (2) registration requirements for brokers and dealers, and (3) registration prerequisites for the sale and purchase of securities. With respect to the last, three methods of securities registration ordinarily exist: notification (a streamlined method for securities with a stable earnings record), qualification (a formalized program similar to the procedures mandated by the '33 Act), and coordination (a regimen that directs the issuer to file with the state a copy of the prospectus filed with the SEC under the '33 Act). State laws frequently exempt from registration the same classes of securities exempted from the '33 Act and additionally often exempt stocks listed on the major stock exchanges. Exempted transactions customarily include private placements, or limited offerings, and isolated nonissuer transactions. State laws generally provide for sanctions and liabilities similar to those imposed under federal law, but the small securities staffs in most states make the possibility of civil liability a more potent deterrent for violations.

In 1956, the National Conference of Commissioners on Uniform State Laws drafted a Uniform Securities Act meant for adoption by the states. This attempt at uniformity for resolving securities questions among the various states has not been wholly successful, however.

Before we leave the issue of state regulation of securities, you should know that in 1996 the Supreme Court—in *Matsushita Electric Industrial Co., Ltd.* v. *Epstein,* 116 S.Ct. 873 (1996)—interpreted the full faith and credit clause of the U.S. Constitution as meaning that federal courts must give class action settlement judgments in a stated court the same preclusive effect that it would have in the state court, notwithstanding the fact that the settlement at issue had released claims under the '33 Act (over which the stated court had no jurisdiction) and claims under the '34 Act were then pending on appeal in a separate action in the federal courts. Among other reasons, this case is interesting because it involved the very type of class action that had galvanized Congress into enacting the PSLRA. Moreover, this case may put a premium on being the first to file, whether in state court or federal court, a tactic the PSLRA had hoped to thwart, at least in the federal courts. The future resolution of these issues warrants your consideration as well.

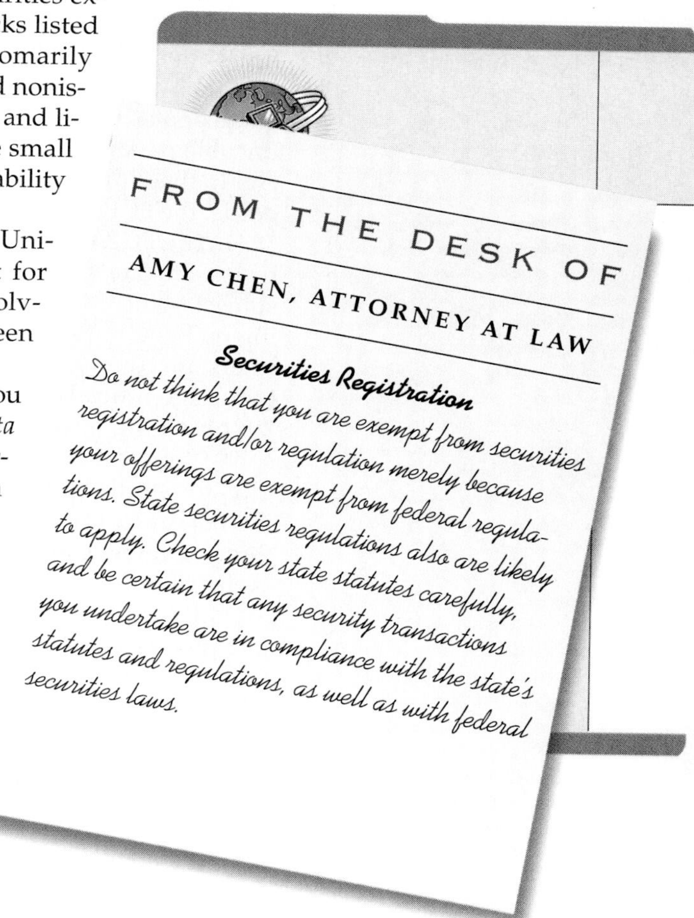

FROM THE DESK OF
AMY CHEN, ATTORNEY AT LAW
Securities Registration
Do not think that you are exempt from securities registration and/or regulation merely because your offerings are exempt from federal regulations. State securities regulations also are likely to apply. Check your state statutes carefully, and be certain that any security transactions you undertake are in compliance with the state's statutes and regulations, as well as with federal securities laws.

THE FOREIGN CORRUPT PRACTICES ACT

One additional topic merits our attention. On 19 December 1977, then-President Jimmy Carter signed into law the Foreign Corrupt Practices Act (FCPA). The FCPA resulted from post-Watergate congressional hearings about questionable payments made to foreign officials by hundreds of U.S. firms, including Exxon, Northrop Corporation, Lockheed Aircraft Company, Gulf Oil, and GTE Corp. Testimony revealed that, in order to land sizable contracts for themselves, companies had given foreign officials large payments, or bribes. In their own defense, these U.S. firms argued that foreign officials often demanded such payments as a condition of doing business and that without such "grease" payments, or sums paid to facilitate transactions by minor governmental functionaries, bureaucratic red tape would have brought business dealings to a complete halt.

Congressional investigators found that such questionable payments often took the form of secret slush funds, dubious transfers of funds or assets between subsidiaries and parent companies, improper invoicing methods (e.g., false payments for goods or services that never were received), and bookkeeping practices designed to camouflage improper payments or procedures. Indeed, these corrupt practices by U.S. corporations even included payments to engineer the overthrow of foreign governments hostile to U.S. business interests and bribes to foreign officials to keep competitors out of certain countries. To compound the improprieties, these same firms often deducted such so-called business expenses from their tax returns.

Since accounting irregularities, including secret funds and falsified or inadequate books, formed the vehicle by which firms most often had effected these questionable payments and bribes, Congress, by enacting the FCPA, attempted to put an end to these practices. Containing both antibribery provisions and accounting standards, the FCPA itself amends §§ 13(a) and 13(b)-2 of the Securities Exchange Act of 1934. The FCPA's antibribery sections provide criminal penalties for actions taken by issuers (i.e., firms subject to the '34 Act) or any domestic concern (even those not subject to the '34 Act) when an officer, director, employee, agent, or stockholder acting on behalf of such businesses corruptly uses the mail or any instrumentality of interstate commerce either to offer or actually to pay money (or anything of value) to foreign officials for the purpose of influencing foreign officials to assist the firm "in obtaining or retaining business for or with, or directing business to, any person."[2] In addition, it is unlawful under the FCPA to offer or to give payments or gifts for similar purposes to any foreign political party (or officials or candidates thereof) or to any person who the U.S. concern knows will transmit the payment or thing of value to any of the classes of persons specifically prohibited from receiving such bribes.[3]

Gifts or payments that are lawful under the written laws and regulations of the foreign country involved or that constitute bona fide reasonable expenditures (such as travel or lodging) incurred by such persons during the performance of a contract with the foreign government do not fall within the FCPA's proscriptions. Moreover, these antibribery provisions do not extend to payments made to these classes of persons when the payments' purpose is to expedite or facilitate the performance of "routine governmental action." Hence, "grease" payments to obtain permits or licenses to do business in the foreign country, visas, work orders, phone service, police protection, or inspections are legal as long as the employee receiving them is not a person known as someone who is acting as a conduit for governmental officials to whom the FCPA forbids corrupt payments or gifts.

However, decisions by foreign officials to award or continue business with a particular party are not included in the definition of routine governmental action.[4] Purely commercial bribery of corporate officials who lack governmental connections and who do not act as conduits for governmental officials thus appears to be legal, but business records, in order to comply with the FCPA's accounting standards described below, should reflect such payments. Recent amendments to the FCPA empower the Attorney General, after consultation with the SEC and others, to issue guidelines describing specific types of conduct that satisfy the strictures of the Act and, when requested by firms, to issue opinions as to whether certain specified prospective conduct by these firms conforms with the act. Once promulgated, these regulations and advisory opinions should greatly facilitate U.S. firms' attempts to comply with the FCPA.

Although all individuals and domestic concerns (whether these latter be corporations, partnerships, sole proprietorships, or any other sort of association) are subject to the FCPA antibribery provisions, only issuers subject to the SEC's jurisdiction must comply with the FCPA's accounting standards. These recordkeeping standards require issuers to do the following:

> (A) *make and keep books, records, and accounts, which, in reasonable detail, accurately and fairly reflect the transactions and dispositions of the assets of the issuer; and*
> (B) *devise and maintain a system of internal accounting controls sufficient to provide reasonable assurances that—*
> (i) *transactions are executed in accordance with management's general or specific authorization;*
> (ii) *transactions are recorded as necessary (i) to permit preparation of financial statements in conformity with generally accepted accounting principles or any other criteria applicable to such statements, and (ii) to maintain accountability for assets;*
> (iii) *access to assets is permitted only in accordance with management's general or specific authorization; and*
> (iv) *the recorded accountability for assets is compared with the existing assets at reasonable intervals and appropriate action is taken with respect to any differences.*[5]

Because they largely eliminate the possibility of secret slush funds for bribing foreign officials, these provisions are beneficial. Yet the statute gives no specific guidelines for setting up a particular internal control system. Rather, it leaves the choice of the particular system to the individual firm. The statute's vagueness therefore has created confusion on the part of some businesspeople as to what type of recordkeeping system will suffice. Given the FCPA's criminal penalties for knowingly failing to comply, this is not an idle worry.

Further compounding such worries is the SEC's promulgation of far-ranging regulations designed to promote the reliability of the information requested in the FCPA's recordkeeping provisions. These regulations prohibit both the falsification of accounting records and misleading statements made by an issuer's directors or officers to auditors or accountants during the preparation of required documents and reports.

The FCPA's imposition of criminal penalties—setting corporate fines of a maximum of $2 million for violations and a maximum of five years' imprisonment and/or $100,000 in fines for willful violations by corporate individuals—and individual civil penalties not to exceed $10,000 should adequately deter U.S. corporations and corporate personnel engaged in international business from such illegal activities. Adding further strength to the criminal penalties is the FCPA's prohibition of a corporation's indemnification of its employees against liability under this Act.[6] Other remedies available under the '34 Act, such as injunctions, also may be used in the enforcement of the FCPA by the Justice Department and the SEC, which share enforcement responsibilities under it.

Critics of the FCPA argue that its provisions and resultant regulations have greatly increased both U.S. businesses' costs of doing business and the enforcement agencies' costs, all of which negatively affect the public. On the other hand, such laws and supplementary regulations carry the attendant advantages of heightened investor information and fewer scandals involving U.S. bribery of foreign officials.

Since the FCPA is of relatively recent vintage, case law interpreting it is sparse. Plus, because of the legal, social, and ethical issues it represents, the FCPA promises to remain a controversial law.

YOU BE THE JUDGE

Foreign Corrupt Practices Act

In 1997, the Foreign Corrupt Practices Act marks the twentieth anniversary of its enactment. As the recent scandals in the Executive Branch and the enforcement actions against Lockheed, Martin Corporation and IBM Corporation indicate, there is little reason to celebrate. On the contrary, the recent opening of previously closed markets (the former Soviet Union and Eastern Europe), the recent emergence of major markets where bribery is commonplace (China and India), and the U.S. public's growing intolerance of corruption and scandal stand as harbingers of more aggressive enforcement of the FCPA. Given these heightened legal risks, some experts have argued for the need for companies to implement a "due diligence" system by which employees can report information relevant to an FCPA inquiry and thus prevent, detect, and deter FCPA violations. As one aspect of such a system, the firm would scrutinize any foreign consultant or agent it proposed to hire as to the agent's possible affiliation with governmental officials.[7]

Suppose that *you* were asked to review the FCPA in order to establish a due diligence system that would make your firm's compliance efforts more efficient. What types of assessments and investigations would *you* require for such a due diligence system?

BUSINESS CONSIDERATIONS What policies should a business institute so as to ensure compliance with the provisions of the FCPA? Do you believe that the FCPA hampers the ability of U.S. firms to compete in a global market?

ETHICAL CONSIDERATIONS Does the FCPA improve the ethical conduct of U.S. firms? Does the FCPA represent a type of "cultural imperialism" in which the United States expects the rest of the world to accede to its view of what is—or is not—ethical?

SOURCE: Wendy C. Schmidt and Jonny J. Frank, *The National Law Journal,* 3 March 1997, p. B16.

http:// RESOURCES FOR BUSINESS LAW STUDENTS

NAME	RESOURCES	WEB ADDRESS
Securities and Exchange Commission (SEC)	The SEC provides information about federal securities laws and investor protection in the securities market.	http://www.sec.gov/
Electronic Data Gathering (EDGAR)	EDGAR is a searchable database of corporate information maintained by the SEC.	http://www.sec.gov/edgarhp.html
Securities Act of 1933	The University of Cincinnati's Center for Corporate Law maintains the Securities Act of 1933.	http://www.law.uc.edu/CCL/33Act/
Securities Exchange Act of 1934	The University of Cincinnati's Center for Corporate Law maintains the Securities Act of 1934.	http://www.law.uc.edu/CCL/34Act/
Foreign Corrupt Practices Act—15 U.S.C. § 78dd-2	The Legal Information Institute, maintained by the Cornell Law School, provides a hypertext and searchable version of 15 U.S.C. § 78dd-2, popularly known as the Foreign Corrupt Practices Act.	http://www.law.cornell.edu/uscode/15/78dd-2.html

SUMMARY

The Securities Act of 1933 and the Securities Exchange Act of 1934 extensively regulate securities. In essence, a "security" involves instruments labeled as stock and that possess all the characteristics typically associated with stock, as well as an investment in an enterprise whereby the investor has no managerial functions but instead expects to profit solely from the efforts of others. The '33 Act basically is a disclosure statute meant to protect the unsophisticated investing public. The '33 Act, in furtherance of this purpose, requires, upon the initial distribution of stock, the issuer's filing of a detailed registration statement with the SEC and the furnishing of a prospectus to virtually all potential investors. Until the registration statement becomes effective, selling and promotional activities remain limited. The '33 Act exempts certain classes of securities from its registration and prospectus requirements: securities issued by federal and state banks, short-term commercial paper, issues by nonprofit organizations, issues by savings and loan associations subject to state or federal regulation, issues by common carriers subject to the jurisdiction of the Surface Transportation Board, certain qualifying employee pension plans, insurance policies and certain annuities subject to regulation by state and federal authorities, and intrastate issues of securities.

The '33 Act, in addition, exempts certain transactions such as private offerings. The '33 Act also contains several antifraud provisions. Civil liability may attend violations of the '33 Act. One section places liability on everyone who signed the registration statement, was named as a director, contributed an expert opinion to the statement, or underwrote the issue. All such persons, except the issuer, may escape liability if they can show they acted with "due diligence." Other sections of the '33 Act establish civil and criminal liability.

The '34 Act regulates the secondary distribution of securities. Its reach therefore is even broader than that of the '33 Act. The '34 Act covers proxy solicitations and tender offers, limits insider trading, forbids short-swing profits, and in general tries to eliminate fraud and manipulative conduct with respect to the sale or purchase of securities. According to the '34 Act, any issuer who trades securities on a national stock exchange must register with the SEC. Like the '33 Act, the '34 Act mandates certain disclosures by the firms that it covers when the securities are listed with national stock exchanges or traded over the counter. Regulation of proxy solicitations is an important facet of the '34 Act. In order to further the democratic aspects of corporations, the '34 Act authorizes the inclusion—in management proxy solicitations—of shareholder proposals that involve "proper subjects." Liability for misleading proxy statements is absolute, as is liability for misleading statements made during tender offers or takeover bids. The '34 Act also prohibits insider trading because of the injury to the investing public that otherwise may ensue. When material inside information is involved, the insider either must publicly disclose the information or refrain from trading in the securities. Under the '34 Act's section on short-swing profits, directors, officers, and beneficial shareholders in certain corporations must refrain from buying or selling securities within a six-month period. Possible liability under the '34 Act is far-reaching, despite the existence of some Supreme Court decisions suggesting less expansive impositions of liability in the future. As well, the Private Securities Litigation Reform Act of 1995 limits class action suits to situations in which shareholders in fact have been the victims of securities fraud and discourages suits brought for frivolous—or entrepreneurial—purposes.

The Securities and Exchange Commission can conduct administrative hearings with respect to securities violations and can seek injunctions to stop continuing violations. State securities laws, "blue sky" laws, usually set up antifraud provisions and registration requirements for brokers and dealers and for the sale of securities. Since 1977, the Foreign Corrupt Practices Act has forbidden U.S. businesses from making payments to foreign officials for the purpose of obtaining foreign business. Noncompliance with the FCPA's antibribery provisions and recordkeeping standards may subject individuals or corporations to civil or criminal penalties.

Discussion Questions

1. What, essentially, is a "security"?
2. Explain the primary purposes of the Securities Act of 1933 and the Securities Exchange Act of 1934.
3. List the types of information the '33 Act requires a registration statement to include.
4. What are "tombstone ads" and "red herring" prospectuses?
5. List the '33 Act's exempt classes of securities and transactions.
6. Explain what a proxy is, and describe the SEC rules surrounding proxy solicitations.
7. What are the '34 Act's provisions regarding insider trading?
8. Discuss the laws regarding short-swing profits and why the '34 Act prohibits these profits.
9. Enumerate the liabilities and remedies possible under both the '33 and '34 Acts.
10. Explain the enforcement powers held by the SEC and how state regulation of securities differs from federal regulation.

Case Problems and Writing Assignments

1. The federal Williams Act and its implementing regulations govern hostile corporate stock tender offers. The Williams Act, among other things, requires that offers remain open for at least 20 business days. The Indiana statute concerning control share acquisitions applies to certain business corporations chartered in Indiana that have specified levels of shares or shareholders within the state and that opt into the state

statute's protection. The Indiana statute provides that the acquisition of "control shares" in such a corporation—shares that, but for the state statute, would bring the acquiring entity's voting power to or above certain threshold levels—does not include voting rights unless a majority of all preexisting disinterested shareholders so agree at their next regularly scheduled meeting. However, by following specified procedures, the stock acquiror can require a special meeting within 50 days.

Dynamics Corporation of America (Dynamics) announced a tender offer that would have raised its ownership interest in CTS Corporation (CTS) above the Indiana statute's threshold. At the same time, Dynamics, alleging federal securities violations by CTS, also filed suit in federal court. After CTS opted into the Indiana statute's protection, Dynamics amended its complaint to challenge the statute's validity under the federal Williams Act and the commerce clause. Was the Indiana takeover statute invalid owing to its preemption (the precedence of federal law over state law) by the Williams Act or its unconstitutionality under the commerce clause? [See *CTS Corporation* v. *Dynamics Corporation of America*, 481 U.S. 69 (1987).]

2. Cousins Home Furnishings, Inc. (Cousins) made a public offering of its stock in December 1983. The stock purchasers later brought a class action against Cousins, its parent company, various officers and directors of Cousins, and two lead underwriters. The plaintiffs alleged the stock offering was misleading in material respects, in violation of §§ 11 and 12 of the '33 Act, § 10(b) of the '34 Act, and certain state laws. The named defendants settled with the plaintiffs for $13.5 million. Employers Insurance of Wausau (EIW), who had insured most of the named defendants, funded $13 million of the settlement. Subrogated to the rights of their insureds, EIW brought this lawsuit seeking contribution from Musick, Peeler & Garrett (MPG), who were the attorneys and accountants involved in the public offering. EIW's complaint alleged these professionals had joint responsibility for the securities violations and were liable for contribution under various theories, including a right to contribution based on Rule 10(b)-5. Should those charged with liability in a Rule 10(b)-5 action have an implied right to contribution against the other parties who have joint responsibility for the violation? Why? [See *Musick, Peeler & Garrett* v. *Employers Insurance of Wausau*, 508 U.S. 286 (1993).]

3. In 1976, Pepsico, Inc., agreed to sell Lee Way Motor Freight, Inc. (Lee Way) to Commercial Lovelace Motor Freight, Inc. (CL). Shortly after taking over Lee Way's operations, CL began soliciting Lee Way employees to participate in a wage reduction program (the Program) that had been in place at CL since 1983. The Program, which was optional for Lee Way's union employees, provided each participating union employee with an interest both in CL's existing company-administered employee stock ownership plan (the CL ESOP) and a profit-sharing plan in return for the individual employee's agreement to a 17.35 percent reduction in the wages due him or her under the union's collective bargaining agreement. CL represented to Lee Way employees that the company probably would fail if they did not enroll in the Program. All the plaintiffs in this action individually elected to participate in the Program. Less than a year later, CL merged with Lee Way and filed for bankruptcy. Lee Way's former assets allegedly were reacquired by Pepsico. In this action, William T. Uselton and 485 former union employees of Lee Way alleged that Pepsico's sale of Lee Way to CL and its subsequent reacquisition of Lee Way's assets upon CL's rapid demise had amounted to a sham transaction designed to disguise Pepsico's intended and ultimately successful liquidation of Lee Way. In their federal securities claim, the plaintiffs alleged that their interests in the CL ESOP had constituted "investment contracts" subject to federal securities regulation pursuant to § 2(l) of the '33 Act. The plaintiffs further submitted that CL's solicitation of Lee Way employees to accept an interest in the CL ESOP as part of the Program had amounted to a sale of an unregistered security and securities fraud in violation of §§ 5 and 17(a) of the '33 Act. Was the CL ESOP—a voluntary, contributory employee benefit plan—a security? Why or why not? [See *Uselton* v. *Commercial Lovelace Motor Freight, Inc.*, 940 F.2d 564 (10th Cir. 1991).]

4. Plaintiffs Billy Lamb and Carmon Willis, along with various other Kentucky growers, produce barley tobacco for use in cigarettes and other tobacco products. Defendants Philip Morris, Inc. (Philip Morris) and B.A.T. Industries (B.A.T.) routinely purchase such tobacco not only from the Kentucky markets serviced by the plaintiffs but also from producers in several foreign countries. Thus, tobacco grown in Kentucky competes directly with tobacco grown abroad; and any purchases from foreign suppliers necessarily reduce the defendants' purchases of domestic tobacco. On 14 May 1982, a Philip Morris subsidiary and a B.A.T. subsidiary entered into a contract with La Fundacion Del Niño (the Children's Foundation) of Caracas, Venezuela. The Children's Foundation's president, the wife of the then-president of Venezuela, signed the agreement on behalf of the Foundation. Under the terms of the agreement,

the two subsidiaries would make periodic donations, totaling approximately $12.5 million, to the Children's Foundation. In exchange, the subsidiaries would obtain price controls on Venezuelan tobacco, would eliminate controls on retail cigarette prices in Venezuela, would receive tax deductions for the donations, and would receive assurances that existing tax rates applicable to tobacco companies would not be increased. In the plaintiffs' view, the donations promised by the defendants' subsidiaries amounted to unlawful inducements designed and intended to restrain trade. The plaintiffs therefore sought redress in the form of treble damages and injunctive relief principally for the former result—the reduction in domestic tobacco prices—which, according to the plaintiffs, constituted violations of federal antitrust laws. The plaintiffs later amended their complaint to include a claim under the Federal Corrupt Practices Act (the FCPA). The district court dismissed the plaintiffs' antitrust claims as barred by the act-of-state doctrine and dismissed the FCPA claim as an impermissible private action. The plaintiffs appealed.

Would the act-of-state doctrine preclude domestic tobacco producers from bringing an antitrust action against tobacco importers based on the claim that the importers' subsidiaries had made contributions to foreign charities in exchange for the foreign government's imposition of price controls on foreign tobacco and the elimination of controls on retail cigarette prices? Would the FCPA in such circumstances create an implied private right of action in favor of these domestic tobacco producers? [See *Lamb* v. *Philip Morris, Inc.*, 915 F.2d 1024 (6th Cir. 1990); *cert. denied* 498 U.S. 1086 (1991).]

5. In October 1984, Mesa Partners II was formed and began accumulating stock in Unocal Corporation (Unocal). By 22 February 1985, Mesa Partners II owned 17 million shares of Unocal's common stock, representing 9.7 percent of the outstanding shares. Unocal then initiated defensive measures designed to discourage a perceived takeover threat by Mesa Partners II. On 25 February 1985, Unocal amended its bylaw concerning the procedures for nominating directors and making shareholder proposals. On 22 March 1985, Mesa Partners II acquired a total of 6.7 million shares of Unocal common stock at $48.10 per share. This transaction increased Mesa Partners II's shares to 23.7 million and its ownership interest to 13.6 percent of Unocal's common stock. On 28 March 1985, Mesa Partners II amended its Schedule 13D statement, adding that it "may seek to obtain control of the company [Unocal] or to participate in the formulation, determination or direction of the basic business decisions of the Company." Mesa Partners II also indicated that it intended to solicit proxies to gain postponement of the annual Unocal shareholders' meeting then scheduled for 29 April 1985. On 8 April 1985, Mesa Partners II made a tender offer to purchase 64 million shares of Unocal common stock at $54 per share. Unocal's board of directors recommended that Unocal's shareholders reject Mesa Partners II's tender offer as inadequate and not in their best interests. On 16 April 1985, Unocal offered to exchange a package of its debt securities for up to 87.2 million shares (approximately one-half of Unocal's outstanding common stock). Unocal stated in its offer that one of its express purposes was "to make it more difficult for Mesa Bidders to complete the Mesa Offer." Unocal therefore expressly excluded Mesa Partners II from participating in its exchange offer.

   On 22 April 1985, in a Delaware state court, Mesa Partners II challenged its exclusion from Unocal's tender offer. The Court of Chancery temporarily restrained Unocal from proceeding with the offer unless it included Mesa Partners II. The Delaware Supreme Court reversed the Court of Chancery and held that Unocal was not prohibited by law from excluding Mesa Partners II from its tender offer. Following the Delaware Supreme Court's decision, representatives of Mesa Partners II contacted Unocal and sought to reopen negotiations. The parties reached an agreement, pursuant to which, the "Mesa Entities" were allowed to participate in Unocal's self-tender offer; Mesa Partners II agreed to terminate its tender offer; and, in addition, Mesa Partners II agreed that it would neither participate in any proxy solicitation nor acquire any additional Unocal shares for a period of 25 years. In addition, Mesa Partners II agreed to strict controls on its ability to sell its Unocal common stock. On the same day, Mesa Partners II exchanged approximately 7.8 million shares of Unocal common stock for negotiable debt securities. On 3 July 1985, Mesa Asset Company (Mesa) sold these debt securities for approximately $589 million. On 3 June 1986, David Colan, a Unocal shareholder, filed a derivative action on behalf of Unocal, alleging violations of § 16(b) by the Mesa defendants. Was the exchange of the Mesa defendants' common stock for negotiable debt securities a "sale" within § 16(b) of the Securities Exchange Act of 1934 and thus violative of § 16(b)? [See *Colan* v. *Mesa Petroleum Co.*, 941 F.2d 933 (9th Cir. 1991), *superseded* at 951 F.2d 1512 (9th Cir. 1991).]

6. **BUSINESS APPLICATION CASE** Sinay, Rosenberg, and Halye purchased Lamson and Session Company (Lamson) common stock. In their complaints, the plaintiffs alleged securities fraud pursuant to § 10(b) of

the '34 Act and Rule 10(b)-5. The plaintiffs did not assert that fraud had been committed individually upon them because they had relied on statements by defendants when they had purchased their shares. Instead, they contended that Lamson and the other defendants had engaged in a course of conduct that artificially had inflated the common stock's market price (that is, the plaintiffs asserted a "fraud-on-the-market" theory). Following several November 1986 acquisitions, Lamson's earnings had increased dramatically. On 24 October 1988, Lamson publicly had disclosed that its performance during the first three quarters had been "gratifying," although it was experiencing a "normal seasonal decline" in its commercial and residential markets that would last "into the first quarter of 1989." On 23 December 1988, Lamson had reported that it was having a "tremendous year." On 21 February 1989, Lamson had stated that it was pleased with the 1988 results and that it planned to continue to develop its position in the domestic and worldwide transportation markets. In an April 1989 interview with the Dow Jones News Service, Schulze, a Lamson officer, had noted that Lamson "does not quarrel with analysts' earnings estimates for 1989 in the area of $1.50 to $1.60. . . ." Schulze further had asserted that Lamson was "counting on new products to offset a weaker construction market for 1989." Notwithstanding these positive forecasts, Lamson's financial condition began to erode in 1989. Owing to prolonged higher interest rates, the construction market failed to rebound after the winter slowdown. Moreover, Lamson experienced severe labor problems at its Midland plant.

The plaintiffs claimed that the defendants knew or should have known that the construction market's decline would be long term and that a major and devastating strike would occur. Therefore, according to the plaintiffs, the defendants, by failing to issue sufficiently cautionary statements concerning Lamson's future, deceived the market. Should the court hold the defendants liable for securities violations based on a corporate officer's statements of honestly held views derived from information currently before the corporation? Why? Assume that your boss at Lamson has asked you to draft a policy that will govern future public statements by corporate personnel. Based on the facts of this case and what you have derived from the *Basic Incorporated* case, how will you respond? [See *Sinay* v. *Lamson & Sessions Co.*, 948 F.2d 1037 (6th Cir. 1991).]

7. **ETHICS APPLICATION CASE** As part of a proposed "freeze-out" merger, in which First American Bank of Virginia would be merged into Virginia Bankshares, Inc. (VBI), a wholly owned subsidiary of First American Bankshares, Inc. (FABI), the Bank's executive committee and board approved a price of $42 per share for the minority stockholders, who, after the merger, would lose their interests in the Bank. Although Virginia law required only that the merger proposal be submitted to a vote at a shareholders' meeting, preceded by the circulation of an informational statement to the shareholders, the Bank directors nevertheless solicited proxies for voting on the proposal. Their solicitation urged the proposal's adoption and stated that the plan had been approved because of its opportunity for the minority shareholders to receive a "high" value for their stock and a "fair" price.

Sandberg, a shareholder, did not give her proxy and, after the approval of the merger, filed suit seeking damages from the Bank's action of soliciting proxies by means of allegedly materially false or misleading statements in violation of § 14(a) of the Securities Exchange Act of 1934 and the Securities and Exchange Commission's Rule 14(a)-9. Among other things, she alleged that the directors had believed they had no alternative but to recommend the merger if they wished to remain on the board. At trial, she obtained a jury instruction that she could prevail without showing her own reliance on the alleged misstatements, as long as they were material and the proxy solicitation was an "essential link" in the merger process. She was awarded an amount equal to the difference between the offered price and her stock's true value. In affirming, the court of appeals held that certain statements in the proxy solicitation, including the one regarding the stock's value, were materially misleading; and that Sandberg (and the other shareholders) could maintain the action even though their votes had not been needed to effectuate the merger.

Was the directors' statement that purported to explain their reasons for recommending a certain corporate action materially misleading within the meaning of Rule 14(a)-9? Could minority shareholders whose votes had not been required by law or any corporate bylaw to authorize the corporate action subject to the proxy solicitation show the causation element needed for an award of damages under § 14(a)? The legalities aside, would it be unethical for a corporation to "freeze out" minority shareholders? Explain fully. [See *Virginia Bankshares, Inc.* v. *Sandberg*, 501 U.S. 1083 (1991).]

8. **IDES CASE** In February 1988, Chrysler Corporation (Chrysler) adopted a shareholder rights plan (the Plan), commonly known as a "poison pill." Under the Plan, Chrysler stockholders received one preferred share purchase right on each outstanding share of Chrysler common stock. Each purchase right could be

exercised following certain triggering events; that is, 10 days after the first public disclosure that a person or group had acquired, or had obtained the right to acquire, beneficial ownership of 30 percent (in 1989, lowered to 20 percent) or more of Chrysler's outstanding common stock, or 10 days after the first public disclosure or actual commencement of a tender or exchange offer intended to result in the offeror's becoming the beneficial owner of 30 percent or more of Chrysler's outstanding common stock. Additionally, the Plan provided that, following certain events, the poison pill preferred purchase rights would entitle holders to exercise "flip-in" rights to buy Chrysler common stock at one-half the market value or, alternatively, "flip-over" rights to buy common shares in an entity whose announced or actual acquisition of Chrysler common stock had triggered the exercise of the purchase rights.

On 14 December 1990, Chrysler issued a press release announcing further amendments to the Plan. This release, which would become the focus of the shareholders' federal securities fraud claim, announced an unsolicited stock purchase by Kirk Kerkorian that gave Kerkorian over 9 percent of Chrysler's outstanding common stock. As a result of the purchase, the press release stated, Chrysler's board of directors had adopted amendments to the company's share purchase rights plan. The amendments reduced from 20 percent to 10 percent the threshold of beneficial ownership at which the rights flip in. The release concluded with a company statement: "The amendments adopted today *are intended to enhance the ability of Chrysler's Board to act in the best interest of all the Company's shareholders if someone should seek to obtain a position of control or substantial influence over Chrysler.*"

Harriet Lewis and other shareholders alleged that the italicized language in the press release constituted fraud in violation of § 10(b) and Rule 10(b)-5. Specifically, Lewis claimed that the corporation's alleged failure to say how management might use the Plan (or "poison pill") to its own advantage represented an actionable omission of a material fact and therefore securities fraud, particularly since the press release had affirmatively portrayed the amendments to the Plan as being in the shareholders' best interests. Moreover, Lewis alleged that Chrysler's failure to disclose the costs of the Plan to the shareholders had violated the securities laws as well. Apply the IDES model in deciding how the appellate court should rule on Lewis's claims. [See *Lewis* v. *Chrysler Corp.*, 949 F.2d 644 (3rd Cir. 1991).]

NOTES

1. *Securities and Exchange Commission* v. *Ralston Purina Co.*, 346 U.S. 119 (1953).
2. 15 U.S.C. § 78(dd-1), (dd-2).
3. Ibid.
4. Ibid.
5. Ibid., § 78(m).
6. Ibid., § 78(ff).
7. Wendy C. Schmidt and Jonny J. Frank, "FCPA Demands Due Diligence in Global Dealings," *The National Law Journal* (3 March 1997), p. B16.

PART 8

IDES PROBLEMS

InterActive is a small, private multimedia software developer specializing in consumer CD-ROMs, especially games. InterActive is a corporation, with three majority and two minority owners, five managers, and twenty employees. InterActive maintains an office and retail store in San Francisco to sell the software the firm develops. InterActive also maintains a "storefront" on the Internet. Despite InterActive's small size and informal atmosphere, it has recently encountered a number of legal problems.

Shelly, a manager for InterActive, learned through a freelancer of a software designer who had written a new three-dimensional modeling language, 3DML (Three Dimensional Modeling Language). This designer was about to sell the exclusive rights to 3DML, and Shelly was invited to bid. Rather than informing other managers at InterActive of the opportunity, Shelly decided to bid on the rights to the language for herself, and she was the highest bidder. With the rights to 3DML, Shelly began her own privately owned business, 3Dwow! (based in Boston, Massachusetts, but operating primarily through an Internet site). In this business, Shelly builds programming tools for 3DML with which other programmers, for a licensing fee, can easily create products, including games. Given the tremendous success of 3Dwow!, Shelly resigned her position with InterActive in order to devote her full time to 3Dwow! The owners and the other managers of InterActive were unaware of 3DML, or Shelly's actions, until her resignation. Citing a variety of reasons, including conflict of interest, InterActive has decided to seek legal recourse against Shelly.

On another issue, a minority owner, Chet, believes that InterActive should seek funds to expand. Chet suggests creating franchises both around the country and on the Internet to sell InterActive products. Chet also suggests that InterActive issue debt securities. The other owners disagree with Chet and instead prefer a slow, steady growth strategy. In addition, InterActive's owners prefer to avoid federal security regulation to the greatest extent possible. Accordingly, they fear Chet's suggestions will require the firm to register with the Securities and Exchange Commission (SEC) and hence open the firm to certain federal regulations that it has managed to avoid. Chet has decided to seek legal action to force the other owners to agree to his ideas for expansion. The owners, on the other hand, believe their rejection of Chet's ideas are valid, and they deny any wrongdoing.

To address these problems, InterActive's majority owners have retained an attorney. In preparation for the firm's first meeting, these owners need to answer the following questions:

IDENTIFY What are the legal and ethical issues surrounding InterActive's relationship with Shelly and Chet? Is Shelly obligated to inform InterActive of any opportunities that arise in the course of her job? Does Chet have the right to sue InterActive if the majority owners refuse to follow his suggestions for growth?

DEFINE What are the meanings of the relevant legal terms associated with these issues?

ENUMERATE What are the legal and ethical principles relevant to these issues? How long does InterActive have to decide whether Shelly has usurped an opportunity from the firm? Does the fact that InterActive is a corporation have any legal bearing on Chet and Shelly's actions? With regard to Chet, does InterActive have any defense that will provide protection to the owners?

SHOW BOTH SIDES Consider all of the facts in light of these questions. Has Shelly acted within the law in creating 3Dwow!? What problems may arise if InterActive pursues legal action? Does Chet have a legitimate legal complaint?

[To review the IDES approach refer to pages 29–30.]

Part 9

GOVERNMENT REGULATION OF BUSINESS

Governmental regulation of business is a controversial area. There are people who believe that governmental regulation is an inappropriate exercise of government power and that the nation would be better served by a return to a *laissez faire* economy. Other people believe that the government does not go far enough in regulating business.

However, for better or for worse, governmental regulation of business is a fact. The government regulates competition through the Sherman, Clayton, Robinson-Patman, and Federal Trade Commission acts; it provides for protection of consumers through various consumer credit acts; it provides for environmental protection; and it provides for protection of both labor and employment.

Governmental regulation is closely related to the social contract theory discussed in the business ethics chapter. It is also an area that creates controversy concerning whether business should be proactive or reactive as it meets its social obligations and expectations. Throughout this section of the text, consider the social contract theory, and consider the benefits and burdens of being either proactive or reactive.

I D E S

Healthtech, a health-care technology firm, has recently encountered legal problems. Healthtech wishes to expand, but in doing so the firm has encountered complaints brought against it under the Sherman and Clayton Acts. Also, advocacy groups have attacked Healthtech's workplace policies, citing the Americans with Disabilities Act and the Civil Rights Act of 1964. To what extent do these statutes affect the actions of Healthtech? In addition, Healthtech has taken a strong antiunion stance in one of its manufacturing plants. What steps can Healthtech legally take pursuant to this stance?

Consider these issues in the context of the chapter materials, and prepare to analyze them using the IDES model:

IDENTIFY the legal issues raised by the questions.

DEFINE all the relevant legal terms and issues involved.

ENUMERATE the legal principles associated with these issues.

SHOW BOTH SIDES by using the facts.

Constitutional Regulation of Business

A G E N D A

In its various activities, CIT is likely to be fairly heavily regulated at both the state and the federal level. The Kochanowskis will want to know *why* the government is able to regulate their efforts and *how* these regulations will affect them. Given the use of the Call-Image videophone, its production may raise some freedom of speech questions. If the government does increase its regulation of videophones, there are likely to be several due process issues raised by this heightened regulation of a particular industry. Most of this potential governmental oversight will subject the firm to administrative regulation.

These and other issues are likely to arise during your study of this chapter. Be prepared! You never know when one of the Kochanowskis will need your help or advice.

O U T L I N E

AN HISTORICAL PERSPECTIVE

In the United States today, government heavily regulates business. Local regulations tell a company where it may conduct business. State regulations cover the selling of securities, loan rates, and highway weight limits. Federal regulations address pollution, the safety of employees, consumer protection, and labor negotiations. And these represent only a few of the regulations that a business faces.

Pervasive governmental regulation of business, however, has not always been the case. As is often mentioned in American history texts, the United States was built on a ***laissez faire*** economy. Business owners ran business and politicians ran government, and the two groups left each other alone. Buyers often were ignored, with ***caveat emptor*** being the rule of the land. Workers remained virtually unprotected. If they did not like their jobs, they could quit. If they did not go to work, they were fired. If they joined a union, they also were fired—and they quite often faced criminal conspiracy charges as well.

Laissez faire
A term meaning "hands-off"; the belief that business operates best when uninhibited by the government.

Caveat emptor
A term meaning "let the buyer beware"; a reference to the fact that the buyer had very few, if any, remedies for defective products.

The nineteenth century was a great time to be an American entrepreneur, especially a wealthy one. These easy times came to an end, however. The general populace viewed too many "captains of industry" as "robber barons." Many people resented the abuse and mistreatment workers suffered. And, given the lack of land remaining for westward migration, people increasingly clamored for reform. Present-day governmental regulation emerged from these tumultuous times.

SHOULD GOVERNMENT REGULATE BUSINESS?

Yet, over the last few decades, people have been asking the question "Should government regulate business?" The answer is either *yes* or *no*, depending on which type of business is at issue, what type of regulation is being discussed, and which level of government is involved. The answer also depends to some degree on whether the business involves international trade, domestic trade, or regional/local trade. In general, such a question involves a number of factors, and the answers may vary over time as the circumstances of the business change.

History shows that society needs some regulation or intervention by government. Governmental regulation typically takes two forms: social regulation (concern for such issues as workplace safety, equal opportunity, environmental protection, and consumer protection) and economic regulation (the behavior of firms, especially the firms' effects on prices, production, industry conditions for entry or exit, and so on). In 1992, 126,501 people worked in the 52 major federal agencies.[1] Obviously, had they not been working in the federal bureaucracy, presumably they could have worked at jobs producing other goods and services. Clearly, then, one must compare the costs—in terms of administration, compliance, and efficiency—of regulation with its perceived benefits.

Many people today believe this balance has tipped too far and has resulted in the overregulation of business. Indeed, the pervasiveness of the government's reach over business activities has led to cries for deregulation and a lessening of this glut of laws. Given the complexities of business at the advent of the twenty-first century, however, no one realistically believes that these laws magically will disappear.

Business's "social contract" requires that it pay heed to the various social and economic issues mentioned above. Somewhere between the extremes of overregulation and underregulation, a happy medium must exist so as to maximize the well-being of business, society, and government. Yet, as we learned in the beginning of this textbook, in the absence of the attainment of this balance, laws can become so burdensome on individuals that such persons can argue that the laws violate the rights guaranteed to individuals by the Constitution. Since the law in many instances views firms as legal, or *juristic,* persons, businesses also can assert various constitutional rights and thus curb what they view as excessive governmental regulation. Hence, just as the Constitution stands as the guardian of individual rights, it in addition represents a significant weapon for businesses to use when they challenge the laws and regulations that affect them.

The Commerce Clause

Perhaps the single most important constitutional provision that affects business is the commerce clause. Article I, Section 8 of the Constitution states that Congress shall have the power "to regulate Commerce with foreign Nations, and among the several States, and with the Indian Tribes." In addition, Article I, Section 8 gives Congress the power to levy taxes. The interplay between these two powers forms the basis for much of the federal government's regulation of business.

The history of the commerce clause has been checkered. The Supreme Court initially had interpreted the clause, next expanded these interpretations, later contracted these interpretations, and then expanded them again. In 1824, the Supreme Court had its first occasion to interpret the commerce clause. Chief Justice Marshall's opinion in *Gibbons* v. *Ogden* defined commerce as "the commercial intercourse between nations, in all its branches . . . regulated by prescribing rules for carrying on that intercourse."[2] Marshall further noted that the federal government can regulate commerce that *affects* other states, even if that commerce is local in nature.

As a result of this interpretation, for nearly three-quarters of a century, federal power to regulate business was broad. The Interstate Commerce Act of 1887 permitted the Interstate Commerce Commission (ICC) to regulate local railroad rates and local railroad safety because such issues directly affected interstate rates and safety.[3] The federal government also could regulate local grain and livestock exchanges because they, too, involved transactions that affected the rest of the nation.

Not all court opinions of the period favored regulation by the federal government, however. In the 1873 Supreme Court decision *In re State Freight Tax,* the Court stated that the commerce clause's phrase *among* meant *between.*[4] As a result, this opinion held that the federal government could regulate only **interstate** commerce. By limiting the definition of commerce, the Court similarly contracted the federal power to regulate business. In its 1888 *Kidd* v. *Pearson* decision, the Court ruled that commerce meant transportation.[5] As a result of these two opinions, federal regulation of business suddenly became restricted to actual interstate **transportation** and did not reach business deals that *affected* interstate business but that were conducted entirely in one state. Such transactions, defined as **intrastate**, therefore remained beyond the scope of federal regulation.

Interstate

Between two or more states; between a point in one state and a point in another state.

Transportation

Carrying or conveying from one place to another; the removal of goods or persons from one place to another.

Intrastate

Begun, carried on, and completed wholly within the boundaries of a single state.

This new, restricted definition of interstate commerce underlay the passage of the Sherman Act in 1890 (see Chapter 40 for a detailed treatment of this act). Indeed, this new definition of the federal authority to regulate business led the Court to narrower interpretations and, consequently, the Court's invalidation of many subsequent federal enactments.

A shift in the Court's narrow view of the exercise of federal power did not occur until 1937. In *NLRB* v. *Jones & Laughlin Steel Corp.,* which overturned 50 years of narrow interpretation, Chief Justice Hughes said:

> *When industries organize themselves on a national scale, making their relation to interstate commerce the dominant factor in their activities, how can it be maintained that their industrial relations constitute a forbidden field into which Congress may not enter when it is necessary to protect interstate commerce from the paralyzing consequences of industrial war?*[6]

Thus, the Court had come full circle. As Justice Jackson noted in *United States* v. *Women's Sportswear Manufacturers Association*, a 1949 case involving a Sherman Act challenge to a local price-fixing arrangement, "If it is interstate commerce that feels the pinch, it does not matter how local the operation which applies the squeeze."[7] In upholding the right of the federal government to regulate the conduct in dispute, Justice Jackson provided us with both a picturesque definition of interstate commerce and the one most courts presently would accept as controlling. This expansive definition of the reach of the federal government under the commerce clause also provided the federal government with a vehicle for ridding society of discrimination and bigotry, as the following case demonstrates.

39.1 HEART OF ATLANTA MOTEL, INC. v. UNITED STATES 379 U.S. 241 (1964)

FACTS The Heart of Atlanta Motel, Inc., had a policy of refusing service to blacks. The federal government challenged this policy as a violation of Title II of the Civil Rights Act of 1964, which prohibits racial, religious, or national origin discrimination by those who offer public accommodations. The government argued that the motel was involved in interstate commerce and that federal intervention therefore was justifiable. The motel argued that it was a purely intrastate business and hence exempt from federal regulation under Title II.

ISSUE Was the motel involved in interstate commerce and therefore subject to federal regulation?

HOLDING Yes. Because the motel served interstate travelers, it was involved in interstate commerce.

REASONING The motel was readily accessible from two interstate highways. It also advertised in national magazines and placed billboards on federal highways. Approximately 75 percent of its guests came from outside the state of Georgia. To allow such discrimination would discourage travel by the black community. The motel was set up to serve interstate travelers; it drew much of its business from interstate travelers; and it was involved in interstate commerce. Hence, Title II gave the government authority to prohibit Heart of Atlanta Motel, Inc.'s discriminatory practice of renting rooms only to white people.

BUSINESS CONSIDERATIONS The legalities aside, why does it make no sense for a business to engage in prejudicial behavior toward members of the public? What steps—if any—should a firm take if it discerns that members of its staff exhibit bigotry toward the firm's clientele?

ETHICAL CONSIDERATIONS What ethical considerations are raised by the facts in this case? In deciding it, did the Court issue an opinion that was both ethical *and* legal?

Exclusive Federal Power

Early on, court constructions viewed three areas as exclusive enclaves of federal regulation: commerce with foreign nations, commercial activities involving Indian tribes (that is, Native Americans), and commerce between the states (that is, interstate commerce). Courts generally have recognized that Congress enjoys **plenary** power over foreign commerce or trade. For instance, the state of Washington does

Plenary
Full; complete; absolute.

not have the authority to sign a treaty regulating tuna-fishing rights with Japan or Canada; only Congress has such power.

Similarly, owing to the unique status that Native Americans have occupied in United States history, only Congress has the power to regulate such commerce. Congress's plenary power in this area stems from the quasi-sovereign status that historically has been accorded to Native American tribes. As such, Native American tribes have virtually complete control over their own reservations and land; the states have little say over reservation affairs. Federal law generally preempts even state or local regulation of off-reservation activities.

As we noted earlier, the phrase "among the several states" has spawned a great deal of litigation concerning when federal power over interstate commerce is plenary. Precedents over the years have established two such areas: (1) Congress's power to regulate the channels and facilities of interstate commerce and (2) Congress's power to regulate activities originating in a single state that have a national economic effect. Under this first prong, Congress can regulate interstate carriers, roads, television and radio stations, and so on. Congress also has the power to exclude from such interstate channels or facilities the goods, persons, or services designated by Congress as harmful to interstate commerce. Congress, then, under this federal police power, can stop the interstate shipment of stolen vehicles, diseased animals, spoiled meat, fungi-ridden fruit, or defective products. Businesses so affected can do little to challenge this exercise of federal power. Besides the channels or facilities of interstate commerce, Congress has plenary power to regulate all commerce or activity that affects more than one state. Note that even intrastate commerce may be subject to such federal control if the intrastate activity has a "substantial effect" on interstate commerce or if Congress rationally could conclude that the activity in question affects interstate commerce.

As the *Heart of Atlanta Motel* case indicates, it takes very little commercial activity to trigger the application of this federal power over commerce. To illustrate, in *Burbank* v. *Lockheed Air Terminal, Inc.*, the Supreme Court struck down a local ordinance that prohibited jet airplane takeoffs during specified hours (11:00 P.M. to 7:00 A.M. local time).[8] The Court invalidated this ordinance because of the need for national uniformity in airplane flight patterns (having this airport "off limits" for several hours could create clogs in air traffic) and because federal law, in the form of agencies concerned with aeronautical and environmental matters, preempted such local or state initiatives.

Clearly, though, this federal power is not boundless. For example, in *U.S.* v. *Lopez*, the Supreme Court invalidated a federal law that had made it a federal criminal offense for anyone to possess a firearm in a school zone.[9] The Court held that the act exceeds Congress's authority under the commerce clause. Why? The possession of a gun in a local school zone in no sense constitutes an economic activity that might, through repetition elsewhere, have a substantial effect on interstate commerce. The Court viewed the argument that possession of firearms in a school zone could lead to violent crime, which, in turn, would hurt the national economy by (1) increasing the costs associated with violent crime; (2) reducing people's willingness to travel to areas they deem unsafe; and (3) threatening the learning environment, which would lead to poorly educated citizens, as demonstrating too tenuous a nexus to interstate commerce for the Court to sustain the law. Although not a business case, this decision may affect business in the future; the decision seems to cut back on 60 years of Supreme Court precedents that had shown broad deference to congressional authority to regulate activities that arguably affect interstate commerce.

Concurrent State Power

In our interdependent domestic economy, virtually all businesses vie for market shares with similar firms in other states. Consequently, Congress's sweeping power to regulate commerce seems practically absolute.

Yet the states enjoy concurrent power with the federal government as to the regulation of commerce within the state. Just as the federal government wishes to promote the welfare of its citizens, so does each state. Hence, state regulation of economic matters is permissible as long as the regulation in question passes muster under a so-called "balancing" test that compares the burdens on interstate commerce caused by the regulation and the importance of the state interest that underlies the regulation.

Therefore, courts generally uphold valid state initiatives in furtherance of local health and safety measures that do not purport merely to protect local economic interests. For example, state regulation of milk products that involves testing or certification of the milk will survive a legal challenge based on the commerce clause unless the state regime discriminates in favor of in-state producers (that is, "local yokels") to the detriment of out-of-state producers and/or the costs of compliance, when compared with the putative benefits of the law, impose an unreasonable, or undue, burden on interstate commerce. In the absence of discrimination against out-of-state firms or the imposition of an undue burden, the states have concurrent power to regulate commerce.

The state's concurrent power to regulate commerce ceases, however, if the state regulation conflicts with federal law. As you may remember, the supremacy clause of Article VI of the Constitution invalidates such state legislation. If Congress expressly prohibits state regulation in a given area or if federal law impliedly preempts the regulatory area, federal law supersedes the state's power to regulate as well.

State powers of taxation can pose special problems under the commerce clause because the states' legitimate interest in increasing their revenues by taxing business entities may burden interstate commerce. As we will see later, such discriminatory taxes, in addition to violating the commerce clause, may pose due process and equal protection problems, too. Although Congress, pursuant to the commerce clause, can authorize or prohibit state taxation that affects interstate commerce, in the absence of such federal legislation, the states can tax corporations and other business entities.

State tax laws that single out—that is, discriminate against—interstate commerce usually violate the commerce clause. Nondiscriminatory taxation schemes—schemes that impose the same type of tax on local business or commerce as imposed on interstate entities—require courts to employ a "balancing" test in which they weigh the state's need for additional revenue against the burden imposed on interstate commerce by such taxes. Although entities of interstate commerce do not remain immune from paying state taxes, such businesses need only pay their fair share; taxation that amounts to undue burdens, unfair discrimination, or multiple taxation generally does not survive challenges brought under the commerce clause (and perhaps not under the due process clause, either).

For a state tax to be legal under the commerce clause, it must be applied to an activity that has a substantial *nexus* (or connection) with the taxing state; it must be fairly apportioned; it must not discriminate against interstate commerce; and it must be fairly related to the services provided by the state. Many courts then look at whether certain *minimum contacts* exist between the person, entity, or transaction taxed and the state levying the tax. If such state *jurisdiction* seems lacking, a violation of due process may have occurred.

Most of the precedents in this area involve state legislative schemes that tax goods shipped in interstate commerce; taxes imposed on firms doing business in a given state; and highway, airport, sales, and use taxes. As a businessperson, you therefore should recognize the possible legal issues that inhere in such state tax laws.

Exclusive State Power

The state's plenary power to regulate commerce covers purely local activities that only remotely affect other states. Given the interdependent nature of our economy and the Supreme Court precedents we have discussed, the instances in which a state has exclusive power over commerce remain comparatively rare.

Facial
Void on its face; totally invalid.

Exhibit 39.1 (p. 1004) provides a useful framework for understanding the analysis courts employ during their disposition of a challenge based on the commerce clause.

Using the foregoing principles, analyze *Chemical Waste Management, Inc.* v. *Hunt.*

39.2 CHEMICAL WASTE MANAGEMENT, INC. v. HUNT — 504 U.S. 334 (1992)

FACTS Chemical Waste Management, Inc. (CWMI), a Delaware corporation with its principal place of business in Oak Brook, Illinois, owns and operates one of the nation's oldest commercial hazardous waste treatment, storage, and land-disposal facilities, located in Emelle, Alabama. Opened in 1977 and acquired by CWMI in 1978, the Emelle facility operates pursuant to permits issued by the U.S. Environmental Protection Agency (EPA) under the Resource Conservation and Recovery Act of 1976 (RCRA) and the Toxic Substances Control Act and by the state of Alabama. Alabama is one of only 16 states that have commercial hazardous waste landfills, and the Emelle facility is the largest of the 21 landfills of this kind located in these 16 states. The wastes and substances being landfilled at the Emelle facility include substances that are inherently dangerous to human health and safety and to the environment. From 1985 to 1989, the tonnage of hazardous waste received per year more than doubled, increasing from 341,000 tons in 1985 to 788,000 tons by 1989. Of this, up to 90 percent of the tonnage permanently buried each year is shipped in from other states. Against this backdrop, Alabama enacted legislation that, among other provisions, included a cap that generally limits the amount of hazardous wastes or substances that may be disposed of in any one-year period. Moreover, the amount of hazardous waste disposed of during the first year under the act's new fees becomes the permanent ceiling in subsequent years. The cap applies to commercial facilities that dispose of more than 100,000 tons of hazardous wastes or substances per year, but only the Emelle facility meets this description. The act also imposes a base fee (of $25.60 per ton on all hazardous wastes and substances to be disposed of at commercial facilities) that the operator of the facility must pay. Finally, the act imposes the additional fee at issue here: "For waste and substances which are generated outside of Alabama and disposed of at a commercial [disposal site] in Alabama, an additional fee shall be levied at the rate of $72.00 per ton." Filing suit in state court, CWMI requested declatory relief and sought to enjoin the enforcement of the act. In addition to its state law claims, CWMI contended that the act violated the commerce, due process, and equal protection clauses of the U.S. Constitution and was preempted by various federal statutes. The trial court declared the base fee and the cap provisions of the act valid and constitutional; but, finding the only basis for the additional fee to be the origin of the waste, the trial court declared this latter fee to be in violation of the commerce clause. The Alabama supreme court affirmed the rulings concerning the base fee and cap provisions but reversed the decision regarding the additional fee. The court held that the fee at issue advanced legitimate local purposes that could not be adequately served by reasonable nondiscriminatory alternatives and therefore was valid under the commerce clause. The U.S. Supreme Court granted certiorari limited to CWMI's commerce clause challenge to the additional fee.

ISSUE Did the Alabama statute that imposed an additional fee on all hazardous waste generated outside of Al-

39.2 CHEMICAL WASTE MANAGEMENT, INC. v. HUNT *(cont.)* 504 U.S. 334 (1992)

abama and disposed of at Alabama facilities violate the commerce clause?

HOLDING Yes. The Alabama statute in question represented economic protectionism that discriminates against out-of-state commerce and violates the commerce clause.

REASONING No state, by raising barriers to the free flow of interstate trade, may attempt to isolate itself from a problem common to several states. The Supreme Court consistently has found parochial legislation of this kind to be constitutionally invalid, whether the ultimate aim of the legislation is, by erecting barriers to allegedly ruinous outside competition, to assure a steady supply of milk; by keeping industry within the state to create jobs; or, by fencing out indigent immigrants, to preserve the state's financial resources from depletion. To this list may be added cases striking down a tax discriminating against interstate commerce, even where such a tax was designed to encourage the use of ethanol and thereby reduce harmful exhaust emissions, or to support inspection of foreign cement to ensure structural integrity. In all these cases, the legislation sought, by the illegitimate means of isolating the state economy, to achieve presumably legitimate goals. The act's additional fee represents **facial** discrimination against hazardous waste generated in states other than Alabama, and the act overall plainly has discouraged the full operation of CWMI's Emelle facility. Such burdensome taxes imposed on interstate commerce alone generally are forbidden, since a state may not tax a transaction or incident more heavily when it crosses state lines than when it occurs entirely within the state. The state, however, argued that the additional fee imposed on out-of-state hazardous waste serves legitimate local purposes related to its citizens' health and safety. At a minimum, such facial discrimination invokes the strictest scrutiny of any purported legitimate local purpose and of the absence of nondiscriminatory alternatives. The state proffered four legitimate local purposes that it argued could not be adequately served by nondiscriminatory alternatives: (1) protection of the health and safety of the citizens of Alabama from toxic substances; (2) conservation of the environment and the state's natural resources; (3) provision for compensatory revenues for the costs and burdens that out-of-state waste generators impose when these firms dump their hazardous waste in Alabama; and (4) reduction of the overall flow of wastes traveling on the state's highways, which creates a great risk to the health and safety of the state's citizens. But, as found by the trial court, "there is absolutely no evidence that waste generated outside Alabama is more dangerous than waste generated in Alabama. . . . [T]he only basis for the additional fee [of $72.00 per ton] is the [out-of-state] origin of the waste." Given such findings, invalidity under the commerce clause necessarily follows; for whatever Alabama's ultimate purpose, it may not be accomplished by discriminating against articles of commerce coming from outside the state unless there is some reason, apart from their origin, to treat them differently. In short, the burden is on the state to show that the discrimination demonstrably is justified by a valid factor unrelated to economic protectionism. Less discriminatory alternatives, however, are available to alleviate this concern, not the least of which is a generally applicable per-ton additional fee on all hazardous waste disposed of within Alabama or a per-mile tax on all vehicles transporting hazardous wastes across Alabama roads or an evenhanded cap on the total tonnage landfilled at Emelle, which would curtail the volume from all sources. In sum, the additional fee clearly is impermissible under the commerce clause of the Constitution. Moreover, Supreme Court decisions regarding quarantine laws do not counsel a different conclusion. While it is true that the Court has not viewed certain quarantine laws as forbidden protectionist measures, even though directed against out-of-state commerce, those laws refrained from discriminating against interstate commerce as such and simply prevented traffic in noxious articles, whatever their origin. However, the record establishes that the hazardous waste at issue in this case is the same regardless of its point of origin. Because no unique threat is posed and because adequate means other than overt discrimination meet Alabama's concerns, the state's legislative scheme is unconstitutional. Accordingly, the decision of the Alabama supreme court is reversed.

BUSINESS CONSIDERATIONS The problem of hazardous waste has galvanized a lot of states into resisting the storage or disposal of such waste on sites in their states. Other states have vied for the opportunity to engage in the disposal of chemical, atomic, and other hazardous waste. What factors should a state take into account when it makes the decision either to resist this type of business activity or to seek it out?

ETHICAL CONSIDERATIONS Do firms that engage in the disposal of hazardous wastes have a heightened ethical responsibility to evaluate (through pre-hire disclosures and continuous monitoring [via blood tests, for example]) the health and well-being of each and every employee? Why or why not?

EXHIBIT 39.1 Commerce Clause Analysis

I. Areas of Exclusive Federal Regulation
   A. Commerce with foreign nations
   B. Commerce involving Indian tribes (that is, Native Americans)
   C. Commerce involving the channels and facilities of interstate commerce
   D. Commerce that is interstate in nature or that originates in a single state but that has a "substantial effect" on interstate commerce
   E. Commerce where Congress has prohibited state regulation or where federal law impliedly preempts the regulatory area

II. Areas of Concurrent Federal and State Regulation
   A. "Balancing" test employed: The burdens on interstate commerce compared to the importance of the state interest underlying the state regulation
   B. State initiatives in furtherance of the state's "police power" (that is, the promotion of the general welfare of the state's citizens) generally permissible unless:
      1. The state regulation imposes an undue, or unreasonable, burden on interstate commerce
      2. The state regulation discriminates in favor of in-state firms and against out-of-state firms
      3. The state regulation conflicts with federal law and thus is invalidated by the supremacy clause

III. Areas of Exclusive State Regulation
   A. Purely local activities with remote effects on other states' commerce

THE EQUAL PROTECTION CLAUSE

Another constitutional provision that acts as a curb on the government's power to regulate business is the equal protection clause. The Fourteenth Amendment states: "[n]or shall any State . . . deny to any person within its jurisdiction the equal protection of the laws." Supreme Court precedents have determined that in most situations the Fifth Amendment's due process clause provides that the *federal* government must guarantee equal protection to all persons as well. Basically, this guarantee means that when the government classifies people, it must treat similarly situated people similarly. In recent years, courts have used the equal protection clause to protect a broad panoply of individual rights. Yet this provision also limits the types of regulations government can impose on businesses.

Invidious
Repugnant; discrimination stemming from bigotry or prejudice.

Whether applied to the protection of individuals' civil rights or businesses' rights, the equal protection clause protects individuals and other entities only from **invidious** discrimination. What constitutes invidious discrimination? All governmental statutes and regulations classify (or discriminate) among groups. This kind of discrimination—mere differentiation—does not necessarily implicate the equal protection clause, however. For example, when the government says professionals or businesses must secure licenses, the government is differentiating (discriminating) among people who need such licenses as a prerequisite for doing business and those who do not. But such differentiation per se does not constitute the discrimination banned by the equal protection clause. Only when such differentiation stems from prejudice, bigotry, or stereotyping on racial, ethnic, gender, or similar bases does illegal discrimination result.

The equal protection clause also prohibits only discrimination that derives from governmental (that is, so-called state) action; it does not reach actions taken by private individuals. Hence, under this clause, one can challenge only those actions taken by federal and state governments (or by any subdivisions or agencies thereof) pursuant to enacted laws or regulations.

Over the years, the Supreme Court has developed various tests for determining the legality of economic regulations challenged under the equal protection clause. Under each of these three possible tests, courts will review the legislative classification at issue with regard to the "fit" that exists between the means the legislative body has used to accomplish a desired end, or objective, and the impact it has on the people affected by the legislation.

Insular
Isolated from others.

Level 1: The Rational Basis Test

Under the traditional, or so-called rational basis, test, the government can distinguish among similarly situated persons if the statutory scheme—or classification—is rationally related to a legitimate state interest (or aim). Courts generally do not second-guess legislators' intent. Courts thus presume that the regulation is valid unless no conceivable justification exists for the law. Simply put, courts allow governmental entities wide latitude when, pursuant to their police power, these regulators enact social and economic regulations; courts only rarely invalidate such measures.

Level 2: The "Compelling State Interest" Test

If a regulatory measure involves invidious discrimination—that is, intentional discrimination against certain racial or ethnic groups—or certain fundamental rights, courts initially will presume such regulations are invalid. Courts will apply strict scrutiny to all such legislation and uphold only those measures necessary to accomplish a compelling state interest. In these instances, the regulating body must show that no alternative, less burdensome ways exist to accomplish the state objective or goal. Regulators only occasionally have successfully justified this type of legislation.

Over the years, the Supreme Court has held that laws that impinge on so-called "suspect" classifications and thus burden the rights of African-Americans, Hispanics, and Asian-Americans must meet this compelling state interest standard. The Court has protected these groups from the application of such laws because these groups represent discrete, **insular** minorities whom other citizens view as unassimilable into American society and whom the government may easily identify because of the groups' immutable physical characteristics.

39.1

CHALLENGING AN APPARENTLY UNCONSTITUTIONAL LAW

The Kochanowskis have recently learned that the federal government has enacted a law requiring all new telecommunication devices to provide auxilliary peripheral devices to better serve users who are disabled. This new law does not apply to any telecommunication devices that were available on the market last year (the year before CIT was established). In order to comply with the law, CIT will need to greatly enhance the audio and visual components, at a significant increase in cost per unit. The family members view this law as unconstitutional and wish to challenge it. The family asks you for your advice in this matter. What will you advise them?

BUSINESS CONSIDERATIONS How should a business react to a proposed change in the law that will affect its current business practices? Should the business immediately begin implementation of methods for complying with the new law, or should the business try to take steps to prevent or delay the effective date of the new law?

ETHICAL CONSIDERATIONS Is it ethical for the government to enact laws that apply to all customers in order to provide needed benefits or protections for a small number who require special accommodations in order to utilize the products covered? Would it be more ethical for the government to refrain from requiring such accommodations, thereby leaving some members of society unable to receive benefits generally available within society?

MANAGEMENT

Disenfranchised
Restricted from enjoying certain constitutional or statutory rights; burdened by systemic prejudice or bigotry.

In order to justify the singling out of such **disenfranchised** groups, the entity enacting the legislation must satisfy the compelling state interest (or level 2) test and the strict scrutiny approach that a court must apply to the law. For example, *Yick Wo* v. *Hopkins* involved a denial of a permit to operate a laundry business.[10] Since all 199 non-Chinese permit seekers had been granted the permit, the egregious denial of the license to Yick Wo, the only Chinese applicant, violated the Fourteenth Amendment. Given the systemic prejudice against Chinese people at the time because of the widely held view that the Chinese were unworthy of citizenship, Yick Wo was a member of a discrete, insular minority who had suffered historical disenfranchisement. His immutable physical characteristics—the shape of his eyes and his skin color, for example—also made him more easily identified and singled out by the government. The city council could not show that its denial of Yick Wo's permit represented the only means of accomplishing the state interest (avoidance of fire hazards) involved here; hence, the city council had failed to show that its treatment of Yick Wo passed muster under the compelling state interest test.

Citing *Yick Wo* v. *Hopkins* and upholding its underlying predicates, the Supreme Court recently—in *Romer* v. *Evans*—held as violative of the equal protection clause a referendum-based amendment to the Colorado state constitution that prohibited all legislative, executive, or judicial action at any level of state or local government designed to protect homosexual persons from discrimination.[11] Finding that the amendment was a status-based enactment divorced from any factual context from which the Court could discern a relationship to a legitimate state interest, the Court concluded that the amendment instead "classifie[d] homosexuals not to further a proper legislative end but to make them unequal to everyone else. This Colorado cannot do. A state [under the equal protection clause] cannot so deem a class of persons a stranger to its laws."[12]

Note that if the facts were different in the *Yick Wo* v. *Hopkins* case and that if all 199 Chinese had obtained their permits and the lone unsuccessful applicant had been white, he presumably could sue under the Fourteenth Amendment for "reverse discrimination." The Supreme Court since 1989 has said that "benign" racial classifications used by the government for affirmative action purposes (for example, a city's deciding to award a certain percentage of city contracts to minority-owned businesses because of the city's desire to correct societal discrimination) will be judged under the strict scrutiny/compelling state interest test as well. *Adarand Constructors, Inc.* v. *Pena,* which involved a challenge to a federal program that granted preferential treatment to minority subcontractors, reinforces this 1989 holding.[13]

In *Adarand,* the Supreme Court held that reviewing courts must subject all racial classifications, imposed by whatever federal, state, or local governmental entity, to the strict scrutiny standard. This case makes it clear that federal racial classifications, like those set up by a state, must serve a compelling governmental interest and must be narrowly tailored to further that interest. Under this standard, only affirmative action plans that respond to specific, provable past discrimination and that are narrowly tailored to eliminate such bias would be legal. Although the Court acknowledged that, practically speaking, it will be hard for the government to meet this test, the Court did not view its decision as dealing a fatal blow to the vast network of federal affirmative action programs that presently exist. Many commentators, however, believe this decision will bring on an avalanche of court challenges to governmental minority preference programs and will fuel the growing political backlash against affirmative action efforts.

Just as the equal protection clause prohibits virtually all legislation that burdens a suspect classification, it also subjects to the compelling state interest test any governmental action that penalizes or unduly burdens a *fundamental right* (that is, rights expressly or impliedly guaranteed in the Constitution). The Supreme Court has struck down laws that forbade a drugstore's selling birth control devices and a doctor's discussing birth control issues with his patients. The Court believed these laws implicate the right of privacy, interpreted by the Court as encompassing the marital relationship and procreation. Similarly, in our earlier example, had Yick Wo been a Presbyterian and the only unsuccessful applicant, he could have argued that the city council's prior, publicly articulated, anti-Presbyterian sentiments led to the penalizing of his First Amendment right of freedom of religion.

Intermediate Level: The Substantially Important State Interest Test

In the 1970s, the Supreme Court flirted with the idea of placing gender-based laws under level 2 analysis, particularly if the challenged legislative enactment unduly burdened women. At that time, many commentators argued that, first, women represent a discrete, insular minority owing to their belated receipt of the right to vote, the existence of Married Women's Property Acts that denied women the capacity to contract, and so on. Second, women represent a group who manifests immutable physical characteristics; in other words, women's secondary sex characteristics ordinarily distinguish women from men and vice versa.

While the Court never accepted these arguments—apparently it believed the discrimination caused by gender-based laws failed to rise to the level of invidiousness found in most level 2 cases—the Court carved out an intermediate tier of analysis for decision makers to use in evaluating challenges to gender-based laws. Accordingly, although classifications based on gender are not "suspect," they deserve more judicial attention than classifications judged under the level 1, rational basis test. Hence, the Court formulated an intermediate tier of analysis and placed classifications based on gender in this "quasi-suspect" classification.

Statutory schemes that encompass quasi-suspect classifications must be "substantially related to an important state interest." If the enacting body cannot meet this test, courts will invalidate the legislation. Thus, older laws that prohibited women from entering certain occupations (say, becoming a barber) nowadays would be decided under this intermediate tier of analysis. Similarly, if Yick Wo had been a woman and the city council's ordinance had said no woman can obtain a permit, the city council would need to show that its prohibition against women advanced a substantially important governmental objective. Otherwise, the ordinance would violate the equal protection clause. Note that men are protected from burdensome laws as well. In *Craig* v. *Boren*, the Supreme Court invalidated an Oklahoma law that allowed females to drink beer at age 18 but prohibited males from drinking beer until age 21.[14]

Relying on these precedents, the Supreme Court recently held that the exclusion of women by the Virginia Military Institute (VMI) violated the equal protection clause. The Court characterized VMI's argument that the alterations to its "adversative" method of training that would be necessary to accommodate women would be so drastic as to destroy VMI's program and its mission to produce "citizen-soldiers" as falling well short of the showing necessary to justify the classification as "substantially related to an important state interest."

Use *City of Dallas* v. *Stanglin* to check your understanding of the equal protection clause.

39.3 CITY OF DALLAS v. STANGLIN 490 U.S. 19 (1989)

FACTS In 1985, the city of Dallas authorized the licensing of "Class E" dance halls to provide a place where younger teenagers could socialize with each other but not be subject to the potentially detrimental influences of older teenagers and young adults. The ordinance restricted admission to Class E dance halls to persons between the ages of fourteen and eighteen. Parents, guardians, law enforcement, and dance hall personnel were excepted from the ordinance's age restriction. The ordinance also limited the hours of operation of Class E dance halls to between 1 P.M. and midnight daily when school was not in session. Charles M. Stanglin operated the Twilight Skating Rink in Dallas and obtained a license for a Class E dance hall. Using movable plastic cones or pylons, he divided the floor of his roller-skating rink into two sections. On one side of the pylons, persons between the ages of fourteen and eighteen dance, while on the other side, persons of all ages skate to the same music. No age or hour restrictions applied to the skating rink. Stanglin did not serve alcohol on the premises, and security personnel were present. Stanglin sued in district court to enjoin enforcement of the age and hour restrictions of the ordinance. He contended that the ordinance violated substantive due process and equal protection under the United States and Texas constitutions and that it unconstitutionally infringed the rights of persons between the ages of fourteen and eighteen to associate with persons outside that age bracket. The trial court, in upholding the ordinance, found that it was rationally related to the city's legitimate interest in ensuring the safety and welfare of children. The Texas court of appeals upheld the ordinance's time restriction, but it struck down the age restriction as violative of the First Amendment associational rights of minors. To support a restriction on the fundamental right of "social association," the court said, "the legislative body must show a compelling interest"; and the regulation "must be accomplished by the least restrictive means." The court recognized the city's interest in "protect[ing] minors from detrimental, corrupting influences," but held that the "[c]ity's stated purposes . . . may be achieved in ways that are less intrusive on minors' freedom to associate." The United States Supreme Court granted certiorari.

ISSUES Did the Dallas ordinance violate any constitutional right of association? Did a rational relationship exist between the ordinance's age restriction and the city's interests?

HOLDINGS No. The Dallas ordinance did not infringe on any constitutionally protected right. Yes. The ordinance served as a rational measure for the furtherance of governmental interests.

REASONING The dispositive question in this case is the level of judicial scrutiny to be applied to the city's ordinance. Unless laws create suspect classifications or impinge upon constitutionally protected rights, it need only be shown that they bear "some rational relationship to a legitimate state purpose." Stanglin does not contend that dance hall patrons are a "suspect classification," but he does urge that the ordinance in question interferes with such patrons' associational rights guaranteed by the First Amendment. While the First Amendment does not in its terms protect a "right of association," Supreme Court precedents have recognized that it embraces such a right in certain circumstances. First, choices to enter into and maintain certain intimate human relationships must be secured against undue intrusion by the state because of the role of such relationships in safeguarding the individual freedom that is central to our constitutional scheme. In this respect, freedom of association receives protection as a fundamental element of personal liberty. Second, the Court has recognized the right to associate for the purpose of engaging in those activities protected by the First Amendment—speech, assembly, petition for redress of grievances, and the exercise of religion. It is clear that dance hall patrons, who may number 1,000 on any given night, are not engaged in "intimate human relationships." The Texas court of appeals, however, erroneously thought that such patrons were engaged in a form of expressive activity protected by the First Amendment. The Dallas ordinance restricts minors between the ages of fourteen and eighteen and certain excepted adults from dancing. These opportunities might be described in common parlance as "associational," but they simply do not involve the sort of expressive association that the First Amendment protects. Thus, this activity involving hundreds of teenagers at this particular dance hall qualifies neither as a form of "intimate association" nor as a form of "expressive association" as earlier Supreme Court precedents have described those terms. The Dallas ordinance therefore implicates no suspect class. The ordinance moreover impinges on no constitutionally protected rights. The question remaining is whether the classification engaged in by the city survives "rational basis" scrutiny under the equal protection clause. As earlier Supreme Court precedents have held:

> *[A] state does not violate the [e]qual [p]rotection [c]lause merely because the classifications made by its laws are imperfect. If the classification has some 'reasonable basis,' it does not offend the Constitution simply because the classification [fails to rise to a] mathematical nicety or because in practice it results in some inequality. . . . [The rational basis standard] is true to the princi-*

39.3 CITY OF DALLAS v. STANGLIN *(cont.)* **490 U.S. 19 (1989)**

ple that the Fourteenth Amendment gives the federal courts no power to impose upon the states the [courts'] views of what constitutes wise economic or social policy.

Similar considerations support the age restriction at issue here, for in the local economic sphere, it is only the invidious discrimination, the wholly arbitrary act, that cannot stand consistently with the Fourteenth Amendment. The city reasonably could conclude that teenagers might be susceptible to corrupting influences if permitted, unaccompanied by parents, to frequent a dance hall with older persons. The city properly could conclude that limiting dance hall contacts between juveniles and adults would make less likely illicit or undesirable juvenile involvement with alcohol, illegal drugs, and promiscuous sex. Consequently, the Dallas ordinance does not infringe on any constitutionally protected right of association; and a rational relationship exists between the age restriction for Class E dance halls and the city's interest in promoting the welfare of teenagers. The judgment of the court of appeals therefore is reversed.

BUSINESS CONSIDERATIONS Some businesses—particularly shopping malls—have instituted policies that regulate the conditions under which individuals below a certain age can have access to business premises. Why have such businesses established these regulations? What advantages and disadvantages inhere in these rules for the businesses that established the rules?

ETHICAL CONSIDERATIONS Is it ethical for businesses to attempt to discourage certain segments of the community (for example, teenagers unaccompanied by their parents, the homeless, and the like) from patronizing the firms' establishments?

THE DUE PROCESS CLAUSE

Besides guaranteeing equal protection, both the Fifth and Fourteenth Amendments protect against deprivations of "life, liberty, or property without due process of law." You probably associate the due process clause with individual rights, and perhaps specifically with the protection of criminals, as mentioned in Chapter 8. Hence, the government cannot deprive us of our lives (for example, by subjecting us to capital punishment) without according us due process. Similarly, the government cannot deprive us of liberty—interpreted by the Court to include one's freedom from physical restraints imposed without due process and in noncriminal contexts to include such issues as involuntary commitments to mental institutions. In the context of business, the term *liberty* also encompasses the right to contract and to engage in gainful employment.

Still, the life and liberty components of the due process clause fade in importance when compared with the property dimension of the provision. The Supreme Court has found few interpretive problems inherent in this third prong of the clause, perhaps because most of us more intuitively understand the concept *property* than we do the intangible concept *liberty*. Thus, the Court not surprisingly has construed the word *property* to include ownership of real estate, personal property, and money; but the Court also has extended the term *property* to entitlements to specific benefits set out under applicable state or federal law. Hence, if state action deprives us of property rights such as public employment, public education, continuing welfare benefits, or continuing public utility services, that deprivation cannot constitutionally occur in the absence of due process. The due process required by notions of fundamental fairness involves two dimensions: procedural protections and substantive considerations.

Procedural Due Process

Before the government can deprive one of life, liberty, or property, one usually must be afforded some kind of hearing. Such hearings generally require notice to the aggrieved party, an opportunity for that person to present his or her side of the story, and an impartial decisionmaker. The government ordinarily can refrain from providing counsel, because counsel usually is not constitutionally required as is the case with indigent criminal defendants. The applicable rules and regulations, however, oftentimes allow counsel to be present. The timing of the hearing—whether it must occur before or after the deprivation of a protected interest—and the extent of the procedural safeguards afforded to the affected individual vary.

Courts generally balance the individual interests involved with the governmental interest in fiscal and administrative efficiency. Prior Supreme Court precedents have held that a hearing must precede, for example, the termination of welfare benefits, the government's seizure and forfeiture of real estate allegedly used in connection with the commission of crimes, termination of public employment, and prejudgment garnishment of wages (a concept discussed in Chapter 30). Evidentiary hearings prior to the termination of benefits need not occur in situations involving disability benefits, some terminations of parental rights, and some license suspensions (for example, failure to take a Breathalyzer test); but postsuspension hearings may be required in such circumstances.

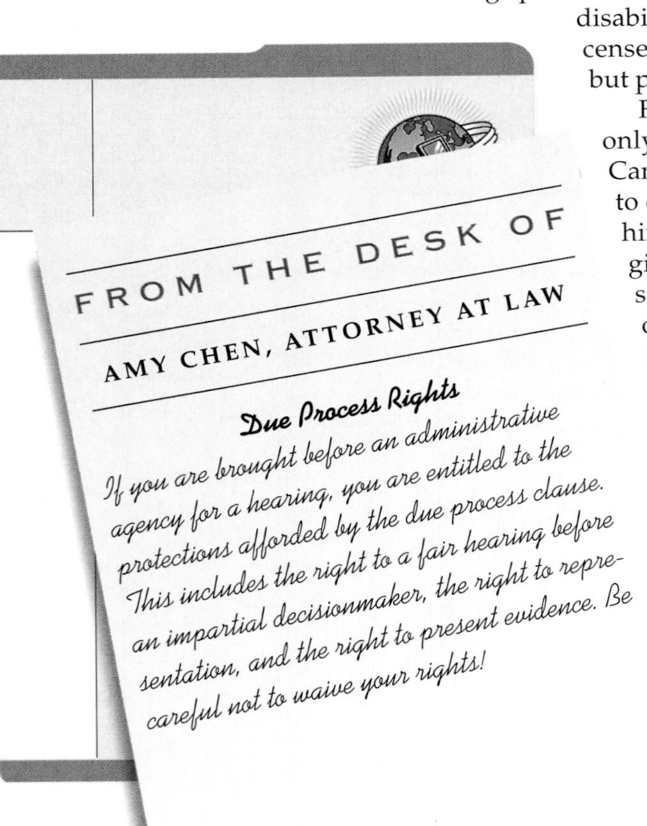

FROM THE DESK OF
AMY CHEN, ATTORNEY AT LAW
Due Process Rights
If you are brought before an administrative agency for a hearing, you are entitled to the protections afforded by the due process clause. This includes the right to a fair hearing before an impartial decisionmaker, the right to representation, and the right to present evidence. Be careful not to waive your rights!

For example, assume a state passes a law saying women can cut only women's hair and men can cut only men's hair. Patrick McCann, who runs a unisex barber shop, flouts the law and continues to cut women's hair. The state licensing board in response notifies him that it plans to revoke his license (state action has occurred), gives him a hearing in which he has an opportunity to present his side of the dispute, and convenes a panel (probably made up of other licensed barbers) that has no apparent biases against McCann. With these procedural steps taken against him, McCann ordinarily will not be able to use the due process clause to challenge the subsequent revocation of his license; the hearing he received apparently fulfilled the requirements of *procedural* due process.

Substantive Due Process

The substantive aspects of due process, however, may hold more promise for McCann. The *substantive* dimension of due process focuses not on providing fundamentally fair procedures but on the content, or the subject matter, of the law. One deprived of life, liberty, or property under arbitrary, irrational, and capricious social or economic laws may challenge such losses under the due process clause. In short, under substantive due process principles, a regulation is invalid if it fails to advance a legitimate governmental interest or if it constitutes an unreasonable means of advancing a legitimate governmental interest.

Owing to its overuse in the first 30 years of the twentieth century, courts for many years viewed substantive due process as a discredited constitutional doctrine. In that earlier period, judges, by substituting their personal views for those of the legislatures that had enacted the laws, struck down a whole host of social and economic legislation. In the mid-1930s, however, the resurrection of the theory began. Today, courts generally defer to legislators' judgments regarding social and economic matters and thus presume such laws are valid unless the challenger can persuade the courts that the laws actually are demonstrably arbitrary and irrational. Judicial deference normally leads to the courts' upholding such laws, as we saw earlier in a Chapter 15 case, *Pacific Mutual Life Insurance Co.* v. *Haslip,* where the Supreme Court upheld a jury award of punitive damages and the state's postverdict procedures for reviewing such awards as reasonable.[16]

Since the mid-1960s, the Supreme Court has used substantive due process primarily as a vehicle for protecting certain fundamental personal rights that are implied by constitutional wording and phraseology. Hence, beginning in the mid-1960s, the Court has struck down on grounds of irrationality and arbitrariness state laws making the use of contraceptives by anyone, including married persons, illegal. Such laws impermissibly infringe on the so-called zone of marital privacy protected by the Court. In coming to this result, the Court viewed such legislation in a fashion virtually identical to strict scrutiny and applied something very akin to the compelling state interest test. The liberty component of the due process clause also guarantees a competent person, who has clearly made his or her wishes known beforehand, the right to terminate unwanted medical treatment.[17] Laws holding otherwise can be challenged on substantive due process grounds.

As you studied this section, you probably noticed the complementary relationship between substantive due process and guarantees of equal protection under the law. Both constitutional guarantees mandate a rational fit between the objectives of the law and the group of people affected thereby. When all persons are subject to a law that deprives them of a life, liberty, or property interest, due process probably applies. When a law classifies certain people for certain purposes, the equal protection doctrine probably becomes the appropriate vehicle for challenging the law.

Under either theory, the Supreme Court since the mid-1930s has required judges to give great deference to legislative prerogatives when judges are called upon to review social legislation that does not involve personal fundamental rights. The same is true of economic legislation: Judges should uphold all such legislation unless the challenger can show the absence of any rational relationship to any legitimate governmental aim or interest.

To check your understanding of this section, ask yourself whether Pat McCann, from our earlier

39.2

MANAGEMENT

CHALLENGING LOCAL LAWS

One city in which CIT has opened a retail outlet has announced that a new city ordinance will go into effect in three months. This new ordinance requires all firms selling interactive videophones to have a switch that be used by either party to a conversation to turn off the video transmission. CIT is the only firm that is currently selling interactive videophones in that state, and the family members believe that CIT has been singled out for discriminatory treatment by this ordinance. They ask you what they can or should do under these circumstances. What will you tell them?

BUSINESS CONSIDERATIONS Suppose that a city ordinance makes conducting business in a particular city too difficult or too expensive for a particular firm. Should the firm move its operation out of the city, or should it seek a variance or exemption from the city?

ETHICAL CONSIDERATIONS Is it ethical for a business to pick and choose where it will operate based on local laws or regulations? What ethical considerations will such a decision raise?

example, could challenge his license revocation under substantive due process. Consider, too, whether McCann could sue under the equal protection clause.

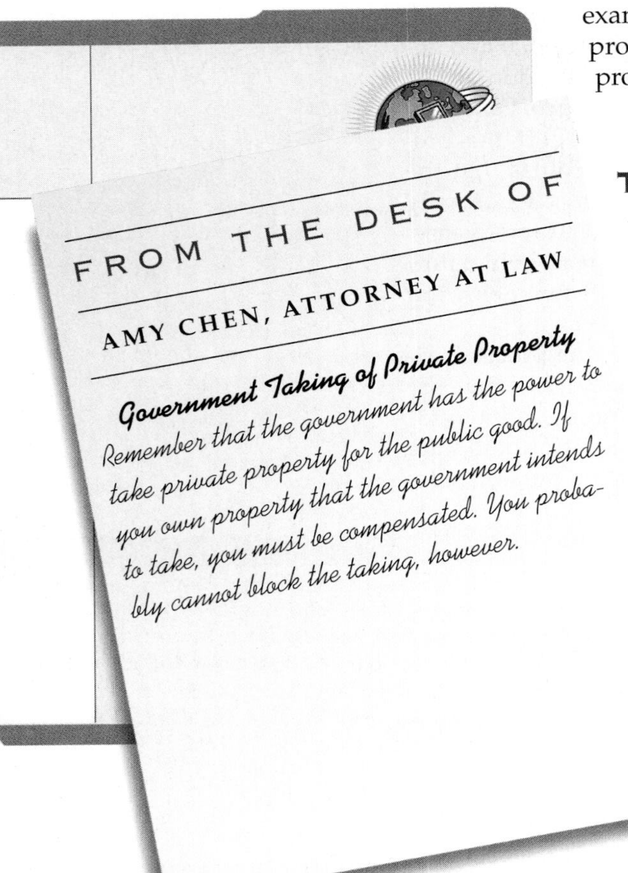

FROM THE DESK OF
AMY CHEN, ATTORNEY AT LAW
Government Taking of Private Property
Remember that the government has the power to take private property for the public good. If you own property that the government intends to take, you must be compensated. You probably cannot block the taking, however.

THE TAKINGS CLAUSE

Besides guaranteeing procedural and substantive due process, the Fifth Amendment also provides that "private property [shall not] be taken for public use, without just compensation." This Fifth Amendment restraint on the power of the federal government moreover applies to the states through the Fourteenth Amendment's due process clause. Under this "takings" clause, the government must take the property for "public use" and must pay "just compensation" to the property owner involved.

In litigation, the disagreement between the parties often centers on whether a *taking* has occurred, in which case the Constitution obligates the government to pay just compensation, or whether the governmental action amounts only to *regulation* under the exercise of its police power, in which case no compensation is owed. While the Court has set out no clear formula for judging when a taking has occurred, any actual appropriation of property will suffice. For example, if the state through formal procedures condemns a business for the purpose of constructing a parking garage on a state college campus, a taking has occurred; and the state will have to pay just compensation to the owner of the property that was razed.

But less-than-complete appropriations of property may suffice as takings as well. For instance, the Court has held that federal dam construction resulting in the repeated flooding of private property and low, direct flights over private property located contiguous to federal or municipal airports constitute takings if the activities in question destroy the property's present use or unreasonably impair the value of the property and the owners' reasonable expectations regarding it.

As the *Lucas* v. *South Carolina Coastal Council* case discussed in Chapter 44 demonstrates, a land use regulation that fails to advance substantially legitimate state interests or that denies an owner the economically viable use of his or her land is a taking subject to the Fifth Amendment.[18] In the absence of such factors, zoning ordinances—the most common type of land use regulations—ordinarily pass muster under the takings clause even if the regulations restrict the use of the property and cause a reduction in its value, so long as the ordinances substantially advance legitimate state interests and do not extinguish fundamental attributes of ownership.

During the attempted taking, the government must afford the affected property owner procedural due process. However, the just compensation paid out by the governmental regulator need reflect only the fair market value of the property; the price paid need not compensate the owner for the sentimental value of the property, the owner's unique need for the property, or the gain the regulating body realizes by virtue of the taking.

Analyze *Dolan* v. *City of Tigard* in light of the principles just discussed.

39.4 DOLAN v. CITY OF TIGARD

512 U.S. 374 (1994)

FACTS The Tigard, Oregon, City Planning Commission conditioned approval of Florence Dolan's application to expand her plumbing and electric supply store and pave her parking lot on her agreeing to dedicate land (1) for a public greenway so as to minimize the Fanno Creek flooding that would result from the increases in the impervious surfaces associated with her development and (2) for a pedestrian/bicycle pathway intended to relieve traffic congestion in the city's central business district. In appealing the Commission's denial of her request for variances from these standards to the Land Use Board of Appeals (LUBA), Dolan alleged that the land dedication requirements were not related to the proposed development and therefore constituted an uncompensated taking of her property under the Fifth Amendment. The LUBA, the state court of appeals, and the state supreme court affirmed the Commission's decision.

ISSUE Did the land dedication requirements imposed on Dolan constitute an unconstitutional taking of her property under the Fifth Amendment?

HOLDING Yes. The city had not shown that it had made an individualized determination that the required dedications related both in nature and extent to the impact of the proposed settlement. The absence of such a connection therefore rendered the city's actions unlawful under the takings clause of the Fifth Amendment.

REASONING The takings clause of the Fifth Amendment of the U.S. Constitution, made applicable to the states through the Fourteenth Amendment, provides: "[N]or shall private property be taken for public use, without just compensation." One of the principal purposes of the takings clause is "to bar Government from forcing some people alone to bear public burdens which, in all fairness and justice, should be borne by the public as a whole." Without question, had the city simply required Dolan to dedicate a strip of land along Fanno Creek for public use, rather than conditioning the grant of her permit to redevelop her property on such a dedication, a taking would have occurred. Such public access would deprive Dolan of the right to exclude others, "one of the most essential sticks in the bundle of rights that are commonly characterized as property." On the other side of the ledger, the authority of state and local governments to engage in land use planning has been sustained against constitutional challenge since 1926. The Supreme Court consistently has held that a land use regulation does not effect a taking if the regulation "substantially advance[s] legitimate state interests" and refrains from denying "an owner the economically viable use of his land." The sort of land use regulations discussed in the Supreme Court precedents just cited, however, differ in two relevant particulars from the present case. First, they involved essentially legislative determinations classifying entire areas of the city, whereas here the city has made an adjudicative decision to condition Dolan's application for a building permit on an individual parcel. Second, the conditions imposed were not simply a limitation on the use Dolan might make of her own parcel, but a requirement that she deed portions of the property to the city. Recent Supreme Court precedents under the Fifth and Fourteenth Amendments circumscribe governmental authority to exact such a condition. Under the well-settled doctrine of unconstitutional conditions, the government lacks the authority to require a person to give up a constitutional right—here, the right to receive just compensation when property is taken for public use—in exchange for a discretionary benefit conferred by the government where the property sought has little or no relationship to the benefit. Apropos of this, Dolan contended that the city has forced her to choose between the building permit and her right under the Fifth Amendment to just compensation for public easements. She argued that the city has failed to identify either any "special benefits" conferred on her or any "special quantifiable burdens" created by her new store that would justify the particular dedications required from her and which are not required from the public at large. In evaluating Dolan's claim, the Court first must determine whether the "essential nexus" exists between the "legitimate state interest" and the permit conditions exacted by the city. If such a nexus exists, the Court then must decide the required degree of connection between the exactions and the projected impact of the proposed developments. The minimization of flooding along Fanno Creek and the reduction of traffic congestion in the central business district qualify as the type of legitimate public purposes upheld by earlier Court decisions. The second part of the analysis requires the Court to determine whether the degree of the exactions demanded by the city's permit conditions bear the required relationship to the projected impact of Dolan's proposed development, since a use restriction may constitute a taking if not reasonably necessary to the effectuation of a substantial government purpose. The states previously have adopted various tests for determining whether the necessary connection between the required dedication and the proposed development suffices for constitutional purposes. But the Court today enunciates a new test: a term such as *rough proportionality* best encapsulates what the Court sees as the requirement of the Fifth Amendment. No precise mathematical calculation is required, but the city must make some sort of individualized determination that the required dedication is related both in nature and in extent to the impact of the proposed development. When one applies this

39.4 DOLAN v. CITY OF TIGARD *(cont.)* 512 U.S. 374 (1994)

test to the city's findings, it becomes apparent that the city's imposition of a permanent recreational easement on Dolan's property that borders Fanno Creek would cause her to lose all her rights to regulate the time in which the public entered onto the city's greenway, regardless of any interference it might impose with regard to her retail store. Her right to exclude would not be regulated; it would be eviscerated. Hence, the findings upon which the city relied do not show the required reasonable relationship between the floodplain easement and Dolan's proposed new building. With respect to the pedestrian/bicycle pathway, the city has not met its burden of demonstrating that the additional number of vehicle and bicycle trips generated by Dolan's development reasonably relates to the city's requirement for a dedication of the pedestrian/bicycle pathway easement. Although no precise mathematical calculation is required, the city must make some effort to quantify its findings in support of the dedication for the pedestrian/bicycle pathway beyond the conclusory statement that the pathway could offset some of the traffic demand generated. The city's failure to meet its burden of proof therefore mandates the reversal of the judgment the supreme court of Oregon previously rendered.

BUSINESS CONSIDERATIONS Was it reasonable for Dolan to expect the city to absorb the adverse effects on the city that arguably would result from Dolan's proposed expansion of her business? How should a business react to a situation in which the business is expected to make a community-benefit "contribution" in exchange for permission to expand or move the business activity?

ETHICAL CONSIDERATIONS If the Court had disposed of this case on ethical—rather than legal—grounds, would its decision have been different? What ethical concerns were raised by this case?

Although we have emphasized only the due process and takings clauses of the Fifth Amendment, as you have learned from earlier chapters, this provision in the Constitution also prohibits *double jeopardy* (being tried twice for the same offense) and compulsory self-incrimination. Thus, the Fifth Amendment's many facets represent an effective curb on illegitimate governmental action taken against individuals or businesses.

THE FIRST AMENDMENT/COMMERCIAL SPEECH

The First Amendment, as you remember, protects individual freedom of speech. Businesses, however, as legal (or *juristic*) persons, arguably enjoy protectable First Amendment rights as well. Indeed, commercial speech—speech that involves commercial transactions, particularly the advertising of business products and services—does qualify for First Amendment protection. Although the Supreme Court has had difficulty in defining the term "commercial speech" with precision, one thing is clear: The parameters of this protection are not coextensive with the boundaries of protected individual speech.

Clearly, the government can—and does—regulate private expression. The First Amendment, though a fundamental right, is not an absolute one. In deciding whether to limit speech, the government engages in yet another balancing test in which it compares such factors as the importance of these rights in a democratic society, the nature of the restriction imposed by the law, the type and importance of the governmental interest the law purports to serve, and the narrowness of the means used to effectuate that interest.

Courts ordinarily view laws that, by punishing some speech and favoring other speech, burden the content of individual speech ("content-based" regulations), as presumptively invalid. Hence, such laws must pass the "strict scrutiny/compelling state interest" (that is, the "least restrictive alternative") test and be narrowly drawn measures designed to achieve such a compelling state interest. Courts in addition can strike down substantially overbroad and vague laws (that is, those that proscribe protected activity and thus "chill" others into refraining from the exercise of constitutionally protected expression). The government, however, may outlaw defamation, advocacy of unlawful action, obscenity, and "fighting words." The government also can subject lawful speech to time, place, and manner regulation (it can require demonstrators to obtain permits, limit the demonstration to a certain venue, and so on).

Thus, because the government can regulate private expression, it comes as no surprise that the government can regulate commercial speech and even ban such speech that is false and misleading. Although the First Amendment protects commercial speech, the greater potential for deception and confusion posed by commercial speech allows the government to regulate even the content of commercial (as opposed to noncommercial) speech so long as the restriction serves and advances a substantial governmental interest and in a manner no more extensive than necessary (that is, "sufficiently tailored") to achieve that governmental objective. For example, in 1994, the Supreme Court held in *Turner Broadcasting System, Inc.* v. *Federal Communications Commission* that the provisions of the federal law that required cable television stations to devote a specified portion of their channels to the transmission of local programming (the "must carry" provisions) were not content-based laws.[19] Hence, the Court rejected the argument that they must be judged under the strict scrutiny/compelling state interest test and instead upheld the challenged provisions because they were sufficiently tailored to serve the important governmental interest relating to the preservation of local broadcasting. The recent challenges to Congress's attempt to regulate "indecent" content on the Internet (specifically, the Communications Decency Act of 1995, which outlaws the electronic transmission of lewd and indecent materials to anyone under age 18 and subjects to criminal penalties any commercial communication service that allows its system to be used for such transmissions) implicate similar issues. This area of the law promises to provide a fertile field for continuing litigation, so try to keep abreast of the Supreme Court's disposition of the legal developments relating to the regulation of telecommunications.

The Supreme Court in *44 Liquormart* v. *Rhode Island* utilizes many of the many principles of law just discussed.

39.3

CITY OFFICIALS CONFISCATE CALL-IMAGE UNITS

Assume that the proposed ordinance requiring a switch that turns off video transmission has taken effect. CIT has decided to add such a switch to its units as soon as practical. In the meantime, the firm has decided to suspend any new sales in that community until the new units are ready. Tom calls the store manager to inform him of this decision and to have him return all of the unsold units in the store to the CIT factory for redistribution to areas where the present units can legally be sold. Tom learns that the city has already confiscated all of the units in the store, however, citing their noncompliance with the city ordinance. Tom asks you if the city can legally do this. What will you tell him?

BUSINESS CONSIDERATIONS What should a business do to protect itself from takings carried out by the government? What sorts of protections are available for the business?

ETHICAL CONSIDERATIONS Is it ethical for the government to take private property for a public purpose? What alternatives might be available that would allow the government to meet its obligation to the public while protecting the property interests of owners?

MANAGEMENT

39.5 44 LIQUORMART, INC. v. RHODE ISLAND

116 S.Ct. 1495 (1996)

FACTS 44 Liquormart, Inc. (44 Liquormart) and Peoples Super Liquor Stores, Inc. (Peoples) are licensed retailers of alcoholic beverages. 44 Liquormart operates a store in Rhode Island and Peoples operates several stores in Massachusetts that are patronized by Rhode Island residents. Peoples uses alcohol price advertising extensively in Massachusetts, where such advertising is permitted, but Rhode Island newspapers and other media outlets have refused to accept such ads. In 1991, 44 Liquormart placed an advertisement in a Rhode Island newspaper. The advertisement did not state the price of any alcoholic beverages. Indeed, it noted that "State law prohibits advertising liquor prices." The ad did, however, state the low prices at which peanuts, potato chips, and Schweppes mixers were being offered, identify various brands of packaged liquor, and include the word "WOW" in large letters next to pictures of vodka and rum bottles. Based on the conclusion that the implied reference to bargain prices for liquor violated the statutory ban on price advertising, the Rhode Island Liquor Control Administrator assessed a $400 fine. After paying the fine, 44 Liquormart, joined by Peoples, sought in federal court a declaratory judgment that the two statutes and the administrator's implementing regulations violate the First Amendment and other provisions of federal law. The parties stipulated that the price advertising ban is vigorously enforced, that Rhode Island permits "all advertising of alcoholic beverages excepting references to price outside the licensed premises," and that the proposed ads do not concern an illegal activity and presumably would not be false or misleading. The parties disagreed, however, about the impact of the ban on the promotion of temperance in Rhode Island. The district court concluded that the price advertising ban was unconstitutional because it did not "directly advance" the state's interest in reducing alcohol consumption and was "more extensive than necessary to serve that interest." The district court reasoned that the party seeking to uphold a restriction on commercial speech carries the burden of justifying it and that the Twenty-first Amendment did not shift or diminish that burden. Acknowledging that it might have been reasonable for the state legislature to "assume a correlation between the price advertising ban and reduced consumption," the court held that more than a rational basis was required to justify the speech restriction and that the state had failed to demonstrate a reasonable fit between its policy objectives and its chosen means. The court of appeals reversed. It found inherent merit in the state's submission that competitive price advertising would lower prices and that lower prices would produce more sales. Moreover, it agreed with the reasoning of the Rhode Island Supreme Court that the Twenty-first Amendment gave the statutes an added presumption of validity. The Supreme Court thereafter granted certiorari.

ISSUES Did Rhode Island's statutory bans on the advertising of liquor prices except at the place of sale violate the First Amendment? Would the Twenty-first Amendment shield this advertising ban from constitutional scrutiny?

HOLDINGS Yes, as to the first issue. The state had failed to carry its heavy burden of justifying its complete ban on advertising; hence, that ban was invalid under the First Amendment. No, as to the second issue. The Twenty-first Amendment was unavailable as a means of saving Rhode Island's price-advertising ban because that amendment does not qualify the First Amendment's prohibition against laws abridging the freedom of speech.

REASONING After reviewing its numerous precedents concerning advertising, the Court submitted that Rhode Island had erred when it had concluded that *all* commercial speech regulations are subject to a similar form of constitutional review simply because they target a similar category of expression. The mere fact that messages propose commercial transactions does not in and of itself dictate the constitutional analysis that should apply to decisions to suppress them. According to the Court, when a state regulates commercial messages to protect consumers from misleading, deceptive, or aggressive sales practices, or requires the disclosure of beneficial consumer information, the purpose of its regulation is consistent with the reasons for according constitutional protection to commercial speech and therefore justifies less than strict review. However, when a state entirely prohibits the dissemination of truthful, nonmisleading commercial messages for reasons unrelated to the preservation of a fair bargaining process, there is far less reason to depart from the rigorous review that the First Amendment generally demands. Sound reasons justify reviewing the latter type of commercial speech regulation more carefully. Most obviously, complete speech bans, unlike content-neutral restrictions on the time, place, or manner of expression, are particularly dangerous because they all but foreclose alternative means of disseminating certain information. Our commercial speech cases have recognized the dangers that attend governmental attempts to single out certain messages for suppression. The special dangers that attend complete bans on truthful, nonmisleading commercial speech cannot be explained away by appeals to the "commonsense distinctions" that

39.5 44 LIQUORMART, INC. v. RHODE ISLAND *(cont.)* 116 S.Ct. 1495 (1996)

exist between commercial and noncommercial speech. Regulations that suppress the truth are no less troubling because they target objectively verifiable information, nor are they less effective because they aim at durable messages. As a result, neither the "greater objectivity" nor the "greater hardiness" of truthful, nonmisleading commercial speech justifies reviewing its complete suppression with added deference. It is the state's interest in protecting consumers from "commercial harms" that provides "the typical reason why commercial speech can be subject to greater governmental regulation than noncommercial speech." Yet bans that target truthful, nonmisleading commercial messages rarely protect consumers from such harms. Instead, such bans often serve only to obscure an "underlying governmental policy" that could be implemented without regulating speech. In this way, these commercial speech bans not only hinder consumer choice, but also impede debate over central issues of public policy. Precisely because bans against truthful, nonmisleading commercial speech rarely seek to protect consumers from either deception or overreaching, they usually rest solely on the offensive assumption that the public will respond "irrationally" to the truth. The First Amendment directs everyone to be especially skeptical of regulations that seek to keep people in the dark for what the government perceives to be their own good. That teaching applies equally to state attempts to deprive consumers of accurate information about their chosen products. In this case, there is no question that Rhode Island's price advertising ban constitutes a blanket prohibition against truthful, nonmisleading speech about a lawful product. There also is no question that the ban serves an end unrelated to consumer protection. Accordingly, any court must review the price advertising ban with "special care" and remain mindful that speech prohibitions of this type rarely survive constitutional review. The state argues that the price advertising prohibition nevertheless should be upheld because it directly advances the state's substantial interest in promoting temperance and because it is no more extensive than necessary. Although there is some confusion as to what Rhode Island means by temperance, the state presumably asserts an interest in reducing alcohol consumption. In evaluating the ban's effectiveness in advancing the state's interest, a court may not sustain a commercial speech regulation if it provides only ineffective or remote support for the government's purpose. For that reason, the state bears the burden of showing not merely that its regulation will advance its interest, but also that it will do so "to a material degree." The need for the state to make such a showing is particularly great given the drastic nature of its chosen means—the wholesale suppression of truthful, nonmisleading information. Accordingly, a court must determine whether the state has shown that the price advertising ban will *significantly* reduce alcohol consumption. And the state has failed to meet its burden in this case. The state also cannot satisfy the requirement that its restriction on speech be no more extensive than necessary. It is perfectly obvious that alternative forms of regulation that would not involve any restriction on speech would be more likely to achieve the state's goal of promoting temperance. As the state's own expert conceded, higher prices can be maintained either by direct regulation or by increased taxation. Per capita purchases could be limited as is the case with prescription drugs. Even educational campaigns focused on the problems of excessive, or even moderate, drinking might prove to be more effective. Furthermore, the Twenty-first Amendment, which repealed the Eighteenth Amendment's prohibitions on liquor and, which delegated the power to regulate commerce in alcoholic beverages to the states, does not qualify the constitutional prohibition against laws abridging the freedom of speech embodied in the First Amendment. The Twenty-first Amendment, therefore, cannot save Rhode Island's ban on liquor price advertising. Rhode Island's failure to carry its heavy burden of justifying its complete ban on price advertising, means that the statutes in question abridge speech in violation of the First Amendment as made applicable to the states by the Due Process Clause of the Fourteenth Amendment. The judgment of the court of appeals therefore must be reversed.

BUSINESS CONSIDERATIONS Some businesses, such as liquor stores, sell products that are more likely to be subject to public concern and scrutiny than others. Should these businesses expect more stringent regulation than businesses not subjected to such public scrutiny? How can these businesses protect themselves in such a situation?

ETHICAL CONSIDERATIONS Is it ethical to single out certain types of businesses for different types or degrees of regulation? How can such treatment be justified ethically?

YOU BE THE JUDGE

First Amendment Rights

Arizona's state constitution, which in article 28 declares English "the official language of the state," requires the state to "act in English and no other language" and authorizes state residents and businesses "to bring [state court] suit[s] to enforce this article." Assume that a Spanish-speaking state employee has challenged this law on First Amendment grounds and that the case has been brought before *your* court. How will *you* decide this case?

BUSINESS CONSIDERATIONS Should businesses that operate in multi-ethnic neighborhoods advertise in more than one language? What benefits might be realized from multilingual advertising? What drawbacks might the business face?

ETHICAL CONSIDERATIONS Is it ethical for a business to refuse to do business with customers unless those customers speak the preferred language of the business owners? From an ethical perspective, how does this compare with a business that refuses to do business with customers who are not of the same race as the business owners?

SOURCE: *Arizonans for Official English* v. *Arizona,* 117 S.Ct. 1055 (1997).

Administrative Agencies

Administrative agencies conduct much of the work of regulating business. Most of us are familiar with the three official branches of the federal government—the legislative, executive, and judicial—but we may tend to overlook the unofficial fourth branch. This so-called administrative branch of government has been especially active since the 1930s. The Great Depression and the presidency of Franklin Delano Roosevelt saw a tremendous growth in the use of administrative agencies as a major means of effecting regulation. Because a great deal of government intervention in the business sphere derives from the actions of administrative agencies, some familiarity with administrative law is essential to understanding governmental regulation of business.

Delegated
Assigned responsibility and/or authority by the person or group normally empowered to exercise the responsibility or authority.

Quasi-legislative
Partly legislative; empowered to enact rules and regulations but not statutes.

Quasi-judicial
Partly judicial; empowered to hold hearings but not trials.

Congress sets up administrative agencies; and since Congress "creates" them, Congress can terminate them. Hence, they are not an independent branch of government. They have only as much authority as is **delegated** to them by the legislature, and as a result they must answer to Congress for their conduct. Congress establishes a basic policy or standard and then authorizes an agency to carry it out.

Once established, the agency will have certain **quasi-legislative** and **quasi-judicial** powers. The agency is allowed to pass rules and regulations within its area of authority and to hold hearings when it believes violations of its rules and regulations have occurred. In so doing, federal administrative agencies must follow the Administrative Procedures Act (APA), which mandates public participation and sets out the rules and procedures that such agencies must follow as they legislate, adjudicate, and enforce their regulations. The power of Congress to abolish any agency and the power of the courts to review any agency's conduct are considered sufficient control devices. It is believed that the agency will not exceed its authority or abuse its discretion as long as these two *official* branches of government keep a watchful eye on the agency's conduct.

Some of the constitutional provisions discussed earlier in the chapter limit the power of administrative agencies. Remember that an agency, in order to ensure procedural due process, must provide fairness in its proceedings. A person involved in a proceeding that affects his or her individual rights (that is, those involving *adjudicative* facts) ordinarily is entitled to a hearing of some sort. Also remember that due process generally includes the right to present witnesses, the right to cross-examine witnesses, the right to an impartial decisionmaker, and possibly other rights as well. Agency proceedings involving only rule making or fact-finding concerning principles of general application (that is, those involving *legislative* facts) usually require fewer procedural safeguards. Notice of the time, place, and purpose of the meeting might satisfy procedural due process in this latter context. Moreover, the agency may enact only rules and regulations that bear a rational relationship to the agency's purpose or function. Under substantive due process doctrines, then, litigants may challenge unreasonable, arbitrary, and capricious administrative rules. Such rules also may deny the persons affected the equal protection of the law.

The respective agencies' enabling statutes ordinarily spell out the methods by which one can seek review of agency decisions. Those dissatisfied with treatment received at the hands of an administrative agency generally may ask a federal district or circuit court of appeals to review the administrative proceedings in question. Judicial review ordinarily focuses on four possible areas of agency error:

1. The agency violated procedural due process.
2. The agency violated substantive due process.
3. The agency otherwise violated the Constitution.
4. The agency exceeded its authority.

http:// RESOURCES FOR BUSINESS LAW STUDENTS

NAME	RESOURCES	WEB ADDRESS
U.S. Constitution	Emory Law School maintains a hypertext and searchable version of the U.S. Constitution.	http://www.law.emory.edu/FEDERAL/usconst.html
The Legal Information Institute (LII)—Decisions of the U.S. Supreme Court	LII, maintained by the Cornell Law School, provides recent Supreme Court decisions (1990–present), as well as various historical decisions and background material on the Court.	http://Supct.law.cornell.edu/Supct/
Oyez Oyez Oyez: A Supreme Court Resource	Oyez Oyez Oyez (pronounced "oh-yay"), maintained by Jerry Goldman and Northwestern University, provides digital recordings (via RealAudio technology) of selected Supreme Court cases ranging from 1955 to the present.	http://oyez.at.nwu.edu/oyez.html
International Association of Constitutional Law	International Association of Constitutional Law provides information and constitutions for countries around the world.	http://www.eur.nl/iacl/const.html

A court, however, will review the proceedings only from the point of view of their legality. As to *questions of fact* (for example, what actually transpired), a court must follow the *substantial evidence rule,* which states that the agency's findings of fact must be upheld if such findings are based on substantial evidence. If instead the judicial review involves *questions of law* (for example, jurisdictional or procedural issues), courts remain free to substitute their judgment for the agencies'; courts need not give deference to the agencies' determinations regarding these issues.

Courts will review *discretionary acts* under the "abuse of discretion" rationale and therefore will invalidate arbitrary, unreasonable, or capricious decisions.

As a result of the restricted nature of judicial review and the pervasive nature of administrative agencies in the business world, this area of regulation has become quite important today. A person who plans to advance very far in business is well advised to study administrative law in further detail.

SUMMARY

Governmental regulation of business is a fact of life in the modern business environment. Whether regulation takes the form of local zoning ordinances, state income taxation, or federal antitrust regulation, businesses today must address it. And the only way to deal with government regulation is to recognize and understand it. Federal regulation of business is based on both the commerce clause of the U.S. Constitution, which authorizes Congress to "regulate commerce among the several states," and Congress's taxing power, also included in the Constitution.

Most regulation derives from the commerce clause. The commerce clause has been interpreted in such a way that federal regulation is permitted only if interstate commerce is involved. To qualify as interstate, the transaction must directly affect citizens of at least two different states or countries. If an interstate connection is present, federal regulation may be applied. The federal government exclusively regulates many aspects of business, but the states have concurrent power to regulate in certain areas. States can exercise exclusive regulatory power over commerce only rarely.

The equal protection clause protects against invidious discrimination. Over the years, the Supreme Court has developed various tests for determining the legality of regulations challenged under this provision of the Constitution.

The Constitution's guarantee of due process has a distinct procedural dimension and a substantive dimension. These aspects guarantee fundamental fairness and freedom from the application of irrational, unreasonable, and arbitrary laws whenever the government deprives anyone of life, liberty, or property.

Under the takings clause of the Fifth Amendment, the government can take property for public use so long as the government pays just compensation to the affected property owner. In addition, the Fifth Amendment's prohibitions on double jeopardy and compulsory self-incrimination also serve as curbs on illegitimate governmental action.

The First Amendment protects commercial speech but to a lesser degree than it does individual speech. The government can ban false and misleading commercial speech and can even regulate other types of commercial speech as long as the restriction serves and advances a substantial governmental interest and in a manner no more extensive than necessary to achieve that governmental objective.

Much of the actual regulation of business is effectuated by administrative agencies. Administrative agencies are created by Congress, and Congress then delegates to the agencies the authority to carry out certain duties. Agencies are involved in a large number of regulatory areas. In carrying out their responsibilities, these agencies are required to assure due process of law, and they are subject to judicial review to ensure that they conduct themselves properly.

Discussion Questions

1. How do you define the phrase *interstate commerce*? Do you accept or reject the Supreme Court's definition of this term? Why?
2. Name and explain the areas of commerce over which the federal government has exclusive jurisdiction. What are the areas of concurrent state and federal regulation? When does the state have exclusive jurisdiction over commerce?
3. Explain in detail the various tests a court must apply when it evaluates a law challenged on equal protection grounds.
4. Discuss the factors courts must take into account in deciding whether a group is a "suspect classification" for purposes of equal protection analysis.
5. Name and explain the various interests protected under the Fifth Amendment.
6. What does *substantive due process* mean? How does a court determine when a violation of this constitutional right has occurred?
7. How does procedural due process differ from substantive due process? What protections must the government provide to individuals and businesses under this aspect of the Fifth and Fourteenth Amendments?
8. What powers does the government enjoy under the takings clause? What rights does an individual or business have under this clause?
9. How does the protection accorded commercial speech differ from the protection granted to individual speech?
10. What powers are possessed by administrative agencies? From what source or sources do administrative agencies derive these powers?

Case Problems and Writing Assignments

1. Silvia Safile Ibanez, a member of the Florida bar since 1983, practices law in Winter Haven, Florida. She also is a certified public accountant (CPA), licensed by the Florida Board of Accountancy (the board) to "practice public accounting." In addition, she is authorized by the Certified Financial Planner Board of Standards, a private organization, to use the trademarked designation "certified financial planner" (CFP). Ibanez referred to these credentials in her advertising and other communications with the public. She placed CPA and CFP next to her name in her Yellow Pages listing (under "Attorneys") and on her business card. She also used those designations at the left side of her "Law Offices" stationery. Notwithstanding the apparently truthful nature of her communication—it is undisputed that neither her CPA license nor her CFP certification has been revoked—the board charged Ibanez with (1) "practicing public accounting" in an unlicensed firm, in violation of the Public Accountancy Act; (2) using a "specialty designation"—CFP—that the board had not approved, in violation of board rules; and (3) appending the CPA designation after her name, thereby "impl[ying] that she abides by the provisions of [the Public Accountancy Act]," in violation of a board rule banning "fraudulent, false, deceptive, or misleading" advertising. At the ensuing disciplinary hearing, Ibanez argued that she was practicing law rather than "public accounting" and therefore was not subject to the board's regulatory jurisdiction. Her use of the CPA and CFP designations, she further maintained, constituted "nonmisleading, truthful, commercial speech" for which she could not be sanctioned. The hearing officer subsequently found in Ibanez's favor on all counts and recommended to the board that, for want of the requisite proof, all charges against Ibanez be dismissed. The board rejected the hearing officer's recommendation and declared Ibanez guilty of "false, deceptive, and misleading" advertising. Did the board's decision to censure Ibanez violate the First Amendment? Explain fully. [See *Ibanez v. Florida Dep't. of Business,* 512 U.S. 136 (1994).]

2. In 1969, Henry H. Amsden was licensed as a land surveyor. Six years later, he became associated with Tyrone Hunter, an unlicensed (but practicing) land surveyor. Such an association was not uncommon, for the apprenticeship allowed newcomers to the profession to gain supervised experience. In 1977, Mr. and Mrs. Whipple hired the Amsden-Hunter duo to survey a 40-acre parcel owned by the Whipples. The tract

then became embroiled in a boundary dispute, and Amsden and Hunter assisted the Whipples in the ensuing litigation. In late 1981, however, the Whipples filed a complaint with the Board of Land Surveyors (the BLS) against the two men. On 24 December, Amsden was notified of the complaint and advised that a hearing would take place on 15 January 1982. The notification letter specified three charges that the BLS would consider: misrepresentation of qualifications, overcharging, and delayed completion of the work. According to Amsden, when the hearings were convened, the BLS, citing jurisdictional problems, declined to consider the question of the reasonableness of the fee billed to the Whipples. Amsden also maintained that in the spring of 1982, before conducting the last of the hearings, BLS members visited the Whipples' property, although Amsden—who was present at, and participated in, all the sessions—was not notified of the field trip. On 1 May 1983, the BLS finally acted on the Whipples' complaint and revoked Amsden's license. The BLS found that Amsden had "failed to exercise adequate supervision or checking over Mr. Hunter, had produced a fraudulent [survey] plan and had acquiesced in the charging of fees which were exorbitant." Amsden then hired a new attorney, who informed the BLS that Amsden had dissolved his professional relationship with Hunter. On 11 May, the lawyer secured an agreement to postpone the effective date of the revocation order. He also proceeded to negotiate a settlement whereby Amsden returned roughly 60 percent of the overall fee to the Whipples. At that point, the BLS restored Amsden's license unconditionally, although the BLS warned him to oversee licensed surveyors more carefully in the future. In January 1984, Amsden filed an action before the Board of Claims (BOC), which reviews BLS decisions. Alleging various due process deprivations and state law torts, Amsden sought damages for loss of business and injury to his professional reputation. Amsden argued, among other things, that the BLS had decided the case against him not on the basis of his conduct, but as a device to force Amsden to abandon his arrangement with Hunter, thereby putting Hunter out of the land-surveying business. Owing to the BLS's masking its true concerns, Amsden contended that he could not defend himself. He also submitted that the BLS as a consequence had misused administrative processes so as to deprive him of his rights. In addition, Amsden claimed that the license revocation had been motivated by the chair's animosity toward him and that certain statements made about the revocation had amounted to slander. The BOC, although it accepted several of Amsden's contentions, believed that the BLS would be entitled to absolute immunity for quasi-judicial acts within the ambit of its ostensible authority and thus denied Amsden any damages. Two years later, Amsden filed suit in federal district court, where he again alleged that the BLS had violated his procedural and substantive due process rights. How should the appellate court rule in this case? Why? [See *Amsden* v. *Moran*, 904 F.2d 748 (1st Cir. 1990).]

3. Montana's Dangerous Drug Tax Act took effect on 1 October 1987. The act imposes a tax "on the possession and storage of dangerous drugs" and expressly provides that the tax is to be "collected only after any state or federal fines or forfeitures have been satisfied." The tax is either 10 percent of the assessed market value of the drugs as determined by the Montana Department of Revenue (DOR) or a specified amount depending on the drug (for example, $100 per ounce for marijuana and $250 per ounce for hashish), whichever is greater. The act directs the state treasurer to allocate the tax proceeds to special funds to support "youth evaluation" and "chemical abuse" programs and "to enforce the drug laws." In addition to imposing reporting responsibilities on law enforcement agencies, the act also authorizes the DOR to adopt rules to administer and enforce the tax. Under those rules, taxpayers must file a return within 72 hours of their arrest. These rules also provide that "[a]t the time of arrest, law enforcement personnel shall complete the dangerous drug information report as required by the department and afford the taxpayer an opportunity to sign it." If the taxpayer refuses to do so, the law enforcement officer is required to file the form within 72 hours of the arrest. The taxpayer has no obligation to file a return or to pay any tax unless and until he or she is arrested. About two weeks after the new Drug Tax Act went into effect, Montana law enforcement officers raided the Kurths' ranch; arrested six members of the extended Kurth family; and confiscated all the marijuana plants, materials, and paraphernalia found at the ranch. This raid put an end to the Kurths' marijuana business and gave rise to four separate legal proceedings. In one of those proceedings, the state filed criminal charges against all six and charged each with conspiracy to possess drugs with intent to sell. Second, the county attorney also filed a civil forfeiture action seeking the recovery of cash and equipment used in the marijuana operation. The third proceeding involved the assessment of the new tax on dangerous drugs wherein the DOR ultimately attempted to collect almost $900,000 in taxes on marijuana plants, harvested marijuana, hash tar and hash oil, interest, and penalties. In administrative proceedings, the Kurths con-

tested these assessments. Those proceedings were automatically stayed in September 1988, however, when the Kurths initiated the fourth legal proceeding triggered by the raid on their ranch: a petition for bankruptcy under Chapter 11 of the Bankruptcy Code. In the bankruptcy proceedings, the Kurths objected to the DOR's proof of claim for unpaid drug taxes and challenged the constitutionality of the Montana tax. The bankruptcy court held that while the assessment of $181,000 on 1,811 ounces of harvested marijuana was authorized by the act, the assessment nonetheless was invalid under the U.S. Constitution as a form of double jeopardy. The court rejected the state's argument that the tax was not a penalty because it was designed to recover law enforcement costs. The district court, holding that the Montana Dangerous Drug Tax Act simply punished the Kurths a second time for the same conduct, affirmed the bankruptcy court's determination. How should the Supreme Court rule in this case? Why? [See *Department of Revenue of Montana* v. *Kurth Ranch,* 511 U.S. 767 (1994).]

4. Feim Azizi illegally entered the United States in early 1986. Soon afterward, the Immigration and Naturalization Service (INS) instituted a deportation proceeding against him, issued an order to show cause, and gave him notice of a hearing. After admitting that he had illegally entered the country, Azizi applied for political asylum. While his application for political asylum was pending, Azizi married Saboet Elmazi, a naturalized U.S. citizen. In January 1987, Mr. Azizi's application for political asylum was denied. The new Mrs. Azizi then filed a petition for an immigrant visa for her husband as an "immediate relative." Under the Immigration Marriage Fraud Amendments, however, an alien who marries a citizen during the pendency of deportation proceedings must reside outside the United States for two years before the INS will consider a petition for an immediate relative visa. In challenging the deportation order of the INS and the denial of the immediate relative visa, the Azizis asserted that they had been denied due process and equal protection. They pointed out that an alien who marries a U.S. citizen while no deportation hearing is pending is given a two-year conditional period to remain in the country; and, if the marriage still is intact at the end of the two years, the conditional status expires. They therefore argued that the deportation order discriminates against people facing deportation hearings in an unfair manner and without any rational basis. Was this rule a denial of due process and equal protection, or was it a legitimate exercise of power by the government? Why? [See *Azizi* v. *Thornburgh,* 908 F.2d 1130 (2nd Cir. 1990).]

5. The Town of Clarkstown, New York (Clarkstown), agreed to allow a private contractor to construct within the town's limits a solid-waste transfer system to separate recyclable from nonrecyclable items and to operate the facility for five years, at which time Clarkstown would buy it for one dollar. To finance the transfer station's cost, the town guaranteed a minimum waste flow to the facility, for which the contractor could charge the hauler a tipping fee, which, at $81 per ton, exceeded the disposal cost of unsorted solid waste on the private market. In order to meet this waste flow guarantee, Clarkstown adopted a flow control ordinance requiring all nonhazardous solid waste within the town to be deposited at the transfer station. While recyclers like C & A Carbone, Inc. (Carbone) might receive solid waste at its own sorting facilities, the ordinance required such recyclers to bring nonrecyclable residue to the transfer station. The ordinance in effect thus forbade such recyclers to ship such waste themselves and required them to pay the tipping fee on trash that already had been sorted. After discovering that Carbone had shipped nonrecyclable waste to out-of-state destinations, Clarkstown sought a state court injunction requiring that this residue be shipped to the transfer station. Finding the ordinance constitutional, the state court granted summary judgment to Clarkstown; and the appellate division affirmed. On appeal, on what constitutional basis should Carbone focus its arguments? [See *C & A Carbone, Inc.* v. *Town of Clarkstown, New York,* 511 U.S. 383 (1994).]

6. **BUSINESS APPLICATION CASE** In 1978, California enacted its Mobile Home Residency Law. The California legislature found that, because of the high cost of moving mobile homes, the potential for damage resulting therefrom, the requirements relating to the installation of mobile homes, and the cost of landscaping or lot preparation, the owner of mobile homes occupied within mobile home parks needs protection from actual or constructive eviction. Hence, the Mobile Home Residency Law limits the bases upon which a park owner may terminate a mobile home owner's tenancy. These include nonpayment of rent, the mobile home owner's violation of law or park rules, and the park owner's desire to change the use of his or her land. While a rental agreement is in effect, however, the park owner generally may not require the removal of a mobile home when it is sold. The park owner may neither charge a transfer fee for the sale nor disapprove of the purchaser, provided that the purchaser has the ability to pay the rent. Consequently, various communities in California adopted mobile home rent control ordinances. In 1988, the voters of Escondido did the same when they

approved Proposition K, the rent control ordinance challenged here. The ordinance sets rents back to their 1986 levels and prohibits rent increases without the approval of the City Council (the council). Park owners may apply to the council for rent increases at any time. In addition, the council must approve any increases it determines to be "just, fair and reasonable." John and Irene Yee owned the Friendly Hills and Sunset Terrace mobile home parks, both of which were located in the city of Escondido. A few months after the adoption of Escondido's rent control ordinance, they filed a lawsuit in which they alleged that the rent control law represented an illegal taking of their property because the rent control ordinance transferred a discrete interest in land—the right to occupy the land indefinitely at a submarket rent—from the park owner to the mobile home owner. The Yees thus contended that what was transferred from the park owner to the mobile home owner was no less than a right of physical occupation of the park owner's land. Should the Supreme Court agree with the Yees' reasoning? In addition, muster arguments for and against this proposition: The Escondido ordinance represents a valid consumer protection measure for adjusting the relative bargaining power between mobile home owners and mobile home park owners. [See *Yee* v. *City of Escondido*, 503 U.S. 519 (1992).]

7. **ETHICS APPLICATION CASE** In September 1992, the operators of Women's Health Center (WHC), an abortion clinic in Melbourne, Florida, sought an injunction against certain anti-abortion protestors. At that time, a Florida state court permanently enjoined Madsen and the other protestors from blocking or interfering with public access to the clinic and from physically abusing persons entering or leaving the clinic. Six months later, WHC, complaining that access to the clinic was still impeded by the protestors' activities and that such activities also had discouraged some potential patients from entering the clinic and had had deleterious physical effects on others, sought to broaden the injunction. The trial court thereupon issued a broader injunction. The court found that, despite the initial injunction, protestors, by congregating on the paved portion of the street leading up to the clinic and by marching in front of the clinic's driveways, continued to impede access to the clinic. The trial court found that as vehicles heading toward the clinic slowed to allow the protestors to move out of the way, "sidewalk counselors" would approach and attempt to give the vehicles' occupants anti-abortion literature. The number of people congregating varied from a handful to 400, and the noise varied from singing and chanting to the use of loudspeakers and bullhorns. A clinic doctor testified that as a result of having to run such a gauntlet to enter the clinic, the patients, owing to heightened anxiety and hypertension, needed a higher level of sedation before they could undergo surgical procedures and thereby faced increased risks from such procedures. The noise caused stress not only for the patients undergoing surgery but also for those recuperating in the recovery rooms. Doctors and clinic workers in turn were not immune even in their homes. The protestors picketed in front of clinic employees' residences, rang the doorbells of neighbors, provided literature identifying the particular clinic employee as a "baby killer," and occasionally confronted the clinic employees' minor children who were home alone. Given this and similar testimony, the state court viewed the original injunction as insufficient "to protect the health, safety and rights of women in Brevard and Seminole County, Florida, and surrounding counties seeking access to [medical and counseling] services." The state court therefore amended its prior order and enjoined a broader array of activities. Although the Florida supreme court had upheld the injunction, the Court of Appeals for the Eleventh Circuit had struck it down. At the U.S. Supreme Court, what constitutional arguments would the parties make? Who should win and why? If you were deciding this case on ethical grounds, with whom would you side—the protestors or the clinic and its personnel? Why? [See *Madsen* v. *Women's Health Center, Inc.*, 512 U.S. 753 (1994), modified at *Schenck* v. *Pro-Choice Network of Western New York*, 117 S.Ct. 885 (1997).]

8. **IDES CASE** Wyoming, a major coal-producing state, does not sell coal, but does impose a severance tax on those who extract it. From 1981 to 1986, Wyoming provided virtually 100 percent of the coal purchased by four Oklahoma electric utilities, including the Grand River Dam Authority (GRDA), a state agency. After the Oklahoma legislature had passed an act requiring coal-fired electric utilities to burn a mixture containing at least 10 percent Oklahoma-mined coal, however, the utilities reduced their purchases of Wyoming coal in favor of Oklahoma coal. In fact, Wyoming's severance tax revenues had declined by approximately $1.2 million after the passage of the Oklahoma statute. The stipulated facts demonstrated that, from 1981 to 1986, Wyoming provided virtually 100 percent of the coal purchased by Oklahoma utilities. In 1987 and 1988, following the effective date of the act, the utilities purchased Oklahoma coal in amounts ranging from 3.4 to 7.4 percent of their annual needs, with a necessarily corresponding reduction in purchases of Wyoming coal. When

Wyoming sued Oklahoma, Oklahoma first argued that Wyoming had no basis for suing and that the trial court accordingly should dismiss the case. Oklahoma furthermore contended that the Oklahoma legislature's requiring the utilities to supply 10 percent of their needs for fuel from Oklahoma coal, which because of its higher sulfur content cannot be the primary source of supply, permitted Oklahoma thereby to conserve Wyoming's cleaner coal for future use. Wyoming thereupon responded that its reserves of low sulfur, clean-burning, sub-bituminous coal from the Powder River Basin are estimated to be in excess of 110 billion tons, thus, at current rates of extraction, providing Wyoming coal for several hundred years. Oklahoma also submitted that the "saving clause" of the Federal Power Act (§ 824(b)(1)), which reserves to the states the regulation of local retail electric rates, whenever electric power has been transmitted and/or sold in interstate commerce, but leaves all other regulatory issues to the federal government, validates the state act because Oklahoma has determined that effective and helpful ways of ensuring lower local utility rates include (1) reducing overdependence on a single source of supply or a single fuel transporter and (2) conserving needed low-sulfur coal for the future. In rebuttal, Wyoming maintained that, despite Oklahoma's arguments, nothing in the federal statute or its legislative history would permit even a partial—much less a total—ban or the interpretation that in-state purchasing quotas imposed on utilities in an effort to regulate utility rates are within the "lawful authority" of the states under the federal act. According to Wyoming, Congress merely left standing whatever valid state laws then existed relating to the exportation of hydroelectric energy; that is, by its plain terms, § 824(b) simply saves from preemption under Part II of the Federal Power Act such state authority as was otherwise "lawful." Apply the IDES model. Was Oklahoma correct that the case merited dismissal at the outset? Why or why not? In challenging this law, what argument(s) should Wyoming make? [See *Wyoming* v. *Oklahoma*, 502 U.S. 437 (1992).]

Notes

1. Bradley R. Schiller, *The Micro Economy Today*, 7th ed. (New York: McGraw-Hill, 1997), p. 294.
2. 9 Wheat (22 U.S.) 1 (1824).
3. 24 Stat. 379 (1887).
4. 15 Wall. (82 U.S.) 232 (1873).
5. 128 U.S. 1 (1888).
6. 301 U.S. 1 (1937).
7. 336 U.S. 460, 464 (1949).
8. 411 U.S. 624 (1973).
9. 514 U.S. 549 (1995).
10. 118 U.S. 356 (1886).
11. 116 S.Ct. 1620 (1996).
12. Ibid. at 1629.
13. 592 U.S. 200 (1995).
14. 429 U.S. 190 (1976).
15. *U.S.* v. *Virginia*, 116 S.Ct. 2264 (1996).
16. 499 U.S. 1 (1991).
17. *Cruzan* v. *Director, Missouri Department of Health*, 497 U.S. 261 (1990).
18. *Lucas* v. *South Carolina Coastal Council*, 112 S.Ct. 2886 (1992).
19. 512 U.S. 622 (1994).

AGENDA

The Kochanowskis have developed a "one-of-a-kind" product, and that puts them in a position to potentially dominate the market. Such market dominance is both good and bad. It may provide the opportunity for large profits, and it may lead to charges of violating various antitrust laws. The family will need to be aware of the scope of the Sherman Act, the Clayton Act, and the Federal Trade Commission Act. They will also need to be aware of various "unfair trade practices." This is all new territory for them, and they may have a significant number of questions.

Be prepared! You never know when one of the Kochanowskis will need your advice or guidance.

ANTITRUST LAW

OUTLINE

THE BASIS OF REGULATORY REFORM

For the first 114 years of U.S. history, business had a fairly free field in which to work. There was little federal regulation and little effective state regulation. The courts and the federal government took a "hands-off" attitude toward business. In such an environment, Cornelius Vanderbilt, buccaneering railroad tycoon of the 1800s, was able to crow, "What do I care about the law? Hain't I got the power?"

The tide began to turn in the late 1800s as the public tired of the irresponsible behavior of some of the so-called robber barons. The press began to call for reforms and for public protection from "big business." Finally, in 1890, a beachhead was established. The assault on business had begun. Government regulation of business was to become a major factor in the management of commercial affairs. All the regulations that affect business today, all the government inputs and interventions that confront the modern businessperson, can be traced back to the cornerstone of business regulation. The law that changed U.S. business so dramatically was the Sherman Antitrust Act.

THE SHERMAN ACT

Congress passed the Sherman Antitrust Act in 1890. The purpose of the act was to preserve the economic ideal of a pure-competition economy. To reach this ideal, the Sherman Act prohibits combinations that restrain trade, and it prohibits attempts to monopolize any area of commerce. Violations of the act can result in fines, imprisonment, injunctive relief, and civil damages.

Section 1: Contracts, Combinations, or Conspiracies in Restraint of Trade

The Sherman Act is a fairly short statute, but its few words cover a great number of actions. Section 1 states:

> *Every contract, combination in the form of trust or otherwise, or conspiracy, in restraint of trade or commerce among the several States, or with foreign nations, is hereby declared to be illegal.*

Because nearly every contract can be viewed as a restraint of trade, if this section were to be interpreted literally, virtually all business dealings that affect interstate commerce would be prohibited. For example, a customer who contracts to buy some item from seller A normally will not buy the same type of item from any of the competitors of seller A. As a result, the courts initially interpreted the Sherman Act very narrowly; this worked in such a way that the act was virtually negated.

The Rule of Reason. The courts eventually found a comfortable middle ground. To give the act the scope that Congress had intended, the courts developed the "rule of reason" as a means of applying the provisions of § 1. Under this test, not every "contract, combination, or conspiracy" is prohibited. Rather, only those contracts, combinations, or conspiracies that unreasonably restrain interstate commerce are prohibited. If a firm can show that its conduct was reasonable, it can avoid a prosecution under § 1.

Standard Oil Co. of New Jersey v. *United States* introduced the rule of reason to the Supreme Court. Although the Court determined the conduct in question was unreasonable, the Court did accept in theory this defense.

40.1 STANDARD OIL CO. OF NEW JERSEY v. UNITED STATES 221 U.S. 1 (1911)

FACTS Standard of Ohio, organized by the Rockefellers in 1870, had acquired all but three or four of the oil refineries in Cleveland by 1872. Standard was able to use its size and economic strength to obtain preferential rates and substantial rebates from the railroads, and, in turn, Standard was able to use this economic advantage to force competitors to either join Standard or be driven out of existence. Standard soon controlled 90 percent of the petroleum industry, which allowed Standard to fix the prices for both crude and refined petroleum. In 1899, Standard Oil of New Jersey was established as a holding company to replace Standard of Ohio. Standard Oil of New Jersey continued to receive preferential treatment from the railroads, and was also alleged to engage in other unfair business practices against competing pipelines. According to the government challenge to Standard's conduct, Standard used these unfair practices to gain control of the pipelines as well, engaged in regional price cutting to suppress competition, set up bogus independents to give the impression of competition, and engaged in industrial espionage. The government brought suit against Standard for violations of the Sherman Act, and Standard defended its conduct by asserting that it had acted within the "rule of reason" for a firm in its industry.

ISSUE Did Standard act in a reasonable manner in its conduct so that it should not be found guilty of violating the Sherman Act?

HOLDING No. While the Court recognized that the rule of reason should provide a defense, Standard's conduct did not fall within that rule.

REASONING The Court examined the historic background leading to the enactment of the Sherman Act, stating that the "dread of enhancement of prices and of the wrongs which it was thought would flow from the undue limitation on competitive conditions caused by contracts or other acts of individuals or corporations, led, as a matter of public policy, to the prohibition or treating as illegal all contracts or acts which were unreasonably restrictive of competitive conditions."

BUSINESS CONSIDERATIONS When a firm is accused of violating a statute or a regulation, should the firm be more concerned with defending its conduct by showing that there was no violation, or should the firm be trying to show that its conduct was reasonable under the circumstances? Is reasonable—but illegal—conduct a proper defense to a charge of criminal conduct?

ETHICAL CONSIDERATIONS Did the Court act ethically by "discovering" that Section 1 of the Sherman Act only prohibited unreasonable restraints of trade? Should the Court have thrown out the law and allowed Congress the opportunity to re-enact a law with more appropriate language?

Both the rule of reason and the economic theory of competition seemed to be invoked by the Court in a recent case.[1] Sears, Roebuck and Company applied for membership with Visa, USA, the association of credit card issuers who offer the Visa card in the United States. The association denied the application by Sears, and Sears filed suit against Visa, USA, alleging that the credit card association was combining or conspiring illegally in an effort to prevent Sears from issuing Visa cards. The Court found that the harm to competition would be greater if the association admitted Sears than it would be if Sears was prevented from joining the association. According to the Court, the credit card industry was better served by having Visa, MasterCard, American Express, Diners/Carte Blanche, and Discover (issued by and through Sears). Competition was keen, and the market was highly competitive. Admitting Sears would reduce the number of competitors, and would seriously harm banks that issue Visa in head-to-head competition with Sears for the potential Visa customers in the market. According to the Court, the association acted in a reasonable manner under the circumstances.

Once it was established, the "rule-of-reason" defense provided business with an opportunity that it lost no time in using to its best advantage. Given a sufficient amount of time to prepare a defense, almost any business can show that its conduct was "reasonable" under the circumstances. Because of the results that the rule of reason produced, the courts had to reevaluate their approach. The amended approach retained the rule of reason but added a new category: The courts declared some conduct to be so lacking in social value as to be an automatic violation of § 1. These actions, called per se violations, tend to contradict directly the economic model of pure competition.

Per se Violations. As noted in the preceding section, the courts restricted the availability of the rule-of-reason defense for alleged Sherman Act violations by the imposition of per se violations. The acts that are deemed to be per se violations are acts that are inherently contradictory to the economic theory of pure competition. If a firm is found guilty of a per se violation, it is not permitted to defend its conduct; it will be found guilty of violation of the Sherman Act by definition.

The per se violations under the Sherman Act, § 1, are as follows:

1. Horizontal price fixing (agreements on price among competitors)
2. Vertical price fixing (agreements on price among suppliers and customers)
3. Horizontal market divisions (agreements among competitors as to who can sell in which region)
4. Group boycotts (agreements among competitors not to sell to a particular buyer or not to buy from a particular seller)

Clearly, few businesses would be careless (or stupid) enough actually to overtly agree to such conduct. As a result, the courts have had to infer such agreements from the conduct of the parties. For example, in the area of price fixing, if the courts find that the parties have acted in a manner that amounts to conscious parallelism, a violation is likely to be found. Conscious parallelism, by itself, is not conclusive proof of a violation of § 1. However, it is to be weighed—and weighed heavily—by the courts in determining whether a § 1 violation is present. Generally, conscious parallelism coupled with some other fact, however slight, is sufficient to support a jury verdict of price fixing in violation of § 1. But if the conduct of the firms amounts only to price leadership, no violation is present. How can anyone distinguish conscious parallelism from price leadership? There is no answer to this problem; it poses a Gordian knot for the court every time it is raised.

The two hypothetical cases that follow show the problem of deciding whether conduct is permitted or prohibited.

> Alpha, Beta, and Gamma are concrete producers in Minnesota, Iowa, and Wisconsin, respectively. All three must compete with Omega, a concrete producer with plants in all three states. Alpha, Beta, and Gamma agree that each company will sell only in its home state so that each can reduce expenses and thus compete more effectively with Omega. Before the agreement, each of the small companies had 10 percent of the market, and Omega had 70 percent. After the agreement, each of the small companies had 17 percent, and Omega had 49 percent. Despite this apparent increase in competition, the conduct of

Alpha, Beta, and Gamma is a per se violation of § 1 of the Sherman Act because it is a horizontal market division.

Al, Bob, and Charlie are cement salesmen in Michigan, Ohio, and Indiana, respectively. They all work for Oscar Concrete, a cement producer with plants in all three states. Oscar tells them that Al is to sell cement only in Michigan, Bob is to sell only in Ohio, and Charlie is to sell only in Indiana. While this is obviously a horizontal market division, since only one firm is involved, it is not a violation of § 1 of the Sherman Act.

Section 2: Monopolizing and Attempts to Monopolize

Section 2 of the Sherman Act is nearly as brief as § 1 and is equally as broad. Section 2 makes the following provision:

> *Every person who shall monopolize, or attempt to monopolize, or combine or conspire with any other person or persons, to monopolize any part of the trade or commerce among the several States, or with foreign nations, shall be deemed guilty of a misdemeanor.*

Note that § 2 can be violated either by one person acting alone or by multiple parties acting in concert. In contrast, § 1 can be violated only by multiple parties acting together. (To avoid confusion, remember that it takes two people to violate § 1; it takes only one person to violate § 2.)

Many people have the mistaken idea that monopolies are prohibited by § 2. In fact, no law prohibits having monopoly power. The prohibition in § 2 is against *monopolizing*, that is, seeking a monopoly or attempting to keep a monopoly once one is attained. Either act is monopolizing and is illegal under § 2. Having a monopoly, however, is not illegal.

If a firm is found to dominate an industry, it may also be found to possess monopoly power. As a rule of thumb, control of 70 percent or more of the relevant market is deemed to be monopoly power. However, defining the relevant market may be difficult. The courts examine the product produced by the challenged firm, substitute goods produced by other firms, and they evaluate the elasticity of demand between the challenged product and the substitutes. If the product in question controls 70 percent or more of this relevant market, the challenged firm possesses monopoly power under the courts' interpretation of § 2 of the Sherman Act.

United States v. *E. I. DuPont de Nemours and Co.* is a landmark in U.S. antitrust law involving relevant product market. Notice how the Court defined the relevant market before making its decision as to the propriety of the challenged firm's conduct.

40.1 SALES/MANAGEMENT

DOES CIT HAVE A MONOPOLY?

The growth of Call-Image has been beyond the wildest dreams of CIT. Videophones currently comprise 20 percent of the domestic telephone market, and CIT controls better than 92 percent of the videophone market. Unfortunately, Amy has recently learned that the firm will be investigated by the Justice Department, which believes that CIT violated Section 2 of the Sherman Act in gaining its dominant position. The family is concerned and has asked you what they should do. What advice will you give them?

BUSINESS CONSIDERATIONS Is there any problem with a business gaining a dominant position in its market? Should a business aim for a lesser degree of control to avoid potential problems under the Sherman Act, or should it maximize its potential, dealing with the Sherman Act problems if or when they arise?

ETHICAL CONSIDERATIONS Section 2 of the Sherman Act prohibits monopolizing, and a "virtual-monopoly" position is defined by the courts as controlling 70 percent or more of the relevant product market. Economic theory states that a monopoly exists when an industry only contains one firm. Is it ethical for the courts to define a virtual-monopoly position differently than economic theory defines monopoly position, when the purpose of the Sherman Act is to provide for industrial conduct that is more in line with economic competition?

40.2 UNITED STATES v. E. I. DUPONT DE NEMOURS AND CO. 351 U.S. 377 (1956)

FACTS In the early 1900s, Jacques Brandenberger, a Swiss chemist, inadvertently discovered cellophane. This initial cellophane was thick, hard, and not perfectly transparent, Nonetheless, Brandenberger obtained patents to cover the process, and then began work to perfect his discovery. In 1917, Brandenberger assigned his patents to La Cellophane Societé Anonyme and joined that organization. In 1923, duPont and La Cellophane organized a U.S. company for the manufacture and sale of plain cellophane. The agreement granted duPont the exclusive right to make and sell cellophane in North and Central America, with La Cellophane retaining exclusive rights for the rest of the world. By 1947, duPont had acquired 75 percent of the cellophane sales in the United States. At that time, the government filed suit against duPont, alleging that duPont was guilty of monopolizing the cellophane market in violation of § 2 of the Sherman Act. Judgment was entered for duPont on all issues, and the government appealed.

ISSUE Was duPont guilty of monopolizing due to its dominance of and control over the cellophane market in the United States?

HOLDING No. Although duPont dominated the cellophane market, with 75 percent of sales, it did not dominate the relevant product market, in which it only had 20 percent of sales.

REASONING Although the government argued that cellophane was a separate and distinct product market, the Court felt that the relevant product market was not cellophane, but all "flexible packaging materials." While recognizing that duPont controlled over 75 percent of the cellophane market, the Court agreed with duPont that its 20 percent share of the flexible packaging materials market was far from dominant, and that duPont was not able to monopolize. The Court reasoned as follows: Monopoly power is the power to control prices or to exclude competition, but duPont's power to control prices is limited by the competition afforded by other flexible wrapping materials; if cellophane is to be treated as an independent relevant market, so must be treated polyethylene, pliofilm, saran, and numerous other wrapping materials similar to cellophane; and except as to permeability to gases, cellophane has no characteristics that are not possessed by a number of other materials. The cellophane market should not be viewed as a monopoly when that product has the competition and interchangeability with other wrappings, which the trial record revealed.

BUSINESS CONSIDERATIONS Should a business only be concerned about competition from products that have virtually the same characteristics, or should it also be concerned about products that share several characteristics? How can a business tell what products are true competitors of its product?

ETHICAL CONSIDERATIONS Is it ethical for a business to base its pricing strategy on the pricing strategy of products with which it competes, or should the firm base its pricing strategy purely on its costs and its expected rate of return? From an ethical perspective, thinking of your constituents, should pricing decisions be based on short-term concerns or long-term concerns?

When a dominant position in the relevant product market is present, there is a presumption that § 2 was, or is, violated. However, a number of defenses exist to rebut this presumption. The dominant firm may argue that it is not attempting to retain its power, or that it acquired its position legally, or that its position was "thrust upon" it. Any of these defenses is sufficient to prevent a § 2 prosecution.

The next hypothetical case shows how the defense can be applied:

> Ralph developed a new product, Kleenzall, which does what other soaps or cleansers do, except that it does it better and is cheaper. Kleenzall is good for washing dishes, clothes, floors, walls, and even hair. Kleenzall is so good a product that Ralph has 95 percent of every cleanser and soap market. The major soap producers sue Ralph for monopolizing the industry in violation of the Sherman Act, § 2. The court, however, finds that Ralph is not guilty. He

did nothing wrong in acquiring his market share. Rather, this monopoly was "thrust upon" him by sheer efficiency. However, if Ralph subsequently takes steps to prevent other firms from entering the cleanser market or acts in any manner that seems to be precluding or preventing competition, he may be found guilty of monopolizing. Possessing his monopoly power is legal, but attempting to retain it is illegal!

Remedies

When a Sherman Act violation is shown, both criminal and civil remedies are available. An individual can be fined up to $100,000 and can receive up to three years in prison; a corporation that is convicted can be fined up to $1 million. Also, an injunction can be issued against the prohibited conduct. As a final disincentive, any harmed parties can recover treble damages plus attorney's fees. This means an injured firm can take its damages, multiply them by three, and then add attorney's fees. In at least one case, damages assessed exceeded $200 million. Needless to say, such damages strongly discourage prohibited conduct.

The Clayton Act

By 1914, Congress realized that the Sherman Act alone was not sufficient to solve the major business problems of the country. The Sherman Act was remedial in nature: If a problem existed, the Sherman Act could be used to help correct the problem. Unfortunately, it is possible (if not probable) that by the time the "remedy" is sought the injured party has suffered irreparable harm or has ceased to exist as a business entity. Nothing, however, was available to prevent a problem from developing. In an effort to correct this regulatory deficiency, Congress decided to enact some preventive legislation. The result was the Clayton Act, which was designed to nip problems "in their incipiency." The Clayton Act has four major provisions, each addressing a different potential problem.

Section 2: Price Discrimination

The first regulating section of the Clayton Act, § 2, prohibits price discrimination. The original § 2 made it illegal for a seller to discriminate in price between different purchasers unless the price difference could be justified by a difference in costs. This provision soon placed a number of sellers in a terrible bind. Major purchasers often demanded special prices from sellers. If the sellers refused, they lost the business; if they agreed, they violated the law. As a result, § 2 was amended in 1936 when the Robinson–Patman Act became law. Under the Robinson–Patman Act, buyers were prohibited from knowingly accepting a discriminatory price. In addition, the act prohibited indirect benefits such as dummy brokerage fees and promotional kickbacks.

A person accused of price discrimination can defend against the charge by showing that he or she is meeting, but not beating, the price being offered by a competitor. The accused can also defend by showing that the lower price is being offered because of obsolescence, seasonal variations, or damage to the goods being sold.

Standard Oil Co. (of Indiana) v. *FTC*, a landmark opinion, involved an allegation of price discrimination and a defense of meeting—but not beating—the competition.

40.3 STANDARD OIL CO. (OF INDIANA) v. FTC 340 U.S. 231 (1951)

FACTS Standard Oil of Indiana was accused by the Federal Trade Commission (FTC) of price discrimination under the Robinson–Patman Act. The basis of the charge was that Standard was selling gasoline to four relatively large "jobbers" in the Detroit area for a lower price than it was selling gasoline to numerous small customers in the same area. Standard denied that it was violating the law, asserting two defenses: that the sales were not subject to regulation because they did not involve interstate commerce, and that the lower price was justified because it was given in good faith to meet an equally low price from a competitor and was given to retain the jobbers as customers. The FTC rejected both defenses and ordered Standard to "cease and desist" from the discrimination. Standard appealed this FTC ruling.

ISSUE Did Standard act in good faith in meeting the price of a competitor, or did Standard illegally discriminate in the prices it charged to different customers in the Detroit area?

HOLDING Standard was acting in good faith in meeting the price of a competitor, and did not illegally discriminate.

REASONING The Court found that Standard had been selling gasoline to the Detroit area jobbers since 1936 in "tank-car" quantities (8,000 to 12,000 gallons), while selling to smaller customers in "tank-wagon" quantities (700 to 800 gallons), with a savings of 1½ cents per gallon. This savings was justified by a lower cost in doing business with the larger quantities. However, in this case, such reduced costs did not reflect all of the price reduction given to the larger jobbers, and the FTC ruled that this meant that the lower price was discriminatory in violation of the law. Standard was able to present evidence that the lower price given to the jobbers was given in good faith and was only given to meet the price offered to the jobbers by a competitor. If Standard was to retain these customers, it had to match the price offered by the competition. The FTC denied that this was a valid defense because competition among the retailers was harmed by the price advantage the jobbers enjoyed over the smaller customers of Standard. The Court ruled that the FTC could not elect to allow the "meeting the price of competition" defense in some cases, but elect to reject it in others. The law specifies that a good faith matching of the price of a competitor in order to retain customers is not price discrimination within the meaning of Robinson–Patman. This is true whether the seller is a small firm, a medium-sized firm, or a very large firm such as Standard Oil. Since Standard was able to establish that it was only meeting the price offered by a competitor, it was not guilty of price discrimination.

BUSINESS CONSIDERATIONS Offering quantity discounts is a good way to encourage customers to place larger orders, allowing them to save money on a per-unit basis. However, it is also a good way to encourage the FTC to investigate the firm for price discrimination. What factors should a business consider in offering a quantity discount to its customers? What should the business do to ensure that it does not violate the law in this area?

ETHICAL CONSIDERATIONS Is it ethical for a firm's largest single customer to demand—or even to expect—treatment, including pricing breaks, that is not generally available to other customers of the firm? What can the firm do in such a situation?

The Robinson–Patman Act also changed the standards needed to show a violation. Under the original § 2, it was necessary to show that general competition had been harmed, but under the Robinson–Patman Act, it is sufficient to prosecute on a showing that a competitor was injured. The following example illustrates this point:

> Bill's Bathtub Boutique is the largest customer of Paula's Porcelain Palace. Bill's biggest competitor is Dan's Discount Tub Store. Bill tells Paula that unless she gives him a 10 percent price reduction, he will take his business elsewhere. If Paula gives Bill this price reduction and does not give the same reduction to Dan, both Bill and Paula will be in violation of the Robinson–Patman Act.

In a recent Puerto Rico case,[2] an interesting Robinson–Patman issue was raised. Caribe BMW purchased new automobiles directly from the manufacturer. Caribe's competitors in the market purchased their new BMWs from a wholly-owned subsidiary of the manufacturer, and were able to purchase at a lower price than that offerred to Caribe. The court ruled that a manufacturer and its wholly-owned subsidiary are a single entity for purposes of applying the Robinson–Patman Act so that there was a discriminatory pricing practice in effect, entitling Caribe to remedies for violation of the act.

Section 3: Exclusive Dealings and Tying Arrangements

The second major prohibition under the Clayton Act is found in § 3. This section bans exclusive-dealing contracts and tying arrangements when their "effect may be to substantially lessen competition or tend to create a monopoly." Notice again the preventive intent of the act: Actual harm need not be shown, merely the likelihood that harm will eventually occur.

In an *exclusive-dealing contract,* one party requires the other party to deal with him, and him alone. For example, the seller tells the buyer that unless the buyer buys only from the seller, and not from the seller's competitors, the seller will not deal with the buyer. For such a demand to be effective, the seller must be in a very powerful market position.

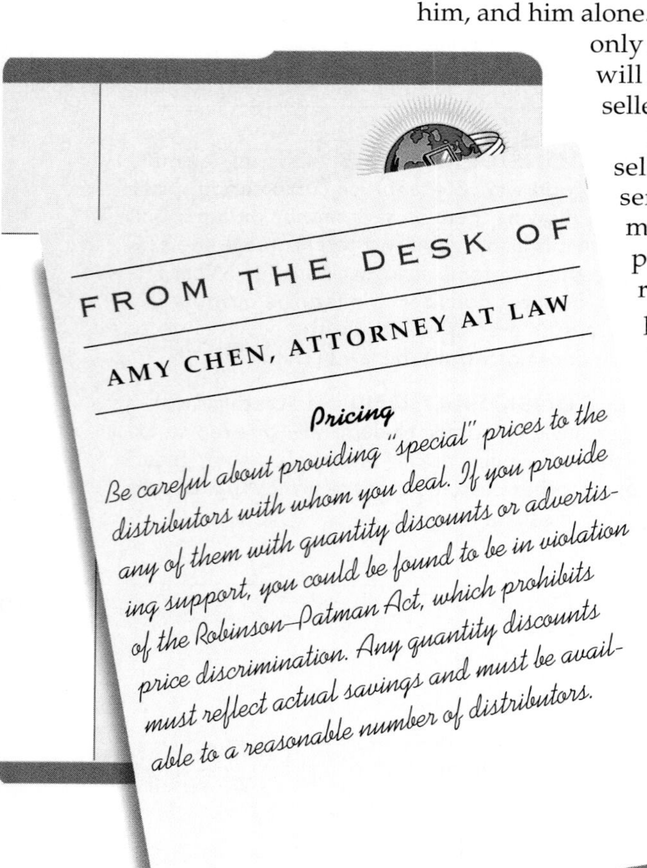

FROM THE DESK OF
AMY CHEN, ATTORNEY AT LAW
Pricing
Be careful about providing "special" prices to the distributors with whom you deal. If you provide any of them with quantity discounts or advertising support, you could be found to be in violation of the Robinson–Patman Act, which prohibits price discrimination. Any quantity discounts must reflect actual savings and must be available to a reasonable number of distributors.

In a *tying arrangement,* one party—usually the seller—refuses to sell one product unless the buyer also takes a second product or service from the seller. For example, a manufacturer of cosmetics might refuse to sell a facial moisturizer unless the buyer agrees to purchase the manufacturer's soap. Usually for this sort of arrangement to work, the seller needs a highly valued, unique product to which he or she can tie a commonly available product. As a defense to a charge that such an arrangement lessens competition or creates a monopoly, the seller may attempt to show that the tied product is tied for quality-control reasons. To do so, the seller must prove that no competitors produce a competing product that works adequately with the controlled product.

The Supreme Court has ruled that a "not insubstantial" amount of commerce must be affected in order to have an illegal tying arrangement.[3] The Ninth Circuit went even further, ruling that there is no requirement for multiple purchasers in order to have an illegal tying arrangement,[4] so long as the effect on commerce is not insubstantial. The amount involved was approximately $100,000 per year for an indeterminant number of years, and the Court ruled that such an amount was sufficiently substantial to allow the trial to proceed even though only one firm was precluded from the market due to the tying arrangement. This could, potentially, open up a number of claims for damages due to tying arrangements by firms that believed there had to be multiple purchasers affected before Section 3 of the Clayton Act was applicable.

Section 7: Antimerger Provisions

The third major section of the Clayton Act, § 7, concerns mergers. As originally written, the only prohibited type of merger was one in which the stock of another firm was acquired with the effect "substantially to lessen competition, or [to] tend to create a monopoly." This prohibition was so narrow that it was rather easily evaded by merging firms.

To broaden the scope of the law, Congress amended § 7 in 1950 by passing the Cellar–Kefauver Act. The amended § 7 prohibits the acquisition of stock or assets of another firm that may tend to have a negative effect on any line of commerce. As a result, firms are now subject to § 7 in almost any type of merger —horizontal, vertical, or conglomerate. A horizontal merger is one between competing firms; a vertical merger is one between a firm and one of its major suppliers or customers; a conglomerate merger is one between firms in two noncompetitive industries.

As a challenge to a merger, the government might argue that a "concentration trend" has been established, or that one of the firms was a "potential entrant" into one of the industries affected by the merger. As a defense to a challenged merger, the merging firms might raise the "failing-company" doctrine, showing that without the merger one of the firms would have gone out of business. The following example illustrates the failing-company doctrine.

> Fred's Stereo is in severe financial difficulty. Irv's Interstate Sound Store, the largest stereo dealer in the region, buys Fred's. Under the failing-company doctrine, if Fred's would have gone bankrupt, the merger with Irv's is probably permissible.

United States v. *Von's Grocery Co.*, a landmark case, illustrates the concentration-trend doctrine as it has been applied in several proposed mergers.

40.2

MANAGEMENT/MANUFACTURING

TYING PRODUCTS

A regional manufacturer of answering machines has approached CIT with what it considers a "can't miss" deal. The manufacturer wants to produce an answering machine that has video as well as audio tape capabilities and that can only be used with Call-Image videophones. According to the president of this company, the two firms can each use the success of the other firm to gain a larger market share in their respective industries. Although the idea is intriguing, the family is afraid there may be some legal implication they have overlooked. They ask you what you think of the idea. What advice will you give them?

BUSINESS CONSIDERATIONS What potential problems could arise under the various antitrust laws from tying your product to the products of another firm? Could this be considered an attempt by each firm to monopolize its respective industry?

ETHICAL CONSIDERATIONS In the United States, basically, a firm must act and then await results if the firm is considering conduct that may or may not violate antitrust provisions. In the European Union, firms can ask for a "negative clearance," seeking advance permission to do something that, eventually, may be determined to violate the Union's rules of competition. Is it more ethical to be allowed to seek advance permission, or to act and then wait to see if the government will challenge the conduct? Why?

40.4 UNITED STATES v. VON'S GROCERY CO. 384 U.S. 270 (1966)

FACTS In 1958, Von's Grocery was the third-largest grocery store chain in the Los Angeles geographic market, while Shopping Bag Food Stores was the sixth largest. By 1960, the combined sales of these two stores was 7.5 percent of the $2.5 billion in retail grocery sales for Los Angeles. Over the previous decade, both stores had grown rapidly: Von's had nearly doubled its number of stores, and its sales had increased fourfold; Shopping Bag had more than doubled its number of stores, and its sales had increased sevenfold; Von's had doubled its market share, with

40.4 UNITED STATES v. VON'S GROCERY CO. *(cont.)* 384 U.S. 270 (1966)

Shopping Bag tripling its share. When the two stores merged in 1960, the resulting chain was the second largest in the L.A. market, with sales of over $172 million per year. From the date of the merger through 1963, the number of single stores in the area decreased from 5,365 to 3,590. In that same period, the number of chains with at least two stores increased from 96 to 150. Despite this trend, the district court rejected the government's argument that there was a concentration trend in the industry and upheld the merger of Von's and Shopping Bag. The government appealed that ruling to the Supreme Court.

ISSUE Did the merger between Von's and Shopping Bag violate § 7 of the Clayton Act as amended by Cellar–Kefauver?

HOLDING Yes. This merger, together with the other evidence from the region, showed a definite concentration trend with a resulting decrease in competition.

REASONING The Court began by explaining the purpose of the antimerger laws:

> *Like the Sherman Act in 1890 and the Clayton Act in 1914, the basic purpose of the 1950 Cellar–Kefauver Act was to prevent economic concentration in the American economy by keeping a large number of small competitors in business. . . .*

The Court then pointed out that Congress wanted to stop concentration trends before competition was destroyed for the small competitors, and that the L.A. retail grocery business was a perfect example of the problems presented by concentration trends. The number of small or single-entity competitors was steadily declining, while the number of chains—especially large chains—was steadily expanding. Von's and Shopping Bag did not merge to save one of the firms or to allow them to compete with a much larger and more powerful firm. Instead they merged to become even more powerful and command an even larger share of the market. While the merger may not have eliminated competition in the market, it portended future mergers among other firms until competition could have been seriously curtailed. The merger violated § 7 of the Clayton Act as amended by Cellar–Kefauver, and the district court was directed to order divestiture without delay.

BUSINESS CONSIDERATIONS Why would a business want to merge with one of its largest competitors? Why would a business be hesitant about merging with one of its largest competitors?

ETHICAL CONSIDERATIONS How does a proposed merger affect each of the four constituent groups of a business? If some of the groups will benefit and some will not benefit from the proposed merger, how should the business decide, from an ethical perspective, whether to proceed with the merger?

Section 8: Interlocking Directorates

The final substantive section of the Clayton Act is § 8. This section prohibits interlocking directorates. In other words, no one may sit on the boards of directors of two or more competing corporations if either of the firms has capital and surplus in excess of $1 million and if a merger between them violates any antitrust law.

THE FEDERAL TRADE COMMISSION ACT

The year 1914 was a very busy year for antitrust regulation. Congress passed not only the Clayton Act but also the Federal Trade Commission Act. The Federal Trade Commission Act did two important things:

1. It created the Federal Trade Commission (FTC) to enforce antitrust laws, especially the Clayton Act.

YOU BE THE JUDGE

Proposed Railroad Merger

The Southern Pacific and the Union Pacific railroads have proposed a merger of the two lines. (They previously proposed merging in 1913, but that merger was blocked in the U.S. Supreme Court.) The merger, if approved, would make the resulting railroad the largest in the United States. It would link 25 western states, Canada, and Mexico. Although some 3,500 workers would lose their jobs, the merged rail lines would employ more than 53,000 people. A number of people involved in agriculture have objected to the proposed merger, alleging that if the two lines merge the impact on farmers and farming in the western states will be detrimental.[5] This case has been brought before *your* court. How will you rule in this case?

BUSINESS CONSIDERATIONS What should be the most important factor for a firm to consider when it is approached regarding a possible merger? When should a board of directors look for firms with whom they can profitably merge?

ETHICAL CONSIDERATIONS From an ethical perspective, how can a firm justify a merger in which 3,500 people will lose their jobs? What factors would offset the lost jobs?

SOURCE: *The Denver Post,* July 4, 1996, p. 1A.

2. In § 5, it provided a broad area of prohibitions to close loopholes left by other statutes.

Section 5 of the act prohibits "unfair methods of competition" and "unfair and deceptive trade practices." This broad language permits the FTC to regulate conduct that technically might be beyond the reach of the other, more specific antitrust statutes. The area of unfair and deceptive trade practices was intentionally made broad and somewhat vague to grant the FTC the leeway to proceed against any commercial practices that seem to be unfair or deceptive under the circumstances. If the statute is specific, businesspeople will find methods to circumvent it, methods that may be unfair or deceptive but within the technical limits of the law. The strength of the law has been its breadth, as well as the willingness of the FTC to attack practices that had been followed for many years.

To further strengthen the FTC position, a violation can be found without proof of any actual deception. A mere showing that there is a "fair possibility" that the public will be deceived is sufficient to establish that the conduct is unfair and deceptive. In addition, if a representation made by a company is ambiguous, with one honest meaning and one deceptive meaning, the FTC will treat it as deceptive and as a material aspect of the transaction so that remedies are available.

If the FTC opposes a business practice as unfair or deceptive, it issues a cease-and-desist order. The business must stop the challenged conduct or face a fine for disobeying the order. The fine is $5,000 per violation. This may sound small, but realize that each day the order is ignored constitutes a separate violation. Thus, ignoring the order for one week costs $35,000 in fines; for a month, $150,000 in fines; and so on.

In recent years, the FTC has become particularly concerned about two business practices: deceptive advertising and "bait-and-switch" advertising. In an effort to force truth in advertising, the FTC has been carefully studying the commercials run by corporations and, in many cases in which the advertising was deemed especially misleading, ordering corrective advertising.

Warner-Lambert Co. v. *FTC* is a well-known case in this area. In it, the FTC attacked Warner-Lambert for the ads it had run for one of its products, Listerine.

40.5 WARNER-LAMBERT CO. v. FTC

562 F.2d 749 (D.C. Cir. 1977)

FACTS Warner-Lambert is the producer of Listerine mouthwash. Listerine has been produced, without a change in the formula, since 1879. From its inception in 1879 to 1972, Listerine was represented in advertising as a beneficial treatment for colds, cold symptoms, and sore throats. In 1972, the Federal Trade Commission issued a cease-and-desist order prohibiting such advertising claims in the future. In addition, the FTC ordered Warner-Lambert to run corrective advertising to remove any lasting impressions implanted with the public that Listerine was an effective cold and sore throat medicine. Warner-Lambert agreed to stop running the challenged ads, but objected to running the corrective ads.

ISSUE Can the FTC require a company to run corrective advertising to remedy the harm done by prior misleading or deceptive advertising?

HOLDING Yes. The FTC can order a company to run corrective advertising in appropriate cases.

REASONING The ingredients in Listerine are not of sufficient quantity to have any therapeutic effect. Even if the quantities were sufficient, gargling with the product would not allow the ingredients to reach the affected areas. Moreover, the germs Listerine reputedly "kills on contact" have no affect on either colds or sore throats. The FTC has the power to shape remedies to fit the problems presented. Corrective advertising, for example, is an appropriate remedy to inform past and future consumers of prior deceptive advertisings and beliefs created by the advertisements. Corrective advertising is not a violation of the First Amendment. Rather, it is a necessary step to remove from the public mind a false belief placed there by the wrong-doer. The court ordered Warner-Lambert to run the corrective advertising, and in it state: "Listerine will not help prevent colds or sore throats or lessen their severity." Furthermore, this correction had to appear in every Listerine advertisement until Warner-Lambert ran $10 million worth of ads for the product.

BUSINESS CONSIDERATIONS Advertising a product carries with it a substantial risk, but also carries the possibility of a substantial return. A good ad can help to boost sales. A bad ad might cost sales. A misleading ad may result in legal action against the firm. What sort of policy should a firm have for deciding how to advertise and how far to "push the envelope" in its advertising?

ETHICAL CONSIDERATIONS Several years ago Isuzu Motors advertised by using a character named "Joe Isuzu" in its ads. Joe Isuzu *never* told the truth, but the truth of his statements *were* scrolled across the bottom of the screen while he talked. Is such an ad unethical, or merely humorous? What should a company using such an ad do if customers start to believe what they are hearing and start to ignore what they should be reading?

Bait-and-switch advertising involves advertising a product at an especially enticing price to get the customer into the store (the "bait") and then talking the customer into buying a more expensive model (the "switch") because the advertised model is sold out or has some alleged defect. An advertiser who refuses to show the advertised item to the customer or who has insufficient quantities on hand to satisfy reasonable customer demand is engaging in an unfair trade practice in violation of § 5 of the FTC Act.

UNFAIR TRADE PRACTICES

Some common law unfair trade practices, such as palming off goods and violating trade secrets, also deserve mention. Palming off involves advertising, designing, or selling goods as if they were the goods of another. The person who is palming off goods is fraudulently taking advantage of the goodwill and brand loyalty of the imitated producer. This practice also frequently involves patent, copyright, or trademark infringements.

Trade secrets are special processes, formulas, and the like that are guarded and treated confidentially by the holder of the trade secret. Employees of a firm that has trade secrets must not betray their loyalty to the firm by revealing the trade secrets to others. To do so is a tort, and the employee can be held liable for any damages suffered by the employer. In addition, the firm or person who receives the information is guilty of appropriating the trade secret, and use of the secret can be stopped by injunction; the recipient of the information will also be liable for damages suffered by the trade secret holder. As we just mentioned, palming off frequently involves the infringement of a patent, a copyright, or a trademark. These three areas, along with a few others, such as service marks and trade names, are protected by federal statutes.

A patent is a federally created and protected monopoly power given to inventors. If a person invents something that is new, useful, and not obvious to a person of ordinary skill in the industry, the inventor is entitled to a patent. In exchange for making the method of production public, the patent grants the inventor an exclusive right to use, make, or sell the product for 17 years. If anyone violates this exclusive right, the patent holder can file an infringement suit. If the court upholds the patent, the infringer will be enjoined from further production and will be liable for damages to the holder of the patent.

A copyright, protected by the Copyright Office of the Library of Congress, is the protection given to writers, artists, and composers. The creator of a book, song, work of art, or similar item has the exclusive right to the profits from the creation for the life of the creator plus 50 years. Any infringement can result in an infringement action in federal court, with injunctive relief and damages being awarded to the holder of the copyright.

A trademark is a mark or symbol used to identify a particular brand name or product. Copying the trademark of a competitor or using a symbol deceptively similar to that of a competitor is a violation of the Lanham Act of 1946, and the violator is subject to an injunction and the imposition of damages.

EXEMPTIONS

Some conduct appears to violate various antitrust laws, and yet the actor is never challenged for the conduct. Many people are confused by this lack of action, questioning why that party is allowed to do something when others are not allowed to do the same thing. The reason is probably that the particular party belongs to a group specifically exempted from antitrust coverage.

Labor unions are exempt from the provisions of the Sherman Act by the Norris–LaGuardia Act, passed in 1932. They are also exempt from the Clayton Act by § 6 of the Clayton Act. The exemption applies only to "labor disputes" and normal union activities.

http:// RESOURCES FOR BUSINESS LAW STUDENTS

NAME	RESOURCES	WEB ADDRESS
Sherman Antitrust Act—15 U.S.C. § 1-7	LII provides a hypertext and searchable version of 15 U.S.C. § 1-7, popularly known as the Sherman Antitrust Act.	http://www.law.cornell.edu/uscode/15/1.html
Clayton Act—15 U.S.C. § 12-25	LII provides a hypertext and searchable version of 15 U.S.C. § 12-25, popularly known as the Clayton Antitrust Act.	http://www.law.cornell.edu/uscode/15/12.html
Robinson–Patman Act—15 U.S.C. § 13	LII provides a hypertext and searchable version of 15 U.S.C. § 13, popularly known as the Robinson–Patman Act.	http://www.law.cornell.edu/uscode/15/13.html
U.S. Department of Justice, Antitrust Division	The Antitrust Division of the U.S. Department of Justice provides press releases, speeches and Congressional testimony, antitrust guidelines, court cases, and international agreements and documents.	http://www.usdoj.gov/atr/atr.htm
U.S. Federal Trade Commission (FTC)	The FTC provides news and press releases, speeches and articles, and facts for consumers and businesses.	http://www.ftc.gov/

Farm cooperatives are also exempt from antitrust coverage so long as they are engaged in the sale of farm produce. (A number of other exemptions exist, but they have little impact on business law.)

Summary

Since 1890, the federal government has regulated business to ensure competition. This legislative effort is referred to as antitrust law. The cornerstone of antitrust law is the Sherman Act, which prohibits joint conduct that unreasonably restricts competition or attempts to monopolize any area of commerce. Some conduct is considered so lacking in social value that it constitutes a per se violation. Other questionable conduct is measured under the rule of reason. If a violation is found, injured parties are entitled to treble damages.

The Sherman Act, however, did not suffice in preventing many violations. Therefore, Congress enacted several other statutes to help protect the competitive ideal. One of these statutes is the Clayton Act, which prohibits price discrimination (by means of the Robinson–Patman Act), exclusive-dealing contracts and tying arrangements, a number of mergers (by means of the Cellar–Kefauver Act), and interlocking directorates. The purpose of the Clayton Act is to stop anticompetitive conduct "in its incipiency." In order to do this, the government can attack conduct within the regulated areas if the effect of such conduct may be to substantially lessen competition in any line of trade or commerce. Notice that the government does not have to prove that competition will be harmed; it merely must show that competition is likely to be harmed. This provides a powerful tool to the government in its antitrust campaigns.

As a means of protecting competition, Congress passed the Federal Trade Commission Act. This act has two major aspects: It created the Federal Trade Commission to act as a watchdog in the antitrust area, and it prohibits unfair and deceptive trade practices. There are numerous other unfair trade practice areas as well, but most of these are regulated under state law.

DISCUSSION QUESTIONS

1. Section 1 of the Sherman Act is intended to protect competition by prohibiting restraints on trade. In order to apply this section, the court uses the so-called "rule of reason." What is the rule of reason, and how does it affect § 1 of the Sherman Act?
2. What is "conscious parallelism," and how does it relate to § 1 of the Sherman Act? What is "price leadership," and how does it relate to § 1 of the Sherman Act? How can a person distinguish conscious parallelism from price leadership?
3. Can a firm totally dominate an industry and not be guilty of monopolizing in violation of § 2 of the Sherman Act? Can a firm be found guilty of monopolizing an industry if it only controls three-quarters of the relevant market?
4. Section 2 of the Clayton Act prohibits price discrimination; however, it has been found to be less effective than originally expected. As a result, the Robinson–Patman Act was passed to supplement the provisions of § 2 of the Clayton Act. What are the major new prohibitions that the Robinson–Patman Act added to § 2 of the Clayton Act?
5. What is the major difference in philosophy between the coverage of the Sherman Act and the coverage of the Clayton Act and the Federal Trade Commission Act? Which philosophy is more effective in protecting competition?
6. What is "bait-and-switch" advertising or selling, and why is such conduct treated as an unfair trade practice under the provisions of the Federal Trade Commission Act? What must a firm show to avoid prosecution if it is accused of bait-and-switch advertising?
7. Anna and Bruce are competitors in the frozen quiche market. After years of competition in which both firms made less profits than they felt they deserved, they agreed to charge the same price for their products and to compete only in quality and advertising. This new arrangement allowed both firms to increase prices slightly, which provided them with a reasonable return on their investments. Without this agreement, at least one of the firms would have failed within a year. The agreement between Anna and Bruce is challenged by the government as violative of the federal antitrust laws. Have they violated any federal antitrust laws? Explain your answer.
8. Samantha is a major shirt manufacturer. She sells shirts at one price but gives a quantity discount on orders of 5,000 shirts or more. Only two of Samantha's customers, out of 600 total customers, can take advantage of this quantity discount. Is Samantha in violation of any antitrust laws? Explain your reasoning.
9. Mort is one of many producers of sugar cane. He developed a new machine for processing sugar cane that was much faster and much cheaper than any other machine available in the country. Mort was willing to lease his machine to sugar processors, but only if the processors bought all their sugar cane from Mort. What antitrust questions are raised by Mort's conduct? If Mort is accused of an antitrust violation, what defenses might he be able to assert?
10. Archaic Airlines advertises that it "gets you there ON TIME more often than any other airline." In fact, Archaic has a very bad record as to arriving on time, with over half of its flights arriving more than 30 minutes late. What might the FTC do to Archaic in regard to this advertising campaign?

CASE PROBLEMS AND WRITING ASSIGNMENTS

1. The Goldfarbs wanted to purchase a home in Fairfax County, Virginia. The financing agency required them to obtain title insurance, which required a title examination. By state law, only a member of the Virginia Bar Association can legally perform the title examination. When the Goldfarbs contacted a local attorney, he quoted them the fee established by the Fairfax County Bar Association, 1 percent of the value of the property. The Goldfarbs decided that this was too expensive, and they began to shop around for a lower fee. However, every attorney they contacted quoted them the same fee, the fee published by the Fairfax County Bar Association. The Goldfarbs eventually retained the first attorney with whom they had spoken, obtained their title examination, and then filed suit against the state and the County Bar Association, alleging an illegal price-fixing arrangement in violation of § 1 of the Sherman Act. Was the imposition of a

minimum fee schedule by the bar association and the adherence to the fee schedule by members of the association an illegal price-fixing agreement? [See *Goldfarb et ux.* v. *Virginia State Bar et al.*, 95 S.Ct. 2004 (1975).]

2. Utah Pie was a local bakery operating in the Salt Lake City area. It began producing frozen pies in 1957, with immediate success. In 1958, Utah Pie built a new plant and gained a competitive edge over its three major competitors—Pet, Continental, and Carnation. Each of the three major competitors independently lowered its prices in the Utah market in an effort to cut into Utah Pie's growing market share. Eventually, each of the three major competitors was selling its frozen pies below cost in the Salt Lake City area. Utah Pie sued all three firms, alleging that their conduct violated the Clayton Act as amended by Robinson–Patman. Did the special prices offered by the three major producers in the Utah market amount to unlawful price discrimination? Explain your answer. [See *Utah Pie Co.* v. *Continental Baking Co.*, 386 U.S. 685 (1967).]

3. Prior to 1988, Nissan advertising was conducted on two distinct levels: national advertising that was developed, placed, and paid for by Nissan; and local advertising that was obtained and paid for by individual Nissan dealerships. The Baltimore-area Nissan dealers used Faulkner, a local advertising firm, to prepare their advertising. Because of the size and importance of the Nissan account, Faulkner worked exclusively on Nissan advertising. In May 1988, Nissan announced a new "local-market advertising" plan that was to take effect 1 October 1988. Under the plan, Nissan was going to increase the wholesale price of its products in order to pay for increased advertising that was to be developed by Nissan and its ad agency. This new advertising was for both national and local use. At the same time, Nissan discontinued its prior habit of providing contributions to local dealers to develop and pay for their advertising campaigns. As a result, the Baltimore Nissan dealers stopped using Faulkner for their advertising, effectively eliminating Faulkner's business. Faulkner has sued Nissan, alleging that this arrangement is an illegal tying contract. How will the court resolve this case? What factors will the court examine in reaching its decision? [See *Faulkner Advertising Associates, Inc.* v. *Nissan Motor Corp.*, 905 F.2d 769 (4th Cir. 1990).]

4. Tampella is a Finnish corporation that manufactures and sells hardrock hydraulic underground drilling rigs (HHUDRs) around the world. Hughes, a Texas-based corporation, owned a French subsidiary, Secoma, that was also involved in the HHUDR industry. In 1989, when Tampella proposed the acquisition of Secoma, the U.S. Justice Department challenged the proposed acquisition under § 7 of the Clayton Act. According to the Justice Department, the acquisition would substantially lessen competition in the HHUDR market in the United States. Between 1986 and 1989, only four firms sold HHUDRs in the United States, and annual sales varied from 22 to 43 units. Each HHUDR unit costs several hundred thousand dollars, and the purchasers are all highly sophisticated and knowledgeable in the industry. Given these factors, does this acquisition violate § 7 of the Clayton Act? Explain your reasoning. [See *U.S.* v. *Baker Hughes, Inc.*, 908 F.2d 981 (D.C. Cir. 1990).]

5. The commercial printing industry in the United States has two major methods for printing: gravure and web offset. Gravure (or rotogravure) printing has nine commercial printing companies in this country. Two of the nine firms, R. R. Donnelley and Sons Company and the Meredith Corporation, reached an agreement in which Donnelley would take over all the commercial printing operations of Meredith. The FTC objected to the agreement, alleging that the effect would be to substantially lessen competition in a line of commerce, commercial printing. Donnelley and Meredith defended the agreement, arguing that limiting the line of commerce to gravure printing is unrealistic and distorts the overall effect on the industry of the proposed takeover. Gravure printing only represents 16 percent of all commercial printing in the country. If the takeover is allowed to stand, Donnelley would be the number one gravure commercial printer in the country, but would still possess only 8 percent of the total commercial printing industry market. Is the FTC definition of the relevant line of commerce appropriate in this case, or has the FTC defined the line of commerce too narrowly? Discuss fully. [See *FTC* v. *R. R. Donnelley & Sons Co.*, 1990-2 Trade Cases [CCH] 69, 240 (20 November 1990).]

6. **BUSINESS APPLICATION CASE** Falls City Industries, Inc. is a regional brewer of Falls City beer. This beer is sold primarily in Kentucky and Indiana. From 1972 to 1978 Falls City sold its beer to Vanco, its only wholesale distributor in Vanderburgh County, Indiana, at a higher price than it sold to its only wholesale distributor in Henderson County, Kentucky. These two counties form a single metropolitan district that extends across the state line separating the two counties. Indiana law requires that all brewers who sell beer in Indiana must sell that beer to all Indiana wholesalers at the same price. The state law also prohibits Indiana wholesalers from selling beer to out-of-state retailers, and prohibits Indiana retailers from purchasing beer from out-of-state wholesalers.

Vanco filed suit against Falls City for price discrimination in violation of Section 2 of the Clayton Act as amended by the Robinson–Patman Act. Falls City insisted that it did not discriminate in that it charged all Indiana wholesalers the same price. How should this case be resolved? What is the likely business impact on beer retailers in the two counties if the different prices are upheld by the court? [See *Falls City Industries, Inc.* v. *Vanco Beverage, Inc.*, 460 U.S. 428 (1983).]

7. **ETHICS APPLICATION CASE** Microsoft, the world's largest producer of software, entered into negotiations to purchase Intuit, the largest producer of personal finance software in the country. The expressed reason for the purchase was the intention of Microsoft to enter the emerging field of electronic commerce. The Justice Department began investigating this planned takeover with an eye to blocking the purchase. The theory being advanced by the Justice Department was that Microsoft was attempting to establish a "vertical foreclosure." The rationale behind this is that Microsoft would effectively dominate "on-line" services if they are allowed to acquire Intuit, effectively precluding competition in this developing area of computer technology.

   How should this case be decided? What ethical issues are raised by the prospect of the world's largest software producer also becoming the world's largest provider of on-line services? [See "Justice Agency Seeks Data from America Online, Lotus and Other Firms," *Wall Street Journal* (1 February 1995), p. B3.]

8. **IDES CASE** The Detroit Auto Dealers Association (DADA) is a trade association in Detroit to which most of the automobile dealers in the Detroit area belong. In 1960 DADA voted to close dealer showrooms on several weekday evenings. In 1973, DADA voted to close dealer showrooms on Saturdays. As a result of these two votes, automobile dealer showrooms in Detroit were virtually all closed at the same times, effectively precluding shopping for new cars during those hours. The Federal Trade Commission viewed this conduct as a restraint of trade, and initiated an administrative action against DADA and its members, alleging a violation of the Sherman Act. According to the FTC, the members of DADA had conspired or combined to set uniform hours for having the showrooms open in restraint of trade. How should this case be resolved? Apply the IDES principles in reaching your decision. [See *Detroit Auto Dealers Association, Inc.* v. *FTC*, 95 F.2d 457 (6th Cir. 1992).]

NOTES

1. *SCFC ILC, Inc.* v. *Visa, USA, Inc.*, 36 F3d 958 (10th Cir. 1994).
2. *Caribe BMW, Inc.* v. *Bayerische Motoren Werke Aktiengesellschaft*, 19 F.3d 745 (1st Cir. 1994).
3. *Jefferson Parish Hospital District #2* v. *Hyde*, 466 U.S. 2, 104 S.Ct. 1551 (1984).
4. *Datagate, Inc.* v. *Hewlett-Packard Co.*, 60 F.3d 1421 (1995).
5. Adriel Bettelheim, "Rail Merger OK'd," *The Denver Post* (4 July 1996), 1A.

A G E N D A

CIT plans to sell Call-Image videophones to customers both directly and indirectly. For direct sales, the firm is considering extending credit to some customers. The Kochanowskis would like to know what consumer protection statutes the family members need to follow if they do extend credit to customers. Tom and Anna also want to know what information they can expect to receive if they seek a credit report on prospective employees. Because a significant number of CIT's customers will be consumers, Tom and Anna are concerned about consumer product safety. Should CIT be apprehensive, or should the firm not worry until or unless its products are inspected by the federal government's Consumer Product Safety Commission? What information concerning warranties should CIT provide with its products?

These and other questions are likely to arise as you study this chapter. Be prepared! You never know when one of the Kochanowskis will need your help or advice.

Consumer Protection

O U T L I N E

INTRODUCTION

For many years, state laws regulated consumer credit activities. But the lack of uniformity among such laws, coupled with the increasing need to protect consumers from fraudulent practices, erroneous information found in credit reports, discrimination in the extension of credit and harassing debt-collection practices, has led to the enactment of numerous federal laws. Product safety also remains a significant issue for the vast majority of the American public. In this chapter, we consider the most noteworthy of these consumer protection laws.[1]

CONSUMER CREDIT

Consumer credit has become a gargantuan business in the United States and increasingly draws the attention of federal lawmakers and regulators. On a given day, we in the United States purchase 500,000 appliances, 40,000 motor vehicles, and 15,000 homes on credit.[2] The ubiquity of such credit transactions in turn has led to a giant industry involving the sale of credit reports by credit bureaus. To generate the two million such reports that are sold every working day, credit bureaus retain information on 90 percent of the adults in our country—some 170 million people.[3]

THE CONSUMER CREDIT PROTECTION ACT

Title I of the Consumer Credit Protection Act of 1968, more commonly known as the Truth in Lending Act (TILA), represents the landmark modern consumer protection law. After its enactment, other federal legislation followed.

TILA, in essence, is a disclosure statute designed to force creditors to inform consumers, via a standardized form and terminology, of the actual costs of credit. This enables consumers to make more informed decisions about credit. Indeed, to comply with TILA, creditors, prior to the consummation of a credit transaction, must provide every consumer with a separate disclosure statement that satisfies the dictates of both TILA and the Federal Reserve Board (FRB), which enforces TILA. Failure to comply with TILA's disclosure provisions subjects the creditor to various civil, criminal, and statutory liabilities.

Although primarily a disclosure statute, TILA also regulates transactions in which a consumer uses his or her home as collateral for a loan, with the exception of transactions involving the purchase or initial construction of a home (that is, home equity or home improvement loans). For situations covered by the statute, TILA allows a three-day cooling-off period, during which the consumer may decide to rescind (that is, cancel) the loan. Congress apparently wanted to allow the consumer the opportunity to reconsider any transaction that may encumber the consumer's title to his or her home. The power of recission potentially lasts for three years from the consummation of the transaction or the sale of the property, whichever occurs first.

Upon its initial enactment, TILA resulted in a great deal of litigation that benefited consumers, much to the chagrin of the lending industry. Largely in response to lobbying efforts by lenders, Congress in 1980 enacted the Truth in Lending Simplification and Reform Act, which the FRB subsequently labeled the "new" truth-in-lending act. Designed avowedly to simplify the disclosures mandated by the 1968 act (which, according to the FRB, resulted in consumer confusion due to the detail required), the 1980 act makes creditor compliance easier. But experts debate whether providing consumers with less information actually furthers the law's overriding purpose of enhancing the consumer's ability to meaningfully shop for credit. Litigation under the new act nonetheless has decreased dramatically. In response to litigation stemming from the part of TILA that deals with home equity loans, Congress in 1995 amended that portion of TILA so as to give lenders some relief from the numerous class action suits that in the mid-1990s had sought the remedy of rescission for the entire class. Hence, these amendments, among other things, provide retroactive and prospective relief from liability for certain types of creditor finance charges.

Regulation Z promulgated by the FRB summarizes the scope of TILA. Therefore, one always should read the statute in conjunction with this regulation. In general, Regulation Z covers persons who regularly offer or extend credit to consumers who seek to use the credit for personal, family, or household purposes and the transaction is subject to a finance charge or, by written agreement, is payable in four or more installments. In the initial disclosure statement, the creditor in a clear and conspicuous manner must provide detailed information in a meaningful sequence to the consumer concerning finance charges (including interest, time differential charges, service charges, points, loan fees, appraisal fees, and certain insurance premiums), any other charges, the creditor's retention of a security interest, and a statement of billing rights that respectively outlines the consumer's rights and the creditor's responsibilities.

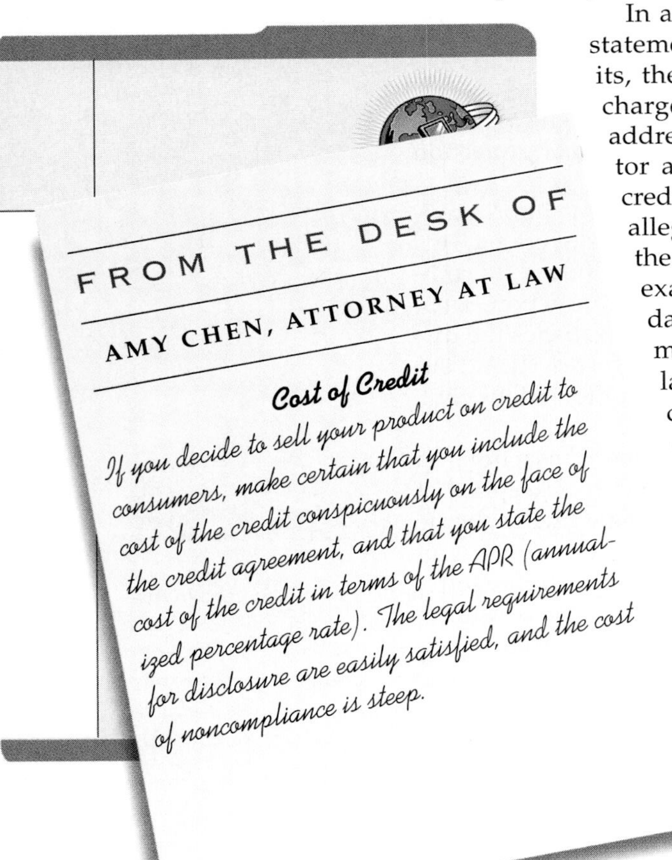

FROM THE DESK OF
AMY CHEN, ATTORNEY AT LAW
Cost of Credit
If you decide to sell your product on credit to consumers, make certain that you include the cost of the credit conspicuously on the face of the credit agreement, and that you state the cost of the credit in terms of the APR (annualized percentage rate). The legal requirements for disclosure are easily satisfied, and the cost of noncompliance is steep.

In addition, creditors must furnish the consumer with periodic statements that disclose various items: the previous balance, credits, the amount of the finance charge, the annual percentage rate charged, the closing date of the billing cycle, the new balance, the address to be used for notice of billing errors, and so on. The creditor also must promptly credit consumer payments and refund credit balances. A consumer must notify a creditor in writing of an alleged billing error within 60 days of the creditor's transmitting the bill to the consumer. TILA and Regulation Z tell the consumer exactly how to satisfy these notification procedures. Within 30 days after receiving notification from the consumer, the creditor must acknowledge in writing the disputed bill or item. And no later than 90 days after receipt of the consumer's notice, the creditor either must correct the disputed bill or, alternatively, explain in writing why the creditor believes the account is correct and supply copies of documented evidence of the consumer's indebtedness.

A creditor who complies with these provisions has no further obligations to the consumer, even if the consumer continues to make substantially the same allegations regarding the alleged error. Until the dispute is settled, however, the creditor may not do the following: try to collect the cost of the disputed item; close or restrict the consumer's account during the controversy, although the creditor can apply the disputed amount to the consumer's credit limit; or make or threaten to make an adverse report that the consumer is in arrears or that his or her bill is delinquent because of nonpayment of the disputed amount. Any creditor who fails to comply with these provisions forfeits the amount in dispute, plus any finance charges, provided the amount does not exceed $50.

These requirements cover "open-ended" credit transactions, such as those accomplished pursuant to credit cards (Visa, Mastercard, American Express, and so forth) or department store revolving charge accounts. If you check a credit card bill, you will notice that it sets out the information required under Regulation Z.

Regulation Z (as well as TILA) also applies to "closed-end" credit transactions, such as consumer loans from finance companies; credit purchases of cars, major appliances, and furniture; and real estate purchases. Different disclosure rules exist for closed-end transactions.

Other provisions of TILA prohibit the issuance of a credit card except in response to an oral or written request or application and limit the liability of the cardholder to $50 in cases of unauthorized use of the card if the cardholder notifies the creditor of an unauthorized use because of the loss or theft of the card. In some circumstances, a person who knowingly and fraudulently uses or traffics in counterfeit access devices (that is, credit cards, plates, codes, account numbers, or any means of account access) and during a one-year period obtains $1,000 in value as a result of this conduct, is subject to a maximum fine of not more than the greater of $100,000 or twice the value obtained by the offense or imprisonment of not more than ten years (or both).

Remedies sought by individuals for creditors' violations of TILA include actual damages and statutory damages of twice the finance charges (but not less than $100 or more than $1,000). Class actions for actual damages as well as statutory damages of an amount equal to the lesser of $500,000 or 1 percent of the creditors' net worth also are possible. Awards of attorneys' fees to successful litigants are available under the statute, too. Criminal penalties for each willful and knowing failure to make the proper disclosures required by the act include fines of not more than $5,000 and one year's imprisonment. Several agencies—the FRB and the Federal Trade Commission (FTC), for example—have responsibility for the administrative enforcement of TILA. Defenses to liability include the expiration of the one-year statute of limitations (for disclosure violations), creditor bona fide clerical errors, and the creditor's timely correction of an error.

Towers World Airways, Inc. v. *PHH Aviation Systems, Inc.* illustrates many of these concepts.

41.1 TOWERS WORLD AIRWAYS, INC. v. PHH AVIATION SYSTEMS, INC.

933 F.2d 174 (2d Cir. 1991)

FACTS In February 1988, PHH Aviation Systems, Inc. (PHH) issued a credit card to Towers World Airways, Inc. (Towers) to purchase fuel and other aircraft-related goods and services for a corporate jet leased by Towers from PHH. World Jet Corporation (World Jet), a subsidiary of United Air Fleet, was responsible for maintaining the aircraft. An officer of Towers designated Fred Jay Schley, an employee of World Jet, as the chief pilot of the leased jet and gave him permission to make purchases with the PHH credit card at least in connection with noncharter flights that were used exclusively by Tower's executives. Notwithstanding United Air Fleet's agreement to pay the cost of fuel on chartered flights, which provided service for other clients, Schley (prior to the cancellation of the card in August 1988) used the credit card to charge $89,025.87 to Towers in connection with such flights. When Towers sought a declaratory judgment that would absolve it of any liability for any charges incurred in connection with chartered flights, the district court denied Towers's petition for declaratory relief and entered judgment for PHH for the full amount in dispute ($89,025.87). The district court held Towers liable for the $89,025.87, pursuant to the terms of the credit agreement between Towers and PHH, which provided that "[the] Aircraft Operator shall be responsible for all purchases made with a Card from the date of its issuance until the Aircraft Operator reports that a card is

41.1 TOWERS WORLD AIRWAYS, INC. v. PHH AVIATION SYSTEMS, INC. *(cont.)* 933 F.2d 174 (2d Cir. 1991)

lost, stolen, misplaced or canceled by calling PHH." The district court held that the Truth in Lending Act (TILA), which limits a cardholder's liability for "unauthorized" uses, was inapplicable to charges incurred by one to whom the cardholder has "voluntarily and knowing allow[ed]" access for another limited purpose. On appeal, Towers conceded liability but contended that summary judgment had been improperly granted on the question of whether the TILA limits its liability to $50.

ISSUE Was Schley's use of the card to incur $89,025.87 in connection with chartered flights unauthorized within the meaning of the TILA provision that limits a cardholder's liability?

HOLDING No. Towers's voluntary relinquishment of the credit card to Schley to enable Schley to make certain airplane fuel purchases created apparent authority in Schley to make additional fuel purchases. Thus, such additional purchases were not unauthorized within the meaning of the statute limiting a cardholder's liability.

REASONING Congress enacted the 1970 amendments to the Truth in Lending Act (TILA) in large measure to protect credit card holders from unauthorized use perpetrated by those able to obtain possession of a card from its original owner. In addition to imposing criminal sanctions for the most egregious cases, those involving fraud, the 1988 amendments enacted a scheme for limiting the liability of cardholders for all charges by third parties made without "actual, implied, or apparent authority" and "from which the cardholder receives no benefit." Where an unauthorized use has occurred, the cardholder faces liability only up to a limit of $50 for the amount charged on the card if certain conditions are satisfied. In determining the liability of cardholders for charges incurred by third-party card bearers, Congress apparently contemplated, and the courts have accepted, primary reliance on principles of agency law. While it remains unclear whether Schley had express or implied authority to make the purchases in question, Towers's consent to Schley's unrestricted access to the PHH card, as well as other conduct and circumstances, gave Schley the apparent authority to make the purchases. Nothing about the PHH card or the circumstances surrounding the purchases gave fuel sellers reason to distinguish the clearly authorized fuel purchases made in connection with noncharter flights from the purchases for chartered flights. It was the industry custom to entrust credit cards used to make airplane-related purchases to the pilot of the plane. By designating Schley as the pilot and subsequently giving him the card, Towers thereby imbued him with more apparent authority than might arise from voluntary relinquishment of a credit card in other contexts. In addition, with Tower's blessing, Schley had used the card, which was inscribed with the registration number of the Gulfstream jet, to purchase fuel on noncharter flights for the same plane. The only difference between those uses expressly authorized and those now claimed to be unauthorized—the identity of the passengers—was insufficient to provide notice to those who sold the fuel that Schley had lacked authority for the charter flight purchases. However, Towers also contended that, despite its own failure to have the card canceled, once PHH, as the card issuer, learned either through Towers or a third party that Schley had lacked authority to make certain charges, any such transaction into which Schley had entered became an unauthorized use even if the fuel sellers reasonably perceived that Schley had had apparent authority to charge fuel purchases. Whether notifying the card issuer that some uses (or users) of a card are unauthorized makes them so has divided those courts that have considered this issue. Granted, both the cardholder and merchants normally regard anyone voluntarily entrusted with a credit card as having the right to make any purchases within the card's contractually specified limits. But to whatever extent a cardholder can limit the authority of a card user by giving notice to a merchant, the cardholder cannot accomplish a similar limitation by giving notice to a card issuer. In arrangements of this sort, it is totally unrealistic to burden the card issuer with the obligation to convey to numerous merchants whatever limitations the cardholder has placed on the card user's authority. Finally, there is no substance to the argument that the court's accepting PHH's construction of the 1970 amendments inadequately protects cardholders against liability for charges made without their consent. However, a cardholder need not do so to prevent unauthorized use by one entrusted with the card. In many cases, the cardholder, simply by repossessing the card, can avoid unwanted charges. Where a card issuer permits a cardholder to cancel the card and thereby any contractual obligation to pay, a cardholder can limit its liability even if it is unable to regain possession of the card by canceling his or her card. Even where the card issuer also requires the return of the card prior to the cancellation of the agreement, a cardholder who has tried and failed to recover a card from an estranged spouse, a dishonest employee, or a disappeared friend likely can prevail on the claim that the card user has stolen the card and that any subsequent charges for that reason are unauthorized. Finally, by foreclosing card issuers from recovering unauthorized charges from cardholders, TILA undoubtedly encourages card issuers to facilitate the cancellation of cards once

41.1 TOWERS WORLD AIRWAYS, INC. v. PHH AVIATION SYSTEMS, INC. (cont.) 933 F.2d 174 (2d Cir. 1991)

a possible unauthorized use has been reported. Because the disputed charges were not unauthorized within the meaning of TILA, PHH was entitled under the agreement to recover the full value of the charges from Towers.

BUSINESS CONSIDERATIONS What pre-hire policies can a business institute in order to avoid an employee's acting as Schley did? Would Schley's actions constitute a basis for Towers's firing him? What other action or actions might Tower want to consider in this situation?

ETHICAL CONSIDERATIONS If a firm has an ethics policy in place, would that deter unethical conduct by its employees? What would an ethics policy offer to the firm that its legal remedies would not necessarily provide?

The Fair Credit Reporting Act

Banks and other lenders, would-be secured creditors (about whom we learned in Chapters 26 through 28), landlords, insurance companies, department stores, and employers often seek information about consumers. Moreover, as we have noted, credit transactions pervade domestic (and international) life. Virtually everyone in our country has a credit card. Therefore, each credit card use becomes part of the credit history of the user. Credit-reporting agencies (or bureaus) in turn summarize this information into credit (or consumer) reports and sell these reports to lenders, landlords, insurers, retailers, and employers. Credit-reporting agencies may be either local or national in scope.

Given the statistics cited earlier, one readily understands the importance of credit bureaus to the U.S. economy. Credit bureaus continually update the information they hold regarding consumers—by some estimates, a total of two billion pieces of information concerning private consumer transactions and two million pieces of public record information (that is, bankruptcies, tax liens, foreclosures, court judgments, and so forth) are reported each month.[4] Although credit-reporting services both facilitate a given consumer's access to various avenues of credit and speed up credit transactions, the centralization of these vast stores of information covering virtually the entire adult population has spawned concerns about the accuracy of the information and the adequacy of the safeguards employed by these agencies to protect the privacy of individual consumers. Indeed, studies have shown that one-half of all credit reports contain erroneous information;[5] and a litany of consumer complaints chronicles the denials of credit based on false information and the difficulties inherent in correcting such records.

Given these abuses, Congress in 1970 passed the Fair Credit Reporting Act (FCRA) as a part of the Consumer Credit Protection Act. Congress enacted the FCRA to require consumer-reporting agencies to adopt reasonable procedures for meeting the needs of commerce for consumer credit, personnel, insurance, and other information in a manner that is fair and equitable to the consumer and ensures the confidentiality, accuracy, relevancy, and proper use of such information. It applies, then, to all persons or entities that collect information concerning a consumer's creditworthiness, credit standing, credit capacity, character, general reputation, personal characteristics, or mode of living when third parties use this information either to deny or to increase the amount charged for credit or insurance used primarily for personal, family, or household purposes.

In addition, the FCRA applies whenever such information is used for the purposes of employment, governmental benefits or licenses, insurance underwriting, or other legitimate business transactions. Credit reports and licenses issued for any other reasons require a court order or the permission of the consumer.

Interestingly, the FCRA does not apply to all such credit reports but only those compiled by any entity that *regularly* engages in the practice of disseminating or evaluating consumer credit or other information concerning consumers for the purpose of furnishing consumer reports to third parties. Thus, the act covers credit reports generated by credit bureaus, whose reports ordinarily set out only financial information about the consumer in question—bank accounts, charge accounts and other indebtedness, creditworthiness, marital status, occupation, income, and perhaps some nonfinancial information. The act also covers credit-reporting bureaus whose reports focus not so much on credit information of the type compiled by credit bureaus but rather involve more personal information typically gathered through interviews with neighbors, colleagues, and the like. In short, whether the report centers respectively on financial matters or investigatory matters pursuant to a prospective employment or landlord/tenant relationship, both types of credit reports raise significant privacy issues.

In placing obligations on third-party users of credit information and those credit agencies or bureaus that report information about consumers, the FCRA attempts to protect such consumers from invasion of privacy and breach of confidentiality. It expressly obligates every consumer-reporting agency to maintain reasonable procedures designed to avoid violations of the act. Among other things, this obligation means that such agencies must report only accurate and up-to-date information and report these data only to those persons or entities eligible to receive the information.

Congress in enacting this legislation unfortunately set out no test for ensuring the relevancy of the information. Thus, while agencies must report information that is accurate and up to date, consumers have little recourse against credit bureaus and credit-reporting bureaus that report irrelevant information (for example, political beliefs or lifestyle issues) that arguably encroaches on the subject's privacy.

Besides setting out limitations on consumer-reporting agencies, the FCRA places on both reporting agencies and users certain obligations regarding the proper disclosure of the information compiled. The limitations on the uses of such information discussed earlier (employment, governmental benefits or licenses, insurance

41.1

MANAGEMENT

CREDIT-REPORTING AGENCIES

CIT recently has fired one of its employees. Following this firing, a credit-reporting agency has contacted the firm and has asked questions about the former employee. Fearing possible liability for the firm under the Fair Credit Reporting Act if the information reported by the firm turns out to be inaccurate or if the information is misused by the agency, Dan believes that CIT should not answer the questions. Tom does not believe that these are legitimate concerns. He thinks that CIT should provide the information, especially since CIT uses this credit-reporting agency when CIT seeks information concerning prospective employees. They ask your opinion on this matter. What will you advise them?

BUSINESS CONSIDERATIONS Should a business establish a policy for providing information concerning employees—or former employees—to credit-reporting agencies? What factors would affect the formation of such a policy?

ETHICAL CONSIDERATIONS Is it ethical for a former employer to provide information about a former employee to a credit-reporting agency? How can the employer, from an ethical perspective, relate the employment performance of a person to the latter's credit-worthiness?

underwriting, or any other legitimate business purpose) fulfill this goal, and the act requires that every consumer-reporting agency undertake reasonable procedures to verify that the users of the information furnished use the report for only these purposes. Reasonable procedures include prospective users' identifying themselves and certifying the purpose for which they are seeking the information. Prospective users also must certify that they will use the information only for this—and no other—purpose.

Users of consumer reports similarly must satisfy certain statutory obligations. Unless the report is an investigative one concerning employment for which the consumer has not yet specifically applied, users of investigative consumer reports must notify the consumer in advance of the preparation of the report that he or she may be the subject of an investigation concerning his or her character, general reputation, personal characteristics, and mode of living. Moreover, whenever a user of a consumer report denies credit, insurance, or employment or charges a higher rate for credit or insurance and bases the denial or increase wholly or in part on the information contained in a credit report, the user must advise the consumer of the adverse action and supply the name and address of the reporting agency that compiled the report. Adverse actions involving only denial of credit or an increased charge for the extension of credit pursuant to information obtained from persons other than a consumer-reporting agency obligate the user, upon request, to disclose to the consumer the nature (but not the source) of the information. In this latter situation, the user also must inform the consumer of his or her statutory right to learn of the information that caused the adverse decision.

Consumers' rights, then, in addition to the FCRA's prohibition on the use of inaccurate and outdated information, include notification of an agency's reliance on adverse information contained in consumer reports. Moreover, by statute the consumer enjoys limited access to any files concerning him or her and the right in certain circumstances to correct erroneous information. The information that the consumer can receive from a consumer credit-reporting agency includes the nature and substance of all information (except medical information) in its files that concern the consumer, the sources of information (except for the sources of information compiled pursuant to investigative reports), and the recipients of any consumer reports that the agency has furnished concerning the consumer for employment purposes within the last two years or for any purpose within the six-month period preceding the request.

Note that under the FCRA the consumer cannot actually see his or her file. But once the consumer receives the information, he or she can dispute the completeness or accuracy of any information contained in the file. When the consumer directly conveys to the reporting agency such questions, the agency within a reasonable time must investigate the information disputed by the consumer unless the agency has reasonable grounds to believe the consumer's claim is frivolous or irrelevant. If the agency's reinvestigation fails to resolve the dispute, the consumer can file a statement that sets forth the nature of the dispute. Unless it has reasonable grounds to believe the statement is frivolous or irrelevant, the agency must clearly note in any subsequent consumer report containing the disputed information that the consumer disputes the information and provide either the consumer's statement or a clear and accurate codification or summary thereof. At the request of the consumer, the agency must send a similar notice to any users that the consumer can identify as having received within the last two years a report concerning employment or having received within the last six months a report for any purpose. The statute expressly mandates that the agency clearly and conspicuously disclose to the consumer his or her right to make such a request.

The FCRA sets out civil remedies for violations of the act. For willful failure to comply with the Act, suits for compensatory or punitive damages are possible; for violations stemming from negligent noncompliance, an injured consumer can recover only compensatory damages. In addition, for either type of violation, the injured party who successfully sues can recover court costs and attorneys' fees.

The FCRA prohibits court actions brought for defamation, invasion of privacy, or negligence with respect to the reporting of information, unless the suit involves false information furnished with malice or with a willful intent to injure the consumer. Any person who under false pretenses knowingly and willfully obtains information concerning a consumer faces a fine of $5,000 and/or one year's imprisonment.

The Federal Trade Commission (FTC), about which you learned in Chapter 40, functions as the principal enforcement agency for violations of the FCRA, because the law views violations of the act as unfair or deceptive trade practices. As such, the FTC can order various administrative remedies (such as cease-and-desist orders) against consumer-reporting agencies, users, or other persons not regulated by other federal agencies (such as the Federal Reserve Board) that themselves have enforcement authority when credit-reporting agencies and users' activities fall within these agencies' regulatory purview.

In *Stevenson* v. *TRW, Inc.*, the judge addressed many of these principles.

41.2 STEVENSON v. TRW, INC. — 987 F.2d 288 (5th Cir. 1993)

FACTS TRW, Inc. (TRW) is one of the nation's largest credit-reporting agencies. John M. Stevenson is a 78-year-old real estate and securities investor. In late 1988, Stevenson began receiving numerous phone calls from bill collectors regarding arrearages in accounts that were not his. In August 1989, Stevenson wrote TRW and obtained a copy of his credit report dated 6 September 1989. On that credit report, the statement "See Reverse Side for Explanation" was printed in red, boldface type and appeared on the bottom, right-hand portion of each page. The boilerplate notice on the reverse side had four paragraphs, the latter of which stated that Stevenson could request that TRW send a corrected report to any of the creditors Stevenson listed on the four blank lines that followed paragraph four. The other paragraphs were printed in red, boldface type; but the fourth paragraph used black, regular-size type. Stevenson discovered many errors in the 6 September report. Some accounts belonged to another John Stevenson living in Arlington, Texas; and some appeared to belong to his estranged son, John Stevenson, Jr. In all, Stevenson disputed approximately sixteen accounts, seven inquiries, and much of the identifying information. Stevenson called TRW to register his complaint and then, on 6 October 1989, wrote TRW's president and CEO and requested the correction of his (Stevenson's) credit report. Stevenson's letter worked its way to TRW's customer relations department by 20 October 1989; and on 1 November 1989, that office began its reinvestigation by sending consumer dispute verification forms (CDVs) to the subscribers that had reported the disputed accounts. The CDVs ask subscribers to check whether the information about a consumer matches the information in TRW's credit report. Subscribers who receive CDVs typically have 20 to 25 working days to respond. If a subscriber fails to respond or indicates that TRW's account information is incorrect, TRW deletes the disputed information. Stevenson understood from TRW that the entire process should take from three to six weeks. As a result of its initial investigation, by 30 November 1989, TRW had removed several of the disputed accounts from the report. TRW also realized that Stevenson's estranged son, by using Stevenson's social security number, apparently had fraudulently obtained some of the disputed accounts. This information led TRW in December 1989 to add a warning statement advising subscribers that Stevenson's identifying information had been used without his consent to obtain credit. By 9 February 1990, TRW claimed that it had removed all the disputed accounts containing "negative" credit information. Inaccurate information, however, either continued to appear on Stevenson's reports or was reentered after TRW had deleted it. As a consequence, Stevenson, filing suit in Texas state court, alleged both common law libel and violation of the Fair Credit Reporting Act (FCRA). TRW removed the case to federal court, where, in a

41.2 STEVENSON v. TRW, INC. *(cont.)* 987 F.2d 288 (5th Cir. 1993)

bench trial, the judge found in favor of Stevenson on both counts. The judge awarded $1 in nominal damages on the libel claim, $30,000 in actual damages for mental anguish, $20,700 in attorneys' fees, and $100,000 in punitive damages.

ISSUE Did TRW, by failing to delete promptly inaccurate or unverifiable entries on Stevenson's credit record and by failing to provide Stevenson clear and conspicuous notice of his rights, negligently and willfully violate the FCRA?

HOLDING Yes and no. TRW, by taking an unreasonably long time to reinvestigate Stevenson's dispute and by failing to delete promptly the information found to be inaccurate or unverifiable, had negligently violated the FCRA. TRW, by failing to disclose clearly and conspicuously to Stevenson his right to have corrected copies of his credit report sent to his creditors, also had negligently violated the act. The district court, however, had erred in finding that TRW's violations were willful. Hence, the findings of negligence, the award of $30,000 in actual damages based on the finding of mental anguish, and the award of $20,700 in attorneys' fees were affirmed; but the findings of willfulness and the punitive damages award were reversed.

REASONING Congress enacted the FCRA to guard against consumer-reporting agencies' use of inaccurate or arbitrary information when they evaluate an individual for credit, insurance, or employment. Congress further required that consumer-reporting agencies "follow reasonable procedures to assure the maximum possible accuracy of the information concerning the individual about whom" a credit report relates. [The trial court found that TRW had done so.] A consumer-reporting agency that negligently fails to comply with the FCRA's requirements is liable for actual damages, costs, and reasonable attorneys' fees. Willful noncompliance renders a consumer-reporting agency additionally liable for punitive damages. Moreover, consumers have the right to see their credit information and to dispute the accuracy or completeness of their credit reports. When it receives a complaint, a consumer-reporting agency must reinvestigate the disputed information "within a reasonable period of time" and "promptly delete" credit information it finds to be inaccurate or unverifiable. According to the FTC, "[a]lthough consumer reporting agencies are able to reinvestigate most disputes within 30 days, a 'reasonable time' for a particular reinvestigation may be shorter or longer depending on the circumstances of the dispute." TRW contends that 10 weeks was a reasonable time to complete its reinvestigation of Stevenson's complicated dispute, especially since his claim involved fraudulently obtained inaccurate accounts. The record, however, contains evidence from which the district court could find that TRW had not deleted unverifiable or inaccurate information promptly. First, TRW did not complete its reinvestigation until 9 February 1990, although TRW's subscribers were supposed to return the CDVs by 4 December 1989. Second, the FCRA requires prompt deletion if the disputed information is inaccurate or unverifiable. Stevenson had disputed incorrect accounts listed with one business, but those accounts appeared on his credit report as late as 22 March 1991. A firm's allowing inaccurate information back onto a credit report after the firm has deleted the information because it is inaccurate is negligent. Additionally, in spite of the complexity of Stevenson's dispute, TRW contacted the subscribers only through the CDVs rather than by calling the subscribers. In short, TRW's claims concerning the complexities associated with Stevenson's claim do not excuse its negligent failure to meet the "prompt deletion" requirement, particularly since the statute places the burden of reinvestigation squarely on TRW. The FCRA authorizes the awarding of actual damages, punitive damages, and reasonable attorneys' fees when the reporting agency willfully fails to comply with any of the FCRA's requirements. To be found in willful noncompliance, a defendant must have "knowingly and intentionally committed an act in conscious disregard for the rights of others." Given the lack of any conscious intention to thwart Stevenson's right to have inaccurate information removed promptly from his report, the district court's finding of willful noncompliance was clearly erroneous. But the district court had not erred in finding that TRW, by sending Stevenson the same boilerplate form it sends everyone, had negligently violated the notice requirement of the FCRA. However, because the notice appears in a paragraph on dispute resolution procedures and is visible, TRW had not knowingly and intentionally obscured the notice in conscious disregard of consumers' rights. The finding of willful noncompliance and the award of punitive damages therefore would be reversed.

BUSINESS CONSIDERATIONS How should TRW revamp both the reinvestigation procedures and the boilerplate form letter that were in issue in this case so as to avoid the types of problems encountered?

ETHICAL CONSIDERATIONS Had the court based its decision concerning TRW's conduct on ethics rather than the law, would the court's decision have been different? What ethical concerns are raised by the conduct of TRW in this case?

THE EQUAL CREDIT OPPORTUNITY ACT

When Congress first passed the Equal Credit Opportunity Act (ECOA) in 1974, it prohibited only discrimination based on sex or marital status whenever creditors extend credit. Congress at that time was responding to evidence showing that creditors more often denied credit to single women than to single men and that married, divorced, and widowed women could not get credit in their own names. Instead, these women had to obtain credit in their husbands' names.

To broaden the protections available to low-income consumers so as to enable them to have access to credit commensurate with the credit opportunities enjoyed by more affluent consumers, Congress in 1976 amended the statute to prohibit, in addition, discrimination based on race, religion, national origin, age (provided the applicant has the capacity to contract), receipt of public assistance benefits, and the good faith exercise of rights under the Consumer Credit Protection Act (that is, TILA). Although part of TILA, ECOA covers more than consumer credit transactions. In short, ECOA covers any creditor who deals with any applicant in any aspect of a credit transaction.

Federal Reserve Board (FRB) Regulation B (extensively revised in 1985), the implementing regulation for ECOA, broadly defines a credit transaction as involving every aspect of an applicant's dealings with a creditor regarding an application for credit or an existing extension of credit including but not limited to information requirements; investigation procedures; standards of creditworthiness; terms of credit; the furnishing of credit information, revocation, alteration, or termination of credit; and collection procedures. ECOA and Regulation B exempt certain transactions, such as those made pursuant to special-purpose credit programs designed to benefit an economically disadvantaged class of persons, from coverage. Partial exemptions also exist for public utility services credit transactions (that is, public utilities can ask questions about an applicant's marital status) and incidental consumer credit transactions, such as those involving physicians, hospitals, and so on.

Since creditors as a precondition of extending credit generally evaluate applicants' creditworthiness, Regulation B sets out rules that creditors must follow in making such evaluations and forms that creditors can use to ensure that they do not discriminate on any of the prohibited bases while they undertake these evaluations. In addition, ECOA requires creditors to give notice to applicants of any actions taken by the creditors concerning the applicants' requests for credit.

Creditor actions typically take three forms: approval of the application; extension of credit under dif-

41.2

FINANCE/MANAGEMENT

EXTENDING CREDIT

CIT has been discussing credit sales to consumers. While Tom and Anna realize that direct sales to consumers—often on credit terms established by the firm—probably will increase sales substantially, they also agree that some of these customers inevitably will default. To minimize the risk of default, John proposes that the firm should extend credit only to consumers who have a minimum family income and a minimum credit bureau rating. All other applicants should be rejected. While the family members agree that this sounds like a good idea, they are concerned that it may violate the law. They ask for your advice. What will you tell them?

BUSINESS CONSIDERATIONS The extension of consumer credit is likely to increase the sales of a business, but it also will increase losses because of bad debts and defaults. When it decides whether to provide credit to its consumer customers, what factors should the firm consider? Should a firm that decides to extend credit to consumer debtors revisit the decision periodically and reevaluate it?

ETHICAL CONSIDERATIONS Is it ethical for a firm to decide not to extend credit to its consumer debtors, thereby possibly precluding lower-income customers from acquiring the product? Is it more ethical to provide such consumer credit, even though the firm may lose some of its profits because of defaults?

ferent terms than those requested; or an adverse action (for example, denial of the application). Regulation B then prescribes a notification regime specifically tailored to the type of action taken. Exhibit 41.1 represents a communication that generally will satisfy these notification requirements. Creditors typically must send such a notification within 30 days of receiving a completed application.

EXHIBIT 41.1 Form C-2—Sample Notice of Action Taken and Statement of Reasons

Dear Applicant:

Thank you for your recent application. Your request for [a loan/a credit card/an increase in your credit limit] was carefully considered, and we regret that we are unable to approve your application at this time, for the following reason(s):

YOUR INCOME:
_____ is below our minimum requirement.
_____ is insufficient to sustain payments on the amount of credit requested.
_____ could not be verified.

YOUR EMPLOYMENT:
_____ is not of sufficient length to qualify.
_____ could not be verified.

YOUR CREDIT HISTORY:
_____ of making payments on time was not satisfactory.
_____ could not be verified.

YOUR APPLICATION:
_____ lacks a sufficient number of credit references.
_____ lacks acceptable types of credit references.
_____ reveals that current obligations are excessive in relation to income.

OTHER: ____

The consumer reporting agency contacted that provided information that influenced our decision in whole or in part was [the name, address, and telephone number of the reporting agency]. The reporting agency is unable to supply specific reasons why we have denied credit to you. You do, however, have a right under the Fair Credit Reporting Act to know the information contained in your credit file. Any questions regarding such information should be directed to [the consumer reporting agency].

If you have any questions regarding this letter, you should contact us at [creditor's name, address, and telephone number].

NOTICE: The federal Equal Credit Opportunity Act prohibits creditors from discriminating against credit applicants on the basis of race, color, religion, national origin, sex, marital status, age (provided the applicant has the capacity to enter into a binding contract); because all or part of the applicant's income derives from any public assistance program; or because the applicant has in good faith exercised any right under the Consumer Credit Protection Act. The federal agency that administers compliance with this law concerning this creditor is [the name and address as specified by the appropriate agency listed in Appendix A].

SOURCE: 12 *Code of Federal Regulations* § 202 (App. C) (1994).

Remedies under ECOA include actual damages and/or punitive damages, to a maximum of $10,000 for individual actions or a maximum of $500,000 (or 1 percent of the creditor's net worth—whichever is greater) for class actions. Equitable relief, attorneys' fees, and costs also may be granted. A two-year statute of limitations generally applies. The usual administrative remedies are available as well. The enforcement agencies in addition can ask the U.S. attorney general to institute civil actions against any creditor who has engaged in a pattern or practice of denying or discouraging credit applicants in violation of the act.

A court recently interpreted ECOA in *Barney* v. *Holzer Clinic, Ltd.*

41.3 BARNEY v. HOLZER CLINIC, LTD. — 902 F.Supp. 139 (S.D. Ohio 1995)

FACTS Teresa and Randy Barney brought a class action against Holzer Clinic, Ltd. (the Clinic). The Barneys alleged that the Clinic's refusals to schedule appointments for and the Clinic's cancellation of the appointments of Medicaid recipients violated the Equal Credit Opportunity Act (ECOA). The Barneys claimed that the Clinic's refusal to schedule an appointment because of a person's status as a Medicaid recipient is a denial of credit because, if an appointment had been scheduled, the Medicaid recipient could receive the benefit of the Clinic's credit policy. The Barneys therefore sought to recover damages for the emotional harm they allegedly had suffered because of the Clinic's acts.

ISSUE Would the denial of medical services to persons who receive Medicaid benefits constitute actionable discrimination under ECOA?

HOLDING No. ECOA applies only to debtor–creditor transactions. Since Medicaid recipients and providers of services to them never enjoy a debtor–creditor relationship, ECOA would be inapplicable to circumstances involving Medicaid services.

REASONING ECOA makes it unlawful for creditors to use certain criteria to evaluate an application for credit in a "credit transaction." One of these criteria is whether "all or part of the applicant's income derives from a public assistance program." At issue in this case is whether the denial of medical services to persons who receive Medicaid benefits constitutes discrimination in a credit transaction. In what appears to be a matter of first impression, the court concludes that under the statutory language it does not. Although ECOA does not define "credit transaction," the regulations promulgated by the Federal Reserve Board (FRB) define a *credit transaction* as "every aspect of an applicant's dealings with a creditor regarding an application for credit or an existing extension of credit." *Credit* in turn is "the right granted by a creditor to a debtor to defer payment of a debt or to incur debt and defer its payment or to purchase property or services and defer payment therefor." From this language, it is clear that there are two parties to a credit transaction—the creditor; and the applicant for credit, who seeks to become a debtor. The clinic, under certain circumstances, thus can be a "creditor." The central question therefore is whether the Barneys can become "debtors." The Barneys contend that they can become debtors because they would owe money for services received. In the alternative, they argue that debt is not a prerequisite for attaining debtor status. The Barneys first submit that they owe money as debtors because, as potential recipients of medical services, they have an implied contract to pay the Clinic for services rendered. This argument, fails, however, because the state has primary and exclusive responsibility to pay for medical services given to Medicaid patients. The source of the state's liability is a contract between the state and the medical service provider. In fact, the service provider is barred by Ohio law from charging the patient at all. Indeed, Medicaid creates an exclusive contract between the service provider and the government; the patient is not a party to an express or implied contract. Simply put, the patient owes nothing to the provider. Accordingly, if the Barneys are to prove that they are applying to become debtors in a credit transaction, they initially must prove that a debtor need not be in debt. Yet the Barneys' argument abuses the English language. The word *debtor,* in any context, refers to one who owes a debt; it is nonsense to believe that one becomes a debtor when one receives services for which someone else must pay. Because the government pays for the costs of Medicaid recipients' medical services, such patients are not debtors under ECOA. Moreover, according to the statute, credit is a right flowing from a creditor "to a debtor." Under this language, the benefit—that is, credit—and the obligation—that is, debt—accrue in the same entity. In the Medicaid system, that entity is the person liable for the debt, which is the government. Here, the government sets its own credit terms; so ECOA does not apply. Finally, the idea that credit can exist without debt does violence to the concept of a

41.3 BARNEY v. HOLZER CLINIC, LTD. *(cont.)* 902 F.Supp. 139 (S.D. Ohio 1995)

credit transaction. A *transaction* involves the exchange of obligations between two parties. Here, there could be no transaction between the Barneys and the Clinic because of the absence of any exchange of obligations. Any transaction that occurs is between the government and the care provider; the patient merely would be a beneficiary of the exchange. Because any construction that ignores the role of debt in the classification of a debtor also reads the concept of transaction completely out of the statute, such a construction cannot stand. In short, debt is an integral part of a credit transaction. The Barneys are not, nor have they applied to become, debtors of the Clinic. Accordingly, they did not participate in a credit transaction; and they consequently are unable to assert any claim under ECOA. Furthermore, the Barneys' interpretation of ECOA is antithetical to the current Medicaid scheme. Under the Barneys' theory, every scheduled visit with the Clinic is a credit transaction because the Clinic routinely allows patients to defer payment of their bills. Thus, denial of service to a Medicaid recipient automatically and always would constitute discrimination in a credit transaction. The Clinic and every medical service provider would be forced into the Medicaid system. Although mandatory provider participation in Medicaid may be preferable, the Barneys have presented no authority that suggests that Congress intended to use the credit laws to implement such a new health-care plan. ECOA simply is not the vehicle that Congress would or did choose to implement such a system. In summary, ECOA applies only when a debtor is liable to a creditor. Because that circumstance fails to arise between a Medicaid recipient and a medical service provider, ECOA does not create a right to service. The existing Medicaid scheme dictates the same result, and any other interpretation is contrary to the direct intent of Congress.

BUSINESS CONSIDERATIONS What effect would a different result here have had on health-care providers? Do you think the court, in deciding this case, took such business factors into account?

ETHICAL CONSIDERATIONS Do you think some businesses treat Medicaid recipients and other persons with lower incomes more shabbily than they do higher-income people? From an ethical perspective, should the income of a customer affect the way that customer is treated?

THE FAIR DEBT COLLECTION PRACTICES ACT

As Title V of the Consumer Credit Protection Act (TILA), Congress in 1977 passed the Fair Debt Collection Practices Act (FDCPA). This part of TILA regulates the activities of those who collect bills owed to others (since 1986 including attorneys). The Act specifically exempts from its coverage the activities of secured parties, process servers, and federal or state employees who are attempting to collect debts pursuant to the performance of their official duties.

Congress intended the law to eliminate abusive, deceptive, and unfair debt-collection practices and thereby to protect consumers. The Act therefore limits the manner in which a **debt collector** can communicate with the debtor. For example, the statute expressly prohibits, without the consumer's consent, any communications made at an unusual or inconvenient time, that is, before 8:00 A.M. and after 9:00 P.M. local time at the debtor's location. The debt collector, moreover, cannot communicate with the debtor at the debtor's place of employment if the debt collector knows or has reason to know that the debtor's employer prohibits the consumer from receiving such communications. In addition, in most circumstances, if the debt collector knows an attorney represents the consumer with respect to the debt, the debt collector can contact only the attorney, not the debtor. A debt collector typically cannot communicate with third parties (for example, the debtor's neighbors, co-workers, or friends) concerning the collection of the debt, either.

Debt collector
A business that collects accounts due and payable but does *not* extend the credit that underlies the debt being collected.

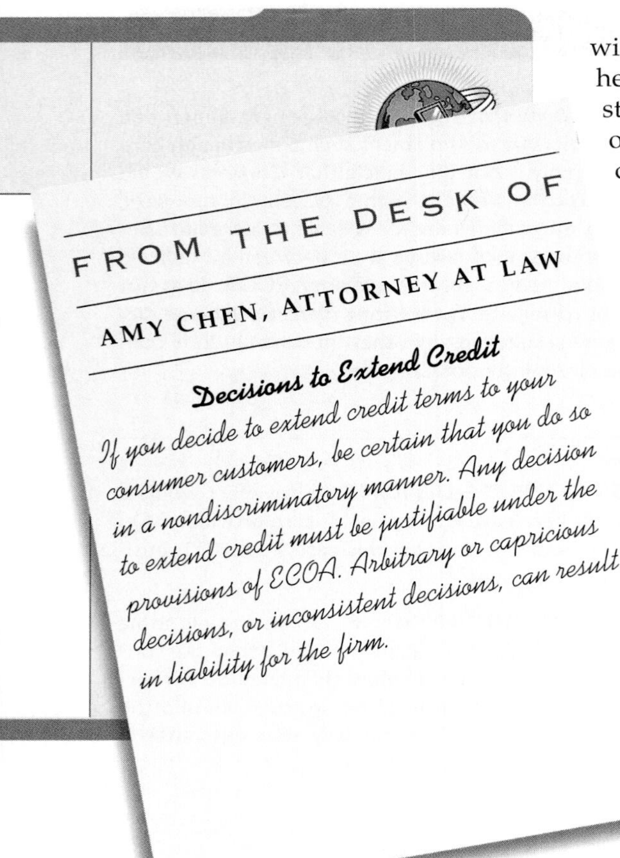

FROM THE DESK OF
AMY CHEN, ATTORNEY AT LAW
Decisions to Extend Credit
If you decide to extend credit terms to your consumer customers, be certain that you do so in a nondiscriminatory manner. Any decision to extend credit must be justifiable under the provisions of ECOA. Arbitrary or capricious decisions, or inconsistent decisions, can result in liability for the firm.

The statute also permits the cessation of further communication with the debtor if he or she in writing notifies the debt collector that he or she refuses to pay the debt and wishes all communications to stop. At that point, the debt collector can advise the consumer only of the termination of further efforts to collect the debt or of the debt collector's intention to invoke any available remedies.

Similarly, debt collectors must refrain from unfair or unconscionable means of debt collection. For example, the debt collector is prohibited from accepting postdated checks, making collect phone calls to debtors, or adding amounts—interest, fees, or expenses—not expressly allowed by the underlying debt agreement or by state law.

So that the debtor can dispute the debt if he or she has grounds to do so, the act requires the bill collector to send the debtor a written verification of the debt. The debtor then has 30 days in which he or she in writing must dispute the debt; otherwise, the debt collector can assume the validity of the debt.

The FTC has primary enforcement responsibilities under the FDCPA. Civil remedies of actual damages plus additional damages, not to exceed $1,000, that the court can set are possible in individual suits. In class actions, $1,000 per person may be awarded; but the total damages so awarded cannot exceed the lesser of $500,000 or 1 percent of the debt collector's net worth.

Under a separate statute, a criminal penalty of $1,000 or a sentence of one year's imprisonment, or both, may be imposed on anyone who, during the course of debt-collection efforts, uses the words *federal*, *national*, or *the United States* to convey the false impression that the communication originates from, or in any way represents, the United States or any of its agencies or instrumentalities. Successful litigants may recover costs and attorneys' fees as well.

Consider these principles as you analyze *Bentley* v. *Great Lakes Collection Bureau*.

41.4 BENTLEY v. GREAT LAKES COLLECTION BUREAU — 6 F.3d 63 (2d Cir. 1993)

FACTS Citicorp Retail Services, Inc. (CRSI) had retained Great Lakes Collection Bureau (Great Lakes) to provide debt-collection services. CRSI's contract with Great Lakes stated that Great Lakes must have CRSI's prior written authorization before Great Lakes attempted to collect on any referred account or implied in any communication to a referred account that CRSI would sue the debtor. In an attempt to collect the $483.43 that Diane W. Bentley owed CRSI, Great Lakes sent her two computer-generated letters (that is, *dunning* letters) dated 30 November 1990 and 18 December 1990. The 30 November 1990 dunning letter included the following language:

> *Your creditor is now taking the necessary steps to recover the outstanding amount of $483.43. They have instructed us to proceed with whatever legal means necessary to enforce collection. This is an attempt to collect and any information obtained will be used for that purpose.*

Great Lakes programs its computer to generate this form letter whenever the agency receives a new account. The 18 December follow-up letter stated in relevant part:

> *This office has been unable to contact you by telephone, therefore your delinquent account has been referred to my desk where a decision must be made as to what*

41.4 BENTLEY v. GREAT LAKES COLLECTION BUREAU *(cont.)* 6 F.3d 63 (2d Cir. 1993)

direction must be taken to enforce collection. Were our client to retain legal counsel in your area, and it was determined that suit should be filed against you, it could result in a judgment. Such judgment might, depending upon the law in your state, include not only the amount of your indebtedness, but the amount of any statutory costs, legal interest, and where applicable, reasonable attorney's fees.

Again, depending upon the law in your state, if such judgment were not thereupon satisfied, it might be collected by attachment of an execution upon your real and personal property.

Garnishment may also be an available remedy to satisfy an unsatisfied judgment, if applicable in the state in which you reside.

We therefore suggest you call our office immediately toll free at [this number] to discuss payment arrangements or mail payment in full in the enclosed envelope.

No legal action has been or is now being taken against you.

In fact, CRSI had not authorized Great Lakes "to proceed with whatever legal means is necessary to enforce collection" as represented in the first letter. And, despite its representations to the contrary in the second letter, Great Lakes had failed to telephone Bentley prior to 18 December and had not referred her account to anyone's desk for a decision regarding her account. Moreover, even in cases where its advice is solicited, Great Lakes recommends legal proceedings to its clients only for approximately 1 percent of the collection accounts referred to it.

ISSUE Did the Great Lakes letter violate the Fair Debt Collection Practices Act's prohibition against the use of any false, deceptive, or misleading representation or means in connection with the collection of a debt?

HOLDING Yes. Various false statements in the two letters Great Lakes had sent to Bentley constituted the types of false, deceptive, or misleading representations that the act condemns.

REASONING The Fair Debt Collection Practices Act (FDCPA) prohibits the use of "any false, deceptive, or misleading representation or means in connection with the collection of any debt." In determining whether a collection letter violates this section of the FDCPA, courts in this jurisdiction apply an objective test based on the understanding of the "least sophisticated consumer." The 16 subsections of this section provide a nonexhaustive list of practices that fall within the statute's ban. These practices include "[t]he threat to take any action that cannot legally be taken or that is not intended to be taken." Here, the two dunning letters contained several admittedly false statements. First, the 30 November dunning letter falsely stated that CRSI had given Great Lakes the authority to initiate legal proceedings against Bentley. It implied that the commencement of legal proceedings was imminent when, in fact, this was not the case. The least sophisticated consumer would interpret this language to mean that legal action was authorized, likely, and imminent. Therefore, these statements are "false, deceptive, [and] misleading" within the meaning of the FDCPA. Second, the 18 December dunning letter falsely stated that Great Lakes had attempted to contact Bentley prior to 18 December and that Bentley's account had been referred to someone's desk, where a decision would be made regarding her account. The reference to the status of Bentley's account was deceptive, implying "personal attention" to her account, when, in fact, no such "desk" existed. The letter therefore violated the FDCPA's strict prohibition against deceptive practices. And because the FDCPA is a strict liability statute, courts may consider the degree of a defendant's culpability only in computing damages, not in assessing whether a violation of the act has occurred. Moreover, the later letter's references to legal remedies, when read in conjunction with the first paragraph of that letter, would convey to the least sophisticated consumer that Great Lakes was authorized to make the decision to institute the legal action that could lead to the supplementary proceedings described. In fact, CRSI retained the authority to decide whether legal proceedings of any kind would be instituted; and the likelihood of such proceedings on a claim for $483.43 was almost nonexistent. The district court's grant of a summary judgment in favor of Great Lakes therefore must be reversed.

BUSINESS CONSIDERATIONS Why would a rational, profit-maximizing firm conduct itself as Great Lakes did here? How should a firm such as Great Lakes act in this type of situation?

ETHICAL CONSIDERATIONS Was the conduct of Great Lakes ethical? How should such a firm, from an ethical perspective, act?

41.3

FINANCE/MANAGEMENT

CREDIT COLLECTION

Several of CIT's credit customers are behind in making their credit payments, and a few have defaulted. All efforts by the firm to collect these amounts have failed, and Tom and Dan think that the firm should hire a collection agency to recover the firm's money. Anna, preferring a low-key approach to collection, wants the firm to write to these customers and remind them of their obligation to repay the debts. The family members all agree that they would like to recover the funds, but they are unsure of the legal implications of various collection efforts. They ask you what they should do. What will you advise them?

BUSINESS CONSIDERATIONS Why would a business be willing to hire a debt-collection agency to recover past due accounts? What should a business consider before it takes such a step?

ETHICAL CONSIDERATIONS Is it ethical for a business to turn its debt collections over to an independent third party who was not involved in the extension of credit? Is it ethical for a firm to accept collections that may have been acquired in an unethical manner by the debt-collection agency?

The Uniform Consumer Credit Code

Designed to replace state laws governing consumer credit, the Uniform Consumer Credit Code (UCCC) resulted from the drafting efforts of the National Conference of Commissioners on Uniform State Laws and was meant to make consistent the widely varying state laws concerning installment sales and loans, revolving charge accounts, home solicitation sales, home improvement loans, and truth-in-lending. Simply put, its drafters wished to do for consumer law what the Uniform Commercial Code had done for commercial law.

First promulgated in 1969 and later revised in 1974, the UCCC has failed to gain wide acceptance. To date, only nine states have enacted it; and many of them have chosen to replace the UCCC's provisions with their own. Still, it represents an additional statutory attempt to benefit consumers.

The Consumer Product Safety Act

The Consumer Product Safety Act of 1972 established the Consumer Product Safety Commission (CPSC). An independent federal regulatory agency, the CPSC consists of five members appointed by the President with the advice and consent of the Senate. The CPSC has authority over a great number of consumer products; but products expressly excluded from the Commission's jurisdiction include tobacco and tobacco products, motor vehicles, pesticides covered under FIFRA, firearms and ammunition, food, and cosmetics.

To help protect the public from injuries from consumer products, the Commission can do the following: set and enforce safety standards; ban hazardous products; collect information on consumer- related injuries; administratively order firms to report publicly defects that could create substantial hazards; force firms to take corrective action (repair, replacement, or refund) with regard to substantially hazardous consumer products in commerce; seek court orders for recalls of imminently hazardous products; conduct research on consumer products; and engage in outreach educational programs for consumers, industry, and local government.

Products banned by the CPSC include certain all-terrain vehicles, unstable refuse bins, lawn darts, tris (a chemical flame-retardant found in children's apparel), products containing asbestos, and paint containing lead. Products subject to CPSC standards include matchbooks, automatic garage door openers, bicycles, cribs, rattles, disposable lighters, toys with small parts, and the like.

For a recent interpretation of the CPSC's powers, consider the *U.S.* v. *Articles of Banned Hazardous Substances* case.

41.5 U.S. v. ARTICLES OF BANNED HAZARDOUS SUBSTANCES 34 F.3d 91 (2d Cir. 1994)

FACTS Linda Weill, an elementary school art teacher, developed a type of finger paint consisting of colored foam dispensed from a self-pressurized canister that she named "Rainbow Foam Paint." Rainbow Foam Paint basically is shaving cream colored with pre-mixed food coloring and is intended for use by children ages three and older. Weill obtained a United States patent for her product in 1986 and formed a company, X-Tra Art, Inc., to distribute the product. Rainbow Foam Paint has been on the market since 1986 and is, according to Weill, purchased primarily by teachers for use in the classroom. The product also is marketed as a children's bath product. On 3 April 1987, the California Department of Health Services approved the product "for purchase by schools for use by children in kindergarten and grades 1–6." Although the product contains hazardous hydrocarbon propellants, such as isobutane and propane, the material safety data sheet provided by the manufacturer indicates that Rainbow Foam Paint, like other aerosol shaving creams containing hydrocarbon propellants, is classified as nonflammable. In 1990, Consumers Union, publisher of *Consumer Reports* magazine, mentioned in its children's magazine *Zillions* that Rainbow Foam Paint was a possible hazard because of flammability. The magazine stated that Rainbow Foam Paint could "catch fire if used near a flame . . . *if* not shaken" and thus was a dangerous toy that needed a *"big, bold"* warning, which it did not have. Weill contacted Consumers Union concerning the article and demanded an immediate retraction. She received a letter from Consumers Union dated 12 December 1990, which stated that the report in *Zillions* had been inaccurate and that Consumers Union intended "to retract it in the next issue" of the magazine since Consumers Union had concluded that "the momentary flash [it] observed . . . presents no hazard." Shortly afterward, Weill nonetheless notified Consumers Union that she intended to sue it for money damages despite the retraction. Thereafter, Consumers Union, in a letter to Weill on 31 December 1990 stated that it would not print a retraction of the *Zillions* report and that Consumers Union was referring the matter to the Consumer Product Safety Commission (CPSC), as Consumers Union believed the product violated the Federal Hazardous Substances Act (FHSA). On 2 January 1991, the CPSC collected 14 cans of Rainbow Foam Paint from an X-Tra Art, Inc., officer. On 9 January 1991, the CPSC extensively tested the product in the upright, sideways, and upside down positions, under the method prescribed in the applicable regulations. Following these tests, the CPSC determined that Rainbow Foam Paint canisters were flammable when placed in the upside down position and may cause substantial personal injury with reasonably foreseeable use. Therefore, the CPSC concluded that Rainbow Foam Paint was a "banned hazardous substance" under the FHSA. The CPSC thereupon requested that Weill stop distributing the product and indicated that she could be fined up to $1,250,000 if she failed to do so. When Weill refused to cease the distribution of the paint, the CPSC notified the U.S. attorney's office, which initiated a seizure order. After protracted litigation, the district court, granting summary judgment for Weill and X-Tra Art, Inc. (the claimants), ruled that Rainbow Foam Paint was not a banned hazardous substance within the meaning of the FHSA because it came within the exemption for adequately labeled art materials. The court rejected the contention that the product should be classified as a toy because it was sold in toy stores. With respect to the argument that warning labels on the product were inadequate because the product was targeted at children too young to read the warning labels, the court stated that, "it must be concluded that the label on Rainbow Foam Paint . . . adequately warns adults who would potentially supervise the use of the product with children." The district court therefore concluded that "Congress may have decided to rely on the premise that [any] danger is alleviated, as a child's access to the product would only be through an adult."

ISSUE Had the CPSC properly classified Rainbow Foam Paint as a hazardous substance under the Consumer Product Safety Act?

HOLDING Yes. The product was a hazardous substance within the meaning of the statute and could not be exempt as an art material under the applicable regulations because its intended child users were too young to read and heed a warning label.

REASONING Courts must review a grant of summary judgment *de novo* and must view all evidence in the light most favorable to the party opposing the motion. The district court did not directly address the question of whether the Rainbow Foam Paint is a hazardous substance within

41.5 U.S. v. ARTICLES OF BANNED HAZARDOUS SUBSTANCES *(cont.)* 34 F.3d 91 (2d Cir. 1994)

the meaning of the statute, and the claimants disputed this classification by the CPSC. A product cannot be a banned hazardous substance unless it first is determined to be a hazardous substance. The statute defines a *hazardous substance* as "[a]ny substance or mixture which . . . is flammable or combustible, . . . if such substance or mixture of substances may cause substantial personal injury or substantial illness during or as a proximate result of any customary or reasonably foreseeable handling or use." After testing the product, the CPSC determined that it was flammable because, when tested according to applicable regulations, it exhibited flashback. In addition to their several arguments that this finding of flammability by the CPSC was flawed, the claimants also contended that Rainbow Foam Paint is not capable of causing substantial injury or illness with customary or reasonably foreseeable use. The government in contrast maintained that it is reasonably foreseeable that young children may try to dispense the paint with the can sideways or upside down and could receive substantial injuries if the product is used in this way near a flame or spark. The claimants disputed that such use is reasonably foreseeable since children normally will be supervised in their use of the product by an adult. In general, a court should defer to the agency's interpretation of the substantial injury requirement if it is not "arbitrary, capricious or manifestly contrary to the statute." *Chevron U.S.A.* Inc. v. *Natural Resources Defense Council,* 467 U.S. 837 [1984]. Here, the statute does not require that the product be likely to cause injury, but only that it "*may* cause substantial injury . . . during or as a proximate result of any customary or reasonably foreseeable handling or use." 15 U.S.C. § 1261(f)(1)(A) [emphasis added]. Thus, as the CPSC had found that Rainbow Foam Paint, under proper testing conditions, could cause flashback in some instances, the product conceivably could "cause substantial injury" during "reasonably foreseeable . . . use" and may properly be characterized as a hazardous substance. Whether the product is a banned hazardous substance, however, depends on whether it is exempt from that definition as art or educational material. The government points out that the proviso authorizing the secretary to exempt certain items specifically makes the exemption contingent on the item's being "intended for use by children who have attained sufficient maturity, and may reasonably be expected, to read and heed such directions and warnings." 15 U.S.C. § 1261(q)(1). The government's reading of this statutory language is reasonable, as even the district court acknowledged in part. The district court ultimately rejected this interpretation, however, because it did not believe the government was advocating that position and because it surmised that Congress may have believed that adult supervision would suffice when a child lacked sufficient maturity to read and heed a warning. The district court's reasoning that the likelihood of adult supervision nullifies the language in the proviso nonetheless is erroneous. Indeed, the statutory language is clear on its face, as the statute provides for an exemption from the definition of banned hazardous substance only if a product intended for use by children is accompanied by a warning that the child users themselves can "read and heed." Thus, a product that is determined to be hazardous within the meaning of the statute cannot be exempt under the regulations—even if it is art material—if its intended child user is too young to read and heed a warning label. This conclusion follows from the determination that the language of §1261(q)(1) focuses on the intended *user* of the product; therefore, the fact that adults purchase Rainbow Foam Paint is irrelevant. Rainbow Foam Paint is intended for use by children as young as three years old, and it cannot reasonably be argued that children who are three years old can "reasonably be expected" to be able to read and heed a proper warning label. Hence, the CPSC's determination, after adequate testing, that Rainbow Foam Paint is a hazardous substance does not appear to be arbitrary or capricious. Accordingly, the CPSC could properly classify the product as a banned hazardous substance because it contains a hazardous substance and is intended for use by children who are too young to read the warnings provided. The district court erred, therefore, in granting summary judgment for the claimants, even if the court correctly had determined that the product was art material. Thus, it is appropriate in this case to reverse the district court's grant of summary judgment to the claimants and to direct the entry of summary judgment for the government.

BUSINESS CONSIDERATIONS Could Weill objectively believe that this case represents misplaced zealotry and over-regulation by the CPSC? What policies should a business establish to protect its interests when it deals with the CPSC?

ETHICAL CONSIDERATIONS Who bears the primary ethical responsibility for seeing that children use toys and other materials safely: the manufacturer or the parents? Is it ethical to sell a patently dangerous toy?

YOU BE THE JUDGE

Debt Collection

Most creditors accept the truism that juries in general do not like bill collectors and that juries oftentimes favor debtors when the juries view the creditors as the proverbial "Goliaths" and the debtors as the "Davids." Yet a Texas jury's award of $11 million against Household Credit Services, Inc. (Household Credit) and the trend this case represents has caused a hue and cry among vendors of consumer credit. Albert and Mary Driscol had sued Household Credit and Allied Adjustment Bureau (Allied), a San Francisco collection agency retained by Household, for a large number of abusive collection practices—ranging from repeated telephone calls at home to a bomb and death threat at work—that allegedly were part and parcel of Allied's efforts to collect the Driscols' delinquent $2,000 Visa bill. The jury found Household joint and severally liable for the actions of Household's agent, Allied. Hence, the verdict effectively makes Household liable for the entire $11 million because Allied has gone out of business and the whereabouts of Allied's principals remain unknown. The real "kicker" here is that the jury premised the bulk of the award not on consumer statutes regulating debt-collection practices but on *common law* causes of action—unreasonable debt-collection efforts, negligence, intentional infliction of emotional distress, and invasion of privacy. Noteworthy, too, is the fact that the jury awarded such a large recovery even though the physical injury present in most common law tort actions was absent here. The unreasonable debt-collection practices allegedly at issue here had subjected the Driscols to mere psychological abuses and threats. As one consumer law specialist notes, "This case is a wake-up call to the commercial collections industry. The technical violations that drive most federal Fair Debt Collection [Practices Act] cases [are] not going to be available against a creditor. But when you are talking about allegations of substantive abuses, [now other remedies] are available, whether these abuses are committed by agencies, creditors or lawyers, and whether the debt is consumer or commercial."

Assume that the Driscols' case has been appealed to *your* court. Will you uphold this verdict, or will you remit [that is, reduce] it?[6]

BUSINESS CONSIDERATIONS Given these new theories of liability, discuss fully what steps a creditor like Household should take so as to reduce its own legal exposure and the exposure resulting from the actions of third-party bill collectors it proposes to hire.

ETHICAL CONSIDERATIONS Would it be ethical for a firm like Household to try to use its "no tolerance" policy (that is, that the company will not permit the debt-collection agencies it hires to engage in overly aggressive tactics)—assuming such a policy were in existence—as a mitigating defense?

SOURCE: *The National Law Journal* (2 September 1996), pp. B1 and B2.

http:// RESOURCES FOR BUSINESS LAW STUDENTS

NAME	RESOURCES	WEB ADDRESS
Consumer Credit Protection Act—15 USC § 1601	Legal Information Institute (LII), maintained by the Cornell Law School, provides a hypertext and searchable version of 15 USC § 1601, the Consumer Credit Protection Act, better known as the Truth in Lending Act.	http://www.law.cornell.edu/uscode/15/1601.html
Federal Reserve Board Regulations	The Federal Reserve Board provides summaries of its regulations, including Regulations B and Z.	http://www.bog.frb.fed.us/frregs.htm
U.S. Consumer Product Safety Commission	U.S. Consumer Product Safety Commission provides consumer news and information, as well as notices on recalls and business contracts.	http://www.cpsc.gov/
The Consumer Law Page	The Consumer Law Page, maintained by The Alexander Law Firm, provides articles, brochures, and reference materials.	http://consumerlawpage.com/

SUMMARY

Various federal and state statutes protect consumers' rights. The Consumer Credit Protection Act of 1968, better known as the Truth in Lending Act (TILA), mandates the disclosure (via a standardized form and terminology) of the actual costs of credit so as to enable consumers to make more informed decisions about credit. Failure to comply with the act's disclosure provisions (or with its implementing regulation, Regulation Z) subjects the creditor to various civil, criminal, and statutory liabilities. The Fair Credit Reporting Act of 1970 requires consumer-reporting agencies to adopt reasonable procedures for guaranteeing the accuracy of information disseminated in credit reports. The act also limits the uses that one can make of such information. Consumers enjoy a variety of rights under the statute, including notification of an agency's reliance on adverse information and mechanisms for disputing the accuracy of information contained in files. Civil, criminal, and administrative remedies are available under the act. The Equal Credit Opportunity Act of 1974 (ECOA) prohibits discrimination based on sex, marital status, race, religion, national origin, age (provided the applicant has the capacity to contract), receipt of public assistance benefits, and the good faith exercise of rights under TILA. Regulation B extensively implements ECOA by, among other things, setting out the rules that creditors must follow when they evaluate the creditworthiness of any applicant and when they provide notification to the consumer of the action taken. The remedies available for violations of ECOA resemble those granted under TILA. The Fair Debt Collection Practices Act of 1974 (FDCPA) regulates the activities of debt collectors. Congress intended the law to eliminate abusive, deceptive, and unfair debt-collection practices and thereby to protect consumers. The act limits the manner in which the debt collector can communicate with the debtor and limits the third parties whom the debt collector can contact about the debt. Remedial awards are similar to those granted under other statutes, but the Federal Trade Commission has primary enforcement responsibilities under the FDCPA. The Uniform Consumer Credit Code represents yet another statute—this time at the state level—that protects consumers. The Consumer Product Safety Act established the Consumer Product Safety Commission (CPSC). The CSPC regulates hazardous products and even can ban those that pose imminent hazards to the public.

DISCUSSION QUESTIONS

1. Explain the disclosures a creditor typically must make to the consumer under the Truth in Lending Act (TILA).
2. Describe the remedies available for creditors' violation of the Truth in Lending Act (TILA).
3. Explain in detail the coverage of the Fair Credit Reporting Act (the FCRA).
4. Delineate the civil remedies that are permitted—and prohibited—by the Fair Credit Reporting Act (the FRCA).
5. Explain what Regulation B of the Equal Credit Opportunity Act (ECOA) requires of creditors for compliance.
6. Outline the general requirements of the Fair Debt Collection Practices Act (FDCPA).
7. Set out the civil and criminal penalties that can result from violations of the Fair Debt Collection Practices Act (FDCPA).
8. Explain the underlying purposes of the Uniform Consumer Credit Code (UCCC).
9. Describe in detail the powers enjoyed by the Consumer Product Safety Commission (CPSC).
10. Mention some of the products subject to the standards set by the Consumer Product Safety Commission and some of the products it has banned.

CASE PROBLEMS AND WRITING ASSIGNMENTS

1. In June 1992, Ocie M. Williams applied for a rural housing assistance loan through the Farmers Home Administration (FHA). Prior to issuing Williams a loan, the FHA requested a credit report from the Credit Bureau of Clanton. The Credit Bureau is a consumer-reporting agency within the terms of the Fair Credit Reporting Act (FCRA). The report prepared by the Credit Bureau disclosed two public record items: (1) an April 1990 mortgage foreclosure notice published in a local paper against Williams by Colonial Bank, which foreclosure had resulted in the sale of the property to another party; and (2) a materialmen's lien filed in April 1990 by William E. Knight in the amount of $14,720. The report indicated that the lien had been paid in June 1990. Upon receiving the credit report, the FHA determined that Williams was not eligible for a loan because of his credit history. When Williams learned of this decision, he approached the Credit Bureau and asked it to reinvestigate the two public record items that had appeared on his credit report. Although Williams acknowledged that a mortgage foreclosure on his property had occurred, he maintained that it should not have been included in his credit report because the bank had effected an improper foreclosure. Similarly, he contended that Knight had lacked any basis for filing the materialmen's lien and that the lien should not have appeared on the credit report, even though the credit report also revealed that the lien had been satisfied. Williams thus admitted that the credit report had accurately reflected the contents of the public records; nonetheless, Williams requested a reinvestigation. When the Credit Bureau did not follow up on Williams's request, he filed suit under the FCRA. In these circumstances, had the Credit Bureau violated the Act? Why or why not? [See *Williams* v. *Colonial Bank*, 826 F.Supp. 415 (M.D. Ala. 1993).]

2. All-terrain vehicles (ATVs) are single-rider, three- or four-wheeled vehicles intended primarily for off-road recreational use on unpaved terrain. In 1989, over 2.75 million ATVs were in use in the United States. Prompted by a surge in ATV-related deaths and injuries, the Consumer Product Safety Commission (CPSC), in May 1985, published an Advance Notice of Proposed Rule-making (ANPR) and set out its intention to pursue a court action declaring three- and four-wheeled ATVs "imminently hazardous consumer products." The ANPR led ultimately to the CPSC and the ATV industry's signing a 1988 consent decree that would be effective for 10 years. This consent decree prohibited the sale of new three-wheeled ATVs and required the distributors to "represent affirmatively" in their advertising "that ATVs with engine sizes [between 70 and 90cc] should be used only by those aged 12 and older" and that ATVs "with engine sizes greater than 90 cc should be used only by those aged 16 and older." The distributors promised to "use their best efforts" to reasonably assure that ATVs would "not [be] purchased by or for the use of any

person" under the specified ages. When undercover CPSC investigations in 1988 and 1989 showed that between 56 and 70 percent of all ATV dealers routinely ignored the age recommendations set out in the consent decree, the CPSC, in 1990 and early 1991, undertook a major review of ATV safety. After considering four regulatory options—including a "youth ban" that would prohibit children under age 16 from riding ATVs of over 90 cc in engine size—in April 1991, a three-member CPSC decided to impose no new restraints and to terminate the rulemaking. In justification of its decision, the CPSC cited its staff's predictions of further declines in ATV injury rates; the difficulty of enforcing the proposed ban; the lack of evidence that the proposed ban more effectively would prevent injuries to children than the recommendations in the consent decree had; and the feasibility of developing ATV safety programs at the state level. In September 1991, four organizations that had participated as *amici curiae* (by filing friends of the court briefs) during the district court's initial consideration of the consent decree challenged as arbitrary and capricious the CPSC's decision to refrain from pursuing, at the present time, a ban on the sale of new adult-size ATVs for use by children under age 16. Should the appellate court set aside the CPSC's agency action as arbitrary and capricious? Why? [See *Consumer Fed. of America* v. *CPSC*, 990 F.2d 1298 (D.C. Cir. 1993).]

3. On 19 October 1987, *John Venesio Graciano, Jr.*, completed a credit application by which he sought to borrow $6,300 from East Cambridge Savings Bank to purchase an automobile. Graciano listed another person's social security number as his and indicated that he worked for New England Tea & Coffee in Malden, Massachusetts. On 27 October 1987, the bank verified Graciano's employment at New England Tea and Coffee and approved his application. Unbeknownst to the bank, Graciano was using someone else's social security number—and that someone else had a very similar name—*John Victor Graziano, Jr.*, the plaintiff in this case. The plaintiff and Graciano had different addresses, different places of employment, and different dates of birth. And, of course, the plaintiff and Graciano had different, albeit similar, names. The bank nonetheless failed to ascertain the true identity and social security number of its loan applicant, Graciano. On 30 October 1987, Graciano signed a promissory note for $4,500 and was given a bank draft in that amount, payable to him and the dealer from whom he was purchasing the automobile. After Graciano failed to make any payments on the note, on 30 June 1988, the matter was referred to the bank's attorney for collection. The attorney sought and, on 14 February 1989, recovered for the bank a judgment against Graciano in the amount of $6,315.64. Prior to and after this judgment, the bank requested consumer reports on Graciano on at least three occasions: 18 July 1988, 11 February 1992, and 25 November 1992. The bank made each request so that the bank could obtain information as to the whereabouts of Graciano and thereby facilitate the bank's efforts to collect its judgment. By entering into the computer system the social security number Graciano falsely had provided to the bank, that is, the plaintiff's social security number, the bank thereafter requested the first report on Graciano. The bank received two reports, one for Graciano and one for the plaintiff. The bank requested the second and third reports after it already knew or should have known that there were two individuals with similar names who were using the same social security number. The plaintiff claimed that he never had requested any credit or taken a loan from the bank. Nor, he asserted, had he ever been a customer of the bank. On 10 December 1992, the plaintiff received a letter from an attorney for the bank, which letter informed the plaintiff that, as he currently owed the bank $8,589.27, the plaintiff should contact the attorney for the purpose of working out an agreeable payment plan. The letter was addressed to the plaintiff's correct address, but the name on the letter was "John V. Graciano." Before being contacted by the bank's attorney, the plaintiff had been aware that someone had been misusing his social security number for employment purposes. Indeed, on 12 March 1991, the plaintiff had advised the Social Security Administration that his number was being misused. Bringing suit against the bank, the plaintiff subsequently claimed that the bank's actions of requesting credit reports—pursuant to its collection efforts—represented a violation of the FCRA because the bank had willfully obtained the plaintiff's consumer reports under false pretenses. Should the court accept the plaintiff's contentions? [See *Graziano* v. *TRW, Inc.*, 877 F.Supp. 53 (D.Mass. 1995).]

4. Transworld Systems, Inc. (TSI), a collection agency, sent David T. Latimer two collection letters, dated 5 August and 19 August 1992. Latimer claimed that the letters violated the Fair Debt Collection Practices Act's (FDCPA's) requirement that consumers be notified of their right to obtain verification of the debt. Latimer stressed that the required verification notice in the 5 August letter is smaller than both the text of the letter and the "Detach and Return with Payment" command. TSI countered that this small size is mitigated by the fact that much of the larger text actually reinforces the required verification language. Latimer

further argued that language contained in the 19 August letter overshadowed the required validation notice (in the 5 August letter). In particular, Latimer complained of the following in that latter letter: "imperative—grace period about to expire. Our client shows an unpaid account in the above stated amount legally due and owing to you." Were the warnings at issue sufficient to comply with the dictates of the FDCPA? Why or why not? [See *Latimer* v. *Transworld Systems, Inc.*, 842 F.Supp. 274 (E.D. Mich. 1993).]

5. On 10 November 1986, Sebastian and Maria Shaumyan entered into a home improvement contract with Sidetex Co., Inc. (Sidetex). The contract provided for Sidetex to install siding, replace windows, and perform other related work at the home jointly owned by the Shaumyans. The contract obligated the Shaumyans to make a deposit and to pay Sidetex in four scheduled progress payments. The contract did not subject the Shaumyans' payments to any finance charges. The total cost of the contracted work, some $14,800, was due and owing upon Sidetex's completion of the final stage of the work. Sidetex commenced work under the contract; and the Shaumyans made the first three scheduled progress payments. Performance was not completed, however, because of a dispute concerning the quality of windows that Sidetex was to install. On 19 October 1987, the Shaumyans filed a lawsuit that alleged a violation of the Equal Credit Opportunity Act (ECOA). They asserted that the insistence of Sidetex's salesman that Mrs. Shaumyan co-sign the home improvement contract had discriminated against both Shaumyans. Was the home improvement contract at issue here a "credit transaction" subject to ECOA? [See *Shaumyan* v. *Sidetex Co., Inc.*, 900 F.2d 16 (1990).]

6. **BUSINESS APPLICATION CASE** Based on her own creditworthiness, Linda J. Pierce obtained a Citibank Chase VISA account with defendant Citibank (South Dakota), N.A. Her husband, Michael Pierce, maintained several accounts with defendant Citicorp Credit Services, Inc. (Citicorp). Citicorp is a corporate affiliate of Citibank. When Citicorp notified Michael Pierce by letter on 11 January 1991, that owing to his delinquent Citibank bankcard account, Citicorp had closed all his accounts, Citicorp included the account number of Linda Pierce among the numbers of the accounts closed. Linda Pierce, who lived with her husband, did not receive notice of the closing of her account; and her name was not included on the notice sent to Michael Pierce. Linda Pierce thereafter continued to receive regular statements on her account and continued to make payments on that account until 15 May 1991, when she learned from a customer service representative of Citibank that the account had been closed. In that telephone conversation, the customer service representative informed Linda Pierce that she could not use her card until the accounts of Michael Pierce were brought current because her account was linked with those of her husband. On 18 July 1991, Linda Pierce sent a registered letter to Citibank and requested a written response within 10 days as to why her account had not been renewed. On 11 September 1991, Citibank renewed her account; reinstated her credit privileges; and, in a letter dated 11 September 1991, informed her that Citicorp appreciated the efforts she had made to return her account to good standing. Linda Pierce thereafter used the account until she filed a petition in bankruptcy on 13 May 1992. Linda Pierce subsequently claimed that Citicorp, and Citibank acting as an agent for Citicorp, by failing to provide her with written notice of the closure or suspension of her charge account, had violated ECOA. Citicorp and Citibank contended that despite the absence of a written notification's being sent to Linda Pierce, she was not entitled to relief because 1) her claim would be barred by the statute of limitations; 2) by receiving actual notice of the cancellation, she had waived her right to written notice; and 3) Citibank's failure to notify her in writing would constitute an inadvertent error permissible under ECOA. Who had the stronger arguments? Why? What intrafirm policies should the banks institute so as to avoid similar litigation in the future? [See *Pierce* v. *Citibank (South Dakota), N.A.*, 843 F.Supp. 646 (D. Or. 1994).]

7. **ETHICS APPLICATION CASE** On 3 February 1989, the Jensens purchased a new 1989 Ford Tempo from Ray Kim Ford, Inc. (Ray Kim Ford). The Jensens signed a retail installment contract that disclosed an annual percentage rate of 15 percent, a finance charge of $7,110.06, an amount financed of $16,636.14, a total of scheduled payments of $23,746.20, and a total sale price of $26,546.20 (including a down payment of $2,800). Eight hundred dollars of the down payment represented the value of the Jensens' trade-in. The Jensens alleged this was only an estimate; they contended that, by agreement, they would owe the difference if the trade-in were worth less, and Ray Kim Ford would refund it if the vehicle were worth more. The Jensens did not allege that this contract failed to make any disclosure that the Truth in Lending Act (TILA) requires. After the trade-in turned out to be worth $1,388.08, or $588.08 more than the estimate, Ray Kim Ford did not make a refund but prepared a second retail installment contract. In net substance, the second contract, by giving almost no benefit to the Jensens for the enhanced value of their trade-in,

increased the total sale price by $588.08. Ray Kim Ford ultimately tendered the $588.08 but only after the Jensens had sued. In their suit, the Jensens alleged that the second contract was a forgery. After Ray Kim Ford had sold it to Citicorp, the Jensens made payments to Citicorp until they noticed the five cents' difference in monthly payments, asked for a copy of the contract, and realized it was not the contract they had signed. The Jensens argued that, under TILA, the second contract represented their credit transaction and that the credit terms had not been disclosed to them. Would TILA provide a civil remedy for such conduct? Why? If the court had based its decision on ethics, would the result differ? Explain. [See *Jensen* v. *Ray Kim Ford, Inc.*, 920 F.2d 3 (7th Cir. 1990).]

8. **IDES CASE** On several occasions between 1988 and 1992, Nachson Draiman used his American Express Platinum Card when he purchased airline tickets through the Travel Dimensions travel agency. Draiman provided Travel Dimensions with his Platinum Card number; and when he needed tickets, he would call and place an order. Travel Dimensions in turn would send the tickets to Draiman and the bill to American Express Travel Related Service Company (American Express). By including the cost of the tickets plus applicable financing charges in its periodic billing statement, American Express then would secure payment from Draiman. On 21 January 1992, Draiman canceled his Platinum Card. Sometime thereafter Draiman deposited an undisclosed sum of money with Travel Dimensions. On 20 July 1992, Draiman purchased four El Al tickets to Israel for a total cost of $8,308. Draiman instructed Travel Dimensions to pay for the El Al tickets by drawing upon his deposited funds. Travel Dimensions did not honor that request—instead it charged the amount against the number that it had for Draiman's Platinum Card. American Express of course knew nothing of Draiman's deposit with, or his instructions to, Travel Dimensions. When American Express received the $8,308 charge from Travel Dimensions, that triggered American Express's reinstatement policy, as set out in these terms in the cardholder agreement:

> *If you ask us to cancel your account, but you continue to use the Card, we will consider such use as your request for reinstatement of your account. If we agree to reinstate your account, this Agreement or any amended or new Agreement we send you will govern your reinstated account.*

American Express does not communicate with cardholders to confirm that it is in fact their desire to revive their accounts. In accordance with its written policy, then, American Express reinstated Draiman's Platinum Card on 26 August 1992, and billed him $8,308. Draiman later actually used the El Al tickets (each of which had his Platinum Card number printed on its face) to travel to Israel. On 15 October 1993, Draiman paid American Express $3,399.98 of the $8,308 total and threatened suit if it tried to collect the $4,908.02 balance. When American Express attempted to collect the debt, Draiman, citing purported violations of the Fair Credit Billing Act, TILA, and other applicable laws, on 11 January 1995, brought the threatened legal action with one twist: Draiman filed not only on his own behalf but also on behalf of a purported class of similarly aggrieved persons. Draiman grounded his lawsuit on two different theories: 1) that American Express, by resuscitating his canceled Platinum Card without his permission, had issued an unsolicited credit card in violation of TILA; and 2) that, owing to Travel Dimensions's unauthorized use of his Platinum Card, he would be entitled to the $50 limitation on liability afforded by TILA in certain circumstances. In analyzing this case, apply the IDES approach. How should the court rule on Draiman's contentions? [See *Draiman* v. *American Express Travel Related Services Co.*, 892 F.Supp. 1096 (N.D. Ill. 1995).]

NOTES

1. See, for example, Jonathan Sheldon, ed., *Fair Credit Reporting Act*, 3rd ed. (Boston: National Consumer Law Center, 1994). This and other National Consumer Law Center publications, such as Ernest L. Sarason, ed., *Truth in Lending* (1986); Gerry Azzata, ed., *Equal Credit Opportunity Act* (1988); and the annual cumulative supplements to these works provide more detailed information on consumer law, as does David G. Epstein and Steve H. Nickles, *Consumer Law in a Nutshell* (Minneapolis: West Publishing Co., 1981) and Howard J. Alperin and Ronald F. Chase, *Consumer Law: Sales Practices and Credit Regulation* (Minneapolis: West Publishing Co., 1986).
2. Jonathan Sheldon, ed., *Fair Credit Reporting Act*, 3rd ed. (Boston: National Consumer Law Center, 1994), p. 31.
3. Ibid.
4. Ibid., p. 32.
5. Ibid.
6. Jacquelyn Lynn, "Creditors, Beware: Juries Find New Basis for Award," *The National Law Journal* (2 September 1996), pp. B1 and B2.

Chapter 42

Environmental Protection

Outline

Introduction
The Environmental Protection Agency
The National Environmental Policy Act
Air Pollution
Water Pollution
Noise Pollution
Land Conservation and Pollution
Wildlife Conservation
Enforcement and Remedies
International Aspects
Summary
Discussion Questions
Case Problems and Writing Assignments

Agenda

CIT will be manufacturing its videophone units at several factories in the United States. The firm wants to make its factories as similar as possible but is concerned that different states may have different environmental protection standards that will force it to adapt each location to the state's particular laws. The family members wish to be viewed as good "neighbors" in any community where CIT operates, and they want to know what they must do to meet this objective. In particular, they want to avoid polluting the community, and they do not wish to be seen as a nuisance in any of their locations. As they open new facilities, they want to ensure that they meet or exceed federal expectations. What sorts of environmentally friendly technologies should they install in their facilities? These and other questions are likely to arise as you study this chapter.

Be prepared! You never know when one of the Kochanowskis will need your help or advice.

INTRODUCTION

Environmental law constitutes an extremely complex, pervasive, and controversial area of the law. Acronym-laden and comprised of highly technical statutes and regulations, environmental law poses genuine challenges to students and legal practitioners alike. Hence, in this chapter we will highlight only some of the most important principles.[1]

During the heyday of environmental protection efforts in the 1970s, the United States, by taking the first steps aimed at halting the destruction of our planet's biodiversity, distinguished itself. The United States did so largely through statutory engraftments onto common law **nuisance** principles. Nuisance laws prohibit interference with the rights of others; however, though providing the framework for modern-day statutory environmental law, such laws proved inadequate to solve the sheer magnitude of the problems these laws must address.

Nuisance
Unlawful use of one's own property so as to injure the rights of another.

THE ENVIRONMENTAL PROTECTION AGENCY

Congress instead chose to opt for a statutory approach that leaves enforcement largely to an administrative agency called the Environmental Protection Agency (EPA), itself established by executive order in 1970. In general, the EPA has the power to enforce environmental laws, adopt regulations, conduct research on pollution, and assist other governmental entities concerned with the environment. To enforce federal environmental laws, the EPA can subject suspected violators to administrative orders and civil penalties and can refer criminal matters to the Department of Justice as well.

The laws Congress passes and the EPA enforces consider the economic aspects of environmental law; take a technological approach to environmental concerns; mandate risk assessment in the implementation of these laws; and use the imposition of liability, sometimes even strict liability, as a hammer to ensure compliance. Early legislation mandated compliance primarily by business and industry, especially the chemical industry. In the last 15 years, however, small businesses and state and local governments increasingly have borne the burden of the compliance costs associated with environmental issues.

Hence the virtual absence of any legislative enactments in the 1990s may indicate the increasing politicization of this area of the law. In general, what seems a simple (and valid) argument—take all steps necessary to save our environment—is complicated by the staggering costs involved. EPA figures (which many critics argue may be underestimated by as much as a multiple of 30) place the costs to local taxpayers for environmental compliance in the year 2000 at over $32 billion (in 1986 dollars), an estimate that does not take into account the costs imposed on businesses and consumers.[2] Another recent article estimates that compliance with all governmental regulations in 1995, including environmental laws, cost U.S. businesses $600 billion (calculated in 1991 dollars).[3] Critics of such environmental regulations question whether the benefits derived from compliance outweigh these gargantuan costs; they suggest the money spent on complying with environmental mandates might be better spent on education, medical research, and the like.[4] Pro-environmentalists, however, argue that we have no choice but to protect our environment. Simply put, it is the only one we have—if we ruin it, we cannot replenish or replace it.

THE NATIONAL ENVIRONMENTAL POLICY ACT

The National Environmental Policy Act of 1969 (NEPA) became effective when then President Nixon signed it into law in 1970. Congress enacted NEPA as a means of furthering a national policy to encourage a productive and harmonious relationship between people and the environment. Congress also viewed NEPA as a vehicle for promoting efforts to eliminate environmental damage and thereby enhance the health and welfare of the citizenry.

In short, § 101 of NEPA declares that it is the federal government's continuing responsibility, in cooperation with state and local governments and other concerned private and public organizations, to use all practicable means, consistent with other essential national policy considerations, to attain the broadest range of beneficial uses of the environment (including the preservation of healthy and aesthetically and culturally pleasing surroundings) while at the same time avoiding the degradation of the environment, risks to health and safety, and other undesirable or unintended consequences. In fulfilling this purpose, NEPA directs that, to the fullest extent possible, all agencies of the federal government live up to these environmental responsibilities.

Environmental Impact Statement

NEPA effectuates this goal primarily by requiring virtually all federal agencies to prepare a detailed environmental impact statement (EIS) whenever the agency proposes legislation, recommends any actions, or undertakes any activities that may affect the environment. Among other things, an EIS must:

- Describe the anticipated impact that the proposed action will have on the environment
- Describe any unavoidable adverse consequences of the action or activity
- Examine the possible alternative methods of achieving the desired goals
- Distinguish between long-term and short-term environmental effects
- Describe the irreversible and irretrievable commitments of resources that will occur if the proposed action is implemented

The statute requires wide dissemination of EISs in draft form to other federal, state, and local agencies; the President; and the Council on Environmental Quality (that is, the CEQ, the importance of which is discussed in the next section).

Given the substantial data gathering necessary for successful compliance with the prerequisites of an EIS, many agencies have tried to exempt themselves from having to prepare this statement. However, the numerous court decisions since 1970 indicate that the following criteria show a need for an EIS: (1) a proposed federal action (2) that is "major" and (3) that has a significant impact on the environment. Courts have made the definitional thresholds for points 1 and 2 law; hence, if a federal agency has control over the proposed action (no matter how small the undertaking, or even if it is regional in scope), coupled with a substantial commitment of resources, the EIS requirement applies. Similarly, court decisions under point 3 have not limited interpretations of the term "environment" solely to the natural environment (lakes, rivers, wetlands, wilderness areas, beaches, and so forth). The broad goals of the act (for example, the preservation of aesthetically and culturally pleasing surroundings, including the historical aspects of our national heritage) support the view that projects covered by NEPA involve more than just proposals that have an impact on various natural habitats. On the other hand, Congress clearly did not intend to require an EIS for every conceivable federal project, even though all such proposed activities in some fashion affect the quality of life of the citizenry.

Hence, considerable litigation has centered around the content of the EIS. CEQ regulations set out detailed requirements that cover the preparation of an EIS. The agency first makes an "environmental assessment" (an EA) of the need for an EIS. An interdisciplinary, interagency evaluation of the need for the proposed action; the likely environmental effects of the proposed action; the alternatives to the proposed action; and the agency, interest group, and public comments received concerning the proposal all factor into the EA as well.

Unless the agency makes a "finding of no significant impact" (that is, a FONSI), the agency, by determining the scope—or subject matter—of the EIS, begins the preparation of the EIS. Court and agency decisions have held that agencies cannot avoid the application of NEPA by breaking up long-term projects—for example, highway, flood control, and hydroelectric projects that cover wide areas—into segments that in and of themselves separately seem to show an absence of environmental risks even though the overall project does. The EIS must adequately discuss the consequences of each alternative, including the alternative that the agency take "no action" on a given problem.

In deciding whether to include a given alternative, courts use a "rule-of-reason" test that gauges whether a reasonable person would view the alternative as sufficiently significant to merit an extended discussion. The EIS need not mention implausible or purely speculative alternatives. Besides the scope of the EIS, the timing of the EIS also has spawned litigation. Agencies contemplating any action that has environmental repercussions must make sure that the preparation of the EIS occurs sufficiently in advance of the commencement of the project so that the EIS makes an important, practical contribution to the decision-making process rather than serving merely as a rationalization or justification for decisions already made by the agency.

Council on Environmental Quality

The responsibility for ensuring the success of the EIS process falls to the Council on Environmental Quality (CEQ). Established by NEPA as an advisory council to the President, the CEQ develops regulations covering EISs and otherwise plays a leading role in developing and recommending to the President national policies that will foster and promote the improvement of the environmental quality of the nation. The CEQ assists and advises the President in the preparation of the Environmental Quality Report, which the President by law submits annually to Congress. By statute, the three-member CEQ can maintain a staff to help keep it abreast of developing environmental issues. Although the EPA represents the primary enforcement agency for federal environmental laws, courts give the CEQ's guidelines and regulations great deference.

Amendments to NEPA in the late 1970s set up a nine-member Science Advisory Board to provide scientific information to the administrator of the EPA (the head of the agency) and various other congressional bodies that address scientific and technical issues affecting the environment. These amendments also give to the EPA administrator the task of coordinating environmental research, development, demonstration, and educational programs so as to minimize unnecessary duplication of programs, projects, and research facilities. Centralizing these responsibilities within the EPA and its staff facilitates the achievement of both NEPA's mandates and the broader environmental objectives and challenges facing the nation.

Robertson v. *Methow Valley Citizens Council*, construing NEPA, follows.

42.1 ROBERTSON v. METHOW VALLEY CITIZENS COUNCIL 490 U.S. 332 (1989)

FACTS The Forest Service is authorized by statute to manage national forests for outdoor recreation, range, timber, watershed, and wildlife and fish purposes. Because its decision to issue a recreational special use permit constitutes major federal action within the meaning of the National Environmental Policy Act of 1969 (NEPA), the preparation of an environmental impact statement (EIS) must precede any such decision. After a Forest Service study designated a particular national forest location as having a high potential for development as a major downhill ski resort, Methow Recreation, Inc. (MRI) applied for a special use permit to develop and operate such a resort on that site and on adjacent private land MRI had acquired. In cooperation with state and local officials, the Service prepared an EIS, which, among other things, considered the effects of various levels of development on wildlife and air quality both onsite and—as required by Council on Environmental Quality (CEQ) regulations—offsite and outlined steps that might be taken to mitigate any adverse effects. The study indicated that these proposed steps were merely conceptual and would "be made more specific as part of the design and implementation stages of the planning process." The study's proposed options regarding offsite mitigation measures primarily were directed to the steps state and local governments might take.

After the regional forester had decided to issue a permit as recommended by the study, the Methow Valley Citizens Council appealed to the chief of the Forest Service, who affirmed. The citizens, owing to their belief that the study had not satisfied NEPA's requirements, then brought suit. The district court's magistrate filed an opinion concluding that the study was adequate; but the court of appeals reversed, holding that the study was inadequate as a matter of law because NEPA imposes a substantive duty on agencies to take action to mitigate the adverse effects of major federal actions, which entails the further duty to include in every EIS a detailed explanation of specific actions that will be employed to mitigate the adverse impact; that if the Forest Service had had difficulty obtaining adequate information to make a reasoned assessment of the project's environmental impact, it had an obligation to make a "worst-case analysis" on the basis of the available information, using reasonable projections of the worst possible consequences; and that the Forest Service's failure to develop a complete mitigation plan violated its own regulations.

ISSUE Did NEPA require federal agencies to include in each EIS: (1) a fully developed plan to mitigate environmental harm and (2) a worst-case analysis of potential environmental harm if relevant information concerning significant environmental effects is unavailable or too costly to obtain?

HOLDING No. NEPA required neither a fully developed plan detailing what steps will be taken to mitigate adverse environmental impacts nor a worst-case analysis.

REASONING NEPA declares a broad national commitment to practicing and promoting environmental quality. The statutory requirement that a federal agency contemplating a major action prepare such an EIS ensures that the agency, in reaching its decision, will have available, and will carefully consider, detailed information concerning significant environmental impacts. Simply by focusing the agency's attention on the environmental consequences of a proposed project, NEPA ensures that important effects will not be overlooked or underestimated only to be discovered after resources have been committed or the die otherwise cast. Moreover, the strong precatory language of the act and the requirement that agencies prepare detailed impact statements inevitably bring pressure to bear on agencies to respond to the needs of environmental quality. Publication of an EIS, both in draft and final form, also gives the public the assurance that the agency in its decision-making process indeed has considered environmental concerns and, perhaps more significantly, provides a springboard for public comment. Moreover, with respect to a development such as that proposed here, where the adverse effects on air quality and the mule deer herd primarily are attributable to predicted offsite development that will be subject to regulation by other governmental bodies, the EIS serves the function of offering those bodies adequate notice of the expected consequences and the opportunity to plan and implement corrective measures in a timely manner. The sweeping policy goals announced in NEPA thus are realized through a set of "action-forcing" procedures that require that agencies take a "hard look" at the environmental consequences and that provide for broad dissemination of relevant environmental information. Although these procedures almost certainly will affect the agency's substantive decision, it now is well settled that NEPA by itself does not mandate particular results but simply prescribes the necessary process. If the adverse environmental effects of the proposed action are adequately identified and evaluated, the agency is not constrained by NEPA from deciding that other values outweigh the environmental costs.

Implicit in NEPA's demand that an agency prepare a detailed statement on "any adverse environmental effects which cannot be avoided should the proposal be implemented" is an understanding that the EIS will discuss the extent to which adverse effects can be avoided. Recognizing the importance of such a discussion in guaranteeing that the agency has taken a "hard look" at the environmental consequences of proposed federal action, the implementing

42.1 ROBERTSON v. METHOW VALLEY CITIZENS COUNCIL *(cont.)* 490 U.S. 332 (1989)

CEQ regulations require that the agency discuss possible mitigation measures whenever the agency defines the scope of the EIS; discusses alternatives to the proposed action and the consequences of that action; and explains its ultimate decision. A fundamental distinction exists, however, between a requirement that mitigation be discussed in sufficient detail to ensure that environmental consequences have been fairly evaluated, on the one hand, and the substantive requirement that a complete mitigation plan be actually formulated and adopted, on the other. In this case, the offsite effects on air quality and the mule deer herd cannot be mitigated unless nonfederal governmental agencies take appropriate action. Since it is those state and local governmental bodies that have jurisdiction over the area in which the adverse effects need to be addressed and since they have the authority to mitigate them, it would be incongruous to conclude that the Forest Service has no power to act until the local agencies have reached a final conclusion on what mitigating measures they consider necessary. Even more significantly, it would be inconsistent with NEPA's reliance on procedural mechanisms—as opposed to substantive, result-based standards—to demand the presence of a fully developed plan that will mitigate environmental harm before an agency can act. Hence, the appellate court had erred in its determination regarding these matters. Moreover, even though the court of appeals recognized that in 1986 the CEQ had replaced the "worst-case" requirement with an amended regulation that retains the duty to describe the consequences of a remote, but potentially severe impact, but grounds the duty in evaluation of scientific opinion rather than in the framework of a conjectural "worst-case analysis," it believed that previous Supreme Court precedents entitled it to disregard the new regulation.

Although less deference to CEQ regulations may be in order in some cases in which the administrative guidelines conflict with the earlier pronouncements of the agency, substantial deference nonetheless is appropriate if there appears to have been good reason for the change. Here, the amendment came only after the prior regulation had been subjected to considerable criticism. Furthermore, the new regulation's requirement that an EIS focus on reasonably foreseeable impacts allows the generation of information and discussion regarding those consequences of greatest concern to the public and of greatest relevance to the agency's decision, rather than the distortion of the decision-making process occasioned by the overemphasis of highly speculative harms. In light of this well-considered basis for change, the new regulation is entitled to substantial deference. Accordingly, the court of appeals erred in concluding that the study is inadequate because it fails to include a worst-case analysis.

BUSINESS CONSIDERATIONS Statistical principles posit that in assessing risk, one tends to minimize low-probability events even if the potential loss from such occurrences is very large. Yet recent scientific evidence suggests that cataclysmic events oftentimes result from an accumulation of errors, each of which at the time may have seemed innocuous. Should businesses in their planning therefore adopt the court of appeals's requirement of a worst-case analysis of the potential environmental harm? Do businesses too easily dismiss the importance of such an analysis even if the analysis were difficult and/or costly to undertake?

ETHICAL CONSIDERATIONS Would the Supreme Court have arrived at a different decision if it had grounded its conclusions on ethics rather than the law? What ethical factors might have influenced the Court's decision?

AIR POLLUTION

The impurities, dirt, and contaminants that a variety of sources emit into the air fall generally into five different classes. The first class is *carbon monoxide*—a colorless, odorless, poisonous gas produced by burning fossil fuels. Discharges from car engines represent the largest source of carbon monoxide. The second class is *particulates*—liquid or solid substances produced by facilities using stationary fuel combustion and other industrial processes. Sources ranging from factories to home furnaces emit such particles. The third class is *sulfur oxides*—corrosive, poisonous gases caused by use of sulfurous fuels. Electrical utility power plants and industrial plants emit most sulfur oxides. The fourth class is *nitrogen oxides*—gases produced by the very hot burning of fuel. These derive from stationary combustion plants, such as steel mills, and transportation vehicles such as trains, trucks, and buses. Once emitted into the atmosphere, sulfur oxides combine with nitrogen oxides to form "acid rain." Finally, the fifth class—*hydrocarbons*—consists of particulates derived from unburned and wasted fuel. Unlike carbon monoxide, hydrocarbons in and of themselves are nontoxic. However, when hydrocarbons combine in the atmosphere with nitrogen oxides, complex secondary pollution—known as smog—often results. Smog, then, causes respiratory difficulties, eye and lung irritation, damage to trees and other vegetation, offensive odors, and haze.

However, it is nearly impossible to gauge with precision the so-called "threshold" or "safe" levels and/or "dangerous" levels of air pollution. Regulators therefore are relegated to setting exposure levels that kick in only when demonstrable adverse effects already have occurred. As a result, risk management continues to be a problematic issue in this area of environmental law.

As we shall see, the Clean Air Act and its amendments reflect this and other complexities: the ever-expanding recognition of the health risks associated with pollution, rapidly changing technologies, a veritable explosion of scientific data relating to air pollution, and industry resistance to policymakers' attempts to redress this problem.

The Clean Air Act

The Clean Air Act represents an oft-amended, lengthy (the statute itself is approximately 300 pages long), technical, complex, and comprehensive approach to combating air pollution. Efforts to regulate air pollution actually began in the 1950s when Congress supplied technical and financial assistance to the states to help control interstate pollution in some circumstances.

The first federal Clean Air Act, enacted in 1963, concentrated on controlling emissions from stationary industrial sources (the so-called "tall-stack" types of facilities). Only four years later, Congress, in the Air Quality Act of 1967, saw the need to pass amendments that address the problem of mobile air emissions from sources such as cars and trucks. The 1967 amendments established atmospheric areas as well as air quality control regions and called for the development of state plans to implement these **ambient** air standards. Under these early enactments, each state retained primary responsibility for ensuring the air quality within its own borders.

Ambient
Pertaining to the surrounding atmosphere or the environment.

The 1970 Amendments

To achieve national air quality standards as well, the 1970 amendments, by establishing timetables for meeting state goals, appreciably strengthened the federal role in combating air pollution. Under these provisions, the administrator of the EPA is responsible for establishing national ambient air quality standards (NAAQSs) for air pollutants that reasonably would be anticipated to endanger the public health or welfare.

The 1970 amendments directed the administrator to establish two kinds of standards: (1) primary standards that, in the judgment of the administrator and allowing for an adequate margin of safety, are necessary in order to protect the public health; and (2) secondary standards that, in the judgment of the administrator, are necessary to protect the public welfare—crops, livestock, buildings, and the like—from any known or anticipated adverse effects associated with the presence of such air pollutants in the ambient air.

These amendments also require each state, after reasonable notice and public hearings, within nine months of the promulgation of any NAAQSs to submit to the EPA a state implementation plan (SIP) setting out how the state proposes to implement and maintain that standard within its air quality control regions (AQCRs). Before the EPA administrator can approve it, the SIP must provide for the establishment and operation of procedures necessary to monitor and control ambient air quality as well as for a program providing for the enforcement of emissions regulations. Any SIP must allow for the attainment of primary standards "as expeditiously as practicable" but in no case later than three years from the date the administrator approves the plan. The state must attain secondary standards within a "reasonable time." Once approved, a SIP has the force of both federal and state law.

The EPA administrator originally promulgated NAAQSs for particulates, sulfur dioxide, carbon monoxide, nitrogen oxide, ozone, and hydrocarbons. In 1978, the EPA administrator also added lead, which can cause retardation and brain damage in children, to this list and in 1983 revoked the hydrocarbon standard.

The 1977 Amendments

Congress realized that the achievement of its national air quality objectives would necessitate strict timetables aimed at forcing cleanup actions on the part of industry and government. Hence, the 1970 amendments contemplated prompt action. But, by 1977, it had become clear that the original timetables were too optimistic. The 1977 Clean Air Act amendments therefore allowed delays in compliance in certain situations. By 1977, Congress also recognized that achievement of the nation's air quality objectives must encompass not only existing stationary sources and motor vehicles but also new stationary sources, new motor vehicles, and hazardous pollutants (such as asbestos, mercury, and vinyl chloride) produced by either existing or new sources. In addition, in 1977, Congress characterized this new undertaking as a federal responsibility; thus, Congress directed the EPA to establish such nationally uniform emission standards.

The 1990 Amendments

The 1990 amendments retain the basic strategies of the 1970 and 1977 amendments but also set new compliance dates for many of the deadlines established under the 1977 amendments that had come and gone.

Title I of these amendments, by mandating overall reductions of emissions within six years, attacks urban air pollution—particularly ozone concentrations.

Title II, by strengthening tailpipe emission standards for all cars and trucks and forcing manufacturers to design a certain number of clean-fuel cars each year, tackles mobile sources of emissions.

Title III requires the EPA to set permissible emission standards for some 190 toxic pollutants. In setting these standards, the administrator must consider the costs associated with achieving that standard, as well as the substances' health and environmental impacts.

Title IV for the first time sets up timetables aimed at specifically limiting emissions of nitrogen oxide and sulfur dioxide, the chief components of acid rain, by the year 2000. Focusing on the major emitting facilities, phase one of this title forces these facilities to achieve sulfur emissions of 2.5 pounds per million BTUs by 1995. Phase two, which must be achieved by the year 2000, cuts the allowable emissions to 1.2 pounds per million BTUs. Interestingly, this title contains economic incentives that allow complying facilities to "bank" or transfer emissions credits so as to use reductions of a given magnitude at one site to justify an increase in emissions levels at another site. As we shall see in the *Chevron U.S.A. Inc.* v. *Natural Resources Defense Council, Inc.*, case that follows, although some litigation has arisen over the mechanics of this trading, it does represent an economic-incentives approach to pollution control (similar to the Clean Water Act's permit process that we shall discuss later) that many environmental economists over the years have championed.

Title V sets up a permit system aimed at controlling emissions by major point sources—buildings, structures, facilities, or installations that emit air pollution. This portion of the amendment gives the EPA and state agencies that control air pollution the authority to regulate atmospheric discharges that may damage the general welfare or health and safety of the citizenry. Although industry groups have criticized the permit system as an unnecessary regulatory impediment to private enterprise, this system highlights the fact that Congress views atmospheric emissions as intrusions on publicly held and environmentally essential ecological systems, rather than as absolute rights, and thus regulable by the appropriate agencies.

Title VI for the first time regulates (and provides for the eventual phaseout of) various chlorofluorocarbons, hydrochlorofluorocarbons, and carbon tetrachlorides that bring about the depletion of the ozone layer. In this fashion, Title VI mirrors Title IV's provisions concerning acid rain.

Title VII strengthens the act's civil and criminal investigation, recordkeeping, and enforcement provisions. These new provisions allow the EPA to impose penalties in a more expeditious fashion and permit citizens' suits that address allegedly unreasonable EPA delays in enforcement and repeated violations by emitters.

The remaining titles set out various miscellaneous provisions, including the institution of a program to monitor and improve air quality standards along the United States/Mexico border; the establishment of an interagency task force to conduct research on air quality; and the retraining of workers laid off or terminated as a consequence of a firm's complying with the Clean Air Act.

Enforcement mechanisms under the Clean Air Act include administrative penalties (not to exceed $25,000 per day per violation), orders issued by the administrator of the EPA, and criminal actions brought by the U.S. Attorney General, including fines of $1,000,000 for each violation and/or imprisonment of up to 15 years in cases where one knowingly releases hazardous air pollutants into the ambient air. In setting civil penalties, the administrator or the courts may take into account the size of the business, the economic impact of the penalty on the business, the violator's full

42.1

MINIMIZING LIABILITY FOR TOXIC SMOKE

One of the CIT manufacturing facilities has been spewing a great deal of smoke recently, thus causing some concern among the family members that the location may be in violation of the Clean Air Act. An industrial engineer has analyzed the location and reported that the smoke consists of asbestos, vinyl chloride, and various other particulates that represent by-products of the production process for Call-Image units. The family members want to take steps to reduce the pollution of the plant and thereby avoid any potential liability for violating environmental statutes. They ask you what they should do in this situation. What advice will you give them?

BUSINESS CONSIDERATIONS Should a business spend more money at the time of plant construction in order to be "ahead of the game" in pollution control and reduction, or should the firm be satisfied with meeting current environmental standards, even though it knows that these standards may change in the future? What factors would influence such a decision?

ETHICAL CONSIDERATIONS Is it ethical for a business to do less than is legally required in the area of environmental protection if the business in so doing is meeting legal requirements and industry standards? Is it ethical for a business, in order to be more environmentally protective, to exceed legal requirements and industry standards—at a cost to the shareholders?

MANUFACTURING/MANAGEMENT

compliance history and good faith efforts to comply, the duration and seriousness of the violation, and so forth. Those mounting successful citizens' suits may receive attorneys' fees and recoup their court costs as well.

According to a 1996 EPA report, the concentrations of five major air pollutants —carbon monoxide, lead, nitrogen dioxide, particulate matter, and sulfur dioxide —declined by an average of about 7 percent in 1995, with the latter pollutant decreasing by 17 percent.[5] The levels of ozone, however, increased by 4 percent, although the overall trend for the last 10 years indicates a reduction in this pollutant.[6] The report also notes that air quality data over the last 25 years show an emissions decline among these six pollutants of about 29 percent while gross domestic product increased by about 99 percent during the same period.[7] The EPA interprets these data as indicative of the fact that the United States can reduce air pollution without sacrificing economic growth.

Chevron U.S.A. Inc. v. *Natural Resources Defense Council, Inc.*, a landmark case, addresses the Clean Air Act.

42.2 CHEVRON U.S.A. INC. v. NATURAL RESOURCES DEFENSE COUNCIL, INC.

467 U.S. 837 (1984)

FACTS The Clean Air Act Amendments of 1977 impose certain requirements on states that have not achieved the national air quality standards established by the Environmental Protection Agency (EPA) pursuant to earlier legislation, including the requirement that such "nonattainment" states establish a permit program regulating "new or modified major stationary sources" of air pollution. Generally, a permit may not be issued for such sources unless stringent conditions are met. EPA regulations promulgated in 1981 to implement the permit requirement allow a state to adopt a plantwide definition of the term "stationary source," under which an existing plant that contains several pollution-emitting devices may install or modify one piece of equipment without meeting the permit conditions if the alteration will not increase the total emissions from the plant, thus allowing a state to treat all the pollution-emitting devices within the same industrial grouping as though they were encased within a single "bubble." The Natural Resources Defense Council, Inc., filed a petition for review in the court of appeals, which set aside the regulations embodying the "bubble concept" as contrary to law. Although recognizing that the amended Clean Air Act does not explicitly define what Congress envisioned as a stationary source to which the permit program should apply and that the legislative history had failed to address the issue, the court concluded that, in view of the purpose of the nonattainment program to improve rather than merely maintain air quality, a plantwide definition was inappropriate.

ISSUE Was the EPA's plantwide definition a permissible construction of the statutory term "stationary source"?

HOLDING Yes. The legislative history indicated that the EPA should have broad discretion as to the implementation of the policies of the 1977 amendments. Moreover, the plantwide definition was fully consistent with the policy of allowing reasonable economic growth; and the EPA had advanced a reasonable explanation for its conclusion that the regulations serve environmental objectives as well.

REASONING The question presented by this and other cases is whether the EPA's decision to allow states to treat all the pollution-emitting devices within the same industrial grouping as though they were encased within a single "bubble" is based on a reasonable construction of the statutory term "stationary source." With regard to judicial review of an agency's construction of the statute that it administers, if Congress has not directly spoken to the precise question at issue, the question for the court is whether the agency's answer represents a permissible construction of the statute. An examination of the legislation and its history supports the conclusion of the court of appeals that Congress did not have a specific intention as to the applicability of the "bubble concept" in these cases. To the extent any congressional "intent" can be discerned from the statutory language, it would appear that the listing of overlapping, illustrative terms was intended to enlarge, rather than to confine, the scope of the EPA's power to regulate particular sources and thus effectuate the policies of the Clean Air Act. Similarly, the legislative history is consistent with the view that the EPA, in implementing the policies of the 1977 amendments, should have broad discretion. The plantwide definition is fully consistent with the policy of allowing reasonable economic growth, and

42.2 CHEVRON U.S.A. INC. v. NATURAL RESOURCES DEFENSE COUNCIL, INC. *(cont.)* 467 U.S. 837 (1984)

the EPA has advanced a reasonable explanation for its conclusion that the regulations serve environmental objectives as well. Policy arguments concerning the bubble concept should be addressed to legislators or administrators, not to judges. The EPA's interpretation of the statute here represents a reasonable accommodation of manifestly competing interests and is entitled to deference. Hence, the decision of the court of appeals to set aside the regulations embodying the bubble concept as contrary to law was erroneous.

BUSINESS CONSIDERATIONS Some commentators have submitted that the "economic-incentives" approach in this case represents the most feasible way to balance the compliance costs incurred by businesses and the protection of the environment. Should businesses follow the economic-incentives approach, or is there a better approach for these firms to follow?

ETHICAL CONSIDERATIONS Does a purely ethical approach to air pollution mandate adherence to a "zero-tolerance" policy? Is it ethical for society to be expected to pay for the "spillover" costs of pollution not paid for by the polluter?

WATER POLLUTION

The Clean Water Act

The Clean Water Act (CWA), like the Clean Air Act, exemplifies the complexities involved in regulating a resource that affects virtually every sphere of human activity. Both also exemplify the so-called "technology-forcing" approach to environmental law.

Passed in 1972 as the Federal Water Pollution Control Amendments (the FWPCA), when Congress amended this act in 1977, Congress changed the name of the act to the Clean Water Act. Both the FWPCA and the CWA owe doctrinal debts to several earlier federal forays into water pollution control, including the Rivers and Harbors Act of 1899, the Water Pollution Control Act of 1948 (and its 1956 amendments), the Water Quality Act of 1965, and the 1970 Water Quality Improvements Act.

Congress in the CWA set as the primary aim of this legislation the restoration and maintenance of the chemical, physical, and biological integrity of the nation's waters as well as national goals for the achievement of this objective. These goals include, within certain timetables, the elimination of discharges of pollutants into navigable rivers; the elimination of the discharge of toxic pollutants in toxic amounts; water quality sufficient to protect fish, shellfish, and wildlife and to provide recreation in and on the water; federal assistance for the construction of publicly owned waste treatment works; the development and implementation of (1) areawide waste treatment management planning procedures designed to control pollutants at their sources in each state and (2) programs to control point and nonpoint sources of pollution; and research efforts aimed at developing the technology necessary to eliminate the discharge of pollutants into the nation's navigable waters, the waters of the continental shelf, and the oceans.

Effluent

Pertaining to an outflow of materials or an emanation.

Under the CWA, the federal role over water policy takes precedence over the states' role, since the administrator of the EPA, in cooperation with the appropriate federal and state agencies, has the responsibility for developing comprehensive programs for preventing, reducing, and eliminating water pollution. For example, the CWA prohibits discharges into navigable waters unless one has a permit to do so. Subsequent EPA regulations and court decisions under the commerce clause make it clear that the term *water* encompasses all waters used in foreign or interstate commerce: rivers, territorial seas, wetlands, interstate lakes, streams, and ponds. The states, by enforcing the federally mandated standards in a manner much like that previously discussed under the Clean Air Act, augment this extensive federal regime. Each state must submit a plan describing how it intends to implement water quality standards applicable to interstate waters and to meet the **effluent** limitation guidelines promulgated by the EPA administrator.

The CWA targets two areas for pollution control and regulation: point sources, such as pipes, ditches, channels, wells, animal feeding operations, or floating vessels that emit water pollutants; and nonpoint sources, such as farms and other agricultural activities, forest lands, mining, and forestry. Congress and the EPA view effluent limitations and ambient water control standards, in conjunction with a permit program, as a technology-based means of eliminating most pollution from point sources. The onus is on the polluter to choose abatement procedures—even costly ones—designed to eliminate water pollution at the source of its discharge. However, Congress and the EPA see technology as having fewer beneficial effects on pollution from nonpoint sources.

Although this view is debatable, the fact that Congress makes distinctions in this fashion has brought about significant legal implications: Point sources must comply with the applicable effluent limitations and must obtain—and satisfy—any and all relevant permits. Nonpoint sources remain exempt from both requirements, although they do have to comply with applicable state management programs.

The CWA attempts, on a case-by-case basis, to resolve questions about whether the point source designation applies to a given polluter. But the CWA itself sets out three mechanisms for regulating discharges from point sources: effluent limitations (ELs), water quality standards (WQSs), and pollution discharge permits issued pursuant to the national pollutant discharge elimination system (NPDES) permit program.

Effluent Limitations. The first of these, ELs, involves industry-specific restrictions on the number of pounds of a given pollutant that a given point source can discharge per day or per week into navigable waters. The CWA mandates the use of technology to reduce the quantities, rates, and concentrations of the chemical and biological effluent released from point sources and has as its ultimate goal the complete eradication of such industrial pollutants. The allowable ELs depend on the industrial processes utilized in a given industry, the available technology, and cost factors.

Water Quality Standards. In contrast to ELs, WQSs derive from the designated uses of the navigable waters involved (for example, fish and wildlife propagation, recreation, agriculture, or industry), as well as their use and value for navigation. The CWA gives the EPA authority to oversee the states' development of minimum ambient standards for particular lakes, rivers, and streams. Then, once a state achieves its desired water standards, the state must comply with EPA-mandated antidegradation standards that ensure the state's continued maintenance of these desired WQSs.

Prior to 1972, pursuant to the FWCPA, federal water pollution control efforts centered on these state WQSs plans and had as their goal the elimination of pollutant discharges into all navigable bodies of water by 1985. Enforcement remained problematic, however, because authorities could not act on a given discharge until the pollution had lowered the quality of the affected water below the water's specified ambient level. Enforcement also faltered when multiple polluters had discharged effluent into the same body of water, since it was hard to prove the contribution each had made to lowering the specified ambient levels of the entire body of water.

The 1972 amendments illustrate Congress's intent to use ELs as the main supplement to the ambient water standards and thus be the primary weapon for controlling point source-generated pollution. These amendments reserve the application of WQSs to those situations wherein compliance with the applicable ELs nevertheless may interfere with the maintenance of water quality in certain areas.

National Pollutant Discharge Elimination System. The NPDES program, however, by forcing each point-source polluter to obtain a permit, forms the linchpin of these federal antipollution efforts. In brief, the NPDES program dictates, as prerequisites for obtaining a permit, that a given point source (other than publicly owned wastewater works), by using within a certain time frame (but no later than 1977) the "best practicable control technology available" (BPT) as defined by the EPA administrator, comply with the ELs. Point sources that discharge nonconventional pollutants, such as ammonia, chlorine, or iron, are subject to a phased-in timetable and the standards of "best available control technology economically achievable" (BAT) by 1983. The ELs for conventional pollutants, such as suspended solids like oil or grease and fecal coliform, must achieve the standard known as "best conventional control technology" (BCT). For discharges of heat from point sources, the 1972 amendments allow a unique variance system designed to ensure the elimination of pollution and the propagation of a balanced, indigenous population of shellfish, fish, and wildlife. These amendments also establish "pretreatment standards" that industrial facilities that discharge into municipal wastewater treatment systems must meet so as to preclude these facilities' evading the NPDES permit program and discharging effluent directly into city sewers. Publicly owned treatment works (POTWs), that is, municipal wastewater treatment facilities, by 1977 must meet the secondary treatment standards or the even more stringent ELs needed to ensure WQSs. Both BPT and BAT allow those setting the ELs to take into account cost considerations when they compute the degree of effluent reduction attainable under either standard, although BAT standards to a lesser degree take cost into account.

In short, the 1972 amendments leave enforcement primarily to the states but allow a variety of federal enforcement mechanisms as well. In permitting citizens to bring lawsuits to enforce the ELs set out in state or federal permits or to enforce EPA orders, the 1972 amendments appreciably strengthened the FWPCA.

Just as Congress had amended the Clean Air Act in 1977, so, too, Congress amended the FWPCA that same year. As mentioned earlier, besides renaming the FWPCA the Clean Water Act, the 1977 amendments authorize the EPA to grant some extensions of the 1977 BPT deadlines on a case-by-case basis. The 1977 amendments also apply the BCT standard to conventional pollutants and therefore replace the BAT standard for all pollutants except toxic and nonconventional ones.

The 1977 amendments reflect an especially stringent approach to toxic pollutants, that is, those that, if ingested, inhaled, or assimilated, can cause death, disease, cancer, physical deformity, behavioral abnormality, or genetic mutation. The CWA requires the administrator of the EPA to publish a list of toxic pollutants, including asbestos, arsenic, copper, cyanide, lead, mercury, polychlorinated biphenyls (PCBs), and vinyl chloride, and, by 1 July 1984, to establish industry-specific ELs that reflect the BAT. Under applicable law, the administrator even can establish a zero tolerance for certain ELs if the EPA deems such actions necessary to provide an ample margin of safety or to attain the applicable WQSs. Moreover, the cost–benefit analysis that the EPA can consider in establishing ELs for conventional pollutants is not available to the agency when it sets ELs reflecting the BAT for toxic and nonconventional pollutants.

In the Water Quality Act of 1987, Congress amended the CWA so as to extend the compliance deadlines for toxic pollutants to 1989 and for some secondary treatment plants to 1988. These amendments also tried to maintain WQSs by requiring the states to identify the navigable bodies of waters within the state that, without additional action to control nonpoint sources of pollution (for example, runoffs from agricultural or urban uses), cannot reasonably be expected to attain or maintain applicable WQSs. The states then must set up a management program and schedules for implementing the best management practices to control pollution added from nonpoint sources to the navigable waters within the state and to improve the quality of such waters.

The NPDES, then, represents the vehicle by which the EPA—or the state—can issue permits to any discharger of any pollutant on the condition that the individual discharger agrees to abide by all ELs and other pollution standards within a certain time period. Those denied an NPDES permit by the EPA can seek court review in a U.S. circuit court of appeals, as can those who have been the object of the EPA's veto of any application permit issued under a state program. Variances under the NPDES-permit program are possible for those facilities that show that they fundamentally differed with respect to the factors considered by the administrator when he or she established the ELs applicable to those facilities and that the alternative requirement (variance) will not result in a nonwater quality environmental impact markedly more adverse than the impact considered by the EPA administrator in establishing the national ELs at issue.

In response to the oil spill caused by the wreck of the Exxon *Valdez* in 1989, Congress passed the Oil Pollution Act of 1990. Although it amends the CWA, the act is modeled after CERCLA, a statute we will discuss shortly, in that it sets up a comprehensive system for removing oil spills caused by vessels or offshore facilities and a trust-fund system approach for paying for the costs and damages from all such spills.

Negligent violations of the CWA can subject violators to a maximum fine of $25,000 per day of violation and/or one year's imprisonment. Knowing violations increase the possible fines to a maximum of $50,000 per day of violation and/or three years' imprisonment. With some exemptions, an individual who knowingly violates the CWA and thereby endangers another shall, upon conviction, face fines of not more than $250,000 and/or 15 years' imprisonment. Organizations convicted of such violations may face fines of $1,000,000. The administrator of the EPA can set civil fines of $25,000 per day of violation but in setting these fines can take into consideration the factors mentioned in the Clean Air Act's civil enforcement provisions. Administrative penalties vary, depending on the type of violation, and range from a maximum of $10,000 per violation and a maximum aggregate amount ranging from $25,000 to $125,000. The citizens' suit provisions and awards are similar to those set out in the Clean Air Act.

Arkansas v. *EPA* illustrates many of the principles discussed here.

42.3 ARKANSAS v. EPA

503 U.S. 91 (1992)

FACTS The Clean Water Act (CWA) provides for two sets of water quality measures: effluent limitations, which are promulgated by the Environmental Protection Agency (EPA); and water quality standards, which are promulgated by the states. The CWA generally prohibits the discharge of effluent into a navigable body of water unless the point source obtains a national pollution discharge elimination system (NPDES) permit from a state with an EPA-approved permit program or from the EPA itself. A Fayetteville, Arkansas, sewage treatment plant received an EPA-issued permit authorizing it to discharge effluent into a stream that ultimately reaches the Illinois River upstream from the Oklahoma border. The State of Oklahoma and other Oklahoma parties, appearing before the EPA to challenge the permit, alleged, among other things, that the discharge violated Oklahoma water quality standards, which allow no degradation of water quality in the upper Illinois River. The EPA's chief judicial officer, remanding the initial affirmance of the permit by the administrative law judge (ALJ), ruled that the act requires an NPDES permit to impose any effluent limitations necessary to comply with applicable state water quality standards and that those standards would be violated only if the record shows by a preponderance of the evidence that the discharge would cause an actual detectable violation of Oklahoma's water quality standards. After making detailed findings of fact, the ALJ concluded that Fayetteville had satisfied the chief judicial officer's standard. Reversing, the court of appeals ruled that the CWA does not allow a permit to be issued where a proposed source would discharge effluent that would contribute to conditions currently constituting a violation of applicable water quality standards. It concluded that the Illinois River already was degraded, that the Fayetteville effluent would reach the river in Oklahoma, and that the effluent would contribute to the river's deterioration even though it would not detectably affect the river's water quality.

ISSUE Did the EPA's finding that discharges from the new source would not cause a detectable violation of Oklahoma's water quality standards satisfy the EPA's duty to protect the interests of the downstream state?

HOLDING Yes. The EPA's action was authorized by the CWA.

REASONING Where an interstate discharge is involved, both the federal common law of nuisance and an affected state's common law are preempted. Affected states may not block a permit but must apply to the EPA administrator, who may disapprove a plan if he or she concludes that the discharge will have an undue impact on interstate waters. The EPA has construed the CWA as requiring that EPA-issued permits comply with the requirements for a permit issued under an approved state plan and with the provision of the CWA that appears to prohibit the issuance of a federal permit over the objection of an affected state unless compliance with the affected state's water quality requirements can be ensured. However, the EPA's requirement that the Fayetteville discharge comply with Oklahoma's water quality standards is a reasonable exercise of the substantial statutory discretion Congress has vested in the agency. EPA regulations, which since 1973 have required that an NPDES permit be denied when compliance with affected states' water quality standards cannot be ensured, are a reasonable exercise of the agency's discretion and are a well-tailored means of reaching the CWA's goal of achieving state water quality standards. The EPA's authority is unconstrained by the limits (set out in some Supreme Court precedents) concerning an affected state's direct input into the permit process, does not conflict with the CWA's legislative history and statutory scheme, and is compatible with the balance among competing policies and interests that Congress struck in the act. Moreover, contrary to the interpretation of the court of appeals, nothing in the CWA mandates a complete ban on discharges into a waterway that itself manifests violations of existing water quality standards. Instead, the CWA vests in the EPA and the states broad authority to develop long-range, areawide programs to alleviate and eliminate existing pollution. The court of appeals therefore exceeded the legitimate scope of judicial review of an agency adjudication when the court failed to give substantial deference to the agency's reasonable, consistently held interpretation of its own regulations, that incorporate the Oklahoma standards. Also, by making its own factual findings when the ALJ's findings were supported by substantial evidence, the court disregarded well-established standards for reviewing agency factual findings. As a result, the court's conclusion that the river's degradation was an important and relevant factor that the EPA had failed to consider was based on its own erroneous interpretation of the controlling law. Had it been properly respectful of the EPA's permissible reading of the CWA—that what matters is not the river's current status, but whether the proposed discharge will have a detectable effect on that status—the court would not have refrained from adjudging the agency's decision as arbitrary and capricious.

BUSINESS CONSIDERATIONS This decision illustrates the deference courts routinely accord to an

42.3 ARKANSAS v. EPA *(cont.)* **503 U.S. 91 (1992)**

administrative agency's (here, the EPA's) interpretations of the laws that fall under its purview. Given this deference, should businesses, in making decisions and planning for the future, be more cognizant of agency interpretations? What policy might a business adopt to help ensure that its conduct is consistent with agency interpretations?

ETHICAL CONSIDERATIONS Is it unethical to allow one state's effluent to contribute to the deterioration of a river in another state even though the effluent will not detectably affect the river's water quality?

Safe Drinking Water Act

Aquifers
Water-bearing strata of permeable rock, sand, or gravel.

As an adjunct to the Clean Water Act, the Safe Drinking Water Act (SDWA), enacted in 1974 and amended in 1986, regulates water supplied by public water systems to home taps. The passage of this legislation stems from congressional awareness of the contaminants that have seeped into groundwater supplies and **aquifers** and that have caused cancer and other serious diseases and organ damage. The more than 200 reported instances of illnesses caused by waterborne microorganisms and parasites—including an outbreak involving the water supply in Milwaukee, Wisconsin—underscore the seriousness of this problem.

Under the SDWA, the EPA must promulgate national primary drinking water regulations (NPDWRs) that in turn set maximum contaminant levels (MCLs) or, alternatively, require specific treatment techniques designed to reduce contaminants to acceptable levels. By using the most economically and technologically feasible treatment techniques available, public water supply operators must try to meet these MCL standards or goals (where no adverse effects on health occur). Variances from these NPDWRs are possible under certain circumstances. The 1986 amendments require the EPA to take more aggressive action to establish standards for 83 specific contaminants, to promulgate a national priority list of known contaminants, and to establish MCL goals and NPDWRs for at least 25 of the contaminants on this list. The 1996 amendments, among other things, for the first time develop a risk-based method to identify drinking water contaminants that could pose a threat to human health.

The 1996 amendments, in addition, require the EPA to publish, by 6 February 1998, a list of contaminants that are known or anticipated to occur in public water systems and may require regulation. An additional list of such contaminants must be published every five years thereafter. Moreover, the newly amended law requires the EPA to determine every five years whether to regulate at least five of the listed contaminants. Under these new amendments, the EPA, when identifying these contaminants, must take into account their danger to sensitive populations such as infants, children, pregnant women, the elderly, and people with illnesses. In its identification method, the EPA will consider factors such as the potential adverse health effects, information on concentrations in drinking water supplies, human exposure via drinking water and other sources, and data uncertainty. This approach will be used to identify and classify contaminants that are not currently regulated and to reevaluate already regulated contaminants. Because microbial contaminants pose unique challenges, the EPA will use a similar but separate approach for their identification.

States may have primary enforcement responsibilities under the SDWA if the states have adopted drinking water regulations no less stringent than the national standards and if they have implemented adequate monitoring, inspection, recordkeeping, and enforcement procedures. If the EPA has primary responsibility, the enforcement provisions of the act resemble those under the Resource Conservation and Recovery Act (RCRA) discussed later in this chapter.

42.2

MANUFACTURING/MANAGEMENT

MINIMIZING LIABILITY FOR WATER POLLUTION

The Kochanowskis have just learned that one of their facilities is discharging effluents into the local drainage system and that this system drains into the primary water reservoir for the community. The effluents from this particular facility contain contaminant concentrations that frequently exceed the standards for the community. They would like to avoid any legal problems or liabilities, and they also want to ensure that they are not harming the community. They ask you what they should do. What will you tell them?

BUSINESS CONSIDERATIONS Should a business attempt to work with local government officials to reduce pollution, or should the business "go it alone" in an effort to act in the most efficient manner possible? Why might working with the local government be advisable? Why might it be unhelpful?

ETHICAL CONSIDERATIONS Is it more ethical for a firm to reveal that it has been polluting, but is taking steps to stop its polluting activities, or for a firm to attempt to hide past pollution, while at the same time it is working to reduce or eliminate pollution in the future? Explain your response.

NOISE POLLUTION

Noise Control Act of 1972

Probably owing to the fact that noise seems less noxious to us than filthy water or sulfurous-smelling air, Congress did not address the issue of noise until 1972 when it passed the federal Noise Control Act. Prior to that time, litigants seeking remedies to limit the increasingly higher decibel levels caused by post–World War II urbanization and mechanization relied on common law nuisance theories.

Compared to many of the other statutes discussed in this chapter, this act is simple and straightforward. Recognizing the noise generated by transportation vehicles and equipment, machinery, and appliances as a growing danger to the health and welfare of U.S. citizens—particularly those residing in urban areas—Congress placed the primary responsibility for controlling such noise on state and local governments. However, Congress expressly noted that federal oversight and action are necessary for noise sources in commerce when control of such sources will require uniform national treatment. Hence, the statute preempts the states' regulation of emissions standards for major noise sources such as construction equipment, transportation equipment, motors or engines, and electrical equipment. For these sources, the EPA must promulgate regulations that are necessary to protect the public health and welfare with an adequate margin of safety. The EPA also has the power to fashion regulations for any nonmajor product for which noise emissions standards are feasible and requisite to protect the public health and welfare. To coordinate federal noise control policies, this legislation furthermore empowers the EPA to file status reports concerning all federal agencies' noise research and noise control programs, to enforce the labeling of products (including imported ones) as to the level of noise emitted by the products, and to prohibit the removal of noise control devices.

The 1978 amendments, called the Quiet Communities Act, reinforce the significant role that state and local governments play in noise control. The amendments provide federal financial and technical assistance aimed at facilitating state and local research related to noise control and developing noise abatement plans. Similar to the remedies we have seen in other statutes, civil and criminal penalties are possible for violations of the Noise Control Act, as are citizens' suits.

LAND CONSERVATION AND POLLUTION

Public domain
Lands that are open to public use.

The protection and preservation of land constitute the most obvious areas of federal environmental regulation. As early as the presidency of Theodore Roosevelt, concern for some protection of the environment and preservation of America's natural resources surfaced in the United States. The **public domain**, that is, land owned and/or controlled by the federal government, today comprises nearly 725 million acres. Hence, federally controlled land, national parks, and wildlife refuges occupy about as much land as the subcontinent of India does. In addition to the federal regulation and control of federal lands, a number of federal statutes regulate private land. The following sections discuss some of the most significant of these regulations.

The Toxic Substances Control Act

The Toxic Substances Control Act (TSCA) passed by Congress in 1976 represents the first statutory enactment that comprehensively addresses toxic chemicals and their impact on health and the environment. Congress passed this law for three reasons: (1) to develop data detailing the effect of chemical substances and mixtures on health and the environment by those who manufacture and process such chemicals (that is, industry); (2) to provide adequate governmental authority to regulate chemicals that present an unreasonable risk of injury to health or the environment and to take steps with regard to those chemicals that are imminent hazards; and (3) to ensure the exercise of this governmental authority in such a fashion as to avoid impediments or unnecessary economic barriers to technological innovation while at the same time to fulfill the primary purpose of the TSCA—that is, the avoidance of unreasonable risk of injury to health or the environment.

Like NEPA, then, it focuses on risk assessment. But note that the TSCA, by giving authority to the EPA to regulate chemicals even before they come onto the market, screens pollutants before (not after, as most other statutes do) those pollutants expose humans and the environment to these substances' effects. The TSCA also permits the government to consider the sum total of the health and environmental hazards caused by a given chemical or mixture.

Despite these lofty purposes, the legislative history of the TSCA shows that Congress chose not to seek a risk-free environment. Granted, Congress requires the administrator of the EPA, after he or she receives notice of the proposed manufacture of any new substances, to subject these chemical substances and mixtures to testing and thereby ensure the development of test data by manufacturers. The TSCA similarly mandates premanufacture notifications for such substances and the regulation of the postmanufacturing distribution of the chemicals.

Yet Congress, by requiring the EPA to test and regulate only those chemicals that pose an "unreasonable risk" of injury to health or the environment, has given the EPA a great deal of discretion, including the consideration of the relative costs of the various test protocols and methodologies that firms, in order to perform the required testing, may need to utilize. In actual practice, the EPA has taken a lax view toward the stringency it will require of companies that provide test data. Similarly, although the EPA can choose among several options, including prohibiting the manufacturing, processing, or distributing of any substance that poses an unreasonable risk, the statute directs the EPA, in arriving at its decision, to use the least burdensome requirements. As a consequence, the EPA has stopped the manufacture and/or distribution of only a minuscule number of chemical substances.

Nevertheless, the statute authorizes the EPA to regulate *imminent hazards*—those that present imminent and unreasonable risks of widespread injury to health or the environment—through emergency judicial relief leading to an injunction and/or seizure of the chemicals or substances. A special section of the TSCA sets out a timetable for phasing out the manufacture of PCBs. Other provisions allow for civil and criminal penalties and carry over the citizens' lawsuit provisions set out in other acts.

The Federal Insecticide, Fungicide, and Rodenticide Act

Given the importance of agriculture in our country's history, it is no surprise that Congress passed a federal Insecticide Act in 1910. Surprisingly, this act was aimed at protecting farmers from becoming victims of unsavory and fraudulent marketing practices rather than at protecting the environment.

In 1947, owing to the proliferation of pesticides and insecticides, Congress responded to those newly emerging, but as yet embryonic, environmental concerns when it passed the Federal Insecticide, Fungicide, and Rodenticide Act (FIFRA). This early version of FIFRA mandated the registration of "economic poisons [pesticides] involved in interstate commerce and the inclusion of labels, warnings, and instructions on such pesticides." The 1962 publication of Rachel Carson's *Silent Spring*, which cataloged the environmental risks and dangers created by pesticides, insecticides, and herbicides, in conjunction with litigation based on the use and sale of DDT, prodded Congress into action.

In 1970, the newly established EPA became responsible for the enforcement of FIFRA; and, in 1972, Congress passed the Federal Environmental Pesticide Control Act (FEPCA). The FEPCA, in amending FIFRA, changes FIFRA's focus from labeling to concerns for the environment. Under FIFRA as amended, all persons who distribute or sell pesticides must register them with the EPA. The EPA will register a pesticide if the administrator determines that the pesticide, when used in accordance with widespread and common practice, will not generally cause unreasonable adverse effects on the environment. The EPA can register any approved pesticide for general use, restricted use (for example, by exterminators), or both. The EPA subsequently can cancel the registration of any pesticide that fails to live up to this standard and can suspend a registration whenever such action is necessary to prevent an imminent hazard.

Although, like NEPA and TSCA, FIFRA is at heart a risk-assessment statute, the 1975 and 1978 amendments make it clear that in determining "unreasonable adverse effects on the environment" the EPA must take into account the benefits, as well as the costs, associated with the use of the pesticide. It is possible, then, for the EPA to register an economically beneficial pesticide even though it might pose harm to health or the environment.

FIFRA sets out several types of unlawful acts, all of which, in general, involve the sale of unregistered or mislabeled pesticides. It also authorizes "stop sale" and/or seizure orders by the EPA. Furthermore, civil and criminal penalties are available under the Act.

Despite the fact that applicants must provide data in support of any application, the EPA has been able to assure the safety of only a handful of the 50,000 pesticides currently on the market. Similarly, the EPA has canceled or suspended the registration of only a few pesticides—for example, DDT, kepone, and chlordane. Critics of FIFRA therefore continue to advocate amendments to the statute that would address these issues.

The Resource Conservation and Recovery Act

Another act passed in 1976, the Resource Conservation and Recovery Act (RCRA), is a broader statute than the TSCA and FIFRA. The RCRA encompasses all types of waste, including hazardous and toxic waste and waste generated by households across the country. The predecessors of the RCRA include the Solid Waste Disposal Act of 1965 and the Resource Recovery Act of 1970. The RCRA, a more comprehensive statute, stemmed from congressional awareness of the environmental problems posed by the generation and disposal of wastes of all types.

Although oftentimes referred to as solid waste, waste actually takes the form of liquids, gases, sludges, and semisolids as well. You undoubtedly recognize the complexities associated with the disposal of the billions of tons of household waste generated annually. At some point, virtually everything we buy ends up in a landfill or at some other type of disposal site. The pollution control efforts that we already have studied—emissions and wastewater sludge, for example—ironically also create waste. Moreover, the characteristics of such waste have changed over the years. The toxic substances considered earlier add yet another dimension to the waste disposal calculus. In short, we presently are paying the price for decades of dumping solid waste on land. We also are running out of room for land-based disposal sites; few communities, owing to fears of groundwater contamination, want to accept other states' waste (as litigation discussed in Chapter 39 demonstrates).

The RCRA indicates Congress's understanding that it may no longer view waste disposal as a purely state or local problem. Rather, Congress sees waste disposal as national in scope and concern and, therefore, worthy of federal assistance in the development and application of new and improved methods of waste reduction and disposal practices as well as potential new energy sources. As yet another technology-forcing statute, the RCRA therefore clothes the EPA with the power to regulate nonhazardous solid waste and to oversee the management and disposal of hazardous waste.

With regard to nonhazardous solid waste, the RCRA provides federal technical and financial assistance to states that voluntarily develop environmentally sound methods of solid waste disposal, including recycling. These state management plans, which resemble the SIPs discussed under the Clean Air Act, must follow EPA guidelines and, among other things, protect ground and surface water from contamination brought on by **leachings** and runoffs. Any approved state plan must distinguish between sanitary landfills and open dumps, the latter of which must be closed or upgraded so as to eliminate health hazards and minimize potential health hazards.

Leachings
Oozings of water containing soil, sediments, chemicals, and other impurities.

By making lawful only dumping into a solid waste facility that complies with the EPA's criteria for a sanitary landfill, Congress apparently intends to abolish open dumping, even in states that do not develop a state solid waste management program. The RCRA also obligates the EPA to publish the names of all the open dump sites in the United States. This public list presumably will spur states to take action to eliminate the environmental and health hazards associated with these sites and also provides the impetus for citizens' suits.

The EPA's powers to regulate hazardous waste under the RCRA far exceed its powers over nonhazardous solid waste. Adopting what one court has called "cradle-to-grave" regulation, the EPA sets out stringent standards covering those who own or operate treatment, storage, or disposal facilities (TSDFs). Such persons or entities must obtain permits issued by the EPA or the states authorized to issue such permits. The RCRA mandates that the EPA identify and list hazardous waste (that is, solid waste that, among other things, can cause or significantly contribute to an increase in serious irreversible illness or pose a substantial present or potential threat to the environment) on the basis of several criteria: toxicity, persistence, degradability in its nature, potential for accumulation in tissue, and other related factors such as flammability or corrosiveness. (Interestingly, the RCRA excludes nuclear waste from its coverage.) EPA regulations thus list certain chemicals, each identified by so-called EPA hazardous waste numbers.

The EPA, aided by the permit, recordkeeping, labeling, container usage, and report provisions of the RCRA, relies on a **manifest** system to track hazardous waste from the cradle to the grave and to ensure that everyone from the generator of the waste, through the transporter, and to the operator of the disposal facility meets and maintains the applicable federal regulatory standards. Since the 1984 amendments to the RCRA, even small generators of hazardous waste must supply this extensive documentation. By setting minimal technological requirements (for example, the provision of two or more liners and a leachate collection system) and groundwater monitoring for both new and existing sanitary landfills, these amendments also phase out land disposal of hazardous wastes, in particular. In addition, the 1984 amendments also broadly regulate leaking underground storage tanks and, like CERCLA (discussed next), set up a federal trust to remediate leaks under certain circumstances. In 1989, Congress initiated in certain northeastern and midwestern states a demonstration program for tracking the disposal of medical waste products.

Manifest
A list or invoice.

Like the Clean Air Act and the Clean Water Act, the permit system established under the RCRA provides the EPA with broad enforcement powers. Civil and criminal penalties are available for violations of the RCRA, as are citizens' suits. Furthermore, under the RCRA, the EPA can seek injunctive relief if the handling, transport, storage, or disposal of solid or hazardous waste presents an imminent and substantial endangerment to health or the environment. The 1984 RCRA amendments extend the coverage of this provision even to past or present generators, transporters, or operators who have contributed or are contributing to an activity that presents such an imminent danger. Subsequent court decisions have construed this as a strict liability provision akin to its counterpart in CERCLA.

The Comprehensive Environmental Response, Compensation, and Liability Act

The Comprehensive Environmental Response, Compensation, and Liability Act (CERCLA), perhaps better known as the "Superfund," was passed in 1980. In this enactment, Congress meant to fill in the gaps left by the TSCA and the RCRA, neither of which had regulated hazardous waste disposal sites, as the infamous Love Canal disaster unfortunately all too aptly demonstrated.

The CERCLA authorizes the administrator of the EPA to regulate "hazardous substances," including those deemed toxic or hazardous under the CWA, the TSCA, or the RCRA, which, when released into the environment, may present substantial danger to the public health or welfare, or the environment. The act specifically excludes petroleum and natural gas from the definition of hazardous substance.

Any owner or operator of a vessel or offshore or onshore facility engaged in the storage, treatment, or disposal of hazardous waste must notify the EPA of any release of hazardous materials. This notification aids the EPA's implementation of a national contingency plan (NCP), which, under the CERCLA, establishes the procedures and standards for responding to releases of hazardous substances, pollutants, and contaminants and for setting priorities dealing with such substances. The act moreover gives the U.S. President authority to undertake any response (including short-term emergency removal and long-term remedial actions) consistent with the NCP and which action the President deems necessary to protect the public health or welfare or the environment. CERCLA also gives the government the injunctive or administrative authority to compel private parties to take steps to abate all imminent and substantial endangerment to the public health or welfare, or the environment, caused by the actual or threatened release of hazardous substances from a facility.

The CERCLA furthermore imposes liability for all costs of removal or remedial action incurred by federal or state governments that are not inconsistent with the NCP; for all other necessary costs of any response incurred by any other person when such costs are consistent with the NCP; and damages to, or loss of natural resources resulting from, the release of hazardous substances.

Recent court decisions have construed this part of the CERCLA as a strict liability standard that can result in joint and several liability among responsible generators, owners, operators, transporters, and so on, up to $50,000,000 *in toto*. For releases or threats of releases caused by willful misconduct or willful negligence, this limitation on liability does not apply. The statute itself sets out defenses to liability for releases or threats of releases caused by acts of God, acts of war, or by an act or omission of a third party who was not an agent or employee (for example, a third party's leachate runoffs). Innocent landowners also escape liability, but the burden of proof necessary to sustain this defense makes it virtually unusable.

Last, the act establishes a Hazardous Substance Superfund to finance governmental cleanups and remedial actions in those situations in which the government cannot identify or find the parties responsible for the damage. The Superfund Amendments and Reauthorization Act of 1986 (SARA), an incredibly complex statute, among other things increases the fund from the $1.6 billion originally enacted to $8.5 billion through 1991. Various excise taxes on petroleum and chemical feedstocks, appropriations from general revenues, and the costs recovered from responsible parties furnish the monies for the Superfund.

To implement a cleanup plan, the EPA, using a scientific model, must place the site on the national priorities list of waste sites that present the greatest danger to the public health or welfare. When the EPA decides remedial action is appropriate for a given site, all "potentially responsible parties" (PRPs)—present and past owners or operators, including, since the passage of SARA, state and local governments; generators; and transporters—are notified.

If no defenses are available to the PRPs, the EPA, through feasibility studies, begins to negotiate with these parties in order to arrive at a settlement of the total costs. Since liability is joint and several, the PRPs usually find it advisable to allocate financial responsibility among themselves and to present their settlement agreement to the EPA for its approval. Special statutory provisions cover settlements, which generally take the form of a consent decree or an administrative order setting forth the terms of the settlement.

Exhibit 42.1 summarizes the environmental acts and statutes enacted from 1895 through 1996 discussed in this chapter.

EXHIBIT 42.1 Representative Environmental Statutes (1895–1996)

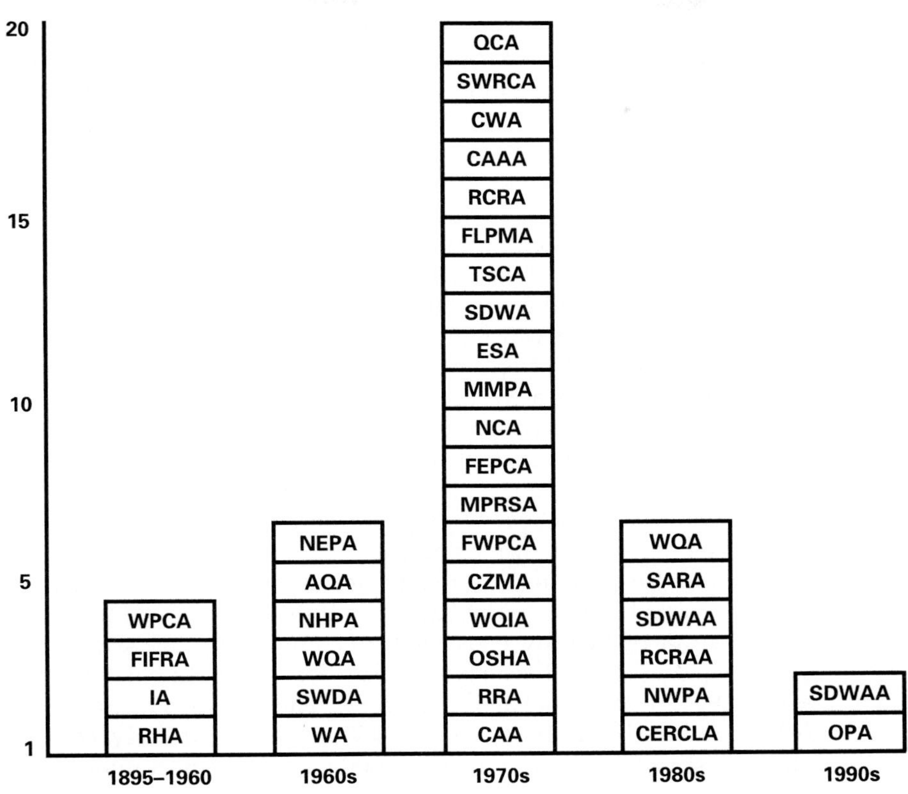

RHA	Rivers and Harbors Act (1899)
IA	Insecticide Act (1910)
FIFRA	Federal Insecticide, Fungicide, and Rodenticide Act (1947)
WPCA	Water Pollution Control Act (1948)
WA	Wilderness Act (1964)
SWDA	Solid Waste Disposal Act (1965)
WQA	Water Quality Act (1965)
NHPA	National Historic Preservation Act (1966)
AQA	Air Quality Act (1967)
NEPA	National Environmental Policy Act (1969)
CAA	Clean Air Act (1970)
RRA	Resource Recovery Act (1970)
OSHA	Occupational Safety and Health Act (1970)
WQIA	Water Quality Improvements Act (1970)
CZMA	Coastal Zone Management Act (1970)
FWPCA	Federal Water Pollution Control Act (1972)
MPRSA	Marine Protection, Research and Sanctuaries Act (1972)
FEPCA	Federal Environmental Pesticide Control Act (1972)
NCA	Noise Control Act (1972)
MMPA	Marine Mammal Protection Act (1972)
ESA	Endangered Species Act (1973)
SDWA	Safe Drinking Water Act (1974)
TSCA	Toxic Substances Control Act (1976)
FLPMA	Federal Land Policy and Management Act (1976)
RCRA	Resource Conservation and Recovery Act (1976)
CAAA	Clean Air Act Amendments (1977)
CWA	Clean Water Act (1977)
SWRCA	Soil and Water Resources Conservation Act (1977)
QCA	Quiet Communities Act (1978)
CERCLA	Comprehensive Environmental Response, Compensation, and Liability Act (1980)
NWPA	Nuclear Waste Policy Act (1982)
RCRAA	Resource Conservation and Recovery Act Amendments (1984)
SDWAA	Safe Drinking Water Act Amendments (1986)
SARA	Superfund Amendments and Reorganization Act (1986)
WQA	Water Quality Act (1987)
OPA	Oil Pollution Act (1990)
SDWAA	Safe Drinking Water Act Amendments (1996)

WILDLIFE CONSERVATION

The Endangered Species Act

The Endangered Species Act of 1973 (ESA) in § 7 states that each federal agency, in consultation with the secretary of the interior, must ensure that no agency action is likely to jeopardize the continued existence of an endangered or threatened species or result in the destruction or adverse modification of any critical habitat of such species. Congress enacted the ESA, the world's first attempt to protect wildlife in a comprehensive manner so as to prevent the extinction of various animals and plants. Indeed, according to scientific estimates, the world loses approximately 100 species per day.[8]

Since 1973, the ESA has helped bring about the stabilization or the improvement of the conditions of 270 threatened or endangered species, including the U.S.'s national symbol, the bald eagle.[9] But the impact of the ESA reaches beyond the borders of the United States because its prohibitions concerning the international trading of wildlife and its protection of the American habitats of migrating birds implicate transnational interests as well.

The national commitment to protecting species and their habitats invokes more than mere sentimentality or altruism—fully 40 percent of all ingredients in prescription medicines (including digitalis and penicillin) derive from plants, animals, and microorganisms.[10] The loss of a species therefore may involve the loss of the medicinal capacity to save thousands of lives.

The provisions of the ESA that preserve genetic diversity help ensure blight- and disease-resistant plants.[11] The harm to wildlife represented by pesticides mirrors the preservation of healthy ecosystems mandated by the Clean Air Act and other statutes discussed in this chapter—clearly a vital national (and international) interest. In 1995, recreational activities in the United States related to wildlife (hunting, fishing, hiking, and so on) totaled $50 billion.[12] Similarly, commercial and recreational fishing resulted in over 100,000 jobs.[13] The declining fish stocks in our nation's navigable waters, lakes, oceans, and contiguous waters and the attendant loss of gainful employment illustrate the economic dimensions of wildlife protection.

Celebrated cases under the ESA wherein dam or road construction projects were halted to protect the habitat of fish or butterflies, for example, have led to public controversies of great magnitude. *Babbitt* v. *Sweet Home Chapter of Communities for a Great Oregon* represents a recent landmark decision in this regard. Note, too, how the Supreme Court, in disposing of this case, relied on the *Chevron U.S.A. Inc.* v. *National Resources Defense Council, Inc.*, decision as a leading precedent.

42.4 BABBITT v. SWEET HOME CHAPTER OF COMMUNITIES FOR A GREAT OREGON

115 S.Ct. 2407 (1995)

FACTS The Endangered Species Act of 1973 (ESA) makes it unlawful for any person to "take" endangered or threatened species and defines *take* to mean to "harass, harm, pursue," "wound," or "kill." In the regulations relating to the ESA, the Secretary of the Interior further defines *harm* to include "significant habitat modification or degradation where it actually kills or injures wildlife." Sweet Home Chapter of Communities for a Great Oregon (Sweet Home) includes small landowners, logging companies, and families dependent on the forest products industries in the

42.4 BABBITT v. SWEET HOME CHAPTER OF COMMUNITIES FOR A GREAT OREGON *(cont.)* 115 S.Ct. 2407 (1995)

Pacific Northwest and the Southeast, as well as organizations that represent these groups' interests. Sweet Home, challenging the statutory validity of the regulation defining "harm," sued Bruce Babbitt, the Secretary of the Interior (Secretary). Sweet Home's complaint for a declaratory judgment challenged the regulation on its face, specifically that the application of the regulation to the red-cockaded woodpecker, an endangered species, and the northern spotted owl, a threatened species, had economically injured its constituent groups. The district court upheld the Secretary's definition, but the court of appeals reversed.

ISSUE In defining "harm" to include habitat modification, had the Secretary reasonably construed Congress's intent?

HOLDING Yes. The Secretary's definition of "harm" rested on a permissible construction of the ESA.

REASONING Section 9(a)(1) of the ESA provides the following protection for endangered species:

> *Except as provided in sections 1535(g)(2) and 1539 of this title, with respect to any endangered species of fish or wildlife listed pursuant to section 1533 of this title it is unlawful for any person subject to the jurisdiction of the United States to . . . (B) take any such species within the United States or the territorial sea of the United States.—16 U.S.C. § 1538(a)(1)*

Section 3(19) of the act defines the statutory term *take:*

> *The term "take" means to harass, harm, pursue, hunt, shoot, wound, kill, trap, capture, or collect, or to attempt to engage in any such conduct.—16 U.S.C. § 1532(19)*

The act does not further define the terms it uses to define "take." The Interior Department regulations that implement the statute, however define the statutory term *harm:*

> *Harm in the definition of "take" in the Act means an act which actually kills or injures wildlife. Such act may include significant habitat modification or degradation where it actually kills or injures wildlife by significantly impairing essential behavioral patterns, including breeding, feeding, or sheltering.—50 CFR § 17.3 (1994)*

This regulation has been in place since 1975.

Sweet Home advanced three arguments to support its submission that Congress did not intend the word "take" in § 9 to include habitat modification, as the Secretary's "harm" regulation provides. First, Sweet Home correctly noted that language in the Senate's original version of the ESA would have defined "take" to include "destruction, modification, or curtailment of [the] habitat or range" of fish or wildlife, but the Senate deleted that language from the bill before enacting it. Second, Sweet Home argued that Congress intended the act's express authorization for the federal government to buy private land in order to prevent habitat degradation in § 5 to be the exclusive check against habitat modification on private property. Third, because the Senate added the term "harm" to the definition of "take" in a floor amendment without debate, Sweet Home claimed that the Court should not interpret the term so expansively as to include habitat modification. Because this case was decided on motions for summary judgment, the Court may appropriately make certain factual assumptions when it frames the legal issue.

First, the Court assumes Sweet Home has no desire to harm either the red-cockaded woodpecker or the spotted owl; the organization merely wishes to continue logging activities that would be entirely proper if not prohibited by the ESA. On the other hand, the Court assumes, for the sake of argument, that those activities will have the effect, even though unintended, of detrimentally changing the natural habitat of both listed species and that, as a consequence, members of those species will be killed or injured. Under Sweet Home's view of the law, the Secretary's only means of forestalling that grave result—even when the actor knows it is certain to occur—is to use his § 5 authority to purchase the lands on which the survival of the species depends. The Secretary, on the other hand, submits that the § 9 prohibition on takings, which Congress defined to include "harm," places on Sweet Home (and other groups) a duty to avoid the harm that such a habitat alteration will cause the birds unless such groups first obtain a permit pursuant to § 10. The text of the act provides three reasons for concluding that the Secretary's interpretation is reasonable. First, an ordinary understanding of the word "harm" supports it. The dictionary definition of the verb form of *harm* is "to cause hurt or damage to: injure" [*Webster's Third New International Dictionary* 1034 (1966)]. In the context of the ESA, that definition naturally encompasses habitat modification that results in actual injury or death to members of an endangered or threatened species. Sweet Home argues that the Secretary should have limited the purview of "harm" to direct applications of force against protected species, but the dictionary definition does not include the word "directly" or suggest in any way that only direct or willful action that leads to injury constitutes "harm."

42.4 BABBITT v. SWEET HOME CHAPTER OF COMMUNITIES FOR A GREAT OREGON *(cont.)*

115 S.Ct. 2407 (1995)

Second, the broad purpose of the ESA supports the Secretary's decision to extend protection against activities that cause the precise harms Congress enacted the statute to avoid. Whereas predecessor statutes enacted in 1966 and 1969 had not contained any sweeping prohibition against the taking of endangered species except on federal lands, the 1973 act applied to all land in the United States and to its territorial seas. As stated in § 2 of the act, among its central purposes is "to provide a means whereby the ecosystems upon which endangered species and threatened species depend may be conserved . . ." —16 U.S.C. § 1531(b). Congress's intent to provide comprehensive protection for endangered and threatened species therefore supports the permissibility of the Secretary's "harm" regulation.

Third, the fact that in 1982 Congress authorized the Secretary to issue permits for takings that § 9(a)(1)(B) otherwise would prohibit, "if such taking is incidental to, and not for the purpose of, the carrying out of an otherwise lawful activity" [§ 10(a)(1)(B)], strongly suggests that Congress understood § 9 to prohibit indirect as well as deliberate takings. No one could seriously request an "incidental" take permit to avert § 9 liability for direct, deliberate action against a member of an endangered or threatened species. Moreover, the Court need not decide whether the statutory definition of "take" compels the Secretary's interpretation of "harm," because the Court's conclusions that Congress did not unambiguously manifest its intent to adopt Sweet Home's view and that the Secretary's interpretation is reasonable suffice to decide this case—see generally *Chevron U.S.A. Inc.* v. *Natural Resources Defense Council, Inc.*, 467 U.S. 837 (1984).

The latitude the ESA gives the Secretary in enforcing the statute, together with the degree of regulatory expertise necessary to its enforcement, establishes that the Court owes some degree of deference to the Secretary's reasonable interpretation. When it enacted the ESA, Congress delegated broad administrative and interpretive power to the Secretary. The task of defining and listing endangered and threatened species requires an expertise and attention to detail that exceeds the normal province of Congress. Fashioning appropriate standards for issuing permits under § 10 for takings that would otherwise violate § 9 necessarily requires the exercise of broad discretion. The proper interpretation of a term such as "harm" involves a complex policy choice. When Congress has entrusted the Secretary with broad discretion, the Court is especially reluctant to substitute its views of wise policy for his (see *Chevron,* 467 U.S., at 865-866). In this case, that reluctance accords with the Court's conclusion, based on the text, structure, and legislative history of the ESA, that the Secretary reasonably construed the intent of Congress when he defined *harm* to include "significant habitat modification or degradation that actually kills or injures wildlife." In the elaboration and enforcement of the ESA, the Secretary and all persons who must comply with the law will confront difficult questions of proximity and degree; for, as all recognize, the act encompasses a vast range of economic and social enterprises and endeavors. These questions must be addressed in the usual course of the law, through case-by-case resolution and adjudication. The judgment of the court of appeals therefore is reversed.

BUSINESS CONSIDERATIONS The Court notes that the ESA "encompasses a vast range of economic and social endeavors and enterprises" that the law must address through "case-by-case resolution and adjudication." Identify these economic and social interests, and explain where a business should strike the balance between these competing interests.

ETHICAL CONSIDERATIONS Does the application of ethics require a "zero-tolerance" policy when economic activity may affect endangered or threatened species? How much harm to endangered or threatened species can be permitted before the conduct in question becomes unethical?

Lujan v. *Defenders of Wildlife* also concerns the ESA. Notice how the constitutional requirement of a "case or controversy" constituted an obstacle to the bringing of a community environmental claim.

42.5 LUJAN v. DEFENDERS OF WILDLIFE

112 U.S. 2130 (1992)

FACTS Section 7(a)(2) of the Endangered Species Act of 1973 (ESA) divides responsibilities regarding the protection of endangered species between the Secretary of the Interior and the Secretary of Commerce and requires each federal agency to consult with the relevant Secretary to ensure that any action funded by the agency is not likely to jeopardize the continued existence or habitat of any endangered or threatened species. Both secretaries initially promulgated a joint regulation extending § 7(a)(2)'s coverage to actions taken in foreign nations, but a subsequent joint rule limited the section's geographic scope to the United States and the high seas. The Defenders of Wildlife (DOW) filed an action seeking a declaratory judgment that the new regulation erred as to § 7(a)(2)'s geographic scope as well as an injunction requiring the Secretary of the Interior, Manuel Lujan, Jr., to promulgate a new rule restoring his initial interpretation. The court of appeals reversed the district court's dismissal of the suit for lack of standing.

ISSUE Did the Defenders of Wildlife (DOW), an association of wildlife conservation and other environmental groups, have standing to seek judicial review of the rule?

HOLDING No. The Defenders of Wildlife lacked standing to seek such review.

REASONING As the party invoking federal jurisdiction, the DOW bears the burden of showing standing by establishing, among other things, that it has suffered an *injury in fact* (a concrete and particularized, actual or imminent invasion of a legally protected interest). Standing is particularly difficult to show here, since third parties rather than the DOW are the object of the government action or inaction to which the DOW objects. Affidavits of members claiming an intent to revisit project sites at some indefinite future time, at which time they presumably will be denied the opportunity to observe endangered animals, fail to suffice, for these affidavits do not demonstrate an "imminent" injury. Similarly, the DOW states purely speculative, nonconcrete injuries when it argues that a lawsuit can be brought by anyone with an interest in studying or seeing endangered animals anywhere on the globe or by anyone with a professional interest in such animals. The court of appeals had erred in holding that the DOW had standing on the ground that the statute's citizen-suit provision confers on all persons the right to file suit to challenge the Secretary's failure to follow the proper consultative procedures, notwithstanding such persons' inability to allege any separate concrete injury flowing from that failure. Courts consistently have held that a plaintiff claiming only a generally available grievance about government, unconnected with a threatened concrete interest of his or her own, does not state an Article III case or controversy. Vindicating the public interest is the function of the Congress and the chief executive. The court of appeals's allowing a statute to permit all citizens to sue, regardless of whether they had suffered any concrete injury, would result in Congress's transferring from the President to the courts the chief executive's most important constitutional duty, to "take Care that the Laws be faithfully executed" (*U.S. Constitution,* Article II, Section 3). The court of appeals's decision therefore was erroneous.

BUSINESS CONSIDERATIONS Some noted jurists have submitted that courts deciding environmental cases should accord standing to the trees, animals, and so forth involved in the litigation. Do you agree? In a related vein, should the courts take a more lenient view toward standing in environmental cases? How might such a change affect the businesses that are involved in the litigation?

ETHICAL CONSIDERATIONS Do so-called "public-interest" groups have an ethical obligation to file lawsuits in opposition to uses of the environment that will degrade it? Some well-known celebrities—pursuant to environmental protection efforts—have trespassed on private property and otherwise have broken the law. Would you characterize these actions as "ethical" or "unethical"?

ENFORCEMENT AND REMEDIES

In the last few years, the EPA has aggressively enforced environmental laws. The EPA during fiscal 1994 brought 220 criminal actions, 1,597 penalty actions, 403 civil referrals to the Department of Justice, and 27 additional civil referrals pursuant to the enforcement of new consent decrees.[14] These EPA actions netted a record $165.2

YOU BE THE JUDGE

Endangered Species Act

A heretofore rarely used 1982 amendment to the Endangered Species Act (ESA) gives private landowners some leeway to take species if such a taking is incidental to the development or harvesting of land, provided that the landowners agree to mitigate the ensuing damage. The Clinton administration has used this portion of the ESA to forge 200 deals (called "Habitat Conservation Plans") with timber companies and private landowners. Known for its pro-environment stand, the Clinton administration has quietly utilized this part of the ESA and has faced few challenges regarding this policy. One such recent Habitat Conservation Plan gave Benjamin Cone, Jr., the right to kill 29 endangered red-cockaded woodpeckers that nest in a North Carolina longleaf pine forest owned by Cone. Under the plan, Cone will underwrite the $45,000 cost of boring artificial woodpecker holes and of establishing new families of birds in the nearby forests owned by persons who welcome the woodpeckers. This plan resulted from Cone's 1995 $1.4 million lawsuit against the government. In that suit, Cone argued that the government, which, because of the woodpeckers' presence, had prohibited his cutting or selling timber on 1,500 acres of his 8,000-acre property, thereby had effected a "taking" of his property. The subsequent deal between Cone and the government made the lawsuit moot—a salutary result, right? Yet critics argue that such a plan relies heavily on the assumption that the birds, who will nest only in trees at least 80 years old (owing to these trees' soft cores), can be moved successfully to these new, man-made cavities drilled in younger trees. (Timber companies, of course, want to harvest these pine trees favored by the woodpeckers before the trees are 80 years old.) Today a mere 4,600 red-cockaded woodpecker groups exist in the 4 million remaining acres of longleaf pines. Studies moreover indicate that while the relocation of females is successful in about 60 percent of the cases, moving male–female pairs to new homes is successful in only one of three attempts.[15]

Assume that an environmental group challenges the plan between the Clinton administration and Cone and that the case is brought before *your* court. How will *you* decide this case? Will you enforce this Habitat Conservation Plan or declare it void?

BUSINESS CONSIDERATIONS Does the Clinton administration's policies in this regard represent a workable compromise between protecting business interests and endangered species? Does the apparent balancing of interests at issue here tip too far in one direction? Explain your responses.

ETHICAL CONSIDERATIONS Some critics of President Clinton question how stationary his "moral compass" is when it comes to political compromises. Do these Habitat Conservation Plans represent a politically expedient response that unethically sacrifices endangered species for the sake of placating anti-environmental voices in Congress and avoiding costly litigation?

SOURCE: Marianne Lavelle, *The National Law Journal* (12 December 1996), pp. A1 and A17.

million in criminal and civil fines.[16] Cost recovery actions at Superfund sites resulted in the return of $206 million to the U.S. Treasury.[17] In addition, the government will realize another $1.4 billion in commitments made by responsible parties pursuant to Superfund cleanups.[18]

International Aspects

Environmental regulation is not only on the rise in the United States, but around the world as well. While some European countries—Germany and the Netherlands, for

http:// RESOURCES FOR BUSINESS LAW STUDENTS

NAME	RESOURCES	WEB ADDRESS
U.S. Environmental Protection Agency (EPA)	The EPA provides educational materials, regulations, publications, news, and text for the National Environmental Policy Act of 1969.	http://www.epa.gov/
Council on Environmental Quality (CEQ)	The CEQ provides, among other services, NEPANet (National Environmental Policy Act), which includes environmental impact statements (EISs) and a library of environmental resources.	http://www.whitehouse.gov/CEQ/

example—have traditionally undertaken regulatory efforts that rival those of the United States, in many other countries environmental laws are nonexistent or at best embryonic. The environmental contamination and degradation found in post–Communist Eastern European countries, besides providing telling examples of what results from lax environmental standards, have discouraged much-needed privatization and foreign investments.

Realizing the need for environmental oversight and modeling its efforts on U.S. legislation, the European Union (EU) has adopted the Eco-audit Management and Audit Scheme (EMAS) Regulation that mandates environmental registers at each plant to catalog pollution emissions, land contamination, and the like; public disclosure of such environmental statements; and external verification of the company's environmental management system. Recently enacted environmental laws covering products now regulate product features (such as shape and recyclability), labeling, packaging, hazardous chemicals, and waste (its generation, transboundary shipment, etc.).[19] These laws also ban certain products such as asbestos, heavy metals, and vinyl chloride.

Such efforts are a harbinger of the future, since South American and Asian nations of necessity soon will recognize the need to enact environmental laws as well. Closer to home, the passage of the North American Free Trade Agreement (NAFTA), about which you learned in Chapter 3, also shows sensitivity to environmental concerns. A subsequent environmental side agreement between the United States and Mexico attempts to address the degradation of the environment along the U.S.–Mexican border. Moreover, the trade talks occurring during the Uruguay Round of the General Agreement on Tariffs and Trade (GATT), also discussed in Chapter 3, involve environmental issues.

SUMMARY

Environmental law involves complicated issues and highly technical statutes. The National Environmental Policy Act of 1969 mandates that virtually all federal agencies prepare detailed EISs whenever any agency undertakes any activities that may affect the environment.

The Clean Air Act, enacted in 1963 and amended subsequently, takes a technology-forcing approach to air pollution. It directs the EPA to establish national ambient air quality standards and state implementation plans that set out how the state proposes to implement and maintain those standards within its air quality regions. The 1990 amendments attack urban air pollution brought on by motor vehicle emissions, toxic pollutants, and acid rain. Among other things, beyond controlling emissions from mobile sources, these amendments set up a permit process aimed at minimizing emissions from major point sources. Civil, criminal, and administrative actions (including citizens' suits) are possible for violations of the act.

The Clean Water Act, so named in 1977 after having been enacted under a different name in 1972, sets out an extensive, joint federal and state comprehensive program for preventing, reducing, and eliminating water pollution. The CWA does so by regulating both point and nonpoint sources. The three mechanisms used to regulate discharges from point sources include: effluent limitations, water quality standards, and the national pollutant discharge elimination system's permit program. States also must comply with EPA-mandated antidegradation standards designed to ensure the maintenance of desirable water quality standards. The CWA sets out a timetable and the technological standards to be used for permit holders' compliance with the act. The act takes an especially stringent approach to toxic pollutants such as asbestos, mercury, lead, PCBs, and so forth. The penalties imposed for violations of the CWA resemble those set out in the Clean Air Act.

The Safe Drinking Water Act of 1974 regulates the water supplied by public water systems to home taps. This act uses EPA-issued national primary drinking water regulations that have as their goal the reduction of contaminant levels in drinking water. States may have primary enforcement responsibilities under the SDWA if they have adopted drinking water regulations no less stringent than the national standards and if they have implemented adequate monitoring, inspection, recordkeeping, and enforcement procedures.

The Noise Control Act of 1972 leaves to the federal government control over noise sources that require national uniformity of treatment or protection of the public health and welfare with an adequate margin of safety. Otherwise, the primary responsibility for controlling noise lies with state and local governments. The remedies granted for violations of this act resemble those permitted under the previous acts.

The Toxic Substances Control Act of 1976, by giving authority to the EPA to regulate chemicals before they come onto the market, screens pollutants before humans and the environment are exposed to these substances' effects. Yet the EPA's laxness regarding the stringency it will require of companies that provide test data, coupled with the congressional mandate requiring the testing and regulation only of chemicals that pose an "unreasonable risk" of injury to health or the environment, has undercut the statute's worthy goals. Besides the civil and criminal penalties set out in other acts, the TSCA, through emergency judicial relief leading to an injunction or seizure of the chemicals at issue, authorizes the EPA to regulate "imminent hazards."

The Federal Insecticide, Fungicide, and Rodenticide Act of 1947 mandates the registration of all insecticides and pesticides with the EPA. The EPA will register only those products that, when used in accordance with widespread and common practice, will not generally cause adverse effects on the environment. The EPA subsequently can cancel the registration of any pesticide that fails to live up to this standard and can suspend a registration whenever such is necessary to prevent an imminent hazard. Civil and criminal penalties, as well as EPA "stop sale" or seizure orders, are available under the FIFRA.

The Resource Conservation and Recovery Act of 1976 requires the EPA to regulate nonhazardous solid waste, typically through approved state management plans.

The EPA's "cradle-to-grave" regulation of hazardous waste involves a permit/manifest system that covers those who own or operate treatment, storage, or disposal facilities. Under the RCRA, the EPA enjoys broad enforcement powers. Anyone involved in the handling, transport, storage, or disposal of solid or hazardous waste that presents an immediate and substantial endangerment to health or the environment faces the imposition of strict liability.

The Comprehensive Environmental Response, Compensation, and Liability Act (or "Superfund"), by regulating hazardous waste disposal sites, fills in the gaps left by the RCRA and the TSCA. Pursuant to the National Contingency Plan, CERCLA authorizes cleanups of hazardous waste sites and makes generators, owners, operators, and transporters of hazardous wastes strictly liable for such response costs. CERCLA also establishes a "Superfund" to finance cleanups whenever the government cannot identify the parties responsible for the damage. The Superfund Amendments and Reauthorization Act of 1986 increases the money allocated to the Superfund.

The Endangered Species Act of 1973, by protecting the critical habitats of wildlife, attempts to conserve endangered or threatened species of plants and animals. Celebrated cases under the ESA wherein dam or road construction projects were halted to protect the habitat of fish or butterflies, for example, have led to public controversies of great magnitude. International efforts to improve the environment in this and other nations are on the rise and therefore bear watching.

Discussion Questions

1. Describe fully when an agency needs to prepare an environmental impact statement (EIS) and the general prerequisites of an EIS.
2. Explain in detail the manner in which the Clean Air Act addresses the problem of air pollution.
3. Explain the following three Clean Water Act mechanisms and their importance to the fulfillment of the act's dictates: effluent limitations, water quality standards, and the national pollutant discharge elimination system's permit program.
4. How does the Safe Drinking Water Act differ from the Clean Water Act?
5. How has Congress allocated the responsibility for noise control among the federal government and state and local governments?
6. Explain Congress's threefold purpose in enacting the Toxic Substances Control Act.
7. How does the Federal Insecticide, Fungicide, and Rodenticide Act differ from the TSCA?
8. How do the Resource Conservation and Recovery Act and the Comprehensive Environmental Response, Compensation, and Liability Act, respectively, regulate waste?
9. Explain some of the more significant economic aspects of the Endangered Species Act.
10. Describe some of the international aspects of environmental law.

Case Problems and Writing Assignments

1. The City of Tacoma, Washington, and a local utility district wanted to build a hydroelectric plant on the Dosewallips River in Washington State. The Washington Department of Ecology, the state environmental agency, conditioned the permit for the project on the maintenance of minimum stream flows that would sufficiently protect salmon and steelhead runs, since the state had designated the river as a fish habitat. In justification of its action, the agency noted that § 303 of the Clean Water Act (CWA) requires each state, subject to federal approval, to institute comprehensive standards establishing the designated uses of the navigable waters involved and the water quality criteria for such waters based on such uses. Under EPA regulations, the standards also must include an antidegradation policy that will maintain existing instream water uses and the level of water quality necessary to protect those uses. Section 401 of the CWA requires states to

provide a water quality certification before a federal license or permit can be issued for any activity that may result in a discharge into intrastate navigable waters. The certification must "set forth any effluent limitations and other limitations . . . necessary to assure that any applicant" will comply with various provisions of the act and "any other appropriate" state law requirement. Under Washington's comprehensive water quality standards, characteristic uses of the river's classification include fish migration, rearing, and spawning. The city and the local utility district argued that the state could impose only water quality limitations specifically tied to a "discharge"; but the agency submitted that, pursuant to § 401, it had the power to condition the grant of the permit on the maintenance of minimum stream flows. Who had the stronger arguments here—the state agency or those who wanted to build the dam? Why? [See *PUD No. 1 of Jefferson County and City of Tacoma* v. *Washington Department of Ecology,* 511 U.S. 700 (1994).]

2. The Oregon Public Utility Commission (Commission) promulgated a rule stating that (1) trains were not required to sound whistles at grade crossings "equipped with operating automatic gates, flashing lights, and audible protective devices"; (2) the Commission was empowered to prohibit whistle sounding at such crossings; and (3) railroads were to provide written notification of such prohibitions to their employees. In 1988, the City of Eugene, Oregon, petitioned the Commission to prohibit whistle sounding by Southern Pacific Transportation Company (Southern Pacific) trains. The Commission then issued an order that banned train whistles at certain crossings in the city between 10 PM and 6 AM. On 13 September 1991, the Commission, having found that the prohibition of routine train whistles in Eugene during nighttime hours would significantly increase the risk of accidents, rescinded this order. Southern Pacific, a California-based railroad that operates freight trains in Oregon and many other states, contended that the federal Noise Control Act (NCA) of 1972, by directing the establishment of standards for railroad noise emissions, preempts the Oregon state law. Under a provision labeled "state and local standards and controls," the NCA sets forth two provisions pertaining to its preemption of state laws:

   > *[A]fter the effective date of a regulation under this section applicable to noise emissions resulting from the operation of any equipment or facility of a surface carrier engaged in interstate commerce by railroad, no State . . . may adopt or enforce any standard applicable to noise emissions resulting from the operation of the . . . equipment . . . unless such standard is identical to a standard . . . prescribed by any regulation under this section.*

   In addition, another provision states:

   > *[N]othing in this section shall diminish or enhance the rights of any State . . . to establish . . . controls on levels of environmental noise . . . if the Administrator . . . determines that such . . . control . . . is necessitated by special local conditions and is not in conflict with regulations promulgated under this section.*

   The Commission maintained that no EPA regulation covering locomotive whistles exists and that the EPA has decided that state and local authorities are best suited to regulate acoustic warning devices such as train whistles. Was this case moot? If not, did the NCA preempt the Oregon regulations regarding the sounding of train whistles? Why? [See *Southern Pacific Transportation Co.* v. *Public Utility Commission of the State of Oregon,* 9 F.3d 807 (9th Cir. 1993).]

3. Owen Electric Steel Company of South Carolina, Inc. (Owen) is engaged in the production of steel. In the course of production, "slag" floats to the surface of the molten metal and is removed. A third-party contractor continuously processes slag at the Owen plant in Cayce, South Carolina. After *curing* (lying on bare soil for six months), the slag becomes amenable for the construction industry's use as a road base material or for other commercial purposes. As an operator of a facility that treats, stores, or disposes of hazardous wastes (TSDF) under the RCRA, Owen must apply for and obtain an EPA permit for the facility. The permit the EPA had mailed to Owen identified the Cayce site's slag processing area (SPA) as a solid waste management unit (SWMU). But Owen claimed that its slag did not constitute "solid waste" under the RCRA (that is, "other discarded material") because the slag ultimately is recycled and used in roadbeds. The EPA countered that, because the slag lies dormant and exposed on the ground for six months before such use, it is "discarded" even if it is later "picked up" and used in another capacity. Whose reasoning was more persuasive, Owen's or the EPA's? Why? [See *Owen Electric Steel Co. of South Carolina, Inc.* v. *Browner,* 37 F.3d 146 (4th Cir. 1994).]

4. KFC Western, Inc. (KFC) owns and operates a "Kentucky Fried Chicken" restaurant on a parcel of property in Los Angeles. In 1988, KFC discovered during the course of a construction project that the property was contaminated with petroleum. The County of Los Angeles Department of Health Services ordered KFC

to attend to the problem, and KFC spent $211,000 removing and disposing of the oil-tainted soil. Three years later, KFC, bringing this suit under the citizen-suit provision of the Resource Conservation Recovery Act (RCRA), sought to recover these cleanup costs from Alan and Margaret Meghrig. KFC claimed that the contaminated soil was a "solid waste" covered by the RCRA, that it had previously posed an "imminent and substantial endangerment to health or the environment," and that the Meghrigs were responsible for the "equitable restitution" of KFC's cleanup costs under the RCRA because, as prior owners of the property, they had contributed to the waste's "past or present handling, storage, treatment, transportation, or disposal." The district court held that the provision of the RCRA at issue neither permits the recovery of past cleanup costs nor does the RCRA authorize a cause of action for the remediation of toxic wastes that fail to pose an "imminent and substantial endangerment to health or the environment" at the time suit is filed. The district court thus dismissed KFC's complaint. The Court of Appeals for the Ninth Circuit reversed and found that a district court would have authority under the RCRA to award restitution of past cleanup costs and that a private party could proceed with a suit under the RCRA if the waste at issue presented an "imminent and substantial endangerment" at the time it was cleaned up. Was the Court of Appeals's determination correct? [*Meghrig* v. *KFC Western, Inc.*, 116 S.Ct. 1251 (1996).]

5. In the late evening of 3 January 1992, or the early morning of 4 January 1992, a number of containers loaded with drums of arsenic trioxide were lost overboard from the vessel *M/V Santa Clara I* during a severe storm in the Atlantic Ocean off the coast of New Jersey. The loss of the drums overboard resulted in a response by the United States, led by the U.S. Coast Guard (Coast Guard) with the support of the U.S. Environmental Protection Agency (EPA), pursuant to the exercise of their apparent authority under Section 104 of the Comprehensive Environmental Response, Compensation, and Liability Act (CERCLA) to respond to a release or a substantial threat of a release of a hazardous substance into the environment. On 20 February 1992, the Coast Guard issued an administrative order to the owner and operator of the *M/V Santa Clara I.* This order, directing the owner and operator to search for, locate, recover, and dispose of the containers and drums of arsenic trioxide, was issued pursuant to the Coast Guard's authority under Section 106 of the CERCLA and Section 311(c) of the Clean Water Act. Although the owner and operator of the ship objected to the government's risk assessment of the arsenic trioxide to the ocean environment, they conducted the mission of locating and recovering the arsenic trioxide drums. Through the concerted efforts of the United States and the owner and operator of the ship, the Coast Guard was able to locate the position of the drums more than 30 miles offshore and under 120 to 130 feet of water. The United States thereafter sued, pursuant to Section 107(a) of the CERCLA, to recover the costs incurred by the government in responding to the loss of the arsenic trioxide from the *M/V Santa Clara I.* Upon the institution of this litigation, the owner and operator filed a counterclaim seeking reimbursement of the costs incurred when they had complied with the administrative cleanup order. Should the court allow this counterclaim? [*U.S.* v. *M/V Santa Clara I*, 819 F.Supp. 507 (D.S.C. 1993).]

6. **BUSINESS APPLICATION CASE** Section 307(b)(1) of the Clean Air Act provides that petitions to review "nationally applicable regulations" issued by the EPA under the act are reviewable only in the U.S. Court of Appeals for the District of Columbia (D.C.) Circuit, while petitions to review "locally or regionally applicable" actions by the agency are reviewable only in the regional courts of appeals. Designed to reduce the amount of acid rain, the regulations create, effective in the year 2000, a national system of tradable pollution permits. Each permit—"allowance" is the term in the regulations—authorizes an electrical utility to emit a ton of sulfur dioxide per year from a specified generating plant owned by the utility. A utility, of course, may have more than one allowance; in fact the average is several thousand. The regulations use a variety of formulas to determine, on the basis of generating capacity, type of fuel, and other factors, how many allowances each of the nation's 2,200-plus electrical generating plants shall be allocated; a table in the regulations sets forth these allocations. The total number of allowances may not exceed 8.95 million; and as the nation's electrical utilities emit more than 8.95 million tons of sulfur dioxide a year, the new program will reduce the total emissions of this pollutant. A novel feature of the program authorizes a utility that can reduce its emissions at very low cost to sell one or more of its allowances to a utility that will incur a much higher cost to reduce its emissions. The program thus helps to minimize the costs associated with limiting emissions.

   Madison Gas and Electric Company (Madison) challenged the allocation of the sulfur-dioxide emission allowances for its Wisconsin electrical generating plants. Madison argued that the allowances are based on an incorrect determination of Madison's generating capacity, one of the factors that determine how many allowances each plant shall receive. The EPA argued that, despite the local incidence of the determination, Madison could challenge the EPA's decision only in the D.C. Circuit because the determination is part of the national acid rain program. The EPA further noted that if courts around the country began giving utilities more allowances, the 8.95 million ceiling might be pierced. Had Madison filed its lawsuit in the correct court? Why? Does the tradable pollution permit system at issue here represent a workable compromise between protecting business from exorbitant compliance costs and protecting the environment, or does the balance represented by this permit system tip too far in one direction? Explain. [See *Madison Gas and Electric Co.* v. *U.S. Environmental Protection Agency,* 4 F.3d 529 (7th Cir. 1993).]

7. **ETHICS APPLICATION CASE** When Helen Frost brought a citizens' suit under the Resource Conservation and Recovery Act and asked for information regarding materials allegedly stored on a classified U.S. Air Force base near Groom Lake, Nevada, the U.S. Air Force invoked the military and state secrets privilege. Should the court recognize this privilege in this case? Would it be unethical to do so? [*Frost* v. *Perry,* 919 F.Supp. 1459 (D. Nev. 1996).]

8. **IDES CASE** The Endangered Species Act of 1973 (ESA) requires the Secretary of the Interior to specify animal species that are "threatened" or "endangered" and designate their "critical habitat." The ESA also requires federal agencies to ensure that any action they authorize, fund, or carry out is not likely to jeopardize a listed species or adversely modify its critical habitat. If an agency determines that a proposed action may adversely affect such a species, it must formally consult with the Fish and Wildlife Service (Service), which in turn must provide the agency with a written statement (the Biological Opinion) explaining how the proposed action will affect the species or its habitat. If the Service concludes that such an action will result in jeopardy or adverse habitat modification, the Biological Opinion must outline any "reasonable and prudent alternatives" that the Service believes will avoid that consequence. If the Biological Opinion concludes that no jeopardy or adverse habitat modification will result, or if it offers reasonable and prudent alternatives, the Service must issue a written statement (known as the "Incidental Take Statement") specifying the terms and conditions under which an agency may take the species.

   The Klamath Project, one of the oldest federal reclamation schemes, consists of a series of lakes, rivers, dams and irrigation canals in northern California and southern Oregon. The project was undertaken by the Secretary of the Interior pursuant to the Reclamation Act of 1902 and is administered by the Bureau of Reclamation (Bureau), which is under the Secretary's jurisdiction. In 1992, the Bureau notified the Service that operation of the project might affect the Lost River sucker and shortnose sucker species of fish that had been listed as endangered in 1988. After formal consultation with the Bureau, the Service issued a Biological Opinion which concluded that the "long-term operation of the Klamath Project was likely to jeopardize the continued existence of the Lost River and shortnose suckers." The Biological Opinion identified "reasonable and prudent alternatives" the Service believed would avoid jeopardy, which alternatives included the maintenance of minimum water levels on Clear Lake and Gerber reservoirs. The Bureau later notified the Service that it intended to operate the project in compliance with the Biological Opinion. The petitioners—two Oregon irrigation districts that receive Klamath Project water and the operators of two ranches within those districts—subsequently filed a lawsuit against the director and regional director of the Service and the Secretary of the Interior. The complaint asserted that there is an absence of any scientifically or commercially available evidence indicating that the populations of endangered suckers in the Clear Lake and Gerber reservoirs have declined, are declining, or will decline as a result of the Bureau's operation of the Klamath Project and that there is an absence of any commercially or scientifically available evidence indicating that the restrictions on lake levels imposed in the Biological Opinion will have any beneficial effect on the populations of suckers in the Clear Lake and Gerber reservoirs. The complaint further asserted that petitioners' uses of the reservoirs and related waterways for recreational, aesthetic, and commercial purposes, as well as for their primary sources of irrigation water, will be "irreparably damaged" by the actions taken by the Service. In essence, the petitioners claimed a competing interest in the water the Biological Opinion declares necessary for the preservation of the suckers.

   The district court, dismissing the complaint for lack of jurisdiction, concluded that petitioners did not have standing because their "recreational, aesthetic, and commercial interests . . . do not fall within the zone of interests sought to be protected by the ESA." Affirming, the Court of Appeals for the Ninth Circuit held that the "zone of interests" test limits the class of persons who may obtain judicial review under the citizen-suit provision of the ESA and that "only plaintiffs who allege an interest in the *preservation* of endangered species fall within the zone of interests protected by the ESA." At the Supreme Court, the petitioners thus raised two questions: first, whether the standing rule known as the "zone of interests" test applies to claims brought under the citizen-suit provision of the ESA; and second, if so, whether the petitioners have standing under that test notwithstanding the fact that the interests they seek to vindicate are economic rather than environmental. How should the Court rule in this case? Why? Use the IDES approach to answer these questions. [*Bennett* v. *Spear,* 117 S.Ct. 1154 (1997).]

NOTES

1. John Henry Davidson and Orlando E. Delogu, *Federal Environmental Regulation,* 2 vols. (Salem, NH: Butterworth Legal Publishers, 1994); Roger W. Findley and Daniel A. Farber, *Environmental Law in a Nutshell,* 2nd ed. (Minneapolis: West Publishing Co., 1988); and William H. Rodgers, Jr., *Handbook on Environmental Law,* 2nd ed. (Minneapolis: West Publishing Co., 1994) provide more detailed and comprehensive information concerning environmental law.
2. Thomas DiLorenzo, "Federal Regulations: Environmentalism's Achilles Heel," *USA Today Magazine* (September 1994), p. 48.
3. Linda Grant, "Shutting Down the Regulatory Machine," *U.S. News & World Report* (13 February 1995), p. 70.
4. Ibid.
5. "Concentrations of Five Major Air Pollutants Drop by Average 7 Percent But Ozone Up 4 Percent," 27 *Environmental Reporter* 1803 (The Bureau of National Affairs, Inc.: Washington, D.C.), 1996.
6. Ibid.
7. Ibid.
8. Tim Eichenberg and Robert Irvin, "Congress Takes Aim at Endangered Species Act," *The National Law Journal* (13 February 1995), p. A21.
9. Ibid.
10. Ibid., pp. A21 and A22.
11. Ibid., p. A22.
12. Ibid.
13. Ibid.
14. Marianne Lavelle, "Feds Settle to Save Act and Species," *The National Law Journal* (12 December 1996), pp. A1 and A17.
15. "EPA Reports Record Number of Enforcement Actions Last Year," *Chemical and Engineering News* (5 December 1994), p. 18.
16. Ibid.
17. Ibid.
18. Ibid.
19. Turner Y. Smith, Jr., "Environmental Regulation on the Rise Worldwide," *The National Law Journal* (19 September 1994), pp. C15 and C16.

Labor and Fair Employment Practices

A G E N D A

As CIT grows and prospers, it will hire more employees. The firm will need to ensure that it complies with all applicable federal and state laws regulating labor. CIT also may have to deal with one or more unions. The firm must be certain that it uses fair employment practices and thus avoids any improper discrimination in its hiring and promotion practices. The firm will need to take steps to protect against sexual harassment, and it must provide a reasonably safe work environment. The firm in addition will have concerns about social security, workers' compensation, and unemployment insurance. Each of these areas requires careful attention to detail and strict compliance with the applicable laws and regulations.

These and other issues are likely to arise during your study of this chapter. Be prepared! You never know when one of the Kochanowskis will need your help or advice.

O U T L I N E

LABOR

Federal Statutes

Unions are a fact of life in the United States today. But this was not always so. Violence and bloody battles between employers and pro-union workers marked the rise of unionism in this country. The courts, moreover, were as hostile as most employers to unions. In fact, in the 1800s and early 1900s, both state and federal courts viewed workers' concerted activities (strikes, **picketing**, and the like) as common law criminal conspiracies, tortious interference with contract, or antitrust violations. Although Congress had passed the Clayton Act in 1914 in part to shield unions from liability under the antitrust laws, subsequent Supreme Court decisions had narrowed this newly won statutory protection.

Picketing
Union activity in which persons stand near a place of work affected by an organizational drive or a strike so as to influence workers regarding union causes.

Norris-LaGuardia Act (1932). Responding to these developments, Congress passed the Norris-LaGuardia Act in 1932. This act immunized certain activities—peaceful refusals to work, **boycotts**, and picketing, for example—from federal court action. The act barred the issuance of federal injunctions in the context of labor disputes as well as the institution of *yellow dog* contracts (that is, promises to refrain from union membership as a condition of employment). It thus allowed employees to organize and to engage in collective bargaining free from court or employer intervention, as long as the concerted activity did not involve **wildcat strikes**, violence, sabotage, trespass, and the like.

Boycotts
Concerted refusals to deal with firms so as to disrupt the business of those firms.

Wildcat strikes
Unauthorized withholdings of services or labor during the term of a contract.

The Norris-LaGuardia Act signaled a policy aimed at keeping the courts out of the labor field. Free from regulation, then, employees and employers, by using the economic weapons appropriate to each side, fought for their respective goals. The unions used strikes, picketing, and boycotts; and the employers used discharges of employees.

The Wagner Act (1935). In 1935, Congress passed the Wagner Act, also called the National Labor Relations Act. This legislation heralded the beginning of an *affirmative*—as opposed to a neutral—approach to labor organizations. In § 7 of the Wagner Act, Congress approved the right of employees to organize themselves and "to form, join, or assist labor organizations, to bargain collectively through representatives of their own choosing, and to engage in concerted activities for the purpose of collective bargaining or other mutual aid or protection." The right to refrain from engaging in concerted activities is protected as well. Buttressing § 7 is § 8, which enumerates employer **unfair labor practices**, such as coercion of or retaliation against employees who exercise their § 7 rights, domination of unions by employers, discrimination in employment (hiring and firing, for instance) designed to discourage union activities, and refusals by employers to bargain collectively and in good faith with employee representatives (that is, with unions). Section 9 sets out the process by which the employees in the appropriate bargaining unit can conduct secret elections for choosing their representative in the collective bargaining process. The Wagner Act also established a new administrative agency, the National Labor Relations Board (NLRB), to oversee such elections and also to investigate and remedy unfair labor practices. Section 10 permits the appropriate federal circuit court of appeals to review any NLRB order. A 1937 case, *NLRB* v. *Jones & Laughlin Steel Corp.*, upheld the constitutionality of the Wagner Act.[1]

Unfair labor practices
Employment or union activities that are prohibited by law as injurious to labor policies.

The Taft-Hartley Act (1947). After the passage of the Wagner Act, unions grew appreciably in size and influence. As a result, the power balance between employees and employers became so pro-union that in 1947 Congress passed legislation meant to counter the perceived excesses of the NLRB and pervasive court deference to its orders.

The Taft-Hartley Act, also called the Labor Management Relations Act (LMRA), attempted to curb union excesses. It amended § 8 of the Wagner Act so as to prohibit certain unfair labor practices by unions, including engaging in **secondary boycotts**, forcing an employer to discriminate against employees on the basis of their union affiliation or lack of union affiliation, refusing to bargain in good faith, requiring an employer to pay for services not actually performed by an employee *(featherbedding)*, and **recognitional picketing**. Congress also amended § 7 to allow employees to refrain from joining a union and participating in its collective activities.

Secondary boycotts
Union activities meant to pressure parties not involved in the labor dispute and to influence the affected employer.

Recognitional picketing
Prohibited picketing in which a union attempts to force recognition of a union different from the currently certified bargaining representative.

In addition, the Taft-Hartley Act, by separating the NLRB's functions, cut back the authority of the board. The Office of General Counsel took on prosecution of the board's unfair labor practices cases, leaving to the five-person board the decision-making (or *adjudicatory*) function. This significantly changed the nature of the NLRB, which had served simultaneously as both prosecutor and decision maker under the Wagner Act.

The Taft-Hartley Act also empowered courts of appeals to set aside NLRB findings concerning unfair labor practices cases, authorized district courts to issue labor injunctions requested by the NLRB for the purpose of stopping unfair labor practices, set out the possibility of fines and imprisonment for anyone resisting NLRB orders, and provided for civil remedies for private parties damaged by secondary boycotts or various union activities.

Other sections protect the employer's right of free speech (by refusing to characterize as unfair labor practices an employer's expressions of its opinions about unionism when they contain no threats of reprisal), preserve the employees' rights to engage in peaceful **informational picketing**, and prohibit *closed shop* agreements (contracts that obligate the employer to hire and retain only union members). *Union shop* clauses (provisions that require an employee, after being hired, to join a union in order to retain his or her job) are legal. The Taft-Hartley Act also created a Federal Mediation and Conciliation Service for settling disputes between labor and management. To foster conciliation efforts further, the act established a cooling-off period that the parties must observe in certain circumstances before strikes can occur. It also preserved the power of states, under their right-to-work laws, to invalidate other union devices designed to consolidate the unions' hold on workers.

Informational picketing
Picketing for the purpose of truthfully advising the public that an employer does not employ members of, or have a contract with, a labor organization.

The Landrum-Griffin Act (1959). By the 1950s, Congress had unearthed substantial corruption among union leadership. Union members had been prejudiced by officers' plundering of union treasuries and by these officers' often tyrannical treatment of the rank-and-file members.

In 1959, Congress responded with the Landrum-Griffin Act, also called the Labor Management Reporting and Disclosure Act (LMRDA). As this latter title suggests, the act requires extensive reporting of financial affairs; allows civil and criminal sanctions for financial wrongdoings by union officers; and, by providing a "bill of rights" for union members regarding elections and meetings, mandates democratic procedures in the conduct of union affairs. In addition, the Landrum-Griffin Act amended portions of the Taft-Hartley Act to outlaw *hot cargo* clauses (provisions in contracts requiring the employer to cease doing business with nonunion companies).

Taken together, these acts cover almost all employers and employees, excluding federal, state, and local government employers and employees; employers covered under the Railway Labor Act; agricultural workers; domestic workers; independent contractors; and most supervisors. Even though government workers are not covered, they can organize themselves under the authority of Executive Order 11491, entitled Labor–Management Relations in the Federal Service, promulgated in 1969. In addition, about two-thirds of the states have enacted laws permitting collective bargaining in the public sector for state and municipal employees. Such executive orders and statutes ordinarily forbid strikes by public employees (such as police officers and firefighters), but such strikes nevertheless have occurred in recent years. The arrival of collective bargaining in the public sector is fairly new, but it promises to have significant implications for the future as our economy becomes more service-oriented and the number of government employees proliferates.

Both *National Labor Relations Board* v. *Health Care & Retirement Corporation of America* and *ABF Freight Systems, Inc.* v. *National Labor Relations Board* involve various facets of the NLRB's interpretive and remedial powers.

43.1 NATIONAL LABOR RELATIONS BOARD v. HEALTH CARE & RETIREMENT CORPORATION OF AMERICA

511 U.S. 571 (1994)

FACTS The National Labor Relations Board's (the Board's) general counsel had issued a complaint alleging that Health Care & Retirement Corporation of America (Health Care), the owner and operator of the Heartland Nursing Home (Heartland) in Urbana, Ohio, had committed unfair labor practices when it disciplined four licensed practical nurses. At Heartland, the director of nursing has overall responsibility for the nursing department. An assistant director of nursing, between nine and eleven staff nurses (including both registered nurses and the four licensed practical nurses involved in this case), and between fifty and fifty-five nurses' aides also work at Heartland. The staff nurses, who are the senior-ranking employees on duty after 5 P.M. during the week and at all times on weekends—approximately 75 percent of the time—have the responsibility to ensure adequate staffing, make daily work assignments, monitor the aides' work to ensure proper performance, counsel and discipline aides, resolve aides' problems and grievances, evaluate aides' performances, and, finally, report to management. In light of these varied activities, Health Care contended that the four nurses involved in this case were supervisors and thus not protected under the Labor Management Relations Act (LMRA). Disagreeing, the administrative law judge (ALJ) concluded that the nurses were not supervisors. The ALJ stated that the nurses' supervisory work did not "equate to responsibly directing the aides in the interest of the employer." The Board stated only that "[t]he judge found, and we agree, that the staff nurses are employees within the meaning of the Act." The U.S. Court of Appeals for the Sixth Circuit reversed, because it had decided in earlier cases that the Board's test for determining the supervisory status of nurses was inconsistent with the statute. Hence, the Court of Appeals held that the four licensed practical nurses involved in this case were supervisors.

ISSUE Was the Board's test for determining if nurses are supervisors rational and consistent with the statutory definition of supervisors under the LMRA?

HOLDING No. The Board's test, which relied on an industry-wide interpretation of the phrase "in the interest of the employer," contravened Supreme Court precedents and had no relation to the ordinary meaning of that language.

REASONING The LMRA defines a supervisor as:

> *Any individual having authority, in the interest of the employer, to hire, transfer, suspend, lay off, recall, promote, discharge, assign, reward, or discipline other employees, or responsibly direct them, or to adjust their grievances, or effectively to recommend such action, if, in connection with the foregoing, exercise of such authority is not of a merely routine or clerical nature, but requires the use of independent judgment.* [29 U.S.C. § 152(11)]

As the Board has stated, the statute requires the resolution of three questions, and each must be answered in the affirmative before the court can deem the employee a supervisor. First, does the employee have authority to engage in one of the twelve listed activities? Second, does the exercise of

43.1 NATIONAL LABOR RELATIONS BOARD v. HEALTH CARE & RETIREMENT CORPORATION OF AMERICA *(cont.)*

511 U.S. 571 (1994)

that authority require "the use of independent judgment"? Third, does the employee hold the authority in the interest of the employer? This case concerns only the third question: the proper interpretation of the phrase "in the interest of the employer." The Board's interpretation, that a nurse's supervisory activity is not exercised in the interest of the employer if it is incidental to the treatment of patients, is similar to an approach the Board took, and the Supreme Court rejected, in *National Labor Relations Board* v. *Yeshiva University,* 444 U.S. 672 (1980) *(Yeshiva)*. There, the Court had to determine whether faculty members at Yeshiva were "managerial employees." Managerial employees are those who "formulate and effectuate management policies by expressing and making operative the decisions of their employer." Like supervisory employees, managerial employees are excluded from the act's coverage. The Board in *Yeshiva,* arguing that the faculty members were not managerial, maintained that faculty authority was "exercised in the faculty's own interest rather than in the interest of the university." To support its position, the Board placed much reliance on the faculty's independent professional role in designing the curriculum and in discharging their professional obligations to the students. The Supreme Court, however, found the Board's reasoning unpersuasive because the Court believed that the faculty's professional interests—as applied to governance at a university like Yeshiva—cannot be separated from those of the institution, since the "business" of a university is education. The Board's reasoning fares no better here than it did in *Yeshiva.* Patient care is the business of a nursing home; and it follows that attending to the needs of nursing home patients, who are the employer's customers, is in the interest of the employer. Thus, the Board's blanket assertion that supervisory authority exercised in connection with patient care somehow is not in the interest of the employer seems unwarranted. Moreover, besides being inconsistent with *Yeshiva,* the Board's test conflicts with the statutory definition of supervisor, which includes the phrase "in the interest of the employer." The welfare of the patient, after all, is no less the object and concern of the employer than it is of the nurses. For purposes of the definition of supervisor in § 2(11), the act does not distinguish professional employees from other employees. The supervisor exclusion applies to "any individual" meeting the statutory requirements, not to "any nonprofessional employee." In addition, the Board relied on the same argument in *Yeshiva,* but to no avail. An examination of the professional's duties (or in this case the duties of the four nonprofessional nurses) to determine whether one or more of the twelve listed activities is performed in a manner that makes the employee a supervisor is, of course, part of the Board's routine and proper adjudicative function. In cases involving nurses, that inquiry no doubt could lead the Board in some cases to conclude that supervisory status has not been demonstrated. The Board has not sought to sustain its decision on that basis here, however. It has chosen instead to rely on an industry-wide interpretation of the phrase "in the interest of the employer" that contravenes Supreme Court precedents and has no relation to the ordinary meaning of that language. Hence, the Court of Appeals was correct in characterizing the Board's test as inconsistent with the statute and Supreme Court precedents.

BUSINESS CONSIDERATIONS What sorts of policies could Health Care have promulgated that would have helped it avoid this litigation? Justify your response.

ETHICAL CONSIDERATIONS Was Health Care's position that these nurses were supervisors unethical? What ethical concerns would classifying these nurses as supervisors raise?

43.2 ABF FREIGHT SYSTEM, INC. v. NATIONAL LABOR RELATIONS BOARD

510 U.S. 317 (1994)

FACTS Michael Manso worked as a casual dock worker at ABF Freight System, Inc.'s (ABF's) trucking terminal in Albuquerque, New Mexico, from the summer of 1987 to August 1989. He was fired three times. The first time, in June 1988, Manso was one of twelve employees discharged in a dispute over a contractual provision relating to "preferential casual" dock workers (that is, those workers "on call" who could be discharged if they failed to be available for

43.2 ABF FREIGHT SYSTEM, INC. v. NATIONAL LABOR RELATIONS BOARD *(cont.)* 510 U.S. 317 (1994)

work two times). The grievance Manso's union filed eventually secured his reinstatement; Manso also filed an unfair labor practice charge against ABF over the incident. Manso's return to work was short-lived. Three supervisors—warning him of likely retaliation from top management—alerted him, for example, to the perception that ABF was "gunning" for him and that "the higher echelon was after [him]." Within six weeks, ABF discharged Manso for a second time on pretextual grounds—ostensibly for failing to respond to a call to work made under a stringent verification procedure ABF recently had imposed on preferential casuals. Once again, a grievance panel ordered Manso reinstated. Manso's third discharge came less than two months later. On 11 August 1989, Manso arrived four minutes late for the 5 A.M. shift. At the time, ABF had no policy regarding lateness. After Manso was late to work, however, ABF decided to discharge preferential casuals—though not other employees—who were late twice without good cause. Six days later, Manso triggered the policy's first application when he arrived at work nearly an hour late for the same shift. Manso had telephoned at 5:25 A.M. to explain that he was having car trouble on the highway and repeated that excuse when he arrived. ABF conducted a prompt investigation; ascertained that he had been lying; and, pursuant to its new policy on lateness, fired him for tardiness. Manso thereupon filed a second unfair labor practice charge. In the hearing before the administrative law judge (ALJ), the ALJ credited most of Manso's testimony about the events surrounding his dismissals but expressly concluded that Manso had lied about the car trouble's making him late to work. Accordingly, although the ALJ decided that ABF illegally had discharged Manso owing to Manso's being a party to the earlier union grievance, the ALJ denied Manso relief for the third discharge based on the ALJ's finding that ABF had dismissed Manso for cause. The National Labor Relations Board (the Board) affirmed the ALJ's finding that Manso's second discharge was unlawful but reversed with respect to the third discharge. Acknowledging that Manso had lied to his employer and that ABF presumably could have discharged him for that dishonesty, the Board nevertheless emphasized that ABF in fact had not discharged him for lying and that the ALJ's conclusion to the contrary was "a plainly erroneous factual statement of [ABF]'s asserted reasons." Instead, Manso's lie had "established only that he did not have a legitimate excuse for the [17 August] lateness." The Board, focusing primarily on ABF's retroactive application of its lateness policy to include Manso's first time late to work, held that ABF had "seized upon" Manso's tardiness "as a pretext to discharge him again and for the same unlawful reasons it [had] discharged him on [19 June]." The Board therefore ordered ABF to reinstate Manso with back pay. The court of appeals enforced the Board's order.

ISSUE Would an employee forfeit the remedy of reinstatement and back pay when an ALJ had found that the employee purposely testified falsely during the administrative hearing?

HOLDING No. Given the Board's broad power to fashion remedial relief, it was not obligated to adopt a rigid rule that would foreclose relief in all comparable cases. Hence, the Board's remedial order in this case did not constitute an abuse of discretion.

REASONING The question for which the Supreme Court granted certiorari is a narrow one. Assuming that the Board correctly found that ABF had discharged Manso unlawfully in August 1989 and that the Board had not abused its discretion in ordering reinstatement even though Manso had given ABF a false reason for being late to work, only the ramifications of Manso's false testimony under oath in a formal proceeding before the ALJ concern the Court. The Board clearly might have decided that such misconduct had disqualified Manso from profiting from the proceeding, or it even might have adopted a flat rule precluding reinstatement when a former employee so testifies. As the case comes before the Court, however, the issue is not whether the Board might adopt such a rule, but whether it must do so. False testimony in a formal proceeding is intolerable; hence, courts must neither reward nor condone such a flagrant affront to the truth-seeking function of adversary proceedings. In any proceeding, whether judicial or administrative, deliberate falsehoods may well affect the dearest concerns of the parties before a tribunal and may put the fact finder and parties "to the disadvantage, hindrance, and delay of ultimately extracting the truth by cross examination, by extraneous investigation, or other collateral means." In short, perjury should be severely sanctioned in appropriate cases. ABF submitted that the false testimony of a former employee who had been the victim of an unfair labor practice always should preclude him from winning reinstatement with back pay. That contention, though, raises countervailing concerns. Most important is Congress's decision to delegate to the Board the primary responsibility for making remedial decisions that best effectuate the policies of the act when the Board has substantiated an unfair labor practice. The act expressly authorizes the Board "to take such affirmative action including reinstatement of employees with or without back pay, as will effectuate the policies of [the Act]." When Congress expressly delegates to an administrative agency the authority to make specific policy

43.2 ABF FREIGHT SYSTEM, INC. v. NATIONAL LABOR RELATIONS BOARD *(cont.)*

510 U.S. 317 (1994)

determinations, courts must give the agency's decision controlling weight unless it is "arbitrary, capricious, or manifestly contrary to the statute." Because this case involves that kind of express delegation, the Board's views merit the greatest deference. Courts must not enter the allowable area of the Board's discretion and must guard against the danger of sliding unconsciously from the narrow confines of law into the more spacious domain of policy. Notwithstanding the seriousness of Manso's ill-advised decision to repeat under oath his false excuse for tardiness, the Court cannot say that the Board's remedial order in this case constituted an abuse of its broad discretion or that the Board was obligated to adopt a rigid rule that would foreclose relief in all comparable cases. The Board's decision to rely on other civil and criminal remedies, rather than a categorical exception to the familiar remedy of reinstatement, is well within its broad discretion. The judgment of the court of appeals therefore is affirmed.

BUSINESS CONSIDERATIONS What should ABF have done differently in order to avoid this case and/or to minimize its problems? Would the institution of certain intra-firm policies have allowed it to fire a problematic employee?

ETHICAL CONSIDERATIONS Had the Court decided this case on ethical—rather than legal—grounds, would its decision have favored Manso or ABF? Why?

Further Issues. Although we cannot describe fully the pervasive regulation of labor embodied in the Wagner, Taft-Hartley, and Landrum-Griffin acts, we will highlight a few of the more important issues.

Questions invariably arise when employees select their bargaining representative. The Wagner Act sets forth the procedures that must be followed during this process. Briefly, these procedures include, upon a required showing of employee interest, the union's petitioning for an election that will lead to its recognition as the exclusive bargaining representative of the employees. The NLRB decides whether the election has been conducted validly and, if so, certifies the union as the exclusive bargaining agent.

The employer, who ordinarily resists the election/representation process, may attempt to "decertify" the union. The employer typically argues that the employees do not constitute an appropriate bargaining unit (that is, the employees have different duties, skills, or responsibilities) or that the union has engaged in unfair labor practices. The NLRB initially adjudicates such complaints, but the circuit courts of appeals can review final NLRB orders. In many cases, the employer prevails.

Not to be outdone, unions usually have alleged unfair labor practices by employers during the certification process. These affairs often become real donnybrooks of contradictory allegations because each side is fighting for the economic power signified by union representation or the lack of such representation.

The certification process may raise property issues as well, because organizers ordinarily wish to distribute union literature to employees in firms where they hope ultimately to hold a certification election. The right to engage in protected activity mandated by the Wagner Act thus clashes with the employer's property rights and the efficient conduct of its business. Board decisions generally invalidate the soliciting of employees and the distributing of literature during working hours and in working areas as long as such restrictions do not unduly interfere with the free exercise of employee rights guaranteed by the Wagner Act. As mentioned earlier, during this process, it is likewise permissible for the employer to state its views about unionism unless these statements convey a threat against pro-union employees or promise a benefit to anti-union employees. The *Lechmere, Inc.* v. *National Labor Relations Board* case involves the Court's resolution of these very issues.

43.3 LECHMERE, INC. v. NATIONAL LABOR RELATIONS BOARD 502 U.S. 527 (1992)

FACTS Lechmere, Inc. (Lechmere), owns and operates a retail store located in a shopping plaza in a large metropolitan area. Lechmere also is part owner of the plaza's parking lot, which is separated from a public highway by a 46-foot-wide grassy strip, almost all of which is public property. In a campaign to organize Lechmere employees, nonemployee union organizers placed handbills on the windshields of cars parked in the employees' part of the parking lot. After Lechmere had denied the organizers access to the lot, they distributed handbills and picketed from the grassy strip. In addition, they were able to contact directly 20 percent of the employees. The union, filing an unfair labor practice charge with the National Labor Relations Board (the Board), alleged that Lechmere, by barring the organizers from its property, had violated the NLRA. An administrative law judge (ALJ), ruling in the union's favor, recommended that the Board order Lechmere to cease and desist from barring the organizers from the parking lot. The Board affirmed, and the court of appeals enforced the Board's order. The Supreme Court granted Lechmere's petition for certiorari.

ISSUE Did Lechmere, by barring nonemployee union organizers from its property, commit an unfair labor practice?

HOLDING No. By its plain terms, the NLRA confers rights only on employees, not on unions or their nonemployee organizers. Thus, as a rule, an employer cannot be compelled to allow nonemployee organizers onto his or her property. Only when reasonable access to employees is infeasible does it become appropriate to balance § 7 and private property rights. Here, the facts did not warrant such a balancing of rights.

REASONING Section 7 of the NLRA in relevant part provides that "employees shall have the right to self-organization, to form, join, or assist labor organizations." Section 8(a)(1) of the act, in turn, makes it an unfair labor practice for an employer "to interfere with, restrain, or coerce employees in the exercise of rights guaranteed in [§ 7]." By its plain terms, then, the NLRA confers rights only on employees, not on unions or their nonemployee organizers. In cases involving employee activities, the Board can balance the conflicting interests of employees to receive information concerning self-organization on the company's property from fellow employees during nonworking time with the employer's right to control the use of its property. Cases involving nonemployee activities, however, do not authorize the Board to engage in that same balancing. By reversing the Board's interpretation of the statute for failing to distinguish between the organizing activities of employees and nonemployees, the Court interpreted § 7 as speaking to the issue of nonemployee access to an employer's property. Section 7 simply does not protect nonemployee union organizers except in the rare case where "the inaccessibility of employees makes ineffective the reasonable attempts by nonemployees to communicate with them through the usual channels." It is only where such access is infeasible (for example, in logging camps or mountain resort hotels) that it becomes necessary to balance the employees and employers' rights. The Board's conclusion in this case that the union had no reasonable means short of trespass to make Lechmere's employees aware of its organizational efforts misapprehends the limited scope of this inaccessibility exception. The employees in this case are presumptively not "beyond the reach" of the union's message. Indeed, the union's success in contacting a substantial percentage of them directly, via mailings, phone calls, and home visits, suggests their accessibility. Such direct contact, of course, is not a necessary element of "reasonably effective" communication; signs or advertising also may suffice. Access to employees, not success in winning them over, is the critical issue—although success, or lack thereof, may be relevant in determining whether reasonable access exists. Because the union in this case had failed to establish the existence of any "unique obstacles" that had frustrated access to Lechmere's employees, the Board erred in concluding that Lechmere, by barring the nonemployee organizers from its property, had committed an unfair labor practice.

43.3 LECHMERE, INC. v. NATIONAL LABOR RELATIONS BOARD *(cont.)* 502 U.S. 527 (1992)

BUSINESS CONSIDERATIONS If you had been the CEO of Lechmere, would you have barred the organizers' access to Lechmere's property? Put differently, did the company's adversarial attitude help—or hurt—the union's organizing efforts?

ETHICAL CONSIDERATIONS Again, assuming you were the CEO and that you were deciding on ethical grounds how to handle access to company property in these circumstances, would your answer differ? Why or why not?

43.1

MANAGEMENT

UNIONS

CIT has been wildly successfull, and the firm has increased its workforce significantly. One of the newly hired workers, a strong union advocate, has started discussing the possibility of forming a union at CIT. Several of the employees, reasoning that a strong bargaining representative will help them, seem to favor forming a union. Others, including a number of the original employees, oppose the formation of a union. They believe that the Kochanowskis have treated the workers fairly and that a union will set up an "us versus them" attitude that will not be in the long-term interests of the firm or the employees. Tom is concerned that this discussion is dividing the loyalty of the workers and is harmful to the firm. He asks you what he can legally do to prevent the formation of a union and what he must legally do if the employees decide to proceed. What will you tell him?

BUSINESS CONSIDERATIONS What should a business do if it learns that its employees are considering petitioning the NLRB for a union-certification election? Should the business take steps to discourage the formation of a union, or should the business wait until after the vote before choosing a course of conduct?

ETHICAL CONSIDERATIONS Is it ethical for a business to take affirmative steps to thwart union-organizing activities if the management of the firm honestly believes that the introduction of a union will have harmful long-term effects on the business?

Once the bargaining representative has been empowered, the Wagner Act requires *good faith bargaining* by both the employer and the union. This, of course, is a nebulous term; in essence, it mandates both sides' meeting and discussing certain issues with as much objectivity as possible. The duty to bargain in good faith does not absolutely presume agreement between the parties. Under this duty, an employer cannot bypass the union to deal directly with the employees.

The Wagner Act requires good faith bargaining over "wages, hours, and other terms and conditions of employment." Basically, then, the duty to bargain covers only those topics that have a direct impact on the employees' job security. Decisions that are not essentially related to conditions of employment but rather are managerial decisions "which lie at the core of entrepreneurial control"[2] fail to suffice as mandatory bargaining subjects. Pay differentials for different shifts, piecework and incentive plans, transfers, fringe benefits, and severance pay are mandatory subjects. Courts have had more trouble classifying bonuses and meals provided by the employer. Managerial decisions to terminate the company's business or to shut down a plant are ordinarily *permissive*, or nonmandatory, subjects. An employer, however, might be forced to bargain about the *effects* of such decisions, such as **severance pay**, which impinge on the conditions of employment.

Although the labor laws view collective bargaining as the parties' meeting, asserting their positions, stating their objections to the other party's position, and disclosing the information necessary for each side to arrive at an informed decision, both sides permissibly can use economic weapons outside the bargaining room. Hence, employee strikes or work stoppages and employer **lockouts** do not in themselves violate the duty to bargain in good faith. An employer's unilateral granting of a wage increase without notice to the union during the process of negotiations does constitute bad faith bargaining, however. On the other hand, such unilateral changes made after bargaining has reached an impasse are legal.

The NLRB can require either side who has refused, directly or indirectly, to bargain in good faith to begin bargaining and to cease and desist from any unfair labor practice that has accompanied the bad faith bargaining. The board also can use such powers for ending violations of any of the employer or union unfair labor practices that have occurred outside the bargaining context.

NLRB orders are not self-enforcing, however; they become law only when imposed by a federal circuit court of appeals. Because litigation is time consuming, these limitations on the NLRB's enforcement powers sometimes make policing the actions of maverick employers or unions difficult. Board hearings and resultant orders, if resisted, bring on court scrutiny. If the court affirms the NLRB order, the court issues an injunction. In the meantime, however, the allegedly unfair labor practices may have continued and may have successfully stifled the employer or employee interests at issue.

Severance pay
Wages paid upon the termination of one's job.

Lockouts
Plant closings or other refusals by employers to furnish work to employees during labor disputes.

State Law

The supremacy clause of the Constitution empowers Congress to pass laws, such as the federal labor laws, that will preempt the states' regulation of labor. Supreme Court decisions construing the labor laws (which are silent on the issue of preemption) have held that federal preemption powers are broad. Because of the NLRB's expertise and a desire for uniformity of case results, federal laws ordinarily will oust the states' jurisdiction in activities that arguably are protected or prohibited by federal labor statutes.

Matters that only peripherally affect the federal statutory scheme or matters that are of deep local concern may constitute legitimate state interests that state law (and courts) therefore may regulate. The law in this area is unsettled and the cases controversial; generally, however, state courts can adjudicate lawsuits involving damages from violence or other criminal or tortious activity, retaliatory discharges, and those causes of action covering all employers and employees exempted under federal statutes.

EMPLOYMENT

Fair Employment Practices Laws

In addition to the extensive federal and state regulation of labor, several federal and state statutes designed to ensure equal employment opportunity for persons historically foreclosed from the workplace have come into existence since 1964.

Civil Rights Act of 1964. Foremost among these laws is the Civil Rights Act of 1964. Title VII of that statute prohibits discrimination in employment on the basis of race, color, religion, sex, or national origin. Under Title VII, an employer cannot lawfully make decisions to hire; discharge; compensate; or establish the terms, conditions, or privileges of employment for any employee based on the categories just enumerated.

In addition, an employer cannot segregate, limit, or classify employees or applicants for employment in discriminatory ways. Moreover, a union cannot discriminate against or refuse to refer for employment or apprenticeship programs any individual because of race, color, religion, sex, or national origin. And employment agencies cannot discriminate with respect to referrals for jobs or use advertisements indicating a discriminatory preference or limitation.

Furthermore, none of the three groups—employers, unions, or employment agencies—can discriminate against any individual because the individual has opposed unlawful employment practices. An employer that relegates blacks to manual labor jobs or an employment agency or labor organization that refers only white males for executive jobs or only women for nursing or secretarial jobs is in violation of Title VII.

Title VII's coverage, in general, extends to employers in interstate commerce that have on their weekly payrolls at least 15 full- or part-time employees[3] for at least 20 weeks per year, to any national or international labor organizations that consist of at least 15 members or that operate a hiring hall, and to employment agencies that regularly procure employees for employers or work opportunities for potential employees. Because of amendments added in 1972, Title VII currently covers most federal, state, and local governmental and educational employees as well.

Title VII authorized the creation of the Equal Employment Opportunity Commission (EEOC), a bipartisan, five-member group appointed by the president. The EEOC presently serves as the enforcement agency for Title VII, the Pregnancy Discrimination Act of 1978, the Equal Pay Act of 1963, the Age Discrimination in Employment Act of 1967, the Rehabilitation Act of 1973, the Americans with Disabilities Act of 1990, the Civil Rights Act of 1991, and other statutes. The EEOC also can bring lawsuits relating to broad patterns and practices of discrimination. Complaints by individual grievants or charges filed by the EEOC or state fair employment or human rights commissions may trigger the EEOC's jurisdiction.

The jurisdictional requirements for successful suits under Title VII are complex. In brief, a charge must be filed within 180 days or 300 days after the alleged discrimination has occurred, the latter time period being applicable in *deferral* states (those that have their own fair employment practices commissions). In deferral states, the local commission has exclusive jurisdiction for 60 days, at which point the EEOC has concurrent jurisdiction over the charge.

If the EEOC has retained jurisdiction for at least 180 days and has decided no reasonable cause exists to file an action on behalf of the grievant, the EEOC may issue a right-to-sue letter to the grievant. Within 90 days of receiving the right-to-sue letter, the grievant must file suit in the appropriate district court or, generally speaking, lose the right to sue.

Practically, however, the process almost never works this quickly (the EEOC's case backlog is almost legendary). Indeed, five to six years may elapse before resolution of the allegations occurs. Moreover, because the process is oriented to grievants and because judges do not expect laypersons to write complaints that resemble legal briefs, courts give grievants considerable leeway in describing and recognizing when discrimination arguably has happened. In addition, the conciliation orientation of the process makes it possible to clear up the grievance before litigation becomes necessary. Still, remember that procedural pitfalls dot this entire area of the law.

Substantive pitfalls also may snare the unaware employer, since many employment practices that seem neutral actually may lead to discrimination. For instance, in the early 1970s, several cases involving testing procedures and mandatory high school diplomas arose. These cases show that selection criteria that seem outwardly neutral may foreclose blacks and other protected persons from jobs merely because statistically fewer blacks than whites are graduated from high school. Selection criteria that require a certain score on an aptitude test or a high school diploma may "operate as 'built-in' headwinds for minority groups and [may be] unrelated to measuring job capability. . . . [Title VII] proscribes not only overt discrimination but also practices that are fair in form, but discriminatory in operation. The touchstone is business necessity. If an employment practice which operates to exclude [minorities] cannot be shown to be related to job performance, the practice is prohibited."[4]

Any job requirement that prevents a disproportionate number of blacks or other minorities from securing employment or promotion has a *disparate impact* (that is, an unequal effect) on minorities and may be illegal. The employer then has the burden of proving that the requirement is job-related. The EEOC has issued guidelines for selecting employees, but these guidelines do not have the force of law. Nonetheless, if courts so wish, they may give these EEOC guidelines considerable deference.

Besides facing liability stemming from disparate impact, employers also may be liable for the *disparate treatment* of their employees. Such cases ordinarily arise when an employer allows whites or males to break rules without punishment but institutes penalties if blacks or women break the same rules. A 1976 case, *McDonald* v. *Santa Fe Trail Transportation Co.,* also held that whites can sue for racial discrimination when they receive disparate treatment.[5] In this case, the employer had accused two whites and one black of misappropriating a shipment of antifreeze. The company fired both white employees but retained the black worker. The Supreme Court concluded that Title VII prohibits all forms of racial discrimination, including **reverse discrimination** of this type.

Reverse discrimination
Claims by whites that they have been subjected to adverse employment decisions because of their race and the application of employment discrimination statutes designed to protect minorities.

The allegations of reverse discrimination that spring from another source—affirmative action plans—pose some of the most controversial issues in the area of fair employment practices involving race. Title VII places on the employer the duty to maintain a racially balanced workforce. Yet if the employer takes affirmative steps—slotting certain apprenticeship openings for blacks, for example—to bring about such racial balance, such actions may adversely affect the white incumbents who wish to take part in these training programs. Two diametrically opposed policies clash here: the interests of the minority candidate who in the past has been disadvantaged because of race and of the white incumbent worker who has taken no part in this discrimination but who now, because the employer is seeking to bring about equality of opportunity for black workers, must lose employment opportunities.

In these situations, whites occasionally have brought suits alleging reverse discrimination. A famous 1978 case, *Regents of the University of California* v. *Bakke,* involved a white student who alleged that the University of California at Davis, by rejecting his application for medical school and admitting 16 minority students with credentials inferior to his, had discriminated against him on the basis of his race, in violation of the Fourteenth Amendment.[6] The Supreme Court, in a very complex opinion, held that university quota systems that absolutely prefer minority candidates (the university had reserved 16 spots out of 100 for minorities) are illegal but that a university in its admissions process may take race into account.

The issue of reverse discrimination becomes even thornier in the private sector, where employers may face charges by the EEOC if they do not aggressively engage in affirmative action and may face suits by white workers alleging reverse discrimination if they do.

In *United Steelworkers of America* v. *Weber,* the Supreme Court addressed this particular issue.[7] In this case, the United Steelworkers of America and Kaiser Aluminum & Chemical Corporation (Kaiser) had entered into a master collective-bargaining agreement covering 15 Kaiser plants. The agreement included an affirmative action plan aimed at eliminating racial imbalances in Kaiser's workforce. This plan reserved for black employees 50 percent of the openings in Kaiser training programs until Kaiser's percentage of skilled black craftworkers equaled the percentage of blacks in the local labor force. Brian Weber, a white worker who had accrued more seniority than some of the black workers selected for the training program, was rejected as a trainee. Weber sued, alleging that Kaiser's affirmative action plan constituted reverse discrimination against white workers and, because of Kaiser's use of race in the selection of apprentices for training programs, violated Title VII's ban on discrimination. The Supreme Court held that a private, voluntary, race-conscious affirmative action plan, such as at issue here, did not violate Title VII's prohibition against racial discrimination. In the Court's view, one of the purposes of Title VII involves opening up job opportunities traditionally closed to blacks; thus, Kaiser's self-evaluation efforts to eliminate its racially imbalanced workforce were appropriate. Moreover, because the Kaiser plan opened up opportunities for blacks without unnecessarily trammeling the interests of white workers, its affirmative action plan was legal. But the Supreme Court's holding in *Adarand Constructors, Inc.* v. *Pena,* a public sector case decided on constitutional grounds (and discussed in Chapter 39), may spawn court challenges to such race-conscious affirmative action plans.[8] Future legal developments therefore warrant your attention.

Bona fide occupational qualification
A defense to charges of discrimination based on religion, sex, or national origin but not to charges of racial discrimination; a situation in which one of these categories is essential to the performance of the job.

MANAGEMENT

43.2

HIRING REQUIREMENTS

From its inception, CIT has had a policy of refusing to hire any nonfamily applicants for full-time employment who are not at least high school graduates. Tom and Anna have included this requirement in the firm's hiring manual because they believe that any high-tech firm—and CIT is high-tech—needs a well-educated workforce if it is to succeed. John recently has noticed this provision in the personnel manual, and he is concerned that this requirement makes CIT vulnerable to lawsuits claiming that the firm is guilty of racial discrimination in its hiring practices. He asks you what he should do in this situation. What advice will you give him? Why?

BUSINESS CONSIDERATIONS Should a business have a policy for any situation in which it decides to change the requirements an applicant must meet in order to be considered for a position? What factors should be included in any such policy? Would a firm's changing its job descriptions or hiring qualifications lead to possible legal vulnerabilities?

ETHICAL CONSIDERATIONS Would it be ethical for a business to establish higher job requirements for a given position than are absolutely necessary to perform the described job? What ethical concerns would such a job description raise? What should a company do to act ethically and legally in this situation?

Besides racial discrimination, Title VII also prohibits religious discrimination. Sincere religious beliefs (or the lack thereof) are protected under Title VII. Typically, cases arise when a job shift necessitates work on the day the employee considers his or her Sabbath. If a person's religion forbids work on Fridays after sundown, for instance, Title VII mandates that the employer make a "reasonable accommodation" to the employee's beliefs unless to do so would pose an "undue hardship" on the conduct of the business.

The 1977 case, *Trans World Airlines, Inc.* v. *Hardison,* however, by holding that an employer does not have to undertake an accommodation that requires more than a minimal expense or that violates a collective-bargaining agreement, has severely undercut the guarantees represented by Title VII.[9] Furthermore, under other provisions of Title VII, educational institutions may make religion a **bona fide occupational qualification** (BFOQ). The University of Notre Dame, for example, can hire only Roman Catholic professors if it so wishes.

Bona fide occupational qualifications also may constitute a limited defense to charges of sex discrimination. For example, it is not a violation of Title VII for a movie director to cast only women in women's roles. Issues implicating the ban on sex discrimination include stereotypes about the ability to perform a job (such as an employer who thinks only men can be telephone "linemen" and only women can be telephone operators), height/weight requirements that are not job-related (women usually are smaller than men), and so-called sex-plus cases. In the last, the employer adds a selection criterion for women that is not added for men (such as when women with pre-school-aged children are not hired but men who have such children are).

One unanswered question under Title VII is whether the theory of comparable worth, which allows employees as part of their proof of sex-based wage discrimination to compare their wages to those of other workers who perform dissimilar jobs of equal value (or intrinsic worth) to the employer, ultimately will enjoy widespread judicial and legislative approval. Legal developments in this area bear watching.

By imposing on employers liability for sexual advances or requests for sexual favors made by the employer's agents and supervisory employees and for sexual misconduct that creates an intimidating, hostile, or offensive working environment for women, recent Title VII cases have protected women from sexual harassment in the workplace. In 1994, a secretary in one of the largest law firms in the country won a $3.5 million judgment against the firm and the partner who allegedly had harassed numerous women over a 14-year period. Although most cases have involved harassment of women by men, men who face harassment from women supervisors have standing to sue under Title VII. Employers thus face potentially large recoveries if they fail to take corrective actions to end sexual harassment once they know, or should have known, that it had occurred. Wise employers should establish and then vigorously enforce anti–sexual harassment policies.

The Pregnancy Discrimination Act of 1978, passed by Congress as an amendment to Title VII, dictates that an employer treat pregnancy in the same fashion as any other disability. To do otherwise constitutes actionable sex discrimination.

Harris v. *Forklift Systems, Inc.* and *International Union, UAW* v. *Johnson Controls, Inc.* illustrate the Court's view of two significant issues under Title VII's proscription of discrimination based on sex.

43.3

HARASSMENT POLICY

CIT employs several drivers, who operate company trucks delivering Call-Image videophones to customers. Each driver is assigned a particular truck. Sam, one of the drivers, took a personal leave day. Another driver was assigned the truck that Sam normally drives. At the end of the day, the other driver informed Tom that Sam had taped several "girlie" pictures to the dashboard of the delivery truck and that the driver found the pictures sexist and insulting. Tom apologized to the driver and promised to look into the situation. Tom later sought your advice as to what liability CIT could face. What would you tell him?

BUSINESS CONSIDERATIONS Should a business establish a strong policy addressing discrimination and harassment before any complaints arise, or should the business wait until there is a problem and then address that particular problem? If the business decides to become proactive, what sorts of conduct should its policy cover?

ETHICAL CONSIDERATIONS Is it ethical for a business to prohibit the free speech of some of its employees if other employees find such speech offensive? How can an employer protect the freedoms and rights of each employee and simultaneously protect all employees from discrimination and harassment?

MANAGEMENT

43.4 HARRIS v. FORKLIFT SYSTEMS, INC. 510 U.S. 17 (1993)

FACTS Teresa Harris worked as a manager at Forklift Systems, Inc. (Forklift), an equipment rental company, from April 1985 until October 1987. Charles Hardy was Forklift's president. Throughout Harris's time at Forklift, Hardy frequently insulted her because of her gender and often made her the target of unwanted sexual innuendos. Hardy told Harris on several occasions, in the presence of other employees, "You're a woman, what do you know" and "We need a man as the rental manager"; at least once, he told her she was "a dumb a__ woman." Again, in front of others, he suggested that the two of them "go to the Holiday Inn to negotiate [Harris's] raise." Hardy occasionally asked Harris and other female employees to retrieve coins from his front pants pocket. He also threw objects on the ground in front of Harris and other women and asked them to pick up the objects. In addition, he made sexual innuendos about Harris and other women's clothing. In mid-August 1987, Harris complained to Hardy about his conduct. Hardy, saying he was surprised that Harris was offended, claimed he was only joking and apologized. He also promised he would stop; and based on this assurance, Harris stayed on the job. But in early September, Hardy began anew. While Harris was arranging a deal with one of Forklift's customers, he asked her, again in front of other employees, "What did you do, promise the guy . . . some [sex] Saturday night?" On 1 October, Harris collected her paycheck and quit. Claiming that Hardy's conduct had created an abusive work environment for her because of her gender, Harris subsequently sued Forklift. The U.S. District Court for the Middle District of Tennessee found this to be "a close case" but held that Hardy's conduct had not created an abusive environment. The court found that some of Hardy's comments "offended [Harris], and would offend the reasonable woman," but that they were not:

> *so severe as to be expected to seriously affect [Harris's] psychological well-being. A reasonable woman manager under like circumstances would have been offended by Hardy, but his conduct would not have risen to the level of interfering with that person's work performance. Neither [did the court] believe that [Harris] was subjectively so offended that she suffered injury. . . . Although Hardy may at times have genuinely offended [Harris], [the court did] not believe that he created a working environment so poisoned as to be intimidating or abusive to [Harris].*

In focusing on the employee's psychological well-being, the district court was following Sixth Circuit precedents. In a brief, unpublished decision, the U.S. Court of Appeals for the Sixth Circuit affirmed.

ISSUE To be actionable as "abusive work environment" sexual harassment, must the defendant's conduct seriously affect the plaintiff's psychological well-being or lead the plaintiff to suffer injury?

HOLDING No. Although Title VII certainly bars conduct that would seriously affect a reasonable person's psychological well-being, the statute is not limited to such conduct. So long as the environment would reasonably be perceived, and is perceived, as hostile or abusive, it need not also be psychologically injurious.

REASONING Title VII of the Civil Rights Act of 1964 makes it "an unlawful employment practice for an employer . . . to discriminate against any individual with respect to his [or her] compensation, terms, conditions, or privileges of employment, because of such individual's race, color, religion, sex, or national origin." As the Supreme Court made clear in *Meritor Savings Bank* v. *Vinson,* 477 U.S. 57, 64 (1986), this language "is not limited to 'economic' or 'tangible' discrimination. The phrase 'terms, conditions, or privileges of employment' evinces a congressional intent to strike at the entire spectrum of disparate treatment of men and women in employment," which includes requiring people to work in a discriminatorily hostile or abusive environment. When the workplace is permeated with discriminatory intimidation, ridicule, and insult "sufficiently severe and pervasive to alter the conditions of the victim's employment and create an abusive working environment," a violation of Title VII has occurred. This standard, reaffirmed in this case, takes a middle path between making actionable any conduct that is merely offensive and requiring the conduct to cause tangible psychological injury. Conduct that is not severe or pervasive enough to create an objectively hostile or abusive work environment—an environment that a reasonable person would find hostile or abusive—is beyond Title VII's purview. Likewise, if the victim fails to objectively perceive the environment to be abusive, the conduct has not actually altered the conditions of the victim's employment; and there is an absence of a Title VII violation. But Title VII comes into play before the harassing conduct leads to a nervous breakdown. A discriminatorily abusive work environment, even one that does not seriously affect employees' psychological well-being, can and often will detract from employees' job performance, discourage employees from remaining on the job, or keep them from advancing in their careers. Moreover, even without regard to these tangible effects, the very fact that the discriminatory conduct was so severe or pervasive that it created a work environment abusive to employees because of their race, gender, religion, or national origin offends Title VII's broad rule of workplace equality. Therefore, in relying on whether the conduct "seriously affect[ed] plaintiff's psychological well-being" or led her to "suffe[r] injury," the district court erred. Such an inquiry may needlessly focus the fact finder's attention on concrete psychological harm, an element Title VII does not require. Certainly Title VII bars conduct that would seriously affect a reasonable person's psychological well-being, but the statute is not limited to such conduct. This is not, and by its nature cannot be, a mathematically precise test. The Court need not answer today all the potential questions it raises nor specifically address the EEOC's new regulations on this subject. Only by looking at all the circumstances can the trier of fact deter-

43.4 HARRIS v. FORKLIFT SYSTEMS, INC. *(cont.)* 510 U.S. 17 (1993)

mine whether an environment is "hostile" or "abusive." These circumstances may include the frequency of the discriminatory conduct; its severity; whether it is physically threatening or humiliating, or a mere offensive utterance; and whether it unreasonably interferes with an employee's psychological well-being. The effect on the employee's well-being, of course, is relevant to determining whether the plaintiff actually found the environment abusive. But while psychological harm, like any other relevant factor, may be taken into account, no single factor is required. The district court's application of incorrect standards may well have influenced its ultimate conclusion, especially given that the court found this to be a "close case." The judgment of the court of appeals therefore is reversed and the case remanded for further proceedings consistent with this opinion.

BUSINESS CONSIDERATIONS The person Harris accused of sexual harassment was the president of the company. Did this fact make it more difficult for the firm to avoid liability under Title VII? What steps could the firm have taken so as to avoid this lawsuit? What should the firm do in the future?

ETHICAL CONSIDERATIONS Argue for or against the following proposition: A company's tolerating a work environment rife with sexual innuendos and insults is just as unethical as a company's tolerating a work environment rife with racial or ethnic slurs.

43.5 INTERNATIONAL UNION, UAW v. JOHNSON CONTROLS, INC. 499 U.S. 187 (1991)

FACTS A primary ingredient in Johnson Control's, Inc.'s (Johnson Controls's) battery-manufacturing process is lead, occupational exposure to which entails health risks, including the risk of harm to a fetus carried by a female employee. After eight of its employees had become pregnant while maintaining blood lead levels exceeding that noted by the Occupational Safety and Health Administration (OSHA) as critical for a worker planning to have a family, Johnson Controls announced a policy barring all women, except those whose infertility could be medically documented, from jobs involving actual or potential lead exposure exceeding the OSHA standard. The International Union UAW (the UAW), a group including employees affected by the company's fetal-protection policy, filed a class action in the district court and claimed that the policy constituted sex discrimination violative of Title VII of the Civil Rights Act of 1964. The district court granted summary judgment for Johnson Controls, and the court of appeals affirmed. The latter court held that the proper standard for evaluating the policy was the business necessity inquiry applied by other circuits; that Johnson Controls was entitled to summary judgment because the UAW had failed to satisfy its burden of persuasion as to each of the elements of the business necessity defense under the relevant Supreme Court precedents; and that even if the proper evaluation standard consisted of bona fide occupational qualification (BFOQ) analysis, Johnson Controls still would deserve summary judgment because its fetal-protection policy was reasonably necessary to further the industrial safety concern that represents the essence of the firm's business.

ISSUE Did Johnson Controls's sex-specific fetal-protection policy, in which the company excluded fertile female employees from certain jobs because of its concern for the health of the fetuses the women might conceive, violate Title VII's ban on sex discrimination?

HOLDING Yes. By excluding women with childbearing capacity from lead-exposed jobs, Johnson Controls's policy created a facial classification based on gender and explicitly discriminated against women on the basis of their sex under Title VII. Moreover, in using the words "capable of bearing children" as the criterion for exclusion, the policy explicitly classified on the basis of potential for pregnancy, which classification must be regarded, under the Pregnancy Discrimination Act, in the same light as explicit sex discrimination.

REASONING The bias in Johnson Controls's policy is obvious. The company gives fertile men, but not fertile women, a choice as to whether they wish to risk their

43.5 INTERNATIONAL UNION, UAW v. JOHNSON CONTROLS, INC. *(cont.)* 499 U.S. 187 (1991)

reproductive health for a particular job. Johnson Controls's fetal-protection policy therefore explicitly discriminates against women on the basis of their sex. The policy excludes women with childbearing capacity from lead-exposed jobs and so creates a facial classification based on gender. Nevertheless, the court of appeals assumed, as did the two appellate courts that already had confronted the issue, that sex-specific fetal-protection policies do not involve facial discrimination. These courts analyzed the policies as though they were facially neutral and had only a discriminatory effect on the employment opportunities of women. Consequently, the courts looked to see if each employer in question had established the business necessity justification for its policy. The business necessity standard is more lenient for the employer than the statutory BFOQ defense. The courts assumed that because the asserted reason for the sex-based exclusion (protecting women's unconceived offspring) ostensibly was benign, the policy was not sex-based discrimination. That assumption, however, was incorrect. First, Johnson Controls's policy classifies on the basis of gender and childbearing capacity rather than fertility alone. The company does not seek to protect the unconceived children of all its employees, male or female. Johnson Controls's policy therefore is facially discriminatory because it requires only a female employee to produce proof that she is not capable of reproducing. The Pregnancy Discrimination Act of 1978 (PDA), in which Congress explicitly provided that, for purposes of Title VII, discrimination "on the basis of sex" includes discrimination "because of or on the basis of pregnancy, childbirth, or related medical conditions" also bolsters this conclusion. According to other Supreme Court precedents, the PDA now has made clear that, for all Title VII purposes, discrimination based on a woman's pregnancy is, on its face, discrimination because of her sex. Its use of the words "capable of bearing children" illustrates that Johnson Controls explicitly classified on the basis of potential for pregnancy. Under the PDA, such a classification must be regarded, for Title VII purposes, in the same light as explicit sex discrimination. Moreover, the beneficence of an employer's purpose does not undermine the conclusion that an explicit, gender-based policy is sex discrimination under § 703(a) and thus may be defended only as a BFOQ. Under § 703(e)(1) of Title VII, an employer may discriminate on the basis of "religion, sex, or national origin in those certain instances where religion, sex, or national origin is a bona fide occupational qualification [BFOQ] reasonably necessary to the normal operation of that particular business or enterprise." Did Johnson Controls's fetal-protection policy represent one of those "certain instances" that come within the BFOQ exception? The BFOQ defense is written narrowly, and this Court has read it narrowly. The statute thus limits the situations in which discrimination is permissible to "certain instances" in which sex discrimination is "reasonably necessary" to the "normal operation" of the "particular" business. This language indicates that these objective, verifiable requirements must concern job-related skills and aptitudes. And while Johnson Controls argues that its fetal-protection policy falls within the so-called third-party safety exception to the BFOQ, Supreme Court cases have stressed that discrimination on the basis of sex because of safety concerns is allowed only in narrow circumstances. In the present case, the unconceived fetuses of Johnson Controls's female employees, however, are neither customers nor third parties whose safety is essential to the business of battery manufacturing. No one can disregard the possibility of injury to future children. The BFOQ, however, is not so broad that it transforms this deep social concern into an essential aspect of battery making. Supreme Court holdings make clear that the safety exception is limited to instances in which sex or pregnancy actually interferes with the employee's ability to perform the job. Johnson Controls suggests, however, that the Court expand the exception to allow fetal-protection policies that mandate particular standards for pregnant or fertile women. But such an expansion contradicts not only the language of the BFOQ and the narrowness of its exception but the plain language and history of the PDA. With the PDA, Congress has made clear that the decision to become pregnant or to work while being either pregnant or capable of becoming pregnant is reserved for each individual woman to make for herself. Thus, the employer must direct its concerns about a woman's ability to perform her job safely and efficiently to these aspects of the woman's job-related activities that fall within the "essence" of the particular business. Johnson Controls's professed moral and ethical concerns about the welfare of the next generation do not suffice to establish a BFOQ of female sterility. Decisions about the welfare of future children must be left to the parents who conceive, bear, support, and raise them rather than to the employers who hire those parents. Although Johnson Controls has attempted to exclude women because of their reproductive capacity, Title VII and the PDA simply do not allow a woman's dismissal because of her failure to submit to sterilization. It is no more appropriate for the courts than it is for individual employers to decide whether a woman's reproductive role is more important to herself and her family than her economic role. Congress has left this choice to the woman as hers to make. Therefore, the judgment of the court of appeals is reversed, and the case is remanded for further proceedings consistent with this opinion.

43.5 INTERNATIONAL UNION, UAW v. JOHNSON CONTROLS, INC. *(cont.)* **499 U.S. 187 (1991)**

BUSINESS CONSIDERATIONS Should Johnson Controls fear the possible tort liability that may result from fertile female employees' giving birth to children who have birth defects? Did the Court, in its discussion of the BFOQ defense, give too little attention to this concern on Johnson Controls's part?

ETHICAL CONSIDERATIONS The Court seemed to pay scant attention to the ethical underpinnings of Johnson Controls's fetal protection policy. Did you agree with the Court's disposition of these ethical considerations? Why or why not?

Title VII's ban on national origin discrimination similarly prevents harassment in the form of ethnic slurs based on the country in which one was born or the country from which one's ancestors came. Repeated ethnic jokes and other derogatory statements directed at one's ethnic origins in a given case may constitute national origin discrimination.

National origin discrimination often takes the form of "covert discrimination." To illustrate, height/weight requirements may foreclose Spanish-surnamed Americans from employment opportunities, as may language difficulties or accents. If an employer fails to hire a worker on the basis of such criteria, the employer must prove that the criteria are job-related.

Narrow BFOQs may exist in national origin cases. It is legal to hire a French person to be a French chef, for example. It also is legal to refuse to hire non-American citizens (because the prohibition against national origin discrimination in Title VII does not include citizenship)[10] unless the discrimination in favor of citizens has the purpose or effect of discrimination on the basis of national origin. The protected categories under Title VII do not include alienage in and of itself. Likewise, it is not a violation of Title VII for an employer to refuse to hire persons who are unable to obtain security clearances because they have relatives in countries that are on unfriendly terms with the United States.

Immigration Reform and Control Act of 1986. On the other hand, the Immigration Reform and Control Act of 1986, although principally aimed at stemming the flow of illegal aliens into the United States, out of fairness also bans immigration-related discrimination based on national origin or citizenship status. This act therefore prohibits an employer's turning away job applicants because they appear to be aliens or noncitizens. Besides being narrower in scope than Title VII (the 1986 act covers only hiring, recruitment of workers for a fee, and discharges), Title VII also preempts this act whenever Title VII covers the conduct in question. The 1986 act's legislative history makes it clear that Congress did not intend this act to expand the rights granted under Title VII.

Equal Pay Act of 1963. In addition to Title VII, several other federal statutes protect various classes of persons. The Equal Pay Act of 1963 prohibits discrimination in wages on the basis of sex. Therefore, men and women performing work in the same establishment under similar working conditions must receive the same rate of pay if the work requires equal skill, equal effort, and equal responsibility. Different wages may be paid if the employer bases the differential on seniority, merit, piecework, or any factor other than sex (for example, participation in training programs).

The Age Discrimination in Employment Act of 1967. The Age Discrimination in Employment Act of 1967 (the ADEA), in general, protects workers from age 40 to age 70 from adverse employment decisions based on age. BFOQs based on safety or human and economic risks—age 55 retirement for police officers, for instance—may be upheld, as may differentiation in age based on a bona fide seniority system and discharges or disciplinary actions undertaken for good cause. The Supreme Court recently held that a plaintiff who alleges discrimination under the ADEA does not have to show, as part of his or her prima facie case, that the employer replaced the plaintiff with a worker under age 40 (*O'Connor* v. *Consolidated Coin Caterers Corporation,* 116 S.Ct. 1307 [1996]). According to the Court, the fact that one person in the protected class has lost out to another person in the protected class is irrelevant, so long as the plaintiff can show that he or she has lost out because of his or her *age.*

The Rehabilitation Act of 1973. The Rehabilitation Act of 1973 directs federal contractors to take affirmative action with respect to "otherwise qualified" handicapped individuals. A handicapped individual includes any person who "has a physical or mental impairment which substantially limits one or more of such person's major life functions, has a record of such impairment, or is regarded as having such an impairment." Federal contractors must make "reasonable accommodation" to such persons' impairments unless to do so would pose an "undue hardship" on the operation of their programs.

The Americans with Disabilities Act of 1990. The Americans with Disabilities Act of 1990 (ADA) seeks to redress discrimination against individuals with disabilities and to guarantee such individuals equal access to public services (including public accommodations and transportation), public services operated by private entities, and telecommunications relay services, to name a few.

Title I, which prohibits employment discrimination, adopts the Rehabilitation Act of 1973's definition of handicap but uses the more up-to-date term *disability.* The ADA, in requiring an employer to provide "reasonable accommodation to the known physical or mental limitations" of a person with a disability unless such accommodation "would impose an undue hardship on the operation of the business" of the covered entity, obviously continues to borrow heavily from the 1973 act. Reasonable accommodation under the ADA includes such actions as making existing facilities accessible to and usable by persons with disabilities, restructuring jobs, and providing part-time or modified work schedules.

However, the act does not require the employer to implement any job accommodation if the employer can demonstrate that the accommodation would impose an "undue hardship" on the operation of the business. The ADA defines *undue hardship* as an action requiring "significant difficulty or expense" with reference to the following factors: (1) the nature and cost of the accommodation; (2) the size, type, and financial resources of the specific facility where the accommodation would have to be made; (3) the size, type, and financial resources of the covered employer; and (4) the covered employer's type of operation, including the composition, structure, and functions of its workforce and the geographic separateness and administrative or fiscal relationship between the specific facility and the covered employer.

The legislative history indicates that the "significant difficulty or expense" standard encompasses any "action that is unduly costly, extensive, substantial, disruptive, or that will fundamentally alter the nature of the program." Significant, too, is the fact that in defining "undue hardship," Congress rejected all attempts to put a cap on the level of difficulty or expense that would constitute an "undue hardship," including an amendment to create a presumption that the cost of any accommodation exceeding 10 percent of the annual salary of the position in question constitutes an "undue hardship."

The employment discrimination provisions under Title I cover employers that have on their weekly payrolls 15 or more full- or part-time employees for each working day in each of 20 or more calendar weeks in the current or preceding calendar year. The ADA subsequently will cover an estimated 3.9 million business establishments and 666,000 employers. Like the Civil Rights Act of 1964, the ADA covers employers, employment agencies, labor organizations, and joint labor/management committees, but exempts religious entities. Thus, the ADA's coverage goes beyond that of the Rehabilitation Act of 1973, which applies only to employers doing business with the federal government. The ADA in addition expressly protects employees or applicants who have completed (or who are participating in) a drug rehabilitation program and no longer are engaging in the use of illegal drugs. Without fear of violating the ADA, employers can, however, impose sanctions against employees who currently are using illegal drugs and may hold such employees (and/or employees who are alcoholics) to the same performance and conduct standards to which it holds other employees, even if the unsatisfactory performance or behavior is related to the employees' drug use or alcoholism. The ADA also protects from discrimination persons who have AIDS or who are HIV-positive.

At the congressional hearings for the ADA, experts testified that it potentially covers about 43 million Americans and that its enactment therefore may cause a flood of litigation. Indeed, the EEOC itself predicted that complainants would file between 12,000 and 15,000 charges during the first year the statute took effect. As with any comparatively new legislation, the overall impact of the ADA remains unclear. In addition to the costs associated with the hiring process and those resulting from the predicted increases in litigation under the act, the expenses of converting existing facilities so as to make them accessible to individuals with disabilities obviously concern many employers, particularly small firms. Yet data from a pre-ADA survey of federal contractors showed that the compliance costs/workplace changes incurred under the Rehabilitation Act of 1973 for half of the companies amounted to zero dollars and for 30 percent of the companies less than $500. In only 8 percent of the cases did the changes cost more than $2,000.

Civil Rights Act of 1991. Congress enacted the Civil Rights Act of 1991 after a two-year struggle. Interestingly, Congress in part passed this act to overturn a series of 1989 and 1991 Supreme Court cases that had significantly eroded the rights of complainants alleging employment discrimination. Thus, the act reflected Congress's displeasure with the present Court's judicial attitude toward civil rights cases. The act, in its amendments of Title VII, therefore reaffirms the holdings of such cases as *Griggs* v. *Duke Power Co.*, 401 U.S. 424 (1971). The new act's amendments to § 1981 of the Civil Rights Act of 1866 also specify that this statute covers all forms of racial discrimination in employment (including racial harassment).

Besides these pro-complainant provisions, the act in addition mandates the impartial use of tests and thus prohibits "race norming" of employment tests. In other words, employers must record and report actual scores and will be unable to modify scores, use different cutoff scores, or otherwise adjust the results of employment-related tests on the basis of race, color, religion, sex, or national origin even if employers have taken these actions so as to assure minority inclusion in the applicant pool. In a similar vein, the act effects no changes in the law regarding what constitutes lawful affirmative action and/or illegal reverse discrimination. It also restricts challenges to court-ordered consent decrees by individuals who had a reasonable opportunity to object to such decrees or whose interests were adequately represented by another party.

The act does broaden the scope of federal antidiscrimination law. It makes clear that Americans employed abroad by U.S.-owned or U.S.-controlled firms can avail themselves of the protection of Title VII, the ADA, and the ADEA, unless compliance with these laws will constitute a violation of the host country's laws. The act moreover extends coverage of the antidiscrimination laws to congressional employees and executive-branch political appointees and sets up discrete internal mechanisms for addressing such claims.

The act furthermore broadens the categories of victims who can seek compensatory and punitive damages based on intentional discrimination, although it provides for caps of $50,000 to $300,000 (depending on the size of the employer's workforce) for discrimination based on the complainant's disability, sex, or religion. Any complainant eligible for compensatory or punitive damages may request a jury trial as well. The act also allows successful complainants to recover expert witness fees in addition to attorneys' fees.

Other amendments deal with the availability of interest payments for delayed awards, extensions of filing deadlines for lawsuits brought against the government, notification by the EEOC to the complainant when the EEOC dismisses charges under the ADEA, and a longer statute of limitations's period for a claimant who brings an action under the ADEA. The act obligates the EEOC to establish a Technical Assistance Training Institute for entities covered by the laws the EEOC enforces. In addition, the act mandates an EEOC outreach/education program for individuals who historically have been the object of employment discrimination. Title II of the act, the Glass Ceiling Act of 1991, sets up a commission to study why impediments to the advancement of women and minorities exist and to make recommendations for eliminating such barriers. Businesses that show substantial efforts to advance such groups to management and decision-making positions in business are eligible to receive national awards recognizing their efforts.[11]

Given the novelty of this landmark legislation, subsequent court decisions will serve to answer the various questions spawned by the Act. In 1994, the Supreme Court [in *Landgraf* v. *USI Film Products,* 511 U.S. 244 (1994)] answered one such question—whether the 1991 act applies retroactively to Title VII cases pending on appeal at the time of the 1991 act's enactment—by holding that it does not. More developments undoubtedly will follow.

Family and Medical Leave Act of 1993. The first major piece of legislation passed under the Clinton Administration was the Family and Medical Leave Act of 1993 (FMLA). Regulations promulgated by the Department of Labor obligate certain employers of 50 or more persons to do the following: formulate a family leave policy, revise employee handbooks and policy manuals so that they are consistent with such a policy, alter any inconsistent policies, and prepare for the paperwork required under the act.

Divided into 6 titles and 26 sections, the FMLA covers public employers of any size and private employers that have on their weekly payrolls 50 or more employees during each of 20 or more calendar work weeks in the current or preceding calendar year. Employees eligible to take leave under the act must have worked for the employer for at least 12 months and for at least 1,250 hours in the 12 months immediately preceding the commencement of any leave taken under the act. Employees who work at job facilities that employ fewer than 50 persons remain ineligible for FMLA leave unless the employer has 50 or more employees working within a 75-mile radius of any work site. Part-time employees count, but laid-off employees do not.

Section 102 of the FMLA provides generally that "an eligible employee shall be entitled to a total of 12 work weeks of leave during any 12 month period" for the following family-related events: (1) the birth of a child; (2) the placement of a child with the employee for adoption or foster care; (3) the care of a seriously ill spouse, child, or parent; and (4) a serious health condition of the employee that makes him or her unable to perform any of the essential functions of his or her job.

The FMLA does not require the employer to pay for any leave taken under the act. However, eligible employees can use any accrued vacation or personal leave for FMLA purposes. Similarly, an eligible employee may elect to use any paid leave—sick, family, or disability leave—in accordance with the terms of the employer's leave policies. In fact, the employer can require employees to exhaust all "banked" personal, sick, and vacation leave as part of the 12 weeks' leave. In such cases, though, the FMLA prohibits employers from imposing more stringent conditions on leave taken under the act than the employers would require under their own leave plans. The act moreover obligates employers to reinstate employees who have availed themselves of FMLA leave to their former position or to one that involves "substantially equivalent skill, effort, responsibility, and authority."

Interestingly, the FMLA exempts the highest-paid 10 percent of salaried employees within the aforementioned 75-mile radius from the right to reinstatement after they have taken a leave. In short, the FMLA allows an employer to refuse restoration of employment to these "key employees" if an employer can show that "substantial and grievous" economic injury would occur if the key employee were restored to his or her original position. The regulations never set forth a precise test for calculating the level of hardship that an employer must sustain before it can deny reinstatement (or restoration) to key employees, however.

Once the employer has determined that a given worker is a key employee, the employer, upon the key employee's request for leave, must notify the employee in writing of this determination. The employer's failure to comply with the specific notification requirements delineated in the regulations will cause the forfeiture of its rights to deny reinstatement (or restoration). Furthermore, the employer cannot require an employee to "requalify" for such benefits as life or disability insurance or profit-sharing plans once the worker completes his or her FMLA leave.

Although the act itself does not specifically define the term *family,* the regulations do and apparently contemplate coverage of a wide spectrum of persons beyond the traditional family unit. The regulations define *spouse* as a husband or wife recognized as such for purposes of marriage under state law (including common law marriages in jurisdictions that recognize these relationships). Partners in homosexual "marriages" presumably do not qualify for benefits and protection under the FMLA. The parental relationship described in the act can be either biological or one that is *in loco parentis;* but parents "in law" are not included. *Son* or *daughter* means a biological, adopted, or foster child, a stepchild, a legal ward, or a child of a person standing *in loco parentis* and who either is under 18 or 18 and older and incapable of self-care owing to mental or physical disability. The regulations define a person who is *in loco parentis* as including anyone with day-to-day responsibilities to care for and financially support a child. A biological or legal relationship specifically is not required under the regulations.

The act defines a *serious health condition* as "an illness, injury, impairment, or physical or mental condition that involves inpatient care in a hospital, hospice, or residential facility or continuing treatment by a health care provider." According to the regulations, a *serious health condition* is one that requires either an overnight stay in a hospital; a period of incapacity requiring an absence from work of more than three days and that involves continuing treatment by a health care provider; or continuing treatment for a chronic or long-term health condition that, if left untreated, likely will result in a period of incapacity for more than three days. Prenatal care and care administered for a long-term or chronic condition that is incurable (such as Alzheimer's disease) and for which condition the person is not receiving active treatment by a health care provider are included as well.

Given this broad threshold for eligibility, many businesspeople fear that the FMLA will be susceptible to abuse by employees who show tendencies toward chronic, unjustified absenteeism. The medical certification requirements set out under the act, however, do provide a hedge against employee abuse of the FMLA's provisions. According to the act, the employer may require the employee to produce medical documentation as to the need for medical leave in many circumstances. The health care providers who provide such certifications ordinarily furnish specific information about the medical facts underlying the condition that has triggered the need for a leave, the commencement date, and the probable duration of the leave. In strictly circumscribing the information an employer can obtain from a certifying health care professional, the act, among other things, prohibits the employer from requesting additional information from such a provider. Rather, if an employer doubts the validity of the certificate produced by the employee, the employer can, at its own expense, require a second opinion by a health-care provider of its choice, so long as the doctor is not "employed on a regular basis by the employer."

The act also allows employees to take *intermittent leave,* that is, "leave taken in separate blocks of time due to a single illness or injury, rather than for one continuous period of time, and may include leave of periods from an hour or more to several weeks." Intermittent leave can include leave taken for medical appointments, chemotherapy, and the like. (The regulations require the employee to give notice to the employer of the need for intermittent leave, but the regulations are more lenient regarding notification for unforeseeable leave.) Employees instead may opt for a *reduced leave* schedule, which the regulations define as a reduction in an employee's usual number of working hours per week or in the hours per work day.

Intermittent or reduced leave taken for the purpose of caring for a family member or for a serious health condition of the employee requires only fulfillment of the applicable certification standards; it is not necessary for the employee to obtain the employer's permission in advance. The employer and employee must agree to any intermittent or reduced leave that the employee takes for the birth or adoption of a child, however.

The act allows an employer to require an employee who has requested intermittent or reduced leave to transfer to another position. The transfer must be temporary, and the new position must reflect equivalent pay and benefits (if not equivalent duties). Employers also have the right, consistent with the leave being taken, to transfer an employee to a part-time position. These transfer provisions give the employer some leeway to place the affected employee in a position that more easily accommodates recurrent and unpredictable absences.

The act requires the employer to post notices regarding the FMLA at the work site. An employer's failure to post these notice requirements at the work site subjects the employer to fines of up to $100 per offense. Furthermore, if the employer has reduced its policies to writing, the employer must include information concerning the FMLA and its entitlements in all employee handbooks. In the absence of such written policies, the employer must provide written guidance as to an employee's rights and obligations under the FMLA whenever an employee requests leave under the act.

Like other federal fair employment practices laws, the FMLA contains antidiscrimination/antiretaliation provisions. Violations of these provisions may result in civil lawsuits, liquidated damages, or administrative remedies.

Other Protections. The Vietnam Era Veterans' Readjustment Assistance Act of 1974, various executive orders, and the Civil Rights Acts of 1866 and 1871 form alternative bases for guaranteeing equal access to the workplace. State law often augments this extensive federal scheme as well.

Occupational Safety and Health Act

Congress passed the Occupational Safety and Health Act, better known as OSHA, in 1970. This act attempts to assure safe and healthful workplace conditions for working men and women. The act does so by authorizing enforcement of the standards developed under the act (through the Occupational Safety and Health Administration); by assisting and encouraging the states' efforts to assure safe and healthful working conditions; and by providing for research, information, education, and training in the field of occupational safety and health, through the National Institute for Occupational Safety and Health (NIOSH).

The act covers most employers and employees, including agricultural employees, nonprofit organizations, and professionals (such as doctors, lawyers, accountants, and brokers). In fact, the act reaches almost any employer that employs at least one employee and whose business in any way affects interstate commerce. Atomic energy workers, however, are exempted.

Because personal illnesses and injuries arising from the workplace produce significant burdens in terms of lost production, lost wages, medical expenses, and disability payments, Congress designed an act meant to highlight the existence of such factors and to provide standards for preventing future illnesses, injuries, and losses. To this end, OSHA sets out methods by which employers can reduce workplace hazards and foster attention to safety. The act further authorizes the secretary of labor to set mandatory occupational safety and health standards for businesses covered under the act and to create an Occupational Safety and Health Review Commission for hearing appeals from OSHA citations and penalties. In *Martin* v. *Occupational Safety and Health Review Commission,* the Supreme Court held that when this "split enforcement" structure (that is, the secretary's powers of enforcement and rule making versus the commission's adjudicatory powers) leads to reasonable but conflicting interpretations of an ambiguous OSHA regulation promulgated by the secretary of labor, courts should defer to the secretary's interpretations.[12]

To help ensure that no employee suffers diminished health, functional capacity, or life expectancy as a result of work experiences, OSHA requires each employer to furnish to its employees a safe and healthful workplace, one that is free from "recognized hazards" that may cause or are likely to cause death or serious physical harm to employees. An example of a recognized hazard might include excessive toxic substances in the air.

OSHA allows inspectors to enter the workplace to inspect for compliance with regulations. Upon an employer's refusal to admit the inspector, OSHA regulations now require a warrant. The refusal in and of itself does not constitute probable cause for the issuance of the warrant. But the standards for demonstrating the need for the warrant are relatively easy to meet and ordinarily do not impede OSHA's functions very much. Employers normally do not know in advance of an inspector's arrival. By writing to the secretary of labor, employees may request an inspection if they believe a violation that threatens physical harm exists.

Inspections typically involve a tour through the business and an examination of each work area for compliance with OSHA standards. After the inspector has informed the employer of the reason for the inspection, the inspector will give the employer a copy of the complaint (if one is involved) or the reason for the inspection if it results from an agency general administrative plan. When an employee has initiated the complaint, OSHA by request will withhold the employee's name. An employer representative and an employee-selected representative generally accompany the inspector on this walk-around tour. The inspector may order the immediate correction of some violations, such as blocked aisles, locked fire exits, or unsanitary conditions. The inspector additionally reviews the records OSHA requires the employer to maintain, including records of deaths, injuries, illnesses, and employee exposure to toxic substances. After the inspection, the inspector and employer engage in a closing conference, during which they discuss probable violations and methods for eliminating these violations. The inspector then files his or her report with the commission.

Citations and proposed penalties may be issued to the employer, and a copy of these will be sent to the complaining party, if there is one. Normally, no citation is issued if a violation of a standard or rule lacks an immediate or direct relationship to safety or health, although a notice of a minimal violation (without a proposed penalty) may be sent to the employer even in these situations. OSHA requires the prominent posting of citations in the workplace.

Penalties, when imposed, are severe: fines of up to $70,000 for each violation may be levied for willful or repeated violations. An employer also will be fined up to $7,000 for each serious violation—one in which there is a "substantial probability" that the consequences of an accident resulting from the violation will be death or serious harm. Employers can defend by showing they did not, and could not with the exercise of "reasonable diligence," know about the condition or hazard. For even nonserious violations (such as a failure to paint steps and banisters or to post citations), fines of up to $7,000 are possible. Prison terms are possible in the event of willful violations that cause an employee's death. The OSHA Commission assesses these penalties in light of the size of the employer's business, the seriousness of the violation, the presence or absence of employer good faith, and the past history of violations.

An employer that wishes to contest any penalties can resort to the procedures established by the commission. In general, these require an investigation and a decision by an administrative law judge. The commission, in turn, can review this decision. An employer that still disagrees with the decision can appeal to the appropriate federal circuit court of appeals for review, as can the secretary of labor if he or she disagrees with the commission's decision.

Upon proof of inability to comply because of the unavailability of materials, equipment, or personnel to effect the changes within the required time, employers may request temporary exemptions from OSHA standards. Permanent exemptions may be granted when the employer's method of protecting employees is as effective as that required by the standard. Needless to say, such exemptions are not granted retroactively.

Other provisions of OSHA protect employees from discrimination or discharge based on filing a complaint, testifying about violations, or exercising any rights guaranteed by the act. The act prohibits employees from stopping work or walking off the job because of "potential unsafe conditions at the workplace" unless the employee, through performance of the assigned work, would subject "himself [or herself] to serious injury or death from a hazardous condition at the workplace."

In *Whirlpool Corp.* v. *Marshall,* the Supreme Court held that the secretary of labor has the authority to promulgate a regulation allowing workers to refuse to perform in hazardous situations.[13] According to the Court, the promulgation of the regulation was a valid exercise of the authority granted the secretary of labor under the Occupational Safety and Health Act, especially given the act's fundamental purpose of preventing occupational deaths and serious injuries.

Social Security

The Social Security Act, first enacted in 1935 as part of President Franklin D. Roosevelt's New Deal policies, has spawned numerous controversies. Current debate about social security centers on fears that the system will become bankrupt and on proposed plans to allay this possibility.

By *social security,* most people mean the federal old-age, survivors', and disability insurance benefits plan. Broad in scope, social security benefits today are payable to workers, their dependents, and their survivors. Through the Supplemental Security Income (SSI) program administered by the Department of Health and Human Services, the federal social security system also makes payments to the blind, the disabled, and the aged who are in need of these benefits. The states also can supplement this pervasive federal scheme if they so choose.

In general, federal social security benefits are computed on the worker's earning records. A *fully insured* worker is one who has worked at least 40 quarters (10 years). To use 1997 as an example, such workers will earn one-quarter of coverage for each $670 in earnings, whether wages, farm wages, or income from self-employment, up to a maximum of four quarters. Fully insured workers who receive retirement benefits include retired workers, 62 years and older; their spouses, or divorced spouses, 62 and older; spouses of any age who care for a child entitled to benefits; and children or grandchildren under 18 (or 19 if a student) or of any age if disabled before age 22. Additionally, survivors' benefits go to certain classes of fully insured workers, as do disability benefits for qualified workers.

Be aware, however, that computing social security benefits involves complicated arithmetical formulas noting the worker's age; date of retirement, disability, or death; and yearly earnings history. Cost-of-living escalators tied to the **consumer price index** in certain circumstances may raise benefits as well. Disability benefits—those granted to a worker who has been disabled at least five months—are computed in a similar manner, subject to some limitations for younger disabled workers.

Consumer price index
Measurement of how the price of a group of consumer goods changes between two time periods.

Additionally, for eligibility, the worker must prove that he or she no longer can engage in substantial gainful employment. The disability must be expected to last at least 12 months or to result in death. Finally, the worker, if near retirement age, must have sufficient quarters of coverage to be considered fully insured and must have worked at least 20 quarters of the last 40 quarters before the disability began. Blind persons and some younger workers who become disabled face less stringent eligibility requirements. Receipt of benefits paid under workers' compensation or other federal, state, or local disability plans may lessen the amount of benefits received from social security.

Monthly payments made to a retired or disabled worker's family or to the survivors of an insured worker are equal to a certain percentage (usually 50 or 75 percent) of the worker's benefits. For example, if a worker were entitled to $379 per month in benefits, the worker's wife or divorced wife who was married to the worker for at least 10 years and is not now married will receive $189.50 or $284.25 in monthly benefits. The act limits the amount one family can receive in total benefits. Similarly, benefits for a nondisabled child who no longer is attending high school normally end at age 18. Lump-sum death benefits to eligible persons cannot exceed $255. In 1997, earnings realized by retired persons between 65 and 69 could not exceed $13,500 without loss of benefits. The Social Security Administration (SSA) will reduce from the benefits of any worker who makes more than this amount one dollar for every three dollars over the limit. Social security coverage extends to most types of employment and self-employment. Among those excluded, however, are employees of the federal government and railroad workers.

Those who have been denied benefits may utilize certain administrative steps to appeal an SSA decision. Usually, such persons file a request for reconsideration within 60 days of the date of the initial determination. The agency then conducts a thorough and independent review of the evidence. After this reconsideration, a person who remains adversely affected can file for a hearing or review by an administrative law judge (ALJ). After the hearing, the ALJ issues a written decision that in understandable language sets out his or her findings of fact. All parties receive copies of this decision. The decision is binding unless appealed to the Appeals Council of the SSA or to a federal district court.

The Federal Insurance Contribution Act (FICA) taxes paid by employees and employers on wages earned by workers not only fund social security retirement benefits but also help provide qualified persons with hospital insurance. Called Medicare, this protection normally is available to persons 65 years and older and to some disabled persons under 65. Medicare (Part A) covers doctors' services, hospital care, some nursing home care, certain home health services, and hospice care. In 1996, the tax rate paid was 6.2 percent on a maximum of $62,700 in employee wages. The Medicare tax rate for that amount of wages is 1.45 percent. In 1993, Congress removed the maximum base amount (formerly $135,000); hence, for 1994 and thereafter, the employer must match the employee's portion. Aside from such costs, the recordkeeping burdens involved with compliance under the Social Security Act also irk many employers.

In addition to receiving Medicare Part A, qualified persons can pay for a government-subsidized plan called Medicare Part B that will cover medical services beyond hospitalization, such as doctors' services and related medical expenses involving outpatient and rehabilitation costs, ambulance services, lab tests, and the like. In order to fill in the gaps in health care protection left by the Medicare program, some persons also purchase Medicare supplemental insurance ("Medigap" insurance) from insurance companies. Another program, Medicaid, provides broad medical assistance to "categorically needy" individuals.

Unemployment Insurance

In addition to retirement, disability, and Medicare benefits, social security covers unemployment insurance through the Federal Unemployment Tax Act (FUTA). Unemployment insurance represents a coordinated federal and state effort to provide economic security for temporarily unemployed workers. The funds used in the unemployment insurance system come from taxes, or "contributions," paid predominantly by employers. In a few states, employees also pay these taxes. Those contributing pay federal taxes, which the government uses to administer the federal/state program, as well as state taxes, which the state uses to finance the payment of weekly benefits to unemployed workers.

Various credits allowed under federal law significantly reduce the amount of taxes paid in federal contributions. Essentially, computation of the taxes is based on a specified percentage of wages paid by the employer/employees. "Wages" include anything paid as compensation for employment and thus may consist of salaries, fees, bonuses, and commissions. Since 1983, the amount of wages subject to federal taxes for unemployment compensation is at most $7,000 for each employee per calendar year. In 1996, the FUTA applies at a rate of 6.2% on the first $7,000 of covered wages paid during the year to each employee. The federal government allows a credit for FUTA sums paid to the state, however. State contribution rates may vary, but most have set a standard rate (such as 5.4 percent). Hence, the amount to be paid to the Internal Revenue Service (IRS) could be as low as 0.8% (6.2% – 5.4%).

State rates, almost without exception, utilize "experience rating" or "merit rating" systems whereby the rate employers pay reflects each individual employer's experience with unemployment. Under such systems, employers whose workers suffer the most involuntary unemployment pay higher rates than employers whose workers suffer less unemployment. Since the aim of unemployment compensation involves the achievement of regular employment and the prevention of unemployment, such systems provide incentives to employers to keep their workforces intact and thereby to perpetuate the goals of these laws.

State provisions regarding the criteria for eligibility and the amount of benefits vary greatly. For instance, in different jurisdictions, unemployment compensation may not be available to employees discharged for cause, to those who quit their jobs without cause, or to those who refuse to seek or accept a job for which they are qualified.

Workers' Compensation

Workers' compensation statutes are not the same as unemployment statutes, although both concern the welfare of workers. Workers' compensation laws in the various states attempt to reimburse workers for injuries or death arising in the employment context. "Compensation" in this area therefore does not refer to wages or salaries but rather to the money paid by the employer to indemnify the worker for employment-related injury or death. The employer usually self-insures; buys insurance; or, as discussed earlier, pays money into a state insurance fund at a "merit" or "experience" rate reflective of the employer's actual incidence of employee injuries. By utilizing administrative proceedings in front of a workers' compensation board, injured workers then receive compensation for their injuries in the form of medical care and disability benefits, the latter often based on a specific statutory scale (such as 60 percent of average weekly wages up to $100 in average weekly wages for 26 weeks).

Workers' compensation acts thus impose *strict liability* on the employer for injuries to employees during the scope of their employment. These laws first arose out of lawmakers' concern for employees injured as a result of increased industrial mechanization, but these acts serve other functions as well. For instance, through such statutes, employees can receive compensation without engaging in costly litigation; and the employer, by passing these costs on to consumers, can recoup the costs of workers' compensation. Both sides benefit, because the employee receives reimbursement for the injuries suffered and the employer's liability to the employee usually ends there; that is, the statutes ordinarily prohibit the employee from suing the employer in a court of law. Such acts, then, are grounded in public policy concerns.

The classes of employees covered by such acts depend on the particular statute involved. Agricultural, domestic, or casual laborers often are not covered because the right to compensation ordinarily depends on the nature of the work performed, the regularity of such work, and/or the status of the worker (that is, whether the worker was working as an independent contractor for someone else when injured).

To be covered, an employee ordinarily must be a *worker*—that is, a person who performs manual labor or similar duties. For this reason, workers' compensation statutes presumably fail to cover directors, officers, or stockholders. Yet under the *dual capacity* doctrine, such persons can receive compensation if, when they suffer injury, they are performing the ordinary duties of the business. For example, a general manager of a tree-pruning service who is injured while pruning trees will be able to recover. If the general manager instead were working as an independent contractor (not for the corporation), he or she normally would be ineligible to receive workers' compensation.

Typically, however, just about any employment-related injury or disease makes the covered employee eligible for workers' compensation. For this reason, even a

http:// RESOURCES FOR BUSINESS LAW STUDENTS

NAME	RESOURCES	WEB ADDRESS
National Labor Relations Board	The National Labor Relations Board provides speeches, publications, Board decisions, and other materials.	http://www.nlrb.gov/
Americans with Disabilities Act (ADA) Document Center	The ADA Document Center provides the full text for the ADA, regulations, guidelines, and other documents.	http://janweb.icdi.wvu.edu/kinder/
Family and Medical Leave Act (FMLA) of 1993	The Department of Labor provides the full text for the FMLA, fact sheets, compliance guides, and regulations.	http://www.dol.gov/dol/esa/
Equal Employment Opportunity Commission (EEOC)	The EEOC provides publications and media releases, fact sheets, and information on the laws enforced by the commission.	http://www.eeoc.gov/
Occupational Safety and Health Administration (OSHA)	OSHA, part of the Department of Labor, provides publications and media releases, program information, software, and data.	http://www.osha.gov/index.html
Social Security Administration (SSA)	The SSA maintains publications, legal information, forms, and other information.	http://www.ssa.gov/

YOU BE THE JUDGE

Hiring Temps

To avoid the skyrocketing costs associated with workers' compensation insurance, some firms have hired employees provided by temporary employment agencies. The firms utilizing these "temps" typically are those that have a high incidence of workplace injuries and concomitant expensive workers' compensation premiums. These companies oftentimes turn to temporary employment agencies, which often have lower insurance costs and which in addition benefit from having a greater pool of workers to insure. The hiring companies, by removing some workers from their rolls, can reduce their annual workers' compensation tab. Once the temporary agency's own experience ratings begin to rise (and, as a consequence, its insurance premiums), it dissolves itself and replaces itself with another experience-free temporary agency. State agencies report that this shell game may be repeated as many as 30 times. Suppose that a state legislature has enacted a law that attempts to close this loophole by preventing a firm that dissolves itself from beginning a new temporary services agency for five years. A newly formed temporary agency challenges this law in *your* court. How will *you* decide this case?[14]

BUSINESS CONSIDERATIONS Why might a business want to dissolve its current form and reorganize under another form and/or name? What might insurance companies do to protect themselves from firms' acting in this manner to avoid increased premiums?

ETHICAL CONSIDERATIONS What ethical concerns would be raised by a business reorganization undertaken to avoid the increased costs associated with its earlier existence? Would it be ethical for insurance companies to refuse to provide insurance coverage to firms until those firms had been in existence for some minimum time period?

SOURCE: *The National Law Journal* (17 March 1997), pp. B1, B2.

negligent employee usually can recover for injuries suffered while he or she was in the employment relationship. Contrast this statutory result with what would occur at common law: The employer could use the employee's contributory negligence as a complete bar to recovery.

Recent decisions allow recoveries for occupational diseases such as asbestosis, for work-related stress, and even for injuries suffered before or after working hours. Although workers' compensation takes the place of an employee's suing the employer for the injuries suffered, employees still can maintain product liability suits against manufacturers or suppliers and also can sue any fellow employees who cause their injuries.

SUMMARY

The Wagner, Taft-Hartley, and Landrum-Griffin acts set out a pervasive federal scheme for the regulation of labor. This blueprint of federal labor law broadly regulates employees' rights to organize and to engage in concerted activities in furtherance of their objectives. Both employees and employers are protected from unfair labor practices. The National Labor Relations Board retains jurisdiction over labor disputes, oversees elections, arbitrates disputes about the duty to bargain, and almost wholly preempts the states' jurisdiction over labor matters, except for criminal violations or torts, retaliatory discharges, and the like.

A host of federal statutes extensively regulates fair employment practices. Title VII of the Civil Rights Act of 1964 prohibits employers, labor organizations, or employment agencies from engaging in employment discrimination based on race, color, religion, sex, or national origin. The Equal Employment Opportunity Commission enforces many of these federal laws and sets out the complex procedures with which a grievant must comply. Employment criteria that have a disparate impact on minorities are illegal unless the employer can show that the criteria are job-related. Employers also may be liable for the disparate treatment of their employees. The issue of reverse discrimination remains controversial in the Title VII context. Limited defenses based on bona fide occupational qualifications (BFOQs) are available for the protected categories of religion, sex, and national origin; a BFOQ never can be based on race, however. The Immigration Reform and Control Act of 1986, the Equal Pay Act of 1963, the Age Discrimination in Employment Act of 1967, the Rehabilitation Act of 1973, the Americans with Disabilities Act of 1990, the Civil Rights Act of 1991, the Family and Medical Leave Act of 1993, and other federal statutes protect qualified individuals against employment discrimination. State law often supplements this comprehensive federal scheme.

The Occupational Safety and Health Act attempts to ensure safe and healthful working conditions for American workers. Inspections of the workplace provide a mechanism for realizing this statutory goal. Warrantless inspections conducted after the owner refuses entry to the inspector are illegal. Workers, in contrast, legally can walk off the job if performance of the work assignment can lead to serious injury or death.

Federal and state social security benefits aid workers, the disabled, the blind, and the aged. Computations of benefits are complex. Those who have been denied benefits may utilize certain administrative steps to appeal such agency decisions.

Unemployment insurance is designed to provide economic security for temporarily unemployed workers. The contributions paid into the insurance fund stem from a specified percentage of wages paid by the employer or employee. State taxable wage bases may differ from the federal figure, and state provisions regarding the criteria for eligibility and the amount of benefits vary greatly.

State workers' compensation statutes attempt to reimburse workers for injuries or death resulting from the employment relationship. In return, such statutes generally prohibit the employee from suing the employer in a court of law. The classes of employees covered in such acts depend on the particular statute involved; but eligible employees may recover for occupational diseases, injuries resulting from the employee's own negligence, and injuries sustained before or after working hours. Workers' compensation statutes ordinarily do not preclude an employee's maintaining either a product liability suit against a manufacturer or a suit against a fellow employee who caused the injuries at issue.

Discussion Questions

1. List a few of the rights guaranteed and the practices prohibited by the Wagner, Taft-Hartley, and Landrum-Griffin acts.
2. Describe a few of the issues and enforcement problems involved in the collective-bargaining process.
3. Explain the boundaries of state regulation of labor.
4. What are the protected classes of employees under Title VII?
5. Define and describe the two methods by which an employee can show liability for discrimination on

the basis of the protected categories set out in Title VII.
6. Why is the issue of reverse discrimination such a difficult problem?
7. Define the term *bona fide occupational qualification.*
8. Name other statutes that guarantee fair employment, and explain how these more recent statutes build on earlier fair employment statutes.
9. Describe a typical OSHA inspection.
10. Name the classes of persons eligible for social security, unemployment insurance, and workers' compensation.

CASE PROBLEMS AND WRITING ASSIGNMENTS

1. Approximately two months before a vote on unionization, the employer, Wiljef Transportation, Inc. (Wiljef), read to its employees a corporate bylaw stating: "Section 2—Corporate Dissolution. Wiljef Transportation, Inc., hereby expresses as a matter of corporate policy that operations will cease and the corporation will be dissolved in the event of unionization of its employees. As hereby authorized by the Board of Directors, this bylaw may be announced to the employees of Wiljef Transportation, Inc. at any time deemed appropriate by the Board." The firm had adopted the bylaw in 1979, and the announcement occurred in 1988. In the ensuing union representation election, the employees rejected unionization. Supreme Court precedents, in addressing the tension between an employer's right to announce the probable consequences of unionization and the employees' right to organize without threat of retaliation, had made the following points. On the one hand, the employer's right to communicate its views to its employees is firmly established in the First Amendment and is recognized in § 8(c) of the NLRA, which provides that "the expressing of any views, argument, or opinion . . . shall not constitute or be evidence of an unfair labor practice . . . if such expression contains no threat of reprisal or force or promise of benefit." On the other hand, the exceptions to the freedom of expression recognized in § 8(c) reflect the right of employees to associate free of coercion by the employer. By declaring that it is an unfair labor practice to interfere with, restrain, or coerce employees who are exercising their right to organize in unions, § 8(a)(1) of the NLRA codifies that right. The difficulty in attempting to reconcile these two rights lies in determining when speech becomes essentially coercive rather than factually informative or predictive so as to fall outside the protection of the First Amendment and thus violate the NLRA. The issue in this case centered on whether the announcement of the bylaw constituted a "permitted prediction" of plant closure or a "proscribed threat." The NLRB had held that the announcement represented a threat in violation of § 8(a)(1) of the NLRA, and Wiljef had appealed to the Court of Appeals for the Seventh Circuit. How should that court rule in this case? [See *Wiljef Transp., Inc.* v. *NLRB,* 946 F.2d 1308 (7th Cir. 1991).]

2. To celebrate a new supplier agreement, New River Industries, Inc. (New River), an acetate fiber manufacturer, announced that it would serve refreshments to its employees. New River issued tickets redeemable in the lunchroom for free ice cream cones. Some employees ridiculed the ice cream cones and suggested writing a letter to "thank" the company for its generosity. Edward Smith drafted a letter, and Jeanie Simpson agreed to type it. Smith posted the letter on an open bulletin board. This letter and several subsequent copies were removed from the open bulletin board and from a locked bulletin board. The final copy had a handwritten notation at the bottom: "United NRI Workers Vote Union on 1 January." Simpson and Smith, both valued employees, were dismissed for violation of plant rules (posting an unauthorized notice that disrupted the workforce and derogating and undermining management and fellow employees). Simpson subsequently filed an unfair labor practice charge with the NLRB. An administrative law judge found that Smith and Simpson had been discharged for union activity in violation of the NLRA and for other "concerted activities." Section 7 of the NLRA provides that an activity, to be protected, must be "for the purpose of collective bargaining or other mutual aid or protection." According to Supreme Court precedents, the "mutual aid or protection" clause of § 7 protects employees who "seek to improve [the] terms and conditions of employment or otherwise improve their lot as employees through channels outside the immediate employee–employer relationship." Did Simpson and Smith's preparation of a sarcastic letter that was critical of the employer's gift of free ice cream cones to employees constitute protected concerted activity within the meaning of the NLRA? Why or why not? [See *New River Indus., Inc.* v. *NLRB,* 945 F.2d 1290 (4th Cir. 1991).]

3. Gene Arline had taught elementary school in Nassau County, Florida, from 1966 until 1979, when she was discharged after having suffered a third relapse of tuberculosis within two years. Arline argued that the school board had dismissed her solely on the basis of her illness, which she contended was a handicap under the Rehabilitation Act of 1973. The school board asserted that a contagious disease was not protectable under the act. Moreover, the board maintained that, in any event, Arline was not a "handicapped" individual because her disease made her "unqualified" to teach. Was Arline a handicapped person under the Rehabilitation Act of 1973? Why or why not? [See *School Board of Nassau County, Florida* v. *Arline,* 480 U.S. 273 (1987), *reh'g denied,* 481 U.S. 1024 (1987).]

4. Sidney Taylor, vice president of Capital City Federal Savings and Loan Association (Capital City), asked Mechelle Vinson to apply for employment with Capital City. Vinson was hired as a teller/trainee, and Taylor became her supervisor at the Northeast Branch. She was promoted successively to teller, head teller, and assistant branch manager. After Vinson had worked at the Northeast Branch for four years, she took an indefinite sick leave and was discharged two months later for excessive use of that leave. Vinson, alleging that Taylor had sexually harassed her, subsequently brought an action under Title VII against Taylor and Capital City. Vinson contended that Taylor had asked her to have sexual relations with him and had claimed that she "owed him" because he had obtained the job for her. She also maintained that after initially declining his invitation, she ultimately had yielded, but only because she had been afraid that continued refusals would jeopardize her employment. She further asserted that she had been forced to submit to sexual advances by Taylor at the Northeast Branch both during and after business hours and that Taylor often had assaulted or raped her. In addition, she said that Taylor had caressed her while she was on the job, that he had followed her into the ladies' room when she had been there alone, and that at times he had exposed himself to her. Capital City argued that, because of its lack of actual knowledge of the conduct, it should not be held liable for its supervisor's sexual harassment. Would you agree? Also, should a successful sexual harassment case be dependent on the alleged victim's suffering a loss of employment or promotions? [See *Meritor Savings Bank* v. *Vinson,* 477 U.S. 57 (1986).]

5. In August 1973, Fort Worth Bank and Trust (the Bank) hired Clara Watson, who is black, as a proof operator. In January 1976, the Bank promoted Watson to a teller position in the Bank's drive-in facility. In February 1980, she sought to become supervisor of tellers in the main lobby; however, the Bank selected a white male for this job. Watson then applied for a position as supervisor of the drive-in bank, but this position went to a white female. In February 1981, after Watson had served for about a year as a commercial teller in the Bank's main lobby and informally as the assistant to the supervisor of tellers, the Bank promoted the man holding that position. Watson applied for the vacancy, but the Bank instead selected the white female who had served as the supervisor of the drive-in bank. Watson then sought the position vacancy created at the drive-in, but a white male won that job. The Bank, which has about 80 employees, had not developed precise and formal criteria for evaluating candidates for the positions for which Watson unsuccessfully had applied. Rather, it had relied on the subjective judgment of supervisors who were acquainted with the candidates and with the nature of the jobs to be filled. All the supervisors involved in denying Watson the four promotions at issue were white. Watson subsequently filed a lawsuit alleging racial discrimination. The district court concluded that Watson had failed to establish a prima facie case of racial discrimination in hiring, since the percentage of blacks in the Bank's workforce approximated the percentage of blacks in the metropolitan area where the Bank is located. The district court addressed Watson's individual claims under the evidentiary standards that apply in a discriminatory treatment case and determined that Watson had established a prima facie case of employment discrimination, but that the Bank, by presenting legitimate and nondiscriminatory reasons for each of the challenged promotion decisions, had met its rebuttal burden. The court also concluded that Watson had failed to show that these reasons had been pretexts for racial discrimination and therefore dismissed Watson's lawsuit. A divided panel of the Court of Appeals for the Fifth Circuit affirmed the district court's conclusions that Watson had failed to prove her claim of racial discrimination. Although Watson argued that the district court should have applied disparate impact analysis, the majority of the court of appeals panel held that a Title VII challenge to an allegedly discretionary promotion system is properly analyzed under the disparate treatment model rather than the disparate impact model. Other courts of appeals, however, had held that disparate impact analysis could be applied to hiring or promotion systems that involve the use of discretionary or subjective criteria. Apropos of these precedents, Watson claimed that subjective selection methods are at least as likely to have discriminatory effects as the kind of objective tests at issue in *Griggs* and other disparate impact

cases. The Bank, however, argued that conventional disparate treatment analysis is adequate to accomplish Congress's purpose in enacting Title VII and that subjective selection practices would be so impossibly difficult to defend under disparate impact analysis that employers would be forced to adopt numerical quotas in order to avoid liability. Whose arguments should the Supreme Court endorse—Watson or the Bank's? Why? [See *Watson* v. *Fort Worth Bank & Trust*, 487 U.S. 977 (1988).]

6. **BUSINESS APPLICATION CASE** The U.S. Customs Service (Service), which has as its primary enforcement mission the interdiction and seizure of illegal drugs smuggled into the country, implemented a drug-screening program requiring urinalysis tests of its employees seeking transfer or promotion to positions having a direct involvement in drug interdiction or requiring the incumbent to carry firearms or to handle classified material. Among other things, the program required that an applicant be notified that his or her selection was contingent upon successful completion of the drug screening; set forth procedures for the collection and analysis of the requisite samples and procedures designed both to ensure against adulteration or substitution of specimens and to limit the intrusion on employee privacy; and provided that test results may not be turned over to any other agency, including criminal prosecutors, without the employee's written consent. The National Treasury Employees Union, a federal employees' union, and one of its officials filed suit on behalf of Service employees seeking covered positions. These plaintiffs alleged that the drug-testing program violated the Fourth Amendment because the program allowed testing without requiring a warrant, probable cause, or any level of individualized suspicion beforehand. The district court agreed and enjoined the program. Vacating the injunction, the court of appeals held that although the program effects a search within the meaning of the Fourth Amendment, such searches are reasonable in light of their limited scope and the Service's strong interest in detecting drug use among employees in the covered positions. Von Raab, the commissioner of the U.S. Customs Service, also argued on behalf of the program that, given the national crisis in law enforcement caused by the smuggling of illicit narcotics, the government has a compelling interest in ensuring that front-line interdiction personnel are physically fit and have unimpeachable integrity and judgment. According to Von Raab, the government also has a compelling interest in preventing the risk to the lives of the citizenry posed by the potential use of deadly force by persons suffering from impaired perception and judgment. In Von Raab's view, these governmental interests outweigh the privacy interests of those seeking promotion to such positions, who have a diminished expectation of privacy with respect to the intrusions occasioned by a urine test by virtue of the special, and obvious physical and ethical, demands of the position. How should the Supreme Court rule in this case? Assume further that your firm is contemplating the institution of a drug-testing program for its employees and that the CEO has asked you to spearhead the development of this program. What interests will you take into account, and how will you reflect these interests in the policy itself? Explain fully. [See *National Treasury Employees Union* v. *Von Raab*, 489 U.S. 656 (1989).]

7. **ETHICS APPLICATION CASE** Transportation Agency of Santa Clara County, California (the Agency), had adopted an affirmative action plan that allowed it to consider sex as one factor whenever it made promotions to positions within traditionally segregated job classifications in which women had been significantly underrepresented. In selecting applicants for the position of road dispatcher, the Agency, in order to promote a female applicant, Diane Joyce, passed over Paul Johnson. Before Joyce, women had held none of the 238 skilled craftworker positions in the Agency. Although both individuals were qualified for the job, Johnson had scored slightly higher on the interview than Joyce. When the Agency nonetheless promoted Joyce, Johnson sued. Johnson argued that the Agency's affirmative action plan, by taking sex into account for promotions, violated Title VII of the Civil Rights Act. Was he correct? Why or why not? Had the Court decided this case on ethical grounds, who would have the stronger argument—the Agency or Johnson? Why? [See *Johnson* v. *Transportation Agency, Santa Clara County, California*, 480 U.S. 616 (1987).]

8. **IDES CASE** The Office of Civil Rights (OCR) of the U.S. Department of Education had employed Debra McWright as an equal opportunity specialist in its Chicago office between 14 February 1977 and 17 March 1983. As an infant, she had contracted polio, which left her with various permanent physical handicaps, including an inability to bear children. The OCR had hired McWright as a "handicapped individual" pursuant to § 501 of the Rehabilitation Act of 1973. In July 1982, McWright informed her immediate supervisor, OCR branch chief Catherine Martin, that she (McWright) was seeking an adoption and would request maternal childcare extended leave if a child were placed with her and her husband. In September, McWright told Martin and Martin's supervisor, Mary

Frances O'Shea, that she had been accepted as an adoptive parent. In November 1982, McWright filed applications for annual leave of four weeks and extended leave without pay (for a total leave time of about four months) but failed to list any particular dates because she did not yet know when the child placement would occur. In December 1982, Martin gave McWright three options: McWright could take immediate annual and extended leave; she could specify a future certain date to begin them; or she could take them on short notice in the future on the condition that she complete her then-pending assignments before taking the time off. McWright considered the first two alternatives unacceptable and therefore agreed to the third. The next day, Martin gave McWright three new civil rights violation case assignments, which, according to McWright, might have taken a year or more to complete. After learning on 5 January 1983 that a child soon would be available, McWright resubmitted her requests for immediate annual and extended leave of approximately four months. Denying her requests, the OCR instead gave McWright four days off with pay after an adoptive son was placed with McWright and her spouse on 11 January. McWright's renewed request for leave informally was approved on the condition that she work at home during the annual leave period. She accepted, began her annual leave the following day, and worked at home. Her request for leave without pay from 10 March to 29 June was approved unconditionally. However, Martin informed McWright that she must complete her pending civil rights violations assignments before her three months' leave could begin; Martin also requested the cancellation of McWright's leave without pay. McWright resigned her position that day. Subsequently filing suit against the OCR, she alleged that it had failed to accommodate her handicap (her inability to bear children) when it had refused to waive two conditions it normally required for maternal childcare leave (but that McWright had been unable to meet): medical certification and specification in advance of the leave period. She further alleged disparate treatment. She claimed that the OCR consistently had granted the extended leave requests of biological mothers, that the OCR had not required biological mothers to complete their pending work beforehand, and that the OCR had not obligated biological mothers to work at home on an uncompensated basis while they were on leave. McWright maintained that the OCR's actions had made her working conditions unreasonable and that her resignation therefore had constituted a constructive discharge (that is, her resignation had been forced on her by the circumstances and was tantamount to the OCR itself's firing her). Should McWright win on appeal? Why or why not? Would the FMLA, had it been enacted, have helped the parties avoid this litigation? Apply the IDES model to answer these questions. [See *McWright* v. *Alexander*, 982 F.2d 222 (7th Cir. 1992).]

NOTES

1. See 301 U.S. 1 (1937).
2. *Fibreboard Paper Products Corp.* v. *NLRB*, 379 U.S. 203, 223 (1964).
3. *Walters* v. *Metropolitan Educational Enterprises, Inc.*, 117 S.Ct. 660 (1997).
4. *Griggs* v. *Duke Power Co.*, 401 U.S. 424, 431–432 (1971).
5. 427 U.S. 273 (1976).
6. 438 U.S. 265 (1978).
7. 443 U.S. 193 (1979), *reh'g denied*, 444 U.S. 889 (1979).
8. 115 S.Ct. 2097 (1995).
9. 432 U.S. 63 (1977).
10. *Espinoza* v. *Farah Mfg. Co., Inc.*, 414 U.S. 86 (1973).
11. See *BNA Employee Relations Weekly* (*Special Supplement: Civil Rights Act of 1991*) (11 November 1991), pp. S1–S6.
12. 449 U.S. 144 (1991).
13. 445 U.S. 1 (1980).
14. "Hiring Temps Not Always a Bargain," *The National Law Journal* (17 March 1997), pp. B1, B2.

PART 9

IDES PROBLEMS

Five years ago, Nobuko Imati founded Healthtech, Inc., to create medical prosthetic devices, although the firm has since expanded into other health-care markets. Healthtech's mission to provide technology products for health-care markets has made the firm a darling of Wall Street investors. Recent legal problems, however, have caused some investors and Nobuko concern.

Healthtech is negotiating a merger with GoodHealth, a corporation specializing in outpatient surgery clinics. GoodHealth is the largest single purchaser of Healthtech's prosthetic devices. One of Healthtech's vice presidents, Simon Jones, is worried the merger may violate provisions of the Sherman and Clayton acts, given that, by some industry estimates, Healthtech currently controls nearly 80 percent of the prosthetics market. Indeed, several of Healthtech's smaller competitors have left the industry in sufficient numbers that the Justice Department is investigating Healthtech for possible Sherman Act violations.

Healthtech also is interested in acquiring Computer, Inc., a computer hardware manufacturer for medical laboratories, in a takeover. Computer's stockholders seem to favor Healthtech's offer, but its board of directors has enacted a poison pill in an effort to prevent the takeover. Nobuko believes that Computer's board members are primarily interested in retaining their positions, although the board members allege that the takeover would be harmful.

Healthtech also faces workplace issues. A disability advocacy group has challenged Healthtech over alleged employment discrimination practices. Although Healthtech has made efforts to employ and promote women and minorities, Healthtech currently has only two disabled employees. The firm has no policy for hiring disabled employees. Healthtech, however, to Nobuko's best understanding, has complied with all relevant provisions of the Americans with Disabilities Act (ADA) and the Civil Rights Act of 1964.

Last year the employees at a Healthtech manufacturing plant in Boston began to discuss unionizing. When the plant management learned of this activity, it took steps to discourage the formation of a union. Several meetings were held with the workers in which plant management discussed the potential negative effects of a union, including the loss of jobs. Several pro-union officials have made threats to pursue legal action against Healthtech unless these meetings stop. In addition, protests outside the plant have become commonplace, causing Healthtech management to fear violence.

Recently Healthtech has formed a corporate legal department headed by Sherman Jackson, an experienced corporate lawyer but a newcomer to the medical technology industry. To help Sherman understand Healthtech's problems, Nobuko needs to explain the legal issues Healthtech faces.

IDENTIFY What are the legal and ethical issues surrounding Healthtech's actions?

DEFINE What are the meanings of the relevant legal terms associated with these issues?

ENUMERATE What are the legal and ethical principles relevant to these issues? What principles, if any, of the Clayton and Sherman acts are relevant? What principles of the ADA or the Civil Rights Act of 1964 are relevant?

SHOW BOTH SIDES Consider all of the facts in light of the preceding questions. Are the steps being taken by the Justice Department, Computer's board of directors, the disability advocacy group, and union officials valid under the law?

[To review the IDES approach refer to pages 29–30.]

PROPERTY PROTECTION

Within the United States, the right to own property is among our most fundamental rights. Preserving the right to pursue and maintain property was a primary concern of our founders; this is evident in the Constitution, especially in the search and seizure limits of the Fourth Amendment and the due process clause of the Fifth Amendment. The Constitution balances the right to own property with the need for government to maintain order and promote the good of society, however. Hence, Congress has the right of eminent domain, or the right to take private lands if they are necessary for public use. Balancing the rights of businesses and individuals with the needs of government is a pressing issue in today's society.

Part 10 examines how local, state, and federal laws treat real and personal property and property rights, as well as the manner in which property is transferred. Moreover, this part examines an increasingly significant type of property—intellectual property—and how the law attempts to address the new challenges technology poses for business.

I D E S

Tom and Anna Kochanowski own and operate Call-Image Technology (CIT), a developer and manufacturer of videophones. CIT and the Kochanowskis have recently encountered a number of legal problems for which the firm needs legal help. If the State of Michigan passes a law curtailing CIT's use of its land, what, if anything, is CIT entitled to as compensation? CIT recently had one of its vans vandalized while it was in the possession of an auto reupholsterer. Who is liable for the vandalism to the CIT van? How can CIT adequately protect its trademarks and patents, both domestically and globally?

Consider these issues in the context of the chapter materials, and prepare to analyze them using the IDES model:

IDENTIFY the legal issues raised by the questions.

DEFINE all the relevant legal terms and issues involved.

ENUMERATE the legal principles associated with these issues.

SHOW BOTH SIDES by using the facts.

A G E N D A

A number of property issues will arise as CIT conducts business. For example, Anna and Tom will need to buy real property to construct manufacturing plants and to lease buildings for warehouse space. What issues must Tom and Anna be familiar with when they engage in these undertakings? What type of deed would CIT prefer? Why? The Kochanowskis have a barn on land they own, and they would like to renovate it into a warehouse. If the land is not zoned for commercial use, can the Kochanowskis lawfully do this? What problems may arise from such a venture?

Tom and Anna plan to purchase some land on which to build a vacation home. They want to be sure that, if something happens to one of them, the property will automatically pass to the surviving spouse. What is the best way to arrange this? Why?

Assume a CIT debtor is a joint owner in an apartment complex—can CIT attach the debtor's interest and force a sale? What issues would affect CIT's rights? Be prepared! You never know when one of the Kochanowskis will call on you for help or advice.

REAL PROPERTY AND JOINT OWNERSH

O U T L I N E

PROPERTY RIGHTS

There are two distinctly different meanings for *property*. First, the term means an object that is subject to ownership, a valuable asset. Second, property means a group of rights and interests that are protected by the law, commonly called "a bundle of rights." A multitude of rights are associated with property ownership. Ownership entitles a person to use the property personally, to give someone else the use of the property, to rent the use of the property to someone else, or to use the property to secure a loan. The owner may sell the property, make improvements to the property, or abandon the property. Courts commonly note that the "bundle of rights" includes the rights to enjoyment and use; to economically exploit the land based on present and potential uses; and to exclude others.

Ownership of real estate normally entitles the owner to continued use and enjoyment of the property in its present condition. For example, suppose you owned a house with a beautiful view of the mountains. If someone purchased an adjacent lot and started constructing a three-story house that would block your view, you can sue for an injunction to prohibit that person from interfering with the view. Such a lawsuit will succeed in some states.[1] Many states also recognize the right of support from adjoining lands; the right to use bodies of water adjacent to the parcel; limited rights to the airspace above the property; the right to things growing on the property; the right to things attached to the property; and the right to things, like minerals, below the surface of the property. Many communities now recognize and protect the right to have sun fall on existing solar collectors.

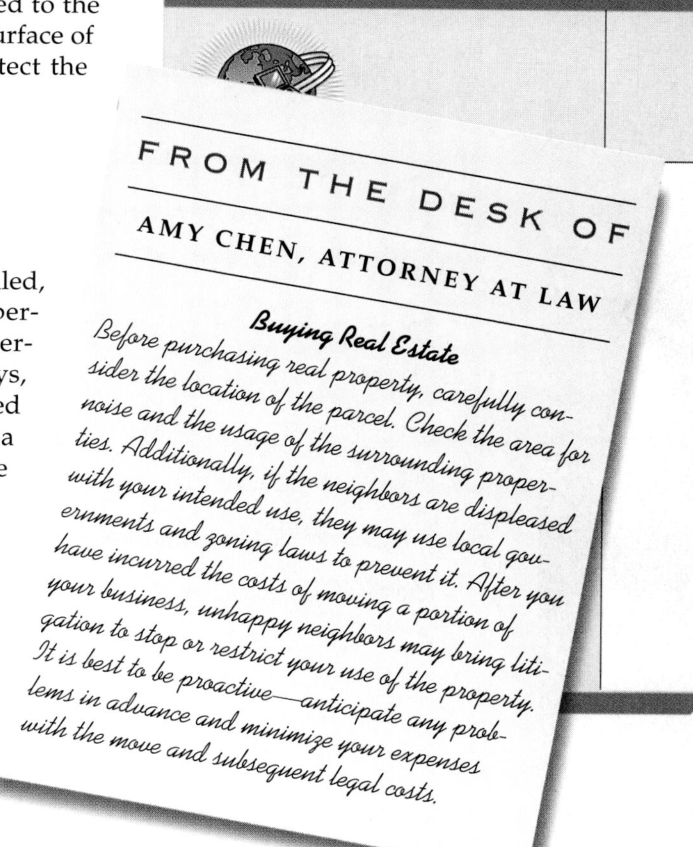

FROM THE DESK OF
AMY CHEN, ATTORNEY AT LAW
Buying Real Estate
Before purchasing real property, carefully consider the location of the parcel. Check the area for noise and the usage of the surrounding properties. Additionally, if the neighbors are displeased with your intended use, they may use local governments and zoning laws to prevent it. After you have incurred the costs of moving a portion of your business, unhappy neighbors may bring litigation to stop or restrict your use of the property. It is best to be proactive—anticipate any problems in advance and minimize your expenses with the move and subsequent legal costs.

REAL PROPERTY DEFINED

Definition of Real Property

This chapter deals with *real property* or, as it is commonly called, *real estate.* Significant differences exist between real and personal property. Real property is land and things that are permanently attached to the land, including buildings, roadways, and storage structures. Property that is permanently attached to buildings is also considered real property and is called a *fixture.* Personal property consists of everything else capable of being owned.

Definition of a Fixture

A *fixture* is property that at one time was movable and independent of real estate but became attached to it. Examples are water heaters, central air-conditioning units, furnaces, built-in ovens, installed dishwashers, bathroom sinks, and copper pipes for plumbing. A builder who is constructing a house will buy a water heater, take it to the construction site, and permanently attach it to the plumbing lines and the gas or electric lines. After the personal property has been attached, it becomes a fixture.

In determining whether an item is a fixture as opposed to personal property, courts will look at the reasonable expectations and understandings of most people. For instance, most people are shocked if they buy a house and, when they move in, discover that the sellers removed the handles on the kitchen cabinets and the plates over the light switches. The same buyers, however, expect the sellers to remove the tables, chairs, and other furniture. Ceiling lights are fixtures; table lamps are household goods. Plants in a flower bed are real property; plants in pots are personal property. Wall-to-wall carpeting is real property; area rugs are personal property. Refrigerators, mirrors, and paintings are generally personal property but may be real property if they are an integral part of the building.

In making this determination, courts also consider how much damage would occur if the property in question were removed.

Common law
A body of law that has developed from prior case decisions, customs, and usage.

Title
Legal ownership of property. Also, evidence of ownership.

The Nature of Plants

Another issue concerns plants: Are they real property (real estate) or personal property? Real estate includes plants that are growing on the land, such as fruit and shade trees, tomatoes, strawberries, artichokes, and trees that are being grown for timber. If a farmer sells land with crops still growing on it, the farmer is clearly selling real estate.

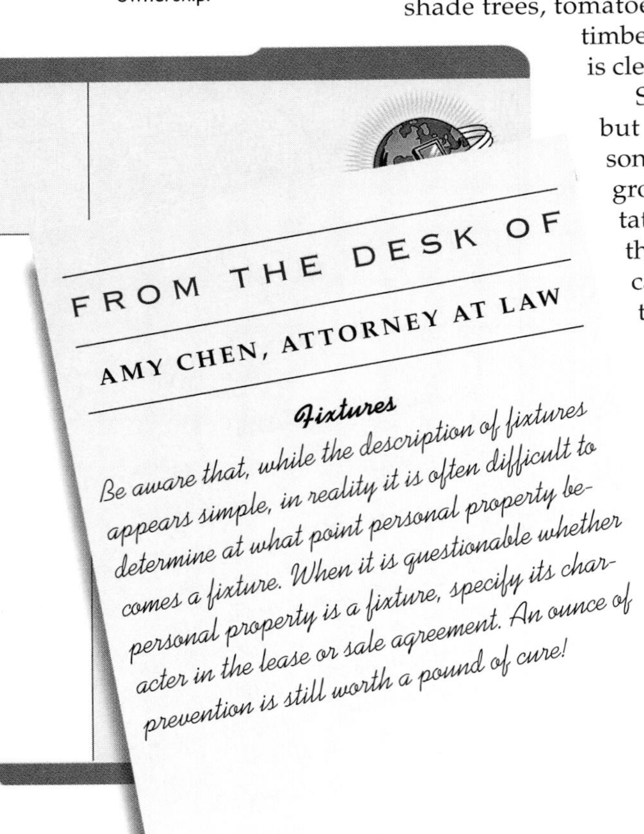

FROM THE DESK OF
AMY CHEN, ATTORNEY AT LAW
Fixtures
Be aware that, while the description of fixtures appears simple, in reality it is often difficult to determine at what point personal property becomes a fixture. When it is questionable whether personal property is a fixture, specify its character in the lease or sale agreement. An ounce of prevention is still worth a pound of cure!

Sometimes a farmer or another landowner may sell the plants but keep the land. In this case, did the landowner sell real or personal property? The **common law** rule is that if the plants were still growing when the **title** passed to the buyer, the sale was of real estate. If the title passed after the plants were severed from the land, the sale was of personal property. This rule is difficult to apply because in many instances the buyer and seller never discuss when title should pass.

Since the common law rule was difficult to apply, the Uniform Commercial Code (UCC) now uses a different test for the situation where the owner is selling the plants but retaining the land. The UCC test is generally much easier to apply. Under it, the determining factor is *who* is going to remove the plants or trees. If the *buyer* is going to remove them, the buyer has purchased real property. If the seller is going to remove them, the sale is of personal property. After defining the difference between real and personal property, the UCC generally is not concerned with real estate, although some sections of the UCC discuss crops and fixtures. A few states still follow the common law rule.

State Governance

Property laws vary from state to state. The laws of a state where the real property is located govern the land, regardless of the residence of the owner. For example, if you live in Wyoming but own land in Florida, Florida law governs your transactions with respect to the Florida real property.

Federal Regulation

Title III of the Americans with Disabilities Act (ADA) regulates property that is open to the public. These properties are commonly called *public accommodations* and include motels, hotels, restaurants, movie theaters, and retail stores. Effective 26 January 1992, under the act, new public accommodations must be designed to accommodate handicapped individuals. Existing structures must be modified if such modification is "readily achievable." The act itself does not specify the types of accommodation necessary, although the Justice Department is drafting regulations to provide guidelines. Court decisions will also provide guidance in interpreting the statute. Critics of the statute claim that the act is ambiguous as to what handicaps must be accommodated and what accommodations are required. Under the statute, disabled Americans can bring private litigation or litigation can be initiated by the Justice Department. Note that the ADA also includes employment provisions that are administered by the EEOC.[2] The ADA is discussed in greater detail in Chapter 43.

ACQUISITION OF REAL PROPERTY

Ownership of land and things growing on the land is a society-based concept. The idea that individuals can own land and trees is prevalent in European countries and the United States; however, it is not universal. A notable exception is found in Native American cultures.

Original Occupancy

Original occupancy (original entry) occurs when the government allows the private ownership of land that was previously owned by the government. In the United States, title may have been acquired by grant from either the U.S. government or other countries that colonized here. Original occupancy may be accomplished under an outright grant to specific people or families, or it may have occurred under homestead entry laws. *Homestead entry laws* are laws that allowed settlers to claim public lands by entering the land, filing an application with the government, and paying any required fees. Homesteading was a popular way to settle large amounts of land during pioneer days in the United States. Land in the United States is not generally available for homesteading today.

Voluntary Transfer by the Owner

The owner of real property may sell, trade, or give title to another by executing (signing) a deed. The recipient can be a private individual, business entity, or government body. In any of these cases, the transfer of title is made by the execution and delivery of a written deed of conveyance. A *deed* is the type of title evidence that is used for real estate, and it indicates who owns the land. A written document is required by the Statute of Frauds. This document must adequately describe the property that is being transferred. Documents that transfer important interests in real estate must also be in writing. An example of this type of document is a mortgage, which is a loan of money secured by real estate.

A deed describes the land being transferred and generally includes the following items:

1. The names of the grantor (transferor) and the grantee (transferee)
2. The amount of consideration, if any, that was paid by the grantee
3. A statement that the grantor intended to make the transfer (commonly called words of conveyance)
4. An adequate description of the property (the street address by itself will not be sufficient; usually this description contains information provided by a private or government survey)
5. A list and description of any ownership rights that are not included in the conveyance (such as mineral rights, oil rights, or **easements**)
6. The quantity of the estate conveyed
7. Any covenants or warranties from the grantor or grantee (some may be implied under the state law; others may be expressed in the deed, such as the grantee can never permit alcohol to be sold on the premises; usually the deed specifies that these covenants are binding on the grantee and his or her heirs and legal transferees)
8. The signature of the grantor or grantors

Easements

Rights to the access and use of someone else's real estate.

Types of Deeds. A *warranty deed* contains a number of implied covenants (or promises) made by the grantor to the effect that a good and marketable title is being conveyed. All the following covenants are included:

1. Covenant of title (the grantor owns the estate or interest that he or she is purporting to convey)
2. Covenant of right to convey (the grantor has the power, authority, and right to transfer this interest in the property)
3. Covenant against encumbrances (there are no encumbrances on the property except for those listed on the deed; encumbrances include easements, mortgages, and similar restrictions on ownership)
4. Covenant of quiet enjoyment (the grantor promises that the grantee's possession or enjoyment of the property will not be disturbed by another person with a lawful claim of title)
5. Covenant to defend (the grantor promises to defend the grantee against any lawful or reasonable claims of a third party against the title of the grantee)

A *grant deed* contains fewer promises than a warranty deed. Basically, it includes only a covenant that the grantor has not conveyed this property interest to anyone else. The grantor also promises that all the encumbrances are listed on the deed.

With a *quitclaim deed,* the grantor makes no promises about his or her interest in the property. The grantor simply releases any interest in the property that he or she *may* possess.

Delivery of the Deed. To complete a transfer of real property, the grantor *must* deliver the deed to the grantee or have it delivered to the grantee by a third person. The delivery establishes the grantor's intention to transfer the property.

Instead of handing the deed directly to the grantee, the grantor may use a third person to make the transfer. Sometimes, as in a real estate sales transaction, it is important to use an impartial third party to assist in the transfer and to protect both the buyer and seller. This third party is charged with the obligation of supervising the transfer, including such activities as collecting the deed, collecting the funds, checking that past utility bills, liens, and tax bills have been paid, prorating real estate taxes, prorating interest payments if a mortgage is being assumed, and assuring that the parties have fulfilled any conditions, such as repairs and inspections of the premises. This procedure is called an **escrow** and is a common method of transferring property in some states. The person who supervises this type of delivery may be an attorney, an *escrow officer* (an employee of a bank or escrow company who oversees the escrow transaction), or another agent.

Escrow
Process of preparing for the exchange of real estate, deed, and other documents managed by a third party.

Recording of the Deed. Recording is accomplished by filing the deed with the proper authority, usually the county clerk or county recorder. The recorder files the deed or a copy of it in a deed book. Deed books usually are arranged in chronological order. The recorder also enters information about the transfer in an index, which is organized by the names of the grantors and grantees or by the location of the property. The index simplifies the task of locating information about a particular parcel. The recording gives the whole world "notice" of the transfer to this grantee. Recording is not a legal prerequisite to the transfer, but it does establish the grantee's interest in the property, and in many states recorded deeds have precedence over unrecorded deeds.

Transfer by Will or Intestate Succession

A person can arrange to leave real property by provisions in a valid will. If a person does not have a valid will, the property will pass by the intestate succession statute of the state where the property is located. This statute will determine who inherits the property if a valid will does not exist. (Wills and intestate succession are discussed in detail in Chapter 46.)

PROTECTION OF REAL PROPERTY

Real property is subject to loss by operation of law; it can also be lost due to actions of the government, of another person, or of nature. This loss is generally involuntary on the part of the owner. To prevent it, the owner should be alert to these potential causes of loss. Obligations of owners of real property are discussed briefly in this chapter.

Involuntary Transfers by Operation of Law

If the owner is in default on a mortgage or trust deed, the owner may lose the property. The lender may institute foreclosure proceedings and take possession of the real estate. The lender must follow the appropriate state laws. Usually, the property will be sold at a foreclosure sale.

In most states, if the owner has not paid a legal judgment, the judgment creditor may ask the court for a writ of execution. Following the applicable state procedures, the sheriff will attach the property and sell it at a judgment sale. (Under state law, some property, both real and personal, may be exempt from attachment under a judgment sale.)

If the owner has not paid people who supplied labor or materials for the premises, these suppliers may also be able to force a sale under state law. These workers may have mechanic's liens for the value of the supplies or services rendered to improve the property. Even if they do not force a sale of the real property, generally they can prevent a voluntary sale by the owner unless they are paid from the proceeds.

Involuntary Transfers by Government Action

Government bodies have the right to take private lands if they are necessary for public use. This is called the right of *eminent domain.* Under this doctrine, the government must have a legitimate public use for the land and must pay the owner a reasonable amount for it.

A different type of taking occurs when the government enacts land use laws. Zoning and planning laws restrict how property may be used. They may prevent certain types of structures from being built on the property; for example, some areas may be limited to single-family residences only. Or certain industries may not be permitted to operate plants in particular areas because of the air pollution these plants would cause. Sometimes these ordinances restrict the number and placement of establishments that sell alcohol. Commonly, bars are not allowed within one-quarter mile of public schools. In order to be valid, zoning and planning laws must be based on a compelling government interest, and the restrictions must be reasonable.

Remand
The return of a case to the lower court for additional hearings.

Noxious
Hurtful and offensive.

The constitutionality of zoning laws was addressed in the landmark Supreme Court case *Lucas* v. *South Carolina Coastal Council*. This case also provides valuable insight into some of the constitutional issues that affect real estate ownership and use.

44.1 LUCAS v. SOUTH CAROLINA COASTAL COUNCIL — 112 S.Ct. 2886 (1992)

FACTS In the late 1970s, David H. Lucas and others were involved in extensive residential development on the Isle of Palms, a barrier island east of Charleston, South Carolina. In 1986, Lucas paid $975,000 for two residential lots for his personal investment, intending to build single-family homes on the lots. At the time, the lots were zoned for single-family residential use and there were no other restrictions on them. In 1988, the state legislature passed the Beachfront Management Act, based on an official report that the beaches named in the act were seriously eroding. The act directed the South Carolina Coastal Council to establish a baseline and permanently prohibited the building of *any* inhabitable structures between the baseline and the ocean. The legislature concluded that the area was not stabilized and setback lines were required to protect people and property from storms, high tides, and beach erosion. No exceptions were allowed under the act. When the baseline was established, Lucas's lots were between the baseline and the ocean, thereby preventing Lucas from building any inhabitable structures on either of his parcels. [In 1990, after this lawsuit was begun, the state legislature amended the act to authorize the council to issue special permits for building or rebuilding of single-family residences.]

ISSUES Did the state take Lucas's property in violation of the Fifth Amendment of the Constitution, which prohibits the taking of property without due process of law? Must the state pay Lucas for the lots because the act deprived him of all economically viable use of the property?

HOLDINGS Yes. There appears to be a taking in violation of the Constitution. The issue of payment is to be decided on **remand**.

REASONING A citizen understands that the state has power over the bundle of rights that he or she acquires when he or she obtains title to property. He or she necessarily expects that uses of the property will be restricted from time to time by the state exercising its police power. A person purchases property subject to these police powers, for example, the power to control harmful and **noxious** uses of the land. *Historically,* the concept of noxious uses was used to define when the exercise of police power would require compensation. Compensation was only required when the legislature was trying to curtail uses that were not noxious.

The state does not have to compensate the property owner every time the state exercises its police power in the interest of protecting the health, safety, morals, or general welfare. However, "the Fifth Amendment is violated when land-use regulation 'does not substantially advance legitimate state interests or denies an owner economically vi-

44.1 LUCAS v. SOUTH CAROLINA COASTAL COUNCIL *(cont.)* 112 S.Ct. 2886 (1992)

able use of his land.'" The state cannot enact a regulation that removes all economic use of the property *after* an owner has acquired it. The court has not clarified what constitutes a legitimate state interest in exercising its police power. Lucas did not contend that the state lacked the power to pass this statute, but he claimed that this action removed all the value of his property and he was entitled to just compensation. Property interests can be regulated; however, at a certain point the regulation will be considered a taking. The court has not described the exact point where a taking occurs, but has instead engaged in individual factual determinations.

The court has traditionally resorted to the existing rules or understandings to interpret regulations that are not takings of property and, consequently, not entitled to compensation. It has established two general categories where compensation is required. The first is when the regulation subjects the owner to a physical invasion of his property. The second is when the regulation denies to the owner all the economically beneficial or productive use of his or her land. In analyzing a total taking, the court will ordinarily examine "among other things, the degree of harm to public lands and resources, or adjacent private property, posed by the claimant's proposed activities, . . . the social value of the claimant's activities and their suitability to the locality in question, . . . the relative ease with which the alleged harm can be avoided through measures taken by the claimant and the government (or adjacent private landowners) alike." The fact that other similarly situated landowners engage in the same use indicates a lack of common law prohibitions; however, new knowledge may change what uses are permitted.

The test of whether a regulation denies all economic uses is rather straightforward. However, it is not always applied consistently. In some cases, it is difficult to determine what is a property interest and/or what is a loss of value. These problems are not posed in this case. The Act required Lucas to leave his land substantially in its natural, undeveloped form. The trial court had concluded that the construction ban left his property valueless. This case is reversed and remanded. In order to show that this prohibition is not a taking, on remand South Carolina must present principles of **nuisance** and property law that would prohibit the building of residences on Lucas's lots under the current conditions. In other words, the State must show that Lucas acquired the property subject to these restrictions. Also, the State must show the court that the decisions of its legislators are correct.

BUSINESS CONSIDERATIONS What could an investor do to avoid Lucas's plight? Should he have known that erosion and/or periodic flooding were probable?

ETHICAL CONSIDERATIONS What role should the government play in protecting citizens who own property in areas subject to erosion and/or flooding? Should the government protect them by prohibiting some types of construction in erosion- or flood-prone areas? What obligations do owners and potential owners have to themselves and others?

Private Restrictions on Land Use

Generally an owner can use property as he or she wishes. Sometimes the government uses **land use regulation** to limit the uses. In addition *restrictive covenants* restrict how land may be used. These are private agreements between landowners on the use of the property and may take the form of building restrictions or covenants, conditions, and restrictions (CC&Rs). These are the techniques used by condominiums and planned developments to control the building on and use of the lots. Restrictive covenants may be enforced by private lawsuits *if* they are lawful. Formerly, restrictive covenants were used to enforce racial segregation. The covenant would state that no owner could sell his or her property to a nonwhite person. The

Nuisance
Unlawful interference with the use of public or private property.

Land use regulation
Laws that regulate the possession, ownership, and use of real property.

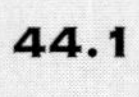

44.1

MANAGEMENT

PROTECTION AGAINST CLAIMS ASSERTED BY MATERIAL PROVIDERS

Tom and Anna decided to have the furnace inspected at the CIT plant before the cold weather began. Following the inspection, the serviceperson informed them that they had a cracked heat exchanger and that the unit must be shut off until it is repaired. Since the system would have to be idled anyway, the Kochanowskis decided to replace the furnace with a new energy-efficient unit installed by Cool Air, Inc. (Cool Air, Inc., is a licensed heating-and-cooling contractor that sells, installs, and services furnaces and air-conditioning units.) Dan has expressed some concern about having the work done by Cool Air, because he believes that this will give Cool Air a claim against the firm and its assets if there are any problems in making payments. However, he recognizes the need for heat in the plant during the winter months. Dan asks you how CIT can be protected against claims asserted by suppliers. What will you tell him?

BUSINESS CONSIDERATIONS Should an installer in a situation like that faced by Cool Air insist on having the family members serve as cosigners on the contract as protection against any possible default by the firm? Should the family members be concerned if they are asked to serve as cosigners on the contract?

ETHICAL CONSIDERATIONS Suppose that the service person knew that the current furnace could be repaired, but that it would not last very long even with repairs. Should he try to talk the customers into purchasing a new furnace in order to protect their long-term interests, or should he make the repairs (a short-term solution) knowing that a new furnace will be needed soon? How should this sort of issue be handled from an ethical perspective?

Supreme Court declared that restrictive covenants based on race are illegal in the landmark decision of *Shelley* v. *Kraemer.*[3]

Adverse Possession

Adverse possession occurs when someone tries to take title and possession of real estate from the owner. A person who has physical possession of real property has better legal rights to that property than anyone else, except for the true owner and people who claim possession through the true owner. If the possession is of an adverse nature and if the possession is for a sufficient length of time, the adverse possessor may actually take ownership from the true owner.

For possession to be adverse, it must be actual, open, and notorious. *Actual* possession means that the adverse possessor is actually on the land and is using the real estate in a reasonable manner for that type of land—as a residence, a farm, a ranch, or a business office. It is not sufficient that the adverse possessor state that he or she is using the land; actual use is required.

For possession to be *open,* it must be obvious that the adverse possessor is on the property. It will not be sufficient if the person stays out of sight during the day and walks around the property only at night. Openness is required to reasonably put the owner and the rest of the world on notice that the adverse possessor is using the property.

Finally, for possession to be *notorious,* it must be adverse or hostile to the true owner. Generally, people who occupy or use the property with the owner's permission, such as co-owners and renters, cannot be adverse possessors.

The required holding period varies from state to state and is specified by state statute. The period may range from five to thirty years. Entry under color of title may affect the holding period. Entering under *color of title* means that the holder thought that he or she had a legal right to take possession of the real property and had title to it. For example, a person with a defective deed would enter under color of title. Some states specify a shorter holding period if the holder entered under color of title and/or if the holder paid real estate taxes. In some states, the payment of real estate taxes is a necessary requirement for adverse possession; in others, color of title is required.

The possession must be continuous for the specified time period. The adverse possessor may leave the property for short periods to go to work, to classes, or on a brief vacation, for example, but he or she may not leave the property for an extended period of time.

The policy behind the doctrine of adverse possession is to encourage the use of land, a very valuable resource. The doctrine tends to encourage the use of land by someone else, if the owner is not using it. As the old adage says, possession may be nine-tenths of the law. This applies only to privately owned real property, however; government land may not be taken by adverse possession.

If renting property is not an option, an owner should periodically check on the property to make sure that no one is using it. If it is being used without permission, take prompt legal steps to remove the occupant.

CALL-IMAGE TECHNOLOGY

44.2

MANAGEMENT

ZONING RESTRICTIONS

The Kochanowskis have a large barn on their residential property. This barn has been vacant for quite some time; and Dan thinks that, with minor renovations, it will make an excellent warehouse from which to ship Call-Image videophones. Anna points out that the property is not zoned for commercial activities and such a use might be criminal without the proper zoning. Dan thinks that, since Call-Image is a family-owned and operated business, such restrictions do not apply. Anna and Dan seek your advice. What will you tell them?

BUSINESS CONSIDERATIONS What are the advantages and disadvantages of renovating the barn into a CIT warehouse? What considerations should a family business take into account in making this sort of decision? Would different factors enter into the decision for a publicly owned corporation?

ETHICAL CONSIDERATIONS Among the factors that might affect any decisions on this issue are: will there be an increase in traffic and/or noise in the neighborhood? How will such a use affect the neighbors? What ethical obligations exist for CIT under these circumstances?

Easements

In some situations a person may be entitled to use the land of another in a particular manner. This right is called an *easement.* An easement is not a right to *own* the property. Rather, it is the right to *use* the property in a particular manner. An easement may belong to a particular person, or it may run with the land. The latter means that the easement belongs to the owner of a particular parcel of land, called the *dominant parcel.* The parcel that is subject to the easement is the *servient parcel.*

An easement may be an *express* easement; that is, it was stated by the person who created the easement. Or an easement can be created by *prescription,* much like adverse possession: A person starts to use the servient parcel openly and, after the state's statutory period, will be entitled to continue the use. An easement can also be created by *necessity.* The most common example of necessity occurs when an owner divides a parcel and deeds a **landlocked** portion to someone else: The only method of access is across the servient estate. A requirement for an easement by necessity is that both parcels were originally one large parcel.

Landlocked
Surrounded by land owned by others.

Easements can also be created by *implication.* Again, this can occur when a parcel is divided, and the owner of the dominant parcel needs to use the servient parcel. However, the proof of need is not required to be as great as it is for an easement by necessity. For example, suppose an owner of a parcel of land decides to sell the northeast corner of the parcel. The owner had previously run a sewer system from this northeast corner to the main sewer line through the rest of the parcel. The buyer can reasonably expect to use the same sewer line when he or she owns the northeast corner. It would be *possible* to run a new sewer line to the northeast corner, but it was implied that the new owner could use the existing one. Easements also are created by *contract,* when an owner of property sells someone a right to use it. For example, an owner may sell an easement to an oil company to come onto the property to drill exploratory oil wells.

The issue in *Silacci* v. *Abramson* concerns whether an easement exists.

44.2 SILACCI v. ABRAMSON

53 Cal.Rptr.2d 37 (Cal.App. 1996)

FACTS The dispute is between neighbors who live in adjoining subdivisions. "The disputed parcel lies where the rear boundaries of the backyards converge. Toro Creek runs through the Silacci lot and that part of Silacci's property which lies across Toro Creek next to Abramson's property line is the portion in dispute." The parcel is about 1,600 square feet in size. David Scott, who previously owned the Abramsons' parcel, placed a three-foot-high picket fence completely around the parcel in question. At the time the land belonged to Carlton. Carlton had given permission to Scott and his other neighbors to take flood-control measures beside Toro Creek. Carlton sold his property and eventually it was owned and developed into Toro Hills Estates. Monterey County required the developer to grant a scenic easement along Toro Creek where there are trails used by hikers and those on horseback. The developer promised that it would not build any structures or gardens that would affect this easement. The developer sold a lot to Bob Franscioni in 1989. "A month after the sale, Chamberlain [the developer] wrote Abramson to say that his rear fence was encroaching on Franscioni's lot. Chamberlain offered to relocate the fence to the correct boundary line. Abramson replied that he believed he was entitled to keep the property located inside of his fence. Later in 1989 Abramson wrote Franscioni suggesting that Franscioni grant him an easement. Franscioni, who had no use for the disputed parcel, talked to Abramson about it and gave him oral permission to use the land. Abramson testified at trial, however, that he did not believe he needed Franscioni's permission, and that he would have continued to use the land without it." Nothing further happened until 1991, when Dinna Silacci purchased the lot from Franscioni. She offered to rent the property to Abramson for $50 per year. She also recorded a consent to use the property "to stop adverse use by Abramson." Abramson did not respond to the offer to lease the property, so she informed him that her son would remove the fence. Dinna Silacci then transferred the property to her son, Robert Silacci, who initiated this lawsuit.

ISSUE Do the Abramsons have the right to continue to use this enclosed yard based on a prescriptive easement?

HOLDING No.

REASONING "Adverse possession is a means to acquire ownership of land. In adverse possession, the claimant must prove open and notorious use, hostile to the true owner, for a period of five years, and he must also show that he has paid taxes [if any] on the parcel of land. Adverse possession, by use of the term 'possession,' implies ownership and title.

By comparison, an easement is merely a right to use the land of another. With an easement, the owner of the burdened land is said to own the servient tenement, and the owner of the easement is said to have the dominant tenement. Every incident of ownership not inconsistent with the enjoyment of the easement is reserved to the owner of the servient tenement. . . .

[The court distinguished some unique cases involving easements where the easement holder had exclusive use.] "An easement, after all, is merely the right to use the land of another for a specific purpose—most often, the right to cross the land of another. An easement acquired by prescription is one acquired by adverse use for a certain period. An easement , however, is not an ownership interest. . . . To permit Abramson to acquire possession of Silacci's land, and to call the acquisition an exclusive prescription easement, perverts the classical distinction in real property law between ownership and use." [The trial court decision that this is a prescriptive easement is overturned. This is not a prescriptive easement. On remand, the Abramsons may pursue the theory of adverse possession. If they do, the court will need to determine the effect of Dinna Silacci's recording of the consent to use.]

BUSINESS CONSIDERATIONS What could the Silaccis have done to avoid becoming embroiled in this problem? How could they have handled the dispute to better protect their interests?

ETHICAL CONSIDERATIONS What ethical rights do the Abramsons have? Why?

The manner and type of use are restricted by the easement. A person who exceeds the amount of use that is permitted under the easement will lose the easement, and his or her rights will be extinguished.

RENTAL OF REAL PROPERTY

Types of Tenancies

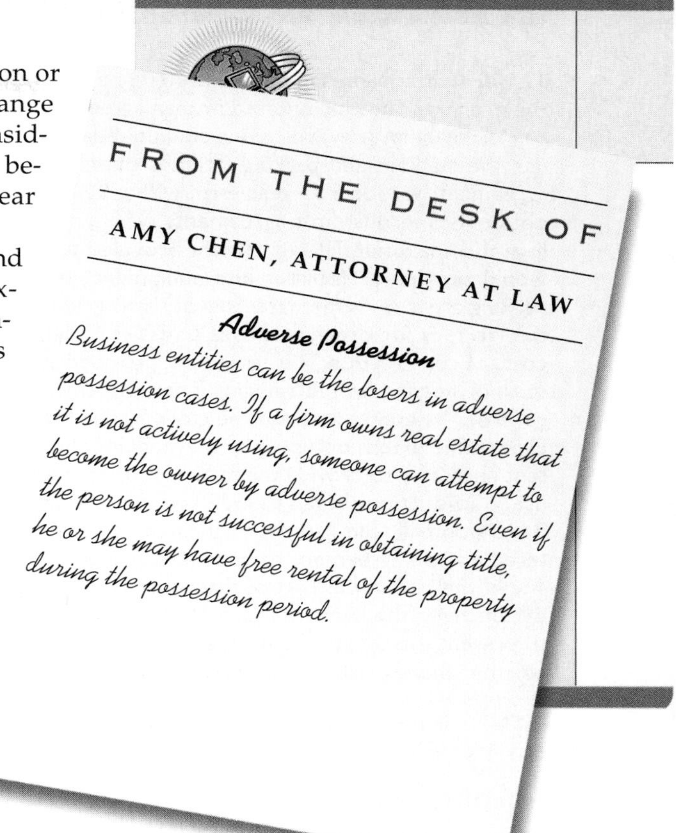

FROM THE DESK OF
AMY CHEN, ATTORNEY AT LAW
Adverse Possession
Business entities can be the losers in adverse possession cases. If a firm owns real estate that it is not actively using, someone can attempt to become the owner by adverse possession. Even if the person is not successful in obtaining title, he or she may have free rental of the property during the possession period.

The owner of real property may decide to allow another person or persons to use the property. If the owner is willing to exchange temporary possession of the property for money or other consideration, there is a rental agreement. Most students are tenants because they live in a university dormitory, an apartment near campus, or rent a house with others.

Tenancies are governed by both the rules of contract law and the rules of real estate law. Several basic types of tenancies exist, which are based on the length of the rental period. These include tenancies for a fixed term, periodic tenancies, tenancies at will, and tenancies at sufferance.

A *tenancy for a fixed term* is a tenancy for a set period of time; the beginning and ending dates are established. Generally, the Statute of Frauds requires a written lease if the tenancy is for one year or longer. Such tenancies automatically end at the set time. (Some states have set a maximum allowable term for a tenancy for a fixed term.) If the tenant has not vacated the premises by the end of the lease period, the landlord can explicitly execute a new lease with the tenant or can elect to treat the tenant's actions as an implicit renewal of the lease for another term of the same length. An implicit renewal cannot exceed one year, however, because of the provisions of the Statute of Frauds.

A *periodic tenancy* starts at a specific time and continues for successive periods until terminated. It may be established to run from year to year, month to month, week to week, or for some similar period. Moreover, either party may terminate it after proper notice. The lease normally specifies how much notice is necessary and to whom the notice should be addressed. The beginning date is specified, but the ending date is not.

A *tenancy at will* is a tenancy that can be terminated any time at the desire of *either* the landlord or the tenant.

A *tenancy at sufferance* is one in which the tenant entered into possession properly and with the landlord's permission, but wrongfully remained in possession after the period of the tenancy.

One issue in *Golden West Baseball Co.* v. *City of Anaheim* was whether an agreement constituted a lease.

44.3 GOLDEN WEST BASEBALL CO. v. CITY OF ANAHEIM 31 Cal.Rptr.2d 378 (Cal.App. 1994)

FACTS Golden West Baseball Co. (club) owns the California Angels baseball team. In 1964, the club was anxious to relocate the Angels from Dodger Stadium, which had been their home stadium. The club wanted their own stadium and also felt that the terraced parking at Dodger stadium was not suitable. In negotiations with Anaheim's mayor, the club said that it would need about 150 acres, a stadium with approximately 45,000 seats, parking for

44.3 GOLDEN WEST BASEBALL CO. v. CITY OF ANAHEIM *(cont.)* 31 Cal.Rptr.2d 378 (Cal.App. 1994)

12,000 automobiles, and adequate ingress and egress from the property. The club entered into an agreement with the city of Anaheim (city) to have a stadium built and then to use the stadium and parking facilities on game days. The agreement was for a 35-year term with a 30-year renewal option. Numerous draft agreements were exchanged before the final draft. The agreement provided that Anaheim would provide all facilities and equipment, including the parking areas on game days. The city also wished to lease the facilities for other purposes to assist in defraying the costs of construction. The agreement provided that the areas not needed would remain under the city's exclusive control. The contract stated the city may use the area "except to the extent occupied by the stadium, and to the extent necessary to provide the minimum parking for stadium use." Negotiations began in 1977 to move the Los Angeles Rams (football team) to the Anaheim Stadium. The city entered into an agreement to build an office complex at the site of the stadium, as part of that negotiation and as an inducement to the Rams to move. The club, however, wanted to prevent the construction. One of its main concerns was whether there would be adequate parking on game days.

ISSUE Is the club's agreement to use the stadium property a lease?

HOLDING No.

REASONING Despite the use of the term "lease agreement," this is not a lease. Labels are some evidence, but are *not* binding on the court. To establish a lease the agreement must show:

1. The parties intend to create a landlord–tenant relationship
2. A description of the parties
3. A description of the premises
4. The rent to be paid
5. Time and manner of payment
6. The term of the lease

Only the parties' intentions are at issue here. A lease gives the lessee the exclusive possession of the premise against everyone, including the owner. That did not occur here. The club had "the use" of the stadium approximately 81 days a year, the exact days vary from year to year. The owner continues to operate the concessions and parking facilities and provide security. Shared use with the owner on these occasions cannot be considered exclusive. The court noted that ambiguities in leases should be resolved according to the same rules used to resolve ambiguities in other contracts. The court determined that portions of the parking lot could be developed without reducing the number of parking spaces below the 12,000 provided in the contract or materially restricting ingress and egress. The parking spaces can be relocated onto adjacent lots owned by the city. This interpretation is consistent with the parties' conduct over the years. In fact, the city has rearranged the parking and traffic flow a number of times over the years without objection by the club. [The court noted that this agreement was not recorded and leases are often recorded.]

BUSINESS CONSIDERATIONS What could the club and the city have done in order to avoid this dispute? Would an alternate form of dispute resolution have better served the parties?

ETHICAL CONSIDERATIONS Was the city's behavior ethical is this situation?

Rights and Duties of Tenants

The tenant rents the right to exclusive possession and control of the premises, which means that the tenant is the only one entitled to be in possession. Generally, the lease specifies that the property can only be used for a particular, stated purpose. Some leases specify that the property can only be used for lawful purposes.

At common law, the landlord is not entitled to enter the premises. The landlord often obtains permission from the tenant to enter the premises either on an ad hoc basis or because such a right is reserved in the lease. Even at common law, the landlord does have the right to enter the premises in case of an emergency.

If the tenant is a business, it may need to install trade fixtures, such as neon signs, commercial refrigeration units, and industrial ovens. If a tenant attaches trade fixtures to the property, the tenant is allowed to remove them before the end of the lease. But if the removal causes any damage, the tenant must repair the damage.

Under a normal lease, the landlord is required to make sure the property is in good condition for the purposes specified in the lease and must maintain the property in good condition. Tenants do not have an obligation to make major improvements or repairs. However, a tenant may contractually agree to make certain modifications or improvements. For example, in exchange for an exceptionally low rent, a tenant might agree to remodel a property at his or her own expense. In such a case, it is wise to specify who will pay for these improvements and who will get the benefit of them at the end of the lease.

Warranty of Habitability. Some states have held that an implied warranty of habitability exists in residential housing leases. That is, the landlord impliedly promises that the premises will be fit for living—for example, that the heating system will work, that there will be running water, and that there will be indoor plumbing. When the courts recognize this warranty, the tenant can use a breach of warranty as a basis for terminating a lease, as a means of reducing the rent, or as a defense for nonpayment of the rent.

Constructive Eviction. Most states recognize an implied covenant that the owner will protect the tenant's right to quiet enjoyment (use) of the premises. Constructive eviction occurs when the owner does not protect this interest of the tenant and allows a material interference with the tenant's enjoyment of the premises. Suppose, for example, that you rent an apartment and that living in the unit next door is a person whose habit of playing drums in the middle of the night is interfering with your sleep. Although your neighbor's behavior is in violation of the lease, the landlord will not enforce the lease provisions. The landlord's behavior constitutes constructive eviction, and you can move out without any further liability to pay rent. However, if you do not take some action promptly, the court may decide that you waived your right to complain about the noise.

Assignment and Subleases. The transfer of the tenant's entire interest in the lease is an *assignment.* If the tenant transfers only part of his or her interest and retains the balance, the transfer is a *sublease.* (Note that this terminology is slightly different from that in Chapter 14.) Ordinarily, assignments and subleases are allowed unless the lease specifically provides that they are not. Most leases do prohibit assignments and subleases without the prior written approval of the landlord.

Rights and Duties of Landlords

Landlords have the right to retake possession of their property at the end of the lease. In most rental situations, the landlord expressly reserves the right to terminate the lease if the tenant breaches any promises contained in it, including the promise to adequately care for the property.

Rent. Rent is the compensation that the landlord receives in exchange for granting the tenant the right to use the landlord's property. Most leases require the tenant to pay the rent in advance. Many landlords require that tenants pay the first and last month's rent in advance, which provides added protection for the landlord. If the tenant is behind in paying the rent, it usually takes a number of weeks to force the tenant to leave the premises. If the tenant has not paid the rent, the landlord has a number of available options. The landlord can sue for the rent that has not been paid or can start procedures to have the tenant evicted (removed) from the premises. In some states, the landlord has a lien on the tenant's personal belongings that are on the premises. This allows a form of self-help called a lockout: the landlord locks the tenant out of the premises while all the tenant's personal property is inside. For example, North Carolina law allows a landlord to gain possession of the property by peaceable means, including lockouts.[4]

States generally select from among the following approaches to determine the amount of self-help allowed to a landlord who is entitled to possession of the premises:

1. A landlord can use necessary and reasonable self-help;
2. A landlord must rely only on the remedies provided by the courts;
3. Or a landlord can gain possession by *peaceable* means.

Damage by the Tenant. The landlord has the right to collect from the tenant for any damage caused by the tenant. For example, if Rudy, a tenant, negligently fills his waterbed, and it leaks and causes substantial damage to the premises, Rudy is liable for the damage. Tenants are also responsible for any damage caused to the premises by their guests. This right to collect for damages exists at common law and is usually stated in the lease. The tenant is responsible for damage caused negligently or intentionally but not for ordinary wear and tear—the deterioration that occurs through ordinary usage.

Security Deposits. For protection, the landlord will usually collect a security deposit. This money is to be used after the tenant has vacated the premises to repair any damage negligently or intentionally caused by the tenant. It is not to be used to clean the premises or to repair normal wear and tear. As such, a security deposit generally cannot be used to repaint walls that have become dirty through normal use. It can be used to replace doors in which holes have been punched, however. Any money that remains should be returned to the tenant within a reasonable period after the tenancy terminates. Some states have statutes that establish when the landlord must return the security deposit.

Duty to Protect a Tenant and His or Her Guests. Landlords generally have the same responsibility to their tenants' guests as they do to the tenants themselves. The landlord does not warrant that the premises are safe, but the landlord does have the duty to warn the tenant of *latent defects*—defects that are not immediately obvious and of which the tenant may not be aware. This duty of the landlord extends only to latent defects that the landlord knew or should have known existed.

Rights After Abandonment by a Tenant. If the tenant wrongfully abandons the premises during the term of the lease, the landlord has various options. The landlord can make a good faith effort to find a suitable tenant, but if one cannot be found, the landlord can leave the premises vacant and collect the rent from the tenant who abandoned the premises. The tenant is legally obligated to pay the rent, and the landlord can obtain a court judgment for the payment. The landlord will be able to collect *if* the tenant can be located and is solvent. If the landlord is able to rerent the premises, he or she is technically renting the premises on the tenant's behalf. If a lower rent is obtained, the tenant is liable for the difference.

As an alternative, the landlord can repossess the premises and rerent them on his or her own behalf. The original tenant who abandoned the premises is relieved of any liability for additional rent. If the landlord is able to rerent the premises for more money, the landlord will benefit. As *Dahl* v. *Comber* indicates, there may be a factual issue whether the rerenting is for the landlord's or the tenant's behalf.

44.4 DAHL v. COMBER

444 A.2d 392 (Me. 1982)

FACTS Dahl constructed a building for Comber's business. This building was leased to Comber for a five-year term. The business had difficult times and defaulted on the lease. Dahl tried to rent the building, but was able to find only temporary tenants.

ISSUE Did Dahl rerent the premises for his own benefit?

HOLDING No. It was rerented for Comber.

REASONING The lower court found that Dahl was rerenting for the benefit of his tenant. The evidence was sufficient to support this conclusion. The lease stated that any surrender had to be in writing and had to be signed by the landlord. When a tenant tries to surrender the premises to the landlord, the landlord can decide whether or not to accept the surrender. The landlord can accept the surrender and then rerent the premises on the landlord's behalf. Or the landlord can refuse the surrender and hold the tenant liable for any shortages in rent. In this case, the landlord was mitigating damages by rerenting the property on the tenant's behalf. Such an action does not extinguish the tenant's underlying responsibility to pay the rent.

BUSINESS CONSIDERATIONS How should a business treat a situation in which a tenant defaults on his or her lease? Should the business actively seek a tenant, or wait for the breaching tenant to find someone to assume the balance of the lease?

ETHICAL CONSIDERATIONS If a tenant breaches a lease, is it ethical for a landlord to wait for the tenant to find someone to assume the lease, knowing that the breaching tenant is liable for the balance of the lease? Is it more ethical for the landlord to actively seek a new tenant, thereby mitigating the damages the breaching tenant faces?

Legislative Trends

Landlord and tenant laws are undergoing change. Two federal statutes address discrimination in housing—the Civil Rights Act of 1866 and the Civil Rights Act of 1968. The 1968 Fair Housing Act, which is contained in the later Civil Rights Act, is the basis for most of the recent litigation and is the more comprehensive of the two acts. As originally passed, it prohibits discrimination based on race, color, religion, or national origin. Discrimination based on sex was added in 1974, and discrimination based on familial status was included in 1988.

Familial status includes having children under eighteen years of age. The 1988 amendment also enhanced the protection by providing three methods for enforcement: (1) the Department of Housing and Urban Development can initiate a lawsuit in federal court or before an administrative law judge, *if* all the parties agree; (2) the person subjected to the discrimination can file a suit in either state or federal court, and the court may award actual damages, punitive damages, or equitable relief; (3) the U.S. attorney general can file a suit if a pattern or practice of discrimination exists. As with most statutes, there are exceptions. For example, single-family units owned by a private investor with less than four houses *may* be exempt from the act as a whole, and housing solely for the elderly (over 62 years of age) is exempt from age discrimination provisions.

44.3

MANAGEMENT/MANUFACTURING

LONG- OR SHORT-TERM LEASE?

CIT wants to rent a new plant in order to expand its production and shipping capacities. The firm has located a parcel that is ideal for its needs: it has good access, adequate space, and a reasonable rent. CIT prefers a relatively long-term lease, due in part to the renovations CIT will need to make to the leased property. The landlord, however, is only willing to sign a five-year lease. He is willing to insert a clause stating that the lease will be renewable for additional periods of five years each, subject to certain conditions. Because the landlord is not willing to meet the terms proposed by CIT, Tom and Anna ask you whether the firm should sign the lease. What advice will you give them?

BUSINESS CONSIDERATIONS What provisions should be included in the lease in order to protect CIT's rights? What concerns should the Kochanowskis have with regard to the renovations? How should they protect themselves and their interests?

ETHICAL CONSIDERATIONS Suppose a prospective tenant explains planned renovations for a rental property during the negotiations. The landlord recognizes that the building will be worth a great deal more in rent with the renovations and decides to negotiate a shorter lease term than was originally anticipated. Does such conduct raise any ethical concerns? Why? How should such a situation be treated, from an ethical perspective?

Some states are very protective of tenants' rights. Other states are more protective of the landlord than of the tenant. Recent examples of protenant legislation include laws that require the payment of interest on security deposits or prevent retaliatory eviction. *Retaliatory eviction* occurs when a landlord evicts a tenant who has filed complaints about violations of law, including building- or health-code violations. To recover for retaliatory eviction, generally, the tenant must prove *all* of the following elements:

1. The tenant's complaint was *bona fide,* reasonable, and serious in nature;
2. The tenant did not create the problem him- or herself;
3. The complaint was filed before the landlord began the eviction proceedings;
4. The primary reason the landlord began the eviction proceedings was to retaliate against the tenant for filing the complaint.

In some states, retaliatory eviction has been prohibited by court decisions and not legislative statutes.

Some states and/or cities have rent control statutes that prohibit landlords from raising the rent. Although rent control is intended to protect tenants, many economists argue that it is ineffective. They argue that instead it creates a shortage of rental housing, because investors choose other investments that provide a higher rate of return. Also, landlords may not provide necessary repairs. After unsatisfactory results, rent controls are being abolished in some areas. Massachusetts voters abolished rent controls in 1994. The California legislature enacted a statute, effective in 1999, allowing landlords to raise the rents on vacant apartments even where there are local rent controls.[5]

JOINT OWNERSHIP OF PROPERTY

Joint ownership exists when two or more people have concurrent title to property; that is, they own the property at the same time. There are five forms of joint ownership: tenancy in common, joint tenancy with rights of survivorship, tenancy by the entireties, community property, and partnership property. (Chapter 34 discusses partnership property; it is not covered in this chapter.) Generally, these forms of joint ownership can exist with personal property as well as with real property. Most of these forms can be created voluntarily by the tenants, or they can be created by someone else for the tenants.

A legal characteristic of most forms of joint ownership is that each of the co-owners (the tenants) has an undivided right to use the whole property. Thus, the parcel described on the deed is not divided equally among the tenants; instead, each

YOU BE THE JUDGE

Rent Control in Santa Monica

Santa Monica, California, may have the toughest rent control law in the United States. Santa Monica is currently governed by members of a political party called Santa Monicans for Renters' Rights (SMRR). (SMRR is pronounced "smur".) Rents there average about $552 a month. By one estimate, this is 30% below market value.

When Santa Monica created its rent control program, it was aware that rent control might encourage landlords to "economize" on maintenance or convert properties to other uses such as condos. To maintain its rent control program, the local rent control board has 250 pages of regulation, a staff of 50, and an annual budget of $4.2 million.

John Rodriguez, a barber and owner of three small apartment buildings, says "They're using our money to give to other people without any proof whatsoever that those people are in need." Until 1986, landlords could not even go out of business. A California law has been enacted that permits landlords, even in Santa Monica, to go out of business.

In 1990, Phyllis Anderson, one Santa Monica landlord, paid each of her tenants $3,500 to vacate their apartments. She still is unable to convert her six-unit apartment building to another use. If she sold her building to someone else, the purchaser would be restricted by the same rules.

Suppose a group of landlords challenges this law in *your* court. How will *you* rule in this case?[6]

BUSINESS CONSIDERATIONS Would you consider investing in rental property in a community where there is rent control? Why or why not? What would you do if you were the owner when rent control was initiated?

ETHICAL CONSIDERATIONS *Should* the government regulate and control how owners use their real property? What ethical issues are raised by such regulation?

SOURCE: *Fortune*, 5 August 1996.

of them has the right to use all the property. If a dispute arises about the use of the property that the tenants are unable to resolve among themselves, they can file their complaint with the court. The primary remedies available to resolve such a dispute are (1) to sell the property and divide the proceeds or (2) to divide the property equitably and give each tenant a separate parcel. Either of these is considered an action for partition. Note that because the usable value of adjoining parcels may differ, the separate segments may differ in size and shape. Exhibit 44.1 summarizes joint ownership of property.

Tenancy in Common

A *tenancy in common* occurs when two or more people own the same property. Each tenant has an undivided right to use the whole property. Usually, a tenancy in common is indicated by words like "Bennett and McCormick, as tenants in common" on the deed or other evidence of title. If the deed simply says "Bennett and McCormick," most courts will presume that they are tenants in common.

EXHIBIT 44.1 Comparison of Forms of Joint Ownership

Remember that because property rights are governed by state law, a wide variation may exist from state to state.

	Tenancy in Common	Joint Tenancy with Rights of Survivorship	Tenancy by the Entireties	Community Property
Requirements for Creation				
Requires equal ownership interests		**	X	X
Restricted to married couples			X	X
Limited to two people			X	X
Restricted to human beings		*	X	X
Applicable to both real and personal property	X	*	*	X
Rights of One Tenant Acting Alone to Transfer or Encumber His or Her Share Without the Consent of the Others				
May use the whole property (undivided right to the whole)	X	X	X	X
May be transferred by will	X			X
May not be transferred by will		X	X	
Will pass to surviving tenants at death, if there is no valid will[b]		X	X	*[a]
Will pass to intestate heirs at death, if there is no valid will	X			*[a]
May be sold during life	X[c]	*		*/**
May be mortgaged or assigned during life	X[c]	*		*
May be transferred by gift during life	X[c]	*		
May be attached by a creditor of a tenant	X	X		

Legend
X The trait applies to the specific form of joint ownership.
* This is true in most states.
** This is true in many situations.

[a] Most community property states have different intestate succession provisions for the passage of separate property and community property. The community property commonly passes to the surviving spouse.

[b] In some types of tenancies, courts would say the interest "remains" with the surviving cotenants instead of "passing" to the surviving cotenants.

[c] Generally, a tenant in common will have this power. However, in many states, if the tenancy in common is between spouses and consists of real estate, the signature of the second spouse will be required.

There is no legal limit on the number of tenants in a tenancy in common. Practically speaking, however, if there are too many tenants, conflicts will probably arise among them regarding the use of the property. Each tenant may sell, assign, or give away his or her interest. A tenant may also will away the interest in a valid will. If the tenant has no valid will, then the interest in the tenancy will pass to his or her heirs under the state intestate succession statute. (Chapter 46 discusses wills and intestate succession in greater detail.) A creditor of an individual tenant can attach his or her interest in the tenancy in common.

Tenants in common do not have to have equal interests in the property. For example, if there are four tenants in common, one may have a one-half interest, one may have a one-quarter interest, and the other two may have a one-eighth interest each.

Joint Tenancy with Rights of Survivorship

A *joint tenancy with rights of survivorship* occurs when two or more people own property together. Again, there is no legal maximum number of tenants. However, the practical question remains: How many cotenants can get along with one another? As in a tenancy in common, each tenant has an undivided right to use the whole property. Generally, each tenant has an equal interest in the property. Joint tenancies differ from tenancies in common in that when one tenant dies, his or her interest passes to the remaining cotenants. The survivors continue to hold an undivided interest in the whole property. Generally, a will does not have any effect on a joint tenancy with rights of survivorship. (There is a movement in the U.S. legal community that advocates changing state laws regarding the ability to will joint tenancies and insurance policies. Some courts are devising theories to this effect.) The interest in the cotenancy property will pass from one tenant to another immediately on death by operation of law. Eventually, the tenant who outlives the others will own the complete interest. In most states, corporations are not allowed to be joint tenants because corporations do not die.

Because of the survivorship feature, joint tenancies often are used as substitutes for wills. Given the potential for disputes during life, however, this practice may be unwise. In addition, if a joint tenant wrongfully causes the death of another joint tenant, he or she will not be allowed to benefit and will be prevented from taking the **decedent**'s interest in most states.

Decedent
A person who has died.

Joint tenancies may be divided during a court action for partition. In most states, a joint tenant can sell, make a gift of, or assign his or her interest during his or her life. A creditor of the joint tenant can attach the interest. A transferee of the joint tenant will take the interest as a tenant in common. A transferee includes a purchaser, a donee, an assignee, or a creditor who obtained rights through the attachment procedure. The transferee does not receive the survivorship rights of a joint tenant because the other joint tenants never agreed to share the risk of survivorship with the transferee.

Tenancy by the Entireties

In a *tenancy by the entireties,* two tenants, who must be husband and wife, share the property. Each tenant is a joint owner in the whole property. This type of ownership has a survivorship feature. If one spouse dies, the survivor receives the whole property. Unlike joint tenants with rights of survivorship, many states allow a tenant who wrongfully caused the death of his or her spouse (cotenant) to benefit and to take title to the whole. Generally, only creditors of the family unit can attach entireties property. One spouse normally cannot unilaterally dispose of his or her interest, unless the parties obtain a legal separation or a divorce. The tenants can, however, agree to sever the tenancy. A valid will does not affect distribution of entireties property. Tenancies by the entireties are not recognized in all states; for example, **community property states** do not have tenancy by the entireties.

Community property states
States in which married couples generally create community property.

Community Property

Community property is recognized in eight states—Arizona, California, Idaho, Louisiana, Nevada, New Mexico, Texas, and Washington—as well as the Commonwealth of Puerto Rico. This discussion emphasizes the general features of community property laws, which vary from state to state. Louisiana community property law is most dissimilar, because it is based on Louisiana's French heritage. The community property laws in the other states are based predominantly on Spanish civil law.[7] Remember, too, that community property laws are also changing. California, for example, recently revised its community property scheme.

Community property is a form of co-ownership that can occur only between husband and wife. It is based on the concept that financially the marriage is a partnership. One-half of most of the property that is acquired or accumulated during marriage belongs to each spouse. Technically, this assumes that one-half of each asset belongs to the husband and one-half belongs to the wife. Thus, most states require that both the husband and the wife sign any deeds to transfer real property. In most states, this requirement does not extend to personal property. In fact, the names of both spouses do not have to appear on the community property or on any title evidence to the property. For example, although a paycheck may bear the name of only one spouse, it is nonetheless community property and, as such, belongs to both spouses. The primary source of community property for most couples is wages and earnings.

This is not meant to imply that a married couple will have only community property. Each may own property separately, just as in **separate property states**.

Separate property states
States in which married couples cannot create community property.

Separate property normally includes the following:

1. Property owned by either spouse before their marriage
2. Property given to one spouse alone by gift, by will, or by intestate succession
3. Property that is acquired with separate property funds

In addition, in some states—California, for example—income, rents, or profits earned from separate property are also separate property; in other states—Idaho, Texas, and Louisiana—this income is community property if received during the marriage. In Louisiana, a husband or wife can file a declaration that this income should be separate property instead of community property. All property other than that previously mentioned is usually community property.

For most purposes, a husband and wife can contractually agree to split their community property into two shares of separate property. However, if they are careless and mix their respective separate properties and/or community properties, it may all become community property. If the property becomes so mixed that it cannot be separated into community and separate property, the courts say that it is hopelessly commingled and treat all of it as community property. Distinguishing separate and community property was an issue in *Potthoff* v. *Potthoff*.

44.5 POTTHOFF v. POTTHOFF — 627 P.2d 708 (C.A.Ariz. 1981)

FACTS Gertrude and Herbert Potthoff were unable to agree on a property settlement in their divorce. They maintained one basic bank account, but Herbert was the only one who could withdraw from the account. Into the account, they deposited funds from Herbert's medical practice, loan proceeds, proceeds from the sale of stock, stock dividends, interest income, and proceeds from the sale of Gertrude's separate property. From this account, they paid

44.5 POTTHOFF v. POTTHOFF *(cont.)* 627 P.2d 708 (C.A.Ariz. 1981)

the expenses of the medical practice, living expenses, costs of investments, and costs of real estate. Before the Potthoffs' marriage, Herbert purchased property on which he built the Palm Grove Shopping Center with his separate funds. He also spent considerable time and effort making it a successful investment.

ISSUES Is the bank account community property? Is the Palm Grove Shopping Center separate property?

HOLDINGS Yes, to both. The bank account is hopelessly commingled; the real property was purchased and improved with separate property funds.

REASONING Due to the various transactions involving separate and community funds and failure to keep accurate banking records, the bank account is commingled. The entire amount becomes community property if the funds become so commingled that the identity of the separate funds are lost, which occurred in this case. The Palm Grove property, however, was purchased before the marriage and was built with separate funds. Thus, it is separate property. Under Arizona law, to the extent that separate property is improved by community funds, the community has a lien on the property for the amount of those funds. To the extent that Herbert's efforts improved the property, this increase in value was community property.

BUSINESS CONSIDERATIONS What businesses are most affected by community property laws? Why? What should business do to minimize losses due to community property interests?

ETHICAL CONSIDERATIONS What ethical obligation does a person owe a spouse? Is it ethical to labor on separate property to the exclusion of community property?

A couple begins to form community property once they are married. In most situations, they stop forming community property once they establish separate residences. In a divorce proceeding, the community property usually is divided.

Community property does not have a survivorship feature. A spouse can will his or her share of the community property to someone else. If the decedent does not have a valid will, most intestate succession statutes provide that the property will pass to the surviving spouse.

The National Conference of Commissioners on Uniform State Laws (NCCUSL) adopted the Uniform Marital Property Act (UMPA).[8] When it is enacted by a state legislature, it modifies the property rights of married couples and makes the state more like a community property state. Wisconsin adopted the UMPA in 1983.[9] A number of other states introduced the bill; however, by 1996, none had adopted the bill.[10]

Distinguishing Among the Forms of Joint Ownership

The words used on the deed or other title evidence are controlling as to whether the tenants are tenants in common, joint tenants with rights of survivorship, or tenants by the entireties. If the language on the deed is not clear, under state law there will be a presumption as to the form of joint ownership. If the tenants are husband and wife, most states will presume that the property is community property or entireties property. If the state recognizes neither form of ownership, it will presume a joint tenancy with the right of survivorship. If the tenants are not related to each other by marriage, most states will presume that they are tenants in common.

http:// RESOURCES FOR BUSINESS LAW STUDENTS

NAME	RESOURCES	WEB ADDRESS
U.S. Department of Housing and Urban Development (HUD)	HUD provides information on real property and planning issues for both consumers and businesses. HUD also provides information on the Fair Housing Act and the Civil Rights Acts.	http://www.hud.gov/
Legal Information Institute (LII)—Land Use Law Materials	LII, maintained by the Cornell Law School, provides an overview of land use law, links to statutes, federal and state judicial court decisions, and other materials.	http://www.law.cornell.edu/topics/land_use.html
The U.S. House of Representatives Internet Law Library—Real Property	The U.S. House of Representatives Internet Law Library provides state, federal, and international legal materials concerning real property.	http://law.house.gov/106.htm
TenantNet	TenantNet, an informal network of tenants and tenant leaders in New York, provides news, information, and resources on landlord–tenant law.	http://tenant.net/

SUMMARY

Property ownership includes title to the property and the right to control possession of the property. Real property consists of land and objects that are built on the land, growing on the land, and/or permanently attached to the land. A fixture is property that was personal in nature before it was permanently attached to a building.

Real property can be acquired by a grant from the government or by transfer from the owner. An owner may trade, sell, give, or will the property or leave it to another person by intestate succession. Lifetime transfers will be described in a deed; the deed will be delivered to the grantee; and, in most cases, the deed will be recorded. Although not legally required, recording protects the grantee and the public.

An owner who is not attentive may lose title to or use of the property. This loss can be caused by unpaid debts, by government restrictions on the use of the land, or by eminent domain. An owner may also lose his or her interest by the adverse possession of another person. Easements can restrict the owner's use of the property.

An owner can enter into a rental agreement called a lease. Under a lease, a tenant is entitled to the exclusive possession of the owner's real estate. The lease is the contract that will govern many terms of the landlord–tenant relationship. Under modern law, the landlord must repair the premises. A tenant who negligently or intentionally damages the property is liable for the cost of those repairs. The landlord can require a security deposit in order to assure that there are funds for making such repairs. The tenant is justified in leaving the premises when there is constructive eviction. A landlord can evict a tenant if the tenant fails to pay the rent. Commercial leases may contain different provisions than the leases of houses or apartments.

Two or more people, called cotenants, can own an interest in the same piece of property at the same time. They may be tenants in common, in which case each tenant owns an undivided right in the whole parcel and there are no survivorship rights. Or they may be joint tenants with rights of survivorship. Such tenants can dispose of their interests during life; at death, their interest will pass to the remaining cotenants by operation of law. Tenants in a tenancy by the entireties must be husband and wife. In community property states, a husband and wife can create community property. Most of the assets that they acquire during their marriage will be community property. The form of ownership is important to a business entity that may desire to purchase the asset from one or more tenants or the business entity may be a creditor that wishes to attach the tenancy property.

Discussion Questions

1. After Al's mother and father died, Al, who is responsible for their estate, decides to sell their home. After locating buyers for the property and entering into a sales contract with them, Al removes the petunias, his father's prize-winning roses, and a load of topsoil that is on the flower beds. The buyers are unhappy about this. Who has the right to these items? Why?
2. Are crops real or personal property? Why is this distinction important?
3. Describe the typical provisions included in a deed.
4. Kim moves onto a piece of real estate in California. He begins to use the property in an open, actual, and notorious manner and continues to do so for five years. He also pays the real estate taxes on this parcel. The applicable holding period is five years. Who owns this parcel? Why? Is it material that Nancy, the original owner, also paid real estate taxes? What are the legal rights of the parties? Why?
5. Jack and Rosie are neighbors. In 1970, Rosie built a fence around her property. However, she did not have the boundary surveyed, and the fence was built four feet into Jack's property. Who owns this four-foot strip of land now? Why?
6. Why is it difficult for a lessee (tenant) to be successful as an adverse possessor?
7. Should a court protect Carmen, a tenant who has complained to the health inspector about rodent infestation in her apartment complex, from eviction? Why or why not?
8. Why might a person want to establish a joint tenancy with another person who is not a relative?
9. How is community property made or acquired in a community property state?
10. Why might a person prefer to establish a tenancy in common instead of a joint tenancy with rights of survivorship?

Case Problems and Writing Assignments

1. The Shaughnesseys purchased a tract of land in 1954. They subdivided 12 acres into lots and retained 4 acres for themselves. In 1967, the Witts purchased the lot next to the one the Shaughnesseys kept. The Witts built a house on this lot and began living there. In 1968, the Witts cleared an area of land that ran along their property. They built a swimming pool, a deck, a playground, a dog run, and built a fence along the property line. Neither owner realized that the Witts had encroached 40 feet onto the Shaughnesseys' property. In 1988, the Shaughnesseys sold their 4-acre lot to the Millers. When a survey showed the encroachment, the Millers demanded that the Witts stop using the property. When the Witts refused, the Millers sued to establish their ownership rights in the property. This is called a suit to quiet title. Who is entitled to the strip of land? Why? [See *Witt* v. *Miller*, 845 S.W.2d 665 (Mo.App. 1993).]
2. Jon and Marion Kubichan owned and occupied a parcel of residential property. During their ownership, they designed and built a fountain pond in their backyard. The Kubichans did not enclose the pond with a fence, but at the time of the accident it was enclosed. The builders had not obtained the permit that was required by a city ordinance. Later, the Kubichans sold the property to Goldman, who then entered into a lease option with the Reids. While the Reids occupied the property, they made changes in the exterior of the pond but not in its interior. A toddler, 22 months old, was visiting the property with his parents and his siblings. He fell into the pond and suffered severe brain damage and quadriplegia. The pond allegedly was deceptive in nature because it appeared much shallower than it was and it lacked safety features. Is either the owner or the tenant liable for creating an unreasonably dangerous condition on the real estate?

Why or why not? [See *Preston* v. *Goldman*, 210 Cal.Rptr. 913 (Cal.App. 1985).]

3. Dorothy Karell purchased 18.917 acres in 1958 and received a warranty deed. Rena West and her partner purchased the adjoining 3.783-acre tract. The 18.917 acres owned by Karell were enclosed by a fence that also enclosed a portion of West's 3.783 acres. Karell rented the property to various tenants from 1958 until 1972. The tenants lived in the house on the 18.917 acres. One or two of the tenants kept livestock or grew crops. In 1970, Karell contracted to sell Howl the sand and topsoil from the land enclosed by the fence. Who owns that portion of the 3.783 acres that is enclosed by the fence? Is Karell liable for the sand and topsoil that were removed by Howl? Why or why not? [See *Karell* v. *West*, 616 S.W.2d 692 (Tex.App. 1981).]

4. Mary Stoiber, a tenant of a residential parcel of real estate, sued for damages from her former landlord, Earley, and the rental agents who managed the property. Stoiber was sued under an unlawful detainer action by Earley. The unlawful detainer action was filed after the Kern County Health Department ordered that the premises be vacated and destroyed within 30 days because of numerous housing code violations. Stoiber alleged that she had complained about the condition of the property to Earley's agents. She further alleged that the faulty plumbing had caused discomfort and annoyance and the flooding had damaged her furnishings. Did Stoiber have a cause of action for breach of the warranty of habitability? What should be her measure of damages? [See *Stoiber* v. *Honeychuck*, 162 Cal. Rptr. 194 (Cal.App. 1980).]

5. **BUSINESS APPLICATIONS CASE** The landlord owned a 36-unit apartment complex. Becker, one of his tenants, slipped and fell against his glass shower door and broke his arm. The shower doors were made of untempered glass. The glass doors were installed before the landlord purchased the premises, and he did not know that the doors were made of untempered glass. One of the witnesses testified that tempered glass and untempered glass look the same except for the small identification mark in one corner. It was agreed that, had the shower door been made of tempered glass, the extent of the injury would have been reduced. Should the landlord be liable for latent defects in rental units if the defects existed when the tenant leased the premises? Why? [See *Becker* v. *IRM Corp.*, 698 P.2d 116 (Cal. 1985).]

6. **BUSINESS APPLICATIONS CASE** Private citizens wanted to enter the common areas of a multibusiness office complex to make antiabortion statements. The protesters carried signs and placards and shouted at prospective patients of Cherry Hill Women's Center, one of the ten tenants on the property. These protesters did not have the permission of the owner of the property. Does the landowner have the right to keep the protesters off the property? Why or why not? [See *Brown* v. *Davis*, 495 A.2d 900 (N.J.Super. 1984).]

7. **ETHICAL APPLICATIONS CASE** A Connecticut statute provided that the lessee be given a five-day notice to quit for nonpayment of rent. A notice to quit informs the tenant to leave the property with his or her belongings. The lease provided that whenever the lease terminated by the lapse of time or by breach of any of the promises in the lease, the tenant waived all rights to notice. Did the lease provisions effectively waive the protections granted by state law? Why or why not? Does this statute treat tenants ethically? [See *Sandrew* v. *Pequot Drug, Inc.*, 495 A.2d 1127 (Conn. App. 1985).]

8. **IDES CASE** Jackson and Chapman purchased a property on or about 5 June 1984. The property was purchased subject to the lease of the Postal Service and other tenants. The Postal Service was notified of the change of ownership of the premises. It then failed to pay rent to anyone for about six months while it waited for an official notice of the change of ownership on its own forms. The landlords filed a forcible entry and detainer action against the Postal Service. Should they win the suit? Why? Use the IDES principles to analyze this case and to reach your conclusions. [See *Jackson* v. *United States Postal Service*, 611 F. Supp. 456 (D.C. Tex. 1985).]

NOTES

1. This is not always the case. In the classic case of *Fontainebleau Hotel Corp.* v. *Forty-Five Twenty-Five, Inc.*, 114 So.2d 367 (Fla. 1959), the court held that there were no rights to sunlight or view.
2. Laura M. Litvan, "The Disabilities Law: Avoid the Pitfalls," *Nation's Business* (January 1994), pp. 25–27.
3. 334 U.S. 1 (1948).
4. See *Spinks* v. *Taylor*, 278 S.E.2d 501 (N.C. 1981).

5. "Slow Death for Rent Control," *Fortune* (5 August 1996), pp. 24, 26.
6. Ibid.
7. For an excellent discussion of the historical basis for community property law in each state, see W. S. McClanahan, *Community Property Law in the United States* (Lawyers Cooperative and Bancroft-Whitney, 1982), ch. 1–3. For an interesting discussion of the origins of community property in Europe and its adoption in other countries, see William Q. DeFuniak and Michael J. Vaughn, *Principles of Community Property,* 2nd ed. (Tucson, AZ: University of Arizona Press, 1971), ch. II.
8. For a copy of the act as adopted by the NCCUSL, see 9A Uniform Laws Annotated (U.L.A.) 97 (1987) and pocket parts.
9. See Wisconsin 1983, Act 186, Effective 1-1-86, W.S.A. 766.001 to 766.97.
10. Information on the current status of adoptions of Uniform State Laws provided by Katie Robinson, Public Affairs Coordinator NCCUSL, during a telephone conversation on 29 May 1997.

A G E N D A

In addition to owning real property, as discussed in Chapter 44, CIT owns personal property. For example, CIT owns the rights to produce and sell its interactive videophone "Call-Image." How can the Kochanowski family protect this asset? What type of property is it? What are the rights and obligations that accompany ownership? How can CIT best protect its property?

CIT was interviewing applicants for positions in its factory. After the applicants left, Dan noticed two umbrellas in the waiting room. What should Dan do with them? In addition, their company leases equipment from an electronics firm. Tom Kochanowski is concerned that CIT may be liable for any damages to the equipment and, consequently, feels this equipment should be insured. Dan disagrees, arguing that, in leases of industrial equipment, the party leasing the equipment assumes the risk relating to damages. Who is correct? Why? When CIT rents extra delivery trucks, what are the legal rights of the lessor and CIT?

Be prepared! You never know when one of the Kochanowskis will ask for your help or advice.

Personal Property and Bailments

O U T L I N E

Ownership of Property

Classifications of Property

The concepts of property rights and joint ownership discussed in the context of real property in Chapter 44 apply to personal property as well. As noted in that chapter, real estate is land and everything constructed on or otherwise permanently attached to the land or to any of the buildings. All property that is not classified as real property is personal property.

Personal property is divided into two categories: tangible and intangible. *Tangible* personal property is property that is movable and can be felt, tasted, or seen. It has texture, color, size, a temperature, and similar characteristics. Examples of tangible personal property include textbooks, pens, briefcases, calculators, computers, and printers.

Intangible personal property cannot be reduced to physical possession; it cannot be held in a person's hand. It may, however, be reduced to legal possession and is often very valuable. Intangible personal possessions include things such as stock ownership, patent rights, copyrights, accounts receivable, and corporate goodwill. A physical thing may just represent *rights.* A good example of this is money—without a government willing and able to stand behind its money, money is just metal or colored paper. Another example of a tangible representation is a patent. The right to use an invention or process is intangible; however, a patent holder applies to the U.S. government and if the application is approved, he or she receives a document from the patent office and a patent number. The valuable right is the right to use and sell the invention. The government paperwork evidences that right. The distinction between tangible and intangible personal property is not significant in most contexts and does not control the parties' legal relationships.

The traditional label for a piece of personal property is a *chattel.* Chattels are divided into chattels real, chattels personal, and chattels personal in action. A *chattel real* involves an interest in land, but the chattel *itself* is personal—for example, a leasehold or other legal right to use land. The owner of the chattel real does not own the land but does have valuable legal rights. *Chattels personal* are tangible, movable personal property such as desks, chairs, chalk, and erasers. A *chattel personal in action,* also called a *chose in action,* is the right to file a lawsuit or to bring legal action.

Components of Ownership

The three components of ownership that are important with respect to real property are also important with respect to personal property. These components are ownership, possession, and title. *Ownership* includes all the rights related to the ownership of property. *Possession* includes the right to control the property by having it in one's custody or by directing who shall have custody of it. The concept of *title* includes both the current legal ownership of the property and the method of its acquisition. Title also refers to the written evidence of ownership that appears on a certificate of title for property, such as a "pink slip" for an automobile or a stock certificate.

ACQUISITION OF PERSONALPROPERTY

Original Possession

Original possession occurs when the owner is the first person to possess the property. In other words, the owner created the ownership rather than receiving it by transfer from another person. One way to obtain ownership by original possession is to create the property through physical or mental labor; an artist, for example, acquires ownership through original possession by creating a painting or a sculpture.

Another way to obtain ownership by original possession is to take something that has never been owned before and reduce it to possession, as when someone pans for gold in a wilderness area and takes possession of any nuggets found. When a person creates property, there is usually no dispute about who actually owns it. Disputes do arise, however, when people are hunting or trapping wild animals. For example, suppose that a group of hunters is about to trap a fox when a farmer spots the fox near some chicken coops and shoots it. A dispute may then ensue about who owns the fox. A court would decide that the farmer owned the fox and its pelt because the hunters had not reduced the fox to their possession. The farmer had taken control over it first.[1]

FROM THE DESK OF

AMY CHEN, ATTORNEY AT LAW

Tax Implications of Bartering

Customers and suppliers sometimes suggest an exchange of goods. Bartering often is promoted as a way to avoid income taxes. Bartering is considered to be an underground economy because transactions cannot be taxed when participants do not report them on their tax returns; therefore, federal and state governments are unaware of the trades. Actually, when a business or individual trades its goods, it receives income in the form of other goods. The fair market value of the goods received should be reported on tax forms.

Voluntary Transfers of Possession

Individuals can also acquire real and personal property by having it transferred to them voluntarily by the previous owner. The transfer can occur by purchase, gift, gift *causa mortis*, inheritance, or intestate succession.

Purchases. The most common way to acquire property owned by another is to *purchase* it. When property is sold by the previous owner, there is an exchange of consideration: The buyer gives up one form of property, often money, and the seller gives up another form of property. Sometimes the parties barter, or exchange goods or services for the property. Bartering is becoming increasingly popular for goods; organizations even exist to assist businesses in locating other businesses with which to barter.

Gifts. A person can also obtain ownership of property through a *gift*. The person who transfers the property is called the *donor* and the person who receives the property is called the *donee*. Three requirements must be satisfied for a valid transfer by gift.

First, the donor (the previous owner) must *intend* to make a gift—that is, to transfer the property without receiving full and fair consideration. In most gift situations, the donor is freely giving up the property without receiving any consideration at all. Sometimes it is difficult to determine whether the intent of the donor was to make a gift or, alternatively, to sell or to lend the property. This is particularly true if the donor has died or if the donor and the donee have had a disagreement. However, if the transfer is to be treated as a valid gift, it must be shown that the donor's intent was to make a gift.

The second requirement for a valid transfer by gift is that the donor *deliver* the gift property to the donee. When the donor hands the gift to the recipient, *actual delivery* occurs. Sometimes actual delivery is not practical because of the situation of the parties or the type of property being transferred. Consequently, courts permit *constructive delivery.* For example, if a hospitalized man has some antique coins in his safe deposit box and wants to give them to his son, he can give his son the keys and a note that will allow the son access to the box, thereby effecting constructive delivery of the gift property.

The third requirement for a valid gift is *acceptance* by the donee. The donee must be willing to take the property from the donor. In most cases, this is not an issue. However, a donee may refuse to accept a gift if the donee feels it will "obligate" him or her to the donor, as when a sales agent making a bid for a contract offers the purchasing agent a two-week vacation in Hawaii. Sometimes a donee may refuse a gift because the gift property has little use or value to the donee or creates legal liabilities for the donee. For instance, a donee might refuse a gift of real estate, such as substandard tenement housing that has many building code violations.

Transfer tax
Tax on the ability to transfer assets.

A transfer by gift may be subject to a **transfer tax** such as a gift tax. If so, usually the donor must pay the tax. Most state and federal gift taxes also apply when the donor receives nominal consideration (i.e., the transfer is for less than full and adequate consideration). For example, if a donor transfers a diamond ring worth $700,000 to a donee for $5, the value of the gift will be treated as the fair market value of the ring ($700,000) less the $5 that was paid for it. Any gift tax is figured on this amount ($699,995) and the donor is obligated to pay the tax. The gift is *not* subject to income tax when it is received by the donee.

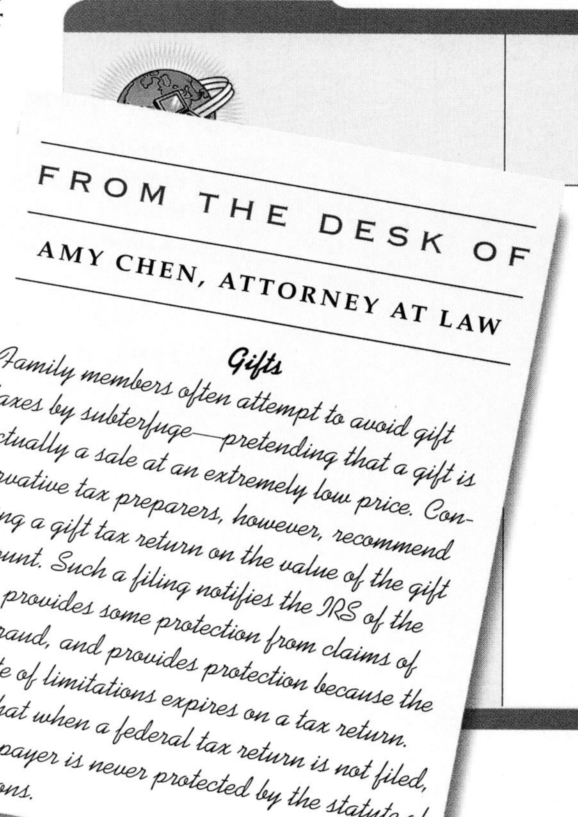

FROM THE DESK OF
AMY CHEN, ATTORNEY AT LAW
Gifts
Family members often attempt to avoid gift taxes by subterfuge—pretending that a gift is actually a sale at an extremely low price. Conservative tax preparers, however, recommend filing a gift tax return on the value of the gift amount. Such a filing notifies the IRS of the gift, provides some protection from claims of tax fraud, and provides protection because the statute of limitations expires on a tax return. Note that when a federal tax return is not filed, the taxpayer is never protected by the statute of limitations.

If the donor intends to make a gift and delivers the property and the donee accepts the property, the transfer is a valid gift. Once transfer of a gift has been completed, it generally cannot be revoked. The donor cannot legally take the property back from the donee, no matter how much the donor wants or needs to have it returned. In most cases a completed gift, also called an *executed gift,* is final. However, the gift can be set aside or revoked if the donee engaged in fraud, duress, or undue influence that resulted in the making of the gift.

A promise to make a gift at some time in the future is not binding on the promisor. The promisor can change his or her mind with impunity. An executory promise to make a gift is enforceable in the case of promissory estoppel, however. This equitable doctrine is applied by the courts to avoid injustice. It is based on the concept that the promisor makes a definite promise that he or she expects, or should reasonably expect, will induce the donee to act or refrain from acting based on the promise. The donor will be held to his or her promise to prevent injustice.

Certain types of property require special formalities before the owner can make gifts of them. To transfer a *chose in action* (a right to bring legal action), the transferor must make an assignment of the right. An

Negotiable instruments
Transferable documents used as credit instruments and as substitutes for money. Examples include checks, drafts, promissory notes, and certificates of deposit.

assignment is a formal transfer of a contract right. (Assignments are discussed in detail in Chapter 14.) To transfer **negotiable instruments**, the transferor must make either an assignment or a negotiation. A *negotiation* is an endorsement or notation on the document that it should be paid to a specific person or that it should be paid to the bearer or holder. The *bearer* or *holder* is the person who is in possession of the document.

Gifts fall into three categories: *inter vivos* gifts, testamentary gifts, or gifts *causa mortis. Inter vivos* gifts are made while the transferor is still alive; they are lifetime gifts. *Testamentary gifts* are completed when the owner dies; they are the types of gifts that a person puts in a will and are commonly called testamentary transfers. These transfers do not actually take place until death. Gifts *causa mortis* must meet special requirements about the donor's intention.

***Gifts* Causa Mortis.** Gifts *causa mortis* occur while the property owner is still alive. The donor is making the gift because he or she expects to die soon. Generally, the donor is contemplating death from a specific cause. The requirements for a gift *causa mortis* are that (1) the donor must intend to make the gift, (2) the gift must be made in contemplation of death, (3) the gift property must be actually or constructively delivered, and (4) the donor must die from the contemplated cause. If the donor does not die from the contemplated cause, the gift will be revoked. In this case, the donor or the donor's estate can reclaim the gift property. Since the donor was motivated, at least in part, by the expectation of death, it is logical that if the donor does not die, he or she should be able to get the property back.

A gift *causa mortis* is a legal concept and is distinct from various tax concepts that require lifetime gifts to be included in the estate for tax purposes.

Inheritances. A person can receive property from the estate of someone who dies. If the person who died has a valid will covering the property, the recipient specified in the will receives the property by inheritance. Like gifts, inheritances may be subject to state and/or federal transfer taxes.

Property Received by Intestate Succession. The property of a person who dies without a valid will is transferred to recipients by intestate succession. The same occurs if property is omitted from an incomplete will. The people who receive this property are specified in the state intestate succession statute. As with other death-time transfers, this transfer may be subject to estate or inheritance taxes. Transfers by wills and intestate succession statutes are discussed in greater detail in Chapter 46.

Involuntary Transfers of Possession

Sometimes the transfer of property or the custody of property to a recipient is not completely voluntary on the part of the true owner. Such a situation occurs when there is accession or confusion or when property is abandoned, lost, or mislaid.

Accession. *Accession* occurs when a person takes property that he or she does not own and adds to it. For example, a person takes some lumber and makes it into a dining room table. The legal question that arises is: Who owns the dining room table? Should it be the person who owned the lumber or the person who worked on the lumber and changed its nature? The court examines a number of factors in making its decision on this question; the most important is whether the worker knew that he or she had no right to the lumber. As with many legal problems, the court weighs the conflicting equities.

YOU BE THE JUDGE

California Farmer Attempts to Sell Water for Nonfarm Use

Under the 1992 Central Valley Project Improvement Act, federal farm water can be sold to cities, such as Los Angeles and Santa Clara. Prior to this act, federal farm water could only be sold from one farming area to another. The Areias Dairy Farms proposes to sell about 32,000 acre-feet of farm water to the Metropolitan Water District of Southern California over a 15-year period. The proposed sale will be worth about $5.6 million to the Areias family, including Assemblyman Rusty Areias. The sale must still be approved by the U.S. Bureau of Reclamation.

A public meeting was scheduled to hear comments on the proposed sale with approximately 400 people in attendance, most of them hostile to the sale. At the meeting, Rusty Areias contended, "I'm not going to pump one gallon more water than I do right now." Metropolitan has indicated that it would prefer to negotiate with districts, instead of individuals; however, attempts to negotiate with the Central California Irrigation District have not been successful. In fact, members of the irrigation district have indicated their opposition to the Areias sale. According to board member Ann Wieser, "A ground water balance has been achieved over the last 100 years . . . That balance is in jeopardy if [Areias] is not putting in his recharge quota. I think this is unreasonable, damaging, and not fair to us." If the Areias contract was challenged in *your* court, how would *you* rule?[2]

BUSINESS CONSIDERATIONS What can other farmers and ranchers in the area do about the proposed sale? What strategies would be most effective? Why?

ETHICAL CONSIDERATIONS *Should* farmers and farm districts be permitted to sell farm water to cities? Should water be different from other types of personal property? What ethical issues are raised here?

SOURCE: Mark Grossi, *The Fresno Bee*, 2 August 1994 and 24 August 1994.

Title *normally* remains with the rightful owner of the lumber and is not transferred to the laborer. Depending on the circumstances, the courts may determine that the laborer is an innocent trespasser. An innocent trespasser does not acquire title simply by adding labor and additional materials. The innocent trespasser *will* acquire title, however, under any one of the following conditions:

1. Because of the work effort, the original property has lost its identity. (The innocent trespasser took iron ore and made it into steel.)
2. A great difference exists in the relative values of the original property and the new property. (The innocent trespasser took a rough diamond and cut and polished it into a beautiful pear shape.)
3. A completely new type of property has been created and the innocent trespasser has added the major portion of it. (The innocent trespasser placed her notebook on a table in the library. After selecting a couple of references, the trespasser sat down and started to write her research paper. Much later the trespasser discovered that she had sat at the wrong table and used someone else's notebook.)

If the innocent trespasser does acquire title by accession, the trespasser is obligated to pay the rightful owner for the value of the property taken. This value will be based on the worth of the property at the time the trespasser took it. These cases are really exceptions to the general rule that the trespasser usually does not acquire title.

If title to the property stays with the original owner, the innocent trespasser can recover for the value of the services rendered in improving the property. If the owner were allowed to keep these improvements without payment, the owner would have an unjust enrichment and the innocent trespasser would suffer an unjust loss. The owner is obligated to pay for the reasonable value of the improvements. This is comparable to the theory underlying quasi contracts, however, there are minor differences.

A *willful trespasser*—one who knows he or she has no right to the property—cannot acquire title to the new property. The transfer of title under such conditions would permit willful trespassers to benefit from their wrongdoings and might even encourage them to try such an action again. A willful trespasser is liable for any damages that he or she caused and will not be entitled to any compensation for improvements made to the property through his or her efforts.

> Suppose, for example, Marti took some bricks she found in a neighbor's yard. Marti knew she was not entitled to the bricks, but since she thought her neighbor did not want them, she decided to go ahead and use them to build a barbecue. Although heavy, the barbecue is movable, and the neighbor is entitled to have it. Marti is not entitled to any money for her labor in building the barbecue. If the neighbor incurs any financial damages because he was planning to use the bricks in another manner, he can recover the damages from Marti.

In rare instances, title may pass to the willful trespasser solely because the owner decides not to contest the trespasser's title. In other words, the owner does not want the improved property. However, the original owner may collect the value of the improved property from the willful trespasser. In our example, if the neighbor decides that he does not want the barbecue, he may allow the title to pass to Marti by default, and he can collect from Marti the value of the brick barbecue instead of the value of the bricks alone. Such action only will occur at the option of the original owner.

Some legal disputes involve cases in which a third party has purchased the property created by the trespasser. Generally, the dispute is between the original owner and the third-party purchaser. To be protected, the third party must be a bona fide purchaser for value. A *bona fide purchaser for value* is a person who buys property in good faith, for a reasonable value, and without actual or constructive knowledge that there are any problems with the transfer. The bona fide purchaser will have the same rights and liabilities as the trespasser. If the original owner could have recovered the property from the trespasser, he or she can obtain it from the bona fide purchaser. Good faith purchasers do have the right to remove any additions or improvements that they have personally made if this can be done without harming the property.

Confusion. *Confusion* occurs when the personal, fungible property of two or more people is mixed together and cannot be separated. *Fungible property* includes things such as sand, gravel, wheat, corn, rye, oil, and gasoline, and generally consists of very small particles or grains. When wheat of the same type and quality belonging to two different farmers is mixed together, confusion occurs: The particles of wheat cannot be separated and returned to their respective owners.

Confusion may be caused by the wrongdoing of one of the owners or may occur without any misconduct. For example, farmers often store their fungible crops, such as corn, in the same storage bin or silo. If confusion occurs *without misconduct,* the farmers receive an undivided interest in the new confused mass. If the corn in the bin is sold, the farmers divide the proceeds in proportion to the amount they put into the bin. If there are any losses, the farmers divide the losses proportionately.

If the confusion is caused by *intentional wrongdoing,* different rules apply. If the new mixture is not divisible, title to the whole mass will pass to the innocent party. Therefore, it is to the wrongdoer's benefit to show that the new mass is divisible. If the wrongdoer can prove that the new mass is divisible and that the mixture has at least the same *unit value* (value per ton, pound, gallon, etc.) as the property belonging to the innocent party, the wrongdoer will be entitled to a share of the new mass. If the wrongdoer can clearly prove how much was added, the court can award the wrongdoer that share. If the wrongdoer can identify only the relative proportion of his or her share, the wrongdoer will be allowed to recover a proportional share. In either case, the proof must be clear and convincing. *Exxon Corp.* v. *West* involved an analysis of this proof.

45.1 EXXON CORP. v. WEST

543 S.W.2d 667 (C.A.Tex. 1976), Cert. Denied, 434 U.S. 875 (1977)

FACTS Exxon had an agreement to take gas from the Wests' property and to pay them a royalty on it. During the contract term, the Texas Railroad Commission authorized the use of this same reservoir under the Wests' property for gas storage purposes. Exxon began injecting gas into the reservoir for storage, which created a mixture of native gas and injected gas.

ISSUE Are the Wests entitled to royalties on all the gas drawn from the reservoir?

HOLDING No. The gas in the reservoir has been confused, but the resulting mass can be divided.

REASONING The court held that Exxon intentionally caused confusion of the injected gas and the native gas. The Wests were entitled to royalties on the native gas. Exxon had the burden of showing how much gas was subject to the royalties. Exxon provided expert testimony by their geologist and their petroleum engineer, who studied and testified about the maximum amount and the probable amount of native gas in the reservoir. Since the Wests did not offer any contradictory testimony, the court held that Exxon's witnesses had to be believed. The amount of native gas did not need to be proved with exact certainty. In such a case, reasonable certainty is sufficient.

BUSINESS CONSIDERATIONS How could Exxon have handled the situation in order to reduce the likelihood of a disagreement with the Wests?

ETHICAL CONSIDERATIONS Is it ethical for Exxon to pump "injected" gas into the reservoir under the Wests' property, knowing that they owe the Wests a royalty for gas pumped from the reservoir? Would it be proper for any company, with knowledge, to inject gas into this reservoir?

Lost or Mislaid Property. *Lost property* is property that has been unintentionally lost by the true owner. The owner does not know where the property was lost or where it may be retrieved. A person who finds lost property has good title to the property. The true owner is the only one with better title to the property than the finder. The finder of lost property generally is entitled to keep possession of it unless a statute or ordinance provides that possession should be given to the police.

Mislaid property is property that was intentionally set somewhere by the owner. The manner of placement and the location of the property indicate whether the owner merely forgot to pick up the property or lost it. The owner of mislaid property usually will be able to remember where the property was left and to reclaim it. The finder of mislaid property has good title against everyone except the true owner.

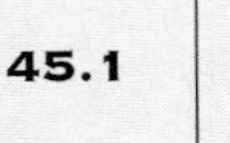
45.1

MANAGEMENT/FINANCE

DESTRUCTION OF PERSONAL PROPERTY

Donna encountered a fairly serious problem at her CPA office last week. Ray Goodall, one of her clients, came to the office for an appointment to review his new business plan and tax strategy. Ray is a computer consultant who designs software systems for his clients. While waiting for Donna, Ray noticed that the office system was using an old version of a virus scan and protection system he had designed. When the secretary left the room, Ray installed the latest version of his virus scan and protection software on the system. He did this without the knowledge or permission of Donna or the secretary. Although Ray meant no harm, and in fact had only the best of intentions, there was a problem with his new software. During his installation, he managed to erase a substantial portion of Donna's client records, which were on the hard drive. Even though a hard copy of all these records exists, a large portion of them had not yet been saved to disks or to magnetic tape. As a result, Donna will have to pay her secretary overtime in order to recreate the files on the computer. Donna would prefer not to sue one of her clients, but she doesn't know what she can or should do. She asks for your advice. What will you tell her?

BUSINESS CONSIDERATIONS How should a business handle a delicate situation such as the one Donna has with Ray? What should a business do to protect itself from being put into this sort of predicament?

ETHICAL CONSIDERATIONS What ethical obligation does Ray owe to Donna? Is it ethical to require employees to use a password in order to prevent nonemployees or unauthorized personnel from gaining access to company computers?

A critical distinction exists between *title to* the property and *possession of* the property. Although the finder of the mislaid property has good title, he or she is not entitled to possession. The owner of the premises where the property is found or the person in charge of the premises is entitled to hold the mislaid property. The reason is that when the true owner remembers where the mislaid property was left, he or she will return to that location to retrieve it. It is logical to leave the personal property on the premises to make it easier for the true owner to reclaim it. Note that the owner of the premises is entitled to *hold* mislaid property, but not lost property. However, if the finder of the lost or mislaid property was a trespasser on the property, the owner of the premises has title to the personal property that was found.

To increase the likelihood that the true owner will be able to reclaim the property, some state statutes and local ordinances require the finder of lost and/or mislaid property to complete certain steps before becoming the final owner. These statutes generally have two requirements:

1. That a specified type of notice be placed in the newspaper
2. That the property be given to the police to be claimed by the true owner

If the property is not claimed within a stated period, the police will allow the finder to claim it.

Abandoned Property. Sometimes an owner is no longer interested in owning a piece of personal property, and may *abandon* it by throwing it away without intending to reclaim it or by relinquishing it to someone else without intending to retake possession. If the property is relinquished to someone else, that person will become the new owner of the property. Generally, this type of transfer will be considered a gift. If the property is thrown away, the person who finds the property and reduces it to possession will acquire title. The property will once again be subject to original possession.

Protection of Personal Property

If an owner of personal property fails to protect the property adequately, it may be taken by someone else. Sometimes this taking is legal, but often it is not. In either case, the owner will suffer a temporary or permanent loss. To protect against such a loss, the owner should be aware of the means—legal or illegal—by which property may be taken, including conversion, escheat, judicial sale, and mortgage foreclosure or repossession of property. The owner should also note that insurance can be purchased to reduce the risk of some losses.

Conversion

Conversion occurs when one person takes the personal property of the owner. It is unauthorized and unjustified interference, whether permanent or temporary, with the owner's use and control of property. According to court opinions, a transitory interference constitutes trespass to personal property rather than conversion. A more lengthy interference—but not necessarily a permanent one—constitutes conversion. Under the theory of conversion, the owner can sue the taker for the return of the property or for money to replace the property. Conversion is the tort equivalent of a number of crimes, including theft, armed robbery, embezzlement, and obtaining property by false pretenses. In a criminal proceeding, the state will protect its interest in having citizens abide by the law. In a civil proceeding, the individual will protect his or her property rights.

Conversion *can* occur when the owner of personal property voluntarily releases the property to another person, who then uses the property in a manner different from that originally authorized. For example, if the owner of an automobile leaves the automobile with a car dealer for repairs and the dealer uses it as a demonstrator, the dealer is liable if the automobile is damaged while a prospective customer is taking it for a test drive.

In *Swish Manufacturing Southeast* v. *Manhattan Fire & Marine Ins. Co.* the court must decide whether or not property was converted.

45.2 SWISH MANUFACTURING SOUTHEAST v. MANHATTAN FIRE & MARINE INS. CO.

675 F.2d 1218 (11th Cir. 1982)

FACTS Swish Manufacturing owned a corporate aircraft. Swish entered into a contract with Wings whereby Wings could lease the aircraft whenever Wings wanted it. Under the lease, Wings could not use the aircraft to transport cargo or for unlawful purposes. Swish received an insurance endorsement on the aircraft that excluded loss due to conversion. Wings took the aircraft to the Bahamas in order to smuggle marijuana. The plane was seized by Bahamian police and was damaged while in their custody.

ISSUE Was the aircraft converted by Wings?

HOLDING Yes.

REASONING The unauthorized use was a conversion. Conversion is the unauthorized assumption and exercise of the right of ownership of someone else's personal property. This exercise is contrary to the owner's right. Misuse or excessive use may be conversion. Unauthorized use that causes damage to a chattel constitutes a conversion. With conversion, the degree of deviation between actual use and permitted use is significant. Here the court found that the deviation was great; consequently, conversion had occurred.

BUSINESS CONSIDERATIONS What could Swish Manufacturing do to reduce the likelihood that this will happen in the future? Is it likely that someone engaged in marijuana smuggling would be honest with the owner of the plane? Note that Swish Manufacturing was at risk of losing the plane under U.S. confiscation statutes because it was utilized in drug trafficking.

ETHICAL CONSIDERATIONS What ethical justification might Wings use to explain its actions?

In a suit for conversion, the owner generally prefers to have the personal property returned and repaired, if necessary. Another option available to the owner under the laws of most states is to force the wrongdoer to keep the personal property and to pay for it. The price will be its value at the time the property was taken. This remedy is performed only at the election of the owner. It is not available at the request of the wrongdoer.

Escheat

When the rightful owner of property cannot be located, the property will *escheat,* or revert, to the state government. The effect of escheat is that the property is given to the government. Usually it is in a third person's custody, and then possession is transferred to the state. The policy behind this doctrine is that the state is more deserving of the property than anyone else if the true owner cannot be found. Escheat tends to occur when a person dies and the heirs or relatives cannot be located. It also can occur when a person does not keep careful financial records and so forgets about small bank accounts, stocks and bonds, or other assets.

Escheat is governed by the appropriate state statute, and the rules vary from state to state. Often, escheated property becomes part of the state's general fund. For a specified period after the escheat, the rightful owner can claim the property from the state. To successfully claim the property, however, the rightful owner will need adequate proof of identity and of a right to the property.

FROM THE DESK OF

AMY CHEN, ATTORNEY AT LAW

Conversions and Thefts

Conversion is a serious problem for business entities. Take legal and practical steps to avoid the loss of inventory, property, and supplies. For example, shoplifting is a serious problem for retailers, while theft from outsiders is a problem for manufacturers. Care should be used to have reliable employees lock premises. Shipments should not be left unprotected on the loading dock for extended periods; consider having security guards and alarms. Employee theft is also a problem. Establish procedures for dealing with theft and inform employees about the consequences.

Judicial Sale

When a person loses a civil lawsuit, the court may order that person to make payment to the other party. This payment is called a *judgment,* and the person entitled to payment is a *judgment creditor.* If the person does not make the required payment, additional action may be necessary. This action commonly consists of an execution of judgment. The person who is entitled to payment procures a writ of execution from the clerk of court's office. With this writ, the sheriff can seize the debtor's property and sell it. This is called a *judicial sale* or a *sheriff's sale.*

After reimbursing the costs of the sheriff's office in seizing and selling this asset and the costs of the execution, the remaining money is then given to the judgment creditor to satisfy the judgment. If the amount received exceeds the expenses and the judgment, the excess is generally transferred to the property owner. However, the treatment of this excess is governed by state law and by the type of judgment. Notices of judicial sales are often included with other legal notices in the newspaper. A purchaser at a judicial sale buys the rights that the seller (the sheriff) had to sell. The sheriff's office generally does not warrant (promise) that it is entitled to sell the property. In addition, the true owner may have a limited period within which he or she may redeem the property, even if it is in the hands of a third-party purchaser. The amount of the payment that is owed to the third party is governed by state law.

Repossession of Property

A lender who wants to protect an interest in a loan may create a security interest in some collateral. If the lender follows the requirements for creating and perfecting a security interest, the lender will have a security interest in the property. If the borrower does not repay the loan under the terms of the contract, the lender can repossess (retake) the property. Usually the lender prefers to have cash and thus will sell the collateral. If the collateral is real estate, the loan is called a *mortgage,* and taking possession of the property is called a *mortgage foreclosure.* A person who buys repossessed property or foreclosed property buys only the seller's legal interest. The purchaser may lose the property if the foreclosure or repossession was wrongful.

Bailments of Personal Property

A *bailment* arises when a person delivers personal property to someone else. The *bailor* is the owner of the property, and the *bailee* is the one who has possession of (but not title to) the property. Whenever an owner allows another person to have custody of the owner's personal property, a bailment exists. It is understood that the bailee is to use the property in a specific way. For example, if the attendants of a parking garage drive a customer's car for any purpose other than parking or safeguarding it, they breach their duty as bailees. It is further understood that the bailee is to return the property at the end of the bailment.

If the bailee is giving up consideration, a contract exists. If Elizabeth rents a car from Zeta Car Rental Company, a bailment relationship exists. Elizabeth is the bailee and Zeta Car Rental Company is the bailor. Their relationship will be governed by *both* the rules of bailments and the rules of contracts. However, a contract is not a requirement for a bailment. A bailment can occur gratuitously. All the following elements are necessary for a bailment:

1. The bailor must retain title.
2. The possession of the property must be delivered to the bailee.
3. The bailee must accept possession.
4. The bailee must have possession of the property for a specific purpose and must have temporary control of the property.
5. The parties must intend that the property will be returned to the bailor unless the bailor directs that the property be delivered to another person.

A bailment is not a sale of personal property. A sale involves a transfer of title and requires an exchange of consideration. A permanent change of possession occurs with the sale. It is not always easy to recognize whether a situation is a bailment. A particularly controversial question is whether parking in a garage constitutes a bailment or the rental of a space to park a car.

Bailee's Duty of Care

Disputes often arise when the property is damaged while in the hands of the bailee. In a lawsuit, the issue concerns whether or not the bailee took proper care of the property. The answer will depend on provisions in local statutes, the language of any bailment contract, and the type of bailment.

Classifications of Bailments

Bailments are divided into types based on who benefits from the bailment relationship. The classification affects the bailee's obligation and his or her liability if any damage occurs to the property. This responsibility is summarized in Exhibit 45.1.

Bailor Benefit Bailments. When the bailment is established solely to benefit the bailor, the bailee will be responsible only for gross negligence in caring for the property. What is considered to be negligence in court will depend on the circumstances and the evidence presented.

Mutual Benefit Bailments. When a bailment is established for the benefit of both the bailor and the bailee, a *mutual benefit bailment* exists. Both parties expect to gain from the bailment relationship. In such bailments, the bailee is responsible for ordinary negligence. A mutual benefit bailment occurs, for example, when the owner of a suit takes it to a dry-cleaning establishment. The owner will benefit by having the suit cleaned and pressed. The dry cleaner will benefit because it is going to be paid. The dry cleaner will be responsible if it carelessly cleans the suit in cleaning fluid that is too hot and causes the suit to shrink.

Bailee Benefit Bailments. When a bailment is established solely for the benefit of the bailee, a *bailee benefit bailment* exists. The bailee will be responsible for slight negligence in caring for the property.

Institute of London v. *Eagle Boats, Ltd.* considers whether the bailee exercised appropriate care of the property.

45.3 INSTITUTE OF LONDON v. EAGLE BOATS, LTD. — 918 F.Supp. 297 (E.D.Mo. 1996)

FACTS Suit was filed by a group of insurance underwriters which had issued a policy on Hoppies Village Marina's (Hoppies) boats, including this one, and had paid Hoppies for its losses and was subrogee of its claim against the defendants. Eagle Boats, Ltd., was voluntarily dissolved in July, 1993, and did not enter a defense in this lawsuit. William Seebold, president of Eagle Boats, did defend this lawsuit.

Seebold was contacted by *Trailer Boats*, a boating magazine, about doing a feature article on a motorboat manufactured by Eagle and including pictures taken on Grand Lake in Oklahoma. At the time of the inquiry a boat owned by Hoppies was in the Eagle Boat repair facility undergoing minor paint repairs. This boat was a 1991 Seebold Eagle 265 Limited Edition motorboat with a 1990 Buccaneer Deluxe Tri-Axle trailer. This boat is considered "to be the 'cadillac' of motorboats in its class." Seebold contacted Paul Hopkins, the owner of Hoppies and Michael Atkinson, the sales manager there. Hopkins agreed to loan this boat and trailer to Eagle Boats, Ltd., and William Seebold, president of Eagle Boats. It was also agreed that the magazine article would include information about the boat, Eagle Boats, Ltd., and Hoppies Village Marina. Seebold would transport the boat to Oklahoma and then return it to Hoppies using Hoppies's trailer.

The night before the magazine demonstration, Seebold parked the boat, trailer, and Eagle's truck in the parking lot of a motel. They were parked near the roadway parallel to the fence across the parking lot from the one dusk-to-dawn light. The trailer did not have a locking device which would lock it onto the truck, which was locked. No one was left to guard the boat and it was not locked in any manner. Although other boats and trailers were in the parking lot, this was the most expensive boat there. It was also the closest to the road. Both the boat and trailer were stolen between 11:00 P.M. and about 5:00 A.M.

45.3 INSTITUTE OF LONDON v. EAGLE BOATS, LTD. *(cont.)* 918 F.Supp. 297 (E.D.Mo. 1996)

Seebold offered evidence that failure to use locks is common in the industry. He testified that at his facility, he simply chains the boats together and locks the chain. He also produced sworn statements by Hopkins and Atkinson that it is common not to use locking devices. Seebold admitted that he could have put a chain around the boat and trailer and locked it to the truck; he did not have a chain with him.

ISSUE Did the bailee fail to exercise proper care over the bailed property?

HOLDING Yes.

REASONING There is no dispute that the parties entered into a bailment relationship. Under Missouri law, the bailor can proceed on alternate legal theories—general negligence of bailee, specific negligence of bailee, or breach of bailment contract. "In a bailment for the mutual benefit of the bailor and bailee, the bailee is not an insurer, and his/her standard of care with respect to the bailed property remains the exercise of ordinary care.

The issue of the bailee's exercise of care is a question of fact and not of law." Under Missouri law, evidence about customary behavior in a business is generally admissible in court but is not controlling. It does not set the standard of care. Even if this evidence is not contradicted, the court can decide that the defendant is negligent. The only steps that he took to protect the boat and trailer were to place them in a spot that he "thought" was inaccessible. The "ease in which the boat/trailer was stolen was due largely to the defendant's failure to take appropriate measures . . ."

BUSINESS CONSIDERATIONS What should the bailee have done to protect the boat and trailer? There were storage units behind the motel, should Seebold have rented one of these? Why or why not?

ETHICAL CONSIDERATIONS Should the bailee treat the boat the same way he would have treated his own boat? Why or why not?

Limitations on a Bailee's Liability

Some states and localities have statutes that provide maximum limits on the liability of the bailee in certain types of bailments.

If the bailment is based on a contract, the terms of the contract may increase or decrease the liability of the bailee. A quasi-public bailee offers services to the public. For example, he or she may operate a common carrier, a garage, a hotel, or a public parking lot. A quasi-public bailee generally will not be permitted to limit his or her liability contractually unless specifically permitted to do so by statute. Even when a statute permits a bailee to restrict liability, any limitation on liability must be reasonable.

EXHIBIT 45.1 The Responsibility of the Bailee

Type of Bailment	Who Will Benefit	The Bailee Will Be Liable For . . .
Bailor benefit	Bailor (owner)	Gross negligence
Mutual benefit	Bailor and bailee	Ordinary negligence
Bailee benefit	Bailee (possessor)	Slight negligence

45.2

MANUFACTURING/MANAGEMENT

SHOULD CIT HAVE INSURANCE ON LEASED PRODUCTION EQUIPMENT?

CIT leases some of its production equipment from a large electronics firm. This equipment is extremely expensive and relatively fragile, and Tom is concerned that the firm will be responsible for any damage to the equipment. He feels that CIT should procure insurance to protect the firm from liability in the event the equipment is damaged. Dan, however, insists that the electronics firm is responsible for maintenance and bears the risk of loss for any damage done to the equipment. He asserts that, since the equipment was leased for industrial use, the electronics firm alone is responsible. They ask you which of their positions is correct. What will you tell them?

BUSINESS CONSIDERATIONS The leasing of equipment creates a bailment, but it also entails a contract for the lease of goods, governed by Article 2A of the UCC. Does Article 2A change the common law treatment of bailments in this sort of situation? Does the lessor or the lessee bear the risk of loss if leased equipment is damaged during the lease, presuming that the equipment is being used by the parties in the manner expected?

ETHICAL CONSIDERATIONS From an ethical perspective, and without regard to who is legally responsible for risk of loss, how should CIT behave in this situation? Is it ethical to underinsure a piece of equipment if the insuring party knows that the other party bears the risk of loss legally? Is it ethical to overinsure a piece of equipment in the hope that the insurer will not notice the overinsurance in the event of a loss?

A private bailee can restrict his or her liability under the terms of the agreement if this restriction does not conflict with the real purpose of the contract between the bailee and the bailor. The bailee must inform the bailor of any limitation on the bailee's liability. Most courts hold that a printed ticket stub or a posted notice on the premises does not adequately inform the bailor of the limitations *unless* the bailor's attention is directed to the sign or the ticket stub.

Termination of a Bailment

A bailment terminates at the end of the period that the parties specify or when a specified condition occurs. If the bailment was for an indefinite time, it may be terminated at the will of either the bailor or the bailee. A bailment terminates when the purpose or performance of the bailment has been completed. If either party causes a material breach of the bailment relationship, the victim can terminate the bailment and the wrongdoer will be liable for any damages he or she caused. The bailment terminates if the bailed property is destroyed or becomes unfit or unsuitable for the purpose of the bailment. Generally, a bailment also terminates by operation of law if death, insanity, or bankruptcy of either party makes performance by the bailee impossible.

Bailee's Duty to Return the Property

A bailee has a general duty to return the bailor's property to the bailor; however, there are exceptions to this rule. The bailee is not liable to the bailor if the property is lost, destroyed, or stolen through no fault of the bailee. The bailee is not liable if the property is taken away by legal process such as an attachment for a sheriff's sale. The bailee is not liable if the property is claimed by someone who has a better legal right to possession than the bailor has.

Sometimes a bailee has a duty to return the property to someone other than the bailor. For example, there may be a duty to "return" the property to a transferee who has bought the property from the bailor. A common business practice involves transferring property to a warehouse or common carrier that has an obligation to hold this property and then transfer it to a purchaser who presents a receipt or bill of lading.

Numbers v. *Suburban Taxi Corp.* addresses the liability of a bailee for failure to return property.

45.4 NUMBERS v. SUBURBAN TAXI CORP. 1995 Minn.App. LEXIS 727 (Minn.App. 1995) (Unpublished opinion)

FACTS Ronald Numbers worked as a taxi driver for Suburban Taxi Corporation. From July 1992 until December 1992, Numbers operated his own cab. In December, the cab needed repairs, so Numbers left it on Suburban's lot for those repairs. Suburban required a $300 deposit before the repairs would be started. Numbers did not deposit this amount. About a month later, when Numbers noticed his cab had been removed, he was informed that the cab had been moved to improve security. In the interim, Numbers leased a cab from Suburban. The leased cab was damaged the first week in a traffic accident. Suburban asked Numbers to pay $950 into a "damage" account for the repair of the leased taxi; Numbers paid some money into the "damage" account but not the full amount. On 23 March 1993, Numbers requested the return of his own cab. Suburban refused, stating that it would not return Numbers' cab until he paid for the damages to the leased vehicle. Numbers never received possession of his cab.

ISSUES Was Suburban the bailee of Numbers' cab? Was Suburban justified in keeping possession of Numbers' cab?

HOLDINGS Yes. No.

REASONING There are three requirements for a bailment: "(1) delivery without transfer of ownership; (2) implied or express acceptance; and (3) an express or implied agreement that the goods be returned. . . . Generally, a bailment is created where the operator of a garage has knowingly and voluntarily assumed control, possession, or custody of the vehicle."

Suburban contends that it did not accept the bailment, because Numbers did not pay the $300 work deposit. However, Suburban did accept the cab: Its conduct indicated a willingness to assume control of the cab while waiting for the deposit. It even moved the cab to another location for the safety of the cab and never requested money for storing the cab on its premises. Suburban had an obligation to return the cab when the repairs were finished, when Numbers requested the return, or when Numbers failed to pay the $300 deposit.

Conversion is "an exercise of dominion over the goods which is inconsistent with and in repudiation of the owner's right to the goods or some act done which destroys or changes their character or deprives the owner of possession permanently or for an indefinite length of time." Refusing to return Numbers' cab until he finished paying for damages to the leased cab was not reasonable. Those damages arise from a completely separate transaction between Suburban and Numbers. Suburban also claimed that it was entitled to keep possession of the cab for storage fees; however, this was not supported by the facts. Suburban converted Numbers' cab.

BUSINESS CONSIDERATIONS How could Suburban have avoided this dispute with Numbers? What business practices would have improved their business relationship? Based on the information provided, what types of relationships do Numbers and Suburban have?

ETHICAL CONSIDERATIONS What ethical duties do Numbers and Suburban owe each other?

http:// RESOURCES FOR BUSINESS LAW STUDENTS

NAME	RESOURCES	WEB ADDRESS
Internal Revenue Service	The Internal Revenue Service, and its publication, the *Digital Daily,* provide tax advice and information on a variety of issues, including personal property issues.	http://www.irs.ustreas.gov/
U.S. Internal Revenue Code—26 USC	Legal Information Institute, maintained by the Cornell Law School, includes the U.S. Internal Revenue Code, 26 USC, in a hypertext and searchable format.	http://www.law.cornell.edu/uscode/26/
Legal Information Institute (LII)—Estate and gift tax law materials	LII provides an overview of estate and gift tax law, including relevant sections from the U.S. Code and Code of Federal Regulation, court cases, and links.	http://www.law.cornell.edu/topics/estate_gift_tax.html

45.3

MANAGEMENT

DISCLAIMERS TO AVOID LIABILITY

Dan was in Chicago recently to meet with a potential client. He drove his rental car to a downtown parking garage in which the parking attendants park the cars and retain the keys. Dan decided he would not need his overcoat, so he left it on the passenger seat of the car. He handed the attendant the keys to the car, took his claim check, and left for his appointment. When Dan returned later that day to reclaim the car, he discovered his overcoat was missing. When Dan complained to the attendants, they denied any knowledge of the loss, and they also pointed to the back of the claim check. The back of the ticket contained the following clause: "The management is not responsible for any personal property or electronic devices left in parked cars. The customer assumes any and all risk of loss for items left in the vehicle."

Dan does not believe that the garage should be able to avoid liability in this manner. He asks you for advice. What will you tell him?

BUSINESS CONSIDERATIONS Is it a good business practice for a firm to use exculpatory clauses, especially those placed on the back of "claim checks," in an effort to avoid liability? What could/should the parking garage do to reduce its customers' potential for loss? What could/should the customers do to reduce their potential for loss?

ETHICAL CONSIDERATIONS Is it ethical for a business to include exculpatory clauses on the back of "claim checks"? Is it ethical for a business to attempt to deny liability for the losses suffered by its customers? Is it ethical for the customers to blame the business for losses caused by the carelessness of the customers?

The bailee does not have to return the property if the bailee has a lien on the property. Many states have statutes that allow the bailee to keep the property in his or her possession until the bailor pays for the bailment; this is called a *possessory lien*. If the bailor fails to make payment, most statutes permit the bailee to sell the property. A common type of bailee's lien is a mechanic's lien, which arises when services have been performed on personal property. For example, if a garage repairs an automobile and the owner does not have the money to pay for the repairs, the garage can keep the automobile until the owner does pay. In most cases, the bailee loses the lien if the bailee willingly releases the goods to the bailor. For example, if the bailor comes to reclaim the property and the bailee releases it without receiving payment. Generally, there is no bailee's lien if the bailor and bailee agree at the beginning that the bailor is going to pay on credit.

SUMMARY

Personal property is classified as tangible and intangible property based on its physical characteristics. Discussions of legal interests in property revolve around ownership rights, title, and possession. Often, one business has title to property, but another business has possession. Title to personal property can be acquired by original possession, by voluntary transfer from the owner to the transferee, or by involuntary transfer from the owner. A transferee of personal property generally will not acquire any better title than the transferor had. This is true even though the transferee thought that the transferor had good title. This limitation on title is especially important in judicial sales, sales of repossessed property, conversion, confusion, and accession.

A bailment is a special legal relationship that occurs when the owner/bailor transfers the possession of personal property to someone else, the bailee. The owner keeps title. After the purpose of the bailment has been completed, generally possession is returned to the owner. Many businesses, such as dry cleaners and repair shops, basically deal in bailment relationships. The bailee's duty of care is affected by whether it is a bailor benefit bailment, a mutual benefit bailment, or a bailee benefit bailment relationship. The bailee's obligation is also influenced by any contract between the bailee and the bailor.

Discussion Questions

1. What are the differences between title and possession?
2. What happens if the donor of a gift *causa mortis* dies but not from the expected cause? Who is likely to complain in such a situation?
3. What are the policies underlying the rules about accession?
4. James takes a piece of rough turquoise stone, polishes it, and sets it in a silver setting in a necklace. James reasonably believes that he found the stone on public land. In reality, he had found it on private land, where the owner, who had mined it, had placed it in a pile for polishing. Who owns the jewelry and why? What are the legal rights of the parties?
5. Twice a year the City of Cedarville has a large trash pickup. At this time, the trash collectors will take nonhazardous waste items they would normally refuse. Charlotte hauls an old washing machine to the curb and adds it to her pile of other debris. Dennis drives by and picks up her washing machine, puts it in his truck, and drives away. Who legally owns the washing machine and why?
6. Is an umbrella on a desk likely to be lost or mislaid property? Why? If the umbrella is on the floor, is it likely to be lost or mislaid property? Why?
7. Ric visits José's Mexican Restaurant for lunch and hangs his coat on the coat rack provided for that purpose. When he is ready to leave, Ric walks out and leaves his coat. Kelly finds the coat. Who is entitled to title of the coat? Why? Who is entitled to possession of the coat? Why?
8. Define escheat. When does it occur? What is its purpose?
9. What are the requirements for a bailment relationship?
10. What legal rights does a bailor have when a bailee has damaged the property or allowed someone else to damage it?

Case Problems and Writing Assignments

1. Kaiser wrote a check to the land title company for $14,692.16, as payment for the home his nephew was buying. He also wrote a check for $2,308 to his nephew for furnishings. The alleged oral loan agreement provided for 300 monthly payments. The nephew issued 44 monthly checks to his uncle after the transaction. A number of these checks carried the notation "for house." After Kaiser's death, the nephew quit making the monthly payments. The nephew claimed the money advanced by Kaiser was a gift, not a loan. Is the nephew correct in his assertion? Why or why not? [See *Estate of Kaiser* v. *Gifford*, 692 S.W.2d 525 (Tex.App. 1 Dist. 1985).]

2. Shepard's personal representative brought a lawsuit for amounts loaned by Shepard to Jacobson. Shepard made the loans by writing checks to Jacobson or his creditors. Some of the checks had the notation "loan" on them. The loans were not evidenced by a note. Shepard had made statements during her life that the debt was forgiven. This evidence was not contradicted. Did Shepard make a valid gift to the debtor of the amount that he owed her? Why? [See *Guardian State Bank & Trust* v. *Jacobson*, 369 N.W.2d 80 (Neb. 1985).]

3. Kenneth Simkin initiated a lawsuit against his former wife, Barbara Norcross. Simkin wanted the return of his sailing vessel, a Morgan sloop. He had left the vessel in good condition tied to a jetty. He had the owner's permission to dock his vessel in this manner. When Simkin returned to his vessel, it was gone. It was later found in the custody of Norcross. Did Simkin abandon his vessel? Did Simkin intend to give the vessel to his former wife? Why? [See *Simkin* v. *Norcross*, 610 F.Supp. 691 (D.C.Fla. 1985).]

4. Vilner, the operator of a restaurant, used the Crocker National Bank's night depository on a regular basis. On the night in question, he unlocked the night depository at Crocker's Novato branch and placed a locked bag containing $7,976.36 in it. After closing the depository, he heard what sounded like a bag dropping into the box. He reopened the depository but did not see his bag. The bag was never recovered. Before that night, the bank had received at least four complaints from customers at other branches that deposits into the night depository were lost. In addition, on two separate occasions, customers had informed Crocker that bags had lodged in the depository at the Novato branch. Crocker did not take any action to correct these problems. Is Crocker liable for not returning the bailed property? Why or why not? [See *Vilner* v. *Crocker Nat'l Bank*, 152 Cal.Rptr. 850 (Cal.App. 1979).]

5. Goldbaum rented two safe deposit boxes at the bank. He stored rare metals and coins in these boxes. The

leases for the boxes stated that "Lessors shall have no liability for loss from fire, water, radiation, the forces of nature. . . ." The bank's sprinkler system failed and water flooded the boxes. Should the bank be liable for the damages? Why? Was the bank a bailee? Why or why not? [See *Goldbaum* v. *Bank Leumi Trust Co. of New York*, 543 F.Supp. 434 (S.D.N.Y. 1982).]

6. **BUSINESS APPLICATIONS CASE** On receiving a shipping order, Delta obtained a cargo container from Imparca, a commercial shipper. The cargo container was loaded and sealed by Delta and then delivered into the possession of Imparca by Delta's agent. The container was placed on a vessel chartered by Imparca, and Imparca issued a clean bill of lading. The bill of lading indicated that the carrier, Imparca, discharged its duties when it delivered the container into the custody of government authorities at the named port. This procedure was required by the laws of the foreign port. The 20-foot cargo container was placed on the dock in Puerto Cabello in the custody of the Instituto Nacional de Puertos (INP). INP was responsible for the operation of this seaport, including stevedoring, warehousing, receiving, and delivering cargo. The goods subsequently disappeared, and the consignee sought recourse from Imparca. Should the carrier be responsible for the disappearance of the goods in this case? Why? [See *Allstate Ins. Co.* v. *Imparca Lines*, 646 F.2d 166 (5th Cir. 1981).]

7. **ETHICAL APPLICATIONS CASE** In 1971, Treasure Salvors located an anchor from the *Nuestra Señora de Atocha*. Since that time, Treasure Salvors has continued to conduct salvage operations in the wreck area and has retrieved numerous artifacts. Frick and a number of other defendants began salvage operations 1,500 yards from the location where a second anchor was discovered. Is Treasure Salvors entitled to conduct its salvage operation free from interference from Frick? Does it have ownership rights in the wreck? Why? What ethical issues are raised in this case? [See *Treasure Salvors, Inc.* v. *Unidentified Wrecked and Abandoned Sailing Vessel*, 640 F.2d 560 (5th Cir. 1981).]

8. **IDES CASE** From 1990 through 1992, the Federal Deposit Insurance Corporation (FDIC) was appointed as the receiver for more than 30 banks principally located or doing business in Massachusetts. Massachusetts claimed title to some of the insurance on deposits in these banks under its abandoned property statute, Mass. Gen. L. ch. 200A. In other words, it contended that the deposit insurance escheated to the state. The statute indicated that escheat should occur when the named depositors failed to communicate with their banks over an extended period of time. Some of the claims arose before the banks' failures and some arose thereafter. Should the Massachusetts statute or the federal Unclaimed Deposits Amendments Act of 1993, 107 Stat. 220, govern? Apply the IDES principle to this case. [See *Massachusetts* v. *FDIC*, 47 F.3d 456, 1995 U.S.App. LEXIS 2310 (1st Cir. 1995).]

NOTES

1. The classic case on this subject is *Pierson* v. *Post*, 3 Cai.R. 175 (N.Y. 1805).
2. Mark Grossi, "Supplier Looks to Buy Farm Water, Then Sell to Cities," *The Fresno Bee* (2 August 1994), p. A1; and Mark Grossi, "Farmers Rip Areias over Bid to Sell Water," *The Fresno Bee* (24 August 1994), pp. A1 and A12.

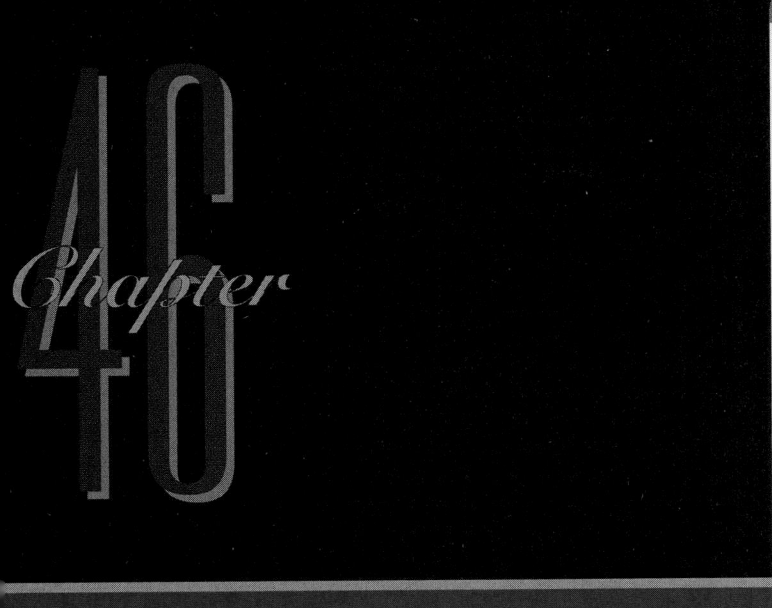

Wills, Estates, and Trusts

Outline

The Transfer of an Estate
Wills
Requirements for a Valid Will
Testamentary Dispositions and Restrictions
Intestate Succession
Probate and Estate Administration
Avoiding Probate
Transfer Taxes
Retirement Plans
Living Wills and Durable Powers of Attorney
Trusts Defined
Express Trusts
Advantages of Trusts
Disadvantages of Trusts
Selection of Trustees and Executors
Duties of Trustees
Implied Trusts
Summary
Discussion Questions
Case Problems and Writing Assignments

Agenda

Like many small business owners, Tom and Anna Kochanowski are concerned about protecting their family in the event that either of them should become incapacitated or die. How should Tom and Anna write their wills to ensure that CIT continues to operate and provide income and security? With a small business, speed is important. Tom and Anna don't want CIT to stop operating for a significant period of time. Tom and Anna also want to provide for their children. Who should be appointed as Lindsay's guardian? Tom has read the book *How to Avoid Probate!* by Norman F. Dacey. As a result, he would like to avoid probate in the administration of his estate. What are the advantages and disadvantages of avoiding probate in Tom's estate? How can Tom and Anna control medical decisions if they become extremely ill and/or incompetent? How can they transfer CIT to family members? What restrictions would be appropriate? Would a trust be proper? Who could serve as the trustee? These and other questions will be raised in this chapter. Be prepared! You never know when one of the Kochanowskis will ask for your advice.

THE TRANSFER OF AN ESTATE

Almost everyone has an estate, no matter how modest it might be. It may consist only of compact disks, a television, and a ten-speed bike; conversely, it may consist of some office buildings, rental houses, sizable money market accounts, and shares in Call-Image Technologies. This chapter deals with critical planning decisions—what happens to an estate when someone dies—and addresses techniques for transferring an estate to family members and friends. The discussion is general because the rules vary significantly from state to state.

Probate codes

State statutes that deal with the estates of incompetents and people who have died with or without a valid will.

Under the U.S. Constitution, property transfers, including wills, are governed by state law. The **probate codes** in the states vary greatly. The *Uniform Probate Code* is a statute drafted by the National Conference of Commissioners on Uniform State Laws (NCCUSL) for adoption by the states as their probate code. Its purposes are to unify state laws and respond to complaints that probate procedures are too complicated, costly, and time consuming. It was first introduced in 1966 and has undergone revision since then. The following states have adopted all or almost all of the Uniform Probate Code: Alaska, Arizona, Colorado, Hawaii, Idaho, Maine, Michigan, Minnesota, Montana, Nebraska, New Jersey, New Mexico, North Dakota, Pennsylvania, South Carolina, South Dakota, and Utah. The District of Columbia, the Virgin Islands and all the other states, except Louisiana, have adopted some sections of the code. Some of these states have adopted whole sections or articles of the code.[1] This chapter discusses many aspects of the Uniform Probate Code that have been widely adopted.

WILLS

Domicile

One's permanent home and principal residence. It is the place to which a person will return after traveling.

In a will, a person indicates who should inherit his or her property at death. The law that controls the validity of a person's will is the law of his or her **domicile**. A will provides an opportunity to name a guardian for any minor children the person may have. In fact, a will is the only way parents can specify who will raise a minor child if they both die. If parents do not use this technique for naming a guardian, the court will appoint one; and the court may not choose the best person. For example, grandparents may no longer be physically or emotionally capable of raising a young child. Because the court is not likely to be aware of these problems, the court may appoint the grandparents as guardians. The parents (and the courts) have the option of dividing the guardian's duties and appointing someone to care for the child's physical needs while appointing someone else to care for his or her financial needs and manage the inheritance. This option is valuable if one person is not competent in caring for *both* the child and the finances, but would be very competent in caring for one of them.

Personal representative

A person who manages the financial affairs of another or an estate.

Residuary clause

A clause that disposes of the remainder (the residual) of an estate.

Intestate share

Portion of the estate that a person is entitled to inherit if there is no valid will.

A will is also the place to name a **personal representative** for the estate. The personal representative nominated in the will is generally the one appointed by the court, if he or she is able to serve. The judge will appoint an alternate if the nominee is dead, disabled, or incompetent. The will should also contain a **residuary clause** for all the property that is not specifically mentioned elsewhere in the will. (It is not advisable to include burial instructions in a will because often the will is not located and read until after the funeral. Such instructions are better contained in a separate document, with copies distributed to the personal representative, close family members, and the attorney.)

Some changes in family relationships affect the validity of a will. Children who are born after a will is executed (signed) receive a share of the estate as after-born children. After-born children generally are entitled to their **intestate share.** If a marriage occurs after a will has been executed, the new spouse also will take a share of the estate. A divorce will change an existing will, too. In most states, a divorce with a property settlement will revoke gifts willed to the ex-spouse; however, a few states, including California, still require a revocation by the **testator** or **testatrix**. (In this chapter, we will use the term *testator* to refer to a man or a woman.)

Testator
A man who makes a will.

Testatrix
A woman who makes a will.

Codicil
A separate written document that modifies an existing will.

To make changes in a will, it is not necessary to write a completely new document. The testator can simply make the desired changes in a **codicil**. The codicil also acts to confirm the unchanged will provisions. Care should be taken to assure that the will and the codicil read together will make sense. To be valid, a codicil must satisfy the same requirements as a will.

The testator may destroy the effect of a will by making a new will and stating in the new will that the old will is revoked. This is commonly called a *revocation clause.* If the new will does not specifically revoke the old will, the courts in some states will try to interpret the two wills together. In such a case, the new will revokes the older will only to the extent that they contain contradictory or inconsistent provisions. A testator can also cancel an old will by physically destroying the signed original, with the intention of revoking it.

Wills can be categorized by the manner in which they are formed. Generally, wills can be *formal, holographic,* or *nuncupative.* Wills also can be categorized by the types of dispositions they contain.

Formal Wills

The most common type of will is called a *formal,* or attested, will. It is generally drafted by an attorney and printed by the attorney's staff. A will prepared by a competent attorney is more likely to achieve the desired results than one prepared by a layperson. Familiarity with the terminology of wills is important because the words used in the will often have a special significance that differs from their ordinary meaning. In addition, each state has its own technical requirements.

A will *can* be a very lengthy document, and it must be executed in strict compliance with the procedures specified in the state statute. Generally, the testator must sign the will at the end of the document in the presence of at least two witnesses. The testator *must* ask these two individuals to act as witnesses to the will. The witnesses must be disinterested persons; that is, they must have no interest in any of the property passing under the will or by intestate succession. The primary purposes of witnesses are to swear that the signatures are valid and to swear that the testator was lucid and seemed competent. In most states, the will also must be dated.

In *Rabsatt* v. *Estate of Savain,* the court addressed the technical requirements for properly signing a will. Notice that the court did not have to address the potential issues of fraud or undue influence.

46.1 RABSATT v. ESTATE OF SAVAIN — 878 F.Supp. 762 (D.V.I., 1995)

FACTS Margarita Savain executed a will on 7 October 1983 (will #1). The will and her trust documents provided that Savain would maintain a life interest in all her property. At her death, the property would pass to her brother, if he were still alive. If he died first, the assets would go to Ruth Robson. [Savain's brother did die first.]

Savain was admitted to the hospital early in May 1992, and she was apparently dying. One of the medicines

46.1 RABSATT v. ESTATE OF SAVAIN *(cont.)* 878 F.Supp. 762 (D.V.I.,1995)

administered to her was Demerol, a narcotic painkiller. As a consequence, there was conflicting information about her state of mind while she was on the medication.

While in the hospital, she signed another will (will #2). In this will, she left all her property to her "good friend" and tenant, John Shack. On 8 May 1992, Shack contacted an attorney. The attorney prepared will #2 according to Shack's instructions and delivered it to the hospital the same day. Shack paid for the preparation of the will. The attorney did not know Savain prior to the signing of the will. The signing of will #2 was witnessed by Shack's employer and a hospital nurse, Ms. Melisano, who was instructed to act as a witness by her supervisor. Melisano said that when she arrived in the hospital room, Shack, his employer (who referred the attorney to Shack), and the attorney were already there. She asked if they had read the will to Savain and they indicated that they had. It was not read again in her presence. Savain signed the document and Melisano signed at the request of the attorney. Savain did not make any statements about the document, although the attesting clause said it was her will. The discussion at the time centered around Savain's return to her home and getting food for her.

On 12 May 1992, Savain executed a third instrument (will #3), naming Ecedro Rabsatt as the sole beneficiary of her estate. Rabsatt had been a close friend of Savain's for a long time. Will #3 was drafted by Rita James, a nonlawyer who used to work as a legal secretary. Savain met with James several weeks prior to entering the hospital to outline the will provisions. James was not paid for preparing will #3. The attesting witnesses were Rabsatt's cousin, Randolph Thomas, and James's **common law husband**, Alvin Canton. Both had a long-time relationship with Rabsatt. Thomas testified that, at the signing, Savain never discussed the fact that the document was her will. He also indicated that Rabsatt, not Savain, asked him to sign the document. Savain died on 24 May 1992.

ISSUE Were wills #2 and/or #3 executed in compliance with the law of the Virgin Islands?

HOLDING No.

REASONING Wills #2 and #3 were not properly executed. V.I. Code Ann., Title 15, § 13, parts 3 and 4 state:

> *(3) The testator, at the time of making such subscription, or at the time of acknowledging the same, shall declare the instrument so subscribed, to be his last will and testament.*
>
> *(4) There shall be at least two attesting witnesses, each of whom shall sign his name as a witness, at the end of the will, at the request of the testator.*

[These provisions were modeled after New York Decedent Estate Law, § 21.]

Savain never declared will #2 to be her will in the presence of the witnesses. The attesting witnesses signed at the request of Shack and the attorney and not at the request of Savain. Neither subsections (3) nor (4) of the statute were satisfied when will #2 was executed. The same is true of will #3, according to Thomas's testimony.

The testatrix must state, in front of the witnesses, that the document is her last will and testament. She must also ask the witnesses to sign the will. Strict compliance with the formalities is required to protect the integrity of wills. Courts want to prevent execution by mental incompetents, prevent execution as a result of undue influence or fraud, and assure that the documents are genuine.

BUSINESS CONSIDERATIONS What role do hospitals, nursing homes, and their employees have in serving as witnesses to the signing of wills? Was it proper for Melisano's supervisor to order that she serve as a witness?

ETHICAL CONSIDERATIONS Did John Shack and his employer behave ethically? Did Ecedro Rabsatt and his friends and relatives behave ethically? Did Melisano have a duty to speak out if Savain seemed incompetent or confused? To whom should she communicate her concerns?

California, Maine, and Wisconsin have a special type of formal will called a *statutory will.* This will is so named because it has been approved by the state legislature, and the language used in the will is specified in the state probate statute. Printing companies in the state can print form wills using the approved language. A form will is sold to an individual testator who fills in the appropriate names and executes the will. Despite its title, a statutory will *is* a formal will, and consequently it must be witnessed by two disinterested witnesses.

Common law husband
A husband who did not participate in the usual wedding ceremony with a legal marriage license. The states that recognize common law marriages generally require that the couple consistently live together and tell people that they are husband and wife.

Holographic Wills

Holographic wills (called olographic wills, in some states) are required to be written, signed, and usually dated in the testator's own handwriting. Although not universally accepted, they are allowed in a number of states, including Alaska, Arizona, Arkansas, California, Idaho, Kentucky, Louisiana, Mississippi, Montana, Nevada, New Jersey, North Carolina, North Dakota, Oklahoma, Pennsylvania, South Dakota, Tennessee, Texas, Utah, Virginia, West Virginia, and Wyoming. Holographic wills also are allowed under the Uniform Probate Code, § 2-503.

A testator who writes a holographic will runs the risk of not expressing his or her intentions properly and not complying with the technical requirements. The testator may be unaware of and hence unable to take advantage of techniques to reduce costs and taxes. An attorney or an accountant with tax expertise may be able to make recommendations that will greatly reduce the taxes.

Most of the states that allow holographic wills require that they be dated. They do not, however, have to be witnessed. Traditionally, holographic wills have to be written completely in the testator's hand with *no* printed or typed matter. Recently, some courts and legislatures have become more lenient about accepting printed matter on a holographic will. For example, the California legislature enacted a statutory change requiring only that the signature and the material provisions be in the testator's handwriting.[2] Also, a court may accept the will if the printed matter is not an integral part of the will. Many of the states that allow holographic wills require that the will be kept with the important papers of the **decedent**. The purpose of this requirement is to assist in establishing the testator's intent to make a will and ascertaining that the document was important to him or her.

Decedent
A person who has died.

The issue in *In re Estate of Krueger* involved the validity of a holographic will.

46.2 IN RE ESTATE OF KRUEGER — 529 N.W.2d 151, 1995 N.D. LEXIS 33 (N.D. 1995)

FACTS Diana Krueger died on 3 May 1992. Her heirs were her four nephews—Fred, William, Rhinhold, and Daniel Bieber. Krueger executed two wills during her life—a holographic will on 8 January 1979 and a formal, attested will prepared by an attorney on 9 March 1990. The 1990 will contained a clause expressly revoking all previous wills, including the holographic will. The original, signed copy of the 1990 will was not located after Krueger's death.

Fred Bieber testified that he and his wife took Krueger home from the hospital on the 14th or 15th of March 1990. While there, Krueger asked Fred to get a box from a closet. Krueger opened the box and took out an envelope that contained the 1979 holographic will. Krueger read the will word for word to Fred. One of the gifts provided that her "Books and Diploma" go to her niece Doris. Krueger crossed out the name of Doris, who had died, and asked Fred to write in "Fred Bieber['s] daughters." Fred did so.

ISSUE Should the holographic will be accepted as valid?

HOLDING No.

REASONING The right to make a will is a statutory right. Unless the testator complies with the statutory formalities, the will is invalid. The holographic will, as altered, does not comply with the North Dakota statute and is not entitled to be probated. The will contains a material provision that is not in the handwriting of the maker. Fred contends that the gift of the books and diplomas is immaterial, in light of the total value of the estate. This is incorrect. Neither the Uniform Probate Code nor the North Dakota Century Code define the term *material provisions*. Consequently, courts attribute their "plain, ordinary, and commonly understood meaning" to this term. To help achieve uniformity, courts in one jurisdiction interpret terms in uniform laws and model acts the same as courts in other jurisdictions. Material provisions of

46.2 IN RE ESTATE OF KRUEGER *(cont.)* 529 N.W.2d 151, 1995 N.D. LEXIS 33 (N.D. 1995)

holographic wills are those provisions that express the testamentary and donative intent of the testator. The insertion of "Fred Bieber['s] daughters" is a material provision that is not in Krueger's handwriting.

There is no evidence that the holographic will was reexecuted after being revoked. In order for a will to be reexecuted, the testator must execute it again in accordance with the statutory formalities. Holographic wills are executed when a testator handwrites a document with testamentary intent and signs the document. There is no evidence that Krueger did this.

BUSINESS CONSIDERATIONS Many businesses today involve family-run enterprises and/or partnerships. Should a closely held business enterprise have a policy of encouraging—or even requiring—its chief operatives to execute a will in order to ensure that the business will pass to predetermined heirs, thus allowing the enterprise to continue?

ETHICAL CONSIDERATIONS What ethical concerns arise with a holographic will?

Nuncupative Wills

Nuncupative, or oral, wills are permitted in a number of states under limited circumstances. Usually, nuncupative wills can be used only to dispose of personal property; this is true in Kansas, Nebraska, Virginia, and Washington. Georgia, however, allows real property to pass in this manner. Some states place a limit on the value of the property transferred by a nuncupative will. The Uniform Probate Code makes no provision for nuncupative wills, and many states do not permit them.

Nuncupative wills also are restricted to certain situations. Generally, an oral will is valid (1) if it is made by a civilian who anticipates death from an injury received the same day or (2) if it is made by a soldier in the field or a sailor on a ship who is in peril or in fear of death. Because of the dangers inherent in military service and duty at sea, some states recognize a separate category of wills called "soldiers' and sailors' wills." These states may exempt soldiers and sailors from the usual requirements for oral or written wills.[3]

A nuncupative will must be heard by two or three disinterested witnesses, at least one of whom must have been asked by the decedent to act as a witness. This requirement is helpful in distinguishing between nuncupative wills and oral instructions to change a written will *or* a plan to change a will. Many statutes require that the nuncupative will be written down within 30 days and/or *probated* (that is, established in probate court as genuine and valid) within six months from the time it was spoken.

Matching Wills

Wills also can be categorized by the types of dispositions they contain. For example, married couples or business partners may have matching provisions in their wills. Matching wills are appropriate when the testators have identical testamentary objectives. For this reason, they are also called *reciprocal* wills. These wills may be mutual, joint, or contractual.

Mutual wills are separate wills in which the testators, usually a husband and wife, have matching provisions in their respective wills. For example, the separate will of each spouse might provide for "the transfer of my assets to my spouse. If my spouse does not survive me, then my assets shall be divided equally among my children."

In *joint wills,* two people sign the same document as their last will and testament. Usually, the dispositive provisions are the same. Joint wills are not recommended. Many state courts have difficulty analyzing the legal relationship between the two signers. The difficulty normally arises after the first person dies and the second person wants to change the will. The issue is whether the second person can modify the will or is contractually obligated to leave it unchanged. This conflict may cause court trials and appeals. As is the case with any lengthy trial and appeal, a large amount of the estate may be expended in trying to resolve the legal rights of the parties.

In *contractual wills,* people enter into a valid contract in which one or more of them promise to make certain dispositions in their wills. This agreement must meet the usual requirements for a valid contract, including consideration and the absence of fraud and undue influence. This arrangement lacks flexibility, but it may be desirable in some situations. If it is desirable, it is preferable to make a separate agreement to avoid the interpretive problems of joint wills.

Requirements for a Valid Will

The requirements for a valid will vary from state to state and apply to formal, holographic, and nuncupative wills. A person must be an adult at the time the will is executed in order for it to be valid. The modern rule is that anyone eighteen or older can execute a valid will. Eighteen is the age used in the Uniform Probate Code and the Model Execution of Wills Act. The Model Act, written by the NCCUSL, is intended as an example for states to follow in drafting their own laws. All states have now adopted the age of 18, with the following exceptions: Alabama (age 19), Louisiana (age 16), and Wyoming (age 19).[4]

A testator must also have **testamentary capacity**. Often wills contain the declaration, "I, Jane Doe, being of sound mind and body. . . ." This statement is *not* necessary. In addition, a person need not be physically healthy to write or sign a valid will. However, *actual* testamentary capacity is required at the time the will is signed. Actual testamentary capacity is narrowly defined by the courts. The common requirements are that the person understands the nature and extent of his or her assets, knows who his or her close relatives are, and understands the purpose of a will.[5] In many states, even a prior adjudication of incompetency will not automatically invalidate a will on the grounds of insanity. If a decedent is suspected of having been incompetent when he or she executed the will, some relatives probably will contest the will. One of the purposes of having disinterested witnesses is so that they will be able to testify about the testator's competency.

Testamentary capacity
Sufficient mental capability or sanity to execute a valid will.

A recent technique developed to assist with this proof is a *self-proved (self-proving) will.* This special type of formal will is accepted under the Uniform Probate Code. The purpose of a self-proved will is to reduce the amount of proof necessary when the testator dies and the will is offered for **probate**.[6] This is achieved by preparing and attaching sworn **affidavits** to the will when it is signed. The sworn affidavit states that the will is signed in compliance with the law. (In some states, the will must be signed by the testator and the witnesses before a notary public or other officer authorized to administer oaths.) The affidavits may include an optional statement that the witnesses believe that the testator is of sound mind and is acting of his or her own volition and without undue influence. Generally, then, the

Probate
The procedure for verifying that a will is authentic and should be implemented.

Affidavit
Written statement made under oath.

witnesses are not needed when the will is actually submitted for probate unless someone contests the will.

As noted earlier, formal and holographic wills must be signed by the testator. Many states require that a proper signature appear at the end of the document.

Testamentary Dispositions and Restrictions

A person has quite a bit of freedom in the dispositions that he or she may make in a will. These provisions are very important to the testator, and the court generally will give effect to them. But a person's ability to make testamentary dispositions has limits. Restrictions vary from state to state, but we will discuss some of the common restrictions. One concerns willing too large a portion of the estate to charity to the detriment of the family. (These prohibitions are called *mortmain,* or fear of death, statutes, and they operate to restrict the types and amounts of charitable gifts.)

Trust

An arrangement in which one person or business holds property and invests it for another.

Honorary trust

An arrangement that does not meet trust requirements and thus is not enforceable, although it may be carried out voluntarily.

Another widely prohibited disposition is a **trust** that is established for too long a period of time. The allowable length of time is specified in the rule against perpetuities, which is discussed briefly in the section of this chapter on private trusts.

In addition, most states do not allow the testator to will money to pets. Animals are not legal beneficiaries under wills or trusts. However, some states do allow the testator to establish an **honorary trust** for the benefit of the animal. Where permitted, the testator is restricted in the amount that may be placed in an honorary trust. The trust is limited to an amount of assets that is not excessive with respect to the animal's reasonable needs.

Community property

A special form of joint ownership between husband and wife permitted in certain states called community property states.

Will provisions can be set aside if they are against public policy. Examples include provisions that encourage beneficiaries to get divorced or that separate children from their parents. Obviously, a person cannot will away someone else's property (for example, the spouse's half of the **community property**) or property that passes by operation of law, as in a joint tenancy with rights of survivorship. (A movement exists in the American legal community that advocates changing state laws so that testators can will joint tenancy property and insurance proceeds.)

If a testator suspects that someone will want to contest the will, a *no-contest clause* may be inserted in it. Basically, such a clause indicates that if a person contests the validity of the will in court, that person will not inherit any assets from the estate. The no-contest clause is used as a threat by the testator, and in that sense it may be effective; however, many states do not enforce no-contest clauses or they make exceptions to them. Regardless of a state's approach to no-contest clauses, if the person is successful in having the will declared invalid, that person can inherit. In other words, the no-contest clause will be invalid along with the rest of the will. Depending on the circumstances, the person may inherit under a prior will or under the state intestate succession statute.

Common law states

States in which married couples cannot create community property.

Heirs

Persons who actually inherit property from the decedent.

Contrary to popular belief, a person is not required to leave assets to family members and other relatives. In **common law states**, there is an exception to this rule for a spouse: A widow or widower who is not willed at least a statutory minimum amount often can *elect against the will* (that is, choose to take a preset minimum percentage of the estate rather than the amount provided by the will). Other family members may be excluded, but a testator should mention them and the fact that they are being excluded. This is often accomplished by leaving them a nominal amount, such as $5 or $10. If the testator fails to do this, the omitted family members can claim that they were *pretermitted* (forgotten) **heirs**. Courts generally will award intestate shares to pretermitted heirs on the grounds that the omission was a mistake. In addition, the omission of a close family member can indicate that the testator was mentally incompetent.

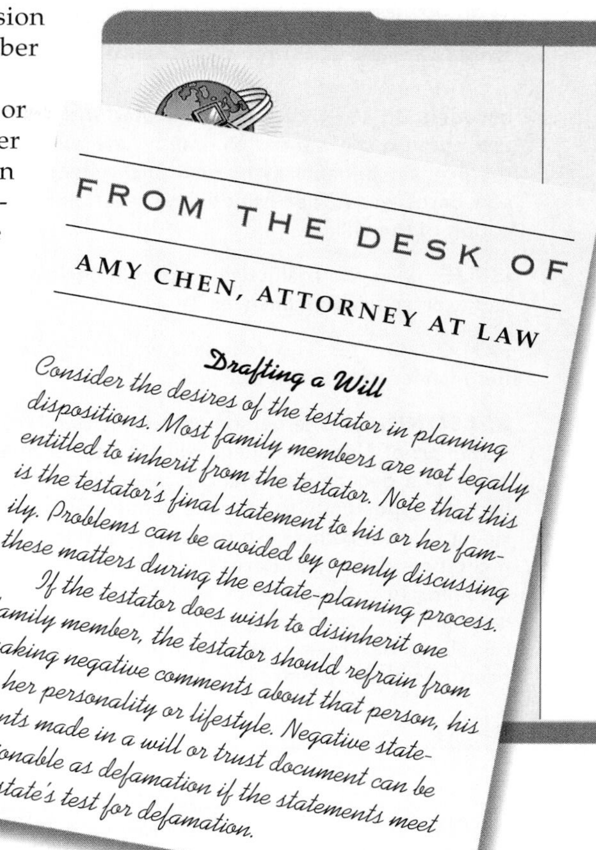

FROM THE DESK OF
AMY CHEN, ATTORNEY AT LAW
Drafting a Will
Consider the desires of the testator in planning dispositions. Most family members are not legally entitled to inherit from the testator. Note that this is the testator's final statement to his or her family. Problems can be avoided by openly discussing these matters during the estate-planning process.
If the testator does wish to disinherit one family member, the testator should refrain from making negative comments about that person, his or her personality or lifestyle. Negative statements made in a will or trust document can be actionable as defamation if the statements meet the state's test for defamation.

Actual heirs may receive their shares under different theories or philosophies. In writing a will, a testator may select between per capita (per head) or per stirpes (per line) distribution of assets. In *per capita* distribution, each beneficiary in the described group receives an equal share, no matter how many generations he or she is below the decedent. For example, in a gift to the decedent's children and grandchildren, each one would receive an equal share. This is true whether the grandchild's parent is alive. In contrast, in a *per stirpes* distribution to the decedent's children and grandchildren, each child of the decedent receives an equal share. If any child has already died, his or her children would equally divide that child's share. If a child is still alive, his or her offspring would not directly receive any assets. This is also called taking by **right of representation**. Exhibit 46.1 illustrates the distinction between a per stirpes and a per capita gift made to children and grandchildren.

The Uniform Probate Code introduced a new type of distribution called *per capita at each generation:* it is also called *per capita with representation*. For this method of distribution, the shares are determined at the first generation at which there are *any* living issue. This generation might be children, grandchildren, or even great-grandchildren. Once the shares are established for each line, then the issue of any deceased line members divide that line member's share. As you might assume, per capita at each generation distribution is really a hybrid between regular per stirpes and per capita distributions. Most states use the per capita at each generation rule in their intestate statutes. If a will or trust does not provide a clear indication about which approach should be used, the courts look to the intestacy statutes of that state. Consequently, most states will use a per capita at each generation approach if the will or trust is ambiguous. Strict per stirpes distribution, by contrast, always divides the shares at the first generational level below the decedent, even though no one at that level is still alive. Exhibit 46.2 illustrates the difference between per capita at each generation and strict per stirpes distributions.

Right of representation
Right of children to inherit in their parent's place, if the parent is deceased.

Wills can be set aside (ignored) by the court if they were signed because of fraud in the inducement, fraud in the execution, duress, or undue influence. (These concepts are used in wills cases in much the same manner as they are used in contract situations.) *Erb* v. *Lee* involved the setting aside of a will on the grounds of undue influence.

46.3 ERB v. LEE 430 N.E.2d 869 (Mass.App. 1982)

FACTS The decedent, approximately eighty-five years of age, hired Bates as her housekeeper in 1969 or 1970. Erb, the decedent's attorney, was appointed her conservator in 1973. Bates began to harass the decedent for money and property, so Erb fired Bates at the decedent's request. Bates called the decedent and harassed her and demanded back wages. About five months later, Bates returned, fired her successor, and again began keeping house for the

46.3 ERB v. LEE (cont.) 430 N.E.2d 869 (Mass.App. 1982)

decedent. In 1974, the decedent met with her attorney, Erb, because she wanted to draft a new will making Bates the primary beneficiary instead of the decedent's grandson. Bates was not present at the meeting or at the execution of the will.

ISSUE Was the trial judge correct in deciding that Bates had exerted undue influence?

HOLDING Yes. The decedent would not have acted in this manner of her own free will.

REASONING The person contesting a will has the burden of proof. Undue influence will not be presumed just because of a decedent's advanced age or because someone had the opportunity to exercise undue influence. The overriding factors in this case were the decedent's weakened mental condition and Bates's threats and harassment, her meddling in the decedent's affairs, her frightening phone calls, and her domineering personality. Bates's failure to testify about her relationship with the decedent may have been construed against her. Furthermore, a person does not have to be physically present when the will is executed to exert undue influence.

BUSINESS CONSIDERATIONS What should a businessperson do to protect himself or herself from charges of undue influence when dealing with a person who is in a vulnerable position due to age or ill health? Does the type of business relationship affect your attitude (i.e., a realtor buying from an elderly owner, a retail store dealing with an infirm customer)?

ETHICAL CONSIDERATIONS Assume that a businessperson is presented with an opportunity to enter into a contract with a person who is possibly vulnerable due to age or illness. Is it ethical for that businessperson to enter the contract without being assured that the other party is properly represented? Should the businessperson require the other party to have someone else present to protect his or her interests? Why or why not?

EXHIBIT 46.1 Testamentary Distributions to Surviving Children and Grandchildren

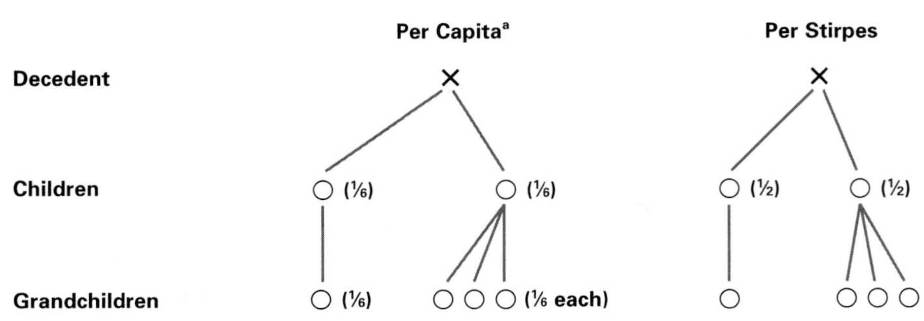

[a] This distribution assumes that the testator provided for per capita distribution to "my children and grandchildren."

EXHIBIT 46.2 Testamentary Distributions to Surviving Children and Grandchildren

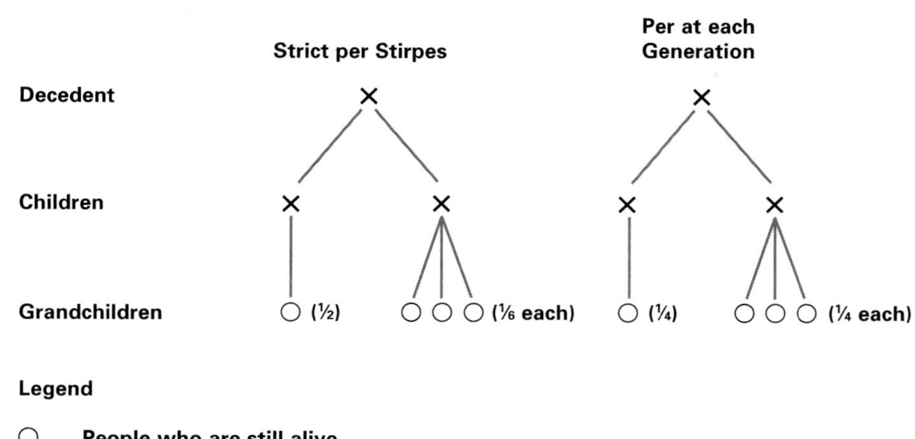

INTESTATE SUCCESSION

For various reasons, people often fail to sign or to execute a valid will. States provide for the transfer of the assets of these people by their intestate succession statute. People who die without a valid will are said to have died *intestate.* Sometimes, especially with holographic wills, people fail to provide for the disposition of *all* their assets. In a properly drafted will, such disposition is assured by the use of a residuary clause that states: "I leave all the rest and residue of my estate to. . . ." Any assets *not* covered by the will provisions pass by intestate succession.

The intestacy statutes vary from state to state. Passage of personal property is governed by the intestate law of the decedent's domicile. Real property is governed by the intestate law where the property is located. Some states have different provisions for the passage of personal property and the passage of real property within their control.

Community property states provide for different chains of distribution for community property and separate property. As mentioned in Chapter 44, community property is a form of joint ownership between husband and wife. In states that allow this form of joint ownership, most property that is acquired during marriage is owned one-half by the husband and one-half by the wife.

Generally, legislators enact a statute to dispose of property in the manner they think most people would desire. For example, under the Uniform Probate Code, if the decedent leaves a surviving spouse but no surviving **issue** or parent(s), the surviving spouse takes all the intestate property.[7] If there are surviving issue who are issue of both the decedent and the surviving spouse, the spouse takes the first

Issue
Lineal descendants, such as children, grandchildren, and great-grandchildren.

$50,000 plus one-half the balance of the estate. The issue would share the rest by per capita at each generation.[8]

These intestate provisions are applicable to separate property states and to separate property in community property states under the Uniform Probate Code. Exhibit 46.3 summarizes the Uniform Probate Code intestate succession provisions for separate property.

PROBATE AND ESTATE ADMINISTRATION

Probate hearings are a series of hearings in probate court in which the judge makes sure that the estate is being properly administered. The judge will conduct a hearing if any interested party contests the validity of the will. The judge confirms whether the will is valid and was properly executed under state law. Even after the judge has accepted the validity of the will, this judicial order can be revoked if it is shown that the will was fraudulently offered for probate. The judge supervises the personal representative in the completion of his or her duties.

The concept of administering an estate is relatively simple. The personal representative of the estate must advertise in newspapers of general circulation in order

EXHIBIT 46.3 Intestate Succession Under the Uniform Probate Code[a]

Survivors	Spouse's Share	Remainder of Estate to Others
Spouse (if there is no issue or parent of decedent)	100%	Not applicable
Spouse and issue, all of whom are also issue of the surviving spouse	First $50,000, plus ½ the balance	To the issue, if they are of the same degree of kinship, equally[b]
Spouse and issue, one or more of whom are not issue of the surviving spouse	½ to the spouse	To the issue, if they are of the same degree of kinship, equally[b]
Spouse and parent(s) (if there is no surviving issue)	First $50,000, plus ½ the balance	To parent or parents equally
Issue of decedent (if there is no surviving spouse)	Not applicable	To the issue, if they are of the same degree of kinship, equally[b]
Parent(s) (if there is no surviving spouse or issue)	Not applicable	To parent or parents equally
Issue of parents (if there is no surviving spouse, issue, or parents)	Not applicable	To the issue of the parents or either parent by representation[b]
Grandparents and issue of grandparents (if there is no surviving spouse, issue, parents, or issue of a parent)	Not applicable	½ to paternal grandparent(s) or to their issue[b] if they are both deceased; ½ to maternal grandparent(s) or to their issue[b] if they are both deceased; if there is no grandparent or issue on one side, that share goes to the other side

[a] This is a representation of the Uniform Probate Code §§ 2-101–2-103. It does not reflect the alternative provisions for community property states.

[b] These transfers are made per capita at each generation.

to locate the creditors of the deceased. If a creditor does not file a claim against the estate in a timely manner, the claim will be barred. The representative will also collect the assets of the decedent, collect money owed to the decedent, pay the lawful debts owed by the decedent, pay the necessary expenses of estate administration, and pay any state and/or federal taxes. It is often necessary to sell assets to make these disbursements. The remaining assets are then distributed to the proper beneficiaries. A court generally will oversee this procedure through probate hearings.

A decedent's estate usually is administered by a personal representative. The representative has fiduciary duties to the lawful beneficiaries of the estate. If the decedent had a valid will that named a representative, that person will be called an *executor.* A court-appointed representative will be called an *administrator.* (Some localities still use the more traditional terminology of calling male representatives executors or administrators, and female representatives executrixes or administratrixes.) The administrator will be appointed following any guidelines provided in the state probate code. Some states require that an executor or an administrator reside in the same state as the decedent. There usually is a minimum age of 18.

These personal representatives are responsible for the proper administration and probate of the estate. They must make sure that the duties mentioned in this section are properly completed. Personal representatives have a significant responsibility for which they receive a fee. They can be **surcharged** from personal funds if they violate their duties by failing to perform as required or by performing incorrectly. Some common examples of wrongdoing include failure to pay taxes, failure to probate the will, failure to sell assets that are declining in value, failure to minimize taxes, failure to sell assets at a fair price, self-dealing, such as selling estate or trust assets to oneself or to a friend, and fraud.

46.1

MANAGEMENT/PERSONAL LAW

PROVIDING FOR THE FAMILY AND CIT

Tom and Anna are both in excellent health, and the continued success and growth of the firm seemingly assures them a comfortable life and a good retirement. Nonetheless, they are concerned about what would happen to their children—and to the firm—if some tragedy were to befall them. They would like to provide for their children (with a minimum tax burden) if anything should happen to them. They would also like to make certain that the firm remains a family-owned enterprise. They have asked you for advice as to what they can or should do to ensure their wishes are carried out. What advice will you give them?

BUSINESS CONSIDERATIONS What might Tom and Anna do to assure that CIT continues to operate as a family-owned business to provide income and security for their family? Would they be better served by establishing a trust or by making provisions in their wills?

ETHICAL CONSIDERATIONS Suppose a person decides to write a will and must decide whether to select distribution of the estate per capita, per stirpes, or per capita at each generation. What ethical issues should be considered in making such a decision? Is it ethical to use either a will or a trust in an effort to delay or avoid taxes?

In many jurisdictions, the judge can reduce the commissions paid to the personal representative and the fees paid to the attorney and accountant if they are excessive. Executors, administrators, and, in many states, attorneys usually are paid based on a percentage of the value of the assets in the estate. In some states, maximum fees are established in the probate code.

Surcharged
Assessed a fee by the court for failure to follow fiduciary duties.

AVOIDING PROBATE

Often, people believe that it is wise to avoid probate. Examples of property that is not subject to probate include entireties property, joint tenancy with rights of survivorship, and life insurance paid to a named beneficiary. (Refer to Exhibit 44.1 on page 1160 for an explanation of the survivorship feature of forms of joint ownership.) New forms of ownership are being originated that also avoid probate, for example, pay-on-death ownership. It is currently available for bank accounts and some government securities; and some states permit pay-on-death registration for securities, for example, Colorado, Minnesota, and Wisconsin.[9] If, during life, a person places assets into a trust with named beneficiaries, these assets will not be probated. Another option of the property owner is to enter into a valid contract that provides, in part, for the passage of property at the owner's death. All these arrangements may serve as substitutes for a valid will and, depending on state law, may escape the technical requirements of the state statute of wills. However, even assets that are not subject to probate may still be subject to an **estate tax** and/or an **inheritance tax**.

Estate tax
A tax assessed on the total net (taxable) value of the estate.

Inheritance tax
A tax assessed on transfers of estate assets at the owner's death. The rates vary depending on the owner's relationship to the recipient.

Avoiding probate of an estate may reduce the amount of time necessary for the administration of that estate. In the case of joint tenancies with rights of survivorship, one owner will have immediate access to these assets at the other owner's death, although some states restrict this immediate access for bank accounts and safe deposit boxes. An important consideration for some people is the additional privacy afforded by avoiding probate. Probate, like most court proceedings, is part of the public record; anyone who is so inclined can read the will and the inventory of assets. Costs usually are involved in the probate of an estate; some, such as fees for filing court documents, are nominal. The amount of some fees may be based on the amount and value of probate assets; avoiding probate or reducing the amount of probate assets eliminates or reduces these costs. Probate costs increase markedly when lawsuits arise concerning the validity of the will, its interpretation, or asset distribution. These *will contests* reduce the amount of assets to be distributed to the beneficiaries. Sometimes these contests are caused by poorly drafted wills or holographic wills. Probate costs and taxes may increase significantly if a person dies intestate or without prudent estate planning.

Avoiding probate has some disadvantages. The extent to which these concerns are disadvantageous will depend on the people involved and the method used to avoid probate. Some of the techniques—for example, establishing and operating out of a trust—require additional paperwork and attention to detail. Avoiding probate may also create a higher inheritance or estate tax liability on the decedent's estate or on the estates of other family members. In probate, the creditors of the decedent are located and paid, and the estate is discharged of all further obligation to them. Without probate, there is no discharge from potential creditors' claims. In addition, the purpose of probate is to protect lawful beneficiaries and creditors. This may be particularly important when beneficiaries are not knowledgeable or are confused. The court can intervene to protect them from unscrupulous people. Unfortunately, this purpose is not always served effectively under some state probate codes and procedures.

Thus, it is not always advantageous to avoid probate. As with any estate-planning decision, consideration must be given to the individuals and the assets involved. One factor that is often overlooked is that an asset's status as a probate or nonprobate asset does *not* avoid estate or inheritance taxation on it.

Legislative sympathy exists for reducing some of the procedures involved in probate. Texas and Washington began permitting executors to perform at least some functions without court supervision. This is called independent administration, as distinguished from the more traditional supervised administration. In Texas, the testator may indicate that the executor is an "independent executor." When this occurs, the executor conducts all duties outside the court, except for probating the will, filing an inventory, appraisal of assets, and list of claims against the estate. The Washington provision is similar and is implemented if the testator executes a "nonintervention will."

The Uniform Probate Code has followed and expanded these examples. Under the Uniform Probate Code, all administrations are unsupervised unless the personal representative or any **interested party** requests a court ruling to the contrary.[10] Supervised administration, however, is still the majority rule.

Interested party
A party with an interest in the estate, such as a beneficiary, heir, or creditor.

The Uniform Probate Code also includes provisions for informal probate with simplified procedures in many situations. A number of states have declined to adopt simplified procedures on the grounds that they do not provide adequate protection from abuses by dishonest and/or incompetent personal representatives.

TRANSFER TAXES

The federal government taxes the owner when he or she exercises the right to transfer property. This may take the form of gift taxes if the owner transfers the asset during lifetime. If the transfer is effective on death, a federal estate tax may be due. Estate taxes treat the entire estate as one unit, subject to certain exclusions, deductions, and credits. See Exhibit 46.4. These tax rates are progressive, as are federal income taxes. The federal transfer tax system consists of an estate tax, a gift tax, and a generation-skipping transfer tax. The system attempts to detect and tax all transfers.

Many states also have gift *and* estate taxes. Other states, however, such as California, have gift and inheritance taxes. In inheritance taxes, each recipient's share or inheritance is taxed separately. Inheritance taxes are based on the recipient's relationship to the decedent and the value of the assets received. A few states do not tax voluntary transfers such as gifts and inheritances.

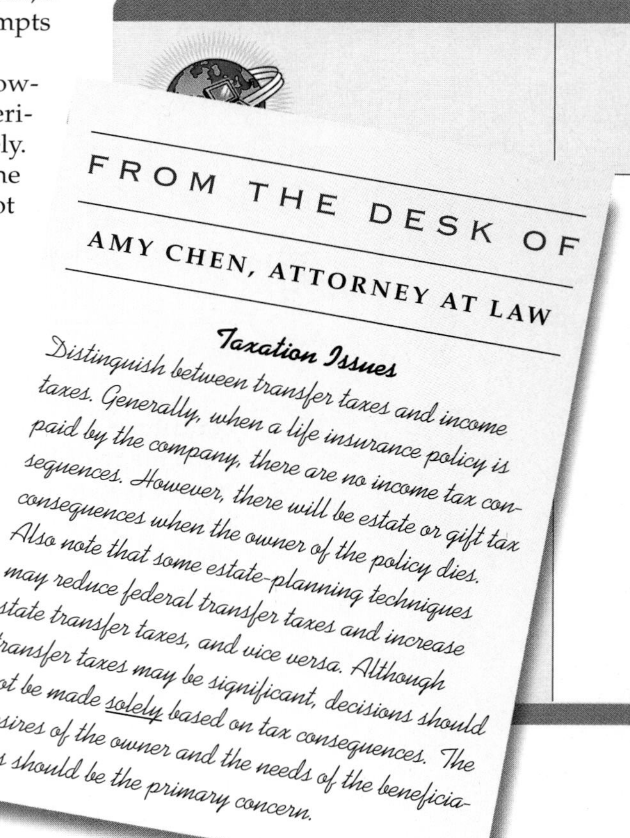

FROM THE DESK OF
AMY CHEN, ATTORNEY AT LAW
Taxation Issues
Distinguish between transfer taxes and income taxes. Generally, when a life insurance policy is paid by the company, there are no income tax consequences. However, there will be estate or gift tax consequences when the owner of the policy dies. Also note that some estate-planning techniques may reduce federal transfer taxes and increase state transfer taxes, and vice versa. Although transfer taxes may be significant, decisions should not be made solely based on tax consequences. The desires of the owner and the needs of the beneficiaries should be the primary concern.

RETIREMENT PLANS

People are living longer. With increased longevity comes increased concerns about income during retirement. Retirement plans are very complex and have both income tax and transfer tax consequences. For many people, their pension or retirement plans may be one of their largest assets.

Some plans are employer plans. One type of an employer plan is a *defined-benefit plan,* where the employer promises to pay the retiree a set benefit based upon a percentage of the employee's average earnings and the number of years worked under the plan. The funds for the employees are pooled together; however, the employer keeps separate records on the amount each employee earns. Payments may be made monthly beginning with retirement, or there may be a lump-sum payment at retirement. The retiree may have a choice, or the plan may require one type of payment. These plans are common for people employed by the military, many unions, and many large companies.

EXHIBIT 46.4 Tentative Federal Estate Tax

Gross Estate
Deduct: Claims, debts, and allowable taxes
Administration and funeral expenses

Adjusted Gross Estate
Deduct: Marital deduction
Charitable deduction

Taxable Estate
Add: Adjusted taxable gifts

Estate Tax Base
Calculate tentative federal estate tax from table below
Deduct: Gift tax payable on adjusted taxable gifts
Unified credit for gift and estate taxes of $192,800
Credit for state death taxes paid (Maximum permitted per IRS table)

Net Federal Estate Tax

A	B	A	B
Taxable Estate[a]	Federal Estate Tax	Taxable Estate	Federal Estate Tax
$ 50,000	$ 10,600	$ 800,000	$ 267,800
100,000	23,800	900,000	306,800
200,000	54,800	1,000,000	345,800
300,000	87,800	1,200,000	427,800
400,000	121,800	1,500,000	555,800
500,000	155,800	2,000,000	780,800
600,000	192,800	3,000,000	1,290,800
700,000	229,800		

[a] Table only shows taxes for certain sized estates.

A *defined-contribution plan* is an employer plan where the employer promises to contribute a certain amount to the plan each year. The contribution is generally a percentage of the worker's earnings. Each employee has a separate account. The money is invested. When an employee retires, the amount the employee receives is based on the amount contributed plus the earnings. At retirement, payments may be periodic or by a lump sum.

Living Wills and Durable Powers of Attorney

People often include a *living will* as part of their estate plan. Despite the use of the title, this document does not dispose of assets at the owner's death. It explains how the individual feels about certain medical treatments, especially life-prolonging treatment, when the patient is very ill and recovery is doubtful. The document often states that the living will requests should be honored "if there is no reasonable expectation of recovery." This is often subject to medical interpretation and the medical experts may not agree on this issue. Living wills are popular because of recent developments in medical research that allow a patient to live with little hope of recovery. Problems arise when a patient is physically incapable of making and/or communicating his or her desires about potential medical treatments. Living wills are legal in most states; but compliance with the state statute, of course, is critical.

Another technique used to control the course of a person's medical treatment is the *durable power of attorney for health care.* This document appoints another person to decide medical care issues for the maker, if the maker becomes incapacitated and is unable to make these decisions.

FROM THE DESK OF
AMY CHEN, ATTORNEY AT LAW
Pension Plans
Pension plans are an effective technique for attracting quality employees. Many individuals no longer believe that social security will provide adequate income during retirement. In addition, individuals who anticipate an active retirement, full of travel and hobbies, will need income and/or assets in excess of social security benefits in order to support this lifestyle.
Family-run companies are at a disadvantage in hiring if they do not offer employee benefits such as retirement plans and health insurance.

TRUSTS DEFINED

A trust is a fiduciary relationship where specific property is transferred to the care of a trustee, or manager. Trusts may be voluntary arrangements created by the property owner, or they may be legal arrangements imposed by the courts or implied by the law in order to reach a fair result. In a trust, legal title and equitable ownership rights are split between two or more people. One person has the legal right to the asset; another person has the beneficial right to the use and enjoyment of the asset.

EXPRESS TRUSTS

Trusts that are created voluntarily by the owner of the property are called *express trusts.* (Trusts that are created by operation of law are discussed in the section of this chapter on implied trusts.) The owner transfers real or personal property to a trustee for the benefit of a named person. During the period of the trust, the trustee manages the property and pays the income to the people specified in the **trust deed**. If the trust is to take effect during the owner's life, it is called an *inter vivos* (lifetime or living) trust. If it is to take effect at death, it is called a *testamentary trust.* Testamentary trusts are usually included as part of the will and do not have a separate trust deed. They must comply with the state's statute of wills.

Trust deed
A legal document that specifies the recipients of a trust, their interests, and how the trust should be managed; also called a deed of trust.

Generally, at least three people are needed for an express trust: a creator, a trustee, and one or more beneficiaries. A creator may also be called a settlor or a trustor. The *creator* is the one who establishes the trust and is usually the person who puts assets into the trust. The *trustee,* who may be a person or a business entity, is in charge of managing the assets. *Corpus, res,* or *principal* are the names used for the assets. The *beneficiaries* are the recipients. Depending on the trust instrument, the beneficiaries may receive the income from the assets, the assets themselves, or both. Consideration is not required to establish a trust.

To be valid, a trust must meet a few requirements. The intention or purpose of the creator must be expressed—for example, by stating that "this trust is established for my children's college educations." In many cases, though, the courts have concluded that the intention of the creator may be inferred from his or her actions if this intention is not stated. Creators commonly establish trusts for one of these purposes: to provide for more than one beneficiary; to protect beneficiaries from themselves and from overreaching by others; and to legally reduce taxes.

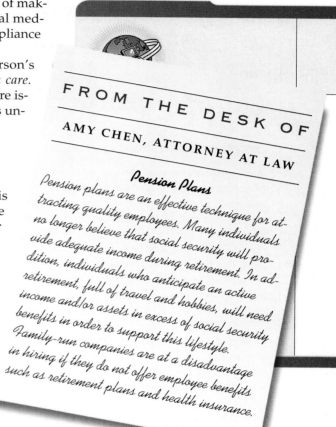

46.2

PERSONAL LAW/MANAGEMENT

PROTECTING AGAINST FINANCIAL HARDSHIPS

Anna's mother suffered from Alzheimer's disease for three years prior to her death. One of Tom's cousins was seriously injured in an industrial accident and spent several years on life-support before dying. As a result, both Anna and Tom have observed the suffering and the financial hardships that a family endures in such a situation. Both are determined to do everything in their power to protect their family from this sort of ordeal. They have each asked you for advice on methods for dealing with these sorts of situations. What advice will you give them?

BUSINESS CONSIDERATIONS What can a closely held firm do to protect itself and its constituents in the event a primary policy maker of the firm suffers from a debilitating disease or injury? Should a business have a policy or procedure in place in the event such a situation arises?

ETHICAL CONSIDERATIONS Suppose a person establishes a durable power of attorney for health care issues. What criteria should the "attorney" use in making decisions? Should the "attorney" only be concerned with the wishes of the "maker," or should the desires of the other family members also be considered?

Under the Statute of Frauds, most trust deeds must be in writing because they cannot possibly be performed within one year. Even if a writing were not required by the Statute of Frauds, it would be foolish to have oral trust provisions. Many potential legal problems do not arise until after the creator has died. Trusts generally contain lengthy and complex provisions about what the trustee can and cannot do; these certainly should be reduced to writing.

A trust may terminate when its purpose is completed or when its term is over. Under some circumstances, the trust may terminate by mutual agreement of all the beneficiaries, or when it becomes uneconomical. Depending on the trust deed, the power to terminate the trust may rest with the trustee, the creator, or someone else. When the trust is terminated, the trust assets are transferred to the specified **remainder beneficiaries**.

Remainder beneficiaries
Persons with an interest in what remains in the trust corpus after use by the income beneficiaries.

A *revocable trust* is one that can be revoked or canceled by the creator. In rare instances, the creator may give this power to another individual. This trust usually becomes permanent and irrevocable at the death of the creator. On the other hand, an *irrevocable trust* is one that may not be terminated during the specified term of the trust. Once the assets are placed in trust, they must remain there for the term of the trust under the conditions specified in the trust deed.

Whether a trust is revocable or irrevocable depends on the trust document. It is always wise to specify this aspect of the trust; otherwise, the trust will be governed by state law. In most states, the trust will be irrevocable unless the creator has stated a contrary intention in the trust deed. In a minority of states, including California, it will be presumed to be revocable unless a contrary intention is expressed.

There are various categories of express trusts, based on the clauses contained in the trust deed. A specific trust may contain provisions in more than one of these categories. This sampling of trust provisions indicates the variety that is possible with trusts.

Private Trusts

A *private trust* is one that is not created for the general public good. The beneficiaries of this type of trust are individual citizens and not society as a whole. A private trust is limited by the time period specified in the *rule against perpetuities.* The rule against perpetuities is really a common law rule that prohibits the remote vesting of trust or property interests. It requires that an interest vest within the time limit set by the rule. The rule does not apply to interests that are already vested, that is, nonforfeitable, even if the beneficiary will not receive the vested interest until far into the future. Section 1 of the Uniform Statutory Rule Against Perpetuities, drafted by the NCCUSL, states the general rule as "A nonvested property interest is invalid unless: (1) when the interest is created, it is certain to vest or terminate no later than 21 years after the death of an individual then alive; or (2) the interest either vests or terminates within ninety years after its creation." The Uniform Statutory Rule Against Perpetuities with 1990 Amendments has been adopted in Alaska, Arizona, California, Colorado, Connecticut, Hawaii, Indiana, Kansas, Montana, New Jersey, New Mexico, North Carolina, North Dakota, South Dakota, Tennessee, and West Virginia. Nine additional states have enacted the Uniform Rule without the 1990 amendments.[11]

Charitable Trusts

A *charitable trust* is one in which money is given to a charity for a public purpose. A qualified charity for tax purposes is a corporation organized for religious, charitable, scientific, literary, or educational purposes, including the encouragement of art and the prevention of cruelty to children or animals. Charities also include the United States or any state or political subdivision or any veterans' organization or its departments or posts.[12] Transfers to charities, either outright or in trust, may pass tax free. However, the strict requirements of the Internal Revenue Service must be met. In addition, the charitable organization must qualify under state and federal rules. An organization that qualifies for federal tax purposes may not qualify for state tax purposes. The opposite is also true. California, for example, requires that the organization be a California charity or a national charity that is going to use the assets in California. To qualify for favorable tax treatment under federal law, a trust with charitable and noncharitable beneficiaries must meet the stringent requirements imposed by the 1969 Tax Reform Act. In most states, charitable trusts are excluded from the *rule against perpetuities.*

If the original charitable purpose cannot be fulfilled, a court of equity may apply the ***cy-pres* doctrine**. The application of the doctrine means that the court will try to follow the transferor's intention as closely as possible. This is usually accomplished by substituting another charitable beneficiary with a similar purpose for the charity initially specified. Before a substitution can occur, it must be shown that the original charity no longer exists or that the original terms no longer apply.

***Cy-pres* doctrine**
Doctrine permitting the court to modify the trust in order to follow the creator's charitable intention as closely as possible.

Additional Types of Express Trusts

A trust that will accumulate income is called an *accumulation trust.* The trustee will not disburse the income to or for the use of the **income beneficiaries** or remainder beneficiaries. The earnings will be reinvested in the trust for the period of time specified. Most states restrict the length of time that a private trust can accumulate income to the identical time period prescribed by the *rule against perpetuities.*

Income beneficiaries
Persons with an income interest in a trust.

A *sprinkling trust* is one that gives the trustee the power to determine which income beneficiaries should receive income each year and how much they should receive. A prudent creator should provide the trustee with some standards to use in making this decision. Income that is not distributed in any particular year is added to the corpus, as in an accumulation trust.

As the name implies, a *spendthrift trust* is established when one or more of the beneficiaries are spendthrifts and need to be protected from their own imprudent spending habits. They are permitted in most but not all states. This type of trust also may be used if the beneficiary is unduly subject to manipulation and/or control by family members and friends. Generally, the beneficiary (1) cannot anticipate the receipt of income or corpus from a spendthrift trust, (2) cannot assign it to creditors or borrow against it, and (3) will not necessarily receive all the income earned in any one year. Income will be paid to the beneficiary only when actually necessary. The trustee often will pay it directly to the creditor for services ordered by the trustee. Under some circumstances, creditors *may* be able to attach the trust assets.

A *discretionary trust* allows the trustee to pay or not to pay the income or principal at his or her discretion. It is commonly used in states that either do not allow or greatly restrict spendthrift trusts. In these situations, the creator generally names an affectionate family member as an alternate beneficiary and, when the primary beneficiary has difficulties with creditors, the trustee makes the distributions to the alternate. It is hoped that the alternate will feel a moral obligation to care for the primary beneficiary.

Advantages of Trusts

One of the advantages of trusts over other methods of transferring assets is the flexibility that trusts permit. With an outright gift, the gift property belongs to the beneficiary. If that transfer turns out to be inappropriate, the transferor cannot change it. With gifts in trust, the trustee maintains control over the assets for a specified period of time under the instructions in the trust deed. For example, a trust can be established for one's children so that each will receive a third of his or her share of the corpus when he or she reaches 25, 30, and 35.

Another aspect of this flexibility is that funding a trust can occur over a period of time. A trust deed can be written to permit the creator to add assets to the trust later. In fact, the trust deed can be written so that other people can add assets to the creator's trust. Moreover, trust income can be paid out to the income beneficiaries equally, based on percentages, or based on need. Beneficiaries can receive the income in a lump sum at the end of the trust or annually, quarterly, monthly, or as needed.

Disadvantages of Trusts

The flexibility of trusts can be an advantage; by the same token, lack of flexibility can be a disadvantage. If a trust is irrevocable and an emergency arises or circumstances change, the trustee generally will be constrained by the trust deed. If the creator did not anticipate this occurrence in the document, the trustee may not be able to modify his or her actions to fit the situation. Another disadvantage of trusts is fees. Rarely is a trustee willing to undertake the responsibility of being a trustee without receiving a fee. *Estate of Gump* involved a suit for fees by the trustee.

46.4 ESTATE OF GUMP — 180 Cal.Rptr. 219 (Cal.App. 1982)

FACTS Wells Fargo Bank was the trustee of a testamentary trust under Gump's will. The trustee filed its eighth annual accounting, which included a request for $32,689 compensation for the trustee. However, the trustee was awarded only $10,000 in fees by the probate court. In accordance with the trust deed, the trustee was managing some real estate occupied by a retail store. The retail store underpaid its rent under the formula provided by the lease.

46.4 ESTATE OF GUMP *(cont.)* 180 Cal.Rptr. 219 (Cal.App. 1982)

The bank negligently accepted the underpayment as full payment of the rent.

ISSUE Did the probate court unduly penalize the negligent trustee?

HOLDING Yes. The probate court did not adequately compensate the trustee, and the penalty imposed was excessive under the circumstances.

REASONING Unless the will provides otherwise, a testamentary trustee is entitled to reasonable compensation for services. The probate court has broad discretion in this matter. Its decision should not be disturbed unless it abuses its discretion. It may properly consider customary charges in the private sector based on the value of trust assets and the success or failure of the trustee's administration. The probate court can charge the trustee for shortages. This may be accomplished by denying part or all of the compensation to be paid in conjunction with the mismanaged trust asset. In this case, the trustee was also assessed a surcharge of $7,300, but the record did not disclose why. Generally, a trustee's liability is limited to the loss actually suffered by the beneficiaries, unless the trustee acted fraudulently or personally benefitted. The appellate court held that neither was the situation in this case, and so the additional charge to the trustee of $7,300 could not be justified.

BUSINESS CONSIDERATIONS What sort of duty is owed by a business that manages the investments of its customers? How should a court measure the business's performance of its duties in those situations?

ETHICAL CONSIDERATIONS Is it ethical for a person to hire a business to manage his or her investments and/or assets, and then to sue that business if the returns on the investments or assets are not as great as expected? When *is* it ethical for the business to be held liable for the "inadequate" returns on the assets?

Trusts may also increase the amount of taxes that must be paid, depending on the nature and terms of the trust. Under the tax codes, trusts are taxed in complex ways. Before establishing a trust, one should determine (1) who will pay income tax on its income, (2) who will have the advantage of any income tax deductions, (3) whether the trust will be subject to gift taxes, (4) whether the trust will be subject to estate and/or inheritance taxes when the creator or a beneficiary dies, and (5) whether the trust will be subject to any generation-skipping transfer taxes. A *generation-skipping transfer tax* is a tax imposed on some trust (and nontrust) transfers to a recipient who is two or more generations younger than the donor. For example, a man who makes a gift to his granddaughter rather than to his daughter makes a generation-skipping transfer. All the tax considerations listed here are complex, with varying tax rates, deductions, exclusions, exemptions, and credits.

Selection of Trustees and Executors

Because trustees and executors have broad powers and broad discretion, it is important to select them wisely. Successor trustees and executors may also be named in a trust or a will in case the first person named is unable or unwilling to serve as the personal representative. If a decedent does not have a valid will naming a suitable executor, the probate court will appoint an administrator for the estate. In such a case, the owner of the assets will have no say in the selection. Trustees may be appointed to invest and protect the estates of the people who are mentally incompetent. Administrators, executors, and trustees may be referred to as *fiduciaries,* since each one has a fiduciary duty to protect the rights of the creator and the beneficiaries.

The legal requirements for who may be a fiduciary are very simple. In most states, the fiduciary must be 18 years of age or older. Some states also require that the fiduciary be a resident of the state. It generally simplifies transactions if the fiduciary does reside in the state.

A common consideration in selecting a fiduciary is whether to select a corporate fiduciary, such as the trust department of a bank, or an individual fiduciary, such as a family member or a friend. A corporate fiduciary usually does not die or dissolve, often has the expertise needed to do a competent job, and does not need to be bonded for the faithful performance of its duties. Although corporate trustees may last forever, individual trust officers do not. Often, a creator or testator will select a bank because of past dealings with a particular trust officer. Remember, however, that the trust officer may leave or die. Moreover, some corporate trust departments do not earn a very good rate of return on the assets that they invest. The same may be true, though, for any individual trustee. Corporate trustees will require a fee, but they may be willing to negotiate and handle the trust for a smaller fee. Many states have statutes that prescribe the maximum fees.

Individual trustees may be willing to serve without fees. They also may have more knowledge about the business and family members than corporate trustees have. In addition, they may be personally concerned for the well-being of the beneficiaries. They may, however, be biased toward certain beneficiaries. In fact, they may be so closely involved with the family that they will be subject to overreaching by family members.

A decision to choose a corporate trustee may be affected by the selection of individuals available to serve in that capacity. A trustee should be honest, mature, competent, impartial, and knowledgeable and should have the ability and time to make sound business decisions. Obviously, the final selection of any personal representative should depend on the facts and circumstances of each case.

Duties of Trustees

The trustee has two primary duties in relation to the property in his or her care. First, the trustee is supposed to preserve and protect the trust corpus. This includes identifying the assets, protecting them, and safeguarding them. The other primary function of the trustee is to make the assets productive. In other words, the trustee is supposed to invest and manage the assets to produce income for the beneficiaries. This task must be accomplished without violating the trustee's other duties.

The trustee has some other, more specific duties. They include an obligation to follow the terms of the trust and a duty of care that must be exercised in administering someone else's property. The rule, as stated by a majority of courts, is that a trustee must exercise the degree of *care, skill, and prudence* that a reasonably prudent businessperson would exercise in dealing with his or her own property. This standard is applied whether the person actually possesses the necessary skill and knowledge.

The trustee also has a duty of loyalty. There are, in reality, two aspects of this duty. One is an obligation not to take advantage of situations involving conflicts of interest. In many instances, the trustee has an obligation to avoid even potential conflicts of interest. Obviously, then, a trustee should not personally enter into a transaction with the trust. Such a transaction usually is a breach of fiduciary duty and consequently is voidable and can be set aside. The other aspect of the duty of loyalty is to be as impartial as possible among the beneficiaries. Impartiality is not always possible because there is a natural conflict between the income beneficiaries and the remainder beneficiaries. (Remainder beneficiaries are also called principal beneficiaries or corpus beneficiaries.) As stated by Justice Putnam of the Supreme Court in the classic decision *Harvard College* v. *Amory* 9 Pick. 446, 461 (1830), "All that can be required of a trustee . . . is that he shall conduct himself faithfully and exercise sound discretion. He is to observe how men of prudence, discretion, and intelligence manage their own affairs, not in regard to speculation, but in regard to the permanent disposition of their funds, considering the probable income, as well as the probable safety of the capital to be invested."

In *Northwestern Mutual Life Insurance Co.* v. *Wiemer,* the trustee breached its duty of loyalty.

46.5 NORTHWESTERN MUTUAL LIFE INSURANCE CO. v. WIEMER 421 N.E.2d 1002 (Ill.App. 1981)

FACTS Mr. and Mrs. Wiemer entered into a trust agreement, with Havana Bank as trustee, to enable them to purchase and work a farm. As part of the financial arrangement, Northwestern Mutual executed a $70,000 first mortgage on the farm; Havana held the second mortgage. After Mr. Wiemer died, Havana took $8,000 from the trust account and paid itself part of its own second mortgage. Consequently, the trust was unable to make the next payment to Northwestern, and Northwestern foreclosed on the first mortgage.

ISSUE Did the trustee breach its trust duties?

HOLDING Yes.

REASONING The trustee was guilty of self-dealing in violation of its duty of loyalty. Havana had drafted the trust document and was trustee under it. Havana knew a payment would be due soon. Havana had three possible options: to apply all the funds to the first mortgage, to pay the regular payment on the first mortgage and pay the rest to itself, or to pay the entire amount to Mrs. Wiemer. Instead, it applied the funds for its own personal gain. This is a classic case of self-dealing and breach of trust. It was also a violation of the trust document, which stated that the first mortgage should be paid first. The court ruled that Mrs. Wiemer was entitled to damages. [Notice that the Wiemers entered into an express trust as part of a loan arrangement and not part of an estate plan.]

BUSINESS CONSIDERATIONS Should a business have a policy regarding potential conflicts of interest such as the one faced by Havana Bank in this case? Should Havana Bank have refused to serve as trustee, since it held a second mortgage on the farm that was central to the trust? Why or why not?

ETHICAL CONSIDERATIONS From an ethical perspective, what should a business do when that business is placed in a position that creates a potential conflict of interest in its dealings with customers or clients? Should the obligation to the customer outweigh the obligations owed to the other constituents of the business?

It is commonly stated that a trustee has a duty not to delegate, but this is really just a cautionary note. Not every act of trust administration must be completed by the trustee personally. A trustee may delegate to others the performance of any act or the exercise of any power when it is consistent with the trustee's general duty of care owed to the beneficiaries. In other words, the trustee may employ agents when a reasonably prudent owner of the same type of property and similar objectives would employ agents. In addition, the trustee must exercise due care in selecting and supervising agents.

The trustee must be careful in selecting trust investments. This generally includes a duty to diversify the types of investments. The statutes in many states list or define what investments a trustee may make. These are often called *legal investments.* A creator, however, may grant a trustee the specific power to invest in nonlegal investments. Such a provision gives the trustee broader investment power, *but* it does not remove the general obligation to invest wisely. Obviously, this duty does not imply that the trustee guarantees that all investments will increase in value or that no money will be lost. Generally, trustees limit themselves to conservative investments. The standard test of whether a trustee has fulfilled this obligation is whether other prudent investors, *at that time,* would have chosen other, better investments; the judgment should not be made in hindsight. The trustee may be surcharged for unwise investment decisions and must pay personally for any losses caused by negligent decisions. The trustee may not offset profits on other investments against these losses.

The trustee has a duty to maintain clear and accurate records regarding the administration of the trust. This obligation, called the *duty to account,* includes recording the location and type of assets and the receipt and expenditure of income. In some jurisdictions, the trustee must file periodic accountings with the court. In others, it is sufficient for the trustee to account to the trust beneficiaries.

The trustee must not mix his or her personal funds with trust funds, a situation known as *commingling of assets.* The trustee may not borrow money or mortgage trust property unless that power was expressly provided in the trust document. The trustee *will* have the incidental authority to carry out ordinary duties.

46.3

MANAGEMENT/PERSONAL LAW

CALL-IMAGE TECHNOLOGY

CREATING A TRUST

Tom and Anna would like to create a trust to provide for the education and support of John and Lindsay until each child reaches the age of 25. They have asked you what they should include in the proposed trust instrument and also what pitfalls or problems they should seek to avoid in creating the trust. What will you tell them?

BUSINESS CONSIDERATIONS Would it be wise to appoint a business associate as the trustee of a trust established to provide for one's children? How much latitude should a trustee be given in administering a trust such as the one proposed by Tom and Anna?

ETHICAL CONSIDERATIONS Is it prudent or ethical to appoint a family member or close family friend as trustee? What ethical issues would such an appointment raise? What advantages might such a person have as the trustee?

Implied Trusts

Express trusts are voluntarily and intentionally created by the owner of the assets. Implied trusts, on the other hand, are created by operation of law. They are either implied by the law or imposed by the courts. Implied trusts may arise in the context of an express trust, but that is not a legal requirement.

Resulting Trusts

A *resulting trust* is based on the owner's presumed intention and occurs when the owner of property disposes of the property but the disposition is not complete. The owner fails to make a complete, effective disposition of all his or her equitable interests. (A disposition will be considered complete if the state rules of trust interpretation determine who receives the interests.) A portion of the owner's interest reverts to the owner or the owner's heirs. A resulting trust will occur only if the owner is acting in good faith. This type of trust most commonly occurs under any one of the following circumstances:

1. The owner does not state who should acquire a beneficial interest, such as a remainder interest; for example, the owner transfers a vacation home to a cousin for 10 years.
2. The owner does not state what should happen under certain unanticipated situations; for example, a child dies before his or her parents.
3. The express trust is not enforceable because it is not in the proper form; for example, the owner fails to name the beneficiaries.
4. The express trust fails completely or in part, because it is illegal, impractical, or impossible *or* because a beneficiary refuses an interest in the trust; for example, a charitable purpose becomes impractical and the court finds *cy-pres* inapplicable.

A resulting trust also may occur when a person purchases real property with his or her own money and puts the title in the name of another person. The law presumes that the purchaser intends that the recipient hold the property as "trustee" for the purchaser. This is often called a *purchase money resulting trust.* The presumption may be rebutted by evidence that the purchaser has a different intention. In many states, the courts will presume that the purchaser intends a gift, *if* the purchaser and transferee are closely related.

Constructive Trusts

A *constructive trust* is actually an equitable remedy. It arises by operation of law and serves to redress a wrong or to prevent an unjust enrichment. A court of equity imposes this trust when a person gains legal title to property but has an equitable duty to transfer the property to someone else. The following are some examples of how this trust can occur:

http:// RESOURCES FOR BUSINESS LAW STUDENTS

NAME	RESOURCES	WEB ADDRESS
Legal Information Institute (LII)—Estates and Trusts Law Materials	LII, maintained by the Cornell Law School, provides an overview of estates and trust law, including relevant sections from the U.S. Code and Code of Federal Regulation, court cases, the Uniform Probate Code, and links.	http://www.law.cornell.edu/topics/estates_trusts.html
The U.S. House of Representatives Internet Law Library—Trusts and Estates	The U.S. House of Representatives Internet Law Library for trusts and estates provides links to cases, essays, statutes, and organizations concerned with estates and trust law.	http://law.house.gov/112.htm
American Bar Association's Section of Real Property, Probate and Trust Law	The Real Property, Probate and Trust Law Section, with more than 30,000 members, publishes the scholarly journal *Real Property, Probate and Trust Law Journal,* and the practical bimonthly magazine *Probate & Property.*	http://www.abanet.org/rppt/home.html

1. A person takes title as a trustee, but the trust is not enforceable; for example, a trustee receives assets under an oral trust that is unenforceable under the Statute of Frauds. To allow the trustee to keep the property would create unjust enrichment.
2. A person obtains property by breaching a fiduciary duty; for example, an employee embezzles company funds.
3. A person is either guilty of a wrong *or* would receive unjust enrichment. Depending on state law, the person may be guilty of fraud, conversion, theft, duress, or murder of the transferor. Some situations may involve mistake. For example, the transferor may own two lots and sell one lot to the transferee, but the deed mistakenly mentions both lots. The court will impose a constructive trust on the second lot for the benefit of the transferor.

Constructive trusts are not limited to these situations. As with other equitable remedies, constructive trusts are created to correct unfair results.

YOU BE THE JUDGE

Accused Murderer's Right to Family Assets and to Serve as Trustee

Dana Ewell's father, mother, and sister were murdered in their home on 19 April 1992, Easter weekend. Dana is accused of hiring Joel P. Radovich, his former college roommate, to murder his family in order to split their $8 million estate. The prosecutor has asked for the death penalty against both men. Both defendants have pleaded not guilty.

After the murders, Dana was made the trustee of the affairs of Glee Mitchell, his 90-year-old maternal grandmother. Investigators contend he spent about $93,000 of estate funds for the care of Glee Mitchell, who resides in a Turlock convalescent home. Initially, he withdrew funds from Mitchell's accounts at the rate of about $1,000 a month for his own use. The rate of withdrawal increased, and, prior to his arrest, he withdrew funds at the rate of about $10,000 a month. Meanwhile, he wrote many checks from the trust account, including checks for more than $15,000 to a Fresno law firm, checks for $5,500 in flying lessons for Radovich, checks for almost $40,000 for his girl friend, Monica Zent, and checks for $2,500 to Neiman Marcus. Checks were also written to the Fresno County Library and the RD Fund for the Blind and for car detailing, doctors, pest control, utility bills, cleaning, and magazine subscriptions. Reports indicate that Dana spent over $160,000 on himself and his friends. He even incurred fees for excessive activity on some of Mitchell's accounts. Spokespersons for Dana indicate that Mitchell was always generous with family members and that Mitchell encouraged Dana to spend even more money on himself.[13] If Dana's conduct was challenged in *your* court, how would *you* rule?

BUSINESS CONSIDERATIONS Does a business or charity have an obligation to scrutinize the source of checks received to determine if the check is drawn on a trust account? Is this an overwhelming burden to place on businesses or charities? Why or why not?

ETHICAL CONSIDERATIONS Is it ethical for a law firm to accept checks drawn on the trust account for services rendered to Dana Ewell as an individual? Is it ethical for Dana's friends to accept gifts from trust assets?

SOURCE: Jerry Bier, *The Fresno Bee,* 26 January 1996; Tom Kertscher, *The Fresno Bee,* 19 June 1995 and 7 April 1995.

SUMMARY

A will states how a person would like to have property pass at his or her death. This property includes business assets, such as patents, copyrights, and ownership interests in business enterprises. For a will to be valid, a person must intend it to be his or her will. The person must have testamentary capacity. The will must conform to the state's statutory requirements. Some legal documents, such as trusts and deeds for property, can act as substitutes for will provisions. In the absence of a valid will, the property passes by intestate succession, which is controlled by state law.

A formal will is drafted by an attorney, the state legislature, or the testator. This is the most common type of will. It must be signed by the testator and witnessed by two disinterested witnesses. Self-proved wills can permit the probate of the will without locating the witnesses. Some states also permit nuncupative (oral) wills and holographic (handwritten) wills.

Most estates are subject to probate proceedings. During the hearings, the probate court oversees the proper administration of the estate by the personal representative. The representative must pay debts, collect assets, pay taxes, and distribute assets to the beneficiaries.

Living wills explain the individual's desires concerning medical treatment, if the maker is unable to speak for himself or herself. Durable powers of attorney allow the maker to designate a person to make medical decisions for him or her. These documents are especially important to health-care providers.

An express trust is an arrangement whereby the owner of assets voluntarily places the legal ownership in a trustee and the equitable ownership in one or more beneficiaries. Creators are motivated to establish trusts for many purposes, including the following: to protect beneficiaries from themselves and creditors, to free beneficiaries from the responsibilities of asset management, to split an asset or estate among multiple beneficiaries, to test a pattern of transfers before finalizing it, to save taxes, and to increase flexibility. The trustee is obligated to manage the trust assets prudently. Trustees are often business entities.

Trusts can be flexible and established to accommodate numerous situations. However, they may be expensive because of trustee's fees and added tax burdens. Care must be utilized in selecting an appropriate trustee, because a trustee has broad discretion in managing the trust. The trustee must exercise due care in selecting investments for the trust. He or she may be surcharged for making careless decisions.

DISCUSSION QUESTIONS

1. How do defined-benefit plans and defined-contribution plans differ?
2. What requirements must be met in order for a formal will to be valid?
3. Why does the omission of a close family member in a will create the appearance of incompetency?
4. Rachael bequeaths the remainder of her estate "to Bank of America in trust to pay all the income to Bill for life, and on Bill's death to transfer the remainder to Bill's issue who are still alive." Bill dies without having any issue. The will has no provision controlling this situation. What will happen? Why?
5. What will be the intestate distribution under the Uniform Probate Code when a husband dies survived by his wife and his mother?
6. Brian has inherited a million dollars from his parents' estate. Brian, who has an extremely low IQ, wants to have his attorney write a will leaving his estate to his gardener and excluding his nieces and nephews. Can such a will be valid? If so, under what circumstances?

7. Distinguish strict per stirpes distributions from per capita at each generation distributions. When will the shares be the same? When will they be different?
8. What are the advantages and disadvantages of living wills?
9. How does the *cy-pres* doctrine work in charitable trusts?
10. Executors and trustees may be asked to serve without fees. Why might they be reluctant to do so? Under what circumstances might they be willing to do so?

CASE PROBLEMS AND WRITING ASSIGNMENTS

1. Roscoe and Mary Liles were married in 1945; they had no children. In 1972, Roscoe executed a will leaving his estate to his wife if she survived him. In 1975, Mary left Roscoe because he threatened her. In 1977, she received a divorce, including a division of their property. Roscoe died in 1978. Should the court accept Roscoe's 1972 will for probate? Why or why not? [See *Estate of Liles*, 435 A.2d 379 (D.C.App. 1981).]
2. In the common law state of Mississippi, a husband and wife separated and established different homes. Neither one filed for a divorce or remarried. Fifteen years after the separation, the wife died testate. Her will provided gifts to three friends. Is her husband entitled to share in her estate because he received insufficient gifts in her will? Should he be so entitled? Why or why not? [See *Tillman* v. *Williams*, 403 So.2d 880 (Miss. 1981).]
3. Clara Hicks resided in a nursing home at the time she executed a will in 1977. She was 87 at that time. The will was read to her at the time of execution, and she indicated her approval of the will provisions leaving a larger share to one particular nephew. That nephew visited her at least once a week and responded to her needs and requests. Dr. Hicks (unrelated), who visited her monthly in the nursing home, testified at trial that he thought that she was competent and that she understood her affairs. Did Clara Hicks have testamentary capacity? Was Clara Hicks subjected to undue influence? Why or why not? [See *Estate of Hicks*, 327 S.E.2d 345 (S.C. 1985).]
4. George Tourville had executed a will in which one of his nephews received 25 percent of the estate; Mary, Tourville's sister and that nephew's mother, received 55 percent; and Eileen, Tourville's other living sister, received 20 percent. The nephew had managed the testator's affairs prior to death. He also helped write the paragraph of the will that left assets to himself and was present when the will was prepared. Was the nephew guilty of exerting undue influence? Why or why not? [See *In re Estate of Tourville*, 366 N.W.2d 380 (Minn.App. 1985).]
5. James Koonce was admitted to the hospital for emphysema and heart trouble. While he was in the hospital, he had an attorney write a will, leaving his estate to his two sisters, Edith K. White and Nannie Sue Mims. He signed the will on 22 October 1974. His physician, who had treated him for 20 years, saw him the day after the signing of the will. In April 1976, Koonce married Hazel Thomas Koonce. He died in September 1978. His sisters filed the will for probate, and Hazel filed a will contest. The physician was permitted to testify at trial. Was the trial court correct in concluding that Koonce was competent to execute a valid will? Why or why not? [See *Koonce* v. *Mims*, 402 So.2d 942 (Ala. 1981).]
6. **BUSINESS APPLICATIONS CASE** Harold Colson died in 1968. In his will, which had been written in 1957, he provided for a scholarship fund to be established and administered by the Wesley United Methodist Church Board of Trustees. The fund was to provide one $500 scholarship per year from trust income to a male member of the congregation who was attending Harvard College. The trust corpus was generating $3,200 of income per year, the tuition at Harvard had risen to $2,600 per year, Harvard was admitting women as well as men, and no member of the congregation had ever applied for the scholarship. The trustees requested a modification of the trust under the *cy-pres* doctrine. The family of the creator petitioned for a cancellation of the old trust. How should the court rule and why? [See *Wesley United Methodist Church* v. *Harvard College*, 316 N.E.2d 620 (Mass. 1974).]
7. **ETHICAL APPLICATIONS CASE** Mary Eickhold signed a will in 1980. It provided that one-half of her farm should go to her brother and one-half to her sister and the residue of her estate should be divided between them. In 1981, she signed a codicil providing that the residue of her estate should go to four of her nephews. The same codicil directed the executor to sell her farm and to divide the proceeds with the rest of the residue. The attorney, who drafted both documents, testified at trial that Mary understood that her brother and sister would still receive the farm. The attorney could not remember whether he explained to her the effect that a sale of the farm would have on this bequest. Was Mary's brother entitled to one-half of the proceeds from the farm? Why or why not? What ethi-

cal implications are raised by this case? [See *Matter of Estate of Eickhold,* 365 N.W.2d 44 (Iowa App. 1985).]

8. **IDES CASE** At the age of 90, Austin Davis signed a will leaving his estate to his step-great-grandchildren. Ten days later, the testator executed a will naming his next-door neighbor as his sole beneficiary. In this will, he specifically revoked his prior wills. The neighbor did not order the will prepared, but she did drive the testator to the attorney's office. The neighbor lived next door to the testator for ten years. During the last year or so, the neighbor was hired to provide meals and general care for the testator. The testator said that his step-great-grandchildren did not care anything about him and that he did not want them to have his money. He also said that he wanted his money to go to someone who helped him. Was the testator competent to execute a will? Did the neighbor exert undue influence? Explain your answer. Use the IDES principles to analyze this case and to answer the questions. [See *Edwards* v. *Vaught,* 681 S.W.2d 322 (Ark. 1984).]

NOTES

1. Information on the current status of adoptions of the Uniform State Laws was provided by Katie Robinson, Public Affairs Coordinator, NCCUSL, during telephone conversations on 29 May 1997.
2. California Probate Code, § 6111(a).
3. 79 American Jurisprudence 2d, Wills, §§ 733, 740 (Rochester, NY: Lawyers' Cooperative, 1962); kept current with periodic updates.
4. *The Book of The States,* 1990–91 ed., Vol. 28 (Lexington: The Council of State Governments, 1990), p. 417.
5. 79 American Jurisprudence 2d, Wills §§ 733, 740 (Rochester, NY: Lawyers' Cooperative, 1962); kept current with periodic updates.
6. See California Probate Code, § 329, for an example of a probate code section permitting self-proving wills.
7. Uniform Probate Code, § 2-102(1).
8. Ibid, §§ 2-102(3), 2-103, and 2-106 as amended in 1990.
9. Denis Clifford, *Make Your Own Living Trust* (Berkeley, CA, Nolo Press, 1993), p. 15/4.
10. Uniform Probate Code, § 3-502.
11. Information on the current status of adoptions of the Uniform State Laws was provided by Katie Robinson, Public Affairs Coordinator, NCCUSL, during a telephone conversation on 29 May 1997.
12. Internal Revenue Code, § 2055.
13. Jerry Bier, "Third Ewell Judge Ousted," *The Fresno Bee* (26 January 1996), pp. B1, B3; Tom Kertscher, "Ewell Allegedly Misused $160,000," *The Fresno Bee* (19 June 1995), pp. A1, A10; Tom Kertscher, "Ewell Uncles Win Round: Aunt Can't Move Money," *The Fresno Bee* (7 April 1995), pp. A1, A14.

Intellectual Property, Computers, and the Law

A G E N D A

CIT is a high-tech operation, and much of its product development is based on patent law. As a result, the family is very concerned both with the protections afforded under patent law and with the effectiveness of a patent in international business operations. The Call-Image name has been registered as a trademark, and the firm would like to protect this trademark to the greatest extent possible. One concern the Kochanowskis have is that, being the first producer in the field, Call-Image may become synonymous with videophones. They therefore may ask what they can do to prevent this from depriving them of their trademarked name. They also are worried that someone will steal their ideas and duplicate their product at a lower price. They will want to know how to prevent this from happening. These and other questions are likely to arise as you study this chapter.

Be prepared! You never know when one of the Kochanowskis will call on you for help or advice.

O U T L I N E

Introduction

In this chapter, we will examine the law's treatment of intellectual property, or the property that comes from the human capacity to create. The body of law that addresses intellectual property derives from a variety of common law, state, and federal statutory and nonstatutory sources. Intellectual property law encompasses several substantive legal areas: copyrights, patents, trademarks, trade secrets, and unfair competition. We will use computers as a special illustration of the importance of intellectual property to U.S. businesses and international competitors.

In the intellectual property arena, several public policies coalesce to serve two goals; these policies both ensure incentives to create so as to guarantee a wider array of products and services in the marketplace and promote competition so as to provide public access to intellectual creations. By granting property rights (sometimes even monopolies) to creators, the law serves the first goal; and by limiting the duration of such exclusive rights and/or circumscribing the rights thereby granted so as to maximize the amount of information found in the public domain, the law facilitates the second goal. This area of the law also seeks to protect creators and businesspeople from injurious trade practices.

In this chapter, then, you will learn how this hodgepodge of disparate legal doctrines affects business. Also, you will see how the law attempts to reconcile the tension between those who, in order to protect investments or ownership rights in intellectual property, want to restrict others from the free use of this type of property, and those who, in furtherance of free markets, argue for largely unrestricted access to such information and inventions.

Copyrights

The U.S. Constitution in Article I, Section 8 authorizes Congress "to promote the progress of science and the useful arts." In conferring statutory protection on artistic works created by writers, artists, and composers, Congress as early as 1790 exercised this constitutional power. The most important of the early copyright laws, the Copyright Act of 1909, remained virtually unchanged until January 1978, when the present copyright statute, the Copyright Act of 1976, became effective. In reality, vestiges of the 1909 Act remain with us, however, since it still covers works created prior to 1 January 1978. The Berne Convention Implementation Act of 1988, which became effective in March 1989, further amended the 1976 act. Under these 1988 amendments, works published after 1 March 1989 do not need a copyright notice. Hence, one first must ascertain which law governs a given copyrighted work and proceed accordingly.

Section 102 of the Copyright Act of 1976 protects any original works of authorship fixed in any tangible medium of expression now known or later developed, from which they can be perceived, reproduced, or otherwise communicated, either directly or with the aid of a machine or a device. Works of authorship include, but are not limited to, (1) literary works; (2) musical works, including any accompanying music; (3) pantomimes and choreographic works; (4) pictorial, graphic, and sculptural works; (5) motion pictures and other audiovisual works; (6) sound recordings; and (7) architectural works. Hence, copyright laws traditionally have protected *only expressions of ideas,* not the ideas themselves. Procedures, plans, methods, systems, concepts, and principles are not copyrightable either.

The Copyright Office of the Library of Congress administers copyrights in the United States. Among other things, the Copyright Office registers copyrights; issues certificates of registration; keeps records of copyright registrations, licenses, and assignments; and oversees deposits of copyrighted materials. Unlike the Patent and Trademark Office's stringent and detailed oversight of patents and trademarks (subjects we shall discuss later), the Copyright Office merely determines whether applications involve copyrightable subject matter and have fulfilled all the registration requirements. In 1995, the Copyright Office registered 609,200 works.[1]

To be copyrightable, the works of authorship listed in § 102 must show originality. Courts have construed this term to involve at the very least minimal creative intellectual activity. Works of authorship moreover must be fixed in tangible form. The notes dancing in a creator's head do not become copyrightable until the songwriter puts the notes and words on paper or records the resultant melody (that is, the creator fixes the song in a tangible medium of expression). Section 101 of the 1976 act defines a work as "fixed" in a tangible medium of expression when its embodiment in a copy or phono record, by or under the authority of the author, is sufficiently permanent to permit it to be perceived, reproduced, or otherwise communicated for a period of more than transitory duration. This provision also states that fixation can occur simultaneously with transmission; therefore, radio or television broadcasts of live sporting events fall under this copyright protection if recordings or tapes of the events are occurring concurrently with the broadcast.

Courts typically grant more limited copyright protection to useful articles (that is, pictorial, graphic, or sculptural works). Only if the creator can show aesthetic or conceptual elements separable from the utilitarian aspects of the article will the article become copyrightable. Bicycle racks or wrought iron benches, for example, that began as pieces of sculpture are primarily utilitarian rather than aesthetic objects. Hence, the creators of these items typically cannot register them for copyright protection. This policy furthers the goal of increasing competition between useful goods and thus benefits the public more than a creator's being granted a statutory monopoly over utilitarian goods. In short, in these instances, copying benefits the public more than would insulating the item from competition.

The Copyright Office similarly will not accept applications involving typeface designs or fonts. Copyright law, however, does protect compilations of materials—for example, collective works (such as anthologies or encyclopedias) or directories, catalogs, and automated databases. But if the research involves only labor (a mere reordering or alphabetizing of materials) and very little creativity, courts treat the compilations like nonfiction, factually based works (history books or biographies) and afford little protection under the copyright laws. Derivative works—for example, a motion picture screenplay based on a novel—are copyrightable as well, as long as one has the right to use the original work and the derivative work varies substantially from the original, or the transformation involves substantial artistic skill, judgment, or labor.

Feist Publications, Inc. v. *Rural Telephone Service Co., Inc.* involves the Supreme Court's interpretation of some of these issues.

47.1 FEIST PUBLICATIONS, INC. v. RURAL TELEPHONE SERVICE CO., INC. 499 U.S. 340 (1991)

FACTS Rural Telephone Service Company, Inc. (Rural) is a certified public utility providing telephone service to several communities in Kansas. Pursuant to state regulation, Rural publishes a typical telephone directory, consisting of white pages and yellow pages. It obtains data for the directory from subscribers, who must provide their names and addresses to obtain telephone service. Feist Publications, Inc. (Feist) is a publishing company that specializes in area-

47.1 FEIST PUBLICATIONS, INC. v. RURAL TELEPHONE SERVICE CO., INC. *(cont.)* 499 U.S. 340 (1991)

wide telephone directories covering a much larger geographic range than directories like Rural's. When Rural refused to license its white pages listings to Feist for a directory covering 11 different telephone service areas, Feist extracted the listings it needed from Rural's directory without Rural's consent. Although Feist altered many of Rural's listings, several remained identical to the listings in Rural's white pages. The district court, granting summary judgment to Rural in its copyright infringement suit, held that telephone directories are copyrightable. The court of appeals affirmed this ruling.

ISSUE Were the names, addresses, and telephone numbers that Feist had copied in compiling its telephone directory white pages copyrightable?

HOLDING No. Rural's white pages were not entitled to copyright protection. Hence, Feist's use of them did not constitute copyright infringement.

REASONING Article I, Section 8, Clause 8 of the Constitution mandates originality as a prerequisite for copyright protection. The constitutional requirement necessitates independent creation plus a modicum of creativity. Since facts do not owe their origin to an act of authorship, they are unoriginal and thus uncopyrightable. Although a compilation of facts may possess the requisite originality because the author typically chooses which facts to include, in what order to place them, and how to arrange them so that readers may use them effectively, copyright protection extends only to those components of the work that are original to the author, not to the facts themselves. This fact/expression dichotomy severely limits the scope of protection in fact-based works. The Copyright Act of 1976 and its predecessor, the Copyright Act of 1909, leave no doubt that originality—rather than effort—is the touchstone of copyright protection in directories and other fact-based works. The 1976 Act explains that copyright extends to "original works of authorship" and that there can be no copyright in facts. A compilation is not copyrightable per se but is copyrightable only if its facts have been "selected, coordinated, or arranged in such a way that the resulting work as a whole constitutes an original work of authorship." Thus, the statute envisions that some ways of selecting, coordinating, and arranging data are not sufficiently original to trigger copyright protection. Even a compilation that is copyrightable receives only limited protection, for the copyright does not extend to facts contained in the compilation.

A fundamental axiom of copyright law holds that no one can copyright facts or ideas. Given these propositions, one can see that Rural's white pages do not meet the constitutional or statutory requirements for copyright protection. While Rural has a valid copyright in the directory as a whole because it contains some original material in the yellow pages, there is nothing original in Rural's white pages. The raw data involve only uncopyrightable facts; and the way in which Rural selected, coordinated, and arranged those facts is not original in any way. Rural's selection of listings—subscribers' names, towns, and telephone numbers—therefore lacks the modicum of creativity necessary to transform mere selection into copyrightable expression. Moreover, there is nothing remotely creative about arranging names alphabetically in a white pages directory. It is an age-old practice, firmly rooted in tradition and so commonplace that it has come to be expected as a matter of course. Hence, the names, towns, and telephone numbers copied by Feist neither were original to Rural nor protected by the copyright in Rural's combined white and yellow pages directory. Because Rural's white pages lack the requisite originality, Feist's use of the listings cannot constitute infringement. The judgment of the court of appeals therefore must be reversed.

BUSINESS CONSIDERATIONS Although the Court in this case reiterates that facts ordinarily are not copyrightable, what business interests was Rural attempting to protect when it instituted this litigation? Would refraining from suing have constituted a more efficient allocation of the firm's resources?

ETHICAL CONSIDERATIONS Had the Court decided this case solely on ethical grounds, would its holding have favored Rural? Why or why not?

Protection and Infringement

A copyright, in essence, consists of a bundle of exclusive rights that enables the copyright owner—usually the author or one to whom the author has transferred rights—to exploit a work for commercial purposes. These exclusive rights include: (1) reproducing the copyrighted work; (2) preparing derivative works (or adaptations) based on the copyrighted work; (3) distributing copies or phono records of the copyrighted work; (4) performing publicly literary, musical, dramatic, and choreographic works, pantomimes, and motion pictures or audiovisual works; and (5) displaying publicly the works themselves or individual images of the works mentioned in (4) as well as pictorial, graphic, or sculptural works.

Therefore, to prove an infringement of a copyrighted work, the owner typically must show by circumstantial evidence (since the existence of direct evidence would be rare) that the defendant had access to the copyrighted work and that the owner's work shows either striking or substantial similarities to the defendant's. Once the trier of fact determines copying has occurred, a finding of unlawful appropriation will result from the plaintiff's showing substantial similarities between the defendant's work and the plaintiff's.

Under the right of reproduction, the Copyright Act itself allows for certain exceptions; for example, reproductions of nondramatic musical works, such as operas or motion picture sound tracks, subject to compulsory licensing under the act, do not constitute infringements if the user complies with certain conditions, including the payment of royalties to the owner. By the same token, the act exempts from the exclusive rights enjoyed by the copyright holder imitations of sound recordings (when the reproductions go beyond a mere "lifting" of the original expression) and reproductions transmitted by public educational or religious broadcasters under certain conditions. Without violating the copyright laws, one also can reproduce pictures of copyrighted useful art (like the bike rack) or architectural works. In addition, in certain circumstances, libraries can make reproductions of works needed to preserve or secure their collections or archives and of works, subject to some limitations, requested by library users.

The copyright holder's exclusive right to distribute the work differs from the exclusive right to reproduce the work. Under this right of distribution, the copyright owner can control the initial sale or distribution of the work to the public but, except in some situations involving the rentals of records, cannot control any subsequent transfers of the work. Sales of pirated works do not constitute "initial sales," so sellers of pirated works may find themselves subject to an infringement action even if the sellers are unaware that the compact disks, tapes, or records were pirated.

The exclusive right of public performance is subject to various exemptions as well. For example, a bar or restaurant that displays a standard-sized television so that its patrons can watch it free of charge does not infringe the copyright of a program broadcast on the television set. Similarly, pupils can perform copyrighted works in the course of face-to-face teaching activities in the classroom, as opposed to performing the work pursuant to a school play open to the public. Record shops, without violating the copyright laws, also can play songs as a means of promoting sales.

Compulsory licensing sections in the act apply to cable television systems' secondary transmissions of primary broadcasts, satellite retransmissions, operators of electronic video game arcades, and operation of jukeboxes (even though, under the Berne Convention, jukeboxes are covered under voluntary—as opposed to compulsory—licenses through 1999).

The American Society of Composers, Authors, and Publishers (ASCAP) and Broadcast Music, Inc. (BMI) act as agents for owners of copyrights and issue licenses on behalf of such authors. After securing a license from ASCAP or BMI, a radio or television station can perform any of the works of any authors these societies represent. Each society, in turn, pays the royalties so received to the authors and monitors the stations' compliance with the licenses granted. This system results in greater efficiencies than one that requires each station to negotiate separately with each artist and for each artist individually to police copyright law compliance. The exceptions for the exclusive right to display the work correlate with those just discussed under the right of public performance.

Anyone who violates any of the copyright owner's exclusive rights provided in the statute or who imports copies or phono records into the United States in violation of the statute is an infringer of the copyright or the right of the author, as the case may be. The courts have imposed liability for infringements that either are direct or contributory—that is, those that induce or materially contribute to another person's direct infringement.

The most common defense that defendants interpose to exonerate themselves from charges of infringement is the "fair use" doctrine. The statute itself states that the fair use of a copyrighted work for purposes of criticism, comment, news reporting, teaching (including multiple copies for classroom use), scholarship, or research is not an infringement of the copyright. The statute then sets out a nonexhaustive list of factors courts shall consider when they determine whether the use made of a work in any particular case is a fair use. These factors include: (1) the purpose and character of the use, including whether such use is of a commercial nature or is for nonprofit educational purposes; (2) the nature of the copyrighted work; (3) the amount and substantiality of the portion used in relation to the copyrighted work as a whole; and (4) the effect of the use on the potential market for or value of the copyrighted work. The statute further states that the fact that a work is unpublished shall not itself bar a finding of fair use if a court, after considering all the above factors, makes such a distinction.

Various professional groups have set out guidelines to ensure that copying done, for example, by libraries and/or by teachers for classroom use, falls either under express statutory exemptions or the fair use doctrine. These efforts underscore the importance of complying with the Copyright Act.

Note how the Supreme Court used many of these factors when it decides *Harper & Row Publishers Inc.* v. *Nation Enterprises.*

47.1

MANAGEMENT

COPYRIGHT INFRINGEMENT

John has come up with what he believes is a tremendous idea for a commercial for Call-Image. He has described it to the rest of the family members, and they also think it could be a very successful ad. In the ad John describes, an extraterrestrial finds itself marooned on earth and it is trying to "call home" to get one of its fellow extraterrestrials to pick it up. As the extraterrestrial dials, the call goes through, and its mother's face appears on the CIT video screen; the voice of the announcer then describes the pleasure of seeing "distant relatives" when one calls home and uses a Call-Image videophone. The family members ask you if this ad involves any copyright infringement problems. What will you tell them?

BUSINESS CONSIDERATIONS Why do businesses use the voices, names, and likenesses of famous people to sell their products? Are these types of ads less effective if the advertiser uses unknown people to show the use of the product?

ETHICAL CONSIDERATIONS Is it ethical for a business to use computer imaging to place famous people who have died into commercials with contemporary stars or contemporary settings? What ethical concerns are raised by the use of the likenesses of deceased celebrities in commercials?

47.2 HARPER & ROW, PUBLISHERS, INC. v. NATION ENTERPRISES 471 U.S. 539 (1985)

FACTS In 1977, former President Ford contracted with Harper & Row, Publishers, Inc. (Harper & Row) to publish his as yet unwritten memoirs. The agreement gave Harper & Row the exclusive first serial right to license prepublication excerpts. Two years later, as the memoirs were nearing completion, Harper & Row, as the copyright holder, negotiated a prepublication licensing agreement with *Time* magazine under which *Time* agreed to pay $25,000 ($12,500 in advance and the balance at publication) in exchange for the right to excerpt 7,500 words from Mr. Ford's account of his pardon of former President Nixon. Shortly before the *Time* article's scheduled release, an unauthorized source provided *The Nation* magazine with the unpublished Ford manuscript. Working directly from this manuscript, an editor of *The Nation* produced a 2,250-word article, at least 300 to 400 words of which consisted of verbatim quotes of copyrighted expression taken from the Ford manuscript. *The Nation* had timed this article so as to "scoop" the *Time* article. As a result of the publication of *The Nation*'s article, *Time* canceled its article and refused to pay the remaining $12,500 to Harper & Row. When Harper & Row sued the publishers of *The Nation,* the district court held that *The Nation*'s use of the copyrighted material constituted an infringement under the act. The court then awarded actual damages of $12,500. The court of appeals reversed and held that *The Nation*'s publication of the 300 to 400 words of copyrightable expression was sanctioned as a "fair use" of the copyrighted material under § 107 of the act.

ISSUE Was *The Nation*'s unauthorized use of quotations from a public figure's unpublished manuscript fair use under the Copyright Act?

HOLDING No. An application of the four factors that the statute sets out as relevant to determine fair use showed that *The Nation*'s use was not a fair use under the Copyright Act.

REASONING Section 107 of the Copyright Act provides that, notwithstanding the provisions of § 106 giving a copyright owner the exclusive right to reproduce the copyrighted work and to prepare derivative works based on the copyrighted work, the fair use of a copyrighted work for purposes such as comment and news reporting is not an infringement of copyright. Section 107 further provides that, in determining whether the use was fair, one shall consider the following factors: (1) the purpose and character of the use, (2) the nature of the copyrighted work, (3) the substantiality of the portion used in relation to the copyrighted work as a whole, and (4) the effect on the potential market for or value of the copyrighted work. In using generous verbatim excerpts of Mr. Ford's unpublished expression to lend authenticity to its account of the forthcoming memoirs, *The Nation* effectively arrogated to itself the right of first publication, an important marketable subsidiary right. Under ordinary circumstances, the author's right to control the first public appearance of his or her undisseminated expression will outweigh a claim of fair use. Moreover, in view of the First Amendment's protections embodied in the act's distinction between copyrightable expression and uncopyrightable facts and ideas and the latitude for scholarship and comment traditionally afforded by fair use, there is no warrant for expanding, as *The Nation*'s publishers contend, the fair use doctrine to what amounts to a public figure exception to copyright law.

Whether verbatim copying from a public figure's manuscript in a given case is or is not fair must be judged according to the traditional equities of fair use. One's taking into account the four factors enumerated in § 107 leads to the conclusion that the use in question here was not fair. The fact that news reporting was the general purpose of *The Nation*'s use is simply one factor. While *The Nation* had every right to be the first to publish the information, it went beyond simply reporting uncopyrightable information and, by making a "news event" out of its unauthorized first publication, actively sought to exploit the value of its infringement. The fact that the publication was commercial as opposed to nonprofit is a separate factor tending to weigh against a finding of fair use. *Fair use* presupposes good faith. Although there may be a greater need to disseminate works of fact than works of fiction, *The Nation*'s taking of copyrighted expression exceeded that necessary to disseminate the facts and infringed the copyright holder's interests in confidentiality and creative control over the first public appearance of the work. Although the verbatim quotations in question constituted an insubstantial portion of the Ford manuscript, they qualitatively embodied Mr. Ford's distinctive expression and played a key role in the infringing article.

As to the effect of *The Nation*'s article on the market for the copyrighted work, *Time*'s cancellation of its projected article and *Time*'s refusal to pay $12,500 directly resulted from the infringing publication. Once a copyright holder establishes a causal connection between the infringement and loss of revenue, the burden shifts to the infringer to show that the damage would have occurred had no taking of copyrighted expression occurred. In short, Harper & Row had established a prima facie case of actual damage that *The Nation*'s publishers failed to rebut. More important, to negate a claim of fair use, one need only show that if the challenged use should become more widespread, it would adversely affect the potential market for the copy-

47.2 HARPER & ROW, PUBLISHERS, INC. v. NATION ENTERPRISES *(cont.)* 471 U.S. 539 (1985)

righted work. Here, *The Nation*'s liberal use of the verbatim excerpts posed substantial potential for damage to the marketability of the first serialization rights in the copyrighted work. Hence, the decision of the court of appeals warrants reversal and a remand to the lower court.

BUSINESS CONSIDERATIONS What should a businessperson do when he or she has an opportunity to gain a competitive advantage by using material that may be subject to the copyright of a competitor? Had you been a part of the editorial board that had to decide whether to "scoop" Harper & Row, would you have voted yes or no?

ETHICAL CONSIDERATIONS Was it unethical for *The Nation* to publish materials supplied to it by an unauthorized source? Should journalists be held to a higher ethical standard than other businesses, especially considering that journalists have the protection of the First Amendment?

The importance of parody in our country's history has led many courts to protect parodic uses of a copyrighted work, despite the owner's unwillingness to grant a license to the parodist. In *Campbell* v. *Acuff-Rose Music, Inc.*, the Supreme Court wrangled with these very issues.

47.3 CAMPBELL v. ACUFF-ROSE MUSIC, INC. 114 U.S. 1164 (1994)

FACTS In 1964, Roy Orbison and William Dees wrote a rock ballad called "Oh, Pretty Woman" and assigned their rights in it to Acuff-Rose Music, Inc. (Acuff-Rose). Acuff-Rose registered the song for copyright protection. A quarter century later, Luther Campbell, a member of the rap music group 2 Live Crew, wrote a song entitled "Pretty Woman." On 5 July 1989, 2 Live Crew's manager informed Acuff-Rose that 2 Live Crew had written a parody of "Oh, Pretty Woman"; that the group would afford all credit for ownership and authorship of the original song to Acuff-Rose, Dees, and Orbison; and that the group would pay a fee for the use it wished to make of the song. Acuff-Rose refused this requested permission. Despite Acuff-Rose's refusal, 2 Live Crew released records, cassette tapes, and compact discs of "Pretty Woman" in a collection of songs entitled "As Clean as They Wanna Be." The albums and compact discs identify the authors of "Pretty Woman" as Orbison and Dees and the publisher as Acuff-Rose. Almost a year later, after the sale of nearly a quarter of a million copies of "As Clean as They Wanna Be," Acuff-Rose sued 2 Live Crew for copyright infringement. Reasoning that the commercial purpose of 2 Live Crew's song was no bar to "fair use"; that 2 Live Crew's version was a parody; that 2 Live Crew had taken only that which was necessary to "conjure up" the original in order to parody it; and that it was extremely unlikely that 2 Live Crew's song would lessen the demand for the original, the district court granted summary judgment for 2 Live Crew. The court of appeals, arguing that the "blatantly commercial purpose" of the 2 Live Crew song prevented this parody from constituting a fair use of a copyrighted work, reversed the lower court's decision.

ISSUE Did 2 Live Crew's commercial parody constitute a fair use of the copyrighted work?

HOLDING Yes. Because the group merely parodied the original song, 2 Live Crew had not infringed on Acuff-Rose's copyright of "Oh, Pretty Woman." Despite its commercial intent, 2 Live Crew, in an effort to satirize the original song, could borrow from "Oh, Pretty Woman" and in so doing not contravene the Copyright Act.

REASONING It is uncontested here that, except for a finding of fair use through parody, 2 Live Crew's song would represent an infringement of Acuff-Rose's rights in "Oh, Pretty Woman" under the Copyright Act of 1976. From the infancy of copyright protection, some opportunity for fair use of copyrighted materials has been thought necessary to

47.3 CAMPBELL v. ACUFF-ROSE MUSIC, INC. *(cont.)* 114 U.S. 1164 (1994)

fulfill copyright's very purpose, "[t]o promote the Progress of Science and useful Arts . . ." (U.S. Constitution, Article I, Section 8, Clause 8). The Copyright Act of 1976 sets some limitations on these exclusive rights but does not establish any hard-and-fast guidelines for courts to use in a fair-use inquiry. The 1976 act merely states that courts should consider four factors: (1) the purpose and character of the use, including whether such use is of a commercial nature or is for nonprofit educational purposes; (2) the nature of the copyrighted work; (3) the amount and substantiality of the portion used in relation to the copyrighted work as a whole; and (4) the effect of the use on the potential market for or value of the copyrighted work. In short, the fair-use doctrine requires courts to avoid a rigid application of the copyright statute when, on occasion, it would stifle the very creativity the law seeks to foster. Such an inquiry involves a case-by-case approach that considers the four statutory factors together, not in isolation.

Under the factor relating to a work's purpose and character, the new work, by adding some sort of new expression, meaning, or message, must transform the original work. Any parody alters the message of the original work on which it is based and, by using the original work, creates a new work that, in part, comments on the original. Although the Court might not assign a high rank to the parodic element here, it is fair to say that one could reasonably perceive 2 Live Crew's song as commenting on the original or criticizing it to some degree. Moreover, the court of appeals erroneously interpreted the Copyright Act of 1976 as indicating that every commercial use of copyrighted material is presumptively unfair. Yet this represents only one consideration that a court, when looking at the "purpose" and "character" criterion, can take into account. When fair use is raised in defense of parody, the threshold question is whether a parodic character may reasonably be perceived. Regardless of 2 Live Crew's desire to sell records, the group's parody constituted a legitimate use of the original copyrighted work. As for the nature of the work, the Court agreed that Orbison's song fell within the type of material protected under the Copyright Act but believed that this factor had little bearing on the case. As for the amount of the copyrighted work used, the Court, citing the *Harper & Row* case, ruled that 2 Live Crew had not drawn too heavily from the original song. Parody's humor, or in any event its comment, necessarily springs from a recognizable allusion to its object through distorted imitation. The art lies in the tension between its known original and its parodic twin. This recognition, in turn, derives from the quotation of the original's most distinctive or memorable features, which the parodist can be sure the audience will know. Hence, 2 Live Crew's quotation of the opening riff and first line of the original song was not excessive. Finally, in examining the potential of the 2 Live Crew work on the market for the original song, the Court rejected the appellate court decision's reliance on *Sony Corp. of America* v. *Universal Studios, Inc.*, a case involving the home copying of television programming. Using the *Sony* case, the appellate court assumed—from an intention to use the work for commercial gain—the likelihood of significant market harm. But no "presumption" or inference of market harm that might find support in *Sony* is applicable to a case involving something beyond mere duplication for commercial purposes. When the second use is transformative, market substitution is at least less certain; and one may not infer market harm so readily. Indeed, as to parody pure and simple, it is more likely that the new work will not affect the market for the original in a way cognizable under this factor, that is, by acting as a substitute for it. This is so because the parody and the original usually serve different market functions. Moreover, no protectable derivative market for criticism exists, since creators of original works generally will refuse to license parodies or lampoons of their work. From the evidence presented at trial, one can draw no conclusion about the likely effect of 2 Live Crew's parodic rap song on the market for a nonparodic, rap version of "Oh, Pretty Woman." For this and the other reasons cited, 2 Live Crew's song represented a fair use of copyrighted material under the Copyright Act of 1976. The erroneous conclusion by the court of appeals that the commercial nature of 2 Live Crew's parody of "Oh, Pretty Woman" rendered it presumptively unfair therefore warrants reversal and remand to the lower court.

BUSINESS CONSIDERATIONS Acuff-Rose presumably thought 2 Live Crew's parody would negatively affect the market for "Oh, Pretty Woman." On what basis did the firm reach this conclusion? Is it possible the parody actually could bring about an appreciation in the value of the original "Oh, Pretty Woman"?

ETHICAL CONSIDERATIONS One of the purposes of parody is to satirize the original. Does "making fun" of the original constitute unethical behavior on the parodist's part? From an ethical perspective, should a parodist be required to obtain permission in advance before he or she produces a parody?

The identity of the owner of a copyright ordinarily poses few problems because the original author usually is the owner. But co-ownership over "joint works" does exist. "Works for hire," or works prepared by an employee within the scope of his or her employment (for example, architectural drawings), or work specifically commissioned for use as an instructional text (for example, this textbook) and considered as works for hire belong, respectively, to the employer or to the person who commissions the works. Works prepared by employees of the U.S. government as a part of that person's official duties enjoy no copyright protection; rather, these works fall within the public domain and generally can be copied at will. By putting the transfer (or assignment) in writing and by recording such actions with the Copyright Office, one can transfer ownership of copyrights.

Since the Berne Convention Implementation Act, which took effect on 1 March 1989, it is not necessary, to ensure copyright protection, that an author put the copyright notice, the copyright symbol, the author's name, and the date of the first publication on the work. However, such notice still is necessary for works copyrighted under the 1976 act and published (that is, released to the public) before 1 March 1989. The 1976 act allows the omission of the required notice in certain limited circumstances, but failure to include the required notice generally results in loss of copyright protection.

Hence, as mentioned earlier, one first must determine which law governs the copyrighted work in question. Registering the work with the Copyright Office remains advisable, however, because registration makes proof of infringement easier in some cases and makes the owner eligible for certain types of damages, court costs, and attorneys' fees.

Under the 1976 act, federal copyright commences with the fixation of the work in a copy or phono record for the first time. The duration of a copyright covered by the 1976 act (that is, works created on or after 1 January 1978) generally is the life of the author plus 50 years. After that time, the law presumes the work has passed into the public domain and therefore is not copyrightable.

Remedies

Civil remedies for infringements include injunctions, the impoundment and destruction of infringing items, and damages. Plaintiffs can choose between actual damages, including the infringer's profits attributable to the infringement if the court, in computing the damages, did not take these into account, or statutory damages ranging from a minimum of $500 to $20,000 for all infringements involved in the action with respect to one work. A court may increase the damages to $100,000 for willful infringements. Similarly, the court may lower the damages to $100 if the infringer can prove it was unaware that its actions constituted an infringement. The court in its discretion can award court costs to either party and may award attorneys' fees to either prevailing plaintiffs or prevailing defendants [see *Fogerty* v. *Fantasy, Inc.*, 510 U.S. 517 (1994)].

Criminal penalties range from a maximum of $10,000 and one year's imprisonment (or both) to a maximum $25,000 and one year's imprisonment (or both) for the first offense involving willful infringement and a maximum of $50,000 and two years' imprisonment (or both) for subsequent offenses.

International Dimensions

As noted earlier, U.S. copyright laws have undergone some changes since the United States became a member of the Berne Convention (the International Union for the

Protection of Literary and Artistic Works) in March 1989. The Berne Convention makes national treatment of copyrights the linchpin of the treaty. In other words, each member nation must automatically extend the protection of its laws to the other signatory nations' nationals and to works originally published in a member nation's jurisdiction. The Berne Convention is not self-executing; each member nation therefore must enact implementing legislation.

The United States has taken a minimalist approach to compliance with the Berne Convention; in other words, it has not accepted *in toto* every provision of the treaty. But since the United States has enacted into law many of the treaty's provisions, it is important to U.S. intellectual property law. Apropos of this, the World Intellectual Property Organization's December 1996 treaties have updated the Berne Convention to reflect the changes in information technology and to set intellectual property standards for the digital age. These new treaties, among other things, have closed some loopholes that had left the U.S. recording industry without copyright protection in the international arena.

The Universal Copyright Convention (UCC), administered by the United Nations, represents another international treaty that covers copyrights. Although it imposes fewer substantive requirements on copyrights than does the Berne Convention, some Berne Convention members also have joined the UCC as a means of establishing relationships concerning copyrights with UCC members who have not signed the Berne Convention.

Recent amendments to GATT (the General Agreement on Tariffs and Trade) expand the protections afforded to copyrighted works, including computer programs. The European Union's (EU's) "Directive on the Legal Protection of Computer Software," slated to cover EU members as of 1 January 1993, represents another promising initiative in the international arena.

Computers

Copyright law also covers computers. Although it was unclear whether computer programs were copyrightable under the 1909 act, the Copyright Office began accepting computer programs for registration as books as early as 1964, despite the misgivings of register officials. At the time of the passage of the 1976 act, the "jury," in the form of the National Commission on New Technological Uses (CONTU), was still out regarding the copyrightability of computer software. However, by adding the phrase "computer program" and certain other provisions exempting the copying of computer programs from the 1976 act's infringement provisions, the Computer Software Copyright Act of 1980 amended the 1976 act. As a result of these amendments, today, few doubts remain as to the copyrightability of computer programs despite the omission of this phrase from the listed categories of proper subject matters for copyright protection.

Under the 1980 amendments, "[a] 'computer program' is a set of statements or instructions to be used directly or indirectly in a computer in order to bring about a certain result." According to the 1980 amendments, computer databases also are copyrightable as "compilations" or "derivative works." Infringements of copyrights—for example, unauthorized copying, distribution, or derivation—do not occur if the owner (that is, a copyright holder) of a copy of a computer program only makes or authorizes the making of a new copy or adaptation when the copy is an essential step in the utilization of the program in conjunction with a machine (that is, for use with the owner's computer) or for archival purposes (that is, for making backup copies in case the original copy is accidentally destroyed). The fair-use doctrine, whereby, for instance, your professor uses computer software for an in-class performance or display, and the right of libraries to reproduce and distribute copyrighted works, including computer software in some circumstances, apparently do not constitute infringements either. The act presently does not differentiate, for infringement purposes, between human-readable or machine-readable copies; copies in either form may constitute infringements unless the copying falls into one of these exemptions.

Yet controversies still abound owing to the fact that the 1976 act continues the longstanding expression/idea dichotomy of copyright law. This duality, that the program as written is protectable but the unique ideas contained in the program are not, of course looms as a significant impediment to software developers who wish to copyright their manuals: It is easy to produce competing products once the ideas underlying the original package become known. Thus, upon the developers' meeting the required statutory criteria, the manuals will be copyrightable, but the formats may not be.

Similarly, the audiovisual display aspects of a video game may be copyrightable whereas the idea—a crazy character that "munches" everything, for instance—behind the game, or the game per se, ordinarily will be ineligible for copyright protection. The same may be true in general of flowcharts, components of machines, and printed circuit boards that do not have computer programs embedded in them: These normally are not copyrightable. The unsettled state of the law in this area merely complicates developers' problems.

The *Apple Computer, Inc.* v. *Franklin Computer Corporation* case—714 F.2d 1240 (3d Cir. 1983), *cert. dismissed,* 464 U.S. 1033 (1984)—represents an early but significant decision regarding the application of the copyright laws to computer software, particularly computer operating systems. Apple Computer, Inc. (Apple) had filed suit against Franklin Computer Corporation (Franklin) for copyright infringement owing to Franklin's copying of 14 of Apple's **operating system computer programs** for use with Franklin's ACE 100 personal computer. Franklin admitted it had copied Apple's programs and **ROM chips (read-only memory chips)** but argued it had done so because it had not been feasible for Franklin to write its own operating system programs. Franklin also asserted that the Apple programs were not copyrightable subject matter because the object code on which the programs had relied was not a "writing"; moreover, according to Franklin, the programs were "processes," "systems," or "methods of operation" unprotected by law. This opinion addressed the important issue of whether the **object code**, which is not readable by people, is a "writing" within the Copyright Act's coverage and hence copyrightable; or instead, given its normal use, whether the object code is a method of operation or a system, which is not copyrightable. In holding that Apple's computer programs, whether in **source code** or in object code embedded in ROM chips, constitute "literary works" protected under the Copyright Act of 1976 from unauthorized copying from either their object code or source code version, the court answered a question that had vexed early software developers. For a more recent disposition of a similar issue, see *Lotus Development Corporation* v. *Borland International, Inc.* [49 F.3d 807 (1st Cir. 1995), *affirmed,* 116 S.Ct. 804 (1996)].

Copyright claims represent a fertile area for litigation. Apple Computer, Inc., Microsoft Corporation, and Hewlett-Packard Company recently have litigated the copyrightability of the visual display aspects of computer user interfaces. Given the huge economic stakes and the ever-changing technology involved in such cases,

Operating system computer programs
Collections of systems software programs designed to help someone else program or use a computer and that allow the computer to execute programs and manage programming tasks.

ROM chips (read-only memory chips)
Computer chips on which the data and information used to run computer operating systems are affixed; chips that can be "read" by a computer program but generally cannot be changed or altered.

Object code
Translation of source code into lower-level language, consisting of numbers and symbols that the computer converts into electronic impulses (machine language).

Source code
Human-readable version of the program that gives instructions to the computer.

companies presumably will continue this zealous protection of their rights through resort to the courts. These developments bear watching.

PATENTS

The same provision of the Constitution that provides the basis for copyright protection furnishes the grounds for patents. Congress's power to promote the progress of science and the useful arts secures for inventors, rather than authors, the exclusive right to their respective discoveries. Today, most experts lump the terms "useful arts," "inventors," and "discoveries" with patent rights and leave the promotion of science through writings to copyright law.

Since the first patent statute in 1790, the statutory categories of patentable subject matter have consisted of (1) any process (the earlier term was "art," but the term "process" now includes a process, art, or method); (2) machine; (3) manufacture; (4) composition of matter, including certain nonnaturally occurring plants, such as hybrids; and (5) any new and useful improvement thereof. The Supreme Court has held that such utility patents may cover genetically engineered living matter as well.

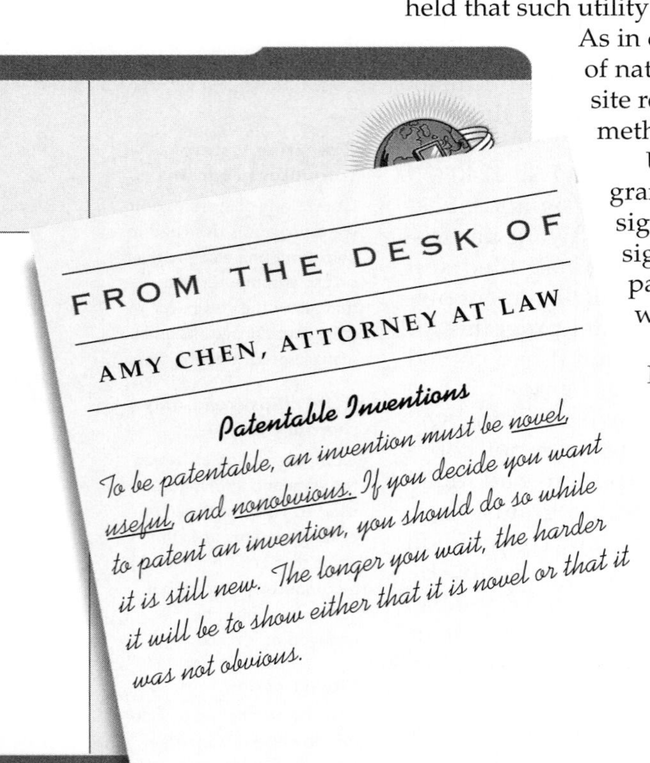
FROM THE DESK OF
AMY CHEN, ATTORNEY AT LAW
Patentable Inventions
To be patentable, an invention must be novel, useful, and nonobvious. If you decide you want to patent an invention, you should do so while it is still new. The longer you wait, the harder it will be to show either that it is novel or that it was not obvious.

As in copyright law, ideas per se are not patentable. Neither are laws of nature (for example, "for every action there is an equal and opposite reaction"), mathematical formulas, scientific truths or principles, methods of doing business, and mental processes.

Utility patents last for 17 years, after which time the monopoly granted to the patentee (that is, the holder of the patent) ends. Design patents (that is, patents involving original, ornamental designs for articles of manufacture) last for only 14 years. Once the patent protection ends, others can make, use, or sell the invention with impunity.

To be patentable, an invention must demonstrate novelty. In other words, prior art must show an absence of anything substantially identical to the claimed invention; the claimed invention therefore must be unanticipated. Public knowledge or use of the invention by others in this country before the application for the patent indicates a lack of novelty. The public use or sale of the invention more than one year prior to the application of the patent thus will result in the denial of a patent.

Just as it is hard to imagine an invention that lacks novelty, so too, it is difficult to imagine as worthy of patent protection an invention that lacks utility. Both the Constitution and the Patent Act of 1952 describe protected discoveries and inventions as "useful" ones. Hence, to deserve protection under the patent laws, the inventor's discovery must provide significant current benefits to society.

Last, an invention must consist of nonobvious subject matter. In other words, if the differences between the subject matter one seeks to patent and prior art are such that the subject matter as a whole will be obvious, at the time the invention is made, to a person having ordinary skill in the art to which the subject matter pertains, the invention does not warrant protection.

These three requirements clearly overlap. The ingenuity that underlies inventions goes beyond the mere carrying forward of an old idea. Yet Thomas Alva Edison, one of our greatest inventors, surely captured another aspect of invention when he noted that it involves 1 percent inspiration and 99 percent perspiration!

By making an application to the U.S. Patent and Trademark Office (PTO), inventors who believe they have met these requirements begin the process of receiving a patent. This application includes a declaration that the applicant first discovered the invention for which he or she solicits the patent; any drawings necessary to explain the patent; detailed descriptions, specifications, and disclosures (including all prior art) of the subject matter the applicant claims as his or her invention; and the required filing fees. The substantive information provided in the specifications should (1) enable any person skilled in the art to make or use the invention after the expiration of the term of the patent and (2) inform the public of the limits of the monopoly asserted by the inventor for the life of the patent.

The Commissioner of Patents and Trademarks will issue a patent if the PTO examiner to whom the Commissioner has given the application approves the application. Applicants who receive rejection notices, usually owing to the examiner's finding prior art or the existence of "double-patenting" (the act prohibits the granting of two patents for the same invention), can appeal to the PTO Board of Patent Appeals and Interferences and then either to the U.S. Court of Appeals for the Federal Circuit or the U.S. District Court for the District of Columbia. Stringent time periods apply to the entire process.

The PTO reports that the number of patents issued jumped from 66,200 in 1980 to 113,600 in 1994.[2] Patents issued in 1994 to international residents accounted for about 43 percent of such patents.[3] In 1994, residents of California received the most domestically issued patents, 10,392 in number.[4]

47.2

MANAGEMENT

PATENT OR TRADE SECRET?

The Kochanowskis have invested a great deal of time, energy, and money in the development of the Call-Image videophone, and they would like to have as much protection for their invention as the law allows. Tom believes that they will receive the greatest protection by applying for patents on the product and then for additional patents on each development as they improve the product. Anna prefers to treat their process as a trade secret and not make the information publicly available. They ask for your advice. What will you tell them?

BUSINESS CONSIDERATIONS What factors should an inventor, in deciding to seek a patent, consider? What drawbacks argue against one's seeking a patent?

ETHICAL CONSIDERATIONS Is it ethical for a firm to copy a patented item and then hope that it can prevail in any litigation that results if the patent holder sues? Is it ethical for a firm to attempt to enforce questionable patents and to use the expense of litigation as a means of preventing competitors from making the product?

Protection and Infringement

Given the economic value of patents, this area of the law tends to invite litigation between parties with adverse interests. Holders of patents (that is, patentees) typically bring patent infringement actions when they believe someone has encroached on or invaded the area covered by the claims the patentee has made concerning the patent. The Patent Act covers direct infringements, indirect infringements, and contributory infringements.

A *direct infringement* involves a party who, without the patent holder's permission, makes, uses, or sells the patented invention in the United States during the term of the patent. For example, Video, Inc. manufactures and sells videophones that directly resemble CIT videophones. In this case, CIT has grounds to bring an action for direct infringement.

The act also covers inducements to infringe, in which another party has directly infringed on the patentee's patent and has actively and knowingly aided and abetted an infringement by a third party. For example, Video, Inc. sells a telephone that, when mixed with other components, infringes on CIT's patent for Call-Image. Video, Inc. then sells the telephones and components to See and Speak, which, following Video, Inc.'s instructions, also manufactures the product. Since Video, Inc. knows that a direct infringement will result from its actions, Video, Inc. has induced See and Speak to infringe on CIT's patent.

Last, the act covers *contributory infringements,* in which another party sells a material component of a patented invention and knows that the component has been specially made or adapted for use in a patented invention and that infringement will occur. For example, Video, Inc. sells a video process specially made for Call-Image (and the process has no substantial, noninfringing use) to See and Speak, and Video, Inc. knows See and Speak will use the process to infringe on the patentee's invention. Video, Inc. is liable as a contributory infringer while See and Speak becomes liable as a direct infringer once it uses the process.

One can engage in a direct infringement even though one is totally ignorant of the existence of a patent, since the issuance of a patent serves as constructive notice to the world of the patent's existence. On the other hand, *indirect infringements* involving inducements or contributory infringements require knowledge on the defendant's part before courts can impose liability.

Persons sued for patent infringement will try to overcome the presumption of validity and prove that the patent is invalid owing to some omitted condition of patentability (for example, novelty); infringement cannot exist in the absence of a valid patent. Abuse of patent provides another defense to infringement actions. For instance, if a patentee uses the patent as a means of engaging in anticompetitive activities and for the purpose of extending its monopoly beyond that granted by Congress, any infringement action brought by the patentee will be unsuccessful. Activities that violate the antitrust laws, such as illegal tie-ins and other activities discussed in Chapter 40, when used in conjunction with a patent, will lead to a finding of noninfringement. Refusing any and all requests to license the patent does not constitute patent misuse, however.

The Supreme Court recently held that when an infringement action involves the interpretation of a patent claim (that is, the portion of the patent document that defines the scope of the patentee's rights), such an interpretation is a question of law exclusively within the province of the court; juries are not empowered to engage in such interpretive activities—*Markman* v. *Westview Instruments, Inc.,* 116 S.Ct. 1384 (1996).

Remedies

Remedies for actionable patent infringement include damages and equitable relief in the form of injunctions. The statute directs courts to award damages in an amount adequate to compensate the patentee for the infringement (such amounts will include lost profits attributable to the infringement) but in no event less than a reasonable royalty representative of the infringer's use of the invention.

The act also allows courts to impose costs and to award reasonable attorneys' fees to the prevailing party in exceptional cases, such as circumstances involving clear fraud and wrongdoing or in circumstances in which the court believes the award of attorneys' fees will prevent gross injustice. But given the enormity of the attorneys' fees in typical patent cases, courts rarely award such fees.

In either jury or nonjury trials, courts have authority to treble the damages assessed. A court's award of damages denies the infringer its ill-gotten gains and also restores to the patentee the benefits he or she would have derived from the monopoly had the infringing sales not occurred. The Patent Act expressly allows courts to use expert testimony for determining the damages or royalties that would be reasonable under the circumstances.

International Dimensions

Given the value of patent rights, patent law (like copyright law) now has international dimensions. Prior to international treaties, an inventor had to patent the invention in each foreign jurisdiction and in accordance with the law of that particular nation.

To overcome these inefficiencies and complexities, the Paris Convention for the Protection of Industrial Property, administered by the World Intellectual Property Organization, came into existence in 1883. About 100 nations, including the United States, are members of the Paris Convention. Like the Berne Convention, the Paris Convention, by emphasizing the concept of national treatment in which each member can determine the nature and extent of the substantive protections afforded to patents, in a given situation may not fully protect patented inventions. Moreover, the Paris Convention has done little to alleviate the need for separate filings in each signatory nation's jurisdiction, and it has no enforcement mechanisms for policing violations of the convention.

Owing to these shortcomings, the Patent Cooperation Treaty (PCT) became effective in 1978. The PCT's procedures—especially the filing system—allow inventors in the 40 or so nations, including the United States, that have signed the treaty to use one filing for securing patent rights in the jurisdictions represented by the signatory nations. The present GATT round and NAFTA, international efforts discussed in Chapter 3, also provide transnational patent protection to inventors. In particular, the recent GATT changes appear to involve reasonable steps that will result in further harmonization of the international treatment of patents.

Computers

Neither the old law nor the significant amendments to the patent laws contemplated the inclusion of computer or program-related inventions within these classifications. As a result, by the 1960s, the PTO and the Court of Customs and Patent Appeals (CCPA) had drawn strict battle lines regarding the patentability of computer programs and other software. The CCPA was for it; the PTO against it.

Although it was clear that computer programs met the first requirement of patentability, that is, that they potentially arose under one of the four categories of patentable subject matter ("process" or "machine," presumably), doubts existed as to whether software fulfilled the remaining conditions of patentability. Those arguing for patentability viewed computer systems consisting of both hardware and software either as a process (a method for operating a machine) or as a physical component of the hardware itself and thus protected by the machine requirement, with the program being one element in the overall apparatus. Other authorities, by characterizing software as ideas standing alone, laws of nature, scientific truths or principles, algorithms (mathematical formulas), mental steps, printed matter, functions of a machine, and/or methods of doing business, however, relegated computer software to areas lying outside patent protection. Indeed, for many years that was the fate that befell program-related invention cases, since questions arose as to whether an invention containing as one of its elements a computer program implementing such an algorithm was patentable.

Preempt
Seize upon to the exclusion of others.

Many precedents relied on the so-called preemption test in which the PTO was obliged to examine whether the patent claim on the software would wholly **preempt** the other uses of the algorithm (that is, calculations, formulas, or equations). If so, the invention fell into one of the categories of nonstatutory subject matter and was unpatentable because the claim merely recited a mathematical algorithm. If, instead, the algorithm was but one of several steps or procedures leading to the transformation of the data into a wholly different state or thing, the invention complied with the statutory subject matter and was patentable.

After several cases in the 1970s holding computer-related inventions unpatentable, the Supreme Court in *Diamond* v. *Diehr* accepted the preemption test and held that the claim was patentable.

47.4 DIAMOND v. DIEHR

450 U.S. 175 (1981)

FACTS Diehr filed a patent application for a process for molding raw, uncured synthetic rubber into cured precision products. Diehr claimed its invention ensured the production of molded articles that were properly cured by a process that fed temperatures inside mold presses into a computer. Repeated calculations of the cure time through use of a mathematical equation enabled the computer to signal a device to open the press at the proper time. Diehr contended that this process of measuring temperatures inside the mold cavity, feeding the information to a digital computer for constant recalculation of the cure time, and the signaling by the computer to open the press were all new in the art. The patent examiner characterized Diehr's claim as being based on a computer program for operating a rubber-molding process and thus rejected it as one predicated on nonstatutory subject matter. However, the Court of Customs and Patent Appeals, owing to its view that Diehr's claim did not constitute a mathematical algorithm or an improved method of calculation but rather an improved process for molding rubber articles (that is, the process had solved a practical problem that had arisen in the molding of rubber products), reversed.

ISSUE Was a process for curing synthetic rubber, which includes in several of its steps the use of a mathematical formula and a programmed digital computer, patentable subject matter?

HOLDING Yes. Because Diehr had not attempted to patent a mathematical formula but instead an industrial process that implements or applies that mathematical formula as a means of transforming or reducing an article to a different state or thing, Diehr's claim constituted patentable subject matter under the Patent Act.

REASONING Answering this issue involved construing § 101 of the patent laws, which provides: "Whoever invents or discovers any new and useful process, machine, manufacture, or composition of matter, or any new and useful improvement thereof, may obtain a patent therefor, subject to the conditions and requirements of this title." Earlier cases had defined a "process" as an act or series of acts performed on the subject matter to be transformed and reduced to a different state or thing. If new and useful, these cases had declared, a process was just as patentable as a piece of machinery; and it mattered not whether the machinery suitable for performing the process was new or patentable. Therefore, industrial processes such as Diehr's were among the types that historically had been eligible to receive the protection of the patent laws. The fact that several steps of the process had used a mathematical equation and a programmed digital computer did not alter this conclusion. Even though mathematical formulas, like laws of nature, natural phenomena, and abstract ideas, are nonpatentable subject matter, Diehr had not sought to patent a mathematical formula; rather, Diehr had requested patent protection for a process of curing synthetic rubber. And, although Diehr's process had employed a well-known mathematical equation, Diehr had not endeavored to preempt (or foreclose from others) the use of that equation except in

47.4 DIAMOND v. DIEHR (cont.) 450 U.S. 175 (1981)

conjunction with all the other steps in the claimed process. In addition, a claim encompassing subject matter otherwise statutory did not become nonstatutory simply because it had used a mathematical formula, computer program, or digital computer. The grafting of § 102's requirement of novelty and § 103's requirement of nonobviousness onto § 101's last phrase was unnecessary; hence, a rejection of patent protection on either of these grounds would not affect the determination of whether the invention fell into a category of protectable subject matter under § 101. Whenever a claim containing a mathematical formula implements or applies that formula in a structure or process that, when considered as a whole, is performing a function the patent laws were designed to protect (that is, transforming or reducing an article to a different state or thing), the claim satisfies § 101. Because Diehr's claim was not an attempt to patent a mathematical formula but rather a claim involving an industrial process for the molding of rubber products, the judgment of the Court of Customs and Patent Appeals was affirmed.

BUSINESS CONSIDERATIONS Although the patent office issues a large number of patents, subsequent litigation ultimately results in the invalidation of a high percentage of these patents. What steps can a business take so as to minimize the chances of this happening? What else can the business do to protect itself from loss if its patents are invalidated?

ETHICAL CONSIDERATIONS Is the government's granting a monopoly (here, a patent) for 14 (or 17) years inherently unethical? What ethical arguments exist in favor of having governmental grants of monopoly power through the issuance of patents to an inventor?

Note that *Diamond* v. *Diehr* involved the question of the patentability of a computer program used as an integral part of a machine. A subsequent CCPA decision, *In re Pardo*,[5] ruled that a **compiler program**, one designed to translate source code to object code, alone may constitute patentable subject matter.

Compiler program
One that converts a high-level programming language into binary or machine code.

TRADEMARKS

From their inception, trademarks have served as a means by which tradespeople and craftspersons identify goods as their own. Indeed, archaeologists have found centuries-old artifacts bearing such trade symbols. In further recognition of the social and economic dimensions of such marks, the medieval guilds used trademarks as a means of controlling quality and fostering customer goodwill. Statutes as early as the thirteenth century codified these ideas. These early statutory developments sought to prohibit "palming off," or one producer's passing off its goods as the goods of a competitor and, through this "free-riding" on the established customer base and goodwill of a competitor, thus taking away sales from the other.

Present-day trademark law, by protecting against consumer confusion as to the origin of goods, advances this goal. In contrast to patents, no analogous constitutional foundation for the protection of trademarks exists. Rather, as we have seen in earlier chapters, the commerce clause provides the basis for the federal regulation of trademarks. However, both federal and state law protect trademarks.

Over the years, an extensive body of state trademark law had developed in the common law, principally through the state common law relating to unfair competition. The 1946 Lanham Act, the most important federal protection of trademarks, provides a structure by which the enforcement of these common law principles can occur through federal oversight and thereby builds on these common law roots. Just as the Lanham Act allows the registration of various marks, so too, some states have statutory registration provisions. The PTO oversees the federal registration of trademarks. The number of trademarks issued jumped from 24,700 in 1980 to 70,100 in 1994.[6]

Protection and Infringement

The Lanham Act defines a trademark as any word, name, symbol, device, or any combination thereof used to identify and distinguish the services of one person from the services of others and to indicate the source of the goods even if the source is unknown. This definition underscores the fact that a trademark always exists pursuant to commercial activity or use and may cover an extensive array of things, including the distinctive features of the product (that is, "trade dress") such as the product's shape, the product's packaging, the logo or artwork on the product, and so on. All these aspects may be worthy of trademark protection.

Well-known trademarks include Coca-Cola, Pepsi, Tide, Chanel, Mercedes-Benz (and its logo), Kodak, Ralph Lauren, and so forth. Service marks—or those that identify and distinguish services rather than products (e.g., McDonald's, United Airlines, or Prudential Insurance); certification marks, or those that identify the goods and services of others as having certain characteristics (e.g., the Good Housekeeping seal of approval or the Underwriters' Laboratories seal); and collective marks, or those that signify membership in a group and the goods or services produced by the group (e.g., the Wool Council, the Beef Council, and so forth)—are protectable under trademark law as well.

To deserve protection, the trademark—whatever its form—must be distinctive. Arbitrary, fanciful, and suggestive terms by definition are distinctive. Calling a brand of gasoline "Mobil" on the one hand seems arbitrary, but this designation also suggests mobility—presumably one of our goals when we put gasoline in our tanks. "Snuggles" as a name for laundry softeners, "Pampers" as a name for disposable diapers, and "Coppertone" as a name for suntan oils clearly meet these tests.

Note that all these marks embody some degree of imaginativeness. Without distinctiveness, identifying the source of the goods and avoiding consumer confusion become decidedly more difficult. Such marks in themselves also serve narrow marketing functions. Purely descriptive marks—adjectives such as "sweet" or "chicken"; geographic designations like "Califor-

47.3

MANAGEMENT

TRADEMARK INFRINGEMENT

A new competitor in the videophone market has recently unveiled its new logo, which is very similar to the trademark CIT has been using since its inception. Dan wants the family to file a trademark infringement suit against this firm. John and Lindsay, expressing concern, point out that CIT does not have a particularly distinctive name or symbol and that the firm's name is used as an adjective for virtually all videophones. They fear that CIT has lost its right to protect its trademark. The family members ask for your advice. What will you tell them?

BUSINESS CONSIDERATIONS How can a business protect its trademark so that the trademark does not become a generic term for the product it is intended to promote? Should a business consider changing its logo periodically so as to make the logo appear "fresh" and "new" to the public?

ETHICAL CONSIDERATIONS What ethical concerns are raised when a firm seems to copy the logo of a more successful rival? What ethical concerns are raised by a firm that attempts to prevent any competitors from using a trademarked logo even remotely similar to its own?

nia" or "New York" in reference to wines; and people's surnames like L.L. Bean and Marriott Hotels used as marks—do not qualify as distinctive until they have acquired "secondary meaning." In other words, when the consumer public no longer views the marks as purely descriptive terms but rather as indicative of the source of the goods or products, the marks have become distinctive. In a similar vein, common geometric shapes, flowers, or slogans, for instance, generally lack the required characteristic of distinctiveness and will not merit trademark status unless the owner can demonstrate secondary meaning.

The Lanham Act specifically provides that the PTO Commissioner may accept as prima facie evidence of distinctiveness proof that the mark has been in substantially exclusive and continuous use in interstate commerce for five years. Even though one cannot place nondistinctive marks on the Principal Register of trademarks, owners, as a means of protecting against international infringements of the mark, often place such marks on the Lanham Act's Supplemental Register.

In *Qualitex Co.* v. *Jacobson Products Co., Inc.*, note how the Supreme Court recognized color alone as a trademark.

47.5 QUALITEX CO. v. JACOBSON PRODUCTS CO., INC. 115 S.Ct. 1300 (1995)

FACTS Qualitex Company (Qualitex) for years has colored the dry cleaning press pads it manufactures with a special shade of green-gold. After Jacobson Products Company, Inc. (Jacobson), a Qualitex rival, began to use a similar shade on its own press pads, Qualitex registered its color as a trademark and added a trademark infringement count to its previously filed lawsuit challenging Jacobson's use of the green-gold color. Qualitex won in the district court, but the Ninth Circuit set aside the judgment on the infringement claim because, in its view, the Lanham Act does not permit registration of color alone as a trademark.

ISSUE Would the Lanham Act permit the registration of a trademark that consists, purely and simply, of a color?

HOLDING Yes. A color sometimes could meet the ordinary legal requirements for a trademark. When it does, no special legal rule would preclude color alone from serving as a trademark.

REASONING The Lanham Act gives a seller or producer the exclusive right to "register" a trademark and to prevent his or her competitors from using that trademark. Both the language of the act and the basic underlying principles of trademark law seem to include color within the universe of things that can qualify as a trademark. The language of the Lanham Act describes that universe in the broadest of terms. It says that trademarks "includ[e] any word, name, symbol, or device, or any combination thereof." Since human beings might use as a "symbol" or "device" almost anything at all that is capable of carrying meaning, this language, read literally, is not restrictive. The Court and the Patent and Trademark Office have authorized for use as a mark a particular shape (of a Coca-Cola bottle), a particular sound (of NBC's three chimes), and even a particular scent (of plumeria blossoms on sewing thread). If a shape, a sound, and a fragrance can act as symbols, so may color. A color also is capable of satisfying the more important part of the statutory definition of a trademark, which requires that a person use or intend to use the mark to identify and distinguish his or her goods, including a unique product, from those manufactured or sold by others and to indicate the source of the goods, even if that source is unknown. Over time, customers may come to treat a particular color on a product or its packaging (say a color that in context seems unusual, such as pink on a firm's industrial bolt) as signifying a brand. And, if so, that color will come to identify and distinguish the goods—that is, to "indicate" their source much in the same way that descriptive words (say "Trim" on nail clippers or "Car-Freshner" on deodorizers), owing to the attainment of a "secondary meaning," can come to indicate a product's origin. Nothing in the basic objectives of trademark law presents any obvious theoretical objection to the use of color alone as a trademark where that color has attained a "secondary meaning" and therefore identifies and distinguishes a particular brand (and thus indicates its "source"). Trademark law thereby encourages the production of quality products and simultaneously discourages those who, by capitalizing on a consumer's inability to evaluate the quality of an item offered for sale, hope to sell inferior products. It is the source-distinguishing ability of a mark—not its ontological status as

47.5 QUALITEX CO. v. JACOBSON PRODUCTS CO., INC. *(cont.)* 115 S.Ct. 1300 (1995)

color, shape, fragrance, word, or sign—that permits it to serve these basic purposes. The "functionality" doctrine of trademark law does not preclude the use of color as a mark, either. This doctrine prevents trademark law, which seeks to promote competition by protecting a firm's reputation, from instead inhibiting legitimate competition by allowing a producer to control a useful product feature. But since color sometimes is unessential to a product's use or purpose and has little effect on cost or quality, the doctrine of "functionality" will not constitute an absolute bar to the use of color alone as a mark. It appears, then, that color alone, at least sometimes, can meet the basic legal requirements for use as a trademark. It can act as a symbol that distinguishes a firm's goods and identifies their source, without serving any other significant function. Indeed, the district court in this case entered findings (accepted by the Ninth Circuit) that show Qualitex's green-gold press pad color has met these requirements. The green-gold color acts as a symbol. Having developed a secondary meaning (customers identified the green-gold color as Qualitex's), it identifies the press pads' source. And, the green-gold color serves no other function.

Accordingly, unless there is some special reason that convincingly militates against the use of a color alone as a trademark, trademark law will protect Qualitex's use of the green-gold color on its press pads. Hence, the Ninth Circuit, in barring Qualitex's use of color as a trademark, erred. For these reasons, the judgment of the Ninth Circuit is reversed.

BUSINESS CONSIDERATIONS Has the Court in this case involved itself in so-called "slippery slope" reasoning? In other words, has the Court failed to take into account the practical business problems spawned by this decision? What are some difficulties businesses might face as they try to abide by this decision?

ETHICAL CONSIDERATIONS Did either Qualitex or Jacobson have a greater claim to the "moral high ground" in this case? Why or why not? What should each firm have done so as to act more ethically?

Generic terms never can qualify for trademark protection. This result derives from the fact that a generic term, that is, one that merely refers to the group of products or services of which this item is a part, cannot identify the specific source or tradesperson from which the goods originate. Trademark law shows numerous examples of words that have passed into generic usage and thereby have lost their trademark status. Aspirin, calico, cellophane, escalator, linoleum, shredded wheat, thermos, yo-yo, and zipper represent a few such formerly trademarked terms.

A deceptive mark, for example, a personal security service that superimposes its logo over the seal of the United States and thereby falsely gives the impression of a connection with the U.S. presidency, cannot obtain trademark status. Neither can an immoral, scandalous, or offensive mark.

Similarly, the Lanham Act specifically precludes trademark status for marks that disparage any person (living or dead), institution, belief, or national symbol; use without consent the name, portrait, or signature of a living person; use the name, portrait, or signature of a deceased U.S. President during the lifetime of his or her spouse without the spouse's consent; and/or so resemble an already registered mark as to be likely to cause confusion, mistake, or deception.

The law recognizes the person or entity that first uses—and then continues to use—the mark in trade and affixes it to goods or services as the owner of the mark. Common law rights of ownership result from such first use. Under federal law, before one can register the mark on the Lanham Act's Principal Register, one must demonstrate prior use or a bona fide good faith intent to use the mark in the future in commerce, the affixation requirement, and use of the mark in interstate commerce.

When the PTO receives the application for registration, it undertakes an examination of the mark similar to that conducted with regard to applications for patents. An examiner checks the application for compliance with the statutory prerequisites and makes sure the proposed mark is not confusingly similar to previously registered marks. Once the examiner completes this investigation, assuming he or she approves the mark, the PTO publishes the mark in its *Official Gazette.*

Anyone who believes the registration may damage himself or herself can, within 30 days, file an opposition with the PTO. Once registration has occurred, one, in some cases, can sue for cancellation of the mark. After exhausting all administrative remedies (including appeals to the Trademark Trial and Appeal Board), aggrieved unsuccessful applicants, or those who unsuccessfully allege opposition or cancellation, can sue in either the Court of Appeals for the Federal Circuit or a U.S. district court. Once granted, registration ordinarily lasts for 10 years and is renewable for 10-year periods so long as the mark remains in commercial use. Registration on the Supplemental Register offers fewer protections but, as discussed earlier, may prove advantageous for those who wish to register marks in countries other than the United States.

The law protects the trademark owner from infringement when the infringer's use will likely cause an appreciable number of consumers to be confused about the source of the goods or services. The factors courts have used to determine the "likelihood of confusion" include, but are not limited to, the following: (1) similarities in the two marks' appearance, sound, connotation, meaning, and impression; (2) similarities in the customer base, sales outlets (that is, "trade channels"), or the character of the sale ("impulse" versus "nonimpulse" sales); (3) the strength of the mark; (4) evidence of actual confusion; and (5) the number and nature of similar marks on similar or related products and services. As in patent law, one can be guilty of contributory infringement as well.

Defenses to infringement include "fair use." As we have noted earlier, one can use one's surname—even if it is the same as another famous, trademarked name like McDonald's, Campbell's, or Hilton—as long as one's use does not create the likelihood of consumer confusion. Abandonment of the mark, whether actual (that is, discontinuation of the use of the mark with the intent not to resume usage) or constructive (acts or omissions by the owner that bring about loss of distinctiveness), constitutes a defense to infringement as well. The Lanham Act expressly provides that nonuse of the mark for two consecutive years constitutes prima facie evidence of an intent to abandon the mark.

The plaintiff's registration of the mark on the Principal Register gives him or her certain advantages in an infringement action, since registration serves as prima facie evidence of the mark's validity and the registrant's exclusive right to use the mark in connection with the goods or services described in the registration. Ordinarily, then, at least until the mark becomes incontestable, defendants challenging the validity of the mark must prove the registrant's noncompliance with the prerequisites of the Lanham Act (or the common law). Incontestability status derives from the registrant's continuous use of the mark in interstate commerce for five consecutive years, the absence of any decision adverse to the registrant's claim of ownership or any pending proceeding, and the registrant's filing an affidavit to this effect with the Commissioner of the PTO.

Attainment of incontestability status gives the registrant of the mark a decided edge. For example, loss of an incontestable mark can occur only through cancellation of the mark, in certain limited statutorily enumerated circumstances, or through the challenger's showing one of the statutorily enumerated defenses to incontestability. Such defenses, among others, include a showing that the mark is generic; registration or incontestability has been obtained fraudulently; the registrant has abandoned the mark; the mark falls within the aforementioned categories prohibited as deceptive marks; or the use of the mark constitutes a violation of the antitrust laws. Moreover, in the context of descriptive products or services, incontestability, in effect, substitutes for proof of secondary meaning. Hence, even though the registrant of a generic mark can never use incontestability to protect the mark, owing to this presumption of secondary meaning, the registrant of a merely descriptive mark can avail himself or herself of the protection represented by the incontestability doctrine. On the other hand, one can assert fair use and certain equitable defenses against even an incontestable mark.

Remedies

The Lanham Act sets out certain statutory remedies for trademark infringement, including the equitable remedies of an injunction or an accounting to recover the profits the defendant unfairly has garnered from the infringing use. In addition, the plaintiff may recover actual damages, and the court in its discretion can treble these damages if the circumstances (for example, willfulness or bad faith on the infringer's part) so dictate. The court similarly can adjust the amount recovered for lost profits to a figure the court considers "just." The court can award court costs and in exceptional cases may award reasonable attorneys' fees to the prevailing party. Special rules apply to counterfeit marks. Treble damages, attorneys' fees, and prejudgment interest awards usually result from the use of such marks.

YOU BE THE JUDGE

Internet Domain Names

So-called "cybersquatters" have registered many well-known trademarks as domain names. Oftentimes, these cybersquatters use the registration to force the affected company to buy the domain name from them. For example, a man named Dennis Toeppen had registered the domain name "panavision.com" and had used it to display an aerial view of Pana, Illinois. When Panavision, the well-known maker of movie equipment, sought to register its name, Toeppen demanded $13,000 from Panavision as the price for his releasing the domain name. A similar case involved Toys "R" Us, Inc.'s seeking to enjoin a domain site called "adultsrus.com" that was used to sell a variety of sexual devices and clothing over the Internet. Suppose that Toys "R" Us, using trademark law, has filed suit in *your* court. How will *you* decide the case?[7]

BUSINESS CONSIDERATIONS How can a business protect itself from individuals who, in an effort to extort money from the firm, attempt to use the name or trademark of the business? Should the business adopt a hard-line approach, or should it try to negotiate each case individually?

ETHICAL CONSIDERATIONS Is it ethical for an individual to register a name that he or she knows is owned by a successful business if he or she intends to sell the registered name to the owner of that name in the larger domain? What ethical issues does such conduct raise?

SOURCE: *The National Law Journal* (27 January 1997), pp. C3 and C4.

International Dimensions

The Paris Convention mentioned earlier in our discussion of patent law applies to trademarks. The "national treatment" rationale of the Paris Convention grants to trademark holders from member nations the same protection a nation grants to its own nationals—no more and no less. Under this rationale, one can register a trademark in another member nation either by complying specifically with that nation's requirements or by registering the mark in one's home country. Member nations then cannot refuse to register any such marks unless the mark is confusingly similar to a preexisting mark, or the mark is nondistinctive, immoral, deceptive, or uses the insignia of a member nation without that nation's consent.

The requirements of U.S. trademark law (for example, use in trade and commerce as a prerequisite to registration and the cancellation provisions of U.S. law) decidedly limit the usefulness of the Paris Convention to many international applicants. The same shortcomings discussed earlier—the lack of substantive guarantees, enforcement mechanisms, and a centralized filing system—have led to the creation of the Madrid Convention and the Trademark Registration Treaty, although neither of these initiatives has attracted very many members. The United States, for example, has refused to sign either treaty. The recent changes under GATT, however, seem promising, since they provide heightened protections against international infringement and piracy of trademarked products.

TRADE SECRETS

Protection

Trade secrecy law provides an alternative method for protecting intellectual property, and a firm therefore can use it to protect "know-how" or other information that gives the firm a differential competitive advantage over its competitors who either do not know or do not use the information. We already have seen some of the limitations on the protection of software under copyright law, in that only the written expression of the software and not the ideas embodied in it are protectable, and patent law, in that strict compliance with statutory requirements is necessary for patentability.

However, various state and common law doctrines, such as trade secrets, unfair competition, and misappropriation, may apply to certain aspects of software—including know-how, information, and ideas—and thus encompass concepts too nebulous for copyright or patent protection. These doctrines may cover computer hardware as well. According to the *Restatement (First) of Torts*, § 757(b), a trade secret may include:

> *[a]ny formula, pattern, device or compilation of information which is used in one's business, and which gives [one] an opportunity to obtain an advantage over competitors who do not know or use it. The subject matter of a trade secret must be secret . . . so that, except by the use of improper means, there would be difficulty in acquiring the information.*

In determining whether given information is a trade secret, courts generally consider:

1. The extent to which the information is known outside the owner's business
2. The extent to which it is known by employees and others involved in the business

3. The extent of measures taken by the owner to guard the secrecy of the information
4. The value of the information to the owner and to its competitors
5. The amount of effort or money expended by the owner in developing the information
6. The ease or difficulty with which others could properly acquire or duplicate the information

To qualify as a trade secret, the know-how, manufacturing processes, customer lists, or other proprietary information must be used continuously in the business. In addition, the business, by ensuring the physical security of the information, limiting disclosure only to those who actually need the information in order to complete their jobs, and putting those who have access to the information on notice that the firm expects them to retain it in confidence, must guard the secrecy of the information. For example, CIT may require employees to sign confidentiality agreements and restrictive covenants, review papers that employees will present publicly, conduct exit interviews with departing employees, and so on. One need only take reasonable precautions—as opposed to those deriving from herculean efforts or gargantuan costs—to guard and/or prevent access to the proprietary information.

Common knowledge is not protectable under trade secrecy law because such knowledge presumably is of little value to the owner of the information. Similarly, if through reverse engineering one can easily acquire or duplicate the information, it may not qualify as a trade secret.

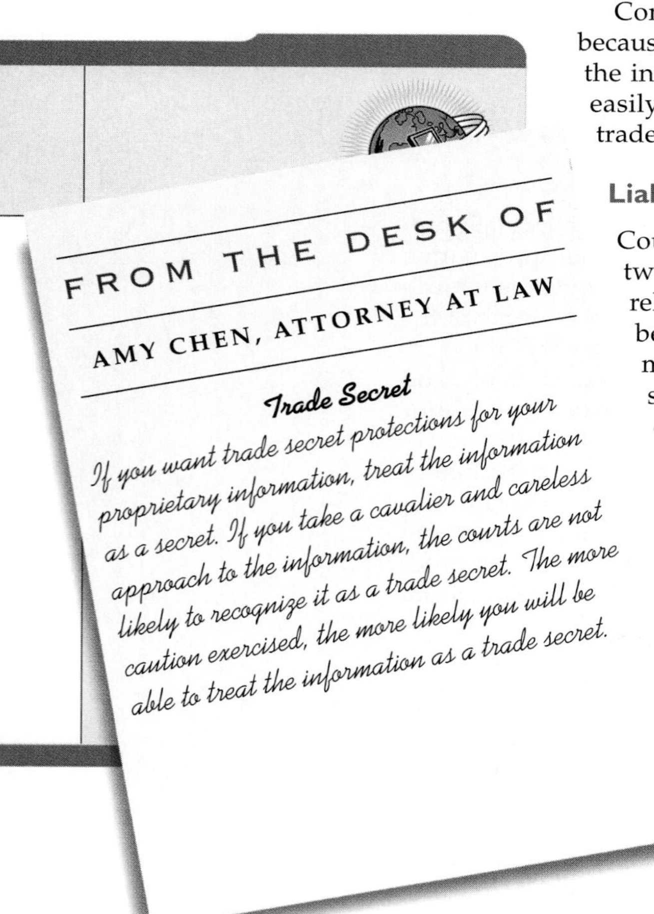

FROM THE DESK OF
AMY CHEN, ATTORNEY AT LAW
Trade Secret
If you want trade secret protections for your proprietary information, treat the information as a secret. If you take a cavalier and careless approach to the information, the courts are not likely to recognize it as a trade secret. The more caution exercised, the more likely you will be able to treat the information as a trade secret.

Liability

Courts ground liability for misappropriation of a trade secret on two principal theories: (1) breach of contractual or confidential relations (note the way in which courts often blur the distinction between contract and tort law) and (2) acquisition of the information through improper means. Under the first line of reasoning, courts will prohibit persons in an agency (including employment) and/or a fiduciary relationship from disclosing or using information acquired in the course of employment. As we saw in Chapter 12, sometimes an employee expressly promises not to compete with the employer for a given period of time in a given geographical area if the employee leaves this particular job. In the absence of such an express contract, courts generally will not imply such a restrictive covenant. But in some circumstances—for example, where a third party learns of confidential information from the employee—the law will imply a confidential relationship between the third party and the owner of the trade secret. In such circumstances, the third party's disclosure or use of the information will represent actionable misappropriation.

The law also imposes liability for impropriety in the methods used to acquire the trade secret. The law will not countenance conduct that falls below generally accepted standards of commercial morality. If a competitor of CIT induces the firm's key engineer to disclose proprietary information, the competitor will have acquired the information through improper means. Liability similarly will result from the acquisition of information through bribery; commercial espionage; or other illegal conduct such as fraud, theft, and trespass. However, as we discussed earlier, information obtained through reverse engineering, independent discovery, or the owner's failure to take reasonable and inexpensive precautions probably does not involve improper means and thus represents a lawful acquisition of information.

Remedies

Remedies for misappropriation of a trade secret include injunctions and actions for damages. Such damages may include the plaintiff's lost profits, the profits made by the defendant, or the royalty amount a reasonable person would have agreed to pay. State criminal laws may apply to misappropriations of trade secrets as well.

On the federal level, the Economic Espionage Act of 1996 (EEA) seeks to punish a broad spectrum of activity that interferes with an owner's proprietary rights in commercial trade secrets. In establishing a comprehensive and systemic approach to trade secret theft and economic espionage, the EEA facilitates investigations and prosecutions by federal authorities. In enacting the EEA, Congress apparently was responding to the losses—estimated at $1.5 billion in 1995[8] alone—resulting from competitors' activities (the "raiding" of employees, for example) and misappropriations by foreign enterprises. Hence, the substantive provisions of the EEA address "economic espionage," including activities in behalf of foreign instrumentalities, and "theft of trade secrets" resulting from certain domestic commercial endeavors. Prohibited activities include misappropriating, concealing, procuring by fraud or deception, possessing, altering or destroying, copying, downloading–uploading, or conveying trade secrets without permission.

The EEA thus seeks to proscribe "traditional" acts of misappropriation, that is, when conversion removes protectable information from the owner's control, as well as "nontraditional" methods—when "the original property never leaves the control of the rightful owner, but the unauthorized duplication or misappropriation effectively destroys the value of what is left with the rightful owners."[9] The sanctions that can be levied against those who engage in such prohibited activities include fines, imprisonment, and criminal forfeiture. Organizations acting in concert with or on behalf of foreign instrumentalities may be fined no more than $10 million. Other organizations may be fined no more than $5 million. Individuals acting in concert with or on behalf of foreign instrumentalities may be fined no more than $500,000 or imprisoned no more than 15 years, or both.[10] Other individuals also may be fined and imprisoned up to 10 years (or both). The criminal forfeiture provision permits the seizure and forfeiture of the property used to facilitate the misappropriation or impermissible possession of a trade secret. The EEA in such provisions thus mirrors the broad seizure powers enjoyed by the government under antidrug enforcement criminal statutes.[11] Try to keep abreast of the developments that stem from this new statute.

Computers

The owner of software who wishes to use trade secret protection may find it advantageous, since trade secret protection avoids the public registration required to devise and enforce rights under the patent and copyright laws. However, because maintaining the secrecy of the proprietary information in question may be difficult and because lack of secrecy constitutes one of the primary defenses to a charge of trade secret misappropriation, the owner of the trade secret should implement various mechanisms to ensure secrecy.

Actions that employers can take to protect trade secrets about software (or hardware) include the creation of nondisclosure, noncompetition, and confidentiality agreements with employees. Employers also should limit physical access to areas where the development of **proprietary** software is taking place as well as to storage areas. All software and documents containing trade secrets should bear proprietary labels, and the software should use **encrypted code** so that only those who have the key for unscrambling it can make the program intelligible. Last, employers should provide constant reminders to employees about secrecy obligations and conduct exit interviews with departing employees regarding the information the company considers proprietary.

Proprietary
Characterized by private, exclusive ownership.

Encrypted code
Code typed in one set of symbols and interpreted by the machine as another; used for security.

The licensing of software, in order to preserve secrecy, mandates special steps by the owner of the software. Besides restricting disclosures by the licensee, the licensor/owner should limit the rights the licensee retains in the software by virtue of the license, prohibit copying except for use or archival purposes, formulate special coding techniques to identify misappropriated software, distribute the software in object code as opposed to source code, and stipulate that the breach of any confidentiality provision will result in the immediate termination of the licensing agreement.

As we have seen, it is easier for a court to discern a relationship between the owner of the trade secret and the person or entity using or disclosing the trade secret than it is for a court to ascribe property concepts to the trade secret. Why? It is difficult to determine where general information, which is unprotectable, leaves off and proprietary information in the form of the trade secret, which is protectable, begins. Courts often derive these relationships impliedly from the parties' status as employer/employee, vendor/buyer, and the like. However, the parties cannot enjoy a confidential relationship unless a protectable trade secret first exists. Once it does, though, the trade secret may last perpetually until the owner loses the differential advantage it affords.

As we learned earlier, the loss of a protectable trade secret may occur through another party's independent discovery of the secret or any other legitimate means, such as reverse engineering or the public dissemination of the knowledge underlying the trade secret through either a failure to keep the information secret or flaws in the methods the owner has employed to ensure secrecy. Mass distribution of software copies to those with whom the software owner has a confidential relationship generally does not eliminate trade secret protection as long as the owner otherwise has taken precautions to preserve secrecy.

Unfair Competition

Our system of law allows, in the name of "competition," rather free-wheeling activities. However, courts will give remedies to those injured by activities such as the solicitation of a former employer's customers or employees, the competition between an employee and his or her employer while the employee still works for the employer, wrongful terminations by the employer, and the "palming off" of one's goods as those of another.

Protection and Remedies

The common law and statutory restrictions on "unfair competition" often form the legal bases on which aggrieved persons in these circumstances sue. Misappropriation, another basis for relief, derives from the common law principles of unfair competition and often becomes a "catch-all" theory used in situations in which patent, copyright, and trade secret law do not cover the aspect of the business in dispute. One note of caution is in order, however. The Supreme Court in several decisions has held that federal law will preempt such state causes of action if they interfere with federal policies.[12]

Palming off, or conduct in which a competitor—by deceptively "palming off" (or "passing off") his or her goods or services as originating from the other firm—tries to divert another firm's patronage or business to itself, represents the oldest theory of unfair competition. The common law recognized the unfairness of one firm's "free-riding" on the effort, investment, and goodwill of another and thus granted injunctions and/or damages to those injured by such palming off.

Since such activities often involved the wrongdoer's misrepresenting or copying the plaintiff's trademark or trade dress, the Lanham Act, in outlawing trademark infringement, basically "federalizes" these common law theories, although it changes them in certain significant ways. Indeed, § 43(a) of the Lanham Act also provides protection to commercial people even in the absence of federal trademark registration; hence, it has carved out broad civil remedies for commercial activities that affect interstate commerce.

Section 43(a) creates three different types of "unfair competition" claims: (1) "palming off" (or "passing off") claims under which the act prohibits any person's falsely designating the origin of particular goods or services if these false designations are likely to cause confusion, mistake, or deception with regard to this person's affiliation or connection to another person's goods, services, or commercial activities; (2) false advertising claims; and (3) product disparagement-type claims (that is, derogatory, false, injurious statements about a competitor's product, service, or title). To recover under § 43(a), the plaintiff must show that the defendant's activities affected interstate commerce; the defendant made material, false, misleading, or deceptive statements or designations that led to a likelihood of confusion among consumers; and actual or the likelihood of injury to the plaintiff.

While consumers ordinarily have no standing to sue (only injured competitors do), § 43(a), by allowing injunctive relief upon the plaintiff's showing a likelihood of damage, indirectly protects consumers' interests; the plaintiff need not show the defendant's actual diversion of patronage or trade. A showing of such a loss of business will be necessary if the plaintiff seeks money damages, however. Otherwise, the remedies ordinarily available for infringement of trademarks apply to § 43(a) claims.

The Federal Trade Commission (FTC), discussed in Chapter 40, has jurisdiction over "unfair or deceptive acts or practices in or affecting commerce." The FTC's enforcement mechanisms, particularly the wide latitude the FTC has in fashioning cease and desist orders, represents yet another avenue for protecting the owners of intellectual property from unfair trade practices. In the international arena, the Paris Convention protects its signatories against unfair trade practices.

Antidilution Statutes. In recent years, the legal system has begun to recognize that competitive injury can result even if the parties are not competitors and even if there is an absence of confusion as to the source of the goods. In other words, the law in some circumstances will protect one who owns strong, distinctive, well-known marks from another's use of an identical or similar mark if such use is likely to tarnish, degrade, or dilute the distinctive power of the mark. Simply put, the states that have enacted these so-called "antidilution" statutes recognize that even nonconfusing uses of identical or similar marks over time may gradually erode the distinctive value of the mark, as well as advertising and other public promotional efforts the mark owner has undertaken to promote product goodwill and to capture, as well as retain, market share.

In granting relief, state courts, as well as federal courts under their diversity jurisdiction, have utilized the dilution doctrine. As we learned in Chapter 39, the law protects truthful, nondeceptive commercial speech. Hence, like the *2 Live Crew* case we studied under copyright law, some cases brought under the dilution theory implicate aspects of the First Amendment, particularly if the defendant's use involves parody.

Celebrated dilution cases have included Pillsbury's seeking to enjoin a company's portraying and marketing Pillsbury's trade figures, "Poppie Fresh" and "Poppin' Fresh," in obscene sexual positions; General Electric's seeking to enjoin an underwear company's using an electric light bulb on its underwear named "Genital Electric"; and Coca-Cola's seeking to enjoin a poster captioned "Enjoy Cocaine" in script similar to that used in the Coca-Cola trademark. These cases illustrate the tension between the owner's desire to protect its mark from tarnishment and the value our society from its inception has placed on parody. Note, too, that only owners of distinctive marks can sue under such statutes, since only they have marks capable of suffering dilution or erosion.

The recently enacted Federal Trademark Dilution Act of 1995 adds to rather than replaces state antidilution statutes. This act codifies as federal law the principle that no one can undertake a diluting use of a famous mark even in circumstances in which there is an absence of the likelihood of customer confusion as to the source of the goods. This statute, then, apparently has ushered in a new era of federal trademark protection, an era that potentially will greatly expand the protection afforded to famous, strong, distinctive marks. Be alert for the legal developments that will result from this congressional enactment.

The Semiconductor Chip Protection Act of 1984

Congress's enactment of the Semiconductor Chip Protection Act of 1984 as an amendment to the copyright laws affords developers of integrated circuits a ten-year monopoly over their resultant semiconductor chips. Although it contains ideas common to copyright, patent, and trade secret law, this act creates a new class of intellectual property law.

Congress directed the legislation at both domestic and international chip pirates who in the past had merely taken chips apart, reconstructed the circuit design on the chip (known as the mask), and then made copies of the original chip. Obviously, as long as copyright law did not protect semiconductor chips (they were deemed utilitarian/useful articles and hence uncopyrightable even though the circuit diagrams might be), the incentive for pirates to reap profits by copying while at the same time avoiding the mammoth costs associated with developing the chips clearly existed. By prohibiting reverse engineering that has as its end purpose the copying of the chip, the act eliminates this result but, by allowing reverse engineering leading to the creation of a new chip, preserves current law.

http:// RESOURCES FOR BUSINESS LAW STUDENTS

NAME	RESOURCES	WEB ADDRESS
Patent and Trademark Office	Patent and Trademark Office (PTO) allows for patent searches; as well, it provides forms, legal materials, and the PTO museum.	http://www.uspto.gov/
World Intellectual Property Organization (WIPO)	The World Intellectual Property Organization maintains the Berne Convention, Paris Convention WIPO Copyright Treaty, and WIPO Performances and Phonograms Treaty, among other resources.	http://www.wipo.org/eng/general/copyrght/bern.htm
Copyright Office, Library of Congress	The Copyright Office provides publications and extensive information on copyright topics, including the basics of copyright law.	http://lcweb.loc.gov/copyright/
Lanham Act	The Legal Information Institute (LII), maintained by the Cornell Law School, provides a hypertext and searchable version of the Lanham Act (Trademark Act of 1946).	http://www.law.cornell.edu/lanham/lanham.table.html

Protection and Remedies

The act itself protects only mask works, or the layouts of the integrated circuits that appear on the chips; it does not protect the semiconductor chips themselves; any other product that performs the function of chips, such as circuit boards; or works embodied in mask works, such as computer programs. Indeed, not all mask works are protected, either. For instance, if the mask work is not "fixed" in a semiconductor chip, as is the case of information merely stored on diskettes, or if the mask work embodies designs that are commonplace and unoriginal, the act is inapplicable. The duration of the protection is ten years from the time of registration or the first commercial exploitation of the mask work, whichever occurs first. The process of registration contains special procedures for protecting proprietary information.

The same remedies generally available under the copyright laws relating to infringement—injunctions, damages, attorneys' fees, and import exclusion and seizure—apply in this context, except that criminal sanctions are unavailable. Some provisions of the act protect the mask works of nonpirating foreign companies under certain circumstances as well.

Although interpretive questions undoubtedly will arise as the first cases begin to appear under this act, note that this statute, at the time of its enactment, represented the first federal intellectual property law in over 100 years.

SUMMARY

Intellectual property encompasses several substantive areas of the law: copyrights, patents, trademarks, trade secrets, and unfair competition. Computers constitute an especially apt illustration of the significance of intellectual property both in the

United States and in the international arena. Intellectual property law strives to serve two oftentimes competing goals: ensuring incentives to create a wider array of products and services in the marketplace while at the same time, by providing public access to intellectual creations, promoting competition. The law serves the first goal when the law grants property rights (sometimes even monopolies) to creators and the second when the law limits the duration of such exclusive rights and/or circumscribes the rights thus granted so as to maximize the amount of information found in the public domain. This area of the law also seeks to protect creators and businesspeople from injurious trade practices.

The copyright laws protect any original works of authorship. To be copyrightable, works of authorship must show originality; and the works must be fixed in a tangible medium of expression. Ideas are not copyrightable. A copyright in essence consists of a bundle of exclusive rights that enables the copyright owner—usually the author or one to whom the author has transferred rights—to exploit a work for commercial purposes. To ensure copyright protection, one must ascertain the governing law: the 1909 Copyright Act, the 1976 Copyright Act, or the Berne Convention. Violations of any of the copyright owner's exclusive rights constitute infringement. The courts have imposed liability for both direct and contributory infringement. The most common defense against charges of infringement is the "fair use" doctrine. Civil remedies for infringement include injunctions, the impoundment and destruction of infringing items, and damages. Criminal penalties also are available.

The Patent Act of 1952 grants to inventors the exclusive right to their respective discoveries that consist of patentable subject matter. The Supreme Court has held that such utility patents may cover genetically engineered living matter as well. As in copyright law, ideas per se are not patentable. Utility patents last for 17 years, while design patents last for only 14 years, after which time the monopoly granted to the patentee ends. At that point, others can make, use, or sell the invention with impunity. To be patentable, an invention must demonstrate novelty, utility, and nonobviousness. Obtaining a patent involves detailed disclosures to the Patent and Trademark Office. Infringements may be either direct or contributory and may consist of inducements to infringe. Persons sued for patent infringement may claim lack of patentability or patent misuse as a defense. Remedies for infringement include injunctive relief as well as damages.

Over the years, an extensive body of state trademark law has developed in the common law, principally through the state common law relating to unfair competition. By providing a structure by which the enforcement of these common principles can occur through federal oversight, the 1946 Lanham Act—the most important federal protection of trademarks—builds on these common law roots. The Lanham Act defines a trademark as any word, name, symbol, device, or any combination thereof used to identify and distinguish the services of one person from the services of others and to indicate the source of the goods, even if the source is unknown. This definition underscores the fact that a trademark always exists pursuant to commercial activity or use and may cover an extensive array of things, including the distinctive features of the product (that is, "trade dress") such as the product's shape, the product's packaging, the logo or artwork on the product, and so on. To deserve protection, the trademark—whatever its form—must be distinctive; generic terms never can qualify for trademark protection. Purely descriptive marks do not qualify as distinctive until they have acquired "secondary meaning."

Under federal law, before one can register the mark on the Lanham Act's Principal Register, one must demonstrate prior use, the affixation requirement, and the use of the mark in interstate commerce. Obtaining a trademark involves registration with the PTO; certain parties can file oppositions to the registration or sue for cancellation of the mark. The law protects the trademark owner from infringements that will result in a likelihood of confusion concerning the source of the goods. Defenses to a cause of action based on infringement include "fair use" and abandonment of the mark. Registration of the mark on the Principal Register gives the owner certain advantages in an infringement action, as does the mark's becoming incontestable. The Lanham Act sets out certain equitable and at law remedies.

Trade secret law protects proprietary information that gives the owner a differential advantage over his or her competitors. To merit protection, the information must be secret and used continuously in the business. The law does not protect as trade secrets either common knowledge or information easily acquired from reverse engineering. Misappropriation can occur through breach of contractual or confidential relations or the use of improper means to acquire the secret. Remedies include injunctions and damages actions. State and federal criminal laws may apply to such misappropriations as well.

In "federalizing" common and state law unfair competition claims, the Lanham Act allows recovery on three bases: (1) "palming off," (2) false advertising, and (3) product disparagement. State and federal "antidilution" laws also protect one who owns strong, distinctive, well-known marks from another's use of an identical or similar mark if such use is likely to tarnish, degrade, or dilute the distinctive power of the mark. As we have seen in other contexts, parody may constitute a defense to actions brought under this theory.

The Federal Trade Commission also has authority to protect the owners of intellectual property from unfair trade practices. Several international treaties regulate intellectual property as well.

Discussion Questions

1. What does the law require before it will grant copyright protection?
2. What factors constitute "fair use" under the Copyright Act?
3. What does the law require before it will grant patent protection?
4. What is a trademark, and what does the law require before it will grant trademark protection?
5. What factors will a court use to determine a "likelihood of confusion" under trademark law?
6. What advantages derive from the registration of a trademark on the Lanham Act's Principal Register?
7. What must one do to protect information as a trade secret? In determining whether information constitutes a trade secret, what factors might a court consider?
8. Name and define the theories on which courts ground liability for misappropriation of a trade secret.
9. Explain in detail how the Lanham Act protects against unfair competition.
10. Explain fully the international protections accorded to various types of intellectual property.

Case Problems and Writing Assignments

1. Sony Corporation of America (Sony) manufactures home video tape recorders (VTRs), that is, Betamaxes, and markets them through retail establishments. Universal City Studios, Inc. (Universal) owns the copyrights on some television programs broadcast on the public airwaves. Universal, bringing an action in federal district court against Sony and the retail establishments that sold Betamaxes, alleged that Betamax consumers had been recording some of Universal's copyrighted works shown on commercially sponsored television and thereby had infringed Universal's copyrights. Universal further claimed that Sony

and the retail establishments, owing to their marketing of the Betamaxes, had become liable for such copyright infringement. Universal sought money damages, an equitable accounting of profits, and an injunction against the manufacture and marketing of the VTRs. The district court denied all of Universal's claims and held that the noncommercial home use recording of material broadcast over the public airwaves constituted a fair use of copyrighted works and thus did not constitute copyright infringement. How should the Supreme Court decide this case? [See *Sony Corporation of America* v. *Universal City Studios, Inc.*, 464 U.S. 417 (1984).]

2. Bonito Boats, Inc. (Bonito) developed a hull design for a fiberglass recreational boat that it marketed under the trade name Bonito Boat Model 5VBR. The manufacturing process involved creating a hardwood model that, when sprayed with fiberglass, created a mold. The mold then served to produce the finished fiberglass boats for sale. Bonito never filed a patent application to protect the utilitarian or design aspects of the hull or the manufacturing process that produced the finished boats. After the Bonito 5VBR had been on the market for six years, the Florida legislature enacted a statute that prohibits the use of a direct molding process to duplicate unpatented boat hulls and forbids the knowing sale of hulls so duplicated. Bonito subsequently filed a state court action alleging that Thunder Craft Boats, Inc. (Thunder Craft), by using the direct molding process to duplicate the Bonito 5VBR fiberglass hull and by knowingly selling such duplicates, had violated the statute. Bonito sought damages, injunctive relief, and an award of attorneys' fees under the Florida law. The trial court granted Thunder Craft's motion to dismiss the complaint on the ground that the statute conflicted with federal patent law and therefore was invalid under the supremacy clause of the U.S. Constitution. The Florida court of appeals and the Florida supreme court affirmed. Was the Florida statute preempted by the supremacy clause? Why or why not? [See *Bonito Boats, Inc.* v. *Thunder Craft Boats, Inc.*, 489 U.S. 141 (1989).]

3. Brooktree Corporation (Brooktree) is a California corporation that designs, manufactures, and sells semiconductor chip products used in computer graphics displays. Advanced Micro Devices, Inc. (AMD) is a competitor and one of the five largest manufacturers of chip products in the United States, with sales almost 30 times that of Brooktree. Brooktree alleged that between 1981 and 1986, it had invested approximately $3.8 million in developing integrated circuit chips that convert digital graphics image information to analog information at high frequencies for display on very high-resolution computer video screens. Brooktree further claimed that its chip had captured this niche market previously dominated by AMD. Brooktree asserted that AMD, in an attempt to recapture AMD's lost market, then introduced pirated chips at lower prices. These pirated chips allegedly consisted of copies of two of Brooktree's chips, which represented 40 percent of Brooktree's sales. Brooktree submitted that AMD's unlawful conduct had caused irreparable injury, including damages of over $2,753,000 in the previous six months; lost sales; and lost ability to expand or go public owing to lost profits. Brooktree further claimed that its total $30 million investment since 1981 was in jeopardy because the firm only recently had reached profitability and thus did not have the strength to weather the loss of sales stemming from AMD's conduct. Finally, Brooktree alleged that AMD's pirating had damaged Brooktree's other products because, in order to keep its cost structure in line, Brooktree had been forced to cut the cost of all its chips.

The jury found AMD liable on all but one of the patent claims and on all the mask work claims; the jury also concluded that AMD's infringement of Brooktree's patents had been willful. The jury then awarded damages of over $25 million to Brooktree. AMD subsequently brought a motion for judgment notwithstanding the verdict (judgment n.o.v.) or, in the alternative, for a new trial, based on several grounds, including the allegations that no reasonable jury could have found that AMD had failed to prove its reverse engineering defense or that Brooktree had proved mask work infringement. Did the circumstances in this case warrant a judgment n.o.v.? Why? [See *Brooktree Corp.* v. *Advanced Micro Devices, Inc.*, 757 F.Supp. 1088 (S.D. Cal. 1990).]

4. When Ashton-Tate Corp. (Ashton-Tate) sued Fox Software, Inc. (Fox) for copyright infringement, Fox used as its affirmative defense Ashton-Tate's alleged misconduct in its dealings with the U.S. Copyright Office. Specifically, Fox claimed that when Ashton-Tate had filed its original applications for copyright, it repeatedly had failed to disclose material information, including the fact that Ashton-Tate had derived its dBase line of computer software programs from JPLDIS, a public-domain computer software program developed by the Jet Propulsion Laboratory, and the fact that the dBase III program had been derived from dBase II. According to Fox, Ashton-Tate's repeated failure to disclose such material information was done knowingly and with an intent to deceive. Fox therefore urged the court to invalidate Ashton-Tate's

copyrights on its dBase line of computer software programs owing to Ashton-Tate's allegedly inequitable conduct. Should the court grant Fox's motion for summary judgment based on Fox's contentions? Why? [See *Ashton-Tate Corp.* v. *Fox Software, Inc.*, 760 F.Supp. 831 (C.D. Cal. 1990).]

5. Robert W. Kearns, the patentee for intermittent windshield wipers (IWWs), sued Chrysler Corporation (Chrysler), Ford Motor Company, General Motors Corporation, and other auto companies for patent infringement. As part of his suit against Chrysler, Kearns asked the court to institute postexpiration injunctive relief. In other words, even though by the time of the trial Kearns's patents had expired, Kearns claimed that Chrysler's infringement had deprived him of the "full value" of his patents during their respective terms, since the infringement in effect had extinguished his exclusive right to sell his patented IWW systems to automobile manufacturers. Kearns therefore urged the court to enjoin Chrysler from manufacturing infringing IWW systems for a period of sufficient duration "to put him in [a] position where the harm [caused by] past infringement during the terms of the patents . . . is rectified." The district court refused to grant such relief because the patents already had expired. The court concluded that nothing in the Patent Act or common law gave Kearns the right to an injunction against practicing the disclosures in an expired patent. Should the appellate court uphold the lower court's decision? Why? [See *Kearns* v. *Chrysler Corp.*, 32 F.3d 1541 (Fed.Cir. 1994).]

6. **BUSINESS APPLICATION CASE** Deere & Company (Deere) is the world's largest supplier of agricultural equipment. For over 100 years, Deere has used a deer design as a trademark for identifying its products and services. Deere owns numerous trademark registrations for different versions of the Deere logo. Although these versions vary slightly, all depict a static, two-dimensional silhouette of a leaping male deer in profile. The Deere logo is a widely recognizable and valuable business asset. MTD Products, Inc. (MTD), an Ohio company, manufactures and sells lawn tractors. In 1993, W.B. Doner & Company (Doner), MTD's advertising agency, decided to create and produce a commercial that would use the Deere logo, without Deere's authorization, for the purpose of comparing Deere's line of lawn tractors to MTD's "Yard-Man" tractor. The intent was to identify Deere as the market leader and convey the message that the Yard-Man was of comparable quality but less costly than a Deere. Doner altered the Deere logo in several respects. For example, the deer in the MTD logo was somewhat differently proportioned than the deer in the Deere logo. The MTD logo also lacked the name "John Deere." More significantly, the deer in the commercial logo was animated and assumed various poses. For instance, the deer, as a two-dimensional cartoon, ran in apparent fear as it was pursued by the Yard-Man lawn tractor and a barking dog. MTD submitted the commercial to ABC, NBC, and CBS for clearance prior to airing, together with substantiation of the various claims made regarding the Yard-Man lawn tractor's quality and cost relative to the corresponding Deere model. Each network ultimately approved the commercial. The commercial ran from the week of 7 March 1994 through the week of 23 May 1994.

   Filing a complaint seeking a preliminary injunction and a temporary restraining order, Deere alleged subsequent violations of the New York antidilution statute and § 43(a) of the Lanham Act, as well as common law claims of unfair competition and unjust enrichment. Following a hearing, the district court denied Deere's application for a temporary restraining order but ultimately found that Deere had demonstrated a likelihood of prevailing on its dilution claim and hence granted preliminary injunctive relief limited to activities within New York. The court later concluded that Deere had not shown a likelihood of success on the merits of its Lanham Act claim. On appeal, MTD argued that the antidilution statute does not prohibit a trademark's commercial uses that fail to confuse consumers or to result in a loss of the trademark's ability to identify a single manufacturer, or to tarnish the trademark's positive connotations. In its cross-appeal, Deere contended that the court should not have limited injunctive relief to New York state. How should the appellate court decide this case? Can an upstart firm ever compete effectively with a well-known firm if the jurisdiction in question has an antidilution statute? Should the parodic nature of the ad immunize MTD from liability? Justify your responses. [See *Deere & Company* v. *MTD Products, Inc.*, 41 F.3d 39 (2d Cir. 1994).]

7. **ETHICAL APPLICATION CASE** Mavety Media Group, Ltd. (Mavety) published *Black Tail*, an adult entertainment magazine featuring photographs of both naked and scantily clad African American women. On 7 June 1990, Mavety filed a PTO application seeking federal registration of its trademark "Black Tail," based on Mavety's bona fide intention to use the mark in connection with goods identified as "magazines." In accordance with the regulation governing the filing of an amendment to allege the first use of the mark, Mavety provided published issues of *Black Tail*. The

examiner ultimately refused registration because the mark consists of or comprises immoral or scandalous matter. The examiner expressly relied on a dictionary reference defining "tail" as "sexual intercourse—usu. considered vulgar." On 15 August 1991, Mavety, responding to the examiner's decision, contended that a substantial composite of the population would not interpret the mark to be a reference to sexual intercourse but rather as a reference to "the rear end," a meaning not usually considered vulgar. Mavety supported its contention with the magazine specimens of record that depicted the use of the mark—for example, on the magazine cover above a photograph of a woman displaying her derriere. Mavety also provided newspaper articles showing that many consumers would interpret "Black Tail" as connoting the full evening dress worn by men at formal occasions and thus the quality, class, and experience of an expensive life-style, consistent with the familiar genre of adult entertainment magazines such as *Playboy* and *Penthouse.* In addition, Mavety argued that the federal trademark register contains numerous marks consisting of words with nonsexual primary meanings that nonetheless have sexual connotations. When the Trademark Trial and Appeal Board (TTAB) of the PTO affirmed the examiner's refusal to register Mavety's mark, Mavety instituted a lawsuit in the Court of Appeals for the Federal Circuit. How should that court rule in this case? Had the court decided this case on ethical (as opposed to legal) grounds, would your answer have differed? Explain fully. [See *In re Mavety Media Group, Ltd.*, 33 F.3d 1367 (Fed. Cir. 1994).]

8. **IDES CASE** Service Merchandise Company, Inc. (Service Merchandise) opened its first store in Nashville, Tennessee, in 1960 and registered its service mark with the U.S. Patent and Trademark Office for the first time in 1977. The firm now owns and operates approximately 304 "Service Merchandise" retail stores across the country, with 37 stores in Texas and 7 stores in the Houston area. Service Jewelry Stores, Inc. (Service Jewelry) is a Texas corporation that owns and operates two jewelry stores in Houston, Texas. Service Merchandise sells a variety of goods; but, by virtually always displaying featured jewelry items in the first several pages of any advertisements, it particularly emphasizes its selection of jewelry. Service Jewelry concentrates solely on jewelry sales and service. It devotes approximately 60 percent of its business to jewelry service or repair and the rest of its business to the retail sale of jewelry; Service Jewelry custom-makes 90 percent of the jewelry it sells. Both Service Merchandise and Service Jewelry's marks begin with the word "Service" in red script letters that are larger than the words following in nonscript letters. Service Jewelry follows the word "Service" with the phrase "Jewelry Store" instead of "Merchandise." The evidence also showed that customers have asked Service Merchandise about its "new store" (which inquiries referred to Service Jewelry's store), and postal authorities have delivered mail intended for Service Jewelry to Service Merchandise. In its suit for trademark infringement, Service Merchandise also asserted the incontestability of the mark. What arguments would you expect Service Jewelry to make in its own behalf, and how should a court rule in this case? Apply the IDES model in answering these questions. [See *Service Merchandise Co., Inc.* v. *Service Jewelry Stores, Inc.*, 737 F.Supp. 983 (S.D. Texas 1990).]

NOTES

1. *Statistical Abstract of the United States,* U.S. Department of Commerce, Bureau of the Census (116th ed.) (Washington, D.C.: 1996), p. 566.
2. Ibid., p. 547.
3. Ibid.
4. Ibid.
5. 684 F.2d 912 (CCPA 1982).
6. *Statistical Abstract of the United States,* U.S. Department of Commerce, Bureau of the Census (116th ed.) (Washington, D.C.: 1996), p. 547.
7. Andrew Baum and Mark Epstein, "New Dilution Act Used to Evict Cybersquatters," *The National Law Journal* (27 January 1997), pp. C3 and C4.
8. Greenlee, "Spies Like Them: How to Protect Your Company from Industrial Spies," 78 *Management Accounting* 31 (December 1996).
9. Chaim A. Levin, "Trade-Secret Thieves Face Fines, Prosecution," *The National Law Journal* (27 January 1997), C13.
10. Ibid.
11. Ibid., C12.
12. *Sears, Roebuck & Co.* v. *Stiffel Co.*, 376 U.S. 225 (1964); *Compco Corporation* v. *Day-Brite Lighting, Inc.*, 376 U.S. 234 (1964); *Bonito Boats, Inc.* v. *Thunder Craft Boats, Inc.*, 489 U.S. 141 (1989).

PART 10

IDES PROBLEMS

Tom and Anna Kochanowski own and operate Call-Image Technology (CIT), a developer and manufacturer of videophones. Recently, CIT has encountered a number of legal problems for which the firm now seeks legal help.

To build a new manufacturing plant, CIT purchased a $50,000 tract of land near Lake Michigan. At the time of the purchase, the land was zoned for commercial and industrial use. Right before construction was to begin, the state of Michigan, citing concerns about the environment and erosion, passed a law forbidding construction of commercial or industrial facilities in "problem" areas near Lake Michigan. CIT's land was one such "problem" area. Tom realizes that this land, given the new law, is essentially worthless to CIT, and he believes the state should compensate the firm for the $50,000 it has spent plus damages for lost use.

On another issue, Tom arranged with Automotive, Inc., to have the seat upholstery on several CIT vans replaced. Automotive specializes in car and truck upholstery. While the vans were in Automotive's possession, one was vandalized, resulting in nearly $2000 in damages. Automotive denies liability, citing signs limiting their liability prominently posted within their office. In addition, Automotive claims Tom agreed to these terms when he left the vans. Tom never saw the signs, and he denies agreeing to such terms. Moreover, Tom believes Automotive's lack of proper security is to blame.

With the rise in popularity of videophones, and Call-Image videophones in particular, CIT, its logo, and the name "Call-Image," have become standard nomenclature in the videophone market. CIT has registered its company name, logo, and product names as trademarks with the U.S. Patent and Trademark Office (PTO). However, Tom and Anna recently have heard people refer to videophones produced by other firms as "call-image phones." Anna fears that this usage shows that their product's name has become a generic term for all videophones, and she believes that if CIT fails to take steps to prevent this, the firm will lose the exclusive right to the name. Also, Tom and Anna want to ensure that their trademarks (and patents, for that matter) are protected globally as well as domestically.

Tom and Anna are scheduled to meet with Amy Chen, their lawyer, to discuss these problems. Before this meeting, Tom and Anna need to clarify these issues.

IDENTIFY What are the legal and ethical issues that arise from the situations CIT faces?

DEFINE What are the meanings of the relevant legal terms associated with these issues?

ENUMERATE What are the legal and ethical principles associated with these issues? Legally speaking, what must the state of Michigan do to curtail CIT's use of its own land? What liability does CIT have for vandalized property that is in the possession of another? What common law principles, statutes, and/or treaties govern patents and trademarks, and how do these relate to CIT?

SHOW BOTH SIDES Consider all the facts that inhere in the preceding questions. Does the state of Michigan have a legitimate reason to curtail CIT's use of its property? Can Automotive forgo its liability for vandalism to other's property while this property is in Automotive's possession? Can competitors of CIT refer to their videophones as "call-image phones"?

[To review the IDES approach, refer to pages 29–30.]

THE CONSTITUTION OF THE UNITED STATES

We the people of the United States, in order to form a more perfect union, establish justice, insure domestic tranquility, provide for the common defense, promote the general welfare, and secure the blessings of liberty to ourselves and our posterity, do ordain and establish this Constitution for the United States of America.

ARTICLE I

Section 1. All legislative powers herein granted shall be vested in a Congress of the United States, which shall consist of a Senate and House of Representatives.

Section 2. 1. The House of Representatives shall be composed of members chosen every second year by the people of the several States, and the electors in each State shall have the qualifications requisite for electors of the most numerous branch of the State legislature.

2. No person shall be a representative who shall not have attained to the age of twenty-five years, and been seven years a citizen of the United States, and who shall not, when elected, be an inhabitant of that State in which he shall be chosen.

3. Representatives and direct taxes shall be apportioned among the several States which may be included within this Union, according to their respective numbers, which shall be determined by adding to the whole number of free persons, including those bound to service for a term of years, and excluding Indians not taxed, three fifths of all other persons.[1] The actual enumeration shall be made within three years after the first meeting of the Congress of the United States, and within every subsequent term of ten years, in such manner as they shall by law direct. The number of representatives shall not exceed one for every thirty thousand, but each State shall have at least one representative; and until such enumeration shall be made, the State of New Hampshire shall be entitled to choose three, Massachusetts eight, Rhode Island and Providence Plantations one, Connecticut five, New York six, New Jersey four, Pennsylvania eight, Delaware one, Maryland six, Virginia ten, North Carolina five, South Carolina five, and Georgia three.

4. When vacancies happen in the representation from any State, the executive authority thereof shall issue writs of election to fill such vacancies.

5. The House of Representatives shall choose their speaker and other officers; and shall have the sole power of impeachment.

Section 3. 1. The Senate of the United States shall be composed of two senators from each State, chosen by the legislature thereof, for six years; and each senator shall have one vote.

2. Immediately after they shall be assembled in consequence of the first election, they shall be divided as equally as may be into three classes. The seats of the senators of the first class shall be vacated at the expiration of the second year, of the second class at the expiration of the fourth year, and of the third class at the expiration of the fourth year, and of the third class at the expiration of the sixth year, so that one third may be chosen every second year; and if vacancies happen by resignation, or otherwise, during the recess of the legislature of any State, the executive thereof may make temporary appointments until the next meeting of the legislature, which shall then fill such vacancies.[2]

3. No person shall be a senator who shall not have attained to the age of thirty years, and been nine years a citizen of the United States, and who shall not, when elected, be an inhabitant of that State for which he shall be chosen.

4. The Vice President of the United States shall be President of the Senate, but shall have no vote, unless they be equally divided.

5. The Senate shall choose their other officers, and also a president pro tempore, in the absence of the Vice President, or when he shall exercise the office of the President of the United States.

6. The Senate shall have the sole power to try all impeachments. When sitting for that purpose, they shall be on oath or affirmation. When the President of the United States is tried, the chief justice shall preside: and no person shall be convicted without the concurrence of two thirds of the members present.

7. Judgment in cases of impeachment shall not extend further than to removal from office, and disqualification to hold and enjoy any office of honor, trust or profit under the United States: but the party convicted shall nevertheless be liable and subject to indictment, trial, judgment and punishment, according to law.

Section 4. 1. The times, places, and manner of holding elections for senators and representatives, shall be prescribed in each State by the legislature thereof; but the Congress may at any time by law make or alter such regulations, except as to the places of choosing senators.

1 See the 14th Amendment.
2 See the 17th Amendment.

2. The Congress shall assemble at least once in every year, and such meeting shall be on the first Monday in December, unless they shall by law appoint a different day.

Section 5. 1. Each House shall be the judge of the elections, returns and qualifications of its own members, and a majority of each shall constitute a quorum to do business; but a smaller number may adjourn from day to day, and may be authorized to compel the attendance of absent members, in such manner, and under such penalties as each House may provide.

2. Each House may determine the rules of its proceedings, punish its members for disorderly behavior, and, with the concurrence of two thirds, expel a member.

3. Each House shall keep a journal of its proceedings, and from time to time publish the same, excepting such parts as may in their judgment require secrecy; and the yeas and nays of the members of either House on any question shall, at the desire of one fifth of those present, be entered on the journal.

4. Neither House, during the session of Congress, shall, without the consent of the other, adjourn for more than three days, nor to any other place than that in which the two Houses shall be sitting.

Section 6. 1. The senators and representatives shall receive a compensation for their services, to be ascertained by law, and paid out of the Treasury of the United States. They shall in all cases, except treason, felony, and breach of the peace, be privileged from arrest during their attendance at the session of their respective Houses, and in going to and returning from the same; and for any speech or debate in either House, they shall not be questioned in any other place.

2. No senator or representative shall, during the time for which he was elected, be appointed to any civil office under the authority of the United States, which shall have been created, or the emoluments whereof shall have been increased during such time; and no person holding any office under the United States shall be a member of either House during his continuance in office.

Section 7. 1. All bills for raising revenue shall originate in the House of Representatives; but the Senate may propose or concur with amendments as on other bills.

2. Every bill which shall have passed the House of Representatives and the Senate, shall, before it becomes a law, be presented to the President of the United States; if he approves he shall sign it, but if not he shall return it, with his objections to that House in which it shall have originated, who shall enter the objections at large on their journal, and proceed to reconsider it. If after such reconsideration two thirds of that House shall agree to pass the bill, it shall be sent, together with the objections, to the other House, by which it shall likewise be reconsidered, and if approved by two thirds of that House, it shall become a law. But in all such cases the votes of both Houses shall be determined by yeas and nays, and the names of the persons voting for and against the bill shall be entered on the journal of each House respectively. If any bill shall not be returned by the President within ten days (Sundays excepted) after it shall have been presented to him, the same shall be a law, in like manner as if he had signed it, unless the Congress by their adjournment prevent its return, in which case it shall not be a law.

3. Every order, resolution, or vote to which the concurrence of the Senate and the House of Representatives may be necessary (except on a question of adjournment) shall be presented to the President of the United States; and before the same shall take effect, shall be approved by him, or being disapproved by him, shall be repassed by two thirds of the Senate and House of Representatives, according to the rules and limitations prescribed in the case of a bill.

Section 8. The Congress shall have the power

1. To lay and collect taxes, duties, imposts, and excises, to pay the debts and provide for the common defense and general welfare of the United States; but all duties, imposts, and excises shall be uniform throughout the United States;

2. To borrow money on the credit of the United States;

3. To regulate commerce with foreign nations, and among the several States, and with the Indian tribes;

4. To establish a uniform rule of naturalization, and uniform laws on the subject of bankruptcies throughout the United States;

5. To coin money, regulate the value thereof, and of foreign coin, and fix the standard of weights and measures;

6. To provide for the punishment of counterfeiting the securities and current coin of the United States;

7. To establish post offices and post roads;

8. To promote the progress of science and useful arts, by securing for limited times to authors and inventors the exclusive rights to their respective writings and discoveries;

9. To constitute tribunals inferior to the Supreme Court;

10. To define and punish piracies and felonies committed on the high seas, and offenses against the law of nations;

11. To declare war, grant letters of marque and reprisal, and make rules concerning captures on land and water;

12. To raise and support armies, but no appropriation of money to that use shall be for a longer term than two years;

13. To provide and maintain a navy;

14. To make rules for the government and regulation of the land and naval forces;

15. To provide for calling forth the militia to execute the laws of the Union, suppress insurrections and repel invasions;

16. To provide for organizing, arming, and disciplining the militia, and for governing such part of them as may be employed in the service of the United States, reserving to the States respectively, the appointment of the officers, and the authority of training the militia according to the discipline prescribed by Congress.

17. To exercise exclusive legislation in all cases whatsoever, over such district (not exceeding ten miles square) as may, by cession of particular States, and the acceptance of Congress, become the seat of the government of the United States, and to exercise like authority over all places purchased by the consent of the legislature of the State in which the same shall be, for the erection of forts, magazines, arsenals, dockyards, and other needful buildings; and

18. To make all laws which shall be necessary and proper for carrying into execution the foregoing powers, and all other powers vested by this Constitution in the government of the United States, or in any department or officer thereof.

Section 9. 1. The migration or importation of such persons as any of the States now existing shall think proper to admit, shall not be prohibited by the Congress prior to the year one thousand eight hundred and eight, but a tax or duty may be imposed on such importation, not exceeding ten dollars for each person.

2. The privilege of the writ of habeas corpus shall not be suspended, unless when in cases of rebellion or invasion the public safety may require it.

3. No bill of attainder or ex post facto law shall be passed.

4. No capitation, or other direct, tax shall be laid, unless in proportion to the census or enumeration hereinbefore directed to be taken.[3]

5. No tax or duty shall be laid on articles exported from any State.

6. No preference shall be given by any regulation of commerce or revenue to the ports of one State over those of another: nor shall vessels bound to, or from, one State be obliged to enter, clear, or pay duties in another.

7. No money shall be drawn from the treasury, but in consequence of appropriations made by law; and a regular statement and account of the receipts and expenditures of all public money shall be published from time to time.

8. No title of nobility shall be granted by the United States: and no person holding any office of profit or trust under them, shall, without the consent of the Congress, accept of any present, emolument, office, or title, of any kind whatever, from any king, prince, or foreign State.

Section 10. 1. No State shall enter into any treaty, alliance, or confederation; grant letters of marque and reprisal; coin money; emit bills of credit; make anything but gold and silver coin a tender in payment of debts; pass any bill of attainder, ex post facto law, or law impairing the obligation of contracts, or grant any title of nobility.

2. No State shall, without the consent of the Congress, lay any imposts or duties on imports or exports, except what may be absolutely necessary for executing its inspection laws: and the net produce of all duties and imposts laid by any State on imports or exports, shall be for the use of the treasury of the United States; and all such laws shall be subject to the revision and control of the Congress.

3. No State shall, without the consent of the Congress, lay any duty of tonnage, keep troops, or ships of war in time of peace, enter into any agreement or compact with another State, or with a foreign power, or engage in war, unless actually invaded, or in such imminent danger as will not admit of delay.

Article II

Section 1. 1. The executive power shall be vested in a President of the United States of America. He shall hold his office during the term of four years, and, together with the Vice President, chosen for the same term, be elected as follows:

2. Each State shall appoint, in such manner as the legislature thereof may direct, a number of electors, equal to the whole number of senators and representatives to which the State may be entitled in the Congress: but no senator or representative, or person holding an office of trust or profit under the United States, shall be appointed an elector.

The electors shall meet in their respective States, and vote by ballot for two persons, of whom one at least shall not be an inhabitant of the same State with themselves. And they shall make a list of all the persons voted for, and of the number of votes for each; which list they shall sign and certify, and transmit sealed to the seat of the government of the United States, directed to the president of the Senate. The president of the Senate shall, in the presence of the Senate and House of Representatives, open all the certificates, and the votes shall then be counted. The person having the greatest number of votes shall be the President, if such number be a majority of the whole number of electors appointed; and if there be more than one who have such majority, and have an equal number of votes, then the House of Representatives shall immediately choose by ballot one of them for President; and if no person have a majority, then from the five highest on the list the said House shall in like manner choose the President. But in choosing the President, the votes shall be taken by States, the representation from each State having one vote; a quorum for this purpose shall consist of a member or members from two thirds of the States, and a majority of all the States shall be necessary to a choice. In every case, after the choice of the President, the person having the greatest number of votes of the electors shall be the Vice President. But if there should remain two or more who have equal votes, the Senate shall choose from them by ballot the Vice President.[4]

3. The Congress may determine the time of choosing the electors, and the day on which they shall give their votes; which day shall be the same throughout the United States.

4. No person except a natural born citizen, or a citizen of the United States, at the time of the adoption of this Constitution, shall be eligible to the office of President; neither shall any person be eligible to that office who shall not have attained to the age of thirty-five years, and been fourteen years a resident within the United States.

5. In the case of removal of the President from office, or of his death, resignation, or inability to discharge the powers and duties of the said office, the same shall devolve on the Vice President, and the Congress may by law provide for the case of removal, death, resignation, or inability, both of the President and Vice President, declaring what officer shall then act as President, and such officer shall act accordingly, until the disability be removed, or a President shall be elected.

6. The President shall, at stated times, receive for his services a compensation, which shall neither be increased nor diminished during the period for which he shall have been elected, and he shall not receive within that period any other emolument from the United States, or any of them.

7. Before he enter on the execution of his office, he shall take the following oath or affirmation:-"I do solemnly swear (or affirm) that I will faithfully execute the office of President of the United States, and will to the best of my ability, preserve, protect and defend the Constitution of the United States."

Section 2. 1. The President shall be commander in chief of the army and navy of the United States, and of the militia of the several States, when called into the actual service of the United States; he may require the opinion, in writing, of the principal officer in each of the executive departments, upon any subject relating to the duties of their respective office, and he shall have power to grant reprieves and pardons for offenses against the United States, except in cases of impeachment.

2. He shall have power, by and with the advice and consent of the Senate, to make treaties, provided two thirds of the senators present concur; and he shall nominate, and by and with the advice and consent of the Senate, shall appoint ambassadors,

3 See the 16th Amendment.

4 Superseded by the 12th Amendment.

other public ministers and consuls, judges of the Supreme Court, and all other officers of the United States, whose appointments are not herein otherwise provided for, and which shall be established by law: but the Congress may by law vest the appointment of such inferior officers, as they think proper, in the President alone, in the courts of law, or in the heads of departments.

3. The President shall have power to fill up all vacancies that may happen during the recess of the Senate, by granting commissions which shall expire at the end of their next session.

Section 3. He shall from time to time give to the Congress information of the state of the Union, and recommend to their consideration such measures as he shall judge necessary and expedient; he may, on extraordinary occasions, convene both Houses, or either of them, and in case of disagreement between them with respect to the time of adjournment, he may adjourn them to such time as he shall think proper; he shall receive ambassadors and other public ministers; he shall take care that the laws be faithfully executed, and shall commission all the officers of the United States.

Section 4. The President, Vice President, and all civil officers of the United States, shall be removed from office on impeachment for, and conviction of, treason, bribery, or other high crimes and misdemeanors.

ARTICLE III

Section 1. The judicial power of the United States shall be vested in one Supreme Court, and in such inferior courts as the Congress may from time to time ordain and establish. The judges, both of the Supreme and inferior courts, shall hold their offices during good behavior, and shall, at stated times, receive for their services, a compensation, which shall not be diminished during their continuance in office.

Section 2. 1. The judicial power shall extend to all cases, in law and equity, arising under this Constitution, the laws of the United States, and treaties made, or which shall be made, under their authority;—to all cases affecting ambassadors, other public ministers and consuls;—to all cases of admiralty and maritime jurisdiction;—to controversies to which the United States shall be a party;-to controversies between two or more States; between a State and citizens of another State;[5]—between citizens of different States;—between citizens of the same State claiming lands under grants of different States, and between a State, or the citizens thereof, and foreign States, citizens or subjects.

2. In all cases affecting ambassadors, other public ministers and consuls, and those in which a State shall be party, the Supreme Court shall have original jurisdiction. In all the other cases before mentioned, the Supreme Court shall have appellate jurisdiction, both as to law and to fact, with such exceptions, and under such regulations as the Congress shall make.

3. The trial of all crimes, except in cases of impeachment, shall be by jury; and such trial shall be held in the State where the said crimes shall have been committed; but when not committed within any State, the trial shall be at such place or places as the Congress may by law have directed.

Section 3. 1. Treason against the United States shall consist only in levying war against them, or in adhering to their enemies, giving them aid and comfort. No person shall be convicted of treason unless on the testimony of two witnesses to the same overt act, or on confession in open court.

2. The Congress shall have power to declare the punishment of treason, but no attainder of treason shall work corruption of blood, or forfeiture except during the life of the person attainted.

ARTICLE IV

Section 1. Full faith and credit shall be given in each State to the public acts, records, and judicial proceedings of every other State. And the Congress may by general laws prescribe the manner in which such acts, records and proceedings shall be proved, and the effect thereof.

Section 2. 1. The citizens of each State shall be entitled to all privileges and immunities of citizens in the several States.[6]

2. A person charged in any State with treason, felony, or other crime, who shall flee from justice, and be found in another State, shall on demand of the executive authority of the State from which he fled, be delivered up to be removed to the State having jurisdiction of the crime.

3. No person held to service or labor in one State under the laws thereof, escaping into another, shall in consequence of any law or regulation therein, be discharged from such service or labor, but shall be delivered up on claim of the party to whom such service or labor may be due.[7]

Section 3. 1. New States may be admitted by the Congress into this Union; but no new State shall be formed or erected within the jurisdiction of any other State, nor any State be formed by the junction of two or more States, or parts of States, without the consent of the legislatures of the States concerned as well as of the Congress.

2. The Congress shall have power to dispose of and make all needful rules and regulations respecting the territory or other property belonging to the United States; and nothing in this Constitution shall be so construed as to prejudice any claims of the United States, or of any particular State.

Section 4. The United States shall guarantee to every State in this Union a republican form of government, and shall protect each of them against invasion; and on application of the legislature, or of the executive (when the legislature cannot be convened) against domestic violence.

ARTICLE V

The Congress, whenever two thirds of both Houses shall deem it necessary, shall propose amendments to this Constitution, or, on the application of the legislature of two thirds of the several States, shall call a convention for proposing amendments, which in either case, shall be valid to all intents and purposes, as part of this Constitution when ratified by the legislatures of three fourths of the several States, or by conventions in three fourths thereof, as the one or the other mode of ratification may be proposed by the Congress; provided that no amendment which may be made prior to the year one thousand eight hundred and eight shall in

5 See the 11th Amendment.

6 See the 14th Amendment, Sec. 1.

7 See the 13th Amendment.

any manner affect the first and fourth clauses in the ninth section of the first article; and that no State, without its consent, shall be deprived of its equal suffrage in the Senate.

Article VI

1. All debts contracted and engagements entered into, before the adoption of this Constitution, shall be as valid against the United States under this Constitution, as under the Confederation.[8]

2. This Constitution, and the laws of the United States which shall be made in pursuance thereof; and all treaties made, or which shall be made, under the authority of the United States, shall be the supreme law of the land; and the judges in every State shall be bound thereby, anything in the Constitution or laws of any State to the contrary notwithstanding.

3. The senators and representatives before mentioned, and the members of the several State legislatures, and all executive and judicial officers, both of the United States and of the several States, shall be bound by oath or affirmation to support this Constitution; but no religious test shall ever be required as a qualification to any office or public trust under the United States.

Article VII

The ratification of the conventions of nine States shall be sufficient for the establishment of this Constitution between the States so ratifying the same.

Done in Convention by the unanimous consent of the States present the seventeenth day of September in the year of our Lord one thousand seven hundred and eighty-seven, and of the independence of the United States of America the twelfth. In witness whereof we have hereunto subscribed our names.

AMENDMENTS

First Ten Amendments passed by Congress Sept. 25, 1789.
Ratified by three-fourths of the States December 15, 1791.

Amendment I

Congress shall make no law respecting an establishment of religion, or prohibiting the free exercise thereof; or abridging the freedom of speech, or of the press; or the right of the people peaceably to assemble, and to petition the government for a redress of grievances.

Amendment II

A well regulated militia, being necessary to the security of a free State, the right of the people to keep and bear arms, shall not be infringed.

Amendment III

No soldier shall, in time of peace be quartered in any house, without the consent of the owner, nor in time of war, but in a manner to be prescribed by law.

Amendment IV

The right of the people to be secure in their persons, houses, papers, and effects, against unreasonable searches and seizures, shall not be violated, and no warrants shall issue, but upon probable cause, supported by oath or affirmation, and particularly describing the place to be searched, and the person or things to be seized.

Amendment V

No person shall be held to answer for a capital, or otherwise infamous crime, unless on a presentment or indictment of a grand jury, except in cases arising in the land or naval forces, or in the militia, when in actual service in time of war or public danger; nor shall any person be subject for the same offense to be twice put in jeopardy of life or limb; nor shall be compelled in any criminal case to be a witness against himself, nor be deprived of life, liberty, or property, without due process of law; nor shall private property be taken for public use without just compensation.

Amendment VI

In all criminal prosecutions, the accused shall enjoy the right to a speedy and public trial, by an impartial jury of the State and district wherein the crime shall have been committed, which district shall have been previously ascertained by law, and to be informed of the nature and cause of the accusation; to be confronted with the witnesses against him; to have compulsory process for obtaining witnesses in his favor, and to have the assistance of counsel for his defense.

Amendment VII

In suits at common law, where the value in controversy shall exceed twenty dollars, the right of trial by jury shall be preserved, and no fact tried by a jury shall be otherwise reexamined in any court of the United States, then according to the rules of the common law.

Amendment VIII

Excessive bail shall not be required, nor excessive fines imposed, nor cruel and unusual punishments inflicted.

Amendment IX

The enumeration in the Constitution of certain rights shall not be construed to deny or disparage others retained by the people.

Amendment X

The powers not delegated to the United States by the Constitution, nor prohibited by it to the States, are reserved to the States respectively, or to the people.

Amendment XI

Passed by Congress March 5, 1794. Ratified January 8, 1798.

The judicial power of the United States shall not be construed to extend to any suit in law or equity, commenced or prosecuted against one of the United States by citizens of another State, or by citizens or subjects of any foreign State.

Amendment XII

Passed by Congress December 12, 1803. Ratified September 25, 1804.

The electors shall meet in their respective States, and vote by ballot for President and Vice President, one of whom, at least, shall not be an inhabitant of the same State with themselves; they shall name in their ballots the person voted for as President, and in distinct ballots, the person voted for as Vice President, and they shall

8 See the 14th Amendment, Sec. 4.

make distinct lists of all persons voted for as President and of all persons voted for as Vice President, and of the number of votes for each, which lists they shall sign and certify, and transmit sealed to the seat of the government of the United States, directed to the President of the Senate;—The President of the Senate shall, in the presence of the Senate and House of Representatives, open all the certificates and the votes shall then be counted;—The person having the greatest number of votes for President, shall be the President, if such number be a majority of the whole number of electors appointed; and if no person have such majority, then from the persons having the highest numbers not exceeding three on the list of those voted for as President, the House of Representatives shall choose immediately, by ballot, the President. But in choosing the President, the votes shall be taken by States, the representation from each State having one vote; a quorum for this purpose shall consist of a member or members from two thirds of the States, and a majority of all the States shall be necessary to a choice. And if the House of Representatives shall not choose a President whenever the right of choice shall devolve upon them, before the fourth day of March next following, then the Vice President shall act as President, as in the case of the death or other constitutional disability of the President. The person having the greatest number of votes as Vice President shall be the Vice President, if such number be a majority of the whole number of electors appointed, and if no person have a majority, then from the two highest numbers on the list, the Senate shall choose the Vice President; a quorum for the purpose shall consist of two thirds of the whole number of Senators, and a majority of the whole number shall be necessary to a choice. But no person constitutionally ineligible to the office of President shall be eligible to that of Vice President of the United States.

Amendment XIII

Passed by Congress February 1, 1865. Ratified December 18, 1865.

Section 1. Neither slavery nor involuntary servitude, except as punishment for crime whereof the party shall have been duly convicted, shall exist within the United States, or any place subject to their jurisdiction.

Section 2. Congress shall have power to enforce this article by appropriate legislation.

Amendment XIV

Passed by Congress June 16, 1866. Ratified July 23, 1868.

Section 1. All persons born or naturalized in the United States, and subject to the jurisdiction thereof, are citizens of the United States and of the State wherein they reside. No State shall make or enforce any law which shall abridge the privileges or immunities of citizens of the United States; nor shall any State deprive any person of life, liberty, or property, without due process of law; nor deny to any person within its jurisdiction the equal protection of the laws.

Section 2. Representatives shall be apportioned among the several States according to their respective numbers, counting the whole number of persons in each State, excluding Indians not taxed. But when the right to vote at any election for the choice of electors for President and Vice President of the United States, representatives in Congress, the executive and judicial officers of a State, or the members of the legislature thereof, is denied to any of the male inhabitants of such State, being twenty-one years of age, and citizens of the United States, or in any way abridged, except for participation in rebellion, or other crime, the basis of representation therein shall be reduced in the proportion which the number of such male citizens shall bear to the whole number of male citizens twenty-one years of age in such State.

Section 3. No person shall be a senator or representative in Congress, or elector of President and Vice President, or hold any office, civil or military, under the United States, or under any State, who having previously taken an oath, as a member of Congress, or as an officer of the United States, or as a member of any State legislature, or as an executive or judicial officer of any State, to support the Constitution of the United States, shall have engaged in insurrection or rebellion against the same, or given aid or comfort to the enemies thereof. But Congress may by a vote of two thirds of each House, remove such disability.

Section 4. The validity of the public debt of the United States, authorized by law, including debts incurred for payment of pensions and bounties for services in suppressing insurrection or rebellion, shall not be questioned. But neither the United States nor any State shall assume or pay any debt or obligation incurred in aid of insurrection or rebellion against the United States, or any claim for the loss or emancipation of any slave; but all such debts, obligations, and claims shall be held illegal and void.

Section 5. The Congress shall have power to enforce, by appropriate legislation, the provisions of this article.

Amendment XV

Passed by Congress February 27, 1869. Ratified March 30, 1870.

Section 1. The right of citizens of the United States to vote shall not be denied or abridged by the United States or by any State on account of race, color, or previous condition of servitude.

Section 2. The Congress shall have power to enforce this article by appropriate legislation.

Amendment XVI

Passed by Congress July 12, 1909. Ratified February 25, 1913.

The Congress shall have power to lay and collect taxes on incomes, from whatever source derived, without apportionment among the several States, and without regard to any census or enumeration.

Amendment XVII

Passed by Congress May 16, 1912. Ratified May 31, 1913.

The Senate of the United States shall be composed of two senators from each State, elected by the people thereof, for six years; and each senator shall have one vote. The electors in each State shall have the qualifications requisite for electors of the most numerous branch of the State legislature.

When vacancies happen in the representation of any State in the Senate, the executive authority of such State shall issue writs of election to fill such vacancies: Provided, That the legislature of any State may empower the executive thereof to make temporary appointments until the people fill the vacancies by election as the legislature may direct.

This amendment shall not be so construed as to affect the election or term of any senator chosen before it becomes valid as part of the Constitution.

Amendment XVIII

Passed by Congress December 17, 1917. Ratified January 29, 1919.

After one year from the ratification of this article, the manufacture, sale, or transportation of intoxicating liquors within, the importation thereof into, or the exportation thereof from the United States and all territory subject to the jurisdiction thereof for beverage purposes is hereby prohibited.

The Congress and the several States shall have concurrent power to enforce this article by appropriate legislation.

This article shall be inoperative unless it shall have been ratified as an amendment to the Constitution by the legislatures of the several States, as provided in the Constitution, within seven years from the date of the submission hereof to the States by Congress.

Amendment XIX

Passed by Congress June 5, 1919. Ratified August 26, 1920.

The right of citizens of the United States to vote shall not be denied or abridged by the United States or by any State on account of sex.

The Congress shall have power by appropriate legislation to enforce the provisions of this article.

Amendment XX

Passed by Congress March 3, 1932. Ratified January 23, 1933.

Section 1. The terms of the President and Vice President shall end at noon on the 20th day of January, and the terms of Senators and Representatives at noon on the 3d day of January, of the years in which such terms would have ended if this article had not been ratified; and the terms of their successors shall then begin.

Section 2. The Congress shall assemble at least once in every year, and such meeting shall begin at noon on the 3d day of January, unless they shall by law appoint a different day.

Section 3. If, at the time fixed for the beginning of the term of the President, the President-elect shall have died, the Vice President-elect shall become President. If a President shall not have been chosen before the time fixed for the beginning of his term, or if the President-elect shall have failed to qualify, then the Vice President-elect shall act as President until a President shall have qualified; and the Congress may by law provide for the case wherein neither a President-elect nor a Vice President-elect shall have qualified, declaring who shall then act as President, or the manner in which one who is to act shall be selected, and such person shall act accordingly until a President or Vice President shall have qualified.

Section 4. The Congress may by law provide for the case of the death of any of the persons from whom the House of Representatives may choose a President whenever the right of choice shall have devolved upon them, and for the case of the death of any of the persons from whom the Senate may choose a Vice President whenever the right of choice shall have devolved upon them.

Section 5. Sections 1 and 2 shall take effect on the 15th day of October following the ratification of this article.

Section 6. This article shall be inoperative unless it shall have been ratified as an amendment to the Constitution by the legislatures of three-fourths of the several States within seven years from the date of its submission.

Amendment XXI

Passed by Congress February 20, 1933. Ratified December 5, 1933.

Section 1. The eighteenth article of amendment to the Constitution of the United States is hereby repealed.

Section 2. The transportation or importation into any State, Territory, or possession of the United States for delivery or use therein of intoxicating liquors in violation of the laws thereof, is hereby prohibited.

Section 3. This article shall be inoperative unless it shall have been ratified as an amendment to the Constitution by conventions in the several States, as provided in the Constitution, within seven years from the date of the submission thereof to the States by the Congress.

Amendment XXII

Passed by Congress March 24, 1947. Ratified February 26, 1951.

Section 1. No person shall be elected to the office of the President more than twice, and no person who has held the office of President, or acted as President, for more than two years of a term to which some other person was elected President shall be elected to the office of the President more than once. But this article shall not apply to any person holding the office of President when this article was proposed by the Congress, and shall not prevent any person who may be holding the office of President, or acting as President, during the term within which this article becomes operative from holding the office of President or acting as President during the remainder of such term.

Section 2. This article shall be inoperative unless it shall have been ratified as an amendment to the Constitution by the legislatures of three-fourths of the several States within seven years from the date of its submission to the States by the Congress.

Amendment XXIII

Passed by Congress June 16, 1960. Ratified April 3, 1961.

Section 1. The District constituting the seat of Government of the United States shall appoint in such manner as the Congress may direct:

A number of electors of President and Vice President equal to the whole number of Senators and Representatives in Congress to which the District would be entitled if it were a State, but in no event more than the least populous State; they shall be in addition to those appointed by the States, but they shall be considered, for the purposes of the election of President and Vice President, to be electors appointed by a State; and they shall meet in the District and perform such duties as provided by the twelfth article of amendment.

Section 2. The Congress shall have power to enforce this article by appropriate legislation.

Amendment XXIV

Passed by Congress August 27, 1962. Ratified February 4, 1964.

Section 1. The right of citizens of the United States to vote in any primary or other election for President or Vice President, for electors for President or Vice President, or for Senator or Representative in Congress, shall not be denied or abridged by the United States or any State by reason of failure to pay any poll tax or other tax.

Section 2. The Congress shall have power to enforce this article by appropriate legislation.

Amendment XXV

Passed by Congress July 6, 1965. Ratified February 23, 1967.

Section 1. In case of the removal of the President from office or of his death or resignation, the Vice President shall become President.

Section 2. Whenever there is a vacancy in the office of the Vice President, the President shall nominate a Vice President who shall take office upon confirmation by a majority vote of both Houses of Congress.

Section 3. Whenever the President transmits to the President pro tempore of the Senate and the Speaker of the House of Representatives his written declaration that he is unable to discharge the powers and duties of his office, and until he transmits to them a written declaration to the contrary, such powers and duties shall be discharged by the Vice President as Acting President.

Section 4. Whenever the Vice President and a majority of either the principal officers of the executive departments or of such other body as Congress may by law provide, transmit to the President pro tempore of the Senate and the Speaker of the House of Representatives their written declaration that the President is unable to discharge the powers and duties of his office, the Vice President shall immediately assume the powers and duties of the office as Acting President.

Thereafter, when the President transmits to the President pro tempore of the Senate and the Speaker of the House of Representatives his written declaration that no inability exists, he shall resume the powers and duties of his office unless the Vice President and a majority of either the principal officers of the executive department or of such other body as Congress may by law provide, transmit within four days to the President pro tempore of the Senate and the Speaker of the House of Representatives their written declaration that the President is unable to discharge the powers and duties of his office. Thereupon Congress shall decide the issue, assembling within forty-eight hours for that purpose if not in session. If the Congress, within twenty-one days after receipt of the latter written declaration, or, if Congress is not in session, within twenty-one days after Congress is required to assemble, determines by two-thirds vote of both Houses that the President is unable to discharge the powers and duties of his office, the Vice President shall continue to discharge the same as Acting President; otherwise, the President shall resume the powers and duties of his office.

Amendment XXVI

Passed by Congress March 23, 1971. Ratified July 5, 1971.

Section 1. The right of citizens of the United States, who are eighteen years of age or older, to vote shall not be denied or abridged by the United States or by any State on account of age.

Amendment XXVII

Passed by Congress September 25, 1789. Ratified May 18, 1992.

No law, varying the compensation for the services of the Senators and Representatives, shall take effect, until an election of Representatives shall have intervened.

UNIFORM COMMERCIAL CODE*

The Code consists of the following articles:

Art.
1. General Provisions
2. Sales
2A. Leases
3. Commercial Paper
4. Bank Deposits and Collections
4A. Funds Transfers
5. Letters of Credit
6. Bulk Transfers (including Alternative B)
7. Warehouse Receipts, Bills of Lading and Other Documents of Title
8. Investment Securities
9. Secured Transactions: Sales of Accounts and Chattel Paper

ARTICLE 1
GENERAL PROVISIONS

PART 1
Short Title, Construction, Application and Subject Matter of the Act

§ 1—101. ***Short Title.***

This Act shall be known and may be cited as Uniform Commercial Code.

§ 1—102. ***Purposes; Rules of Construction; Variation by Agreement.***

(1) This Act shall be liberally construed and applied to promote its underlying purposes and policies.

(2) Underlying purposes and policies of this Act are

(a) to simplify, clarify and modernize the law governing commercial transactions;

(b) to permit the continued expansion of commercial practices through custom, usage and agreement of the parties;

(c) to make uniform the law among the various jurisdictions.

(3) The effect of provisions of this Act may be varied by agreement, except as otherwise provided in this Act and except that the obligations of good faith, diligence, reasonableness and care prescribed by this Act may not be disclaimed by agreement but the parties may by agreement determine the standards by

* The Code has been adopted in every state except Louisiana. It has also been adopted for Guam, the Virgin Islands, and the District of Columbia. Louisiana has adopted Articles 1, 3, 4, 7, 8, and 9 of the Code.

In 1972, a group of Amendments to the Code was recommended. These have now been adopted in all states and for Guam. The changes made by the 1972 Amendments to the UCC are confined mainly to Article 9 on secured transactions.

In 1977, Article 8 of the Code, relating to investment securities, was amended. This amended version was adopted by all states except Alabama. The Uniform Law Commissioners have adopted a 1994 Article 8 (Revised), in order to regulate the indirect holding system of securities. The following states have adopted this version: Alabama, Alaska, Arizona, Arkansas, California, Colorado, Idaho, Illinois, Indiana, Iowa, Kansas, Kentucky, Louisiana, Maryland, Massachusetts, Minnesota, Mississippi, Nebraska, New Mexico, Oklahoma, Oregon, Pennsylvania, Texas, Utah, Vermont, Virginia, Washington, West Virginia, and Wyoming.

Article 2A on leases was completed by the Uniform Law Commissioners in 1987 and amended in 1990. The 1987 act has been adopted by Florida and South Dakota. As of November 1994, the 1987 act with 1990 amendments has been adopted by Alabama, Alaska, Arizona, Arkansas, California, Colorado, Delaware, District of Columbia, Georgia, Hawaii, Idaho, Illinois, Indiana, Iowa, Kansas, Kentucky, Maine, Maryland, Massachusetts, Michigan, Minnesota, Mississippi, Missouri, Montana, Nebraska, Nevada, New Hampshire, New Jersey, New Mexico, New York, North Carolina, North Dakota, Ohio, Oklahoma, Oregon, Pennsylvania, Rhode Island, Tennessee, Texas, Utah, Vermont, Virginia, Washington, West Virginia, Wisconsin, and Wyoming.

Article 4A, Funds Transfers, has been adopted in all states, including the District of Columbia, as of February 1996.

The 1988 Article 6, Bulk Sales, Alternative A (repeal) has been adopted in Alabama, Alaska, Arkansas, Colorado, Connecticut, Delaware, Florida, Idaho, Illinois, Iowa, Kansas, Kentucky, Maine, Massachusetts, Minnesota, Mississippi, Montana, Nebraska, Nevada, New Hampshire, New Jersey, New Mexico, North Dakota, Ohio, Oregon, Pennsylvania, South Dakota, Texas, Utah, Vermont, Washington, West Virginia, and Wyoming. Alternative B (revision) has been adopted in Arizona, California, Hawaii, and Oklahoma. Louisiana never adopted Article 6.

The 1990 Article 3, Negotiable Instruments (Revised) and the 1990 Article 4 (Revised), Bank Collections, have been adopted in Alabama, Alaska, Arizona, Arkansas, California, Colorado, Connecticut, Delaware, District of Columbia, Florida, Georgia, Hawaii, Idaho, Illinois, Indiana, Iowa, Kansas, Kentucky, Louisiana, Maine, Michigan, Minnesota, Mississippi, Missouri, Montana, Nebraska, Nevada, New Hampshire, New Jersey, New Mexico, North Carolina, North Dakota, Ohio, Oklahoma, Oregon, Pennsylvania, South Dakota, Tennessee, Texas, Utah, Vermont, Virginia, Washington, West Virginia, Wisconsin, and Wyoming.

Revised Article 5 (1995) has been adopted by 14 states as of January 1997: Arizona, California, Colorado, Connecticut, Hawaii, Idaho, Illinois, Indiana, Iowa, Kansas, Mississippi, Nebraska, Oklahoma, and West Virginia.

which the performance of such obligations is to be measured if such standards are not manifestly unreasonable.

(4) The presence in certain provisions of this Act of the words "unless otherwise agreed" or words of similar import does not imply that the effect of other provisions may not be varied by agreement under subsection (3).

(5) In this Act unless the context otherwise requires

(a) words in the singular number include the plural, and in the plural include the singular;

(b) words of the masculine gender include the feminine and the neuter, and when the sense so indicates words of the neuter gender may refer to any gender.

§ 1—103. *Supplementary General Principles of Law Applicable.*

Unless displaced by the particular provisions of this Act, the principles of law and equity, including the law merchant and the law relative to capacity to contract, principal and agent, estoppel, fraud, misrepresentation, duress, coercion, mistake, bankruptcy, or other validating or invalidating cause shall supplement its provisions.

§ 1—104. *Construction Against Implicit Repeal.*

This Act being a general act intended as a unified coverage of its subject matter, no part of it shall be deemed to be impliedly repealed by subsequent legislation if such construction can reasonably be avoided.

§ 1—105. *Territorial Application of the Act; Parties' Power to Choose Applicable Law.*

(1) Except as provided hereafter in this section, when a transaction bears a reasonable relation to this state and also to another state or nation the parties may agree that the law either of this state or of such other state or nation shall govern their rights and duties. Failing such agreement this Act applies to transactions bearing an appropriate relation to this state.

(2) Where one of the following provisions of this Act specifies the applicable law, that provision governs and a contrary agreement is effective only to the extent permitted by the law (including the conflict of laws rules) so specified:

Rights of creditors against sold goods. Section 2—402.

Applicability of the Article on Leases. Sections 2A—105 and 2A—106.

Applicability of the Article on Bank Deposits and Collections. Section 4—102.

Governing law in the Article on Funds Transfers. Section 4A—507.

Letters of Credit, Section 5—116.

Bulk sales subject to the Article on Bulk Sales. Section 6—103.

Applicability of the Article on Investment Securities. Section 8—106.

Perfection provisions of the Article on Secured Transactions. Section 9—103.

§ 1—106. *Remedies to Be Liberally Administered.*

(1) The remedies provided by this Act shall be liberally administered to the end that the aggrieved party may be put in as good a position as if the other party had fully performed but neither consequential or special nor penal damages may be had except as specifically provided in this Act or by other rule of law.

(2) Any right or obligation declared by this Act is enforceable by action unless the provision declaring it specifies a different and limited effect.

§ 1—107. *Waiver or Renunciation of Claim or Right After Breach.*

Any claim or right arising out of an alleged breach can be discharged in whole or in part without consideration by a written waiver or renunciation signed and delivered by the aggrieved party.

§ 1—108. *Severability.*

If any provision or clause of this Act or application thereof to any person or circumstances is held invalid, such invalidity shall not affect other provisions or applications of the Act which can be given effect without the invalid provision or application, and to this end the provisions of this Act are declared to be severable.

§ 1—109. *Section Captions.*

Section captions are parts of this Act.

PART 2
General Definitions and Principles of Interpretation

§ 1—201. *General Definitions.*

Subject to additional definitions contained in the subsequent Articles of this Act which are applicable to specific Articles or Parts thereof, and unless the context otherwise requires, in this Act:

(1) "Action" in the sense of a judicial proceeding includes recoupment, counterclaim, set-off, suit in equity and any other proceedings in which rights are determined.

(2) "Aggrieved party" means a party entitled to resort to a remedy.

(3) "Agreement" means the bargain of the parties in fact as found in their language or by implication from other circumstances including course of dealing or usage of trade or course of performance as provided in this Act (Sections 1—205 and 2—208). Whether an agreement has legal consequences is determined by the provisions of this Act, if applicable; otherwise by the law of contracts (Section 1—103). (Compare "Contract.")

(4) "Bank" means any person engaged in the business of banking.

(5) "Bearer" means the person in possession of an instrument, document of title, or certificated security payable to bearer or indorsed in blank.

(6) "Bill of lading" means a document evidencing the receipt of goods for shipment issued by a person engaged in the business of transporting or forwarding goods, and includes an airbill. "Airbill" means a document serving for air transportation as a bill of lading does for marine or rail transportation, and includes an air consignment note or air waybill.

(7) "Branch" includes a separately incorporated foreign branch of a bank.

(8) "Burden of establishing" a fact means the burden of persuading the triers of fact that the existence of the fact is more probable than its non-existence.

(9) "Buyer in ordinary course of business" means a person who in good faith and without knowledge that the sale to him is in violation of the ownership rights or security interest of a third party in the goods buys in ordinary course from a person in the business of selling goods of that kind but does not include a pawnbroker. All persons who sell minerals or the like (including oil and

gas) at wellhead or minehead shall be deemed to be persons in the business of selling goods of that kind. "Buying" may be for cash or by exchange of other property or on secured or unsecured credit and includes receiving goods or documents of title under a pre-existing contract for sale but does not include a transfer in bulk or as security for or in total or partial satisfaction of a money debt.

(10) "Conspicuous": A term or clause is conspicuous when it is so written that a reasonable person against whom it is to operate ought to have noticed it. A printed heading in capitals (as: NON-NEGOTIABLE BILL OF LADING) is conspicuous. Language in the body of a form is "conspicuous" if it is in larger or other contrasting type or color. But in a telegram any stated term is "conspicuous." Whether a term or clause is "conspicuous" or not is for decision by the court.

(11) "Contract" means the total legal obligation which results from the parties' agreement as affected by this Act and any other applicable rules of law. (Compare "Agreement.")

(12) "Creditor" includes a general creditor, a secured creditor, a lien creditor and any representative of creditors, including an assignee for the benefit of creditors, a trustee in bankruptcy, a receiver in equity and an executor or administrator of an insolvent debtor's or assignor's estate.

(13) "Defendant" includes a person in the position of defendant in a cross-action or counterclaim.

(14) "Delivery" with respect to instruments, documents of title, chattel paper, or certificated securities means voluntary transfer of possession.

(15) "Document of title" includes bill of lading, dock warrant, dock receipt, warehouse receipt or order for the delivery of goods, and also any other document which in the regular course of business or financing is treated as adequately evidencing that the person in possession of it is entitled to receive, hold and dispose of the document and the goods it covers. To be a document of title a document must purport to be issued by or addressed to a bailee and purport to cover goods in the bailee's possession which are either identified or are fungible portions of an identified mass.

(16) "Fault" means wrongful act, omission or breach.

(17) "Fungible" with respect to goods or securities means goods or securities of which any unit is, by nature or usage of trade, the equivalent of any other like unit. Goods which are not fungible shall be deemed fungible for the purposes of this Act to the extent that under a particular agreement or document unlike units are treated as equivalents.

(18) "Genuine" means free of forgery or counterfeiting.

(19) "Good faith" means honesty in fact in the conduct or transaction concerned.

(20) "Holder" with respect to a negotiable instrument, means the person in possession if the instrument is payable to bearer or, in the cases of an instrument payable to an identified person, if the identified person is in possession. "Holder" with respect to a document of title means the person in possession if the goods are deliverable to bearer or to the order of the person in possession.

(21) To "honor" is to pay or to accept and pay, or where a credit so engages to purchase or discount a draft complying with the terms of the credit.

(22) "Insolvency proceedings" includes any assignment for the benefit of creditors or other proceedings intended to liquidate or rehabilitate the estate of the person involved.

(23) A person is "insolvent" who either has ceased to pay his debts in the ordinary course of business or cannot pay his debts as they become due or is insolvent within the meaning of the federal bankruptcy law.

(24) "Money" means a medium of exchange authorized or adopted by a domestic or foreign government and includes a monetary unit of account established by an intergovernmental organization or by agreement between two or more nations.

(25) A person has "notice" of a fact when

(a) he has actual knowledge of it; or

(b) he has received a notice or notification of it; or

(c) from all the facts and circumstances known to him at the time in question he has reason to know that it exists.

A person "knows" or has "knowledge" of a fact when he has actual knowledge of it. "Discover" or "learn" or a word or phrase of similar import refers to knowledge rather than to reason to know. The time and circumstances under which a notice or notification may cease to be effective are not determined by this Act.

(26) A person "notifies" or "gives" a notice or notification to another by taking such steps as may be reasonably required to inform the other in ordinary course whether or not such other actually comes to know of it. A person "receives" a notice or notification when

(a) it comes to his attention; or

(b) it is duly delivered at the place of business through which the contract was made or at any other place held out by him as the place for receipt of such communications.

(27) Notice, knowledge or a notice or notification received by an organization is effective for a particular transaction from the time when it is brought to the attention of the individual conducting that transaction, and in any event from the time when it would have been brought to his attention if the organization had exercised due diligence. An organization exercises due diligence if it maintains reasonable routines for communicating significant information to the person conducting the transaction and there is reasonable compliance with the routines. Due diligence does not require an individual acting for the organization to communicate information unless such communication is part of his regular duties or unless he has reason to know of the transaction and that the transaction would be materially affected by the information.

(28) "Organization" includes a corporation, government or governmental subdivision or agency, business trust, estate, trust, partnership or association, two or more persons having a joint or common interest, or any other legal or commercial entity.

(29) "Party," as distinct from "third party," means a person who has engaged in a transaction or made an agreement within this Act.

(30) "Person" includes an individual or an organization (See Section 1—102).

(31) "Presumption" or "presumed" means that the trier of fact must find the existence of the fact presumed unless and until evidence is introduced which would support a finding of its nonexistence.

(32) "Purchase" includes taking by sale, discount, negotiation, mortgage, pledge, lien, issue or re-issue, gift or any other voluntary transaction creating an interest in property.

(33) "Purchaser" means a person who takes by purchase.

(34) "Remedy" means any remedial right to which an aggrieved party is entitled with or without resort to a tribunal.

(35) "Representative" includes an agent, an officer of a corporation or association, and a trustee, executor or administrator of an estate, or any other person empowered to act for another.

(36) "Rights" includes remedies.

(37) "Security interest" means an interest in personal property or fixtures which secures payment or performance of an obligation. The retention or reservation of title by a seller of goods notwithstanding shipment or delivery to the buyer (Section 2—401) is limited in effect to a reservation of a "security interest." The term also includes any interest of a buyer of accounts or chattel paper which is subject to Article 9. The special property interest of a buyer of goods on identification of those goods to a contract for sale under Section 2—401 is not a "security interest," but a buyer may also acquire a "security interest" by complying with Article 9. Unless a consignment is intended as security, reservation of title thereunder is not a "security interest," but a consignment is in any event subject to the provisions on consignment sales (Section 2—326).

Whether a transaction creates a lease or security interest is determined by the facts of each case; however, a transaction creates a security interest if the consideration the lessee is to pay the lessor for the right to possession and use of the goods is an obligation for the term of the lease not subject to termination by the lessee, and

(a) the original term of the lease is equal to or greater than the remaining economic life of the goods,

(b) the lessee is bound to renew the lease for the remaining economic life of the goods or is bound to become the owner of the goods,

(c) the lessee has an option to renew the lease for the remaining economic life of the goods for no additional consideration or nominal additional consideration upon compliance with the lease agreement, or

(d) the lessee has an option to become the owner of the goods for no additional consideration or nominal additional consideration upon compliance with the lease agreement.

A transaction does not create a security interest merely because it provides that

(a) the present value of the consideration the lessee is obligated to pay the lessor for the right to possession and use of the goods is substantially equal to or is greater than the fair market value of the goods at the time the lease is entered into,

(b) the lessee assumes risk of loss of the goods, or agrees to pay taxes, insurance, filing, recording, or registration fees, or service or maintenance costs with respect to the goods,

(c) the lessee has an option to renew the lease or to become the owner of the goods,

(d) the lessee has an option to renew the lease for a fixed rent that is equal to or greater than the reasonably predictable fair market rent for the use of the goods for the term of the renewal at the time the option is to be performed, or

(e) the lessee has an option to become the owner of the goods for a fixed price that is equal to or greater than the reasonably predictable fair market value of the goods at the time the option is to be performed.

For purposes of this subsection (37):

(x) Additional consideration is not nominal if (i) when the option to renew the lease is granted to the lessee the rent is stated to be the fair market rent for the use of the goods for the term of the renewal determined at the time the option is to be performed, or (ii) when the option to become the owner of the goods is granted to the lessee the price is stated to be the fair market value of the goods determined at the time the option is to be performed. Additional consideration is nominal if it is less than the lessee's reasonably predictable cost of performing under the lease agreement if the option is not exercised;

(y) "Reasonably predictable" and "remaining economic life of the goods" are to be determined with reference to the facts and circumstances at the time the transaction is entered into; and

(z) "Present value" means the amount as of a date certain of one or more sums payable in the future, discounted to the date certain. The discount is determined by the interest rate specified by the parties if the rate is not manifestly unreasonable at the time the transaction is entered into; otherwise, the discount is determined by a commercially reasonable rate that takes into account the facts and circumstances of each case at the time the transaction was entered into.

(38) "Send" in connection with any writing or notice means to deposit in the mail or deliver for transmission by any other usual means of communication with postage or cost of transmission provided for and properly addressed and in the case of an instrument to an address specified thereon or otherwise agreed, or if there be none to any address reasonable under the circumstances. The receipt of any writing or notice within the time at which it would have arrived if properly sent has the effect of a proper sending.

(39) "Signed" includes any symbol executed or adopted by a party with present intention to authenticate a writing.

(40) "Surety" includes guarantor.

(41) "Telegram" includes a message transmitted by radio, teletype, cable, any mechanical method of transmission, or the like.

(42) "Term" means that portion of an agreement which relates to a particular matter.

(43) "Unauthorized" signature means one made without actual, implied or apparent authority and includes a forgery.

(44) "Value." Except as otherwise provided with respect to negotiable instruments and bank collections (Sections 3—303, 4—208 and 4—209) a person gives "value" for rights if he acquires them

(a) in return for a binding commitment to extend credit or for the extension of immediately available credit whether or not drawn upon and whether or not a chargeback is provided for in the event of difficulties in collection; or

(b) as security for or in total or partial satisfaction of a preexisting claim; or

(c) by accepting delivery pursuant to a preexisting contract for purchase; or

(d) generally, in return for any consideration sufficient to support a simple contract.

(45) "Warehouse receipt" means a receipt issued by a person engaged in the business of storing goods for hire.

(46) "Written" or "writing" includes printing, typewriting or any other intentional reduction to tangible form.

§1—202. Prima Facie Evidence by Third Party Documents.

A document in due form purporting to be a bill of lading, policy or certificate of insurance, official weigher's or inspector's certificate, consular invoice, or any other document authorized or required by the contract to be issued by a third party shall be prima facie evidence of its own authenticity and genuineness and of the facts stated in the document by the third party.

§ 1—203. Obligation of Good Faith.

Every contract or duty within this Act imposes an obligation of good faith in its performance or enforcement.

§ 1—204. Time; Reasonable Time; "Seasonably."

(1) Whenever this Act requires any action to be taken within a reasonable time, any time which is not manifestly unreasonable may be fixed by agreement.

(2) What is a reasonable time for taking any action depends on the nature, purpose and circumstances of such action.

(3) An action is taken "seasonably" when it is taken at or within the time agreed or if no time is agreed at or within a reasonable time.

§ 1—205. Course of Dealing and Usage of Trade.

(1) A course of dealing is a sequence of previous conduct between the parties to a particular transaction which is fairly to be regarded as establishing a common basis of understanding for interpreting their expressions and other conduct.

(2) A usage of trade is any practice or method of dealing having such regularity of observance in a place, vocation or trade as to justify an expectation that it will be observed with respect to the transaction in question. The existence and scope of such a usage are to be proved as facts. If it is established that such a usage is embodied in a written trade code or similar writing the interpretation of the writing is for the court.

(3) A course of dealing between parties and any usage of trade in the vocation or trade in which they are engaged or of which they are or should be aware give particular meaning to and supplement or qualify terms of an agreement.

(4) The express terms of an agreement and an applicable course of dealing or usage of trade shall be construed wherever reasonable as consistent with each other; but when such construction is unreasonable express terms control both course of dealing and usage of trade and course of dealing controls usage trade.

(5) An applicable usage of trade in the place where any part of performance is to occur shall be used in interpreting the agreement as to that part of the performance.

(6) Evidence of a relevant usage of trade offered by one party is not admissible unless and until he has given the other party such notice as the court finds sufficient to prevent unfair surprise to the latter.

§ 1—206. Statute of Frauds for Kinds of Personal Property Not Otherwise Covered.

(1) Except in the cases described in subsection (2) of this section a contract for the sale of personal property is not enforceable by way of action or defense beyond five thousand dollars in amount or value of remedy unless there is some writing which indicates that a contract for sale has been made between the parties at a defined or stated price, reasonably identifies the subject matter, and is signed by the party against whom enforcement is sought or by his authorized agent.

(2) Subsection (1) of this section does not apply to contracts for the sale of goods (Section 2—201) nor of securities (Section 8—319) nor to security agreements (Section 9—203).

§ 1—207. Performance or Acceptance Under Reservation of Rights.

(1) A party who with explicit reservation of rights performs or promises performance or assents to performance in a manner demanded or offered by the other party does not thereby prejudice the rights reserved. Such words as "without prejudice," "under protest" or the like are sufficient.

(2) Subsection (1) does not apply to an accord and satisfaction.

§ 1—208. Option to Accelerate at Will.

A term providing that one party or his successor in interest may accelerate payment or performance or require collateral or additional collateral "at will" or "when he deems himself insecure" or in words of similar import shall be construed to mean that he shall have power to do so only if he in good faith believes that the prospect of payment or performance is impaired. The burden of establishing lack of good faith is on the party against whom the power has been exercised.

§ 1—209. Subordinated Obligations.

An obligation may be issued as subordinated to payment of another obligation of the person obligated, or a creditor may subordinate his right to payment of an obligation by agreement with either the person obligated or another creditor of the person obligated. Such a subordination does not create a security interest as against either the common debtor or a subordinated creditor. This section shall be construed as declaring the law as it existed prior to the enactment of this section and not as modifying it. Added 1966.

ARTICLE 2
SALES

PART 1
Short Title, General Construction and Subject Matter

§ 2—101. Short Title.

This Article shall be known and may be cited as Uniform Commercial Code—Sales.

§ 2—102. Scope; Certain Security and Other Transactions Excluded From This Article.

Unless the context otherwise requires, this Article applies to transactions in goods; it does not apply to any transaction which although in the form of an unconditional contract to sell or present sale is intended to operate only as a security transaction nor does this Article impair or repeal any statute regulating sales to consumers, farmers or other specified classes of buyers.

§ 2—103. Definitions and Index of Definitions.

(1) In this Article unless the context otherwise requires

(a) "Buyer" means a person who buys or contracts to buy goods.

(b) "Good faith" in the case of a merchant means honesty in fact and the observance of reasonable commercial standards of fair dealing in the trade.

(c) "Receipt" of goods means taking physical possession of them.

(d) "Seller" means a person who sells or contracts to sell goods.

(2) Other definitions applying to this Article or to specified Parts thereof, and the sections in which they appear are:

"Acceptance." Section 2—606.
"Banker's credit." Section 2—325.
"Between merchants." Section 2—104.
"Cancellation." Section 2—106(4).
"Commercial unit." Section 2—105.
"Confirmed credit." Section 2—325.
"Conforming to contract." Section 2—106.
"Contract for sale." Section 2—106.
"Cover." Section 2—712.
"Entrusting." Section 2—403.
"Financing agency." Section 2—104.
"Future goods." Section 2—105.
"Goods." Section 2—105.
"Identification." Section 2—501.
"Installment contract." Section 2—612.
"Letter of Credit." Section 2—325.
"Lot." Section 2—105.
"Merchant." Section 2—104.
"Overseas." Section 2—323.
"Person in position of seller." Section 2—707.
"Present sale." Section 2—106.
"Sale." Section 2—106.
"Sale on approval." Section 2—326.
"Sale or return." Section 2—326.
"Termination." Section 2—106.

(3) The following definitions in other Articles apply to this Article:

"Check." Section 3—104.
"Consignee." Section 7—102.
"Consignor." Section 7—102.
"Consumer goods." Section 9—109.
"Dishonor." Section 3—507.
"Draft." Section 3—104.

(4) In addition Article 1 contains general definitions and principles of construction and interpretation applicable throughout this Article.

§ 2—104. *Definitions: "Merchant"; "Between Merchants"; "Financing Agency."*

(1) "Merchant" means a person who deals in goods of the kind or otherwise by his occupation holds himself out as having knowledge or skill peculiar to the practices or goods involved in the transaction or to whom such knowledge or skill may be attributed by his employment of an agent or broker or other intermediary who by his occupation holds himself out as having such knowledge or skill.

(2) "Financing agency" means a bank, finance company or other person who in the ordinary course of business makes advances against goods or documents of title or who by arrangement with either the seller or the buyer intervenes in ordinary course to make or collect payment due or claimed under the contract for sale, as by purchasing or paying the seller's draft or making advances against it or by merely taking it for collection whether or not documents of title accompany the draft. "Financing agency" includes also a bank or other person who similarly intervenes between persons who are in the position of seller and buyer in respect to the goods (Section 2—707).

(3) "Between merchants" means in any transaction with respect to which both parties are chargeable with the knowledge or skill of merchants.

§ 2—105. *Definitions: Transferability; "Goods"; "Future" Goods; "Lot"; "Commercial Unit."*

(1) "Goods" means all things (including specially manufactured goods) which are movable at the time of identification to the contract for sale other than the money in which the price is to be paid, investment securities (Article 8) and things in action. "Goods" also includes the unborn young of animals and growing crops and other identified things attached to realty as described in the section on goods to be severed from realty (Section 2—107).

(2) Goods must be both existing and identified before any interest in them can pass. Goods which are not both existing and identified are "future" goods. A purported present sale of future goods or of any interest therein operates as a contract to sell.

(3) There may be a sale of a part interest in existing identified goods.

(4) An undivided share in an identified bulk of fungible goods is sufficiently identified to be sold although the quantity of the bulk is not determined. Any agreed proportion of such a bulk or any quantity thereof agreed upon by number, weight or other measure may to the extent of the seller's interest in the bulk be sold to the buyer who then becomes an owner in common.

(5) "Lot" means a parcel or a single article which is the subject matter of a separate sale or delivery, whether or not it is sufficient to perform the contract.

(6) "Commercial unit" means such a unit of goods as by commercial usage is a single whole for purposes of sale and division of which materially impairs its character or value on the market or in use. A commercial unit may be a single article (as a machine) or a set of articles (as a suite of furniture or an assortment of sizes) or a quantity (as a bale, gross, or carload) or any other unit treated in use or in the relevant market as a single whole.

§ 2—106. *Definitions: "Contract"; "Agreement"; "Contract for Sale"; "Sale"; "Present Sale"; "Conforming" to Contract; "Termination"; "Cancellation."*

(1) In this Article unless the context otherwise requires "contract" and "agreement" are limited to those relating to the present or future sale of goods. "Contract for sale" includes both a present sale of goods and a contract to sell goods at a future time. A "sale" consists in the passing of title from the seller to the buyer for a price (Section 2—401). A "present sale" means a sale which is accomplished by the making of the contract.

(2) Goods or conduct including any part of a performance are "conforming" or conform to the contract when they are in accordance with the obligations under the contract.

(3) "Termination" occurs when either party pursuant to a power created by agreement or law puts an end to the contract otherwise than for its breach. On "termination" all obligations which are still executory on both sides are discharged but any right based on prior breach or performance survives.

(4) "Cancellation" occurs when either party puts an end to the contract for breach by the other and its effect is the same as

that of "termination" except that the cancelling party also retains any remedy for breach of the whole contract or any unperformed balance.

§ 2—107. *Goods to Be Severed From Realty: Recording.*

(1) A contract for the sale of minerals or the like (including oil and gas) or a structure or its materials to be removed from realty is a contract for the sale of goods within this Article if they are to be severed by the seller but until severance a purported present sale thereof which is not effective as a transfer of an interest in land is effective only as a contract to sell.

(2) A contract for the sale apart from the land of growing crops or other things attached to realty and capable of severance without material harm thereto but not described in subsection (1) or of timber to be cut is a contract for the sale of goods within this Article whether the subject matter is to be severed by the buyer or by the seller even though it forms part of the realty at the time of contracting, and the parties can by identification effect a present sale before severance.

(3) The provisions of this section are subject to any third party rights provided by the law relating to realty records, and the contract for sale may be executed and recorded as a document transferring an interest in land and shall then constitute notice to third parties of the buyer's rights under the contract for sale.

PART 2

Form, Formation and Readjustment of Contract

§ 2—201. *Formal Requirements; Statute of Frauds.*

(1) Except as otherwise provided in this section a contract for the sale of goods for the price of $500 or more is not enforceable by way of action or defense unless there is some writing sufficient to indicate that a contract for sale has been made between the parties and signed by the party against whom enforcement is sought or by his authorized agent or broker. A writing is not insufficient because it omits or incorrectly states a term agreed upon but the contract is not enforceable under this paragraph beyond the quantity of goods shown in such writing.

(2) Between merchants if within a reasonable time a writing in confirmation of the contract and sufficient against the sender is received and the party receiving it has reason to know its contents, its satisfies the requirements of subsection (1) against such party unless written notice of objection to its contents is given within ten days after it is received.

(3) A contract which does not satisfy the requirements of subsection (1) but which is valid in other respects is enforceable

(a) if the goods are to be specially manufactured for the buyer and are not suitable for sale to others in the ordinary course of the seller's business and the seller, before notice of repudiation is received and under circumstances which reasonably indicate that the goods are for the buyer, has made either a substantial beginning of their manufacture or commitments for their procurement; or

(b) if the party against whom enforcement is sought admits in his pleading, testimony or otherwise in court that a contract for sale was made, but the contract is not enforceable under this provision beyond the quantity of goods admitted; or

(c) with respect to goods for which payment has been made and accepted or which have been received and accepted (Sec. 2—606).

§ 2—202. *Final Written Expression: Parol or Extrinsic Evidence.*

Terms with respect to which the confirmatory memoranda of the parties agree or which are otherwise set forth in a writing intended by the parties as a final expression of their agreement with respect to such terms as are included therein may not be contradicted by evidence of any prior agreement or of a contemporaneous oral agreement but may be explained or supplemented

(a) by course of dealing or usage of trade (Section 1—205) or by course of performance (Section 2—208); and

(b) by evidence of consistent additional terms unless the court finds the writing to have been intended also as a complete and exclusive statement of the terms of the agreement.

§ 2—203. *Seals Inoperative.*

The affixing of a seal to a writing evidencing a contract for sale or an offer to buy or sell goods does not constitute the writing a sealed instrument and the law with respect to sealed instruments does not apply to such a contract or offer.

§ 2—204. *Formation in General.*

(1) A contract for sale of goods may be made in any manner sufficient to show agreement, including conduct by both parties which recognizes the existence of such a contract.

(2) An agreement sufficient to constitute a contract for sale may be found even though the moment of its making is undetermined.

(3) Even though one or more terms are left open a contract for sale does not fail for indefiniteness if the parties have intended to make a contract and there is a reasonably certain basis for giving an appropriate remedy.

§ 2—205. *Firm Offers.*

An offer by a merchant to buy or sell goods in a signed writing which by its terms gives assurance that it will be held open is not revocable, for lack of consideration, during the time stated or if no time is stated for a reasonable time, but in no event may such period of irrevocability exceed three months; but any such term of assurance on a form supplied by the offeree must be separately signed by the offeror.

§ 2—206. *Offer and Acceptance in Formation of Contract.*

(1) Unless other unambiguously indicated by the language or circumstances

(a) an offer to make a contract shall be construed as inviting acceptance in any manner and by any medium reasonable in the circumstances;

(b) an order or other offer to buy goods for prompt or current shipment shall be construed as inviting acceptance either by a prompt promise to ship or by the prompt or current shipment of conforming or non-conforming goods, but such a shipment of non-conforming goods does not constitute an acceptance if the seller seasonably notifies the buyer that the shipment is offered only as an accommodation to the buyer.

(2) Where the beginning of a requested performance is a reasonable mode of acceptance an offeror who is not notified of acceptance within a reasonable time may treat the offer as having lapsed before acceptance.

§ 2—207. *Additional Terms in Acceptance or Confirmation.*

(1) A definite and seasonable expression of acceptance or a written confirmation which is sent within a reasonable time oper-

ates as an acceptance even though it states terms additional to or different from those offered or agreed upon, unless acceptance is expressly made conditional on assent to the additional or different terms.

(2) The additional terms are to be construed as proposals for addition to the contract. Between merchants such terms become part of the contract unless:

(a) the offer expressly limits acceptance to the terms of the offer;

(b) they materially alter it; or

(c) notification of objection to them has already been given or is given within a reasonable time after notice of them is received.

(3) Conduct by both parties which recognizes the existence of a contract is sufficient to establish a contract for sale although the writings of the parties do not otherwise establish a contract. In such case the terms of the particular contract consist of those terms on which the writings of the parties agree, together with any supplementary terms incorporated under any other provisions of this Act.

§ 2—208. *Course of Performance or Practical Construction.*

(1) Where the contract for sale involves repeated occasions for performance by either party with knowledge of the nature of the performance and opportunity for objection to it by the other, any course of performance accepted or acquiesced in without objection shall be relevant to determine the meaning of the agreement.

(2) The express terms of the agreement and any such course of performance, as well as any course of dealing and usage of trade, shall be construed whenever reasonable as consistent with each other; but when such construction is unreasonable, express terms shall control course of performance and course of performance shall control both course of dealing and usage of trade (Section 1—205).

(3) Subject to the provisions of the next section on modification and waiver, such course of performance shall be relevant to show a waiver or modification of any term inconsistent with such course of performance.

§ 2—209. *Modification, Rescission and Waiver.*

(1) An agreement modifying a contract within this Article needs no consideration to be binding.

(2) A signed agreement which excludes modification or rescission except by a signed writing cannot be otherwise modified or rescinded, but except as between merchants such a requirement on a form supplied by the merchant must be separately signed by the other party.

(3) The requirements of the statute of frauds section of this Article (Section 2—201) must be satisfied if the contract as modified is within its provisions.

(4) Although an attempt at modification or rescission does not satisfy the requirements of subsection (2) or (3) it can operate as a waiver.

(5) A party who has made a waiver affecting an executory portion of the contract may retract the waiver by reasonable notification received by the other party that strict performance will be required of any term waived, unless the retraction would be unjust in view of a material change of position in reliance on the waiver.

§ 2—210. *Delegation of Performance; Assignment of Rights.*

(1) A party may perform his duty through a delegate unless otherwise agreed or unless the other party has a substantial interest in having his original promisor perform or control the acts required by the contract. No delegation of performance relieves the party delegating of any duty to perform or any liability for breach.

(2) Unless otherwise agreed all rights of either seller or buyer can be assigned except where the assignment would materially change the duty of the other party, or increase materially the burden or risk imposed on him by his contract, or impair materially his chance of obtaining return performance. A right to damages for breach of the whole contract or a right arising out of the assignor's due performance of his entire obligation can be assigned despite agreement otherwise.

(3) Unless the circumstances indicate the contrary a prohibition of assignment of "the contract" is to be construed as barring only the delegation to the assignee of the assignor's performance.

(4) An assignment of "the contract" or of "all my rights under the contract" or an assignment in similar general terms is an assignment of rights and unless the language or the circumstances (as in an assignment for security) indicate the contrary, it is a delegation of performance of the duties of the assignor and its acceptance by the assignee constitutes a promise by him to perform those duties. This promise is enforceable by either the assignor or the other party to the original contract.

(5) The other party may treat any assignment which delegates performance as creating reasonable grounds for insecurity and may without prejudice to his rights against the assignor demand assurances from the assignee (Section 2—609).

PART 3

General Obligation and Construction of Contract

§ 2—301. *General Obligations of Parties.*

The obligation of the seller is to transfer and deliver and that of the buyer is to accept and pay in accordance with the contract.

§ 2—302. *Unconscionable Contract or Clause.*

(1) If the court as a matter of law finds the contract or any clause of the contract to have been unconscionable at the time it was made the court may refuse to enforce the contract, or it may enforce the remainder of the contract without the unconscionable clause, or it may so limit the application of any unconscionable clause as to avoid any unconscionable result.

(2) When it is claimed or appears to the court that the contract or any clause thereof may be unconscionable the parties shall be afforded a reasonable opportunity to present evidence as to its commercial setting, purpose and effect to aid the court in making the determination.

§ 2—303. *Allocations or Division of Risks.*

Where this Article allocates a risk or a burden as between the parties "unless otherwise agreed," the agreement may not only shift the allocation but may also divide the risk or burden.

§ 2—304. *Price Payable in Money, Goods, Realty, or Otherwise.*

(1) The price can be made payable in money or otherwise. If it is payable in whole or in part in goods each party is a seller of the goods which he is to transfer.

(2) Even though all or part of the price is payable in an interest in realty the transfer of the goods and the seller's obligations

with reference to them are subject to this Article, but not the transfer of the interest in realty or the transferor's obligations in connection therewith.

§ 2—305. *Open Price Term.*

(1) The parties if they so intend can conclude a contract for sale even though the price is not settled. In such a case the price is a reasonable price at the time for delivery if

(a) nothing is said as to price; or

(b) the price is left to be agreed by the parties and they fail to agree; or

(c) the price is to be fixed in terms of some agreed market or other standard as set or recorded by a third person or agency and it is not so set or recorded.

(2) A price to be fixed by the seller or by the buyer means a price for him to fix in good faith.

(3) When a price left to be fixed otherwise than by agreement of the parties fails to be fixed through fault of one party the other may at his option treat the contract as cancelled or himself fix a reasonable price.

(4) Where, however, the parties intend not to be bound unless the price be fixed or agreed and it is not fixed or agreed there is no contract. In such a case the buyer must return any goods already received or if unable so to do must pay their reasonable value at the time of delivery and the seller must return any portion of the price paid on account.

§ 2—306. *Output, Requirements and Exclusive Dealings.*

(1) A term which measures the quantity by the output of the seller or the requirements of the buyer means such actual output or requirements as may occur in good faith, except that no quantity unreasonably disproportionate to any stated estimate or in the absence of a stated estimate to any normal or otherwise comparable prior output or requirements may be tendered or demanded.

(2) A lawful agreement by either the seller or the buyer for exclusive dealing in the kind of goods concerned imposes unless otherwise agreed an obligation by the seller to use best efforts to supply the goods and by the buyer to use best efforts to promote their sale.

§ 2—307. *Delivery in Single Lot or Several Lots.*

Unless otherwise agreed all goods called for by a contract for sale must be tendered in a single delivery and payment is due only on such tender but where the circumstances give either party the right to make or demand delivery in lots the price if it can be apportioned may be demanded for each lot.

§ 2—308. *Absence of Specified Place for Delivery.*

Unless otherwise agreed

(a) the place for delivery of goods is the seller's place of business or if he has none his residence; but

(b) in a contract for sale of identified goods which to the knowledge of the parties at the time of contracting are in some other place, that place is the place for their delivery; and

(c) documents of title may be delivered through customary banking channels.

§ 2—309. *Absence of Specific Time Provisions; Notice of Termination.*

(1) The time for shipment or delivery or any other action under a contract if not provided in this Article or agreed upon shall be a reasonable time.

(2) Where the contract provides for successive performances but is indefinite in duration it is valid for a reasonable time but unless otherwise agreed may be terminated at any time by either party.

(3) Termination of a contract by one party except on the happening of an agreed event requires that reasonable notification be received by the other party and an agreement dispensing with notification is invalid if its operation would be unconscionable.

§ 2—310. *Open Time for Payment or Running of Credit; Authority to Ship Under Reservation.*

Unless otherwise agreed

(a) payment is due at the time and place at which the buyer is to receive the goods even though the place of shipment is the place of delivery; and

(b) if the seller is authorized to send the goods he may ship them under reservation, and may tender the documents of title, but the buyer may inspect the goods after their arrival before payment is due unless such inspection is inconsistent with the terms of the contract (Section 2—513); and

(c) if delivery is authorized and made by way of documents of title otherwise than by subsection (b) then payment is due at the time and place at which the buyer is to receive the documents regardless of where the goods are to be received; and

(d) where the seller is required or authorized to ship the goods on credit the credit period runs from the time of shipment but post-dating the invoice or delaying its dispatch will correspondingly delay the starting of the credit period.

§ 2—311. *Options and Cooperation Respecting Performance.*

(1) An agreement for sale which is otherwise sufficiently definite (subsection (3) of Section 2—204) to be a contract is not made invalid by the fact that it leaves particulars of performance to be specified by one of the parties. Any such specification must be made in good faith and within limits set by commercial reasonableness.

(2) Unless otherwise agreed specifications relating to assortment of the goods are at the buyer's option and except as otherwise provided in subsections (1)(c) and (3) of Section 2—319 specifications or arrangements relating to shipment are at the seller's option.

(3) Where such specification would materially affect the other party's performance but is not seasonably made or where one party's cooperation is necessary to the agreed performance of the other but is not seasonably forthcoming, the other party in addition to all other remedies

(a) is excused for any resulting delay in his own performance; and

(b) may also either proceed to perform in any reasonable manner or after the time for a material part of his own performance treat the failure to specify or to cooperate as a breach by failure to deliver or accept the goods.

§ 2—312. *Warranty of Title and Against Infringement; Buyer's Obligation Against Infringement.*

(1) Subject to subsection (2) there is in a contract for sale a warranty by the seller that

(a) the title conveyed shall be good, and its transfer rightful; and

(b) the goods shall be delivered free from any security interest or other lien or encumbrance of which the buyer at the time of contracting has no knowledge.

(2) A warranty under subsection (1) will be excluded or modified only by specific language or by circumstances which give the buyer reason to know that the person selling does not claim title in himself or that he is purporting to sell only such right or title as he or a third person may have.

(3) Unless otherwise agreed a seller who is a merchant regularly dealing in goods of the kind warrants that the goods shall be delivered free of the rightful claim of any third person by way of infringement or the like but a buyer who furnishes specifications to the seller must hold the seller harmless against any such claim which arises out of compliance with the specifications.

§ 2—313. *Express Warranties by Affirmation, Promise, Description, Sample.*

(1) Express warranties by the seller are created as follows:

(a) Any affirmation of fact or promise made by the seller to the buyer which relates to the goods and becomes part of the basis of the bargain creates an express warranty that the goods shall conform to the affirmation or promise.

(b) Any description of the goods which is made part of the basis of the bargain creates an express warranty that the goods shall conform to the description.

(c) Any sample or model which is made part of the basis of the bargain creates an express warranty that the whole of the goods shall conform to the sample or model.

(2) It is not necessary to the creation of an express warranty that the seller use formal words such as "warrant" or "guarantee" or that he have a specific intention to make a warranty, but an affirmation merely of the value of the goods or a statement purporting to be merely the seller's opinion or commendation of the goods does not create a warranty.

§ 2—314. *Implied Warranty: Merchantability; Usage of Trade.*

(1) Unless excluded or modified (Section 2—316), a warranty that the goods shall be merchantable is implied in a contract for their sale if the seller is a merchant with respect to goods of that kind. Under this section the serving for value of food or drink to be consumed either on the premises or elsewhere is a sale.

(2) Goods to be merchantable must be at least such as

(a) pass without objection in the trade under the contract description; and

(b) in the case of fungible goods, are of fair average quality within the description; and

(c) are fit for the ordinary purposes for which such goods are used; and

(d) run, within the variations permitted by the agreement, of even kind, quality and quantity within each unit and among all units involved; and

(e) are adequately contained, packaged, and labeled as the agreement may require; and

(f) conform to the promises or affirmations of fact made on the container or label if any.

(3) Unless excluded or modified (Section 2—316) other implied warranties may arise from course of dealing or usage of trade.

§ 2—315. *Implied Warranty: Fitness for Particular Purpose.*

Where the seller at the time of contracting has reason to know any particular purpose for which the goods are required and that the buyer is relying on the seller's skill or judgment to select or furnish suitable goods, there is unless excluded or modified under the next section an implied warranty that the goods shall be fit for such purpose.

§ 2—316. *Exclusion or Modification of Warranties.*

(1) Words or conduct relevant to the creation of an express warranty and words or conduct tending to negate or limit warranty shall be construed wherever reasonable as consistent with each other; but subject to the provisions of this Article on parol or extrinsic evidence (Section 2—202) negation or limitation is inoperative to the extent that such construction is unreasonable.

(2) Subject to subsection (3), to exclude or modify the implied warranty of merchantability or any part of it the language must mention merchantability and in case of a writing must be conspicuous, and to exclude or modify any implied warranty of fitness the exclusion must be by a writing and conspicuous. Language to exclude all implied warranties of fitness is sufficient if it states, for example, that "There are no warranties which extend beyond the description on the face hereof."

(3) Notwithstanding subsection (2)

(a) unless the circumstances indicate otherwise, all implied warranties are excluded by expressions like "as is," "with all faults" or other language which in common understanding calls the buyer's attention to the exclusion of warranties and makes plain that there is no implied warranty; and

(b) when the buyer before entering into the contract has examined the goods or the sample or model as fully as he desired or has refused to examine the goods there is no implied warranty with regard to defects which an examination ought in the circumstances to have revealed to him; and

(c) an implied warranty can also be excluded or modified by course of dealing or course of performance or usage of trade.

(4) Remedies for breach of warranty can be limited in accordance with the provisions of this Article on liquidation or limitation of damages and on contractual modification of remedy (Sections 2—718 and 2—719).

§ 2—317. *Cumulation and Conflict of Warranties Express or Implied.*

Warranties whether express or implied shall be construed as consistent with each other and as cumulative, but if such construction is unreasonable the intention of the parties shall determine which warranty is dominant. In ascertaining that intention the following rules apply:

(a) Exact or technical specifications displace an inconsistent sample or model or general language of description.

(b) A sample from an existing bulk displaces inconsistent general language of description.

(c) Express warranties displace inconsistent implied warranties other than an implied warranty of fitness for a particular purpose.

§ 2—318. *Third Party Beneficiaries of Warranties Express or Implied.*

Alternative A

A seller's warranty whether express or implied extends to any natural person who is in the family or household of his buyer or who is a guest in his home if it is reasonable to expect that such person may use, consume or be affected by the goods and who is injured in person by breach of the warranty. A seller may not exclude or limit the operation of this section.

Alternative B

A seller's warranty whether express or implied extends to any natural person who may reasonably be expected to use, consume or be affected by the goods and who is injured in person by breach of the warranty. A seller may not exclude or limit the operation of this section.

Alternative C

A seller's warranty whether express or implied extends to any person who may reasonably be expected to use, consume or be affected by the goods and who is injured by breach of the warranty. A seller may not exclude or limit the operation of this section with respect to injury to the person of an individual to whom the warranty extends. As amended 1966.

§ 2—319. *F.O.B. and F.A.S. Terms.*

(1) Unless otherwise agreed the term F.O.B. (which means "free on board") at a named place, even though used only in connection with the stated price, is a delivery term under which

(a) when the term is F.O.B. the place of shipment, the seller must at that place ship the goods in the manner provided in this Article (Section 2—504) and bear the expense and risk of putting them into the possession of the carrier; or

(b) when the term is F.O.B. the place of destination, the seller must at his own expense and risk transport the goods to that place and there tender delivery of them in the manner provided in this Article (Section 2—503);

(c) when under either (a) or (b) the term is also F.O.B. vessel, car or other vehicle, the seller must in addition at his own expense and risk load the goods on board. If the term is F.O.B. vessel the buyer must name the vessel and in an appropriate case the seller must comply with the provisions of this Article on the form of bill of lading (Section 2—323).

(2) Unless otherwise agreed the term F.A.S. vessel (which means "free alongside") at a named port, even though used only in connection with the stated price, is a delivery term under which the seller must

(a) at his own expense and risk deliver the goods alongside the vessel in the manner usual in that port or on a dock designated and provided by the buyer; and

(b) obtain and tender a receipt for the goods in exchange for which the carrier is under a duty to issue a bill of lading.

(3) Unless otherwise agreed in any case falling within subsection (1)(a) or (c) or subsection (2) the buyer must seasonably give any needed instructions for making delivery, including when the term is F.A.S. or F.O.B. the loading berth of the vessel and in an appropriate case its name and sailing date. The seller may treat the failure of needed instructions as a failure of cooperation under this Article (Section 2—311). He may also at his option move the goods in any reasonable manner preparatory to delivery or shipment.

(4) Under the term F.O.B. vessel or F.A.S. unless otherwise agreed the buyer must make payment against tender of the required documents and the seller may not tender nor the buyer demand delivery of the goods in substitution for the documents.

§ 2—320. *C.I.F. and C. & F. Terms.*

(1) The term C.I.F. means that the price includes in a lump sum the cost of the goods and the insurance and freight to the named destination. The term C. & F. or C.F. means that the price so includes cost and freight to the named destination.

(2) Unless otherwise agreed and even though used only in connection with the stated price and destination, the term C.I.F. destination or its equivalent requires the seller at his own expense and risk to

(a) put the goods into the possession of a carrier at the port for shipment and obtain a negotiable bill or bills of lading covering the entire transportation to the named destination; and

(b) load the goods and obtain a receipt from the carrier (which may be contained in the bill of lading) showing that the freight has been paid or provided for; and

(c) obtain a policy or certificate of insurance, including any war risk insurance, of a kind and on terms then current at the port of shipment in the usual amount, in the currency of the contract, shown to cover the same goods covered by the bill of lading and providing for payment of loss to the order of the buyer or for the account of whom it may concern; but the seller may add to the price the amount of the premium for any such war risk insurance; and

(d) prepare an invoice of the goods and procure any other documents required to effect shipment or to comply with the contract; and

(e) forward and tender with commercial promptness all the documents in due form and with any indorsement necessary to perfect the buyer's rights.

(3) Unless otherwise agreed the term C. & F. or its equivalent has the same effect and imposes upon the seller the same obligations and risks as a C.I.F. term except the obligation as to insurance.

(4) Under the term C.I.F. or C. & F. unless otherwise agreed the buyer must make payment against tender of the required documents and the seller may not tender nor the buyer demand delivery of the goods in substitution for the documents.

§ 2—321. *C.I.F. or C. & F.: "Net Landed Weights"; "Payment on Arrival"; Warranty of Condition on Arrival.*

Under a contract containing a term C.I.F. or C. & F.

(1) Where the price is based on or is to be adjusted according to "net landed weights," "delivered weights," "out turn" quantity or quality or the like, unless otherwise agreed the seller must reasonably estimate the price. The payment due on tender of the documents called for by the contract is the amount so estimated, but after final adjustment of the price a settlement must be made with commercial promptness.

(2) An agreement described in subsection (1) or any warranty of quality or condition of the goods on arrival places upon the seller the risk of ordinary deterioration, shrinkage and the like in transportation but has no effect on the place or time of identification to the contract for sale or delivery or on the passing of the risk of loss.

(3) Unless otherwise agreed where the contract provides for payment on or after arrival of the goods the seller must before payment allow such preliminary inspection as is feasible; but if the goods are lost delivery of the documents and payment are due when the goods should have arrived.

§ 2—322. *Delivery "Ex-Ship."*

(1) Unless otherwise agreed a term for delivery of goods "ex-ship" (which means from the carrying vessel) or in equivalent language is not restricted to a particular ship and requires de-

livery from a ship which has reached a place at the named port of destination where goods of the kind are usually discharged.

(2) Under such a term unless otherwise agreed

(a) the seller must discharge all liens arising out of the carriage and furnish the buyer with a direction which puts the carrier under a duty to deliver the goods; and

(b) the risk of loss does not pass to the buyer until the goods leave the ship's tackle or are otherwise properly unloaded.

§ 2—323. *Form of Bill of Lading Required in 1270Overseas Shipment; "Overseas."*

(1) Where the contract contemplates overseas shipment and contains a term C.I.F. or C. & F. or F.O.B. vessel, the seller unless otherwise agreed must obtain a negotiable bill of lading stating that the goods have been loaded on board or, in the case of a term C.I.F. or C. & F., received for shipment.

(2) Where in a case within subsection (1) a bill of lading has been issued in a set of parts, unless otherwise agreed if the documents are not to be sent from abroad the buyer may demand tender of the full set; otherwise only one part of the bill of lading need be tendered. Even if the agreement expressly requires a full set

(a) due tender of a single part is acceptable within the provisions of this Article on cure of improper delivery (subsection (1) of Section 2—508); and

(b) even though the full set is demanded, if the documents are sent from abroad the person tendering an incomplete set may nevertheless require payment upon furnishing an indemnity which the buyer in good faith deems adequate.

(3) A shipment by water or by air or a contract contemplating such shipment is "overseas" insofar as by usage of trade or agreement it is subject to the commercial, financing or shipping practices characteristic of international deep water commerce.

§ 2—324. *"No Arrival, No Sale" Term.*

Under a term "no arrival, no sale" or terms of like meaning, unless otherwise agreed,

(a) the seller must properly ship conforming goods and if they arrive by any means he must tender them on arrival but he assumes no obligation that the goods will arrive unless he has caused the non-arrival; and

(b) where without fault of the seller the goods are in part lost or have so deteriorated as no longer to conform to the contract or arrive after the contract time, the buyer may proceed as if there had been casualty to identified goods (Section 2—613).

§ 2—325. *"Letter of Credit" Term; "Confirmed Credit."*

(1) Failure of the buyer seasonably to furnish an agreed letter of credit is a breach of the contract for sale.

(2) The delivery to seller of a proper letter of credit suspends the buyer's obligation to pay. If the letter of credit is dishonored, the seller may on seasonable notification to the buyer require payment directly from him.

(3) Unless otherwise agreed the term "letter of credit" or "banker's credit" in a contract for sale means an irrevocable credit issued by a financing agency of good repute and, where the shipment is overseas, of good international repute. The term "confirmed credit" means that the credit must also carry the direct obligation of such an agency which does business in the seller's financial market.

§ 2—326. *Sale on Approval and Sale or Return; Consignment Sales and Rights of Creditors.*

(1) Unless otherwise agreed, if delivered goods may be returned by the buyer even though they conform to the contract, the transaction is

(a) a "sale on approval" if the goods are delivered primarily for use, and

(b) a "sale or return" if the goods are delivered primarily for resale.

(2) Except as provided in subsection (3), goods held on approval are not subject to the claims of the buyer's creditors until acceptance; goods held on sale or return are subject to such claims while in the buyer's possession.

(3) Where goods are delivered to a person for sale and such person maintains a place of business at which he deals in goods of the kind involved, under a name other than the name of the person making delivery, then with respect to claims of creditors of the person conducting the business the goods are deemed to be on sale or return. The provisions of this subsection are applicable even though an agreement purports to reserve title to the person making delivery until payment or resale or uses such words as "on consignment" or "on memorandum." However, this subsection is not applicable if the person making delivery

(a) complies with an applicable law providing for a consignor's interest or the like to be evidenced by a sign, or

(b) establishes that the person conducting the business is generally known by his creditors to be substantially engaged in selling the goods of others, or

(c) complies with the filing provisions of the Article on Secured Transactions (Article 9).

(4) Any "or return" term of a contract for sale is to be treated as a separate contract for sale within the statute of frauds section of this Article (Section 2—201) and as contradicting the sale aspect of the contract within the provisions of this Article on parol or extrinsic evidence (Section 2—202).

§ 2—327. *Special Incidents of Sale on Approval and Sale or Return.*

(1) Under a sale on approval unless otherwise agreed

(a) although the goods are identified to the contract the risk of loss and the title do not pass to the buyer until acceptance; and

(b) use of the goods consistent with the purpose of trial is not acceptance but failure seasonably to notify the seller of election to return the goods is acceptance, and if the goods conform to the contract acceptance of any part is acceptance of the whole; and

(c) after due notification of election to return, the return is at the seller's risk and expense but a merchant buyer must follow any reasonable instructions.

(2) Under a sale or return unless otherwise agreed

(a) the option to return extends to the whole or any commercial unit of the goods while in substantially their original condition, but must be exercised seasonably; and

(b) the return is at the buyer's risk and expense.

§ 2—328. *Sale by Auction.*

(1) In a sale by auction if goods are put up in lots each lot is the subject of a separate sale.

(2) A sale by auction is complete when the auctioneer so announces by the fall of the hammer or in other customary manner.

Where a bid is made while the hammer is falling in acceptance of a prior bid the auctioneer may in his discretion reopen the bidding or declare the goods sold under the bid on which the hammer was falling.

(3) Such a sale is with reserve unless the goods are in explicit terms put up without reserve. In an auction with reserve the auctioneer may withdraw the goods at any time until he announces completion of the sale. In an auction without reserve, after the auctioneer calls for bids on an article or lot, that article or lot cannot be withdrawn unless no bid is made within a reasonable time. In either case a bidder may retract his bid until the auctioneer's announcement of completion of the sale, but a bidder's retraction does not revive any previous bid.

(4) If the auctioneer knowingly receives a bid on the seller's behalf or the seller makes or procures such as bid, and notice has not been given that liberty for such bidding is reserved, the buyer may at his option avoid the sale or take the goods at the price of the last good faith bid prior to the completion of the sale. This subsection shall not apply to any bid at a forced sale.

PART 4

Title, Creditors and Good Faith Purchasers

§ 2—401. Passing of Title; Reservation for Security; Limited Application of This Section.

Each provision of this Article with regard to the rights, obligations and remedies of the seller, the buyer, purchasers or other third parties applies irrespective of title to the goods except where the provision refers to such title. Insofar as situations are not covered by the other provisions of this Article and matters concerning title became material the following rules apply:

(1) Title to goods cannot pass under a contract for sale prior to their identification to the contract (Section 2—501), and unless otherwise explicitly agreed the buyer acquires by their identification a special property as limited by this Act. Any retention or reservation by the seller of the title (property) in goods shipped or delivered to the buyer is limited in effect to a reservation of a security interest. Subject to these provisions and to the provisions of the Article on Secured Transactions (Article 9), title to goods passes from the seller to the buyer in any manner and on any conditions explicitly agreed on by the parties.

(2) Unless otherwise explicitly agreed title passes to the buyer at the time and place at which the seller completes his performance with reference to the physical delivery of the goods, despite any reservation of a security interest and even though a document of title is to be delivered at a different time or place; and in particular and despite any reservation of a security interest by the bill of lading

(a) if the contract requires or authorizes the seller to send the goods to the buyer but does not require him to deliver them at destination, title passes to the buyer at the time and place of shipment; but

(b) if the contract requires delivery at destination, title passes on tender there.

(3) Unless otherwise explicitly agreed where delivery is to be made without moving the goods,

(a) if the seller is to deliver a document of title, title passes at the time when and the place where he delivers such documents; or

(b) if the goods are at the time of contracting already identified and no documents are to be delivered, title passes at the time and place of contracting.

(4) A rejection or other refusal by the buyer to receive or retain the goods, whether or not justified, or a justified revocation of acceptance revests title to the goods in the seller. Such revesting occurs by operation of law and is not a "sale."

§ 2—402. Rights of Seller's Creditors Against Sold Goods.

(1) Except as provided in subsections (2) and (3), rights of unsecured creditors of the seller with respect to goods which have been identified to a contract for sale are subject to the buyer's rights to recover the goods under this Article (Sections 2—502 and 2—716).

(2) A creditor of the seller may treat a sale or an identification of goods to a contract for sale as void if as against him a retention of possession by the seller is fraudulent under any rule of law of the state where the goods are situated, except that retention of possession in good faith and current course of trade by a merchant-seller for a commercially reasonable time after a sale or identification is not fraudulent.

(3) Nothing in this Article shall be deemed to impair the rights of creditors of the seller

(a) under the provisions of the Article on Secured Transactions (Article 9); or

(b) where identification to the contract or delivery is made not in current course of trade but in satisfaction of or as security for a pre-existing claim for money, security or the like and is made under circumstances which under any rule of law of the state where the goods are situated would apart from this Article constitute the transaction a fraudulent transfer or voidable preference.

§ 2—403. Power to Transfer; Good Faith Purchase of Goods; "Entrusting."

(1) A purchaser of goods acquires all title which his transferor had or had power to transfer except that a purchaser of a limited interest acquires rights only to the extent of the interest purchased. A person with voidable title has power to transfer a good title to a good faith purchaser for value. When goods have been delivered under a transaction of purchase the purchaser has such power even though

(a) the transferor was deceived as to the identity of the purchaser, or

(b) the delivery was in exchange for a check which is later dishonored, or

(c) it was agreed that the transaction was to be a "cash sale," or

(d) the delivery was procured through fraud punishable as larcenous under the criminal law.

(2) Any entrusting of possession of goods to a merchant who deals in goods of that kind gives him power to transfer all rights of the entruster to a buyer in ordinary course of business.

(3) "Entrusting" includes any delivery and any acquiescence in retention of possession regardless of any condition expressed between the parties to the delivery or acquiescence and regardless of whether the procurement of the entrusting or the possessor's disposition of the goods have been such as to be larcenous under the criminal law.

(4) The rights of other purchasers of goods and of lien creditors are governed by the Articles on Secured Transactions (Article 9), Bulk Transfers (Article 6) and Documents of Title (Article 7).

PART 5
Performance

§ 2—501. *Insurable Interest in Goods; Manner of Identification of Goods.*

(1) The buyer obtains a special property and an insurable interest in goods by identification of existing goods as goods to which the contract refers even though the goods so identified are non-conforming and he has an option to return or reject them. Such identification can be made at any time and in any manner explicitly agreed to by the parties. In the absence of explicit agreement identification occurs

(a) when the contract is made if it is for the sale of goods already existing and identified;

(b) if the contract is for the sale of future goods other than those described in paragraph (c), when goods are shipped, marked or otherwise designated by the seller as goods to which the contract refers;

(c) when the crops are planted or otherwise become growing crops or the young are conceived if the contract is for the sale of unborn young to be born within twelve months after contracting or for the sale of crops to be harvested within twelve months or the next normal harvest season after contracting whichever is longer.

(2) The seller retains an insurable interest in goods so long as title to or any security interest in the goods remains in him and where the identification is by the seller alone he may until default or insolvency or notification to the buyer that the identification is final substitute other goods for those identified.

(3) Nothing in this section impairs any insurable interest recognized under any other statute or rule of law.

§ 2—502. *Buyer's Right to Goods on Seller's Insolvency.*

(1) Subject to subsection (2) and even though the goods have not been shipped a buyer who has paid a part or all of the price of goods in which he has a special property under the provisions of the immediately preceding section may on making and keeping good a tender of any unpaid portion of their price recover them from the seller if the seller becomes insolvent within ten days after receipt of the first installment on their price.

(2) If the identification creating his special property has been made by the buyer he acquires the right to recover the goods only if they conform to the contract for sale.

§ 2—503. *Manner of Seller's Tender of Delivery.*

(1) Tender of delivery requires that the seller put and hold conforming goods at the buyer's disposition and give the buyer any notification reasonably necessary to enable him to take delivery. The manner, time and place for tender are determined by the agreement and this Article, and in particular

(a) tender must be at a reasonable hour, and if it is of goods they must be kept available for the period reasonably necessary to enable the buyer to take possession; but

(b) unless otherwise agreed the buyer must furnish facilities reasonably suited to the receipt of the goods.

(2) Where the case is within the next section respecting shipment tender requires that the seller comply with its provisions.

(3) Where the seller is required to deliver at a particular destination tender requires that he comply with subsection (1) and also in any appropriate case tender documents as described in subsections (4) and (5) of this section.

(4) Where goods are in the possession of a bailee and are to be delivered without being moved

(a) tender requires that the seller either tender a negotiable document of title covering such goods or procure acknowledgment by the bailee of the buyer's right to possession of the goods; but

(b) tender to the buyer of a non-negotiable document of title or of a written direction to the bailee to deliver is sufficient tender unless the buyer seasonably objects, and receipt by the bailee of notification of the buyer's rights fixes those rights as against the bailee and all third persons; but risk of loss of the goods and of any failure by the bailee to honor the non-negotiable document of title or to obey the direction remains on the seller until the buyer has had a reasonable time to present the document or direction, and a refusal by the bailee to honor the document or to obey the direction defeats the tender.

(5) Where the contract requires the seller to deliver documents

(a) he must tender all such documents in correct form, except as provided in this Article with respect to bills of lading in a set (subsection (2) of Section 2—323); and

(b) tender through customary banking channels is sufficient and dishonor of a draft accompanying the documents constitutes non-acceptance or rejection.

§ 2—504. *Shipment by Seller.*

Where the seller is required or authorized to send the goods to the buyer and the contract does not require him to deliver them at a particular destination, then unless otherwise agreed he must

(a) put the goods in the possession of such a carrier and make such a contract for their transportation as may be reasonable having regard to the nature of the goods and other circumstances of the case; and

(b) obtain and promptly deliver or tender in due form any document necessary to enable the buyer to obtain possession of the goods or otherwise required by the agreement or by usage of trade; and

(c) promptly notify the buyer of the shipment.

Failure to notify the buyer under paragraph (c) or to make a proper contract under paragraph (a) is a ground for rejection only if material delay or loss ensues.

§ 2—505. *Seller's Shipment under Reservation.*

(1) Where the seller has identified goods to the contract by or before shipment:

(a) his procurement of a negotiable bill of lading to his own order or otherwise reserves in him a security interest in the goods. His procurement of the bill to the order of a financing agency or of the buyer indicates in addition only the seller's expectation of transferring that interest to the person named.

(b) a non-negotiable bill of lading to himself or his nominee reserves possession of the goods as security but except in a case of conditional delivery (subsection (2) of Section 2—507) a non-negotiable bill of lading naming the buyer as consignee reserves no security interest even though the seller retains possession of the bill of lading.

(2) When shipment by the seller with reservation of a security interest is in violation of the contract for sale it constitutes an improper contract for transportation within the preceding section but impairs neither the rights given to the buyer by shipment and identification of the goods to the contract nor the seller's powers as a holder of a negotiable document.

§ 2—506. *Rights of Financing Agency.*

(1) A financing agency by paying or purchasing for value a draft which relates to a shipment of goods acquires to the extent of the payment or purchase and in addition to its own rights under the draft and any document of title securing it any rights of the shipper in the goods including the right to stop delivery and the shipper's right to have the draft honored by the buyer.

(2) The right to reimbursement of a financing agency which has in good faith honored or purchased the draft under commitment to or authority from the buyer is not impaired by subsequent discovery of defects with reference to any relevant document which was apparently regular on its face.

§ 2—507. *Effect of Seller's Tender; Delivery on Condition.*

(1) Tender of delivery is a condition to the buyer's duty to accept the goods and, unless otherwise agreed, to his duty to pay for them. Tender entitles the seller to acceptance of the goods and to payment according to the contract.

(2) Where payment is due and demanded on the delivery to the buyer of goods or documents of title, his right as against the seller to retain or dispose of them is conditional upon his making the payment due.

§ 2—508. *Cure by Seller of Improper Tender or Delivery; Replacement.*

(1) Where any tender or delivery by the seller is rejected because non-conforming and the time for performance has not yet expired, the seller may seasonably notify the buyer of his intention to cure and may then within the contract time make a conforming delivery.

(2) Where the buyer rejects a non-conforming tender which the seller had reasonable grounds to believe would be acceptable with or without money allowance the seller may if he seasonably notifies the buyer have a further reasonable time to substitute a conforming tender.

§ 2—509. *Risk of Loss in the Absence of Breach.*

(1) Where the contract requires or authorizes the seller to ship the goods by carrier

(a) if it does not require him to deliver them at a particular destination, the risk of loss passes to the buyer when the goods are duly delivered to the carrier even though the shipment is under reservation (Section 2—505); but

(b) if it does require him to deliver them at a particular destination and the goods are there duly tendered while in the possession of the carrier, the risk of loss passes to the buyer when the goods are there duly so tendered as to enable the buyer to take delivery.

(2) Where the goods are held by a bailee to be delivered without being moved, the risk of loss passes to the buyer

(a) on his receipt of a negotiable document of title covering the goods; or

(b) on acknowledgment by the bailee of the buyer's right to possession of the goods; or

(c) after his receipt of a non-negotiable document of title or other written direction to deliver, as provided in subsection (4)(b) of Section 2—503.

(3) In any case not within subsection (1) or (2), the risk of loss passes to the buyer on his receipt of the goods if the seller is a merchant; otherwise the risk passes to the buyer on tender of delivery.

(4) The provisions of this section are subject to contrary agreement of the parties and to the provisions of this Article on sale on approval (Section 2—327) and on effect of breach on risk of loss (Section 2—510).

§ 2—510. *Effect of Breach on Risk of Loss.*

(1) Where a tender or delivery of goods so fails to conform to the contract as to give a right of rejection the risk of their loss remains on the seller until cure or acceptance.

(2) Where the buyer rightfully revokes acceptance he may to the extent of any deficiency in his effective insurance coverage treat the risk of loss as having rested on the seller from the beginning.

(3) Where the buyer as to conforming goods already identified to the contract for sale repudiates or is otherwise in breach before risk of their loss has passed to him, the seller may to the extent of any deficiency in his effective insurance coverage treat the risk of loss as resting on the buyer for a commercially reasonable time.

§ 2—511. *Tender of Payment by Buyer; Payment by Check.*

(1) Unless otherwise agreed tender of payment is a condition to the seller's duty to tender and complete any delivery.

(2) Tender of payment is sufficient when made by any means or in any manner current in the ordinary course of business unless the seller demands payment in legal tender and gives any extension of time reasonably necessary to procure it.

(3) Subject to the provisions of this Act on the effect of an instrument on an obligation (Section 3—802), payment by check is conditional and is defeated as between the parties by dishonor of the check on due presentment.

§ 2—512. *Payment by Buyer Before Inspection.*

(1) Where the contract requires payment before inspection non-conformity of the goods does not excuse the buyer from so making payment unless

(a) the non-conformity appears without inspection; or

(b) despite tender of the required documents the circumstances would justify injunction against honor under the provisions of this Act (Section 5—114).

(2) Payment pursuant to subsection (1) does not constitute an acceptance of goods or impair the buyer's right to inspect or any of his

remedies.

§ 2—513. *Buyer's Right to Inspection of Goods.*

(1) Unless otherwise agreed and subject to subsection (3), where goods are tendered or delivered or identified to the contract for sale, the buyer has a right before payment or acceptance to inspect them at any reasonable place and time and in any reasonable manner. When the seller is required or authorized to send the goods to the buyer, the inspection may be after their arrival.

(2) Expenses of inspection must be borne by the buyer but may be recovered from the seller if the goods do not conform and are rejected.

(3) Unless otherwise agreed and subject to the provisions of this Article on C.I.F. contracts (subsection (3) of Section 2—321), the buyer is not entitled to inspect the goods before payment of the price when the contract provides

(a) for delivery "C.O.D." or on other like terms; or

(b) for payment against documents of title, except where such payment is due only after the goods are to become available for inspection.

(4) A place or method of inspection fixed by the parties is presumed to be exclusive but unless otherwise expressly agreed it does not postpone identification or shift the place for delivery or for passing the risk of loss. If compliance becomes impossible, inspection shall be as provided in this section unless the place or method fixed was clearly intended as an indispensable condition failure of which avoids the contract.

§ 2—514. *When Documents Deliverable on Acceptance; When on Payment.*

Unless otherwise agreed documents against which a draft is drawn are to be delivered to the drawee on acceptance of the draft if it is payable more than three days after presentment; otherwise, only on payment.

§ 2—515. *Preserving Evidence of Goods in Dispute.*

In furtherance of the adjustment of any claim or dispute

(a) either party on reasonable notification to the other and for the purpose of ascertaining the facts and preserving evidence has the right to inspect, test and sample the goods including such of them as may be in the possession or control of the other; and

(b) the parties may agree to a third party inspection or survey to determine the conformity or condition of the goods and may agree that the findings shall be binding upon them in any subsequent litigation or adjustment.

PART 6
Breach, Repudiation and Excuse

§ 2—601. *Buyer's Rights on Improper Delivery.*

Subject to the provisions of this Article on breach in installment contracts (Section 2—612) and unless otherwise agreed under the sections on contractual limitations of remedy (Sections 2—718 and 2—719), if the goods or the tender of delivery fail in any respect to conform to the contract, the buyer may

(a) reject the whole; or

(b) accept the whole; or

(c) accept any commercial unit or units and reject the rest.

§ 2—602. *Manner and Effect of Rightful Rejection.*

(1) Rejection of goods must be within a reasonable time after their delivery or tender. It is ineffective unless the buyer seasonably notifies the seller.

(2) Subject to the provisions of the two following sections on rejected goods (Sections 2—603 and 2—604),

(a) after rejection any exercise of ownership by the buyer with respect to any commercial unit is wrongful as against the seller; and

(b) if the buyer has before rejection taken physical possession of goods in which he does not have a security interest under the provisions of this Article (subsection (3) of Section 2—711), he is under a duty after rejection to hold them with reasonable care at the seller's disposition for a time sufficient to permit the seller to remove them; but

(c) the buyer has no further obligations with regard to goods rightfully rejected.

(3) The seller's rights with respect to goods wrongfully rejected are governed by the provisions of this Article on Seller's remedies in general (Section 2—703).

§ 2—603. *Merchant Buyer's Duties as to Rightfully Rejected Goods.*

(1) Subject to any security interest in the buyer (subsection (3) of Section 2—711), when the seller has no agent or place of business at the market of rejection a merchant buyer is under a duty after rejection of goods in his possession or control to follow any reasonable instructions received from the seller with respect to the goods and in the absence of such instructions to make reasonable efforts to sell them for the seller's account if they are perishable or threaten to decline in value speedily. Instructions are not reasonable if on demand indemnity for expenses is not forthcoming.

(2) When the buyer sells goods under subsection (1), he is entitled to reimbursement from the seller or out of the proceeds for reasonable expenses of caring for and selling them, and if the expenses include no selling commission then to such commission as is usual in the trade or if there is none to a reasonable sum not exceeding ten per cent on the gross proceeds.

(3) In complying with this section the buyer is held only to good faith and good faith conduct hereunder is neither acceptance nor conversion nor the basis of an action for damages.

§ 2—604. *Buyer's Options as to Salvage of Rightfully Rejected Goods.*

Subject to the provisions of the immediately preceding section on perishables if the seller gives no instructions within a reasonable time after notification of rejection the buyer may store the rejected goods for the seller's account or reship them to him or resell them for the seller's account with reimbursement as provided in the preceding section. Such action is not acceptance or conversion.

§ 2—605. *Waiver of Buyer's Objections by Failure to Particularize.*

(1) The buyer's failure to state in connection with rejection a particular defect which is ascertainable by reasonable inspection precludes him from relying on the unstated defect to justify rejection or to establish breach

(a) where the seller could have cured it if stated seasonably; or

(b) between merchants when the seller has after rejection made a request in writing for a full and final written statement of all defects on which the buyer proposes to rely.

(2) Payment against documents made without reservation of rights precludes recovery of the payment for defects apparent on the face of the documents.

§ 2—606. *What Constitutes Acceptance of Goods.*

(1) Acceptance of goods occurs when the buyer

(a) after a reasonable opportunity to inspect the goods signifies to the seller that the goods are conforming or that he will take or retain them in spite of their non-conformity; or

(b) fails to make an effective rejection (subsection (1) of Section 2—602), but such acceptance does not occur until the buyer has had a reasonable opportunity to inspect them; or

(c) does any act inconsistent with the seller's ownership; but if such act is wrongful as against the seller it is an acceptance only if ratified by him.

(2) Acceptance of a part of any commercial unit is acceptance of that entire unit.

§ 2—607. *Effect of Acceptance; Notice of Breach; Burden of Establishing Breach After Acceptance; Notice of Claim or Litigation to Person Answerable Over.*

(1) The buyer must pay at the contract rate for any goods accepted.

(2) Acceptance of goods by the buyer precludes rejection of the goods accepted and if made with knowledge of a non-conformity cannot be revoked because of it unless the acceptance was on the reasonable assumption that the non-conformity would be seasonably cured but acceptance does not of itself impair any other remedy provided by this Article for non-conformity.

(3) Where a tender has been accepted

(a) the buyer must within a reasonable time after he discovers or should have discovered any breach notify the seller of breach or be barred from any remedy; and

(b) if the claim is one for infringement or the like (subsection (3) of Section 2—312) and the buyer is sued as a result of such a breach he must so notify the seller within a reasonable time after he receives notice of the litigation or be barred from any remedy over for liability established by the litigation.

(4) The burden is on the buyer to establish any breach with respect to the goods accepted.

(5) Where the buyer is sued for breach of a warranty or other obligation for which his seller is answerable over

(a) he may give his seller written notice of the litigation. If the notice states that the seller may come in and defend and that if the seller does not do so he will be bound in any action against him by his buyer by any determination of fact common to the two litigations, then unless the seller after seasonable receipt of the notice does come in and defend he is so bound.

(b) if the claim is one for infringement or the like (subsection (3) of Section 2—312) the original seller may demand in writing that his buyer turn over to him control of the litigation including settlement or else be barred from any remedy over and if he also agrees to bear all expense and to satisfy any adverse judgment, then unless the buyer after seasonable receipt of the demand does turn over control the buyer is so barred.

(6) The provisions of subsections (3), (4) and (5) apply to any obligation of a buyer to hold the seller harmless against infringement or the like (subsection (3) of Section 2—312).

§ 2—608. *Revocation of Acceptance in Whole or in Part.*

(1) The buyer may revoke his acceptance of a lot or commercial unit whose non-conformity substantially impairs its value to him if he has accepted it

(a) on the reasonable assumption that its non-conformity would be cured and it has not been seasonably cured; or

(b) without discovery of such non-conformity if his acceptance was reasonably induced either by the difficulty of discovery before acceptance or by the seller's assurances.

(2) Revocation of acceptance must occur within a reasonable time after the buyer discovers or should have discovered the ground for it and before any substantial change in condition of the goods which is not caused by their own defects. It is not effective until the buyer notifies the seller of it.

(3) A buyer who so revokes has the same rights and duties with regard to the goods involved as if he had rejected them.

§ 2—609. *Right to Adequate Assurance of Performance.*

(1) A contract for sale imposes an obligation on each party that the other's expectation of receiving due performance will not be impaired. When reasonable grounds for insecurity arise with respect to the performance of either party the other may in writing demand adequate assurance of due performance and until he receives such assurance may if commercially reasonable suspend any performance for which he has not already received the agreed return.

(2) Between merchants the reasonableness of grounds for insecurity and the adequacy of any assurance offered shall be determined according to commercial standards.

(3) Acceptance of any improper delivery or payment does not prejudice the party's right to demand adequate assurance of future performance.

(4) After receipt of a justified demand failure to provide within a reasonable time not exceeding thirty days such assurance of due performance as is adequate under the circumstances of the particular case is a repudiation of the contract.

§ 2—610. *Anticipatory Repudiation.*

When either party repudiates the contract with respect to a performance not yet due the loss of which will substantially impair the value of the contract to the other, the aggrieved party may

(a) for a commercially reasonable time await performance by the repudiating party; or

(b) resort to any remedy for breach (Section 2—703 or Section 2—711), even though he has notified the repudiating party that he would await the latter's performance and has urged retraction; and

(c) in either case suspend his own performance or proceed in accordance with the provisions of this Article on the seller's right to identify goods to the contract notwithstanding breach or to salvage unfinished goods (Section 2—704).

§ 2—611. *Retraction of Anticipatory Repudiation.*

(1) Until the repudiating party's next performance is due he can retract his repudiation unless the aggrieved party has since the repudiation cancelled or materially changed his position or otherwise indicated that he considers the repudiation final.

(2) Retraction may be by any method which clearly indicates to the aggrieved party that the repudiating party intends to perform, but must include any assurance justifiably demanded under the provisions of this Article (Section 2—609).

(3) Retraction reinstates the repudiating party's rights under the contract with due excuse and allowance to the aggrieved party for any delay occasioned by the repudiation.

§ 2—612. *"Installment Contract"; Breach.*

(1) An "installment contract" is one which requires or authorizes the delivery of goods in separate lots to be separately accepted, even though the contract contains a clause "each delivery is a separate contract" or its equivalent.

(2) The buyer may reject any installment which is non-conforming if the non-conformity substantially impairs the value of that installment and cannot be cured or if the non-conformity is a

defect in the required documents; but if the non-conformity does not fall within subsection (3) and the seller gives adequate assurance of its cure the buyer must accept that installment.

(3) Whenever non-conformity or default with respect to one or more installments substantially impairs the value of the whole contract there is a breach of the whole. But the aggrieved party reinstates the contract if he accepts a non-conforming installment without seasonably notifying of cancellation or if he brings an action with respect only to past installments or demands performance as to future installments.

§ 2—613. *Casualty to Identified Goods.*

Where the contract requires for its performance goods identified when the contract is made, and the goods suffer casualty without fault of either party before the risk of loss passes to the buyer, or in a proper case under a "no arrival, no sale" term (Section 2—324) then

(a) if the loss is total the contract is avoided; and

(b) if the loss is partial or the goods have so deteriorated as no longer to conform to the contract the buyer may nevertheless demand inspection and at his option either treat the contract as voided or accept the goods with due allowance from the contract price for the deterioration or the deficiency in quantity but without further right against the seller.

§ 2—614. *Substituted Performance.*

(1) Where without fault of either party the agreed berthing, loading, or unloading facilities fail or an agreed type of carrier becomes unavailable or the agreed manner of delivery otherwise becomes commercially impracticable but a commercially reasonable substitute is available, such substitute performance must be tendered and accepted.

(2) If the agreed means or manner of payment fails because of domestic or foreign governmental regulation, the seller may withhold or stop delivery unless the buyer provides a means or manner of payment which is commercially a substantial equivalent. If delivery has already been taken, payment by the means or in the manner provided by the regulation discharges the buyer's obligation unless the regulation is discriminatory, oppressive or predatory.

§ 2—615. *Excuse by Failure of Presupposed Conditions.*

Except so far as a seller may have assumed a greater obligation and subject to the preceding section on substituted performance:

(a) Delay in delivery or non-delivery in whole or in part by a seller who complies with paragraphs (b) and (c) is not a breach of his duty under a contract for sale if performance as agreed has been made impracticable by the occurrence of a contingency the nonoccurrence of which was a basic assumption on which the contract was made or by compliance in good faith with any applicable foreign or domestic governmental regulation or order whether or not it later proves to be invalid.

(b) Where the causes mentioned in paragraph (a) affect only a part of the seller's capacity to perform, he must allocate production and deliveries among his customers but may at his option include regular customers not then under contract as well as his own requirements for further manufacture. He may so allocate in any manner which is fair and reasonable.

(c) The seller must notify the buyer seasonably that there will be delay or non-delivery and, when allocation is required under paragraph (b), of the estimated quota thus made available for the buyer.

§ 2—616. *Procedure on Notice Claiming Excuse.*

(1) Where the buyer receives notification of a material or indefinite delay or an allocation justified under the preceding section he may by written notification to the seller as to any delivery concerned, and where the prospective deficiency substantially impairs the value of the whole contract under the provisions of this Article relating to breach of installment contracts (Section 2—612), then also as to the whole,

(a) terminate and thereby discharge any unexecuted portion of the contract; or

(b) modify the contract by agreeing to take his available quota in substitution.

(2) If after receipt of such notification from the seller the buyer fails so to modify the contract within a reasonable time not exceeding thirty days the contract lapses with respect to any deliveries affected.

(3) The provisions of this section may not be negated by agreement except in so far as the seller has assumed a greater obligation under the preceding section.

PART 7
Remedies

§ 2—701. *Remedies for Breach of Collateral Contracts Not Impaired.*

Remedies for breach of any obligation or promise collateral or ancillary to a contract for sale are not impaired by the provisions of this Article.

§ 2—702. *Seller's Remedies on Discovery of Buyer's Insolvency.*

(1) Where the seller discovers the buyer to be insolvent he may refuse delivery except for cash including payment for all goods theretofore delivered under the contract, and stop delivery under this Article (Section 2—705).

(2) Where the seller discovers that the buyer has received goods on credit while insolvent he may reclaim the goods upon demand made within ten days after the receipt, but if misrepresentation of solvency has been made to the particular seller in writing within three months before delivery the ten day limitation does not apply. Except as provided in this subsection the seller may not base a right to reclaim goods on the buyer's fraudulent or innocent misrepresentation of solvency or of intent to pay.

(3) The seller's right to reclaim under subsection (2) is subject to the rights of a buyer in ordinary course or other good faith purchaser under this Article (Section 2—403). Successful reclamation of goods excludes all other remedies with respect to them.

§ 2—703. *Seller's Remedies in General.*

Where the buyer wrongfully rejects or revokes acceptance of goods or fails to make a payment due on or before delivery or repudiates with respect to a part or the whole, then with respect to any goods directly affected and, if the breach is of the whole contract (Section 2—612), then also with respect to the whole undelivered balance, the aggrieved seller may

(a) withhold delivery of such goods;

(b) stop delivery by any bailee as hereafter provided (Section 2—705);

(c) proceed under the next section respecting goods still unidentified to the contract;

(d) resell and recover damages as hereafter provided (Section 2—706);

(e) recover damages for non-acceptance (Section 2—708) or in a proper case the price (Section 2—709);

(f) cancel.

§ 2—704. *Seller's Right to Identify Goods to the Contract Notwithstanding Breach or to Salvage Unfinished Goods.*

(1) An aggrieved seller under the preceding section may

(a) identify to the contract conforming goods not already identified if at the time he learned of the breach they are in his possession or control;

(b) treat as the subject of resale goods which have demonstrably been intended for the particular contract even though those goods are unfinished.

(2) Where the goods are unfinished an aggrieved seller may in the exercise of reasonable commercial judgment for the purposes of avoiding loss and of effective realization either complete the manufacture and wholly identify the goods to the contract or cease manufacture and resell for scrap or salvage value or proceed in any other reasonable manner.

§ 2—705. *Seller's Stoppage of Delivery in Transit or Otherwise.*

(1) The seller may stop delivery of goods in the possession of a carrier or other bailee when he discovers the buyer to be insolvent (Section 2—702) and may stop delivery of carload, truckload, planeload or larger shipments of express or freight when the buyer repudiates or fails to make a payment due before delivery or if for any other reason the seller has a right to withhold or reclaim the goods.

(2) As against such buyer the seller may stop delivery until

(a) receipt of the goods by the buyer; or

(b) acknowledgment to the buyer by any bailee of the goods except a carrier that the bailee holds the goods for the buyer; or

(c) such acknowledgment to the buyer by a carrier by reshipment or as warehouseman; or

(d) negotiation to the buyer of any negotiable document of title covering the goods.

(3) (a) To stop delivery the seller must so notify as to enable the bailee by reasonable diligence to prevent delivery of the goods.

(b) After such notification the bailee must hold and deliver the goods according to the directions of the seller but the seller is liable to the bailee for any ensuing charges or damages.

(c) If a negotiable document of title has been issued for goods the bailee is not obliged to obey a notification to stop until surrender of the document.

(d) A carrier who has issued a non-negotiable bill of lading is not obliged to obey a notification to stop received from a person other than the consignor.

§ 2—706. *Seller's Resale Including Contract for Resale.*

(1) Under the conditions stated in Section 2—703 on seller's remedies, the seller may resell the goods concerned or the undelivered balance thereof. Where the resale is made in good faith and in a commercially reasonable manner the seller may recover the difference between the resale price and the contract price together with any incidental damages allowed under the provisions of this Article (Section 2—710), but less expenses saved in consequence of the buyer's breach.

(2) Except as otherwise provided in subsection (3) or unless otherwise agreed resale may be at public or private sale including sale by way of one or more contracts to sell or of identification to an existing contract of the seller. Sale may be as a unit or in parcels and at any time and place and on any terms but every aspect of the sale including the method, manner, time, place and terms must be commercially reasonable. The resale must be reasonably identified as referring to the broken contract, but it is not necessary that the goods be in existence or that any or all of them have been identified to the contract before the breach.

(3) Where the resale is at private sale the seller must give the buyer reasonable notification of his intention to resell.

(4) Where the resale is at public sale

(a) only identified goods can be sold except where there is a recognized market for a public sale of futures in goods of the kind; and

(b) it must be made at a usual place or market for public sale if one is reasonably available and except in the case of goods which are perishable or threaten to decline in value speedily the seller must give the buyer reasonable notice of the time and place of the resale; and

(c) if the goods are not to be within the view of those attending the sale the notification of sale must state the place where the goods are located and provide for their reasonable inspection by prospective bidders; and

(d) the seller may buy.

(5) A purchaser who buys in good faith at a resale takes the goods free of any rights of the original buyer even though the seller fails to comply with one or more of the requirements of this section.

(6) The seller is not accountable to the buyer for any profit made on any resale. A person in the position of a seller (Section 2—707) or a buyer who has rightfully rejected or justifiably revoked acceptance must account for any excess over the amount of his security interest, as hereinafter defined (subsection (3) of Section 2—711).

§ 2—707. *"Person in the Position of a Seller."*

(1) A "person in the position of a seller" includes as against a principal an agent who has paid or become responsible for the price of goods on behalf of his principal or anyone who otherwise holds a security interest or other right in goods similar to that of a seller.

(2) A person in the position of a seller may as provided in this Article withhold or stop delivery (Section 2—705) and resell (Section 2—706) and recover incidental damages (Section 2—710).

§ 2—708. *Seller's Damages for Non-Acceptance or Repudiation.*

(1) Subject to subsection (2) and to the provisions of this Article with respect to proof of market price (Section 2—723), the measure of damages for non-acceptance or repudiation by the buyer is the difference between the market price at the time and place for tender and the unpaid contract price together with any

incidental damages provided in this Article (Section 2—710), but less expenses saved in consequence of the buyer's breach.

(2) If the measure of damages provided in subsection (1) is inadequate to put the seller in as good a position as performance would have done then the measure of damages is the profit (including reasonable overhead) which the seller would have made from full performance by the buyer, together with any incidental damages provided in this Article (Section 2—710), due allowance for costs reasonably incurred and due credit for payments or proceeds of resale.

§ 2—709. *Action for the Price.*

(1) When the buyer fails to pay the price as it becomes due the seller may recover, together with any incidental damages under the next section, the price

(a) of goods accepted or of conforming goods lost or damaged within a commercially reasonable time after risk of their loss has passed to the buyer; and

(b) of goods identified to the contract if the seller is unable after reasonable effort to resell them at a reasonable price or the circumstances reasonably indicate that such effort will be unavailing.

(2) Where the seller sues for the price he must hold for the buyer any goods which have been identified to the contract and are still in his control except that if resale becomes possible he may resell them at any time prior to the collection of the judgment. The net proceeds of any such resale must be credited to the buyer and payment of the judgment entitles him to any goods not resold.

(3) After the buyer has wrongfully rejected or revoked acceptance of the goods or has failed to make a payment due or has repudiated (Section 2—610), a seller who is held not entitled to the price under this section shall nevertheless be awarded damages for non-acceptance under the preceding section.

§ 2—710. *Seller's Incidental Damages.*

Incidental damages to an aggrieved seller include any commercially reasonable charges, expenses or commissions incurred in stopping delivery, in the transportation, care and custody of goods after the buyer's breach, in connection with return or resale of the goods or otherwise resulting from the breach.

§ 2—711. *Buyer's Remedies in General; Buyer's Security Interest in Rejected Goods.*

(1) Where the seller fails to make delivery or repudiates or the buyer rightfully rejects or justifiably revokes acceptance then with respect to any goods involved, and with respect to the whole if the breach goes to the whole contract (Section 2—612), the buyer may cancel and whether or not he has done so may in addition to recovering so much of the price as has been paid

(a) "cover" and have damages under the next section as to all the goods affected whether or not they have been identified to the contract; or

(b) recover damages for non-delivery as provided in this Article (Section 2—713).

(2) Where the seller fails to deliver or repudiates the buyer may also

(a) if the goods have been identified recover them as provided in this Article (Section 2—502); or

(b) in a proper case obtain specific performance or replevy the goods as provided in this Article (Section 2—716).

(3) On rightful rejection or justifiable revocation of acceptance a buyer has a security interest in goods in his possession or control for any payments made on their price and any expenses reasonably incurred in their inspection, receipt, transportation, care and custody and may hold such goods and resell them in like manner as an aggrieved seller (Section 2—706).

§ 2—712. *"Cover"; Buyer's Procurement of Substitute Goods.*

(1) After a breach within the preceding section the buyer may "cover" by making in good faith and without unreasonable delay any reasonable purchase of or contract to purchase goods in substitution for those due from the seller.

(2) The buyer may recover from the seller as damages the difference between the cost of cover and the contract price together with any incidental or consequential damages as hereinafter defined (Section 2—715), but less expenses saved in consequence of the seller's breach.

(3) Failure of the buyer to effect cover within this section does not bar him from any other remedy.

§ 2—713. *Buyer's Damages for Non-Delivery or Repudiation.*

(1) Subject to the provisions of this Article with respect to proof of market price (Section 2—723), the measure of damages for non-delivery or repudiation by the seller is the difference between the market price at the time when the buyer learned of the breach and the contract price together with any incidental and consequential damages provided in this Article (Section 2—715), but less expenses saved in consequence of the seller's breach.

(2) Market price is to be determined as of the place for tender or, in cases of rejection after arrival or revocation of acceptance, as of the place of arrival.

§ 2—714. *Buyer's Damages for Breach in Regard to Accepted Goods.*

(1) Where the buyer has accepted goods and given notification (subsection (3) of Section 2—607) he may recover as damages for any non-conformity of tender the loss resulting in the ordinary course of events from the seller's breach as determined in any manner which is reasonable.

(2) The measure of damages for breach of warranty is the difference at the time and place of acceptance between the value of the goods accepted and the value they would have had if they had been as warranted, unless special circumstances show proximate damages of a different amount.

(3) In a proper case any incidental and consequential damages under the next section may also be recovered.

§ 2—715. *Buyer's Incidental and Consequential Damages.*

(1) Incidental damages resulting from the seller's breach include expenses reasonably incurred in inspection, receipt, transportation and care and custody of goods rightfully rejected, any commercially reasonable charges, expenses or commissions in connection with effecting cover and any other reasonable expense incident to the delay or other breach.

(2) Consequential damages resulting from the seller's breach include

(a) any loss resulting from general or particular requirements and needs of which the seller at the time of contracting had reason to know and which could not reasonably be prevented by cover or otherwise; and

(b) injury to person or property proximately resulting from any breach of warranty.

§ 2—716. *Buyer's Right to Specific Performance or Replevin.*

(1) Specific performance may be decreed where the goods are unique or in other proper circumstances.

(2) The decree for specific performance may include such terms and conditions as to payment of the price, damages, or other relief as the court may deem just.

(3) The buyer has a right of replevin for goods identified to the contract if after reasonable effort he is unable to effect cover for such goods or the circumstances reasonably indicate that such effort will be unavailing or if the goods have been shipped under reservation and satisfaction of the security interest in them has been made or tendered.

§ 2—717. *Deduction of Damages From the Price.*

The buyer on notifying the seller of his intention to do so may deduct all or any part of the damages resulting from any breach of the contract from any part of the price still due under the same contract.

§ 2—718. *Liquidation or Limitation of Damages; Deposits.*

(1) Damages for breach by either party may be liquidated in the agreement but only at an amount which is reasonable in the light of the anticipated or actual harm caused by the breach, the difficulties of proof of loss, and the inconvenience or nonfeasibility of otherwise obtaining an adequate remedy. A term fixing unreasonably large liquidated damages is void as a penalty.

(2) Where the seller justifiably withholds delivery of goods because of the buyer's breach, the buyer is entitled to restitution of any amount by which the sum of his payments exceeds

(a) the amount to which the seller is entitled by virtue of terms liquidating the seller's damages in accordance with subsection (1), or

(b) in the absence of such terms, twenty percent of the value of the total performance for which the buyer is obligated under the contract or $500, whichever is smaller.

(3) The buyer's right to restitution under subsection (2) is subject to offset to the extent that the seller establishes

(a) a right to recover damages under the provisions of this Article other than subsection (1), and

(b) the amount or value of any benefits received by the buyer directly or indirectly by reason of the contract.

(4) Where a seller has received payment in goods their reasonable value or the proceeds of their resale shall be treated as payments for the purposes of subsection (2); but if the seller has notice of the buyer's breach before reselling goods received in part performance, his resale is subject to the conditions laid down in this Article on resale by an aggrieved seller (Section 2—706).

§ 2—719. *Contractual Modification or Limitation of Remedy.*

(1) Subject to the provisions of subsections (2) and (3) of this section and of the preceding section on liquidation and limitation of damages,

(a) the agreement may provide for remedies in addition to or in substitution for those provided in this Article and may limit or alter the measure of damages recoverable under this Article, as by limiting the buyer's remedies to return of the goods and repayment of the price or to repair and replacement of non-conforming goods or parts; and

(b) resort to a remedy as provided is optional unless the remedy is expressly agreed to be exclusive, in which case it is the sole remedy.

(2) Where circumstances cause an exclusive or limited remedy to fail of its essential purpose, remedy may be had as provided in this Act.

(3) Consequential damages may be limited or excluded unless the limitation or exclusion is unconscionable. Limitation of consequential damages for injury to the person in the case of consumer goods is prima facie unconscionable but limitation of damages where the loss is commercial is not.

§ 2—720. *Effect of "Cancellation" or "Rescission" on Claims for Antecedent Breach.*

Unless the contrary intention clearly appears, expressions of "cancellation" or "rescission" of the contract or the like shall not be construed as a renunciation or discharge of any claim in damages for an antecedent breach.

§ 2—721. *Remedies for Fraud.*

Remedies for material misrepresentation or fraud include all remedies available under this Article for non-fraudulent breach. Neither rescission or a claim for rescission of the contract for sale nor rejection or return of the goods shall bar or be deemed inconsistent with a claim for damages or other remedy.

§ 2—722. *Who Can Sue Third Parties for Injury to Goods.*

Where a third party so deals with goods which have been identified to a contract for sale as to cause actionable injury to a party to that contract

(a) a right of action against the third party is in either party to the contract for sale who has title to or a security interest or a special property or an insurable interest in the goods; and if the goods have been destroyed or converted a right of action is also in the party who either bore the risk of loss under the contract for sale or has since the injury assumed that risk as against the other;

(b) if at the time of the injury the party plaintiff did not bear the risk of loss as against the other party to the contract for sale and there is no arrangement between them for disposition of the recovery, his suit or settlement is, subject to his own interest, as a fiduciary for the other party to the contract;

(c) either party may with the consent of the other sue for the benefit of whom it may concern.

§ 2—723. *Proof of Market Price: Time and Place.*

(1) If an action based on anticipatory repudiation comes to trial before the time for performance with respect to some or all of the goods, any damages based on market price (Section 2—708 or Section 2—713) shall be determined according to the price of such goods prevailing at the time when the aggrieved party learned of the repudiation.

(2) If evidence of a price prevailing at the times or places described in this Article is not readily available the price prevailing within any reasonable time before or after the time described or at any other place which in commercial judgment or under usage of trade would serve as a reasonable substitute for the one described may be used, making any proper allowance for the cost of transporting the goods to or from such other place.

(3) Evidence of a relevant price prevailing at a time or place other than the one described in this Article offered by one party is not admissible unless and until he has given the other party such notice as the court finds sufficient to prevent unfair surprise.

§ 2—724. *Admissibility of Market Quotations.*

Whenever the prevailing price or value of any goods regularly bought and sold in any established commodity market is in issue, reports in official publications or trade journals or in newspapers or periodicals of general circulation published as the reports of such market shall be admissible in evidence. The circumstances of the preparation of such a report may be shown to affect its weight but not its admissibility.

§ 2—725. *Statute of Limitations in Contracts for Sale.*

(1) An action for breach of any contract for sale must be commenced within four years after the cause of action has accrued. By the original agreement the parties may reduce the period of limitation to not less than one year but may not extend it.

(2) A cause of action accrues when the breach occurs, regardless of the aggrieved party's lack of knowledge of the breach. A breach of warranty occurs when tender of delivery is made, except that where a warranty explicitly extends to future performance of the goods and discovery of the breach must await the time of such performance the cause of action accrues when the breach is or should have been discovered.

(3) Where an action commenced within the time limited by subsection (1) is so terminated as to leave available a remedy by another action for the same breach such other action may be commenced after the expiration of the time limited and within six months after the termination of the first action unless the termination resulted from voluntary discontinuance or from dismissal for failure or neglect to prosecute.

(4) This section does not alter the law on tolling of the statute of limitations nor does it apply to causes of action which have accrued before this Act becomes effective.

ARTICLE 2A
LEASES

PART 1
General Provisions

§ 2A—101. *Short Title.*

This Article shall be known and may be cited as the Uniform Commercial Code—Leases.

§ 2A—102. *Scope.*

This Article applies to any transaction, regardless of form, that creates a lease.

§ 2A—103. *Definitions and Index of Definitions.*

(1) In this Article unless the context otherwise requires:

(a) "Buyer in ordinary course of business" means a person who in good faith and without knowledge that the sale to him [or her] is in violation of the ownership rights or security interest or leasehold interest of a third party in the goods buys in ordinary course from a person in the business of selling goods of that kind but does not include a pawnbroker. "Buying" may be for cash or by exchange of other property or on secured or unsecured credit and includes receiving goods or documents of title under a pre-existing contract for sale but does not include a transfer in bulk or as security for or in total or partial satisfaction of a money debt.

(b) "Cancellation" occurs when either party puts an end to the lease contract for default by the other party.

(c) "Commercial unit" means such a unit of goods as by commercial usage is a single whole for purposes of lease and division of which materially impairs its character or value on the market or in use. A commercial unit may be a single article, as a machine, or a set of articles, as a suite of furniture or a line of machinery, or a quantity, as a gross or carload, or any other unit treated in use or in the relevant market as a single whole.

(d) "Conforming" goods or performance under a lease contract means goods or performance that are in accordance with the obligations under the lease contract.

(e) "Consumer lease" means a lease that a lessor regularly engaged in the business of leasing or selling makes to a lessee who is an individual and who takes under the lease primarily for a personal, family, or household purpose, if the total payments to be made under the lease contract, excluding payments for options to renew or buy, do not exceed $25,000.

(f) "Fault" means wrongful act, omission, breach, or default.

(g) "Finance lease" means a lease with respect in which (i) the lessor does not select, manufacture or supply the goods; (ii) the lessor acquires the goods or the right to possession and use of the goods in connection with the lease; and (iii) either the lessee receives a copy of the contract evidencing the lessor's purchase of the goods on or before signing the lease contract, or the lessee's approval of the contract evidencing the lessor's purchase of the goods is a condition to effectiveness of the lease contract.

(h) "Goods" means all things that are movable at the time of identification to the lease contract, or are fixtures (Section 2A—309), but the term does not include money, documents, instruments, accounts, chattel paper, general intangibles, or minerals or the like, including oil and gas, before extraction. The term also includes the unborn young of animals.

(i) "Installment lease contract" means a lease contract that authorizes or requires the delivery of goods in separate lots to be separately accepted, even though the lease contract contains a clause "each delivery is a separate lease" or its equivalent.

(j) "Lease" means a transfer of the right to possession and use of goods for a term in return for consideration, but a sale, including a sale on approval or a sale or return, or retention or creation of a security interest is not a lease. Unless the context clearly indicates otherwise, the term includes a sublease.

(k) "Lease agreement" means the bargain, with respect to the lease, of the lessor and the lessee in fact as found in their language or by implication from other circumstances including course of dealing or usage of trade or course of performance as provided in this Article. Unless the context clearly indicates otherwise, the term includes a sublease agreement.

(l) "Lease contract" means the total legal obligation that results from the lease agreement as affected by this Article and any other applicable rules of law. Unless the context clearly indicates otherwise, the term includes a sublease contract.

(m) "Leasehold interest" means the interest of the lessor or the lessee under a lease contract.

(n) "Lessee" means a person who acquires the right to possession and use of goods under a lease. Unless the context clearly indicates otherwise, the term includes a sublessee.

(o) "Lessee in ordinary course of business" means a person who in good faith and without knowledge that the lease to him [or her] is in violation of the ownership rights or security interest or leasehold interest of a third party in the goods, leases in ordinary course from a person in the business of selling or leasing goods of that kind but does not include a pawnbroker. "Leasing" may be for cash or by exchange of other property or on secured or unsecured credit and includes receiving goods or documents of title under a pre-existing lease contract but does not include a transfer in bulk or as security for or in total or partial satisfaction of a money debt.

(p) "Lessor" means a person who transfers the right to possession and use of goods under a lease. Unless the context clearly indicates otherwise, the term includes a sublessor.

(q) "Lessor's residual interest" means the lessor's interest in the goods after expiration, termination, or cancellation of the lease contract.

(r) "Lien" means a charge against or interest in goods to secure payment of a debt or performance of an obligation, but the term does not include a security interest.

(s) "Lot" means a parcel or a single article that is the subject matter of a separate lease or delivery, whether or not it is sufficient to perform the lease contract.

(t) "Merchant lessee" means a lessee that is a merchant with respect to goods of the kind subject to the lease.

(u) "Present value" means the amount as of a date certain of one or more sums payable in the future, discounted to the date certain. The discount is determined by the interest rate specified by the parties if the rate was not manifestly unreasonable at the time the transaction was entered into; otherwise, the discount is determined by a commercially reasonable rate that takes into account the facts and circumstances of each case at the time the transaction was entered into.

(v) "Purchase" includes taking by sale, lease, mortgage, security interest, pledge, gift, or any other voluntary transaction creating an interest in goods.

(w) "Sublease" means a lease of goods the right to possession and use of which was acquired by the lessor as a lessee under an existing lease.

(x) "Supplier" means a person from whom a lessor buys or leases goods to be leased under a finance lease.

(y) "Supply contract" means a contract under which a lessor buys or leases goods to be leased.

(z) "Termination" occurs when either party pursuant to a power created by agreement or law puts an end to the lease contract otherwise than for default.

(2) Other definitions applying to this Article and the sections in which they appear are:

"Accessions." Section 2A—310(1).
"Construction mortgage." Section 2A—309(1)(d).
"Encumbrance." Section 2A—309(1)(e).
"Fixtures." Section 2A—309(1)(a).
"Fixture filing." Section 2A—309(1)(b).
"Purchase money lease." Section 2A—309(1)(c).

(3) The following definitions in other Articles apply to this Article:

"Accounts." Section 9—106.
"Between merchants." Section 2—104(3).
"Buyer." Section 2—103(1)(a).
"Chattel paper." Section 9—105(1)(b).
"Consumer goods." Section 9—109(1).
"Documents." Section 9—105(1)(f).
"Entrusting." Section 2—403(3).
"General intangibles." Section 9—106.
"Good faith." Section 2—103(1)(b).
"Instrument." Section 9—105(1)(i).
"Merchant." Section 2—104(1).
"Mortgage." Section 9—105(1)(j).
"Pursuant to commitment." Section 9—105(1)(k).
"Receipt." Section 2—103(1)(c).
"Sale." Section 2—106(1).
"Sale on Approval." Section 2—326.
"Sale or Return." Section 2—326.
"Seller." Section 2—103(1)(d).

(4) In addition Article 1 contains general definitions and principles of construction and interpretation applicable throughout this Article.

§ 2A—104. *Leases Subject to Other Statutes.*

(1) A lease, although subject to this Article, is also subject to any applicable:

(a) certificate of title statute of this State: (list any certificate of title statutes covering automobiles, trailers, mobile homes, boats, farm tractors, and the like);

(b) certificate of title statute of another jurisdiction (Section 2A—105); or

(c) consumer protection statute of this State.

(2) In case of conflict between the provisions of this Article, other than Sections 2A—105, 2A—304(3) and 2A—305(3), and any statute referred to in subsection (1), the provisions of that statute control.

(3) Failure to comply with an applicable law has only the effect specified therein.

As amended in 1990.

§ 2A—105. *Territorial Application of Article to Goods Covered by Certificate of Title.*

Subject to the provisions of Sections 2A—304(3) and 2A—305(3), with respect to goods covered by a certificate of title issued under a statute of this State or of another jurisdiction, compliance and the effect of compliance or noncompliance with a certificate of title statute are governed by the law (including the conflict of laws rules) of the jurisdiction issuing the certificate until the earlier of (a) surrender of the certificate, or (b) four months after the goods are removed from that jurisdiction and thereafter until a new certificate of title is issued by another jurisdiction.

§ 2A—106. *Limitation on Power of Parties to Consumer Lease to Choose Applicable Law and Judicial Forum.*

(1) If the law chosen by the parties to a consumer lease is that of a jurisdiction other than a jurisdiction in which the lessee resides at the time the lease agreement becomes enforceable or within 30 days thereafter or in which the goods are to be used, the choice is not enforceable.

(2) If the judicial forum chosen by the parties to a consumer lease is a forum that would not otherwise have jurisdiction over the lessee, the choice is not enforceable.

§ 2A—107. *Waiver or Renunciation of Claim or Right After Default.*

Any claim or right arising out of an alleged default or breach of warranty may be discharged in whole or in part without consideration by a written waiver or renunciation signed and delivered by the aggrieved party.

§ 2A—108. Unconscionability.

(1) If the court as a matter of law finds a lease contract or any clause of a lease contract to have been unconscionable at the time it was made the court may refuse to enforce the lease contract, or it may enforce the remainder of the lease contract without the unconscionable clause, or it may so limit the application of any unconscionable clause as to avoid any unconscionable result.

(2) With respect to a consumer lease, if the court as a matter of law finds that a lease contract or any clause of a lease contract has been induced by unconscionable conduct or that unconscionable conduct has occurred in the collection of a claim arising from a lease contract, the court may grant appropriate relief.

(3) Before making a finding of unconscionability under subsection (1) or (2), the court, on its own motion or that of a party, shall afford the parties a reasonable opportunity to present evidence as to the setting, purpose, and effect of the lease contract or clause thereof, or of the conduct.

(4) In an action in which the lessee claims unconscionability with respect to a consumer lease:

(a) If the court finds unconscionability under subsection (1) or (2), the court shall award reasonable attorney's fees to the lessee.

(b) If the court does not find unconscionability and the lessee claiming unconscionability has brought or maintained an action he [or she] knew to be groundless, the court shall award reasonable attorney's fees to the party against whom the claim is made.

(c) In determining attorney's fees, the amount of the recovery on behalf of the claimant under subsections (1) and (2) is not controlling.

§ 2A—109. Option to Accelerate at Will.

(1) A term providing that one party or his [or her] successor in interest may accelerate payment or performance or require collateral or additional collateral "at will" or "when he [or she] deems himself [or herself] insecure" or in words of similar import must be construed to mean that he [or she] has power to do so only if he [or she] in good faith believes that the prospect of payment or performance is impaired.

(2) With respect to a consumer lease, the burden of establishing good faith under subsection (1) is on the party who exercised the power; otherwise the burden of establishing lack of good faith is on the party against whom the power has been exercised.

PART 2
Formation and Construction of Lease Contract

§ 2A—201. Statute of Frauds.

(1) A lease contract is not enforceable by way of action or defense unless:

(a) the total payments to be made under the lease contract, excluding payments for options to renew or buy, are less than $1,000; or

(b) there is a writing, signed by the party against whom enforcement is sought or by that party's authorized agent, sufficient to indicate that a lease contract has been made between the parties and to describe the goods leased and the lease term.

(2) Any description of leased goods or of the lease term is sufficient and satisfies subsection (1)(b), whether or not it is specific, if it reasonably identifies what is described.

(3) A writing is not insufficient because it omits or incorrectly states a term agreed upon, but the lease contract is not enforceable under subsection (1)(b) beyond the lease term and the quantity of goods shown in this writing.

(4) A lease contract that does not satisfy the requirements of subsection (1), but which is valid in other respects, is enforceable:

(a) if the goods are to be specially manufactured or obtained for the lessee and are not suitable for lease or sale to others in the ordinary course of the lessor's business, and the lessor, before notice of repudiation is received and under circumstances that reasonably indicate that the goods are for the lessee, has made either a substantial beginning of their manufacture or commitments for their procurement;

(b) if the party against whom enforcement is sought admits in that party's pleading, testimony or otherwise in court that a lease contract was made, but the lease contract is not enforceable under this provision beyond the quantity of goods admitted; or

(c) with respect to goods that have been received and accepted by the lessee.

(5) The lease term under a lease contract referred to in subsection (4) is:

(a) if there is a writing signed by the party against whom enforcement is sought or by that party's authorized agent specifying the lease term, the term so specified;

(b) if the party against whom enforcement is sought admits in that party's pleading, testimony, or otherwise in court a lease term, the term so admitted; or

(c) a reasonable lease term.

§ 2A—202. Final Written Expression: Parol or Extrinsic Evidence.

Terms with respect to which the confirmatory memoranda of the parties agree or which are otherwise set forth in a writing intended by the parties as a final expression of their agreement with respect to such terms as are included therein may not be contradicted by evidence of any prior agreement or of a contemporaneous oral agreement but may be explained or supplemented:

(a) by course of dealing or usage of trade or by course of performance; and

(b) by evidence of consistent additional terms unless the court finds the writing to have been intended also as a complete and exclusive statement of the terms of the agreement.

§ 2A—203. Seals Inoperative.

The affixing of a seal to a writing evidencing a lease contract or an offer to enter into a lease contract does not render the writing a sealed instrument and the law with respect to sealed instruments does not apply to the lease contract or offer.

§ 2A—204. Formation in General.

(1) A lease contract may be made in any manner sufficient to show agreement, including conduct by both parties which recognizes the existence of a lease contract.

(2) An agreement sufficient to constitute a lease contract may be found although the moment of its making is undetermined.

(3) Although one or more terms are left open, a lease contract does not fail for indefiniteness if the parties have intended

to make a lease contract and there is a reasonably certain basis for giving an appropriate remedy.

§ 2A—205. Firm Offers.

An offer by a merchant to lease goods to or from another person in a signed writing that by its terms gives assurance it will be held open is not revocable, for lack of consideration, during the time stated or, if no time is stated, for a reasonable time, but in no event may the period of irrevocability exceed 3 months. Any such term of assurance on a form supplied by the offeree must be separately signed by the offeror.

§ 2A—206. Offer and Acceptance in Formation of Lease Contract.

(1) Unless otherwise unambiguously indicated by the language or circumstances, an offer to make a lease contract must be construed as inviting acceptance in any manner and by any medium reasonable in the circumstances.

(2) If the beginning of a requested performance is a reasonable mode of acceptance, an offeror who is not notified of acceptance within a reasonable time may treat the offer as having lapsed before acceptance.

§ 2A—207. Course of Performance or Practical Construction.

(1) If a lease contract involves repeated occasions for performance by either party with knowledge of the nature of the performance and opportunity for objection to it by the other, any course of performance accepted or acquiesced in without objection is relevant to determine the meaning of the lease agreement.

(2) The express terms of a lease agreement and any course of performance, as well as any course of dealing and usage of trade, must be construed whenever reasonable as consistent with each other; but if that construction is unreasonable, express terms control course of performance, course of performance controls both course of dealing and usage of trade, and course of dealing controls usage of trade.

(3) Subject to the provisions of Section 2A—208 on modification and waiver, course of performance is relevant to show a waiver or modification of any term inconsistent with the course of performance.

§ 2A—208. Modification, Rescission and Waiver.

(1) An agreement modifying a lease contract needs no consideration to be binding.

(2) A signed lease agreement that excludes modification or rescission except by a signed writing may not be otherwise modified or rescinded, but, except as between merchants, such a requirement on a form supplied by a merchant must be separately signed by the other party.

(3) Although an attempt at modification or rescission does not satisfy the requirements of subsection (2), it may operate as a waiver.

(4) A party who has made a waiver affecting an executory portion of a lease contract may retract the waiver by reasonable notification received by the other party that strict performance will be required of any term waived, unless the retraction would be unjust in view of a material change of position in reliance on the waiver.

§ 2A—209. Lessee under Finance Lease as Beneficiary of Supply Contract.

(1) The benefit of the supplier's promises to the lessor under the supply contract and of all warranties, whether express or implied, including those of any third party provided in connection with or as part of the supply contract, extends to the lessee to the extent of the lessee's leasehold interest under a finance lease related to the supply contract, but is subject to the terms warranty and of the supply contract and all defenses or claims arising therefrom.

(2) The extension of the benefit of supplier's promises to the lessee does not: (a) modify the rights and obligations of the parties to the supply contract, whether arising therefrom or otherwise, or (b) impose any duty or liability under the supply contract on the lessee.

(3) Any modification or rescission of the supply contract by the supplier and the lessor is effective against the lessee unless, prior to the modification or rescission, the supplier has received notice that the lessee has entered into a finance lease related to the supply contract. If the supply contract is modified or rescinded after the lessee enters the finance lease, the lessee has a cause of action against the lessor, and against the supplier if the supplier has notice if the lessees's entering the finance lease when the supply contract is modified or rescinded. The lessee's recovery from such action shall put the lessee in as good a position as if the modification or rescission had not occurred.

§ 2A—210. Express Warranties.

(1) Express warranties by the lessor are created as follows:

(a) Any affirmation of fact or promise made by the lessor to the lessee which relates to the goods and becomes part of the basis of the bargain creates an express warranty that the goods will conform to the affirmation or promise.

(b) Any description of the goods which is made part of the basis of the bargain creates an express warranty that the goods will conform to the description.

(c) Any sample or model that is made part of the basis of the bargain creates an express warranty that the whole of the goods will conform to the sample or model.

(2) It is not necessary to the creation of an express warranty that the lessor use formal words, such as "warrant" or "guarantee," or that the lessor have a specific intention to make a warranty, but an affirmation merely of the value of the goods or a statement purporting to be merely the lessor's opinion or commendation of the goods does not create a warranty.

§ 2A—211. Warranties Against Interference and Against Infringement; Lessee's Obligation Against Infringement.

(1) There is in a lease contract a warranty that for the lease term no person holds a claim to or interest in the goods that arose from an act or omission of the lessor, other than a claim by way of infringement or the like, which will interfere with the lessee's enjoyment of its leasehold interest.

(2) Except in a finance lease there is in a lease contract by a lessor who is a merchant regularly dealing in goods of the kind a warranty that the goods are delivered free of the rightful claim of any person by way of infringement or the like.

(3) A lessee who furnishes specifications to a lessor or a supplier shall hold the lessor and the supplier harmless against any claim by way of infringement or the like that arises out of compliance with the specifications.

§ 2A—212. Implied Warranty of Merchantability.

(1) Except in a finance lease, a warranty that the goods will be merchantable is implied in a lease contract if the lessor is a merchant with respect to goods of that kind.

(2) Goods to be merchantable must be at least such as

(a) pass without objection in the trade under the description in the lease agreement;

(b) in the case of fungible goods, are of fair average quality within the description;

(c) are fit for the ordinary purposes for which goods of that type are used;

(d) run, within the variation permitted by the lease agreement, of even kind, quality, and quantity within each unit and among all units involved;

(e) are adequately contained, packaged, and labeled as the lease agreement may require; and

(f) conform to any promises or affirmations of fact made on the container or label.

(3) Other implied warranties may arise from course of dealing or usage of trade.

§ 2A—213. *Implied Warranty of Fitness for Particular Purpose.*

Except in a finance of lease, if the lessor at the time the lease contract is made has reason to know of any particular purpose for which the goods are required and that the lessee is relying on the lessor's skill or judgment to select or furnish suitable goods, there is in the lease contract an implied warranty that the goods will be fit for that purpose.

§ 2A—214. *Exclusion or Modification of Warranties.*

(1) Words or conduct relevant to the creation of an express warranty and words or conduct tending to negate or limit a warranty must be construed wherever reasonable as consistent with each other; but, subject to the provisions of Section 2A—202 on parol or extrinsic evidence, negation or limitation is inoperative to the extent that the construction is unreasonable.

(2) Subject to subsection (3), to exclude or modify the implied warranty of merchantability or any part of it the language must mention "merchantability," be by a writing, and be conspicuous. Subject to subsection (3), to exclude or modify any implied warranty of fitness the exclusion must be by a writing and be conspicuous. Language to exclude all implied warranties of fitness is sufficient if it is conspicuous and states, for example, "There is no warranty that the goods will be fit for a particular purpose."

(3) Notwithstanding subsection (2), but subject to subsection (4),

(a) unless the circumstances indicate otherwise, all implied warranties are excluded by expressions like "as is" or "with all faults" or by other language that in common understanding calls the lessee's attention to the exclusion of warranties and makes plain that there is no implied warranty, and is conspicuous;

(b) if the lessee before entering into the lease contract has examined the goods or the sample or model as fully as desired or has refused to examine the goods, there is no implied warranty with regard to defects that an examination ought in the circumstances to have revealed; and

(c) an implied warranty may also be excluded or modified by course of dealing, course of performance, or usage of trade.

(4) To exclude or modify a warranty against interference or against infringement (Section 2A—211) or any part of it, the language must be specific, be by a writing, and be conspicuous, unless the circumstances, including course of performance, course of dealing, or usage of trade, give the lessee reason to know that the goods are being leased subject to a claim or interest of any person.

§ 2A—215. *Cumulation and Conflict of Warranties Express or Implied.*

Warranties, whether express or implied, must be construed as consistent with each other and as cumulative, but if that construction is unreasonable, the intention of the parties determines which warranty is dominant. In ascertaining that intention the following rules apply:

(a) Exact or technical specifications displace an inconsistent sample or model or general language of description.

(b) A sample from an existing bulk displaces inconsistent general language of description.

(c) Express warranties displace inconsistent implied warranties other than an implied warranty of fitness for a particular purpose.

§ 2A—216. *Third-Party Beneficiaries of Express and Implied Warranties.*

Alternative A

A warranty to or for the benefit of a lessee under this Article, whether express or implied, extends to any natural person who is in the family or household of the lessee or who is a guest in the lessee's home if it is reasonable to expect that such person may use, consume, or be affected by the goods and who is injured in person by breach of the warranty. This section does not displace principles of law and equity that extend a warranty to or for the benefit of a lessee to other persons. The operation of this section may not be excluded, modified, or limited, but an exclusion, modification, or limitation of the warranty, including any with respect to rights and remedies, effective against the lessee is also effective against any beneficiary designated under this section.

Alternative B

A warranty to or for the benefit of a lessee under this Article, whether express or implied, extends to any natural person who may reasonably be expected to use, consume, or be affected by the goods and who is injured in person by breach of the warranty. This section does not displace principles of law and equity that extend a warranty to or for the benefit of a lessee to other persons. The operation of this section may not be excluded, modified, or limited, but an exclusion, modification, or limitation of the warranty, including any with respect to rights and remedies, effective against the lessee is also effective against the beneficiary designated under this section.

Alternative C

A warranty to or for the benefit of a lessee under this Article, whether express or implied, extends to any person who may reasonably be expected to use, consume, or be affected by the goods and who is injured by breach of the warranty. The operation of this section may not be excluded, modified, or limited with respect to injury to the person of an individual to whom the warranty extends, but an exclusion, modification, or limitation of the warranty, including any with respect to rights and remedies, effective against the lessee is also effective against the beneficiary designated under this section.

§ 2A—217. *Identification.*

Identification of goods as goods to which a lease contract refers may be made at any time and in any manner explicitly agreed to by the parties. In the absence of explicit agreement, identification occurs:

(a) when the lease contract is made if the lease contract is for a lease of goods that are existing and identified;

(b) when the goods are shipped, marked, or otherwise designated by the lessor as goods to which the lease contract refers, if the lease contract is for a lease of goods that are not existing and identified; or

(c) when the young are conceived, if the lease contract is for a lease of unborn young of animals.

§ 2A—218. *Insurance and Proceeds.*

(1) A lessee obtains an insurable interest when existing goods are identified to the lease contract even though the goods identified are nonconforming and the lessee has an option to reject them.

(2) If a lessee has an insurable interest only by reason of the lessor's identification of the goods, the lessor, until default or insolvency or notification to the lessee that identification is final, may substitute other goods for those identified.

(3) Notwithstanding a lessee's insurable interest under subsections (1) and (2), the lessor retains an insurable interest until an option to buy has been exercised by the lessee and risk of loss has passed to the lessee.

(4) Nothing in this section impairs any insurable interest recognized under any other statute or rule of law.

(5) The parties by agreement may determine that one or more parties have an obligation to obtain and pay for insurance covering the goods and by agreement may determine the beneficiary of the proceeds of the insurance.

§ 2A—219. *Risk of Loss.*

(1) Except in the case of a finance lease, risk of loss is retained by the lessor and does not pass to the lessee. In the case of a finance lease, risk of loss passes to the lessee.

(2) Subject to the provisions of this Article on the effect of default on risk of loss (Section 2A—220), if risk of loss is to pass to the lessee and the time of passage is not stated, the following rules apply:

(a) If the lease contract requires or authorizes the goods to be shipped by carrier

(i) and it does not require delivery at a particular destination, the risk of loss passes to the lessee when the goods are duly delivered to the carrier; but

(ii) if it does require delivery at a particular destination and the goods are there duly tendered while in the possession of the carrier, the risk of loss passes to the lessee when the goods are there duly so tendered as to enable the lessee to take delivery.

(b) If the goods are held by a bailee to be delivered without being moved, the risk of loss passes to the lessee on acknowledgment by the bailee of the lessee's right to possession of the goods.

(c) In any case not within subsection (a) or (b), the risk of loss passes to the lessee on the lessee's receipt of the goods if the lessor, or, in the case of a finance lease, the supplier, is a merchant; otherwise the risk passes to the lessee on tender of delivery.

§ 2A—220. *Effect of Default on Risk of Loss.*

(1) Where risk of loss is to pass to the lessee and the time of passage is not stated:

(a) If a tender or delivery of goods so fails to conform to the lease contract as to give a right of rejection, the risk of their loss remains with the lessor, or, in the case of a finance lease, the supplier, until cure or acceptance.

(b) If the lessee rightfully revokes acceptance, he [or she], to the extent of any deficiency in his [or her] effective insurance coverage, may treat the risk of loss as having remained with the lessor from the beginning.

(2) Whether or not risk of loss is to pass to the lessee, if the lessee as to conforming goods already identified to a lease contract repudiates or is otherwise in default under the lease contract, the lessor, or, in the case of a finance lease, the supplier, to the extent of any deficiency in his [or her] effective insurance coverage may treat the risk of loss as resting on the lessee for a commercially reasonable time.

§ 2A—221. *Casualty to Identified Goods.*

If a lease contract requires goods identified when the lease contract is made, and the goods suffer casualty without fault of the lessee, the lessor or the supplier before delivery, or the goods suffer casualty before risk of loss passes to the lessee pursuant to the lease agreement or Section 2A—219, then:

(a) if the loss is total, the lease contract is avoided; and

(b) if the loss is partial or the goods have so deteriorated as to no longer conform to the lease contract, the lessee may nevertheless demand inspection and at his [or her] option either treat the lease contract as avoided or, except in a finance lease that is not a consumer lease, accept the goods with due allowance from the rent payable for the balance of the lease term for the deterioration or the deficiency in quantity but without further right against the lessor.

PART 3
Effect Of Lease Contract

§ 2A—301. *Enforceability of Lease Contract.*

Except as otherwise provided in this Article, a lease contract is effective and enforceable according to its terms between the parties, against purchasers of the goods and against creditors of the parties.

§ 2A—302. *Title to and Possession of Goods.*

Except as otherwise provided in this Article, each provision of this Article applies whether the lessor or a third party has title to the goods, and whether the lessor, the lessee, or a third party has possession of the goods, notwithstanding any statute or rule of law that possession or the absence of possession is fraudulent.

§ 2A—303. *Alienability of Party's Interest Under Lease Contract or of Lessor's Residual Interest in Goods; Delegation of Performance; Assignment of Rights.*

(1) Any interest of a party under a lease contract and the lessor's residual interest in the goods may be transferred unless

(a) the transfer is voluntary and the lease contract prohibits the transfer; or

(b) the transfer materially changes the duty of or materially increases the burden or risk imposed on the other party to the lease contract, and within a reasonable time after notice of the transfer the other party demands that the transferee comply with subsection (2) and the transferee fails to comply.

(2) Within a reasonable time after demand pursuant to subsection (1)(b), the transferee shall:

(a) cure or provide adequate assurance that he [or she] will promptly cure any default other than one arising from the transfer;

(b) compensate or provide adequate assurance that he [or she] will promptly compensate the other party to the lease contract and any other person holding an interest in the lease contract, except the party whose interest is being transferred, for any loss to that party resulting from the transfer;

(c) provide adequate assurance of future due performance under the lease contract; and

(d) assume the lease contract.

(3) Demand pursuant to subsection (1)(b) is without prejudice to the other party's rights against the transferee and the party whose interest is transferred.

(4) An assignment of "the lease" or of "all my rights under the lease" or an assignment in similar general terms is a transfer of rights, and unless the language or the circumstances, as in an assignment for security, indicate the contrary, the assignment is a delegation of duties by the assignor to the assignee and acceptance by the assignee constitutes a promise by him [or her] to perform those duties. This promise is enforceable by either the assignor or the other party to the lease contract.

(5) Unless otherwise agreed by the lessor and the lessee, no delegation of performance relieves the assignor as against the other party of any duty to perform or any liability for default.

(6) A right to damages for default with respect to the whole lease contract or a right arising out of the assignor's due performance of his [or her] entire obligation can be assigned despite agreement otherwise.

(7) To prohibit the transfer of an interest of a party under a lease contract, the language of prohibition must be specific, by a writing, and conspicuous.

§ 2A—304. *Subsequent Lease of Goods by Lessor.*

(1) Subject to Section 2A—303, a subsequent lessee from a lessor of goods under an existing lease contract obtains, to the extent of the leasehold interest transferred, the leasehold interest in the goods that the lessor had or had power to transfer, and except as provided in subsection (2) and Section 2A—527(4), takes subject to the existing lease contract. A lessor with voidable title has power to transfer a good leasehold interest to a good faith subsequent lessee for value, but only to the extent set forth in the preceding sentence. If goods have been delivered under a transaction of purchase the lessor has that power even though:

(a) the lessor's transferor was deceived as to the identity of the lessor;

(b) the delivery was in exchange for a check which is later dishonored;

(c) it was agreed that the transaction was to be a "cash sale"; or

(d) the delivery was procured through fraud punishable as larcenous under the criminal law.

(2) A subsequent lessee in the ordinary course of business from a lessor who is a merchant dealing in goods of that kind to whom the goods were entrusted by the existing lessee before the interest of the subsequent lessee became enforceable against the lessor obtains, to the extent of the leasehold interest transferred, all of that lessor's and the existing lessee's rights to the goods, and takes free of the existing lease contract.

(3) A subsequent lessee from the lessor of goods that are subject to an existing lease contract and are covered by a certificate of title issued under a statute of this State or of another jurisdiction takes no greater rights than those provided both by this section and by the certificate of title statute.

§ 2A—305. *Sale or Sublease of Goods by Lessee.*

(1) Subject to the provisions of Section 2A—303, a buyer or sublessee from the lessee of goods under an existing lease contract obtains, to the extent of the interest transferred, the leasehold interest in the goods that the lessee had or had power to transfer, and except as provided in subsection (2) and Section 2A—511(4), takes subject to the existing lease contract. A lessee with a voidable leasehold interest has power to transfer a good leasehold interest to a good faith buyer for value or a good faith sublessee for value, but only to the extent set forth in the preceding sentence. When goods have been delivered under a transaction of lease the lessee has that power even though:

(a) the lessor was deceived as to the identity of the lessee;

(b) the delivery was in exchange for a check which is later dishonored; or

(c) the delivery was procured through fraud punishable as larcenous under the criminal law.

(2) A buyer in the ordinary course of business or a sublessee in the ordinary course of business from a lessee who is a merchant dealing in goods of that kind to whom the goods were entrusted by the lessor obtains, to the extent of the interest transferred, all of the lessor's and lessee's rights to the goods, and takes free of the existing lease contract.

(3) A buyer or sublessee from the lessee of goods that are subject to an existing lease contract and are covered by a certificate of title issued under a statute of this State or of another jurisdiction takes no greater rights than those provided both by this section and by the certificate of title statute.

§ 2A—306. *Priority of Certain Liens Arising by Operation of Law.*

If a person in the ordinary course of his [or her] business furnishes services or materials with respect to goods subject to a lease contract, a lien upon those goods in the possession of that person given by statute or rule of law for those materials or services takes priority over any interest of the lessor or lessee under the lease contract or this Article unless the lien is created by statute and the statute provides otherwise or unless the lien is created by rule of law and the rule of law provides otherwise.

§ 2A—307. *Priority of Liens Arising by Attachment or Levy on, Security Interests in, and Other Claims to Goods.*

(1) Except as otherwise provided in Section 2A—306, a creditor of a lessee takes subject to the lease contract.

(2) Except as otherwise provided in subsections (3) and (4) and in Sections 2A—306 and 2A—308, a creditor of a lessor takes subject to the lease contract:

(a) unless the creditor holds a lien that attached to the goods before the lease contract became enforceable,

(b) unless the creditor holds a security interest in the goods that under the Article on Secured Transactions (Article 9) would have priority over any other security interest in the goods perfected by a filing covering the goods and made at the time the lease contract became enforceable, whether or not any other security interest existed.

(3) A lessee in the ordinary course of business takes the leasehold interest free of a security interest in the goods created by the lessor even though the security interest is perfected and the lessee knows of its existence.

(4) A lessee other than a lessee in the ordinary course of business takes the leasehold interest free of a security interest to the extent that it secures future advances made after the secured party acquires knowledge of the lease or more than 45 days after the lease contract becomes enforceable, whichever first occurs,

unless the future advances are made pursuant to a commitment entered into without knowledge of the lease and before the expiration of the 45-day period.

§ *2A—308. Special Rights of Creditors.*

(1) A creditor of a lessor in possession of goods subject to a lease contract may treat the lease contract as void if as against the creditor retention of possession by the lessor is fraudulent under any statute or rule of law, but retention of possession in good faith and current course of trade by the lessor for a commercially reasonable time after the lease contract becomes enforceable is not fraudulent.

(2) Nothing in this Article impairs the rights of creditors of a lessor if the lease contract (a) becomes enforceable, not in current course of trade but in satisfaction of or as security for a pre-existing claim for money, security, or the like, and (b) is made under circumstances which under any statute or rule of law apart from this Article would constitute the transaction a fraudulent transfer or voidable preference.

(3) A creditor of a seller may treat a sale or an identification of goods to a contract for sale as void if as against the creditor retention of possession by the seller is fraudulent under any statute or rule of law, but retention of possession of the goods pursuant to a lease contract entered into by the seller as lessee and the buyer as lessor in connection with the sale or identification of the goods is not fraudulent if the buyer bought for value and in good faith.

§ *2A—309. Lessor's and Lessee's Rights When Goods Become Fixtures.*

(1) In this section:

(a) goods are "fixtures" when they become so related to particular real estate that an interest in them arises under real estate law;

(b) a "fixture filing" is the filing, in the office where a mortgage on the real estate would be filed or recorded, of a financing statement covering goods that are or are to become fixtures and conforming to the requirements of subsection (5) of Section 9—402;

(c) a lease is a "purchase money lease" unless the lessee has possession or use of the goods or the right to possession or use of the goods before the lease agreement is enforceable;

(d) a mortgage is a "construction mortgage" to the extent it secures an obligation incurred for the construction of an improvement on land including the acquisition cost of the land, if the recorded writing so indicates; and

(e) "encumbrance" includes real estate mortgages and other liens on real estate and all other rights in real estate that are not ownership interests.

(2) Under this Article a lease may be of goods that are fixtures or may continue in goods that become fixtures, but no lease exists under this Article of ordinary building materials incorporated into an improvement on land.

(3) This Article does not prevent creation of a lease of fixtures pursuant to real estate law.

(4) The perfected interest of a lessor of fixtures has priority over a conflicting interest of an encumbrancer or owner of the real estate if:

(a) the lease is a purchase money lease, the conflicting interest of the encumbrancer or owner arises before the goods become fixtures, the interest of the lessor is perfected by a fixture filing before the goods become fixtures or within ten days thereafter, and the lessee has an interest of record in the real estate or is in possession of the real estate; or

(b) the interest of the lessor is perfected by a fixture filing before the interest of the encumbrancer or owner is of record, the lessor's interest has priority over any conflicting interest of a predecessor in title of the encumbrancer or owner, and the lessee has an interest of record in the real estate or is in possession of the real estate.

(5) The interest of a lessor of fixtures, whether or not perfected, has priority over the conflicting interest of an encumbrancer or owner of the real estate if:

(a) the fixtures are readily removable factory or office machines, readily removable equipment that is not primarily used or leased for use in the operation of the real estate, or readily removable replacements of domestic appliances that are goods subject to a consumer lease, and before the goods become fixtures the lease contract is enforceable; or

(b) the conflicting interest is a lien on the real estate obtained by legal or equitable proceedings after the lease contract is enforceable; or

(c) the encumbrancer or owner has consented in writing to the lease or has disclaimed an interest in the goods as fixtures; or

(d) the lessee has a right to remove the goods as against the encumbrancer or owner. If the lessee's right to remove terminates, the priority of the interest of the lessor continues for a reasonable time.

(6) Notwithstanding paragraph (a) of subsection (4) but otherwise subject to subsections (4) and (5), the interest of a lessor of fixtures, including the lessor's residual interest, is subordinate to the conflicting interest of an encumbrancer of the real estate under a construction mortgage recorded before the goods become fixtures if the goods become fixtures before the completion of the construction. To the extent given to refinance a construction mortgage, the conflicting interest of an encumbrancer of the real estate under a mortgage has this priority to the same extent as the encumbrancer of the real estate under the construction mortgage.

(7) In cases not within the preceding subsections, priority between the interest of a lessor of fixtures, including the lessor's residual interest, and the conflicting interest of an encumbrancer or owner of the real estate who is not the lessee is determined by the priority rules governing conflicting interests in real estate.

(8) If the interest of a lessor has priority over all conflicting interests of all owners and encumbrancers of the real estate, the lessor or the lessee may (a) on default, expiration, termination, or cancellation of the lease agreement by the other party but subject to the provisions of the lease agreement and this Article, or (b) if necessary to enforce his [or her] other rights and remedies of the lessor or lessee under this Article, remove the goods from the real estate, free and clear of all conflicting interests of all owners and encumbrancers of the real estate, but he [or she] must reimburse any encumbrancer or owner of the real estate who is not the lessee and who has not otherwise agreed for the cost of repair of any physical injury, but not for any diminution in value of the real estate caused by the absence of the goods removed or by any necessity of replacing them. A person entitled to reimbursement may refuse permission to remove until the party seeking removal gives adequate security for the performance of this obligation.

(9) Even though the lease agreement does not create a security interest, the interest of a lessor of fixtures is perfected by fil-

ing a financing statement as a fixture filing for leased goods that are or are to become fixtures in accordance with the relevant provisions of the Article on Secured Transactions (Article 9).

§ 2A—310. *Lessor's and Lessee's Rights When Goods Become Accessions.*

(1) Goods are "accessions" when they are installed in or affixed to other goods.

(2) The interest of a lessor or a lessee under a lease contract entered into before the goods became accessions is superior to all interests in the whole except as stated in subsection (4).

(3) The interest of a lessor or a lessee under a lease contract entered into at the time or after the goods became accessions is superior to all subsequently acquired interests in the whole except as stated in subsection (4) but is subordinate to interests in the whole existing at the time the lease contract was made unless the holders of such interests in the whole have in writing consented to the lease or disclaimed an interest in the goods as part of the whole.

(4) The interest of a lessor or a lessee under a lease contract described in subsection (2) or (3) is subordinate to the interest of

(a) a buyer in the ordinary course of business or a lessee in the ordinary course of business of any interest in the whole acquired after the goods became accessions; or

(b) a creditor with a security interest in the whole perfected before the lease contract was made to the extent that the creditor makes subsequent advances without knowledge of the lease contract.

(5) When under subsections (2) or (3) and (4) a lessor or a lessee of accessions holds an interest that is superior to all interests in the whole, the lessor or the lessee may (a) on default, expiration, termination, or cancellation of the lease contract by the other party but subject to the provisions of the lease contract and this Article, or (b) if necessary to enforce his [or her] other rights and remedies under this Article, remove the goods from the whole, free and clear of all interests in the whole, but he [or she] must reimburse any holder of an interest in the whole who is not the lessee and who has not otherwise agreed for the cost of repair of any physical injury but not for any diminution in value of the whole caused by the absence of the goods removed or by any necessity for replacing them. A person entitled to reimbursement may refuse permission to remove until the party seeking removal gives adequate security for the performance of this obligation.

PART 4

Performance Of Lease Contract: Repudiated, Substituted And Excused

§ 2A—401. *Insecurity: Adequate Assurance of Performance.*

(1) A lease contract imposes an obligation on each party that the other's expectation of receiving due performance will not be impaired.

(2) If reasonable grounds for insecurity arise with respect to the performance of either party, the insecure party may demand in writing adequate assurance of due performance. Until the insecure party receives that assurance, if commercially reasonable the insecure party may suspend any performance for which he [or she] has not already received the agreed return.

(3) A repudiation of the lease contract occurs if assurance of due performance adequate under the circumstances of the particular case is not provided to the insecure party within a reasonable time, not to exceed 30 days after receipt of a demand by the other party.

(4) Between merchants, the reasonableness of grounds for insecurity and the adequacy of any assurance offered must be determined according to commercial standards.

(5) Acceptance of any non-conforming delivery or payment does not prejudice the aggrieved party's right to demand adequate assurance of future performance.

§ 2A—402. *Anticipatory Repudiation.*

If either party repudiates a lease contract with respect to a performance not yet due under the lease contract, the loss of which performance will substantially impair the value of the lease contract to the other, the aggrieved party may:

(a) for a commercially reasonable time, await retraction of repudiation and performance by the repudiating party;

(b) make demand pursuant to Section 2A—401 and await assurance of future performance adequate under the circumstances of the particular case; or

(c) resort to any right or remedy upon default under the lease contract or this Article, even though the aggrieved party has notified the repudiating party that the aggrieved party would await the repudiating party's performance and assurance and has urged retraction. In addition, whether or not the aggrieved party is pursuing one of the foregoing remedies, the aggrieved party may suspend performance or, if the aggrieved party is the lessor, proceed in accordance with the provisions of this Article on the lessor's right to identify goods to the lease contract notwithstanding default or to salvage unfinished goods (Section 2A—524).

§ 2A—403. *Retraction of Anticipatory Repudiation.*

(1) Until the repudiating party's next performance is due, the repudiating party can retract the repudiation unless, since the repudiation, the aggrieved party has cancelled the lease contract or materially changed the aggrieved party's position or otherwise indicated that the aggrieved party considers the repudiation final.

(2) Retraction may be by any method that clearly indicates to the aggrieved party that the repudiating party intends to perform under the lease contract and includes any assurance demanded under Section 2A—401.

(3) Retraction reinstates a repudiating party's rights under a lease contract with due excuse and allowance to the aggrieved party for any delay occasioned by the repudiation.

§ 2A—404. *Substituted Performance.*

(1) If without fault of the lessee, the lessor and the supplier, the agreed berthing, loading, or unloading facilities fail or the agreed type of carrier becomes unavailable or the agreed manner of delivery otherwise becomes commercially impracticable, but a commercially reasonable substitute is available, the substitute performance must be tendered and accepted.

(2) If the agreed means or manner of payment fails because of domestic or foreign governmental regulation:

(a) the lessor may withhold or stop delivery or cause the supplier to withhold or stop delivery unless the lessee provides a means or manner of payment that is commercially a substantial equivalent; and

(b) if delivery has already been taken, payment by the means or in the manner provided by the regulation discharges the lessee's obligation unless the regulation is discriminatory, oppressive, or predatory.

§ 2A—405. *Excused Performance.*

Subject to Section 2A—404 on substituted performance, the following rules apply:

(a) Delay in delivery or nondelivery in whole or in part by a lessor or a supplier who complies with paragraphs (b) and (c) is not a default under the lease contract if performance as agreed has been made impracticable by the occurrence of a contingency the nonoccurrence of which was a basic assumption on which the lease contract was made or by compliance in good faith with any applicable foreign or domestic governmental regulation or order, whether or not the regulation or order later proves to be invalid.

(b) If the causes mentioned in paragraph (a) affect only part of the lessor's or the supplier's capacity to perform, he [or she] shall allocate production and deliveries among his [or her] customers but at his [or her] option may include regular customers not then under contract for sale or lease as well as his [or her] own requirements for further manufacture. He [or she] may so allocate in any manner that is fair and reasonable.

(c) The lessor seasonably shall notify the lessee and in the case of a finance lease the supplier seasonably shall notify the lessor and the lessee, if known, that there will be delay or nondelivery and, if allocation is required under paragraph (b), of the estimated quota thus made available for the lessee.

§ 2A—406. *Procedure on Excused Performance.*

(1) If the lessee receives notification of a material or indefinite delay or an allocation justified under Section 2A—405, the lessee may by written notification to the lessor as to any goods involved, and with respect to all of the goods if under an installment lease contract the value of the whole lease contract is substantially impaired (Section 2A—510):

(a) terminate the lease contract (Section 2A—505(2)); or

(b) except in a finance lease that is not a consumer lease, modify the lease contract by accepting the available quota in substitution, with due allowance from the rent payable for the balance of the lease term for the deficiency but without further right against the lessor.

(2) If, after receipt of a notification from the lessor under Section 2A—405, the lessee fails so to modify the lease agreement within a reasonable time not exceeding 30 days, the lease contract lapses with respect to any deliveries affected.

§ 2A—407. *Irrevocable Promises: Finance Leases.*

(1) In the case of a finance lease that is not a consumer lease the lessee's promises under the lease contract become irrevocable and independent upon the lessee's acceptance of the goods.

(2) A promise that has become irrevocable and independent under subsection (1):

(a) is effective and enforceable between the parties, and by or against third parties including assignees of the parties, and

(b) is not subject to cancellation, termination, modification, repudiation, excuse, or substitution without the consent of the party to whom the promise runs.

PART 5

Default

A. In General

§ 2A—501. *Default: Procedure.*

(1) Whether the lessor or the lessee is in default under a lease contract is determined by the lease agreement and this Article.

(2) If the lessor or the lessee is in default under the lease contract, the party seeking enforcement has rights and remedies as provided in this Article and, except as limited by this Article, as provided in the lease agreement.

(3) If the lessor or the lessee is in default under the lease contract, the party seeking enforcement may reduce the party's claim to judgment, or otherwise enforce the lease contract by self-help or any available judicial procedure or nonjudicial procedure, including administrative proceeding, arbitration, or the like, in accordance with this Article.

(4) Except as otherwise provided in this Article or the lease agreement, the rights and remedies referred to in subsections (2) and (3) are cumulative.

(5) If the lease agreement covers both real property and goods, the party seeking enforcement may proceed under this Part as to the goods, or under other applicable law as to both the real property and the goods in accordance with his [or her] rights and remedies in respect of the real property, in which case this Part does not apply.

§ 2A—502. *Notice After Default.*

Except as otherwise provided in this Article or the lease agreement, the lessor or lessee in default under the lease contract is not entitled to notice of default or notice of enforcement from the other party to the lease agreement.

§ 2A—503. *Modification or Impairment of Rights and Remedies.*

(1) Except as otherwise provided in this Article, the lease agreement may include rights and remedies for default in addition to or in substitution for those provided in this Article and may limit or alter the measure of damages recoverable under this Article.

(2) Resort to a remedy provided under this Article or in the lease agreement is optional unless the remedy is expressly agreed to be exclusive. If circumstances cause an exclusive or limited remedy to fail of its essential purpose, or provision for an exclusive remedy is unconscionable, remedy may be had as provided in this Article.

(3) Consequential damages may be liquidated under Section 2A—504, or may otherwise be limited, altered, or excluded unless the limitation, alteration, or exclusion is unconscionable. Limitation, alteration, or exclusion of consequential damages for injury to the person in the case of consumer goods is prima facie unconscionable but limitation, alteration, or exclusion of damages where the loss is commercial is not prima facie unconscionable.

(4) Rights and remedies on default by the lessor or the lessee with respect to any obligation or promise collateral or ancillary to the lease contract are not impaired by this Article.

§ 2A—504. *Liquidation of Damages.*

(1) Damages payable by either party for default, or any other act or omission, including indemnity for loss or diminution of anticipated tax benefits or loss or damage to lessor's residual interest, may be liquidated in the lease agreement but only at an amount or by a formula that is reasonable in light of the then anticipated harm caused by the default or other act or omission.

(2) If the lease agreement provides for liquidation of damages, and such provision does not comply with subsection (1), or

such provision is an exclusive or limited remedy that circumstances cause to fail of its essential purpose, remedy may be had as provided in this Article.

(3) If the lessor justifiably withholds or stops delivery of goods because of the lessee's default or insolvency (Section 2A—525 or 2A—526), the lessee is entitled to restitution of any amount by which the sum of his [or her] payments exceeds:

(a) the amount to which the lessor is entitled by virtue of terms liquidating the lessor's damages in accordance with subsection (1); or

(b) in the absence of those terms, 20 percent of the then present value of the total rent the lessee was obligated to pay for the balance of the lease term, or, in the case of a consumer lease, the lesser of such amount or $500.

(4) A lessee's right to restitution under subsection (3) is subject to offset to the extent the lessor establishes:

(a) a right to recover damages under the provisions of this Article other than subsection (1); and

(b) the amount or value of any benefits received by the lessee directly or indirectly by reason of the lease contract.

§ 2A—505. *Cancellation and Termination and Effect of Cancellation, Termination, Rescission, or Fraud on Rights and Remedies.*

(1) On cancellation of the lease contract, all obligations that are still executory on both sides are discharged, but any right based on prior default or performance survives, and the cancelling party also retains any remedy for default of the whole lease contract or any unperformed balance.

(2) On termination of the lease contract, all obligations that are still executory on both sides are discharged but any right based on prior default or performance survives.

(3) Unless the contrary intention clearly appears, expressions of "cancellation," "rescission," or the like of the lease contract may not be construed as a renunciation or discharge of any claim in damages for an antecedent default.

(4) Rights and remedies for material misrepresentation or fraud include all rights and remedies available under this Article for default.

(5) Neither rescission nor a claim for rescission of the lease contract nor rejection or return of the goods may bar or be deemed inconsistent with a claim for damages or other right or remedy.

§ 2A—506. *Statute of Limitations.*

(1) An action for default under a lease contract, including breach of warranty or indemnity, must be commenced within 4 years after the cause of action accrued. By the original lease contract the parties may reduce the period of limitation to not less than one year.

(2) A cause of action for default accrues when the act or omission on which the default or breach of warranty is based is or should have been discovered by the aggrieved party, or when the default occurs, whichever is later. A cause of action for indemnity accrues when the act or omission on which the claim for indemnity is based is or should have been discovered by the indemnified party, whichever is later.

(3) If an action commenced within the time limited by subsection (1) is so terminated as to leave available a remedy by another action for the same default or breach of warranty or indemnity, the other action may be commenced after the expiration of the time limited and within 6 months after the termination of the first action unless the termination resulted from voluntary discontinuance or from dismissal for failure or neglect to prosecute.

(4) This section does not alter the law on tolling of the statute of limitations nor does it apply to causes of action that have accrued before this Article becomes effective.

§ 2A—507. *Proof of Market Rent: Time and Place.*

(1) Damages based on market rent (Section 2A—519 or 2A—528) are determined according to the rent for the use of the goods concerned for a lease term identical to the remaining lease term of the original lease agreement and prevailing at the time of default.

(2) If evidence of rent for the use of the goods concerned for a lease term identical to the remaining lease term of the original lease agreement and prevailing at the times or places described in this Article is not readily available, the rent prevailing within any reasonable time before or after the time described or at any other place or for a different lease term which in commercial judgment or under usage of trade would serve as a reasonable substitute for the one described may be used, making any proper allowance for the difference, including the cost of transporting the goods to or from the other place.

(3) Evidence of a relevant rent prevailing at a time or place or for a lease term other than the one described in this Article offered by one party is not admissible unless and until he [or she] has given the other party notice the court finds sufficient to prevent unfair surprise.

(4) If the prevailing rent or value of any goods regularly leased in any established market is in issue, reports in official publications or trade journals or in newspapers or periodicals of general circulation published as the reports of that market are admissible in evidence. The circumstances of the preparation of the report may be shown to affect its weight but not its admissibility.

B. Default by Lessor

§ 2A—508. *Lessee's Remedies.*

(1) If a lessor fails to deliver the goods in conformity to the lease contract (Section 2A—509) or repudiates the lease contract (Section 2A—402), or a lessee rightfully rejects the goods (Section 2A—509) or justifiably revokes acceptance of the goods (Section 2A—517), then with respect to any goods involved, and with respect to all of the goods if under an installment lease contract the value of the whole lease contract is substantially impaired (Section 2A—510), the lessor is in default under the lease contract and the lessee may:

(a) cancel the lease contract (Section 2A—505(1));

(b) recover so much of the rent and security as has been paid but in the case of an installment lease contract the recovery is that which is just under the circumstances;

(c) cover and recover damages as to all goods affected whether or not they have been identified to the lease contract (Sections 2A—518 and 2A—520), or recover damages for nondelivery (Sections 2A—519 and 2A—520);

(2) If a lessor fails to deliver the goods in conformity to the lease contract or repudiates the lease contract, the lessee may also:

(a) if the goods have been identified, recover them (Section 2A—522); or

(b) in a proper case, obtain specific performance or replevy the goods (Section 2A—521).

(3) If a lessor is otherwise in default under a lease contract, the lessee may exercise the rights and pursue the remedies provided in the lease contract and this Article.

(4) If a lessor has breached a warranty, whether express or implied, the lessee may recover damages (Section 2A—519(4)).

(5) On rightful rejection or justifiable revocation of acceptance, a lessee has a security interest in goods in the lessee's possession or control for any rent and security that has been paid and any expenses reasonably incurred in their inspection, receipt, transportation, and care and custody and may hold those goods and dispose of them in good faith and in a commercially reasonable manner, subject to Section 2A—527(5).

(6) Subject to the provisions of Section 2A—407, a lessee, on notifying the lessor of the lessee's intention to do so, may deduct all or any part of the damages resulting from any default under the lease contract from any part of the rent still due under the same lease contract.

§ 2A—509. *Lessee's Rights on Improper Delivery; Rightful Rejection.*

(1) Subject to the provisions of Section 2A—510 on default in installment lease contracts, if the goods or the tender or delivery fail in any respect to conform to the lease contract, the lessee may reject or accept the goods or accept any commercial unit or units and reject the rest of the goods.

(2) Rejection of goods is ineffective unless it is within a reasonable time after tender or delivery of the goods and the lessee seasonably notifies the lessor.

§ 2A—510. *Installment Lease Contracts: Rejection and Default.*

(1) Under an installment lease contract a lessee may reject any delivery that is non-conforming if the non-conformity substantially impairs the value of that delivery and cannot be cured or the non-conformity is a defect in the required documents; but if the non-conformity does not fall within subsection (2) and the lessor or the supplier gives adequate assurance of its cure, the lessee must accept that delivery.

(2) Whenever non-conformity or default with respect to one or more deliveries substantially impairs the value of the installment lease contract as a whole there is a default with respect to the whole. But, the aggrieved party reinstates the installment lease contract as a whole if the aggrieved party accepts a non-conforming delivery without seasonably notifying of cancellation or brings an action with respect only to past deliveries or demands performance as to future deliveries.

§ 2A—511. *Merchant Lessee's Duties as to Rightfully Rejected Goods.*

(1) Subject to any security interest of a lessee (Section 2A—508(5)), if a lessor or a supplier has no agent or place of business at the market of rejection, a merchant lessee, after rejection of goods in his [or her] possession or control, shall follow any reasonable instructions received from the lessor or the supplier with respect to the goods. In the absence of those instructions, a merchant lessee shall make reasonable efforts to sell, lease, or otherwise dispose of the goods for the lessor's account if they threaten to decline in value speedily. Instructions are not reasonable if on demand indemnity for expenses is not forthcoming.

(2) If a merchant lessee (subsection (1)) or any other lessee (Section 2A—512) disposes of goods, he [or she] is entitled to reimbursement either from the lessor or the supplier or out of the proceeds for reasonable expenses of caring for and disposing of the goods and, if the expenses include no disposition commission, to such commission as is usual in the trade, or if there is none, to a reasonable sum not exceeding 10 percent of the gross proceeds.

(3) In complying with this section or Section 2A—512, the lessee is held only to good faith. Good faith conduct hereunder is neither acceptance or conversion nor the basis of an action for damages.

(4) A purchaser who purchases in good faith from a lessee pursuant to this section or Section 2A—512 takes the goods free of any rights of the lessor and the supplier even though the lessee fails to comply with one or more of the requirements of this Article.

§ 2A—512. *Lessee's Duties as to Rightfully Rejected Goods.*

(1) Except as otherwise provided with respect to goods that threaten to decline in value speedily (Section 2A—511) and subject to any security interest of a lessee (Section 2A—508(5)):

(a) the lessee, after rejection of goods in the lessee's possession, shall hold them with reasonable care at the lessor's or the supplier's disposition for a reasonable time after the lessee's seasonable notification of rejection;

(b) if the lessor or the supplier gives no instructions within a reasonable time after notification of rejection, the lessee may store the rejected goods for the lessor's or the supplier's account or ship them to the lessor or the supplier or dispose of them for the lessor's or the supplier's account with reimbursement in the manner provided in Section 2A—511; but

(c) the lessee has no further obligations with regard to goods rightfully rejected.

(2) Action by the lessee pursuant to subsection (1) is not acceptance or conversion.

§ 2A—513. *Cure by Lessor of Improper Tender or Delivery; Replacement.*

(1) If any tender or delivery by the lessor or the supplier is rejected because non-conforming and the time for performance has not yet expired, the lessor or the supplier may seasonably notify the lessee of the lessor's or the supplier's intention to cure and may then make a conforming delivery within the time provided in the lease contract.

(2) If the lessee rejects a non-conforming tender that the lessor or the supplier had reasonable grounds to believe would be acceptable with or without money allowance, the lessor or the supplier may have a further reasonable time to substitute a conforming tender if he [or she] seasonably notifies the lessee.

§ 2A—514. *Waiver of Lessee's Objections.*

(1) In rejecting goods, a lessee's failure to state a particular defect that is ascertainable by reasonable inspection precludes the lessee from relying on the defect to justify rejection or to establish default:

(a) if, stated seasonably, the lessor or the supplier could have cured it (Section 2A—513); or

(b) between merchants if the lessor or the supplier after rejection has made a request in writing for a full and final written statement of all defects on which the lessee proposes to rely.

(2) A lessee's failure to reserve rights when paying rent or other consideration against documents precludes recovery of the payment for defects apparent on the face of the documents.

§ 2A—515. *Acceptance of Goods.*

(1) Acceptance of goods occurs after the lessee has had a reasonable opportunity to inspect the goods and

(a) the lessee signifies or acts with respect to the goods in a manner that signifies to the lessor or the supplier that the goods are conforming or that the lessee will take or retain them in spite of their non-conformity; or

(b) the lessee fails to make an effective rejection of the goods (Section 2A—509(2)).

(2) Acceptance of a part of any commercial unit is acceptance of that entire unit.

§ 2A—516. *Effect of Acceptance of Goods; Notice of Default; Burden of Establishing Default after Acceptance; Notice of Claim or Litigation to Person Answerable Over.*

(1) A lessee must pay rent for any goods accepted in accordance with the lease contract, with due allowance for goods rightfully rejected or not delivered.

(2) A lessee's acceptance of goods precludes rejection of the goods accepted. In the case of a finance lease, if made with knowledge of a non-conformity, acceptance cannot be revoked because of it. In any other case, if made with knowledge of a non-conformity, acceptance cannot be revoked because of it unless the acceptance was on the reasonable assumption that the non-conformity would be seasonably cured. Acceptance does not of itself impair any other remedy provided by this Article or the lease agreement for non-conformity.

(3) If a tender has been accepted:

(a) within a reasonable time after the lessee discovers or should have discovered any default, the lessee shall notify the lessor and the supplier, or be barred from any remedy.

(b) except in the case of a consumer lease, within a reasonable time after the lessee receives notice of litigation for infringement or the like (Section 2A—211) the lessee shall notify the lessor or be barred from any remedy over for liability established by the litigation; and

(c) the burden is on the lessee to establish any default.

(4) If a lessee is sued for breach of a warranty or other obligation for which a lessor or a supplier is answerable over:

(a) The lessee may give the lessor or the supplier written notice of the litigation. If the notice states that the lessor or the supplier may come in and defend and that if the lessor or the supplier does not do so he [or she] will be bound in any action against him [or her] by the lessee by any determination of fact common to the two litigations, then unless the lessor or the supplier after seasonable receipt of the notice does come in and defend he [or she] is so bound.

(b) The lessor or the supplier may demand in writing that the lessee turn over control of the litigation including settlement if the claim is one for infringement or the like (Section 2A—211) or else be barred from any remedy over. If the demand states that the lessor or the supplier agrees to bear all expense and to satisfy any adverse judgment, then unless the lessee after seasonable receipt of the demand does turn over control the lessee is so barred.

(5) The provisions of subsections (3) and (4) apply to any obligation of a lessee to hold the lessor or the supplier harmless against infringement or the like (Section 2A—211).

§ 2A—517. *Revocation of Acceptance of Goods.*

(1) A lessee may revoke acceptance of a lot or commercial unit whose non-conformity substantially impairs its value to the lessee if he [or she] has accepted it:

(a) except in the case of a finance lease, on the reasonable assumption that its non-conformity would be cured and it has not been seasonably cured; or

(b) without discovery of the non-conformity if the lessee's acceptance was reasonably induced either by the lessor's assurances or, except in the case of a finance lease, by the difficulty of discovery before acceptance.

(2) Revocation of acceptance must occur within a reasonable time after the lessee discovers or should have discovered the ground for it and before any substantial change in condition of the goods which is not caused by the non-conformity. Revocation is not effective until the lessee notifies the lessor.

(3) A lessee who so revokes has the same rights and duties with regard to the goods involved as if the lessee had rejected them.

§ 2A—518. *Cover; Substitute Goods.*

(1) After default by a lessor under the lease contract (Section 2A—508(1)), the lessee may cover by making in good faith and without unreasonable delay any purchase or lease of or contract to purchase or lease goods in substitution for those due from the lessor.

(2) Except as otherwise provided with respect to damages liquidated in the lease agreement (Section 2A—504) or determined by agreement of the parties (Section 1—102(3)), if a lessee's cover is by lease agreement substantially similar to the original lease agreement and the lease agreement is made in good faith and in a commercially reasonable manner, the lessee may recover from the lessor as damages (a) the present value, as of the date of default, of the difference between the total rent for the lease term of the new lease agreement and the total rent for the remaining lease term of the original lease agreement and (b) any incidental or consequential damages less expenses saved in consequence of the lessor's default.

(3) If a lessee's cover does not qualify for treatment under subsection (2), the lessee may recover from the lessor as if the lessee had elected not to cover and Section 2A—519 governs.

§ 2A—519. *Lessee's Damages for Non-Delivery, Repudiation, Default, and Breach of Warranty in Regard to Accepted Goods.*

(1) If a lessee elects not to cover or a lessee elects to cover and the cover does not qualify for treatment under Section 2A—518(2), the measure of damages for non-delivery or repudiation by the lessor or for rejection or revocation of acceptance by the lessee is the present value as of the date of the default of the difference between the then market rent and the original rent, computed for the remaining lease term of the original lease agreement together with incidental and consequential damages, less expenses saved in consequence of the lessor's default.

(2) Market rent is to be determined as of the place for tender or, in cases of rejection after arrival or revocation of acceptance, as of the place of arrival.

(3) If the lessee has accepted goods and given notification (Section 2A—516(3)), the measure of damages for non-conforming tender or delivery by a lessor is the loss resulting in the ordinary course of events from the lessor's default as determined in any manner that is reasonable together with incidental and consequential damages, less expenses saved in consequence of the lessor's default.

(4) The measure of damages for breach of warranty is the present value at the time and place of acceptance of the difference between the value of the use of the goods accepted and the value if they had been as warranted for the lease term, unless special circumstances show proximate damages of a different amount, together with incidental and consequential damages, less expenses saved in consequence of the lessor's default or breach of warranty.

§ 2A—520. Lessee's Incidental and Consequential Damages.

(1) Incidental damages resulting from a lessor's default include expenses reasonably incurred in inspection, receipt, transportation, and care and custody of goods rightfully rejected or goods the acceptance of which is justifiably revoked, any commercially reasonable charges, expenses or commissions in connection with effecting cover, and any other reasonable expense incident to the default.

(2) Consequential damages resulting from a lessor's default include:

(a) any loss resulting from general or particular requirements and needs of which the lessor at the time of contracting had reason to know and which could not reasonably be prevented by cover or otherwise; and

(b) injury to person or property proximately resulting from any breach of warranty.

§ 2A—521. Lessee's Right to Specific Performance or Replevin.

(1) Specific performance may be decreed if the goods are unique or in other proper circumstances.

(2) A decree for specific performance may include any terms and conditions as to payment of the rent, damages, or other relief that the court deems just.

(3) A lessee has a right of replevin, detinue, sequestration, claim and delivery, or the like for goods identified to the lease contract if after reasonable effort the lessee is unable to effect cover for those goods or the circumstances reasonably indicate that the effort will be unavailing.

§ 2A—522. Lessee's Right to Goods on Lessor's Insolvency.

(1) Subject to subsection (2) and even though the goods have not been shipped, a lessee who has paid a part or all of the rent and security for goods identified to a lease contract (Section 2A—217) on making and keeping good a tender of any unpaid portion of the rent and security due under the lease contract may recover the goods identified from the lessor if the lessor becomes insolvent within 10 days after receipt of the first installment of rent and security.

(2) A lessee acquires the right to recover goods identified to a lease contract only if they conform to the lease contract.

C. Default by Lessee

§ 2A—523. Lessor's Remedies.

(1) If a lessee wrongfully rejects or revokes acceptance of goods or fails to make a payment when due or repudiates with respect to a part or the whole, then, with respect to any goods involved, and with respect to all of the goods if under an installment lease contract the value of the whole lease contract is substantially impaired (Section 2A—510), the lessee is in default under the lease contract and the lessor may:

(a) cancel the lease contract (Section 2A—505(1));

(b) proceed respecting goods not identified to the lease contract (Section 2A—524);

(c) withhold delivery of the goods and take possession of goods previously delivered (Section 2A—525);

(d) stop delivery of the goods by any bailee (Section 2A—526);

(e) dispose of the goods and recover damages (Section 2A—527), or retain the goods and recover damages (Section 2A—528), or in a proper case recover rent (Section 2A—529);

(2) If a lessee is otherwise in default under a lease contract, the lessor may exercise the rights and remedies provided in the lease contract and this Article.

§ 2A—524. Lessor's Right to Identify Goods to Lease Contract.

(1) A lessor aggrieved under Section 2A—523(1) may:

(a) identify to the lease contract conforming goods not already identified if at the time the lessor learned of the default they were in the lessor's or the supplier's possession or control; and

(b) dispose of goods (Section 2A—527(1)) that demonstrably have been intended for the particular lease contract even though those goods are unfinished.

(2) If the goods are unfinished, in the exercise of reasonable commercial judgment for the purposes of avoiding loss and of effective realization, an aggrieved lessor or the supplier may either complete manufacture and wholly identify the goods to the lease contract or cease manufacture and lease, sell, or otherwise dispose of the goods for scrap or salvage value or proceed in any other reasonable manner.

§ 2A—525. Lessor's Right to Possession of Goods.

(1) If a lessor discovers the lessee to be insolvent, the lessor may refuse to deliver the goods.

(2) The lessor has on default by the lessee under the lease contract the right to take possession of the goods. If the lease contract so provides, the lessor may require the lessee to assemble the goods and make them available to the lessor at a place to be designated by the lessor which is reasonably convenient to both parties. Without removal, the lessor may render unusable any goods employed in trade or business, and may dispose of goods on the lessee's premises (Section 2A—527).

(3) The lessor may proceed under subsection (2) without judicial process if that can be done without breach of the peace or the lessor may proceed by action.

§ 2A—526. Lessor's Stoppage of Delivery in Transit or Otherwise.

(1) A lessor may stop delivery of goods in the possession of a carrier or other bailee if the lessor discovers the lessee to be insolvent and may stop delivery of carload, truckload, planeload, or larger shipments of express or freight if the lessee repudiates or fails to make a payment due before delivery, whether for rent, security or otherwise under the lease contract, or for any other reason the lessor has a right to withhold or take possession of the goods.

(2) In pursuing its remedies under subsection (1), the lessor may stop delivery until

(a) receipt of the goods by the lessee;

(b) acknowledgment to the lessee by any bailee of the goods, except a carrier, that the bailee holds the goods for the lessee; or

(c) such an acknowledgment to the lessee by a carrier via reshipment or as warehouseman.

(3) (a) To stop delivery, a lessor shall so notify as to enable the bailee by reasonable diligence to prevent delivery of the goods.

(b) After notification, the bailee shall hold and deliver the goods according to the directions of the lessor, but the lessor is liable to the bailee for any ensuing charges or damages.

(c) A carrier who has issued a nonnegotiable bill of lading is not obliged to obey a notification to stop received from a person other than the consignor.

§ *2A—527. Lessor's Rights to Dispose of Goods.*

(1) After a default by a lessee under the lease contract of the type described in Section 2A—523(1) or after the lessor refuses to deliver or take possession of goods (Section 2A—525 or 2A—526), the lessor may dispose of the goods concerned or the undelivered balance thereof by lease, sale, or otherwise.

(2) If the disposition is by lease agreement substantially similar to the original lease contract and the new lease contract is made in good faith and in a commercially reasonable manner, the lessor may recover from the lessee as damages (a) accrued and unpaid rent as of the date of (b) the present value as of the date of default of the difference between the total rent for the remaining lease term of the original lease contract and the total rent for the lease term of the new lease contract, and (c) any incidental damages allowed under Section 2A—530, less expenses saved in consequence of the lessee's default.

(3) If the lessor's disposition is by lease contract that for any reason does not qualify for treatment under subsection (2), or is by sale or otherwise, the lessor may recover from the lessee as if the lessor had elected not to dispose of the goods and Section 2A—528 governs.

(4) A subsequent buyer or lessee who buys or leases from the lessor in good faith for value as a result of a disposition under this section takes the goods free of the original lease contract and any rights of the original lessee even though the lessor fails to comply with one or more of the requirements of this Article.

(5) The lessor is not accountable to the lessee for any profit made on any disposition. A lessee who has rightfully rejected or justifiably revoked acceptance shall account to the lessor for any excess over the amount of the lessee's security interest (Section 2A—508(5)).

§ *2A—528. Lessor's Damages for Non-Acceptance, Failure to Pay, Repudiation, or Other Default.*

(1) Except as otherwise provided with respect to damages liquidated in the lease agreement (Section 2A—504) or determined by agreement of the parties (Section 1—102(3)), if a lessor elects to dispose of the goods and disposition is by lease agreement that for any reason does not qualify for treatment under Section 2A—527(2), or is by sale or otherwise, the lessor may recover from the lessee as damages for non-acceptance or repudiation by the lessee (a) accrued and unpaid rent as of the date of default, (b) the present value as of the date of default of the difference between the total rent for the remaining lease term of the original lease agreement and the market rent at the time and place for tender computed for the same lease term, and (c) any incidental damages allowed under Section 2A—530, less expenses saved in consequence of the lessee's default.

(2) If the measure of damages provided in subsection (1) is inadequate to put a lessor in as good a position as performance would have, the measure of damages is the profit, including reasonable overhead, the lessor would have made from full performance by the lessee, together with any incidental damages allowed under Section 2A—530, due allowance for costs reasonably incurred and due credit for payments or proceeds of disposition.

§ *2A—529. Lessor's Action for the Rent.*

(1) After default by the lessee under the lease contract (Section 2A—523(1)) if the lessor complies with subsection (2), the lessor may recover from the lessee as damages:

(a) for goods accepted by the lessee and for conforming goods lost or damaged within a commercially reasonable time after risk of loss passes to the lessee (Section 2A—219), (i) accrued and unpaid rent as of the date of default, (ii) the present value as of the date of default of the rent for the remaining lease term of the lease agreement, and (iii) any incidental damages allowed under Section 2A—530, less expenses saved in consequence of the lessee's default; and

(b) for goods identified to the lease contract if the lessor is unable after reasonable effort to dispose of them at a reasonable price or the circumstances reasonably indicate that effort will be unavailing, (i) accrued and unpaid rent as of the date of default, (ii) the present value as of the date of default of the rent for the remaining lease term of the lease agreement, and (iii) any incidental damages allowed under Section 2A—530, less expenses saved in consequence of the lessee's default.

(2) Except as provided in subsection (3), the lessor shall hold for the lessee for the remaining lease term of the lease agreement any goods that have been identified to the lease contract and are in the lessor's control.

(3) The lessor may dispose of the goods at any time before collection of the judgment for damages obtained pursuant to subsection (1) and the lessor may proceed against the lessee for damages pursuant to Section 2A—527 or Section 2A—528.

(4) Payment of the judgment for damages obtained pursuant to subsection (1) entitles the lessee to use and possession of the goods not then disposed of for the remaining lease term of the lease agreement.

(5) After a lessee has wrongfully rejected or revoked acceptance of goods, has failed to pay rent then due, or has repudiated (Section 2A—402), a lessor who is held not entitled to rent under this section must nevertheless be awarded damages for non-acceptance under Sections 2A—527 and 2A—528.

§ *2A—530. Lessor's Incidental Damages.*

Incidental damages to an aggrieved lessor include any commercially reasonable charges, expenses, or commissions incurred in stopping delivery, in the transportation, care and custody of goods after the lessee's default, in connection with return or disposition of the goods, or otherwise resulting from the default.

§ *2A—531. Standing to Sue Third Parties for Injury to Goods.*

(1) If a third party so deals with goods that have been identified to a lease contract as to cause actionable injury to a party to the lease contract (a) the lessor has a right of action against the third party, and (b) the lessee also has a right of action against the third party if the lessee:

(i) has a security interest in the goods;

(ii) has an insurable interest in the goods; or

(iii) bears the risk of loss under the lease contract or has since the injury assumed that risk as against the lessor and the goods have been converted or destroyed.

(2) If at the time of the injury the party plaintiff did not bear the risk of loss as against the other party to the lease contract and there is no arrangement between them for disposition of the recovery, his [or her] suit or settlement, subject to his [or her] own interest, is as a fiduciary for the other party to the lease contract.

(3) Either party with the consent of the other may sue for the benefit of whom it may concern.

§ 2A—532. *Lessor's Rights to Residual Interest.*

In addition to any other recovery permitted by this Article or other law, the lessor may recover from the lessee an amount that will fully compensate the lessor for any loss of or damage to the lessor's residual interest in the goods caused by the default of the lessee. As added in 1990.

REVISED ARTICLE 3
NEGOTIABLE INSTRUMENTS

PART 1
General Provisions and Definitions

§ 3—101. *Short Title.*

This Article may be cited as Uniform Commercial Code—Negotiable Instruments.

§ 3—102. *Subject Matter.*

(a) This Article applies to negotiable instruments. It does not apply to money, to payment orders governed by Article 4A, or to securities governed by Article 8.

(b) If there is conflict between this Article and Article 4 or 9, Articles 4 and 9 govern.

(c) Regulations of the Board of Governors of the Federal Reserve System and operating circulars of the Federal Reserve Banks supersede any inconsistent provision of this Article to the extent of the inconsistency.

§ 3—103. *Definitions.*

(a) In this Article:

(1) "Acceptor" means a drawee who has accepted a draft.

(2) "Drawee" means a person ordered in a draft to make payment.

(3) "Drawer" means a person who signs or is identified in a draft as a person ordering payment.

(4) "Good faith" means honesty in fact and the observance of reasonable commercial standards of fair dealing.

(5) "Maker" means a person who signs or is identified in a note as a person undertaking to pay.

(6) "Order" means a written instruction to pay money signed by the person giving the instruction. The instruction may be addressed to any person, including the person giving the instruction, or to one or more persons jointly or in the alternative but not in succession. An authorization to pay is not an order unless the person authorized to pay is also instructed to pay.

(7) "Ordinary care" in the case of a person engaged in business means observance of reasonable commercial standards, prevailing in the area in which the person is located, with respect to the business in which the person is engaged. In the case of a bank that takes an instrument for processing for collection or payment by automated means, reasonable commercial standards do not require the bank to examine the instrument if the failure to examine does not violate the bank's prescribed procedures and the bank's procedures do not vary unreasonably from general banking usage not disapproved by this Article or Article 4.

(8) "Party" means a party to an instrument.

(9) "Promise" means a written undertaking to pay money signed by the person undertaking to pay. An acknowledgment of an obligation by the obligor is not a promise unless the obligor also undertakes to pay the obligation.

(10) "Prove" with respect to a fact means to meet the burden of establishing the fact (Section 1—201(8)).

(11) "Remitter" means a person who purchases an instrument from its issuer if the instrument is payable to an identified person other than the purchaser.

(b);(c) [Other definitions' section references deleted.]

(d) In addition, Article 1 contains general definitions and principles of construction and interpretation applicable throughout this Article.

§ 3—104. *Negotiable Instrument.*

(a) Except as provided in subsections (c) and (d), "negotiable instrument" means an unconditional promise or order to pay a fixed amount of money, with or without interest or other charges described in the promise or order, if it:

(1) is payable to bearer or to order at the time it is issued or first comes into possession of a holder;

(2) is payable on demand or at a definite time; and

(3) does not state any other undertaking or instruction by the person promising or ordering payment to do any act in addition to the payment of money, but the promise or order may contain (i) an undertaking or power to give, maintain, or protect collateral to secure payment, (ii) an authorization or power to the holder to confess judgment or realize on or dispose of collateral, or (iii) a waiver of the benefit of any law intended for the advantage or protection of an obligor.

(b) "Instrument" means a negotiable instrument.

(c) An order that meets all of the requirements of subsection (a), except paragraph (1), and otherwise falls within the definition of "check" in subsection (f) is a negotiable instrument and a check.

(d) A promise or order other than a check is not an instrument if, at the time it is issued or first comes into possession of a holder, it contains a conspicuous statement, however expressed, to the effect that the promise or order is not negotiable or is not an instrument governed by this Article.

(e) An instrument is a "note" if it is a promise and is a "draft" if it is an order. If an instrument falls within the definition of both "note" and "draft," a person entitled to enforce the instrument may treat it as either.

(f) "Check" means (i) a draft, other than a documentary draft, payable on demand and drawn on a bank or (ii) a cashier's check or teller's check. An instrument may be a check even though it is described on its face by another term, such as "money order."

(g) "Cashier's check" means a draft with respect to which the drawer and drawee are the same bank or branches of the same bank.

(h) "Teller's check" means a draft drawn by a bank (i) on another bank, or (ii) payable at or through a bank.

(i) "Traveler's check" means an instrument that (i) is payable on demand, (ii) is drawn on or payable at or through a bank, (iii) is designated by the term "traveler's check" or by a substantially similar term, and (iv) requires, as a condition to payment, a countersignature by a person whose specimen signature appears on the instrument.

(j) "Certificate of deposit" means an instrument containing an acknowledgment by a bank that a sum of money has been received by the bank and a promise by the bank to repay the sum of money. A certificate of deposit is a note of the bank.

§ 3—105. *Issue of Instrument.*

(a) "Issue" means the first delivery of an instrument by the maker or drawer, whether to a holder or nonholder, for the purpose of giving rights on the instrument to any person.

(b) An unissued instrument, or an unissued incomplete instrument that is completed, is binding on the maker or drawer, but nonissuance is a defense. An instrument that is conditionally issued or is issued for a special purpose is binding on the maker or drawer, but failure of the condition or special purpose to be fulfilled is a defense.

(c) "Issuer" applies to issued and unissued instruments and means a maker or drawer of an instrument.

§ 3—106. *Unconditional Promise or Order.*

(a) Except as provided in this section, for the purposes of Section 3—104(a), a promise or order is unconditional unless it states (i) an express condition to payment, (ii) that the promise or order is subject to or governed by another writing, or (iii) that rights or obligations with respect to the promise or order are stated in another writing. A reference to another writing does not of itself make the promise or order conditional.

(b) A promise or order is not made conditional (i) by a reference to another writing for a statement of rights with respect to collateral, prepayment, or acceleration, or (ii) because payment is limited to resort to a particular fund or source.

(c) If a promise or order requires, as a condition to payment, a countersignature by a person whose specimen signature appears on the promise or order, the condition does not make the promise or order conditional for the purposes of Section 3—104(a). If the person whose specimen signature appears on an instrument fails to countersign the instrument, the failure to countersign is a defense to the obligation of the issuer, but the failure does not prevent a transferee of the instrument from becoming a holder of the instrument.

(d) If a promise or order at the time it is issued or first comes into possession of a holder contains a statement, required by applicable statutory or administrative law, to the effect that the rights of a holder or transferee are subject to claims or defenses that the issuer could assert against the original payee, the promise or order is not thereby made conditional for the purposes of Section 3—104(a); but if the promise or order is an instrument, there cannot be a holder in due course of the instrument.

§ 3—107. *Instrument Payable in Foreign Money.*

Unless the instrument otherwise provides, an instrument that states the amount payable in foreign money may be paid in the foreign money or in an equivalent amount in dollars calculated by using the current bank-offered spot rate at the place of payment for the purchase of dollars on the day on which the instrument is paid.

§ 3—108. *Payable on Demand or at Definite Time.*

(a) A promise or order is "payable on demand" if it (i) states that it is payable on demand or at sight, or otherwise indicates that it is payable at the will of the holder, or (ii) does not state any time of payment.

(b) A promise or order is "payable at a definite time" if it is payable on elapse of a definite period of time after sight or acceptance or at a fixed date or dates or at a time or times readily ascertainable at the time the promise or order is issued, subject to rights of (i) prepayment, (ii) acceleration, (iii) extension at the option of the holder, or (iv) extension to a further definite time at the option of the maker or acceptor or automatically upon or after a specified act or event.

(c) If an instrument, payable at a fixed date, is also payable upon demand made before the fixed date, the instrument is payable on demand until the fixed date and, if demand for payment is not made before that date, becomes payable at a definite time on the fixed date.

§ 3—109. *Payable to Bearer or to Order.*

(a) A promise or order is payable to bearer if it:

(1) states that it is payable to bearer or to the order of bearer or otherwise indicates that the person in possession of the promise or order is entitled to payment;

(2) does not state a payee; or

(3) states that it is payable to or to the order of cash or otherwise indicates that it is not payable to an identified person.

(b) A promise or order that is not payable to bearer is payable to order if it is payable (i) to the order of an identified person or (ii) to an identified person or order. A promise or order that is payable to order is payable to the identified person.

(c) An instrument payable to bearer may become payable to an identified person if it is specially indorsed pursuant to Section

3—205(a). An instrument payable to an identified person may become payable to bearer if it is indorsed in blank pursuant to Section 3—205(b).

§ 3—110. *Identification of Person to Whom Instrument Is Payable.*

(a) The person to whom an instrument is initially payable is determined by the intent of the person, whether or not authorized, signing as, or in the name or behalf of, the issuer of the instrument. The instrument is payable to the person intended by the signer even if that person is identified in the instrument by a name or other identification that is not that of the intended person. If more than one person signs in the name or behalf of the issuer of an instrument and all the signers do not intend the same person as payee, the instrument is payable to any person intended by one or more of the signers.

(b) If the signature of the issuer of an instrument is made by automated means, such as a check-writing machine, the payee of the instrument is determined by the intent of the person who supplied the name or identification of the payee, whether or not authorized to do so.

(c) A person to whom an instrument is payable may be identified in any way, including by name, identifying number, office, or account number. For the purpose of determining the holder of an instrument, the following rules apply:

(1) If an instrument is payable to an account and the account is identified only by number, the instrument is payable to the person to whom the account is payable. If an instrument is payable to an account identified by number and by the name of a person, the instrument is payable to the named person, whether or not that person is the owner of the account identified by number.

(2) If an instrument is payable to:

(i) a trust, an estate, or a person described as trustee or representative of a trust or estate, the instrument is payable to the trustee, the representative, or a successor of either, whether or not the beneficiary or estate is also named;

(ii) a person described as agent or similar representative of a named or identified person, the instrument is payable to the represented person, the representative, or a successor of the representative;

(iii) a fund or organization that is not a legal entity, the instrument is payable to a representative of the members of the fund or organization; or

(iv) an office or to a person described as holding an office, the instrument is payable to the named person, the incumbent of the office, or a successor to the incumbent.

(d) If an instrument is payable to two or more persons alternatively, it is payable to any of them and may be negotiated, discharged, or enforced by any or all of them in possession of the instrument. If an instrument is payable to two or more persons not alternatively, it is payable to all of them and may be negotiated, discharged, or enforced only by all of them. If an instrument payable to two or more persons is ambiguous as to whether it is payable to the persons alternatively, the instrument is payable to the persons alternatively.

§ *3—111. Place of Payment.*

Except as otherwise provided for items in Article 4, an instrument is payable at the place of payment stated in the instrument. If no place of payment is stated, an instrument is payable at the address of the drawee or maker stated in the instrument. If no address is stated, the place of payment is the place of business of the drawee or maker. If a drawee or maker has more than one place of business, the place of payment is any place of business of the drawee or maker chosen by the person entitled to enforce the instrument. If the drawee or maker has no place of business, the place of payment is the residence of the drawee or maker.

§ *3—112. Interest.*

(a) Unless otherwise provided in the instrument, (i) an instrument is not payable with interest, and (ii) interest on an interest-bearing instrument is payable from the date of the instrument.

(b) Interest may be stated in an instrument as a fixed or variable amount of money or it may be expressed as a fixed or variable rate or rates. The amount or rate of interest may be stated or described in the instrument in any manner and may require reference to information not contained in the instrument. If an instrument provides for interest, but the amount of interest payable cannot be ascertained from the description, interest is payable at the judgment rate in effect at the place of payment of the instrument and at the time interest first accrues.

§ *3—113. Date of Instrument.*

(a) An instrument may be antedated or postdated. The date stated determines the time of payment if the instrument is payable at a fixed period after date. Except as provided in Section 4—401(c), an instrument payable on demand is not payable before the date of the instrument.

(b) If an instrument is undated, its date is the date of its issue or, in the case of an unissued instrument, the date it first comes into possession of a holder.

§ *3—114. Contradictory Terms of Instrument.*

If an instrument contains contradictory terms, typewritten terms prevail over printed terms, handwritten terms prevail over both, and words prevail over numbers.

§ *3—115. Incomplete Instrument.*

(a) "Incomplete instrument" means a signed writing, whether or not issued by the signer, the contents of which show at the time of signing that it is incomplete but that the signer intended it to be completed by the addition of words or numbers.

(b) Subject to subsection (c), if an incomplete instrument is an instrument under Section 3—104, it may be enforced according to its terms if it is not completed, or according to its terms as augmented by completion. If an incomplete instrument is not an instrument under Section 3—104, but, after completion, the requirements of Section 3—104 are met, the instrument may be enforced according to its terms as augmented by completion.

(c) If words or numbers are added to an incomplete instrument without authority of the signer, there is an alteration of the incomplete instrument under Section 3—407.

(d) The burden of establishing that words or numbers were added to an incomplete instrument without authority of the signer is on the person asserting the lack of authority.

§ *3—116. Joint and Several Liability; Contribution.*

(a) Except as otherwise provided in the instrument, two or more persons who have the same liability on an instrument as makers, drawers, acceptors, indorsers who indorse as joint payees, or anomalous indorsers are jointly and severally liable in the capacity in which they sign.

(b) Except as provided in Section 3—419(e) or by agreement of the affected parties, a party having joint and several liability who pays the instrument is entitled to receive from any party having the same joint and several liability contribution in accordance with applicable law.

(c) Discharge of one party having joint and several liability by a person entitled to enforce the instrument does not affect the right under subsection (b) of a party having the same joint and several liability to receive contribution from the party discharged.

§ *3—117. Other Agreements Affecting Instrument.*

Subject to applicable law regarding exclusion of proof of contemporaneous or previous agreements, the obligation of a party to an instrument to pay the instrument may be modified, supplemented, or nullified by a separate agreement of the obligor and a person entitled to enforce the instrument, if the instrument is issued or the obligation is incurred in reliance on the agreement or as part of the same transaction giving rise to the agreement. To the extent an obligation is modified, supplemented, or nullified by an agreement under this section, the agreement is a defense to the obligation.

§ 3—118. *Statute of Limitations.*

(a) Except as provided in subsection (e), an action to enforce the obligation of a party to pay a note payable at a definite time must be commenced within six years after the due date or dates stated in the note or, if a due date is accelerated, within six years after the accelerated due date.

(b) Except as provided in subsection (d) or (e), if demand for payment is made to the maker of a note payable on demand, an action to enforce the obligation of a party to pay the note must be commenced within six years after the demand. If no demand for payment is made to the maker, an action to enforce the note is barred if neither principal nor interest on the note has been paid for a continuous period of 10 years.

(c) Except as provided in subsection (d), an action to enforce the obligation of a party to an unaccepted draft to pay the draft must be commenced within three years after dishonor of the draft or 10 years after the date of the draft, whichever period expires first.

(d) An action to enforce the obligation of the acceptor of a certified check or the issuer of a teller's check, cashier's check, or traveler's check must be commenced within three years after demand for payment is made to the acceptor or issuer, as the case may be.

(e) An action to enforce the obligation of a party to a certificate of deposit to pay the instrument must be commenced within six years after demand for payment is made to the maker, but if the instrument states a due date and the maker is not required to pay before that date, the six-year period begins when a demand for payment is in effect and the due date has passed.

(f) An action to enforce the obligation of a party to pay an accepted draft, other than a certified check, must be commenced (i) within six years after the due date or dates stated in the draft or acceptance if the obligation of the acceptor is payable at a definite time, or (ii) within six years after the date of the acceptance if the obligation of the acceptor is payable on demand.

(g) Unless governed by other law regarding claims for indemnity or contribution, an action (i) for conversion of an instrument, for money had and received, or like action based on conversion, (ii) for breach of warranty, or (iii) to enforce an obligation, duty, or right arising under this Article and not governed by this section must be commenced within three years after the [cause of action] accrues.

§ 3—119. *Notice of Right to Defend Action.*

In an action for breach of an obligation for which a third person is answerable over pursuant to this Article or Article 4, the defendant may give the third person written notice of the litigation, and the person notified may then give similar notice to any other person who is answerable over. If the notice states (i) that the person notified may come in and defend and (ii) that failure to do so will bind the person notified in an action later brought by the person giving the notice as to any determination of fact common to the two litigations, the person notified is so bound unless after seasonable receipt of the notice the person notified does come in and defend.

PART 2
Negotiation, Transfer, and Indorsement

§ 3—201. *Negotiation.*

(a) "Negotiation" means a transfer of possession, whether voluntary or involuntary, of an instrument by a person other than the issuer to a person who thereby becomes its holder.

(b) Except for negotiation by a remitter, if an instrument is payable to an identified person, negotiation requires transfer of possession of the instrument and its indorsement by the holder. If an instrument is payable to bearer, it may be negotiated by transfer of possession alone.

§ 3—202. *Negotiation Subject to Rescission.*

(a) Negotiation is effective even if obtained (i) from an infant, a corporation exceeding its powers, or a person without capacity, (ii) by fraud, duress, or mistake, or (iii) in breach of duty or as part of an illegal transaction.

(b) To the extent permitted by other law, negotiation may be rescinded or may be subject to other remedies, but those remedies may not be asserted against a subsequent holder in due course or a person paying the instrument in good faith and without knowledge of facts that are a basis for rescission or other remedy.

§ 3—203. *Transfer of Instrument; Rights Acquired by Transfer.*

(a) An instrument is transferred when it is delivered by a person other than its issuer for the purpose of giving to the person receiving delivery the right to enforce the instrument.

(b) Transfer of an instrument, whether or not the transfer is a negotiation, vests in the transferee any right of the transferor to enforce the instrument, including any right as a holder in due course, but the transferee cannot acquire rights of a holder in due course by a transfer, directly or indirectly, from a holder in due course if the transferee engaged in fraud or illegality affecting the instrument.

(c) Unless otherwise agreed, if an instrument is transferred for value and the transferee does not become a holder because of lack of indorsement by the transferor, the transferee has a specifically enforceable right to the unqualified indorsement of the transferor, but negotiation of the instrument does not occur until the indorsement is made.

(d) If a transferor purports to transfer less than the entire instrument, negotiation of the instrument does not occur. The transferee obtains no rights under this Article and has only the rights of a partial assignee.

§ 3—204. *Indorsement.*

(a) "Indorsement" means a signature, other than that of a signer as maker, drawer, or acceptor, that alone or accompanied by other words is made on an instrument for the purpose of (i) negotiating the instrument, (ii) restricting payment of the instrument, or (iii) incurring indorser's liability on the instrument, but regardless of the intent of the signer, a signature and its accompanying words is an indorsement unless the accompanying words, terms of the instrument, place of the signature, or other circumstances unambiguously indicate that the signature was made for a purpose other than indorsement. For the purpose of determining whether a signature is made on an instrument, a paper affixed to the instrument is a part of the instrument.

(b) "Indorser" means a person who makes an indorsement.

(c) For the purpose of determining whether the transferee of an instrument is a holder, an indorsement that transfers a security interest in the instrument is effective as an unqualified indorsement of the instrument.

(d) If an instrument is payable to a holder under a name that is not the name of the holder, indorsement may be made by the holder in the name stated in the instrument or in the holder's name or both, but signature in both names may be required by a person paying or taking the instrument for value or collection.

§ 3—205. *Special Indorsement; Blank Indorsement; Anomalous Indorsement.*

(a) If an indorsement is made by the holder of an instrument, whether payable to an identified person or payable to bearer, and the indorsement identifies a person to whom it makes the instrument payable, it is a "special indorsement." When specially indorsed, an instrument becomes payable to the identified person and may be negotiated only by the indorsement of that person. The principles stated in Section 3—110 apply to special indorsements.

(b) If an indorsement is made by the holder of an instrument and it is not a special indorsement, it is a "blank indorsement." When indorsed in blank, an instrument becomes payable to bearer and may be negotiated by transfer of possession alone until specially indorsed.

(c) The holder may convert a blank indorsement that consists only of a signature into a special indorsement by writing, above the signature of the indorser, words identifying the person to whom the instrument is made payable.

(d) "Anomalous indorsement" means an indorsement made by a person who is not the holder of the instrument. An anomalous indorsement does not affect the manner in which the instrument may be negotiated.

§ 3—206. *Restrictive Indorsement.*

(a) An indorsement limiting payment to a particular person or otherwise prohibiting further transfer or negotiation of the instrument is not effective to prevent further transfer or negotiation of the instrument.

(b) An indorsement stating a condition to the right of the indorsee to receive payment does not affect the right of the indorsee to enforce the instrument. A person paying the instrument or taking it for value or collection may disregard the condition, and the rights and liabilities of that person are not affected by whether the condition has been fulfilled.

(c) If an instrument bears an indorsement (i) described in Section 4—201(b), or (ii) in blank or to a particular bank using the words "for deposit," "for collection," or other words indicating a purpose of having the instrument collected by a bank for the indorser or for a particular account, the following rules apply:

(1) A person, other than a bank, who purchases the instrument when so indorsed converts the instrument unless the amount paid for the instrument is received by the indorser or applied consistently with the indorsement.

(2) A depositary bank that purchases the instrument or takes it for collection when so indorsed converts the instrument unless the amount paid by the bank with respect to the instrument is received by the indorser or applied consistently with the indorsement.

(3) A payor bank that is also the depositary bank or that takes the instrument for immediate payment over the counter from a person other than a collecting bank converts the instrument unless the proceeds of the instrument are received by the indorser or applied consistently with the indorsement.

(4) Except as otherwise provided in paragraph (3), a payor bank or intermediary bank may disregard the indorsement and is not liable if the proceeds of the instrument are not received by the indorser or applied consistently with the indorsement.

(d) Except for an indorsement covered by subsection (c), if an instrument bears an indorsement using words to the effect that payment is to be made to the indorsee as agent, trustee, or other fiduciary for the benefit of the indorser or another person, the following rules apply:

(1) Unless there is notice of breach of fiduciary duty as provided in Section 3—307, a person who purchases the instrument from the indorsee or takes the instrument from the indorsee for collection or payment may pay the proceeds of payment or the value given for the instrument to the indorsee without regard to whether the indorsee violates a fiduciary duty to the indorser.

(2) A subsequent transferee of the instrument or person who pays the instrument is neither given notice nor otherwise affected by the restriction in the indorsement unless the transferee or payor knows that the fiduciary dealt with the instrument or its proceeds in breach of fiduciary duty.

(e) The presence on an instrument of an indorsement to which this section applies does not prevent a purchaser of the instrument from becoming a holder in due course of the instrument unless the purchaser is a converter under subsection (c) or has notice or knowledge of breach of fiduciary duty as stated in subsection (d).

(f) In an action to enforce the obligation of a party to pay the instrument, the obligor has a defense if payment would violate an indorsement to which this section applies and the payment is not permitted by this section.

§ 3—207. *Reacquisition.*

Reacquisition of an instrument occurs if it is transferred to a former holder, by negotiation or otherwise. A former holder who reacquires the instrument may cancel indorsements made after the reacquirer first became a holder of the instrument. If the cancellation causes the instrument to be payable to the reacquirer or to bearer, the reacquirer may negotiate the instrument. An indorser whose indorsement is canceled is discharged, and the discharge is effective against any subsequent holder.

PART 3
Enforcement of Instruments

§ 3—301. *Person Entitled to Enforce Instrument.*

"Person entitled to enforce" an instrument means (i) the holder of the instrument, (ii) a nonholder in possession of the instrument who has the rights of a holder, or (iii) a person not in possession of the instrument who is entitled to enforce the instrument pursuant to Section 3—309 or 3—418(d). A person may be a person entitled to enforce the instrument even though the person is not the owner of the instrument or is in wrongful possession of the instrument.

§ 3—302. *Holder in Due Course.*

(a) Subject to subsection (c) and Section 3—106(d), "holder in due course" means the holder of an instrument if:

(1) the instrument when issued or negotiated to the holder does not bear such apparent evidence of forgery or alteration or is not otherwise so irregular or incomplete as to call into question its authenticity; and

(2) the holder took the instrument (i) for value, (ii) in good faith, (iii) without notice that the instrument is overdue or has

been dishonored or that there is an uncured default with respect to payment of another instrument issued as part of the same series, (iv) without notice that the instrument contains an unauthorized signature or has been altered, (v) without notice of any claim to the instrument described in Section 3—306, and (vi) without notice that any party has a defense or claim in recoupment described in Section 3—305(a).

(b) Notice of discharge of a party, other than discharge in an insolvency proceeding, is not notice of a defense under subsection (a), but discharge is effective against a person who became a holder in due course with notice of the discharge. Public filing or recording of a document does not of itself constitute notice of a defense, claim in recoupment, or claim to the instrument.

(c) Except to the extent a transferor or predecessor in interest has rights as a holder in due course, a person does not acquire rights of a holder in due course of an instrument taken (i) by legal process or by purchase in an execution, bankruptcy, or creditor's sale or similar proceeding, (ii) by purchase as part of a bulk transaction not in ordinary course of business of the transferor, or (iii) as the successor in interest to an estate or other organization.

(d) If, under Section 3—303(a)(1), the promise of performance that is the consideration for an instrument has been partially performed, the holder may assert rights as a holder in due course of the instrument only to the fraction of the amount payable under the instrument equal to the value of the partial performance divided by the value of the promised performance.

(e) If (i) the person entitled to enforce an instrument has only a security interest in the instrument and (ii) the person obliged to pay the instrument has a defense, claim in recoupment, or claim to the instrument that may be asserted against the person who granted the security interest, the person entitled to enforce the instrument may assert rights as a holder in due course only to an amount payable under the instrument which, at the time of enforcement of the instrument, does not exceed the amount of the unpaid obligation secured.

(f) To be effective, notice must be received at a time and in a manner that gives a reasonable opportunity to act on it.

(g) This section is subject to any law limiting status as a holder in due course in particular classes of transactions.

§ 3—303. *Value and Consideration.*

(a) An instrument is issued or transferred for value if:

(1) the instrument is issued or transferred for a promise of performance, to the extent the promise has been performed;

(2) the transferee acquires a security interest or other lien in the instrument other than a lien obtained by judicial proceeding;

(3) the instrument is issued or transferred as payment of, or as security for, an antecedent claim against any person, whether or not the claim is due;

(4) the instrument is issued or transferred in exchange for a negotiable instrument; or

(5) the instrument is issued or transferred in exchange for the incurring of an irrevocable obligation to a third party by the person taking the instrument.

(b) "Consideration" means any consideration sufficient to support a simple contract. The drawer or maker of an instrument has a defense if the instrument is issued without consideration. If an instrument is issued for a promise of performance, the issuer has a defense to the extent performance of the promise is due and the promise has not been performed. If an instrument is issued for value as stated in subsection (a), the instrument is also issued for consideration.

§ 3—304. *Overdue Instrument.*

(a) An instrument payable on demand becomes overdue at the earliest of the following times:

(1) on the day after the day demand for payment is duly made;

(2) if the instrument is a check, 90 days after its date; or

(3) if the instrument is not a check, when the instrument has been outstanding for a period of time after its date which is unreasonably long under the circumstances of the particular case in light of the nature of the instrument and usage of the trade.

(b) With respect to an instrument payable at a definite time the following rules apply:

(1) If the principal is payable in installments and a due date has not been accelerated, the instrument becomes overdue upon default under the instrument for nonpayment of an installment, and the instrument remains overdue until the default is cured.

(2) If the principal is not payable in installments and the due date has not been accelerated, the instrument becomes overdue on the day after the due date.

(3) If a due date with respect to principal has been accelerated, the instrument becomes overdue on the day after the accelerated due date.

(c) Unless the due date of principal has been accelerated, an instrument does not become overdue if there is default in payment of interest but no default in payment of principal.

§ 3—305. *Defenses and Claims in Recoupment.*

(a) Except as stated in subsection (b), the right to enforce the obligation of a party to pay an instrument is subject to the following:

(1) a defense of the obligor based on (i) infancy of the obligor to the extent it is a defense to a simple contract, (ii) duress, lack of legal capacity, or illegality of the transaction which, under other law, nullifies the obligation of the obligor, (iii) fraud that induced the obligor to sign the instrument with neither knowledge nor reasonable opportunity to learn of its character or its essential terms, or (iv) discharge of the obligor in insolvency proceedings;

(2) a defense of the obligor stated in another section of this Article or a defense of the obligor that would be available if the person entitled to enforce the instrument were enforcing a right to payment under a simple contract; and

(3) a claim in recoupment of the obligor against the original payee of the instrument if the claim arose from the transaction that gave rise to the instrument; but the claim of the obligor may be asserted against a transferee of the instrument only to reduce the amount owing on the instrument at the time the action is brought.

(b) The right of a holder in due course to enforce the obligation of a party to pay the instrument is subject to defenses of the obligor stated in subsection (a)(1), but is not subject to defenses of the obligor stated in subsection (a)(2) or claims in recoupment stated in subsection (a)(3) against a person other than the holder.

(c) Except as stated in subsection (d), in an action to enforce the obligation of a party to pay the instrument, the obligor may not assert against the person entitled to enforce the instrument a defense, claim in recoupment, or claim to the instrument (Section 3—306) of another person, but the other person's claim to the instrument may be asserted by the obligor if the other person is joined in the action and personally asserts the claim against the person entitled to enforce the instrument. An obligor is not obliged to pay the instrument if the person seeking enforcement of the instrument does not have rights of a holder in due course and the obligor proves that the instrument is a lost or stolen instrument.

(d) In an action to enforce the obligation of an accommodation party to pay an instrument, the accommodation party may assert against the person entitled to enforce the instrument any defense or claim in recoupment under subsection (a) that the accommodated party could assert against the person entitled to enforce the instrument, except the defenses of discharge in insolvency proceedings, infancy, and lack of legal capacity.

§ 3—306. *Claims to an Instrument.*

A person taking an instrument, other than a person having rights of a holder in due course, is subject to a claim of a property or possessory right in the instrument or its proceeds, including a claim to rescind a negotiation and to recover the instrument or its proceeds. A person having rights of a holder in due course takes free of the claim to the instrument.

§ 3—307. *Notice of Breach of Fiduciary Duty.*

(a) In this section:

(1) "Fiduciary" means an agent, trustee, partner, corporate officer or director, or other representative owing a fiduciary duty with respect to an instrument.

(2) "Represented person" means the principal, beneficiary, partnership, corporation, or other person to whom the duty stated in paragraph (1) is owed.

(b) If (i) an instrument is taken from a fiduciary for payment or collection or for value, (ii) the taker has knowledge of the fiduciary status of the fiduciary, and (iii) the represented person makes a claim to the instrument or its proceeds on the basis that the transaction of the fiduciary is a breach of fiduciary duty, the following rules apply:

(1) Notice of breach of fiduciary duty by the fiduciary is notice of the claim of the represented person.

(2) In the case of an instrument payable to the represented person or the fiduciary as such, the taker has notice of the breach of fiduciary duty if the instrument is (i) taken in payment of or as security for a debt known by the taker to be the personal debt of the fiduciary, (ii) taken in a transaction known by the taker to be for the personal benefit of the fiduciary, or (iii) deposited to an account other than an account of the fiduciary, as such, or an account of the represented person.

(3) If an instrument is issued by the represented person or the fiduciary as such, and made payable to the fiduciary personally, the taker does not have notice of the breach of fiduciary duty unless the taker knows of the breach of fiduciary duty.

(4) If an instrument is issued by the represented person or the fiduciary as such, to the taker as payee, the taker has notice of the breach of fiduciary duty if the instrument is (i) taken in payment of or as security for a debt known by the taker to be the personal debt of the fiduciary, (ii) taken in a transaction known by the taker to be for the personal benefit of the fiduciary, or (iii) deposited to an account other than an account of the fiduciary, as such, or an account of the represented person.

§ 3—308. *Proof of Signatures and Status as Holder in Due Course.*

(a) In an action with respect to an instrument, the authenticity of, and authority to make, each signature on the instrument is admitted unless specifically denied in the pleadings. If the validity of a signature is denied in the pleadings, the burden of establishing validity is on the person claiming validity, but the signature is presumed to be authentic and authorized unless the action is to enforce the liability of the purported signer and the signer is dead or incompetent at the time of trial of the issue of validity of the signature. If an action to enforce the instrument is brought against a person as the undisclosed principal of a person who signed the instrument as a party to the instrument, the plaintiff has the burden of establishing that the defendant is liable on the instrument as a represented person under Section 3—402(a).

(b) If the validity of signatures is admitted or proved and there is compliance with subsection (a), a plaintiff producing the instrument is entitled to payment if the plaintiff proves entitlement to enforce the instrument under Section 3—301, unless the defendant proves a defense or claim in recoupment. If a defense or claim in recoupment is proved, the right to payment of the plaintiff is subject to the defense or claim, except to the extent the plaintiff proves that the plaintiff has rights of a holder in due course which are not subject to the defense or claim.

§ 3—309. *Enforcement of Lost, Destroyed, or Stolen Instrument.*

(a) A person not in possession of an instrument is entitled to enforce the instrument if (i) the person was in possession of the instrument and entitled to enforce it when loss of possession occurred, (ii) the loss of possession was not the result of a transfer by the person or a lawful seizure, and (iii) the person cannot reasonably obtain possession of the instrument because the instrument was destroyed, its whereabouts cannot be determined, or it is in the wrongful possession of an unknown person or a person that cannot be found or is not amenable to service of process.

(b) A person seeking enforcement of an instrument under subsection (a) must prove the terms of the instrument and the person's right to enforce the instrument. If that proof is made, Section 3—308 applies to the case as if the person seeking enforcement had produced the instrument. The court may not enter judgment in favor of the person seeking enforcement unless it finds that the person required to pay the instrument is adequately protected against loss that might occur by reason of a claim by another person to enforce the instrument. Adequate protection may be provided by any reasonable means.

§ 3—310. *Effect of Instrument on Obligation for Which Taken.*

(a) Unless otherwise agreed, if a certified check, cashier's check, or teller's check is taken for an obligation, the obligation is discharged to the same extent discharge would result if an amount of money equal to the amount of the instrument were taken in payment of the obligation. Discharge of the obligation does not affect any liability that the obligor may have as an indorser of the instrument.

(b) Unless otherwise agreed and except as provided in subsection (a), if a note or an uncertified check is taken for an obligation, the obligation is suspended to the same extent the obligation would be discharged if an amount of money equal to the amount of the instrument were taken, and the following rules apply:

(1) In the case of an uncertified check, suspension of the obligation continues until dishonor of the check or until it is paid or certified. Payment or certification of the check results in discharge of the obligation to the extent of the amount of the check.

(2) In the case of a note, suspension of the obligation continues until dishonor of the note or until it is paid. Payment of the note results in discharge of the obligation to the extent of the payment.

(3) Except as provided in paragraph (4), if the check or note is dishonored and the obligee of the obligation for which the instrument was taken is the person entitled to enforce the instrument, the obligee may enforce either the instrument or the obligation. In the case of an instrument of a third person which is negotiated to the obligee by the obligor, discharge of the obligor on the instrument also discharges the obligation.

(4) If the person entitled to enforce the instrument taken for an obligation is a person other than the obligee, the obligee may not enforce the obligation to the extent the obligation is suspended. If the obligee is the person entitled to enforce the instrument but no longer has possession of it because it was lost, stolen, or destroyed, the obligation may not be enforced to the extent of the amount payable on the instrument, and to that extent the obligee's rights against the obligor are limited to enforcement of the instrument.

(c) If an instrument other than one described in subsection (a) or (b) is taken for an obligation, the effect is (i) that stated in subsection (a) if the instrument is one on which a bank is liable as maker or acceptor, or (ii) that stated in subsection (b) in any other case.

§ 3—311. *Accord and Satisfaction by Use of Instrument.*

(a) If a person against whom a claim is asserted proves that (i) that person in good faith tendered an instrument to the claimant as full satisfaction of the claim, (ii) the amount of the claim was unliquidated or subject to a bona fide dispute, and (iii) the claimant obtained payment of the instrument, the following subsections apply.

(b) Unless subsection (c) applies, the claim is discharged if the person against whom the claim is asserted proves that the instrument or an accompanying written communication contained a conspicuous statement to the effect that the instrument was tendered as full satisfaction of the claim.

(c) Subject to subsection (d), a claim is not discharged under subsection (b) if either of the following applies:

(1) The claimant, if an organization, proves that (i) within a reasonable time before the tender, the claimant sent a conspicuous statement to the person against whom the claim is asserted that communications concerning disputed debts, including an instrument tendered as full satisfaction of a debt, are to be sent to a designated person, office, or place, and (ii) the instrument or accompanying communication was not received by that designated person, office, or place.

(2) The claimant, whether or not an organization, proves that within 90 days after payment of the instrument, the claimant tendered repayment of the amount of the instrument to the person against whom the claim is asserted. This paragraph does not apply if the claimant is an organization that sent a statement complying with paragraph (1)(i).

(d) A claim is discharged if the person against whom the claim is asserted proves that within a reasonable time before collection of the instrument was initiated, the claimant, or an agent of the claimant having direct responsibility with respect to the disputed obligation, knew that the instrument was tendered in full satisfaction of the claim.

§ 3—312. *Lost, Destroyed, or Stolen Cashier's Check, Teller's Check, or Certified Check.*

(a) In this section:

(1) "Check" means a cashier's check, teller's check, or certified check.

(2) "Claimant" means a person who claims the right to receive the amount of a cashier's check, teller's check, or certified check that was lost, destroyed, or stolen.

(3) "Declaration of loss" means a written statement, made under penalty of perjury, to the effect that (i) the declarer lost possession of a check, (ii) the declarer is the drawer or payee of the check, in the case of a certified check, or the remitter or payee of the check, in the case of a cashier's check or teller's check, (iii) the loss of possession was not the result of a transfer by the declarer or a lawful seizure, and (iv) the declarer cannot reasonably obtain possession of the check because the check was destroyed, its whereabouts cannot be determined, or it is in the wrongful possession of an unknown person or a person that cannot be found or is not amenable to service of process.

(4) "Obligated bank" means the issuer of a cashier's check or teller's check or the acceptor of a certified check.

(b) A claimant may assert a claim to the amount of a check by a communication to the obligated bank describing the check with reasonable certainty and requesting payment of the amount of the check, if (i) the claimant is the drawer or payee of a certified check or the remitter or payee of a cashier's check or teller's check, (ii) the communication contains or is accompanied by a declaration of loss of the claimant with respect to the check, (iii) the communication is received at a time and in a manner affording the bank a reasonable time to act on it before the check is paid, and (iv) the claimant provides reasonable identification if requested by the obligated bank. Delivery of a declaration of loss is a warranty of the truth of the statements made in the declaration. If a claim is asserted in compliance with this subsection, the following rules apply:

(1) The claim becomes enforceable at the later of (i) the time the claim is asserted, or (ii) the 90th day following the date of the check, in the case of a cashier's check or teller's check, or the 90th day following the date of the acceptance, in the case of a certified check.

(2) Until the claim becomes enforceable, it has no legal effect and the obligated bank may pay the check or, in the case of a teller's check, may permit the drawee to pay the check. Payment to a person entitled to enforce the check discharges all liability of the obligated bank with respect to the check.

(3) If the claim becomes enforceable before the check is presented for payment, the obligated bank is not obliged to pay the check.

(4) When the claim becomes enforceable, the obligated bank becomes obliged to pay the amount of the check to the claimant if payment of the check has not been made to a person entitled to enforce the check. Subject to Section 4—302(a)(1), payment to the

claimant discharges all liability of the obligated bank with respect to the check.

(c) If the obligated bank pays the amount of a check to a claimant under subsection (b)(4) and the check is presented for payment by a person having rights of a holder in due course, the claimant is obliged to (i) refund the payment to the obligated bank if the check is paid, or (ii) pay the amount of the check to the person having rights of a holder in due course if the check is dishonored.

(d) If a claimant has the right to assert a claim under subsection (b) and is also a person entitled to enforce a cashier's check, teller's check, or certified check which is lost, destroyed, or stolen, the claimant may assert rights with respect to the check either under this section or Section 3—309.

PART 4
Liability of Parties

§ 3—401. *Signature.*

(a) A person is not liable on an instrument unless (i) the person signed the instrument, or (ii) the person is represented by an agent or representative who signed the instrument and the signature is binding on the represented person under Section 3—402.

(b) A signature may be made (i) manually or by means of a device or machine, and (ii) by the use of any name, including a trade or assumed name, or by a word, mark, or symbol executed or adopted by a person with present intention to authenticate a writing.

§ 3—402. *Signature by Representative.*

(a) If a person acting, or purporting to act, as a representative signs an instrument by signing either the name of the represented person or the name of the signer, the represented person is bound by the signature to the same extent the represented person would be bound if the signature were on a simple contract. If the represented person is bound, the signature of the representative is the "authorized signature of the represented person" and the represented person is liable on the instrument, whether or not identified in the instrument.

(b) If a representative signs the name of the representative to an instrument and the signature is an authorized signature of the represented person, the following rules apply:

(1) If the form of the signature shows unambiguously that the signature is made on behalf of the represented person who is identified in the instrument, the representative is not liable on the instrument.

(2) Subject to subsection (c), if (i) the form of the signature does not show unambiguously that the signature is made in a representative capacity or (ii) the represented person is not identified in the instrument, the representative is liable on the instrument to a holder in due course that took the instrument without notice that the representative was not intended to be liable on the instrument. With respect to any other person, the representative is liable on the instrument unless the representative proves that the original parties did not intend the representative to be liable on the instrument.

(c) If a representative signs the name of the representative as drawer of a check without indication of the representative status and the check is payable from an account of the represented person who is identified on the check, the signer is not liable on the check if the signature is an authorized signature of the represented person.

§ 3—403. *Unauthorized Signature.*

(a) Unless otherwise provided in this Article or Article 4, an unauthorized signature is ineffective except as the signature of the unauthorized signer in favor of a person who in good faith pays the instrument or takes it for value. An unauthorized signature may be ratified for all purposes of this Article.

(b) If the signature of more than one person is required to constitute the authorized signature of an organization, the signature of the organization is unauthorized if one of the required signatures is lacking.

(c) The civil or criminal liability of a person who makes an unauthorized signature is not affected by any provision of this Article which makes the unauthorized signature effective for the purposes of this Article.

§ 3—404. *Impostors; Fictitious Payees.*

(a) If an impostor, by use of the mails or otherwise, induces the issuer of an instrument to issue the instrument to the impostor, or to a person acting in concert with the impostor, by impersonating the payee of the instrument or a person authorized to act for the payee, an indorsement of the instrument by any person in the name of the payee is effective as the indorsement of the payee in favor of a person who, in good faith, pays the instrument or takes it for value or for collection.

(b) If (i) a person whose intent determines to whom an instrument is payable (Section 3—110(a) or (b)) does not intend the person identified as payee to have any interest in the instrument, or (ii) the person identified as payee of an instrument is a fictitious person, the following rules apply until the instrument is negotiated by special indorsement:

(1) Any person in possession of the instrument is its holder.

(2) An indorsement by any person in the name of the payee stated in the instrument is effective as the indorsement of the payee in favor of a person who, in good faith, pays the instrument or takes it for value or for collection.

(c) Under subsection (a) or (b), an indorsement is made in the name of a payee if (i) it is made in a name substantially similar to that of the payee or (ii) the instrument, whether or not indorsed, is deposited in a depositary bank to an account in a name substantially similar to that of the payee.

(d) With respect to an instrument to which subsection (a) or (b) applies, if a person paying the instrument or taking it for value or for collection fails to exercise ordinary care in paying or taking the instrument and that failure substantially contributes to loss resulting from payment of the instrument, the person bearing the loss may recover from the person failing to exercise ordinary care to the extent the failure to exercise ordinary care contributed to the loss.

§ 3—405. *Employer's Responsibility for Fraudulent Indorsement by Employee.*

(a) In this section:

(1) "Employee" includes an independent contractor and employee of an independent contractor retained by the employer.

(2) "Fraudulent indorsement" means (i) in the case of an instrument payable to the employer, a forged indorsement purporting to be that of the employer, or (ii) in the case of an instrument

with respect to which the employer is the issuer, a forged indorsement purporting to be that of the person identified as payee.

(3) "Responsibility" with respect to instruments means authority (i) to sign or indorse instruments on behalf of the employer, (ii) to process instruments received by the employer for bookkeeping purposes, for deposit to an account, or for other disposition, (iii) to prepare or process instruments for issue in the name of the employer, (iv) to supply information determining the names or addresses of payees of instruments to be issued in the name of the employer, (v) to control the disposition of instruments to be issued in the name of the employer, or (vi) to act otherwise with respect to instruments in a responsible capacity. "Responsibility" does not include authority that merely allows an employee to have access to instruments or blank or incomplete instrument forms that are being stored or transported or are part of incoming or outgoing mail, or similar access.

(b) For the purpose of determining the rights and liabilities of a person who, in good faith, pays an instrument or takes it for value or for collection, if an employer entrusted an employee with responsibility with respect to the instrument and the employee or a person acting in concert with the employee makes a fraudulent indorsement of the instrument, the indorsement is effective as the indorsement of the person to whom the instrument is payable if it is made in the name of that person. If the person paying the instrument or taking it for value or for collection fails to exercise ordinary care in paying or taking the instrument and that failure substantially contributes to loss resulting from the fraud, the person bearing the loss may recover from the person failing to exercise ordinary care to the extent the failure to exercise ordinary care contributed to the loss.

(c) Under subsection (b), an indorsement is made in the name of the person to whom an instrument is payable if (i) it is made in a name substantially similar to the name of that person or (ii) the instrument, whether or not indorsed, is deposited in a depositary bank to an account in a name substantially similar to the name of that person.

§ 3—406. *Negligence Contributing to Forged Signature or Alteration of Instrument.*

(a) A person whose failure to exercise ordinary care substantially contributes to an alteration of an instrument or to the making of a forged signature on an instrument is precluded from asserting the alteration or the forgery against a person who, in good faith, pays the instrument or takes it for value or for collection.

(b) Under subsection (a), if the person asserting the preclusion fails to exercise ordinary care in paying or taking the instrument and that failure substantially contributes to loss, the loss is allocated between the person precluded and the person asserting the preclusion according to the extent to which the failure of each to exercise ordinary care contributed to the loss.

(c) Under subsection (a), the burden of proving failure to exercise ordinary care is on the person asserting the preclusion. Under subsection (b), the burden of proving failure to exercise ordinary care is on the person precluded.

§ 3—407. *Alteration.*

(a) "Alteration" means (i) an unauthorized change in an instrument that purports to modify in any respect the obligation of a party, or (ii) an unauthorized addition of words or numbers or other change to an incomplete instrument relating to the obligation of a party.

(b) Except as provided in subsection (c), an alteration fraudulently made discharges a party whose obligation is affected by the alteration unless that party assents or is precluded from asserting the alteration. No other alteration discharges a party, and the instrument may be enforced according to its original terms.

(c) A payor bank or drawee paying a fraudulently altered instrument or a person taking it for value, in good faith and without notice of the alteration, may enforce rights with respect to the instrument (i) according to its original terms, or (ii) in the case of an incomplete instrument altered by unauthorized completion, according to its terms as completed.

§ 3—408. *Drawee Not Liable on Unaccepted Draft.*

A check or other draft does not of itself operate as an assignment of funds in the hands of the drawee available for its payment, and the drawee is not liable on the instrument until the drawee accepts it.

§ 3—409. *Acceptance of Draft; Certified Check.*

(a) "Acceptance" means the drawee's signed agreement to pay a draft as presented. It must be written on the draft and may consist of the drawee's signature alone. Acceptance may be made at any time and becomes effective when notification pursuant to instructions is given or the accepted draft is delivered for the purpose of giving rights on the acceptance to any person.

(b) A draft may be accepted although it has not been signed by the drawer, is otherwise incomplete, is overdue, or has been dishonored.

(c) If a draft is payable at a fixed period after sight and the acceptor fails to date the acceptance, the holder may complete the acceptance by supplying a date in good faith.

(d) "Certified check" means a check accepted by the bank on which it is drawn. Acceptance may be made as stated in subsection (a) or by a writing on the check which indicates that the check is certified. The drawee of a check has no obligation to certify the check, and refusal to certify is not dishonor of the check.

§ 3—410. *Acceptance Varying Draft.*

(a) If the terms of a drawee's acceptance vary from the terms of the draft as presented, the holder may refuse the acceptance and treat the draft as dishonored. In that case, the drawee may cancel the acceptance.

(b) The terms of a draft are not varied by an acceptance to pay at a particular bank or place in the United States, unless the acceptance states that the draft is to be paid only at that bank or place.

(c) If the holder assents to an acceptance varying the terms of a draft, the obligation of each drawer and indorser that does not expressly assent to the acceptance is discharged.

§ 3—411. *Refusal to Pay Cashier's Checks, Teller's Checks, and Certified Checks.*

(a) In this section, "obligated bank" means the acceptor of a certified check or the issuer of a cashier's check or teller's check bought from the issuer.

(b) If the obligated bank wrongfully (i) refuses to pay a cashier's check or certified check, (ii) stops payment of a teller's check, or (iii) refuses to pay a dishonored teller's check, the person asserting the right to enforce the check is entitled to compensation for expenses and loss of interest resulting from the nonpayment and may recover consequential damages if the obligated bank refuses to pay after receiving notice of particular circumstances giving rise to the damages.

(c) Expenses or consequential damages under subsection (b) are not recoverable if the refusal of the obligated bank to pay occurs because

(i) the bank suspends payments, (ii) the obligated bank asserts a claim or defense of the bank that it has reasonable grounds to believe is available against the person entitled to enforce the instrument, (iii) the obligated bank has a reasonable doubt whether the person demanding payment is the person entitled to enforce the instrument, or (iv) payment is prohibited by law.

§ 3—412. *Obligation of Issuer of Note or Cashier's Check.*

The issuer of a note or cashier's check or other draft drawn on the drawer is obliged to pay the instrument (i) according to its terms at the time it was issued or, if not issued, at the time it first came into possession of a holder, or (ii) if the issuer signed an incomplete instrument, according to its terms when completed, to the extent stated in Sections 3—115 and 3—407. The obligation is owed to a person entitled to enforce the instrument or to an indorser who paid the instrument under Section 3—415.

§ 3—413. *Obligation of Acceptor.*

(a) The acceptor of a draft is obliged to pay the draft (i) according to its terms at the time it was accepted, even though the acceptance states that the draft is payable "as originally drawn" or equivalent terms, (ii) if the acceptance varies the terms of the draft, according to the terms of the draft as varied, or (iii) if the acceptance is of a draft that is an incomplete instrument, according to its terms when completed, to the extent stated in Sections 3—115 and 3—407. The obligation is owed to a person entitled to enforce the draft or to the drawer or an indorser who paid the draft under Section 3—414 or 3—415.

(b) If the certification of a check or other acceptance of a draft states the amount certified or accepted, the obligation of the acceptor is that amount. If (i) the certification or acceptance does not state an amount, (ii) the amount of the instrument is subsequently raised, and (iii) the instrument is then negotiated to a holder in due course, the obligation of the acceptor is the amount of the instrument at the time it was taken by the holder in due course.

§ 3—414. *Obligation of Drawer.*

(a) This section does not apply to cashier's checks or other drafts drawn on the drawer.

(b) If an unaccepted draft is dishonored, the drawer is obliged to pay the draft (i) according to its terms at the time it was issued or, if not issued, at the time it first came into possession of a holder, or (ii) if the drawer signed an incomplete instrument, according to its terms when completed, to the extent stated in Sections 3—115 and 3—407. The obligation is owed to a person entitled to enforce the draft or to an indorser who paid the draft under Section 3—415.

(c) If a draft is accepted by a bank, the drawer is discharged, regardless of when or by whom acceptance was obtained.

(d) If a draft is accepted and the acceptor is not a bank, the obligation of the drawer to pay the draft if the draft is dishonored by the acceptor is the same as the obligation of an indorser under Section 3—415(a) and (c).

(e) If a draft states that it is drawn "without recourse" or otherwise disclaims liability of the drawer to pay the draft, the drawer is not liable under subsection (b) to pay the draft if the draft is not a check. A disclaimer of the liability stated in subsection (b) is not effective if the draft is a check.

(f) If (i) a check is not presented for payment or given to a depositary bank for collection within 30 days after its date, (ii) the drawee suspends payments after expiration of the 30-day period without paying the check, and (iii) because of the suspension of payments, the drawer is deprived of funds maintained with the drawee to cover payment of the check, the drawer to the extent deprived of funds may discharge its obligation to pay the check by assigning to the person entitled to enforce the check the rights of the drawer against the drawee with respect to the funds.

§ 3—415. *Obligation of Indorser.*

(a) Subject to subsections (b), (c), and (d) and to Section 3—419(d), if an instrument is dishonored, an indorser is obliged to pay the amount due on the instrument (i) according to the terms of the instrument at the time it was indorsed, or (ii) if the indorser indorsed an incomplete instrument, according to its terms when completed, to the extent stated in Sections 3—115 and 3—407. The obligation of the indorser is owed to a person entitled to enforce the instrument or to a subsequent indorser who paid the instrument under this section.

(b) If an indorsement states that it is made "without recourse" or otherwise disclaims liability of the indorser, the indorser is not liable under subsection (a) to pay the instrument.

(c) If notice of dishonor of an instrument is required by Section 3—503 and notice of dishonor complying with that section is not given to an indorser, the liability of the indorser under subsection (a) is discharged.

(d) If a draft is accepted by a bank after an indorsement is made, the liability of the indorser under subsection (a) is discharged.

(e) If an indorser of a check is liable under subsection (a) and the check is not presented for payment, or given to a depositary bank for collection, within 30 days after the day the indorsement was made, the liability of the indorser under subsection (a) is discharged.

§ 3—416. *Transfer Warranties.*

(a) A person who transfers an instrument for consideration warrants to the transferee and, if the transfer is by indorsement, to any subsequent transferee that:

(1) the warrantor is a person entitled to enforce the instrument;

(2) all signatures on the instrument are authentic and authorized;

(3) the instrument has not been altered;

(4) the instrument is not subject to a defense or claim in recoupment of any party which can be asserted against the warrantor; and

(5) the warrantor has no knowledge of any insolvency proceeding commenced with respect to the maker or acceptor or, in the case of an unaccepted draft, the drawer.

(b) A person to whom the warranties under subsection (a) are made and who took the instrument in good faith may recover from the warrantor as damages for breach of warranty an amount equal to the loss suffered as a result of the breach, but not more than the amount of the instrument plus expenses and loss of interest incurred as a result of the breach.

(c) The warranties stated in subsection (a) cannot be disclaimed with respect to checks. Unless notice of a claim for breach of warranty is given to the warrantor within 30 days after the claimant has reason to know of the breach and the identity of the warrantor, the liability of the warrantor under subsection (b) is discharged to the extent of any loss caused by the delay in giving notice of the claim.

(d) A [cause of action] for breach of warranty under this section accrues when the claimant has reason to know of the breach.

§ 3—417. *Presentment Warranties.*

(a) If an unaccepted draft is presented to the drawee for payment or acceptance and the drawee pays or accepts the draft, (i) the person obtaining payment or acceptance, at the time of presentment, and (ii) a previous transferor of the draft, at the time of transfer, warrant to the drawee making payment or accepting the draft in good faith that:

(1) the warrantor is, or was, at the time the warrantor transferred the draft, a person entitled to enforce the draft or authorized to obtain payment or acceptance of the draft on behalf of a person entitled to enforce the draft;

(2) the draft has not been altered; and

(3) the warrantor has no knowledge that the signature of the drawer of the draft is unauthorized.

(b) A drawee making payment may recover from any warrantor damages for breach of warranty equal to the amount paid by the drawee less the amount the drawee received or is entitled to receive from the drawer because of the payment. In addition, the drawee is entitled to compensation for expenses and loss of interest resulting from the breach. The right of the drawee to recover damages under this subsection is not affected by any failure of the drawee to exercise ordinary care in making payment. If the drawee accepts the draft, breach of warranty is a defense to the obligation of the acceptor. If the acceptor makes payment with respect to the draft, the acceptor is entitled to recover from any warrantor for breach of warranty the amounts stated in this subsection.

(c) If a drawee asserts a claim for breach of warranty under subsection (a) based on an unauthorized indorsement of the draft or an alteration of the draft, the warrantor may defend by proving that the indorsement is effective under Section 3—404 or 3—405 or the drawer is precluded under Section 3—406 or 4—406 from asserting against the drawee the unauthorized indorsement or alteration.

(d) If (i) a dishonored draft is presented for payment to the drawer or an indorser or (ii) any other instrument is presented for payment to a party obliged to pay the instrument, and (iii) payment is received, the following rules apply:

(1) The person obtaining payment and a prior transferor of the instrument warrant to the person making payment in good faith that the warrantor is, or was, at the time the warrantor transferred the instrument, a person entitled to enforce the instrument or authorized to obtain payment on behalf of a person entitled to enforce the instrument.

(2) The person making payment may recover from any warrantor for breach of warranty an amount equal to the amount paid plus expenses and loss of interest resulting from the breach.

(e) The warranties stated in subsections (a) and (d) cannot be disclaimed with respect to checks. Unless notice of a claim for breach of warranty is given to the warrantor within 30 days after the claimant has reason to know of the breach and the identity of the warrantor, the liability of the warrantor under subsection (b) or (d) is discharged to the extent of any loss caused by the delay in giving notice of the claim.

(f) A [cause of action] for breach of warranty under this section accrues when the claimant has reason to know of the breach.

§ 3—418. *Payment or Acceptance by Mistake.*

(a) Except as provided in subsection (c), if the drawee of a draft pays or accepts the draft and the drawee acted on the mistaken belief that (i) payment of the draft had not been stopped pursuant to Section 4—403 or (ii) the signature of the drawer of the draft was authorized, the drawee may recover the amount of the draft from the person to whom or for whose benefit payment was made or, in the case of acceptance, may revoke the acceptance. Rights of the drawee under this subsection are not affected by failure of the drawee to exercise ordinary care in paying or accepting the draft.

(b) Except as provided in subsection (c), if an instrument has been paid or accepted by mistake and the case is not covered by subsection (a), the person paying or accepting may, to the extent permitted by the law governing mistake and restitution, (i) recover the payment from the person to whom or for whose benefit payment was made or (ii) in the case of acceptance, may revoke the acceptance.

(c) The remedies provided by subsection (a) or (b) may not be asserted against a person who took the instrument in good faith and for value or who in good faith changed position in reliance on the payment or acceptance. This subsection does not limit remedies provided by Section 3—417 or 4—407.

(d) Notwithstanding Section 4—215, if an instrument is paid or accepted by mistake and the payor or acceptor recovers payment or revokes acceptance under subsection (a) or (b), the instrument is deemed not to have been paid or accepted and is treated as dishonored, and the person from whom payment is recovered has rights as a person entitled to enforce the dishonored instrument.

§ 3—419. *Instruments Signed for Accommodation.*

(a) If an instrument is issued for value given for the benefit of a party to the instrument ("accommodated party") and another party to the instrument ("accommodation party") signs the instrument for the purpose of incurring liability on the instrument without being a direct beneficiary of the value given for the instrument, the instrument is signed by the accommodation party "for accommodation."

(b) An accommodation party may sign the instrument as maker, drawer, acceptor, or indorser and, subject to subsection (d), is obliged to pay the instrument in the capacity in which the accommodation party signs. The obligation of an accommodation party may be enforced notwithstanding any statute of frauds and whether or not the accommodation party receives consideration for the accommodation.

(c) A person signing an instrument is presumed to be an accommodation party and there is notice that the instrument is signed for accommodation if the signature is an anomalous indorsement or is accompanied by words indicating that the signer is acting as surety or guarantor with respect to the obligation of another party to the instrument. Except as provided in Section 3—605, the obligation of an accommodation party to pay the instrument is not affected by the fact that the person enforcing the obligation had notice when the instrument was taken by that person that the accommodation party signed the instrument for accommodation.

(d) If the signature of a party to an instrument is accompanied by words indicating unambiguously that the party is guaranteeing collection rather than payment of the obligation of another party to the instrument, the signer is obliged to pay the amount due on the instrument to a person entitled to enforce the instrument only if (i) execution of judgment against the other party has been returned unsatisfied, (ii) the other party is insolvent or in an insolvency proceeding, (iii) the other party cannot be served with process, or (iv) it is otherwise apparent that payment cannot be obtained from the other party.

(e) An accommodation party who pays the instrument is entitled to reimbursement from the accommodated party and is entitled to enforce the instrument against the accommodated party. An accommodated party who pays the instrument has no right of recourse against, and is not entitled to contribution from, an accommodation party.

§ 3—420. *Conversion of Instrument.*

(a) The law applicable to conversion of personal property applies to instruments. An instrument is also converted if it is taken by transfer, other than a negotiation, from a person not entitled to enforce the instrument or a bank makes or obtains payment with respect to the instrument for a person not entitled to enforce the instrument or receive payment. An action for conversion of an instrument may not be brought by (i) the issuer or acceptor of the instrument or (ii) a payee or indorsee who did not receive delivery of the instrument either directly or through delivery to an agent or a co-payee.

(b) In an action under subsection (a), the measure of liability is presumed to be the amount payable on the instrument, but recovery may not exceed the amount of the plaintiff's interest in the instrument.

(c) A representative, other than a depositary bank, who has in good faith dealt with an instrument or its proceeds on behalf of one who was not the person entitled to enforce the instrument is not liable in conversion to that person beyond the amount of any proceeds that it has not paid out.

PART 5
Dishonor

§ 3—501. *Presentment.*

(a) "Presentment" means a demand made by or on behalf of a person entitled to enforce an instrument (i) to pay the instrument made to the drawee or a party obliged to pay the instrument or, in the case of a note or accepted draft payable at a bank, to the bank, or (ii) to accept a draft made to the drawee.

(b) The following rules are subject to Article 4, agreement of the parties, and clearing-house rules and the like:

(1) Presentment may be made at the place of payment of the instrument and must be made at the place of payment if the instrument is payable at a bank in the United States; may be made by any commercially reasonable means, including an oral, written, or electronic communication; is effective when the demand for payment or acceptance is received by the person to whom presentment is made; and is effective if made to any one of two or more makers, acceptors, drawees, or other payors.

(2) Upon demand of the person to whom presentment is made, the person making presentment must (i) exhibit the instrument, (ii) give reasonable identification and, if presentment is made on behalf of another person, reasonable evidence of authority to do so, and (. . .) sign a receipt on the instrument for any payment made or surrender the instrument if full payment is made.

(3) Without dishonoring the instrument, the party to whom presentment is made may (i) return the instrument for lack of a necessary indorsement, or (ii) refuse payment or acceptance for failure of the presentment to comply with the terms of the instrument, an agreement of the parties, or other applicable law or rule.

(4) The party to whom presentment is made may treat presentment as occurring on the next business day after the day of presentment if the party to whom presentment is made has established a cut-off hour not earlier than 2 p.m. for the receipt and processing of instruments presented for payment or acceptance and presentment is made after the cut-off hour.

§ 3—502. *Dishonor.*

(a) Dishonor of a note is governed by the following rules:

(1) If the note is payable on demand, the note is dishonored if presentment is duly made to the maker and the note is not paid on the day of presentment.

(2) If the note is not payable on demand and is payable at or through a bank or the terms of the note require presentment, the note is dishonored if presentment is duly made and the note is not paid on the day it becomes payable or the day of presentment, whichever is later.

(3) If the note is not payable on demand and paragraph (2) does not apply, the note is dishonored if it is not paid on the day it becomes payable.

(b) Dishonor of an unaccepted draft other than a documentary draft is governed by the following rules:

(1) If a check is duly presented for payment to the payor bank otherwise than for immediate payment over the counter, the check is dishonored if the payor bank makes timely return of the check or sends timely notice of dishonor or nonpayment under Section 4—301 or 4—302, or becomes accountable for the amount of the check under Section 4—302.

(2) If a draft is payable on demand and paragraph (1) does not apply, the draft is dishonored if presentment for payment is duly made to the drawee and the draft is not paid on the day of presentment.

(3) If a draft is payable on a date stated in the draft, the draft is dishonored if (i) presentment for payment is duly made to the drawee and payment is not made on the day the draft becomes payable or the day of presentment, whichever is later, or (ii) presentment for acceptance is duly made before the day the draft becomes payable and the draft is not accepted on the day of presentment.

(4) If a draft is payable on elapse of a period of time after sight or acceptance, the draft is dishonored if presentment for acceptance is duly made and the draft is not accepted on the day of presentment.

(c) Dishonor of an unaccepted documentary draft occurs according to the rules stated in subsection (b)(2), (3), and (4), except that payment or acceptance may be delayed without dishonor until no later than the close of the third business day of the drawee following the day on which payment or acceptance is required by those paragraphs.

(d) Dishonor of an accepted draft is governed by the following rules:

(1) If the draft is payable on demand, the draft is dishonored if presentment for payment is duly made to the acceptor and the draft is not paid on the day of presentment.

(2) If the draft is not payable on demand, the draft is dishonored if presentment for payment is duly made to the acceptor and payment is not made on the day it becomes payable or the day of presentment, whichever is later.

(e) In any case in which presentment is otherwise required for dishonor under this section and presentment is excused under Section 3—504, dishonor occurs without presentment if the instrument is not duly accepted or paid.

(f) If a draft is dishonored because timely acceptance of the draft was not made and the person entitled to demand acceptance consents to a late acceptance, from the time of acceptance the draft is treated as never having been dishonored.

§ 3—503. *Notice of Dishonor.*

(a) The obligation of an indorser stated in Section 3—415(a) and the obligation of a drawer stated in Section 3—414(d) may not be enforced unless (i) the indorser or drawer is given notice of dishonor of the instrument complying with this section or (ii) notice of dishonor is excused under Section 3—504(b).

(b) Notice of dishonor may be given by any person; may be given by any commercially reasonable means, including an oral, written, or electronic communication; and is sufficient if it reasonably identifies the instrument and indicates that the instrument has been dishonored or has not been paid or accepted. Return of an instrument given to a bank for collection is sufficient notice of dishonor.

(c) Subject to Section 3—504(c), with respect to an instrument taken for collection by a collecting bank, notice of dishonor must be given (i) by the bank before midnight of the next banking day following the banking day on which the bank receives notice of dishonor of the instrument, or (ii) by any other person within 30 days following the day on which the person receives notice of dishonor. With respect to any other instrument, notice of dishonor must be given within 30 days following the day on which dishonor occurs.

§ 3—504. *Excused Presentment and Notice of Dishonor.*

(a) Presentment for payment or acceptance of an instrument is excused if (i) the person entitled to present the instrument cannot with reasonable diligence make presentment, (ii) the maker or acceptor has repudiated an obligation to pay the instrument or is dead or in insolvency proceedings, (iii) by the terms of the instrument presentment is not necessary to enforce the obligation of indorsers or the drawer, (iv) the drawer or indorser whose obligation is being enforced has waived presentment or otherwise has no reason to expect or right to require that the instrument be paid or accepted, or (v) the drawer instructed the drawee not to pay or accept the draft or the drawee was not obligated to the drawer to pay the draft.

(b) Notice of dishonor is excused if (i) by the terms of the instrument notice of dishonor is not necessary to enforce the obligation of a party to pay the instrument, or (ii) the party whose obligation is being enforced waived notice of dishonor. A waiver of presentment is also a waiver of notice of dishonor.

(c) Delay in giving notice of dishonor is excused if the delay was caused by circumstances beyond the control of the person giving the notice and the person giving the notice exercised reasonable diligence after the cause of the delay ceased to operate.

§ 3—505. *Evidence of Dishonor.*

(a) The following are admissible as evidence and create a presumption of dishonor and of any notice of dishonor stated:

(1) a document regular in form as provided in subsection (b) which purports to be a protest;

(2) a purported stamp or writing of the drawee, payor bank, or presenting bank on or accompanying the instrument stating that acceptance or payment has been refused unless reasons for the refusal are stated and the reasons are not consistent with dishonor;

(3) a book or record of the drawee, payor bank, or collecting bank, kept in the usual course of business which shows dishonor, even if there is no evidence of who made the entry.

(b) A protest is a certificate of dishonor made by a United States consul or vice consul, or a notary public or other person authorized to administer oaths by the law of the place where dishonor occurs. It may be made upon information satisfactory to that person. The protest must identify the instrument and certify either that presentment has been made or, if not made, the reason why it was not made, and that the instrument has been dishonored by nonacceptance or nonpayment. The protest may also certify that notice of dishonor has been given to some or all parties.

PART 6
Discharge and Payment

§ 3—601. *Discharge and Effect of Discharge.*

(a) The obligation of a party to pay the instrument is discharged as stated in this Article or by an act or agreement with the party which would discharge an obligation to pay money under a simple contract.

(b) Discharge of the obligation of a party is not effective against a person acquiring rights of a holder in due course of the instrument without notice of the discharge.

§ 3—602. *Payment.*

(a) Subject to subsection (b), an instrument is paid to the extent payment is made (i) by or on behalf of a party obliged to pay the instrument, and (ii) to a person entitled to enforce the instrument. To the extent of the payment, the obligation of the party obliged to pay the instrument is discharged even though payment is made with knowledge of a claim to the instrument under Section 3—306 by another person.

(b) The obligation of a party to pay the instrument is not discharged under subsection (a) if:

(1) a claim to the instrument under Section 3—306 is enforceable against the party receiving payment and (i) payment is made with knowledge by the payor that payment is prohibited by injunction or similar process of a court of competent jurisdiction, or (ii) in the case of an instrument other than a cashier's check, teller's check, or certified check, the party making payment accepted, from the person having a claim to the instrument, indemnity against loss resulting from refusal to pay the person entitled to enforce the instrument; or

(2) the person making payment knows that the instrument is a stolen instrument and pays a person it knows is in wrongful possession of the instrument.

§ 3—603. *Tender of Payment.*

(a) If tender of payment of an obligation to pay an instrument is made to a person entitled to enforce the instrument, the effect of tender is governed by principles of law applicable to tender of payment under a simple contract.

(b) If tender of payment of an obligation to pay an instrument is made to a person entitled to enforce the instrument and the tender is refused, there is discharge, to the extent of the amount of the tender, of the obligation of an indorser or accommodation party having a right of recourse with respect to the obligation to which the tender relates.

(c) If tender of payment of an amount due on an instrument is made to a person entitled to enforce the instrument, the obligation of the obligor to pay interest after the due date on the amount tendered is discharged. If presentment is required with respect to an instrument and the obligor is able and ready to pay on the due date at every place of payment stated in the instrument, the obligor is deemed to have made tender of payment on the due date to the person entitled to enforce the instrument.

§ 3—604. *Discharge by Cancellation or Renunciation.*

(a) A person entitled to enforce an instrument, with or without consideration, may discharge the obligation of a party to pay the instrument (i) by an intentional voluntary act, such as surrender of the instrument to the party, destruction, mutilation, or cancellation of the instrument, cancellation or striking out of the party's signature, or the addition of words to the instrument indicating discharge, or (ii) by agreeing not to sue or otherwise renouncing rights against the party by a signed writing.

(b) Cancellation or striking out of an indorsement pursuant to subsection (a) does not affect the status and rights of a party derived from the indorsement.

§ 3—605. *Discharge of Indorsers and Accommodation Parties.*

(a) In this section, the term "indorser" includes a drawer having the obligation described in Section 3—414(d).

(b) Discharge, under Section 3—604, of the obligation of a party to pay an instrument does not discharge the obligation of an indorser or accommodation party having a right of recourse against the discharged party.

(c) If a person entitled to enforce an instrument agrees, with or without consideration, to an extension of the due date of the obligation of a party to pay the instrument, the extension discharges an indorser or accommodation party having a right of recourse against the party whose obligation is extended to the extent the indorser or accommodation party proves that the extension caused loss to the indorser or accommodation party with respect to the right of recourse.

(d) If a person entitled to enforce an instrument agrees, with or without consideration, to a material modification of the obligation of a party other than an extension of the due date, the modification discharges the obligation of an indorser or accommodation party having a right of recourse against the person whose obligation is modified to the extent the modification causes loss to the indorser or accommodation party with respect to the right of recourse. The loss suffered by the indorser or accommodation party as a result of the modification is equal to the amount of the right of recourse unless the person enforcing the instrument proves that no loss was caused by the modification or that the loss caused by the modification was an amount less than the amount of the right of recourse.

(e) If the obligation of a party to pay an instrument is secured by an interest in collateral and a person entitled to enforce the instrument impairs the value of the interest in collateral, the obligation of an indorser or accommodation party having a right of recourse against the obligor is discharged to the extent of the impairment. The value of an interest in collateral is impaired to the extent (i) the value of the interest is reduced to an amount less than the amount of the right of recourse of the party asserting discharge, or (ii) the reduction in value of the interest causes an increase in the amount by which the amount of the right of recourse exceeds the value of the interest. The burden of proving impairment is on the party asserting discharge.

(f) If the obligation of a party is secured by an interest in collateral not provided by an accommodation party and a person entitled to enforce the instrument impairs the value of the interest in collateral, the obligation of any party who is jointly and severally liable with respect to the secured obligation is discharged to the extent the impairment causes the party asserting discharge to pay more than that party would have been obliged to pay, taking into account rights of contribution, if impairment had not occurred. If the party asserting discharge is an accommodation party not entitled to discharge under subsection (e), the party is deemed to have a right to contribution based on joint and several liability rather than a right to reimbursement. The burden of proving impairment is on the party asserting discharge.

(g) Under subsection (e) or (f), impairing value of an interest in collateral includes (i) failure to obtain or maintain perfection or recordation of the interest in collateral, (ii) release of collateral without substitution of collateral of equal value, (iii) failure to perform a duty to preserve the value of collateral owed, under Article 9 or other law, to a debtor or surety or other person secondarily liable, or (iv) failure to comply with applicable law in disposing of collateral.

(h) An accommodation party is not discharged under subsection (c), (d), or (e) unless the person entitled to enforce the instrument knows of the accommodation or has notice under Section 3—419(c) that the instrument was signed for accommodation.

(i) A party is not discharged under this section if (i) the party asserting discharge consents to the event or conduct that is the basis of the discharge, or (ii) the instrument or a separate agreement of the party provides for waiver of discharge under this section either specifically or by general language indicating that parties waive defenses based on suretyship or impairment of collateral.

ADDENDUM TO REVISED ARTICLE 3

Notes to Legislative Counsel

1. If revised Article 3 is adopted in your state, the reference in Section 2—511 to Section 3—802 should be changed to Section 3—310.

2. If revised Article 3 is adopted in your state and the Uniform Fiduciaries Act is also in effect in your state, you may want to consider amending Uniform Fiduciaries Act § 9 to conform to Section 3—307(b)(2)(iii) and (4)(iii). See Official Comment 3 to Section 3—307.

REVISED ARTICLE 4
BANK DEPOSITS AND COLLECTIONS

PART 1
General Provisions and Definitions

§ 4—101. *Short Title.*

This Article may be cited as Uniform Commercial Code—Bank Deposits and Collections.

§ 4—102. *Applicability.*

(a) To the extent that items within this Article are also within Articles 3 and 8, they are subject to those Articles. If there is conflict, this Article governs Article 3, but Article 8 governs this Article.

(b) The liability of a bank for action or non-action with respect to an item handled by it for purposes of presentment, payment, or collection is governed by the law of the place where the bank is located. In the case of action or non-action by or at a branch or separate office of a bank, its liability is governed by the law of the place where the branch or separate office is located.

§ 4—103. *Variation by Agreement; Measure of Damages; Action Constituting Ordinary Care.*

(a) The effect of the provisions of this Article may be varied by agreement, but the parties to the agreement cannot disclaim a bank's responsibility for its lack of good faith or failure to exercise ordinary care or limit the measure of damages for the lack or failure. However, the parties may determine by agreement the standards by which the bank's responsibility is to be measured if those standards are not manifestly unreasonable.

(b) Federal Reserve regulations and operating circulars, clearing-house rules, and the like have the effect of agreements under subsection (a), whether or not specifically assented to by all parties interested in items handled.

(c) Action or non-action approved by this Article or pursuant to Federal Reserve regulations or operating circulars is the exercise of ordinary care and, in the absence of special instructions, action or non-action consistent with clearing-house rules and the like or with a general banking usage not disapproved by this Article, is prima facie the exercise of ordinary care.

(d) The specification or approval of certain procedures by this Article is not disapproval of other procedures that may be reasonable under the circumstances.

(e) The measure of damages for failure to exercise ordinary care in handling an item is the amount of the item reduced by an amount that could not have been realized by the exercise of ordinary care. If there is also bad faith it includes any other damages the party suffered as a proximate consequence.

§ 4—104. *Definitions and Index of Definitions.*

(a) In this Article, unless the context otherwise requires:

(1) "Account" means any deposit or credit account with a bank, including a demand, time, savings, passbook, share draft, or like account, other than an account evidenced by a certificate of deposit;

(2) "Afternoon" means the period of a day between noon and midnight;

(3) "Banking day" means the part of a day on which a bank is open to the public for carrying on substantially all of its banking functions;

(4) "Clearing-house" means an association of banks or other payors regularly clearing items;

(5) "Customer" means a person having an account with a bank or for whom a bank has agreed to collect items, including a bank that maintains an account at another bank;

(6) "Documentary draft" means a draft to be presented for acceptance or payment if specified documents, certificated securities (Section 8—102) or instructions for uncertificated securities (Section 8—102), or other certificates, statements, or the like are to be received by the drawee or other payor before acceptance or payment of the draft;

(7) "Draft" means a draft as defined in Section 3—104 or an item, other than an instrument, that is an order;

(8) "Drawee" means a person ordered in a draft to make payment;

(9) "Item" means an instrument or a promise or order to pay money handled by a bank for collection or payment. The term does not include a payment order governed by Article 4A or a credit or debit card slip;

(10) "Midnight deadline" with respect to a bank is midnight on its next banking day following the banking day on which it receives the relevant item or notice or from which the time for taking action commences to run, whichever is later;

(11) "Settle" means to pay in cash, by clearing-house settlement, in a charge or credit or by remittance, or otherwise as agreed. A settlement may be either provisional or final;

(12) "Suspends payments" with respect to a bank means that it has been closed by order of the supervisory authorities, that a public officer has been appointed to take it over, or that it ceases or refuses to make payments in the ordinary course of business.

(b);(c) [Other definitions' section references deleted.]

(d) In addition, Article 1 contains general definitions and principles of construction and interpretation applicable throughout this Article.

§ 4—105. *"Bank"; "Depositary Bank"; "Payor Bank"; "Intermediary Bank"; "Collecting Bank"; "Presenting Bank."*

In this Article:

(1) "Bank" means a person engaged in the business of banking, including a savings bank, savings and loan association, credit union, or trust company;

(2) "Depositary bank" means the first bank to take an item even though it is also the payor bank, unless the item is presented for immediate payment over the counter;

(3) "Payor bank" means a bank that is the drawee of a draft;

(4) "Intermediary bank" means a bank to which an item is transferred in course of collection except the depositary or payor bank;

(5) "Collecting bank" means a bank handling an item for collection except the payor bank;

(6) "Presenting bank" means a bank presenting an item except a payor bank.

§ 4—106. *Payable Through or Payable at Bank: Collecting Bank.*

(a) If an item states that it is "payable through" a bank identified in the item, (i) the item designates the bank as a collecting bank and does not by itself authorize the bank to pay the item, and

(ii) the item may be presented for payment only by or through the bank.

Alternative A

(b) If an item states that it is "payable at" a bank identified in the item, the item is equivalent to a draft drawn on the bank.

Alternative B

(b) If an item states that it is "payable at" a bank identified in the item, (i) the item designates the bank as a collecting bank and does not by itself authorize the bank to pay the item, and (ii) the item may be presented for payment only by or through the bank.

(c) If a draft names a nonbank drawee and it is unclear whether a bank named in the draft is a co-drawee or a collecting bank, the bank is a collecting bank.

§ *4—107.* ***Separate Office of Bank.***

A branch or separate office of a bank is a separate bank for the purpose of computing the time within which and determining the place at or to which action may be taken or notices or orders shall be given under this Article and under Article 3.

§ *4—108.* ***Time of Receipt of Items.***

(a) For the purpose of allowing time to process items, prove balances, and make the necessary entries on its books to determine its position for the day, a bank may fix an afternoon hour of 2 p.m. or later as a cutoff hour for the handling of money and items and the making of entries on its books.

(b) An item or deposit of money received on any day after a cutoff hour so fixed or after the close of the banking day may be treated as being received at the opening of the next banking day.

§ *4—109.* ***Delays.***

(a) Unless otherwise instructed, a collecting bank in a good faith effort to secure payment of a specific item drawn on a payor other than a bank, and with or without the approval of any person involved, may waive, modify, or extend time limits imposed or permitted by this [act] for a period not exceeding two additional banking days without discharge of drawers or indorsers or liability to its transferor or a prior party.

(b) Delay by a collecting bank or payor bank beyond time limits prescribed or permitted by this [act] or by instructions is excused if (i) the delay is caused by interruption of communication or computer facilities, suspension of payments by another bank, war, emergency conditions, failure of equipment, or other circumstances beyond the control of the bank, and (ii) the bank exercises such diligence as the circumstances require.

§ *4—110.* ***Electronic Presentment.***

(a) "Agreement for electronic presentment" means an agreement, clearing-house rule, or Federal Reserve regulation or operating circular, providing that presentment of an item may be made by transmission of an image of an item or information describing the item ("presentment notice") rather than delivery of the item itself. The agreement may provide for procedures governing retention, presentment, payment, dishonor, and other matters concerning items subject to the agreement.

(b) Presentment of an item pursuant to an agreement for presentment is made when the presentment notice is received.

(c) If presentment is made by presentment notice, a reference to "item" or "check" in this Article means the presentment notice unless the context otherwise indicates.

§ *4—111.* ***Statute of Limitations.***

An action to enforce an obligation, duty, or right arising under this Article must be commenced within three years after the [cause of action] accrues.

PART 2

Collection of Items: Depositary and Collecting Banks

§ *4—201.* ***Status of Collecting Bank As Agent and Provisional Status of Credits; Applicability of Article; Item Indorsed "Pay Any Bank."***

(a) Unless a contrary intent clearly appears and before the time that a settlement given by a collecting bank for an item is or becomes final, the bank, with respect to an item, is an agent or sub-agent of the owner of the item and any settlement given for the item is provisional. This provision applies regardless of the form of indorsement or lack of indorsement and even though credit given for the item is subject to immediate withdrawal as of right or is in fact withdrawn; but the continuance of ownership of an item by its owner and any rights of the owner to proceeds of the item are subject to rights of a collecting bank, such as those resulting from outstanding advances on the item and rights of recoupment or setoff. If an item is handled by banks for purposes of presentment, payment, collection, or return, the relevant provisions of this Article apply even though action of the parties clearly establishes that a particular bank has purchased the item and is the owner of it.

(b) After an item has been indorsed with the words "pay any bank" or the like, only a bank may acquire the rights of a holder until the item has been:

(1) returned to the customer initiating collection; or

(2) specially indorsed by a bank to a person who is not a bank.

§ *4—202.* ***Responsibility for Collection or Return; When Action Timely.***

(a) A collecting bank must exercise ordinary care in:

(1) presenting an item or sending it for presentment;

(2) sending notice of dishonor or nonpayment or returning an item other than a documentary draft to the bank's transferor after learning that the item has not been paid or accepted, as the case may be;

(3) settling for an item when the bank receives final settlement; and

(4) notifying its transferor of any loss or delay in transit within a reasonable time after discovery thereof.

(b) A collecting bank exercises ordinary care under subsection (a) by taking proper action before its midnight deadline following receipt of an item, notice, or settlement. Taking proper action within a reasonably longer time may constitute the exercise of ordinary care, but the bank has the burden of establishing timeliness.

(c) Subject to subsection (a)(1), a bank is not liable for the insolvency, neglect, misconduct, mistake, or default of another bank or person or for loss or destruction of an item in the possession of others or in transit.

§ *4—203.* ***Effect of Instructions.***

Subject to Article 3 concerning conversion of instruments (Section 3—420) and restrictive indorsements (Section 3—206), only a collecting bank's transferor can give instructions that affect the bank or constitute notice to it, and a collecting bank is not liable to prior parties for any action taken pursuant to the instructions or in accordance with any agreement with its transferor.

§ 4—204. *Methods of Sending and Presenting; Sending Directly to Payor Bank.*

(a) A collecting bank shall send items by a reasonably prompt method, taking into consideration relevant instructions, the nature of the item, the number of those items on hand, the cost of collection involved, and the method generally used by it or others to present those items.

(b) A collecting bank may send:

(1) an item directly to the payor bank;

(2) an item to a nonbank payor if authorized by its transferor; and

(3) an item other than documentary drafts to a nonbank payor, if authorized by Federal Reserve regulation or operating circular, clearing-house rule, or the like.

(c) Presentment may be made by a presenting bank at a place where the payor bank or other payor has requested that presentment be made.

§ 4—205. *Depositary Bank Holder of Unindorsed Item.*

If a customer delivers an item to a depositary bank for collection:

(1) the depositary bank becomes a holder of the item at the time it receives the item for collection if the customer at the time of delivery was a holder of the item, whether or not the customer indorses the item, and, if the bank satisfies the other requirements of Section 3—302, it is a holder in due course; and

(2) the depositary bank warrants to collecting banks, the payor bank or other payor, and the drawer that the amount of the item was paid to the customer or deposited to the customer's account.

§ 4—206. *Transfer Between Banks.*

Any agreed method that identifies the transferor bank is sufficient for the item's further transfer to another bank.

§ 4—207. *Transfer Warranties.*

(a) A customer or collecting bank that transfers an item and receives a settlement or other consideration warrants to the transferee and to any subsequent collecting bank that:

(1) the warrantor is a person entitled to enforce the item;

(2) all signatures on the item are authentic and authorized;

(3) the item has not been altered;

(4) the item is not subject to a defense or claim in recoupment (Section 3—305(a)) of any party that can be asserted against the warrantor; and

(5) the warrantor has no knowledge of any insolvency proceeding commenced with respect to the maker or acceptor or, in the case of an unaccepted draft, the drawer.

(b) If an item is dishonored, a customer or collecting bank transferring the item and receiving settlement or other consideration is obliged to pay the amount due on the item (i) according to the terms of the item at the time it was transferred, or (ii) if the transfer was of an incomplete item, according to its terms when completed as stated in Sections 3—115 and 3—407. The obligation of a transferor is owed to the transferee and to any subsequent collecting bank that takes the item in good faith. A transferor cannot disclaim its obligation under this subsection by an indorsement stating that it is made "without recourse" or otherwise disclaiming liability.

(c) A person to whom the warranties under subsection (a) are made and who took the item in good faith may recover from the warrantor as damages for breach of warranty an amount equal to the loss suffered as a result of the breach, but not more than the amount of the item plus expenses and loss of interest incurred as a result of the breach.

(d) The warranties stated in subsection (a) cannot be disclaimed with respect to checks. Unless notice of a claim for breach of warranty is given to the warrantor within 30 days after the claimant has reason to know of the breach and the identity of the warrantor, the warrantor is discharged to the extent of any loss caused by the delay in giving notice of the claim.

(e) A cause of action for breach of warranty under this section accrues when the claimant has reason to know of the breach.

§ 4—208. *Presentment Warranties.*

(a) If an unaccepted draft is presented to the drawee for payment or acceptance and the drawee pays or accepts the draft, (i) the person obtaining payment or acceptance, at the time of presentment, and (ii) a previous transferor of the draft, at the time of transfer, warrant to the drawee that pays or accepts the draft in good faith that:

(1) the warrantor is, or was, at the time the warrantor transferred the draft, a person entitled to enforce the draft or authorized to obtain payment or acceptance of the draft on behalf of a person entitled to enforce the draft;

(2) the draft has not been altered; and

(3) the warrantor has no knowledge that the signature of the purported drawer of the draft is unauthorized.

(b) A drawee making payment may recover from a warrantor damages for breach of warranty equal to the amount paid by the drawee less the amount the drawee received or is entitled to receive from the drawer because of the payment. In addition, the drawee is entitled to compensation for expenses and loss of interest resulting from the breach. The right of the drawee to recover damages under this subsection is not affected by any failure of the drawee to exercise ordinary care in making payment. If the drawee accepts the draft (i) breach of warranty is a defense to the obligation of the acceptor, and (ii) if the acceptor makes payment with respect to the draft, the acceptor is entitled to recover from a warrantor for breach of warranty the amounts stated in this subsection.

(c) If a drawee asserts a claim for breach of warranty under subsection (a) based on an unauthorized indorsement of the draft or an alteration of the draft, the warrantor may defend by proving that the indorsement is effective under Section 3—404 or 3—405 or the drawer is precluded under Section 3—406 or 4—406 from asserting against the drawee the unauthorized indorsement or alteration.

(d) If (i) a dishonored draft is presented for payment to the drawer or an indorser or (ii) any other item is presented for payment to a party obliged to pay the item, and the item is paid, the person obtaining payment and a prior transferor of the item warrant to the person making payment in good faith that the warrantor is, or was, at the time the warrantor transferred the item, a person entitled to enforce the item or authorized to obtain payment on behalf of a person entitled to enforce the item. The person making payment may recover from any warrantor for breach of warranty an amount equal to the amount paid plus expenses and loss of interest resulting from the breach.

(e) The warranties stated in subsections (a) and (d) cannot be disclaimed with respect to checks. Unless notice of a claim for breach of warranty is given to the warrantor within 30 days after the claimant has reason to know of the breach and the identity of the warrantor, the warrantor is discharged to the extent of any loss caused by the delay in giving notice of the claim.

(f) A cause of action for breach of warranty under this section accrues when the claimant has reason to know of the breach.

§ 4—209. *Encoding and Retention Warranties.*

(a) A person who encodes information on or with respect to an item after issue warrants to any subsequent collecting bank and to the payor bank or other payor that the information is correctly encoded. If the customer of a depositary bank encodes, that bank also makes the warranty.

(b) A person who undertakes to retain an item pursuant to an agreement for electronic presentment warrants to any subsequent collecting bank and to the payor bank or other payor that retention and presentment of the item comply with the agreement. If a customer of a depositary bank undertakes to retain an item, that bank also makes this warranty.

(c) A person to whom warranties are made under this section and who took the item in good faith may recover from the warrantor as damages for breach of warranty an amount equal to the loss suffered as a result of the breach, plus expenses and loss of interest incurred as a result of the breach.

§ 4—210. *Security Interest of Collecting Bank in Items, Accompanying Documents and Proceeds.*

(a) A collecting bank has a security interest in an item and any accompanying documents or the proceeds of either:

(1) in case of an item deposited in an account, to the extent to which credit given for the item has been withdrawn or applied;

(2) in case of an item for which it has given credit available for withdrawal as of right, to the extent of the credit given, whether or not the credit is drawn upon or there is a right of charge-back; or

(3) if it makes an advance on or against the item.

(b) If credit given for several items received at one time or pursuant to a single agreement is withdrawn or applied in part, the security interest remains upon all the items, any accompanying documents or the proceeds of either. For the purpose of this section, credits first given are first withdrawn.

(c) Receipt by a collecting bank of a final settlement for an item is a realization on its security interest in the item, accompanying documents, and proceeds. So long as the bank does not receive final settlement for the item or give up possession of the item or accompanying documents for purposes other than collection, the security interest continues to that extent and is subject to Article 9, but:

(1) no security agreement is necessary to make the security interest enforceable (Section 9—203(1)(a));

(2) no filing is required to perfect the security interest; and

(3) the security interest has priority over conflicting perfected security interests in the item, accompanying documents, or proceeds.

§ 4—211. *When Bank Gives Value for Purposes of Holder in Due Course.*

For purposes of determining its status as a holder in due course, a bank has given value to the extent it has a security interest in an item, if the bank otherwise complies with the requirements of Section 3—302 on what constitutes a holder in due course.

§ 4—212. *Presentment by Notice of Item Not Payable by, Through, or at Bank; Liability of Drawer or Indorser.*

(a) Unless otherwise instructed, a collecting bank may present an item not payable by, through, or at a bank by sending to the party to accept or pay a written notice that the bank holds the item for acceptance or payment. The notice must be sent in time to be received on or before the day when presentment is due and the bank must meet any requirement of the party to accept or pay under Section 3—501 by the close of the bank's next banking day after it knows of the requirement.

(b) If presentment is made by notice and payment, acceptance, or request for compliance with a requirement under Section 3—501 is not received by the close of business on the day after maturity or, in the case of demand items, by the close of business on the third banking day after notice was sent, the presenting bank may treat the item as dishonored and charge any drawer or indorser by sending it notice of the facts.

§ 4—213. *Medium and Time of Settlement by Bank.*

(a) With respect to settlement by a bank, the medium and time of settlement may be prescribed by Federal Reserve regulations or circulars, clearing-house rules, and the like, or agreement. In the absence of such prescription:

(1) the medium of settlement is cash or credit to an account in a Federal Reserve bank of or specified by the person to receive settlement; and

(2) the time of settlement is:

(i) with respect to tender of settlement by cash, a cashier's check, or teller's check, when the cash or check is sent or delivered;

(ii) with respect to tender of settlement by credit in an account in a Federal Reserve Bank, when the credit is made;

(iii) with respect to tender of settlement by a credit or debit to an account in a bank, when the credit or debit is made or, in the case of tender of settlement by authority to charge an account, when the authority is sent or delivered; or

(iv) with respect to tender of settlement by a funds transfer, when payment is made pursuant to Section 4A—406(a) to the person receiving settlement.

(b) If the tender of settlement is not by a medium authorized by subsection (a) or the time of settlement is not fixed by subsection (a), no settlement occurs until the tender of settlement is accepted by the person receiving settlement.

(c) If settlement for an item is made by cashier's check or teller's check and the person receiving settlement, before its midnight deadline:

(1) presents or forwards the check for collection, settlement is final when the check is finally paid; or

(2) fails to present or forward the check for collection, settlement is final at the midnight deadline of the person receiving settlement.

(d) If settlement for an item is made by giving authority to charge the account of the bank giving settlement in the bank receiving settlement, settlement is final when the charge is made by the bank receiving settlement if there are funds available in the account for the amount of the item.

§ 4—214. *Right of Charge-Back or Refund; Liability of Collecting Bank: Return of Item.*

(a) If a collecting bank has made provisional settlement with its customer for an item and fails by reason of dishonor, suspension of payments by a bank, or otherwise to receive settlement for the item which is or becomes final, the bank may revoke the settlement given by it, charge back the amount of any credit given for the item to its customer's account, or obtain refund from its customer, whether or not it is able to return the item, if by its midnight deadline or within a longer reasonable time after it learns the facts it returns the item or sends notification of the facts. If the return or notice is delayed beyond the bank's midnight deadline or a longer reasonable time after it learns the facts, the bank may revoke the settlement, charge back the credit, or obtain refund from its customer, but it is liable for any loss resulting from the delay. These rights to revoke, charge back, and obtain refund terminate if and when a settlement for the item received by the bank is or becomes final.

(b) A collecting bank returns an item when it is sent or delivered to the bank's customer or transferor or pursuant to its instructions.

(c) A depositary bank that is also the payor may charge back the amount of an item to its customer's account or obtain refund in accordance with the section governing return of an item received by a payor bank for credit on its books (Section 4—301).

(d) The right to charge back is not affected by:

(1) previous use of a credit given for the item; or

(2) failure by any bank to exercise ordinary care with respect to the item, but a bank so failing remains liable.

(e) A failure to charge back or claim refund does not affect other rights of the bank against the customer or any other party.

(f) If credit is given in dollars as the equivalent of the value of an item payable in foreign money, the dollar amount of any charge-back or refund must be calculated on the basis of the bank-offered spot rate for the foreign money prevailing on the day when the person entitled to the charge-back or refund learns that it will not receive payment in ordinary course.

§ 4—215. *Final Payment of Item by Payor Bank; When Provisional Debits and Credits Become Final; When Certain Credits Become Available for Withdrawal.*

(a) An item is finally paid by a payor bank when the bank has first done any of the following:

(1) paid the item in cash;

(2) settled for the item without having a right to revoke the settlement under statute, clearing-house rule, or agreement; or

(3) made a provisional settlement for the item and failed to revoke the settlement in the time and manner permitted by statute, clearing-house rule, or agreement.

(b) If provisional settlement for an item does not become final, the item is not finally paid.

(c) If provisional settlement for an item between the presenting and payor banks is made through a clearing house or by debits or credits in an account between them, then to the extent that provisional debits or credits for the item are entered in accounts between the presenting and payor banks or between the presenting and successive prior collecting banks seriatim, they become final upon final payment of the item by the payor bank.

(d) If a collecting bank receives a settlement for an item which is or becomes final, the bank is accountable to its customer for the amount of the item and any provisional credit given for the item in an account with its customer becomes final.

(e) Subject to (i) applicable law stating a time for availability of funds and (ii) any right of the bank to apply the credit to an obligation of the customer, credit given by a bank for an item in a customer's account becomes available for withdrawal as of right:

(1) if the bank has received a provisional settlement for the item, when the settlement becomes final and the bank has had a reasonable time to receive return of the item and the item has not been received within that time;

(2) if the bank is both the depositary bank and the payor bank, and the item is finally paid, at the opening of the bank's second banking day following receipt of the item.

(f) Subject to applicable law stating a time for availability of funds and any right of a bank to apply a deposit to an obligation of the depositor, a deposit of money becomes available for withdrawal as of right at the opening of the bank's next banking day after receipt of the deposit.

§ 4—216. *Insolvency and Preference.*

(a) If an item is in or comes into the possession of a payor or collecting bank that suspends payment and the item has not been finally paid, the item must be returned by the receiver, trustee, or agent in charge of the closed bank to the presenting bank or the closed bank's customer.

(b) If a payor bank finally pays an item and suspends payments without making a settlement for the item with its customer or the presenting bank which settlement is or becomes final, the owner of the item has a preferred claim against the payor bank.

(c) If a payor bank gives or a collecting bank gives or receives a provisional settlement for an item and thereafter suspends payments, the suspension does not prevent or interfere with the settlement's becoming final if the finality occurs automatically upon the lapse of certain time or the happening of certain events.

(d) If a collecting bank receives from subsequent parties settlement for an item, which settlement is or becomes final and the bank suspends payments without making a settlement for the item with its customer which settlement is or becomes final, the owner of the item has a preferred claim against the collecting bank.

PART 3
Collection of Items: Payor Banks

§ 4—301. *Deferred Posting; Recovery of Payment by Return of Items; Time of Dishonor; Return of Items by Payor Bank.*

(a) If a payor bank settles for a demand item other than a documentary draft presented otherwise than for immediate payment over the counter before midnight of the banking day of receipt, the payor bank may revoke the settlement and recover the settlement if, before it has made final payment and before its midnight deadline, it

(1) returns the item; or

(2) sends written notice of dishonor or nonpayment if the item is unavailable for return.

(b) If a demand item is received by a payor bank for credit on its books, it may return the item or send notice of dishonor and may revoke any credit given or recover the amount thereof withdrawn by its customer, if it acts within the time limit and in the manner specified in subsection (a).

(c) Unless previous notice of dishonor has been sent, an item is dishonored at the time when for purposes of dishonor it is returned or notice sent in accordance with this section.

(d) An item is returned:

(1) as to an item presented through a clearing house, when it is delivered to the presenting or last collecting bank or to the clearinghouse or is sent or delivered in accordance with clearinghouse rules; or

(2) in all other cases, when it is sent or delivered to the bank's customer or transferor or pursuant to instructions.

§ 4—302. *Payor Bank's Responsibility for Late Return of Item.*

(a) If an item is presented to and received by a payor bank, the bank is accountable for the amount of:

(1) a demand item, other than a documentary draft, whether properly payable or not, if the bank, in any case in which it is not also the depositary bank, retains the item beyond midnight of the banking day of receipt without settling for it or, whether or not it is also the depositary bank, does not pay or return the item or send notice of dishonor until after its midnight deadline; or

(2) any other properly payable item unless, within the time allowed for acceptance or payment of that item, the bank either accepts or pays the item or returns it and accompanying documents.

(b) The liability of a payor bank to pay an item pursuant to subsection (a) is subject to defenses based on breach of a presentment warranty (Section 4—208) or proof that the person seeking enforcement of the liability presented or transferred the item for the purpose of defrauding the payor bank.

§ 4—303. *When Items Subject to Notice, Stop-Payment Order, Legal Process, or Setoff; Order in Which Items May Be Charged or Certified.*

(a) Any knowledge, notice, or stop-payment order received by, legal process served upon, or setoff exercised by a payor bank comes too late to terminate, suspend, or modify the bank's right or duty to pay an item or to charge its customer's account for the item if the knowledge, notice, stop-payment order, or legal process is received or served and a reasonable time for the bank to act thereon expires or the setoff is exercised after the earliest of the following:

(1) the bank accepts or certifies the item;

(2) the bank pays the item in cash;

(3) the bank settles for the item without having a right to revoke the settlement under statute, clearing-house rule, or agreement;

(4) the bank becomes accountable for the amount of the item under Section 4—302 dealing with the payor bank's responsibility for late return of items; or

(5) with respect to checks, a cutoff hour no earlier than one hour after the opening of the next banking day after the banking day on which the bank received the check and no later than the close of that next banking day or, if no cutoff hour is fixed, the close of the next banking day after the banking day on which the bank received the check.

(b) Subject to subsection (a), items may be accepted, paid, certified, or charged to the indicated account of its customer in any order.

PART 4
Relationship Between Payor Bank and its Customer

§ 4—401. *When Bank May Charge Customer's Account.*

(a) A bank may charge against the account of a customer an item that is properly payable from the account even though the charge creates an overdraft. An item is properly payable if it is authorized by the customer and is in accordance with any agreement between the customer and bank.

(b) A customer is not liable for the amount of an overdraft if the customer neither signed the item nor benefited from the proceeds of the item.

(c) A bank may charge against the account of a customer a check that is otherwise properly payable from the account, even though payment was made before the date of the check, unless the customer has given notice to the bank of the postdating describing the check with reasonable certainty. The notice is effective for the period stated in Section 4—403(b) for stop-payment orders, and must be received at such time and in such manner as to afford the bank a reasonable opportunity to act on it before the bank takes any action with respect to the check described in Section 4—303. If a bank charges against the account of a customer a check before the date stated in the notice of postdating, the bank is liable for damages for the loss resulting from its act. The loss may include damages for dishonor of subsequent items under Section 4—402.

(d) A bank that in good faith makes payment to a holder may charge the indicated account of its customer according to:

(1) the original terms of the altered item; or

(2) the terms of the completed item, even though the bank knows the item has been completed unless the bank has notice that the completion was improper.

§ 4—402. *Bank's Liability to Customer for Wrongful Dishonor; Time of Determining Insufficiency of Account.*

(a) Except as otherwise provided in this Article, a payor bank wrongfully dishonors an item if it dishonors an item that is properly payable, but a bank may dishonor an item that would create an overdraft unless it has agreed to pay the overdraft.

(b) A payor bank is liable to its customer for damages proximately caused by the wrongful dishonor of an item. Liability is limited to actual damages proved and may include damages for an arrest or prosecution of the customer or other consequential damages. Whether any consequential damages are proximately caused by the wrongful dishonor is a question of fact to be determined in each case.

(c) A payor bank's determination of the customer's account balance on which a decision to dishonor for insufficiency of available funds is based may be made at any time between the time the item is received by the payor bank and the time that the payor bank returns the item or gives notice in lieu of return, and no more than one determination need be made. If, at the election of the payor bank, a subsequent balance determination is made for the purpose of reevaluating the bank's decision to dishonor the item, the account balance at that time is determinative of whether a dishonor for insufficiency of available funds is wrongful.

§ 4—403. *Customer's Right to Stop Payment; Burden of Proof of Loss.*

(a) A customer or any person authorized to draw on the account if there is more than one person may stop payment of any item drawn on the customer's account or close the account by an order to the bank describing the item or account with reasonable certainty received at a time and in a manner that affords the bank a reasonable opportunity to act on it before any action by the bank with respect to the item described in Section 4—303. If the signature of more than one person is required to draw on an account, any of these persons may stop payment or close the account.

(b) A stop-payment order is effective for six months, but it lapses after 14 calendar days if the original order was oral and was not confirmed in writing within that period. A stop-payment order may be renewed for additional six-month periods by a writing given to the bank within a period during which the stop-payment order is effective.

(c) The burden of establishing the fact and amount of loss resulting from the payment of an item contrary to a stop-payment order or order to close an account is on the customer. The loss from payment of an item contrary to a stop-payment order may include damages for dishonor of subsequent items under Section 4—402.

§ 4—404. *Bank Not Obliged to Pay Check More Than Six Months Old.*

A bank is under no obligation to a customer having a checking account to pay a check, other than a certified check, which is presented more than six months after its date, but it may charge its customer's account for a payment made thereafter in good faith.

§ 4—405. *Death or Incompetence of Customer.*

(a) A payor or collecting bank's authority to accept, pay, or collect an item or to account for proceeds of its collection, if otherwise effective, is not rendered ineffective by incompetence of a customer of either bank existing at the time the item is issued or its collection is undertaken if the bank does not know of an adjudication of incompetence. Neither death nor incompetence of a customer revokes the authority to accept, pay, collect, or account until the bank knows of the fact of death or of an adjudication of incompetence and has reasonable opportunity to act on it.

(b) Even with knowledge, a bank may for 10 days after the date of death pay or certify checks drawn on or before the date unless ordered to stop payment by a person claiming an interest in the account.

§ 4—406. *Customer's Duty to Discover and Report Unauthorized Signature or Alteration.*

(a) A bank that sends or makes available to a customer a statement of account showing payment of items for the account shall either return or make available to the customer the items paid or provide information in the statement of account sufficient to allow the customer reasonably to identify the items paid. The statement of account provides sufficient information if the item is described by item number, amount, and date of payment.

(b) If the items are not returned to the customer, the person retaining the items shall either retain the items or, if the items are destroyed, maintain the capacity to furnish legible copies of the items until the expiration of seven years after receipt of the items. A customer may request an item from the bank that paid the item, and that bank must provide in a reasonable time either the item or, if the item has been destroyed or is not otherwise obtainable, a legible copy of the item.

(c) If a bank sends or makes available a statement of account or items pursuant to subsection (a), the customer must exercise reasonable promptness in examining the statement or the items to determine whether any payment was not authorized because of an alteration of an item or because a purported signature by or on behalf of the customer was not authorized. If, based on the statement or items provided, the customer should reasonably have discovered the unauthorized payment, the customer must promptly notify the bank of the relevant facts.

(d) If the bank proves that the customer failed, with respect to an item, to comply with the duties imposed on the customer by subsection (c), the customer is precluded from asserting against the bank:

(1) the customer's unauthorized signature or any alteration on the item, if the bank also proves that it suffered a loss by reason of the failure; and

(2) the customer's unauthorized signature or alteration by the same wrongdoer on any other item paid in good faith by the bank if the payment was made before the bank received notice from the customer of the unauthorized signature or alteration and after the customer had been afforded a reasonable period of time, not exceeding 30 days, in which to examine the item or statement of account and notify the bank.

(e) If subsection (d) applies and the customer proves that the bank failed to exercise ordinary care in paying the item and that the failure substantially contributed to loss, the loss is allocated between the customer precluded and the bank asserting the preclusion according to the extent to which the failure of the customer to comply with subsection (c) and the failure of the bank to exercise ordinary care contributed to the loss. If the customer proves that the bank did not pay the item in good faith, the preclusion under subsection (d) does not apply.

(f) Without regard to care or lack of care of either the customer or the bank, a customer who does not within one year after the statement or items are made available to the customer (subsection (a)) discover and report the customer's unauthorized signature on or any alteration on the item is precluded from asserting against the bank the unauthorized signature or alteration. If there is a preclusion under this subsection, the payor bank may not recover for breach or warranty under Section 4—208 with respect to the unauthorized signature or alteration to which the preclusion applies.

§ 4—407. *Payor Bank's Right to Subrogation on Improper Payment.*

If a payor has paid an item over the order of the drawer or maker to stop payment, or after an account has been closed, or otherwise under circumstances giving a basis for objection by the drawer or maker, to prevent unjust enrichment and only to the extent necessary to prevent loss to the bank by reason of its payment of the item, the payor bank is subrogated to the rights

(1) of any holder in due course on the item against the drawer or maker;

(2) of the payee or any other holder of the item against the drawer or maker either on the item or under the transaction out of which the item arose; and

(3) of the drawer or maker against the payee or any other holder of the item with respect to the transaction out of which the item arose.

PART 5
Collection of Documentary Drafts

§ 4—501. *Handling of Documentary Drafts; Duty to Send for Presentment and to Notify Customer of Dishonor.*

A bank that takes a documentary draft for collection shall present or send the draft and accompanying documents for presentment and, upon learning that the draft has not been paid or accepted in due course, shall seasonably notify its customer of the fact even though it may have discounted or bought the draft or extended credit available for withdrawal as of right.

§ 4—502. *Presentment of "On Arrival" Drafts.*

If a draft or the relevant instructions require presentment "on arrival," "when goods arrive" or the like, the collecting bank need not present until in its judgment a reasonable time for arrival of the goods has expired. Refusal to pay or accept because the goods have not arrived is not dishonor; the bank must notify its transferor of the refusal but need not present the draft again until it is instructed to do so or learns of the arrival of the goods.

§ 4—503. *Responsibility of Presenting Bank for Documents and Goods; Report of Reasons for Dishonor; Referee in Case of Need.*

Unless otherwise instructed and except as provided in Article 5, a bank presenting a documentary draft:

(1) must deliver the documents to the drawee on acceptance of the draft if it is payable more than three days after presentment, otherwise, only on payment; and

(2) upon dishonor, either in the case of presentment for acceptance or presentment for payment, may seek and follow instructions from any referee in case of need designated in the draft or, if the presenting bank does not choose to utilize the referee's services, it must use diligence and good faith to ascertain the reason for dishonor, must notify its transferor of the dishonor and of the results of its effort to ascertain the reasons therefor, and must request instructions.

However, the presenting bank is under no obligation with respect to goods represented by the documents except to follow any reasonable instructions seasonably received; it has a right to reimbursement for any expense incurred in following instructions and to prepayment of or indemnity for those expenses.

§ 4—504. *Privilege of Presenting Bank to Deal With Goods; Security Interest for Expenses.*

(a) A presenting bank that, following the dishonor of a documentary draft, has seasonably requested instructions but does not receive them within a reasonable time may store, sell, or otherwise deal with the goods in any reasonable manner.

(b) For its reasonable expenses incurred by action under subsection (a) the presenting bank has a lien upon the goods or their proceeds, which may be foreclosed in the same manner as an unpaid seller's lien.

ARTICLE 4A
FUNDS TRANSFERS

PART 1
Subject Matter and Definitions

§ *4A—101. Short Title.*

This Article may be cited as Uniform Commercial Code—Funds Transfers.

§ *4A—102. Subject Matter.*

Except as otherwise provided in Section 4A—108, this Article applies to funds transfers defined in Section 4A—104.

§ *4A—103. Payment Order—Definitions.*

(a) In this Article:

(1) "Payment order" means an instruction of a sender to a receiving bank, transmitted orally, electronically, or in writing, to pay, or to cause another bank to pay, a fixed or determinable amount of money to a beneficiary if:

(i) the instruction does not state a condition to payment to the beneficiary other than time of payment,

(ii) the receiving bank is to be reimbursed by debiting an account of, or otherwise receiving payment from, the sender, and

(iii) the instruction is transmitted by the sender directly to the receiving bank or to an agent, funds-transfer system, or communication system for transmittal to the receiving bank.

(2) "Beneficiary" means the person to be paid by the beneficiary's bank.

(3) "Beneficiary's bank" means the bank identified in a payment order in which an account of the beneficiary is to be credited pursuant to the order or which otherwise is to make payment to the beneficiary if the order does not provide for payment to an account.

(4) "Receiving bank" means the bank to which the sender's instruction is addressed.

(5) "Sender" means the person giving the instruction to the receiving bank.

(b) If an instruction complying with subsection (a)(1) is to make more than one payment to a beneficiary, the instruction is a separate payment order with respect to each payment.

(c) A payment order is issued when it is sent to the receiving bank.

§ *4A—104. Funds Transfer—Definitions.*

In this Article:

(a) "Funds transfer" means the series of transactions, beginning with the originator's payment order, made for the purpose of making payment to the beneficiary of the order. The term includes any payment order issued by the originator's bank or an intermediary bank intended to carry out the originator's payment order. A funds transfer is completed by acceptance by the beneficiary's bank of a payment order for the benefit of the beneficiary of the originator's payment order.

(b) "Intermediary bank" means a receiving bank other than the originator's bank or the beneficiary's bank.

(c) "Originator" means the sender of the first payment order in a funds transfer.

(d) "Originator's bank" means (i) the receiving bank to which the payment order of the originator is issued if the originator is not a bank, or (ii) the originator if the originator is a bank.

§ *4A—105. Other Definitions.*

(a) In this Article:

(1) "Authorized account" means a deposit account of a customer in a bank designated by the customer as a source of payment of payment orders issued by the customer to the bank. If a customer does not so designate an account, any account of the customer is an authorized account if payment of a payment order from that account is not inconsistent with a restriction on the use of that account.

(2) "Bank" means a person engaged in the business of banking and includes a savings bank, savings and loan association, credit union, and trust company. A branch or separate office of a bank is a separate bank for purposes of this Article.

(3) "Customer" means a person, including a bank, having an account with a bank or from whom a bank has agreed to receive payment orders.

(4) "Funds-transfer business day" of a receiving bank means the part of a day during which the receiving bank is open for the receipt, processing, and transmittal of payment orders and cancellations and amendments of payment orders.

(5) "Funds-transfer system" means a wire transfer network, automated clearing house, or other communication system of a clearing house or other association of banks through which a payment order by a bank may be transmitted to the bank to which the order is addressed.

(6) "Good faith" means honesty in fact and the observance of reasonable commercial standards of fair dealing.

(7) "Prove" with respect to a fact means to meet the burden of establishing the fact (Section 1—201(8)).

(b) Other definitions applying to this Article and the sections in which they appear are:

"Acceptance" Section 4A—209
"Beneficiary" Section 4A—103
"Beneficiary's bank" Section 4A—103
"Executed" Section 4A—301
"Execution date" Section 4A—301
"Funds transfer" Section 4A—104
"Funds-transfer system rule" Section 4A—501
"Intermediary bank" Section 4A—104
"Originator" Section 4A—104
"Originator's bank" Section 4A—104
"Payment by beneficiary's bank to beneficiary" Section 4A—405
"Payment by originator to beneficiary"Section 4A—406
"Payment by sender to receiving bank" Section 4A—403
"Payment date" Section 4A—401
"Payment order" Section 4A—103
"Receiving bank" Section 4A—103
"Security procedure" Section 4A—201
"Sender" Section 4A—103

(c) The following definitions in Article 4 apply to this Article:

"Clearinghouse" Section 4—104
"Item" Section 4—104
"Suspends payments" Section 4—104

(d) In addition, Article 1 contains general definitions and principles of construction and interpretation applicable throughout this Article.

§ *4A—106. Time Payment Order Is Received.*

(a) The time of receipt of a payment order or communication cancelling or amending a payment order is determined by the rules applicable to receipt of a notice stated in Section 1—201(27). A receiving bank may fix a cut-off time or times on a funds-transfer business day for the receipt and processing of payment orders and communications cancelling or amending payment orders. Different cut-off times may apply to payment orders, cancellations, or amendments, or to different categories of payment orders, cancellations, or amendments. A cut-off time may apply to senders generally or different cut-off times may apply to different senders or categories of payment orders. If a payment order or communication cancelling or amending a payment order is received after the close of a funds-transfer business day or after the appropriate cut-off time on a funds-transfer business day, the receiving bank may treat the payment order or communication as received at the opening of the next funds-transfer business day.

(b) If this Article refers to an execution date or payment date or states a day on which a receiving bank is required to take action, and the date or day does not fall on a funds-transfer business day, the next day that is a funds-transfer business day is treated as the date or day stated, unless the contrary is stated in this Article.

§ *4A—107. Federal Reserve Regulations and Operating Circulars.*

Regulations of the Board of Governors of the Federal Reserve System and operating circulars of the Federal Reserve Banks supersede any inconsistent provision of this Article to the extent of the inconsistency.

§ *4A—108. Exclusion of Consumer Transactions Governed by Federal Law.*

This Article does not apply to a funds transfer any part of which is governed by the Electronic Fund Transfer Act of 1978 (Title XX, Public Law 95—630, 92 Stat. 3728, 15 U.S.C. § 1693 et seq.) as amended from time to time.

PART 2
Issue and Acceptance of Payment Order

§ *4A—201. Security Procedure.*

"Security procedure" means a procedure established by agreement of a customer and a receiving bank for the purpose of (i) verifying that a payment order or communication amending or cancelling a payment order is that of the customer, or (ii) detecting error in the transmission or the content of the payment order or communication. A security procedure may require the use of algorithms or other codes, identifying words or numbers, encryption, callback procedures, or similar security devices. Comparison of a signature on a payment order or communication with an authorized specimen signature of the customer is not by itself a security procedure.

§ *4A—202. Authorized and Verified Payment Orders.*

(a) A payment order received by the receiving bank is the authorized order of the person identified as sender if that person authorized the order or is otherwise bound by it under the law of agency.

(b) If a bank and its customer have agreed that the authenticity of payment orders issued to the bank in the name of the customer as sender will be verified pursuant to a security procedure, a payment order received by the receiving bank is effective as the order of the customer, whether or not authorized, if (i) the security procedure is a commercially reasonable method of providing security against unauthorized payment orders, and (ii) the bank proves that it accepted the payment order in good faith and in compliance with the security procedure and any written agreement or instruction of the customer restricting acceptance of payment orders issued in the name of the customer. The bank is not required to follow an instruction that violates a written agreement with the customer or notice of which is not received at a time and in a manner affording the bank a reasonable opportunity to act on it before the payment order is accepted.

(c) Commercial reasonableness of a security procedure is a question of law to be determined by considering the wishes of the customer expressed to the bank, the circumstances of the customer known to the bank, including the size, type, and frequency of payment orders normally issued by the customer to the bank, alternative security procedures offered to the customer, and security procedures in general use by customers and receiving banks similarly situated. A security procedure is deemed to be commercially reasonable if (i) the security procedure was chosen by the customer after the bank offered, and the customer refused, a security procedure that was commercially reasonable for that customer, and (ii) the customer expressly agreed in writing to be bound by any payment order, whether or not authorized, issued in its name and accepted by the bank in compliance with the security procedure chosen by the customer.

(d) The term "sender" in this Article includes the customer in whose name a payment order is issued if the order is the authorized order of the customer under subsection (a), or it is effective as the order of the customer under subsection (b).

(e) This section applies to amendments and cancellations of payment orders to the same extent it applies to payment orders.

(f) Except as provided in this section and in Section 4A—203(a)(1), rights and obligations arising under this section or Section 4A—203 may not be varied by agreement.

§ 4A—203. *Unenforceability of Certain Verified Payment Orders.*

(a) If an accepted payment order is not, under Section 4A—202(a), an authorized order of a customer identified as sender, but is effective as an order of the customer pursuant to Section 4A—202(b), the following rules apply:

(1) By express written agreement, the receiving bank may limit the extent to which it is entitled to enforce or retain payment of the payment order.

(2) The receiving bank is not entitled to enforce or retain payment of the payment order if the customer proves that the order was not caused, directly or indirectly, by a person (i) entrusted at any time with duties to act for the customer with respect to payment orders or the security procedure, or (ii) who obtained access to transmitting facilities of the customer or who obtained, from a source controlled by the customer and without authority of the receiving bank, information facilitating breach of the security procedure, regardless of how the information was obtained or whether the customer was at fault. Information includes any access device, computer software, or the like.

(b) This section applies to amendments of payment orders to the same extent it applies to payment orders.

§ 4A—204. *Refund of Payment and Duty of Customer to Report with Respect to Unauthorized Payment Order.*

(a) If a receiving bank accepts a payment order issued in the name of its customer as sender which is (i) not authorized and not effective as the order of the customer under Section 4A—202, or (ii) not enforceable, in whole or in part, against the customer under Section 4A—203, the bank shall refund any payment of the payment order received from the customer to the extent the bank is not entitled to enforce payment and shall pay interest on the refundable amount calculated from the date the bank received payment to the date of the refund. However, the customer is not entitled to interest from the bank on the amount to be refunded if the customer fails to exercise ordinary care to determine that the order was not authorized by the customer and to notify the bank of the relevant facts within a reasonable time not exceeding 90 days after the date the customer received notification from the bank that the order was accepted or that the customer's account was debited with respect to the order. The bank is not entitled to any recovery from the customer on account of a failure by the customer to give notification as stated in this section.

(b) Reasonable time under subsection (a) may be fixed by agreement as stated in Section 1—204(1), but the obligation of a receiving bank to refund payment as stated in subsection (a) may not otherwise be varied by agreement.

§ 4A—205. *Erroneous Payment Orders.*

(a) If an accepted payment order was transmitted pursuant to a security procedure for the detection of error and the payment order (i) erroneously instructed payment to a beneficiary not intended by the sender, (ii) erroneously instructed payment in an amount greater than the amount intended by the sender, or (iii) was an erroneously transmitted duplicate of a payment order previously sent by the sender, the following rules apply:

(1) If the sender proves that the sender or a person acting on behalf of the sender pursuant to Section 4A—206 complied with the security procedure and that the error would have been detected if the receiving bank had also complied, the sender is not obliged to pay the order to the extent stated in paragraphs (2) and (3).

(2) If the funds transfer is completed on the basis of an erroneous payment order described in clause (i) or (iii) of subsection (a), the sender is not obliged to pay the order and the receiving bank is entitled to recover from the beneficiary any amount paid to the beneficiary to the extent allowed by the law governing mistake and restitution.

(3) If the funds transfer is completed on the basis of a payment order described in clause (ii) of subsection (a), the sender is not obliged to pay the order to the extent the amount received by the beneficiary is greater than the amount intended by the sender. In that case, the receiving bank is entitled to recover from the beneficiary the excess amount received to the extent allowed by the law governing mistake and restitution.

(b) If (i) the sender of an erroneous payment order described in subsection (a) is not obliged to pay all or part of the order, and (ii) the sender receives notification from the receiving bank that the order was accepted by the bank or that the sender's account was debited with respect to the order, the sender has a duty to exercise ordinary care, on the basis of information available to the sender, to discover the error with respect to the order and to advise the bank of the relevant facts within a reasonable time, not exceeding 90 days, after the bank's notification was received by the sender. If the bank proves that the sender failed to perform that duty, the sender is liable to the bank for the loss the bank proves it incurred as a result of the failure, but the liability of the sender may not exceed the amount of the sender's order.

(c) This section applies to amendments to payment orders to the same extent it applies to payment orders.

§ 4A—206. *Transmission of Payment Order through Funds-Transfer or Other Communication System.*

(a) If a payment order addressed to a receiving bank is transmitted to a funds-transfer system or other third party communication system for transmittal to the bank, the system is deemed to be an agent of the sender for the purpose of transmitting the payment order to the bank. If there is a discrepancy between the terms of the payment order transmitted to the system and the terms of the payment order transmitted by the system to the bank, the terms of the payment order of the sender are those transmitted by the system. This section does not apply to a funds-transfer system of the Federal Reserve Banks.

(b) This section applies to cancellations and amendments to payment orders to the same extent it applies to payment orders.

§ 4A—207. *Misdescription of Beneficiary.*

(a) Subject to subsection (b), if, in a payment order received by the beneficiary's bank, the name, bank account number, or other identification of the beneficiary refers to a nonexistent or unidentifiable person or account, no person has rights as a beneficiary of the order and acceptance of the order cannot occur.

(b) If a payment order received by the beneficiary's bank identifies the beneficiary both by name and by an identifying or bank account number and the name and number identify different persons, the following rules apply:

(1) Except as otherwise provided in subsection (c), if the beneficiary's bank does not know that the name and number refer to different persons, it may rely on the number as the proper identification of the beneficiary of the order. The beneficiary's bank need not determine whether the name and number refer to the same person.

(2) If the beneficiary's bank pays the person identified by name or knows that the name and number identify different persons, no person has rights as beneficiary except the person paid by the beneficiary's bank if that person was entitled to receive payment from the originator of the funds transfer. If no person has rights as beneficiary, acceptance of the order cannot occur.

(c) If (i) a payment order described in subsection (b) is accepted, (ii) the originator's payment order described the beneficiary inconsistently by name and number, and (iii) the beneficiary's bank pays the person identified by number as permitted by subsection (b)(1), the following rules apply:

(1) If the originator is a bank, the originator is obliged to pay its order.

(2) If the originator is not a bank and proves that the person identified by number was not entitled to receive payment from the originator, the originator is not obliged to pay its order unless the originator's bank proves that the originator, before acceptance of the originator's order, had notice that payment of a payment order issued by the originator might be made by the beneficiary's bank on the basis of an identifying or bank account number even if it identifies a person different from the named beneficiary. Proof of notice may be made by any admissible evidence. The originator's bank satisfies the burden of proof if it proves that the originator, before the payment order was accepted, signed a writing stating the information to which the notice relates.

(d) In a case governed by subsection (b)(1), if the beneficiary's bank rightfully pays the person identified by number and that person was not entitled to receive payment from the originator, the amount paid may be recovered from that person to the extent allowed by the law governing mistake and restitution as follows:

(1) If the originator is obliged to pay its payment order as stated in subsection (c), the originator has the right to recover.

(2) If the originator is not a bank and is not obliged to pay its payment order, the originator's bank has the right to recover.

§ 4A—208. *Misdescription of Intermediary Bank or Beneficiary's Bank.*

(a) This subsection applies to a payment order identifying an intermediary bank or the beneficiary's bank only by an identifying number.

(1) The receiving bank may rely on the number as the proper identification of the intermediary or beneficiary's bank and need not determine whether the number identifies a bank.

(2) The sender is obliged to compensate the receiving bank for any loss and expenses incurred by the receiving bank as a result of its reliance on the number in executing or attempting to execute the order.

(b) This subsection applies to a payment order identifying an intermediary bank or the beneficiary's bank both by name and an identifying number if the name and number identify different persons.

(1) If the sender is a bank, the receiving bank may rely on the number as the proper identification of the intermediary or beneficiary's bank if the receiving bank, when it executes the sender's order, does not know that the name and number identify different persons. The receiving bank need not determine whether the name and number refer to the same person or whether the number refers to a bank. The sender is obliged to compensate the receiving bank for any loss and expenses incurred by the receiving bank as a result of its reliance on the number in executing or attempting to execute the order.

(2) If the sender is not a bank and the receiving bank proves that the sender, before the payment order was accepted, had notice that the receiving bank might rely on the number as the proper identification of the intermediary or beneficiary's bank even if it identifies a person different from the bank identified by name, the rights and obligations of the sender and the receiving bank are governed by subsection (b)(1), as though the sender were a bank. Proof of notice may be made by any admissible evidence. The receiving bank satisfies the burden of proof if it proves that the sender, before the payment order was accepted, signed a writing stating the information to which the notice relates.

(3) Regardless of whether the sender is a bank, the receiving bank may rely on the name as the proper identification of the intermediary or beneficiary's bank if the receiving bank, at the time it executes the sender's order, does not know that the name and number identify different persons. The receiving bank need not determine whether the name and number refer to the same person.

(4) If the receiving bank knows that the name and number identify different persons, reliance on either the name or the number in executing the sender's payment order is a breach of the obligation stated in Section 4A—302(a)(1).

§ 4A—209. *Acceptance of Payment Order.*

(a) Subject to subsection (d), a receiving bank other than the beneficiary's bank accepts a payment order when it executes the order.

(b) Subject to subsections (c) and (d), a beneficiary's bank accepts a payment order at the earliest of the following times:

(1) When the bank (i) pays the beneficiary as stated in Section 4A—405(a) or 4A—405(b), or (ii) notifies the beneficiary of receipt of the order or that the account of the beneficiary has been credited with respect to the order unless the notice indicates that the bank is rejecting the order or that funds with respect to the order may not be withdrawn or used until receipt of payment from the sender of the order;

(2) When the bank receives payment of the entire amount of the sender's order pursuant to Section 4A—403(a)(1) or 4A—403(a)(2); or

(3) The opening of the next funds-transfer business day of the bank following the payment date of the order if, at that time, the amount of the sender's order is fully covered by a withdrawable credit balance in an authorized account of the sender or the bank has otherwise received full payment from the sender, unless the order was rejected before that time or is rejected within (i) one hour after that time, or (ii) one hour after the opening of the next business day of the sender following the payment date if that time is later. If notice of rejection is received by the sender after the payment date and the authorized account of the sender does not bear interest, the bank is obliged to pay interest to the sender on the amount of the order for the number of days elapsing after the payment date to the day the sender receives notice or learns that the order was not accepted, counting that day as an elapsed day. If the withdrawable credit balance during that period falls below the amount of the order, the amount of interest payable is reduced accordingly.

(c) Acceptance of a payment order cannot occur before the order is received by the receiving bank. Acceptance does not occur under subsection (b)(2) or (b)(3) if the beneficiary of the payment order does not have an account with the receiving bank, the account has been closed, or the receiving bank is not permitted by law to receive credits for the beneficiary's account.

(d) A payment order issued to the originator's bank cannot be accepted until the payment date if the bank is the beneficiary's bank, or the execution date if the bank is not the beneficiary's bank. If the originator's bank executes the originator's payment order before the execution date or pays the beneficiary of the originator's payment order before the payment date and the payment order is subsequently cancelled pursuant to Section 4A—211(b), the bank may recover from the beneficiary any payment received to the extent allowed by the law governing mistake and restitution.

§ 4A—210. *Rejection of Payment Order.*

(a) A payment order is rejected by the receiving bank by a notice of rejection transmitted to the sender orally, electronically, or in writing. A notice of rejection need not use any particular words and is sufficient if it indicates that the receiving bank is rejecting the order or will not execute or pay the order. Rejection is effective when the notice is given if transmission is by a means that is reasonable in the circumstances. If notice of rejection is given by a means that is not reasonable, rejection is effective when the notice is received. If an agreement of the sender and receiving bank establishes the means to be used to reject a payment order, (i) any means complying with the agreement is reasonable and (ii) any means not complying is not reasonable unless no significant delay in receipt of the notice resulted from the use of the noncomplying means.

(b) This subsection applies if a receiving bank other than the beneficiary's bank fails to execute a payment order despite the existence on the execution date of a withdrawable credit balance in an authorized account of the sender sufficient to cover the order. If the sender does not receive notice of rejection of the order on the execution date and the authorized account of the sender does not bear interest, the bank is obliged to pay interest to the sender on the amount of the order for the number of days elapsing after the execution date to the earlier of the day the order is cancelled pursuant to Section 4A—211(d) or the day the sender receives notice or learns that the order was not executed, counting the final day of the period as an elapsed day. If the withdrawable credit balance during that period falls below the amount of the order, the amount of interest is reduced accordingly.

(c) If a receiving bank suspends payments, all unaccepted payment orders issued to it are are deemed rejected at the time the bank suspends payments.

(d) Acceptance of a payment order precludes a later rejection of the order. Rejection of a payment order precludes a later acceptance of the order.

§ 4A—211. *Cancellation and Amendment of Payment Order.*

(a) A communication of the sender of a payment order cancelling or amending the order may be transmitted to the receiving bank orally, electronically, or in writing. If a security procedure is in effect between the sender and the receiving bank, the communication is not effective to cancel or amend the order unless the communication is verified pursuant to the security procedure or the bank agrees to the cancellation or amendment.

(b) Subject to subsection (a), a communication by the sender cancelling or amending a payment order is effective to cancel or amend the order if notice of the communication is received at a time and in a manner affording the receiving bank a reasonable opportunity to act on the communication before the bank accepts the payment order.

(c) After a payment order has been accepted, cancellation or amendment of the order is not effective unless the receiving bank agrees or a funds-transfer system rule allows cancellation or amendment without agreement of the bank.

(1) With respect to a payment order accepted by a receiving bank other than the beneficiary's bank, cancellation or amendment is not effective unless a conforming cancellation or amendment of the payment order issued by the receiving bank is also made.

(2) With respect to a payment order accepted by the beneficiary's bank, cancellation or amendment is not effective unless the order was issued in execution of an unauthorized payment order, or because of a mistake by a sender in the funds transfer which resulted in the issuance of a payment order (i) that is a duplicate of a payment order previously issued by the sender, (ii) that orders payment to a beneficiary not entitled to receive payment from the originator, or (iii) that orders payment in an amount greater than the amount the beneficiary was entitled to

receive from the originator. If the payment order is cancelled or amended, the beneficiary's bank is entitled to recover from the beneficiary any amount paid to the beneficiary to the extent allowed by the law governing mistake and restitution.

(d) An unaccepted payment order is cancelled by operation of law at the close of the fifth funds-transfer business day of the receiving bank after the execution date or payment date of the order.

(e) A cancelled payment order cannot be accepted. If an accepted payment order is cancelled, the acceptance is nullified and no person has any right or obligation based on the acceptance. Amendment of a payment order is deemed to be cancellation of the original order at the time of amendment and issue of a new payment order in the amended form at the same time.

(f) Unless otherwise provided in an agreement of the parties or in a funds-transfer system rule, if the receiving bank, after accepting a payment order, agrees to cancellation or amendment of the order by the sender or is bound by a funds-transfer system rule allowing cancellation or amendment without the bank's agreement, the sender, whether or not cancellation or amendment is effective, is liable to the bank for any loss and expenses, including reasonable attorney's fees, incurred by the bank as a result of the cancellation or amendment or attempted cancellation or amendment.

(g) A payment order is not revoked by the death or legal incapacity of the sender unless the receiving bank knows of the death or of an adjudication of incapacity by a court of competent jurisdiction and has reasonable opportunity to act before acceptance of the order.

(h) A funds-transfer system rule is not effective to the extent it conflicts with subsection (c)(2).

§ 4A—212. *Liability and Duty of Receiving Bank Regarding Unaccepted Payment Order.*

If a receiving bank fails to accept a payment order that it is obliged by express agreement to accept, the bank is liable for breach of the agreement to the extent provided in the agreement or in this Article, but does not otherwise have any duty to accept a payment order or, before acceptance, to take any action, or refrain from taking action, with respect to the order except as provided in this Article or by express agreement. Liability based on acceptance arises only when acceptance occurs as stated in Section 4A—209, and liability is limited to that provided in this Article. A receiving bank is not the agent of the sender or beneficiary of the payment order it accepts, or of any other party to the funds transfer, and the bank owes no duty to any party to the funds transfer except as provided in this Article or by express agreement.

PART 3
Execution of Sender's Payment Order by Receiving Bank

§ 4A—301. *Execution and Execution Date.*

(a) A payment order is "executed" by the receiving bank when it issues a payment order intended to carry out the payment order received by the bank. A payment order received by the beneficiary's bank can be accepted but cannot be executed.

(b) "Execution date" of a payment order means the day on which the receiving bank may properly issue a payment order in execution of the sender's order. The execution date may be determined by instruction of the sender but cannot be earlier than the day the order is received and, unless otherwise determined, is the day the order is received. If the sender's instruction states a payment date, the execution date is the payment date or an earlier date on which execution is reasonably necessary to allow payment to the beneficiary on the payment date.

§ 4A—302. *Obligations of Receiving Bank in Execution of Payment Order.*

(a) Except as provided in subsections (b) through (d), if the receiving bank accepts a payment order pursuant to Section 4A—209(a), the bank has the following obligations in executing the order:

(1) The receiving bank is obliged to issue, on the execution date, a payment order complying with the sender's order and to follow the sender's instructions concerning (i) any intermediary bank or funds-transfer system to be used in carrying out the funds transfer, or (ii) the means by which payment orders are to be transmitted in the funds transfer. If the originator's bank issues a payment order to an intermediary bank, the originator's bank is obliged to instruct the intermediary bank according to the instruction of the originator. An intermediary bank in the funds transfer is similarly bound by an instruction given to it by the sender of the payment order it accepts.

(2) If the sender's instruction states that the funds transfer is to be carried out telephonically or by wire transfer or otherwise indicates that the funds transfer is to be carried out by the most expeditious means, the receiving bank is obliged to transmit its payment order by the most expeditious available means, and to instruct any intermediary bank accordingly. If a sender's instruction states a payment date, the receiving bank is obliged to transmit its payment order at a time and by means reasonably necessary to allow payment to the beneficiary on the payment date or as soon thereafter as is feasible.

(b) Unless otherwise instructed, a receiving bank executing a payment order may (i) use any funds-transfer system if use of that system is reasonable in the circumstances, and (ii) issue a payment order to the beneficiary's bank or to an intermediary bank through which a payment order conforming to the sender's order can expeditiously be issued to the beneficiary's bank if the receiving bank exercises ordinary care in the selection of the intermediary bank. A receiving bank is not required to follow an instruction of the sender designating a funds-transfer system to be used in carrying out the funds transfer if the receiving bank, in good faith, determines that it is not feasible to follow the instruction or that following the instruction would unduly delay completion of the funds transfer.

(c) Unless subsection (a)(2) applies or the receiving bank is otherwise instructed, the bank may execute a payment order by transmitting its payment order by first class mail or by any means reasonable in the circumstances. If the receiving bank is instructed to execute the sender's order by transmitting its payment order by a particular means, the receiving bank may issue its payment order by the means stated or by any means as expeditious as the means stated.

(d) Unless instructed by the sender, (i) the receiving bank may not obtain payment of its charges for services and expenses in connection with the execution of the sender's order by issuing a payment order in an amount equal to the amount of the sender's order less the amount of the charges, and (ii) may not instruct a subsequent receiving bank to obtain payment of its charges in the same manner.

§ *4A—303. Erroneous Execution of Payment Order.*

(a) A receiving bank that (i) executes the payment order of the sender by issuing a payment order in an amount greater than the amount of the sender's order, or (ii) issues a payment order in execution of the sender's order and then issues a duplicate order, is entitled to payment of the amount of the sender's order under Section 4A—402(c) if that subsection is otherwise satisfied. The bank is entitled to recover from the beneficiary of the erroneous order the excess payment received to the extent allowed by the law governing mistake and restitution.

(b) A receiving bank that executes the payment order of the sender by issuing a payment order in an amount less than the amount of the sender's order is entitled to payment of the amount of the sender's order under Section 4A—402(c) if (i) that subsection is otherwise satisfied and (ii) the bank corrects its mistake by issuing an additional payment order for the benefit of the beneficiary of the sender's order. If the error is not corrected, the issuer of the erroneous order is entitled to receive or retain payment from the sender of the order it accepted only to the extent of the amount of the erroneous order. This subsection does not apply if the receiving bank executes the sender's payment order by issuing a payment order in an amount less than the amount of the sender's order for the purpose of obtaining payment of its charges for services and expenses pursuant to instruction of the sender.

(c) If a receiving bank executes the payment order of the sender by issuing a payment order to a beneficiary different from the beneficiary of the sender's order and the funds transfer is completed on the basis of that error, the sender of the payment order that was erroneously executed and all previous senders in the funds transfer are not obliged to pay the payment orders they issued. The issuer of the erroneous order is entitled to recover from the beneficiary of the order the payment received to the extent allowed by the law governing mistake and restitution.

§ *4A—304. Duty of Sender to Report Erroneously Executed Payment Order.*

If the sender of a payment order that is erroneously executed as stated in Section 4A—303 receives notification from the receiving bank that the order was executed or that the sender's account was debited with respect to the order, the sender has a duty to exercise ordinary care to determine, on the basis of information available to the sender, that the order was erroneously executed and to notify the bank of the relevant facts within a reasonable time not exceeding 90 days after the notification from the bank was received by the sender. If the sender fails to perform that duty, the bank is not obliged to pay interest on any amount refundable to the sender under Section 4A—402(d) for the period before the bank learns of the execution error. The bank is not entitled to any recovery from the sender on account of a failure by the sender to perform the duty stated in this section.

§ *4A—305. Liability for Late or Improper Execution or Failure to Execute Payment Order.*

(a) If a funds transfer is completed but execution of a payment order by the receiving bank in breach of Section 4A—302 results in delay in payment to the beneficiary, the bank is obliged to pay interest to either the originator or the beneficiary of the funds transfer for the period of delay caused by the improper execution. Except as provided in subsection (c), additional damages are not recoverable.

(b) If execution of a payment order by a receiving bank in breach of Section 4A—302 results in (i) noncompletion of the funds transfer, (ii) failure to use an intermediary bank designated by the originator, or (iii) issuance of a payment order that does not comply with the terms of the payment order of the originator, the bank is liable to the originator for its expenses in the funds transfer and for incidental expenses and interest losses, to the extent not covered by subsection (a), resulting from the improper execution. Except as provided in subsection (c), additional damages are not recoverable.

(c) In addition to the amounts payable under subsections (a) and (b), damages, including consequential damages, are recoverable to the extent provided in an express written agreement of the receiving bank.

(d) If a receiving bank fails to execute a payment order it was obliged by express agreement to execute, the receiving bank is liable to the sender for its expenses in the transaction and for incidental expenses and interest losses resulting from the failure to execute. Additional damages, including consequential damages, are recoverable to the extent provided in an express written agreement of the receiving bank, but are not otherwise recoverable.

(e) Reasonable attorney's fees are recoverable if demand for compensation under subsection (a) or (b) is made and refused before an action is brought on the claim. If a claim is made for breach of an agreement under subsection (d) and the agreement does not provide for damages, reasonable attorney's fees are recoverable if demand for compensation under subsection (d) is made and refused before an action is brought on the claim.

(f) Except as stated in this section, the liability of a receiving bank under subsections (a) and (b) may not be varied by agreement.

PART 4
Payment

§ *4A—401. Payment Date.*

"Payment date" of a payment order means the day on which the amount of the order is payable to the beneficiary by the beneficiary's bank. The payment date may be determined by instruction of the sender but cannot be earlier than the day the order is received by the beneficiary's bank and, unless otherwise determined, is the day the order is received by the beneficiary's bank.

§ *4A—402. Obligation of Sender to Pay Receiving Bank.*

(a) This section is subject to Sections 4A—205 and 4A—207.

(b) With respect to a payment order issued to the beneficiary's bank, acceptance of the order by the bank obliges the sender to pay the bank the amount of the order, but payment is not due until the payment date of the order.

(c) This subsection is subject to subsection (e) and to Section 4A—303. With respect to a payment order issued to a receiving bank other than the beneficiary's bank, acceptance of the order by the receiving bank obliges the sender to pay the bank the amount of the sender's order. Payment by the sender is not due until the execution date of the sender's order. The obligation of that sender to pay its payment order is excused if the funds transfer is not completed by acceptance by the beneficiary's bank of a payment order instructing payment to the beneficiary of that sender's payment order.

(d) If the sender of a payment order pays the order and was not obliged to pay all or part of the amount paid, the bank receiving payment is obliged to refund payment to the extent the sender was not obliged to pay. Except as provided in Sections 4A—204 and 4A—304, interest is payable on the refundable amount from the date of payment.

(e) If a funds transfer is not completed as stated in subsection (c) and an intermediary bank is obliged to refund payment as stated in subsection (d) but is unable to do so because not permitted by applicable law or because the bank suspends payments, a sender in the funds transfer that executed a payment order in compliance with an instruction, as stated in Section 4A—302(a)(1), to route the funds transfer through that intermediary bank is entitled to receive or retain payment from the sender of the payment order that it accepted. The first sender in the funds transfer that issued an instruction requiring routing through that intermediary bank is subrogated to the right of the bank that paid the intermediary bank to refund as stated in subsection (d).

(f) The right of the sender of a payment order to be excused from the obligation to pay the order as stated in subsection (c) or to receive refund under subsection (d) may not be varied by agreement.

§ 4A—403. *Payment by Sender to Receiving Bank.*

(a) Payment of the sender's obligation under Section 4A—402 to pay the receiving bank occurs as follows:

(1) If the sender is a bank, payment occurs when the receiving bank receives final settlement of the obligation through a Federal Reserve Bank or through a funds-transfer system.

(2) If the sender is a bank and the sender (i) credited an account of the receiving bank with the sender, or (ii) caused an account of the receiving bank in another bank to be credited, payment occurs when the credit is withdrawn or, if not withdrawn, at midnight of the day on which the credit is withdrawable and the receiving bank learns of that fact.

(3) If the receiving bank debits an account of the sender with the receiving bank, payment occurs when the debit is made to the extent the debit is covered by a withdrawable credit balance in the account.

(b) If the sender and receiving bank are members of a funds-transfer system that nets obligations multilaterally among participants, the receiving bank receives final settlement when settlement is complete in accordance with the rules of the system. The obligation of the sender to pay the amount of a payment order transmitted through the funds-transfer system may be satisfied, to the extent permitted by the rules of the system, by setting off and applying against the sender's obligation the right of the sender to receive payment from the receiving bank of the amount of any other payment order transmitted to the sender by the receiving bank through the funds-transfer system. The aggregate balance of obligations owed by each sender to each receiving bank in the funds-transfer system may be satisfied, to the extent permitted by the rules of the system, by setting off and applying against that balance the aggregate balance of obligations owed to the sender by other members of the system. The aggregate balance is determined after the right of setoff stated in the second sentence of this subsection has been exercised.

(c) If two banks transmit payment orders to each other under an agreement that settlement of the obligations of each bank to the other under Section 4A—402 will be made at the end of the day or other period, the total amount owed with respect to all orders transmitted by one bank shall be set off against the total amount owed with respect to all orders transmitted by the other bank. To the extent of the setoff, each bank has made payment to the other.

(d) In a case not covered by subsection (a), the time when payment of the sender's obligation under Section 4A—402(b) or 4A—402(c) occurs is governed by applicable principles of law that determine when an obligation is satisfied.

§ 4A—404. *Obligation of Beneficiary's Bank to Pay and Give Notice to Beneficiary.*

(a) Subject to Sections 4A—211(e), 4A—405(d), and 4A—405(e), if a beneficiary's bank accepts a payment order, the bank is obliged to pay the amount of the order to the beneficiary of the order. Payment is due on the payment date of the order, but if acceptance occurs on the payment date after the close of the funds-transfer business day of the bank, payment is due on the next funds-transfer business day. If the bank refuses to pay after demand by the beneficiary and receipt of notice of particular circumstances that will give rise to consequential damages as a result of nonpayment, the beneficiary may recover damages resulting from the refusal to pay to the extent the bank had notice of the damages, unless the bank proves that it did not pay because of a reasonable doubt concerning the right of the beneficiary to payment.

(b) If a payment order accepted by the beneficiary's bank instructs payment to an account of the beneficiary, the bank is obliged to notify the beneficiary of receipt of the order before midnight of the next funds-transfer business day following the payment date. If the payment order does not instruct payment to an account of the beneficiary, the bank is required to notify the beneficiary only if notice is required by the order. Notice may be given by first class mail or any other means reasonable in the circumstances. If the bank fails to give the required notice, the bank is obliged to pay interest to the beneficiary on the amount of the payment order from the day notice should have been given until the day the beneficiary learned of receipt of the payment order by the bank. No other damages are recoverable. Reasonable attorney's fees are also recoverable if demand for interest is made and refused before an action is brought on the claim.

(c) The right of a beneficiary to receive payment and damages as stated in subsection (a) may not be varied by agreement or a funds-transfer system rule. The right of a beneficiary to be notified as stated in subsection (b) may be varied by agreement of the beneficiary or by a funds-transfer system rule if the beneficiary is notified of the rule before initiation of the funds transfer.

§ 4A—405. *Payment by Beneficiary's Bank to Beneficiary.*

(a) If the beneficiary's bank credits an account of the beneficiary of a payment order, payment of the bank's obligation under Section 4A—404(a) occurs when and to the extent (i) the beneficiary is notified of the right to withdraw the credit, (ii) the bank lawfully applies the credit to a debt of the beneficiary, or (iii) funds with respect to the order are otherwise made available to the beneficiary by the bank.

(b) If the beneficiary's bank does not credit an account of the beneficiary of a payment order, the time when payment of the bank's obligation under Section 4A—404(a) occurs is governed by principles of law that determine when an obligation is satisfied.

(c) Except as stated in subsections (d) and (e), if the beneficiary's bank pays the beneficiary of a payment order under a condition to payment or agreement of the beneficiary giving the bank the right to recover payment from the beneficiary if the bank does not receive payment of the order, the condition to payment or agreement is not enforceable.

(d) A funds-transfer system rule may provide that payments made to beneficiaries of funds transfers made through the system are provisional until receipt of payment by the beneficiary's bank of the payment order it accepted. A beneficiary's bank that makes a payment that is provisional under the rule is entitled to refund from the beneficiary if (i) the rule requires that both the beneficiary and the originator be given notice of the provisional nature of the payment before the funds transfer is initiated, (ii) the beneficiary, the beneficiary's bank, and the originator's bank agreed to be bound by the rule, and (iii) the beneficiary's bank did not receive payment of the payment order that it accepted. If the beneficiary is obliged to refund payment to the beneficiary's bank, acceptance of the payment order by the beneficiary's bank is nullified and no payment by the originator of the funds transfer to the beneficiary occurs under Section 4A—406.

(e) This subsection applies to a funds transfer that includes a payment order transmitted over a funds-transfer system that (i) nets obligations multilaterally among participants, and (ii) has in effect a loss-sharing agreement among participants for the purpose of providing funds necessary to complete settlement of the obligations of one or more participants that do not meet their settlement obligations. If the beneficiary's bank in the funds transfer accepts a payment order and the system fails to complete settlement pursuant to its rules with respect to any payment order in the funds transfer, (i) the acceptance by the beneficiary's bank is nullified and no person has any right or obligation based on the acceptance, (ii) the beneficiary's bank is entitled to recover payment from the beneficiary, (iii) no payment by the originator to the beneficiary occurs under Section 4A—406, and (iv) subject to Section 4A—402(e), each sender in the funds transfer is excused from its obligation to pay its payment order under Section 4A—402(c) because the funds transfer has not been completed.

§ *4A—406. Payment by Originator to Beneficiary; Discharge of Underlying Obligation.*

(a) Subject to Sections 4A—211(e), 4A—405(d), and 4A—405(e), the originator of a funds transfer pays the beneficiary of the originator's payment order (i) at the time a payment order for the benefit of the beneficiary is accepted by the beneficiary's bank in the funds transfer and (ii) in an amount equal to the amount of the order accepted by the beneficiary's bank, but not more than the amount of the originator's order.

(b) If payment under subsection (a) is made to satisfy an obligation, the obligation is discharged to the same extent discharge would result from payment to the beneficiary of the same amount in money, unless (i) the payment under subsection (a) was made by a means prohibited by the contract of the beneficiary with respect to the obligation, (ii) the beneficiary, within a reasonable time after receiving notice of receipt of the order by the beneficiary's bank, notified the originator of the beneficiary's refusal of the payment, (iii) funds with respect to the order were not withdrawn by the beneficiary or applied to a debt of the beneficiary, and (iv) the beneficiary would suffer a loss that could reasonably have been avoided if payment had been made by a means complying with the contract. If payment by the originator does not result in discharge under this section, the originator is subrogated to the rights of the beneficiary to receive payment from the beneficiary's bank under Section 4A—404(a).

(c) For the purpose of determining whether discharge of an obligation occurs under subsection (b), if the beneficiary's bank accepts a payment order in an amount equal to the amount of the originator's payment order less charges of one or more receiving banks in the funds transfer, payment to the beneficiary is deemed to be in the amount of the originator's order unless upon demand by the beneficiary the originator does not pay the beneficiary the amount of the deducted charges.

(d) Rights of the originator or of the beneficiary of a funds transfer under this section may be varied only by agreement of the originator and the beneficiary.

PART 5
Miscellaneous Provisions

§ *4A—501. Variation by Agreement and Effect of Funds-Transfer System Rule.*

(a) Except as otherwise provided in this Article, the rights and obligations of a party to a funds transfer may be varied by agreement of the affected party.

(b) "Funds-transfer system rule" means a rule of an association of banks (i) governing transmission of payment orders by means of a funds-transfer system of the association or rights and obligations with respect to those orders, or (ii) to the extent the rule governs rights and obligations between banks that are parties to a funds transfer in which a Federal Reserve Bank, acting as an intermediary bank, sends a payment order to the beneficiary's bank. Except as otherwise provided in this Article, a funds-transfer system rule governing rights and obligations between participating banks using the system may be effective even if the rule conflicts with this Article and indirectly affects another party to the funds transfer who does not consent to the rule. A funds-transfer system rule may also govern rights and obligations of parties other than participating banks using the system to the extent stated in Sections 4A—404(c), 4A—405(d), and 4A—507(c).

§ *4A—502. Creditor Process Served on Receiving Bank; Setoff by Beneficiary's Bank.*

(a) As used in this section, "creditor process" means levy, attachment, garnishment, notice of lien, sequestration, or similar process issued by or on behalf of a creditor or other claimant with respect to an account.

(b) This subsection applies to creditor process with respect to an authorized account of the sender of a payment order if the creditor process is served on the receiving bank. For the purpose of determining rights with respect to the creditor process, if the receiving bank accepts the payment order the balance in the authorized account is deemed to be reduced by the amount of the payment order to the extent the bank did not otherwise receive payment of the order, unless the creditor process is served at a time and in a manner affording the bank a reasonable opportunity to act on it before the bank accepts the payment order.

(c) If a beneficiary's bank has received a payment order for payment to the beneficiary's account in the bank, the following rules apply:

(1) The bank may credit the beneficiary's account. The amount credited may be set off against an obligation owed by the beneficiary to the bank or may be applied to satisfy creditor process served on the bank with respect to the account.

(2) The bank may credit the beneficiary's account and allow withdrawal of the amount credited unless creditor process with respect to the account is served at a time and in a manner affording the bank a reasonable opportunity to act to prevent withdrawal.

(3) If creditor process with respect to the beneficiary's account has been served and the bank has had a reasonable opportunity to act on it, the bank may not reject the payment order except for a reason unrelated to the service of process.

(d) Creditor process with respect to a payment by the originator to the beneficiary pursuant to a funds transfer may be served only on the beneficiary's bank with respect to the debt owed by that bank to the beneficiary. Any other bank served with the creditor process is not obliged to act with respect to the process.

§ 4A—503. *Injunction or Restraining Order with Respect to Funds Transfer.*

For proper cause and in compliance with applicable law, a court may restrain (i) a person from issuing a payment order to initiate a funds transfer, (ii) an originator's bank from executing the payment order of the originator, or (iii) the beneficiary's bank from releasing funds to the beneficiary or the beneficiary from withdrawing the funds. A court may not otherwise restrain a person from issuing a payment order, paying or receiving payment of a payment order, or otherwise acting with respect to a funds transfer.

§ 4A—504. *Order in Which Items and Payment Orders May Be Charged to Account; Order of Withdrawals from Account.*

(a) If a receiving bank has received more than one payment order of the sender or one or more payment orders and other items that are payable from the sender's account, the bank may charge the sender's account with respect to the various orders and items in any sequence.

(b) In determining whether a credit to an account has been withdrawn by the holder of the account or applied to a debt of the holder of the account, credits first made to the account are first withdrawn or applied.

§ 4A—505. *Preclusion of Objection to Debit of Customer's Account.*

If a receiving bank has received payment from its customer with respect to a payment order issued in the name of the customer as sender and accepted by the bank, and the customer received notification reasonably identifying the order, the customer is precluded from asserting that the bank is not entitled to retain the payment unless the customer notifies the bank of the customer's objection to the payment within one year after the notification was received by the customer.

§ 4A—506. *Rate of Interest.*

(a) If, under this Article, a receiving bank is obliged to pay interest with respect to a payment order issued to the bank, the amount payable may be determined (i) by agreement of the sender and receiving bank, or (ii) by a funds-transfer system rule if the payment order is transmitted through a funds-transfer system.

(b) If the amount of interest is not determined by an agreement or rule as stated in subsection (a), the amount is calculated by multiplying the applicable Federal Funds rate by the amount on which interest is payable, and then multiplying the product by the number of days for which interest is payable. The applicable Federal Funds rate is the average of the Federal Funds rates published by the Federal Reserve Bank of New York for each of the days for which interest is payable divided by 360. The Federal Funds rate for any day on which a published rate is not available is the same as the published rate for the next preceding day for which there is a published rate. If a receiving bank that accepted a payment order is required to refund payment to the sender of the order because the funds transfer was not completed, but the failure to complete was not due to any fault by the bank, the interest payable is reduced by a percentage equal to the reserve requirement on deposits of the receiving bank.

§ 4A—507. *Choice of Law.*

(a) The following rules apply unless the affected parties otherwise agree or subsection (c) applies:

(1) The rights and obligations between the sender of a payment order and the receiving bank are governed by the law of the jurisdiction in which the receiving bank is located.

(2) The rights and obligations between the beneficiary's bank and the beneficiary are governed by the law of the jurisdiction in which the beneficiary's bank is located.

(3) The issue of when payment is made pursuant to a funds transfer by the originator to the beneficiary is governed by the law of the jurisdiction in which the beneficiary's bank is located.

(b) If the parties described in each paragraph of subsection (a) have made an agreement selecting the law of a particular jurisdiction to govern rights and obligations between each other, the law of that jurisdiction governs those rights and obligations, whether or not the payment order or the funds transfer bears a reasonable relation to that jurisdiction.

(c) A funds-transfer system rule may select the law of a particular jurisdiction to govern (i) rights and obligations between participating banks with respect to payment orders transmitted or processed through the system, or (ii) the rights and obligations of some or all parties to a funds transfer any part of which is carried out by means of the system. A choice of law made pursuant to clause (i) is binding on participating banks. A choice of law made pursuant to clause (ii) is binding on the originator, other sender, or a receiving bank having notice that the funds-transfer system might be used in the funds transfer and of the choice of law by the system when the originator, other sender, or receiving bank issued or accepted a payment order. The beneficiary of a funds transfer is bound by the choice of law if, when the funds transfer is initiated, the beneficiary has notice that the funds-transfer system might be used in the funds transfer and of the choice of law by the system. The law of a jurisdiction selected pursuant to this subsection may govern, whether or not that law bears a reasonable relation to the matter in issue.

(d) In the event of inconsistency between an agreement under subsection (b) and a choice-of-law rule under subsection (c), the agreement under subsection (b) prevails.

(e) If a funds transfer is made by use of more than one funds-transfer system and there is inconsistency between choice-of-law rules of the systems, the matter in issue is governed by the law of the selected jurisdiction that has the most significant relationship to the matter in issue.

ARTICLE 5
LETTERS OF CREDIT

§ 5—101. *Short Title.*

This Article shall be known and may be cited as Uniform Commercial Code—Letters of Credit.

§ 5—102. *Scope.*

(1) This Article applies

(a) to a credit issued by a bank if the credit requires a documentary draft or a documentary demand for payment; and

(b) to a credit issued by a person other than a bank if the credit requires that the draft or demand for payment be accompanied by a document of title; and

(c) to a credit issued by a bank or other person if the credit is not within subparagraphs (a) or (b) but conspicuously states that it is a letter of credit or is conspicuously so entitled.

(2) Unless the engagement meets the requirements of subsection (1), this Article does not apply to engagements to make advances or to honor drafts or demands for payment, to authorities to pay or purchase, to guarantees or to general agreements.

(3) This Article deals with some but not all of the rules and concepts of letters of credit as such rules or concepts have developed prior to this act or may hereafter develop. The fact that this Article states a rule does not by itself require, imply or negate application of the same or a converse rule to a situation not provided for or to a person not specified by this Article.

§ 5—103. *Definitions.*

(1) In this Article unless the context otherwise requires

(a) "Credit" or "letter of credit" means an engagement by a bank or other person made at the request of a customer and of a kind within the scope of this Article (Section 5—102) that the issuer will honor drafts or other demands for payment upon compliance with the conditions specified in the credit. A credit may be either revocable or irrevocable. The engagement may be either an agreement to honor or a statement that the bank or other person is authorized to honor.

(b) A "documentary draft" or a "documentary demand for payment" is one honor of which is conditioned upon the presentation of a document or documents. "Document" means any paper including document of title, security, invoice, certificate, notice of default and the like.

(c) An "issuer" is a bank or other person issuing a credit.

(d) A "beneficiary" of a credit is a person who is entitled under its terms to draw or demand payment.

(e) An "advising bank" is a bank which gives notification of the issuance of a credit by another bank.

(f) A "confirming bank" is a bank which engages either that it will itself honor a credit already issued by another bank or that such a credit will be honored by the issuer or a third bank.

(g) A "customer" is a buyer or other person who causes an issuer to issue a credit. The term also includes a bank which procures issuance or confirmation on behalf of that bank's customer.

(2) Other definitions applying to this Article and the sections in which they appear are:

"Notation of Credit". Section 5—108.
"Presenter". Section 5—112(3).

(3) Definitions in other Articles applying to this Article and the sections in which they appear are:

"Accept" or "Acceptance". Section 3—410.
"Contract for sale". Section 2—106.
"Draft". Section 3—104.
"Holder in due course". Section 3—302.
"Midnight deadline". Section 4—104.
"Security". Section 8—102.

(4) In addition, Article 1 contains general definitions and principles of construction and interpretation applicable throughout this Article.

§ 5—104. *Formal Requirements; Signing.*

(1) Except as otherwise required in subsection (1)(c) of Section 5—102 on scope, no particular form of phrasing is required for a credit. A credit must be in writing and signed by the issuer and a confirmation must be in writing and signed by the confirming bank. A modification of the terms of a credit or confirmation must be signed by the issuer or confirming bank.

(2) A telegram may be a sufficient signed writing if it identifies its sender by an authorized authentication. The authentication may be in code and the authorized naming of the issuer in an advice of credit is a sufficient signing.

§ 5—105. *Consideration.*

No consideration is necessary to establish a credit or to enlarge or otherwise modify its terms.

§ 5—106. *Time and Effect of Establishment of Credit.*

(1) Unless otherwise agreed a credit is established

(a) as regards the customer as soon as a letter of credit is sent to him or the letter of credit or an authorized written advice of its issuance is sent to the beneficiary; and

(b) as regards the beneficiary when he receives a letter of credit or an authorized written advice of its issuance.

(2) Unless otherwise agreed once an irrevocable credit is established as regards the customer it can be modified or revoked only with the consent of the customer and once it is established as regards the beneficiary it can be modified or revoked only with his consent.

(3) Unless otherwise agreed after a revocable credit is established it may be modified or revoked by the issuer without notice to or consent from the customer or beneficiary.

(4) Notwithstanding any modification or revocation of a revocable credit any person authorized to honor or negotiate under the terms of the original credit is entitled to reimbursement for or honor of any draft or demand for payment duly honored or negotiated before receipt of notice of the modification or revo-

cation and the issuer in turn is entitled to reimbursement from its customer.

§ 5—107. *Advice of Credit; Confirmation; Error in Statement of Terms.*

(1) Unless otherwise specified an advising bank by advising a credit issued by another bank does not assume any obligation to honor drafts drawn or demands for payment made under the credit but it does assume obligation for the accuracy of its own statement.

(2) A confirming bank by confirming a credit becomes directly obligated on the credit to the extent of its confirmation as though it were its issuer and acquires the rights of an issuer.

(3) Even though an advising bank incorrectly advises the terms of a credit it has been authorized to advise the credit is established as against the issuer to the extent of its original terms.

(4) Unless otherwise specified the customer bears as against the issuer all risks of transmission and reasonable translation or interpretation of any message relating to a credit.

§ 5—108. *"Notation Credit"; Exhaustion of Credit.*

(1) A credit which specifies that any person purchasing or paying drafts drawn or demands for payment made under it must note the amount of the draft or demand on the letter or advice of credit is a "notation credit".

(2) Under a notation credit

(a) a person paying the beneficiary or purchasing a draft or demand for payment from him acquires a right to honor only if the appropriate notation is made and by transferring or forwarding for honor the documents under the credit such a person warrants to the issuer that the notation has been made; and

(b) unless the credit or a signed statement that an appropriate notation has been made accompanies the draft or demand for payment the issuer may delay honor until evidence of notation has been procured which is satisfactory to it but its obligation and that of its customer continue for a reasonable time not exceeding thirty days to obtain such evidence.

(3) If the credit is not a notation credit

(a) the issuer may honor complying drafts or demands for payment presented to it in the order in which they are presented and is discharged pro tanto by honor of any such draft or demand;

(b) as between competing good faith purchasers of complying drafts or demands the person first purchasing his priority over a subsequent purchaser even though the later purchased draft or demand has been first honored.

§ 5—109. *Issuer's Obligation to Its Customer.*

(1) An issuer's obligation to its customer includes good faith and observance of any general banking usage but unless otherwise agreed does not include liability or responsibility

(a) for performance of the underlying contract for sale or other transaction between the customer and the beneficiary; or

(b) for any act or omission of any person other than itself or its own branch or for loss or destruction of a draft, demand or document in transit or in the possession of others; or

(c) based on knowledge or lack of knowledge of any usage of any particular trade.

(2) An issuer must examine documents with care so as to ascertain that on their face they appear to comply with the terms of the credit but unless otherwise agreed assumes no liability or responsibility for the genuineness, falsification or effect of any document which appears on such examination to be regular on its face.

(3) A non-bank issuer is not bound by any banking usage of which it has no knowledge.

§ 5—110. *Availability of Credit in Portions; Presenter's Reservation of Lien or Claim.*

(1) Unless otherwise specified a credit may be used in portions in the discretion of the beneficiary.

(2) Unless otherwise specified a person by presenting a documentary draft or demand for payment under a credit relinquishes upon its honor all claims to the documents and a person by transferring such draft or demand or causing such presentment authorizes such relinquishment. An explicit reservation of claim makes the draft or demand noncomplying.

§ 5—111. *Warranties on Transfer and Presentment.*

(1) Unless otherwise agreed the beneficiary by transferring or presenting a documentary draft or demand for payment warrants to all interested parties that the necessary conditions of the credit have been complied with. This is in addition to any warranties arising under Articles 3, 4, 7 and 8.

(2) Unless otherwise agreed a negotiating, advising, confirming, collecting or issuing bank presenting or transferring a draft or demand for payment under a credit warrants only the matters warranted by a collecting bank under Article 4 and any such bank transferring a document warrants only the matters warranted by an intermediary under Articles 7 and 8.

§ 5—112. *Time Allowed for Honor or Rejection; Withholding Honor or Rejection by Consent; "Presenter".*

(1) A bank to which a documentary draft or demand for payment is presented under a credit may without dishonor of the draft, demand or credit

(a) defer honor until the close of the third banking day following receipt of the documents; and

(b) further defer honor if the presenter has expressly or impliedly consented thereto.

Failure to honor within the time here specified constitutes dishonor of the draft or demand and of the credit [except as otherwise provided in subsection (4) of Section 5—114 on conditional payment].

(2) Upon dishonor the bank may unless otherwise instructed fulfill its duty to return the draft or demand and the documents by holding them at the disposal of the presenter and sending him an advice to that effect.

(3) "Presenter" means any person presenting a draft or demand for payment for honor under a credit even though that person is a confirming bank or other correspondent which is acting under an issuer's authorization.

§ 5—113. *Indemnities*

(1) A bank seeking to obtain (whether for itself or another) honor, negotiation or reimbursement under a credit may give an indemnity to induce such honor, negotiation or reimbursement.

(2) An indemnity agreement inducing honor, negotiation or reimbursement

(a) unless otherwise explicitly agreed applies to defects in the documents but not in the goods; and

(b) unless a longer time is explicitly agreed expires at the end of ten business days following receipt of the documents by the ultimate customer unless notice of objection is sent before such expiration date. The ultimate customer may send notice of objection to the person from whom he received the documents and any bank receiving such notice is under a duty to send notice to its transferor before its midnight deadline.

§ 5—114. *Issuer's Duty and Privilege to Honor; Right to Reimbursement.*

(1) An issuer must honor a draft or demand for payment which complies with the terms of the relevant credit regardless of whether the goods or documents conform to the underlying contract for sale or other contract between the customer and the beneficiary. The issuer is not excused from honor of such a draft or demand by reason of an additional general term that all documents must be satisfactory to the issuer, but an issuer may require that specified documents must be satisfactory to it.

(2) Unless otherwise agreed when documents appear on their face to comply with the terms of a credit but a required document does not in fact conform to the warranties made on negotiation or transfer of a document of title (Section 7—507) or of a certificated security (Section 8—306) or is forged or fraudulent or there is fraud in the transaction:

(a) the issuer must honor the draft or demand for payment if honor is demanded by a negotiating bank or other holder of the draft or demand which has taken the draft or demand under the credit and under circumstances which would make it a holder in due course (Section 3—302) and in an appropriate case would make it a person to whom a document of title has been duly negotiated (Section 7—502) or a bona fide purchaser of a certificated security (Section 8—302); and

(b) in all other cases as against its customer, an issuer acting in good faith may honor the draft or demand for payment despite notification from the customer of fraud, forgery or other defect not apparent on the face of the documents but a court of appropriate jurisdiction may enjoin such honor.

(3) Unless otherwise agreed an issuer which has duly honored a draft or demand for payment is entitled to immediate reimbursement of any payment made under the credit and to be put in effectively available funds not later than the day before maturity of any acceptance made under the credit.

[(4) When a credit provides for payment by the issuer on receipt of notice that the required documents are in the possession of a correspondent or other agent of the issuer

(a) any payment made on receipt of such notice is conditional; and

(b) the issuer may reject documents which do not comply with the credit if it does so within three banking days following its receipt of the documents; and

(c) in the event of such rejection, the issuer is entitled by charge back or otherwise to return of the payment made.]

[(5) In the case covered by subsection (4) failure to reject documents within the time specified in sub-paragraph (b) constitutes acceptance of the documents and makes the payment final in favor of the beneficiary.]

§ 5—115. *Remedy for Improper Dishonor or Anticipatory Repudiation.*

(1) When an issuer wrongfully dishonors a draft or demand for payment presented under a credit the person entitled to honor has with respect to any documents the rights of a person in the position of a seller (Section 2—707) and may recover from the issuer the face amount of the draft or demand together with incidental damages under Section 2—710 on seller's incidental damages and interest but less any amount realized by resale or other use or disposition of the subject matter of the transaction. In the event no resale or other utilization is made the documents, goods or other subject matter involved in the transaction must be turned over to the issuer on payment of judgment.

(2) When an issuer wrongfully cancels or otherwise repudiates a credit before presentment of a draft or demand for payment drawn under it the beneficiary has the rights of a seller after anticipatory repudiation by the buyer under Section 2—610 if he learns of the repudiation in time reasonably to avoid procurement of the required documents. Otherwise the beneficiary has an immediate right of action for wrongful dishonor.

§ 5—116. *Transfer and Assignment.*

(1) The right to draw under a credit can be transferred or assigned only when the credit is expressly designated as transferable or assignable.

(2) Even through the credit specifically states that it is nontransferable or nonassignable the beneficiary may before performance of the conditions of the credit assign his right to proceeds. Such an assignment is an assignment of an account under Article 9 on Secured Transactions and is governed by that Article except that

(a) the assignment is ineffective until the letter of credit or advice of credit is delivered to the assignee which delivery constitutes perfection of the security interest under Article 9; and

(b) the issuer may honor drafts or demands for payment drawn under the credit until it receives a notification of the assignment signed by the beneficiary which reasonably identifies the credit involved in the assignment and contains a request to pay the assignee; and

(c) after what reasonably appears to be such a notification has been received the issuer may without dishonor refuse to accept or pay even to a person otherwise entitled to honor until the letter of credit or advice of credit is exhibited to the issuer.

(3) Except where the beneficiary has effectively assigned his right to draw or his right to proceeds, nothing in this section limits his right to transfer or negotiate drafts or demands drawn under the credit.

§ 5—117. *Insolvency of Bank Holding Funds for Documentary Credit.*

(1) Where an issuer or an advising or confirming bank or a bank which has for a customer procured issuance of a credit by another bank becomes insolvent before final payment under the credit and the credit is one to which this Article is made applicable by paragraphs (a) or (b) of Section 5—102(1) on scope, the receipt or allocation of funds or collateral to secure or meet obligations under the credit shall have the following results:

(a) to the extent of any funds or collateral turned over after or before the insolvency as indemnity against or specifically for the purpose of payment of drafts or demands for payment drawn under the designated credit, the drafts or demands are entitled to payment in preference over depositors or other general creditors of the issuer or bank; and

(b) on expiration of the credit or surrender of the beneficiary's rights under it unused any person who has given such funds or collateral is similarly entitled to return thereof; and

(c) a charge to a general or current account with a bank if specifically consented to for the purpose of indemnity against or payment of drafts or demands for payment drawn under the designated credit falls under the same rules as if the funds had been drawn out in cash and then turned over with specific instructions.

(2) After honor or reimbursement under this section the customer or other person for whose account the insolvent bank has acted is entitled to receive the documents involved.

ARTICLE 6
BULK TRANSFERS

§ 6—101. *Short Title.*

This Article shall be known and may be cited as Uniform Commercial Code—Bulk Transfers.

§ 6—102. *"Bulk Transfers"; Transfers of Equipment; Enterprises Subject to This Article; Bulk Transfers Subject to This Article.*

(1) A "bulk transfer" is any transfer in bulk and not in the ordinary course of the transferor's business of a major part of the materials, supplies, merchandise or other inventory (Section 9—109) of an enterprise subject to this Article.

(2) A transfer of a substantial part of the equipment (Section 9—109) of such an enterprise is a bulk transfer if it is made in connection with a bulk transfer of inventory, but not otherwise.

(3) The enterprises subject to this Article are all those whose principal business is the sale of merchandise from stock, including those who manufacture what they sell.

(4) Except as limited by the following section all bulk transfers of goods located within this state are subject to this Article.

§ 6—103. *Transfers Excepted From This Article.*

The following transfers are not subject to this Article:

(1) Those made to give security for the performance of an obligation;

(2) General assignments for the benefit of all the creditors of the transferor, and subsequent transfers by the assignee thereunder;

(3) Transfers in settlement or realization of a lien or other security interests;

(4) Sales by executors, administrators, receivers, trustees in bankruptcy, or any public officer under judicial process;

(5) Sales made in the course of judicial or administrative proceedings for the dissolution or reorganization of a corporation and of which notice is sent to the creditors of the corporation pursuant to order of the court or administrative agency;

(6) Transfers to a person maintaining a known place of business in this State who becomes bound to pay the debts of the transferor in full and gives public notice of that fact, and who is solvent after becoming so bound;

(7) A transfer to a new business enterprise organized to take over and continue the business, if public notice of the transaction is given and the new enterprise assumes the debts of the transferor and he receives nothing from the transaction except an interest in the new enterprise junior to the claims of creditors;

(8) Transfers of property which is exempt from execution.

Public notice under subsection (6) or subsection (7) may be given by publishing once a week for two consecutive weeks in a newspaper of general circulation where the transferor had its principal place of business in this state an advertisement including the names and addresses of the transferor and transferee and the effective date of the transfer.

§ 6—104. *Schedule of Property, List of Creditors.*

(1) Except as provided with respect to auction sales (Section 6—108), a bulk transfer subject to this Article is ineffective against any creditor of the transferor unless:

(a) The transferee requires the transferor to furnish a list of his existing creditors prepared as stated in this section; and

(b) The parties prepare a schedule of the property transferred sufficient to identify it; and

(c) The transferee preserves the list and schedule for six months next following the transfer and permits inspection of either or both and copying therefrom at all reasonable hours by any creditor of the transferor, or files the list and schedule in (a public office to be here identified).

(2) The list of creditors must be signed and sworn to or affirmed by the transferor or his agent. It must contain the names and business addresses of all creditors of the transferor, with the amounts when known, and also the names of all persons who are known to the transferor to assert claims against him even though such claims are disputed. If the transferor is the obligor of an outstanding issue of bonds, debentures or the like as to which there is an indenture trustee, the list of creditors need include only the name and address of the indenture trustee and the aggregate outstanding principal amount of the issue.

(3) Responsibility for the completeness and accuracy of the list of creditors rests on the transferor, and the transfer is not rendered ineffective by errors or omissions therein unless the transferee is shown to have had knowledge.

§ 6—105. *Notice to Creditors.*

In addition to the requirements of the preceding section, any bulk transfer subject to this Article except one made by auction sale (Section 6—108) is ineffective against any creditor of the transferor unless at least ten days before he takes possession of the goods or pays for them, whichever happens first, the transferee gives notice of the transfer in the manner and to the persons hereafter provided (Section 6—107).

§ 6—106. *Application of the Proceeds.*

In addition to the requirements of the two preceding sections:

(1) Upon every bulk transfer subject to this Article for which new consideration becomes payable except those made by sale at auction it is the duty of the transferee to assure that such consideration is applied so far as necessary to pay those debts of the transferor which are either shown on the list furnished by the transferor (Section 6—104) or filed in writing in the place stated in the notice (Section 6—107) within thirty days after the mailing of such notice. This duty of the transferee runs to all the holders of such debts, and may be enforced by any of them for the benefit of all.

(2) If any of said debts are in dispute the necessary sum may be withheld from distribution until the dispute is settled or adjudicated.

(3) If the consideration payable is not enough to pay all of the said debts in full distribution shall be made pro rata.]

Optional Subsection (4)

[(4) The transferee may within ten days after he takes possession of the goods pay the consideration into the (specify court) in the county where the transferor had its principal place of business in this state and thereafter may discharge his duty under this section by giving notice by registered or certified mail to all the persons to whom the duty runs that the consideration has been paid into that court and that they should file their claims there. On motion of any interested party, the court may order the distribution of the consideration to the persons entitled to it.]

§ 6—107. *The Notice.*

(1) The notice to creditors (Section 6—105) shall state:

(a) that a bulk transfer is about to be made; and

(b) the names and business addresses of the transferor and transferee, and all other business names and addresses used by the transferor within three years last past so far as known to the transferee; and

(c) whether or not all the debts of the transferor are to be paid in full as they fall due as a result of the transaction, and if so, the address to which creditors should send their bills.

(2) If the debts of the transferor are not to be paid in full as they fall due or if the transferee is in doubt on that point then the notice shall state further:

(a) the location and general description of the property to be transferred and the estimated total of the transferor's debts;

(b) the address where the schedule of property and list of creditors (Section 6—104) may be inspected;

(c) whether the transfer is to pay existing debts and if so the amount of such debts and to whom owing;

(d) whether the transfer is for new consideration and if so the amount of such consideration and the time and place of payment; [and]

[(e) if for new consideration the time and place where creditors of the transferor are to file their claims.]

(3) The notice in any case shall be delivered personally or sent by registered or certified mail to all the persons shown on the list of creditors furnished by the transferor (Section 6—104) and to all other persons who are known to the transferee to hold or assert claims against the transferor.

§ 6—108. *Auction Sales; "Auctioneer."*

(1) A bulk transfer is subject to this Article even though it is by sale at auction, but only in the manner and with the results stated in this section.

(2) The transferor shall furnish a list of his creditors and assist in the preparation of a schedule of the property to be sold, both prepared as before stated (Section 6—104).

(3) The person or persons other than the transferor who direct, control or are responsible for the auction are collectively called the "auctioneer". The auctioneer shall:

(a) receive and retain the list of creditors and prepare and retain the schedule of property for the period stated in this Article (Section 6—104);

(b) give notice of the auction personally or by registered or certified mail at least ten days before it occurs to all persons shown on the list of creditors and to all other persons who are known to him to hold or assert claims against the transferor; [and]

[(c) assure that the net proceeds of the auction are applied as provided in this Article (Section 6—106).]

(4) Failure of the auctioneer to perform any of these duties does not affect the validity of the sale or the title of the purchasers, but if the auctioneer knows that the auction constitutes a bulk transfer such failure renders the auctioneer liable to the creditors of the transferor as a class for the sums owing to them from the transferor up to but not exceeding the net proceeds of the auction. If the auctioneer consists of several persons their liability is joint and several.

§ 6—109. *What Creditors Protected; [Credit for Payment to Particular Creditors].*

(1) The creditors of the transferor mentioned in this Article are those holding claims based on transactions or events occurring before the bulk transfer, but creditors who become such after notice to creditors is given (Sections 6—105 and 6—107) are not entitled to notice.

[(2) Against the aggregate obligation imposed by the provisions of this Article concerning the application of the proceeds (Section 6—106 and subsection (3)(c) of 6—108) the transferee or auctioneer is entitled to credit for sums paid to particular creditors of the transferor, not exceeding the sums believed in good faith at the time of the payment to be properly payable to such creditors.]

§ 6—110. *Subsequent Transfers.*

When the title of a transferee to property is subject to a defect by reason of his noncompliance with the requirements of this Article, then:

(1) a purchaser of any of such property from such transferee who pays no value or who takes with notice of such noncompliance takes subject to such defect, but

(2) a purchaser for value in good faith and without such notice takes free of such defect.

§ 6—111. *Limitation of Actions and Levies.*

No action under this Article shall be brought nor levy made more than six months after the date on which the transferee took possession of the goods unless the transfer has been concealed. If the transfer has been concealed, actions may be brought or levies made within six months after its discovery.

ARTICLE 6
ALTERNATIVE B

§ 6—101. *Short Title.*

This Article shall be known and may be cited as Uniform Commercial Code—Bulk Sales.

§ 6—102. *Definitions and Index of Definitions.*

(1) In this Article, unless the context otherwise requires:

(a) "Assets" means the inventory that is the subject of a bulk sale and any tangible and intangible personal property used or held for use primarily in, or arising from, the seller's business and sold in connection with that inventory, but the term does not include:

(i) fixtures (Section 9—313(1)(a)) other than readily removable factory and office machines;

(ii) the lessee's interest in a lease of real property; or

(iii) property to the extent it is generally exempt from creditor process under nonbankruptcy law.

(b) "Auctioneer" means a person whom the seller engages to direct, conduct, control, or be responsible for a sale by auction.

(c) "Bulk sale" means:

(i) in the case of a sale by auction or a sale or series of sales conducted by a liquidator on the seller's behalf, a sale or series of sales not in the ordinary course of the seller's business of more than half of the seller's inventory, as measured by value on the date of the bulk-sale agreement, if on that date the auctioneer or liquidator has notice, or after reasonable inquiry would have had notice, that the seller will not continue to operate the same or a similar kind of business after the sale or series of sales; and

(ii) in all other cases, a sale not in the ordinary course of the seller's business of more than half the seller's inventory, as measured by value on the date of the bulk-sale agreement, if on that date the buyer has notice, or after reasonable inquiry would have had notice, that the seller will not continue to operate the same or a similar kind of business after the sale.

(d) "Claim" means a right to payment from the seller, whether or not the right is reduced to judgment, liquidated, fixed, matured, disputed, secured, legal, or equitable. The term includes costs of collection and attorney's fees only to the extent that the laws of this state permit the holder of the claim to recover them in an action against the obligor.

(e) "Claimant" means a person holding a claim incurred in the seller's business other than:

(i) an unsecured and unmatured claim for employment compensation and benefits, including commissions and vacation, severance, and sick-leave pay;

(ii) a claim for injury to an individual or to property, or for breach of warranty, unless:

(A) a right of action for the claim has accrued;

(B) the claim has been asserted against the seller; and

(C) the seller knows the identity of the person asserting the claim and the basis upon which the person has asserted it; and

(States to Select One Alternative)

Alternative A

[(iii) a claim for taxes owing to a governmental unit.]

Alternative B

[(iii) a claim for taxes owing to a governmental unit, if:

(A) a statute governing the enforcement of the claim permits or requires notice of the bulk sale to be given to the governmental unit in a manner other than by compliance with the requirements of this Article; and

(B) notice is given in accordance with the statute.]

(f) "Creditor" means a claimant or other person holding a claim.

(g)(i) "Date of the bulk sale" means:

(A) if the sale is by auction or is conducted by a liquidator on the seller's behalf, the date on which more than ten percent of the net proceeds is paid to or for the benefit of the seller; and

(B) in all other cases, the later of the date on which:

(I) more than ten percent of the net contract price is paid to or for the benefit of the seller; or

(II) more than ten percent of the assets, as measured by value, are transferred to the buyer.

(ii) For purposes of this subsection:

(A) delivery of a negotiable instrument (Section 3—104(1)) to or for the benefit of the seller in exchange for assets constitutes payment of the contract price pro tanto;

(B) to the extent that the contract price is deposited in an escrow, the contract price is paid to or for the benefit of the seller when the seller acquires the unconditional right to receive the deposit or when the deposit is delivered to the seller or for the benefit of the seller, whichever is earlier; and

(C) an asset is transferred when a person holding an unsecured claim can no longer obtain through judicial proceedings rights to the asset that are superior to those of the buyer arising as a result of the bulk sale. A person holding an unsecured claim can obtain those superior rights to a tangible asset at least until the buyer has an unconditional right, under the bulk-sale agreement, to possess the asset, and a person holding an unsecured claim can obtain those superior rights to an intangible asset at least until the buyer has an unconditional right, under the bulk-sale agreement, to use the asset.

(h) "Date of the bulk-sale agreement" means:

(i) in the case of a sale by auction or conducted by a liquidator (subsection (c)(i)), the date on which the seller engages the auctioneer or liquidator; and

(ii) in all other cases, the date on which a bulk-sale agreement becomes enforceable between the buyer and the seller.

(i) "Debt" means liability on a claim.

(j) "Liquidator" means a person who is regularly engaged in the business of disposing of assets for businesses contemplating liquidation or dissolution.

(k) "Net contract price" means the new consideration the buyer is obligated to pay for the assets less:

(i) the amount of any proceeds of the sale of an asset, to the extent the proceeds are applied in partial or total satisfaction of a debt secured by the asset; and

(ii) the amount of any debt to the extent it is secured by a security interest or lien that is enforceable against the asset before and after it has been sold to a buyer. If a debt is secured by an asset and other property of the seller, the amount of the debt secured by a security interest or lien that is enforceable against the asset is determined by multiplying the debt by a fraction, the numerator of which is the value of the new consideration for the asset on the date of the bulk sale and the denominator of which is the value of all property securing the debt on the date of the bulk sale.

(l) "Net proceeds" means the new consideration received for assets sold at a sale by auction or a sale conducted by a liquidator on the seller's behalf less:

(i) commissions and reasonable expenses of the sale;

(ii) the amount of any proceeds of the sale of an asset, to the extent the proceeds are applied in partial or total satisfaction of a debt secured by the asset; and

(iii) the amount of any debt to the extent it is secured by a security interest or lien that is enforceable against the asset before and after it has been sold to a buyer. If a debt is secured by an asset and other property of the seller, the amount of the debt secured by a security interest or lien that is enforceable against the asset is determined by multiplying the debt by a fraction, the numerator of which is the value of the new consideration for the asset on the date of the bulk sale and the denominator of which is the value of all property securing the debt on the date of the bulk sale.

(m) A sale is "in the ordinary course of the seller's business" if the sale comports with usual or customary practices in the kind of business in which the seller is engaged or with the seller's own usual or customary practices.

(n) "United States" includes its territories and possessions and the Commonwealth of Puerto Rico.

(o) "Value" means fair market value.

(p) "Verified" means signed and sworn to or affirmed.

(2) The following definitions in other Articles apply to this Article:

(a) "Buyer." Section 2—103(1)(a).

(b) "Equipment." Section 9—109(2).

(c) "Inventory." Section 9—109(4).

(d) "Sale." Section 2—106(1).

(e) "Seller." Section 2—103(1)(d).

(3) In addition, Article 1 contains general definitions and principles of construction and interpretation applicable throughout this Article.

§ 6—103. *Applicability of Article.*

(1) Except as otherwise provided in subsection (3), this Article applies to a bulk sale if:

(a) the seller's principal business is the sale of inventory from stock; and

(b) on the date of the bulk-sale agreement the seller is located in this state or, if the seller is located in a jurisdiction that is not a part of the United States, the seller's major executive office in the United States is in this state.

(2) A seller is deemed to be located at his [or her] place of business. If a seller has more than one place of business, the seller is deemed located at his [or her] chief executive office.

(3) This Article does not apply to:

(a) a transfer made to secure payment or performance of an obligation;

(b) a transfer of collateral to a secured party pursuant to Section 9—503;

(c) a sale of collateral pursuant to Section 9—504;

(d) retention of collateral pursuant to Section 9—505;

(e) a sale of an asset encumbered by a security interest or lien if (i) all the proceeds of the sale are applied in partial or total satisfaction of the debt secured by the security interest or lien or (ii) the security interest or lien is enforceable against the asset after it has been sold to the buyer and the net contract price is zero;

(f) a general assignment for the benefit of creditors or to a subsequent transfer by the assignee;

(g) a sale by an executor, administrator, receiver, trustee in bankruptcy, or any public officer under judicial process;

(h) a sale made in the course of judicial or administrative proceedings for the dissolution or reorganization of an organization;

(i) a sale to a buyer whose principal place of business is in the United States and who:

(i) not earlier than 21 days before the date of the bulk sale, (A) obtains from the seller a verified and dated list of claimants of whom the seller has notice three days before the seller sends or delivers the list to the buyer or (B) conducts a reasonable inquiry to discover the claimants;

(ii) assumes in full the debts owed to claimants of whom the buyer has knowledge on the date the buyer receives the list of claimants from the seller or on the date the buyer completes the reasonable inquiry, as the case may be;

(iii) is not insolvent after the assumption; and

(iv) gives written notice of the assumption not later than 30 days after the date of the bulk sale by sending or delivering a notice to the claimants identified in subparagraph (ii) or by filing a notice in the office of the [Secretary of State];

(j) a sale to a buyer whose principal place of business is in the United States and who:

(i) assumes in full the debts that were incurred in the seller's business before the date of the bulk sale;

(ii) is not insolvent after the assumption; and

(iii) gives written notice of the assumption not later than 30 days after the date of the bulk sale by sending or delivering a notice to each creditor whose debt is assumed or by filing a notice in the office of the [Secretary of State];

(k) a sale to a new organization that is organized to take over and continue the business of the seller and that has its principal place of business in the United States if:

(i) the buyer assumes in full the debts that were incurred in the seller's business before the date of the bulk sale;

(ii) the seller receives nothing from the sale except an interest in the new organization that is subordinate to the claims against the organization arising from the assumption; and

(iii) the buyer gives written notice of the assumption not later than 30 days after the date of the bulk sale by sending or delivering a notice to each creditor whose debt is assumed or by filing a notice in the office of the [Secretary of State];

(l) a sale of assets having:

(i) a value, net of liens and security interests, of less than $10,000. If a debt is secured by assets and other property of the seller, the net value of the assets is determined by subtracting from their value an amount equal to the product of the debt multiplied by a fraction, the numerator of which is the value of the assets on the date of the bulk sale and the denominator of which is the value of all property securing the debt on the date of the bulk sale; or

(ii) a value of more than $25,000,000 on the date of the bulk-sale agreement; or

(m) a sale required by, and made pursuant to, statute.

(4) The notice under subsection (3)(i)(iv) must state: (i) that a sale that may constitute a bulk sale has been or will be made; (ii) the date or prospective date of the bulk sale; (iii) the individual, partnership, or corporate names and the addresses of the seller and buyer; (iv) the address to which inquiries about the sale may be made, if different from the seller's address; and (v) that the buyer has assumed or will assume in full the debts owed to claimants of whom the buyer has knowledge on the date the buyer receives the list of claimants from the seller or completes a reasonable inquiry to discover the claimants.

(5) The notice under subsections (3)(j)(iii) and (3)(k)(iii) must state: (i) that a sale that may constitute a bulk sale has been or will be made; (ii) the date or prospective date of the bulk sale; (iii) the individual, partnership, or corporate names and the addresses of the seller and buyer; (iv) the address to which inquiries about the sale may be made, if different from the seller's address; and (v) that the buyer has assumed or will assume the debts that were incurred in the seller's business before the date of the bulk sale.

(6) For purposes of subsection (3)(l), the value of assets is presumed to be equal to the price the buyer agrees to pay for the assets. However, in a sale by auction or a sale conducted by a liquidator on the seller's behalf, the value of assets is presumed to be the amount the auctioneer or liquidator reasonably estimates the assets will bring at auction or upon liquidation.

§ 6—104. *Obligations of Buyer.*

(1) In a bulk sale as defined in Section 6—102(1)(c)(ii) the buyer shall:

(a) obtain from the seller a list of all business names and addresses used by the seller within three years before the date the list is sent or delivered to the buyer;

(b) unless excused under subsection (2), obtain from the seller a verified and dated list of claimants of whom the seller has notice three days before the seller sends or delivers the list to the buyer and including, to the extent known by the seller, the address of and the amount claimed by each claimant;

(c) obtain from the seller or prepare a schedule of distribution (Section 6—106(1));

(d) give notice of the bulk sale in accordance with Section 6—105;

(e) unless excused under Section 6—106(4), distribute the net contract price in accordance with the undertakings of the buyer in the schedule of distribution; and

(f) unless excused under subsection (2), make available the list of claimants (subsection (1)(b)) by:

(i) promptly sending or delivering a copy of the list without charge to any claimant whose written request is received by the buyer no later than six months after the date of the bulk sale;

(ii) permitting any claimant to inspect and copy the list at any reasonable hour upon request received by the buyer no later than six months after the date of the bulk sale; or

(iii) filing a copy of the list in the office of the [Secretary of State] no later than the time for giving a notice of the bulk sale (Section 6—105(5)). A list filed in accordance with this subparagraph must state the individual, partnership, or corporate name and a mailing address of the seller.

(2) A buyer who gives notice in accordance with Section 6—105(2) is excused from complying with the requirements of subsections (1)(b) and (1)(f).

§ 6—105. *Notice to Claimants.*

(1) Except as otherwise provided in subsection (2), to comply with Section 6—104(1)(d) the buyer shall send or deliver a written notice of the bulk sale to each claimant on the list of claimants (Section 6—104(1)(b)) and to any other claimant of which the buyer has knowledge at the time the notice of the bulk sale is sent or delivered.

(2) A buyer may comply with Section 6—104(1)(d) by filing a written notice of the bulk sale in the office of the [Secretary of State] if:

(a) on the date of the bulk-sale agreement the seller has 200 or more claimants, exclusive of claimants holding secured or matured claims for employment compensation and benefits, including commissions and vacation, severance, and sick-leave pay; or

(b) the buyer has received a verified statement from the seller stating that, as of the date of the bulk-sale agreement, the number of claimants, exclusive of claimants holding secured or matured claims for employment compensation and benefits, including commissions and vacation, severance, and sick-leave pay, is 200 or more.

(3) The written notice of the bulk sale must be accompanied by a copy of the schedule of distribution (Section 6—106(1)) and state at least:

(a) that the seller and buyer have entered into an agreement for a sale that may constitute a bulk sale under the laws of the State of __________;

(b) the date of the agreement;

(c) the date on or after which more than ten percent of the assets were or will be transferred;

(d) the date on or after which more than ten percent of the net contract price was or will be paid, if the date is not stated in the schedule of distribution;

(e) the name and a mailing address of the seller;

(f) any other business name and address listed by the seller pursuant to Section 6—104(1)(a);

(g) the name of the buyer and an address of the buyer from which information concerning the sale can be obtained;

(h) a statement indicating the type of assets or describing the assets item by item;

(i) the manner in which the buyer will make available the list of claimants (Section 6—104(1)(f)), if applicable; and

(j) if the sale is in total or partial satisfaction of an antecedent debt owed by the seller, the amount of the debt to be satisfied and the name of the person to whom it is owed.

(4) For purposes of subsections (3)(e) and (3)(g), the name of a person is the person's individual, partnership, or corporate name.

(5) The buyer shall give notice of the bulk sale not less than 45 days before the date of the bulk sale and, if the buyer gives notice in accordance with subsection (1), not more than 30 days after obtaining the list of claimants.

(6) A written notice substantially complying with the requirements of subsection (3) is effective even though it contains minor errors that are not seriously misleading.

(7) A form substantially as follows is sufficient to comply with subsection (3):

Notice of Sale

(1) ______, whose address is ______, is described in this notice as the "seller."

(2) ______, whose address is ______, is described in this notice as the "buyer."

(3) The seller has disclosed to the buyer that within the past three years the seller has used other business names, operated at other addresses, or both, as follows: ______.

(4) The seller and the buyer have entered into an agreement dated ______, for a sale that may constitute a bulk sale under the laws of the State of ______.

(5) The date on or after which more than ten percent of the assets that are the subject of the sale were or will be transferred is ______, and [if not stated in the schedule of distribution] the date on or after which more than ten percent of the net contract price was or will be paid is ______.

(6) The following assets are the subject of the sale: ______.

(7) [If applicable] The buyer will make available to claimants of the seller a list of the seller's claimants in the following manner: ______.

(8) [If applicable] The sale is to satisfy $ ______ of an antecedent debt owed by the seller to ______.

(9) A copy of the schedule of distribution of the net contract price accompanies this notice.

[End of Notice]

§ 6—106. *Schedule of Distribution.*

(1) The seller and buyer shall agree on how the net contract price is to be distributed and set forth their agreement in a written schedule of distribution.

(2) The schedule of distribution may provide for distribution to any person at any time, including distribution of the entire net contract price to the seller.

(3) The buyer's undertakings in the schedule of distribution run only to the seller. However, a buyer who fails to distribute the net contract price in accordance with the buyer's undertakings in the schedule of distribution is liable to a creditor only as provided in Section 6—107(1).

(4) If the buyer undertakes in the schedule of distribution to distribute any part of the net contract price to a person other than the seller, and, after the buyer has given notice in accordance with Section 6—105, some or all of the anticipated net contract price is or becomes unavailable for distribution as a consequence of the buyer's or seller's having complied with an order of court, legal process, statute, or rule of law, the buyer is excused from any obligation arising under this Article or under any contract with the seller to distribute the net contract price in accordance with the buyer's undertakings in the schedule if the buyer:

(a) distributes the net contract price remaining available in accordance with any priorities for payment stated in the schedule of distribution and, to the extent that the price is insufficient to pay all the debts having a given priority, distributes the price pro rata among those debts shown in the schedule as having the same priority;

(b) distributes the net contract price remaining available in accordance with an order of court;

(c) commences a proceeding for interpleader in a court of competent jurisdiction and is discharged from the proceeding; or

(d) reaches a new agreement with the seller for the distribution of the net contract price remaining available, sets forth the new agreement in an amended schedule of distribution, gives notice of the amended schedule, and distributes the net contract price remaining available in accordance with the buyer's undertakings in the amended schedule.

(5) The notice under subsection (4)(d) must identify the buyer and the seller, state the filing number, if any, of the original notice, set forth the amended schedule, and be given in accordance with subsection (1) or (2) of Section 6—105, whichever is applicable, at least 14 days before the buyer distributes any part of the net contract price remaining available.

(6) If the seller undertakes in the schedule of distribution to distribute any part of the net contract price, and, after the buyer has given notice in accordance with Section 6—105, some or all of the anticipated net contract price is or becomes unavailable for distribution as a consequence of the buyer's or seller's having complied with an order of court, legal process, statute, or rule of law, the seller and any person in control of the seller are excused from any obligation arising under this Article or under any agreement with the buyer to distribute the net contract price in accordance with the seller's undertakings in the schedule if the seller:

(a) distributes the net contract price remaining available in accordance with any priorities for payment stated in the schedule of distribution and, to the extent that the price is insufficient to pay all the debts having a given priority, distributes the price pro rata among those debts shown in the schedule as having the same priority;

(b) distributes the net contract price remaining available in accordance with an order of court;

(c) commences a proceeding for interpleader in a court of competent jurisdiction and is discharged from the proceeding; or

(d) prepares a written amended schedule of distribution of the net contract price remaining available for distribution, gives notice of the amended schedule, and distributes the net contract price remaining available in accordance with the amended schedule.

(7) The notice under subsection (6)(d) must identify the buyer and the seller, state the filing number, if any, of the original notice, set forth the amended schedule, and be given in accordance with subsection (1) or (2) of Section 6—105, whichever is applicable, at least 14 days before the seller distributes any part of the net contract price remaining available.

§ 6—107. *Liability for Noncompliance.*

(1) Except as provided in subsection (3), and subject to the limitation in subsection (4):

(a) a buyer who fails to comply with the requirements of Section 6—104(1)(e) with respect to a creditor is liable to the creditor for damages in the amount of the claim, reduced by any amount that the creditor would not have realized if the buyer had complied; and

(b) a buyer who fails to comply with the requirements of any other subsection of Section 6—104 with respect to a claimant is liable to the claimant for damages in the amount of the claim, reduced by any amount that the claimant would not have realized if the buyer had complied.

(2) In an action under subsection (1), the creditor has the burden of establishing the validity and amount of the claim, and the buyer has the burden of establishing the amount that the creditor would not have realized if the buyer had complied.

(3) A buyer who:

(a) made a good faith and commercially reasonable effort to comply with the requirements of Section 6—104(1) or to exclude the sale from the application of this Article under Section 6—103(3); or

(b) on or after the date of the bulk-sale agreement, but before the date of the bulk sale, held a good faith and commercially reasonable belief that this Article does not apply to the particular sale is not liable to creditors for failure to comply with the requirements of Section 6—104. The buyer has the burden of establishing the good faith and commercial reasonableness of the effort or belief.

(4) In a single bulk sale the cumulative liability of the buyer for failure to comply with the requirements of Section 6—104(1) may not exceed an amount equal to:

(a) if the assets consist only of inventory and equipment, twice the net contract price, less the amount of any part of the net contract price paid to or applied for the benefit of the seller or a creditor; or

(b) if the assets include property other than inventory and equipment, twice the net value of the inventory and equipment less the amount of the portion of any part of the net contract price paid to or applied for the benefit of the seller or a creditor which is allocable to the inventory and equipment.

(5) For the purposes of subsection (4)(b), the "net value" of an asset is the value of the asset less (i) the amount of any proceeds of the sale of an asset, to the extent the proceeds are applied

in partial or total satisfaction of a debt secured by the asset and (ii) the amount of any debt to the extent it is secured by a security interest or lien that is enforceable against the asset before and after it has been sold to a buyer. If a debt is secured by an asset and other property of the seller, the amount of the debt secured by a security interest or lien that is enforceable against the asset is determined by multiplying the debt by a fraction, the numerator of which is the value of the asset on the date of the bulk sale and the denominator of which is the value of all property securing the debt on the date of the bulk sale. The portion of a part of the net contract price paid to or applied for the benefit of the seller or a creditor that is "allocable to the inventory and equipment" is the portion that bears the same ratio to that part of the net contract price as the net value of the inventory and equipment bears to the net value of all of the assets.

(6) A payment made by the buyer to a person to whom the buyer is, or believes he [or she] is, liable under subsection (1) reduces pro tanto the buyer's cumulative liability under subsection (4).

(7) No action may be brought under subsection (1)(b) by or on behalf of a claimant whose claim is unliquidated or contingent.

(8) A buyer's failure to comply with the requirements of Section 6—104(1) does not (i) impair the buyer's rights in or title to the assets, (ii) render the sale ineffective, void, or voidable, (iii) entitle a creditor to more than a single satisfaction of his [or her] claim, or (iv) create liability other than as provided in this Article.

(9) Payment of the buyer's liability under subsection (1) discharges pro tanto the seller's debt to the creditor.

(10) Unless otherwise agreed, a buyer has an immediate right of reimbursement from the seller for any amount paid to a creditor in partial or total satisfaction of the buyer's liability under subsection (1).

(11) If the seller is an organization, a person who is in direct or indirect control of the seller, and who knowingly, intentionally, and without legal justification fails, or causes the seller to fail, to distribute the net contract price in accordance with the schedule of distribution is liable to any creditor to whom the seller undertook to make payment under the schedule for damages caused by the failure.

§ 6—108. *Bulk Sales by Auction; Bulk Sales Conducted by Liquidator.*

(1) Sections 6—104, 6—105, 6—106, and 6—107 apply to a bulk sale by auction and a bulk sale conducted by a liquidator on the seller's behalf with the following modifications:

(a) "buyer" refers to auctioneer or liquidator, as the case may be;

(b) "net contract price" refers to net proceeds of the auction or net proceeds of the sale, as the case may be;

(c) the written notice required under Section 6—105(3) must be accompanied by a copy of the schedule of distribution (Section 6—106(1)) and state at least:

(i) that the seller and the auctioneer or liquidator have entered into an agreement for auction or liquidation services that may constitute an agreement to make a bulk sale under the laws of the State of __________;

(ii) the date of the agreement;

(iii) the date on or after which the auction began or will begin or the date on or after which the liquidator began or will begin to sell assets on the seller's behalf;

(iv) the date on or after which more than ten percent of the net proceeds of the sale were or will be paid, if the date is not stated in the schedule of distribution;

(v) the name and a mailing address of the seller;

(vi) any other business name and address listed by the seller pursuant to Section 6—104(1)(a);

(vii) the name of the auctioneer or liquidator and an address of the auctioneer or liquidator from which information concerning the sale can be obtained;

(viii) a statement indicating the type of assets or describing the assets item by item;

(ix) the manner in which the auctioneer or liquidator will make available the list of claimants (Section 6—104(1)(f)), if applicable; and

(x) if the sale is in total or partial satisfaction of an antecedent debt owed by the seller, the amount of the debt to be satisfied and the name of the person to whom it is owed; and

(d) in a single bulk sale the cumulative liability of the auctioneer or liquidator for failure to comply with the requirements of this section may not exceed the amount of the net proceeds of the sale allocable to inventory and equipment sold less the amount of the portion of any part of the net proceeds paid to or applied for the benefit of a creditor which is allocable to the inventory and equipment.

(2) A payment made by the auctioneer or liquidator to a person to whom the auctioneer or liquidator is, or believes he [or she] is, liable under this section reduces pro tanto the auctioneer's or liquidator's cumulative liability under subsection (1)(d).

(3) A form substantially as follows is sufficient to comply with subsection (1)(c):

Notice of Sale

(1) ______, whose address is ______, is described in this notice as the "seller."

(2) ______, whose address is ______, is described in this notice as the "auctioneer" or "liquidator."

(3) The seller has disclosed to the auctioneer or liquidator that within the past three years the seller has used other business names, operated at other addresses, or both, as follows: ______.

(4) The seller and the auctioneer or liquidator have entered into an agreement dated for auction or liquidation services that may constitute an agreement to make a bulk sale under the laws of the State of ______.

(5) The date on or after which the auction began or will begin or the date on or after which the liquidator began or will begin to sell assets on the seller's behalf is ______, and [if not stated in the schedule of distribution] the date on or after which more than ten percent of the net proceeds of the sale were or will be paid is ______.

(6) The following assets are the subject of the sale: ______.

(7) [If applicable] The auctioneer or liquidator will make available to claimants of the seller a list of the seller's claimants in the following manner: ______.

(8) [If applicable] The sale is to satisfy $______ of an antecedent debt owed by the seller to ______.

(9) A copy of the schedule of distribution of the net proceeds accompanies this notice.

[End of Notice]

(4) A person who buys at a bulk sale by auction or conducted by a liquidator need not comply with the requirements of Section 6—104(1) and is not liable for the failure of an auctioneer or liquidator to comply with the requirements of this section.

§ 6—109. *What Constitutes Filing; Duties of Filing Officer; Information from Filing Officer.*

(1) Presentation of a notice or list of claimants for filing and tender of the filing fee or acceptance of the notice or list by the filing officer constitutes filing under this Article.

(2) The filing officer shall:

(a) mark each notice or list with a file number and with the date and hour of filing;

(b) hold the notice or list or a copy for public inspection;

(c) index the notice or list according to each name given for the seller and for the buyer; and

(d) note in the index the file number and the addresses of the seller and buyer given in the notice or list.

(3) If the person filing a notice or list furnishes the filing officer with a copy, the filing officer upon request shall note upon the copy the file number and date and hour of the filing of the original and send or deliver the copy to the person.

(4) The fee for filing and indexing and for stamping a copy furnished by the person filing to show the date and place of filing is $_______ for the first page and $_______ for each additional page. The fee for indexing each name beyond the first two is $ _______.

(5) Upon request of any person, the filing officer shall issue a certificate showing whether any notice or list with respect to a particular seller or buyer is on file on the date and hour stated in the certificate. If a notice or list is on file, the certificate must give the date and hour of filing of each notice or list and the name and address of each seller, buyer, auctioneer, or liquidator. The fee for the certificate is $_______ if the request for the certificate is in the standard form prescribed by the [Secretary of State] and otherwise is $_______. Upon request of any person, the filing officer shall furnish a copy of any filed notice or list for a fee of $_______.

(6) The filing officer shall keep each notice or list for two years after it is filed.

§ 6—110. *Limitation of Actions.*

(1) Except as provided in subsection (2), an action under this Article against a buyer, auctioneer, or liquidator must be commenced within one year after the date of the bulk sale.

(2) If the buyer, auctioneer, or liquidator conceals the fact that the sale has occurred, the limitation is tolled and an action under this Article may be commenced within the earlier of (i) one year after the person bringing the action discovers that the sale has occurred or (ii) one year after the person bringing the action should have discovered that the sale has occurred, but no later than two years after the date of the bulk sale. Complete noncompliance with the requirements of this Article does not of itself constitute concealment.

(3) An action under Section 6—107(11) must be commenced within one year after the alleged violation occurs.

ARTICLE 7
WAREHOUSE RECEIPTS, BILLS OF LADING AND OTHER DOCUMENTS OF TITLE

PART 1
General

§ 7—101. *Short Title.*

This Article shall be known and may be cited as Uniform Commercial Code—Documents of Title.

§ 7—102. *Definitions and Index of Definitions.*

(1) In this Article, unless the context otherwise requires:

(a) "Bailee" means the person who by a warehouse receipt, bill of lading or other document of title acknowledges possession of goods and contracts to deliver them.

(b) "Consignee" means the person named in a bill to whom or to whose order the bill promises delivery.

(c) "Consignor" means the person named in a bill as the person from whom the goods have been received for shipment.

(d) "Delivery order" means a written order to deliver goods directed to a warehouseman, carrier or other person who in the ordinary course of business issues warehouse receipts or bills of lading.

(e) "Document" means document of title as defined in the general definitions in Article 1 (Section 1—201).

(f) "Goods" means all things which are treated as movable for the purposes of a contract of storage or transportation.

(g) "Issuer" means a bailee who issues a document except that in relation to an unaccepted delivery order it means the person who orders the possessor of goods to deliver. Issuer includes any person for whom an agent or employee purports to act in issuing a document if the agent or employee has real or apparent authority to issue documents, notwithstanding that the issuer received no goods or that the goods were misdescribed or that in any other respect the agent or employee violated his instructions.

(h) "Warehouseman" is a person engaged in the business of storing goods for hire.

(2) Other definitions applying to this Article or to specified Parts thereof, and the sections in which they appear are:

"Duly negotiate." Section 7—501.

"Person entitled under the document." Section 7—403(4).

(3) Definitions in other Articles applying to this Article and the sections in which they appear are:

"Contract for sale." Section 2—106.

"Overseas." Section 2—323.

"Receipt" of goods. Section 2—103.

(4) In addition Article 1 contains general definitions and principles of construction and interpretation applicable throughout this Article.

§ 7—103. *Relation of Article to Treaty, Statute, Tariff, Classification or Regulation.*

To the extent that any treaty or statute of the United States, regulatory statute of this State or tariff, classification or regulation filed or issued pursuant thereto is applicable, the provisions of this Article are subject thereto.

§ 7—104. *Negotiable and Nonnegotiable Warehouse Receipt, Bill of Lading or Other Document of Title.*

(1) A warehouse receipt, bill of lading or other document of title is negotiable

(a) if by its terms the goods are to be delivered to bearer or to the order of a named person; or

(b) where recognized in overseas trade, if it runs to a named person or assigns.

(2) Any other document is nonnegotiable. A bill of lading in which it is stated that the goods are consigned to a named person is not made negotiable by a provision that the goods are to be delivered only against a written order signed by the same or another named person.

§ 7—105. *Construction Against Negative Implication.*

The omission from either Part 2 or Part 3 of this Article of a provision corresponding to a provision made in the other Part does not imply that a corresponding rule of law is not applicable.

PART 2

Warehouse Receipts: Special Provisions

§ 7—201. *Who May Issue a Warehouse Receipt; Storage Under Government Bond.*

(1) A warehouse receipt may be issued by any warehouseman.

(2) Where goods including distilled spirits and agricultural commodities are stored under a statute requiring a bond against withdrawal or a license for the issuance of receipts in the nature of warehouse receipts, a receipt issued for the goods has like effect as a warehouse receipt even though issued by a person who is the owner of the goods and is not a warehouseman.

§ 7—202. *Form of Warehouse Receipt; Essential Terms; Optional Terms.*

(1) A warehouse receipt need not be in any particular form.

(2) Unless a warehouse receipt embodies within its written or printed terms each of the following, the warehouseman is liable for damages caused by the omission to a person injured thereby:

(a) the location of the warehouse where the goods are stored;

(b) the date of issue of the receipt;

(c) the consecutive number of the receipt;

(d) a statement whether the goods received will be delivered to the bearer, to a specified person, or to a specified person or his order;

(e) the rate of storage and handling charges, except that where goods are stored under a field warehousing arrangement a statement of that fact is sufficient on a nonnegotiable receipt;

(f) a description of the goods or of the packages containing them;

(g) the signature of the warehouseman, which may be made by his authorized agent;

(h) if the receipt is issued for goods of which the warehouseman is owner, either solely or jointly or in common with others, the fact of such ownership; and

(i) a statement of the amount of advances made and of liabilities incurred for which the warehouseman claims a lien or security interest (Section 7—209). If the precise amount of such advances made or of such liabilities incurred is, at the time of the issue of the receipt, unknown to the warehouseman or to his agent who issues it, a statement of the fact that advances have been made or liabilities incurred and the purpose thereof is sufficient.

(3) A warehouseman may insert in his receipt any other terms which are not contrary to the provisions of this Act and do not impair his obligation of delivery (Section 7—403) or his duty of care (Section 7—204). Any contrary provisions shall be ineffective.

§ 7—203. *Liability for Nonreceipt or Misdescription.*

A party to or purchaser for value in good faith of a document of title other than a bill of lading relying in either case upon the description therein of the goods may recover from the issuer damages caused by the nonreceipt or misdescription of the goods, except to the extent that the document conspicuously indicates that the issuer does not know whether any part or all of the goods in fact were received or conform to the description, as where the description is in terms of marks or labels or kind, quantity or condition, or the receipt or description is qualified by "contents, condition and quality unknown", "said to contain" or the like, if such indication be true, or the party or purchaser otherwise has notice.

§ 7—204. *Duty of Care; Contractual Limitation of Warehouseman's Liability.*

(1) A warehouseman is liable for damages for loss of or injury to the goods caused by his failure to exercise such care in regard to them as a reasonably careful man would exercise under like circumstances but unless otherwise agreed he is not liable for damages which could not have been avoided by the exercise of such care.

(2) Damages may be limited by a term in the warehouse receipt or storage agreement limiting the amount of liability in case of loss or damage, and setting forth a specific liability per article or item, or value per unit of weight, beyond which the warehouseman shall not be liable; provided, however, that such liability may on written request of the bailor at the time of signing such storage agreement or within a reasonable time after receipt of the warehouse receipt be increased on part or all of the goods thereunder, in which event increased rates may be charged based on such increased valuation, but that no such increase shall be permitted contrary to a lawful limitation of liability contained in the warehouseman's tariff, if any. No such limitation is effective with respect to the warehouseman's liability for conversion to his own use.

(3) Reasonable provisions as to the time and manner of presenting claims and instituting actions based on the bailment may be included in the warehouse receipt or tariff.

(4) This section does not impair or repeal . . .

§ 7—205. *Title Under Warehouse Receipt Defeated in Certain Cases.*

A buyer in the ordinary course of business of fungible goods sold and delivered by a warehouseman who is also in the business of buying and selling such goods takes free of any claim under a warehouse receipt even though it has been duly negotiated.

§ 7—206. *Termination of Storage at Warehouseman's Option.*

(1) A warehouseman may on notifying the person on whose account the goods are held and any other person known to claim an interest in the goods require payment of any charges and removal of the goods from the warehouse at the termination of the period of storage fixed by the document, or, if no period is fixed, within a stated period not less than thirty days after the notification. If the goods are not removed before the date specified in the notification, the warehouseman may sell them in accordance with the provisions of the section on enforcement of a warehouseman's lien (Section 7—210).

(2) If a warehouseman in good faith believes that the goods are about to deteriorate or decline in value to less than the

amount of his lien within the time prescribed in subsection (1) for notification, advertisement and sale, the warehouseman may specify in the notification any reasonable shorter time for removal of the goods and in case the goods are not removed, may sell them at public sale held not less than one week after a single advertisement or posting.

(3) If as a result of a quality or condition of the goods of which the warehouseman had no notice at the time of deposit the goods are a hazard to other property or to the warehouse or to persons, the warehouseman may sell the goods at public or private sale without advertisement on reasonable notification to all persons known to claim an interest in the goods. If the warehouseman after a reasonable effort is unable to sell the goods he may dispose of them in any lawful manner and shall incur no liability by reason of such disposition.

(4) The warehouseman must deliver the goods to any person entitled to them under this Article upon due demand made at any time prior to sale or other disposition under this section.

(5) The warehouseman may satisfy his lien from the proceeds of any sale or disposition under this section but must hold the balance for delivery on the demand of any person to whom he would have been bound to deliver the goods.

§ 7—207. *Goods Must Be Kept Separate; Fungible Goods.*

(1) Unless the warehouse receipt otherwise provides, a warehouseman must keep separate the goods covered by each receipt so as to permit at all times identification and delivery of those goods except that different lots of fungible goods may be commingled.

(2) Fungible goods so commingled are owned in common by the persons entitled thereto and the warehouseman is severally liable to each owner for that owner's share. Where because of overissue a mass of fungible goods is insufficient to meet all the receipts which the warehouseman has issued against it, the persons entitled include all holders to whom overissued receipts have been duly negotiated.

§ 7—208. *Altered Warehouse Receipts.*

Where a blank in a negotiable warehouse receipt has been filled in without authority, a purchaser for value and without notice of the want of authority may treat the insertion as authorized. Any other unauthorized alteration leaves any receipt enforceable against the issuer according to its original tenor.

§ 7—209. *Lien of Warehouseman.*

(1) A warehouseman has a lien against the bailor on the goods covered by a warehouse receipt or on the proceeds thereof in his possession for charges for storage or transportation (including demurrage and terminal charges), insurance, labor, or charges present or future in relation to the goods, and for expenses necessary for preservation of the goods or reasonably incurred in their sale pursuant to law. If the person on whose account the goods are held is liable for like charges or expenses in relation to other goods whenever deposited and it is stated in the receipt that a lien is claimed for charges and expenses in relation to other goods, the warehouseman also has a lien against him for such charges and expenses whether or not the other goods have been delivered by the warehouseman. But against a person to whom a negotiable warehouse receipt is duly negotiated a warehouseman's lien is limited to charges in an amount or at a rate specified on the receipt or if no charges are so specified then to a reasonable charge for storage of the goods covered by the receipt subsequent to the date of the receipt.

(2) The warehouseman may also reserve a security interest against the bailor for a maximum amount specified on the receipt for charges other than those specified in subsection (1), such as for money advanced and interest. Such a security interest is governed by the Article on Secured Transactions (Article 9).

(3) (a) A warehouseman's lien for charges and expenses under subsection (1) or a security interest under subsection (2) is also effective against any person who so entrusted the bailor with possession of the goods that a pledge of them by him to a good faith purchaser for value would have been valid but is not effective against a person as to whom the document confers no right in the goods covered by it under Section 7—503.

(b) A warehouseman's lien on household goods for charges and expenses in relation to the goods under subsection (1) is also effective against all persons if the depositor was the legal possessor of the goods at the time of deposit. "Household goods" means furniture, furnishings and personal effects used by the depositor in a dwelling.

(4) A warehouseman loses his lien on any goods which he voluntarily delivers or which he unjustifiably refuses to deliver.

§ 7—210. *Enforcement of Warehouseman's Lien.*

(1) Except as provided in subsection (2), a warehouseman's lien may be enforced by public or private sale of the goods in bloc or in parcels, at any time or place and on any terms which are commercially reasonable, after notifying all persons known to claim an interest in the goods. Such notification must include a statement of the amount due, the nature of the proposed sale and the time and place of any public sale. The fact that a better price could have been obtained by a sale at a different time or in a different method from that selected by the warehouseman is not of itself sufficient to establish that the sale was not made in a commercially reasonable manner. If the warehouseman either sells the goods in the usual manner in any recognized market therefor, or if he sells at the price current in such market at the time of his sale, or if he has otherwise sold in conformity with commercially reasonable practices among dealers in the type of goods sold, he has sold in a commercially reasonable manner. A sale of more goods than apparently necessary to be offered to ensure satisfaction of the obligation is not commercially reasonable except in cases covered by the preceding sentence.

(2) A warehouseman's lien on goods other than goods stored by a merchant in the course of his business may be enforced only as follows:

(a) All persons known to claim an interest in the goods must be notified.

(b) The notification must be delivered in person or sent by registered or certified letter to the last known address of any person to be notified.

(c) The notification must include an itemized statement of the claim, a description of the goods subject to the lien, a demand for payment within a specified time not less than ten days after receipt of the notification, and a conspicuous statement that unless the claim is paid within the time the goods will be advertised for sale and sold by auction at a specified time and place.

(d) The sale must conform to the terms of the notification.

(e) The sale must be held at the nearest suitable place to that where the goods are held or stored.

(f) After the expiration of the time given in the notification, an advertisement of the sale must be published once a week for two weeks consecutively in a newspaper of general circulation where the sale is to be held. The advertisement must include a description of the goods, the name of the person on whose account they are being held, and the time and place of the sale. The sale must take place at least fifteen days after the first publication. If there is no newspaper of general circulation where the sale is to be held, the advertisement must be posted at least ten days before the sale in not less than six conspicuous places in the neighborhood of the proposed sale.

(3) Before any sale pursuant to this section any person claiming a right in the goods may pay the amount necessary to satisfy the lien and the reasonable expenses incurred under this section. In that event the goods must not be sold, but must be retained by the warehouseman subject to the terms of the receipt and this Article.

(4) The warehouseman may buy at any public sale pursuant to this section.

(5) A purchaser in good faith of goods sold to enforce a warehouseman's lien takes the goods free of any rights of persons against whom the lien was valid, despite noncompliance by the warehouseman with the requirements of this section.

(6) The warehouseman may satisfy his lien from the proceeds of any sale pursuant to this section but must hold the balance, if any, for delivery on demand to any person to whom he would have been bound to deliver the goods.

(7) The rights provided by this section shall be in addition to all other rights allowed by law to a creditor against his debtor.

(8) Where a lien is on goods stored by a merchant in the course of his business the lien may be enforced in accordance with either subsection (1) or (2).

(9) The warehouseman is liable for damages caused by failure to comply with the requirements for sale under this section and in case of willful violation is liable for conversion.

PART 3
Bills of Lading: Special Provisions

§ 7—301. *Liability for Nonreceipt or Misdescription; "Said to Contain"; "Shipper's Load and Count"; Improper Handling.*

(1) A consignee of a nonnegotiable bill who has given value in good faith or a holder to whom a negotiable bill has been duly negotiated relying in either case upon the description therein of the goods, or upon the date therein shown, may recover from the issuer damages caused by the misdating of the bill or the nonreceipt or misdescription of the goods, except to the extent that the document indicates that the issuer does not know whether any part of all of the goods in fact were received or conform to the description, as where the description is in terms of marks or labels or kind, quantity, or condition or the receipt or description is qualified by "contents or condition of contents of packages unknown", "said to contain", "shipper's weight, load and count" or the like, if such indication be true.

(2) When goods are loaded by an issuer who is a common carrier, the issuer must count the packages of goods if package freight and ascertain the kind and quantity if bulk freight. In such cases "shipper's weight, load and count" or other words indicating that the description was made by the shipper are ineffective except as to freight concealed by packages.

(3) When bulk freight is loaded by a shipper who makes available to the issuer adequate facilities for weighing such freight, an issuer who is a common carrier must ascertain the kind and quantity within a reasonable time after receiving the written request of the shipper to do so. In such cases "shipper's weight" or other words of like purport are ineffective.

(4) The issuer may by inserting in the bill the words "shipper's weight, load and count" or other words of like purport indicate that the goods were loaded by the shipper; and if such statement be true the issuer shall not be liable for damages caused by the improper loading. But their omission does not imply liability for such damages.

(5) The shipper shall be deemed to have guaranteed to the issuer the accuracy at the time of shipment of the description, marks, labels, number, kind, quantity, condition and weight, as furnished by him; and the shipper shall indemnify the issuer against damage caused by inaccuracies in such particulars. The right of the issuer to such indemnity shall in no way limit his responsibility and liability under the contract of carriage to any person other than the shipper.

§ 7—302. *Through Bills of Lading and Similar Documents.*

(1) The issuer of a through bill of lading or other document embodying an undertaking to be performed in part by persons acting as its agents or by connecting carriers is liable to anyone entitled to recover on the document for any breach by such other persons or by a connecting carrier of its obligation under the document but to the extent that the bill covers an undertaking to be performed overseas or in territory not contiguous to the continental United States or an undertaking including matters other than transportation this liability may be varied by agreement of the parties.

(2) Where goods covered by a through bill of lading or other document embodying an undertaking to be performed in part by persons other than the issuer are received by any such person, he is subject with respect to his own performance while the goods are in his possession to the obligation of the issuer. His obligation is discharged by delivery of the goods to another such person pursuant to the document, and does not include liability for breach by any other such persons or by the issuer.

(3) The issuer of such through bill of lading or other document shall be entitled to recover from the connecting carrier or such other person in possession of the goods when the breach of the obligation under the document occurred, the amount it may be required to pay to anyone entitled to recover on the document therefor, as may be evidenced by any receipt, judgment, or transcript thereof, and the amount of any expense reasonably incurred by it in defending any action brought by anyone entitled to recover on the document therefor.

§ 7—303. *Diversion; Reconsignment; Change of Instructions.*

(1) Unless the bill of lading otherwise provides, the carrier may deliver the goods to a person or destination other than that stated in the bill or may otherwise dispose of the goods on instructions from

(a) the holder of a negotiable bill; or

(b) the consignor on a nonnegotiable bill notwithstanding contrary instructions from the consignee; or

(c) the consignee on a nonnegotiable bill in the absence of contrary instructions from the consignor, if the goods have arrived at the billed destination or if the consignee is in possession of the bill; or

(d) the consignee on a nonnegotiable bill if he is entitled as against the consignor to dispose of them.

(2) Unless such instructions are noted on a negotiable bill of lading, a person to whom the bill is duly negotiated can hold the bailee according to the original terms.

§ 7—304. *Bills of Lading in a Set.*

(1) Except where customary in overseas transportation, a bill of lading must not be issued in a set of parts. The issuer is liable for damages caused by violation of this subsection.

(2) Where a bill of lading is lawfully drawn in a set of parts, each of which is numbered and expressed to be valid only if the goods have not been delivered against any other part, the whole of the parts constitute one bill.

(3) Where a bill of lading is lawfully issued in a set of parts and different parts are negotiated to different persons, the title of the holder to whom the first due negotiation is made prevails as to both the document and the goods even though any later holder may have received the goods from the carrier in good faith and discharged the carrier's obligation by surrender of his part.

(4) Any person who negotiates or transfers a single part of a bill of lading drawn in a set is liable to holders of that part as if it were the whole set.

(5) The bailee is obliged to deliver in accordance with Part 4 of this Article against the first presented part of a bill of lading lawfully drawn in a set. Such delivery discharges the bailee's obligation on the whole bill.

§ 7—305. *Destination Bills.*

(1) Instead of issuing a bill of lading to the consignor at the place of shipment a carrier may at the request of the consignor procure the bill to be issued at destination or at any other place designated in the request.

(2) Upon request of anyone entitled as against the carrier to control the goods while in transit and on surrender of any outstanding bill of lading or other receipt covering such goods, the issuer may procure a substitute bill to be issued at any place designated in the request.

§ 7—306. *Altered Bills of Lading.*

An unauthorized alteration or filling in of a blank in a bill of lading leaves the bill enforceable according to its original tenor.

§ 7—307. *Lien of Carrier.*

(1) A carrier has a lien on the goods covered by a bill of lading for charges subsequent to the date of its receipt of the goods for storage or transportation (including demurrage and terminal charges) and for expenses necessary for preservation of the goods incident to their transportation or reasonably incurred in their sale pursuant to law. But against a purchaser for value of a negotiable bill of lading a carrier's lien is limited to charges stated in the bill or the applicable tariffs, or if no charges are stated then to a reasonable charge.

(2) A lien for charges and expenses under subsection (1) on goods which the carrier was required by law to receive for transportation is effective against the consignor or any person entitled to the goods unless the carrier had notice that the consignor lacked authority to subject the goods to such charges and expenses. Any other lien under subsection (1) is effective against the consignor and any person who permitted the bailor to have control or possession of the goods unless the carrier had notice that the bailor lacked such authority.

(3) A carrier loses his lien on any goods which he voluntarily delivers or which he unjustifiably refuses to deliver.

§ 7—308. *Enforcement of Carrier's Lien.*

(1) A carrier's lien may be enforced by public or private sale of the goods, in bloc or in parcels, at any time or place and on any terms which are commercially reasonable, after notifying all persons known to claim an interest in the goods. Such notification must include a statement of the amount due, the nature of the proposed sale and the time and place of any public sale. The fact that a better price could have been obtained by a sale at a different time or in a different method from that selected by the carrier is not of itself sufficient to establish that the sale was not made in a commercially reasonable manner. If the carrier either sells the goods in the usual manner in any recognized market therefor or if he sells at the price current in such market at the time of his sale or if he has otherwise sold in conformity with commercially reasonable practices among dealers in the type of goods sold he has sold in a commercially reasonable manner. A sale of more goods than apparently necessary to be offered to ensure satisfaction of the obligation is not commercially reasonable except in cases covered by the preceding sentence.

(2) Before any sale pursuant to this section any person claiming a right in the goods may pay the amount necessary to satisfy the lien and the reasonable expenses incurred under this section. In that event the goods must not be sold, but must be retained by the carrier subject to the terms of the bill and this Article.

(3) The carrier may buy at any public sale pursuant to this section.

(4) A purchaser in good faith of goods sold to enforce a carrier's lien takes the goods free of any rights of persons against whom the lien was valid, despite noncompliance by the carrier with the requirements of this section.

(5) The carrier may satisfy his lien from the proceeds of any sale pursuant to this section but must hold the balance, if any, for delivery on demand to any person to whom he would have been bound to deliver the goods.

(6) The rights provided by this section shall be in addition to all other rights allowed by law to a creditor against his debtor.

(7) A carrier's lien may be enforced in accordance with either subsection (1) or the procedure set forth in subsection (2) of Section 7—210.

(8) The carrier is liable for damages caused by failure to comply with the requirements for sale under this section and in case of willful violation is liable for conversion.

§ 7—309. *Duty of Care; Contractual Limitation of Carrier's Liability.*

(1) A carrier who issues a bill of lading whether negotiable or nonnegotiable must exercise the degree of care in relation to the goods which a reasonably careful man would exercise under like circumstances. This subsection does not repeal or change any law or rule of law which imposes liability upon a common carrier for damages not caused by its negligence.

(2) Damages may be limited by a provision that the carrier's liability shall not exceed a value stated in the document if the carrier's rates are dependent upon value and the consignor by the carrier's tariff is afforded an opportunity to declare a higher value or a value as lawfully provided in the tariff, or where no tariff is filed he is otherwise advised of such opportunity; but no

such limitation is effective with respect to the carrier's liability for conversion to its own use.

(3) Reasonable provisions as to the time and manner of presenting claims and instituting actions based on the shipment may be included in a bill of lading or tariff.

PART 4
Warehouse Receipts and Bills of Lading: General Obligations

§ 7—401. *Irregularities in Issue of Receipt or Bill or Conduct of Issuer.*

The obligations imposed by this Article on an issuer apply to a document of title regardless of the fact that

(a) the document may not comply with the requirements of this Article or of any other law or regulation regarding its issue, form or content; or

(b) the issuer may have violated laws regulating the conduct of his business; or

(c) the goods covered by the document were owned by the bailee at the time the document was issued; or

(d) the person issuing the document does not come within the definition of warehouseman if it purports to be a warehouse receipt.

§ 7—402. *Duplicate Receipt or Bill; Overissue.*

Neither a duplicate nor any other document of title purporting to cover goods already represented by an outstanding document of the same issuer confers any right in the goods, except as provided in the case of bills in a set, overissue of documents for fungible goods and substitutes for lost, stolen or destroyed documents. But the issuer is liable for damages caused by his overissue or failure to identify a duplicate document as such by conspicuous notation on its face.

§ 7—403. *Obligation of Warehouseman or Carrier to Deliver; Excuse.*

(1) The bailee must deliver the goods to a person entitled under the document who complies with subsections (2) and (3), unless and to the extent that the bailee establishes any of the following:

(a) delivery of the goods to a person whose receipt was rightful as against the claimant;

(b) damage to or delay, loss or destruction of the goods for which the bailee is not liable [, but the burden of establishing negligence in such cases is on the person entitled under the document];

(c) previous sale or other disposition of the goods in lawful enforcement of a lien or on warehouseman's lawful termination of storage;

(d) the exercise by a seller of his right to stop delivery pursuant to the provisions of the Article on Sales (Section 2—705);

(e) a diversion, reconsignment or other disposition pursuant to the provisions of this Article (Section 7—303) or tariff regulating such right;

(f) release, satisfaction or any other fact affording a personal defense against the claimant;

(g) any other lawful excuse.

(2) A person claiming goods covered by a document of title must satisfy the bailee's lien where the bailee so requests or where the bailee is prohibited by law from delivering the goods until the charges are paid.

(3) Unless the person claiming is one against whom the document confers no right under Sec. 7—503(1), he must surrender for cancellation or notation of partial deliveries any outstanding negotiable document covering the goods, and the bailee must cancel the document or conspicuously note the partial delivery thereon or be liable to any person to whom the document is duly negotiated.

(4) "Person entitled under the document" means holder in the case of a negotiable document, or the person to whom delivery is to be made by the terms of or pursuant to written instructions under a nonnegotiable document.

§ 7—404. *No Liability for Good Faith Delivery Pursuant to Receipt or Bill.*

A bailee who in good faith including observance of reasonable commercial standards has received goods and delivered or otherwise disposed of them according to the terms of the document of title or pursuant to this Article is not liable therefor. This rule applies even though the person from whom he received the goods had no authority to procure the document or to dispose of the goods and even though the person to whom he delivered the goods had no authority to receive them.

PART 5
Warehouse Receipts and Bills of Lading: Negotiation and Transfer

§ 7—501. *Form of Negotiation and Requirements of "Due Negotiation."*

(1) A negotiable document of title running to the order of a named person is negotiated by his indorsement and delivery. After his indorsement in blank or to bearer any person can negotiate it by delivery alone.

(2) (a) A negotiable document of title is also negotiated by delivery alone when by its original terms it runs to bearer.

(b) When a document running to the order of a named person is delivered to him the effect is the same as if the document had been negotiated.

(3) Negotiation of a negotiable document of title after it has been indorsed to a specified person requires indorsement by the special indorsee as well as delivery.

(4) A negotiable document of title is "duly negotiated" when it is negotiated in the manner stated in this section to a holder who purchases it in good faith without notice of any defense against or claim to it on the part of any person and for value, unless it is established that the negotiation is not in the regular course of business or financing or involves receiving the document in settlement or payment of a money obligation.

(5) Indorsement of a nonnegotiable document neither makes it negotiable nor adds to the transferee's rights.

(6) The naming in a negotiable bill of a person to be notified of the arrival of the goods does not limit the negotiability of the bill nor constitute notice to a purchaser thereof of any interest of such person in the goods.

§ 7—502. *Rights Acquired by Due Negotiation.*

(1) Subject to the following section and to the provisions of Section 7—205 on fungible goods, a holder to whom a negotiable document of title has been duly negotiated acquires thereby:

(a) title to the document;

(b) title to the goods;

(c) all rights accruing under the law of agency or estoppel, including rights to goods delivered to the bailee after the document was issued; and

(d) the direct obligation of the issuer to hold or deliver the goods according to the terms of the document free of any defense or claim by him except those arising under the terms of the document or under this Article. In the case of a delivery order the bailee's obligation accrues only upon acceptance and the obligation acquired by the holder is that the issuer and any indorser will procure the acceptance of the bailee.

(2) Subject to the following section, title and rights so acquired are not defeated by any stoppage of the goods represented by the document or by surrender of such goods by the bailee, and are not impaired even though the negotiation or any prior negotiation constituted a breach of duty or even though any person has been deprived of possession of the document by misrepresentation, fraud, accident, mistake, duress, loss, theft or conversion, or even though a previous sale or other transfer of the goods or document has been made to a third person.

§ 7—503. *Document of Title to Goods Defeated in Certain Cases.*

(1) A document of title confers no right in goods against a person who before issuance of the document had a legal interest or a perfected security interest in them and who neither

(a) delivered or entrusted them or any document of title covering them to the bailor or his nominee with actual or apparent authority to ship, store or sell or with power to obtain delivery under this Article (Section 7—403) or with power of disposition under this Act (Sections 2—403 and 9—307) or other statute or rule of law; nor

(b) acquiesced in the procurement by the bailor or his nominee of any document of title.

(2) Title to goods based upon an unaccepted delivery order is subject to the rights of anyone to whom a negotiable warehouse receipt or bill of lading covering the goods has been duly negotiated. Such a title may be defeated under the next section to the same extent as the rights of the issuer or a transferee from the issuer.

(3) Title to goods based upon a bill of lading issued to a freight forwarder is subject to the rights of anyone to whom a bill issued by the freight forwarder is duly negotiated; but delivery by the carrier in accordance with Part 4 of this Article pursuant to its own bill of lading discharges the carrier's obligation to deliver.

§ 7—504. *Rights Acquired in the Absence of Due Negotiation; Effect of Diversion; Seller's Stoppage of Delivery.*

(1) A transferee of a document, whether negotiable or nonnegotiable, to whom the document has been delivered but not duly negotiated, acquires the title and rights which his transferor had or had actual authority to convey.

(2) In the case of a nonnegotiable document, until but not after the bailee receives notification of the transfer, the rights of the transferee may be defeated

(a) by those creditors of the transferor who could treat the sale as void under Section 2—402; or

(b) by a buyer from the transferor in ordinary course of business if the bailee has delivered the goods to the buyer or received notification of his rights; or

(c) as against the bailee by good faith dealings of the bailee with the transferor.

(3) A diversion or other change of shipping instructions by the consignor in a nonnegotiable bill of lading which causes the bailee not to deliver to the consignee defeats the consignee's title to the goods if they have been delivered to a buyer in ordinary course of business and in any event defeats the consignee's rights against the bailee.

(4) Delivery pursuant to a nonnegotiable document may be stopped by a seller under Section 2—705, and subject to the requirement of due notification there provided. A bailee honoring the seller's instructions is entitled to be indemnified by the seller against any resulting loss or expense.

§ 7—505. *Indorser Not a Guarantor for Other Parties.*

The indorsement of a document of title issued by a bailee does not make the indorser liable for any default by the bailee or by previous indorsers.

§ 7—506. *Delivery Without Indorsement: Right to Compel Indorsement.*

The transferee of a negotiable document of title has a specifically enforceable right to have his transferor supply any necessary indorsement but the transfer becomes a negotiation only as of the time the indorsement is supplied.

§ 7—507. *Warranties on Negotiation or Transfer of Receipt or Bill.*

Where a person negotiates or transfers a document of title for value otherwise than as a mere intermediary under the next following section, then unless otherwise agreed he warrants to his immediate purchaser only in addition to any warranty made in selling the goods

(a) that the document is genuine; and

(b) that he has no knowledge of any fact which would impair its validity or worth; and

(c) that his negotiation or transfer is rightful and fully effective with respect to the title to the document and the goods it represents.

§ 7—508. *Warranties of Collecting Bank as to Documents.*

A collecting bank or other intermediary known to be entrusted with documents on behalf of another or with collection of a draft or other claim against delivery of documents warrants by such delivery of the documents only its own good faith and authority. This rule applies even though the intermediary has purchased or made advances against the claim or draft to be collected.

§ 7—509. *Receipt or Bill: When Adequate Compliance With Commercial Contract.*

The question whether a document is adequate to fulfill the obligations of a contract for sale or the conditions of a credit is governed by the Articles on Sales (Article 2) and on Letters of Credit (Article 5).

PART 6

Warehouse Receipts and Bills of Lading: Miscellaneous Provisions

§ 7—601. *Lost and Missing Documents.*

(1) If a document has been lost, stolen or destroyed, a court may order delivery of the goods or issuance of a substitute document and the bailee may without liability to any person comply with such order. If the document was negotiable the claimant must post security approved by the court to indemnify any person who may suffer loss as a result of non-surrender of the document. If the document was not negotiable, such security may be

required at the discretion of the court. The court may also in its discretion order payment of the bailee's reasonable costs and counsel fees.

(2) A bailee who without court order delivers goods to a person claiming under a missing negotiable document is liable to any person injured thereby, and if the delivery is not in good faith becomes liable for conversion. Delivery in good faith is not conversion if made in accordance with a filed classification or tariff or, where no classification or tariff is filed, if the claimant posts security with the bailee in an amount at least double the value of the goods at the time of posting to indemnify any person injured by the delivery who files a notice of claim within one year after the delivery.

§ 7—602. ***Attachment of Goods Covered by a Negotiable Document.***

Except where the document was originally issued upon delivery of the goods by a person who had no power to dispose of them, no lien attaches by virtue of any judicial process to goods in the possession of a bailee for which a negotiable document of title is outstanding unless the document be first surrendered to the bailee or its negotiation enjoined, and the bailee shall not be compelled to deliver the goods pursuant to process until the document is surrendered to him or impounded by the court. One who purchases the document for value without notice of the process or injunction takes free of the lien imposed by judicial process.

§ 7—603. ***Conflicting Claims; Interpleader.***

If more than one person claims title or possession of the goods, the bailee is excused from delivery until he has had a reasonable time to ascertain the validity of the adverse claims or to bring an action to compel all claimants to interplead and may compel such interpleader, either in defending an action for nondelivery of the goods, or by original action, whichever is appropriate.

ARTICLE 8
INVESTMENT SECURITIES

PART 1
Short Title and General Matters

§ 8—101. ***Short Title.***

This Article shall be known and may be cited as Uniform Commercial Code—Investment Securities.

§ 8—102. ***Definitions and Index of Definitions.***

(1) In this Article, unless the context otherwise requires:

(a) A "certificated security" is a share, participation, or other interest in property of or an enterprise of the issuer or an obligation of the issuer which is

(i) represented by an instrument issued in bearer or registered form;

(ii) of a type commonly dealt in on securities exchanges or markets or commonly recognized in any area in which it is issued or dealt in as a medium for investment; and

(iii) either one of a class or series or by its terms divisible into a class or series of shares, participations, interests, or obligations.

(b) An "uncertificated security" is a share, participation, or other interest in property or an enterprise of the issuer or an obligation of the issuer which is

(i) not represented by an instrument and the transfer of which is registered upon books maintained for that purpose by or on behalf of the issuer;

(ii) of a type commonly dealt in on securities exchanges or markets; and

(iii) either one of a class or series or by its terms divisible into a class or series of shares, participations, interests, or obligations.

(c) A "security" is either a certificated or an uncertificated security. If a security is certificated, the terms "security" and "certificated security" may mean either the intangible interest, the instrument representing that interest, or both, as the context requires. A writing that is a certificated security is governed by this Article and not by Article 3, even though it also meets the requirements of that Article. This Article does not apply to money. If a certificated security has been retained by or surrendered to the issuer or its transfer agent for reasons other than registration of transfer, other temporary purpose, payment, exchange, or acquisition by the issuer, that security shall be treated as an uncertificated security for purposes of this Article.

(d) A certificated security is in "registered form" if

(i) it specifies a person entitled to the security or the rights it represents; and

(ii) its transfer may be registered upon books maintained for that purpose by or on behalf of the issuer, or the security so states.

(e) A certificated security is in "bearer form" if it runs to bearer according to its terms and not by reason of any indorsement.

(2) A "subsequent purchaser" is a person who takes other than by original issue.

(3) A "clearing corporation" is a corporation registered as a "clearing agency" under the federal securities laws or a corporation:

(a) at least 90 percent of whose capital stock is held by or for one or more organizations, none of which, other than a national securities exchange or association, holds in excess of 20 percent of the capital stock of the corporation, and each of which is

(i) subject to supervision or regulation pursuant to the provisions of federal or state banking laws or state insurance laws,

(ii) a broker or dealer or investment company registered under the federal securities laws, or

(iii) a national securities exchange or association registered under the federal securities laws; and

(b) any remaining capital stock of which is held by individuals who have purchased it at or prior to the time of their taking office as directors of the corporation and who have purchased only so much of the capital stock as is necessary to permit them to qualify as directors.

(4) A "custodian bank" is a bank or trust company that is supervised and examined by state or federal authority having supervision over banks and is acting as custodian for a clearing corporation.

(5) Other definitions applying to this Article or to specified Parts thereof and the sections in which they appear are:

"Adverse claim." Section 8—302.

"Bona fide purchaser." Section 8—302.

"Broker." Section 8—303.
"Debtor." Section 9—105.
"Financial intermediary." Section 8—313.
"Guarantee of the signature." Section 8—402.
"Initial transaction statement." Section 8—408.
"Instruction." Section 8—308.
"Intermediary bank." Section 4—105.
"Issuer." Section 8—201.
"Overissue." Section 8—104.
"Secured Party." Section 9—105.
"Security Agreement." Section 9—105.

(6) In addition, Article 1 contains general definitions and principles of construction and interpretation applicable throughout this Article.

Amended in 1962, 1973 and 1977.

§ 8—103. ***Issuer's Lien.***

A lien upon a security in favor of an issuer thereof is valid against a purchaser only if:

(a) the security is certificated and the right of the issuer to the lien is noted conspicuously thereon; or

(b) the security is uncertificated and a notation of the right of the issuer to the lien is contained in the initial transaction statement sent to the purchaser or, if his interest is transferred to him other than by registration of transfer, pledge, or release, the initial transaction statement sent to the registered owner or the registered pledgee.

Amended in 1977.

§ 8—104. ***Effect of Overissue; "Overissue."***

(1) The provisions of this Article which validate a security or compel its issue or reissue do not apply to the extent that validation, issue, or reissue would result in overissue; but if:

(a) an identical security which does not constitute an overissue is reasonably available for purchase, the person entitled to issue or validation may compel the issuer to purchase the security for him and either to deliver a certificated security or to register the transfer of an uncertificated security to him, against surrender of any certificated security he holds; or

(b) a security is not so available for purchase, the person entitled to issue or validation may recover from the issuer the price he or the last purchaser for value paid for it with interest from the date of his demand.

(2) "Overissue" means the issue of securities in excess of the amount the issuer has corporate power to issue.

Amended in 1977.

§ 8—105. ***Certificated Securities Negotiable; Statements and Instructions Not Negotiable; Presumptions.***

(1) Certificated securities governed by this Article are negotiable instruments.

(2) Statements (Section 8—408), notices, or the like, sent by the issuer of uncertificated securities and instructions (Section 8—308) are neither negotiable instruments nor certificated securities.

(3) In any action on a security:

(a) unless specifically denied in the pleadings, each signature on a certificated security, in a necessary indorsement, on an initial transaction statement, or on an instruction, is admitted;

(b) if the effectiveness of a signature is put in issue, the burden of establishing it is on the party claiming under the signature, but the signature is presumed to be genuine or authorized;

(c) if signatures on a certificated security are admitted or established, production of the security entitles a holder to recover on it unless the defendant establishes a defense or a defect going to the validity of the security;

(d) if signatures on an initial transaction statement are admitted or established, the facts stated in the statement are presumed to be true as of the time of its issuance; and

(e) after it is shown that a defense or defect exists, the plaintiff has the burden of establishing that he or some person under whom he claims is a person against whom the defense or defect is ineffective (Section 8—202).

Amended in 1977.

§ 8—106. ***Applicability.***

The law (including the conflict of laws rules) of the jurisdiction of organization of the issuer governs the validity of a security, the effectiveness of registration by the issuer, and the rights and duties of the issuer with respect to:

(a) registration of transfer of a certificated security;

(b) registration of transfer, pledge, or release of an uncertificated security; and

(c) sending of statements of uncertificated securities.

Amended in 1977.

§ 8—107. ***Securities Transferable; Action for Price.***

(1) Unless otherwise agreed and subject to any applicable law or regulation respecting short sales, a person obligated to transfer securities may transfer any certificated security of the specified issue in bearer form or registered in the name of the transferee, or indorsed to him or in blank, or he may transfer an equivalent uncertificated security to the transferee or a person designated by the transferee.

(2) If the buyer fails to pay the price as it comes due under a contract of sale, the seller may recover the price of:

(a) certificated securities accepted by the buyer;

(b) uncertificated securities that have been transferred to the buyer or a person designated by the buyer; and

(c) other securities if efforts at their resale would be unduly burdensome or if there is no readily available market for their resale.

Amended in 1977.

§ 8—108. ***Registration of Pledge and Release of Uncertificated Securities.***

A security interest in an uncertificated security may be evidenced by the registration of pledge to the secured party or a person designated by him. There can be no more than one registered pledge of an uncertificated security at any time. The registered owner of an uncertificated security is the person in whose name the security is registered, even if the security is subject to a registered pledge. The rights of a registered pledgee of an uncertificated security under this Article are terminated by the registration of release.

Added in 1977.

PART 2
Issue-Issuer

§ 8—201. ***"Issuer."***

(1) With respect to obligations on or defenses to a security, "issuer" includes a person who:

(a) places or authorizes the placing of his name on a certificated security (otherwise than as authenticating trustee, registrar, transfer agent, or the like) to evidence that it represents a share, participation, or other interest in his property or in an enterprise, or to evidence his duty to perform an obligation represented by the certificated security;

(b) creates shares, participations, or other interests in his property or in an enterprise or undertakes obligations, which shares, participations, interests, or obligations are uncertificated securities;

(c) directly or indirectly creates fractional interests in his rights or property, which fractional interests are represented by certificated securities; or

(d) becomes responsible for or in place of any other person described as an issuer in this section.

(2) With respect to obligations on or defenses to a security, a guarantor is an issuer to the extent of his guaranty, whether or not his obligation is noted on a certificated security or on statements of uncertificated securities sent pursuant to Section 8—408.

(3) With respect to registration of transfer, pledge, or release (Part 4 of this Article), "issuer" means a person on whose behalf transfer books are maintained.

Amended in 1977.

§ 8—202. *Issuer's Responsibility and Defenses; Notice of Defect or Defense.*

(1) Even against a purchaser for value and without notice, the terms of a security include:

(a) if the security is certificated, those stated on the security;

(b) if the security is uncertificated, those contained in the initial transaction statement sent to such purchaser or, if his interest is transferred to him other than by registration of transfer, pledge, or release, the initial transaction statement sent to the registered owner or registered pledgee; and

(c) those made part of the security by reference, on the certificated security or in the initial transaction statement, to another instrument, indenture, or document or to a constitution, statute, ordinance, rule, regulation, order or the like, to the extent that the terms referred to do not conflict with the terms stated on the certificated security or contained in the statement. A reference under this paragraph does not of itself charge a purchaser for value with notice of a defect going to the validity of the security, even though the certificated security or statement expressly states that a person accepting it admits notice.

(2) A certificated security in the hands of a purchaser for value or an uncertificated security as to which an initial transaction statement has been sent to a purchaser for value, other than a security issued by a government or governmental agency or unit, even though issued with a defect going to its validity, is valid with respect to the purchaser if he is without notice of the particular defect unless the defect involves a violation of constitutional provisions, in which case the security is valid with respect to a subsequent purchaser for value and without notice of the defect. This subsection applies to an issuer that is a government or governmental agency or unit only if either there has been substantial compliance with the legal requirements governing the issue or the issuer has received a substantial consideration for the issue as a whole or for the particular security and a stated purpose of the issue is one for which the issuer has power to borrow money or issue the security.

(3) Except as provided in the case of certain unauthorized signatures (Section 8—205), lack of genuineness of a certificated security or an initial transaction statement is a complete defense, even against a purchaser for value and without notice.

(4) All other defenses of the issuer of a certificated or uncertificated security, including nondelivery and conditional delivery of a certificated security, are ineffective against a purchaser for value who has taken without notice of the particular defense.

(5) Nothing in this section shall be construed to affect the right of a party to a "when, as and if issued" or a "when distributed" contract to cancel the contract in the event of a material change in the character of the security that is the subject of the contract or in the plan or arrangement pursuant to which the security is to be issued or distributed.

Amended in 1977.

§ 8—203. *Staleness as Notice of Defects or Defenses.*

(1) After an act or event creating a right to immediate performance of the principal obligation represented by a certificated security or that sets a date on or after which the security is to be presented or surrendered for redemption or exchange, a purchaser is charged with notice of any defect in its issue or defense of the issuer if:

(a) the act or event is one requiring the payment of money, the delivery of certificated securities, the registration of transfer of uncertificated securities, or any of these on presentation or surrender of the certificated security, the funds or securities are available on the date set for payment or exchange, and he takes the security more than one year after that date; and

(b) the act or event is not covered by paragraph (a) and he takes the security more than 2 years after the date set for surrender or presentation or the date on which performance became due.

(2) A call that has been revoked is not within subsection (1).

Amended in 1977.

§ 8—204. *Effect of Issuer's Restrictions on Transfer.*

A restriction on transfer of a security imposed by the issuer, even if otherwise lawful, is ineffective against any person without actual knowledge of it unless:

(a) the security is certificated and the restriction is noted conspicuously thereon; or

(b) the security is uncertificated and a notation of the restriction is contained in the initial transaction statement sent to the person or, if his interest is transferred to him other than by registration of transfer, pledge, or release, the initial transaction statement sent to the registered owner or the registered pledgee.

Amended in 1977.

§ 8—205. *Effect of Unauthorized Signature on Certificated Security or Initial Transaction Statement.*

An unauthorized signature placed on a certificated security prior to or in the course of issue or placed on an initial transaction statement is ineffective, but the signature is effective in favor of a purchaser for value of the certificated security or a purchaser for value of an uncertificated security to whom the initial transaction statement has been sent, if the purchaser is without notice of the lack of authority and the signing has been done by:

(a) an authenticating trustee, registrar, transfer agent, or other person entrusted by the issuer with the signing of the security, of similar securities, or of initial transaction statements or the immediate preparation for signing of any of them; or

(b) an employee of the issuer, or of any of the foregoing, entrusted with responsible handling of the security or initial transaction statement.

Amended in 1977.

§ 8—206. *Completion or Alteration of Certificated Security or Initial Transaction Statement.*

(1) If a certificated security contains the signatures necessary to its issue or transfer but is incomplete in any other respect:

(a) any person may complete it by filling in the blanks as authorized; and

(b) even though the blanks are incorrectly filled in, the security as completed is enforceable by a purchaser who took it for value and without notice of the incorrectness.

(2) A complete certificated security that has been improperly altered, even though fraudulently, remains enforceable, but only according to its original terms.

(3) If an initial transaction statement contains the signatures necessary to its validity, but is incomplete in any other respect:

(a) any person may complete it by filling in the blanks as authorized; and

(b) even though the blanks are incorrectly filled in, the statement as completed is effective in favor of the person to whom it is sent if he purchased the security referred to therein for value and without notice of the incorrectness.

(4) A complete initial transaction statement that has been improperly altered, even though fraudulently, is effective in favor of a purchaser to whom it has been sent, but only according to its original terms.

Amended in 1977.

§ 8—207. *Rights and Duties of Issuer With Respect to Registered Owners and Registered Pledgees.*

(1) Prior to due presentment for registration of transfer of a certificated security in registered form, the issuer or indenture trustee may treat the registered owner as the person exclusively entitled to vote, to receive notifications, and otherwise to exercise all the rights and powers of an owner.

(2) Subject to the provisions of subsections (3), (4), and (6), the issuer or indenture trustee may treat the registered owner of an uncertificated security as the person exclusively entitled to vote, to receive notifications, and otherwise to exercise all the rights and powers of an owner.

(3) The registered owner of an uncertificated security that is subject to a registered pledge is not entitled to registration of transfer prior to the due presentment to the issuer of a release instruction. The exercise of conversion rights with respect to a convertible uncertificated security is a transfer within the meaning of this section.

(4) Upon due presentment of a transfer instruction from the registered pledgee of an uncertificated security, the issuer shall:

(a) register the transfer of the security to the new owner free of pledge, if the instruction specifies a new owner (who may be the registered pledgee) and does not specify a pledgee;

(b) register the transfer of the security to the new owner subject to the interest of the existing pledgee, if the instruction specifies a new owner and the existing pledgee; or

(c) register the release of the security from the existing pledge and register the pledge of the security to the other pledgee, if the instruction specifies the existing owner and another pledgee.

(5) Continuity of perfection of a security interest is not broken by registration of transfer under subsection (4)(b) or by registration of release and pledge under subsection (4)(c), if the security interest is assigned.

(6) If an uncertificated security is subject to a registered pledge:

(a) any uncertificated securities issued in exchange for or distributed with respect to the pledged security shall be registered subject to the pledge;

(b) any certificated securities issued in exchange for or distributed with respect to the pledged security shall be delivered to the registered pledgee; and

(c) any money paid in exchange for or in redemption of part or all of the security shall be paid to the registered pledgee.

(7) Nothing in this Article shall be construed to affect the liability of the registered owner of a security for calls, assessments, or the like.

Amended in 1977.

§ 8—208. *Effect of Signature of Authenticating Trustee, Registrar, or Transfer Agent.*

(1) A person placing his signature upon a certificated security or an initial transaction statement as authenticating trustee, registrar, transfer agent, or the like, warrants to a purchaser for value of the certificated security or a purchaser for value of an uncertificated security to whom the initial transaction statement has been sent, if the purchaser is without notice of the particular defect, that:

(a) the certificated security or initial transaction statement is genuine;

(b) his own participation in the issue or registration of the transfer, pledge, or release of the security is within his capacity and within the scope of the authority received by him from the issuer; and

(c) he has reasonable grounds to believe the security is in the form and within the amount the issuer is authorized to issue.

(2) Unless otherwise agreed, a person by so placing his signature does not assume responsibility for the validity of the security in other respects.

Amended in 1962 and 1977.

PART 3
Transfer

§ 8—301. *Rights Acquired by Purchaser.*

(1) Upon transfer of a security to a purchaser (Section 8—313), the purchaser acquires the rights in the security which his transferor had or had actual authority to convey unless the purchaser's rights are limited by Section 8—302(4).

(2) A transferee of a limited interest acquires rights only to the extent of the interest transferred. The creation or release of a security interest in a security is the transfer of a limited interest in that security.

Amended in 1977.

§ 8—302. *"Bona Fide Purchaser";*
"Adverse Claim"; Title Acquired by Bona Fide Purchaser.

(1) A "bona fide purchaser" is a purchaser for value in good faith and without notice of any adverse claim:

(a) who takes delivery of a certificated security in bearer form or in registered form, issued or indorsed to him or in blank;

(b) to whom the transfer, pledge, or release of an uncertificated security is registered on the books of the issuer; or

(c) to whom a security is transferred under the provisions of paragraph (c), (d)(i), or (g) of Section 8—313(1).

(2) "Adverse claim" includes a claim that a transfer was or would be wrongful or that a particular adverse person is the owner of or has an interest in the security.

(3) A bona fide purchaser in addition to acquiring the rights of a purchaser (Section 8—301) also acquires his interest in the security free of any adverse claim.

(4) Notwithstanding Section 8—301(1), the transferee of a particular certificated security who has been a party to any fraud or illegality affecting the security, or who as a prior holder of that certificated security had notice of an adverse claim, cannot improve his position by taking from a bona fide purchaser.

Amended in 1977.

§ 8—303. "Broker".

"Broker" means a person engaged for all or part of his time in the business of buying and selling securities, who in the transaction concerned acts for, buys a security from, or sells a security to, a customer. Nothing in this Article determines the capacity in which a person acts for purposes of any other statute or rule to which the person is subject.

§ 8—304. Notice to Purchaser of Adverse Claims.

(1) A purchaser (including a broker for the seller or buyer, but excluding an intermediary bank) of a certificated security is charged with notice of adverse claims if:

(a) the security, whether in bearer or registered form, has been indorsed "for collection" or "for surrender" or for some other purpose not involving transfer; or

(b) the security is in bearer form and has on it an unambiguous statement that it is the property of a person other than the transferor. The mere writing of a name on a security is not such a statement.

(2) A purchaser (including a broker for the seller or buyer, but excluding an intermediary bank) to whom the transfer, pledge, or release of an uncertificated security is registered is charged with notice of adverse claims as to which the issuer has a duty under Section 8—403(4) at the time of registration and which are noted in the initial transaction statement sent to the purchaser or, if his interest is transferred to him other than by registration of transfer, pledge, or release, the initial transaction statement sent to the registered owner or the registered pledgee.

(3) The fact that the purchaser (including a broker for the seller or buyer) of a certificated or uncertificated security has notice that the security is held for a third person or is registered in the name of or indorsed by a fiduciary does not create a duty of inquiry into the rightfulness of the transfer or constitute constructive notice of adverse claims. However, if the purchaser (excluding an intermediary bank) has knowledge that the proceeds are being used or that the transaction is for the individual benefit of the fiduciary or otherwise in breach of duty, the purchaser is charged with notice of adverse claims.

Amended in 1977.

§ 8—305. Staleness as Notice of Adverse Claims.

An act or event that creates a right to immediate performance of the principal obligation represented by a certificated security or sets a date on or after which a certificated security is to be presented or surrendered for redemption or exchange does not itself constitute any notice of adverse claims except in the case of a transfer:

(a) after one year from any date set for presentment or surrender for redemption or exchange; or

(b) after 6 months from any date set for payment of money against presentation or surrender of the security if funds are available for payment on that date.

Amended in 1977.

§ 8—306. Warranties on Presentment and Transfer of Certificated Securities; Warranties of Originators of Instructions.

(1) A person who presents a certificated security for registration of transfer or for payment or exchange warrants to the issuer that he is entitled to the registration, payment, or exchange. But, a purchaser for value and without notice of adverse claims who receives a new, reissued, or re-registered certificated security on registration of transfer or receives an initial transaction statement confirming the registration of transfer of an equivalent uncertificated security to him warrants only that he has no knowledge of any unauthorized signature (Section 8—311) in a necessary indorsement.

(2) A person by transferring a certificated security to a purchaser for value warrants only that:

(a) his transfer is effective and rightful;

(b) the security is genuine and has not been materially altered; and

(c) he knows of no fact which might impair the validity of the security.

(3) If a certificated security is delivered by an intermediary known to be entrusted with delivery of the security on behalf of another or with collection of a draft or other claim against delivery, the intermediary by delivery warrants only his own good faith and authority, even though he has purchased or made advances against the claim to be collected against the delivery.

(4) A pledgee or other holder for security who redelivers a certificated security received, or after payment and on order of the debtor delivers that security to a third person, makes only the warranties of an intermediary under subsection (3).

(5) A person who originates an instruction warrants to the issuer that:

(a) he is an appropriate person to originate the instruction; and

(b) at the time the instruction is presented to the issuer he will be entitled to the registration of transfer, pledge, or release.

(6) A person who originates an instruction warrants to any person specially guaranteeing his signature (subsection 8—312(3)) that:

(a) he is an appropriate person to originate the instruction; and

(b) at the time the instruction is presented to the issuer

(i) he will be entitled to the registration of transfer, pledge, or release; and

(ii) the transfer, pledge, or release requested in the instruction will be registered by the issuer free from all liens, security interests, restrictions, and claims other than those specified in the instruction.

(7) A person who originates an instruction warrants to a purchaser for value and to any person guaranteeing the instruction (Section 8—312(6)) that:

(a) he is an appropriate person to originate the instruction;

(b) the uncertificated security referred to therein is valid; and

(c) at the time the instruction is presented to the issuer

(i) the transferor will be entitled to the registration of transfer, pledge, or release;

(ii) the transfer, pledge, or release requested in the instruction will be registered by the issuer free from all liens, security interests, restrictions, and claims other than those specified in the instruction; and

(iii) the requested transfer, pledge, or release will be rightful.

(8) If a secured party is the registered pledgee or the registered owner of an uncertificated security, a person who originates an instruction of release or transfer to the debtor or, after payment and on order of the debtor, a transfer instruction to a third person, warrants to the debtor or the third person only that he is an appropriate person to originate the instruction and, at the time the instruction is presented to the issuer, the transferor will be entitled to the registration of release or transfer. If a transfer instruction to a third person who is a purchaser for value is originated on order of the debtor, the debtor makes to the purchaser the warranties of paragraphs (b), (c)(ii) and (c)(iii) of subsection (7).

(9) A person who transfers an uncertificated security to a purchaser for value and does not originate an instruction in connection with the transfer warrants only that:

(a) his transfer is effective and rightful; and

(b) the uncertificated security is valid.

(10) A broker gives to his customer and to the issuer and a purchaser the applicable warranties provided in this section and has the rights and privileges of a purchaser under this section. The warranties of and in favor of the broker, acting as an agent are in addition to applicable warranties given by and in favor of his customer.

Amended in 1962 and 1977.

§ 8—307. *Effect of Delivery Without Indorsement; Right to Compel Indorsement.*

If a certificated security in registered form has been delivered to a purchaser without a necessary indorsement he may become a bona fide purchaser only as of the time the indorsement is supplied; but against the transferor, the transfer is complete upon delivery and the purchaser has a specifically enforceable right to have any necessary indorsement supplied.

Amended in 1977.

§ 8—308. *Indorsements; Instructions.*

(1) An indorsement of a certificated security in registered form is made when an appropriate person signs on it or on a separate document an assignment or transfer of the security or a power to assign or transfer it or his signature is written without more upon the back of the security.

(2) An indorsement may be in blank or special. An indorsement in blank includes an indorsement to bearer. A special indorsement specifies to whom the security is to be transferred, or who has power to transfer it. A holder may convert a blank indorsement into a special indorsement.

(3) An indorsement purporting to be only of part of a certificated security representing units intended by the issuer to be separately transferable is effective to the extent of the indorsement.

(4) An "instruction" is an order to the issuer of an uncertificated security requesting that the transfer, pledge, or release from pledge of the uncertificated security specified therein be registered.

(5) An instruction originated by an appropriate person is:

(a) a writing signed by an appropriate person; or

(b) a communication to the issuer in any form agreed upon in a writing signed by the issuer and an appropriate person.

If an instruction has been originated by an appropriate person but is incomplete in any other respect, any person may complete it as authorized and the issuer may rely on it as completed even though it has been completed incorrectly.

(6) "An appropriate person" in subsection (1) means the person specified by the certificated security or by special indorsement to be entitled to the security.

(7) "An appropriate person" in subsection (5) means:

(a) for an instruction to transfer or pledge an uncertificated security which is then not subject to a registered pledge, the registered owner; or

(b) for an instruction to transfer or release an uncertificated security which is then subject to a registered pledge, the registered pledgee.

(8) In addition to the persons designated in subsections (6) and (7), "an appropriate person" in subsections (1) and (5) includes:

(a) if the person designated is described as a fiduciary but is no longer serving in the described capacity, either that person or his successor;

(b) if the persons designated are described as more than one person as fiduciaries and one or more are no longer serving in the described capacity, the remaining fiduciary or fiduciaries, whether or not a successor has been appointed or qualified;

(c) if the person designated is an individual and is without capacity to act by virtue of death, incompetence, infancy, or otherwise, his executor, administrator, guardian, or like fiduciary;

(d) if the persons designated are described as more than one person as tenants by the entirety or with right of survivorship and by reason of death all cannot sign, the survivor or survivors;

(e) a person having power to sign under applicable law or controlling instrument; and

(f) to the extent that the person designated or any of the foregoing persons may act through an agent, his authorized agent.

(9) Unless otherwise agreed, the indorser of a certificated security by his indorsement or the originator of an instruction by his origination assumes no obligation that the security will be honored by the issuer but only the obligations provided in Section 8—306.

(10) Whether the person signing is appropriate is determined as of the date of signing and an indorsement made by or an instruction originated by him does not become unauthorized for the purposes of this Article by virtue of any subsequent change of circumstances.

(11) Failure of a fiduciary to comply with a controlling instrument or with the law of the state having jurisdiction of the fiduciary relationship, including any law requiring the fiduciary to obtain court approval of the transfer, pledge, or release, does not render his indorsement or an instruction originated by him unauthorized for the purposes of this Article.

Amended in 1962 and 1977.

§ 8—309. *Effect of Indorsement Without Delivery.*

An indorsement of a certificated security, whether special or in blank, does not constitute a transfer until delivery of the certificated security on which it appears or, if the indorsement is on a separate document, until delivery of both the document and the certificated security.

Amended in 1977.

§ 8—310. *Indorsement of Certificated Security in Bearer Form.*

An indorsement of a certificated security in bearer form may give notice of adverse claims (Section 8—304) but does not otherwise affect any right to registration the holder possesses.

Amended in 1977.

§ 8—311. *Effect of Unauthorized Indorsement or Instruction.*

Unless the owner or pledgee has ratified an unauthorized indorsement or instruction or is otherwise precluded from asserting its ineffectiveness:

(a) he may assert its ineffectiveness against the issuer or any purchaser, other than a purchaser for value and without notice of adverse claims, who has in good faith received a new, reissued, or re-registered certificated security on registration of transfer or received an initial transaction statement confirming the registration of transfer, pledge, or release of an equivalent uncertificated security to him; and

(b) an issuer who registers the transfer of a certificated security upon the unauthorized indorsement or who registers the transfer, pledge, or release of an uncertificated security upon the unauthorized instruction is subject to liability for improper registration (Section 8—404).

Amended in 1977.

§ 8—312. *Effect of Guaranteeing Signature, Indorsement or Instruction.*

(1) Any person guaranteeing a signature of an indorser of a certificated security warrants that at the time of signing:

(a) the signature was genuine;

(b) the signer was an appropriate person to indorse (Section 8—308); and

(c) the signer had legal capacity to sign.

(2) Any person guaranteeing a signature of the originator of an instruction warrants that at the time of signing:

(a) the signature was genuine;

(b) the signer was an appropriate person to originate the instruction (Section 8—308) if the person specified in the instruction as the registered owner or registered pledgee of the uncertificated security was, in fact, the registered owner or registered pledgee of the security, as to which fact the signature guarantor makes no warranty;

(c) the signer had legal capacity to sign; and

(d) the taxpayer identification number, if any, appearing on the instruction as that of the registered owner or registered pledgee was the taxpayer identification number of the signer or of the owner or pledgee for whom the signer was acting.

(3) Any person specially guaranteeing the signature of the originator of an instruction makes not only the warranties of a signature guarantor (subsection (2)) but also warrants that at the time the instruction is presented to the issuer:

(a) the person specified in the instruction as the registered owner or registered pledgee of the uncertificated security will be the registered owner or registered pledgee; and

(b) the transfer, pledge, or release of the uncertificated security requested in the instruction will be registered by the issuer free from all liens, security interests, restrictions, and claims other than those specified in the instruction.

(4) The guarantor under subsections (1) and (2) or the special guarantor under subsection (3) does not otherwise warrant the rightfulness of the particular transfer, pledge, or release.

(5) Any person guaranteeing an indorsement of a certificated security makes not only the warranties of a signature guarantor under subsection (1) but also warrants the rightfulness of the particular transfer in all respects.

(6) Any person guaranteeing an instruction requesting the transfer, pledge, or release of an uncertificated security makes not only the warranties of a special signature guarantor under subsection (3) but also warrants the rightfulness of the particular transfer, pledge, or release in all respects.

(7) No issuer may require a special guarantee of signature (subsection (3)), a guarantee of indorsement (subsection (5)), or a guarantee of instruction (subsection (6)) as a condition to registration of transfer, pledge, or release.

(8) The foregoing warranties are made to any person taking or dealing with the security in reliance on the guarantee, and the guarantor is liable to the person for any loss resulting from breach of the warranties.

Amended in 1977.

§ 8—313. *When Transfer to Purchaser Occurs; Financial Intermediary as Bona Fide Purchaser; "Financial Intermediary".*

(1) Transfer of a security or a limited interest (including a security interest) therein to a purchaser occurs only:

(a) at the time he or a person designated by him acquires possession of a certificated security;

(b) at the time the transfer, pledge, or release of an uncertificated security is registered to him or a person designated by him;

(c) at the time his financial intermediary acquires possession of a certificated security specially indorsed to or issued in the name of the purchaser;

(d) at the time a financial intermediary, not a clearing corporation, sends him confirmation of the purchase and also by book entry or otherwise identifies as belonging to the purchaser

(i) a specific certificated security in the financial intermediary's possession;

(ii) a quantity of securities that constitute or are part of a fungible bulk of certificated securities in the financial intermediary's possession or of uncertificated securities registered in the name of the financial intermediary; or

(iii) a quantity of securities that constitute or are part of a fungible bulk of securities shown on the account of the financial intermediary on the books of another financial intermediary;

(e) with respect to an identified certificated security to be delivered while still in the possession of a third person, not a financial intermediary, at the time that person acknowledges that he holds for the purchaser;

(f) with respect to a specific uncertificated security the pledge or transfer of which has been registered to a third person, not a financial intermediary, at the time that person acknowledges that he holds for the purchaser;

(g) at the time appropriate entries to the account of the purchaser or a person designated by him on the books of a clearing corporation are made under Section 8—320;

(h) with respect to the transfer of a security interest where the debtor has signed a security agreement containing a description of the security, at the time a written notification, which, in the case of the creation of the security interest, is signed by the debtor (which may be a copy of the security agreement) or which, in the case of the release or assignment of the security interest created pursuant to this paragraph, is signed by the secured party, is received by

(i) a financial intermediary on whose books the interest of the transferor in the security appears;

(ii) a third person, not a financial intermediary, in possession of the security, if it is certificated;

(iii) a third person, not a financial intermediary, who is the registered owner of the security, if it is uncertificated and not subject to a registered pledge; or

(iv) a third person, not a financial intermediary, who is the registered pledgee of the security, if it is uncertificated and subject to a registered pledge;

(i) with respect to the transfer of a security interest where the transferor has signed a security agreement containing a description of the security, at the time new value is given by the secured party; or

(j) with respect to the transfer of a security interest where the secured party is a financial intermediary and the security has already been transferred to the financial intermediary under paragraphs (a), (b), (c), (d), or (g), at the time the transferor has signed a security agreement containing a description of the security and value is given by the secured party.

(2) The purchaser is the owner of a security held for him by a financial intermediary, but cannot be a bona fide purchaser of a security so held except in the circumstances specified in paragraphs (c), (d)(i), and (g) of subsection (1). If a security so held is part of a fungible bulk, as in the circumstances specified in paragraphs (d)(ii) and (d)(iii) of subsection (1), the purchaser is the owner of a proportionate property interest in the fungible bulk.

(3) Notice of an adverse claim received by the financial intermediary or by the purchaser after the financial intermediary takes delivery of a certificated security as a holder for value or after the transfer, pledge, or release of an uncertificated security has been registered free of the claim to a financial intermediary who has given value is not effective either as to the financial intermediary or as to the purchaser. However, as between the financial intermediary and the purchaser the purchaser may demand transfer of an equivalent security as to which no notice of adverse claim has been received.

(4) A "financial intermediary" is a bank, broker, clearing corporation, or other person (or the nominee of any of them) which in the ordinary course of its business maintains security accounts for its customers and is acting in that capacity. A financial intermediary may have a security interest in securities held in account for its customer.

Amended in 1962 and 1977.

§ 8—314. *Duty to Transfer, When Completed.*

(1) Unless otherwise agreed, if a sale of a security is made on an exchange or otherwise through brokers:

(a) the selling customer fulfills his duty to transfer at the time he:

(i) places a certificated security in the possession of the selling broker or a person designated by the broker;

(ii) causes an uncertificated security to be registered in the name of the selling broker or a person designated by the broker;

(iii) if requested, causes an acknowledgment to be made to the selling broker that a certificated or uncertificated security is held for the broker; or

(iv) places in the possession of the selling broker or of a person designated by the broker a transfer instruction for an uncertificated security, providing the issuer does not refuse to register the requested transfer if the instruction is presented to the issuer for registration within 30 days thereafter; and

(b) the selling broker, including a correspondent broker acting for a selling customer, fulfills his duty to transfer at the time he:

(i) places a certificated security in the possession of the buying broker or a person designated by the buying broker;

(ii) causes an uncertificated security to be registered in the name of the buying broker or a person designated by the buying broker;

(iii) places in the possession of the buying broker or of a person designated by the buying broker a transfer instruction for an uncertificated security, providing the issuer does not refuse to register the requested transfer if the instruction is presented to the issuer for registration within 30 days thereafter; or

(iv) effects clearance of the sale in accordance with the rules of the exchange on which the transaction took place.

(2) Except as provided in this section or unless otherwise agreed, a transferor's duty to transfer a security under a contract of purchase is not fulfilled until he:

(a) places a certificated security in form to be negotiated by the purchaser in the possession of the purchaser or of a person designated by the purchaser;

(b) causes an uncertificated security to be registered in the name of the purchaser or a person designated by the purchaser; or

(c) if the purchaser requests, causes an acknowledgment to be made to the purchaser that a certificated or uncertificated security is held for the purchaser.

(3) Unless made on an exchange, a sale to a broker purchasing for his own account is within subsection (2) and not within subsection (1).

Amended in 1977.

§ 8—315. *Action Against Transferee Based Upon Wrongful Transfer.*

(1) Any person against whom the transfer of a security is wrongful for any reason, including his incapacity, as against anyone except a bona fide purchaser, may:

(a) reclaim possession of the certificated security wrongfully transferred;

(b) obtain possession of any new certificated security representing all or part of the same rights;

(c) compel the origination of an instruction to transfer to him or a person designated by him an uncertificated security constituting all or part of the same rights; or

(d) have damages.

(2) If the transfer is wrongful because of an unauthorized indorsement of a certificated security, the owner may also reclaim or obtain possession of the security or a new certificated security, even from a bona fide purchaser, if the ineffectiveness of the purported indorsement can be asserted against him under the provisions of this Article on unauthorized indorsements (Section 8—311).

(3) The right to obtain or reclaim possession of a certificated security or to compel the origination of a transfer instruction may be specifically enforced and the transfer of a certificated or uncer-

tificated security enjoined and a certificated security impounded pending the litigation.

Amended in 1977.

§ 8—316. *Purchaser's Right to Requisites for Registration of Transfer, Pledge, or Release on Books.*

Unless otherwise agreed, the transferor of a certificated security or the transferor, pledgor, or pledgee of an uncertificated security on due demand must supply his purchaser with any proof of his authority to transfer, pledge, or release or with any other requisite necessary to obtain registration of the transfer, pledge, or release of the security; but if the transfer, pledge, or release is not for value, a transferor, pledgor, or pledgee need not do so unless the purchaser furnishes the necessary expenses. Failure within a reasonable time to comply with a demand made gives the purchaser the right to reject or rescind the transfer, pledge, or release.

Amended in 1977.

§ 8—317. *Creditors' Rights.*

(1) Subject to the exceptions in subsections (3) and (4), no attachment or levy upon a certificated security or any share or other interest represented thereby which is outstanding is valid until the security is actually seized by the officer making the attachment or levy, but a certificated security which has been surrendered to the issuer may be reached by a creditor by legal process at the issuer's chief executive office in the United States.

(2) An uncertificated security registered in the name of the debtor may not be reached by a creditor except by legal process at the issuer's chief executive office in the United States.

(3) The interest of a debtor in a certificated security that is in the possession of a secured party not a financial intermediary or in an uncertificated security registered in the name of a secured party not a financial intermediary (or in the name of a nominee of the secured party) may be reached by a creditor by legal process upon the secured party.

(4) The interest of a debtor in a certificated security that is in the possession of or registered in the name of a financial intermediary or in an uncertificated security registered in the name of a financial intermediary may be reached by a creditor by legal process upon the financial intermediary on whose books the interest of the debtor appears.

(5) Unless otherwise provided by law, a creditor's lien upon the interest of a debtor in a security obtained pursuant to subsection (3) or (4) is not a restraint on the transfer of the security, free of the lien, to a third party for new value; but in the event of a transfer, the lien applies to the proceeds of the transfer in the hands of the secured party or financial intermediary, subject to any claims having priority.

(6) A creditor whose debtor is the owner of a security is entitled to aid from courts of appropriate jurisdiction, by injunction or otherwise, in reaching the security or in satisfying the claim by means allowed at law or in equity in regard to property that cannot readily be reached by ordinary legal process.

Amended in 1977.

§ 8—318. *No Conversion by Good Faith Conduct.*

An agent or bailee who in good faith (including observance of reasonable commercial standards if he is in the business of buying, selling, or otherwise dealing with securities) has received certificated securities and sold, pledged, or delivered them or has sold or caused the transfer or pledge of uncertificated securities over which he had control according to the instructions of his principal, is not liable for conversion or for participation in breach of fiduciary duty although the principal had no right so to deal with the securities.

Amended in 1977.

§ 8—319. *Statute of Frauds.*

A contract for the sale of securities is not enforceable by way of action or defense unless:

(a) there is some writing signed by the party against whom enforcement is sought or by his authorized agent or broker, sufficient to indicate that a contract has been made for sale of a stated quantity of described securities at a defined or stated price;

(b) delivery of a certificated security or transfer instruction has been accepted, or transfer of an uncertificated security has been registered and the transferee has failed to send written objection to the issuer within 10 days after receipt of the initial transaction statement confirming the registration, or payment has been made, but the contract is enforceable under this provision only to the extent of the delivery, registration, or payment;

(c) within a reasonable time a writing in confirmation of the sale or purchase and sufficient against the sender under paragraph (a) has been received by the party against whom enforcement is sought and he has failed to send written objection to its contents within 10 days after its receipt; or

(d) the party against whom enforcement is sought admits in his pleading, testimony, or otherwise in court that a contract was made for the sale of a stated quantity of described securities at a defined or stated price.

Amended in 1977.

§ 8—320. *Transfer or Pledge Within Central Depository System.*

(1) In addition to other methods, a transfer, pledge, or release of a security or any interest therein may be effected by the making of appropriate entries on the books of a clearing corporation reducing the account of the transferor, pledgor, or pledgee and increasing the account of the transferee, pledgee, or pledgor by the amount of the obligation or the number of shares or rights transferred, pledged, or released, if the security is shown on the account of a transferor, pledgor, or pledgee on the books of the clearing corporation; is subject to the control of the clearing corporation; and

(a) if certificated,

(i) is in the custody of the clearing corporation, another clearing corporation, a custodian bank, or a nominee of any of them; and

(ii) is in bearer form or indorsed in blank by an appropriate person or registered in the name of the clearing corporation, a custodian bank, or a nominee of any of them; or

(b) if uncertificated, is registered in the name of the clearing corporation, another clearing corporation, a custodian bank, or a nominee of any of them.

(2) Under this section entries may be made with respect to like securities or interests therein as a part of a fungible bulk and may refer merely to a quantity of a particular security without reference to the name of the registered owner, certificate or bond number, or the like, and, in appropriate cases, may be on a net basis taking into account other transfers, pledges, or releases of the same security.

(3) A transfer under this section is effective (Section 8—313) and the purchaser acquires the rights of the transferor (Section 8—301). A pledge or release under this section is the transfer of a limited interest. If a pledge or the creation of a security interest is intended, the security interest is perfected at the time when both value is given by the pledgee and the appropriate entries are made (Section 8—321). A transferee or pledgee under this section may be a bona fide purchaser (Section 8—302).

(4) A transfer or pledge under this section is not a registration of transfer under Part 4.

(5) That entries made on the books of the clearing corporation as provided in subsection (1) are not appropriate does not affect the validity or effect of the entries or the liabilities or obligations of the clearing corporation to any person adversely affected thereby.

Added in 1962; amended in 1977.

§ *8—321.* ***Enforceability, Attachment, Perfection and Termination of Security Interests.***

(1) A security interest in a security is enforceable and can attach only if it is transferred to the secured party or a person designated by him pursuant to a provision of Section 8—313(1).

(2) A security interest so transferred pursuant to agreement by a transferor who has rights in the security to a transferee who has given value is a perfected security interest, but a security interest that has been transferred solely under paragraph (i) of Section 8—313(1) becomes unperfected after 21 days unless, within that time, the requirements for transfer under any other provision of Section 8—313(1) are satisfied.

(3) A security interest in a security is subject to the provisions of Article 9, but:

(a) no filing is required to perfect the security interest; and

(b) no written security agreement signed by the debtor is necessary to make the security interest enforceable, except as provided in paragraph (h), (i), or (j) of Section 8—313(1). The secured party has the rights and duties provided under Section 9—207, to the extent they are applicable, whether or not the security is certificated, and, if certificated, whether or not it is in his possession.

(4) Unless otherwise agreed, a security interest in a security is terminated by transfer to the debtor or a person designated by him pursuant to a provision of Section 8—313(1). If a security is thus transferred, the security interest, if not terminated, becomes unperfected unless the security is certificated and is delivered to the debtor for the purpose of ultimate sale or exchange or presentation, collection, renewal, or registration of transfer. In that case, the security interest becomes unperfected after 21 days unless, within that time, the security (or securities for which it has been exchanged) is transferred to the secured party or a person designated by him pursuant to a provision of Section 8—313(1).

Added in 1977.

PART 4
Registration

§ *8—401.* ***Duty of Issuer to Register Transfer, Pledge, or Release.***

(1) If a certificated security in registered form is presented to the issuer with a request to register transfer or an instruction is presented to the issuer with a request to register transfer, pledge, or release, the issuer shall register the transfer, pledge, or release as requested if:

(a) the security is indorsed or the instruction was originated by the appropriate person or persons (Section 8—308);

(b) reasonable assurance is given that those indorsements or instructions are genuine and effective (Section 8—402);

(c) the issuer has no duty as to adverse claims or has discharged the duty (Section 8—403);

(d) any applicable law relating to the collection of taxes has been complied with; and

(e) the transfer, pledge, or release is in fact rightful or is to a bona fide purchaser.

(2) If an issuer is under a duty to register a transfer, pledge, or release of a security, the issuer is also liable to the person presenting a certificated security or an instruction for registration or his principal for loss resulting from any unreasonable delay in registration or from failure or refusal to register the transfer, pledge, or release.

Amended in 1977.

§ *8—402.* ***Assurance that Indorsements and Instructions Are Effective.***

(1) The issuer may require the following assurance that each necessary indorsement of a certificated security or each instruction (Section 8—308) is genuine and effective:

(a) in all cases, a guarantee of the signature (Section 8—312(1) or (2)) of the person indorsing a certificated security or originating an instruction including, in the case of an instruction, a warranty of the taxpayer identification number or, in the absence thereof, other reasonable assurance of identity;

(b) if the indorsement is made or the instruction is originated by an agent, appropriate assurance of authority to sign;

(c) if the indorsement is made or the instruction is originated by a fiduciary, appropriate evidence of appointment or incumbency;

(d) if there is more than one fiduciary, reasonable assurance that all who are required to sign have done so; and

(e) if the indorsement is made or the instruction is originated by a person not covered by any of the foregoing, assurance appropriate to the case corresponding as nearly as may be to the foregoing.

(2) A "guarantee of the signature" in subsection (1) means a guarantee signed by or on behalf of a person reasonably believed by the issuer to be responsible. The issuer may adopt standards with respect to responsibility if they are not manifestly unreasonable.

(3) "Appropriate evidence of appointment or incumbency" in subsection (1) means:

(a) in the case of a fiduciary appointed or qualified by a court, a certificate issued by or under the direction or supervision of that court or an officer thereof and dated within 60 days before the date of presentation for transfer, pledge, or release; or

(b) in any other case, a copy of a document showing the appointment or a certificate issued by or on behalf of a person reasonably believed by the issuer to be responsible or, in the absence of that document or certificate, other evidence reasonably deemed by the issuer to be appropriate. The issuer may adopt standards with respect to the evidence if they are not manifestly unreasonable. The issuer is not charged with notice of the contents of any document obtained pursuant to this paragraph (b) except to the extent that the contents relate directly to the appointment or incumbency.

(4) The issuer may elect to require reasonable assurance beyond that specified in this section, but if it does so and, for a purpose other than that specified in subsection (3)(b), both requires and obtains a copy of a will, trust, indenture, articles of co-partnership, by-laws, or other controlling instrument, it is charged with notice of all matters contained therein affecting the transfer, pledge, or release.

Amended in 1977.

§ 8—403. *Issuer's Duty as to Adverse Claims.*

(1) An issuer to whom a certificated security is presented for registration shall inquire into adverse claims if:

(a) a written notification of an adverse claim is received at a time and in a manner affording the issuer a reasonable opportunity to act on it prior to the issuance of a new, reissued, or re-registered certificated security, and the notification identifies the claimant, the registered owner, and the issue of which the security is a part, and provides an address for communications directed to the claimant; or

(b) the issuer is charged with notice of an adverse claim from a controlling instrument it has elected to require under Section 8—402(4).

(2) The issuer may discharge any duty of inquiry by any reasonable means, including notifying an adverse claimant by registered or certified mail at the address furnished by him or, if there be no such address, at his residence or regular place of business that the certificated security has been presented for registration of transfer by a named person, and that the transfer will be registered unless within 30 days from the date of mailing the notification, either:

(a) an appropriate restraining order, injunction, or other process issues from a court of competent jurisdiction; or

(b) there is filed with the issuer an indemnity bond, sufficient in the issuer's judgment to protect the issuer and any transfer agent, registrar, or other agent of the issuer involved from any loss it or they may suffer by complying with the adverse claim.

(3) Unless an issuer is charged with notice of an adverse claim from a controlling instrument which it has elected to require under Section 8—402(4) or receives notification of an adverse claim under subsection (1), if a certificated security presented for registration is indorsed by the appropriate person or persons the issuer is under no duty to inquire into adverse claims. In particular:

(a) an issuer registering a certificated security in the name of a person who is a fiduciary or who is described as a fiduciary is not bound to inquire into the existence, extent, or correct description of the fiduciary relationship; and thereafter the issuer may assume without inquiry that the newly registered owner continues to be the fiduciary until the issuer receives written notice that the fiduciary is no longer acting as such with respect to the particular security;

(b) an issuer registering transfer on an indorsement by a fiduciary is not bound to inquire whether the transfer is made in compliance with a controlling instrument or with the law of the state having jurisdiction of the fiduciary relationship, including any law requiring the fiduciary to obtain court approval of the transfer; and

(c) the issuer is not charged with notice of the contents of any court record or file or other recorded or unrecorded document even though the document is in its possession and even though the transfer is made on the indorsement of a fiduciary to the fiduciary himself or to his nominee.

(4) An issuer is under no duty as to adverse claims with respect to an uncertificated security except:

(a) claims embodied in a restraining order, injunction, or other legal process served upon the issuer if the process was served at a time and in a manner affording the issuer a reasonable opportunity to act on it in accordance with the requirements of subsection (5);

(b) claims of which the issuer has received a written notification from the registered owner or the registered pledgee if the notification was received at a time and in a manner affording the issuer a reasonable opportunity to act on it in accordance with the requirements of subsection (5);

(c) claims (including restrictions on transfer not imposed by the issuer) to which the registration of transfer to the present registered owner was subject and were so noted in the initial transaction statement sent to him; and

(d) claims as to which an issuer is charged with notice from a controlling instrument it has elected to require under Section 8—402(4).

(5) If the issuer of an uncertificated security is under a duty as to an adverse claim, he discharges that duty by:

(a) including a notation of the claim in any statements sent with respect to the security under Sections 8—408(3), (6), and (7); and

(b) refusing to register the transfer or pledge of the security unless the nature of the claim does not preclude transfer or pledge subject thereto.

(6) If the transfer or pledge of the security is registered subject to an adverse claim, a notation of the claim must be included in the initial transaction statement and all subsequent statements sent to the transferee and pledgee under Section 8—408.

(7) Notwithstanding subsections (4) and (5), if an uncertificated security was subject to a registered pledge at the time the issuer first came under a duty as to a particular adverse claim, the issuer has no duty as to that claim if transfer of the security is requested by the registered pledgee or an appropriate person acting for the registered pledgee unless:

(a) the claim was embodied in legal process which expressly provides otherwise;

(b) the claim was asserted in a written notification from the registered pledgee;

(c) the claim was one as to which the issuer was charged with notice from a controlling instrument it required under Section 8—402(4) in connection with the pledgee's request for transfer; or

(d) the transfer requested is to the registered owner.

Amended in 1977.

§ 8—404. *Liability and Non-Liability for Registration.*

(1) Except as provided in any law relating to the collection of taxes, the issuer is not liable to the owner, pledgee, or any other person suffering loss as a result of the registration of a transfer, pledge, or release of a security if:

(a) there were on or with a certificated security the necessary indorsements or the issuer had received an instruction originated by an appropriate person (Section 8—308); and

(b) the issuer had no duty as to adverse claims or has discharged the duty (Section 8—403).

(2) If an issuer has registered a transfer of a certificated security to a person not entitled to it, the issuer on demand shall deliver a like security to the true owner unless:

(a) the registration was pursuant to subsection (1);

(b) the owner is precluded from asserting any claim for registering the transfer under Section 8—405(1); or

(c) the delivery would result in overissue, in which case the issuer's liability is governed by Section 8—104.

(3) If an issuer has improperly registered a transfer, pledge, or release of an uncertificated security, the issuer on demand from the injured party shall restore the records as to the injured party to the condition that would have obtained if the improper registration had not been made unless:

(a) the registration was pursuant to subsection (1); or

(b) the registration would result in overissue, in which case the issuer's liability is governed by Section 8—104.

Amended in 1977.

§ 8—405. *Lost, Destroyed, and Stolen Certificated Securities.*

(1) If a certificated security has been lost, apparently destroyed, or wrongfully taken, and the owner fails to notify the issuer of that fact within a reasonable time after he has notice of it and the issuer registers a transfer of the security before receiving notification, the owner is precluded from asserting against the issuer any claim for registering the transfer under Section 8—404 or any claim to a new security under this section.

(2) If the owner of a certificated security claims that the security has been lost, destroyed, or wrongfully taken, the issuer shall issue a new certificated security or, at the option of the issuer, an equivalent uncertificated security in place of the original security if the owner:

(a) so requests before the issuer has notice that the security has been acquired by a bona fide purchaser;

(b) files with the issuer a sufficient indemnity bond; and

(c) satisfies any other reasonable requirements imposed by the issuer.

(3) If, after the issue of a new certificated or uncertificated security, a bona fide purchaser of the original certificated security presents it for registration of transfer, the issuer shall register the transfer unless registration would result in overissue, in which event the issuer's liability is governed by Section 8—104. In addition to any rights on the indemnity bond, the issuer may recover the new certificated security from the person to whom it was issued or any person taking under him except a bona fide purchaser or may cancel the uncertificated security unless a bona fide purchaser or any person taking under a bona fide purchaser is then the registered owner or registered pledgee thereof.

Amended in 1977.

§ 8—406. *Duty of Authenticating Trustee, Transfer Agent, or Registrar.*

(1) If a person acts as authenticating trustee, transfer agent, registrar, or other agent for an issuer in the registration of transfers of its certificated securities or in the registration of transfers, pledges, and releases of its uncertificated securities, in the issue of new securities, or in the cancellation of surrendered securities:

(a) he is under a duty to the issuer to exercise good faith and due diligence in performing his functions; and

(b) with regard to the particular functions he performs, he has the same obligation to the holder or owner of a certificated security or to the owner or pledgee of an uncertificated security and has the same rights and privileges as the issuer has in regard to those functions.

(2) Notice to an authenticating trustee, transfer agent, registrar or other agent is notice to the issuer with respect to the functions performed by the agent.

Amended in 1977.

§ 8—407. *Exchangeability of Securities.*

(1) No issuer is subject to the requirements of this section unless it regularly maintains a system for issuing the class of securities involved under which both certificated and uncertificated securities are regularly issued to the category of owners, which includes the person in whose name the new security is to be registered.

(2) Upon surrender of a certificated security with all necessary indorsements and presentation of a written request by the person surrendering the security, the issuer, if he has no duty as to adverse claims or has discharged the duty (Section 8—403), shall issue to the person or a person designated by him an equivalent uncertificated security subject to all liens, restrictions, and claims that were noted on the certificated security.

(3) Upon receipt of a transfer instruction originated by an appropriate person who so requests, the issuer of an uncertificated security shall cancel the uncertificated security and issue an equivalent certificated security on which must be noted conspicuously any liens and restrictions of the issuer and any adverse claims (as to which the issuer has a duty under Section 8—403(4)) to which the uncertificated security was subject. The certificated security shall be registered in the name of and delivered to:

(a) the registered owner, if the uncertificated security was not subject to a registered pledge; or

(b) the registered pledgee, if the uncertificated security was subject to a registered pledge.

Added in 1977.

§ 8—408. *Statements of Uncertificated Securities.*

(1) Within 2 business days after the transfer of an uncertificated security has been registered, the issuer shall send to the new registered owner and, if the security has been transferred subject to a registered pledge, to the registered pledgee a written statement containing:

(a) a description of the issue of which the uncertificated security is a part;

(b) the number of shares or units transferred;

(c) the name and address and any taxpayer identification number of the new registered owner and, if the security has been transferred subject to a registered pledge, the name and address and any taxpayer identification number of the registered pledgee;

(d) a notation of any liens and restrictions of the issuer and any adverse claims (as to which the issuer has a duty under Section 8—403(4)) to which the uncertificated security is or may be subject at the time of registration or a statement that there are none of those liens, restrictions, or adverse claims; and

(e) the date the transfer was registered.

(2) Within 2 business days after the pledge of an uncertificated security has been registered, the issuer shall send to the registered owner and the registered pledgee a written statement containing:

(a) a description of the issue of which the uncertificated security is a part;

(b) the number of shares or units pledged;

(c) the name and address and any taxpayer identification number of the registered owner and the registered pledgee;

(d) a notation of any liens and restrictions of the issuer and any adverse claims (as to which the issuer has a duty under Section 8—403(4)) to which the uncertificated security is or may be subject at the time of registration or a statement that there are none of those liens, restrictions, or adverse claims; and

(e) the date the pledge was registered.

(3) Within 2 business days after the release from pledge of an uncertificated security has been registered, the issuer shall send to the registered owner and the pledgee whose interest was released a written statement containing:

(a) a description of the issue of which the uncertificated security is a part;

(b) the number of shares or units released from pledge;

(c) the name and address and any taxpayer identification number of the registered owner and the pledgee whose interest was released;

(d) a notation of any liens and restrictions of the issuer and any adverse claims (as to which the issuer has a duty under Section 8—403(4)) to which the uncertificated security is or may be subject at the time of registration or a statement that there are none of those liens, restrictions, or adverse claims; and

(e) the date the release was registered.

(4) An "initial transaction statement" is the statement sent to:

(a) the new registered owner and, if applicable, to the registered pledgee pursuant to subsection (1);

(b) the registered pledgee pursuant to subsection (2); or

(c) the registered owner pursuant to subsection (3).

Each initial transaction statement shall be signed by or on behalf of the issuer and must be identified as "Initial Transaction Statement".

(5) Within 2 business days after the transfer of an uncertificated security has been registered, the issuer shall send to the former registered owner and the former registered pledgee, if any, a written statement containing:

(a) a description of the issue of which the uncertificated security is a part;

(b) the number of shares or units transferred;

(c) the name and address and any taxpayer identification number of the former registered owner and of any former registered pledgee; and

(d) the date the transfer was registered.

(6) At periodic intervals no less frequent than annually and at any time upon the reasonable written request of the registered owner, the issuer shall send to the registered owner of each uncertificated security a dated written statement containing:

(a) a description of the issue of which the uncertificated security is a part;

(b) the name and address and any taxpayer identification number of the registered owner;

(c) the number of shares or units of the uncertificated security registered in the name of the registered owner on the date of the statement;

(d) the name and address and any taxpayer identification number of any registered pledgee and the number of shares or units subject to the pledge; and

(e) a notation of any liens and restrictions of the issuer and any adverse claims (as to which the issuer has a duty under Section 8—403(4)) to which the uncertificated security is or may be subject or a statement that there are none of those liens, restrictions, or adverse claims.

(7) At periodic intervals no less frequent than annually and at any time upon the reasonable written request of the registered pledgee, the issuer shall send to the registered pledgee of each uncertificated security a dated written statement containing:

(a) a description of the issue of which the uncertificated security is a part;

(b) the name and address and any taxpayer identification number of the registered owner;

(c) the name and address and any taxpayer identification number of the registered pledgee;

(d) the number of shares or units subject to the pledge; and

(e) a notation of any liens and restrictions of the issuer and any adverse claims (as to which the issuer has a duty under Section 8—403(4)) to which the uncertificated security is or may be subject or a statement that there are none of those liens, restrictions, or adverse claims.

(8) If the issuer sends the statements described in subsections (6) and (7) at periodic intervals no less frequent than quarterly, the issuer is not obliged to send additional statements upon request unless the owner or pledgee requesting them pays to the issuer the reasonable cost of furnishing them.

(9) Each statement sent pursuant to this section must bear a conspicuous legend reading substantially as follows: "This statement is merely a record of the rights of the addressee as of the time of its issuance. Delivery of this statement, of itself, confers no rights on the recipient. This statement is neither a negotiable instrument nor a security."

Added in 1977.

ARTICLE 9
SECURED TRANSACTIONS; SALES OF ACCOUNTS AND CHATTEL PAPER

PART 1
Short Title, Applicability and Definitions

§ 9—101. *Short Title.*

This Article shall be known and may be cited as Uniform Commercial Code—Secured Transactions.

§ 9—102. *Policy and Subject Matter of Article.*

(1) Except as otherwise provided in Section 9—104 on excluded transactions, this Article applies

(a) to any transaction (regardless of its form) which is intended to create a security interest in personal property or fixtures including goods, documents, instruments, general intangibles, chattel paper or accounts; and also

(b) to any sale of accounts or chattel paper.

(2) This Article applies to security interests created by contract including pledge, assignment, chattel mortgage, chattel trust, trust deed, factor's lien, equipment trust, conditional sale, trust receipt, other lien or title retention contract and lease or consignment

intended as security. This Article does not apply to statutory liens except as provided in Section 9—310.

(3) The application of this Article to a security interest in a secured obligation is not affected by the fact that the obligation is itself secured by a transaction or interest to which this Article does not apply.

§ 9—103. *Perfection of Security Interest in Multiple State Transactions.*

(1) Documents, instruments and ordinary goods.

(a) This subsection applies to documents, instruments, rights to proceeds of written letters of credit, and goods other than those covered by a certificate of title described in subsection (2), mobile goods described in subsection (3), and minerals described in subsection (5).

(b) Except as otherwise provided in this subsection, perfection and the effect of perfection or non-perfection of a security interest in collateral are governed by the law of the jurisdiction where the collateral is when the last event occurs on which is based the assertion that the security interest is perfected or unperfected.

(c) If the parties to a transaction creating a purchase money security interest in goods in one jurisdiction understand at the time that the security interest attaches that the goods will be kept in another jurisdiction, then the law of the other jurisdiction governs the perfection and the effect of perfection or non-perfection of the security interest from the time it attaches until thirty days after the debtor receives possession of the goods and thereafter if the goods are taken to the other jurisdiction before the end of the thirty-day period.

(d) When collateral is brought into and kept in this state while subject to a security interest perfected under the law of the jurisdiction from which the collateral was removed, the security interest remains perfected, but if action is required by Part 3 of this Article to perfect the security interest,

(i) if the action is not taken before the expiration of the period of perfection in the other jurisdiction or the end of four months after the collateral is brought into this state, whichever period first expires, the security interest becomes unperfected at the end of that period and is thereafter deemed to have been unperfected as against a person who became a purchaser after removal;

(ii) if the action is taken before the expiration of the period specified in subparagraph (i), the security interest continues perfected thereafter;

(iii) for the purpose of priority over a buyer of consumer goods (subsection (2) of Section 9—307), the period of the effectiveness of a filing in the jurisdiction from which the collateral is removed is governed by the rules with respect to perfection in subparagraphs (i) and (ii).

(2) Certificate of title.

(a) This subsection applies to goods covered by a certificate of title issued under a statute of this state or of another jurisdiction under the law of which indication of a security interest on the certificate is required as a condition of perfection.

(b) Except as otherwise provided in this subsection, perfection and the effect of perfection or non-perfection of the security interest are governed by the law (including the conflict of laws rules) of the jurisdiction issuing the certificate until four months after the goods are removed from that jurisdiction and thereafter until the goods are registered in another jurisdiction, but in any event not beyond surrender of the certificate. After the expiration of that period, the goods are not covered by the certificate of title within the meaning of this section.

(c) Except with respect to the rights of a buyer described in the next paragraph, a security interest, perfected in another jurisdiction otherwise than by notation on a certificate of title, in goods brought into this state and thereafter covered by a certificate of title issued by this state is subject to the rules stated in paragraph (d) of subsection (1).

(d) If goods are brought into this state while a security interest therein is perfected in any manner under the law of the jurisdiction from which the goods are removed and a certificate of title is issued by this state and the certificate does not show that the goods are subject to the security interest or that they may be subject to security interests not shown on the certificate, the security interest is subordinate to the rights of a buyer of the goods who is not in the business of selling goods of that kind to the extent that he gives value and receives delivery of the goods after issuance of the certificate and without knowledge of the security interest.

(3) Accounts, general intangibles and mobile goods.

(a) This subsection applies to accounts (other than an account described in subsection (5) on minerals) and general intangibles (other than uncertificated securities) and to goods which are mobile and which are of a type normally used in more than one jurisdiction, such as motor vehicles, trailers, rolling stock, airplanes, shipping containers, road building and construction machinery and commercial harvesting machinery and the like, if the goods are equipment or are inventory leased or held for lease by the debtor to others, and are not covered by a certificate of title described in subsection (2).

(b) The law (including the conflict of laws rules) of the jurisdiction in which the debtor is located governs the perfection and the effect of perfection or non-perfection of the security interest.

(c) If, however, the debtor is located in a jurisdiction which is not a part of the United States, and which does not provide for perfection of the security interest by filing or recording in that jurisdiction, the law of the jurisdiction in the United States in which the debtor has its major executive office in the United States governs the perfection and the effect of perfection or non-perfection of the security interest through filing. In the alternative, if the debtor is located in a jurisdiction which is not a part of the United States or Canada and the collateral is accounts or general intangibles for money due or to become due, the security interest may be perfected by notification to the account debtor. As used in this paragraph, "United States" includes its territories and possessions and the Commonwealth of Puerto Rico.

(d) A debtor shall be deemed located at his place of business if he has one, at his chief executive office if he has more than one place of business, otherwise at his residence. If, however, the debtor is a foreign air carrier under the Federal Aviation Act of 1958, as amended, it shall be deemed located at the designated office of the agent upon whom service of process may be made on behalf of the foreign air carrier.

(e) A security interest perfected under the law of the jurisdiction of the location of the debtor is perfected until the expiration of four months after a change of the debtor's location to another jurisdiction, or until perfection would have ceased by the law of the first jurisdiction, whichever period first expires. Unless perfected in the new jurisdiction before the end of that period, it becomes unperfected thereafter and is deemed to have been unperfected as against a person who became a purchaser after the change.

(4) Chattel paper.

The rules stated for goods in subsection (1) apply to a possessory security interest in chattel paper. The rules stated for accounts in subsection (3) apply to a nonpossessory security interest in chattel paper, but the security interest may not be perfected by notification to the account debtor.

(5) Minerals.

Perfection and the effect of perfection or non-perfection of a security interest which is created by a debtor who has an interest in minerals or the like (including oil and gas) before extraction and which attaches thereto as extracted, or which attaches to an account resulting from the sale thereof at the wellhead or minehead are governed by the law (including the conflict of laws rules) of the jurisdiction wherein the wellhead or minehead is located.

(6) Uncertificated securities

The law (including the conflict of laws rules) of the jurisdiction of organization of the issuer governs the perfection and the effect of perfection or non-perfection of a security interest in uncertificated securities.

§ 9—104. *Transactions Excluded From Article.*

This Article does not apply

(a) to a security interest subject to any statute of the United States, to the extent that such statute governs the rights of parties to and third parties affected by transactions in particular types of property; or

(b) to a landlord's lien; or

(c) to a lien given by statute or other rule of law for services or materials except as provided in Section 9—310 on priority of such liens; or

(d) to a transfer of a claim for wages, salary or other compensation of an employee; or

(e) to a transfer by a government or governmental subdivision or agency; or

(f) to a sale of accounts or chattel paper as part of a sale of the business out of which they arose, or an assignment of accounts or chattel paper which is for the purpose of collection only, or a transfer of a right to payment under a contract to an assignee who is also to do the performance under the contract or a transfer of a single account to an assignee in whole or partial satisfaction of a preexisting indebtedness; or

(g) to a transfer of an interest in or claim in or under any policy of insurance, except as provided with respect to proceeds (Section 9—306) and priorities in proceeds (Section 9—312); or

(h) to a right represented by a judgment (other than a judgment taken on a right to payment which was collateral); or

(i) to any right of set-off; or

(j) except to the extent that provision is made for fixtures in Section 9—313, to the creation or transfer of an interest in or lien on real estate, including a lease or rents thereunder; or

(k) to a transfer in whole or in part of any claim arising out of tort; or

(l) to a transfer of an interest in any deposit account (subsection (1) of Section 9—105), except as provided with respect to proceeds (Section 9—306) and priorities in proceeds (Section 9—312).

§ 9—105. *Definitions and Index of Definitions.*

(1) In this Article unless the context otherwise requires:

(a) "Account debtor" means the person who is obligated on an account, chattel paper or general intangible;

(b) "Chattel paper" means a writing or writings which evidence both a monetary obligation and a security interest in or a lease of specific goods, but a charter or other contract involving the use or hire of a vessel is not chattel paper. When a transaction is evidenced both by such a security agreement or a lease and by an instrument or a series of instruments, the group of writings taken together constitutes chattel paper;

(c) "Collateral" means the property subject to a security interest, and includes accounts and chattel paper which have been sold;

(d) "Debtor" means the person who owes payment or other performance of the obligation secured, whether or not he owns or has rights in the collateral, and includes the seller of accounts or chattel paper. Where the debtor and the owner of the collateral are not the same person, the term "debtor" means the owner of the collateral in any provision of the Article dealing with the collateral, the obligor in any provision dealing with the obligation, and may include both where the context so requires;

(e) "Deposit account" means a demand, time, savings, passbook or like account maintained with a bank, savings and loan association, credit union or like organization, other than an account evidenced by a certificate of deposit;

(f) "Document" means document of title as defined in the general definitions of Article 1 (Section 1—201), and a receipt of the kind described in subsection (2) of Section 7—201;

(g) "Encumbrance" includes real estate mortgages and other liens on real estate and all other rights in real estate that are not ownership interests;

(h) "Goods" includes all things which are movable at the time the security interest attaches or which are fixtures (Section 9—313), but does not include money, documents, instruments, investment property, commodity contracts accounts, chattel paper, general intangibles, or minerals or the like (including oil and gas) before extraction. "Goods" also includes standing timber which is to be cut and removed under a conveyance or contract for sale, the unborn young of animals, and growing crops;

(i) "Instrument" means a negotiable instrument (defined in Section 3—104), or a certificated security (defined in Section 8—102) or any other writing which evidences a right to the payment of money and is not itself a security agreement or lease and is of a type which is in ordinary course of business transferred by delivery with any necessary indorsement or assignment;

(j) "Mortgage" means a consensual interest created by a real estate mortgage, a trust deed on real estate, or the like;

(k) An advance is made "pursuant to commitment" if the secured party has bound himself to make it, whether or not a subsequent event of default or other event not within his control has relieved or may relieve him from his obligation;

(l) "Security agreement" means an agreement which creates or provides for a security interest;

(m) "Secured party" means a lender, seller or other person in whose favor there is a security interest, including a person to whom accounts or chattel paper have been sold. When the holders of obligations issued under an indenture of trust, equipment trust agreement or the like are represented by a trustee or other person, the representative is the secured party;

(n) "Transmitting utility" means any person primarily engaged in the railroad, street railway or trolley bus business, the electric or electronics communications transmission business, the transmission of goods by pipeline, or the transmission or the production and transmission of electricity, steam, gas or water, or the provision of sewer service.

(2) Other definitions applying to this Article and the sections in which they appear are:

"Account." Section 9—106.
"Attach." Section 9—203.
"Construction mortgage." Section 9—313(1).
"Consumer goods." Section 9—109(1).
"Control." Section 9—115.
"Equipment." Section 9—109(2).
"Farm products." Section 9—109(3).
"Fixture." Section 9—313(1).
"Fixture filing." Section 9—313(1).
"General intangibles." Section 9—106.
"Inventory." Section 9—109(4).
"Investment property." Section 9—115.
"Lien creditor." Section 9—301(3).
"Proceeds." Section 9—306(1).
"Purchase money security interest." Section 9—107.
"United States." Section 9—103.

(3) The following definitions in other Articles apply to this Article:

"Check." Section 3—104.
"Contract for sale." Section 2—106.
"Holder in due course." Section 3—302.
"Note." Section 3—104.
"Sale." Section 2—106.

(4) In addition Article 1 contains general definitions and principles of construction and interpretation applicable throughout this Article.

§ 9—106. *Definitions: "Account"; "General Intangibles."*

"Account" means any right to payment for goods sold or leased or for services rendered which is not evidenced by an instrument or chattel paper, whether or not it has been earned by performance. "General intangibles" means any personal property (including things in action) other than goods, accounts, chattel paper, documents, instruments, investment property, rights to proceeds of written letters of credit, and money. All rights to payment earned or unearned under a charter or other contract involving the use or hire of a vessel and all rights incident to the charter or contract are accounts.

§ 9—107. *Definitions: "Purchase Money Security Interest."*

A security interest is a "purchase money security interest" to the extent that it is

(a) taken or retained by the seller of the collateral to secure all or part of its price; or

(b) taken by a person who by making advances or incurring an obligation gives value to enable the debtor to acquire rights in or the use of collateral if such value is in fact so used.

§ 9—108. *When After-Acquired Collateral Not Security for Antecedent Debt.*

Where a secured party makes an advance, incurs an obligation, releases a perfected security interest, or otherwise gives new value which is to be secured in whole or in part by after-acquired property his security interest in the after-acquired collateral shall be deemed to be taken for new value and not as security for an antecedent debt if the debtor acquires his rights in such collateral either in the ordinary course of his business or under a contract of purchase made pursuant to the security agreement within a reasonable time after new value is given.

§ 9—109. *Classification of Goods; "Consumer Goods"; "Equipment";*

"Farm Products"; "Inventory."

Goods are

(1) "consumer goods" if they are used or bought for use primarily for personal, family or household purposes;

(2) "equipment" if they are used or bought for use primarily in business (including farming or a profession) or by a debtor who is a non-profit organization or a governmental subdivision or agency or if the goods are not included in the definitions of inventory, farm products or consumer goods;

(3) "farm products" if they are crops or livestock or supplies used or produced in farming operations or if they are products of crops or livestock in their unmanufactured states (such as ginned cotton, wool-clip, maple syrup, milk and eggs), and if they are in the possession of a debtor engaged in raising, fattening, grazing or other farming operations. If goods are farm products they are neither equipment nor inventory;

(4) "inventory" if they are held by a person who holds them for sale or lease or to be furnished under contracts of service or if he has so furnished them, or if they are raw materials, work in process or materials used or consumed in a business. Inventory of a person is not to be classified as his equipment.

§ 9—110. *Sufficiency of Description.*

For purposes of this Article any description of personal property or real estate is sufficient whether or not it is specific if it reasonably identifies what is described.

§ 9—111. *Applicability of Bulk Transfer Laws.*

The creation of a security interest is not a bulk transfer under Article 6 (see Section 6—103).

§ 9—112. *Where Collateral Is Not Owned by Debtor.*

Unless otherwise agreed, when a secured party knows that collateral is owned by a person who is not the debtor, the owner of the collateral is entitled to receive from the secured party any surplus under Section 9—502(2) or under Section 9—504(1), and is not liable for the debt or for any deficiency after resale, and he has the same right as the debtor

(a) to receive statements under Section 9—208;

(b) to receive notice of and to object to a secured party's proposal to retain the collateral in satisfaction of the indebtedness under Section 9—505;

(c) to redeem the collateral under Section 9—506;

(d) to obtain injunctive or other relief under Section 9—507(1); and

(e) to recover losses caused to him under Section 9—208(2).

§ 9—113. *Security Interests Arising Under Article on Sales or Under Article on Leases.*

A security interest arising solely under the Article on Sales (Article 2) or the Article on Leases is subject to the provisions of this Article except that to the extent that and so long as the debtor does not have or does not lawfully obtain possession of the goods

(a) no security agreement is necessary to make the security interest enforceable; and

(b) no filing is required to perfect the security interest; and

(c) the rights of the secured party on default by the debtor are governed (i) by the Article on Sales (Article 2) in the case of a security interest arising solely under such Article or (ii) by the Article on Leases (Article 2A) in the case of a security interest arising solely under such Article.

§ 9—114. *Consignment.*

(1) A person who delivers goods under a consignment which is not a security interest and who would be required to file under this Article by paragraph (3)(c) of Section 2—326 has priority over a secured party who is or becomes a creditor of the consignee and who would have a perfected security interest in the goods if they were the property of the consignee, and also has priority with respect to identifiable cash proceeds received on or before delivery of the goods to a buyer, if

(a) the consignor complies with the filing provision of the Article on Sales with respect to consignments (paragraph (3)(c) of Section 2—326) before the consignee receives possession of the goods; and

(b) the consignor gives notification in writing to the holder of the security interest if the holder has filed a financing statement covering the same types of goods before the date of the filing made by the consignor; and

(c) the holder of the security interest receives the notification within five years before the consignee receives possession of the goods; and

(d) the notification states that the consignor expects to deliver goods on consignment to the consignee, describing the goods by item or type.

(2) In the case of a consignment which is not a security interest and in which the requirements of the preceding subsection have not been met, a person who delivers goods to another is subordinate to a person who would have a perfected security interest in the goods if they were the property of the debtor.

PART 2
Validity of Security Agreement and Rights of Parties Thereto

§ 9—201. *General Validity of Security Agreement.*

Except as otherwise provided by this Act a security agreement is effective according to its terms between the parties, against purchasers of the collateral and against creditors. Nothing in this Article validates any charge or practice illegal under any statute or regulation thereunder governing usury, small loans, retail installment sales, or the like, or extends the application of any such statute or regulation to any transaction not otherwise subject thereto.

§ 9—202. *Title to Collateral Immaterial.*

Each provision of this Article with regard to rights, obligations and remedies applies whether title to collateral is in the secured party or in the debtor.

§ 9—203. *Attachment and Enforceability of Security Interest; Proceeds; Formal Requisites.*

(1) Subject to the provisions of Section 4—208 on the security interest of a collecting bank, Section 8—321 on security interests in securities and Section 9—113 on a security interest arising under the Article on Sales, a security interest is not enforceable against the debtor or third parties with respect to the collateral and does not attach unless:

(a) the collateral is in the possession of the secured party pursuant to agreement, or the debtor has signed a security agreement which contains a description of the collateral and in addition, when the security interest covers crops growing or to be grown or timber to be cut, a description of the land concerned;

(b) value has been given; and

(c) the debtor has rights in the collateral.

(2) A security interest attaches when it becomes enforceable against the debtor with respect to the collateral. Attachment occurs as soon as all of the events specified in subsection (1) have taken place unless explicit agreement postpones the time of attaching.

(3) Unless otherwise agreed a security agreement gives the secured party the rights to proceeds provided by Section 9—306.

(4) A transaction, although subject to this Article, is also subject to . . . .*, and in the case of conflict between the provisions of this Article and any such statute, the provisions of such statute control. Failure to comply with any applicable statute has only the effect which is specified therein.

§ 9—204. *After-Acquired Property; Future Advances.*

(1) Except as provided in subsection (2), a security agreement may provide that any or all obligations covered by the security agreement are to be secured by after-acquired collateral.

(2) No security interest attaches under an after-acquired property clause to consumer goods other than accessions (Section 9—314) when given as additional security unless the debtor acquires rights in them within ten days after the secured party gives value.

(3) Obligations covered by a security agreement may include future advances or other value whether or not the advances or value are given pursuant to commitment (subsection (1) of Section 9—105).

§ 9—205. *Use or Disposition of Collateral Without Accounting Permissible.*

A security interest is not invalid or fraudulent against creditors by reason of liberty in the debtor to use, commingle or dispose of all or part of the collateral (including returned or repossessed goods) or to collect or compromise accounts or chattel paper, or to accept the return of goods or make repossessions, or to use, commingle or dispose of proceeds, or by reason of the failure of the secured party to require the debtor to account for proceeds or replace collateral. This section does not relax the requirements of possession where perfection of a security interest depends upon possession of the collateral by the secured party or by a bailee.

§ 9—206. *Agreement Not to Assert Defenses Against Assignee; Modification of Sales Warranties Where Security Agreement Exists.*

(1) Subject to any statute or decision which establishes a different rule for buyers or lessees of consumer goods, an agreement by a buyer or lessee that he will not assert against an assignee any claim or defense which he may have against the seller or lessor is enforceable by an assignee who takes his assignment for value, in good faith and without notice of a claim or defense, except as to

defenses of a type which may be asserted against a holder in due course of a negotiable instrument under the Article on Commercial Paper (Article 3). A buyer who as part of one transaction signs both a negotiable instrument and a security agreement makes such an agreement.

(2) When a seller retains a purchase money security interest in goods the Article on Sales (Article 2) governs the sale and any disclaimer, limitation or modification of the seller's warranties.

§ 9—207. *Rights and Duties When Collateral is in Secured Party's Possession*

(1) A secured party must use reasonable care in the custody and preservation of collateral in his possession. In the case of an instrument or chattel paper reasonable care includes taking necessary steps to preserve rights against prior parties unless otherwise agreed.

(2) Unless otherwise agreed, when collateral is in the secured party's possession

(a) reasonable expenses (including the cost of any insurance and payment of taxes or other charges) incurred in the custody, preservation, use or operation of the collateral are chargeable to the debtor and are secured by the collateral;

(b) the risk of accidental loss or damage is on the debtor to the extent of any deficiency in any effective insurance coverage;

(c) the secured party may hold as additional security any increase or profits (except money) received from the collateral, but money so received, unless remitted to the debtor, shall be applied in reduction of the secured obligation;

(d) the secured party must keep the collateral identifiable but fungible collateral may be commingled;

(e) the secured party may repledge the collateral upon terms which do not impair the debtor's right to redeem it.

(3) A secured party is liable for any loss caused by his failure to meet any obligation imposed by the preceding subsections but does not lose his security interest.

(4) A secured party may use or operate the collateral for the purpose of preserving the collateral or its value or pursuant to the order of a court of appropriate jurisdiction or, except in the case of consumer goods, in the manner and to the extent provided in the security agreement.

§ 9—208. *Request for Statement of Account or List of Collateral.*

(1) A debtor may sign a statement indicating what he believes to be the aggregate amount of unpaid indebtedness as of a specified date and may send it to the secured party with a request that the statement be approved or corrected and returned to the debtor. When the security agreement or any other record kept by the secured party identifies the collateral a debtor may similarly request the secured party to approve or correct a list of the collateral.

(2) The secured party must comply with such a request within two weeks after receipt by sending a written correction or approval. If the secured party claims a security interest in all of a particular type of collateral owned by the debtor he may indicate that fact in his reply and need not approve or correct an itemized list of such collateral. If the secured party without reasonable excuse fails to comply he is liable for any loss caused to the debtor thereby; and if the debtor has properly included in his request a good faith statement of the obligation or a list of the collateral or both the secured party may claim a security interest only as shown in the statement against persons misled by his failure to comply. If he no longer has an interest in the obligation or collateral at the time the request is received he must disclose the name and address of any successor in interest known to him and he is liable for any loss caused to the debtor as a result of failure to disclose. A successor in interest is not subject to this section until a request is received by him.

(3) A debtor is entitled to such a statement once every six months without charge. The secured party may require payment of a charge not exceeding $10 for each additional statement furnished.

PART 3
Rights of Third Parties; Perfected and Unperfected Security Interests; Rules of Priority

§ 9—301. *Persons Who Take Priority Over Unperfected Security Interests; Rights of "Lien Creditor."*

(1) Except as otherwise provided in subsection (2), an unperfected security interest is subordinate to the rights of

(a) persons entitled to priority under Section 9—312;

(b) a person who becomes a lien creditor before the security interest is perfected;

(c) in the case of goods, instruments, documents, and chattel paper, a person who is not a secured party and who is a transferee in bulk or other buyer not in ordinary course of business or is a buyer of farm products in ordinary course of business, to the extent that he gives value and receives delivery of the collateral without knowledge of the security interest and before it is perfected;

(d) in the case of accounts, general intangibles, and investment property a person who is not a secured party and who is a transferee to the extent that he gives value without knowledge of the security interest and before it is perfected.

(2) If the secured party files with respect to a purchase money security interest before or within ten days after the debtor receives possession of the collateral, he takes priority over the rights of a transferee in bulk or of a lien creditor which arise between the time the security interest attaches and the time of filing.

(3) A "lien creditor" means a creditor who has acquired a lien on the property involved by attachment, levy or the like and includes an assignee for benefit of creditors from the time of assignment, and a trustee in bankruptcy from the date of the filing of the petition or a receiver in equity from the time of appointment.

(4) A person who becomes a lien creditor while a security interest is perfected takes subject to the security interest only to the extent that it secures advances made before he becomes a lien creditor or within 45 days thereafter or made without knowledge of the lien or pursuant to a commitment entered into without knowledge of the lien.

§ 9—302. *When Filing Is Required to Perfect Security Interest; Security Interests to Which Filing Provisions of This Article Do Not Apply.*

(1) A financing statement must be filed to perfect all security interests except the following:

(a) a security interest in collateral in possession of the secured party under Section 9—305;

(b) a security interest temporarily perfected in instruments, certificated securities, or documents without delivery under

Section 9—304 or in proceeds for a 10-day period under Section 9—306;

(c) a security interest created by an assignment of a beneficial interest in a trust or a decedent's estate;

(d) a purchase money security interest in consumer goods; but filing is required for a motor vehicle required to be registered; and fixture filing is required for priority over conflicting interests in fixtures to the extent provided in Section 9—313;

(e) an assignment of accounts which does not alone or in conjunction with other assignments to the same assignee transfer a significant part of the outstanding accounts of the assignor;

(f) a security interest of a collecting bank (Section 4—208) or arising under the Article on Sales (see Section 9—113) or covered in subsection (3) of this section;

(g) an assignment for the benefit of all the creditors of the transferor, and subsequent transfers by the assignee thereunder.

(2) If a secured party assigns a perfected security interest, no filing under this Article is required in order to continue the perfected status of the security interest against creditors of and transferees from the original debtor.

(3) The filing of a financing statement otherwise required by this Article is not necessary or effective to perfect a security interest in property subject to

(a) a statute or treaty of the United States which provides for a national or international registration or a national or international certificate of title or which specifies a place of filing different from that specified in this Article for filing of the security interest; or

(b) the following statutes of this state; [list any certificate of title statute covering automobiles, trailers, mobile homes, boats, farm tractors, or the like, and any central filing statute.]; but during any period in which collateral is inventory held for sale by a person who is in the business of selling goods of that kind, the filing provisions of this Article (Part 4) apply to a security interest in that collateral created by him as debtor; or

(c) a certificate of title statute of another jurisdiction under the law of which indication of a security interest on the certificate is required as a condition of perfection (subsection (2) of Section 9—103).

(4) Compliance with a statute or treaty described in subsection (3) is equivalent to the filing of a financing statement under this Article, and a security interest in property subject to the statute or treaty can be perfected only by compliance therewith except as provided in Section 9—103 on multiple state transactions. Duration and renewal of perfection of a security interest perfected by compliance with the statute or treaty are governed by the provisions of the statute or treaty; in other respects the security interest is subject to this Article.

Amended in 1972 and 1977.

§ 9—303. *When Security Interest Is Perfected; Continuity of Perfection.*

(1) A security interest is perfected when it has attached and when all of the applicable steps required for perfection have been taken. Such steps are specified in Sections 9—302, 9—304, 9—305 and 9—306. If such steps are taken before the security interest attaches, it is perfected at the time when it attaches.

(2) If a security interest is originally perfected in any way permitted under this Article and is subsequently perfected in some other way under this Article, without an intermediate period when it was unperfected, the security interest shall be deemed to be perfected continuously for the purposes of this Article.

§ 9—304. *Perfection of Security Interest in Instruments, Documents, and Goods Covered by Documents; Perfection by Permissive Filing; Temporary Perfection Without Filing or Transfer of Possession.*

(1) A security interest in chattel paper or negotiable documents may be perfected by filing. A security interest in money or instruments (other than certificated securities or instruments which constitute part of chattel paper) can be perfected only by the secured party's taking possession, except as provided in subsections (4) and (5) of this section and subsections (2) and (3) of Section 9—306 on proceeds.

(2) During the period that goods are in the possession of the issuer of a negotiable document therefor, a security interest in the goods is perfected by perfecting a security interest in the document, and any security interest in the goods otherwise perfected during such period is subject thereto.

(3) A security interest in goods in the possession of a bailee other than one who has issued a negotiable document therefor is perfected by issuance of a document in the name of the secured party or by the bailee's receipt of notification of the secured party's interest or by filing as to the goods.

(4) A security interest in instruments, certificated securities, or negotiable documents is perfected without filing or the taking of possession for a period of 21 days from the time it attaches to the extent that it arises for new value given under a written security agreement.

(5) A security interest remains perfected for a period of 21 days without filing where a secured party having a perfected security interest in an instrument a certificated security (other than) a negotiable document or goods in possession of a bailee other than one who has issued a negotiable document therefor

(a) makes available to the debtor the goods or documents representing the goods for the purpose of ultimate sale or exchange or for the purpose of loading, unloading, storing, shipping, transshipping, manufacturing, processing or otherwise dealing with them in a manner preliminary to their sale or exchange, but priority between conflicting security interests in the goods is subject to subsection (3) of Section 9—312; or

(b) delivers the instrument or certificated security to the debtor for the purpose of ultimate sale or exchange or of presentation, collection, renewal or registration of transfer.

(6) After the 21-day period in subsections (4) and (5) perfection depends upon compliance with applicable provisions of this Article.

§ 9—305. *When Possession by Secured Party Perfects Security Interest Without Filing.*

A security interest in letters of credit and advices of credit (subsection (2)(a) of Section 5—116), goods, instruments (other than certificated securities), money, negotiable documents, or chattel paper may be perfected by the secured party's taking possession of the collateral. If such collateral other than goods covered by a negotiable document is held by a bailee, the secured party is deemed to have possession from the time the bailee receives notification of the secured party's interest. A security interest is perfected by possession from the time possession is taken without a relation back and continues only so long as possession is retained, unless otherwise specified in this Article. The security interest may be otherwise perfected as provided in this Article before or after the period of possession by the secured party.

§ 9—306. *"Proceeds"; Secured Party's Rights on Disposition of Collateral.*

(1) "Proceeds" includes whatever is received upon the sale, exchange, collection or other disposition of collateral or proceeds. Insurance payable by reason of loss or damage to the collateral is proceeds, except to the extent that it is payable to a person other than a party to the security agreement. Money, checks, deposit accounts, and the like are "cash proceeds." All other proceeds are "noncash proceeds."

(2) Except where this Article otherwise provides, a security interest continues in collateral notwithstanding sale, exchange or other disposition thereof unless the disposition was authorized by the secured party in the security agreement or otherwise, and also continues in any identifiable proceeds including collections received by the debtor.

(3) The security interest in proceeds is a continuously perfected security interest if the interest in the original collateral was perfected but it ceases to be a perfected security interest and becomes unperfected ten days after receipt of the proceeds by the debtor unless

(a) a filed financing statement covers the original collateral and the proceeds are collateral in which a security interest may be perfected by filing in the office or offices where the financing statement has been filed and, if the proceeds are acquired with cash proceeds, the description of collateral in the financing statement indicates the types of property constituting the proceeds; or

(b) a filed financing statement covers the original collateral and the proceeds are identifiable cash proceeds; or

(c) the security interest in the proceeds is perfected before the expiration of the ten-day period.

Except as provided in this section, a security interest in proceeds can be perfected only by the methods or under the circumstances permitted in this Article for original collateral of the same type.

(4) In the event of insolvency proceedings instituted by or against a debtor, a secured party with a perfected security interest in proceeds has a perfected security interest only in the following proceeds:

(a) in identifiable noncash proceeds and in separate deposit accounts containing only proceeds;

(b) in identifiable cash proceeds in the form of money which is neither commingled with other money nor deposited in a deposit account prior to the insolvency proceedings;

(c) in identifiable cash proceeds in the form of checks and the like which are not deposited in a deposit account prior to the insolvency proceedings; and

(d) in all cash and deposit accounts of the debtor in which proceeds have been commingled with other funds, but the perfected security interest under this paragraph (d) is

(i) subject to any right to set-off; and

(ii) limited to an amount not greater than the amount of any cash proceeds received by the debtor within ten days before the institution of the insolvency proceedings less the sum of (I) the payments to the secured party on account of cash proceeds received by the debtor during such period and (II) the cash proceeds received by the debtor during such period to which the secured party is entitled under paragraphs (a) through (c) of this subsection (4).

(5) If a sale of goods results in an account or chattel paper which is transferred by the seller to a secured party, and if the goods are returned to or are repossessed by the seller or the secured party, the following rules determine priorities:

(a) If the goods were collateral at the time of sale, for an indebtedness of the seller which is still unpaid, the original security interest attaches again to the goods and continues as a perfected security interest if it was perfected at the time when the goods were sold. If the security interest was originally perfected by a filing which is still effective, nothing further is required to continue the perfected status; in any other case, the secured party must take possession of the returned or repossessed goods or must file.

(b) An unpaid transferee of the chattel paper has a security interest in the goods against the transferor. Such security interest is prior to a security interest asserted under paragraph (a) to the extent that the transferee of the chattel paper was entitled to priority under Section 9—308.

(c) An unpaid transferee of the account has a security interest in the goods against the transferor. Such security interest is subordinate to a security interest asserted under paragraph (a).

(d) A security interest of an unpaid transferee asserted under paragraph (b) or (c) must be perfected for protection against creditors of the transferor and purchasers of the returned or repossessed goods.

§ 9—307. *Protection of Buyers of Goods.*

(1) A buyer in ordinary course of business (subsection (9) of Section 1—201) other than a person buying farm products from a person engaged in farming operations takes free of a security interest created by his seller even though the security interest is perfected and even though the buyer knows of its existence [subject to the Food Security Act of 1985 (7 U.S.C. Section 1631)].

(2) In the case of consumer goods, a buyer takes free of a security interest even though perfected if he buys without knowledge of the security interest, for value and for his own personal, family or household purposes unless prior to the purchase the secured party has filed a financing statement covering such goods.

(3) A buyer other than a buyer in ordinary course of business (subsection (1) of this section) takes free of a security interest to the extent that it secures future advances made after the secured party acquires knowledge of the purchase, or more than 45 days after the purchase, whichever first occurs, unless made pursuant to a commitment entered into without knowledge of the purchase and before the expiration of the 45-day period.

§ 9—308. *Purchase of Chattel Paper and Instruments.*

A purchaser of chattel paper or an instrument who gives new value and takes possession of it in the ordinary course of his business has priority over a security interest in the chattel paper or instrument

(a) which is perfected under Section 9—304 (permissive filing and temporary perfection) or under Section 9—306 (perfection as to proceeds) if he acts without knowledge that the specific paper or instrument is subject to a security interest; or

(b) which is claimed merely as proceeds of inventory subject to a security interest (Section 9—306) even though he knows that the specific paper or instrument is subject to the security interest.

§ 9—309. *Protection of Purchasers of Instruments, Documents and Securities.*

Nothing in this Article limits the rights of a holder in due course of a negotiable instrument (Section 3—302) or a holder to whom a negotiable document of title has been duly negotiated (Section 7—501) or a bona fide purchaser of a security (Section 8—302) and the holders or purchasers take priority over an earlier security interest even though perfected. Filing under this Article does not constitute notice of the security interest to such holders or purchasers.

§ 9—310. *Priority of Certain Liens Arising by Operation of Law.*

When a person in the ordinary course of his business furnishes services or materials with respect to goods subject to a security interest, a lien upon goods in the possession of such person given by statute or rule of law for such materials or services takes priority over a perfected security interest unless the lien is statutory and the statute expressly provides otherwise.

§ 9—311. *Alienability of Debtor's Rights: Judicial Process.*

The debtor's rights in collateral may be voluntarily or involuntarily transferred (by way of sale, creation of a security interest, attachment, levy, garnishment or other judicial process) notwithstanding a provision in the security agreement prohibiting any transfer or making the transfer constitute a default.

§ 9—312. *Priorities Among Conflicting Security Interests in the Same Collateral.*

(1) The rules of priority stated in other sections of this Part and in the following sections shall govern when applicable: Section 4—208 with respect to the security interests of collecting banks in items being collected, accompanying documents and proceeds; Section 9—103 on security interests related to other jurisdictions; Section 9—114 on consignments.

(2) A perfected security interest in crops for new value given to enable the debtor to produce the crops during the production season and given not more than three months before the crops become growing crops by planting or otherwise takes priority over an earlier perfected security interest to the extent that such earlier interest secures obligations due more than six months before the crops become growing crops by planting or otherwise, even though the person giving new value had knowledge of the earlier security interest.

(3) A perfected purchase money security interest in inventory has priority over a conflicting security interest in the same inventory and also has priority in identifiable cash proceeds received on or before the delivery of the inventory to a buyer if

(a) the purchase money security interest is perfected at the time the debtor receives possession of the inventory; and

(b) the purchase money secured party gives notification in writing to the holder of the conflicting security interest if the holder had filed a financing statement covering the same types of inventory (i) before the date of the filing made by the purchase money secured party, or (ii) before the beginning of the 21-day period where the purchase money security interest is temporarily perfected without filing or possession (subsection (5) of Section 9—304); and

(c) the holder of the conflicting security interest receives the notification within five years before the debtor receives possession of the inventory; and

(d) the notification states that the person giving the notice has or expects to acquire a purchase money security interest in inventory of the debtor, describing such inventory by item or type.

(4) A purchase money security interest in collateral other than inventory has priority over a conflicting security interest in the same collateral or its proceeds if the purchase money security interest is perfected at the time the debtor receives possession of the collateral or within ten days thereafter.

(5) In all cases not governed by other rules stated in this section (including cases of purchase money security interests which do not qualify for the special priorities set forth in subsections (3) and (4) of this section), priority between conflicting security interests in the same collateral shall be determined according to the following rules:

(a) Conflicting security interests rank according to priority in time of filing or perfection. Priority dates from the time a filing is first made covering the collateral or the time the security interest is first perfected, whichever is earlier, provided that there is no period thereafter when there is neither filing nor perfection.

(b) So long as conflicting security interests are unperfected, the first to attach has priority.

(6) For the purposes of subsection (5) a date of filing or perfection as to collateral is also a date of filing or perfection as to proceeds.

(7) If future advances are made while a security interest is perfected by filing, the taking of possession, or under Section 8—321 on securities, the security interest has the same priority for the purposes of subsection (5) with respect to the future advances as it does with respect to the first advance. If a commitment is made before or while the security interest is so perfected, the security interest has the same priority with respect to advances made pursuant thereto. In other cases a perfected security interest has priority from the date the advance is made.

§ 9—313. *Priority of Security Interests in Fixtures.*

(1) In this section and in the provisions of Part 4 of this Article referring to fixture filing, unless the context otherwise requires

(a) goods are "fixtures" when they become so related to particular real estate that an interest in them arises under real estate law

(b) a "fixture filing" is the filing in the office where a mortgage on the real estate would be filed or recorded of a financing statement covering goods which are or are to become fixtures and conforming to the requirements of subsection (5) of Section 9—402

(c) a mortgage is a "construction mortgage" to the extent that it secures an obligation incurred for the construction of an improvement on land including the acquisition cost of the land, if the recorded writing so indicates.

(2) A security interest under this Article may be created in goods which are fixtures or may continue in goods which become fixtures, but no security interest exists under this Article in ordinary building materials incorporated into an improvement on land.

(3) This Article does not prevent creation of an encumbrance upon fixtures pursuant to real estate law.

(4) A perfected security interest in fixtures has priority over the conflicting interest of an encumbrancer or owner of the real estate where

(a) the security interest is a purchase money security interest, the interest of the encumbrancer or owner arises before the goods become fixtures, the security interest is perfected by a fixture filing before the goods become fixtures or within ten days thereafter, and the debtor has an interest of record in the real estate or is in possession of the real estate; or

(b) the security interest is perfected by a fixture filing before the interest of the encumbrancer or owner is of record, the security interest has priority over any conflicting interest of a predecessor in title of the encumbrancer or owner, and the debtor has an interest of record in the real estate or is in possession of the real estate; or

(c) the fixtures are readily removable factory or office machines or readily removable replacements of domestic appliances which are consumer goods, and before the goods become fixtures the security interest is perfected by any method permitted by this Article; or

(d) the conflicting interest is a lien on the real estate obtained by legal or equitable proceedings after the security interest was perfected by any method permitted by this Article.

(5) A security interest in fixtures, whether or not perfected, has priority over the conflicting interest of an encumbrancer or owner of the real estate where

(a) the encumbrancer or owner has consented in writing to the security interest or has disclaimed an interest in the goods as fixtures; or

(b) the debtor has a right to remove the goods as against the encumbrancer or owner. If the debtor's right terminates, the priority of the security interest continues for a reasonable time.

(6) Notwithstanding paragraph (a) of subsection (4) but otherwise subject to subsections (4) and (5), a security interest in fixtures is subordinate to a construction mortgage recorded before the goods become fixtures if the goods become fixtures before the completion of the construction. To the extent that it is given to refinance a construction mortgage, a mortgage has this priority to the same extent as the construction mortgage.

(7) In cases not within the preceding subsections, a security interest in fixtures is subordinate to the conflicting interest of an encumbrancer or owner of the related real estate who is not the debtor.

(8) When the secured party has priority over all owners and encumbrancers of the real estate, he may, on default, subject to the provisions of Part 5, remove his collateral from the real estate but he must reimburse any encumbrancer or owner of the real estate who is not the debtor and who has not otherwise agreed for the cost of repair of any physical injury, but not for any diminution in value of the real estate caused by the absence of the goods removed or by any necessity of replacing them. A person entitled to reimbursement may refuse permission to remove until the secured party gives adequate security for the performance of this obligation.

§ 9—314. *Accessions.*

(1) A security interest in goods which attaches before they are installed in or affixed to other goods takes priority as to the goods installed or affixed (called in this section "accessions") over the claims of all persons to the whole except as stated in subsection (3) and subject to Section 9—315(1).

(2) A security interest which attaches to goods after they become part of a whole is valid against all persons subsequently acquiring interests in the whole except as stated in subsection (3) but is invalid against any person with an interest in the whole at the time the security interest attaches to the goods who has not in writing consented to the security interest or disclaimed an interest in the goods as part of the whole.

(3) The security interests described in subsections (1) and (2) do not take priority over

(a) a subsequent purchaser for value of any interest in the whole; or

(b) a creditor with a lien on the whole subsequently obtained by judicial proceedings; or

(c) a creditor with a prior perfected security interest in the whole to the extent that he makes subsequent advances if the subsequent purchase is made, the lien by judicial proceedings obtained or the subsequent advance under the prior perfected security interest is made or contracted for without knowledge of the security interest and before it is perfected. A purchaser of the whole at a foreclosure sale other than the holder of a perfected security interest purchasing at his own foreclosure sale is a subsequent purchaser within this section.

(4) When under subsections (1) or (2) and (3) a secured party has an interest in accessions which has priority over the claims of all persons who have interests in the whole, he may on default subject to the provisions of Part 5 remove his collateral from the whole but he must reimburse any encumbrancer or owner of the whole who is not the debtor and who has not otherwise agreed for the cost of repair of any physical injury but not for any diminution in value of the whole caused by the absence of the goods removed or by any necessity for replacing them. A person entitled to reimbursement may refuse permission to remove until the secured party gives adequate security for the performance of this obligation.

§ 9—315. *Priority When Goods Are Commingled or Processed.*

(1) If a security interest in goods was perfected and subsequently the goods or a part thereof have become part of a product or mass, the security interest continues in the product or mass if

(a) the goods are so manufactured, processed, assembled or commingled that their identity is lost in the product or mass; or

(b) a financing statement covering the original goods also covers the product into which the goods have been manufactured, processed or assembled.

In a case to which paragraph (b) applies, no separate security interest in that part of the original goods which has been manufactured, processed or assembled into the product may be claimed under Section 9—314.

(2) When under subsection (1) more than one security interest attaches to the product or mass, they rank equally according to the ratio that the cost of the goods to which each interest originally attached bears to the cost of the total product or mass.

§ 9—316. *Priority Subject to Subordination.*

Nothing in this Article prevents subordination by agreement by any person entitled to priority.

§ 9—317. *Secured Party Not Obligated on Contract of Debtor.*

The mere existence of a security interest or authority given to the debtor to dispose of or use collateral does not impose contract or tort liability upon the secured party for the debtor's acts or omissions.

§ 9—318. *Defenses Against Assignee; Modification of Contract After Notification of Assignment; Term Prohibiting Assignment Ineffective; Identification and Proof of Assignment.*

(1) Unless an account debtor has made an enforceable agreement not to assert defenses or claims arising out of a sale as provided in Section 9—206 the rights of an assignee are subject to

(a) all the terms of the contract between the account debtor and assignor and any defense or claim arising therefrom; and

(b) any other defense or claim of the account debtor against the assignor which accrues before the account debtor receives notification of the assignment.

(2) So far as the right to payment or a part thereof under an assigned contract has not been fully earned by performance, and notwithstanding notification of the assignment, any modification of or substitution for the contract made in good faith and in accordance with reasonable commercial standards is effective against an assignee unless the account debtor has otherwise agreed but the assignee acquires corresponding rights under the modified or substituted contract. The assignment may provide that such modification or substitution is a breach by the assignor.

(3) The account debtor is authorized to pay the assignor until the account debtor receives notification that the amount due or to become due has been assigned and that payment is to be made to the assignee. A notification which does not reasonably identify the rights assigned is ineffective. If requested by the account debtor, the assignee must seasonably furnish reasonable proof that the assignment has been made and unless he does so the account debtor may pay the assignor.

(4) A term in any contract between an account debtor and an assignor is ineffective if it prohibits assignment of an account or prohibits creation of a security interest in a general intangible for money due or to become due or requires the account debtor's consent to such assignment or security interest.

PART 4
Filing

§ 9—401. *Place of Filing; Erroneous Filing; Removal of Collateral.*

First Alternative Subsection (1)

(1) The proper place to file in order to perfect a security interest is as follows:

(a) when the collateral is timber to be cut or is minerals or the like (including oil and gas) or accounts subject to subsection (5) of Section 9—103, or when the financing statement is filed as a fixture filing (Section 9—313) and the collateral is goods which are or are to become fixtures, then in the office where a mortgage on the real estate would be filed or recorded;

(b) in all other cases, in the office of the [Secretary of State].

Second Alternative Subsection (1)

(1) The proper place to file in order to perfect a security interest is as follows:

(a) when the collateral is equipment used in farming operations, or farm products, or accounts or general intangibles arising from or relating to the sale of farm products by a farmer, or consumer goods, then in the office of the ______ in the county of the debtor's residence or if the debtor is not a resident of this state then in the office of the ______ in the county where the goods are kept, and in addition when the collateral is crops growing or to be grown in the office of the ______in the county where the land is located;

(b) when the collateral is timber to be cut or is minerals or the like (including oil and gas) or accounts subject to subsection (5) of Section 9—103, or when the financing statement is filed as a fixture filing (Section 9—313) and the collateral is goods which are or are to become fixtures, then in the office where a mortgage on the real estate would be filed or recorded;

(c) in all other cases, in the office of the [Secretary of State].

Third Alternative Subsection (1)

(1) The proper place to file in order to perfect a security interest is as follows:

(a) when the collateral is equipment used in farming operations, or farm products, or accounts or general intangibles arising from or relating to the sale of farm products by a farmer, or consumer goods, then in the office of the ______ in the county of the debtor's residence or if the debtor is not a resident of this state then in the office of the ______ in the county where the goods are kept, and in addition when the collateral is crops growing or to be grown in the office of the ______ in the county where the land is located;

(b) when the collateral is timber to be cut or is minerals or the like (including oil and gas) or accounts subject to subsection (5) of Section 9—103, or when the financing statement is filed as a fixture filing (Section 9—313) and the collateral is goods which are or are to become fixtures, then in the office where a mortgage on the real estate would be filed or recorded;

(c) in all other cases, in the office of the [Secretary of State] and in addition, if

the debtor has a place of business in only one county of this state, also in the office of ______ of such county, or, if the debtor has no place of business in this state, but resides in the state, also in the office of ______ of the county in which he resides.

(2) A filing which is made in good faith in an improper place or not in all of the places required by this section is nevertheless effective with regard to any collateral as to which the filing complied with the requirements of this Article and is also effective with regard to collateral covered by the financing statement against any person who has knowledge of the contents of such financing statement.

(3) A filing which is made in the proper place in this state continues effective even though the debtor's residence or place of business or the location of the collateral or its use, whichever controlled the original filing, is thereafter changed.

Alternative Subsection (3)

[(3) A filing which is made in the proper county continues effective for four months after a change to another county of the debtor's residence or place of business or the location of the collateral, whichever controlled the original filing. It becomes ineffective thereafter unless a copy of the financing statement signed by the secured party is filed in the new county within said period. The security interest may also be perfected in the new county after the expiration of the four-month period; in such case perfection dates from the time of perfection in the new county. A change in the use of the collateral does not impair the effectiveness of the original filing.]

(4) The rules stated in Section 9—103 determine whether filing is necessary in this state.

(5) Notwithstanding the preceding subsections, and subject to subsection (3) of Section 9—302, the proper place to file in order to perfect a security interest in collateral, including fixtures, of a transmitting utility is the office of the [Secretary of State].

This filing constitutes a fixture filing (Section 9—313) as to the collateral described therein which is or is to become fixtures.

(6) For the purposes of this section, the residence of an organization is its place of business if it has one or its chief executive office if it has more than one place of business.

§ 9—402. *Formal Requisites of Financing Statement; Amendments; Mortgage as Financing Statement.*

(1) A financing statement is sufficient if it gives the names of the debtor and the secured party, is signed by the debtor, gives an address of the secured party from which information concerning the security interest may be obtained, gives a mailing address of the debtor and contains a statement indicating the types, or describing the items, of collateral. A financing statement may be filed before a security agreement is made or a security interest otherwise attaches. When the financing statement covers crops growing or to be grown, the statement must also contain a description of the real estate concerned. When the financing statement covers timber to be cut or covers minerals or the like (including oil and gas) or accounts subject to subsection (5) of Section 9—103, or when the financing statement is filed as a fixture filing (Section 9—313) and the collateral is goods which are or are to become fixtures, the statement must also comply with subsection (5). A copy of the security agreement is sufficient as a financing statement if it contains the above information and is signed by the debtor. A carbon, photographic or other reproduction of a security agreement or a financing statement is sufficient as a financing statement if the security agreement so provides or if the original has been filed in this state.

(2) A financing statement which otherwise complies with subsection (1) is sufficient when it is signed by the secured party instead of the debtor if it is filed to perfect a security interest in

(a) collateral already subject to a security interest in another jurisdiction when it is brought into this state, or when the debtor's location is changed to this state. Such a financing statement must state that the collateral was brought into this state or that the debtor's location was changed to this state under such circumstances; or

(b) proceeds under Section 9—306 if the security interest in the original collateral was perfected. Such a financing statement must describe the original collateral; or

(c) collateral as to which the filing has lapsed; or

(d) collateral acquired after a change of name, identity or corporate structure of the debtor (subsection (7)).

(3) A form substantially as follows is sufficient to comply with subsection (1):

Name of debtor (or assignor)________________
Address ________________
Name of secured party (or assignee) ________________
Address ________________

1. This financing statement covers the following types (or items) of property:

(Describe)

2. (If collateral is crops) The above described crops are growing or are to be grown on:

(Describe Real Estate)

3. (If applicable) The above goods are to become fixtures on *

*Where appropriate substitute either "The above timber is standing on _______" or "The above minerals or the like (including oil and gas) or accounts will be financed at the wellhead or minehead of the well or mine located on _______."

(Describe Real Estate) ________________ and this financing statement is to be filed [for record] in the real estate records. (If the debtor does not have an interest of record) The name of a record owner is________________

4. (If products of collateral are claimed) Products of the collateral are also covered.

(use whichever is applicable)
____
Signature of Debtor (or Assignor)
____
Signature of Secured Party (or Assignee)

(4) A financing statement may be amended by filing a writing signed by both the debtor and the secured party. An amendment does not extend the period of effectiveness of a financing statement. If any amendment adds collateral, it is effective as to the added collateral only from the filing date of the amendment. In this Article, unless the context otherwise requires, the term "financing statement" means the original financing statement and any amendments.

(5) A financing statement covering timber to be cut or covering minerals or the like (including oil and gas) or accounts subject to subsection (5) of Section 9—103, or a financing statement filed as a fixture filing (Section 9—313) where the debtor is not a transmitting utility, must show that it covers this type of collateral, must recite that it is to be filed [for record] in the real estate records, and the financing statement must contain a description of the real estate [sufficient if it were contained in a mortgage of the real estate to give constructive notice of the mortgage under the law of this state]. If the debtor does not have an interest of record in the real estate, the financing statement must show the name of a record owner.

(6) A mortgage is effective as a financing statement filed as a fixture filing from the date of its recording if

(a) the goods are described in the mortgage by item or type; and

(b) the goods are or are to become fixtures related to the real estate described in the mortgage; and

(c) the mortgage complies with the requirements for a financing statement in this section other than a recital that it is to be filed in the real estate records; and

(d) the mortgage is duly recorded.

No fee with reference to the financing statement is required other than the regular recording and satisfaction fees with respect to the mortgage.

(7) A financing statement sufficiently shows the name of the debtor if it gives the individual, partnership or corporate name of the debtor, whether or not it adds other trade names or names of partners. Where the debtor so changes his name or in the case of an organization its name, identity or corporate structure that a filed financing statement becomes seriously misleading, the filing is not effective to perfect a security interest in collateral acquired by the debtor more than four months after the change, unless a new appropriate financing statement is filed before the expiration of that time. A filed financing statement remains effective with respect to collateral transferred by the debtor even though the secured party knows of or consents to the transfer.

(8) A financing statement substantially complying with the requirements of this section is effective even though it contains minor errors which are not seriously misleading.

§ 9—403. *What Constitutes Filing; Duration of Filing; Effect of Lapsed Filing; Duties of Filing Officer.*

(1) Presentation for filing of a financing statement and tender of the filing fee or acceptance of the statement by the filing officer constitutes filing under this Article.

(2) Except as provided in subsection (6) a filed financing statement is effective for a period of five years from the date of filing. The effectiveness of a filed financing statement lapses on the expiration of the five year period unless a continuation statement is filed prior to the lapse. If a security interest perfected by filing exists at the time insolvency proceedings are commenced by or against the debtor, the security interest remains perfected until termination of the insolvency proceedings and thereafter for a period of sixty days or until expiration of the five year period, whichever occurs later. Upon lapse the security interest becomes unperfected, unless it is perfected without filing. If the security interest becomes unperfected upon lapse, it is deemed to have been unperfected as against a person who became a purchaser or lien creditor before lapse.

(3) A continuation statement may be filed by the secured party within six months prior to the expiration of the five year period specified in subsection (2). Any such continuation statement must be signed by the secured party, identify the original statement by file number and state that the original statement is still effective. A continuation statement signed by a person other than the secured party of record must be accompanied by a separate written statement of assignment signed by the secured party of record and complying with subsection (2) of Section 9—405, including payment of the required fee. Upon timely filing of the continuation statement, the effectiveness of the original statement is continued for five years after the last date to which the filing was effective whereupon it lapses in the same manner as provided in subsection (2) unless another continuation statement is filed prior to such lapse. Succeeding continuation statements may be filed in the same manner to continue the effectiveness of the original statement. Unless a statute on disposition of public records provides otherwise, the filing officer may remove a lapsed statement from the files and destroy it immediately if he has retained a microfilm or other photographic record, or in other cases after one year after the lapse. The filing officer shall so arrange matters by physical annexation of financing statements to continuation statements or other related filings, or by other means, that if he physically destroys the financing statements of a period more than five years past, those which have been continued by a continuation statement or which are still effective under subsection (6) shall be retained.

(4) Except as provided in subsection (7) a filing officer shall mark each statement with a file number and with the date and hour of filing and shall hold the statement or a microfilm or other photographic copy thereof for public inspection. In addition the filing officer shall index the statement according to the name of the debtor and shall note in the index the file number and the address of the debtor given in the statement.

(5) The uniform fee for filing and indexing and for stamping a copy furnished by the secured party to show the date and place of filing for an original financing statement or for a continuation statement shall be $______ if the statement is in the standard form prescribed by the [Secretary of State] and otherwise shall be $______, plus in each case, if the financing statement is subject to subsection (5) of Section 9—402, $______. The uniform fee for each name more than one required to be indexed shall be $______. The secured party may at his option show a trade name for any person and an extra uniform indexing fee of $______ shall be paid with respect thereto.

(6) If the debtor is a transmitting utility (subsection (5) of Section 9—401) and a filed financing statement so states, it is effective until a termination statement is filed. A real estate mortgage which is effective as a fixture filing under subsection (6) of Section 9—402 remains effective as a fixture filing until the mortgage is released or satisfied of record or its effectiveness otherwise terminates as to the real estate.

(7) When a financing statement covers timber to be cut or covers minerals or the like (including oil and gas) or accounts subject to subsection (5) of Section 9—103, or is filed as a fixture filing, [it shall be filed for record and] the filing officer shall index it under the names of the debtor and any owner of record shown on the financing statement in the same fashion as if they were the mortgagors in a mortgage of the real estate described, and, to the extent that the law of this state provides for indexing of mortgages under the name of the mortgagee, under the name of the secured party as if he were the mortgagee thereunder, or where indexing is by description in the same fashion as if the financing statement were a mortgage of the real estate described.

§ 9—404. *Termination Statement.*

(1) If a financing statement covering consumer goods is filed on or after ______, then within one month or within ten days following written demand by the debtor after there is no outstanding secured obligation and no commitment to make advances, incur obligations or otherwise give value, the secured party must file with each filing officer with whom the financing statement was filed, a termination statement to the effect that he no longer claims a security interest under the financing statement, which shall be identified by file number. In other cases whenever there is no outstanding secured obligation and no commitment to make advances, incur obligations or otherwise give value, the secured party must on written demand by the debtor send the debtor, for each filing officer with whom the financing statement was filed, a termination statement to the effect that he no longer claims a security interest under the financing statement, which shall be identified by file number. A termination statement signed by a person other than the secured party of record must be accompanied by a separate written statement of assignment signed by the secured party of record complying with subsection (2) of Section 9—405, including payment of the required fee. If the affected secured party fails to file such a termination statement as required by this subsection, or to send such a termination statement within ten days after proper demand therefor, he shall be liable to the debtor for one hundred dollars, and in addition for any loss caused to the debtor by such failure.

(2) On presentation to the filing officer of such a termination statement he must note it in the index. If he has received the termination statement in duplicate, he shall return one copy of the termination statement to the secured party stamped to show the time of receipt thereof. If the filing officer has a microfilm or other photographic record of the financing statement, and of any related continuation statement, statement of assignment and statement of release, he may remove the originals from the files at any time after receipt of the termination statement, or if he has no

such record, he may remove them from the files at any time after one year after receipt of the termination statement.

(3) If the termination statement is in the standard form prescribed by the [Secretary of State], the uniform fee for filing and indexing the termination statement shall be $______, and otherwise shall be $______, plus in each case an additional fee of $______ for each name more than one against which the termination statement is required to be indexed.

§ 9—405. ***Assignment of Security Interest; Duties of Filing Officer; Fees.***

(1) A financing statement may disclose an assignment of a security interest in the collateral described in the financing statement by indication in the financing statement of the name and address of the assignee or by an assignment itself or a copy thereof on the face or back of the statement. On presentation to the filing officer of such a financing statement the filing officer shall mark the same as provided in Section 9—403(4). The uniform fee for filing, indexing and furnishing filing data for a financing statement so indicating an assignment shall be $______ if the statement is in the standard form prescribed by the [Secretary of State] and otherwise shall be $______, plus in each case an additional fee of $______ for each name more than one against which the financing statement is required to be indexed.

(2) A secured party may assign of record all or part of his rights under a financing statement by the filing in the place where the original financing statement was filed of a separate written statement of assignment signed by the secured party of record and setting forth the name of the secured party of record and the debtor, the file number and the date of filing of the financing statement and the name and address of the assignee and containing a description of the collateral assigned. A copy of the assignment is sufficient as a separate statement if it complies with the preceding sentence. On presentation to the filing officer of such a separate statement, the filing officer shall mark such separate statement with the date and hour of the filing. He shall note the assignment on the index of the financing statement, or in the case of a fixture filing, or a filing covering timber to be cut, or covering minerals or the like (including oil and gas) or accounts subject to subsection (5) of Section 9—103, he shall index the assignment under the name of the assignor as grantor and, to the extent that the law of this state provides for indexing the assignment of a mortgage under the name of the assignee, he shall index the assignment of the financing statement under the name of the assignee. The uniform fee for filing, indexing and furnishing filing data about such a separate statement of assignment shall be $______ if the statement is in the standard form prescribed by the [Secretary of State] and otherwise shall be $______, plus in each case an additional fee of $______ for each name more than one against which the statement of assignment is required to be indexed. Notwithstanding the provisions of this subsection, an assignment of record of a security interest in a fixture contained in a mortgage effective as a fixture filing (subsection (6) of Section 9—402) may be made only by an assignment of the mortgage in the manner provided by the law of this state other than this Act.

(3) After the disclosure or filing of an assignment under this section, the assignee is the secured party of record.

§ 9—406. ***Release of Collateral; Duties of Filing Officer; Fees.***

A secured party of record may by his signed statement release all or a part of any collateral described in a filed financing statement. The statement of release is sufficient if it contains a description of the collateral being released, the name and address of the debtor, the name and address of the secured party, and the file number of the financing statement. A statement of release signed by a person other than the secured party of record must be accompanied by a separate written statement of assignment signed by the secured party of record and complying with subsection (2) of Section 9—405, including payment of the required fee. Upon presentation of such a statement of release to the filing officer he shall mark the statement with the hour and date of filing and shall note the same upon the margin of the index of the filing of the financing statement. The uniform fee for filing and noting such a statement of release shall be $______ if the statement is in the standard form prescribed by the [Secretary of State] and otherwise shall be $______, plus in each case an additional fee of $______ for each name more than one against which the statement of release is required to be indexed.

§ 9—407. ***Information From Filing Officer.***

[(1) If the person filing any financing statement, termination statement, statement of assignment, or statement of release, furnishes the filing officer a copy thereof, the filing officer shall upon request note upon the copy the file number and date and hour of the filing of the original and deliver or send the copy to such person.]

[(2) Upon request of any person, the filing officer shall issue his certificate showing whether there is on file on the date and hour stated therein, any presently effective financing statement naming a particular debtor and any statement of assignment thereof and if there is, giving the date and hour of filing of each such statement and the names and addresses of each secured party therein. The uniform fee for such a certificate shall be $______ if the request for the certificate is in the standard form prescribed by the [Secretary of State] and otherwise shall be $______. Upon request the filing officer shall furnish a copy of any filed financing statement or statement of assignment for a uniform fee of $______ per page.]

§ 9—408. ***Financing Statements Covering Consigned or Leased Goods.***

A consignor or lessor of goods may file a financing statement using the terms "consignor," "consignee," "lessor," "lessee" or the like instead of the terms specified in Section 9—402. The provisions of this Part shall apply as appropriate to such a financing statement but its filing shall not of itself be a factor in determining whether or not the consignment or lease is intended as security (Section 1—201(37)). However, if it is determined for other reasons that the consignment or lease is so intended, a security interest of the consignor or lessor which attaches to the consigned or leased goods is perfected by such filing.

PART 5
Default

§ 9—501. ***Default; Procedure When Security Agreement Covers Both Real and Personal Property.***

(1) When a debtor is in default under a security agreement, a secured party has the rights and remedies provided in this Part and except as limited by subsection (3) those provided in the security agreement. He may reduce his claim to judgment, foreclose or otherwise enforce the security interest by any available judicial procedure. If the collateral is documents the secured party may

proceed either as to the documents or as to the goods covered thereby. A secured party in possession has the rights, remedies and duties provided in Section 9—207. The rights and remedies referred to in this subsection are cumulative.

(2) After default, the debtor has the rights and remedies provided in this Part, those provided in the security agreement and those provided in Section 9—207.

(3) To the extent that they give rights to the debtor and impose duties on the secured party, the rules stated in the subsections referred to below may not be waived or varied except as provided with respect to compulsory disposition of collateral (subsection (3) of Section 9—504 and Section 9—505) and with respect to redemption of collateral (Section 9—506) but the parties may by agreement determine the standards by which the fulfillment of these rights and duties is to be measured if such standards are not manifestly unreasonable:

(a) subsection (2) of Section 9—502 and subsection (2) of Section 9—504 insofar as they require accounting for surplus proceeds of collateral;

(b) subsection (3) of Section 9—504 and subsection (1) of Section 9—505 which deal with disposition of collateral;

(c) subsection (2) of Section 9—505 which deals with acceptance of collateral as discharge of obligation;

(d) Section 9—506 which deals with redemption of collateral; and

(e) subsection (1) of Section 9—507 which deals with the secured party's liability for failure to comply with this Part.

(4) If the security agreement covers both real and personal property, the secured party may proceed under this Part as to the personal property or he may proceed as to both the real and the personal property in accordance with his rights and remedies in respect of the real property in which case the provisions of this Part do not apply.

(5) When a secured party has reduced his claim to judgment the lien of any levy which may be made upon his collateral by virtue of any execution based upon the judgment shall relate back to the date of the perfection of the security interest in such collateral. A judicial sale, pursuant to such execution, is a foreclosure of the security interest by judicial procedure within the meaning of this section, and the secured party may purchase at the sale and thereafter hold the collateral free of any other requirements of this Article.

§ 9—502. *Collection Rights of Secured Party.*

(1) When so agreed and in any event on default the secured party is entitled to notify an account debtor or the obligor on an instrument to make payment to him whether or not the assignor was theretofore making collections on the collateral, and also to take control of any proceeds to which he is entitled under Section 9—306.

(2) A secured party who by agreement is entitled to charge back uncollected collateral or otherwise to full or limited recourse against the debtor and who undertakes to collect from the account debtors or obligors must proceed in a commercially reasonable manner and may deduct his reasonable expenses of realization from the collections. If the security agreement secures an indebtedness, the secured party must account to the debtor for any surplus, and unless otherwise agreed, the debtor is liable for any deficiency. But, if the underlying transaction was a sale of accounts or chattel paper, the debtor is entitled to any surplus or is liable for any deficiency only if the security agreement so provides.

§ 9—503. *Secured Party's Right to Take Possession After Default.*

Unless otherwise agreed a secured party has on default the right to take possession of the collateral. In taking possession a secured party may proceed without judicial process if this can be done without breach of the peace or may proceed by action. If the security agreement so provides the secured party may require the debtor to assemble the collateral and make it available to the secured party at a place to be designated by the secured party which is reasonably convenient to both parties. Without removal a secured party may render equipment unusable, and may dispose of collateral on the debtor's premises under Section 9—504.

§ 9—504. *Secured Party's Right to Dispose of Collateral After Default; Effect of Disposition.*

(1) A secured party after default may sell, lease or otherwise dispose of any or all of the collateral in its then condition or following any commercially reasonable preparation or processing. Any sale of goods is subject to the Article on Sales (Article 2). The proceeds of disposition shall be applied in the order following to

(a) the reasonable expenses of retaking, holding, preparing for sale or lease, selling, leasing and the like and, to the extent provided for in the agreement and not prohibited by law, the reasonable attorneys' fees and legal expenses incurred by the secured party;

(b) the satisfaction of indebtedness secured by the security interest under which the disposition is made;

(c) the satisfaction of indebtedness secured by any subordinate security interest in the collateral if written notification of demand therefor is received before distribution of the proceeds is completed. If requested by the secured party, the holder of a subordinate security interest must seasonably furnish reasonable proof of his interest, and unless he does so, the secured party need not comply with his demand.

(2) If the security interest secures an indebtedness, the secured party must account to the debtor for any surplus, and, unless otherwise agreed, the debtor is liable for any deficiency. But if the underlying transaction was a sale of accounts or chattel paper, the debtor is entitled to any surplus or is liable for any deficiency only if the security agreement so provides.

(3) Disposition of the collateral may be by public or private proceedings and may be made by way of one or more contracts. Sale or other disposition may be as a unit or in parcels and at any time and place and on any terms but every aspect of the disposition including the method, manner, time, place and terms must be commercially reasonable. Unless collateral is perishable or threatens to decline speedily in value or is of a type customarily sold on a recognized market, reasonable notification of the time and place of any public sale or reasonable notification of the time after which any private sale or other intended disposition is to be made shall be sent by the secured party to the debtor, if he has not signed after default a statement renouncing or modifying his right to notification of sale. In the case of consumer goods no other notification need be sent. In other cases notification shall be sent to any other secured party from whom the secured party has received (before sending his notification to the debtor or before the debtor's renunciation of his rights) written notice of a claim of an interest in the collateral. The secured party may buy at any

public sale and if the collateral is of a type customarily sold in a recognized market or is of a type which is the subject of widely distributed standard price quotations he may buy at private sale.

(4) When collateral is disposed of by a secured party after default, the disposition transfers to a purchaser for value all of the debtor's rights therein, discharges the security interest under which it is made and any security interest or lien subordinate thereto. The purchaser takes free of all such rights and interests even though the secured party fails to comply with the requirements of this Part or of any judicial proceedings

(a) in the case of a public sale, if the purchaser has no knowledge of any defects in the sale and if he does not buy in collusion with the secured party, other bidders or the person conducting the sale; or

(b) in any other case, if the purchaser acts in good faith.

(5) A person who is liable to a secured party under a guaranty, indorsement, repurchase agreement or the like and who receives a transfer of collateral from the secured party or is subrogated to his rights has thereafter the rights and duties of the secured party. Such a transfer of collateral is not a sale or disposition of the collateral under this Article.

§ 9—505. *Compulsory Disposition of Collateral; Acceptance of the Collateral as Discharge of Obligation.*

(1) If the debtor has paid sixty percent of the cash price in the case of a purchase money security interest in consumer goods or sixty percent of the loan in the case of another security interest in consumer goods, and has not signed after default a statement renouncing or modifying his rights under this Part a secured party who has taken possession of collateral must dispose of it under Section 9—504 and if he fails to do so within ninety days after he takes possession the debtor at his option may recover in conversion or under Section 9—507(1) on secured party's liability.

(2) In any other case involving consumer goods or any other collateral a secured party in possession may, after default, propose to retain the collateral in satisfaction of the obligation. Written notice of such proposal shall be sent to the debtor if he has not signed after default a statement renouncing or modifying his rights under this subsection. In the case of consumer goods no other notice need be given. In other cases notice shall be sent to any other secured party from whom the secured party has received (before sending his notice to the debtor or before the debtor's renunciation of his rights) written notice of a claim of an interest in the collateral. If the secured party receives objection in writing from a person entitled to receive notification within twenty-one days after the notice was sent, the secured party must dispose of the collateral under Section 9—504. In the absence of such written objection the secured party may retain the collateral in satisfaction of the debtor's obligation. Amended in 1972.

§ 9—506. *Debtor's Right to Redeem Collateral.*

At any time before the secured party has disposed of collateral or entered into a contract for its disposition under Section 9—504 or before the obligation has been discharged under Section 9—505(2) the debtor or any other secured party may unless otherwise agreed in writing after default redeem the collateral by tendering fulfillment of all obligations secured by the collateral as well as the expenses reasonably incurred by the secured party in retaking, holding and preparing the collateral for disposition, in arranging for the sale, and to the extent provided in the agreement and not prohibited by law, his reasonable attorneys' fees and legal expenses.

§ 9—507. *Secured Party's Liability for Failure to Comply With This Part.*

(1) If it is established that the secured party is not proceeding in accordance with the provisions of this Part disposition may be ordered or restrained on appropriate terms and conditions. If the disposition has occurred the debtor or any person entitled to notification or whose security interest has been made known to the secured party prior to the disposition has a right to recover from the secured party any loss caused by a failure to comply with the provisions of this Part. If the collateral is consumer goods, the debtor has a right to recover in any event an amount not less than the credit service charge plus 10 percent of the principal amount of the debt or the time price differential plus 10 percent of the cash price.

(2) The fact that a better price could have been obtained by a sale at a different time or in a different method from that selected by the secured party is not of itself sufficient to establish that the sale was not made in a commercially reasonable manner. If the secured party either sells the collateral in the usual manner in any recognized market therefor or if he sells at the price current in such market at the time of his sale or if he has otherwise sold in conformity with reasonable commercial practices among dealers in the type of property sold he has sold in a commercially reasonable manner. The principles stated in the two preceding sentences with respect to sales also apply as may be appropriate to other types of disposition. A disposition which has been approved in any judicial proceeding or by any bona fide creditors' committee or representative of creditors shall conclusively be deemed to be commercially reasonable, but this sentence does not indicate that any such approval must be obtained in any case nor does it indicate that any disposition not so approved is not commercially reasonable.

GLOSSARY

A fortiori All the more; said of a conclusion that follows with even greater logical necessity than another already accepted in the argument.
Acceleration clauses Clauses in contracts that advance the date for payment based on the occurrence of a condition or the breach of a duty.
Acceptance The agreement by the maker or the drawee to accept and/or pay a negotiable instrument upon presentment.
Accessory to the crime A situation in which one person assists another in the commission of a crime, without being the primary actor.
Accommodation Something supplied for a convenience or to satisfy a need.
Accounts Rights to payments for goods sold or leased or for services rendered that are not evidenced by an instrument or chattel paper.
Actionable Furnishing legal grounds for an action.
Adduced Given as proof.
Administrators The persons who have been empowered by an appropriate court to handle the estate of a deceased person.
Admission A statement acknowledging the truth of an allegation and accepted in court as evidence against the party making the admission.
Advisory opinion A formal opinion by a judge, court, or law officer on a question of law submitted by a legislative body or a government official but not presented in an actual case.
Affidavit Written statement made under oath.
Affirmative defense A defense to a cause of action that the defendant must raise.
Aid and abet To help, assist, or facilitate the commission of a crime; to promote the accomplishment of a crime.
Alienation The transfer of ownership to another.
Ambient Pertaining to the surrounding atmosphere or the environment.
Ambiguities Uncertainties regarding the meanings of expressions used in contractual agreements.
Ambiguity Subject to two or more reasonable interpretations.
Amoral Being neither moral nor immoral; lying outside the sphere to which moral judgments apply.
Appellants Persons who appeal the decision of the lower court.
Appellate court A court that has the power to review the decisions of lower courts.
Aquifers Water-bearing strata of permeable rock, sand, or gravel.
Arbitration The submission for determination of a disputed matter to private unofficial persons selected in a manner provided by law or agreement, with the substitution of their award or decision for the judgment of a court.
Arbitrator An independent person chosen by the parties or appointed by statute and to whom the issues are submitted for settlement outside of court.
Arraigned Called before a court to enter a plea on an indictment or criminal complaint.
Assault A threat to touch someone in an undesired manner (a battery).
Assignable Legally capable of being transferred from one person to another.
Assignment for the benefit of creditors An assignment in trust made by debtors for the payment of their debts.
At will Having no specific date or circumstance to bring about a dissolution.
Attachment Seizure of the defendant's property.
Bail Technique for the release of a person charged with a crime while ensuring his or her presence in the court at future hearings by the posting of money or property.
Bailee One to whom goods are delivered with the understanding that they will be returned at a future time.
Bankruptcy An area of law designed to give an "honest debtor" a fresh start; the proceedings undertaken against a person or a firm under the bankruptcy laws.
Bar In the legal sense, to prevent or to stop.
Battery Unauthorized touching of another person without legal justification or that person's consent.
Beneficial owner One who does not have title to the property but who has rights in the property; the equitable, as opposed to the legal, owner of the property.

Beyond a reasonable doubt The degree of proof required in a criminal trial, which is proof to a moral certainty; there is no other reasonable interpretation.

Boilerplate Standard contract language found in all instruments of a like nature.

Bona fide In good faith; honest; without deceit; innocent.

Bona fide occupational qualification A defense to charges of discrimination based on religion, sex, or national origin but not to charges of racial discrimination; a situation in which one of these categories is essential to the performance of the job.

Bona fide purchaser A person who purchases in good faith, for value, and without notice of any defects or defenses affecting the sale or transaction.

Boycotts Concerted refusals to deal with firms so as to disrupt the business of those firms.

Cancellation Any action shown on the face of a contract that indicates an intent to destroy the obligation of the contract.

Capital Business assets or property of a permanent nature used in carrying on a business.

Capital contribution Money or assets invested by the business owners for commencing and/or promoting an enterprise.

Carriage The transportation of goods or people from one location to another.

Carrier A third party hired to deliver the goods from the seller to the buyer.

Case and controversy A case brought before the court where the plaintiff and defendant are really opposed to one another on significant issues.

Cases and controversies Claims brought before the court in regular proceedings to protect or enforce rights or to prevent or punish wrongs.

Caucusing Meditation technique in which the mediator meets with each party separately.

Caveat emptor A term meaning "let the buyer beware"; a reference to the fact that the buyer had very few, if any, remedies for defective products.

Censured Formally reprimanded for specific conduct.

Certiorari A writ used by a superior court to direct an inferior court to send it the records and proceedings in a case for review.

Charging order A court order permitting a creditor to receive profits from the operation of a business; especially common in partnership situations.

Chattel paper A writing that evidences both a monetary obligation and a security interest in specific goods.

Chattels Articles of personal (as opposed to real) property.

Choses in action A personal right not reduced to possession but recoverable in a suit at law.

Circumscribe Limit the range of activity associated with something.

CISG The United Nations Convention on Contracts for the International Sale of Goods.

Civil rights The rights in the first 10 amendments to the U.S. Constitution (the Bill of Rights) and due process and equal protection under the Fourteenth Amendment.

Class action lawsuit A lawsuit involving a group of plaintiffs or defendants who are in substantially the same situation.

Clearinghouse An association of banks and financial institutions that "clear" items between banks.

Codicil A separate written document that modifies an existing will.

Common carrier A company in the business of transporting goods or people for a fee and holding itself out as serving the general public.

Common law Unwritten law, which is based on custom, usage, and court decisions; different from statute law, which consists of laws passed by legislatures.

Common law husband A husband who did not participate in the usual wedding ceremony with a legal marriage license. The states that recognize common law marriages generally require that the couple consistently live together and tell people that they are husband and wife.

Common law states States in which married couples cannot create community property.

Community property A special form of joint ownership between husband and wife permitted in certain states called community property states.

Community property states States in which married couples generally create community property.

Commutative justice The attempt to give all persons equal treatment based on the assumption that equal treatment is appropriate. Individual differences are not considered.

Comparative negligence A defense in a negligence suit that reduces the plaintiff's award based on the plaintiff's own negligence.

Compiler program One that converts a high-level programming language into binary or machine code.

Complaint In civil practice, the plaintiff's first pleading. It informs the defendant that he or she is being sued.

Concessionaires Operators of refreshment centers.

Conclusive presumption An inference of the truth or falsity of a fact from which a result must follow as a matter of law.

Conditional sales contracts Sales contracts in which the transfer of title is subject to a condition, most commonly the payment of the full purchase price by the buyer.

Confirmation A written memorandum of the agreement; a notation that provides written evidence that an agreement was made.

Conglomerate mergers Mergers between noncompeting firms in different industries.

Consequential damages Damages or losses that occur as a result of the initial wrong but that are not direct and immediate.

Consignee A person to whom goods are shipped for sale and who generally can return all unsold goods to the consignor.

Consignor A person who ships goods to another party.

Conspicuous Easy to see or perceive; obvious.

Conspiracy An unlawful situation in which two or more people plan to engage in an illegal act or to use illegal means to achieve a lawful objective.

Constructive Inferred; amounting to or involving the act assumed.

Constructive trust A trust imposed by law to prevent the unjust enrichment of the person in possession of the property (the purported owner).

Consumer price index Measurement of how the price of a group of consumer goods changes between two time periods.

Contingency fee A fee stipulated to be paid to an attorney only if the case is settled or won or based on some other contingency or event.

Contracts of adhesion Contracts in which the terms are not open to negotiation; so-called take-it-or-leave-it contracts.

Convention An agreement between nations; a treaty.

Conversion The unauthorized and wrongful exercise of dominion and control over the personal property of another to the detriment of that other person.

Convert Change.

Cooperatives Groups of individuals, commonly laborers or farmers, who unite in a common enterprise and share the profits proportionately.

Corporation An artificial person or legal entity created by or under the authority of a state or nation, composed of a group of persons known as stockholders or shareholders.

Counterclaimed Presented a cause of action in opposition to the plaintiff's.

Court of Common Pleas Title used for some trial courts of general jurisdiction.

Creditor beneficiary A third party who is entitled to performance because the promisee has a contractual obligation with him or her.

Criminal law The body of law dealing with public wrongs called crimes.

Currency transaction report (CTR) A report businesses must file if a customer brings $10,000 or more in cash to the business.

Cy-pres doctrine Doctrine permitting the court to modify the trust in order to follow the creator's charitable intention as closely as possible.

Debt collector A business that collects accounts due and payable but does *not* extend the credit that underlies the debt being collected.

Decedent A person who has died.

Declaratory judgment A decision by a court that merely sets out the rights of the parties without ordering either party to perform any actions.

Default A failure to do what should be done, especially in the performance of a contractual obligation, without legal excuse or justification for the nonperformance.

Defendant A person who answers a lawsuit; the person whose behavior is the subject of the complaint.

Defenses A legal reason, excuse, or justification for the conduct of the party.

Defraud To deprive a person of property or of any interest, estate, or right by fraud, deceit, or artifice.

Delegated Assigned responsibility and/or authority by the person or group normally empowered to exercise the responsibility or authority.

Delivered Intentional transfer of physical possession of some thing or right to another person.

Deterrent A danger, difficulty, or other consideration that stops or prevents a person from acting.

Dictum An observation or remark by a judge, which is not necessarily involved in the case or essential to its resolution. An aside written by the judge.
Discharge Release from obligation or liability.
Discretion The right to use one's own judgment in selecting between alternatives.
Discretionary Having the freedom to make certain decisions.
Disenfranchised Restricted from enjoying certain constitutional or statutory rights; burdened by systemic prejudice or bigotry.
Disgorge Give up ill-gotten or illicit gains.
Dishonor A refusal to accept or to pay a negotiable instrument upon proper presentment.
Distributive justice The attempt to "distribute" justice in a way that considers inequalities among individuals.
Document of title Written evidence of ownership or of rights to something.
Domicile One's permanent home and principal residence. It is the place to which a person will return after traveling.
Double jeopardy A rule of criminal law that states that a person will not be tried in court more than once for the same criminal offense.
Draft An order for a third person to pay a sum certain in money without conditions, either at a preset time in the future or "on demand."
Due process The proper exercise of judicial authority as established by general concepts of law and morality.
Duress When one party enters into a contract due to a wrongful threat of force.
Easements Rights to the access and use of someone else's real estate; limited rights to use and enjoy the land of another.
Effluent Pertaining to an outflow of materials or an emanation.
Emancipation Freedom from the control or power of another; release from parental care; or the attainment of legal independence.
Employment at will An employment relationship in which, owing to the absence of any contractual obligation to remain in the relationship, either party can terminate the relationship at any time and for any reason not prohibited by law.
Encrypted code Code typed in one set of symbols and interpreted by the machine as another; used for security.
Encumbrancer The holder of a claim relating to real or personal property.
Entrustment The delivery of goods to a merchant who regularly deals in goods of the type delivered.
Equal protection The assurance that any person before the court will be treated the same as every other person before the court.
Equitable Arising from the branch of the legal system designed to provide a remedy where no remedy existed at common law; a system designed to provide fairness when there was no suitable remedy "at law."
Escrow Process of preparing for the exchange of real estate, deed, and other documents managed by a third party.
Estate tax A tax assessed on the total net (taxable) value of the estate.
Estoppel A legal bar (or impediment) that prevents a person from claiming or denying certain facts as a result of the person's previous conduct.
European Union The EU, formerly called the Common Market, creates a free-trade zone among the member nations of Europe.
***Ex post facto* law** A law passed after an occurrence or act that retrospectively changes the legal consequences of such act.
Exculpatory clauses Parts of agreements in which a prospective plaintiff agrees in advance not to seek to hold the prospective defendant liable for certain losses for which the prospective defendant otherwise would be liable.
Executors The persons named and appointed in a will by the testator to carry out the administration of the estate as established by the will.
Exemplary damages Punitive damages; damages imposed in a case to punish the defendant.
Expert A person with a high degree of skill or with a specialized knowledge.
Express Actually stated; communicated from one party to another.
Extinguished Destroyed, wiped out.
Facial Void on its face; totally invalid.
Fact-finding A process in which an arbitrator investigates a dispute and issues findings of fact and a nonbinding report.
Fair market value The current price for selling an asset between informed willing buyers and informed willing sellers.
Fiat An order issued by legal authority.

Fictitious payee A recipient of payments who has no right to the payments.
Fiduciary One who holds a special position of trust or confidence and who thereby is expected to act with the utmost good faith and loyalty.
Fiduciary duty The legal duty to exercise the highest degree of loyalty and good faith in handling the affairs of the person to whom the duty is owed.
Field warehousing A method of perfection in a secured transaction in which the creditor takes "possession" of a portion of the debtor's storage area.
First impression Case is presented to the court for an initial decision when the case presents an entirely novel question of law for the court's decision. It is not governed by any existing precedent.
Foreclose Cut off an existing ownership right in property.
Foreign corporation A corporation that received its articles of incorporation in another state.
Foreseeability The knowledge or notice that a result is likely to occur if a certain act occurs.
Forfeiture The loss of a right or privilege as a penalty for certain conduct.
Forum The court conducting the trial.
Forum shopping Choosing the court or place of jurisdiction that will be most favorable to the litigant.
Franchising Special privileges granted by a corporation that allow the franchisee to conduct business under the corporate name of the franchisor.
Fraud When one party enters into a contract due to a false statement of material fact.
Free enterprise The carrying on of free, legitimate business for profit.
Frivolous lawsuit A lawsuit that is clearly insufficient and is begun presumably to annoy, harass, or embarrass the opponent.
Fungible Virtually identical; interchangeable; descriptive of things that belong to a class and that are not identifiable individually.
Garnish Receive the debtor's assets that are in the hands of a third party; a remedy given to satisfy a debt owed.
Garnishment A legal proceeding in which assets of a debtor that are in the hands of a third person are ordered held by the third person or turned over to the creditor in full or partial satisfaction of the debt.
General intangibles Personal property other than goods, accounts, chattel paper, instruments, documents, or money; for example, goodwill, literary rights, patents, or copyrights.
Goods Movable, identifiable items of personal property.
Goodwill The good name and reputation of a business and the resulting ability to attract clients; the fixed and favorable consideration of customers arising from established and well-conducted business.
Grand jury A jury whose duty it is to receive complaints of criminal conduct and to return a bill of indictment if convinced a trial should be held.
Greenmail The process by which a firm threatens a corporate takeover by buying a significant portion of a corporation's stock and then selling it back to the corporation at a premium when the corporation's directors and executives, fearing for their positions, agree to buy the firm out.
Group bias Presumption that jurors are biased merely because they belong to an identifiable group based on race, religion, ethnicity, or gender.
Guarantor One who promises to answer for the payment of a debt or the performance of an obligation if the person liable in the first instance fails to make payment or to perform.
Guardian A person legally responsible for taking care of another who lacks the legal capacity to do so.
Habeas corpus The name given to a variety of writs issued to bring a party before a court or judge.
Hacker An outsider who gains unauthorized access to a computer or computer network.
Heirs Persons who actually inherit property from the decedent.
Holder A person who receives possession of a negotiable instrument by means of a negotiation.
Honorary trust An arrangement that does not meet trust requirements and thus is not enforceable, although it may be carried out voluntarily.
Illusory Fallacious; nominal as opposed to substantial; of false appearance.
Immemorial antiquity Goes back to earliest memory.
Impeach To question the truthfulness of a witness by means of some evidence.
Implied consent A concurrence of wills manifested by signs, actions, or facts, or by inaction or silence, which raises a presumption that agreement has been given.
Implied Presumed to be present under the circumstances; tacit.
In pari delicto Equally at fault or equally wrong.

In personam jurisdiction Authority over a specific person or corporation within the control of the court.

In propria persona In this context—in one's own proper person and not being represented by legal counsel. Here it has the same meaning as pro se.

In rem jurisdiction Authority over property or status within the control of the court.

Income beneficiaries Persons with an income interest in a trust.

Indemnify To reimburse a party for a loss suffered by that party for the benefit of another.

Independent contractor A person hired to perform a task but not subject to the specific control of the hiring party.

Indeterminant sentencing Criminal punishment, which does not have exact limits or maximum sentences.

Indictment A written accusation of criminal conduct issued to a court by a grand jury.

Indorsed Signature placed on the back of a negotiable instrument in order to properly negotiate to the next holder.

Informational picketing Picketing for the purpose of truthfully advising the public that an employer does not employ members of, or have a contract with, a labor organization.

Inheritance tax A tax assessed on transfers of estate assets at the owner's death. The rates vary depending on the owner's relationship to the recipient.

Injunction A writ issued by the court of equity ordering a person to do or not do a specified act.

Injunction *pendente lite* A preliminary injunction pending a suit.

Injunctive actions Lawsuits asking a court of equity to order a person to do or to refrain from doing some specified act.

Innately dangerous Dangerous as an existing characteristic; dangerous from the beginning.

Insolvency Inability to pay one's debts as they become due.

Insular Isolated from others.

Insureds Persons or entities covered under an insurance policy.

Interested party A party with an interest in the estate, such as a beneficiary, heir, or creditor.

Interpretation The process of discovering the meaning of a contract; the defining, discovering, and explaining of unclear language.

Interstate Between two or more states; between a point in one state and a point in another state.

Intervention Generally, a group of relatives and friends confront a person who drinks or uses drugs and explains to the user how serious and detrimental the use is.

Intestate share Portion of the estate that a person is entitled to inherit if there is no valid will.

Intra vires Acts within the scope of the power of a corporation.

Intrastate Begun, carried on, and completed wholly within the boundaries of a single state.

Investment securities Bonds, notes, certificates, and other instruments or contracts from which one expects to receive a return primarily from the efforts of others.

Invidious Repugnant; discrimination stemming from bigotry or prejudice.

Issue Lineal descendants, such as children, grandchildren, and great-grandchildren.

Issuer One who officially distributes an item or document.

Joint venture A commercial or maritime enterprise undertaken by several persons jointly; an association of two or more persons to carry out a single business enterprise for profit.

Judgment non obstante veredicto (judgment n.o.v.) Literally, judgment notwithstanding the verdict; a judgment entered by the court in favor of the plaintiff in circumstances in which the jury has rendered a verdict for the defendant (or vice versa).

Judgment proof Inability to pay a civil judgment if ordered to do so by the court.

Judicial questions Questions that are proper for a court to decide.

Judicial restraint A judicial policy of refusing to hear and decide certain types of cases.

Judicial review The power of the courts to say what the law is.

Junior secured parties Any secured parties whose security interests are subordinate to that of the foreclosing secured party.

Knocking down The acceptance of a bid by an auctioneer, signified by the falling of the gavel after the announcement that the goods are "Going, going, gone."

Laissez-faire A term meaning "hands-off"; the belief that business operates best when uninhibited by the government.

Landlocked Surrounded by land owned by others.

Land use regulation Laws that regulate the possession, ownership, and use of real property.

Lapse The expiration or the loss of an opportunity because of the passage of a time limit within which the opportunity had to be exercised.

Law merchant Those rules of trade and commerce used by merchants in England after 1066.

Leachings Oozings of water containing soil, sediments, chemicals, and other impurities.

Leases Contracts that grant the right to use and occupy realty.

Letters of credit Agreements made at the request of a customer that, upon another party's compliance with the conditions specified in the documents, the bank will honor drafts or other demands for payment.

Libel Any written or printed statement that tends to expose a person to public ridicule or to injure a person's reputation.

License A permission granted by a competent authority to do some act that, without such authorization, would be illegal or a trespass or a tort.

Lien creditor One whose debt is secured by a claim on specific property.

Limited partner A limited-partnership member who furnishes certain funds to the partnership and whose liability is restricted to the funds furnished.

Liquidate To collect assets, settle with creditors and debtors, and apportion any remaining assets.

Liquidated damages An amount expressly stipulated by the parties as the proper measure of damages if a breach occurs; cannot be a penalty.

Liquidation preferences Priorities given to creditors and owners when the enterprise is terminated and the assets are distributed.

Lockouts Plant closings or other refusals by employers to furnish work to employees during labor disputes.

Logotypes Identifying symbols.

Mala prohibita Wrong because it is prohibited.

Mandamus A type of writ that issues from a court of superior jurisdiction commanding the performance of a particular act specified therein.

Manifest A list or invoice.

Manual subscription Autograph; the act of physically writing one's name in longhand.

Market value The current price the stock will sell for on a stock exchange.

Marshal To arrange assets or claims in such a way as to secure the proper application of the assets to the claims.

Mechanic's lien Given to certain builders, artisans, and providers of material, a statutory protection that grants a lien on the building and the land improved by such persons.

Mens rea A guilty mind; a guilty or wrongful purpose; a criminal intent.

Mercantile Having to do with business, commerce, or trade.

Merchant A person who deals in goods of the kind, or otherwise, through his or her occupation, holds himself or herself out as having knowledge or skill peculiar to the practice or goods involved in the transaction.

Midnight deadline Midnight of the next business day after the day on which an item is received.

Mining partnership An association of several owners of a mine for cooperation in working the mine.

Money A legally recognized medium of exchange authorized or adopted by a government.

Monopoly The power of a firm to carry on a business or a trade to the exclusion of all competitors.

Moot Arguable; a point not properly submitted to the court for a resolution. Not capable of resolution.

Moot case A case not properly submitted to a court for resolution because it seeks to determine an abstract question that does not arise upon existing facts or rights.

Mortgage insurance Insurance that will provide funds to pay the mortgage balance on a home if the insured dies.

Mortgages Conditional transfers of property as security for a debt.

Motions Requests to a judge to take certain action. These requests are generally in writing.

Mutual assent The parties must agree to be bound by exactly the same terms.

NAFTA The North American Free Trade Agreement is a treaty among the United States, Canada, and Mexico designed to create a free trade zone within North America.

Negative clearance Permission given by the EU Commission to a firm or firms to act in a manner that appears to violate EU competition laws.

Negligence Failure to do something a reasonable person would do, or doing something a reasonable and prudent person would not do.

Negligence per se Inherent negligence; negligence without a need for further proof.
Negotiable A document that is transferable either by endorsement and delivery or by delivery alone.
Negotiable instruments Transferable documents used as credit instruments and as substitutes for money; governed by Article 3 of the UCC. Examples include checks, drafts, promissory notes, and certificates of deposit.
Nolo contendere A plea in a criminal proceeding that has the same effect as a plea of guilty but that cannot be used as evidence of guilt.
Nonjusticiable Not subject to the jurisdiction of a court; not a proper question for a court.
Novations By mutual agreement, substitutions of new contracts in place of preexisting ones, whether between the same parties or with new parties replacing one or more of the original parties.
Noxious Hurtful and offensive.
Nuisance Unlawful use of one's own property so as to injure the rights of another; unlawful interference with the use of public or private property.
Object code Translation of source code into lower-level language, consisting of numbers and symbols that the computer converts into electronic impulses (machine language).
Objective Capable of being observed and verified without being distorted by personal feelings and prejudices.
Obviousness of hazard The hazard in the product is obvious, such as a sharp knife.
Oligopoly An economic condition in which a small number of firms dominate a market but no one firm controls it.
Operating system computer programs Collections of systems software programs designed to help someone else program or use a computer and which allow the computer to execute programs and manage programming tasks.
Operation of law Certain automatic results that must occur following certain actions or facts because of established legal principles and not as the result of any voluntary choice by the parties involved.
Option A privilege existing in one person, for the giving of consideration, which allows him or her to accept an offer at any time during a specified period.
Output contract A contract that calls for the buyer to purchase all the seller's production during the term of the contract.
Outsiders Directors who are not shareholders or officers.
Overdraft A check or draft written by the drawer for an amount in excess of the amount on account, and accepted by the drawee.
Par value The face value assigned to a stock and printed on the stock certificate.
Parol evidence Oral statements.
Parol evidence rule A rule stating that when contracts are in writing, only the writing can be used to show the terms of the contract.
Perjuries False statements made under oath during court proceedings.
Personal representative A person who manages the financial affairs of another or an estate.
Petit jurors Ordinary jurors comprising the panel for the trial of a civil or criminal action.
Picketing Union activity in which persons stand near a place of work affected by an organizational drive or a strike so as to influence workers regarding union causes.
Plaintiff A person who files a lawsuit; the person who complains to the court.
Pledge A debtor's delivery of collateral to a creditor, who will possess the collateral until the debt is paid.
Plenary Full; complete; absolute.
Poison pill Any strategy adopted by the directors of a target firm in order to decrease their firm's attractiveness to an acquiring firm during an attempted hostile takeover.
Political questions Questions concerning government, the state, or politics that would encroach on executive or legislative powers.
Post-loss Obligations of insurance companies after a covered loss has actually occurred.
Precedents Prior court cases that control the decision in court.
Preempt Seize upon to the exclusion of others.
Prejudicial Causing harm, injurious, disadvantageous, or detrimental.
Prepayment clauses Contract clauses that allow the debtor to pay the debt before it is due without penalty.
Presentment A demand by a holder for the maker or the drawee of a negotiable instrument to accept and/or pay the instrument.
Preventive law Law designed to prevent harm or wrongdoing before it occurs.

Prima facie At first sight; on its face; something presumed to be true because of its appearance unless disproved by evidence to the contrary.
Prima facie case A case that is obvious on its face. It may be rebutted by evidence to the contrary.
Privilege A particular benefit or advantage beyond the common advantages of other citizens; an exceptional right, power, franchise, or immunity held by a person, class, or company.
Privity of contract Direct contractual relationship with another party.
Pro se Appearing in his or her own behalf, in person.
Probate The procedure for verifying that a will is authentic and should be implemented.
Probate codes State statutes that deal with the estates of incompetents and people who have died with or without a valid will.
Procedural law Methods of enforcing rights or obtaining compensation for the violation of rights.
Professionals In the sense used here, a member of a "learned profession," such as a doctor, a lawyer, or an accountant.
Profits The gain made in the enterprise, after deducting the costs incurred for labor, materials, rents, and all other expenses.
Promisee One to whom a promise or commitment has been made.
Promisors Those who make a promise or commitment.
Promissory estoppel A doctrine that prohibits a promisor from denying the making of a promise or from escaping the liability for that promise because of the justifiable reliance of the promisee that the promise would be kept.
Promissory note A written promise to pay a sum certain in money without conditions, either at a preset time in the future or "on demand."
Proprietary Characterized by private, exclusive ownership.
Proprietorship A business with legal rights or exclusive title vested in one individual; a solely owned business.
Prothonotary Title used in some states to designate the chief clerk of courts.
Proximate cause An act that naturally and foreseeably leads to harm or injury to another.
Proxy A person appointed and designated to act for another, especially at a public meeting.
Public domain Lands that are open to public use.
Public policy The general attitude of the public toward certain conduct; the public sense of morality, good conduct, and acceptable behavior to which citizens must conform.
Purported Gave the impression authority was present. Often this is a false impression.
Quantifiable Capable of exact statement; measurable, normally in numbers.
Quantum meruit An equitable remedy allowing one to recover the reasonable value of the services rendered.
Quasi in rem jurisdiction Authority obtained through property under the control of the court.
Quasi-judicial Partly judicial; empowered to hold hearings but not trials.
Quasi-legislative Partly legislative; empowered to enact rules and regulations but not statutes.
Ratification Accepting an act that was unauthorized when committed and becoming bound to that act upon its acceptance.
Rebuttable presumption A legal assumption that will be followed until a stronger proof or presumption is presented.
Receiver An unbiased person appointed by a court to receive, preserve, and manage the funds and property of a party.
Recognitional picketing Prohibited picketing in which a union attempts to force recognition of a union different from the currently certified bargaining representative.
Reformation Equitable remedy whereby a court corrects a written instrument in order to remove a mistake and to make the agreement conform to the terms to which the parties originally had agreed.
Registered agent Person designated by a corporation to receive service of process within the state.
Rejection A refusal to accept what is offered.
Relative Not capable of exact statement or measurable; comparative.
Remainder beneficiaries Persons with an interest in what remains in the trust corpus after use by the income beneficiaries.
Remand The return of a case to the lower court for additional hearings.
Remedies Methods for enforcing rights or preventing the violation of rights.
Replevin A personal action brought to recover possession of goods unlawfully taken; similar to specific

performance, but the object of the contract is not unique; it must be currently unavailable.

Replevy Acquire possession of goods unlawfully held by another.

Repudiation Rejection of an offered or available right or privilege, or of a duty or relation.

Requirements contract A contract in which the seller agrees to provide as much of a product or service as the buyer needs during the contract term.

Res judicata A rule of civil law that states that a person will not be sued more than once for the same civil wrong.

Rescission An annulment or cancellation; a termination of the contract through the restoration of the parties to the status quo.

Reservation of title An attempt by the seller to retain title until the buyer has fully performed the contract.

Residuary clause A clause that disposes of the remainder (the residual) of an estate.

Respondeat superior Doctrine asserting that an employer is liable for the tortious acts of employees while they are acting within the scope of their employment.

Restitutionary An equitable basis by which the law restores an injured party to the position he or she would have enjoyed had a loss not occurred.

Retainer Advance payment made to an attorney.

Reverse To overturn the lower court's decision.

Reverse discrimination Claims by whites that they have been subjected to adverse employment decisions because of their race and the application of employment discrimination statutes designed to protect minorities.

Revests Vests again; is acquired a second time.

Revocation The cancellation, rescission, or annulment of something previously done or offered.

Right of representation Right of children to inherit in their parent's place, if the parent is deceased.

Ripe Fully ready for adjudication.

ROM chips (read-only memory chips) Computer chips on which the data and information used to run computer operating systems are affixed; chips that can be "read" by a computer program but generally cannot be changed or altered.

Royalty fee Payment made in exchange for the granting of a right or a license.

Scienter Guilty knowledge; specifically, one party's prior knowledge of the cause of a subsequent injury to another person.

Seasonably Timely; something occurring in a prompt or timely manner.

Secondary boycotts Union activities meant to pressure parties not involved in the labor dispute and to influence the affected employer.

Secondary liability Conditional responsibility; liability following denial of primary liability.

Secured transactions Credit arrangements, covered by Article 9 of the UCC, in which the creditor retains a security interest in certain assets of the debtor.

Securities exchanges Organized secondary markets in which investors buy and sell securities at central locations.

Security interest An interest in the personal property of another as a means of securing payment or performance of a contractual obligation.

Separate property states States in which married couples cannot create community property.

Service marks Distinctive symbols designating the services offered by a particular business or individual.

Service of process Delivery of a writ or notice to the person named so as to inform that person of the nature of the legal dispute.

Severance pay Wages paid upon the termination of one's job.

Shuttle mediation Mediation technique in which the mediator physically separates the parties during the session and then runs messages between them.

Slander Any oral statement that tends to expose a person to public ridicule or to injure a person's reputation.

Solicitation A situation in which one person convinces another to engage in criminal activity.

Source code Human-readable version of the program that gives instructions to the computer.

Sovereign Above or superior to all others; that from which all authority flows.

Specific performance An equitable remedy granted when monetary damages would be insufficient and the object of the contract is unique and in which the court orders performance of the contract exactly as agreed.

Stale checks Checks a bank may dishonor due to their age (over six months old) without regard to the drawer's account balance.

Standing Legal involvement; the right to sue.

Stare decisis To abide by, or adhere to, decided cases; policy of courts to stand by decided cases and not to disturb a settled point of law.

Stated capital The amount of consideration received by the corporation for all shares of the corporation.
Statute of Frauds A statute requiring that specified types of contracts be in writing in order to be enforceable.
Statutory Created by statute; imposed by law.
Stay Suspend.
Stipend A fixed sum of money paid periodically for services or to defray costs.
Strict liability Liability for an action simply because it occurred and caused damage, and not because it is the fault of the person who must pay.
Sua sponte Voluntarily, without prompting or suggestion, of his or her own will or motion.
Subject matter jurisdiction The power of a court to hear certain kinds of legal questions.
Subjective Capable of being observed and verified through individual feelings and emotions.
Subpoena duces tecum A court order to produce evidence at a trial.
Subrogated Placed in the position of another; given the rights that another person previously held.
Substantially impairs Makes worth a great deal less, seriously harms or injures, or reduces in value.
Substantive law The portion of the law that creates, defines, and regulates rights, in contrast to law that grants remedies or enforces rights.
Suit Lawsuit; the formal legal proceeding used to resolve a legal dispute.
Summary judgment Owing to an absence of any genuine issue of fact, a judgment rendered in favor of one party before trial and on the basis of the pleadings.
Summons A writ requiring the sheriff to notify the person named that the person must appear in court to answer a complaint.
Supervening Coming or happening as something additional or unexpected.
Surcharged Assessed a fee by the court for failure to follow fiduciary duties.
Surety A person who promises to pay or to perform in the event the principal debtor fails to do so.
Suspend To cause to cease for a time; to become inoperative for a time; to stop temporarily.
Tenancy in partnership A special form of ownership of property, found only in partnerships, in which each partner has an equal right to possess and to use partnership assets for partnership purposes and which carries a right of survivorship.
Tender An offer to perform; an offer to satisfy an obligation.
Testamentary Pertaining to a will.
Testamentary capacity Sufficient mental capability or sanity to execute a valid will.
Testator A man who makes a will.
Testatrix A woman who makes a will.
Things in action A personal right; an intangible claim not yet reduced to possession, but recoverable in a suit at law.
Time price differential sales contracts Contracts with a difference in price based on the date of payment, with one price for an immediate payment and another for a payment at a later date.
Title Legal ownership of property. Also, evidence of ownership.
Tortfeasor A wrongdoer; one who commits a tort.
Tortious Relating to private or civil wrongs or injuries.
Trademarks Distinctive marks or symbols used to identify a particular company as the source of its products.
Transfer tax Tax on the ability to transfer assets.
Transportation Carrying or conveying from one place to another; the removal of goods or persons from one place to another.
Treble damages A statutory remedy that allows the successful plaintiff to recover three times the damages suffered as a result of the injury.
Trust An arrangement in which legal title, indicated on the deed or other evidence of ownership, is separated from the equitable or beneficial ownership; an arrangement in which one person or business holds property and invests it for another.
Trust deed A legal document that specifies the recipients of a trust, their interests, and how the trust should be managed; also called a deed of trust.
Trustee in bankruptcy The person appointed by the bankruptcy court to act as trustee of the debtor's property for the benefit and protection of the creditors.
Trustees Persons in whom a power is vested under an express or implied agreement in order to exercise the power for the benefit of another.
U.S.C. Abbreviation for the United States Code (statutes).
Ultra vires Acts beyond the scope of the power of a corporation.
Uncollateralized Having no underlying security to guarantee performance.

Unconscionability Condition of being so unreasonably favorable to one party, or so one-sided, as to shock the conscience.
Unconscionable Blatantly unfair and one-sided; so unfair as to shock the conscience.
Underwriters Persons or institutions that, by agreeing to sell securities to the public and to buy those not sold, insure the sale of corporate securities.
Unfair labor practices Employment or union activities that are prohibited by law as injurious to labor policies.
Uniform Commercial Code State statutory provisions covering various aspects of commercial law in the United States.
United Nations Convention on Contracts for the International Sale of Goods A treaty developed by the United Nations and intended to provide uniform treatment for contracts involving the international sales of goods.
Unsecured creditor A general creditor; a creditor whose claim is not secured by collateral.
Vacated Set aside; nullified; rendered void.
Vested interest A fixed interest or right to something, even though actual possession may be postponed until later.
Vicarious liability Legal responsibility for the wrong committed by another person.
Virus A computer program that destroys, damages, rearranges, or replaces computer data.
Voir dire The examination of potential jurors to determine their competence to serve on the jury.
Waiver The voluntary surrender of a legal right; the intentional surrender of a right.
Warehouseman A person engaged in the business of receiving and storing the goods of others for a fee.
Warranties Representations that become part of the contract and that are made by a seller of goods at the time of the sale and that concern the character, quality, or nature of the goods.
Wildcat strikes Unauthorized withholdings of services or labor during the term of a contract.
Winding up Paying the accounts and liquidating the assets of a business for the purpose of making distributions and dissolving the concern.
Workers' compensation Payments to injured workers based on the provisions in the state workers' compensation statute.
Writ A writing issued by a court in the form of a letter ordering some designated activity.
Writ of execution A court-issued writing that enforces a judgment or decree.
Wrongful death Unlawful death. It does not necessarily involve a crime.

CASE INDEX

Key: a = annotated and/or case citation; *b* = brief case; *c* = case problem

C

D

E

SUBJECT INDEX

Key: e = exhibit; *t* = table

B

J

N

T

U

THE CALL-IMAGE TECHNOLOGY (CIT) BUSINESS APPLICATION THREAD CASE

CIT NEEDS YOU!

Call Image Technology (CIT), a hypothetical videophone company, needs a consultant with training in business law matters to help the company avoid legal problems, correctly identify legal problems should they arise, and communicate these problems in an intelligent manner to CIT's attorney. CIT needs your help!

YOU NEED CIT!

The legal problems CIT faces involve the different functional areas of business—management, manufacturing, finance and accounting, sales, marketing, and international business. Hence, this text and this course will help you not only to understand the law but to apply these concepts to your field of study.

HOW THE CIT BUSINESS APPLICATION THREAD CASE WORKS

Chapters begin with an **agenda** that highlights the major legal issues relevant to CIT. Within chapters, **application boxes** address particular legal issues and call for your help (for an example, see the facing page). Chapters also contain **memos,** offering practical legal advice on business issues.

LIST OF THE PEOPLE AND PRODUCTS BEHIND CIT

CALL-IMAGE CIT's core product—a videophone that enables parties in a conversation to speak with and see each other simultaneously.

ANNA KOCHANOWSKI A founder of CIT and a former engineer for a major fiber optics firm; primary designer of Call-Image; full-time CIT employee.

TOM KOCHANOWSKI A founder of CIT and a 25-year veteran of the business world; works primarily in marketing and sales; part-time CIT employee.

AMY CHEN A lawyer who provides legal advice and performs legal functions for CIT.

DONNA KOCHANOWSKI Anna and Tom's 27-year-old daughter; a certified public accountant (CPA); offers financial advice to CIT; part-time CIT employee.

JULIO RODRIGUEZ Donna Kochanowski's fiancé; a CPA; offers financial advice to CIT; not a CIT employee.

DAN KOCHANOWSKI Anna and Tom's 23-year-old son; an engineer who assists in all aspects of CIT; full-time CIT employee.

JOHN KOCHANOWSKI Anna and Tom's 20-year-old son; college student; part-time CIT employee.

LINDSAY KOCHANOWSKI Anna and Tom's 16-year-old daughter; attends high school; part-time CIT employee.